RESENTED
TO

_____

BY

_____

ON

_____

NRSV

CLASSICS
DEVOTIONAL
BIBLE

WITH DAILY READINGS FROM
MEN AND WOMEN WHOSE FAITH
INFLUENCED THE WORLD

NRSV

CLASSICS

DEVOTIONAL

BIBLE

WITH DAILY READINGS FROM

MEN AND WOMEN WHOSE FAITH

INFLUENCED THE WORLD

NEW REVISED
STANDARD VERSION

Zondervan Publishing House

Grand Rapids, Michigan 49530, U.S.A.

TABLE OF CONTENTS

INTRODUCTION

elcome to the *NRSV Classics Devotional Bible!* If you are like most people today, your life is full—perhaps even too full. With so many things to do and so many demands on your time, finding time to read and reflect on the Bible can be difficult at times. The *NRSV Classics Devotional Bible* gives you a convenient Bible reading/devotional plan. Drawing from the writings of nearly 2000 years of church history, the *NRSV Classics Devotional Bible* offers a wonderful selection of devotions that will take you into the thoughts of well-known Christian authors, thinkers, theologians, hymn writers, poets, and pastors. We earnestly hope these meditations will provide you with new perspective and inspiration.

Even though the Bible was written approximately 2000 years ago, it contains themes not unlike today—struggling between good and evil, dealing with suffering and loss, celebrating in laughter and joy, seeing God's promises fulfilled. As you read, you will discover how relevant God's Word is to your life today! Several features make the *NRSV Classics Devotional Bible* an exceptional devotional guide:

THE BIBLE

The *NRSV Classics Devotional Bible* features the complete text of the New Revised Standard Version of the Bible.

THE DEVOTIONS

Your *NRSV Classics Devotional Bible* contains devotions for Monday through Friday, plus special devotions for every weekend. This devotional Bible contains 312 devotions—one for every weekday and weekend of the year. Each devotion is placed close to the Scripture reading for that day, encouraging you to read the devotion and the related Bible verses. The top of each devotion provides both a "Verse" and a "Passage." The subject of each devotion is tied to the designated Scripture verse. And the passage provides the context, or Scripture that surrounds the verse.

Regardless of what day of the week you begin, simply turn to a devotion for that day. For the next day, look to the bottom of the devotion for the page number of the next day's devotion. For example, if you start on a Monday, you could turn to the first devotion in the book of Genesis. Glance at the bottom of Monday's devotion and you will see the page number for Tuesday's devotion—and so on as you keep reading on through Friday.

Friday's devotion will direct you to a "Weekend." The bottom of the "Weekend" will send you to the next Monday devotion. As you follow this format, you will find yourself well on your way—through a year of spending precious time in God's Word and growing closer to him.

THE BOOK INTRODUCTIONS

At the beginning of each book of the Bible, you will find an interesting and informative introduction. These introductions succinctly highlight the practical themes of each book. Each introduction also provides you with interesting facts and helpful background, as well as a practical application to encourage you as you read that particular book and the devotions within it.

READING PLANS

Do you need a structure to follow for reading your Bible in a disciplined way? Several reading plans (see page 1563) should provide just what you need, including ways to read the entire Bible.

Now that you've become acquainted with your *NRSV Classics Devotional Bible*, open it and use it every day. You will never be sorry you took the time.

AUTHOR BIOGRAPHIES

You will very likely recognize many of the names of the people who contributed to the *NRSV Classics Devotional Bible*. The detailed author biographies, found on page 1537, provide interesting and helpful information about each author, as well as a list of the pages where the author's devotion appears.

SUBJECT INDEX

At the back of your *NRSV Classics Devotional Bible*, on page 1533, you'll find a guide for locating information within this Bible. If you're looking for Biblical perspectives on creation, or faith, or God's love, or prayer, or peace, or truth, or worship, or death, or any of over 175 other topics, this is the place to find it.

SUMMARY OF TIME ERAS

hen Jesus Christ gathered his disciples at Cesarea Phillipi, he spoke about an event of primary importance to the accomplishment of God's eternal purpose. There Jesus said, "I will build my church" (Matthew 16.18). During the brief period of Jesus' ministry on earth, he spoke of three essential prophecies. First, he spoke of his own death and resurrection. Second, he prophesied about his future return to earth with all of its tumult and glory. And third, he spoke of the building of the church. The first he fully accomplished with all of its profound effect on human history and individual lives. The second is yet to come. And the third is in process today, with each believer involved in some way with Christ in this work.

Of course, the building of the church has not been without its tumult as well. In fact, like all construction projects, the process of building the church has caused quite a disturbance. Church history can be read both as a document of this upheaval and as a record of the loving kindness and patience of the purposeful God. Scripture assures, however, that "Christ loved the church and gave himself up for her, in order to make her holy by cleansing her with the washing of water by the word, so as to present the church to himself in splendor, without a spot or wrinkle or anything of the kind—yes, so that she may be holy and without blemish" (Ephesians 5.25–27). These verses richly describe the church's future.

The apostle Paul fully embraced the demanding work of building the church. "According to the grace of God given to me," he wrote, "like a skilled master builder I laid a foundation" (1 Corinthians 3.10). Then he seriously cautions those who would follow to build on the foundation: "that foundation is Jesus Christ" (1 Corinthians 3.11). His warning echoes through 1900 years of history: "Each builder must choose with care how to build on it" (v. 10). And so the age of the church began. While some built with gold, silver, and precious stones, others built with wood, hay, and straw (v. 12). And when Christ returns, "the work of each builder will become visible, for the Day will disclose it" (v. 13). In the meantime the church is the repository of the documents, writings, and records of some of the laborers who have gone before. The *Classics Devotional Bible* is a selection of these writings placed alongside the text of the Bible. This allows the reader to find the relevance of these works to the record of Scripture and enjoy both for the sake of the building up of the church.

While reading these selections, the reader can trace the path of church history through five main eras of the Christian church. The following briefly charts this path using authors and sources—most of which are included in this Bible—for milestones and landmarks along the way.

100   500

THE EARLY CHURCH ERA

Little but legend has remained of the history and fate of Christ's original disciples. After the Lord's crucifixion and resurrection, the defining event of the first century, as far as the church is concerned, was the destruction of Jerusalem by the Roman general Titus in A.D. 70. At that time the believers joined the Jews in their dispersal and the church at Jerusalem was no more. Any records or artifacts of the church's first years were burned by the Romans with the rest of the city. The surviving founders of that inaugural church were absorbed into the ancient world, and the single Christian church composed predominately of Jews disappeared. This was followed by 400 to 500 years of organizational, liturgical, and theological development.

The second generation of Christians immediately met opposition in various arenas. Written between A.D. 70 and 100, *The Epistle of Barnabas* attempts to show Christ in types and figures of the Old Testament. In its stridently polemical attack on Judaism, it succeeds in finding convincing testimonies for the Christian faith in the Old Testament. Ignatius of Antioch (d. c. 116) encountered a different source of conflict: Roman paganism. He was condemned to be devoured by wild beasts during the reign of the Roman emperor Trajan. While traveling to his death in Rome, Ignatius wrote seven letters that show he wanted nothing to stand in the way of his martyrdom. He is the prototypical martyr. His letters also show the development of early church structure, speak of the Virgin Birth of Jesus, emphasize the physical resurrection of Christ, and describe the church as *catholic* in reference to her universal quality. The first theological writer for the church was Irenaeus of Lyons (c. 175–195) who lived in southern France. The title of his primary work, *Against Heresies*, indicates his field of work. While refuting the gnostic heresies, Irenaeus cited the Old Testament, the four gospels, and other apostolic writings as the canon of Scripture. He also affirmed both creation and redemption as acts of God.

While wrestling with influences that threatened the young church, these and many other individuals developed the beliefs and practices that are still the structural constitution of the church today. Soon these began to be codified for the benefit of all the believers. The profession of faith called the *Athanasian Creed* was named after Athanasius (c. 295–373). This great defender of the faith strove against the teaching of Arius who advocated that Christ was not eternal but was created by the Father. This view threatened to turn the faith into a philosophy mixed with pagan thought. In A.D. 325 Emperor Constantine called the Council of Nicea to settle this issue. In *The Three Orations against the Arians* (c. 335), Athanasius emphasized the necessity for the Word to be as eternal as God if he was to form the divine image in man. The creed named for him is composed of two parts devoted respectively to the doctrines of the Trinity and Incarnation. Adherence to these, it declares, is necessary for salvation.

Other early documents include *The Didache*, a summary of moral principles, instructions on the organization of Christian communities, and rules on worship. It contains the oldest recorded eucharistic prayers, and orders on baptism, fasting, prayer, as well as the treatment of bishops, deacons, and prophets. *The Epistle to Diognetus*, a document from the second or third century, explains why paganism and Judaism cannot be accepted, describes Christians as the soul of the world, and declares that Christianity is the unique revelation of God and of God's love.

No event or precise date formally ends the church's early era, though one shining individual illuminates the transition to medieval times—Augustine of Hippo (354–430). This son of a pagan father and Christian mother in North Africa is a figure of major importance to the church. In his *Confessions* (c. 397) he presents a Biblical understanding of a person's life under grace. In his *City of God* (c. 413–26) he is the first to give a Biblical view of history, time, and the state. He established the doctrine of the church, gave a clear statement concerning the person of Christ, and made the grace of God a major theme of theology in the West.

500   1500

THE MEDIEVAL ERA

The centuries between approximately A.D. 500 and the commencement of the Protestant Reformation are frequently referred to as the Dark Ages. But for the church of God, they were anything but dark. In reality, some of the brightest minds of the day applied themselves to her theological and ecclesiastical advancement. And had it not been for the cache of documents protected within the walls of European and Middle Eastern monasteries, and the diligence of monastic scholars and copyists, the treasury of knowledge, art, and philosophy of the classical ages would have perished. It is difficult for Protestants to appreciate this era. Indeed the church's testimony did slowly dim as these centuries wore on and the ecclesiastical bushel basket of Romanism descended over her lamp. Yet we must not forget that it was at this time that the monk Anselm of Canterbury (c. 1033–1109) asked *and answered* the question posed by his most famous work: *Why Did God Become Man?* It was Benedict of Nursia (c. 480–c. 547) who wrote the *Benedictine Rule*, which not only established a balanced way of life for the monasteries that were to prove so vital to the preservation of human culture, it also became a basis of organizational thought until modern times. Another leading monk, Bernard of Clairvaux (1090–1153), made the act of loving God the foundation of his life and teaching. How precious it is still to find this tendency in a believer. It is he who wrote our beloved hymn "Jesus the very thought of thee with sweetness fills my soul." Bernard also challenged Christians to lead lives of true devotion to God and was a forerunner to our Reformers. The philosopher, theologian, and mystic Bonaventura (1221–1274) was more akin in thought to Augustine and the Protestant Reformers than he was to his contemporaries in Rome.

Not all Reformers were Protestant, but it was the Protestants who were most successful. The Spanish poet and monk John of the Cross (1542–1591) suffered greatly with his benefactor Teresa of Avila (1515–1582) for joining her in attempting to reform the monastic system. The result was some of the world's great poetic literature and the record of a true Christian mystic. The Dutch writer, scholar, and Renaissance intellectual Desiderius Erasmus

(c. 1466–1536) wrote, "It has long been my cherished wish to cleanse the Lord's temple of barbarous ignorance and to adorn it with treasures from afar, such as may kindle in generous hearts a warm love for the Scriptures." The great work of his life was an edition of the Greek New Testament text (1516) which became a touchstone for successive generations of scholars and a source for Bible translations in the common vernacular. These translations went far to fulfill the cherished wishes of Erasmus. Two women must also be mentioned: Julian of Norwich (c. 1342–c. 1413), whose *Sixteen Revelations of Divine Love* became the first book to be published in English by a female author; and Catherine of Siena (1347–1380), an illiterate Florentine nun who worked for ecclesiastical reform and became prominent among the church's mystics.

Readers of history know that the medieval era was a difficult time in the human drama. And it was at this time that the full weight of the hope of humanity was carried by the Christian church.

1500   1700

THE REFORMATION ERA

If the earth's gravity had shifted as much as the church's theology did during the Reformation, the globe may have spun off its axis. Combine this with the political, cultural, and social changes that were simultaneously operating in Europe and the result is a true revolution.

In fact the religious, political, cultural, and social realms were quite inter-connected. This is seen clearly in the person of John Calvin (1509–1564), the French Protestant Reformer who labored in Geneva, Switzerland. His major work, *Institutes of the Christian Religion*, is considered one of the most influential in world literature. While laboring to organize evangelical churches, Calvin developed a highly adaptable model of church government. Meanwhile, social institutions were deteriorating. Many new institutions developed under the influence of Calvin's model and his "presbyterian" example even extended to influence modern democratic political theory. When John Calvin's contemporary, the Biblical translator, religious reformer, and writer William Tyndale (c. 1492–1536), left England to commence his work he said to a learned man, "If God spare my life, ere many years I will cause a boy that driveth the plough shall know more of the Scripture than thou dost." Considering that the Bible had been exclusively in a Latin translation for 1000 years and that Tyndale's proverbial ploughboy was an illiterate, the fact that Tyndale succeeded reveals not only his genius but also the harvest of cultural transformation caused by his English translation of the Bible. It is not commonly known that many of the finest passages of the King James Version of the Bible were taken unchanged from Tyndale's seminal work. These passages are treasures of the English language to this day.

These Reformers were struggling to free the human spirit from the bondage of religious darkness, but antiquated social systems and illiteracy were being overthrown as well. Simultaneously, the political world was in upheaval while emerging from its dominance by the church at Rome. Thomas Cranmer (1489–1556) was Archbishop of Canterbury and a leader of the English Reformation. As such he became embroiled in the maneuvers of Henry VIII to rid England of the influence of Rome. Cranmer himself renounced allegiance to the pope, directed that the pope's name be erased from every prayer book in England, and pronounced the king of England head of the English church. Cranmer was a brilliant editor, translator, and composer of prayers and formulae. His labor produced *The Book of Common Prayer* (1548), which is in use to this day in churches of the Anglican Communion. Political and religious shifts in England caused Cranmer to be condemned as a heretic; thus he joined the many martyrs of his time when he was burned at the stake in 1556.

An example of the quality of the people God enlisted to accomplish the Church's reformation is Blaise Pascal (1623–1662), one of the great minds in Western intellectual history. A Frenchman, Pascal was an eminent mathematician and physicist and one of the greatest mystical writers in Christian literature. At 19 he invented the first practical calculating machine. Later he verified the theory of atmospheric pressure and formulated the mathematical theory of probability, a fundamental element of modern theoretical physics. Pascal was an adherent of the Roman Catholic reform movement known as Jansenism. His *Provincial Letters* (1657), a classic in the literature of irony and satire, demanded a reemphasis on Augustine's doctrine of grace within the Catholic church. Yet God also gave the church John Bunyan (1628–1688), the impoverished son of a tinker who authored *The Pilgrim's Progress* while in prison. One of the most famous religious allegories in the English language, *The Pilgrim's Progress* became the most widely read book in English after the Bible.

Another descendant of peasants grew up to be perhaps the most crucial figure in modern European history—Martin Luther of Germany (1483–1546). We have noted that there were reform-minded individuals working in the church for centuries. But this German theologian appeared at the confluence of the flow of history to directly initiate the Protestant Reformation and thereby influence politics, economics, education, and language as well. Luther held the chair of Biblical theology at University of Wittenberg in 1512. This was his final station in his journey toward understanding that God's free grace is the unique source of salvation. On October 31, 1517, he published his Ninety-five Theses, which opposed certain beliefs and practices of the Catholic church. With Luther as its leader and innovator, the Reformation burst forth. Luther was a preacher, professor, theologian, linguist, educator, and political theorist. God places his treasure in earthen vessels and Martin Luther was the gifted and versatile man of the hour chosen to usher in a truly new era in human history.

1700　　　1900

THE POST-REFORMATION ERA

When the English mystic poet William Blake (1757–1827) wrote, "I will not cease from Mental Fight,/Nor shall my Sword sleep in my hand/Till we have built Jerusalem/In England's green and pleasant Land," he may indeed have been prophesying of the hopes of the post-Reformers. These individuals toiled to establish the truth of the gospel in their homelands and also to spread it to the entire world. They were preachers, missionaries, hymn writers, and revivalists. They included William Law (1688–1761), a preacher of the Church

of England whose book *A Serious Call to a Devout and Holy Life* o̶
ethics and mysticism influenced John Wesley and George Whit
iconoclast George Fox (1624–1691), founder of the Society of Fri
stressed the priesthood of all believers and advocated a simple life-s
Jonathan Edwards (1703–1758), who presided over the revival know
Great Awakening, which engulfed all New England.

Hymns like "Sweet Hour of Prayer" by Fanny Crosby (1820–1915),
I Survey the Wondrous Cross" by Issac Watts (1674–1748), "For the Brea
For the Wine" by Horatius Bonar (1808–1889), and "In The Deep, Deep
ter" by Christina Rossetti (1830–1894), and the rich African-American spir
als still ring in our churches and feed our devotion to God. Native-America
are indebted to the sacrifice of missionary David Brainerd (1718–1747). The
faithful in China still stand on the foundation laid by James Hudson Taylor
(1832–1905) and the China Inland Mission. And the world is a far better place
for the labor of William Booth (1829–1912) and his Salvation Army. The Quaker John Woolman (1720–1772) and the former slaves Frederick Douglass
(1817–1895) and Sojourner Truth (c. 1797–1883) insisted that the church heed
her Scriptures and her conscience in the fight for the abolition of slavery.

The great lights of this era, like John Wesley (1703–1791), George Whitefield (1714–1770), and Charles H. Spurgeon (1834–1892), must share their
place on history's pages with countless other saints. The sacrifices of these
lesser-known servants of God salted and preserved the earth and its inhabitants by spreading and establishing the truth of the gospel of Jesus Christ as
the unique source of salvation and the strengthening fiber of the human race.

1900   PRESENT

THE MODERN ERA

As we pass into the next millennium, we leave behind a century marked by
two world wars, which all the world hopes never to repeat. Oswald Chambers
(1874–1917), who labored for the Lord at the huge encampment of the
Mediterranean Expeditionary Force at Zeitoun, Egypt, during World War I,
sought to minister the hope of the message of Jesus Christ "in the full blaze
of the intellectual problems and actual difficulties of the times in which we
live." Modern times have posed this challenge to all Christians. This century
has seen Karl Barth (1886–1968), the Swiss theologian teacher and writer who
was driven to reconsider his liberal theological training when his teachers
supported German militarism. He challenged German National Socialism
with a series of pamphlets entitled *Theological Existence Today* and was
forced to flee Germany in 1935. We witnessed the testimony of Dietrich Bonhoeffer (1906–1945), who refused to cooperate with Hitler's interference in
church affairs. With Barth and others, he helped found the Confessing Church
in Germany, began an illegal seminary, and early-on identified himself with
the resistance against Nazism. As a result this German theologian was arrested and became a modern Christian martyr.

Peter Marshall (1902–1949), a Scottish emigrant to America, rose up to
serve as chaplain to the United States Senate; and the Roman Catholic con-

...has Merton (1915–1968) wrote eloquently about modern society
...vert ...nd the walls of a Trappist monastery.
from age has been filled with writers, preachers, and scholars, like F. F.
...(1910–990), the Scotsman who was the preeminent evangelical scholar
...post-World War II era; Francis Schaeffer (1912–1984), who together with
...vife Edith founded an international study and ministry community in the
...iss Alps and wrote a total of 23 books; and Evelyn Underhill (1875–1941),
...nose classic evaluation of spirituality, *Mysticism: A Study in the Nature
...nd Development of Man's Spiritual Consciousness*, examined the church
from the first through the nineteenth centuries.

But our era has also witnessed the contributions of activists as well. Preeminent among these was Martin Luther King, Jr. (1929–1968), the son of a
Baptist minister who was catapulted into national prominence as a leader for
civil rights. He led a massive civil rights campaign, organized drives for black
voter registration, desegregation, and better education and housing throughout the South. Dag Hammarskjöld (1905–61), the Swedish economist and
diplomat, was elected secretary-general of the United Nations and was
posthumously awarded the 1961 Nobel Peace Prize. His legacy to the church
and the world is his book of meditations, *Markings*. And William Temple
(1881–1944) effectively lead the Anglican Communion with a passionate concern for national and social righteousness.

The church of God is a steadfast presence in a capricious world. As this
century marred by conflict closes, we hope for more than peace. We hope for
Jesus Christ, the Prince of Peace, and pray that he will continue the cleansing
of his church "by cleansing her with the washing of water by the word, so as
to present the church to himself in splendor, without a spot or wrinkle or anything of the kind—yes, so that she may be holy and without blemish" (Ephesians 5.26–27).

TO THE READER

his preface is addressed to you by the Committee of translators, who wish to explain, as briefly as possible, the origin and character of our work. The publication of our revision is yet another step in the long, continual process of making the Bible available in the form of the English language that is most widely current in our day. To summarize in a single sentence: the New Revised Standard Version of the Bible is an authorized revision of the Revised Standard Version, published in 1952, which was a revision of the American Standard Version, published in 1901, which, in turn, embodied earlier revisions of the King James Version, published in 1611.

In the course of time, the King James Version came to be regarded as "the Authorized Version." With good reason it has been termed "the noblest monument of English prose," and it has entered, as no other book has, into the making of the personal character and the public institutions of the English-speaking peoples. We owe to it an incalculable debt.

Yet the King James Version has serious defects. By the middle of the nineteenth century, the development of biblical studies and the discovery of many biblical manuscripts more ancient than those on which the King James Version was based made it apparent that these defects were so many as to call for revision. The task was begun, by authority of the Church of England, in 1870. The (British) Revised Version of the Bible was published in 1881-1885; and the American Standard Version, its variant embodying the preferences of the American scholars associated with the work, was published, as was mentioned above, in 1901. In 1928 the copyright of the latter was acquired by the International Council of Religious Education and thus passed into the ownership of the Churches of the United States and Canada that were associated in this Council through their boards of education and publication.

The Council appointed a committee of scholars to have charge of the text of the American Standard Version and to undertake inquiry concerning the need for further revision. After studying the questions whether or not revision should be undertaken, and if so, what its nature and extent should be, in 1937 the Council authorized a revision. The scholars who served as members of the Committee worked in two sections, one dealing with the Old Testament and one with the New Testament. In 1946 the Revised Standard Version of the New Testament was published. The publication of the Revised Standard Version of the Bible, containing the Old and New Testaments, took place on September 30, 1952. A translation of the *Apocryphal/Deuterocanonical* Books of the Old Testament followed in 1957. In 1977 this collection was issued in an expanded edition, containing three additional texts received by Eastern Orthodox communions (3 and 4 Maccabees and Psalm 151). Thereafter the Revised Standard Version gained the distinction of being officially authorized for use by all major Christian churches: Protestant, Anglican, Roman Catholic, and Eastern Orthodox.

The Revised Standard Version Bible Committee is a continuing body, comprising about thirty members, both men and women. Ecumenical in representation, it includes scholars affiliated with various Protestant denominations, as well as several Roman Catholic members, an Eastern Orthodox member, and a Jewish member who serves in the Old Testament section. For a period of time the Committee included several members from Canada and from England.

Because no translation of the Bible is perfect or is acceptable to all groups of readers, and because discoveries of older manuscripts and further investigation of linguistic features of the text continue to become available, renderings of the Bible have proliferated. During the years following the publication of the Revised Standard Version, twenty-six other English translations and revisions of the Bible were produced by committees and by individual scholars—not to mention twenty-five other translations and revisions of the New Testament alone. One of the latter was the second edition of the RSV New Testament, issued in 1971, twenty-five years after its initial publication.

Following the publication of the RSV Old Testament in 1952, significant advances were made in the discovery and interpretation of documents in Semitic languages related to Hebrew. In addition to the information that had become available in the late 1940s from the Dead Sea texts of Isaiah and Habakkuk, subsequent acquisitions from the same area brought to light many other early copies of all the books of the Hebrew Scriptures (except Esther), though most of these copies are fragmentary. During the same period early Greek manuscript copies of books of the New Testament also became available.

In order to take these discoveries into account, along with recent studies of documents in

Semitic languages related to Hebrew, in 1974 the Policies Committee of the Revised Standard Version, which is a standing committee of the National Council of the Churches of Christ in the U.S.A., authorized the preparation of a revision of the entire RSV Bible.

For the Old Testament the Committee has made use of the *Biblia Hebraica Stuttgartensia* (1977; ed. sec. emendata, 1983). This is an edition of the Hebrew and Aramaic text as current early in the Christian era and fixed by Jewish scholars (the "Masoretes") of the sixth to the ninth centuries. The vowel signs, which were added by the Masoretes, are accepted in the main, but where a more probable and convincing reading can be obtained by assuming different vowels, this has been done. No notes are given in such cases, because the vowel points are less ancient and reliable than the consonants. When an alternative reading given by the Masoretes is translated in a footnote, this is identified by the words "Another reading is."

Departures from the consonantal text of the best manuscripts have been made only where it seems clear that errors in copying had been made before the text was standardized. Most of the corrections adopted are based on the ancient versions (translations into Greek, Aramaic, Syriac, and Latin), which were made prior to the time of the work of the Masoretes and which therefore may reflect earlier forms of the Hebrew text. In such instances a footnote specifies the version or versions from which the correction has been derived and also gives a translation of the Masoretic Text. Where it was deemed appropriate to do so, information is supplied in footnotes from subsidiary Jewish traditions concerning other textual readings (the *Tiqqune Sopherim*, "emendations of the scribes"). These are identified in the footnotes as "Ancient Heb tradition."

Occasionally it is evident that the text has suffered in transmission and that none of the versions provides a satisfactory restoration. Here we can only follow the best judgment of competent scholars as to the most probable reconstruction of the original text. Such reconstructions are indicated in footnotes by the abbreviation Cn ("Correction"), and a translation of the Masoretic Text is added.

For the New Testament the Committee has based its work on the most recent edition of *The Greek New Testament*, prepared by an interconfessional and international committee and published by the United Bible Societies (1966; 3rd ed. corrected, 1983; information concerning changes to be introduced into the critical apparatus of the forthcoming 4th edition was available to the Committee). As in that edition, double brackets are used to enclose a few passages that are generally regarded to be later additions to the text, but which we have retained because of their evident antiquity and their importance in the textual tradition. Only in very rare instances have we replaced the text or the punctuation of the Bible Societies' edition by an alternative that seemed to us to be superior. Here and there in the footnotes the phrase, "Other ancient authorities read," identifies alternative readings preserved by Greek manuscripts and early versions. In both Testaments, alternative renderings of the text are indicated by the word "Or."

As for the style of English adopted for the present revision, among the mandates given to the Committee in 1980 by the Division of Education and Ministry of the National Council of Churches of Christ (which now holds the copyright of the RSV Bible) was the directive to continue in the tradition of the King James Bible, but to introduce such changes as are warranted on the basis of accuracy, clarity, euphony, and current English usage. Within the constraints set by the original texts and by the mandates of the Division, the Committee has followed the maxim, "As literal as possible, as free as necessary." As a consequence, the New Revised Standard Version (NRSV) remains essentially a literal translation. Paraphrastic renderings have been adopted only sparingly, and then chiefly to compensate for a deficiency in the English language—the lack of a common gender third person singular pronoun.

During the almost half a century since the publication of the RSV, many in the churches have become sensitive to the danger of linguistic sexism arising from the inherent bias of the English language towards the masculine gender, a bias that in the case of the Bible has often restricted or obscured the meaning of the original text. The mandates from the Division specified that, in references to men and women, masculine-oriented language should be eliminated as far as this can be done without altering passages that reflect the historical situation of ancient patriarchal culture. As can be appreciated, more than once the Committee found that the several mandates stood in tension and even in conflict. The various concerns had to be balanced case by case in order to provide a faithful and acceptable rendering without using contrived English. Only very occasionally has the pronoun "he" or "him" been retained in passages where the reference may have been to a woman as well as to a man; for example, in several legal texts in Leviticus and Deuteronomy. In such instances of formal, legal language, the options of either putting the passage in the plural or of introducing additional nouns to avoid masculine pronouns in English seemed to the Committee to obscure the historic structure and literary character of the original. In the vast majority of cases, however, inclusiveness has been attained by simple rephrasing or by introducing plural forms when this does not distort the meaning of the passage. Of course, in narrative and in parable no attempt was made to generalize the sex of individual persons.

Another aspect of style will be detected by readers who compare the more stately English rendering of the Old Testament with the less formal rendering adopted for the New Testament. For example, the traditional distinction between *shall* and *will* in English has been retained in the Old Testament as appropriate in rendering a document that embodies what may be termed the classic form of Hebrew, while in the New Testament the abandonment of such distinctions in the usage of the future tense in English reflects the more colloquial nature of the koine Greek used by most New Testament authors except when they are quoting the Old Testament.

Careful readers will notice that here and there in the Old Testament the word LORD (or in certain cases GOD) is printed in capital letters. This represents the traditional manner in English versions of rendering the Divine Name, the "Tetragrammaton" (see the notes on Exodus 3.14, 15), following the precedent of the ancient Greek and Latin translators and the long established practice in the reading of the Hebrew Scriptures in the synagogue. While it is almost if not quite certain that the Name was originally pronounced "Yahweh," this pronunciation was not indicated when the Masoretes added vowel sounds to the consonantal Hebrew text. To the four consonants YHWH of the Name, which had come to be regarded as too sacred to be pronounced, they attached vowel signs indicating that in its place should be read the Hebrew word *Adonai* meaning "Lord" (or *Elohim* meaning "God"). Ancient Greek translators employed the word *Kyrios* ("Lord") for the Name. The Vulgate likewise used the Latin word *Dominus* ("Lord"). The form "Jehovah" is of late medieval origin; it is a combination of the consonants of the Divine Name and the vowels attached to it by the Masoretes but belonging to an entirely different word. Although the American Standard Version (1901) had used "Jehovah" to render the Tetragrammaton (the sound of Y being represented by J and the sound of W by V, as in Latin), for two reasons the Committees that produced the RSV and the NRSV returned to the more familiar usage of the King James Version. (1) The word "Jehovah" does not accurately represent any form of the Name ever used in Hebrew. (2) The use of any proper name for the one and only God, as though there were other gods from whom the true God had to be distinguished, began to be discontinued in Judaism before the Christian era and is inappropriate for the universal faith of the Christian Church.

It will be seen that in the Psalms and in other prayers addressed to God the archaic second person singular pronouns *(thee, thou, thine)* and verb forms *(art, hast, hadst)* are no longer used. Although some readers may regret this change, it should be pointed out that in the original languages neither the Old Testament nor the New makes any linguistic distinction between addressing a human being and addressing the Deity. Furthermore, in the tradition of the King James Version one will not expect to find the use of capital letters for pronouns that refer to the Deity—such capitalization is an unnecessary innovation that has only recently been introduced into a few English translations of the Bible. Finally, we have left to the discretion of the licensed publishers such matters as section headings, cross-references, and clues to the pronunciation of proper names.

This new version seeks to preserve all that is best in the English Bible as it has been known and used through the years. It is intended for use in public reading and congregational worship, as well as in private study, instruction, and meditation. We have resisted the temptation to introduce terms and phrases that merely reflect current moods, and have tried to put the message of the Scriptures in simple, enduring words and expressions that are worthy to stand in the great tradition of the King James Bible and its predecessors.

In traditional Judaism and Christianity, the Bible has been more than a historical document to be preserved or a classic of literature to be cherished and admired; it is recognized as the unique record of God's dealings with people over the ages. The Old Testament sets forth the call of a special people to enter into covenant relation with the God of justice and steadfast love and to bring God's law to the nations. The New Testament records the life and work of Jesus Christ, the one in whom "the Word became flesh," as well as describes the rise and spread of the early Christian Church. The Bible carries its full message, not to those who regard it simply as a noble literary heritage of the past or who wish to use it to enhance political purposes and advance otherwise desirable goals, but to all persons and communities who read it so that they may discern and understand what God is saying to them. That message must not be disguised in phrases that are no longer clear, or hidden under words that have changed or lost their meaning; it must be presented in language that is direct and plain and meaningful to people today. It is the hope and prayer of the translators that this version of the Bible may continue to hold a large place in congregational life and to speak to all readers, young and old alike, helping them to understand and believe and respond to its message.

For the Committee,
BRUCE M. METZGER

OLD
TESTAMENT

GENESIS

T HE BOOK OF GENESIS IS ABOUT MANY BEGINNINGS—THE BEGINNING OF THE UNIVERSE, THE BEGINNING OF THE HUMAN RACE, THE BEGINNING OF SIN, AND THE BEGINNING OF GOD'S PROMISES AND PLAN FOR SALVATION. GENESIS IS MAINLY A STORY OF RELATIONSHIPS—BETWEEN GOD AND HIS PEOPLE, BETWEEN GOD AND NATURE, AND BETWEEN HIS PEOPLE AND OTHERS. GENESIS REMINDS US OF THE BEAUTIFUL WAYS IN WHICH GOD INITIATES AND ENTERS INTO COVENANTS WITH ALL OF HIS CHOSEN PEOPLE, AND HOW HE PLEDGES HIS LOVE AND FAITHFULNESS TO US.

Six Days of Creation and the Sabbath

1 In the beginning when God created[a] the heavens and the earth, 2the earth was a formless void and darkness covered the face of the deep, while a wind from God[b] swept over the face of the waters. 3Then God said, "Let there be light"; and there was light. 4And God saw that the light was good; and God separated the light from the darkness. 5God called the light Day, and the darkness he called Night. And there was evening and there was morning, the first day.

6 And God said, "Let there be a dome in the midst of the waters, and let it separate the waters from the waters." 7So God made the dome and separated the waters that were under the dome from the waters that were above the dome. And it was so. 8God called the dome Sky. And there was evening and there was morning, the second day.

9 And God said, "Let the waters under the sky be gathered together into one place, and let the dry land appear." And it was so. 10God called the dry land Earth, and the waters that were gathered together he called Seas. And God saw that it was good. 11Then God said, "Let the earth put forth vegetation: plants yielding seed, and fruit trees of every kind on earth that bear fruit with the seed in it." And it was so. 12The earth

a Or when God began to create or In the beginning God created   b Or while the spirit of God or while a mighty wind

brought forth vegetation: plants yielding seed of every kind, and trees of every kind bearing fruit with the seed in it. And God saw that it was good. 13 And there was evening and there was morning, the third day.

14 And God said, "Let there be lights in the dome of the sky to separate the day from the night; and let them be for signs and for seasons and for days and years, 15 and let them be lights in the dome of the sky to give light upon the earth." And it was so. 16 God made the two great lights—the greater light to

---

MONDAY

EVOLUTION IS MISTAKEN FOR EXPLANATION
G. K. Chesterton

VERSE: Genesis 1.1   PASSAGE: Genesis 1.1—2.3

 have noticed that if you put a word like God into the same sentence with a word like dog, these abrupt and angular words affect people like pistol shots. Whether you say that God made the dog or the dog made God does not seem to matter; that is only one of the sterile disputations of the too subtle theologians. But so long as you begin with a long word like evolution the rest will roll harmlessly past . . .

Most modern histories of mankind begin with the word evolution, and with a rather wordy exposition of evolution, for much the same reason that operated in this case. There is something slow and soothing and gradual about the word and even about the idea. As a matter of fact, it is not, touching these primary things, a very practical word or a very profitable idea. Nobody can imagine how nothing could turn into something. Nobody can get an inch nearer to it by explaining how something could turn into something else. It is really far more logical to start by saying "In the beginning God created heaven and earth" even if you only mean "In the beginning some unthinkable power began some unthinkable process." For God is by its nature a name of mystery, and nobody ever supposed that man could imagine how a world was created any more than he could create one. But evolution really is mistaken for explanation. It has the fatal quality of leaving on many minds the impression that they do understand it and everything else; just as many of them live under a sort of illusion that they have read [The] Origin of Species.

ADDITIONAL SCRIPTURE READING:
Job 38.4–38; Psalm 104.1–26; John 1.1–10

Go to page 4 for your next devotional reading.

1900   Present

rule the day and the lesser light to rule the night—and the stars. [17]God set them in the dome of the sky to give light upon the earth, [18]to rule over the day and over the night, and to separate the light from the darkness. And God saw that it was good. [19]And there was evening and there was morning, the fourth day.

20 And God said, "Let the waters bring forth swarms of living creatures, and let birds fly above the earth across the dome of the sky." [21]So God created the great sea monsters and every living creature that moves, of every kind, with which the waters swarm, and every winged bird of every kind. And God saw that it was good. [22]God blessed them, saying, "Be fruitful and multiply and fill the waters in the seas, and let birds multiply on the earth." [23]And there was evening and there was morning, the fifth day.

24 And God said, "Let the earth bring forth living creatures of every kind: cattle and creeping things and wild animals of the earth of every kind." And it was so. [25]God made the wild animals of the earth of every kind, and the cattle of every kind, and everything that creeps upon the ground of every kind. And God saw that it was good.

26 Then God said, "Let us make humankind[c] in our image, according to our likeness; and let them have dominion over the fish of the sea, and over the birds of the air, and over the cattle, and over all the wild animals of the earth,[d] and over every creeping thing that creeps upon the earth."

27   So God created humankind[c] in his image,
     in the image of God he created them;[e]
     male and female he created them.

[28]God blessed them, and God said to them, "Be fruitful and multiply, and fill the earth and subdue it; and have dominion over the fish of the sea and over the birds of the air and over every living thing that moves upon the earth." [29]God said, "See, I have given you every plant yielding seed that is upon the face of all the earth, and every tree with seed in its fruit; you shall have them for food.

[30]And to every beast of the earth, and to every bird of the air, and to everything that creeps on the earth, everything that has the breath of life, I have given every green plant for food." And it was so. [31]God saw everything that he had made, and indeed, it was very good. And there was evening and there was morning, the sixth day.

2 Thus the heavens and the earth were finished, and all their multitude. [2]And on the seventh day God finished the work that he had done, and he rested on the seventh day from all the work that he had done. [3]So God blessed the seventh day and hallowed it, because on it God rested from all the work that he had done in creation.

4 These are the generations of the heavens and the earth when they were created.

Another Account of the Creation

In the day that the LORD God made the earth and the heavens, [5]when no plant of the field was yet in the earth and no herb of the field had yet sprung up—for the LORD God had not caused it to rain upon the earth, and there was no one to till the ground; [6]but a stream would rise from the earth, and water the whole face of the ground— [7]then the LORD God formed man from the dust of the ground,[f] and breathed into his nostrils the breath of life; and the man became a living being. [8]And the LORD God planted a garden in Eden, in the east; and there he put the man whom he had formed. [9]Out of the ground the LORD God made to grow every tree that is pleasant to the sight and good for food, the tree of life also in the midst of the

---

THE BIBLE SHOWS HOW THE WORLD PROGRESSES.
IT BEGINS WITH A GARDEN, BUT ENDS WITH A
HOLY CITY.   —*Phillips Brooks*

---

garden, and the tree of the knowledge of good and evil.

10 A river flows out of Eden to water the garden, and from there it divides and becomes four branches. [11]The name of

---

c Heb *adam*   d Syr: Heb *and over all the earth*   e Heb *him*   f Or *formed a man* (Heb *adam*) of
dust from the ground (Heb *adamah*)

the first is Pishon; it is the one that flows around the whole land of Havilah, where there is gold; 12and the gold of that land is good; bdellium and onyx stone are there. 13The name of the second river is Gihon; it is the one that flows around the whole land of Cush. 14The name of the third river is Tigris, which flows east of Assyria. And the fourth river is the Euphrates.

15 The LORD God took the man and put him in the garden of Eden to till it and keep it. 16And the LORD God commanded the man, "You may freely eat of every tree of the garden; 17but of the tree of the knowledge of good and evil you shall not eat, for in the day that you eat of it you shall die."

18 Then the LORD God said, "It is not good that the man should be alone; I

TUESDAY

FROM PARADISE LOST, BOOK VIII
John Milton

VERSE: Genesis 2.7   PASSAGE: Genesis 2.4–25

[Adam, to the archangel Raphael]:

or man to tell how human life began
Is hard; for who himself beginning knew?
Desire with thee still longer to converse
Induced me. As new-waked from soundest sleep
Soft on the flow'ry herb I found me laid
In balmy sweat, which with his beams the sun
Soon dried, and on the reeking moisture fed.
Straight toward heav'n my wond'ring eyes I turned,
And gazed a while the ample sky, till raised
By quick instinctive motion up I sprung,
As thitherward endeavoring, and upright
Stood on my feet; about me round I saw
Hill, dale, and shady woods, and sunny plains,
And liquid lapse of murmuring streams; by these,
Creatures that lived, and moved, and walked, or flew,
Birds on the branches warbling; all things smiled,
With fragrance and with joy my heart o'erflowed.
Myself I then perused, and limb by limb
Surveyed, and sometimes went, and sometimes ran
With supple joints, as lively vigor led:
But who I was, or where, or from what cause,
Knew not . . .

ADDITIONAL SCRIPTURE READING:
Job 10.8–12; Isaiah 29.16; 42.5

Go to page 6 for your next devotional reading.

1500   1700

will make him a helper as his partner."
¹⁹So out of the ground the LORD God
formed every animal of the field and
every bird of the air, and brought them
to the man to see what he would call
them; and whatever the man called
every living creature, that was its name.
²⁰The man gave names to all cattle, and
to the birds of the air, and to every animal of the field; but for the man^g there
was not found a helper as his partner.
²¹So the LORD God caused a deep sleep
to fall upon the man, and he slept; then
he took one of his ribs and closed up its
place with flesh. ²²And the rib that the
LORD God had taken from the man he
made into a woman and brought her to
the man. ²³Then the man said,

"This at last is bone of my bones
    and flesh of my flesh;
this one shall be called Woman,^h
    for out of Manⁱ this one was
        taken."

²⁴Therefore a man leaves his father and
his mother and clings to his wife, and
they become one flesh. ²⁵And the man
and his wife were both naked, and were
not ashamed.

The First Sin and Its Punishment

3 Now the serpent was more
crafty than any other wild animal that the LORD God had made. He
said to the woman, "Did God say, 'You
shall not eat from any tree in the garden'?" ²The woman said to the serpent,
"We may eat of the fruit of the trees in
the garden; ³but God said, 'You shall not
eat of the fruit of the tree that is in the
middle of the garden, nor shall you
touch it, or you shall die.' " ⁴But the serpent said to the woman, "You will not
die; ⁵for God knows that when you eat
of it your eyes will be opened, and you
will be like God,^j knowing good and
evil." ⁶So when the woman saw that the
tree was good for food, and that it was a
delight to the eyes, and that the tree was
to be desired to make one wise, she took
of its fruit and ate; and she also gave
some to her husband, who was with her,
and he ate. ⁷Then the eyes of both were
opened, and they knew that they were
naked; and they sewed fig leaves together and made loincloths for themselves.

⁸ They heard the sound of the LORD
God walking in the garden at the time of
the evening breeze, and the man and his
wife hid themselves from the presence
of the LORD God among the trees of the
garden. ⁹But the LORD God called to the
man, and said to him, "Where are you?"
¹⁰He said, "I heard the sound of you in
the garden, and I was afraid, because I

AS IN PARADISE, GOD WALKS IN THE HOLY SCRIP-
TURES, SEEKING MAN.   —*Ambrose*

---

was naked; and I hid myself." ¹¹He said,
"Who told you that you were naked?
Have you eaten from the tree of which I
commanded you not to eat?" ¹²The man
said, "The woman whom you gave to be
with me, she gave me fruit from the
tree, and I ate." ¹³Then the LORD God
said to the woman, "What is this that
you have done?" The woman said, "The
serpent tricked me, and I ate." ¹⁴The
LORD God said to the serpent,

"Because you have done this,
    cursed are you among all animals
    and among all wild creatures;
upon your belly you shall go,
    and dust you shall eat
    all the days of your life.
¹⁵   I will put enmity between you and
      the woman,
    and between your offspring and
      hers;
he will strike your head,
    and you will strike his heel."
¹⁶To the woman he said,
"I will greatly increase your pangs
    in childbearing;
in pain you shall bring forth
    children,
yet your desire shall be for your
    husband,
and he shall rule over you."
¹⁷And to the man^k he said,
"Because you have listened to the
    voice of your wife,
and have eaten of the tree
about which I commanded you,
    'You shall not eat of it,'
cursed is the ground because of you;
in toil you shall eat of it all the
    days of your life;

---

g Or *for Adam*   *h* Heb *ishshah*   *i* Heb *ish*   *j* Or *gods*   *k* Or *to Adam*

OF RESISTING TEMPTATION
Thomas à Kempis

VERSE: Genesis 3.1   **PASSAGE:** Genesis 3.1–9

 o long as we live in this world we can not be without tribulation and temptation . . .

Every one therefore ought to be careful about his temptations, and to watch in prayer, lest the devil find an occasion to deceive him; who never sleepeth, but goeth about seeking whom he may devour (see 1 Peter 5.8).

No man is so perfect and holy, but he hath sometimes temptations; and altogether without them we can not be.

Nevertheless, temptations are often very profitable to us, though they be troublesome and grievous; for in them a man is humbled, purified, and instructed.

All saints passed through many tribulations and temptations, and profited thereby.

And they that could not bear temptations, became reprobate, and fell away.

There is no order so holy, nor place so secret, where there be not temptations, or adversities . . .

Some suffer great temptations in the beginning of their conversion; others at the end.

Others again are much troubled almost through the whole of their life.

Some are easily tempted, according to the wisdom and equity of the divine appointment, which weigheth the states and worth of men, and ordaineth all things for the welfare of his own chosen ones.

We ought not therefore to despair when we are tempted, but so much the more fervently to pray unto God, that he will grant us help in all tribulations; who, surely, according to the words of St. Paul, will give with the temptation a way of escape, that we may be able to bear it.

Let us therefore humble our souls under the hand of God in all temptations and tribulations, for he will save and exalt the humble in spirit.

ADDITIONAL SCRIPTURE READING:
Matthew 4.1–11; 1 Corinthians 10.13

Go to page 12 for your next devotional reading.

500   1500

18 thorns and thistles it shall bring
forth for you;
and you shall eat the plants of
the field.
19 By the sweat of your face
you shall eat bread
until you return to the ground,
for out of it you were taken;
you are dust,
and to dust you shall return."

20 The man named his wife Eve,[l] because she was the mother of all living. 21 And the LORD God made garments of skins for the man[m] and for his wife, and clothed them.

22 Then the LORD God said, "See, the man has become like one of us, knowing good and evil; and now, he might reach out his hand and take also from the tree of life, and eat, and live forever"— 23 therefore the LORD God sent him forth from the garden of Eden, to till the ground from which he was taken. 24 He drove out the man; and at the east of the garden of Eden he placed the cherubim, and a sword flaming and turning to guard the way to the tree of life.

Cain Murders Abel

4 Now the man knew his wife Eve, and she conceived and bore Cain, saying, "I have produced[n] a man with the help of the LORD." 2 Next she bore his brother Abel. Now Abel was a keeper of sheep, and Cain a tiller of the ground. 3 In the course of time Cain brought to the LORD an offering of the fruit of the ground, 4 and Abel for his part brought of the firstlings of his flock, their fat portions. And the LORD had regard for Abel and his offering, 5 but for Cain and his offering he had no regard. So Cain was very angry, and his countenance fell. 6 The LORD said to Cain, "Why are you angry, and why has your countenance fallen? 7 If you do well, will you not be accepted? And if you do not do well, sin is lurking at the door; its desire is for you, but you must master it."

8 Cain said to his brother Abel, "Let us go out to the field."[o] And when they were in the field, Cain rose up against his brother Abel, and killed him. 9 Then

the LORD said to Cain, "Where is your brother Abel?" He said, "I do not know; am I my brother's keeper?" 10 And the LORD said, "What have you done? Listen; your brother's blood is crying out to me from the ground! 11 And now you are cursed from the ground, which has opened its mouth to receive your brother's blood from your hand. 12 When you till the ground, it will no longer yield to you its strength; you will be a fugitive and a wanderer on the earth." 13 Cain said to the LORD, "My punishment is greater than I can bear! 14 Today you have driven me away from the soil, and I shall be hidden from your face; I shall be a fugitive and a wanderer on the earth, and anyone who meets me may kill me." 15 Then the LORD said to him, "Not so![p] Whoever kills Cain will suffer a sevenfold vengeance." And the LORD put a mark on Cain, so that no one who came upon him would kill him. 16 Then Cain went away from the presence of the LORD, and settled in the land of Nod,[q] east of Eden.

Beginnings of Civilization

17 Cain knew his wife, and she conceived and bore Enoch; and he built a city, and named it Enoch after his son Enoch. 18 To Enoch was born Irad; and Irad was the father of Mehujael, and Mehujael the father of Methushael, and Methushael the father of Lamech. 19 Lamech took two wives; the name of the one was Adah, and the name of the other Zillah. 20 Adah bore Jabal; he was the ancestor of those who live in tents and have livestock. 21 His brother's name was Jubal; he was the ancestor of all those who play the lyre and pipe. 22 Zillah bore Tubal-cain, who made all kinds of bronze and iron tools. The sister of Tubal-cain was Naamah.

23 Lamech said to his wives:
"Adah and Zillah, hear my voice;
you wives of Lamech, listen to
what I say:
I have killed a man for wounding
me,
a young man for striking me.
24 If Cain is avenged sevenfold,

---

l In Heb *Eve* resembles the word for *living*   *m* Or *for Adam*   *n* The verb in Heb resembles the word for *Cain*   *o* Sam Gk Syr Compare Vg: MT lacks *Let us go out to the field*   *p* Gk Syr Vg: Heb *Therefore*   *q* That is *Wandering*

truly Lamech seventy-sevenfold."

25 Adam knew his wife again, and she bore a son and named him Seth, for she said, "God has appointed[r] for me another child instead of Abel, because Cain killed him." 26To Seth also a son was born, and he named him Enosh. At that time people began to invoke the name of the LORD.

Adam's Descendants to Noah and His Sons

5 This is the list of the descendants of Adam. When God created humankind,[s] he made them[t] in the likeness of God. 2Male and female he created them, and he blessed them and named them "Humankind"[s] when they were created.

3 When Adam had lived one hundred thirty years, he became the father of a son in his likeness, according to his image, and named him Seth. 4The days of Adam after he became the father of Seth were eight hundred years; and he had other sons and daughters. 5Thus all the days that Adam lived were nine hundred thirty years; and he died.

6 When Seth had lived one hundred five years, he became the father of Enosh. 7Seth lived after the birth of Enosh eight hundred seven years, and had other sons and daughters. 8Thus all the days of Seth were nine hundred twelve years; and he died.

9 When Enosh had lived ninety years, he became the father of Kenan. 10Enosh lived after the birth of Kenan eight hundred fifteen years, and had other sons and daughters. 11Thus all the days of Enosh were nine hundred five years; and he died.

12 When Kenan had lived seventy years, he became the father of Mahalalel. 13Kenan lived after the birth of Mahalalel eight hundred and forty years, and had other sons and daughters. 14Thus all the days of Kenan were nine hundred and ten years; and he died.

15 When Mahalalel had lived sixty-five years, he became the father of Jared. 16Mahalalel lived after the birth of Jared eight hundred thirty years, and had other sons and daughters. 17Thus all the days of Mahalalel were eight hundred ninety-five years; and he died.

18 When Jared had lived one hundred sixty-two years he became the father of Enoch. 19Jared lived after the birth of Enoch eight hundred years, and had other sons and daughters. 20Thus all the days of Jared were nine hundred sixty-two years; and he died.

21 When Enoch had lived sixty-five years, he became the father of Methuselah. 22Enoch walked with God after the birth of Methuselah three hundred years, and had other sons and daughters. 23Thus all the days of Enoch were three hundred sixty-five years. 24Enoch walked with God; then he was no more, because God took him.

25 When Methuselah had lived one hundred eighty-seven years, he became the father of Lamech. 26Methuselah lived after the birth of Lamech seven hundred eighty-two years, and had other sons and daughters. 27Thus all the days of Methuselah were nine hundred sixty-nine years; and he died.

28 When Lamech had lived one hundred eighty-two years, he became the father of a son; 29he named him Noah, saying, "Out of the ground that the LORD has cursed this one shall bring us relief from our work and from the toil of our hands." 30Lamech lived after the birth of Noah five hundred ninety-five years, and had other sons and daughters. 31Thus all the days of Lamech were seven hundred seventy-seven years; and he died.

32 After Noah was five hundred years old, Noah became the father of Shem, Ham, and Japheth.

The Wickedness of Humankind

6 When people began to multiply on the face of the ground, and daughters were born to them, 2the sons of God saw that they were fair; and they took wives for themselves of all that they chose. 3Then the LORD said, "My spirit shall not abide[u] in mortals forever, for they are flesh; their days shall be one hundred twenty years." 4The Nephilim were on the earth in those days—and also afterward—when the sons of God

---

r The verb in Heb resembles the word for *Seth*   s Heb *adam*   t Heb *him*   u Meaning of Heb uncertain

went in to the daughters of humans, who bore children to them. These were the heroes that were of old, warriors of renown.

5 The LORD saw that the wickedness of humankind was great in the earth, and that every inclination of the thoughts of their hearts was only evil continually. 6And the LORD was sorry that he had made humankind on the earth, and it grieved him to his heart. 7So the LORD said, "I will blot out from the earth the human beings I have created—people together with animals and creeping things and birds of the air, for I am sorry that I have made them." 8But Noah found favor in the sight of the LORD.

Noah Pleases God

9 These are the descendants of Noah. Noah was a righteous man, blameless in his generation; Noah walked with God. 10And Noah had three sons, Shem, Ham, and Japheth.

11 Now the earth was corrupt in God's sight, and the earth was filled with violence. 12And God saw that the earth was corrupt; for all flesh had corrupted its ways upon the earth. 13And God said to Noah, "I have determined to make an end of all flesh, for the earth is filled with violence because of them; now I am going to destroy them along with the earth. 14Make yourself an ark of cypressv wood; make rooms in the ark, and cover it inside and out with pitch. 15This is how you are to make it: the length of the ark three hundred cubits, its width fifty cubits, and its height thirty cubits. 16Make a roofw for the ark, and finish it to a cubit above; and put the door of the ark in its side; make it with lower, second, and third decks. 17For my part, I am going to bring a flood of waters on the earth, to destroy from under heaven all flesh in which is the breath of life; everything that is on the earth shall die. 18But I will establish my covenant with you; and you shall come into the ark, you, your sons, your wife, and your sons' wives with you. 19And of every living thing, of all flesh, you shall bring two of every kind into the ark, to keep them alive with you; they shall be male and female. 20Of the birds according to their kinds, and of the animals according to their kinds, of every creeping thing of the ground according to its kind, two of every kind shall come in to you, to keep them alive. 21Also take with you every kind of food that is eaten, and store it up; and it shall serve as food for you and for them." 22Noah did this; he did all that God commanded him.

The Great Flood

7 Then the LORD said to Noah, "Go into the ark, you and all your household, for I have seen that you alone are righteous before me in this generation. 2Take with you seven pairs of all clean animals, the male and its mate; and a pair of the animals that are not clean, the male and its mate; 3and seven pairs of the birds of the air also, male and female, to keep their kind alive on the face of all the earth. 4For in seven days I will send rain on the earth for forty days and forty nights; and every living thing that I have made I will blot out from the face of the ground." 5And Noah did all that the LORD had commanded him.

6 Noah was six hundred years old when the flood of waters came on the earth. 7And Noah with his sons and his wife and his sons' wives went into the ark to escape the waters of the flood. 8Of clean animals, and of animals that are not clean, and of birds, and of everything that creeps on the ground, 9two and two, male and female, went into the ark with Noah, as God had commanded Noah. 10And after seven days the waters of the flood came on the earth.

11 In the six hundredth year of Noah's life, in the second month, on the seventeenth day of the month, on that day all the fountains of the great deep burst forth, and the windows of the heavens were opened. 12The rain fell on the earth forty days and forty nights. 13On the very same day Noah with his sons, Shem and Ham and Japheth, and Noah's wife and the three wives of his sons entered the ark, 14they and every wild animal of every kind, and all domestic animals of every kind, and every creeping thing that creeps on the

---

v Meaning of Heb uncertain   w Or window

earth, and every bird of every kind—every bird, every winged creature. 15They went into the ark with Noah, two and two of all flesh in which there was the breath of life. 16And those that entered, male and female of all flesh, went in as God had commanded him; and the LORD shut him in.

17 The flood continued forty days on the earth; and the waters increased, and bore up the ark, and it rose high above the earth. 18The waters swelled and increased greatly on the earth; and the ark floated on the face of the waters. 19The waters swelled so mightily on the earth that all the high mountains under the whole heaven were covered; 20the waters swelled above the mountains, covering them fifteen cubits deep. 21And all flesh died that moved on the earth, birds, domestic animals, wild animals, all swarming creatures that swarm on the earth, and all human beings; 22everything on dry land in whose nostrils was the breath of life died. 23He blotted out every living thing that was on the face of the ground, human beings and animals and creeping things and birds of the air; they were blotted out from the earth. Only Noah was left, and those that were with him in the ark. 24And the waters swelled on the earth for one hundred fifty days.

The Flood Subsides

8 But God remembered Noah and all the wild animals and all the domestic animals that were with him in the ark. And God made a wind blow over the earth, and the waters subsided; 2the fountains of the deep and the windows of the heavens were closed, the rain from the heavens was restrained, 3and the waters gradually receded from the earth. At the end of one hundred fifty days the waters had abated; 4and in the seventh month, on the seventeenth day of the month, the ark came to rest on the mountains of Ararat. 5The waters continued to abate until the tenth month; in the tenth month, on the first day of the month, the tops of the mountains appeared.

6 At the end of forty days Noah opened the window of the ark that he had made 7and sent out the raven; and it went to and fro until the waters were dried up from the earth. 8Then he sent out the dove from him, to see if the waters had subsided from the face of the ground; 9but the dove found no place to set its foot, and it returned to him to the ark, for the waters were still on the face of the whole earth. So he put out his hand and took it and brought it into the ark with him. 10He waited another seven days, and again he sent out the dove from the ark; 11and the dove came back to him in the evening, and there in its beak was a freshly plucked olive leaf; so Noah knew that the waters had subsided from the earth. 12Then he waited another seven days, and sent out the dove; and it did not return to him any more.

13 In the six hundred first year, in the first month, on the first day of the month, the waters were dried up from the earth; and Noah removed the covering of the ark, and looked, and saw that the face of the ground was drying. 14In the second month, on the twenty-seventh day of the month, the earth was dry. 15Then God said to Noah, 16"Go out of the ark, you and your wife, and your sons and your sons' wives with you. 17Bring out with you every living thing that is with you of all flesh—birds and animals and every creeping thing that creeps on the earth—so that they may abound on the earth, and be fruitful and multiply on the earth." 18So Noah went out with his sons and his wife and his sons' wives. 19And every animal, every creeping thing, and every bird, everything that moves on the earth, went out of the ark by families.

God's Promise to Noah

20 Then Noah built an altar to the LORD, and took of every clean animal and of every clean bird, and offered burnt offerings on the altar. 21And when the LORD smelled the pleasing odor, the LORD said in his heart, "I will never again curse the ground because of humankind, for the inclination of the human heart is evil from youth; nor will I ever again destroy every living creature as I have done.

22   As long as the earth endures,
     seedtime and harvest, cold and
      heat,

THE GLORY OF THE RAINBOW
Charles Haddon Spurgeon

VERSE: Genesis 9.13   **PASSAGE:** Genesis 9.12–17

ooking from the little wooden bridge which passes over the brow of the beautiful waterfall of Handeck, on a bright day one will see a circular rainbow surrounding the fall like a coronet of gems. Every hue is there from the red to where the violet fades into the sky.

This fair vision reminded me of the mystic rainbow which the seer of Patmos beheld around the throne (see Revelation 4.3). It was seen by John as a *complete circle;* we see but half on earth. The upper arch of manifest glory we rejoice to gaze upon, but the lower and foundational arch of the eternal purpose, upon which the visible display of grace is founded, is reserved for our contemplation in another world.

I compared the little stream to the church of God, which in peaceful times flows on like a village brook, quiet and obscure, blessed and blessing others, but yet little known or considered by the sons of men. But when the church advances over the steeps of opposition and is dashed down the crags of persecution, then her glory is revealed. Then it is that the eternal God glorifies her with the rainbow of his everlasting grace, makes the beauty of her holiness to shine forth, and reveals a heavenly radiance, which all behold with astonishment.

The majestic rainbow of the divine presence encircles the chosen people when tribulation, affliction, and distress break them, as the stream is broken by the precipitous rocks on which it boldly casts itself, that its current may advance in its predestined channel. When forebodings foretell the coming of evil times for the church, remember that before the Spirit revealed to the beloved disciple the terrible beasts, the thundering trumpets, the falling stars, and the dreadful vials, he bade him mark with attention that the covenant rainbow was round about the throne. All is well, for God is true.

ADDITIONAL SCRIPTURE READING:
Ezekiel 1.28; Revelation 4.2–3; 10.1

Go to page 15 for your next devotional reading.

1700   1900

summer and winter, day and night, shall not cease."

The Covenant with Noah

9 God blessed Noah and his sons, and said to them, "Be fruitful and multiply, and fill the earth. 2The fear and dread of you shall rest on every animal of the earth, and on every bird of the air, on everything that creeps on the ground, and on all the fish of the sea; into your hand they are delivered. 3Every moving thing that lives shall be food for you; and just as I gave you the green plants, I give you everything. 4Only, you shall not eat flesh with its life, that is, its blood. 5For your own lifeblood I will surely require a reckoning: from every animal I will require it and from human beings, each one for the blood of another, I will require a reckoning for human life.

6   Whoever sheds the blood of a
          human,
     by a human shall that person's
          blood be shed;
     for in his own image
     God made humankind.

7And you, be fruitful and multiply, abound on the earth and multiply in it."

8 Then God said to Noah and to his sons with him, 9"As for me, I am establishing my covenant with you and your descendants after you, 10and with every living creature that is with you, the birds, the domestic animals, and every animal of the earth with you, as many as came out of the ark.x 11I establish my covenant with you, that never again shall all flesh be cut off by the waters of a flood, and never again shall there be a flood to destroy the earth." 12God said, "This is the sign of the covenant that I make between me and you and every living creature that is with you, for all future generations: 13I have set my bow in the clouds, and it shall be a sign of the covenant between me and the earth. 14When I bring clouds over the earth and the bow is seen in the clouds, 15I will remember my covenant that is between me and you and every living creature of all flesh; and the waters shall never again become a flood to destroy all flesh. 16When the bow is in the clouds, I will see it and remember the everlasting covenant between God and every living creature of all flesh that is on the earth." 17God said to Noah, "This is the sign of the covenant that I have established between me and all flesh that is on the earth."

Noah and His Sons

18 The sons of Noah who went out of the ark were Shem, Ham, and Japheth. Ham was the father of Canaan. 19These three were the sons of Noah; and from these the whole earth was peopled.

20 Noah, a man of the soil, was the first to plant a vineyard. 21He drank some of the wine and became drunk, and he lay uncovered in his tent. 22And Ham, the father of Canaan, saw the nakedness of his father, and told his two brothers outside. 23Then Shem and Japheth took a garment, laid it on both their shoulders, and walked backward and covered the nakedness of their father; their faces were turned away, and they did not see their father's nakedness. 24When Noah awoke from his wine and knew what his youngest son had done to him, 25he said,

     "Cursed be Canaan;
          lowest of slaves shall he be to his
               brothers."

26He also said,

     "Blessed by the LORD my God be
          Shem;
     and let Canaan be his slave.
27   May God make space fory Japheth,
          and let him live in the tents of
               Shem;
     and let Canaan be his slave."

28 After the flood Noah lived three hundred fifty years. 29All the days of Noah were nine hundred fifty years; and he died.

Nations Descended from Noah

10 These are the descendants of Noah's sons, Shem, Ham, and Japheth; children were born to them after the flood.

2 The descendants of Japheth: Gomer, Magog, Madai, Javan, Tubal, Meshech, and Tiras. 3The descendants of Gomer: Ashkenaz, Riphath, and Togarmah. 4The descendants of Javan: Elishah, Tarshish,

---

x Gk: Heb adds *every animal of the earth*   y Heb *yapht*, a play on *Japheth*

Kittim, and Rodanim.^{z} ^{5}From these the coastland peoples spread. These are the descendants of Japheth^a in their lands, with their own language, by their families, in their nations.

6 The descendants of Ham: Cush, Egypt, Put, and Canaan. ^{7}The descendants of Cush: Seba, Havilah, Sabtah, Raamah, and Sabteca. The descendants of Raamah: Sheba and Dedan. ^{8}Cush became the father of Nimrod; he was the first on earth to become a mighty warrior. ^{9}He was a mighty hunter before the LORD; therefore it is said, "Like Nimrod a mighty hunter before the LORD." ^{10}The beginning of his kingdom was Babel, Erech, and Accad, all of them in the land of Shinar. ^{11}From that land he went into Assyria, and built Nineveh, Rehoboth-ir, Calah, and ^{12}Resen between Nineveh and Calah; that is the great city. ^{13}Egypt became the father of Ludim, Anamim, Lehabim, Naphtuhim, ^{14}Pathrusim, Casluhim, and Caphtorim, from which the Philistines come.^{b}

15 Canaan became the father of Sidon his firstborn, and Heth, ^{16}and the Jebusites, the Amorites, the Girgashites, ^{17}the Hivites, the Arkites, the Sinites, ^{18}the Arvadites, the Zemarites, and the Hamathites. Afterward the families of the Canaanites spread abroad. ^{19}And the territory of the Canaanites extended from Sidon, in the direction of Gerar, as far as Gaza, and in the direction of Sodom, Gomorrah, Admah, and Zeboiim, as far as Lasha. ^{20}These are the descendants of Ham, by their families, their languages, their lands, and their nations.

21 To Shem also, the father of all the children of Eber, the elder brother of Japheth, children were born. ^{22}The descendants of Shem: Elam, Asshur, Arpachshad, Lud, and Aram. ^{23}The descendants of Aram: Uz, Hul, Gether, and Mash. ^{24}Arpachshad became the father of Shelah; and Shelah became the father of Eber. ^{25}To Eber were born two sons: the name of the one was Peleg,^{c} for in his days the earth was divided, and his brother's name was Joktan. ^{26}Joktan became the father of Almodad, Sheleph,

Hazarmaveth, Jerah, ^{27}Hadoram, Uzal, Diklah, ^{28}Obal, Abimael, Sheba, ^{29}Ophir, Havilah, and Jobab; all these were the descendants of Joktan. ^{30}The territory in which they lived extended from Mesha in the direction of Sephar, the hill country of the east. ^{31}These are the descendants of Shem, by their families, their languages, their lands, and their nations.

32 These are the families of Noah's sons, according to their genealogies, in their nations; and from these the nations spread abroad on the earth after the flood.

The Tower of Babel

11 Now the whole earth had one language and the same words. ^{2}And as they migrated from the east,^{d} they came upon a plain in the land of Shinar and settled there. ^{3}And they said to one another, "Come, let us make bricks, and burn them thoroughly." And they had brick for stone, and bitumen for mortar. ^{4}Then they said, "Come, let us build ourselves a city, and a tower with its top in the heavens, and let us make a name for ourselves; otherwise we shall be scattered abroad upon the face of the whole earth." ^{5}The LORD came down to see the city and the tower, which mortals had built. ^{6}And the LORD said, "Look, they are one people, and they have all one language; and this is only the beginning of what they will do; nothing that they propose to do will now be impossible for them. ^{7}Come, let us go down, and confuse their language there, so that they will not understand one another's speech." ^{8}So the LORD scattered them abroad from there over the face of all the earth, and they left off building the city. ^{9}Therefore it was called Babel, because there the LORD confused^e the language of all the earth; and from there the LORD scattered them abroad over the face of all the earth.

Descendants of Shem

10 These are the descendants of Shem. When Shem was one hundred years old, he became the father of Arpachshad two

---

z Heb Mss Sam Gk See 1 Chr 1.7: MT *Dodanim* a Compare verses 20, 31. Heb lacks *These are the descendants of Japheth* b Cn: Heb *Casluhim, from which the Philistines come, and Caphtorim* c That is *Division* d Or *migrated eastward* e Heb *balal*, meaning *to confuse*

years after the flood; [11]and Shem lived after the birth of Arpachshad five hundred years, and had other sons and daughters.

12 When Arpachshad had lived thirty-five years, he became the father of Shelah; [13]and Arpachshad lived after the birth of Shelah four hundred three years, and had other sons and daughters.

14 When Shelah had lived thirty years, he became the father of Eber; [15]and Shelah lived after the birth of Eber four hundred three years, and had other sons and daughters.

16 When Eber had lived thirty-four years, he became the father of Peleg; [17]and Eber lived after the birth of Peleg four hundred thirty years, and had other sons and daughters.

18 When Peleg had lived thirty years, he became the father of Reu; [19]and Peleg lived after the birth of Reu two hundred nine years, and had other sons and daughters.

20 When Reu had lived thirty-two years, he became the father of Serug; [21]and Reu lived after the birth of Serug two hundred seven years, and had other sons and daughters.

22 When Serug had lived thirty years, he became the father of Nahor; [23]and Serug lived after the birth of Nahor two hundred years, and had other sons and daughters.

24 When Nahor had lived twenty-nine years, he became the father of Terah; [25]and Nahor lived after the birth of Terah one hundred nineteen years, and had other sons and daughters.

26 When Terah had lived seventy years, he became the father of Abram, Nahor, and Haran.

Descendants of Terah

27 Now these are the descendants of Terah. Terah was the father of Abram, Nahor, and Haran; and Haran was the father of Lot. [28]Haran died before his father Terah in the land of his birth, in Ur of the Chaldeans. [29]Abram and Nahor took wives; the name of Abram's wife was Sarai, and the name of Nahor's wife was Milcah. She was the daughter of Haran the father of Milcah and Iscah.

[30]Now Sarai was barren; she had no child.

31 Terah took his son Abram and his grandson Lot son of Haran, and his daughter-in-law Sarai, his son Abram's wife, and they went out together from Ur of the Chaldeans to go into the land of Canaan; but when they came to Haran, they settled there. [32]The days of Terah were two hundred five years; and Terah died in Haran.

The Call of Abram

12 Now the LORD said to Abram, "Go from your country and your kindred and your father's house to the land that I will show you. [2]I will make of you a great nation, and I will bless you, and make your name great, so that you will be a blessing. [3]I will bless those who bless you, and the one who curses you I will curse; and in you all the families of the earth shall be blessed."[f]

4 So Abram went, as the LORD had told him; and Lot went with him. Abram was seventy-five years old when he departed from Haran. [5]Abram took his wife Sarai and his brother's son Lot, and all the possessions that they had gathered, and the persons whom they had acquired in Haran; and they set forth to go to the land of Canaan. When they had come to the land of Canaan, [6]Abram passed through the land to the place at Shechem, to the oaks[g] of Moreh. At that time the Canaanites were in the land. [7]Then the LORD appeared to Abram, and said, "To your offspring[h] I will give this land." So he built there an altar to the LORD, who had appeared to him. [8]From there he moved on to the hill country on the east of Bethel, and pitched his tent, with Bethel on the west and Ai on the east; and there he built an altar to the LORD and invoked the name of the LORD. [9]And Abram journeyed on by stages toward the Negeb.

Abram and Sarai in Egypt

10 Now there was a famine in the land. So Abram went down to Egypt to reside there as an alien, for the famine was severe in the land. [11]When he was about to enter Egypt, he said to his wife Sarai, "I know well that you are a

f Or by you all the families of the earth shall bless themselves   g Or terebinth   h Heb seed

woman beautiful in appearance; ¹²and when the Egyptians see you, they will say, 'This is his wife'; then they will kill me, but they will let you live. ¹³Say you are my sister, so that it may go well with me because of you, and that my life may be spared on your account." ¹⁴When Abram entered Egypt the Egyptians saw that the woman was very beautiful. ¹⁵When the officials of Pharaoh saw her, they praised her to Pharaoh. And the woman was taken into Pharaoh's house. ¹⁶And for her sake he dealt well with Abram; and he had sheep, oxen, male

FRIDAY

WORSHIP
Oswald Chambers

VERSE: Genesis 12.8   PASSAGE: Genesis 12.1–9

 orship is giving God the best that he has given you. Be careful what you do with the best you have. Whenever you get a blessing from God, give it back to him as a love gift. Take time to meditate before God and offer the blessing back to him in a deliberate act of worship. If you hoard it for yourself, it will turn into spiritual dry rot, as the manna did when it was hoarded (see Exodus 16.20). God will never allow you to keep a spiritual blessing completely for yourself. It must be given back to him so that he can make it a blessing to others.

Bethel is the symbol of fellowship with God; Ai is the symbol of the world. Abram "pitched his tent" between the two. The lasting value of our public service for God is measured by the depth of the intimacy of our private times of fellowship and oneness with him. Rushing in and out of worship is wrong every time—there is always plenty of time to worship God. Days set apart for quiet can be a trap, detracting from the need to have daily quiet time with God. That is why we must "pitch our tents" where we will always have quiet times with him, however noisy our times with the world may be. There are not three levels of spiritual life—worship, waiting, and work. Yet some of us seem to jump like spiritual frogs from worship to waiting, and from waiting to work. God's idea is that the three should go together as one. They were always together in the life of our Lord and in perfect harmony. It is a discipline that must be developed; it will not happen overnight.

ADDITIONAL SCRIPTURE READING:
Genesis 8.20; 13.4, 18; 26.25; Hebrews 12.28

Go to page 17 for your next devotional reading.

1900   Present

donkeys, male and female slaves, female donkeys, and camels.

17 But the LORD afflicted Pharaoh and his house with great plagues because of Sarai, Abram's wife. 18So Pharaoh called Abram, and said, "What is this you have done to me? Why did you not tell me that she was your wife? 19Why did you say, 'She is my sister,' so that I took her for my wife? Now then, here is your wife, take her, and be gone." 20And Pharaoh gave his men orders concerning him; and they set him on the way, with his wife and all that he had.

Abram and Lot Separate

13 So Abram went up from Egypt, he and his wife, and all that he had, and Lot with him, into the Negeb.

2 Now Abram was very rich in livestock, in silver, and in gold. 3He journeyed on by stages from the Negeb as far as Bethel, to the place where his tent had been at the beginning, between Bethel and Ai, 4to the place where he had made an altar at the first; and there Abram called on the name of the LORD. 5Now Lot, who went with Abram, also had flocks and herds and tents, 6so that the land could not support both of them living together; for their possessions were so great that they could not live together, 7and there was strife between the herders of Abram's livestock and the herders of Lot's livestock. At that time the Canaanites and the Perizzites lived in the land.

8 Then Abram said to Lot, "Let there be no strife between you and me, and between your herders and my herders; for we are kindred. 9Is not the whole land before you? Separate yourself from me. If you take the left hand, then I will go to the right; or if you take the right hand, then I will go to the left." 10Lot looked about him, and saw that the plain of the Jordan was well watered everywhere like the garden of the LORD, like the land of Egypt, in the direction of Zoar; this was before the LORD had destroyed Sodom and Gomorrah. 11So Lot chose for himself all the plain of the Jordan, and Lot journeyed eastward; thus they separated from each other. 12Abram settled in the land of Canaan, while Lot settled among the cities of the Plain and moved his tent as far as Sodom. 13Now the people of Sodom were wicked, great sinners against the LORD.

14 The LORD said to Abram, after Lot had separated from him, "Raise your eyes now, and look from the place where you are, northward and southward and eastward and westward; 15for all the land that you see I will give to you and to your offspring[i] forever. 16I will make your offspring like the dust of the earth; so that if one can count the dust of the earth, your offspring also can be counted. 17Rise up, walk through the length and the breadth of the land, for I will give it to you." 18So Abram moved his tent, and came and settled by the oaks[j] of Mamre, which are at Hebron; and there he built an altar to the LORD.

Lot's Captivity and Rescue

14 In the days of King Amraphel of Shinar, King Arioch of Ellasar, King Chedorlaomer of Elam, and King Tidal of Goiim, 2these kings made war with King Bera of Sodom, King Birsha of Gomorrah, King Shinab of Admah, King Shemeber of Zeboiim, and the king of Bela (that is, Zoar). 3All these joined forces in the Valley of Siddim (that is, the Dead Sea).[k] 4Twelve years they had served Chedorlaomer, but in the thirteenth year they rebelled. 5In the fourteenth year Chedorlaomer and the kings who were with him came and subdued the Rephaim in Ashteroth-karnaim, the Zuzim in Ham, the Emim in Shaveh-kiriathaim, 6and the Horites in the hill country of Seir as far as El-paran on the edge of the wilderness; 7then they turned back and came to En-mishpat (that is, Kadesh), and subdued all the country of the Amalekites, and also the Amorites who lived in Hazazon-tamar. 8Then the king of Sodom, the king of Gomorrah, the king of Admah, the king of Zeboiim, and the king of Bela (that is, Zoar) went out, and they joined battle in the Valley of Siddim 9with King Chedorlaomer of Elam, King Tidal of Goiim, King Amraphel of Shinar, and King Arioch of Ellasar, four kings against five. 10Now the Valley of Siddim was full of

i Heb seed   j Or terebinths   k Heb Salt Sea

WEEKEND

THE GOOD OR THE BEST?
Oswald Chambers

VERSE: Genesis 13.9   **PASSAGE:** Genesis 13.8–18

s soon as you begin to live the life of faith in God, fascinating and physically gratifying possibilities will open up before you. These things are yours by right, but if you are living the life of faith you will exercise your right to waive your rights, and let God make your choice for you. God sometimes allows you to get into a place of testing where your own welfare would be the appropriate thing to consider, if you were not living the life of faith. But if you are, you will joyfully waive your right and allow God to make your choice for you. This is the discipline God uses to transform the natural into the spiritual through obedience to his voice.

Whenever our *right* becomes the guiding factor of our lives, it dulls our spiritual insight. The greatest enemy of the life of faith in God is not sin, but good choices which are not quite good enough. The good is always the enemy of the best. In this passage, it would seem that the wisest thing in the world for Abram to do would be to choose. It was his right, and the people around him would consider him to be a fool for not choosing.

Many of us do not continue to grow spiritually because we prefer to choose on the basis of our rights, instead of relying on God to make the choice for us. We have to learn to walk according to the standard which has its eyes focused on God. And God says to us, as he did to Abram, "... *walk before me* ..." (Genesis 17.1).

ADDITIONAL SCRIPTURE READING:
Genesis 6.9; 17.1; 2 Kings 20.2–3

Go to page 25 for your next devotional reading.

1900   Present

bitumen pits; and as the kings of Sodom and Gomorrah fled, some fell into them, and the rest fled to the hill country. [11]So the enemy took all the goods of Sodom and Gomorrah, and all their provisions, and went their way; [12]they also took Lot, the son of Abram's brother, who lived in Sodom, and his goods, and departed.

13 Then one who had escaped came and told Abram the Hebrew, who was living by the oaks[1] of Mamre the Amorite, brother of Eshcol and of Aner; these were allies of Abram. [14]When Abram heard that his nephew had been taken captive, he led forth his trained men, born in his house, three hundred eighteen of them, and went in pursuit as far as Dan. [15]He divided his forces against them by night, he and his servants, and routed them and pursued them to Hobah, north of Damascus. [16]Then he brought back all the goods, and also brought back his nephew Lot with his goods, and the women and the people.

Abram Blessed by Melchizedek

17 After his return from the defeat of Chedorlaomer and the kings who were with him, the king of Sodom went out to meet him at the Valley of Shaveh (that is, the King's Valley). [18]And King Melchizedek of Salem brought out bread and wine; he was priest of God Most High.[m] [19]He blessed him and said,
"Blessed be Abram by God Most
        High,[m]
    maker of heaven and earth;
20   and blessed be God Most High,[m]
    who has delivered your enemies
        into your hand!"
And Abram gave him one-tenth of everything. [21]Then the king of Sodom said to Abram, "Give me the persons, but take the goods for yourself." [22]But Abram said to the king of Sodom, "I have sworn to the LORD, God Most High,[m] maker of heaven and earth, [23]that I would not take a thread or a sandal-thong or anything that is yours, so that you might not say, 'I have made Abram rich.' [24]I will take nothing but what the young men have eaten, and the share of the men who went with me—Aner, Eshcol, and Mamre. Let them take their share."

God's Covenant with Abram

15 After these things the word of the LORD came to Abram in a vision, "Do not be afraid, Abram, I am your shield; your reward shall be very great." [2]But Abram said, "O Lord GOD, what will you give me, for I continue childless, and the heir of my house is Eliezer of Damascus?"[n] [3]And Abram said, "You have given me no offspring, and so a slave born in my house is to be my heir." [4]But the word of the LORD came to him, "This man shall not be your heir; no one but your very own issue shall be your heir." [5]He brought him outside and said, "Look toward heaven and count the stars, if you are able to count them." Then he said to him, "So shall your descendants be." [6]And he believed the LORD; and the LORD[o] reckoned it to him as righteousness.

7 Then he said to him, "I am the LORD who brought you from Ur of the Chaldeans, to give you this land to possess." [8]But he said, "O Lord GOD, how am I to know that I shall possess it?" [9]He said to him, "Bring me a heifer three years old, a female goat three years old, a ram three years old, a turtledove, and a young pigeon." [10]He brought him all these and cut them in two, laying each half over against the other; but he did not cut the birds in two. [11]And when birds of prey came down on the carcasses, Abram drove them away.

12 As the sun was going down, a deep sleep fell upon Abram, and a deep and terrifying darkness descended upon him. [13]Then the LORD[o] said to Abram, "Know this for certain, that your offspring shall be aliens in a land that is not theirs, and shall be slaves there, and they shall be oppressed for four hundred years; [14]but I will bring judgment on the nation that they serve, and afterward they shall come out with great possessions. [15]As for yourself, you shall go to your ancestors in peace; you shall be buried in a good old age. [16]And they shall come back here in the fourth generation; for the iniquity of the Amorites is not yet complete."

17 When the sun had gone down and it was dark, a smoking fire pot and a

---

l Or *terebinths*   *m* Heb *El Elyon*   *n* Meaning of Heb uncertain   *o* Heb *he* flaming torch passed between these pieces. [18]On that day the LORD made a covenant with Abram, saying, "To your descendants I give this land, from the river of Egypt to the great river, the river Euphrates, [19]the land of the Kenites, the Kenizzites, the Kadmonites, [20]the Hittites, the Perizzites, the Rephaim, [21]the Amorites, the Canaanites, the Girgashites, and the Jebusites."

The Birth of Ishmael

16 Now Sarai, Abram's wife, bore him no children. She had an Egyptian slave-girl whose name was Hagar, [2]and Sarai said to Abram, "You see that the LORD has prevented me from bearing children; go in to my slave-girl; it may be that I shall obtain children by her." And Abram listened to the voice of Sarai. [3]So, after Abram had lived ten years in the land of Canaan, Sarai, Abram's wife, took Hagar the Egyptian, her slave-girl, and gave her to her husband Abram as a wife. [4]He went in to Hagar, and she conceived; and when she saw that she had conceived, she looked with contempt on her mistress. [5]Then Sarai said to Abram, "May the wrong done to me be on you! I gave my slave-girl to your embrace, and when she saw that she had conceived, she looked on me with contempt. May the LORD judge between you and me!" [6]But Abram said to Sarai, "Your slave-girl is in your power; do to her as you please." Then Sarai dealt harshly with her, and she ran away from her.

7 The angel of the LORD found her by a spring of water in the wilderness, the spring on the way to Shur. [8]And he said, "Hagar, slave-girl of Sarai, where have you come from and where are you going?" She said, "I am running away from my mistress Sarai." [9]The angel of the LORD said to her, "Return to your mistress, and submit to her." [10]The angel of the LORD also said to her, "I will so greatly multiply your offspring that they cannot be counted for multitude." [11]And the angel of the LORD said to her, "Now you have conceived and shall bear a son;

you shall call him Ishmael,[p] for the LORD has given heed to your affliction.
12   He shall be a wild ass of a man, with his hand against everyone, and everyone's hand against him; and he shall live at odds with all his kin."

[13]So she named the LORD who spoke to her, "You are El-roi";[q] for she said, "Have I really seen God and remained alive after seeing him?"[r] [14]Therefore the well was called Beer-lahai-roi;[s] it lies between Kadesh and Bered.

15 Hagar bore Abram a son; and Abram named his son, whom Hagar bore, Ishmael. [16]Abram was eighty-six years old when Hagar bore him[t] Ishmael.

The Sign of the Covenant

17 When Abram was ninety-nine years old, the LORD appeared to Abram, and said to him, "I am God Almighty;[u] walk before me, and be blameless. [2]And I will make my covenant between me and you, and will make you exceedingly numerous." [3]Then Abram fell on his face; and God said to him, [4]"As for me, this is my covenant with you: You shall be the ancestor of a multitude of nations. [5]No longer shall your name be Abram;[v] but your name shall be Abraham;[w] for I have made you the ancestor of a multitude of nations. [6]I will make you exceedingly fruitful; and I will make nations of you, and kings shall come from you. [7]I will establish my covenant between me and you, and your offspring after you throughout their generations, for an everlasting covenant, to be God to you and to your offspring[x] after you. [8]And I will give to you, and to your offspring after you, the land where you are now an alien, all the land of Canaan, for a perpetual holding; and I will be their God."

9 God said to Abraham, "As for you, you shall keep my covenant, you and your offspring after you throughout their generations. [10]This is my covenant, which you shall keep, between me and you and your offspring after you: Every male among you shall be circumcised.

p That is God hears   q Perhaps God of seeing or God who sees   r Meaning of Heb uncertain
s That is the Well of the Living One who sees me   t Heb Abram   u Traditional rendering of Heb El Shaddai   v That is exalted ancestor   w Here taken to mean ancestor of a multitude   x Heb seed

11You shall circumcise the flesh of your foreskins, and it shall be a sign of the covenant between me and you. 12Throughout your generations every male among you shall be circumcised when he is eight days old, including the slave born in your house and the one bought with your money from any foreigner who is not of your offspring. 13Both the slave born in your house and the one bought with your money must be circumcised. So shall my covenant be in your flesh an everlasting covenant. 14Any uncircumcised male who is not circumcised in the flesh of his foreskin shall be cut off from his people; he has broken my covenant."

15 God said to Abraham, "As for Sarai your wife, you shall not call her Sarai, but Sarah shall be her name. 16I will bless her, and moreover I will give you a son by her. I will bless her, and she shall give rise to nations; kings of peoples shall come from her." 17Then Abraham fell on his face and laughed, and said to himself, "Can a child be born to a man who is a hundred years old? Can Sarah, who is ninety years old, bear a child?" 18And Abraham said to God, "O that Ishmael might live in your sight!" 19God said, "No, but your wife Sarah shall bear you a son, and you shall name him Isaac.y I will establish my covenant with him as an everlasting covenant for his offspring after him. 20As for Ishmael, I have heard you; I will bless him and make him fruitful and exceedingly numerous; he shall be the father of twelve princes, and I will make him a great nation. 21But my covenant I will establish with Isaac, whom Sarah shall bear to you at this season next year." 22And when he had finished talking with him, God went up from Abraham.

23 Then Abraham took his son Ishmael and all the slaves born in his house or bought with his money, every male among the men of Abraham's house, and he circumcised the flesh of their foreskins that very day, as God had said to him. 24Abraham was ninety-nine years old when he was circumcised in the flesh of his foreskin. 25And his son Ishmael was thirteen years old when he was circumcised in the flesh of his fore-

skin. 26That very day Abraham and his son Ishmael were circumcised; 27and all the men of his house, slaves born in the house and those bought with money from a foreigner, were circumcised with him.

A Son Promised to Abraham and Sarah

18 The LORD appeared to Abrahamz by the oaksa of Mamre, as he sat at the entrance of his tent in the heat of the day. 2He looked up and saw three men standing near him. When he saw them, he ran from the tent entrance to meet them, and bowed down to the ground. 3He said, "My lord, if I find favor with you, do not pass by your servant. 4Let a little water be brought, and wash your feet, and rest yourselves under the tree. 5Let me bring a little bread, that you may refresh yourselves, and after that you may pass on—since you have come to your servant." So they said, "Do as you have said." 6And Abraham hastened into the tent to Sarah, and said, "Make ready quickly three measuresb of choice flour, knead it, and make cakes." 7Abraham ran to the herd, and took a calf, tender and good, and gave it to the servant, who hastened to prepare it. 8Then he took curds and milk and the calf that he had prepared, and set it before them; and he stood by them under the tree while they ate.

9 They said to him, "Where is your wife Sarah?" And he said, "There, in the tent." 10Then one said, "I will surely return to you in due season, and your wife Sarah shall have a son." And Sarah was listening at the tent entrance behind him. 11Now Abraham and Sarah were old, advanced in age; it had ceased to be with Sarah after the manner of women. 12So Sarah laughed to herself, saying, "After I have grown old, and my husband is old, shall I have pleasure?" 13The LORD said to Abraham, "Why did Sarah laugh, and say, 'Shall I indeed bear a child, now that I am old?' 14Is anything too wonderful for the LORD? At the set time I will return to you, in due season, and Sarah shall have a son." 15But Sarah denied, saying, "I did not laugh"; for she was afraid. He said, "Oh yes, you did laugh."

y That is he laughs   z Heb him   a Or terebinths   b Heb seahs

Judgment Pronounced on Sodom

16 Then the men set out from there, and they looked toward Sodom; and Abraham went with them to set them on their way. 17The LORD said, "Shall I hide from Abraham what I am about to do, 18seeing that Abraham shall become a great and mighty nation, and all the nations of the earth shall be blessed in him? c 19No, for I have chosen d him, that he may charge his children and his household after him to keep the way of the LORD by doing righteousness and justice; so that the LORD may bring about for Abraham what he has promised him." 20Then the LORD said, "How great is the outcry against Sodom and Gomorrah and how very grave their sin! 21I must go down and see whether they have done altogether according to the outcry that has come to me; and if not, I will know."

22 So the men turned from there, and went toward Sodom, while Abraham remained standing before the LORD.e 23Then Abraham came near and said, "Will you indeed sweep away the righteous with the wicked? 24Suppose there are fifty righteous within the city; will you then sweep away the place and not forgive it for the fifty righteous who are in it? 25Far be it from you to do such a thing, to slay the righteous with the wicked, so that the righteous fare as the wicked! Far be that from you! Shall not the Judge of all the earth do what is just?" 26And the LORD said, "If I find at Sodom fifty righteous in the city, I will forgive the whole place for their sake." 27Abraham answered, "Let me take it upon myself to speak to the Lord, I who am but dust and ashes. 28Suppose five of the fifty righteous are lacking? Will you destroy the whole city for lack of five?" And he said, "I will not destroy it if I find forty-five there." 29Again he spoke to him, "Suppose forty are found there." He answered, "For the sake of forty I will not do it." 30Then he said, "Oh do not let the Lord be angry if I speak. Suppose thirty are found there." He answered, "I will not do it, if I find thirty there." 31He said, "Let me take it upon myself to speak to the Lord. Suppose twenty are found there." He answered, "For the sake of twenty I will not destroy it." 32Then he said, "Oh do not let the Lord be angry if I speak just once more. Suppose ten are found there." He answered, "For the sake of ten I will not destroy it." 33And the LORD went his way, when he had finished speaking to Abraham; and Abraham returned to his place.

The Depravity of Sodom

19 The two angels came to Sodom in the evening, and Lot was sitting in the gateway of Sodom. When Lot saw them, he rose to meet them, and bowed down with his face to the ground. 2He said, "Please, my lords, turn aside to your servant's house and spend the night, and wash your feet; then you can rise early and go on your way." They said, "No; we will spend the night in the square." 3But he urged them strongly; so they turned aside to him and entered his house; and he made them a feast, and baked unleavened bread, and they ate. 4But before they lay down, the men of the city, the men of Sodom, both young and old, all the people to the last man, surrounded the house; 5and they called to Lot, "Where are the men who came to you tonight? Bring them out to us, so that we may know them." 6Lot went out of the door to the men, shut the door after him, 7and said, "I beg you, my brothers, do not act so wickedly. 8Look, I have two daughters who have not known a man; let me bring them out to you, and do to them as you please; only do nothing to these men, for they have come under the shelter of my roof." 9But they replied, "Stand back!" And they said, "This fellow came here as an alien, and he would play the judge! Now we will deal worse with you than with them." Then they pressed hard against the man Lot, and came near the door to break it down. 10But the men inside reached out their hands and brought Lot into the house with them, and shut the door. 11And they struck with blindness the men who were at the door of the house,

---

c Or and all the nations of the earth shall bless themselves by him   d Heb known   e Another ancient tradition reads while the LORD remained standing before Abraham

both small and great, so that they were unable to find the door.

Sodom and Gomorrah Destroyed

12 Then the men said to Lot, "Have you anyone else here? Sons-in-law, sons, daughters, or anyone you have in the city—bring them out of the place. 13For we are about to destroy this place, because the outcry against its people has become great before the LORD, and the LORD has sent us to destroy it." 14So Lot went out and said to his sons-in-law, who were to marry his daughters, "Up, get out of this place; for the LORD is about to destroy the city." But he seemed to his sons-in-law to be jesting.

15 When morning dawned, the angels urged Lot, saying, "Get up, take your wife and your two daughters who are here, or else you will be consumed in the punishment of the city." 16But he lingered; so the men seized him and his wife and his two daughters by the hand, the LORD being merciful to him, and they brought him out and left him outside the city. 17When they had brought them outside, they^f said, "Flee for your life; do not look back or stop anywhere in the Plain; flee to the hills, or else you will be consumed." 18And Lot said to them, "Oh, no, my lords; 19your servant has found favor with you, and you have shown me great kindness in saving my life; but I cannot flee to the hills, for fear the disaster will overtake me and I die. 20Look, that city is near enough to flee to, and it is a little one. Let me escape there—is it not a little one?—and my life will be saved!" 21He said to him, "Very well, I grant you this favor too, and will not overthrow the city of which you have spoken. 22Hurry, escape there, for I can do nothing until you arrive there." Therefore the city was called Zoar.^g 23The sun had risen on the earth when Lot came to Zoar.

24 Then the LORD rained on Sodom and Gomorrah sulfur and fire from the LORD out of heaven; 25and he overthrew those cities, and all the Plain, and all the inhabitants of the cities, and what grew on the ground. 26But Lot's wife, behind him, looked back, and she became a pillar of salt.

27 Abraham went early in the morning to the place where he had stood before the LORD; 28and he looked down toward Sodom and Gomorrah and toward all the land of the Plain and saw the smoke of the land going up like the smoke of a furnace.

29 So it was that, when God destroyed the cities of the Plain, God remembered Abraham, and sent Lot out of the midst of the overthrow, when he overthrew the cities in which Lot had settled.

The Shameful Origin of Moab and Ammon

30 Now Lot went up out of Zoar and settled in the hills with his two daughters, for he was afraid to stay in Zoar; so he lived in a cave with his two daughters. 31And the firstborn said to the younger, "Our father is old, and there is not a man on earth to come in to us after the manner of all the world. 32Come, let us make our father drink wine, and we will lie with him, so that we may preserve offspring through our father." 33So they made their father drink wine that night; and the firstborn went in, and lay with her father; he did not know when she lay down or when she rose. 34On the next day, the firstborn said to the younger, "Look, I lay last night with my father; let us make him drink wine tonight also; then you go in and lie with him, so that we may preserve offspring through our father." 35So they made their father drink wine that night also; and the younger rose, and lay with him; and he did not know when she lay down or when she rose. 36Thus both the daughters of Lot became pregnant by their father. 37The firstborn bore a son, and named him Moab; he is the ancestor of the Moabites to this day. 38The younger also bore a son and named him Ben-ammi; he is the ancestor of the Ammonites to this day.

Abraham and Sarah at Gerar

20 From there Abraham journeyed toward the region of the Negeb, and settled between Kadesh and Shur. While residing in Gerar as an alien, 2Abraham said of his wife Sarah,

f Gk Syr Vg: Heb he   g That is Little

"She is my sister." And King Abimelech of Gerar sent and took Sarah. 3But God came to Abimelech in a dream by night, and said to him, "You are about to die because of the woman whom you have taken; for she is a married woman." 4Now Abimelech had not approached her; so he said, "Lord, will you destroy an innocent people? 5Did he not himself say to me, 'She is my sister'? And she herself said, 'He is my brother.' I did this in the integrity of my heart and the innocence of my hands." 6Then God said to him in the dream, "Yes, I know that you did this in the integrity of your heart; furthermore it was I who kept you from sinning against me. Therefore I did not let you touch her. 7Now then, return the man's wife; for he is a prophet, and he will pray for you and you shall live. But if you do not restore her, know that you shall surely die, you and all that are yours."

8 So Abimelech rose early in the morning, and called all his servants and told them all these things; and the men were very much afraid. 9Then Abimelech called Abraham, and said to him, "What have you done to us? How have I sinned against you, that you have brought such great guilt on me and my kingdom? You have done things to me that ought not to be done." 10And Abimelech said to Abraham, "What were you thinking of, that you did this thing?" 11Abraham said, "I did it because I thought, There is no fear of God at all in this place, and they will kill me because of my wife. 12Besides, she is indeed my sister, the daughter of my father but not the daughter of my mother; and she became my wife. 13And when God caused me to wander from my father's house, I said to her, 'This is the kindness you must do me: at every place to which we come, say of me, He is my brother.' " 14Then Abimelech took sheep and oxen, and male and female slaves, and gave them to Abraham, and restored his wife Sarah to him. 15Abimelech said, "My land is before you; settle where it pleases you." 16To Sarah he said, "Look, I have given your brother a thousand pieces of silver; it is your exoneration before all who are with you; you are

completely vindicated." 17Then Abraham prayed to God; and God healed Abimelech, and also healed his wife and female slaves so that they bore children. 18For the LORD had closed fast all the wombs of the house of Abimelech because of Sarah, Abraham's wife.

The Birth of Isaac

21 The LORD dealt with Sarah as he had said, and the LORD did for Sarah as he had promised. 2Sarah conceived and bore Abraham a son in his old age, at the time of which God had spoken to him. 3Abraham gave the name Isaac to his son whom Sarah bore him. 4And Abraham circumcised his son Isaac when he was eight days old, as God had commanded him. 5Abraham was a hundred years old when his son Isaac was born to him. 6Now Sarah said, "God has brought laughter for me; everyone who hears will laugh with me." 7And she said, "Who would ever have said to Abraham that Sarah would nurse children? Yet I have borne him a son in his old age."

Hagar and Ishmael Sent Away

8 The child grew, and was weaned; and Abraham made a great feast on the day that Isaac was weaned. 9But Sarah saw the son of Hagar the Egyptian, whom she had borne to Abraham, playing with her son Isaac.h 10So she said to Abraham, "Cast out this slave woman with her son; for the son of this slave woman shall not inherit along with my son Isaac." 11The matter was very distressing to Abraham on account of his son. 12But God said to Abraham, "Do not be distressed because of the boy and because of your slave woman; whatever Sarah says to you, do as she tells you, for it is through Isaac that offspring shall be named for you. 13As for the son of the slave woman, I will make a nation of him also, because he is your offspring." 14So Abraham rose early in the morning, and took bread and a skin of water, and gave it to Hagar, putting it on her shoulder, along with the child, and sent her away. And she departed, and wandered about in the wilderness of Beer-sheba.

15 When the water in the skin was

h Gk Vg: Heb lacks with her son Isaac

gone, she cast the child under one of the bushes. [16]Then she went and sat down opposite him a good way off, about the distance of a bowshot; for she said, "Do not let me look on the death of the child." And as she sat opposite him, she lifted up her voice and wept. [17]And God heard the voice of the boy; and the angel of God called to Hagar from heaven, and said to her, "What troubles you, Hagar? Do not be afraid; for God has heard the voice of the boy where he is. [18]Come, lift up the boy and hold him fast with your hand, for I will make a great nation of him." [19]Then God opened her eyes and she saw a well of water. She went, and filled the skin with water, and gave the boy a drink.

20 God was with the boy, and he grew up; he lived in the wilderness, and became an expert with the bow. [21]He lived in the wilderness of Paran; and his mother got a wife for him from the land of Egypt.

Abraham and Abimelech Make a Covenant

22 At that time Abimelech, with Phicol the commander of his army, said to Abraham, "God is with you in all that you do; [23]now therefore swear to me here by God that you will not deal falsely with me or with my offspring or with my posterity, but as I have dealt loyally with you, you will deal with me and with the land where you have resided as an alien." [24]And Abraham said, "I swear it."

25 When Abraham complained to Abimelech about a well of water that Abimelech's servants had seized, [26]Abimelech said, "I do not know who has done this; you did not tell me, and I have not heard of it until today." [27]So Abraham took sheep and oxen and gave them to Abimelech, and the two men made a covenant. [28]Abraham set apart seven ewe lambs of the flock. [29]And Abimelech said to Abraham, "What is the meaning of these seven ewe lambs that you have set apart?" [30]He said, "These seven ewe lambs you shall accept from my hand, in order that you may be a witness for me that I dug this well." [31]Therefore that place was called

Beer-sheba;[i] because there both of them swore an oath. [32]When they had made a covenant at Beer-sheba, Abimelech, with Phicol the commander of his army, left and returned to the land of the Philistines. [33]Abraham[j] planted a tamarisk tree in Beer-sheba, and called there on the name of the LORD, the Everlasting God.[k] [34]And Abraham resided as an alien many days in the land of the Philistines.

The Command to Sacrifice Isaac

22 After these things God tested Abraham. He said to him, "Abraham!" And he said, "Here I am." [2]He said, "Take your son, your only son Isaac, whom you love, and go to the land of Moriah, and offer him there as a burnt offering on one of the mountains that I shall show you." [3]So Abraham rose early in the morning, saddled his donkey, and took two of his young men with him, and his son Isaac; he cut the wood for the burnt offering, and set out and went to the place in the distance that God had shown him. [4]On the third day Abraham looked up and saw the place far away. [5]Then Abraham said to his young men, "Stay here with the donkey; the boy and I will go over there; we will worship, and then we will come back to you." [6]Abraham took the wood of the burnt offering and laid it on his son Isaac, and he himself carried the fire and the knife. So the two of them walked on together. [7]Isaac said to his father Abraham, "Father!" And he said, "Here I am, my son." He said, "The fire and the wood are here, but where is the lamb for a burnt offering?" [8]Abraham said, "God himself will provide the lamb for a burnt offering, my son." So the two of them walked on together.

9 When they came to the place that God had shown him, Abraham built an altar there and laid the wood in order. He bound his son Isaac, and laid him on the altar, on top of the wood. [10]Then Abraham reached out his hand and took the knife to kill[l] his son. [11]But the angel of the LORD called to him from heaven, and said, "Abraham, Abraham!" And he said, "Here I am." [12]He said, "Do not lay your hand on the boy or do anything to

---

i That is *Well of seven* or *Well of the oath*   *j* Heb *He*   *k* Or *the* LORD, *El Olam*   *l* Or *to slaughter*

him; for now I know that you fear God, since you have not withheld your son, your only son, from me." ¹³And Abraham looked up and saw a ram, caught in a thicket by its horns. Abraham went and took the ram and offered it up as a burnt offering instead of his son. ¹⁴So Abraham called that place "The LORD will provide";ᵐ as it is said to this day, "On the mount of the LORD it shall be provided."ⁿ

15 The angel of the LORD called to Abraham a second time from heaven, ¹⁶and said, "By myself I have sworn, says the LORD: Because you have done this, and have not withheld your son, your only son, ¹⁷I will indeed bless you, and I will make your offspring as numerous as the stars of heaven and as the sand that is on the seashore. And your offspring shall possess the gate of their enemies, ¹⁸and by your offspring shall all the nations of the earth gain blessing for themselves, because you

m Or will see; Heb traditionally transliterated *Jehovah Jireh*   n Or *he shall be seen*

MONDAY

THE LOVE OF GOD
Dwight L. Moody

VERSE: Genesis 22.14   **PASSAGE:** Genesis 22.1–14

 remember that for the first few years after I was converted, I had a good deal more love for Christ than for God the Father. I looked upon God as the stern judge, while I regarded Christ as the mediator who had come between me and that stern judge to appease his wrath. But when I got a little better acquainted with my Bible, those views all fled.

After I became a father and woke up to the realization of what it cost God to have his Son die, I began to see that God was to be loved just as much as his Son was. Why, it took more love for God to give his Son to die than it would to die himself. You would a thousand times sooner die yourself in your son's place than have him taken away. If the executioner was about to take your son to the gallows, you would say, "Let me die in his stead; let my son be spared."

Oh, think of the love God must have had for this world that he gave his only begotten Son to die for it. And that is what I want you to understand. "The Father himself loves you, because you have loved me . . ." (John 16.27). If a man has loved Christ, God will set his love upon him.

ADDITIONAL SCRIPTURE READING:
Deuteronomy 7.7–8; 1 John 4.19

Go to page 52 for your next devotional reading.

1900   Present

have obeyed my voice." ¹⁹So Abraham returned to his young men, and they arose and went together to Beer-sheba; and Abraham lived at Beer-sheba.

The Children of Nahor

20 Now after these things it was told Abraham, "Milcah also has borne children, to your brother Nahor: ²¹Uz the firstborn, Buz his brother, Kemuel the father of Aram, ²²Chesed, Hazo, Pildash, Jidlaph, and Bethuel." ²³Bethuel became the father of Rebekah. These eight Milcah bore to Nahor, Abraham's brother. ²⁴Moreover, his concubine, whose name was Reumah, bore Tebah, Gaham, Tahash, and Maacah.

Sarah's Death and Burial

23 Sarah lived one hundred twenty-seven years; this was the length of Sarah's life. ²And Sarah died at Kiriath-arba (that is, Hebron) in the land of Canaan; and Abraham went in to mourn for Sarah and to weep for her. ³Abraham rose up from beside his dead, and said to the Hittites, ⁴"I am a stranger and an alien residing among you; give me property among you for a burying place, so that I may bury my dead out of my sight." ⁵The Hittites answered Abraham, ⁶"Hear us, my lord; you are a mighty prince among us. Bury your dead in the choicest of our burial places; none of us will withhold from you any burial ground for burying your dead." ⁷Abraham rose and bowed to the Hittites, the people of the land. ⁸He said to them, "If you are willing that I should bury my dead out of my sight, hear me, and entreat for me Ephron son of Zohar, ⁹so that he may give me the cave of Machpelah, which he owns; it is at the end of his field. For the full price let him give it to me in your presence as a possession for a burying place." ¹⁰Now Ephron was sitting among the Hittites; and Ephron the Hittite answered Abraham in the hearing of the Hittites, of all

who went in at the gate of his city, ¹¹"No, my lord, hear me; I give you the field, and I give you the cave that is in it; in the presence of my people I give it to you; bury your dead." ¹²Then Abraham bowed down before the people of the land. ¹³He said to Ephron in the hearing of the people of the land, "If you only will listen to me! I will give the price of the field; accept it from me, so that I may bury my dead there." ¹⁴Ephron answered Abraham, ¹⁵"My lord, listen to me; a piece of land worth four hundred shekels of silver—what is that between you and me? Bury your dead." ¹⁶Abraham agreed with Ephron; and Abraham weighed out for Ephron the silver that he had named in the hearing of the Hittites, four hundred shekels of silver, according to the weights current among the merchants.

17 So the field of Ephron in Machpelah, which was to the east of Mamre, the field with the cave that was in it and all the trees that were in the field, throughout its whole area, passed ¹⁸to Abraham as a possession in the presence of the Hittites, in the presence of all who went in at the gate of his city. ¹⁹After this, Abraham buried Sarah his wife in the cave of the field of Machpelah facing Mamre (that is, Hebron) in the land of Canaan. ²⁰The field and the cave that is in it passed from the Hittites into Abraham's possession as a burying place.

The Marriage of Isaac and Rebekah

24 Now Abraham was old, well advanced in years; and the LORD had blessed Abraham in all things. ²Abraham said to his servant, the oldest of his house, who had charge of all that he had, "Put your hand under my thigh ³and I will make you swear by the LORD, the God of heaven and earth, that you will not get a wife for my son from the daughters of the Canaanites, among whom I live, ⁴but will go to my country and to my kindred and get a wife for my son Isaac." ⁵The servant said to him, "Perhaps the woman may not be willing to follow me to this land; must I then take your son back to the land from which you came?" ⁶Abraham said to him, "See to it that you do not take my son back there. ⁷The LORD, the God of heaven, who took me from my father's house and from the land of my birth, and who spoke to me and swore to me, 'To your offspring I will give this land,' he will send his angel before you, and you shall take a wife for my son from there. [8]But if the woman is not willing to follow you, then you will be free from this oath of mine; only you must not take my son back there." [9]So the servant put his hand under the thigh of Abraham his master and swore to him concerning this matter.

10 Then the servant took ten of his master's camels and departed, taking all kinds of choice gifts from his master; and he set out and went to Aram-naharaim, to the city of Nahor. [11]He made the camels kneel down outside the city by the well of water; it was toward evening, the time when women go out to draw water. [12]And he said, "O LORD, God of my master Abraham, please grant me success today and show steadfast love to my master Abraham. [13]I am standing here by the spring of water, and the daughters of the townspeople are coming out to draw water. [14]Let the girl to whom I shall say, 'Please offer your jar that I may drink,' and who shall say, 'Drink, and I will water your camels'— let her be the one whom you have appointed for your servant Isaac. By this I shall know that you have shown steadfast love to my master."

15 Before he had finished speaking, there was Rebekah, who was born to Bethuel son of Milcah, the wife of Nahor, Abraham's brother, coming out with her water jar on her shoulder. [16]The girl was very fair to look upon, a virgin, whom no man had known. She went down to the spring, filled her jar, and came up. [17]Then the servant ran to meet her and said, "Please let me sip a little water from your jar." [18]"Drink, my lord," she said, and quickly lowered her jar upon her hand and gave him a drink. [19]When she had finished giving him a drink, she said, "I will draw for your camels also, until they have finished drinking." [20]So she quickly emptied her jar into the trough and ran again to the well to draw, and she drew for all his camels. [21]The man gazed at her in silence to learn whether or not the LORD had made his journey successful.

22 When the camels had finished drinking, the man took a gold nose-ring weighing a half shekel, and two bracelets for her arms weighing ten gold shekels, [23]and said, "Tell me whose daughter you are. Is there room in your father's house for us to spend the night?" [24]She said to him, "I am the daughter of Bethuel son of Milcah, whom she bore to Nahor." [25]She added, "We have plenty of straw and fodder and a place to spend the night." [26]The man bowed his head and worshiped the LORD [27]and said, "Blessed be the LORD, the God of my master Abraham, who has not forsaken his steadfast love and his faithfulness toward my master. As for me, the LORD has led me on the way to the house of my master's kin."

28 Then the girl ran and told her mother's household about these things. [29]Rebekah had a brother whose name was Laban; and Laban ran out to the man, to the spring. [30]As soon as he had seen the nose-ring, and the bracelets on his sister's arms, and when he heard the words of his sister Rebekah, "Thus the man spoke to me," he went to the man; and there he was, standing by the camels at the spring. [31]He said, "Come in, O blessed of the LORD. Why do you stand outside when I have prepared the house and a place for the camels?" [32]So the man came into the house; and Laban unloaded the camels, and gave him straw and fodder for the camels, and water to wash his feet and the feet of the men who were with him. [33]Then food was set before him to eat; but he said, "I will not eat until I have told my errand." He said, "Speak on."

34 So he said, "I am Abraham's servant. [35]The LORD has greatly blessed my master, and he has become wealthy; he has given him flocks and herds, silver and gold, male and female slaves, camels and donkeys. [36]And Sarah my master's wife bore a son to my master when she was old; and he has given him all that he has. [37]My master made me swear, saying, 'You shall not take a wife for my son from the daughters of the Canaanites, in whose land I live; [38]but you shall go to my father's house, to my

kindred, and get a wife for my son.' 39I said to my master, 'Perhaps the woman will not follow me.' 40But he said to me, 'The LORD, before whom I walk, will send his angel with you and make your way successful. You shall get a wife for my son from my kindred, from my father's house. 41Then you will be free from my oath, when you come to my kindred; even if they will not give her to you, you will be free from my oath.'

42 "I came today to the spring, and said, 'O LORD, the God of my master Abraham, if now you will only make successful the way I am going! 43I am standing here by the spring of water; let the young woman who comes out to draw, to whom I shall say, "Please give me a little water from your jar to drink," 44and who will say to me, "Drink, and I will draw for your camels also"—let her be the woman whom the LORD has appointed for my master's son.'

45 "Before I had finished speaking in my heart, there was Rebekah coming out with her water jar on her shoulder; and she went down to the spring, and drew. I said to her, 'Please let me drink.' 46She quickly let down her jar from her shoulder, and said, 'Drink, and I will also water your camels.' So I drank, and she also watered the camels. 47Then I asked her, 'Whose daughter are you?' She said, 'The daughter of Bethuel, Nahor's son, whom Milcah bore to him.' So I put the ring on her nose, and the bracelets on her arms. 48Then I bowed my head and worshiped the LORD, and blessed the LORD, the God of my master Abraham, who had led me by the right way to obtain the daughter of my master's kinsman for his son. 49Now then, if you will deal loyally and truly with my master, tell me; and if not, tell me, so that I may turn either to the right hand or to the left."

50 Then Laban and Bethuel answered, "The thing comes from the LORD; we cannot speak to you anything bad or good. 51Look, Rebekah is before you, take her and go, and let her be the wife of your master's son, as the LORD has spoken."

52 When Abraham's servant heard their words, he bowed himself to the ground before the LORD. 53And the servant brought out jewelry of silver and of gold, and garments, and gave them to Rebekah; he also gave to her brother and to her mother costly ornaments. 54Then he and the men who were with him ate and drank, and they spent the night there. When they rose in the morning, he said, "Send me back to my master." 55Her brother and her mother said, "Let the girl remain with us a while, at least ten days; after that she may go." 56But he said to them, "Do not delay me, since the LORD has made my journey successful; let me go that I may go to my master." 57They said, "We will call the girl, and ask her." 58And they called Rebekah, and said to her, "Will you go with this man?" She said, "I will." 59So they sent away their sister Rebekah and her nurse along with Abraham's servant and his men. 60And they blessed Rebekah and said to her,

"May you, our sister, become
    thousands of myriads;
may your offspring gain possession
    of the gates of their foes."

61Then Rebekah and her maids rose up, mounted the camels, and followed the man; thus the servant took Rebekah, and went his way.

62 Now Isaac had come fromᵒ Beer-lahai-roi, and was settled in the Negeb. 63Isaac went out in the evening to walkᵖ in the field; and looking up, he saw camels coming. 64And Rebekah looked up, and when she saw Isaac, she slipped quickly from the camel, 65and said to the servant, "Who is the man over there, walking in the field to meet us?" The servant said, "It is my master." So she took her veil and covered herself. 66And the servant told Isaac all the things that

---

GOD ALWAYS GIVES HIS VERY BEST TO THOSE WHO LEAVE THE CHOICE WITH HIM.

—James Hudson Taylor

---

he had done. 67Then Isaac brought her into his mother Sarah's tent. He took Rebekah, and she became his wife; and he loved her. So Isaac was comforted after his mother's death.

---

o Syr Tg: Heb *from coming to*   p Meaning of Heb word is uncertain

Abraham Marries Keturah

25 Abraham took another wife, whose name was Keturah. [2]She bore him Zimran, Jokshan, Medan, Midian, Ishbak, and Shuah. [3]Jokshan was the father of Sheba and Dedan. The sons of Dedan were Asshurim, Letushim, and Leummim. [4]The sons of Midian were Ephah, Epher, Hanoch, Abida, and Eldaah. All these were the children of Keturah. [5]Abraham gave all he had to Isaac. [6]But to the sons of his concubines Abraham gave gifts, while he was still living, and he sent them away from his son Isaac, eastward to the east country.

The Death of Abraham

[7] This is the length of Abraham's life, one hundred seventy-five years. [8]Abraham breathed his last and died in a good old age, an old man and full of years, and was gathered to his people. [9]His sons Isaac and Ishmael buried him in the cave of Machpelah, in the field of Ephron son of Zohar the Hittite, east of Mamre, [10]the field that Abraham purchased from the Hittites. There Abraham was buried, with his wife Sarah. [11]After the death of Abraham God blessed his son Isaac. And Isaac settled at Beer-lahai-roi.

Ishmael's Descendants

[12] These are the descendants of Ishmael, Abraham's son, whom Hagar the Egyptian, Sarah's slave-girl, bore to Abraham. [13]These are the names of the sons of Ishmael, named in the order of their birth: Nebaioth, the firstborn of Ishmael; and Kedar, Adbeel, Mibsam, [14]Mishma, Dumah, Massa, [15]Hadad, Tema, Jetur, Naphish, and Kedemah. [16]These are the sons of Ishmael and these are their names, by their villages and by their encampments, twelve princes according to their tribes. [17](This is the length of the life of Ishmael, one hundred thirty-seven years; he breathed his last and died, and was gathered to his people.) [18]They settled from Havilah to Shur, which is opposite Egypt in the direction of Assyria; he settled down*q* alongside of*r* all his people.

The Birth and Youth of Esau and Jacob

[19] These are the descendants of Isaac, Abraham's son: Abraham was the father of Isaac, [20]and Isaac was forty years old when he married Rebekah, daughter of Bethuel the Aramean of Paddan-aram, sister of Laban the Aramean. [21]Isaac prayed to the LORD for his wife, because she was barren; and the LORD granted his prayer, and his wife Rebekah conceived. [22]The children struggled together within her; and she said, "If it is to be this way, why do I live?"*s* So she went to inquire of the LORD. [23]And the LORD said to her,

"Two nations are in your womb,
    and two peoples born of you shall
        be divided;
the one shall be stronger than the
        other,
    the elder shall serve the younger."

[24]When her time to give birth was at hand, there were twins in her womb. [25]The first came out red, all his body like a hairy mantle; so they named him Esau. [26]Afterward his brother came out, with his hand gripping Esau's heel; so he was named Jacob.*t* Isaac was sixty years old when she bore them.

[27] When the boys grew up, Esau was a skillful hunter, a man of the field, while Jacob was a quiet man, living in tents. [28]Isaac loved Esau, because he was fond of game; but Rebekah loved Jacob.

Esau Sells His Birthright

[29] Once when Jacob was cooking a stew, Esau came in from the field, and he was famished. [30]Esau said to Jacob, "Let me eat some of that red stuff, for I am famished!" (Therefore he was called Edom.*u*) [31]Jacob said, "First sell me your birthright." [32]Esau said, "I am about to die; of what use is a birthright to me?" [33]Jacob said, "Swear to me first."*v* So he swore to him, and sold his birthright to Jacob. [34]Then Jacob gave Esau bread and lentil stew, and he ate and drank, and rose and went his way. Thus Esau despised his birthright.

q Heb he fell   r Or down in opposition to   s Syr: Meaning of Heb uncertain   t That is He takes by the heel or He supplants   u That is Red   v Heb today

Isaac and Abimelech

26 Now there was a famine in the land, besides the former famine that had occurred in the days of Abraham. And Isaac went to Gerar, to King Abimelech of the Philistines. 2The LORD appeared to Isaac[w] and said, "Do not go down to Egypt; settle in the land that I shall show you. 3Reside in this land as an alien, and I will be with you, and will bless you; for to you and to your descendants I will give all these lands, and I will fulfill the oath that I swore to your father Abraham. 4I will make your offspring as numerous as the stars of heaven, and will give to your offspring all these lands; and all the nations of the earth shall gain blessing for themselves through your offspring, 5because Abraham obeyed my voice and kept my charge, my commandments, my statutes, and my laws."

6 So Isaac settled in Gerar. 7When the men of the place asked him about his wife, he said, "She is my sister"; for he was afraid to say, "My wife," thinking, "or else the men of the place might kill me for the sake of Rebekah, because she is attractive in appearance." 8When Isaac had been there a long time, King Abimelech of the Philistines looked out of a window and saw him fondling his wife Rebekah. 9So Abimelech called for Isaac, and said, "So she is your wife! Why then did you say, 'She is my sister'?" Isaac said to him, "Because I thought I might die because of her." 10Abimelech said, "What is this you have done to us? One of the people might easily have lain with your wife, and you would have brought guilt upon us." 11So Abimelech warned all the people, saying, "Whoever touches this man or his wife shall be put to death."

12 Isaac sowed seed in that land, and in the same year reaped a hundredfold. The LORD blessed him, 13and the man became rich; he prospered more and more until he became very wealthy. 14He had possessions of flocks and herds, and a great household, so that the Philistines envied him. 15(Now the Philistines had stopped up and filled with earth all the wells that his father's servants had dug in the days of his father

Abraham.) 16And Abimelech said to Isaac, "Go away from us; you have become too powerful for us."

17 So Isaac departed from there and camped in the valley of Gerar and settled there. 18Isaac dug again the wells of water that had been dug in the days of his father Abraham; for the Philistines had stopped them up after the death of Abraham; and he gave them the names that his father had given them. 19But when Isaac's servants dug in the valley and found there a well of spring water, 20the herders of Gerar quarreled with Isaac's herders, saying, "The water is ours." So he called the well Esek,[x] because they contended with him. 21Then they dug another well, and they quarreled over that one also; so he called it Sitnah.[y] 22He moved from there and dug another well, and they did not quarrel over it; so he called it Rehoboth,[z] saying, "Now the LORD has made room for us, and we shall be fruitful in the land."

23 From there he went up to Beersheba. 24And that very night the LORD appeared to him and said, "I am the God of your father Abraham; do not be afraid, for I am with you and will bless you and make your offspring numerous for my servant Abraham's sake." 25So he built an altar there, called on the name of the LORD, and pitched his tent there. And there Isaac's servants dug a well.

26 Then Abimelech went to him from Gerar, with Ahuzzath his adviser and Phicol the commander of his army. 27Isaac said to them, "Why have you come to me, seeing that you hate me and have sent me away from you?" 28They said, "We see plainly that the LORD has been with you; so we say, let there be an oath between you and us, and let us make a covenant with you 29so that you will do us no harm, just as we have not touched you and have done to you nothing but good and have sent you away in peace. You are now the blessed of the LORD." 30So he made them a feast, and they ate and drank. 31In the morning they rose early and exchanged oaths; and Isaac set them on their way, and they departed from him in peace. 32That same day Isaac's servants came and told him about the well

---

w Heb *him*   *x* That is *Contention*   *y* That is *Enmity*   *z* That is *Broad places* or *Room*

that they had dug, and said to him, "We have found water!" 33He called it Shibah;*a* therefore the name of the city is Beer-sheba*b* to this day.

Esau's Hittite Wives

34 When Esau was forty years old, he married Judith daughter of Beeri the Hittite, and Basemath daughter of Elon the Hittite; 35and they made life bitter for Isaac and Rebekah.

Isaac Blesses Jacob

27 When Isaac was old and his eyes were dim so that he could not see, he called his elder son Esau and said to him, "My son"; and he answered, "Here I am." 2He said, "See, I am old; I do not know the day of my death. 3Now then, take your weapons, your quiver and your bow, and go out to the field, and hunt game for me. 4Then prepare for me savory food, such as I like, and bring it to me to eat, so that I may bless you before I die."

5 Now Rebekah was listening when Isaac spoke to his son Esau. So when Esau went to the field to hunt for game and bring it, 6Rebekah said to her son Jacob, "I heard your father say to your brother Esau, 7'Bring me game, and prepare for me savory food to eat, that I may bless you before the LORD before I die.' 8Now therefore, my son, obey my word as I command you. 9Go to the flock, and get me two choice kids, so that I may prepare from them savory food for your father, such as he likes; 10and you shall take it to your father to eat, so that he may bless you before he dies." 11But Jacob said to his mother Rebekah, "Look, my brother Esau is a hairy man, and I am a man of smooth skin. 12Perhaps my father will feel me, and I shall seem to be mocking him, and bring a curse on myself and not a blessing." 13His mother said to him, "Let your curse be on me, my son; only obey my word, and go, get them for me." 14So he went and got them and brought them to his mother; and his mother prepared savory food, such as his father loved. 15Then Rebekah took the best garments of her elder son Esau, which were with her in the house, and put them on her younger son Jacob; 16and she put the skins of the kids on his hands and on the smooth part of his neck. 17Then she handed the savory food, and the bread that she had prepared, to her son Jacob.

18 So he went in to his father, and said, "My father"; and he said, "Here I am; who are you, my son?" 19Jacob said to his father, "I am Esau your firstborn. I have done as you told me; now sit up and eat of my game, so that you may bless me." 20But Isaac said to his son, "How is it that you have found it so quickly, my son?" He answered, "Because the LORD your God granted me success." 21Then Isaac said to Jacob, "Come near, that I may feel you, my son, to know whether you are really my son Esau or not." 22So Jacob went up to his father Isaac, who felt him and said, "The voice is Jacob's voice, but the hands are the hands of Esau." 23He did not recognize him, because his hands were hairy like his brother Esau's hands; so he blessed him. 24He said, "Are you really my son Esau?" He answered, "I am." 25Then he said, "Bring it to me, that I may eat of my son's game and bless you." So he brought it to him, and he ate; and he brought him wine, and he drank. 26Then his father Isaac said to him, "Come near and kiss me, my son." 27So he came near and kissed him; and he smelled the smell of his garments, and blessed him, and said,

"Ah, the smell of my son
    is like the smell of a field that
        the LORD has blessed.
28 May God give you of the dew of
        heaven,
    and of the fatness of the earth,
        and plenty of grain and wine.
29 Let peoples serve you,
        and nations bow down to you.
    Be lord over your brothers,
        and may your mother's sons bow
            down to you.
    Cursed be everyone who curses
        you,
    and blessed be everyone who
        blesses you!"

Esau's Lost Blessing

30 As soon as Isaac had finished blessing Jacob, when Jacob had scarcely

---

a A word resembling the word for *oath*   *b* That is *Well of the oath* or *Well of seven*

gone out from the presence of his father Isaac, his brother Esau came in from his hunting. 31He also prepared savory food, and brought it to his father. And he said to his father, "Let my father sit up and eat of his son's game, so that you may bless me." 32His father Isaac said to him, "Who are you?" He answered, "I am your firstborn son, Esau." 33Then Isaac trembled violently, and said, "Who was it then that hunted game and brought it to me, and I ate it all*c* before you came, and I have blessed him?—yes, and blessed he shall be!" 34When Esau heard his father's words, he cried out with an exceedingly great and bitter cry, and said to his father, "Bless me, me also, father!" 35But he said, "Your brother came deceitfully, and he has taken away your blessing." 36Esau said, "Is he not rightly named Jacob?*d* For he has supplanted me these two times. He took away my birthright; and look, now he has taken away my blessing." Then he said, "Have you not reserved a blessing for me?" 37Isaac answered Esau, "I have already made him your lord, and I have given him all his brothers as servants, and with grain and wine I have sustained him. What then can I do for you, my son?" 38Esau said to his father, "Have you only one blessing, father? Bless me, me also, father!" And Esau lifted up his voice and wept.

39 Then his father Isaac answered him:

"See, away from*e* the fatness of the
   earth shall your home be,
   and away from*f* the dew of
   heaven on high.
40 By your sword you shall live,
   and you shall serve your brother;
but when you break loose,*g*
   you shall break his yoke from
   your neck."

Jacob Escapes Esau's Fury

41 Now Esau hated Jacob because of the blessing with which his father had blessed him, and Esau said to himself, "The days of mourning for my father are approaching; then I will kill my brother Jacob." 42But the words of her elder son Esau were told to Rebekah; so she sent and called her younger son Jacob and said to him, "Your brother Esau is consoling himself by planning to kill you. 43Now therefore, my son, obey my voice; flee at once to my brother Laban in Haran, 44and stay with him a while, until your brother's fury turns away— 45until your brother's anger against you turns away, and he forgets what you have done to him; then I will send, and bring you back from there. Why should I lose both of you in one day?"

46 Then Rebekah said to Isaac, "I am weary of my life because of the Hittite women. If Jacob marries one of the Hittite women such as these, one of the women of the land, what good will my life be to me?"

28 Then Isaac called Jacob and blessed him, and charged him, "You shall not marry one of the Canaanite women. 2Go at once to Paddan-aram to the house of Bethuel, your mother's father; and take as wife from there one of the daughters of Laban, your mother's brother. 3May God Almighty*h* bless you and make you fruitful and numerous, that you may become a company of peoples. 4May he give to you the blessing of Abraham, to you and to your offspring with you, so that you may take possession of the land where you now live as an alien—land that God gave to Abraham." 5Thus Isaac sent Jacob away; and he went to Paddan-aram, to Laban son of Bethuel the Aramean, the brother of Rebekah, Jacob's and Esau's mother.

Esau Marries Ishmael's Daughter

6 Now Esau saw that Isaac had blessed Jacob and sent him away to Paddan-aram to take a wife from there, and that as he blessed him he charged him, "You shall not marry one of the Canaanite women," 7and that Jacob had obeyed his father and his mother and gone to Paddan-aram. 8So when Esau saw that the Canaanite women did not please his father Isaac, 9Esau went to Ishmael and took Mahalath daughter of Abraham's son Ishmael, and sister of Nebaioth, to be his wife in addition to the wives he had.

---

c Cn: Heb *of all*   *d* That is *He supplants* or *He takes by the heel*   *e* Or *See, of*   *f* Or *and of*
g Meaning of Heb uncertain   *h* Traditional rendering of Heb *El Shaddai*

Jacob's Dream at Bethel

10 Jacob left Beer-sheba and went toward Haran. 11He came to a certain place and stayed there for the night, because the sun had set. Taking one of the stones of the place, he put it under his head and lay down in that place. 12And he dreamed that there was a ladder[i] set up on the earth, the top of it reaching to heaven; and the angels of God were ascending and descending on it. 13And the LORD stood beside him[j] and said, "I am the LORD, the God of Abraham your father and the God of Isaac; the land on which you lie I will give to you and to your offspring; 14and your offspring shall be like the dust of the earth, and you shall spread abroad to the west and to the east and to the north and to the south; and all the families of the earth shall be blessed[k] in you and in your offspring. 15Know that I am with you and will keep you wherever you go, and will bring you back to this land; for I will not leave you until I have done what I have promised you." 16Then Jacob woke from his sleep and said, "Surely the LORD is in this place—and I did not know it!" 17And he was afraid, and said, "How awesome is this place! This is none other than the house of God, and this is the gate of heaven."

18 So Jacob rose early in the morning, and he took the stone that he had put under his head and set it up for a pillar and poured oil on the top of it. 19He called that place Bethel;[l] but the name of the city was Luz at the first. 20Then Jacob made a vow, saying, "If God will be with me, and will keep me in this way that I go, and will give me bread to eat and clothing to wear, 21so that I come again to my father's house in peace, then the LORD shall be my God, 22and this stone, which I have set up for a pillar, shall be God's house; and of all that you give me I will surely give one-tenth to you."

Jacob Meets Rachel

29 Then Jacob went on his journey, and came to the land of the people of the east. 2As he looked, he saw a well in the field and three flocks of sheep lying there beside it; for out of that well the flocks were watered. The stone on the well's mouth was large, 3and when all the flocks were gathered there, the shepherds would roll the stone from the mouth of the well, and water the sheep, and put the stone back in its place on the mouth of the well.

4 Jacob said to them, "My brothers, where do you come from?" They said, "We are from Haran." 5He said to them, "Do you know Laban son of Nahor?" They said, "We do." 6He said to them, "Is it well with him?" "Yes," they replied, "and here is his daughter Rachel, coming with the sheep." 7He said, "Look, it is still broad daylight; it is not time for the animals to be gathered together. Water the sheep, and go, pasture them." 8But they said, "We cannot until all the flocks are gathered together, and the stone is rolled from the mouth of the well; then we water the sheep."

9 While he was still speaking with them, Rachel came with her father's sheep; for she kept them. 10Now when Jacob saw Rachel, the daughter of his mother's brother Laban, and the sheep of his mother's brother Laban, Jacob went up and rolled the stone from the well's mouth, and watered the flock of his mother's brother Laban. 11Then Jacob kissed Rachel, and wept aloud. 12And Jacob told Rachel that he was her father's kinsman, and that he was Rebekah's son; and she ran and told her father.

13 When Laban heard the news about his sister's son Jacob, he ran to meet him; he embraced him and kissed him, and brought him to his house. Jacob[m] told Laban all these things, 14and Laban said to him, "Surely you are my bone and my flesh!" And he stayed with him a month.

Jacob Marries Laban's Daughters

15 Then Laban said to Jacob, "Because you are my kinsman, should you therefore serve me for nothing? Tell me, what shall your wages be?" 16Now Laban had two daughters; the name of the elder was Leah, and the name of the younger was Rachel. 17Leah's eyes were lovely,[n] and Rachel was graceful and

---

i Or *stairway* or *ramp*   j Or *stood above it*   k Or *shall bless themselves*   l That is *House of God*
m Heb *He*   n Meaning of Heb uncertain

beautiful. 18Jacob loved Rachel; so he said, "I will serve you seven years for your younger daughter Rachel." 19Laban said, "It is better that I give her to you than that I should give her to any other man; stay with me." 20So Jacob served seven years for Rachel, and they seemed to him but a few days because of the love he had for her.

21 Then Jacob said to Laban, "Give me my wife that I may go in to her, for my time is completed." 22So Laban gathered together all the people of the place, and made a feast. 23But in the evening he took his daughter Leah and brought her to Jacob; and he went in to her. 24(Laban gave his maid Zilpah to his daughter Leah to be her maid.) 25When morning came, it was Leah! And Jacob said to Laban, "What is this you have done to me? Did I not serve with you for Rachel? Why then have you deceived me?" 26Laban said, "This is not done in our country—giving the younger before the firstborn. 27Complete the week of this one, and we will give you the other also in return for serving me another seven years." 28Jacob did so, and completed her week; then Laban gave him his daughter Rachel as a wife. 29(Laban gave his maid Bilhah to his daughter Rachel to be her maid.) 30So Jacob went in to Rachel also, and he loved Rachel more than Leah. He served Labano for another seven years.

31 When the LORD saw that Leah was unloved, he opened her womb; but Rachel was barren. 32Leah conceived and bore a son, and she named him Reuben;p for she said, "Because the LORD has looked on my affliction; surely now my husband will love me." 33She conceived again and bore a son, and said, "Because the LORD has heardq that I am hated, he has given me this son also"; and she named him Simeon. 34Again she conceived and bore a son, and said, "Now this time my husband will be joinedr to me, because I have borne him three sons"; therefore he was named Levi. 35She conceived again and bore a son, and said, "This time I will praises the LORD"; therefore she named him Judah; then she ceased bearing.

30 When Rachel saw that she bore Jacob no children, she envied her sister; and she said to Jacob, "Give me children, or I shall die!" 2Jacob became very angry with Rachel and said, "Am I in the place of God, who has withheld from you the fruit of the womb?" 3Then she said, "Here is my maid Bilhah; go in to her, that she may bear upon my knees and that I too may have children through her." 4So she gave him her maid Bilhah as a wife; and Jacob went in to her. 5And Bilhah conceived and bore Jacob a son. 6Then Rachel said, "God has judged me, and has also heard my voice and given me a son"; therefore she named him Dan.t 7Rachel's maid Bilhah conceived again and bore Jacob a second son. 8Then Rachel said, "With mighty wrestlings I have wrestledu with my sister, and have prevailed"; so she named him Naphtali.

9 When Leah saw that she had ceased bearing children, she took her maid Zilpah and gave her to Jacob as a wife. 10Then Leah's maid Zilpah bore Jacob a son. 11And Leah said, "Good fortune!" so she named him Gad.v 12Leah's maid Zilpah bore Jacob a second son. 13And Leah said, "Happy am I! For the women will call me happy"; so she named him Asher.w

14 In the days of wheat harvest Reuben went and found mandrakes in the field, and brought them to his mother Leah. Then Rachel said to Leah, "Please give me some of your son's mandrakes." 15But she said to her, "Is it a small matter that you have taken away my husband? Would you take away my son's mandrakes also?" Rachel said, "Then he may lie with you tonight for your son's mandrakes." 16When Jacob came from the field in the evening, Leah went out to meet him, and said, "You must come in to me; for I have hired you with my son's mandrakes." So he lay with her that night. 17And God heeded Leah, and she conceived and bore Jacob a fifth son. 18Leah said, "God has given me my hirex because I gave my maid to my husband"; so she named him Issachar. 19And Leah conceived again, and she bore Jacob a sixth son. 20Then Leah said,

o Heb him   p That is See, a son   q Heb shama   r Heb lawah   s Heb hodah   t That is He judged   u Heb niphtal   v That is Fortune   w That is Happy   x Heb sakar

"God has endowed me with a good dowry; now my husband will honor me, because I have borne him six sons"; so she named him Zebulun. ²¹Afterwards she bore a daughter, and named her Dinah.

22 Then God remembered Rachel, and God heeded her and opened her womb. ²³She conceived and bore a son, and said, "God has taken away my reproach"; ²⁴and she named him Joseph,ᶻ saying, "May the LORD add to me another son!"

Jacob Prospers at Laban's Expense

25 When Rachel had borne Joseph, Jacob said to Laban, "Send me away, that I may go to my own home and country. ²⁶Give me my wives and my children for whom I have served you, and let me go; for you know very well the service I have given you." ²⁷But Laban said to him, "If you will allow me to say so, I have learned by divination that the LORD has blessed me because of you; ²⁸name your wages, and I will give it." ²⁹Jacob said to him, "You yourself know how I have served you, and how your cattle have fared with me. ³⁰For you had little before I came, and it has increased abundantly; and the LORD has blessed you wherever I turned. But now when shall I provide for my own household also?" ³¹He said, "What shall I give you?" Jacob said, "You shall not give me anything; if you will do this for me, I will again feed your flock and keep it: ³²let me pass through all your flock today, removing from it every speckled and spotted sheep and every black lamb, and the spotted and speckled among the goats; and such shall be my wages. ³³So my honesty will answer for me later, when you come to look into my wages with you. Every one that is not speckled and spotted among the goats and black among the lambs, if found with me, shall be counted stolen." ³⁴Laban said, "Good! Let it be as you have said." ³⁵But that day Laban removed the male goats that were striped and spotted, and all the female goats that were speckled and spotted, every one that had white on it, and every lamb that was black, and put them in charge of his sons; ³⁶and he set

a distance of three days' journey between himself and Jacob, while Jacob was pasturing the rest of Laban's flock.

37 Then Jacob took fresh rods of poplar and almond and plane, and peeled white streaks in them, exposing the white of the rods. ³⁸He set the rods that he had peeled in front of the flocks in the troughs, that is, the watering places, where the flocks came to drink. And since they bred when they came to drink, ³⁹the flocks bred in front of the rods, and so the flocks produced young that were striped, speckled, and spotted. ⁴⁰Jacob separated the lambs, and set the faces of the flocks toward the striped and the completely black animals in the flock of Laban; and he put his own droves apart, and did not put them with Laban's flock. ⁴¹Whenever the stronger of the flock were breeding, Jacob laid the rods in the troughs before the eyes of the flock, that they might breed among the rods, ⁴²but for the feebler of the flock he did not lay them there; so the feebler were Laban's, and the stronger Jacob's. ⁴³Thus the man grew exceedingly rich, and had large flocks, and male and female slaves, and camels and donkeys.

Jacob Flees with Family and Flocks

31 Now Jacob heard that the sons of Laban were saying, "Jacob has taken all that was our father's; he has gained all this wealth from what belonged to our father." ²And Jacob saw that Laban did not regard him as favorably as he did before. ³Then the LORD said to Jacob, "Return to the land of your ancestors and to your kindred, and I will be with you." ⁴So Jacob sent and called Rachel and Leah into the field where his flock was, ⁵and said to them, "I see that your father does not regard me as favorably as he did before. But the God of my father has been with me. ⁶You know that I have served your father with all my strength; ⁷yet your father has cheated me and changed my wages ten times, but God did not permit him to harm me. ⁸If he said, 'The speckled shall be your wages,' then all the flock bore speckled; and if he said, 'The striped shall be your wages,' then all the flock bore striped. ⁹Thus God has taken

y Heb zabal   z That is He adds

away the livestock of your father, and given them to me.

10 During the mating of the flock I once had a dream in which I looked up and saw that the male goats that leaped upon the flock were striped, speckled, and mottled. 11Then the angel of God said to me in the dream, 'Jacob,' and I said, 'Here I am!' 12And he said, 'Look up and see that all the goats that leap on the flock are striped, speckled, and mottled; for I have seen all that Laban is doing to you. 13I am the God of Bethel,a where you anointed a pillar and made a vow to me. Now leave this land at once and return to the land of your birth.' " 14Then Rachel and Leah answered him, "Is there any portion or inheritance left to us in our father's house? 15Are we not regarded by him as foreigners? For he has sold us, and he has been using up the money given for us. 16All the property that God has taken away from our father belongs to us and to our children; now then, do whatever God has said to you."

17 So Jacob arose, and set his children and his wives on camels; 18and he drove away all his livestock, all the property that he had gained, the livestock in his possession that he had acquired in Paddan-aram, to go to his father Isaac in the land of Canaan.

19 Now Laban had gone to shear his sheep, and Rachel stole her father's household gods. 20And Jacob deceived Laban the Aramean, in that he did not tell him that he intended to flee. 21So he fled with all that he had; starting out he crossed the Euphrates,b and set his face toward the hill country of Gilead.

Laban Overtakes Jacob

22 On the third day Laban was told that Jacob had fled. 23So he took his kinsfolk with him and pursued him for seven days until he caught up with him in the hill country of Gilead. 24But God came to Laban the Aramean in a dream by night, and said to him, "Take heed that you say not a word to Jacob, either good or bad."

25 Laban overtook Jacob. Now Jacob had pitched his tent in the hill country, and Laban with his kinsfolk camped in the hill country of Gilead. 26Laban said

to Jacob, "What have you done? You have deceived me, and carried away my daughters like captives of the sword. 27Why did you flee secretly and deceive me and not tell me? I would have sent you away with mirth and songs, with tambourine and lyre. 28And why did you not permit me to kiss my sons and my daughters farewell? What you have done is foolish. 29It is in my power to do you harm; but the God of your father spoke to me last night, saying, 'Take heed that you speak to Jacob neither good nor bad.' 30Even though you had to go because you longed greatly for your father's house, why did you steal my gods?" 31Jacob answered Laban, "Because I was afraid, for I thought that you would take your daughters from me by force. 32But anyone with whom you find your gods shall not live. In the presence of our kinsfolk, point out what I have that is yours, and take it." Now Jacob did not know that Rachel had stolen the gods.c

33 So Laban went into Jacob's tent, and into Leah's tent, and into the tent of the two maids, but he did not find them. And he went out of Leah's tent, and entered Rachel's. 34Now Rachel had taken the household gods and put them in the camel's saddle, and sat on them. Laban felt all about in the tent, but did not find them. 35And she said to her father, "Let not my lord be angry that I cannot rise before you, for the way of women is upon me." So he searched, but did not find the household gods.

36 Then Jacob became angry, and upbraided Laban. Jacob said to Laban, "What is my offense? What is my sin, that you have hotly pursued me? 37Although you have felt about through all my goods, what have you found of all your household goods? Set it here before my kinsfolk and your kinsfolk, so that they may decide between us two. 38These twenty years I have been with you; your ewes and your female goats have not miscarried, and I have not eaten the rams of your flocks. 39That which was torn by wild beasts I did not bring to you; I bore the loss of it myself; of my hand you required it, whether stolen by day or stolen by night. 40It was like this

a Cn: Meaning of Heb uncertain   b Heb the river   c Heb them with me: by day the heat consumed me, and the cold by night, and my sleep fled from my eyes. 41These twenty years I have been in your house; I served you fourteen years for your two daughters, and six years for your flock, and you have changed my wages ten times. 42If the God of my father, the God of Abraham and the Fear*d* of Isaac, had not been on my side, surely now you would have sent me away empty-handed. God saw my affliction and the labor of my hands, and rebuked you last night."

Laban and Jacob Make a Covenant

43 Then Laban answered and said to Jacob, "The daughters are my daughters, the children are my children, the flocks are my flocks, and all that you see is mine. But what can I do today about these daughters of mine, or about their children whom they have borne? 44Come now, let us make a covenant, you and I; and let it be a witness between you and me." 45So Jacob took a stone, and set it up as a pillar. 46And Jacob said to his kinsfolk, "Gather stones," and they took stones, and made a heap; and they ate there by the heap. 47Laban called it Jegar-sahadutha:*e* but Jacob called it Galeed.*f* 48Laban said, "This heap is a witness between you and me today." Therefore he called it Galeed, 49and the pillar*g* Mizpah,*h* for he said, "The LORD watch between you and me, when we are absent one from the other. 50If you ill-treat my daughters, or if you take wives in addition to my daughters, though no one else is with us, remember that God is witness between you and me."

51 Then Laban said to Jacob, "See this heap and see the pillar, which I have set between you and me. 52This heap is a witness, and the pillar is a witness, that I will not pass beyond this heap to you, and you will not pass beyond this heap and this pillar to me, for harm. 53May the God of Abraham and the God of Nahor"—the God of their father— "judge between us." So Jacob swore by the Fear*d* of his father Isaac, 54and Jacob offered a sacrifice on the height and

called his kinsfolk to eat bread; and they ate bread and tarried all night in the hill country.

55*i* Early in the morning Laban rose up, and kissed his grandchildren and his daughters and blessed them; then he departed and returned home.

32 Jacob went on his way and the angels of God met him; 2and when Jacob saw them he said, "This is God's camp!" So he called that place Mahanaim.*j*

Jacob Sends Presents to Appease Esau

3 Jacob sent messengers before him to his brother Esau in the land of Seir, the country of Edom, 4instructing them, "Thus you shall say to my lord Esau: Thus says your servant Jacob, 'I have lived with Laban as an alien, and stayed until now; 5and I have oxen, donkeys, flocks, male and female slaves; and I have sent to tell my lord, in order that I may find favor in your sight.' "

6 The messengers returned to Jacob, saying, "We came to your brother Esau, and he is coming to meet you, and four hundred men are with him." 7Then Jacob was greatly afraid and distressed; and he divided the people that were with him, and the flocks and herds and camels, into two companies, 8thinking, "If Esau comes to the one company and destroys it, then the company that is left will escape."

9 And Jacob said, "O God of my father Abraham and God of my father Isaac, O LORD who said to me, 'Return to your country and to your kindred, and I will do you good,' 10I am not worthy of the least of all the steadfast love and all the faithfulness that you have shown to your servant, for with only my staff I crossed this Jordan; and now I have become two companies. 11Deliver me, please, from the hand of my brother, from the hand of Esau, for I am afraid of him; he may come and kill us all, the mothers with the children. 12Yet you have said, 'I will surely do you good, and make your offspring as the sand of the

d Meaning of Heb uncertain   *e* In Aramaic *The heap of witness*   *f* In Hebrew *The heap of witness*
g Compare Sam: MT lacks *the pillar*   *h* That is *Watchpost*   *i* Ch 32.1 in Heb   *j* Here taken to mean *Two camps*

sea, which cannot be counted because of their number.' "

13 So he spent that night there, and from what he had with him he took a present for his brother Esau, 14two hundred female goats and twenty male goats, two hundred ewes and twenty rams, 15thirty milch camels and their colts, forty cows and ten bulls, twenty female donkeys and ten male donkeys. 16These he delivered into the hand of his servants, every drove by itself, and said to his servants, "Pass on ahead of me, and put a space between drove and drove." 17He instructed the foremost, "When Esau my brother meets you, and asks you, 'To whom do you belong? Where are you going? And whose are these ahead of you?' 18then you shall say, 'They belong to your servant Jacob; they are a present sent to my lord Esau; and moreover he is behind us.' " 19He likewise instructed the second and the third and all who followed the droves, "You shall say the same thing to Esau when you meet him, 20and you shall say, 'Moreover your servant Jacob is behind us.' " For he thought, "I may appease him with the present that goes ahead of me, and afterwards I shall see his face; perhaps he will accept me." 21So the present passed on ahead of him; and he himself spent that night in the camp.

Jacob Wrestles at Peniel

22 The same night he got up and took his two wives, his two maids, and his eleven children, and crossed the ford of the Jabbok. 23He took them and sent them across the stream, and likewise everything that he had. 24Jacob was left alone; and a man wrestled with him until daybreak. 25When the man saw that he did not prevail against Jacob, he struck him on the hip socket; and Jacob's hip was put out of joint as he wrestled with him. 26Then he said, "Let me go, for the day is breaking." But Jacob said, "I will not let you go, unless you bless me." 27So he said to him, "What is your name?" And he said, "Jacob." 28Then the mank said, "You shall no longer be called Jacob, but Israel,l for you have striven with God and with humans,m and have

prevailed." 29Then Jacob asked him, "Please tell me your name." But he said, "Why is it that you ask my name?" And there he blessed him. 30So Jacob called the place Peniel,n saying, "For I have seen God face to face, and yet my life is preserved." 31The sun rose upon him as he passed Penuel, limping because of his hip. 32Therefore to this day the Israelites do not eat the thigh muscle that is on the hip socket, because he struck Jacob on the hip socket at the thigh muscle.

Jacob and Esau Meet

33 Now Jacob looked up and saw Esau coming, and four hundred men with him. So he divided the children among Leah and Rachel and the two maids. 2He put the maids with their children in front, then Leah with her children, and Rachel and Joseph last of all. 3He himself went on ahead of them, bowing himself to the ground seven times, until he came near his brother.

4 But Esau ran to meet him, and embraced him, and fell on his neck and kissed him, and they wept. 5When Esau looked up and saw the women and children, he said, "Who are these with you?" Jacob said, "The children whom God has graciously given your servant." 6Then the maids drew near, they and their children, and bowed down; 7Leah likewise and her children drew near and bowed down; and finally Joseph and Rachel drew near, and they bowed down. 8Esau said, "What do you mean by all this company that I met?" Jacob answered, "To find favor with my lord." 9But Esau said, "I have enough, my brother; keep what you have for yourself." 10Jacob said, "No, please; if I find favor with you, then accept my present from my hand; for truly to see your face is like seeing the face of God—since you have received me with such favor. 11Please accept my gift that is brought to you, because God has dealt graciously with me, and because I have everything I want." So he urged him, and he took it.

12 Then Esau said, "Let us journey on our way, and I will go alongside you." 13But Jacob said to him, "My lord knows

k Heb he   l That is The one who strives with God or God strives   m Or with divine and human beings   n That is The face of God

that the children are frail and that the
flocks and herds, which are nursing, are
a care to me; and if they are overdriven
for one day, all the flocks will die. 14 Let
my lord pass on ahead of his servant,
and I will lead on slowly, according to
the pace of the cattle that are before me
and according to the pace of the children, until I come to my lord in Seir."

15 So Esau said, "Let me leave with
you some of the people who are with
me." But he said, "Why should my lord
be so kind to me?" 16 So Esau returned
that day on his way to Seir. 17 But Jacob
journeyed to Succoth,[o] and built himself
a house, and made booths for his cattle;
therefore the place is called Succoth.

Jacob Reaches Shechem

18 Jacob came safely to the city of
Shechem, which is in the land of
Canaan, on his way from Paddan-aram;
and he camped before the city. 19 And
from the sons of Hamor, Shechem's
father, he bought for one hundred pieces
of money[p] the plot of land on which he
had pitched his tent. 20 There he erected
an altar and called it El-Elohe-Israel.[q]

The Rape of Dinah

34 Now Dinah the daughter of
Leah, whom she had borne to
Jacob, went out to visit the women of
the region. 2 When Shechem son of
Hamor the Hivite, prince of the region,
saw her, he seized her and lay with her
by force. 3 And his soul was drawn to
Dinah daughter of Jacob; he loved the
girl, and spoke tenderly to her. 4 So Shechem spoke to his father Hamor, saying,
"Get me this girl to be my wife."

5 Now Jacob heard that Shechem[r]
had defiled his daughter Dinah; but his
sons were with his cattle in the field, so
Jacob held his peace until they came.
6 And Hamor the father of Shechem
went out to Jacob to speak with him,
7 just as the sons of Jacob came in from
the field. When they heard of it, the men
were indignant and very angry, because
he had committed an outrage in Israel
by lying with Jacob's daughter, for such
a thing ought not to be done.

8 But Hamor spoke with them, saying, "The heart of my son Shechem
longs for your daughter; please give her
to him in marriage. 9 Make marriages
with us; give your daughters to us, and
take our daughters for yourselves. 10 You
shall live with us; and the land shall be
open to you; live and trade in it, and get
property in it." 11 Shechem also said to
her father and to her brothers, "Let me
find favor with you, and whatever you
say to me I will give. 12 Put the marriage
present and gift as high as you like, and I
will give whatever you ask me; only
give me the girl to be my wife."

13 The sons of Jacob answered Shechem and his father Hamor deceitfully,
because he had defiled their sister
Dinah. 14 They said to them, "We cannot
do this thing, to give our sister to one
who is uncircumcised, for that would be
a disgrace to us. 15 Only on this condition will we consent to you: that you
will become as we are and every male
among you be circumcised. 16 Then we
will give our daughters to you, and we
will take your daughters for ourselves,
and we will live among you and become
one people. 17 But if you will not listen to
us and be circumcised, then we will
take our daughter and be gone."

18 Their words pleased Hamor and
Hamor's son Shechem. 19 And the young
man did not delay to do the thing,
because he was delighted with Jacob's
daughter. Now he was the most honored
of all his family. 20 So Hamor and his son
Shechem came to the gate of their city
and spoke to the men of their city, saying, 21 "These people are friendly with
us; let them live in the land and trade in
it, for the land is large enough for them;
let us take their daughters in marriage,
and let us give them our daughters.
22 Only on this condition will they agree
to live among us, to become one people:
that every male among us be circumcised as they are circumcised. 23 Will not
their livestock, their property, and all
their animals be ours? Only let us agree
with them, and they will live among
us." 24 And all who went out of the city
gate heeded Hamor and his son Shechem; and every male was circumcised,
all who went out of the gate of his city.

o That is *Booths* p Heb *one hundred qesitah* q That is *God, the God of Israel* r Heb *he*

Dinah's Brothers Avenge Their Sister

25 On the third day, when they were still in pain, two of the sons of Jacob, Simeon and Levi, Dinah's brothers, took their swords and came against the city unawares, and killed all the males. 26They killed Hamor and his son Shechem with the sword, and took Dinah out of Shechem's house, and went away. 27And the other sons of Jacob came upon the slain, and plundered the city, because their sister had been defiled. 28They took their flocks and their herds, their donkeys, and whatever was in the city and in the field. 29All their wealth, all their little ones and their wives, all that was in the houses, they captured and made their prey. 30Then Jacob said to Simeon and Levi, "You have brought trouble on me by making me odious to the inhabitants of the land, the Canaanites and the Perizzites; my numbers are few, and if they gather themselves against me and attack me, I shall be destroyed, both I and my household." 31But they said, "Should our sister be treated like a whore?"

Jacob Returns to Bethel

35 God said to Jacob, "Arise, go up to Bethel, and settle there. Make an altar there to the God who appeared to you when you fled from your brother Esau." 2So Jacob said to his household and to all who were with him, "Put away the foreign gods that are among you, and purify yourselves, and change your clothes; 3then come, let us go up to Bethel, that I may make an altar there to the God who answered me in the day of my distress and has been with me wherever I have gone." 4So they gave to Jacob all the foreign gods that they had, and the rings that were in their ears; and Jacob hid them under the oak that was near Shechem.

5 As they journeyed, a terror from God fell upon the cities all around them, so that no one pursued them. 6Jacob came to Luz (that is, Bethel), which is in the land of Canaan, he and all the people who were with him, 7and there he built an altar and called the place El-bethel,s

because it was there that God had revealed himself to him when he fled from his brother. 8And Deborah, Rebekah's nurse, died, and she was buried under an oak below Bethel. So it was called Allon-bacuth.t

9 God appeared to Jacob again when he came from Paddan-aram, and he blessed him. 10God said to him, "Your name is Jacob; no longer shall you be called Jacob, but Israel shall be your name." So he was called Israel. 11God said to him, "I am God Almighty:u be fruitful and multiply; a nation and a company of nations shall come from you, and kings shall spring from you. 12The land that I gave to Abraham and Isaac I will give to you, and I will give the land to your offspring after you." 13Then God went up from him at the place where he had spoken with him. 14Jacob set up a pillar in the place where he had spoken with him, a pillar of stone; and he poured out a drink offering on it, and poured oil on it. 15So Jacob called the place where God had spoken with him Bethel.

The Birth of Benjamin and the Death of Rachel

16 Then they journeyed from Bethel; and when they were still some distance from Ephrath, Rachel was in childbirth, and she had hard labor. 17When she was in her hard labor, the midwife said to her, "Do not be afraid; for now you will have another son." 18As her soul was departing (for she died), she named him Ben-oni;v but his father called him Benjamin.w 19So Rachel died, and she was buried on the way to Ephrath (that is, Bethlehem), 20and Jacob set up a pillar at her grave; it is the pillar of Rachel's tomb, which is there to this day. 21Israel journeyed on, and pitched his tent beyond the tower of Eder.

22 While Israel lived in that land, Reuben went and lay with Bilhah his father's concubine; and Israel heard of it.

Now the sons of Jacob were twelve. 23The sons of Leah: Reuben (Jacob's firstborn), Simeon, Levi, Judah, Issachar, and Zebulun. 24The sons of Rachel: Joseph and Benjamin. 25The sons of Bilhah,

---

s That is God of Bethel   t That is Oak of weeping   u Traditional rendering of Heb El Shaddai
v That is Son of my sorrow   w That is Son of the right hand or Son of the South

Rachel's maid: Dan and Naphtali. 26The sons of Zilpah, Leah's maid: Gad and Asher. These were the sons of Jacob who were born to him in Paddan-aram.

The Death of Isaac

27 Jacob came to his father Isaac at Mamre, or Kiriath-arba (that is, Hebron), where Abraham and Isaac had resided as aliens. 28Now the days of Isaac were one hundred eighty years. 29And Isaac breathed his last; he died and was gathered to his people, old and full of days; and his sons Esau and Jacob buried him.

Esau's Descendants

36 These are the descendants of Esau (that is, Edom). 2Esau took his wives from the Canaanites: Adah daughter of Elon the Hittite, Oholibamah daughter of Anah son^x of Zibeon the Hivite, 3and Basemath, Ishmael's daughter, sister of Nebaioth. 4Adah bore Eliphaz to Esau; Basemath bore Reuel; 5and Oholibamah bore Jeush, Jalam, and Korah. These were the sons of Esau who were born to him in the land of Canaan.

6 Then Esau took his wives, his sons, his daughters, and all the members of his household, his cattle, all his livestock, and all the property he had acquired in the land of Canaan; and he moved to a land some distance from his brother Jacob. 7For their possessions were too great for them to live together; the land where they were staying could not support them because of their livestock. 8So Esau settled in the hill country of Seir; Esau is Edom.

9 These are the descendants of Esau, ancestor of the Edomites, in the hill country of Seir. 10These are the names of Esau's sons: Eliphaz son of Adah the wife of Esau; Reuel, the son of Esau's wife Basemath. 11The sons of Eliphaz were Teman, Omar, Zepho, Gatam, and Kenaz. 12(Timna was a concubine of Eliphaz, Esau's son; she bore Amalek to Eliphaz.) These were the sons of Adah, Esau's wife. 13These were the sons of Reuel: Nahath, Zerah, Shammah, and Mizzah. These were the sons of Esau's wife, Basemath. 14These were the sons of Esau's wife Oholibamah, daughter of

Anah son^y of Zibeon: she bore to Esau Jeush, Jalam, and Korah.

Clans and Kings of Edom

15 These are the clans^z of the sons of Esau. The sons of Eliphaz the firstborn of Esau: the clans^z Teman, Omar, Zepho, Kenaz, 16Korah, Gatam, and Amalek; these are the clans^z of Eliphaz in the land of Edom; they are the sons of Adah. 17These are the sons of Esau's son Reuel: the clans^z Nahath, Zerah, Shammah, and Mizzah; these are the clans^z of Reuel in the land of Edom; they are the sons of Esau's wife Basemath. 18These are the sons of Esau's wife Oholibamah: the clans^z Jeush, Jalam, and Korah; these are the clans^z born of Esau's wife Oholibamah, the daughter of Anah. 19These are the sons of Esau (that is, Edom), and these are their clans.^{z}

20 These are the sons of Seir the Horite, the inhabitants of the land: Lotan, Shobal, Zibeon, Anah, 21Dishon, Ezer, and Dishan; these are the clans^z of the Horites, the sons of Seir in the land of Edom. 22The sons of Lotan were Hori and Heman; and Lotan's sister was Timna. 23These are the sons of Shobal: Alvan, Manahath, Ebal, Shepho, and Onam. 24These are the sons of Zibeon: Aiah and Anah; he is the Anah who found the springs^a in the wilderness, as he pastured the donkeys of his father Zibeon. 25These are the children of Anah: Dishon and Oholibamah daughter of Anah. 26These are the sons of Dishon: Hemdan, Eshban, Ithran, and Cheran. 27These are the sons of Ezer: Bilhan, Zaavan, and Akan. 28These are the sons of Dishan: Uz and Aran. 29These are the clans^z of the Horites: the clans^z Lotan, Shobal, Zibeon, Anah, 30Dishon, Ezer, and Dishan; these are the clans^z of the Horites, clan by clan^b in the land of Seir.

31 These are the kings who reigned in the land of Edom, before any king reigned over the Israelites. 32Bela son of Beor reigned in Edom, the name of his city being Dinhabah. 33Bela died, and Jobab son of Zerah of Bozrah succeeded him as king. 34Jobab died, and Husham of the land of the Temanites succeeded

x Sam Gk Syr: Heb *daughter*   y Gk Syr: Heb *daughter*   z Or *chiefs*   a Meaning of Heb uncertain
b Or *chief by chief*

him as king. 35Husham died, and Hadad son of Bedad, who defeated Midian in the country of Moab, succeeded him as king, the name of his city being Avith. 36Hadad died, and Samlah of Masrekah succeeded him as king. 37Samlah died, and Shaul of Rehoboth on the Euphrates succeeded him as king. 38Shaul died, and Baal-hanan son of Achbor succeeded him as king. 39Baal-hanan son of Achbor died, and Hadar succeeded him as king, the name of his city being Pau; his wife's name was Mehetabel, the daughter of Matred, daughter of Me-zahab.

40 These are the names of the clansc of Esau, according to their families and their localities by their names: the clansc Timna, Alvah, Jetheth, 41Oholibamah, Elah, Pinon, 42Kenaz, Teman, Mibzar, 43Magdiel, and Iram; these are the clansc of Edom (that is, Esau, the father of Edom), according to their settlements in the land that they held.

Joseph Dreams of Greatness

37 Jacob settled in the land where his father had lived as an alien, the land of Canaan. 2This is the story of the family of Jacob.

Joseph, being seventeen years old, was shepherding the flock with his brothers; he was a helper to the sons of Bilhah and Zilpah, his father's wives; and Joseph brought a bad report of them to their father. 3Now Israel loved Joseph more than any other of his children, because he was the son of his old age; and he had made him a long robe with sleeves.d 4But when his brothers saw that their father loved him more than all his brothers, they hated him, and could not speak peaceably to him.

CRUELTY IS A DETESTED SPORT THAT OWES ITS PLEASURES TO ANOTHER'S PAIN.

—*William Cowper*

---

5 Once Joseph had a dream, and when he told it to his brothers, they hated him even more. 6He said to them, "Listen to this dream that I dreamed. 7There we were, binding sheaves in the field. Suddenly my sheaf rose and stood upright; then your sheaves gathered around it, and bowed down to my sheaf." 8His brothers said to him, "Are you indeed to reign over us? Are you indeed to have dominion over us?" So they hated him even more because of his dreams and his words.

9 He had another dream, and told it to his brothers, saying, "Look, I have had another dream: the sun, the moon, and eleven stars were bowing down to me." 10But when he told it to his father and to his brothers, his father rebuked him, and said to him, "What kind of dream is this that you have had? Shall we indeed come, I and your mother and your brothers, and bow to the ground before you?" 11So his brothers were jealous of him, but his father kept the matter in mind.

Joseph Is Sold by His Brothers

12 Now his brothers went to pasture their father's flock near Shechem. 13And Israel said to Joseph, "Are not your brothers pasturing the flock at Shechem? Come, I will send you to them." He answered, "Here I am." 14So he said to him, "Go now, see if it is well with your brothers and with the flock; and bring word back to me." So he sent him from the valley of Hebron.

He came to Shechem, 15and a man found him wandering in the fields; the man asked him, "What are you seeking?" 16"I am seeking my brothers," he said; "tell me, please, where they are pasturing the flock." 17The man said, "They have gone away, for I heard them say, 'Let us go to Dothan.' " So Joseph went after his brothers, and found them at Dothan. 18They saw him from a distance, and before he came near to them, they conspired to kill him. 19They said to one another, "Here comes this dreamer. 20Come now, let us kill him and throw him into one of the pits; then we shall say that a wild animal has devoured him, and we shall see what will become of his dreams." 21But when Reuben heard it, he delivered him out of their hands, saying, "Let us not take his life." 22Reuben said to them, "Shed no blood; throw him into this pit here in the wilderness, but lay no hand on him"— that he might rescue him out of their

---

c Or *chiefs*   d Traditional rendering (compare Gk): *a coat of many colors*; Meaning of Heb uncertain

hand and restore him to his father. 23So when Joseph came to his brothers, they stripped him of his robe, the long robe with sleeves*e* that he wore; 24and they took him and threw him into a pit. The pit was empty; there was no water in it.

25 Then they sat down to eat; and looking up they saw a caravan of Ishmaelites coming from Gilead, with their camels carrying gum, balm, and resin, on their way to carry it down to Egypt. 26Then Judah said to his brothers, "What profit is it if we kill our brother and conceal his blood? 27Come, let us sell him to the Ishmaelites, and not lay our hands on him, for he is our brother, our own flesh." And his brothers agreed. 28When some Midianite traders passed by, they drew Joseph up, lifting him out of the pit, and sold him to the Ishmaelites for twenty pieces of silver. And they took Joseph to Egypt.

29 When Reuben returned to the pit and saw that Joseph was not in the pit, he tore his clothes. 30He returned to his brothers, and said, "The boy is gone; and I, where can I turn?" 31Then they took Joseph's robe, slaughtered a goat, and dipped the robe in the blood. 32They had the long robe with sleeves*e* taken to their father, and they said, "This we have found; see now whether it is your son's robe or not." 33He recognized it, and said, "It is my son's robe! A wild animal has devoured him; Joseph is without doubt torn to pieces." 34Then Jacob tore his garments, and put sackcloth on his loins, and mourned for his son many days. 35All his sons and all his daughters sought to comfort him; but he refused to be comforted, and said, "No, I shall go down to Sheol to my son, mourning." Thus his father bewailed him. 36Meanwhile the Midianites had sold him in Egypt to Potiphar, one of Pharaoh's officials, the captain of the guard.

Judah and Tamar

38 It happened at that time that Judah went down from his brothers and settled near a certain Adullamite whose name was Hirah. 2There Judah saw the daughter of a certain Canaanite whose name was Shua; he married her and went in to her. 3She conceived and bore a son; and he named him Er. 4Again she conceived and bore a son whom she named Onan. 5Yet again she bore a son, and she named him Shelah. She*f* was in Chezib when she bore him. 6Judah took a wife for Er his firstborn; her name was Tamar. 7But Er, Judah's firstborn, was wicked in the sight of the LORD, and the LORD put him to death. 8Then Judah said to Onan, "Go in to your brother's wife and perform the duty of a brother-in-law to her; raise up offspring for your brother." 9But since Onan knew that the offspring would not be his, he spilled his semen on the ground whenever he went in to his brother's wife, so that he would not give offspring to his brother. 10What he did was displeasing in the sight of the LORD, and he put him to death also. 11Then Judah said to his daughter-in-law Tamar, "Remain a widow in your father's house until my son Shelah grows up"—for he feared that he too would die, like his brothers. So Tamar went to live in her father's house.

12 In course of time the wife of Judah, Shua's daughter, died; when Judah's time of mourning was over,*g* he went up to Timnah to his sheepshearers, he and his friend Hirah the Adullamite. 13When Tamar was told, "Your father-in-law is going up to Timnah to shear his sheep," 14she put off her widow's garments, put on a veil, wrapped herself up, and sat down at the entrance to Enaim, which is on the road to Timnah. She saw that Shelah was grown up, yet she had not been given to him in marriage. 15When Judah saw her, he thought her to be a prostitute, for she had covered her face. 16He went over to her at the roadside, and said, "Come, let me come in to you," for he did not know that she was his daughter-in-law. She said, "What will you give me, that you may come in to me?" 17He answered, "I will send you a kid from the flock." And she said, "Only if you give me a pledge, until you send it." 18He said, "What pledge shall I give you?" She replied, "Your signet and your cord, and the staff that is in your hand." So he gave them to her, and went in to her, and she conceived by him. 19Then she got up and

went away, and taking off her veil she put on the garments of her widowhood. 20 When Judah sent the kid by his friend the Adullamite, to recover the pledge from the woman, he could not find her. 21He asked the townspeople, "Where is the temple prostitute who was at Enaim by the wayside?" But they said, "No prostitute has been here." 22So he returned to Judah, and said, "I have not found her; moreover the townspeople said, 'No prostitute has been here.' " 23Judah replied, "Let her keep the things as her own, otherwise we will be laughed at; you see, I sent this kid, and you could not find her."

24 About three months later Judah was told, "Your daughter-in-law Tamar has played the whore; moreover she is pregnant as a result of whoredom." And Judah said, "Bring her out, and let her be burned." 25As she was being brought out, she sent word to her father-in-law, "It was the owner of these who made me pregnant." And she said, "Take note, please, whose these are, the signet and the cord and the staff." 26Then Judah acknowledged them and said, "She is more in the right than I, since I did not give her to my son Shelah." And he did not lie with her again.

27 When the time of her delivery came, there were twins in her womb. 28While she was in labor, one put out a hand; and the midwife took and bound on his hand a crimson thread, saying, "This one came out first." 29But just then he drew back his hand, and out came his brother; and she said, "What a breach you have made for yourself!" Therefore he was named Perez.h 30Afterward his brother came out with the crimson thread on his hand; and he was named Zerah.i

Joseph and Potiphar's Wife

39 Now Joseph was taken down to Egypt, and Potiphar, an officer of Pharaoh, the captain of the guard, an Egyptian, bought him from the Ishmaelites who had brought him down there. 2The LORD was with Joseph, and he became a successful man; he was in the house of his Egyptian master. 3His master saw that the LORD was with him,

and that the LORD caused all that he did to prosper in his hands. 4So Joseph found favor in his sight and attended him; he made him overseer of his house and put him in charge of all that he had. 5From the time that he made him overseer in his house and over all that he had, the LORD blessed the Egyptian's house for Joseph's sake; the blessing of the LORD was on all that he had, in house and field. 6So he left all that he had in Joseph's charge; and, with him there, he had no concern for anything but the food that he ate.

Now Joseph was handsome and good-looking. 7And after a time his master's wife cast her eyes on Joseph and said, "Lie with me." 8But he refused and said to his master's wife, "Look, with me here, my master has no concern about anything in the house, and he has put everything that he has in my hand. 9He is not greater in this house than I am, nor has he kept back anything from me except yourself, because you are his wife. How then could I do this great wickedness, and sin against God?" 10And although she spoke to Joseph day after day, he would not consent to lie beside her or to be with her. 11One day, however, when he went into the house to do his work, and while no one else was in the house, 12she caught hold of his garment, saying, "Lie with me!" But he left his garment in her hand, and fled and ran outside. 13When she saw that he had left his garment in her hand and had fled outside, 14she called out to the members of her household and said to them, "See, my husbandj has brought among us a Hebrew to insult us! He came in to me to lie with me, and I cried out with a loud voice; 15and when he heard me raise my voice and cry out, he left his garment beside me, and fled outside." 16Then she kept his garment by her until his master came home, 17and she told him the same story, saying, "The Hebrew servant, whom you have brought among us, came in to me to insult me; 18but as soon as I raised my voice and cried out, he left his garment beside me, and fled outside."

19 When his master heard the words that his wife spoke to him, saying,

---

h That is A breach   i That is Brightness; perhaps alluding to the crimson thread   j Heb he

"This is the way your servant treated me," he became enraged. 20And Joseph's master took him and put him into the prison, the place where the king's prisoners were confined; he remained there in prison. 21But the LORD was with Joseph and showed him steadfast love; he gave him favor in the sight of the chief jailer. 22The chief jailer committed to Joseph's care all the prisoners who were in the prison, and whatever was done there, he was the one who did it. 23The chief jailer paid no heed to anything that was in Joseph's care, because the LORD was with him; and whatever he did, the LORD made it prosper.

The Dreams of Two Prisoners

40 Some time after this, the cupbearer of the king of Egypt and his baker offended their lord the king of Egypt. 2Pharaoh was angry with his two officers, the chief cupbearer and the chief baker, 3and he put them in custody in the house of the captain of the guard, in the prison where Joseph was confined. 4The captain of the guard charged Joseph with them, and he waited on them; and they continued for some time in custody. 5One night they both dreamed—the cupbearer and the baker of the king of Egypt, who were confined in the prison—each his own dream, and each dream with its own meaning. 6When Joseph came to them in the morning, he saw that they were troubled. 7So he asked Pharaoh's officers, who were with him in custody in his master's house, "Why are your faces downcast today?" 8They said to him, "We have had dreams, and there is no one to interpret them." And Joseph said to them, "Do not interpretations belong to God? Please tell them to me."

9 So the chief cupbearer told his dream to Joseph, and said to him, "In my dream there was a vine before me, 10and on the vine there were three branches. As soon as it budded, its blossoms came out and the clusters ripened into grapes. 11Pharaoh's cup was in my hand; and I took the grapes and pressed them into Pharaoh's cup, and placed the cup in Pharaoh's hand." 12Then Joseph said to him, "This is its interpretation: the three branches are three days;

13within three days Pharaoh will lift up your head and restore you to your office; and you shall place Pharaoh's cup in his hand, just as you used to do when you were his cupbearer. 14But remember me when it is well with you; please do me the kindness to make mention of me to Pharaoh, and so get me out of this place. 15For in fact I was stolen out of the land of the Hebrews; and here also I have done nothing that they should have put me into the dungeon."

16 When the chief baker saw that the interpretation was favorable, he said to Joseph, "I also had a dream: there were three cake baskets on my head, 17and in the uppermost basket there were all sorts of baked food for Pharaoh, but the birds were eating it out of the basket on my head." 18And Joseph answered, "This is its interpretation: the three baskets are three days; 19within three days Pharaoh will lift up your head—from you!—and hang you on a pole; and the birds will eat the flesh from you."

20 On the third day, which was Pharaoh's birthday, he made a feast for all his servants, and lifted up the head of the chief cupbearer and the head of the chief baker among his servants. 21He restored the chief cupbearer to his cupbearing, and he placed the cup in Pharaoh's hand; 22but the chief baker he hanged, just as Joseph had interpreted to them. 23Yet the chief cupbearer did not remember Joseph, but forgot him.

Joseph Interprets Pharaoh's Dream

41 After two whole years, Pharaoh dreamed that he was standing by the Nile, 2and there came up out of the Nile seven sleek and fat cows, and they grazed in the reed grass. 3Then seven other cows, ugly and thin, came up out of the Nile after them, and stood by the other cows on the bank of the Nile. 4The ugly and thin cows ate up the seven sleek and fat cows. And Pharaoh awoke. 5Then he fell asleep and dreamed a second time; seven ears of grain, plump and good, were growing on one stalk. 6Then seven ears, thin and blighted by the east wind, sprouted after them. 7The thin ears swallowed up the seven plump and full ears. Pharaoh awoke, and it was a dream. 8In the morning his spirit was troubled; so he sent and called for all the magicians of Egypt and all its wise men. Pharaoh told them his dreams, but there was no one who could interpret them to Pharaoh.

9 Then the chief cupbearer said to Pharaoh, "I remember my faults today. 10Once Pharaoh was angry with his servants, and put me and the chief baker in custody in the house of the captain of the guard. 11We dreamed on the same night, he and I, each having a dream with its own meaning. 12A young Hebrew was there with us, a servant of the captain of the guard. When we told him, he interpreted our dreams to us, giving an interpretation to each according to his dream. 13As he interpreted to us, so it turned out; I was restored to my office, and the baker was hanged."

14 Then Pharaoh sent for Joseph, and he was hurriedly brought out of the dungeon. When he had shaved himself and changed his clothes, he came in before Pharaoh. 15And Pharaoh said to Joseph, "I have had a dream, and there is no one who can interpret it. I have heard it said of you that when you hear a dream you can interpret it." 16Joseph answered Pharaoh, "It is not I; God will give Pharaoh a favorable answer." 17Then Pharaoh said to Joseph, "In my dream I was standing on the banks of the Nile; 18and seven cows, fat and sleek, came up out of the Nile and fed in the reed grass. 19Then seven other cows came up after them, poor, very ugly, and thin. Never had I seen such ugly ones in all the land of Egypt. 20The thin and ugly cows ate up the first seven fat cows, 21but when they had eaten them no one would have known that they had done so, for they were still as ugly as before. Then I awoke. 22I fell asleep a second time[k] and I saw in my dream seven ears of grain, full and good, growing on one stalk, 23and seven ears, withered, thin, and blighted by the east wind, sprouting after them; 24and the thin ears swallowed up the seven good ears. But when I told it to the magicians, there was no one who could explain it to me."

25 Then Joseph said to Pharaoh, "Pharaoh's dreams are one and the same; God has revealed to Pharaoh what

he is about to do. 26The seven good cows are seven years, and the seven good ears are seven years; the dreams are one. 27The seven lean and ugly cows that came up after them are seven years, as are the seven empty ears blighted by the east wind. They are seven years of famine. 28It is as I told Pharaoh; God has shown to Pharaoh what he is about to do. 29There will come seven years of great plenty throughout all the land of Egypt. 30After them there will arise seven years of famine, and all the plenty will be forgotten in the land of Egypt; the famine will consume the land. 31The plenty will no longer be known in the land because of the famine that will follow, for it will be very grievous. 32And the doubling of Pharaoh's dream means that the thing is fixed by God, and God will shortly bring it about. 33Now therefore let Pharaoh select a man who is discerning and wise, and set him over the land of Egypt. 34Let Pharaoh proceed to appoint overseers over the land, and take one-fifth of the produce of the land of Egypt during the seven plenteous years. 35Let them gather all the food of these good years that are coming, and lay up grain under the authority of Pharaoh for food in the cities, and let them keep it. 36That food shall be a reserve for the land against the seven years of famine that are to befall the land of Egypt, so that the land may not perish through the famine."

Joseph's Rise to Power

37 The proposal pleased Pharaoh and all his servants. 38Pharaoh said to his servants, "Can we find anyone else like this—one in whom is the spirit of God?" 39So Pharaoh said to Joseph, "Since God has shown you all this, there is no one so discerning and wise as you. 40You shall be over my house, and all my people shall order themselves as you command; only with regard to the throne will I be greater than you." 41And Pharaoh said to Joseph, "See, I have set you over all the land of Egypt." 42Removing his signet ring from his hand, Pharaoh put it on Joseph's hand; he arrayed him in garments of fine linen, and put a gold chain around his neck. 43He had him

---

k Gk Syr Vg: Heb lacks *I fell asleep a second time*

ride in the chariot of his second-in-command; and they cried out in front of him, "Bow the knee!"[1] Thus he set him over all the land of Egypt. [44]Moreover Pharaoh said to Joseph, "I am Pharaoh, and without your consent no one shall lift up hand or foot in all the land of Egypt." [45]Pharaoh gave Joseph the name Zaphenath-paneah; and he gave him Asenath daughter of Potiphera, priest of On, as his wife. Thus Joseph gained authority over the land of Egypt.

46 Joseph was thirty years old when he entered the service of Pharaoh king of Egypt. And Joseph went out from the presence of Pharaoh, and went through all the land of Egypt. [47]During the seven plenteous years the earth produced abundantly. [48]He gathered up all the food of the seven years when there was plenty[m] in the land of Egypt, and stored up food in the cities; he stored up in every city the food from the fields around it. [49]So Joseph stored up grain in such abundance—like the sand of the sea—that he stopped measuring it; it was beyond measure.

50 Before the years of famine came, Joseph had two sons, whom Asenath daughter of Potiphera, priest of On, bore to him. [51]Joseph named the firstborn Manasseh,[n] "For," he said, "God has made me forget all my hardship and all my father's house." [52]The second he named Ephraim,[o] "For God has made me fruitful in the land of my misfortunes."

53 The seven years of plenty that prevailed in the land of Egypt came to an end; [54]and the seven years of famine began to come, just as Joseph had said. There was famine in every country, but throughout the land of Egypt there was bread. [55]When all the land of Egypt was famished, the people cried to Pharaoh for bread. Pharaoh said to all the Egyptians, "Go to Joseph; what he says to you, do." [56]And since the famine had spread over all the land, Joseph opened all the storehouses,[p] and sold to the Egyptians, for the famine was severe in the land of Egypt. [57]Moreover, all the world came to Joseph in Egypt to buy grain, because the famine became severe throughout the world.

Joseph's Brothers Go to Egypt

[42] When Jacob learned that there was grain in Egypt, he said to his sons, "Why do you keep looking at one another? [2]I have heard," he said, "that there is grain in Egypt; go down and buy grain for us there, that we may live and not die." [3]So ten of Joseph's brothers went down to buy grain in Egypt. [4]But Jacob did not send Joseph's brother Benjamin with his brothers, for he feared that harm might come to him. [5]Thus the sons of Israel were among the other people who came to buy grain, for the famine had reached the land of Canaan.

6 Now Joseph was governor over the land; it was he who sold to all the people of the land. And Joseph's brothers came and bowed themselves before him with their faces to the ground. [7]When Joseph saw his brothers, he recognized them, but he treated them like strangers and spoke harshly to them. "Where do you come from?" he said. They said, "From the land of Canaan, to buy food." [8]Although Joseph had recognized his brothers, they did not recognize him. [9]Joseph also remembered the dreams that he had dreamed about them. He said to them, "You are spies; you have come to see the nakedness of the land!" [10]They said to him, "No, my lord; your servants have come to buy food. [11]We are all sons of one man; we are honest men; your servants have never been spies." [12]But he said to them, "No, you have come to see the nakedness of the land!" [13]They said, "We, your servants, are twelve brothers, the sons of a certain man in the land of Canaan; the youngest, however, is now with our father, and one is no more." [14]But Joseph said to them, "It is just as I have said to you; you are spies! [15]Here is how you shall be tested: as Pharaoh lives, you shall not leave this place unless your youngest brother comes here! [16]Let one of you go and bring your brother, while the rest of you remain in prison, in order that your

---

1 Abrek, apparently an Egyptian word similar in sound to the Hebrew word meaning *to kneel*   *m* Sam Gk: MT *the seven years that were*   *n* That is *Making to forget*   *o* From a Hebrew word meaning *to be fruitful*   *p* Gk Vg Compare Syr: Heb *opened all that was in* (or, *among*) *them*

words may be tested, whether there is truth in you; or else, as Pharaoh lives, surely you are spies." 17And he put them all together in prison for three days.

18 On the third day Joseph said to them, "Do this and you will live, for I fear God: 19if you are honest men, let one of your brothers stay here where you are imprisoned. The rest of you shall go and carry grain for the famine of your households, 20and bring your youngest brother to me. Thus your words will be verified, and you shall not die." And they agreed to do so. 21They said to one another, "Alas, we are paying the penalty for what we did to our brother; we saw his anguish when he pleaded with us, but we would not listen. That is why this anguish has come upon us." 22Then Reuben answered them, "Did I not tell you not to wrong the boy? But you would not listen. So now there comes a reckoning for his blood." 23They did not know that Joseph understood them, since he spoke with them through an interpreter. 24He turned away from them and wept; then he returned and spoke to them. And he picked out Simeon and had him bound before their eyes. 25Joseph then gave orders to fill their bags with grain, to return every man's money to his sack, and to give them provisions for their journey. This was done for them.

Joseph's Brothers Return to Canaan

26 They loaded their donkeys with their grain, and departed. 27When one of them opened his sack to give his donkey fodder at the lodging place, he saw his money at the top of the sack. 28He said to his brothers, "My money has been put back; here it is in my sack!" At this they lost heart and turned trembling to one another, saying, "What is this that God has done to us?"

29 When they came to their father Jacob in the land of Canaan, they told him all that had happened to them, saying, 30"The man, the lord of the land, spoke harshly to us, and charged us with spying on the land. 31But we said to him, 'We are honest men, we are not spies. 32We are twelve brothers, sons of our father; one is no more, and the youngest is now with our father in the land of Canaan.' 33Then the man, the lord of the land, said to us, 'By this I shall know that you are honest men: take grain for the famine of your households, and go your way. 34Bring your youngest brother to me, and I shall know that you are not spies but honest men. Then I will release your brother to you, and you may trade in the land.' "

35 As they were emptying their sacks, there in each one's sack was his bag of money. When they and their father saw their bundles of money, they were dismayed. 36And their father Jacob said to them, "I am the one you have bereaved of children: Joseph is no more, and Simeon is no more, and now you would take Benjamin. All this has happened to me!" 37Then Reuben said to his father, "You may kill my two sons if I do not bring him back to you. Put him in my hands, and I will bring him back to you." 38But he said, "My son shall not go down with you, for his brother is dead, and he alone is left. If harm should come to him on the journey that you are to make, you would bring down my gray hairs with sorrow to Sheol."

The Brothers Come Again, Bringing Benjamin

43 Now the famine was severe in the land. 2And when they had eaten up the grain that they had brought from Egypt, their father said to them, "Go again, buy us a little more food." 3But Judah said to him, "The man solemnly warned us, saying, 'You shall not see my face unless your brother is with you.' 4If you will send our brother with us, we will go down and buy you food; 5but if you will not send him, we will not go down, for the man said to us, 'You shall not see my face, unless your brother is with you.' " 6Israel said, "Why did you treat me so badly as to tell the man that you had another brother?" 7They replied, "The man questioned us carefully about ourselves and our kindred, saying, 'Is your father still alive? Have you another brother?' What we told him was in answer to these questions. Could we in any way know that he would say, 'Bring your brother down'?" 8Then Judah said to his father

Israel, "Send the boy with me, and let us be on our way, so that we may live and not die—you and we and also our little ones. ⁹I myself will be surety for him; you can hold me accountable for him. If I do not bring him back to you and set him before you, then let me bear the blame forever. ¹⁰If we had not delayed, we would now have returned twice."

11 Then their father Israel said to them, "If it must be so, then do this: take some of the choice fruits of the land in your bags, and carry them down as a present to the man—a little balm and a little honey, gum, resin, pistachio nuts, and almonds. ¹²Take double the money with you. Carry back with you the money that was returned in the top of your sacks; perhaps it was an oversight. ¹³Take your brother also, and be on your way again to the man; ¹⁴may God Almighty*q* grant you mercy before the man, so that he may send back your other brother and Benjamin. As for me, if I am bereaved of my children, I am bereaved." ¹⁵So the men took the present, and they took double the money with them, as well as Benjamin. Then they went on their way down to Egypt, and stood before Joseph.

16 When Joseph saw Benjamin with them, he said to the steward of his house, "Bring the men into the house, and slaughter an animal and make ready, for the men are to dine with me at noon." ¹⁷The man did as Joseph said, and brought the men to Joseph's house. ¹⁸Now the men were afraid because they were brought to Joseph's house, and they said, "It is because of the money, replaced in our sacks the first time, that we have been brought in, so that he may have an opportunity to fall upon us, to make slaves of us and take our donkeys." ¹⁹So they went up to the steward of Joseph's house and spoke with him at the entrance to the house. ²⁰They said, "Oh, my lord, we came down the first time to buy food; ²¹and when we came to the lodging place we opened our sacks, and there was each one's money in the top of his sack, our money in full weight. So we have brought it back with us. ²²Moreover we have brought down with us additional money to buy food.

We do not know who put our money in our sacks." ²³He replied, "Rest assured, do not be afraid; your God and the God of your father must have put treasure in your sacks for you; I received your money." Then he brought Simeon out to them. ²⁴When the steward*r* had brought the men into Joseph's house, and given them water, and they had washed their feet, and when he had given their donkeys fodder, ²⁵they made the present ready for Joseph's coming at noon, for they had heard that they would dine there.

26 When Joseph came home, they brought him the present that they had carried into the house, and bowed to the ground before him. ²⁷He inquired about their welfare, and said, "Is your father well, the old man of whom you spoke? Is he still alive?" ²⁸They said, "Your servant our father is well; he is still alive." And they bowed their heads and did obeisance. ²⁹Then he looked up and saw his brother Benjamin, his mother's son, and said, "Is this your youngest brother, of whom you spoke to me? God be gracious to you, my son!" ³⁰With that, Joseph hurried out, because he was overcome with affection for his brother, and he was about to weep. So he went into a private room and wept there. ³¹Then he washed his face and came out; and controlling himself he said, "Serve the meal." ³²They served him by himself, and them by themselves, and the Egyptians who ate with him by themselves, because the Egyptians could not eat with the Hebrews, for that is an abomination to the Egyptians. ³³When they were seated before him, the firstborn according to his birthright and the youngest according to his youth, the men looked at one another in amazement. ³⁴Portions were taken to them from Joseph's table, but Benjamin's portion was five times as much as any of theirs. So they drank and were merry with him.

Joseph Detains Benjamin

44 Then he commanded the steward of his house, "Fill the men's sacks with food, as much as they can carry, and put each man's money in

the top of his sack. ²Put my cup, the silver cup, in the top of the sack of the youngest, with his money for the grain." And he did as Joseph told him. ³As soon as the morning was light, the men were sent away with their donkeys. ⁴When they had gone only a short distance from the city, Joseph said to his steward, "Go, follow after the men; and when you overtake them, say to them, 'Why have you returned evil for good? Why have you stolen my silver cup?ˢ ⁵Is it not from this that my lord drinks? Does he not indeed use it for divination? You have done wrong in doing this.' "

6 When he overtook them, he repeated these words to them. ⁷They said to him, "Why does my lord speak such words as these? Far be it from your servants that they should do such a thing! ⁸Look, the money that we found at the top of our sacks, we brought back to you from the land of Canaan; why then would we steal silver or gold from your lord's house? ⁹Should it be found with any one of your servants, let him die; moreover the rest of us will become my lord's slaves." ¹⁰He said, "Even so; in accordance with your words, let it be: he with whom it is found shall become my slave, but the rest of you shall go free." ¹¹Then each one quickly lowered his sack to the ground, and each opened his sack. ¹²He searched, beginning with the eldest and ending with the youngest; and the cup was found in Benjamin's sack. ¹³At this they tore their clothes. Then each one loaded his donkey, and they returned to the city.

14 Judah and his brothers came to Joseph's house while he was still there; and they fell to the ground before him. ¹⁵Joseph said to them, "What deed is this that you have done? Do you not know that one such as I can practice divination?" ¹⁶And Judah said, "What can we say to my lord? What can we speak? How can we clear ourselves? God has found out the guilt of your servants; here we are then, my lord's slaves, both we and also the one in whose possession the cup has been found." ¹⁷But he said, "Far be it from me that I should do so! Only the one in whose possession the cup was found shall be my slave; but as for you, go up in peace to your father."

Judah Pleads for Benjamin's Release

18 Then Judah stepped up to him and said, "O my lord, let your servant please speak a word in my lord's ears, and do not be angry with your servant; for you are like Pharaoh himself. ¹⁹My lord asked his servants, saying, 'Have you a father or a brother?' ²⁰And we said to my lord, 'We have a father, an old man, and a young brother, the child of his old age. His brother is dead; he alone is left of his mother's children, and his father loves him.' ²¹Then you said to your servants, 'Bring him down to me, so that I may set my eyes on him.' ²²We said to my lord, 'The boy cannot leave his father, for if he should leave his father, his father would die.' ²³Then you said to your servants, 'Unless your youngest brother comes down with you, you shall see my face no more.' ²⁴When we went back to your servant my father we told him the words of my lord. ²⁵And when our father said, 'Go again, buy us a little food,' ²⁶we said, 'We cannot go down. Only if our youngest brother goes with us, will we go down; for we cannot see the man's face unless our youngest brother is with us.' ²⁷Then your servant my father said to us, 'You know that my wife bore me two sons; ²⁸one left me, and I said, Surely he has been torn to pieces; and I have never seen him since. ²⁹If you take this one also from me, and harm comes to him, you will bring down my gray hairs in sorrow to Sheol.' ³⁰Now therefore, when I come to your servant my father and the boy is not with us, then, as his life is bound up in the boy's life, ³¹when he sees that the boy is not with us, he will die; and your servants will bring down the gray hairs of your servant our father with sorrow to Sheol. ³²For your servant became surety for the boy to my father, saying, 'If I do not bring him back to you, then I will bear the blame in the sight of my father all my life.' ³³Now therefore, please let your servant remain as a slave to my lord in place of the boy; and let the boy go back with his brothers. ³⁴For

s Gk Compare Vg: Heb lacks *Why have you stolen my silver cup?*

how can I go back to my father if the boy is not with me? I fear to see the suffering that would come upon my father."

Joseph Reveals Himself to His Brothers

45 Then Joseph could no longer control himself before all those who stood by him, and he cried out, "Send everyone away from me." So no one stayed with him when Joseph made himself known to his brothers. 2And he wept so loudly that the Egyptians heard it, and the household of Pharaoh heard it. 3Joseph said to his brothers, "I am Joseph. Is my father still alive?" But his brothers could not answer him, so dismayed were they at his presence.

4 Then Joseph said to his brothers, "Come closer to me." And they came closer. He said, "I am your brother, Joseph, whom you sold into Egypt. 5And now do not be distressed, or angry with yourselves, because you sold me here; for God sent me before you to preserve life. 6For the famine has been in the land these two years; and there are five more years in which there will be neither plowing nor harvest. 7God sent me before you to preserve for you a remnant on earth, and to keep alive for you many survivors. 8So it was not you who sent me here, but God; he has made me a father to Pharaoh, and lord of all his house and ruler over all the land of Egypt. 9Hurry and go up to my father and say to him, 'Thus says your son Joseph, God has made me lord of all Egypt; come down to me, do not delay. 10You shall settle in the land of Goshen, and you shall be near me, you and your children and your children's children, as well as your flocks, your herds, and all that you have. 11I will provide for you there—since there are five more years of famine to come—so that you and your household, and all that you have, will not come to poverty.' 12And now your eyes and the eyes of my brother Benjamin see that it is my own mouth that speaks to you. 13You must tell my father how greatly I am honored in Egypt, and all that you have seen. Hurry and bring my father down here." 14Then he fell

upon his brother Benjamin's neck and wept, while Benjamin wept upon his neck. 15And he kissed all his brothers and wept upon them; and after that his brothers talked with him.

16 When the report was heard in Pharaoh's house, "Joseph's brothers have come," Pharaoh and his servants were pleased. 17Pharaoh said to Joseph, "Say to your brothers, 'Do this: load your animals and go back to the land of Canaan. 18Take your father and your households and come to me, so that I may give you the best of the land of Egypt, and you may enjoy the fat of the land.' 19You are further charged to say, 'Do this: take wagons from the land of Egypt for your little ones and for your wives, and bring your father, and come. 20Give no thought to your possessions, for the best of all the land of Egypt is yours.' "

21 The sons of Israel did so. Joseph gave them wagons according to the instruction of Pharaoh, and he gave them provisions for the journey. 22To each one of them he gave a set of garments; but to Benjamin he gave three hundred pieces of silver and five sets of garments. 23To his father he sent the following: ten donkeys loaded with the good things of Egypt, and ten female donkeys loaded with grain, bread, and provision for his father on the journey. 24Then he sent his brothers on their way, and as they were leaving he said to them, "Do not quarrel*t* along the way."

25 So they went up out of Egypt and came to their father Jacob in the land of Canaan. 26And they told him, "Joseph is still alive! He is even ruler over all the land of Egypt." He was stunned; he could not believe them. 27But when they told him all the words of Joseph that he had said to them, and when he saw the wagons that Joseph had sent to carry him, the spirit of their father Jacob revived. 28Israel said, "Enough! My son Joseph is still alive. I must go and see him before I die."

Jacob Brings His Whole Family to Egypt

46 When Israel set out on his journey with all that he had and came to Beer-sheba, he offered

t Or *be agitated*

sacrifices to the God of his father Isaac. ²God spoke to Israel in visions of the night, and said, "Jacob, Jacob." And he said, "Here I am." ³Then he said, "I am God,ᵘ the God of your father; do not be afraid to go down to Egypt, for I will make of you a great nation there. ⁴I myself will go down with you to Egypt, and I will also bring you up again; and Joseph's own hand shall close your eyes."

5 Then Jacob set out from Beer-sheba;

u Heb *the God*

TUESDAY

HIS CARE IS INFINITELY SUPERIOR
Hannah Whitall Smith

VERSE: Genesis 45.8   **PASSAGE:** Genesis 45.1–28

 am afraid there are some, even of God's own children, who scarcely think that he is equal to themselves in tenderness, and love, and thoughtful care; and who, in their secret thoughts, charge him with a neglect and indifference of which they would feel themselves incapable. The truth really is that his care is infinitely superior to any possibilities of human care; and that he, who counts the very hairs of our heads, and suffers not a sparrow to fall without him, takes note of the minutest matters that can affect the lives of his children, and regulates them all according to his own perfect will, let their origin be what they may (see Matthew 6.26; Luke 21.18).

The instances of this are numberless. Take Joseph. What could have seemed more apparently on the face of it to be the result of sin, and utterly contrary to the will of God, than the action of his brethren in selling him into slavery? And yet Joseph, in speaking of it said, "As for you, ye thought evil against me; but God meant it unto good." "Now therefore be not grieved, nor angry with yourselves, that ye sold me hither: for God did send me before you to preserve life" (Genesis 50.20; 45.5, KJV). It was undoubtedly sin in Joseph's brethren, but by the time it had reached Joseph it had become God's will for him, and was, in truth, though he did not see it then, the greatest blessing of his whole life. And thus we see how God can make even "the wrath of man to praise him," and how all things, even the sins of others, "shall work together for good to them that love him" (Romans 8.28, KJV).

ADDITIONAL SCRIPTURE READING:
Genesis 50.20; Romans 8.28–39

Go to page 56 for your next devotional reading.

1700   1900

and the sons of Israel carried their father Jacob, their little ones, and their wives, in the wagons that Pharaoh had sent to carry him. 6They also took their livestock and the goods that they had acquired in the land of Canaan, and they came into Egypt, Jacob and all his offspring with him, 7his sons, and his sons' sons with him, his daughters, and his sons' daughters; all his offspring he brought with him into Egypt.

8 Now these are the names of the Israelites, Jacob and his offspring, who came to Egypt. Reuben, Jacob's firstborn, 9and the children of Reuben: Hanoch, Pallu, Hezron, and Carmi. 10The children of Simeon: Jemuel, Jamin, Ohad, Jachin, Zohar, and Shaul,v the son of a Canaanite woman. 11The children of Levi: Gershon, Kohath, and Merari. 12The children of Judah: Er, Onan, Shelah, Perez, and Zerah (but Er and Onan died in the land of Canaan); and the children of Perez were Hezron and Hamul. 13The children of Issachar: Tola, Puvah, Jashub,w and Shimron. 14The children of Zebulun: Sered, Elon, and Jahleel 15(these are the sons of Leah, whom she bore to Jacob in Paddan-aram, together with his daughter Dinah; in all his sons and his daughters numbered thirty-three). 16The children of Gad: Ziphion, Haggi, Shuni, Ezbon, Eri, Arodi, and Areli. 17The children of Asher: Imnah, Ishvah, Ishvi, Beriah, and their sister Serah. The children of Beriah: Heber and Malchiel 18(these are the children of Zilpah, whom Laban gave to his daughter Leah; and these she bore to Jacob—sixteen persons). 19The children of Jacob's wife Rachel: Joseph and Benjamin. 20To Joseph in the land of Egypt were born Manasseh and Ephraim, whom Asenath daughter of Potiphera, priest of On, bore to him. 21The children of Benjamin: Bela, Becher, Ashbel, Gera, Naaman, Ehi, Rosh, Muppim, Huppim, and Ard 22(these are the children of Rachel, who were born to Jacob—fourteen persons in all). 23The children of Dan: Hashum.x 24The children of Naphtali: Jahzeel, Guni, Jezer, and Shillem 25(these are the children of Bilhah, whom Laban gave to his daughter Rachel, and these she bore to Jacob—seven persons in all). 26All the

persons belonging to Jacob who came into Egypt, who were his own offspring, not including the wives of his sons, were sixty-six persons in all. 27The children of Joseph, who were born to him in Egypt, were two; all the persons of the house of Jacob who came into Egypt were seventy.

Jacob Settles in Goshen

28 Israely sent Judah ahead to Joseph to lead the way before him into Goshen. When they came to the land of Goshen, 29Joseph made ready his chariot and went up to meet his father Israel in Goshen. He presented himself to him, fell on his neck, and wept on his neck a good while. 30Israel said to Joseph, "I can die now, having seen for myself that you are still alive." 31Joseph said to his brothers and to his father's household, "I will go up and tell Pharaoh, and will say to him, 'My brothers and my father's household, who were in the land of Canaan, have come to me. 32The men are shepherds, for they have been keepers of livestock; and they have brought their flocks, and their herds, and all that they have.' 33When Pharaoh calls you, and says, 'What is your occupation?' 34you shall say, 'Your servants have been keepers of livestock from our youth even until now, both we and our ancestors'—in order that you may settle in the land of Goshen, because all shepherds are abhorrent to the Egyptians."

47 So Joseph went and told Pharaoh, "My father and my brothers, with their flocks and herds and all that they possess, have come from the land of Canaan; they are now in the land of Goshen." 2From among his brothers he took five men and presented them to Pharaoh. 3Pharaoh said to his brothers, "What is your occupation?" And they said to Pharaoh, "Your servants are shepherds, as our ancestors were." 4They said to Pharaoh, "We have come to reside as aliens in the land; for there is no pasture for your servants' flocks because the famine is severe in the land of Canaan. Now, we ask you, let your servants settle in the land of Goshen." 5Then Pharaoh said to Joseph, "Your father and your brothers have

v Or Saul   w Compare Sam Gk Num 26.24; 1 Chr 7.1: MT Iob   x Gk: Heb Hushim   y Heb He

come to you. ⁶The land of Egypt is before you; settle your father and your brothers in the best part of the land; let them live in the land of Goshen; and if you know that there are capable men among them, put them in charge of my livestock."

7 Then Joseph brought in his father Jacob, and presented him before Pharaoh, and Jacob blessed Pharaoh. ⁸Pharaoh said to Jacob, "How many are the years of your life?" ⁹Jacob said to Pharaoh, "The years of my earthly sojourn are one hundred thirty; few and hard have been the years of my life. They do not compare with the years of the life of my ancestors during their long sojourn." ¹⁰Then Jacob blessed Pharaoh, and went out from the presence of Pharaoh. ¹¹Joseph settled his father and his brothers, and granted them a holding in the land of Egypt, in the best part of the land, in the land of Rameses, as Pharaoh had instructed. ¹²And Joseph provided his father, his brothers, and all his father's household with food, according to the number of their dependents.

The Famine in Egypt

13 Now there was no food in all the land, for the famine was very severe. The land of Egypt and the land of Canaan languished because of the famine. ¹⁴Joseph collected all the money to be found in the land of Egypt and in the land of Canaan, in exchange for the grain that they bought; and Joseph brought the money into Pharaoh's house. ¹⁵When the money from the land of Egypt and from the land of Canaan was spent, all the Egyptians came to Joseph, and said, "Give us food! Why should we die before your eyes? For our money is gone." ¹⁶And Joseph answered, "Give me your livestock, and I will give you food in exchange for your livestock, if your money is gone." ¹⁷So they brought their livestock to Joseph; and Joseph gave them food in exchange for the horses, the flocks, the herds, and the donkeys. That year he supplied them with food in exchange for all their livestock. ¹⁸When that year was ended, they came to him the following year, and said to him, "We can not hide from my lord

that our money is all spent; and the herds of cattle are my lord's. There is nothing left in the sight of my lord but our bodies and our lands. ¹⁹Shall we die before your eyes, both we and our land? Buy us and our land in exchange for food. We with our land will become slaves to Pharaoh; just give us seed, so that we may live and not die, and that the land may not become desolate."

20 So Joseph bought all the land of Egypt for Pharaoh. All the Egyptians sold their fields, because the famine was severe upon them; and the land became Pharaoh's. ²¹As for the people, he made slaves of themᶻ from one end of Egypt to the other. ²²Only the land of the priests he did not buy; for the priests had a fixed allowance from Pharaoh, and lived on the allowance that Pharaoh gave them; therefore they did not sell their land. ²³Then Joseph said to the people, "Now that I have this day bought you and your land for Pharaoh, here is seed for you; sow the land. ²⁴And at the harvests you shall give one-fifth to Pharaoh, and four-fifths shall be your own, as seed for the field and as food for yourselves and your households, and as food for your little ones." ²⁵They said, "You have saved our lives; may it please my lord, we will be slaves to Pharaoh." ²⁶So Joseph made it a statute concerning the land of Egypt, and it stands to this day, that Pharaoh should have the fifth. The land of the priests alone did not become Pharaoh's.

The Last Days of Jacob

27 Thus Israel settled in the land of Egypt, in the region of Goshen; and they gained possessions in it, and were fruitful and multiplied exceedingly. ²⁸Jacob lived in the land of Egypt seventeen years; so the days of Jacob, the years of his life, were one hundred forty-seven years.

29 When the time of Israel's death drew near, he called his son Joseph and said to him, "If I have found favor with you, put your hand under my thigh and promise to deal loyally and truly with me. Do not bury me in Egypt. ³⁰When I lie down with my ancestors, carry me out of Egypt and bury me in their burial place." He answered, "I will do as you

---

z Sam Gk Compare Vg: MT *He removed them to the cities*

have said." 31And he said, "Swear to me"; and he swore to him. Then Israel bowed himself on the head of his bed.

Jacob Blesses Joseph's Sons

48 After this Joseph was told, "Your father is ill." So he took with him his two sons, Manasseh and Ephraim. 2When Jacob was told, "Your son Joseph has come to you," hea summoned his strength and sat up in bed. 3And Jacob said to Joseph, "God Almightyb appeared to me at Luz in the land of Canaan, and he blessed me, 4and said to me, 'I am going to make you fruitful and increase your numbers; I will make of you a company of peoples, and will give this land to your offspring after you for a perpetual holding.' 5Therefore your two sons, who were born to you in the land of Egypt before I came to you in Egypt, are now mine; Ephraim and Manasseh shall be mine, just as Reuben and Simeon are. 6As for the offspring born to you after them, they shall be yours. They shall be recorded under the names of their brothers with regard to their inheritance. 7For when I came from Paddan, Rachel, alas, died in the land of Canaan on the way, while there was still some distance to go to Ephrath; and I buried her there on the way to Ephrath" (that is, Bethlehem).

8 When Israel saw Joseph's sons, he said, "Who are these?" 9Joseph said to his father, "They are my sons, whom God has given me here." And he said, "Bring them to me, please, that I may bless them." 10Now the eyes of Israel were dim with age, and he could not see well. So Joseph brought them near him; and he kissed them and embraced them. 11Israel said to Joseph, "I did not expect to see your face; and here God has let me see your children also." 12Then Joseph removed them from his father's knees,c and he bowed himself with his face to the earth. 13Joseph took them both, Ephraim in his right hand toward Israel's left, and Manasseh in his left hand toward Israel's right, and brought them near him. 14But Israel stretched out his right hand and laid it on the head of Ephraim, who was the younger, and his left hand on the head of Manasseh, crossing his hands, for Manasseh was the firstborn. 15He blessed Joseph, and said,
"The God before whom my
     ancestors Abraham and Isaac
     walked,
the God who has been my shepherd
     all my life to this day,
16   the angel who has redeemed me
     from all harm, bless the boys;
and in them let my name be
     perpetuated, and the name of
     my ancestors Abraham and
     Isaac;
and let them grow into a multitude
     on the earth."

17 When Joseph saw that his father laid his right hand on the head of Ephraim, it displeased him; so he took his father's hand, to remove it from Ephraim's head to Manasseh's head. 18Joseph said to his father, "Not so, my father! Since this one is the firstborn, put your right hand on his head." 19But his father refused, and said, "I know, my son, I know; he also shall become a people, and he also shall be great. Nevertheless his younger brother shall be greater than he, and his offspring shall become a multitude of nations." 20So he blessed them that day, saying,
"By youd Israel will invoke
     blessings, saying,
'God make youd like Ephraim and
     like Manasseh.' "
So he put Ephraim ahead of Manasseh. 21Then Israel said to Joseph, "I am about to die, but God will be with you and will bring you again to the land of your ancestors. 22I now give to you one portione more than to your brothers, the portione that I took from the hand of the Amorites with my sword and with my bow."

Jacob's Last Words to His Sons

49 Then Jacob called his sons, and said: "Gather around, that I may tell you what will happen to you in days to come.
2   Assemble and hear, O sons of
     Jacob;
     listen to Israel your father.

³ Reuben, you are my firstborn,
   my might and the first fruits of
      my vigor,
   excelling in rank and excelling in
      power.
⁴ Unstable as water, you shall no
      longer excel
   because you went up onto your
      father's bed;
   then you defiled it—you*f* went
      up onto my couch!

⁵ Simeon and Levi are brothers;

weapons of violence are their
   swords.
⁶ May I never come into their
   council;
   may I not be joined to their
      company—
   for in their anger they killed men,
   and at their whim they
      hamstrung oxen.
⁷ Cursed be their anger, for it is fierce,
   and their wrath, for it is cruel!
   I will divide them in Jacob,
   and scatter them in Israel.

f Gk Syr Tg: Heb *he*

WEDNESDAY

THE ANGELS WILL DELIVER US
Origen

VERSE: Genesis 48.16   **PASSAGE:** Genesis 48.8–16

hen anyone prays, the angels that minister to God and watch over mankind gather round about him and join with him in his prayer (see Hebrews 1.14). Nor is that all. Every Christian—each of the "little ones" who are in the church—has an angel of his own, who "always see the face of my Father in heaven" (see Matthew 18.10), and who looks upon the Godhead of the Creator. This angel prays with us and works with us, as far as he can, to obtain the things for which we ask.

"The angel of the Lord," so it is written, "encamps around those who fear him and he delivers them" (see Psalm 34.7), while Jacob speaks of "the angel who has delivered me from all harm" (see Genesis 48.16): and what he says is true not of himself only but of all those who set their trust in God. It would seem, then, that when a number of the faithful meet together genuinely for the glory of Christ, since they all fear the Lord, each of them will have, encamped beside him, his own angel whom God has appointed to guard him and care for him. So, when the saints are assembled, there will be a double church, one of men and one of angels.

ADDITIONAL SCRIPTURE READING:
Genesis 32.1; Psalm 34.7; Daniel 3.28

Go to page 62 for your next devotional reading.

100 ✠ 500

8 Judah, your brothers shall praise
    you;
  your hand shall be on the neck of
    your enemies;
  your father's sons shall bow
    down before you.
9 Judah is a lion's whelp;
  from the prey, my son, you have
    gone up.
  He crouches down, he stretches out
    like a lion,
  like a lioness—who dares rouse
    him up?
10 The scepter shall not depart from
    Judah,
  nor the ruler's staff from between
    his feet,
  until tribute comes to him;^{g}
  and the obedience of the peoples
    is his.
11 Binding his foal to the vine
  and his donkey's colt to the
    choice vine,
  he washes his garments in wine
  and his robe in the blood of
    grapes;
12 his eyes are darker than wine,
  and his teeth whiter than milk.

13 Zebulun shall settle at the shore of
    the sea;
  he shall be a haven for ships,
  and his border shall be at Sidon.

14 Issachar is a strong donkey,
  lying down between the
    sheepfolds;
15 he saw that a resting place was
    good,
  and that the land was pleasant;
  so he bowed his shoulder to the
    burden,
  and became a slave at forced
    labor.

16 Dan shall judge his people
  as one of the tribes of Israel.
17 Dan shall be a snake by the
    roadside,
  a viper along the path,
  that bites the horse's heels
  so that its rider falls backward.

18 I wait for your salvation, O LORD.

19 Gad shall be raided by raiders,
  but he shall raid at their heels.

20 Asher's^h food shall be rich,
  and he shall provide royal
    delicacies.

21 Naphtali is a doe let loose
  that bears lovely fawns.^{i}

22 Joseph is a fruitful bough,
  a fruitful bough by a spring;
  his branches run over the wall.^{j}
23 The archers fiercely attacked him;
  they shot at him and pressed him
    hard.
24 Yet his bow remained taut,
  and his arms^k were made agile
  by the hands of the Mighty One of
    Jacob,
  by the name of the Shepherd, the
    Rock of Israel,
25 by the God of your father, who will
    help you,
  by the Almighty^l who will bless
    you
  with blessings of heaven above,
  blessings of the deep that lies
    beneath,
  blessings of the breasts and of the
    womb.
26 The blessings of your father
  are stronger than the blessings of
    the eternal mountains,
  the bounties^m of the everlasting
    hills;
  may they be on the head of Joseph,
  on the brow of him who was set
    apart from his brothers.

27 Benjamin is a ravenous wolf,
  in the morning devouring the
    prey,
  and at evening dividing the
    spoil."

28 All these are the twelve tribes of
Israel, and this is what their father said
to them when he blessed them, blessing
each one of them with a suitable blessing.

---

g Or until Shiloh comes or until he comes to Shiloh or (with Syr) until he comes to whom it belongs
h Gk Vg Syr: Heb From Asher   i Or that gives beautiful words   j Meaning of Heb uncertain
k Heb the arms of his hands   l Traditional rendering of Heb Shaddai   m Cn Compare Gk: Heb of
my progenitors to the boundaries

Jacob's Death and Burial

29 Then he charged them, saying to them, "I am about to be gathered to my people. Bury me with my ancestors—in the cave in the field of Ephron the Hittite, 30in the cave in the field at Machpelah, near Mamre, in the land of Canaan, in the field that Abraham bought from Ephron the Hittite as a burial site. 31There Abraham and his wife Sarah were buried; there Isaac and his wife Rebekah were buried; and there I buried Leah— 32the field and the cave that is in it were purchased from the Hittites." 33When Jacob ended his charge to his sons, he drew up his feet into the bed, breathed his last, and was gathered to his people.

50 Then Joseph threw himself on his father's face and wept over him and kissed him. 2Joseph commanded the physicians in his service to embalm his father. So the physicians embalmed Israel; 3they spent forty days in doing this, for that is the time required for embalming. And the Egyptians wept for him seventy days.

4 When the days of weeping for him were past, Joseph addressed the household of Pharaoh, "If now I have found favor with you, please speak to Pharaoh as follows: 5My father made me swear an oath; he said, 'I am about to die. In the tomb that I hewed out for myself in the land of Canaan, there you shall bury me.' Now therefore let me go up, so that I may bury my father; then I will return." 6Pharaoh answered, "Go up, and bury your father, as he made you swear to do."

7 So Joseph went up to bury his father. With him went up all the servants of Pharaoh, the elders of his household, and all the elders of the land of Egypt, 8as well as all the household of Joseph, his brothers, and his father's household. Only their children, their flocks, and their herds were left in the land of Goshen. 9Both chariots and charioteers went up with him. It was a very great company. 10When they came to the threshing floor of Atad, which is beyond the Jordan, they held there a very great and sorrowful lamentation; and he

observed a time of mourning for his father seven days. 11When the Canaanite inhabitants of the land saw the mourning on the threshing floor of Atad, they said, "This is a grievous mourning on the part of the Egyptians." Therefore the place was named Abel-mizraim;[n] it is beyond the Jordan. 12Thus his sons did for him as he had instructed them. 13They carried him to the land of Canaan and buried him in the cave of the field at Machpelah, the field near Mamre, which Abraham bought as a burial site from Ephron the Hittite. 14After he had buried his father, Joseph returned to Egypt with his brothers and all who had gone up with him to bury his father.

Joseph Forgives His Brothers

15 Realizing that their father was dead, Joseph's brothers said, "What if Joseph still bears a grudge against us and pays us back in full for all the wrong that we did to him?" 16So they approached[o] Joseph, saying, "Your father gave this instruction before he died, 17'Say to Joseph: I beg you, forgive the crime of your brothers and the wrong they did in harming you.' Now therefore please forgive the crime of the servants of the God of your father." Joseph wept when they spoke to him. 18Then his brothers also wept,[p] fell down before him, and said, "We are here as your slaves." 19But Joseph said to them, "Do not be afraid! Am I in the place of God? 20Even though you intended to do harm to me, God intended it for good, in order to preserve a numerous people, as he is doing today. 21So have no fear; I myself will provide for you and your little ones." In this way he reassured them, speaking kindly to them.

Joseph's Last Days and Death

22 So Joseph remained in Egypt, he and his father's household; and Joseph lived one hundred ten years. 23Joseph saw Ephraim's children of the third generation; the children of Machir son of Manasseh were also born on Joseph's knees. 24 Then Joseph said to his brothers, "I am about to die; but God will surely come to you, and bring you up out of

---

n That is mourning (or meadow) of Egypt   o Gk Syr: Heb they commanded   p Cn: Heb also came

this land to the land that he swore to Abraham, to Isaac, and to Jacob." [25] So Joseph made the Israelites swear, saying, "When God comes to you, you shall carry up my bones from here." [26] And Joseph died, being one hundred ten years old; he was embalmed and placed in a coffin in Egypt.

EXODUS

I N EXODUS, THE AUTHOR MOSES UN-
FOLDS A REVELATION OF GOD'S NAME,
HIS ATTRIBUTES, HIS REDEMPTION, HIS
LAW AND HIS WORSHIP. HE TELLS THE EXCITING
STORIES OF HOW GOD DELIVERS HIS PEOPLE FROM
SLAVERY IN EGYPT AND HOW HE GIVES THEM THE
LAW AT MOUNT SINAI AND INSTRUCTS THEM TO
BUILD THE TABERNACLE. THE BOOK OF EXODUS
DEMONSTRATES THE DEPTH OF GOD'S SAVING
LOVE FOR HIS PEOPLE, AND YET HOW HIS HOLINESS
DEMANDS THEIR OBEDIENCE. THE TEN COM-
MANDMENTS EMBODY HIS CONCERN FOR OUR
WELFARE AND HOLINESS YET TODAY.

1 These are the names of the sons of Israel who came to Egypt with Jacob, each with his household: 2Reuben, Simeon, Levi, and Judah, 3Issachar, Zebulun, and Benjamin, 4Dan and Naphtali, Gad and Asher. 5The total number of people born to Jacob was seventy. Joseph was already in Egypt. 6Then Joseph died, and all his brothers, and that whole generation. 7But the Israelites were fruitful and prolific; they multiplied and grew exceedingly strong, so that the land was filled with them.

The Israelites Are Oppressed

8 Now a new king arose over Egypt, who did not know Joseph. 9He said to his people, "Look, the Israelite people are more numerous and more powerful than we. 10Come, let us deal shrewdly with them, or they will increase and, in the event of war, join our enemies and fight against us and escape from the land." 11Therefore they set taskmasters over them to oppress them with forced labor. They built supply cities, Pithom and Rameses, for Pharaoh. 12But the more they were oppressed, the more they multiplied and spread, so that the Egyptians came to dread the Israelites. 13The Egyptians became ruthless in imposing tasks on the Israelites, 14and made their lives bitter with hard service in mortar and brick and in every kind of field labor. They were ruthless in all the tasks that they imposed on them.

15 The king of Egypt said to the Hebrew midwives, one of whom was named Shiphrah and the other Puah, 16"When you act as midwives to the

Hebrew women, and see them on the birthstool, if it is a boy, kill him; but if it is a girl, she shall live." 17But the midwives feared God; they did not do as the king of Egypt commanded them, but they let the boys live. 18So the king of Egypt summoned the midwives and said to them, "Why have you done this, and allowed the boys to live?" 19The midwives said to Pharaoh, "Because the Hebrew women are not like the Egyptian women; for they are vigorous and give birth before the midwife comes to them." 20So God dealt well with the midwives; and the people multiplied and became very strong. 21And because the midwives feared God, he gave them families. 22Then Pharaoh commanded all his people, "Every boy that is born to the Hebrews[a] you shall throw into the Nile, but you shall let every girl live."

Birth and Youth of Moses

2 Now a man from the house of Levi went and married a Levite woman. 2The woman conceived and bore a son; and when she saw that he was a fine baby, she hid him three months. 3When she could hide him no longer she got a papyrus basket for him, and plastered it with bitumen and pitch; she put the child in it and placed it among the reeds on the bank of the river. 4His sister stood at a distance, to see what would happen to him.

5 The daughter of Pharaoh came down to bathe at the river, while her attendants walked beside the river. She saw the basket among the reeds and sent her maid to bring it. 6When she opened it, she saw the child. He was crying, and she took pity on him. "This must be one of the Hebrews' children," she said. 7Then his sister said to Pharaoh's daughter, "Shall I go and get you a nurse from the Hebrew women to nurse the child for you?" 8Pharaoh's daughter said to her, "Yes." So the girl went and called the child's mother. 9Pharaoh's daughter said to her, "Take this child and nurse it for me, and I will give you your wages." So the woman took the child and nursed it. 10When the child grew up, she brought him to Pharaoh's daughter, and

she took him as her son. She named him Moses,[b] "because," she said, "I drew him out[c] of the water."

Moses Flees to Midian

11 One day, after Moses had grown up, he went out to his people and saw their forced labor. He saw an Egyptian beating a Hebrew, one of his kinsfolk. 12He looked this way and that, and seeing no one he killed the Egyptian and hid him in the sand. 13When he went out the next day, he saw two Hebrews fighting; and he said to the one who was in the wrong, "Why do you strike your fellow Hebrew?" 14He answered, "Who made you a ruler and judge over us? Do you mean to kill me as you killed the Egyptian?" Then Moses was afraid and thought, "Surely the thing is known." 15When Pharaoh heard of it, he sought to kill Moses.

But Moses fled from Pharaoh. He settled in the land of Midian, and sat down by a well. 16The priest of Midian had seven daughters. They came to draw water, and filled the troughs to water their father's flock. 17But some shepherds came and drove them away. Moses got up and came to their defense and watered their flock. 18When they returned to their father Reuel, he said, "How is it that you have come back so soon today?" 19They said, "An Egyptian helped us against the shepherds; he even drew water for us and watered the flock." 20He said to his daughters, "Where is he? Why did you leave the man? Invite him to break bread." 21Moses agreed to stay with the man, and he gave Moses his daughter Zipporah in marriage. 22She bore a son, and he named him Gershom; for he said, "I have been an alien[d] residing in a foreign land."

23 After a long time the king of Egypt died. The Israelites groaned under their slavery, and cried out. Out of the slavery their cry for help rose up to God. 24God heard their groaning, and God remembered his covenant with Abraham, Isaac, and Jacob. 25God looked upon the Israelites, and God took notice of them.

---

a Sam Gk Tg: Heb lacks *to the Hebrews*   *b* Heb *Mosheh*   *c* Heb *mashah*   *d* Heb *ger*

FROM A LITANY OF ATLANTA
W. E. B. Du Bois

VERSE: Exodus 2.23   **PASSAGE:** Exodus 2.11–25

 city lay in travail, God our Lord, and from her loins sprang twin Murder and Black Hate. Red was the midnight; clang, crack and cry of death and fury filled the air and trembled underneath the stars when church spires pointed silently to thee. And all this was to sate the greed of greedy men who hide behind the veil of vengeance!

Bend us thine ear, O Lord!

In the pale, still morning we looked upon the deed. We stopped our ears and held our leaping hands, but they—did they not wag their heads and leer and cry with bloody jaws: *Cease from Crime!* The word was mockery, for thus they train a hundred crimes while we do cure one.

Turn again our captivity, O Lord!

Behold this maimed and broken thing; dear God, it was an humble black man who toiled and sweat to save a bit from the pittance paid him. They told him: *Work and Rise.* He worked. Did this man sin? Nay, but some one told how some one said another did—one whom he had never seen nor known. Yet for that man's crime this man lieth maimed and murdered, his wife naked to shame, his children, to poverty and evil.

Hear us, O heavenly Father!

Doth not this justice of hell stink in thy nostrils, O God? How long shall the mounting flood of innocent blood roar in thine ears and pound in our hearts for vengeance? Pile the pale frenzy of blood-crazed brutes who do such deeds high on thine altar, Jehovah Jireh, and burn it in hell forever and forever!

Forgive us, good Lord; we know not what we say!

Bewildered we are, and passion-tossed, mad with the madness of a mobbed and mocked and murdered people; straining at the armposts of thy throne, we raise our shackled hands and charge thee, God, by the bones of our stolen fathers, by the tears of our dead mothers, by the very blood of thy crucified Christ: *What meaneth this?* Tell us the plan; give us the sign!

Keep not thou silence, O God!

ADDITIONAL SCRIPTURE READING:
Exodus 1.14; Psalms 5.1–3; 22.19–24

Go to page 70 for your next devotional reading.

1900   Present

Moses at the Burning Bush

3 Moses was keeping the flock of his father-in-law Jethro, the priest of Midian; he led his flock beyond the wilderness, and came to Horeb, the mountain of God. 2There the angel of the LORD appeared to him in a flame of fire out of a bush; he looked, and the bush was blazing, yet it was not consumed. 3Then Moses said, "I must turn aside and look at this great sight, and see why the bush is not burned up." 4When the LORD saw that he had turned aside to see, God called to him out of the bush, "Moses, Moses!" And he said, "Here I am." 5Then he said, "Come no closer! Remove the sandals from your feet, for the place on which you are standing is holy ground." 6He said further, "I am the God of your father, the God of Abraham, the God of Isaac, and the God of Jacob." And Moses hid his face, for he was afraid to look at God.

7 Then the LORD said, "I have observed the misery of my people who are in Egypt; I have heard their cry on account of their taskmasters. Indeed, I know their sufferings, 8and I have come down to deliver them from the Egyptians, and to bring them up out of that land to a good and broad land, a land flowing with milk and honey, to the country of the Canaanites, the Hittites, the Amorites, the Perizzites, the Hivites, and the Jebusites. 9The cry of the Israelites has now come to me; I have also seen how the Egyptians oppress them. 10So come, I will send you to Pharaoh to bring my people, the Israelites, out of Egypt." 11But Moses said to God, "Who am I that I should go to Pharaoh, and bring the Israelites out of Egypt?" 12He said, "I will be with you; and this shall be the sign for you that it is I who sent you: when you have brought the people out of Egypt, you shall worship God on this mountain."

The Divine Name Revealed

13 But Moses said to God, "If I come to the Israelites and say to them, 'The God of your ancestors has sent me to you,' and they ask me, 'What is his name?' what shall I say to them?" 14God said to Moses, "I AM WHO I AM."e He said further, "Thus you shall say to the Israelites, 'I AM has sent me to you.' " 15God also said to Moses, "Thus you shall say to the Israelites, 'The LORD,f the God of your ancestors, the God of Abraham, the God of Isaac, and the God of Jacob, has sent me to you':

This is my name forever,
  and this my title for all generations.
16Go and assemble the elders of Israel, and say to them, 'The LORD, the God of your ancestors, the God of Abraham, of Isaac, and of Jacob, has appeared to me, saying: I have given heed to you and to what has been done to you in Egypt. 17I declare that I will bring you up out of the misery of Egypt, to the land of the Canaanites, the Hittites, the Amorites, the Perizzites, the Hivites, and the Jebusites, a land flowing with milk and honey.' 18They will listen to your voice; and you and the elders of Israel shall go to the king of Egypt and say to him, 'The LORD, the God of the Hebrews, has met with us; let us now go a three days' journey into the wilderness, so that we may sacrifice to the LORD our God.' 19I know, however, that the king of Egypt will not let you go unless compelled by a mighty hand.g 20So I will stretch out my hand and strike Egypt with all my wonders that I will perform in it; after that he will let you go. 21I will bring this people into such favor with the Egyptians that, when you go, you will not go empty-handed; 22each woman shall ask her neighbor and any woman living in the neighbor's house for jewelry of silver and of gold, and clothing, and you shall put them on your sons and on your daughters; and so you shall plunder the Egyptians."

Moses' Miraculous Power

4 Then Moses answered, "But suppose they do not believe me or listen to me, but say, 'The LORD did not appear to you.' " 2The LORD said to him, "What is that in your hand?" He said, "A staff." 3And he said, "Throw it on the ground." So he threw the staff on

---

e Or I AM WHAT I AM or I WILL BE WHAT I WILL BE   f The word "LORD" when spelled with capital letters stands for the divine name, YHWH, which is here connected with the verb hayah, "to be"   g Gk Vg: Heb no, not by a mighty hand

the ground, and it became a snake; and Moses drew back from it. ⁴Then the LORD said to Moses, "Reach out your hand, and seize it by the tail"—so he reached out his hand and grasped it, and it became a staff in his hand— ⁵"so that they may believe that the LORD, the God of their ancestors, the God of Abraham, the God of Isaac, and the God of Jacob, has appeared to you."

6 Again, the LORD said to him, "Put your hand inside your cloak." He put his hand into his cloak; and when he took it out, his hand was leprous,ʰ as white as snow. ⁷Then God said, "Put your hand back into your cloak"—so he put his hand back into his cloak, and when he took it out, it was restored like the rest of his body— ⁸"If they will not believe you or heed the first sign, they may believe the second sign. ⁹If they will not believe even these two signs or heed you, you shall take some water from the Nile and pour it on the dry ground; and the water that you shall take from the Nile will become blood on the dry ground."

10 But Moses said to the LORD, "O my Lord, I have never been eloquent, neither in the past nor even now that you have spoken to your servant; but I am slow of speech and slow of tongue." ¹¹Then the LORD said to him, "Who gives speech to mortals? Who makes them mute or deaf, seeing or blind? Is it not I, the LORD? ¹²Now go, and I will be with your mouth and teach you what you are to speak." ¹³But he said, "O my Lord, please send someone else." ¹⁴Then the anger of the LORD was kindled against Moses and he said, "What of your brother Aaron the Levite? I know that he can speak fluently; even now he is coming out to meet you, and when he sees you his heart will be glad. ¹⁵You shall speak to him and put the words in his mouth; and I will be with your mouth and with his mouth, and will teach you what you shall do. ¹⁶He indeed shall speak for you to the people; he shall serve as a mouth for you, and you shall serve as God for him. ¹⁷Take in your hand this staff, with which you shall perform the signs."

Moses Returns to Egypt

18 Moses went back to his father-in-law Jethro and said to him, "Please let me go back to my kindred in Egypt and see whether they are still living." And Jethro said to Moses, "Go in peace." ¹⁹The LORD said to Moses in Midian, "Go back to Egypt; for all those who were seeking your life are dead." ²⁰So Moses took his wife and his sons, put them on a donkey, and went back to the land of Egypt; and Moses carried the staff of God in his hand.

21 And the LORD said to Moses, "When you go back to Egypt, see that you perform before Pharaoh all the wonders that I have put in your power; but I will harden his heart, so that he will not let the people go. ²²Then you shall say to Pharaoh, 'Thus says the LORD: Israel is my firstborn son. ²³I said to you, "Let my son go that he may worship me." But you refused to let him go; now I will kill your firstborn son.' "

24 On the way, at a place where they spent the night, the LORD met him and tried to kill him. ²⁵But Zipporah took a flint and cut off her son's foreskin, and touched Moses'ⁱ feet with it, and said, "Truly you are a bridegroom of blood to me!" ²⁶So he let him alone. It was then she said, "A bridegroom of blood by circumcision."

27 The LORD said to Aaron, "Go into the wilderness to meet Moses." So he went; and he met him at the mountain of God and kissed him. ²⁸Moses told Aaron all the words of the LORD with which he had sent him, and all the signs with which he had charged him. ²⁹Then Moses and Aaron went and assembled all the elders of the Israelites. ³⁰Aaron spoke all the words that the LORD had spoken to Moses, and performed the signs in the sight of the people. ³¹The people believed; and when they heard that the LORD had given heed to the Israelites and that he had seen their misery, they bowed down and worshiped.

Bricks without Straw

5 Afterward Moses and Aaron went to Pharaoh and said, "Thus says the LORD, the God of Israel,

_____
ʰ A term for several skin diseases; precise meaning uncertain   ⁱ Heb his

'Let my people go, so that they may celebrate a festival to me in the wilderness.' " 2But Pharaoh said, "Who is the LORD, that I should heed him and let Israel go? I do not know the LORD, and I will not let Israel go." 3Then they said, "The God of the Hebrews has revealed himself to us; let us go a three days' journey into the wilderness to sacrifice to the LORD our God, or he will fall upon us with pestilence or sword." 4But the king of Egypt said to them, "Moses and Aaron, why are you taking the people away from their work? Get to your labors!" 5Pharaoh continued, "Now they are more numerous than the people of the land*j* and yet you want them to stop working!" 6That same day Pharaoh commanded the taskmasters of the people, as well as their supervisors, 7"You shall no longer give the people straw to make bricks, as before; let them go and gather straw for themselves. 8But you shall require of them the same quantity of bricks as they have made previously; do not diminish it, for they are lazy; that is why they cry, 'Let us go and offer sacrifice to our God.' 9Let heavier work be laid on them; then they will labor at it and pay no attention to deceptive words."

10 So the taskmasters and the supervisors of the people went out and said to the people, "Thus says Pharaoh, 'I will not give you straw. 11Go and get straw yourselves, wherever you can find it; but your work will not be lessened in the least.' " 12So the people scattered throughout the land of Egypt, to gather stubble for straw. 13The taskmasters were urgent, saying, "Complete your work, the same daily assignment as when you were given straw." 14And the supervisors of the Israelites, whom Pharaoh's taskmasters had set over them, were beaten, and were asked, "Why did you not finish the required quantity of bricks yesterday and today, as you did before?"

15 Then the Israelite supervisors came to Pharaoh and cried, "Why do you treat your servants like this? 16No straw is given to your servants, yet they say to us, 'Make bricks!' Look how your servants are beaten! You are unjust to your own people."*k* 17He said, "You are lazy, lazy; that is why you say, 'Let us go and sacrifice to the LORD.' 18Go now, and work; for no straw shall be given you, but you shall still deliver the same number of bricks." 19The Israelite supervisors saw that they were in trouble when they were told, "You shall not lessen your daily number of bricks." 20As they left Pharaoh, they came upon Moses and Aaron who were waiting to meet them. 21They said to them, "The LORD look upon you and judge! You have brought us into bad odor with Pharaoh and his officials, and have put a sword in their hand to kill us."

22 Then Moses turned again to the LORD and said, "O LORD, why have you mistreated this people? Why did you ever send me? 23Since I first came to Pharaoh to speak in your name, he has mistreated this people, and you have done nothing at all to deliver your people."

Israel's Deliverance Assured

6 Then the LORD said to Moses, "Now you shall see what I will do to Pharaoh: Indeed, by a mighty hand he will let them go; by a mighty hand he will drive them out of his land."

2 God also spoke to Moses and said to him: "I am the LORD. 3I appeared to Abraham, Isaac, and Jacob as God Almighty,*l* but by my name 'The LORD'*m* I did not make myself known to them. 4I also established my covenant with them, to give them the land of Canaan, the land in which they resided as aliens. 5I have also heard the groaning of the Israelites whom the Egyptians are holding as slaves, and I have remembered my covenant. 6Say therefore to the Israelites, 'I am the LORD, and I will free you from the burdens of the Egyptians and deliver you from slavery to them. I will redeem you with an outstretched arm and with mighty acts of judgment. 7I will take you as my people, and I will be your God. You shall know that I am the LORD your God, who has freed you from the burdens of the Egyptians. 8I will bring you into the land that I swore to give to Abraham, Isaac, and Jacob; I will

---

j Sam: Heb *The people of the land are now many your people*   *l* Traditional rendering of Heb *El Shaddai*   *k* Gk Compare Syr Vg: Heb *beaten, and the sin of*   *m* Heb *YHWH*; see note at 3.15

give it to you for a possession. I am the LORD.' " 9Moses told this to the Israelites; but they would not listen to Moses, because of their broken spirit and their cruel slavery.

10 Then the LORD spoke to Moses, 11"Go and tell Pharaoh king of Egypt to let the Israelites go out of his land." 12But Moses spoke to the LORD, "The Israelites have not listened to me; how then shall Pharaoh listen to me, poor speaker that I am?"n 13Thus the LORD spoke to Moses and Aaron, and gave them orders regarding the Israelites and Pharaoh king of Egypt, charging them to free the Israelites from the land of Egypt.

The Genealogy of Moses and Aaron

14 The following are the heads of their ancestral houses: the sons of Reuben, the firstborn of Israel: Hanoch, Pallu, Hezron, and Carmi; these are the families of Reuben. 15The sons of Simeon: Jemuel, Jamin, Ohad, Jachin, Zohar, and Shaul,o the son of a Canaanite woman; these are the families of Simeon. 16The following are the names of the sons of Levi according to their genealogies: Gershon,p Kohath, and Merari, and the length of Levi's life was one hundred thirty-seven years. 17The sons of Gershon:p Libni and Shimei, by their families. 18The sons of Kohath: Amram, Izhar, Hebron, and Uzziel, and the length of Kohath's life was one hundred thirty-three years. 19The sons of Merari: Mahli and Mushi. These are the families of the Levites according to their genealogies. 20Amram married Jochebed his father's sister and she bore him Aaron and Moses, and the length of Amram's life was one hundred thirty-seven years. 21The sons of Izhar: Korah, Nepheg, and Zichri. 22The sons of Uzziel: Mishael, Elzaphan, and Sithri. 23Aaron married Elisheba, daughter of Amminadab and sister of Nahshon, and she bore him Nadab, Abihu, Eleazar, and Ithamar. 24The sons of Korah: Assir, Elkanah, and Abiasaph; these are the families of the Korahites. 25Aaron's son Eleazar married one of the daughters of Putiel, and she bore him Phinehas. These are the heads of the ancestral houses of the Levites by their families.

26 It was this same Aaron and Moses to whom the LORD said, "Bring the Israelites out of the land of Egypt, company by company." 27It was they who spoke to Pharaoh king of Egypt to bring the Israelites out of Egypt, the same Moses and Aaron.

Moses and Aaron Obey God's Commands

28 On the day when the LORD spoke to Moses in the land of Egypt, 29he said to him, "I am the LORD; tell Pharaoh king of Egypt all that I am speaking to you." 30But Moses said in the LORD's presence, "Since I am a poor speaker,q why would Pharaoh listen to me?"

7 The LORD said to Moses, "See, I have made you like God to Pharaoh, and your brother Aaron shall be your prophet. 2You shall speak all that I command you, and your brother Aaron shall tell Pharaoh to let the Israelites go out of his land. 3But I will harden Pharaoh's heart, and I will multiply my signs and wonders in the land of Egypt. 4When Pharaoh does not listen to you, I will lay my hand upon Egypt and bring my people the Israelites, company by company, out of the land of Egypt by great acts of judgment. 5The Egyptians shall know that I am the LORD, when I stretch out my hand against Egypt and bring the Israelites out from among them." 6Moses and Aaron did so; they did just as the LORD commanded them. 7Moses was eighty years old and Aaron eighty-three when they spoke to Pharaoh.

Aaron's Miraculous Rod

8 The LORD said to Moses and Aaron, 9"When Pharaoh says to you, 'Perform a wonder,' then you shall say to Aaron, 'Take your staff and throw it down before Pharaoh, and it will become a snake.' " 10So Moses and Aaron went to Pharaoh and did as the LORD had commanded; Aaron threw down his staff before Pharaoh and his officials, and it became a snake. 11Then Pharaoh summoned the wise men and the sorcerers; and they also, the magicians of Egypt,

n Heb me! I am uncircumcised of lips   o Or Saul
uncircumcised of lips; see 6.12   p Also spelled Gershom; see 2.22   q Heb am

did the same by their secret arts. 12Each one threw down his staff, and they became snakes; but Aaron's staff swallowed up theirs. 13Still Pharaoh's heart was hardened, and he would not listen to them, as the LORD had said.

The First Plague: Water Turned to Blood

14 Then the LORD said to Moses, "Pharaoh's heart is hardened; he refuses to let the people go. 15Go to Pharaoh in the morning, as he is going out to the water; stand by at the river bank to meet him, and take in your hand the staff that was turned into a snake. 16Say to him, 'The LORD, the God of the Hebrews, sent me to you to say, "Let my people go, so that they may worship me in the wilderness." But until now you have not listened. 17Thus says the LORD, "By this you shall know that I am the LORD." See, with the staff that is in my hand I will strike the water that is in the Nile, and it shall be turned to blood. 18The fish in the river shall die, the river itself shall stink, and the Egyptians shall be unable to drink water from the Nile.' " 19The LORD said to Moses, "Say to Aaron, 'Take your staff and stretch out your hand over the waters of Egypt—over its rivers, its canals, and its ponds, and all its pools of water—so that they may become blood; and there shall be blood throughout the whole land of Egypt, even in vessels of wood and in vessels of stone.' "

20 Moses and Aaron did just as the LORD commanded. In the sight of Pharaoh and of his officials he lifted up the staff and struck the water in the river, and all the water in the river was turned into blood, 21and the fish in the river died. The river stank so that the Egyptians could not drink its water, and there was blood throughout the whole land of Egypt. 22But the magicians of Egypt did the same by their secret arts; so Pharaoh's heart remained hardened, and he would not listen to them, as the LORD had said. 23Pharaoh turned and went into his house, and he did not take even this to heart. 24And all the Egyptians had to dig along the Nile for water

to drink, for they could not drink the water of the river.

25 Seven days passed after the LORD had struck the Nile.

The Second Plague: Frogs

8 r Then the LORD said to Moses, "Go to Pharaoh and say to him, 'Thus says the LORD: Let my people go, so that they may worship me. 2If you refuse to let them go, I will plague your whole country with frogs. 3The river shall swarm with frogs; they shall come up into your palace, into your bedchamber and your bed, and into the houses of your officials and of your people,s and into your ovens and your kneading bowls. 4The frogs shall come up on you and on your people and on all your officials.' " 5,t And the LORD said to Moses, "Say to Aaron, 'Stretch out your hand with your staff over the rivers, the canals, and the pools, and make frogs come up on the land of Egypt.' " 6So Aaron stretched out his hand over the waters of Egypt; and the frogs came up and covered the land of Egypt. 7But the magicians did the same by their secret arts, and brought frogs up on the land of Egypt.

8 Then Pharaoh called Moses and Aaron, and said, "Pray to the LORD to take away the frogs from me and my people, and I will let the people go to sacrifice to the LORD." 9Moses said to Pharaoh, "Kindly tell me when I am to pray for you and for your officials and for your people, that the frogs may be removed from you and your houses and be left only in the Nile." 10And he said, "Tomorrow." Moses said, "As you say! So that you may know that there is no one like the LORD our God, 11the frogs shall leave you and your houses and your officials and your people; they shall be left only in the Nile." 12Then Moses and Aaron went out from Pharaoh; and Moses cried out to the LORD concerning the frogs that he had brought upon Pharaoh.u 13And the LORD did as Moses requested: the frogs died in the houses, the courtyards, and the fields. 14And they gathered them together in heaps, and the land stank. 15But when Pharaoh

r Ch 7.26 in Heb   s Gk: Heb upon your people   t Ch 8.1 in Heb   u Or frogs, as he had agreed
with Pharaoh

saw that there was a respite, he hardened his heart, and would not listen to them, just as the LORD had said.

The Third Plague: Gnats

16 Then the LORD said to Moses, "Say to Aaron, 'Stretch out your staff and strike the dust of the earth, so that it may become gnats throughout the whole land of Egypt.' " 17And they did so; Aaron stretched out his hand with his staff and struck the dust of the earth, and gnats came on humans and animals alike; all the dust of the earth turned into gnats throughout the whole land of Egypt. 18The magicians tried to produce gnats by their secret arts, but they could not. There were gnats on both humans and animals. 19And the magicians said to Pharaoh, "This is the finger of God!" But Pharaoh's heart was hardened, and he would not listen to them, just as the LORD had said.

The Fourth Plague: Flies

20 Then the LORD said to Moses, "Rise early in the morning and present yourself before Pharaoh, as he goes out to the water, and say to him, 'Thus says the LORD: Let my people go, so that they may worship me. 21For if you will not let my people go, I will send swarms of flies on you, your officials, and your people, and into your houses; and the houses of the Egyptians shall be filled with swarms of flies; so also the land where they live. 22But on that day I will set apart the land of Goshen, where my people live, so that no swarms of flies shall be there, that you may know that I the LORD am in this land. 23Thus I will make a distinctionv between my people and your people. This sign shall appear tomorrow.' " 24The LORD did so, and great swarms of flies came into the house of Pharaoh and into his officials' houses; in all of Egypt the land was ruined because of the flies.

25 Then Pharaoh summoned Moses and Aaron, and said, "Go, sacrifice to your God within the land." 26But Moses said, "It would not be right to do so; for the sacrifices that we offer to the LORD our God are offensive to the Egyptians. If we offer in the sight of the Egyptians

sacrifices that are offensive to them, will they not stone us? 27We must go a three days' journey into the wilderness and sacrifice to the LORD our God as he commands us." 28So Pharaoh said, "I will let you go to sacrifice to the LORD your God in the wilderness, provided you do not go very far away. Pray for me." 29Then Moses said, "As soon as I leave you, I will pray to the LORD that the swarms of flies may depart tomorrow from Pharaoh, from his officials, and from his people; only do not let Pharaoh again deal falsely by not letting the people go to sacrifice to the LORD."

30 So Moses went out from Pharaoh and prayed to the LORD. 31And the LORD did as Moses asked: he removed the swarms of flies from Pharaoh, from his officials, and from his people; not one remained. 32But Pharaoh hardened his heart this time also, and would not let the people go.

The Fifth Plague: Livestock Diseased

9 Then the LORD said to Moses, "Go to Pharaoh, and say to him, 'Thus says the LORD, the God of the Hebrews: Let my people go, so that they may worship me. 2For if you refuse to let them go and still hold them, 3the hand of the LORD will strike with a deadly pestilence your livestock in the field: the horses, the donkeys, the camels, the herds, and the flocks. 4But the LORD will make a distinction between the livestock of Israel and the livestock of Egypt, so that nothing shall die of all that belongs to the Israelites.' " 5The LORD set a time, saying, "Tomorrow the LORD will do this thing in the land." 6And on the next day the LORD did so; all the livestock of the Egyptians died, but of the livestock of the Israelites not one died. 7Pharaoh inquired and found that not one of the livestock of the Israelites was dead. But the heart of Pharaoh was hardened, and he would not let the people go.

The Sixth Plague: Boils

8 Then the LORD said to Moses and Aaron, "Take handfuls of soot from the kiln, and let Moses throw it in the air in

v Gk Vg: Heb will set redemption

the sight of Pharaoh. ⁹It shall become fine dust all over the land of Egypt, and shall cause festering boils on humans and animals throughout the whole land of Egypt." ¹⁰So they took soot from the kiln, and stood before Pharaoh, and Moses threw it in the air, and it caused festering boils on humans and animals. ¹¹The magicians could not stand before Moses because of the boils, for the boils afflicted the magicians as well as all the Egyptians. ¹²But the LORD hardened the heart of Pharaoh, and he would not listen to them, just as the LORD had spoken to Moses.

The Seventh Plague: Thunder and Hail

13 Then the LORD said to Moses, "Rise up early in the morning and present yourself before Pharaoh, and say to him, 'Thus says the LORD, the God of the Hebrews: Let my people go, so that they may worship me. ¹⁴For this time I will send all my plagues upon you yourself, and upon your officials, and upon your people, so that you may know that there is no one like me in all the earth. ¹⁵For by now I could have stretched out my hand and struck you and your people with pestilence, and you would have been cut off from the earth. ¹⁶But this is why I have let you live: to show you my power, and to make my name resound through all the earth. ¹⁷You are still exalting yourself against my people, and will not let them go. ¹⁸Tomorrow at this time I will cause the heaviest hail to fall that has ever fallen in Egypt from the day it was founded until now. ¹⁹Send, therefore, and have your livestock and everything that you have in the open field brought to a secure place; every human or animal that is in the open field and is not brought under shelter will die when the hail comes down upon them.' " ²⁰Those officials of Pharaoh who feared the word of the LORD hurried their slaves and livestock off to a secure place. ²¹Those who did not regard the word of the LORD left their slaves and livestock in the open field.

22 The LORD said to Moses, "Stretch out your hand toward heaven so that hail may fall on the whole land of Egypt, on humans and animals and all the plants of the field in the land of Egypt." ²³Then Moses stretched out his staff toward heaven, and the LORD sent thunder and hail, and fire came down on the earth. And the LORD rained hail on the land of Egypt; ²⁴there was hail with fire flashing continually in the midst of it, such heavy hail as had never fallen in all the land of Egypt since it became a nation. ²⁵The hail struck down everything that was in the open field throughout all the land of Egypt, both human and animal; the hail also struck down all the plants of the field, and shattered every tree in the field. ²⁶Only in the land of Goshen, where the Israelites were, there was no hail.

27 Then Pharaoh summoned Moses and Aaron, and said to them, "This time I have sinned; the LORD is in the right, and I and my people are in the wrong. ²⁸Pray to the LORD! Enough of God's thunder and hail! I will let you go; you need stay no longer." ²⁹Moses said to him, "As soon as I have gone out of the city, I will stretch out my hands to the LORD; the thunder will cease, and there will be no more hail, so that you may know that the earth is the LORD's. ³⁰But as for you and your officials, I know that you do not yet fear the LORD God." ³¹(Now the flax and the barley were ruined, for the barley was in the ear and the flax was in bud. ³²But the wheat and the spelt were not ruined, for they are late in coming up.) ³³So Moses left Pharaoh, went out of the city, and stretched out his hands to the LORD; then the thunder and the hail ceased, and the rain no longer poured down on the earth. ³⁴But when Pharaoh saw that the rain and the hail and the thunder had ceased, he sinned once more and hardened his heart, he and his officials. ³⁵So the heart of Pharaoh was hardened, and he would not let the Israelites go, just as the LORD had spoken through Moses.

The Eighth Plague: Locusts

10 Then the LORD said to Moses, "Go to Pharaoh; for I have hardened his heart and the heart of his officials, in order that I may show these signs of mine among them, ²and that you may tell your children and grandchildren how I have made fools of the

GO DOWN, MOSES
African-American Spiritual

VERSE: Exodus 10.3   PASSAGE: Exodus 10.1–20

hen Israel was in Egypt's land,
Let my people go,
Oppressed so hard they could not stand,
Let my people go.

Go down, Moses,
Way down in Egypt land,
Tell de Pharaoh
To let my people go.

Thus saith the Lord, bold Moses said,
Let my people go.
If not I'll smite your firstborn dead,
Let my people go.

No more shall they in bondage toil . . .
Let my people go.
Let them come out with Egypt's spoil . . .
Let my people go.

The Lord told Moses what to do . . .
Let my people go.
To lead the children of Israel through . . .
Let my people go.

As I stood by the waterside . . .
Let my people go.
At the command of God, it did divide . . .
Let my people go.

When they reached the other shore . . .
Let my people go.
They sang a song of triumph o'er . . .
Let my people go.

ADDITIONAL SCRIPTURE READING:
Exodus 4.21–23; James 4.10; 1 Peter 5.6

Go to page 72 for your next devotional reading.

1700   1900

Egyptians and what signs I have done among them—so that you may know that I am the LORD."

3 So Moses and Aaron went to Pharaoh, and said to him, "Thus says the LORD, the God of the Hebrews, 'How long will you refuse to humble yourself before me? Let my people go, so that they may worship me. ⁴For if you refuse to let my people go, tomorrow I will bring locusts into your country. ⁵They shall cover the surface of the land, so that no one will be able to see the land. They shall devour the last remnant left you after the hail, and they shall devour every tree of yours that grows in the field. ⁶They shall fill your houses, and the houses of all your officials and of all the Egyptians—something that neither your parents nor your grandparents have seen, from the day they came on earth to this day.' " Then he turned and went out from Pharaoh.

7 Pharaoh's officials said to him, "How long shall this fellow be a snare to us? Let the people go, so that they may worship the LORD their God; do you not yet understand that Egypt is ruined?" ⁸So Moses and Aaron were brought back to Pharaoh, and he said to them, "Go, worship the LORD your God! But which ones are to go?" ⁹Moses said, "We will go with our young and our old; we will go with our sons and daughters and with our flocks and herds, because we have the LORD's festival to celebrate." ¹⁰He said to them, "The LORD indeed will be with you, if ever I let your little ones go with you! Plainly, you have some evil purpose in mind. ¹¹No, never! Your men may go and worship the LORD, for that is what you are asking." And they were driven out from Pharaoh's presence.

12 Then the LORD said to Moses, "Stretch out your hand over the land of Egypt, so that the locusts may come upon it and eat every plant in the land, all that the hail has left." ¹³So Moses stretched out his staff over the land of Egypt, and the LORD brought an east wind upon the land all that day and all that night; when morning came, the east wind had brought the locusts. ¹⁴The locusts came upon all the land of Egypt and settled on the whole country of Egypt, such a dense swarm of locusts as had never been before, nor ever shall be again. ¹⁵They covered the surface of the whole land, so that the land was black; and they ate all the plants in the land and all the fruit of the trees that the hail had left; nothing green was left, no tree, no plant in the field, in all the land of Egypt. ¹⁶Pharaoh hurriedly summoned Moses and Aaron and said, "I have sinned against the LORD your God, and against you. ¹⁷Do forgive my sin just this once, and pray to the LORD your God that at the least he remove this deadly thing from me." ¹⁸So he went out from Pharaoh and prayed to the LORD. ¹⁹The LORD changed the wind into a very strong west wind, which lifted the locusts and drove them into the Red Sea;ʷ not a single locust was left in all the country of Egypt. ²⁰But the LORD hardened Pharaoh's heart, and he would not let the Israelites go.

The Ninth Plague: Darkness

21 Then the LORD said to Moses, "Stretch out your hand toward heaven so that there may be darkness over the land of Egypt, a darkness that can be felt." ²²So Moses stretched out his hand toward heaven, and there was dense darkness in all the land of Egypt for three days. ²³People could not see one another, and for three days they could not move from where they were; but all the Israelites had light where they lived. ²⁴Then Pharaoh summoned Moses, and said, "Go, worship the LORD. Only your flocks and your herds shall remain behind. Even your children may go with you." ²⁵But Moses said, "You must also let us have sacrifices and burnt offerings to sacrifice to the LORD our God. ²⁶Our livestock also must go with us; not a hoof shall be left behind, for we must choose some of them for the worship of the LORD our God, and we will not know what to use to worship the LORD until we arrive there." ²⁷But the LORD hardened Pharaoh's heart, and he was unwilling to let them go. ²⁸Then Pharaoh said to him, "Get away from me! Take care that you do not see my face again, for on the day you see my face you shall die." ²⁹Moses said, "Just as

w Or *Sea of Reeds*

WEEKEND

EVIL'S COMPROMISE
G. Campbell Morgan

VERSE: Exodus 10.26   **PASSAGE:** Exodus 10.21–29

 ot a hoof shall be left behind." This was the final word of Moses in a persistent conflict against anything in the nature of compromise. Pharaoh had attempted to bring this about since after the fourth plague. Note the stages of these attempts. At the beginning he had declared that these people should not go to sacrifice to Jehovah their God. After the plague of flies, the fourth, he suggested that they might sacrifice, but they could do it without going away from the land (Exodus 8.25). This Moses at once refused. Then Pharaoh suggested that if they must go, it should not be very far away (8.28). On this Moses entreated for him, and the plague was removed, but he would not let them go. He proposed later, after the eighth plague (that of locusts), that they should leave the women and children behind (10.8–11). Moses refused. After the ninth plague (that of the darkness), he suggested that the cattle be left (10.24). Then Moses spoke this final word: "Not a hoof shall be left behind."

That is the true attitude of the man of faith. Evil is always suggesting some compromise. To listen to it, is to remain enslaved. The only way into liberty is to leave the land of evil; to go accompanied by the women and the children; and to take all property also. It is when that attitude is assumed, that men pass out from all bondage, and find the liberty which is in the purpose of God for them.

ADDITIONAL SCRIPTURE READING:
Hosea 5.5–6; 1 Timothy 6.11

Go to page 74 for your next devotional reading.

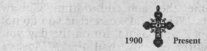

1900   Present

you say! I will never see your face again."

Warning of the Final Plague

11 The LORD said to Moses, "I will bring one more plague upon Pharaoh and upon Egypt; afterwards he will let you go from here; indeed, when he lets you go, he will drive you away. ²Tell the people that every man is to ask his neighbor and every woman is to ask her neighbor for objects of silver and gold." ³The LORD gave the people favor in the sight of the Egyptians. Moreover, Moses himself was a man of great importance in the land of Egypt, in the sight of Pharaoh's officials and in the sight of the people.

4 Moses said, "Thus says the LORD: About midnight I will go out through Egypt. ⁵Every firstborn in the land of Egypt shall die, from the firstborn of Pharaoh who sits on his throne to the firstborn of the female slave who is behind the handmill, and all the firstborn of the livestock. ⁶Then there will be a loud cry throughout the whole land of Egypt, such as has never been or will ever be again. ⁷But not a dog shall growl at any of the Israelites—not at people, not at animals—so that you may know that the LORD makes a distinction between Egypt and Israel. ⁸Then all these officials of yours shall come down to me, and bow low to me, saying, 'Leave us, you and all the people who follow you.' After that I will leave." And in hot anger he left Pharaoh.

9 The LORD said to Moses, "Pharaoh will not listen to you, in order that my wonders may be multiplied in the land of Egypt." ¹⁰Moses and Aaron performed all these wonders before Pharaoh; but the LORD hardened Pharaoh's heart, and he did not let the people of Israel go out of his land.

The First Passover Instituted

12 The LORD said to Moses and Aaron in the land of Egypt: ²This month shall mark for you the beginning of months; it shall be the first month of the year for you. ³Tell the whole congregation of Israel that on the tenth of this month they are to take a lamb for each family, a lamb for each household. ⁴If a household is too small for a whole lamb, it shall join its closest neighbor in obtaining one; the lamb shall be divided in proportion to the number of people who eat of it. ⁵Your lamb shall be without blemish, a year-old male; you may take it from the sheep or from the goats. ⁶You shall keep it until the fourteenth day of this month; then the whole assembled congregation of Israel shall slaughter it at twilight. ⁷They shall take some of the blood and put it on the two doorposts and the lintel of the houses in which they eat it. ⁸They shall eat the lamb that same night; they shall eat it roasted over the fire with unleavened bread and bitter herbs. ⁹Do not eat any of it raw or boiled in water, but roasted over the fire, with its head, legs, and inner organs. ¹⁰You shall let none of it remain until the morning; anything that remains until the morning you shall burn. ¹¹This is how you shall eat it: your loins girded, your sandals on your feet, and your staff in your hand; and you shall eat it hurriedly. It is the passover of the LORD. ¹²For I will pass through the land of Egypt that night, and I will strike down every firstborn in the land of Egypt, both human beings and animals; on all the gods of Egypt I will execute judgments: I am the LORD. ¹³The blood shall be a sign for you on the houses where you live: when I see the blood, I will pass over you, and no plague shall destroy you when I strike the land of Egypt.

14 This day shall be a day of remembrance for you. You shall celebrate it as a festival to the LORD; throughout your generations you shall observe it as a perpetual ordinance. ¹⁵Seven days you shall eat unleavened bread; on the first day you shall remove leaven from your houses, for whoever eats leavened bread from the first day until the seventh day shall be cut off from Israel. ¹⁶On the first day you shall hold a solemn assembly, and on the seventh day a solemn assembly; no work shall be done on those days; only what everyone must eat, that alone may be prepared by you. ¹⁷You shall observe the festival of unleavened bread, for on this very day I brought your companies out of the land of Egypt: you shall observe this day throughout your

generations as a perpetual ordinance. ¹⁸In the first month, from the evening of the fourteenth day until the evening of the twenty-first day, you shall eat unleavened bread. ¹⁹For seven days no leaven shall be found in your houses; for whoever eats what is leavened shall be cut off from the congregation of Israel,

---

MONDAY

JUST AS I AM
Charlotte Elliot

VERSE: Exodus 12.3   PASSAGE: Exodus 12.1–30

ust as I am, without one plea,
But that thy blood was shed for me,
And that thou bidd'st me come to thee,
O Lamb of God, I come, I come.

Just as I am, and waiting not
To rid my soul of one dark blot,
To thee whose blood can cleanse each spot,
O Lamb of God, I come, I come.

Just as I am, though tossed about
With many a conflict, many a doubt;
Fightings and fears within, without,
O Lamb of God, I come, I come.

Just as I am, poor, wretched, blind;
Sight, riches, healing of the mind,
Yea, all I need, in thee to find,
O Lamb of God, I come, I come.

Just as I am: thou wilt receive;
Wilt welcome, pardon, cleanse, relieve;
Because thy promise I believe,
O Lamb of God, I come, I come.

Just as I am, thy love unknown
Has broken every barrier down;
Now to be thine, yea, thine alone,
O Lamb of God, I come, I come.

ADDITIONAL SCRIPTURE READING:
Mark 14.12; John 1.29; 1 Corinthians 5.7

Go to page 78 for your next devotional reading.

1700   1900

whether an alien or a native of the land. 20You shall eat nothing leavened; in all your settlements you shall eat unleavened bread.

21 Then Moses called all the elders of Israel and said to them, "Go, select lambs for your families, and slaughter the passover lamb. 22Take a bunch of hyssop, dip it in the blood that is in the basin, and touch the lintel and the two doorposts with the blood in the basin. None of you shall go outside the door of your house until morning. 23For the LORD will pass through to strike down the Egyptians; when he sees the blood on the lintel and on the two doorposts, the LORD will pass over that door and will not allow the destroyer to enter your houses to strike you down. 24You shall observe this rite as a perpetual ordinance for you and your children. 25When you come to the land that the LORD will give you, as he has promised, you shall keep this observance. 26And when your children ask you, 'What do you mean by this observance?' 27you shall say, 'It is the passover sacrifice to the LORD, for he passed over the houses of the Israelites in Egypt, when he struck down the Egyptians but spared our houses.' " And the people bowed down and worshiped.

28 The Israelites went and did just as the LORD had commanded Moses and Aaron.

The Tenth Plague: Death of the Firstborn

29 At midnight the LORD struck down all the firstborn in the land of Egypt, from the firstborn of Pharaoh who sat on his throne to the firstborn of the prisoner who was in the dungeon, and all the firstborn of the livestock. 30Pharaoh arose in the night, he and all his officials and all the Egyptians; and there was a loud cry in Egypt, for there was not a house without someone dead. 31Then he summoned Moses and Aaron in the night, and said, "Rise up, go away from my people, both you and the Israelites! Go, worship the LORD, as you said. 32Take your flocks and your herds, as you said, and be gone. And bring a blessing on me too!"

The Exodus: From Rameses to Succoth

33 The Egyptians urged the people to hasten their departure from the land, for they said, "We shall all be dead." 34So the people took their dough before it was leavened, with their kneading bowls wrapped up in their cloaks on their shoulders. 35The Israelites had done as Moses told them; they had asked the Egyptians for jewelry of silver and gold, and for clothing, 36and the LORD had given the people favor in the sight of the Egyptians, so that they let them have what they asked. And so they plundered the Egyptians.

37 The Israelites journeyed from Rameses to Succoth, about six hundred thousand men on foot, besides children. 38A mixed crowd also went up with them, and livestock in great numbers, both flocks and herds. 39They baked unleavened cakes of the dough that they had brought out of Egypt; it was not leavened, because they were driven out of Egypt and could not wait, nor had they prepared any provisions for themselves.

40 The time that the Israelites had lived in Egypt was four hundred thirty years. 41At the end of four hundred thirty years, on that very day, all the companies of the LORD went out from the land of Egypt. 42That was for the LORD a night of vigil, to bring them out of the land of Egypt. That same night is a vigil to be kept for the LORD by all the Israelites throughout their generations.

Directions for the Passover

43 The LORD said to Moses and Aaron: This is the ordinance for the passover: no foreigner shall eat of it, 44but any slave who has been purchased may eat of it after he has been circumcised; 45no bound or hired servant may eat of it. 46It shall be eaten in one house; you shall not take any of the animal outside the house, and you shall not break any of its bones. 47The whole congregation of Israel shall celebrate it. 48If an alien who resides with you wants to celebrate the passover to the LORD, all his males shall be circumcised; then he may draw near to celebrate it; he shall be regarded as a native of the land. But no uncircumcised person shall eat of it;

⁴⁹there shall be one law for the native and for the alien who resides among you. 50 All the Israelites did just as the LORD had commanded Moses and Aaron. ⁵¹That very day the LORD brought the Israelites out of the land of Egypt, company by company.

13 The LORD said to Moses: ²Consecrate to me all the firstborn; whatever is the first to open the womb among the Israelites, of human beings and animals, is mine.

The Festival of Unleavened Bread

3 Moses said to the people, "Remember this day on which you came out of Egypt, out of the house of slavery, because the LORD brought you out from there by strength of hand; no leavened bread shall be eaten. ⁴Today, in the month of Abib, you are going out. ⁵When the LORD brings you into the land of the Canaanites, the Hittites, the Amorites, the Hivites, and the Jebusites, which he swore to your ancestors to give you, a land flowing with milk and honey, you shall keep this observance in this month. ⁶Seven days you shall eat unleavened bread, and on the seventh day there shall be a festival to the LORD. ⁷Unleavened bread shall be eaten for seven days; no leavened bread shall be seen in your possession, and no leaven shall be seen among you in all your territory. ⁸You shall tell your child on that day, 'It is because of what the LORD did for me when I came out of Egypt.' ⁹It shall serve for you as a sign on your hand and as a reminder on your forehead, so that the teaching of the LORD may be on your lips; for with a strong hand the LORD brought you out of Egypt. ¹⁰You shall keep this ordinance at its proper time from year to year.

The Consecration of the Firstborn

11 "When the LORD has brought you into the land of the Canaanites, as he swore to you and your ancestors, and has given it to you, ¹²you shall set apart to the LORD all that first opens the womb. All the firstborn of your livestock that are males shall be the LORD's. ¹³But every firstborn donkey you shall redeem with a sheep; if you do not redeem it, you must break its neck. Every firstborn male among your children you shall redeem. ¹⁴When in the future your child asks you, 'What does this mean?' you shall answer, 'By strength of hand the LORD brought us out of Egypt, from the house of slavery. ¹⁵When Pharaoh stubbornly refused to let us go, the LORD killed all the firstborn in the land of Egypt, from human firstborn to the firstborn of animals. Therefore I sacrifice to the LORD every male that first opens the womb, but every firstborn of my sons I redeem.' ¹⁶It shall serve as a sign on your hand and as an emblemˣ on your forehead that by strength of hand the LORD brought us out of Egypt."

The Pillars of Cloud and Fire

17 When Pharaoh let the people go, God did not lead them by way of the land of the Philistines, although that was nearer; for God thought, "If the people face war, they may change their minds and return to Egypt." ¹⁸So God led the people by the roundabout way of the wilderness toward the Red Sea.ʸ The Israelites went up out of the land of Egypt prepared for battle. ¹⁹And Moses took with him the bones of Joseph who had required a solemn oath of the Israelites, saying, "God will surely take notice of you, and then you must carry my bones with you from here." ²⁰They set out from Succoth, and camped at Etham, on the edge of the wilderness. ²¹The LORD went in front of them in a pillar of cloud by day, to lead them along the way, and in a pillar of fire by night, to give them light, so that they might travel by day and by night. ²²Neither the pillar of cloud by day nor the pillar of fire by night left its place in front of the people.

Crossing the Red Sea

14 Then the LORD said to Moses: ²Tell the Israelites to turn back and camp in front of Pi-hahiroth, between Migdol and the sea, in front of Baal-zephon; you shall camp opposite it, by the sea. ³Pharaoh will say of the Israelites, "They are wandering aimlessly in the land; the wilderness has closed in on them." ⁴I will harden Pharaoh's heart,

x Or as a frontlet; Meaning of Heb uncertain   y Or Sea of Reeds and he will pursue them, so that I will gain glory for myself over Pharaoh and all his army; and the Egyptians shall know that I am the LORD. And they did so.

5 When the king of Egypt was told that the people had fled, the minds of Pharaoh and his officials were changed toward the people, and they said, "What have we done, letting Israel leave our service?" 6So he had his chariot made ready, and took his army with him; 7he took six hundred picked chariots and all the other chariots of Egypt with officers over all of them. 8The LORD hardened the heart of Pharaoh king of Egypt and he pursued the Israelites, who were going out boldly. 9The Egyptians pursued them, all Pharaoh's horses and chariots, his chariot drivers and his army; they overtook them camped by the sea, by Pi-hahiroth, in front of Baal-zephon.

10 As Pharaoh drew near, the Israelites looked back, and there were the Egyptians advancing on them. In great fear the Israelites cried out to the LORD. 11They said to Moses, "Was it because there were no graves in Egypt that you have taken us away to die in the wilderness? What have you done to us, bringing us out of Egypt? 12Is this not the very thing we told you in Egypt, 'Let us alone and let us serve the Egyptians'? For it would have been better for us to serve the Egyptians than to die in the wilderness." 13But Moses said to the people, "Do not be afraid, stand firm, and see the deliverance that the LORD will accomplish for you today; for the Egyptians whom you see today you shall never see again. 14The LORD will fight for you, and you have only to keep still."

15 Then the LORD said to Moses, "Why do you cry out to me? Tell the Israelites to go forward. 16But you lift up your staff, and stretch out your hand over the sea and divide it, that the Israelites may go into the sea on dry ground. 17Then I will harden the hearts of the Egyptians so that they will go in after them; and so I will gain glory for myself over Pharaoh and all his army, his chariots, and his chariot drivers. 18And the Egyptians shall know that I am the

LORD, when I have gained glory for myself over Pharaoh, his chariots, and his chariot drivers."

19 The angel of God who was going before the Israelite army moved and went behind them; and the pillar of cloud moved from in front of them and took its place behind them. 20It came between the army of Egypt and the army of Israel. And so the cloud was there with the darkness, and it lit up the night; one did not come near the other all night.

21 Then Moses stretched out his hand over the sea. The LORD drove the sea back by a strong east wind all night, and turned the sea into dry land; and the waters were divided. 22The Israelites went into the sea on dry ground, the waters forming a wall for them on their right and on their left. 23The Egyptians pursued, and went into the sea after them, all of Pharaoh's horses, chariots, and chariot drivers. 24At the morning watch the LORD in the pillar of fire and cloud looked down upon the Egyptian army, and threw the Egyptian army into panic. 25He clogged^z their chariot wheels so that they turned with difficulty. The Egyptians said, "Let us flee from the Israelites, for the LORD is fighting for them against Egypt."

The Pursuers Drowned

26 Then the LORD said to Moses, "Stretch out your hand over the sea, so that the water may come back upon the Egyptians, upon their chariots and chariot drivers." 27So Moses stretched out his hand over the sea, and at dawn the sea returned to its normal depth. As the Egyptians fled before it, the LORD tossed the Egyptians into the sea. 28The waters returned and covered the chariots and the chariot drivers, the entire army of Pharaoh that had followed them into the sea; not one of them remained. 29But the Israelites walked on dry ground through the sea, the waters forming a wall for them on their right and on their left.

30 Thus the LORD saved Israel that day from the Egyptians; and Israel saw the Egyptians dead on the seashore. 31Israel saw the great work that the

z Sam Gk Syr: MT removed

LORD did against the Egyptians. So the
people feared the LORD and believed in
the LORD and in his servant Moses.

The Song of Moses

 15 Then Moses and the Israelites sang this song to the LORD:

TUESDAY

THE DEATH OF EVIL
Martin Luther King, Jr.

VERSE: Exodus 14.30   PASSAGE: Exodus 14.13–31

hen the children of Israel were held under the gripping yoke of Egyptian slavery, Egypt symbolized evil in the form of humiliating oppression, ungodly exploitation, and crushing domination, and the Israelites symbolized goodness in the form of devotion and dedication to the God of Abraham, Isaac, and Jacob. Egypt struggled to maintain her oppressive yoke, and Israel struggled to gain freedom. Pharaoh stubbornly refused to respond to the cry of Moses, even when plague after plague threatened his domain. This tells us something about evil that we must never forget, namely that evil is recalcitrant and determined, and never voluntarily relinquishes its hold short of a persistent, almost fanatical resistance. But there is a checkpoint in the universe: evil cannot permanently organize itself. So after a long and trying struggle, the Israelites, through the providence of God, crossed the Red Sea. But like the old guard that never surrenders, the Egyptians, in a desperate attempt to prevent the Israelites from escaping, had their armies go in the Red Sea behind them. As soon as the Egyptians got into the dried-up sea the parted waters swept back upon them, and the turbulence and momentum of the tidal waves soon drowned all of them. When the Israelites looked back, all they could see was here and there a poor drowned body beaten upon the seashore. For the Israelites, this was a great moment. It was the end of a frightful period in their history. It was a joyous daybreak that had come to end the long night of their captivity. The meaning of this story is not found in the drowning of Egyptian soldiers, for no one should rejoice at the death or defeat of a human being. Rather, this story symbolizes the death of evil and of inhuman oppression and unjust exploitation.

ADDITIONAL SCRIPTURE READING:
Joshua 3.14–17; Psalm 44.4–8

Go to page 92 for your next devotional reading.

1900   Present

"I will sing to the LORD, for he has
    triumphed gloriously;
  horse and rider he has thrown
    into the sea.
2 The LORD is my strength and my
    might,*a*
  and he has become my salvation;
  this is my God, and I will praise
    him,
  my father's God, and I will exalt
    him.
3 The LORD is a warrior;
  the LORD is his name.

4 "Pharaoh's chariots and his army
  he cast into the sea;
  his picked officers were sunk in
    the Red Sea.*b*
5 The floods covered them;
  they went down into the depths
    like a stone.
6 Your right hand, O LORD, glorious
    in power—
  your right hand, O LORD,
    shattered the enemy.
7 In the greatness of your majesty
  you overthrew your
    adversaries;
  you sent out your fury, it
    consumed them like stubble.
8 At the blast of your nostrils the
    waters piled up,
  the floods stood up in a heap;
  the deeps congealed in the heart
    of the sea.
9 The enemy said, 'I will pursue, I
    will overtake,
  I will divide the spoil, my desire
    shall have its fill of them.
  I will draw my sword, my hand
    shall destroy them.'
10 You blew with your wind, the sea
    covered them;
  they sank like lead in the mighty
    waters.

11 "Who is like you, O LORD, among
    the gods?
  Who is like you, majestic in
    holiness,
  awesome in splendor, doing
    wonders?
12 You stretched out your right hand,
  the earth swallowed them.

13 "In your steadfast love you led the
    people whom you redeemed;
  you guided them by your
    strength to your holy abode.
14 The peoples heard, they trembled;
  pangs seized the inhabitants of
    Philistia.
15 Then the chiefs of Edom were
    dismayed;
  trembling seized the leaders of
    Moab;
  all the inhabitants of Canaan
    melted away.
16 Terror and dread fell upon them;
  by the might of your arm, they
    became still as a stone
  until your people, O LORD, passed
    by,
  until the people whom you
    acquired passed by.
17 You brought them in and planted
    them on the mountain of
    your own possession,
  the place, O LORD, that you made
    your abode,
  the sanctuary, O LORD, that your
    hands have established.
18 The LORD will reign forever and
    ever."

19 When the horses of Pharaoh with
his chariots and his chariot drivers went
into the sea, the LORD brought back the
waters of the sea upon them; but the
Israelites walked through the sea on dry
ground.

The Song of Miriam

20 Then the prophet Miriam, Aaron's
sister, took a tambourine in her hand;
and all the women went out after her
with tambourines and with dancing.
21 And Miriam sang to them:
  "Sing to the LORD, for he has
    triumphed gloriously;
  horse and rider he has thrown into
    the sea."

Bitter Water Made Sweet

22 Then Moses ordered Israel to set out
from the Red Sea,*b* and they went into
the wilderness of Shur. They went three
days in the wilderness and found no
water. 23 When they came to Marah,
they could not drink the water of Marah
because it was bitter. That is why it was

a Or *song*   *b* Or *Sea of Reeds*

called Marah.*c* **24**And the people complained against Moses, saying, "What shall we drink?" **25**He cried out to the LORD; and the LORD showed him a piece of wood;*d* he threw it into the water, and the water became sweet.

There the LORD*e* made for them a statute and an ordinance and there he put them to the test. **26**He said, "If you will listen carefully to the voice of the LORD your God, and do what is right in his sight, and give heed to his commandments and keep all his statutes, I will not bring upon you any of the diseases that I brought upon the Egyptians; for I am the LORD who heals you."

27 Then they came to Elim, where there were twelve springs of water and seventy palm trees; and they camped there by the water.

Bread from Heaven

16 The whole congregation of the Israelites set out from Elim; and Israel came to the wilderness of Sin, which is between Elim and Sinai, on the fifteenth day of the second month after they had departed from the land of Egypt. **2**The whole congregation of the Israelites complained against Moses and Aaron in the wilderness. **3**The Israelites said to them, "If only we had died by the hand of the LORD in the land of Egypt, when we sat by the fleshpots and ate our fill of bread; for you have brought us out into this wilderness to kill this whole assembly with hunger."

4 Then the LORD said to Moses, "I am going to rain bread from heaven for you, and each day the people shall go out and gather enough for that day. In that way I will test them, whether they will follow my instruction or not. **5**On the sixth day, when they prepare what they bring in, it will be twice as much as they gather on other days." **6**So Moses and Aaron said to all the Israelites, "In the evening you shall know that it was the LORD who brought you out of the land of Egypt, **7**and in the morning you shall see the glory of the LORD, because he has heard your complaining against the LORD. For what are we, that you complain against us?" **8**And Moses said, "When the LORD gives you meat to eat in the evening and your fill of bread in the morning, because the LORD has heard the complaining that you utter against him—what are we? Your complaining is not against us but against the LORD."

9 Then Moses said to Aaron, "Say to the whole congregation of the Israelites, 'Draw near to the LORD, for he has heard your complaining.'" **10**And as Aaron spoke to the whole congregation of the Israelites, they looked toward the wilderness, and the glory of the LORD appeared in the cloud. **11**The LORD spoke to Moses and said, **12**"I have heard the complaining of the Israelites; say to them, 'At twilight you shall eat meat, and in the morning you shall have your fill of bread; then you shall know that I am the LORD your God.'"

WHENEVER YOU FIND YOURSELF DISPOSED TO UNEASINESS OR MURMURING AT ANYTHING THAT IS THE EFFECT OF GOD'S PROVIDENCE, LOOK UPON YOURSELF AS DENYING EITHER THE WISDOM OR GOODNESS OF GOD.   —*William Law*

---

13 In the evening quails came up and covered the camp; and in the morning there was a layer of dew around the camp. **14**When the layer of dew lifted, there on the surface of the wilderness was a fine flaky substance, as fine as frost on the ground. **15**When the Israelites saw it, they said to one another, "What is it?"*f* For they did not know what it was. Moses said to them, "It is the bread that the LORD has given you to eat. **16**This is what the LORD has commanded: 'Gather as much of it as each of you needs, an omer to a person according to the number of persons, all providing for those in their own tents.'" **17**The Israelites did so, some gathering more, some less. **18**But when they measured it with an omer, those who gathered much had nothing over, and those who gathered little had no shortage; they gathered as much as each of them needed. **19**And Moses said to them, "Let no one leave any of it over until morning." **20**But they did not listen to Moses; some left part of it until morning, and it bred worms and became foul. And Moses

---

c That is *Bitterness*   *d* Or *a tree*   *e* Heb *he*   *f* Or *"It is manna"* (Heb *man hu,* see verse 31)

was angry with them. 21Morning by morning they gathered it, as much as each needed; but when the sun grew hot, it melted.

22 On the sixth day they gathered twice as much food, two omers apiece. When all the leaders of the congregation came and told Moses, 23he said to them, "This is what the LORD has commanded: 'Tomorrow is a day of solemn rest, a holy sabbath to the LORD; bake what you want to bake and boil what you want to boil, and all that is left over put aside to be kept until morning.' " 24So they put it aside until morning, as Moses commanded them; and it did not become foul, and there were no worms in it. 25Moses said, "Eat it today, for today is a sabbath to the LORD; today you will not find it in the field. 26Six days you shall gather it; but on the seventh day, which is a sabbath, there will be none."

27 On the seventh day some of the people went out to gather, and they found none. 28The LORD said to Moses, "How long will you refuse to keep my commandments and instructions? 29See! The LORD has given you the sabbath, therefore on the sixth day he gives you food for two days; each of you stay where you are; do not leave your place on the seventh day." 30So the people rested on the seventh day.

31 The house of Israel called it manna; it was like coriander seed, white, and the taste of it was like wafers made with honey. 32Moses said, "This is what the LORD has commanded: 'Let an omer of it be kept throughout your generations, in order that they may see the food with which I fed you in the wilderness, when I brought you out of the land of Egypt.' " 33And Moses said to Aaron, "Take a jar, and put an omer of manna in it, and place it before the LORD, to be kept throughout your generations." 34As the LORD commanded Moses, so Aaron placed it before the covenant,g for safekeeping. 35The Israelites ate manna forty years, until they came to a habitable land; they ate manna, until they came to the border of the land of Canaan. 36An omer is a tenth of an ephah.

Water from the Rock

17 From the wilderness of Sin the whole congregation of the Israelites journeyed by stages, as the LORD commanded. They camped at Rephidim, but there was no water for the people to drink. 2The people quarreled with Moses, and said, "Give us water to drink." Moses said to them, "Why do you quarrel with me? Why do you test the LORD?" 3But the people thirsted there for water; and the people complained against Moses and said, "Why did you bring us out of Egypt, to kill us and our children and livestock with thirst?" 4So Moses cried out to the LORD, "What shall I do with this people? They are almost ready to stone me." 5The LORD said to Moses, "Go on ahead of the people, and take some of the elders of Israel with you; take in your hand the staff with which you struck the Nile, and go. 6I will be standing there in front of you on the rock at Horeb. Strike the rock, and water will come out of it, so that the people may drink." Moses did so, in the sight of the elders of Israel. 7He called the place Massahh and Meribah,i because the Israelites quarreled and tested the LORD, saying, "Is the LORD among us or not?"

Amalek Attacks Israel and Is Defeated

8 Then Amalek came and fought with Israel at Rephidim. 9Moses said to Joshua, "Choose some men for us and go out, fight with Amalek. Tomorrow I will stand on the top of the hill with the staff of God in my hand." 10So Joshua did as Moses told him, and fought with Amalek, while Moses, Aaron, and Hur went up to the top of the hill. 11Whenever Moses held up his hand, Israel prevailed; and whenever he lowered his hand, Amalek prevailed. 12But Moses' hands grew weary; so they took a stone and put it under him, and he sat on it. Aaron and Hur held up his hands, one on one side, and the other on the other side; so his hands were steady until the sun set. 13And Joshua defeated Amalek and his people with the sword.

14 Then the LORD said to Moses,

g Or treaty or testimony; Heb eduth   h That is Test   i That is Quarrel

"Write this as a reminder in a book and recite it in the hearing of Joshua: I will utterly blot out the remembrance of Amalek from under heaven." [15]And Moses built an altar and called it, The LORD is my banner. [16]He said, "A hand upon the banner of the LORD![j] The LORD will have war with Amalek from generation to generation."

Jethro's Advice

18 Jethro, the priest of Midian, Moses' father-in-law, heard of all that God had done for Moses and for his people Israel, how the LORD had brought Israel out of Egypt. [2]After Moses had sent away his wife Zipporah, his father-in-law Jethro took her back, [3]along with her two sons. The name of the one was Gershom (for he said, "I have been an alien[k] in a foreign land"), [4]and the name of the other, Eliezer[l] (for he said, "The God of my father was my help, and delivered me from the sword of Pharaoh"). [5]Jethro, Moses' father-in-law, came into the wilderness where Moses was encamped at the mountain of God, bringing Moses' sons and wife to him. [6]He sent word to Moses, "I, your father-in-law Jethro, am coming to you, with your wife and her two sons." [7]Moses went out to meet his father-in-law; he bowed down and kissed him; each asked after the other's welfare, and they went into the tent. [8]Then Moses told his father-in-law all that the LORD had done to Pharaoh and to the Egyptians for Israel's sake, all the hardship that had beset them on the way, and how the LORD had delivered them. [9]Jethro rejoiced for all the good that the LORD had done to Israel, in delivering them from the Egyptians.

10 Jethro said, "Blessed be the LORD, who has delivered you from the Egyptians and from Pharaoh. [11]Now I know that the LORD is greater than all gods, because he delivered the people from the Egyptians,[m] when they dealt arrogantly with them." [12]And Jethro, Moses' father-in-law, brought a burnt offering and sacrifices to God; and Aaron came with all the elders of Israel to eat bread with Moses' father-in-law in the presence of God.

13 The next day Moses sat as judge for the people, while the people stood around him from morning until evening. [14]When Moses' father-in-law saw all that he was doing for the people, he said, "What is this that you are doing for the people? Why do you sit alone, while all the people stand around you from morning until evening?" [15]Moses said to his father-in-law, "Because the people come to me to inquire of God. [16]When they have a dispute, they come to me and I decide between one person and another, and I make known to them the statutes and instructions of God." [17]Moses' father-in-law said to him, "What you are doing is not good. [18]You will surely wear yourself out, both you and these people with you. For the task is too heavy for you; you cannot do it alone. [19]Now listen to me. I will give you counsel, and God be with you! You should represent the people before God, and you should bring their cases before God; [20]teach them the statutes and instructions and make known to them the way they are to go and the things they are to do. [21]You should also look for able men among all the people, men who fear God, are trustworthy, and hate dishonest gain; set such men over them as officers over thousands, hundreds, fifties, and tens. [22]Let them sit as judges for the people at all times; let them bring every important case to you, but decide every minor case themselves. So it will be easier for you, and they will bear the burden with you. [23]If you do this, and God so commands you, then you will be able to endure, and all these people will go to their home in peace."

24 So Moses listened to his father-in-law and did all that he had said. [25]Moses chose able men from all Israel and appointed them as heads over the people, as officers over thousands, hundreds, fifties, and tens. [26]And they judged the people at all times; hard cases they brought to Moses, but any minor case they decided themselves. [27]Then Moses let his father-in-law depart, and he went off to his own country.

---

[j] Cn: Meaning of Heb uncertain   [k] Heb ger   [l] Heb Eli, my God; ezer, help   [m] The clause because . . . Egyptians has been transposed from verse 10

The Israelites Reach Mount Sinai

19 On the third new moon after the Israelites had gone out of the land of Egypt, on that very day, they came into the wilderness of Sinai. ²They had journeyed from Rephidim, entered the wilderness of Sinai, and camped in the wilderness; Israel camped there in front of the mountain. ³Then Moses went up to God; the LORD called to him from the mountain, saying, "Thus you shall say to the house of Jacob, and tell the Israelites: ⁴You have seen what I did to the Egyptians, and how I bore you on eagles' wings and brought you to myself. ⁵Now therefore, if you obey my voice and keep my covenant, you shall be my treasured possession out of all the peoples. Indeed, the whole earth is mine, ⁶but you shall be for me a priestly kingdom and a holy nation. These are the words that you shall speak to the Israelites."

7 So Moses came, summoned the elders of the people, and set before them all these words that the LORD had commanded him. ⁸The people all answered as one: "Everything that the LORD has spoken we will do." Moses reported the words of the people to the LORD. ⁹Then the LORD said to Moses, "I am going to come to you in a dense cloud, in order that the people may hear when I speak with you and so trust you ever after."

The People Consecrated

When Moses had told the words of the people to the LORD, ¹⁰the LORD said to Moses: "Go to the people and consecrate them today and tomorrow. Have them wash their clothes ¹¹and prepare for the third day, because on the third day the LORD will come down upon Mount Sinai in the sight of all the people. ¹²You shall set limits for the people all around, saying, 'Be careful not to go up the mountain or to touch the edge of it. Any who touch the mountain shall be put to death. ¹³No hand shall touch them, but they shall be stoned or shot with arrows;ⁿ whether animal or human being, they shall not live.' When the trumpet sounds a long blast, they may go up on the mountain." ¹⁴So Moses went down from the mountain to the people. He consecrated the people, and they washed their clothes. ¹⁵And he said to the people, "Prepare for the third day; do not go near a woman."

16 On the morning of the third day there was thunder and lightning, as well as a thick cloud on the mountain, and a blast of a trumpet so loud that all the people who were in the camp trembled. ¹⁷Moses brought the people out of the camp to meet God. They took their stand at the foot of the mountain. ¹⁸Now Mount Sinai was wrapped in smoke, because the LORD had descended upon it in fire; the smoke went up like the smoke of a kiln, while the whole mountain shook violently. ¹⁹As the blast of the trumpet grew louder and louder, Moses would speak and God would answer him in thunder. ²⁰When the LORD descended upon Mount Sinai, to the top of the mountain, the LORD summoned Moses to the top of the mountain, and Moses went up. ²¹Then the LORD said to Moses, "Go down and warn the people not to break through to the LORD to look; otherwise many of them will perish. ²²Even the priests who approach the LORD must consecrate themselves or the LORD will break out against them." ²³Moses said to the LORD, "The people are not permitted to come up to Mount Sinai; for you yourself warned us, saying, 'Set limits around the mountain and keep it holy.' " ²⁴The LORD said to him, "Go down, and come up bringing Aaron with you; but do not let either the priests or the people break through to come up to the LORD; otherwise he will break out against them." ²⁵So Moses went down to the people and told them.

The Ten Commandments

20 Then God spoke all these words:

2 I am the LORD your God, who brought you out of the land of Egypt, out of the house of slavery; ³you shall have no other gods beforeᵒ me.

4 You shall not make for yourself an idol, whether in the form of anything that is in heaven above, or that is on the earth beneath, or that is in the water under the earth. ⁵You shall not bow

---

n Heb lacks *with arrows*   o Or *besides*

down to them or worship them; for I the LORD your God am a jealous God, punishing children for the iniquity of parents, to the third and the fourth generation of those who reject me, 6but showing steadfast love to the thousandth generationᵖ of those who love me and keep my commandments.

WHERE WOULD YOU BE IF GOD TOOK AWAY ALL YOUR CHRISTIAN WORK? TOO OFTEN IT IS OUR CHRISTIAN WORK THAT IS WORSHIPED AND NOT GOD. —Oswald Chambers

---

7 You shall not make wrongful use of the name of the LORD your God, for the LORD will not acquit anyone who misuses his name.

8 Remember the sabbath day, and keep it holy. 9Six days you shall labor and do all your work. 10But the seventh day is a sabbath to the LORD your God; you shall not do any work—you, your son or your daughter, your male or female slave, your livestock, or the alien resident in your towns. 11For in six days the LORD made heaven and earth, the sea, and all that is in them, but rested the seventh day; therefore the LORD blessed the sabbath day and consecrated it.

12 Honor your father and your mother, so that your days may be long in the land that the LORD your God is giving you.

13 You shall not murder.q

14 You shall not commit adultery.

15 You shall not steal.

16 You shall not bear false witness against your neighbor.

17 You shall not covet your neighbor's house; you shall not covet your neighbor's wife, or male or female slave, or ox, or donkey, or anything that belongs to your neighbor.

18 When all the people witnessed the thunder and lightning, the sound of the trumpet, and the mountain smoking, they were afraidʳ and trembled and stood at a distance, 19and said to Moses, "You speak to us, and we will listen; but do not let God speak to us, or we will die." 20Moses said to the people, "Do not be afraid; for God has come only to test you and to put the fear of him upon you so that you do not sin." 21Then the people stood at a distance, while Moses drew near to the thick darkness where God was.

The Law concerning the Altar

22 The LORD said to Moses: Thus you shall say to the Israelites: "You have seen for yourselves that I spoke with you from heaven. 23You shall not make gods of silver alongside me, nor shall you make for yourselves gods of gold. 24You need make for me only an altar of earth and sacrifice on it your burnt offerings and your offerings of well-being, your sheep and your oxen; in every place where I cause my name to be remembered I will come to you and bless you. 25But if you make for me an altar of stone, do not build it of hewn stones; for if you use a chisel upon it you profane it. 26You shall not go up by steps to my altar, so that your nakedness may not be exposed on it."

The Law concerning Slaves

21 These are the ordinances that you shall set before them:

2 When you buy a male Hebrew slave, he shall serve six years, but in the seventh he shall go out a free person, without debt. 3If he comes in single, he shall go out single; if he comes in married, then his wife shall go out with him. 4If his master gives him a wife and she bears him sons or daughters, the wife and her children shall be her master's and he shall go out alone. 5But if the slave declares, "I love my master, my wife, and my children; I will not go out a free person," 6then his master shall bring him before God.s He shall be brought to the door or the doorpost; and his master shall pierce his ear with an awl; and he shall serve him for life.

7 When a man sells his daughter as a slave, she shall not go out as the male slaves do. 8If she does not please her master, who designated her for himself, then he shall let her be redeemed; he shall have no right to sell her to a foreign people, since he has dealt unfairly with

---

p Or to thousands   q Or kill   r Sam Gk Syr Vg: MT they saw   s Or to the judges

her. ⁹If he designates her for his son, he shall deal with her as with a daughter. ¹⁰If he takes another wife to himself, he shall not diminish the food, clothing, or marital rights of the first wife.ᵗ ¹¹And if he does not do these three things for her, she shall go out without debt, without payment of money.

The Law concerning Violence

12 Whoever strikes a person mortally shall be put to death. ¹³If it was not premeditated, but came about by an act of God, then I will appoint for you a place to which the killer may flee. ¹⁴But if someone willfully attacks and kills another by treachery, you shall take the killer from my altar for execution.

15 Whoever strikes father or mother shall be put to death.

16 Whoever kidnaps a person, whether that person has been sold or is still held in possession, shall be put to death.

17 Whoever curses father or mother shall be put to death.

18 When individuals quarrel and one strikes the other with a stone or fist so that the injured party, though not dead, is confined to bed, ¹⁹but recovers and walks around outside with the help of a staff, then the assailant shall be free of liability, except to pay for the loss of time, and to arrange for full recovery.

20 When a slaveowner strikes a male or female slave with a rod and the slave dies immediately, the owner shall be punished. ²¹But if the slave survives a day or two, there is no punishment; for the slave is the owner's property.

22 When people who are fighting injure a pregnant woman so that there

---

---

is a miscarriage, and yet no further harm follows, the one responsible shall be fined what the woman's husband demands, paying as much as the judges determine. ²³If any harm follows, then you shall give life for life, ²⁴eye for eye, tooth for tooth, hand for hand, foot for foot, ²⁵burn for burn, wound for wound, stripe for stripe.

26 When a slaveowner strikes the eye of a male or female slave, destroying it, the owner shall let the slave go, a free person, to compensate for the eye. ²⁷If the owner knocks out a tooth of a male or female slave, the slave shall be let go, a free person, to compensate for the tooth.

Laws concerning Property

28 When an ox gores a man or a woman to death, the ox shall be stoned, and its flesh shall not be eaten; but the owner of the ox shall not be liable. ²⁹If the ox has been accustomed to gore in the past, and its owner has been warned but has not restrained it, and it kills a man or a woman, the ox shall be stoned, and its owner also shall be put to death. ³⁰If a ransom is imposed on the owner, then the owner shall pay whatever is imposed for the redemption of the victim's life. ³¹If it gores a boy or a girl, the owner shall be dealt with according to this same rule. ³²If the ox gores a male or female slave, the owner shall pay to the slaveowner thirty shekels of silver, and the ox shall be stoned.

33 If someone leaves a pit open, or digs a pit and does not cover it, and an ox or a donkey falls into it, ³⁴the owner of the pit shall make restitution, giving money to its owner, but keeping the dead animal.

35 If someone's ox hurts the ox of another, so that it dies, then they shall sell the live ox and divide the price of it; and the dead animal they shall also divide. ³⁶But if it was known that the ox was accustomed to gore in the past, and its owner has not restrained it, the owner shall restore ox for ox, but keep the dead animal.

Laws of Restitution

22 ᵘ When someone steals an ox or a sheep, and slaughters it or sells it, the thief shall pay five oxen

---

t Heb of her   u Ch 21.37 in Heb

for an ox, and four sheep for a sheep.^{v} The thief shall make restitution, but if unable to do so, shall be sold for the theft. ^{4}When the animal, whether ox or donkey or sheep, is found alive in the thief's possession, the thief shall pay double.

2^w If a thief is found breaking in, and is beaten to death, no bloodguilt is incurred; ^{3}but if it happens after sunrise, bloodguilt is incurred.

5 When someone causes a field or vineyard to be grazed over, or lets livestock loose to graze in someone else's field, restitution shall be made from the best in the owner's field or vineyard.

6 When fire breaks out and catches in thorns so that the stacked grain or the standing grain or the field is consumed, the one who started the fire shall make full restitution.

7 When someone delivers to a neighbor money or goods for safekeeping, and they are stolen from the neighbor's house, then the thief, if caught, shall pay double. ^{8}If the thief is not caught, the owner of the house shall be brought before God,^{x} to determine whether or not the owner had laid hands on the neighbor's goods.

9 In any case of disputed ownership involving ox, donkey, sheep, clothing, or any other loss, of which one party says, "This is mine," the case of both parties shall come before God;^{x} the one whom God condemns^y shall pay double to the other.

10 When someone delivers to another a donkey, ox, sheep, or any other animal for safekeeping, and it dies or is injured or is carried off, without anyone seeing it, ^{11}an oath before the LORD shall decide between the two of them that the one has not laid hands on the property of the other; the owner shall accept the oath, and no restitution shall be made. ^{12}But if it was stolen, restitution shall be made to its owner. ^{13}If it was mangled by beasts, let it be brought as evidence; restitution shall not be made for the mangled remains.

14 When someone borrows an animal from another and it is injured or dies, the owner not being present, full restitution shall be made. ^{15}If the owner was present, there shall be no restitution; if it was hired, only the hiring fee is due.

Social and Religious Laws

16 When a man seduces a virgin who is not engaged to be married, and lies with her, he shall give the bride-price for her and make her his wife. ^{17}But if her father refuses to give her to him, he shall pay an amount equal to the bride-price for virgins.

18 You shall not permit a female sorcerer to live.

19 Whoever lies with an animal shall be put to death.

20 Whoever sacrifices to any god, other than the LORD alone, shall be devoted to destruction.

21 You shall not wrong or oppress a resident alien, for you were aliens in the land of Egypt. ^{22}You shall not abuse any widow or orphan. ^{23}If you do abuse them, when they cry out to me, I will surely heed their cry; ^{24}my wrath will burn, and I will kill you with the sword, and your wives shall become widows and your children orphans.

25 If you lend money to my people, to the poor among you, you shall not deal with them as a creditor; you shall not exact interest from them. ^{26}If you take your neighbor's cloak in pawn, you shall restore it before the sun goes down; ^{27}for it may be your neighbor's only clothing to use as cover; in what else shall that person sleep? And if your neighbor cries out to me, I will listen, for I am compassionate.

28 You shall not revile God, or curse a leader of your people.

29 You shall not delay to make offerings from the fullness of your harvest and from the outflow of your presses.^{z} The firstborn of your sons you shall give to me. ^{30}You shall do the same with your oxen and with your sheep: seven days it shall remain with its mother; on the eighth day you shall give it to me.

31 You shall be people consecrated to me; therefore you shall not eat any meat that is mangled by beasts in the field; you shall throw it to the dogs.

---

v Verses 2, 3, and 4 rearranged thus: 3b, 4, 2, 3a w Ch 22.1 in Heb x Or *before the judges*
y Or *the judges condemn* z Meaning of Heb uncertain

Justice for All

23 You shall not spread a false report. You shall not join hands with the wicked to act as a malicious witness. 2 You shall not follow a majority in wrongdoing; when you bear witness in a lawsuit, you shall not side with the majority so as to pervert justice; 3 nor shall you be partial to the poor in a lawsuit.

4 When you come upon your enemy's ox or donkey going astray, you shall bring it back.

5 When you see the donkey of one who hates you lying under its burden and you would hold back from setting it free, you must help to set it free.*a*

6 You shall not pervert the justice due to your poor in their lawsuits. 7 Keep far from a false charge, and do not kill the innocent and those in the right, for I will not acquit the guilty. 8 You shall take no bribe, for a bribe blinds the officials, and subverts the cause of those who are in the right.

9 You shall not oppress a resident alien; you know the heart of an alien, for you were aliens in the land of Egypt.

Sabbatical Year and Sabbath

10 For six years you shall sow your land and gather in its yield; 11 but the seventh year you shall let it rest and lie fallow, so that the poor of your people may eat; and what they leave the wild animals may eat. You shall do the same with your vineyard, and with your olive orchard.

12 Six days you shall do your work, but on the seventh day you shall rest, so that your ox and your donkey may have relief, and your homeborn slave and the resident alien may be refreshed. 13 Be attentive to all that I have said to you. Do not invoke the names of other gods; do not let them be heard on your lips.

The Annual Festivals

14 Three times in the year you shall hold a festival for me. 15 You shall observe the festival of unleavened bread; as I commanded you, you shall eat unleavened bread for seven days at the appointed time in the month of Abib, for in it you came out of Egypt. No one shall appear before me empty-handed.

16 You shall observe the festival of harvest, of the first fruits of your labor, of what you sow in the field. You shall observe the festival of ingathering at the end of the year, when you gather in from the field the fruit of your labor. 17 Three times in the year all your males shall appear before the Lord GOD.

18 You shall not offer the blood of my sacrifice with anything leavened, or let the fat of my festival remain until the morning.

19 The choicest of the first fruits of your ground you shall bring into the house of the LORD your God.

You shall not boil a kid in its mother's milk.

The Conquest of Canaan Promised

20 I am going to send an angel in front of you, to guard you on the way and to bring you to the place that I have prepared. 21 Be attentive to him and listen to his voice; do not rebel against him, for he will not pardon your transgression; for my name is in him. 22 But if you listen attentively to his voice and do all that I say, then I will be an enemy to your enemies and a foe to your foes.

23 When my angel goes in front of you, and brings you to the Amorites, the Hittites, the Perizzites, the Canaanites, the Hivites, and the Jebusites, and I blot them out, 24 you shall not bow down to their gods, or worship them, or follow their practices, but you shall utterly demolish them and break their pillars in pieces. 25 You shall worship the LORD your God, and I*b* will bless your bread and your water; and I will take sickness away from among you. 26 No one shall miscarry or be barren in your land; I will fulfill the number of your days. 27 I will send my terror in front of you, and will throw into confusion all the people against whom you shall come, and I will make all your enemies turn their backs to you. 28 And I will send the pestilence*c* in front of you, which shall drive out the Hivites,

a Meaning of Heb uncertain   *b* Gk Vg: Heb *he*   *c* Or *hornets*: Meaning of Heb uncertain

the Canaanites, and the Hittites from before you. 29I will not drive them out from before you in one year, or the land would become desolate and the wild animals would multiply against you. 30Little by little I will drive them out from before you, until you have increased and possess the land. 31I will set your borders from the Red Sea*d* to the sea of the Philistines, and from the wilderness to the Euphrates; for I will hand over to you the inhabitants of the land, and you shall drive them out before you. 32You shall make no covenant with them and their gods. 33They shall not live in your land, or they will make you sin against me; for if you worship their gods, it will surely be a snare to you.

The Blood of the Covenant

24 Then he said to Moses, "Come up to the LORD, you and Aaron, Nadab, and Abihu, and seventy of the elders of Israel, and worship at a distance. 2Moses alone shall come near the LORD; but the others shall not come near, and the people shall not come up with him."

3 Moses came and told the people all the words of the LORD and all the ordinances; and all the people answered with one voice, and said, "All the words that the LORD has spoken we will do." 4And Moses wrote down all the words of the LORD. He rose early in the morning, and built an altar at the foot of the mountain, and set up twelve pillars, corresponding to the twelve tribes of Israel. 5He sent young men of the people of Israel, who offered burnt offerings and sacrificed oxen as offerings of well-being to the LORD. 6Moses took half of the blood and put it in basins, and half of the blood he dashed against the altar. 7Then he took the book of the covenant, and read it in the hearing of the people; and they said, "All that the LORD has spoken we will do, and we will be obedient." 8Moses took the blood and dashed it on the people, and said, "See the blood of the covenant that the LORD has made with you in accordance with all these words."

On the Mountain with God

9 Then Moses and Aaron, Nadab, and Abihu, and seventy of the elders of Israel went up, 10and they saw the God of Israel. Under his feet there was something like a pavement of sapphire stone, like the very heaven for clearness. 11God*e* did not lay his hand on the chief men of the people of Israel; also they beheld God, and they ate and drank.

12 The LORD said to Moses, "Come up to me on the mountain, and wait there; and I will give you the tablets of stone, with the law and the commandment, which I have written for their instruction." 13So Moses set out with his assistant Joshua, and Moses went up into the mountain of God. 14To the elders he had said, "Wait here for us, until we come to you again; for Aaron and Hur are with you; whoever has a dispute may go to them."

15 Then Moses went up on the mountain, and the cloud covered the mountain. 16The glory of the LORD settled on Mount Sinai, and the cloud covered it for six days; on the seventh day he called to Moses out of the cloud. 17Now the appearance of the glory of the LORD was like a devouring fire on the top of the mountain in the sight of the people of Israel. 18Moses entered the cloud, and went up on the mountain. Moses was on the mountain for forty days and forty nights.

Offerings for the Tabernacle

25 The LORD said to Moses: 2Tell the Israelites to take for me an offering; from all whose hearts prompt them to give you shall receive the offering for me. 3This is the offering that you shall receive from them: gold, silver, and bronze, 4blue, purple, and crimson yarns and fine linen, goats' hair, 5tanned rams' skins, fine leather,*f* acacia wood, 6oil for the lamps, spices for the anointing oil and for the fragrant incense, 7onyx stones and gems to be set in the ephod and for the breastpiece. 8And have them make me a sanctuary, so that I may dwell among them. 9In accordance with all that I show you con-

d Or *Sea of Reeds*   *e* Heb *He*   *f* Meaning of Heb uncertain cerning the pattern of the tabernacle and of all its furniture, so you shall make it.

The Ark of the Covenant

10 They shall make an ark of acacia wood; it shall be two and a half cubits long, a cubit and a half wide, and a cubit and a half high. 11 You shall overlay it with pure gold, inside and outside you shall overlay it, and you shall make a molding of gold upon it all around. 12 You shall cast four rings of gold for it and put them on its four feet, two rings on the one side of it, and two rings on the other side. 13 You shall make poles of acacia wood, and overlay them with gold. 14 And you shall put the poles into the rings on the sides of the ark, by which to carry the ark. 15 The poles shall remain in the rings of the ark; they shall not be taken from it. 16 You shall put into the ark the covenant*g* that I shall give you.

17 Then you shall make a mercy seat*h* of pure gold; two cubits and a half shall be its length, and a cubit and a half its width. 18 You shall make two cherubim of gold; you shall make them of hammered work, at the two ends of the mercy seat.*i* 19 Make one cherub at the one end, and one cherub at the other; of one piece with the mercy seat*i* you shall make the cherubim at its two ends. 20 The cherubim shall spread out their wings above, overshadowing the mercy seat*i* with their wings. They shall face one to another; the faces of the cherubim shall be turned toward the mercy seat.*i* 21 You shall put the mercy seat*i* on the top of the ark; and in the ark you shall put the covenant*g* that I shall give you. 22 There I will meet with you, and from above the mercy seat,*i* from between the two cherubim that are on the ark of the covenant,*g* I will deliver to you all my commands for the Israelites.

The Table for the Bread of the Presence

23 You shall make a table of acacia wood, two cubits long, one cubit wide, and a cubit and a half high. 24 You shall overlay it with pure gold, and make a molding of gold around it. 25 You shall make around it a rim a handbreadth

wide, and a molding of gold around the rim. 26 You shall make for it four rings of gold, and fasten the rings to the four corners at its four legs. 27 The rings that hold the poles used for carrying the table shall be close to the rim. 28 You shall make the poles of acacia wood, and overlay them with gold, and the table shall be carried with these. 29 You shall make its plates and dishes for incense, and its flagons and bowls with which to pour drink offerings; you shall make them of pure gold. 30 And you shall set the bread of the Presence on the table before me always.

The Lampstand

31 You shall make a lampstand of pure gold. The base and the shaft of the lampstand shall be made of hammered work; its cups, its calyxes, and its petals shall be of one piece with it; 32 and there shall be six branches going out of its sides, three branches of the lampstand out of one side of it and three branches of the lampstand out of the other side of it; 33 three cups shaped like almond blossoms, each with calyx and petals, on one branch, and three cups shaped like almond blossoms, each with calyx and petals, on the other branch—so for the six branches going out of the lampstand. 34 On the lampstand itself there shall be four cups shaped like almond blossoms, each with its calyxes and petals. 35 There shall be a calyx of one piece with it under the first pair of branches, a calyx of one piece with it under the next pair of branches, and a calyx of one piece with it under the last pair of branches—so for the six branches that go out of the lampstand. 36 Their calyxes and their branches shall be of one piece with it, the whole of it one hammered piece of pure gold. 37 You shall make the seven lamps for it; and the lamps shall be set up so as to give light on the space in front of it. 38 Its snuffers and trays shall be of pure gold. 39 It, and all these utensils, shall be made from a talent of pure gold. 40 And see that you make them according to the pattern for them, which is being shown you on the mountain.

g Or *treaty,* or *testimony*; Heb *eduth*   *h* Or *a cover*   *i* Or *the cover*

The Tabernacle

26 Moreover you shall make the tabernacle with ten curtains of fine twisted linen, and blue, purple, and crimson yarns; you shall make them with cherubim skillfully worked into them. ²The length of each curtain shall be twenty-eight cubits, and the width of each curtain four cubits; all the curtains shall be of the same size. ³Five curtains shall be joined to one another; and the other five curtains shall be joined to one another. ⁴You shall make loops of blue on the edge of the outermost curtain in the first set; and likewise you shall make loops on the edge of the outermost curtain in the second set. ⁵You shall make fifty loops on the one curtain, and you shall make fifty loops on the edge of the curtain that is in the second set; the loops shall be opposite one another. ⁶You shall make fifty clasps of gold, and join the curtains to one another with the clasps, so that the tabernacle may be one whole.

7 You shall also make curtains of goats' hair for a tent over the tabernacle; you shall make eleven curtains. ⁸The length of each curtain shall be thirty cubits, and the width of each curtain four cubits; the eleven curtains shall be of the same size. ⁹You shall join five curtains by themselves, and six curtains by themselves, and the sixth curtain you shall double over at the front of the tent. ¹⁰You shall make fifty loops on the edge of the curtain that is outermost in one set, and fifty loops on the edge of the curtain that is outermost in the second set.

11 You shall make fifty clasps of bronze, and put the clasps into the loops, and join the tent together, so that it may be one whole. ¹²The part that remains of the curtains of the tent, the half curtain that remains, shall hang over the back of the tabernacle. ¹³The cubit on the one side, and the cubit on the other side, of what remains in the length of the curtains of the tent, shall hang over the sides of the tabernacle, on this side and that side, to cover it. ¹⁴You shall make for the tent a covering of tanned rams' skins and an outer covering of fine leather.*j*

j Meaning of Heb uncertain

The Framework

15 You shall make upright frames of acacia wood for the tabernacle. ¹⁶Ten cubits shall be the length of a frame, and a cubit and a half the width of each frame. ¹⁷There shall be two pegs in each frame to fit the frames together; you shall make these for all the frames of the tabernacle. ¹⁸You shall make the frames for the tabernacle: twenty frames for the south side; ¹⁹and you shall make forty bases of silver under the twenty frames, two bases under the first frame for its two pegs, and two bases under the next frame for its two pegs; ²⁰and for the second side of the tabernacle, on the north side twenty frames, ²¹and their forty bases of silver, two bases under the first frame, and two bases under the next frame; ²²and for the rear of the tabernacle westward you shall make six frames. ²³You shall make two frames for corners of the tabernacle in the rear; ²⁴they shall be separate beneath, but joined at the top, at the first ring; it shall be the same with both of them; they shall form the two corners. ²⁵And so there shall be eight frames, with their bases of silver, sixteen bases; two bases under the first frame, and two bases under the next frame.

26 You shall make bars of acacia wood, five for the frames of the one side of the tabernacle, ²⁷and five bars for the frames of the other side of the tabernacle, and five bars for the frames of the side of the tabernacle at the rear westward. ²⁸The middle bar, halfway up the frames, shall pass through from end to end. ²⁹You shall overlay the frames with gold, and shall make their rings of gold to hold the bars; and you shall overlay the bars with gold. ³⁰Then you shall erect the tabernacle according to the plan for it that you were shown on the mountain.

The Curtain

31 You shall make a curtain of blue, purple, and crimson yarns, and of fine twisted linen; it shall be made with cherubim skillfully worked into it. ³²You shall hang it on four pillars of acacia overlaid with gold, which have

hooks of gold and rest on four bases of silver. 33 You shall hang the curtain under the clasps, and bring the ark of the covenant[k] in there, within the curtain; and the curtain shall separate for you the holy place from the most holy. 34 You shall put the mercy seat[l] on the ark of the covenant[k] in the most holy place. 35 You shall set the table outside the curtain, and the lampstand on the south side of the tabernacle opposite the table; and you shall put the table on the north side.

36 You shall make a screen for the entrance of the tent, of blue, purple, and crimson yarns, and of fine twisted linen, embroidered with needlework. 37 You shall make for the screen five pillars of acacia, and overlay them with gold; their hooks shall be of gold, and you shall cast five bases of bronze for them.

The Altar of Burnt Offering

27 You shall make the altar of acacia wood, five cubits long and five cubits wide; the altar shall be square, and it shall be three cubits high. 2 You shall make horns for it on its four corners; its horns shall be of one piece with it, and you shall overlay it with bronze. 3 You shall make pots for it to receive its ashes, and shovels and basins and forks and firepans; you shall make all its utensils of bronze. 4 You shall also make for it a grating, a network of bronze; and on the net you shall make four bronze rings at its four corners. 5 You shall set it under the ledge of the altar so that the net shall extend halfway down the altar. 6 You shall make poles for the altar, poles of acacia wood, and overlay them with bronze; 7 the poles shall be put through the rings, so that the poles shall be on the two sides of the altar when it is carried. 8 You shall make it hollow, with boards. They shall be made just as you were shown on the mountain.

The Court and Its Hangings

9 You shall make the court of the tabernacle. On the south side the court shall have hangings of fine twisted linen one hundred cubits long for that side; 10 its twenty pillars and their twenty bases shall be of bronze, but the hooks of the pillars and their bands shall be of silver. 11 Likewise for its length on the north side there shall be hangings one hundred cubits long, their pillars twenty and their bases twenty, of bronze, but the hooks of the pillars and their bands shall be of silver. 12 For the width of the court on the west side there shall be fifty cubits of hangings, with ten pillars and ten bases. 13 The width of the court on the front to the east shall be fifty cubits. 14 There shall be fifteen cubits of hangings on the one side, with three pillars and three bases. 15 There shall be fifteen cubits of hangings on the other side, with three pillars and three bases. 16 For the gate of the court there shall be a screen twenty cubits long, of blue, purple, and crimson yarns, and of fine twisted linen, embroidered with needlework; it shall have four pillars and with them four bases. 17 All the pillars around the court shall be banded with silver; their hooks shall be of silver, and their bases of bronze. 18 The length of the court shall be one hundred cubits, the width fifty, and the height five cubits, with hangings of fine twisted linen and bases of bronze. 19 All the utensils of the tabernacle for every use, and all its pegs and all the pegs of the court, shall be of bronze.

The Oil for the Lamp

20 You shall further command the Israelites to bring you pure oil of beaten olives for the light, so that a lamp may be set up to burn regularly. 21 In the tent of meeting, outside the curtain that is before the covenant,[k] Aaron and his sons shall tend it from evening to morning before the LORD. It shall be a perpetual ordinance to be observed throughout their generations by the Israelites.

Vestments for the Priesthood

28 Then bring near to you your brother Aaron, and his sons with him, from among the Israelites, to serve me as priests—Aaron and Aaron's sons, Nadab and Abihu, Eleazar and Ithamar. 2 You shall make sacred vestments for the glorious adornment of your brother Aaron. 3 And you shall speak to

k Or treaty, or testimony; Heb eduth   l Or the cover

OIL AND THE LIGHT OF THE LAMPSTAND
A. B. Simpson

VERSE: Exodus 27.20   PASSAGE: Exodus 27.20–21

 he two figures of light and oil are beautiful and interesting in their natural symbolism . . .

Light is that which makes the human face so full of loveliness. It is that which gives us everything beautiful in all the wonders of the natural world.

Nor have we only the light that comes from without. We have also the light that comes from within—the sense of sight and the power of insight that bring into our consciousness and perception the objects of nature around us.

We find this figure of light through all of God's Word. It was the most marked symbol of his presence. He appeared in the Garden of Eden in the light of the *shekinah*. He appeared to Abraham in the lamp that passed between the pieces of the sacrifice (see Genesis 15.17). He appeared to the migrating children of Israel in the pillar of fire (see Exodus 13.21). And he appeared to Moses in the burning bush (see Exodus 3.2).

Jesus uses this figure of himself. He claimed to be the light of the world, of his own children especially (see John 8.12). The Holy Spirit is also the source of light. And the vision of the Apocalypse closes with the light that is brighter than the sun and a rainbow gathering up all its beautiful effulgence around the throne forever.

Likewise the figure of oil expresses many interesting thoughts. It is the source of artificial light. It contains in itself the elements of life and healing and, in contact with fire, the elements of light.

We find it employed for many other purposes than light. It was used in connection with the consecration of the priesthood and in healing, but it was especially set apart for the lighting of God's sanctuary. And it was specifically prescribed by God himself and by the most awful sanctions guarded from being counterfeited. If anyone should endeavor to imitate or counterfeit it, he was to be cut off from among the people. Its ingredients were compounded together in some mysterious way for its sacred use, to light God's holy sanctuary.

ADDITIONAL SCRIPTURE READING:
Leviticus 24.1–3; Matthew 25.1–13

Go to page 97 for your next devotional reading.

1900   Present

all who have ability, whom I have endowed with skill, that they make Aaron's vestments to consecrate him for my priesthood. [4]These are the vestments that they shall make: a breastpiece, an ephod, a robe, a checkered tunic, a turban, and a sash. When they make these sacred vestments for your brother Aaron and his sons to serve me as priests, [5]they shall use gold, blue, purple, and crimson yarns, and fine linen.

The Ephod

6 They shall make the ephod of gold, of blue, purple, and crimson yarns, and of fine twisted linen, skillfully worked. [7]It shall have two shoulder-pieces attached to its two edges, so that it may be joined together. [8]The decorated band on it shall be of the same workmanship and materials, of gold, of blue, purple, and crimson yarns, and of fine twisted linen. [9]You shall take two onyx stones, and engrave on them the names of the sons of Israel, [10]six of their names on the one stone, and the names of the remaining six on the other stone, in the order of their birth. [11]As a gem-cutter engraves signets, so you shall engrave the two stones with the names of the sons of Israel; you shall mount them in settings of gold filigree. [12]You shall set the two stones on the shoulder-pieces of the ephod, as stones of remembrance for the sons of Israel; and Aaron shall bear their names before the LORD on his two shoulders for remembrance. [13]You shall make settings of gold filigree, [14]and two chains of pure gold, twisted like cords; and you shall attach the corded chains to the settings.

The Breastplate

15 You shall make a breastpiece of judgment, in skilled work; you shall make it in the style of the ephod; of gold, of blue and purple and crimson yarns, and of fine twisted linen you shall make it. [16]It shall be square and doubled, a span in length and a span in width. [17]You shall set in it four rows of stones. A row of carnelian,[m] chrysolite, and emerald shall be the first row; [18]and the second row a turquoise, a sapphire[n]

and a moonstone; [19]and the third row a jacinth, an agate, and an amethyst; [20]and the fourth row a beryl, an onyx, and a jasper; they shall be set in gold filigree. [21]There shall be twelve stones with names corresponding to the names of the sons of Israel; they shall be like signets, each engraved with its name, for the twelve tribes. [22]You shall make for the breastpiece chains of pure gold, twisted like cords; [23]and you shall make for the breastpiece two rings of gold, and put the two rings on the two edges of the breastpiece. [24]You shall put the two cords of gold in the two rings at the edges of the breastpiece; [25]the two ends of the two cords you shall attach to the two settings, and so attach it in front to the shoulder-pieces of the ephod. [26]You shall make two rings of gold, and put them at the two ends of the breastpiece, on its inside edge next to the ephod. [27]You shall make two rings of gold, and attach them in front to the lower part of the two shoulder-pieces of the ephod, at its joining above the decorated band of the ephod. [28]The breastpiece shall be bound by its rings to the rings of the ephod with a blue cord, so that it may lie on the decorated band of the ephod, and so that the breastpiece shall not come loose from the ephod. [29]So Aaron shall bear the names of the sons of Israel in the breastpiece of judgment on his heart when he goes into the holy place, for a continual remembrance before the LORD. [30]In the breastpiece of judgment you shall put the Urim and the Thummim, and they shall be on Aaron's heart when he goes in before the LORD; thus Aaron shall bear the judgment of the Israelites on his heart before the LORD continually.

Other Priestly Vestments

31 You shall make the robe of the ephod all of blue. [32]It shall have an opening for the head in the middle of it, with a woven binding around the opening, like the opening in a coat of mail,[o] so that it may not be torn. [33]On its lower hem you shall make pomegranates of blue, purple, and crimson yarns, all around the lower hem, with bells of gold

m The identity of several of these stones is uncertain   n Or *lapis lazuli*   o Meaning of Heb uncertain

between them all around— 34a golden bell and a pomegranate alternating all around the lower hem of the robe. 35Aaron shall wear it when he ministers, and its sound shall be heard when he goes into the holy place before the LORD, and when he comes out, so that he may not die.

36 You shall make a rosette of pure gold, and engrave on it, like the engraving of a signet, "Holy to the LORD." 37You shall fasten it on the turban with a blue cord; it shall be on the front of the turban. 38It shall be on Aaron's forehead, and Aaron shall take on himself any guilt incurred in the holy offering that the Israelites consecrate as their sacred donations; it shall always be on his forehead, in order that they may find favor before the LORD.

39 You shall make the checkered tunic of fine linen, and you shall make a turban of fine linen, and you shall make a sash embroidered with needlework.

40 For Aaron's sons you shall make tunics and sashes and headdresses; you shall make them for their glorious adornment. 41You shall put them on your brother Aaron, and on his sons with him, and shall anoint them and ordain them and consecrate them, so that they may serve me as priests. 42You shall make for them linen undergarments to cover their naked flesh; they shall reach from the hips to the thighs; 43Aaron and his sons shall wear them when they go into the tent of meeting, or when they come near the altar to minister in the holy place; or they will bring guilt on themselves and die. This shall be a perpetual ordinance for him and for his descendants after him.

The Ordination of the Priests

29 Now this is what you shall do to them to consecrate them, so that they may serve me as priests. Take one young bull and two rams without blemish, 2and unleavened bread, unleavened cakes mixed with oil, and unleavened wafers spread with oil. You shall make them of choice wheat flour. 3You shall put them in one basket and bring them in the basket, and bring the bull and the two rams. 4You shall bring

Aaron and his sons to the entrance of the tent of meeting, and wash them with water. 5Then you shall take the vestments, and put on Aaron the tunic and the robe of the ephod, and the ephod, and the breastpiece, and gird him with the decorated band of the ephod; 6and you shall set the turban on his head, and put the holy diadem on the turban. 7You shall take the anointing oil, and pour it on his head and anoint him. 8Then you shall bring his sons, and put tunics on them, 9and you shall gird them with sashes[p] and tie headdresses on them; and the priesthood shall be theirs by a perpetual ordinance. You shall then ordain Aaron and his sons.

10 You shall bring the bull in front of the tent of meeting. Aaron and his sons shall lay their hands on the head of the bull, 11and you shall slaughter the bull before the LORD, at the entrance of the tent of meeting, 12and shall take some of the blood of the bull and put it on the horns of the altar with your finger, and all the rest of the blood you shall pour out at the base of the altar. 13You shall take all the fat that covers the entrails, and the appendage of the liver, and the two kidneys with the fat that is on them, and turn them into smoke on the altar. 14But the flesh of the bull, and its skin, and its dung, you shall burn with fire outside the camp; it is a sin offering.

15 Then you shall take one of the rams, and Aaron and his sons shall lay their hands on the head of the ram, 16and you shall slaughter the ram, and shall take its blood and dash it against all sides of the altar. 17Then you shall cut the ram into its parts, and wash its entrails and its legs, and put them with its parts and its head, 18and turn the whole ram into smoke on the altar; it is a burnt offering to the LORD; it is a pleasing odor, an offering by fire to the LORD.

19 You shall take the other ram; and Aaron and his sons shall lay their hands on the head of the ram, 20and you shall slaughter the ram, and take some of its blood and put it on the lobe of Aaron's right ear and on the lobes of the right ears of his sons, and on the thumbs of their right hands, and on the big toes of their right feet, and dash the rest of the

p Gk: Heb *sashes, Aaron and his sons*

blood against all sides of the altar. 21 Then you shall take some of the blood that is on the altar, and some of the anointing oil, and sprinkle it on Aaron and his vestments and on his sons and his sons' vestments with him; then he and his vestments shall be holy, as well as his sons and his sons' vestments.

22 You shall also take the fat of the ram, the fat tail, the fat that covers the entrails, the appendage of the liver, the two kidneys with the fat that is on them, and the right thigh (for it is a ram of ordination), 23 and one loaf of bread, one cake of bread made with oil, and one wafer, out of the basket of unleavened bread that is before the Lord; 24 and you shall place all these on the palms of Aaron and on the palms of his sons, and raise them as an elevation offering before the Lord. 25 Then you shall take them from their hands, and turn them into smoke on the altar on top of the burnt offering of pleasing odor before the Lord; it is an offering by fire to the Lord.

26 You shall take the breast of the ram of Aaron's ordination and raise it as an elevation offering before the Lord; and it shall be your portion. 27 You shall consecrate the breast that was raised as an elevation offering and the thigh that was raised as an elevation offering from the ram of ordination, from that which belonged to Aaron and his sons. 28 These things shall be a perpetual ordinance for Aaron and his sons from the Israelites, for this is an offering; and it shall be an offering by the Israelites from their sacrifice of offerings of well-being, their offering to the Lord.

29 The sacred vestments of Aaron shall be passed on to his sons after him; they shall be anointed in them and ordained in them. 30 The son who is priest in his place shall wear them seven days, when he comes into the tent of meeting to minister in the holy place.

31 You shall take the ram of ordination, and boil its flesh in a holy place; 32 and Aaron and his sons shall eat the flesh of the ram and the bread that is in the basket, at the entrance of the tent of meeting. 33 They themselves shall eat the food by which atonement is made, to ordain and consecrate them, but no

one else shall eat of them, because they are holy. 34 If any of the flesh for the ordination, or of the bread, remains until the morning, then you shall burn the remainder with fire; it shall not be eaten, because it is holy.

35 Thus you shall do to Aaron and to his sons, just as I have commanded you; through seven days you shall ordain them. 36 Also every day you shall offer a bull as a sin offering for atonement. Also you shall offer a sin offering for the altar, when you make atonement for it, and shall anoint it, to consecrate it. 37 Seven days you shall make atonement for the altar, and consecrate it, and the altar shall be most holy; whatever touches the altar shall become holy.

The Daily Offerings

38 Now this is what you shall offer on the altar: two lambs a year old regularly each day. 39 One lamb you shall offer in the morning, and the other lamb you shall offer in the evening; 40 and with the first lamb one-tenth of a measure of choice flour mixed with one-fourth of a hin of beaten oil, and one-fourth of a hin of wine for a drink offering. 41 And the other lamb you shall offer in the evening, and shall offer with it a grain offering and its drink offering, as in the morning, for a pleasing odor, an offering by fire to the Lord. 42 It shall be a regular burnt offering throughout your generations at the entrance of the tent of meeting before the Lord, where I will meet with you, to speak to you there. 43 I will meet with the Israelites there, and it shall be sanctified by my glory; 44 I will consecrate the tent of meeting and the altar; Aaron also and his sons I will consecrate, to serve me as priests. 45 I will dwell among the Israelites, and I will be their God. 46 And they shall know that I am the Lord their God, who brought them out of the land of Egypt that I might dwell among them; I am the Lord their God.

The Altar of Incense

30 You shall make an altar on which to offer incense; you shall make it of acacia wood. 2 It shall be one cubit long, and one cubit wide; it shall be square, and shall be two cubits high; its horns shall be of one piece with it. 3You shall overlay it with pure gold, its top, and its sides all around and its horns; and you shall make for it a molding of gold all around. 4And you shall make two golden rings for it; under its molding on two opposite sides of it you shall make them, and they shall hold the poles with which to carry it. 5You shall make the poles of acacia wood, and overlay them with gold. 6You shall place it in front of the curtain that is above the ark of the covenant,[q] in front of the mercy seat[r] that is over the covenant,[q] where I will meet with you. 7Aaron shall offer fragrant incense on it; every morning when he dresses the lamps he shall offer it, 8and when Aaron sets up the lamps in the evening, he shall offer it, a regular incense offering before the LORD throughout your generations. 9You shall not offer unholy incense on it, or a burnt offering, or a grain offering; and you shall not pour a drink offering on it. 10Once a year Aaron shall perform the rite of atonement on its horns. Throughout your generations he shall perform the atonement for it once a year with the blood of the atoning sin offering. It is most holy to the LORD.

The Half Shekel for the Sanctuary

11 The LORD spoke to Moses: 12When you take a census of the Israelites to register them, at registration all of them shall give a ransom for their lives to the LORD, so that no plague may come upon them for being registered. 13This is what each one who is registered shall give: half a shekel according to the shekel of the sanctuary (the shekel is twenty gerahs), half a shekel as an offering to the LORD. 14Each one who is registered, from twenty years old and upward, shall give the LORD's offering. 15The rich shall not give more, and the poor shall not give less, than the half shekel, when you bring this offering to the LORD to make atonement for your lives. 16You shall take the atonement money from the Israelites and shall designate it for the service of the tent of meeting; before the LORD it will be a reminder to the Israelites of the ransom given for your lives.

The Bronze Basin

17 The LORD spoke to Moses: 18You shall make a bronze basin with a bronze stand for washing. You shall put it between the tent of meeting and the altar, and you shall put water in it; 19with the water[s] Aaron and his sons shall wash their hands and their feet. 20When they go into the tent of meeting, or when they come near the altar to minister, to make an offering by fire to the LORD, they shall wash with water, so that they may not die. 21They shall wash their hands and their feet, so that they may not die: it shall be a perpetual ordinance for them, for him and for his descendants throughout their generations.

The Anointing Oil and Incense

22 The LORD spoke to Moses: 23Take the finest spices: of liquid myrrh five hundred shekels, and of sweet-smelling cinnamon half as much, that is, two hundred fifty, and two hundred fifty of aromatic cane, 24and five hundred of cassia—measured by the sanctuary shekel—and a hin of olive oil; 25and you shall make of these a sacred anointing oil blended as by the perfumer; it shall be a holy anointing oil. 26With it you shall anoint the tent of meeting and the ark of the covenant,[q] 27and the table and all its utensils, and the lampstand and its utensils, and the altar of incense, 28and the altar of burnt offering with all its utensils, and the basin with its stand; 29you shall consecrate them, so that they may be most holy; whatever touches them will become holy. 30You shall anoint Aaron and his sons, and consecrate them, in order that they may serve me as priests. 31You shall say to the Israelites, "This shall be my holy anointing oil throughout your generations. 32It shall not be used in any ordinary anointing of the body, and you shall make no other like it in composition; it is holy, and it shall be holy to you. 33Whoever compounds any like it or whoever puts any of it on an unqualified person shall be cut off from the people."

34 The LORD said to Moses: Take sweet spices, stacte, and onycha, and

q Or *treaty*, or *testimony*; Heb *eduth* *r* Or *the cover* *s* Heb *it*

AN UNPRETENTIOUS AND GHASTLY ALTAR
A. B. Simpson

VERSE: Exodus 30.28   PASSAGE: Exodus 30.22–29

he altar of burnt offering in the ancient tabernacle court was the first object a person would notice upon entering the curtain that surrounded that ancient sanctuary. It stood just inside the entryway, accessible to all the people . . .

Its place at the entrance of the tabernacle teaches us that Christ's sacrifice, of which it is the type, stands at the very entrance of all our access to and communion with God.

Then again, the relation which it bore to the inner sections of the sanctuary, and that its blood was necessary in order to enter the inner shrine, shows us that Christ's blood is the only passport now to the presence of God, either on earth or in heaven. With it, we are accepted either on earth or in heaven to the very presence of God.

Further, it was accessible to the highest and the lowest, to every class of people. This indicates the fullness and graciousness of the great atonement that Christ has made for the sins of the whole world, sufficient for all, though effectual only for those who believe.

These are the chief lessons of the altar. There was nothing ornamental about it. It was unpretentious and ghastly looking. It was made of brass to bear the heaviest burdens and to sustain the streams of gore that bathed it and the ceaseless fires that burned upon it.

It was a place of suffering and blood, and it bore the constant mark of sin. So the cross of Calvary, the death of Christ and the whole doctrine of the atonement have nothing very sentimental about them. The culture of man does not like it; the philosophy of the world would get rid of it if it could. But God has made his people prize the precious blood of Jesus Christ above all price and honor and love.

ADDITIONAL SCRIPTURE READING:
Exodus 27.1–8; Hebrews 9.11–28

Go to page 102 for your next devotional reading.

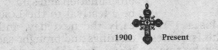

1900   Present

galbanum, sweet spices with pure frankincense (an equal part of each), 35and make an incense blended as by the perfumer, seasoned with salt, pure and holy; 36and you shall beat some of it into powder, and put part of it before the covenant[t] in the tent of meeting where I shall meet with you; it shall be for you most holy. 37When you make incense according to this composition, you shall not make it for yourselves; it shall be regarded by you as holy to the LORD. 38Whoever makes any like it to use as perfume shall be cut off from the people.

Bezalel and Oholiab

31 The LORD spoke to Moses: 2See, I have called by name Bezalel son of Uri son of Hur, of the tribe of Judah: 3and I have filled him with divine spirit,[u] with ability, intelligence, and knowledge in every kind of craft, 4to devise artistic designs, to work in gold, silver, and bronze, 5in cutting stones for setting, and in carving wood, in every kind of craft. 6Moreover, I have appointed with him Oholiab son of Ahisamach, of the tribe of Dan; and I have given skill to all the skillful, so that they may make all that I have commanded you: 7the tent of meeting, and the ark of the covenant,[t] and the mercy seat[v] that is on it, and all the furnishings of the tent, 8the table and its utensils, and the pure lampstand with all its utensils, and the altar of incense, 9and the altar of burnt offering with all its utensils, and the basin with its stand, 10and the finely worked vestments, the holy vestments for the priest Aaron and the vestments of his sons, for their service as priests, 11and the anointing oil and the fragrant incense for the holy place. They shall do just as I have commanded you.

The Sabbath Law

12 The LORD said to Moses: 13You yourself are to speak to the Israelites: "You shall keep my sabbaths, for this is a sign between me and you throughout your generations, given in order that you may know that I, the LORD, sanctify you. 14You shall keep the sabbath,

because it is holy for you; everyone who profanes it shall be put to death; whoever does any work on it shall be cut off from among the people. 15Six days shall work be done, but the seventh day is a sabbath of solemn rest, holy to the LORD; whoever does any work on the sabbath day shall be put to death. 16Therefore the Israelites shall keep the sabbath, observing the sabbath throughout their generations, as a perpetual covenant. 17It is a sign forever between me and the people of Israel that in six days the LORD made heaven and earth, and on the seventh day he rested, and was refreshed."

The Two Tablets of the Covenant

18 When God[w] finished speaking with Moses on Mount Sinai, he gave him the two tablets of the covenant,[t] tablets of stone, written with the finger of God.

The Golden Calf

32 When the people saw that Moses delayed to come down from the mountain, the people gathered around Aaron, and said to him, "Come, make gods for us, who shall go before us; as for this Moses, the man who brought us up out of the land of Egypt, we do not know what has become of him." 2Aaron said to them, "Take off the gold rings that are on the ears of your wives, your sons, and your daughters, and bring them to me." 3So all the people took off the gold rings from their ears, and brought them to Aaron. 4He took the gold from them, formed it in a mold,[x] and cast an image of a calf; and they said, "These are your gods, O Israel, who brought you up out of the land of Egypt!" 5When Aaron saw this, he built an altar before it; and Aaron made proclamation and said, "Tomorrow shall be a festival to the LORD." 6They rose early the next day, and offered burnt offerings and brought sacrifices of well-being; and the people sat down to eat and drink, and rose up to revel.

7 The LORD said to Moses, "Go down at once! Your people, whom you brought up out of the land of Egypt, have

acted perversely; **8**they have been quick to turn aside from the way that I commanded them; they have cast for themselves an image of a calf, and have worshiped it and sacrificed to it, and said, 'These are your gods, O Israel, who brought you up out of the land of Egypt!' " **9**The LORD said to Moses, "I have seen this people, how stiff-necked they are. **10**Now let me alone, so that my wrath may burn hot against them and I may consume them; and of you I will make a great nation."

11 But Moses implored the LORD his God, and said, "O LORD, why does your wrath burn hot against your people, whom you brought out of the land of Egypt with great power and with a mighty hand? **12**Why should the Egyptians say, 'It was with evil intent that he brought them out to kill them in the mountains, and to consume them from the face of the earth'? Turn from your fierce wrath; change your mind and do not bring disaster on your people. **13**Remember Abraham, Isaac, and Israel, your servants, how you swore to them by your own self, saying to them, 'I will multiply your descendants like the stars of heaven, and all this land that I have promised I will give to your descendants, and they shall inherit it forever.' " **14**And the LORD changed his mind about the disaster that he planned to bring on his people.

15 Then Moses turned and went down from the mountain, carrying the two tablets of the covenant*y* in his hands, tablets that were written on both sides, written on the front and on the back. **16**The tablets were the work of God, and the writing was the writing of God, engraved upon the tablets. **17**When Joshua heard the noise of the people as they shouted, he said to Moses, "There is a noise of war in the camp." **18**But he said,

> "It is not the sound made by
>   victors,
> or the sound made by losers;
> it is the sound of revelers that I
>   hear."

19As soon as he came near the camp and saw the calf and the dancing, Moses' anger burned hot, and he threw the tablets from his hands and broke them at the foot of the mountain. **20**He took the calf that they had made, burned it with fire, ground it to powder, scattered it on the water, and made the Israelites drink it.

21 Moses said to Aaron, "What did this people do to you that you have brought so great a sin upon them?" **22**And Aaron said, "Do not let the anger of my lord burn hot; you know the people, that they are bent on evil. **23**They said to me, 'Make us gods, who shall go before us; as for this Moses, the man who brought us up out of the land of Egypt, we do not know what has become of him.' **24**So I said to them, 'Whoever has gold, take it off'; so they gave it to me, and I threw it into the fire, and out came this calf!"

25 When Moses saw that the people were running wild (for Aaron had let them run wild, to the derision of their enemies), **26**then Moses stood in the gate of the camp, and said, "Who is on the LORD's side? Come to me!" And all the sons of Levi gathered around him. **27**He said to them, "Thus says the LORD, the God of Israel, 'Put your sword on your side, each of you! Go back and forth from gate to gate throughout the camp, and each of you kill your brother, your friend, and your neighbor.' " **28**The sons of Levi did as Moses commanded, and about three thousand of the people fell on that day. **29**Moses said, "Today you have ordained yourselves*z* for the service of the LORD, each one at the cost of a son or a brother, and so have brought a blessing on yourselves this day."

30 On the next day Moses said to the people, "You have sinned a great sin. But now I will go up to the LORD; perhaps I can make atonement for your sin." **31**So Moses returned to the LORD and said, "Alas, this people has sinned a great sin; they have made for themselves gods of gold. **32**But now, if you will only forgive their sin—but if not, blot me out of the book that you have written." **33**But the LORD said to Moses, "Whoever has sinned against me I will blot out of my book. **34**But now go, lead the people to the place about which I have spoken to you; see, my angel shall go in front of you. Nevertheless, when the day comes for punishment, I will punish them for their sin."

35 Then the LORD sent a plague on the people, because they made the calf— the one that Aaron made.

The Command to Leave Sinai

33 The LORD said to Moses, "Go, leave this place, you and the people whom you have brought up out of the land of Egypt, and go to the land of which I swore to Abraham, Isaac, and Jacob, saying, 'To your descendants I will give it.' ²I will send an angel before you, and I will drive out the Canaanites, the Amorites, the Hittites, the Perizzites, the Hivites, and the Jebusites. ³Go up to a land flowing with milk and honey; but I will not go up among you, or I would consume you on the way, for you are a stiff-necked people."

4 When the people heard these harsh words, they mourned, and no one put on ornaments. ⁵For the LORD had said to Moses, "Say to the Israelites, 'You are a stiff-necked people; if for a single moment I should go up among you, I would consume you. So now take off your ornaments, and I will decide what to do to you.' " ⁶Therefore the Israelites stripped themselves of their ornaments, from Mount Horeb onward.

The Tent outside the Camp

7 Now Moses used to take the tent and pitch it outside the camp, far off from the camp; he called it the tent of meeting. And everyone who sought the LORD would go out to the tent of meeting, which was outside the camp. ⁸Whenever Moses went out to the tent, all the people would rise and stand, each of them, at the entrance of their tents and watch Moses until he had gone into the tent. ⁹When Moses entered the tent, the pillar of cloud would descend and stand at the entrance of the tent, and the LORD would speak with Moses. ¹⁰When all the people saw the pillar of cloud standing at the entrance of the tent, all the people would rise and bow down, all of them, at the entrance of their tent. ¹¹Thus the LORD used to speak to Moses face to face, as one speaks to a friend.

a Heb *YHWH;* see note at 3.15

Then he would return to the camp; but his young assistant, Joshua son of Nun, would not leave the tent.

Moses' Intercession

12 Moses said to the LORD, "See, you have said to me, 'Bring up this people'; but you have not let me know whom you will send with me. Yet you have said, 'I know you by name, and you have also found favor in my sight.' ¹³Now if I have found favor in your sight, show me your ways, so that I may know you and find favor in your sight. Consider too that this nation is your people." ¹⁴He said, "My presence will go with you, and I will give you rest." ¹⁵And he said to him, "If your presence will not go, do not carry us up from here. ¹⁶For how shall it be known that I have found favor in your sight, I and your people, unless you go with us? In this way, we shall be distinct, I and your people, from every people on the face of the earth."

17 The LORD said to Moses, "I will do the very thing that you have asked; for you have found favor in my sight, and I know you by name." ¹⁸Moses said, "Show me your glory, I pray." ¹⁹And he said, "I will make all my goodness pass before you, and will proclaim before you the name, 'The LORD';*a* and I will be gracious to whom I will be gracious, and will show mercy on whom I will show mercy. ²⁰But," he said, "you cannot see my face; for no one shall see me and live." ²¹And the LORD continued, "See, there is a place by me where you shall stand on the rock; ²²and while my glory passes by I will put you in a cleft of the rock, and I will cover you with my hand until I have passed by; ²³then I will take away my hand, and you shall see my back; but my face shall not be seen."

Moses Makes New Tablets

34 The LORD said to Moses, "Cut two tablets of stone like the former ones, and I will write on the tablets the words that were on the former tablets, which you broke. ²Be ready in the morning, and come up in the morning to Mount Sinai and present yourself there to me, on the top of the mountain. ³No one shall come up with you, and do not let anyone be seen throughout all the mountain; and do not let flocks or herds graze in front of that mountain." 4So Moses cut two tablets of stone like the former ones; and he rose early in the morning and went up on Mount Sinai, as the LORD had commanded him, and took in his hand the two tablets of stone. 5The LORD descended in the cloud and stood with him there, and proclaimed the name, "The LORD."b 6The LORD passed before him, and proclaimed,

"The LORD, the LORD,
a God merciful and gracious,
slow to anger,
and abounding in steadfast love and
faithfulness,
7   keeping steadfast love for the
thousandth generation,c
forgiving iniquity and transgression
and sin,
yet by no means clearing the guilty,
but visiting the iniquity of the
parents
upon the children
and the children's children,
to the third and the fourth
generation."

8And Moses quickly bowed his head toward the earth, and worshiped. 9He said, "If now I have found favor in your sight, O Lord, I pray, let the Lord go with us. Although this is a stiff-necked people, pardon our iniquity and our sin, and take us for your inheritance."

The Covenant Renewed

10 He said: I hereby make a covenant. Before all your people I will perform marvels, such as have not been performed in all the earth or in any nation; and all the people among whom you live shall see the work of the LORD; for it is an awesome thing that I will do with you. 11 Observe what I command you today. See, I will drive out before you the Amorites, the Canaanites, the Hittites, the Perizzites, the Hivites, and the Jebusites. 12Take care not to make a covenant with the inhabitants of the land to which you are going, or it will become a snare among you. 13You shall tear down

their altars, break their pillars, and cut down their sacred polesd 14(for you shall worship no other god, because the LORD, whose name is Jealous, is a jealous God). 15You shall not make a covenant with the inhabitants of the land, for when they prostitute themselves to their gods and sacrifice to their gods, someone among them will invite you, and you will eat of the sacrifice. 16And you will take wives from among their daughters for your sons, and their daughters who prostitute themselves to their gods will make your sons also prostitute themselves to their gods.

17 You shall not make cast idols.

18 You shall keep the festival of unleavened bread. Seven days you shall eat unleavened bread, as I commanded you, at the time appointed in the month of Abib; for in the month of Abib you came out from Egypt.

19 All that first opens the womb is mine, all your malee livestock, the firstborn of cow and sheep. 20The firstborn of a donkey you shall redeem with a lamb, or if you will not redeem it you shall break its neck. All the firstborn of your sons you shall redeem.

No one shall appear before me empty-handed.

21 Six days you shall work, but on the seventh day you shall rest; even in plowing time and in harvest time you shall rest. 22You shall observe the festival of weeks, the first fruits of wheat harvest, and the festival of ingathering at the turn of the year. 23Three times in the year all your males shall appear before the LORD God, the God of Israel. 24For I will cast out nations before you, and enlarge your borders; no one shall covet your land when you go up to appear before the LORD your God three times in the year.

25 You shall not offer the blood of my sacrifice with leaven, and the sacrifice of the festival of the passover shall not be left until the morning.

26 The best of the first fruits of your ground you shall bring to the house of the LORD your God.

You shall not boil a kid in its mother's milk.

b Heb YHWH; see note at 3.15   c Or for thousands   d Heb Asherim   e Gk Theodotion Vg Tg:
Meaning of Heb uncertain

THE GLORY ON MOSES—THE GLORY IN US

George MacDonald

VERSE: Exodus 34.29   PASSAGE: Exodus 34.29–35

hen Moses came out from speaking with God, his face was radiant; its shining was a wonder to the people, and a power upon them. But the radiance began at once to diminish and die away, as was natural, for it was not indigenous in Moses. Therefore Moses put a veil upon his face that they might not see it fade. As to whether this was right or wise, opinion may differ: it is not my business to discuss the question. When he went again into the tabernacle, he took off his veil, talked with God with open face, and again put on the veil when he came out.

Paul says that the veil which obscured the face of Moses lies now upon the hearts of the Jews, so that they cannot understand him, but that when they turn to the Lord (go into the tabernacle with Moses) the veil shall be taken away, and they shall see God. Then will they understand that the glory is indeed faded upon the face of Moses, but by reason of the glory of Jesus that overshines it.

Paul says that the sight of the Lord will take that veil from their hearts (see 2 Corinthians 3.14–16). His light will burn it away. His presence gives liberty. Where he is, there is no more heaviness, no more bondage, no more wilderness or Mount Sinai. The Son makes free with sonship.

Paul's idea is, that when we take into our understanding, our heart, our conscience, our being, the glory of God—namely Jesus Christ as he shows himself to our eyes, our hearts, our consciences—he works upon us, and will keep working, till we are changed to the very likeness we have thus mirrored in us; for with his likeness he comes himself, and dwells in us. He will work until the same likeness is wrought out and perfected in us, the image, namely, of the humanity of God, in which image we were made at first, but which could never be developed in us except by the indwelling of the perfect likeness. By the power of Christ thus received and at home in us, we are changed—the glory in him becoming glory in us, his glory changing us to glory.

ADDITIONAL SCRIPTURE READING:
1 Corinthians 13.12; 2 Corinthians 3.7–18

Go to page 104 for your next devotional reading.

1700   1900

27 The LORD said to Moses: Write these words; in accordance with these words I have made a covenant with you and with Israel. 28He was there with the LORD forty days and forty nights; he neither ate bread nor drank water. And he wrote on the tablets the words of the covenant, the ten commandments.*f*

The Shining Face of Moses

29 Moses came down from Mount Sinai. As he came down from the mountain with the two tablets of the covenant*g* in his hand, Moses did not know that the skin of his face shone because he had been talking with God. 30When Aaron and all the Israelites saw Moses, the skin of his face was shining, and they were afraid to come near him. 31But Moses called to them; and Aaron and all the leaders of the congregation returned to him, and Moses spoke with them. 32Afterward all the Israelites came near, and he gave them in commandment all that the LORD had spoken with him on Mount Sinai. 33When Moses had finished speaking with them, he put a veil on his face; 34but whenever Moses went in before the LORD to speak with him, he would take the veil off, until he came out; and when he came out, and told the Israelites what he had been commanded, 35the Israelites would see the face of Moses, that the skin of his face was shining; and Moses would put the veil on his face again, until he went in to speak with him.

Sabbath Regulations

35 Moses assembled all the congregation of the Israelites and said to them: These are the things that the LORD has commanded you to do:
2 Six days shall work be done, but on the seventh day you shall have a holy sabbath of solemn rest to the LORD; whoever does any work on it shall be put to death. 3You shall kindle no fire in all your dwellings on the sabbath day.

Preparations for Making the Tabernacle

4 Moses said to all the congregation of the Israelites: This is the thing that the LORD has commanded: 5Take from among you an offering to the LORD; let whoever is of a generous heart bring the LORD's offering: gold, silver, and bronze; 6blue, purple, and crimson yarns, and fine linen; goats' hair, 7tanned rams' skins, and fine leather;*h* acacia wood, 8oil for the light, spices for the anointing oil and for the fragrant incense, 9and onyx stones and gems to be set in the ephod and the breastpiece.

10 All who are skillful among you shall come and make all that the LORD has commanded: the tabernacle, 11its tent and its covering, its clasps and its frames, its bars, its pillars, and its bases; 12the ark with its poles, the mercy seat,*i* and the curtain for the screen; 13the table with its poles and all its utensils, and the bread of the Presence; 14the lampstand also for the light, with its utensils and its lamps, and the oil for the light; 15and the altar of incense, with its poles, and the anointing oil and the fragrant incense, and the screen for the entrance, the entrance of the tabernacle; 16the altar of burnt offering, with its grating of bronze, its poles, and all its utensils, the basin with its stand; 17the hangings of the court, its pillars and its bases, and the screen for the gate of the court; 18the pegs of the tabernacle and the pegs of the court, and their cords; 19the finely worked vestments for ministering in the holy place, the holy vestments for the priest Aaron, and the vestments of his sons, for their service as priests.

Offerings for the Tabernacle

20 Then all the congregation of the Israelites withdrew from the presence of Moses. 21And they came, everyone whose heart was stirred, and everyone whose spirit was willing, and brought the LORD's offering to be used for the tent of meeting, and for all its service, and for the sacred vestments. 22So they came, both men and women; all who were of a willing heart brought brooches and earrings and signet rings and pendants, all sorts of gold objects, everyone bringing an offering of gold to the LORD. 23And everyone who possessed blue or purple or crimson yarn or fine linen or goats' hair or tanned rams' skins or fine

f Heb *words*   *g* Or *treaty,* or *testimony;* Heb *eduth*   *h* Meaning of Heb uncertain   *i* Or *the cover*

WEEKEND

THE ANOINTING OIL
Charles H. Spurgeon

VERSE: Exodus 35.8   **PASSAGE:** Exodus 35.4–29

uch use was made of this anointing oil under the law, and that which it represents is of primary importance under the gospel. The Holy Spirit, who anoints us for all holy service, is indispensable to us if we would serve the Lord acceptably. Without his aid our religious services are but a vain oblation, and our inward experience is a dead thing . . . To go before the Lord without anointing is as though some common Levite had thrust himself into the priest's office—his ministrations would have been sins rather than services. May we never venture into hallowed exercises without sacred anointings . . .

Choice spices were compounded with rarest art of the apothecary to form the anointing oil, to show forth to us how rich are all the influences of the Holy Spirit. All good things are found in the divine Comforter. Matchless consolation, infallible instruction, immortal quickening, spiritual energy, and divine sanctification all lie compounded with other excellencies in that sacred eye salve, the heavenly anointing oil of the Holy Spirit. It imparts a delightful fragrance to the character and person of the man on whom it is poured. Nothing like it can be found in all the treasuries of the rich, or the secrets of the wise. It is not to be imitated. It comes alone from God, and it is freely given, through Jesus Christ, to every waiting soul. Let us seek it, for we may have it, may have it this very evening. O Lord, anoint us, your servants.

ADDITIONAL SCRIPTURE READING:
Exodus 25.1–40; 30.23–25

Go to page 116 for your next devotional reading.

1700   1900

leather,ⁱ brought them. ²⁴Everyone who could make an offering of silver or bronze brought it as the LORD's offering; and everyone who possessed acacia wood of any use in the work, brought it. ²⁵All the skillful women spun with their hands, and brought what they had spun in blue and purple and crimson yarns and fine linen; ²⁶all the women whose hearts moved them to use their skill spun the goats' hair. ²⁷And the leaders brought onyx stones and gems to be set in the ephod and the breastpiece, ²⁸and spices and oil for the light, and for the anointing oil, and for the fragrant incense. ²⁹All the Israelite men and women whose hearts made them willing to bring anything for the work that the LORD had commanded by Moses to be done, brought it as a freewill offering to the LORD.

Bezalel and Oholiab

30 Then Moses said to the Israelites: See, the LORD has called by name Bezalel son of Uri son of Hur, of the tribe of Judah; ³¹he has filled him with divine spirit,ᵏ with skill, intelligence, and knowledge in every kind of craft, ³²to devise artistic designs, to work in gold, silver, and bronze, ³³in cutting stones for setting, and in carving wood, in every kind of craft. ³⁴And he has inspired him to teach, both him and Oholiab son of Ahisamach, of the tribe of Dan. ³⁵He has filled them with skill to do every kind of work done by an artisan or by a designer or by an embroiderer in blue, purple, and crimson yarns, and in fine linen, or by a weaver—by any sort of artisan or skilled designer.

36 Bezalel and Oholiab and every skillful one to whom the LORD has given skill and understanding to know how to do any work in the construction of the sanctuary shall work in accordance with all that the LORD has commanded.

2 Moses then called Bezalel and Oholiab and every skillful one to whom the LORD had given skill, everyone whose heart was stirred to come to do the work; ³and they received from Moses all the freewill offerings that the Israelites had brought for doing the work on the

sanctuary. They still kept bringing him freewill offerings every morning, ⁴so that all the artisans who were doing every sort of task on the sanctuary came, each from the task being performed, ⁵and said to Moses, "The people are bringing much more than enough for doing the work that the LORD has commanded us to do." ⁶So Moses gave command, and word was proclaimed throughout the camp: "No man or woman is to make anything else as an offering for the sanctuary." So the people were restrained from bringing; ⁷for what they had already brought was more than enough to do all the work.

Construction of the Tabernacle

8 All those with skill among the workers made the tabernacle with ten curtains; they were made of fine twisted linen, and blue, purple, and crimson yarns, with cherubim skillfully worked into them. ⁹The length of each curtain was twenty-eight cubits, and the width of each curtain four cubits; all the curtains were of the same size.

10 He joined five curtains to one another, and the other five curtains he joined to one another. ¹¹He made loops of blue on the edge of the outermost curtain of the first set; likewise he made them on the edge of the outermost curtain of the second set; ¹²he made fifty loops on the one curtain, and he made fifty loops on the edge of the curtain that was in the second set; the loops were opposite one another. ¹³And he made fifty clasps of gold, and joined the curtains one to the other with clasps; so the tabernacle was one whole.

14 He also made curtains of goats' hair for a tent over the tabernacle; he made eleven curtains. ¹⁵The length of each curtain was thirty cubits, and the width of each curtain four cubits; the eleven curtains were of the same size. ¹⁶He joined five curtains by themselves, and six curtains by themselves. ¹⁷He made fifty loops on the edge of the outermost curtain of the one set, and fifty loops on the edge of the other connecting curtain. ¹⁸He made fifty clasps of bronze to join the tent together so that it might be one whole. ¹⁹And he made for

---

ⁱ Meaning of Heb uncertain   ᵏ Or *the spirit of God*

the tent a covering of tanned rams' skins and an outer covering of fine leather.[1]

20 Then he made the upright frames for the tabernacle of acacia wood. [21]Ten cubits was the length of a frame, and a cubit and a half the width of each frame. [22]Each frame had two pegs for fitting together; he did this for all the frames of the tabernacle. [23]The frames for the tabernacle he made in this way: twenty frames for the south side; [24]and he made forty bases of silver under the twenty frames, two bases under the first frame for its two pegs, and two bases under the next frame for its two pegs. [25]For the second side of the tabernacle, on the north side, he made twenty frames [26]and their forty bases of silver, two bases under the first frame and two bases under the next frame. [27]For the rear of the tabernacle westward he made six frames. [28]He made two frames for corners of the tabernacle in the rear. [29]They were separate beneath, but joined at the top, at the first ring; he made two of them in this way, for the two corners. [30]There were eight frames with their bases of silver: sixteen bases, under every frame two bases.

31 He made bars of acacia wood, five for the frames of the one side of the tabernacle, [32]and five bars for the frames of the other side of the tabernacle, and five bars for the frames of the tabernacle at the rear westward. [33]He made the middle bar to pass through from end to end halfway up the frames. [34]And he overlaid the frames with gold, and made rings of gold for them to hold the bars, and overlaid the bars with gold.

35 He made the curtain of blue, purple, and crimson yarns, and fine twisted linen, with cherubim skillfully worked into it. [36]For it he made four pillars of acacia, and overlaid them with gold; their hooks were of gold, and he cast for them four bases of silver. [37]He also made a screen for the entrance to the tent, of blue, purple, and crimson yarns, and fine twisted linen, embroidered with needlework; [38]and its five pillars with their hooks. He overlaid their capitals and their bases with gold, but their five bases were of bronze.

Making the Ark of the Covenant

37 Bezalel made the ark of acacia wood; it was two and a half cubits long, a cubit and a half wide, and a cubit and a half high. [2]He overlaid it with pure gold inside and outside, and made a molding of gold around it. [3]He cast for it four rings of gold for its four feet, two rings on its one side and two rings on its other side. [4]He made poles of acacia wood, and overlaid them with gold, [5]and put the poles into the rings on the sides of the ark, to carry the ark. [6]He made a mercy seat[m] of pure gold; two cubits and a half was its length, and a cubit and a half its width. [7]He made two cherubim of hammered gold; at the two ends of the mercy seat[n] he made them, [8]one cherub at the one end, and one cherub at the other end; of one piece with the mercy seat[n] he made the cherubim at its two ends. [9]The cherubim spread out their wings above, overshadowing the mercy seat[n] with their wings. They faced one another; the faces of the cherubim were turned toward the mercy seat.[n]

Making the Table for the Bread of the Presence

10 He also made the table of acacia wood, two cubits long, one cubit wide, and a cubit and a half high. [11]He overlaid it with pure gold, and made a molding of gold around it. [12]He made around it a rim a handbreadth wide, and made a molding of gold around the rim. [13]He cast for it four rings of gold, and fastened the rings to the four corners at its four legs. [14]The rings that held the poles used for carrying the table were close to the rim. [15]He made the poles of acacia wood to carry the table, and overlaid them with gold. [16]And he made the vessels of pure gold that were to be on the table, its plates and dishes for incense, and its bowls and flagons with which to pour drink offerings.

Making the Lampstand

17 He also made the lampstand of pure gold. The base and the shaft of the lampstand were made of hammered work; its cups, its calyxes, and its petals

---

l Meaning of Heb uncertain   *m* Or *a cover*   *n* Or *the cover* were of one piece with it. ¹⁸There were six branches going out of its sides, three branches of the lampstand out of one side of it and three branches of the lampstand out of the other side of it; ¹⁹three cups shaped like almond blossoms, each with calyx and petals, on one branch, and three cups shaped like almond blossoms, each with calyx and petals, on the other branch—so for the six branches going out of the lampstand. ²⁰On the lampstand itself there were four cups shaped like almond blossoms, each with its calyxes and petals. ²¹There was a calyx of one piece with it under the first pair of branches, a calyx of one piece with it under the next pair of branches, and a calyx of one piece with it under the last pair of branches. ²²Their calyxes and their branches were of one piece with it, the whole of it one hammered piece of pure gold. ²³He made its seven lamps and its snuffers and its trays of pure gold. ²⁴He made it and all its utensils of a talent of pure gold.

Making the Altar of Incense

25 He made the altar of incense of acacia wood, one cubit long, and one cubit wide; it was square, and was two cubits high; its horns were of one piece with it. ²⁶He overlaid it with pure gold, its top, and its sides all around, and its horns; and he made for it a molding of gold all around, ²⁷and made two golden rings for it under its molding, on two opposite sides of it, to hold the poles with which to carry it. ²⁸And he made the poles of acacia wood, and overlaid them with gold.

Making the Anointing Oil and the Incense

29 He made the holy anointing oil also, and the pure fragrant incense, blended as by the perfumer.

Making the Altar of Burnt Offering

38 He made the altar of burnt offering also of acacia wood; it was five cubits long, and five cubits wide; it was square, and three cubits high. ²He made horns for it on its four corners; its horns were of one piece with it, and he overlaid it with bronze. ³He made all the utensils of the altar, the pots, the shovels, the basins, the forks, and the firepans: all its utensils he made of bronze. ⁴He made for the altar a grating, a network of bronze, under its ledge, extending halfway down. ⁵He cast four rings on the four corners of the bronze grating to hold the poles; ⁶he made the poles of acacia wood, and overlaid them with bronze. ⁷And he put the poles through the rings on the sides of the altar, to carry it with them; he made it hollow, with boards.

8 He made the basin of bronze with its stand of bronze, from the mirrors of the women who served at the entrance to the tent of meeting.

Making the Court of the Tabernacle

9 He made the court; for the south side the hangings of the court were of fine twisted linen, one hundred cubits long; ¹⁰its twenty pillars and their twenty bases were of bronze, but the hooks of the pillars and their bands were of silver. ¹¹For the north side there were hangings one hundred cubits long; its twenty pillars and their twenty bases were of bronze, but the hooks of the pillars and their bands were of silver. ¹²For the west side there were hangings fifty cubits long, with ten pillars and ten bases; the hooks of the pillars and their bands were of silver. ¹³And for the front to the east, fifty cubits. ¹⁴The hangings for one side of the gate were fifteen cubits, with three pillars and three bases. ¹⁵And so for the other side; on each side of the gate of the court were hangings of fifteen cubits, with three pillars and three bases. ¹⁶All the hangings around the court were of fine twisted linen. ¹⁷The bases for the pillars were of bronze, but the hooks of the pillars and their bands were of silver; the overlaying of their capitals was also of silver, and all the pillars of the court were banded with silver. ¹⁸The screen for the entrance to the court was embroidered with needlework in blue, purple, and crimson yarns and fine twisted linen. It was twenty cubits long and, along the width of it, five cubits high, corresponding to the hangings of the court. ¹⁹There were four pillars; their four bases were of bronze, their hooks of silver, and the

overlaying of their capitals and their bands of silver. ²⁰All the pegs for the tabernacle and for the court all around were of bronze.

Materials of the Tabernacle

21 These are the records of the tabernacle, the tabernacle of the covenant,^o which were drawn up at the commandment of Moses, the work of the Levites being under the direction of Ithamar son of the priest Aaron. ²²Bezalel son of Uri son of Hur, of the tribe of Judah, made all that the LORD commanded Moses; ²³and with him was Oholiab son of Ahisamach, of the tribe of Dan, engraver, designer, and embroiderer in blue, purple, and crimson yarns, and in fine linen.

24 All the gold that was used for the work, in all the construction of the sanctuary, the gold from the offering, was twenty-nine talents and seven hundred thirty shekels, measured by the sanctuary shekel. ²⁵The silver from those of the congregation who were counted was one hundred talents and one thousand seven hundred seventy-five shekels, measured by the sanctuary shekel; ²⁶a beka a head (that is, half a shekel, measured by the sanctuary shekel), for everyone who was counted in the census, from twenty years old and upward, for six hundred three thousand, five hundred fifty men. ²⁷The hundred talents of silver were for casting the bases of the sanctuary, and the bases of the curtain; one hundred bases for the hundred talents, a talent for a base. ²⁸Of the thousand seven hundred seventy-five shekels he made hooks for the pillars, and overlaid their capitals and made bands for them. ²⁹The bronze that was contributed was seventy talents, and two thousand four hundred shekels; ³⁰with it he made the bases for the entrance of the tent of meeting, the bronze altar and the bronze grating for it and all the utensils of the altar, ³¹the bases all around the court, and the bases of the gate of the court, all the pegs of the tabernacle, and all the pegs around the court.

Making the Vestments for the Priesthood

39 Of the blue, purple, and crimson yarns they made finely worked vestments, for ministering in the holy place; they made the sacred vestments for Aaron; as the LORD had commanded Moses.

2 He made the ephod of gold, of blue, purple, and crimson yarns, and of fine twisted linen. ³Gold leaf was hammered out and cut into threads to work into the blue, purple, and crimson yarns and into the fine twisted linen, in skilled design. ⁴They made for the ephod shoulder-pieces, joined to it at its two edges. ⁵The decorated band on it was of the same materials and workmanship, of gold, of blue, purple, and crimson yarns, and of fine twisted linen; as the LORD had commanded Moses.

6 The onyx stones were prepared, enclosed in settings of gold filigree and engraved like the engravings of a signet, according to the names of the sons of Israel. ⁷He set them on the shoulder-pieces of the ephod, to be stones of remembrance for the sons of Israel; as the LORD had commanded Moses.

8 He made the breastpiece, in skilled work, like the work of the ephod, of gold, of blue, purple, and crimson yarns, and of fine twisted linen. ⁹It was square; the breastpiece was made double, a span in length and a span in width when doubled. ¹⁰They set in it four rows of stones. A row of carnelian,^p chrysolite, and emerald was the first row; ¹¹and the second row, a turquoise, a sapphire,^q and a moonstone; ¹²and the third row, a jacinth, an agate, and an amethyst; ¹³and the fourth row, a beryl, an onyx, and a jasper; they were enclosed in settings of gold filigree. ¹⁴There were twelve stones with names corresponding to the names of the sons of Israel; they were like signets, each engraved with its name, for the twelve tribes. ¹⁵They made on the breastpiece chains of pure gold, twisted like cords; ¹⁶and they made two settings of gold filigree and two gold rings, and put the two rings on the two edges of the breastpiece; ¹⁷and they put the two cords of gold in the two rings at the

o Or *treaty,* or *testimony*; Heb *eduth*   p The identification of several of these stones is uncertain
q Or *lapis lazuli*

edges of the breastpiece. 18Two ends of the two cords they had attached to the two settings of filigree; in this way they attached it in front to the shoulderpieces of the ephod. 19Then they made two rings of gold, and put them at the two ends of the breastpiece, on its inside edge next to the ephod. 20They made two rings of gold, and attached them in front to the lower part of the two shoulder-pieces of the ephod, at its joining above the decorated band of the ephod. 21They bound the breastpiece by its rings to the rings of the ephod with a blue cord, so that it should lie on the decorated band of the ephod, and that the breastpiece should not come loose from the ephod; as the LORD had commanded Moses.

22 He also made the robe of the ephod woven all of blue yarn; 23and the opening of the robe in the middle of it was like the opening in a coat of mail,r with a binding around the opening, so that it might not be torn. 24On the lower hem of the robe they made pomegranates of blue, purple, and crimson yarns, and of fine twisted linen. 25They also made bells of pure gold, and put the bells between the pomegranates on the lower hem of the robe all around, between the pomegranates; 26a bell and a pomegranate, a bell and a pomegranate all around on the lower hem of the robe for ministering; as the LORD had commanded Moses.

27 They also made the tunics, woven of fine linen, for Aaron and his sons, 28and the turban of fine linen, and the headdresses of fine linen, and the linen undergarments of fine twisted linen, 29and the sash of fine twisted linen, and of blue, purple, and crimson yarns, embroidered with needlework; as the LORD had commanded Moses.

30 They made the rosette of the holy diadem of pure gold, and wrote on it an inscription, like the engraving of a signet, "Holy to the LORD." 31They tied to it a blue cord, to fasten it on the turban above; as the LORD had commanded Moses.

The Work Completed

32 In this way all the work of the tabernacle of the tent of meeting was finished; the Israelites had done everything just as the LORD had commanded Moses. 33Then they brought the tabernacle to Moses, the tent and all its utensils, its hooks, its frames, its bars, its pillars, and its bases; 34the covering of tanned rams' skins and the covering of fine leather,r and the curtain for the screen; 35the ark of the covenants with its poles and the mercy seat;t 36the table with all its utensils, and the bread of the Presence; 37the pure lampstand with its lamps set on it and all its utensils, and the oil for the light; 38the golden altar, the anointing oil and the fragrant incense, and the screen for the entrance of the tent; 39the bronze altar, and its grating of bronze, its poles, and all its utensils; the basin with its stand; 40the hangings of the court, its pillars, and its bases, and the screen for the gate of the court, its cords, and its pegs; and all the utensils for the service of the tabernacle, for the tent of meeting; 41the finely worked vestments for ministering in the holy place, the sacred vestments for the priest Aaron, and the vestments of his sons to serve as priests. 42The Israelites had done all of the work just as the LORD had commanded Moses. 43When Moses saw that they had done all the work just as the LORD had commanded, he blessed them.

The Tabernacle Erected and Its Equipment Installed

40 The LORD spoke to Moses: 2On the first day of the first month you shall set up the tabernacle of the tent of meeting. 3You shall put in it the ark of the covenant,s and you shall screen the ark with the curtain. 4You shall bring in the table, and arrange its setting; and you shall bring in the lampstand, and set up its lamps. 5You shall put the golden altar for incense before the ark of the covenant,s and set up the screen for the entrance of the tabernacle. 6You shall set the altar of burnt offering before the entrance of the tabernacle of the tent of meeting, 7and place the basin between the tent of meeting and the altar, and put water in it. 8You shall set up the court all around, and hang up the screen for the gate of the court. 9Then

r Meaning of Heb uncertain   s Or treaty, or testimony; Heb eduth   t Or the cover you shall take the anointing oil, and anoint the tabernacle and all that is in it, and consecrate it and all its furniture, so that it shall become holy. ¹⁰You shall also anoint the altar of burnt offering and all its utensils, and consecrate the altar, so that the altar shall be most holy. ¹¹You shall also anoint the basin with its stand, and consecrate it. ¹²Then you shall bring Aaron and his sons to the entrance of the tent of meeting, and shall wash them with water, ¹³and put on Aaron the sacred vestments, and you shall anoint him and consecrate him, so that he may serve me as priest. ¹⁴You shall bring his sons also and put tunics on them, ¹⁵and anoint them, as you anointed their father, that they may serve me as priests: and their anointing shall admit them to a perpetual priesthood throughout all generations to come.

16 Moses did everything just as the LORD had commanded him. ¹⁷In the first month in the second year, on the first day of the month, the tabernacle was set up. ¹⁸Moses set up the tabernacle; he laid its bases, and set up its frames, and put in its poles, and raised up its pillars; ¹⁹and he spread the tent over the tabernacle, and put the covering of the tent over it; as the LORD had commanded Moses. ²⁰He took the covenant*u* and put it into the ark, and put the poles on the ark, and set the mercy seat*v* above the ark; ²¹and he brought the ark into the tabernacle, and set up the curtain for screening, and screened the ark of the covenant;*u* as the LORD had commanded Moses. ²²He put the table in the tent of meeting, on the north side of the tabernacle, outside the curtain, ²³and set the bread in order on it before the LORD; as the LORD had commanded Moses. ²⁴He put the lampstand in the tent of meet-

ing, opposite the table on the south side of the tabernacle, ²⁵and set up the lamps before the LORD; as the LORD had commanded Moses. ²⁶He put the golden altar in the tent of meeting before the curtain, ²⁷and offered fragrant incense on it; as the LORD had commanded Moses. ²⁸He also put in place the screen for the entrance of the tabernacle. ²⁹He set the altar of burnt offering at the entrance of the tabernacle of the tent of meeting, and offered on it the burnt offering and the grain offering as the LORD had commanded Moses. ³⁰He set the basin between the tent of meeting and the altar, and put water in it for washing, ³¹with which Moses and Aaron and his sons washed their hands and their feet. ³²When they went into the tent of meeting, and when they approached the altar, they washed; as the LORD had commanded Moses. ³³He set up the court around the tabernacle and the altar, and put up the screen at the gate of the court. So Moses finished the work.

The Cloud and the Glory

34 Then the cloud covered the tent of meeting, and the glory of the LORD filled the tabernacle. ³⁵Moses was not able to enter the tent of meeting because the cloud settled upon it, and the glory of the LORD filled the tabernacle. ³⁶Whenever the cloud was taken up from the tabernacle, the Israelites would set out on each stage of their journey; ³⁷but if the cloud was not taken up, then they did not set out until the day that it was taken up. ³⁸For the cloud of the LORD was on the tabernacle by day, and fire was in the cloud*w* by night, before the eyes of all the house of Israel at each stage of their journey.

---

u Or *treaty*, or *testimony*; Heb *eduth*   *v* Or *the cover*   *w* Heb *it*

LEVITICUS

OSES WRITES LEVITICUS WHILE THE ISRAELITES ARE IN THE DESERT, BEFORE THEY ENTER THE PROMISED LAND. THE BOOK'S KEY THOUGHT IS STATED IN 11.45—"YOU SHALL BE HOLY, FOR I AM HOLY." THE LAWS IN THE BOOK WERE GIVEN TO HELP THE ISRAELITES WORSHIP AND LIVE AS GOD'S HOLY PEOPLE. EVEN THOUGH THE NEW COVENANT HAS FREED US FROM THE INTRICACIES OF THE LEVITICAL LAW, LEVITICUS REMINDS US THAT EVERY PART OF OUR LIVES IS IMPORTANT TO GOD, AND THAT WE ARE TO LOVE AND SERVE HIM IN HOLINESS.

The Burnt Offering

1 The LORD summoned Moses and spoke to him from the tent of meeting, saying: 2Speak to the people of Israel and say to them: When any of you bring an offering of livestock to the LORD, you shall bring your offering from the herd or from the flock.

3 If the offering is a burnt offering from the herd, you shall offer a male without blemish; you shall bring it to the entrance of the tent of meeting, for acceptance in your behalf before the LORD. 4You shall lay your hand on the head of the burnt offering, and it shall be acceptable in your behalf as atonement for you. 5The bull shall be slaughtered before the LORD; and Aaron's sons the priests shall offer the blood, dashing the blood against all sides of the altar that is at the entrance of the tent of meeting. 6The burnt offering shall be flayed and cut up into its parts. 7The sons of the priest Aaron shall put fire on the altar and arrange wood on the fire. 8Aaron's sons the priests shall arrange the parts, with the head and the suet, on the wood that is on the fire on the altar; 9but its entrails and its legs shall be washed with water. Then the priest shall turn the whole into smoke on the altar as a burnt offering, an offering by fire of pleasing odor to the LORD.

10 If your gift for a burnt offering is from the flock, from the sheep or goats, your offering shall be a male without blemish. 11It shall be slaughtered on the north side of the altar before the LORD, and Aaron's sons the priests shall dash its blood against all sides of the altar. 12It

shall be cut up into its parts, with its head and its suet, and the priest shall arrange them on the wood that is on the fire on the altar; 13but the entrails and the legs shall be washed with water. Then the priest shall offer the whole and turn it into smoke on the altar; it is a burnt offering, an offering by fire of pleasing odor to the LORD.

14 If your offering to the LORD is a burnt offering of birds, you shall choose your offering from turtledoves or pigeons. 15The priest shall bring it to the altar and wring off its head, and turn it into smoke on the altar; and its blood shall be drained out against the side of the altar. 16He shall remove its crop with its contents*a* and throw it at the east side of the altar, in the place for ashes. 17He shall tear it open by its wings without severing it. Then the priest shall turn it into smoke on the altar, on the wood that is on the fire; it is a burnt offering, an offering by fire of pleasing odor to the LORD.

Grain Offerings

2 When anyone presents a grain offering to the LORD, the offering shall be of choice flour; the worshiper shall pour oil on it, and put frankincense on it, 2and bring it to Aaron's sons the priests. After taking from it a handful of the choice flour and oil, with all its frankincense, the priest shall turn this token portion into smoke on the altar, an offering by fire of pleasing odor to the LORD. 3And what is left of the grain offering shall be for Aaron and his sons, a most holy part of the offerings by fire to the LORD.

4 When you present a grain offering baked in the oven, it shall be of choice flour: unleavened cakes mixed with oil, or unleavened wafers spread with oil. 5If your offering is grain prepared on a griddle, it shall be of choice flour mixed with oil, unleavened; 6break it in pieces, and pour oil on it; it is a grain offering. 7If your offering is grain prepared in a pan, it shall be made of choice flour in oil. 8You shall bring to the LORD the grain offering that is prepared in any of these ways; and when it is presented to the priest, he shall take it to the altar.

9The priest shall remove from the grain offering its token portion and turn this into smoke on the altar, an offering by fire of pleasing odor to the LORD. 10And what is left of the grain offering shall be for Aaron and his sons; it is a most holy part of the offerings by fire to the LORD.

11 No grain offering that you bring to the LORD shall be made with leaven, for you must not turn any leaven or honey into smoke as an offering by fire to the LORD. 12You may bring them to the LORD as an offering of choice products, but they shall not be offered on the altar for a pleasing odor. 13You shall not omit from your grain offerings the salt of the covenant with your God; with all your offerings you shall offer salt.

14 If you bring a grain offering of first fruits to the LORD, you shall bring as the grain offering of your first fruits coarse new grain from fresh ears, parched with fire. 15You shall add oil to it and lay frankincense on it; it is a grain offering. 16And the priest shall turn a token portion of it into smoke—some of the coarse grain and oil with all its frankincense; it is an offering by fire to the LORD.

Offerings of Well-Being

3 If the offering is a sacrifice of well-being, if you offer an animal of the herd, whether male or female, you shall offer one without blemish before the LORD. 2You shall lay your hand on the head of the offering and slaughter it at the entrance of the tent of meeting; and Aaron's sons the priests shall dash the blood against all sides of the altar. 3You shall offer from the sacrifice of well-being, as an offering by fire to the LORD, the fat that covers the entrails and all the fat that is around the entrails; 4the two kidneys with the fat that is on them at the loins, and the appendage of the liver, which he shall remove with the kidneys. 5Then Aaron's sons shall turn these into smoke on the altar, with the burnt offering that is on the wood on the fire, as an offering by fire of pleasing odor to the LORD.

6 If your offering for a sacrifice of well-being to the LORD is from the flock, male or female, you shall offer one without

a Meaning of Heb uncertain

blemish. [7]If you present a sheep as your offering, you shall bring it before the LORD [8]and lay your hand on the head of the offering. It shall be slaughtered before the tent of meeting, and Aaron's sons shall dash its blood against all sides of the altar. [9]You shall present its fat from the sacrifice of well-being, as an offering by fire to the LORD: the whole broad tail, which shall be removed close to the backbone, the fat that covers the entrails, and all the fat that is around the entrails; [10]the two kidneys with the fat that is on them at the loins, and the appendage of the liver, which you shall remove with the kidneys. [11]Then the priest shall turn these into smoke on the altar as a food offering by fire to the LORD.

12 If your offering is a goat, you shall bring it before the LORD [13]and lay your hand on its head; it shall be slaughtered before the tent of meeting; and the sons of Aaron shall dash its blood against all sides of the altar. [14]You shall present as your offering from it, as an offering by fire to the LORD, the fat that covers the entrails, and all the fat that is around the entrails; [15]the two kidneys with the fat that is on them at the loins, and the appendage of the liver, which you shall remove with the kidneys. [16]Then the priest shall turn these into smoke on the altar as a food offering by fire for a pleasing odor.

All fat is the LORD's. [17]It shall be a perpetual statute throughout your generations, in all your settlements: you must not eat any fat or any blood.

Sin Offerings

4 The LORD spoke to Moses, saying, [2]Speak to the people of Israel, saying: When anyone sins unintentionally in any of the LORD's commandments about things not to be done, and does any one of them:

3 If it is the anointed priest who sins, thus bringing guilt on the people, he shall offer for the sin that he has committed a bull of the herd without blemish as a sin offering to the LORD. [4]He shall bring the bull to the entrance of the tent of meeting before the LORD and lay his hand on the head of the bull; the bull shall be slaughtered before the LORD. [5]The anointed priest shall take

some of the blood of the bull and bring it into the tent of meeting. [6]The priest shall dip his finger in the blood and sprinkle some of the blood seven times before the LORD in front of the curtain of the sanctuary. [7]The priest shall put some of the blood on the horns of the altar of fragrant incense that is in the tent of meeting before the LORD; and the rest of the blood of the bull he shall pour out at the base of the altar of burnt offering, which is at the entrance of the tent of meeting. [8]He shall remove all the fat from the bull of sin offering: the fat that covers the entrails and all the fat that is around the entrails; [9]the two kidneys with the fat that is on them at the loins; and the appendage of the liver, which he shall remove with the kidneys, [10]just as these are removed from the ox of the sacrifice of well-being. The priest shall turn them into smoke upon the altar of burnt offering. [11]But the skin of the bull and all its flesh, as well as its head, its legs, its entrails, and its dung— [12]all the rest of the bull—he shall carry out to a clean place outside the camp, to the ash heap, and shall burn it on a wood fire; at the ash heap it shall be burned.

13 If the whole congregation of Israel errs unintentionally and the matter escapes the notice of the assembly, and they do any one of the things that by the LORD's commandments ought not to be done and incur guilt; [14]when the sin that they have committed becomes known, the assembly shall offer a bull of the herd for a sin offering and bring it before the tent of meeting. [15]The elders of the congregation shall lay their hands on the head of the bull before the LORD, and the bull shall be slaughtered before the LORD. [16]The anointed priest shall bring some of the blood of the bull into the tent of meeting, [17]and the priest shall dip his finger in the blood and sprinkle it seven times before the LORD, in front of the curtain. [18]He shall put some of the blood on the horns of the altar that is before the LORD in the tent of meeting; and the rest of the blood he shall pour out at the base of the altar of burnt offering that is at the entrance of the tent of meeting. [19]He shall remove all its fat and turn it into smoke on the altar. [20]He shall do with the bull just as is done

with the bull of sin offering; he shall do the same with this. The priest shall make atonement for them, and they shall be forgiven. ²¹He shall carry the bull outside the camp, and burn it as he burned the first bull; it is the sin offering for the assembly.

22 When a ruler sins, doing unintentionally any one of all the things that by commandments of the Lord his God ought not to be done and incurs guilt, ²³once the sin that he has committed is made known to him, he shall bring as his offering a male goat without blemish. ²⁴He shall lay his hand on the head of the goat; it shall be slaughtered at the spot where the burnt offering is slaughtered before the Lord; it is a sin offering. ²⁵The priest shall take some of the blood of the sin offering with his finger and put it on the horns of the altar of burnt offering, and pour out the rest of its blood at the base of the altar of burnt offering. ²⁶All its fat he shall turn into smoke on the altar, like the fat of the sacrifice of well-being. Thus the priest shall make atonement on his behalf for his sin, and he shall be forgiven.

27 If anyone of the ordinary people among you sins unintentionally in doing any one of the things that by the Lord's commandments ought not to be done and incurs guilt, ²⁸when the sin that you have committed is made known to you, you shall bring a female goat without blemish as your offering, for the sin that you have committed. ²⁹You shall lay your hand on the head of the sin offering; and the sin offering shall be slaughtered at the place of the burnt offering. ³⁰The priest shall take some of its blood with his finger and put it on the horns of the altar of burnt offering, and he shall pour out the rest of its blood at the base of the altar. ³¹He shall remove all its fat, as the fat is removed from the offering of well-being, and the priest shall turn it into smoke on the altar for a pleasing odor to the Lord. Thus the priest shall make atonement on your behalf, and you shall be forgiven.

32 If the offering you bring as a sin offering is a sheep, you shall bring a female without blemish. ³³You shall lay your hand on the head of the sin offering; and it shall be slaughtered as a sin offer-

ing at the spot where the burnt offering is slaughtered. ³⁴The priest shall take some of the blood of the sin offering with his finger and put it on the horns of the altar of burnt offering, and pour out the rest of its blood at the base of the altar. ³⁵You shall remove all its fat, as the fat of the sheep is removed from the sacrifice of well-being, and the priest shall turn it into smoke on the altar, with the offerings by fire to the Lord. Thus the priest shall make atonement on your behalf for the sin that you have committed, and you shall be forgiven.

5 When any of you sin in that you have heard a public adjuration to testify and—though able to testify as one who has seen or learned of the matter—do not speak up, you are subject to punishment. ²Or when any of you touch any unclean thing—whether the carcass of an unclean beast or the carcass of unclean livestock or the carcass of an unclean swarming thing—and are unaware of it, you have become unclean, and are guilty. ³Or when you touch human uncleanness—any uncleanness by which one can become unclean—and are unaware of it, when you come to know it, you shall be guilty. ⁴Or when any of you utter aloud a rash oath for a bad or a good purpose, whatever people utter in an oath, and are unaware of it, when you come to know it, you shall in any of these be guilty. ⁵When you realize your guilt in any of these, you shall confess the sin that you have committed. ⁶And you shall bring to the Lord, as your penalty for the sin that you have committed, a female from the flock, a sheep or a goat, as a sin offering; and the priest shall make atonement on your behalf for your sin.

7 But if you cannot afford a sheep, you shall bring to the Lord, as your penalty for the sin that you have committed, two turtledoves or two pigeons, one for a sin offering and the other for a burnt offering. ⁸You shall bring them to the priest, who shall offer first the one for the sin offering, wringing its head at the nape without severing it. ⁹He shall sprinkle some of the blood of the sin offering on the side of the altar, while the rest of the blood shall be drained out at the base of the altar; it is a sin offering. ¹⁰And the

second he shall offer for a burnt offering according to the regulation. Thus the priest shall make atonement on your behalf for the sin that you have committed, and you shall be forgiven. 11 But if you cannot afford two turtledoves or two pigeons, you shall bring as your offering for the sin that you have committed one-tenth of an ephah of choice flour for a sin offering; you shall not put oil on it or lay frankincense on it, for it is a sin offering. 12 You shall bring it to the priest, and the priest shall scoop up a handful of it as its memorial portion, and turn this into smoke on the altar, with the offerings by fire to the LORD; it is a sin offering. 13 Thus the priest shall make atonement on your behalf for whichever of these sins you have committed, and you shall be forgiven. Like the grain offering, the rest shall be for the priest.

Offerings with Restitution

14 The LORD spoke to Moses, saying: 15 When any of you commit a trespass and sin unintentionally in any of the holy things of the LORD, you shall bring, as your guilt offering to the LORD, a ram without blemish from the flock, convertible into silver by the sanctuary shekel; it is a guilt offering. 16 And you shall make restitution for the holy thing in which you were remiss, and shall add one-fifth to it and give it to the priest. The priest shall make atonement on your behalf with the ram of the guilt offering, and you shall be forgiven. 17 If any of you sin without knowing it, doing any of the things that by the LORD's commandments ought not to be done, you have incurred guilt, and are subject to punishment. 18 You shall bring to the priest a ram without blemish from the flock, or the equivalent, as a guilt offering; and the priest shall make atonement on your behalf for the error that you committed unintentionally, and you shall be forgiven. 19 It is a guilt offering; you have incurred guilt before the LORD.

6 b The LORD spoke to Moses, saying: 2 When any of you sin and commit a trespass against the LORD by deceiving a neighbor in a matter of a deposit or a pledge, or by robbery, or if you have defrauded a neighbor, 3 or have found something lost and lied about it— if you swear falsely regarding any of the various things that one may do and sin thereby— 4 when you have sinned and realize your guilt, and would restore what you took by robbery or by fraud or the deposit that was committed to you, or the lost thing that you found, 5 or anything else about which you have sworn falsely, you shall repay the principal amount and shall add one-fifth to it. You shall pay it to its owner when you realize your guilt. 6 And you shall bring to the priest, as your guilt offering to the LORD, a ram without blemish from the flock, or its equivalent, for a guilt offering. 7 The priest shall make atonement on your behalf before the LORD, and you shall be forgiven for any of the things that one may do and incur guilt thereby.

Instructions concerning Sacrifices

8 c The LORD spoke to Moses, saying: 9 Command Aaron and his sons, saying: This is the ritual of the burnt offering. The burnt offering itself shall remain on the hearth upon the altar all night until the morning, while the fire on the altar shall be kept burning. 10 The priest shall put on his linen vestments after putting on his linen undergarments next to his body; and he shall take up the ashes to which the fire has reduced the burnt offering on the altar, and place them beside the altar. 11 Then he shall take off his vestments and put on other garments, and carry the ashes out to a clean place outside the camp. 12 The fire on the altar shall be kept burning; it shall not go out. Every morning the priest shall add wood to it, lay out the burnt offering on it, and turn into smoke the fat pieces of the offerings of well-being. 13 A perpetual fire shall be kept burning on the altar; it shall not go out.

14 This is the ritual of the grain offering: The sons of Aaron shall offer it before the LORD, in front of the altar. 15 They shall take from it a handful of the choice flour and oil of the grain offering, with all the frankincense that is on the offering, and they shall turn its memorial portion into smoke on the

b Ch 5.20 in Heb   c Ch 6.1 in Heb

RESTITUTION AND SALVATION
William Booth

VERSE: Leviticus 6.4–5   PASSAGE: Leviticus 5.14—6.7

 he entrance to the heavenly kingdom was closed against me by an evil act of the past which required restitution. In a boyish trading affair I had managed to make a profit out of my companions, whilst giving them to suppose that what I did was all in the way of a generous fellowship. As a testimonial of their gratitude they had given me a silver pencil case. Merely to return their gift would have been comparatively easy, but to confess the deception I had practiced upon them was a humiliation to which for some days I could not bring myself.

I remember, as if it were but yesterday, the spot in the corner of a room under the chapel, the hour, the resolution to end the matter, the rising up and rushing forth, the finding of the young fellow I had chiefly wronged, the acknowledgment of my sin, the return of the pencil case—the instant rolling away from my heart of the guilty burden, the peace that came in its place, and the going forth to serve my God and my generation from that hour.

It was in the open street that this great change passed over me, and if I could only have possessed the flagstone on which I stood at that happy moment, the sight of it occasionally might have been as useful to me as the stones carried up long ago from the bed of the Jordan were to the Israelites who had passed over them dry-shod.

Since that night, for it was near upon eleven o'clock when the happy change was realized, the business of my life has been not only to make a holy character but to live a life of loving activity in the service of God and man. I have ever felt that true religion consists not only in being holy myself, but in assisting my crucified Lord in his work of saving men and women, making them into his soldiers, keeping them faithful to death, and so getting them into heaven.

ADDITIONAL SCRIPTURE READING:
Exodus 22.3; Matthew 5.23–26; Philippians 4.7

Go to page 120 for your next devotional reading.

1700   1900

altar as a pleasing odor to the LORD. ¹⁶Aaron and his sons shall eat what is left of it; it shall be eaten as unleavened cakes in a holy place; in the court of the tent of meeting they shall eat it. ¹⁷It shall not be baked with leaven. I have given it as their portion of my offerings by fire; it is most holy, like the sin offering and the guilt offering. ¹⁸Every male among the descendants of Aaron shall eat of it, as their perpetual due throughout your generations, from the LORD's offerings by fire; anything that touches them shall become holy.

19 The LORD spoke to Moses, saying: ²⁰This is the offering that Aaron and his sons shall offer to the LORD on the day when he is anointed: one-tenth of an ephah of choice flour as a regular offering, half of it in the morning and half in the evening. ²¹It shall be made with oil on a griddle; you shall bring it well soaked, as a grain offering of baked ᵈ pieces, and you shall present it as a pleasing odor to the LORD. ²²And so the priest, anointed from among Aaron's descendants as a successor, shall prepare it; it is the LORD's—a perpetual due—to be turned entirely into smoke. ²³Every grain offering of a priest shall be wholly burned; it shall not be eaten.

24 The LORD spoke to Moses, saying: ²⁵Speak to Aaron and his sons, saying: This is the ritual of the sin offering. The sin offering shall be slaughtered before the LORD at the spot where the burnt offering is slaughtered; it is most holy. ²⁶The priest who offers it as a sin offering shall eat of it; it shall be eaten in a holy place, in the court of the tent of meeting. ²⁷Whatever touches its flesh shall become holy; and when any of its blood is spattered on a garment, you shall wash the bespattered part in a holy place. ²⁸An earthen vessel in which it was boiled shall be broken; but if it is boiled in a bronze vessel, that shall be scoured and rinsed in water. ²⁹Every male among the priests shall eat of it; it is most holy. ³⁰But no sin offering shall be eaten from which any blood is brought into the tent of meeting for atonement in the holy place; it shall be burned with fire.

ᵈ Meaning of Heb uncertain

7 This is the ritual of the guilt offering. It is most holy; ²at the spot where the burnt offering is slaughtered, they shall slaughter the guilt offering, and its blood shall be dashed against all sides of the altar. ³All its fat shall be offered: the broad tail, the fat that covers the entrails, ⁴the two kidneys with the fat that is on them at the loins, and the appendage of the liver, which shall be removed with the kidneys. ⁵The priest shall turn them into smoke on the altar as an offering by fire to the LORD; it is a guilt offering. ⁶Every male among the priests shall eat of it; it shall be eaten in a holy place; it is most holy.

7 The guilt offering is like the sin offering, there is the same ritual for them; the priest who makes atonement with it shall have it. ⁸So, too, the priest who offers anyone's burnt offering shall keep the skin of the burnt offering that he has offered. ⁹And every grain offering baked in the oven, and all that is prepared in a pan or on a griddle, shall belong to the priest who offers it. ¹⁰But every other grain offering, mixed with oil or dry, shall belong to all the sons of Aaron equally.

Further Instructions

11 This is the ritual of the sacrifice of the offering of well-being that one may offer to the LORD. ¹²If you offer it for thanksgiving, you shall offer with the thank offering unleavened cakes mixed with oil, unleavened wafers spread with oil, and cakes of choice flour well soaked in oil. ¹³With your thanksgiving sacrifice of well-being you shall bring your offering with cakes of leavened bread. ¹⁴From this you shall offer one cake from each offering, as a gift to the LORD; it shall belong to the priest who dashes the blood of the offering of well-being. ¹⁵And the flesh of your thanksgiving sacrifice of well-being shall be eaten on the day it is offered; you shall not leave any of it until morning. ¹⁶But if the sacrifice you offer is a votive offering or a freewill offering, it shall be eaten on the day that you offer your sacrifice, and what is left of it shall be eaten the next day; ¹⁷but what is left of the flesh of the sacrifice shall be burned up

on the third day. [18]If any of the flesh of your sacrifice of well-being is eaten on the third day, it shall not be acceptable, nor shall it be credited to the one who offers it; it shall be an abomination, and the one who eats of it shall incur guilt.

19 Flesh that touches any unclean thing shall not be eaten; it shall be burned up. As for other flesh, all who are clean may eat such flesh. [20]But those who eat flesh from the LORD's sacrifice of well-being while in a state of uncleanness shall be cut off from their kin. [21]When any one of you touches any unclean thing—human uncleanness or an unclean animal or any unclean creature—and then eats flesh from the LORD's sacrifice of well-being, you shall be cut off from your kin.

22 The LORD spoke to Moses, saying: [23]Speak to the people of Israel, saying: You shall eat no fat of ox or sheep or goat. [24]The fat of an animal that died or was torn by wild animals may be put to any other use, but you must not eat it. [25]If any one of you eats the fat from an animal of which an offering by fire may be made to the LORD, you who eat it shall be cut off from your kin. [26]You must not eat any blood whatever, either of bird or of animal, in any of your settlements. [27]Any one of you who eats any blood shall be cut off from your kin.

28 The LORD spoke to Moses, saying: [29]Speak to the people of Israel, saying: Any one of you who would offer to the LORD your sacrifice of well-being must yourself bring to the LORD your offering from your sacrifice of well-being. [30]Your own hands shall bring the LORD's offering by fire; you shall bring the fat with the breast, so that the breast may be raised as an elevation offering before the LORD. [31]The priest shall turn the fat into smoke on the altar, but the breast shall belong to Aaron and his sons. [32]And the right thigh from your sacrifices of well-being you shall give to the priest as an offering; [33]the one among the sons of Aaron who offers the blood and fat of the offering of well-being shall have the right thigh for a portion. [34]For I have taken the breast of the elevation offering, and the thigh that is offered, from the people of Israel, from their sacrifices of well-being, and have given them to

Aaron the priest and to his sons, as a perpetual due from the people of Israel. [35]This is the portion allotted to Aaron and to his sons from the offerings made by fire to the LORD, once they have been brought forward to serve the LORD as priests; [36]these the LORD commanded to be given them, when he anointed them, as a perpetual due from the people of Israel throughout their generations.

37 This is the ritual of the burnt offering, the grain offering, the sin offering, the guilt offering, the offering of ordination, and the sacrifice of well-being, [38]which the LORD commanded Moses on Mount Sinai, when he commanded the people of Israel to bring their offerings to the LORD, in the wilderness of Sinai.

The Rites of Ordination

8 The LORD spoke to Moses, saying: [2]Take Aaron and his sons with him, the vestments, the anointing oil, the bull of sin offering, the two rams, and the basket of unleavened bread; [3]and assemble the whole congregation at the entrance of the tent of meeting. [4]And Moses did as the LORD commanded him. When the congregation was assembled at the entrance of the tent of meeting, [5]Moses said to the congregation, "This is what the LORD has commanded to be done."

6 Then Moses brought Aaron and his sons forward, and washed them with water. [7]He put the tunic on him, fastened the sash around him, clothed him with the robe, and put the ephod on him. He then put the decorated band of the ephod around him, tying the ephod to him with it. [8]He placed the breastpiece on him, and in the breastpiece he put the Urim and the Thummim. [9]And he set the turban on his head, and on the turban, in front, he set the golden ornament, the holy crown, as the LORD commanded Moses.

10 Then Moses took the anointing oil and anointed the tabernacle and all that was in it, and consecrated them. [11]He sprinkled some of it on the altar seven times, and anointed the altar and all its utensils, and the basin and its base, to consecrate them. [12]He poured some of the anointing oil on Aaron's head and

anointed him, to consecrate him. [13]And Moses brought forward Aaron's sons, and clothed them with tunics, and fastened sashes around them, and tied headdresses on them, as the LORD commanded Moses.

14 He led forward the bull of sin offering; and Aaron and his sons laid their hands upon the head of the bull of sin offering, [15]and it was slaughtered. Moses took the blood and with his finger put some on each of the horns of the altar, purifying the altar; then he poured out the blood at the base of the altar. Thus he consecrated it, to make atonement for it. [16]Moses took all the fat that was around the entrails, and the appendage of the liver, and the two kidneys with their fat, and turned them into smoke on the altar. [17]But the bull itself, its skin and flesh and its dung, he burned with fire outside the camp, as the LORD commanded Moses.

18 Then he brought forward the ram of burnt offering. Aaron and his sons laid their hands on the head of the ram, [19]and it was slaughtered. Moses dashed the blood against all sides of the altar. [20]The ram was cut into its parts, and Moses turned into smoke the head and the parts and the suet. [21]And after the entrails and the legs were washed with water, Moses turned into smoke the whole ram on the altar; it was a burnt offering for a pleasing odor, an offering by fire to the LORD, as the LORD commanded Moses.

22 Then he brought forward the second ram, the ram of ordination. Aaron and his sons laid their hands on the head of the ram, [23]and it was slaughtered. Moses took some of its blood and put it on the lobe of Aaron's right ear and on the thumb of his right hand and on the big toe of his right foot. [24]After Aaron's sons were brought forward, Moses put some of the blood on the lobes of their right ears and on the thumbs of their right hands and on the big toes of their right feet; and Moses dashed the rest of the blood against all sides of the altar. [25]He took the fat—the broad tail, all the fat that was around the entrails, the appendage of the liver, and the two kidneys with their fat—and the right thigh. [26]From the basket of unleavened bread that was before the LORD, he took one cake of unleavened bread, one cake of bread with oil, and one wafer, and placed them on the fat and on the right thigh. [27]He placed all these on the palms of Aaron and on the palms of his sons, and raised them as an elevation offering before the LORD. [28]Then Moses took them from their hands and turned them into smoke on the altar with the burnt offering. This was an ordination offering for a pleasing odor, an offering by fire to the LORD. [29]Moses took the breast and raised it as an elevation offering before the LORD; it was Moses' portion of the ram of ordination, as the LORD commanded Moses.

30 Then Moses took some of the anointing oil and some of the blood that was on the altar and sprinkled them on Aaron and his vestments, and also on his sons and their vestments. Thus he consecrated Aaron and his vestments, and also his sons and their vestments.

31 And Moses said to Aaron and his sons, "Boil the flesh at the entrance of the tent of meeting, and eat it there with the bread that is in the basket of ordination offerings, as I was commanded, 'Aaron and his sons shall eat it'; [32]and what remains of the flesh and the bread you shall burn with fire. [33]You shall not go outside the entrance of the tent of meeting for seven days, until the day when your period of ordination is completed. For it will take seven days to ordain you; [34]as has been done today, the LORD has commanded to be done to make atonement for you. [35]You shall remain at the entrance of the tent of meeting day and night for seven days, keeping the LORD's charge so that you do not die; for so I am commanded." [36]Aaron and his sons did all the things that the LORD commanded through Moses.

Aaron's Priesthood Inaugurated

9 On the eighth day Moses summoned Aaron and his sons and the elders of Israel. [2]He said to Aaron, "Take a bull calf for a sin offering and a ram for a burnt offering, without blemish, and offer them before the LORD. [3]And say to the people of Israel, 'Take a male goat for a sin offering; a calf and a lamb, yearlings without blemish, for a burnt offering; 4and an ox and a ram for an offering of well-being to sacrifice before the LORD; and a grain offering mixed with oil. For today the LORD will appear to you.' " 5They brought what Moses commanded to the front of the tent of meeting; and the whole congregation drew near and stood before the LORD. 6And Moses said, "This is the

TUESDAY

SIN AND THE GLORY OF GOD
William Temple

VERSE: Leviticus 9.7, 22　　　　　　　　PASSAGE: Leviticus 9.1–24

 e tend to think of sin as consisting of acts which are done in defiance of conscience or are, whether we know it or not, contrary to God's command. Some people even say that so long as a man follows his conscience he cannot be committing sin. (The theologian would say that he is certainly not committing "formal sin" but he may be committing "material sin.") Certainly a man should follow his conscience; but that is not the whole of his duty. Still more important is it to enlighten conscience itself, lest "the light in you is darkness" (Matthew 6.23). The greatest crimes in history have been perpetrated at the bidding of conscience—such as the Spanish Inquisition. The disciples were warned to expect a time when *those who kill you will think that by doing so they are offering worship to God* (John 16.2). A sin committed against the light is more wicked than another; the man who does it is more guilty. But sin is something much wider and deeper than guilt. Everything which is other than God would have it be is sin. "All have sinned and fall short of the glory of God" (Romans 3.23); that is the definition of sin—to fall short of the glory of God! It is not enough that we should be as good as the people about us; nothing is enough except that we should be as good as God—"Be perfect, therefore, as your heavenly Father is perfect" (Matthew 5.48). But we shall not set ourselves that standard, to say nothing of attaining it, if we are left to our own resources. And we do not know what the perfection of God is until we have seen it in Christ. Unless we *believe on* him we are bound to be wrong in our whole idea about sin; for apart from that faith we have neither the stimulus nor the capacity to frame the true standard.

ADDITIONAL SCRIPTURE READING:
Leviticus 19.1–2; 1 Peter 1.14–16

Go to page 130 for your next devotional reading.

1900　　Present

thing that the LORD commanded you to do, so that the glory of the LORD may appear to you." 7Then Moses said to Aaron, "Draw near to the altar and sacrifice your sin offering and your burnt offering, and make atonement for yourself and for the people; and sacrifice the offering of the people, and make atonement for them; as the LORD has commanded."

8 Aaron drew near to the altar, and slaughtered the calf of the sin offering, which was for himself. 9The sons of Aaron presented the blood to him, and he dipped his finger in the blood and put it on the horns of the altar; and the rest of the blood he poured out at the base of the altar. 10But the fat, the kidneys, and the appendage of the liver from the sin offering he turned into smoke on the altar, as the LORD commanded Moses; 11and the flesh and the skin he burned with fire outside the camp.

12 Then he slaughtered the burnt offering. Aaron's sons brought him the blood, and he dashed it against all sides of the altar. 13And they brought him the burnt offering piece by piece, and the head, which he turned into smoke on the altar. 14He washed the entrails and the legs and, with the burnt offering, turned them into smoke on the altar.

15 Next he presented the people's offering. He took the goat of the sin offering that was for the people, and slaughtered it, and presented it as a sin offering like the first one. 16He presented the burnt offering, and sacrificed it according to regulation. 17He presented the grain offering, and, taking a handful of it, he turned it into smoke on the altar, in addition to the burnt offering of the morning.

18 He slaughtered the ox and the ram as a sacrifice of well-being for the people. Aaron's sons brought him the blood, which he dashed against all sides of the altar, 19and the fat of the ox and of the ram—the broad tail, the fat that covers the entrails, the two kidneys and the fat on them,*e* and the appendage of the liver. 20They first laid the fat on the breasts, and the fat was turned into smoke on the altar; 21and the breasts and the right thigh Aaron raised as an elevation offering before the LORD, as Moses had commanded.

22 Aaron lifted his hands toward the people and blessed them; and he came down after sacrificing the sin offering, the burnt offering, and the offering of well-being. 23Moses and Aaron entered the tent of meeting, and then came out and blessed the people; and the glory of the LORD appeared to all the people. 24Fire came out from the LORD and consumed the burnt offering and the fat on the altar; and when all the people saw it, they shouted and fell on their faces.

Nadab and Abihu

10 Now Aaron's sons, Nadab and Abihu, each took his censer, put fire in it, and laid incense on it; and they offered unholy fire before the LORD, such as he had not commanded them. 2And fire came out from the presence of the LORD and consumed them, and they died before the LORD. 3Then Moses said to Aaron, "This is what the LORD meant when he said,

'Through those who are near me
    I will show myself holy,
and before all the people
    I will be glorified.' "

And Aaron was silent.

4 Moses summoned Mishael and Elzaphan, sons of Uzziel the uncle of Aaron, and said to them, "Come forward, and carry your kinsmen away from the front of the sanctuary to a place outside the camp." 5They came forward and carried them by their tunics out of the camp, as Moses had ordered. 6And Moses said to Aaron and to his sons Eleazar and Ithamar, "Do not dishevel your hair, and do not tear your vestments, or you will die and wrath will strike all the congregation; but your kindred, the whole house of Israel, may mourn the burning that the LORD has sent. 7You shall not go outside the entrance of the tent of meeting, or you will die; for the anointing oil of the LORD is on you." And they did as Moses had ordered.

8 And the LORD spoke to Aaron: 9Drink no wine or strong drink, neither you nor your sons, when you enter the tent of meeting, that you may not die; it

e Gk: Heb *the broad tail, and that which covers, and the kidneys*

is a statute forever throughout your generations. 10You are to distinguish between the holy and the common, and between the unclean and the clean; 11and you are to teach the people of Israel all the statutes that the LORD has spoken to them through Moses.

12 Moses spoke to Aaron and to his remaining sons, Eleazar and Ithamar: Take the grain offering that is left from the LORD's offerings by fire, and eat it unleavened beside the altar, for it is most holy; 13you shall eat it in a holy place, because it is your due and your sons' due, from the offerings by fire to the LORD; for so I am commanded. 14But the breast that is elevated and the thigh that is raised, you and your sons and daughters as well may eat in any clean place; for they have been assigned to you and your children from the sacrifices of the offerings of well-being of the people of Israel. 15The thigh that is raised and the breast that is elevated they shall bring, together with the offerings by fire of the fat, to raise for an elevation offering before the LORD; they are to be your due and that of your children forever, as the LORD has commanded.

16 Then Moses made inquiry about the goat of the sin offering, and—it had already been burned! He was angry with Eleazar and Ithamar, Aaron's remaining sons, and said, 17"Why did you not eat the sin offering in the sacred area? For it is most holy, and God/ has given it to you that you may remove the guilt of the congregation, to make atonement on their behalf before the LORD. 18Its blood was not brought into the inner part of the sanctuary. You should certainly have eaten it in the sanctuary, as I commanded." 19And Aaron spoke to Moses, "See, today they offered their sin offering and their burnt offering before the LORD; and yet such things as these have befallen me! If I had eaten the sin offering today, would it have been agreeable to the LORD?" 20And when Moses heard that, he agreed.

Clean and Unclean Foods

11 The LORD spoke to Moses and Aaron, saying to them: 2Speak to the people of Israel, saying:

From among all the land animals, these are the creatures that you may eat. 3Any animal that has divided hoofs and is cleft-footed and chews the cud—such you may eat. 4But among those that chew the cud or have divided hoofs, you shall not eat the following: the camel, for even though it chews the cud, it does not have divided hoofs; it is unclean for you. 5The rock badger, for even though it chews the cud, it does not have divided hoofs; it is unclean for you. 6The hare, for even though it chews the cud, it does not have divided hoofs; it is unclean for you. 7The pig, for even though it has divided hoofs and is cleft-footed, it does not chew the cud; it is unclean for you. 8Of their flesh you shall not eat, and their carcasses you shall not touch; they are unclean for you.

9 These you may eat, of all that are in the waters. Everything in the waters that has fins and scales, whether in the seas or in the streams—such you may eat. 10But anything in the seas or the streams that does not have fins and scales, of the swarming creatures in the waters and among all the other living creatures that are in the waters—they are detestable to you 11and detestable they shall remain. Of their flesh you shall not eat, and their carcasses you shall regard as detestable. 12Everything in the waters that does not have fins and scales is detestable to you.

13 These you shall regard as detestable among the birds. They shall not be eaten; they are an abomination: the eagle, the vulture, the osprey, 14the buzzard, the kite of any kind; 15every raven of any kind; 16the ostrich, the nighthawk, the sea gull, the hawk of any kind; 17the little owl, the cormorant, the great owl, 18the water hen, the desert owl,g the carrion vulture, 19the stork, the heron of any kind, the hoopoe, and the bat.h

20 All winged insects that walk upon all fours are detestable to you. 21But among the winged insects that walk on all fours you may eat those that have jointed legs above their feet, with which to leap on the ground. 22Of them you may eat: the locust according to its kind, the bald locust according to its kind, the

---

f Heb he   g Or pelican   h Identification of several of the birds in verses 13-19 is uncertain

cricket according to its kind, and the grasshopper according to its kind. 23But all other winged insects that have four feet are detestable to you.

Unclean Animals

24 By these you shall become unclean; whoever touches the carcass of any of them shall be unclean until the evening, 25and whoever carries any part of the carcass of any of them shall wash his clothes and be unclean until the evening. 26Every animal that has divided hoofs but is not cleft-footed or does not chew the cud is unclean for you; everyone who touches one of them shall be unclean. 27All that walk on their paws, among the animals that walk on all fours, are unclean for you; whoever touches the carcass of any of them shall be unclean until the evening, 28and the one who carries the carcass shall wash his clothes and be unclean until the evening; they are unclean for you.

29 These are unclean for you among the creatures that swarm upon the earth: the weasel, the mouse, the great lizard according to its kind, 30the gecko, the land crocodile, the lizard, the sand lizard, and the chameleon. 31These are unclean for you among all that swarm; whoever touches one of them when they are dead shall be unclean until the evening. 32And anything upon which any of them falls when they are dead shall be unclean, whether an article of wood or cloth or skin or sacking, any article that is used for any purpose; it shall be dipped into water, and it shall be unclean until the evening, and then it shall be clean. 33And if any of them falls into any earthen vessel, all that is in it shall be unclean, and you shall break the vessel. 34Any food that could be eaten shall be unclean if water from any such vessel comes upon it; and any liquid that could be drunk shall be unclean if it was in any such vessel. 35Everything on which any part of the carcass falls shall be unclean; whether an oven or stove, it shall be broken in pieces; they are unclean, and shall remain unclean for you. 36But a spring or a cistern holding water shall be clean, while whatever touches the carcass in it shall be unclean. 37If any part of their carcass falls upon any seed set aside for sowing, it is clean; 38but if water is put on the seed and any part of their carcass falls on it, it is unclean for you.

39 If an animal of which you may eat dies, anyone who touches its carcass shall be unclean until the evening. 40Those who eat of its carcass shall wash their clothes and be unclean until the evening; and those who carry the carcass shall wash their clothes and be unclean until the evening.

41 All creatures that swarm upon the earth are detestable; they shall not be eaten. 42Whatever moves on its belly, and whatever moves on all fours, or whatever has many feet, all the creatures that swarm upon the earth, you shall not eat; for they are detestable. 43You shall not make yourselves detestable with any creature that swarms; you shall not defile yourselves with them, and so become unclean. 44For I am the LORD your God; sanctify yourselves therefore, and be holy, for I am holy. You shall not defile yourselves with any swarming creature that moves on the earth. 45For I am the LORD who brought you up from the land of Egypt, to be your God; you shall be holy, for I am holy.

46 This is the law pertaining to land animal and bird and every living creature that moves through the waters and every creature that swarms upon the earth, 47to make a distinction between the unclean and the clean, and between the living creature that may be eaten and the living creature that may not be eaten.

Purification of Women after Childbirth

12 The LORD spoke to Moses, saying: 2Speak to the people of Israel, saying:

If a woman conceives and bears a male child, she shall be ceremonially unclean seven days; as at the time of her menstruation, she shall be unclean. 3On the eighth day the flesh of his foreskin shall be circumcised. 4Her time of blood purification shall be thirty-three days; she shall not touch any holy thing, or come into the sanctuary, until the days of her purification are completed. 5If she bears a female child, she shall be unclean two weeks, as in her menstruation; her time of blood purification shall be sixty-six days.

6 When the days of her purification are completed, whether for a son or for a daughter, she shall bring to the priest at the entrance of the tent of meeting a lamb in its first year for a burnt offering, and a pigeon or a turtledove for a sin offering. 7He shall offer it before the LORD, and make atonement on her behalf; then she shall be clean from her flow of blood. This is the law for her who bears a child, male or female. 8If she cannot afford a sheep, she shall take two turtledoves or two pigeons, one for a burnt offering and the other for a sin offering; and the priest shall make atonement on her behalf, and she shall be clean.

Leprosy, Varieties and Symptoms

13 The LORD spoke to Moses and Aaron, saying:

2 When a person has on the skin of his body a swelling or an eruption or a spot, and it turns into a leprous*i* disease on the skin of his body, he shall be brought to Aaron the priest or to one of his sons the priests. 3The priest shall examine the disease on the skin of his body, and if the hair in the diseased area has turned white and the disease appears to be deeper than the skin of his body, it is a leprous*i* disease; after the priest has examined him he shall pronounce him ceremonially unclean. 4But if the spot is white in the skin of his body, and appears no deeper than the skin, and the hair in it has not turned white, the priest shall confine the diseased person for seven days. 5The priest shall examine him on the seventh day, and if he sees that the disease is checked and the disease has not spread in the skin, then the priest shall confine him seven days more. 6The priest shall examine him again on the seventh day, and if the disease has abated and the disease has not spread in the skin, the priest shall pronounce him clean; it is only an eruption; and he shall wash his clothes, and be clean. 7But if the eruption spreads in the skin after he has shown himself to the priest for his cleansing, he shall appear again before the priest. 8The priest shall

make an examination, and if the eruption has spread in the skin, the priest shall pronounce him unclean; it is a leprous*i* disease.

9 When a person contracts a leprous*i* disease, he shall be brought to the priest. 10The priest shall make an examination, and if there is a white swelling in the skin that has turned the hair white, and there is quick raw flesh in the swelling, 11it is a chronic leprous*i* disease in the skin of his body. The priest shall pronounce him unclean; he shall not confine him, for he is unclean. 12But if the disease breaks out in the skin, so that it covers all the skin of the diseased person from head to foot, so far as the priest can see, 13then the priest shall make an examination, and if the disease has covered all his body, he shall pronounce him clean of the disease; since it has all turned white, he is clean. 14But if raw flesh ever appears on him, he shall be unclean; 15the priest shall examine the raw flesh and pronounce him unclean. Raw flesh is unclean, for it is a leprous*i* disease. 16But if the raw flesh again turns white, he shall come to the priest; 17the priest shall examine him, and if the disease has turned white, the priest shall pronounce the diseased person clean. He is clean.

18 When there is on the skin of one's body a boil that has healed, 19and in the place of the boil there appears a white swelling or a reddish-white spot, it shall be shown to the priest. 20The priest shall make an examination, and if it appears deeper than the skin and its hair has turned white, the priest shall pronounce him unclean; this is a leprous*i* disease, broken out in the boil. 21But if the priest examines it and the hair on it is not white, nor is it deeper than the skin but has abated, the priest shall confine him seven days. 22If it spreads in the skin, the priest shall pronounce him unclean; it is diseased. 23But if the spot remains in one place and does not spread, it is the scar of the boil; the priest shall pronounce him clean.

24 Or, when the body has a burn on the skin and the raw flesh of the burn becomes a spot, reddish-white or white, 25the priest shall examine it. If the hair

i A term for several skin diseases; precise meaning uncertain in the spot has turned white and it appears deeper than the skin, it is a leprous[j] disease; it has broken out in the burn, and the priest shall pronounce him unclean. This is a leprous[j] disease. 26But if the priest examines it and the hair in the spot is not white, and it is no deeper than the skin but has abated, the priest shall confine him seven days. 27The priest shall examine him the seventh day; if it is spreading in the skin, the priest shall pronounce him unclean. This is a leprous[j] disease. 28But if the spot remains in one place and does not spread in the skin but has abated, it is a swelling from the burn, and the priest shall pronounce him clean; for it is the scar of the burn.

29 When a man or woman has a disease on the head or in the beard, 30the priest shall examine the disease. If it appears deeper than the skin and the hair in it is yellow and thin, the priest shall pronounce him unclean; it is an itch, a leprous[j] disease of the head or the beard. 31If the priest examines the itching disease, and it appears no deeper than the skin and there is no black hair in it, the priest shall confine the person with the itching disease for seven days. 32On the seventh day the priest shall examine the itch; if the itch has not spread, and there is no yellow hair in it, and the itch appears to be no deeper than the skin, 33he shall shave, but the itch he shall not shave. The priest shall confine the person with the itch for seven days more. 34On the seventh day the priest shall examine the itch; if the itch has not spread in the skin and it appears to be no deeper than the skin, the priest shall pronounce him clean. He shall wash his clothes and be clean. 35But if the itch spreads in the skin after he was pronounced clean, 36the priest shall examine him. If the itch has spread in the skin, the priest need not seek for the yellow hair; he is unclean. 37But if in his eyes the itch is checked, and black hair has grown in it, the itch is healed, he is clean; and the priest shall pronounce him clean.

38 When a man or a woman has spots on the skin of the body, white spots, 39the priest shall make an examination, and if the spots on the skin of the body are of a dull white, it is a rash that has broken out on the skin; he is clean.

40 If anyone loses the hair from his head, he is bald but he is clean. 41If he loses the hair from his forehead and temples, he has baldness of the forehead but he is clean. 42But if there is on the bald head or the bald forehead a reddish-white diseased spot, it is a leprous[j] disease breaking out on his bald head or his bald forehead. 43The priest shall examine him; if the diseased swelling is reddish-white on his bald head or on his bald forehead, which resembles a leprous[j] disease in the skin of the body, 44he is leprous,[j] he is unclean. The priest shall pronounce him unclean; the disease is on his head.

45 The person who has the leprous[j] disease shall wear torn clothes and let the hair of his head be disheveled; and he shall cover his upper lip and cry out, "Unclean, unclean." 46He shall remain unclean as long as he has the disease; he is unclean. He shall live alone; his dwelling shall be outside the camp.

47 Concerning clothing: when a leprous[j] disease appears in it, in woolen or linen cloth, 48in warp or woof of linen or wool, or in a skin or in anything made of skin, 49if the disease shows greenish or reddish in the garment, whether in warp or woof or in skin or in anything made of skin, it is a leprous[j] disease and shall be shown to the priest. 50The priest shall examine the disease, and put the diseased article aside for seven days. 51He shall examine the disease on the seventh day. If the disease has spread in the cloth, in warp or woof, or in the skin, whatever be the use of the skin, this is a spreading leprous[j] disease; it is unclean. 52He shall burn the clothing, whether diseased in warp or woof, woolen or linen, or anything of skin, for it is a spreading leprous[j] disease; it shall be burned in fire.

53 If the priest makes an examination, and the disease has not spread in the clothing, in warp or woof or in anything of skin, 54the priest shall command them to wash the article in which the disease appears, and he shall put it aside seven days more. 55The priest shall

j A term for several skin diseases; precise meaning uncertain examine the diseased article after it has been washed. If the diseased spot has not changed color, though the disease has not spread, it is unclean; you shall burn it in fire, whether the leprous*k* spot is on the inside or on the outside.

56 If the priest makes an examination, and the disease has abated after it is washed, he shall tear the spot out of the cloth, in warp or woof, or out of skin. 57If it appears again in the garment, in warp or woof, or in anything of skin, it is spreading; you shall burn with fire that in which the disease appears. 58But the cloth, warp or woof, or anything of skin from which the disease disappears when you have washed it, shall then be washed a second time, and it shall be clean.

59 This is the ritual for a leprous*k* disease in a cloth of wool or linen, either in warp or woof, or in anything of skin, to decide whether it is clean or unclean.

Purification of Lepers and Leprous Houses

14 The LORD spoke to Moses, saying: 2This shall be the ritual for the leprous*k* person at the time of his cleansing:

He shall be brought to the priest; 3the priest shall go out of the camp, and the priest shall make an examination. If the disease is healed in the leprous*k* person, 4the priest shall command that two living clean birds and cedarwood and crimson yarn and hyssop be brought for the one who is to be cleansed. 5The priest shall command that one of the birds be slaughtered over fresh water in an earthen vessel. 6He shall take the living bird with the cedarwood and the crimson yarn and the hyssop, and dip them and the living bird in the blood of the bird that was slaughtered over the fresh water. 7He shall sprinkle it seven times upon the one who is to be cleansed of the leprous*k* disease; then he shall pronounce him clean, and he shall let the living bird go into the open field. 8The one who is to be cleansed shall wash his clothes, and shave off all his hair, and bathe himself in water, and he shall be clean. After that he shall come into the camp, but shall live outside his tent

seven days. 9On the seventh day he shall shave all his hair: of head, beard, eyebrows; he shall shave all his hair. Then he shall wash his clothes, and bathe his body in water, and he shall be clean.

10 On the eighth day he shall take two male lambs without blemish, and one ewe lamb in its first year without blemish, and a grain offering of three-tenths of an ephah of choice flour mixed with oil, and one log*l* of oil. 11The priest who cleanses shall set the person to be cleansed, along with these things, before the LORD, at the entrance of the tent of meeting. 12The priest shall take one of the lambs, and offer it as a guilt offering, along with the log*l* of oil, and raise them as an elevation offering before the LORD. 13He shall slaughter the lamb in the place where the sin offering and the burnt offering are slaughtered in the holy place; for the guilt offering, like the sin offering, belongs to the priest: it is most holy. 14The priest shall take some of the blood of the guilt offering and put it on the lobe of the right ear of the one to be cleansed, and on the thumb of the right hand, and on the big toe of the right foot. 15The priest shall take some of the log*l* of oil and pour it into the palm of his own left hand, 16and dip his right finger in the oil that is in his left hand and sprinkle some oil with his finger seven times before the LORD. 17Some of the oil that remains in his hand the priest shall put on the lobe of the right ear of the one to be cleansed, and on the thumb of the right hand, and on the big toe of the right foot, on top of the blood of the guilt offering. 18The rest of the oil that is in the priest's hand he shall put on the head of the one to be cleansed. Then the priest shall make atonement on his behalf before the LORD: 19the priest shall offer the sin offering, to make atonement for the one to be cleansed from his uncleanness. Afterward he shall slaughter the burnt offering; 20and the priest shall offer the burnt offering and the grain offering on the altar. Thus the priest shall make atonement on his behalf and he shall be clean.

21 But if he is poor and cannot afford so much, he shall take one male lamb for a guilt offering to be elevated, to

---

k A term for several skin diseases; precise meaning uncertain   *l* A liquid measure

make atonement on his behalf, and one-tenth of an ephah of choice flour mixed with oil for a grain offering and a log^m of oil; 22also two turtledoves or two pigeons, such as he can afford, one for a sin offering and the other for a burnt offering. 23On the eighth day he shall bring them for his cleansing to the priest, to the entrance of the tent of meeting, before the LORD; 24and the priest shall take the lamb of the guilt offering and the log^m of oil, and the priest shall raise them as an elevation offering before the LORD. 25The priest shall slaughter the lamb of the guilt offering and shall take some of the blood of the guilt offering, and put it on the lobe of the right ear of the one to be cleansed, and on the thumb of the right hand, and on the big toe of the right foot. 26The priest shall pour some of the oil into the palm of his own left hand, 27and shall sprinkle with his right finger some of the oil that is in his left hand seven times before the LORD. 28The priest shall put some of the oil that is in his hand on the lobe of the right ear of the one to be cleansed, and on the thumb of the right hand, and the big toe of the right foot, where the blood of the guilt offering was placed. 29The rest of the oil that is in the priest's hand he shall put on the head of the one to be cleansed, to make atonement on his behalf before the LORD. 30And he shall offer, of the turtledoves or pigeons such as he can afford, 31one^n for a sin offering and the other for a burnt offering, along with a grain offering; and the priest shall make atonement before the LORD on behalf of the one being cleansed. 32This is the ritual for the one who has a leprous^o disease, who cannot afford the offerings for his cleansing.

33 The LORD spoke to Moses and Aaron, saying:

34 When you come into the land of Canaan, which I give you for a possession, and I put a leprous^o disease in a house in the land of your possession, 35the owner of the house shall come and tell the priest, saying, "There seems to me to be some sort of disease in my house." 36The priest shall command that they empty the house before the priest goes to examine the disease, or all that is in the house will become unclean; and afterward the priest shall go in to inspect the house. 37He shall examine the disease; if the disease is in the walls of the house with greenish or reddish spots, and if it appears to be deeper than the surface, 38the priest shall go outside to the door of the house and shut up the house seven days. 39The priest shall come again on the seventh day and make an inspection; if the disease has spread in the walls of the house, 40the priest shall command that the stones in which the disease appears be taken out and thrown into an unclean place outside the city. 41He shall have the inside of the house scraped thoroughly, and the plaster that is scraped off shall be dumped in an unclean place outside the city. 42They shall take other stones and put them in the place of those stones, and take other plaster and plaster the house.

43 If the disease breaks out again in the house, after he has taken out the stones and scraped the house and plastered it, 44the priest shall go and make inspection; if the disease has spread in the house, it is a spreading leprous^o disease in the house; it is unclean. 45He shall have the house torn down, its stones and timber and all the plaster of the house, and taken outside the city to an unclean place. 46All who enter the house while it is shut up shall be unclean until the evening; 47and all who sleep in the house shall wash their clothes; and all who eat in the house shall wash their clothes.

48 If the priest comes and makes an inspection, and the disease has not spread in the house after the house was plastered, the priest shall pronounce the house clean; the disease is healed. 49For the cleansing of the house he shall take two birds, with cedarwood and crimson yarn and hyssop, 50and shall slaughter one of the birds over fresh water in an earthen vessel, 51and shall take the cedarwood and the hyssop and the crimson yarn, along with the living bird, and dip them in the blood of the slaughtered

---

m A liquid measure n Gk Syr: Heb afford, 31such as he can afford, one o A term for several skin diseases; precise meaning uncertain

bird and the fresh water, and sprinkle the house seven times. [52]Thus he shall cleanse the house with the blood of the bird, and with the fresh water, and with the living bird, and with the cedarwood and hyssop and crimson yarn; [53]and he shall let the living bird go out of the city into the open field; so he shall make atonement for the house, and it shall be clean.

[54] This is the ritual for any leprous[p] disease: for an itch, [55]for leprous[p] diseases in clothing and houses, [56]and for a swelling or an eruption or a spot, [57]to determine when it is unclean and when it is clean. This is the ritual for leprous[p] diseases.

Concerning Bodily Discharges

15 The LORD spoke to Moses and Aaron, saying: [2]Speak to the people of Israel and say to them:

When any man has a discharge from his member,[q] his discharge makes him ceremonially unclean. [3]The uncleanness of his discharge is this: whether his member[q] flows with his discharge, or his member[q] is stopped from discharging, it is uncleanness for him. [4]Every bed on which the one with the discharge lies shall be unclean; and everything on which he sits shall be unclean. [5]Anyone who touches his bed shall wash his clothes, and bathe in water, and be unclean until the evening. [6]All who sit on anything on which the one with the discharge has sat shall wash their clothes, and bathe in water, and be unclean until the evening. [7]All who touch the body of the one with the discharge shall wash their clothes, and bathe in water, and be unclean until the evening. [8]If the one with the discharge spits on persons who are clean, then they shall wash their clothes, and bathe in water, and be unclean until the evening. [9]Any saddle on which the one with the discharge rides shall be unclean. [10]All who touch anything that was under him shall be unclean until the evening, and all who carry such a thing shall wash their clothes, and bathe in water, and be unclean until the evening. [11]All those whom the one with the discharge touches without his hav-

ing rinsed his hands in water shall wash their clothes, and bathe in water, and be unclean until the evening. [12]Any earthen vessel that the one with the discharge touches shall be broken; and every vessel of wood shall be rinsed in water.

[13] When the one with a discharge is cleansed of his discharge, he shall count seven days for his cleansing; he shall wash his clothes and bathe his body in fresh water, and he shall be clean. [14]On the eighth day he shall take two turtledoves or two pigeons and come before the LORD to the entrance of the tent of meeting and give them to the priest. [15]The priest shall offer them, one for a sin offering and the other for a burnt offering; and the priest shall make atonement on his behalf before the LORD for his discharge.

[16] If a man has an emission of semen, he shall bathe his whole body in water, and be unclean until the evening. [17]Everything made of cloth or of skin on which the semen falls shall be washed with water, and be unclean until the evening. [18]If a man lies with a woman and has an emission of semen, both of them shall bathe in water, and be unclean until the evening.

[19] When a woman has a discharge of blood that is her regular discharge from her body, she shall be in her impurity for seven days, and whoever touches her shall be unclean until the evening. [20]Everything upon which she lies during her impurity shall be unclean; everything also upon which she sits shall be unclean. [21]Whoever touches her bed shall wash his clothes, and bathe in water, and be unclean until the evening. [22]Whoever touches anything upon which she sits shall wash his clothes, and bathe in water, and be unclean until the evening; [23]whether it is the bed or anything upon which she sits, when he touches it he shall be unclean until the evening. [24]If any man lies with her, and her impurity falls on him, he shall be unclean seven days; and every bed on which he lies shall be unclean.

[25] If a woman has a discharge of blood for many days, not at the time of her impurity, or if she has a discharge

p A term for several skin diseases; precise meaning uncertain   q Heb *flesh* beyond the time of her impurity, all the days of the discharge she shall continue in uncleanness; as in the days of her impurity, she shall be unclean. ²⁶Every bed on which she lies during all the days of her discharge shall be treated as the bed of her impurity; and everything on which she sits shall be unclean, as in the uncleanness of her impurity. ²⁷Whoever touches these things shall be unclean, and shall wash his clothes, and bathe in water, and be unclean until the evening. ²⁸If she is cleansed of her discharge, she shall count seven days, and after that she shall be clean. ²⁹On the eighth day she shall take two turtledoves or two pigeons and bring them to the priest at the entrance of the tent of meeting. ³⁰The priest shall offer one for a sin offering and the other for a burnt offering; and the priest shall make atonement on her behalf before the LORD for her unclean discharge.

31 Thus you shall keep the people of Israel separate from their uncleanness, so that they do not die in their uncleanness by defiling my tabernacle that is in their midst.

32 This is the ritual for those who have a discharge: for him who has an emission of semen, becoming unclean thereby, ³³for her who is in the infirmity of her period, for anyone, male or female, who has a discharge, and for the man who lies with a woman who is unclean.

The Day of Atonement

16 The LORD spoke to Moses after the death of the two sons of Aaron, when they drew near before the LORD and died. ²The LORD said to Moses:

Tell your brother Aaron not to come just at any time into the sanctuary inside the curtain before the mercy seat*ʳ* that is upon the ark, or he will die; for I appear in the cloud upon the mercy seat.*ʳ* ³Thus shall Aaron come into the holy place: with a young bull for a sin offering and a ram for a burnt offering. ⁴He shall put on the holy linen tunic, and shall have the linen undergarments next to his body, fasten the linen sash, and wear the linen turban; these are the holy vestments. He shall bathe his body in water, and then

put them on. ⁵He shall take from the congregation of the people of Israel two male goats for a sin offering, and one ram for a burnt offering.

6 Aaron shall offer the bull as a sin offering for himself, and shall make atonement for himself and for his house. ⁷He shall take the two goats and set them before the LORD at the entrance of the tent of meeting; ⁸and Aaron shall cast lots on the two goats, one lot for the LORD and the other lot for Azazel.*ˢ* ⁹Aaron shall present the goat on which the lot fell for the LORD, and offer it as a sin offering; ¹⁰but the goat on which the lot fell for Azazel*ˢ* shall be presented alive before the LORD to make atonement over it, that it may be sent away into the wilderness to Azazel.*ˢ*

11 Aaron shall present the bull as a sin offering for himself, and shall make atonement for himself and for his house; he shall slaughter the bull as a sin offering for himself. ¹²He shall take a censer full of coals of fire from the altar before the LORD, and two handfuls of crushed sweet incense, and he shall bring it inside the curtain ¹³and put the incense on the fire before the LORD, that the cloud of the incense may cover the mercy seat*ʳ* that is upon the covenant,*ᵗ* or he will die. ¹⁴He shall take some of the blood of the bull, and sprinkle it with his finger on the front of the mercy seat,*ʳ* and before the mercy seat*ʳ* he shall sprinkle the blood with his finger seven times.

15 He shall slaughter the goat of the sin offering that is for the people and bring its blood inside the curtain, and do with its blood as he did with the blood of the bull, sprinkling it upon the mercy seat*ʳ* and before the mercy seat.*ʳ* ¹⁶Thus he shall make atonement for the sanctuary, because of the uncleannesses of the people of Israel, and because of their transgressions, all their sins; and so he shall do for the tent of meeting, which remains with them in the midst of their uncleannesses. ¹⁷No one shall be in the tent of meeting from the time he enters to make atonement in the sanctuary until he comes out and has made atonement for himself and for his house and for all the assembly of Israel. ¹⁸Then he

---

r Or *the cover*   *s* Traditionally rendered *a scapegoat*   *t* Or *treaty*, or *testament*; Heb *eduth*

shall go out to the altar that is before the LORD and make atonement on its behalf, and shall take some of the blood of the bull and of the blood of the goat, and put it on each of the horns of the altar. ¹⁹He shall sprinkle some of the blood on it

---

WEDNESDAY

OF THE SCAPEGOAT
Epistle of Barnabas

VERSE: Leviticus 16.8   PASSAGE: Leviticus 16.2–34

 otice the directions he gave. *Take a couple of goats, unblemished and well-matched; bring them for an offering, and let the priest take one of them for a burnt-offering.* And what are they to do with the other? *The other,* he declares, *is accursed.* (Now see how plainly the type of Jesus appears.) *Spit on it, all of you; thrust your goads into it, wreathe its head with scarlet wool, and so let it be driven out into the desert.* This is done, and the goat-ward leads the animal into the desert, where he takes off the wool and leaves it there, on the bush we call a bramble (the plant we usually eat the berries of, if we come across it in the countryside; nothing has such tasty fruit as a bramble). Now what does that signify? Notice that the first goat is for the altar, and the other is accursed; and that it is the accursed one that wears the wreath. That is because they shall see him on that day clad to the ankles in his red woollen robe, and will say, "Is not this he whom we once crucified, and mocked and pierced and spat upon? Yes, this is the man who told us that he was the son of God." But how will he resemble the goat? The point of there being two similar goats, both of them fair and alike, is that when they see him coming on the day, they are going to be struck with terror at the manifest parallel between him and the goat. In this ordinance, then, you are to see typified the future sufferings of Jesus.

But why should they put the wool on the thorns? This too is a type of Jesus, meant for the church's instruction. For if one wanted to take the scarlet wool for himself, it would cost him much suffering, since the thorns were fearsome and could only be mastered with anguish. Similarly, says he, those who would behold me and possess my kingdom must go through affliction and suffering before they can reach me.

ADDITIONAL SCRIPTURE READING:
Numbers 29.7–11; Hebrews 9.1–14, 24–26

Go to page 132 for your next devotional reading.

100   500

with his finger seven times, and cleanse it and hallow it from the uncleannesses of the people of Israel. 20 When he has finished atoning for the holy place and the tent of meeting and the altar, he shall present the live goat. 21Then Aaron shall lay both his hands on the head of the live goat, and confess over it all the iniquities of the people of Israel, and all their transgressions, all their sins, putting them on the head of the goat, and sending it away into the wilderness by means of someone designated for the task.u 22The goat shall bear on itself all their iniquities to a barren region; and the goat shall be set free in the wilderness.

23 Then Aaron shall enter the tent of meeting, and shall take off the linen vestments that he put on when he went into the holy place, and shall leave them there. 24He shall bathe his body in water in a holy place, and put on his vestments; then he shall come out and offer his burnt offering and the burnt offering of the people, making atonement for himself and for the people. 25The fat of the sin offering he shall turn into smoke on the altar. 26The one who sets the goat free for Azazelv shall wash his clothes and bathe his body in water, and afterward may come into the camp. 27The bull of the sin offering and the goat of the sin offering, whose blood was brought in to make atonement in the holy place, shall be taken outside the camp; their skin and their flesh and their dung shall be consumed in fire. 28The one who burns them shall wash his clothes and bathe his body in water, and afterward may come into the camp.

29 This shall be a statute to you forever: In the seventh month, on the tenth day of the month, you shall deny yourselves,w and shall do no work, neither the citizen nor the alien who resides among you. 30For on this day atonement shall be made for you, to cleanse you; from all your sins you shall be clean before the LORD. 31It is a sabbath of complete rest to you, and you shall deny yourselves;w it is a statute forever. 32The priest who is anointed and consecrated as priest in his father's place shall make atonement, wearing the linen vest-

ments, the holy vestments. 33He shall make atonement for the sanctuary, and he shall make atonement for the tent of meeting and for the altar, and he shall make atonement for the priests and for all the people of the assembly. 34This shall be an everlasting statute for you, to make atonement for the people of Israel once in the year for all their sins. And Moses did as the LORD had commanded him.

The Slaughtering of Animals

17 The LORD spoke to Moses: 2 Speak to Aaron and his sons and to all the people of Israel and say to them: This is what the LORD has commanded. 3If anyone of the house of Israel slaughters an ox or a lamb or a goat in the camp, or slaughters it outside the camp, 4and does not bring it to the entrance of the tent of meeting, to present it as an offering to the LORD before the tabernacle of the LORD, he shall be held guilty of bloodshed; he has shed blood, and he shall be cut off from the people. 5This is in order that the people of Israel may bring their sacrifices that they offer in the open field, that they may bring them to the LORD, to the priest at the entrance of the tent of meeting, and offer them as sacrifices of well-being to the LORD. 6The priest shall dash the blood against the altar of the LORD at the entrance of the tent of meeting, and turn the fat into smoke as a pleasing odor to the LORD, 7so that they may no longer offer their sacrifices for goat-demons, to whom they prostitute themselves. This shall be a statute forever to them throughout their generations.

8 And say to them further: Anyone of the house of Israel or of the aliens who reside among them who offers a burnt offering or sacrifice, 9and does not bring it to the entrance of the tent of meeting, to sacrifice it to the LORD, shall be cut off from the people.

Eating Blood Prohibited

10 If anyone of the house of Israel or of the aliens who reside among them eats any blood, I will set my face against that person who eats blood, and will cut that person off from the people. 11For

the life of the flesh is in the blood; and I have given it to you for making atonement for your lives on the altar; for, as life, it is the blood that makes atonement. [12]Therefore I have said to the people of Israel: No person among you shall eat blood, nor shall any alien who resides among you eat blood. [13]And anyone of the people of Israel, or of the aliens who reside among them, who hunts down an animal or bird that may be eaten shall pour out its blood and cover it with earth.

[14] For the life of every creature—its blood is its life; therefore I have said to the people of Israel: You shall not eat the blood of any creature, for the life of every creature is its blood; whoever eats it shall be cut off. [15]All persons, citizens or aliens, who eat what dies of itself or

THURSDAY

NOT WITHOUT BLOOD
Andrew Murray

VERSE: Leviticus 17.11   PASSAGE: Leviticus 17.10–12

 od has made more than one covenant with man, but ever, not without blood! And why? . . . The life is in the blood. The blood shed is the token of death, life taken away . . . The shed blood sprinkled upon the altar, or the person, is the proof that death has been endured, that the penalty of the transgressions, for which atonement is being made, has been borne. In some cases the hands were laid upon the head of the sacrifice, confessing over it, and laying upon it, the sin to be atoned for. The shed blood upon the altar was the pledge that God accepted the death of the substitute: the sins were covered by the blood, and the guilty one restored to God's favor . . .

Not without blood! This is the wondrous note that rings through all Scripture, from Abel's sacrifice at the gate of paradise to the song of the ransomed in Revelation (see Genesis 4.4; Revelation 7.14). God is willing to receive fallen man back again to his fellowship, to admit him to his heart and his love, to make a covenant with him, to give full assurance of all this; but—not without blood. Even his own Son, the almighty and all-perfect One, the gift of his eternal love, even he could only redeem us, by the sacrifice of himself . . .

Not without blood! In earth and heaven, in each moment of our life, in each thought and act of worship, this word reigns supreme. There can be no fellowship with God, but in the blood, in the death, of his blessed Son.

ADDITIONAL SCRIPTURE READING:
Deuteronomy 12.23–27; Hebrews 9.18–22

Go to page 135 for your next devotional reading.

1700   1900

what has been torn by wild animals, shall wash their clothes, and bathe themselves in water, and be unclean until the evening; then they shall be clean. 16But if they do not wash themselves or bathe their body, they shall bear their guilt.

Sexual Relations

18 The LORD spoke to Moses, saying:
2 Speak to the people of Israel and say to them: I am the LORD your God. 3You shall not do as they do in the land of Egypt, where you lived, and you shall not do as they do in the land of Canaan, to which I am bringing you. You shall not follow their statutes. 4My ordinances you shall observe and my statutes you shall keep, following them: I am the LORD your God. 5You shall keep my statutes and my ordinances; by doing so one shall live: I am the LORD.

6 None of you shall approach anyone near of kin to uncover nakedness: I am the LORD. 7You shall not uncover the nakedness of your father, which is the nakedness of your mother; she is your mother, you shall not uncover her nakedness. 8You shall not uncover the nakedness of your father's wife; it is the nakedness of your father. 9You shall not uncover the nakedness of your sister, your father's daughter or your mother's daughter, whether born at home or born abroad. 10You shall not uncover the nakedness of your son's daughter or of your daughter's daughter, for their nakedness is your own nakedness. 11You shall not uncover the nakedness of your father's wife's daughter, begotten by your father, since she is your sister. 12You shall not uncover the nakedness of your father's sister; she is your father's flesh. 13You shall not uncover the nakedness of your mother's sister, for she is your mother's flesh. 14You shall not uncover the nakedness of your father's brother, that is, you shall not approach his wife; she is your aunt. 15You shall not uncover the nakedness of your daughter-in-law: she is your son's wife; you shall not uncover her nakedness. 16You shall not uncover the nakedness of your brother's wife; it is

your brother's nakedness. 17You shall not uncover the nakedness of a woman and her daughter, and you shall not take*x* her son's daughter or her daughter's daughter to uncover her nakedness; they are your*y* flesh; it is depravity. 18And you shall not take*x* a woman as a rival to her sister, uncovering her nakedness while her sister is still alive.

19 You shall not approach a woman to uncover her nakedness while she is in her menstrual uncleanness. 20You shall not have sexual relations with your kinsman's wife, and defile yourself with her. 21You shall not give any of your offspring to sacrifice them*z* to Molech, and so profane the name of your God: I am the LORD. 22You shall not lie with a male as with a woman; it is an abomination. 23You shall not have sexual relations with any animal and defile yourself with it, nor shall any woman give herself to an animal to have sexual relations with it: it is perversion.

24 Do not defile yourselves in any of these ways, for by all these practices the nations I am casting out before you have defiled themselves. 25Thus the land became defiled; and I punished it for its iniquity, and the land vomited out its inhabitants. 26But you shall keep my statutes and my ordinances and commit none of these abominations, either the citizen or the alien who resides among you 27(for the inhabitants of the land, who were before you, committed all of these abominations, and the land became defiled); 28otherwise the land will vomit you out for defiling it, as it vomited out the nation that was before you. 29For whoever commits any of these abominations shall be cut off from their people. 30So keep my charge not to commit any of these abominations that were done before you, and not to defile yourselves by them: I am the LORD your God.

Ritual and Moral Holiness

19 The LORD spoke to Moses, saying:
2 Speak to all the congregation of the people of Israel and say to them: You shall be holy, for I the LORD your God am holy. 3You shall each revere your

---

x Or *marry*   y Gk: Heb lacks *your*   z Heb *to pass them over*

mother and father, and you shall keep my sabbaths: I am the LORD your God. 4Do not turn to idols or make cast images for yourselves: I am the LORD your God.

5 When you offer a sacrifice of well-being to the LORD, offer it in such a way that it is acceptable in your behalf. 6It shall be eaten on the same day you offer it, or on the next day; and anything left over until the third day shall be consumed in fire. 7If it is eaten at all on the third day, it is an abomination; it will not be acceptable. 8All who eat it shall be subject to punishment, because they have profaned what is holy to the LORD; and any such person shall be cut off from the people.

9 When you reap the harvest of your land, you shall not reap to the very edges of your field, or gather the gleanings of your harvest. 10You shall not strip your vineyard bare, or gather the fallen grapes of your vineyard; you shall leave them for the poor and the alien: I am the LORD your God.

11 You shall not steal; you shall not deal falsely; and you shall not lie to one another. 12And you shall not swear falsely by my name, profaning the name of your God: I am the LORD.

13 You shall not defraud your neighbor; you shall not steal; and you shall not keep for yourself the wages of a laborer until morning. 14You shall not revile the deaf or put a stumbling block before the blind; you shall fear your God: I am the LORD.

15 You shall not render an unjust judgment; you shall not be partial to the poor or defer to the great: with justice you shall judge your neighbor. 16You shall not go around as a slanderera among your people, and you shall not

---

HOW SELDOM WE WEIGH OUR NEIGHBOR IN THE SAME BALANCE WITH OURSELVES.

—*Thomas à Kempis*

---

profit by the bloodb of your neighbor: I am the LORD.

17 You shall not hate in your heart

anyone of your kin; you shall reprove your neighbor, or you will incur guilt yourself. 18You shall not take vengeance or bear a grudge against any of your people, but you shall love your neighbor as yourself: I am the LORD.

19 You shall keep my statutes. You shall not let your animals breed with a different kind; you shall not sow your field with two kinds of seed; nor shall you put on a garment made of two different materials.

20 If a man has sexual relations with a woman who is a slave, designated for another man but not ransomed or given her freedom, an inquiry shall be held. They shall not be put to death, since she has not been freed; 21but he shall bring a guilt offering for himself to the LORD, at the entrance of the tent of meeting, a ram as guilt offering. 22And the priest shall make atonement for him with the ram of guilt offering before the LORD for his sin that he committed; and the sin he committed shall be forgiven him.

23 When you come into the land and plant all kinds of trees for food, then you shall regard their fruit as forbidden;c three years it shall be forbiddend to you, it must not be eaten. 24In the fourth year all their fruit shall be set apart for rejoicing in the LORD. 25But in the fifth year you may eat of their fruit, that their yield may be increased for you: I am the LORD your God.

26 You shall not eat anything with its blood. You shall not practice augury or witchcraft. 27You shall not round off the hair on your temples or mar the edges of your beard. 28You shall not make any gashes in your flesh for the dead or tattoo any marks upon you: I am the LORD.

29 Do not profane your daughter by making her a prostitute, that the land not become prostituted and full of depravity. 30You shall keep my sabbaths and reverence my sanctuary: I am the LORD.

31 Do not turn to mediums or wizards; do not seek them out, to be defiled by them: I am the LORD your God.

32 You shall rise before the aged, and defer to the old; and you shall fear your God: I am the LORD.

---

a Meaning of Heb uncertain   b Heb *stand against the blood*   c Heb *as their uncircumcision*
d Heb *uncircumcision*

THE PROBLEM OF SELF-LOVE
François Fénelon

VERSE: Leviticus 19.18   **PASSAGE:** Leviticus 19.11–18

 elf-love must be uprooted, and the love of God take its place in our hearts before we can see ourselves as we are. Then the same principle that enables us to see our imperfections will destroy them. When the light of truth has risen within us, then we see clearly what is there. Then we love ourselves without partiality, without flattery, as we love our neighbor. In the meantime, God spares us by revealing our weakness to us just in proportion as our strength to support the view of it increases. We discover our imperfections one by one as we are able to cure them. Without this merciful preparation that adapts our strength to the light within, we should be in despair. Those who correct others ought to watch the moment when God touches their hearts; they must bear a fault with patience till they perceive his spirit reproaching them within. Then they must follow his providence that gently reproaches them, so that they may feel that it is less God than their own hearts that condemns them. When we blame with impatience because we are displeased with the fault, it is a human censure and not the disapprobation of God. It is a sensitive self-love that cannot forgive the self-love of others. The more self-love we have, the more severe are our censures. There is nothing so vexatious as the collisions between one excessive self-love and another still more violent and sensitive. The passions of others are infinitely ridiculous to those who are under the dominion of their own. The ways of God are very different. He is ever full of kindness for us, he gives us strength, he regards us with pity and condescension, he remembers our weakness, he waits for us. The less we love ourselves, the more considerate we are of others. We wait for providence to give the occasion, and grace to open their hearts to receive it. If you would gather the fruit before its time, you lose it entirely.

ADDITIONAL SCRIPTURE READING:
Mark 12.31–34; Luke 10.27–37; Romans 13.9–10

Go to page 138 for your next devotional reading.

1500   1700

33 When an alien resides with you in your land, you shall not oppress the alien. 34The alien who resides with you shall be to you as the citizen among you; you shall love the alien as yourself, for you were aliens in the land of Egypt: I am the LORD your God.

35 You shall not cheat in measuring length, weight, or quantity. 36You shall have honest balances, honest weights, an honest ephah, and an honest hin: I am the LORD your God, who brought you out of the land of Egypt. 37You shall keep all my statutes and all my ordinances, and observe them: I am the LORD.

Penalties for Violations of Holiness

20 The LORD spoke to Moses, saying: 2Say further to the people of Israel:

Any of the people of Israel, or of the aliens who reside in Israel, who give any of their offspring to Molech shall be put to death; the people of the land shall stone them to death. 3I myself will set my face against them, and will cut them off from the people, because they have given of their offspring to Molech, defiling my sanctuary and profaning my holy name. 4And if the people of the land should ever close their eyes to them, when they give of their offspring to Molech, and do not put them to death, 5I myself will set my face against them and against their family, and will cut them off from among their people, them and all who follow them in prostituting themselves to Molech.

6 If any turn to mediums and wizards, prostituting themselves to them, I will set my face against them, and will cut them off from the people. 7Consecrate yourselves therefore, and be holy; for I am the LORD your God. 8Keep my statutes, and observe them; I am the LORD; I sanctify you. 9All who curse father or mother shall be put to death; having cursed father or mother, their blood is upon them.

10 If a man commits adultery with the wife ofe his neighbor, both the adulterer and the adulteress shall be put to death. 11The man who lies with his father's wife has uncovered his father's nakedness; both of them shall be put to

death; their blood is upon them. 12If a man lies with his daughter-in-law, both of them shall be put to death; they have committed perversion, their blood is upon them. 13If a man lies with a male as with a woman, both of them have committed an abomination; they shall be put to death; their blood is upon them. 14If a man takes a wife and her mother also, it is depravity; they shall be burned to death, both he and they, that there may be no depravity among you. 15If a man has sexual relations with an animal, he shall be put to death; and you shall kill the animal. 16If a woman approaches any animal and has sexual relations with it, you shall kill the woman and the animal; they shall be put to death, their blood is upon them.

17 If a man takes his sister, a daughter of his father or a daughter of his mother, and sees her nakedness, and she sees his nakedness, it is a disgrace, and they shall be cut off in the sight of their people; he has uncovered his sister's nakedness, he shall be subject to punishment. 18If a man lies with a woman having her sickness and uncovers her nakedness, he has laid bare her flow and she has laid bare her flow of blood; both of them shall be cut off from their people. 19You shall not uncover the nakedness of your mother's sister or of your father's sister, for that is to lay bare one's own flesh; they shall be subject to punishment. 20If a man lies with his uncle's wife, he has uncovered his uncle's nakedness; they shall be subject to punishment; they shall die childless. 21If a man takes his brother's wife, it is impurity; he has uncovered his brother's nakedness; they shall be childless.

22 You shall keep all my statutes and all my ordinances, and observe them, so that the land to which I bring you to settle in may not vomit you out. 23You shall not follow the practices of the nation that I am driving out before you. Because they did all these things, I abhorred them. 24But I have said to you: You shall inherit their land, and I will give it to you to possess, a land flowing with milk and honey. I am the LORD your God; I have separated you from the peoples. 25You shall therefore make a

e Heb repeats if a man commits adultery with the wife of

distinction between the clean animal and the unclean, and between the unclean bird and the clean; you shall not bring abomination on yourselves by animal or by bird or by anything with which the ground teems, which I have set apart for you to hold unclean. 26You shall be holy to me; for I the LORD am holy, and I have separated you from the other peoples to be mine.

27 A man or a woman who is a medium or a wizard shall be put to death; they shall be stoned to death, their blood is upon them.

The Holiness of Priests

21 The LORD said to Moses: Speak to the priests, the sons of Aaron, and say to them:

No one shall defile himself for a dead person among his relatives, 2except for his nearest kin: his mother, his father, his son, his daughter, his brother; 3likewise, for a virgin sister, close to him because she has had no husband, he may defile himself for her. 4But he shall not defile himself as a husband among his people and so profane himself. 5They shall not make bald spots upon their heads, or shave off the edges of their beards, or make any gashes in their flesh. 6They shall be holy to their God, and not profane the name of their God; for they offer the LORD's offerings by fire, the food of their God; therefore they shall be holy. 7They shall not marry a prostitute or a woman who has been defiled; neither shall they marry a woman divorced from her husband. For they are holy to their God, 8and you shall treat them as holy, since they offer the food of your God; they shall be holy to you, for I the LORD, I who sanctify you, am holy. 9When the daughter of a priest profanes herself through prostitution, she profanes her father; she shall be burned to death.

10 The priest who is exalted above his fellows, on whose head the anointing oil has been poured and who has been consecrated to wear the vestments, shall not dishevel his hair, nor tear his vestments. 11He shall not go where there is a dead body; he shall not defile himself even for his father or mother.

12He shall not go outside the sanctuary and thus profane the sanctuary of his God; for the consecration of the anointing oil of his God is upon him: I am the LORD. 13He shall marry only a woman who is a virgin. 14A widow, or a divorced woman, or a woman who has been defiled, a prostitute, these he shall not marry. He shall marry a virgin of his own kin, 15that he may not profane his offspring among his kin; for I am the LORD; I sanctify him.

16 The LORD spoke to Moses, saying: 17Speak to Aaron and say: No one of your offspring throughout their generations who has a blemish may approach to offer the food of his God. 18For no one who has a blemish shall draw near, one who is blind or lame, or one who has a mutilated face or a limb too long, 19or one who has a broken foot or a broken hand, 20or a hunchback, or a dwarf, or a man with a blemish in his eyes or an itching disease or scabs or crushed testicles. 21No descendant of Aaron the priest who has a blemish shall come near to offer the LORD's offerings by fire; since he has a blemish, he shall not come near to offer the food of his God. 22He may eat the food of his God, of the most holy as well as of the holy. 23But he shall not come near the curtain or approach the altar, because he has a blemish, that he may not profane my sanctuaries; for I am the LORD; I sanctify them. 24Thus Moses spoke to Aaron and to his sons and to all the people of Israel.

The Use of Holy Offerings

22 The LORD spoke to Moses, saying: 2Direct Aaron and his sons to deal carefully with the sacred donations of the people of Israel, which they dedicate to me, so that they may not profane my holy name; I am the LORD. 3Say to them: If anyone among all your offspring throughout your generations comes near the sacred donations, which the people of Israel dedicate to the LORD, while he is in a state of uncleanness, that person shall be cut off from my presence: I am the LORD. 4No one of Aaron's offspring who has a leprous*f* disease or suffers a discharge may eat of the sacred donations until he is

f A term for several skin diseases; precise meaning uncertain

WEEKEND

THE PILLAR OF THE CLOUD
Cardinal John Henry Newman

VERSE: Exodus 13.21   **PASSAGE:** Exodus 13.17–22

ead, kindly light, amid the circling gloom,
    Lead thou me on!
The night is dark, and I am far from home—
    Lead thou me on!
Keep thou my feet; I do not ask to see
The distant scene,—one step enough for me.

I was not ever thus, nor prayed that thou
    Shouldest lead me on!
I loved to choose and see my path; but now
    Lead thou me on!
I loved the garish day, and, spite of fears,
Pride ruled my will: remember not past years.

So long thy power hast blest me, sure it still
    Will lead me on,
O'er moor and fen, o'er crag and torrent, till
    The night is gone;
And with the morn those angel faces smile
Which I have loved long since, and lost awhile.

ADDITIONAL SCRIPTURE READING:
Exodus 14.19–24; Numbers 9.15–23; Psalm 105.39–45

Go to page 143 for your next devotional reading.

1700   1900

clean. Whoever touches anything made unclean by a corpse or a man who has had an emission of semen, 5and whoever touches any swarming thing by which he may be made unclean or any human being by whom he may be made unclean—whatever his uncleanness may be— 6the person who touches any such shall be unclean until evening and shall not eat of the sacred donations unless he has washed his body in water. 7When the sun sets he shall be clean; and afterward he may eat of the sacred donations, for they are his food. 8That which died or was torn by wild animals he shall not eat, becoming unclean by it: I am the LORD. 9They shall keep my charge, so that they may not incur guilt and die in the sanctuary8 for having profaned it: I am the LORD; I sanctify them.

10 No lay person shall eat of the sacred donations. No bound or hired servant of the priest shall eat of the sacred donations; 11but if a priest acquires anyone by purchase, the person may eat of them; and those that are born in his house may eat of his food. 12If a priest's daughter marries a layman, she shall not eat of the offering of the sacred donations; 13but if a priest's daughter is widowed or divorced, without offspring, and returns to her father's house, as in her youth, she may eat of her father's food. No lay person shall eat of it. 14If a man eats of the sacred donation unintentionally, he shall add one-fifth of its value to it, and give the sacred donation to the priest. 15No one shall profane the sacred donations of the people of Israel, which they offer to the LORD, 16causing them to bear guilt requiring a guilt offering, by eating their sacred donations: for I am the LORD; I sanctify them.

Acceptable Offerings

17 The LORD spoke to Moses, saying: 18Speak to Aaron and his sons and all the people of Israel and say to them: When anyone of the house of Israel or of the aliens residing in Israel presents an offering, whether in payment of a vow or as a freewill offering that is offered to the LORD as a burnt offering, 19to be acceptable in your behalf it shall be a male without blemish, of the cattle or the sheep or the goats. 20You shall not offer anything that has a blemish, for it will not be acceptable in your behalf.

21 When anyone offers a sacrifice of well-being to the LORD, in fulfillment of a vow or as a freewill offering, from the herd or from the flock, to be acceptable it must be perfect; there shall be no blemish in it. 22Anything blind, or injured, or maimed, or having a discharge or an itch or scabs—these you shall not offer to the LORD or put any of them on the altar as offerings by fire to the LORD. 23An ox or a lamb that has a limb too long or too short you may present for a freewill offering; but it will not be accepted for a vow. 24Any animal that has its testicles bruised or crushed or torn or cut, you shall not offer to the LORD; such you shall not do within your land, 25nor shall you accept any such animals from a foreigner to offer as food to your God; since they are mutilated, with a blemish in them, they shall not be accepted in your behalf.

26 The LORD spoke to Moses, saying: 27When an ox or a sheep or a goat is born, it shall remain seven days with its mother, and from the eighth day on it shall be acceptable as the LORD's offering by fire. 28But you shall not slaughter, from the herd or the flock, an animal with its young on the same day. 29When you sacrifice a thanksgiving offering to the LORD, you shall sacrifice it so that it may be acceptable in your behalf. 30It shall be eaten on the same day; you shall not leave any of it until morning: I am the LORD.

31 Thus you shall keep my commandments and observe them: I am the LORD. 32You shall not profane my holy name, that I may be sanctified among the people of Israel: I am the LORD; I sanctify you, 33I who brought you out of the land of Egypt to be your God: I am the LORD.

Appointed Festivals

23 The LORD spoke to Moses, saying: 2Speak to the people of Israel and say to them: These are the appointed festivals of the LORD that you shall proclaim as holy convocations, my appointed festivals.

g Vg: Heb incur guilt for it and die in it

The Sabbath, Passover, and Unleavened Bread

3 Six days shall work be done; but the seventh day is a sabbath of complete rest, a holy convocation; you shall do no work: it is a sabbath to the LORD throughout your settlements.

4 These are the appointed festivals of the LORD, the holy convocations, which you shall celebrate at the time appointed for them. 5In the first month, on the fourteenth day of the month, at twilight,h there shall be a passover offering to the LORD, 6and on the fifteenth day of the same month is the festival of unleavened bread to the LORD; seven days you shall eat unleavened bread. 7On the first day you shall have a holy convocation; you shall not work at your occupations. 8For seven days you shall present the LORD's offerings by fire; on the seventh day there shall be a holy convocation: you shall not work at your occupations.

The Offering of First Fruits

9 The LORD spoke to Moses: 10Speak to the people of Israel and say to them: When you enter the land that I am giving you and you reap its harvest, you shall bring the sheaf of the first fruits of your harvest to the priest. 11He shall raise the sheaf before the LORD, that you may find acceptance; on the day after the sabbath the priest shall raise it. 12On the day when you raise the sheaf, you shall offer a lamb a year old, without blemish, as a burnt offering to the LORD. 13And the grain offering with it shall be two-tenths of an ephah of choice flour mixed with oil, an offering by fire of pleasing odor to the LORD; and the drink offering with it shall be of wine, one-fourth of a hin. 14You shall eat no bread or parched grain or fresh ears until that very day, until you have brought the offering of your God: it is a statute forever throughout your generations in all your settlements.

The Festival of Weeks

15 And from the day after the sabbath, from the day on which you bring the sheaf of the elevation offering, you

shall count off seven weeks; they shall be complete. 16You shall count until the day after the seventh sabbath, fifty days; then you shall present an offering of new grain to the LORD. 17You shall bring from your settlements two loaves of bread as an elevation offering, each made of two-tenths of an ephah; they shall be of choice flour, baked with leaven, as first fruits to the LORD. 18You shall present with the bread seven lambs a year old without blemish, one young bull, and two rams; they shall be a burnt offering to the LORD, along with their grain offering and their drink offerings, an offering by fire of pleasing odor to the LORD. 19You shall also offer one male goat for a sin offering, and two male lambs a year old as a sacrifice of well-being. 20The priest shall raise them with the bread of the first fruits as an elevation offering before the LORD, together with the two lambs; they shall be holy to the LORD for the priest. 21On that same day you shall make proclamation; you shall hold a holy convocation; you shall not work at your occupations. This is a statute forever in all your settlements throughout your generations.

22 When you reap the harvest of your land, you shall not reap to the very edges of your field, or gather the gleanings of your harvest; you shall leave them for the poor and for the alien: I am the LORD your God.

The Festival of Trumpets

23 The LORD spoke to Moses, saying: 24Speak to the people of Israel, saying: In the seventh month, on the first day of the month, you shall observe a day of complete rest, a holy convocation commemorated with trumpet blasts. 25You shall not work at your occupations; and you shall present the LORD's offering by fire.

The Day of Atonement

26 The LORD spoke to Moses, saying: 27Now, the tenth day of this seventh month is the day of atonement; it shall be a holy convocation for you: you shall deny yourselvesi and present the LORD's offering by fire; 28and you shall do no work during that entire day; for it is a

h Heb between the two evenings   i Or shall fast

day of atonement, to make atonement on your behalf before the LORD your God. 29For anyone who does not practice self-denial[j] during that entire day shall be cut off from the people. 30And anyone who does any work during that entire day, such a one I will destroy from the midst of the people. 31You shall do no work: it is a statute forever throughout your generations in all your settlements. 32It shall be to you a sabbath of complete rest, and you shall deny yourselves;[k] on the ninth day of the month at evening, from evening to evening you shall keep your sabbath.

The Festival of Booths

33 The LORD spoke to Moses, saying: 34Speak to the people of Israel, saying: On the fifteenth day of this seventh month, and lasting seven days, there shall be the festival of booths[l] to the LORD. 35The first day shall be a holy convocation; you shall not work at your occupations. 36Seven days you shall present the LORD's offerings by fire; on the eighth day you shall observe a holy convocation and present the LORD's offerings by fire; it is a solemn assembly; you shall not work at your occupations.

37 These are the appointed festivals of the LORD, which you shall celebrate as times of holy convocation, for presenting to the LORD offerings by fire— burnt offerings and grain offerings, sacrifices and drink offerings, each on its proper day— 38apart from the sabbaths of the LORD, and apart from your gifts, and apart from all your votive offerings, and apart from all your freewill offerings, which you give to the LORD.

39 Now, the fifteenth day of the seventh month, when you have gathered in the produce of the land, you shall keep the festival of the LORD, lasting seven days; a complete rest on the first day, and a complete rest on the eighth day. 40On the first day you shall take the fruit of majestic[m] trees, branches of palm trees, boughs of leafy trees, and willows of the brook; and you shall rejoice before the LORD your God for seven days. 41You shall keep it as a festival to the LORD seven days in the year; you shall keep it

in the seventh month as a statute forever throughout your generations. 42You shall live in booths for seven days; all that are citizens in Israel shall live in booths, 43so that your generations may know that I made the people of Israel live in booths when I brought them out of the land of Egypt: I am the LORD your God.

44 Thus Moses declared to the people of Israel the appointed festivals of the LORD.

The Lamp

24 The LORD spoke to Moses, saying: 2Command the people of Israel to bring you pure oil of beaten olives for the lamp, that a light may be kept burning regularly. 3Aaron shall set it up in the tent of meeting, outside the curtain of the covenant,[n] to burn from evening to morning before the LORD regularly; it shall be a statute forever throughout your generations. 4He shall set up the lamps on the lampstand of pure gold[o] before the LORD regularly.

The Bread for the Tabernacle

5 You shall take choice flour, and bake twelve loaves of it; two-tenths of an ephah shall be in each loaf. 6You shall place them in two rows, six in a row, on the table of pure gold.[p] 7You shall put pure frankincense with each row, to be a token offering for the bread, as an offering by fire to the LORD. 8Every sabbath day Aaron shall set them in order before the LORD regularly as a commitment of the people of Israel, as a covenant forever. 9They shall be for Aaron and his descendants, who shall eat them in a holy place, for they are most holy portions for him from the offerings by fire to the LORD, a perpetual due.

Blasphemy and Its Punishment

10 A man whose mother was an Israelite and whose father was an Egyptian came out among the people of Israel; and the Israelite woman's son and a certain Israelite began fighting in the camp. 11The Israelite woman's son blasphemed the Name in a curse. And they brought him to Moses—now his mother's name was Shelomith, daughter of Dibri, of the

---

j Or does not fast   k Or shall fast   l Or tabernacles: Heb succoth   m Meaning of Heb uncertain
n Or treaty, or testament; Heb eduth   o Heb pure lampstand   p Heb pure table

tribe of Dan— ¹²and they put him in custody, until the decision of the LORD should be made clear to them.

13 The LORD said to Moses, saying: ¹⁴Take the blasphemer outside the camp; and let all who were within hearing lay their hands on his head, and let the whole congregation stone him. ¹⁵And speak to the people of Israel, saying: Anyone who curses God shall bear the sin. ¹⁶One who blasphemes the name of the LORD shall be put to death; the whole congregation shall stone the blasphemer. Aliens as well as citizens, when they blaspheme the Name, shall be put to death. ¹⁷Anyone who kills a human being shall be put to death. ¹⁸Anyone who kills an animal shall make restitution for it, life for life. ¹⁹Anyone who maims another shall suffer the same injury in return: ²⁰fracture for fracture, eye for eye, tooth for tooth; the injury inflicted is the injury to be suffered. ²¹One who kills an animal shall make restitution for it; but one who kills a human being shall be put to death. ²²You shall have one law for the alien and for the citizen: for I am the LORD your God. ²³Moses spoke thus to the people of Israel; and they took the blasphemer outside the camp, and stoned him to death. The people of Israel did as the LORD had commanded Moses.

The Sabbatical Year

25 The LORD spoke to Moses on Mount Sinai, saying: ²Speak to the people of Israel and say to them: When you enter the land that I am giving you, the land shall observe a sabbath for the LORD. ³Six years you shall sow your field, and six years you shall prune your vineyard, and gather in their yield; ⁴but in the seventh year there shall be a sabbath of complete rest for the land, a sabbath for the LORD: you shall not sow your field or prune your vineyard. ⁵You shall not reap the aftergrowth of your harvest or gather the grapes of your unpruned vine: it shall be a year of complete rest for the land. ⁶You may eat what the land yields during its sabbath—you, your male and female slaves, your hired and your bound laborers who

live with you; ⁷for your livestock also, and for the wild animals in your land all its yield shall be for food.

The Year of Jubilee

8 You shall count off seven weeks^q of years, seven times seven years, so that the period of seven weeks of years gives forty-nine years. ⁹Then you shall have the trumpet sounded loud; on the tenth day of the seventh month—on the day of atonement—you shall have the trumpet sounded throughout all your land. ¹⁰And you shall hallow the fiftieth year and you shall proclaim liberty throughout the land to all its inhabitants. It shall be a jubilee for you: you shall return, every one of you, to your property and every one of you to your family. ¹¹That fiftieth year shall be a jubilee for you: you shall not sow, or reap the aftergrowth, or harvest the unpruned vines. ¹²For it is a jubilee; it shall be holy to you: you shall eat only what the field itself produces.

13 In this year of jubilee you shall return, every one of you, to your property. ¹⁴When you make a sale to your neighbor or buy from your neighbor, you shall not cheat one another. ¹⁵When you buy from your neighbor, you shall pay only for the number of years since the jubilee; the seller shall charge you only for the remaining crop years. ¹⁶If the years are more, you shall increase the price, and if the years are fewer, you shall diminish the price; for it is a certain number of harvests that are being sold to you. ¹⁷You shall not cheat one another, but you shall fear your God; for I am the LORD your God.

18 You shall observe my statutes and faithfully keep my ordinances, so that you may live on the land securely. ¹⁹The land will yield its fruit, and you will eat your fill and live on it securely. ²⁰Should you ask, "What shall we eat in the seventh year, if we may not sow or gather in our crop?" ²¹I will order my blessing for you in the sixth year, so that it will yield a crop for three years. ²²When you sow in the eighth year, you will be eating from the old crop; until the ninth year, when its produce comes in, you shall eat the old. ²³The land shall not be

q Or sabbaths

UNCEASING DEPENDENCE—CONTINUAL PEACE

François Fénelon

VERSE: Leviticus 25.21   PASSAGE: Leviticus 25.18–22

o not dwell upon remote events; this anxiety about the future is contrary to a religious state of mind. When God bestows any blessings upon you, look only to him in the comfort that you receive, and take every day of the manna that he sends you, as the Israelites did, without making yourself any provision for the morrow.

A life of faith produces two things. First, it enables us to see God in everything. Secondly, it holds the mind in a state of readiness for whatever may be his will. We must trust to God for whatever depends upon him, and only think of being faithful ourselves in the performance of our duties. This continual, unceasing dependence, this state of entire peace and acquiescence of the soul in whatever may happen, is the true, silent martyrdom of self. It is so slow, and gradual, and internal, that they who experience it are hardly conscious of it.

When God deprives you of any blessing, he can replace it either by other instruments or by himself. The very stones can in his hands become the children of Abraham. Sufficient for the day is the evil thereof; the morrow will take care of itself (see Matthew 6.34). He who has fed you today will take care of you tomorrow.

We shall sooner see the manna fall from heaven in the desert than the children of God shall want support.

Meditation

I sleep, but my heart waketh.

We sleep in peace in the arms of God when we yield ourselves up to his providence in a delightful consciousness of his tender mercies; no more restless uncertainties, no more anxious desires, no more impatience at the place we are in; for it is God who has put us there and who holds us in his arms. Can we be unsafe where he has placed us, and where he watches over us as a parent watches a child? This confiding repose, in which earthly care sleeps, is the true vigilance of the heart; yielding itself up to God, with no other support than him, it thus watches while we sleep. This is the love of him that will not sleep even in death. Amen.

ADDITIONAL SCRIPTURE READING:
Jeremiah 17.7–8; John 14.1; Philippians 4.6–7

Go to page 163 for your next devotional reading.

1500   1700

sold in perpetuity, for the land is mine; with me you are but aliens and tenants. 24Throughout the land that you hold, you shall provide for the redemption of the land.

25 If anyone of your kin falls into difficulty and sells a piece of property, then the next of kin shall come and redeem what the relative has sold. 26If the person has no one to redeem it, but then prospers and finds sufficient means to do so, 27the years since its sale shall be computed and the difference shall be refunded to the person to whom it was sold, and the property shall be returned. 28But if there are not sufficient means to recover it, what was sold shall remain with the purchaser until the year of jubilee; in the jubilee it shall be released, and the property shall be returned.

29 If anyone sells a dwelling house in a walled city, it may be redeemed until a year has elapsed since its sale; the right of redemption shall be one year. 30If it is not redeemed before a full year has elapsed, a house that is in a walled city shall pass in perpetuity to the purchaser, throughout the generations; it shall not be released in the jubilee. 31But houses in villages that have no walls around them shall be classed as open country; they may be redeemed, and they shall be released in the jubilee. 32As for the cities of the Levites, the Levites shall forever have the right of redemption of the houses in the cities belonging to them. 33Such property as may be redeemed from the Levites—houses sold in a city belonging to them—shall be released in the jubilee; because the houses in the cities of the Levites are their possession among the people of Israel. 34But the open land around their cities may not be sold; for that is their possession for all time.

35 If any of your kin fall into difficulty and become dependent on you,r you shall support them; they shall live with you as though resident aliens. 36Do not take interest in advance or otherwise make a profit from them, but fear your God; let them live with you. 37You shall not lend them your money at interest taken in advance, or provide them food at a profit. 38I am the LORD your God,

who brought you out of the land of Egypt, to give you the land of Canaan, to be your God.

39 If any who are dependent on you become so impoverished that they sell themselves to you, you shall not make them serve as slaves. 40They shall remain with you as hired or bound laborers. They shall serve with you until the year of the jubilee. 41Then they and their children with them shall be free from your authority; they shall go back to their own family and return to their ancestral property. 42For they are my servants, whom I brought out of the land of Egypt; they shall not be sold as slaves are sold. 43You shall not rule over them with harshness, but shall fear your God. 44As for the male and female slaves whom you may have, it is from the nations around you that you may acquire male and female slaves. 45You may also acquire them from among the aliens residing with you, and from their families that are with you, who have been born in your land; and they may be your property. 46You may keep them as a possession for your children after you, for them to inherit as property. These you may treat as slaves, but as for your fellow Israelites, no one shall rule over the other with harshness.

47 If resident aliens among you prosper, and if any of your kin fall into difficulty with one of them and sell themselves to an alien, or to a branch of the alien's family, 48after they have sold themselves they shall have the right of redemption; one of their brothers may redeem them, 49or their uncle or their uncle's son may redeem them, or anyone of their family who is of their own flesh may redeem them; or if they prosper they may redeem themselves. 50They shall compute with the purchaser the total from the year when they sold themselves to the alien until the jubilee year; the price of the sale shall be applied to the number of years: the time they were with the owner shall be rated as the time of a hired laborer. 51If many years remain, they shall pay for their redemption in proportion to the purchase price; 52and if few years remain until the jubilee year, they shall compute thus:

r Meaning of Heb uncertain

according to the years involved they shall make payment for their redemption. 53 As a laborer hired by the year they shall be under the alien's authority, who shall not, however, rule with harshness over them in your sight. 54 And if they have not been redeemed in any of these ways, they and their children with them shall go free in the jubilee year. 55 For to me the people of Israel are servants; they are my servants whom I brought out from the land of Egypt: I am the LORD your God.

Rewards for Obedience

26 You shall make for yourselves no idols and erect no carved images or pillars, and you shall not place figured stones in your land, to worship at them; for I am the LORD your God. 2 You shall keep my sabbaths and reverence my sanctuary: I am the LORD.

3 If you follow my statutes and keep my commandments and observe them faithfully, 4 I will give you your rains in their season, and the land shall yield its produce, and the trees of the field shall yield their fruit. 5 Your threshing shall overtake the vintage, and the vintage shall overtake the sowing; you shall eat your bread to the full, and live securely in your land. 6 And I will grant peace in the land, and you shall lie down, and no one shall make you afraid; I will remove dangerous animals from the land, and no sword shall go through your land. 7 You shall give chase to your enemies, and they shall fall before you by the sword. 8 Five of you shall give chase to a hundred, and a hundred of you shall give chase to ten thousand; your enemies shall fall before you by the sword. 9 I will look with favor upon you and make you fruitful and multiply you; and I will maintain my covenant with you. 10 You shall eat old grain long stored, and you shall have to clear out the old to make way for the new. 11 I will place my dwelling in your midst, and I shall not abhor you. 12 And I will walk among you, and will be your God, and you shall be my people. 13 I am the LORD your God who brought you out of the land of Egypt, to be their slaves no more; I have broken the bars of your yoke and made you walk erect.

Penalties for Disobedience

14 But if you will not obey me, and do not observe all these commandments, 15 if you spurn my statutes, and abhor my ordinances, so that you will not observe all my commandments, and you break my covenant, 16 I in turn will do this to you: I will bring terror on you; consumption and fever that waste the eyes and cause life to pine away. You shall sow your seed in vain, for your enemies shall eat it. 17 I will set my face against you, and you shall be struck down by your enemies; your foes shall rule over you, and you shall flee though no one pursues you. 18 And if in spite of this you will not obey me, I will continue to punish you sevenfold for your sins. 19 I will break your proud glory, and I will make your sky like iron and your earth like copper. 20 Your strength shall be spent to no purpose: your land shall not yield its produce, and the trees of the land shall not yield their fruit.

21 If you continue hostile to me, and will not obey me, I will continue to plague you sevenfold for your sins. 22 I will let loose wild animals against you, and they shall bereave you of your children and destroy your livestock; they shall make you few in number, and your roads shall be deserted.

23 If in spite of these punishments you have not turned back to me, but continue hostile to me, 24 then I too will continue hostile to you: I myself will strike you sevenfold for your sins. 25 I will bring the sword against you, executing vengeance for the covenant; and if you withdraw within your cities, I will send pestilence among you, and you shall be delivered into enemy hands. 26 When I break your staff of bread, ten women shall bake your bread in a single oven, and they shall dole out your bread by weight; and though you eat, you shall not be satisfied.

27 But if, despite this, you disobey me, and continue hostile to me, 28 I will continue hostile to you in fury; I in turn will punish you myself sevenfold for your sins. 29 You shall eat the flesh of your sons, and you shall eat the flesh of your daughters. 30 I will destroy your high places and cut down your incense altars; I will heap your carcasses on the

carcasses of your idols. I will abhor you. [31]I will lay your cities waste, will make your sanctuaries desolate, and I will not smell your pleasing odors. [32]I will devastate the land, so that your enemies who come to settle in it shall be appalled at it. [33]And you I will scatter among the nations, and I will unsheathe the sword against you; your land shall be a desolation, and your cities a waste.

34 Then the land shall enjoy[s] its sabbath years as long as it lies desolate, while you are in the land of your enemies; then the land shall rest, and enjoy[s] its sabbath years. [35]As long as it lies desolate, it shall have the rest it did not have on your sabbaths when you were living on it. [36]And as for those of you who survive, I will send faintness into their hearts in the lands of their enemies; the sound of a driven leaf shall put them to flight, and they shall flee as one flees from the sword, and they shall fall though no one pursues. [37]They shall stumble over one another, as if to escape a sword, though no one pursues; and you shall have no power to stand against your enemies. [38]You shall perish among the nations, and the land of your enemies shall devour you. [39]And those of you who survive shall languish in the land of your enemies because of their iniquities; also they shall languish because of the iniquities of their ancestors.

40 But if they confess their iniquity and the iniquity of their ancestors, in that they committed treachery against me and, moreover, that they continued hostile to me— [41]so that I, in turn, continued hostile to them and brought them into the land of their enemies; if then their uncircumcised heart is humbled and they make amends for their iniquity, [42]then will I remember my covenant with Jacob; I will remember also my covenant with Isaac and also my covenant with Abraham, and I will remember the land. [43]For the land shall be deserted by them, and enjoy[s] its sabbath years by lying desolate without them, while they shall make amends for their iniquity, because they dared to spurn my ordinances, and they abhorred my statutes. [44]Yet for all that, when

they are in the land of their enemies, I will not spurn them, or abhor them so as to destroy them utterly and break my covenant with them; for I am the LORD their God; [45]but I will remember in their favor the covenant with their ancestors whom I brought out of the land of Egypt in the sight of the nations, to be their God: I am the LORD.

46 These are the statutes and ordinances and laws that the LORD established between himself and the people of Israel on Mount Sinai through Moses.

Votive Offerings

27 The LORD spoke to Moses, saying: [2]Speak to the people of Israel and say to them: When a person makes an explicit vow to the LORD concerning the equivalent for a human being, [3]the equivalent for a male shall be: from twenty to sixty years of age the equivalent shall be fifty shekels of silver by the sanctuary shekel. [4]If the person is a female, the equivalent is thirty shekels. [5]If the age is from five to twenty years of age, the equivalent is twenty shekels for a male and ten shekels for a female. [6]If the age is from one month to five years, the equivalent for a male is five shekels of silver, and for a female the equivalent is three shekels of silver. [7]And if the person is sixty years old or over, then the equivalent for a male is fifteen shekels, and for a female ten shekels. [8]If any cannot afford the equivalent, they shall be brought before the priest and the priest shall assess them; the priest shall assess them according to what each one making a vow can afford.

9 If it concerns an animal that may be brought as an offering to the LORD, any such that may be given to the LORD shall be holy. [10]Another shall not be exchanged or substituted for it, either good for bad or bad for good; and if one animal is substituted for another, both that one and its substitute shall be holy. [11]If it concerns any unclean animal that may not be brought as an offering to the LORD, the animal shall be presented before the priest. [12]The priest shall assess it: whether good or bad, according to the assessment of the priest, so it shall be. [13]But if it is to be redeemed,

---

s Or make up for

one-fifth must be added to the assessment.

14 If a person consecrates a house to the LORD, the priest shall assess it: whether good or bad, as the priest assesses it, so it shall stand. 15And if the one who consecrates the house wishes to redeem it, one-fifth shall be added to its assessed value, and it shall revert to the original owner.

16 If a person consecrates to the LORD any inherited landholding, its assessment shall be in accordance with its seed requirements: fifty shekels of silver to a homer of barley seed. 17If the person consecrates the field as of the year of jubilee, that assessment shall stand; 18but if the field is consecrated after the jubilee, the priest shall compute the price for it according to the years that remain until the year of jubilee, and the assessment shall be reduced. 19And if the one who consecrates the field wishes to redeem it, then one-fifth shall be added to its assessed value, and it shall revert to the original owner; 20but if the field is not redeemed, or if it has been sold to someone else, it shall no longer be redeemable. 21But when the field is released in the jubilee, it shall be holy to the LORD as a devoted field; it becomes the priest's holding. 22If someone consecrates to the LORD a field that has been purchased, which is not a part of the inherited landholding, 23the priest shall compute for it the proportionate assessment up to the year of jubilee, and the assessment shall be paid as of that day, a sacred donation to the LORD. 24In the year of jubilee the field shall return to the one from whom it was bought, whose holding the land is. 25All assessments shall be by the sanctuary shekel: twenty gerahs shall make a shekel.

26 A firstling of animals, however, which as a firstling belongs to the LORD, cannot be consecrated by anyone; whether ox or sheep, it is the LORD's. 27If it is an unclean animal, it shall be ransomed at its assessment, with one-fifth added; if it is not redeemed, it shall be sold at its assessment.

28 Nothing that a person owns that has been devoted to destruction for the LORD, be it human or animal, or inherited landholding, may be sold or redeemed; every devoted thing is most holy to the LORD. 29No human beings who have been devoted to destruction can be ransomed; they shall be put to death.

30 All tithes from the land, whether the seed from the ground or the fruit from the tree, are the LORD's; they are holy to the LORD. 31If persons wish to redeem any of their tithes, they must add one-fifth to them. 32All tithes of herd and flock, every tenth one that passes under the shepherd's staff, shall be holy to the LORD. 33Let no one inquire whether it is good or bad, or make substitution for it; if one makes substitution for it, then both it and the substitute shall be holy and cannot be redeemed.

34 These are the commandments that the LORD gave to Moses for the people of Israel on Mount Sinai.

NUMBERS

T HE BOOK OF NUMBERS GETS ITS NAME FROM THE TWO NUMBERINGS, OR COUNT- INGS, OF THE PEOPLE OF ISRAEL DURING THEIR YEARS OF WANDERING IN THE DESERT. NUMBERS PRESENTS AN ACCOUNT OF THAT WANDERING FOLLOWING THE ESTABLISHMENT OF THE COVENANT AT SINAI. IT TELLS OF THE MUR- MURING AND REBELLION OF GOD'S PEOPLE AND OF THEIR SUBSEQUENT JUDGMENT. THROUGHOUT THE YEARS IN THE DESERT ONE THING BECAME CLEAR TO ISRAEL—GOD'S CONSTANT CARE FOR THEM. NOT ONLY DID HE MEET THEIR NEEDS BUT HE ALSO LOVED AND CONTINUALLY FORGAVE HIS PEOPLE.

The First Census of Israel

1 The LORD spoke to Moses in the wilderness of Sinai, in the tent of meeting, on the first day of the second month, in the second year after they had come out of the land of Egypt, saying: 2Take a census of the whole congrega- tion of Israelites, in their clans, by ancestral houses, according to the num- ber of names, every male individually; 3from twenty years old and upward, everyone in Israel able to go to war. You and Aaron shall enroll them, company by company. 4A man from each tribe shall be with you, each man the head of his ancestral house. 5These are the names of the men who shall assist you:

From Reuben, Elizur son of Shedeur.

6 From Simeon, Shelumiel son of Zurishaddai.
7 From Judah, Nahshon son of Amminadab.
8 From Issachar, Nethanel son of Zuar.
9 From Zebulun, Eliab son of Helon.
10 From the sons of Joseph:
from Ephraim, Elishama son of Ammihud;
from Manasseh, Gamaliel son of Pedahzur.
11 From Benjamin, Abidan son of Gideoni.
12 From Dan, Ahiezer son of Ammishaddai.
13 From Asher, Pagiel son of Ochran.
14 From Gad, Eliasaph son of Deuel.
15 From Naphtali, Ahira son of Enan.
16These were the ones chosen from the

congregation, the leaders of their ancestral tribes, the heads of the divisions of Israel.

17 Moses and Aaron took these men who had been designated by name, 18and on the first day of the second month they assembled the whole congregation together. They registered themselves in their clans, by their ancestral houses, according to the number of names from twenty years old and upward, individually, 19as the LORD commanded Moses. So he enrolled them in the wilderness of Sinai.

20 The descendants of Reuben, Israel's firstborn, their lineage, in their clans, by their ancestral houses, according to the number of names, individually, every male from twenty years old and upward, everyone able to go to war: 21those enrolled of the tribe of Reuben were forty-six thousand five hundred.

22 The descendants of Simeon, their lineage, in their clans, by their ancestral houses, those of them that were numbered, according to the number of names, individually, every male from twenty years old and upward, everyone able to go to war: 23those enrolled of the tribe of Simeon were fifty-nine thousand three hundred.

24 The descendants of Gad, their lineage, in their clans, by their ancestral houses, according to the number of the names, from twenty years old and upward, everyone able to go to war: 25those enrolled of the tribe of Gad were forty-five thousand six hundred fifty.

26 The descendants of Judah, their lineage, in their clans, by their ancestral houses, according to the number of names, from twenty years old and upward, everyone able to go to war: 27those enrolled of the tribe of Judah were seventy-four thousand six hundred.

28 The descendants of Issachar, their lineage, in their clans, by their ancestral houses, according to the number of names, from twenty years old and upward, everyone able to go to war: 29those enrolled of the tribe of Issachar were fifty-four thousand four hundred.

30 The descendants of Zebulun, their lineage, in their clans, by their ancestral houses, according to the number of names, from twenty years old and upward, everyone able to go to war: 31those enrolled of the tribe of Zebulun were fifty-seven thousand four hundred.

32 The descendants of Joseph, namely, the descendants of Ephraim, their lineage, in their clans, by their ancestral houses, according to the number of names, from twenty years old and upward, everyone able to go to war: 33those enrolled of the tribe of Ephraim were forty thousand five hundred.

34 The descendants of Manasseh, their lineage, in their clans, by their ancestral houses, according to the number of names, from twenty years old and upward, everyone able to go to war: 35those enrolled of the tribe of Manasseh were thirty-two thousand two hundred.

36 The descendants of Benjamin, their lineage, in their clans, by their ancestral houses, according to the number of names, from twenty years old and upward, everyone able to go to war: 37those enrolled of the tribe of Benjamin were thirty-five thousand four hundred.

38 The descendants of Dan, their lineage, in their clans, by their ancestral houses, according to the number of names, from twenty years old and upward, everyone able to go to war: 39those enrolled of the tribe of Dan were sixty-two thousand seven hundred.

40 The descendants of Asher, their lineage, in their clans, by their ancestral houses, according to the number of names, from twenty years old and upward, everyone able to go to war: 41those enrolled of the tribe of Asher were forty-one thousand five hundred.

42 The descendants of Naphtali, their lineage, in their clans, by their ancestral houses, according to the number of names, from twenty years old and upward, everyone able to go to war: 43those enrolled of the tribe of Naphtali were fifty-three thousand four hundred.

44 These are those who were enrolled, whom Moses and Aaron enrolled with the help of the leaders of Israel, twelve men, each representing his ancestral house. 45So the whole number of the Israelites, by their ancestral houses, from twenty years old and upward, everyone able to go to war in Israel— 46their whole number was six

hundred three thousand five hundred fifty. 47The Levites, however, were not numbered by their ancestral tribe along with them.

48 The LORD had said to Moses: 49Only the tribe of Levi you shall not enroll, and you shall not take a census of them with the other Israelites. 50Rather you shall appoint the Levites over the tabernacle of the covenant,a and over all its equipment, and over all that belongs to it; they are to carry the tabernacle and all its equipment, and they shall tend it, and shall camp around the tabernacle. 51When the tabernacle is to set out, the Levites shall take it down; and when the tabernacle is to be pitched, the Levites shall set it up. And any outsider who comes near shall be put to death. 52The other Israelites shall camp in their respective regimental camps, by companies; 53but the Levites shall camp around the tabernacle of the covenant,a that there may be no wrath on the congregation of the Israelites; and the Levites shall perform the guard duty of the tabernacle of the covenant.a 54The Israelites did so; they did just as the LORD commanded Moses.

The Order of Encampment and Marching

2 The LORD spoke to Moses and Aaron, saying: 2The Israelites shall camp each in their respective regiments, under ensigns by their ancestral houses; they shall camp facing the tent of meeting on every side. 3Those to camp on the east side toward the sunrise shall be of the regimental encampment of Judah by companies. The leader of the people of Judah shall be Nahshon son of Amminadab, 4with a company as enrolled of seventy-four thousand six hundred. 5Those to camp next to him shall be the tribe of Issachar. The leader of the Issacharites shall be Nethanel son of Zuar, 6with a company as enrolled of fifty-four thousand four hundred. 7Then the tribe of Zebulun: The leader of the Zebulunites shall be Eliab son of Helon, 8with a company as enrolled of fifty-seven thousand four hundred. 9The total enrollment of the camp of Judah, by companies, is one hundred eighty-six

thousand four hundred. They shall set out first on the march.

10 On the south side shall be the regimental encampment of Reuben by companies. The leader of the Reubenites shall be Elizur son of Shedeur, 11with a company as enrolled of forty-six thousand five hundred. 12And those to camp next to him shall be the tribe of Simeon. The leader of the Simeonites shall be Shelumiel son of Zurishaddai, 13with a company as enrolled of fifty-nine thousand three hundred. 14Then the tribe of Gad: The leader of the Gadites shall be Eliasaph son of Reuel, 15with a company as enrolled of forty-five thousand six hundred fifty. 16The total enrollment of the camp of Reuben, by companies, is one hundred fifty-one thousand four hundred fifty. They shall set out second.

17 The tent of meeting, with the camp of the Levites, shall set out in the center of the camps; they shall set out just as they camp, each in position, by their regiments.

18 On the west side shall be the regimental encampment of Ephraim by companies. The leader of the people of Ephraim shall be Elishama son of Ammihud, 19with a company as enrolled of forty thousand five hundred. 20Next to him shall be the tribe of Manasseh. The leader of the people of Manasseh shall be Gamaliel son of Pedahzur, 21with a company as enrolled of thirty-two thousand two hundred. 22Then the tribe of Benjamin: The leader of the Benjaminites shall be Abidan son of Gideoni, 23with a company as enrolled of thirty-five thousand four hundred. 24The total enrollment of the camp of Ephraim, by companies, is one hundred eight thousand one hundred. They shall set out third on the march.

25 On the north side shall be the regimental encampment of Dan by companies. The leader of the Danites shall be Ahiezer son of Ammishaddai, 26with a company as enrolled of sixty-two thousand seven hundred. 27Those to camp next to him shall be the tribe of Asher. The leader of the Asherites shall be Pagiel son of Ochran, 28with a company as enrolled of forty-one thousand five hundred. 29Then the tribe of Naphtali: The

a Or treaty, or testimony; Heb eduth

leader of the Naphtalites shall be Ahira son of Enan, 30with a company as enrolled of fifty-three thousand four hundred. 31The total enrollment of the camp of Dan is one hundred fifty-seven thousand six hundred. They shall set out last, by companies.b

32 This was the enrollment of the Israelites by their ancestral houses; the total enrollment in the camps by their companies was six hundred three thousand five hundred fifty. 33Just as the LORD had commanded Moses, the Levites were not enrolled among the other Israelites.

34 The Israelites did just as the LORD had commanded Moses: They camped by regiments, and they set out the same way, everyone by clans, according to ancestral houses.

The Sons of Aaron

3 This is the lineage of Aaron and Moses at the time when the LORD spoke with Moses on Mount Sinai. 2These are the names of the sons of Aaron: Nadab the firstborn, and Abihu, Eleazar, and Ithamar; 3these are the names of the sons of Aaron, the anointed priests, whom he ordained to minister as priests. 4Nadab and Abihu died before the LORD when they offered unholy fire before the LORD in the wilderness of Sinai, and they had no children. Eleazar and Ithamar served as priests in the lifetime of their father Aaron.

The Duties of the Levites

5 Then the LORD spoke to Moses, saying: 6Bring the tribe of Levi near, and set them before Aaron the priest, so that they may assist him. 7They shall perform duties for him and for the whole congregation in front of the tent of meeting, doing service at the tabernacle; 8they shall be in charge of all the furnishings of the tent of meeting, and attend to the duties for the Israelites as they do service at the tabernacle. 9You shall give the Levites to Aaron and his descendants; they are unreservedly given to him from among the Israelites. 10But you shall make a register of Aaron and his descendants; it is they who shall

attend to the priesthood, and any outsider who comes near shall be put to death.

11 Then the LORD spoke to Moses, saying: 12I hereby accept the Levites from among the Israelites as substitutes for all the firstborn that open the womb among the Israelites. The Levites shall be mine, 13for all the firstborn are mine; when I killed all the firstborn in the land of Egypt, I consecrated for my own all the firstborn in Israel, both human and animal; they shall be mine. I am the LORD.

A Census of the Levites

14 Then the LORD spoke to Moses in the wilderness of Sinai, saying: 15Enroll the Levites by ancestral houses and by clans. You shall enroll every male from a month old and upward. 16So Moses enrolled them according to the word of the LORD, as he was commanded. 17The following were the sons of Levi, by their names: Gershon, Kohath, and Merari. 18These are the names of the sons of Gershon by their clans: Libni and Shimei. 19The sons of Kohath by their clans: Amram, Izhar, Hebron, and Uzziel. 20The sons of Merari by their clans: Mahli and Mushi. These are the clans of the Levites, by their ancestral houses.

21 To Gershon belonged the clan of the Libnites and the clan of the Shimeites; these were the clans of the Gershonites. 22Their enrollment, counting all the males from a month old and upward, was seven thousand five hundred. 23The clans of the Gershonites were to camp behind the tabernacle on the west, 24with Eliasaph son of Lael as head of the ancestral house of the Gershonites. 25The responsibility of the sons of Gershon in the tent of meeting was to be the tabernacle, the tent with its covering, the screen for the entrance of the tent of meeting, 26the hangings of the court, the screen for the entrance of the court that is around the tabernacle and the altar, and its cords—all the service pertaining to these.

27 To Kohath belonged the clan of the Amramites, the clan of the Izharites, the clan of the Hebronites, and the clan of the Uzzielites; these are the clans of

b Compare verses 9, 16, 24: Heb by their regiments

the Kohathites. 28Counting all the males, from a month old and upward, there were eight thousand six hundred, attending to the duties of the sanctuary. 29The clans of the Kohathites were to camp on the south side of the tabernacle, 30with Elizaphan son of Uzziel as head of the ancestral house of the clans of the Kohathites. 31Their responsibility was to be the ark, the table, the lampstand, the altars, the vessels of the sanctuary with which the priests minister, and the screen—all the service pertaining to these. 32Eleazar son of Aaron the priest was to be chief over the leaders of the Levites, and to have oversight of those who had charge of the sanctuary.

33 To Merari belonged the clan of the Mahlites and the clan of the Mushites: these are the clans of Merari. 34Their enrollment, counting all the males from a month old and upward, was six thousand two hundred. 35The head of the ancestral house of the clans of Merari was Zuriel son of Abihail; they were to camp on the north side of the tabernacle. 36The responsibility assigned to the sons of Merari was to be the frames of the tabernacle, the bars, the pillars, the bases, and all their accessories—all the service pertaining to these; 37also the pillars of the court all around, with their bases and pegs and cords.

38 Those who were to camp in front of the tabernacle on the east—in front of the tent of meeting toward the east— were Moses and Aaron and Aaron's sons, having charge of the rites within the sanctuary, whatever had to be done for the Israelites; and any outsider who came near was to be put to death. 39The total enrollment of the Levites whom Moses and Aaron enrolled at the commandment of the LORD, by their clans, all the males from a month old and upward, was twenty-two thousand.

The Redemption of the Firstborn

40 Then the LORD said to Moses: Enroll all the firstborn males of the Israelites, from a month old and upward, and count their names. 41But you shall accept the Levites for me—I am the LORD—as substitutes for all the firstborn among the Israelites, and the livestock

of the Levites as substitutes for all the firstborn among the livestock of the Israelites. 42So Moses enrolled all the firstborn among the Israelites, as the LORD commanded him. 43The total enrollment, all the firstborn males from a month old and upward, counting the number of names, was twenty-two thousand two hundred seventy-three.

44 Then the LORD spoke to Moses, saying: 45Accept the Levites as substitutes for all the firstborn among the Israelites, and the livestock of the Levites as substitutes for their livestock; and the Levites shall be mine. I am the LORD. 46As the price of redemption of the two hundred seventy-three of the firstborn of the Israelites, over and above the number of the Levites, 47you shall accept five shekels apiece, reckoning by the shekel of the sanctuary, a shekel of twenty gerahs. 48Give to Aaron and his sons the money by which the excess number of them is redeemed. 49So Moses took the redemption money from those who were over and above those redeemed by the Levites; 50from the firstborn of the Israelites he took the money, one thousand three hundred sixty-five shekels, reckoned by the shekel of the sanctuary; 51and Moses gave the redemption money to Aaron and his sons, according to the word of the LORD, as the LORD had commanded Moses.

The Kohathites

4 The LORD spoke to Moses and Aaron, saying: 2Take a census of the Kohathites separate from the other Levites, by their clans and their ancestral houses, 3from thirty years old up to fifty years old, all who qualify to do work relating to the tent of meeting. 4The service of the Kohathites relating to the tent of meeting concerns the most holy things.

5 When the camp is to set out, Aaron and his sons shall go in and take down the screening curtain, and cover the ark of the covenantc with it; 6then they shall put on it a covering of fine leather,d and spread over that a cloth all of blue, and shall put its poles in place. 7Over the table of the bread of the Presence they shall spread a blue cloth, and

c Or treaty, or testimony; Heb eduth   d Meaning of Heb uncertain put on it the plates, the dishes for incense, the bowls, and the flagons for the drink offering; the regular bread also shall be on it; 8then they shall spread over them a crimson cloth, and cover it with a covering of fine leather,e and shall put its poles in place. 9They shall take a blue cloth, and cover the lampstand for the light, with its lamps, its snuffers, its trays, and all the vessels for oil with which it is supplied; 10and they shall put it with all its utensils in a covering of fine leather,e and put it on the carrying frame. 11Over the golden altar they shall spread a blue cloth, and cover it with a covering of fine leather,e and shall put its poles in place; 12and they shall take all the utensils of the service that are used in the sanctuary, and put them in a blue cloth, and cover them with a covering of fine leather,e and put them on the carrying frame. 13They shall take away the ashes from the altar, and spread a purple cloth over it; 14and they shall put on it all the utensils of the altar, which are used for the service there, the firepans, the forks, the shovels, and the basins, all the utensils of the altar; and they shall spread on it a covering of fine leather,e and shall put its poles in place. 15When Aaron and his sons have finished covering the sanctuary and all the furnishings of the sanctuary, as the camp sets out, after that the Kohathites shall come to carry these, but they must not touch the holy things, or they will die. These are the things of the tent of meeting that the Kohathites are to carry.

16 Eleazar son of Aaron the priest shall have charge of the oil for the light, the fragrant incense, the regular grain offering, and the anointing oil, the oversight of all the tabernacle and all that is in it, in the sanctuary and in its utensils.

17 Then the LORD spoke to Moses and Aaron, saying: 18You must not let the tribe of the clans of the Kohathites be destroyed from among the Levites. 19This is how you must deal with them in order that they may live and not die when they come near to the most holy things: Aaron and his sons shall go in and assign each to a particular task or burden. 20But the Kohathites f must not go in to look on the holy things even for a moment; otherwise they will die.

The Gershonites and Merarites

21 Then the LORD spoke to Moses, saying: 22Take a census of the Gershonites also, by their ancestral houses and by their clans; 23from thirty years old up to fifty years old you shall enroll them, all who qualify to do work in the tent of meeting. 24This is the service of the clans of the Gershonites, in serving and bearing burdens: 25They shall carry the curtains of the tabernacle, and the tent of meeting with its covering, and the outer covering of fine leathere that is on top of it, and the screen for the entrance of the tent of meeting, 26and the hangings of the court, and the screen for the entrance of the gate of the court that is around the tabernacle and the altar, and their cords, and all the equipment for their service; and they shall do all that needs to be done with regard to them. 27All the service of the Gershonites shall be at the command of Aaron and his sons, in all that they are to carry, and in all that they have to do; and you shall assign to their charge all that they are to carry. 28This is the service of the clans of the Gershonites relating to the tent of meeting, and their responsibilities are to be under the oversight of Ithamar son of Aaron the priest.

29 As for the Merarites, you shall enroll them by their clans and their ancestral houses; 30from thirty years old up to fifty years old you shall enroll them, everyone who qualifies to do the work of the tent of meeting. 31This is what they are charged to carry, as the whole of their service in the tent of meeting: the frames of the tabernacle, with its bars, pillars, and bases, 32and the pillars of the court all around with their bases, pegs, and cords, with all their equipment and all their related service; and you shall assign by name the objects that they are required to carry. 33This is the service of the clans of the Merarites, the whole of their service relating to the tent of meeting, under the hand of Ithamar son of Aaron the priest.

e Meaning of Heb uncertain   f Heb they

Census of the Levites

34 So Moses and Aaron and the leaders of the congregation enrolled the Kohathites, by their clans and their ancestral houses, 35from thirty years old up to fifty years old, everyone who qualified for work relating to the tent of meeting; 36and their enrollment by clans was two thousand seven hundred fifty. 37This was the enrollment of the clans of the Kohathites, all who served at the tent of meeting, whom Moses and Aaron enrolled according to the commandment of the LORD by Moses.

38 The enrollment of the Gershonites, by their clans and their ancestral houses, 39from thirty years old up to fifty years old, everyone who qualified for work relating to the tent of meeting— 40their enrollment by their clans and their ancestral houses was two thousand six hundred thirty. 41This was the enrollment of the clans of the Gershonites, all who served at the tent of meeting, whom Moses and Aaron enrolled according to the commandment of the LORD.

42 The enrollment of the clans of the Merarites, by their clans and their ancestral houses, 43from thirty years old up to fifty years old, everyone who qualified for work relating to the tent of meeting— 44their enrollment by their clans was three thousand two hundred. 45This is the enrollment of the clans of the Merarites, whom Moses and Aaron enrolled according to the commandment of the LORD by Moses.

46 All those who were enrolled of the Levites, whom Moses and Aaron and the leaders of Israel enrolled, by their clans and their ancestral houses, 47from thirty years old up to fifty years old, everyone who qualified to do the work of service and the work of bearing burdens relating to the tent of meeting, 48their enrollment was eight thousand five hundred eighty. 49According to the commandment of the LORD through Moses they were appointed to their several tasks of serving or carrying; thus they were enrolled by him, as the LORD commanded Moses.

Unclean Persons

5 The LORD spoke to Moses, saying: 2Command the Israelites to put out of the camp everyone who is leprous,g or has a discharge, and everyone who is unclean through contact with a corpse; 3you shall put out both male and female, putting them outside the camp; they must not defile their camp, where I dwell among them. 4The Israelites did so, putting them outside the camp; as the LORD had spoken to Moses, so the Israelites did.

Confession and Restitution

5 The LORD spoke to Moses, saying: 6Speak to the Israelites: When a man or a woman wrongs another, breaking faith with the LORD, that person incurs guilt 7and shall confess the sin that has been committed. The person shall make full restitution for the wrong, adding one-fifth to it, and giving it to the one who was wronged. 8If the injured party has no next of kin to whom restitution may be made for the wrong, the restitution for wrong shall go to the LORD for the priest, in addition to the ram of atonement with which atonement is made for the guilty party. 9Among all the sacred donations of the Israelites, every gift that they bring to the priest shall be his. 10The sacred donations of all are their own; whatever anyone gives to the priest shall be his.

Concerning an Unfaithful Wife

11 The LORD spoke to Moses, saying: 12Speak to the Israelites and say to them: If any man's wife goes astray and is unfaithful to him, 13if a man has had intercourse with her but it is hidden from her husband, so that she is undetected though she has defiled herself, and there is no witness against her since she was not caught in the act; 14if a spirit of jealousy comes on him, and he is jealous of his wife who has defiled herself; or if a spirit of jealousy comes on him, and he is jealous of his wife, though she has not defiled herself; 15then the man shall bring his wife to the priest. And he shall bring the offering required for her, one-tenth of an

g A term for several skin diseases; precise meaning uncertain ephah of barley flour. He shall pour no oil on it and put no frankincense on it, for it is a grain offering of jealousy, a grain offering of remembrance, bringing iniquity to remembrance.

16 Then the priest shall bring her near, and set her before the LORD; 17 the priest shall take holy water in an earthen vessel, and take some of the dust that is on the floor of the tabernacle and put it into the water. 18 The priest shall set the woman before the LORD, dishevel the woman's hair, and place in her hands the grain offering of remembrance, which is the grain offering of jealousy. In his own hand the priest shall have the water of bitterness that brings the curse. 19 Then the priest shall make her take an oath, saying, "If no man has lain with you, if you have not turned aside to uncleanness while under your husband's authority, be immune to this water of bitterness that brings the curse. 20 But if you have gone astray while under your husband's authority, if you have defiled yourself and some man other than your husband has had intercourse with you," 21—let the priest make the woman take the oath of the curse and say to the woman—"the LORD make you an execration and an oath among your people, when the LORD makes your uterus drop, your womb discharge; 22 now may this water that brings the curse enter your bowels and make your womb discharge, your uterus drop!" And the woman shall say, "Amen. Amen."

23 Then the priest shall put these curses in writing, and wash them off into the water of bitterness. 24 He shall make the woman drink the water of bitterness that brings the curse, and the water that brings the curse shall enter her and cause bitter pain. 25 The priest shall take the grain offering of jealousy out of the woman's hand, and shall elevate the grain offering before the LORD and bring it to the altar; 26 and the priest shall take a handful of the grain offering, as its memorial portion, and turn it into smoke on the altar, and afterward shall make the woman drink the water. 27 When he has made her drink the water, then, if she has defiled herself and has been unfaithful to her husband, the water that brings the curse shall enter into her and cause bitter pain, and her womb shall discharge, her uterus drop, and the woman shall become an execration among her people. 28 But if the woman has not defiled herself and is clean, then she shall be immune and be able to conceive children.

29 This is the law in cases of jealousy, when a wife, while under her husband's authority, goes astray and defiles herself, 30 or when a spirit of jealousy comes on a man and he is jealous of his wife; then he shall set the woman before the LORD, and the priest shall apply this entire law to her. 31 The man shall be free from iniquity, but the woman shall bear her iniquity.

The Nazirites

6 The LORD spoke to Moses, saying: 2 Speak to the Israelites and say to them: When either men or women make a special vow, the vow of a nazirite,[h] to separate themselves to the LORD, 3 they shall separate themselves from wine and strong drink; they shall drink no wine vinegar or other vinegar, and shall not drink any grape juice or eat grapes, fresh or dried. 4 All their days as nazirites[i] they shall eat nothing that is produced by the grapevine, not even the seeds or the skins.

5 All the days of their nazirite vow no razor shall come upon the head; until the time is completed for which they separate themselves to the LORD, they shall be holy; they shall let the locks of the head grow long.

6 All the days that they separate themselves to the LORD they shall not go near a corpse. 7 Even if their father or mother, brother or sister, should die, they may not defile themselves; because their consecration to God is upon the head. 8 All their days as nazirites[i] they are holy to the LORD.

9 If someone dies very suddenly nearby, defiling the consecrated head, then they shall shave the head on the day of their cleansing; on the seventh day they shall shave it. 10 On the eighth day they shall bring two turtledoves or two young pigeons to the priest at the entrance of

---

h That is one separated or one consecrated   i That is those separated or those consecrated

the tent of meeting, [11]and the priest shall offer one as a sin offering and the other as a burnt offering, and make atonement for them, because they incurred guilt by reason of the corpse. They shall sanctify the head that same day, [12]and separate themselves to the LORD for their days as nazirites,[j] and bring a male lamb a year old as a guilt offering. The former time shall be void, because the consecrated head was defiled.

13 This is the law for the nazirites[j] when the time of their consecration has been completed: they shall be brought to the entrance of the tent of meeting, [14]and they shall offer their gift to the LORD, one male lamb a year old without blemish as a burnt offering, one ewe lamb a year old without blemish as a sin offering, one ram without blemish as an offering of well-being, [15]and a basket of unleavened bread, cakes of choice flour mixed with oil and unleavened wafers spread with oil, with their grain offering and their drink offerings. [16]The priest shall present them before the LORD and offer their sin offering and burnt offering, [17]and shall offer the ram as a sacrifice of well-being to the LORD, with the basket of unleavened bread; the priest also shall make the accompanying grain offering and drink offering. [18]Then the nazirites[j] shall shave the consecrated head at the entrance of the tent of meeting, and shall take the hair from the consecrated head and put it on the fire under the sacrifice of well-being. [19]The priest shall take the shoulder of the ram, when it is boiled, and one unleavened cake out of the basket, and one unleavened wafer, and shall put them in the palms of the nazirites,[j] after they have shaved the consecrated head. [20]Then the priest shall elevate them as an elevation offering before the LORD; they are a holy portion for the priest, together with the breast that is elevated and the thigh that is offered. After that the nazirites[j] may drink wine.

21 This is the law for the nazirites[j] who take a vow. Their offering to the LORD must be in accordance with the nazirite[k] vow, apart from what else they can afford. In accordance with whatever vow they take, so they shall do, following the law for their consecration.

The Priestly Benediction

22 The LORD spoke to Moses, saying: [23]Speak to Aaron and his sons, saying, Thus you shall bless the Israelites: You shall say to them,

24　The LORD bless you and keep you;
25　the LORD make his face to shine
　　　upon you, and be gracious to
　　　you;
26　the LORD lift up his countenance
　　　upon you, and give you
　　　peace.

27 So they shall put my name on the Israelites, and I will bless them.

Offerings of the Leaders

7 On the day when Moses had finished setting up the tabernacle, and had anointed and consecrated it with all its furnishings, and had anointed and consecrated the altar with all its utensils, [2]the leaders of Israel, heads of their ancestral houses, the leaders of the tribes, who were over those who were enrolled, made offerings. [3]They brought their offerings before the LORD, six covered wagons and twelve oxen, a wagon for every two of the leaders, and for each one an ox; they presented them before the tabernacle. [4]Then the LORD said to Moses: [5]Accept these from them, that they may be used in doing the service of the tent of meeting, and give them to the Levites, to each according to his service. [6]So Moses took the wagons and the oxen, and gave them to the Levites. [7]Two wagons and four oxen he gave to the Gershonites, according to their service; [8]and four wagons and eight oxen he gave to the Merarites, according to their service, under the direction of Ithamar son of Aaron the priest. [9]But to the Kohathites he gave none, because they were charged with the care of the holy things that had to be carried on the shoulders.

10 The leaders also presented offerings for the dedication of the altar at the time when it was anointed; the leaders presented their offering before the altar. [11]The LORD said to Moses: They shall

---

j That is those separated or those consecrated　　k That is one separated or one consecrated

present their offerings, one leader each day, for the dedication of the altar.

12 The one who presented his offering the first day was Nahshon son of Amminadab, of the tribe of Judah; 13his offering was one silver plate weighing one hundred thirty shekels, one silver basin weighing seventy shekels, according to the shekel of the sanctuary, both of them full of choice flour mixed with oil for a grain offering; 14one golden dish weighing ten shekels, full of incense; 15one young bull, one ram, one male lamb a year old, for a burnt offering; 16one male goat for a sin offering; 17and for the sacrifice of well-being, two oxen, five rams, five male goats, and five male lambs a year old. This was the offering of Nahshon son of Amminadab.

18 On the second day Nethanel son of Zuar, the leader of Issachar, presented an offering; 19he presented for his offering one silver plate weighing one hundred thirty shekels, one silver basin weighing seventy shekels, according to the shekel of the sanctuary, both of them full of choice flour mixed with oil for a grain offering; 20one golden dish weighing ten shekels, full of incense; 21one young bull, one ram, one male lamb a year old, as a burnt offering; 22one male goat as a sin offering; 23and for the sacrifice of well-being, two oxen, five rams, five male goats, and five male lambs a year old. This was the offering of Nethanel son of Zuar.

24 On the third day Eliab son of Helon, the leader of the Zebulunites: 25his offering was one silver plate weighing one hundred thirty shekels, one silver basin weighing seventy shekels, according to the shekel of the sanctuary, both of them full of choice flour mixed with oil for a grain offering; 26one golden dish weighing ten shekels, full of incense; 27one young bull, one ram, one male lamb a year old, for a burnt offering; 28one male goat for a sin offering; 29and for the sacrifice of well-being, two oxen, five rams, five male goats, and five male lambs a year old. This was the offering of Eliab son of Helon.

30 On the fourth day Elizur son of Shedeur, the leader of the Reubenites: 31his offering was one silver plate weighing one hundred thirty shekels, one sil-

ver basin weighing seventy shekels, according to the shekel of the sanctuary, both of them full of choice flour mixed with oil for a grain offering; 32one golden dish weighing ten shekels, full of incense; 33one young bull, one ram, one male lamb a year old, for a burnt offering; 34one male goat for a sin offering; 35and for the sacrifice of well-being, two oxen, five rams, five male goats, and five male lambs a year old. This was the offering of Elizur son of Shedeur.

36 On the fifth day Shelumiel son of Zurishaddai, the leader of the Simeonites: 37his offering was one silver plate weighing one hundred thirty shekels, one silver basin weighing seventy shekels, according to the shekel of the sanctuary, both of them full of choice flour mixed with oil for a grain offering; 38one golden dish weighing ten shekels, full of incense; 39one young bull, one ram, one male lamb a year old, for a burnt offering; 40one male goat for a sin offering; 41and for the sacrifice of well-being, two oxen, five rams, five male goats, and five male lambs a year old. This was the offering of Shelumiel son of Zurishaddai.

42 On the sixth day Eliasaph son of Deuel, the leader of the Gadites: 43his offering was one silver plate weighing one hundred thirty shekels, one silver basin weighing seventy shekels, according to the shekel of the sanctuary, both of them full of choice flour mixed with oil for a grain offering; 44one golden dish weighing ten shekels, full of incense; 45one young bull, one ram, one male lamb a year old, for a burnt offering; 46one male goat for a sin offering; 47and for the sacrifice of well-being, two oxen, five rams, five male goats, and five male lambs a year old. This was the offering of Eliasaph son of Deuel.

48 On the seventh day Elishama son of Ammihud, the leader of the Ephraimites: 49his offering was one silver plate weighing one hundred thirty shekels, one silver basin weighing seventy shekels, according to the shekel of the sanctuary, both of them full of choice flour mixed with oil for a grain offering; 50one golden dish weighing ten shekels, full of incense; 51one young bull, one ram, one male lamb a year old,

for a burnt offering; 52one male goat for a sin offering; 53and for the sacrifice of well-being, two oxen, five rams, five male goats, and five male lambs a year old. This was the offering of Elishama son of Ammihud.

54 On the eighth day Gamaliel son of Pedahzur, the leader of the Manassites: 55his offering was one silver plate weighing one hundred thirty shekels, one silver basin weighing seventy shekels, according to the shekel of the sanctuary, both of them full of choice flour mixed with oil for a grain offering; 56one golden dish weighing ten shekels, full of incense; 57one young bull, one ram, one male lamb a year old, for a burnt offering; 58one male goat for a sin offering; 59and for the sacrifice of well-being, two oxen, five rams, five male goats, and five male lambs a year old. This was the offering of Gamaliel son of Pedahzur.

60 On the ninth day Abidan son of Gideoni, the leader of the Benjaminites: 61his offering was one silver plate weighing one hundred thirty shekels, one silver basin weighing seventy shekels, according to the shekel of the sanctuary, both of them full of choice flour mixed with oil for a grain offering; 62one golden dish weighing ten shekels, full of incense; 63one young bull, one ram, one male lamb a year old, for a burnt offering; 64one male goat for a sin offering; 65and for the sacrifice of well-being, two oxen, five rams, five male goats, and five male lambs a year old. This was the offering of Abidan son of Gideoni.

66 On the tenth day Ahiezer son of Ammishaddai, the leader of the Danites: 67his offering was one silver plate weighing one hundred thirty shekels, one silver basin weighing seventy shekels, according to the shekel of the sanctuary, both of them full of choice flour mixed with oil for a grain offering; 68one golden dish weighing ten shekels, full of incense; 69one young bull, one ram, one male lamb a year old, for a burnt offering; 70one male goat for a sin offering; 71and for the sacrifice of well-being, two oxen, five rams, five male goats, and five male lambs a year old. This was the offering of Ahiezer son of Ammishaddai.

72 On the eleventh day Pagiel son of Ochran, the leader of the Asherites:

73his offering was one silver plate weighing one hundred thirty shekels, one silver basin weighing seventy shekels, according to the shekel of the sanctuary, both of them full of choice flour mixed with oil for a grain offering; 74one golden dish weighing ten shekels, full of incense; 75one young bull, one ram, one male lamb a year old, for a burnt offering; 76one male goat for a sin offering; 77and for the sacrifice of well-being, two oxen, five rams, five male goats, and five male lambs a year old. This was the offering of Pagiel son of Ochran.

78 On the twelfth day Ahira son of Enan, the leader of the Naphtalites: 79his offering was one silver plate weighing one hundred thirty shekels, one silver basin weighing seventy shekels, according to the shekel of the sanctuary, both of them full of choice flour mixed with oil for a grain offering; 80one golden dish weighing ten shekels, full of incense; 81one young bull, one ram, one male lamb a year old, for a burnt offering; 82one male goat for a sin offering; 83and for the sacrifice of well-being, two oxen, five rams, five male goats, and five male lambs a year old. This was the offering of Ahira son of Enan.

84 This was the dedication offering for the altar, at the time when it was anointed, from the leaders of Israel: twelve silver plates, twelve silver basins, twelve golden dishes, 85each silver plate weighing one hundred thirty shekels and each basin seventy, all the silver of the vessels two thousand four hundred shekels according to the shekel of the sanctuary, 86the twelve golden dishes, full of incense, weighing ten shekels apiece according to the shekel of the sanctuary, all the gold of the dishes being one hundred twenty shekels; 87all the livestock for the burnt offering twelve bulls, twelve rams, twelve male lambs a year old, with their grain offering; and twelve male goats for a sin offering; 88and all the livestock for the sacrifice of well-being twenty-four bulls, the rams sixty, the male goats sixty, the male lambs a year old sixty. This was the dedication offering for the altar, after it was anointed.

89 When Moses went into the tent of

meeting to speak with the LORD,[1] he would hear the voice speaking to him from above the mercy seat[m] that was on the ark of the covenant[n] from between the two cherubim; thus it spoke to him.

The Seven Lamps

8 The LORD spoke to Moses, saying: [2]Speak to Aaron and say to him: When you set up the lamps, the seven lamps shall give light in front of the lampstand. [3]Aaron did so; he set up its lamps to give light in front of the lampstand, as the LORD had commanded Moses. [4]Now this was how the lampstand was made, out of hammered work of gold. From its base to its flowers, it was hammered work; according to the pattern that the LORD had shown Moses, so he made the lampstand.

Consecration and Service of the Levites

5 The LORD spoke to Moses, saying: [6]Take the Levites from among the Israelites and cleanse them. [7]Thus you shall do to them, to cleanse them: sprinkle the water of purification on them, have them shave their whole body with a razor and wash their clothes, and so cleanse themselves. [8]Then let them take a young bull and its grain offering of choice flour mixed with oil, and you shall take another young bull for a sin offering. [9]You shall bring the Levites before the tent of meeting, and assemble the whole congregation of the Israelites. [10]When you bring the Levites before the LORD, the Israelites shall lay their hands on the Levites, [11]and Aaron shall present the Levites before the LORD as an elevation offering from the Israelites, that they may do the service of the LORD. [12]The Levites shall lay their hands on the heads of the bulls, and he shall offer the one for a sin offering and the other for a burnt offering to the LORD, to make atonement for the Levites. [13]Then you shall have the Levites stand before Aaron and his sons, and you shall present them as an elevation offering to the LORD. 14 Thus you shall separate the Levites from among the other Israelites, and the Levites shall be mine. [15]There-

after the Levites may go in to do service at the tent of meeting, once you have cleansed them and presented them as an elevation offering. [16]For they are unreservedly given to me from among the Israelites; I have taken them for myself, in place of all that open the womb, the firstborn of all the Israelites. [17]For all the firstborn among the Israelites are mine, both human and animal. On the day that I struck down all the firstborn in the land of Egypt I consecrated them for myself, [18]but I have taken the Levites in place of all the firstborn among the Israelites. [19]Moreover, I have given the Levites as a gift to Aaron and his sons from among the Israelites, to do the service for the Israelites at the tent of meeting, and to make atonement for the Israelites, in order that there may be no plague among the Israelites for coming too close to the sanctuary.

20 Moses and Aaron and the whole congregation of the Israelites did with the Levites accordingly; the Israelites did with the Levites just as the LORD had commanded Moses concerning them. [21]The Levites purified themselves from sin and washed their clothes; then Aaron presented them as an elevation offering before the LORD, and Aaron made atonement for them to cleanse them. [22]Thereafter the Levites went in to do their service in the tent of meeting in attendance on Aaron and his sons. As the LORD had commanded Moses concerning the Levites, so they did with them.

23 The LORD spoke to Moses, saying: [24]This applies to the Levites: from twenty-five years old and upward they shall begin to do duty in the service of the tent of meeting; [25]and from the age of fifty years they shall retire from the duty of the service and serve no more. [26]They may assist their brothers in the tent of meeting in carrying out their duties, but they shall perform no service. Thus you shall do with the Levites in assigning their duties.

The Passover at Sinai

9 The LORD spoke to Moses in the wilderness of Sinai, in the first month of the second year after they had

---

[1] Heb *him*   [m] Or *the cover*   [n] Or *treaty*, or *testimony*; Heb *eduth*

come out of the land of Egypt, saying:
2 Let the Israelites keep the passover at
its appointed time. 3 On the fourteenth
day of this month, at twilight,[o] you shall
keep it at its appointed time; according
to all its statutes and all its regulations
you shall keep it. 4 So Moses told the
Israelites that they should keep the
passover. 5 They kept the passover in
the first month, on the fourteenth day
of the month, at twilight,[o] in the wilderness of Sinai. Just as the LORD had commanded Moses, so the Israelites did.
6 Now there were certain people who
were unclean through touching a corpse,
so that they could not keep the passover
on that day. They came before Moses
and Aaron on that day, 7 and said to him,
"Although we are unclean through
touching a corpse, why must we be kept
from presenting the LORD's offering at
its appointed time among the Israelites?" 8 Moses spoke to them, "Wait, so
that I may hear what the LORD will command concerning you."

9 The LORD spoke to Moses, saying:
10 Speak to the Israelites, saying: Anyone
of you or your descendants who is
unclean through touching a corpse, or is
away on a journey, shall still keep the
passover to the LORD. 11 In the second
month on the fourteenth day, at twilight,[o] they shall keep it; they shall eat it
with unleavened bread and bitter herbs.
12 They shall leave none of it until morning, nor break a bone of it; according to
all the statute for the passover they shall
keep it. 13 But anyone who is clean and is
not on a journey, and yet refrains from
keeping the passover, shall be cut off
from the people for not presenting the
LORD's offering at its appointed time;
such a one shall bear the consequences
for the sin. 14 Any alien residing among
you who wishes to keep the passover to
the LORD shall do so according to the
statute of the passover and according to
its regulation; you shall have one statute
for both the resident alien and the
native.

The Cloud and the Fire

15 On the day the tabernacle was set
up, the cloud covered the tabernacle, the
tent of the covenant;[p] and from evening
until morning it was over the tabernacle, having the appearance of fire. 16 It
was always so: the cloud covered it by
day[q] and the appearance of fire by night.
17 Whenever the cloud lifted from over
the tent, then the Israelites would set
out; and in the place where the cloud
settled down, there the Israelites would
camp. 18 At the command of the LORD
the Israelites would set out, and at the
command of the LORD they would
camp. As long as the cloud rested over
the tabernacle, they would remain in
camp. 19 Even when the cloud continued
over the tabernacle many days, the Israelites would keep the charge of the
LORD, and would not set out. 20 Sometimes the cloud would remain a few
days over the tabernacle, and according
to the command of the LORD they would
remain in camp; then according to the
command of the LORD they would set
out. 21 Sometimes the cloud would
remain from evening until morning; and
when the cloud lifted in the morning,
they would set out, or if it continued for
a day and a night, when the cloud lifted
they would set out. 22 Whether it was
two days, or a month, or a longer time,
that the cloud continued over the tabernacle, resting upon it, the Israelites
would remain in camp and would not
set out; but when it lifted they would
set out. 23 At the command of the LORD
they would camp, and at the command
of the LORD they would set out. They
kept the charge of the LORD, at the command of the LORD by Moses.

The Silver Trumpets

10 The LORD spoke to Moses,
saying: 2 Make two silver
trumpets; you shall make them of hammered work; and you shall use them for
summoning the congregation, and for
breaking camp. 3 When both are blown,
the whole congregation shall assemble
before you at the entrance of the tent of
meeting. 4 But if only one is blown, then
the leaders, the heads of the tribes of
Israel, shall assemble before you. 5 When
you blow an alarm, the camps on the
east side shall set out; 6 when you blow a

o Heb *between the two evenings* p Or *treaty*, or *testimony*; Heb *eduth* q Gk Syr Vg: Heb lacks *by day* second alarm, the camps on the south side shall set out. An alarm is to be blown whenever they are to set out. [7]But when the assembly is to be gathered, you shall blow, but you shall not sound an alarm. [8]The sons of Aaron, the priests, shall blow the trumpets; this shall be a perpetual institution for you throughout your generations. [9]When you go to war in your land against the adversary who oppresses you, you shall sound an alarm with the trumpets, so that you may be remembered before the LORD your God and be saved from your enemies. [10]Also on your days of rejoicing, at your appointed festivals, and at the beginnings of your months, you shall blow the trumpets over your burnt offerings and over your sacrifices of well-being; they shall serve as a reminder on your behalf before the LORD your God: I am the LORD your God.

Departure from Sinai

11 In the second year, in the second month, on the twentieth day of the month, the cloud lifted from over the tabernacle of the covenant.[r] [12]Then the Israelites set out by stages from the wilderness of Sinai, and the cloud settled down in the wilderness of Paran. [13]They set out for the first time at the command of the LORD by Moses. [14]The standard of the camp of Judah set out first, company by company, and over the whole company was Nahshon son of Amminadab. [15]Over the company of the tribe of Issachar was Nethanel son of Zuar; [16]and over the company of the tribe of Zebulun was Eliab son of Helon.

17 Then the tabernacle was taken down, and the Gershonites and the Merarites, who carried the tabernacle, set out. [18]Next the standard of the camp of Reuben set out, company by company; and over the whole company was Elizur son of Shedeur. [19]Over the company of the tribe of Simeon was Shelumiel son of Zurishaddai, [20]and over the company of the tribe of Gad was Eliasaph son of Deuel.

21 Then the Kohathites, who carried the holy things, set out; and the tabernacle was set up before their arrival. [22]Next the standard of the Ephraimite camp set out, company by company, and over the whole company was Elishama son of Ammihud. [23]Over the company of the tribe of Manasseh was Gamaliel son of Pedahzur, [24]and over the company of the tribe of Benjamin was Abidan son of Gideoni.

25 Then the standard of the camp of Dan, acting as the rear guard of all the camps, set out, company by company, and over the whole company was Ahiezer son of Ammishaddai. [26]Over the company of the tribe of Asher was Pagiel son of Ochran, [27]and over the company of the tribe of Naphtali was Ahira son of Enan. [28]This was the order of march of the Israelites, company by company, when they set out.

29 Moses said to Hobab son of Reuel the Midianite, Moses' father-in-law, "We are setting out for the place of which the LORD said, 'I will give it to you'; come with us, and we will treat you well; for the LORD has promised good to Israel." [30]But he said to him, "I will not go, but I will go back to my own land and to my kindred." [31]He said, "Do not leave us, for you know where we should camp in the wilderness, and you will serve as eyes for us. [32]Moreover, if you go with us, whatever good the LORD does for us, the same we will do for you."

33 So they set out from the mount of the LORD three days' journey with the ark of the covenant of the LORD going before them three days' journey, to seek out a resting place for them, [34]the cloud of the LORD being over them by day when they set out from the camp.

35 Whenever the ark set out, Moses would say,

"Arise, O LORD, let your enemies
        be scattered,
    and your foes flee before you."

[36]And whenever it came to rest, he would say,

"Return, O LORD of the ten
        thousand thousands of
        Israel."[s]

Complaining in the Desert

11 Now when the people complained in the hearing of the LORD about their misfortunes, the LORD

r Or treaty, or testimony; Heb eduth   s Meaning of Heb uncertain

heard it and his anger was kindled. Then the fire of the LORD burned against them, and consumed some outlying parts of the camp. 2But the people cried out to Moses; and Moses prayed to the LORD, and the fire abated. 3So that place was called Taberah,t because the fire of the LORD burned against them.

4 The rabble among them had a strong craving; and the Israelites also wept again, and said, "If only we had meat to eat! 5We remember the fish we used to eat in Egypt for nothing, the cucumbers, the melons, the leeks, the onions, and the garlic; 6but now our strength is dried up, and there is nothing at all but this manna to look at."

7 Now the manna was like coriander seed, and its color was like the color of gum resin. 8The people went around and gathered it, ground it in mills or beat it in mortars, then boiled it in pots and made cakes of it; and the taste of it was like the taste of cakes baked with oil. 9When the dew fell on the camp in the night, the manna would fall with it.

10 Moses heard the people weeping throughout their families, all at the entrances of their tents. Then the LORD became very angry, and Moses was displeased. 11So Moses said to the LORD, "Why have you treated your servant so badly? Why have I not found favor in your sight, that you lay the burden of all this people on me? 12Did I conceive all this people? Did I give birth to them, that you should say to me, 'Carry them in your bosom, as a nurse carries a sucking child,' to the land that you promised on oath to their ancestors? 13Where am I to get meat to give to all this people? For they come weeping to me and say, 'Give us meat to eat!' 14I am not able to carry all this people alone, for they are too heavy for me. 15If this is the way you are going to treat me, put me to death at once—if I have found favor in your sight—and do not let me see my misery."

The Seventy Elders

16 So the LORD said to Moses, "Gather for me seventy of the elders of Israel, whom you know to be the elders of the people and officers over them; bring them to the tent of meeting, and have them take their place there with you. 17I will come down and talk with you there; and I will take some of the spirit that is on you and put it on them; and they shall bear the burden of the people along with you so that you will not bear it all by yourself. 18And say to the people: Consecrate yourselves for tomorrow, and you shall eat meat; for you have wailed in the hearing of the LORD, saying, 'If only we had meat to eat! Surely it was better for us in Egypt.' Therefore the LORD will give you meat, and you shall eat. 19You shall eat not only one day, or two days, or five days, or ten days, or twenty days, 20but for a whole month—until it comes out of your nostrils and becomes loathsome to you—because you have rejected the LORD who is among you, and have wailed before him, saying, 'Why did we ever leave Egypt?' " 21But Moses said, "The people I am with number six hundred thousand on foot; and you say, 'I will give them meat, that they may eat for a whole month'! 22Are there enough flocks and herds to slaughter for them? Are there enough fish in the sea to catch for them?" 23The LORD said to Moses, "Is the LORD's power limited?u Now you shall see whether my word will come true for you or not."

24 So Moses went out and told the people the words of the LORD; and he gathered seventy elders of the people, and placed them all around the tent. 25Then the LORD came down in the cloud and spoke to him, and took some of the spirit that was on him and put it on the seventy elders; and when the spirit rested upon them, they prophesied. But they did not do so again.

26 Two men remained in the camp, one named Eldad, and the other named Medad, and the spirit rested on them; they were among those registered, but they had not gone out to the tent, and so they prophesied in the camp. 27And a young man ran and told Moses, "Eldad and Medad are prophesying in the camp." 28And Joshua son of Nun, the assistant of Moses, one of his chosen men,v said, "My lord Moses, stop them!" 29But Moses said to him, "Are

t That is Burning   u Heb LORD's hand too short?   v Or of Moses from his youth

TUESDAY

THOSE WHO MURMUR
Charles H. Spurgeon

VERSE: Numbers 12.1–2 **PASSAGE:** Numbers 12.1–16

 here are murmurers among Christians now, as there were in the camp of Israel. There are those who, when the rod falls, cry out against the afflictive dispensation. They ask, "Why am I afflicted? What have I done to be chastened like this?"

Allow me a word with you who murmur. Why should you murmur against the dispensations of your heavenly Father? Can he treat you more harshly than you deserve? Consider what a rebel you once were, but he pardoned you! Surely, if he in his wisdom sees fit to chasten you, you should not complain. Does not that proud, rebellious spirit of yours prove that your heart is not thoroughly sanctified? Those murmuring words are contrary to the holy, submissive nature of God's children. Is not the correction needed? But if you murmur against the chastening, take heed, for it will go hard with murmurers.

But know one thing—"He doth not afflict willingly, nor grieve the children of men" (Lamentations 3.33, KJV). All his corrections are sent in love, to purify you, and to draw you nearer to himself. Surely it must help you bear the chastening if you are able to recognize your Father's hand. For "whom the Lord loveth he chasteneth, and scourgeth every son whom he receiveth. If ye endure chastening, God dealeth with you as with sons" (Hebrews 12.6–7). "Neither murmur ye as some of them also murmured and were destroyed of the destroyer" (1 Corinthians 10.10).

ADDITIONAL SCRIPTURE READING:
Romans 8.12–14; 2 Corinthians 7.1

Go to page 165 for your next devotional reading.

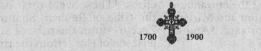

1700   1900

you jealous for my sake? Would that all the LORD's people were prophets, and that the LORD would put his spirit on them!" 30And Moses and the elders of Israel returned to the camp.

The Quails

31 Then a wind went out from the LORD, and it brought quails from the sea and let them fall beside the camp, about a day's journey on this side and a day's journey on the other side, all around the camp, about two cubits deep on the ground. 32So the people worked all that day and night and all the next day, gathering the quails; the least anyone gathered was ten homers; and they spread them out for themselves all around the camp. 33But while the meat was still between their teeth, before it was consumed, the anger of the LORD was kindled against the people, and the LORD struck the people with a very great plague. 34So that place was called Kibroth-hattaavah,w because there they buried the people who had the craving. 35From Kibroth-hattaavah the people journeyed to Hazeroth.

Aaron and Miriam Jealous of Moses

12 While they were at Hazeroth, Miriam and Aaron spoke against Moses because of the Cushite woman whom he had married (for he had indeed married a Cushite woman); 2and they said, "Has the LORD spoken only through Moses? Has he not spoken through us also?" And the LORD heard it. 3Now the man Moses was very humble,x more so than anyone else on the face of the earth. 4Suddenly the LORD said to Moses, Aaron, and Miriam, "Come out, you three, to the tent of meeting." So the three of them came out. 5Then the LORD came down in a pillar of cloud, and stood at the entrance of the tent, and called Aaron and Miriam; and they both came forward. 6And he said, "Hear my words:

When there are prophets among you,
I the LORD make myself known to them in visions;
I speak to them in dreams.

7   Not so with my servant Moses;
he is entrusted with all my house.
8   With him I speak face to face—
clearly, not in riddles;
and he beholds the form of the LORD.

Why then were you not afraid to speak against my servant Moses?" 9And the anger of the LORD was kindled against them, and he departed.

10 When the cloud went away from over the tent, Miriam had become leprous,y as white as snow. And Aaron turned towards Miriam and saw that she was leprous. 11Then Aaron said to Moses, "Oh, my lord, do not punish usz for a sin that we have so foolishly committed. 12Do not let her be like one stillborn, whose flesh is half consumed when it comes out of its mother's womb." 13And Moses cried to the LORD, "O God, please heal her." 14But the LORD said to Moses, "If her father had but spit in her face, would she not bear her shame for seven days? Let her be shut out of the camp for seven days, and after that she may be brought in again." 15So Miriam was shut out of the camp for seven days; and the people did not set out on the march until Miriam had been brought in again. 16After that the people set out from Hazeroth, and camped in the wilderness of Paran.

Spies Sent into Canaan

13 The LORD said to Moses, 2"Send men to spy out the land of Canaan, which I am giving to the Israelites; from each of their ancestral tribes you shall send a man, every one a leader among them." 3So Moses sent them from the wilderness of Paran, according to the command of the LORD, all of them leading men among the Israelites. 4These were their names: From the tribe of Reuben, Shammua son of Zaccur; 5from the tribe of Simeon, Shaphat son of Hori; 6from the tribe of Judah, Caleb son of Jephunneh; 7from the tribe of Issachar, Igal son of Joseph; 8from the tribe of Ephraim, Hoshea son of Nun; 9from the tribe of Benjamin, Palti son of Raphu; 10from the tribe of Zebulun, Gad-

---

w That is Graves of craving   x Or devout   y A term for several skin diseases; precise meaning uncertain   z Heb do not lay sin upon us

diel son of Sodi; [11]from the tribe of Joseph (that is, from the tribe of Manasseh), Gaddi son of Susi; [12]from the tribe of Dan, Ammiel son of Gemalli; [13]from the tribe of Asher, Sethur son of Michael; [14]from the tribe of Naphtali, Nahbi son of Vophsi; [15]from the tribe of Gad, Geuel son of Machi. [16]These were the names of the men whom Moses sent to spy out the land. And Moses changed the name of Hoshea son of Nun to Joshua.

[17] Moses sent them to spy out the land of Canaan, and said to them, "Go up there into the Negeb, and go up into the hill country, [18]and see what the land is like, and whether the people who live in it are strong or weak, whether they are few or many, [19]and whether the land they live in is good or bad, and whether the towns that they live in are unwalled or fortified, [20]and whether the land is rich or poor, and whether there are trees in it or not. Be bold, and bring some of the fruit of the land." Now it was the season of the first ripe grapes.

[21] So they went up and spied out the land from the wilderness of Zin to Rehob, near Lebo-hamath. [22]They went up into the Negeb, and came to Hebron; and Ahiman, Sheshai, and Talmai, the Anakites, were there. (Hebron was built seven years before Zoan in Egypt.) [23]And they came to the Wadi Eshcol, and cut down from there a branch with a single cluster of grapes, and they carried it on a pole between two of them. They also brought some pomegranates and figs. [24]That place was called the Wadi Eshcol,[a] because of the cluster that the Israelites cut down from there.

a That is Cluster

WEDNESDAY

TRUSTING HIM TO KEEP YOU
Andrew Murray

VERSE: Numbers 13.31   PASSAGE: Numbers 13.26–33

ear souls! how little they know that the abiding in Christ is just meant for the weak, and so beautifully suited to their feebleness. It is not the doing of some great thing, and does not demand that we first lead a very holy and devoted life. No, it is simply weakness entrusting itself to a Mighty One to be kept—the unfaithful one casting self on One who is altogether trustworthy and true. Abiding in him is not a work that we have to do as the condition for enjoying his salvation, but a consenting to let him do all for us, and in us, and through us. It is a work he does for us—the fruit and the power of his redeeming love. Our part is simply to yield, to trust, and to wait for what he has engaged to perform.

ADDITIONAL SCRIPTURE READING:
Deuteronomy 1.27–32; John 15.1–7

Go to page 170 for your next devotional reading.

1700   1900

The Report of the Spies

25 At the end of forty days they returned from spying out the land. 26And they came to Moses and Aaron and to all the congregation of the Israelites in the wilderness of Paran, at Kadesh; they brought back word to them and to all the congregation, and showed them the fruit of the land. 27And they told him, "We came to the land to which you sent us; it flows with milk and honey, and this is its fruit. 28Yet the people who live in its land are strong, and the towns are fortified and very large; and besides, we saw the descendants of Anak there. 29The Amalekites live in the land of the Negeb; the Hittites, the Jebusites, and the Amorites live in the hill country; and the Canaanites live by the sea, and along the Jordan."

30 But Caleb quieted the people before Moses, and said, "Let us go up at once and occupy it, for we are well able to overcome it." 31Then the men who had gone up with him said, "We are not able to go up against this people, for they are stronger than we." 32So they brought to the Israelites an unfavorable report of the land that they had spied out, saying, "The land that we have gone through as spies is a land that devours its inhabitants; and all the people that we saw in it are of great size. 33There we saw the Nephilim (the Anakites come from the Nephilim); and to ourselves we seemed like grasshoppers, and so we seemed to them."

The People Rebel

14 Then all the congregation raised a loud cry, and the people wept that night. 2And all the Israelites complained against Moses and Aaron; the whole congregation said to them, "Would that we had died in the land of Egypt! Or would that we had died in this wilderness! 3Why is the LORD bringing us into this land to fall by the sword? Our wives and our little ones will become booty; would it not be better for us to go back to Egypt?" 4So they said to one another, "Let us choose a captain, and go back to Egypt."

5 Then Moses and Aaron fell on their faces before all the assembly of the congregation of the Israelites. 6And Joshua son of Nun and Caleb son of Jephunneh, who were among those who had spied out the land, tore their clothes 7and said to all the congregation of the Israelites, "The land that we went through as spies is an exceedingly good land. 8If the LORD is pleased with us, he will bring us into this land and give it to us, a land that flows with milk and honey. 9Only, do not rebel against the LORD; and do not fear the people of the land, for they are no more than bread for us; their protection is removed from them, and the LORD is with us; do not fear them." 10But the whole congregation threatened to stone them.

Then the glory of the LORD appeared at the tent of meeting to all the Israelites. 11And the LORD said to Moses, "How long will this people despise me? And how long will they refuse to believe in me, in spite of all the signs that I have done among them? 12I will strike them with pestilence and disinherit them, and I will make of you a nation greater and mightier than they."

Moses Intercedes for the People

13 But Moses said to the LORD, "Then the Egyptians will hear of it, for in your might you brought up this people from among them, 14and they will tell the inhabitants of this land. They have heard that you, O LORD, are in the midst of this people; for you, O LORD, are seen face to face, and your cloud stands over them and you go in front of them, in a pillar of cloud by day and in a pillar of fire by night. 15Now if you kill this people all at one time, then the nations who have heard about you will say, 16'It is because the LORD was not able to bring this people into the land he swore to give them that he has slaughtered them in the wilderness.' 17And now, therefore, let the power of the LORD be great in the way that you promised when you spoke, saying,

18 'The LORD is slow to anger,
  and abounding in steadfast love,
  forgiving iniquity and
    transgression,
  but by no means clearing the
    guilty,
  visiting the iniquity of the parents

upon the children
to the third and the fourth
generation.'
19Forgive the iniquity of this people according to the greatness of your steadfast love, just as you have pardoned this people, from Egypt even until now."

20 Then the LORD said, "I do forgive, just as you have asked; 21nevertheless— as I live, and as all the earth shall be filled with the glory of the LORD— 22none of the people who have seen my glory and the signs that I did in Egypt and in the wilderness, and yet have tested me these ten times and have not obeyed my voice, 23shall see the land that I swore to give to their ancestors; none of those who despised me shall see it. 24But my servant Caleb, because he has a different spirit and has followed me wholeheartedly, I will bring into the land into which he went, and his descendants shall possess it. 25Now, since the Amalekites and the Canaanites live in the valleys, turn tomorrow and set out for the wilderness by the way to the Red Sea."[b]

An Attempted Invasion is Repulsed

26 And the LORD spoke to Moses and to Aaron, saying: 27How long shall this wicked congregation complain against me? I have heard the complaints of the Israelites, which they complain against me. 28Say to them, "As I live," says the LORD, "I will do to you the very things I heard you say: 29your dead bodies shall fall in this very wilderness; and of all your number, included in the census, from twenty years old and upward, who have complained against me, 30not one of you shall come into the land in which I swore to settle you, except Caleb son of Jephunneh and Joshua son of Nun. 31But your little ones, who you said would become booty, I will bring in, and they shall know the land that you have despised. 32But as for you, your dead bodies shall fall in this wilderness. 33And your children shall be shepherds in the wilderness for forty years, and shall suffer for your faithlessness, until the last of your dead bodies lies in the wilderness. 34According to the number of the days in which you spied out the

land, forty days, for every day a year, you shall bear your iniquity, forty years, and you shall know my displeasure." 35I the LORD have spoken; surely I will do thus to all this wicked congregation gathered together against me: in this wilderness they shall come to a full end, and there they shall die.

HE THAT COMPLAINS OR MURMURS IS NOT PERFECT, NOR IS HE EVEN A GOOD CHRISTIAN.

—*John of the Cross*

---

36 And the men whom Moses sent to spy out the land, who returned and made all the congregation complain against him by bringing a bad report about the land— 37the men who brought an unfavorable report about the land died by a plague before the LORD. 38But Joshua son of Nun and Caleb son of Jephunneh alone remained alive, of those men who went to spy out the land.

39 When Moses told these words to all the Israelites, the people mourned greatly. 40They rose early in the morning and went up to the heights of the hill country, saying, "Here we are. We will go up to the place that the LORD has promised, for we have sinned." 41But Moses said, "Why do you continue to transgress the command of the LORD? That will not succeed. 42Do not go up, for the LORD is not with you; do not let yourselves be struck down before your enemies. 43For the Amalekites and the Canaanites will confront you there, and you shall fall by the sword; because you have turned back from following the LORD, the LORD will not be with you." 44But they presumed to go up to the heights of the hill country, even though the ark of the covenant of the LORD, and Moses, had not left the camp. 45Then the Amalekites and the Canaanites who lived in that hill country came down and defeated them, pursuing them as far as Hormah.

Various Offerings

15 The LORD spoke to Moses, saying: 2Speak to the Israelites and say to them: When you come

b Or *Sea of Reeds*

into the land you are to inhabit, which I am giving you, 3and you make an offering by fire to the LORD from the herd or from the flock—whether a burnt offering or a sacrifice, to fulfill a vow or as a freewill offering or at your appointed festivals—to make a pleasing odor for the LORD, 4then whoever presents such an offering to the LORD shall present also a grain offering, one-tenth of an ephah of choice flour, mixed with one-fourth of a hin of oil. 5Moreover, you shall offer one-fourth of a hin of wine as a drink offering with the burnt offering or the sacrifice, for each lamb. 6For a ram, you shall offer a grain offering, two-tenths of an ephah of choice flour mixed with one-third of a hin of oil; 7and as a drink offering you shall offer one-third of a hin of wine, a pleasing odor to the LORD. 8When you offer a bull as a burnt offering or a sacrifice, to fulfill a vow or as an offering of well-being to the LORD, 9then you shall present with the bull a grain offering, three-tenths of an ephah of choice flour, mixed with half a hin of oil, 10and you shall present as a drink offering half a hin of wine, as an offering by fire, a pleasing odor to the LORD.

11 Thus it shall be done for each ox or ram, or for each of the male lambs or the kids. 12According to the number that you offer, so you shall do with each and every one. 13Every native Israelite shall do these things in this way, in presenting an offering by fire, a pleasing odor to the LORD. 14An alien who lives with you, or who takes up permanent residence among you, and wishes to offer an offering by fire, a pleasing odor to the LORD, shall do as you do. 15As for the assembly, there shall be for both you and the resident alien a single statute, a perpetual statute throughout your generations; you and the alien shall be alike before the LORD. 16You and the alien who resides with you shall have the same law and the same ordinance.

17 The LORD spoke to Moses, saying: 18Speak to the Israelites and say to them: After you come into the land to which I am bringing you, 19whenever you eat of the bread of the land, you shall present a donation to the LORD. 20From your first batch of dough you shall present a loaf as a donation; you

shall present it just as you present a donation from the threshing floor. 21Throughout your generations you shall give to the LORD a donation from the first of your batch of dough.

22 But if you unintentionally fail to observe all these commandments that the LORD has spoken to Moses— 23everything that the LORD has commanded you by Moses, from the day the LORD gave commandment and thereafter, throughout your generations— 24then if it was done unintentionally without the knowledge of the congregation, the whole congregation shall offer one young bull for a burnt offering, a pleasing odor to the LORD, together with its grain offering and its drink offering, according to the ordinance, and one male goat for a sin offering. 25The priest shall make atonement for all the congregation of the Israelites, and they shall be forgiven; it was unintentional, and they have brought their offering, an offering by fire to the LORD, and their sin offering before the LORD, for their error. 26All the congregation of the Israelites shall be forgiven, as well as the aliens residing among them, because the whole people was involved in the error.

27 An individual who sins unintentionally shall present a female goat a year old for a sin offering. 28And the priest shall make atonement before the LORD for the one who commits an error, when it is unintentional, to make atonement for the person, who then shall be forgiven. 29For both the native among the Israelites and the alien residing among them—you shall have the same law for anyone who acts in error. 30But whoever acts high-handedly, whether a native or an alien, affronts the LORD, and shall be cut off from among the people. 31Because of having despised the word of the LORD and broken his commandment, such a person shall be utterly cut off and bear the guilt.

Penalty for Violating the Sabbath

32 When the Israelites were in the wilderness, they found a man gathering sticks on the sabbath day. 33Those who found him gathering sticks brought him to Moses, Aaron, and to the whole congregation. 34They put him in custody,

because it was not clear what should be done to him. 35Then the LORD said to Moses, "The man shall be put to death; all the congregation shall stone him outside the camp." 36The whole congregation brought him outside the camp and stoned him to death, just as the LORD had commanded Moses.

Fringes on Garments

37 The LORD said to Moses: 38Speak to the Israelites, and tell them to make fringes on the corners of their garments throughout their generations and to put a blue cord on the fringe at each corner. 39You have the fringe so that, when you see it, you will remember all the commandments of the LORD and do them, and not follow the lust of your own heart and your own eyes. 40So you shall remember and do all my commandments, and you shall be holy to your God. 41I am the LORD your God, who brought you out of the land of Egypt, to be your God: I am the LORD your God.

Revolt of Korah, Dathan, and Abiram

16 Now Korah son of Izhar son of Kohath son of Levi, along with Dathan and Abiram sons of Eliab, and On son of Peleth—descendants of Reuben—took 2two hundred fifty Israelite men, leaders of the congregation, chosen from the assembly, well-known men,c and they confronted Moses. 3They assembled against Moses and against Aaron, and said to them, "You have gone too far! All the congregation are holy, every one of them, and the LORD is among them. So why then do you exalt yourselves above the assembly of the LORD?" 4When Moses heard it, he fell on his face. 5Then he said to Korah and all his company, "In the morning the LORD will make known who is his, and who is holy, and who will be allowed to approach him; the one whom he will choose he will allow to approach him. 6Do this: take censers, Korah and all yourd company, 7and tomorrow put fire in them, and lay incense on them before the LORD; and the man whom the LORD chooses shall be the holy one. You Levites have gone too far!" 8Then Moses

said to Korah, "Hear now, you Levites! 9Is it too little for you that the God of Israel has separated you from the congregation of Israel, to allow you to approach him in order to perform the duties of the LORD's tabernacle, and to stand before the congregation and serve them? 10He has allowed you to approach him, and all your brother Levites with you; yet you seek the priesthood as well! 11Therefore you and all your company have gathered together against the LORD. What is Aaron that you rail against him?"

12 Moses sent for Dathan and Abiram sons of Eliab; but they said, "We will not come! 13Is it too little that you have brought us up out of a land flowing with milk and honey to kill us in the wilderness, that you must also lord it over us? 14It is clear you have not brought us into a land flowing with milk and honey, or given us an inheritance of fields and vineyards. Would you put out the eyes of these men? We will not come!"

15 Moses was very angry and said to the LORD, "Pay no attention to their offering. I have not taken one donkey from them, and I have not harmed any one of them." 16And Moses said to Korah, "As for you and all your company, be present tomorrow before the LORD, you and they and Aaron; 17and let each one of you take his censer, and put incense on it, and each one of you present his censer before the LORD, two hundred fifty censers; you also, and Aaron, each his censer." 18So each man took his censer, and they put fire in the censers and laid incense on them, and they stood at the entrance of the tent of meeting with Moses and Aaron. 19Then Korah assembled the whole congregation against them at the entrance of the tent of meeting. And the glory of the LORD appeared to the whole congregation.

20 Then the LORD spoke to Moses and to Aaron, saying: 21Separate yourselves from this congregation, so that I may consume them in a moment. 22They fell on their faces, and said, "O God, the God of the spirits of all flesh, shall one person

c Cn: Heb and they confronted Moses, and two hundred fifty men . . . well-known men   d Heb his

JEALOUSY AND THE GRACE OF REPENTANCE
Clement of Rome

VERSE: Numbers 16.1   **PASSAGE:** Numbers 16.1–3, 22–35

nd Cain said to Abel his brother, 'Let us go out to the field.' And it came to pass, while they were in the field, that Cain rose up against Abel his brother and killed him" (see Genesis 4.8). You see, brothers, jealousy and envy brought about a brother's murder. Because of jealousy our father Jacob ran away from the presence of Esau his brother. Jealousy caused Joseph to be persecuted nearly to death, and to be sold into slavery. Jealousy compelled Moses to flee from the presence of Pharaoh, king of Egypt, when he was asked by his own countryman, "Who made you a judge or ruler over us? Do you want to kill me, just as you killed the Egyptian yesterday?" (see Exodus 2.14). Because of jealousy Aaron and Miriam were excluded from the camp. Jealousy brought Dathan and Abiram down alive into *hades*, because they revolted against Moses, the servant of God. Because of jealousy David not only was envied by the Philistines, but also was persecuted by Saul, king of Israel.

But to pass from the examples of ancient times, let us come to those champions who lived nearest to our time. Let us set before us the noble examples which belong to our own generation. Because of jealousy and envy the greatest and most righteous pillars were persecuted, and fought to the death. Let us set before our eyes the good apostles . . .

We write these things, dear friends, not only to admonish you, but also to remind ourselves. For we are in the same arena, and the same contest awaits us. Therefore let us abandon empty and futile thoughts, and let us conform to the glorious and holy rule of our tradition; indeed, let us note what is good and what is pleasing and what is acceptable in the sight of him who made us. Let us fix our eyes on the blood of Christ and understand how precious it is to his Father, because, being poured out for our salvation, it won for the whole world the grace of repentance.

ADDITIONAL SCRIPTURE READING:
Job 5.2; Philippians 4.8–9; James 3.16

Go to page 183 for your next devotional reading.

sin and you become angry with the whole congregation?"

23 And the LORD spoke to Moses, saying: 24Say to the congregation: Get away from the dwellings of Korah, Dathan, and Abiram. 25So Moses got up and went to Dathan and Abiram; the elders of Israel followed him. 26He said to the congregation, "Turn away from the tents of these wicked men, and touch nothing of theirs, or you will be swept away for all their sins." 27So they got away from the dwellings of Korah, Dathan, and Abiram; and Dathan and Abiram came out and stood at the entrance of their tents, together with their wives, their children, and their little ones. 28And Moses said, "This is how you shall know that the LORD has sent me to do all these works; it has not been of my own accord: 29If these people die a natural death, or if a natural fate comes on them, then the LORD has not sent me. 30But if the LORD creates something new, and the ground opens its mouth and swallows them up, with all that belongs to them, and they go down alive into Sheol, then you shall know that these men have despised the LORD."

31 As soon as he finished speaking all these words, the ground under them was split apart. 32The earth opened its mouth and swallowed them up, along with their households—everyone who belonged to Korah and all their goods. 33So they with all that belonged to them went down alive into Sheol; the earth closed over them, and they perished from the midst of the assembly. 34All Israel around them fled at their outcry, for they said, "The earth will swallow us too!" 35And fire came out from the LORD and consumed the two hundred fifty men offering the incense.

36e Then the LORD spoke to Moses, saying: 37Tell Eleazar son of Aaron the priest to take the censers out of the blaze; then scatter the fire far and wide. 38For the censers of these sinners have become holy at the cost of their lives. Make them into hammered plates as a covering for the altar, for they presented them before the LORD and they became holy. Thus they shall be a sign to the Israelites. 39So Eleazar the priest took

the bronze censers that had been presented by those who were burned; and they were hammered out as a covering for the altar— 40a reminder to the Israelites that no outsider, who is not of the descendants of Aaron, shall approach to offer incense before the LORD, so as not to become like Korah and his company—just as the LORD had said to him through Moses.

41 On the next day, however, the whole congregation of the Israelites rebelled against Moses and against Aaron, saying, "You have killed the people of the LORD." 42And when the congregation had assembled against them, Moses and Aaron turned toward the tent of meeting; the cloud had covered it and the glory of the LORD appeared. 43Then Moses and Aaron came to the front of the tent of meeting, 44and the LORD spoke to Moses, saying, 45"Get away from this congregation, so that I may consume them in a moment." And they fell on their faces. 46Moses said to Aaron, "Take your censer, put fire on it from the altar and lay incense on it, and carry it quickly to the congregation and make atonement for them. For wrath has gone out from the LORD; the plague has begun." 47So Aaron took it as Moses had ordered, and ran into the middle of the assembly, where the plague had already begun among the people. He put on the incense, and made atonement for the people. 48He stood between the dead and the living; and the plague was stopped. 49Those who died by the plague were fourteen thousand seven hundred, besides those who died in the affair of Korah. 50When the plague was stopped, Aaron returned to Moses at the entrance of the tent of meeting.

The Budding of Aaron's Rod

17f The LORD spoke to Moses, saying: 2Speak to the Israelites, and get twelve staffs from them, one for each ancestral house, from all the leaders of their ancestral houses. Write each man's name on his staff, 3and write Aaron's name on the staff of Levi. For there shall be one staff for the head of each ancestral house. 4Place them in the tent of meeting before the covenant,g

e Ch 17.1 in Heb   f Ch 17.16 in Heb   g Or treaty, or testimony; Heb eduth where I meet with you. 5And the staff of the man whom I choose shall sprout; thus I will put a stop to the complaints of the Israelites that they continually make against you. 6Moses spoke to the Israelites; and all their leaders gave him staffs, one for each leader, according to their ancestral houses, twelve staffs; and the staff of Aaron was among theirs. 7So Moses placed the staffs before the LORD in the tent of the covenant.h

8 When Moses went into the tent of the covenanth on the next day, the staff of Aaron for the house of Levi had sprouted. It put forth buds, produced blossoms, and bore ripe almonds. 9Then Moses brought out all the staffs from before the LORD to all the Israelites; and they looked, and each man took his staff. 10And the LORD said to Moses, "Put back the staff of Aaron before the covenant,h to be kept as a warning to rebels, so that you may make an end of their complaints against me, or else they will die." 11Moses did so; just as the LORD commanded him, so he did.

12 The Israelites said to Moses, "We are perishing; we are lost, all of us are lost! 13Everyone who approaches the tabernacle of the LORD will die. Are we all to perish?"

Responsibility of Priests and Levites

18 The LORD said to Aaron: You and your sons and your ancestral house with you shall bear responsibility for offenses connected with the sanctuary, while you and your sons alone shall bear responsibility for offenses connected with the priesthood. 2So bring with you also your brothers of the tribe of Levi, your ancestral tribe, in order that they may be joined to you, and serve you while you and your sons with you are in front of the tent of the covenant.h 3They shall perform duties for you and for the whole tent. But they must not approach either the utensils of the sanctuary or the altar, otherwise both they and you will die. 4They are attached to you in order to perform the duties of the tent of meeting, for all the service of the tent; no outsider shall approach you. 5You yourselves shall per-

form the duties of the sanctuary and the duties of the altar, so that wrath may never again come upon the Israelites. 6It is I who now take your brother Levites from among the Israelites; they are now yours as a gift, dedicated to the LORD, to perform the service of the tent of meeting. 7But you and your sons with you shall diligently perform your priestly duties in all that concerns the altar and the area behind the curtain. I give your priesthood as a gift;i any outsider who approaches shall be put to death.

The Priests' Portion

8 The LORD spoke to Aaron: I have given you charge of the offerings made to me, all the holy gifts of the Israelites; I have given them to you and your sons as a priestly portion due you in perpetuity. 9This shall be yours from the most holy things, reserved from the fire: every offering of theirs that they render to me as a most holy thing, whether grain offering, sin offering, or guilt offering, shall belong to you and your sons. 10As a most holy thing you shall eat it; every male may eat it; it shall be holy to you. 11This also is yours: I have given to you, together with your sons and daughters, as a perpetual due, whatever is set aside from the gifts of all the elevation offerings of the Israelites; everyone who is clean in your house may eat them. 12All the best of the oil and all the best of the wine and of the grain, the choice produce that they give to the LORD, I have given to you. 13The first fruits of all that is in their land, which they bring to the LORD, shall be yours; everyone who is clean in your house may eat of it. 14Every devoted thing in Israel shall be yours. 15The first issue of the womb of all creatures, human and animal, which is offered to the LORD, shall be yours; but the firstborn of human beings you shall redeem, and the firstborn of unclean animals you shall redeem. 16Their redemption price, reckoned from one month of age, you shall fix at five shekels of silver, according to the shekel of the sanctuary (that is, twenty gerahs). 17But the firstborn of a cow, or the firstborn of a sheep, or the firstborn of a goat, you shall not redeem; they are

h Or treaty, or testimony; Heb eduth   i Heb as a service of gift holy. You shall dash their blood on the altar, and shall turn their fat into smoke as an offering by fire for a pleasing odor to the LORD; [18]but their flesh shall be yours, just as the breast that is elevated and as the right thigh are yours. [19]All the holy offerings that the Israelites present to the LORD I have given to you, together with your sons and daughters, as a perpetual due; it is a covenant of salt forever before the LORD for you and your descendants as well. [20]Then the LORD said to Aaron: You shall have no allotment in their land, nor shall you have any share among them; I am your share and your possession among the Israelites.

21 To the Levites I have given every tithe in Israel for a possession in return for the service that they perform, the service in the tent of meeting. [22]From now on the Israelites shall no longer approach the tent of meeting, or else they will incur guilt and die. [23]But the Levites shall perform the service of the tent of meeting, and they shall bear responsibility for their own offenses; it shall be a perpetual statute throughout your generations. But among the Israelites they shall have no allotment, [24]because I have given to the Levites as their portion the tithe of the Israelites, which they set apart as an offering to the LORD. Therefore I have said of them that they shall have no allotment among the Israelites.

25 Then the LORD spoke to Moses, saying: [26]You shall speak to the Levites, saying: When you receive from the Israelites the tithe that I have given you from them for your portion, you shall set apart an offering from it to the LORD, a tithe of the tithe. [27]It shall be reckoned to you as your gift, the same as the grain of the threshing floor and the fullness of the wine press. [28]Thus you also shall set apart an offering to the LORD from all the tithes that you receive from the Israelites; and from them you shall give the LORD's offering to the priest Aaron. [29]Out of all the gifts to you, you shall set apart every offering due to the LORD; the best of all of them is the part to be consecrated. [30]Say also to them: When you have set apart the best of it, then the rest

shall be reckoned to the Levites as produce of the threshing floor, and as produce of the wine press. [31]You may eat it in any place, you and your households; for it is your payment for your service in the tent of meeting. [32]You shall incur no guilt by reason of it, when you have offered the best of it. But you shall not profane the holy gifts of the Israelites, on pain of death.

Ceremony of the Red Heifer

19 The LORD spoke to Moses and Aaron, saying: [2]This is a statute of the law that the LORD has commanded: Tell the Israelites to bring you a red heifer without defect, in which there is no blemish and on which no yoke has been laid. [3]You shall give it to the priest Eleazar, and it shall be taken outside the camp and slaughtered in his presence. [4]The priest Eleazar shall take some of its blood with his finger and sprinkle it seven times towards the front of the tent of meeting. [5]Then the heifer shall be burned in his sight; its skin, its flesh, and its blood, with its dung, shall be burned. [6]The priest shall take cedarwood, hyssop, and crimson material, and throw them into the fire in which the heifer is burning. [7]Then the priest shall wash his clothes and bathe his body in water, and afterwards he may come into the camp; but the priest shall remain unclean until evening. [8]The one who burns the heifer[j] shall wash his clothes in water and bathe his body in water; he shall remain unclean until evening. [9]Then someone who is clean shall gather up the ashes of the heifer, and deposit them outside the camp in a clean place; and they shall be kept for the congregation of the Israelites for the water for cleansing. It is a purification offering. [10]The one who gathers the ashes of the heifer shall wash his clothes and be unclean until evening.

This shall be a perpetual statute for the Israelites and for the alien residing among them. [11]Those who touch the dead body of any human being shall be unclean seven days. [12]They shall purify themselves with the water on the third day and on the seventh day, and so be

[j] Heb it

clean; but if they do not purify themselves on the third day and on the seventh day, they will not become clean. 13All who touch a corpse, the body of a human being who has died, and do not purify themselves, defile the tabernacle of the LORD; such persons shall be cut off from Israel. Since water for cleansing was not dashed on them, they remain unclean; their uncleanness is still on them.

14 This is the law when someone dies in a tent: everyone who comes into the tent, and everyone who is in the tent, shall be unclean seven days. 15And every open vessel with no cover fastened on it is unclean. 16Whoever in the open field touches one who has been killed by a sword, or who has died naturally,k or a human bone, or a grave, shall be unclean seven days. 17For the unclean they shall take some ashes of the burnt purification offering, and running water shall be added in a vessel; 18then a clean person shall take hyssop, dip it in the water, and sprinkle it on the tent, on all the furnishings, on the persons who were there, and on whoever touched the bone, the slain, the corpse, or the grave. 19The clean person shall sprinkle the unclean ones on the third day and on the seventh day, thus purifying them on the seventh day. Then they shall wash their clothes and bathe themselves in water, and at evening they shall be clean. 20Any who are unclean but do not purify themselves, those persons shall be cut off from the assembly, for they have defiled the sanctuary of the LORD. Since the water for cleansing has not been dashed on them, they are unclean.

21 It shall be a perpetual statute for them. The one who sprinkles the water for cleansing shall wash his clothes, and whoever touches the water for cleansing shall be unclean until evening. 22Whatever the unclean person touches shall be unclean, and anyone who touches it shall be unclean until evening.

The Waters of Meribah

20 The Israelites, the whole congregation, came into the wilderness of Zin in the first month, and the people stayed in Kadesh. Miriam died there, and was buried there.

2 Now there was no water for the congregation; so they gathered together against Moses and against Aaron. 3The people quarreled with Moses and said, "Would that we had died when our kindred died before the LORD! 4Why have you brought the assembly of the LORD into this wilderness for us and our livestock to die here? 5Why have you brought us up out of Egypt, to bring us to this wretched place? It is no place for grain, or figs, or vines, or pomegranates; and there is no water to drink." 6Then Moses and Aaron went away from the assembly to the entrance of the tent of meeting; they fell on their faces, and the glory of the LORD appeared to them. 7The LORD spoke to Moses, saying: 8Take the staff, and assemble the congregation, you and your brother Aaron, and command the rock before their eyes to yield its water. Thus you shall bring water out of the rock for them; thus you shall provide drink for the congregation and their livestock.

9 So Moses took the staff from before the LORD, as he had commanded him. 10Moses and Aaron gathered the assembly together before the rock, and he said to them, "Listen, you rebels, shall we bring water for you out of this rock?" 11Then Moses lifted up his hand and struck the rock twice with his staff; water came out abundantly, and the congregation and their livestock drank. 12But the LORD said to Moses and Aaron, "Because you did not trust in me, to show my holiness before the eyes of the Israelites, therefore you shall not bring this assembly into the land that I have given them." 13These are the waters of Meribah,l where the people of Israel quarreled with the LORD, and by which he showed his holiness.

Passage through Edom Refused

14 Moses sent messengers from Kadesh to the king of Edom, "Thus says your brother Israel: You know all the adversity that has befallen us: 15how our ancestors went down to Egypt, and we lived in Egypt a long time; and the

---

k Heb lacks *naturally*　　l That is *Quarrel*

Egyptians oppressed us and our ancestors; **16**and when we cried to the LORD, he heard our voice, and sent an angel and brought us out of Egypt; and here we are in Kadesh, a town on the edge of your territory. **17**Now let us pass through your land. We will not pass through field or vineyard, or drink water from any well; we will go along the King's Highway, not turning aside to the right hand or to the left until we have passed through your territory."

18 But Edom said to him, "You shall not pass through, or we will come out with the sword against you." **19**The Israelites said to him, "We will stay on the highway; and if we drink of your water, we and our livestock, then we will pay for it. It is only a small matter; just let us pass through on foot." **20**But he said, "You shall not pass through." And Edom came out against them with a large force, heavily armed. **21**Thus Edom refused to give Israel passage through their territory; so Israel turned away from them.

The Death of Aaron

22 They set out from Kadesh, and the Israelites, the whole congregation, came to Mount Hor. **23**Then the LORD said to Moses and Aaron at Mount Hor, on the border of the land of Edom, **24**"Let Aaron be gathered to his people. For he shall not enter the land that I have given to the Israelites, because you rebelled against my command at the waters of Meribah. **25**Take Aaron and his son Eleazar, and bring them up Mount Hor; **26**strip Aaron of his vestments, and put them on his son Eleazar. But Aaron shall be gathered to his people,*m* and shall die there." **27**Moses did as the LORD had commanded; they went up Mount Hor in the sight of the whole congregation. **28**Moses stripped Aaron of his vestments, and put them on his son Eleazar; and Aaron died there on the top of the mountain. Moses and Eleazar came down from the mountain. **29**When all the congregation saw that Aaron had died, all the house of Israel mourned for Aaron thirty days.

The Bronze Serpent

21 When the Canaanite, the king of Arad, who lived in the Negeb, heard that Israel was coming by the way of Atharim, he fought against Israel and took some of them captive. **2**Then Israel made a vow to the LORD and said, "If you will indeed give this people into our hands, then we will utterly destroy their towns." **3**The LORD listened to the voice of Israel, and handed over the Canaanites; and they utterly destroyed them and their towns; so the place was called Hormah.*n*

4 From Mount Hor they set out by the way to the Red Sea,*o* to go around the land of Edom; but the people became impatient on the way. **5**The people spoke against God and against Moses, "Why have you brought us up out of Egypt to die in the wilderness? For there is no food and no water, and we detest this miserable food." **6**Then the LORD sent poisonous*p* serpents among the people, and they bit the people, so that many Israelites died. **7**The people came to Moses and said, "We have sinned by speaking against the LORD and against you; pray to the LORD to take away the serpents from us." So Moses prayed for the people. **8**And the LORD said to Moses, "Make a poisonous*q* serpent, and set it on a pole; and everyone who is bitten shall look at it and live." **9**So Moses made a serpent of bronze, and put it upon a pole; and whenever a serpent bit someone, that person would look at the serpent of bronze and live.

The Journey to Moab

10 The Israelites set out, and camped in Oboth. **11**They set out from Oboth, and camped at Iye-abarim, in the wilderness bordering Moab toward the sunrise. **12**From there they set out, and camped in the Wadi Zered. **13**From there they set out, and camped on the other side of the Arnon, in*r* the wilderness that extends from the boundary of the Amorites; for the Arnon is the boundary of Moab, between Moab and the Amorites. **14**Wherefore it is said in the Book of the Wars of the LORD,

"Waheb in Suphah and the wadis,

---

m Heb lacks *to his people*   *n* Heb *Destruction*   *o* Or *Sea of Reeds*   *p* Or *fiery*; Heb *seraphim*
q Or *fiery*; Heb *seraph*   *r* Gk: Heb *which is in*

The Arnon [15]and the slopes of the wadis
that extend to the seat of Ar,
and lie along the border of Moab."[s]

16 From there they continued to Beer;[t] that is the well of which the LORD said to Moses, "Gather the people together, and I will give them water." [17]Then Israel sang this song:

"Spring up, O well!—Sing to it!—
18   the well that the leaders sank,
that the nobles of the people dug,
with the scepter, with the staff."

From the wilderness to Mattanah, [19]from Mattanah to Nahaliel, from Nahaliel to Bamoth, [20]and from Bamoth to the valley lying in the region of Moab by the top of Pisgah that overlooks the wasteland.[u]

King Sihon Defeated

21 Then Israel sent messengers to King Sihon of the Amorites, saying, [22]"Let me pass through your land; we will not turn aside into field or vineyard; we will not drink the water of any well; we will go by the King's Highway until we have passed through your territory." [23]But Sihon would not allow Israel to pass through his territory. Sihon gathered all his people together, and went out against Israel to the wilderness; he came to Jahaz, and fought against Israel. [24]Israel put him to the sword, and took possession of his land from the Arnon to the Jabbok, as far as to the Ammonites; for the boundary of the Ammonites was strong. [25]Israel took all these towns, and Israel settled in all the towns of the Amorites, in Heshbon, and in all its villages. [26]For Heshbon was the city of King Sihon of the Amorites, who had fought against the former king of Moab and captured all his land as far as the Arnon. [27]Therefore the ballad singers say,

"Come to Heshbon, let it be built;
let the city of Sihon be established.
28   For fire came out from Heshbon,
flame from the city of Sihon.
It devoured Ar of Moab,
and swallowed up[v] the heights of the Arnon.
29   Woe to you, O Moab!
You are undone, O people of Chemosh!
He has made his sons fugitives,
and his daughters captives,
to an Amorite king, Sihon.
30   So their posterity perished
from Heshbon[w] to Dibon,
and we laid waste until fire
spread to Medeba."[x]

31 Thus Israel settled in the land of the Amorites. [32]Moses sent to spy out Jazer; and they captured its villages, and dispossessed the Amorites who were there.

King Og Defeated

33 Then they turned and went up the road to Bashan; and King Og of Bashan came out against them, he and all his people, to battle at Edrei. [34]But the LORD said to Moses, "Do not be afraid of him; for I have given him into your hand, with all his people, and all his land. You shall do to him as you did to King Sihon of the Amorites, who ruled in Heshbon." [35]So they killed him, his sons, and all his people, until there was no survivor left; and they took possession of his land.

Balak Summons Balaam to Curse Israel

22 The Israelites set out, and camped in the plains of Moab across the Jordan from Jericho. [2]Now Balak son of Zippor saw all that Israel had done to the Amorites. [3]Moab was in great dread of the people, because they were so numerous; Moab was overcome with fear of the people of Israel. [4]And Moab said to the elders of Midian, "This horde will now lick up all that is around us, as an ox licks up the grass of the field." Now Balak son of Zippor was king of Moab at that time. [5]He sent messengers to Balaam son of Beor at Pethor, which is on the Euphrates, in the land of Amaw,[y] to summon him, saying, "A people has come out of Egypt; they have spread over the face of the earth, and they have settled next to me. [6]Come now, curse this people for

s Meaning of Heb uncertain   t That is Well   u Or Jeshimon   v Gk: Heb and the lords of
w Gk: Heb we have shot at them; Heshbon has perished   x Compare Sam Gk: Meaning of MT
uncertain   y Or land of his kinsfolk

me, since they are stronger than I; perhaps I shall be able to defeat them and drive them from the land; for I know that whomever you bless is blessed, and whomever you curse is cursed."

7 So the elders of Moab and the elders of Midian departed with the fees for divination in their hand; and they came to Balaam, and gave him Balak's message. ⁸He said to them, "Stay here tonight, and I will bring back word to you, just as the LORD speaks to me"; so the officials of Moab stayed with Balaam. ⁹God came to Balaam and said, "Who are these men with you?" ¹⁰Balaam said to God, "King Balak son of Zippor of Moab, has sent me this message: ¹¹'A people has come out of Egypt and has spread over the face of the earth; now come, curse them for me; perhaps I shall be able to fight against them and drive them out.'" ¹²God said to Balaam, "You shall not go with them; you shall not curse the people, for they are blessed." ¹³So Balaam rose in the morning, and said to the officials of Balak, "Go to your own land, for the LORD has refused to let me go with you." ¹⁴So the officials of Moab rose and went to Balak, and said, "Balaam refuses to come with us."

15 Once again Balak sent officials, more numerous and more distinguished than these. ¹⁶They came to Balaam and said to him, "Thus says Balak son of Zippor: 'Do not let anything hinder you from coming to me; ¹⁷for I will surely do you great honor, and whatever you say to me I will do; come, curse this people for me.'" ¹⁸But Balaam replied to the servants of Balak, "Although Balak were to give me his house full of silver and gold, I could not go beyond the command of the LORD my God, to do less or more. ¹⁹You remain here, as the others did, so that I may learn what more the LORD may say to me." ²⁰That night God came to Balaam and said to him, "If the men have come to summon you, get up and go with them; but do only what I tell you to do." ²¹So Balaam got up in the morning, saddled his donkey, and went with the officials of Moab.

Balaam, the Donkey, and the Angel

22 God's anger was kindled because he was going, and the angel of the LORD took his stand in the road as his adversary. Now he was riding on the donkey, and his two servants were with him. ²³The donkey saw the angel of the LORD standing in the road, with a drawn sword in his hand; so the donkey turned off the road, and went into the field; and Balaam struck the donkey, to turn it back onto the road. ²⁴Then the angel of the LORD stood in a narrow path between the vineyards, with a wall on either side. ²⁵When the donkey saw the angel of the LORD, it scraped against the wall, and scraped Balaam's foot against the wall; so he struck it again. ²⁶Then the angel of the LORD went ahead, and stood in a narrow place, where there was no way to turn either to the right or to the left. ²⁷When the donkey saw the angel of the LORD, it lay down under Balaam; and Balaam's anger was kindled, and he struck the donkey with his staff. ²⁸Then the LORD opened the mouth of the donkey, and it said to Balaam, "What have I done to you, that you have struck me these three times?" ²⁹Balaam said to the donkey, "Because you have made a fool of me! I wish I had a sword in my hand! I would kill you right now!" ³⁰But the donkey said to Balaam, "Am I not your donkey, which you have ridden all your life to this day? Have I been in the habit of treating you this way?" And he said, "No."

31 Then the LORD opened the eyes of Balaam, and he saw the angel of the LORD standing in the road, with his drawn sword in his hand; and he bowed down, falling on his face. ³²The angel of the LORD said to him, "Why have you struck your donkey these three times? I have come out as an adversary, because your way is perverseᶻ before me. ³³The donkey saw me, and turned away from me these three times. If it had not turned away from me, surely just now I would have killed you and let it live." ³⁴Then Balaam said to the angel of the LORD, "I have sinned, for I did not know that you were standing in the road to oppose me. Now therefore, if it is displeasing to you, I will return home." ³⁵The angel of the LORD said to Balaam, "Go with the men; but speak only what

z Meaning of Heb uncertain

I tell you to speak." So Balaam went on with the officials of Balak.

36 When Balak heard that Balaam had come, he went out to meet him at Ir-moab, on the boundary formed by the Arnon, at the farthest point of the boundary. 37Balak said to Balaam, "Did I not send to summon you? Why did you not come to me? Am I not able to honor you?" 38Balaam said to Balak, "I have come to you now, but do I have power to say just anything? The word God puts in my mouth, that is what I must say." 39Then Balaam went with Balak, and they came to Kiriath-huzoth. 40Balak sacrificed oxen and sheep, and sent them to Balaam and to the officials who were with him.

Balaam's First Oracle

41 On the next day Balak took Balaam and brought him up to Bamoth-baal; and from there he could see part of the people of Israel.*a* **23** 1Then Balaam said to Balak, "Build me seven altars here, and prepare seven bulls and seven rams for me." 2Balak did as Balaam had said; and Balak and Balaam offered a bull and a ram on each altar. 3Then Balaam said to Balak, "Stay here beside your burnt offerings while I go aside. Perhaps the LORD will come to meet me. Whatever he shows me I will tell you." And he went to a bare height. 4 Then God met Balaam; and Balaam said to him, "I have arranged the seven altars, and have offered a bull and a ram on each altar." 5The LORD put a word in Balaam's mouth, and said, "Return to Balak, and this is what you must say." 6So he returned to Balak,*b* who was standing beside his burnt offerings with all the officials of Moab. 7Then Balaam*c* uttered his oracle, saying:

"Balak has brought me from Aram,
    the king of Moab from the
    eastern mountains:
'Come, curse Jacob for me;
Come, denounce Israel!'
8 How can I curse whom God has
    not cursed?
How can I denounce those whom
    the LORD has not denounced?
9 For from the top of the crags I see
    him,

from the hills I behold him;
Here is a people living alone,
    and not reckoning itself among
    the nations!
10 Who can count the dust of Jacob,
    or number the dust-cloud*d* of
    Israel?
Let me die the death of the upright,
    and let my end be like his!"

11 Then Balak said to Balaam, "What have you done to me? I brought you to curse my enemies; but now you have done nothing but bless them." 12He answered, "Must I not take care to say what the LORD puts into my mouth?"

Balaam's Second Oracle

13 So Balak said to him, "Come with me to another place from which you may see them; you shall see only part of them, and shall not see them all; then curse them for me from there." 14So he took him to the field of Zophim, to the top of Pisgah. He built seven altars, and offered a bull and a ram on each altar. 15Balaam said to Balak, "Stand here beside your burnt offerings, while I meet the LORD over there." 16The LORD met Balaam, put a word into his mouth, and said, "Return to Balak, and this is what you shall say." 17When he came to him, he was standing beside his burnt offerings with the officials of Moab. Balak said to him, "What has the LORD said?" 18Then Balaam uttered his oracle, saying:

"Rise, Balak, and hear;
    listen to me, O son of Zippor:
19 God is not a human being, that he
    should lie,
or a mortal, that he should
    change his mind.
Has he promised, and will he not
    do it?
Has he spoken, and will he not
    fulfill it?
20 See, I received a command to bless;
    he has blessed, and I cannot
    revoke it.
21 He has not beheld misfortune in
    Jacob;
nor has he seen trouble in Israel.
The LORD their God is with them,
    acclaimed as a king among them.
22 God, who brings them out of Egypt,

---

a Heb lacks *of Israel*   *b* Heb *him*   *c* Heb *he*   *d* Or *fourth part*

is like the horns of a wild ox for
them.
23 Surely there is no enchantment
against Jacob,
no divination against Israel;
now it shall be said of Jacob and
Israel,
'See what God has done!'
24 Look, a people rising up like a
lioness,
and rousing itself like a lion!
It does not lie down until it has
eaten the prey
and drunk the blood of the
slain."
25 Then Balak said to Balaam, "Do
not curse them at all, and do not bless
them at all." 26But Balaam answered
Balak, "Did I not tell you, 'Whatever the
LORD says, that is what I must do'?"
27 So Balak said to Balaam, "Come
now, I will take you to another place;
perhaps it will please God that you may
curse them for me from there." 28So
Balak took Balaam to the top of Peor,
which overlooks the wasteland.e 29Ba-
laam said to Balak, "Build me seven
altars here, and prepare seven bulls and
seven rams for me." 30So Balak did as
Balaam had said, and offered a bull and
a ram on each altar.

Balaam's Third Oracle

24 Now Balaam saw that it
pleased the LORD to bless Isra-
el, so he did not go, as at other times, to
look for omens, but set his face toward
the wilderness. 2Balaam looked up and
saw Israel camping tribe by tribe. Then
the spirit of God came upon him, 3and
he uttered his oracle, saying:
"The oracle of Balaam son of Beor,
the oracle of the man whose eye
is clear,f
4 the oracle of one who hears the
words of God,
who sees the vision of the
Almighty,g
who falls down, but with eyes
uncovered:
5 how fair are your tents, O Jacob,
your encampments, O Israel!
6 Like palm groves that stretch far
away,

like gardens beside a river,
like aloes that the LORD has
planted,
like cedar trees beside the waters.
7 Water shall flow from his buckets,
and his seed shall have abundant
water,
his king shall be higher than Agag,
and his kingdom shall be exalted.
8 God who brings him out of Egypt,
is like the horns of a wild ox for
him;
he shall devour the nations that are
his foes
and break their bones.
He shall strike with his arrows.h
9 He crouched, he lay down like a
lion,
and like a lioness; who will rouse
him up?
Blessed is everyone who blesses
you,
and cursed is everyone who
curses you."
10 Then Balak's anger was kindled
against Balaam, and he struck his hands
together. Balak said to Balaam, "I summoned you to curse my enemies, but
instead you have blessed them these
three times. 11Now be off with you! Go
home! I said, 'I will reward you richly,'
but the LORD has denied you any
reward." 12And Balaam said to Balak,
"Did I not tell your messengers whom
you sent to me, 13'If Balak should give
me his house full of silver and gold, I
would not be able to go beyond the word
of the LORD, to do either good or bad of
my own will; what the LORD says, that
is what I will say'? 14So now, I am going
to my people; let me advise you what
this people will do to your people in
days to come."

Balaam's Fourth Oracle

15 So he uttered his oracle, saying:
"The oracle of Balaam son of Beor,
the oracle of the man whose eye
is clear,f
16 the oracle of one who hears the
words of God,
and knows the knowledge of the
Most High,i

e Or overlooks Jeshimon   f Or closed or open   g Traditional rendering of Heb Shaddai
h Meaning of Heb uncertain   i Or of Elyon

who sees the vision of the
    Almighty,*j*
    who falls down, but with his eyes
        uncovered:
17 I see him, but not now;
    I behold him, but not near—
    a star shall come out of Jacob,
    and a scepter shall rise out of
        Israel;
    it shall crush the borderlands*k* of
        Moab,
    and the territory*l* of all the
        Shethites.
18 Edom will become a possession,
    Seir a possession of its enemies,*m*
    while Israel does valiantly.
19 One out of Jacob shall rule,
    and destroy the survivors of Ir."
20 Then he looked on Amalek, and
uttered his oracle, saying:
    "First among the nations was
        Amalek,
    but its end is to perish forever."
21 Then he looked on the Kenite, and
uttered his oracle, saying:
    "Enduring is your dwelling place,
    and your nest is set in the rock;
22 yet Kain is destined for burning.
    How long shall Asshur take you
        away captive?"
23 Again he uttered his oracle, saying:
    "Alas, who shall live when God
        does this?
24   But ships shall come from Kittim
    and shall afflict Asshur and Eber;
    and he also shall perish forever."
25 Then Balaam got up and went
back to his place, and Balak also went
his way.

Worship of Baal of Peor

25 While Israel was staying at
Shittim, the people began to
have sexual relations with the women of
Moab. 2These invited the people to the
sacrifices of their gods, and the people
ate and bowed down to their gods. 3Thus
Israel yoked itself to the Baal of Peor, and
the LORD's anger was kindled against
Israel. 4The LORD said to Moses, "Take
all the chiefs of the people, and impale
them in the sun before the LORD, in order
that the fierce anger of the LORD may
turn away from Israel." 5And Moses said
to the judges of Israel, "Each of you shall
kill any of your people who have yoked
themselves to the Baal of Peor."

6 Just then one of the Israelites came
and brought a Midianite woman into his
family, in the sight of Moses and in the
sight of the whole congregation of the
Israelites, while they were weeping at
the entrance of the tent of meeting.
7When Phinehas son of Eleazar, son of
Aaron the priest, saw it, he got up and
left the congregation. Taking a spear in
his hand, 8he went after the Israelite
man into the tent, and pierced the two
of them, the Israelite and the woman,
through the belly. So the plague was
stopped among the people of Israel.
9Nevertheless those that died by the
plague were twenty-four thousand.

10 The LORD spoke to Moses, saying:
11"Phinehas son of Eleazar, son of Aaron
the priest, has turned back my wrath
from the Israelites by manifesting such
zeal among them on my behalf that in
my jealousy I did not consume the Israelites. 12Therefore say, 'I hereby grant
him my covenant of peace. 13It shall be
for him and for his descendants after
him a covenant of perpetual priesthood,
because he was zealous for his God, and
made atonement for the Israelites.' "

14 The name of the slain Israelite
man, who was killed with the Midianite
woman, was Zimri son of Salu, head of
an ancestral house belonging to the Simeonites. 15The name of the Midianite
woman who was killed was Cozbi
daughter of Zur, who was the head of a
clan, an ancestral house in Midian.

16 The LORD said to Moses, 17"Harass
the Midianites, and defeat them; 18for
they have harassed you by the trickery
with which they deceived you in the
affair of Peor, and in the affair of Cozbi,
the daughter of a leader of Midian, their
sister; she was killed on the day of the
plague that resulted from Peor."

A Census of the New Generation

26 After the plague the LORD said
to Moses and to Eleazar son of
Aaron the priest, 2"Take a census of the
whole congregation of the Israelites,

---

j Traditional rendering of Heb *Shaddai*   *k* Or *forehead*   *l* Some Mss read *skull*   *m* Heb *Seir, its*
enemies, a possession

from twenty years old and upward, by their ancestral houses, everyone in Israel able to go to war." [3]Moses and Eleazar the priest spoke with them in the plains of Moab by the Jordan opposite Jericho, saying, [4]"Take a census of the people,[n] from twenty years old and upward," as the LORD commanded Moses.

The Israelites, who came out of the land of Egypt, were:

5 Reuben, the firstborn of Israel. The descendants of Reuben: of Hanoch, the clan of the Hanochites; of Pallu, the clan of the Palluites; [6]of Hezron, the clan of the Hezronites; of Carmi, the clan of the Carmites. [7]These are the clans of the Reubenites; the number of those enrolled was forty-three thousand seven hundred thirty. [8]And the descendants of Pallu: Eliab. [9]The descendants of Eliab: Nemuel, Dathan, and Abiram. These are the same Dathan and Abiram, chosen from the congregation, who rebelled against Moses and Aaron in the company of Korah, when they rebelled against the LORD, [10]and the earth opened its mouth and swallowed them up along with Korah, when that company died, when the fire devoured two hundred fifty men; and they became a warning. [11]Notwithstanding, the sons of Korah did not die.

12 The descendants of Simeon by their clans: of Nemuel, the clan of the Nemuelites; of Jamin, the clan of the Jaminites; of Jachin, the clan of the Jachinites; [13]of Zerah, the clan of the Zerahites; of Shaul, the clan of the Shaulites.[o] [14]These are the clans of the Simeonites, twenty-two thousand two hundred.

15 The children of Gad by their clans: of Zephon, the clan of the Zephonites; of Haggi, the clan of the Haggites; of Shuni, the clan of the Shunites; [16]of Ozni, the clan of the Oznites; of Eri, the clan of the Erites; [17]of Arod, the clan of the Arodites; of Areli, the clan of the Arelites. [18]These are the clans of the Gadites: the number of those enrolled was forty thousand five hundred.

19 The sons of Judah: Er and Onan; Er and Onan died in the land of Canaan. [20]The descendants of Judah by their clans were: of Shelah, the clan of the

Shelanites; of Perez, the clan of the Perezites; of Zerah, the clan of the Zerahites. [21]The descendants of Perez were: of Hezron, the clan of the Hezronites; of Hamul, the clan of the Hamulites. [22]These are the clans of Judah: the number of those enrolled was seventy-six thousand five hundred.

23 The descendants of Issachar by their clans: of Tola, the clan of the Tolaites; of Puvah, the clan of the Punites; [24]of Jashub, the clan of the Jashubites; of Shimron, the clan of the Shimronites. [25]These are the clans of Issachar: sixty-four thousand three hundred enrolled.

26 The descendants of Zebulun by their clans: of Sered, the clan of the Seredites; of Elon, the clan of the Elonites; of Jahleel, the clan of the Jahleelites. [27]These are the clans of the Zebulunites; the number of those enrolled was sixty thousand five hundred.

28 The sons of Joseph by their clans: Manasseh and Ephraim. [29]The descendants of Manasseh: of Machir, the clan of the Machirites; and Machir was the father of Gilead; of Gilead, the clan of the Gileadites. [30]These are the descendants of Gilead: of Iezer, the clan of the Iezerites; of Helek, the clan of the Helekites; [31]and of Asriel, the clan of the Asrielites; and of Shechem, the clan of the Shechemites; [32]and of Shemida, the clan of the Shemidaites; and of Hepher, the clan of the Hepherites. [33]Now Zelophehad son of Hepher had no sons, but daughters: and the names of the daughters of Zelophehad were Mahlah, Noah, Hoglah, Milcah, and Tirzah. [34]These are the clans of Manasseh; the number of those enrolled was fifty-two thousand seven hundred.

35 These are the descendants of Ephraim according to their clans: of Shuthelah, the clan of the Shuthelahites; of Becher, the clan of the Becherites; of Tahan, the clan of the Tahanites. [36]And these are the descendants of Shuthelah: of Eran, the clan of the Eranites. [37]These are the clans of the Ephraimites: the number of those enrolled was thirty-two thousand five hundred. These are the descendants of Joseph by their clans.

n Heb lacks take a census of the people: Compare verse 2   o Or Saul . . . Saulites

38 The descendants of Benjamin by their clans: of Bela, the clan of the Belaites; of Ashbel, the clan of the Ashbelites; of Ahiram, the clan of the Ahiramites; 39of Shephupham, the clan of the Shuphamites; of Hupham, the clan of the Huphamites. 40And the sons of Bela were Ard and Naaman: of Ard, the clan of the Ardites; of Naaman, the clan of the Naamites. 41These are the descendants of Benjamin by their clans; the number of those enrolled was forty-five thousand six hundred.

42 These are the descendants of Dan by their clans: of Shuham, the clan of the Shuhamites. These are the clans of Dan by their clans. 43All the clans of the Shuhamites: sixty-four thousand four hundred enrolled.

44 The descendants of Asher by their families: of Imnah, the clan of the Imnites; of Ishvi, the clan of the Ishvites; of Beriah, the clan of the Beriites. 45Of the descendants of Beriah: of Heber, the clan of the Heberites; of Malchiel, the clan of the Malchielites. 46And the name of the daughter of Asher was Serah. 47These are the clans of the Asherites: the number of those enrolled was fifty-three thousand four hundred.

48 The descendants of Naphtali by their clans: of Jahzeel, the clan of the Jahzeelites; of Guni, the clan of the Gunites; 49of Jezer, the clan of the Jezerites; of Shillem, the clan of the Shillemites. 50These are the Naphtalites*p* by their clans: the number of those enrolled was forty-five thousand four hundred.

51 This was the number of the Israelites enrolled: six hundred and one thousand seven hundred thirty.

52 The LORD spoke to Moses, saying: 53To these the land shall be apportioned for inheritance according to the number of names. 54To a large tribe you shall give a large inheritance, and to a small tribe you shall give a small inheritance; every tribe shall be given its inheritance according to its enrollment. 55But the land shall be apportioned by lot; according to the names of their ancestral tribes they shall inherit. 56Their inheritance shall be apportioned according to lot between the larger and the smaller.

57 This is the enrollment of the Levites by their clans: of Gershon, the clan of the Gershonites; of Kohath, the clan of the Kohathites; of Merari, the clan of the Merarites. 58These are the clans of Levi: the clan of the Libnites, the clan of the Hebronites, the clan of the Mahlites, the clan of the Mushites, the clan of the Korahites. Now Kohath was the father of Amram. 59The name of Amram's wife was Jochebed daughter of Levi, who was born to Levi in Egypt; and she bore to Amram: Aaron, Moses, and their sister Miriam. 60To Aaron were born Nadab, Abihu, Eleazar, and Ithamar. 61But Nadab and Abihu died when they offered unholy fire before the LORD. 62The number of those enrolled was twenty-three thousand, every male one month old and upward; for they were not enrolled among the Israelites because there was no allotment given to them among the Israelites.

63 These were those enrolled by Moses and Eleazar the priest, who enrolled the Israelites in the plains of Moab by the Jordan opposite Jericho. 64Among these there was not one of those enrolled by Moses and Aaron the priest, who had enrolled the Israelites in the wilderness of Sinai. 65For the LORD had said of them, "They shall die in the wilderness." Not one of them was left, except Caleb son of Jephunneh and Joshua son of Nun.

The Daughters of Zelophehad

27 Then the daughters of Zelophehad came forward. Zelophehad was son of Hepher son of Gilead son of Machir son of Manasseh son of Joseph, a member of the Manassite clans. The names of his daughters were: Mahlah, Noah, Hoglah, Milcah, and Tirzah. 2They stood before Moses, Eleazar the priest, the leaders, and all the congregation, at the entrance of the tent of meeting, and they said, 3"Our father died in the wilderness; he was not among the company of those who gathered themselves together against the LORD in the company of Korah, but died for his own sin; and he had no sons. 4Why should the name of our father be taken away from his clan because he

---

p Heb clans of Naphtali

had no son? Give to us a possession among our father's brothers." 5 Moses brought their case before the LORD. 6And the LORD spoke to Moses, saying: 7The daughters of Zelo- phehad are right in what they are saying; you shall indeed let them possess an inheritance among their father's brothers and pass the inheritance of their father on to them. 8You shall also

FRIDAY

OUR TIMES ARE AT HIS SOVEREIGN DISPOSAL
John Owen

VERSE: Numbers 27.13   **PASSAGE:** Numbers 27.12–23

 ome desire to live that they may see more of that glorious work of God for his church, which they believe he will accomplish. So Moses prayed that he might not die in the wilderness, but go over Jordan, and see the good land, and that goodly mountain and Lebanon, the seat of the church and of the worship of God; which yet God thought meet to deny unto him. And this denial of the request of Moses, made on the highest consideration possible, is instructive unto all in the like case. Others may judge themselves to have some work to do in the world, wherein they suppose that the glory of God and good of the church are concerned; and therefore would be spared for a season. Paul knew not clearly whether it were not best for him to abide a while longer in the flesh on this account (see Philippians 1.21–25); and David often deprecates the present season of death because of the work which he had to do for God in the world. Others rise no higher than their own private interests or concerns with respect unto their persons, their families, their relations, and goods in this world. They would see these things in a better or more settled condition before they die, and then they shall be most willing so to do. But it is the love of life that lies at the bottom of all these desires in men; which of itself will never forsake them. But no man can die cheerfully or comfortably who lives not in a constant resignation of the time and season of his death unto the will of God, as well as himself with respect unto death itself. Our times are in his hand, at his sovereign disposal; and his will in all things must be complied withal. Without this resolution, without this resignation, no man can enjoy the least solid peace in this world.

ADDITIONAL SCRIPTURE READING:
Psalm 73.24–26; Luke 2.28–30; 2 Corinthians 5.8–9

Go to page 192 for your next devotional reading.

1500   1700

say to the Israelites, "If a man dies, and
has no son, then you shall pass his
inheritance on to his daughter. 9 If he
has no daughter, then you shall give his
inheritance to his brothers. 10 If he has
no brothers, then you shall give his
inheritance to his father's brothers.
11 And if his father has no brothers, then
you shall give his inheritance to the
nearest kinsman of his clan, and he
shall possess it. It shall be for the Israelites a statute and ordinance, as the
LORD commanded Moses."

Joshua Appointed Moses' Successor

12 The LORD said to Moses, "Go up
this mountain of the Abarim range, and
see the land that I have given to the
Israelites. 13 When you have seen it, you
also shall be gathered to your people, as
your brother Aaron was, 14 because you
rebelled against my word in the wilderness of Zin when the congregation
quarreled with me.[q] You did not show
my holiness before their eyes at the
waters." (These are the waters of Meribath-kadesh in the wilderness of Zin.)
15 Moses spoke to the LORD, saying,
16 "Let the LORD, the God of the spirits
of all flesh, appoint someone over the
congregation 17 who shall go out before
them and come in before them, who
shall lead them out and bring them in,
so that the congregation of the LORD
may not be like sheep without a shepherd." 18 So the LORD said to Moses,
"Take Joshua son of Nun, a man in
whom is the spirit, and lay your hand
upon him; 19 have him stand before Eleazar the priest and all the congregation,
and commission him in their sight.
20 You shall give him some of your
authority, so that all the congregation of
the Israelites may obey. 21 But he shall
stand before Eleazar the priest, who
shall inquire for him by the decision of
the Urim before the LORD; at his word
they shall go out, and at his word they
shall come in, both he and all the Israelites with him, the whole congregation."
22 So Moses did as the LORD commanded
him. He took Joshua and had him stand
before Eleazar the priest and the whole
congregation; 23 he laid his hands on
him and commissioned him—as the
LORD had directed through Moses.

Daily Offerings

28 The LORD spoke to Moses,
saying: 2 Command the Israelites, and say to them: My offering, the
food for my offerings by fire, my pleasing odor, you shall take care to offer to
me at its appointed time. 3 And you shall
say to them, This is the offering by fire
that you shall offer to the LORD: two
male lambs a year old without blemish,
daily, as a regular offering. 4 One lamb
you shall offer in the morning, and the
other lamb you shall offer at twilight;[r]
5 also one-tenth of an ephah of choice
flour for a grain offering, mixed with
one-fourth of a hin of beaten oil. 6 It is a
regular burnt offering, ordained at
Mount Sinai for a pleasing odor, an offering by fire to the LORD. 7 Its drink offering shall be one-fourth of a hin for each
lamb; in the sanctuary you shall pour
out a drink offering of strong drink to
the LORD. 8 The other lamb you shall
offer at twilight[r] with a grain offering
and a drink offering like the one in the
morning; you shall offer it as an offering
by fire, a pleasing odor to the LORD.

Sabbath Offerings

9 On the sabbath day: two male
lambs a year old without blemish, and
two-tenths of an ephah of choice flour
for a grain offering, mixed with oil, and
its drink offering— 10 this is the burnt
offering for every sabbath, in addition to
the regular burnt offering and its drink
offering.

Monthly Offerings

11 At the beginnings of your months
you shall offer a burnt offering to the
LORD: two young bulls, one ram, seven
male lambs a year old without blemish;
12 also three-tenths of an ephah of choice
flour for a grain offering, mixed with oil,
for each bull; and two-tenths of choice
flour for a grain offering, mixed with oil,
for the one ram; 13 and one-tenth of
choice flour mixed with oil as a grain
offering for every lamb—a burnt offering
of pleasing odor, an offering by fire to
the LORD. 14 Their drink offerings shall

q Heb lacks *with me* r Heb *between the two evenings*

be half a hin of wine for a bull, one-third of a hin for a ram, and one-fourth of a hin for a lamb. This is the burnt offering of every month throughout the months of the year. 15And there shall be one male goat for a sin offering to the LORD; it shall be offered in addition to the regular burnt offering and its drink offering.

Offerings at Passover

16 On the fourteenth day of the first month there shall be a passover offering to the LORD. 17And on the fifteenth day of this month is a festival; seven days shall unleavened bread be eaten. 18On the first day there shall be a holy convocation. You shall not work at your occupations. 19You shall offer an offering by fire, a burnt offering to the LORD: two young bulls, one ram, and seven male lambs a year old; see that they are without blemish. 20Their grain offering shall be of choice flour mixed with oil: three-tenths of an ephah shall you offer for a bull, and two-tenths for a ram; 21one-tenth shall you offer for each of the seven lambs; 22also one male goat for a sin offering, to make atonement for you. 23You shall offer these in addition to the burnt offering of the morning, which belongs to the regular burnt offering. 24In the same way you shall offer daily, for seven days, the food of an offering by fire, a pleasing odor to the LORD; it shall be offered in addition to the regular burnt offering and its drink offering. 25And on the seventh day you shall have a holy convocation; you shall not work at your occupations.

Offerings at the Festival of Weeks

26 On the day of the first fruits, when you offer a grain offering of new grain to the LORD at your festival of weeks, you shall have a holy convocation; you shall not work at your occupations. 27You shall offer a burnt offering, a pleasing odor to the LORD: two young bulls, one ram, seven male lambs a year old. 28Their grain offering shall be of choice flour mixed with oil, three-tenths of an ephah for each bull, two-tenths for one ram, 29one-tenth for each of the seven lambs; 30with one male goat, to make atonement for you. 31In addition to the

regular burnt offering with its grain offering, you shall offer them and their drink offering. They shall be without blemish.

Offerings at the Festival of Trumpets

29 On the first day of the seventh month you shall have a holy convocation; you shall not work at your occupations. It is a day for you to blow the trumpets, 2and you shall offer a burnt offering, a pleasing odor to the LORD: one young bull, one ram, seven male lambs a year old without blemish. 3Their grain offering shall be of choice flour mixed with oil, three-tenths of one ephah for the bull, two-tenths for the ram, 4and one-tenth for each of the seven lambs; 5with one male goat for a sin offering, to make atonement for you. 6These are in addition to the burnt offering of the new moon and its grain offering, and the regular burnt offering and its grain offering, and their drink offerings, according to the ordinance for them, a pleasing odor, an offering by fire to the LORD.

Offerings on the Day of Atonement

7 On the tenth day of this seventh month you shall have a holy convocation, and deny yourselves;s you shall do no work. 8You shall offer a burnt offering to the LORD, a pleasing odor: one young bull, one ram, seven male lambs a year old. They shall be without blemish. 9Their grain offering shall be of choice flour mixed with oil, three-tenths of an ephah for the bull, two-tenths for the one ram, 10one-tenth for each of the seven lambs; 11with one male goat for a sin offering, in addition to the sin offering of atonement, and the regular burnt offering and its grain offering, and their drink offerings.

Offerings at the Festival of Booths

12 On the fifteenth day of the seventh month you shall have a holy convocation; you shall not work at your occupations. You shall celebrate a festival to the LORD seven days. 13You shall offer a burnt offering, an offering by fire, a pleasing odor to the LORD: thirteen

s Or and fast

young bulls, two rams, fourteen male lambs a year old. They shall be without blemish. 14Their grain offering shall be of choice flour mixed with oil, three-tenths of an ephah for each of the thirteen bulls, two-tenths for each of the two rams, 15and one-tenth for each of the fourteen lambs; 16also one male goat for a sin offering, in addition to the regular burnt offering, its grain offering and its drink offering.

17 On the second day: twelve young bulls, two rams, fourteen male lambs a year old without blemish, 18with the grain offering and the drink offerings for the bulls, for the rams, and for the lambs, as prescribed in accordance with their number; 19also one male goat for a sin offering, in addition to the regular burnt offering and its grain offering, and their drink offerings.

20 On the third day: eleven bulls, two rams, fourteen male lambs a year old without blemish, 21with the grain offering and the drink offerings for the bulls, for the rams, and for the lambs, as prescribed in accordance with their number; 22also one male goat for a sin offering, in addition to the regular burnt offering and its grain offering and its drink offering.

23 On the fourth day: ten bulls, two rams, fourteen male lambs a year old without blemish, 24with the grain offering and the drink offerings for the bulls, for the rams, and for the lambs, as prescribed in accordance with their number; 25also one male goat for a sin offering, in addition to the regular burnt offering, its grain offering and its drink offering.

26 On the fifth day: nine bulls, two rams, fourteen male lambs a year old without blemish, 27with the grain offering and the drink offerings for the bulls, for the rams, and for the lambs, as prescribed in accordance with their number; 28also one male goat for a sin offering, in addition to the regular burnt offering and its grain offering and its drink offering.

29 On the sixth day: eight bulls, two rams, fourteen male lambs a year old without blemish, 30with the grain offering and the drink offerings for the bulls,

for the rams, and for the lambs, as prescribed in accordance with their number; 31also one male goat for a sin offering, in addition to the regular burnt offering, its grain offering, and its drink offerings.

32 On the seventh day: seven bulls, two rams, fourteen male lambs a year old without blemish, 33with the grain offering and the drink offerings for the bulls, for the rams, and for the lambs, as prescribed in accordance with their number; 34also one male goat for a sin offering, besides the regular burnt offering, its grain offering, and its drink offering.

35 On the eighth day you shall have a solemn assembly; you shall not work at your occupations. 36You shall offer a burnt offering, an offering by fire, a pleasing odor to the LORD: one bull, one ram, seven male lambs a year old without blemish, 37and the grain offering and the drink offerings for the bull, for the ram, and for the lambs, as prescribed in accordance with their number; 38also one male goat for a sin offering, in addition to the regular burnt offering and its grain offering and its drink offering.

39 These you shall offer to the LORD at your appointed festivals, in addition to your votive offerings and your freewill offerings, as your burnt offerings, your grain offerings, your drink offerings, and your offerings of well-being.

40t So Moses told the Israelites everything just as the LORD had commanded Moses.

Vows Made by Women

30 Then Moses said to the heads of the tribes of the Israelites: This is what the LORD has commanded. 2When a man makes a vow to the LORD, or swears an oath to bind himself by a pledge, he shall not break his word; he shall do according to all that proceeds out of his mouth.

3 When a woman makes a vow to the LORD, or binds herself by a pledge, while within her father's house, in her youth, 4and her father hears of her vow or her pledge by which she has bound herself, and says nothing to her; then all her

vows shall stand, and any pledge by which she has bound herself shall stand. 5But if her father expresses disapproval to her at the time that he hears of it, no vow of hers, and no pledge by which she has bound herself, shall stand; and the LORD will forgive her, because her father had expressed to her his disapproval.

6 If she marries, while obligated by her vows or any thoughtless utterance of her lips by which she has bound herself, 7and her husband hears of it and says nothing to her at the time that he hears, then her vows shall stand, and her pledges by which she has bound herself shall stand. 8But if, at the time that her husband hears of it, he expresses disapproval to her, then he shall nullify the vow by which she was obligated, or the thoughtless utterance of her lips, by which she bound herself; and the LORD will forgive her. 9(But every vow of a widow or of a divorced woman, by which she has bound herself, shall be binding upon her.) 10And if she made a vow in her husband's house, or bound herself by a pledge with an oath, 11and her husband heard it and said nothing to her, and did not express disapproval to her, then all her vows shall stand, and any pledge by which she bound herself shall stand. 12But if her husband nullifies them at the time that he hears them, then whatever proceeds out of her lips concerning her vows, or concerning her pledge of herself, shall not stand. Her husband has nullified them, and the LORD will forgive her. 13Any vow or any binding oath to deny herself,u her husband may allow to stand, or her husband may nullify. 14But if her husband says nothing to her from day to day,v then he validates all her vows, or all her pledges, by which she is obligated; he has validated them, because he said nothing to her at the time that he heard of them. 15But if he nullifies them some time after he has heard of them, then he shall bear her guilt.

16 These are the statutes that the LORD commanded Moses concerning a husband and his wife, and a father and his daughter while she is still young and in her father's house.

War against Midian

31 The LORD spoke to Moses, saying, 2"Avenge the Israelites on the Midianites; afterward you shall be gathered to your people." 3So Moses said to the people, "Arm some of your number for the war, so that they may go against Midian, to execute the LORD's vengeance on Midian. 4You shall send a thousand from each of the tribes of Israel to the war." 5So out of the thousands of Israel, a thousand from each tribe were conscripted, twelve thousand armed for battle. 6Moses sent them to the war, a thousand from each tribe, along with Phinehas son of Eleazar the priest,w with the vessels of the sanctuary and the trumpets for sounding the alarm in his hand. 7They did battle against Midian, as the LORD had commanded Moses, and killed every male. 8They killed the kings of Midian: Evi, Rekem, Zur, Hur, and Reba, the five kings of Midian, in addition to others who were slain by them; and they also killed Balaam son of Beor with the sword. 9The Israelites took the women of Midian and their little ones captive; and they took all their cattle, their flocks, and all their goods as booty. 10All their towns where they had settled, and all their encampments, they burned, 11but they took all the spoil and all the booty, both people and animals. 12Then they brought the captives and the booty and the spoil to Moses, to Eleazar the priest, and to the congregation of the Israelites, at the camp on the plains of Moab by the Jordan at Jericho.

Return from the War

13 Moses, Eleazar the priest, and all the leaders of the congregation went to meet them outside the camp. 14Moses became angry with the officers of the army, the commanders of thousands and the commanders of hundreds, who had come from service in the war. 15Moses said to them, "Have you allowed all the women to live? 16These women here, on Balaam's advice, made the Israelites act treacherously against the LORD in the affair of Peor, so that the plague came among the congregation of the LORD.

---

u Or *to fast*   v Or *from that day to the next*   w Gk: Heb adds *to the war*

17Now therefore, kill every male among the little ones, and kill every woman who has known a man by sleeping with him. 18But all the young girls who have not known a man by sleeping with him, keep alive for yourselves. 19Camp outside the camp seven days; whoever of you has killed any person or touched a corpse, purify yourselves and your captives on the third and on the seventh day. 20You shall purify every garment, every article of skin, everything made of goats' hair, and every article of wood."

21 Eleazar the priest said to the troops who had gone to battle: "This is the statute of the law that the LORD has commanded Moses: 22gold, silver, bronze, iron, tin, and lead— 23everything that can withstand fire, shall be passed through fire, and it shall be clean. Nevertheless it shall also be purified with the water for purification; and whatever cannot withstand fire, shall be passed through the water. 24You must wash your clothes on the seventh day, and you shall be clean; afterward you may come into the camp."

Disposition of Captives and Booty

25 The LORD spoke to Moses, saying, 26"You and Eleazar the priest and the heads of the ancestral houses of the congregation make an inventory of the booty captured, both human and animal. 27Divide the booty into two parts, between the warriors who went out to battle and all the congregation. 28From the share of the warriors who went out to battle, set aside as tribute for the LORD, one item out of every five hundred, whether persons, oxen, donkeys, sheep, or goats. 29Take it from their half and give it to Eleazar the priest as an offering to the LORD. 30But from the Israelites' half you shall take one out of every fifty, whether persons, oxen, donkeys, sheep, or goats—all the animals— and give them to the Levites who have charge of the tabernacle of the LORD."

31 Then Moses and Eleazar the priest did as the LORD had commanded Moses: 32 The booty remaining from the spoil that the troops had taken totaled six hundred seventy-five thousand sheep, 33seventy-two thousand oxen, 34sixty-one thousand donkeys, 35and

thirty-two thousand persons in all, women who had not known a man by sleeping with him.

36 The half-share, the portion of those who had gone out to war, was in number three hundred thirty-seven thousand five hundred sheep and goats, 37and the LORD's tribute of sheep and goats was six hundred seventy-five. 38The oxen were thirty-six thousand, of which the LORD's tribute was seventy-two. 39The donkeys were thirty thousand five hundred, of which the LORD's tribute was sixty-one. 40The persons were sixteen thousand, of which the LORD's tribute was thirty-two persons. 41Moses gave the tribute, the offering for the LORD, to Eleazar the priest, as the LORD had commanded Moses.

42 As for the Israelites' half, which Moses separated from that of the troops, 43the congregation's half was three hundred thirty-seven thousand five hundred sheep and goats, 44thirty-six thousand oxen, 45thirty thousand five hundred donkeys, 46and sixteen thousand persons. 47From the Israelites' half Moses took one of every fifty, both of persons and of animals, and gave them to the Levites who had charge of the tabernacle of the LORD; as the LORD had commanded Moses.

48 Then the officers who were over the thousands of the army, the commanders of thousands and the commanders of hundreds, approached Moses, 49and said to Moses, "Your servants have counted the warriors who are under our command, and not one of us is missing. 50And we have brought the LORD's offering, what each of us found, articles of gold, armlets and bracelets, signet rings, earrings, and pendants, to make atonement for ourselves before the LORD." 51Moses and Eleazar the priest received the gold from them, all in the form of crafted articles. 52And all the gold of the offering that they offered to the LORD, from the commanders of thousands and the commanders of hundreds, was sixteen thousand seven hundred fifty shekels. 53(The troops had all taken plunder for themselves.) 54So Moses and Eleazar the priest received the gold from the commanders of thousands and of hundreds, and brought it

into the tent of meeting as a memorial for the Israelites before the LORD.

Conquest and Division of Transjordan

32 Now the Reubenites and the Gadites owned a very great number of cattle. When they saw that the land of Jazer and the land of Gilead was a good place for cattle, 2the Gadites and the Reubenites came and spoke to Moses, to Eleazar the priest, and to the leaders of the congregation, saying, 3"Ataroth, Dibon, Jazer, Nimrah, Heshbon, Elealeh, Sebam, Nebo, and Beon— 4the land that the LORD subdued before the congregation of Israel—is a land for cattle; and your servants have cattle." 5They continued, "If we have found favor in your sight, let this land be given to your servants for a possession; do not make us cross the Jordan."

6 But Moses said to the Gadites and to the Reubenites, "Shall your brothers go to war while you sit here? 7Why will you discourage the hearts of the Israelites from going over into the land that the LORD has given them? 8Your fathers did this, when I sent them from Kadeshbarnea to see the land. 9When they went up to the Wadi Eshcol and saw the land, they discouraged the hearts of the Israelites from going into the land that the LORD had given them. 10The LORD's anger was kindled on that day and he swore, saying, 11'Surely none of the people who came up out of Egypt, from twenty years old and upward, shall see the land that I swore to give to Abraham, to Isaac, and to Jacob, because they have not unreservedly followed me— 12none except Caleb son of Jephunneh the Kenizzite and Joshua son of Nun, for they have unreservedly followed the LORD.' 13And the LORD's anger was kindled against Israel, and he made them wander in the wilderness for forty years, until all the generation that had done evil in the sight of the LORD had disappeared. 14And now you, a brood of sinners, have risen in place of your fathers, to increase the LORD's fierce anger against Israel! 15If you turn away from following him, he will again abandon

them in the wilderness; and you will destroy all this people."

16 Then they came up to him and said, "We will build sheepfolds here for our flocks, and towns for our little ones, 17but we will take up arms as a vanguard[x] before the Israelites, until we have brought them to their place. Meanwhile our little ones will stay in the fortified towns because of the inhabitants of the land. 18We will not return to our homes until all the Israelites have obtained their inheritance. 19We will not inherit with them on the other side of the Jordan and beyond, because our inheritance has come to us on this side of the Jordan to the east."

20 So Moses said to them, "If you do this—if you take up arms to go before the LORD for the war, 21and all those of you who bear arms cross the Jordan before the LORD, until he has driven out his enemies from before him 22and the land is subdued before the LORD—then after that you may return and be free of obligation to the LORD and to Israel, and this land shall be your possession before the LORD. 23But if you do not do this, you have sinned against the LORD; and be sure your sin will find you out. 24Build towns for your little ones, and folds for your flocks; but do what you have promised."

25 Then the Gadites and the Reubenites said to Moses, "Your servants will do as my lord commands. 26Our little ones, our wives, our flocks, and all our livestock shall remain there in the towns of Gilead; 27but your servants will cross over, everyone armed for war, to do battle for the LORD, just as my lord orders."

28 So Moses gave command concerning them to Eleazar the priest, to Joshua son of Nun, and to the heads of the ancestral houses of the Israelite tribes. 29And Moses said to them, "If the Gadites and the Reubenites, everyone armed for battle before the LORD, will cross over the Jordan with you and the land shall be subdued before you, then you shall give them the land of Gilead for a possession; 30but if they will not cross over with you armed, they shall have possessions among you in the land of

x Cn: Heb *hurrying*

Canaan." 31The Gadites and the Reubenites answered, "As the LORD has spoken to your servants, so we will do. 32We will cross over armed before the LORD into the land of Canaan, but the possession of our inheritance shall remain with us on this side of*y* the Jordan."

33 Moses gave to them—to the Gadites and to the Reubenites and to the half-tribe of Manasseh son of Joseph—the kingdom of King Sihon of the Amorites and the kingdom of King Og of Bashan, the land and its towns, with the territories of the surrounding towns. 34And the Gadites rebuilt Dibon, Ataroth, Aroer, 35Atroth-shophan, Jazer, Jogbehah, 36Beth-nimrah, and Bethharan, fortified cities, and folds for sheep. 37And the Reubenites rebuilt Heshbon, Elealeh, Kiriathaim, 38Nebo, and Baal-meon (some names being changed), and Sibmah; and they gave names to the towns that they rebuilt. 39The descendants of Machir son of Manasseh went to Gilead, captured it, and dispossessed the Amorites who were there; 40so Moses gave Gilead to Machir son of Manasseh, and he settled there. 41Jair son of Manasseh went and captured their villages, and renamed them Havvoth-jair.*z* 42And Nobah went and captured Kenath and its villages, and renamed it Nobah after himself.

The Stages of Israel's Journey from Egypt

33 These are the stages by which the Israelites went out of the land of Egypt in military formation under the leadership of Moses and Aaron. 2Moses wrote down their starting points, stage by stage, by command of the LORD; and these are their stages according to their starting places. 3They set out from Rameses in the first month, on the fifteenth day of the first month; on the day after the passover the Israelites went out boldly in the sight of all the Egyptians, 4while the Egyptians were burying all their firstborn, whom the LORD had struck down among them. The LORD executed judgments even against their gods.

5 So the Israelites set out from Rameses, and camped at Succoth. 6They set out from Succoth, and camped at Etham, which is on the edge of the wilderness. 7They set out from Etham, and turned back to Pi-hahiroth, which faces Baalzephon; and they camped before Migdol. 8They set out from Pi-hahiroth, passed through the sea into the wilderness, went a three days' journey in the wilderness of Etham, and camped at Marah. 9They set out from Marah and came to Elim; at Elim there were twelve springs of water and seventy palm trees, and they camped there. 10They set out from Elim and camped by the Red Sea.*a* 11They set out from the Red Sea*a* and camped in the wilderness of Sin. 12They set out from the wilderness of Sin and camped at Dophkah. 13They set out from Dophkah and camped at Alush. 14They set out from Alush and camped at Rephidim, where there was no water for the people to drink. 15They set out from Rephidim and camped in the wilderness of Sinai. 16They set out from the wilderness of Sinai and camped at Kibroth-hattaavah. 17They set out from Kibroth-hattaavah and camped at Hazeroth. 18They set out from Hazeroth and camped at Rithmah. 19They set out from Rithmah and camped at Rimmon-perez. 20They set out from Rimmon-perez and camped at Libnah. 21They set out from Libnah and camped at Rissah. 22They set out from Rissah and camped at Kehelathah. 23They set out from Kehelathah and camped at Mount Shepher. 24They set out from Mount Shepher and camped at Haradah. 25They set out from Haradah and camped at Makheloth. 26They set out from Makheloth and camped at Tahath. 27They set out from Tahath and camped at Terah. 28They set out from Terah and camped at Mithkah. 29They set out from Mithkah and camped at Hashmonah. 30They set out from Hashmonah and camped at Moseroth. 31They set out from Moseroth and camped at Bene-jaakan. 32They set out from Benejaakan and camped at Hor-haggidgad. 33They set out from Hor-haggidgad and camped at Jotbathah. 34They set out from Jotbathah and camped at Abronah. 35They set out from Abronah and camped at Ezion-geber. 36They set out

y Heb *beyond*   *z* That is *the villages of Jair*   *a* Or *Sea of Reeds* from Ezion-geber and camped in the wilderness of Zin (that is, Kadesh). 37 They set out from Kadesh and camped at Mount Hor, on the edge of the land of Edom.

38 Aaron the priest went up Mount Hor at the command of the LORD and died there in the fortieth year after the Israelites had come out of the land of Egypt, on the first day of the fifth month. 39 Aaron was one hundred twenty-three years old when he died on Mount Hor.

40 The Canaanite, the king of Arad, who lived in the Negeb in the land of Canaan, heard of the coming of the Israelites.

41 They set out from Mount Hor and camped at Zalmonah. 42 They set out from Zalmonah and camped at Punon. 43 They set out from Punon and camped at Oboth. 44 They set out from Oboth and camped at Iye-abarim, in the territory of Moab. 45 They set out from Iyim and camped at Dibon-gad. 46 They set out from Dibon-gad and camped at Almon-diblathaim. 47 They set out from Almon-diblathaim and camped in the mountains of Abarim, before Nebo. 48 They set out from the mountains of Abarim and camped in the plains of Moab by the Jordan at Jericho; 49 they camped by the Jordan from Beth-jeshimoth as far as Abel-shittim in the plains of Moab.

Directions for the Conquest of Canaan

50 In the plains of Moab by the Jordan at Jericho, the LORD spoke to Moses, saying: 51 Speak to the Israelites, and say to them: When you cross over the Jordan into the land of Canaan, 52 you shall drive out all the inhabitants of the land from before you, destroy all their figured stones, destroy all their cast images, and demolish all their high places. 53 You shall take possession of the land and settle in it, for I have given you the land to possess. 54 You shall apportion the land by lot according to your clans; to a large one you shall give a large inheritance, and to a small one you shall give a small inheritance; the inheritance shall belong to the person on whom the lot falls;

according to your ancestral tribes you shall inherit. 55 But if you do not drive out the inhabitants of the land from before you, then those whom you let remain shall be as barbs in your eyes and thorns in your sides; they shall trouble you in the land where you are settling. 56 And I will do to you as I thought to do to them.

The Boundaries of the Land

34 The LORD spoke to Moses, saying: 2 Command the Israelites, and say to them: When you enter the land of Canaan (this is the land that shall fall to you for an inheritance, the land of Canaan, defined by its boundaries), 3 your south sector shall extend from the wilderness of Zin along the side of Edom. Your southern boundary shall begin from the end of the Dead Sea[b] on the east; 4 your boundary shall turn south of the ascent of Akrabbim, and cross to Zin, and its outer limit shall be south of Kadesh-barnea; then it shall go on to Hazar-addar, and cross to Azmon; 5 the boundary shall turn from Azmon to the Wadi of Egypt, and its termination shall be at the Sea.

6 For the western boundary, you shall have the Great Sea and its[c] coast; this shall be your western boundary.

7 This shall be your northern boundary: from the Great Sea you shall mark out your line to Mount Hor; 8 from Mount Hor you shall mark it out to Lebo-hamath, and the outer limit of the boundary shall be at Zedad; 9 then the boundary shall extend to Ziphron, and its end shall be at Hazar-enan; this shall be your northern boundary.

10 You shall mark out your eastern boundary from Hazar-enan to Shepham; 11 and the boundary shall continue down from Shepham to Riblah on the east side of Ain; and the boundary shall go down, and reach the eastern slope of the sea of Chinnereth; 12 and the boundary shall go down to the Jordan, and its end shall be at the Dead Sea.[b] This shall be your land with its boundaries all around.

13 Moses commanded the Israelites, saying: This is the land that you shall inherit by lot, which the LORD has commanded to give to the nine tribes and to

b Heb Salt Sea   c Syr: Heb lacks its

WEEKEND

ROCK MOUNT SINAI
African-American Spiritual

VERSE: Exodus 19.18   **PASSAGE:** Exodus 19.16–25

rock, Mount Sinai,
Rock, Mount Sinai,
Rock, Mount Sinai, in that mornin'.
O, when you hear, my coffin soun',
Then you may know my body's boun'.
O, rock, Mount Sinai.

O, come on, Moses, don't you get los',
Smote the water an' come on the cross,
O, rock, Mount Sinai.

O, David, David, is a shepherd boy,
David killed Goliath and shouted for joy.
He killed Goliath, killed Goliath in that morning.
O, rock, Mount Sinai.

When I get to heaven, going to sit right down;
Going to ask my Lord for a starry crown.
O, rock, Mount Sinai.

O, Pilate's wife she dreamt a dream,
When the dream was over she said to Pilate:
O, give me a little water to wash my han',
So they won't be stained with the innocent man.

ADDITIONAL SCRIPTURE READING:
1 Samuel 17.1–46; Matthew 27.19–24

Go to page 201 for your next devotional reading.

1700   1900

the half-tribe; [14]for the tribe of the Reubenites by their ancestral houses and the tribe of the Gadites by their ancestral houses have taken their inheritance, and also the half-tribe of Manasseh; [15]the two tribes and the half-tribe have taken their inheritance beyond the Jordan at Jericho eastward, toward the sunrise.

Tribal Leaders

16 The LORD spoke to Moses, saying: [17]These are the names of the men who shall apportion the land to you for inheritance: the priest Eleazar and Joshua son of Nun. [18]You shall take one leader of every tribe to apportion the land for inheritance. [19]These are the names of the men: Of the tribe of Judah, Caleb son of Jephunneh. [20]Of the tribe of the Simeonites, Shemuel son of Ammihud. [21]Of the tribe of Benjamin, Elidad son of Chislon. [22]Of the tribe of the Danites a leader, Bukki son of Jogli. [23]Of the Josephites: of the tribe of the Manassites a leader, Hanniel son of Ephod, [24]and of the tribe of the Ephraimites a leader, Kemuel son of Shiphtan. [25]Of the tribe of the Zebulunites a leader, Eli-zaphan son of Parnach. [26]Of the tribe of the Issacharites a leader, Paltiel son of Azzan. [27]And of the tribe of the Asherites a leader, Ahihud son of Shelomi. [28]Of the tribe of the Naphtalites a leader, Pedahel son of Ammihud. [29]These were the ones whom the LORD commanded to apportion the inheritance for the Israelites in the land of Canaan.

Cities for the Levites

35 In the plains of Moab by the Jordan at Jericho, the LORD spoke to Moses, saying: [2]Command the Israelites to give, from the inheritance that they possess, towns for the Levites to live in; you shall also give to the Levites pasture lands surrounding the towns. [3]The towns shall be theirs to live in, and their pasture lands shall be for their cattle, for their livestock, and for all their animals. [4]The pasture lands of the towns, which you shall give to the Levites, shall reach from the wall of the town outward a thousand cubits all around. [5]You shall measure, outside the town, for the east side two thousand cubits, for the south side two thousand cubits, for the west side two thousand cubits, and for the north side two thousand cubits, with the town in the middle; this shall belong to them as pasture land for their towns.

6 The towns that you give to the Levites shall include the six cities of refuge, where you shall permit a slayer to flee, and in addition to them you shall give forty-two towns. [7]The towns that you give to the Levites shall total forty-eight, with their pasture lands. [8]And as for the towns that you shall give from the possession of the Israelites, from the larger tribes you shall take many, and from the smaller tribes you shall take few; each, in proportion to the inheritance that it obtains, shall give of its towns to the Levites.

Cities of Refuge

9 The LORD spoke to Moses, saying: [10]Speak to the Israelites, and say to them: When you cross the Jordan into the land of Canaan, [11]then you shall select cities to be cities of refuge for you, so that a slayer who kills a person without intent may flee there. [12]The cities shall be for you a refuge from the avenger, so that the slayer may not die until there is a trial before the congregation.

13 The cities that you designate shall be six cities of refuge for you: [14]you shall designate three cities beyond the Jordan, and three cities in the land of Canaan, to be cities of refuge. [15]These six cities shall serve as refuge for the Israelites, for the resident or transient alien among them, so that anyone who kills a person without intent may flee there.

Concerning Murder and Blood Revenge

16 But anyone who strikes another with an iron object, and death ensues, is a murderer; the murderer shall be put to death. [17]Or anyone who strikes another with a stone in hand that could cause death, and death ensues, is a murderer; the murderer shall be put to death. [18]Or anyone who strikes another with a weapon of wood in hand that could cause death, and death ensues, is a murderer; the murderer shall be put to

death. 19The avenger of blood is the one who shall put the murderer to death; when they meet, the avenger of blood shall execute the sentence. 20Likewise, if someone pushes another from hatred, or hurls something at another, lying in wait, and death ensues, 21or in enmity strikes another with the hand, and death ensues, then the one who struck the blow shall be put to death; that person is a murderer; the avenger of blood shall put the murderer to death, when they meet.

22 But if someone pushes another suddenly without enmity, or hurls any object without lying in wait, 23or, while handling any stone that could cause death, unintentionally[d] drops it on another and death ensues, though they were not enemies, and no harm was intended, 24then the congregation shall judge between the slayer and the avenger of blood, in accordance with these ordinances; 25and the congregation shall rescue the slayer from the avenger of blood. Then the congregation shall send the slayer back to the original city of refuge. The slayer shall live in it until the death of the high priest who was anointed with the holy oil. 26But if the slayer shall at any time go outside the bounds of the original city of refuge, 27and is found by the avenger of blood outside the bounds of the city of refuge, and is killed by the avenger, no blood-guilt shall be incurred. 28For the slayer must remain in the city of refuge until the death of the high priest; but after the death of the high priest the slayer may return home.

29 These things shall be a statute and ordinance for you throughout your generations wherever you live.

30 If anyone kills another, the murderer shall be put to death on the evidence of witnesses; but no one shall be put to death on the testimony of a single witness. 31Moreover you shall accept no ransom for the life of a murderer who is subject to the death penalty; a murderer must be put to death. 32Nor shall you accept ransom for one who has fled to a city of refuge, enabling the fugitive to return to live in the land before the death of the high priest. 33You shall not pollute the land in which you live; for blood pollutes the land, and no expiation can be made for the land, for the blood that is shed in it, except by the blood of the one who shed it. 34You shall not defile the land in which you live, which I also dwell; for I the LORD dwell among the Israelites.

Marriage of Female Heirs

36 The heads of the ancestral houses of the clans of the descendants of Gilead son of Machir son of Manasseh, of the Josephite clans, came forward and spoke in the presence of Moses and the leaders, the heads of the ancestral houses of the Israelites; 2they said, "The LORD commanded my lord to give the land for inheritance by lot to the Israelites; and my lord was commanded by the LORD to give the inheritance of our brother Zelophehad to his daughters. 3But if they are married into another Israelite tribe, then their inheritance will be taken from the inheritance of our ancestors and added to the inheritance of the tribe into which they marry; so it will be taken away from the allotted portion of our inheritance. 4And when the jubilee of the Israelites comes, then their inheritance will be added to the inheritance of the tribe into which they have married; and their inheritance will be taken from the inheritance of our ancestral tribe."

5 Then Moses commanded the Israelites according to the word of the LORD, saying, "The descendants of the tribe of Joseph are right in what they are saying. 6This is what the LORD commands concerning the daughters of Zelophehad, 'Let them marry whom they think best; only it must be into a clan of their father's tribe that they are married, 7so that no inheritance of the Israelites shall be transferred from one tribe to another; for all Israelites shall retain the inheritance of their ancestral tribes. 8Every daughter who possesses an inheritance in any tribe of the Israelites shall marry one from the clan of her father's tribe, so that all Israelites may continue to possess their ancestral inheritance. 9No inheritance shall be transferred from one tribe to another; for each of the

d Heb without seeing

tribes of the Israelites shall retain its own inheritance.' "

10 The daughters of Zelophehad did as the LORD had commanded Moses. 11Mahlah, Tirzah, Hoglah, Milcah, and Noah, the daughters of Zelophehad, married sons of their father's brothers. 12They were married into the clans of the descendants of Manasseh son of Joseph, and their inheritance remained in the tribe of their father's clan.

13 These are the commandments and the ordinances that the LORD commanded through Moses to the Israelites in the plains of Moab by the Jordan at Jericho.

DEUTERONOMY

 FTER FORTY YEARS THE ISRAELITES
WERE ABOUT TO ENTER CANAAN.
BEFORE THEY DID, MOSES WANTED
TO REMIND THEM OF ALL THAT GOD HAD
DONE FOR THEM AND TO ENCOURAGE THEM
TO KEEP OBEYING THE LAWS GOD HAD GIVEN
THEM. MOSES REMINDED THE PEOPLE OF
GOD'S GOODNESS TO THEM THROUGH THEIR
JOURNEY AND HIS GIVING THEM THE LAND OF
CANAAN. ABOVE ALL, MOSES WANTED HIS
PEOPLE TO SEE HOW MUCH GOD LOVED
THEM AND HOW THEY WERE TO RETURN
THAT LOVE TO THEIR POWERFUL GOD.

Events at Horeb Recalled

1 These are the words that Moses spoke to all Israel beyond the Jordan—in the wilderness, on the plain opposite Suph, between Paran and Tophel, Laban, Hazeroth, and Di-zahab. 2(By the way of Mount Seir it takes eleven days to reach Kadesh-barnea from Horeb.) 3In the fortieth year, on the first day of the eleventh month, Moses spoke to the Israelites just as the LORD had commanded him to speak to them. 4This was after he had defeated King Sihon of the Amorites, who reigned in Heshbon, and King Og of Bashan, who reigned in Ashtaroth and*a* in Edrei. 5Beyond the Jordan in the land of Moab, Moses undertook to expound this law as follows:

6 The LORD our God spoke to us at Horeb, saying, "You have stayed long enough at this mountain. 7Resume your journey, and go into the hill country of the Amorites as well as into the neighboring regions—the Arabah, the hill country, the Shephelah, the Negeb, and the seacoast—the land of the Canaanites and the Lebanon, as far as the great river, the river Euphrates. 8See, I have set the land before you; go in and take possession of the land that I*b* swore to your ancestors, to Abraham, to Isaac, and to Jacob, to give to them and to their descendants after them."

a Gk Syr Vg Compare Josh 12.4: Heb lacks *and*   *b* Sam Gk: MT *the LORD*

Appointment of Tribal Leaders

9 At that time I said to you, "I am unable by myself to bear you. 10The LORD your God has multiplied you, so that today you are as numerous as the stars of heaven. 11May the LORD, the God of your ancestors, increase you a thousand times more and bless you, as he has promised you! 12But how can I bear the heavy burden of your disputes all by myself? 13Choose for each of your tribes individuals who are wise, discerning, and reputable to be your leaders." 14You answered me, "The plan you have proposed is a good one." 15So I took the leaders of your tribes, wise and reputable individuals, and installed them as leaders over you, commanders of thousands, commanders of hundreds, commanders of fifties, commanders of tens, and officials, throughout your tribes. 16I charged your judges at that time: "Give the members of your community a fair hearing, and judge rightly between one person and another, whether citizen or resident alien. 17You must not be partial in judging: hear out the small and the great alike; you shall not be intimidated by anyone, for the judgment is God's. Any case that is too hard for you, bring to me, and I will hear it." 18So I charged you at that time with all the things that you should do.

Israel's Refusal to Enter the Land

19 Then, just as the LORD our God had ordered us, we set out from Horeb and went through all that great and terrible wilderness that you saw, on the way to the hill country of the Amorites, until we reached Kadesh-barnea. 20I said to you, "You have reached the hill country of the Amorites, which the LORD our God is giving us. 21See, the LORD your God has given the land to you; go up, take possession, as the LORD, the God of your ancestors, has promised you; do not fear or be dismayed." 22 All of you came to me and said, "Let us send men ahead of us to explore the land for us and bring back a report to us regarding the route by which we should go up and the cities we will come to." 23The plan seemed good to me, and I selected twelve of you, one from each tribe. 24They set out and went up into the hill country, and when they reached the Valley of Eshcol they spied it out 25and gathered some of the land's produce, which they brought down to us. They brought back a report to us, and said, "It is a good land that the LORD our God is giving us."

26 But you were unwilling to go up. You rebelled against the command of the LORD your God; 27you grumbled in your tents and said, "It is because the LORD hates us that he has brought us out of the land of Egypt, to hand us over to the Amorites to destroy us. 28Where are we headed? Our kindred have made our hearts melt by reporting, 'The people are stronger and taller than we; the cities are large and fortified up to heaven! We actually saw there the offspring of the Anakim!' " 29I said to you, "Have no dread or fear of them. 30The LORD your God, who goes before you, is the one who will fight for you, just as he did for you in Egypt before your very eyes, 31and in the wilderness, where you saw how the LORD your God carried you, just as one carries a child, all the way that you traveled until you reached this place. 32But in spite of this, you have no trust in the LORD your God, 33who goes before you on the way to seek out a place for you to camp, in fire by night, and in the cloud by day, to show you the route you should take."

The Penalty for Israel's Rebellion

34 When the LORD heard your words, he was wrathful and swore: 35"Not one of these—not one of this evil generation—shall see the good land that I swore to give to your ancestors, 36except Caleb son of Jephunneh. He shall see it, and to him and to his descendants I will give the land on which he set foot, because of his complete fidelity to the LORD." 37Even with me the LORD was angry on your account, saying, "You also shall not enter there. 38Joshua son of Nun, your assistant, shall enter there; encourage him, for he is the one who will secure Israel's possession of it. 39And as for your little ones, who you thought would become booty, your children, who today do not yet know right from wrong, they shall enter there; to them I will give it, and they shall take

possession of it. [40]But as for you, journey back into the wilderness, in the direction of the Red Sea."[c]

41 You answered me, "We have sinned against the LORD! We are ready to go up and fight, just as the LORD our God commanded us." So all of you strapped on your battle gear, and thought it easy to go up into the hill country. [42]The LORD said to me, "Say to them, 'Do not go up and do not fight, for I am not in the midst of you; otherwise you will be defeated by your enemies.' " [43]Although I told you, you would not listen. You rebelled against the command of the LORD and presumptuously went up into the hill country. [44]The Amorites who lived in that hill country then came out against you and chased you as bees do. They beat you down in Seir as far as Hormah. [45]When you returned and wept before the LORD, the LORD would neither heed your voice nor pay you any attention.

The Desert Years

46 After you had stayed at Kadesh as many days as you did, [1]we journeyed back into the wilderness, in the direction of the Red Sea,[c] as the LORD had told me and skirted Mount Seir for many days. [2]Then the LORD said to me: [3]"You have been skirting this hill country long enough. Head north, [4]and charge the people as follows: You are about to pass through the territory of your kindred, the descendants of Esau, who live in Seir. They will be afraid of you, so, be very careful [5]not to engage in battle with them, for I will not give you even so much as a foot's length of their land, since I have given Mount Seir to Esau as a possession. [6]You shall purchase food from them for money, so that you may eat; and you shall also buy water from them for money, so that you may drink. [7]Surely the LORD your God has blessed you in all your undertakings; he knows your going through this great wilderness. These forty years the LORD your God has been with you; you have lacked nothing." [8]So we passed by our kin, the descendants of Esau who live in Seir, leaving behind the route of the Ara-

bah, and leaving behind Elath and Ezion-geber.

When we had headed out along the route of the wilderness of Moab, [9]the LORD said to me: "Do not harass Moab or engage them in battle, for I will not give you any of its land as a possession, since I have given Ar as a possession to the descendants of Lot." [10](The Emim—a large and numerous people, as tall as the Anakim—had formerly inhabited it. [11]Like the Anakim, they are usually reckoned as Rephaim, though the Moabites call them Emim. [12]Moreover, the Horim had formerly inhabited Seir, but the descendants of Esau dispossessed them, destroying them and settling in their place, as Israel has done in the land that the LORD gave them as a possession.) [13]"Now then, proceed to cross over the Wadi Zered."

So we crossed over the Wadi Zered. [14]And the length of time we had traveled from Kadesh-barnea until we crossed the Wadi Zered was thirty-eight years, until the entire generation of warriors had perished from the camp, as the LORD had sworn concerning them. [15]Indeed, the LORD's own hand was against them, to root them out from the camp, until all had perished.

16 Just as soon as all the warriors had died off from among the people, [17]the LORD spoke to me, saying, [18]"Today you are going to cross the boundary of Moab at Ar. [19]When you approach the frontier of the Ammonites, do not harass them or engage them in battle, for I will not give the land of the Ammonites to you as a possession, because I have given it to the descendants of Lot." [20](It also is usually reckoned as a land of Rephaim. Rephaim formerly inhabited it, though the Ammonites call them Zamzummim, [21]a strong and numerous people, as tall as the Anakim. But the LORD destroyed them from before the Ammonites so that they could dispossess them and settle in their place. [22]He did the same for the descendants of Esau, who live in Seir, by destroying the Horim before them so that they could dispossess them and settle in their place even to this day. [23]As for the Avvim, who had lived in settlements in the

vicinity of Gaza, the Caphtorim, who came from Caphtor, destroyed them and settled in their place.) 24"Proceed on your journey and cross the Wadi Arnon. See, I have handed over to you King Sihon the Amorite of Heshbon, and his land. Begin to take possession by engaging him in battle. 25This day I will begin to put the dread and fear of you upon the peoples everywhere under heaven; when they hear report of you, they will tremble and be in anguish because of you."

Defeat of King Sihon

26 So I sent messengers from the wilderness of Kedemoth to King Sihon of Heshbon with the following terms of peace: 27"If you let me pass through your land, I will travel only along the road; I will turn aside neither to the right nor to the left. 28You shall sell me food for money, so that I may eat, and supply me water for money, so that I may drink. Only allow me to pass through on foot— 29just as the descendants of Esau who live in Seir have done for me and likewise the Moabites who live in Ar—until I cross the Jordan into the land that the LORD our God is giving us." 30But King Sihon of Heshbon was not willing to let us pass through, for the LORD your God had hardened his spirit and made his heart defiant in order to hand him over to you, as he has now done.

31 The LORD said to me, "See, I have begun to give Sihon and his land over to you. Begin now to take possession of his land." 32So when Sihon came out against us, he and all his people for battle at Jahaz, 33the LORD our God gave him over to us; and we struck him down, along with his offspring and all his people. 34At that time we captured all his towns, and in each town we utterly destroyed men, women, and children. We left not a single survivor. 35Only the livestock we kept as spoil for ourselves, as well as the plunder of the towns that we had captured. 36From Aroer on the edge of the Wadi Arnon (including the town that is in the wadi itself) as far as Gilead, there was no citadel too high for us. The LORD our God gave everything to us. 37You did not encroach, however, on the land of the

Ammonites, avoiding the whole upper region of the Wadi Jabbok as well as the towns of the hill country, just asd the LORD our God had charged.

Defeat of King Og

3 When we headed up the road to Bashan, King Og of Bashan came out against us, he and all his people, for battle at Edrei. 2The LORD said to me, "Do not fear him, for I have handed him over to you, along with his people and his land. Do to him as you did to King Sihon of the Amorites, who reigned in Heshbon." 3So the LORD our God also handed over to us King Og of Bashan and all his people. We struck him down until not a single survivor was left. 4At that time we captured all his towns; there was no citadel that we did not take from them—sixty towns, the whole region of Argob, the kingdom of Og in Bashan. 5All these were fortress towns with high walls, double gates, and bars, besides a great many villages. 6And we utterly destroyed them, as we had done to King Sihon of Heshbon, in each city utterly destroying men, women, and children. 7But all the livestock and the plunder of the towns we kept as spoil for ourselves.

8 So at that time we took from the two kings of the Amorites the land beyond the Jordan, from the Wadi Arnon to Mount Hermon 9(the Sidonians call Hermon Sirion, while the Amorites call it Senir), 10all the towns of the tableland, the whole of Gilead, and all of Bashan, as far as Salecah and Edrei, towns of Og's kingdom in Bashan. 11(Now only King Og of Bashan was left of the remnant of the Rephaim. In fact his bed, an iron bed, can still be seen in Rabbah of the Ammonites. By the common cubit it is nine cubits long and four cubits wide.) 12As for the land that we took possession of at that time, I gave to the Reubenites and Gadites the territory north of Aroer,e that is on the edge of the Wadi Arnon, as well as half the hill country of Gilead with its towns, 13and I gave to the half-tribe of Manasseh the rest of Gilead and all of Bashan, Og's kingdom. (The whole region of Argob: all that portion of Bashan used to be called a land of

d Gk Tg: Heb and all   e Heb territory from Aroer

Rephaim; 14Jair the Manassite acquired the whole region of Argob as far as the border of the Geshurites and the Maacathites, and he named them—that is, Bashan—after himself, Havvoth-jair,ᶠ as it is to this day.) 15To Machir I gave Gilead. 16And to the Reubenites and the Gadites I gave the territory from Gilead as far as the Wadi Arnon, with the middle of the wadi as a boundary, and up to the Jabbok, the wadi being boundary of the Ammonites; 17the Arabah also, with the Jordan and its banks, from Chinnereth down to the sea of the Arabah, the Dead Sea,ᵍ with the lower slopes of Pisgah on the east.

18 At that time, I charged you as follows: "Although the LORD your God has given you this land to occupy, all your troops shall cross over armed as the vanguard of your Israelite kin. 19Only your wives, your children, and your livestock—I know that you have much livestock—shall stay behind in the towns that I have given to you. 20When the LORD gives rest to your kindred, as to you, and they too have occupied the land that the LORD your God is giving them beyond the Jordan, then each of you may return to the property that I have given to you." 21And I charged Joshua as well at that time, saying: "Your own eyes have seen everything that the LORD your God has done to these two kings; so the LORD will do to all the kingdoms into which you are about to cross. 22Do not fear them, for it is the LORD your God who fights for you."

Moses Views Canaan from Pisgah

23 At that time, too, I entreated the LORD, saying: 24"O Lord GOD, you have only begun to show your servant your greatness and your might; what god in heaven or on earth can perform deeds and mighty acts like yours! 25Let me cross over to see the good land beyond the Jordan, that good hill country and the Lebanon." 26But the LORD was angry with me on your account and would not heed me. The LORD said to me, "Enough from you! Never speak to me of this matter again! 27Go up to the top of Pisgah and look around you to the west, to the north, to the south, and to the east.

Look well, for you shall not cross over this Jordan. 28But charge Joshua, and encourage and strengthen him, because it is he who shall cross over at the head of this people and who shall secure their possession of the land that you will see." 29So we remained in the valley opposite Beth-peor.

Moses Commands Obedience

4 So now, Israel, give heed to the statutes and ordinances that I am teaching you to observe, so that you may live to enter and occupy the land that the LORD, the God of your ancestors, is giving you. 2You must neither add anything to what I command you nor take away anything from it, but keep the commandments of the LORD your God with which I am charging you. 3You have seen for yourselves what the LORD did with regard to the Baal of Peor—how the LORD your God destroyed from among you everyone who followed the Baal of Peor, 4while those of you who held fast to the LORD your God are all alive today.

5 See, just as the LORD my God has charged me, I now teach you statutes and ordinances for you to observe in the land that you are about to enter and occupy. 6You must observe them diligently, for this will show your wisdom and discernment to the peoples, who, when they hear all these statutes, will say, "Surely this great nation is a wise and discerning people!" 7For what other great nation has a god so near to it as the LORD our God is whenever we call to him? 8And what other great nation has statutes and ordinances as just as this entire law that I am setting before you today?

9 But take care and watch yourselves closely, so as neither to forget the things that your eyes have seen nor to let them slip from your mind all the days of your life; make them known to your children and your children's children— 10how you once stood before the LORD your God at Horeb, when the LORD said to me, "Assemble the people for me, and I will let them hear my words, so that they may learn to fear me as long as they live on the earth, and may teach

ᶠ That is Settlement of Jair   ᵍ Heb Salt Sea

their children so"; **11**you approached and stood at the foot of the mountain while the mountain was blazing up to the very heavens, shrouded in dark clouds. **12**Then the LORD spoke to you out of the fire. You heard the sound of words but saw no form; there was only a voice. **13**He declared to you his covenant, which he charged you to observe, that is, the ten commandments;*h* and he wrote them on two stone tablets. **14**And the LORD charged me at that time to teach you statutes and ordinances for you to observe in the land that you are about to cross into and occupy.

15 Since you saw no form when the

h Heb *the ten words*

MONDAY

THE PERIL OF PRAYER
A. W. Tozer

VERSE: Deuteronomy 4.7   PASSAGE: Deuteronomy 4.1–14

 othing is so vital as prayer, yet a reputation for being a mighty prayer warrior is probably the most perilous of all reputations to have. No form of selfishness is so deeply and dangerously sinful as that which glories in being a man of prayer. It comes near to being self-worship; and that while in the very act of worshiping God.

What then shall we do?

We must deny self, take up the cross and count ourselves expendable.

We must cease to exercise the world's judgments and try to think God's thoughts after him.

We must reckon ourselves dead to gain and glory and allow ourselves to become inextricably involved with the cross of Christ and the high honor of God.

Then our prayers will be something like this: *O God, let thy glory be revealed once more to men: through me if it please thee, or without me or apart from me, it matters not. Restore thy church to the place of moral beauty that becomes her as the bride of Christ: through me, or apart from me; only let this prayer be answered. O God, honor whom thou wilt. Let me be used or overlooked or ignored or forgotten.*

Prayer is still the greatest power on earth if it is practiced in the true fear of God. It is our solemn obligation to see that it is so practiced.

ADDITIONAL SCRIPTURE READING:
Psalm 145.18–19; Jeremiah 29.12–13

Go to page 206 for your next devotional reading.

1900   Present

LORD spoke to you at Horeb out of the fire, take care and watch yourselves closely, 16so that you do not act corruptly by making an idol for yourselves, in the form of any figure—the likeness of male or female, 17the likeness of any animal that is on the earth, the likeness of any winged bird that flies in the air, 18the likeness of anything that creeps on the ground, the likeness of any fish that is in the water under the earth. 19And when you look up to the heavens and see the sun, the moon, and the stars, all the host of heaven, do not be led astray and bow down to them and serve them, things that the LORD your God has allotted to all the peoples everywhere under heaven. 20But the LORD has taken you and brought you out of the iron-smelter, out of Egypt, to become a people of his very own possession, as you are now.

21 The LORD was angry with me because of you, and he vowed that I should not cross the Jordan and that I should not enter the good land that the LORD your God is giving for your possession. 22For I am going to die in this land without crossing over the Jordan, but you are going to cross over to take possession of that good land. 23So be careful not to forget the covenant that the LORD your God made with you, and not to make for yourselves an idol in the form of anything that the LORD your God has forbidden you. 24For the LORD your God is a devouring fire, a jealous God.

25 When you have had children and children's children, and become complacent in the land, if you act corruptly by making an idol in the form of anything, thus doing what is evil in the sight of the LORD your God, and provoking him to anger, 26I call heaven and earth to witness against you today that you will soon utterly perish from the land that you are crossing the Jordan to occupy; you will not live long on it, but will be utterly destroyed. 27The LORD will scatter you among the peoples; only a few of you will be left among the nations where the LORD will lead you. 28There you will serve other gods made by human hands, objects of wood and stone that neither see, nor hear, nor eat, nor smell. 29From there you will seek the LORD your God, and you will find him if you search after him with all your heart and soul. 30In your distress, when all these things have happened to you in time to come, you will return to the LORD your God and heed him. 31Because the LORD your God is a merciful God, he will neither abandon you nor destroy you; he will not forget the covenant with your ancestors that he swore to them.

32 For ask now about former ages, long before your own, ever since the day that God created human beings on the earth; ask from one end of heaven to the other: has anything so great as this ever happened or has its like ever been heard of? 33Has any people ever heard the voice of a god speaking out of a fire, as you have heard, and lived? 34Or has any god ever attempted to go and take a nation for himself from the midst of another nation, by trials, by signs and wonders, by war, by a mighty hand and an outstretched arm, and by terrifying displays of power, as the LORD your God did for you in Egypt before your very eyes? 35To you it was shown so that you would acknowledge that the LORD is God; there is no other besides him. 36From heaven he made you hear his voice to discipline you. On earth he showed you his great fire, while you heard his words coming out of the fire. 37And because he loved your ancestors, he chose their descendants after them. He brought you out of Egypt with his own presence, by his great power, 38driving out before you nations greater and mightier than yourselves, to bring you in, giving you their land for a possession, as it is still today. 39So acknowledge today and take to heart that the LORD is God in heaven above and on the earth beneath; there is no other. 40Keep his statutes and his commandments, which I am commanding you today for your own well-being and that of your descendants after you, so that you may long remain in the land that the LORD your God is giving you for all time.

Cities of Refuge East of the Jordan

41 Then Moses set apart on the east side of the Jordan three cities 42to which a homicide could flee, someone who unintentionally kills another person,

the two not having been at enmity before; the homicide could flee to one of these cities and live: 43Bezer in the wilderness on the tableland belonging to the Reubenites, Ramoth in Gilead belonging to the Gadites, and Golan in Bashan belonging to the Manassites.

Transition to the Second Address

44 This is the law that Moses set before the Israelites. 45These are the decrees and the statutes and ordinances that Moses spoke to the Israelites when they had come out of Egypt, 46beyond the Jordan in the valley opposite Beth-peor, in the land of King Sihon of the Amorites, who reigned at Heshbon, whom Moses and the Israelites defeated when they came out of Egypt. 47They occupied his land and the land of King Og of Bashan, the two kings of the Amorites on the eastern side of the Jordan: 48from Aroer, which is on the edge of the Wadi Arnon, as far as Mount Sirion[i] (that is, Hermon), 49together with all the Arabah on the east side of the Jordan as far as the Sea of the Arabah, under the slopes of Pisgah.

The Ten Commandments

5 Moses convened all Israel, and said to them:

Hear, O Israel, the statutes and ordinances that I am addressing to you today; you shall learn them and observe them diligently. 2The LORD our God made a covenant with us at Horeb. 3Not with our ancestors did the LORD make this covenant, but with us, who are all of us here alive today. 4The LORD spoke with you face to face at the mountain, out of the fire. 5(At that time I was standing between the LORD and you to declare to you the words[j] of the LORD; for you were afraid because of the fire and did not go up the mountain.) And he said:

6 I am the LORD your God, who brought you out of the land of Egypt, out of the house of slavery; 7you shall have no other gods before[k] me.

8 You shall not make for yourself an idol, whether in the form of anything that is in heaven above, or that is on the earth beneath, or that is in the water under the earth. 9You shall not bow down to them or worship them; for I the LORD your God am a jealous God, punishing children for the iniquity of parents, to the third and fourth generation of those who reject me, 10but showing steadfast love to the thousandth generation[l] of those who love me and keep my commandments.

11 You shall not make wrongful use of the name of the LORD your God, for the LORD will not acquit anyone who misuses his name.

12 Observe the sabbath day and keep it holy, as the LORD your God commanded you. 13Six days you shall labor and do all your work. 14But the seventh day is a sabbath to the LORD your God; you shall not do any work—you, or your son or your daughter, or your male or female slave, or your ox or your donkey, or any of your livestock, or the resident alien in your towns, so that your male and female slave may rest as well as you. 15Remember that you were a slave in the land of Egypt, and the LORD your God brought you out from there with a mighty hand and an outstretched arm; therefore the LORD your God commanded you to keep the sabbath day.

16 Honor your father and your mother, as the LORD your God commanded you, so that your days may be long and that it may go well with you in the land that the LORD your God is giving you.

17 You shall not murder.[m]

18 Neither shall you commit adultery.

19 Neither shall you steal.

20 Neither shall you bear false witness against your neighbor.

21 Neither shall you covet your neighbor's wife.

Neither shall you desire your neighbor's house, or field, or male or female slave, or ox, or donkey, or anything that belongs to your neighbor.

Moses the Mediator of God's Will

22 These words the LORD spoke with a loud voice to your whole assembly at the mountain, out of the fire, the cloud, and the thick darkness, and he added no more. He wrote them on two stone

i Syr: Heb Sion   j Q Mss Sam Gk Syr Vg Tg: MT word   k Or besides   l Or to thousands
m Or kill

tablets, and gave them to me. 23When you heard the voice out of the darkness, while the mountain was burning with fire, you approached me, all the heads of your tribes and your elders; 24and you said, "Look, the LORD our God has shown us his glory and greatness, and we have heard his voice out of the fire. Today we have seen that God may speak to someone and the person may still live. 25So now why should we die? For this great fire will consume us; if we hear the voice of the LORD our God any longer, we shall die. 26For who is there of all flesh that has heard the voice of the living God speaking out of fire, as we have, and remained alive? 27Go near, you yourself, and hear all that the LORD our God will say. Then tell us everything that the LORD our God tells you, and we will listen and do it."

28 The LORD heard your words when you spoke to me, and the LORD said to me: "I have heard the words of this people, which they have spoken to you; they are right in all that they have spoken. 29If only they had such a mind as this, to fear me and to keep all my commandments always, so that it might go well with them and with their children forever! 30Go say to them, 'Return to your tents.' 31But you, stand here by me, and I will tell you all the commandments, the statutes and the ordinances, that you shall teach them, so that they may do them in the land that I am giving them to possess." 32You must therefore be careful to do as the LORD your God has commanded you; you shall not turn to the right or to the left. 33You must follow exactly the path that the LORD your God has commanded you, so that you may live, and that it may go well with you, and that you may live long in the land that you are to possess.

The Great Commandment

6 Now this is the commandment—the statutes and the ordinances—that the LORD your God charged me to teach you to observe in the land that you are about to cross into and occupy, 2so that you and your children and your children's children may fear the LORD your God all the days of your life, and keep all his decrees and his commandments that I am commanding you, so that your days may be long. 3Hear therefore, O Israel, and observe them diligently, so that it may go well with you, and so that you may multiply greatly in a land flowing with milk and honey, as the LORD, the God of your ancestors, has promised you.

4 Hear, O Israel: The LORD is our God, the LORD alone.n 5You shall love the LORD your God with all your heart, and with all your soul, and with all your might. 6Keep these words that I am commanding you today in your heart. 7Recite them to your children and talk about them when you are at home and when you are away, when you lie down and when you rise. 8Bind them as a sign on your hand, fix them as an emblemo on your forehead, 9and write them on the doorposts of your house and on your gates.

Caution against Disobedience

10 When the LORD your God has brought you into the land that he swore to your ancestors, to Abraham, to Isaac, and to Jacob, to give you—a land with fine, large cities that you did not build, 11houses filled with all sorts of goods that you did not fill, hewn cisterns that you did not hew, vineyards and olive groves that you did not plant—and when you have eaten your fill, 12take care that you do not forget the LORD, who brought you out of the land of Egypt, out of the house of slavery. 13The LORD your God you shall fear; him you shall serve, and by his name alone you shall swear. 14Do not follow other gods, any of the gods of the peoples who are all around you, 15because the LORD your God, who is present with you, is a jealous God. The anger of the LORD your God would be kindled against you and he would destroy you from the face of the earth.

n Or The LORD our God is one LORD, or The LORD our God, the LORD is one, or The LORD is our God, the LORD is one   o Or as a frontlet

16 Do not put the LORD your God to the test, as you tested him at Massah. 17You must diligently keep the commandments of the LORD your God, and his decrees, and his statutes that he has commanded you. 18Do what is right and good in the sight of the LORD, so that it may go well with you, and so that you may go in and occupy the good land that the LORD swore to your ancestors to give you, 19thrusting out all your enemies from before you, as the LORD has promised.

20 When your children ask you in time to come, "What is the meaning of the decrees and the statutes and the ordinances that the LORD our God has commanded you?" 21then you shall say to your children, "We were Pharaoh's slaves in Egypt, but the LORD brought us out of Egypt with a mighty hand. 22The LORD displayed before our eyes great and awesome signs and wonders against Egypt, against Pharaoh and all his household. 23He brought us out from there in order to bring us in, to give us the land that he promised on oath to our ancestors. 24Then the LORD commanded us to observe all these statutes, to fear the LORD our God, for our lasting good, so as to keep us alive, as is now the case. 25If we diligently observe this entire commandment before the LORD our God, as he has commanded us, we will be in the right."

A Chosen People

7 When the LORD your God brings you into the land that you are about to enter and occupy, and he clears away many nations before you—the Hittites, the Girgashites, the Amorites, the Canaanites, the Perizzites, the Hivites, and the Jebusites, seven nations mightier and more numerous than you— 2and when the LORD your God gives them over to you and you defeat them, then you must utterly destroy them. Make no covenant with them and show them no mercy. 3Do not intermarry with them, giving your daughters to their sons or taking their daughters for your sons, 4for that would turn away your children from following me, to serve other gods. Then the anger of the LORD would be kindled against you, and he would destroy you quickly. 5But this is how you must deal with them: break down their altars, smash their pillars, hew down their sacred poles,*p* and burn their idols with fire. 6For you are a people holy to the LORD your God; the LORD your God has chosen you out of all the peoples on earth to be his people, his treasured possession.

7 It was not because you were more numerous than any other people that the LORD set his heart on you and chose you—for you were the fewest of all peoples. 8It was because the LORD loved you and kept the oath that he swore to your ancestors, that the LORD has brought you out with a mighty hand, and redeemed you from the house of slavery, from the hand of Pharaoh king of Egypt. 9Know therefore that the LORD your God is God, the faithful God who maintains covenant loyalty with those who love him and keep his commandments, to a thousand generations, 10and who repays in their own person those who reject him. He does not delay but repays in their own person those who reject him. 11Therefore, observe diligently the commandment—the statutes and the ordinances—that I am commanding you today.

Blessings for Obedience

12 If you heed these ordinances, by diligently observing them, the LORD your God will maintain with you the covenant loyalty that he swore to your ancestors; 13he will love you, bless you, and multiply you; he will bless the fruit of your womb and the fruit of your ground, your grain and your wine and your oil, the increase of your cattle and the issue of your flock, in the land that he swore to your ancestors to give you. 14You shall be the most blessed of peoples, with neither sterility nor barrenness among you or your livestock. 15The LORD will turn away from you every illness; all the dread diseases of Egypt that you experienced, he will not inflict on you, but he will lay them on all who hate you. 16You shall devour all the peoples that the LORD your God is giving over to you, showing them no pity; you

p Heb *Asherim*

GOD NEVER FORSAKES US
Martin Luther

VERSE: Deuteronomy 7.18   **PASSAGE:** Deuteronomy 7.17–24

hen God . . . delivered the children of Israel out the long, wearisome, and heavy captivity in Egypt, and led them into the land of promise, he called Moses, to whom he afterwards gave his brother Aaron as an assistant. And though Pharaoh at first set himself hard against them, and plagued the people worse than before, yet he was forced in the end to let Israel go. And when he hunted after them with all his host, the Lord drowned Pharaoh with all his power in the Red Sea, and so delivered his people.

Again, in the time of Eli the priest, when matters stood very evil in Israel, the Philistines pressing hard upon them, and taking away the Ark of God into their land, and when Eli, in great sorrow of heart, fell backwards from his chair and broke his neck, and it seemed as if Israel were utterly undone. God raised up Samuel the prophet, and through him restored Israel, and the Philistines were overthrown.

Afterwards, when Saul was sore pressed by the Philistines, so that for anguish of heart he despaired and thrust himself through, three of his sons and many people dying with him, every man thought that now there was an end of Israel. But shortly after, when David was chosen king over all Israel, then came the golden time. For David, the chosen of God, not only saved Israel out of the enemies' hands, but also forced to obedience all kings and people that set themselves against him, and helped the kingdom up again in such manner, that in his and Solomon's time it was in full flourish, power, and glory.

Even so, when Judah was carried captive to Babylon, then God selected the prophets Ezekiel, Haggai, and Zechariah, who comforted men in their distress and captivity; making not only promise of their return into the land of Judah, but also that Christ should come in his due time.

Hence we may see that God never forsakes his people, nor even the wicked; though, by reason of their sins, he suffer them a long time to be severely punished and plagued as also, in this our time, he has graciously delivered us . . . God of his mercy grant we may thankfully acknowledge this.

ADDITIONAL SCRIPTURE READING:
Psalm 46.7–11; Isaiah 43.1–5; Matthew 28.20

Go to page 208 for your next devotional reading.

1500   1700

shall not serve their gods, for that would be a snare to you.

17 If you say to yourself, "These nations are more numerous than I; how can I dispossess them?" 18do not be afraid of them. Just remember what the LORD your God did to Pharaoh and to all Egypt, 19the great trials that your eyes saw, the signs and wonders, the mighty hand and the outstretched arm by which the LORD your God brought you out. The LORD your God will do the same to all the peoples of whom you are afraid. 20Moreover, the LORD your God will send the pestilenceq against them, until even the survivors and the fugitives are destroyed. 21Have no dread of them, for the LORD your God, who is present with you, is a great and awesome God. 22The LORD your God will clear away these nations before you little by little; you will not be able to make a quick end of them, otherwise the wild animals would become too numerous for you. 23But the LORD your God will give them over to you, and throw them into great panic, until they are destroyed. 24He will hand their kings over to you and you shall blot out their name from under heaven; no one will be able to stand against you, until you have destroyed them. 25The images of their gods you shall burn with fire. Do not covet the silver or the gold that is on them and take it for yourself, because you could be ensnared by it; for it is abhorrent to the LORD your God. 26Do not bring an abhorrent thing into your house, or you will be set apart for destruction like it. You must utterly detest and abhor it, for it is set apart for destruction.

A Warning Not to Forget God in Prosperity

8 This entire commandment that I command you today you must diligently observe, so that you may live and increase, and go in and occupy the land that the LORD promised on oath to your ancestors. 2Remember the long way that the LORD your God has led you these forty years in the wilderness, in order to humble you, testing you to know what was in your heart, whether or not you would keep his commandments. 3He humbled you by letting you hunger, then by feeding you with manna, with which neither you nor your ancestors were acquainted, in order to make you understand that one does not live by bread alone, but by every word that comes from the mouth of the LORD.r 4The clothes on your back did not wear out and your feet did not swell these forty years. 5Know then in your heart that as a parent disciplines a child so the LORD your God disciplines you. 6Therefore keep the commandments of the LORD your God, by walking in his ways and by fearing him. 7For the LORD your God is bringing you into a good land, a land with flowing streams, with springs and underground waters welling up in valleys and hills, 8a land of wheat and barley, of vines and fig trees and pomegranates, a land of olive trees and honey, 9a land where you may eat bread without scarcity, where you will lack nothing, a land whose stones are iron and from whose hills you may mine copper. 10You shall eat your fill and bless the LORD your God for the good land that he has given you.

11 Take care that you do not forget the LORD your God, by failing to keep his commandments, his ordinances, and his statutes, which I am commanding you today. 12When you have eaten your fill and have built fine houses and live in them, 13and when your herds and flocks have multiplied, and your silver and gold is multiplied, and all that you have is multiplied, 14then do not exalt yourself, forgetting the LORD your God, who brought you out of the land of Egypt, out of the house of slavery, 15who led you through the great and terrible wilderness, an arid wasteland with poisonouss snakes and scorpions. He made water flow for you from flint rock, 16and fed you in the wilderness with manna that your ancestors did not know, to humble you and to test you, and in the end to do you good. 17Do not say to yourself, "My power and the might of my own hand have gotten me this wealth." 18But remember the LORD your God, for it is

q Or hornets: Meaning of Heb uncertain   r Or by anything that the LORD decrees   s Or fiery; Heb seraph he who gives you power to get wealth, so that he may confirm his covenant that he swore to your ancestors, as he is doing today. ¹⁹If you do forget the LORD your God and follow other gods to serve and worship them, I solemnly warn you today that you shall surely perish. ²⁰Like the nations that the LORD is destroying before you, so shall you perish, because you would not obey the voice of the LORD your God.

The Consequences of Rebelling against God

9 Hear, O Israel! You are about to cross the Jordan today, to go in and dispossess nations larger and mightier than you, great cities, fortified to the heavens, ²a strong and tall people, the offspring of the Anakim, whom you know. You have heard it said of them, "Who can stand up to the Anakim?" ³Know then today that the LORD your

---

WEDNESDAY

NOT BY BREAD ALONE
F. B. Meyer

VERSE: Deuteronomy 8.3   PASSAGE: Deuteronomy 8.3

he Old Testament must be worth our study since it was our Savior's Bible, deeply pondered and often quoted. And the New demands it, since it is so full of what he said and did, not only in his earthly life but through the medium of his holy apostles and prophets.

The advantages of a deep knowledge of the Bible are more than can be numbered here. It is the storehouse of the promises. It is the sword of the Spirit, before which temptation flees. It is the all-sufficient equipment of Christian usefulness. It is the believer's guidebook and directory in all possible circumstances. Words fail to tell how glad, how strong, how useful shall be the daily life of those who can say with the prophet: "Thy words were found, and I did eat them; and thy word was unto me the joy and rejoicing of mine heart" (Jeremiah 15.16, KJV).

But there is one thing, which may be said last, because it is most important and should linger in the memory and heart, though all the other exhortations of this chapter should pass away as a summer brook. It is this. It is useless to dream of making headway in the knowledge of Scripture unless we are prepared to practice each new and clearly-defined duty which looms out before our view.

ADDITIONAL SCRIPTURE READING:
Psalm 119.105; Jeremiah 15.16; Matthew 4.1–4

Go to page 231 for your next devotional reading.

1700   1900

God is the one who crosses over before you as a devouring fire; he will defeat them and subdue them before you, so that you may dispossess and destroy them quickly, as the LORD has promised you.

4 When the LORD your God thrusts them out before you, do not say to yourself, "It is because of my righteousness that the LORD has brought me in to occupy this land"; it is rather because of the wickedness of these nations that the LORD is dispossessing them before you. 5It is not because of your righteousness or the uprightness of your heart that you are going in to occupy their land; but because of the wickedness of these nations the LORD your God is dispossessing them before you, in order to fulfill the promise that the LORD made on oath to your ancestors, to Abraham, to Isaac, and to Jacob.

6 Know, then, that the LORD your God is not giving you this good land to occupy because of your righteousness; for you are a stubborn people. 7Remember and do not forget how you provoked the LORD your God to wrath in the wilderness; you have been rebellious against the LORD from the day you came out of the land of Egypt until you came to this place.

8 Even at Horeb you provoked the LORD to wrath, and the LORD was so angry with you that he was ready to destroy you. 9When I went up the mountain to receive the stone tablets, the tablets of the covenant that the LORD made with you, I remained on the mountain forty days and forty nights; I neither ate bread nor drank water. 10And the LORD gave me the two stone tablets written with the finger of God; on them were all the words that the LORD had spoken to you at the mountain out of the fire on the day of the assembly. 11At the end of forty days and forty nights the LORD gave me the two stone tablets, the tablets of the covenant. 12Then the LORD said to me, "Get up, go down quickly from here, for your people whom you have brought from Egypt have acted corruptly. They have been quick to turn from the way that I commanded them; they have cast an image

for themselves." 13Furthermore the LORD said to me, "I have seen that this people is indeed a stubborn people. 14Let me alone that I may destroy them and blot out their name from under heaven; and I will make of you a nation mightier and more numerous than they."

15 So I turned and went down from the mountain, while the mountain was ablaze; the two tablets of the covenant were in my two hands. 16Then I saw that you had indeed sinned against the LORD your God, by casting for yourselves an image of a calf; you had been quick to turn from the way that the LORD had commanded you. 17So I took hold of the two tablets and flung them from my two hands, smashing them before your eyes. 18Then I lay prostrate before the LORD as before, forty days and forty nights; I neither ate bread nor drank water, because of all the sin you had committed, provoking the LORD by doing what was evil in his sight. 19For I was afraid that the anger that the LORD bore against you was so fierce that he would destroy you. But the LORD listened to me that time also. 20The LORD was so angry with Aaron that he was ready to destroy him, but I interceded also on behalf of Aaron at that same time. 21Then I took the sinful thing you had made, the calf, and burned it with fire and crushed it, grinding it thoroughly, until it was reduced to dust; and I threw the dust of it into the stream that runs down the mountain.

22 At Taberah also, and at Massah, and at Kibroth-hattaavah, you provoked the LORD to wrath. 23And when the LORD sent you from Kadesh-barnea, saying, "Go up and occupy the land that I have given you," you rebelled against the command of the LORD your God, neither trusting him nor obeying him. 24You have been rebellious against the LORD as long as he has*t* known you.

25 Throughout the forty days and forty nights that I lay prostrate before the LORD when the LORD intended t destroy you, 26I prayed to the LORD a said, "Lord GOD, do not destroy the ple who are your very own posses whom you redeemed in your grea whom you brought out of Egy

t Sam Gk: MT *I have*

a mighty hand. 27Remember your servants, Abraham, Isaac, and Jacob; pay no attention to the stubbornness of this people, their wickedness and their sin, 28otherwise the land from which you have brought us might say, 'Because the LORD was not able to bring them into the land that he promised them, and because he hated them, he has brought them out to let them die in the wilderness.' 29For they are the people of your very own possession, whom you brought out by your great power and by your outstretched arm."

The Second Pair of Tablets

10 At that time the LORD said to me, "Carve out two tablets of stone like the former ones, and come up to me on the mountain, and make an ark of wood. 2I will write on the tablets the words that were on the former tablets, which you smashed, and you shall put them in the ark." 3So I made an ark of acacia wood, cut two tablets of stone like the former ones, and went up the mountain with the two tablets in my hand. 4Then he wrote on the tablets the same words as before, the ten commandmentsu that the LORD had spoken to you on the mountain out of the fire on the day of the assembly; and the LORD gave them to me. 5So I turned and came down from the mountain, and put the tablets in the ark that I had made; and there they are, as the LORD commanded me.

6 (The Israelites journeyed from Beeroth-bene-jaakanv to Moserah. There Aaron died, and there he was buried; his son Eleazar succeeded him as priest. 7From there they journeyed to Gudgodah, and from Gudgodah to Jotbathah, a land with flowing streams. 8At that time the LORD set apart the tribe of Levi to carry the ark of the covenant of the LORD, to stand before the LORD to minister to him, and to bless in his name, to ... 9Therefore Levi has no allotment ... heritage with his kindred; ... his inheritance, as the LORD ... omised him.) ... ed on the mountain forty ... ty nights, as I had done the ... nd once again the LORD lis-

tened to me. The LORD was unwilling to destroy you. 11The LORD said to me, "Get up, go on your journey at the head of the people, that they may go in and occupy the land that I swore to their ancestors to give them."

The Essence of the Law

12 So now, O Israel, what does the LORD your God require of you? Only to fear the LORD your God, to walk in all his ways, to love him, to serve the LORD your God with all your heart and with all your soul, 13and to keep the commandments of the LORD your Godw and his decrees that I am commanding today, for your own well-being. 14Although heaven and the heaven of heavens belong to the LORD your God, the earth with all that is in it, 15yet the LORD set his heart in love on your ancestors alone and chose you, their descendants after them, out of all the peoples, as it is today. 16Circumcise, then, the foreskin of your heart, and do not be stubborn any longer. 17For the LORD your God is God of gods and Lord of lords, the great God, mighty and awesome, who is not partial and takes no bribe, 18who executes justice for the orphan and the widow, and who loves the strangers, providing them food and clothing. 19You shall also love the stranger, for you were strangers in the land of Egypt. 20You shall fear the LORD your God; him alone you shall worship; to him you shall hold fast, and by his name you shall swear. 21He is your praise; he is your God, who has done for you these great and awesome things that your own eyes have seen. 22Your ancestors went down to Egypt seventy persons; and now the LORD your God has made you as numerous as the stars in heaven.

Rewards for Obedience

11 You shall love the LORD your God, therefore, and keep his charge, his decrees, his ordinances, and his commandments always. 2Remember today that it was not your children (who have not known or seen the discipline of the LORD your God), but it is you who must acknowledge his greatness, his mighty hand and his outstretched arm, 3his signs and his deeds that he did in Egypt to Pharaoh, the king of Egypt, and to all his land; 4what he did to the Egyptian army, to their horses and chariots, how he made the water of the Red Sea*x* flow over them as they pursued you, so that the LORD has destroyed them to this day; 5what he did to you in the wilderness, until you came to this place; 6and what he did to Dathan and Abiram, sons of Eliab son of Reuben, how in the midst of all Israel the earth opened its mouth and swallowed them up, along with their households, their tents, and every living being in their company; 7for it is your own eyes that have seen every great deed that the LORD did.

8 Keep, then, this entire commandment that I am commanding you today, so that you may have strength to go in and occupy the land that you are crossing over to occupy, 9and so that you may live long in the land that the LORD swore to your ancestors to give them and to their descendants, a land flowing with milk and honey. 10For the land that you are about to enter to occupy is not like the land of Egypt, from which you have come, where you sow your seed and irrigate by foot like a vegetable garden. 11But the land that you are crossing over to occupy is a land of hills and valleys, watered by rain from the sky, 12a land that the LORD your God looks after. The eyes of the LORD your God are always on it, from the beginning of the year to the end of the year.

13 If you will only heed his every commandment*y* that I am commanding you today—loving the LORD your God, and serving him with all your heart and with all your soul— 14then he*z* will give the rain for your land in its season, the early rain and the later rain, and you will gather in your grain, your wine, and your oil; 15and he*z* will give grass in your fields for your livestock, and you will eat your fill. 16Take care, or you will be seduced into turning away, serving other gods and worshiping them, 17for then the anger of the LORD will be kindled against you and he will shut up the heavens, so that there will be no rain

and the land will yield no fruit; then you will perish quickly off the good land that the LORD is giving you.

18 You shall put these words of mine in your heart and soul, and you shall bind them as a sign on your hand, and fix them as an emblem*a* on your forehead. 19Teach them to your children, talking about them when you are at home and when you are away, when you lie down and when you rise. 20Write them on the doorposts of your house and on your gates, 21so that your days and the days of your children may be multiplied in the land that the LORD swore to your ancestors to give them, as long as the heavens are above the earth.

22 If you will diligently observe this entire commandment that I am commanding you, loving the LORD your God, walking in all his ways, and holding fast to him, 23then the LORD will drive out all these nations before you, and you will dispossess nations larger and mightier than yourselves. 24Every place on which you set foot shall be yours; your territory shall extend from the wilderness to the Lebanon and from the River, the river Euphrates, to the Western Sea. 25No one will be able to stand against you; the LORD your God will put the fear and dread of you on all the land on which you set foot, as he promised you.

26 See, I am setting before you today a blessing and a curse: 27the blessing, if you obey the commandments of the LORD your God that I am commanding you today; 28and the curse, if you do not obey the commandments of the LORD your God, but turn from the way that I am commanding you today, to follow other gods that you have not known.

29 When the LORD your God has brought you into the land that you are entering to occupy, you shall set the blessing on Mount Gerizim and the curse on Mount Ebal. 30As you know, they are beyond the Jordan, some distance to the west, in the land of the Canaanites who live in the Arabah, opposite Gilgal, beside the oak*b* of Moreh.

31 When you cross the Jordan to go in to occupy the land that the LORD your

---

x Or *Sea of Reeds*   *y* Compare Gk: Heb *my commandments*   *z* Sam Gk Vg: MT *I*   *a* Or *as a frontlet*   *b* Gk Syr: Compare Gen 12.6; Heb *oaks* or *terebinths*

God is giving you, and when you occupy it and live in it, 32you must diligently observe all the statutes and ordinances that I am setting before you today.

Pagan Shrines to Be Destroyed

12 These are the statutes and ordinances that you must diligently observe in the land that the LORD, the God of your ancestors, has given you to occupy all the days that you live on the earth. 2 You must demolish completely all the places where the nations whom you are about to dispossess served their gods, on the mountain heights, on the hills, and under every leafy tree. 3Break down their altars, smash their pillars, burn their sacred poles*c* with fire, and hew down the idols of their gods, and thus blot out their name from their places. 4You shall not worship the LORD your God in such ways. 5But you shall seek the place that the LORD your God will choose out of all your tribes as his habitation to put his name there. You shall go there, 6bringing there your burnt offerings and your sacrifices, your tithes and your donations, your votive gifts, your freewill offerings, and the firstlings of your herds and flocks. 7And you shall eat there in the presence of the LORD your God, you and your households together, rejoicing in all the undertakings in which the LORD your God has blessed you.

8 You shall not act as we are acting here today, all of us according to our own desires, 9for you have not yet come into the rest and the possession that the LORD your God is giving you. 10When you cross over the Jordan and live in the land that the LORD your God is allotting to you, and when he gives you rest from your enemies all around so that you live in safety, 11then you shall bring everything that I command you to the place that the LORD your God will choose as a dwelling for his name: your burnt offerings and your sacrifices, your tithes and your donations, and all your choice votive gifts that you vow to the LORD. 12And you shall rejoice before the LORD your God, you together with your sons and your daughters, your male and

female slaves, and the Levites who reside in your towns (since they have no allotment or inheritance with you).

A Prescribed Place of Worship

13 Take care that you do not offer your burnt offerings at any place you happen to see. 14But only at the place that the LORD will choose in one of your tribes—there you shall offer your burnt offerings and there you shall do everything I command you.

15 Yet whenever you desire you may slaughter and eat meat within any of your towns, according to the blessing that the LORD your God has given you; the unclean and the clean may eat of it, as they would of gazelle or deer. 16The blood, however, you must not eat; you shall pour it out on the ground like water. 17Nor may you eat within your towns the tithe of your grain, your wine, and your oil, the firstlings of your herds and your flocks, any of your votive gifts that you vow, your freewill offerings, or your donations; 18these you shall eat in the presence of the LORD your God at the place that the LORD your God will choose, you together with your son and your daughter, your male and female slaves, and the Levites resident in your towns, rejoicing in the presence of the LORD your God in all your undertakings. 19Take care that you do not neglect the Levite as long as you live in your land.

20 When the LORD your God enlarges your territory, as he has promised you, and you say, "I am going to eat some meat," because you wish to eat meat, you may eat meat whenever you have the desire. 21If the place where the LORD your God will choose to put his name is too far from you, and you slaughter as I have commanded you any of your herd or flock that the LORD has given you, then you may eat within your towns whenever you desire. 22Indeed, just as gazelle or deer is eaten, so you may eat it; the unclean and the clean alike may eat it. 23Only be sure that you do not eat the blood; for the blood is the life, and you shall not eat the life with the meat. 24Do not eat it; you shall pour it out on the ground like water. 25Do not eat it, so that all may go well with you and your

c Heb *Asherim*

children after you, because you do what is right in the sight of the LORD. 26But the sacred donations that are due from you, and your votive gifts, you shall bring to the place that the LORD will choose. 27You shall present your burnt offerings, both the meat and the blood, on the altar of the LORD your God; the blood of your other sacrifices shall be poured out beside[d] the altar of the LORD your God, but the meat you may eat.

28 Be careful to obey all these words that I command you today,[e] so that it may go well with you and with your children after you forever, because you will be doing what is good and right in the sight of the LORD your God.

Warning against Idolatry

29 When the LORD your God has cut off before you the nations whom you are about to enter to dispossess them, when you have dispossessed them and live in their land, 30take care that you are not snared into imitating them, after they have been destroyed before you: do not inquire concerning their gods, saying, "How did these nations worship their gods? I also want to do the same." 31You must not do the same for the LORD your God, because every abhorrent thing that the LORD hates they have done for their gods. They would even burn their sons and their daughters in the fire to their gods. 32f You must diligently observe everything that I command you; do not add to it or take anything from it.

13 [g] If prophets or those who divine by dreams appear among you and promise you omens or portents, 2and the omens or the portents declared by them take place, and they say, "Let us follow other gods" (whom you have not known) "and let us serve them," 3you must not heed the words of those prophets or those who divine by dreams; for the LORD your God is testing you, to know whether you indeed love the LORD your God with all your heart and soul. 4The LORD your God you shall follow, him alone you shall fear, his commandments you shall keep, his voice you shall obey, him you shall serve, and to him you shall hold fast.

5But those prophets or those who divine by dreams shall be put to death for having spoken treason against the LORD your God—who brought you out of the land of Egypt and redeemed you from the house of slavery—to turn you from the way in which the LORD your God commanded you to walk. So you shall purge the evil from your midst.

6 If anyone secretly entices you—even if it is your brother, your father's son or[h] your mother's son, or your own son or daughter, or the wife you embrace, or your most intimate friend—saying, "Let us go worship other gods," whom neither you nor your ancestors have known, 7any of the gods of the peoples that are around you, whether near you or far away from you, from one end of the earth to the other, 8you must not yield to or heed any such persons. Show them no pity or compassion and do not shield them. 9But you shall surely kill them; your own hand shall be first against them to execute them, and afterwards the hand of all the people. 10Stone them to death for trying to turn you away from the LORD your God, who brought you out of the land of Egypt, out of the house of slavery. 11Then all Israel shall hear and be afraid, and never again do any such wickedness.

12 If you hear it said about one of the towns that the LORD your God is giving you to live in, 13that scoundrels from among you have gone out and led the inhabitants of the town astray, saying, "Let us go and worship other gods," whom you have not known, 14then you shall inquire and make a thorough investigation. If the charge is established that such an abhorrent thing has been done among you, 15you shall put the inhabitants of that town to the sword, utterly destroying it and everything in it—even putting its livestock to the sword. 16All of its spoil you shall gather into its public square; then burn the town and all its spoil with fire, as a whole burnt offering to the LORD your God. It shall remain a perpetual ruin, never to be rebuilt. 17Do not let anything devoted to destruction stick to your hand, so that the LORD may turn

d Or on   e Gk Sam Syr: MT lacks today   f Ch 13.1 in Heb   g Ch 13.2 in Heb   h Sam Gk
Compare Tg: MT lacks your father's son or

from his fierce anger and show you compassion, and in his compassion multiply you, as he swore to your ancestors, 18if you obey the voice of the LORD your God by keeping all his commandments that I am commanding you today, doing what is right in the sight of the LORD your God.

Pagan Practices Forbidden

14 You are children of the LORD your God. You must not lacerate yourselves or shave your forelocks for the dead. 2For you are a people holy to the LORD your God; it is you the LORD has chosen out of all the peoples on earth to be his people, his treasured possession.

Clean and Unclean Foods

3 You shall not eat any abhorrent thing. 4These are the animals you may eat: the ox, the sheep, the goat, 5the deer, the gazelle, the roebuck, the wild goat, the ibex, the antelope, and the mountain-sheep. 6Any animal that divides the hoof and has the hoof cleft in two, and chews the cud, among the animals, you may eat. 7Yet of those that chew the cud or have the hoof cleft you shall not eat these: the camel, the hare, and the rock badger, because they chew the cud but do not divide the hoof; they are unclean for you. 8And the pig, because it divides the hoof but does not chew the cud, is unclean for you. You shall not eat their meat, and you shall not touch their carcasses.

9 Of all that live in water you may eat these: whatever has fins and scales you may eat. 10And whatever does not have fins and scales you shall not eat; it is unclean for you.

11 You may eat any clean birds. 12But these are the ones that you shall not eat: the eagle, the vulture, the osprey, 13the buzzard, the kite of any kind; 14every raven of any kind; 15the ostrich, the nighthawk, the sea gull, the hawk of any kind; 16the little owl and the great owl, the water hen 17and the desert owl,i the carrion vulture and the cormorant, 18the stork, the heron of any kind; the hoopoe and the bat.j 19And all winged insects are unclean for you; they shall not be

eaten. 20You may eat any clean winged creature.

21 You shall not eat anything that dies of itself; you may give it to aliens residing in your towns for them to eat, or you may sell it to a foreigner. For you are a people holy to the LORD your God.

You shall not boil a kid in its mother's milk.

Regulations concerning Tithes

22 Set apart a tithe of all the yield of your seed that is brought in yearly from the field. 23In the presence of the LORD your God, in the place that he will choose as a dwelling for his name, you shall eat the tithe of your grain, your wine, and your oil, as well as the firstlings of your herd and flock, so that you may learn to fear the LORD your God always. 24But if, when the LORD your God has blessed you, the distance is so great that you are unable to transport it, because the place where the LORD your God will choose to set his name is too far away from you, 25then you may turn it into money. With the money secure in hand, go to the place that the LORD your God will choose; 26spend the money for whatever you wish—oxen, sheep, wine, strong drink, or whatever you desire. And you shall eat there in the presence of the LORD your God, you and your household rejoicing together. 27As for the Levites resident in your towns, do not neglect them, because they have no allotment or inheritance with you.

28 Every third year you shall bring out the full tithe of your produce for that year, and store it within your towns; 29the Levites, because they have no allotment or inheritance with you, as well as the resident aliens, the orphans, and the widows in your towns, may come and eat their fill so that the LORD your God may bless you in all the work that you undertake.

Laws concerning the Sabbatical Year

15 Every seventh year you shall grant a remission of debts. 2And this is the manner of the remission: every creditor shall remit the claim that is held against a neighbor, not exact-

---

i Or pelican   j Identification of several of the birds in verses 12-18 is uncertain

ing it of a neighbor who is a member of the community, because the LORD's remission has been proclaimed. 3Of a foreigner you may exact it, but you must remit your claim on whatever any member of your community owes you. 4There will, however, be no one in need among you, because the LORD is sure to bless you in the land that the LORD your God is giving you as a possession to occupy, 5if only you will obey the LORD your God by diligently observing this entire commandment that I command you today. 6When the LORD your God has blessed you, as he promised you, you will lend to many nations, but you will not borrow; you will rule over many nations, but they will not rule over you.

7 If there is among you anyone in need, a member of your community in any of your towns within the land that the LORD your God is giving you, do not be hard-hearted or tight-fisted toward your needy neighbor. 8You should rather open your hand, willingly lending enough to meet the need, whatever it may be. 9Be careful that you do not entertain a mean thought, thinking, "The seventh year, the year of remission, is near," and therefore view your needy neighbor with hostility and give nothing; your neighbor might cry to the LORD against you, and you would incur guilt. 10Give liberally and be ungrudging when you do so, for on this account the LORD your God will bless you in all your work and in all that you undertake. 11Since there will never cease to be some in need on the earth, I therefore command you, "Open your hand to the poor and needy neighbor in your land."

THE SAYING IS, THAT HE WHO GIVES TO THE POOR, LENDS TO THE LORD. BUT IT MAY BE SAID, NOT IMPROPERLY, THE LORD LENDS TO US TO GIVE TO THE POOR.   —*William Penn*

---

12 If a member of your community, whether a Hebrew man or a Hebrew woman, is sold*k* to you and works for you six years, in the seventh year you shall set that person free. 13And when you send a male slave*l* out from you a

free person, you shall not send him out empty-handed. 14Provide liberally out of your flock, your threshing floor, and your wine press, thus giving to him some of the bounty with which the LORD your God has blessed you. 15Remember that you were a slave in the land of Egypt, and the LORD your God redeemed you; for this reason I lay this command upon you today. 16But if he says to you, "I will not go out from you," because he loves you and your household, since he is well off with you, 17then you shall take an awl and thrust it through his earlobe into the door, and he shall be your slave*m* forever. You shall do the same with regard to your female slave.*n*

18 Do not consider it a hardship when you send them out from you free persons, because for six years they have given you services worth the wages of hired laborers; and the LORD your God will bless you in all that you do.

The Firstborn of Livestock

19 Every firstling male born of your herd and flock you shall consecrate to the LORD your God; you shall not do work with your firstling ox nor shear the firstling of your flock. 20You shall eat it, you together with your household, in the presence of the LORD your God year by year at the place that the LORD will choose. 21But if it has any defect—any serious defect, such as lameness or blindness—you shall not sacrifice it to the LORD your God; 22within your towns you may eat it, the unclean and the clean alike, as you would a gazelle or deer. 23Its blood, however, you must not eat; you shall pour it out on the ground like water.

The Passover Reviewed

16 Observe the month*o* of Abib by keeping the passover to the LORD your God, for in the month of Abib the LORD your God brought you out of Egypt by night. 2You shall offer the passover sacrifice to the LORD your God, from the flock and the herd, at the place that the LORD will choose as a dwelling for his name. 3You must not

---

k Or *sells himself or herself*   *l* Heb *him*   *m* Or *bondman*   *n* Or *bondwoman*   *o* Or *new moon*

eat with it anything leavened. For seven
days you shall eat unleavened bread
with it—the bread of affliction—because
you came out of the land of Egypt in
great haste, so that all the days of your
life you may remember the day of your
departure from the land of Egypt. 4 No
leaven shall be seen with you in all your
territory for seven days; and none of the
meat of what you slaughter on the
evening of the first day shall remain
until morning. 5 You are not permitted
to offer the passover sacrifice within any
of your towns that the LORD your God is
giving you. 6 But at the place that the
LORD your God will choose as a dwelling
for his name, only there shall you offer
the passover sacrifice, in the evening at
sunset, the time of day when you
departed from Egypt. 7 You shall cook it
and eat it at the place that the LORD your
God will choose; the next morning you
may go back to your tents. 8 For six days
you shall continue to eat unleavened
bread, and on the seventh day there
shall be a solemn assembly for the LORD
your God, when you shall do no work.

The Festival of Weeks Reviewed

9 You shall count seven weeks; begin
to count the seven weeks from the time
the sickle is first put to the standing
grain. 10 Then you shall keep the festival
of weeks to the LORD your God, contributing a freewill offering in proportion to the blessing that you have
received from the LORD your God.
11 Rejoice before the LORD your God—
you and your sons and your daughters,
your male and female slaves, the Levites
resident in your towns, as well as the
strangers, the orphans, and the widows
who are among you—at the place that
the LORD your God will choose as a
dwelling for his name. 12 Remember that
you were a slave in Egypt, and diligently
observe these statutes.

The Festival of Booths Reviewed

13 You shall keep the festival of
booths[p] for seven days, when you have
gathered in the produce from your
threshing floor and your wine press.
14 Rejoice during your festival, you and
your sons and your daughters, your male
and female slaves, as well as the Levites,
the strangers, the orphans, and the widows resident in your towns. 15 Seven
days you shall keep the festival to the
LORD your God at the place that the
LORD will choose; for the LORD your
God will bless you in all your produce
and in all your undertakings, and you
shall surely celebrate.

16 Three times a year all your males
shall appear before the LORD your God at
the place that he will choose: at the festival of unleavened bread, at the festival
of weeks, and at the festival of booths.[p]
They shall not appear before the LORD
empty-handed; 17 all shall give as they
are able, according to the blessing of the
LORD your God that he has given you.

Municipal Judges and Officers

18 You shall appoint judges and officials throughout your tribes, in all your
towns that the LORD your God is giving
you, and they shall render just decisions
for the people. 19 You must not distort
justice; you must not show partiality;
and you must not accept bribes, for a
bribe blinds the eyes of the wise and
subverts the cause of those who are in
the right. 20 Justice, and only justice, you
shall pursue, so that you may live and
occupy the land that the LORD your God
is giving you.

Forbidden Forms of Worship

21 You shall not plant any tree as a
sacred pole[q] beside the altar that you
make for the LORD your God; 22 nor shall
you set up a stone pillar—things that
the LORD your God hates.

17 You must not sacrifice to the
LORD your God an ox or a
sheep that has a defect, anything seriously wrong; for that is abhorrent to the
LORD your God.

2 If there is found among you, in one
of your towns that the LORD your God is
giving you, a man or woman who does
what is evil in the sight of the LORD your
God, and transgresses his covenant 3 by
going to serve other gods and worshiping them—whether the sun or the moon
or any of the host of heaven, which I
have forbidden— 4 and if it is reported to
you or you hear of it, and you make a

p Or *tabernacles*; Heb *succoth* q Heb *Asherah*

thorough inquiry, and the charge is proved true that such an abhorrent thing has occurred in Israel, 5then you shall bring out to your gates that man or that woman who has committed this crime and you shall stone the man or woman to death. 6On the evidence of two or three witnesses the death sentence shall be executed; a person must not be put to death on the evidence of only one witness. 7The hands of the witnesses shall be the first raised against the person to execute the death penalty, and afterward the hands of all the people. So you shall purge the evil from your midst.

Legal Decisions by Priests and Judges

8 If a judicial decision is too difficult for you to make between one kind of bloodshed and another, one kind of legal right and another, or one kind of assault and another—any such matters of dispute in your towns—then you shall immediately go up to the place that the LORD your God will choose, 9where you shall consult with the levitical priests and the judge who is in office in those days; they shall announce to you the decision in the case. 10Carry out exactly the decision that they announce to you from the place that the LORD will choose, diligently observing everything they instruct you. 11You must carry out fully the law that they interpret for you or the ruling that they announce to you; do not turn aside from the decision that they announce to you, either to the right or to the left. 12As for anyone who presumes to disobey the priest appointed to minister there to the LORD your God, or the judge, that person shall die. So you shall purge the evil from Israel. 13All the people will hear and be afraid, and will not act presumptuously again.

Limitations of Royal Authority

14 When you have come into the land that the LORD your God is giving you, and have taken possession of it and settled in it, and you say, "I will set a king over me, like all the nations that are around me," 15you may indeed set over you a king whom the LORD your God will choose. One of your own com-

munity you may set as king over you; you are not permitted to put a foreigner over you, who is not of your own community. 16Even so, he must not acquire many horses for himself, or return the people to Egypt in order to acquire more horses, since the LORD has said to you, "You must never return that way again." 17And he must not acquire many wives for himself, or else his heart will turn away; also silver and gold he must not acquire in great quantity for himself. 18When he has taken the throne of his kingdom, he shall have a copy of this law written for him in the presence of the levitical priests. 19It shall remain with him and he shall read in it all the days of his life, so that he may learn to fear the LORD his God, diligently observing all the words of this law and these statutes, 20neither exalting himself above other members of the community nor turning aside from the commandment, either to the right or to the left, so that he and his descendants may reign long over his kingdom in Israel.

Privileges of Priests and Levites

18 The levitical priests, the whole tribe of Levi, shall have no allotment or inheritance within Israel. They may eat the sacrifices that are the LORD's portion.r 2but they shall have no inheritance among the other members of the community; the LORD is their inheritance, as he promised them.

3 This shall be the priests' due from the people, from those offering a sacrifice, whether an ox or a sheep: they shall give to the priest the shoulder, the two jowls, and the stomach. 4The first fruits of your grain, your wine, and your oil, as well as the first of the fleece of your sheep, you shall give him. 5For the LORD your God has chosen Levis out of all your tribes, to stand and minister in the name of the LORD, him and his sons for all time.

6 If a Levite leaves any of your towns, from wherever he has been residing in Israel, and comes to the place that the LORD will choose (and he may come whenever he wishes), 7then he may minister in the name of the LORD his God, like all his fellow-Levites who

r Meaning of Heb uncertain   s Heb him

stand to minister there before the LORD. 8They shall have equal portions to eat, even though they have income from the sale of family possessions.t

Child-Sacrifice, Divination, and Magic Prohibited

9 When you come into the land that the LORD your God is giving you, you must not learn to imitate the abhorrent practices of those nations. 10No one shall be found among you who makes a son or daughter pass through fire, or who practices divination, or is a soothsayer, or an augur, or a sorcerer, 11or one who casts spells, or who consults ghosts or spirits, or who seeks oracles from the dead. 12For whoever does these things is abhorrent to the LORD; it is because of such abhorrent practices that the LORD your God is driving them out before you. 13You must remain completely loyal to the LORD your God. 14Although these nations that you are about to dispossess do give heed to soothsayers and diviners, as for you, the LORD your God does not permit you to do so.

A New Prophet Like Moses

15 The LORD your God will raise up for you a prophetu like me from among your own people; you shall heed such a prophet.v 16This is what you requested of the LORD your God at Horeb on the day of the assembly when you said: "If I hear the voice of the LORD my God any more, or ever again see this great fire, I will die." 17Then the LORD replied to me: "They are right in what they have said. 18I will raise up for them a prophetu like you from among their own people; I will put my words in the mouth of the prophet,w who shall speak to them everything that I command. 19Anyone who does not heed the words that the prophetx shall speak in my name, I myself will hold accountable. 20But any prophet who speaks in the name of other gods, or who presumes to speak in my name a word that I have not commanded the prophet to speak—that prophet shall die." 21You may say to yourself, "How can we recognize a word that the LORD has not spoken?" 22If a prophet speaks in the name

of the LORD but the thing does not take place or prove true, it is a word that the LORD has not spoken. The prophet has spoken it presumptuously; do not be frightened by it.

Laws concerning the Cities of Refuge

19 When the LORD your God has cut off the nations whose land the LORD your God is giving you, and you have dispossessed them and settled in their towns and in their houses, 2you shall set apart three cities in the land that the LORD your God is giving you to possess. 3You shall calculate the distancesy and divide into three regions the land that the LORD your God gives you as a possession, so that any homicide can flee to one of them.

4 Now this is the case of a homicide who might flee there and live, that is, someone who has killed another person unintentionally when the two had not been at enmity before: 5Suppose someone goes into the forest with another to cut wood, and when one of them swings the ax to cut down a tree, the head slips from the handle and strikes the other person who then dies; the killer may flee to one of these cities and live. 6But if the distance is too great, the avenger of blood in hot anger might pursue and overtake and put the killer to death, although a death sentence was not deserved, since the two had not been at enmity before. 7Therefore I command you: You shall set apart three cities.

8 If the LORD your God enlarges your territory, as he swore to your ancestors—and he will give you all the land that he promised your ancestors to give you, 9provided you diligently observe this entire commandment that I command you today, by loving the LORD your God and walking always in his ways—then you shall add three more cities to these three, 10so that the blood of an innocent person may not be shed in the land that the LORD your God is giving you as an inheritance, thereby bringing bloodguilt upon you.

11 But if someone at enmity with another lies in wait and attacks and

t Meaning of Heb uncertain   u Or prophets   v Or such prophets   w Or mouths of the prophets
x Heb he   y Or prepare roads to them

takes the life of that person, and flees into one of these cities, [12]then the elders of the killer's city shall send to have the culprit taken from there and handed over to the avenger of blood to be put to death. [13]Show no pity; you shall purge the guilt of innocent blood from Israel, so that it may go well with you.

Property Boundaries

14 You must not move your neighbor's boundary marker, set up by former generations, on the property that will be allotted to you in the land that the LORD your God is giving you to possess.

Law concerning Witnesses

15 A single witness shall not suffice to convict a person of any crime or wrongdoing in connection with any offense that may be committed. Only on the evidence of two or three witnesses shall a charge be sustained. [16]If a malicious witness comes forward to accuse someone of wrongdoing, [17]then both parties to the dispute shall appear before the LORD, before the priests and the judges who are in office in those days, [18]and the judges shall make a thorough inquiry. If the witness is a false witness, having testified falsely against another, [19]then you shall do to the false witness just as the false witness had meant to do to the other. So you shall purge the evil from your midst. [20]The rest shall hear and be afraid, and a crime such as this shall never again be committed among you. [21]Show no pity: life for life, eye for eye, tooth for tooth, hand for hand, foot for foot.

Rules of Warfare

20 When you go out to war against your enemies, and see horses and chariots, an army larger than your own, you shall not be afraid of them; for the LORD your God is with you, who brought you up from the land of Egypt. [2]Before you engage in battle, the priest shall come forward and speak to the troops, [3]and shall say to them: "Hear, O Israel! Today you are drawing near to do battle against your enemies. Do not lose heart, or be afraid, or panic, or be in dread of them; [4]for it is the LORD your God who goes with you, to fight for

you against your enemies, to give you victory." [5]Then the officials shall address the troops, saying, "Has anyone built a new house but not dedicated it? He should go back to his house, or he might die in the battle and another dedicate it. [6]Has anyone planted a vineyard but not yet enjoyed its fruit? He should go back to his house, or he might die in the battle and another be first to enjoy its fruit. [7]Has anyone become engaged to a woman but not yet married her? He should go back to his house, or he might die in the battle and another marry her." [8]The officials shall continue to address the troops, saying, "Is anyone afraid or disheartened? He should go back to his house, or he might cause the heart of his comrades to melt like his own." [9]When the officials have finished addressing the troops, then the commanders shall take charge of them.

10 When you draw near to a town to fight against it, offer it terms of peace. [11]If it accepts your terms of peace and surrenders to you, then all the people in it shall serve you at forced labor. [12]If it does not submit to you peacefully, but makes war against you, then you shall besiege it; [13]and when the LORD your God gives it into your hand, you shall put all its males to the sword. [14]You may, however, take as your booty the women, the children, livestock, and everything else in the town, all its spoil. You may enjoy the spoil of your enemies, which the LORD your God has given you. [15]Thus you shall treat all the towns that are very far from you, which are not towns of the nations here. [16]But as for the towns of these peoples that the LORD your God is giving you as an inheritance, you must not let anything that breathes remain alive. [17]You shall annihilate them—the Hittites and the Amorites, the Canaanites and the Perizzites, the Hivites and the Jebusites—just as the LORD your God has commanded, [18]so that they may not teach you to do all the abhorrent things that they do for their gods, and you thus sin against the LORD your God.

19 If you besiege a town for a long time, making war against it in order to take it, you must not destroy its trees by wielding an ax against them. Although

you may take food from them, you must not cut them down. Are trees in the field human beings that they should come under siege from you? 20You may destroy only the trees that you know do not produce food; you may cut them down for use in building siegeworks against the town that makes war with you, until it falls.

Law concerning Murder by Persons Unknown

21 If, in the land that the LORD your God is giving you to possess, a body is found lying in open country, and it is not known who struck the person down, 2then your elders and your judges shall come out to measure the distances to the towns that are near the body. 3The elders of the town nearest the body shall take a heifer that has never been worked, one that has not pulled in the yoke; 4the elders of that town shall bring the heifer down to a wadi with running water, which is neither plowed nor sown, and shall break the heifer's neck there in the wadi. 5Then the priests, the sons of Levi, shall come forward, for the LORD your God has chosen them to minister to him and to pronounce blessings in the name of the LORD, and by their decision all cases of dispute and assault shall be settled. 6All the elders of that town nearest the body shall wash their hands over the heifer whose neck was broken in the wadi, 7and they shall declare: "Our hands did not shed this blood, nor were we witnesses to it. 8Absolve, O LORD, your people Israel, whom you redeemed; do not let the guilt of innocent blood remain in the midst of your people Israel." Then they will be absolved of bloodguilt. 9So you shall purge the guilt of innocent blood from your midst, because you must do what is right in the sight of the LORD.

Female Captives

10 When you go out to war against your enemies, and the LORD your God hands them over to you and you take them captive, 11suppose you see among the captives a beautiful woman whom you desire and want to marry, 12and so

you bring her home to your house: she shall shave her head, pare her nails, 13discard her captive's garb, and shall remain in your house a full month, mourning for her father and mother; after that you may go in to her and be her husband, and she shall be your wife. 14But if you are not satisfied with her, you shall let her go free and not sell her for money. You must not treat her as a slave, since you have dishonored her.

The Right of the Firstborn

15 If a man has two wives, one of them loved and the other disliked, and if both the loved and the disliked have borne him sons, the firstborn being the son of the one who is disliked, 16then on the day when he wills his possessions to his sons, he is not permitted to treat the son of the loved as the firstborn in preference to the son of the disliked, who is the firstborn. 17He must acknowledge as firstborn the son of the one who is disliked, giving him a double portionz of all that he has; since he is the first issue of his virility, the right of the firstborn is his.

Rebellious Children

18 If someone has a stubborn and rebellious son who will not obey his father and mother, who does not heed them when they discipline him, 19then his father and his mother shall take hold of him and bring him out to the elders of his town at the gate of that place. 20They shall say to the elders of his town, "This son of ours is stubborn and rebellious. He will not obey us. He is a glutton and a drunkard." 21Then all the men of the town shall stone him to death. So you shall purge the evil from your midst; and all Israel will hear, and be afraid.

Miscellaneous Laws

22 When someone is convicted of a crime punishable by death and is executed, and you hang him on a tree, 23his corpse must not remain all night upon the tree; you shall bury him that same day, for anyone hung on a tree is under God's curse. You must not defile the

z Heb two-thirds

land that the LORD your God is giving you for possession.

22 You shall not watch your neighbor's ox or sheep straying away and ignore them; you shall take them back to their owner. 2If the owner does not reside near you or you do not know who the owner is, you shall bring it to your own house, and it shall remain with you until the owner claims it; then you shall return it. 3You shall do the same with a neighbor's donkey; you shall do the same with a neighbor's garment; and you shall do the same with anything else that your neighbor loses and you find. You may not withhold your help.

4 You shall not see your neighbor's donkey or ox fallen on the road and ignore it; you shall help to lift it up.

5 A woman shall not wear a man's apparel, nor shall a man put on a woman's garment; for whoever does such things is abhorrent to the LORD your God.

6 If you come on a bird's nest, in any tree or on the ground, with fledglings or eggs, with the mother sitting on the fledglings or on the eggs, you shall not take the mother with the young. 7Let the mother go, taking only the young for yourself, in order that it may go well with you and you may live long.

8 When you build a new house, you shall make a parapet for your roof; otherwise you might have bloodguilt on your house, if anyone should fall from it.

9 You shall not sow your vineyard with a second kind of seed, or the whole yield will have to be forfeited, both the crop that you have sown and the yield of the vineyard itself.

10 You shall not plow with an ox and a donkey yoked together.

11 You shall not wear clothes made of wool and linen woven together.

12 You shall make tassels on the four corners of the cloak with which you cover yourself.

Laws concerning Sexual Relations

13 Suppose a man marries a woman, but after going in to her, he dislikes her, 14and makes up charges against her, slandering her by saying, "I married this woman; but when I lay with her, I did not find evidence of her virginity." 15The father of the young woman and her mother shall then submit the evidence of the young woman's virginity to the elders of the city at the gate. 16The father of the young woman shall say to the elders: "I gave my daughter in marriage to this man but he dislikes her; 17now he has made up charges against her, saying, 'I did not find evidence of your daughter's virginity.' But here is the evidence of my daughter's virginity." Then they shall spread out the cloth before the elders of the town. 18The elders of that town shall take the man and punish him; 19they shall fine him one hundred shekels of silver (which they shall give to the young woman's father) because he has slandered a virgin of Israel. She shall remain his wife; he shall not be permitted to divorce her as long as he lives.

20 If, however, this charge is true, that evidence of the young woman's virginity was not found, 21then they shall bring the young woman out to the entrance of her father's house and the men of her town shall stone her to death, because she committed a disgraceful act in Israel by prostituting herself in her father's house. So you shall purge the evil from your midst.

22 If a man is caught lying with the wife of another man, both of them shall die, the man who lay with the woman as well as the woman. So you shall purge the evil from Israel.

23 If there is a young woman, a virgin already engaged to be married, and a man meets her in the town and lies with her, 24you shall bring both of them to the gate of that town and stone them to death, the young woman because she did not cry for help in the town and the man because he violated his neighbor's wife. So you shall purge the evil from your midst.

25 But if the man meets the engaged woman in the open country, and the man seizes her and lies with her, then only the man who lay with her shall die. 26You shall do nothing to the young woman; the young woman has not committed an offense punishable by death, because this case is like that of someone who attacks and murders a neighbor.

27Since he found her in the open country, the engaged woman may have cried for help, but there was no one to rescue her.

28 If a man meets a virgin who is not engaged, and seizes her and lies with her, and they are caught in the act, 29the man who lay with her shall give fifty shekels of silver to the young woman's father, and she shall become his wife. Because he violated her he shall not be permitted to divorce her as long as he lives.

30a A man shall not marry his father's wife, thereby violating his father's rights.b

Those Excluded from the Assembly

23 No one whose testicles are crushed or whose penis is cut off shall be admitted to the assembly of the LORD.

2 Those born of an illicit union shall not be admitted to the assembly of the LORD. Even to the tenth generation, none of their descendants shall be admitted to the assembly of the LORD.

3 No Ammonite or Moabite shall be admitted to the assembly of the LORD. Even to the tenth generation, none of their descendants shall be admitted to the assembly of the LORD, 4because they did not meet you with food and water on your journey out of Egypt, and because they hired against you Balaam son of Beor, from Pethor of Mesopotamia, to curse you. 5(Yet the LORD your God refused to heed Balaam; the LORD your God turned the curse into a blessing for you, because the LORD your God loved you.) 6You shall never promote their welfare or their prosperity as long as you live.

7 You shall not abhor any of the Edomites, for they are your kin. You shall not abhor any of the Egyptians, because you were an alien residing in their land. 8The children of the third generation that are born to them may be admitted to the assembly of the LORD.

Sanitary, Ritual, and Humanitarian Precepts

9 When you are encamped against your enemies you shall guard against any impropriety.

10 If one of you becomes unclean because of a nocturnal emission, then he shall go outside the camp; he must not come within the camp. 11When evening comes, he shall wash himself with water, and when the sun has set, he may come back into the camp.

12 You shall have a designated area outside the camp to which you shall go. 13With your utensils you shall have a trowel; when you relieve yourself outside, you shall dig a hole with it and then cover up your excrement. 14Because the LORD your God travels along with your camp, to save you and to hand over your enemies to you, therefore your camp must be holy, so that he may not see anything indecent among you and turn away from you.

15 Slaves who have escaped to you from their owners shall not be given back to them. 16They shall reside with you, in your midst, in any place they choose in any one of your towns, wherever they please; you shall not oppress them.

17 None of the daughters of Israel shall be a temple prostitute; none of the sons of Israel shall be a temple prostitute. 18You shall not bring the fee of a prostitute or the wages of a male prostitutec into the house of the LORD your God in payment for any vow, for both of these are abhorrent to the LORD your God.

19 You shall not charge interest on loans to another Israelite, interest on money, interest on provisions, interest on anything that is lent. 20On loans to a foreigner you may charge interest, but on loans to another Israelite you may not charge interest, so that the LORD your God may bless you in all your undertakings in the land that you are about to enter and possess.

21 If you make a vow to the LORD your God, do not postpone fulfilling it; for the LORD your God will surely require it of you, and you would incur guilt. 22But if you refrain from vowing, you will not incur guilt. 23Whatever your lips utter you must diligently perform, just as you have freely vowed to the LORD your God with your own mouth.

24 If you go into your neighbor's

a Ch 23.1 in Heb   b Heb uncovering his father's skirt   c Heb a dog

vineyard, you may eat your fill of grapes, as many as you wish, but you shall not put any in a container.

25 If you go into your neighbor's standing grain, you may pluck the ears with your hand, but you shall not put a sickle to your neighbor's standing grain.

Laws concerning Marriage and Divorce

24 Suppose a man enters into marriage with a woman, but she does not please him because he finds something objectionable about her, and so he writes her a certificate of divorce, puts it in her hand, and sends her out of his house; she then leaves his house 2and goes off to become another man's wife. 3Then suppose the second man dislikes her, writes her a bill of divorce, puts it in her hand, and sends her out of his house (or the second man who married her dies); 4her first husband, who sent her away, is not permitted to take her again to be his wife after she has been defiled; for that would be abhorrent to the LORD, and you shall not bring guilt on the land that the LORD your God is giving you as a possession.

Miscellaneous Laws

5 When a man is newly married, he shall not go out with the army or be charged with any related duty. He shall be free at home one year, to be happy with the wife whom he has married.

6 No one shall take a mill or an upper millstone in pledge, for that would be taking a life in pledge.

7 If someone is caught kidnaping another Israelite, enslaving or selling the Israelite, then that kidnaper shall die. So you shall purge the evil from your midst.

8 Guard against an outbreak of a leprousd skin disease by being very careful; you shall carefully observe whatever the levitical priests instruct you, just as I have commanded them. 9Remember what the LORD your God did to Miriam on your journey out of Egypt.

10 When you make your neighbor a loan of any kind, you shall not go into the house to take the pledge. 11You shall wait outside, while the person to whom

you are making the loan brings the pledge out to you. 12If the person is poor, you shall not sleep in the garment given you ase the pledge. 13You shall give the pledge back by sunset, so that your neighbor may sleep in the cloak and bless you; and it will be to your credit before the LORD your God.

14 You shall not withhold the wages of poor and needy laborers, whether other Israelites or aliens who reside in your land in one of your towns. 15You shall pay them their wages daily before sunset, because they are poor and their livelihood depends on them; otherwise they might cry to the LORD against you, and you would incur guilt.

16 Parents shall not be put to death for their children, nor shall children be put to death for their parents; only for their own crimes may persons be put to death.

17 You shall not deprive a resident alien or an orphan of justice; you shall not take a widow's garment in pledge. 18Remember that you were a slave in Egypt and the LORD your God redeemed you from there; therefore I command you to do this.

19 When you reap your harvest in your field and forget a sheaf in the field, you shall not go back to get it; it shall be left for the alien, the orphan, and the widow, so that the LORD your God may bless you in all your undertakings. 20When you beat your olive trees, do not strip what is left; it shall be for the alien, the orphan, and the widow.

21 When you gather the grapes of your vineyard, do not glean what is left; it shall be for the alien, the orphan, and the widow. 22Remember that you were a slave in the land of Egypt; therefore I am commanding you to do this.

25 Suppose two persons have a dispute and enter into litigation, and the judges decide between them, declaring one to be in the right and the other to be in the wrong. 2If the one in the wrong deserves to be flogged, the judge shall make that person lie down and be beaten in his presence with the number of lashes proportionate to the offense. 3Forty lashes may be given but not more; if more lashes than these

---

d A term for several skin diseases; precise meaning uncertain   e Heb lacks the garment given you as

are given, your neighbor will be degraded in your sight.

4 You shall not muzzle an ox while it is treading out the grain.

Levirate Marriage

5 When brothers reside together, and one of them dies and has no son, the wife of the deceased shall not be married outside the family to a stranger. Her husband's brother shall go in to her, taking her in marriage, and performing the duty of a husband's brother to her, 6and the firstborn whom she bears shall succeed to the name of the deceased brother, so that his name may not be blotted out of Israel. 7But if the man has no desire to marry his brother's widow, then his brother's widow shall go up to the elders at the gate and say, "My husband's brother refuses to perpetuate his brother's name in Israel; he will not perform the duty of a husband's brother to me." 8Then the elders of his town shall summon him and speak to him. If he persists, saying, "I have no desire to marry her," 9then his brother's wife shall go up to him in the presence of the elders, pull his sandal off his foot, spit in his face, and declare, "This is what is done to the man who does not build up his brother's house." 10Throughout Israel his family shall be known as "the house of him whose sandal was pulled off."

Various Commands

11 If men get into a fight with one another, and the wife of one intervenes to rescue her husband from the grip of his opponent by reaching out and seizing his genitals, 12you shall cut off her hand; show no pity.

13 You shall not have in your bag two kinds of weights, large and small. 14You shall not have in your house two kinds of measures, large and small. 15You shall have only a full and honest weight; you shall have only a full and honest measure, so that your days may be long in the land that the LORD your God is giving you. 16For all who do such things, all who act dishonestly, are abhorrent to the LORD your God.

17 Remember what Amalek did to you on your journey out of Egypt, 18how he attacked you on the way, when you were faint and weary, and struck down all who lagged behind you; he did not fear God. 19Therefore when the LORD your God has given you rest from all your enemies on every hand, in the land that the LORD your God is giving you as an inheritance to possess, you shall blot out the remembrance of Amalek from under heaven; do not forget.

First Fruits and Tithes

26 When you have come into the land that the LORD your God is giving you as an inheritance to possess, and you possess it, and settle in it, 2you shall take some of the first of all the fruit of the ground, which you harvest from the land that the LORD your God is giving you, and you shall put it in a basket and go to the place that the LORD your God will choose as a dwelling for his name. 3You shall go to the priest who is in office at that time, and say to him, "Today I declare to the LORD your God that I have come into the land that the LORD swore to our ancestors to give us." 4When the priest takes the basket from your hand and sets it down before the altar of the LORD your God, 5you shall make this response before the LORD your God: "A wandering Aramean was my ancestor; he went down into Egypt and lived there as an alien, few in number, and there he became a great nation, mighty and populous. 6When the Egyptians treated us harshly and afflicted us, by imposing hard labor on us, 7we cried to the LORD, the God of our ancestors; the LORD heard our voice and saw our affliction, our toil, and our oppression. 8The LORD brought us out of Egypt with a mighty hand and an outstretched arm, with a terrifying display of power, and with signs and wonders; 9and he brought us into this place and gave us this land, a land flowing with milk and honey. 10So now I bring the first of the fruit of the ground that you, O LORD, have given me." You shall set it down before the LORD your God and bow down before the LORD your God. 11Then you, together with the Levites and the aliens who reside among you, shall celebrate with all the bounty that the LORD your God has given to you and to your house.

12 When you have finished paying all the tithe of your produce in the third year (which is the year of the tithe), giving it to the Levites, the aliens, the orphans, and the widows, so that they may eat their fill within your towns, 13then you shall say before the LORD your God: "I have removed the sacred portion from the house, and I have given it to the Levites, the resident aliens, the orphans, and the widows, in accordance with your entire commandment that you commanded me; I have neither transgressed nor forgotten any of your commandments; 14I have not eaten of it while in mourning; I have not removed any of it while I was unclean; and I have not offered any of it to the dead. I have obeyed the LORD my God, doing just as you commanded me. 15Look down from your holy habitation, from heaven, and bless your people Israel and the ground that you have given us, as you swore to our ancestors—a land flowing with milk and honey."

Concluding Exhortation

16 This very day the LORD your God is commanding you to observe these statutes and ordinances; so observe them diligently with all your heart and with all your soul. 17Today you have obtained the LORD's agreement: to be your God; and for you to walk in his ways, to keep his statutes, his commandments, and his ordinances, and to obey him. 18Today the LORD has obtained your agreement: to be his treasured people, as he promised you, and to keep his commandments; 19for him to set you high above all nations that he has made, in praise and in fame and in honor; and for you to be a people holy to the LORD your God, as he promised.

The Inscribed Stones and Altar on Mount Ebal

27 Then Moses and the elders of Israel charged all the people as follows: Keep the entire commandment that I am commanding you today. 2On the day that you cross over the Jordan into the land that the LORD your God is giving you, you shall set up large stones and cover them with plaster. 3You shall write on them all the words of this law when you have crossed over, to enter the land that the LORD your God is giving you, a land flowing with milk and honey, as the LORD, the God of your ancestors, promised you. 4So when you have crossed over the Jordan, you shall set up these stones, about which I am commanding you today, on Mount Ebal, and you shall cover them with plaster. 5And you shall build an altar there to the LORD your God, an altar of stones on which you have not used an iron tool. 6You must build the altar of the LORD your God of unhewn*f* stones. Then offer up burnt offerings on it to the LORD your God, 7make sacrifices of well-being, and eat them there, rejoicing before the LORD your God. 8You shall write on the stones all the words of this law very clearly.

9 Then Moses and the levitical priests spoke to all Israel, saying: Keep silence and hear, O Israel! This very day you have become the people of the LORD your God. 10Therefore obey the LORD your God, observing his commandments and his statutes that I am commanding you today.

Twelve Curses

11 The same day Moses charged the people as follows: 12When you have crossed over the Jordan, these shall stand on Mount Gerizim for the blessing of the people: Simeon, Levi, Judah, Issachar, Joseph, and Benjamin. 13And these shall stand on Mount Ebal for the curse: Reuben, Gad, Asher, Zebulun, Dan, and Naphtali. 14Then the Levites shall declare in a loud voice to all the Israelites:

15 "Cursed be anyone who makes an idol or casts an image, anything abhorrent to the LORD, the work of an artisan, and sets it up in secret." All the people shall respond, saying, "Amen!"

16 "Cursed be anyone who dishonors father or mother." All the people shall say, "Amen!"

17 "Cursed be anyone who moves a neighbor's boundary marker." All the people shall say, "Amen!"

18 "Cursed be anyone who misleads

f Heb *whole*

a blind person on the road." All the people shall say, "Amen!"

19 "Cursed be anyone who deprives the alien, the orphan, and the widow of justice." All the people shall say, "Amen!"

20 "Cursed be anyone who lies with his father's wife, because he has violated his father's rights."g All the people shall say, "Amen!"

21 "Cursed be anyone who lies with any animal." All the people shall say, "Amen!"

22 "Cursed be anyone who lies with his sister, whether the daughter of his father or the daughter of his mother." All the people shall say, "Amen!"

23 "Cursed be anyone who lies with his mother-in-law." All the people shall say, "Amen!"

24 "Cursed be anyone who strikes down a neighbor in secret." All the people shall say, "Amen!"

25 "Cursed be anyone who takes a bribe to shed innocent blood." All the people shall say, "Amen!"

26 "Cursed be anyone who does not uphold the words of this law by observing them." All the people shall say, "Amen!"

Blessings for Obedience

28 If you will only obey the LORD your God, by diligently observing all his commandments that I am commanding you today, the LORD your God will set you high above all the nations of the earth; 2all these blessings shall come upon you and overtake you, if you obey the LORD your God:

3 Blessed shall you be in the city, and blessed shall you be in the field.

4 Blessed shall be the fruit of your womb, the fruit of your ground, and the fruit of your livestock, both the increase of your cattle and the issue of your flock.

5 Blessed shall be your basket and your kneading bowl.

6 Blessed shall you be when you come in, and blessed shall you be when you go out.

7 The LORD will cause your enemies who rise against you to be defeated before you; they shall come out against you one way, and flee before you seven

ways. 8The LORD will command the blessing upon you in your barns, and in all that you undertake; he will bless you in the land that the LORD your God is giving you. 9The LORD will establish you as his holy people, as he has sworn to you, if you keep the commandments of the LORD your God and walk in his ways. 10All the peoples of the earth shall see that you are called by the name of the LORD, and they shall be afraid of you. 11The LORD will make you abound in prosperity, in the fruit of your womb, in the fruit of your livestock, and in the fruit of your ground in the land that the LORD swore to your ancestors to give you. 12The LORD will open for you his rich storehouse, the heavens, to give the rain of your land in its season and to bless all your undertakings. You will lend to many nations, but you will not borrow. 13The LORD will make you the head, and not the tail; you shall be only at the top, and not at the bottom—if you obey the commandments of the LORD your God, which I am commanding you today, by diligently observing them, 14and if you do not turn aside from any of the words that I am commanding you today, either to the right or to the left, following other gods to serve them.

Warnings against Disobedience

15 But if you will not obey the LORD your God by diligently observing all his commandments and decrees, which I am commanding you today, then all these curses shall come upon you and overtake you:

16 Cursed shall you be in the city, and cursed shall you be in the field.

17 Cursed shall be your basket and your kneading bowl.

18 Cursed shall be the fruit of your womb, the fruit of your ground, the increase of your cattle and the issue of your flock.

19 Cursed shall you be when you come in, and cursed shall you be when you go out.

20 The LORD will send upon you disaster, panic, and frustration in everything you attempt to do, until you are destroyed and perish quickly, on account of the evil of your deeds,

g Heb uncovered his father's skirt

because you have forsaken me. 21The LORD will make the pestilence cling to you until it has consumed you off the land that you are entering to possess. 22The LORD will afflict you with consumption, fever, inflammation, with fiery heat and drought, and with blight and mildew; they shall pursue you until you perish. 23The sky over your head shall be bronze, and the earth under you iron. 24The LORD will change the rain of your land into powder, and only dust shall come down upon you from the sky until you are destroyed.

25 The LORD will cause you to be defeated before your enemies; you shall go out against them one way and flee before them seven ways. You shall become an object of horror to all the kingdoms of the earth. 26Your corpses shall be food for every bird of the air and animal of the earth, and there shall be no one to frighten them away. 27The LORD will afflict you with the boils of Egypt, with ulcers, scurvy, and itch, of which you cannot be healed. 28The LORD will afflict you with madness, blindness, and confusion of mind; 29you shall grope about at noon as blind people grope in darkness, but you shall be unable to find your way; and you shall be continually abused and robbed, without anyone to help. 30You shall become engaged to a woman, but another man shall lie with her. You shall build a house, but not live in it. You shall plant a vineyard, but not enjoy its fruit. 31Your ox shall be butchered before your eyes, but you shall not eat of it. Your donkey shall be stolen in front of you, and shall not be restored to you. Your sheep shall be given to your enemies, without anyone to help you. 32Your sons and daughters shall be given to another people, while you look on; you will strain your eyes looking for them all day but be powerless to do anything. 33A people whom you do not know shall eat up the fruit of your ground and of all your labors; you shall be continually abused and crushed, 34and driven mad by the sight that your eyes shall see. 35The LORD will strike you on the knees and on the legs with grievous boils of which you cannot be healed, from the sole of your foot to the crown of your head. 36The LORD will bring you, and the king

whom you set over you, to a nation that neither you nor your ancestors have known, where you shall serve other gods, of wood and stone. 37You shall become an object of horror, a proverb, and a byword among all the peoples where the LORD will lead you.

38 You shall carry much seed into the field but shall gather little in, for the locust shall consume it. 39You shall plant vineyards and dress them, but you shall neither drink the wine nor gather the grapes, for the worm shall eat them. 40You shall have olive trees throughout all your territory, but you shall not anoint yourself with the oil, for your olives shall drop off. 41You shall have sons and daughters, but they shall not remain yours, for they shall go into captivity. 42All your trees and the fruit of your ground the cicada shall take over. 43Aliens residing among you shall ascend above you higher and higher, while you shall descend lower and lower. 44They shall lend to you but you shall not lend to them; they shall be the head and you shall be the tail.

45 All these curses shall come upon you, pursuing and overtaking you until you are destroyed, because you did not obey the LORD your God, by observing the commandments and the decrees that he commanded you. 46They shall be among you and your descendants as a sign and a portent forever.

47 Because you did not serve the LORD your God joyfully and with gladness of heart for the abundance of everything, 48therefore you shall serve your enemies whom the LORD will send against you, in hunger and thirst, in nakedness and lack of everything. He will put an iron yoke on your neck until he has destroyed you. 49The LORD will

---

WE CAN STAND AFFLICTION BETTER THAN WE CAN PROSPERITY, FOR IN PROSPERITY WE FORGET GOD.   —Dwight L. Moody

---

bring a nation from far away, from the end of the earth, to swoop down on you like an eagle, a nation whose language you do not understand, 50a grim-faced nation showing no respect to the old or favor to the young. 51It shall consume the fruit of your livestock and the fruit of your ground until you are destroyed, leaving you neither grain, wine, and oil, nor the increase of your cattle and the issue of your flock, until it has made you perish. 52It shall besiege you in all your towns until your high and fortified walls, in which you trusted, come down throughout your land; it shall besiege you in all your towns throughout the land that the LORD your God has given you. 53In the desperate straits to which the enemy siege reduces you, you will eat the fruit of your womb, the flesh of your own sons and daughters whom the LORD your God has given you. 54Even the most refined and gentle of men among you will begrudge food to his own brother, to the wife whom he embraces, and to the last of his remaining children, 55giving to none of them any of the flesh of his children whom he is eating, because nothing else remains to him, in the desperate straits to which the enemy siege will reduce you in all your towns. 56She who is the most refined and gentle among you, so gentle and refined that she does not venture to set the sole of her foot on the ground, will begrudge food to the husband whom she embraces, to her own son, and to her own daughter, 57begrudging even the afterbirth that comes out from between her thighs, and the children that she bears, because she is eating them in secret for lack of anything else, in the desperate straits to which the enemy siege will reduce you in your towns.

58 If you do not diligently observe all the words of this law that are written in this book, fearing this glorious and awesome name, the LORD your God, 59then the LORD will overwhelm both you and your offspring with severe and lasting afflictions and grievous and lasting maladies. 60He will bring back upon you all the diseases of Egypt, of which you were in dread, and they shall cling to you. 61Every other malady and affliction, even though not recorded in the book of this law, the LORD will inflict on you until you are destroyed. 62Although once you were as numerous as the stars in heaven, you shall be left few in number, because you did not obey the LORD

your God. 63And just as the LORD took delight in making you prosperous and numerous, so the LORD will take delight in bringing you to ruin and destruction; you shall be plucked off the land that you are entering to possess. 64The LORD will scatter you among all peoples, from one end of the earth to the other; and there you shall serve other gods, of wood and stone, which neither you nor your ancestors have known. 65Among those nations you shall find no ease, no resting place for the sole of your foot. There the LORD will give you a trembling heart, failing eyes, and a languishing spirit. 66Your life shall hang in doubt before you; night and day you shall be in dread, with no assurance of your life. 67In the morning you shall say, "If only it were evening!" and at evening you shall say, "If only it were morning!"—because of the dread that your heart shall feel and the sights that your eyes shall see. 68The LORD will bring you back in ships to Egypt, by a route that I promised you would never see again; and there you shall offer yourselves for sale to your enemies as male and female slaves, but there will be no buyer.

29 h These are the words of the covenant that the LORD commanded Moses to make with the Israelites in the land of Moab, in addition to the covenant that he had made with them at Horeb.

The Covenant Renewed in Moab

2i Moses summoned all Israel and said to them: You have seen all that the LORD did before your eyes in the land of Egypt, to Pharaoh and to all his servants and to all his land, 3the great trials that your eyes saw, the signs, and those great wonders. 4But to this day the LORD has not given you a mind to understand, or eyes to see, or ears to hear. 5I have led you forty years in the wilderness. The clothes on your back have not worn out, and the sandals on your feet have not worn out; 6you have not eaten bread, and you have not drunk wine or strong drink—so that you may know that I am the LORD your God. 7When you came to this place, King Sihon of Heshbon and King Og of Bashan came out against us

h Ch 28.69 in Heb   i Ch 29.1 in Heb

for battle, but we defeated them. 8We took their land and gave it as an inheritance to the Reubenites, the Gadites, and the half-tribe of Manasseh. 9Therefore diligently observe the words of this covenant, in order that you may succeed[j] in everything that you do.

10 You stand assembled today, all of you, before the LORD your God—the leaders of your tribes,[k] your elders, and your officials, all the men of Israel, 11your children, your women, and the aliens who are in your camp, both those who cut your wood and those who draw your water— 12to enter into the covenant of the LORD your God, sworn by an oath, which the LORD your God is making with you today; 13in order that he may establish you today as his people, and that he may be your God, as he promised you and as he swore to your ancestors, to Abraham, to Isaac, and to Jacob. 14I am making this covenant, sworn by an oath, not only with you who stand here with us today before the LORD our God, 15but also with those who are not here with us today. 16You know how we lived in the land of Egypt, and how we came through the midst of the nations through which you passed. 17You have seen their detestable things, the filthy idols of wood and stone, of silver and gold, that were among them. 18It may be that there is among you a man or woman, or a family or tribe, whose heart is already turning away from the LORD our God to serve the gods of those nations. It may be that there is among you a root sprouting poisonous and bitter growth. 19All who hear the words of this oath and bless themselves, thinking in their hearts, "We are safe even though we go our own stubborn ways" (thus bringing disaster on moist and dry alike)[l]— 20the LORD will be unwilling to pardon them, for the LORD's anger and passion will smoke against them. All the curses written in this book will descend on them, and the LORD will blot out their names from under heaven. 21The LORD will single them out from all the tribes of Israel for calamity, in accordance with all the curses of the covenant written in this book of the law. 22The next generation, your children who rise up after you, as well as the foreigner who comes from a distant country, will see the devastation of that land and the afflictions with which the LORD has afflicted it— 23all its soil burned out by sulfur and salt, nothing planted, nothing sprouting, unable to support any vegetation, like the destruction of Sodom and Gomorrah, Admah and Zeboiim, which the LORD destroyed in his fierce anger— 24they and indeed all the nations will wonder, "Why has the LORD done thus to this land? What caused this great display of anger?" 25They will conclude, "It is because they abandoned the covenant of the LORD, the God of their ancestors, which he made with them when he brought them out of the land of Egypt. 26They turned and served other gods, worshiping them, gods whom they had not known and whom he had not allotted to them; 27so the anger of the LORD was kindled against that land, bringing on it every curse written in this book. 28The LORD uprooted them from their land in anger, fury, and great wrath, and cast them into another land, as is now the case." 29The secret things belong to the LORD our God, but the revealed things belong to us and to our children forever, to observe all the words of this law.

God's Fidelity Assured

30 When all these things have happened to you, the blessings and the curses that I have set before you, if you call them to mind among all the nations where the LORD your God has driven you, 2and return to the LORD your God, and you and your children obey him with all your heart and with all your soul, just as I am commanding you today, 3then the LORD your God will restore your fortunes and have compassion on you, gathering you again from all the peoples among whom the LORD your God has scattered you. 4Even if you are exiled to the ends of the world,[m] from there the LORD your God will gather you, and from there he will bring you back. 5The LORD your God will bring you into the land that your ancestors

j Or deal wisely   k Gk Syr: Heb your leaders, your tribes   l Meaning of Heb uncertain   m Heb of heaven possessed, and you will possess it; he will make you more prosperous and numerous than your ancestors.

6 Moreover, the Lord your God will circumcise your heart and the heart of your descendants, so that you will love the Lord your God with all your heart and with all your soul, in order that you may live. 7The Lord your God will put all these curses on your enemies and on the adversaries who took advantage of you. 8Then you shall again obey the Lord, observing all his commandments that I am commanding you today, 9and the Lord your God will make you abundantly prosperous in all your undertakings, in the fruit of your body, in the fruit of your livestock, and in the fruit of your soil. For the Lord will again take delight in prospering you, just as he delighted in prospering your ancestors, 10when you obey the Lord your God by observing his commandments and decrees that are written in this book of the law, because you turn to the Lord your God with all your heart and with all your soul.

Exhortation to Choose Life

11 Surely, this commandment that I am commanding you today is not too hard for you, nor is it too far away. 12It is not in heaven, that you should say, "Who will go up to heaven for us, and get it for us so that we may hear it and observe it?" 13Neither is it beyond the sea, that you should say, "Who will cross to the other side of the sea for us, and get it for us so that we may hear it and observe it?" 14No, the word is very near to you; it is in your mouth and in your heart for you to observe.

15 See, I have set before you today life and prosperity, death and adversity. 16If you obey the commandments of the Lord your God[n] that I am commanding you today, by loving the Lord your God, walking in his ways, and observing his commandments, decrees, and ordinances, then you shall live and become numerous, and the Lord your God will bless you in the land that you are entering to possess. 17But if your heart turns away and you do not hear, but are led astray to bow down to other gods and serve them, 18I declare to you today that you shall perish; you shall not live long in the land that you are crossing the Jordan to enter and possess. 19I call heaven and earth to witness against you today that I have set before you life and death, blessings and curses. Choose life so that you and your descendants may live, 20loving the Lord your God, obeying him, and holding fast to him; for that means life to you and length of days, so that you may live in the land that the Lord swore to give to your ancestors, to Abraham, to Isaac, and to Jacob.

Joshua Becomes Moses' Successor

31 When Moses had finished speaking all[o] these words to all Israel, 2he said to them: "I am now one hundred twenty years old. I am no longer able to get about, and the Lord has told me, 'You shall not cross over this Jordan.' 3The Lord your God himself will cross over before you. He will destroy these nations before you, and you shall dispossess them. Joshua also will cross over before you, as the Lord promised. 4The Lord will do to them as he did to Sihon and Og, the kings of the Amorites, and to their land, when he destroyed them. 5The Lord will give them over to you and you shall deal with them in full accord with the command that I have given to you. 6Be strong and bold; have no fear or dread of them, because it is the Lord your God who goes with you; he will not fail you or forsake you."

7 Then Moses summoned Joshua and said to him in the sight of all Israel: "Be strong and bold, for you are the one who will go with this people into the land that the Lord has sworn to their ancestors to give them; and you will put them in possession of it. 8It is the Lord who goes before you. He will be with you; he will not fail you or forsake you. Do not fear or be dismayed."

The Law to Be Read Every Seventh Year

9 Then Moses wrote down this law, and gave it to the priests, the sons of

---

n Gk: Heb lacks *If you obey the commandments of the* Lord *your God*   o Q Ms Gk: MT *Moses went and spoke*

Levi, who carried the ark of the covenant of the LORD, and to all the elders of Israel. [10]Moses commanded them: "Every seventh year, in the scheduled

p Or *tabernacles*; Heb *succoth*

year of remission, during the festival of booths,[p] [11]when all Israel comes to appear before the LORD your God at the place that he will choose, you shall read

---

THURSDAY

THE BROOM OF THE LAW AND THE DUST OF SIN
John Bunyan

VERSE: Deuteronomy 30.14   PASSAGE: Deuteronomy 30.11–21

hen he took him by the hand, and led him into a very large parlor that was full of dust, because it was never swept; the which, after he had reviewed a little while, the Interpreter called for a man to sweep. Now when he began to sweep, the dust began so abundantly to fly about that Christian had almost therewith been choked. Then said the Interpreter to a damsel that stood by, Bring hither the water and sprinkle the room; which when she had done, it was swept and cleansed with pleasure.

Then said Christian, What means this?

The Interpreter answered: This parlor is the heart of a man that was never sanctified by the sweet grace of the gospel: the dust is his original sin and inward corruptions that have defiled the whole man. He that began to sweep at first is the law; but she that brought water and did sprinkle it is the gospel. Now, whereas thou sawest that so soon as the first began to sweep, the dust did so fly about that the room by him could not be cleansed, but that thou wast almost choked therewith: this is to shew thee that the law, instead of cleansing the heart (by its working) from sin, doth revive, put strength into, and increase it in the soul, even as it doth discover and forbid it, but doth not give power to subdue.

Again, as thou sawest the damsel sprinkle the room with water, upon which it was cleansed with pleasure; this is to shew thee that when the gospel comes in the sweet and precious influences thereof to the heart, then, I say, even as thou sawest the damsel lay the dust by sprinkling the floor with water, so is sin vanquished and subdued, and the soul made clean, through the faith of it, and consequently fit for the King of glory to inhabit.

ADDITIONAL SCRIPTURE READING:
Psalm 51.2–10; Ezekiel 36.25–27; 1 John 1.6–10

Go to page 235 for your next devotional reading.

1500   1700

this law before all Israel in their hearing. [12]Assemble the people—men, women, and children, as well as the aliens residing in your towns—so that they may hear and learn to fear the LORD your God and to observe diligently all the words of this law, [13]and so that their children, who have not known it, may hear and learn to fear the LORD your God, as long as you live in the land that you are crossing over the Jordan to possess."

Moses and Joshua Receive God's Charge

14 The LORD said to Moses, "Your time to die is near; call Joshua and present yourselves in the tent of meeting, so that I may commission him." So Moses and Joshua went and presented themselves in the tent of meeting, [15]and the LORD appeared at the tent in a pillar of cloud; the pillar of cloud stood at the entrance to the tent.

16 The LORD said to Moses, "Soon you will lie down with your ancestors. Then this people will begin to prostitute themselves to the foreign gods in their midst, the gods of the land into which they are going; they will forsake me, breaking my covenant that I have made with them. [17]My anger will be kindled against them in that day. I will forsake them and hide my face from them; they will become easy prey, and many terrible troubles will come upon them. In that day they will say, 'Have not these troubles come upon us because our God is not in our midst?' [18]On that day I will surely hide my face on account of all the evil they have done by turning to other gods. [19]Now therefore write this song, and teach it to the Israelites; put it in their mouths, in order that this song may be a witness for me against the Israelites. [20]For when I have brought them into the land flowing with milk and honey, which I promised on oath to their ancestors, and they have eaten their fill and grown fat, they will turn to other gods and serve them, despising me and breaking my covenant. [21]And when many terrible troubles come upon them, this song will confront them as a witness, because it will not be lost from the mouths of their descendants. For I know what they are inclined to do even now,

before I have brought them into the land that I promised them on oath." [22]That very day Moses wrote this song and taught it to the Israelites.

23 Then the LORD commissioned Joshua son of Nun and said, "Be strong and bold, for you shall bring the Israelites into the land that I promised them; I will be with you."

24 When Moses had finished writing down in a book the words of this law to the very end, [25]Moses commanded the Levites who carried the ark of the covenant of the LORD, saying, [26]"Take this book of the law and put it beside the ark of the covenant of the LORD your God; let it remain there as a witness against you. [27]For I know well how rebellious and stubborn you are. If you already have been so rebellious toward the LORD while I am still alive among you, how much more after my death! [28]Assemble to me all the elders of your tribes and your officials, so that I may recite these words in their hearing and call heaven and earth to witness against them. [29]For I know that after my death you will surely act corruptly, turning aside from the way that I have commanded you. In time to come trouble will befall you, because you will do what is evil in the sight of the LORD, provoking him to anger through the work of your hands."

The Song of Moses

30 Then Moses recited the words of this song, to the very end, in the hearing of the whole assembly of Israel:

32 Give ear, O heavens, and I
 will speak;
 let the earth hear the words of
  my mouth.
2 May my teaching drop like the
 rain,
 my speech condense like the
  dew;
 like gentle rain on grass,
 like showers on new growth.
3 For I will proclaim the name of the
 LORD;
 ascribe greatness to our God!

4 The Rock, his work is perfect,
 and all his ways are just.
A faithful God, without deceit,
 just and upright is he;

5   yet his degenerate children have
      dealt falsely with him,*q*
    a perverse and crooked
      generation.
6   Do you thus repay the LORD,
      O foolish and senseless people?
    Is not he your father, who created
      you,
    who made you and established
      you?
7   Remember the days of old,
      consider the years long past;
    ask your father, and he will inform
      you;
    your elders, and they will tell
      you.
8   When the Most High*r* apportioned
      the nations,
    when he divided humankind,
    he fixed the boundaries of the
      peoples
    according to the number of the
      gods;*s*
9   the LORD's own portion was his
      people,
    Jacob his allotted share.

10 He sustained*t* him in a desert land,
      in a howling wilderness waste;
    he shielded him, cared for him,
      guarded him as the apple of his
      eye.
11 As an eagle stirs up its nest,
      and hovers over its young;
    as it spreads its wings, takes them
      up,
    and bears them aloft on its
      pinions,
12 the LORD alone guided him;
      no foreign god was with him.
13 He set him atop the heights of the
      land,
    and fed him with*u* produce of the
      field;
    he nursed him with honey from the
      crags,
      with oil from flinty rock;
14 curds from the herd, and milk from
      the flock,
    with fat of lambs and rams;
    Bashan bulls and goats,
      together with the choicest
      wheat—

    you drank fine wine from the
      blood of grapes.
15 Jacob ate his fill;*v*
    Jeshurun grew fat, and kicked.
    You grew fat, bloated, and
      gorged!
    He abandoned God who made him,
      and scoffed at the Rock of his
      salvation.
16 They made him jealous with
      strange gods,
    with abhorrent things they
      provoked him.
17 They sacrificed to demons, not
      God,
    to deities they had never known,
    to new ones recently arrived,
      whom your ancestors had not
      feared.
18 You were unmindful of the Rock
      that bore you;*w*
    you forgot the God who gave you
      birth.

19 The LORD saw it, and was jealous;*x*
    he spurned*y* his sons and
      daughters.
20 He said: I will hide my face from
      them,
    I will see what their end will be;
    for they are a perverse generation,
      children in whom there is no
      faithfulness.
21 They made me jealous with what is
      no god,
    provoked me with their idols.
    So I will make them jealous with
      what is no people,
    provoke them with a foolish
      nation.
22 For a fire is kindled by my anger,
      and burns to the depths of Sheol;
    it devours the earth and its
      increase,
    and sets on fire the foundations
      of the mountains.
23 I will heap disasters upon them,
      spend my arrows against them:
24 wasting hunger,
      burning consumption,
      bitter pestilence.
    The teeth of beasts I will send
      against them,

---

q Meaning of Heb uncertain   *r* Traditional rendering of Heb *Elyon*   *s* Q Ms Compare Gk Tg: MT
the Israelites   *t* Sam Gk Compare Tg: MT *found*   *u* Sam Gk Syr Tg: MT *he ate*   *v* Q Mss Sam
Gk: MT lacks *Jacob ate his fill*   *w* Or *that begot you*   *x* Q Mss Gk: MT lacks *was jealous*
y Cn: Heb *he spurned because of provocation*

with venom of things crawling in
the dust.
25 In the street the sword shall bereave,
and in the chambers terror,
for young man and woman alike,
nursing child and old gray head.
26 I thought to scatter them[z]
and blot out the memory of them
from humankind;
27 but I feared provocation by the
enemy,
for their adversaries might
misunderstand
and say, "Our hand is triumphant;
it was not the LORD who did all
this."

28 They are a nation void of sense;
there is no understanding in
them.
29 If they were wise, they would
understand this;
they would discern what the end
would be.
30 How could one have routed a
thousand,
and two put a myriad to flight,
unless their Rock had sold them,
the LORD had given them up?
31 Indeed their rock is not like our
Rock;
our enemies are fools.[z]
32 Their vine comes from the
vinestock of Sodom,
from the vineyards of Gomorrah;
their grapes are grapes of poison,
their clusters are bitter;
33 their wine is the poison of serpents,
the cruel venom of asps.

34 Is not this laid up in store with me,
sealed up in my treasuries?
35 Vengeance is mine, and
recompense,
for the time when their foot shall
slip;
because the day of their calamity is
at hand,
their doom comes swiftly.

36 Indeed the LORD will vindicate his
people,
have compassion on his servants,

when he sees that their power is
gone,
neither bond nor free remaining.
37 Then he will say: Where are their
gods,
the rock in which they took
refuge,
38 who ate the fat of their sacrifices,
and drank the wine of their
libations?
Let them rise up and help you,
let them be your protection!

39 See now that I, even I, am he;
there is no god besides me.
I kill and I make alive;
I wound and I heal;
and no one can deliver from my
hand.
40 For I lift up my hand to heaven,
and swear: As I live forever,
41 when I whet my flashing sword,
and my hand takes hold on
judgment;
I will take vengeance on my
adversaries,
and will repay those who hate me.
42 I will make my arrows drunk with
blood,
and my sword shall devour
flesh—
with the blood of the slain and the
captives,
from the long-haired enemy.

43 Praise, O heavens,[a] his people,
worship him, all you gods![b]
For he will avenge the blood of his
children,[c]
and take vengeance on his
adversaries;
he will repay those who hate him,[b]
and cleanse the land for his
people.[d]
44 Moses came and recited all the
words of this song in the hearing of the
people, he and Joshua[e] son of Nun.
45 When Moses had finished reciting all
these words to all Israel, 46 he said to
them: "Take to heart all the words that
I am giving in witness against you
today; give them as a command to your
children, so that they may diligently

z Gk: Meaning of Heb uncertain   a Q Ms Gk: MT nations   b Q Ms Gk: MT lacks this line
c Q Ms Gk: MT his servants   d Q Ms Sam Gk Vg: MT his land his people   e Sam Gk Syr Vg:
MT Hoshea

observe all the words of this law. ⁴⁷This is no trifling matter for you, but rather your very life; through it you may live long in the land that you are crossing over the Jordan to possess."

Moses' Death Foretold

48 On that very day the LORD addressed Moses as follows: ⁴⁹"Ascend this mountain of the Abarim, Mount Nebo, which is in the land of Moab,

FRIDAY

FROM SINNERS IN THE HANDS OF AN ANGRY GOD
Jonathan Edwards

VERSE: Deuteronomy 32.35   **PASSAGE:** Deuteronomy 32.34–43

ll wicked men's pains and *contrivance* which they use to escape hell, while they continue to reject Christ, and so remain wicked men, do not secure them from hell one moment. Almost every natural man that hears of hell, flatters himself that he shall escape it; he depends upon himself for his own security; he flatters himself in what he has done, in what he is now doing, or what he intends to do. Every one lays out matters in his own mind how he shall avoid damnation, and flatters himself that he contrives well for himself, and that his schemes will not fail. They hear indeed that there are but few saved, and that the greater part of men that have died heretofore are gone to hell; but each one imagines that he lays out matters better for his own escape than others have done. He does not intend to come to that place of torment; he says within himself, that he intends to take effectual care, and to order matters so for himself as not to fail . . .

If we could speak with them and inquire of them, one by one, whether they expected, when alive, and when they used to hear about hell, ever to be the subjects of that misery: we doubtless, should hear one and another reply, "No, I never intended to come here: I had laid out matters otherwise in my mind; I thought my scheme good. I intended to take effectual care; but it came upon me unexpected; I did not look for it at that time, and in that manner; it came as a thief: Death outwitted me: God's wrath was too quick for me. Oh, my cursed foolishness! I was flattering myself, and pleasing myself with vain dreams of what I would do hereafter; and when I was saying, Peace and safety, then suddenly destruction came upon me" (see 1 Thessalonians 5.3).

ADDITIONAL SCRIPTURE READING:
Proverbs 16.9; Luke 12.19–21; 16.19–31

Go to page 240 for your next devotional reading.

1700   1900

across from Jericho, and view the land of Canaan, which I am giving to the Israelites for a possession; 50you shall die there on the mountain that you ascend and shall be gathered to your kin, as your brother Aaron died on Mount Hor and was gathered to his kin; 51because both of you broke faith with me among the Israelites at the waters of Meribath-kadesh in the wilderness of Zin, by failing to maintain my holiness among the Israelites. 52Although you may view the land from a distance, you shall not enter it—the land that I am giving to the Israelites."

Moses' Final Blessing on Israel

33 This is the blessing with which Moses, the man of God, blessed the Israelites before his death. 2He said:

> The LORD came from Sinai,
> and dawned from Seir upon us;*f*
> he shone forth from Mount Paran.
> With him were myriads of holy ones;*g*
> at his right, a host of his own.*h*
> 3 Indeed, O favorite among*i* peoples,
> all his holy ones were in your charge;
> they marched at your heels,
> accepted direction from you.
> 4 Moses charged us with the law,
> as a possession for the assembly of Jacob.
> 5 There arose a king in Jeshurun,
> when the leaders of the people assembled—
> the united tribes of Israel.

> 6 May Reuben live, and not die out,
> even though his numbers are few.

7And this he said of Judah:

> O LORD, give heed to Judah,
> and bring him to his people;
> strengthen his hands for him,*j*
> and be a help against his adversaries.

8And of Levi he said:

> Give to Levi*k* your Thummim,
> and your Urim to your loyal one,
> whom you tested at Massah,
> with whom you contended at the waters of Meribah;
> 9 who said of his father and mother,
> "I regard them not";
> he ignored his kin,
> and did not acknowledge his children.
> For they observed your word,
> and kept your covenant.
> 10 They teach Jacob your ordinances,
> and Israel your law;
> they place incense before you,
> and whole burnt offerings on your altar.
> 11 Bless, O LORD, his substance,
> and accept the work of his hands;
> crush the loins of his adversaries,
> of those that hate him, so that they do not rise again.

12Of Benjamin he said:

> The beloved of the LORD rests in safety—
> the High God*l* surrounds him all day long—
> the beloved*m* rests between his shoulders.

13And of Joseph he said:

> Blessed by the LORD be his land,
> with the choice gifts of heaven above,
> and of the deep that lies beneath;
> 14 with the choice fruits of the sun,
> and the rich yield of the months;
> 15 with the finest produce of the ancient mountains,
> and the abundance of the everlasting hills;
> 16 with the choice gifts of the earth and its fullness,
> and the favor of the one who dwells on Sinai.*n*
> Let these come on the head of Joseph,
> on the brow of the prince among his brothers.
> 17 A firstborn*o* bull—majesty is his!

---

f Gk Syr Vg Compare Tg: Heb *upon them*   *g* Cn Compare Gk Sam Syr Vg: MT *He came from Riboboth-kodesh,*   *h* Cn Compare Gk: meaning of Heb uncertain   *i* Or *O lover of the*   *j* Cn: Heb *with his hands he contended*   *k* Q Ms Gk: MT lacks *Give to Levi*   *l* Heb *above him*   *m* Heb *he*   *n* Cn: Heb *in the bush*   *o* Q Ms Gk Syr Vg: MT *His firstborn*

His horns are the horns of a wild
ox;
with them he gores the peoples,
driving them to^p the ends of the
earth;
such are the myriads of Ephraim,
such the thousands of Manasseh.

18 And of Zebulun he said:
Rejoice, Zebulun, in your going out;
and Issachar, in your tents.
19 They call peoples to the mountain;
there they offer the right
sacrifices;
for they suck the affluence of the
seas
and the hidden treasures of the
sand.

20 And of Gad he said:
Blessed be the enlargement of Gad!
Gad lives like a lion;
he tears at arm and scalp.
21 He chose the best for himself,
for there a commander's
allotment was reserved;
he came at the head of the people,
he executed the justice of the
LORD,
and his ordinances for Israel.

22 And of Dan he said:
Dan is a lion's whelp
that leaps forth from Bashan.

23 And of Naphtali he said:
O Naphtali, sated with favor,
full of the blessing of the LORD,
possess the west and the south.

24 And of Asher he said:
Most blessed of sons be Asher;
may he be the favorite of his
brothers,
and may he dip his foot in oil.
25 Your bars are iron and bronze;
and as your days, so is your
strength.

26 There is none like God,
O Jeshurun,
who rides through the heavens to
your help,
majestic through the skies.

27 He subdues the ancient gods,^q
shatters^r the forces of old;^s
he drove out the enemy before you,
and said, "Destroy!"

NOR CAN WE FALL BELOW THE ARMS OF GOD,
HOW LOW SOEVER IT BE WE FALL.   —*William Penn*

---

28 So Israel lives in safety,
untroubled is Jacob's abode^t
in a land of grain and wine,
where the heavens drop down
dew.
29 Happy are you, O Israel! Who is
like you,
a people saved by the LORD,
the shield of your help,
and the sword of your triumph!
Your enemies shall come fawning
to you,
and you shall tread on their
backs.

Moses Dies and Is Buried in the Land of Moab

34 Then Moses went up from the plains of Moab to Mount Nebo, to the top of Pisgah, which is opposite Jericho, and the LORD showed him the whole land: Gilead as far as Dan, 2 all Naphtali, the land of Ephraim and Manasseh, all the land of Judah as far as the Western Sea, 3 the Negeb, and the Plain—that is, the valley of Jericho, the city of palm trees—as far as Zoar. 4 The LORD said to him, "This is the land of which I swore to Abraham, to Isaac, and to Jacob, saying, 'I will give it to your descendants'; I have let you see it with your eyes, but you shall not cross over there." 5 Then Moses, the servant of the LORD, died there in the land of Moab, at the LORD's command. 6 He was buried in a valley in the land of Moab, opposite Beth-peor, but no one knows his burial place to this day. 7 Moses was one hundred twenty years old when he died; his sight was unimpaired and his vigor had not abated. 8 The Israelites wept for Moses in the plains of Moab thirty days; then the period of mourning for Moses was ended.

---

p Cn: Heb *the peoples, together*   q Or *The eternal God is a dwelling place*   r Cn: Heb *from underneath*   s Or *the everlasting arms*   t Or *fountain*

9 Joshua son of Nun was full of the spirit of wisdom, because Moses had laid his hands on him; and the Israelites obeyed him, doing as the LORD had commanded Moses.

10 Never since has there arisen a prophet in Israel like Moses, whom the LORD knew face to face. 11He was unequaled for all the signs and wonders that the LORD sent him to perform in the land of Egypt, against Pharaoh and all his servants and his entire land, 12and for all the mighty deeds and all the terrifying displays of power that Moses performed in the sight of all Israel.

JOSHUA

AMED AFTER ITS LEADING CHAR-
ACTER, JOSHUA, WHOM GOD AP-
POINTED LEADER OF ISRAEL BEFORE
MOSES' DEATH, THE BOOK OF JOSHUA BEGINS
WITH THE TRIBES STILL CAMPED ON THE EAST
SIDE OF THE JORDAN RIVER. THIS BOOK
TELLS THE STORY OF HOW, WITH GOD'S
HELP, THE PEOPLE CROSSED THE JORDAN
RIVER AND TOOK POSSESSION OF THE PROM-
ISED LAND. JOSHUA REMINDS THE PEOPLE OF
GOD'S COVENANT PROMISES TO THEM AND
URGES THEM TO SERVE ONLY THE LORD.

God's Commission to Joshua

1 After the death of Moses the servant of the LORD, the LORD spoke to Joshua son of Nun, Moses' assistant, saying, 2"My servant Moses is dead. Now proceed to cross the Jordan, you and all this people, into the land that I am giving to them, to the Israelites. 3Every place that the sole of your foot will tread upon I have given to you, as I promised to Moses. 4From the wilderness and the Lebanon as far as the great river, the river Euphrates, all the land of the Hittites, to the Great Sea in the west shall be your territory. 5No one shall be able to stand against you all the days of your life. As I was with Moses, so I will be with you; I will not fail you or forsake you. 6Be strong and courageous; for you shall put this peo-ple in possession of the land that I swore to their ancestors to give them. 7Only be strong and very courageous, being careful to act in accordance with all the law that my servant Moses com-manded you; do not turn from it to the right hand or to the left, so that you may be successful wherever you go. 8This book of the law shall not depart out of your mouth; you shall meditate on it day and night, so that you may be careful to act in accordance with all that is written in it. For then you shall make your way prosperous, and then you shall be successful. 9I hereby com-mand you: Be strong and courageous; do not be frightened or dismayed, for the LORD your God is with you wherever you go."

WEEKEND

JEPHTHAH'S DAUGHTER
Lord George Gordon Noel Byron

VERSE: Judges 11.30–31　　　　**PASSAGE:** Judges 11.30–38

ince our country, our God—Oh, my sire!
Demand that thy daughter expire;
Since thy triumph was bought by thy vow—
Strike the bosom that's bared for thee now!

And the voice of my mourning is o'er,
And the mountains behold me no more:
If the hand that I love lay me low,
There cannot be pain in the blow!

And of this, oh, my father! be sure—
That the blood of thy child is as pure
As the blessing I beg ere it flow,
And the last thought that soothes me below.

Though the virgins of Salem lament,
Be the judge and the hero unbent!
I have won the great battle for thee,
And my father and country are free!

When this blood of thy giving hath gushed,
When the voice that thou lovest is hushed,
Let my memory still be thy pride,
And forget not I smiled as I died!

ADDITIONAL SCRIPTURE READING:
Leviticus 27.28–29; Numbers 30.2–5; 1 Samuel 1.22–28

Go to page 243 for your next devotional reading.

1700　　1900

Preparations for the Invasion

10 Then Joshua commanded the officers of the people, 11"Pass through the camp, and command the people: 'Prepare your provisions; for in three days

---

I STUDY MY BIBLE AS I GATHER APPLES. FIRST, I SHAKE THE WHOLE TREE THAT THE RIPEST MIGHT FALL. THEN I SHAKE EACH LIMB, AND WHEN I HAVE SHAKEN EACH LIMB, I SHAKE EACH BRANCH AND EVERY TWIG. THEN I LOOK UNDER EVERY LEAF.

—Martin Luther

---

you are to cross over the Jordan, to go in to take possession of the land that the LORD your God gives you to possess.' "

12 To the Reubenites, the Gadites, and the half-tribe of Manasseh Joshua said, 13"Remember the word that Moses the servant of the LORD commanded you, saying, 'The LORD your God is providing you a place of rest, and will give you this land.' 14Your wives, your little ones, and your livestock shall remain in the land that Moses gave you beyond the Jordan. But all the warriors among you shall cross over armed before your kindred and shall help them, 15until the LORD gives rest to your kindred as well as to you, and they too take possession of the land that the LORD your God is giving them. Then you shall return to your own land and take possession of it, the land that Moses the servant of the LORD gave you beyond the Jordan to the east."

16 They answered Joshua: "All that you have commanded us we will do, and wherever you send us we will go. 17Just as we obeyed Moses in all things, so we will obey you. Only may the LORD your God be with you, as he was with Moses! 18Whoever rebels against your orders and disobeys your words, whatever you command, shall be put to death. Only be strong and courageous."

Spies Sent to Jericho

2 Then Joshua son of Nun sent two men secretly from Shittim as spies, saying, "Go, view the land, especially Jericho." So they went, and entered the house of a prostitute whose name was Rahab, and spent the night there. 2The king of Jericho was told, "Some Israelites have come here tonight to search out the land." 3Then the king of Jericho sent orders to Rahab, "Bring out the men who have come to you, who entered your house, for they have come only to search out the whole land." 4But the woman took the two men and hid them. Then she said, "True, the men came to me, but I did not know where they came from. 5And when it was time to close the gate at dark, the men went out. Where the men went I do not know. Pursue them quickly, for you can overtake them." 6She had, however, brought them up to the roof and hidden them with the stalks of flax that she had laid out on the roof. 7So the men pursued them on the way to the Jordan as far as the fords. As soon as the pursuers had gone out, the gate was shut.

8 Before they went to sleep, she came up to them on the roof 9and said to the men: "I know that the LORD has given you the land, and that dread of you has fallen on us, and that all the inhabitants of the land melt in fear before you. 10For we have heard how the LORD dried up the water of the Red Sea*a* before you when you came out of Egypt, and what you did to the two kings of the Amorites that were beyond the Jordan, to Sihon and Og, whom you utterly destroyed. 11As soon as we heard it, our hearts melted, and there was no courage left in any of us because of you. The LORD your God is indeed God in heaven above and on earth below. 12Now then, since I have dealt kindly with you, swear to me by the LORD that you in turn will deal kindly with my family. Give me a sign of good faith 13that you will spare my father and mother, my brothers and sisters, and all who belong to them, and deliver our lives from death." 14The men said to her, "Our life for yours! If you do not tell this business of ours, then we will deal kindly and faithfully with you when the LORD gives us the land."

15 Then she let them down by a rope through the window, for her house was on the outer side of the city wall and she resided within the wall itself. 16She said

---

a Or Sea of Reeds

to them, "Go toward the hill country, so that the pursuers may not come upon you. Hide yourselves there three days, until the pursuers have returned; then afterward you may go your way." 17The men said to her, "We will be released from this oath that you have made us swear to you 18if we invade the land and you do not tie this crimson cord in the window through which you let us down, and you do not gather into your house your father and mother, your brothers, and all your family. 19If any of you go out of the doors of your house into the street, they shall be responsible for their own death, and we shall be innocent; but if a hand is laid upon any who are with you in the house, we shall bear the responsibility for their death. 20But if you tell this business of ours, then we shall be released from this oath that you made us swear to you." 21She said, "According to your words, so be it." She sent them away and they departed. Then she tied the crimson cord in the window.

22 They departed and went into the hill country and stayed there three days, until the pursuers returned. The pursuers had searched all along the way and found nothing. 23Then the two men came down again from the hill country. They crossed over, came to Joshua son of Nun, and told him all that had happened to them. 24They said to Joshua, "Truly the LORD has given all the land into our hands; moreover all the inhabitants of the land melt in fear before us."

Israel Crosses the Jordan

3 Early in the morning Joshua rose and set out from Shittim with all the Israelites, and they came to the Jordan. They camped there before crossing over. 2At the end of three days the officers went through the camp 3and commanded the people, "When you see the ark of the covenant of the LORD your God being carried by the levitical priests, then you shall set out from your place. Follow it, 4so that you may know the way you should go, for you have not passed this way before. Yet there shall be a space between you and it, a distance of about two thousand cubits; do not come any nearer to it." 5Then Joshua

said to the people, "Sanctify yourselves; for tomorrow the LORD will do wonders among you." 6To the priests Joshua said, "Take up the ark of the covenant, and pass on in front of the people." So they took up the ark of the covenant and went in front of the people.

7 The LORD said to Joshua, "This day I will begin to exalt you in the sight of all Israel, so that they may know that I will be with you as I was with Moses. 8You are the one who shall command the priests who bear the ark of the covenant, 'When you come to the edge of the waters of the Jordan, you shall stand still in the Jordan.'" 9Joshua then said to the Israelites, "Draw near and hear the words of the LORD your God." 10Joshua said, "By this you shall know that among you is the living God who without fail will drive out from before you the Canaanites, Hittites, Hivites, Perizzites, Girgashites, Amorites, and Jebusites: 11the ark of the covenant of the Lord of all the earth is going to pass before you into the Jordan. 12So now select twelve men from the tribes of Israel, one from each tribe. 13When the soles of the feet of the priests who bear the ark of the LORD, the Lord of all the earth, rest in the waters of the Jordan, the waters of the Jordan flowing from above shall be cut off; they shall stand in a single heap."

14 When the people set out from their tents to cross over the Jordan, the priests bearing the ark of the covenant were in front of the people. 15Now the Jordan overflows all its banks throughout the time of harvest. So when those who bore the ark had come to the Jordan, and the feet of the priests bearing the ark were dipped in the edge of the water, 16the waters flowing from above stood still, rising up in a single heap far off at Adam, the city that is beside Zarethan, while those flowing toward the sea of the Arabah, the Dead Sea,b were wholly cut off. Then the people crossed over opposite Jericho. 17While all Israel were crossing over on dry ground, the priests who bore the ark of the covenant of the LORD stood on dry ground in the middle of the Jordan, until the entire nation finished crossing over the Jordan.

b Heb *Salt Sea*

Twelve Stones Set Up at Gilgal

 4 When the entire nation had finished crossing over the Jordan, the LORD said to Joshua: 2"Select twelve men from the people, one from each tribe, 3and command them, 'Take twelve stones from here out of the middle of the Jordan, from the place where the priests' feet stood, carry them over with you, and lay them down in the place where you camp tonight.' " 4Then Joshua summoned the twelve men from the Israelites, whom he had appointed, one from each tribe. 5Joshua said to them, "Pass on before the ark of the LORD your God into the middle of the Jordan, and each of you take up a stone on his shoulder, one for each of the tribes of the Israelites, 6so that this may be a sign among you. When your children ask in time to come, 'What do those stones mean to you?' 7then you shall tell them that the waters of the Jordan were cut off in front of the ark of the covenant of the LORD. When it crossed over the Jordan, the waters of the Jordan

---

MONDAY

STEP INTO THE WATERS
Hannah Whitall Smith

VERSE: Joshua 3.13   **PASSAGE:** Joshua 3.7–17

A man was obliged to descend into a deep well by sliding down a fixed rope which was supposed to be of ample length. But to his dismay he came to the end of it before his feet had touched the bottom. He had not the strength to climb up again, and to let go and drop seemed to him but to be dashed to pieces in the depths below. He held on until his strength was utterly exhausted, and then dropped, as he thought, to his death. He fell—just three inches—and found himself safe on the rock bottom.

Are you afraid to take this step? Does it seem too sudden, too much like a leap in the dark? Do you not know that the step of faith always "falls on the seeming void, but finds the rock beneath"? If ever you are to enter this glorious land, flowing with milk and honey, you must sooner or later step into the brimming waters, for there is no other path; and to do it now may save you months and even years of disappointment and grief. Hear the word of the Lord,—

"Have not I commanded thee? Be strong and of a good courage; be not afraid, neither be thou dismayed: for the Lord thy God is with thee, whithersoever thou goest" (Joshua 1.9, KJV).

ADDITIONAL SCRIPTURE READING:
Genesis 28.15; Joshua 1.6–7; Psalm 27.1

Go to page 255 for your next devotional reading.

1700   1900

were cut off. So these stones shall be to the Israelites a memorial forever."

8 The Israelites did as Joshua commanded. They took up twelve stones out of the middle of the Jordan, according to the number of the tribes of the Israelites, as the LORD told Joshua, carried them over with them to the place where they camped, and laid them down there. 9(Joshua set up twelve stones in the middle of the Jordan, in the place where the feet of the priests bearing the ark of the covenant had stood; and they are there to this day.)

10 The priests who bore the ark remained standing in the middle of the Jordan, until everything was finished that the LORD commanded Joshua to tell the people, according to all that Moses had commanded Joshua. The people crossed over in haste. 11As soon as all the people had finished crossing over, the ark of the LORD, and the priests, crossed over in front of the people. 12The Reubenites, the Gadites, and the half-tribe of Manasseh crossed over armed before the Israelites, as Moses had ordered them. 13About forty thousand armed for war crossed over before the LORD to the plains of Jericho for battle.

14 On that day the LORD exalted Joshua in the sight of all Israel; and they stood in awe of him, as they had stood in awe of Moses, all the days of his life.

15 The LORD said to Joshua, 16"Command the priests who bear the ark of the covenant,c to come up out of the Jordan." 17Joshua therefore commanded the priests, "Come up out of the Jordan." 18When the priests bearing the ark of the covenant of the LORD came up from the middle of the Jordan, and the soles of the priests' feet touched dry ground, the waters of the Jordan returned to their place and overflowed all its banks, as before.

19 The people came up out of the Jordan on the tenth day of the first month, and they camped in Gilgal on the east border of Jericho. 20Those twelve stones, which they had taken out of the Jordan, Joshua set up in Gilgal, 21saying to the Israelites, "When your children ask their parents in time to come, 'What do these stones mean?' 22then you shall let

your children know, 'Israel crossed over the Jordan here on dry ground.' 23For the LORD your God dried up the waters of the Jordan for you until you crossed over, as the LORD your God did to the Red Sea,d which he dried up for us until we crossed over, 24so that all the peoples of the earth may know that the hand of the LORD is mighty, and so that you may fear the LORD your God forever."

The New Generation Circumcised

5 When all the kings of the Amorites beyond the Jordan to the west, and all the kings of the Canaanites by the sea, heard that the LORD had dried up the waters of the Jordan for the Israelites until they had crossed over, their hearts melted, and there was no longer any spirit in them, because of the Israelites.

2 At that time the LORD said to Joshua, "Make flint knives and circumcise the Israelites a second time." 3So Joshua made flint knives, and circumcised the Israelites at Gibeath-haaraloth.e 4This is the reason why Joshua circumcised them: all the males of the people who came out of Egypt, all the warriors, had died during the journey through the wilderness after they had come out of Egypt. 5Although all the people who came out had been circumcised, yet all the people born on the journey through the wilderness after they had come out of Egypt had not been circumcised. 6For the Israelites traveled forty years in the wilderness, until all the nation, the warriors who came out of Egypt, perished, not having listened to the voice of the LORD. To them the LORD swore that he would not let them see the land that he had sworn to their ancestors to give us, a land flowing with milk and honey. 7So it was their children, whom he raised up in their place, that Joshua circumcised; for they were uncircumcised, because they had not been circumcised on the way.

8 When the circumcising of all the nation was done, they remained in their places in the camp until they were healed. 9The LORD said to Joshua, "Today I have rolled away from you the

---

c Or treaty, or testimony; Heb eduth   d Or Sea of Reeds   e That is the Hill of the Foreskins

disgrace of Egypt." And so that place is called Gilgal[f] to this day.

The Passover at Gilgal

10 While the Israelites were camped in Gilgal they kept the passover in the evening on the fourteenth day of the month in the plains of Jericho. [11]On the day after the passover, on that very day, they ate the produce of the land, unleavened cakes and parched grain. [12]The manna ceased on the day they ate the produce of the land, and the Israelites no longer had manna; they ate the crops of the land of Canaan that year.

Joshua's Vision

13 Once when Joshua was by Jericho, he looked up and saw a man standing before him with a drawn sword in his hand. Joshua went to him and said to him, "Are you one of us, or one of our adversaries?" [14]He replied, "Neither; but as commander of the army of the LORD I have now come." And Joshua fell on his face to the earth and worshiped, and he said to him, "What do you command your servant, my lord?" [15]The commander of the army of the LORD said to Joshua, "Remove the sandals from your feet, for the place where you stand is holy." And Joshua did so.

Jericho Taken and Destroyed

6 Now Jericho was shut up inside and out because of the Israelites; no one came out and no one went in. [2]The LORD said to Joshua, "See, I have handed Jericho over to you, along with its king and soldiers. [3]You shall march around the city, all the warriors circling the city once. Thus you shall do for six days, [4]with seven priests bearing seven trumpets of rams' horns before the ark. On the seventh day you shall march around the city seven times, the priests blowing the trumpets. [5]When they make a long blast with the ram's horn, as soon as you hear the sound of the trumpet, then all the people shall shout with a great shout; and the wall of the city will fall down flat, and all the people shall charge straight ahead." [6]So Joshua son of Nun summoned the priests and said to them, "Take up the ark of the covenant, and have seven priests carry seven trumpets of rams' horns in front of the ark of the LORD." [7]To the people he said, "Go forward and march around the city; have the armed men pass on before the ark of the LORD."

8 As Joshua had commanded the people, the seven priests carrying the seven trumpets of rams' horns before the LORD went forward, blowing the trumpets, with the ark of the covenant of the LORD following them. [9]And the armed men went before the priests who blew the trumpets; the rear guard came after the ark, while the trumpets blew continually. [10]To the people Joshua gave this command: "You shall not shout or let your voice be heard, nor shall you utter a word, until the day I tell you to shout. Then you shall shout." [11]So the ark of the LORD went around the city, circling it once; and they came into the camp, and spent the night in the camp.

12 Then Joshua rose early in the morning, and the priests took up the ark of the LORD. [13]The seven priests carrying the seven trumpets of rams' horns before the ark of the LORD passed on, blowing the trumpets continually. The armed men went before them, and the rear guard came after the ark of the LORD, while the trumpets blew continually. [14]On the second day they marched around the city once and then returned to the camp. They did this for six days.

15 On the seventh day they rose early, at dawn, and marched around the city in the same manner seven times. It was only on that day that they marched around the city seven times. [16]And at the seventh time, when the priests had blown the trumpets, Joshua said to the people, "Shout! For the LORD has given you the city. [17]The city and all that is in it shall be devoted to the LORD for destruction. Only Rahab the prostitute and all who are with her in her house shall live because she hid the messengers we sent. [18]As for you, keep away from the things devoted to destruction, so as not to covet[g] and take any of the devoted things and make the camp of Israel an object for destruction, bringing trouble upon it. [19]But all silver and gold, and vessels of bronze and iron, are sacred to the

f Related to Heb galal to roll   g Gk: Heb devote to destruction Compare 7.21

LORD; they shall go into the treasury of the LORD." [20]So the people shouted, and the trumpets were blown. As soon as the people heard the sound of the trumpets, they raised a great shout, and the wall fell down flat; so the people charged straight ahead into the city and captured it. [21]Then they devoted to destruction by the edge of the sword all in the city, both men and women, young and old, oxen, sheep, and donkeys.

[22] Joshua said to the two men who had spied out the land, "Go into the prostitute's house, and bring the woman out of it and all who belong to her, as you swore to her." [23]So the young men who had been spies went in and brought Rahab out, along with her father, her mother, her brothers, and all who belonged to her—they brought all her kindred out—and set them outside the camp of Israel. [24]They burned down the city, and everything in it; only the silver and gold, and the vessels of bronze and iron, they put into the treasury of the house of the LORD. [25]But Rahab the prostitute, with her family and all who belonged to her, Joshua spared. Her family[h] has lived in Israel ever since. For she hid the messengers whom Joshua sent to spy out Jericho.

[26] Joshua then pronounced this oath, saying,

"Cursed before the LORD be anyone
    who tries
    to build this city—this Jericho!
At the cost of his firstborn he shall
    lay its foundation,
and at the cost of his youngest he
    shall set up its gates!"

[27] So the LORD was with Joshua; and his fame was in all the land.

The Sin of Achan and Its Punishment

7 But the Israelites broke faith in regard to the devoted things: Achan son of Carmi son of Zabdi son of Zerah, of the tribe of Judah, took some of the devoted things; and the anger of the LORD burned against the Israelites.

[2] Joshua sent men from Jericho to Ai, which is near Beth-aven, east of Bethel, and said to them, "Go up and spy out the land." And the men went up and spied out Ai. [3]Then they returned to Joshua and said to him, "Not all the people need go up; about two or three thousand men should go up and attack Ai. Since they are so few, do not make the whole people toil up there." [4]So about three thousand of the people went up there; and they fled before the men of Ai. [5]The men of Ai killed about thirty-six of them, chasing them from outside the gate as far as Shebarim and killing them on the slope. The hearts of the people melted and turned to water.

[6] Then Joshua tore his clothes, and fell to the ground on his face before the ark of the LORD until the evening, he and the elders of Israel; and they put dust on their heads. [7]Joshua said, "Ah, Lord GOD! Why have you brought this people across the Jordan at all, to hand us over to the Amorites so as to destroy us? Would that we had been content to settle beyond the Jordan! [8]O Lord, what can I say, now that Israel has turned their backs to their enemies! [9]The Canaanites and all the inhabitants of the land will hear of it, and surround us, and cut off our name from the earth. Then what will you do for your great name?"

[10] The LORD said to Joshua, "Stand up! Why have you fallen upon your face? [11]Israel has sinned; they have transgressed my covenant that I imposed on them. They have taken some of the devoted things; they have stolen, they have acted deceitfully, and they have put them among their own belongings. [12]Therefore the Israelites are unable to stand before their enemies; they turn their backs to their enemies, because they have become a thing devoted for destruction themselves. I will be with you no more, unless you destroy the devoted things from among you. [13]Proceed to sanctify the people, and say, 'Sanctify yourselves for tomorrow; for thus says the LORD, the God of Israel, "There are devoted things among you, O Israel; you will be unable to stand before your enemies until you take away the devoted things from among you." [14]In the morning therefore you shall come forward tribe by tribe. The tribe that the LORD takes shall come near by clans, the clan that the LORD takes shall

_h_ Heb _She_

come near by households, and the household that the LORD takes shall come near one by one. 15And the one who is taken as having the devoted things shall be burned with fire, together with all that he has, for having transgressed the covenant of the LORD, and for having done an outrageous thing in Israel.' "

16 So Joshua rose early in the morning, and brought Israel near tribe by tribe, and the tribe of Judah was taken. 17He brought near the clans of Judah, and the clan of the Zerahites was taken; and he brought near the clan of the Zerahites, family by family,*i* and Zabdi was taken. 18And he brought near his household one by one, and Achan son of Carmi son of Zabdi son of Zerah, of the tribe of Judah, was taken. 19Then Joshua said to Achan, "My son, give glory to the LORD God of Israel and make confession to him. Tell me now what you have done; do not hide it from me." 20And Achan answered Joshua, "It is true; I am the one who sinned against the LORD God of Israel. This is what I did: 21when I saw among the spoil a beautiful mantle from Shinar, and two hundred shekels of silver, and a bar of gold weighing fifty shekels, then I coveted them and took them. They now lie hidden in the ground inside my tent, with the silver underneath."

RICHES HAVE MADE MORE COVETOUS MEN THAN COVETOUSNESS HATH MADE RICH MEN.

—*Thomas Fuller*

---

22 So Joshua sent messengers, and they ran to the tent; and there it was, hidden in his tent with the silver underneath. 23They took them out of the tent and brought them to Joshua and all the Israelites; and they spread them out before the LORD. 24Then Joshua and all Israel with him took Achan son of Zerah, with the silver, the mantle, and the bar of gold, with his sons and daughters, with his oxen, donkeys, and sheep, and his tent and all that he had; and they brought them up to the Valley of Achor. 25Joshua said, "Why did you bring trouble on us? The LORD is bringing trouble

on you today." And all Israel stoned him to death; they burned them with fire, cast stones on them, 26and raised over him a great heap of stones that remains to this day. Then the LORD turned from his burning anger. Therefore that place to this day is called the Valley of Achor.*j*

Ai Captured by a Stratagem and Destroyed

8 Then the LORD said to Joshua, "Do not fear or be dismayed; take all the fighting men with you, and go up now to Ai. See, I have handed over to you the king of Ai with his people, his city, and his land. 2You shall do to Ai and its king as you did to Jericho and its king; only its spoil and its livestock you may take as booty for yourselves. Set an ambush against the city, behind it."

3 So Joshua and all the fighting men set out to go up against Ai. Joshua chose thirty thousand warriors and sent them out by night 4with the command, "You shall lie in ambush against the city, behind it; do not go very far from the city, but all of you stay alert. 5I and all the people who are with me will approach the city. When they come out against us, as before, we shall flee from them. 6They will come out after us until we have drawn them away from the city; for they will say, 'They are fleeing from us, as before.' While we flee from them, 7you shall rise up from the ambush and seize the city; for the LORD your God will give it into your hand. 8And when you have taken the city, you shall set the city on fire, doing as the LORD has ordered; see, I have commanded you." 9So Joshua sent them out; and they went to the place of ambush, and lay between Bethel and Ai, to the west of Ai; but Joshua spent that night in the camp.*k*

10 In the morning Joshua rose early and mustered the people, and went up, with the elders of Israel, before the people to Ai. 11All the fighting men who were with him went up, and drew near before the city, and camped on the north side of Ai, with a ravine between them and Ai. 12Taking about five thousand men, he set them in ambush between Bethel and Ai, to the west of the city.

---

i Mss Syr: MT *man by man*   *j* That is *Trouble*   *k* Heb *among the people*

13So they stationed the forces, the main encampment that was north of the city and its rear guard west of the city. But Joshua spent that night in the valley. 14When the king of Ai saw this, he and all his people, the inhabitants of the city, hurried out early in the morning to the meeting place facing the Arabah to meet Israel in battle; but he did not know that there was an ambush against him behind the city. 15And Joshua and all Israel made a pretense of being beaten before them, and fled in the direction of the wilderness. 16So all the people who were in the city were called together to pursue them, and as they pursued Joshua they were drawn away from the city. 17There was not a man left in Ai or Bethel who did not go out after Israel; they left the city open, and pursued Israel.

18 Then the LORD said to Joshua, "Stretch out the sword that is in your hand toward Ai; for I will give it into your hand." And Joshua stretched out the sword that was in his hand toward the city. 19As soon as he stretched out his hand, the troops in ambush rose quickly out of their place and rushed forward. They entered the city, took it, and at once set the city on fire. 20So when the men of Ai looked back, the smoke of the city was rising to the sky. They had no power to flee this way or that, for the people who fled to the wilderness turned back against the pursuers. 21When Joshua and all Israel saw that the ambush had taken the city and that the smoke of the city was rising, then they turned back and struck down the men of Ai. 22And the others came out from the city against them; so they were surrounded by Israelites, some on one side, and some on the other; and Israel struck them down until no one was left who survived or escaped. 23But the king of Ai was taken alive and brought to Joshua.

24 When Israel had finished slaughtering all the inhabitants of Ai in the open wilderness where they pursued them, and when all of them to the very last had fallen by the edge of the sword, all Israel returned to Ai, and attacked it with the edge of the sword. 25The total of those who fell that day, both men and women, was twelve thousand—all the people of Ai. 26For Joshua did not draw back his hand, with which he stretched out the sword, until he had utterly destroyed all the inhabitants of Ai. 27Only the livestock and the spoil of that city Israel took as their booty, according to the word of the LORD that he had issued to Joshua. 28So Joshua burned Ai, and made it forever a heap of ruins, as it is to this day. 29And he hanged the king of Ai on a tree until evening; and at sunset Joshua commanded, and they took his body down from the tree, threw it down at the entrance of the gate of the city, and raised over it a great heap of stones, which stands there to this day.

Joshua Renews the Covenant

30 Then Joshua built on Mount Ebal an altar to the LORD, the God of Israel, 31just as Moses the servant of the LORD had commanded the Israelites, as it is written in the book of the law of Moses, "an altar of unhewn1 stones, on which no iron tool has been used"; and they offered on it burnt offerings to the LORD, and sacrificed offerings of well-being. 32And there, in the presence of the Israelites, Joshuam wrote on the stones a copy of the law of Moses, which he had written. 33All Israel, alien as well as citizen, with their elders and officers and their judges, stood on opposite sides of the ark in front of the levitical priests who carried the ark of the covenant of the LORD, half of them in front of Mount Gerizim and half of them in front of Mount Ebal, as Moses the servant of the LORD had commanded at the first, that they should bless the people of Israel. 34And afterward he read all the words of the law, blessings and curses, according to all that is written in the book of the law. 35There was not a word of all that Moses commanded that Joshua did not read before all the assembly of Israel, and the women, and the little ones, and the aliens who resided among them.

The Gibeonites Save Themselves by Trickery

9 Now when all the kings who were beyond the Jordan in the hill country and in the lowland all along the coast of the Great Sea toward Leba-

1 Heb whole   m Heb he

non—the Hittites, the Amorites, the Canaanites, the Perizzites, the Hivites, and the Jebusites—heard of this, [2]they gathered together with one accord to fight Joshua and Israel.

3 But when the inhabitants of Gibeon heard what Joshua had done to Jericho and to Ai, [4]they on their part acted with cunning: they went and prepared provisions,[n] and took worn-out sacks for their donkeys, and wineskins, worn-out and torn and mended, [5]with worn-out, patched sandals on their feet, and worn-out clothes; and all their provisions were dry and moldy. [6]They went to Joshua in the camp at Gilgal, and said to him and to the Israelites, "We have come from a far country; so now make a treaty with us." [7]But the Israelites said to the Hivites, "Perhaps you live among us; then how can we make a treaty with you?" [8]They said to Joshua, "We are your servants." And Joshua said to them, "Who are you? And where do you come from?" [9]They said to him, "Your servants have come from a very far country, because of the name of the LORD your God; for we have heard a report of him, of all that he did in Egypt, [10]and of all that he did to the two kings of the Amorites who were beyond the Jordan, King Sihon of Heshbon, and King Og of Bashan who lived in Ashtaroth. [11]So our elders and all the inhabitants of our country said to us, 'Take provisions in your hand for the journey; go to meet them, and say to them, "We are your servants; come now, make a treaty with us."' [12]Here is our bread; it was still warm when we took it from our houses as our food for the journey, on the day we set out to come to you, but now, see, it is dry and moldy; [13]these wineskins were new when we filled them, and see, they are burst; and these garments and sandals of ours are worn out from the very long journey." [14]So the leaders[o] partook of their provisions, and did not ask direction from the LORD. [15]And Joshua made peace with them, guaranteeing their lives by a treaty; and the leaders of the congregation swore an oath to them.

16 But when three days had passed after they had made a treaty with them, they heard that they were their neighbors and were living among them. [17]So the Israelites set out and reached their cities on the third day. Now their cities were Gibeon, Chephirah, Beeroth, and Kiriath-jearim. [18]But the Israelites did not attack them, because the leaders of the congregation had sworn to them by the LORD, the God of Israel. Then all the congregation murmured against the leaders. [19]But all the leaders said to all the congregation, "We have sworn to them by the LORD, the God of Israel, and now we must not touch them. [20]This is what we will do to them: We will let them live, so that wrath may not come upon us, because of the oath that we swore to them." [21]The leaders said to them, "Let them live." So they became hewers of wood and drawers of water for all the congregation, as the leaders had decided concerning them.

22 Joshua summoned them, and said to them, "Why did you deceive us, saying, 'We are very far from you,' while in fact you are living among us? [23]Now therefore you are cursed, and some of you shall always be slaves, hewers of wood and drawers of water for the house of my God." [24]They answered Joshua, "Because it was told to your servants for a certainty that the LORD your God had commanded his servant Moses to give you all the land, and to destroy all the inhabitants of the land before you; so we were in great fear for our lives because of you, and did this thing. [25]And now we are in your hand: do as it seems good and right in your sight to do to us." [26]This is what he did for them: he saved them from the Israelites; and they did not kill them. [27]But on that day Joshua made them hewers of wood and drawers of water for the congregation and for the altar of the LORD, to continue to this day, in the place that he should choose.

The Sun Stands Still

10 When King Adoni-zedek of Jerusalem heard how Joshua had taken Ai, and had utterly destroyed it, doing to Ai and its king as he had done to Jericho and its king, and how the inhabitants of Gibeon had made peace with Israel and were among them, [2]he[p] became greatly frightened, because

n Cn: Meaning of Heb uncertain   o Gk: Heb men   p Heb they

Gibeon was a large city, like one of the royal cities, and was larger than Ai, and all its men were warriors. 3So King Adoni-zedek of Jerusalem sent a message to King Hoham of Hebron, to King Piram of Jarmuth, to King Japhia of Lachish, and to King Debir of Eglon, saying, 4"Come up and help me, and let us attack Gibeon; for it has made peace with Joshua and with the Israelites." 5Then the five kings of the Amorites— the king of Jerusalem, the king of Hebron, the king of Jarmuth, the king of Lachish, and the king of Eglon—gathered their forces, and went up with all their armies and camped against Gibeon, and made war against it.

6 And the Gibeonites sent to Joshua at the camp in Gilgal, saying, "Do not abandon your servants; come up to us quickly, and save us, and help us; for all the kings of the Amorites who live in the hill country are gathered against us." 7So Joshua went up from Gilgal, he and all the fighting force with him, all the mighty warriors. 8The LORD said to Joshua, "Do not fear them, for I have handed them over to you; not one of them shall stand before you." 9So Joshua came upon them suddenly, having marched up all night from Gilgal. 10And the LORD threw them into a panic before Israel, who inflicted a great slaughter on them at Gibeon, chased them by the way of the ascent of Beth-horon, and struck them down as far as Azekah and Makkedah. 11As they fled before Israel, while they were going down the slope of Beth-horon, the LORD threw down huge stones from heaven on them as far as Azekah, and they died; there were more who died because of the hailstones than the Israelites killed with the sword.

12 On the day when the LORD gave the Amorites over to the Israelites, Joshua spoke to the LORD; and he said in the sight of Israel,

"Sun, stand still at Gibeon,
    and Moon, in the valley of
        Aijalon."
13   And the sun stood still, and the
        moon stopped,
    until the nation took vengeance
        on their enemies.
Is this not written in the Book of Jashar?

The sun stopped in midheaven, and did not hurry to set for about a whole day. 14There has been no day like it before or since, when the LORD heeded a human voice; for the LORD fought for Israel.

15 Then Joshua returned, and all Israel with him, to the camp at Gilgal.

Five Kings Defeated

16 Meanwhile, these five kings fled and hid themselves in the cave at Makkedah. 17And it was told Joshua, "The five kings have been found, hidden in the cave at Makkedah." 18Joshua said, "Roll large stones against the mouth of the cave, and set men by it to guard them; 19but do not stay there yourselves; pursue your enemies, and attack them from the rear. Do not let them enter their towns, for the LORD your God has given them into your hand." 20When Joshua and the Israelites had finished inflicting a very great slaughter on them, until they were wiped out, and when the survivors had entered into the fortified towns, 21all the people returned safe to Joshua in the camp at Makkedah; no one dared to speakq against any of the Israelites.

22 Then Joshua said, "Open the mouth of the cave, and bring those five kings out to me from the cave." 23They did so, and brought the five kings out to him from the cave, the king of Jerusalem, the king of Hebron, the king of Jarmuth, the king of Lachish, and the king of Eglon. 24When they brought the kings out to Joshua, Joshua summoned all the Israelites, and said to the chiefs of the warriors who had gone with him, "Come near, put your feet on the necks of these kings." Then they came near and put their feet on their necks. 25And Joshua said to them, "Do not be afraid or dismayed; be strong and courageous; for thus the LORD will do to all the enemies against whom you fight." 26Afterward Joshua struck them down and put them to death, and he hung them on five trees. And they hung on the trees until evening. 27At sunset Joshua commanded, and they took them down from the trees and threw them into the cave where they had hidden themselves; they

q Heb moved his tongue

set large stones against the mouth of the cave, which remain to this very day.

28 Joshua took Makkedah on that day, and struck it and its king with the edge of the sword; he utterly destroyed every person in it; he left no one remaining. And he did to the king of Makkedah as he had done to the king of Jericho.

29 Then Joshua passed on from Makkedah, and all Israel with him, to Libnah, and fought against Libnah. 30 The LORD gave it also and its king into the hand of Israel; and he struck it with the edge of the sword, and every person in it; he left no one remaining in it; and he did to its king as he had done to the king of Jericho.

31 Next Joshua passed on from Libnah, and all Israel with him, to Lachish, and laid siege to it, and assaulted it. 32 The LORD gave Lachish into the hand of Israel, and he took it on the second day, and struck it with the edge of the sword, and every person in it, as he had done to Libnah.

33 Then King Horam of Gezer came up to help Lachish; and Joshua struck him and his people, leaving him no survivors.

34 From Lachish Joshua passed on with all Israel to Eglon; and they laid siege to it, and assaulted it; 35 and they took it that day, and struck it with the edge of the sword; and every person in it he utterly destroyed that day, as he had done to Lachish.

36 Then Joshua went up with all Israel from Eglon to Hebron; they assaulted it, 37 and took it, and struck it with the edge of the sword, and its king and its towns, and every person in it; he left no one remaining, just as he had done to Eglon, and utterly destroyed it with every person in it.

38 Then Joshua, with all Israel, turned back to Debir and assaulted it, 39 and he took it with its king and all its towns; they struck them with the edge of the sword, and utterly destroyed every person in it; he left no one remaining; just as he had done to Hebron, and, as he had done to Libnah and its king, so he did to Debir and its king.

40 So Joshua defeated the whole land, the hill country and the Negeb and the lowland and the slopes, and all their kings; he left no one remaining, but utterly destroyed all that breathed, as the LORD God of Israel commanded. 41 And Joshua defeated them from Kadesh-barnea to Gaza, and all the country of Goshen, as far as Gibeon. 42 Joshua took all these kings and their land at one time, because the LORD God of Israel fought for Israel. 43 Then Joshua returned, and all Israel with him, to the camp at Gilgal.

The United Kings of Northern Canaan Defeated

11 When King Jabin of Hazor heard of this, he sent to King Jobab of Madon, to the king of Shimron, to the king of Achshaph, 2 and to the kings who were in the northern hill country, and in the Arabah south of Chinneroth, and in the lowland, and in Naphoth-dor on the west, 3 to the Canaanites in the east and the west, the Amorites, the Hittites, the Perizzites, and the Jebusites in the hill country, and the Hivites under Hermon in the land of Mizpah. 4 They came out, with all their troops, a great army, in number like the sand on the seashore, with very many horses and chariots. 5 All these kings joined their forces, and came and camped together at the waters of Merom, to fight with Israel.

6 And the LORD said to Joshua, "Do not be afraid of them, for tomorrow at this time I will hand over all of them, slain, to Israel; you shall hamstring their horses, and burn their chariots with fire." 7 So Joshua came suddenly upon them with all his fighting force, by the waters of Merom, and fell upon them. 8 And the LORD handed them over to Israel, who attacked them and chased them as far as Great Sidon and Misrephoth-maim, and eastward as far as the valley of Mizpeh. They struck them down, until they had left no one remaining. 9 And Joshua did to them as the LORD commanded him; he hamstrung their horses, and burned their chariots with fire.

10 Joshua turned back at that time, and took Hazor, and struck its king down with the sword. Before that time Hazor was the head of all those kingdoms. 11 And they put to the sword all

who were in it, utterly destroying them; there was no one left who breathed, and he burned Hazor with fire. 12And all the towns of those kings, and all their kings, Joshua took, and struck them with the edge of the sword, utterly destroying them, as Moses the servant of the LORD had commanded. 13But Israel burned none of the towns that stood on mounds except Hazor, which Joshua did burn. 14All the spoil of these towns, and the livestock, the Israelites took for their booty; but all the people they struck down with the edge of the sword, until they had destroyed them, and they did not leave any who breathed. 15As the LORD had commanded his servant Moses, so Moses commanded Joshua, and so Joshua did; he left nothing undone of all that the LORD had commanded Moses.

Summary of Joshua's Conquests

16 So Joshua took all that land: the hill country and all the Negeb and all the land of Goshen and the lowland and the Arabah and the hill country of Israel and its lowland, 17from Mount Halak, which rises toward Seir, as far as Baal-gad in the valley of Lebanon below Mount Hermon. He took all their kings, struck them down, and put them to death. 18Joshua made war a long time with all those kings. 19There was not a town that made peace with the Israelites, except the Hivites, the inhabitants of Gibeon; all were taken in battle. 20For it was the LORD's doing to harden their hearts so that they would come against Israel in battle, in order that they might be utterly destroyed, and might receive no mercy, but be exterminated, just as the LORD had commanded Moses.

21 At that time Joshua came and wiped out the Anakim from the hill country, from Hebron, from Debir, from Anab, and from all the hill country of Judah, and from all the hill country of Israel; Joshua utterly destroyed them with their towns. 22None of the Anakim was left in the land of the Israelites; some remained only in Gaza, in Gath, and in Ashdod. 23So Joshua took the whole land, according to all that the LORD had spoken to Moses; and Joshua

gave it for an inheritance to Israel according to their tribal allotments. And the land had rest from war.

The Kings Conquered by Moses

12 Now these are the kings of the land, whom the Israelites defeated, whose land they occupied beyond the Jordan toward the east, from the Wadi Arnon to Mount Hermon, with all the Arabah eastward: 2King Sihon of the Amorites who lived at Heshbon, and ruled from Aroer, which is on the edge of the Wadi Arnon, and from the middle of the valley as far as the river Jabbok, the boundary of the Ammonites, that is, half of Gilead, 3and the Arabah to the Sea of Chinneroth eastward, and in the direction of Beth-jeshimoth, to the sea of the Arabah, the Dead Sea,r southward to the foot of the slopes of Pisgah; 4and King Ogs of Bashan, one of the last of the Rephaim, who lived at Ashtaroth and at Edrei 5and ruled over Mount Hermon and Salecah and all Bashan to the boundary of the Geshurites and the Maacathites, and over half of Gilead to the boundary of King Sihon of Heshbon. 6Moses, the servant of the LORD, and the Israelites defeated them; and Moses the servant of the LORD gave their land for a possession to the Reubenites and the Gadites and the half-tribe of Manasseh.

The Kings Conquered by Joshua

7 The following are the kings of the land whom Joshua and the Israelites defeated on the west side of the Jordan, from Baal-gad in the valley of Lebanon to Mount Halak, that rises toward Seir (and Joshua gave their land to the tribes of Israel as a possession according to their allotments, 8in the hill country, in the lowland, in the Arabah, in the slopes, in the wilderness, and in the Negeb, the land of the Hittites, Amorites, Canaanites, Perizzites, Hivites, and Jebusites):

9	the king of Jericho	one
	the king of Ai, which is next to Bethel	one
10	the king of Jerusalem	one
	the king of Hebron	one
11	the king of Jarmuth	one

---

r Heb *Salt Sea*   s Gk: Heb *the boundary of King Og*

the king of Lachish one
12 the king of Eglon one
the king of Gezer one
13 the king of Debir one
the king of Geder one
14 the king of Hormah one
the king of Arad one
15 the king of Libnah one
the king of Adullam one
16 the king of Makkedah one
the king of Bethel one
17 the king of Tappuah one
the king of Hepher one
18 the king of Aphek one
the king of Lasharon one
19 the king of Madon one
the king of Hazor one
20 the king of Shimron-meron one
the king of Achshaph one
21 the king of Taanach one
the king of Megiddo one
22 the king of Kedesh one
the king of Jokneam in Carmel one
23 the king of Dor in Naphath-dor one
the king of Goiim in Galilee,ᵗ one
24 the king of Tirzah one
thirty-one kings in all.

The Parts of Canaan Still Unconquered

13 Now Joshua was old and advanced in years; and the LORD said to him, "You are old and advanced in years, and very much of the land still remains to be possessed. ²This is the land that still remains: all the regions of the Philistines, and all those of the Geshurites ³(from the Shihor, which is east of Egypt, northward to the boundary of Ekron, it is reckoned as Canaanite; there are five rulers of the Philistines, those of Gaza, Ashdod, Ashkelon, Gath, and Ekron), and those of the Avvim ⁴in the south; all the land of the Canaanites, and Mearah that belongs to the Sidonians, to Aphek, to the boundary of the Amorites, ⁵and the land of the Gebalites, and all Lebanon, toward the east, from Baal-gad below Mount Hermon to Lebo-hamath, ⁶all the inhabitants of the hill country from Lebanon to Misrephoth-maim, even all the Sidonians. I will myself drive them out from before the Israelites; only allot the land to Israel for an inheritance, as I have commanded

you. ⁷Now therefore divide this land for an inheritance to the nine tribes and the half-tribe of Manasseh."

The Territory East of the Jordan

8 With the other half-tribe of Manasseh ᵘ the Reubenites and the Gadites received their inheritance, which Moses gave them, beyond the Jordan eastward, as Moses the servant of the LORD gave them: ⁹from Aroer, which is on the edge of the Wadi Arnon, and the town that is in the middle of the valley, and all the tableland fromᵛ Medeba as far as Dibon; ¹⁰and all the cities of King Sihon of the Amorites, who reigned in Heshbon, as far as the boundary of the Ammonites; ¹¹and Gilead, and the region of the Geshurites and Maacathites, and all Mount Hermon, and all Bashan to Salecah; ¹²all the kingdom of Og in Bashan, who reigned in Ashtaroth and in Edrei (he alone was left of the survivors of the Rephaim); these Moses had defeated and driven out. ¹³Yet the Israelites did not drive out the Geshurites or the Maacathites; but Geshur and Maacath live within Israel to this day.

14 To the tribe of Levi alone Moses gave no inheritance; the offerings by fire to the LORD God of Israel are their inheritance, as he said to them.

The Territory of Reuben

15 Moses gave an inheritance to the tribe of the Reubenites according to their clans. ¹⁶Their territory was from Aroer, which is on the edge of the Wadi Arnon, and the town that is in the middle of the valley, and all the tableland by Medeba; ¹⁷with Heshbon, and all its towns that are in the tableland; Dibon, and Bamoth-baal, and Beth-baal-meon, ¹⁸and Jahaz, and Kedemoth, and Mephaath, ¹⁹and Kiriathaim, and Sibmah, and Zereth-shahar on the hill of the valley, ²⁰and Beth-peor, and the slopes of Pisgah, and Beth-jeshimoth, ²¹that is, all the towns of the tableland, and all the kingdom of King Sihon of the Amorites, who reigned in Heshbon, whom Moses defeated with the leaders of Midian, Evi and Rekem and Zur and Hur and Reba, as princes of Sihon, who lived in the land. ²²Along with the rest of those they

t Gk: Heb Gilgal   u Cn: Heb With it   v Compare Gk: Heb lacks from

put to death, the Israelites also put to the sword Balaam son of Beor, who practiced divination. 23And the border of the Reubenites was the Jordan and its banks. This was the inheritance of the Reubenites according to their families, with their towns and villages.

The Territory of Gad

24 Moses gave an inheritance also to the tribe of the Gadites, according to their families. 25Their territory was Jazer, and all the towns of Gilead, and half the land of the Ammonites, to Aroer, which is east of Rabbah, 26and from Heshbon to Ramath-mizpeh and Betonim, and from Mahanaim to the territory of Debir,w 27and in the valley Beth-haram, Beth-nimrah, Succoth, and Zaphon, the rest of the kingdom of King Sihon of Heshbon, the Jordan and its banks, as far as the lower end of the Sea of Chinnereth, eastward beyond the Jordan. 28This is the inheritance of the Gadites according to their clans, with their towns and villages.

The Territory of the Half-Tribe of Manasseh (East)

29 Moses gave an inheritance to the half-tribe of Manasseh; it was allotted to the half-tribe of the Manassites according to their families. 30Their territory extended from Mahanaim, through all Bashan, the whole kingdom of King Og of Bashan, and all the settlements of Jair, which are in Bashan, sixty towns, 31and half of Gilead, and Ashtaroth, and Edrei, the towns of the kingdom of Og in Bashan; these were allotted to the people of Machir son of Manasseh according to their clans—for half the Machirites.

32 These are the inheritances that Moses distributed in the plains of Moab, beyond the Jordan east of Jericho. 33But to the tribe of Levi Moses gave no inheritance; the LORD God of Israel is their inheritance, as he said to them.

The Distribution of Territory West of the Jordan

14 These are the inheritances that the Israelites received in the land of Canaan, which the priest Eleazar, and Joshua son of Nun, and the heads of the families of the tribes of the Israelites distributed to them. 2Their inheritance was by lot, as the LORD had commanded Moses for the nine and one-half tribes. 3For Moses had given an inheritance to the two and one-half tribes beyond the Jordan; but to the Levites he gave no inheritance among them. 4For the people of Joseph were two tribes, Manasseh and Ephraim; and no portion was given to the Levites in the land, but only towns to live in, with their pasture lands for their flocks and herds. 5The Israelites did as the LORD commanded Moses; they allotted the land.

Hebron Allotted to Caleb

6 Then the people of Judah came to Joshua at Gilgal; and Caleb son of Jephunneh the Kenizzite said to him, "You know what the LORD said to Moses the man of God in Kadesh-barnea concerning you and me. 7I was forty years old when Moses the servant of the LORD sent me from Kadesh-barnea to spy out the land; and I brought him an honest report. 8But my companions who went up with me made the heart of the people melt; yet I wholeheartedly followed the LORD my God. 9And Moses swore on that day, saying, 'Surely the land on which your foot has trodden shall be an inheritance for you and your children forever, because you have wholeheartedly followed the LORD my God.' 10And now, as you see, the LORD has kept me alive, as he said, these forty-five years since the time that the LORD spoke this word to Moses, while Israel was journeying through the wilderness; and here I am today, eighty-five years old. 11I am still as strong today as I was on the day that Moses sent me; my strength now is as my strength was then, for war, and for going and coming. 12So now give me this hill country of which the LORD spoke on that day; for you heard on that day how the Anakim were there, with great fortified cities; it may be that the LORD will be with me, and I shall drive them out, as the LORD said."

13 Then Joshua blessed him, and gave Hebron to Caleb son of Jephunneh for an inheritance. 14So Hebron became the inheritance of Caleb son of Jephunneh

w Gk Syr Vg: Heb Lidebir

the Kenizzite to this day, because he wholeheartedly followed the LORD, the God of Israel. 15Now the name of Hebron formerly was Kiriath-arba;ˣ this Arba wasʸ the greatest man among the Anakim. And the land had rest from war.

The Territory of Judah

 15 The lot for the tribe of the people of Judah according to their families reached southward to the boundary of Edom, to the wilderness of Zin at the farthest south. 2And their south boundary ran from the end of the Dead Sea,ᶻ from the bay that faces southward; 3it goes out southward of the ascent of Akrabbim, passes along to Zin, and goes up south of Kadesh-barnea, along by Hezron, up to Addar, makes a turn to Karka, 4passes along to Azmon, goes out by the Wadi of Egypt, and comes to its end at the sea. This shall be

x That is *the city of Arba*   y Heb lacks *this Arba was*   z Heb *Salt Sea*

TUESDAY

"MORE TO FOLLOW"
Charles H. Spurgeon

VERSE: Joshua 14.9   PASSAGE: Joshua 14.6–12

 benevolent person gave Mr. Rowland Hill a hundred pounds to dispense to a poor minister a bit at a time, thinking it was too much to send him all at once. Mr. Hill forwarded five pounds in a letter, with only these words within the envelope, "More to follow." In a few days' time, the good man received another letter; this second messenger contained another five pounds, with the same motto, "And more to follow." A day or two after came a third and a fourth, and still the same promise, "And more to follow." Till the whole sum had been received, the astonished minister was made familiar with the cheering words, "And more to follow."

Every blessing that comes from God is sent with the same message, "And more to follow." "I forgive you your sins, but there's more to follow." "I justify you in the righteousness of Christ, but there's more to follow." "I adopt you into my family, but there's more to follow." "I educated you for heaven, but there's more to follow." "I give you grace upon grace, but there's more to follow." "I will uphold you in the hour of death, and as you are passing into the world of spirits, my mercy shall still continue with you, and when you land in the world to come there shall still be *more to follow*."

ADDITIONAL SCRIPTURE READING:
Matthew 7.11; 25.14–30; Revelation 2.26–28

Go to page 259 for your next devotional reading.

1700   1900

your south boundary. ⁵And the east boundary is the Dead Sea,ᵃ to the mouth of the Jordan. And the boundary on the north side runs from the bay of the sea at the mouth of the Jordan; ⁶and the boundary goes up to Beth-hoglah, and passes along north of Beth-arabah; and the boundary goes up to the Stone of Bohan, Reuben's son; ⁷and the boundary goes up to Debir from the Valley of Achor, and so northward, turning toward Gilgal, which is opposite the ascent of Adummim, which is on the south side of the valley; and the boundary passes along to the waters of En-shemesh, and ends at En-rogel; ⁸then the boundary goes up by the valley of the son of Hinnom at the southern slope of the Jebusites (that is, Jerusalem); and the boundary goes up to the top of the mountain that lies over against the valley of Hinnom, on the west, at the northern end of the valley of Rephaim; ⁹then the boundary extends from the top of the mountain to the spring of the Waters of Nephtoah, and from there to the towns of Mount Ephron; then the boundary bends around to Baalah (that is, Kiriath-jearim); ¹⁰and the boundary circles west of Baalah to Mount Seir, passes along to the northern slope of Mount Jearim (that is, Chesalon), and goes down to Beth-shemesh, and passes along by Timnah; ¹¹the boundary goes out to the slope of the hill north of Ekron, then the boundary bends around to Shikkeron, and passes along to Mount Baalah, and goes out to Jabneel; then the boundary comes to an end at the sea. ¹²And the west boundary was the Mediterranean with its coast. This is the boundary surrounding the people of Judah according to their families.

Caleb Occupies His Portion

13 According to the commandment of the LORD to Joshua, he gave to Caleb son of Jephunneh a portion among the people of Judah, Kiriath-arba,ᵇ that is, Hebron (Arba was the father of Anak). ¹⁴And Caleb drove out from there the three sons of Anak: Sheshai, Ahiman, and Talmai, the descendants of Anak. ¹⁵From there he went up against the inhabitants of Debir; now the name of Debir formerly was Kiriath-sepher. ¹⁶And Caleb said, "Whoever attacks Kiriath-sepher and takes it, to him I will give my daughter Achsah as wife." ¹⁷Othniel son of Kenaz, the brother of Caleb, took it; and he gave him his daughter Achsah as wife. ¹⁸When she came to him, she urged him to ask her father for a field. As she dismounted from her donkey, Caleb said to her, "What do you wish?" ¹⁹She said to him, "Give me a present; since you have set me in the land of the Negeb, give me springs of water as well." So Caleb gave her the upper springs and the lower springs.

The Towns of Judah

20 This is the inheritance of the tribe of the people of Judah according to their families. ²¹The towns belonging to the tribe of the people of Judah in the extreme south, toward the boundary of Edom, were Kabzeel, Eder, Jagur, ²²Kinah, Dimonah, Adadah, ²³Kedesh, Hazor, Ithnan, ²⁴Ziph, Telem, Bealoth, ²⁵Hazor-hadattah, Kerioth-hezron (that is, Hazor), ²⁶Amam, Shema, Moladah, ²⁷Hazar-gaddah, Heshmon, Beth-pelet, ²⁸Hazar-shual, Beer-sheba, Biziothiah, ²⁹Baalah, Iim, Ezem, ³⁰Eltolad, Chesil, Hormah, ³¹Ziklag, Madmannah, Sansannah, ³²Lebaoth, Shilhim, Ain, and Rimmon: in all, twenty-nine towns, with their villages.

33 And in the lowland, Eshtaol, Zorah, Ashnah, ³⁴Zanoah, En-gannim, Tappuah, Enam, ³⁵Jarmuth, Adullam, Socoh, Azekah, ³⁶Shaaraim, Adithaim, Gederah, Gederothaim: fourteen towns with their villages.

37 Zenan, Hadashah, Migdal-gad, ³⁸Dilan, Mizpeh, Jokthe-el, ³⁹Lachish, Bozkath, Eglon, ⁴⁰Cabbon, Lahmam, Chitlish, ⁴¹Gederoth, Beth-dagon, Naamah, and Makkedah: sixteen towns with their villages.

42 Libnah, Ether, Ashan, ⁴³Iphtah, Ashnah, Nezib, ⁴⁴Keilah, Achzib, and Mareshah: nine towns with their villages.

45 Ekron, with its dependencies and its villages; ⁴⁶from Ekron to the sea, all that were near Ashdod, with their villages.

ᵃ Heb *Salt Sea*   ᵇ That is *the city of Arba*

47 Ashdod, its towns and its villages; Gaza, its towns and its villages; to the Wadi of Egypt, and the Great Sea with its coast.

48 And in the hill country, Shamir, Jattir, Socoh, 49Dannah, Kiriath-sannah (that is, Debir), 50Anab, Eshtemoh, Anim, 51Goshen, Holon, and Giloh: eleven towns with their villages.

52 Arab, Dumah, Eshan, 53Janim, Beth-tappuah, Aphekah, 54Humtah, Kiriath-arba (that is, Hebron), and Zior: nine towns with their villages.

55 Maon, Carmel, Ziph, Juttah, 56Jezreel, Jokdeam, Zanoah, 57Kain, Gibeah, and Timnah: ten towns with their villages.

58 Halhul, Beth-zur, Gedor, 59Maarath, Beth-anoth, and Eltekon: six towns with their villages.

60 Kiriath-baal (that is, Kiriath-jearim) and Rabbah: two towns with their villages.

61 In the wilderness, Beth-arabah, Middin, Secacah, 62Nibshan, the City of Salt, and En-gedi: six towns with their villages.

63 But the people of Judah could not drive out the Jebusites, the inhabitants of Jerusalem; so the Jebusites live with the people of Judah in Jerusalem to this day.

The Territory of Ephraim

16 The allotment of the Josephites went from the Jordan by Jericho, east of the waters of Jericho, into the wilderness, going up from Jericho into the hill country to Bethel; 2then going from Bethel to Luz, it passes along to Ataroth, the territory of the Archites; 3then it goes down westward to the territory of the Japhletites, as far as the territory of Lower Beth-horon, then to Gezer, and it ends at the sea.

4 The Josephites—Manasseh and Ephraim—received their inheritance.

5 The territory of the Ephraimites by their families was as follows: the boundary of their inheritance on the east was Ataroth-addar as far as Upper Beth-horon, 6and the boundary goes from there to the sea; on the north is Michmethath; then on the east the boundary makes a turn toward Taanath-shiloh, and passes along beyond it on the east to

Janoah, 7then it goes down from Janoah to Ataroth and to Naarah, and touches Jericho, ending at the Jordan. 8From Tappuah the boundary goes westward to the Wadi Kanah, and ends at the sea. Such is the inheritance of the tribe of the Ephraimites by their families, 9together with the towns that were set apart for the Ephraimites within the inheritance of the Manassites, all those towns with their villages. 10They did not, however, drive out the Canaanites who lived in Gezer: so the Canaanites have lived within Ephraim to this day but have been made to do forced labor.

The Other Half-Tribe of Manasseh (West)

17 Then allotment was made to the tribe of Manasseh, for he was the firstborn of Joseph. To Machir the firstborn of Manasseh, the father of Gilead, were allotted Gilead and Bashan, because he was a warrior. 2And allotments were made to the rest of the tribe of Manasseh, by their families, Abiezer, Helek, Asriel, Shechem, Hepher, and Shemida; these were the male descendants of Manasseh son of Joseph, by their families.

3 Now Zelophehad son of Hepher son of Gilead son of Machir son of Manasseh had no sons, but only daughters; and these are the names of his daughters: Mahlah, Noah, Hoglah, Milcah, and Tirzah. 4They came before the priest Eleazar and Joshua son of Nun and the leaders, and said, "The LORD commanded Moses to give us an inheritance along with our male kin." So according to the commandment of the LORD he gave them an inheritance among the kinsmen of their father. 5Thus there fell to Manasseh ten portions, besides the land of Gilead and Bashan, which is on the other side of the Jordan, 6because the daughters of Manasseh received an inheritance along with his sons. The land of Gilead was allotted to the rest of the Manassites.

7 The territory of Manasseh reached from Asher to Michmethath, which is east of Shechem; then the boundary goes along southward to the inhabitants of En-tappuah. 8The land of Tappuah belonged to Manasseh, but the town of

Tappuah on the boundary of Manasseh belonged to the Ephraimites. ⁹Then the boundary went down to the Wadi Kanah. The towns here, to the south of the wadi, among the towns of Manasseh, belong to Ephraim. Then the boundary of Manasseh goes along the north side of the wadi and ends at the sea. ¹⁰The land to the south is Ephraim's and that to the north is Manasseh's, with the sea forming its boundary; on the north Asher is reached, and on the east Issachar. ¹¹Within Issachar and Asher, Manasseh had Beth-shean and its villages, Ibleam and its villages, the inhabitants of Dor and its villages, the inhabitants of En-dor and its villages, the inhabitants of Taanach and its villages, and the inhabitants of Megiddo and its villages (the third is Naphath).*c* ¹²Yet the Manassites could not take possession of those towns; but the Canaanites continued to live in that land. ¹³But when the Israelites grew strong, they put the Canaanites to forced labor, but did not utterly drive them out.

The Tribe of Joseph Protests

14 The tribe of Joseph spoke to Joshua, saying, "Why have you given me but one lot and one portion as an inheritance, since we are a numerous people, whom all along the LORD has blessed?" ¹⁵And Joshua said to them, "If you are a numerous people, go up to the forest, and clear ground there for yourselves in the land of the Perizzites and the Rephaim, since the hill country of Ephraim is too narrow for you." ¹⁶The tribe of Joseph said, "The hill country is not enough for us; yet all the Canaanites who live in the plain have chariots of iron, both those in Beth-shean and its villages and those in the Valley of Jezreel." ¹⁷Then Joshua said to the house of Joseph, to Ephraim and Manasseh, "You are indeed a numerous people, and have great power; you shall not have one lot only, ¹⁸but the hill country shall be yours, for though it is a forest, you shall clear it and possess it to its farthest borders; for you shall drive out the Canaanites, though they have chariots of iron, and though they are strong."

c Meaning of Heb uncertain

The Territories of the Remaining Tribes

18 Then the whole congregation of the Israelites assembled at Shiloh, and set up the tent of meeting there. The land lay subdued before them.

2 There remained among the Israelites seven tribes whose inheritance had not yet been apportioned. ³So Joshua said to the Israelites, "How long will you be slack about going in and taking possession of the land that the LORD, the God of your ancestors, has given you? ⁴Provide three men from each tribe, and I will send them out that they may begin to go throughout the land, writing a description of it with a view to their inheritances. Then come back to me. ⁵They shall divide it into seven portions, Judah continuing in its territory on the south, and the house of Joseph in their territory on the north. ⁶You shall describe the land in seven divisions and bring the description here to me; and I will cast lots for you here before the LORD our God. ⁷The Levites have no portion among you, for the priesthood of the LORD is their heritage; and Gad and Reuben and the half-tribe of Manasseh have received their inheritance beyond the Jordan eastward, which Moses the servant of the LORD gave them."

8 So the men started on their way; and Joshua charged those who went to write the description of the land, saying, "Go throughout the land and write a description of it, and come back to me; and I will cast lots for you here before the LORD in Shiloh." ⁹So the men went and traversed the land and set down in a book a description of it by towns in seven divisions; then they came back to Joshua in the camp at Shiloh, ¹⁰and Joshua cast lots for them in Shiloh before the LORD; and there Joshua apportioned the land to the Israelites, to each a portion.

The Territory of Benjamin

11 The lot of the tribe of Benjamin according to its families came up, and the territory allotted to it fell between the tribe of Judah and the tribe of Joseph. ¹²On the north side their boundary

began at the Jordan; then the boundary goes up to the slope of Jericho on the north, then up through the hill country westward; and it ends at the wilderness of Beth-aven. ¹³From there the boundary passes along southward in the direction of Luz, to the slope of Luz (that is, Beth-el), then the boundary goes down to Ata- roth-addar, on the mountain that lies south of Lower Beth-horon. ¹⁴Then the boundary goes in another direction, turning on the western side southward from the mountain that lies to the south, opposite Beth-horon, and it ends at Kiriath-baal (that is, Kiriath-jearim), a town belonging to the tribe of Judah.

WEDNESDAY

THE CONCLUSION OF THE TASK
F. B. Meyer

VERSE: Joshua 18.3   PASSAGE: Joshua 18.1–10

oshua rebuked the inertness of the people. He said to the children of Israel, "How long are ye slack to go in to possess the land, which the LORD God of your fathers hath given you?" (18.3, KJV). At that point the twenty-one commissioners arose to walk through the land and surveyed it . . . It may be that the account of what they had seen was the means under God of arousing the people from the apathy into which they had sunk.

Too long have we been slack to go in to possess that fullness of the Holy Spirit that might be in us as a living spring, making us perfectly satisfied. There is a knowledge of Jesus, a partici- pation in his victory, a realization of blessedness, which are as much beyond the ordinary experience of Christians as Canaan was better than the wilderness. But how sad, that of all this we know so little.

How much we miss! The nomad life could not afford those seven tribes so much lasting enjoyment as their own freehold in Canaan. But the comparison is utterly inadequate to portray the loss to which we subject ourselves in refusing to appropri- ate and enjoy the blessedness that is laid up for us in Jesus. Let us come to our Joshua at Shiloh, and ask him to lead us into each of these.

ADDITIONAL SCRIPTURE READING:
Proverbs 2.2–6; Hosea 6.3; Philippians 3.13–14

Go to page 270 for your next devotional reading.

1700   1900

This forms the western side. 15The southern side begins at the outskirts of Kiriath-jearim; and the boundary goes from there to Ephron,*d* to the spring of the Waters of Nephtoah; 16then the boundary goes down to the border of the mountain that overlooks the valley of the son of Hinnom, which is at the north end of the valley of Rephaim; and it then goes down the valley of Hinnom, south of the slope of the Jebusites, and downward to En-rogel; 17then it bends in a northerly direction going on to En-shemesh, and from there it goes to Geliloth, which is opposite the ascent of Adummim; then it goes down to the Stone of Bohan, Reuben's son; 18and passing on to the north of the slope of Beth-arabah*e* it goes down to the Arabah; 19then the boundary passes on to the north of the slope of Beth-hoglah; and the boundary ends at the northern bay of the Dead Sea,*f* at the south end of the Jordan: this is the southern border. 20The Jordan forms its boundary on the eastern side. This is the inheritance of the tribe of Benjamin, according to its families, boundary by boundary all around.

21 Now the towns of the tribe of Benjamin according to their families were Jericho, Beth-hoglah, Emek-keziz, 22Betharabah, Zemaraim, Bethel, 23Avvim, Parah, Ophrah, 24Chephar-ammoni, Ophni, and Geba—twelve towns with their villages; 25Gibeon, Ramah, Beeroth, 26Mizpeh, Chephirah, Mozah, 27Rekem, Irpeel, Taralah, 28Zela, Haeleph, Jebus*g* (that is, Jerusalem), Gibeah*h* and Kiriath-jearim*i*—fourteen towns with their villages. This is the inheritance of the tribe of Benjamin according to its families.

The Territory of Simeon

19 The second lot came out for Simeon, for the tribe of Simeon, according to its families; its inheritance lay within the inheritance of the tribe of Judah. 2It had for its inheritance Beer-sheba, Sheba, Moladah, 3Hazarshual, Balah, Ezem, 4Eltolad, Bethul, Hormah, 5Ziklag, Beth-marcaboth, Hazar-susah, 6Beth-lebaoth, and Sharuhen—thirteen towns with their villages; 7Ain, Rimmon, Ether, and Ashan—four

towns with their villages; 8together with all the villages all around these towns as far as Baalath-beer, Ramah of the Negeb. This was the inheritance of the tribe of Simeon according to its families. 9The inheritance of the tribe of Simeon formed part of the territory of Judah; because the portion of the tribe of Judah was too large for them, the tribe of Simeon obtained an inheritance within their inheritance.

The Territory of Zebulun

10 The third lot came up for the tribe of Zebulun, according to its families. The boundary of its inheritance reached as far as Sarid; 11then its boundary goes up westward, and on to Maralah, and touches Dabbesheth, then the wadi that is east of Jokneam; 12from Sarid it goes in the other direction eastward toward the sunrise to the boundary of Chisloth-tabor; from there it goes to Daberath, then up to Japhia; 13from there it passes along on the east toward the sunrise to Gath-hepher, to Eth-kazin, and going on to Rimmon it bends toward Neah; 14then on the north the boundary makes a turn to Hannathon, and it ends at the valley of Iphtah-el; 15and Kattath, Nahalal, Shimron, Idalah, and Bethlehem—twelve towns with their villages. 16This is the inheritance of the tribe of Zebulun, according to its families—these towns with their villages.

The Territory of Issachar

17 The fourth lot came out for Issachar, for the tribe of Issachar, according to its families. 18Its territory included Jezreel, Chesulloth, Shunem, 19Hapharaim, Shion, Anaharath, 20Rabbith, Kishion, Ebez, 21Remeth, En-gannim, Enhaddah, Beth-pazzez; 22the boundary also touches Tabor, Shahazumah, and Beth-shemesh, and its boundary ends at the Jordan—sixteen towns with their villages. 23This is the inheritance of the tribe of Issachar, according to its families—the towns with their villages.

The Territory of Asher

24 The fifth lot came out for the tribe of Asher according to its families. 25Its

---

d Cn See 15.9. Heb *westward*   *e* Gk: Heb *to the slope over against the Arabah*   *f* Heb *Salt Sea*
g Gk Syr Vg: Heb *the Jebusite*   *h* Heb *Gibeath*   *i* Gk: Heb *Kiriath*

boundary included Helkath, Hali, Beten, Achshaph, 26Allammelech, Amad, and Mishal; on the west it touches Carmel and Shihor-libnath, 27then it turns eastward, goes to Beth-dagon, and touches Zebulun and the valley of Iphtah-el northward to Beth-emek and Neiel; then it continues in the north to Cabul, 28Ebron, Rehob, Hammon, Kanah, as far as Great Sidon; 29then the boundary turns to Ramah, reaching to the fortified city of Tyre; then the boundary turns to Hosah, and it ends at the sea; Mahalab,*j* 30Ummah, Aphek, and Rehob— twenty-two towns with their villages. 31This is the inheritance of the tribe of Asher according to its families—these towns with their villages.

The Territory of Naphtali

32 The sixth lot came out for the tribe of Naphtali, for the tribe of Naphtali, according to its families. 33And its boundary ran from Heleph, from the oak in Zaanannim, and Adami-nekeb, and Jabneel, as far as Lakkum; and it ended at the Jordan; 34then the boundary turns westward to Aznoth-tabor, and goes from there to Hukkok, touching Zebulun at the south, and Asher on the west, and Judah on the east at the Jordan. 35The fortified towns are Ziddim, Zer, Hammath, Rakkath, Chinnereth, 36Adamah, Ramah, Hazor, 37Kedesh, Edrei, En-hazor, 38Iron, Migdal-el, Horem, Beth-anath, and Beth-shemesh—nineteen towns with their villages. 39This is the inheritance of the tribe of Naphtali according to its families—the towns with their villages.

The Territory of Dan

40 The seventh lot came out for the tribe of Dan, according to its families. 41The territory of its inheritance included Zorah, Eshtaol, Ir-shemesh, 42Shaalabbin, Aijalon, Ithlah, 43Elon, Timnah, Ekron, 44Eltekeh, Gibbethon, Baalath, 45Jehud, Bene-berak, Gath-rimmon, 46Me-jarkon, and Rakkon at the border opposite Joppa. 47When the territory of the Danites was lost to them, the Danites went up and fought against Leshem, and after capturing it and putting it to the sword, they took possession of it and

settled in it, calling Leshem, Dan, after their ancestor Dan. 48This is the inheritance of the tribe of Dan, according to their families—these towns with their villages.

Joshua's Inheritance

49 When they had finished distributing the several territories of the land as inheritances, the Israelites gave an inheritance among them to Joshua son of Nun. 50By command of the LORD they gave him the town that he asked for, Timnath-serah in the hill country of Ephraim; he rebuilt the town, and settled in it.

51 These are the inheritances that the priest Eleazar and Joshua son of Nun and the heads of the families of the tribes of the Israelites distributed by lot at Shiloh before the LORD, at the entrance of the tent of meeting. So they finished dividing the land.

The Cities of Refuge

20 Then the LORD spoke to Joshua, saying, 2"Say to the Israelites, 'Appoint the cities of refuge, of which I spoke to you through Moses, 3so that anyone who kills a person without intent or by mistake may flee there; they shall be for you a refuge from the avenger of blood. 4The slayer shall flee to one of these cities and shall stand at the entrance of the gate of the city, and explain the case to the elders of that city; then the fugitive shall be taken into the city, and given a place, and shall remain with them. 5And if the avenger of blood is in pursuit, they shall not give up the slayer, because the neighbor was killed by mistake, there having been no enmity between them before. 6The slayer shall remain in that city until there is a trial before the congregation, until the death of the one who is high priest at the time: then the slayer may return home, to the town in which the deed was done.' "

7 So they set apart Kedesh in Galilee in the hill country of Naphtali, and Shechem in the hill country of Ephraim, and Kiriath-arba (that is, Hebron) in the hill country of Judah. 8And beyond the Jordan east of Jericho, they appointed

j Cn Compare Gk: Heb *Mehebel*

Bezer in the wilderness on the tableland, from the tribe of Reuben, and Ramoth in Gilead, from the tribe of Gad, and Golan in Bashan, from the tribe of Manasseh. ⁹These were the cities designated for all the Israelites, and for the aliens residing among them, that anyone who killed a person without intent could flee there, so as not to die by the hand of the avenger of blood, until there was a trial before the congregation.

Cities Allotted to the Levites

21 Then the heads of the families of the Levites came to the priest Eleazar and to Joshua son of Nun and to the heads of the families of the tribes of the Israelites; ²they said to them at Shiloh in the land of Canaan, "The LORD commanded through Moses that we be given towns to live in, along with their pasture lands for our livestock." ³So by command of the LORD the Israelites gave to the Levites the following towns and pasture lands out of their inheritance.

4 The lot came out for the families of the Kohathites. So those Levites who were descendants of Aaron the priest received by lot thirteen towns from the tribes of Judah, Simeon, and Benjamin. 5 The rest of the Kohathites received by lot ten towns from the families of the tribe of Ephraim, from the tribe of Dan, and the half-tribe of Manasseh.

6 The Gershonites received by lot thirteen towns from the families of the tribe of Issachar, from the tribe of Asher, from the tribe of Naphtali, and from the half-tribe of Manasseh in Bashan. 7 The Merarites according to their families received twelve towns from the tribe of Reuben, the tribe of Gad, and the tribe of Zebulun.

8 These towns and their pasture lands the Israelites gave by lot to the Levites, as the LORD had commanded through Moses.

9 Out of the tribe of Judah and the tribe of Simeon they gave the following towns mentioned by name, ¹⁰which went to the descendants of Aaron, one of the families of the Kohathites who belonged to the Levites, since the lot fell to them first. ¹¹They gave them Kiriath-arba (Arba being the father of Anak),

that is Hebron, in the hill country of Judah, along with the pasture lands around it. ¹²But the fields of the town and its villages had been given to Caleb son of Jephunneh as his holding.

13 To the descendants of Aaron the priest they gave Hebron, the city of refuge for the slayer, with its pasture lands, Libnah with its pasture lands, ¹⁴Jattir with its pasture lands, Eshtemoa with its pasture lands, ¹⁵Holon with its pasture lands, Debir with its pasture lands, ¹⁶Ain with its pasture lands, Juttah with its pasture lands, and Beth-shemesh with its pasture lands—nine towns out of these two tribes. ¹⁷Out of the tribe of Benjamin: Gibeon with its pasture lands, Geba with its pasture lands, ¹⁸Anathoth with its pasture lands, and Almon with its pasture lands—four towns. ¹⁹The towns of the descendants of Aaron—the priests—were thirteen in all, with their pasture lands.

20 As to the rest of the Kohathites belonging to the Kohathite families of the Levites, the towns allotted to them were out of the tribe of Ephraim. ²¹To them were given Shechem, the city of refuge for the slayer, with its pasture lands in the hill country of Ephraim, Gezer with its pasture lands, ²²Kibzaim with its pasture lands, and Beth-horon with its pasture lands—four towns. ²³Out of the tribe of Dan: Elteke with its pasture lands, Gibbethon with its pasture lands, ²⁴Aijalon with its pasture lands, Gath-rimmon with its pasture lands—four towns. ²⁵Out of the half-tribe of Manasseh: Taanach with its pasture lands, and Gath-rimmon with its pasture lands—two towns. ²⁶The towns of the families of the rest of the Kohathites were ten in all, with their pasture lands.

27 To the Gershonites, one of the families of the Levites, were given out of the half-tribe of Manasseh, Golan in Bashan with its pasture lands, the city of refuge for the slayer, and Beeshterah with its pasture lands—two towns. ²⁸Out of the tribe of Issachar: Kishion with its pasture lands, Daberath with its pasture lands, ²⁹Jarmuth with its pasture lands, En-gannim with its pasture lands—four towns. ³⁰Out of the tribe of Asher: Mishal with its pasture lands, Abdon with its pasture lands, ³¹Helkath with its pasture lands,

and Rehob with its pasture lands—four towns. 32Out of the tribe of Naphtali: Kedesh in Galilee with its pasture lands, the city of refuge for the slayer, Hammoth-dor with its pasture lands, and Kartan with its pasture lands—three towns. 33The towns of the several families of the Gershonites were in all thirteen, with their pasture lands.

34 To the rest of the Levites—the Merarite families—were given out of the tribe of Zebulun: Jokneam with its pasture lands, Kartah with its pasture lands, 35Dimnah with its pasture lands, Nahalal with its pasture lands—four towns. 36Out of the tribe of Reuben: Bezer with its pasture lands, Jahzah with its pasture lands, 37Kedemoth with its pasture lands, and Mephaath with its pasture lands— four towns. 38Out of the tribe of Gad: Ramoth in Gilead with its pasture lands, the city of refuge for the slayer, Mahanaim with its pasture lands, 39Heshbon with its pasture lands, Jazer with its pasture lands—four towns in all. 40As for the towns of the several Merarite families, that is, the remainder of the families of the Levites, those allotted to them were twelve in all.

41 The towns of the Levites within the holdings of the Israelites were in all forty-eight towns with their pasture lands. 42Each of these towns had its pasture lands around it; so it was with all these towns.

43 Thus the LORD gave to Israel all the land that he swore to their ancestors that he would give them; and having taken possession of it, they settled there. 44And the LORD gave them rest on every side just as he had sworn to their ancestors; not one of all their enemies had withstood them, for the LORD had given all their enemies into their hands. 45Not one of all the good promises that the LORD had made to the house of Israel had failed; all came to pass.

The Eastern Tribes Return to Their Territory

22 Then Joshua summoned the Reubenites, the Gadites, and the half-tribe of Manasseh, 2and said to them, "You have observed all that Moses the servant of the LORD com-

manded you, and have obeyed me in all that I have commanded you; 3you have not forsaken your kindred these many days, down to this day, but have been careful to keep the charge of the LORD your God. 4And now the LORD your God has given rest to your kindred, as he promised them; therefore turn and go to your tents in the land where your possession lies, which Moses the servant of the LORD gave you on the other side of the Jordan. 5Take good care to observe the commandment and instruction that Moses the servant of the LORD commanded you, to love the LORD your God, to walk in all his ways, to keep his commandments, and to hold fast to him, and to serve him with all your heart and with all your soul." 6So Joshua blessed them and sent them away, and they went to their tents.

7 Now to the one half of the tribe of Manasseh Moses had given a possession in Bashan; but to the other half Joshua had given a possession beside their fellow Israelites in the land west of the Jordan. And when Joshua sent them away to their tents and blessed them, 8he said to them, "Go back to your tents with much wealth, and with very much livestock, with silver, gold, bronze, and iron, and with a great quantity of clothing; divide the spoil of your enemies with your kindred." 9So the Reubenites and the Gadites and the half-tribe of Manasseh returned home, parting from the Israelites at Shiloh, which is in the land of Canaan, to go to the land of Gilead, their own land of which they had taken possession by command of the LORD through Moses.

A Memorial Altar East of the Jordan

10 When they came to the regionk near the Jordan that lies in the land of Canaan, the Reubenites and the Gadites and the half-tribe of Manasseh built there an altar by the Jordan, an altar of great size. 11The Israelites heard that the Reubenites and the Gadites and the half-tribe of Manasseh had built an altar at the frontier of the land of Canaan, in the regionl near the Jordan, on the side that belongs to the Israelites. 12And when the people of Israel heard of it, the whole

k Or to Geliloth   l Or at Geliloth

assembly of the Israelites gathered at Shiloh, to make war against them.

13 Then the Israelites sent the priest Phinehas son of Eleazar to the Reubenites and the Gadites and the half-tribe of Manasseh, in the land of Gilead, 14and with him ten chiefs, one from each of the tribal families of Israel, every one of them the head of a family among the clans of Israel. 15They came to the Reubenites, the Gadites, and the half-tribe of Manasseh, in the land of Gilead, and they said to them, 16"Thus says the whole congregation of the LORD, 'What is this treachery that you have committed against the God of Israel in turning away today from following the LORD, by building yourselves an altar today in rebellion against the LORD? 17Have we not had enough of the sin at Peor from which even yet we have not cleansed ourselves, and for which a plague came upon the congregation of the LORD, 18that you must turn away today from following the LORD! If you rebel against the LORD today, he will be angry with the whole congregation of Israel tomorrow. 19But now, if your land is unclean, cross over into the LORD's land where the LORD's tabernacle now stands, and take for yourselves a possession among us; only do not rebel against the LORD, or rebel against us*m* by building yourselves an altar other than the altar of the LORD our God. 20Did not Achan son of Zerah break faith in the matter of the devoted things, and wrath fell upon all the congregation of Israel? And he did not perish alone for his iniquity!' "

21 Then the Reubenites, the Gadites, and the half-tribe of Manasseh said in answer to the heads of the families of Israel, 22"The LORD, God of gods! The LORD, God of gods! He knows; and let Israel itself know! If it was in rebellion or in breach of faith toward the LORD, do not spare us today 23for building an altar to turn away from following the LORD; or if we did so to offer burnt offerings or grain offerings or offerings of well-being on it, may the LORD himself take vengeance. 24No! We did it from fear that in time to come your children might say to our children, 'What have you to do with the LORD, the God of

Israel? 25For the LORD has made the Jordan a boundary between us and you, you Reubenites and Gadites; you have no portion in the LORD.' So your children might make our children cease to worship the LORD. 26Therefore we said, 'Let us now build an altar, not for burnt offering, nor for sacrifice, 27but to be a witness between us and you, and between the generations after us, that we do perform the service of the LORD in his presence with our burnt offerings and sacrifices and offerings of well-being; so that your children may never say to our children in time to come, "You have no portion in the LORD." ' 28And we thought, If this should be said to us or to our descendants in time to come, we could say, 'Look at this copy of the altar of the LORD, which our ancestors made, not for burnt offerings, nor for sacrifice, but to be a witness between us and you.' 29Far be it from us that we should rebel against the LORD, and turn away this day from following the LORD by building an altar for burnt offering, grain offering, or sacrifice, other than the altar of the LORD our God that stands before his tabernacle!"

30 When the priest Phinehas and the chiefs of the congregation, the heads of the families of Israel who were with him, heard the words that the Reubenites and the Gadites and the Manassites spoke, they were satisfied. 31The priest Phinehas son of Eleazar said to the Reubenites and the Gadites and the Manassites, "Today we know that the LORD is among us, because you have not committed this treachery against the LORD; now you have saved the Israelites from the hand of the LORD."

32 Then the priest Phinehas son of Eleazar and the chiefs returned from the Reubenites and the Gadites in the land of Gilead to the land of Canaan, to the Israelites, and brought back word to them. 33The report pleased the Israelites; and the Israelites blessed God and spoke no more of making war against them, to destroy the land where the Reubenites and the Gadites were settled. 34The Reubenites and the Gadites called the altar Witness;*n* "For," said

m Or *make rebels of us*   *n* Cn Compare Syr: Heb lacks *Witness*

they, "it is a witness between us that the LORD is God."

Joshua Exhorts the People

23 A long time afterward, when the LORD had given rest to Israel from all their enemies all around, and Joshua was old and well advanced in years, ²Joshua summoned all Israel, their elders and heads, their judges and officers, and said to them, "I am now old and well advanced in years; ³and you have seen all that the LORD your God has done to all these nations for your sake, for it is the LORD your God who has fought for you. ⁴I have allotted to you as an inheritance for your tribes those nations that remain, along with all the nations that I have already cut off, from the Jordan to the Great Sea in the west. ⁵The LORD your God will push them back before you, and drive them out of your sight; and you shall possess their land, as the LORD your God promised you. ⁶Therefore be very steadfast to observe and do all that is written in the book of the law of Moses, turning aside from it neither to the right nor to the left, ⁷so that you may not be mixed with these nations left here among you, or make mention of the names of their gods, or swear by them, or serve them, or bow yourselves down to them, ⁸but hold fast to the LORD your God, as you have done to this day. ⁹For the LORD has driven out before you great and strong nations; and as for you, no one has been able to withstand you to this day. ¹⁰One of you puts to flight a thousand, since it is the LORD your God who fights for you, as he promised you. ¹¹Be very careful, therefore, to love the LORD your God. ¹²For if you turn back, and join the survivors of these nations left here among you, and intermarry with them, so that you marry their women and they yours, ¹³know assuredly that the LORD your God will not continue to drive out these nations before you; but they shall be a snare and a trap for you, a scourge on your sides, and thorns in your eyes, until you perish from this good land that the LORD your God has given you.

14 "And now I am about to go the way of all the earth, and you know in your hearts and souls, all of you, that not one thing has failed of all the good things that the LORD your God promised concerning you; all have come to pass for you, not one of them has failed. ¹⁵But just as all the good things that the LORD your God promised concerning you have been fulfilled for you, so the LORD will bring upon you all the bad things, until he has destroyed you from this good land that the LORD your God has given you. ¹⁶If you transgress the covenant of the LORD your God, which he enjoined on you, and go and serve other gods and bow down to them, then the anger of the LORD will be kindled against you, and you shall perish quickly from the good land that he has given to you."

The Tribes Renew the Covenant

24 Then Joshua gathered all the tribes of Israel to Shechem, and summoned the elders, the heads, the judges, and the officers of Israel; and they presented themselves before God. ²And Joshua said to all the people, "Thus says the LORD, the God of Israel: Long ago your ancestors—Terah and his sons Abraham and Nahor—lived beyond the Euphrates and served other gods. ³Then I took your father Abraham from beyond the River and led him through all the land of Canaan and made his offspring many. I gave him Isaac; ⁴and to Isaac I gave Jacob and Esau. I gave Esau the hill country of Seir to possess, but Jacob and his children went down to Egypt. ⁵Then I sent Moses and Aaron, and I plagued Egypt with what I did in its midst; and afterwards I brought you out. ⁶When I brought your ancestors out of Egypt, you came to the sea; and the Egyptians pursued your ancestors with chariots and horsemen to the Red Sea.ᵒ ⁷When they cried out to the LORD, he put darkness between you and the Egyptians, and made the sea come upon them and cover them; and your eyes saw what I did to Egypt. Afterwards you lived in the wilderness a long time. ⁸Then I brought you to the land of the Amorites, who lived on the other side of the Jordan; they fought with you, and I handed them over to you, and you took possession of their land, and I destroyed

o Or Sea of Reeds

them before you. ⁹Then King Balak son of Zippor of Moab, set out to fight against Israel. He sent and invited Balaam son of Beor to curse you, ¹⁰but I would not listen to Balaam; therefore he blessed you; so I rescued you out of his hand. ¹¹When you went over the Jordan and came to Jericho, the citizens of Jericho fought against you, and also the Amorites, the Perizzites, the Canaanites, the Hittites, the Girgashites, the Hivites, and the Jebusites; and I handed them over to you. ¹²I sent the hornet*p* ahead of you, which drove out before you the two kings of the Amorites; it was not by your sword or by your bow. ¹³I gave you a land on which you had not labored, and towns that you had not built, and you live in them; you eat the fruit of vineyards and oliveyards that you did not plant.

14 "Now therefore revere the LORD, and serve him in sincerity and in faithfulness; put away the gods that your ancestors served beyond the River and in Egypt, and serve the LORD. ¹⁵Now if you are unwilling to serve the LORD, choose this day whom you will serve, whether the gods your ancestors served in the region beyond the River or the gods of the Amorites in whose land you are living; but as for me and my household, we will serve the LORD."

16 Then the people answered, "Far be it from us that we should forsake the LORD to serve other gods; ¹⁷for it is the LORD our God who brought us and our ancestors up from the land of Egypt, out of the house of slavery, and who did those great signs in our sight. He protected us along all the way that we went, and among all the peoples through whom we passed; ¹⁸and the LORD drove out before us all the peoples, the Amorites who lived in the land. Therefore we also will serve the LORD, for he is our God."

19 But Joshua said to the people, "You cannot serve the LORD, for he is a holy God. He is a jealous God; he will not forgive your transgressions or your sins. ²⁰If you forsake the LORD and serve foreign gods, then he will turn and do you harm, and consume you, after having done you good." ²¹And the people said to Joshua, "No, we will serve the LORD!" ²²Then Joshua said to the people, "You are witnesses against yourselves that you have chosen the LORD, to serve him." And they said, "We are witnesses." ²³He said, "Then put away the foreign gods that are among you, and incline your hearts to the LORD, the God of Israel." ²⁴The people said to Joshua, "The LORD our God we will serve, and him we will obey." ²⁵So Joshua made a covenant with the people that day, and made statutes and ordinances for them at Shechem. ²⁶Joshua wrote these words in the book of the law of God; and he took a large stone, and set it up there under the oak in the sanctuary of the LORD. ²⁷Joshua said to all the people, "See, this stone shall be a witness against us; for it has heard all the words of the LORD that he spoke to us; therefore it shall be a witness against you, if you deal falsely with your God." ²⁸So Joshua sent the people away to their inheritances.

Death of Joshua and Eleazar

29 After these things Joshua son of Nun, the servant of the LORD, died, being one hundred ten years old. ³⁰They buried him in his own inheritance at Timnath-serah, which is in the hill country of Ephraim, north of Mount Gaash.

31 Israel served the LORD all the days of Joshua, and all the days of the elders who outlived Joshua and had known all the work that the LORD did for Israel.

32 The bones of Joseph, which the Israelites had brought up from Egypt, were buried at Shechem, in the portion of ground that Jacob had bought from the children of Hamor, the father of Shechem, for one hundred pieces of money;*q* it became an inheritance of the descendants of Joseph.

33 Eleazar son of Aaron died; and they buried him at Gibeah, the town of his son Phinehas, which had been given him in the hill country of Ephraim.

p Meaning of Heb uncertain   *q* Heb one hundred qesitah

JUDGES

THE BOOK OF JUDGES TELLS THE ACCOUNT OF ISRAEL'S FREQUENT FAILURES AND APOSTASY, WHICH IN TURN PROVOKES GOD'S CHASTENING. IT ALSO TELLS OF THE PEOPLE'S URGENT APPEALS TO GOD IN TIMES OF CRISIS, MOVING HIM TO RAISE UP LEADERS (JUDGES) THROUGH WHOM HE THROWS OFF OPPRESSION AND RESTORES THE LAND TO PEACE. JUDGES REMINDS US TO LET GO OF OUR REBELLION AND FIND JOY IN GOD'S FIRM BUT LOVING AND FORGIVING PRESENCE.

Israel's Failure to Complete the Conquest of Canaan

1 After the death of Joshua, the Israelites inquired of the LORD, "Who shall go up first for us against the Canaanites, to fight against them?" ²The LORD said, "Judah shall go up. I hereby give the land into his hand." ³Judah said to his brother Simeon, "Come up with me into the territory allotted to me, that we may fight against the Canaanites; then I too will go with you into the territory allotted to you." So Simeon went with him. ⁴Then Judah went up and the LORD gave the Canaanites and the Perizzites into their hand; and they defeated ten thousand of them at Bezek. ⁵They came upon Adoni-bezek at Bezek, and fought against him, and defeated the Canaanites and the Per-izzites. ⁶Adoni-bezek fled; but they pursued him, and caught him, and cut off his thumbs and big toes. ⁷Adoni-bezek said, "Seventy kings with their thumbs and big toes cut off used to pick up scraps under my table; as I have done, so God has paid me back." They brought him to Jerusalem, and he died there.

8 Then the people of Judah fought against Jerusalem and took it. They put it to the sword and set the city on fire. ⁹Afterward the people of Judah went down to fight against the Canaanites who lived in the hill country, in the Negeb, and in the lowland. ¹⁰Judah went against the Canaanites who lived in Hebron (the name of Hebron was formerly Kiriath-arba); and they defeated Sheshai and Ahiman and Talmai.

11 From there they went against the

inhabitants of Debir (the name of Debir was formerly Kiriath-sepher). [12]Then Caleb said, "Whoever attacks Kiriath-sepher and takes it, I will give him my daughter Achsah as wife." [13]And Othniel son of Kenaz, Caleb's younger brother, took it; and he gave him his daughter Achsah as wife. [14]When she came to him, she urged him to ask her father for a field. As she dismounted from her donkey, Caleb said to her, "What do you wish?" [15]She said to him, "Give me a present; since you have set me in the land of the Negeb, give me also Gulloth-mayim."[a] So Caleb gave her Upper Gulloth and Lower Gulloth.

16 The descendants of Hobab[b] the Kenite, Moses' father-in-law, went up with the people of Judah from the city of palms into the wilderness of Judah, which lies in the Negeb near Arad. Then they went and settled with the Amalekites.[c] [17]Judah went with his brother Simeon, and they defeated the Canaanites who inhabited Zephath, and devoted it to destruction. So the city was called Hormah. [18]Judah took Gaza with its territory, Ashkelon with its territory, and Ekron with its territory. [19]The Lord was with Judah, and he took possession of the hill country, but could not drive out the inhabitants of the plain, because they had chariots of iron. [20]Hebron was given to Caleb, as Moses had said; and he drove out from it the three sons of Anak. [21]But the Benjaminites did not drive out the Jebusites who lived in Jerusalem; so the Jebusites have lived in Jerusalem among the Benjaminites to this day.

22 The house of Joseph also went up against Bethel; and the Lord was with them. [23]The house of Joseph sent out spies to Bethel (the name of the city was formerly Luz). [24]When the spies saw a man coming out of the city, they said to him, "Show us the way into the city, and we will deal kindly with you." [25]So he showed them the way into the city; and they put the city to the sword, but they let the man and all his family go. [26]So the man went to the land of the Hittites and built a city, and named it Luz; that is its name to this day.

27 Manasseh did not drive out the inhabitants of Beth-shean and its villages, or Taanach and its villages, or the inhabitants of Dor and its villages, or the inhabitants of Ibleam and its villages, or the inhabitants of Megiddo and its villages; but the Canaanites continued to live in that land. [28]When Israel grew strong, they put the Canaanites to forced labor, but did not in fact drive them out.

29 And Ephraim did not drive out the Canaanites who lived in Gezer; but the Canaanites lived among them in Gezer.

30 Zebulun did not drive out the inhabitants of Kitron, or the inhabitants of Nahalol; but the Canaanites lived among them, and became subject to forced labor.

31 Asher did not drive out the inhabitants of Acco, or the inhabitants of Sidon, or of Ahlab, or of Achzib, or of Helbah, or of Aphik, or of Rehob; [32]but the Asherites lived among the Canaanites, the inhabitants of the land; for they did not drive them out.

33 Naphtali did not drive out the inhabitants of Beth-shemesh, or the inhabitants of Beth-anath, but lived among the Canaanites, the inhabitants of the land; nevertheless the inhabitants of Beth-shemesh and of Beth-anath became subject to forced labor for them.

34 The Amorites pressed the Danites back into the hill country; they did not allow them to come down to the plain. [35]The Amorites continued to live in Har-heres, in Aijalon, and in Shaalbim, but the hand of the house of Joseph rested heavily on them, and they became subject to forced labor. [36]The border of the Amorites ran from the ascent of Akrabbim, from Sela and upward.

Israel's Disobedience

2 Now the angel of the Lord went up from Gilgal to Bochim, and said, "I brought you up from Egypt, and brought you into the land that I had promised to your ancestors. I said, 'I will never break my covenant with you. [2]For your part, do not make a covenant with the inhabitants of this land; tear down their altars.' But you have not obeyed my command. See what you have done! [3]So now I say, I will not drive them out before

_____

a That is Basins of Water   b Gk: Heb lacks Hobab   c See 1 Sam 15.6: Heb people you; but they shall become adversaries[d] to you, and their gods shall be a snare to you." 4When the angel of the LORD spoke these words to all the Israelites, the people lifted up their voices and wept. 5So they named that place Bochim,[e] and there they sacrificed to the LORD.

Death of Joshua

6 When Joshua dismissed the people, the Israelites all went to their own inheritances to take possession of the land. 7The people worshiped the LORD all the days of Joshua, and all the days of the elders who outlived Joshua, who had seen all the great work that the LORD had done for Israel. 8Joshua son of Nun, the servant of the LORD, died at the age of one hundred ten years. 9So they buried him within the bounds of his inheritance in Timnath-heres, in the hill country of Ephraim, north of Mount Gaash. 10Moreover, that whole generation was gathered to their ancestors, and another generation grew up after them, who did not know the LORD or the work that he had done for Israel.

Israel's Unfaithfulness

11 Then the Israelites did what was evil in the sight of the LORD and worshiped the Baals; 12and they abandoned the LORD, the God of their ancestors, who had brought them out of the land of Egypt; they followed other gods, from among the gods of the peoples who were all around them, and bowed down to them; and they provoked the LORD to anger. 13They abandoned the LORD, and worshiped Baal and the Astartes. 14So the anger of the LORD was kindled against Israel, and he gave them over to plunderers who plundered them, and he sold them into the power of their enemies all around, so that they could no longer withstand their enemies. 15Whenever they marched out, the hand of the LORD was against them to bring misfortune, as the LORD had warned them and sworn to them; and they were in great distress.

16 Then the LORD raised up judges, who delivered them out of the power of those who plundered them. 17Yet they did not listen even to their judges; for

they lusted after other gods and bowed down to them. They soon turned aside from the way in which their ancestors had walked, who had obeyed the commandments of the LORD; they did not follow their example. 18Whenever the LORD raised up judges for them, the LORD was with the judge, and he delivered them from the hand of their enemies all the days of the judge; for the LORD would be moved to pity by their groaning because of those who persecuted and oppressed them. 19But whenever the judge died, they would relapse and behave worse than their ancestors, following other gods, worshiping them and bowing down to them. They would not drop any of their practices or their stubborn ways. 20So the anger of the LORD was kindled against Israel; and he said, "Because this people have transgressed my covenant that I commanded their ancestors, and have not obeyed my voice, 21I will no longer drive out before them any of the nations that Joshua left when he died." 22In order to test Israel, whether or not they would take care to walk in the way of the LORD as their ancestors did, 23the LORD had left those nations, not driving them out at once, and had not handed them over to Joshua.

Nations Remaining in the Land

3 Now these are the nations that the LORD left to test all those in Israel who had no experience of any war in Canaan 2(it was only that successive generations of Israelites might know war, to teach those who had no experience of it before): 3the five lords of the Philistines, and all the Canaanites, and the Sidonians, and the Hivites who lived on Mount Lebanon, from Mount Baal-hermon as far as Lebo-hamath. 4They were for the testing of Israel, to know whether Israel would obey the commandments of the LORD, which he commanded their ancestors by Moses. 5So the Israelites lived among the Canaanites, the Hittites, the Amorites, the Perizzites, the Hivites, and the Jebusites; 6and they took their daughters as wives for themselves, and their own daughters they gave to their sons; and they worshiped their gods.

d OL Vg Compare Gk: Heb *sides*   e That is *Weepers*

Othniel

7 The Israelites did what was evil in the sight of the LORD, forgetting the LORD their God, and worshiping the Baals and the Asherahs. 8 Therefore the anger of the LORD was kindled against Israel, and he sold them into the hand of King Cushan-rishathaim of Aram-naharaim; and the

THURSDAY

A PERSONAL PRAYER FOR OBEDIENCE
John Baillie

VERSE: Judges 2.17   PASSAGE: Judges 2.16–19

 oly God, to whose service I long ago dedicated my soul and life, I grieve and lament before thee that I am still so prone to sin and so little inclined to obedience:

So much attached to the pleasures of sense, so negligent of things spiritual:

So prompt to gratify my body, so slow to nourish my soul:

So greedy for present delight, so indifferent to lasting blessedness:

So fond of idleness, so indisposed for labor:

So soon at play, so late at prayer:

So brisk in the service of self, so slack in the service of others;

So eager to get, so reluctant to give:

So lofty in my profession, so low in my practice:

So full of good intentions, so backward to fulfill them:

So severe with my neighbors, so indulgent with myself:

So eager to find fault, so resentful at being found fault with:

So little able for great tasks, so discontented with small ones:

So weak in adversity, so swollen and self-satisfied in prosperity:

So helpless apart from thee, and yet so little willing to be bound to thee.

O merciful heart of God, grant me yet again thy forgiveness. Hear my sorrowful tale and in thy great mercy blot it out from the book of thy remembrance. Give me faith so to lay hold of thine own holiness and so to rejoice in the righteousness of Christ my Savior that, resting on his merits rather than on my own, I may more and more become conformed to his likeness, my will becoming one with his in obedience to thine. All this I ask for his holy name's sake. Amen.

ADDITIONAL SCRIPTURE READING:
John 17.16—26; 2 Corinthians 3.18; Ephesians 4.22–24

Go to page 272 for your next devotional reading.

1900   Present

Israelites served Cushan-rishathaim eight years. 9But when the Israelites cried out to the LORD, the LORD raised up a deliverer for the Israelites, who delivered them, Othniel son of Kenaz, Caleb's younger brother. 10The spirit of the LORD came upon him, and he judged Israel; he went out to war, and the LORD gave King Cushan-rishathaim of Aram into his hand; and his hand prevailed over Cushan-rishathaim. 11So the land had rest forty years. Then Othniel son of Kenaz died.

Ehud

12 The Israelites again did what was evil in the sight of the LORD; and the LORD strengthened King Eglon of Moab against Israel, because they had done what was evil in the sight of the LORD. 13In alliance with the Ammonites and the Amalekites, he went and defeated Israel; and they took possession of the city of palms. 14So the Israelites served King Eglon of Moab eighteen years.

15 But when the Israelites cried out to the LORD, the LORD raised up for them a deliverer, Ehud son of Gera, the Benjaminite, a left-handed man. The Israelites sent tribute by him to King Eglon of Moab. 16Ehud made for himself a sword with two edges, a cubit in length; and he fastened it on his right thigh under his clothes. 17Then he presented the tribute to King Eglon of Moab. Now Eglon was a very fat man. 18When Ehud had finished presenting the tribute, he sent the people who carried the tribute on their way. 19But he himself turned back at the sculptured stones near Gilgal, and said, "I have a secret message for you, O king." So the king said,f "Silence!" and all his attendants went out from his presence. 20Ehud came to him, while he was sitting alone in his cool roof chamber, and said, "I have a message from God for you." So he rose from his seat. 21Then Ehud reached with his left hand, took the sword from his right thigh, and thrust it into Eglon'sg belly; 22the hilt also went in after the blade, and the fat closed over the blade, for he did not draw the sword out of his belly; and the dirt came out.h 23Then Ehud went out

into the vestibule,i and closed the doors of the roof chamber on him, and locked them. 24 After he had gone, the servants came. When they saw that the doors of the roof chamber were locked, they thought, "He must be relieving himselfj in the cool chamber." 25So they waited until they were embarrassed. When he still did not open the doors of the roof chamber, they took the key and opened them. There was their lord lying dead on the floor.

26 Ehud escaped while they delayed, and passed beyond the sculptured stones, and escaped to Seirah. 27When he arrived, he sounded the trumpet in the hill country of Ephraim; and the Israelites went down with him from the hill country, having him at their head. 28He said to them, "Follow after me; for the LORD has given your enemies the Moabites into your hand." So they went down after him, and seized the fords of the Jordan against the Moabites, and allowed no one to cross over. 29At that time they killed about ten thousand of the Moabites, all strong, able-bodied men; no one escaped. 30So Moab was subdued that day under the hand of Israel. And the land had rest eighty years.

Shamgar

31 After him came Shamgar son of Anath, who killed six hundred of the Philistines with an oxgoad. He too delivered Israel.

Deborah and Barak

4 The Israelites again did what was evil in the sight of the LORD, after Ehud died. 2So the LORD sold them into the hand of King Jabin of Canaan, who reigned in Hazor; the commander of his army was Sisera, who lived in Harosheth-ha-goiim. 3Then the Israelites cried out to the LORD for help; for he had nine hundred chariots of iron, and had oppressed the Israelites cruelly twenty years.

4 At that time Deborah, a prophetess, wife of Lappidoth, was judging Israel. 5She used to sit under the palm of Deborah between Ramah and Bethel in the

---

f Heb he said   g Heb his   h With Tg Vg: Meaning of Heb uncertain   i Meaning of Heb uncertain
j Heb covering his feet

hill country of Ephraim; and the Israelites came up to her for judgment. ⁶She sent and summoned Barak son of Abinoam from Kedesh in Naphtali, and said to him, "The LORD, the God of Israel, commands you, 'Go, take position at Mount Tabor, bringing ten thousand from the tribe of Naphtali and the tribe of Zebulun. ⁷I will draw out Sisera, the general of Jabin's army, to meet you by the Wadi Kishon with his chariots and his troops; and I will give him into your hand.' "

⁸Barak said to her, "If you will go with me, I will go; but if you will not go with me, I will not go." ⁹And she said, "I will surely go with you; nevertheless, the road on which you are going will not lead to your glory, for the LORD will sell Sisera into the hand of a woman." Then Deborah got up and went with Barak to Kedesh. ¹⁰Barak summoned Zebulun and Naphtali to Kedesh; and ten thousand warriors went up behind him; and Deborah went up with him.

FRIDAY

GOD'S IMPARTIALITY
G. Campbell Morgan

VERSE: Judges 4.4   PASSAGE: Judges 4.1–10

 n the light of subsequent Jewish prejudice against women as leaders, the story of Deborah is full of interest, as it reveals the fact that there never was any such prejudice in the mind of God. Whereas motherhood in all the sanctity and beauty of that great word, is the special function and glory of womanhood, yet when a woman is specially gifted for the exercise of prophetic and administrative work, she is not barred by any Divine law from such work. Deborah was a prophetess in the full sense of that word; that is, she was the inspired mouthpiece of the Word of God to her people. She also judged Israel, and whatever that meant in the case of the men who exercised that office, it also meant in her case. She was a savior, a deliverer; she administered the affairs of the people, and led them out of the circumstances of difficulty into which their sin had brought them . . . Ever and anon in the long history of God's patient dealing with men, we find him raising up some woman to lead, to guide, to inspire; and always there is this same element of enthusiasm and force. The one great message of the story seems to be that it warns us to take heed that we do not imagine ourselves to be wiser than God. When he calls and equips a woman to high service, let us beware lest we dishonor him by refusing to recognize her, or cooperate with her.

ADDITIONAL SCRIPTURE READING:
Judges 5.12–15; 2 Kings 22.14–20; Luke 2.36–38

Go to page 277 for your next devotional reading.

1900   Present

11 Now Heber the Kenite had separated from the other Kenites,[k] that is, the descendants of Hobab the father-in-law of Moses, and had encamped as far away as Elon-bezaanannim, which is near Kedesh.

12 When Sisera was told that Barak son of Abinoam had gone up to Mount Tabor, 13Sisera called out all his chariots, nine hundred chariots of iron, and all the troops who were with him, from Harosheth-ha-goiim to the Wadi Kishon. 14Then Deborah said to Barak, "Up! For this is the day on which the LORD has given Sisera into your hand. The LORD is indeed going out before you." So Barak went down from Mount Tabor with ten thousand warriors following him. 15And the LORD threw Sisera and all his chariots and all his army into a panic[l] before Barak; Sisera got down from his chariot and fled away on foot, 16while Barak pursued the chariots and the army to Harosheth-ha-goiim. All the army of Sisera fell by the sword; no one was left.

17 Now Sisera had fled away on foot to the tent of Jael wife of Heber the Kenite; for there was peace between King Jabin of Hazor and the clan of Heber the Kenite. 18Jael came out to meet Sisera, and said to him, "Turn aside, my lord, turn aside to me; have no fear." So he turned aside to her into the tent, and she covered him with a rug. 19Then he said to her, "Please give me a little water to drink; for I am thirsty." So she opened a skin of milk and gave him a drink and covered him. 20He said to her, "Stand at the entrance of the tent, and if anybody comes and asks you, 'Is anyone here?' say, 'No.' " 21But Jael wife of Heber took a tent peg, and took a hammer in her hand, and went softly to him and drove the peg into his temple, until it went down into the ground—he was lying fast asleep from weariness—and he died. 22Then, as Barak came in pursuit of Sisera, Jael went out to meet him, and said to him, "Come, and I will show you the man whom you are seeking." So he went into her tent; and there was Sisera lying dead, with the tent peg in his temple.

23 So on that day God subdued King Jabin of Canaan before the Israelites. 24Then the hand of the Israelites bore harder and harder on King Jabin of Canaan, until they destroyed King Jabin of Canaan.

The Song of Deborah

5 Then Deborah and Barak son of Abinoam sang on that day, saying:

2   "When locks are long in Israel,
        when the people offer themselves
        willingly—
        bless[m] the LORD!

3   "Hear, O kings; give ear, O princes;
        to the LORD I will sing,
    I will make melody to the LORD,
        the God of Israel.

4   "LORD, when you went out from
        Seir,
    when you marched from the
        region of Edom,
    the earth trembled,
        and the heavens poured,
        the clouds indeed poured water.
5   The mountains quaked before the
        LORD, the One of Sinai,
    before the LORD, the God of Israel.

6   "In the days of Shamgar son of
        Anath,
        in the days of Jael, caravans
        ceased
    and travelers kept to the byways.
7   The peasantry prospered in Israel,
        they grew fat on plunder,
    because you arose, Deborah,
        arose as a mother in Israel.
8   When new gods were chosen,
        then war was in the gates.
    Was shield or spear to be seen
        among forty thousand in Israel?
9   My heart goes out to the
        commanders of Israel
    who offered themselves willingly
        among the people.
    Bless the LORD.

10   "Tell of it, you who ride on white
        donkeys,
    you who sit on rich carpets[n]
    and you who walk by the way.

---

k Heb from the Kain   l Heb adds to the sword; compare verse 16   m Or You who offer yourselves willingly among the people, bless   n Meaning of Heb uncertain

11 To the sound of musicians[o] at the
        watering places,
    there they repeat the triumphs of
        the LORD,
    the triumphs of his peasantry in
        Israel.

    "Then down to the gates marched
        the people of the LORD.

12 "Awake, awake, Deborah!
        Awake, awake, utter a song!
    Arise, Barak, lead away your
        captives,
        O son of Abinoam.
13 Then down marched the remnant
        of the noble;
    the people of the LORD marched
        down for him[p] against the
        mighty.
14 From Ephraim they set out[q] into
        the valley,[r]
    following you, Benjamin, with
        your kin;
    from Machir marched down the
        commanders,
    and from Zebulun those who
        bear the marshal's staff;
15 the chiefs of Issachar came with
        Deborah,
    and Issachar faithful to Barak;
    into the valley they rushed out at
        his heels.
    Among the clans of Reuben
    there were great searchings of
        heart.
16 Why did you tarry among the
        sheepfolds,
    to hear the piping for the flocks?
    Among the clans of Reuben
    there were great searchings of
        heart.
17 Gilead stayed beyond the Jordan;
    and Dan, why did he abide with
        the ships?
    Asher sat still at the coast of the
        sea,
    settling down by his landings.
18 Zebulun is a people that scorned
        death;
    Naphtali too, on the heights of
        the field.

19 "The kings came, they fought;

    then fought the kings of Canaan,
    at Taanach, by the waters of
        Megiddo;
    they got no spoils of silver.
20 The stars fought from heaven,
    from their courses they fought
        against Sisera.
21 The torrent Kishon swept them
        away,
    the onrushing torrent, the torrent
        Kishon.
    March on, my soul, with might!

22 "Then loud beat the horses' hoofs
    with the galloping, galloping of
        his steeds.

23 "Curse Meroz, says the angel of the
        LORD,
    curse bitterly its inhabitants,
    because they did not come to the
        help of the LORD,
    to the help of the LORD against
        the mighty.

24 "Most blessed of women be Jael,
        the wife of Heber the Kenite,
    of tent-dwelling women most
        blessed.
25 He asked water and she gave him
        milk,
    she brought him curds in a lordly
        bowl.
26 She put her hand to the tent peg
        and her right hand to the
        workmen's mallet;
    she struck Sisera a blow,
    she crushed his head,
    she shattered and pierced his
        temple.
27 He sank, he fell,
        he lay still at her feet;
    at her feet he sank, he fell;
    where he sank, there he fell dead.

28 "Out of the window she peered,
        the mother of Sisera gazed[s]
        through the lattice:
    'Why is his chariot so long in
        coming?
    Why tarry the hoofbeats of his
        chariots?'
29 Her wisest ladies make answer,

o Meaning of Heb uncertain   p Gk: Heb me   q Cn: Heb From Ephraim their root   r Gk: Heb in
Amalek   s Gk Compare Tg: Heb exclaimed

indeed, she answers the question herself:

30 'Are they not finding and dividing
       the spoil?—
    A girl or two for every man;
    spoil of dyed stuffs for Sisera,
       spoil of dyed stuffs embroidered,
    two pieces of dyed work
       embroidered for my neck as
       spoil?'

31 "So perish all your enemies,
       O LORD!
    But may your friends be like the
       sun as it rises in its might."

And the land had rest forty years.

The Midianite Oppression

6 The Israelites did what was evil in the sight of the LORD, and the LORD gave them into the hand of Midian seven years. 2 The hand of Midian prevailed over Israel; and because of Midian the Israelites provided for themselves hiding places in the mountains, caves and strongholds. 3 For whenever the Israelites put in seed, the Midianites and the Amalekites and the people of the east would come up against them. 4 They would encamp against them and destroy the produce of the land, as far as the neighborhood of Gaza, and leave no sustenance in Israel, and no sheep or ox or donkey. 5 For they and their livestock would come up, and they would even bring their tents, as thick as locusts; neither they nor their camels could be counted; so they wasted the land as they came in. 6 Thus Israel was greatly impoverished because of Midian; and the Israelites cried out to the LORD for help.

7 When the Israelites cried to the LORD on account of the Midianites, 8 the LORD sent a prophet to the Israelites; and he said to them, "Thus says the LORD, the God of Israel: I led you up from Egypt, and brought you out of the house of slavery; 9 and I delivered you from the hand of the Egyptians, and from the hand of all who oppressed you, and drove them out before you, and gave you their land; 10 and I said to you, 'I am the LORD your God; you shall not pay reverence to the gods of the Amorites, in whose land you live.' But you have not given heed to my voice.'"

The Call of Gideon

11 Now the angel of the LORD came and sat under the oak at Ophrah, which belonged to Joash the Abiezrite, as his son Gideon was beating out wheat in the wine press, to hide it from the Midianites. 12 The angel of the LORD appeared to him and said to him, "The LORD is with you, you mighty warrior." 13 Gideon answered him, "But sir, if the LORD is with us, why then has all this happened to us? And where are all his wonderful deeds that our ancestors recounted to us, saying, 'Did not the LORD bring us up from Egypt?' But now the LORD has cast us off, and given us into the hand of Midian." 14 Then the LORD turned to him and said, "Go in this might of yours and deliver Israel from the hand of Midian; I hereby commission you." 15 He responded, "But sir, how can I deliver Israel? My clan is the weakest in Manasseh, and I am the least in my family." 16 The LORD said to him, "But I will be with you, and you shall strike down the Midianites, every one of them." 17 Then he said to him, "If now I have found favor with you, then show me a sign that it is you who speak with me. 18 Do not depart from here until I come to you, and bring out my present, and set it before you." And he said, "I will stay until you return."

19 So Gideon went into his house and prepared a kid, and unleavened cakes from an ephah of flour; the meat he put in a basket, and the broth he put in a pot, and brought them to him under the oak and presented them. 20 The angel of God said to him, "Take the meat and the unleavened cakes, and put them on this rock, and pour out the broth." And he did so. 21 Then the angel of the LORD reached out the tip of the staff that was in his hand, and touched the meat and the unleavened cakes; and fire sprang up from the rock and consumed the meat and the unleavened cakes; and the angel of the LORD vanished from his sight. 22 Then Gideon perceived that it was the angel of the LORD; and Gideon said, "Help me, Lord GOD! For I have seen the angel of the LORD face to face." 23 But the

LORD said to him, "Peace be to you; do not fear, you shall not die." 24Then Gideon built an altar there to the LORD, and called it, The LORD is peace. To this day it still stands at Ophrah, which belongs to the Abiezrites.

25 That night the LORD said to him, "Take your father's bull, the second bull seven years old, and pull down the altar of Baal that belongs to your father, and cut down the sacred pole*t* that is beside it; 26and build an altar to the LORD your God on the top of the stronghold here, in proper order; then take the second bull, and offer it as a burnt offering with the wood of the sacred pole*t* that you shall cut down." 27So Gideon took ten of his servants, and did as the LORD had told him; but because he was too afraid of his family and the townspeople to do it by day, he did it by night.

Gideon Destroys the Altar of Baal

28 When the townspeople rose early in the morning, the altar of Baal was broken down, and the sacred pole*t* beside it was cut down, and the second bull was offered on the altar that had been built. 29So they said to one another, "Who has done this?" After searching and inquiring, they were told, "Gideon son of Joash did it." 30Then the townspeople said to Joash, "Bring out your son, so that he may die, for he has pulled down the altar of Baal and cut down the sacred pole*t* beside it." 31But Joash said to all who were arrayed against him, "Will you contend for Baal? Or will you defend his cause? Whoever contends for him shall be put to death by morning. If he is a god, let him contend for himself, because his altar has been pulled down." 32Therefore on that day Gideon*u* was called Jerubbaal, that is to say, "Let Baal contend against him," because he pulled down his altar.

33 Then all the Midianites and the Amalekites and the people of the east came together, and crossing the Jordan they encamped in the Valley of Jezreel. 34But the spirit of the LORD took possession of Gideon; and he sounded the trumpet, and the Abiezrites were called out to follow him. 35He sent messengers throughout all Manasseh, and they too were called out to follow him. He also sent messengers to Asher, Zebulun, and Naphtali, and they went up to meet them.

The Sign of the Fleece

36 Then Gideon said to God, "In order to see whether you will deliver Israel by my hand, as you have said, 37I am going to lay a fleece of wool on the threshing floor; if there is dew on the fleece alone, and it is dry on all the ground, then I shall know that you will deliver Israel by my hand, as you have said." 38And it was so. When he rose early next morning and squeezed the fleece, he wrung enough dew from the fleece to fill a bowl with water. 39Then Gideon said to God, "Do not let your anger burn against me, let me speak one more time; let me, please, make trial with the fleece just once more; let it be dry only on the fleece, and on all the ground let there be dew." 40And God did so that night. It was dry on the fleece only, and on all the ground there was dew.

Gideon Surprises and Routs the Midianites

7 Then Jerubbaal (that is, Gideon) and all the troops that were with him rose early and encamped beside the spring of Harod; and the camp of Midian was north of them, below*v* the hill of Moreh, in the valley.

2 The LORD said to Gideon, "The troops with you are too many for me to give the Midianites into their hand. Israel would only take the credit away from me, saying, 'My own hand has delivered me.' 3Now therefore proclaim this in the hearing of the troops, 'Whoever is fearful and trembling, let him return home.' " Thus Gideon sifted them out;*w* twenty-two thousand returned, and ten thousand remained.

4 Then the LORD said to Gideon, "The troops are still too many; take them down to the water and I will sift them out for you there. When I say, 'This one shall go with you,' he shall go with you; and when I say, 'This one shall not go with you,' he shall not go." 5So he brought the troops down to the

---

t Heb *Asherah*   *u* Heb *he*   *v* Heb *from*   *w* Cn: Heb *home, and depart from Mount Gilead'* "

WEEKEND

FOR GOD'S GRACE IN OUR HELPLESSNESS
Peter Marshall

VERSE: Judges 7.2   **PASSAGE:** Judges 7.1–8, 20–21

 e know, our Father, that at this desperate hour in world affairs, we need thee. We need thy strength, thy guidance, thy wisdom.

There are problems far greater than any wisdom of man can solve. What shall our leaders do in such an hour?

May thy wisdom and thy power come upon the President of these United States, the Senators and Congressmen, to whom have been entrusted leadership. May the responsibility lie heavily on their hearts, until they are ready to acknowledge their helplessness and turn to thee. Give to them the honesty, the courage, and the moral integrity to confess that they don't know what to do. Only then can they lead us as a nation beyond human wisdom to thee, who alone hast the answer.

Lead us to this high adventure. Remind us that a "mighty fortress is our God"—not a hiding place where we can escape for an easy life, but rather an arsenal of courage and strength—the mightiest of all, who will march beside us into the battle for righteousness and world brotherhood.

O our God, may we never recover from our feeling of helplessness and our need of thee! In the strong name of Jesus, our Lord, we pray. Amen.

ADDITIONAL SCRIPTURE READING:
2 Chronicles 14.11; Zechariah 4.6; 2 Corinthians 4.6–7

Go to page 297 for your next devotional reading.

water; and the LORD said to Gideon, "All those who lap the water with their tongues, as a dog laps, you shall put to one side; all those who kneel down to drink, putting their hands to their mouths,[x] you shall put to the other side." [6]The number of those that lapped was three hundred; but all the rest of the troops knelt down to drink water. [7]Then the LORD said to Gideon, "With the three hundred that lapped I will deliver you, and give the Midianites into your hand. Let all the others go to their homes." [8]So he took the jars of the troops from their hands,[y] and their trumpets; and he sent all the rest of Israel back to their own tents, but retained the three hundred. The camp of Midian was below him in the valley.

9 That same night the LORD said to him, "Get up, attack the camp; for I have given it into your hand. [10]But if you fear to attack, go down to the camp with your servant Purah; [11]and you shall hear what they say, and afterward your hands shall be strengthened to attack the camp." Then he went down with his servant Purah to the outposts of the armed men that were in the camp. [12]The Midianites and the Amalekites and all the people of the east lay along the valley as thick as locusts; and their camels were without number, countless as the sand on the seashore. [13]When Gideon arrived, there was a man telling a dream to his comrade; and he said, "I had a dream, and in it a cake of barley bread tumbled into the camp of Midian, and came to the tent, and struck it so that it fell; it turned upside down, and the tent collapsed." [14]And his comrade answered, "This is no other than the sword of Gideon son of Joash, a man of Israel; into his hand God has given Midian and all the army."

15 When Gideon heard the telling of the dream and its interpretation, he worshiped; and he returned to the camp of Israel, and said, "Get up; for the LORD has given the army of Midian into your hand." [16]After he divided the three hundred men into three companies, and put trumpets into the hands of all of them, and empty jars, with torches inside the jars, [17]he said to them, "Look at me, and do the same; when I come to the outskirts of the camp, do as I do. [18]When I blow the trumpet, I and all who are with me, then you also blow the trumpets around the whole camp, and shout, 'For the LORD and for Gideon!' "

19 So Gideon and the hundred who were with him came to the outskirts of the camp at the beginning of the middle watch, when they had just set the watch; and they blew the trumpets and smashed the jars that were in their hands. [20]So the three companies blew the trumpets and broke the jars, holding in their left hands the torches, and in their right hands the trumpets to blow; and they cried, "A sword for the LORD and for Gideon!" [21]Every man stood in his place all around the camp, and all the men in camp ran; they cried out and fled. [22]When they blew the three hundred trumpets, the LORD set every man's sword against his fellow and against all the army; and the army fled as far as Beth-shittah toward Zererah,[z] as far as the border of Abel-meholah, by Tabbath. [23]And the men of Israel were called out from Naphtali and from Asher and from all Manasseh, and they pursued after the Midianites.

24 Then Gideon sent messengers throughout all the hill country of Ephraim, saying, "Come down against the Midianites and seize the waters against them, as far as Beth-barah, and also the Jordan." So all the men of Ephraim were called out, and they seized the waters as far as Beth-barah, and also the Jordan. [25]They captured the two captains of Midian, Oreb and Zeeb; they killed Oreb at the rock of Oreb, and Zeeb they killed at the wine press of Zeeb, as they pursued the Midianites. They brought the heads of Oreb and Zeeb to Gideon beyond the Jordan.

Gideon's Triumph and Vengeance

8 Then the Ephraimites said to him, "What have you done to us, not to call us when you went to fight against the Midianites?" And they upbraided him violently. [2]So he said to them, "What have I done now in com-

---

x Heb places the words *putting their hands to their mouths* after the word *lapped* in verse 6
y Cn: Heb *So the people took provisions in their hands*   z Another reading is *Zeredah*

parison with you? Is not the gleaning of the grapes of Ephraim better than the vintage of Abiezer? 3God has given into your hands the captains of Midian, Oreb and Zeeb; what have I been able to do in comparison with you?" When he said this, their anger against him subsided.

4 Then Gideon came to the Jordan and crossed over, he and the three hundred who were with him, exhausted and famished.a 5So he said to the people of Succoth, "Please give some loaves of bread to my followers, for they are exhausted, and I am pursuing Zebah and Zalmunna, the kings of Midian." 6But the officials of Succoth said, "Do you already have in your possession the hands of Zebah and Zalmunna, that we should give bread to your army?" 7Gideon replied, "Well then, when the LORD has given Zebah and Zalmunna into my hand, I will trample your flesh on the thorns of the wilderness and on briers." 8From there he went up to Penuel, and made the same request of them; and the people of Penuel answered him as the people of Succoth had answered. 9So he said to the people of Penuel, "When I come back victorious, I will break down this tower."

10 Now Zebah and Zalmunna were in Karkor with their army, about fifteen thousand men, all who were left of all the army of the people of the east; for one hundred twenty thousand men bearing arms had fallen. 11So Gideon went up by the caravan route east of Nobah and Jogbehah, and attacked the army; for the army was off its guard. 12Zebah and Zalmunna fled; and he pursued them and took the two kings of Midian, Zebah and Zalmunna, and threw all the army into a panic.

13 When Gideon son of Joash returned from the battle by the ascent of Heres, 14he caught a young man, one of the people of Succoth, and questioned him; and he listed for him the officials and elders of Succoth, seventy-seven people. 15Then he came to the people of Succoth, and said, "Here are Zebah and Zalmunna, about whom you taunted me, saying, 'Do you already have in your possession the hands of Zebah and Zalmunna, that we should give bread to your troops who are exhausted?' " 16So he took the elders of the city and he took thorns of the wilderness and briers and with them he trampledb the people of Succoth. 17He also broke down the tower of Penuel, and killed the men of the city.

18 Then he said to Zebah and Zalmunna, "What about the men whom you killed at Tabor?" They answered, "As you are, so were they, every one of them; they resembled the sons of a king." 19And he replied, "They were my brothers, the sons of my mother; as the LORD lives, if you had saved them alive, I would not kill you." 20So he said to Jether his firstborn, "Go kill them!" But the boy did not draw his sword, for he was afraid, because he was still a boy. 21Then Zebah and Zalmunna said, "You come and kill us; for as the man is, so is his strength." So Gideon proceeded to kill Zebah and Zalmunna; and he took the crescents that were on the necks of their camels.

Gideon's Idolatry

22 Then the Israelites said to Gideon, "Rule over us, you and your son and your grandson also; for you have delivered us out of the hand of Midian." 23Gideon said to them, "I will not rule over you, and my son will not rule over you; the LORD will rule over you." 24Then Gideon said to them, "Let me make a request of you; each of you give me an earring he has taken as booty." (For the enemyc had golden earrings, because they were Ishmaelites.) 25"We will willingly give them," they answered. So they spread a garment, and each threw into it an earring he had taken as booty. 26The weight of the golden earrings that he requested was one thousand seven hundred shekels of gold (apart from the crescents and the pendants and the purple garments worn by the kings of Midian, and the collars that were on the necks of their camels). 27Gideon made an ephod of it and put it in his town, in Ophrah; and all Israel prostituted themselves to it there, and it became a snare to Gideon and to his family. 28So Midian was subdued before the Israelites, and they lifted up their

a Gk: Heb pursuing   b With verse 7, Compare Gk: Heb he taught   c Heb they

heads no more. So the land had rest forty years in the days of Gideon.

Death of Gideon

29 Jerubbaal son of Joash went to live in his own house. 30Now Gideon had seventy sons, his own offspring, for he had many wives. 31His concubine who was in Shechem also bore him a son, and he named him Abimelech. 32Then Gideon son of Joash died at a good old age, and was buried in the tomb of his father Joash at Ophrah of the Abiezrites.

33 As soon as Gideon died, the Israelites relapsed and prostituted themselves with the Baals, making Baal-berith their god. 34The Israelites did not remember the LORD their God, who had rescued them from the hand of all their enemies on every side; 35and they did not exhibit loyalty to the house of Jerubbaal (that is, Gideon) in return for all the good that he had done to Israel.

Abimelech Attempts to Establish a Monarchy

9 Now Abimelech son of Jerubbaal went to Shechem to his mother's kinsfolk and said to them and to the whole clan of his mother's family, 2"Say in the hearing of all the lords of Shechem, 'Which is better for you, that all seventy of the sons of Jerubbaal rule over you, or that one rule over you?' Remember also that I am your bone and your flesh." 3So his mother's kinsfolk spoke all these words on his behalf in the hearing of all the lords of Shechem; and their hearts inclined to follow Abimelech, for they said, "He is our brother." 4They gave him seventy pieces of silver out of the temple of Baal-berith with which Abimelech hired worthless and reckless fellows, who followed him. 5He went to his father's house at Ophrah, and killed his brothers the sons of Jerubbaal, seventy men, on one stone; but Jotham, the youngest son of Jerubbaal, survived, for he hid himself. 6Then all the lords of Shechem and all Beth-millo came together, and they went and made Abimelech king, by the oak of the pillard at Shechem.

d Cn: Meaning of Heb uncertain

The Parable of the Trees

7 When it was told to Jotham, he went and stood on the top of Mount Gerizim, and cried aloud and said to them, "Listen to me, you lords of Shechem, so that God may listen to you.
8   The trees once went out
        to anoint a king over themselves.
     So they said to the olive tree,
        'Reign over us.'
9   The olive tree answered them,
        'Shall I stop producing my rich oil
        by which gods and mortals are
           honored,
        and go to sway over the trees?'
10   Then the trees said to the fig tree,
        'You come and reign over us.'
11   But the fig tree answered them,
        'Shall I stop producing my
           sweetness
        and my delicious fruit,
        and go to sway over the trees?'
12   Then the trees said to the vine,
        'You come and reign over us.'
13   But the vine said to them,
        'Shall I stop producing my wine
        that cheers gods and mortals,
        and go to sway over the trees?'
14   So all the trees said to the bramble,
        'You come and reign over us.'
15   And the bramble said to the trees,
        'If in good faith you are anointing
           me king over you,
        then come and take refuge in
           my shade;
        but if not, let fire come out of the
           bramble
        and devour the cedars of
           Lebanon.'
16 "Now therefore, if you acted in good faith and honor when you made Abimelech king, and if you have dealt well with Jerubbaal and his house, and have done to him as his actions deserved— 17for my father fought for you, and risked his life, and rescued you from the hand of Midian; 18but you have risen up against my father's house this day, and have killed his sons, seventy men on one stone, and have made Abimelech, the son of his slave woman, king over the lords of Shechem, because he is your kinsman— 19if, I say, you have acted in good faith and honor with Jerubbaal and with his house this day, then rejoice in

Abimelech, and let him also rejoice in you; **20** but if not, let fire come out from Abimelech, and devour the lords of Shechem, and Beth-millo; and let fire come out from the lords of Shechem, and from Beth-millo, and devour Abimelech." **21** Then Jotham ran away and fled, going to Beer, where he remained for fear of his brother Abimelech.

The Downfall of Abimelech

22 Abimelech ruled over Israel three years. **23** But God sent an evil spirit between Abimelech and the lords of Shechem; and the lords of Shechem dealt treacherously with Abimelech. **24** This happened so that the violence done to the seventy sons of Jerubbaal might be avenged*e* and their blood be laid on their brother Abimelech, who killed them, and on the lords of Shechem, who strengthened his hands to kill his brothers. **25** So, out of hostility to him, the lords of Shechem set ambushes on the mountain tops. They robbed all who passed by them along that way; and it was reported to Abimelech.

26 When Gaal son of Ebed moved into Shechem with his kinsfolk, the lords of Shechem put confidence in him. **27** They went out into the field and gathered the grapes from their vineyards, trod them, and celebrated. Then they went into the temple of their god, ate and drank, and ridiculed Abimelech. **28** Gaal son of Ebed said, "Who is Abimelech, and who are we of Shechem, that we should serve him? Did not the son of Jerubbaal and Zebul his officer serve the men of Hamor father of Shechem? Why then should we serve him? **29** If only this people were under my command! Then I would remove Abimelech; I would say*f* to him, 'Increase your army, and come out.' "

30 When Zebul the ruler of the city heard the words of Gaal son of Ebed, his anger was kindled. **31** He sent messengers to Abimelech at Arumah,*g* saying, "Look, Gaal son of Ebed and his kinsfolk have come to Shechem, and they are stirring up*h* the city against you. **32** Now therefore, go by night, you and the troops that are with you, and lie in wait in the fields. **33** Then early in the morning, as soon as the sun rises, get up and rush on the city; and when he and the troops that are with him come out against you, you may deal with them as best you can."

34 So Abimelech and all the troops with him got up by night and lay in wait against Shechem in four companies. **35** When Gaal son of Ebed went out and stood in the entrance of the gate of the city, Abimelech and the troops with him rose from the ambush. **36** And when Gaal saw them, he said to Zebul, "Look, people are coming down from the mountain tops!" And Zebul said to him, "The shadows on the mountains look like people to you." **37** Gaal spoke again and said, "Look, people are coming down from Tabbur-erez, and one company is coming from the direction of Elon-meonenim."*i* **38** Then Zebul said to him, "Where is your boast*j* now, you who said, 'Who is Abimelech, that we should serve him?' Are not these the troops you made light of? Go out now and fight with them." **39** So Gaal went out at the head of the lords of Shechem, and fought with Abimelech. **40** Abimelech chased him, and he fled before him. Many fell wounded, up to the entrance of the gate. **41** So Abimelech resided at Arumah; and Zebul drove out Gaal and his kinsfolk, so that they could not live on at Shechem.

42 On the following day the people went out into the fields. When Abimelech was told, **43** he took his troops and divided them into three companies, and lay in wait in the fields. When he looked and saw the people coming out of the city, he rose against them and killed them. **44** Abimelech and the company that was*k* with him rushed forward and stood at the entrance of the gate of the city, while the two companies rushed on all who were in the fields and killed them. **45** Abimelech fought against the city all that day; he took the city, and killed the people that were in it; and he razed the city and sowed it with salt.

46 When all the lords of the Tower of Shechem heard of it, they entered the stronghold of the temple of El-berith.

e Heb *might come*   *f* Gk: Heb *and he said*   *g* Cn See 9.41. Heb *Tormah*   *h* Cn: Heb *are besieging*
i That is *Diviners' Oak*   *j* Heb *mouth*   *k* Vg and some Gk Mss: Heb *companies that were*

47Abimelech was told that all the lords of the Tower of Shechem were gathered together. **48**So Abimelech went up to Mount Zalmon, he and all the troops that were with him. Abimelech took an ax in his hand, cut down a bundle of brushwood, and took it up and laid it on his shoulder. Then he said to the troops with him, "What you have seen me do, do quickly, as I have done." **49**So every one of the troops cut down a bundle and following Abimelech put it against the stronghold, and they set the stronghold on fire over them, so that all the people of the Tower of Shechem also died, about a thousand men and women.

50 Then Abimelech went to Thebez, and encamped against Thebez, and took it. **51**But there was a strong tower within the city, and all the men and women and all the lords of the city fled to it and shut themselves in; and they went to the roof of the tower. **52**Abimelech came to the tower, and fought against it, and came near to the entrance of the tower to burn it with fire. **53**But a certain woman threw an upper millstone on Abimelech's head, and crushed his skull. **54**Immediately he called to the young man who carried his armor and said to him, "Draw your sword and kill me, so people will not say about me, 'A woman killed him.'" So the young man thrust him through, and he died. **55**When the Israelites saw that Abimelech was dead, they all went home. **56**Thus God repaid Abimelech for the crime he committed against his father in killing his seventy brothers; **57**and God also made all the wickedness of the people of Shechem fall back on their heads, and on them came the curse of Jotham son of Jerubbaal.

Tola and Jair

10 After Abimelech, Tola son of Puah son of Dodo, a man of Issachar, who lived at Shamir in the hill country of Ephraim, rose to deliver Israel. **2**He judged Israel twenty-three years. Then he died, and was buried at Shamir.

3 After him came Jair the Gileadite, who judged Israel twenty-two years. **4**He had thirty sons who rode on thirty donkeys; and they had thirty towns, which are in the land of Gilead, and are called Havvoth-jair to this day. **5**Jair died, and was buried in Kamon.

Oppression by the Ammonites

6 The Israelites again did what was evil in the sight of the LORD, worshiping the Baals and the Astartes, the gods of Aram, the gods of Sidon, the gods of Moab, the gods of the Ammonites, and the gods of the Philistines. Thus they abandoned the LORD, and did not worship him. **7**So the anger of the LORD was kindled against Israel, and he sold them into the hand of the Philistines and into the hand of the Ammonites, **8**and they crushed and oppressed the Israelites that year. For eighteen years they oppressed all the Israelites that were beyond the Jordan in the land of the Amorites, which is in Gilead. **9**The Ammonites also crossed the Jordan to fight against Judah and against Benjamin and against the house of Ephraim; so that Israel was greatly distressed.

10 So the Israelites cried to the LORD, saying, "We have sinned against you, because we have abandoned our God and have worshiped the Baals." **11**And the LORD said to the Israelites, "Did I not deliver you[1] from the Egyptians and from the Amorites, from the Ammonites and from the Philistines? **12**The Sidonians also, and the Amalekites, and the Maonites, oppressed you; and you cried to me, and I delivered you out of their hand. **13**Yet you have abandoned me and worshiped other gods; therefore I will deliver you no more. **14**Go and cry to the gods whom you have chosen; let them deliver you in the time of your distress." **15**And the Israelites said to the LORD, "We have sinned; do to us whatever seems good to you; but deliver us this day!" **16**So they put away the foreign gods from among them and worshiped the LORD; and he could no longer bear to see Israel suffer.

17 Then the Ammonites were called to arms, and they encamped in Gilead; and the Israelites came together, and they encamped at Mizpah. **18**The commanders of the people of Gilead said to one another, "Who will begin the fight

1 Heb lacks *Did I not deliver you*

against the Ammonites? He shall be head over all the inhabitants of Gilead."

Jephthah

11 Now Jephthah the Gileadite, the son of a prostitute, was a mighty warrior. Gilead was the father of Jephthah. ²Gilead's wife also bore him sons; and when his wife's sons grew up, they drove Jephthah away, saying to him, "You shall not inherit anything in our father's house; for you are the son of another woman." ³Then Jephthah fled from his brothers and lived in the land of Tob. Outlaws collected around Jephthah and went raiding with him.

4 After a time the Ammonites made war against Israel. ⁵And when the Ammonites made war against Israel, the elders of Gilead went to bring Jephthah from the land of Tob. ⁶They said to Jephthah, "Come and be our commander, so that we may fight with the Ammonites." ⁷But Jephthah said to the elders of Gilead, "Are you not the very ones who rejected me and drove me out of my father's house? So why do you come to me now when you are in trouble?" ⁸The elders of Gilead said to Jephthah, "Nevertheless, we have now turned back to you, so that you may go with us and fight with the Ammonites, and become head over us, over all the inhabitants of Gilead." ⁹Jephthah said to the elders of Gilead, "If you bring me home again to fight with the Ammonites, and the LORD gives them over to me, I will be your head." ¹⁰And the elders of Gilead said to Jephthah, "The LORD will be witness between us; we will surely do as you say." ¹¹So Jephthah went with the elders of Gilead, and the people made him head and commander over them; and Jephthah spoke all his words before the LORD at Mizpah.

12 Then Jephthah sent messengers to the king of the Ammonites and said, "What is there between you and me, that you have come to me to fight against my land?" ¹³The king of the Ammonites answered the messengers of Jephthah, "Because Israel, on coming from Egypt, took away my land from the Arnon to the Jabbok and to the Jordan; now therefore restore it peaceably."

¹⁴Once again Jephthah sent messengers to the king of the Ammonites ¹⁵and said to him: "Thus says Jephthah: Israel did not take away the land of Moab or the land of the Ammonites, ¹⁶but when they came up from Egypt, Israel went through the wilderness to the Red Sea*ᵐ* and came to Kadesh. ¹⁷Israel then sent messengers to the king of Edom, saying, 'Let us pass through your land'; but the king of Edom would not listen. They also sent to the king of Moab, but he would not consent. So Israel remained at Kadesh. ¹⁸Then they journeyed through the wilderness, went around the land of Edom and the land of Moab, arrived on the east side of the land of Moab, and camped on the other side of the Arnon. They did not enter the territory of Moab, for the Arnon was the boundary of Moab. ¹⁹Israel then sent messengers to King Sihon of the Amorites, king of Heshbon; and Israel said to him, 'Let us pass through your land to our country.' ²⁰But Sihon did not trust Israel to pass through his territory; so Sihon gathered all his people together, and encamped at Jahaz, and fought with Israel. ²¹Then the LORD, the God of Israel, gave Sihon and all his people into the hand of Israel, and they defeated them; so Israel occupied all the land of the Amorites, who inhabited that country. ²²They occupied all the territory of the Amorites from the Arnon to the Jabbok and from the wilderness to the Jordan. ²³So now the LORD, the God of Israel, has conquered the Amorites for the benefit of his people Israel. Do you intend to take their place? ²⁴Should you not possess what your god Chemosh gives you to possess? And should we not be the ones to possess everything that the LᴄRD our God has conquered for our benefit? ²⁵Now are you any better than King Balak son of Zippor of Moab? Did he ever enter into conflict with Israel, or did he ever go to war with them? ²⁶While Israel lived in Heshbon and its villages, and in Aroer and its villages, and in all the towns that are along the Arnon, three hundred years, why did you not recover them within that time? ²⁷It is not I who have sinned against you, but you are the one who does me wrong by making war

---

m Or Sea of Reeds

on me. Let the LORD, who is judge, decide today for the Israelites or for the Ammonites." 28But the king of the Ammonites did not heed the message that Jephthah sent him.

Jephthah's Vow

29 Then the spirit of the LORD came upon Jephthah, and he passed through Gilead and Manasseh. He passed on to Mizpah of Gilead, and from Mizpah of Gilead he passed on to the Ammonites. 30And Jephthah made a vow to the LORD, and said, "If you will give the Ammonites into my hand, 31then whoever comes out of the doors of my house to meet me, when I return victorious from the Ammonites, shall be the LORD's, to be offered up by me as a burnt offering." 32So Jephthah crossed over to the Ammonites to fight against them; and the LORD gave them into his hand. 33He inflicted a massive defeat on them from Aroer to the neighborhood of Minnith, twenty towns, and as far as Abel-keramim. So the Ammonites were subdued before the people of Israel.

Jephthah's Daughter

34 Then Jephthah came to his home at Mizpah; and there was his daughter coming out to meet him with timbrels and with dancing. She was his only child; he had no son or daughter except her. 35When he saw her, he tore his clothes, and said, "Alas, my daughter! You have brought me very low; you have become the cause of great trouble to me. For I have opened my mouth to the LORD, and I cannot take back my vow." 36She said to him, "My father, if you have opened your mouth to the LORD, do to me according to what has gone out of your mouth, now that the LORD has given you vengeance against your enemies, the Ammonites." 37And she said to her father, "Let this thing be done for me: Grant me two months, so that I may go and wander[n] on the mountains, and bewail my virginity, my companions and I." 38"Go," he said and sent her away for two months. So she departed, she and her companions, and bewailed her virginity on the moun-

tains. 39At the end of two months, she returned to her father, who did with her according to the vow he had made. She had never slept with a man. So there arose an Israelite custom that 40for four days every year the daughters of Israel would go out to lament the daughter of Jephthah the Gileadite.

Intertribal Dissension

12 The men of Ephraim were called to arms, and they crossed to Zaphon and said to Jephthah, "Why did you cross over to fight against the Ammonites, and did not call us to go with you? We will burn your house down over you!" 2Jephthah said to them, "My people and I were engaged in conflict with the Ammonites who oppressed us[o] severely. But when I called you, you did not deliver me from their hand. 3When I saw that you would not deliver me, I took my life in my hand, and crossed over against the Ammonites, and the LORD gave them into my hand. Why then have you come up to me this day, to fight against me?" 4Then Jephthah gathered all the men of Gilead and fought with Ephraim; and the men of Gilead defeated Ephraim, because they said, "You are fugitives from Ephraim, you Gileadites—in the heart of Ephraim and Manasseh."[p] 5Then the Gileadites took the fords of the Jordan against the Ephraimites. Whenever one of the fugitives of Ephraim said, "Let me go over," the men of Gilead would say to him, "Are you an Ephraimite?" When he said, "No," 6they said to him, "Then say Shibboleth," and he said, "Sibboleth," for he could not pronounce it right. Then they seized him and killed him at the fords of the Jordan. Forty-two thousand of the Ephraimites fell at that time.

7 Jephthah judged Israel six years. Then Jephthah the Gileadite died, and was buried in his town in Gilead.[q]

Ibzan, Elon, and Abdon

8 After him Ibzan of Bethlehem judged Israel. 9He had thirty sons. He gave his thirty daughters in marriage outside his clan and brought in thirty

---

n Cn: Heb go down o Gk OL, Syr H: Heb lacks who oppressed us p Meaning of Heb uncertain: Gk omits because . . . Manasseh q Gk: Heb in the towns of Gilead

young women from outside for his sons. He judged Israel seven years. ¹⁰Then Ibzan died, and was buried at Bethlehem.

11 After him Elon the Zebulunite judged Israel; and he judged Israel ten years. ¹²Then Elon the Zebulunite died, and was buried at Aijalon in the land of Zebulun.

13 After him Abdon son of Hillel the Pirathonite judged Israel. ¹⁴He had forty sons and thirty grandsons, who rode on seventy donkeys; he judged Israel eight years. ¹⁵Then Abdon son of Hillel the Pirathonite died, and was buried at Pirathon in the land of Ephraim, in the hill country of the Amalekites.

The Birth of Samson

13 The Israelites again did what was evil in the sight of the LORD, and the LORD gave them into the hand of the Philistines forty years.

2 There was a certain man of Zorah, of the tribe of the Danites, whose name was Manoah. His wife was barren, having borne no children. ³And the angel of the LORD appeared to the woman and said to her, "Although you are barren, having borne no children, you shall conceive and bear a son. ⁴Now be careful not to drink wine or strong drink, or to eat anything unclean, ⁵for you shall conceive and bear a son. No razor is to come on his head, for the boy shall be a nazirite^r to God from birth. It is he who shall begin to deliver Israel from the hand of the Philistines." ⁶Then the woman came and told her husband, "A man of God came to me, and his appearance was like that of an angel^s of God, most awe-inspiring; I did not ask him where he came from, and he did not tell me his name; ⁷but he said to me, 'You shall conceive and bear a son. So then drink no wine or strong drink, and eat nothing unclean, for the boy shall be a nazirite^r to God from birth to the day of his death.' "

8 Then Manoah entreated the LORD, and said, "O LORD, I pray, let the man of God whom you sent come to us again and teach us what we are to do concerning the boy who will be born." ⁹God listened to Manoah, and the angel of God came again to the woman as she sat in the field; but her husband Manoah was not with her. ¹⁰So the woman ran quickly and told her husband, "The man who came to me the other day has appeared to me." ¹¹Manoah got up and followed his wife, and came to the man and said to him, "Are you the man who spoke to this woman?" And he said, "I am." ¹²Then Manoah said, "Now when your words come true, what is to be the boy's rule of life; what is he to do?" ¹³The angel of the LORD said to Manoah, "Let the woman give heed to all that I said to her. ¹⁴She may not eat of anything that comes from the vine. She is not to drink wine or strong drink, or eat any unclean thing. She is to observe everything that I commanded her."

15 Manoah said to the angel of the LORD, "Allow us to detain you, and prepare a kid for you." ¹⁶The angel of the LORD said to Manoah, "If you detain me, I will not eat your food; but if you want to prepare a burnt offering, then offer it to the LORD." (For Manoah did not know that he was the angel of the LORD.) ¹⁷Then Manoah said to the angel of the LORD, "What is your name, so that we may honor you when your words come true?" ¹⁸But the angel of the LORD said to him, "Why do you ask my name? It is too wonderful."

19 So Manoah took the kid with the grain offering, and offered it on the rock to the LORD, to him who works^t wonders.^u ²⁰When the flame went up toward heaven from the altar, the angel of the LORD ascended in the flame of the altar while Manoah and his wife looked on; and they fell on their faces to the ground. ²¹The angel of the LORD did not appear again to Manoah and his wife. Then Manoah realized that it was the angel of the LORD. ²²And Manoah said to his wife, "We shall surely die, for we have seen God." ²³But his wife said to him, "If the LORD had meant to kill us, he would not have accepted a burnt offering and a grain offering at our hands, or shown us all these things, or now announced to us such things as these."

24 The woman bore a son, and named him Samson. The boy grew, and

r That is one separated or one consecrated   s Or the angel   t Gk Vg: Heb and working
u Heb wonders, while Manoah and his wife looked on

the LORD blessed him. 25The spirit of the LORD began to stir him in Mahaneh-dan, between Zorah and Eshtaol.

Samson's Marriage

14 Once Samson went down to Timnah, and at Timnah he saw a Philistine woman. 2Then he came up, and told his father and mother, "I saw a Philistine woman at Timnah; now get her for me as my wife." 3But his father and mother said to him, "Is there not a woman among your kin, or among all our\ *v* people, that you must go to take a wife from the uncircumcised Philistines?" But Samson said to his father, "Get her for me, because she pleases me." 4His father and mother did not know that this was from the LORD; for he was seeking a pretext to act against the Philistines. At that time the Philistines had dominion over Israel.

5 Then Samson went down with his father and mother to Timnah. When he came to the vineyards of Timnah, suddenly a young lion roared at him. 6The spirit of the LORD rushed on him, and he tore the lion apart barehanded as one might tear apart a kid. But he did not tell his father or his mother what he had done. 7Then he went down and talked with the woman, and she pleased Samson. 8After a while he returned to marry her, and he turned aside to see the carcass of the lion, and there was a swarm of bees in the body of the lion, and honey. 9He scraped it out into his hands, and went on, eating as he went. When he came to his father and mother, he gave some to them, and they ate it. But he did not tell them that he had taken the honey from the carcass of the lion.

10 His father went down to the woman, and Samson made a feast there as the young men were accustomed to do. 11When the people saw him, they brought thirty companions to be with him. 12Samson said to them, "Let me now put a riddle to you. If you can explain it to me within the seven days of the feast, and find it out, then I will give you thirty linen garments and thirty festal garments. 13But if you cannot explain it to me, then you shall give me thirty linen garments and thirty festal gar-

ments." So they said to him, "Ask your riddle; let us hear it." 14He said to them,
"Out of the eater came something
      to eat.
Out of the strong came something
      sweet."
But for three days they could not explain the riddle.

15 On the fourth\ *w* day they said to Samson's wife, "Coax your husband to explain the riddle to us, or we will burn you and your father's house with fire. Have you invited us here to impoverish us?" 16So Samson's wife wept before him, saying, "You hate me; you do not really love me. You have asked a riddle of my people, but you have not explained it to me." He said to her, "Look, I have not told my father or my mother. Why should I tell you?" 17She wept before him the seven days that their feast lasted; and because she nagged him, on the seventh day he told her. Then she explained the riddle to her people. 18The men of the town said to him on the seventh day before the sun went down,
"What is sweeter than honey?
What is stronger than a lion?"
And he said to them,
"If you had not plowed with my
      heifer,
you would not have found out my
      riddle."
19Then the spirit of the LORD rushed on him, and he went down to Ashkelon. He killed thirty men of the town, took their spoil, and gave the festal garments to those who had explained the riddle. In hot anger he went back to his father's house. 20And Samson's wife was given to his companion, who had been his best man.

Samson Defeats the Philistines

15 After a while, at the time of the wheat harvest, Samson went to visit his wife, bringing along a kid. He said, "I want to go into my wife's room." But her father would not allow him to go in. 2Her father said, "I was sure that you had rejected her; so I gave her to your companion. Is not her younger sister prettier than she? Why not take her instead?" 3Samson said to them, "This

v Cn: Heb *my*   *w* Gk Syr: Heb *seventh*

time, when I do mischief to the Philistines, I will be without blame." [4]So Samson went and caught three hundred foxes, and took some torches; and he turned the foxes[x] tail to tail, and put a torch between each pair of tails. [5]When he had set fire to the torches, he let the foxes go into the standing grain of the Philistines, and burned up the shocks and the standing grain, as well as the vineyards and[y] olive groves. [6]Then the Philistines asked, "Who has done this?" And they said, "Samson, the son-in-law of the Timnite, because he has taken Samson's wife and given her to his companion." So the Philistines came up, and burned her and her father. [7]Samson said to them, "If this is what you do, I swear I will not stop until I have taken revenge on you." [8]He struck them down hip and thigh with great slaughter; and he went down and stayed in the cleft of the rock of Etam.

9 Then the Philistines came up and encamped in Judah, and made a raid on Lehi. [10]The men of Judah said, "Why have you come up against us?" They said, "We have come up to bind Samson, to do to him as he did to us." [11]Then three thousand men of Judah went down to the cleft of the rock of Etam, and they said to Samson, "Do you not know that the Philistines are rulers over us? What then have you done to us?" He replied, "As they did to me, so I have done to them." [12]They said to him, "We have come down to bind you, so that we may give you into the hands of the Philistines." Samson answered them, "Swear to me that you yourselves will not attack me." [13]They said to him, "No, we will only bind you and give you into their hands; we will not kill you." So they bound him with two new ropes, and brought him up from the rock.

14 When he came to Lehi, the Philistines came shouting to meet him; and the spirit of the LORD rushed on him, and the ropes that were on his arms became like flax that has caught fire, and his bonds melted off his hands. [15]Then he found a fresh jawbone of a donkey, reached down and took it, and with it he killed a thousand men. [16]And Samson said,

"With the jawbone of a donkey,
    heaps upon heaps,
with the jawbone of a donkey
    I have slain a thousand men."

[17]When he had finished speaking, he threw away the jawbone; and that place was called Ramath-lehi.[z]

18 By then he was very thirsty, and he called on the LORD, saying, "You have granted this great victory by the hand of your servant. Am I now to die of thirst, and fall into the hands of the uncircumcised?" [19]So God split open the hollow place that is at Lehi, and water came from it. When he drank, his spirit returned, and he revived. Therefore it was named En-hakkore,[a] which is at Lehi to this day. [20]And he judged Israel in the days of the Philistines twenty years.

Samson and Delilah

16 Once Samson went to Gaza, where he saw a prostitute and went in to her. [2]The Gazites were told,[b] "Samson has come here." So they circled around and lay in wait for him all night at the city gate. They kept quiet all night, thinking, "Let us wait until the light of the morning; then we will kill him." [3]But Samson lay only until midnight. Then at midnight he rose up, took hold of the doors of the city gate and the two posts, pulled them up, bar and all, put them on his shoulders, and carried them to the top of the hill that is in front of Hebron.

4 After this he fell in love with a woman in the valley of Sorek, whose name was Delilah. [5]The lords of the Philistines came to her and said to her, "Coax him, and find out what makes his strength so great, and how we may overpower him, so that we may bind him in order to subdue him; and we will each give you eleven hundred pieces of silver." [6]So Delilah said to Samson, "Please tell me what makes your strength so great, and how you could be bound, so that one could subdue you." [7]Samson said to her, "If they bind me with seven fresh bowstrings that are not

x Heb them   y Gk Tg Vg: Heb lacks and   z That is The Hill of the Jawbone   a That is The Spring of the One who Called   b Gk: Heb lacks were told

dried out, then I shall become weak, and be like anyone else." ⁸Then the lords of the Philistines brought her seven fresh bowstrings that had not dried out, and she bound him with them. ⁹While men were lying in wait in an inner chamber, she said to him, "The Philistines are upon you, Samson!" But he snapped the bowstrings, as a strand of fiber snaps when it touches the fire. So the secret of his strength was not known.

10 Then Delilah said to Samson, "You have mocked me and told me lies; please tell me how you could be bound." ¹¹He said to her, "If they bind me with new ropes that have not been used, then I shall become weak, and be like anyone else." ¹²So Delilah took new ropes and bound him with them, and said to him, "The Philistines are upon you, Samson!" (The men lying in wait were in an inner chamber.) But he snapped the ropes off his arms like a thread.

13 Then Delilah said to Samson, "Until now you have mocked me and told me lies; tell me how you could be bound." He said to her, "If you weave the seven locks of my head with the web and make it tight with the pin, then I shall become weak, and be like anyone else." ¹⁴So while he slept, Delilah took the seven locks of his head and wove them into the web,ᶜ and made them tight with the pin. Then she said to him, "The Philistines are upon you, Samson!" But he awoke from his sleep, and pulled away the pin, the loom, and the web.

15 Then she said to him, "How can you say, 'I love you,' when your heart is not with me? You have mocked me three times now and have not told me what makes your strength so great." ¹⁶Finally, after she had nagged him with her words day after day, and pestered him, he was tired to death. ¹⁷So he told her his whole secret, and said to her, "A razor has never come upon my head; for I have been a naziriteᵈ to God from my mother's womb. If my head were shaved, then my strength would leave me; I would become weak, and be like anyone else."

18 When Delilah realized that he had told her his whole secret, she sent and called the lords of the Philistines, saying, "This time come up, for he has told his whole secret to me." Then the lords of the Philistines came up to her, and brought the money in their hands. ¹⁹She let him fall asleep on her lap; and she called a man, and had him shave off the seven locks of his head. He began to weaken,ᵉ and his strength left him.

TO KEEP YOUR SECRET IS WISDOM; BUT TO EXPECT OTHERS TO KEEP IT IS FOOLISH.

—*Samuel Johnson*

---

²⁰Then she said, "The Philistines are upon you, Samson!" When he awoke from his sleep, he thought, "I will go out as at other times, and shake myself free." But he did not know that the LORD had left him. ²¹So the Philistines seized him and gouged out his eyes. They brought him down to Gaza and bound him with bronze shackles; and he ground at the mill in the prison. ²²But the hair of his head began to grow again after it had been shaved.

Samson's Death

23 Now the lords of the Philistines gathered to offer a great sacrifice to their god Dagon, and to rejoice; for they said, "Our god has given Samson our enemy into our hand." ²⁴When the people saw him, they praised their god; for they said, "Our god has given our enemy into our hand, the ravager of our country, who has killed many of us." ²⁵And when their hearts were merry, they said, "Call Samson, and let him entertain us." So they called Samson out of the prison, and he performed for them. They made him stand between the pillars; ²⁶and Samson said to the attendant who held him by the hand, "Let me feel the pillars on which the house rests, so that I may lean against them." ²⁷Now the house was full of men and women; all the lords of the Philistines were there, and on the roof there were about three thousand men and women, who looked on while Samson performed.

28 Then Samson called to the LORD

---

c Compare Gk: in verses 13-14, Heb lacks *and make it tight . . . into the web*　　d That is *one separated or one consecrated*　　e Gk: Heb *She began to torment him* and said, "Lord GOD, remember me and strengthen me only this once, O God, so that with this one act of revenge I may pay back the Philistines for my two eyes."*f* 29 And Samson grasped the two middle pillars on which the house rested, and he leaned his weight against them, his right hand on the one and his left hand on the other. 30 Then Samson said, "Let me die with the Philistines." He strained with all his might; and the house fell on the lords and all the people who were in it. So those he killed at his death were more than those he had killed during his life. 31 Then his brothers and all his family came down and took him and brought him up and buried him between Zorah and Eshtaol in the tomb of his father Manoah. He had judged Israel twenty years.

Micah and the Levite

17 There was a man in the hill country of Ephraim whose name was Micah. 2 He said to his mother, "The eleven hundred pieces of silver that were taken from you, about which you uttered a curse, and even spoke it in my hearing,—that silver is in my possession; I took it; but now I will return it to you."*g* And his mother said, "May my son be blessed by the LORD!" 3 Then he returned the eleven hundred pieces of silver to his mother; and his mother said, "I consecrate the silver to the LORD from my hand for my son, to make an idol of cast metal." 4 So when he returned the money to his mother, his mother took two hundred pieces of silver, and gave it to the silversmith, who made it into an idol of cast metal; and it was in the house of Micah. 5 This man Micah had a shrine, and he made an ephod and teraphim, and installed one of his sons, who became his priest. 6 In those days there was no king in Israel; all the people did what was right in their own eyes.

7 Now there was a young man of Bethlehem in Judah, of the clan of Judah. He was a Levite residing there. 8 This man left the town of Bethlehem in Judah, to live wherever he could find a place. He came to the house of Micah in the hill country of Ephraim to carry on his work.*h* 9 Micah said to him, "From where do you come?" He replied, "I am a Levite of Bethlehem in Judah, and I am going to live wherever I can find a place." 10 Then Micah said to him, "Stay with me, and be to me a father and a priest, and I will give you ten pieces of silver a year, a set of clothes, and your living."*i* 11 The Levite agreed to stay with the man; and the young man became to him like one of his sons. 12 So Micah installed the Levite, and the young man became his priest, and was in the house of Micah. 13 Then Micah said, "Now I know that the LORD will prosper me, because the Levite has become my priest."

The Migration of Dan

18 In those days there was no king in Israel. And in those days the tribe of the Danites was seeking for itself a territory to live in; for until then no territory among the tribes of Israel had been allotted to them. 2 So the Danites sent five valiant men from the whole number of their clan, from Zorah and from Eshtaol, to spy out the land and to explore it; and they said to them, "Go, explore the land." When they came to the hill country of Ephraim, to the house of Micah, they stayed there. 3 While they were at Micah's house, they recognized the voice of the young Levite; so they went over and asked him, "Who brought you here? What are you doing in this place? What is your business here?" 4 He said to them, "Micah did such and such for me, and he hired me, and I have become his priest." 5 Then they said to him, "Inquire of God that we may know whether the mission we are undertaking will succeed." 6 The priest replied, "Go in peace. The mission you are on is under the eye of the LORD."

7 The five men went on, and when they came to Laish, they observed the people who were there living securely, after the manner of the Sidonians, quiet and unsuspecting, lacking*j* nothing on

---

f Or *so that I may be avenged upon the Philistines for one of my two eyes* *g* The words *but now I will return it to you* are transposed from the end of verse 3 in Heb *h* Or *Ephraim, continuing his journey* *i* Heb *living, and the Levite went* *j* Cn Compare 18.10: Meaning of Heb uncertain

earth, and possessing wealth.*k* Furthermore, they were far from the Sidonians and had no dealings with Aram.*l* 8When they came to their kinsfolk at Zorah and Eshtaol, they said to them, "What do you report?" 9They said, "Come, let us go up against them; for we have seen the land, and it is very good. Will you do nothing? Do not be slow to go, but enter in and possess the land. 10When you go, you will come to an unsuspecting people. The land is broad—God has indeed given it into your hands—a place where there is no lack of anything on earth."

11 Six hundred men of the Danite clan, armed with weapons of war, set out from Zorah and Eshtaol, 12and went up and encamped at Kiriath-jearim in Judah. On this account that place is called Mahaneh-dan*m* to this day; it is west of Kiriath-jearim. 13From there they passed on to the hill country of Ephraim, and came to the house of Micah.

14 Then the five men who had gone to spy out the land (that is, Laish) said to their comrades, "Do you know that in these buildings there are an ephod, teraphim, and an idol of cast metal? Now therefore consider what you will do." 15So they turned in that direction and came to the house of the young Levite, at the home of Micah, and greeted him. 16While the six hundred men of the Danites, armed with their weapons of war, stood by the entrance of the gate, 17the five men who had gone to spy out the land proceeded to enter and take the idol of cast metal, the ephod, and the teraphim.*n* The priest was standing by the entrance of the gate with the six hundred men armed with weapons of war. 18When the men went into Micah's house and took the idol of cast metal, the ephod, and the teraphim, the priest said to them, "What are you doing?" 19They said to him, "Keep quiet! Put your hand over your mouth, and come with us, and be to us a father and a priest. Is it better for you to be priest to the house of one person, or to be priest to a tribe and clan in Israel?" 20Then the priest accepted the offer. He took the ephod, the teraphim, and the idol, and went along with the people.

21 So they resumed their journey, putting the little ones, the livestock, and the goods in front of them. 22When they were some distance from the home of Micah, the men who were in the houses near Micah's house were called out, and they overtook the Danites. 23They shouted to the Danites, who turned around and said to Micah, "What is the matter that you come with such a company?" 24He replied, "You take my gods that I made, and the priest, and go away, and what have I left? How then can you ask me, 'What is the matter?' " 25And the Danites said to him, "You had better not let your voice be heard among us or else hot-tempered fellows will attack you, and you will lose your life and the lives of your household." 26Then the Danites went their way. When Micah saw that they were too strong for him, he turned and went back to his home.

The Danites Settle in Laish

27 The Danites, having taken what Micah had made, and the priest who belonged to him, came to Laish, to a people quiet and unsuspecting, put them to the sword, and burned down the city. 28There was no deliverer, because it was far from Sidon and they had no dealings with Aram.*o* It was in the valley that belongs to Beth-rehob. They rebuilt the city, and lived in it. 29They named the city Dan, after their ancestor Dan, who was born to Israel; but the name of the city was formerly Laish. 30Then the Danites set up the idol for themselves. Jonathan son of Gershom, son of Moses,*p* and his sons were priests to the tribe of the Danites until the time the land went into captivity. 31So they maintained as their own Micah's idol that he had made, as long as the house of God was at Shiloh.

The Levite's Concubine

19 In those days, when there was no king in Israel, a certain Levite, residing in the remote parts of

---

k Meaning of Heb uncertain   *l* Symmachus: Heb *with anyone*   *m* That is *Camp of Dan*
n Compare 17.4, 5; 18.14: Heb *teraphim and the cast metal*   *o* Cn Compare verse 7: Heb *with anyone*
p Another reading is *son of Manasseh*

the hill country of Ephraim, took to himself a concubine from Bethlehem in Judah. 2But his concubine became angry with*q* him, and she went away from him to her father's house at Bethlehem in Judah, and was there some four months. 3Then her husband set out after her, to speak tenderly to her and bring her back. He had with him his servant and a couple of donkeys. When he reached*r* her father's house, the girl's father saw him and came with joy to meet him. 4His father-in-law, the girl's father, made him stay, and he remained with him three days; so they ate and drank, and he*s* stayed there. 5On the fourth day they got up early in the morning, and he prepared to go; but the girl's father said to his son-in-law, "Fortify yourself with a bit of food, and after that you may go." 6So the two men sat and ate and drank together; and the girl's father said to the man, "Why not spend the night and enjoy yourself?" 7When the man got up to go, his father-in-law kept urging him until he spent the night there again. 8On the fifth day he got up early in the morning to leave; and the girl's father said, "Fortify yourself." So they lingered*t* until the day declined, and the two of them ate and drank.*u* 9When the man with his concubine and his servant got up to leave, his father-in-law, the girl's father, said to him, "Look, the day has worn on until it is almost evening. Spend the night. See, the day has drawn to a close. Spend the night here and enjoy yourself. Tomorrow you can get up early in the morning for your journey, and go home."

10 But the man would not spend the night; he got up and departed, and arrived opposite Jebus (that is, Jerusalem). He had with him a couple of saddled donkeys, and his concubine was with him. 11When they were near Jebus, the day was far spent, and the servant said to his master, "Come now, let us turn aside to this city of the Jebusites, and spend the night in it." 12But his master said to him, "We will not turn aside into a city of foreigners, who do not belong to the people of Israel; but we

will continue on to Gibeah." 13Then he said to his servant, "Come, let us try to reach one of these places, and spend the night at Gibeah or at Ramah." 14So they passed on and went their way; and the sun went down on them near Gibeah, which belongs to Benjamin. 15They turned aside there, to go in and spend the night at Gibeah. He went in and sat down in the open square of the city, but no one took them in to spend the night.

16 Then at evening there was an old man coming from his work in the field. The man was from the hill country of Ephraim, and he was residing in Gibeah. (The people of the place were Benjaminites.) 17When the old man looked up and saw the wayfarer in the open square of the city, he said, "Where are you going and where do you come from?" 18He answered him, "We are passing from Bethlehem in Judah to the remote parts of the hill country of Ephraim, from which I come. I went to Bethlehem in Judah; and I am going to my home.*v* Nobody has offered to take me in. 19We your servants have straw and fodder for our donkeys, with bread and wine for me and the woman and the young man along with us. We need nothing more." 20The old man said, "Peace be to you. I will care for all your wants; only do not spend the night in the square." 21So he brought him into his house, and fed the donkeys; they washed their feet, and ate and drank.

Gibeah's Crime

22 While they were enjoying themselves, the men of the city, a perverse lot, surrounded the house, and started pounding on the door. They said to the old man, the master of the house, "Bring out the man who came into your house, so that we may have intercourse with him." 23And the man, the master of the house, went out to them and said to them, "No, my brothers, do not act so wickedly. Since this man is my guest, do not do this vile thing. 24Here are my virgin daughter and his concubine; let me bring them out now. Ravish them and do whatever you want to them; but

---

q Gk OL: Heb *prostituted herself against*   *r* Gk: Heb *she brought him*   *s* Compare verse 7 and Gk: Heb *they*   *t* Cn: Heb *Linger*   *u* Gk: Heb lacks *and drank*   *v* Gk Compare 19.29. Heb *to the house of the* Lord

against this man do not do such a vile thing." 25But the men would not listen to him. So the man seized his concubine, and put her out to them. They wantonly raped her, and abused her all through the night until the morning. And as the dawn began to break, they let her go. 26As morning appeared, the woman came and fell down at the door of the man's house where her master was, until it was light.

27 In the morning her master got up, opened the doors of the house, and when he went out to go on his way, there was his concubine lying at the door of the house, with her hands on the threshold. 28"Get up," he said to her, "we are going." But there was no answer. Then he put her on the donkey; and the man set out for his home. 29When he had entered his house, he took a knife, and grasping his concubine he cut her into twelve pieces, limb by limb, and sent her throughout all the territory of Israel. 30Then he commanded the men whom he sent, saying, "Thus shall you say to all the Israelites, 'Has such a thing ever happenedʷ since the day that the Israelites came up from the land of Egypt until this day? Consider it, take counsel, and speak out.' "

The Other Tribes Attack Benjamin

20 Then all the Israelites came out, from Dan to Beer-sheba, including the land of Gilead, and the congregation assembled in one body before the LORD at Mizpah. 2The chiefs of all the people, of all the tribes of Israel, presented themselves in the assembly of the people of God, four hundred thousand foot-soldiers bearing arms. 3(Now the Benjaminites heard that the people of Israel had gone up to Mizpah.) And the Israelites said, "Tell us, how did this criminal act come about?" 4The Levite, the husband of the woman who was murdered, answered, "I came to Gibeah that belongs to Benjamin, I and my concubine, to spend the night. 5The lords of Gibeah rose up against me, and surrounded the house at night. They intended to kill me, and they raped my concubine until she died. 6Then I took

my concubine and cut her into pieces, and sent her throughout the whole extent of Israel's territory; for they have committed a vile outrage in Israel. 7So now, you Israelites, all of you, give your advice and counsel here."

8 All the people got up as one, saying, "We will not any of us go to our tents, nor will any of us return to our houses. 9But now this is what we will do to Gibeah: we will go upˣ against it by lot. 10We will take ten men of a hundred throughout all the tribes of Israel, and a hundred of a thousand, and a thousand of ten thousand, to bring provisions for the troops, who are going to repayʸ Gibeah of Benjamin for all the disgrace that they have done in Israel." 11So all the men of Israel gathered against the city, united as one.

12 The tribes of Israel sent men through all the tribe of Benjamin, saying, "What crime is this that has been committed among you? 13Now then, hand over those scoundrels in Gibeah, so that we may put them to death, and purge the evil from Israel." But the Benjaminites would not listen to their kinsfolk, the Israelites. 14The Benjaminites came together out of the towns to Gibeah, to go out to battle against the Israelites. 15On that day the Benjaminites mustered twenty-six thousand armed men from their towns, besides the inhabitants of Gibeah. 16Of all this force, there were seven hundred picked men who were left-handed; every one could sling a stone at a hair, and not miss. 17And the Israelites, apart from Benjamin, mustered four hundred thousand armed men, all of them warriors.

18 The Israelites proceeded to go up to Bethel, where they inquired of God, "Which of us shall go up first to battle against the Benjaminites?" And the LORD answered, "Judah shall go up first." 19 Then the Israelites got up in the morning, and encamped against Gibeah. 20The Israelites went out to battle against Benjamin; and the Israelites drew up the battle line against them at Gibeah. 21The Benjaminites came out of Gibeah, and struck down on that day twenty-two thousand of the Israelites.

w Compare Gk: Heb 30And all who saw it said, "Such a thing has not happened or been seen
x Gk: Heb lacks we will go up   y Compare Gk: Meaning of Heb uncertain

23z The Israelites went up and wept before the LORD until the evening; and they inquired of the LORD, "Shall we again draw near to battle against our kinsfolk the Benjaminites?" And the LORD said, "Go up against them." 22 The Israelites took courage, and again formed the battle line in the same place where they had formed it on the first day.

24 So the Israelites advanced against the Benjaminites the second day. 25 Benjamin moved out against them from Gibeah the second day, and struck down eighteen thousand of the Israelites, all of them armed men. 26 Then all the Israelites, the whole army, went back to Bethel and wept, sitting there before the LORD; they fasted that day until evening. Then they offered burnt offerings and sacrifices of well-being before the LORD. 27 And the Israelites inquired of the LORD (for the ark of the covenant of God was there in those days, 28 and Phinehas son of Eleazar, son of Aaron, ministered before it in those days), saying, "Shall we go out once more to battle against our kinsfolk the Benjaminites, or shall we desist?" The LORD answered, "Go up, for tomorrow I will give them into your hand."

29 So Israel stationed men in ambush around Gibeah. 30 Then the Israelites went up against the Benjaminites on the third day, and set themselves in array against Gibeah, as before. 31 When the Benjaminites went out against the army, they were drawn away from the city. As before they began to inflict casualties on the troops, along the main roads, one of which goes up to Bethel and the other to Gibeah, as well as in the open country, killing about thirty men of Israel. 32 The Benjaminites thought, "They are being routed before us, as previously." But the Israelites said, "Let us retreat and draw them away from the city toward the roads." 33 The main body of the Israelites drew back its battle line to Baal-tamar, while those Israelites who were in ambush rushed out of their place west[a] of Geba. 34 There came against Gibeah ten thousand picked men out of all Israel, and the battle was fierce. But the Ben-jaminites did not realize that disaster was close upon them.

35 The LORD defeated Benjamin before Israel; and the Israelites destroyed twenty-five thousand one hundred men of Benjamin that day, all of them armed.

36 Then the Benjaminites saw that they were defeated.[b]

The Israelites gave ground to Benjamin, because they trusted to the troops in ambush that they had stationed against Gibeah. 37 The troops in ambush rushed quickly upon Gibeah. Then they put the whole city to the sword. 38 Now the agreement between the main body of Israel and the men in ambush was that when they sent up a cloud of smoke out of the city 39 the main body of Israel should turn in battle. But Benjamin had begun to inflict casualties on the Israelites, killing about thirty of them; so they thought, "Surely they are defeated before us, as in the first battle." 40 But when the cloud, a column of smoke, began to rise out of the city, the Benjaminites looked behind them—and there was the whole city going up in smoke toward the sky! 41 Then the main body of Israel turned, and the Benjaminites were dismayed, for they saw that disaster was close upon them. 42 Therefore they turned away from the Israelites in the direction of the wilderness; but the battle overtook them, and those who came out of the city[c] were slaughtering them in between.[d] 43 Cutting down[e] the Benjaminites, they pursued them from Nohah[f] and trod them down as far as a place east of Gibeah. 44 Eighteen thousand Benjaminites fell, all of them courageous fighters. 45 When they turned and fled toward the wilderness to the rock of Rimmon, five thousand of them were cut down on the main roads, and they were pursued as far as Gidom, and two thousand of them were slain. 46 So all who fell that day of Benjamin were twenty-five thousand arms-bearing men, all of them courageous fighters. 47 But six hundred turned and fled toward the wilderness to the rock of Rimmon, and remained at the rock of Rimmon for four months.

z Verses 22 and 23 are transposed   a Gk Vg: Heb in the plain   b This sentence is continued by verse 45.   c Compare Vg and some Gk Mss: Heb cities   d Compare Syr: Meaning of Heb uncertain   e Gk: Heb Surrounding   f Gk: Heb pursued them at their resting place

48 Meanwhile, the Israelites turned back against the Benjaminites, and put them to the sword—the city, the people, the animals, and all that remained. Also the remaining towns they set on fire.

The Benjaminites Saved from Extinction

21 Now the Israelites had sworn at Mizpah, "No one of us shall give his daughter in marriage to Benjamin." 2 And the people came to Bethel, and sat there until evening before God, and they lifted up their voices and wept bitterly. 3 They said, "O LORD, the God of Israel, why has it come to pass that today there should be one tribe lacking in Israel?" 4 On the next day, the people got up early, and built an altar there, and offered burnt offerings and sacrifices of well-being. 5 Then the Israelites said, "Which of all the tribes of Israel did not come up in the assembly to the LORD?" For a solemn oath had been taken concerning whoever did not come up to the LORD to Mizpah, saying, "That one shall be put to death." 6 But the Israelites had compassion for Benjamin their kin, and said, "One tribe is cut off from Israel this day. 7 What shall we do for wives for those who are left, since we have sworn by the LORD that we will not give them any of our daughters as wives?"

8 Then they said, "Is there anyone from the tribes of Israel who did not come up to the LORD to Mizpah?" It turned out that no one from Jabesh-gilead had come to the camp, to the assembly. 9 For when the roll was called among the people, not one of the inhabitants of Jabesh-gilead was there. 10 So the congregation sent twelve thousand soldiers there and commanded them, "Go, put the inhabitants of Jabesh-gilead to the sword, including the women and the little ones. 11 This is what you shall do; every male and every woman that has lain with a male you shall devote to destruction." 12 And they found among the inhabitants of Jabesh-gilead four hundred young virgins who had never slept with a man and brought them to the camp at Shiloh, which is in the land of Canaan.

13 Then the whole congregation sent word to the Benjaminites who were at the rock of Rimmon, and proclaimed peace to them. 14 Benjamin returned at that time; and they gave them the women whom they had saved alive of the women of Jabesh-gilead; but they did not suffice for them.

15 The people had compassion on Benjamin because the LORD had made a breach in the tribes of Israel. 16 So the elders of the congregation said, "What shall we do for wives for those who are left, since there are no women left in Benjamin?" 17 And they said, "There must be heirs for the survivors of Benjamin, in order that a tribe may not be blotted out from Israel. 18 Yet we cannot give any of our daughters to them as wives." For the Israelites had sworn, "Cursed be anyone who gives a wife to Benjamin." 19 So they said, "Look, the yearly festival of the LORD is taking place at Shiloh, which is north of Bethel, on the east of the highway that goes up from Bethel to Shechem, and south of Lebonah." 20 And they instructed the Benjaminites, saying, "Go and lie in wait in the vineyards, 21 and watch; when the young women of Shiloh come out to dance in the dances, then come out of the vineyards and each of you carry off a wife for himself from the young women of Shiloh, and go to the land of Benjamin. 22 Then if their fathers or their brothers come to complain to us, we will say to them, 'Be generous and allow us to have them; because we did not capture in battle a wife for each man. But neither did you incur guilt by giving your daughters to them.' " 23 The Benjaminites did so; they took wives for each of them from the dancers whom they abducted. Then they went and returned to their territory, and rebuilt the towns, and lived in them. 24 So the Israelites departed from there at that time by tribes and families, and they went out from there to their own territories.

25 In those days there was no king in Israel; all the people did what was right in their own eyes.

RUTH

THIS BOOK TELLS THE STORY OF RUTH, A YOUNG MOABITE WOMAN AND GREAT-GRANDMOTHER OF KING DAVID. SET IN THE TIME OF THE JUDGES, THE BOOK OF RUTH GIVES A SERIES OF INTIMATE GLANCES INTO THE PRIVATE LIVES OF THE MEMBERS OF AN ISRAELITE FAMILY AND PRESENTS A DELIGHTFUL ACCOUNT OF TRUE FAITH AND PIETY. IN THIS POWERFUL STORY OF LOVE AND DEVOTION, LOOK FOR GOD AT WORK TO BRING FULLNESS IN THE LIVES OF THOSE WHO FEEL EMPTY.

Elimelech's Family Goes to Moab

1 In the days when the judges ruled, there was a famine in the land, and a certain man of Bethlehem in Judah went to live in the country of Moab, he and his wife and two sons. ²The name of the man was Elimelech and the name of his wife Naomi, and the names of his two sons were Mahlon and Chilion; they were Ephrathites from Bethlehem in Judah. They went into the country of Moab and remained there. ³But Elimelech, the husband of Naomi, died, and she was left with her two sons. ⁴These took Moabite wives; the name of the one was Orpah and the name of the other Ruth. When they had lived there about ten years, ⁵both Mahlon and Chilion also died, so that the woman was left without her two sons and her husband.

Naomi and Her Moabite Daughters-in-Law

6 Then she started to return with her daughters-in-law from the country of Moab, for she had heard in the country of Moab that the LORD had considered his people and given them food. ⁷So she set out from the place where she had been living, she and her two daughters-in-law, and they went on their way to go back to the land of Judah. ⁸But Naomi said to her two daughters-in-law, "Go back each of you to your mother's house. May the LORD deal kindly with you, as you have dealt with the dead and with me. ⁹The LORD grant that you may find security, each of you in the house of your husband." Then she kissed them, and they wept aloud. ¹⁰They said to her, "No, we will return with you to your

people." 11But Naomi said, "Turn back, my daughters, why will you go with me? Do I still have sons in my womb that they may become your husbands? 12Turn back, my daughters, go your way, for I am too old to have a husband. Even if I thought there was hope for me, even if I should have a husband tonight and bear sons, 13would you then wait until they were grown? Would you then refrain from marrying? No, my daughters, it has been far more bitter for me than for you, because the hand of the LORD has turned against me." 14Then they wept aloud again. Orpah kissed her mother-in-law, but Ruth clung to her.

15 So she said, "See, your sister-in-law has gone back to her people and to her gods; return after your sister-in-law." 16But Ruth said,

"Do not press me to leave you
    or to turn back from following
      you!
Where you go, I will go;
    where you lodge, I will lodge;
your people shall be my people,
    and your God my God.
17   Where you die, I will die—
    there will I be buried.
May the LORD do thus and so to
    me,
    and more as well,
if even death parts me from you!"

18When Naomi saw that she was determined to go with her, she said no more to her.

19 So the two of them went on until they came to Bethlehem. When they came to Bethlehem, the whole town was stirred because of them; and the women said, "Is this Naomi?" 20She said to them,

"Call me no longer Naomi,a
    call me Mara,b
    for the Almightyc has dealt
      bitterly with me.
21   I went away full,
    but the LORD has brought me
      back empty;
why call me Naomi
    when the LORD has dealt harshly
      withd me,
and the Almightyc has brought
    calamity upon me?"

22 So Naomi returned together with Ruth the Moabite, her daughter-in-law, who came back with her from the country of Moab. They came to Bethlehem at the beginning of the barley harvest.

Ruth Meets Boaz

2 Now Naomi had a kinsman on her husband's side, a prominent rich man, of the family of Elimelech, whose name was Boaz. 2And Ruth the Moabite said to Naomi, "Let me go to the field and glean among the ears of grain, behind someone in whose sight I may find favor." She said to her, "Go, my daughter." 3So she went. She came and gleaned in the field behind the reapers. As it happened, she came to the part of the field belonging to Boaz, who was of the family of Elimelech. 4Just then Boaz came from Bethlehem. He said to the reapers, "The LORD be with you." They answered, "The LORD bless you." 5Then Boaz said to his servant who was in charge of the reapers, "To whom does this young woman belong?" 6The servant who was in charge of the reapers answered, "She is the Moabite who came back with Naomi from the country of Moab. 7She said, 'Please, let me glean and gather among the sheaves behind the reapers.' So she came, and she has been on her feet from early this morning until now, without resting even for a moment."e

8 Then Boaz said to Ruth, "Now listen, my daughter, do not go to glean in another field or leave this one, but keep close to my young women. 9Keep your eyes on the field that is being reaped, and follow behind them. I have ordered the young men not to bother you. If you get thirsty, go to the vessels and drink from what the young men have drawn." 10Then she fell prostrate, with her face to the ground, and said to him, "Why have I found favor in your sight, that you should take notice of me, when I am a foreigner?" 11But Boaz answered her, "All that you have done for your mother-in-law since the death of your husband has been fully told me, and how you left your father and mother and your native land and came to a people

a That is Pleasant   b That is Bitter   c Traditional rendering of Heb Shaddai   d Or has testified against   e Compare Gk Vg: Meaning of Heb uncertain

that you did not know before. [12]May the LORD reward you for your deeds, and may you have a full reward from the LORD, the God of Israel, under whose wings you have come for refuge!" [13]Then she said, "May I continue to find favor in your sight, my lord, for you have comforted me and spoken kindly to your servant, even though I am not one of your servants."

14 At mealtime Boaz said to her, "Come here, and eat some of this bread, and dip your morsel in the sour wine."

So she sat beside the reapers, and he heaped up for her some parched grain. She ate until she was satisfied, and she had some left over. [15]When she got up to glean, Boaz instructed his young men, "Let her glean even among the standing sheaves, and do not reproach her. [16]You must also pull out some handfuls for her from the bundles, and leave them for her to glean, and do not rebuke her."

17 So she gleaned in the field until evening. Then she beat out what she had gleaned, and it was about an ephah

MONDAY

HAPPENSTANCE
Charles H. Spurgeon

VERSE: Ruth 2.3   **PASSAGE:** Ruth 2.2–20

t seemed nothing but an accidental happenstance, but how divinely was it planned! Ruth had gone forth with her [mother-in-law's] blessing under the care of her [mother-in-law's] God to humble but honorable toil, and the providence of God was guiding her every step. Little did she know that amid the sheaves she would find a husband, that he would make her the joint owner of all those broad acres, and that she, a poor foreigner, would become one of the progenitors of the great Messiah. God is very good to those who trust in him and often surprises them with unlooked for blessings. Little do we know what may happen to us tomorrow, but this sweet fact may cheer us, that no good thing shall be withheld. Chance is banished from the faith of Christians, for they see the hand of God in everything. The trivial events of today or tomorrow may involve consequences of the highest importance. O Lord, deal as graciously with your servants as you did with Ruth.

How blessed would it be, if, in wandering in the field of meditation tonight, our [happenstance] should be to "light" on the place where our next Kinsman will reveal himself to us! O Spirit of God, guide us to him. We would sooner glean in his field than bear away the whole harvest from any other.

ADDITIONAL SCRIPTURE READING:
2 Kings 8.5–6; Matthew 10.29; Luke 10.30–33

Go to page 301 for your next devotional reading.

1700   1900

of barley. ¹⁸She picked it up and came into the town, and her mother-in-law saw how much she had gleaned. Then she took out and gave her what was left over after she herself had been satisfied. ¹⁹Her mother-in-law said to her, "Where did you glean today? And where have you worked? Blessed be the man who took notice of you." So she told her mother-in-law with whom she had worked, and said, "The name of the man with whom I worked today is Boaz." ²⁰Then Naomi said to her daughter-in-law, "Blessed be he by the LORD, whose kindness has not forsaken the living or the dead!" Naomi also said to her, "The man is a relative of ours, one of our nearest kin."ᶠ ²¹Then Ruth the Moabite said, "He even said to me, 'Stay close by my servants, until they have finished all my harvest.' " ²²Naomi said to Ruth, her daughter-in-law, "It is better, my daughter, that you go out with his young women, otherwise you might be bothered in another field." ²³So she stayed close to the young women of Boaz, gleaning until the end of the barley and wheat harvests; and she lived with her mother-in-law.

Ruth and Boaz at the Threshing Floor

3 Naomi her mother-in-law said to her, "My daughter, I need to seek some security for you, so that it may be well with you. ²Now here is our kinsman Boaz, with whose young women you have been working. See, he is winnowing barley tonight at the threshing floor. ³Now wash and anoint yourself, and put on your best clothes and go down to the threshing floor; but do not make yourself known to the man until he has finished eating and drinking. ⁴When he lies down, observe the place where he lies; then, go and uncover his feet and lie down; and he will tell you what to do." ⁵She said to her, "All that you tell me I will do."

6 So she went down to the threshing floor and did just as her mother-in-law had instructed her. ⁷When Boaz had eaten and drunk, and he was in a contented mood, he went to lie down at the end of the heap of grain. Then she came

stealthily and uncovered his feet, and lay down. ⁸At midnight the man was startled, and turned over, and there, lying at his feet, was a woman! ⁹He said, "Who are you?" And she answered, "I am Ruth, your servant; spread your cloak over your servant, for you are next-of-kin."ᶠ ¹⁰He said, "May you be blessed by the LORD, my daughter; this last instance of your loyalty is better than the first; you have not gone after young men, whether poor or rich. ¹¹And now, my daughter, do not be afraid, I will do for you all that you ask, for all the assembly of my people know that you are a worthy woman. ¹²But now, though it is true that I am a near kinsman, there is another kinsman more closely related than I. ¹³Remain this night, and in the morning, if he will act as next-of-kinᶠ for you, good; let him do it. If he is not willing to act as next-of-kinᶠ for you, then, as the LORD lives, I will act as next-of-kinᶠ for you. Lie down until the morning."

14 So she lay at his feet until morning, but got up before one person could recognize another; for he said, "It must not be known that the woman came to the threshing floor." ¹⁵Then he said, "Bring the cloak you are wearing and hold it out." So she held it, and he measured out six measures of barley, and put it on her back; then he went into the city. ¹⁶She came to her mother-in-law, who said, "How did things go with you,ᵍ my daughter?" Then she told her all that the man had done for her, ¹⁷saying, "He gave me these six measures of barley, for he said, 'Do not go back to your mother-in-law empty-handed.' " ¹⁸She replied, "Wait, my daughter, until you learn how the matter turns out, for the man will not rest, but will settle the matter today."

The Marriage of Boaz and Ruth

4 No sooner had Boaz gone up to the gate and sat down there than the next-of-kin,ᶠ of whom Boaz had spoken, came passing by. So Boaz said, "Come over, friend; sit down here." And he went over and sat down. ²Then Boaz took ten men of the elders of the city, and said, "Sit down here"; so they sat down. ³He then said to the next-of-kin,ᶠ

ᶠ Or *one with the right to redeem*   ᵍ Or *"Who are you,*

"Naomi, who has come back from the country of Moab, is selling the parcel of land that belonged to our kinsman Elimelech. ⁴So I thought I would tell you of it, and say: Buy it in the presence of those sitting here, and in the presence of the elders of my people. If you will redeem it, redeem it; but if you will not, tell me, so that I may know; for there is no one prior to you to redeem it, and I come after you." So he said, "I will redeem it." ⁵Then Boaz said, "The day you acquire the field from the hand of Naomi, you are also acquiring Ruth^h the Moabite, the widow of the dead man, to maintain the dead man's name on his inheritance." ⁶At this, the next-of-kinⁱ said, "I cannot redeem it for myself without damaging my own inheritance. Take my right of redemption yourself, for I cannot redeem it."

7 Now this was the custom in former times in Israel concerning redeeming and exchanging: to confirm a transaction, the one took off a sandal and gave it to the other; this was the manner of attesting in Israel. ⁸So when the next-of-kinⁱ said to Boaz, "Acquire it for yourself," he took off his sandal. ⁹Then Boaz said to the elders and all the people, "Today you are witnesses that I have acquired from the hand of Naomi all that belonged to Elimelech and all that belonged to Chilion and Mahlon. ¹⁰I have also acquired Ruth the Moabite, the wife of Mahlon, to be my wife, to maintain the dead man's name on his inheritance, in order that the name of the dead may not be cut off from his kindred and from the gate of his native place; today you are witnesses." ¹¹Then all the people who were at the gate, along with the elders, said, "We are witnesses. May the LORD make the woman who is coming into your house like Rachel and Leah, who together built up the house of Israel. May you produce children in Ephrathah and bestow a name in Bethlehem; ¹²and, through the children that the LORD will give you by this young woman, may your house be like the house of Perez, whom Tamar bore to Judah."

The Genealogy of David

13 So Boaz took Ruth and she became his wife. When they came together, the LORD made her conceive, and she bore a son. ¹⁴Then the women said to Naomi, "Blessed be the LORD, who has not left you this day without next-of-kin;ⁱ and may his name be renowned in Israel! ¹⁵He shall be to you a restorer of life and a nourisher of your old age; for your daughter-in-law who loves you,

---

O FOR A THOUSAND TONGUES TO SING MY GREAT
REDEEMER'S PRAISE!   —*Charles Wesley*

---

who is more to you than seven sons, has borne him." ¹⁶Then Naomi took the child and laid him in her bosom, and became his nurse. ¹⁷The women of the neighborhood gave him a name, saying, "A son has been born to Naomi." They named him Obed; he became the father of Jesse, the father of David.

18 Now these are the descendants of Perez: Perez became the father of Hezron, ¹⁹Hezron of Ram, Ram of Amminadab, ²⁰Amminadab of Nahshon, Nahshon of Salmon, ²¹Salmon of Boaz, Boaz of Obed, ²²Obed of Jesse, and Jesse of David.

---

h OL Vg: Heb *from the hand of Naomi and from Ruth*   i Or *one with the right to redeem*

1 SAMUEL

HE BOOK OF 1 SAMUEL RECORDS THE LIVES OF SAMUEL AND SAUL, AND MUCH OF THE LIFE OF DAVID. HERE YOU WILL FIND THE STORY OF ISRAEL'S FIRST KING, SAUL. BUT SAUL DISOBEYED GOD, WHO IN TURN REJECTED HIM AS KING. THE PROPHET SAMUEL SECRETLY ANOINTED DAVID TO TAKE SAUL'S PLACE. THE REST OF THE BOOK RECORDS THE STRUGGLES BETWEEN SAUL AND DAVID. AS YOU READ THIS BOOK, NOTE HOW GOD PROTECTS AND BLESSES THOSE WHO FOLLOW HIM OBEDIENTLY, AND HOW THOSE WHO DISREGARD HIM INEVITABLY FACE DIFFICULTIES.

Samuel's Birth and Dedication

1 There was a certain man of Ramathaim, a Zuphite[a] from the hill country of Ephraim, whose name was Elkanah son of Jeroham son of Elihu son of Tohu son of Zuph, an Ephraimite. 2He had two wives; the name of the one was Hannah, and the name of the other Peninnah. Peninnah had children, but Hannah had no children.

3 Now this man used to go up year by year from his town to worship and to sacrifice to the LORD of hosts at Shiloh, where the two sons of Eli, Hophni and Phinehas, were priests of the LORD. 4On the day when Elkanah sacrificed, he would give portions to his wife Peninnah and to all her sons and daughters; 5but to Hannah he gave a double portion,[b] because he loved her, though the LORD had closed her womb. 6Her rival used to provoke her severely, to irritate her, because the LORD had closed her womb. 7So it went on year by year; as often as she went up to the house of the LORD, she used to provoke her. Therefore Hannah wept and would not eat. 8Her husband Elkanah said to her, "Hannah, why do you weep? Why do you not eat? Why is your heart sad? Am I not more to you than ten sons?"

9 After they had eaten and drunk at Shiloh, Hannah rose and presented herself before the LORD.[c] Now Eli the priest was sitting on the seat beside the doorpost of the temple of the LORD. 10She was

a Compare Gk and 1 Chr 6.35-36: Heb *Ramathaim-zophim*   b Syr: Meaning of Heb uncertain
c Gk: Heb lacks *and presented herself before the LORD*

deeply distressed and prayed to the Lord, and wept bitterly. [11]She made this vow: "O Lord of hosts, if only you will look on the misery of your servant, and remember me, and not forget your servant, but will give to your servant a male child, then I will set him before you as a nazirite[d] until the day of his death. He shall drink neither wine nor intoxicants,[e] and no razor shall touch his head."

d That is *one separated* or *one consecrated the Lord all the days of his life*

e Cn Compare Gk Q Ms 1.22: MT *then I will give him to*

TUESDAY

PERSEVERANCE IN PRAYER
John Calvin

VERSE: 1 Samuel 1.10   **PASSAGE:** 1 Samuel 1.9–20

e must not wish to bind God to certain circumstances, because . . . we are taught not to put on him any law, nor to impose upon him any condition. For, before making any prayer for ourselves, before all things, we ask that his will be done; whereby we submit beforehand our will to his, in order that, as if it were caught and retained by a rein, our will may not presume to wish to range and to submit him under our will. If, having the heart formed in this obedience, we permit ourselves to be governed according to the good pleasure of the divine providence, we shall easily learn to persevere in prayer and wait with patience upon the Lord, while deferring the fulfillment of our desires to the hour set by his will; being assured that, although he does not show himself to us, yet he is always present to us and at his own time will reveal that he did not at all have his ears deaf to our prayers, though they seemed to men to be despised by him.

And even if at the end, after long waiting, our mind cannot understand the profit of our praying, and our senses feel no fruit thereof, nevertheless our faith will certify unto us what our mind and sense will not be able to perceive, that is, we shall have obtained [from God] all that which was good for us, for he will make us in poverty to possess abundance and in affliction to have consolation. For, even if all things should fail us, yet God will never leave us, inasmuch as he cannot disappoint the expectation and patience of his own.

ADDITIONAL SCRIPTURE READING:
Psalms 50.14–15; 91.15–16; James 5.16

Go to page 305 for your next devotional reading.

1500   1700

12 As she continued praying before the LORD, Eli observed her mouth. ¹³Hannah was praying silently; only her lips moved, but her voice was not heard; therefore Eli thought she was drunk. ¹⁴So Eli said to her, "How long will you make a drunken spectacle of yourself? Put away your wine." ¹⁵But Hannah answered, "No, my lord, I am a woman deeply troubled; I have drunk neither wine nor strong drink, but I have been pouring out my soul before the LORD. ¹⁶Do not regard your servant as a worthless woman, for I have been speaking out of my great anxiety and vexation all this time." ¹⁷Then Eli answered, "Go in peace; the God of Israel grant the petition you have made to him." ¹⁸And she said, "Let your servant find favor in your sight." Then the woman went to her quarters,ᶠ ate and drank with her husband,ᵍ and her countenance was sad no longer.ʰ

19 They rose early in the morning and worshiped before the LORD; then they went back to their house at Ramah. Elkanah knew his wife Hannah, and the LORD remembered her. ²⁰In due time Hannah conceived and bore a son. She named him Samuel, for she said, "I have asked him of the LORD."

21 The man Elkanah and all his household went up to offer to the LORD the yearly sacrifice, and to pay his vow. ²²But Hannah did not go up, for she said to her husband, "As soon as the child is weaned, I will bring him, that he may appear in the presence of the LORD, and remain there forever; I will offer him as a naziriteⁱ for all time."ʲ ²³Her husband Elkanah said to her, "Do what seems best to you, wait until you have weaned him; only—may the LORD establish his word."ᵏ So the woman remained and nursed her son, until she weaned him. ²⁴When she had weaned him, she took him up with her, along with a three-year-old bull,ˡ an ephah of flour, and a skin of wine. She brought him to the house of the LORD at Shiloh; and the child was young. ²⁵Then they slaugh-

tered the bull, and they brought the child to Eli. ²⁶And she said, "Oh, my lord! As you live, my lord, I am the woman who was standing here in your presence, praying to the LORD. ²⁷For this child I prayed; and the LORD has granted me the petition that I made to him. ²⁸Therefore I have lent him to the LORD; as long as he lives, he is given to the LORD."

She left him there forᵐ the LORD.

Hannah's Prayer

2 Hannah prayed and said,
"My heart exults in the LORD;
my strength is exalted in my God.ⁿ
My mouth derides my enemies,
because I rejoice in myᵒ victory.

2 "There is no Holy One like the LORD,
no one besides you;
there is no Rock like our God.
3 Talk no more so very proudly,
let not arrogance come from your mouth;
for the LORD is a God of knowledge,
and by him actions are weighed.
4 The bows of the mighty are broken,
but the feeble gird on strength.
5 Those who were full have hired themselves out for bread,
but those who were hungry are fat with spoil.
The barren has borne seven,
but she who has many children is forlorn.
6 The LORD kills and brings to life;
he brings down to Sheol and raises up.
7 The LORD makes poor and makes rich;
he brings low, he also exalts.
8 He raises up the poor from the dust;
he lifts the needy from the ash heap,
to make them sit with princes
and inherit a seat of honor.ᵖ

ᶠ Gk: Heb went her way   g Gk: Heb lacks and drank with her husband   h Gk: Meaning of Heb uncertain   i That is one separated or one consecrated   j Cn Compare Q Ms: MT lacks I will offer him as a nazirite for all time   k MT: Q Ms Gk Compare Syr that which goes out of your mouth   l Q Ms Gk Syr: MT three bulls   m Gk (Compare Q Ms) and Gk at 2.11: MT And he (that is, Elkanah) worshiped there before   n Gk: Heb the LORD   o Q Ms: MT your   p Gk (Compare Q Ms) adds He grants the vow of the one who vows, and blesses the years of the just

For the pillars of the earth are the
LORD's,
and on them he has set the
world.

9 "He will guard the feet of his
faithful ones,
but the wicked shall be cut off in
darkness;
for not by might does one prevail.
10 The LORD! His adversaries shall be
shattered;
the Most High*q* will thunder in
heaven.
The LORD will judge the ends of the
earth;
he will give strength to his king,
and exalt the power of his
anointed."

Eli's Wicked Sons

11 Then Elkanah went home to
Ramah, while the boy remained to minister to the LORD, in the presence of the
priest Eli.

12 Now the sons of Eli were
scoundrels; they had no regard for the
LORD 13or for the duties of the priests to
the people. When anyone offered sacrifice, the priest's servant would come,
while the meat was boiling, with a
three-pronged fork in his hand, 14and he
would thrust it into the pan, or kettle, or
caldron, or pot; all that the fork brought
up the priest would take for himself.*r*
This is what they did at Shiloh to all the
Israelites who came there. 15Moreover,
before the fat was burned, the priest's
servant would come and say to the one
who was sacrificing, "Give meat for the
priest to roast; for he will not accept
boiled meat from you, but only raw."
16And if the man said to him, "Let them
burn the fat first, and then take whatever you wish," he would say, "No, you
must give it now; if not, I will take it by
force." 17Thus the sin of the young men
was very great in the sight of the LORD;
for they treated the offerings of the LORD
with contempt.

The Child Samuel at Shiloh

18 Samuel was ministering before
the LORD, a boy wearing a linen ephod.
19His mother used to make for him a little robe and take it to him each year,
when she went up with her husband to
offer the yearly sacrifice. 20Then Eli
would bless Elkanah and his wife, and
say, "May the LORD repay*s* you with
children by this woman for the gift that
she made to*t* the LORD"; and then they
would return to their home.

21 And*u* the LORD took note of Hannah; she conceived and bore three sons
and two daughters. And the boy Samuel
grew up in the presence of the LORD.

Prophecy against Eli's Household

22 Now Eli was very old. He heard all
that his sons were doing to all Israel, and
how they lay with the women who
served at the entrance to the tent of
meeting. 23He said to them, "Why do
you do such things? For I hear of your
evil dealings from all these people. 24No,
my sons; it is not a good report that I
hear the people of the LORD spreading
abroad. 25If one person sins against
another, someone can intercede for the
sinner with the LORD;*v* but if someone
sins against the LORD, who can make
intercession?" But they would not listen
to the voice of their father; for it was the
will of the LORD to kill them.

26 Now the boy Samuel continued to
grow both in stature and in favor with
the LORD and with the people.

27 A man of God came to Eli and said
to him, "Thus the LORD has said, 'I
revealed*w* myself to the family of your
ancestor in Egypt when they were
slaves*x* to the house of Pharaoh. 28I
chose him out of all the tribes of Israel
to be my priest, to go up to my altar, to
offer incense, to wear an ephod before
me; and I gave to the family of your
ancestor all my offerings by fire from the
people of Israel. 29Why then look with
greedy eye*y* at my sacrifices and my
offerings that I commanded, and honor
your sons more than me by fattening
yourselves on the choicest parts of every

---

q Cn Heb *against him he*   *r* Gk Syr Vg: Heb *with it*   *s* Q Ms Gk: MT *give*   *t* Q Ms Gk: MT *for*
the petition that she asked of   *u* Q Ms Gk: MT *When*   *v* Gk Compare Q Ms: MT *another, God will*
mediate for him   *w* Gk Tg Syr: Heb *Did I reveal*   *x* Q Ms Gk: MT lacks *slaves*   *y* Q Ms Gk: MT
then kick

offering of my people Israel?' 30There-
fore the LORD the God of Israel declares:
'I promised that your family and the
family of your ancestor should go in and
out before me forever'; but now the
LORD declares: 'Far be it from me; for
those who honor me I will honor, and
those who despise me shall be treated
with contempt. 31See, a time is coming
when I will cut off your strength and the
strength of your ancestor's family, so
that no one in your family will live to
old age. 32Then in distress you will look
with greedy eyez on all the prosperity
that shall be bestowed upon Israel; and
no one in your family shall ever live to
old age. 33The only one of you whom I
shall not cut off from my altar shall be
spared to weep out hisa eyes and grieve
hisb heart; all the members of your
household shall die by the sword.c 34The
fate of your two sons, Hophni and Phinehas, shall be the sign to you—both of
them shall die on the same day. 35I will
raise up for myself a faithful priest, who
shall do according to what is in my heart
and in my mind. I will build him a sure
house, and he shall go in and out before
my anointed one forever. 36Everyone
who is left in your family shall come to
implore him for a piece of silver or a loaf
of bread, and shall say, Please put me in
one of the priest's places, that I may eat
a morsel of bread.' "

IF YOU SAY THAT MAN IS TOO LITTLE FOR GOD TO
SPEAK TO HIM, YOU MUST BE VERY BIG TO BE
ABLE TO JUDGE.   —Blaise Pascal

Samuel's Calling and Prophetic Activity

3 Now the boy Samuel was ministering to the LORD under Eli.
The word of the LORD was rare in those
days; visions were not widespread.
2 At that time Eli, whose eyesight
had begun to grow dim so that he could
not see, was lying down in his room;
3the lamp of God had not yet gone out,
and Samuel was lying down in the temple of the LORD, where the ark of God

was. 4Then the LORD called, "Samuel!
Samuel!"d and he said, "Here I am!"
5and ran to Eli, and said, "Here I am, for
you called me." But he said, "I did not
call; lie down again." So he went and lay
down. 6The LORD called again, "Samuel!" Samuel got up and went to Eli, and
said, "Here I am, for you called me." But
he said, "I did not call, my son; lie down
again." 7Now Samuel did not yet know
the LORD, and the word of the LORD had
not yet been revealed to him. 8The LORD
called Samuel again, a third time. And
he got up and went to Eli, and said,
"Here I am, for you called me." Then Eli
perceived that the LORD was calling the
boy. 9Therefore Eli said to Samuel, "Go,
lie down; and if he calls you, you shall
say, 'Speak, LORD, for your servant is listening.' " So Samuel went and lay down
in his place.
10 Now the LORD came and stood
there, calling as before, "Samuel! Samuel!" And Samuel said, "Speak, for your
servant is listening." 11Then the LORD
said to Samuel, "See, I am about to do
something in Israel that will make both
ears of anyone who hears of it tingle.
12On that day I will fulfill against Eli all
that I have spoken concerning his
house, from beginning to end. 13For I
have told him that I am about to punish
his house forever, for the iniquity that
he knew, because his sons were blaspheming God,e and he did not restrain
them. 14Therefore I swear to the house
of Eli that the iniquity of Eli's house
shall not be expiated by sacrifice or
offering forever."
15 Samuel lay there until morning;
then he opened the doors of the house of
the LORD. Samuel was afraid to tell the
vision to Eli. 16But Eli called Samuel and
said, "Samuel, my son." He said, "Here I
am." 17Eli said, "What was it that he
told you? Do not hide it from me. May
God do so to you and more also, if you
hide anything from me of all that he told
you." 18So Samuel told him everything
and hid nothing from him. Then he said,
"It is the LORD; let him do what seems
good to him."
19 As Samuel grew up, the LORD was

---

z Q Ms Gk: MT will kick   a Q Ms Gk: MT your   b Q Ms Gk: Heb your   c Q Ms See Gk: MT die
like mortals   d Q Ms Gk See 3.10: MT the LORD called Samuel   e Another reading is for
themselves

with him and let none of his words fall to the ground. 20 And all Israel from Dan to Beer-sheba knew that Samuel was a trustworthy prophet of the LORD. 21 The LORD continued to appear at Shiloh, for the LORD revealed himself to Samuel at Shiloh by the word of the LORD.

 4 1 And the word of Samuel came to all Israel.

The Ark of God Captured

In those days the Philistines mustered for war against Israel, f and Israel went out to battle against them; g they encamped at Ebenezer, and the Philistines encamped at Aphek. 2 The Philistines drew up in line against Israel, and when the battle was joined, h Israel was defeated by the Philistines, who killed about

---

f Gk: Heb lacks In those days the Philistines mustered for war against Israel   g Gk: Heb against the Philistines   h Meaning of Heb uncertain

---

WEDNESDAY

I WONDER IF THAT IS GOD'S VOICE?
Oswald Chambers

VERSE: 1 Samuel 3.10   **PASSAGE:** 1 Samuel 3.1–14

od never speaks to us in dramatic ways, but in ways that are easy to misunderstand. Then we say, "I wonder if that is God's voice?" Isaiah said that the Lord spoke to him "with a strong hand," that is, by the pressure of circumstances (Isaiah 8.11). Without the sovereign hand of God himself, nothing touches our lives. Do we discern his hand at work, or do we see things as mere occurrences?

Get into the habit of saying, "Speak, LORD," and life will become a romance (1 Samuel 3.9). Every time circumstances press in on you, say, "Speak, LORD," and make time to listen. Chastening is more than a means of discipline—it is meant to get me to the point of saying, "Speak, LORD." Think back to a time when God spoke to you. Do you remember what he said? Was it Luke 11.13, or was it 1 Thessalonians 5.23? As we listen, our ears become more sensitive, and, like Jesus, we shall hear God all the time.

Should I tell my "Eli" what God has shown to me? This is where the dilemma of obedience hits us. We disobey God by becoming amateur providences and thinking, "I must shield 'Eli,'" who represents the best people we know. God did not tell Samuel to tell Eli—he had to decide that for himself. God's message to you may hurt your "Eli," but trying to prevent suffering in another's life will prove to be an obstruction between your soul and God.

ADDITIONAL SCRIPTURE READING:
Genesis 46.2–3; Exodus 3.4–6; Acts 22.6–10

Go to page 314 for your next devotional reading.

1900   Present

four thousand men on the field of battle.
3 When the troops came to the camp, the
elders of Israel said, "Why has the LORD
put us to rout today before the Philistines? Let us bring the ark of the covenant of the LORD here from Shiloh, so
that he may come among us and save us
from the power of our enemies." 4 So the
people sent to Shiloh, and brought from
there the ark of the covenant of the
LORD of hosts, who is enthroned on the
cherubim. The two sons of Eli, Hophni
and Phinehas, were there with the ark of
the covenant of God.

5 When the ark of the covenant of the
LORD came into the camp, all Israel gave
a mighty shout, so that the earth
resounded. 6 When the Philistines heard
the noise of the shouting, they said,
"What does this great shouting in the
camp of the Hebrews mean?" When
they learned that the ark of the LORD
had come to the camp, 7 the Philistines
were afraid; for they said, "Gods have[i]
come into the camp." They also said,
"Woe to us! For nothing like this has
happened before. 8 Woe to us! Who can
deliver us from the power of these
mighty gods? These are the gods who
struck the Egyptians with every sort of
plague in the wilderness. 9 Take courage,
and be men, O Philistines, in order not
to become slaves to the Hebrews as they
have been to you; be men and fight."

10 So the Philistines fought; Israel
was defeated, and they fled, everyone to
his home. There was a very great slaughter, for there fell of Israel thirty thousand foot soldiers. 11 The ark of God was
captured; and the two sons of Eli, Hophni and Phinehas, died.

Death of Eli

12 A man of Benjamin ran from the
battle line, and came to Shiloh the same
day, with his clothes torn and with earth
upon his head. 13 When he arrived, Eli
was sitting upon his seat by the road
watching, for his heart trembled for the
ark of God. When the man came into
the city and told the news, all the city
cried out. 14 When Eli heard the sound of
the outcry, he said, "What is this
uproar?" Then the man came quickly
and told Eli. 15 Now Eli was ninety-eight

years old and his eyes were set, so that
he could not see. 16 The man said to Eli,
"I have just come from the battle; I fled
from the battle today." He said, "How
did it go, my son?" 17 The messenger
replied, "Israel has fled before the Philistines, and there has also been a great
slaughter among the troops; your two
sons also, Hophni and Phinehas, are
dead, and the ark of God has been captured." 18 When he mentioned the ark of
God, Eli[j] fell over backward from his
seat by the side of the gate; and his neck
was broken and he died, for he was an
old man, and heavy. He had judged Israel forty years.

19 Now his daughter-in-law, the wife
of Phinehas, was pregnant, about to give
birth. When she heard the news that the
ark of God was captured, and that her
father-in-law and her husband were
dead, she bowed and gave birth; for her
labor pains overwhelmed her. 20 As she
was about to die, the women attending
her said to her, "Do not be afraid, for you
have borne a son." But she did not
answer or give heed. 21 She named the
child Ichabod, meaning, "The glory has
departed from Israel," because the ark of
God had been captured and because of
her father-in-law and her husband. 22 She
said, "The glory has departed from Israel,
for the ark of God has been captured."

The Philistines and the Ark

5 When the Philistines captured
the ark of God, they brought it
from Ebenezer to Ashdod; 2 then the Philistines took the ark of God and brought
it into the house of Dagon and placed it
beside Dagon. 3 When the people of Ashdod rose early the next day, there was
Dagon, fallen on his face to the ground
before the ark of the LORD. So they took
Dagon and put him back in his place.
4 But when they rose early on the next
morning, Dagon had fallen on his face to
the ground before the ark of the LORD,
and the head of Dagon and both his
hands were lying cut off upon the
threshold; only the trunk of[k] Dagon was
left to him. 5 This is why the priests of
Dagon and all who enter the house
of Dagon do not step on the threshold of
Dagon in Ashdod to this day.

i Or A god has   j Heb he   k Heb lacks the trunk of

6 The hand of the Lord was heavy upon the people of Ashdod, and he terrified and struck them with tumors, both in Ashdod and in its territory. 7And when the inhabitants of Ashdod saw how things were, they said, "The ark of the God of Israel must not remain with us; for his hand is heavy on us and on our god Dagon." 8So they sent and gathered together all the lords of the Philistines, and said, "What shall we do with the ark of the God of Israel?" The inhabitants of Gath replied, "Let the ark of God be moved on to us."*l* So they moved the ark of the God of Israel to Gath.*m* 9But after they had brought it to Gath,*n* the hand of the Lord was against the city, causing a very great panic; he struck the inhabitants of the city, both young and old, so that tumors broke out on them. 10So they sent the ark of the God of Israel*o* to Ekron. But when the ark of God came to Ekron, the people of Ekron cried out, "Why*p* have they brought around to us*q* the ark of the God of Israel to kill us*q* and our*r* people?" 11They sent therefore and gathered together all the lords of the Philistines, and said, "Send away the ark of the God of Israel, and let it return to its own place, that it may not kill us and our people." For there was a deathly panic*s* throughout the whole city. The hand of God was very heavy there; 12those who did not die were stricken with tumors, and the cry of the city went up to heaven.

The Ark Returned to Israel

6 The ark of the Lord was in the country of the Philistines seven months. 2Then the Philistines called for the priests and the diviners and said, "What shall we do with the ark of the Lord? Tell us what we should send with it to its place." 3They said, "If you send away the ark of the God of Israel, do not send it empty, but by all means return him a guilt offering. Then you will be healed and will be ransomed;*t* will not his hand then turn from you?" 4And they said, "What is the guilt offering that we shall return to him?" They answered,

"Five gold tumors and five gold mice, according to the number of the lords of the Philistines; for the same plague was upon all of you and upon your lords. 5So you must make images of your tumors and images of your mice that ravage the land, and give glory to the God of Israel; perhaps he will lighten his hand on you and your gods and your land. 6Why should you harden your hearts as the Egyptians and Pharaoh hardened their hearts? After he had made fools of them, did they not let the people go, and they departed? 7Now then, get ready a new cart and two milch cows that have never borne a yoke, and yoke the cows to the cart, but take their calves home, away from them. 8Take the ark of the Lord and place it on the cart, and put in a box at its side the figures of gold, which you are returning to him as a guilt offering. Then send it off, and let it go its way. 9And watch; if it goes up on the way to its own land, to Beth-shemesh, then it is he who has done us this great harm; but if not, then we shall know that it is not his hand that struck us; it happened to us by chance."

10 The men did so; they took two milch cows and yoked them to the cart, and shut up their calves at home. 11They put the ark of the Lord on the cart, and the box with the gold mice and the images of their tumors. 12The cows went straight in the direction of Beth-shemesh along one highway, lowing as they went; they turned neither to the right nor to the left, and the lords of the Philistines went after them as far as the border of Beth-shemesh.

13 Now the people of Beth-shemesh were reaping their wheat harvest in the valley. When they looked up and saw the ark, they went with rejoicing to meet it.*u* 14The cart came into the field of Joshua of Beth-shemesh, and stopped there. A large stone was there; so they split up the wood of the cart and offered the cows as a burnt offering to the Lord. 15The Levites took down the ark of the Lord and the box that was beside it, in which were the gold objects, and set them upon the large stone. Then the

---

l Gk Compare Q Ms: MT *They answered, "Let the ark of the God of Israel be brought around to Gath."*
m Gk: Heb lacks *to Gath*   *n* Q Ms: MT lacks *to Gath*   *o* Q Ms Gk: MT lacks *of Israel*   *p* Q Ms
Gk: MT lacks *Why*   *q* Heb *me*   *r* Heb *my*   *s* Q Ms reads *a panic from the Lord*   *t* Q Ms Gk:
MT *and it will be known to you*   *u* Gk: Heb *rejoiced to see it*

people of Beth-shemesh offered burnt offerings and presented sacrifices on that day to the LORD. 16When the five lords of the Philistines saw it, they returned that day to Ekron.

17 These are the gold tumors, which the Philistines returned as a guilt offering to the LORD: one for Ashdod, one for Gaza, one for Ashkelon, one for Gath, one for Ekron; 18also the gold mice, according to the number of all the cities of the Philistines belonging to the five lords, both fortified cities and unwalled villages. The great stone, beside which they set down the ark of the LORD, is a witness to this day in the field of Joshua of Beth-shemesh.

The Ark at Kiriath-jearim

19 The descendants of Jeconiah did not rejoice with the people of Beth-shemesh when they greeted*v* the ark of the LORD; and he killed seventy men of them.*w* The people mourned because the LORD had made a great slaughter among the people. 20Then the people of Beth-shemesh said, "Who is able to stand before the LORD, this holy God? To whom shall he go so that we may be rid of him?" 21So they sent messengers to the inhabitants of Kiriath-jearim, saying, "The Philistines have returned the ark of the LORD. Come down and take it up to you." 1And the people of Kiriath-jearim came and took up the ark of the LORD, and brought it to the house of Abinadab on the hill. They consecrated his son, Eleazar, to have charge of the ark of the LORD.

2 From the day that the ark was lodged at Kiriath-jearim, a long time passed, some twenty years, and all the house of Israel lamented*x* after the LORD.

Samuel as Judge

3 Then Samuel said to all the house of Israel, "If you are returning to the LORD with all your heart, then put away the foreign gods and the Astartes from among you. Direct your heart to the LORD, and serve him only, and he will deliver you out of the hand of the Philistines." 4So Israel put away the Baals and the Astartes, and they served the LORD only.

5 Then Samuel said, "Gather all Israel at Mizpah, and I will pray to the LORD for you." 6So they gathered at Mizpah, and drew water and poured it out before the LORD. They fasted that day, and said, "We have sinned against the LORD." And Samuel judged the people of Israel at Mizpah.

7 When the Philistines heard that the people of Israel had gathered at Mizpah, the lords of the Philistines went up against Israel. And when the people of Israel heard of it they were afraid of the Philistines. 8The people of Israel said to Samuel, "Do not cease to cry out to the LORD our God for us, and pray that he may save us from the hand of the Philistines." 9So Samuel took a sucking lamb and offered it as a whole burnt offering to the LORD; Samuel cried out to the LORD for Israel, and the LORD answered him. 10As Samuel was offering up the burnt offering, the Philistines drew near to attack Israel; but the LORD thundered with a mighty voice that day against the Philistines and threw them into confusion; and they were routed before Israel. 11And the men of Israel went out of Mizpah and pursued the Philistines, and struck them down as far as beyond Beth-car.

12 Then Samuel took a stone and set it up between Mizpah and Jeshanah,*y* and named it Ebenezer;*z* for he said, "Thus far the LORD has helped us." 13So the Philistines were subdued and did not again enter the territory of Israel; the hand of the LORD was against the Philistines all the days of Samuel. 14The towns that the Philistines had taken from Israel were restored to Israel, from Ekron to Gath; and Israel recovered their territory from the hand of the Philistines. There was peace also between Israel and the Amorites.

15 Samuel judged Israel all the days of his life. 16He went on a circuit year by year to Bethel, Gilgal, and Mizpah; and he judged Israel in all these places. 17Then he would come back to Ramah, for his home was there; he administered

---

v Gk: Heb *And he killed some of the people of Beth-shemesh, because they looked into*   w Heb *killed seventy men, fifty thousand men*   x Meaning of Heb uncertain   y Gk Syr: Heb *Shen*   z That is *Stone of Help*

justice there to Israel, and built there an altar to the LORD.

Israel Demands a King

8 When Samuel became old, he made his sons judges over Israel. 2 The name of his firstborn son was Joel, and the name of his second, Abijah; they were judges in Beer-sheba. 3 Yet his sons did not follow in his ways, but turned aside after gain; they took bribes and perverted justice.

4 Then all the elders of Israel gathered together and came to Samuel at Ramah, 5 and said to him, "You are old and your sons do not follow in your ways; appoint for us, then, a king to govern us, like other nations." 6 But the thing displeased Samuel when they said, "Give us a king to govern us." Samuel prayed to the LORD, 7 and the LORD said to Samuel, "Listen to the voice of the people in all that they say to you; for they have not rejected you, but they have rejected me from being king over them. 8 Just as they have done to me,*a* from the day I brought them up out of Egypt to this day, forsaking me and serving other gods, so also they are doing to you. 9 Now then, listen to their voice; only—you shall solemnly warn them, and show them the ways of the king who shall reign over them."

10 So Samuel reported all the words of the LORD to the people who were asking him for a king. 11 He said, "These will be the ways of the king who will reign over you: he will take your sons and appoint them to his chariots and to be his horsemen, and to run before his chariots; 12 and he will appoint for himself commanders of thousands and commanders of fifties, and some to plow his ground and to reap his harvest, and to make his implements of war and the equipment of his chariots. 13 He will take your daughters to be perfumers and cooks and bakers. 14 He will take the best of your fields and vineyards and olive orchards and give them to his courtiers. 15 He will take one-tenth of your grain and of your vineyards and give it to his officers and his courtiers. 16 He will take your male and female slaves, and the best of your cattle*b* and

donkeys, and put them to his work. 17 He will take one-tenth of your flocks, and you shall be his slaves. 18 And in that day you will cry out because of your king, whom you have chosen for yourselves; but the LORD will not answer you in that day."

Israel's Request for a King Granted

19 But the people refused to listen to the voice of Samuel; they said, "No! but we are determined to have a king over us, 20 so that we also may be like other nations, and that our king may govern us and go out before us and fight our battles." 21 When Samuel had heard all the words of the people, he repeated them in the ears of the LORD. 22 The LORD said to Samuel, "Listen to their voice and set a king over them." Samuel then said to the people of Israel, "Each of you return home."

Saul Chosen to Be King

9 There was a man of Benjamin whose name was Kish son of Abiel son of Zeror son of Becorath son of Aphiah, a Benjaminite, a man of wealth. 2 He had a son whose name was Saul, a handsome young man. There was not a man among the people of Israel more handsome than he; he stood head and shoulders above everyone else.

3 Now the donkeys of Kish, Saul's father, had strayed. So Kish said to his son Saul, "Take one of the boys with you; go and look for the donkeys." 4 He passed through the hill country of Ephraim and passed through the land of Shalishah, but they did not find them. And they passed through the land of Shaalim, but they were not there. Then he passed through the land of Benjamin, but they did not find them.

5 When they came to the land of Zuph, Saul said to the boy who was with him, "Let us turn back, or my father will stop worrying about the donkeys and worry about us." 6 But he said to him, "There is a man of God in this town; he is a man held in honor. Whatever he says always comes true. Let us go there now; perhaps he will tell us about the journey on which we have set out." 7 Then Saul replied to the boy, "But

a Gk: Heb lacks *to me*   *b* Gk: Heb *young men*

if we go, what can we bring the man? For the bread in our sacks is gone, and there is no present to bring to the man of God. What have we?" 8The boy answered Saul again, "Here, I have with me a quarter shekel of silver; I will give it to the man of God, to tell us our way." 9(Formerly in Israel, anyone who went to inquire of God would say, "Come, let us go to the seer"; for the one who is now called a prophet was formerly called a seer.) 10Saul said to the boy, "Good; come, let us go." So they went to the town where the man of God was.

11 As they went up the hill to the town, they met some girls coming out to draw water, and said to them, "Is the seer here?" 12They answered, "Yes, there he is just ahead of you. Hurry; he has come just now to the town, because the people have a sacrifice today at the shrine. 13As soon as you enter the town, you will find him, before he goes up to the shrine to eat. For the people will not eat until he comes, since he must bless the sacrifice; afterward those eat who are invited. Now go up, for you will meet him immediately." 14So they went up to the town. As they were entering the town, they saw Samuel coming out toward them on his way up to the shrine.

15 Now the day before Saul came, the LORD had revealed to Samuel: 16"Tomorrow about this time I will send to you a man from the land of Benjamin, and you shall anoint him to be ruler over my people Israel. He shall save my people from the hand of the Philistines; for I have seen the suffering ofc my people, because their outcry has come to me." 17When Samuel saw Saul, the LORD told him, "Here is the man of whom I spoke to you. He it is who shall rule over my people." 18Then Saul approached Samuel inside the gate, and said, "Tell me, please, where is the house of the seer?" 19Samuel answered Saul, "I am the seer; go up before me to the shrine, for today you shall eat with me, and in the morning I will let you go and will tell you all that is on your mind. 20As for your donkeys that were

lost three days ago, give no further thought to them, for they have been found. And on whom is all Israel's desire fixed, if not on you and on all your ancestral house?" 21Saul answered, "I am only a Benjaminite, from the least of the tribes of Israel, and my family is the humblest of all the families of the tribe of Benjamin. Why then have you spoken to me in this way?"

22 Then Samuel took Saul and his servant-boy and brought them into the hall, and gave them a place at the head of those who had been invited, of whom there were about thirty. 23And Samuel said to the cook, "Bring the portion I gave you, the one I asked you to put aside." 24The cook took up the thigh and what went with itd and set them before Saul. Samuel said, "See, what was kept is set before you. Eat; for it is sete before you at the appointed time, so that you might eat with the guests."f

So Saul ate with Samuel that day. 25When they came down from the shrine into the town, a bed was spread for Saulg on the roof, and he lay down to sleep.h 26Then at the break of dawni Samuel called to Saul upon the roof, "Get up, so that I may send you on your way." Saul got up, and both he and Samuel went out into the street.

Samuel Anoints Saul

27 As they were going down to the outskirts of the town, Samuel said to Saul, "Tell the boy to go on before us, and when he has passed on, stop here yourself for a while, that I may make known to you the word of God."

10 1Samuel took a vial of oil and poured it on his head, and kissed him; he said, "The LORD has anointed you ruler over his people Israel. You shall reign over the people of the LORD and you will save them from the hand of their enemies all around. Now this shall be the sign to you that the LORD has anointed you rulerj over his heritage: 2When you depart from me today you will meet two men by Rachel's tomb in the territory of Benja-

---

c Gk: Heb lacks the suffering of   d Meaning of Heb uncertain   e Q Ms Gk: MT it was kept
f Cn: Heb it was kept for you, saying, I have invited the people   g Gk: Heb and he spoke with Saul
h Gk: Heb lacks and he lay down to sleep   i Gk: Heb and they arose early and at break of dawn
j Gk: Heb lacks over his people Israel. You shall . . . anointed you ruler

min at Zelzah; they will say to you, 'The
donkeys that you went to seek are
found, and now your father has stopped
worrying about them and is worrying
about you, saying: What shall I do about
my son?' 3Then you shall go on from
there further and come to the oak of
Tabor; three men going up to God at
Bethel will meet you there, one carrying
three kids, another carrying three loaves
of bread, and another carrying a skin of
wine. 4They will greet you and give you
two loaves of bread, which you shall
accept from them. 5After that you shall
come to Gibeath-elohim,[k] at the place
where the Philistine garrison is; there,
as you come to the town, you will meet
a band of prophets coming down from
the shrine with harp, tambourine, flute,
and lyre playing in front of them; they
will be in a prophetic frenzy. 6Then the
spirit of the LORD will possess you, and
you will be in a prophetic frenzy along
with them and be turned into a different
person. 7Now when these signs meet
you, do whatever you see fit to do, for
God is with you. 8And you shall go
down to Gilgal ahead of me; then I will
come down to you to present burnt
offerings and offer sacrifices of well-being.
Seven days you shall wait, until I
come to you and show you what you
shall do."

Saul Prophesies

9 As he turned away to leave Samuel,
God gave him another heart; and all
these signs were fulfilled that day.
10When they were going from there[l] to
Gibeah,[m] a band of prophets met him;
and the spirit of God possessed him, and
he fell into a prophetic frenzy along with
them. 11When all who knew him before
saw how he prophesied with the prophets,
the people said to one another,
"What has come over the son of Kish? Is
Saul also among the prophets?" 12A man
of the place answered, "And who is their
father?" Therefore it became a proverb,
"Is Saul also among the prophets?"
13When his prophetic frenzy had ended,
he went home.[n]
14 Saul's uncle said to him and to the
boy, "Where did you go?" And he
replied, "To seek the donkeys; and when
we saw they were not to be found, we
went to Samuel." 15Saul's uncle said,
"Tell me what Samuel said to you."
16Saul said to his uncle, "He told us that
the donkeys had been found." But about
the matter of the kingship, of which
Samuel had spoken, he did not tell him
anything.

Saul Proclaimed King

17 Samuel summoned the people to
the LORD at Mizpah 18and said to them,[o]
"Thus says the LORD, the God of Israel,
'I brought up Israel out of Egypt, and I
rescued you from the hand of the Egyptians
and from the hand of all the kingdoms
that were oppressing you.' 19But
today you have rejected your God, who
saves you from all your calamities and
your distresses; and you have said, 'No!
but set a king over us.' Now therefore
present yourselves before the LORD by
your tribes and by your clans."
20 Then Samuel brought all the
tribes of Israel near, and the tribe of Benjamin
was taken by lot. 21He brought
the tribe of Benjamin near by its families,
and the family of the Matrites was
taken by lot. Finally he brought the family
of the Matrites near man by man,[p]
and Saul the son of Kish was taken by
lot. But when they sought him, he could
not be found. 22So they inquired again of
the LORD, "Did the man come here?"[q]
and the LORD said, "See, he has hidden
himself among the baggage." 23Then
they ran and brought him from there.
When he took his stand among the people,
he was head and shoulders taller
than any of them. 24Samuel said to all
the people, "Do you see the one whom
the LORD has chosen? There is no one
like him among all the people." And all
the people shouted, "Long live the
king!"
25 Samuel told the people the rights
and duties of the kingship; and he wrote
them in a book and laid it up before the
LORD. Then Samuel sent all the people
back to their homes. 26Saul also went to
his home at Gibeah, and with him went

k Or *the Hill of God* *l* Gk: Heb *they came there* *m* Or *the hill* *n* Cn: Heb *he came to the shrine* *o* Heb *to the people of Israel* *p* Gk: Heb lacks *Finally . . . man by man* *q* Gk: Heb *Is there yet a man to come here?*

warriors whose hearts God had touched. [27]But some worthless fellows said, "How can this man save us?" They despised him and brought him no present. But he held his peace.

Now Nahash, king of the Ammonites, had been grievously oppressing the Gadites and the Reubenites. He would gouge out the right eye of each of them and would not grant Israel a deliverer. No one was left of the Israelites across the Jordan whose right eye Nahash, king of the Ammonites, had not gouged out. But there were seven thousand men who had escaped from the Ammonites and had entered Jabesh-gilead.[r]

Saul Defeats the Ammonites

11 About a month later,[s] Nahash the Ammonite went up and besieged Jabesh-gilead; and all the men of Jabesh said to Nahash, "Make a treaty with us, and we will serve you." [2]But Nahash the Ammonite said to them, "On this condition I will make a treaty with you, namely that I gouge out everyone's right eye, and thus put disgrace upon all Israel." [3]The elders of Jabesh said to him, "Give us seven days' respite that we may send messengers through all the territory of Israel. Then, if there is no one to save us, we will give ourselves up to you." [4]When the messengers came to Gibeah of Saul, they reported the matter in the hearing of the people; and all the people wept aloud.

[5] Now Saul was coming from the field behind the oxen; and Saul said, "What is the matter with the people, that they are weeping?" So they told him the message from the inhabitants of Jabesh. [6]And the spirit of God came upon Saul in power when he heard these words, and his anger was greatly kindled. [7]He took a yoke of oxen, and cut them in pieces and sent them throughout all the territory of Israel by messengers, saying, "Whoever does not come out after Saul and Samuel, so shall it be done to his oxen!" Then the dread of the LORD fell upon the people, and they came out as one. [8]When he mustered them at Bezek, those from Israel were

three hundred thousand, and those from Judah seventy[t] thousand. [9]They said to the messengers who had come, "Thus shall you say to the inhabitants of Jabesh-gilead: 'Tomorrow, by the time the sun is hot, you shall have deliverance.'" When the messengers came and told the inhabitants of Jabesh, they rejoiced. [10]So the inhabitants of Jabesh said, "Tomorrow we will give ourselves up to you, and you may do to us whatever seems good to you." [11]The next day Saul put the people in three companies. At the morning watch they came into the camp and cut down the Ammonites until the heat of the day; and those who survived were scattered, so that no two of them were left together.

[12] The people said to Samuel, "Who is it that said, 'Shall Saul reign over us?' Give them to us so that we may put them to death." [13]But Saul said, "No one shall be put to death this day, for today the LORD has brought deliverance to Israel."

[14] Samuel said to the people, "Come, let us go to Gilgal and there renew the kingship." [15]So all the people went to Gilgal, and there they made Saul king before the LORD in Gilgal. There they sacrificed offerings of well-being before the LORD, and there Saul and all the Israelites rejoiced greatly.

Samuel's Farewell Address

12 Samuel said to all Israel, "I have listened to you in all that you have said to me, and have set a king over you. [2]See, it is the king who leads you now; I am old and gray, but my sons are with you. I have led you from my youth until this day. [3]Here I am; testify against me before the LORD and before his anointed. Whose ox have I taken? Or whose donkey have I taken? Or whom have I defrauded? Whom have I oppressed? Or from whose hand have I taken a bribe to blind my eyes with it? Testify against me[u] and I will restore it to you." [4]They said, "You have not defrauded us or oppressed us or taken anything from the hand of anyone." [5]He said to them, "The LORD is witness

r Q Ms Compare Josephus, *Antiquities* VI.v.1 (68-71): MT lacks *Now Nahash . . . entered Jabesh-gilead*.
s Q Ms Gk: MT lacks *About a month later*   t Q Ms Gk: MT *thirty*   u Gk: Heb lacks *Testify against me*

against you, and his anointed is witness this day, that you have not found anything in my hand." And they said, "He is witness."

6 Samuel said to the people, "The LORD is witness, who[v] appointed Moses and Aaron and brought your ancestors up out of the land of Egypt. [7]Now therefore take your stand, so that I may enter into judgment with you before the LORD, and I will declare to you[w] all the saving deeds of the LORD that he performed for you and for your ancestors. [8]When Jacob went into Egypt and the Egyptians oppressed them,[x] then your ancestors cried to the LORD and the LORD sent Moses and Aaron, who brought forth your ancestors out of Egypt, and settled them in this place. [9]But they forgot the LORD their God; and he sold them into the hand of Sisera, commander of the army of King Jabin of[y] Hazor, and into the hand of the Philistines, and into the hand of the king of Moab; and they fought against them. [10]Then they cried to the LORD, and said, 'We have sinned, because we have forsaken the LORD, and have served the Baals and the Astartes; but now rescue us out of the hand of our enemies, and we will serve you.' [11]And the LORD sent Jerubbaal and Barak,[z] and Jephthah, and Samson,[a] and rescued you out of the hand of your enemies on every side; and you lived in safety. [12]But when you saw that King Nahash of the Ammonites came against you, you said to me, 'No, but a king shall reign over us,' though the LORD your God was your king. [13]See, here is the king whom you have chosen, for whom you have asked; see, the LORD has set a king over you. [14]If you will fear the LORD and serve him and heed his voice and not rebel against the commandment of the LORD, and if both you and the king who reigns over you will follow the LORD your God, it will be well; [15]but if you will not heed the voice of the LORD, but rebel against the commandment of the LORD, then the hand of the LORD will be against you and your king.[b] [16]Now therefore take your stand and see this great thing that the LORD

will do before your eyes. [17]Is it not the wheat harvest today? I will call upon the LORD, that he may send thunder and rain; and you shall know and see that the wickedness that you have done in the sight of the LORD is great in demanding a king for yourselves." [18]So Samuel called upon the LORD, and the LORD sent thunder and rain that day; and all the people greatly feared the LORD and Samuel.

19 All the people said to Samuel, "Pray to the LORD your God for your servants, so that we may not die; for we have added to all our sins the evil of demanding a king for ourselves." [20]And Samuel said to the people, "Do not be afraid; you have done all this evil, yet do not turn aside from following the LORD, but serve the LORD with all your heart; [21]and do not turn aside after useless things that cannot profit or save, for they are useless. [22]For the LORD will not cast away his people, for his great name's sake, because it has pleased the LORD to make you a people for himself. [23]Moreover as for me, far be it from me that I should sin against the LORD by ceasing to pray for you; and I will instruct you in the good and the right way. [24]Only fear the LORD, and serve him faithfully with all your heart; for consider what great things he has done for you. [25]But if you still do wickedly, you shall be swept away, both you and your king."

Saul's Unlawful Sacrifice

13 Saul was . . .[c] years old when he began to reign; and he reigned . . . and two[d] years over Israel.

2 Saul chose three thousand out of Israel; two thousand were with Saul in Michmash and the hill country of Bethel, and a thousand were with Jonathan in Gibeah of Benjamin; the rest of the people he sent home to their tents. [3]Jonathan defeated the garrison of the Philistines that was at Geba; and the Philistines heard of it. And Saul blew the trumpet throughout all the land, saying, "Let the Hebrews hear!" [4]When all Israel

---

v Gk: Heb lacks *is witness, who*   w Gk: Heb lacks *and I will declare to you*   x Gk: Heb lacks *and the Egyptians oppressed them*   y Gk: Heb lacks *King Jabin of*   z Gk Syr: Heb *Bedan*   a Gk: Heb *Samuel*   b Gk: Heb *and your ancestors*   c The number is lacking in the Heb text (the verse is lacking in the Septuagint).   d *Two* is not the entire number; something has dropped out.

heard that Saul had defeated the garrison of the Philistines, and also that Israel had become odious to the Philistines, the people were called out to join Saul at Gilgal.

5 The Philistines mustered to fight

THURSDAY

THE ONLY REAL APOSTOLIC LIFE
Evelyn Underhill

VERSE: 1 Samuel 12.19   **PASSAGE:** 1 Samuel 12.19–25

 hat then is a real man of prayer? He is one who deliberately wills and steadily desires that his intercourse with God and other souls shall be controlled and actuated at every point by God himself; one who has so far developed and educated his spiritual sense, that his supernatural environment is more real and solid to him than his natural environment. A man of prayer is not necessarily a person who says a number of offices, or abounds in detailed intercessions; but he is a child of God, who is and knows himself to be in the deeps of his soul attached to God, and is wholly and entirely guided by the creative Spirit in his prayer and his work. This is not merely a bit of pious language. It is a description, as real and concrete as I can make it, of the only really apostolic life. Every Christian starts with a chance of it; but only a few develop it. The laity distinguish in a moment the clergy who have it from the clergy who have it not: there is nothing that you can do for God or for the souls of men, which exceeds in importance the achievement of that spiritual temper and attitude.

It is only through adoration and attention that we make our personal discoveries about him . . . I think that if you have only as little as half an hour to give each morning to your private prayer, it is not too much to make up your minds to spend half that time in such adoration. For it is the central service asked by God of human souls; and its neglect is responsible for much lack of spiritual depth and power.

In the flood tide of such adoring prayer, the soul is released from the strife and confusions of temporal life; it is lifted far beyond all petty controversies, petty worries and vanities—and none of us escapes these things. It is carried into God, hidden in him.

ADDITIONAL SCRIPTURE READING:
Psalm 19.12–14; Luke 11.1–4; Romans 8.26–27

Go to page 319 for your next devotional reading.

1900   Present

with Israel, thirty thousand chariots, and six thousand horsemen, and troops like the sand on the seashore in multitude; they came up and encamped at Michmash, to the east of Beth-aven. 6When the Israelites saw that they were in distress (for the troops were hard pressed), the people hid themselves in caves and in holes and in rocks and in tombs and in cisterns. 7Some Hebrews crossed the Jordan to the land of Gad and Gilead. Saul was still at Gilgal, and all the people followed him trembling.

8 He waited seven days, the time appointed by Samuel; but Samuel did not come to Gilgal, and the people began to slip away from Saul.e 9So Saul said, "Bring the burnt offering here to me, and the offerings of well-being." And he offered the burnt offering. 10As soon as he had finished offering the burnt offering, Samuel arrived; and Saul went out to meet him and salute him. 11Samuel said, "What have you done?" Saul replied, "When I saw that the people were slipping away from me, and that you did not come within the days appointed, and that the Philistines were mustering at Michmash, 12I said, 'Now the Philistines will come down upon me at Gilgal, and I have not entreated the favor of the LORD'; so I forced myself, and offered the burnt offering." 13Samuel said to Saul, "You have done foolishly; you have not kept the commandment of the LORD your God, which he commanded you. The LORD would have established your kingdom over Israel forever, 14but now your kingdom will not continue; the LORD has sought out a man after his own heart; and the LORD has appointed him to be ruler over his people, because you have not kept what the LORD commanded you." 15And Samuel left and went on his way from Gilgal.f The rest of the people followed Saul to join the army; they went up from Gilgal toward Gibeah of Benjamin.g

Preparations for Battle

Saul counted the people who were present with him, about six hundred men. 16Saul, his son Jonathan, and the people who were present with them stayed in Geba of Benjamin; but the Philistines encamped at Michmash. 17And raiders came out of the camp of the Philistines in three companies; one company turned toward Ophrah, to the land of Shual, 18another company turned toward Beth-horon, and another company turned toward the mountainh that looks down upon the valley of Zeboim toward the wilderness.

19 Now there was no smith to be found throughout all the land of Israel; for the Philistines said, "The Hebrews must not make swords or spears for themselves"; 20so all the Israelites went down to the Philistines to sharpen their plowshares, mattocks, axes, or sickles;i 21The charge was two-thirds of a shekelj for the plowshares and for the mattocks, and one-third of a shekel for sharpening the axes and for setting the goads.k 22So on the day of the battle neither sword nor spear was to be found in the possession of any of the people with Saul and Jonathan; but Saul and his son Jonathan had them.

Jonathan Surprises and Routs the Philistines

23 Now a garrison of the Philistines had gone out to the pass of Michmash. 14 1One day Jonathan son of Saul said to the young man who carried his armor, "Come, let us go over to the Philistine garrison on the other side." But he did not tell his father. 2Saul was staying in the outskirts of Gibeah under the pomegranate tree that is at Migron; the troops that were with him were about six hundred men, 3along with Ahijah son of Ahitub, Ichabod's brother, son of Phinehas son of Eli, the priest of the LORD in Shiloh, carrying an ephod. Now the people did not know that Jonathan had gone. 4In the pass,l by which Jonathan tried to go over to the Philistine garrison, there was a rocky crag on one side and a rocky crag on the other; the name of the one was Bozez, and the name of the other Seneh. 5One crag rose on the north in front of Michmash, and the other on the south in front of Geba.

---

e Heb him   f Gk: Heb went up from Gilgal to Gibeah of Benjamin   g Gk: Heb lacks The rest . . . of Benjamin   h Cn Compare Gk: Heb toward the border   i Gk: Heb plowshare   j Heb was a pim   k Cn: Meaning of Heb uncertain   l Heb Between the passes

6 Jonathan said to the young man who carried his armor, "Come, let us go over to the garrison of these uncircumcised; it may be that the LORD will act for us; for nothing can hinder the LORD from saving by many or by few." 7His armor-bearer said to him, "Do all that your mind inclines to.m I am with you; as your mind is, so is mine."n 8Then Jonathan said, "Now we will cross over to those men and will show ourselves to them. 9If they say to us, 'Wait until we come to you,' then we will stand still in our place, and we will not go up to them. 10But if they say, 'Come up to us,' then we will go up; for the LORD has given them into our hand. That will be the sign for us." 11So both of them showed themselves to the garrison of the Philistines; and the Philistines said, "Look, Hebrews are coming out of the holes where they have hidden themselves." 12The men of the garrison hailed Jonathan and his armor-bearer, saying, "Come up to us, and we will show you something." Jonathan said to his armor-bearer, "Come up after me; for the LORD has given them into the hand of Israel." 13Then Jonathan climbed up on his hands and feet, with his armor-bearer following after him. The Philistineso fell before Jonathan, and his armor-bearer, coming after him, killed them. 14In that first slaughter Jonathan and his armor-bearer killed about twenty men within an area about half a furrow long in an acrep of land. 15There was a panic in the camp, in the field, and among all the people; the garrison and even the raiders trembled; the earth quaked; and it became a very great panic.

16 Saul's lookouts in Gibeah of Benjamin were watching as the multitude was surging back and forth.q 17Then Saul said to the troops that were with him, "Call the roll and see who has gone from us." When they had called the roll, Jonathan and his armor-bearer were not there. 18Saul said to Ahijah, "Bring the arkr of God here." For at that time the arkr of God went with the Israelites. 19While Saul was talking to the priest,

the tumult in the camp of the Philistines increased more and more; and Saul said to the priest, "Withdraw your hand." 20Then Saul and all the people who were with him rallied and went into the battle; and every sword was against the other, so that there was very great confusion. 21Now the Hebrews who previously had been with the Philistines and had gone up with them into the camp turned and joined the Israelites who were with Saul and Jonathan. 22Likewise, when all the Israelites who had gone into hiding in the hill country of Ephraim heard that the Philistines were fleeing, they too followed closely after them in the battle. 23So the LORD gave Israel the victory that day.

The battle passed beyond Beth-aven, and the troops with Saul numbered altogether about ten thousand men. The battle spread out over the hill country of Ephraim.

Saul's Rash Oath

24 Now Saul committed a very rash act on that day.s He had laid an oath on the troops, saying, "Cursed be anyone who eats food before it is evening and I have been avenged on my enemies." So none of the troops tasted food. 25All the troopst came upon a honeycomb; and there was honey on the ground. 26When the troops came upon the honeycomb, the honey was dripping out; but they did not put their hands to their mouths, for they feared the oath. 27But Jonathan had not heard his father charge the troops with the oath; so he extended the staff that was in his hand, and dipped the tip of it in the honeycomb, and put his hand to his mouth; and his eyes brightened. 28Then one of the soldiers said, "Your father strictly charged the troops with an oath, saying, 'Cursed be anyone who eats food this day.' And so the troops are faint." 29Then Jonathan said, "My father has troubled the land; see how my eyes have brightened because I tasted a little of this honey. 30How much better if today the troops had eaten freely of the spoil taken from their enemies; for now

m Gk: Heb Do all that is in your mind. Turn   n Gk: Heb lacks so is mine   o Heb They
p Heb yoke   q Gk: Heb they went and there   r Gk the ephod   s Gk: Heb The Israelites were
distressed that day   t Heb land

the slaughter among the Philistines has not been great."

31 After they had struck down the Philistines that day from Michmash to Aijalon, the troops were very faint; 32so the troops flew upon the spoil, and took sheep and oxen and calves, and slaughtered them on the ground; and the troops ate them with the blood. 33Then it was reported to Saul, "Look, the troops are sinning against the LORD by eating with the blood." And he said, "You have dealt treacherously; roll a large stone before me here."u 34Saul said, "Disperse yourselves among the troops, and say to them, 'Let all bring their oxen or their sheep, and slaughter them here, and eat; and do not sin against the LORD by eating with the blood.'" So all of the troops brought their oxen with them that night, and slaughtered them there. 35And Saul built an altar to the LORD; it was the first altar that he built to the LORD.

Jonathan in Danger of Death

36 Then Saul said, "Let us go down after the Philistines by night and despoil them until the morning light; let us not leave one of them." They said, "Do whatever seems good to you." But the priest said, "Let us draw near to God here." 37So Saul inquired of God, "Shall I go down after the Philistines? Will you give them into the hand of Israel?" But he did not answer him that day. 38Saul said, "Come here, all you leaders of the people; and let us find out how this sin has arisen today. 39For as the LORD lives who saves Israel, even if it is in my son Jonathan, he shall surely die!" But there was no one among all the people who answered him. 40He said to all Israel, "You shall be on one side, and I and my son Jonathan will be on the other side." The people said to Saul, "Do what seems good to you." 41Then Saul said, "O LORD God of Israel, why have you not answered your servant today? If this guilt is in me or in my son Jonathan, O LORD God of Israel, give Urim; but if this guilt is in your people Israel,v give Thummim." And Jonathan and Saul were indicated by the lot, but the people were cleared. 42Then Saul said, "Cast the lot between me and my son Jonathan." And Jonathan was taken.

43 Then Saul said to Jonathan, "Tell me what you have done." Jonathan told him, "I tasted a little honey with the tip of the staff that was in my hand; here I am, I will die." 44Saul said, "God do so to me and more also; you shall surely die, Jonathan!" 45Then the people said to Saul, "Shall Jonathan die, who has accomplished this great victory in Israel? Far from it! As the LORD lives, not one hair of his head shall fall to the ground; for he has worked with God today." So the people ransomed Jonathan, and he did not die. 46Then Saul withdrew from pursuing the Philistines; and the Philistines went to their own place.

Saul's Continuing Wars

47 When Saul had taken the kingship over Israel, he fought against all his enemies on every side—against Moab, against the Ammonites, against Edom, against the kings of Zobah, and against the Philistines; wherever he turned he routed them. 48He did valiantly, and struck down the Amalekites, and rescued Israel out of the hands of those who plundered them.

49 Now the sons of Saul were Jonathan, Ishvi, and Malchishua; and the names of his two daughters were these: the name of the firstborn was Merab, and the name of the younger, Michal. 50The name of Saul's wife was Ahinoam daughter of Ahimaaz. And the name of the commander of his army was Abner son of Ner, Saul's uncle; 51Kish was the father of Saul, and Ner the father of Abner was the son of Abiel.

52 There was hard fighting against the Philistines all the days of Saul; and when Saul saw any strong or valiant warrior, he took him into his service.

Saul Defeats the Amalekites but Spares Their King

15 Samuel said to Saul, "The LORD sent me to anoint you king over his people Israel; now therefore listen to the words of the LORD. 2Thus says the LORD of hosts, 'I will punish the Amalekites for what they did in opposing

the Israelites when they came up out of Egypt. ³Now go and attack Amalek, and utterly destroy all that they have; do not spare them, but kill both man and woman, child and infant, ox and sheep, camel and donkey.' "

4 So Saul summoned the people, and numbered them in Telaim, two hundred thousand foot soldiers, and ten thousand soldiers of Judah. ⁵Saul came to the city of the Amalekites and lay in wait in the valley. ⁶Saul said to the Kenites, "Go! Leave! Withdraw from among the Amalekites, or I will destroy you with them; for you showed kindness to all the people of Israel when they came up out of Egypt." So the Kenites withdrew from the Amalekites. ⁷Saul defeated the Amalekites, from Havilah as far as Shur, which is east of Egypt. ⁸He took King Agag of the Amalekites alive, but utterly destroyed all the people with the edge of the sword. ⁹Saul and the people spared Agag, and the best of the sheep and of the cattle and of the fatlings, and the lambs, and all that was valuable, and would not utterly destroy them; all that was despised and worthless they utterly destroyed.

Saul Rejected as King

10 The word of the LORD came to Samuel: ¹¹"I regret that I made Saul king, for he has turned back from following me, and has not carried out my commands." Samuel was angry; and he cried out to the LORD all night. ¹²Samuel rose early in the morning to meet Saul, and Samuel was told, "Saul went to Carmel, where he set up a monument for himself, and on returning he passed on down to Gilgal." ¹³When Samuel came to Saul, Saul said to him, "May you be blessed by the LORD; I have carried out the command of the LORD." ¹⁴But Samuel said, "What then is this bleating of sheep in my ears, and the lowing of cattle that I hear?" ¹⁵Saul said, "They have brought them from the Amalekites; for the people spared the best of the sheep and the cattle, to sacrifice to the LORD your God; but the rest we have utterly destroyed." ¹⁶Then Samuel said to Saul, "Stop! I will tell you what the LORD said to me last night." He replied, "Speak."

17 Samuel said, "Though you are little in your own eyes, are you not the head of the tribes of Israel? The LORD anointed you king over Israel. ¹⁸And the LORD sent you on a mission, and said, 'Go, utterly destroy the sinners, the Amalekites, and fight against them until they are consumed.' ¹⁹Why then did you not obey the voice of the LORD? Why did you swoop down on the spoil, and do what was evil in the sight of the

---

JUSTICE IS THE INSURANCE WE HAVE ON OUR LIVES, AND OBEDIENCE IS THE PREMIUM WE PAY FOR IT.   —*William Penn*

LORD?" ²⁰Saul said to Samuel, "I have obeyed the voice of the LORD, I have gone on the mission on which the LORD sent me, I have brought Agag the king of Amalek, and I have utterly destroyed the Amalekites. ²¹But from the spoil the people took sheep and cattle, the best of the things devoted to destruction, to sacrifice to the LORD your God in Gilgal." ²²And Samuel said,

"Has the LORD as great delight in
     burnt offerings and sacrifices,
as in obedience to the voice of
     the LORD?
Surely, to obey is better than
     sacrifice,
     and to heed than the fat of rams.
23   For rebellion is no less a sin than
     divination,
     and stubbornness is like iniquity
       and idolatry.
Because you have rejected the word
     of the LORD,
     he has also rejected you from
       being king."

24 Saul said to Samuel, "I have sinned; for I have transgressed the commandment of the LORD and your words, because I feared the people and obeyed their voice. ²⁵Now therefore, I pray, pardon my sin, and return with me, so that I may worship the LORD." ²⁶Samuel said to Saul, "I will not return with you; for you have rejected the word of the LORD, and the LORD has rejected you from being king over Israel." ²⁷As Samuel turned to go away, Saul caught hold of the hem of his robe, and it tore. ²⁸And Samuel said to him, "The LORD has

torn the kingdom of Israel from you this very day, and has given it to a neighbor of yours, who is better than you. [29]Moreover the Glory of Israel will not recant[w] or change his mind; for he is not a mortal, that he should change his mind." [30]Then Saul[x] said, "I have sinned; yet honor me now before the elders of my people and before Israel, and return with me, so that I may worship the LORD your God." [31]So Samuel turned back after Saul; and Saul worshiped the LORD.

32 Then Samuel said, "Bring Agag king of the Amalekites here to me." And Agag came to him haltingly.[y] Agag said, "Surely this is the bitterness of death."[z] [33]But Samuel said,

"As your sword has made women childless,
so your mother shall be childless among women."

And Samuel hewed Agag in pieces before the LORD in Gilgal.

34 Then Samuel went to Ramah; and Saul went up to his house in Gibeah of Saul. [35]Samuel did not see Saul again until the day of his death, but Samuel

w Q Ms Gk: MT deceive   x Heb he   y Cn Compare Gk: Meaning of Heb uncertain   z Q Ms Gk: MT Surely the bitterness of death is past

---

FRIDAY

GOD'S GREAT DELIGHT
Matthew Henry

VERSE: 1 Samuel 15.22   **PASSAGE:** 1 Samuel 15.10–23

ere we are plainly told . . . that humble, sincere, and conscientious obedience to the will of God is more pleasing and acceptable to him than *all burnt offerings and sacrifices*. A careful conformity to moral precepts recommends us to God more than all ceremonial observances (see Micah 6.6–8; Hosea 6.6). Obedience was the law of innocency, but sacrifice supposes sin come into the world and is but a feeble attempt to take that away which obedience would have prevented. It is much easier to bring a bullock or lamb to be burnt upon the altar than to bring *every high thought into obedience* to God and the will subject to his will. Nothing is so provoking to God as disobedience, setting up our wills in competition with his. This is here called *rebellion* and *stubbornness*, and is said to be as bad as *witchcraft* and *idolatry* (v. 23, KJV). It is as bad to set up other gods as to live in disobedience to the true God . . . Those are unfit and unworthy to rule over men who are not willing that God should rule over them.

ADDITIONAL SCRIPTURE READING:
Jeremiah 7.23; Hosea 6.6

Go to page 322 for your next devotional reading.

1700   1900

grieved over Saul. And the LORD was sorry that he had made Saul king over Israel.

David Anointed as King

16 The LORD said to Samuel, "How long will you grieve over Saul? I have rejected him from being king over Israel. Fill your horn with oil and set out; I will send you to Jesse the Bethlehemite, for I have provided for myself a king among his sons." 2Samuel said, "How can I go? If Saul hears of it, he will kill me." And the LORD said, "Take a heifer with you, and say, 'I have come to sacrifice to the LORD.' 3Invite Jesse to the sacrifice, and I will show you what you shall do; and you shall anoint for me the one whom I name to you." 4Samuel did what the LORD commanded, and came to Bethlehem. The elders of the city came to meet him trembling, and said, "Do you come peaceably?" 5He said, "Peaceably; I have come to sacrifice to the LORD; sanctify yourselves and come with me to the sacrifice." And he sanctified Jesse and his sons and invited them to the sacrifice.

6 When they came, he looked on Eliab and thought, "Surely the LORD's anointed is now before the LORD."*a* 7But the LORD said to Samuel, "Do not look on his appearance or on the height of his stature, because I have rejected him; for the LORD does not see as mortals see; they look on the outward appearance, but the LORD looks on the heart." 8Then Jesse called Abinadab, and made him pass before Samuel. He said, "Neither has the LORD chosen this one." 9Then Jesse made Shammah pass by. And he said, "Neither has the LORD chosen this one." 10Jesse made seven of his sons pass before Samuel, and Samuel said to Jesse, "The LORD has not chosen any of these." 11Samuel said to Jesse, "Are all your sons here?" And he said, "There remains yet the youngest, but he is keeping the sheep." And Samuel said to Jesse, "Send and bring him; for we will not sit down until he comes here." 12He sent and brought him in. Now he was ruddy, and had beautiful eyes, and was handsome. The LORD said, "Rise and anoint him; for this is the one." 13Then Samuel took the horn of oil, and anointed him in the presence of his brothers; and the spirit of the LORD came mightily upon David from that day forward. Samuel then set out and went to Ramah.

David Plays the Lyre for Saul

14 Now the spirit of the LORD departed from Saul, and an evil spirit from the LORD tormented him. 15And Saul's servants said to him, "See now, an evil spirit from God is tormenting you. 16Let our lord now command the servants who attend you to look for someone who is skillful in playing the lyre; and when the evil spirit from God is upon you, he will play it, and you will feel better." 17So Saul said to his servants, "Provide for me someone who can play well, and bring him to me." 18One of the young men answered, "I have seen a son of Jesse the Bethlehemite who is skillful in playing, a man of valor, a warrior, prudent in speech, and a man of good presence; and the LORD is with him." 19So Saul sent messengers to Jesse, and said, "Send me your son David who is with the sheep." 20Jesse took a donkey loaded with bread, a skin of wine, and a kid, and sent them by his son David to Saul. 21And David came to Saul, and entered his service. Saul loved him greatly, and he became his armor-bearer. 22Saul sent to Jesse, saying, "Let David remain in my service, for he has found favor in my sight." 23And whenever the evil spirit from God came upon Saul, David took the lyre and played it with his hand, and Saul would be relieved and feel better, and the evil spirit would depart from him.

David and Goliath

17 Now the Philistines gathered their armies for battle; they were gathered at Socoh, which belongs to Judah, and encamped between Socoh and Azekah, in Ephes-dammim. 2Saul and the Israelites gathered and encamped in the valley of Elah, and formed ranks against the Philistines. 3The Philistines stood on the mountain on the one side, and Israel stood on the mountain on the other side, with a valley between them.

a Heb *him*

4And there came out from the camp of the Philistines a champion named Goliath, of Gath, whose height was six[b] cubits and a span. 5He had a helmet of bronze on his head, and he was armed with a coat of mail; the weight of the coat was five thousand shekels of bronze. 6He had greaves of bronze on his legs and a javelin of bronze slung between his shoulders. 7The shaft of his spear was like a weaver's beam, and his spear's head weighed six hundred shekels of iron; and his shield-bearer went before him. 8He stood and shouted to the ranks of Israel, "Why have you come out to draw up for battle? Am I not a Philistine, and are you not servants of Saul? Choose a man for yourselves, and let him come down to me. 9If he is able to fight with me and kill me, then we will be your servants; but if I prevail against him and kill him, then you shall be our servants and serve us." 10And the Philistine said, "Today I defy the ranks of Israel! Give me a man, that we may fight together." 11When Saul and all Israel heard these words of the Philistine, they were dismayed and greatly afraid.

12 Now David was the son of an Ephrathite of Bethlehem in Judah, named Jesse, who had eight sons. In the days of Saul the man was already old and advanced in years.[c] 13The three eldest sons of Jesse had followed Saul to the battle; the names of his three sons who went to the battle were Eliab the firstborn, and next to him Abinadab, and the third Shammah. 14David was the youngest; the three eldest followed Saul, 15but David went back and forth from Saul to feed his father's sheep at Bethlehem. 16For forty days the Philistine came forward and took his stand, morning and evening.

17 Jesse said to his son David, "Take for your brothers an ephah of this parched grain and these ten loaves, and carry them quickly to the camp to your brothers; 18also take these ten cheeses to the commander of their thousand. See how your brothers fare, and bring some token from them."

19 Now Saul, and they, and all the men of Israel, were in the valley of Elah, fighting with the Philistines. 20David rose early in the morning, left the sheep with a keeper, took the provisions, and went as Jesse had commanded him. He came to the encampment as the army was going forth to the battle line, shouting the war cry. 21Israel and the Philistines drew up for battle, army against army. 22David left the things in charge of the keeper of the baggage, ran to the ranks, and went and greeted his brothers. 23As he talked with them, the champion, the Philistine of Gath, Goliath by name, came up out of the ranks of the Philistines, and spoke the same words as before. And David heard him.

24 All the Israelites, when they saw the man, fled from him and were very much afraid. 25The Israelites said, "Have you seen this man who has come up? Surely he has come up to defy Israel. The king will greatly enrich the man who kills him, and will give him his daughter and make his family free in Israel." 26David said to the men who stood by him, "What shall be done for the man who kills this Philistine, and takes away the reproach from Israel? For who is this uncircumcised Philistine that he should defy the armies of the living God?" 27The people answered him in the same way, "So shall it be done for the man who kills him."

28 His eldest brother Eliab heard him talking to the men; and Eliab's anger was kindled against David. He said, "Why have you come down? With whom have you left those few sheep in the wilderness? I know your presumption and the evil of your heart; for you have come down just to see the battle." 29David said, "What have I done now? It was only a question." 30He turned away from him toward another and spoke in the same way; and the people answered him again as before.

31 When the words that David spoke were heard, they repeated them before Saul; and he sent for him. 32David said to Saul, "Let no one's heart fail because of him; your servant will go and fight with this Philistine." 33Saul said to David, "You are not able to go against this Philistine to fight with him; for you are just a boy, and he has been a warrior from his youth." 34But David said to

b MT: Q Ms Gk *four*   c Gk Syr: Heb *among men*

WEEKEND

GOD'S OPPORTUNITY IN DISGUISE
C. H. Parkhurst

VERSE: 1 Samuel 17.34   **PASSAGE:** 1 Samuel 17.12–50

 t is a source of inspiration and strength to come in touch with the youthful David, trusting God. Through faith in God he conquered a lion and a bear, and afterwards overthrew the mighty Goliath. When that lion came to despoil that flock, it came as a wondrous *opportunity* to David. If he had failed or faltered he would have missed God's opportunity for him and probably would never have come to be God's chosen king of Israel.

One would not think that a lion was a special blessing from God; one would think that only an occasion of alarm. The lion was *God's opportunity in disguise.* Every difficulty that presents itself to us, if we receive it in the right way, is God's opportunity. Every temptation that comes is God's opportunity.

When the "lion" comes, recognize it as God's opportunity no matter how rough the exterior . . . May God open our eyes to see him, whether in temptations, trials, dangers, or misfortunes.

ADDITIONAL SCRIPTURE READING:
Matthew 26.41; Luke 11.4; 1 Corinthians 10.13

Go to page 330 for your next devotional reading.

1700 ✝ 1900

Saul, "Your servant used to keep sheep for his father; and whenever a lion or a bear came, and took a lamb from the flock, 35I went after it and struck it down, rescuing the lamb from its mouth; and if it turned against me, I would catch it by the jaw, strike it down, and kill it. 36Your servant has killed both lions and bears; and this uncircumcised Philistine shall be like one of them, since he has defied the armies of the living God." 37David said, "The LORD, who saved me from the paw of the lion and from the paw of the bear, will save me from the hand of this Philistine." So Saul said to David, "Go, and may the LORD be with you!"

38 Saul clothed David with his armor; he put a bronze helmet on his head and clothed him with a coat of mail. 39David strapped Saul's sword over the armor, and he tried in vain to walk, for he was not used to them. Then David said to Saul, "I cannot walk with these; for I am not used to them." So David removed them. 40Then he took his staff in his hand, and chose five smooth stones from the wadi, and put them in his shepherd's bag, in the pouch; his sling was in his hand, and he drew near to the Philistine.

41 The Philistine came on and drew near to David, with his shield-bearer in front of him. 42When the Philistine looked and saw David, he disdained him, for he was only a youth, ruddy and handsome in appearance. 43The Philistine said to David, "Am I a dog, that you come to me with sticks?" And the Philistine cursed David by his gods. 44The Philistine said to David, "Come to me, and I will give your flesh to the birds of the air and to the wild animals of the field." 45But David said to the Philistine, "You come to me with sword and spear and javelin; but I come to you in the name of the LORD of hosts, the God of the armies of Israel, whom you have defied. 46This very day the LORD will deliver you into my hand, and I will strike you down and cut off your head; and I will give the dead bodies of the Philistine army this very day to the birds of the air and to the wild animals of the earth, so that all the earth may

know that there is a God in Israel, 47and that all this assembly may know that the LORD does not save by sword and spear; for the battle is the LORD's and he will give you into our hand."

48 When the Philistine drew nearer to meet David, David ran quickly toward the battle line to meet the Philistine. 49David put his hand in his bag, took out a stone, slung it, and struck the Philistine on his forehead; the stone sank into his forehead, and he fell face down on the ground.

50 So David prevailed over the Philistine with a sling and a stone, striking down the Philistine and killing him; there was no sword in David's hand. 51Then David ran and stood over the Philistine; he grasped his sword, drew it out of its sheath, and killed him; then he cut off his head with it.

When the Philistines saw that their champion was dead, they fled. 52The troops of Israel and Judah rose up with a shout and pursued the Philistines as far as Gathᵈ and the gates of Ekron, so that the wounded Philistines fell on the way from Shaaraim as far as Gath and Ekron. 53The Israelites came back from chasing the Philistines, and they plundered their camp. 54David took the head of the Philistine and brought it to Jerusalem; but he put his armor in his tent.

55 When Saul saw David go out against the Philistine, he said to Abner, the commander of the army, "Abner, whose son is this young man?" Abner said, "As your soul lives, O king, I do not know." 56The king said, "Inquire whose son the stripling is." 57On David's return from killing the Philistine, Abner took him and brought him before Saul, with the head of the Philistine in his hand. 58Saul said to him, "Whose son are you, young man?" And David answered, "I am the son of your servant Jesse the Bethlehemite."

Jonathan's Covenant with David

18 When Davidᵉ had finished speaking to Saul, the soul of Jonathan was bound to the soul of David, and Jonathan loved him as his own soul. 2Saul took him that day and would not let him return to his father's

house. ³Then Jonathan made a covenant with David, because he loved him as his own soul. ⁴Jonathan stripped himself of the robe that he was wearing, and gave it to David, and his armor, and even his sword and his bow and his belt. ⁵David went out and was successful wherever Saul sent him; as a result, Saul set him over the army. And all the people, even the servants of Saul, approved.

6 As they were coming home, when David returned from killing the Philistine, the women came out of all the towns of Israel, singing and dancing, to meet King Saul, with tambourines, with songs of joy, and with musical instruments.*f* ⁷And the women sang to one another as they made merry,

"Saul has killed his thousands,
　　and David his ten thousands."
⁸Saul was very angry, for this saying displeased him. He said, "They have ascribed to David ten thousands, and to me they have ascribed thousands; what more can he have but the kingdom?" ⁹So Saul eyed David from that day on.

Saul Tries to Kill David

10 The next day an evil spirit from God rushed upon Saul, and he raved within his house, while David was playing the lyre, as he did day by day. Saul had his spear in his hand; ¹¹and Saul threw the spear, for he thought, "I will pin David to the wall." But David eluded him twice.

12 Saul was afraid of David, because the LORD was with him but had departed from Saul. ¹³So Saul removed him from his presence, and made him a commander of a thousand; and David marched out and came in, leading the army. ¹⁴David had success in all his undertakings; for the LORD was with him. ¹⁵When Saul saw that he had great success, he stood in awe of him. ¹⁶But all Israel and Judah loved David; for it was he who marched out and came in leading them.

David Marries Michal

17 Then Saul said to David, "Here is my elder daughter Merab; I will give her to you as a wife; only be valiant for me

and fight the LORD's battles." For Saul thought, "I will not raise a hand against him; let the Philistines deal with him." ¹⁸David said to Saul, "Who am I and who are my kinsfolk, my father's family in Israel, that I should be son-in-law to the king?" ¹⁹But at the time when Saul's daughter Merab should have been given to David, she was given to Adriel the Meholathite as a wife.

20 Now Saul's daughter Michal loved David. Saul was told, and the thing pleased him. ²¹Saul thought, "Let me give her to him that she may be a snare for him and that the hand of the Philistines may be against him." Therefore Saul said to David a second time,*g* "You shall now be my son-in-law." ²²Saul commanded his servants, "Speak to David in private and say, 'See, the king is delighted with you, and all his servants love you; now then, become the king's son-in-law.' " ²³So Saul's servants reported these words to David in private. And David said, "Does it seem to you a little thing to become the king's son-in-law, seeing that I am a poor man and of no repute?" ²⁴The servants of Saul told him, "This is what David said." ²⁵Then Saul said, "Thus shall you say to David, 'The king desires no marriage present except a hundred foreskins of the Philistines, that he may be avenged on the king's enemies.' " Now Saul planned to make David fall by the hand of the Philistines. ²⁶When his servants told David these words, David was well pleased to be the king's son-in-law. Before the time had expired, ²⁷David rose and went, along with his men, and killed one hundred*h* of the Philistines; and David brought their foreskins, which were given in full number to the king, that he might become the king's son-in-law. Saul gave him his daughter Michal as a wife. ²⁸But when Saul realized that the LORD was with David, and that Saul's daughter Michal loved him, ²⁹Saul was still more afraid of David. So Saul was David's enemy from that time forward.

30 Then the commanders of the Philistines came out to battle; and as often as they came out, David had more suc-

---

f Or *triangles,* or *three-stringed instruments* 　　*g* Heb *by two* 　　*h* Gk Compare 2 Sam 3.14: Heb *two hundred*

cess than all the servants of Saul, so that his fame became very great.

Jonathan Intercedes for David

19 Saul spoke with his son Jonathan and with all his servants about killing David. But Saul's son Jonathan took great delight in David. 2Jonathan told David, "My father Saul is trying to kill you; therefore be on guard tomorrow morning; stay in a secret place and hide yourself. 3I will go out and stand beside my father in the field where you are, and I will speak to my father about you; if I learn anything I will tell you." 4Jonathan spoke well of David to his father Saul, saying to him, "The king should not sin against his servant David, because he has not sinned against you, and because his deeds have been of good service to you; 5for he took his life in his hand when he attacked the Philistine, and the LORD brought about a great victory for all Israel. You saw it, and rejoiced; why then will you sin against an innocent person by killing David without cause?" 6Saul heeded the voice of Jonathan; Saul swore, "As the LORD lives, he shall not be put to death." 7So Jonathan called David and related all these things to him. Jonathan then brought David to Saul, and he was in his presence as before.

Michal Helps David Escape from Saul

8 Again there was war, and David went out to fight the Philistines. He launched a heavy attack on them, so that they fled before him. 9Then an evil spirit from the LORD came upon Saul, as he sat in his house with his spear in his hand, while David was playing music. 10Saul sought to pin David to the wall with the spear; but he eluded Saul, so that he struck the spear into the wall. David fled and escaped that night.

11 Saul sent messengers to David's house to keep watch over him, planning to kill him in the morning. David's wife Michal told him, "If you do not save your life tonight, tomorrow you will be killed." 12So Michal let David down through the window; he fled away and

escaped. 13Michal took an idolⁱ and laid it on the bed; she put a net^j of goats' hair on its head, and covered it with the clothes. 14When Saul sent messengers to take David, she said, "He is sick." 15Then Saul sent the messengers to see David for themselves. He said, "Bring him up to me in the bed, that I may kill him." 16When the messengers came in, the idol^k was in the bed, with the covering^j of goats' hair on its head. 17Saul said to Michal, "Why have you deceived me like this, and let my enemy go, so that he has escaped?" Michal answered Saul, "He said to me, 'Let me go; why should I kill you?'"

David Joins Samuel in Ramah

18 Now David fled and escaped; he came to Samuel at Ramah, and told him all that Saul had done to him. He and Samuel went and settled at Naioth. 19Saul was told, "David is at Naioth in Ramah." 20Then Saul sent messengers to take David. When they saw the company of the prophets in a frenzy, with Samuel standing in charge of^j them, the spirit of God came upon the messengers of Saul, and they also fell into a prophetic frenzy. 21When Saul was told, he sent other messengers, and they also fell into a frenzy. Saul sent messengers again the third time, and they also fell into a frenzy. 22Then he himself went to Ramah. He came to the great well that is in Secu;^l he asked, "Where are Samuel and David?" And someone said, "They are at Naioth in Ramah." 23He went there, toward Naioth in Ramah; and the spirit of God came upon him. As he was going, he fell into a prophetic frenzy, until he came to Naioth in Ramah. 24He too stripped off his clothes, and he too fell into a frenzy before Samuel. He lay naked all that day and all that night. Therefore it is said, "Is Saul also among the prophets?"

The Friendship of David and Jonathan

20 David fled from Naioth in Ramah. He came before Jonathan and said, "What have I done? What is my guilt? And what is my sin against

i Heb took the teraphim   j Meaning of Heb uncertain   k Heb the teraphim   l Gk reads to the well of the threshing floor on the bare height

your father that he is trying to take my life?" ²He said to him, "Far from it! You shall not die. My father does nothing either great or small without disclosing it to me; and why should my father hide this from me? Never!" ³But David also swore, "Your father knows well that you like me; and he thinks, 'Do not let Jonathan know this, or he will be grieved.' But truly, as the LORD lives and as you yourself live, there is but a step between me and death." ⁴Then Jonathan said to David, "Whatever you say, I will do for you." ⁵David said to Jonathan, "Tomorrow is the new moon, and I should not fail to sit with the king at the meal; but let me go, so that I may hide in the field until the third evening. ⁶If your father misses me at all, then say, 'David earnestly asked leave of me to run to Bethlehem his city; for there is a yearly sacrifice there for all the family.' ⁷If he says, 'Good!' it will be well with your servant; but if he is angry, then know that evil has been determined by him. ⁸Therefore deal kindly with your servant, for you have brought your servant into a sacred covenant^m with you. But if there is guilt in me, kill me yourself; why should you bring me to your father?" ⁹Jonathan said, "Far be it from you! If I knew that it was decided by my father that evil should come upon you, would I not tell you?" ¹⁰Then David said to Jonathan, "Who will tell me if your father answers you harshly?" ¹¹Jonathan replied to David, "Come, let us go out into the field." So they both went out into the field.

12 Jonathan said to David, "By the LORD, the God of Israel! When I have sounded out my father, about this time tomorrow, or on the third day, if he is well disposed toward David, shall I not then send and disclose it to you? ¹³But if my father intends to do you harm, the LORD do so to Jonathan, and more also, if I do not disclose it to you, and send you away, so that you may go in safety. May the LORD be with you, as he has been with my father. ¹⁴If I am still alive, show me the faithful love of the LORD; but if I die,^{n} ¹⁵never cut off your faithful love from my house, even if the LORD were to cut off every one of the enemies of

David from the face of the earth." ¹⁶Thus Jonathan made a covenant with the house of David, saying, "May the LORD seek out the enemies of David." ¹⁷Jonathan made David swear again by his love for him; for he loved him as he loved his own life.

18 Jonathan said to him, "Tomorrow is the new moon; you will be missed, because your place will be empty. ¹⁹On the day after tomorrow, you shall go a long way down; go to the place where you hid yourself earlier, and remain beside the stone there.^{n} ²⁰I will shoot three arrows to the side of it, as though I shot at a mark. ²¹Then I will send the boy, saying, 'Go, find the arrows.' If I say to the boy, 'Look, the arrows are on this side of you, collect them,' then you are to come, for, as the LORD lives, it is safe for you and there is no danger. ²²But if I say to the young man, 'Look, the arrows are beyond you,' then go; for the LORD has sent you away. ²³As for the matter about which you and I have spoken, the LORD is witness^o between you and me forever."

24 So David hid himself in the field. When the new moon came, the king sat at the feast to eat. ²⁵The king sat upon his seat, as at other times, upon the seat by the wall. Jonathan stood, while Abner sat by Saul's side; but David's place was empty.

26 Saul did not say anything that day; for he thought, "Something has befallen him; he is not clean, surely he is not clean." ²⁷But on the second day, the day after the new moon, David's place was empty. And Saul said to his son Jonathan, "Why has the son of Jesse not come to the feast, either yesterday or today?" ²⁸Jonathan answered Saul, "David earnestly asked leave of me to go to Bethlehem; ²⁹he said, 'Let me go; for our family is holding a sacrifice in the city, and my brother has commanded me to be there. So now, if I have found favor in your sight, let me get away, and see my brothers.' For this reason he has not come to the king's table."

30 Then Saul's anger was kindled against Jonathan. He said to him, "You son of a perverse, rebellious woman! Do I not know that you have chosen the son

m Heb *a covenant of the LORD*　　n Meaning of Heb uncertain　　o Gk: Heb lacks *witness*

of Jesse to your own shame, and to the shame of your mother's nakedness? 31For as long as the son of Jesse lives upon the earth, neither you nor your kingdom shall be established. Now send and bring him to me, for he shall surely die." 32Then Jonathan answered his father Saul, "Why should he be put to death? What has he done?" 33But Saul threw his spear at him to strike him; so Jonathan knew that it was the decision of his father to put David to death. 34Jonathan rose from the table in fierce anger and ate no food on the second day of the month, for he was grieved for David, and because his father had disgraced him.

35 In the morning Jonathan went out into the field to the appointment with David, and with him was a little boy. 36He said to the boy, "Run and find the arrows that I shoot." As the boy ran, he shot an arrow beyond him. 37When the boy came to the place where Jonathan's arrow had fallen, Jonathan called after the boy and said, "Is the arrow not beyond you?" 38Jonathan called after the boy, "Hurry, be quick, do not linger." So Jonathan's boy gathered up the arrows and came to his master. 39But the boy knew nothing; only Jonathan and David knew the arrangement. 40Jonathan gave his weapons to the boy and said to him, "Go and carry them to the city." 41As soon as the boy had gone, David rose from beside the stone heap*p* and prostrated himself with his face to the ground. He bowed three times, and they kissed each other, and wept with each other; David wept the more.*q* 42Then Jonathan said to David, "Go in peace, since both of us have sworn in the name of the LORD, saying, 'The LORD shall be between me and you, and between my descendants and your descendants, forever.'" He got up and left; and Jonathan went into the city.*r*

David and the Holy Bread

21 *s* David came to Nob to the priest Ahimelech. Ahimelech came trembling to meet David, and said to him, "Why are you alone, and no one with you?" 2David said to the priest Ahimelech, "The king has charged me

with a matter, and said to me, 'No one must know anything of the matter about which I send you, and with which I have charged you.' I have made an appointment*t* with the young men for such and such a place. 3Now then, what have you at hand? Give me five loaves of bread, or whatever is here." 4The priest answered David, "I have no ordinary bread at hand, only holy bread—provided that the young men have kept themselves from women." 5David answered the priest, "Indeed women have been kept from us as always when I go on an expedition; the vessels of the young men are holy even when it is a common journey; how much more today will their vessels be holy?" 6So the priest gave him the holy bread; for there was no bread there except the bread of the Presence, which is removed from before the LORD, to be replaced by hot bread on the day it is taken away.

7 Now a certain man of the servants of Saul was there that day, detained before the LORD; his name was Doeg the Edomite, the chief of Saul's shepherds.

8 David said to Ahimelech, "Is there no spear or sword here with you? I did not bring my sword or my weapons with me, because the king's business required haste." 9The priest said, "The sword of Goliath the Philistine, whom you killed in the valley of Elah, is here wrapped in a cloth behind the ephod; if you will take that, take it, for there is none here except that one." David said, "There is none like it; give it to me."

David Flees to Gath

10 David rose and fled that day from Saul; he went to King Achish of Gath. 11The servants of Achish said to him, "Is this not David the king of the land? Did they not sing to one another of him in dances,

'Saul has killed his thousands,
    and David his ten thousands'?"

12David took these words to heart and was very much afraid of King Achish of Gath. 13So he changed his behavior before them; he pretended to be mad when in their presence.*u* He scratched marks on the doors of the gate, and let

p Gk: Heb *from beside the south*   q Vg: Meaning of Heb uncertain   r This sentence is 21.1 in Heb
s Ch 21.2 in Heb   t Q Ms Vg Compare Gk: Meaning of MT uncertain   u Heb *in their hands*

his spittle run down his beard. 14Achish said to his servants, "Look, you see the man is mad; why then have you brought him to me? 15Do I lack madmen, that you have brought this fellow to play the madman in my presence? Shall this fellow come into my house?"

David and His Followers at Adullam

22 David left there and escaped to the cave of Adullam; when his brothers and all his father's house heard of it, they went down there to him. 2Everyone who was in distress, and everyone who was in debt, and everyone who was discontented gathered to him; and he became captain over them. Those who were with him numbered about four hundred.

3 David went from there to Mizpeh of Moab. He said to the king of Moab, "Please let my father and mother come^v to you, until I know what God will do for me." 4He left them with the king of Moab, and they stayed with him all the time that David was in the stronghold. 5Then the prophet Gad said to David, "Do not remain in the stronghold; leave, and go into the land of Judah." So David left, and went into the forest of Hereth.

Saul Slaughters the Priests at Nob

6 Saul heard that David and those who were with him had been located. Saul was sitting at Gibeah, under the tamarisk tree on the height, with his spear in his hand, and all his servants were standing around him. 7Saul said to his servants who stood around him, "Hear now, you Benjaminites; will the son of Jesse give every one of you fields and vineyards, will he make you all commanders of thousands and commanders of hundreds? 8Is that why all of you have conspired against me? No one discloses to me when my son makes a league with the son of Jesse, none of you is sorry for me or discloses to me that my son has stirred up my servant against me, to lie in wait, as he is doing today." 9Doeg the Edomite, who was in charge of Saul's servants, answered, "I saw the son of Jesse coming to Nob, to Ahimelech son of Ahitub; 10he inquired

of the LORD for him, gave him provisions, and gave him the sword of Goliath the Philistine."

11 The king sent for the priest Ahimelech son of Ahitub and for all his father's house, the priests who were at Nob; and all of them came to the king. 12Saul said, "Listen now, son of Ahitub." He answered, "Here I am, my lord." 13Saul said to him, "Why have you conspired against me, you and the son of Jesse, by giving him bread and a sword, and by inquiring of God for him, so that he has risen against me, to lie in wait, as he is doing today?"

14 Then Ahimelech answered the king, "Who among all your servants is so faithful as David? He is the king's son-in-law, and is quick^w to do your bidding, and is honored in your house. 15Is today the first time that I have inquired of God for him? By no means! Do not let the king impute anything to his servant or to any member of my father's house; for your servant has known nothing of all this, much or little." 16The king said, "You shall surely die, Ahimelech, you and all your father's house." 17The king said to the guard who stood around him, "Turn and kill the priests of the LORD, because their hand also is with David; they knew that he fled, and did not disclose it to me." But the servants of the king would not raise their hand to attack the priests of the LORD. 18Then the king said to Doeg, "You, Doeg, turn and attack the priests." Doeg the Edomite turned and attacked the priests; on that day he killed eighty-five who wore the linen ephod. 19Nob, the city of the priests, he put to the sword; men and women, children and infants, oxen, donkeys, and sheep, he put to the sword.

20 But one of the sons of Ahimelech son of Ahitub, named Abiathar, escaped and fled after David. 21Abiathar told David that Saul had killed the priests of the LORD. 22David said to Abiathar, "I knew on that day, when Doeg the Edomite was there, that he would surely tell Saul. I am responsible^x for the lives of all your father's house. 23Stay with me, and do not be afraid; for the one who seeks my life seeks your life; you will be safe with me."

v Syr Vg: Heb come out   w Heb and turns aside   x Gk Vg: Meaning of Heb uncertain

David Saves the City of Keilah

23 Now they told David, "The Philistines are fighting against Keilah, and are robbing the threshing floors." 2David inquired of the LORD, "Shall I go and attack these Philistines?" The LORD said to David, "Go and attack the Philistines and save Keilah." 3But David's men said to him, "Look, we are afraid here in Judah; how much more then if we go to Keilah against the armies of the Philistines?" 4Then David inquired of the LORD again. The LORD answered him, "Yes, go down to Keilah; for I will give the Philistines into your hand." 5So David and his men went to Keilah, fought with the Philistines, brought away their livestock, and dealt them a heavy defeat. Thus David rescued the inhabitants of Keilah.

6 When Abiathar son of Ahimelech fled to David at Keilah, he came down with an ephod in his hand. 7Now it was told Saul that David had come to Keilah. And Saul said, "God has given^y him into my hand; for he has shut himself in by entering a town that has gates and bars." 8Saul summoned all the people to war, to go down to Keilah, to besiege David and his men. 9When David learned that Saul was plotting evil against him, he said to the priest Abiathar, "Bring the ephod here." 10David said, "O LORD, the God of Israel, your servant has heard that Saul seeks to come to Keilah, to destroy the city on my account. 11And now, will^z Saul come down as your servant has heard? O LORD, the God of Israel, I beseech you, tell your servant." The LORD said, "He will come down." 12Then David said, "Will the men of Keilah surrender me and my men into the hand of Saul?" The LORD said, "They will surrender you." 13Then David and his men, who were about six hundred, set out and left Keilah; they wandered wherever they could go. When Saul was told that David had escaped from Keilah, he gave up the expedition. 14David remained in the strongholds in the wilderness, in the hill country of the Wilderness of Ziph. Saul sought him every day, but the LORD^a did not give him into his hand.

David Eludes Saul in the Wilderness

15 David was in the Wilderness of Ziph at Horesh when he learned that^b Saul had come out to seek his life. 16Saul's son Jonathan set out and came to David at Horesh; there he strengthened his hand through the LORD.^{c} 17He said to him, "Do not be afraid; for the hand of my father Saul shall not find you; you shall be king over Israel, and I shall be second to you; my father Saul also knows that this is so." 18Then the two of them made a covenant before the LORD; David remained at Horesh, and Jonathan went home.

19 Then some Ziphites went up to Saul at Gibeah and said, "David is hiding among us in the strongholds of Horesh, on the hill of Hachilah, which is south of Jeshimon. 20Now, O king, whenever you wish to come down, do so; and our part will be to surrender him into the king's hand." 21Saul said, "May you be blessed by the LORD for showing me compassion! 22Go and make sure once more; find out exactly where he is, and who has seen him there; for I am told that he is very cunning. 23Look around and learn all the hiding places where he lurks, and come back to me with sure information. Then I will go with you; and if he is in the land, I will search him out among all the thousands of Judah." 24So they set out and went to Ziph ahead of Saul.

David and his men were in the wilderness of Maon, in the Arabah to the south of Jeshimon. 25Saul and his men went to search for him. When David was told, he went down to the rock and stayed in the wilderness of Maon. When Saul heard that, he pursued David into the wilderness of Maon. 26Saul went on one side of the mountain, and David and his men on the other side of the mountain. David was hurrying to get away from Saul, while Saul and his men were closing in on David and his men to capture them. 27Then a messenger came to Saul, saying, "Hurry and come; for the Philistines have made a raid on the land." 28So Saul stopped pursuing David, and went against the Philistines; therefore

y Gk Tg: Heb *made a stranger of*   z Q Ms Compare Gk: MT *Will the men of Keilah surrender me into his hand? Will*   a Q Ms Gk: MT *God*   b Or *saw that*   c Compare Q Ms Gk: MT *God*

that place was called the Rock of Escape.*d* **29***e* David then went up from there, and lived in the strongholds of En-gedi.

David Spares Saul's Life

 24 When Saul returned from following the Philistines, he was told, "David is in the wilderness of En-gedi." 2Then Saul took three thousand chosen men out of all Israel, and went to look for David and his men in the direction of the Rocks of the Wild Goats. 3He came to the sheepfolds beside the road, where there was a cave; and Saul went in to relieve himself.*f* Now David and

his men were sitting in the innermost parts of the cave. 4The men of David said to him, "Here is the day of which the LORD said to you, 'I will give your enemy into your hand, and you shall do to him as it seems good to you.'" Then David went and stealthily cut off a corner of Saul's cloak. 5Afterward David was stricken to the heart because he had cut off a corner of Saul's cloak. 6He said to his men, "The LORD forbid that I should do this thing to my lord, the LORD's anointed, to raise my hand against him; for he is the LORD's anointed." 7So David scolded his men severely and did not permit them to attack Saul.

d Or *Rock of Division*; Meaning of Heb uncertain   *e* Ch 24.1 in Heb   *f* Heb *to cover his feet*

MONDAY

GOD'S SURE WORD
Martin Luther

VERSE: 1 Samuel 24.11   **PASSAGE:** 1 Samuel 24.1–19

any strange things, according to human sense and reason, are written in the books of the kings; they seem to be slight and simple books, but in the spirit they are of great weight. David endured much; Saul persecuted and plagued him ten whole years; yet David remained constant in faith, and believed that the kingdom pertained unto him. I should have gone my way, and said: Lord! thou hast deceived me; wilt thou make me a king, and sufferest me in this sort to be tormented, persecuted, and plagued? But David was like a strong wall. He was also a good and a godly man; he refused to lay hands on the king when he had fit opportunity; for he had God's word, and that made him remain so steadfast; he was sure that God's word and promise never would or could fail him . . .

So it often happens, that the good are punished for the sake of the wicked and ungodly. The Son of God himself was not spared.

ADDITIONAL SCRIPTURE READING:
1 Samuel 26.17–25; Psalm 25.20–21

Go to page 346 for your next devotional reading.

1500   1700

Then Saul got up and left the cave, and went on his way.

8 Afterwards David also rose up and went out of the cave and called after Saul, "My lord the king!" When Saul looked behind him, David bowed with his face to the ground, and did obeisance. [9]David said to Saul, "Why do you listen to the words of those who say, 'David seeks to do you harm'? [10]This very day your eyes have seen how the LORD gave you into my hand in the cave; and some urged me to kill you, but I spared[g] you. I said, 'I will not raise my hand against my lord; for he is the LORD's anointed.' [11]See, my father, see the corner of your cloak in my hand; for by the fact that I cut off the corner of your cloak, and did not kill you, you may know for certain that there is no wrong or treason in my hands. I have not sinned against you, though you are hunting me to take my life. [12]May the LORD judge between me and you! May the LORD avenge me on you; but my hand shall not be against you. [13]As the ancient proverb says, 'Out of the wicked comes forth wickedness'; but my hand shall not be against you. [14]Against whom has the king of Israel come out? Whom do you pursue? A dead dog? A single flea? [15]May the LORD therefore be judge, and give sentence between me and you. May he see to it, and plead my cause, and vindicate me against you."

16 When David had finished speaking these words to Saul, Saul said, "Is this your voice, my son David?" Saul lifted up his voice and wept. [17]He said to David, "You are more righteous than I; for you have repaid me good, whereas I have repaid you evil. [18]Today you have explained how you have dealt well with me, in that you did not kill me when the LORD put me into your hands. [19]For who has ever found an enemy, and sent the enemy safely away? So may the LORD reward you with good for what you have done to me this day. [20]Now I know that you shall surely be king, and that the kingdom of Israel shall be established in your hand. [21]Swear to me therefore by the LORD that you will not cut off my descendants after me, and that you will not wipe out my name from my father's

house." [22]So David swore this to Saul. Then Saul went home; but David and his men went up to the stronghold.

Death of Samuel

25 Now Samuel died; and all Israel assembled and mourned for him. They buried him at his home in Ramah.

Then David got up and went down to the wilderness of Paran.

David and the Wife of Nabal

2 There was a man in Maon, whose property was in Carmel. The man was very rich; he had three thousand sheep and a thousand goats. He was shearing his sheep in Carmel. [3]Now the name of the man was Nabal, and the name of his wife Abigail. The woman was clever and beautiful, but the man was surly and mean; he was a Calebite. [4]David heard in the wilderness that Nabal was shearing his sheep. [5]So David sent ten young men; and David said to the young men, "Go up to Carmel, and go to Nabal, and greet him in my name. [6]Thus you shall salute him: 'Peace be to you, and peace be to your house, and peace be to all that you have. [7]I hear that you have shearers; now your shepherds have been with us, and we did them no harm, and they missed nothing, all the time they were in Carmel. [8]Ask your young men, and they will tell you. Therefore let my young men find favor in your sight; for we have come on a feast day. Please give whatever you have at hand to your servants and to your son David.' "

9 When David's young men came, they said all this to Nabal in the name of David; and then they waited. [10]But Nabal answered David's servants, "Who is David? Who is the son of Jesse? There are many servants today who are breaking away from their masters. [11]Shall I take my bread and my water and the meat that I have butchered for my shearers, and give it to men who come from I do not know where?" [12]So David's young men turned away, and came back and told him all this. [13]David said to his men, "Every man strap on his sword!" And every one of them strapped on his sword; David also strapped on his sword;

g Gk Syr Tg Vg: Heb *it* (my eye) *spared*

and about four hundred men went up after David, while two hundred remained with the baggage.

14 But one of the young men told Abigail, Nabal's wife, "David sent messengers out of the wilderness to salute our master; and he shouted insults at them. 15 Yet the men were very good to us, and we suffered no harm, and we never missed anything when we were in the fields, as long as we were with them; 16 they were a wall to us both by night and by day, all the while we were with them keeping the sheep. 17 Now therefore know this and consider what you should do; for evil has been decided against our master and against all his house; he is so ill-natured that no one can speak to him."

18 Then Abigail hurried and took two hundred loaves, two skins of wine, five sheep ready dressed, five measures of parched grain, one hundred clusters of raisins, and two hundred cakes of figs. She loaded them on donkeys 19 and said to her young men, "Go on ahead of me; I am coming after you." But she did not tell her husband Nabal. 20 As she rode on the donkey and came down under cover of the mountain, David and his men came down toward her; and she met them. 21 Now David had said, "Surely it was in vain that I protected all that this fellow has in the wilderness, so that nothing was missed of all that belonged to him; but he has returned me evil for good. 22 God do so to David[h] and more also, if by morning I leave so much as one male of all who belong to him."

23 When Abigail saw David, she hurried and alighted from the donkey, and fell before David on her face, bowing to the ground. 24 She fell at his feet and said, "Upon me alone, my lord, be the guilt; please let your servant speak in your ears, and hear the words of your servant. 25 My lord, do not take seriously this ill-natured fellow, Nabal; for as his name is, so is he; Nabal[i] is his name, and folly is with him; but I, your servant, did not see the young men of my lord, whom you sent.

26 "Now then, my lord, as the LORD lives, and as you yourself live, since the LORD has restrained you from bloodguilt

and from taking vengeance with your own hand, now let your enemies and those who seek to do evil to my lord be like Nabal. 27 And now let this present that your servant has brought to my lord be given to the young men who follow my lord. 28 Please forgive the trespass of your servant; for the LORD will certainly make my lord a sure house, because my lord is fighting the battles of the LORD; and evil shall not be found in you so long as you live. 29 If anyone should rise up to pursue you and to seek your life, the life of my lord shall be bound in the bundle of the living under the care of the LORD your God; but the lives of your enemies he shall sling out as from the hollow of a sling. 30 When the LORD has done to my lord according to all the good that he has spoken concerning you, and has appointed you prince over Israel, 31 my lord shall have no cause of grief, or pangs of conscience, for having shed blood without cause or for having saved himself. And when the LORD has dealt well with my lord, then remember your servant."

32 David said to Abigail, "Blessed be the LORD, the God of Israel, who sent you to meet me today! 33 Blessed be your good sense, and blessed be you, who have kept me today from bloodguilt and from avenging myself by my own hand! 34 For as surely as the LORD the God of Israel lives, who has restrained me from hurting you, unless you had hurried and come to meet me, truly by morning there would not have been left to Nabal so much as one male." 35 Then David received from her hand what she had brought him; he said to her, "Go up to your house in peace; see, I have heeded your voice, and I have granted your petition."

36 Abigail came to Nabal; he was holding a feast in his house, like the feast of a king. Nabal's heart was merry within him, for he was very drunk; so she told him nothing at all until the morning light. 37 In the morning, when the wine had gone out of Nabal, his wife told him these things, and his heart died within him; he became like a stone. 38 About ten days later the LORD struck Nabal, and he died.

---

h Gk Compare Syr: Heb the enemies of David　　i That is Fool

39 When David heard that Nabal was dead, he said, "Blessed be the LORD who has judged the case of Nabal's insult to me, and has kept back his servant from evil; the LORD has returned the evildoing of Nabal upon his own head." Then David sent and wooed Abigail, to make her his wife. 40When David's servants came to Abigail at Carmel, they said to her, "David has sent us to you to take you to him as his wife." 41She rose and bowed down, with her face to the ground, and said, "Your servant is a slave to wash the feet of the servants of my lord." 42Abigail got up hurriedly and rode away on a donkey; her five maids attended her. She went after the messengers of David and became his wife.

43 David also married Ahinoam of Jezreel; both of them became his wives. 44Saul had given his daughter Michal, David's wife, to Palti son of Laish, who was from Gallim.

David Spares Saul's Life a Second Time

26 Then the Ziphites came to Saul at Gibeah, saying, "David is in hiding on the hill of Hachilah, which is opposite Jeshimon."*j* 2So Saul rose and went down to the Wilderness of Ziph, with three thousand chosen men of Israel, to seek David in the Wilderness of Ziph. 3Saul encamped on the hill of Hachilah, which is opposite Jeshimon*j* beside the road. But David remained in the wilderness. When he learned that Saul had come after him into the wilderness, 4David sent out spies, and learned that Saul had indeed arrived. 5Then David set out and came to the place where Saul had encamped; and David saw the place where Saul lay, with Abner son of Ner, the commander of his army. Saul was lying within the encampment, while the army was encamped around him.

6 Then David said to Ahimelech the Hittite, and to Joab's brother Abishai son of Zeruiah, "Who will go down with me into the camp to Saul?" Abishai said, "I will go down with you." 7So David and Abishai went to the army by night; there Saul lay sleeping within the

encampment, with his spear stuck in the ground at his head; and Abner and the army lay around him. 8Abishai said to David, "God has given your enemy

---

PLENTEOUS GRACE WITH THEE IS FOUND,

GRACE TO COVER ALL MY SIN;

LET THE HEALING STREAMS ABOUND,

MAKE AND KEEP ME PURE WITHIN.

—*Charles Wesley*

---

into your hand today; now therefore let me pin him to the ground with one stroke of the spear; I will not strike him twice." 9But David said to Abishai, "Do not destroy him; for who can raise his hand against the LORD's anointed, and be guiltless?" 10David said, "As the LORD lives, the LORD will strike him down; or his day will come to die; or he will go down into battle and perish. 11The LORD forbid that I should raise my hand against the LORD's anointed; but now take the spear that is at his head, and the water jar, and let us go." 12So David took the spear that was at Saul's head and the water jar, and they went away. No one saw it, or knew it, nor did anyone awake; for they were all asleep, because a deep sleep from the LORD had fallen upon them.

13 Then David went over to the other side, and stood on top of a hill far away, with a great distance between them. 14David called to the army and to Abner son of Ner, saying, "Abner! Will you not answer?" Then Abner replied, "Who are you that calls to the king?" 15David said to Abner, "Are you not a man? Who is like you in Israel? Why then have you not kept watch over your lord the king? For one of the people came in to destroy your lord the king. 16This thing that you have done is not good. As the LORD lives, you deserve to die, because you have not kept watch over your lord, the LORD's anointed. See now, where is the king's spear, or the water jar that was at his head?"

17 Saul recognized David's voice, and said, "Is this your voice, my son David?" David said, "It is my voice, my lord,

j Or *opposite the wasteland*

O king." 18And he added, "Why does my lord pursue his servant? For what have I done? What guilt is on my hands? 19Now therefore let my lord the king hear the words of his servant. If it is the LORD who has stirred you up against me, may he accept an offering; but if it is mortals, may they be cursed before the LORD, for they have driven me out today from my share in the heritage of the LORD, saying, 'Go, serve other gods.' 20Now therefore, do not let my blood fall to the ground, away from the presence of the LORD; for the king of Israel has come out to seek a single flea, like one who hunts a partridge in the mountains."

21 Then Saul said, "I have done wrong; come back, my son David, for I will never harm you again, because my life was precious in your sight today; I have been a fool, and have made a great mistake." 22David replied, "Here is the spear, O king! Let one of the young men come over and get it. 23The LORD rewards everyone for his righteousness and his faithfulness; for the LORD gave you into my hand today, but I would not raise my hand against the LORD's anointed. 24As your life was precious today in my sight, so may my life be precious in the sight of the LORD, and may he rescue me from all tribulation." 25Then Saul said to David, "Blessed be you, my son David! You will do many things and will succeed in them." So David went his way, and Saul returned to his place.

David Serves King Achish of Gath

27 David said in his heart, "I shall now perish one day by the hand of Saul; there is nothing better for me than to escape to the land of the Philistines; then Saul will despair of seeking me any longer within the borders of Israel, and I shall escape out of his hand." 2So David set out and went over, he and the six hundred men who were with him, to King Achish son of Maoch of Gath. 3David stayed with Achish at Gath, he and his troops, every man with his household, and David with his two wives, Ahinoam of Jezreel, and Abigail of Carmel, Nabal's widow. 4When Saul was told that David had fled to Gath, he no longer sought for him.

5 Then David said to Achish, "If I have found favor in your sight, let a place be given me in one of the country towns, so that I may live there; for why should your servant live in the royal city with you?" 6So that day Achish gave him Ziklag; therefore Ziklag has belonged to the kings of Judah to this day. 7The length of time that David lived in the country of the Philistines was one year and four months.

8 Now David and his men went up and made raids on the Geshurites, the Girzites, and the Amalekites; for these were the landed settlements from Telamk on the way to Shur and on to the land of Egypt. 9David struck the land, leaving neither man nor woman alive, but took away the sheep, the oxen, the donkeys, the camels, and the clothing, and came back to Achish. 10When Achish asked, "Against whoml have you made a raid today?" David would say, "Against the Negeb of Judah," or "Against the Negeb of the Jerahmeelites," or, "Against the Negeb of the Kenites." 11David left neither man nor woman alive to be brought back to Gath, thinking, "They might tell about us, and say, 'David has done so and so.' " Such was his practice all the time he lived in the country of the Philistines. 12Achish trusted David, thinking, "He has made himself utterly abhorrent to his people Israel; therefore he shall always be my servant."

28 In those days the Philistines gathered their forces for war, to fight against Israel. Achish said to David, "You know, of course, that you and your men are to go out with me in the army." 2David said to Achish, "Very well, then you shall know what your servant can do." Achish said to David, "Very well, I will make you my bodyguard for life."

Saul Consults a Medium

3 Now Samuel had died, and all Israel had mourned for him and buried him in Ramah, his own city. Saul had expelled the mediums and the wizards from the land. 4The Philistines assembled, and came and encamped at Shunem. Saul gathered all Israel, and they encamped at

k Compare Gk 15.4: Heb *from of old*   l Q Ms Gk Vg: MT lacks *whom*

Gilboa. 5When Saul saw the army of the Philistines, he was afraid, and his heart trembled greatly. 6When Saul inquired of the LORD, the LORD did not answer him, not by dreams, or by Urim, or by prophets. 7Then Saul said to his servants, "Seek out for me a woman who is a medium, so that I may go to her and inquire of her." His servants said to him, "There is a medium at Endor."

8 So Saul disguised himself and put on other clothes and went there, he and two men with him. They came to the woman by night. And he said, "Consult a spirit for me, and bring up for me the one whom I name to you." 9The woman said to him, "Surely you know what Saul has done, how he has cut off the mediums and the wizards from the land. Why then are you laying a snare for my life to bring about my death?" 10But Saul swore to her by the LORD, "As the LORD lives, no punishment shall come upon you for this thing." 11Then the woman said, "Whom shall I bring up for you?" He answered, "Bring up Samuel for me." 12When the woman saw Samuel, she cried out with a loud voice; and the woman said to Saul, "Why have you deceived me? You are Saul!" 13The king said to her, "Have no fear; what do you see?" The woman said to Saul, "I see a divine beingm coming up out of the ground." 14He said to her, "What is his appearance?" She said, "An old man is coming up; he is wrapped in a robe." So Saul knew that it was Samuel, and he bowed with his face to the ground, and did obeisance.

15 Then Samuel said to Saul, "Why have you disturbed me by bringing me up?" Saul answered, "I am in great distress, for the Philistines are warring against me, and God has turned away from me and answers me no more, either by prophets or by dreams; so I have summoned you to tell me what I should do." 16Samuel said, "Why then do you ask me, since the LORD has turned from you and become your enemy? 17The LORD has done to you just as he spoke by me; for the LORD has torn the kingdom out of your hand, and given it to your neighbor, David. 18Because you did not obey the voice of the LORD, and did not carry out

his fierce wrath against Amalek, therefore the LORD has done this thing to you today. 19Moreover the LORD will give Israel along with you into the hands of the Philistines; and tomorrow you and your sons shall be with me; the LORD will also give the army of Israel into the hands of the Philistines."

20 Immediately Saul fell full length on the ground, filled with fear because of the words of Samuel; and there was no strength in him, for he had eaten nothing all day and all night. 21The woman came to Saul, and when she saw that he was terrified, she said to him, "Your servant has listened to you; I have taken my life in my hand, and have listened to what you have said to me. 22Now therefore, you also listen to your servant; let me set a morsel of bread before you. Eat, that you may have strength when you go on your way." 23He refused, and said, "I will not eat." But his servants, together with the woman, urged him; and he listened to their words. So he got up from the ground and sat on the bed. 24Now the woman had a fatted calf in the house. She quickly slaughtered it, and she took flour, kneaded it, and baked unleavened cakes. 25She put them before Saul and his servants, and they ate. Then they rose and went away that night.

The Philistines Reject David

29 Now the Philistines gathered all their forces at Aphek, while the Israelites were encamped by the fountain that is in Jezreel. 2As the lords of the Philistines were passing on by hundreds and by thousands, and David and his men were passing on in the rear with Achish, 3the commanders of the Philistines said, "What are these Hebrews doing here?" Achish said to the commanders of the Philistines, "Is this not David, the servant of King Saul of Israel, who has been with me now for days and years? Since he deserted to me I have found no fault in him to this day." 4But the commanders of the Philistines were angry with him; and the commanders of the Philistines said to him, "Send the man back, so that he may return to the place that you have assigned to him; he shall not go down with us to battle, or

m Or a god; or gods

else he may become an adversary to us in the battle. For how could this fellow reconcile himself to his lord? Would it not be with the heads of the men here? 5Is this not David, of whom they sing to one another in dances,

'Saul has killed his thousands,
    and David his ten thousands'?"

6 Then Achish called David and said to him, "As the LORD lives, you have been honest, and to me it seems right that you should march out and in with me in the campaign; for I have found nothing wrong in you from the day of your coming to me until today. Nevertheless the lords do not approve of you. 7So go back now; and go peaceably; do nothing to displease the lords of the Philistines." 8David said to Achish, "But what have I done? What have you found in your servant from the day I entered your service until now, that I should not go and fight against the enemies of my lord the king?" 9Achish replied to David, "I know that you are as blameless in my sight as an angel of God; nevertheless, the commanders of the Philistines have said, 'He shall not go up with us to the battle.' 10Now then rise early in the morning, you and the servants of your lord who came with you, and go to the place that I appointed for you. As for the evil report, do not take it to heart, for you have done well before me.n Start early in the morning, and leave as soon as you have light." 11So David set out with his men early in the morning, to return to the land of the Philistines. But the Philistines went up to Jezreel.

David Avenges the Destruction of Ziklag

30 Now when David and his men came to Ziklag on the third day, the Amalekites had made a raid on the Negeb and on Ziklag. They had attacked Ziklag, burned it down, 2and taken captive the women and allo who were in it, both small and great; they killed none of them, but carried them off, and went their way. 3When David and his men came to the city, they found it burned down, and their wives and sons and daughters taken captive. 4Then David and the people who

were with him raised their voices and wept, until they had no more strength to weep. 5David's two wives also had been taken captive, Ahinoam of Jezreel, and Abigail the widow of Nabal of Carmel. 6David was in great danger; for the people spoke of stoning him, because all the people were bitter in spirit for their sons and daughters. But David strengthened himself in the LORD his God.

7 David said to the priest Abiathar son of Ahimelech, "Bring me the ephod." So Abiathar brought the ephod to David. 8David inquired of the LORD, "Shall I pursue this band? Shall I overtake them?" He answered him, "Pursue; for you shall surely overtake and shall surely rescue." 9So David set out, he and the six hundred men who were with him. They came to the Wadi Besor, where those stayed who were left behind. 10But David went on with the pursuit, he and four hundred men; two hundred stayed behind, too exhausted to cross the Wadi Besor.

11 In the open country they found an Egyptian, and brought him to David. They gave him bread and he ate; they gave him water to drink; 12they also gave him a piece of fig cake and two clusters of raisins. When he had eaten, his spirit revived; for he had not eaten bread or drunk water for three days and three nights. 13Then David said to him, "To whom do you belong? Where are you from?" He said, "I am a young man of Egypt, servant to an Amalekite. My master left me behind because I fell sick three days ago. 14We had made a raid on the Negeb of the Cherethites and on that which belongs to Judah and on the Negeb of Caleb; and we burned Ziklag down." 15David said to him, "Will you take me down to this raiding party?" He said, "Swear to me by God that you will not kill me, or hand me over to my master, and I will take you down to them."

16 When he had taken him down, they were spread out all over the ground, eating and drinking and dancing, because of the great amount of spoil they had taken from the land of the Philistines and from the land of Judah. 17David attacked them from twilight until the evening of the next day. Not

n Gk: Heb lacks and go to the place . . . done well before me   o Gk: Heb lacks and all one of them escaped, except four hundred young men, who mounted camels and fled. 18David recovered all that the Amalekites had taken; and David rescued his two wives. 19Nothing was missing, whether small or great, sons or daughters, spoil or anything that had been taken; David brought back everything. 20David also captured all the flocks and herds, which were driven ahead of the other cattle; people said, "This is David's spoil."

21 Then David came to the two hundred men who had been too exhausted to follow David, and who had been left at the Wadi Besor. They went out to meet David and to meet the people who were with him. When David drew near to the people he saluted them. 22Then all the corrupt and worthless fellows among the men who had gone with David said, "Because they did not go with us, we will not give them any of the spoil that we have recovered, except that each man may take his wife and children, and leave." 23But David said, "You shall not do so, my brothers, with what the LORD has given us; he has preserved us and handed over to us the raiding party that attacked us. 24Who would listen to you in this matter? For the share of the one who goes down into the battle shall be the same as the share of the one who stays by the baggage; they shall share alike." 25From that day forward he made it a statute and an ordinance for Israel; it continues to the present day.

26 When David came to Ziklag, he sent part of the spoil to his friends, the elders of Judah, saying, "Here is a present for you from the spoil of the enemies of the LORD"; 27it was for those in Bethel, in Ramoth of the Negeb, in Jattir, 28in Aroer, in Siphmoth, in Eshtemoa, 29in Racal, in the towns of the Jerahmeelites, in the towns of the Kenites, 30in Hormah, in Bor-ashan, in Athach, 31in Hebron, all the places where David and his men had roamed.

The Death of Saul and His Sons

31 Now the Philistines fought against Israel; and the men of Israel fled before the Philistines, and many fellp on Mount Gilboa. 2The Philistines overtook Saul and his sons; and the Philistines killed Jonathan and Abinadab and Malchishua, the sons of Saul. 3The battle pressed hard upon Saul; the archers found him, and he was badly wounded by them. 4Then Saul said to his armor-bearer, "Draw your sword and thrust me through with it, so that these uncircumcised may not come and thrust me through, and make sport of me." But his armor-bearer was unwilling; for he was terrified. So Saul took his own sword and fell upon it. 5When his armor-bearer saw that Saul was dead, he also fell upon his sword and died with him. 6So Saul and his three sons and his armor-bearer and all his men died together on the same day. 7When the men of Israel who were on the other side of the valley and those beyond the Jordan saw that the men of Israel had fled and that Saul and his sons were dead, they forsook their towns and fled; and the Philistines came and occupied them.

8 The next day, when the Philistines came to strip the dead, they found Saul and his three sons fallen on Mount Gilboa. 9They cut off his head, stripped off his armor, and sent messengers throughout the land of the Philistines to carry the good news to the houses of their idols and to the people. 10They put his armor in the temple of Astarte;q and they fastened his body to the wall of Beth-shan. 11But when the inhabitants of Jabesh-gilead heard what the Philistines had done to Saul, 12all the valiant men set out, traveled all night long, and took the body of Saul and the bodies of his sons from the wall of Beth-shan. They came to Jabesh and burned them there. 13Then they took their bones and buried them under the tamarisk tree in Jabesh, and fasted seven days.

p Heb *and they fell slain*   q Heb plural

2 SAMUEL

T his book tells the story of David's reign over Israel. Although God called David a man after his own heart (Acts 13.22), David knew sin and failure. The book of 2 Samuel tells the story of David's adultery and testifies to the power of God's faithfulness and forgiving love. Look for God's hand at work as the nation prospers under David's rule. And take comfort that as you lay your sins before God, he will forgive you and use you once again in his service.

David Mourns for Saul and Jonathan

1 After the death of Saul, when David had returned from defeating the Amalekites, David remained two days in Ziklag. ²On the third day, a man came from Saul's camp, with his clothes torn and dirt on his head. When he came to David, he fell to the ground and did obeisance. ³David said to him, "Where have you come from?" He said to him, "I have escaped from the camp of Israel." ⁴David said to him, "How did things go? Tell me!" He answered, "The army fled from the battle, but also many of the army fell and died; and Saul and his son Jonathan also died." ⁵Then David asked the young man who was reporting to him, "How do you know that Saul and his son Jonathan died?" ⁶The young man reporting to him said, "I happened to be on Mount Gilboa; and there was Saul leaning on his spear, while the chariots and the horsemen drew close to him. ⁷When he looked behind him, he saw me, and called to me. I answered, 'Here sir.' ⁸And he said to me, 'Who are you?' I answered him, 'I am an Amalekite.' ⁹He said to me, 'Come, stand over me and kill me; for convulsions have seized me, and yet my life still lingers.' ¹⁰So I stood over him, and killed him, for I knew that he could not live after he had fallen. I took the crown that was on his head and the armlet that was on his arm, and I have brought them here to my lord."

11 Then David took hold of his clothes and tore them; and all the men who were with him did the same. ¹²They mourned and wept, and fasted until evening for Saul and for his son

Jonathan, and for the army of the LORD and for the house of Israel, because they had fallen by the sword. ¹³David said to the young man who had reported to him, "Where do you come from?" He answered, "I am the son of a resident alien, an Amalekite." ¹⁴David said to him, "Were you not afraid to lift your hand to destroy the LORD's anointed?" ¹⁵Then David called one of the young men and said, "Come here and strike him down." So he struck him down and he died. ¹⁶David said to him, "Your blood be on your head; for your own mouth has testified against you, saying, 'I have killed the LORD's anointed.' "

17 David intoned this lamentation over Saul and his son Jonathan. ¹⁸(He ordered that The Song of the Bow*a* be taught to the people of Judah; it is written in the Book of Jashar.) He said:

19   Your glory, O Israel, lies slain upon
         your high places!
      How the mighty have fallen!
20   Tell it not in Gath,
         proclaim it not in the streets of
         Ashkelon;
      or the daughters of the Philistines
         will rejoice,
      the daughters of the
         uncircumcised will exult.

21   You mountains of Gilboa,
         let there be no dew or rain upon
         you,
      nor bounteous fields!*b*
      For there the shield of the mighty
         was defiled,
      the shield of Saul, anointed with
         oil no more.

22   From the blood of the slain,
         from the fat of the mighty,
      the bow of Jonathan did not turn
         back,
      nor the sword of Saul return
         empty.

23   Saul and Jonathan, beloved and
         lovely!
      In life and in death they were not
         divided;
      they were swifter than eagles,
      they were stronger than lions.

24   O daughters of Israel, weep over
         Saul,
      who clothed you with crimson,
         in luxury,
      who put ornaments of gold on
         your apparel.

25   How the mighty have fallen
         in the midst of the battle!

      Jonathan lies slain upon your high
         places.
26   I am distressed for you, my
         brother Jonathan;
      greatly beloved were you to me;
      your love to me was wonderful,
         passing the love of women.

27   How the mighty have fallen,
         and the weapons of war perished!

David Anointed King of Judah

2 After this David inquired of the LORD, "Shall I go up into any of the cities of Judah?" The LORD said to him, "Go up." David said, "To which shall I go up?" He said, "To Hebron." ²So David went up there, along with his two wives, Ahinoam of Jezreel, and Abigail the widow of Nabal of Carmel. ³David brought up the men who were with him, every one with his household; and they settled in the towns of Hebron. ⁴Then the people of Judah came, and there they anointed David king over the house of Judah.

When they told David, "It was the people of Jabesh-gilead who buried Saul," ⁵David sent messengers to the people of Jabesh-gilead, and said to them, "May you be blessed by the LORD, because you showed this loyalty to Saul your lord, and buried him! ⁶Now may the LORD show steadfast love and faithfulness to you! And I too will reward you because you have done this thing. ⁷Therefore let your hands be strong, and be valiant; for Saul your lord is dead, and the house of Judah has anointed me king over them."

Ishbaal King of Israel

8 But Abner son of Ner, commander of Saul's army, had taken Ishbaal*c* son of

---

a Heb *that The Bow*   *b* Meaning of Heb uncertain   *c* Gk Compare 1 Chr 8.33; 9.39: Heb *Ish-bosheth*, "man of shame"

Saul, and brought him over to Mahanaim. ⁹He made him king over Gilead, the Ashurites, Jezreel, Ephraim, Benjamin, and over all Israel. ¹⁰Ishbaal,ᵈ Saul's son, was forty years old when he began to reign over Israel, and he reigned two years. But the house of Judah followed David. ¹¹The time that David was king in Hebron over the house of Judah was seven years and six months.

The Battle of Gibeon

12 Abner son of Ner, and the servants of Ishbaalᵈ son of Saul, went out from Mahanaim to Gibeon. ¹³Joab son of Zeruiah, and the servants of David, went out and met them at the pool of Gibeon. One group sat on one side of the pool, while the other sat on the other side of the pool. ¹⁴Abner said to Joab, "Let the young men come forward and have a contest before us." Joab said, "Let them come forward." ¹⁵So they came forward and were counted as they passed by, twelve for Benjamin and Ishbaalᵈ son of Saul, and twelve of the servants of David. ¹⁶Each grasped his opponent by the head, and thrust his sword in his opponent's side; so they fell down together. Therefore that place was called Helkath-hazzurim,ᵉ which is at Gibeon. ¹⁷The battle was very fierce that day; and Abner and the men of Israel were beaten by the servants of David.

18 The three sons of Zeruiah were there, Joab, Abishai, and Asahel. Now Asahel was as swift of foot as a wild gazelle. ¹⁹Asahel pursued Abner, turning neither to the right nor to the left as he followed him. ²⁰Then Abner looked back and said, "Is it you, Asahel?" He answered, "Yes, it is." ²¹Abner said to him, "Turn to your right or to your left, and seize one of the young men, and take his spoil." But Asahel would not turn away from following him. ²²Abner said again to Asahel, "Turn away from following me; why should I strike you to the ground? How then could I show my face to your brother Joab?" ²³But he refused to turn away. So Abner struck him in the stomach with the butt of his spear, so that the spear came out at his back. He fell there, and died where he

lay. And all those who came to the place where Asahel had fallen and died, stood still.

24 But Joab and Abishai pursued Abner. As the sun was going down they came to the hill of Ammah, which lies before Giah on the way to the wilderness of Gibeon. ²⁵The Benjaminites rallied around Abner and formed a single band; they took their stand on the top of a hill. ²⁶Then Abner called to Joab, "Is the sword to keep devouring forever? Do you not know that the end will be bitter? How long will it be before you order your people to turn from the pursuit of their kinsmen?" ²⁷Joab said, "As God lives, if you had not spoken, the people would have continued to pursue their kinsmen, not stopping until morning." ²⁸Joab sounded the trumpet and all the people stopped; they no longer pursued Israel or engaged in battle any further.

29 Abner and his men traveled all that night through the Arabah; they crossed the Jordan, and, marching the whole forenoon,ᶠ they came to Mahanaim. ³⁰Joab returned from the pursuit of Abner; and when he had gathered all the people together, there were missing of David's servants nineteen men besides Asahel. ³¹But the servants of David had killed of Benjamin three hundred sixty of Abner's men. ³²They took up Asahel and buried him in the tomb of his father, which was at Bethlehem. Joab and his men marched all night, and the day broke upon them at Hebron.

Abner Defects to David

3 There was a long war between the house of Saul and the house of David; David grew stronger and stronger, while the house of Saul became weaker and weaker.

2 Sons were born to David at Hebron: his firstborn was Amnon, of Ahinoam of Jezreel; ³his second, Chileab, of Abigail the widow of Nabal of Carmel; the third, Absalom son of Maacah, daughter of King Talmai of Geshur; ⁴the fourth, Adonijah son of Haggith; the fifth, Shephatiah son of Abital; ⁵and the sixth, Ithream, of David's wife Eglah. These were born to David in Hebron.

ᵈ Gk Compare 1 Chr 8.33; 9.39: Heb *Ish-bosheth*, "man of shame"   ᵉ That is *Field of Sword-edges*
ᶠ Meaning of Heb uncertain

6 While there was war between the house of Saul and the house of David, Abner was making himself strong in the house of Saul. 7Now Saul had a concubine whose name was Rizpah daughter of Aiah. And Ishbaal*g* said to Abner, "Why have you gone in to my father's concubine?" 8The words of Ishbaal*h* made Abner very angry; he said, "Am I a dog's head for Judah? Today I keep showing loyalty to the house of your father Saul, to his brothers, and to his friends, and have not given you into the hand of David; and yet you charge me now with a crime concerning this woman. 9So may God do to Abner and so may he add to it! For just what the LORD has sworn to David, that will I accomplish for him, 10to transfer the kingdom from the house of Saul, and set up the throne of David over Israel and over Judah, from Dan to Beer-sheba." 11And Ishbaal*g* could not answer Abner another word, because he feared him.

12 Abner sent messengers to David at Hebron,*i* saying, "To whom does the land belong? Make your covenant with me, and I will give you my support to bring all Israel over to you." 13He said, "Good; I will make a covenant with you. But one thing I require of you: you shall never appear in my presence unless you bring Saul's daughter Michal when you come to see me." 14Then David sent messengers to Saul's son Ishbaal,*j* saying, "Give me my wife Michal, to whom I became engaged at the price of one hundred foreskins of the Philistines." 15Ishbaal*j* sent and took her from her husband Paltiel the son of Laish. 16But her husband went with her, weeping as he walked behind her all the way to Bahurim. Then Abner said to him, "Go back home!" So he went back.

17 Abner sent word to the elders of Israel, saying, "For some time past you have been seeking David as king over you. 18Now then bring it about; for the LORD has promised David: Through my servant David I will save my people Israel from the hand of the Philistines, and from all their enemies." 19Abner also spoke directly to the Benjaminites; then

Abner went to tell David at Hebron all that Israel and the whole house of Benjamin were ready to do.

20 When Abner came with twenty men to David at Hebron, David made a feast for Abner and the men who were with him. 21Abner said to David, "Let me go and rally all Israel to my lord the king, in order that they may make a covenant with you, and that you may reign over all that your heart desires." So David dismissed Abner, and he went away in peace.

Abner Is Killed by Joab

22 Just then the servants of David arrived with Joab from a raid, bringing much spoil with them. But Abner was not with David at Hebron, for David*k* had dismissed him, and he had gone away in peace. 23When Joab and all the army that was with him came, it was told Joab, "Abner son of Ner came to the king, and he has dismissed him, and he has gone away in peace." 24Then Joab went to the king and said, "What have you done? Abner came to you; why did you dismiss him, so that he got away? 25You know that Abner son of Ner came to deceive you, and to learn your comings and goings and to learn all that you are doing."

26 When Joab came out from David's presence, he sent messengers after Abner, and they brought him back from the cistern of Sirah; but David did not know about it. 27When Abner returned to Hebron, Joab took him aside in the gateway to speak with him privately, and there he stabbed him in the stomach. So he died for shedding*l* the blood of Asahel, Joab's*m* brother. 28Afterward, when David heard of it, he said, "I and my kingdom are forever guiltless before the LORD for the blood of Abner son of Ner. 29May the guilt*n* fall on the head of Joab, and on all his father's house; and may the house of Joab never be without one who has a discharge, or who is leprous,*o* or who holds a spindle, or who falls by the sword, or who lacks food!" 30So Joab and his brother Abishai murdered Abner because

g Heb And he   h Gk Compare 1 Chr 8.33; 9.39: Heb Ish-bosheth, "man of shame"   i Gk: Heb where he was   j Heb Ish-bosheth   k Heb he   l Heb lacks shedding   m Heb his   n Heb May it   o A term for several skin diseases; precise meaning uncertain

he had killed their brother Asahel in the battle at Gibeon.

31 Then David said to Joab and to all the people who were with him, "Tear your clothes, and put on sackcloth, and mourn over Abner." And King David followed the bier. 32 They buried Abner at Hebron. The king lifted up his voice and wept at the grave of Abner, and all the people wept. 33 The king lamented for Abner, saying,

"Should Abner die as a fool dies?
34   Your hands were not bound,
        your feet were not fettered;
      as one falls before the wicked
        you have fallen."

And all the people wept over him again. 35 Then all the people came to persuade David to eat something while it was still day; but David swore, saying, "So may God do to me, and more, if I taste bread or anything else before the sun goes down!" 36 All the people took notice of it, and it pleased them; just as everything the king did pleased all the people. 37 So all the people and all Israel understood that day that the king had no part in the killing of Abner son of Ner. 38 And the king said to his servants, "Do you not know that a prince and a great man has fallen this day in Israel? 39 Today I am powerless, even though anointed king; these men, the sons of Zeruiah, are too violent for me. The LORD pay back the one who does wickedly in accordance with his wickedness!"

Ishbaal Assassinated

4 When Saul's son Ishbaal[p] heard that Abner had died at Hebron, his courage failed, and all Israel was dismayed. 2 Saul's son had two captains of raiding bands; the name of the one was Baanah, and the name of the other Rechab. They were sons of Rimmon a Benjaminite from Beeroth—for Beeroth is considered to belong to Benjamin. 3 (Now the people of Beeroth had fled to Gittaim and are there as resident aliens to this day).

4 Saul's son Jonathan had a son who was crippled in his feet. He was five years old when the news about Saul and Jonathan came from Jezreel. His nurse picked him up and fled; and, in her haste to flee, it happened that he fell and became lame. His name was Mephibosheth.[q]

5 Now the sons of Rimmon the Beerothite, Rechab and Baanah, set out, and about the heat of the day they came to the house of Ishbaal,[r] while he was taking his noonday rest. 6 They came inside the house as though to take wheat, and they struck him in the stomach; then Rechab and his brother Baanah escaped.[s] 7 Now they had come into the house while he was lying on his couch in his bedchamber; they attacked him, killed him, and beheaded him. Then they took his head and traveled by way of the Arabah all night long. 8 They brought the head of Ishbaal[r] to David at Hebron and said to the king, "Here is the head of Ishbaal,[r] son of Saul, your enemy, who sought your life; the LORD has avenged my lord the king this day on Saul and on his offspring."

9 David answered Rechab and his brother Baanah, the sons of Rimmon the Beerothite, "As the LORD lives, who has redeemed my life out of every adversity, 10 when the one who told me, 'See, Saul is dead,' thought he was bringing good news, I seized him and killed him at Ziklag—this was the reward I gave him for his news. 11 How much more then, when wicked men have killed a righteous man on his bed in his own house! And now shall I not require his blood at your hand, and destroy you from the earth?" 12 So David commanded the young men, and they killed them; they cut off their hands and feet, and hung their bodies beside the pool at Hebron. But the head of Ishbaal[r] they took and buried in the tomb of Abner at Hebron.

David Anointed King of All Israel

5 Then all the tribes of Israel came to David at Hebron, and said, "Look, we are your bone and flesh. 2 For some time, while Saul was king over us, it was you who led out Israel and brought it in. The LORD said to you: It is you who shall be shepherd of my people Israel, you who shall be ruler over Israel." 3 So all the elders of Israel

---

p Heb lacks *Ishbaal*   q In 1 Chr 8.34 and 9.40, *Merib-baal*   r Heb *Ish-bosheth*   s Meaning of Heb of verse 6 uncertain

came to the king at Hebron; and King David made a covenant with them at Hebron before the LORD, and they anointed David king over Israel. ⁴David was thirty years old when he began to reign, and he reigned forty years. ⁵At Hebron he reigned over Judah seven years and six months; and at Jerusalem he reigned over all Israel and Judah thirty-three years.

Jerusalem Made Capital of the United Kingdom

6 The king and his men marched to Jerusalem against the Jebusites, the inhabitants of the land, who said to David, "You will not come in here, even the blind and the lame will turn you back"—thinking, "David cannot come in here." ⁷Nevertheless David took the stronghold of Zion, which is now the city of David. ⁸David had said on that day, "Whoever would strike down the Jebusites, let him get up the water shaft to attack the lame and the blind, those whom David hates."ᵗ Therefore it is said, "The blind and the lame shall not come into the house." ⁹David occupied the stronghold, and named it the city of David. David built the city all around from the Millo inward. ¹⁰And David became greater and greater, for the LORD, the God of hosts, was with him.

11 King Hiram of Tyre sent messengers to David, along with cedar trees, and carpenters and masons who built David a house. ¹²David then perceived that the LORD had established him king over Israel, and that he had exalted his kingdom for the sake of his people Israel.

13 In Jerusalem, after he came from Hebron, David took more concubines and wives; and more sons and daughters were born to David. ¹⁴These are the names of those who were born to him in Jerusalem: Shammua, Shobab, Nathan, Solomon, ¹⁵Ibhar, Elishua, Nepheg, Japhia, ¹⁶Elishama, Eliada, and Eliphelet.

Philistine Attack Repulsed

17 When the Philistines heard that David had been anointed king over Israel, all the Philistines went up in search of David; but David heard about it and went down to the stronghold. ¹⁸Now the Philistines had come and spread out in the valley of Rephaim. ¹⁹David inquired of the LORD, "Shall I go up against the Philistines? Will you give them into my hand?" The LORD said to David, "Go up; for I will certainly give the Philistines into your hand." ²⁰So David came to Baal-perazim, and David defeated them there. He said, "The LORD has burst forth againstᵘ my enemies before me, like a bursting flood." Therefore that place is called Baal-perazim.ᵛ ²¹The Philistines abandoned their idols there, and David and his men carried them away.

22 Once again the Philistines came up, and were spread out in the valley of Rephaim. ²³When David inquired of the LORD, he said, "You shall not go up; go around to their rear, and come upon them opposite the balsam trees. ²⁴When you hear the sound of marching in the tops of the balsam trees, then be on the alert; for then the LORD has gone out before you to strike down the army of the Philistines." ²⁵David did just as the LORD had commanded him; and he struck down the Philistines from Geba all the way to Gezer.

David Brings the Ark to Jerusalem

6 David again gathered all the chosen men of Israel, thirty thousand. ²David and all the people with him set out and went from Baale-judah, to bring up from there the ark of God, which is called by the name of the LORD of hosts who is enthroned on the cherubim. ³They carried the ark of God on a new cart, and brought it out of the house of Abinadab, which was on the hill. Uzzah and Ahio,ʷ the sons of Abinadab, were driving the new cart ⁴with the ark of God;ˣ and Ahioʷ went in front of the ark. ⁵David and all the house of Israel were dancing before the LORD with all their might, with songsʸ and lyres and harps and tambourines and castanets and cymbals.

6 When they came to the threshing floor of Nacon, Uzzah reached out his

---

t Another reading is *those who hate David*   u Heb *paraz*   v That is *Lord of Bursting Forth*
w Or *and his brother*   x Compare Gk: Heb *and brought it out of the house of Abinadab, which was on the hill with the ark of God*   y Q Ms Gk 1 Chr 13.8: Heb *fir trees*

hand to the ark of God and took hold of it, for the oxen shook it. 7 The anger of the LORD was kindled against Uzzah; and God struck him there because he reached out his hand to the ark;z and he died there beside the ark of God. 8 David was angry because the LORD had burst forth with an outburst upon Uzzah; so that place is called Perez-uzzah,a to this day. 9 David was afraid of the LORD that day; he said, "How can the ark of the LORD come into my care?" 10 So David was unwilling to take the ark of the LORD into his care in the city of David; instead David took it to the house of Obed-edom the Gittite. 11 The ark of the LORD remained in the house of Obed-edom the Gittite three months; and the LORD blessed Obed-edom and all his household.

12 It was told King David, "The LORD has blessed the household of Obed-edom and all that belongs to him, because of the ark of God." So David went and brought up the ark of God from the house of Obed-edom to the city of David with rejoicing; 13 and when those who bore the ark of the LORD had gone six paces, he sacrificed an ox and a fatling. 14 David danced before the LORD with all his might; David was girded with a linen ephod. 15 So David and all the house of Israel brought up the ark of the LORD with shouting, and with the sound of the trumpet.

16 As the ark of the LORD came into the city of David, Michal daughter of Saul looked out of the window, and saw King David leaping and dancing before the LORD; and she despised him in her heart.

17 They brought in the ark of the LORD, and set it in its place, inside the tent that David had pitched for it; and David offered burnt offerings and offerings of well-being before the LORD. 18 When David had finished offering the burnt offerings and the offerings of well-being, he blessed the people in the name of the LORD of hosts, 19 and distributed food among all the people, the whole multitude of Israel, both men and women, to each a cake of bread, a por-

tion of meat,b and a cake of raisins. Then all the people went back to their homes.

20 David returned to bless his household. But Michal the daughter of Saul came out to meet David, and said, "How the king of Israel honored himself today, uncovering himself today before the eyes of his servants' maids, as any vulgar fellow might shamelessly uncover himself!" 21 David said to Michal, "It was before the LORD, who chose me in place of your father and all his household, to appoint me as prince over Israel, the people of the LORD, that I have danced before the LORD. 22 I will make myself yet more contemptible than this, and I will be abased in my own eyes; but by the maids of whom you have spoken, by them I shall be held in honor." 23 And Michal the daughter of Saul had no child to the day of her death.

God's Covenant with David

7 Now when the king was settled in his house, and the LORD had given him rest from all his enemies around him, 2 the king said to the prophet Nathan, "See now, I am living in a house of cedar, but the ark of God stays in a tent." 3 Nathan said to the king, "Go, do all that you have in mind; for the LORD is with you."

4 But that same night the word of the LORD came to Nathan: 5 Go and tell my servant David: Thus says the LORD: Are you the one to build me a house to live in? 6 I have not lived in a house since the day I brought up the people of Israel from Egypt to this day, but I have been moving about in a tent and a tabernacle. 7 Wherever I have moved about among all the people of Israel, did I ever speak a word with any of the tribal leadersc of Israel, whom I commanded to shepherd my people Israel, saying, "Why have you not built me a house of cedar?" 8 Now therefore thus you shall say to my servant David: Thus says the LORD of hosts: I took you from the pasture, from following the sheep to be prince over my people Israel; 9 and I have been with you wherever you went, and have cut off all your enemies from before you; and I will make for you a great name, like the

z 1 Chr 13.10 Compare Q Ms: Meaning of Heb uncertain   a That is *Bursting Out Against Uzzah*
b Vg: Meaning of Heb uncertain   c Or *any of the tribes*

name of the great ones of the earth. [10]And I will appoint a place for my people Israel and will plant them, so that they may live in their own place, and be disturbed no more; and evildoers shall afflict them no more, as formerly, [11]from the time that I appointed judges over my people Israel; and I will give you rest from all your enemies. Moreover the LORD declares to you that the LORD will make you a house. [12]When your days are fulfilled and you lie down with your ancestors, I will raise up your offspring after you, who shall come forth from your body, and I will establish his kingdom. [13]He shall build a house for my name, and I will establish the throne of his kingdom forever. [14]I will be a father to him, and he shall be a son to me. When he commits iniquity, I will punish him with a rod such as mortals use, with blows inflicted by human beings. [15]But I will not take[d] my steadfast love from him, as I took it from Saul, whom I put away from before you. [16]Your house and your kingdom shall be made sure forever before me;[e] your throne shall be established forever. [17]In accordance with all these words and with all this vision, Nathan spoke to David.

David's Prayer

18 Then King David went in and sat before the LORD, and said, "Who am I, O Lord GOD, and what is my house, that you have brought me thus far? [19]And yet this was a small thing in your eyes, O Lord GOD; you have spoken also of your servant's house for a great while to come. May this be instruction for the people,[f] O Lord GOD! [20]And what more can David say to you? For you know your servant, O Lord GOD! [21]Because of your promise, and according to your own heart, you have wrought all this greatness, so that your servant may know it. [22]Therefore you are great, O LORD God; for there is no one like you, and there is no God besides you, according to all that we have heard with our ears. [23]Who is like your people, like Israel? Is there another[g] nation on earth

whose God went to redeem it as a people, and to make a name for himself, doing great and awesome things for them,[h] by driving out[i] before his people nations and their gods?[j] [24]And you established your people Israel for yourself to be your people forever; and you, O LORD, became their God. [25]And now, O LORD God, as for the word that you have spoken concerning your servant and concerning his house, confirm it forever; do as you have promised. [26]Thus your name will be magnified forever in the saying, 'The LORD of hosts is God over Israel'; and the house of your servant David will be established before you. [27]For you, O LORD of hosts, the God of Israel, have made this revelation to your servant, saying, 'I will build you a house'; therefore your servant has found courage to pray this prayer to you. [28]And now, O Lord GOD, you are God, and your words are true, and you have promised this good thing to your servant; [29]now therefore may it please you to bless the house of your servant, so that it may continue forever before you; for you, O Lord GOD, have spoken, and with your blessing shall the house of your servant be blessed forever."

David's Wars

8 Some time afterward, David attacked the Philistines and subdued them; David took Methegammah out of the hand of the Philistines.

2 He also defeated the Moabites and, making them lie down on the ground, measured them off with a cord; he measured two lengths of cord for those who were to be put to death, and one length[k] for those who were to be spared. And the Moabites became servants to David and brought tribute.

3 David also struck down King Hadadezer son of Rehob of Zobah, as he went to restore his monument[l] at the river Euphrates. [4]David took from him one thousand seven hundred horsemen, and twenty thousand foot soldiers. David hamstrung all the chariot horses,

---

d Gk Syr Vg 1 Chr 17.13: Heb *shall not depart*   e Gk Heb Mss: MT *before you*; Compare 2 Sam 7.26, 29   f Meaning of Heb uncertain   g Gk: Heb *one*   h Heb *you*   i Gk 1 Chr 17.21: Heb *for your land*   j Cn: Heb *before your people, whom you redeemed for yourself from Egypt, nations and its gods*   k Heb *one full length*   l Compare 1 Sam 15.12 and 2 Sam 18.18

but left enough for a hundred chariots. ⁵When the Arameans of Damascus came to help King Hadadezer of Zobah, David killed twenty-two thousand men of the Arameans. ⁶Then David put garrisons among the Arameans of Damascus; and

---

TUESDAY

THE BLESSINGS OF HIS COVENANT
Oswald Chambers

VERSE: 2 Samuel 7.28   **PASSAGE:** 2 Samuel 7.18–29

t is the will of God that human beings should get into a right-standing relationship with him, and his covenants are designed for this purpose. Why doesn't God save me? He has accomplished and provided for my salvation, but I have not yet entered into a relationship with him. Why doesn't God do everything we ask? He has done it. The point is—will I step into that covenant relationship? All the great blessings of God are finished and complete, but they are not mine until I enter into a relationship with him on the basis of his covenant.

Waiting for God to act is fleshly unbelief. It means that I have no faith in him. I wait for him to do something in me so I may trust in that. But God won't do it, because that is not the basis of the God-and-man relationship. Man must go beyond the physical body and feelings in his covenant with God, just as God goes beyond himself in reaching out with his covenant to man. It is a question of faith in God—a very rare thing. We only have faith in our feelings. I don't believe God until he puts something tangible in my hand, so that I know I have it. Then I say, "Now I believe." There is no faith exhibited in that. God says, "Turn to me and be saved . . . " (Isaiah 45.22).

When I have really transacted business with God on the basis of his covenant, letting everything else go, there is no sense of personal achievement—no human ingredient in it at all. Instead, there is a complete overwhelming sense of being brought into union with God, and my life is transformed and radiates peace and joy.

ADDITIONAL SCRIPTURE READING:
Jeremiah 31.31–34; Hebrews 8

Go to page 349 for your next devotional reading.

1900   Present

the Arameans became servants to David and brought tribute. The LORD gave victory to David wherever he went. [7]David took the gold shields that were carried by the servants of Hadadezer, and brought them to Jerusalem. [8]From Betah and from Berothai, towns of Hadadezer, King David took a great amount of bronze.

9 When King Toi of Hamath heard that David had defeated the whole army of Hadadezer, [10]Toi sent his son Joram to King David, to greet him and to congratulate him because he had fought against Hadadezer and defeated him. Now Hadadezer had often been at war with Toi. Joram brought with him articles of silver, gold, and bronze; [11]these also King David dedicated to the LORD, together with the silver and gold that he dedicated from all the nations he subdued, [12]from Edom, Moab, the Ammonites, the Philistines, Amalek, and from the spoil of King Hadadezer son of Rehob of Zobah.

13 David won a name for himself. When he returned, he killed eighteen thousand Edomites[m] in the Valley of Salt. [14]He put garrisons in Edom; throughout all Edom he put garrisons, and all the Edomites became David's servants. And the LORD gave victory to David wherever he went.

David's Officers

15 So David reigned over all Israel; and David administered justice and equity to all his people. [16]Joab son of Zeruiah was over the army; Jehoshaphat son of Ahilud was recorder; [17]Zadok son of Ahitub and Ahimelech son of Abiathar were priests; Seraiah was secretary; [18]Benaiah son of Jehoiada was over[n] the Cherethites and the Pelethites; and David's sons were priests.

David's Kindness to Mephibosheth

9 David asked, "Is there still anyone left of the house of Saul to whom I may show kindness for Jonathan's sake?" [2]Now there was a servant of the house of Saul whose name was Ziba, and he was summoned to David. The king said to him, "Are you Ziba?"

And he said, "At your service!" [3]The king said, "Is there anyone remaining of the house of Saul to whom I may show the kindness of God?" Ziba said to the king, "There remains a son of Jonathan; he is crippled in his feet." [4]The king said to him, "Where is he?" Ziba said to the king, "He is in the house of Machir son of Ammiel, at Lo-debar." [5]Then King David sent and brought him from the house of Machir son of Ammiel, at Lo-debar. [6]Mephibosheth[o] son of Jonathan son of Saul came to David, and fell on his face and did obeisance. David said, "Mephibosheth!"[o] He answered, "I am your servant." [7]David said to him, "Do not be afraid, for I will show you kindness for the sake of your father Jonathan; I will restore to you all the land of your grandfather Saul, and you yourself shall eat at my table always." [8]He did obeisance and said, "What is your servant, that you should look upon a dead dog such as I?"

9 Then the king summoned Saul's servant Ziba, and said to him, "All that belonged to Saul and to all his house I have given to your master's grandson. [10]You and your sons and your servants shall till the land for him, and shall bring in the produce, so that your master's grandson may have food to eat; but your master's grandson Mephibosheth[o] shall always eat at my table." Now Ziba had fifteen sons and twenty servants. [11]Then Ziba said to the king, "According to all that my lord the king commands his servant, so your servant will do." Mephibosheth[o] ate at David's[p] table, like one of the king's sons. [12]Mephibosheth[o] had a young son whose name was Mica. And all who lived in Ziba's house became Mephibosheth's[q] servants. [13]Mephibosheth[o] lived in Jerusalem, for he always ate at the king's table. Now he was lame in both his feet.

The Ammonites and Arameans Are Defeated

10 Some time afterward, the king of the Ammonites died, and his son Hanun succeeded him.

---

m Gk: Heb *returned from striking down eighteen thousand Arameans*   n Syr Tg Vg 20.23; 1 Chr
18.17: Heb lacks *was over*   o Or *Merib-baal*: See 4.4 note   p Gk: Heb *my*   q Or *Merib-baal's*: See
4.4 note

²David said, "I will deal loyally with Hanun son of Nahash, just as his father dealt loyally with me." So David sent envoys to console him concerning his father. When David's envoys came into the land of the Ammonites, ³the princes of the Ammonites said to their lord Hanun, "Do you really think that David is honoring your father just because he has sent messengers with condolences to you? Has not David sent his envoys to you to search the city, to spy it out, and to overthrow it?" ⁴So Hanun seized David's envoys, shaved off half the beard of each, cut off their garments in the middle at their hips, and sent them away. ⁵When David was told, he sent to meet them, for the men were greatly ashamed. The king said, "Remain at Jericho until your beards have grown, and then return."

6 When the Ammonites saw that they had become odious to David, the Ammonites sent and hired the Arameans of Beth-rehob and the Arameans of Zobah, twenty thousand foot soldiers, as well as the king of Maacah, one thousand men, and the men of Tob, twelve thousand men. ⁷When David heard of it, he sent Joab and all the army with the warriors. ⁸The Ammonites came out and drew up in battle array at the entrance of the gate; but the Arameans of Zobah and of Rehob, and the men of Tob and Maacah, were by themselves in the open country.

9 When Joab saw that the battle was set against him both in front and in the rear, he chose some of the picked men of Israel, and arrayed them against the Arameans; ¹⁰the rest of his men he put in the charge of his brother Abishai, and he arrayed them against the Ammonites. ¹¹He said, "If the Arameans are too strong for me, then you shall help me; but if the Ammonites are too strong for you, then I will come and help you. ¹²Be strong, and let us be courageous for the sake of our people, and for the cities of our God; and may the LORD do what seems good to him." ¹³So Joab and the people who were with him moved forward into battle against the Arameans; and they fled before him. ¹⁴When the Ammonites saw that the Arameans fled,

they likewise fled before Abishai, and entered the city. Then Joab returned from fighting against the Ammonites, and came to Jerusalem.

15 But when the Arameans saw that they had been defeated by Israel, they gathered themselves together. ¹⁶Hadadezer sent and brought out the Arameans who were beyond the Euphrates; and they came to Helam, with Shobach the commander of the army of Hadadezer at their head. ¹⁷When it was told David, he gathered all Israel together, and crossed the Jordan, and came to Helam. The Arameans arrayed themselves against David and fought with him. ¹⁸The Arameans fled before Israel; and David killed of the Arameans seven hundred chariot teams, and forty thousand horsemen,ʳ and wounded Shobach the commander of their army, so that he died there. ¹⁹When all the kings who were servants of Hadadezer saw that they had been defeated by Israel, they made peace with Israel, and became subject to them. So the Arameans were afraid to help the Ammonites any more.

David Commits Adultery with Bathsheba

11 In the spring of the year, the time when kings go out to battle, David sent Joab with his officers and all Israel with him; they ravaged the Ammonites, and besieged Rabbah. But David remained at Jerusalem.

2 It happened, late one afternoon, when David rose from his couch and was walking about on the roof of the king's house, that he saw from the roof a woman bathing; the woman was very beautiful. ³David sent someone to inquire about the woman. It was reported, "This is Bathsheba daughter of Eliam, the wife of Uriah the Hittite." ⁴So David sent messengers to get her, and she came to him, and he lay with her. (Now she was purifying herself after her period.) Then she returned to her house. ⁵The woman conceived; and she sent and told David, "I am pregnant."

6 So David sent word to Joab, "Send me Uriah the Hittite." And Joab sent Uriah to David. ⁷When Uriah came to him, David asked how Joab and the peo-

ʳ 1 Chr 19.18 and some Gk Mss read *foot soldiers*

ple fared, and how the war was going. ⁸Then David said to Uriah, "Go down to your house, and wash your feet." Uriah went out of the king's house, and there followed him a present from the king. ⁹But Uriah slept at the entrance of the king's house with all the servants of his lord, and did not go down to his house. ¹⁰When they told David, "Uriah did not go down to his house," David said to Uriah, "You have just come from a journey. Why did you not go down to your

house?" ¹¹Uriah said to David, "The ark and Israel and Judah remain in booths;ˢ and my lord Joab and the servants of my lord are camping in the open field; shall I then go to my house, to eat and to drink, and to lie with my wife? As you live, and as your soul lives, I will not do such a thing." ¹²Then David said to Uriah, "Remain here today also, and tomorrow I will send you back." So Uriah remained in Jerusalem that day. On the next day, ¹³David invited him to eat and drink in

s Or at Succoth

WEDNESDAY

TEMPTATION'S REACH
Charles H. Spurgeon

VERSE: 2 Samuel 11.2   PASSAGE: 2 Samuel 11.1–27

 e are never out of the reach of temptation. Both at home and abroad we are liable to meet with allurements to evil; the morning opens with peril, and the shades of evening find us still in jeopardy . . . Those who think themselves secure are more exposed to danger than any others. The armor-bearer of sin is self-confidence . . . When I see the King of Israel sluggishly leaving his couch at the close of the day, and falling at once into temptation, let me take warning, and set holy watchfulness to guard the door.

Is it possible that the king had climbed to his housetop for retirement and devotion? If so, what a caution is given us to count no place, however secret, a sanctuary from sin! Since our hearts are so like a tinderbox and sparks so plentiful, we had better use all diligence in all places to prevent a blaze. Satan can climb housetops and enter closets, and even if we could shut out that foul fiend, our own corruptions are enough to work our ruin unless grace prevents. Reader, beware of evening temptations. Do not be secure. The sun is down but sin is up. We need a watchman for the night as well as a guardian for the day. O blessed Spirit, keep us from all evil this night. Amen.

ADDITIONAL SCRIPTURE READING:
Psalm 32.1–5; Mark 14.38

Go to page 359 for your next devotional reading.

1700   1900

his presence and made him drunk; and in the evening he went out to lie on his couch with the servants of his lord, but he did not go down to his house.

David Has Uriah Killed

14 In the morning David wrote a letter to Joab, and sent it by the hand of Uriah. 15In the letter he wrote, "Set Uriah in the forefront of the hardest fighting, and then draw back from him, so that he may be struck down and die." 16As Joab was besieging the city, he assigned Uriah to the place where he knew there were valiant warriors. 17The men of the city came out and fought with Joab; and some of the servants of David among the people fell. Uriah the Hittite was killed as well. 18Then Joab sent and told David all the news about the fighting; 19and he instructed the messenger, "When you have finished telling the king all the news about the fighting, 20then, if the king's anger rises, and if he says to you, 'Why did you go so near the city to fight? Did you not know that they would shoot from the wall? 21Who killed Abimelech son of Jerubbaal?t Did not a woman throw an upper millstone on him from the wall, so that he died at Thebez? Why did you go so near the wall?' then you shall say, 'Your servant Uriah the Hittite is dead too.' "

22 So the messenger went, and came and told David all that Joab had sent him to tell. 23The messenger said to David, "The men gained an advantage over us, and came out against us in the field; but we drove them back to the entrance of the gate. 24Then the archers shot at your servants from the wall; some of the king's servants are dead; and your servant Uriah the Hittite is dead also." 25David said to the messenger, "Thus you shall say to Joab, 'Do not let this matter trouble you, for the sword devours now one and now another; press your attack on the city, and overthrow it.' And encourage him."

26 When the wife of Uriah heard that her husband was dead, she made lamentation for him. 27When the mourning was over, David sent and brought her to his house, and she became his wife, and bore him a son.

t Gk Syr Judg 7.1: Heb *Jerubbesheth*

Nathan Condemns David

But the thing that David had done displeased the LORD, 1and the LORD sent Nathan to David. He came to him, and said to him, "There were two men in a certain city, the one rich and the other poor. 2The rich man had very many flocks and herds; 3but the poor man had nothing but one little ewe lamb, which he had bought. He brought it up, and it grew up with him and with his children; it used to eat of his meager fare, and drink from his cup, and lie in his bosom, and it was like a daughter to him. 4Now there came a traveler to the rich man, and he was loath to take one of his own flock or herd to prepare for the wayfarer who had come to him, but he took the poor man's lamb, and prepared that for the guest who had come to him." 5Then David's anger was greatly kindled against the man. He said to Nathan, "As the LORD lives, the man who has done this deserves to die; 6he shall restore the lamb fourfold, because he did this thing, and because he had no pity."

7 Nathan said to David, "You are the man! Thus says the LORD, the God of Israel: I anointed you king over Israel, and I rescued you from the hand of Saul; 8I gave you your master's house, and your master's wives into your bosom, and gave you the house of Israel and of Judah; and if that had been too little, I would have added as much more. 9Why have you despised the word of the LORD, to do what is evil in his sight? You have struck down Uriah the Hittite with the sword, and have taken his wife to be your wife, and have killed him with the sword of the Ammonites. 10Now therefore the sword shall never depart from your house, for you have despised me, and have taken the wife of Uriah the Hittite to be your wife. 11Thus says the LORD: I will raise up trouble against you from within your own house; and I will take your wives before your eyes, and give them to your neighbor, and he shall lie with your wives in the sight of this very sun. 12For you did it secretly; but I will do this thing before all Israel, and before the sun." 13David said to Nathan, "I have sinned against the LORD."

Nathan said to David, "Now the LORD has put away your sin; you shall not die. [14]Nevertheless, because by this deed you have utterly scorned the LORD,[u] the child that is born to you shall die." [15]Then Nathan went to his house.

Bathsheba's Child Dies

The LORD struck the child that Uriah's wife bore to David, and it became very ill. [16]David therefore pleaded with God for the child; David fasted, and went in and lay all night on the ground. [17]The elders of his house stood beside him, urging him to rise from the ground; but he would not, nor did he eat food with them. [18]On the seventh day the child died. And the servants of David were afraid to tell him that the child was dead; for they said, "While the child was still alive, we spoke to him, and he did not listen to us; how then can we tell him the child is dead? He may do himself some harm." [19]But when David saw that his servants were whispering together, he perceived that the child was dead; and David said to his servants, "Is the child dead?" They said, "He is dead."

[20] Then David rose from the ground, washed, anointed himself, and changed his clothes. He went into the house of the LORD, and worshiped; he then went to his own house; and when he asked, they set food before him and he ate. [21]Then his servants said to him, "What is this thing that you have done? You fasted and wept for the child while it was alive; but when the child died, you rose and ate food." [22]He said, "While the child was still alive, I fasted and wept; for I said, 'Who knows? The LORD may be gracious to me, and the child may live.' [23]But now he is dead; why should I fast? Can I bring him back again? I shall go to him, but he will not return to me."

Solomon Is Born

[24] Then David consoled his wife Bathsheba, and went to her, and lay with her; and she bore a son, and he named him Solomon. The LORD loved him, [25]and sent a message by the prophet Nathan; so he named him Jedidiah,[v] because of the LORD.

The Ammonites Crushed

[26] Now Joab fought against Rabbah of the Ammonites, and took the royal city. [27]Joab sent messengers to David, and said, "I have fought against Rabbah; moreover, I have taken the water city. [28]Now, then, gather the rest of the people together, and encamp against the city, and take it; or I myself will take the city, and it will be called by my name." [29]So David gathered all the people together and went to Rabbah, and fought against it and took it. [30]He took the crown of Milcom[w] from his head; the weight of it was a talent of gold, and in it was a precious stone; and it was placed on David's head. He also brought forth the spoil of the city, a very great amount. [31]He brought out the people who were in it, and set them to work with saws and iron picks and iron axes, or sent them to the brickworks. Thus he did to all the cities of the Ammonites. Then David and all the people returned to Jerusalem.

Amnon and Tamar

13 Some time passed. David's son Absalom had a beautiful sister whose name was Tamar; and David's son Amnon fell in love with her. [2]Amnon was so tormented that he made himself ill because of his sister Tamar, for she was a virgin and it seemed impossible to Amnon to do anything to her. [3]But Amnon had a friend whose name was Jonadab, the son of David's brother Shimeah; and Jonadab was a very crafty man. [4]He said to him, "O son of the king, why are you so haggard morning after morning? Will you not tell me?" Amnon said to him, "I love Tamar, my brother Absalom's sister." [5]Jonadab said to him, "Lie down on your bed, and pretend to be ill; and when your father comes to see you, say to him, 'Let my sister Tamar come and give me something to eat, and prepare the food in my sight, so that I may see it and eat it from her hand.' " [6]So Amnon lay down, and pretended to be ill; and when the king came to see him, Amnon said to the king, "Please let my sister Tamar come and make a couple of cakes

---

u Ancient scribal tradition: Compare 1 Sam 25.22 note: Heb *scorned the enemies of the LORD*   v That is *Beloved of the LORD*   w Gk See 1 Kings 11.5, 33: Heb *their kings*

in my sight, so that I may eat from her hand."

7 Then David sent home to Tamar, saying, "Go to your brother Amnon's house, and prepare food for him." 8So Tamar went to her brother Amnon's house, where he was lying down. She took dough, kneaded it, made cakes in his sight, and baked the cakes. 9Then she took the pan and set them^x out before him, but he refused to eat. Amnon said, "Send out everyone from me." So everyone went out from him. 10Then Amnon said to Tamar, "Bring the food into the chamber, so that I may eat from your hand." So Tamar took the cakes she had made, and brought them into the chamber to Amnon her brother. 11But when she brought them near him to eat, he took hold of her, and said to her, "Come, lie with me, my sister." 12She answered him, "No, my brother, do not force me; for such a thing is not done in Israel; do not do anything so vile! 13As for me, where could I carry my shame? And as for you, you would be as one of the scoundrels in Israel. Now therefore, I beg you, speak to the king; for he will not withhold me from you." 14But he would not listen to her; and being stronger than she, he forced her and lay with her.

15 Then Amnon was seized with a very great loathing for her; indeed, his loathing was even greater than the lust he had felt for her. Amnon said to her, "Get out!" 16But she said to him, "No, my brother;^y for this wrong in sending me away is greater than the other that you did to me." But he would not listen to her. 17He called the young man who served him and said, "Put this woman out of my presence, and bolt the door after her." 18(Now she was wearing a long robe with sleeves; for this is how the virgin daughters of the king were clothed in earlier times.^z) So his servant put her out, and bolted the door after her. 19But Tamar put ashes on her head, and tore the long robe that she was wearing; she put her hand on her head, and went away, crying aloud as she went.

20 Her brother Absalom said to her,

"Has Amnon your brother been with you? Be quiet for now, my sister; he is your brother; do not take this to heart." So Tamar remained, a desolate woman, in her brother Absalom's house. 21When King David heard of all these things, he became very angry, but he would not punish his son Amnon, because he loved him, for he was his firstborn.^a 22But Absalom spoke to Amnon neither good nor bad; for Absalom hated Amnon, because he had raped his sister Tamar.

Absalom Avenges the Violation of His Sister

23 After two full years Absalom had sheepshearers at Baal-hazor, which is near Ephraim, and Absalom invited all the king's sons. 24Absalom came to the king, and said, "Your servant has sheepshearers; will the king and his servants please go with your servant?" 25But the king said to Absalom, "No, my son, let us not all go, or else we will be burdensome to you." He pressed him, but he would not go but gave him his blessing. 26Then Absalom said, "If not, please let my brother Amnon go with us." The king said to him, "Why should he go with you?" 27But Absalom pressed him until he let Amnon and all the king's sons go with him. Absalom made a feast like a king's feast.^b 28Then Absalom commanded his servants, "Watch when Amnon's heart is merry with wine, and when I say to you, 'Strike Amnon,' then kill him. Do not be afraid; have I not myself commanded you? Be courageous and valiant." 29So the servants of Absalom did to Amnon as Absalom had commanded. Then all the king's sons rose, and each mounted his mule and fled.

30 While they were on the way, the report came to David that Absalom had killed all the king's sons, and not one of them was left. 31The king rose, tore his garments, and lay on the ground; and all his servants who were standing by tore their garments. 32But Jonadab, the son of David's brother Shimeah, said, "Let not my lord suppose that they have killed all the young men the king's sons;

x Heb and poured   y Cn Compare Gk Vg: Meaning of Heb uncertain   z Cn: Heb were clothed in robes   a Q Ms Gk: MT lacks but he would not punish . . . firstborn   b Gk Compare Q Ms: MT lacks Absalom made a feast like a king's feast

Amnon alone is dead. This has been determined by Absalom from the day Amnon*c* raped his sister Tamar. 33Now therefore, do not let my lord the king take it to heart, as if all the king's sons were dead; for Amnon alone is dead."

34 But Absalom fled. When the young man who kept watch looked up, he saw many people coming from the Horonaim road*d* by the side of the mountain. 35Jonadab said to the king, "See, the king's sons have come; as your servant said, so it has come about." 36As soon as he had finished speaking, the king's sons arrived, and raised their voices and wept; and the king and all his servants also wept very bitterly.

37 But Absalom fled, and went to Talmai son of Ammihud, king of Geshur. David mourned for his son day after day. 38Absalom, having fled to Geshur, stayed there three years. 39And the heart of*e* the king went out, yearning for Absalom; for he was now consoled over the death of Amnon.

Absalom Returns to Jerusalem

14 Now Joab son of Zeruiah perceived that the king's mind was on Absalom. 2Joab sent to Tekoa and brought from there a wise woman. He said to her, "Pretend to be a mourner; put on mourning garments, do not anoint yourself with oil, but behave like a woman who has been mourning many days for the dead. 3Go to the king and speak to him as follows." And Joab put the words into her mouth.

4 When the woman of Tekoa came to the king, she fell on her face to the ground and did obeisance, and said, "Help, O king!" 5The king asked her, "What is your trouble?" She answered, "Alas, I am a widow; my husband is dead. 6Your servant had two sons, and they fought with one another in the field; there was no one to part them, and one struck the other and killed him. 7Now the whole family has risen against your servant. They say, 'Give up the man who struck his brother, so that we may kill him for the life of his brother whom he murdered, even if we destroy the heir as well.' Thus they would

quench my one remaining ember, and leave to my husband neither name nor remnant on the face of the earth."

8 Then the king said to the woman, "Go to your house, and I will give orders concerning you." 9The woman of Tekoa said to the king, "On me be the guilt, my lord the king, and on my father's house; let the king and his throne be guiltless." 10The king said, "If anyone says anything to you, bring him to me, and he shall never touch you again." 11Then she said, "Please, may the king keep the LORD your God in mind, so that the avenger of blood may kill no more, and my son not be destroyed." He said, "As the LORD lives, not one hair of your son shall fall to the ground."

12 Then the woman said, "Please let your servant speak a word to my lord the king." He said, "Speak." 13The woman said, "Why then have you planned such a thing against the people of God? For in giving this decision the king convicts himself, inasmuch as the king does not bring his banished one home again. 14We must all die; we are like water spilled on the ground, which cannot be gathered up. But God will not take away a life; he will devise plans so as not to keep an outcast banished forever from his presence.*f* 15Now I have come to say this to my lord the king because the people have made me afraid; your servant thought, 'I will speak to the king; it may be that the king will perform the request of his servant. 16For the king will hear, and deliver his servant from the hand of the man who would cut both me and my son off from the heritage of God.' 17Your servant thought, 'The word of my lord the king will set me at rest'; for my lord the king is like the angel of God, discerning good and evil. The LORD your God be with you!"

18 Then the king answered the woman, "Do not withhold from me anything I ask you." The woman said, "Let my lord the king speak." 19The king said, "Is the hand of Joab with you in all this?" The woman answered and said, "As surely as you live, my lord the king, one cannot turn right or left from anything that my lord the king has said.

c Heb *he*   *d* Cn Compare Gk: Heb *the road behind him*   *e* Q Ms Gk: MT *And David*   *f* Meaning of Heb uncertain

For it was your servant Joab who commanded me; it was he who put all these words into the mouth of your servant. 20In order to change the course of affairs your servant Joab did this. But my lord has wisdom like the wisdom of the angel of God to know all things that are on the earth."

21 Then the king said to Joab, "Very well, I grant this; go, bring back the young man Absalom." 22Joab prostrated himself with his face to the ground and did obeisance, and blessed the king; and Joab said, "Today your servant knows that I have found favor in your sight, my lord the king, in that the king has granted the request of his servant." 23So Joab set off, went to Geshur, and brought Absalom to Jerusalem. 24The king said, "Let him go to his own house; he is not to come into my presence." So Absalom went to his own house, and did not come into the king's presence.

David Forgives Absalom

25 Now in all Israel there was no one to be praised so much for his beauty as Absalom; from the sole of his foot to the crown of his head there was no blemish in him. 26When he cut the hair of his head (for at the end of every year he used to cut it; when it was heavy on him, he cut it), he weighed the hair of his head, two hundred shekels by the king's weight. 27There were born to Absalom three sons, and one daughter whose name was Tamar; she was a beautiful woman.

28 So Absalom lived two full years in Jerusalem, without coming into the king's presence. 29Then Absalom sent for Joab to send him to the king; but Joab would not come to him. He sent a second time, but Joab would not come. 30Then he said to his servants, "Look, Joab's field is next to mine, and he has barley there; go and set it on fire." So Absalom's servants set the field on fire. 31Then Joab rose and went to Absalom at his house, and said to him, "Why have your servants set my field on fire?" 32Absalom answered Joab, "Look, I sent word to you: Come here, that I may send you to the king with the question, 'Why have I come from Geshur? It

would be better for me to be there still.' Now let me go into the king's presence; if there is guilt in me, let him kill me!" 33Then Joab went to the king and told him; and he summoned Absalom. So he came to the king and prostrated himself with his face to the ground before the king; and the king kissed Absalom.

Absalom Usurps the Throne

15 After this Absalom got himself a chariot and horses, and fifty men to run ahead of him. 2Absalom used to rise early and stand beside the road into the gate; and when anyone brought a suit before the king for judgment, Absalom would call out and say, "From what city are you?" When the person said, "Your servant is of such and such a tribe in Israel," 3Absalom would say, "See, your claims are good and right; but there is no one deputed by the king to hear you." 4Absalom said moreover, "If only I were judge in the land! Then all who had a suit or cause might come to me, and I would give them justice." 5Whenever people came near to do obeisance to him, he would put out his hand and take hold of them, and kiss them. 6Thus Absalom did to every Israelite who came to the king for judgment; so Absalom stole the hearts of the people of Israel.

7 At the end of four*g* years Absalom said to the king, "Please let me go to Hebron and pay the vow that I have made to the LORD. 8For your servant made a vow while I lived at Geshur in Aram: If the LORD will indeed bring me back to Jerusalem, then I will worship the LORD in Hebron."*h* 9The king said to him, "Go in peace." So he got up, and went to Hebron. 10But Absalom sent secret messengers throughout all the tribes of Israel, saying, "As soon as you hear the sound of the trumpet, then shout: Absalom has become king at Hebron!" 11Two hundred men from Jerusalem went with Absalom; they were invited guests, and they went in their innocence, knowing nothing of the matter. 12While Absalom was offering the sacrifices, he sent for*i* Ahithophel the Gilonite, David's counselor, from his city Giloh. The conspiracy grew in

---

g Gk Syr: Heb *forty*   *h* Gk Mss: Heb lacks *in Hebron*   *i* Or *he sent*

strength, and the people with Absalom kept increasing.

David Flees from Jerusalem

13 A messenger came to David, saying, "The hearts of the Israelites have gone after Absalom." [14] Then David said to all his officials who were with him at Jerusalem, "Get up! Let us flee, or there will be no escape for us from Absalom. Hurry, or he will soon overtake us, and bring disaster down upon us, and attack the city with the edge of the sword." [15] The king's officials said to the king, "Your servants are ready to do whatever our lord the king decides." [16] So the king left, followed by all his household, except ten concubines whom he left behind to look after the house. [17] The king left, followed by all the people; and they stopped at the last house. [18] All his officials passed by him; and all the Cherethites, and all the Pelethites, and all the six hundred Gittites who had followed him from Gath, passed on before the king.

19 Then the king said to Ittai the Gittite, "Why are you also coming with us? Go back, and stay with the king; for you are a foreigner, and also an exile from your home. [20] You came only yesterday, and shall I today make you wander about with us, while I go wherever I can? Go back, and take your kinsfolk with you; and may the LORD show[j] steadfast love and faithfulness to you." [21] But Ittai answered the king, "As the LORD lives, and as my lord the king lives, wherever my lord the king may be, whether for death or for life, there also your servant will be." [22] David said to Ittai, "Go then, march on." So Ittai the Gittite marched on, with all his men and all the little ones who were with him. [23] The whole country wept aloud as all the people passed by; the king crossed the Wadi Kidron, and all the people moved on toward the wilderness.

24 Abiathar came up, and Zadok also, with all the Levites, carrying the ark of the covenant of God. They set down the ark of God, until the people had all passed out of the city. [25] Then the king said to Zadok, "Carry the ark of God back into the city. If I find favor in the eyes of the LORD, he will bring me back and let me see both it and the place where it stays. [26] But if he says, 'I take no pleasure in you,' here I am, let him do to me what seems good to him." [27] The king also said to the priest Zadok, "Look,[k] go back to the city in peace, you and Abiathar,[l] with your two sons, Ahimaaz your son, and Jonathan son of Abiathar. [28] See, I will wait at the fords of the wilderness until word comes from you to inform me." [29] So Zadok and Abiathar carried the ark of God back to Jerusalem, and they remained there.

30 But David went up the ascent of the Mount of Olives, weeping as he went, with his head covered and walking barefoot; and all the people who were with him covered their heads and went up, weeping as they went. [31] David was told that Ahithophel was among the conspirators with Absalom. And David said, "O LORD, I pray you, turn the counsel of Ahithophel into foolishness."

Hushai Becomes David's Spy

32 When David came to the summit, where God was worshiped, Hushai the Archite came to meet him with his coat torn and earth on his head. [33] David said to him, "If you go on with me, you will be a burden to me. [34] But if you return to the city and say to Absalom, 'I will be your servant, O king; as I have been your father's servant in time past, so now I will be your servant,' then you will defeat for me the counsel of Ahithophel. [35] The priests Zadok and Abiathar will be with you there. So whatever you hear from the king's house, tell it to the priests Zadok and Abiathar. [36] Their two sons are with them there, Zadok's son Ahimaaz and Abiathar's son Jonathan; and by them you shall report to me everything you hear." [37] So Hushai, David's friend, came into the city, just as Absalom was entering Jerusalem.

David's Adversaries

16 When David had passed a little beyond the summit, Ziba the servant of Mephibosheth[m] met him, with a couple of donkeys saddled,

---

j Gk Compare 2.6: Heb lacks *may the LORD show*   k Gk: Heb *Are you a seer* or *Do you see?*
l Cn: Heb lacks *and Abiathar*   m Or *Merib-baal*: See 4.4 note

carrying two hundred loaves of bread, one hundred bunches of raisins, one hundred of summer fruits, and one skin of wine. 2The king said to Ziba, "Why have you brought these?" Ziba answered, "The donkeys are for the king's household to ride, the bread and summer fruit for the young men to eat, and the wine is for those to drink who faint in the wilderness." 3The king said, "And where is your master's son?" Ziba said to the king, "He remains in Jerusalem; for he said, 'Today the house of Israel will give me back my grandfather's kingdom.' " 4Then the king said to Ziba, "All that belonged to Mephibosheth*n* is now yours." Ziba said, "I do obeisance; let me find favor in your sight, my lord the king."

Shimei Curses David

5 When King David came to Bahurim, a man of the family of the house of Saul came out whose name was Shimei son of Gera; he came out cursing. 6He threw stones at David and at all the servants of King David; now all the people and all the warriors were on his right and on his left. 7Shimei shouted while he cursed, "Out! Out! Murderer! Scoundrel! 8The LORD has avenged on all of you the blood of the house of Saul, in whose place you have reigned; and the LORD has given the kingdom into the hand of your son Absalom. See, disaster has overtaken you; for you are a man of blood."

9 Then Abishai son of Zeruiah said to the king, "Why should this dead dog curse my lord the king? Let me go over and take off his head." 10But the king said, "What have I to do with you, you sons of Zeruiah? If he is cursing because the LORD has said to him, 'Curse David,' who then shall say, 'Why have you done so?' " 11David said to Abishai and to all his servants, "My own son seeks my life; how much more now may this Benjaminite! Let him alone, and let him curse; for the LORD has bidden him. 12It may be that the LORD will look on my distress,*o* and the LORD will repay me with good for this cursing of me today."

13So David and his men went on the road, while Shimei went along on the hillside opposite him and cursed as he went, throwing stones and flinging dust at him. 14The king and all the people who were with him arrived weary at the Jordan;*p* and there he refreshed himself.

The Counsel of Ahithophel

15 Now Absalom and all the Israelites*q* came to Jerusalem; Ahithophel was with him. 16When Hushai the Archite, David's friend, came to Absalom, Hushai said to Absalom, "Long live the king! Long live the king!" 17Absalom said to Hushai, "Is this your loyalty to your friend? Why did you not go with your friend?" 18Hushai said to Absalom, "No; but the one whom the LORD and this people and all the Israelites have chosen, his I will be, and with him I will remain. 19Moreover, whom should I serve? Should it not be his son? Just as I have served your father, so I will serve you."

20 Then Absalom said to Ahithophel, "Give us your counsel; what shall we do?" 21Ahithophel said to Absalom, "Go in to your father's concubines, the ones he has left to look after the house; and all Israel will hear that you have made yourself odious to your father, and the hands of all who are with you will be strengthened." 22So they pitched a tent for Absalom upon the roof; and Absalom went in to his father's concubines in the sight of all Israel. 23Now in those days the counsel that Ahithophel gave was as if one consulted the oracle*r* of God; so all the counsel of Ahithophel was esteemed, both by David and by Absalom.

17 Moreover Ahithophel said to Absalom, "Let me choose twelve thousand men, and I will set out and pursue David tonight. 2I will come upon him while he is weary and discouraged, and throw him into a panic; and all the people who are with him will flee. I will strike down only the king, 3and I will bring all the people back to you as a bride comes home to her husband. You seek the life of only one man,*s* and all the people will be at peace."

---

n Or Merib-baal: See 4.4 note   o Gk Vg: Heb iniquity   p Gk: Heb lacks at the Jordan   q Gk: Heb all the people, the men of Israel   r Heb word   s Gk: Heb like the return of the whole (is) the man whom you seek

[4]The advice pleased Absalom and all the elders of Israel.

The Counsel of Hushai

5 Then Absalom said, "Call Hushai the Archite also, and let us hear too what he has to say." [6]When Hushai came to Absalom, Absalom said to him, "This is what Ahithophel has said; shall we do as he advises? If not, you tell us." [7]Then Hushai said to Absalom, "This time the counsel that Ahithophel has given is not good." [8]Hushai continued, "You know that your father and his men are warriors, and that they are enraged, like a bear robbed of her cubs in the field. Besides, your father is expert in war; he will not spend the night with the troops. [9]Even now he has hidden himself in one of the pits, or in some other place. And when some of our troops[t] fall at the first attack, whoever hears it will say, 'There has been a slaughter among the troops who follow Absalom.' [10]Then even the valiant warrior, whose heart is like the heart of a lion, will utterly melt with fear; for all Israel knows that your father is a warrior, and that those who are with him are valiant warriors. [11]But my counsel is that all Israel be gathered to you, from Dan to Beer-sheba, like the sand by the sea for multitude, and that you go to battle in person. [12]So we shall come upon him in whatever place he may be found, and we shall light on him as the dew falls on the ground; and he will not survive, nor will any of those with him. [13]If he withdraws into a city, then all Israel will bring ropes to that city, and we shall drag it into the valley, until not even a pebble is to be found there." [14]Absalom and all the men of Israel said, "The counsel of Hushai the Archite is better than the counsel of Ahithophel." For the LORD had ordained to defeat the good counsel of Ahithophel, so that the LORD might bring ruin on Absalom.

Hushai Warns David to Escape

15 Then Hushai said to the priests Zadok and Abiathar, "Thus and so did Ahithophel counsel Absalom and the elders of Israel; and thus and so I have counseled. [16]Therefore send quickly and tell David, 'Do not lodge tonight at the fords of the wilderness, but by all means cross over; otherwise the king and all the people who are with him will be swallowed up.' " [17]Jonathan and Ahimaaz were waiting at En-rogel; a servant-girl used to go and tell them, and they would go and tell King David; for they could not risk being seen entering the city. [18]But a boy saw them, and told Absalom; so both of them went away quickly, and came to the house of a man at Bahurim, who had a well in his courtyard; and they went down into it. [19]The man's wife took a covering, stretched it over the well's mouth, and spread out grain on it; and nothing was known of it. [20]When Absalom's servants came to the woman at the house, they said, "Where are Ahimaaz and Jonathan?" The woman said to them, "They have crossed over the brook[u] of water." And when they had searched and could not find them, they returned to Jerusalem.

21 After they had gone, the men came up out of the well, and went and told King David. They said to David, "Go and cross the water quickly; for thus and so has Ahithophel counseled against you." [22]So David and all the people who were with him set out and crossed the Jordan; by daybreak not one was left who had not crossed the Jordan.

23 When Ahithophel saw that his counsel was not followed, he saddled his donkey and went off home to his own city. He set his house in order, and hanged himself; he died and was buried in the tomb of his father.

24 Then David came to Mahanaim, while Absalom crossed the Jordan with all the men of Israel. [25]Now Absalom had set Amasa over the army in the place of Joab. Amasa was the son of a man named Ithra the Ishmaelite,[v] who had married Abigal daughter of Nahash, sister of Zeruiah, Joab's mother. [26]The Israelites and Absalom encamped in the land of Gilead.

27 When David came to Mahanaim, Shobi son of Nahash from Rabbah of the Ammonites, and Machir son of Ammiel from Lo-debar, and Barzillai the Gileadite from Rogelim, [28]brought beds, basins, and earthen vessels, wheat, barley, meal,

---

t Gk Mss: Heb some of them   u Meaning of Heb uncertain   v 1 Chr 2.17: Heb Israelite

parched grain, beans and lentils,w
29honey and curds, sheep, and cheese
from the herd, for David and the people
with him to eat; for they said, "The
troops are hungry and weary and thirsty
in the wilderness."

The Defeat and Death of Absalom

18 Then David mustered the men who were with him, and set over them commanders of thousands and commanders of hundreds. 2And David divided the army into three groups:x one third under the command of Joab, one third under the command of Abishai son of Zeruiah, Joab's brother, and one third under the command of Ittai the Gittite. The king said to the men, "I myself will also go out with you." 3But the men said, "You shall not go out. For if we flee, they will not care about us. If half of us die, they will not care about us. But you are worth ten thousand of us;y therefore it is better that you send us help from the city." 4The king said to them, "Whatever seems best to you I will do." So the king stood at the side of the gate, while all the army marched out by hundreds and by thousands. 5The king ordered Joab and Abishai and Ittai, saying, "Deal gently for my sake with the young man Absalom." And all the people heard when the king gave orders to all the commanders concerning Absalom.

6 So the army went out into the field against Israel; and the battle was fought in the forest of Ephraim. 7The men of Israel were defeated there by the servants of David, and the slaughter there was great on that day, twenty thousand men. 8The battle spread over the face of all the country; and the forest claimed more victims that day than the sword.

9 Absalom happened to meet the servants of David. Absalom was riding on his mule, and the mule went under the thick branches of a great oak. His head caught fast in the oak, and he was left hangingz between heaven and earth, while the mule that was under him went on. 10A man saw it, and told Joab, "I saw Absalom hanging in an oak."

11Joab said to the man who told him, "What, you saw him! Why then did you not strike him there to the ground? I would have been glad to give you ten pieces of silver and a belt." 12But the man said to Joab, "Even if I felt in my hand the weight of a thousand pieces of silver, I would not raise my hand against the king's son; for in our hearing the king commanded you and Abishai and Ittai, saying: For my sake protect the young man Absalom! 13On the other hand, if I had dealt treacherously against his lifea (and there is nothing hidden from the king), then you yourself would have stood aloof." 14Joab said, "I will not waste time like this with you." He took three spears in his hand, and thrust them into the heart of Absalom, while he was still alive in the oak. 15And ten young men, Joab's armor-bearers, surrounded Absalom and struck him, and killed him.

16 Then Joab sounded the trumpet, and the troops came back from pursuing Israel, for Joab restrained the troops. 17They took Absalom, threw him into a great pit in the forest, and raised over him a very great heap of stones. Meanwhile all the Israelites fled to their homes. 18Now Absalom in his lifetime had taken and set up for himself a pillar that is in the King's Valley, for he said, "I have no son to keep my name in remembrance"; he called the pillar by his own name. It is called Absalom's Monument to this day.

David Hears of Absalom's Death

19 Then Ahimaaz son of Zadok said, "Let me run, and carry tidings to the king that the LORD has delivered him from the power of his enemies." 20Joab said to him, "You are not to carry tidings today; you may carry tidings another day, but today you shall not do so, because the king's son is dead." 21Then Joab said to a Cushite, "Go, tell the king what you have seen." The Cushite bowed before Joab, and ran. 22Ahimaaz son of Zadok said again to Joab, "Come what may, let me also run after the Cushite." And Joab said, "Why

---

w Heb and lentils and parched grain   x Gk: Heb sent forth the army   y Gk Vg Symmachus: Heb for now there are ten thousand such as we   z Gk Syr Tg: Heb was put   a Another reading is at the risk of my life

will you run, my son, seeing that you have no reward[b] for the tidings?" [23]"Come what may," he said, "I will run." So he said to him, "Run." Then Ahimaaz ran by the way of the Plain, and outran the Cushite.

24 Now David was sitting between the two gates. The sentinel went up to the roof of the gate by the wall, and when he looked up, he saw a man running alone. [25]The sentinel shouted and told the king. The king said, "If he is alone, there are tidings in his mouth." He kept coming, and drew near. [26]Then the sentinel saw another man running; and the sentinel called to the gatekeeper and said, "See, another man running alone!" The king said, "He also is bring-

ing tidings." [27]The sentinel said, "I think the running of the first one is like the running of Ahimaaz son of Zadok." The king said, "He is a good man, and comes with good tidings."

28 Then Ahimaaz cried out to the king, "All is well!" He prostrated himself before the king with his face to the ground, and said, "Blessed be the LORD your God, who has delivered up the men who raised their hand against my lord the king." [29]The king said, "Is it well with the young man Absalom?" Ahimaaz answered, "When Joab sent your servant,[c] I saw a great tumult, but I do not know what it was." [30]The king said, "Turn aside, and stand here." So he turned aside, and stood still.

b Meaning of Heb uncertain   c Heb the king's servant, your servant

---

THURSDAY

IF ONLY . . .
G. Campbell Morgan

VERSE: 2 Samuel 18.33   **PASSAGE:** 2 Samuel 18.1–33

 n this hour David's cup of sorrow was filled to the full. Everything in the story leads up to, and culminates in, this wail of anguish over his dead boy. It is very brief, but it thrills with agony. Five times he repeated the words, "my son." This surely had a deeper note in it than that of the merely half-conscious repetition of words occasioned by personal grief. The father recognized how much he was responsible for his son. It is as though he had said: "He is indeed my son, his weaknesses are my weaknesses, his passions are my passions, his sins are my sins." Out of all that sense there came the deepest cry of all: "Would I had died instead of you!" Here surely David reached the profoundest moment of his suffering. May none of us ever experimentally enter into its awful consciousness! In order that we may not, we need to ponder all the story carefully, and learn the solemn lessons it teaches of parental responsibility.

ADDITIONAL SCRIPTURE READING:
Psalm 116.1–7; Romans 9.1–5

Go to page 367 for your next devotional reading.

1900   Present

31 Then the Cushite came; and the Cushite said, "Good tidings for my lord the king! For the LORD has vindicated you this day, delivering you from the power of all who rose up against you." ³²The king said to the Cushite, "Is it well with the young man Absalom?" The Cushite answered, "May the enemies of my lord the king, and all who rise up to do you harm, be like that young man."

David Mourns for Absalom

33ᵈ The king was deeply moved, and went up to the chamber over the gate, and wept; and as he went, he said, "O my son Absalom, my son, my son Absalom! Would I had died instead of you, O Absalom, my son, my son!"

19 It was told Joab, "The king is weeping and mourning for Absalom." ²So the victory that day was turned into mourning for all the troops; for the troops heard that day, "The king is grieving for his son." ³The troops stole into the city that day as soldiers steal in who are ashamed when they flee in battle. ⁴The king covered his face, and the king cried with a loud voice, "O my son Absalom, O Absalom, my son, my son!" ⁵Then Joab came into the house to the king, and said, "Today you have covered with shame the faces of all your officers who have saved your life today, and the lives of your sons and your daughters, and the lives of your wives and your concubines, ⁶for love of those who hate you and for hatred of those who love you. You have made it clear today that commanders and officers are nothing to you; for I perceive that if Absalom were alive and all of us were dead today, then you would be pleased. ⁷So go out at once and speak kindly to your servants; for I swear by the LORD, if you do not go, not a man will stay with you this night; and this will be worse for you than any disaster that has come upon you from your youth until now." ⁸Then the king got up and took his seat in the gate. The troops were all told, "See, the king is sitting in the gate"; and all the troops came before the king.

David Recalled to Jerusalem

Meanwhile, all the Israelites had fled to their homes. ⁹All the people were disputing throughout all the tribes of Israel, saying, "The king delivered us from the hand of our enemies, and saved us from the hand of the Philistines; and now he has fled out of the land because of Absalom. ¹⁰But Absalom, whom we anointed over us, is dead in battle. Now therefore why do you say nothing about bringing the king back?"

11 King David sent this message to the priests Zadok and Abiathar, "Say to the elders of Judah, 'Why should you be the last to bring the king back to his house? The talk of all Israel has come to the king.ᵉ ¹²You are my kin, you are my bone and my flesh; why then should you be the last to bring back the king?' ¹³And say to Amasa, 'Are you not my bone and my flesh? So may God do to me, and more, if you are not the commander of my army from now on, in place of Joab.' " ¹⁴Amasaᶠ swayed the hearts of all the people of Judah as one, and they sent word to the king, "Return, both you and all your servants." ¹⁵So the king came back to the Jordan; and Judah came to Gilgal to meet the king and to bring him over the Jordan.

16 Shimei son of Gera, the Benjaminite, from Bahurim, hurried to come down with the people of Judah to meet King David; ¹⁷with him were a thousand people from Benjamin. And Ziba, the servant of the house of Saul, with his fifteen sons and his twenty servants, rushed down to the Jordan ahead of the king, ¹⁸while the crossing was taking place,ᵍ to bring over the king's household, and to do his pleasure.

David's Mercy to Shimei

Shimei son of Gera fell down before the king, as he was about to cross the Jordan, ¹⁹and said to the king, "May my lord not hold me guilty or remember how your servant did wrong on the day my lord the king left Jerusalem; may the king not bear it in mind. ²⁰For your servant knows that I have sinned; therefore, see, I have come this day, the first of all the house of Joseph to come down

---

ᵈ Ch 19.1 in Heb   ᵉ Gk: Heb to the king, to his house   ᶠ Heb He   ᵍ Cn: Heb the ford crossed

to meet my lord the king." ²¹Abishai son of Zeruiah answered, "Shall not Shimei be put to death for this, because he cursed the LORD's anointed?" ²²But David said, "What have I to do with you, you sons of Zeruiah, that you should today become an adversary to me? Shall anyone be put to death in Israel this day? For do I not know that I am this day king over Israel?" ²³The king said to Shimei, "You shall not die." And the king gave him his oath.

David and Mephibosheth Meet

24 Mephibosheth^h grandson of Saul came down to meet the king; he had not taken care of his feet, or trimmed his beard, or washed his clothes, from the day the king left until the day he came back in safety. ²⁵When he came from Jerusalem to meet the king, the king said to him, "Why did you not go with me, Mephibosheth?"^h ²⁶He answered, "My lord, O king, my servant deceived me; for your servant said to him, 'Saddle a donkey for me,^i so that I may ride on it and go with the king.' For your servant is lame. ²⁷He has slandered your servant to my lord the king. But my lord the king is like the angel of God; do therefore what seems good to you. ²⁸For all my father's house were doomed to death before my lord the king; but you set your servant among those who eat at your table. What further right have I, then, to appeal to the king?" ²⁹The king said to him, "Why speak any more of your affairs? I have decided: you and Ziba shall divide the land." ³⁰Mephibosheth^h said to the king, "Let him take it all, since my lord the king has arrived home safely."

David's Kindness to Barzillai

31 Now Barzillai the Gileadite had come down from Rogelim; he went on with the king to the Jordan, to escort him over the Jordan. ³²Barzillai was a very aged man, eighty years old. He had provided the king with food while he stayed at Mahanaim, for he was a very wealthy man. ³³The king said to Barzillai, "Come over with me, and I will provide for you in Jerusalem at my side." ³⁴But Barzillai said to the king, "How

many years have I still to live, that I should go up with the king to Jerusalem? ³⁵Today I am eighty years old; can I discern what is pleasant and what is not? Can your servant taste what he eats or what he drinks? Can I still listen to the voice of singing men and singing women? Why then should your servant be an added burden to my lord the king? ³⁶Your servant will go a little way over the Jordan with the king. Why should the king recompense me with such a reward? ³⁷Please let your servant return, so that I may die in my own town, near the graves of my father and my mother. But here is your servant Chimham; let him go over with my lord the king; and do for him whatever seems good to you." ³⁸The king answered, "Chimham shall go over with me, and I will do for him whatever seems good to you; and all that you desire of me I will do for you." ³⁹Then all the people crossed over the Jordan, and the king crossed over; the king kissed Barzillai and blessed him, and he returned to his own home. ⁴⁰The king went on to Gilgal, and Chimham went on with him; all the people of Judah, and also half the people of Israel, brought the king on his way.

41 Then all the people of Israel came to the king, and said to him, "Why have our kindred the people of Judah stolen you away, and brought the king and his household over the Jordan, and all David's men with him?" ⁴²All the people of Judah answered the people of Israel, "Because the king is near of kin to us. Why then are you angry over this matter? Have we eaten at all at the king's expense? Or has he given us any gift?" ⁴³But the people of Israel answered the people of Judah, "We have ten shares in the king, and in David also we have more than you. Why then did you despise us? Were we not the first to speak of bringing back our king?" But the words of the people of Judah were fiercer than the words of the people of Israel.

The Rebellion of Sheba

20 Now a scoundrel named Sheba son of Bichri, a Benjaminite, happened to be there. He sounded the trumpet and cried out,

---

h Or *Merib-baal*: See 4.4 note   i Gk Syr Vg: Heb *said, 'I will saddle a donkey for myself*

"We have no portion in David,
no share in the son of Jesse!
Everyone to your tents, O Israel!"
2So all the people of Israel withdrew from David and followed Sheba son of Bichri; but the people of Judah followed their king steadfastly from the Jordan to Jerusalem.

3 David came to his house at Jerusalem; and the king took the ten concubines whom he had left to look after the house, and put them in a house under guard, and provided for them, but did not go in to them. So they were shut up until the day of their death, living as if in widowhood.

4 Then the king said to Amasa, "Call the men of Judah together to me within three days, and be here yourself." 5So Amasa went to summon Judah; but he delayed beyond the set time that had been appointed him. 6David said to Abishai, "Now Sheba son of Bichri will do us more harm than Absalom; take your lord's servants and pursue him, or he will find fortified cities for himself, and escape from us." 7Joab's men went out after him, along with the Cherethites, the Pelethites, and all the warriors; they went out from Jerusalem to pursue Sheba son of Bichri. 8When they were at the large stone that is in Gibeon, Amasa came to meet them. Now Joab was wearing a soldier's garment and over it was a belt with a sword in its sheath fastened at his waist; as he went forward it fell out. 9Joab said to Amasa, "Is it well with you, my brother?" And Joab took Amasa by the beard with his right hand to kiss him. 10But Amasa did not notice the sword in Joab's hand; Joab struck him in the belly so that his entrails poured out on the ground, and he died. He did not strike a second blow.

Then Joab and his brother Abishai pursued Sheba son of Bichri. 11And one of Joab's men took his stand by Amasa, and said, "Whoever favors Joab, and whoever is for David, let him follow Joab." 12Amasa lay wallowing in his blood on the highway, and the man saw that all the people were stopping. Since he saw that all who came by him were stopping, he carried Amasa from the highway into a field, and threw a garment over him. 13Once he was removed from the highway, all the people went on after Joab to pursue Sheba son of Bichri.

14 Sheba[j] passed through all the tribes of Israel to Abel of Beth-maacah;[k] and all the Bichrites[l] assembled, and followed him inside. 15Joab's forces[m] came and besieged him in Abel of Beth-maacah; they threw up a siege ramp against the city, and it stood against the rampart. Joab's forces were battering the wall to break it down. 16Then a wise woman called from the city, "Listen! Listen! Tell Joab, 'Come here, I want to speak to you.' " 17He came near her; and the woman said, "Are you Joab?" He answered, "I am." Then she said to him, "Listen to the words of your servant." He answered, "I am listening." 18Then she said, "They used to say in the old days, 'Let them inquire at Abel'; and so they would settle a matter. 19I am one of those who are peaceable and faithful in Israel; you seek to destroy a city that is a mother in Israel; why will you swallow up the heritage of the LORD?" 20Joab answered, "Far be it from me, far be it, that I should swallow up or destroy! 21That is not the case! But a man of the hill country of Ephraim, called Sheba son of Bichri, has lifted up his hand against King David; give him up alone, and I will withdraw from the city." The woman said to Joab, "His head shall be thrown over the wall to you." 22Then the woman went to all the people with her wise plan. And they cut off the head of Sheba son of Bichri, and threw it out to Joab. So he blew the trumpet, and they dispersed from the city, and all went to their homes, while Joab returned to Jerusalem to the king.

23 Now Joab was in command of all the army of Israel;[n] Benaiah son of Jehoiada was in command of the Cherethites and the Pelethites; 24Adoram was in charge of the forced labor; Jehoshaphat son of Ahilud was the recorder; 25Sheva was secretary; Zadok and Abiathar were priests; 26and Ira the Jairite was also David's priest.

---

j Heb He   k Compare 20.15: Heb and Beth-maacah   l Compare Gk Vg: Heb Berites
m Heb They   n Cn: Heb Joab to all the army, Israel

David Avenges the Gibeonites

21 Now there was a famine in the days of David for three years, year after year; and David inquired of the LORD. The LORD said, "There is bloodguilt on Saul and on his house, because he put the Gibeonites to death." 2So the king called the Gibeonites and spoke to them. (Now the Gibeonites were not of the people of Israel, but of the remnant of the Amorites; although the people of Israel had sworn to spare them, Saul had tried to wipe them out in his zeal for the people of Israel and Judah.) 3David said to the Gibeonites, "What shall I do for you? How shall I make expiation, that you may bless the heritage of the LORD?" 4The Gibeonites said to him, "It is not a matter of silver or gold between us and Saul or his house; neither is it for us to put anyone to death in Israel." He said, "What do you say that I should do for you?" 5They said to the king, "The man who consumed us and planned to destroy us, so that we should have no place in all the territory of Israel— 6let seven of his sons be handed over to us, and we will impale them before the LORD at Gibeon on the mountain of the LORD."*o* The king said, "I will hand them over."

7 But the king spared Mephibosheth,*p* the son of Saul's son Jonathan, because of the oath of the LORD that was between them, between David and Jonathan son of Saul. 8The king took the two sons of Rizpah daughter of Aiah, whom she bore to Saul, Armoni and Mephibosheth;*p* and the five sons of Merab*q* daughter of Saul, whom she bore to Adriel son of Barzillai the Meholathite; 9he gave them into the hands of the Gibeonites, and they impaled them on the mountain before the LORD. The seven of them perished together. They were put to death in the first days of harvest, at the beginning of barley harvest.

10 Then Rizpah the daughter of Aiah took sackcloth, and spread it on a rock for herself, from the beginning of harvest until rain fell on them from the heavens; she did not allow the birds of the air to come on the bodies*r* by day, or the wild animals by night. 11When David was told what Rizpah daughter of Aiah, the concubine of Saul, had done, 12David went and took the bones of Saul and the bones of his son Jonathan from the people of Jabesh-gilead, who had stolen them from the public square of Beth-shan, where the Philistines had hung them up, on the day the Philistines killed Saul on Gilboa. 13He brought up from there the bones of Saul and the bones of his son Jonathan; and they gathered the bones of those who had been impaled. 14They buried the bones of Saul and of his son Jonathan in the land of Benjamin in Zela, in the tomb of his father Kish; they did all that the king commanded. After that, God heeded supplications for the land.

Exploits of David's Men

15 The Philistines went to war again with Israel, and David went down together with his servants. They fought against the Philistines, and David grew weary. 16Ishbi-benob, one of the descendants of the giants, whose spear weighed three hundred shekels of bronze, and who was fitted out with new weapons,*s* said he would kill David. 17But Abishai son of Zeruiah came to his aid, and attacked the Philistine and killed him. Then David's men swore to him, "You shall not go out with us to battle any longer, so that you do not quench the lamp of Israel."

18 After this a battle took place with the Philistines, at Gob; then Sibbecai the Hushathite killed Saph, who was one of the descendants of the giants. 19Then there was another battle with the Philistines at Gob; and Elhanan son of Jaare-oregim, the Bethlehemite, killed Goliath the Gittite, the shaft of whose spear was like a weaver's beam. 20There was again war at Gath, where there was a man of great size, who had six fingers on each hand, and six toes on each foot, twenty-four in number; he too was descended from the giants. 21When he taunted Israel, Jonathan son of David's brother Shimei, killed him. 22These four were descended from the giants in Gath;

o Cn Compare Gk and 21.9: Heb *at Gibeah of Saul, the chosen of the* LORD   *p* Or *Merib-baal: See 4.4* note   *q* Two Heb Mss Syr Compare Gk: MT *Michal*   *r* Heb *them*   *s* Heb *was belted anew*

they fell by the hands of David and his servants.

David's Song of Thanksgiving

22 David spoke to the LORD the words of this song on the day when the LORD delivered him from the hand of all his enemies, and from the hand of Saul. 2He said:

The LORD is my rock, my fortress,
and my deliverer,
3 　my God, my rock, in whom I
take refuge,
my shield and the horn of my
salvation,
my stronghold and my refuge,
my savior; you save me from
violence.
4 I call upon the LORD, who is
worthy to be praised,
and I am saved from my enemies.

5 　For the waves of death
encompassed me,
the torrents of perdition assailed
me;
6 the cords of Sheol entangled me,
the snares of death confronted
me.

7 In my distress I called upon the
LORD;
to my God I called.
From his temple he heard my
voice,
and my cry came to his ears.

8 　Then the earth reeled and rocked;
the foundations of the heavens
trembled
and quaked, because he was
angry.
9 Smoke went up from his nostrils,
and devouring fire from his
mouth;
glowing coals flamed forth from
him.
10 He bowed the heavens, and came
down;
thick darkness was under his
feet.
11 He rode on a cherub, and flew;
he was seen upon the wings of
the wind.
12 He made darkness around him a
canopy,

thick clouds, a gathering of
water.
13 Out of the brightness before him
coals of fire flamed forth.
14 The LORD thundered from heaven;
the Most High uttered his voice.
15 He sent out arrows, and scattered
them
—lightning, and routed them.
16 Then the channels of the sea were
seen,
the foundations of the world
were laid bare
at the rebuke of the LORD,
at the blast of the breath of his
nostrils.

17 He reached from on high, he took
me,
he drew me out of mighty
waters.
18 He delivered me from my strong
enemy,
from those who hated me;
for they were too mighty for me.
19 They came upon me in the day of
my calamity,
but the LORD was my stay.
20 He brought me out into a broad
place;
he delivered me, because he
delighted in me.

21 　The LORD rewarded me according
to my righteousness;
according to the cleanness of my
hands he recompensed me.
22 For I have kept the ways of the
LORD,
and have not wickedly departed
from my God.
23 For all his ordinances were before
me,
and from his statutes I did not
turn aside.
24 I was blameless before him,
and I kept myself from guilt.
25 Therefore the LORD has
recompensed me according
to my righteousness,
according to my cleanness in his
sight.

26 With the loyal you show yourself
loyal;

with the blameless you show
yourself blameless;
27 with the pure you show yourself
pure,
and with the crooked you show
yourself perverse.
28 You deliver a humble people,
but your eyes are upon the
haughty to bring them down.
29 Indeed, you are my lamp, O LORD,
the LORD lightens my darkness.
30 By you I can crush a troop,
and by my God I can leap over a
wall.
31 This God—his way is perfect;
the promise of the LORD proves
true;
he is a shield for all who take
refuge in him.

32 For who is God, but the LORD?
And who is a rock, except our
God?
33 The God who has girded me with
strength[t]
has opened wide my path.[u]
34 He made my[v] feet like the feet of
deer,
and set me secure on the heights.
35 He trains my hands for war,
so that my arms can bend a bow
of bronze.
36 You have given me the shield of
your salvation,
and your help[w] has made me
great.
37 You have made me stride freely,
and my feet do not slip;
38 I pursued my enemies and
destroyed them,
and did not turn back until they
were consumed.
39 I consumed them; I struck them
down, so that they did not
rise;
they fell under my feet.
40 For you girded me with strength for
the battle;
you made my assailants sink
under me.
41 You made my enemies turn their
backs to me,
those who hated me, and I
destroyed them.

42 They looked, but there was no one
to save them;
they cried to the LORD, but he did
not answer them.
43 I beat them fine like the dust of the
earth,
I crushed them and stamped
them down like the mire of
the streets.

44 You delivered me from strife with
the peoples;[x]
you kept me as the head of the
nations;
people whom I had not known
served me.
45 Foreigners came cringing to me;
as soon as they heard of me, they
obeyed me.
46 Foreigners lost heart,
and came trembling out of their
strongholds.

47 The LORD lives! Blessed be my
rock,
and exalted be my God, the rock
of my salvation,
48 the God who gave me vengeance
and brought down peoples under
me,
49 who brought me out from my
enemies;
you exalted me above my
adversaries,
you delivered me from the
violent.

50 For this I will extol you, O LORD,
among the nations,
and sing praises to your name.
51 He is a tower of salvation for his
king,

THE FETTERS OF MY TONGUE DO THOU UNBIND,

THAT I MAY HAVE THE POWER TO SING OF THEE,

AND SOUND THY PRAISES EVERLASTINGLY.

—*William Wordsworth*

---

and shows steadfast love to his
anointed,
to David and his descendants
forever.

---

t Q Ms Gk Syr Vg Compare Ps 18.32: MT *God is my strong refuge*   *u* Meaning of Heb uncertain
v Another reading is *his*   *w* Q Ms: MT *your answering*   *x* Gk: Heb *from strife with my people*

The Last Words of David

23 Now these are the last words of David:

The oracle of David, son of Jesse,
  the oracle of the man whom God
    exalted,[y]
the anointed of the God of Jacob,
  the favorite of the Strong One of
    Israel:

2 The spirit of the LORD speaks
    through me,
  his word is upon my tongue.
3 The God of Israel has spoken,
    the Rock of Israel has said to me:
  One who rules over people justly,
    ruling in the fear of God,
4 is like the light of morning,
    like the sun rising on a cloudless
      morning,
  gleaming from the rain on the
    grassy land.

5 Is not my house like this with
    God?
  For he has made with me an
    everlasting covenant,
  ordered in all things and secure.
  Will he not cause to prosper
    all my help and my desire?
6 But the godless are[z] all like thorns
    that are thrown away;
  for they cannot be picked up
    with the hand;
7 to touch them one uses an iron bar
    or the shaft of a spear.
  And they are entirely consumed
    in fire on the spot.[a]

David's Mighty Men

8 These are the names of the warriors whom David had: Josheb-basshebeth a Tahchemonite; he was chief of the Three;[b] he wielded his spear[c] against eight hundred whom he killed at one time. 9 Next to him among the three warriors was Eleazar son of Dodo son of Ahohi. He was with David when they defied the Philistines who were gathered there for battle. The Israelites withdrew, 10but he stood his ground. He struck down the Philistines until his arm grew weary, though his hand clung to the sword. The LORD brought about a great victory that day. Then the people came back to him—but only to strip the dead.

11 Next to him was Shammah son of Agee, the Hararite. The Philistines gathered together at Lehi, where there was a plot of ground full of lentils; and the army fled from the Philistines. 12But he took his stand in the middle of the plot, defended it, and killed the Philistines; and the LORD brought about a great victory.

13 Towards the beginning of harvest three of the thirty[d] chiefs went down to join David at the cave of Adullam, while a band of Philistines was encamped in the valley of Rephaim. 14David was then in the stronghold; and the garrison of the Philistines was then at Bethlehem. 15David said longingly, "O that someone would give me water to drink from the well of Bethlehem that is by the gate!" 16Then the three warriors broke through the camp of the Philistines, drew water from the well of Bethlehem that was by the gate, and brought it to David. But he would not drink of it; he poured it out to the LORD, 17for he said, "The LORD forbid that I should do this. Can I drink the blood of the men who went at the risk of their lives?" Therefore he would not drink it. The three warriors did these things.

18 Now Abishai son of Zeruiah, the brother of Joab, was chief of the Thirty.[e] With his spear he fought against three hundred men and killed them, and won a name beside the Three. 19He was the most renowned of the Thirty,[f] and became their commander; but he did not attain to the Three.

20 Benaiah son of Jehoiada was a valiant warrior[g] from Kabzeel, a doer of great deeds; he struck down two sons of Ariel[h] of Moab. He also went down and killed a lion in a pit on a day when snow had fallen. 21And he killed an Egyptian, a handsome man. The Egyptian had a spear in his hand; but Benaiah went against him with a staff, snatched the spear out of the Egyptian's hand, and

---

y Q Ms: MT *who was raised on high*   z Heb *But worthlessness*   a Heb *in sitting*   b Gk Vg
Compare 1 Chr 11.11: Meaning of Heb uncertain   c 1 Chr 11.11: Meaning of Heb uncertain
d Heb adds *head*   e Two Heb Mss Syr: MT *Three*   f Syr Compare 1 Chr 11.25: Heb *Was he the most renowned of the Three?*   g Another reading is *the son of Ish-hai*   h Gk: Heb lacks *sons of*

killed him with his own spear. 22Such were the things Benaiah son of Jehoiada did, and won a name beside the three warriors. 23He was renowned among the Thirty, but he did not attain to the Three. And David put him in charge of his bodyguard.

24 Among the Thirty were Asahel brother of Joab; Elhanan son of Dodo of Bethlehem; 25Shammah of Harod; Elika of Harod; 26Helez the Paltite; Ira son of Ikkesh of Tekoa; 27Abiezer of Anathoth; Mebunnai the Hushathite; 28Zalmon the Ahohite; Maharai of Netophah; 29Heleb son of Baanah of Netophah; Ittai son of Ribai of Gibeah of the Benjaminites; 30Benaiah of Pirathon; Hiddai of the torrents of Gaash; 31Abi-albon the Arbathite; Azmaveth of Bahurim; 32Eliahba of Shaalbon; the sons of Jashen: Jonathan 33son of*i* Shammah the Hararite; Ahiam son of Sharar the Hararite;

i Gk: Heb lacks *son of*

FRIDAY

POURED-OUT SATISFACTION
Oswald Chambers

VERSE: 2 Samuel 23.16   PASSAGE: 2 Samuel 23.13–17

 can never sanctify to God that with which I long to satisfy myself. If I am going to satisfy myself with the blessings of God, they will corrupt me; I have to sacrifice them, pour them out, do with them what any commonsense man would say is an absurd waste. Take it in the case of friendship, or of blessing, or of spiritual experiences; as soon as I long to hold any of these for myself I cannot sanctify them to the Lord. David had the right idea when he poured out the water before the Lord.

What has been like water from the well of Bethlehem to you recently? Love, friendship, spiritual blessing? Then at the peril of your soul, you take it to satisfy yourself. If you do, you cannot pour out before the Lord. How am I to pour out spiritual gifts, or natural friendship, or love? How can I give them to the Lord? In one way only—in the determination of my mind, and that takes about two seconds. If I hold spiritual blessings or friendship for myself they will corrupt me, no matter how beautiful they are. I have to pour them out before the Lord, give them to him in my mind, though it looks as if I am wasting them; even as when David poured the water out on the sand, to be instantly sucked up.

ADDITIONAL SCRIPTURE READING:
Numbers 28.7; Philippians 2.17–18; 2 Timothy 4.6–7

Go to page 373 for your next devotional reading.

1900   Present

34Eliphelet son of Ahasbai of Maacah; Eliam son of Ahithophel the Gilonite; 35Hezro*i* of Carmel; Paarai the Arbite; 36Igal son of Nathan of Zobah; Bani the Gadite; 37Zelek the Ammonite; Naharai of Beeroth, the armor-bearer of Joab son of Zeruiah; 38Ira the Ithrite; Gareb the Ithrite; 39Uriah the Hittite—thirty-seven in all.

David's Census of Israel and Judah

24 Again the anger of the LORD was kindled against Israel, and he incited David against them, saying, "Go, count the people of Israel and Judah." 2So the king said to Joab and the commanders of the army,*k* who were with him, "Go through all the tribes of Israel, from Dan to Beer-sheba, and take a census of the people, so that I may know how many there are." 3But Joab said to the king, "May the LORD your God increase the number of the people a hundredfold, while the eyes of my lord the king can still see it! But why does my lord the king want to do this?" 4But the king's word prevailed against Joab and the commanders of the army. So Joab and the commanders of the army went out from the presence of the king to take a census of the people of Israel. 5They crossed the Jordan, and began from*l* Aroer and from the city that is in the middle of the valley, toward Gad and on to Jazer. 6Then they came to Gilead, and to Kadesh in the land of the Hittites;*m* and they came to Dan, and from Dan*n* they went around to Sidon, 7and came to the fortress of Tyre and to all the cities of the Hivites and Canaanites; and they went out to the Negeb of Judah at Beer-sheba. 8So when they had gone through all the land, they came back to Jerusalem at the end of nine months and twenty days. 9Joab reported to the king the number of those who had been recorded: in Israel there were eight hundred thousand soldiers able to draw the sword, and those of Judah were five hundred thousand.

Judgment on David's Sin

10 But afterward, David was stricken to the heart because he had numbered the people. David said to the LORD, "I have sinned greatly in what I have done. But now, O LORD, I pray you, take away the guilt of your servant; for I have done very foolishly." 11When David rose in the morning, the word of the LORD came to the prophet Gad, David's seer, saying, 12"Go and say to David: Thus says the LORD: Three things I offer*o* you; choose one of them, and I will do it to you." 13So Gad came to David and told him; he asked him, "Shall three*p* years of famine come to you on your land? Or will you flee three months before your foes while they pursue you? Or shall there be three days' pestilence in your land? Now consider, and decide what answer I shall return to the one who sent me." 14Then David said to Gad, "I am in great distress; let us fall into the hand of the LORD, for his mercy is great; but let me not fall into human hands."

15 So the LORD sent a pestilence on Israel from that morning until the appointed time; and seventy thousand of the people died, from Dan to Beer-sheba. 16But when the angel stretched out his hand toward Jerusalem to destroy it, the LORD relented concerning the evil, and said to the angel who was bringing destruction among the people, "It is enough; now stay your hand." The angel of the LORD was then by the threshing floor of Araunah the Jebusite. 17When David saw the angel who was destroying the people, he said to the LORD, "I alone have sinned, and I alone have done wickedly; but these sheep, what have they done? Let your hand, I pray, be against me and against my father's house."

David's Altar on the Threshing Floor

18 That day Gad came to David and said to him, "Go up and erect an altar to the LORD on the threshing floor of Araunah the Jebusite." 19Following Gad's instructions, David went up, as the LORD had commanded. 20When Araunah looked down, he saw the king and his servants coming toward him; and Araunah went out and prostrated himself

---

j Another reading is *Hezrai*   *k* 1 Chr 21.2 Gk: Heb *to Joab the commander of the army*   *l* Gk Mss: Heb *encamped in Aroer south of*   *m* Gk: Heb *to the land of Tahtim-hodshi*   *n* Cn Compare Gk: Heb *they came to Dan-jaan and*   *o* Or *hold over*   *p* 1 Chr 21.12 Gk: Heb *seven*

before the king with his face to the ground. 21 Araunah said, "Why has my lord the king come to his servant?" David said, "To buy the threshing floor from you in order to build an altar to the LORD, so that the plague may be averted from the people." 22 Then Araunah said to David, "Let my lord the king take and offer up what seems good to him; here are the oxen for the burnt offering, and the threshing sledges and the yokes of the oxen for the wood. 23 All this, O king, Araunah gives to the king." And Arau-

nah said to the king, "May the LORD your God respond favorably to you."

24 But the king said to Araunah, "No, but I will buy them from you for a price; I will not offer burnt offerings to the LORD my God that cost me nothing." So David bought the threshing floor and the oxen for fifty shekels of silver. 25 David built there an altar to the LORD, and offered burnt offerings and offerings of well-being. So the LORD answered his supplication for the land, and the plague was averted from Israel.

1 KINGS

THE BOOKS OF 1 AND 2 KINGS WERE ORIGINALLY ONE LITERARY WORK, CALLED "KINGS." BEGINNING WITH SOLOMON'S REIGN, 1 KINGS RECORDS THE HISTORY OF ISRAEL THROUGH THE DIVIDED KINGDOM TO THE DEATH OF KING AHAZ. IN GENERAL, 1 AND 2 KINGS DESCRIBES THE HISTORY OF THE KINGS OF ISRAEL AND JUDAH IN THE LIGHT OF GOD'S COVENANTS. AS YOU READ THE ACCOUNTS, NOTE THE POSITIVE EXAMPLES TO FOLLOW AND THE MISTAKES TO AVOID AS YOU SEEK TO SERVE GOD IN YOUR LIFE.

The Struggle for the Succession

1 King David was old and advanced in years; and although they covered him with clothes, he could not get warm. 2So his servants said to him, "Let a young virgin be sought for my lord the king, and let her wait on the king, and be his attendant; let her lie in your bosom, so that my lord the king may be warm." 3So they searched for a beautiful girl throughout all the territory of Israel, and found Abishag the Shunammite, and brought her to the king. 4The girl was very beautiful. She became the king's attendant and served him, but the king did not know her sexually.

5 Now Adonijah son of Haggith exalted himself, saying, "I will be king"; he prepared for himself chariots and horsemen, and fifty men to run before him. 6His father had never at any time displeased him by asking, "Why have you done thus and so?" He was also a very handsome man, and he was born next after Absalom. 7He conferred with Joab son of Zeruiah and with the priest Abiathar, and they supported Adonijah. 8But the priest Zadok, and Benaiah son of Jehoiada, and the prophet Nathan, and Shimei, and Rei, and David's own warriors did not side with Adonijah.

9 Adonijah sacrificed sheep, oxen, and fatted cattle by the stone Zoheleth, which is beside En-rogel, and he invited all his brothers, the king's sons, and all the royal officials of Judah, 10but he did not invite the prophet Nathan or Benaiah or the warriors or his brother Solomon.

11 Then Nathan said to Bathsheba, Solomon's mother, "Have you not heard

that Adonijah son of Haggith has become king and our lord David does not know it? ¹²Now therefore come, let me give you advice, so that you may save your own life and the life of your son Solomon. ¹³Go in at once to King David, and say to him, 'Did you not, my lord the king, swear to your servant, saying: Your son Solomon shall succeed me as king, and he shall sit on my throne? Why then is Adonijah king?' ¹⁴Then while you are still there speaking with the king, I will come in after you and confirm your words."

15 So Bathsheba went to the king in his room. The king was very old; Abishag the Shunammite was attending the king. ¹⁶Bathsheba bowed and did obeisance to the king, and the king said, "What do you wish?" ¹⁷She said to him, "My lord, you swore to your servant by the LORD your God, saying: Your son Solomon shall succeed me as king, and he shall sit on my throne. ¹⁸But now suddenly Adonijah has become king, though you, my lord the king, do not know it. ¹⁹He has sacrificed oxen, fatted cattle, and sheep in abundance, and has invited all the children of the king, the priest Abiathar, and Joab the commander of the army; but your servant Solomon he has not invited. ²⁰But you, my lord the king—the eyes of all Israel are on you to tell them who shall sit on the throne of my lord the king after him. ²¹Otherwise it will come to pass, when my lord the king sleeps with his ancestors, that my son Solomon and I will be counted offenders."

22 While she was still speaking with the king, the prophet Nathan came in. ²³The king was told, "Here is the prophet Nathan." When he came in before the king, he did obeisance to the king, with his face to the ground. ²⁴Nathan said, "My lord the king, have you said, 'Adonijah shall succeed me as king, and he shall sit on my throne'? ²⁵For today he has gone down and has sacrificed oxen, fatted cattle, and sheep in abundance, and has invited all the king's children, Joab the commander[a] of the army, and the priest Abiathar, who are now eating and drinking before him, and saying, 'Long live King Adonijah!' ²⁶But he did

not invite me, your servant, and the priest Zadok, and Benaiah son of Jehoiada, and your servant Solomon. ²⁷Has this thing been brought about by my lord the king and you have not let your servants know who should sit on the throne of my lord the king after him?"

The Accession of Solomon

28 King David answered, "Summon Bathsheba to me." So she came into the king's presence, and stood before the king. ²⁹The king swore, saying, "As the LORD lives, who has saved my life from every adversity, ³⁰as I swore to you by the LORD, the God of Israel, 'Your son Solomon shall succeed me as king, and he shall sit on my throne in my place,' so will I do this day." ³¹Then Bathsheba bowed with her face to the ground, and did obeisance to the king, and said, "May my lord King David live forever!"

32 King David said, "Summon to me the priest Zadok, the prophet Nathan, and Benaiah son of Jehoiada." When they came before the king, ³³the king said to them, "Take with you the servants of your lord, and have my son Solomon ride on my own mule, and bring him down to Gihon. ³⁴There let the priest Zadok and the prophet Nathan anoint him king over Israel; then blow the trumpet, and say, 'Long live King Solomon!' ³⁵You shall go up following him. Let him enter and sit on my throne; he shall be king in my place; for I have appointed him to be ruler over Israel and over Judah." ³⁶Benaiah son of Jehoiada answered the king, "Amen! May the LORD, the God of my lord the king, so ordain. ³⁷As the LORD has been with my lord the king, so may he be with Solomon, and make his throne greater than the throne of my lord King David."

38 So the priest Zadok, the prophet Nathan, and Benaiah son of Jehoiada, and the Cherethites and the Pelethites, went down and had Solomon ride on King David's mule, and led him to Gihon. ³⁹There the priest Zadok took the horn of oil from the tent and anointed Solomon. Then they blew the trumpet, and all the people said, "Long live King Solomon!" ⁴⁰And all the people went up following him, playing on pipes

a Gk: Heb the commanders

and rejoicing with great joy, so that the earth quaked at their noise.

41 Adonijah and all the guests who were with him heard it as they finished feasting. When Joab heard the sound of the trumpet, he said, "Why is the city in an uproar?" 42While he was still speaking, Jonathan son of the priest Abiathar arrived. Adonijah said, "Come in, for you are a worthy man and surely you bring good news." 43Jonathan answered Adonijah, "No, for our lord King David has made Solomon king; 44the king has sent with him the priest Zadok, the prophet Nathan, and Benaiah son of Jehoiada, and the Cherethites and the Pelethites; and they had him ride on the king's mule; 45the priest Zadok and the prophet Nathan have anointed him king at Gihon; and they have gone up from there rejoicing, so that the city is in an uproar. This is the noise that you heard. 46Solomon now sits on the royal throne. 47Moreover the king's servants came to congratulate our lord King David, saying, 'May God make the name of Solomon more famous than yours, and make his throne greater than your throne.' The king bowed in worship on the bed 48and went on to pray thus, 'Blessed be the LORD, the God of Israel, who today has granted one of my offspring*b* to sit on my throne and permitted me to witness it.' "

49 Then all the guests of Adonijah got up trembling and went their own ways. 50Adonijah, fearing Solomon, got up and went to grasp the horns of the altar. 51Solomon was informed, "Adonijah is afraid of King Solomon; see, he has laid hold of the horns of the altar, saying, 'Let King Solomon swear to me first that he will not kill his servant with the sword.' " 52So Solomon responded, "If he proves to be a worthy man, not one of his hairs shall fall to the ground; but if wickedness is found in him, he shall die." 53Then King Solomon sent to have him brought down from the altar. He came to do obeisance to King Solomon; and Solomon said to him, "Go home."

David's Instruction to Solomon

2 When David's time to die drew near, he charged his son Solomon, saying: 2"I am about to go the way of all the earth. Be strong, be courageous, 3and keep the charge of the LORD your God, walking in his ways and keeping his statutes, his commandments, his ordinances, and his testimonies, as it is written in the law of Moses, so that you may prosper in all that you do and wherever you turn. 4Then the LORD will establish his word that he spoke concerning me: 'If your heirs take heed to their way, to walk before me in faithfulness with all their heart and with all their soul, there shall not fail you a successor on the throne of Israel.'

5 "Moreover you know also what Joab son of Zeruiah did to me, how he dealt with the two commanders of the armies of Israel, Abner son of Ner, and Amasa son of Jether, whom he murdered, retaliating in time of peace for blood that had been shed in war, and putting the blood of war on the belt around his waist, and on the sandals on his feet. 6Act therefore according to your wisdom, but do not let his gray head go down to Sheol in peace. 7Deal loyally, however, with the sons of Barzillai the Gileadite, and let them be among those who eat at your table; for with such loyalty they met me when I fled from your brother Absalom. 8There is also with you Shimei son of Gera, the Benjaminite from Bahurim, who cursed me with a terrible curse on the day when I went to Mahanaim; but when he came down to meet me at the Jordan, I swore to him by the LORD, 'I will not put you to death with the sword.' 9Therefore do not hold him guiltless, for you are a wise man; you will know what you ought to do to him, and you must bring his gray head down with blood to Sheol."

Death of David

10 Then David slept with his ancestors, and was buried in the city of David. 11The time that David reigned over Israel was forty years; he reigned seven years in Hebron, and thirty-three years in Jerusalem. 12So Solomon sat on the throne of his father David; and his kingdom was firmly established.

Solomon Consolidates His Reign

13 Then Adonijah son of Haggith

b Gk: Heb one

CROSSING THE BAR
Alfred, Lord Tennyson

VERSE: 1 Kings 2.10   **PASSAGE:** 1 Kings 2.10–12

unset and evening star,
     And one clear call for me!
And may there be no moaning of the bar,
     When I put out to sea,

But such a tide as moving seems asleep,
     Too full for sound and foam,
When that which drew from out the boundless deep
     Turns again home.

Twilight and evening bell,
     And after that the dark!
And may there be no sadness of farewell,
     When I embark;

For though from out our bourn of time and place
     The flood may bear me far,
I hope to see my Pilot face to face
     When I have crossed the bar.

ADDITIONAL SCRIPTURE READING:
Luke 12.35–40; 1 Corinthians 13.12; 1 John 3.2

Go to page 379 for your next devotional reading.

1700   1900

374

...athsheba, Solomon's mother.
...d, "Do you come peaceably?"
..."Peaceably." 14Then he said,
..."have a word with you?" She said,
...n." 15He said, "You know that the
...dom was mine, and that all Israel
...ected me to reign; however, the king-
...m has turned about and become my
...other's, for it was his from the LORD.
...And now I have one request to make
of you; do not refuse me." She said to
him, "Go on." 17He said, "Please ask
King Solomon—he will not refuse you—
to give me Abishag the Shunammite as
my wife." 18Bathsheba said, "Very well;
I will speak to the king on your behalf."

19 So Bathsheba went to King Solomon, to speak to him on behalf of Adonijah. The king rose to meet her, and bowed down to her; then he sat on his throne, and had a throne brought for the king's mother, and she sat on his right. 20Then she said, "I have one small request to make of you; do not refuse me." And the king said to her, "Make your request, my mother; for I will not refuse you." 21She said, "Let Abishag the Shunammite be given to your brother Adonijah as his wife." 22King Solomon answered his mother, "And why do you ask Abishag the Shunammite for Adonijah? Ask for him the kingdom as well! For he is my elder brother; ask not only for him but also for the priest Abiathar and for Joab son of Zeruiah!" 23Then King Solomon swore by the LORD, "So may God do to me, and more also, for Adonijah has devised this scheme at the risk of his life! 24Now therefore as the LORD lives, who has established me and placed me on the throne of my father David, and who has made me a house as he promised, today Adonijah shall be put to death." 25So King Solomon sent Benaiah son of Jehoiada; he struck him down, and he died.

26 The king said to the priest Abiathar, "Go to Anathoth, to your estate; for you deserve death. But I will not at this time put you to death, because you carried the ark of the Lord GOD before my father David, and because you shared in all the hardships my father endured." 27So Solomon banished Abiathar from being priest to the LORD, thus fulfilling the word of the LORD that he had spoken concerning the house of Eli in Shiloh.

28 When the news came to Joab—for Joab had supported Adonijah though he had not supported Absalom—Joab fled to the tent of the LORD and grasped the horns of the altar. 29When it was told King Solomon, "Joab has fled to the tent of the LORD and now is beside the altar," Solomon sent Benaiah son of Jehoiada, saying, "Go, strike him down." 30So Benaiah came to the tent of the LORD and said to him, "The king commands, 'Come out.' " But he said, "No, I will die here." Then Benaiah brought the king word again, saying, "Thus said Joab, and thus he answered me." 31The king replied to him, "Do as he has said, strike him down and bury him; and thus take away from me and from my father's house the guilt for the blood that Joab shed without cause. 32The LORD will bring back his bloody deeds on his own head, because, without the knowledge of my father David, he attacked and killed with the sword two men more righteous and better than himself, Abner son of Ner, commander of the army of Israel, and Amasa son of Jether, commander of the army of Judah. 33So shall their blood come back on the head of Joab and on the head of his descendants forever; but to David, and to his descendants, and to his house, and to his throne, there shall be peace from the LORD forevermore." 34Then Benaiah son of Jehoiada went up and struck him down and killed him; and he was buried at his own house near the wilderness. 35The king put Benaiah son of Jehoiada over the army in his place, and the king put the priest Zadok in the place of Abiathar.

36 Then the king sent and summoned Shimei, and said to him, "Build yourself a house in Jerusalem, and live there, and do not go out from there to any place whatever. 37For on the day you go out, and cross the Wadi Kidron, know for certain that you shall die; your blood shall be on your own head." 38And Shimei said to the king, "The sentence is fair; as my lord the king has said, so will your servant do." So Shimei lived in Jerusalem many days.

39 But it happened at the end of three years that two of Shimei's slaves ran

away to King Achish son of Maacah of Gath. When it was told Shimei, "Your slaves are in Gath," ⁴⁰Shimei arose and saddled a donkey, and went to Achish in Gath, to search for his slaves; Shimei went and brought his slaves from Gath. ⁴¹When Solomon was told that Shimei had gone from Jerusalem to Gath and returned, ⁴²the king sent and summoned Shimei, and said to him, "Did I not make you swear by the LORD, and solemnly adjure you, saying, 'Know for certain that on the day you go out and go to any place whatever, you shall die'? And you said to me, 'The sentence is fair; I accept.' ⁴³Why then have you not kept your oath to the LORD and the commandment with which I charged you?" ⁴⁴The king also said to Shimei, "You know in your own heart all the evil that you did to my father David; so the LORD will bring back your evil on your own head. ⁴⁵But King Solomon shall be blessed, and the throne of David shall be established before the LORD forever." ⁴⁶Then the king commanded Benaiah son of Jehoiada; and he went out and struck him down, and he died.

So the kingdom was established in the hand of Solomon.

Solomon's Prayer for Wisdom

3 Solomon made a marriage alliance with Pharaoh king of Egypt; he took Pharaoh's daughter and brought her into the city of David, until he had finished building his own house and the house of the LORD and the wall around Jerusalem. ²The people were sacrificing at the high places, however, because no house had yet been built for the name of the LORD.

3 Solomon loved the LORD, walking in the statutes of his father David; only, he sacrificed and offered incense at the high places. ⁴The king went to Gibeon to sacrifice there, for that was the principal high place; Solomon used to offer a thousand burnt offerings on that altar. ⁵At Gibeon the LORD appeared to Solomon in a dream by night; and God said, "Ask what I should give you." ⁶And Solomon said, "You have shown great and steadfast love to your servant my father David, because he walked before you in faithfulness, in righteousness,

and in uprightness of heart toward you; and you have kept for him this great and steadfast love, and have given him a son to sit on his throne today. ⁷And now, O LORD my God, you have made your servant king in place of my father David, although I am only a little child; I do not know how to go out or come in. ⁸And your servant is in the midst of the people whom you have chosen, a great people, so numerous they cannot be numbered or counted. ⁹Give your servant therefore an understanding mind to govern your people, able to discern between good and evil; for who can govern this your great people?"

10 It pleased the Lord that Solomon had asked this. ¹¹God said to him, "Because you have asked this, and have not asked for yourself long life or riches, or for the life of your enemies, but have asked for yourself understanding to discern what is right, ¹²I now do according to your word. Indeed I give you a wise and discerning mind; no one like you has been before you and no one like you shall arise after you. ¹³I give you also what you have not asked, both riches and honor all your life; no other king shall compare with you. ¹⁴If you will walk in my ways, keeping my statutes and my commandments, as your father David walked, then I will lengthen your life."

15 Then Solomon awoke; it had been a dream. He came to Jerusalem where he stood before the ark of the covenant of the LORD. He offered up burnt offerings and offerings of well-being, and provided a feast for all his servants.

Solomon's Wisdom in Judgment

16 Later, two women who were prostitutes came to the king and stood before him. ¹⁷The one woman said, "Please, my lord, this woman and I live in the same house; and I gave birth while she was in the house. ¹⁸Then on the third day after I gave birth, this woman also gave birth. We were together; there was no one else with us in the house, only the two of us were in the house. ¹⁹Then this woman's son died in the night, because she lay on him. ²⁰She got up in the middle of the night and took my son from beside me while your

servant slept. She laid him at her breast, and laid her dead son at my breast. 21When I rose in the morning to nurse my son, I saw that he was dead; but when I looked at him closely in the morning, clearly it was not the son I had borne." 22But the other woman said, "No, the living son is mine, and the dead son is yours." The first said, "No, the dead son is yours, and the living son is mine." So they argued before the king.

23 Then the king said, "The one says, 'This is my son that is alive, and your son is dead'; while the other says, 'Not so! Your son is dead, and my son is the living one.' " 24So the king said, "Bring me a sword," and they brought a sword before the king. 25The king said, "Divide the living boy in two; then give half to the one, and half to the other." 26But the woman whose son was alive said to the king—because compassion for her son burned within her—"Please, my lord, give her the living boy; certainly do not kill him!" The other said, "It shall be neither mine nor yours; divide it." 27Then the king responded: "Give the first woman the living boy; do not kill him. She is his mother." 28All Israel heard of the judgment that the king had rendered; and they stood in awe of the king, because they perceived that the wisdom of God was in him, to execute justice.

Solomon's Administrative Officers

4 King Solomon was king over all Israel, 2and these were his high officials: Azariah son of Zadok was the priest; 3Elihoreph and Ahijah sons of Shisha were secretaries; Jehoshaphat son of Ahilud was recorder; 4Benaiah son of Jehoiada was in command of the army; Zadok and Abiathar were priests; 5Azariah son of Nathan was over the officials; Zabud son of Nathan was priest and king's friend; 6Ahishar was in charge of the palace; and Adoniram son of Abda was in charge of the forced labor.

7 Solomon had twelve officials over all Israel, who provided food for the king and his household; each one had to make provision for one month in the year. 8These were their names: Ben-hur, in the hill country of Ephraim; 9Bendeker, in Makaz, Shaalbim, Beth-shemesh, and Elon-beth-hanan; 10Benhesed, in Arubboth (to him belonged Socoh and all the land of Hepher); 11Benabinadab, in all Naphath-dor (he had Taphath, Solomon's daughter, as his wife); 12Baana son of Ahilud, in Taanach, Megiddo, and all Beth-shean, which is beside Zarethan below Jezreel, and from Beth-shean to Abel-meholah, as far as the other side of Jokmeam; 13Ben-geber, in Ramoth-gilead (he had the villages of Jair son of Manasseh, which are in Gilead, and he had the region of Argob, which is in Bashan, sixty great cities with walls and bronze bars); 14Ahinadab son of Iddo, in Mahanaim; 15Ahimaaz, in Naphtali (he had taken Basemath, Solomon's daughter, as his wife); 16Baana son of Hushai, in Asher and Bealoth; 17Jehoshaphat son of Paruah, in Issachar; 18Shimei son of Ela, in Benjamin; 19Geber son of Uri, in the land of Gilead, the country of King Sihon of the Amorites and of King Og of Bashan. And there was one official in the land of Judah.

Magnificence of Solomon's Rule

20 Judah and Israel were as numerous as the sand by the sea; they ate and drank and were happy. 21cSolomon was sovereign over all the kingdoms from the Euphrates to the land of the Philistines, even to the border of Egypt; they brought tribute and served Solomon all the days of his life.

22 Solomon's provision for one day was thirty cors of choice flour, and sixty cors of meal, 23ten fat oxen, and twenty pasture-fed cattle, one hundred sheep, besides deer, gazelles, roebucks, and fatted fowl. 24For he had dominion over all the region west of the Euphrates from Tiphsah to Gaza, over all the kings west of the Euphrates; and he had peace on all sides. 25During Solomon's lifetime Judah and Israel lived in safety, from Dan even to Beer-sheba, all of them under their vines and fig trees. 26Solomon also had forty thousand stalls of horses for his chariots, and twelve thousand horsemen. 27Those officials supplied provisions for King Solomon and

c Ch 5.1 in Heb

for all who came to King Solomon's table, each one in his month; they let nothing be lacking. 28They also brought to the required place barley and straw for the horses and swift steeds, each according to his charge.

Fame of Solomon's Wisdom

29 God gave Solomon very great wisdom, discernment, and breadth of understanding as vast as the sand on the seashore, 30so that Solomon's wisdom surpassed the wisdom of all the people of the east, and all the wisdom of Egypt. 31He was wiser than anyone else, wiser than Ethan the Ezrahite, and Heman, Calcol, and Darda, children of Mahol; his fame spread throughout all the surrounding nations. 32He composed three thousand proverbs, and his songs numbered a thousand and five. 33He would speak of trees, from the cedar that is in the Lebanon to the hyssop that grows in the wall; he would speak of animals, and birds, and reptiles, and fish. 34People came from all the nations to hear the wisdom of Solomon; they came from all the kings of the earth who had heard of his wisdom.

Preparations and Materials for the Temple

5 d Now King Hiram of Tyre sent his servants to Solomon, when he heard that they had anointed him king in place of his father; for Hiram had always been a friend to David. 2Solomon sent word to Hiram, saying, 3"You know that my father David could not build a house for the name of the LORD his God because of the warfare with which his enemies surrounded him, until the LORD put them under the soles of his feet.e 4But now the LORD my God has given me rest on every side; there is neither adversary nor misfortune. 5So I intend to build a house for the name of the LORD my God, as the LORD said to my father David, 'Your son, whom I will set on your throne in your place, shall build the house for my name.' 6Therefore command that cedars from the Lebanon be cut for me. My servants will join your servants, and I will give you whatever wages you set for your ser-

vants; for you know that there is no one among us who knows how to cut timber like the Sidonians."

7 When Hiram heard the words of Solomon, he rejoiced greatly, and said, "Blessed be the LORD today, who has given to David a wise son to be over this great people." 8Hiram sent word to Solomon, "I have heard the message that you have sent to me; I will fulfill all your needs in the matter of cedar and cypress timber. 9My servants shall bring it down to the sea from the Lebanon; I will make it into rafts to go by sea to the place you indicate. I will have them broken up there for you to take away. And you shall meet my needs by providing food for my household." 10So Hiram supplied Solomon's every need for timber of cedar and cypress. 11Solomon in turn gave Hiram twenty thousand cors of wheat as food for his household, and twenty cors of fine oil. Solomon gave this to Hiram year by year. 12So the LORD gave Solomon wisdom, as he promised him. There was peace between Hiram and Solomon; and the two of them made a treaty.

13 King Solomon conscripted forced labor out of all Israel; the levy numbered thirty thousand men. 14He sent them to the Lebanon, ten thousand a month in shifts; they would be a month in the Lebanon and two months at home; Adoniram was in charge of the forced labor. 15Solomon also had seventy thousand laborers and eighty thousand stonecutters in the hill country, 16besides Solomon's three thousand three hundred supervisors who were over the work, having charge of the people who did the work. 17At the king's command, they quarried out great, costly stones in order to lay the foundation of the house with dressed stones. 18So Solomon's builders and Hiram's builders and the Gebalites did the stonecutting and prepared the timber and the stone to build the house.

Solomon Builds the Temple

6 In the four hundred eightieth year after the Israelites came out of the land of Egypt, in the fourth year of Solomon's reign over Israel, in the month of Ziv, which is the second month, he began to build the house of

d Ch 5.15 in Heb   e Gk Tg Vg: Heb my feet or his feet

the LORD. 2The house that King Solomon built for the LORD was sixty cubits long, twenty cubits wide, and thirty cubits high. 3The vestibule in front of the nave of the house was twenty cubits wide, across the width of the house. Its depth was ten cubits in front of the house. 4For the house he made windows with recessed frames.f 5He also built a structure against the wall of the house, running around the walls of the house, both the nave and the inner sanctuary; and he made side chambers all around. 6The lowest storyg was five cubits wide, the middle one was six cubits wide, and the third was seven cubits wide; for around the outside of the house he made offsets on the wall in order that the supporting beams should not be inserted into the walls of the house.

7 The house was built with stone finished at the quarry, so that neither hammer nor ax nor any tool of iron was heard in the temple while it was being built.

8 The entrance for the middle story was on the south side of the house: one went up by winding stairs to the middle story, and from the middle story to the third. 9So he built the house, and finished it; he roofed the house with beams and planks of cedar. 10He built the structure against the whole house, each storyh five cubits high, and it was joined to the house with timbers of cedar.

11 Now the word of the LORD came to Solomon, 12"Concerning this house that you are building, if you will walk in my statutes, obey my ordinances, and keep all my commandments by walking in them, then I will establish my promise with you, which I made to your father David. 13I will dwell among the children of Israel, and will not forsake my people Israel."

14 So Solomon built the house, and finished it. 15He lined the walls of the house on the inside with boards of cedar; from the floor of the house to the rafters of the ceiling, he covered them on the inside with wood; and he covered the floor of the house with boards of cypress. 16He built twenty cubits of the rear of the house with boards of cedar from the floor to the rafters, and he built this within as an inner sanctuary, as the most holy place. 17The house, that is, the nave in front of the inner sanctuary, was forty cubits long. 18The cedar within the house had carvings of gourds and open flowers; all was cedar, no stone was seen. 19The inner sanctuary he prepared in the innermost part of the house, to set there the ark of the covenant of the LORD. 20The interior of the inner sanctuary was twenty cubits long, twenty cubits wide, and twenty cubits high; he overlaid it with pure gold. He also overlaid the altar with cedar.i 21Solomon overlaid the inside of the house with pure gold, then he drew chains of gold across, in front of the inner sanctuary, and overlaid it with gold. 22Next he overlaid the whole house with gold, in order that the whole house might be perfect; even the whole altar that belonged to the inner sanctuary he overlaid with gold.

The Furnishings of the Temple

23 In the inner sanctuary he made two cherubim of olivewood, each ten cubits high. 24Five cubits was the length of one wing of the cherub, and five cubits the length of the other wing of the cherub; it was ten cubits from the tip of one wing to the tip of the other. 25The other cherub also measured ten cubits; both cherubim had the same measure and the same form. 26The height of one cherub was ten cubits, and so was that of the other cherub. 27He put the cherubim in the innermost part of the house; the wings of the cherubim were spread out so that a wing of one was touching the one wall, and a wing of the other cherub was touching the other wall; their other wings toward the center of the house were touching wing to wing. 28He also overlaid the cherubim with gold.

29 He carved the walls of the house all around about with carved engravings of cherubim, palm trees, and open flowers, in the inner and outer rooms. 30The floor of the house he overlaid with gold, in the inner and outer rooms.

31 For the entrance to the inner sanctuary he made doors of olivewood; the lintel and the doorposts were five-sided.i

f Gk: Meaning of Heb uncertain   g Gk: Heb structure   h Heb lacks each story   i Meaning of Heb uncertain

32He covered the two doors of olive-wood with carvings of cherubim, palm trees, and open flowers; he overlaid them with gold, and spread gold on the cherubim and on the palm trees.

33 So also he made for the entrance to the nave doorposts of olivewood, four-sided each, 34and two doors of cypress wood; the two leaves of the one door were folding, and the two leaves of the other door were folding. 35He carved cherubim, palm trees, and open flowers, overlaying them with gold evenly applied upon the carved work. 36He built the inner court with three courses of dressed stone to one course of cedar beams.

37 In the fourth year the foundation of the house of the LORD was laid, in the month of Ziv. 38In the eleventh year, in the month of Bul, which is the eighth month, the house was finished in all its parts, and according to all its specifications. He was seven years in building it.

Solomon's Palace and Other Buildings

7 Solomon was building his own house thirteen years, and he finished his entire house.

2 He built the House of the Forest of the Lebanon one hundred cubits long, fifty cubits wide, and thirty cubits high, built on four rows of cedar pillars, with cedar beams on the pillars. 3It was roofed with cedar on the forty-five rafters, fifteen in each row, which were on the pillars. 4There were window frames in the three rows, facing each other in the three rows. 5All the door-

---

MONDAY

ALL THE FLOWERS OF HIS FIELD
Charles H. Spurgeon

VERSE: 1 Kings 6.18   **PASSAGE:** 1 Kings 6.18–35

You can buy complete sets of all the flowers of the Alpine district at the hotel near the foot of the Rosenlaui glacier, very neatly pressed and enclosed in cases. Some of the flowers are very common, but they must be included, or the flora would not be completely represented. The botanist is as careful to see that the common ones are there as he is to note that the rarer specimens are not excluded.

Our blessed Lord will be sure to make a perfect collection of the flowers in his field, and even the ordinary believer, the everyday worker, the common convert, will not be forgotten. To Jesus' eye, there is beauty in all his plants, and each one is needed to perfect the flora of Paradise. May I be found among his flowers, if only as one out of myriad daisies, who with sweet simplicity shall look up and wonder at his love forever.

ADDITIONAL SCRIPTURE READING:
Romans 12.4–8; 1 Corinthians 12.14–18, 22

Go to page 384 for your next devotional reading.

1700   1900

ways and doorposts had four-sided frames, opposite, facing each other in the three rows.

6 He made the Hall of Pillars fifty cubits long and thirty cubits wide. There was a porch in front with pillars, and a canopy in front of them.

7 He made the Hall of the Throne where he was to pronounce judgment, the Hall of Justice, covered with cedar from floor to floor.

8 His own house where he would reside, in the other court back of the hall, was of the same construction. Solomon also made a house like this hall for Pharaoh's daughter, whom he had taken in marriage.

9 All these were made of costly stones, cut according to measure, sawed with saws, back and front, from the foundation to the coping, and from outside to the great court. 10The foundation was of costly stones, huge stones, stones of eight and ten cubits. 11There were costly stones above, cut to measure, and cedarwood. 12The great court had three courses of dressed stone to one layer of cedar beams all around; so had the inner court of the house of the LORD, and the vestibule of the house.

Products of Hiram the Bronzeworker

13 Now King Solomon invited and received Hiram from Tyre. 14He was the son of a widow of the tribe of Naphtali, whose father, a man of Tyre, had been an artisan in bronze; he was full of skill, intelligence, and knowledge in working bronze. He came to King Solomon, and did all his work.

15 He cast two pillars of bronze. Eighteen cubits was the height of the one, and a cord of twelve cubits would encircle it; the second pillar was the same.*j* 16He also made two capitals of molten bronze, to set on the tops of the pillars; the height of the one capital was five cubits, and the height of the other capital was five cubits. 17There were nets of checker work with wreaths of chain work for the capitals on the tops of the pillars; seven*k* for the one capital, and seven*k* for the other capital. 18He made

the columns with two rows around each latticework to cover the capitals that were above the pomegranates; he did the same with the other capital. 19Now the capitals that were on the tops of the pillars in the vestibule were of lily-work, four cubits high. 20The capitals were on the two pillars and also above the rounded projection that was beside the latticework; there were two hundred pomegranates in rows all around; and so with the other capital. 21He set up the pillars at the vestibule of the temple; he set up the pillar on the south and called it Jachin; and he set up the pillar on the north and called it Boaz. 22On the tops of the pillars was lily-work. Thus the work of the pillars was finished.

23 Then he made the molten sea; it was round, ten cubits from brim to brim, and five cubits high. A line of thirty cubits would encircle it completely. 24Under its brim were panels all around it, each of ten cubits, surrounding the sea; there were two rows of panels, cast when it was cast. 25It stood on twelve oxen, three facing north, three facing west, three facing south, and three facing east; the sea was set on them. The hindquarters of each were toward the inside. 26Its thickness was a handbreadth; its brim was made like the brim of a cup, like the flower of a lily; it held two thousand baths.*l*

27 He also made the ten stands of bronze; each stand was four cubits long, four cubits wide, and three cubits high. 28This was the construction of the stands: they had borders; the borders were within the frames; 29on the borders that were set in the frames were lions, oxen, and cherubim. On the frames, both above and below the lions and oxen, there were wreaths of beveled work. 30Each stand had four bronze wheels and axles of bronze; at the four corners were supports for a basin. The supports were cast with wreaths at the side of each. 31Its opening was within the crown whose height was one cubit; its opening was round, as a pedestal is made; it was a cubit and a half wide. At its opening there were carvings; its borders were four-sided, not round. 32The four wheels

---

j Cn: Heb *and a cord of twelve cubits encircled the second pillar;* Compare Jer 52.21   *k* Heb: Gk *a net*
l A Heb measure of volume

were underneath the borders; the axles of the wheels were in the stands; and the height of a wheel was a cubit and a half. 33The wheels were made like a chariot wheel; their axles, their rims, their spokes, and their hubs were all cast. 34There were four supports at the four corners of each stand; the supports were of one piece with the stands. 35On the top of the stand there was a round band half a cubit high; on the top of the stand, its stays and its borders were of one piece with it. 36On the surfaces of its stays and on its borders he carved cherubim, lions, and palm trees, where each had space, with wreaths all around. 37In this way he made the ten stands; all of them were cast alike, with the same size and the same form.

38 He made ten basins of bronze; each basin held forty baths,m each basin measured four cubits; there was a basin for each of the ten stands. 39He set five of the stands on the south side of the house, and five on the north side of the house; he set the sea on the southeast corner of the house.

40 Hiram also made the pots, the shovels, and the basins. So Hiram finished all the work that he did for King Solomon on the house of the LORD: 41the two pillars, the two bowls of the capitals that were on the tops of the pillars, the two latticeworks to cover the two bowls of the capitals that were on the tops of the pillars; 42the four hundred pomegranates for the two latticeworks, two rows of pomegranates for each latticework, to cover the two bowls of the capitals that were on the pillars; 43the ten stands, the ten basins on the stands; 44the one sea, and the twelve oxen underneath the sea.

45 The pots, the shovels, and the basins, all these vessels that Hiram made for King Solomon for the house of the LORD were of burnished bronze. 46In the plain of the Jordan the king cast them, in the clay ground between Succoth and Zarethan. 47Solomon left all the vessels unweighed, because there were so many of them; the weight of the bronze was not determined.

48 So Solomon made all the vessels that were in the house of the LORD: the golden altar, the golden table for the bread of the Presence, 49the lampstands of pure gold, five on the south side and five on the north, in front of the inner sanctuary; the flowers, the lamps, and the tongs, of gold; 50the cups, snuffers, basins, dishes for incense, and firepans, of pure gold; the sockets for the doors of the innermost part of the house, the most holy place, and for the doors of the nave of the temple, of gold.

51 Thus all the work that King Solomon did on the house of the LORD was finished. Solomon brought in the things that his father David had dedicated, the silver, the gold, and the vessels, and stored them in the treasuries of the house of the LORD.

Dedication of the Temple

8 Then Solomon assembled the elders of Israel and all the heads of the tribes, the leaders of the ancestral houses of the Israelites, before King Solomon in Jerusalem, to bring up the ark of the covenant of the LORD out of the city of David, which is Zion. 2All the people of Israel assembled to King Solomon at the festival in the month Ethanim, which is the seventh month. 3And all the elders of Israel came, and the priests carried the ark. 4So they brought up the ark of the LORD, the tent of meeting, and all the holy vessels that were in the tent; the priests and the Levites brought them up. 5King Solomon and all the congregation of Israel, who had assembled before him, were with him before the ark, sacrificing so many sheep and oxen that they could not be counted or numbered. 6Then the priests brought the ark of the covenant of the LORD to its place, in the inner sanctuary of the house, in the most holy place, underneath the wings of the cherubim. 7For the cherubim spread out their wings over the place of the ark, so that the cherubim made a covering above the ark and its poles. 8The poles were so long that the ends of the poles were seen from the holy place in front of the inner sanctuary; but they could not be seen from outside; they are there to this day. 9There was nothing in the ark except the two tablets of stone that

m A Heb measure of volume

Moses had placed there at Horeb, where the LORD made a covenant with the Israelites, when they came out of the land of Egypt. 10And when the priests came out of the holy place, a cloud filled the house of the LORD, 11so that the priests could not stand to minister because of the cloud; for the glory of the LORD filled the house of the LORD.

12 Then Solomon said,

"The LORD has said that he would
    dwell in thick darkness.
13 I have built you an exalted house,
    a place for you to dwell in
        forever."

Solomon's Speech

14 Then the king turned around and blessed all the assembly of Israel, while all the assembly of Israel stood. 15He said, "Blessed be the LORD, the God of Israel, who with his hand has fulfilled what he promised with his mouth to my father David, saying, 16'Since the day that I brought my people Israel out of Egypt, I have not chosen a city from any of the tribes of Israel in which to build a house, that my name might be there; but I chose David to be over my people Israel.' 17My father David had it in mind to build a house for the name of the LORD, the God of Israel. 18But the LORD said to my father David, 'You did well to consider building a house for my name; 19nevertheless you shall not build the house, but your son who shall be born to you shall build the house for my name.' 20Now the LORD has upheld the promise that he made; for I have risen in the place of my father David; I sit on the throne of Israel, as the LORD promised, and have built the house for the name of the LORD, the God of Israel. 21There I have provided a place for the ark, in which is the covenant of the LORD that he made with our ancestors when he brought them out of the land of Egypt."

Solomon's Prayer of Dedication

22 Then Solomon stood before the altar of the LORD in the presence of all the assembly of Israel, and spread out his hands to heaven. 23He said, "O LORD, God of Israel, there is no God like you in heaven above or on earth beneath, keep-ing covenant and steadfast love for your servants who walk before you with all their heart, 24the covenant that you kept for your servant my father David as you declared to him; you promised with your mouth and have this day fulfilled with your hand. 25Therefore, O LORD, God of Israel, keep for your servant my father David that which you promised him, saying, 'There shall never fail you a successor before me to sit on the throne of Israel, if only your children look to their way, to walk before me as you have walked before me.' 26Therefore, O God of Israel, let your word be confirmed, which you promised to your servant my father David.

27 "But will God indeed dwell on the earth? Even heaven and the highest heaven cannot contain you, much less this house that I have built! 28Regard your servant's prayer and his plea, O LORD my God, heeding the cry and the prayer that your servant prays to you today; 29that your eyes may be open night and day toward this house, the place of which you said, 'My name shall be there,' that you may heed the prayer that your servant prays toward this place. 30Hear the plea of your servant and of your people Israel when they pray toward this place; O hear in heaven your dwelling place; heed and forgive.

31 "If someone sins against a neighbor and is given an oath to swear, and comes and swears before your altar in this house, 32then hear in heaven, and act, and judge your servants, condemning the guilty by bringing their conduct on their own head, and vindicating the righteous by rewarding them according to their righteousness.

33 "When your people Israel, having sinned against you, are defeated before an enemy but turn again to you, confess your name, pray and plead with you in this house, 34then hear in heaven, forgive the sin of your people Israel, and bring them again to the land that you gave to their ancestors.

35 "When heaven is shut up and there is no rain because they have sinned against you, and then they pray toward this place, confess your name, and turn from their sin, because you punish[n]

n Or *when you answer*

them, 36then hear in heaven, and forgive the sin of your servants, your people Israel, when you teach them the good way in which they should walk; and grant rain on your land, which you have given to your people as an inheritance.

37 "If there is famine in the land, if there is plague, blight, mildew, locust, or caterpillar; if their enemy besieges them in any° of their cities; whatever plague, whatever sickness there is; 38whatever prayer, whatever plea there is from any individual or from all your people Israel, all knowing the afflictions of their own hearts so that they stretch out their hands toward this house; 39then hear in heaven your dwelling place, forgive, act, and render to all whose hearts you know—according to all their ways, for only you know what is in every human heart— 40so that they may fear you all the days that they live in the land that you gave to our ancestors.

41 "Likewise when a foreigner, who is not of your people Israel, comes from a distant land because of your name 42— for they shall hear of your great name, your mighty hand, and your outstretched arm—when a foreigner comes and prays toward this house, 43then hear in heaven your dwelling place, and do according to all that the foreigner calls to you, so that all the peoples of the earth may know your name and fear you, as do your people Israel, and so that they may know that your name has been invoked on this house that I have built.

44 "If your people go out to battle against their enemy, by whatever way you shall send them, and they pray to the LORD toward the city that you have chosen and the house that I have built for your name, 45then hear in heaven their prayer and their plea, and maintain their cause.

46 "If they sin against you—for there is no one who does not sin—and you are angry with them and give them to an enemy, so that they are carried away captive to the land of the enemy, far off or near; 47yet if they come to their senses in the land to which they have been taken captive, and repent, and

plead with you in the land of their captors, saying, 'We have sinned, and have done wrong; we have acted wickedly'; 48if they repent with all their heart and soul in the land of their enemies, who took them captive, and pray to you toward their land, which you gave to their ancestors, the city that you have chosen, and the house that I have built for your name; 49then hear in heaven your dwelling place their prayer and their plea, maintain their cause 50and forgive your people who have sinned against you, and all their transgressions that they have committed against you; and grant them compassion in the sight of their captors, so that they may have compassion on them 51(for they are your people and heritage, which you brought out of Egypt, from the midst of the iron-smelter). 52Let your eyes be open to the plea of your servant, and to the plea of your people Israel, listening to them whenever they call to you. 53For you have separated them from among all the peoples of the earth, to be your heritage, just as you promised through Moses, your servant, when you brought our ancestors out of Egypt, O Lord GOD."

Solomon Blesses the Assembly

54 Now when Solomon finished offering all this prayer and this plea to the LORD, he arose from facing the altar of the LORD, where he had knelt with hands outstretched toward heaven; 55he stood and blessed all the assembly of Israel with a loud voice:

56 "Blessed be the LORD, who has given rest to his people Israel according to all that he promised; not one word has failed of all his good promise, which he spoke through his servant Moses. 57The LORD our God be with us, as he was with our ancestors; may he not leave us or abandon us, 58but incline our hearts to him, to walk in all his ways, and to keep his commandments, his statutes, and his ordinances, which he commanded our ancestors. 59Let these words of mine, with which I pleaded before the LORD, be near to the LORD our God day and night, and may he maintain the cause of his servant

o Gk Syr: Heb in the land

and the cause of his people Israel, as each day requires; [60]so that all the peoples of the earth may know that the LORD is God; there is no other. [61]Therefore devote yourselves completely to the LORD our God, walking in his statutes and keeping his commandments, as at this day."

TUESDAY

PRAYERS
Book of Common Prayer

VERSE: 1 Kings 8.54   **PASSAGE:** 1 Kings 8.54–61

A Collect for Peace

 ost holy God, the source of all good desires, all right judgments, and all just works: Give to us, your servants, that peace which the world cannot give, so that our minds may be fixed on the doing of your will, and that we, being delivered from the fear of all enemies, may live in peace and quietness; through the mercies of Christ Jesus our Savior. *Amen.*

A Collect for Aid Against Perils

Be our light in the darkness, O Lord, and in your great mercy defend us from all perils and dangers of this night; for the love of your only Son, our Savior Jesus Christ. *Amen.*

A Collect for Protection

O God, the life of all who live, the light of the faithful, the strength of those who labor, and the repose of the dead: We thank you for the blessings of the day that is past, and humbly ask for your protection through the coming night. Bring us in safety to the morning hours; through him who died and rose again for us, your Son our Savior Jesus Christ. *Amen.*

A Collect for the Presence of Christ

Lord Jesus, stay with us, for evening is at hand and the day is past; be our companion in the way, kindle our hearts, and awaken hope, that we may know you as you are revealed in Scripture and the breaking of bread. Grant this for the sake of your love. *Amen.*

ADDITIONAL SCRIPTURE READING:
Matthew 6.6–8; Luke 11.1–4; Romans 8.26–27

Go to page 387 for your next devotional reading.

1500   1700

Solomon Offers Sacrifices

62 Then the king, and all Israel with him, offered sacrifice before the LORD. 63Solomon offered as sacrifices of well-being to the LORD twenty-two thousand oxen and one hundred twenty thousand sheep. So the king and all the people of Israel dedicated the house of the LORD. 64The same day the king consecrated the middle of the court that was in front of the house of the LORD; for there he offered the burnt offerings and the grain offerings and the fat pieces of the sacrifices of well-being, because the bronze altar that was before the LORD was too small to receive the burnt offerings and the grain offerings and the fat pieces of the sacrifices of well-being.

65 So Solomon held the festival at that time, and all Israel with him—a great assembly, people from Lebo-hamath to the Wadi of Egypt—before the LORD our God, seven days.p 66On the eighth day he sent the people away; and they blessed the king, and went to their tents, joyful and in good spirits because of all the goodness that the LORD had shown to his servant David and to his people Israel.

God Appears Again to Solomon

9 When Solomon had finished building the house of the LORD and the king's house and all that Solomon desired to build, 2the LORD appeared to Solomon a second time, as he had appeared to him at Gibeon. 3The LORD said to him, "I have heard your prayer and your plea, which you made before me; I have consecrated this house that you have built, and put my name there forever; my eyes and my heart will be there for all time. 4As for you, if you will walk before me, as David your father walked, with integrity of heart and uprightness, doing according to all that I have commanded you, and keeping my statutes and my ordinances, 5then I will establish your royal throne over Israel forever, as I promised your father David, saying, 'There shall not fail you a successor on the throne of Israel.'

6 "If you turn aside from following me, you or your children, and do not keep my commandments and my statutes that I have set before you, but go and serve other gods and worship them, 7then I will cut Israel off from the land that I have given them; and the house that I have consecrated for my name I will cast out of my sight; and Israel will become a proverb and a taunt among all peoples. 8This house will become a heap of ruins;q everyone passing by it will be astonished, and will hiss; and they will say, 'Why has the LORD done such a thing to this land and to this house?' 9Then they will say, 'Because they have forsaken the LORD their God, who brought their ancestors out of the land of Egypt, and embraced other gods, worshiping them and serving them; therefore the LORD has brought this disaster upon them.'"

10 At the end of twenty years, in which Solomon had built the two houses, the house of the LORD and the king's house, 11King Hiram of Tyre having supplied Solomon with cedar and cypress timber and gold, as much as he desired, King Solomon gave to Hiram twenty cities in the land of Galilee. 12But when Hiram came from Tyre to see the cities that Solomon had given him, they did not please him. 13Therefore he said, "What kind of cities are these that you have given me, my brother?" So they are called the land of Cabulr to this day. 14But Hiram had sent to the king one hundred twenty talents of gold.

Other Acts of Solomon

15 This is the account of the forced labor that King Solomon conscripted to build the house of the LORD and his own house, the Millo and the wall of Jerusalem, Hazor, Megiddo, Gezer 16(Pharaoh king of Egypt had gone up and captured Gezer and burned it down, had killed the Canaanites who lived in the city, and had given it as dowry to his daughter, Solomon's wife; 17so Solomon rebuilt Gezer), Lower Beth-horon, 18Baalath, Tamar in the wilderness, within the land, 19as well as all of Solomon's storage cities, the cities for his chariots, the cities for his cavalry, and whatever Solomon desired to build, in Jerusalem,

p Compare Gk: Heb seven days and seven days, fourteen days   q Syr Old Latin: Heb will become high   r Perhaps meaning a land good for nothing

in Lebanon, and in all the land of his dominion. 20All the people who were left of the Amorites, the Hittites, the Perizzites, the Hivites, and the Jebusites, who were not of the people of Israel— 21their descendants who were still left in the land, whom the Israelites were unable to destroy completely— these Solomon conscripted for slave labor, and so they are to this day. 22But of the Israelites Solomon made no slaves; they were the soldiers, they were his officials, his commanders, his captains, and the commanders of his chariotry and cavalry.

23 These were the chief officers who were over Solomon's work: five hundred fifty, who had charge of the people who carried on the work.

24 But Pharaoh's daughter went up from the city of David to her own house that Solomon had built for her; then he built the Millo.

25 Three times a year Solomon used to offer up burnt offerings and sacrifices of well-being on the altar that he built for the LORD, offering incenses before the LORD. So he completed the house.

Solomon's Commercial Activity

26 King Solomon built a fleet of ships at Ezion-geber, which is near Eloth on the shore of the Red Sea,t in the land of Edom. 27Hiram sent his servants with the fleet, sailors who were familiar with the sea, together with the servants of Solomon. 28They went to Ophir, and imported from there four hundred twenty talents of gold, which they delivered to King Solomon.

Visit of the Queen of Sheba

10 When the queen of Sheba heard of the fame of Solomon (fame due tou the name of the LORD), she came to test him with hard questions. 2She came to Jerusalem with a very great retinue, with camels bearing spices, and very much gold, and precious stones; and when she came to Solomon, she told him all that was on her mind. 3Solomon answered all her questions; there was nothing hidden from the king that he could not explain

to her. 4When the queen of Sheba had observed all the wisdom of Solomon, the house that he had built, 5the food of his table, the seating of his officials, and the attendance of his servants, their clothing, his valets, and his burnt offerings that he offered at the house of the LORD, there was no more spirit in her.

6 So she said to the king, "The report was true that I heard in my own land of your accomplishments and of your wisdom, 7but I did not believe the reports until I came and my own eyes had seen it. Not even half had been told me; your wisdom and prosperity far surpass the report that I had heard. 8Happy are your wives!v Happy are these your servants, who continually attend you and hear your wisdom! 9Blessed be the LORD your God, who has delighted in you and set you on the throne of Israel! Because the LORD loved Israel forever, he has made you king to execute justice and righteousness." 10Then she gave the king one hundred twenty talents of gold, a great quantity of spices, and precious stones; never again did spices come in such quantity as that which the queen of Sheba gave to King Solomon.

11 Moreover, the fleet of Hiram, which carried gold from Ophir, brought from Ophir a great quantity of almug wood and precious stones. 12From the almug wood the king made supports for the house of the LORD, and for the king's house, lyres also and harps for the singers; no such almug wood has come or been seen to this day.

13 Meanwhile King Solomon gave to the queen of Sheba every desire that she expressed, as well as what he gave her out of Solomon's royal bounty. Then she returned to her own land, with her servants.

14 The weight of gold that came to Solomon in one year was six hundred sixty-six talents of gold, 15besides that which came from the traders and from the business of the merchants, and from all the kings of Arabia and the governors of the land. 16King Solomon made two hundred large shields of beaten gold; six hundred shekels of gold went into each large shield. 17He made three hundred

s Gk: Heb offering incense with it that was   t Or Sea of Reeds   u Meaning of Heb uncertain
v Gk Syr: Heb men

shields of beaten gold; three minas of gold went into each shield; and the king put them in the House of the Forest of Lebanon. [18]The king also made a great ivory throne, and overlaid it with the finest gold. [19]The throne had six steps. The top of the throne was rounded in the back, and on each side of the seat were arm rests and two lions standing beside the arm rests, [20]while twelve lions were standing, one on each end of a step on the six steps. Nothing like it was ever made in any kingdom. [21]All King Solomon's drinking vessels were of gold, and all the vessels of the House of the Forest of Lebanon were of pure gold; none were of silver—it was not consid-

ered as anything in the days of Solomon. [22]For the king had a fleet of ships of Tarshish at sea with the fleet of Hiram. Once every three years the fleet of ships of Tarshish used to come bringing gold, silver, ivory, apes, and peacocks.*w*

23 Thus King Solomon excelled all the kings of the earth in riches and in wisdom. [24]The whole earth sought the presence of Solomon to hear his wisdom, which God had put into his mind. [25]Every one of them brought a present, objects of silver and gold, garments, weaponry, spices, horses, and mules, so much year by year.

26 Solomon gathered together chariots and horses; he had fourteen hundred

w Or *baboons*

I DID NOT BELIEVE UNTIL I CAME AND SAW
George Whitefield

VERSE: 1 Kings 10.7   **PASSAGE:** 1 Kings 10.6–9

ut I must stop: the glories of the upper world crowd in so fast upon my soul, that I am lost in the contemplation of them. Brethren, the redemption spoken of is unutterable; we cannot here find it out; eye hath not seen, nor ear heard, nor has it entered into the hearts of the most holy men living to conceive, how great it is. Were I to entertain you whole ages with an account of it, when you come to heaven, you must say, with the queen of Sheba, "Not half, no, not one thousandth part was told us." All we can do here, is to go upon mount Pisgah, and, by the eye of faith, take a distant view of the promised land: we may see it, as Abraham did Christ, afar off, and rejoice in it; but here we only know in part. Blessed be God, there is a time coming, when we shall know God, even as we are known, and God be all in all. Lord Jesus, accomplish the number of thine elect! Lord Jesus, hasten thy kingdom!

ADDITIONAL SCRIPTURE READING:
Isaiah 64.4; 1 Corinthians 2.9–10; 1 Peter 1.12

Go to page 398 for your next devotional reading.

1700   1900

chariots and twelve thousand horses, which he stationed in the chariot cities and with the king in Jerusalem. 27 The king made silver as common in Jerusalem as stones, and he made cedars as numerous as the sycamores of the Shephelah. 28 Solomon's import of horses was from Egypt and Kue, and the king's traders received them from Kue at a price. 29 A chariot could be imported from Egypt for six hundred shekels of silver, and a horse for one hundred fifty; so through the king's traders they were exported to all the kings of the Hittites and the kings of Aram.

Solomon's Errors

11 King Solomon loved many foreign women along with the daughter of Pharaoh: Moabite, Ammonite, Edomite, Sidonian, and Hittite women, 2 from the nations concerning which the LORD had said to the Israelites, "You shall not enter into marriage with them, neither shall they with you; for they will surely incline your heart to follow their gods"; Solomon clung to these in love. 3 Among his wives were seven hundred princesses and three hundred concubines; and his wives turned away his heart. 4 For when Solomon was old, his wives turned away his heart after other gods; and his heart was not true to the LORD his God, as was the heart of his father David. 5 For Solomon followed Astarte the goddess of the Sidonians, and Milcom the abomination of the Ammonites. 6 So Solomon did what was evil in the sight of the LORD, and did not completely follow the LORD, as his father David had done. 7 Then Solomon built a high place for Chemosh the abomination of Moab, and for Molech the abomination of the Ammonites, on the mountain east of Jerusalem. 8 He did the same for all his foreign wives, who offered incense and sacrificed to their gods.

9 Then the LORD was angry with Solomon, because his heart had turned away from the LORD, the God of Israel, who had appeared to him twice, 10 and had commanded him concerning this matter, that he should not follow other gods; but he did not observe what the LORD commanded. 11 Therefore the LORD

said to Solomon, "Since this has been your mind and you have not kept my covenant and my statutes that I have commanded you, I will surely tear the kingdom from you and give it to your servant. 12 Yet for the sake of your father David I will not do it in your lifetime; I will tear it out of the hand of your son. 13 I will not, however, tear away the entire kingdom; I will give one tribe to your son, for the sake of my servant David and for the sake of Jerusalem, which I have chosen."

Adversaries of Solomon

14 Then the LORD raised up an adversary against Solomon, Hadad the Edomite; he was of the royal house in Edom. 15 For when David was in Edom, and Joab the commander of the army went up to bury the dead, he killed every male in Edom 16 (for Joab and all Israel remained there six months, until he had eliminated every male in Edom); 17 but Hadad fled to Egypt with some Edomites who were servants of his father. He was a young boy at that time. 18 They set out from Midian and came to Paran; they took people with them from Paran and came to Egypt, to Pharaoh king of Egypt, who gave him a house, assigned him an allowance of food, and gave him land. 19 Hadad found great favor in the sight of Pharaoh, so that he gave him his sister-in-law for a wife, the sister of Queen Tahpenes. 20 The sister of Tahpenes gave birth by him to his son Genubath, whom Tahpenes weaned in Pharaoh's house; Genubath was in Pharaoh's house among the children of Pharaoh. 21 When Hadad heard in Egypt that David slept with his ancestors and that Joab the commander of the army was dead, Hadad said to Pharaoh, "Let me depart, that I may go to my own country." 22 But Pharaoh said to him, "What do you lack with me that you now seek to go to your own country?" And he said, "No, do let me go."

23 God raised up another adversary against Solomon, x Rezon son of Eliada, who had fled from his master, King Hadadezer of Zobah. 24 He gathered followers around him and became leader of a marauding band, after the slaughter by

x Heb *him*

David; they went to Damascus, settled there, and made him king in Damascus. 25He was an adversary of Israel all the days of Solomon, making trouble as Hadad did; he despised Israel and reigned over Aram.

Jeroboam's Rebellion

26 Jeroboam son of Nebat, an Ephraimite of Zeredah, a servant of Solomon, whose mother's name was Zeruah, a widow, rebelled against the king. 27The following was the reason he rebelled against the king. Solomon built the Millo, and closed up the gap in the wally of the city of his father David. 28The man Jeroboam was very able, and when Solomon saw that the young man was industrious he gave him charge over all the forced labor of the house of Joseph. 29About that time, when Jeroboam was leaving Jerusalem, the prophet Ahijah the Shilonite found him on the road. Ahijah had clothed himself with a new garment. The two of them were alone in the open country 30when Ahijah laid hold of the new garment he was wearing and tore it into twelve pieces. 31He then said to Jeroboam: Take for yourself ten pieces; for thus says the LORD, the God of Israel, "See, I am about to tear the kingdom from the hand of Solomon, and will give you ten tribes. 32One tribe will remain his, for the sake of my servant David and for the sake of Jerusalem, the city that I have chosen out of all the tribes of Israel. 33This is because he hasz forsaken me, worshiped Astarte the goddess of the Sidonians, Chemosh the god of Moab, and Milcom the god of the Ammonites, and hasz not walked in my ways, doing what is right in my sight and keeping my statutes and my ordinances, as his father David did. 34Nevertheless I will not take the whole kingdom away from him but will make him ruler all the days of his life, for the sake of my servant David whom I chose and who did keep my commandments and my statutes; 35but I will take the kingdom away from his son and give it to you—that is, the ten tribes. 36Yet to his son I will give one tribe, so that my servant David may always have a lamp before me in Jerusalem, the city where I

have chosen to put my name. 37I will take you, and you shall reign over all that your soul desires; you shall be king over Israel. 38If you will listen to all that I command you, walk in my ways, and do what is right in my sight by keeping my statutes and my commandments, as David my servant did, I will be with you, and will build you an enduring house, as I built for David, and I will give Israel to you. 39For this reason I will punish the descendants of David, but not forever." 40Solomon sought therefore to kill Jeroboam; but Jeroboam promptly fled to Egypt, to King Shishak of Egypt, and remained in Egypt until the death of Solomon.

Death of Solomon

41 Now the rest of the acts of Solomon, all that he did as well as his wisdom, are they not written in the Book of the Acts of Solomon? 42The time that Solomon reigned in Jerusalem over all Israel was forty years. 43Solomon slept with his ancestors and was buried in the city of his father David; and his son Rehoboam succeeded him.

The Northern Tribes Secede

12 Rehoboam went to Shechem, for all Israel had come to Shechem to make him king. 2When Jeroboam son of Nebat heard of it (for he was still in Egypt), where he had fled from King Solomon), then Jeroboam returned froma Egypt. 3And they sent and called him; and Jeroboam and all the assembly of Israel came and said to Rehoboam, 4"Your father made our yoke heavy. Now therefore lighten the hard service of your father and his heavy yoke that he placed on us, and we will serve you." 5He said to them, "Go away for three days, then come again to me." So the people went away.

6 Then King Rehoboam took counsel with the older men who had attended his father Solomon while he was still alive, saying, "How do you advise me to answer this people?" 7They answered him, "If you will be a servant to this people today and serve them, and speak good words to them when you answer them, then they will be your servants

y Heb lacks in the wall   z Gk Syr Vg: Heb they have   a Gk Vg Compare 2 Chr 10.2: Heb lived in forever." **8**But he disregarded the advice that the older men gave him, and consulted with the young men who had grown up with him and now attended him. **9**He said to them, "What do you advise that we answer this people who have said to me, 'Lighten the yoke that your father put on us'?" **10**The young men who had grown up with him said to him, "Thus you should say to this people who spoke to you, 'Your father made our yoke heavy, but you must lighten it for us'; thus you should say to them, 'My little finger is thicker than my father's loins. **11**Now, whereas my father laid on you a heavy yoke, I will add to your yoke. My father disciplined you with whips, but I will discipline you with scorpions.' "

12 So Jeroboam and all the people came to Rehoboam the third day, as the king had said, "Come to me again the third day." **13**The king answered the people harshly. He disregarded the advice that the older men had given him **14**and spoke to them according to the advice of the young men, "My father made your yoke heavy, but I will add to your yoke; my father disciplined you with whips, but I will discipline you with scorpions." **15**So the king did not listen to the people, because it was a turn of affairs brought about by the LORD that he might fulfill his word, which the LORD had spoken by Ahijah the Shilonite to Jeroboam son of Nebat.

16 When all Israel saw that the king would not listen to them, the people answered the king,

"What share do we have in David?
   We have no inheritance in the
      son of Jesse.
To your tents, O Israel!
   Look now to your own house,
      O David."

So Israel went away to their tents. **17**But Rehoboam reigned over the Israelites who were living in the towns of Judah. **18**When King Rehoboam sent Adoram, who was taskmaster over the forced labor, all Israel stoned him to death. King Rehoboam then hurriedly mounted his chariot to flee to Jerusalem. **19**So

Israel has been in rebellion against the house of David to this day.

First Dynasty: Jeroboam Reigns over Israel

20 When all Israel heard that Jeroboam had returned, they sent and called him to the assembly and made him king over all Israel. There was no one who followed the house of David, except the tribe of Judah alone.

21 When Rehoboam came to Jerusalem, he assembled all the house of Judah and the tribe of Benjamin, one hundred eighty thousand chosen troops to fight against the house of Israel, to restore the kingdom to Rehoboam son of Solomon. **22**But the word of God came to Shemaiah the man of God: **23**Say to King Rehoboam of Judah, son of Solomon, and to all the house of Judah and Benjamin, and to the rest of the people, **24**"Thus says the LORD, You shall not go up or fight against your kindred the people of Israel. Let everyone go home, for this thing is from me." So they heeded the word of the LORD and went home again, according to the word of the LORD.

Jeroboam's Golden Calves

25 Then Jeroboam built Shechem in the hill country of Ephraim, and resided there; he went out from there and built Penuel. **26**Then Jeroboam said to himself, "Now the kingdom may well revert to the house of David. **27**If this people continues to go up to offer sacrifices in the house of the LORD at Jerusalem, the heart of this people will turn again to their master, King Rehoboam of Judah; they will kill me and return to King Rehoboam of Judah." **28**So the king took counsel, and made two calves of gold. He said to the people,*b* "You have gone up to Jerusalem long enough. Here are your gods, O Israel, who brought you up out of the land of Egypt." **29**He set one in Bethel, and the other he put in Dan. **30**And this thing became a sin, for the people went to worship before the one at Bethel and before the other as far as Dan.*c* **31**He also made houses*d* on high places, and appointed priests from

---

b Gk: Heb *to them*   *c* Compare Gk: Heb *went to the one as far as Dan*   *d* Gk Vg Compare 13.32:
Heb *a house*

among all the people, who were not Levites. 32Jeroboam appointed a festival on the fifteenth day of the eighth month like the festival that was in Judah, and he offered sacrifices on the altar; so he did in Bethel, sacrificing to the calves that he had made. And he placed in Bethel the priests of the high places that he had made. 33He went up to the altar that he had made in Bethel on the fifteenth day in the eighth month, in the month that he alone had devised; he appointed a festival for the people of Israel, and he went up to the altar to offer incense.

A Man of God from Judah

13 While Jeroboam was standing by the altar to offer incense, a man of God came out of Judah by the word of the LORD to Bethel 2and proclaimed against the altar by the word of the LORD, and said, "O altar, altar, thus says the LORD: 'A son shall be born to the house of David, Josiah by name; and he shall sacrifice on you the priests of the high places who offer incense on you, and human bones shall be burned on you.' " 3He gave a sign the same day, saying, "This is the sign that the LORD has spoken: 'The altar shall be torn down, and the ashes that are on it shall be poured out.' " 4When the king heard what the man of God cried out against the altar at Bethel, Jeroboam stretched out his hand from the altar, saying, "Seize him!" But the hand that he stretched out against him withered so that he could not draw it back to himself. 5The altar also was torn down, and the ashes poured out from the altar, according to the sign that the man of God had given by the word of the LORD.

WE OUGHT TO ACT WITH GOD IN THE GREATEST SIMPLICITY, SPEAKING TO HIM FRANKLY AND PLAINLY, AND IMPLORING HIS ASSISTANCE IN OUR AFFAIRS, JUST AS THEY HAPPEN.

—*Brother Lawrence*

6The king said to the man of God, "Entreat now the favor of the LORD your God, and pray for me, so that my hand may be restored to me." So the man of God entreated the LORD; and the king's hand was restored to him, and became as it was before. 7Then the king said to the man of God, "Come home with me and dine, and I will give you a gift." 8But the man of God said to the king, "If you give me half your kingdom, I will not go in with you; nor will I eat food or drink water in this place. 9For thus I was commanded by the word of the LORD: You shall not eat food, or drink water, or return by the way that you came." 10So he went another way, and did not return by the way that he had come to Bethel.

11 Now there lived an old prophet in Bethel. One of his sons came and told him all that the man of God had done that day in Bethel; the words also that he had spoken to the king, they told to their father. 12Their father said to them, "Which way did he go?" And his sons showed him the way that the man of God who came from Judah had gone. 13Then he said to his sons, "Saddle a donkey for me." So they saddled a donkey for him, and he mounted it. 14He went after the man of God, and found him sitting under an oak tree. He said to him, "Are you the man of God who came from Judah?" He answered, "I am." 15Then he said to him, "Come home with me and eat some food." 16But he said, "I cannot return with you, or go in with you; nor will I eat food or drink water with you in this place; 17for it was said to me by the word of the LORD: You shall not eat food or drink water there, or return by the way that you came." 18Then the other[e] said to him, "I also am a prophet as you are, and an angel spoke to me by the word of the LORD: Bring him back with you into your house so that he may eat food and drink water." But he was deceiving him. 19Then the man of God[e] went back with him, and ate food and drank water in his house.

20 As they were sitting at the table, the word of the LORD came to the prophet who had brought him back; 21and he proclaimed to the man of God who came from Judah, "Thus says the LORD: Because you have disobeyed the word of the LORD, and have not kept the commandment that the LORD your God

---

e Heb he

commanded you, 22but have come back and have eaten food and drunk water in the place of which he said to you, 'Eat no food, and drink no water,' your body shall not come to your ancestral tomb." 23After the man of God*f* had eaten food and had drunk, they saddled for him a donkey belonging to the prophet who had brought him back. 24Then as he went away, a lion met him on the road and killed him. His body was thrown in the road, and the donkey stood beside it; the lion also stood beside the body. 25People passed by and saw the body thrown in the road, with the lion standing by the body. And they came and told it in the town where the old prophet lived.

26 When the prophet who had brought him back from the way heard of it, he said, "It is the man of God who disobeyed the word of the LORD; therefore the LORD has given him to the lion, which has torn him and killed him according to the word that the LORD spoke to him." 27Then he said to his sons, "Saddle a donkey for me." So they saddled one, 28and he went and found the body thrown in the road, with the donkey and the lion standing beside the body. The lion had not eaten the body or attacked the donkey. 29The prophet took up the body of the man of God, laid it on the donkey, and brought it back to the city,*g* to mourn and to bury him. 30He laid the body in his own grave; and they mourned over him, saying, "Alas, my brother!" 31After he had buried him, he said to his sons, "When I die, bury me in the grave in which the man of God is buried; lay my bones beside his bones. 32For the saying that he proclaimed by the word of the LORD against the altar in Bethel, and against all the houses of the high places that are in the cities of Samaria, shall surely come to pass."

33 Even after this event Jeroboam did not turn from his evil way, but made priests for the high places again from among all the people; any who wanted to be priests he consecrated for the high places. 34This matter became sin to the house of Jeroboam, so as to cut it off and to destroy it from the face of the earth.

Judgment on the House of Jeroboam

14 At that time Abijah son of Jeroboam fell sick. 2Jeroboam said to his wife, "Go, disguise yourself, so that it will not be known that you are the wife of Jeroboam, and go to Shiloh; for the prophet Ahijah is there, who said of me that I should be king over this people. 3Take with you ten loaves, some cakes, and a jar of honey, and go to him; he will tell you what shall happen to the child."

4 Jeroboam's wife did so; she set out and went to Shiloh, and came to the house of Ahijah. Now Ahijah could not see, for his eyes were dim because of his age. 5But the LORD said to Ahijah, "The wife of Jeroboam is coming to inquire of you concerning her son; for he is sick. Thus and thus you shall say to her."

When she came, she pretended to be another woman. 6But when Ahijah heard the sound of her feet, as she came in at the door, he said, "Come in, wife of Jeroboam; why do you pretend to be another? For I am charged with heavy tidings for you. 7Go, tell Jeroboam, 'Thus says the LORD, the God of Israel: Because I exalted you from among the people, made you leader over my people Israel, 8and tore the kingdom away from the house of David to give it to you; yet you have not been like my servant David, who kept my commandments and followed me with all his heart, doing only that which was right in my sight, 9but you have done evil above all those who were before you and have gone and made for yourself other gods, and cast images, provoking me to anger, and have thrust me behind your back; 10therefore, I will bring evil upon the house of Jeroboam. I will cut off from Jeroboam every male, both bond and free in Israel, and will consume the house of Jeroboam, just as one burns up dung until it is all gone. 11Anyone belonging to Jeroboam who dies in the city, the dogs shall eat; and anyone who dies in the open country, the birds of the air shall eat; for the LORD has spoken.' 12Therefore set out, go to your house. When your feet enter the city, the child shall die. 13All Israel shall mourn for him and bury him; for he alone of Jeroboam's family shall come to

f Heb he   g Gk: Heb he came to the town of the old prophet the grave, because in him there is found something pleasing to the LORD, the God of Israel, in the house of Jeroboam. [14]Moreover the LORD will raise up for himself a king over Israel, who shall cut off the house of Jeroboam today, even right now![h] 15 "The LORD will strike Israel, as a reed is shaken in the water; he will root up Israel out of this good land that he gave to their ancestors, and scatter them beyond the Euphrates, because they have made their sacred poles,[i] provoking the LORD to anger. [16]He will give Israel up because of the sins of Jeroboam, which he sinned and which he caused Israel to commit."

17 Then Jeroboam's wife got up and went away, and she came to Tirzah. As she came to the threshold of the house, the child died. [18]All Israel buried him and mourned for him, according to the word of the LORD, which he spoke by his servant the prophet Ahijah.

Death of Jeroboam

19 Now the rest of the acts of Jeroboam, how he warred and how he reigned, are written in the Book of the Annals of the Kings of Israel. [20]The time that Jeroboam reigned was twenty-two years; then he slept with his ancestors, and his son Nadab succeeded him.

Rehoboam Reigns over Judah

21 Now Rehoboam son of Solomon reigned in Judah. Rehoboam was forty-one years old when he began to reign, and he reigned seventeen years in Jerusalem, the city that the LORD had chosen out of all the tribes of Israel, to put his name there. His mother's name was Naamah the Ammonite. [22]Judah did what was evil in the sight of the LORD; they provoked him to jealousy with their sins that they committed, more than all that their ancestors had done. [23]For they also built for themselves high places, pillars, and sacred poles[i] on every high hill and under every green tree; [24]there were also male temple prostitutes in the land. They committed all the abominations of the nations that the LORD drove out before the people of Israel.

25 In the fifth year of King Rehoboam, King Shishak of Egypt came up against Jerusalem; [26]he took away the treasures of the house of the LORD and the treasures of the king's house; he took everything. He also took away all the shields of gold that Solomon had made; [27]so King Rehoboam made shields of bronze instead, and committed them to the hands of the officers of the guard, who kept the door of the king's house. [28]As often as the king went into the house of the LORD, the guard carried them and brought them back to the guardroom.

29 Now the rest of the acts of Rehoboam, and all that he did, are they not written in the Book of the Annals of the Kings of Judah? [30]There was war between Rehoboam and Jeroboam continually. [31]Rehoboam slept with his ancestors and was buried with his ancestors in the city of David. His mother's name was Naamah the Ammonite. His son Abijam succeeded him.

Abijam Reigns over Judah: Idolatry and War

15 Now in the eighteenth year of King Jeroboam son of Nebat, Abijam began to reign over Judah. [2]He reigned for three years in Jerusalem. His mother's name was Maacah daughter of Abishalom. [3]He committed all the sins that his father did before him; his heart was not true to the LORD his God, like the heart of his father David. [4]Nevertheless for David's sake the LORD his God gave him a lamp in Jerusalem, setting up his son after him, and establishing Jerusalem; [5]because David did what was right in the sight of the LORD, and did not turn aside from anything that he commanded him all the days of his life, except in the matter of Uriah the Hittite. [6]The war begun between Rehoboam and Jeroboam continued all the days of his life. [7]The rest of the acts of Abijam, and all that he did, are they not written in the Book of the Annals of the Kings of Judah? There was war between Abijam and Jeroboam. [8]Abijam slept with his ancestors, and they buried him in the city of David. Then his son Asa succeeded him.

---

h Meaning of Heb uncertain   *i* Heb *Asherim*

Asa Reigns over Judah

9 In the twentieth year of King Jeroboam of Israel, Asa began to reign over Judah; 10he reigned forty-one years in Jerusalem. His mother's name was Maacah daughter of Abishalom. 11Asa did what was right in the sight of the LORD, as his father David had done. 12He put away the male temple prostitutes out of the land, and removed all the idols that his ancestors had made. 13He also removed his mother Maacah from being queen mother, because she had made an abominable image for Asherah; Asa cut down her image and burned it at the Wadi Kidron. 14But the high places were not taken away. Nevertheless the heart of Asa was true to the LORD all his days. 15He brought into the house of the LORD the votive gifts of his father and his own votive gifts—silver, gold, and utensils.

Alliance with Aram against Israel

16 There was war between Asa and King Baasha of Israel all their days. 17King Baasha of Israel went up against Judah, and built Ramah, to prevent anyone from going out or coming in to King Asa of Judah. 18Then Asa took all the silver and the gold that were left in the treasures of the house of the LORD and the treasures of the king's house, and gave them into the hands of his servants. King Asa sent them to King Benhadad son of Tabrimmon son of Hezion of Aram, who resided in Damascus, saying, 19"Let there be an alliance between me and you, like that between my father and your father: I am sending you a present of silver and gold; go, break your alliance with King Baasha of Israel, so that he may withdraw from me." 20Benhadad listened to King Asa, and sent the commanders of his armies against the cities of Israel. He conquered Ijon, Dan, Abel-beth-maacah, and all Chinneroth, with all the land of Naphtali. 21When Baasha heard of it, he stopped building Ramah and lived in Tirzah. 22Then King Asa made a proclamation to all Judah, none was exempt: they carried away the stones of Ramah and its timber, with which Baasha had been building; with them King Asa built Geba of Benjamin

and Mizpah. 23Now the rest of all the acts of Asa, all his power, all that he did, and the cities that he built, are they not written in the Book of the Annals of the Kings of Judah? But in his old age he was diseased in his feet. 24Then Asa slept with his ancestors, and was buried with his ancestors in the city of his father David; his son Jehoshaphat succeeded him.

Nadab Reigns over Israel

25 Nadab son of Jeroboam began to reign over Israel in the second year of King Asa of Judah; he reigned over Israel two years. 26He did what was evil in the sight of the LORD, walking in the way of his ancestor and in the sin that he caused Israel to commit.

27 Baasha son of Ahijah, of the house of Issachar, conspired against him; and Baasha struck him down at Gibbethon, which belonged to the Philistines; for Nadab and all Israel were laying siege to Gibbethon. 28So Baasha killed Nadab[j] in the third year of King Asa of Judah, and succeeded him. 29As soon as he was king, he killed all the house of Jeroboam; he left to the house of Jeroboam not one that breathed, until he had destroyed it, according to the word of the LORD that he spoke by his servant Ahijah the Shilonite— 30because of the sins of Jeroboam that he committed and that he caused Israel to commit, and because of the anger to which he provoked the LORD, the God of Israel.

31 Now the rest of the acts of Nadab, and all that he did, are they not written in the Book of the Annals of the Kings of Israel? 32There was war between Asa and King Baasha of Israel all their days.

Second Dynasty: Baasha Reigns over Israel

33 In the third year of King Asa of Judah, Baasha son of Ahijah began to reign over all Israel at Tirzah; he reigned twenty-four years. 34He did what was evil in the sight of the LORD, walking in the way of Jeroboam and in the sin that he caused Israel to commit.

16 The word of the LORD came to Jehu son of Hanani against Baasha, saying, 2"Since I exalted you out

j Heb him

of the dust and made you leader over my people Israel, and you have walked in the way of Jeroboam, and have caused my people Israel to sin, provoking me to anger with their sins, 3therefore, I will consume Baasha and his house, and I will make your house like the house of Jeroboam son of Nebat. 4Anyone belonging to Baasha who dies in the city the dogs shall eat; and anyone of his who dies in the field the birds of the air shall eat."

5 Now the rest of the acts of Baasha, what he did, and his power, are they not written in the Book of the Annals of the Kings of Israel? 6Baasha slept with his ancestors, and was buried at Tirzah; and his son Elah succeeded him. 7Moreover the word of the LORD came by the prophet Jehu son of Hanani against Baasha and his house, both because of all the evil that he did in the sight of the LORD, provoking him to anger with the work of his hands, in being like the house of Jeroboam, and also because he destroyed it.

Elah Reigns over Israel

8 In the twenty-sixth year of King Asa of Judah, Elah son of Baasha began to reign over Israel in Tirzah; he reigned two years. 9But his servant Zimri, commander of half his chariots, conspired against him. When he was at Tirzah, drinking himself drunk in the house of Arza, who was in charge of the palace at Tirzah, 10Zimri came in and struck him down and killed him, in the twenty-seventh year of King Asa of Judah, and succeeded him.

11 When he began to reign, as soon as he had seated himself on his throne, he killed all the house of Baasha; he did not leave him a single male of his kindred or his friends. 12Thus Zimri destroyed all the house of Baasha, according to the word of the LORD, which he spoke against Baasha by the prophet Jehu— 13because of all the sins of Baasha and the sins of his son Elah that they committed, and that they caused Israel to commit, provoking the LORD God of Israel to anger with their idols. 14Now the rest of the acts of Elah, and all that he did, are they not written in the Book of the Annals of the Kings of Israel?

Third Dynasty: Zimri Reigns over Israel

15 In the twenty-seventh year of King Asa of Judah, Zimri reigned seven days in Tirzah. Now the troops were encamped against Gibbethon, which belonged to the Philistines, 16and the troops who were encamped heard it said, "Zimri has conspired, and he has killed the king"; therefore all Israel made Omri, the commander of the army, king over Israel that day in the camp. 17So Omri went up from Gibbethon, and all Israel with him, and they besieged Tirzah. 18When Zimri saw that the city was taken, he went into the citadel of the king's house; he burned down the king's house over himself with fire, and died— 19because of the sins that he committed, doing evil in the sight of the LORD, walking in the way of Jeroboam, and for the sin that he committed, causing Israel to sin. 20Now the rest of the acts of Zimri, and the conspiracy that he made, are they not written in the Book of the Annals of the Kings of Israel?

Fourth Dynasty: Omri Reigns over Israel

21 Then the people of Israel were divided into two parts; half of the people followed Tibni son of Ginath, to make him king, and half followed Omri. 22But the people who followed Omri overcame the people who followed Tibni son of Ginath; so Tibni died, and Omri became king. 23In the thirty-first year of King Asa of Judah, Omri began to reign over Israel; he reigned for twelve years, six of them in Tirzah.

Samaria the New Capital

24 He bought the hill of Samaria from Shemer for two talents of silver; he fortified the hill, and called the city that he built, Samaria, after the name of Shemer, the owner of the hill.

25 Omri did what was evil in the sight of the LORD; he did more evil than all who were before him. 26For he walked in all the way of Jeroboam son of Nebat, and in the sins that he caused Israel to commit, provoking the LORD, the God of Israel, to anger by their idols. 27Now the rest of the acts of Omri that

he did, and the power that he showed, are they not written in the Book of the Annals of the Kings of Israel? 28Omri slept with his ancestors, and was buried in Samaria; his son Ahab succeeded him.

Ahab Reigns over Israel

29 In the thirty-eighth year of King Asa of Judah, Ahab son of Omri began to reign over Israel; Ahab son of Omri reigned over Israel in Samaria twenty-two years. 30Ahab son of Omri did evil in the sight of the LORD more than all who were before him.

Ahab Marries Jezebel and Worships Baal

31 And as if it had been a light thing for him to walk in the sins of Jeroboam son of Nebat, he took as his wife Jezebel daughter of King Ethbaal of the Sidonians, and went and served Baal, and worshiped him. 32He erected an altar for Baal in the house of Baal, which he built in Samaria. 33Ahab also made a sacred pole.k Ahab did more to provoke the anger of the LORD, the God of Israel, than had all the kings of Israel who were before him. 34In his days Hiel of Bethel built Jericho; he laid its foundation at the cost of Abiram his firstborn, and set up its gates at the cost of his youngest son Segub, according to the word of the LORD, which he spoke by Joshua son of Nun.

Elijah Predicts a Drought

17 Now Elijah the Tishbite, of Tishbel in Gilead, said to Ahab, "As the LORD the God of Israel lives, before whom I stand, there shall be neither dew nor rain these years, except by my word." 2The word of the LORD came to him, saying, 3"Go from here and turn eastward, and hide yourself by the Wadi Cherith, which is east of the Jordan. 4You shall drink from the wadi, and I have commanded the ravens to feed you there." 5So he went and did according to the word of the LORD; he went and lived by the Wadi Cherith, which is east of the Jordan. 6The ravens brought him bread and meat in the morning, and bread and meat in the evening; and he drank from the wadi. 7But

after a while the wadi dried up, because there was no rain in the land.

The Widow of Zarephath

8 Then the word of the LORD came to him, saying, 9"Go now to Zarephath, which belongs to Sidon, and live there; for I have commanded a widow there to feed you." 10So he set out and went to Zarephath. When he came to the gate of the town, a widow was there gathering sticks; he called to her and said, "Bring me a little water in a vessel, so that I may drink." 11As she was going to bring it, he called to her and said, "Bring me a morsel of bread in your hand." 12But she said, "As the LORD your God lives, I have nothing baked, only a handful of meal in a jar, and a little oil in a jug; I am now gathering a couple of sticks, so that I may go home and prepare it for myself and my son, that we may eat it, and die." 13Elijah said to her, "Do not be afraid; go and do as you have said; but first make me a little cake of it and bring it to me, and afterwards make something for yourself and your son. 14For thus says the LORD the God of Israel: The jar of meal will not be emptied and the jug of oil will not fail until the day that the LORD sends rain on the earth." 15She went and did as Elijah said, so that she as well as he and her household ate for many days. 16The jar of meal was not emptied, neither did the jug of oil fail, according to the word of the LORD that he spoke by Elijah.

Elijah Revives the Widow's Son

17 After this the son of the woman, the mistress of the house, became ill; his illness was so severe that there was no breath left in him. 18She then said to Elijah, "What have you against me, O man of God? You have come to me to bring my sin to remembrance, and to cause the death of my son!" 19But he said to her, "Give me your son." He took him from her bosom, carried him up into the upper chamber where he was lodging, and laid him on his own bed. 20He cried out to the LORD, "O LORD my God, have you brought calamity even upon the widow with whom I am staying, by killing her son?" 21Then he stretched

k Heb Asherah   l Gk: Heb of the settlers

himself upon the child three times, and cried out to the LORD, "O LORD my God, let this child's life come into him again." 22The LORD listened to the voice of Elijah; the life of the child came into him again, and he revived. 23Elijah took the child, brought him down from the upper chamber into the house, and gave him to his mother; then Elijah said, "See, your son is alive." 24So the woman said to Elijah, "Now I know that you are a man of God, and that the word of the LORD in your mouth is truth."

Elijah's Message to Ahab

18 After many days the word of the LORD came to Elijah, in the third year of the drought,m saying, "Go, present yourself to Ahab; I will send rain on the earth." 2So Elijah went to present himself to Ahab. The famine was severe in Samaria. 3Ahab summoned Obadiah, who was in charge of the palace. (Now Obadiah revered the LORD greatly; 4when Jezebel was killing off the prophets of the LORD, Obadiah took a hundred prophets, hid them fifty to a cave, and provided them with bread and water.) 5Then Ahab said to Obadiah, "Go through the land to all the springs of water and to all the wadis; perhaps we may find grass to keep the horses and mules alive, and not lose some of the animals." 6So they divided the land between them to pass through it; Ahab went in one direction by himself, and Obadiah went in another direction by himself.

7 As Obadiah was on the way, Elijah met him; Obadiah recognized him, fell on his face, and said, "Is it you, my lord Elijah?" 8He answered him, "It is I. Go, tell your lord that Elijah is here." 9And he said, "How have I sinned, that you would hand your servant over to Ahab, to kill me? 10As the LORD your God lives, there is no nation or kingdom to which my lord has not sent to seek you; and when they would say, 'He is not here,' he would require an oath of the kingdom or nation, that they had not found you. 11But now you say, 'Go, tell your lord that Elijah is here.' 12As soon as I have gone from you, the spirit of the LORD will carry you I know not where;

so, when I come and tell Ahab and he cannot find you, he will kill me, although I your servant have revered the LORD from my youth. 13Has it not been told my lord what I did when Jezebel killed the prophets of the LORD, how I hid a hundred of the LORD's prophets fifty to a cave, and provided them with bread and water? 14Yet now you say, 'Go, tell your lord that Elijah is here'; he will surely kill me." 15Elijah said, "As the LORD of hosts lives, before whom I stand, I will surely show myself to him today." 16So Obadiah went to meet Ahab, and told him; and Ahab went to meet Elijah.

17 When Ahab saw Elijah, Ahab said to him, "Is it you, you troubler of Israel?" 18He answered, "I have not troubled Israel; but you have, and your father's house, because you have forsaken the commandments of the LORD and followed the Baals. 19Now therefore have all Israel assemble for me at Mount Carmel, with the four hundred fifty prophets of Baal and the four hundred prophets of Asherah, who eat at Jezebel's table."

Elijah's Triumph over the Priests of Baal

20 So Ahab sent to all the Israelites, and assembled the prophets at Mount Carmel. 21Elijah then came near to all the people, and said, "How long will you go limping with two different opinions? If the LORD is God, follow him; but if Baal, then follow him." The people did not answer him a word. 22Then Elijah said to the people, "I, even I only, am left a prophet of the LORD; but Baal's prophets number four hundred fifty. 23Let two bulls be given to us; let them choose one bull for themselves, cut it in pieces, and lay it on the wood, but put no fire to it; I will prepare the other bull and lay it on the wood, but put no fire to it. 24Then you call on the name of your god and I will call on the name of the LORD; the god who answers by fire is indeed God." All the people answered, "Well spoken!" 25Then Elijah said to the prophets of Baal, "Choose for yourselves one bull and prepare it first, for you are many; then call on the name of your god, but put no fire to it." 26So they took

m Heb lacks of the drought

the bull that was given them, prepared it, and called on the name of Baal from morning until noon, crying, "O Baal, answer us!" But there was no voice, and no answer. They limped about the altar that they had made. ²⁷At noon Elijah mocked them, saying, "Cry aloud! Surely he is a god; either he is meditating, or he has wandered away, or he is on a journey, or perhaps he is asleep and must be awakened." ²⁸Then they cried aloud and, as was their custom, they cut themselves with swords and lances until the blood gushed out over them. ²⁹As midday passed, they raved on until the time of the offering of the oblation,

THURSDAY

THE COURAGE OF OBEDIENCE
James Hudson Taylor

VERSE: 1 Kings 18.24　　　　　　**PASSAGE:** 1 Kings 18.19–39

ant of trust is at the root of almost all our sins and all our weaknesses; and how shall we escape it but by looking to him and observing his faithfulness? The man who holds God's faithfulness will not be foolhardy or reckless, but he will be ready for every emergency. The man who holds God's faithfulness will dare to obey him, however impolitic it may appear. Abraham held God's faithfulness and offered up Isaac, "accounting that God was able to raise him . . . from the dead" (Hebrews 11.19, KJV). Moses held God's faithfulness and led the millions of Israel into the waste, howling wilderness. "And what shall I more say? for the time would fail me to tell" of those who, holding God's faithfulness, had faith, and by it "subdued kingdoms, wrought righteousness, obtained promises . . . out of weakness were made strong, waxed valiant in fight, turned to flight the armies of the aliens" (11.33–34).

Satan, too, has his creed: Doubt God's faithfulness. "Hath God said? Are you not mistaken as to his commands? He could not really mean just that. You take an extreme view, give too literal a meaning to the words." How constantly, and alas, how successfully are such arguments used to prevent wholehearted trust in God, wholehearted consecration to God! How many estimate difficulties in the light of their own resources, and thus attempt little and often fail in the little they attempt! All God's giants have been weak men, who did great things for God because they reckoned on his being with them.

ADDITIONAL SCRIPTURE READING:
Genesis 3.1–5; Matthew 4.1–10; Mark 11.22–24

Go to page 410 for your next devotional reading.

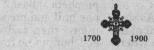

1700　　1900

but there was no voice, no answer, and no response.

30 Then Elijah said to all the people, "Come closer to me"; and all the people came closer to him. First he repaired the altar of the LORD that had been thrown down; 31Elijah took twelve stones, according to the number of the tribes of the sons of Jacob, to whom the word of the LORD came, saying, "Israel shall be your name"; 32with the stones he built an altar in the name of the LORD. Then he made a trench around the altar, large enough to contain two measures of seed. 33Next he put the wood in order, cut the bull in pieces, and laid it on the wood. He said, "Fill four jars with water and pour it on the burnt offering and on the wood." 34Then he said, "Do it a second time"; and they did it a second time. Again he said, "Do it a third time"; and they did it a third time, 35so that the water ran all around the altar, and filled the trench also with water.

36 At the time of the offering of the oblation, the prophet Elijah came near and said, "O LORD, God of Abraham, Isaac, and Israel, let it be known this day that you are God in Israel, that I am your servant, and that I have done all these things at your bidding. 37Answer me, O LORD, answer me, so that this people may know that you, O LORD, are God, and that you have turned their hearts back." 38Then the fire of the LORD fell and consumed the burnt offering, the wood, the stones, and the dust, and even licked up the water that was in the trench. 39When all the people saw it, they fell on their faces and said, "The LORD indeed is God; the LORD indeed is God." 40Elijah said to them, "Seize the prophets of Baal; do not let one of them escape." Then they seized them; and Elijah brought them down to the Wadi Kishon, and killed them there.

The Drought Ends

41 Elijah said to Ahab, "Go up, eat and drink; for there is a sound of rushing rain." 42So Ahab went up to eat and to drink. Elijah went up to the top of Carmel; there he bowed himself down upon the earth and put his face between his knees. 43He said to his servant, "Go up now, look toward the sea." He went up

and looked, and said, "There is nothing." Then he said, "Go again seven times." 44At the seventh time he said, "Look, a little cloud no bigger than a person's hand is rising out of the sea." Then he said, "Go say to Ahab, 'Harness your chariot and go down before the rain stops you.' " 45In a little while the heavens grew black with clouds and wind; there was a heavy rain. Ahab rode off and went to Jezreel. 46But the hand of the LORD was on Elijah; he girded up his loins and ran in front of Ahab to the entrance of Jezreel.

Elijah Flees from Jezebel

19 Ahab told Jezebel all that Elijah had done, and how he had killed all the prophets with the sword. 2Then Jezebel sent a messenger to Elijah, saying, "So may the gods do to me, and more also, if I do not make your life like the life of one of them by this time tomorrow." 3Then he was afraid; he got up and fled for his life, and came to Beersheba, which belongs to Judah; he left his servant there.

4 But he himself went a day's journey into the wilderness, and came and sat down under a solitary broom tree. He asked that he might die: "It is enough; now, O LORD, take away my life, for I am no better than my ancestors." 5Then he lay down under the broom tree and fell asleep. Suddenly an angel touched him and said to him, "Get up and eat." 6He looked, and there at his head was a cake baked on hot stones, and a jar of water. He ate and drank, and lay down again. 7The angel of the LORD came a second time, touched him, and said, "Get up and eat, otherwise the journey will be too much for you." 8He got up, and ate and drank; then he went in the strength of that food forty days and forty nights to Horeb the mount of God. 9At that place he came to a cave, and spent the night there.

Then the word of the LORD came to him, saying, "What are you doing here, Elijah?" 10He answered, "I have been very zealous for the LORD, the God of hosts; for the Israelites have forsaken your covenant, thrown down your altars, and killed your prophets with the sword. I alone am left, and they are seeking my life, to take it away."

Elijah Meets God at Horeb

11 He said, "Go out and stand on the mountain before the LORD, for the LORD is about to pass by." Now there was a great wind, so strong that it was splitting mountains and breaking rocks in pieces before the LORD, but the LORD was not in the wind; and after the wind an earthquake, but the LORD was not in the earthquake; 12and after the earthquake a fire, but the LORD was not in the fire; and after the fire a sound of sheer silence. 13When Elijah heard it, he wrapped his face in his mantle and went out and stood at the entrance of the cave. Then there came a voice to him that said, "What are you doing here, Elijah?" 14He answered, "I have been very zealous for the LORD, the God of hosts; for the Israelites have forsaken your covenant, thrown down your altars, and killed your prophets with the sword. I alone am left, and they are seeking my life, to take it away." 15Then the LORD said to him, "Go, return on your way to the wilderness of Damascus; when you arrive, you shall anoint Hazael as king over Aram. 16Also you shall anoint Jehu son of Nimshi as king over Israel; and you shall anoint Elisha son of Shaphat of Abel-meholah as prophet in your place. 17Whoever escapes from the sword of Hazael, Jehu shall kill; and whoever escapes from the sword of Jehu, Elisha shall kill. 18Yet I will leave seven thousand in Israel, all the knees that have not bowed to Baal, and every mouth that has not kissed him."

Elisha Becomes Elijah's Disciple

19 So he set out from there, and found Elisha son of Shaphat, who was plowing. There were twelve yoke of oxen ahead of him, and he was with the twelfth. Elijah passed by him and threw his mantle over him. 20He left the oxen, ran after Elijah, and said, "Let me kiss my father and my mother, and then I will follow you." Then Elijah*n* said to him, "Go back again; for what have I done to you?" 21He returned from following him, took the yoke of oxen, and

slaughtered them; using the equipment from the oxen, he boiled their flesh, and gave it to the people, and they ate. Then he set out and followed Elijah, and became his servant.

Ahab's Wars with the Arameans

20 King Ben-hadad of Aram gathered all his army together; thirty-two kings were with him, along with horses and chariots. He marched against Samaria, laid siege to it, and attacked it. 2Then he sent messengers into the city to King Ahab of Israel, and said to him: "Thus says Ben-hadad: 3Your silver and gold are mine; your fairest wives and children also are mine." 4The king of Israel answered, "As you say, my lord, O king, I am yours, and all that I have." 5The messengers came again and said: "Thus says Ben-hadad: I sent to you, saying, 'Deliver to me your silver and gold, your wives and children'; 6nevertheless I will send my servants to you tomorrow about this time, and they shall search your house and the houses of your servants, and lay hands on whatever pleases them,*o* and take it away."

7 Then the king of Israel called all the elders of the land, and said, "Look now! See how this man is seeking trouble; for he sent to me for my wives, my children, my silver, and my gold; and I did not refuse him." 8Then all the elders and all the people said to him, "Do not listen or consent." 9So he said to the messengers of Ben-hadad, "Tell my lord the king: All that you first demanded of your servant I will do; but this thing I cannot do." The messengers left and brought him word again. 10Ben-hadad sent to him and said, "The gods do so to me, and more also, if the dust of Samaria will provide a handful for each of the people who follow me." 11The king of Israel answered, "Tell him: One who puts on armor should not brag like one who takes it off." 12When Ben-hadad heard this message—now he had been drinking with the kings in the booths— he said to his men, "Take your positions!" And they took their positions against the city.

n Heb he   *o* Gk Syr Vg: Heb you

Prophetic Opposition to Ahab

13 Then a certain prophet came up to King Ahab of Israel and said, "Thus says the LORD, Have you seen all this great multitude? Look, I will give it into your hand today; and you shall know that I am the LORD." 14 Ahab said, "By whom?" He said, "Thus says the LORD, By the young men who serve the district governors." Then he said, "Who shall begin the battle?" He answered, "You." 15 Then he mustered the young men who served the district governors, two hundred thirty-two; after them he mustered all the people of Israel, seven thousand.

16 They went out at noon, while Ben-hadad was drinking himself drunk in the booths, he and the thirty-two kings allied with him. 17 The young men who served the district governors went out first. Ben-hadad had sent out scouts,[p] and they reported to him, "Men have come out from Samaria." 18 He said, "If they have come out for peace, take them alive; if they have come out for war, take them alive."

19 But these had already come out of the city: the young men who served the district governors, and the army that followed them. 20 Each killed his man; the Arameans fled and Israel pursued them, but King Ben-hadad of Aram escaped on a horse with the cavalry. 21 The king of Israel went out, attacked the horses and chariots, and defeated the Arameans with a great slaughter.

22 Then the prophet approached the king of Israel and said to him, "Come, strengthen yourself, and consider well what you have to do; for in the spring the king of Aram will come up against you."

The Arameans Are Defeated

23 The servants of the king of Aram said to him, "Their gods are gods of the hills, and so they were stronger than we; but let us fight against them in the plain, and surely we shall be stronger than they. 24 Also do this: remove the kings, each from his post, and put commanders in place of them; 25 and muster an army like the army that you have lost, horse for horse, and chariot for chariot; then

we will fight against them in the plain, and surely we shall be stronger than they." He heeded their voice, and did so.

26 In the spring Ben-hadad mustered the Arameans and went up to Aphek to fight against Israel. 27 After the Israelites had been mustered and provisioned, they went out to engage them; the people of Israel encamped opposite them like two little flocks of goats, while the Arameans filled the country. 28 A man of God approached and said to the king of Israel, "Thus says the LORD: Because the Arameans have said, 'The LORD is a god of the hills but he is not a god of the valleys,' therefore I will give all this great multitude into your hand, and you shall know that I am the LORD." 29 They encamped opposite one another seven days. Then on the seventh day the battle began; the Israelites killed one hundred thousand Aramean foot soldiers in one day. 30 The rest fled into the city of Aphek; and the wall fell on twenty-seven thousand men that were left.

Ben-hadad also fled, and entered the city to hide. 31 His servants said to him, "Look, we have heard that the kings of the house of Israel are merciful kings; let us put sackcloth around our waists and ropes on our heads, and go out to the king of Israel; perhaps he will spare your life." 32 So they tied sackcloth around their waists, put ropes on their heads, went to the king of Israel, and said, "Your servant Ben-hadad says, 'Please let me live.'" And he said, "Is he still alive? He is my brother." 33 Now the men were watching for an omen; they quickly took it up from him and said, "Yes, Ben-hadad is your brother." Then he said, "Go and bring him." So Ben-hadad came out to him; and he had him come up into the chariot. 34 Ben-hadad[q] said to him, "I will restore the towns that my father took from your father; and you may establish bazaars for yourself in Damascus, as my father did in Samaria." The king of Israel responded,[r] "I will let you go on those terms." So he made a treaty with him and let him go.

A Prophet Condemns Ahab

35 At the command of the LORD a certain member of a company of

p Heb lacks scouts   q Heb He   r Heb lacks The king of Israel responded

prophets[s] said to another, "Strike me!" But the man refused to strike him. 36Then he said to him, "Because you have not obeyed the voice of the LORD, as soon as you have left me, a lion will kill you." And when he had left him, a lion met him and killed him. 37Then he found another man and said, "Strike me!" So the man hit him, striking and wounding him. 38Then the prophet departed, and waited for the king along the road, disguising himself with a bandage over his eyes. 39As the king passed by, he cried to the king and said, "Your servant went out into the thick of the battle; then a soldier turned and brought a man to me, and said, 'Guard this man; if he is missing, your life shall be given for his life, or else you shall pay a talent of silver.' 40While your servant was busy here and there, he was gone." The king of Israel said to him, "So shall your judgment be; you yourself have decided it." 41Then he quickly took the bandage away from his eyes. The king of Israel recognized him as one of the prophets. 42Then he said to him, "Thus says the LORD, 'Because you have let the man go whom I had devoted to destruction, therefore your life shall be for his life, and your people for his people.' " 43The king of Israel set out toward home, resentful and sullen, and came to Samaria.

Naboth's Vineyard

21 Later the following events took place: Naboth the Jezreelite had a vineyard in Jezreel, beside the palace of King Ahab of Samaria. 2And Ahab said to Naboth, "Give me your vineyard, so that I may have it for a vegetable garden, because it is near my house; I will give you a better vineyard for it; or, if it seems good to you, I will give you its value in money." 3But Naboth said to Ahab, "The LORD forbid that I should give you my ancestral inheritance." 4Ahab went home resentful and sullen because of what Naboth the Jezreelite had said to him; for he had said, "I will not give you my ancestral inheritance." He lay down on his bed, turned away his face, and would not eat.

5 His wife Jezebel came to him and said, "Why are you so depressed that you will not eat?" 6He said to her, "Because I spoke to Naboth the Jezreelite and said to him, 'Give me your vineyard for money; or else, if you prefer, I will give you another vineyard for it'; but he answered, 'I will not give you my vineyard.' " 7His wife Jezebel said to him, "Do you now govern Israel? Get up, eat some food, and be cheerful; I will give you the vineyard of Naboth the Jezreelite."

8 So she wrote letters in Ahab's name and sealed them with his seal; she sent the letters to the elders and the nobles who lived with Naboth in his city. 9She wrote in the letters, "Proclaim a fast, and seat Naboth at the head of the assembly; 10seat two scoundrels opposite him, and have them bring a charge against him, saying, 'You have cursed God and the king.' Then take him out, and stone him to death." 11The men of his city, the elders and the nobles who lived in his city, did as Jezebel had sent word to them. Just as it was written in the letters that she had sent to them, 12they proclaimed a fast and seated Naboth at the head of the assembly. 13The two scoundrels came in and sat opposite him; and the scoundrels brought a charge against Naboth, in the presence of the people, saying, "Naboth cursed God and the king." So they took him outside the city, and stoned him to death. 14Then they sent to Jezebel, saying, "Naboth has been stoned; he is dead."

15 As soon as Jezebel heard that Naboth had been stoned and was dead, Jezebel said to Ahab, "Go, take possession of the vineyard of Naboth the Jezreelite, which he refused to give you for money; for Naboth is not alive, but dead." 16As soon as Ahab heard that Naboth was dead, Ahab set out to go down to the vineyard of Naboth the Jezreelite, to take possession of it.

Elijah Pronounces God's Sentence

17 Then the word of the LORD came to Elijah the Tishbite, saying: 18Go down to meet King Ahab of Israel, who rules[t] in Samaria; he is now in the vineyard of Naboth, where he has gone to take possession. 19You shall say to him, "Thus

s Heb of the sons of the prophets   t Heb who is

says the LORD: Have you killed, and also taken possession?" You shall say to him, "Thus says the LORD: In the place where dogs licked up the blood of Naboth, dogs will also lick up your blood."

20 Ahab said to Elijah, "Have you found me, O my enemy?" He answered, "I have found you. Because you have sold yourself to do what is evil in the sight of the LORD, 21I will bring disaster on you; I will consume you, and will cut off from Ahab every male, bond or free, in Israel; 22and I will make your house like the house of Jeroboam son of Nebat, and like the house of Baasha son of Ahijah, because you have provoked me to anger and have caused Israel to sin. 23Also concerning Jezebel the LORD said, 'The dogs shall eat Jezebel within the bounds of Jezreel.' 24Anyone belonging to Ahab who dies in the city the dogs shall eat; and anyone of his who dies in the open country the birds of the air shall eat."

25 (Indeed, there was no one like Ahab, who sold himself to do what was evil in the sight of the LORD, urged on by his wife Jezebel. 26He acted most abominably in going after idols, as the Amorites had done, whom the LORD drove out before the Israelites.)

27 When Ahab heard those words, he tore his clothes and put sackcloth over his bare flesh; he fasted, lay in the sackcloth, and went about dejectedly. 28Then the word of the LORD came to Elijah the Tishbite: 29"Have you seen how Ahab has humbled himself before me? Because he has humbled himself before me, I will not bring the disaster in his days; but in his son's days I will bring the disaster on his house."

Joint Campaign with Judah against Aram

22 For three years Aram and Israel continued without war. 2But in the third year King Jehoshaphat of Judah came down to the king of Israel. 3The king of Israel said to his servants, "Do you know that Ramoth-gilead belongs to us, yet we are doing nothing to take it out of the hand of the king of Aram?" 4He said to Jehoshaphat, "Will you go with me to battle at Ramoth-gilead?" Jehoshaphat replied to the king of Israel, "I am as you are; my people are your people, my horses are your horses."

5 But Jehoshaphat also said to the king of Israel, "Inquire first for the word of the LORD." 6Then the king of Israel gathered the prophets together, about four hundred of them, and said to them, "Shall I go to battle against Ramoth-gilead, or shall I refrain?" They said, "Go up; for the LORD will give it into the hand of the king." 7But Jehoshaphat said, "Is there no other prophet of the LORD here of whom we may inquire?" 8The king of Israel said to Jehoshaphat, "There is still one other by whom we may inquire of the LORD, Micaiah son of Imlah; but I hate him, for he never prophesies anything favorable about me, but only disaster." Jehoshaphat said, "Let the king not say such a thing." 9Then the king of Israel summoned an officer and said, "Bring quickly Micaiah son of Imlah." 10Now the king of Israel and King Jehoshaphat of Judah were sitting on their thrones, arrayed in their robes, at the threshing floor at the entrance of the gate of Samaria; and all the prophets were prophesying before them. 11Zedekiah son of Chenaanah made for himself horns of iron, and he said, "Thus says the LORD: With these you shall gore the Arameans until they are destroyed." 12All the prophets were prophesying the same and saying, "Go up to Ramoth-gilead and triumph; the LORD will give it into the hand of the king."

Micaiah Predicts Failure

13 The messenger who had gone to summon Micaiah said to him, "Look, the words of the prophets with one accord are favorable to the king; let your word be like the word of one of them, and speak favorably." 14But Micaiah said, "As the LORD lives, whatever the LORD says to me, that I will speak."

15 When he had come to the king, the king said to him, "Micaiah, shall we go to Ramoth-gilead to battle, or shall we refrain?" He answered him, "Go up and triumph; the LORD will give it into the hand of the king." 16But the king said to him, "How many times must I make you swear to tell me nothing but

the truth in the name of the LORD?"
17Then Micaiahu said, "I saw all Israel
scattered on the mountains, like sheep
that have no shepherd; and the LORD
said, 'These have no master; let each
one go home in peace.' " 18The king of
Israel said to Jehoshaphat, "Did I not tell
you that he would not prophesy anything favorable about me, but only
disaster?"

19 Then Micaiahu said, "Therefore
hear the word of the LORD: I saw the
LORD sitting on his throne, with all the
host of heaven standing beside him to
the right and to the left of him. 20And
the LORD said, 'Who will entice Ahab, so
that he may go up and fall at Ramoth-
gilead?' Then one said one thing, and
another said another, 21until a spirit
came forward and stood before the
LORD, saying, 'I will entice him.'
22'How?' the LORD asked him. He
replied, 'I will go out and be a lying spirit in the mouth of all his prophets.'
Then the LORDu said, 'You are to entice
him, and you shall succeed; go out and
do it.' 23So you see, the LORD has put a
lying spirit in the mouth of all these
your prophets; the LORD has decreed
disaster for you."

24 Then Zedekiah son of Chenaanah
came up to Micaiah, slapped him on the
cheek, and said, "Which way did the
spirit of the LORD pass from me to speak
to you?" 25Micaiah replied, "You will
find out on that day when you go in to
hide in an inner chamber." 26The king of
Israel then ordered, "Take Micaiah, and
return him to Amon the governor of the
city and to Joash the king's son, 27and
say, 'Thus says the king: Put this fellow
in prison, and feed him on reduced
rations of bread and water until I come
in peace.' " 28Micaiah said, "If you
return in peace, the LORD has not spoken by me." And he said, "Hear, you
peoples, all of you!"

Defeat and Death of Ahab

29 So the king of Israel and King
Jehoshaphat of Judah went up to
Ramoth-gilead. 30The king of Israel said
to Jehoshaphat, "I will disguise myself
and go into battle, but you wear your
robes." So the king of Israel disguised

himself and went into battle. 31Now the
king of Aram had commanded the thirty-two captains of his chariots, "Fight
with no one small or great, but only
with the king of Israel." 32When the captains of the chariots saw Jehoshaphat,
they said, "It is surely the king of Israel." So they turned to fight against him;
and Jehoshaphat cried out. 33When the
captains of the chariots saw that it was
not the king of Israel, they turned back
from pursuing him. 34But a certain man
drew his bow and unknowingly struck
the king of Israel between the scale
armor and the breastplate; so he said to
the driver of his chariot, "Turn around,
and carry me out of the battle, for I am
wounded." 35The battle grew hot that
day, and the king was propped up in his
chariot facing the Arameans, until at
evening he died; the blood from the
wound had flowed into the bottom of
the chariot. 36Then about sunset a shout
went through the army, "Every man to
his city, and every man to his country!"

37 So the king died, and was brought
to Samaria; they buried the king in
Samaria. 38They washed the chariot by
the pool of Samaria; the dogs licked up
his blood, and the prostitutes washed
themselves in it,v according to the word
of the LORD that he had spoken. 39Now
the rest of the acts of Ahab, and all that
he did, and the ivory house that he built,
and all the cities that he built, are they
not written in the Book of the Annals of
the Kings of Israel? 40So Ahab slept with
his ancestors; and his son Ahaziah succeeded him.

Jehoshaphat Reigns over Judah

41 Jehoshaphat son of Asa began to
reign over Judah in the fourth year of
King Ahab of Israel. 42Jehoshaphat was
thirty-five years old when he began to
reign, and he reigned twenty-five years
in Jerusalem. His mother's name was
Azubah daughter of Shilhi. 43He walked
in all the way of his father Asa; he did
not turn aside from it, doing what was
right in the sight of the LORD; yet the
high places were not taken away, and the
people still sacrificed and offered incense
on the high places. 44Jehoshaphat also
made peace with the king of Israel.

u Heb he   v Heb lacks in it

45 Now the rest of the acts of Jehoshaphat, and his power that he showed, and how he waged war, are they not written in the Book of the Annals of the Kings of Judah? 46The remnant of the male temple prostitutes who were still in the land in the days of his father Asa, he exterminated.

47 There was no king in Edom; a deputy was king. 48Jehoshaphat made ships of the Tarshish type to go to Ophir for gold; but they did not go, for the ships were wrecked at Ezion-geber. 49Then Ahaziah son of Ahab said to Jehoshaphat, "Let my servants go with your servants in the ships," but Jehoshaphat was not willing. 50Jehoshaphat slept with his ancestors and was buried with his ancestors in the city of his father David; his son Jehoram succeeded him.

Ahaziah Reigns over Israel

51 Ahaziah son of Ahab began to reign over Israel in Samaria in the seventeenth year of King Jehoshaphat of Judah; he reigned two years over Israel. 52He did what was evil in the sight of the LORD, and walked in the way of his father and mother, and in the way of Jeroboam son of Nebat, who caused Israel to sin. 53He served Baal and worshiped him; he provoked the LORD, the God of Israel, to anger, just as his father had done.

2 KINGS

HE BOOK OF 2 KINGS CONTINUES
THE HISTORY OF ISRAEL AND
JUDAH BEGUN IN 1 KINGS. IT
INCLUDES THE FASCINATING STORIES OF
THE GREAT PROPHETS ELIJAH AND ELISHA.
LOOK FOR THE PROPHET'S WARNINGS
THAT GOD WOULD PUNISH THE PEOPLE IF
THEY DID NOT REPENT OF THEIR SINS, AND
NOTE THE TERRIBLE LOSSES GOD'S PEOPLE
ENDURED BECAUSE OF THEIR SIN.

Elijah Denounces Ahaziah

1 After the death of Ahab, Moab rebelled against Israel.

2 Ahaziah had fallen through the lattice in his upper chamber in Samaria, and lay injured; so he sent messengers, telling them, "Go, inquire of Baal-zebub, the god of Ekron, whether I shall recover from this injury." ³But the angel of the LORD said to Elijah the Tishbite, "Get up, go to meet the messengers of the king of Samaria, and say to them, 'Is it because there is no God in Israel that you are going to inquire of Baal-zebub, the god of Ekron?' ⁴Now therefore thus says the LORD, 'You shall not leave the bed to which you have gone, but you shall surely die.' " So Elijah went.

5 The messengers returned to the king, who said to them, "Why have you returned?" ⁶They answered him, "There came a man to meet us, who said to us, 'Go back to the king who sent you, and say to him: Thus says the LORD: Is it because there is no God in Israel that you are sending to inquire of Baal-zebub, the god of Ekron? Therefore you shall not leave the bed to which you have gone, but shall surely die.' " ⁷He said to them, "What sort of man was he who came to meet you and told you these things?" ⁸They answered him, "A hairy man, with a leather belt around his waist." He said, "It is Elijah the Tishbite."

9 Then the king sent to him a captain of fifty with his fifty men. He went up to Elijah, who was sitting on the top of a hill, and said to him, "O man of God, the king says, 'Come down.' " ¹⁰But Eli-

jah answered the captain of fifty, "If I am a man of God, let fire come down from heaven and consume you and your fifty." Then fire came down from heaven, and consumed him and his fifty.

11 Again the king sent to him another captain of fifty with his fifty. He went up[a] and said to him, "O man of God, this is the king's order: Come down quickly!" 12But Elijah answered them, "If I am a man of God, let fire come down from heaven and consume you and your fifty." Then the fire of God came down from heaven and consumed him and his fifty.

13 Again the king sent the captain of a third fifty with his fifty. So the third captain of fifty went up, and came and fell on his knees before Elijah, and entreated him, "O man of God, please let my life, and the life of these fifty servants of yours, be precious in your sight. 14Look, fire came down from heaven and consumed the two former captains of fifty men with their fifties; but now let my life be precious in your sight." 15Then the angel of the LORD said to Elijah, "Go down with him; do not be afraid of him." So he set out and went down with him to the king, 16and said to him, "Thus says the LORD: Because you have sent messengers to inquire of Baalzebub, the god of Ekron,—is it because there is no God in Israel to inquire of his word?—therefore you shall not leave the bed to which you have gone, but you shall surely die."

Death of Ahaziah

17 So he died according to the word of the LORD that Elijah had spoken. His brother,[b] Jehoram succeeded him as king in the second year of King Jehoram son of Jehoshaphat of Judah, because Ahaziah had no son. 18Now the rest of the acts of Ahaziah that he did, are they not written in the Book of the Annals of the Kings of Israel?

Elijah Ascends to Heaven

2 Now when the LORD was about to take Elijah up to heaven by a whirlwind, Elijah and Elisha were on their way from Gilgal. 2Elijah said to Elisha, "Stay here; for the LORD has sent me as far as Bethel." But Elisha said, "As the LORD lives, and as you yourself live, I will not leave you." So they went down to Bethel. 3The company of prophets[c] who were in Bethel came out to Elisha, and said to him, "Do you know that today the LORD will take your master away from you?" And he said, "Yes, I know; keep silent."

4 Elijah said to him, "Elisha, stay here; for the LORD has sent me to Jericho." But he said, "As the LORD lives, and as you yourself live, I will not leave you." So they came to Jericho. 5The company of prophets[c] who were at Jericho drew near to Elisha, and said to him, "Do you know that today the LORD will take your master away from you?" And he answered, "Yes, I know; be silent."

6 Then Elijah said to him, "Stay here; for the LORD has sent me to the Jordan." But he said, "As the LORD lives, and as you yourself live, I will not leave you." So the two of them went on. 7Fifty men of the company of prophets[c] also went, and stood at some distance from them, as they both were standing by the Jordan. 8Then Elijah took his mantle and rolled it up, and struck the water; the water was parted to the one side and to the other, until the two of them crossed on dry ground.

9 When they had crossed, Elijah said to Elisha, "Tell me what I may do for you, before I am taken from you." Elisha said, "Please let me inherit a double share of your spirit." 10He responded, "You have asked a hard thing; yet, if you see me as I am being taken from you, it will be granted you; if not, it will not." 11As they continued walking and talking, a chariot of fire and horses of fire separated the two of them, and Elijah ascended in a whirlwind into heaven. 12Elisha kept watching and crying out, "Father, father! The chariots of Israel and its horsemen!" But when he could no longer see him, he grasped his own clothes and tore them in two pieces.

Elisha Succeeds Elijah

13 He picked up the mantle of Elijah that had fallen from him, and went back

---

a Gk Compare verses 9, 13: Heb He answered   b Gk Syr: Heb lacks His brother   c Heb sons of the prophets

and stood on the bank of the Jordan. [14]He took the mantle of Elijah that had fallen from him, and struck the water, saying, "Where is the LORD, the God of Elijah?" When he had struck the water, the water was parted to the one side and to the other, and Elisha went over.

15 When the company of prophets[d] who were at Jericho saw him at a distance, they declared, "The spirit of Elijah rests on Elisha." They came to meet him and bowed to the ground before him. [16]They said to him, "See now, we have fifty strong men among your servants; please let them go and seek your master; it may be that the spirit of the LORD has caught him up and thrown him down on some mountain or into some valley." He responded, "No, do not send them." [17]But when they urged him until he was ashamed, he said, "Send them." So they sent fifty men who searched for three days but did not find him. [18]When they came back to him (he had remained at Jericho), he said to them, "Did I not say to you, Do not go?"

Elisha Performs Miracles

19 Now the people of the city said to Elisha, "The location of this city is good, as my lord sees; but the water is bad, and the land is unfruitful." [20]He said, "Bring me a new bowl, and put salt in it." So they brought it to him. [21]Then he went to the spring of water and threw the salt into it, and said, "Thus says the LORD, I have made this water wholesome; from now on neither death nor miscarriage shall come from it." [22]So the water has been wholesome to this day, according to the word that Elisha spoke.

23 He went up from there to Bethel; and while he was going up on the way, some small boys came out of the city and jeered at him, saying, "Go away, baldhead! Go away, baldhead!" [24]When he turned around and saw them, he cursed them in the name of the LORD. Then two she-bears came out of the woods and mauled forty-two of the boys. [25]From there he went on to Mount Carmel, and then returned to Samaria.

d Heb sons of the prophets

Jehoram Reigns over Israel

3 In the eighteenth year of King Jehoshaphat of Judah, Jehoram son of Ahab became king over Israel in Samaria; he reigned twelve years. [2]He did what was evil in the sight of the LORD, though not like his father and mother, for he removed the pillar of Baal that his father had made. [3]Nevertheless he clung to the sin of Jeroboam son of Nebat, which he caused Israel to commit; he did not depart from it.

War with Moab

4 Now King Mesha of Moab was a sheep breeder, who used to deliver to the king of Israel one hundred thousand lambs, and the wool of one hundred thousand rams. [5]But when Ahab died, the king of Moab rebelled against the king of Israel. [6]So King Jehoram marched out of Samaria at that time and mustered all Israel. [7]As he went he sent word to King Jehoshaphat of Judah, "The king of Moab has rebelled against me; will you go with me to battle against Moab?" He answered, "I will; I am with you, my people are your people, my horses are your horses." [8]Then he asked, "By which way shall we march?" Jehoram answered, "By the way of the wilderness of Edom."

9 So the king of Israel, the king of Judah, and the king of Edom set out; and when they had made a roundabout march of seven days, there was no water for the army or for the animals that were with them. [10]Then the king of Israel said, "Alas! The LORD has summoned us, three kings, only to be handed over to Moab." [11]But Jehoshaphat said, "Is there no prophet of the LORD here, through whom we may inquire of the LORD?" Then one of the servants of the king of Israel answered, "Elisha son of Shaphat, who used to pour water on the hands of Elijah, is here." [12]Jehoshaphat said, "The word of the LORD is with him." So the king of Israel and Jehoshaphat and the king of Edom went down to him.

13 Elisha said to the king of Israel, "What have I to do with you? Go to your father's prophets or to your mother's."

But the king of Israel said to him, "No; it is the LORD who has summoned us, three kings, only to be handed over to Moab." 14Elisha said, "As the LORD of hosts lives, whom I serve, were it not that I have regard for King Jehoshaphat of Judah, I would give you neither a look nor a glance. 15But get me a musician." And then, while the musician was playing, the power of the LORD came on him. 16And he said, "Thus says the LORD, 'I will make this wadi full of pools.' 17For thus says the LORD, 'You shall see neither wind nor rain, but the wadi shall be filled with water, so that you shall drink, you, your cattle, and your animals.' 18This is only a trifle in the sight of the LORD, for he will also hand Moab over to you. 19You shall conquer every fortified city and every choice city; every good tree you shall fell, all springs of water you shall stop up, and every good piece of land you shall ruin with stones." 20The next day, about the time of the morning offering, suddenly water began to flow from the direction of Edom, until the country was filled with water.

21 When all the Moabites heard that the kings had come up to fight against them, all who were able to put on armor, from the youngest to the oldest, were called out and were drawn up at the frontier. 22When they rose early in the morning, and the sun shone upon the water, the Moabites saw the water opposite them as red as blood. 23They said, "This is blood; the kings must have fought together, and killed one another. Now then, Moab, to the spoil!" 24But when they came to the camp of Israel, the Israelites rose up and attacked the Moabites, who fled before them; as they entered Moab they continued the attack.e 25The cities they overturned, and on every good piece of land everyone threw a stone, until it was covered; every spring of water they stopped up, and every good tree they felled. Only at Kir-hareseth did the stone walls remain, until the slingers surrounded and attacked it. 26When the king of Moab saw that the battle was going against him, he took with him seven hundred swordsmen to break through, opposite the king of Edom; but they could not. 27Then he took his first-born son who was to succeed him, and offered him as a burnt offering on the wall. And great wrath came upon Israel, so they withdrew from him and returned to their own land.

Elisha and the Widow's Oil

4 Now the wife of a member of the company of prophetsf cried to Elisha, "Your servant my husband is dead; and you know that your servant feared the LORD, but a creditor has come to take my two children as slaves." 2Elisha said to her, "What shall I do for you? Tell me, what do you have in the house?" She answered, "Your servant has nothing in the house, except a jar of oil." 3He said, "Go outside, borrow vessels from all your neighbors, empty vessels and not just a few. 4Then go in, and shut the door behind you and your children, and start pouring into all these vessels; when each is full, set it aside." 5So she left him and shut the door behind her and her children; they kept bringing vessels to her, and she kept pouring. 6When the vessels were full, she said to her son, "Bring me another vessel." But he said to her, "There are no more." Then the oil stopped flowing. 7She came and told the man of God, and he said, "Go sell the oil and pay your debts, and you and your children can live on the rest."

Elisha Raises the Shunammite's Son

8 One day Elisha was passing through Shunem, where a wealthy woman lived, who urged him to have a meal. So whenever he passed that way, he would stop there for a meal. 9She said to her husband, "Look, I am sure that this man who regularly passes our way is a holy man of God. 10Let us make a small roof chamber with walls, and put there for him a bed, a table, a chair, and a lamp, so that he can stay there whenever he comes to us."

11 One day when he came there, he went up to the chamber and lay down there. 12He said to his servant Gehazi, "Call the Shunammite woman." When he had called her, she stood before him. 13He said to him, "Say to her, Since you have taken all this trouble for us, what

e Compare Gk Syr: Meaning of Heb uncertain   f Heb the sons of the prophets may be done for you? Would you have a word spoken on your behalf to the king or to the commander of the army?" She answered, "I live among my own people." 14He said, "What then may be done for her?" Gehazi answered, "Well, she has no son, and her husband is old." 15He said, "Call her." When he had called her, she stood at the door. 16He said, "At this season, in due time, you shall embrace a son." She replied, "No, my lord, O man of God; do not deceive your servant."

17 The woman conceived and bore a son at that season, in due time, as Elisha had declared to her.

18 When the child was older, he went out one day to his father among the reapers. 19He complained to his father, "Oh, my head, my head!" The father said to his servant, "Carry him to his mother." 20He carried him and brought him to his mother; the child sat on her lap until noon, and he died. 21She went up and laid him on the bed of the man of God, closed the door on him, and left. 22Then she called to her husband, and said, "Send me one of the servants and one of the donkeys, so that I may quickly go to the man of God and come back again." 23He said, "Why go to him today? It is neither new moon nor sabbath." She said, "It will be all right." 24Then she saddled the donkey and said to her servant, "Urge the animal on; do not hold back for me unless I tell you."

FRIDAY

THE PASSING OF THE IMPRESSION OF GOD
Watchman Nee

VERSE: 2 Kings 4.9   **PASSAGE:** 2 Kings 4.8–10

 always like to think of the words of that "great woman" of Shunem. Speaking of the prophet, whom she had observed but whom she did not know well, she said: "I am sure that this man who regularly passes our way is a holy man of God" (2 Kings 4.9). It was not what Elisha said or did that conveyed that impression, but what he was. By his merely passing by she could detect something; she could *see*. What are people sensing about us? We may leave many kinds of impressions: we may leave the impression that we are clever, that we are gifted, that *we* are this or that or the other. But no, the impression left by Elisha was an impression of God himself.

This matter of our impact upon others turns upon one thing, and that is the working of the Cross in us with regard to the pleasure of the heart of God. It demands that I seek his pleasure, that I seek to satisfy him only, and I do not mind how much it costs me to do so.

ADDITIONAL SCRIPTURE READING:
1 Kings 17.18–24; 1 Timothy 6.11–12

Go to page 413 for your next devotional reading.

Go to page 413 for your next devotional reading.

1900   Present

25 So she set out, and came to the man of God at Mount Carmel.

When the man of God saw her coming, he said to Gehazi his servant, "Look, there is the Shunammite woman; 26 run at once to meet her, and say to her, Are you all right? Is your husband all right? Is the child all right?" She answered, "It is all right." 27 When she came to the man of God at the mountain, she caught hold of his feet. Gehazi approached to push her away. But the man of God said, "Let her alone, for she is in bitter distress; the LORD has hidden it from me and has not told me." 28 Then she said, "Did I ask my lord for a son? Did I not say, Do not mislead me?" 29 He said to Gehazi, "Gird up your loins, and take my staff in your hand, and go. If you meet anyone, give no greeting, and if anyone greets you, do not answer; and lay my staff on the face of the child." 30 Then the mother of the child said, "As the LORD lives, and as you yourself live, I will not leave without you." So he rose up and followed her. 31 Gehazi went on ahead and laid the staff on the face of the child, but there was no sound or sign of life. He came back to meet him and told him, "The child has not awakened."

32 When Elisha came into the house, he saw the child lying dead on his bed. 33 So he went in and closed the door on the two of them, and prayed to the LORD. 34 Then he got up on the bed[g] and lay upon the child, putting his mouth upon his mouth, his eyes upon his eyes, and his hands upon his hands; and while he lay bent over him, the flesh of the child became warm. 35 He got down, walked once to and fro in the room, then got up again and bent over him; the child sneezed seven times, and the child opened his eyes. 36 Elisha[h] summoned Gehazi and said, "Call the Shunammite woman." So he called her. When she came to him, he said, "Take your son." 37 She came and fell at his feet, bowing to the ground; then she took her son and left.

Elisha Purifies the Pot of Stew

38 When Elisha returned to Gilgal, there was a famine in the land. As the company of prophets was[i] sitting before him, he said to his servant, "Put the large pot on, and make some stew for the company of prophets."[i] 39 One of them went out into the field to gather herbs; he found a wild vine and gathered from it a lapful of wild gourds, and came and cut them up into the pot of stew, not knowing what they were. 40 They served some for the men to eat. But while they were eating the stew, they cried out, "O man of God, there is death in the pot!" They could not eat it. 41 He said, "Then bring some flour." He threw it into the pot, and said, "Serve the people and let them eat." And there was nothing harmful in the pot.

Elisha Feeds One Hundred Men

42 A man came from Baal-shalishah, bringing food from the first fruits to the man of God: twenty loaves of barley and fresh ears of grain in his sack. Elisha said, "Give it to the people and let them eat." 43 But his servant said, "How can I set this before a hundred people?" So he repeated, "Give it to the people and let them eat, for thus says the LORD, 'They shall eat and have some left.' " 44 He set it before them, they ate, and had some left, according to the word of the LORD.

The Healing of Naaman

5 Naaman, commander of the army of the king of Aram, was a great man and in high favor with his master, because by him the LORD had given victory to Aram. The man, though a mighty warrior, suffered from leprosy.[k] 2 Now the Arameans on one of their raids had taken a young girl captive from the land of Israel, and she served Naaman's wife. 3 She said to her mistress, "If only my lord were with the prophet who is in Samaria! He would cure him of his leprosy."[k] 4 So Naaman[h] went in and told his lord just what the girl from the land of Israel had said. 5 And the king of Aram said, "Go then, and I will send along a letter to the king of Israel."

He went, taking with him ten talents of silver, six thousand shekels of gold, and ten sets of garments. 6 He brought

---

g Heb lacks *on the bed*   h Heb *he*   i Heb *sons of the prophets were*   j Heb *sons of the prophets*
k A term for several skin diseases; precise meaning uncertain

the letter to the king of Israel, which read, "When this letter reaches you, know that I have sent to you my servant Naaman, that you may cure him of his leprosy."[1] [7]When the king of Israel read the letter, he tore his clothes and said, "Am I God, to give death or life, that this man sends word to me to cure a man of his leprosy?[1] Just look and see how he is trying to pick a quarrel with me."

8 But when Elisha the man of God heard that the king of Israel had torn his clothes, he sent a message to the king, "Why have you torn your clothes? Let him come to me, that he may learn that there is a prophet in Israel." [9]So Naaman came with his horses and chariots, and halted at the entrance of Elisha's house. [10]Elisha sent a messenger to him, saying, "Go, wash in the Jordan seven times, and your flesh shall be restored and you shall be clean." [11]But Naaman became angry and went away, saying, "I thought that for me he would surely come out, and stand and call on the name of the LORD his God, and would wave his hand over the spot, and cure the leprosy![1] [12]Are not Abana[m] and Pharpar, the rivers of Damascus, better than all the waters of Israel? Could I not wash in them, and be clean?" He turned and went away in a rage. [13]But his servants approached and said to him, "Father, if the prophet had commanded you to do something difficult, would you not have done it? How much more, when all he said to you was, 'Wash, and be clean'?" [14]So he went down and immersed himself seven times in the Jordan, according to the word of the man of God; his flesh was restored like the flesh of a young boy, and he was clean.

15 Then he returned to the man of God, he and all his company; he came and stood before him and said, "Now I know that there is no God in all the earth except in Israel; please accept a present from your servant." [16]But he said, "As the LORD lives, whom I serve, I will accept nothing!" He urged him to accept, but he refused. [17]Then Naaman said, "If not, please let two mule-loads

of earth be given to your servant; for your servant will no longer offer burnt offering or sacrifice to any god except the LORD. [18]But may the LORD pardon your servant on one count: when my master goes into the house of Rimmon to worship there, leaning on my arm, and I bow down in the house of Rimmon, when I do bow down in the house of Rimmon, may the LORD pardon your servant on this one count." [19]He said to him, "Go in peace."

Gehazi's Greed

But when Naaman had gone from him a short distance, [20]Gehazi, the servant of Elisha the man of God, thought, "My master has let that Aramean Naaman off too lightly by not accepting from him what he offered. As the LORD lives, I will run after him and get something out of him." [21]So Gehazi went after Naaman. When Naaman saw someone running after him, he jumped down from the chariot to meet him and said, "Is everything all right?" [22]He replied, "Yes, but my master has sent me to say, 'Two members of a company of prophets[n] have just come to me from the hill country of Ephraim; please give them a talent of silver and two changes of clothing.' " [23]Naaman said, "Please accept two talents." He urged him, and tied up two talents of silver in two bags, with two changes of clothing, and gave them to two of his servants, who carried them in front of Gehazi.[o] [24]When he came to the citadel, he took the bags[p] from them, and stored them inside; he dismissed the men, and they left.

25 He went in and stood before his master; and Elisha said to him, "Where have you been, Gehazi?" He answered, "Your servant has not gone anywhere at all." [26]But he said to him, "Did I not go with you in spirit when someone left his chariot to meet you? Is this a time to accept money and to accept clothing, olive orchards and vineyards, sheep and oxen, and male and female slaves? [27]Therefore the leprosy[1] of Naaman shall cling to you, and to your descendants forever." So he left his presence leprous,[1] as white as snow.

---

[1] A term for several skin diseases; precise meaning uncertain   [m] Another reading is *Amana*
[n] Heb *sons of the prophets*   [o] Heb *him*   [p] Heb lacks *the bags*

WEEKEND

UNCONDITIONAL SURRENDER
Dwight L. Moody

VERSE: 2 Kings 5.15   **PASSAGE:** 2 Kings 5.1–15

 he history of Naaman in 2 Kings 5.15 shows what Naaman's faith led him to believe. "Then he returned to the man of God, he and all his company; he came and stood before him and said, 'Now I know that there is no God in all the earth except in Israel . . . ' " I want particularly to call your attention to the words "I know."

There is no hesitation about it, no qualifying the expression. Naaman doesn't now say, "I think"; no, he says, "I know there is a God who has power to forgive sins and to cleanse the leprosy."

Then there is another thought. Naaman left only one thing in Samaria, and that was his sin, his leprosy. The only thing God wishes you to leave with him is your sin; and yet it is the only thing you seem not to care about giving up . . .

How long did it take Naaman to be cured? The seventh time he went down, away went the leprosy! Read the great conversions recorded in the Bible—Saul of Tarsus, Zacchaeus, and a host of others; how long did it take the Lord to bring them about (see Acts 9.1–36; Luke 9.1–8)? They were effected in a minute. We are born in iniquity, shaped in it, dead in trespasses and sin; but when spiritual life comes it comes in a moment, and we are freed both from sin and death.

ADDITIONAL SCRIPTURE READING:
Isaiah 43.10–11; Daniel 6.26–27

Go to page 424 for your next devotional reading.

1900   Present

The Miracle of the Ax Head

6 Now the company of prophets[q] said to Elisha, "As you see, the place where we live under your charge is too small for us. ²Let us go to the Jordan, and let us collect logs there, one for each of us, and build a place there for us to live." He answered, "Do so." ³Then one of them said, "Please come with your servants." And he answered, "I will." ⁴So he went with them. When they came to the Jordan, they cut down trees. ⁵But as one was felling a log, his ax head fell into the water; he cried out, "Alas, master! It was borrowed." ⁶Then the man of God said, "Where did it fall?" When he showed him the place, he cut off a stick, and threw it in there, and made the iron float. ⁷He said, "Pick it up." So he reached out his hand and took it.

The Aramean Attack Is Thwarted

8 Once when the king of Aram was at war with Israel, he took counsel with his officers. He said, "At such and such a place shall be my camp." ⁹But the man of God sent word to the king of Israel, "Take care not to pass this place, because the Arameans are going down there." ¹⁰The king of Israel sent word to the place of which the man of God spoke. More than once or twice he warned such a place[r] so that it was on the alert.

11 The mind of the king of Aram was greatly perturbed because of this; he called his officers and said to them, "Now tell me who among us sides with the king of Israel?" ¹²Then one of his officers said, "No one, my lord king. It is Elisha, the prophet in Israel, who tells the king of Israel the words that you speak in your bedchamber." ¹³He said, "Go and find where he is; I will send and seize him." He was told, "He is in Dothan." ¹⁴So he sent horses and chariots there and a great army; they came by night, and surrounded the city.

15 When an attendant of the man of God rose early in the morning and went out, an army with horses and chariots was all around the city. His servant said, "Alas, master! What shall we do?" ¹⁶He

replied, "Do not be afraid, for there are more with us than there are with them." ¹⁷Then Elisha prayed: "O LORD, please open his eyes that he may see." So the LORD opened the eyes of the servant, and he saw; the mountain was full of horses and chariots of fire all around Elisha. ¹⁸When the Arameans[s] came down against him, Elisha prayed to the LORD, and said, "Strike this people, please, with blindness." So he struck them with blindness as Elisha had asked. ¹⁹Elisha said to them, "This is not the way, and this is not the city; follow me, and I will bring you to the man whom you seek." And he led them to Samaria.

20 As soon as they entered Samaria, Elisha said, "O LORD, open the eyes of these men so that they may see." The LORD opened their eyes, and they saw that they were inside Samaria. ²¹When the king of Israel saw them he said to Elisha, "Father, shall I kill them? Shall I kill them?" ²²He answered, "No! Did you capture with your sword and your bow those whom you want to kill? Set food and water before them so that they may eat and drink; and let them go to their master." ²³So he prepared for them a great feast; after they ate and drank, he sent them on their way, and they went to their master. And the Arameans no longer came raiding into the land of Israel.

Ben-hadad's Siege of Samaria

24 Some time later King Ben-hadad of Aram mustered his entire army; he marched against Samaria and laid siege to it. ²⁵As the siege continued, famine in Samaria became so great that a donkey's head was sold for eighty shekels of silver, and one-fourth of a kab of dove's dung for five shekels of silver. ²⁶Now as the king of Israel was walking on the city wall, a woman cried out to him, "Help, my lord king!" ²⁷He said, "No! Let the LORD help you. How can I help you? From the threshing floor or from the wine press?" ²⁸But then the king asked her, "What is your complaint?" She answered, "This woman said to me, 'Give up your son; we will eat him today, and we will eat my son tomor-

q Heb sons of the prophets   r Heb warned it   s Heb they

row.' ²⁹So we cooked my son and ate him. The next day I said to her, 'Give up your son and we will eat him.' But she has hidden her son." ³⁰When the king heard the words of the woman he tore his clothes—now since he was walking on the city wall, the people could see that he had sackcloth on his body underneath— ³¹and he said, "So may God do to me, and more, if the head of Elisha son of Shaphat stays on his shoulders today." ³²So he dispatched a man from his presence.

Now Elisha was sitting in his house, and the elders were sitting with him. Before the messenger arrived, Elisha said to the elders, "Are you aware that this murderer has sent someone to take off my head? When the messenger comes, see that you shut the door and hold it closed against him. Is not the sound of his master's feet behind him?" ³³While he was still speaking with them, the king*t* came down to him and said, "This trouble is from the LORD! Why should I hope in the LORD any longer?" **7** ¹But Elisha said, "Hear the word of the LORD: thus says the LORD, Tomorrow about this time a measure of choice meal shall be sold for a shekel, and two measures of barley for a shekel, at the gate of Samaria." ²Then the captain on whose hand the king leaned said to the man of God, "Even if the LORD were to make windows in the sky, could such a thing happen?" But he said, "You shall see it with your own eyes, but you shall not eat from it."

The Arameans Flee

3 Now there were four leprous*u* men outside the city gate, who said to one another, "Why should we sit here until we die? ⁴If we say, 'Let us enter the city,' the famine is in the city, and we shall die there; but if we sit here, we shall also die. Therefore, let us desert to the Aramean camp; if they spare our lives, we shall live; and if they kill us, we shall but die." ⁵So they arose at twilight to go to the Aramean camp; but when they came to the edge of the Aramean camp, there was no one there at all. ⁶For the Lord had caused the Aramean army to hear the sound of chariots, and of horses, the sound of a great army, so that they said to one another, "The king of Israel has hired the kings of the Hittites and the kings of Egypt to fight against us." ⁷So they fled away in the twilight and abandoned their tents, their horses, and their donkeys leaving the camp just as it was, and fled for their lives. ⁸When these leprous*u* men had come to the edge of the camp, they went into a tent, ate and drank, carried off silver, gold, and clothing, and went and hid them. Then they came back, entered another tent, carried off things from it, and went and hid them.

9 Then they said to one another, "What we are doing is wrong. This is a day of good news; if we are silent and wait until the morning light, we will be found guilty; therefore let us go and tell the king's household." ¹⁰So they came and called to the gatekeepers of the city, and told them, "We went to the Aramean camp, but there was no one to be seen or heard there, nothing but the horses tied, the donkeys tied, and the tents as they were." ¹¹Then the gatekeepers called out and proclaimed it to the king's household. ¹²The king got up in the night, and said to his servants, "I will tell you what the Arameans have prepared against us. They know that we are starving; so they have left the camp to hide themselves in the open country, thinking, 'When they come out of the city, we shall take them alive and get into the city.' " ¹³One of his servants said, "Let some men take five of the remaining horses, since those left here will suffer the fate of the whole multitude of Israel that have perished already;*v* let us send and find out." ¹⁴So they took two mounted men, and the king sent them after the Aramean army, saying, "Go and find out." ¹⁵So they went after them as far as the Jordan; the whole way was littered with garments and equipment that the Arameans had thrown away in their haste. So the messengers returned, and told the king.

16 Then the people went out, and plundered the camp of the Arameans. So a measure of choice meal was sold for a

---

t See 7.2: Heb *messenger*   *u* A term for several skin diseases; precise meaning uncertain
v Compare Gk Syr Vg: Meaning of Heb uncertain

shekel, and two measures of barley for a shekel, according to the word of the LORD. 17Now the king had appointed the captain on whose hand he leaned to have charge of the gate; the people trampled him to death in the gate, just as the man of God had said when the king came down to him. 18For when the man of God had said to the king, "Two measures of barley shall be sold for a shekel, and a measure of choice meal for a shekel, about this time tomorrow in the gate of Samaria," 19the captain had answered the man of God, "Even if the LORD were to make windows in the sky, could such a thing happen?" And he had answered, "You shall see it with your own eyes, but you shall not eat from it." 20It did indeed happen to him; the people trampled him to death in the gate.

The Shunammite Woman's Land Restored

8 Now Elisha had said to the woman whose son he had restored to life, "Get up and go with your household, and settle wherever you can; for the LORD has called for a famine, and it will come on the land for seven years." 2So the woman got up and did according to the word of the man of God; she went with her household and settled in the land of the Philistines seven years. 3At the end of the seven years, when the woman returned from the land of the Philistines, she set out to appeal to the king for her house and her land. 4Now the king was talking with Gehazi the servant of the man of God, saying, "Tell me all the great things that Elisha has done." 5While he was telling the king how Elisha had restored a dead person to life, the woman whose son he had restored to life appealed to the king for her house and her land. Gehazi said, "My lord king, here is the woman, and here is her son whom Elisha restored to life." 6When the king questioned the woman, she told him. So the king appointed an official for her, saying, "Restore all that was hers, together with all the revenue of the fields from the day that she left the land until now."

Death of Ben-hadad

7 Elisha went to Damascus while King Ben-hadad of Aram was ill. When it was told him, "The man of God has come here," 8the king said to Hazael, "Take a present with you and go to meet the man of God. Inquire of the LORD through him, whether I shall recover from this illness." 9So Hazael went to meet him, taking a present with him, all kinds of goods of Damascus, forty camel loads. When he entered and stood before him, he said, "Your son King Ben-hadad of Aram has sent me to you, saying, 'Shall I recover from this illness?' " 10Elisha said to him, "Go, say to him, 'You shall certainly recover'; but the LORD has shown me that he shall certainly die." 11He fixed his gaze and stared at him, until he was ashamed. Then the man of God wept. 12Hazael asked, "Why does my lord weep?" He answered, "Because I know the evil that you will do to the people of Israel; you will set their fortresses on fire, you will kill their young men with the sword, dash in pieces their little ones, and rip up their pregnant women." 13Hazael said, "What is your servant, who is a mere dog, that he should do this great thing?" Elisha answered, "The LORD has shown me that you are to be king over Aram." 14Then he left Elisha, and went to his master Ben-hadad,w who said to him, "What did Elisha say to you?" And he answered, "He told me that you would certainly recover." 15But the next day he took the bed-cover and dipped it in water and spread it over the king's face, until he died. And Hazael succeeded him.

Jehoram Reigns over Judah

16 In the fifth year of King Joram son of Ahab of Israel,x Jehoram son of King Jehoshaphat of Judah began to reign. 17He was thirty-two years old when he became king, and he reigned eight years in Jerusalem. 18He walked in the way of the kings of Israel, as the house of Ahab had done, for the daughter of Ahab was his wife. He did what was evil in the sight of the LORD. 19Yet the LORD would not destroy Judah, for the sake of his ser-

w Heb lacks Ben-hadad   x Gk Syr: Heb adds Jehoshaphat being king of Judah, vant David, since he had promised to give a lamp to him and to his descendants forever.

20 In his days Edom revolted against the rule of Judah, and set up a king of their own. 21 Then Joram crossed over to Zair with all his chariots. He set out by night and attacked the Edomites and their chariot commanders who had surrounded him;y but his army fled home. 22 So Edom has been in revolt against the rule of Judah to this day. Libnah also revolted at the same time. 23 Now the rest of the acts of Joram, and all that he did, are they not written in the Book of the Annals of the Kings of Judah? 24 So Joram slept with his ancestors, and was buried with them in the city of David; his son Ahaziah succeeded him.

Ahaziah Reigns over Judah

25 In the twelfth year of King Joram son of Ahab of Israel, Ahaziah son of King Jehoram of Judah began to reign. 26 Ahaziah was twenty-two years old when he began to reign; he reigned one year in Jerusalem. His mother's name was Athaliah, a granddaughter of King Omri of Israel. 27 He also walked in the way of the house of Ahab, doing what was evil in the sight of the LORD, as the house of Ahab had done, for he was son-in-law to the house of Ahab.

28 He went with Joram son of Ahab to wage war against King Hazael of Aram at Ramoth-gilead, where the Arameans wounded Joram. 29 King Joram returned to be healed in Jezreel of the wounds that the Arameans had inflicted on him at Ramah, when he fought against King Hazael of Aram. King Ahaziah son of Jehoram of Judah went down to see Joram son of Ahab in Jezreel, because he was wounded.

Anointing of Jehu

9 Then the prophet Elisha called a member of the company of prophetsz and said to him, "Gird up your loins; take this flask of oil in your hand, and go to Ramoth-gilead. 2 When you arrive, look there for Jehu son of Jehoshaphat, son of Nimshi; go in and get him to leave his companions, and take him into an inner chamber. 3 Then

take the flask of oil, pour it on his head, and say, 'Thus says the LORD: I anoint you king over Israel.' Then open the door and flee; do not linger."

4 So the young man, the young prophet, went to Ramoth-gilead. 5 He arrived while the commanders of the army were in council, and he announced, "I have a message for you, commander." "For which one of us?" asked Jehu. "For you, commander." 6 So Jehua got up and went inside; the young man poured the oil on his head, saying to him, "Thus says the LORD the God of Israel: I anoint you king over the people of the LORD, over Israel. 7 You shall strike down the house of your master Ahab, so that I may avenge on Jezebel the blood of my servants the prophets, and the blood of all the servants of the LORD. 8 For the whole house of Ahab shall perish; I will cut off from Ahab every male, bond or free, in Israel. 9 I will make the house of Ahab like the house of Jeroboam son of Nebat, and like the house of Baasha son of Ahijah. 10 The dogs shall eat Jezebel in the territory of Jezreel, and no one shall bury her." Then he opened the door and fled.

11 When Jehu came back to his master's officers, they said to him, "Is everything all right? Why did that madman come to you?" He answered them, "You know the sort and how they babble." 12 They said, "Liar! Come on, tell us!" So he said, "This is just what he said to me: 'Thus says the LORD, I anoint you king over Israel.' " 13 Then hurriedly they all took their cloaks and spread them for him on the barey steps; and they blew the trumpet, and proclaimed, "Jehu is king."

Joram of Israel Killed

14 Thus Jehu son of Jehoshaphat son of Nimshi conspired against Joram. Joram with all Israel had been on guard at Ramoth-gilead against King Hazael of Aram; 15 but King Joram had returned to be healed in Jezreel of the wounds that the Arameans had inflicted on him, when he fought against King Hazael of Aram. So Jehu said, "If this is your wish, then let no one slip out of the city to go and tell the news in Jezreel." 16 Then

y Meaning of Heb uncertain   z Heb sons of the prophets   a Heb he

Jehu mounted his chariot and went to Jezreel, where Joram was lying ill. King Ahaziah of Judah had come down to visit Joram.

17 In Jezreel, the sentinel standing on the tower spied the company of Jehu arriving, and said, "I see a company." Joram said, "Take a horseman; send him to meet them, and let him say, 'Is it peace?' " 18So the horseman went to meet him; he said, "Thus says the king, 'Is it peace?' " Jehu responded, "What have you to do with peace? Fall in behind me." The sentinel reported, saying, "The messenger reached them, but he is not coming back." 19Then he sent out a second horseman, who came to them and said, "Thus says the king, 'Is it peace?' " Jehu answered, "What have you to do with peace? Fall in behind me." 20Again the sentinel reported, "He reached them, but he is not coming back. It looks like the driving of Jehu son of Nimshi; for he drives like a maniac."

21 Joram said, "Get ready." And they got his chariot ready. Then King Joram of Israel and King Ahaziah of Judah set out, each in his chariot, and went to meet Jehu; they met him at the property of Naboth the Jezreelite. 22When Joram saw Jehu, he said, "Is it peace, Jehu?" He answered, "What peace can there be, so long as the many whoredoms and sorceries of your mother Jezebel continue?" 23Then Joram reined about and fled, saying to Ahaziah, "Treason, Ahaziah!" 24Jehu drew his bow with all his strength, and shot Joram between the shoulders, so that the arrow pierced his heart; and he sank in his chariot. 25Jehu said to his aide Bidkar, "Lift him out, and throw him on the plot of ground belonging to Naboth the Jezreelite; for remember, when you and I rode side by side behind his father Ahab how the LORD uttered this oracle against him: 26'For the blood of Naboth and for the blood of his children that I saw yesterday, says the LORD, I swear I will repay you on this very plot of ground.' Now therefore lift him out and throw him on the plot of ground, in accordance with the word of the LORD."

Ahaziah of Judah Killed

27 When King Ahaziah of Judah saw this, he fled in the direction of Beth-haggan. Jehu pursued him, saying, "Shoot him also!" And they shot him b in the chariot at the ascent to Gur, which is by Ibleam. Then he fled to Megiddo, and died there. 28His officers carried him in a chariot to Jerusalem, and buried him in his tomb with his ancestors in the city of David.

29 In the eleventh year of Joram son of Ahab, Ahaziah began to reign over Judah.

Jezebel's Violent Death

30 When Jehu came to Jezreel, Jezebel heard of it; she painted her eyes, and adorned her head, and looked out of the window. 31As Jehu entered the gate, she said, "Is it peace, Zimri, murderer of your master?" 32He looked up to the window and said, "Who is on my side? Who?" Two or three eunuchs looked out at him. 33He said, "Throw her down." So they threw her down; some of her blood spattered on the wall and on the horses, which trampled on her. 34Then he went in and ate and drank; he said, "See to that cursed woman and bury her; for she is a king's daughter." 35But when they went to bury her, they found no more of her than the skull and the feet and the palms of her hands. 36When they came back and told him, he said, "This is the word of the LORD, which he spoke by his servant Elijah the Tishbite, 'In the territory of Jezreel the dogs shall eat the flesh of Jezebel; 37the corpse of Jezebel shall be like dung on the field in the territory of Jezreel, so that no one can say, This is Jezebel.' "

Massacre of Ahab's Descendants

10 Now Ahab had seventy sons in Samaria. So Jehu wrote letters and sent them to Samaria, to the rulers of Jezreel,c to the elders, and to the guardians of the sons ofd Ahab, saying, 2"Since your master's sons are with you and you have at your disposal chariots and horses, a fortified city, and weapons, 3select the son of your master who is the best qualified, set him on his

b Syr Vg Compare Gk: Heb lacks and they shot him lacks of the sons of   c Or of the city; Vg Compare Gk   d Gk: Heb father's throne, and fight for your master's house." 4But they were utterly terrified and said, "Look, two kings could not withstand him; how then can we stand?" 5So the steward of the palace, and the governor of the city, along with the elders and the guardians, sent word to Jehu: "We are your servants; we will do anything you say. We will not make anyone king; do whatever you think right." 6Then he wrote them a second letter, saying, "If you are on my side, and if you are ready to obey me, take the heads of your master's sons and come to me at Jezreel tomorrow at this time." Now the king's sons, seventy persons, were with the leaders of the city, who were charged with their upbringing. 7When the letter reached them, they took the king's sons and killed them, seventy persons; they put their heads in baskets and sent them to him at Jezreel. 8When the messenger came and told him, "They have brought the heads of the king's sons," he said, "Lay them in two heaps at the entrance of the gate until the morning." 9Then in the morning when he went out, he stood and said to all the people, "You are innocent. It was I who conspired against my master and killed him; but who struck down all these? 10Know then that there shall fall to the earth nothing of the word of the LORD, which the LORD spoke concerning the house of Ahab; for the LORD has done what he said through his servant Elijah." 11So Jehu killed all who were left of the house of Ahab in Jezreel, all his leaders, close friends, and priests, until he left him no survivor.

12 Then he set out and went to Samaria. On the way, when he was at Beth-eked of the Shepherds, 13Jehu met relatives of King Ahaziah of Judah and said, "Who are you?" They answered, "We are kin of Ahaziah; we have come down to visit the royal princes and the sons of the queen mother." 14He said, "Take them alive." They took them alive, and slaughtered them at the pit of Beth-eked, forty-two in all; he spared none of them.

15 When he left there, he met Jehonadab son of Rechab coming to meet him; he greeted him, and said to him, "Is your heart as true to mine as mine is to yours?"e Jehonadab answered, "It is." Jehu said,f "If it is, give me your hand." So he gave him his hand. Jehu took him up with him into the chariot. 16He said, "Come with me, and see my zeal for the LORD." So heg had him ride in his chariot. 17When he came to Samaria, he killed all who were left to Ahab in Samaria, until he had wiped them out, according to the word of the LORD that he spoke to Elijah.

Slaughter of Worshipers of Baal

18 Then Jehu assembled all the people and said to them, "Ahab offered Baal small service; but Jehu will offer much more. 19Now therefore summon to me all the prophets of Baal, all his worshipers, and all his priests; let none be missing, for I have a great sacrifice to offer to Baal; whoever is missing shall not live." But Jehu was acting with cunning in order to destroy the worshipers of Baal. 20Jehu decreed, "Sanctify a solemn assembly for Baal." So they proclaimed it. 21Jehu sent word throughout all Israel; all the worshipers of Baal came, so that there was no one left who did not come. They entered the temple of Baal, until the temple of Baal was filled from wall to wall. 22He said to the keeper of the wardrobe, "Bring out the vestments for all the worshipers of Baal." So he brought out the vestments for them. 23Then Jehu entered the temple of Baal with Jehonadab son of Rechab; he said to the worshipers of Baal, "Search and see that there is no worshiper of the LORD here among you, but only worshipers of Baal." 24Then they proceeded to offer sacrifices and burnt offerings.

Now Jehu had stationed eighty men outside, saying, "Whoever allows any of those to escape whom I deliver into your hands shall forfeit his life." 25As soon as he had finished presenting the burnt offering, Jehu said to the guards and to the officers, "Come in and kill them; let no one escape." So they put them to the sword. The guards and the officers threw them out, and then went into the citadel

---

e Gk: Heb *Is it right with your heart, as my heart is with your heart?*   f Gk: Heb lacks *Jehu said*
g Gk Syr Tg: Heb *they*

of the temple of Baal. 26They brought out the pillar*h* that was in the temple of Baal, and burned it. 27Then they demolished the pillar of Baal, and destroyed the temple of Baal, and made it a latrine to this day.

28 Thus Jehu wiped out Baal from Israel. 29But Jehu did not turn aside from the sins of Jeroboam son of Nebat, which he caused Israel to commit—the golden calves that were in Bethel and in Dan. 30The LORD said to Jehu, "Because you have done well in carrying out what I consider right, and in accordance with all that was in my heart have dealt with the house of Ahab, your sons of the fourth generation shall sit on the throne of Israel." 31But Jehu was not careful to follow the law of the LORD the God of Israel with all his heart; he did not turn from the sins of Jeroboam, which he caused Israel to commit.

Death of Jehu

32 In those days the LORD began to trim off parts of Israel. Hazael defeated them throughout the territory of Israel: 33from the Jordan eastward, all the land of Gilead, the Gadites, the Reubenites, and the Manassites, from Aroer, which is by the Wadi Arnon, that is, Gilead and Bashan. 34Now the rest of the acts of Jehu, all that he did, and all his power, are they not written in the Book of the Annals of the Kings of Israel? 35So Jehu slept with his ancestors, and they buried him in Samaria. His son Jehoahaz succeeded him. 36The time that Jehu reigned over Israel in Samaria was twenty-eight years.

Athaliah Reigns over Judah

11 Now when Athaliah, Ahaziah's mother, saw that her son was dead, she set about to destroy all the royal family. 2But Jehosheba, King Joram's daughter, Ahaziah's sister, took Joash son of Ahaziah, and stole him away from among the king's children who were about to be killed; she put*i* him and his nurse in a bedroom. Thus she*j* hid him from Athaliah, so that he was not killed; 3he remained with her six years, hidden in the house of the

LORD, while Athaliah reigned over the land.

Jehoiada Anoints the Child Joash

4 But in the seventh year Jehoiada summoned the captains of the Carites and of the guards and had them come to him in the house of the LORD. He made a covenant with them and put them under oath in the house of the LORD; then he showed them the king's son. 5He commanded them, "This is what you are to do: one-third of you, those who go off duty on the sabbath and guard the king's house 6(another third being at the gate Sur and a third at the gate behind the guards), shall guard the palace; 7and your two divisions that come on duty in force on the sabbath and guard the house of the LORD*k* 8shall surround the king, each with weapons in hand; and whoever approaches the ranks is to be killed. Be with the king in his comings and goings."

9 The captains did according to all that the priest Jehoiada commanded; each brought his men who were to go off duty on the sabbath, with those who were to come on duty on the sabbath, and came to the priest Jehoiada. 10The priest delivered to the captains the spears and shields that had been King David's, which were in the house of the LORD; 11the guards stood, every man with his weapons in his hand, from the south side of the house to the north side of the house, around the altar and the house, to guard the king on every side. 12Then he brought out the king's son, put the crown on him, and gave him the covenant;*l* they proclaimed him king, and anointed him; they clapped their hands and shouted, "Long live the king!"

Death of Athaliah

13 When Athaliah heard the noise of the guard and of the people, she went into the house of the LORD to the people; 14when she looked, there was the king standing by the pillar, according to custom, with the captains and the trumpeters beside the king, and all the people of the land rejoicing and blowing trum-

---

h Gk Vg Syr Tg: Heb *pillars*   *i* With 2 Chr 22.11: Heb lacks *she put*   *j* Gk Syr Vg Compare 2 Chr 22.11: Heb *they*   *k* Heb *the LORD to the king*   *l* Or *treaty* or *testimony*; Heb *eduth*

pets. Athaliah tore her clothes and cried, "Treason! Treason!" 15Then the priest Jehoiada commanded the captains who were set over the army, "Bring her out between the ranks, and kill with the sword anyone who follows her." For the priest said, "Let her not be killed in the house of the LORD." 16So they laid hands on her; she went through the horses' entrance to the king's house, and there she was put to death.

17 Jehoiada made a covenant between the LORD and the king and people, that they should be the LORD's people; also between the king and the people. 18Then all the people of the land went to the house of Baal, and tore it down; his altars and his images they broke in pieces, and they killed Mattan, the priest of Baal, before the altars. The priest posted guards over the house of the LORD. 19He took the captains, the Carites, the guards, and all the people of the land; then they brought the king down from the house of the LORD, marching through the gate of the guards to the king's house. He took his seat on the throne of the kings. 20So all the people of the land rejoiced; and the city was quiet after Athaliah had been killed with the sword at the king's house.

21mJehoashn was seven years old when he began to reign.

The Temple Repaired

12 In the seventh year of Jehu, Jehoash began to reign; he reigned forty years in Jerusalem. His mother's name was Zibiah of Beersheba. 2Jehoash did what was right in the sight of the LORD all his days, because the priest Jehoiada instructed him. 3Nevertheless the high places were not taken away; the people continued to sacrifice and make offerings on the high places.

4 Jehoash said to the priests, "All the money offered as sacred donations that is brought into the house of the LORD, the money for which each person is assessed—the money from the assessment of persons—and the money from the voluntary offerings brought into the house of the LORD, 5let the priests receive from each of the donors; and let

them repair the house wherever any need of repairs is discovered." 6But by the twenty-third year of King Jehoash the priests had made no repairs on the house. 7Therefore King Jehoash summoned the priest Jehoiada with the other priests and said to them, "Why are you not repairing the house? Now therefore do not accept any more money from your donors but hand it over for the repair of the house." 8So the priests agreed that they would neither accept more money from the people nor repair the house.

9 Then the priest Jehoiada took a chest, made a hole in its lid, and set it beside the altar on the right side as one entered the house of the LORD; the priests who guarded the threshold put in it all the money that was brought into the house of the LORD. 10Whenever they saw that there was a great deal of money in the chest, the king's secretary and the high priest went up, counted the money that was found in the house of the LORD, and tied it up in bags. 11They would give the money that was weighed out into the hands of the workers who had the oversight of the house of the LORD; then they paid it out to the carpenters and the builders who worked on the house of the LORD, 12to the masons and the stonecutters, as well as to buy timber and quarried stone for making repairs on the house of the LORD, as well as for any outlay for repairs of the house. 13But for the house of the LORD no basins of silver, snuffers, bowls, trumpets, or any vessels of gold, or of silver, were made from the money that was brought into the house of the LORD, 14for that was given to the workers who were repairing the house of the LORD with it. 15They did not ask an accounting from those into whose hand they delivered the money to pay out to the workers, for they dealt honestly. 16The money from the guilt offerings and the money from the sin offerings was not brought into the house of the LORD; it belonged to the priests.

Hazael Threatens Jerusalem

17 At that time King Hazael of Aram went up, fought against Gath, and took it. But when Hazael set his face to go up

m Ch 12.1 in Heb   n Another spelling is Joash; see verse 19 against Jerusalem, 18King Jehoash of Judah took all the votive gifts that Jehoshaphat, Jehoram, and Ahaziah, his ancestors, the kings of Judah, had dedicated, as well as his own votive gifts, all the gold that was found in the treasuries of the house of the LORD and of the king's house, and sent these to King Hazael of Aram. Then Hazael withdrew from Jerusalem.

Death of Joash

19 Now the rest of the acts of Joash, and all that he did, are they not written in the Book of the Annals of the Kings of Judah? 20His servants arose, devised a conspiracy, and killed Joash in the house of Millo, on the way that goes down to Silla. 21It was Jozacar son of Shimeath and Jehozabad son of Shomer, his servants, who struck him down, so that he died. He was buried with his ancestors in the city of David; then his son Amaziah succeeded him.

Jehoahaz Reigns over Israel

13 In the twenty-third year of King Joash son of Ahaziah of Judah, Jehoahaz son of Jehu began to reign over Israel in Samaria; he reigned seventeen years. 2He did what was evil in the sight of the LORD, and followed the sins of Jeroboam son of Nebat, which he caused Israel to sin; he did not depart from them. 3The anger of the LORD was kindled against Israel, so that he gave them repeatedly into the hand of King Hazael of Aram, then into the hand of Ben-hadad son of Hazael. 4But Jehoahaz entreated the LORD, and the LORD heeded him; for he saw the oppression of Israel, how the king of Aram oppressed them. 5Therefore the LORD gave Israel a savior, so that they escaped from the hand of the Arameans; and the people of Israel lived in their homes as formerly. 6Nevertheless they did not depart from the sins of the house of Jeroboam, which he caused Israel to sin, but walkedo in them; the sacred polep also remained in Samaria. 7So Jehoahaz was left with an army of not more than fifty horsemen, ten chariots and ten thousand footmen; for the king of Aram had destroyed them and made them like the dust at thresh-

ing. 8Now the rest of the acts of Jehoahaz and all that he did, including his might, are they not written in the Book of the Annals of the Kings of Israel? 9So Jehoahaz slept with his ancestors, and they buried him in Samaria; then his son Joash succeeded him.

Jehoash Reigns over Israel

10 In the thirty-seventh year of King Joash of Judah, Jehoash son of Jehoahaz began to reign over Israel in Samaria; he reigned sixteen years. 11He also did what was evil in the sight of the LORD; he did not depart from all the sins of Jeroboam son of Nebat, which he caused Israel to sin, but he walked in them. 12Now the rest of the acts of Joash, and all that he did, as well as the might with which he fought against King Amaziah of Judah, are they not written in the Book of the Annals of the Kings of Israel? 13So Joash slept with his ancestors, and Jeroboam sat upon his throne; Joash was buried in Samaria with the kings of Israel.

Death of Elisha

14 Now when Elisha had fallen sick with the illness of which he was to die, King Joash of Israel went down to him, and wept before him, crying, "My father, my father! The chariots of Israel and its horsemen!" 15Elisha said to him, "Take a bow and arrows"; so he took a bow and arrows. 16Then he said to the king of Israel, "Draw the bow"; and he drew it. Elisha laid his hands on the king's hands. 17Then he said, "Open the window eastward"; and he opened it. Elisha said, "Shoot"; and he shot. Then he said, "The LORD's arrow of victory, the arrow of victory over Aram! For you shall fight the Arameans in Aphek until you have made an end of them." 18He continued, "Take the arrows"; and he took them. He said to the king of Israel, "Strike the ground with them"; he struck three times, and stopped. 19Then the man of God was angry with him, and said, "You should have struck five or six times; then you would have struck down Aram until you had made an end of it, but now you will strike down Aram only three times."

20 So Elisha died, and they buried

o Gk Syr Tg Vg: Heb *he walked*   p Heb *Asherah*

him. Now bands of Moabites used to invade the land in the spring of the year. 21As a man was being buried, a marauding band was seen and the man was thrown into the grave of Elisha; as soon as the man touched the bones of Elisha, he came to life and stood on his feet.

Israel Recaptures Cities from Aram

22 Now King Hazael of Aram oppressed Israel all the days of Jehoahaz. 23But the LORD was gracious to them and had compassion on them; he turned toward them, because of his covenant with Abraham, Isaac, and Jacob, and would not destroy them; nor has he banished them from his presence until now.

THE DEW OF COMPASSION IS A TEAR.

—*Lord George Gordon Noel Byron*

---

24 When King Hazael of Aram died, his son Ben-hadad succeeded him. 25Then Jehoash son of Jehoahaz took again from Ben-hadad son of Hazael the towns that he had taken from his father Jehoahaz in war. Three times Joash defeated him and recovered the towns of Israel.

Amaziah Reigns over Judah

14 In the second year of King Joash son of Joahaz of Israel, King Amaziah son of Joash of Judah, began to reign. 2He was twenty-five years old when he began to reign, and he reigned twenty-nine years in Jerusalem. His mother's name was Jehoaddin of Jerusalem. 3He did what was right in the sight of the LORD, yet not like his ancestor David; in all things he did as his father Joash had done. 4But the high places were not removed; the people still sacrificed and made offerings on the high places. 5As soon as the royal power was firmly in his hand he killed his servants who had murdered his father the king. 6But he did not put to death the children of the murderers; according to what is written in the book of the law of Moses, where the LORD commanded, "The parents shall not be put to death for the children, or the children be put to death for the parents; but all shall be put to death for their own sins."

7 He killed ten thousand Edomites in the Valley of Salt and took Sela by storm; he called it Jokthe-el, which is its name to this day.

8 Then Amaziah sent messengers to King Jehoash son of Jehoahaz, son of Jehu, of Israel, saying, "Come, let us look one another in the face." 9King Jehoash of Israel sent word to King Amaziah of Judah, "A thornbush on Lebanon sent to a cedar on Lebanon, saying, 'Give your daughter to my son for a wife'; but a wild animal of Lebanon passed by and trampled down the thornbush. 10You have indeed defeated Edom, and your heart has lifted you up. Be content with your glory, and stay at home; for why should you provoke trouble so that you fall, you and Judah with you?"

11 But Amaziah would not listen. So King Jehoash of Israel went up; he and King Amaziah of Judah faced one another in battle at Beth-shemesh, which belongs to Judah. 12Judah was defeated by Israel; everyone fled home. 13King Jehoash of Israel captured King Amaziah of Judah son of Jehoash, son of Ahaziah, at Beth-shemesh; he came to Jerusalem, and broke down the wall of Jerusalem from the Ephraim Gate to the Corner Gate, a distance of four hundred cubits. 14He seized all the gold and silver, and all the vessels that were found in the house of the LORD and in the treasuries of the king's house, as well as hostages; then he returned to Samaria.

15 Now the rest of the acts that Jehoash did, his might, and how he fought with King Amaziah of Judah, are they not written in the Book of the Annals of the Kings of Israel? 16Jehoash slept with his ancestors, and was buried in Samaria with the kings of Israel; then his son Jeroboam succeeded him.

17 King Amaziah son of Joash of Judah lived fifteen years after the death of King Jehoash son of Jehoahaz of Israel. 18Now the rest of the deeds of Amaziah, are they not written in the Book of the Annals of the Kings of Judah? 19They made a conspiracy against him in Jerusalem, and he fled to Lachish. But they sent after him to Lachish, and killed him there. 20They brought him on horses; he was buried in Jerusalem with his ancestors in the city of David. 21All

the people of Judah took Azariah, who was sixteen years old, and made him king to succeed his father Amaziah. 22He rebuilt Elath and restored it to Judah, after King Amaziah*q* slept with his ancestors.

Jeroboam II Reigns over Israel

23 In the fifteenth year of King Amaziah son of Joash of Judah, King Jeroboam son of Joash of Israel began to reign in Samaria; he reigned forty-one years. 24He did what was evil in the sight of the LORD; he did not depart from all the sins of Jeroboam son of Nebat, which he caused Israel to sin. 25He restored the border of Israel from Lebo-hamath as far as the Sea of the Arabah, according to the word of the LORD, the God of Israel, which he spoke by his servant Jonah son of Amittai, the prophet, who was from Gath-hepher. 26For the LORD saw that the distress of Israel was very bitter; there was no one left, bond or free, and no one to help Israel. 27But the LORD had not said that he would blot out the name of Israel from under heaven, so he

q Heb *the king*

MONDAY

COMPLETE OBEDIENCE
Charles G. Finney

VERSE: 2 Kings 14.4   **PASSAGE:** 2 Kings 14.1–7

 hosoever keeps the whole law yet offends at one point is guilty of all (see James 2.10). He is rightly subject to the whole penalty. If he habitually disobeys God in one thing, then he doesn't obey him in anything, because obedience to God consists in an attitude of the heart. It is willingness to obey God, to let him rule everything. So if a person habitually disobeys God in one thing, his state of heart renders obedience in anything else impossible, because a person can't in one area obey God out of respect for his authority while in another area refuse obedience.

Obedience to God is an obedient state of heart, a preference for God's authority and commandments over everything else. If a person therefore appears to obey in some areas yet he knowingly disobeys in others, he is deceived. He offends in one point, and this proves he is guilty of all; in other words, he doesn't obey from the heart at all . . . If a person refuses to obey God's law, even a single duty, he . . . has no true faith, and his outwardly spiritual acts are loathsome.

ADDITIONAL SCRIPTURE READING:
2 Chronicles 25.1–2; Zechariah 1.4–6

Go to page 429 for your next devotional reading.

1700   1900

saved them by the hand of Jeroboam son of Joash.

28 Now the rest of the acts of Jeroboam, and all that he did, and his might, how he fought, and how he recovered for Israel Damascus and Hamath, which had belonged to Judah, are they not written in the Book of the Annals of the Kings of Israel? 29Jeroboam slept with his ancestors, the kings of Israel; his son Zechariah succeeded him.

Azariah Reigns over Judah

15 In the twenty-seventh year of King Jeroboam of Israel King Azariah son of Amaziah of Judah began to reign. 2He was sixteen years old when he began to reign, and he reigned fifty-two years in Jerusalem. His mother's name was Jecoliah of Jerusalem. 3He did what was right in the sight of the LORD, just as his father Amaziah had done. 4Nevertheless the high places were not taken away; the people still sacrificed and made offerings on the high places. 5The LORD struck the king, so that he was leprous[r] to the day of his death, and lived in a separate house. Jotham the king's son was in charge of the palace, governing the people of the land. 6Now the rest of the acts of Azariah, and all that he did, are they not written in the Book of the Annals of the Kings of Judah? 7Azariah slept with his ancestors; they buried him with his ancestors in the city of David; his son Jotham succeeded him.

Zechariah Reigns over Israel

8 In the thirty-eighth year of King Azariah of Judah, Zechariah son of Jeroboam reigned over Israel in Samaria six months. 9He did what was evil in the sight of the LORD, as his ancestors had done. He did not depart from the sins of Jeroboam son of Nebat, which he caused Israel to sin. 10Shallum son of Jabesh conspired against him, and struck him down in public and killed him, and reigned in place of him. 11Now the rest of the deeds of Zechariah are written in the Book of the Annals of the Kings of Israel. 12This was the promise of the LORD that he gave to Jehu, "Your sons

shall sit on the throne of Israel to the fourth generation." And so it happened.

Shallum Reigns over Israel

13 Shallum son of Jabesh began to reign in the thirty-ninth year of King Uzziah of Judah; he reigned one month in Samaria. 14Then Menahem son of Gadi came up from Tirzah and came to Samaria; he struck down Shallum son of Jabesh in Samaria and killed him; he reigned in place of him. 15Now the rest of the deeds of Shallum, including the conspiracy that he made, are written in the Book of the Annals of the Kings of Israel. 16At that time Menahem sacked Tiphsah, all who were in it and its territory from Tirzah on; because they did not open it to him, he sacked it. He ripped open all the pregnant women in it.

Menahem Reigns over Israel

17 In the thirty-ninth year of King Azariah of Judah, Menahem son of Gadi began to reign over Israel; he reigned ten years in Samaria. 18He did what was evil in the sight of the LORD; he did not depart all his days from any of the sins of Jeroboam son of Nebat, which he caused Israel to sin. 19King Pul of Assyria came against the land; Menahem gave Pul a thousand talents of silver, so that he might help him confirm his hold on the royal power. 20Menahem exacted the money from Israel, that is, from all the wealthy, fifty shekels of silver from each one, to give to the king of Assyria. So the king of Assyria turned back, and did not stay there in the land. 21Now the rest of the deeds of Menahem, and all that he did, are they not written in the Book of the Annals of the Kings of Israel? 22Menahem slept with his ancestors, and his son Pekahiah succeeded him.

Pekahiah Reigns over Israel

23 In the fiftieth year of King Azariah of Judah, Pekahiah son of Menahem began to reign over Israel in Samaria; he reigned two years. 24He did what was evil in the sight of the LORD; he did not turn away from the sins of Jeroboam son of Nebat, which he caused Israel to sin. 25Pekah son of Remaliah, his captain,

---

r A term for several skin diseases; precise meaning uncertain

conspired against him with fifty of the Gileadites, and attacked him in Samaria, in the citadel of the palace along with Argob and Arieh; he killed him, and reigned in place of him. 26Now the rest of the deeds of Pekahiah, and all that he did, are written in the Book of the Annals of the Kings of Israel.

Pekah Reigns over Israel

27 In the fifty-second year of King Azariah of Judah, Pekah son of Remaliah began to reign over Israel in Samaria; he reigned twenty years. 28He did what was evil in the sight of the LORD; he did not depart from the sins of Jeroboam son of Nebat, which he caused Israel to sin. 29 In the days of King Pekah of Israel, King Tiglath-pileser of Assyria came and captured Ijon, Abel-beth-maacah, Janoah, Kedesh, Hazor, Gilead, and Galilee, all the land of Naphtali; and he carried the people captive to Assyria. 30Then Hoshea son of Elah made a conspiracy against Pekah son of Remaliah, attacked him, and killed him; he reigned in place of him, in the twentieth year of Jotham son of Uzziah. 31Now the rest of the acts of Pekah, and all that he did, are written in the Book of the Annals of the Kings of Israel.

Jotham Reigns over Judah

32 In the second year of King Pekah son of Remaliah of Israel, King Jotham son of Uzziah of Judah began to reign. 33He was twenty-five years old when he began to reign and reigned sixteen years in Jerusalem. His mother's name was Jerusha daughter of Zadok. 34He did what was right in the sight of the LORD, just as his father Uzziah had done. 35Nevertheless the high places were not removed; the people still sacrificed and made offerings on the high places. He built the upper gate of the house of the LORD. 36Now the rest of the acts of Jotham, and all that he did, are they not written in the Book of the Annals of the Kings of Judah? 37In those days the LORD began to send King Rezin of Aram and Pekah son of Remaliah against Judah. 38Jotham slept with his ancestors, and was buried with his ancestors in the city

of David, his ancestor; his son Ahaz succeeded him.

Ahaz Reigns over Judah

16 In the seventeenth year of Pekah son of Remaliah, King Ahaz son of Jotham of Judah began to reign. 2Ahaz was twenty years old when he began to reign; he reigned sixteen years in Jerusalem. He did not do what was right in the sight of the LORD his God, as his ancestor David had done, 3but he walked in the way of the kings of Israel. He even made his son pass through fire, according to the abominable practices of the nations whom the LORD drove out before the people of Israel. 4He sacrificed and made offerings on the high places, on the hills, and under every green tree.

5 Then King Rezin of Aram and King Pekah son of Remaliah of Israel came up to wage war on Jerusalem; they besieged Ahaz but could not conquer him. 6At that time the king of Edom[s] recovered Elath for Edom,[t] and drove the Judeans from Elath; and the Edomites came to Elath, where they live to this day. 7Ahaz sent messengers to King Tiglath-pileser of Assyria, saying, "I am your servant and your son. Come up, and rescue me from the hand of the king of Aram and from the hand of the king of Israel, who are attacking me." 8Ahaz also took the silver and gold found in the house of the LORD and in the treasures of the king's house, and sent a present to the king of Assyria. 9The king of Assyria listened to him; the king of Assyria marched up against Damascus, and took it, carrying its people captive to Kir; then he killed Rezin.

10 When King Ahaz went to Damascus to meet King Tiglath-pileser of Assyria, he saw the altar that was at Damascus. King Ahaz sent to the priest Uriah a model of the altar, and its pattern, exact in all its details. 11The priest Uriah built the altar; in accordance with all that King Ahaz had sent from Damascus, just so did the priest Uriah build it, before King Ahaz arrived from Damascus. 12When the king came from Damascus, the king viewed the altar. Then the king drew near to the altar,

_s_ Cn: Heb _King Rezin of Aram_   _t_ Cn: Heb _Aram_

went up on it, ¹³and offered his burnt offering and his grain offering, poured his drink offering, and dashed the blood of his offerings of well-being against the altar. ¹⁴The bronze altar that was before the LORD he removed from the front of the house, from the place between his altar and the house of the LORD, and put it on the north side of his altar. ¹⁵King Ahaz commanded the priest Uriah, saying, "Upon the great altar offer the morning burnt offering, and the evening grain offering, and the king's burnt offering, and his grain offering, with the burnt offering of all the people of the land, their grain offering, and their drink offering; then dash against it all the blood of the burnt offering, and all the blood of the sacrifice; but the bronze altar shall be for me to inquire by." ¹⁶The priest Uriah did everything that King Ahaz commanded.

17 Then King Ahaz cut off the frames of the stands, and removed the laver from them; he removed the sea from the bronze oxen that were under it, and put it on a pediment of stone. ¹⁸The covered portal for use on the sabbath that had been built inside the palace, and the outer entrance for the king he removed from^u the house of the LORD. He did this because of the king of Assyria. ¹⁹Now the rest of the acts of Ahaz that he did, are they not written in the Book of the Annals of the Kings of Judah? ²⁰Ahaz slept with his ancestors, and was buried with his ancestors in the city of David; his son Hezekiah succeeded him.

Hoshea Reigns over Israel

17 In the twelfth year of King Ahaz of Judah, Hoshea son of Elah began to reign in Samaria over Israel; he reigned nine years. ²He did what was evil in the sight of the LORD, yet not like the kings of Israel who were before him. ³King Shalmaneser of Assyria came up against him; Hoshea became his vassal, and paid him tribute. ⁴But the king of Assyria found treachery in Hoshea; for he had sent messengers to King So of Egypt, and offered no tribute to the king of Assyria, as he had done year by year; therefore the king of Assyria confined him and imprisoned him.

Israel Carried Captive to Assyria

5 Then the king of Assyria invaded all the land and came to Samaria; for three years he besieged it. ⁶In the ninth year of Hoshea the king of Assyria captured Samaria; he carried the Israelites away to Assyria. He placed them in Halah, on the Habor, the river of Gozan, and in the cities of the Medes.

7 This occurred because the people of Israel had sinned against the LORD their God, who had brought them up out of the land of Egypt from under the hand of Pharaoh king of Egypt. They had worshiped other gods ⁸and walked in the customs of the nations whom the LORD drove out before the people of Israel, and in the customs that the kings of Israel had introduced.^v ⁹The people of Israel secretly did things that were not right against the LORD their God. They built for themselves high places at all their towns, from watchtower to fortified city; ¹⁰they set up for themselves pillars and sacred poles^w on every high hill and under every green tree; ¹¹there they made offerings on all the high places, as the nations did whom the LORD carried away before them. They did wicked things, provoking the LORD to anger; ¹²they served idols, of which the LORD had said to them, "You shall not do this." ¹³Yet the LORD warned Israel and Judah by every prophet and every seer, saying, "Turn from your evil ways and keep my commandments and my statutes, in accordance with all the law that I commanded your ancestors and that I sent to you by my servants the prophets." ¹⁴They would not listen but were stubborn, as their ancestors had been, who did not believe in the LORD their God. ¹⁵They despised his statutes, and his covenant that he made with their ancestors, and the warnings that he gave them. They went after false idols and became false; they followed the nations that were around them, concerning whom the LORD had commanded them that they should not do as they did. ¹⁶They rejected all the commandments of the LORD their God and made for themselves cast images of two calves; they made a sacred pole,^x worshiped all the host of heaven, and served Baal.

u Cn: Heb lacks *from*   v Meaning of Heb uncertain   w Heb *Asherim*   x Heb *Asherah*

17They made their sons and their daughters pass through fire; they used divination and augury; and they sold themselves to do evil in the sight of the LORD, provoking him to anger. 18Therefore the LORD was very angry with Israel and removed them out of his sight; none was left but the tribe of Judah alone.

19 Judah also did not keep the commandments of the LORD their God but walked in the customs that Israel had introduced. 20The LORD rejected all the descendants of Israel; he punished them and gave them into the hand of plunderers, until he had banished them from his presence.

21 When he had torn Israel from the house of David, they made Jeroboam son of Nebat king. Jeroboam drove Israel from following the LORD and made them commit great sin. 22The people of Israel continued in all the sins that Jeroboam committed; they did not depart from them 23until the LORD removed Israel out of his sight, as he had foretold through all his servants the prophets. So Israel was exiled from their own land to Assyria until this day.

Assyria Resettles Samaria

24 The king of Assyria brought people from Babylon, Cuthah, Avva, Hamath, and Sepharvaim, and placed them in the cities of Samaria in place of the people of Israel; they took possession of Samaria, and settled in its cities. 25When they first settled there, they did not worship the LORD; therefore the LORD sent lions among them, which killed some of them. 26So the king of Assyria was told, "The nations that you have carried away and placed in the cities of Samaria do not know the law of the god of the land; therefore he has sent lions among them; they are killing them, because they do not know the law of the god of the land." 27Then the king of Assyria commanded, "Send there one of the priests whom you carried away from there; let himy go and live there, and teach them the law of the god of the land." 28So one of the priests whom they had carried away from Samaria came and lived in Bethel; he taught them how they should worship the LORD.

29 But every nation still made gods of its own and put them in the shrines of the high places that the people of Samaria had made, every nation in the cities in which they lived; 30the people of Babylon made Succoth-benoth, the people of Cuth made Nergal, the people of Hamath made Ashima; 31the Avvites made Nibhaz and Tartak; the Sepharvites burned their children in the fire to Adrammelech and Anammelech, the gods of Sepharvaim. 32They also worshiped the LORD and appointed from among themselves all sorts of people as priests of the high places, who sacrificed for them in the shrines of the high places. 33So they worshiped the LORD but also served their own gods, after the manner of the nations from among whom they had been carried away. 34To this day they continue to practice their former customs.

They do not worship the LORD and they do not follow the statutes or the ordinances or the law or the commandment that the LORD commanded the children of Jacob, whom he named Israel. 35The LORD had made a covenant with them and commanded them, "You shall not worship other gods or bow yourselves to them or serve them or sacrifice to them, 36but you shall worship the LORD, who brought you out of the land of Egypt with great power and with an outstretched arm; you shall bow yourselves to him, and to him you shall sacrifice. 37The statutes and the ordinances and the law and the commandment that he wrote for you, you shall always be careful to observe. You shall not worship other gods; 38you shall not forget the covenant that I have made with you. You shall not worship other gods, 39but you shall worship the LORD your God; he will deliver you out of the hand of all your enemies." 40They would not listen, however, but they continued to practice their former custom.

41 So these nations worshiped the LORD, but also served their carved images; to this day their children and their children's children continue to do as their ancestors did.

y Syr Vg: Heb them

Hezekiah's Reign over Judah

18 In the third year of King Hoshea son of Elah of Israel, Hezekiah son of King Ahaz of Judah began to reign. ²He was twenty-five years old when he began to reign; he reigned twenty-nine years in Jerusalem. His mother's name was Abi daughter of Zechariah. ³He did what was right in the sight of the LORD just as his ancestor David had done. ⁴He removed the high places, broke down the pillars, and cut down the sacred pole.ᶻ He broke in pieces the bronze serpent that Moses had made, for until those days the people of Israel had made offerings to it; it was called Nehushtan. ⁵He trusted in the LORD the God of Israel; so that there was no one like him among all the kings of Judah after him, or among those who were before him. ⁶For he held fast to the LORD; he did not depart from following him but kept the commandments that the LORD commanded Moses. ⁷The

z Heb *Asherah*

TUESDAY

THE ROD, THE SERPENT AND HOLINESS
Horatius Bonar

VERSE: 2 Kings 18.4   **PASSAGE:** 2 Kings 18.1–7

Against evil, divine truth is quick and powerful. It acts like some chemical ingredient that precipitates all impurities and leaves the water clear. It works like a spell of disenchantment against the evil one, casting him out, and casting him down. It is "the sword of the Spirit," with whose keen edge we cut our way through hostile thousands. It is the rod of Moses, by which we divide the Red Sea, and defeat Amalek, and bring water from the desert rock (see Exodus 14.16; 17.6). What evil, what enemy, within or without, is there that can withstand this unconquered and unconquerable Word? Satan's object at present is to undermine that Word and to disparage its perfection. Let us the more magnify it, and the more make constant use of it. It is indeed only a fragment of man's language, made up of human letters and syllables; but it is furnished with superhuman virtue.

That rod in the hand of Moses, what was it? A piece of common wood. Yet it cut the Red Sea in two. That serpent on the pole, what was it? A bit of brass. Yet it healed thousands (see Numbers 21.9). Why all this? Because that wood and that brass were connected with omnipotence, conductors of the heavenly electricity.

ADDITIONAL SCRIPTURE READING:
Numbers 21.8–9; John 3.14–15

Go to page 456 for your next devotional reading.

1700   1900

LORD was with him; wherever he went, he prospered. He rebelled against the king of Assyria and would not serve him. 8He attacked the Philistines as far as Gaza and its territory, from watchtower to fortified city.

9 In the fourth year of King Hezekiah, which was the seventh year of King Hoshea son of Elah of Israel, King Shalmaneser of Assyria came up against Samaria, besieged it, 10and at the end of three years, took it. In the sixth year of Hezekiah, which was the ninth year of King Hoshea of Israel, Samaria was taken. 11The king of Assyria carried the Israelites away to Assyria, settled them in Halah, on the Habor, the river of Gozan, and in the cities of the Medes, 12because they did not obey the voice of the LORD their God but transgressed his covenant—all that Moses the servant of the LORD had commanded; they neither listened nor obeyed.

Sennacherib Invades Judah

13 In the fourteenth year of King Hezekiah, King Sennacherib of Assyria came up against all the fortified cities of Judah and captured them. 14King Hezekiah of Judah sent to the king of Assyria at Lachish, saying, "I have done wrong; withdraw from me; whatever you impose on me I will bear." The king of Assyria demanded of King Hezekiah of Judah three hundred talents of silver and thirty talents of gold. 15Hezekiah gave him all the silver that was found in the house of the LORD and in the treasuries of the king's house. 16At that time Hezekiah stripped the gold from the doors of the temple of the LORD, and from the doorposts that King Hezekiah of Judah had overlaid and gave it to the king of Assyria. 17The king of Assyria sent the Tartan, the Rabsaris, and the Rabshakeh with a great army from Lachish to King Hezekiah at Jerusalem. They went up and came to Jerusalem. When they arrived, they came and stood by the conduit of the upper pool, which is on the highway to the Fuller's Field. 18When they called for the king, there came out to them Eliakim son of Hilkiah, who was in charge of the palace, and Shebnah the secretary, and Joah son of Asaph, the recorder.

19 The Rabshakeh said to them, "Say to Hezekiah: Thus says the great king, the king of Assyria: On what do you base this confidence of yours? 20Do you think that mere words are strategy and power for war? On whom do you now rely, that you have rebelled against me? 21See, you are relying now on Egypt, that broken reed of a staff, which will pierce the hand of anyone who leans on it. Such is Pharaoh king of Egypt to all who rely on him. 22But if you say to me, 'We rely on the LORD our God,' is it not he whose high places and altars Hezekiah has removed, saying to Judah and to Jerusalem, 'You shall worship before this altar in Jerusalem'? 23Come now, make a wager with my master the king of Assyria: I will give you two thousand horses, if you are able on your part to set riders on them. 24How then can you repulse a single captain among the least of my master's servants, when you rely on Egypt for chariots and for horsemen? 25Moreover, is it without the LORD that I have come up against this place to destroy it? The LORD said to me, Go up against this land, and destroy it."

26 Then Eliakim son of Hilkiah, and Shebnah, and Joah said to the Rabshakeh, "Please speak to your servants in the Aramaic language, for we understand it; do not speak to us in the language of Judah within the hearing of the people who are on the wall." 27But the Rabshakeh said to them, "Has my master sent me to speak these words to your master and to you, and not to the people sitting on the wall, who are doomed with you to eat their own dung and to drink their own urine?"

28 Then the Rabshakeh stood and called out in a loud voice in the language of Judah, "Hear the word of the great king, the king of Assyria! 29Thus says the king: 'Do not let Hezekiah deceive you, for he will not be able to deliver you out of my hand. 30Do not let Hezekiah make you rely on the LORD by saying, The LORD will surely deliver us, and this city will not be given into the hand of the king of Assyria.' 31Do not listen to Hezekiah; for thus says the king of Assyria: 'Make your peace with me and come out to me; then every one of you will eat from your own vine and

your own fig tree, and drink water from your own cistern, ³²until I come and take you away to a land like your own land, a land of grain and wine, a land of bread and vineyards, a land of olive oil and honey, that you may live and not die. Do not listen to Hezekiah when he misleads you by saying, The LORD will deliver us. ³³Has any of the gods of the nations ever delivered its land out of the hand of the king of Assyria? ³⁴Where are the gods of Hamath and Arpad? Where are the gods of Sepharvaim, Hena, and Ivvah? Have they delivered Samaria out of my hand? ³⁵Who among all the gods of the countries have delivered their countries out of my hand, that the LORD should deliver Jerusalem out of my hand?' "

36 But the people were silent and answered him not a word, for the king's command was, "Do not answer him." ³⁷Then Eliakim son of Hilkiah, who was in charge of the palace, and Shebna the secretary, and Joah son of Asaph, the recorder, came to Hezekiah with their clothes torn and told him the words of the Rabshakeh.

Hezekiah Consults Isaiah

19 When King Hezekiah heard it, he tore his clothes, covered himself with sackcloth, and went into the house of the LORD. ²And he sent Eliakim, who was in charge of the palace, and Shebna the secretary, and the senior priests, covered with sackcloth, to the prophet Isaiah son of Amoz. ³They said to him, "Thus says Hezekiah, This day is a day of distress, of rebuke, and of disgrace; children have come to the birth, and there is no strength to bring them forth. ⁴It may be that the LORD your God heard all the words of the Rabshakeh, whom his master the king of Assyria has sent to mock the living God, and will rebuke the words that the LORD your God has heard; therefore lift up your prayer for the remnant that is left." ⁵When the servants of King Hezekiah came to Isaiah, ⁶Isaiah said to them, "Say to your master, 'Thus says the LORD: Do not be afraid because of the words that you have heard, with which the servants of the king of Assyria have

reviled me. ⁷I myself will put a spirit in him, so that he shall hear a rumor and return to his own land; I will cause him to fall by the sword in his own land.' "

Sennacherib's Threat

8 The Rabshakeh returned, and found the king of Assyria fighting against Libnah; for he had heard that the king had left Lachish. ⁹When the king*a* heard concerning King Tirhakah of Ethiopia,*b* "See, he has set out to fight against you," he sent messengers again to Hezekiah, saying, ¹⁰"Thus shall you speak to King Hezekiah of Judah: Do not let your God on whom you rely deceive you by promising that Jerusalem will not be given into the hand of the king of Assyria. ¹¹See, you have heard what the kings of Assyria have done to all lands, destroying them utterly. Shall you be delivered? ¹²Have the gods of the nations delivered them, the nations that my predecessors destroyed, Gozan, Haran, Rezeph, and the people of Eden who were in Telassar? ¹³Where is the king of Hamath, the king of Arpad, the king of the city of Sepharvaim, the king of Hena, or the king of Ivvah?"

Hezekiah's Prayer

14 Hezekiah received the letter from the hand of the messengers and read it; then Hezekiah went up to the house of the LORD and spread it before the LORD. ¹⁵And Hezekiah prayed before the LORD, and said: "O LORD the God of Israel, who are enthroned above the cherubim, you are God, you alone, of all the kingdoms of the earth; you have made heaven and earth. ¹⁶Incline your ear, O LORD, and hear; open your eyes, O LORD, and see; hear the words of Sennacherib, which he has sent to mock the living God. ¹⁷Truly, O LORD, the kings of Assyria have laid waste the nations and their lands, ¹⁸and have hurled their gods into the fire, though they were no gods but the work of human hands—wood and stone—and so they were destroyed. ¹⁹So now, O LORD our God, save us, I pray you, from his hand, so that all the kingdoms of the earth may know that you, O LORD, are God alone."

20 Then Isaiah son of Amoz sent to

a Heb *he*   *b* Or *Nubia*; Heb *Cush*

Hezekiah, saying, "Thus says the LORD, the God of Israel: I have heard your prayer to me about King Sennacherib of Assyria. 21This is the word that the LORD has spoken concerning him:

She despises you, she scorns you—
    virgin daughter Zion;
she tosses her head—behind your
    back,
    daughter Jerusalem.

22 "Whom have you mocked and
    reviled?
    Against whom have you raised
    your voice
and haughtily lifted your eyes?
    Against the Holy One of Israel!
23 By your messengers you have
    mocked the Lord,
    and you have said, 'With my
    many chariots
I have gone up the heights of the
    mountains,
    to the far recesses of Lebanon;
I felled its tallest cedars,
    its choicest cypresses;
I entered its farthest retreat,
    its densest forest.
24 I dug wells
    and drank foreign waters,
I dried up with the sole of my foot
    all the streams of Egypt.'

25 "Have you not heard
    that I determined it long ago?
I planned from days of old
    what now I bring to pass,
    that you should make fortified
    cities
    crash into heaps of ruins,
26 while their inhabitants, shorn of
    strength,
    are dismayed and confounded;
they have become like plants of the
    field
    and like tender grass,
like grass on the housetops,
    blighted before it is grown.

27 "But I know your risingᶜ and your
    sitting,
    your going out and coming in,
    and your raging against me.
28 Because you have raged against me

and your arrogance has come to
    my ears,
I will put my hook in your nose
    and my bit in your mouth;
I will turn you back on the way
    by which you came.

29 "And this shall be the sign for you: This year you shall eat what grows of itself, and in the second year what springs from that; then in the third year sow, reap, plant vineyards, and eat their fruit. 30The surviving remnant of the house of Judah shall again take root downward, and bear fruit upward; 31for from Jerusalem a remnant shall go out, and from Mount Zion a band of survivors. The zeal of the LORD of hosts will do this.

32 "Therefore thus says the LORD concerning the king of Assyria: He shall not come into this city, shoot an arrow there, come before it with a shield, or cast up a siege ramp against it. 33By the way that he came, by the same he shall return; he shall not come into this city, says the LORD. 34For I will defend this city to save it, for my own sake and for the sake of my servant David."

Sennacherib's Defeat and Death

35 That very night the angel of the LORD set out and struck down one hundred eighty-five thousand in the camp of the Assyrians; when morning dawned, they were all dead bodies. 36Then King Sennacherib of Assyria left, went home, and lived at Nineveh. 37As he was worshiping in the house of his god Nisroch, his sons Adrammelech and Sharezer killed him with the sword, and they escaped into the land of Ararat. His son Esar-haddon succeeded him.

Hezekiah's Illness

20 In those days Hezekiah became sick and was at the point of death. The prophet Isaiah son of Amoz came to him, and said to him, "Thus says the LORD: Set your house in order, for you shall die; you shall not recover." 2Then Hezekiah turned his face to the wall and prayed to the LORD: 3"Remember now, O LORD, I implore you, how I have walked before you in

c Gk Compare Isa 37.27 Q Ms: MT lacks rising

faithfulness with a whole heart, and have done what is good in your sight." Hezekiah wept bitterly. [4]Before Isaiah had gone out of the middle court, the word of the LORD came to him: [5]"Turn back, and say to Hezekiah prince of my people, Thus says the LORD, the God of your ancestor David: I have heard your prayer, I have seen your tears; indeed, I will heal you; on the third day you shall go up to the house of the LORD. [6]I will add fifteen years to your life. I will deliver you and this city out of the hand of the king of Assyria; I will defend this city for my own sake and for my servant David's sake." [7]Then Isaiah said, "Bring a lump of figs. Let them take it and apply it to the boil, so that he may recover."

8 Hezekiah said to Isaiah, "What shall be the sign that the LORD will heal me, and that I shall go up to the house of the LORD on the third day?" [9]Isaiah said, "This is the sign to you from the LORD, that the LORD will do the thing that he has promised: the shadow has now advanced ten intervals; shall it retreat ten intervals?" [10]Hezekiah answered, "It is normal for the shadow to lengthen ten intervals; rather let the shadow retreat ten intervals." [11]The prophet Isaiah cried to the LORD; and he brought the shadow back the ten intervals, by which the sun[d] had declined on the dial of Ahaz.

Envoys from Babylon

12 At that time King Merodach-baladan son of Baladan of Babylon sent envoys with letters and a present to Hezekiah, for he had heard that Hezekiah had been sick. [13]Hezekiah welcomed them;[e] he showed them all his treasure house, the silver, the gold, the spices, the precious oil, his armory, all that was found in his storehouses; there was nothing in his house or in all his realm that Hezekiah did not show them. [14]Then the prophet Isaiah came to King Hezekiah, and said to him, "What did these men say? From where did they come to you?" Hezekiah answered, "They have come from a far country, from Babylon." [15]He said, "What have they seen in your house?" Hezekiah

answered, "They have seen all that is in my house; there is nothing in my storehouses that I did not show them."

16 Then Isaiah said to Hezekiah, "Hear the word of the LORD: [17]Days are coming when all that is in your house, and that which your ancestors have stored up until this day, shall be carried to Babylon; nothing shall be left, says the LORD. [18]Some of your own sons who are born to you shall be taken away; they shall be eunuchs in the palace of the king of Babylon." [19]Then Hezekiah said to Isaiah, "The word of the LORD that you have spoken is good." For he thought, "Why not, if there will be peace and security in my days?"

Death of Hezekiah

20 The rest of the deeds of Hezekiah, all his power, how he made the pool and the conduit and brought water into the city, are they not written in the Book of the Annals of the Kings of Judah? [21]Hezekiah slept with his ancestors; and his son Manasseh succeeded him.

Manasseh Reigns over Judah

21 Manasseh was twelve years old when he began to reign; he reigned fifty-five years in Jerusalem. His mother's name was Hephzibah. [2]He did what was evil in the sight of the LORD, following the abominable practices of the nations that the LORD drove out before the people of Israel. [3]For he rebuilt the high places that his father Hezekiah had destroyed; he erected altars for Baal, made a sacred pole,[f] as King Ahab of Israel had done, worshiped all the host of heaven, and served them. [4]He built altars in the house of the LORD, of which the LORD had said, "In Jerusalem I will put my name." [5]He built altars for all the host of heaven in the two courts of the house of the LORD. [6]He made his son pass through fire; he practiced soothsaying and augury, and dealt with mediums and with wizards. He did much evil in the sight of the LORD, provoking him to anger. [7]The carved image of Asherah that he had made he set in the house of which the LORD said to David and to his son

d Syr See Isa 38.8 and Tg: Heb it   e Gk Vg Syr: Heb When Hezekiah heard about them
f Heb Asherah

Solomon, "In this house, and in Jerusalem, which I have chosen out of all the tribes of Israel, I will put my name forever; 8I will not cause the feet of Israel to wander any more out of the land that I gave to their ancestors, if only they will be careful to do according to all that I have commanded them, and according to all the law that my servant Moses commanded them." 9But they did not listen; Manasseh misled them to do more evil than the nations had done that the LORD destroyed before the people of Israel.

10 The LORD said by his servants the prophets, 11"Because King Manasseh of Judah has committed these abominations, has done things more wicked than all that the Amorites did, who were before him, and has caused Judah also to sin with his idols; 12therefore thus says the LORD, the God of Israel, I am bringing upon Jerusalem and Judah such evil that the ears of everyone who hears of it will tingle. 13I will stretch over Jerusalem the measuring line for Samaria, and the plummet for the house of Ahab; I will wipe Jerusalem as one wipes a dish, wiping it and turning it upside down. 14I will cast off the remnant of my heritage, and give them into the hand of their enemies; they shall become a prey and a spoil to all their enemies, 15because they have done what is evil in my sight and have provoked me to anger, since the day their ancestors came out of Egypt, even to this day."

16 Moreover Manasseh shed very much innocent blood, until he had filled Jerusalem from one end to another, besides the sin that he caused Judah to sin so that they did what was evil in the sight of the LORD.

17 Now the rest of the acts of Manasseh, all that he did, and the sin that he committed, are they not written in the Book of the Annals of the Kings of Judah? 18Manasseh slept with his ancestors, and was buried in the garden of his house, in the garden of Uzza. His son Amon succeeded him.

Amon Reigns over Judah

19 Amon was twenty-two years old when he began to reign; he reigned two years in Jerusalem. His mother's name

was Meshullemeth daughter of Haruz of Jotbah. 20He did what was evil in the sight of the LORD, as his father Manasseh had done. 21He walked in all the way in which his father walked, served the idols that his father served, and worshiped them; 22he abandoned the LORD, the God of his ancestors, and did not walk in the way of the LORD. 23The servants of Amon conspired against him, and killed the king in his house. 24But the people of the land killed all those who had conspired against King Amon, and the people of the land made his son Josiah king in place of him. 25Now the rest of the acts of Amon that he did, are they not written in the Book of the Annals of the Kings of Judah? 26He was buried in his tomb in the garden of Uzza; then his son Josiah succeeded him.

Josiah Reigns over Judah

22 Josiah was eight years old when he began to reign; he reigned thirty-one years in Jerusalem. His mother's name was Jedidah daughter of Adaiah of Bozkath. 2He did what was right in the sight of the LORD, and walked in all the way of his father David; he did not turn aside to the right or to the left.

Hilkiah Finds the Book of the Law

3 In the eighteenth year of King Josiah, the king sent Shaphan son of Azaliah, son of Meshullam, the secretary, to the house of the LORD, saying, 4"Go up to the high priest Hilkiah, and have him count the entire sum of the money that has been brought into the house of the LORD, which the keepers of the threshold have collected from the people; 5let it be given into the hand of the workers who have the oversight of the house of the LORD; let them give it to the workers who are at the house of the LORD, repairing the house, 6that is, to the carpenters, to the builders, to the masons; and let them use it to buy timber and quarried stone to repair the house. 7But no accounting shall be asked from them for the money that is delivered into their hand, for they deal honestly."

8 The high priest Hilkiah said to Shaphan the secretary, "I have found the

book of the law in the house of the LORD." When Hilkiah gave the book to Shaphan, he read it. ⁹Then Shaphan the secretary came to the king, and reported to the king, "Your servants have emptied out the money that was found in the house, and have delivered it into the hand of the workers who have oversight of the house of the LORD." ¹⁰Shaphan the secretary informed the king, "The priest Hilkiah has given me a book." Shaphan then read it aloud to the king.

11 When the king heard the words of the book of the law, he tore his clothes. ¹²Then the king commanded the priest Hilkiah, Ahikam son of Shaphan, Achbor son of Micaiah, Shaphan the secretary, and the king's servant Asaiah, saying, ¹³"Go, inquire of the LORD for me, for the people, and for all Judah, concerning the words of this book that has been found; for great is the wrath of the LORD that is kindled against us, because our ancestors did not obey the words of this book, to do according to all that is written concerning us."

14 So the priest Hilkiah, Ahikam, Achbor, Shaphan, and Asaiah went to the prophetess Huldah the wife of Shallum son of Tikvah, son of Harhas, keeper of the wardrobe; she resided in Jerusalem in the Second Quarter, where they consulted her. ¹⁵She declared to them, "Thus says the LORD, the God of Israel: Tell the man who sent you to me, ¹⁶Thus says the LORD, I will indeed bring disaster on this place and on its inhabitants—all the words of the book that the king of Judah has read. ¹⁷Because they have abandoned me and have made offerings to other gods, so that they have provoked me to anger with all the work of their hands, therefore my wrath will be kindled against this place, and it will not be quenched. ¹⁸But as to the king of Judah, who sent you to inquire of the LORD, thus shall you say to him, Thus says the LORD, the God of Israel: Regarding the words that you have heard, ¹⁹because your heart was penitent, and you humbled yourself before the LORD, when you heard how I spoke against this place, and against its inhabitants, that they should become a desolation and a curse, and because you

have torn your clothes and wept before me, I also have heard you, says the LORD. ²⁰Therefore, I will gather you to your ancestors, and you shall be gathered to your grave in peace; your eyes shall not see all the disaster that I will bring on this place." They took the message back to the king.

Josiah's Reformation

23 Then the king directed that all the elders of Judah and Jerusalem should be gathered to him. ²The king went up to the house of the LORD, and with him went all the people of Judah, all the inhabitants of Jerusalem, the priests, the prophets, and all the people, both small and great; he read in their hearing all the words of the book of the covenant that had been found in the house of the LORD. ³The king stood by the pillar and made a covenant before the LORD, to follow the LORD, keeping his commandments, his decrees, and his statutes, with all his heart and all his soul, to perform the words of this covenant that were written in this book. All the people joined in the covenant.

4 The king commanded the high priest Hilkiah, the priests of the second order, and the guardians of the threshold, to bring out of the temple of the LORD all the vessels made for Baal, for Asherah, and for all the host of heaven; he burned them outside Jerusalem in the fields of the Kidron, and carried their ashes to Bethel. ⁵He deposed the idolatrous priests whom the kings of Judah had ordained to make offerings in the high places at the cities of Judah and around Jerusalem; those also who made offerings to Baal, to the sun, the moon, the constellations, and all the host of the heavens. ⁶He brought out the image ofᵍ Asherah from the house of the LORD, outside Jerusalem, to the Wadi Kidron, burned it at the Wadi Kidron, beat it to dust and threw the dust of it upon the graves of the common people. ⁷He broke down the houses of the male temple prostitutes that were in the house of the LORD, where the women did weaving for Asherah. ⁸He brought all the priests out of the towns of Judah, and defiled the

g Heb lacks *image of*

high places where the priests had made offerings, from Geba to Beer-sheba; he broke down the high places of the gates that were at the entrance of the gate of Joshua the governor of the city, which were on the left at the gate of the city. 9The priests of the high places, however, did not come up to the altar of the LORD in Jerusalem, but ate unleavened bread among their kindred. 10He defiled Topheth, which is in the valley of Ben-hinnom, so that no one would make a son or a daughter pass through fire as an offering to Molech. 11He removed the horses that the kings of Judah had dedicated to the sun, at the entrance to the house of the LORD, by the chamber of the eunuch Nathan-melech, which was in the precincts;h then he burned the chariots of the sun with fire. 12The altars on the roof of the upper chamber of Ahaz, which the kings of Judah had made, and the altars that Manasseh had made in the two courts of the house of the LORD, he pulled down from there and broke in pieces, and threw the rubble into the Wadi Kidron. 13The king defiled the high places that were east of Jerusalem, to the south of the Mount of Destruction, which King Solomon of Israel had built for Astarte the abomination of the Sidonians, for Chemosh the abomination of Moab, and for Milcom the abomination of the Ammonites. 14He broke the pillars in pieces, cut down the sacred poles,i and covered the sites with human bones.

15 Moreover, the altar at Bethel, the high place erected by Jeroboam son of Nebat, who caused Israel to sin—he pulled down that altar along with the high place. He burned the high place, crushing it to dust; he also burned the sacred pole.j 16As Josiah turned, he saw the tombs there on the mount; and he sent and took the bones out of the tombs, and burned them on the altar, and defiled it, according to the word of the LORD that the man of God proclaimed,k when Jeroboam stood by the altar at the festival; he turned and looked up at the tomb of the man of God who had predicted these things. 17Then he said, "What is that monument that I

see?" The people of the city told him, "It is the tomb of the man of God who came from Judah and predicted these things that you have done against the altar at Bethel." 18He said, "Let him rest; let no one move his bones." So they let his bones alone, with the bones of the prophet who came out of Samaria. 19Moreover, Josiah removed all the shrines of the high places that were in the towns of Samaria, which kings of Israel had made, provoking the LORD to anger; he did to them just as he had done at Bethel. 20He slaughtered on the altars all the priests of the high places who were there, and burned human bones on them. Then he returned to Jerusalem.

The Passover Celebrated

21 The king commanded all the people, "Keep the passover to the LORD your God as prescribed in this book of the covenant." 22No such passover had been kept since the days of the judges who judged Israel, even during all the days of the kings of Israel and of the kings of Judah; 23but in the eighteenth year of King Josiah this passover was kept to the LORD in Jerusalem.

24 Moreover Josiah put away the mediums, wizards, teraphim,l idols, and all the abominations that were seen in the land of Judah and in Jerusalem, so that he established the words of the law that were written in the book that the priest Hilkiah had found in the house of the LORD. 25Before him there was no king like him, who turned to the LORD with all his heart, with all his soul, and with all his might, according to all the law of Moses; nor did any like him arise after him.

26 Still the LORD did not turn from the fierceness of his great wrath, by which his anger was kindled against Judah, because of all the provocations with which Manasseh had provoked him. 27The LORD said, "I will remove Judah also out of my sight, as I have removed Israel; and I will reject this city that I have chosen, Jerusalem, and the house of which I said, My name shall be there."

---

h Meaning of Heb uncertain   i Heb Asherim   j Heb Asherah   k Gk: Heb proclaimed, who had predicted these things   l Or household gods

Josiah Dies in Battle

28 Now the rest of the acts of Josiah, and all that he did, are they not written in the Book of the Annals of the Kings of Judah? 29In his days Pharaoh Neco king of Egypt went up to the king of Assyria to the river Euphrates. King Josiah went to meet him; but when Pharaoh Neco met him at Megiddo, he killed him. 30His servants carried him dead in a chariot from Megiddo, brought him to Jerusalem, and buried him in his own tomb. The people of the land took Jehoahaz son of Josiah, anointed him, and made him king in place of his father.

Reign and Captivity of Jehoahaz

31 Jehoahaz was twenty-three years old when he began to reign; he reigned three months in Jerusalem. His mother's name was Hamutal daughter of Jeremiah of Libnah. 32He did what was evil in the sight of the LORD, just as his ancestors had done. 33Pharaoh Neco confined him at Riblah in the land of Hamath, so that he might not reign in Jerusalem, and imposed tribute on the land of one hundred talents of silver and a talent of gold. 34Pharaoh Neco made Eliakim son of Josiah king in place of his father Josiah, and changed his name to Jehoiakim. But he took Jehoahaz away; he came to Egypt, and died there. 35Jehoiakim gave the silver and the gold to Pharaoh, but he taxed the land in order to meet Pharaoh's demand for money. He exacted the silver and the gold from the people of the land, from all according to their assessment, to give it to Pharaoh Neco.

Jehoiakim Reigns over Judah

36 Jehoiakim was twenty-five years old when he began to reign; he reigned eleven years in Jerusalem. His mother's name was Zebidah daughter of Pedaiah of Rumah. 37He did what was evil in the sight of the LORD, just as all his ancestors had done.

Judah Overrun by Enemies

24 In his days King Nebuchadnezzar of Babylon came up; Jehoiakim became his servant for three years; then he turned and rebelled against him. 2The LORD sent against him bands of the Chaldeans, bands of the Arameans, bands of the Moabites, and bands of the Ammonites; he sent them against Judah to destroy it, according to the word of the LORD that he spoke by his servants the prophets. 3Surely this came upon Judah at the command of the LORD, to remove them out of his sight, for the sins of Manasseh, for all that he had committed, 4and also for the innocent blood that he had shed; for he filled Jerusalem with innocent blood, and the LORD was not willing to pardon. 5Now the rest of the deeds of Jehoiakim, and all that he did, are they not written in the Book of the Annals of the Kings of Judah? 6So Jehoiakim slept with his ancestors; then his son Jehoiachin succeeded him. 7The king of Egypt did not come again out of his land, for the king of Babylon had taken over all that belonged to the king of Egypt from the Wadi of Egypt to the River Euphrates.

Reign and Captivity of Jehoiachin

8 Jehoiachin was eighteen years old when he began to reign; he reigned three months in Jerusalem. His mother's name was Nehushta daughter of Elnathan of Jerusalem. 9He did what was evil in the sight of the LORD, just as his father had done.

10 At that time the servants of King Nebuchadnezzar of Babylon came up to Jerusalem, and the city was besieged. 11King Nebuchadnezzar of Babylon came to the city, while his servants were besieging it; 12King Jehoiachin of Judah gave himself up to the king of Babylon, himself, his mother, his servants, his officers, and his palace officials. The king of Babylon took him prisoner in the eighth year of his reign.

Capture of Jerusalem

13 He carried off all the treasures of the house of the LORD, and the treasures of the king's house; he cut in pieces all the vessels of gold in the temple of the LORD, which King Solomon of Israel had made, all this as the LORD had foretold. 14He carried away all Jerusalem, all the officials, all the warriors, ten thousand captives, all the artisans and the smiths; no one remained, except the poorest

people of the land. 15He carried away Jehoiachin to Babylon; the king's mother, the king's wives, his officials, and the elite of the land, he took into captivity from Jerusalem to Babylon. 16The king of Babylon brought captive to Babylon all the men of valor, seven thousand, the artisans and the smiths, one thousand, all of them strong and fit for war. 17The king of Babylon made Mattaniah, Jehoiachin's uncle, king in his place, and changed his name to Zedekiah.

Zedekiah Reigns over Judah

18 Zedekiah was twenty-one years old when he began to reign; he reigned eleven years in Jerusalem. His mother's name was Hamutal daughter of Jeremiah of Libnah. 19He did what was evil in the sight of the LORD, just as Jehoiakim had done. 20Indeed, Jerusalem and Judah so angered the LORD that he expelled them from his presence.

The Fall and Captivity of Judah

Zedekiah rebelled against the king of Babylon. 1And in the ninth year of his reign, in the tenth month, on the tenth day of the month, King Nebuchadnezzar of Babylon came with all his army against Jerusalem, and laid siege to it; they built siegeworks against it all around. 2So the city was besieged until the eleventh year of King Zedekiah. 3On the ninth day of the fourth month the famine became so severe in the city that there was no food for the people of the land. 4Then a breach was made in the city wall;m the king with all the soldiers fledn by night by the way of the gate between the two walls, by the king's garden, though the Chaldeans were all around the city. They went in the direction of the Arabah. 5But the army of the Chaldeans pursued the king, and overtook him in the plains of Jericho; all his army was scattered, deserting him. 6Then they captured the king and brought him up to the king of Babylon at Riblah, who passed sentence on him. 7They slaughtered the sons of Zedekiah before his eyes, then put out the eyes of Zedekiah; they bound him in fetters and took him to Babylon.

8 In the fifth month, on the seventh day of the month—which was the nineteenth year of King Nebuchadnezzar, king of Babylon—Nebuzaradan, the captain of the bodyguard, a servant of the king of Babylon, came to Jerusalem. 9He burned the house of the LORD, the king's house, and all the houses of Jerusalem; every great house he burned down. 10All the army of the Chaldeans who were with the captain of the guard broke down the walls around Jerusalem. 11Nebuzaradan the captain of the guard carried into exile the rest of the people who were left in the city and the deserters who had defected to the king of Babylon—all the rest of the population. 12But the captain of the guard left some of the poorest people of the land to be vinedressers and tillers of the soil.

13 The bronze pillars that were in the house of the LORD, as well as the stands and the bronze sea that were in the house of the LORD, the Chaldeans broke in pieces, and carried the bronze to Babylon. 14They took away the pots, the shovels, the snuffers, the dishes for incense, and all the bronze vessels used in the temple service, 15as well as the firepans and the basins. What was made of gold the captain of the guard took away for the gold, and what was made of silver, for the silver. 16As for the two pillars, the one sea, and the stands, which Solomon had made for the house of the LORD, the bronze of all these vessels was beyond weighing. 17The height of the one pillar was eighteen cubits, and on it was a bronze capital; the height of the capital was three cubits; latticework and pomegranates, all of bronze, were on the capital all around. The second pillar had the same, with the latticework.

18 The captain of the guard took the chief priest Seraiah, the second priest Zephaniah, and the three guardians of the threshold; 19from the city he took an officer who had been in command of the soldiers, and five men of the king's council who were found in the city; the secretary who was the commander of the army who mustered the people of the land; and sixty men of the people of the land who were found in the city. 20Nebuzaradan the captain of the guard

m Heb lacks wall   n Gk Compare Jer 39.4; 52.7: Heb lacks the king and lacks fled

took them, and brought them to the king of Babylon at Riblah. 21The king of Babylon struck them down and put them to death at Riblah in the land of Hamath. So Judah went into exile out of its land.

Gedaliah Made Governor of Judah

22 He appointed Gedaliah son of Ahikam son of Shaphan as governor over the people who remained in the land of Judah, whom King Nebuchadnezzar of Babylon had left. 23Now when all the captains of the forces and their men heard that the king of Babylon had appointed Gedaliah as governor, they came with their men to Gedaliah at Mizpah, namely, Ishmael son of Nethaniah, Johanan son of Kareah, Seraiah son of Tanhumeth the Netophathite, and Jaazaniah son of the Maacathite. 24Gedaliah swore to them and their men, saying, "Do not be afraid because of the Chaldean officials; live in the land, serve the king of Babylon, and it shall be well with you." 25But in the seventh month, Ishmael son of Nethaniah son of Elishama, of the royal family, came with ten men; they struck down Gedaliah so that he died, along with the Judeans and Chaldeans who were with him at Mizpah. 26Then all the people, high and low,o and the captains of the forces set out and went to Egypt; for they were afraid of the Chaldeans.

Jehoiachin Released from Prison

27 In the thirty-seventh year of the exile of King Jehoiachin of Judah, in the twelfth month, on the twenty-seventh day of the month, King Evil-merodach of Babylon, in the year that he began to reign, released King Jehoiachin of Judah from prison; 28he spoke kindly to him, and gave him a seat above the other seats of the kings who were with him in Babylon. 29So Jehoiachin put aside his prison clothes. Every day of his life he dined regularly in the king's presence. 30For his allowance, a regular allowance was given him by the king, a portion every day, as long as he lived.

o Or young and old

1 CHRONICLES

HE BOOK OF 1 CHRONICLES WAS WRITTEN FOR THE EXILES WHO HAD RETURNED TO ISRAEL AFTER THE BABYLONIAN CAPTIVITY TO REMIND THEM THAT THEY WERE STILL GOD'S CHOSEN PEOPLE. THE BURNING ISSUE WAS THE QUESTION OF CONTINUITY WITH THE PAST: IS GOD STILL INTERESTED IN US? ARE HIS COVENANTS STILL IN FORCE? DO WE STILL FIT INTO HIS PLAN? BE ENCOURAGED BY GOD'S AFFIRMATION THAT HIS PEOPLE BELONG TO HIM, AND THEN RESPOND TO HIM WITH WORSHIP AND THANKSGIVING.

From Adam to Abraham

1 Adam, Seth, Enosh; 2Kenan, Mahalalel, Jared; 3Enoch, Methuselah, Lamech; 4Noah, Shem, Ham, and Japheth.

5 The descendants of Japheth: Gomer, Magog, Madai, Javan, Tubal, Meshech, and Tiras. 6The descendants of Gomer: Ashkenaz, Diphath,a and Togarmah. 7The descendants of Javan: Elishah, Tarshish, Kittim, and Rodanim.b

8 The descendants of Ham: Cush, Egypt, Put, and Canaan. 9The descendants of Cush: Seba, Havilah, Sabta, Raama, and Sabteca. The descendants of Raamah: Sheba and Dedan. 10Cush became the father of Nimrod; he was the first to be a mighty one on the earth.

11 Egypt became the father of Ludim, Anamim, Lehabim, Naphtuhim, 12Pathrusim, Casluhim, and Caphtorim, from whom the Philistines come.c

13 Canaan became the father of Sidon his firstborn, and Heth, 14and the Jebusites, the Amorites, the Girgashites, 15the Hivites, the Arkites, the Sinites, 16the Arvadites, the Zemarites, and the Hamathites.

17 The descendants of Shem: Elam, Asshur, Arpachshad, Lud, Aram, Uz, Hul, Gether, and Meshech.d 18Arpachshad became the father of Shelah; and Shelah became the father of Eber. 19To Eber were born two sons: the name of the one was Peleg (for in his days the earth was divided), and the name of his

brother Joktan. [20]Joktan became the father of Almodad, Sheleph, Hazarmaveth, Jerah, [21]Hadoram, Uzal, Diklah, [22]Ebal, Abimael, Sheba, [23]Ophir, Havilah, and Jobab; all these were the descendants of Joktan.

24 Shem, Arpachshad, Shelah; [25]Eber, Peleg, Reu; [26]Serug, Nahor, Terah; [27]Abram, that is, Abraham.

From Abraham to Jacob

28 The sons of Abraham: Isaac and Ishmael. [29]These are their genealogies: the firstborn of Ishmael, Nebaioth; and Kedar, Adbeel, Mibsam, [30]Mishma, Dumah, Massa, Hadad, Tema, [31]Jetur, Naphish, and Kedemah. These are the sons of Ishmael. [32]The sons of Keturah, Abraham's concubine: she bore Zimran, Jokshan, Medan, Midian, Ishbak, and Shuah. The sons of Jokshan: Sheba and Dedan. [33]The sons of Midian: Ephah, Epher, Hanoch, Abida, and Eldaah. All these were the descendants of Keturah.

34 Abraham became the father of Isaac. The sons of Isaac: Esau and Israel. [35]The sons of Esau: Eliphaz, Reuel, Jeush, Jalam, and Korah. [36]The sons of Eliphaz: Teman, Omar, Zephi, Gatam, Kenaz, Timna, and Amalek. [37]The sons of Reuel: Nahath, Zerah, Shammah, and Mizzah.

38 The sons of Seir: Lotan, Shobal, Zibeon, Anah, Dishon, Ezer, and Dishan. [39]The sons of Lotan: Hori and Homam; and Lotan's sister was Timna. [40]The sons of Shobal: Alian, Manahath, Ebal, Shephi, and Onam. The sons of Zibeon: Aiah and Anah. [41]The sons of Anah: Dishon. The sons of Dishon: Hamran, Eshban, Ithran, and Cheran. [42]The sons of Ezer: Bilhan, Zaavan, and Jaakan.*e* The sons of Dishan:*f* Uz and Aran.

43 These are the kings who reigned in the land of Edom before any king reigned over the Israelites: Bela son of Beor, whose city was called Dinhabah. [44]When Bela died, Jobab son of Zerah of Bozrah succeeded him. [45]When Jobab died, Husham of the land of the Temanites succeeded him. [46]When Husham died, Hadad son of Bedad, who defeated Midian in the country of Moab, succeeded him; and the name of his city was

Avith. [47]When Hadad died, Samlah of Masrekah succeeded him. [48]When Samlah died, Shaul*g* of Rehoboth on the Euphrates succeeded him. [49]When Shaul*g* died, Baal-hanan son of Achbor succeeded him. [50]When Baal-hanan died, Hadad succeeded him; the name of his city was Pai, and his wife's name Mehetabel daughter of Matred, daughter of Me-zahab. [51]And Hadad died.

The clans*h* of Edom were: clans*h* Timna, Aliah,*i* Jetheth, [52]Oholibamah, Elah, Pinon, [53]Kenaz, Teman, Mibzar, [54]Magdiel, and Iram; these are the clans*h* of Edom.

The Sons of Israel and the Descendants of Judah

2 These are the sons of Israel: Reuben, Simeon, Levi, Judah, Issachar, Zebulun, [2]Dan, Joseph, Benjamin, Naphtali, Gad, and Asher. [3]The sons of Judah: Er, Onan, and Shelah; these three the Canaanite woman Bathshua bore to him. Now Er, Judah's firstborn, was wicked in the sight of the LORD, and he put him to death. [4]His daughter-in-law Tamar also bore him Perez and Zerah. Judah had five sons in all.

5 The sons of Perez: Hezron and Hamul. [6]The sons of Zerah: Zimri, Ethan, Heman, Calcol, and Dara,*i* five in all. [7]The sons of Carmi: Achar, the troubler of Israel, who transgressed in the matter of the devoted thing; [8]and Ethan's son was Azariah.

9 The sons of Hezron, who were born to him: Jerahmeel, Ram, and Chelubai. [10]Ram became the father of Amminadab, and Amminadab became the father of Nahshon, prince of the sons of Judah. [11]Nahshon became the father of Salma, Salma of Boaz, [12]Boaz of Obed, Obed of Jesse. [13]Jesse became the father of Eliab his firstborn, Abinadab the second, Shimea the third, [14]Nethanel the fourth, Raddai the fifth, [15]Ozem the sixth, David the seventh; [16]and their sisters were Zeruiah and Abigail. The sons of Zeruiah: Abishai, Joab, and Asahel, three. [17]Abigail bore Amasa, and the father of Amasa was Jether the Ishmaelite.

18 Caleb son of Hezron had children

---

e Or *and Akan;* See Gen 36.27   *f* See 1.38: Heb *Dishon*   *g* Or *Saul*   *h* Or *chiefs*   *i* Or *Alvah;*
See Gen 36.40   *j* Or *Darda;* Compare Syr Tg some Gk Mss; See 1 Kings 4.31

by his wife Azubah, and by Jerioth; these were her sons: Jesher, Shobab, and Ardon. ¹⁹When Azubah died, Caleb married Ephrath, who bore him Hur. ²⁰Hur became the father of Uri, and Uri became the father of Bezalel.

21 Afterward Hezron went in to the daughter of Machir father of Gilead, whom he married when he was sixty years old; and she bore him Segub; ²²and Segub became the father of Jair, who had twenty-three towns in the land of Gilead. ²³But Geshur and Aram took from them Havvoth-jair, Kenath and its villages, sixty towns. All these were descendants of Machir, father of Gilead. ²⁴After the death of Hezron, in Caleb-ephrathah, Abijah wife of Hezron bore him Ashhur, father of Tekoa.

25 The sons of Jerahmeel, the firstborn of Hezron: Ram his firstborn, Bunah, Oren, Ozem, and Ahijah. ²⁶Jerahmeel also had another wife, whose name was Atarah; she was the mother of Onam. ²⁷The sons of Ram, the firstborn of Jerahmeel: Maaz, Jamin, and Eker. ²⁸The sons of Onam: Shammai and Jada. The sons of Shammai: Nadab and Abishur. ²⁹The name of Abishur's wife was Abihail, and she bore him Ahban and Molid. ³⁰The sons of Nadab: Seled and Appaim; and Seled died childless. ³¹The son^k of Appaim: Ishi. The son^k of Ishi: Sheshan. The son^k of Sheshan: Ahlai. ³²The sons of Jada, Shammai's brother: Jether and Jonathan; and Jether died childless. ³³The sons of Jonathan: Peleth and Zaza. These were the descendants of Jerahmeel. ³⁴Now Sheshan had no sons, only daughters; but Sheshan had an Egyptian slave, whose name was Jarha. ³⁵So Sheshan gave his daughter in marriage to his slave Jarha; and she bore him Attai. ³⁶Attai became the father of Nathan, and Nathan of Zabad. ³⁷Zabad became the father of Ephlal, and Ephlal of Obed. ³⁸Obed became the father of Jehu, and Jehu of Azariah. ³⁹Azariah became the father of Helez, and Helez of Eleasah. ⁴⁰Eleasah became the father of Sismai, and Sismai of Shallum. ⁴¹Shallum became the father of Jekamiah, and Jekamiah of Elishama.

42 The sons of Caleb brother of Jerahmeel: Mesha^l his firstborn, who was father of Ziph. The sons of Mareshah father of Hebron. ⁴³The sons of Hebron: Korah, Tappuah, Rekem, and Shema. ⁴⁴Shema became father of Raham, father of Jorkeam; and Rekem became the father of Shammai. ⁴⁵The son of Shammai: Maon; and Maon was the father of Beth-zur. ⁴⁶Ephah also, Caleb's concubine, bore Haran, Moza, and Gazez; and Haran became the father of Gazez. ⁴⁷The sons of Jahdai: Regem, Jotham, Geshan, Pelet, Ephah, and Shaaph. ⁴⁸Maacah, Caleb's concubine, bore Sheber and Tirhanah. ⁴⁹She also bore Shaaph father of Madmannah, Sheva father of Machbenah and father of Gibea; and the daughter of Caleb was Achsah. ⁵⁰These were the descendants of Caleb.

The sons^m of Hur the firstborn of Ephrathah: Shobal father of Kiriath-jearim, ⁵¹Salma father of Bethlehem, and Hareph father of Beth-gader. ⁵²Shobal father of Kiriath-jearim had other sons: Haroeh, half of the Menuhoth. ⁵³And the families of Kiriath-jearim: the Ithrites, the Puthites, the Shumathites, and the Mishraites; from these came the Zorathites and the Eshtaolites. ⁵⁴The sons of Salma: Bethlehem, the Netophathites, Atroth-beth-joab, and half of the Manahathites, the Zorites. ⁵⁵The families also of the scribes that lived at Jabez: the Tirathites, the Shimeathites, and the Sucathites. These are the Kenites who came from Hammath, father of the house of Rechab.

Descendants of David and Solomon

3 These are the sons of David who were born to him in Hebron: the firstborn Amnon, by Ahinoam the Jezreelite; the second Daniel, by Abigail the Carmelite; ²the third Absalom, son of Maacah, daughter of King Talmai of Geshur; the fourth Adonijah, son of Haggith; ³the fifth Shephatiah, by Abital; the sixth Ithream, by his wife Eglah; ⁴six were born to him in Hebron, where he reigned for seven years and six months. And he reigned thirty-three years in Jerusalem. ⁵These were born to him in Jerusalem: Shimea, Shobab, Nathan, and Solomon, four by Bathshua, daughter of Ammiel; ⁶then Ibhar, Elishama, Eliphelet, ⁷Nogah, Nepheg,

k Heb sons   l Gk reads Mareshah   m Gk Vg: Heb son

Japhia, [8]Elishama, Eliada, and Eliphelet, nine. [9]All these were David's sons, besides the sons of the concubines; and Tamar was their sister.

10 The descendants of Solomon: Rehoboam, Abijah his son, Asa his son, Jehoshaphat his son, [11]Joram his son, Ahaziah his son, Joash his son, [12]Amaziah his son, Azariah his son, Jotham his son, [13]Ahaz his son, Hezekiah his son, Manasseh his son, [14]Amon his son, Josiah his son. [15]The sons of Josiah: Johanan the firstborn, the second Jehoiakim, the third Zedekiah, the fourth Shallum. [16]The descendants of Jehoiakim: Jeconiah his son, Zedekiah his son; [17]and the sons of Jeconiah, the captive: Shealtiel his son, [18]Malchiram, Pedaiah, Shenazzar, Jekamiah, Hoshama, and Nedabiah; [19]The sons of Pedaiah: Zerubbabel and Shimei; and the sons of Zerubbabel: Meshullam and Hananiah, and Shelomith was their sister; [20]and Hashubah, Ohel, Berechiah, Hasadiah, and Jushabhesed, five. [21]The sons of Hananiah: Pelatiah and Jeshaiah, his son[n] Rephaiah, his son[n] Arnan, his son[n] Obadiah, his son[n] Shecaniah. [22]The son[o] of Shecaniah: Shemaiah. And the sons of Shemaiah: Hattush, Igal, Bariah, Neariah, and Shaphat, six. [23]The sons of Neariah: Elioenai, Hizkiah, and Azrikam, three. [24]The sons of Elioenai: Hodaviah, Eliashib, Pelaiah, Akkub, Johanan, Delaiah, and Anani, seven.

Descendants of Judah

4 The sons of Judah: Perez, Hezron, Carmi, Hur, and Shobal. [2]Reaiah son of Shobal became the father of Jahath, and Jahath became the father of Ahumai and Lahad. These were the families of the Zorathites. [3]These were the sons[p] of Etam: Jezreel, Ishma, and Idbash; and the name of their sister was Hazzelelponi, [4]and Penuel was the father of Gedor, and Ezer the father of Hushah. These were the sons of Hur, the firstborn of Ephrathah, the father of Bethlehem. [5]Ashhur father of Tekoa had two wives, Helah and Naarah; [6]Naarah bore him Ahuzzam, Hepher, Temeni,

and Haahashtari.[q] These were the sons of Naarah. [7]The sons of Helah: Zereth, Izhar,[r] and Ethnan. [8]Koz became the father of Anub, Zobebah, and the families of Aharhel son of Harum. [9]Jabez was honored more than his brothers; and his mother named him Jabez, saying, "Because I bore him in pain." [10]Jabez called on the God of Israel, saying, "Oh that you would bless me and enlarge my border, and that your hand might be with me, and that you would keep me from hurt and harm!" And God granted what he asked. [11]Chelub the brother of Shuhah became the father of Mehir, who was the father of Eshton. [12]Eshton became the father of Beth-rapha, Paseah, and Tehinnah the father of Ir-nahash. These are the men of Recah. [13]The sons of Kenaz: Othniel and Seraiah; and the sons of Othniel: Hathath and Meonothai.[s] [14]Meonothai became the father of Ophrah; and Seraiah became the father of Joab father of Ge-harashim,[t] so-called because they were artisans. [15]The sons of Caleb son of Jephunneh: Iru, Elah, and Naam; and the son[o] of Elah: Kenaz. [16]The sons of Jehallelel: Ziph, Ziphah, Tiria, and Asarel. [17]The sons of Ezrah: Jether, Mered, Epher, and Jalon. These are the sons of Bithiah, daughter of Pharaoh, whom Mered married;[u] and she conceived and bore[v] Miriam, Shammai, and Ishbah father of Eshtemoa. [18]And his Judean wife bore Jered father of Gedor, Heber father of Soco, and Jekuthiel father of Zanoah. [19]The sons of the wife of Hodiah, the sister of Naham, were the fathers of Keilah the Garmite and Eshtemoa the Maacathite. [20]The sons of Shimon: Amnon, Rinnah, Benhanan, and Tilon. The sons of Ishi: Zoheth and Ben-zoheth. [21]The sons of Shelah son of Judah: Er father of Lecah, Laadah father of Mareshah, and the families of the guild of linen workers at Beth-ashbea; [22]and Jokim, and the men of Cozeba, and Joash, and Saraph, who married into Moab but returned to Lehem[w] (now the records[x] are ancient). [23]These were the potters and inhabitants of Netaim and Gederah; they lived there with the king in his service.

---

n Gk Compare Syr Vg: Heb sons of   o Heb sons   p Gk Compare Vg: Heb the father
q Or Ahashtari   r Another reading is Zohar   s Gk Vg: Heb lacks and Meonothai   t That is
Valley of artisans   u The clause: These are . . . married is transposed from verse 18   v Heb lacks
and bore   w Vg Compare Gk: Heb and Jashubi-lehem   x Or matters

Descendants of Simeon

24 The sons of Simeon: Nemuel, Jamin, Jarib, Zerah, Shaul;[y] 25 Shallum was his son, Mibsam his son, Mishma his son. 26 The sons of Mishma: Hammuel his son, Zaccur his son, Shimei his son. 27 Shimei had sixteen sons and six daughters; but his brothers did not have many children, nor did all their family multiply like the Judeans. 28 They lived in Beer-sheba, Moladah, Hazar-shual, 29 Bilhah, Ezem, Tolad, 30 Bethuel, Hormah, Ziklag, 31 Beth-marcaboth, Hazar-susim, Beth-biri, and Shaaraim. These were their towns until David became king. 32 And their villages were Etam, Ain, Rimmon, Tochen, and Ashan, five towns, 33 along with all their villages that were around these towns as far as Baal. These were their settlements. And they kept a genealogical record.

34 Meshobab, Jamlech, Joshah son of Amaziah, 35 Joel, Jehu son of Joshibiah son of Seraiah son of Asiel, 36 Elioenai, Jaakobah, Jeshohaiah, Asaiah, Adiel, Jesimiel, Benaiah, 37 Ziza son of Shiphi son of Allon son of Jedaiah son of Shimri son of Shemaiah— 38 these mentioned by name were leaders in their families, and their clans increased greatly. 39 They journeyed to the entrance of Gedor, to the east side of the valley, to seek pasture for their flocks, 40 where they found rich, good pasture, and the land was very broad, quiet, and peaceful; for the former inhabitants there belonged to Ham. 41 These, registered by name, came in the days of King Hezekiah of Judah, and attacked their tents and the Meunim who were found there, and exterminated them to this day, and settled in their place, because there was pasture there for their flocks. 42 And some of them, five hundred men of the Simeonites, went to Mount Seir, having as their leaders Pelatiah, Neariah, Rephaiah, and Uzziel, sons of Ishi; 43 they destroyed the remnant of the Amalekites that had escaped, and they have lived there to this day.

Descendants of Reuben

5 The sons of Reuben the firstborn of Israel. (He was the firstborn, but because he defiled his father's

bed his birthright was given to the sons of Joseph son of Israel, so that he is not enrolled in the genealogy according to the birthright; 2 though Judah became prominent among his brothers and a ruler came from him, yet the birthright belonged to Joseph.) 3 The sons of Reuben, the firstborn of Israel: Hanoch, Pallu, Hezron, and Carmi. 4 The sons of Joel: Shemaiah his son, Gog his son, Shimei his son, 5 Micah his son, Reaiah his son, Baal his son, 6 Beerah his son, whom King Tilgath-pilneser of Assyria carried away into exile; he was a chieftain of the Reubenites. 7 And his kindred by their families, when the genealogy of their generations was reckoned: the chief, Jeiel, and Zechariah, 8 and Bela son of Azaz, son of Shema, son of Joel, who lived in Aroer, as far as Nebo and Baal-meon. 9 He also lived to the east as far as the beginning of the desert this side of the Euphrates, because their cattle had multiplied in the land of Gilead. 10 And in the days of Saul they made war on the Hagrites, who fell by their hand; and they lived in their tents throughout all the region east of Gilead.

Descendants of Gad

11 The sons of Gad lived beside them in the land of Bashan as far as Salecah: 12 Joel the chief, Shapham the second, Janai, and Shaphat in Bashan. 13 And their kindred according to their clans: Michael, Meshullam, Sheba, Jorai, Jacan, Zia, and Eber, seven. 14 These were the sons of Abihail son of Huri, son of Jaroah, son of Gilead, son of Michael, son of Jeshishai, son of Jahdo, son of Buz; 15 Ahi son of Abdiel, son of Guni, was chief in their clan; 16 and they lived in Gilead, in Bashan and in its towns, and in all the pasture lands of Sharon to their limits. 17 All of these were enrolled by genealogies in the days of King Jotham of Judah, and in the days of King Jeroboam of Israel.

18 The Reubenites, the Gadites, and the half-tribe of Manasseh had valiant warriors, who carried shield and sword, and drew the bow, expert in war, forty-four thousand seven hundred sixty, ready for service. 19 They made war on the Hagrites, Jetur, Naphish, and Nodab;

---

y   Or *Saul*

20and when they received help against them, the Hagrites and all who were with them were given into their hands, for they cried to God in the battle, and he granted their entreaty because they trusted in him. 21They captured their livestock: fifty thousand of their camels, two hundred fifty thousand sheep, two thousand donkeys, and one hundred thousand captives. 22Many fell slain, because the war was of God. And they lived in their territory until the exile.

The Half-Tribe of Manasseh

23 The members of the half-tribe of Manasseh lived in the land; they were very numerous from Bashan to Baal-hermon, Senir, and Mount Hermon. 24These were the heads of their clans: Epher,z Ishi, Eliel, Azriel, Jeremiah, Hodaviah, and Jahdiel, mighty warriors, famous men, heads of their clans. 25But they transgressed against the God of their ancestors, and prostituted themselves to the gods of the peoples of the land, whom God had destroyed before them. 26So the God of Israel stirred up the spirit of King Pul of Assyria, the spirit of King Tilgath-pilneser of Assyria, and he carried them away, namely, the Reubenites, the Gadites, and the half-tribe of Manasseh, and brought them to Halah, Habor, Hara, and the river Gozan, to this day.

Descendants of Levi

6a The sons of Levi: Gershom,b Kohath, and Merari. 2The sons of Kohath: Amram, Izhar, Hebron, and Uzziel. 3The children of Amram: Aaron, Moses, and Miriam. The sons of Aaron: Nadab, Abihu, Eleazar, and Ithamar. 4Eleazar became the father of Phinehas, Phinehas of Abishua, 5Abishua of Bukki, Bukki of Uzzi, 6Uzzi of Zerahiah, Zerahiah of Meraioth, 7Meraioth of Amariah, Amariah of Ahitub, 8Ahitub of Zadok, Zadok of Ahimaaz, 9Ahimaaz of Azariah, Azariah of Johanan, 10and Johanan of Azariah (it was he who served as priest in the house that Solomon built in Jerusalem). 11Azariah became the father of Amariah, Amariah

of Ahitub, 12Ahitub of Zadok, Zadok of Shallum, 13Shallum of Hilkiah, Hilkiah of Azariah, 14Azariah of Seraiah, Seraiah of Jehozadak; 15and Jehozadak went into exile when the LORD sent Judah and Jerusalem into exile by the hand of Nebuchadnezzar.

16c The sons of Levi: Gershom, Kohath, and Merari. 17These are the names of the sons of Gershom: Libni and Shimei. 18The sons of Kohath: Amram, Izhar, Hebron, and Uzziel. 19The sons of Merari: Mahli and Mushi. These are the clans of the Levites according to their ancestry. 20Of Gershom: Libni his son, Jahath his son, Zimmah his son, 21Joah his son, Iddo his son, Zerah his son, Jeatherai his son. 22The sons of Kohath: Amminadab his son, Korah his son, Assir his son, 23Elkanah his son, Ebiasaph his son, Assir his son, 24Tahath his son, Uriel his son, Uzziah his son, and Shaul his son. 25The sons of Elkanah: Amasai and Ahimoth, 26Elkanah his son, Zophai his son, Nahath his son, 27Eliab his son, Jeroham his son, Elkanah his son. 28The sons of Samuel: Joeld his firstborn, the second Abijah.e 29The sons of Merari: Mahli, Libni his son, Shimei his son, Uzzah his son, 30Shimea his son, Haggiah his son, and Asaiah his son.

Musicians Appointed by David

31 These are the men whom David put in charge of the service of song in the house of the LORD, after the ark came to rest there. 32They ministered with song before the tabernacle of the tent of meeting, until Solomon had built the house of the LORD in Jerusalem; and they performed their service in due order. 33These are the men who served; and their sons were: Of the Kohathites: Heman, the singer, son of Joel, son of Samuel, 34son of Elkanah, son of Jeroham, son of Eliel, son of Toah, 35son of Zuph, son of Elkanah, son of Mahath, son of Amasai, 36son of Elkanah, son of Joel, son of Azariah, son of Zephaniah, 37son of Tahath, son of Assir, son of Ebiasaph, son of Korah, 38son of Izhar, son of Kohath, son of Levi, son of Israel; 39and his brother Asaph, who stood on

z Gk Vg: Heb and Epher   a Ch 5.27 in Heb   b Heb Gershon, variant of Gershom; See 6.16
c Ch 6.1 in Heb   d Gk Syr Compare verse 33 and 1 Sam 8.2: Heb lacks Joel   e Heb reads Vashni,
and Abijah for the second Abijah, taking the second as a proper name

his right, namely, Asaph son of Berechiah, son of Shimea, 40son of Michael, son of Baaseiah, son of Malchijah, 41son of Ethni, son of Zerah, son of Adaiah, 42son of Ethan, son of Zimmah, son of Shimei, 43son of Jahath, son of Gershom, son of Levi. 44On the left were their kindred the sons of Merari: Ethan son of Kishi, son of Abdi, son of Malluch, 45son of Hashabiah, son of Amaziah, son of Hilkiah, 46son of Amzi, son of Bani, son of Shemer, 47son of Mahli, son of Mushi, son of Merari, son of Levi; 48and their kindred the Levites were appointed for all the service of the tabernacle of the house of God.

49 But Aaron and his sons made offerings on the altar of burnt offering and on the altar of incense, doing all the work of the most holy place, to make atonement for Israel, according to all that Moses the servant of God had commanded. 50These are the sons of Aaron: Eleazar his son, Phinehas his son, Abishua his son, 51Bukki his son, Uzzi his son, Zerahiah his son, 52Meraioth his son, Amariah his son, Ahitub his son, 53Zadok his son, Ahimaaz his son.

Settlements of the Levites

54 These are their dwelling places according to their settlements within their borders: to the sons of Aaron of the families of Kohathites—for the lot fell to them first— 55to them they gave Hebron in the land of Judah and its surrounding pasture lands, 56but the fields of the city and its villages they gave to Caleb son of Jephunneh. 57To the sons of Aaron they gave the cities of refuge: Hebron, Libnah with its pasture lands, Jattir, Eshtemoa with its pasture lands, 58Hilen f with its pasture lands, Debir with its pasture lands, 59Ashan with its pasture lands, and Beth-shemesh with its pasture lands. 60From the tribe of Benjamin, Geba with its pasture lands, Alemeth with its pasture lands, and Anathoth with its pasture lands. All their towns throughout their families were thirteen.

61 To the rest of the Kohathites were given by lot out of the family of the tribe, out of the half-tribe, the half of Manasseh, ten towns. 62To the Gershomites according to their families were allotted thirteen towns out of the tribes of Issachar, Asher, Naphtali, and Manasseh in Bashan. 63To the Merarites according to their families were allotted twelve towns out of the tribes of Reuben, Gad, and Zebulun. 64So the people of Israel gave the Levites the towns with their pasture lands. 65They also gave them by lot out of the tribes of Judah, Simeon, and Benjamin these towns that are mentioned by name.

66 And some of the families of the sons of Kohath had towns of their territory out of the tribe of Ephraim. 67They were given the cities of refuge: Shechem with its pasture lands in the hill country of Ephraim, Gezer with its pasture lands, 68Jokmeam with its pasture lands, Beth-horon with its pasture lands, 69Aijalon with its pasture lands, Gath-rimmon with its pasture lands; 70and out of the half-tribe of Manasseh, Aner with its pasture lands, and Bileam with its pasture lands, for the rest of the families of the Kohathites.

71 To the Gershomites: out of the half-tribe of Manasseh: Golan in Bashan with its pasture lands and Ashtaroth with its pasture lands; 72and out of the tribe of Issachar: Kedesh with its pasture lands, Daberath g with its pasture lands, 73Ramoth with its pasture lands, and Anem with its pasture lands; 74out of the tribe of Asher: Mashal with its pasture lands, Abdon with its pasture lands, 75Hukok with its pasture lands, and Rehob with its pasture lands; 76and out of the tribe of Naphtali: Kedesh in Galilee with its pasture lands, Hammon with its pasture lands, and Kiriathaim with its pasture lands. 77To the rest of the Merarites out of the tribe of Zebulun: Rimmono with its pasture lands, Tabor with its pasture lands, 78and across the Jordan from Jericho, on the east side of the Jordan, out of the tribe of Reuben: Bezer in the steppe with its pasture lands, Jahzah with its pasture lands, 79Kedemoth with its pasture lands, and Mephaath with its pasture lands; 80and out of the tribe of Gad: Ramoth in Gilead with its pasture lands, Mahanaim with its pasture lands, 81Heshbon with its pasture lands, and Jazer with its pasture lands.

f Other readings Hilez, Holon; See Josh 21.15   g Or Dobrath

Descendants of Issachar

7 The sons[h] of Issachar: Tola, Puah, Jashub, and Shimron, four. 2The sons of Tola: Uzzi, Rephaiah, Jeriel, Jahmai, Ibsam, and Shemuel, heads of their ancestral houses, namely of Tola, mighty warriors of their generations, their number in the days of David being twenty-two thousand six hundred. 3The son[i] of Uzzi: Izrahiah. And the sons of Izrahiah: Michael, Obadiah, Joel, and Isshiah, five, all of them chiefs; 4and along with them, by their generations, according to their ancestral houses, were units of the fighting force, thirty-six thousand, for they had many wives and sons. 5Their kindred belonging to all the families of Issachar were in all eighty-seven thousand mighty warriors, enrolled by genealogy.

Descendants of Benjamin

6 The sons of Benjamin: Bela, Becher, and Jediael, three. 7The sons of Bela: Ezbon, Uzzi, Uzziel, Jerimoth, and Iri, five, heads of ancestral houses, mighty warriors; and their enrollment by genealogies was twenty-two thousand thirty-four. 8The sons of Becher: Zemirah, Joash, Eliezer, Elioenai, Omri, Jeremoth, Abijah, Anathoth, and Alemeth. All these were the sons of Becher; 9and their enrollment by genealogies, according to their generations, as heads of their ancestral houses, mighty warriors, was twenty thousand two hundred. 10The sons of Jediael: Bilhan. And the sons of Bilhan: Jeush, Benjamin, Ehud, Chenaanah, Zethan, Tarshish, and Ahishahar. 11All these were the sons of Jediael according to the heads of their ancestral houses, mighty warriors, seventeen thousand two hundred, ready for service in war. 12And Shuppim and Huppim were the sons of Ir, Hushim the son[i] of Aher.

Descendants of Naphtali

13 The descendants of Naphtali: Jahziel, Guni, Jezer, and Shallum, the descendants of Bilhah.

Descendants of Manasseh

14 The sons of Manasseh: Asriel, whom his Aramean concubine bore; she bore Machir the father of Gilead. 15And Machir took a wife for Huppim and for Shuppim. The name of his sister was Maacah. And the name of the second was Zelophehad; and Zelophehad had daughters. 16Maacah the wife of Machir bore a son, and she named him Peresh; the name of his brother was Sheresh; and his sons were Ulam and Rekem. 17The son[i] of Ulam: Bedan. These were the sons of Gilead son of Machir, son of Manasseh. 18And his sister Hammolecheth bore Ishhod, Abiezer, and Mahlah. 19The sons of Shemida were Ahian, Shechem, Likhi, and Aniam.

Descendants of Ephraim

20 The sons of Ephraim: Shuthelah, and Bered his son, Tahath his son, Eleadah his son, Tahath his son, 21Zabad his son, Shuthelah his son, and Ezer and Elead. Now the people of Gath, who were born in the land, killed them, because they came down to raid their cattle. 22And their father Ephraim mourned many days, and his brothers came to comfort him. 23Ephraim[j] went in to his wife, and she conceived and bore a son; and he named him Beriah, because disaster[k] had befallen his house. 24His daughter was Sheerah, who built both Lower and Upper Beth-horon, and Uzzen-sheerah. 25Rephah was his son, Resheph his son, Telah his son, Tahan his son, 26Ladan his son, Ammihud his son, Elishama his son, 27Nun[l] his son, Joshua his son. 28Their possessions and settlements were Bethel and its towns, and eastward Naaran, and westward Gezer and its towns, Shechem and its towns, as far as Ayyah and its towns; 29also along the borders of the Manassites, Beth-shean and its towns, Taanach and its towns, Megiddo and its towns, Dor and its towns. In these lived the sons of Joseph son of Israel.

Descendants of Asher

30 The sons of Asher: Imnah, Ishvah, Ishvi, Beriah, and their sister Serah. 31The sons of Beriah: Heber and Malchiel, who was the father of Birzaith. 32Heber became the father of Japh-

h Syr Compare Vg: Heb *And to the sons Non*; see Ex 33.11   i Heb *sons*   j Heb *He*   k Heb *beraah*   l Here spelled

let, Shomer, Hotham, and their sister Shua. [33]The sons of Japhlet: Pasach, Bimhal, and Ashvath. These are the sons of Japhlet. [34]The sons of Shemer: Ahi, Rohgah, Hubbah, and Aram. [35]The sons of Helem[m] his brother: Zophah, Imna, Shelesh, and Amal. [36]The sons of Zophah: Suah, Harnepher, Shual, Beri, Imrah, [37]Bezer, Hod, Shamma, Shilshah, Ithran, and Beera. [38]The sons of Jether: Jephunneh, Pispa, and Ara. [39]The sons of Ulla: Arah, Hanniel, and Rizia. [40]All of these were men of Asher, heads of ancestral houses, select mighty warriors, chief of the princes. Their number enrolled by genealogies, for service in war, was twenty-six thousand men.

Descendants of Benjamin

8 Benjamin became the father of Bela his firstborn, Ashbel the second, Aharah the third, [2]Nohah the fourth, and Rapha the fifth. [3]And Bela had sons: Addar, Gera, Abihud,[n] [4]Abishua, Naaman, Ahoah, [5]Gera, Shephuphan, and Huram. [6]These are the sons of Ehud (they were heads of ancestral houses of the inhabitants of Geba, and they were carried into exile to Manahath): [7]Naaman,[o] Ahijah, and Gera, that is, Heglam,[p] who became the father of Uzza and Ahihud. [8]And Shaharaim had sons in the country of Moab after he had sent away his wives Hushim and Baara. [9]He had sons by his wife Hodesh: Jobab, Zibia, Mesha, Malcam, [10]Jeuz, Sachia, and Mirmah. These were his sons, heads of ancestral houses. [11]He also had sons by Hushim: Abitub and Elpaal. [12]The sons of Elpaal: Eber, Misham, and Shemed, who built Ono and Lod with its towns, [13]and Beriah and Shema (they were heads of ancestral houses of the inhabitants of Aijalon, who put to flight the inhabitants of Gath); [14]and Ahio, Shashak, and Jeremoth. [15]Zebadiah, Arad, Eder, [16]Michael, Ishpah, and Joha were sons of Beriah. [17]Zebadiah, Meshullam, Hizki, Heber, [18]Ishmerai, Izliah, and Jobab were the sons of Elpaal. [19]Jakim, Zichri, Zabdi, [20]Elienai, Zillethai, Eliel, [21]Adaiah, Beraiah, and Shimrath were the sons of Shimei. [22]Ishpan,

Eber, Eliel, [23]Abdon, Zichri, Hanan, [24]Hananiah, Elam, Anthothijah, [25]Iphdeiah, and Penuel were the sons of Shashak. [26]Shamsherai, Shehariah, Athaliah, [27]Jaareshiah, Elijah, and Zichri were the sons of Jeroham. [28]These were heads of ancestral houses, according to their generations, chiefs. These lived in Jerusalem.

[29] Jeiel[q] the father of Gibeon lived in Gibeon, and the name of his wife was Maacah. [30]His firstborn son: Abdon, then Zur, Kish, Baal,[r] Nadab, [31]Gedor, Ahio, Zecher, [32]and Mikloth, who became the father of Shimeah. Now these also lived opposite their kindred in Jerusalem, with their kindred. [33]Ner became the father of Kish, Kish of Saul,[s] Saul[s] of Jonathan, Malchishua, Abinadab, and Esh-baal; [34]and the son of Jonathan was Merib-baal; and Merib-baal became the father of Micah. [35]The sons of Micah: Pithon, Melech, Tarea, and Ahaz. [36]Ahaz became the father of Jehoaddah; and Jehoaddah became the father of Alemeth, Azmaveth, and Zimri; Zimri became the father of Moza. [37]Moza became the father of Binea; Raphah was his son, Eleasah his son, Azel his son. [38]Azel had six sons, and these are their names: Azrikam, Bocheru, Ishmael, Sheariah, Obadiah, and Hanan; all these were the sons of Azel. [39]The sons of his brother Eshek: Ulam his firstborn, Jeush the second, and Eliphelet the third. [40]The sons of Ulam were mighty warriors, archers, having many children and grandchildren, one hundred fifty. All these were Benjaminites.

9 So all Israel was enrolled by genealogies; and these are written in the Book of the Kings of Israel. And Judah was taken into exile in Babylon because of their unfaithfulness. [2]Now the first to live again in their possessions in their towns were Israelites, priests, Levites, and temple servants.

Inhabitants of Jerusalem after the Exile

[3] And some of the people of Judah, Benjamin, Ephraim, and Manasseh lived

---

in Jerusalem: 4Uthai son of Ammihud, son of Omri, son of Imri, son of Bani, from the sons of Perez son of Judah. 5And of the Shilonites: Asaiah the firstborn, and his sons. 6Of the sons of Zerah: Jeuel and their kin, six hundred ninety. 7Of the Benjaminites: Sallu son of Meshullam, son of Hodaviah, son of Hassenuah, 8Ibneiah son of Jeroham, Elah son of Uzzi, son of Michri, and Meshullam son of Shephatiah, son of Reuel, son of Ibnijah; 9and their kindred according to their generations, nine hundred fifty-six. All these were heads of families according to their ancestral houses.

Priestly Families

10 Of the priests: Jedaiah, Jehoiarib, Jachin, 11and Azariah son of Hilkiah, son of Meshullam, son of Zadok, son of Meraioth, son of Ahitub, the chief officer of the house of God; 12and Adaiah son of Jeroham, son of Pashhur, son of Malchijah, and Maasai son of Adiel, son of Jahzerah, son of Meshullam, son of Meshillemith, son of Immer; 13besides their kindred, heads of their ancestral houses, one thousand seven hundred sixty, qualified for the work of the service of the house of God.

Levitical Families

14 Of the Levites: Shemaiah son of Hasshub, son of Azrikam, son of Hashabiah, of the sons of Merari; 15and Bakbakkar, Heresh, Galal, and Mattaniah son of Mica, son of Zichri, son of Asaph; 16and Obadiah son of Shemaiah, son of Galal, son of Jeduthun, and Berechiah son of Asa, son of Elkanah, who lived in the villages of the Netophathites.

17 The gatekeepers were: Shallum, Akkub, Talmon, Ahiman; and their kindred Shallum was the chief, 18stationed previously in the king's gate on the east side. These were the gatekeepers of the camp of the Levites. 19Shallum son of Kore, son of Ebiasaph, son of Korah, and his kindred of his ancestral house, the Korahites, were in charge of the work of the service, guardians of the thresholds of the tent, as their ancestors had been in charge of the camp of the LORD, guardians of the entrance. 20And Phinehas son of Eleazar was chief over them

in former times; the LORD was with him. 21Zechariah son of Meshelemiah was gatekeeper at the entrance of the tent of meeting. 22All these, who were chosen as gatekeepers at the thresholds, were two hundred twelve. They were enrolled by genealogies in their villages. David and the seer Samuel established them in their office of trust. 23So they and their descendants were in charge of the gates of the house of the LORD, that is, the house of the tent, as guards. 24The gatekeepers were on the four sides, east, west, north, and south; 25and their kindred who were in their villages were obliged to come in every seven days, in turn, to be with them; 26for the four chief gatekeepers, who were Levites, were in charge of the chambers and the treasures of the house of God. 27And they would spend the night near the house of God; for on them lay the duty of watching, and they had charge of opening it every morning.

28 Some of them had charge of the utensils of service, for they were required to count them when they were brought in and taken out. 29Others of them were appointed over the furniture, and over all the holy utensils, also over the choice flour, the wine, the oil, the incense, and the spices. 30Others, of the sons of the priests, prepared the mixing of the spices, 31and Mattithiah, one of the Levites, the firstborn of Shallum the Korahite, was in charge of making the flat cakes. 32Also some of their kindred of the Kohathites had charge of the rows of bread, to prepare them for each sabbath.

33 Now these are the singers, the heads of ancestral houses of the Levites, living in the chambers of the temple free from other service, for they were on duty day and night. 34These were heads of ancestral houses of the Levites, according to their generations; these leaders lived in Jerusalem.

The Family of King Saul

35 In Gibeon lived the father of Gibeon, Jeiel, and the name of his wife was Maacah. 36His firstborn son was Abdon, then Zur, Kish, Baal, Ner, Nadab, 37Gedor, Ahio, Zechariah, and Mikloth; 38and Mikloth became the father of Shimeam; and these also lived opposite

their kindred in Jerusalem, with their kindred. **39**Ner became the father of Kish, Kish of Saul, Saul of Jonathan, Malchishua, Abinadab, and Esh-baal; **40**and the son of Jonathan was Merib-baal; and Merib-baal became the father of Micah. **41**The sons of Micah: Pithon, Melech, Tahrea, and Ahaz;*t* **42**and Ahaz became the father of Jarah, and Jarah of Alemeth, Azmaveth, and Zimri; and Zimri became the father of Moza. **43**Moza became the father of Binea; and Rephaiah was his son, Eleasah his son, Azel his son. **44**Azel had six sons, and these are their names: Azrikam, Boche-ru, Ishmael, Sheariah, Obadiah, and Hanan; these were the sons of Azel.

Death of Saul and His Sons

10 Now the Philistines fought against Israel; and the men of Israel fled before the Philistines, and fell slain on Mount Gilboa. **2**The Philistines overtook Saul and his sons; and the Philistines killed Jonathan and Abinadab and Malchishua, sons of Saul. **3**The battle pressed hard on Saul; and the archers found him, and he was wounded by the archers. **4**Then Saul said to his armor-bearer, "Draw your sword, and thrust me through with it, so that these uncircumcised may not come and make sport of me." But his armor-bearer was unwilling, for he was terrified. So Saul took his own sword and fell on it. **5**When his armor-bearer saw that Saul was dead, he also fell on his sword and died. **6**Thus Saul died; he and his three sons and all his house died together. **7**When all the men of Israel who were in the valley saw that the army*u* had fled and that Saul and his sons were dead, they abandoned their towns and fled; and the Philistines came and occupied them.

8 The next day when the Philistines came to strip the dead, they found Saul and his sons fallen on Mount Gilboa. **9**They stripped him and took his head and his armor, and sent messengers throughout the land of the Philistines to carry the good news to their idols and to the people. **10**They put his armor in the temple of their gods, and fastened his head in the temple of Dagon. **11**But when all Jabesh-gilead heard everything that the Philistines had done to Saul, **12**all the valiant warriors got up and took away the body of Saul and the bodies of his sons, and brought them to Jabesh. Then they buried their bones under the oak in Jabesh, and fasted seven days.

13 So Saul died for his unfaithfulness; he was unfaithful to the LORD in that he did not keep the command of the LORD; moreover, he had consulted a medium, seeking guidance, **14**and did not seek guidance from the LORD. Therefore the LORD*v* put him to death and turned the kingdom over to David son of Jesse.

David Anointed King of All Israel

11 Then all Israel gathered together to David at Hebron and said, "See, we are your bone and flesh. **2**For some time now, even while Saul was king, it was you who commanded the army of Israel. The LORD your God said to you: It is you who shall be shepherd of my people Israel, you who shall be ruler over my people Israel." **3**So all the elders of Israel came to the king at Hebron, and David made a covenant with them at Hebron before the LORD. And they anointed David king over Israel, according to the word of the LORD by Samuel.

Jerusalem Captured

4 David and all Israel marched to Jerusalem, that is Jebus, where the Jebusites were, the inhabitants of the land. **5**The inhabitants of Jebus said to David, "You will not come in here." Nevertheless David took the stronghold of Zion, now the city of David. **6**David had said, "Whoever attacks the Jebusites first shall be chief and commander." And Joab son of Zeruiah went up first, so he became chief. **7**David resided in the stronghold; therefore it was called the city of David. **8**He built the city all around, from the Millo in complete circuit; and Joab repaired the rest of the city. **9**And David became greater and greater, for the LORD of hosts was with him.

David's Mighty Men and Their Exploits

10 Now these are the chiefs of David's warriors, who gave him strong

---

t Compare 8.35: Heb lacks *and Ahaz*   *u* Heb *they*   *v* Heb *he* support in his kingdom, together with all Israel, to make him king, according to the word of the LORD concerning Israel. [11] This is an account of David's mighty warriors: Jashobeam, son of Hachmoni,[w] was chief of the Three;[x] he wielded his spear against three hundred whom he killed at one time.

12 And next to him among the three warriors was Eleazar son of Dodo, the Ahohite. [13] He was with David at Pasdammim when the Philistines were gathered there for battle. There was a plot of ground full of barley. Now the people had fled from the Philistines, [14] but he and David took their stand in the middle of the plot, defended it, and killed the Philistines; and the LORD saved them by a great victory.

15 Three of the thirty chiefs went down to the rock to David at the cave of Adullam, while the army of Philistines was encamped in the valley of Rephaim. [16] David was then in the stronghold; and the garrison of the Philistines was then at Bethlehem. [17] David said longingly, "O that someone would give me water to drink from the well of Bethlehem that is by the gate!" [18] Then the Three broke through the camp of the Philistines, and drew water from the well of Bethlehem that was by the gate, and they brought it to David. But David would not drink of it; he poured it out to the LORD, [19] and said, "My God forbid that I should do this. Can I drink the blood of these men? For at the risk of their lives they brought it." Therefore he would not drink it. The three warriors did these things.

20 Now Abishai,[y] the brother of Joab, was chief of the Thirty.[z] With his spear he fought against three hundred and killed them, and won a name beside the Three. [21] He was the most renowned[a] of the Thirty,[z] and became their commander; but he did not attain to the Three. [22] Benaiah son of Jehoiada was a valiant man[b] of Kabzeel, a doer of great deeds; he struck down two sons of[c] Ariel of Moab. He also went down and killed a lion in a pit on a day when snow had fallen. [23] And he killed an Egyptian,

a man of great stature, five cubits tall. The Egyptian had in his hand a spear like a weaver's beam; but Benaiah went against him with a staff, snatched the spear out of the Egyptian's hand, and killed him with his own spear. [24] Such were the things Benaiah son of Jehoiada did, and he won a name beside the three warriors. [25] He was renowned among the Thirty, but he did not attain to the Three. And David put him in charge of his bodyguard.

26 The warriors of the armies were Asahel brother of Joab, Elhanan son of Dodo of Bethlehem, [27] Shammoth of Harod,[d] Helez the Pelonite, [28] Ira son of Ikkesh of Tekoa, Abiezer of Anathoth, [29] Sibbecai the Hushathite, Ilai the Ahohite, [30] Maharai of Netophah, Heled son of Baanah of Netophah, [31] Ithai son of Ribai of Gibeah of the Benjaminites, Benaiah of Pirathon, [32] Hurai of the wadis of Gaash, Abiel the Arbathite, [33] Azmaveth of Baharum, Eliahba of Shaalbon, [34] Hashem[e] the Gizonite, Jonathan son of Shagee the Hararite, [35] Ahiam son of Sachar the Hararite, Eliphal son of Ur, [36] Hepher the Mecherathite, Ahijah the Pelonite, [37] Hezro of Carmel, Naarai son of Ezbai, [38] Joel the brother of Nathan, Mibhar son of Hagri, [39] Zelek the Ammonite, Naharai of Beeroth, the armor-bearer of Joab son of Zeruiah, [40] Ira the Ithrite, Gareb the Ithrite, [41] Uriah the Hittite, Zabad son of Ahlai, [42] Adina son of Shiza the Reubenite, a leader of the Reubenites, and thirty with him, [43] Hanan son of Maacah, and Joshaphat the Mithnite, [44] Uzzia the Ashterathite, Shama and Jeiel sons of Hotham the Aroerite, [45] Jediael son of Shimri, and his brother Joha the Tizite, [46] Eliel the Mahavite, and Jeribai and Joshaviah sons of Elnaam, and Ithmah the Moabite, [47] Eliel, and Obed, and Jaasiel the Mezobaite.

David's Followers in the Wilderness

12 The following are those who came to David at Ziklag, while he could not move about freely because of Saul son of Kish; they were

---

w Or *a Hachmonite*   x Compare 2 Sam 23.8: Heb *Thirty* or *captains*   y Gk Vg Tg Compare 2 Sam 23.18: Heb *Abshai*   z Syr: Heb *Three*   a Compare 2 Sam 23.19: Heb *more renowned among the two*   b Syr: Heb *the son of a valiant man*   c See 2 Sam 23.20: Heb lacks *sons of*   d Compare 2 Sam 23.25: Heb *the Harorite*   e Compare Gk and 2 Sam 23.32: Heb *the sons of Hashem* among the mighty warriors who helped him in war. ²They were archers, and could shoot arrows and sling stones with either the right hand or the left; they were Benjaminites, Saul's kindred. ³The chief was Ahiezer, then Joash, both sons of Shemaah of Gibeah; also Jeziel and Pelet sons of Azmaveth; Beracah, Jehu of Anathoth, ⁴Ishmaiah of Gibeon, a warrior among the Thirty and a leader over the Thirty; Jeremiah,ᶠ Jahaziel, Johanan, Jozabad of Gederah, ⁵Eluzai,ᵍ Jerimoth, Bealiah, Shemariah, Shephatiah the Haruphite; ⁶Elkanah, Isshiah, Azarel, Joezer, and Jashobeam, the Korahites; ⁷and Joelah and Zebadiah, sons of Jeroham of Gedor.

8 From the Gadites there went over to David at the stronghold in the wilderness mighty and experienced warriors, expert with shield and spear, whose faces were like the faces of lions, and who were swift as gazelles on the mountains: ⁹Ezer the chief, Obadiah second, Eliab third, ¹⁰Mishmannah fourth, Jeremiah fifth, ¹¹Attai sixth, Eliel seventh, ¹²Johanan eighth, Elzabad ninth, ¹³Jeremiah tenth, Machbannai eleventh. ¹⁴These Gadites were officers of the army, the least equal to a hundred and the greatest to a thousand. ¹⁵These are the men who crossed the Jordan in the first month, when it was overflowing all its banks, and put to flight all those in the valleys, to the east and to the west.

16 Some Benjaminites and Judahites came to the stronghold to David. ¹⁷David went out to meet them and said to them, "If you have come to me in friendship, to help me, then my heart will be knit to you; but if you have come to betray me to my adversaries, though my hands have done no wrong, then may the God of our ancestors see and give judgment." ¹⁸Then the spirit came upon Amasai, chief of the Thirty, and he said,

"We are yours, O David;
    and with you, O son of Jesse!
Peace, peace to you,
    and peace to the one who helps
        you!
For your God is the one who
    helps you."

Then David received them, and made them officers of his troops.

19 Some of the Manassites deserted to David when he came with the Philistines for the battle against Saul. (Yet he did not help them, for the rulers of the Philistines took counsel and sent him away, saying, "He will desert to his master Saul at the cost of our heads.") ²⁰As he went to Ziklag these Manassites deserted to him: Adnah, Jozabad, Jediael, Michael, Jozabad, Elihu, and Zillethai, chiefs of the thousands in Manasseh. ²¹They helped David against the band of raiders,ʰ for they were all warriors and commanders in the army. ²²Indeed from day to day people kept coming to David to help him, until there was a great army, like an army of God.

David's Army at Hebron

23 These are the numbers of the divisions of the armed troops who came to David in Hebron to turn the kingdom of Saul over to him, according to the word of the LORD. ²⁴The people of Judah bearing shield and spear numbered six thousand eight hundred armed troops. ²⁵Of the Simeonites, mighty warriors, seven thousand one hundred. ²⁶Of the Levites four thousand six hundred. ²⁷Jehoiada, leader of the house of Aaron, and with him three thousand seven hundred. ²⁸Zadok, a young warrior, and twenty-two commanders from his own ancestral house. ²⁹Of the Benjaminites, the kindred of Saul, three thousand, of whom the majority had continued to keep their allegiance to the house of Saul. ³⁰Of the Ephraimites, twenty thousand eight hundred, mighty warriors, notables in their ancestral houses. ³¹Of the half-tribe of Manasseh, eighteen thousand, who were expressly named to come and make David king. ³²Of Issachar, those who had understanding of the times, to know what Israel ought to do, two hundred chiefs, and all their kindred under their command. ³³Of Zebulun, fifty thousand seasoned troops, equipped for battle with all the weapons of war, to help Davidⁱ with singleness of purpose. ³⁴Of Naphtali, a thousand commanders, with whom there were thirty-seven thousand armed with shield and

ᶠ Heb verse 5   ᵍ Heb verse 6   ʰ Or *as officers of his troops*   ⁱ Gk: Heb lacks *David* spear. 35Of the Danites, twenty-eight thousand six hundred equipped for battle. 36Of Asher, forty thousand seasoned troops ready for battle. 37Of the Reubenites and Gadites and the half-tribe of Manasseh from beyond the Jordan, one hundred twenty thousand armed with all the weapons of war.

38 All these, warriors arrayed in battle order, came to Hebron with full intent to make David king over all Israel; likewise all the rest of Israel were of a single mind to make David king. 39They were there with David for three days, eating and drinking, for their kindred had provided for them. 40And also their neighbors, from as far away as Issachar and Zebulun and Naphtali, came bringing food on donkeys, camels, mules, and oxen—abundant provisions of meal, cakes of figs, clusters of raisins, wine, oil, oxen, and sheep, for there was joy in Israel.

The Ark Brought from Kiriath-jearim

13 David consulted with the commanders of the thousands and of the hundreds, with every leader. 2David said to the whole assembly of Israel, "If it seems good to you, and if it is the will of the LORD our God, let us send abroad to our kindred who remain in all the land of Israel, including the priests and Levites in the cities that have pasture lands, that they may come together to us. 3Then let us bring again the ark of our God to us; for we did not turn to it in the days of Saul." 4The whole assembly agreed to do so, for the thing pleased all the people.

5 So David assembled all Israel from the Shihor of Egypt to Lebo-hamath, to bring the ark of God from Kiriath-jearim. 6And David and all Israel went up to Baalah, that is, to Kiriath-jearim, which belongs to Judah, to bring up from there the ark of God, the LORD, who is enthroned on the cherubim, which is called by his*j* name. 7They carried the ark of God on a new cart, from the house of Abinadab, and Uzzah and Ahio*k* were driving the cart. 8David and all Israel were dancing before God with all their might, with song and lyres and harps and tambourines and cymbals and trumpets.

9 When they came to the threshing floor of Chidon, Uzzah put out his hand to hold the ark, for the oxen shook it. 10The anger of the LORD was kindled against Uzzah; he struck him down because he put out his hand to the ark; and he died there before God. 11David was angry because the LORD had burst out against Uzzah; so that place is called Perez-uzzah*l* to this day. 12David was afraid of God that day; he said, "How can I bring the ark of God into my care?" 13So David did not take the ark into his care into the city of David; he took it instead to the house of Obed-edom the Gittite. 14The ark of God remained with the household of Obed-edom in his house three months, and the LORD blessed the household of Obed-edom and all that he had.

David Established at Jerusalem

14 King Hiram of Tyre sent messengers to David, along with cedar logs, and masons and carpenters to build a house for him. 2David then perceived that the LORD had established him as king over Israel, and that his kingdom was highly exalted for the sake of his people Israel.

3 David took more wives in Jerusalem, and David became the father of more sons and daughters. 4These are the names of the children whom he had in Jerusalem: Shammua, Shobab, and Nathan; Solomon, 5Ibhar, Elishua, and Elpelet; 6Nogah, Nepheg, and Japhia; 7Elishama, Beeliada, and Eliphelet.

Defeat of the Philistines

8 When the Philistines heard that David had been anointed king over all Israel, all the Philistines went up in search of David; and David heard of it and went out against them. 9Now the Philistines had come and made a raid in the valley of Rephaim. 10David inquired of God, "Shall I go up against the Philistines? Will you give them into my hand?" The LORD said to him, "Go up, and I will give them into your hand." 11So he went up to Baal-perazim, and David defeated them there. David said,

---

j Heb lacks *his*   *k* Or *and his brother*   *l* That is *Bursting Out Against Uzzah*

"God has burst out[m] against my enemies by my hand, like a bursting flood." Therefore that place is called Baal-perazim.[n] 12They abandoned their gods there, and at David's command they were burned.

13 Once again the Philistines made a raid in the valley. 14When David again inquired of God, God said to him, "You shall not go up after them; go around and come on them opposite the balsam trees. 15When you hear the sound of marching in the tops of the balsam trees, then go out to battle; for God has gone out before you to strike down the army of the Philistines." 16David did as God had commanded him, and they struck down the Philistine army from Gibeon to Gezer. 17The fame of David went out into all lands, and the LORD brought the fear of him on all nations.

The Ark Brought to Jerusalem

15 David[o] built houses for himself in the city of David, and he prepared a place for the ark of God and pitched a tent for it. 2Then David commanded that no one but the Levites were to carry the ark of God, for the LORD had chosen them to carry the ark of the LORD and to minister to him forever. 3David assembled all Israel in Jerusalem to bring up the ark of the LORD to its place, which he had prepared for it. 4Then David gathered together the descendants of Aaron and the Levites: 5of the sons of Kohath, Uriel the chief, with one hundred twenty of his kindred; 6of the sons of Merari, Asaiah the chief, with two hundred twenty of his kindred; 7of the sons of Gershom, Joel the chief, with one hundred thirty of his kindred; 8of the sons of Elizaphan, Shemaiah the chief, with two hundred of his kindred; 9of the sons of Hebron, Eliel the chief, with eighty of his kindred; 10of the sons of Uzziel, Amminadab the chief, with one hundred twelve of his kindred.

11 David summoned the priests Zadok and Abiathar, and the Levites Uriel, Asaiah, Joel, Shemaiah, Eliel, and Amminadab. 12He said to them, "You are the heads of families of the Levites; sanctify yourselves, you and your kindred, so that you may bring up the ark of the LORD, the God of Israel, to the place that I have prepared for it. 13Because you did not carry it the first time,[p] the LORD our God burst out against us, because we did not give it proper care." 14So the priests and the Levites sanctified themselves to bring up the ark of the LORD, the God of Israel. 15And the Levites carried the ark of God on their shoulders with the poles, as Moses had commanded according to the word of the LORD.

16 David also commanded the chiefs of the Levites to appoint their kindred as the singers to play on musical instruments, on harps and lyres and cymbals, to raise loud sounds of joy. 17So the Levites appointed Heman son of Joel; and of his kindred Asaph son of Berechiah; and of the sons of Merari, their kindred, Ethan son of Kushaiah; 18and with them their kindred of the second order, Zechariah, Jaaziel, Shemiramoth, Jehiel, Unni, Eliab, Benaiah, Maaseiah, Mattithiah, Eliphelehu, and Mikneiah, and the gatekeepers Obed-edom and Jeiel. 19The singers Heman, Asaph, and Ethan were to sound bronze cymbals; 20Zechariah, Aziel, Shemiramoth, Jehiel, Unni, Eliab, Maaseiah, and Benaiah were to play harps according to Alamoth; 21but Mattithiah, Eliphelehu, Mikneiah, Obed-edom, Jeiel, and Azaziah were to lead with lyres according to the Sheminith. 22Chenaniah, leader of the Levites in music, was to direct the music, for he understood it. 23Berechiah and Elkanah were to be gatekeepers for the ark. 24Shebaniah, Joshaphat, Nethanel, Amasai, Zechariah, Benaiah, and Eliezer, the priests, were to blow the trumpets before the ark of God. Obed-edom and Jehiah also were to be gatekeepers for the ark.

25 So David and the elders of Israel, and the commanders of the thousands, went to bring up the ark of the covenant of the LORD from the house of Obed-edom with rejoicing. 26And because God helped the Levites who were carrying the ark of the covenant of the LORD, they sacrificed seven bulls and seven rams. 27David was clothed with a robe of fine linen, as also were all the Levites who were carrying the ark, and the

---

m Heb *paraz*   *n* That is *Lord of Bursting Out*   *o* Heb *He*   *p* Meaning of Heb uncertain

singers, and Chenaniah the leader of the music of the singers; and David wore a linen ephod. 28So all Israel brought up the ark of the covenant of the LORD with shouting, to the sound of the horn, trumpets, and cymbals, and made loud music on harps and lyres.

29 As the ark of the covenant of the LORD came to the city of David, Michal daughter of Saul looked out of the window, and saw King David leaping and dancing; and she despised him in her heart.

The Ark Placed in the Tent

16 They brought in the ark of God, and set it inside the tent that David had pitched for it; and they offered burnt offerings and offerings of well-being before God. 2When David had finished offering the burnt offerings and the offerings of well-being, he blessed the people in the name of the LORD; 3and he distributed to every person in Israel—man and woman alike—to each a loaf of bread, a portion of meat,q and a cake of raisins.

4 He appointed certain of the Levites as ministers before the ark of the LORD, to invoke, to thank, and to praise the LORD, the God of Israel. 5Asaph was the chief, and second to him Zechariah, Jeiel, Shemiramoth, Jehiel, Mattithiah, Eliab, Benaiah, Obed-edom, and Jeiel, with harps and lyres; Asaph was to sound the cymbals, 6and the priests Benaiah and Jahaziel were to blow trumpets regularly, before the ark of the covenant of God.

David's Psalm of Thanksgiving

7 Then on that day David first appointed the singing of praises to the LORD by Asaph and his kindred.

8 O give thanks to the LORD, call on
     his name,
   make known his deeds among
     the peoples.
9 Sing to him, sing praises to him,
   tell of all his wonderful works.
10 Glory in his holy name;
   let the hearts of those who seek
     the LORD rejoice.

11 Seek the LORD and his strength,
   seek his presence continually.
12 Remember the wonderful works he
     has done,
   his miracles, and the judgments
     he uttered,
13 O offspring of his servant Israel,r
   children of Jacob, his chosen ones.

14 He is the LORD our God;
   his judgments are in all the earth.
15 Remember his covenant forever,
   the word that he commanded, for
     a thousand generations,
16 the covenant that he made with
     Abraham,
   his sworn promise to Isaac,
17 which he confirmed to Jacob as a
     statute,
   to Israel as an everlasting
     covenant,
18 saying, "To you I will give the land
     of Canaan
   as your portion for an
     inheritance."

19 When they were few in number,
   of little account, and strangers in
     the land,s
20 wandering from nation to nation,
   from one kingdom to another
     people,
21 he allowed no one to oppress them;
   he rebuked kings on their
     account,
22 saying, "Do not touch my anointed
     ones;
   do my prophets no harm."

23 Sing to the LORD, all the earth.
   Tell of his salvation from day to
     day.
24 Declare his glory among the
     nations,
   his marvelous works among all
     the peoples.
25 For great is the LORD, and greatly to
     be praised;
   he is to be revered above all gods.
26 For all the gods of the peoples are
     idols,
   but the LORD made the heavens.
27 Honor and majesty are before him;
   strength and joy are in his place.

q Compare Gk Syr Vg: Meaning of Heb uncertain
s Heb in it

r Another reading is Abraham (compare Ps 105.6)

THE FOUNDATION OF A PREVIOUS RELIGION
Blaise Pascal

VERSE: 1 Chronicles 16.8   **PASSAGE:** 1 Chronicles 16.7–36

 see Christianity founded on a previous religion, in which I find the following facts.

(I am not speaking here of the miracles of Moses, Christ and the apostles, because they do not at first appear convincing, and I want here only to bring as evidence all those foundations of Christianity which are beyond doubt and cannot be called in doubt by anyone whatever.)

It is certain that in certain parts of the world we can see a peculiar people, separated from the other peoples of the world, and this is called the Jewish people.

I see then makers of religions in several parts of the world and throughout the ages, but their morality fails to satisfy me and their proofs fail to give me pause. Thus I should have refused alike the Moslem religion, that of China, of the ancient Romans, and of the Egyptians solely because, none of them bearing the stamp of truth more than another, nor anything which forces me to choose it, reason cannot incline towards one rather than another.

But as I consider this shifting and odd variety of customs and beliefs in different ages, I find in one corner of the world a peculiar people, separated from all the other peoples of the earth, who are the most ancient of all and whose history is earlier by several centuries than the oldest histories we have.

I find then this great and numerous people, descended from one man, worshiping one God, and living according to a law which they claim to have received from his hand. They maintain that they are the only people in the world to whom God has revealed his mysteries; that all men are corrupt and in disgrace with God, that they have all been abandoned to their senses and their own minds; and that this is the reason for the strange aberrations and continual changes of religions and customs among them, whereas these people remain unshakable in their conduct; but that God will not leave the other peoples for ever in darkness, that a redeemer will come, for all; that they are in the world to proclaim him to men; that they have been expressly created to be the forerunners and heralds of this great coming, and to call all peoples to unite with them in looking forward to this redeemer.

ADDITIONAL SCRIPTURE READING:
Deuteronomy 14.2; Titus 2.11–14; 1 Peter 2.9–12

Go to page 469 for your next devotional reading.

1500   1700

28 Ascribe to the LORD, O families of
        the peoples,
     ascribe to the LORD glory and
        strength.
29 Ascribe to the LORD the glory due
        his name;
     bring an offering, and come
        before him.
     Worship the LORD in holy splendor;
30   tremble before him, all the earth.
     The world is firmly established;
        it shall never be moved.
31 Let the heavens be glad, and let the
        earth rejoice,
     and let them say among the
        nations, "The LORD is king!"
32 Let the sea roar, and all that fills it;
     let the field exult, and everything
        in it.
33 Then shall the trees of the forest
        sing for joy
     before the LORD, for he comes to
        judge the earth.
34 O give thanks to the LORD, for he is
        good;
     for his steadfast love endures
        forever.

35 Say also:
     "Save us, O God of our salvation,
        and gather and rescue us from
           among the nations,
     that we may give thanks to your
        holy name,
        and glory in your praise.

THE CRY OF A YOUNG RAVEN IS NOTHING BUT
THE NATURAL CRY OF A CREATURE, BUT YOUR
CRY, IF IT BE SINCERE, IS THE RESULT OF A WORK
OF GRACE IN YOUR HEART.   —C. H. Spurgeon

---

36 Blessed be the LORD, the God of
        Israel,
     from everlasting to everlasting."
     Then all the people said "Amen!" and
     praised the LORD.

Regular Worship Maintained

37 David left Asaph and his kinsfolk
there before the ark of the covenant of
the LORD to minister regularly before
the ark as each day required, 38 and also

Obed-edom and his[t] sixty-eight kinsfolk; while Obed-edom son of Jeduthun
and Hosah were to be gatekeepers.
39 And he left the priest Zadok and his
kindred the priests before the tabernacle
of the LORD in the high place that was at
Gibeon, 40 to offer burnt offerings to the
LORD on the altar of burnt offering regularly, morning and evening, according to
all that is written in the law of the LORD
that he commanded Israel. 41 With them
were Heman and Jeduthun, and the rest
of those chosen and expressly named to
render thanks to the LORD, for his steadfast love endures forever. 42 Heman and
Jeduthun had with them trumpets and
cymbals for the music, and instruments
for sacred song. The sons of Jeduthun
were appointed to the gate.

43 Then all the people departed to
their homes, and David went home to
bless his household.

God's Covenant with David

17 Now when David settled in
his house, David said to the
prophet Nathan, "I am living in a house
of cedar, but the ark of the covenant of
the LORD is under a tent." 2 Nathan said
to David, "Do all that you have in mind,
for God is with you."

3 But that same night the word of the
LORD came to Nathan, saying: 4 Go and
tell my servant David: Thus says the
LORD: You shall not build me a house to
live in. 5 For I have not lived in a house
since the day I brought out Israel to this
very day, but I have lived in a tent and a
tabernacle.[u] 6 Wherever I have moved
about among all Israel, did I ever speak a
word with any of the judges of Israel,
whom I commanded to shepherd my
people, saying, Why have you not built
me a house of cedar? 7 Now therefore
thus you shall say to my servant David:
Thus says the LORD of hosts: I took you
from the pasture, from following the
sheep, to be ruler over my people Israel;
8 and I have been with you wherever you
went, and have cut off all your enemies
before you; and I will make for you a
name, like the name of the great ones of
the earth. 9 I will appoint a place for my
people Israel, and will plant them, so
that they may live in their own place,

---

t Gk Syr Vg: Heb *their*   u Gk 2 Sam 7.6: Heb *but I have been from tent to tent and from tabernacle*

and be disturbed no more; and evildoers shall wear them down no more, as they did formerly, 10from the time that I appointed judges over my people Israel; and I will subdue all your enemies.

Moreover I declare to you that the LORD will build you a house. 11When your days are fulfilled to go to be with your ancestors, I will raise up your offspring after you, one of your own sons, and I will establish his kingdom. 12He shall build a house for me, and I will establish his throne forever. 13I will be a father to him, and he shall be a son to me. I will not take my steadfast love from him, as I took it from him who was before you, 14but I will confirm him in my house and in my kingdom forever, and his throne shall be established forever. 15In accordance with all these words and all this vision, Nathan spoke to David.

David's Prayer

16 Then King David went in and sat before the LORD, and said, "Who am I, O LORD God, and what is my house, that you have brought me thus far? 17And even this was a small thing in your sight, O God; you have also spoken of your servant's house for a great while to come. You regard me as someone of high rank,ᵛ O LORD God! 18And what more can David say to you for honoring your servant? You know your servant. 19For your servant's sake, O LORD, and according to your own heart, you have done all these great deeds, making known all these great things. 20There is no one like you, O LORD, and there is no God besides you, according to all that we have heard with our ears. 21Who is like your people Israel, one nation on the earth whom God went to redeem to be his people, making for yourself a name for great and terrible things, in driving out nations before your people whom you redeemed from Egypt? 22And you made your people Israel to be your people forever; and you, O LORD, became their God.

23 "And now, O LORD, as for the word that you have spoken concerning your servant and concerning his house,

let it be established forever, and do as you have promised. 24Thus your name will be established and magnified forever in the saying, 'The LORD of hosts, the God of Israel, is Israel's God'; and the house of your servant David will be established in your presence. 25For you, my God, have revealed to your servant that you will build a house for him; therefore your servant has found it possible to pray before you. 26And now, O LORD, you are God, and you have promised this good thing to your servant; 27therefore may it please you to bless the house of your servant, that it may continue forever before you. For you, O LORD, have blessed and are blessedʷ forever."

David's Kingdom Established and Extended

18 Some time afterward, David attacked the Philistines and subdued them; he took Gath and its villages from the Philistines.

2 He defeated Moab, and the Moabites became subject to David and brought tribute.

3 David also struck down King Hadadezer of Zobah, toward Hamath,ᵛ as he went to set up a monument at the river Euphrates. 4David took from him one thousand chariots, seven thousand cavalry, and twenty thousand foot soldiers. David hamstrung all the chariot horses, but left one hundred of them. 5When the Arameans of Damascus came to help King Hadadezer of Zobah, David killed twenty-two thousand Arameans. 6Then David put garrisonsˣ in Aram of Damascus; and the Arameans became subject to David, and brought tribute. The LORD gave victory to David wherever he went. 7David took the gold shields that were carried by the servants of Hadadezer, and brought them to Jerusalem. 8From Tibhath and from Cun, cities of Hadadezer, David took a vast quantity of bronze; with it Solomon made the bronze sea and the pillars and the vessels of bronze.

9 When King Tou of Hamath heard that David had defeated the whole army of King Hadadezer of Zobah, 10he sent

---

v Meaning of Heb uncertain   w Or and it is blessed   x Gk Vg 2 Sam 8.6 Compare Syr: Heb lacks garrisons

his son Hadoram to King David, to greet him and to congratulate him, because he had fought against Hadadezer and defeated him. Now Hadadezer had often been at war with Tou. He sent all sorts of articles of gold, of silver, and of bronze; 11these also King David dedicated to the LORD, together with the silver and gold that he had carried off from all the nations, from Edom, Moab, the Ammonites, the Philistines, and Amalek.

12 Abishai son of Zeruiah killed eighteen thousand Edomites in the Valley of Salt. 13He put garrisons in Edom; and all the Edomites became subject to David. And the LORD gave victory to David wherever he went.

David's Administration

14 So David reigned over all Israel; and he administered justice and equity to all his people. 15Joab son of Zeruiah was over the army; Jehoshaphat son of Ahilud was recorder; 16Zadok son of Ahitub and Ahimelech son of Abiathar were priests; Shavsha was secretary; 17Benaiah son of Jehoiada was over the Cherethites and the Pelethites; and David's sons were the chief officials in the service of the king.

Defeat of the Ammonites and Arameans

19 Some time afterward, King Nahash of the Ammonites died, and his son succeeded him. 2David said, "I will deal loyally with Hanun son of Nahash, for his father dealt loyally with me." So David sent messengers to console him concerning his father. When David's servants came to Hanun in the land of the Ammonites, to console him, 3the officials of the Ammonites said to Hanun, "Do you think, because David has sent consolers to you, that he is honoring your father? Have not his servants come to you to search and to overthrow and to spy out the land?" 4So Hanun seized David's servants, shaved them, cut off their garments in the middle at their hips, and sent them away; 5and they departed. When David was told about the men, he sent messengers to them, for they felt greatly humiliated. The king said,

"Remain at Jericho until your beards have grown, and then return."

6 When the Ammonites saw that they had made themselves odious to David, Hanun and the Ammonites sent a thousand talents of silver to hire chariots and cavalry from Mesopotamia, from Aram-maacah and from Zobah. 7They hired thirty-two thousand chariots and the king of Maacah with his army, who came and camped before Medeba. And the Ammonites were mustered from their cities and came to battle. 8When David heard of it, he sent Joab and all the army of the warriors. 9The Ammonites came out and drew up in battle array at the entrance of the city, and the kings who had come were by themselves in the open country.

10 When Joab saw that the line of battle was set against him both in front and in the rear, he chose some of the picked men of Israel and arrayed them against the Arameans; 11the rest of his troops he put in the charge of his brother Abishai, and they were arrayed against the Ammonites. 12He said, "If the Arameans are too strong for me, then you shall help me; but if the Ammonites are too strong for you, then I will help you. 13Be strong, and let us be courageous for our people and for the cities of our God; and may the LORD do what seems good to him." 14So Joab and the troops who were with him advanced toward the Arameans for battle; and they fled before him. 15When the Ammonites saw that the Arameans fled, they likewise fled before Abishai, Joab's brother, and entered the city. Then Joab came to Jerusalem.

16 But when the Arameans saw that they had been defeated by Israel, they sent messengers and brought out the Arameans who were beyond the Euphrates, with Shophach the commander of the army of Hadadezer at their head. 17When David was informed, he gathered all Israel together, crossed the Jordan, came to them, and drew up his forces against them. When David set the battle in array against the Arameans, they fought with him. 18The Arameans fled before Israel; and David killed seven thousand Aramean charioteers and forty thousand foot soldiers, and also killed Shophach the commander of their army.

19When the servants of Hadadezer saw that they had been defeated by Israel, they made peace with David, and became subject to him. So the Arameans were not willing to help the Ammonites any more.

Siege and Capture of Rabbah

20 In the spring of the year, the time when kings go out to battle, Joab led out the army, ravaged the country of the Ammonites, and came and besieged Rabbah. But David remained at Jerusalem. Joab attacked Rabbah, and overthrew it. 2David took the crown of Milcomʸ from his head; he found that it weighed a talent of gold, and in it was a precious stone; and it was placed on David's head. He also brought out the booty of the city, a very great amount. 3He brought out the people who were in it, and set them to workᶻ with saws and iron picks and axes.ᵃ Thus David did to all the cities of the Ammonites. Then David and all the people returned to Jerusalem.

Exploits against the Philistines

4 After this, war broke out with the Philistines at Gezer; then Sibbecai the Hushathite killed Sippai, who was one of the descendants of the giants; and the Philistines were subdued. 5Again there was war with the Philistines; and Elhanan son of Jair killed Lahmi the brother of Goliath the Gittite, the shaft of whose spear was like a weaver's beam. 6Again there was war at Gath, where there was a man of great size, who had six fingers on each hand, and six toes on each foot, twenty-four in number; he also was descended from the giants. 7When he taunted Israel, Jonathan son of Shimea, David's brother, killed him. 8These were descended from the giants in Gath; they fell by the hand of David and his servants.

The Census and Plague

21 Satan stood up against Israel, and incited David to count the people of Israel. 2So David said to Joab and the commanders of the army, "Go, number Israel, from Beer-sheba to Dan, and bring me a report, so that I may know their number." 3But Joab said, "May the LORD increase the number of his people a hundredfold! Are they not, my lord the king, all of them my lord's servants? Why then should my lord require this? Why should he bring guilt on Israel?" 4But the king's word prevailed against Joab. So Joab departed and went throughout all Israel, and came back to Jerusalem. 5Joab gave the total count of the people to David. In all Israel there were one million one hundred thousand men who drew the sword, and in Judah four hundred seventy thousand who drew the sword. 6But he did not include Levi and Benjamin in the numbering, for the king's command was abhorrent to Joab.

7 But God was displeased with this thing, and he struck Israel. 8David said to God, "I have sinned greatly in that I have done this thing. But now, I pray you, take away the guilt of your servant; for I have done very foolishly." 9The LORD spoke to Gad, David's seer, saying, 10"Go and say to David, 'Thus says the LORD: Three things I offer you; choose one of them, so that I may do it to you.'" 11So Gad came to David and said to him, "Thus says the LORD, 'Take your choice: 12either three years of famine; or three months of devastation by your foes, while the sword of your enemies overtakes you; or three days of the sword of the LORD, pestilence on the land, and the angel of the LORD destroying throughout all the territory of Israel.' Now decide what answer I shall return to the one who sent me." 13Then David said to Gad, "I am in great distress; let me fall into the hand of the LORD, for his mercy is very great; but let me not fall into human hands."

14 So the LORD sent a pestilence on Israel; and seventy thousand persons fell in Israel. 15And God sent an angel to Jerusalem to destroy it; but when he was about to destroy it, the LORD took note and relented concerning the calamity; he said to the destroying angel, "Enough! Stay your hand." The angel of the LORD was then standing by the threshing floor of Ornan the Jebusite.

y Gk Vg See 1 Kings 11.5, 33: MT of their king   z Compare 2 Sam 12.31: Heb and he sawed
a Compare 2 Sam 12.31: Heb saws

16David looked up and saw the angel of the LORD standing between earth and heaven, and in his hand a drawn sword stretched out over Jerusalem. Then David and the elders, clothed in sackcloth, fell on their faces. 17And David said to God, "Was it not I who gave the command to count the people? It is I who have sinned and done very wickedly. But these sheep, what have they done? Let your hand, I pray, O LORD my God, be against me and against my father's house; but do not let your people be plagued!"

David's Altar and Sacrifice

18 Then the angel of the LORD commanded Gad to tell David that he should go up and erect an altar to the LORD on the threshing floor of Ornan the Jebusite. 19So David went up following Gad's instructions, which he had spoken in the name of the LORD. 20Ornan turned and saw the angel; and while his four sons who were with him hid themselves, Ornan continued to thresh wheat. 21As David came to Ornan, Ornan looked and saw David; he went out from the threshing floor, and did obeisance to David with his face to the ground. 22David said to Ornan, "Give me the site of the threshing floor that I may build on it an altar to the LORD—give it to me at its full price—so that the plague may be averted from the people." 23Then Ornan said to David, "Take it; and let my lord the king do what seems good to him; see, I present the oxen for burnt offerings, and the threshing sledges for the wood, and the wheat for a grain offering. I give it all." 24But King David said to Ornan, "No; I will buy them for the full price. I will not take for the LORD what is yours, nor offer burnt offerings that cost me nothing." 25So David paid Ornan six hundred shekels of gold by weight for the site. 26David built there an altar to the LORD and presented burnt offerings and offerings of well-being. He called upon the LORD, and he answered him with fire from heaven on the altar of burnt offering. 27Then the LORD commanded the angel, and he put his sword back into its sheath.

The Place Chosen for the Temple

28 At that time, when David saw that the LORD had answered him at the threshing floor of Ornan the Jebusite, he made his sacrifices there. 29For the tabernacle of the LORD, which Moses had made in the wilderness, and the altar of burnt offering were at that time in the high place at Gibeon; 30but David could not go before it to inquire of God, for he was afraid of the sword of the **22** angel of the LORD. 1Then David said, "Here shall be the house of the LORD God and here the altar of burnt offering for Israel."

David Prepares to Build the Temple

2 David gave orders to gather together the aliens who were residing in the land of Israel, and he set stonecutters to prepare dressed stones for building the house of God. 3David also provided great stores of iron for nails for the doors of the gates and for clamps, as well as bronze in quantities beyond weighing, 4and cedar logs without number—for the Sidonians and Tyrians brought great quantities of cedar to David. 5For David said, "My son Solomon is young and inexperienced, and the house that is to be built for the LORD must be exceedingly magnificent, famous and glorified throughout all lands; I will therefore make preparation for it." So David provided materials in great quantity before his death.

David's Charge to Solomon and the Leaders

6 Then he called for his son Solomon and charged him to build a house for the LORD, the God of Israel. 7David said to Solomon, "My son, I had planned to build a house to the name of the LORD my God. 8But the word of the LORD came to me, saying, 'You have shed much blood and have waged great wars; you shall not build a house to my name, because you have shed so much blood in my sight on the earth. 9See, a son shall be born to you; he shall be a man of peace. I will give him peace from all his enemies on every side; for his name shall be Solomon,b and I will give peacec and

b Heb *Shelomoh*   c Heb *shalom*

quiet to Israel in his days. [10]He shall build a house for my name. He shall be a son to me, and I will be a father to him, and I will establish his royal throne in Israel forever.' [11]Now, my son, the LORD be with you, so that you may succeed in building the house of the LORD your God, as he has spoken concerning you. [12]Only, may the LORD grant you discretion and understanding, so that when he gives you charge over Israel you may keep the law of the LORD your God. [13]Then you will prosper if you are careful to observe the statutes and the ordinances that the LORD commanded Moses for Israel. Be strong and of good courage. Do not be afraid or dismayed. [14]With great pains I have provided for the house of the LORD one hundred thousand talents of gold, one million talents of silver, and bronze and iron beyond weighing, for there is so much of it; timber and stone too I have provided. To these you must add more. [15]You have an abundance of workers: stonecutters, masons, carpenters, and all kinds of artisans without number, skilled in working [16]gold, silver, bronze, and iron. Now begin the work, and the LORD be with you."

17 David also commanded all the leaders of Israel to help his son Solomon, saying, [18]"Is not the LORD your God with you? Has he not given you peace on every side? For he has delivered the inhabitants of the land into my hand; and the land is subdued before the LORD and his people. [19]Now set your mind and heart to seek the LORD your God. Go and build the sanctuary of the LORD God so that the ark of the covenant of the LORD and the holy vessels of God may be brought into a house built for the name of the LORD."

Families of the Levites and Their Functions

23 When David was old and full of days, he made his son Solomon king over Israel.

2 David assembled all the leaders of Israel and the priests and the Levites. [3]The Levites, thirty years old and upward, were counted, and the total was thirty-eight thousand. [4]"Twenty-four thousand of these," David said, "shall have charge of the work in the house of the LORD, six thousand shall be officers and judges, [5]four thousand gatekeepers, and four thousand shall offer praises to the LORD with the instruments that I have made for praise." [6]And David organized them in divisions corresponding to the sons of Levi: Gershon,[d] Kohath, and Merari.

7 The sons of Gershon[e] were Ladan and Shimei. [8]The sons of Ladan: Jehiel the chief, Zetham, and Joel, three. [9]The sons of Shimei: Shelomoth, Haziel, and Haran, three. These were the heads of families of Ladan. [10]And the sons of Shimei: Jahath, Zina, Jeush, and Beriah. These four were the sons of Shimei. [11]Jahath was the chief, and Zizah the second; but Jeush and Beriah did not have many sons, so they were enrolled as a single family.

12 The sons of Kohath: Amram, Izhar, Hebron, and Uzziel, four. [13]The sons of Amram: Aaron and Moses. Aaron was set apart to consecrate the most holy things, so that he and his sons forever should make offerings before the LORD, and minister to him and pronounce blessings in his name forever; [14]but as for Moses the man of God, his sons were to be reckoned among the tribe of Levi. [15]The sons of Moses: Gershom and Eliezer. [16]The sons of Gershom: Shebuel the chief. [17]The sons of Eliezer: Rehabiah the chief; Eliezer had no other sons, but the sons of Rehabiah were very numerous. [18]The sons of Izhar: Shelomith the chief. [19]The sons of Hebron: Jeriah the chief, Amariah the second, Jahaziel the third, and Jekameam the fourth. [20]The sons of Uzziel: Micah the chief and Isshiah the second.

21 The sons of Merari: Mahli and Mushi. The sons of Mahli: Eleazar and Kish. [22]Eleazar died having no sons, but only daughters; their kindred, the sons of Kish, married them. [23]The sons of Mushi: Mahli, Eder, and Jeremoth, three.

24 These were the sons of Levi by their ancestral houses, the heads of families as they were enrolled according to the number of the names of the individuals from twenty years old and upward who were to do the work for the service of the house of the LORD. [25]For David

---

d Or Gershom; See 1 Chr 6.1, note, and 23.15   e Vg Compare Gk Syr: Heb to the Gershonite

said, "The LORD, the God of Israel, has given rest to his people; and he resides in Jerusalem forever. 26 And so the Levites no longer need to carry the tabernacle or any of the things for its service"— 27 for according to the last words of David these were the number of the Levites from twenty years old and upward— 28 "but their duty shall be to assist the descendants of Aaron for the service of the house of the LORD, having the care of the courts and the chambers, the cleansing of all that is holy, and any work for the service of the house of God; 29 to assist also with the rows of bread, the choice flour for the grain offering, the wafers of unleavened bread, the baked offering, the offering mixed with oil, and all measures of quantity or size. 30 And they shall stand every morning, thanking and praising the LORD, and likewise at evening, 31 and whenever burnt offerings are offered to the LORD on sabbaths, new moons, and appointed festivals, according to the number required of them, regularly before the LORD. 32 Thus they shall keep charge of the tent of meeting and the sanctuary, and shall attend the descendants of Aaron, their kindred, for the service of the house of the LORD."

Divisions of the Priests

24 The divisions of the descendants of Aaron were these. The sons of Aaron: Nadab, Abihu, Eleazar, and Ithamar. 2 But Nadab and Abihu died before their father, and had no sons; so Eleazar and Ithamar became the priests. 3 Along with Zadok of the sons of Eleazar, and Ahimelech of the sons of Ithamar, David organized them according to the appointed duties in their service. 4 Since more chief men were found among the sons of Eleazar than among the sons of Ithamar, they organized them under sixteen heads of ancestral houses of the sons of Eleazar, and eight of the sons of Ithamar. 5 They organized them by lot, all alike, for there were officers of the sanctuary and officers of God among both the sons of Eleazar and the sons of Ithamar. 6 The scribe Shemaiah son of Nethanel, a Levite, recorded them

in the presence of the king, and the officers, and Zadok the priest, and Ahimelech son of Abiathar, and the heads of ancestral houses of the priests and of the Levites; one ancestral house being chosen for Eleazar and one chosen for Ithamar.

7 The first lot fell to Jehoiarib, the second to Jedaiah, 8 the third to Harim, the fourth to Seorim, 9 the fifth to Malchijah, the sixth to Mijamin, 10 the seventh to Hakkoz, the eighth to Abijah, 11 the ninth to Jeshua, the tenth to Shecaniah, 12 the eleventh to Eliashib, the twelfth to Jakim, 13 the thirteenth to Huppah, the fourteenth to Jeshebeab, 14 the fifteenth to Bilgah, the sixteenth to Immer, 15 the seventeenth to Hezir, the eighteenth to Happizzez, 16 the nineteenth to Pethahiah, the twentieth to Jehezkel, 17 the twenty-first to Jachin, the twenty-second to Gamul, 18 the twenty-third to Delaiah, the twenty-fourth to Maaziah. 19 These had as their appointed duty in their service to enter the house of the LORD according to the procedure established for them by their ancestor Aaron, as the LORD God of Israel had commanded him.

Other Levites

20 And of the rest of the sons of Levi: of the sons of Amram, Shubael; of the sons of Shubael, Jehdeiah. 21 Of Rehabiah: of the sons of Rehabiah, Isshiah the chief. 22 Of the Izharites, Shelomoth; of the sons of Shelomoth, Jahath. 23 The sons of Hebron:f Jeriah the chief,g Amariah the second, Jahaziel the third, Jekameam the fourth. 24 The sons of Uzziel, Micah; of the sons of Micah, Shamir. 25 The brother of Micah, Isshiah; of the sons of Isshiah, Zechariah. 26 The sons of Merari: Mahli and Mushi. The sons of Jaaziah: Beno.h 27 The sons of Merari: of Jaaziah, Beno,h Shoham, Zaccur, and Ibri. 28 Of Mahli: Eleazar, who had no sons. 29 Of Kish, the sons of Kish: Jerahmeel. 30 The sons of Mushi: Mahli, Eder, and Jerimoth. These were the sons of the Levites according to their ancestral houses. 31 These also cast lots corresponding to their kindred, the descendants of Aaron, in the presence of King

f See 23.19: Heb lacks Hebron   g See 23.19: Heb lacks the chief   h Or his son: Meaning of Heb uncertain

David, Zadok, Ahimelech, and the heads of ancestral houses of the priests and of the Levites, the chief as well as the youngest brother.

The Temple Musicians

25 David and the officers of the army also set apart for the service the sons of Asaph, and of Heman, and of Jeduthun, who should prophesy with lyres, harps, and cymbals. The list of those who did the work and of their duties was: 2Of the sons of Asaph: Zaccur, Joseph, Nethaniah, and Asarelah, sons of Asaph, under the direction of Asaph, who prophesied under the direction of the king. 3Of Jeduthun, the sons of Jeduthun: Gedaliah, Zeri, Jeshaiah, Shimei,[i] Hashabiah, and Mattithiah, six, under the direction of their father Jeduthun, who prophesied with the lyre in thanksgiving and praise to the LORD. 4Of Heman, the sons of Heman: Bukkiah, Mattaniah, Uzziel, Shebuel, and Jerimoth, Hananiah, Hanani, Eliathah, Giddalti, and Romamti-ezer, Joshbekashah, Mallothi, Hothir, Mahazioth. 5All these were the sons of Heman the king's seer, according to the promise of God to exalt him; for God had given Heman fourteen sons and three daughters. 6They were all under the direction of their father for the music in the house of the LORD with cymbals, harps, and lyres for the service of the house of God. Asaph, Jeduthun, and Heman were under the order of the king. 7They and their kindred, who were trained in singing to the LORD, all of whom were skillful, numbered two hundred eighty-eight. 8And they cast lots for their duties, small and great, teacher and pupil alike.

9 The first lot fell for Asaph to Joseph; the second to Gedaliah, to him and his brothers and his sons, twelve; 10the third to Zaccur, his sons and his brothers, twelve; 11the fourth to Izri, his sons and his brothers, twelve; 12the fifth to Nethaniah, his sons and his brothers, twelve; 13the sixth to Bukkiah, his sons and his brothers, twelve; 14the seventh to Jesarelah,[j] his sons and his brothers, twelve; 15the eighth to Jeshaiah, his sons and his brothers, twelve; 16the ninth to Mattaniah, his sons and his brothers, twelve;

17the tenth to Shimei, his sons and his brothers, twelve; 18the eleventh to Azarel, his sons and his brothers, twelve; 19the twelfth to Hashabiah, his sons and his brothers, twelve; 20to the thirteenth, Shubael, his sons and his brothers, twelve; 21to the fourteenth, Mattithiah, his sons and his brothers, twelve; 22to the fifteenth, to Jeremoth, his sons and his brothers, twelve; 23to the sixteenth, to Hananiah, his sons and his brothers, twelve; 24to the seventeenth, to Joshbekashah, his sons and his brothers, twelve; 25to the eighteenth, to Hanani, his sons and his brothers, twelve; 26to the nineteenth, to Mallothi, his sons and his brothers, twelve; 27to the twentieth, to Eliathah, his sons and his brothers, twelve; 28to the twenty-first, to Hothir, his sons and his brothers, twelve; 29to the twenty-second, to Giddalti, his sons and his brothers, twelve; 30to the twenty-third, to Mahazioth, his sons and his brothers, twelve; 31to the twenty-fourth, to Romamti-ezer, his sons and his brothers, twelve.

The Gatekeepers

26 As for the divisions of the gatekeepers: of the Korahites, Meshelemiah son of Kore, of the sons of Asaph. 2Meshelemiah had sons: Zechariah the firstborn, Jediael the second, Zebadiah the third, Jathniel the fourth, 3Elam the fifth, Jehohanan the sixth, Eliehoenai the seventh. 4Obed-edom had sons: Shemaiah the firstborn, Jehozabad the second, Joah the third, Sachar the fourth, Nethanel the fifth, 5Ammiel the sixth, Issachar the seventh, Peullethai the eighth; for God blessed him. 6Also to his son Shemaiah sons were born who exercised authority in their ancestral houses, for they were men of great ability. 7The sons of Shemaiah: Othni, Rephael, Obed, and Elzabad, whose brothers were able men, Elihu and Semachiah. 8All these, sons of Obed-edom with their sons and brothers, were able men qualified for the service; sixty-two of Obed-edom. 9Meshelemiah had sons and brothers, able men, eighteen. 10Hosah, of the sons of Merari, had sons: Shimri the chief (for though he was not the firstborn, his father made

him chief), 11Hilkiah the second, Tebali-
ah the third, Zechariah the fourth: all
the sons and brothers of Hosah totaled
thirteen.

12 These divisions of the gatekeepers, corresponding to their leaders, had
duties, just as their kindred did, ministering in the house of the Lord; 13and
they cast lots by ancestral houses, small
and great alike, for their gates. 14The lot
for the east fell to Shelemiah. They cast
lots also for his son Zechariah, a prudent
counselor, and his lot came out for the
north. 15Obed-edom's came out for the
south, and to his sons was allotted the
storehouse. 16For Shuppim and Hosah it
came out for the west, at the gate of
Shallecheth on the ascending road.
Guard corresponded to guard. 17On the
east there were six Levites each day,k on
the north four each day, on the south
four each day, as well as two and two at
the storehouse; 18and for the colonnadel
on the west there were four at the road
and two at the colonnade.l 19These were
the divisions of the gatekeepers among
the Korahites and the sons of Merari.

The Treasurers, Officers, and Judges

20 And of the Levites, Ahijah had
charge of the treasuries of the house of
God and the treasuries of the dedicated
gifts. 21The sons of Ladan, the sons of
the Gershonites belonging to Ladan, the
heads of families belonging to Ladan the
Gershonite: Jehieli.m
22 The sons of Jehieli, Zetham and
his brother Joel, were in charge of the
treasuries of the house of the Lord. 23Of
the Amramites, the Izharites, the
Hebronites, and the Uzzielites: 24She-
buel son of Gershom, son of Moses, was
chief officer in charge of the treasuries.
25His brothers: from Eliezer were his son
Rehabiah, his son Jeshaiah, his son
Joram, his son Zichri, and his son Shelomoth. 26This Shelomoth and his brothers were in charge of all the treasuries of
the dedicated gifts that King David, and
the heads of families, and the officers of
the thousands and the hundreds, and the
commanders of the army, had dedicated.
27From booty won in battles they dedicated gifts for the maintenance of the

house of the Lord. 28Also all that Samuel the seer, and Saul son of Kish, and
Abner son of Ner, and Joab son of Zeruiah had dedicated—all dedicated gifts
were in the care of Shelomothn and his
brothers.

29 Of the Izharites, Chenaniah and
his sons were appointed to outside
duties for Israel, as officers and judges.
30Of the Hebronites, Hashabiah and his
brothers, one thousand seven hundred
men of ability, had the oversight of Israel west of the Jordan for all the work of
the Lord and for the service of the king.
31Of the Hebronites, Jerijah was chief of
the Hebronites. (In the fortieth year of
David's reign search was made, of whatever genealogy or family, and men of
great ability among them were found at
Jazer in Gilead.) 32King David appointed
him and his brothers, two thousand
seven hundred men of ability, heads of
families, to have the oversight of the
Reubenites, the Gadites, and the half-
tribe of the Manassites for everything
pertaining to God and for the affairs of
the king.

The Military Divisions

27 This is the list of the people of
Israel, the heads of families,
the commanders of the thousands and
the hundreds, and their officers who
served the king in all matters concerning the divisions that came and went,
month after month throughout the year,
each division numbering twenty-four
thousand.
2 Jashobeam son of Zabdiel was in
charge of the first division in the first
month; in his division were twenty-four
thousand. 3He was a descendant of
Perez, and was chief of all the commanders of the army for the first month.
4Dodai the Ahohite was in charge of the
division of the second month; Mikloth
was the chief officer of his division. In
his division were twenty-four thousand.
5The third commander, for the third
month, was Benaiah son of the priest
Jehoiada, as chief; in his division were
twenty-four thousand. 6This is the
Benaiah who was a mighty man of the
Thirty and in command of the Thirty;

k Gk: Heb lacks *each day*   l Heb *parbar*: meaning uncertain   m The Hebrew text of verse 21 is
confused   n Gk Compare 26.28: Heb *Shelomith*

his son Ammizabad was in charge of his division.[o] 7Asahel brother of Joab was fourth, for the fourth month, and his son Zebadiah after him; in his division were twenty-four thousand. 8The fifth commander, for the fifth month, was Shamhuth, the Izrahite; in his division were twenty-four thousand. 9Sixth, for the sixth month, was Ira son of Ikkesh the Tekoite; in his division were twenty-four thousand. 10Seventh, for the seventh month, was Helez the Pelonite, of the Ephraimites; in his division were twenty-four thousand. 11Eighth, for the eighth month, was Sibbecai the Hushathite, of the Zerahites; in his division were twenty-four thousand. 12Ninth, for the ninth month, was Abiezer of Anathoth, a Benjaminite; in his division were twenty-four thousand. 13Tenth, for the tenth month, was Maharai of Netophah, of the Zerahites; in his division were twenty-four thousand. 14Eleventh, for the eleventh month, was Benaiah of Pirathon, of the Ephraimites; in his division were twenty-four thousand. 15Twelfth, for the twelfth month, was Heldai the Netophathite, of Othniel; in his division were twenty-four thousand.

Leaders of Tribes

16 Over the tribes of Israel, for the Reubenites, Eliezer son of Zichri was chief officer; for the Simeonites, Shephatiah son of Maacah; 17for Levi, Hashabiah son of Kemuel; for Aaron, Zadok; 18for Judah, Elihu, one of David's brothers; for Issachar, Omri son of Michael; 19for Zebulun, Ishmaiah son of Obadiah; for Naphtali, Jerimoth son of Azriel; 20for the Ephraimites, Hoshea son of Azaziah; for the half-tribe of Manasseh, Joel son of Pedaiah; 21for the half-tribe of Manasseh in Gilead, Iddo son of Zechariah; for Benjamin, Jaasiel son of Abner; 22for Dan, Azarel son of Jeroham. These were the leaders of the tribes of Israel. 23David did not count those below twenty years of age, for the LORD had promised to make Israel as numerous as the stars of heaven. 24Joab son of Zeruiah began to count them, but did not finish; yet wrath came upon Israel for this, and the number was not

entered into the account of the Annals of King David.

Other Civic Officials

25 Over the king's treasuries was Azmaveth son of Adiel. Over the treasuries in the country, in the cities, in the villages and in the towers, was Jonathan son of Uzziah. 26Over those who did the work of the field, tilling the soil, was Ezri son of Chelub. 27Over the vineyards was Shimei the Ramathite. Over the produce of the vineyards for the wine cellars was Zabdi the Shiphmite. 28Over the olive and sycamore trees in the Shephelah was Baal-hanan the Gederite. Over the stores of oil was Joash. 29Over the herds that pastured in Sharon was Shitrai the Sharonite. Over the herds in the valleys was Shaphat son of Adlai. 30Over the camels was Obil the Ishmaelite. Over the donkeys was Jehdeiah the Meronothite. Over the flocks was Jaziz the Hagrite. 31All these were stewards of King David's property.

32 Jonathan, David's uncle, was a counselor, being a man of understanding and a scribe; Jehiel son of Hachmoni attended the king's sons. 33Ahithophel was the king's counselor, and Hushai the Archite was the king's friend. 34After Ahithophel came Jehoiada son of Benaiah, and Abiathar. Joab was commander of the king's army.

Solomon Instructed to Build the Temple

28 David assembled at Jerusalem all the officials of Israel, the officials of the tribes, the officers of the divisions that served the king, the commanders of the thousands, the commanders of the hundreds, the stewards of all the property and cattle of the king and his sons, together with the palace officials, the mighty warriors, and all the warriors. 2Then King David rose to his feet and said: "Hear me, my brothers and my people. I had planned to build a house of rest for the ark of the covenant of the LORD, for the footstool of our God; and I made preparations for building. 3But God said to me, 'You shall not build a house for my name, for you are a warrior and have shed blood.'

o Gk Vg: Heb Ammizabad was his division

4Yet the LORD God of Israel chose me from all my ancestral house to be king over Israel forever; for he chose Judah as leader, and in the house of Judah my father's house, and among my father's sons he took delight in making me king over all Israel. 5And of all my sons, for the LORD has given me many, he has chosen my son Solomon to sit upon the throne of the kingdom of the LORD over Israel. 6He said to me, 'It is your son Solomon who shall build my house and my courts, for I have chosen him to be a son to me, and I will be a father to him. 7I will establish his kingdom forever if he continues resolute in keeping my commandments and my ordinances, as he is today.' 8Now therefore in the sight of all Israel, the assembly of the LORD, and in the hearing of our God, observe and search out all the commandments of the LORD your God; that you may possess this good land, and leave it for an inheritance to your children after you forever.

9 "And you, my son Solomon, know the God of your father, and serve him with single mind and willing heart; for the LORD searches every mind, and understands every plan and thought. If you seek him, he will be found by you; but if you forsake him, he will abandon you forever. 10Take heed now, for the LORD has chosen you to build a house as the sanctuary; be strong, and act."

11 Then David gave his son Solomon the plan of the vestibule of the temple, and of its houses, its treasuries, its upper rooms, and its inner chambers, and of the room for the mercy seat;p 12and the plan of all that he had in mind: for the courts of the house of the LORD, all the surrounding chambers, the treasuries of the house of God, and the treasuries for dedicated gifts; 13for the divisions of the priests and of the Levites, and all the work of the service in the house of the LORD; for all the vessels for the service in the house of the LORD, 14the weight of gold for all golden vessels for each service, the weight of silver vessels for each service, 15the weight of the golden lampstands and their lamps, the weight of gold for each lampstand and its lamps, the weight of silver for a lampstand and

its lamps, according to the use of each in the service, 16the weight of gold for each table for the rows of bread, the silver for the silver tables, 17and pure gold for the forks, the basins, and the cups; for the golden bowls and the weight of each; for the silver bowls and the weight of each; 18for the altar of incense made of refined gold, and its weight; also his plan for the golden chariot of the cherubim that spread their wings and covered the ark of the covenant of the LORD.

19 "All this, in writing at the LORD's direction, he made clear to me—the plan of all the works."

20 David said further to his son Solomon, "Be strong and of good courage, and act. Do not be afraid or dismayed; for the LORD God, my God, is with you. He will not fail you or forsake you, until all the work for the service of the house of the LORD is finished. 21Here are the divisions of the priests and the Levites for all the service of the house of God; and with you in all the work will be every volunteer who has skill for any kind of service; also the officers and all the people will be wholly at your command."

Offerings for Building the Temple

29 King David said to the whole assembly, "My son Solomon, whom alone God has chosen, is young and inexperienced, and the work is great; for the templeq will not be for mortals but for the LORD God. 2So I have provided for the house of my God, so far as I was able, the gold for the things of gold, the silver for the things of silver, and the bronze for the things of bronze, the iron for the things of iron, and wood for the things of wood, besides great quantities of onyx and stones for setting, antimony, colored stones, all sorts of precious stones, and marble in abundance. 3Moreover, in addition to all that I have provided for the holy house, I have a treasure of my own of gold and silver, and because of my devotion to the house of my God I give it to the house of my God: 4three thousand talents of gold, of the gold of Ophir, and seven thousand talents of refined silver, for overlaying the walls of the house,

5and for all the work to be done by artisans, gold for the things of gold and silver for the things of silver. Who then will offer willingly, consecrating themselves today to the LORD?"

6 Then the leaders of ancestral houses made their freewill offerings, as did also the leaders of the tribes, the commanders of the thousands and of the hundreds, and the officers over the king's work. 7They gave for the service of the house of God five thousand talents and ten thousand darics of gold, ten thousand talents of silver, eighteen thousand talents of bronze, and one hundred thousand talents of iron. 8Whoever had precious stones gave them to the treasury of the house of the LORD, into the care of Jehiel the Gershonite. 9Then the people rejoiced because these had given willingly, for with single mind they had offered freely to the LORD; King David also rejoiced greatly.

David's Praise to God

10 Then David blessed the LORD in the presence of all the assembly; David said: "Blessed are you, O LORD, the God of our ancestor Israel, forever and ever. 11Yours, O LORD, are the greatness, the power, the glory, the victory, and the majesty; for all that is in the heavens and on the earth is yours; yours is the kingdom, O LORD, and you are exalted as head above all. 12Riches and honor come from you, and you rule over all. In your hand are power and might; and it is in your hand to make great and to give strength to all. 13And now, our God, we give thanks to you and praise your glorious name.

14 "But who am I, and what is my people, that we should be able to make this freewill offering? For all things come from you, and of your own have we given you. 15For we are aliens and transients before you, as were all our ancestors; our days on the earth are like a shadow, and there is no hope. 16O LORD our God, all this abundance that we have provided for building you a house for your holy name comes from your hand and is all your own. 17I know, my God, that you search the heart, and take pleasure in uprightness; in the uprightness of my heart I have freely offered all these things, and now I have seen your people, who are present here, offering freely and joyously to you. 18O LORD, the God of Abraham, Isaac, and Israel, our ancestors, keep forever such purposes and thoughts in the hearts of your people, and direct their hearts toward you. 19Grant to my son Solomon that with single mind he may keep your commandments, your decrees, and your statutes, performing all of them, and that he may build the temple*r* for which I have made provision."

20 Then David said to the whole assembly, "Bless the LORD your God." And all the assembly blessed the LORD, the God of their ancestors, and bowed their heads and prostrated themselves before the LORD and the king. 21On the next day they offered sacrifices and burnt offerings to the LORD, a thousand bulls, a thousand rams, and a thousand lambs, with their libations, and sacrifices in abundance for all Israel; 22and they ate and drank before the LORD on that day with great joy.

Solomon Anointed King

They made David's son Solomon king a second time; they anointed him as the LORD's prince, and Zadok as priest. 23Then Solomon sat on the throne of the LORD, succeeding his father David as king; he prospered, and all Israel obeyed him. 24All the leaders and the mighty warriors, and also all the sons of King David, pledged their allegiance to King Solomon. 25The LORD highly exalted Solomon in the sight of all Israel, and bestowed upon him such royal majesty as had not been on any king before him in Israel.

Summary of David's Reign

26 Thus David son of Jesse reigned over all Israel. 27The period that he reigned over Israel was forty years; he reigned seven years in Hebron, and thirty-three years in Jerusalem. 28He died in a good old age, full of days, riches, and honor; and his son Solomon succeeded him. 29Now the acts of King David, from first to last, are written in the

r Heb *fortress*

records of the seer Samuel, and in the records of the prophet Nathan, and in the records of the seer Gad, ³⁰with accounts of all his rule and his might and of the events that befell him and Israel and all the kingdoms of the earth.

THURSDAY

IT IS NOT MY VICTORY
Francis Schaeffer

VERSE: 1 Chronicles 29.11   **PASSAGE:** 1 Chronicles 29.10–13

ow we must understand too, in the framework of the Scripture, that since the fall everything is under the covenant of grace. The covenant of works is destroyed by the deliberate, free, unconditioned choice of Adam and Eve. In its place, by the grace of God, with the promises begun in Genesis 3.15, man was immediately given the promise of the work of the Messiah, coming in the future. Thus from the time of the fall onwards, everything rests upon the finished work of the Lord Jesus Christ on the cross, not upon ourselves, not *in* ourselves. Hence if there is any real victory in my life, it must not be thought of as *my* victory or *my* perfection. Such a notion does not fit the scriptural picture of man, nor God's dealing with us since man has sinned. It is not my victory, it is always Christ's work and Christ's holiness. When I begin to think and to grow in the idea of *my* victory, there is really no true victory. To the extent that I am thinking about *my* sanctification, there is no real sanctification. I must see it always as Jesus Christ's.

Indeed, it is only as we consciously bring each victory to his feet, and keep it there as we think of it—and especially as we speak of it—that we can avoid the pride of that victory, which can be worse than the sin over which we claim to have had the victory. The greater the victory, the greater the need of placing it consciously (and as we speak of it, vocally) at his feet.

ADDITIONAL SCRIPTURE READING:
Psalm 98.1–2; 1 Corinthians 15.57–58

Go to page 472 for your next devotional reading.

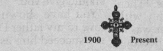

1900   Present

2 CHRONICLES

T HE BOOK OF 2 CHRONICLES CONTINUES THE HISTORY OF DAVID'S ROYAL LINE. THIS BOOK, LIKE 1 CHRONICLES, TEACHES THAT THE PEOPLE'S RELATIONSHIP TO GOD WAS CRUCIAL TO THEIR DAILY LIVING. NOTICE HOW WHEN THE AUTHOR WRITES ABOUT THE KINGS, HE MEASURES THEM ON THE BASIS OF THEIR FAITHFULNESS TO GOD. THE REIGNS OF EVIL KINGS ARE REPORTED BY THE AUTHOR BRIEFLY, WHILE THE REIGNS OF GOOD KINGS ARE DESCRIBED IN MORE DETAIL.

Solomon Requests Wisdom

1 Solomon son of David established himself in his kingdom; the LORD his God was with him and made him exceedingly great.

2 Solomon summoned all Israel, the commanders of the thousands and of the hundreds, the judges, and all the leaders of all Israel, the heads of families. ³Then Solomon, and the whole assembly with him, went to the high place that was at Gibeon; for God's tent of meeting, which Moses the servant of the LORD had made in the wilderness, was there. ⁴(But David had brought the ark of God up from Kiriath-jearim to the place that David had prepared for it; for he had pitched a tent for it in Jerusalem.) ⁵Moreover the bronze altar that Bezalel son of Uri, son of Hur, had made, was there in front of the tabernacle of the LORD. And Solomon and the assembly inquired at it. ⁶Solomon went up there to the bronze altar before the LORD, which was at the tent of meeting, and offered a thousand burnt offerings on it.

7 That night God appeared to Solomon, and said to him, "Ask what I should give you." ⁸Solomon said to God, "You have shown great and steadfast love to my father David, and have made me succeed him as king. ⁹O LORD God, let your promise to my father David now be fulfilled, for you have made me king over a people as numerous as the dust of the earth. ¹⁰Give me now wisdom and knowledge to go out and come in before this people, for who can rule this great people of yours?" ¹¹God answered Solomon, "Because this was

in your heart, and you have not asked for possessions, wealth, honor, or the life of those who hate you, and have not even asked for long life, but have asked for wisdom and knowledge for yourself that you may rule my people over whom I have made you king, ¹²wisdom and knowledge are granted to you. I will also give you riches, possessions, and honor, such as none of the kings had who were before you, and none after you shall have the like." ¹³So Solomon came from*a* the high place at Gibeon, from the tent of meeting, to Jerusalem. And he reigned over Israel.

Solomon's Military and Commercial Activity

14 Solomon gathered together chariots and horses; he had fourteen hundred chariots and twelve thousand horses, which he stationed in the chariot cities and with the king in Jerusalem. ¹⁵The king made silver and gold as common in Jerusalem as stone, and he made cedar as plentiful as the sycamore of the Shephelah. ¹⁶Solomon's horses were imported from Egypt and Kue; the king's traders received them from Kue at the prevailing price. ¹⁷They imported from Egypt, and then exported, a chariot for six hundred shekels of silver, and a horse for one hundred fifty; so through them these were exported to all the kings of the Hittites and the kings of Aram.

Preparations for Building the Temple

2 *b* Solomon decided to build a temple for the name of the LORD, and a royal palace for himself. ²*c*Solomon conscripted seventy thousand laborers and eighty thousand stonecutters in the hill country, with three thousand six hundred to oversee them.

Alliance with Huram of Tyre

3 Solomon sent word to King Huram of Tyre: "Once you dealt with my father David and sent him cedar to build himself a house to live in. ⁴I am now about to build a house for the name of the LORD my God and dedicate it to him for offering fragrant incense before him, and

for the regular offering of the rows of bread, and for burnt offerings morning and evening, on the sabbaths and the new moons and the appointed festivals of the LORD our God, as ordained forever for Israel. ⁵The house that I am about to build will be great, for our God is greater than other gods. ⁶But who is able to build him a house, since heaven, even highest heaven, cannot contain him? Who am I to build a house for him, except as a place to make offerings before him? ⁷So now send me an artisan skilled to work in gold, silver, bronze, and iron, and in purple, crimson, and blue fabrics, trained also in engraving, to join the skilled workers who are with me in Judah and Jerusalem, whom my father David provided. ⁸Send me also cedar, cypress, and algum timber from Lebanon, for I know that your servants are skilled in cutting Lebanon timber. My servants will work with your servants ⁹to prepare timber for me in abundance, for the house I am about to build will be great and wonderful. ¹⁰I will provide for your servants, those who cut the timber, twenty thousand cors of crushed wheat, twenty thousand cors of barley, twenty thousand baths*d* of wine, and twenty thousand baths of oil."

11 Then King Huram of Tyre answered in a letter that he sent to Solomon, "Because the LORD loves his people he has made you king over them." ¹²Huram also said, "Blessed be the LORD God of Israel, who made heaven and earth, who has given King David a wise son, endowed with discretion and understanding, who will build a temple for the LORD, and a royal palace for himself.

13 "I have dispatched Huram-abi, a skilled artisan, endowed with understanding, ¹⁴the son of one of the Danite women, his father a Tyrian. He is trained to work in gold, silver, bronze, iron, stone, and wood, and in purple, blue, and crimson fabrics and fine linen, and to do all sorts of engraving and execute any design that may be assigned him, with your artisans, the artisans of my lord, your father David. ¹⁵Now, as for the wheat, barley, oil, and wine, of which my lord has spoken, let him send

---

a Gk Vg: Heb *to*   *b* Ch 1.18 in Heb   *c* Ch 2.1 in Heb   *d* A Hebrew measure of volume

them to his servants. ¹⁶We will cut whatever timber you need from Lebanon, and bring it to you as rafts by sea to Joppa; you will take it up to Jerusalem."

17 Then Solomon took a census of all the aliens who were residing in the land of Israel, after the census that his father David had taken; and there were found to be one hundred fifty-three thousand six hundred. ¹⁸Seventy thousand of them he assigned as laborers, eighty thousand as stonecutters in the hill

---

FRIDAY

THE TEMPLE HE HAD SPOKEN OF WAS HIS BODY
Evelyn Underhill

VERSE: 2 Chronicles 2.7   **PASSAGE:** 2 Chronicles 2.1–10

t sometimes happens that one goes to see a cathedral which is famous for the splendor of its glass; only to discover that, seen from outside, the windows give us no hint whatever of that which awaits us within. They all look alike; dull, thick, and grubby . . . Then we open the door, and go inside . . . and at once we are surrounded by a radiance, a beauty, that lie beyond the fringe of speech. The universal light of God in which we live and move, and yet which in its reality always escapes us, pours through those windows . . . and shows us things of which we never dreamed before.

In the same way, the deep mysteries of the being of God . . . cannot be seen by us, until they have passed through a human medium, a human life. Nor can that life, and all that it means as a revelation of God, his eternal truth and beauty, be realized by us from the outside . . . It is only within the place of prayer, recollection, worship and love . . . that we can cleanse our vision . . . and fully and truly receive the revelation of reality which is made to us in Christ . . .

For here, a light we can bear to look at . . . comes to us from a light we cannot bear to look at even whilst we worship it . . . What we see is not very sensational . . . First we see a baby, and a long hidden growth; and then the unmeasured outpouring and self spending of an other-worldly love and mercy, teaching, healing, rescuing and transforming, but never trying to get anything for itself . . . consummated at last in the most generous and lonely of deaths, issuing in a victory which has given life ever since to men's souls.

ADDITIONAL SCRIPTURE READING:
1 Corinthians 6.19–20; Ephesians 2.19–22; 1 Peter 2.5

Go to page 478 for your next devotional reading.

1900   Present

country, and three thousand six hundred as overseers to make the people work.

Solomon Builds the Temple

3 Solomon began to build the house of the LORD in Jerusalem on Mount Moriah, where the LORD had appeared to his father David, at the place that David had designated, on the threshing floor of Ornan the Jebusite. 2He began to build on the second day of the second month of the fourth year of his reign. 3These are Solomon's measurements*e* for building the house of God: the length, in cubits of the old standard, was sixty cubits, and the width twenty cubits. 4The vestibule in front of the nave of the house was twenty cubits long, across the width of the house;*f* and its height was one hundred twenty cubits. He overlaid it on the inside with pure gold. 5The nave he lined with cypress, covered it with fine gold, and made palms and chains on it. 6He adorned the house with settings of precious stones. The gold was gold from Parvaim. 7So he lined the house with gold—its beams, its thresholds, its walls, and its doors; and he carved cherubim on the walls.

8 He made the most holy place; its length, corresponding to the width of the house, was twenty cubits, and its width was twenty cubits; he overlaid it with six hundred talents of fine gold. 9The weight of the nails was fifty shekels of gold. He overlaid the upper chambers with gold.

10 In the most holy place he made two carved cherubim and overlaid*g* them with gold. 11The wings of the cherubim together extended twenty cubits: one wing of the one, five cubits long, touched the wall of the house, and its other wing, five cubits long, touched the wing of the other cherub; 12and of this cherub, one wing, five cubits long, touched the wall of the house, and the other wing, also five cubits long, was joined to the wing of the first cherub. 13The wings of these cherubim extended twenty cubits; the cherubim*h* stood on their feet, facing the nave. 14And Solomon*i* made the curtain of blue and pur-

ple and crimson fabrics and fine linen, and worked cherubim into it.

15 In front of the house he made two pillars thirty-five cubits high, with a capital of five cubits on the top of each. 16He made encircling*i* chains and put them on the tops of the pillars; and he made one hundred pomegranates, and put them on the chains. 17He set up the pillars in front of the temple, one on the right, the other on the left; the one on the right he called Jachin, and the one on the left, Boaz.

Furnishings of the Temple

4 He made an altar of bronze, twenty cubits long, twenty cubits wide, and ten cubits high. 2Then he made the molten sea; it was round, ten cubits from rim to rim, and five cubits high. A line of thirty cubits would encircle it completely. 3Under it were panels all around, each of ten cubits, surrounding the sea; there were two rows of panels, cast when it was cast. 4It stood on twelve oxen, three facing north, three facing west, three facing south, and three facing east; the sea was set on them. The hindquarters of each were toward the inside. 5Its thickness was a handbreadth; its rim was made like the rim of a cup, like the flower of a lily; it held three thousand baths.*k* 6He also made ten basins in which to wash, and set five on the right side, and five on the left. In these they were to rinse what was used for the burnt offering. The sea was for the priests to wash in.

7 He made ten golden lampstands as prescribed, and set them in the temple, five on the south side and five on the north. 8He also made ten tables and placed them in the temple, five on the right side and five on the left. And he made one hundred basins of gold. 9He made the court of the priests, and the great court, and doors for the court; he overlaid their doors with bronze. 10He set the sea at the southeast corner of the house.

11 And Huram made the pots, the shovels, and the basins. Thus Huram finished the work that he did for King Solomon on the house of God: 12the two

---

e Syr: Heb *foundations*   *f* Compare 1 Kings 6.3: Meaning of Heb uncertain   *g* Heb *they overlaid*
h Heb *they*   *i* Heb *he*   *j* Cn: Heb *in the inner sanctuary*   *k* A Hebrew measure of volume

pillars, the bowls, and the two capitals on the top of the pillars; and the two latticeworks to cover the two bowls of the capitals that were on the top of the pillars; 13the four hundred pomegranates for the two latticeworks, two rows of pomegranates for each latticework, to cover the two bowls of the capitals that were on the pillars. 14He made the stands, the basins on the stands, 15the one sea, and the twelve oxen underneath it. 16The pots, the shovels, the forks, and all the equipment for these Huram-abi made of burnished bronze for King Solomon for the house of the LORD. 17In the plain of the Jordan the king cast them, in the clay ground between Succoth and Zeredah. 18Solomon made all these things in great quantities, so that the weight of the bronze was not determined.

19 So Solomon made all the things that were in the house of God: the golden altar, the tables for the bread of the Presence, 20the lampstands and their lamps of pure gold to burn before the inner sanctuary, as prescribed; 21the flowers, the lamps, and the tongs, of purest gold; 22the snuffers, basins, ladles, and firepans, of pure gold. As for the entrance to the temple: the inner doors to the most holy place and the doors of the nave of the temple were of gold.

5 Thus all the work that Solomon did for the house of the LORD was finished. Solomon brought in the things that his father David had dedicated, and stored the silver, the gold, and all the vessels in the treasuries of the house of God.

The Ark Brought into the Temple

2 Then Solomon assembled the elders of Israel and all the heads of the tribes, the leaders of the ancestral houses of the people of Israel, in Jerusalem, to bring up the ark of the covenant of the LORD out of the city of David, which is Zion. 3And all the Israelites assembled before the king at the festival that is in the seventh month. 4And all the elders of Israel came, and the Levites carried the ark. 5So they brought up the ark, the tent of meeting, and all the holy vessels that were in the

tent; the priests and the Levites brought them up. 6King Solomon and all the congregation of Israel, who had assembled before him, were before the ark, sacrificing so many sheep and oxen that they could not be numbered or counted. 7Then the priests brought the ark of the covenant of the LORD to its place, in the inner sanctuary of the house, in the most holy place, underneath the wings of the cherubim. 8For the cherubim spread out their wings over the place of the ark, so that the cherubim made a covering above the ark and its poles. 9The poles were so long that the ends of the poles were seen from the holy place in front of the inner sanctuary; but they could not be seen from outside; they are there to this day. 10There was nothing in the ark except the two tablets that Moses put there at Horeb, where the LORD made a covenant[1] with the people of Israel after they came out of Egypt.

11 Now when the priests came out of the holy place (for all the priests who were present had sanctified themselves, without regard to their divisions), 12all the levitical singers, Asaph, Heman, and Jeduthun, their sons and kindred, arrayed in fine linen, with cymbals, harps, and lyres, stood east of the altar with one hundred twenty priests who were trumpeters. 13It was the duty of the trumpeters and singers to make themselves heard in unison in praise and thanksgiving to the LORD, and when the song was raised, with trumpets and cymbals and other musical instruments, in praise to the LORD,

"For he is good,
    for his steadfast love endures
        forever,"

the house, the house of the LORD, was filled with a cloud, 14so that the priests could not stand to minister because of the cloud; for the glory of the LORD filled the house of God.

Dedication of the Temple

6 Then Solomon said, "The LORD has said that he would reside in thick darkness. 2I have built you an exalted house, a place for you to reside in forever."

3 Then the king turned around and

---

1 Heb lacks *a covenant*

blessed all the assembly of Israel, while all the assembly of Israel stood. 4And he said, "Blessed be the LORD, the God of Israel, who with his hand has fulfilled what he promised with his mouth to my father David, saying, 5'Since the day that I brought my people out of the land of Egypt, I have not chosen a city from any of the tribes of Israel in which to build a house, so that my name might be there, and I chose no one as ruler over my people Israel; 6but I have chosen Jerusalem in order that my name may be there, and I have chosen David to be over my people Israel.' 7My father David had it in mind to build a house for the name of the LORD, the God of Israel. 8But the LORD said to my father David, 'You did well to consider building a house for my name; 9nevertheless you shall not build the house, but your son who shall be born to you shall build the house for my name.' 10Now the LORD has fulfilled his promise that he made; for I have succeeded my father David, and sit on the throne of Israel, as the LORD promised, and have built the house for the name of the LORD, the God of Israel. 11There I have set the ark, in which is the covenant of the LORD that he made with the people of Israel."

Solomon's Prayer of Dedication

12 Then Solomonm stood before the altar of the LORD in the presence of the whole assembly of Israel, and spread out his hands. 13Solomon had made a bronze platform five cubits long, five cubits wide, and three cubits high, and had set it in the court; and he stood on it. Then he knelt on his knees in the presence of the whole assembly of Israel, and spread out his hands toward heaven. 14He said, "O LORD, God of Israel, there is no God like you, in heaven or on earth, keeping covenant in steadfast love with your servants who walk before you with all their heart— 15you who have kept for your servant, my father David, what you promised to him. Indeed, you promised with your mouth and this day have fulfilled with your hand. 16Therefore, O LORD, God of Israel, keep for your servant, my father David, that which you

promised him, saying, 'There shall never fail you a successor before me to sit on the throne of Israel, if only your children keep to their way, to walk in my law as you have walked before me.' 17Therefore, O LORD, God of Israel, let your word be confirmed, which you promised to your servant David.

18 "But will God indeed reside with mortals on earth? Even heaven and the highest heaven cannot contain you, how much less this house that I have built! 19Regard your servant's prayer and his plea, O LORD my God, heeding the cry and the prayer that your servant prays to you. 20May your eyes be open day and night toward this house, the place where you promised to set your name, and may you heed the prayer that your servant prays toward this place. 21And hear the plea of your servant and of your people Israel, when they pray toward this place; may you hear from heaven your dwelling place; hear and forgive.

22 "If someone sins against another and is required to take an oath and comes and swears before your altar in this house, 23may you hear from heaven, and act, and judge your servants, repaying the guilty by bringing their conduct on their own head, and vindicating those who are in the right by rewarding them in accordance with their righteousness.

24 "When your people Israel, having sinned against you, are defeated before an enemy but turn again to you, confess your name, pray and plead with you in this house, 25may you hear from heaven, and forgive the sin of your people Israel, and bring them again to the land that you gave to them and to their ancestors.

26 "When heaven is shut up and there is no rain because they have sinned against you, and then they pray toward this place, confess your name, and turn from their sin, because you

---

AFFLICTIONS ARE BUT THE SHADOW OF GOD'S WINGS.   —George MacDonald

---

punish them, 27may you hear in heaven, forgive the sin of your servants, your people Israel, when you teach them the good way in which they should walk; and send down rain upon your land, which you have given to your people as an inheritance.

28 "If there is famine in the land, if there is plague, blight, mildew, locust, or caterpillar; if their enemies besiege them in any of the settlements of the lands; whatever suffering, whatever sickness there is; 29whatever prayer, whatever plea from any individual or from all your people Israel, all knowing their own suffering and their own sorrows so that they stretch out their hands toward this house; 30may you hear from heaven, your dwelling place, forgive, and render to all whose heart you know, according to all their ways, for only you know the human heart. 31Thus may they fear you and walk in your ways all the days that they live in the land that you gave to our ancestors.

32 "Likewise when foreigners, who are not of your people Israel, come from a distant land because of your great name, and your mighty hand, and your outstretched arm, when they come and pray toward this house, 33may you hear from heaven your dwelling place, and do whatever the foreigners ask of you, in order that all the peoples of the earth may know your name and fear you, as do your people Israel, and that they may know that your name has been invoked on this house that I have built.

34 "If your people go out to battle against their enemies, by whatever way you shall send them, and they pray to you toward this city that you have chosen and the house that I have built for your name, 35then hear from heaven their prayer and their plea, and maintain their cause.

36 "If they sin against you—for there is no one who does not sin—and you are angry with them and give them to an enemy, so that they are carried away captive to a land far or near; 37then if they come to their senses in the land to which they have been taken captive, and repent, and plead with you in the land of their captivity, saying, 'We have sinned, and have done wrong; we have acted wickedly'; 38if they repent with all their heart and soul in the land of their captivity, to which they were taken cap-

tive, and pray toward their land, which you gave to their ancestors, the city that you have chosen, and the house that I have built for your name, 39then hear from heaven your dwelling place their prayer and their pleas, maintain their cause and forgive your people who have sinned against you. 40Now, O my God, let your eyes be open and your ears attentive to prayer from this place.

41   "Now rise up, O LORD God, and go
          to your resting place,
      you and the ark of your might.
    Let your priests, O LORD God, be
          clothed with salvation,
      and let your faithful rejoice in
          your goodness.
42   O LORD God, do not reject your
          anointed one.
      Remember your steadfast love
          for your servant David."

Solomon Dedicates the Temple

7 When Solomon had ended his prayer, fire came down from heaven and consumed the burnt offering and the sacrifices; and the glory of the LORD filled the temple. 2The priests could not enter the house of the LORD, because the glory of the LORD filled the LORD's house. 3When all the people of Israel saw the fire come down and the glory of the LORD on the temple, they bowed down on the pavement with their faces to the ground, and worshiped and gave thanks to the LORD, saying,

"For he is good,
    for his steadfast love endures
        forever."

4 Then the king and all the people offered sacrifice before the LORD. 5King Solomon offered as a sacrifice twenty-two thousand oxen and one hundred twenty thousand sheep. So the king and all the people dedicated the house of God. 6The priests stood at their posts; the Levites also, with the instruments for music to the LORD that King David had made for giving thanks to the LORD—for his steadfast love endures forever—whenever David offered praises by their ministry. Opposite them the priests sounded trumpets; and all Israel stood.

7 Solomon consecrated the middle of the court that was in front of the house of the LORD; for there he offered the

burnt offerings and the fat of the offerings of well-being because the bronze altar Solomon had made could not hold the burnt offering and the grain offering and the fat parts.

8 At that time Solomon held the festival for seven days, and all Israel with him, a very great congregation, from Lebo-hamath to the Wadi of Egypt. 9On the eighth day they held a solemn assembly; for they had observed the dedication of the altar seven days and the festival seven days. 10On the twenty-third day of the seventh month he sent the people away to their homes, joyful and in good spirits because of the goodness that the LORD had shown to David and to Solomon and to his people Israel.

11 Thus Solomon finished the house of the LORD and the king's house; all that Solomon had planned to do in the house of the LORD and in his own house he successfully accomplished.

God's Second Appearance to Solomon

12 Then the LORD appeared to Solomon in the night and said to him: "I have heard your prayer, and have chosen this place for myself as a house of sacrifice. 13When I shut up the heavens so that there is no rain, or command the locust to devour the land, or send pestilence among my people, 14if my people who are called by my name humble themselves, pray, seek my face, and turn from their wicked ways, then I will hear from heaven, and will forgive their sin and heal their land. 15Now my eyes will be open and my ears attentive to the prayer that is made in this place. 16For now I have chosen and consecrated this house so that my name may be there forever; my eyes and my heart will be there for all time. 17As for you, if you walk before me, as your father David walked, doing according to all that I have commanded you and keeping my statutes and my ordinances, 18then I will establish your royal throne, as I made covenant with your father David saying, 'You shall never lack a successor to rule over Israel.'

19 "But if you[n] turn aside and forsake my statutes and my commandments that I have set before you, and go and serve other gods and worship them, 20then I will pluck you[o] up from the land that I have given you;[o] and this house, which I have consecrated for my name, I will cast out of my sight, and will make it a proverb and a byword among all peoples. 21And regarding this house, now exalted, everyone passing by will be astonished, and say, 'Why has the LORD done such a thing to this land and to this house?' 22Then they will say, 'Because they abandoned the LORD the God of their ancestors who brought them out of the land of Egypt, and they adopted other gods, and worshiped them and served them; therefore he has brought all this calamity upon them.' "

Various Activities of Solomon

8 At the end of twenty years, during which Solomon had built the house of the LORD and his own house, 2Solomon rebuilt the cities that Huram had given to him, and settled the people of Israel in them.

3 Solomon went to Hamath-zobah, and captured it. 4He built Tadmor in the wilderness and all the storage towns that he built in Hamath. 5He also built Upper Beth-horon and Lower Beth-horon, fortified cities, with walls, gates, and bars, 6and Baalath, as well as all Solomon's storage towns, and all the towns for his chariots, the towns for his cavalry, and whatever Solomon desired to build, in Jerusalem, in Lebanon, and in all the land of his dominion. 7All the people who were left of the Hittites, the Amorites, the Perizzites, the Hivites, and the Jebusites, who were not of Israel, 8from their descendants who were still left in the land, whom the people of Israel had not destroyed—these Solomon conscripted for forced labor, as is still the case today. 9But of the people of Israel Solomon made no slaves for his work; they were soldiers, and his officers, the commanders of his chariotry and cavalry. 10These were the chief officers of King Solomon, two hundred fifty of them, who exercised authority over the people.

11 Solomon brought Pharaoh's daughter from the city of David to the house

---

n The word *you* in this verse is plural   o Heb *them*

WEEKEND

A Morning Watch
Jacob Boehme

Verse: 2 Chronicles 7.14   **Passage:** 2 Chronicles 7.11–22

On Waking

iving Lord, you have watched over me, and put your hand on my head, during the long, dark hours of night. Your holy angels have protected me from all harm and pain. To you, Lord, I owe life itself. Continue to watch over me and bless me during the hours of day.

On Rising

Rule over me this day, O God, leading me on the path of righteousness. Put your Word in my mind and your truth in my heart, that this day I neither think nor feel anything except what is good and honest. Protect me from all lies and falsehood, helping me to discern deception wherever I meet it. Let my eyes always look straight ahead on the road you wish me to tread, that I might not be tempted by any distraction. And make my eyes pure, that no false desires may be awakened within me.

On Going to Work

Give me, dear Lord, a pure heart and a wise mind, that I may carry out my work according to your will. Save me from all false desires, from pride, greed, envy and anger, and let me accept joyfully every task you set before me. Let me seek to serve the poor, the sad and those unable to work. Help me to discern honestly my own gifts that I may do the things of which I am capable, and happily and humbly leave the rest to others. Above all, remind me constantly that I have nothing except what you give me, and can do nothing except what you enable me to do.

Additional Scripture Reading:
2 Chronicles 6.29–30; Psalm 139.23–24; Lamentations 3.40–41

Go to page 493 for your next devotional reading.

1500   1700

that he had built for her, for he said, "My wife shall not live in the house of King David of Israel, for the places to which the ark of the Lord has come are holy."

12 Then Solomon offered up burnt offerings to the Lord on the altar of the Lord that he had built in front of the vestibule, 13as the duty of each day required, offering according to the commandment of Moses for the sabbaths, the new moons, and the three annual festivals—the festival of unleavened bread, the festival of weeks, and the festival of booths. 14According to the ordinance of his father David, he appointed the divisions of the priests for their service, and the Levites for their offices of praise and ministry alongside the priests as the duty of each day required, and the gatekeepers in their divisions for the several gates; for so David the man of God had commanded. 15They did not turn away from what the king had commanded the priests and Levites regarding anything at all, or regarding the treasuries.

16 Thus all the work of Solomon was accomplished from[p] the day the foundation of the house of the Lord was laid until the house of the Lord was finished completely.

17 Then Solomon went to Eziongeber and Eloth on the shore of the sea, in the land of Edom. 18Huram sent him, in the care of his servants, ships and servants familiar with the sea. They went to Ophir, together with the servants of Solomon, and imported from there four hundred fifty talents of gold and brought it to King Solomon.

Visit of the Queen of Sheba

9 When the queen of Sheba heard of the fame of Solomon, she came to Jerusalem to test him with hard questions, having a very great retinue and camels bearing spices and very much gold and precious stones. When she came to Solomon, she discussed with him all that was on her mind. 2Solomon answered all her questions; there was nothing hidden from Solomon that he could not explain to her. 3When the queen of Sheba had observed the wisdom of Solomon, the house that he

had built, 4the food of his table, the seating of his officials, and the attendance of his servants, and their clothing, his valets, and their clothing, and his burnt offerings[q] that he offered at the house of the Lord, there was no more spirit left in her.

5 So she said to the king, "The report was true that I heard in my own land of your accomplishments and of your wisdom, 6but I did not believe the[r] reports until I came and my own eyes saw it. Not even half of the greatness of your wisdom had been told to me; you far surpass the report that I had heard. 7Happy are your people! Happy are these your servants, who continually attend you and hear your wisdom! 8Blessed be the Lord your God, who has delighted in you and set you on his throne as king for the Lord your God. Because your God loved Israel and would establish them forever, he has made you king over them, that you may execute justice and righteousness." 9Then she gave the king one hundred twenty talents of gold, a very great quantity of spices, and precious stones: there were no spices such as those that the queen of Sheba gave to King Solomon.

10 Moreover the servants of Huram and the servants of Solomon who brought gold from Ophir brought algum wood and precious stones. 11From the algum wood, the king made steps[s] for the house of the Lord and for the king's house, lyres also and harps for the singers; there never was seen the like of them before in the land of Judah.

12 Meanwhile King Solomon granted the queen of Sheba every desire that she expressed, well beyond what she had brought to the king. Then she returned to her own land, with her servants.

Solomon's Great Wealth

13 The weight of gold that came to Solomon in one year was six hundred sixty-six talents of gold, 14besides that which the traders and merchants brought; and all the kings of Arabia and the governors of the land brought gold and silver to Solomon. 15King Solomon made two hundred large shields of beaten

p Gk Syr Vg: Heb to   q Gk Syr Vg 1 Kings 10.5: Heb ascent   r Heb their   s Gk Vg: Meaning of Heb uncertain

gold; six hundred shekels of beaten gold went into each large shield. 16He made three hundred shields of beaten gold; three hundred shekels of gold went into each shield; and the king put them in the House of the Forest of Lebanon. 17The king also made a great ivory throne, and overlaid it with pure gold. 18The throne had six steps and a footstool of gold, which were attached to the throne, and on each side of the seat were arm rests and two lions standing beside the arm rests, 19while twelve lions were standing, one on each end of a step on the six steps. The like of it was never made in any kingdom. 20All King Solomon's drinking vessels were of gold, and all the vessels of the House of the Forest of Lebanon were of pure gold; silver was not considered as anything in the days of Solomon. 21For the king's ships went to Tarshish with the servants of Huram; once every three years the ships of Tarshish used to come bringing gold, silver, ivory, apes, and peacocks.*t*

22 Thus King Solomon excelled all the kings of the earth in riches and in wisdom. 23All the kings of the earth sought the presence of Solomon to hear his wisdom, which God had put into his mind. 24Every one of them brought a present, objects of silver and gold, garments, weaponry, spices, horses, and mules, so much year by year. 25Solomon had four thousand stalls for horses and chariots, and twelve thousand horses, which he stationed in the chariot cities and with the king in Jerusalem. 26He ruled over all the kings from the Euphrates to the land of the Philistines, and to the border of Egypt. 27The king made silver as common in Jerusalem as stone, and cedar as plentiful as the sycamore of the Shephelah. 28Horses were imported for Solomon from Egypt and from all lands.

Death of Solomon

29 Now the rest of the acts of Solomon, from first to last, are they not written in the history of the prophet Nathan, and in the prophecy of Ahijah the Shilonite, and in the visions of the seer Iddo concerning Jeroboam son of Nebat? 30Solomon reigned in Jerusalem over all Israel forty years. 31Solomon slept with his ancestors and was buried in the city of his father David; and his son Rehoboam succeeded him.

The Revolt against Rehoboam

10 Rehoboam went to Shechem, for all Israel had come to Shechem to make him king. 2When Jeroboam son of Nebat heard of it (for he was in Egypt, where he had fled from King Solomon), then Jeroboam returned from Egypt. 3They sent and called him; and Jeroboam and all Israel came and said to Rehoboam, 4"Your father made our yoke heavy. Now therefore lighten the hard service of your father and his heavy yoke that he placed on us, and we will serve you." 5He said to them, "Come to me again in three days." So the people went away.

6 Then King Rehoboam took counsel with the older men who had attended his father Solomon while he was still alive, saying, "How do you advise me to answer this people?" 7They answered him, "If you will be kind to this people and please them, and speak good words to them, then they will be your servants forever." 8But he rejected the advice that the older men gave him, and consulted the young men who had grown up with him and now attended him. 9He said to them, "What do you advise that we answer this people who have said to me, 'Lighten the yoke that your father put on us'?" 10The young men who had grown up with him said to him, "Thus should you speak to the people who said to you, 'Your father made our yoke heavy, but you must lighten it for us'; tell them, 'My little finger is thicker than my father's loins. 11Now, whereas my father laid on you a heavy yoke, I will add to your yoke. My father disciplined you with whips, but I will discipline you with scorpions.' "

12 So Jeroboam and all the people came to Rehoboam the third day, as the king had said, "Come to me again the third day." 13The king answered them harshly. King Rehoboam rejected the advice of the older men; 14he spoke to them in accordance with the advice of the young men, "My father made your

t Or *baboons*

yoke heavy, but I will add to it; my father disciplined you with whips, but I will discipline you with scorpions." 15So the king did not listen to the people, because it was a turn of affairs brought about by God so that the LORD might fulfill his word, which he had spoken by Ahijah the Shilonite to Jeroboam son of Nebat.

16 When all Israel saw that the king would not listen to them, the people answered the king,

"What share do we have in David?
  We have no inheritance in the
  son of Jesse.
Each of you to your tents, O Israel!
  Look now to your own house,
  O David."

So all Israel departed to their tents. 17But Rehoboam reigned over the people of Israel who were living in the cities of Judah. 18When King Rehoboam sent Hadoram, who was taskmaster over the forced labor, the people of Israel stoned him to death. King Rehoboam hurriedly mounted his chariot to flee to Jerusalem. 19So Israel has been in rebellion against the house of David to this day.

Judah and Benjamin Fortified

11 When Rehoboam came to Jerusalem, he assembled one hundred eighty thousand chosen troops of the house of Judah and Benjamin to fight against Israel, to restore the kingdom to Rehoboam. 2But the word of the LORD came to Shemaiah the man of God: 3Say to King Rehoboam of Judah, son of Solomon, and to all Israel in Judah and Benjamin, 4"Thus says the LORD: You shall not go up or fight against your kindred. Let everyone return home, for this thing is from me." So they heeded the word of the LORD and turned back from the expedition against Jeroboam.

5 Rehoboam resided in Jerusalem, and he built cities for defense in Judah. 6He built up Bethlehem, Etam, Tekoa, 7Beth-zur, Soco, Adullam, 8Gath, Mareshah, Ziph, 9Adoraim, Lachish, Azekah, 10Zorah, Aijalon, and Hebron, fortified cities that are in Judah and in Benjamin. 11He made the fortresses strong, and put commanders in them, and stores of food, oil, and wine. 12He also put large shields and spears in all the cities, and made them very strong. So he held Judah and Benjamin.

Priests and Levites Support Rehoboam

13 The priests and the Levites who were in all Israel presented themselves to him from all their territories. 14The Levites had left their common lands and their holdings and had come to Judah and Jerusalem, because Jeroboam and his sons had prevented them from serving as priests of the LORD, 15and had appointed his own priests for the high places, and for the goat-demons, and for the calves that he had made. 16Those who had set their hearts to seek the LORD God of Israel came after them from all the tribes of Israel to Jerusalem to sacrifice to the LORD, the God of their ancestors. 17They strengthened the kingdom of Judah, and for three years they made Rehoboam son of Solomon secure, for they walked for three years in the way of David and Solomon.

Rehoboam's Marriages

18 Rehoboam took as his wife Mahalath daughter of Jerimoth son of David, and of Abihail daughter of Eliab son of Jesse. 19She bore him sons: Jeush, Shemariah, and Zaham. 20After her he took Maacah daughter of Absalom, who bore him Abijah, Attai, Ziza, and Shelomith. 21Rehoboam loved Maacah daughter of Absalom more than all his other wives and concubines (he took eighteen wives and sixty concubines, and became the father of twenty-eight sons and sixty daughters). 22Rehoboam appointed Abijah son of Maacah as chief prince among his brothers, for he intended to make him king. 23He dealt wisely, and distributed some of his sons through all the districts of Judah and Benjamin, in all the fortified cities; he gave them abundant provisions, and found many wives for them.

Egypt Attacks Judah

12 When the rule of Rehoboam was established and he grew strong, he abandoned the law of the LORD, he and all Israel with him. 2In the fifth year of King Rehoboam, because they had been unfaithful to the LORD,

King Shishak of Egypt came up against Jerusalem [3]with twelve hundred chariots and sixty thousand cavalry. A countless army came with him from Egypt—Libyans, Sukkiim, and Ethiopians.[u] [4]He took the fortified cities of Judah and came as far as Jerusalem. [5]Then the prophet Shemaiah came to Rehoboam and to the officers of Judah, who had gathered at Jerusalem because of Shishak, and said to them, "Thus says the LORD: You abandoned me, so I have abandoned you to the hand of Shishak." [6]Then the officers of Israel and the king humbled themselves and said, "The LORD is in the right." [7]When the LORD saw that they humbled themselves, the word of the LORD came to Shemaiah, saying: "They have humbled themselves; I will not destroy them, but I will grant them some deliverance, and my wrath shall not be poured out on Jerusalem by the hand of Shishak. [8]Nevertheless they shall be his servants, so that they may know the difference between serving me and serving the kingdoms of other lands."

[9] So King Shishak of Egypt came up against Jerusalem; he took away the treasures of the house of the LORD and the treasures of the king's house; he took everything. He also took away the shields of gold that Solomon had made; [10]but King Rehoboam made in place of them shields of bronze, and committed them to the hands of the officers of the guard, who kept the door of the king's house. [11]Whenever the king went into the house of the LORD, the guard would come along bearing them, and would then bring them back to the guardroom. [12]Because he humbled himself the wrath of the LORD turned from him, so as not to destroy them completely; moreover, conditions were good in Judah.

Death of Rehoboam

[13] So King Rehoboam established himself in Jerusalem and reigned. Rehoboam was forty-one years old when he began to reign; he reigned seventeen years in Jerusalem, the city that the LORD had chosen out of all the tribes of Israel to put his name there. His mother's name was Naamah the Ammonite. [14]He did evil, for he did not set his heart to seek the LORD.

[15] Now the acts of Rehoboam, from first to last, are they not written in the records of the prophet Shemaiah and of the seer Iddo, recorded by genealogy? There were continual wars between Rehoboam and Jeroboam. [16]Rehoboam slept with his ancestors and was buried in the city of David; and his son Abijah succeeded him.

Abijah Reigns over Judah

13 In the eighteenth year of King Jeroboam, Abijah began to reign over Judah. [2]He reigned for three years in Jerusalem. His mother's name was Micaiah daughter of Uriel of Gibeah.

Now there was war between Abijah and Jeroboam. [3]Abijah engaged in battle, having an army of valiant warriors, four hundred thousand picked men; and Jeroboam drew up his line of battle against him with eight hundred thousand picked mighty warriors. [4]Then Abijah stood on the slope of Mount Zemaraim that is in the hill country of Ephraim, and said, "Listen to me, Jeroboam and all Israel! [5]Do you not know that the LORD God of Israel gave the kingship over Israel forever to David and his sons by a covenant of salt? [6]Yet Jeroboam son of Nebat, a servant of Solomon son of David, rose up and rebelled against his lord; [7]and certain worthless scoundrels gathered around him and defied Rehoboam son of Solomon, when Rehoboam was young and irresolute and could not withstand them.

[8] "And now you think that you can withstand the kingdom of the LORD in the hand of the sons of David, because you are a great multitude and have with you the golden calves that Jeroboam made as gods for you. [9]Have you not driven out the priests of the LORD, the descendants of Aaron, and the Levites, and made priests for yourselves like the peoples of other lands? Whoever comes to be consecrated with a young bull or seven rams becomes a priest of what are no gods. [10]But as for us, the LORD is our God, and we have not abandoned him. We have priests ministering to the LORD

---

u Or Nubians; Heb Cushites

who are descendants of Aaron, and Levites for their service. 11They offer to the LORD every morning and every evening burnt offerings and fragrant incense, set out the rows of bread on the table of pure gold, and care for the golden lampstand so that its lamps may burn every evening; for we keep the charge of the LORD our God, but you have abandoned him. 12See, God is with us at our head, and his priests have their battle trumpets to sound the call to battle against you. O Israelites, do not fight against the LORD, the God of your ancestors; for you cannot succeed."

13 Jeroboam had sent an ambush around to come on them from behind; thus his troopsv were in front of Judah, and the ambush was behind them. 14When Judah turned, the battle was in front of them and behind them. They cried out to the LORD, and the priests blew the trumpets. 15Then the people of Judah raised the battle shout. And when the people of Judah shouted, God defeated Jeroboam and all Israel before Abijah and Judah. 16The Israelites fled before Judah, and God gave them into their hands. 17Abijah and his army defeated them with great slaughter; five hundred thousand picked men of Israel fell slain. 18Thus the Israelites were subdued at that time, and the people of Judah prevailed, because they relied on the LORD, the God of their ancestors. 19Abijah pursued Jeroboam, and took cities from him: Bethel with its villages and Jeshanah with its villages and Ephronw with its villages. 20Jeroboam did not recover his power in the days of Abijah; the LORD struck him down, and he died. 21But Abijah grew strong. He took fourteen wives, and became the father of twenty-two sons and sixteen daughters. 22The rest of the acts of Abijah, his behavior and his deeds, are written in the story of the prophet Iddo.

Asa Reigns

14 x So Abijah slept with his ancestors, and they buried him in the city of David. His son Asa succeeded him. In his days the land had rest for ten years. 2yAsa did what was good and right in the sight of the LORD his God. 3He took away the foreign altars and the high places, broke down the pillars, hewed down the sacred poles,z 4and commanded Judah to seek the LORD, the God of their ancestors, and to keep the law and the commandment. 5He also removed from all the cities of Judah the high places and the incense altars. And the kingdom had rest under him. 6He built fortified cities in Judah while the land had rest. He had no war in those years, for the LORD gave him peace. 7He said to Judah, "Let us build these cities, and surround them with walls and towers, gates and bars; the land is still ours because we have sought the LORD our God; we have sought him, and he has given us peace on every side." So they built and prospered. 8Asa had an army of three hundred thousand from Judah, armed with large shields and spears, and two hundred eighty thousand troops from Benjamin who carried shields and drew bows; all these were mighty warriors.

Ethiopian Invasion Repulsed

9 Zerah the Ethiopiana came out against them with an army of a million men and three hundred chariots, and came as far as Mareshah. 10Asa went out to meet him, and they drew up their lines of battle in the valley of Zephathah at Mareshah. 11Asa cried to the LORD his God, "O LORD, there is no difference for you between helping the mighty and the weak. Help us, O LORD our God, for we rely on you, and in your name we have come against this multitude. O LORD, you are our God; let no mortal prevail against you." 12So the LORD defeated the Ethiopiansb before Asa and before Judah, and the Ethiopiansb fled. 13Asa and the army with him pursued them as far as Gerar, and the Ethiopiansb fell until no one remained alive; for they were broken before the LORD and his army. The people of Judahc carried away a great quantity of booty. 14They defeated all the cities around Gerar, for the fear of the LORD was on them. They plundered all the cities; for there was much plunder in them. 15They also attacked the

---

v Heb they   w Another reading is Ephrain   x Ch 13.23 in Heb   y Ch 14.1 in Heb
z Heb Asherim   a Or Nubian; Heb Cushite   b Or Nubians; Heb Cushites   c Heb They

tents of those who had livestock,^{d} and carried away sheep and goats in abundance, and camels. Then they returned to Jerusalem.

15 The spirit of God came upon Azariah son of Oded. ^{2}He went out to meet Asa and said to him, "Hear me, Asa, and all Judah and Benjamin: The LORD is with you, while you are with him. If you seek him, he will be found by you, but if you abandon him, he will abandon you. ^{3}For a long time Israel was without the true God, and without a teaching priest, and without law; ^{4}but when in their distress they turned to the LORD, the God of Israel, and sought him, he was found by them. ^{5}In those times it was not safe for anyone to go or come, for great disturbances afflicted all the inhabitants of the lands. ^{6}They were broken in pieces, nation against nation and city against city, for God troubled them with every sort of distress. ^{7}But you, take courage! Do not let your hands be weak, for your work shall be rewarded."

8 When Asa heard these words, the prophecy of Azariah son of Oded,^{e} he took courage, and put away the abominable idols from all the land of Judah and Benjamin and from the towns that he had taken in the hill country of Ephraim. He repaired the altar of the LORD that was in front of the vestibule of the house of the LORD.^{f} ^{9}He gathered all Judah and Benjamin, and those from Ephraim, Manasseh, and Simeon who were residing as aliens with them, for great numbers had deserted to him from Israel when they saw that the LORD his God was with him. ^{10}They were gathered at Jerusalem in the third month of the fifteenth year of the reign of Asa. ^{11}They sacrificed to the LORD on that day, from the booty that they had brought, seven hundred oxen and seven thousand sheep. ^{12}They entered into a covenant to seek the LORD, the God of their ancestors, with all their heart and with all their soul. ^{13}Whoever would not seek the LORD, the God of Israel, should be put to death, whether young or old, man or woman. ^{14}They took an oath to the LORD with a loud voice, and with

shouting, and with trumpets, and with horns. ^{15}All Judah rejoiced over the oath; for they had sworn with all their heart, and had sought him with their whole desire, and he was found by them, and the LORD gave them rest all around.

16 King Asa even removed his mother Maacah from being queen mother because she had made an abominable image for Asherah. Asa cut down her image, crushed it, and burned it at the Wadi Kidron. ^{17}But the high places were not taken out of Israel. Nevertheless the heart of Asa was true all his days. ^{18}He brought into the house of God the votive gifts of his father and his own votive gifts—silver, gold, and utensils. ^{19}And there was no more war until the thirty-fifth year of the reign of Asa.

Alliance with Aram Condemned

16 In the thirty-sixth year of the reign of Asa, King Baasha of Israel went up against Judah, and built Ramah, to prevent anyone from going out or coming into the territory of^g King Asa of Judah. ^{2}Then Asa took silver and gold from the treasures of the house of the LORD and the king's house, and sent them to King Ben-hadad of Aram, who resided in Damascus, saying, ^{3}"Let there be an alliance between me and you, like that between my father and your father; I am sending to you silver and gold; go, break your alliance with King Baasha of Israel, so that he may withdraw from me." ^{4}Ben-hadad listened to King Asa, and sent the commanders of his armies against the cities of Israel. They conquered Ijon, Dan, Abel-maim, and all the store-cities of Naphtali. ^{5}When Baasha heard of it, he stopped building Ramah, and let his work cease. ^{6}Then King Asa brought all Judah, and they carried away the stones of Ramah and its timber, with which Baasha had been building, and with them he built up Geba and Mizpah.

7 At that time the seer Hanani came to King Asa of Judah, and said to him, "Because you relied on the king of Aram, and did not rely on the LORD your God, the army of the king of Aram has escaped you. ^{8}Were not the Ethiopians^h

---

d Meaning of Heb uncertain e Compare Syr Vg: Heb *the prophecy, the prophet Obed* f Heb *the vestibule of the LORD* g Heb lacks *the territory of* h Or *Nubians;* Heb *Cushites*

and the Libyans a huge army with exceedingly many chariots and cavalry? Yet because you relied on the LORD, he gave them into your hand. ⁹For the eyes of the LORD range throughout the entire earth, to strengthen those whose heart is true to him. You have done foolishly in this; for from now on you will have wars." ¹⁰Then Asa was angry with the seer, and put him in the stocks, in prison, for he was in a rage with him because of this. And Asa inflicted cruelties on some of the people at the same time.

Asa's Disease and Death

11 The acts of Asa, from first to last, are written in the Book of the Kings of Judah and Israel. ¹²In the thirty-ninth year of his reign Asa was diseased in his feet, and his disease became severe; yet even in his disease he did not seek the LORD, but sought help from physicians. ¹³Then Asa slept with his ancestors, dying in the forty-first year of his reign. ¹⁴They buried him in the tomb that he had hewn out for himself in the city of David. They laid him on a bier that had been filled with various kinds of spices prepared by the perfumer's art; and they made a very great fire in his honor.

Jehoshaphat's Reign

17 His son Jehoshaphat succeeded him, and strengthened himself against Israel. ²He placed forces in all the fortified cities of Judah, and set garrisons in the land of Judah, and in the cities of Ephraim that his father Asa had taken. ³The LORD was with Jehoshaphat, because he walked in the earlier ways of his father;ⁱ he did not seek the Baals, ⁴but sought the God of his father and walked in his commandments, and not according to the ways of Israel. ⁵Therefore the LORD established the kingdom in his hand. All Judah brought tribute to Jehoshaphat, and he had great riches and honor. ⁶His heart was courageous in the ways of the LORD; and furthermore he removed the high places and the sacred polesʲ from Judah.

7 In the third year of his reign he sent his officials, Ben-hail, Obadiah, Zechariah, Nethanel, and Micaiah, to teach in the cities of Judah. ⁸With them were the Levites, Shemaiah, Nethaniah, Zebadiah, Asahel, Shemiramoth, Jehonathan, Adonijah, Tobijah, and Tob-adonijah; and with these Levites, the priests Elishama and Jehoram. ⁹They taught in Judah, having the book of the law of the LORD with them; they went around through all the cities of Judah and taught among the people.

10 The fear of the LORD fell on all the kingdoms of the lands around Judah, and they did not make war against Jehoshaphat. ¹¹Some of the Philistines brought Jehoshaphat presents, and silver for tribute; and the Arabs also brought him seven thousand seven hundred rams and seven thousand seven hundred male goats. ¹²Jehoshaphat grew steadily greater. He built fortresses and storage cities in Judah. ¹³He carried out great works in the cities of Judah. He had soldiers, mighty warriors, in Jerusalem. ¹⁴This was the muster of them by ancestral houses: Of Judah, the commanders of the thousands: Adnah the commander, with three hundred thousand mighty warriors, ¹⁵and next to him Jehohanan the commander, with two hundred eighty thousand, ¹⁶and next to him Amasiah son of Zichri, a volunteer for the service of the LORD, with two hundred thousand mighty warriors. ¹⁷Of Benjamin: Eliada, a mighty warrior, with two hundred thousand armed with bow and shield, ¹⁸and next to him Jehozabad with one hundred eighty thousand armed for war. ¹⁹These were in the service of the king, besides those whom the king had placed in the fortified cities throughout all Judah.

Micaiah Predicts Failure

18 Now Jehoshaphat had great riches and honor; and he made a marriage alliance with Ahab. ²After some years he went down to Ahab in Samaria. Ahab slaughtered an abundance of sheep and oxen for him and for the people who were with him, and induced him to go up against Ramoth-gilead. ³King Ahab of Israel said to King Jehoshaphat of Judah, "Will you go with me to Ramoth-gilead?" He answered him, "I

ⁱ Another reading is *his father David*   ʲ Heb *Asherim*

am with you, my people are your people. We will be with you in the war."

4 But Jehoshaphat also said to the king of Israel, "Inquire first for the word of the LORD." ⁵Then the king of Israel gathered the prophets together, four hundred of them, and said to them, "Shall we go to battle against Ramoth-gilead, or shall I refrain?" They said, "Go up; for God will give it into the hand of the king." ⁶But Jehoshaphat said, "Is there no other prophet of the LORD here of whom we may inquire?" ⁷The king of Israel said to Jehoshaphat, "There is still one other by whom we may inquire of the LORD, Micaiah son of Imlah; but I hate him, for he never prophesies anything favorable about me, but only disaster." Jehoshaphat said, "Let the king not say such a thing." ⁸Then the king of Israel summoned an officer and said, "Bring quickly Micaiah son of Imlah." ⁹Now the king of Israel and King Jehoshaphat of Judah were sitting on their thrones, arrayed in their robes; and they were sitting at the threshing floor at the entrance of the gate of Samaria; and all the prophets were prophesying before them. ¹⁰Zedekiah son of Chenaanah made for himself horns of iron, and he said, "Thus says the LORD: With these you shall gore the Arameans until they are destroyed." ¹¹All the prophets were prophesying the same and saying, "Go up to Ramoth-gilead and triumph; the LORD will give it into the hand of the king."

12 The messenger who had gone to summon Micaiah said to him, "Look, the words of the prophets with one accord are favorable to the king; let your word be like the word of one of them, and speak favorably." ¹³But Micaiah said, "As the LORD lives, whatever my God says, that I will speak."

14 When he had come to the king, the king said to him, "Micaiah, shall we go to Ramoth-gilead to battle, or shall I refrain?" He answered, "Go up and triumph; they will be given into your hand." ¹⁵But the king said to him, "How many times must I make you swear to tell me nothing but the truth in the name of the LORD?" ¹⁶Then Micaiah^k said, "I saw all Israel scattered on the mountains, like sheep without a shepherd; and the LORD said, 'These have no master; let each one go home in peace.'" ¹⁷The king of Israel said to Jehoshaphat, "Did I not tell you that he would not prophesy anything favorable about me, but only disaster?"

18 Then Micaiah^k said, "Therefore hear the word of the LORD: I saw the LORD sitting on his throne, with all the host of heaven standing to the right and to the left of him. ¹⁹And the LORD said, 'Who will entice King Ahab of Israel, so that he may go up and fall at Ramoth-gilead?' Then one said one thing, and another said another, ²⁰until a spirit came forward and stood before the LORD, saying, 'I will entice him.' The LORD asked him, 'How?' ²¹He replied, 'I will go out and be a lying spirit in the mouth of all his prophets.' Then the LORD^k said, 'You are to entice him, and you shall succeed; go out and do it.' ²²So you see, the LORD has put a lying spirit in the mouth of these your prophets; the LORD has decreed disaster for you."

23 Then Zedekiah son of Chenaanah came up to Micaiah, slapped him on the cheek, and said, "Which way did the spirit of the LORD pass from me to speak to you?" ²⁴Micaiah replied, "You will find out on that day when you go in to hide in an inner chamber." ²⁵The king of Israel then ordered, "Take Micaiah, and return him to Amon the governor of the city and to Joash the king's son; ²⁶and say, 'Thus says the king: Put this fellow in prison, and feed him on reduced rations of bread and water until I return in peace.'" ²⁷Micaiah said, "If you return in peace, the LORD has not spoken by me." And he said, "Hear, you peoples, all of you!"

Defeat and Death of Ahab

28 So the king of Israel and King Jehoshaphat of Judah went up to Ramoth-gilead. ²⁹The king of Israel said to Jehoshaphat, "I will disguise myself and go into battle, but you wear your robes." So the king of Israel disguised himself, and they went into battle. ³⁰Now the king of Aram had commanded the captains of his chariots, "Fight with no one small or great, but only

---

k Heb *he*

with the king of Israel." [31]When the captains of the chariots saw Jehoshaphat, they said, "It is the king of Israel." So they turned to fight against him; and Jehoshaphat cried out, and the LORD helped him. God drew them away from him, [32]for when the captains of the chariots saw that it was not the king of Israel, they turned back from pursuing him. [33]But a certain man drew his bow and unknowingly struck the king of Israel between the scale armor and the breastplate; so he said to the driver of his chariot, "Turn around, and carry me out of the battle, for I am wounded." [34]The battle grew hot that day, and the king of Israel propped himself up in his chariot facing the Arameans until evening; then at sunset he died.

19 King Jehoshaphat of Judah returned in safety to his house in Jerusalem. [2]Jehu son of Hanani the seer went out to meet him and said to King Jehoshaphat, "Should you help the wicked and love those who hate the LORD? Because of this, wrath has gone out against you from the LORD. [3]Nevertheless, some good is found in you, for you destroyed the sacred poles[l] out of the land, and have set your heart to seek God."

The Reforms of Jehoshaphat

4 Jehoshaphat resided at Jerusalem; then he went out again among the people, from Beer-sheba to the hill country of Ephraim, and brought them back to the LORD, the God of their ancestors. [5]He appointed judges in the land in all the fortified cities of Judah, city by city, [6]and said to the judges, "Consider what you are doing, for you judge not on behalf of human beings but on the LORD's behalf; he is with you in giving judgment. [7]Now, let the fear of the LORD be upon you; take care what you do, for there is no perversion of justice with the LORD our God, or partiality, or taking of bribes."

8 Moreover in Jerusalem Jehoshaphat appointed certain Levites and priests and heads of families of Israel, to give judgment for the LORD and to decide disputed cases. They had their seat at Jeru-

salem. [9]He charged them: "This is how you shall act: in the fear of the LORD, in faithfulness, and with your whole heart; [10]whenever a case comes to you from your kindred who live in their cities, concerning bloodshed, law or commandment, statutes or ordinances, then you shall instruct them, so that they may not incur guilt before the LORD and wrath may not come on you and your kindred. Do so, and you will not incur guilt. [11]See, Amariah the chief priest is over you in all matters of the LORD; and Zebadiah son of Ishmael, the governor of the house of Judah, in all the king's matters; and the Levites will serve you as officers. Deal courageously, and may the LORD be with the good!"

Invasion from the East

20 After this the Moabites and Ammonites, and with them some of the Meunites,[m] came against Jehoshaphat for battle. [2]Messengers[n] came and told Jehoshaphat, "A great multitude is coming against you from Edom,[o] from beyond the sea; already they are at Hazazon-tamar" (that is, Engedi). [3]Jehoshaphat was afraid; he set himself to seek the LORD, and proclaimed a fast throughout all Judah. [4]Judah assembled to seek help from the LORD; from all the towns of Judah they came to seek the LORD.

Jehoshaphat's Prayer and Victory

5 Jehoshaphat stood in the assembly of Judah and Jerusalem, in the house of the LORD, before the new court, [6]and said, "O LORD, God of our ancestors, are you not God in heaven? Do you not rule over all the kingdoms of the nations? In your hand are power and might, so that no one is able to withstand you. [7]Did you not, O our God, drive out the inhabitants of this land before your people Israel, and give it forever to the descendants of your friend Abraham? [8]They have lived in it, and in it have built you a sanctuary for your name, saying, [9]'If disaster comes upon us, the sword, judgment,[p] or pestilence, or famine, we will stand before this house, and before you, for your name is in this house, and cry

---

l Heb *Asheroth*   *m* Compare 26.7: Heb *Ammonites*   *n* Heb *They*   *o* One Ms: MT *Aram*
p Or *the sword of judgment*

to you in our distress, and you will hear and save.' ¹⁰See now, the people of Ammon, Moab, and Mount Seir, whom you would not let Israel invade when they came from the land of Egypt, and whom they avoided and did not destroy— ¹¹they reward us by coming to drive us out of your possession that you have given us to inherit. ¹²O our God, will you not execute judgment upon them? For we are powerless against this great multitude that is coming against us. We do not know what to do, but our eyes are on you."

13 Meanwhile all Judah stood before the LORD, with their little ones, their wives, and their children. ¹⁴Then the spirit of the LORD came upon Jahaziel son of Zechariah, son of Benaiah, son of Jeiel, son of Mattaniah, a Levite of the sons of Asaph, in the middle of the assembly. ¹⁵He said, "Listen, all Judah and inhabitants of Jerusalem, and King Jehoshaphat: Thus says the LORD to you: 'Do not fear or be dismayed at this great multitude; for the battle is not yours but God's. ¹⁶Tomorrow go down against them; they will come up by the ascent of Ziz; you will find them at the end of the valley, before the wilderness of Jeruel. ¹⁷This battle is not for you to fight; take your position, stand still, and see the victory of the LORD on your behalf, O Judah and Jerusalem.' Do not fear or be dismayed; tomorrow go out against them, and the LORD will be with you."

18 Then Jehoshaphat bowed down with his face to the ground, and all Judah and the inhabitants of Jerusalem fell down before the LORD, worshiping the LORD. ¹⁹And the Levites, of the Kohathites and the Korahites, stood up to praise the LORD, the God of Israel, with a very loud voice.

20 They rose early in the morning and went out into the wilderness of Tekoa; and as they went out, Jehoshaphat stood and said, "Listen to me, O Judah and inhabitants of Jerusalem! Believe in the LORD your God and you will be established; believe his prophets." ²¹When he had taken counsel with the people, he appointed those who were to sing to the LORD and praise him

in holy splendor, as they went before the army, saying,

"Give thanks to the LORD,
    for his steadfast love endures
        forever."

²²As they began to sing and praise, the LORD set an ambush against the Ammonites, Moab, and Mount Seir, who had come against Judah, so that they were routed. ²³For the Ammonites and Moab attacked the inhabitants of Mount Seir, destroying them utterly; and when they had made an end of the inhabitants of Seir, they all helped to destroy one another.

24 When Judah came to the watchtower of the wilderness, they looked toward the multitude; they were corpses lying on the ground; no one had escaped. ²⁵When Jehoshaphat and his people came to take the booty from them, they found livestock⁹ in great numbers, goods, clothing, and precious things, which they took for themselves until they could carry no more. They spent three days taking the booty, because of its abundance. ²⁶On the fourth day they assembled in the Valley of Beracah, for there they blessed the LORD; therefore that place has been called the Valley of Beracahʳ to this day. ²⁷Then all the people of Judah and Jerusalem, with Jehoshaphat at their head, returned to Jerusalem with joy, for the LORD had enabled them to rejoice over their enemies. ²⁸They came to Jerusalem, with harps and lyres and trumpets, to the house of the LORD. ²⁹The fear of God came on all the kingdoms of the countries when they heard that the LORD had fought against the enemies of Israel. ³⁰And the realm of Jehoshaphat was quiet, for his God gave him rest all around.

The End of Jehoshaphat's Reign

31 So Jehoshaphat reigned over Judah. He was thirty-five years old when he began to reign; he reigned twenty-five years in Jerusalem. His mother's name was Azubah daughter of Shilhi. ³²He walked in the way of his father Asa and did not turn aside from it, doing what was right in the sight of the LORD. ³³Yet the high places were not removed; the

q Gk: Heb *among them*   r That is *Blessing*

people had not yet set their hearts upon the God of their ancestors.

34 Now the rest of the acts of Jehoshaphat, from first to last, are written in the Annals of Jehu son of Hanani, which are recorded in the Book of the Kings of Israel.

35 After this King Jehoshaphat of Judah joined with King Ahaziah of Israel, who did wickedly. ³⁶He joined him in building ships to go to Tarshish; they built the ships in Ezion-geber. ³⁷Then Eliezer son of Dodavahu of Mareshah prophesied against Jehoshaphat, saying, "Because you have joined with Ahaziah, the LORD will destroy what you have made." And the ships were wrecked and were not able to go to Tarshish.

Jehoram's Reign

21 Jehoshaphat slept with his ancestors and was buried with his ancestors in the city of David; his son Jehoram succeeded him. ²He had brothers, the sons of Jehoshaphat: Azariah, Jehiel, Zechariah, Azariah, Michael, and Shephatiah; all these were the sons of King Jehoshaphat of Judah.ˢ ³Their father gave them many gifts, of silver, gold, and valuable possessions, together with fortified cities in Judah; but he gave the kingdom to Jehoram, because he was the firstborn. ⁴When Jehoram had ascended the throne of his father and was established, he put all his brothers to the sword, and also some of the officials of Israel. ⁵Jehoram was thirty-two years old when he began to reign; he reigned eight years in Jerusalem. ⁶He walked in the way of the kings of Israel, as the house of Ahab had done; for the daughter of Ahab was his wife. He did what was evil in the sight of the LORD. ⁷Yet the LORD would not destroy the house of David because of the covenant that he had made with David, and since he had promised to give a lamp to him and to his descendants forever.

Revolt of Edom

8 In his days Edom revolted against the rule of Judah and set up a king of their own. ⁹Then Jehoram crossed over with his commanders and all his chariots. He set out by night and attacked the Edom-

ites, who had surrounded him and his chariot commanders. ¹⁰So Edom has been in revolt against the rule of Judah to this day. At that time Libnah also revolted against his rule, because he had forsaken the LORD, the God of his ancestors.

Elijah's Letter

11 Moreover he made high places in the hill country of Judah, and led the inhabitants of Jerusalem into unfaithfulness, and made Judah go astray. ¹²A letter came to him from the prophet Elijah, saying: "Thus says the LORD, the God of your father David: Because you have not walked in the ways of your father Jehoshaphat or in the ways of King Asa of Judah, ¹³but have walked in the way of the kings of Israel, and have led Judah and the inhabitants of Jerusalem into unfaithfulness, as the house of Ahab led Israel into unfaithfulness, and because you also have killed your brothers, members of your father's house, who were better than yourself, ¹⁴see, the LORD will bring a great plague on your people, your children, your wives, and all your possessions, ¹⁵and you yourself will have a severe sickness with a disease of your bowels, until your bowels come out, day after day, because of the disease."

16 The LORD aroused against Jehoram the anger of the Philistines and of the Arabs who are near the Ethiopians.ᵗ ¹⁷They came up against Judah, invaded it, and carried away all the possessions they found that belonged to the king's house, along with his sons and his wives, so that no son was left to him except Jehoahaz, his youngest son.

Disease and Death of Jehoram

18 After all this the LORD struck him in his bowels with an incurable disease. ¹⁹In course of time, at the end of two years, his bowels came out because of the disease, and he died in great agony. His people made no fire in his honor, like the fires made for his ancestors. ²⁰He was thirty-two years old when he began to reign; he reigned eight years in Jerusalem. He departed with no one's regret. They buried him in the city of David, but not in the tombs of the kings.

s Gk Syr: Heb *Israel*   t Or *Nubians*; Heb *Cushites*

Ahaziah's Reign

22 The inhabitants of Jerusalem made his youngest son Ahaziah king as his successor; for the troops who came with the Arabs to the camp had killed all the older sons. So Ahaziah son of Jehoram reigned as king of Judah. ²Ahaziah was forty-two years old when he began to reign; he reigned one year in Jerusalem. His mother's name was Athaliah, a granddaughter of Omri. ³He also walked in the ways of the house of Ahab, for his mother was his counselor in doing wickedly. ⁴He did what was evil in the sight of the LORD, as the house of Ahab had done; for after the death of his father they were his counselors, to his ruin. ⁵He even followed their advice, and went with Jehoram son of King Ahab of Israel to make war against King Hazael of Aram at Ramoth-gilead. The Arameans wounded Joram, ⁶and he returned to be healed in Jezreel of the wounds that he had received at Ramah, when he fought King Hazael of Aram. And Ahaziah son of King Jehoram of Judah went down to see Joram son of Ahab in Jezreel, because he was sick.

7 But it was ordained by God that the downfall of Ahaziah should come about through his going to visit Joram. For when he came there he went out with Jehoram to meet Jehu son of Nimshi, whom the LORD had anointed to destroy the house of Ahab. ⁸When Jehu was executing judgment on the house of Ahab, he met the officials of Judah and the sons of Ahaziah's brothers, who attended Ahaziah, and he killed them. ⁹He searched for Ahaziah, who was captured while hiding in Samaria and was brought to Jehu, and put to death. They buried him, for they said, "He is the grandson of Jehoshaphat, who sought the LORD with all his heart." And the house of Ahaziah had no one able to rule the kingdom.

Athaliah Seizes the Throne

10 Now when Athaliah, Ahaziah's mother, saw that her son was dead, she set about to destroy all the royal family of the house of Judah. ¹¹But Jehoshabeath, the king's daughter, took

Joash son of Ahaziah, and stole him away from among the king's children who were about to be killed; she put him and his nurse in a bedroom. Thus Jehoshabeath, daughter of King Jehoram and wife of the priest Jehoiada—because she was a sister of Ahaziah—hid him from Athaliah, so that she did not kill him; ¹²he remained with them six years, hidden in the house of God, while Athaliah reigned over the land.

23 But in the seventh year Jehoiada took courage, and entered into a compact with the commanders of the hundreds, Azariah son of Jeroham, Ishmael son of Jehohanan, Azariah son of Obed, Maaseiah son of Adaiah, and Elishaphat son of Zichri. ²They went around through Judah and gathered the Levites from all the towns of Judah, and the heads of families of Israel, and they came to Jerusalem. ³Then the whole assembly made a covenant with the king in the house of God. Jehoiadaᵘsaid to them, "Here is the king's son! Let him reign, as the LORD promised concerning the sons of David. ⁴This is what you are to do: one-third of you, priests and Levites, who come on duty on the sabbath, shall be gatekeepers, ⁵one-third shall be at the king's house, and one-third at the Gate of the Foundation; and all the people shall be in the courts of the house of the LORD. ⁶Do not let anyone enter the house of the LORD except the priests and ministering Levites; they may enter, for they are holy, but all the otherᵛ people shall observe the instructions of the LORD. ⁷The Levites shall surround the king, each with his weapons in his hand; and whoever enters the house shall be killed. Stay with the king in his comings and goings."

Joash Crowned King

8 The Levites and all Judah did according to all that the priest Jehoiada commanded; each brought his men, who were to come on duty on the sabbath, with those who were to go off duty on the sabbath; for the priest Jehoiada did not dismiss the divisions. ⁹The priest Jehoiada delivered to the captains the spears and the large and small shields

that had been King David's, which were in the house of God; 10and he set all the people as a guard for the king, everyone with weapon in hand, from the south side of the house to the north side of the house, around the altar and the house. 11Then he brought out the king's son, put the crown on him, and gave him the covenant;w they proclaimed him king, and Jehoiada and his sons anointed him; and they shouted, "Long live the king!"

Athaliah Murdered

12 When Athaliah heard the noise of the people running and praising the king, she went into the house of the LORD to the people; 13and when she looked, there was the king standing by his pillar at the entrance, and the captains and the trumpeters beside the king, and all the people of the land rejoicing and blowing trumpets, and the singers with their musical instruments leading in the celebration. Athaliah tore her clothes, and cried, "Treason! Treason!" 14Then the priest Jehoiada brought out the captains who were set over the army, saying to them, "Bring her out between the ranks; anyone who follows her is to be put to the sword." For the priest said, "Do not put her to death in the house of the LORD." 15So they laid hands on her; she went into the entrance of the Horse Gate of the king's house, and there they put her to death.

16 Jehoiada made a covenant between himself and all the people and the king that they should be the LORD's people. 17Then all the people went to the house of Baal, and tore it down; his altars and his images they broke in pieces, and they killed Mattan, the priest of Baal, in front of the altars. 18Jehoiada assigned the care of the house of the LORD to the levitical priests whom David had organized to be in charge of the house of the LORD, to offer burnt offerings to the LORD, as it is written in the law of Moses, with rejoicing and with singing, according to the order of David. 19He stationed the gatekeepers at the gates of the house of the LORD so that no one should enter who was in any way unclean. 20And he took the captains, the nobles, the governors of the people, and all the people of the land,

and they brought the king down from the house of the LORD, marching through the upper gate to the king's house. They set the king on the royal throne. 21So all the people of the land rejoiced, and the city was quiet after Athaliah had been killed with the sword.

Joash Repairs the Temple

24 Joash was seven years old when he began to reign; he reigned forty years in Jerusalem; his mother's name was Zibiah of Beersheba. 2Joash did what was right in the sight of the LORD all the days of the priest Jehoiada. 3Jehoiada got two wives for him, and he became the father of sons and daughters.

4 Some time afterward Joash decided to restore the house of the LORD. 5He assembled the priests and the Levites and said to them, "Go out to the cities of Judah and gather money from all Israel to repair the house of your God, year by year; and see that you act quickly." But the Levites did not act quickly. 6So the king summoned Jehoiada the chief, and said to him, "Why have you not required the Levites to bring in from Judah and Jerusalem the tax levied by Moses, the servant of the LORD, onx the congregation of Israel for the tent of the covenant?"w 7For the children of Athaliah, that wicked woman, had broken into the house of God, and had even used all the dedicated things of the house of the LORD for the Baals.

8 So the king gave command, and they made a chest, and set it outside the gate of the house of the LORD. 9A proclamation was made throughout Judah and Jerusalem to bring in for the LORD the tax that Moses the servant of God laid on Israel in the wilderness. 10All the leaders and all the people rejoiced and brought their tax and dropped it into the chest until it was full. 11Whenever the chest was brought to the king's officers by the Levites, when they saw that there was a large amount of money in it, the king's secretary and the officer of the chief priest would come and empty the chest and take it and return it to its place. So they did day after day, and collected money in abundance. 12The king

---

w Or treaty, or testimony; Heb eduth   x Compare Vg: Heb and

and Jehoiada gave it to those who had charge of the work of the house of the LORD, and they hired masons and carpenters to restore the house of the LORD, and also workers in iron and bronze to repair the house of the LORD. 13So those who were engaged in the work labored, and the repairing went forward at their hands, and they restored the house of God to its proper condition and strengthened it. 14When they had finished, they brought the rest of the money to the king and Jehoiada, and with it were made utensils for the house of the LORD, utensils for the service and for the burnt offerings, and ladles, and vessels of gold and silver. They offered burnt offerings in the house of the LORD regularly all the days of Jehoiada.

Apostasy of Joash

15 But Jehoiada grew old and full of days, and died; he was one hundred thirty years old at his death. 16And they buried him in the city of David among the kings, because he had done good in Israel, and for God and his house.

17 Now after the death of Jehoiada the officials of Judah came and did obeisance to the king; then the king listened to them. 18They abandoned the house of the LORD, the God of their ancestors, and served the sacred polesʸ and the idols. And wrath came upon Judah and Jerusalem for this guilt of theirs. 19Yet he sent prophets among them to bring them back to the LORD; they testified against them, but they would not listen.

20 Then the spirit of God took possession ofᶻ Zechariah son of the priest Jehoiada; he stood above the people and said to them, "Thus says God: Why do you transgress the commandments of the LORD, so that you cannot prosper? Because you have forsaken the LORD, he has also forsaken you." 21But they conspired against him, and by command of the king they stoned him to death in the court of the house of the LORD. 22King Joash did not remember the kindness that Jehoiada, Zechariah's father, had shown him; but killed his son. As he was dying, he said, "May the LORD see and avenge!"

Death of Joash

23 At the end of the year the army of Aram came up against Joash. They came to Judah and Jerusalem, and destroyed all the officials of the people from among them, and sent all the booty they took to the king of Damascus. 24Although the army of Aram had come with few men, the LORD delivered into their hand a very great army, because they had abandoned the LORD, the God of their ancestors. Thus they executed judgment on Joash.

25 When they had withdrawn, leaving him severely wounded, his servants conspired against him because of the blood of the sonᵃ of the priest Jehoiada, and they killed him on his bed. So he died; and they buried him in the city of David, but they did not bury him in the tombs of the kings. 26Those who conspired against him were Zabad son of Shimeath the Ammonite, and Jehozabad son of Shimrith the Moabite. 27Accounts of his sons, and of the many oracles against him, and of the rebuildingᵇ of the house of God are written in the Commentary on the Book of the Kings. And his son Amaziah succeeded him.

Reign of Amaziah

25 Amaziah was twenty-five years old when he began to reign, and he reigned twenty-nine years in Jerusalem. His mother's name was Jehoaddan of Jerusalem. 2He did what was right in the sight of the LORD, yet not with a true heart. 3As soon as the royal power was firmly in his hand he killed his servants who had murdered his father the king. 4But he did not put their children to death, according to what is written in the law, in the book of Moses, where the LORD commanded, "The parents shall not be put to death for the children, or the children be put to death for the parents; but all shall be put to death for their own sins."

Slaughter of the Edomites

5 Amaziah assembled the people of Judah, and set them by ancestral houses under commanders of the thousands and of the hundreds for all Judah and Benjamin. He mustered those twenty

y Heb Asherim   z Heb clothed itself with   a Gk Vg: Heb sons   b Heb founding

THE MARTYRDOM OF JOHN HUSS

John Foxe

VERSE: 2 Chronicles 24.21   **PASSAGE:** 2 Chronicles 24.17–22

 ohn Huss was summoned . . . arrested, and committed prisoner . . . While Huss was in confinement, the Council acted the part of inquisitors . . .

John Huss's answer was this: "I did appeal unto the pope; who being dead, and the cause of my matter remaining undetermined, I appealed likewise unto his successor John XXIII: before whom when, by the space of two years, I could not be admitted by my advocates to defend my cause, I appealed unto the high judge Christ."

When John Huss had spoken these words, it was demanded of him whether he had received absolution of the pope or no? He answered, "No." Then again, whether it were lawful for him to appeal unto Christ or no? Whereunto John Huss answered: "Verily I do affirm here before you all, that there is no more just or effectual appeal, than that appeal which is made unto Christ, forasmuch as the law doth determine, that to appeal is no other thing than in a cause of grief or wrong done by an inferior judge, to implore and require aid at a higher Judge's hand. Who is then a higher Judge than Christ? Who, I say, can know or judge the matter more justly, or with more equity? when in him there is found no deceit, neither can he be deceived; or, who can better help the miserable and oppressed than he?" While John Huss, with a devout and sober countenance, was speaking and pronouncing those words, he was derided and mocked by all the whole council.

These excellent sentences were esteemed as so many expressions of treason, and tended to inflame his adversaries. Accordingly, the bishops appointed by the council stripped him of his priestly garments, degraded him, put a paper miter on his head, on which was painted devils, with this inscription, "A ringleader of heretics." Which when he saw, he said: "My Lord Jesus Christ, for my sake, did wear a crown of thorns; why should not I then, for his sake, again wear this light crown, be it ever so ignominious? Truly I will do it, and that willingly."

ADDITIONAL SCRIPTURE READING:
Jeremiah 38.3–6; Acts 5.34–40

Go to page 500 for your next devotional reading.

1500   1700

years old and upward, and found that they were three hundred thousand picked troops fit for war, able to handle spear and shield. ⁶He also hired one hundred thousand mighty warriors from Israel for one hundred talents of silver. ⁷But a man of God came to him and said, "O king, do not let the army of Israel go with you, for the LORD is not with Israel—all these Ephraimites. ⁸Rather, go by yourself and act; be strong in battle, or God will fling you down before the enemy; for God has power to help or to overthrow." ⁹Amaziah said to the man of God, "But what shall we do about the hundred talents that I have given to the army of Israel?" The man of God answered, "The LORD is able to give you much more than this." ¹⁰Then Amaziah discharged the army that had come to him from Ephraim, letting them go home again. But they became very angry with Judah, and returned home in fierce anger.

11 Amaziah took courage, and led out his people; he went to the Valley of Salt, and struck down ten thousand men of Seir. ¹²The people of Judah captured another ten thousand alive, took them to the top of Sela, and threw them down from the top of Sela, so that all of them were dashed to pieces. ¹³But the men of the army whom Amaziah sent back, not letting them go with him to battle, fell on the cities of Judah from Samaria to Beth-horon; they killed three thousand people in them, and took much booty.

14 Now after Amaziah came from the slaughter of the Edomites, he brought the gods of the people of Seir, set them up as his gods, and worshiped them, making offerings to them. ¹⁵The LORD was angry with Amaziah and sent to him a prophet, who said to him, "Why have you resorted to a people's gods who could not deliver their own people from your hand?" ¹⁶But as he was speaking the king*c* said to him, "Have we made you a royal counselor? Stop! Why should you be put to death?" So the prophet stopped, but said, "I know that God has determined to destroy you, because you have done this and have not listened to my advice."

Israel Defeats Judah

17 Then King Amaziah of Judah took counsel and sent to King Joash son of Jehoahaz son of Jehu of Israel, saying, "Come, let us look one another in the face." ¹⁸King Joash of Israel sent word to King Amaziah of Judah, "A thornbush on Lebanon sent to a cedar on Lebanon, saying, 'Give your daughter to my son for a wife'; but a wild animal of Lebanon passed by and trampled down the thornbush. ¹⁹You say, 'See, I have defeated Edom,' and your heart has lifted you up in boastfulness. Now stay at home; why should you provoke trouble so that you fall, you and Judah with you?"

20 But Amaziah would not listen—it was God's doing, in order to hand them over, because they had sought the gods of Edom. ²¹So King Joash of Israel went up; he and King Amaziah of Judah faced one another in battle at Beth-shemesh, which belongs to Judah. ²²Judah was defeated by Israel; everyone fled home. ²³King Joash of Israel captured King Amaziah of Judah, son of Joash, son of Ahaziah, at Beth-shemesh; he brought him to Jerusalem, and broke down the wall of Jerusalem from the Ephraim Gate to the Corner Gate, a distance of four hundred cubits. ²⁴He seized all the gold and silver, and all the vessels that were found in the house of God, and Obed-edom with them; he seized also the treasuries of the king's house, also hostages; then he returned to Samaria.

Death of Amaziah

25 King Amaziah son of Joash of Judah, lived fifteen years after the death of King Joash son of Jehoahaz of Israel. ²⁶Now the rest of the deeds of Amaziah, from first to last, are they not written in the Book of the Kings of Judah and Israel? ²⁷From the time that Amaziah turned away from the LORD they made a conspiracy against him in Jerusalem, and he fled to Lachish. But they sent after him to Lachish, and killed him there. ²⁸They brought him back on horses; he was buried with his ancestors in the city of David.

c Heb he

Reign of Uzziah

26 Then all the people of Judah took Uzziah, who was sixteen years old, and made him king to succeed his father Amaziah. ²He rebuilt Eloth and restored it to Judah, after the king slept with his ancestors. ³Uzziah was sixteen years old when he began to reign, and he reigned fifty-two years in Jerusalem. His mother's name was Jecoliah of Jerusalem. ⁴He did what was right in the sight of the LORD, just as his father Amaziah had done. ⁵He set himself to seek God in the days of Zechariah, who instructed him in the fear of God; and as long as he sought the LORD, God made him prosper.

6 He went out and made war against the Philistines, and broke down the wall of Gath and the wall of Jabneh and the wall of Ashdod; he built cities in the territory of Ashdod and elsewhere among the Philistines. ⁷God helped him against the Philistines, against the Arabs who lived in Gur-baal, and against the Meunites. ⁸The Ammonites paid tribute to Uzziah, and his fame spread even to the border of Egypt, for he became very strong. ⁹Moreover Uzziah built towers in Jerusalem at the Corner Gate, at the Valley Gate, and at the Angle, and fortified them. ¹⁰He built towers in the wilderness and hewed out many cisterns, for he had large herds, both in the Shephelah and in the plain, and he had farmers and vinedressers in the hills and in the fertile lands, for he loved the soil. ¹¹Moreover Uzziah had an army of soldiers, fit for war, in divisions according to the numbers in the muster made by the secretary Jeiel and the officer Maaseiah, under the direction of Hananiah, one of the king's commanders. ¹²The whole number of the heads of ancestral houses of mighty warriors was two thousand six hundred. ¹³Under their command was an army of three hundred seven thousand five hundred, who could make war with mighty power, to help the king against the enemy. ¹⁴Uzziah provided for all the army the shields, spears, helmets, coats of mail, bows, and stones for slinging. ¹⁵In Jerusalem he set up machines, invented by skilled workers, on the towers and the corners for shooting arrows and large stones. And his fame spread far, for he was marvelously helped until he became strong.

Pride and Apostasy

16 But when he had become strong he grew proud, to his destruction. For he was false to the LORD his God, and entered the temple of the LORD to make offering on the altar of incense. ¹⁷But the priest Azariah went in after him, with eighty priests of the LORD who were men of valor; ¹⁸they withstood King Uzziah, and said to him, "It is not for you, Uzziah, to make offering to the LORD, but for the priests the descendants of Aaron, who are consecrated to make offering. Go out of the sanctuary; for you have done wrong, and it will bring you no honor from the LORD God." ¹⁹Then Uzziah was angry. Now he had a censer in his hand to make offering, and when he became angry with the priests a leprous^d disease broke out on his forehead, in the presence of the priests in the house of the LORD, by the altar of incense. ²⁰When the chief priest Azariah, and all the priests, looked at him, he was leprous^d in his forehead. They hurried him out, and he himself hurried to get out, because the LORD had struck him. ²¹King Uzziah was leprous^d to the day of his death, and being leprous^d lived in a separate house, for he was excluded from the house of the LORD. His son Jotham was in charge of the palace of the king, governing the people of the land.

22 Now the rest of the acts of Uzziah, from first to last, the prophet Isaiah son of Amoz wrote. ²³Uzziah slept with his ancestors; they buried him near his ancestors in the burial field that belonged to the kings, for they said, "He is leprous."^d His son Jotham succeeded him.

Reign of Jotham

27 Jotham was twenty-five years old when he began to reign; he reigned sixteen years in Jerusalem. His mother's name was Jerushah daughter of Zadok. ²He did what was right in the sight of the LORD just as his father Uzziah had done—only he did not

d A term for several skin diseases; precise meaning uncertain invade the temple of the LORD. But the people still followed corrupt practices. [3]He built the upper gate of the house of the LORD, and did extensive building on the wall of Ophel. [4]Moreover he built cities in the hill country of Judah, and forts and towers on the wooded hills. [5]He fought with the king of the Ammonites and prevailed against them. The Ammonites gave him that year one hundred talents of silver, ten thousand cors of wheat and ten thousand of barley. The Ammonites paid him the same amount in the second and the third years. [6]So Jotham became strong because he ordered his ways before the LORD his God. [7]Now the rest of the acts of Jotham, and all his wars and his ways, are written in the Book of the Kings of Israel and Judah. [8]He was twenty-five years old when he began to reign; he reigned sixteen years in Jerusalem. [9]Jotham slept with his ancestors, and they buried him in the city of David; and his son Ahaz succeeded him.

Reign of Ahaz

28 Ahaz was twenty years old when he began to reign; he reigned sixteen years in Jerusalem. He did not do what was right in the sight of the LORD, as his ancestor David had done, [2]but he walked in the ways of the kings of Israel. He even made cast images for the Baals; [3]and he made offerings in the valley of the son of Hinnom, and made his sons pass through fire, according to the abominable practices of the nations whom the LORD drove out before the people of Israel. [4]He sacrificed and made offerings on the high places, on the hills, and under every green tree.

Aram and Israel Defeat Judah

5 Therefore the LORD his God gave him into the hand of the king of Aram, who defeated him and took captive a great number of his people and brought them to Damascus. He was also given into the hand of the king of Israel, who defeated him with great slaughter. [6]Pekah son of Remaliah killed one hundred twenty thousand in Judah in one day, all of them valiant warriors, because they had abandoned the LORD,

the God of their ancestors. [7]And Zichri, a mighty warrior of Ephraim, killed the king's son Maaseiah, Azrikam the commander of the palace, and Elkanah the next in authority to the king.

Intervention of Oded

8 The people of Israel took captive two hundred thousand of their kin, women, sons, and daughters; they also took much booty from them and brought the booty to Samaria. [9]But a prophet of the LORD was there, whose name was Oded; he went out to meet the army that came to Samaria, and said to them, "Because the LORD, the God of your ancestors, was angry with Judah, he gave them into your hand, but you have killed them in a rage that has reached up to heaven. [10]Now you intend to subjugate the people of Judah and Jerusalem, male and female, as your slaves. But what have you except sins against the LORD your God? [11]Now hear me, and send back the captives whom you have taken from your kindred, for the fierce wrath of the LORD is upon you." [12]Moreover, certain chiefs of the Ephraimites, Azariah son of Johanan, Berechiah son of Meshillemoth, Jehizkiah son of Shallum, and Amasa son of Hadlai, stood up against those who were coming from the war, [13]and said to them, "You shall not bring the captives in here, for you propose to bring on us guilt against the LORD in addition to our present sins and guilt. For our guilt is already great, and there is fierce wrath against Israel." [14]So the warriors left the captives and the booty before the officials and all the assembly. [15]Then those who were mentioned by name got up and took the captives, and with the booty they clothed all that were naked among them; they clothed them, gave them sandals, provided them with food and drink, and anointed them; and carrying all the feeble among them on donkeys, they brought them to their kindred at Jericho, the city of palm trees. Then they returned to Samaria.

Assyria Refuses to Help Judah

16 At that time King Ahaz sent to the king[e] of Assyria for help. [17]For the

---

e Gk Syr Vg Compare 2 Kings 16.7: Heb *kings*

Edomites had again invaded and defeated Judah, and carried away captives. 18And the Philistines had made raids on the cities in the Shephelah and the Negeb of Judah, and had taken Beth-shemesh, Aijalon, Gederoth, Soco with its villages, Timnah with its villages, and Gimzo with its villages; and they settled there. 19For the LORD brought Judah low because of King Ahaz of Israel, for he had behaved without restraint in Judah and had been faithless to the LORD. 20So King Tilgath-pilneser of Assyria came against him, and oppressed him instead of strengthening him. 21For Ahaz plundered the house of the LORD and the houses of the king and of the officials, and gave tribute to the king of Assyria; but it did not help him.

Apostasy and Death of Ahaz

22 In the time of his distress he became yet more faithless to the LORD—this same King Ahaz. 23For he sacrificed to the gods of Damascus, which had defeated him, and said, "Because the gods of the kings of Aram helped them, I will sacrifice to them so that they may help me." But they were the ruin of him, and of all Israel. 24Ahaz gathered together the utensils of the house of God, and cut in pieces the utensils of the house of God. He shut up the doors of the house of the LORD and made himself altars in every corner of Jerusalem. 25In every city of Judah he made high places to make offerings to other gods, provoking to anger the LORD, the God of his ancestors. 26Now the rest of his acts and all his ways, from first to last, are written in the Book of the Kings of Judah and Israel. 27Ahaz slept with his ancestors, and they buried him in the city, in Jerusalem; but they did not bring him into the tombs of the kings of Israel. His son Hezekiah succeeded him.

Reign of Hezekiah

29 Hezekiah began to reign when he was twenty-five years old; he reigned twenty-nine years in Jerusalem. His mother's name was Abijah daughter of Zechariah. 2He did what was right in the sight of the LORD, just as his ancestor David had done.

The Temple Cleansed

3 In the first year of his reign, in the first month, he opened the doors of the house of the LORD and repaired them. 4He brought in the priests and the Levites and assembled them in the square on the east. 5He said to them, "Listen to me, Levites! Sanctify yourselves, and sanctify the house of the LORD, the God of your ancestors, and carry out the filth from the holy place. 6For our ancestors have been unfaithful and have done what was evil in the sight of the LORD our God; they have forsaken him, and have turned away their faces from the dwelling of the LORD, and turned their backs. 7They also shut the doors of the vestibule and put out the lamps, and have not offered incense or made burnt offerings in the holy place to the God of Israel. 8Therefore the wrath of the LORD came upon Judah and Jerusalem, and he has made them an object of horror, of astonishment, and of hissing, as you see with your own eyes. 9Our fathers have fallen by the sword and our sons and our daughters and our wives are in captivity for this. 10Now it is in my heart to make a covenant with the LORD, the God of Israel, so that his fierce anger may turn away from us. 11My sons, do not now be negligent, for the LORD has chosen you to stand in his presence to minister to him, and to be his ministers and make offerings to him."

12 Then the Levites arose, Mahath son of Amasai, and Joel son of Azariah, of the sons of the Kohathites; and of the sons of Merari, Kish son of Abdi, and Azariah son of Jehallelel; and of the Gershonites, Joah son of Zimmah, and Eden son of Joah; 13and of the sons of Elizaphan, Shimri and Jeuel; and of the sons of Asaph, Zechariah and Mattaniah; 14and of the sons of Heman, Jehuel and Shimei; and of the sons of Jeduthun, Shemaiah and Uzziel. 15They gathered their brothers, sanctified themselves, and went in as the king had commanded, by the words of the LORD, to cleanse the house of the LORD. 16The priests went into the inner part of the house of the LORD to cleanse it, and they brought out all the unclean things that they found in the temple of the LORD into the court of the house of the LORD; and the Levites took them and carried them out

to the Wadi Kidron. 17They began to sanctify on the first day of the first month, and on the eighth day of the month they came to the vestibule of the LORD; then for eight days they sanctified the house of the LORD, and on the sixteenth day of the first month they finished. 18Then they went inside to King Hezekiah and said, "We have cleansed all the house of the LORD, the altar of burnt offering and all its utensils, and the table for the rows of bread and all its utensils. 19All the utensils that King Ahaz repudiated during his reign when he was faithless, we have made ready and sanctified; see, they are in front of the altar of the LORD."

Temple Worship Restored

20 Then King Hezekiah rose early, assembled the officials of the city, and went up to the house of the LORD. 21They brought seven bulls, seven rams, seven lambs, and seven male goats for a sin offering for the kingdom and for the sanctuary and for Judah. He commanded the priests the descendants of Aaron to offer them on the altar of the LORD. 22So they slaughtered the bulls, and the priests received the blood and dashed it against the altar; they slaughtered the rams and their blood was dashed against the altar; they also slaughtered the lambs and their blood was dashed against the altar. 23Then the male goats for the sin offering were brought to the king and the assembly; they laid their hands on them, 24and the priests slaughtered them and made a sin offering with their blood at the altar, to make atonement for all Israel. For the king commanded that the burnt offering and the sin offering should be made for all Israel.

25 He stationed the Levites in the house of the LORD with cymbals, harps, and lyres, according to the commandment of David and of Gad the king's seer and of the prophet Nathan, for the commandment was from the LORD through his prophets. 26The Levites stood with the instruments of David, and the priests with the trumpets. 27Then Hezekiah commanded that the burnt offering be offered on the altar. When the burnt offering began, the song to the LORD began also, and the trumpets, accompanied by the instruments of King David of Israel. 28The whole assembly worshiped, the singers sang, and the trumpeters sounded; all this continued until the burnt offering was finished. 29When the offering was finished, the king and all who were present with him bowed down and worshiped. 30King Hezekiah and the officials commanded the Levites to sing praises to the LORD with the words of David and of the seer Asaph. They sang praises with gladness, and they bowed down and worshiped.

31 Then Hezekiah said, "You have now consecrated yourselves to the LORD; come near, bring sacrifices and thank offerings to the house of the LORD." The assembly brought sacrifices and thank offerings; and all who were of a willing heart brought burnt offerings. 32The number of the burnt offerings that the assembly brought was seventy bulls, one hundred rams, and two hundred lambs; all these were for a burnt offering to the LORD. 33The consecrated offerings were six hundred bulls and three thousand sheep. 34But the priests were too few and could not skin all the burnt offerings, so, until other priests had sanctified themselves, their kindred, the Levites, helped them until the work was finished—for the Levites were more conscientious*f* than the priests in sanctifying themselves. 35Besides the great number of burnt offerings there was the fat of the offerings of well-being, and there were the drink offerings for the burnt offerings. Thus the service of the house of the LORD was restored. 36And Hezekiah and all the people rejoiced because of what God had done for the people; for the thing had come about suddenly.

The Great Passover

30 Hezekiah sent word to all Israel and Judah, and wrote letters also to Ephraim and Manasseh, that they should come to the house of the LORD at Jerusalem, to keep the passover to the LORD the God of Israel. 2For the king and his officials and all the assembly in Jerusalem had taken counsel to keep the passover in the second month 3(for they

f Heb *upright in heart*

could not keep it at its proper time because the priests had not sanctified themselves in sufficient number, nor had the people assembled in Jerusalem). **4**The plan seemed right to the king and all the assembly. **5**So they decreed to make a proclamation throughout all Israel, from Beer-sheba to Dan, that the people should come and keep the passover to the LORD the God of Israel, at Jerusalem; for they had not kept it in great numbers as prescribed. **6**So couriers went throughout all Israel and Judah with letters from the king and his officials, as the king had commanded, saying, "O people of Israel, return to the LORD, the God of Abraham, Isaac, and Israel, so that he may turn again to the remnant of you who have escaped from the hand of the kings of Assyria. **7**Do not be like your ancestors and your kindred, who were faithless to the LORD God of their ancestors, so that he made them a desolation, as you see. **8**Do not now be stiff-necked as your ancestors were, but yield yourselves to the LORD and come to his sanctuary, which he has sanctified forever, and serve the LORD your God, so that his fierce anger may turn away from you. **9**For as you return to the LORD, your kindred and your children will find compassion with their captors, and return to this land. For the LORD your God is gracious and merciful, and will not turn away his face from you, if you return to him."

10 So the couriers went from city to city through the country of Ephraim and Manasseh, and as far as Zebulun; but they laughed them to scorn, and mocked them. **11**Only a few from Asher, Manasseh, and Zebulun humbled themselves and came to Jerusalem. **12**The hand of God was also on Judah to give them one heart to do what the king and the officials commanded by the word of the LORD.

13 Many people came together in Jerusalem to keep the festival of unleavened bread in the second month, a very large assembly. **14**They set to work and removed the altars that were in Jerusalem, and all the altars for offering incense they took away and threw into the Wadi Kidron. **15**They slaughtered the passover lamb on the fourteenth day of

the second month. The p[riests and the] Levites were ashamed, an[d sancti-] fied themselves and broug[ht offer-] ings into the house of the [LORD. They] took their accustomed po[sts, according] to the law of Moses the ma[n of God; the] priests dashed the bloo[d that they] received[g] from the hands o[f the Levites.] **17**For there were many in t[he assembly] who had not sanctified [themselves;] therefore the Levites had t[o slaughter] the passover lamb for every[one who was] not clean, to make it holy t[o the LORD.] **18**For a multitude of the peop[le, many of] them from Ephraim, Manass[eh, Issa-] char, and Zebulun, had not c[leansed] themselves, yet they ate the pa[ssover] otherwise than as prescribed. But H[eze-] kiah prayed for them, saying, "The go[od] LORD pardon all **19**who set their hearts [to] seek God, the LORD the God of their ancestors, even though not in accordance with the sanctuary's rules of cleanness." **20**The LORD heard Hezekiah, and healed the people. **21**The people of Israel who were present at Jerusalem kept the festival of unleavened bread seven days with great gladness; and the Levites and the priests praised the LORD day by day, accompanied by loud instruments for the LORD. **22**Hezekiah spoke encouragingly to all the Levites who showed good skill in the service of the LORD. So the people ate the food of the festival for seven days, sacrificing offerings of well-being and giving thanks to the LORD the God of their ancestors.

23 Then the whole assembly agreed together to keep the festival for another seven days; so they kept it for another seven days with gladness. **24**For King Hezekiah of Judah gave the assembly a thousand bulls and seven thousand sheep for offerings, and the officials gave the assembly a thousand bulls and ten thousand sheep. The priests sanctified themselves in great numbers. **25**The whole assembly of Judah, the priests and the Levites, and the whole assembly that came out of Israel, and the resident aliens who came out of the land of Israel, and the resident aliens who lived in Judah, rejoiced. **26**There was great joy in Jerusalem, for since the time of Solomon son of King David of Israel there had

g Heb lacks *that they received*

500

ng like this in Jerusalem.
priests and the Levites stood
been essed the people, and their
27 T heard; their prayer came to his
velling in heaven.

Shrines Destroyed

Now when all this was finished, all Israel who were
nt went out to the cities of Judah

b Asherim

and broke down the pillars, hewed down
the sacred poles,[h] and pulled down the
high places and the altars throughout all
Judah and Benjamin, and in Ephraim
and Manasseh, until they had destroyed
them all. Then all the people of Israel
returned to their cities, all to their individual properties.

2 Hezekiah appointed the divisions of
the priests and of the Levites, division

TUESDAY

THE SEEKER'S COVENANT
Matthew Henry

VERSE: 2 Chronicles 30.6   **PASSAGE:** 2 Chronicles 30.1–20

ield yourselves unto the Lord" (2 Chronicles 30.8, KJV).
Before you can come into communion with him you
must come into covenant with him. *Give the hand to
the Lord* (so the word is), that is, "Consent to take him
for your God." "The doors of the sanctuary are now opened, and
you have liberty to enter; the temple service is now revived, and
you are welcome to join in it. You are children of Israel. The God
you are called to return to is the God of Abraham, Isaac, and
Jacob, a God in covenant with your first fathers. Your late fathers
that forsook him and trespassed against him have been given up
to desolation; their apostasy and idolatry have been their ruin, as
you see (v. 7). You yourselves are but a *remnant* narrowly *escaped
out of the hands of the kings of Assyria*. If you return to God in a
way of duty, he will return to you in a way of mercy."
. . . Could anything be expressed more pathetically, more mov-
ingly? Could there be a better cause, or could it be better pleaded?
. . . In the worst of times God has had a remnant; so he had here
. . . A command was given to the men of Judah to attend this
solemnity; and they universally obeyed it. They did it with one
heart, were all of a mind in it, and *the hand of God gave* them that
one heart (v. 12, KJV) . . . For this is the one thing needful, that we
seek God, his favor, his honor, and that we set our hearts to do it.

ADDITIONAL SCRIPTURE READING:
Isaiah 55.6–7; Joel 2.12–14; James 4.8

Go to page 506 for your next devotional reading.

1700   1900

by division, everyone according to his service, the priests and the Levites, for burnt offerings and offerings of well-being, to minister in the gates of the camp of the LORD and to give thanks and praise. 3The contribution of the king from his own possessions was for the burnt offerings: the burnt offerings of morning and evening, and the burnt offerings for the sabbaths, the new moons, and the appointed festivals, as it is written in the law of the LORD. 4He commanded the people who lived in Jerusalem to give the portion due to the priests and the Levites, so that they might devote themselves to the law of the LORD. 5As soon as the word spread, the people of Israel gave in abundance the first fruits of grain, wine, oil, honey, and of all the produce of the field; and they brought in abundantly the tithe of everything. 6The people of Israel and Judah who lived in the cities of Judah also brought in the tithe of cattle and sheep, and the tithe of the dedicated things that had been consecrated to the LORD their God, and laid them in heaps. 7In the third month they began to pile up the heaps, and finished them in the seventh month. 8When Hezekiah and the officials came and saw the heaps, they blessed the LORD and his people Israel. 9Hezekiah questioned the priests and the Levites about the heaps. 10The chief priest Azariah, who was of the house of Zadok, answered him, "Since they began to bring the contributions into the house of the LORD, we have had enough to eat and have plenty to spare; for the LORD has blessed his people, so that we have this great supply left over."

Reorganization of Priests and Levites

11 Then Hezekiah commanded them to prepare store-chambers in the house of the LORD; and they prepared them. 12Faithfully they brought in the contributions, the tithes and the dedicated things. The chief officer in charge of them was Conaniah the Levite, with his brother Shimei as second; 13while Jehiel, Azaziah, Nahath, Asahel, Jerimoth, Jozabad, Eliel, Ismachiah, Mahath, and Benaiah were overseers assisting Conaniah and his brother Shimei, by the appointment of King Hezekiah and the chief officer of the ho 14Kore son of Imnah the Lev the east gate, was in charg freewill offerings to God, the contribution reserved and the most holy offeri Miniamin, Jeshua, Shemaia and Shecaniah were faithful him in the cities of the priest ute the portions to their kind young alike, by divisions, 16e enrolled by genealogy, males years old and upwards, all who the house of the LORD as the duty day required, for their service acco to their offices, by their divisions. 17 enrollment of the priests was according to their ancestral houses; that of the Levites from twenty years old and upwards was according to their offices, by their divisions. 18The priests were enrolled with all their little children, their wives, their sons, and their daughters, the whole multitude; for they were faithful in keeping themselves holy. 19And for the descendants of Aaron, the priests, who were in the fields of common land belonging to their towns, town by town, the people designated by name were to distribute portions to every male among the priests and to everyone among the Levites who was enrolled.

20 Hezekiah did this throughout all Judah; he did what was good and right and faithful before the LORD his God. 21And every work that he undertook in the service of the house of God, and in accordance with the law and the commandments, to seek his God, he did with all his heart; and he prospered.

Sennacherib's Invasion

32 After these things and these acts of faithfulness, King Sennacherib of Assyria came and invaded Judah and encamped against the fortified cities, thinking to win them for himself. 2When Hezekiah saw that Sennacherib had come and intended to fight against Jerusalem, 3he planned with his officers and his warriors to stop the flow of the springs that were outside the city; and they helped him. 4A great many people were gathered, and they stopped all the springs and the wadi that flowed

e land, saying, "Why should
an kings come and find water
thì nce?" 5Hezekiah[i] set to work
...ly and built up the entire wall
s broken down, and raised tow-
t,[j] and outside it he built another
...e also strengthened the Millo in
...ty of David, and made weapons
...hields in abundance. 6He appointed
...bat commanders over the people,
... gathered them together to him in
... square at the gate of the city and
...oke encouragingly to them, saying,
"Be strong and of good courage. Do not
be afraid or dismayed before the king of
Assyria and all the horde that is with
him; for there is one greater with us
than with him. 8With him is an arm of
flesh; but with us is the LORD our God,
to help us and to fight our battles." The
people were encouraged by the words of
King Hezekiah of Judah.

9 After this, while King Sennacherib
of Assyria was at Lachish with all his
forces, he sent his servants to Jerusalem
to King Hezekiah of Judah and to all the
people of Judah that were in Jerusalem,
saying, 10"Thus says King Sennacherib
of Assyria: On what are you relying, that
you undergo the siege of Jerusalem? 11Is
not Hezekiah misleading you, handing
you over to die by famine and by thirst,
when he tells you, 'The LORD our God
will save us from the hand of the king of
Assyria'? 12Was it not this same Hezekiah who took away his high places and
his altars and commanded Judah and
Jerusalem, saying, 'Before one altar you
shall worship, and upon it you shall
make your offerings'? 13Do you not
know what I and my ancestors have
done to all the peoples of other lands?
Were the gods of the nations of those
lands at all able to save their lands out of
my hand? 14Who among all the gods of
those nations that my ancestors utterly
destroyed was able to save his people
from my hand, that your God should be
able to save you from my hand? 15Now
therefore do not let Hezekiah deceive
you or mislead you in this fashion, and
do not believe him, for no god of any
nation or kingdom has been able to save
his people from my hand or from the
hand of my ancestors. How much less
will your God save you out of my hand!"

16 His servants said still more against
the Lord GOD and against his servant
Hezekiah. 17He also wrote letters to
throw contempt on the LORD the God of
Israel and to speak against him, saying,
"Just as the gods of the nations in other
lands did not rescue their people from
my hands, so the God of Hezekiah will
not rescue his people from my hand."
18They shouted it with a loud voice in
the language of Judah to the people of
Jerusalem who were on the wall, to
frighten and terrify them, in order that
they might take the city. 19They spoke of
the God of Jerusalem as if he were like
the gods of the peoples of the earth,
which are the work of human hands.

Sennacherib's Defeat and Death

20 Then King Hezekiah and the
prophet Isaiah son of Amoz prayed
because of this and cried to heaven.
21And the LORD sent an angel who cut
off all the mighty warriors and commanders and officers in the camp of the
king of Assyria. So he returned in disgrace to his own land. When he came
into the house of his god, some of his
own sons struck him down there with
the sword. 22So the LORD saved Hezekiah
and the inhabitants of Jerusalem from
the hand of King Sennacherib of Assyria
and from the hand of all his enemies; he
gave them rest[k] on every side. 23Many
brought gifts to the LORD in Jerusalem
and precious things to King Hezekiah of
Judah, so that he was exalted in the sight
of all nations from that time onward.

Hezekiah's Sickness

24 In those days Hezekiah became
sick and was at the point of death. He
prayed to the LORD, and he answered
him and gave him a sign. 25But Hezekiah did not respond according to the benefit done to him, for his heart was proud.
Therefore wrath came upon him and
upon Judah and Jerusalem. 26Then Hezekiah humbled himself for the pride of
his heart, both he and the inhabitants of
Jerusalem, so that the wrath of the LORD
did not come upon them in the days of
Hezekiah.

---

i Heb He   j Vg: Heb and raised on the towers   k Gk Vg: Heb guided them

Hezekiah's Prosperity and Achievements

27 Hezekiah had very great riches and honor; and he made for himself treasuries for silver, for gold, for precious stones, for spices, for shields, and for all kinds of costly objects; 28 storehouses also for the yield of grain, wine, and oil; and stalls for all kinds of cattle, and sheepfolds.[1] 29 He likewise provided cities for himself, and flocks and herds in abundance; for God had given him very great possessions. 30 This same Hezekiah closed the upper outlet of the waters of Gihon and directed them down to the west side of the city of David. Hezekiah prospered in all his works. 31 So also in the matter of the envoys of the officials of Babylon, who had been sent to him to inquire about the sign that had been done in the land, God left him to himself, in order to test him and to know all that was in his heart.

32 Now the rest of the acts of Hezekiah, and his good deeds, are written in the vision of the prophet Isaiah son of Amoz in the Book of the Kings of Judah and Israel. 33 Hezekiah slept with his ancestors, and they buried him on the ascent to the tombs of the descendants of David; and all Judah and the inhabitants of Jerusalem did him honor at his death. His son Manasseh succeeded him.

Reign of Manasseh

33 Manasseh was twelve years old when he began to reign; he reigned fifty-five years in Jerusalem. 2 He did what was evil in the sight of the LORD, according to the abominable practices of the nations whom the LORD drove out before the people of Israel. 3 For he rebuilt the high places that his father Hezekiah had pulled down, and erected altars to the Baals, made sacred poles,[m] worshiped all the host of heaven, and served them. 4 He built altars in the house of the LORD, of which the LORD had said, "In Jerusalem shall my name be forever." 5 He built altars for all the host of heaven in the two courts of the house of the LORD. 6 He made his son pass through fire in the valley of the son of Hinnom, practiced soothsaying and

augury and sorcery, and dealt with mediums and with wizards. He did much evil in the sight of the LORD, provoking him to anger. 7 The carved image of the idol that he had made he set in the house of God, of which God said to David and to his son Solomon, "In this house, and in Jerusalem, which I have chosen out of all the tribes of Israel, I will put my name forever; 8 I will never again remove the feet of Israel from the land that I appointed for your ancestors, if only they will be careful to do all that I have commanded them, all the law, the statutes, and the ordinances given through Moses." 9 Manasseh misled Judah and the inhabitants of Jerusalem, so that they did more evil than the nations whom the LORD had destroyed before the people of Israel.

Manasseh Restored after Repentance

10 The LORD spoke to Manasseh and to his people, but they gave no heed. 11 Therefore the LORD brought against them the commanders of the army of the king of Assyria, who took Manasseh captive in manacles, bound him with fetters, and brought him to Babylon. 12 While he was in distress he entreated the favor of the LORD his God and humbled himself greatly before the God of his ancestors. 13 He prayed to him, and God received his entreaty, heard his plea, and restored him again to Jerusalem and to his kingdom. Then Manasseh knew that the LORD indeed was God.

14 Afterward he built an outer wall for the city of David west of Gihon, in the valley, reaching the entrance at the Fish Gate; he carried it around Ophel, and raised it to a very great height. He also put commanders of the army in all the fortified cities in Judah. 15 He took away the foreign gods and the idol from the house of the LORD, and all the altars that he had built on the mountain of the house of the LORD and in Jerusalem, and he threw them out of the city. 16 He also restored the altar of the LORD and offered on it sacrifices of well-being and of thanksgiving; and he commanded Judah to serve the LORD the God of Israel. 17 The people, however, still sacrificed at

---

1 Gk Vg: Heb *flocks for folds*   *m* Heb *Asheroth*

the high places, but only to the LORD their God.

Death of Manasseh

18 Now the rest of the acts of Manasseh, his prayer to his God, and the words of the seers who spoke to him in the name of the LORD God of Israel, these are in the Annals of the Kings of Israel. 19His prayer, and how God received his entreaty, all his sin and his faithlessness, the sites on which he built high places and set up the sacred poles[n] and the images, before he humbled himself, these are written in the records of the seers.[o] 20So Manasseh slept with his ancestors, and they buried him in his house. His son Amon succeeded him.

Amon's Reign and Death

21 Amon was twenty-two years old when he began to reign; he reigned two years in Jerusalem. 22He did what was evil in the sight of the LORD, as his father Manasseh had done. Amon sacrificed to all the images that his father Manasseh had made, and served them. 23He did not humble himself before the LORD, as his father Manasseh had humbled himself, but this Amon incurred more and more guilt. 24His servants conspired against him and killed him in his house. 25But the people of the land killed all those who had conspired against King Amon; and the people of the land made his son Josiah king to succeed him.

Reign of Josiah

34 Josiah was eight years old when he began to reign; he reigned thirty-one years in Jerusalem. 2He did what was right in the sight of the LORD, and walked in the ways of his ancestor David; he did not turn aside to the right or to the left. 3For in the eighth year of his reign, while he was still a boy, he began to seek the God of his ancestor David, and in the twelfth year he began to purge Judah and Jerusalem of the high places, the sacred poles,[n] and the carved and the cast images. 4In his presence they pulled down the altars of the Baals; he demolished the incense altars that stood above them. He broke

down the sacred poles[n] and the carved and the cast images; he made dust of them and scattered it over the graves of those who had sacrificed to them. 5He also burned the bones of the priests on their altars, and purged Judah and Jerusalem. 6In the towns of Manasseh, Ephraim, and Simeon, and as far as Naphtali, in their ruins[p] all around, 7he broke down the altars, beat the sacred poles[n] and the images into powder, and demolished all the incense altars throughout all the land of Israel. Then he returned to Jerusalem.

Discovery of the Book of the Law

8 In the eighteenth year of his reign, when he had purged the land and the house, he sent Shaphan son of Azaliah, Maaseiah the governor of the city, and Joah son of Joahaz, the recorder, to repair the house of the LORD his God. 9They came to the high priest Hilkiah and delivered the money that had been brought into the house of God, which the Levites, the keepers of the threshold, had collected from Manasseh and Ephraim and from all the remnant of Israel and from all Judah and Benjamin and from the inhabitants of Jerusalem. 10They delivered it to the workers who had the oversight of the house of the LORD, and the workers who were working in the house of the LORD gave it for repairing and restoring the house. 11They gave it to the carpenters and the builders to buy quarried stone, and timber for binders, and beams for the buildings that the kings of Judah had let go to ruin. 12The people did the work faithfully. Over them were appointed the Levites Jahath and Obadiah, of the sons of Merari, along with Zechariah and Meshullam, of the sons of the Kohathites, to have oversight. Other Levites, all skillful with instruments of music, 13were over the burden bearers and directed all who did work in every kind of service; and some of the Levites were scribes, and officials, and gatekeepers.

14 While they were bringing out the money that had been brought into the house of the LORD, the priest Hilkiah found the book of the law of the LORD given through Moses. 15Hilkiah said to

---

n Heb *Asherim*   o One Ms Gk: MT *of Hozai*   p Meaning of Heb uncertain

the secretary Shaphan, "I have found the book of the law in the house of the LORD"; and Hilkiah gave the book to Shaphan. 16Shaphan brought the book to the king, and further reported to the king, "All that was committed to your servants they are doing. 17They have emptied out the money that was found in the house of the LORD and have delivered it into the hand of the overseers and the workers." 18The secretary Shaphan informed the king, "The priest Hilkiah has given me a book." Shaphan then read it aloud to the king.

19 When the king heard the words of the law he tore his clothes. 20Then the king commanded Hilkiah, Ahikam son of Shaphan, Abdon son of Micah, the secretary Shaphan, and the king's servant Asaiah: 21"Go, inquire of the LORD for me and for those who are left in Israel and in Judah, concerning the words of the book that has been found; for the wrath of the LORD that is poured out on us is great, because our ancestors did not keep the word of the LORD, to act in accordance with all that is written in this book."

The Prophet Huldah Consulted

22 So Hilkiah and those whom the king had sent went to the prophet Huldah, the wife of Shallum son of Tokhath son of Hasrah, keeper of the wardrobe (who lived in Jerusalem in the Second Quarter) and spoke to her to that effect. 23She declared to them, "Thus says the LORD, the God of Israel: Tell the man who sent you to me, 24Thus says the LORD: I will indeed bring disaster upon this place and upon its inhabitants, all the curses that are written in the book that was read before the king of Judah. 25Because they have forsaken me and have made offerings to other gods, so that they have provoked me to anger with all the works of their hands, my wrath will be poured out on this place and will not be quenched. 26But as to the king of Judah, who sent you to inquire of the LORD, thus shall you say to him: Thus says the LORD, the God of Israel: Regarding the words that you have heard, 27because your heart was penitent and you humbled yourself before God when you heard his words against

this place and its inhabit... have humbled yourself b... have torn your clothes an... me, I also have heard ... LORD. 28I will gather you ... tors and you shall be gat... grave in peace; your eyes s... the disaster that I will ... place and its inhabitants... the message back to the ki...

The Covenant Renewed

29 Then the king sent w... ered together all the elders o... Jerusalem. 30The king went ... house of the LORD, with all the p... Judah, the inhabitants of Jerusalem... priests and the Levites, all the pe... both great and small; he read in th... hearing all the words of the book of the covenant that had been found in the house of the LORD. 31The king stood in his place and made a covenant before the LORD, to follow the LORD, keeping his commandments, his decrees, and his statutes, with all his heart and all his soul, to perform the words of the covenant that were written in this book. 32Then he made all who were present in Jerusalem and in Benjamin pledge themselves to it. And the inhabitants of Jerusalem acted according to the covenant of God, the God of their ancestors. 33Josiah took away all the abominations from all the territory that belonged to the people of Israel, and made all who were in Israel worship the LORD their God. All his days they did not turn away from following the LORD the God of their ancestors.

Celebration of the Passover

35 Josiah kept a passover to the LORD in Jerusalem; they slaughtered the passover lamb on the fourteenth day of the first month. 2He appointed the priests to their offices and encouraged them in the service of the house of the LORD. 3He said to the Levites who taught all Israel and who were holy to the LORD, "Put the holy ark in the house that Solomon son of David, king of Israel, built; you need no longer carry it on your shoulders. Now serve the LORD your God and his people Israel. 4Make preparations by your ancestral

THE TERRIFYING OF THE CONSCIENCE AND THE PREACHING OF THE LAW

Martin Luther

VERSE: 2 Chronicles 34.21   **PASSAGE:** 2 Chronicles 34.14–21

e must preach the law for the sake of the evil and wicked, but for the most part it lights upon the good and godly who, although they need it not, except so far as may concern the old Adam, yet accept it. The preaching of the gospel we must have for the sake of the good and godly, yet it falls among the wicked and ungodly, who take it to themselves, whereas it profits them not; for they abuse it, and are thereby made confident. It is even as when it rains in the water or on a desert wilderness, while meantime the good pastures and grounds are parched and dried up. The ungodly suck only a fleshly liberty out of the gospel, and become worse thereby; therefore not the gospel but the law belongs to them. Even as when my little son John offends, if then I should not whip him but call him to the table to me and give him sugarplums, I should thereby make him worse, yea, quite spoil him.

The gospel is like a fresh, mild, and cool air in the extreme heat of summer, a solace and comfort in the anguish of the conscience. But as this heat proceeds from the rays of the sun, so likewise the terrifying of the conscience must proceed from the preaching of the law, to the end that we may know we have offended against the laws of God.

Now, when the mind is refreshed and quickened again by the cool air of the gospel, we must not then be idle, or lie down and sleep. That is, when our consciences are settled in peace, quieted and comforted through God's Spirit, we must prove our faith by such good works as God has commanded. But so long as we live in this vale of misery, we shall be plagued and vexed with flies, with beetles, and with vermin, that is, with the devil, the world, and our own flesh. Yet we must press through, and not suffer ourselves to recoil.

ADDITIONAL SCRIPTURE READING:
Job 27.6; Acts 24.16; Hebrews 10.22–24

Go to page 519 for your next devotional reading.

1500   1700

houses by your divisions, following the written directions of King David of Israel and the written directions of his son Solomon. 5Take position in the holy place according to the groupings of the ancestral houses of your kindred the people, and let there be Levites for each division of an ancestral house.q 6Slaughter the passover lamb, sanctify yourselves, and on behalf of your kindred make preparations, acting according to the word of the LORD by Moses."

7 Then Josiah contributed to the people, as passover offerings for all that were present, lambs and kids from the flock to the number of thirty thousand, and three thousand bulls; these were from the king's possessions. 8His officials contributed willingly to the people, to the priests, and to the Levites. Hilkiah, Zechariah, and Jehiel, the chief officers of the house of God, gave to the priests for the passover offerings two thousand six hundred lambs and kids and three hundred bulls. 9Conaniah also, and his brothers Shemaiah and Nethanel, and Hashabiah and Jeiel and Jozabad, the chiefs of the Levites, gave to the Levites for the passover offerings five thousand lambs and kids and five hundred bulls.

10 When the service had been prepared for, the priests stood in their place, and the Levites in their divisions according to the king's command. 11They slaughtered the passover lamb, and the priests dashed the blood that they receivedr from them, while the Levites did the skinning. 12They set aside the burnt offerings so that they might distribute them according to the groupings of the ancestral houses of the people, to offer to the LORD, as it is written in the book of Moses. And they did the same with the bulls. 13They roasted the passover lamb with fire according to the ordinance; and they boiled the holy offerings in pots, in caldrons, and in pans, and carried them quickly to all the people. 14Afterward they made preparations for themselves and for the priests, because the priests the descendants of Aaron were occupied in offering the burnt offerings and the fat parts until

night; so the Levites made preparations for themselves and for the priests, the descendants of Aaron. 15The singers, the descendants of Asaph, were in their place according to the command of David, and Asaph, and Heman, and the king's seer Jeduthun. The gatekeepers were at each gate; they did not need to interrupt their service, for their kindred the Levites made preparations for them.

16 So all the service of the LORD was prepared that day, to keep the passover and to offer burnt offerings on the altar of the LORD, according to the command of King Josiah. 17The people of Israel who were present kept the passover at that time, and the festival of unleavened bread seven days. 18No passover like it had been kept in Israel since the days of the prophet Samuel; none of the kings of Israel had kept such a passover as was kept by Josiah, by the priests and the Levites, by all Judah and Israel who were present, and by the inhabitants of Jerusalem. 19In the eighteenth year of the reign of Josiah this passover was kept.

Defeat by Pharaoh Neco and Death of Josiah

20 After all this, when Josiah had set the temple in order, King Neco of Egypt went up to fight at Carchemish on the Euphrates, and Josiah went out against him. 21But Necos sent envoys to him, saying, "What have I to do with you, king of Judah? I am not coming against you today, but against the house with which I am at war; and God has commanded me to hurry. Cease opposing God, who is with me, so that he will not destroy you." 22But Josiah would not turn away from him, but disguised himself in order to fight with him. He did not listen to the words of Neco from the mouth of God, but joined battle in the plain of Megiddo. 23The archers shot King Josiah; and the king said to his servants, "Take me away, for I am badly wounded." 24So his servants took him out of the chariot and carried him in his second chariott and brought him to Jerusalem. There he died, and was buried in the tombs of his ancestors. All Judah and Jerusalem mourned for Josiah. 25Jer-

q Meaning of Heb uncertain   r Heb lacks that they received   s Heb he   t Or the chariot of his deputy

emiah also uttered a lament for Josiah, and all the singing men and singing women have spoken of Josiah in their laments to this day. They made these a custom in Israel; they are recorded in the Laments. 26Now the rest of the acts of Josiah and his faithful deeds in accordance with what is written in the law of the LORD, 27and his acts, first and last, are written in the Book of the Kings of Israel and Judah.

Reign of Jehoahaz

36 The people of the land took Jehoahaz son of Josiah and made him king to succeed his father in Jerusalem. 2Jehoahaz was twenty-three years old when he began to reign; he reigned three months in Jerusalem. 3Then the king of Egypt deposed him in Jerusalem and laid on the land a tribute of one hundred talents of silver and one talent of gold. 4The king of Egypt made his brother Eliakim king over Judah and Jerusalem, and changed his name to Jehoiakim; but Neco took his brother Jehoahaz and carried him to Egypt.

Reign and Captivity of Jehoiakim

5 Jehoiakim was twenty-five years old when he began to reign; he reigned eleven years in Jerusalem. He did what was evil in the sight of the LORD his God. 6Against him King Nebuchadnezzar of Babylon came up, and bound him with fetters to take him to Babylon. 7Nebuchadnezzar also carried some of the vessels of the house of the LORD to Babylon and put them in his palace in Babylon. 8Now the rest of the acts of Jehoiakim, and the abominations that he did, and what was found against him, are written in the Book of the Kings of Israel and Judah; and his son Jehoiachin succeeded him.

Reign and Captivity of Jehoiachin

9 Jehoiachin was eight years old when he began to reign; he reigned three months and ten days in Jerusalem. He did what was evil in the sight of the LORD. 10In the spring of the year King Nebuchadnezzar sent and brought him to Babylon, along with the precious vessels of the house of the LORD, and made his brother Zedekiah king over Judah and Jerusalem.

Reign of Zedekiah

11 Zedekiah was twenty-one years old when he began to reign; he reigned eleven years in Jerusalem. 12He did what was evil in the sight of the LORD his God. He did not humble himself before the prophet Jeremiah who spoke from the mouth of the LORD. 13He also rebelled against King Nebuchadnezzar, who had made him swear by God; he stiffened his neck and hardened his heart against turning to the LORD, the God of Israel. 14All the leading priests and the people also were exceedingly unfaithful, following all the abominations of the nations; and they polluted the house of the LORD that he had consecrated in Jerusalem.

The Fall of Jerusalem

15 The LORD, the God of their ancestors, sent persistently to them by his messengers, because he had compassion on his people and on his dwelling place; 16but they kept mocking the messengers of God, despising his words, and scoffing at his prophets, until the wrath of the LORD against his people became so great that there was no remedy.

17 Therefore he brought up against them the king of the Chaldeans, who killed their youths with the sword in the house of their sanctuary, and had no compassion on young man or young woman, the aged or the feeble; he gave them all into his hand. 18All the vessels of the house of God, large and small, and the treasures of the house of the LORD, and the treasures of the king and of his officials, all these he brought to Babylon. 19They burned the house of God, broke down the wall of Jerusalem, burned all its palaces with fire, and destroyed all its precious vessels. 20He took into exile in Babylon those who had escaped from the sword, and they became servants to him and to his sons until the establishment of the kingdom of Persia, 21to fulfill the word of the LORD by the mouth of Jeremiah, until the land had made up for its sabbaths. All the days that it lay desolate it kept sabbath, to fulfill seventy years.

Cyrus Proclaims Liberty for the Exiles

22 In the first year of King Cyrus of Persia, in fulfillment of the word of the LORD spoken by Jeremiah, the LORD stirred up the spirit of King Cyrus of Persia so that he sent a herald throughout all his kingdom and also declared in a written edict: 23 "Thus sa of Persia: The LORD, the has given me all the kin earth, and he has charge him a house at Jerusalem Judah. Whoever is among people, may the LORD his him! Let him go up."

EZRA

ZRA TELLS OF THE RETURN OF THE JEWS FROM EXILE IN BABYLON AND ALSO OF THE REBUILDING OF THE TEMPLE. THE PEOPLE COMPLETED AND DEDICATED THE TEMPLE IN 516 B.C. AFTER BEING DELAYED FOR 18 YEARS BY THEIR ENEMIES FROM THE NORTH. AS YOU READ THIS BOOK, TAKE COMFORT IN THE STORY OF ORDINARY PEOPLE RESTORED BY GOD, AND REJOICE IN THE GOD WHO ALWAYS GIVES YOU A SECOND CHANCE TO TRUST AND FOLLOW HIM.

End of the Babylonian Captivity

 1 In the first year of King Cyrus of Persia, in order that the word of the LORD by the mouth of Jeremiah might be accomplished, the LORD stirred up the spirit of King Cyrus of Persia so that he sent a herald throughout all his kingdom, and also in a written edict declared:

2 "Thus says King Cyrus of Persia: The LORD, the God of heaven, has given me all the kingdoms of the earth, and he has charged me to build him a house at Jerusalem in Judah. 3 Any of those among you who are of his people—may their God be with them!—are now permitted to go up to Jerusalem in Judah, and rebuild the house of the LORD, the God of Israel—he is the God who is in Jerusalem; 4 and let all survivors, in whatever place they reside, be assisted by the people of their place with silver and gold, with goods and with animals, besides freewill offerings for the house of God in Jerusalem."

5 The heads of the families of Judah and Benjamin, and the priests and the Levites—everyone whose spirit God had stirred—got ready to go up and rebuild the house of the LORD in Jerusalem. 6 All their neighbors aided them with silver vessels, with gold, with goods, with animals, and with valuable gifts, besides all that was freely offered. 7 King Cyrus himself brought out the vessels of the house of the LORD that Nebuchadnezzar had carried away from Jerusalem and placed in the house of his gods. 8 King Cyrus of Persia had them released into the charge of Mithredath the treasurer,

who counted them out to Sheshbazzar the prince of Judah. ⁹And this was the inventory: gold basins, thirty; silver basins, one thousand; knives,ᵃ twenty-nine; ¹⁰gold bowls, thirty; other silver bowls, four hundred ten; other vessels, one thousand; ¹¹the total of the gold and silver vessels was five thousand four hundred. All these Sheshbazzar brought up, when the exiles were brought up from Babylonia to Jerusalem.

List of the Returned Exiles

2 Now these were the people of the province who came from those captive exiles whom King Nebuchadnezzar of Babylon had carried captive to Babylonia; they returned to Jerusalem and Judah, all to their own towns. ²They came with Zerubbabel, Jeshua, Nehemiah, Seraiah, Reelaiah, Mordecai, Bilshan, Mispar, Bigvai, Rehum, and Baanah.

The number of the Israelite people: ³the descendants of Parosh, two thousand one hundred seventy-two. ⁴Of Shephatiah, three hundred seventy-two. ⁵Of Arah, seven hundred seventy-five. ⁶Of Pahath-moab, namely the descendants of Jeshua and Joab, two thousand eight hundred twelve. ⁷Of Elam, one thousand two hundred fifty-four. ⁸Of Zattu, nine hundred forty-five. ⁹Of Zaccai, seven hundred sixty. ¹⁰Of Bani, six hundred forty-two. ¹¹Of Bebai, six hundred twenty-three. ¹²Of Azgad, one thousand two hundred twenty-two. ¹³Of Adonikam, six hundred sixty-six. ¹⁴Of Bigvai, two thousand fifty-six. ¹⁵Of Adin, four hundred fifty-four. ¹⁶Of Ater, namely of Hezekiah, ninety-eight. ¹⁷Of Bezai, three hundred twenty-three. ¹⁸Of Jorah, one hundred twelve. ¹⁹Of Hashum, two hundred twenty-three. ²⁰Of Gibbar, ninety-five. ²¹Of Bethlehem, one hundred twenty-three. ²²The people of Netophah, fifty-six. ²³Of Anathoth, one hundred twenty-eight. ²⁴The descendants of Azmaveth, forty-two. ²⁵Of Kiriatharim, Chephirah, and Beeroth, seven hundred forty-three. ²⁶Of Ramah and Geba, six hundred twenty-one. ²⁷The people of Michmas, one hundred twenty-two. ²⁸Of Bethel and Ai, two hundred twenty-three. ²⁹The descendants of Nebo, fifty-

two. ³⁰Of Magbish, one hu... six. ³¹Of the other Elam, or... two hundred fifty-four. ... three hundred twenty. ³³Of ... and Ono, seven hundred t... ³⁴Of Jericho, three hundred ... ³⁵Of Senaah, three thousand s... thirty.

36 The priests: the desce... Jedaiah, of the house of Jesh... hundred seventy-three. ³⁷Of Im... thousand fifty-two. ³⁸Of Pash... thousand two hundred forty-sev... Harim, one thousand seventeen.

40 The Levites: the descendant... Jeshua and Kadmiel, of the descendan... of Hodaviah, seventy-four. ⁴¹The singers: the descendants of Asaph, one hundred twenty-eight. ⁴²The descendants of the gatekeepers: of Shallum, of Ater, of Talmon, of Akkub, of Hatita, and of Shobai, in all one hundred thirty-nine.

43 The temple servants: the descendants of Ziha, Hasupha, Tabbaoth, ⁴⁴Keros, Siaha, Padon, ⁴⁵Lebanah, Hagabah, Akkub, ⁴⁶Hagab, Shamlai, Hanan, ⁴⁷Giddel, Gahar, Reaiah, ⁴⁸Rezin, Nekoda, Gazzam, ⁴⁹Uzza, Paseah, Besai, ⁵⁰Asnah, Meunim, Nephisim, ⁵¹Bakbuk, Hakupha, Harhur, ⁵²Bazluth, Mehida, Harsha, ⁵³Barkos, Sisera, Temah, ⁵⁴Neziah, and Hatipha.

55 The descendants of Solomon's servants: Sotai, Hassophereth, Peruda, ⁵⁶Jaalah, Darkon, Giddel, ⁵⁷Shephatiah, Hattil, Pochereth-hazzebaim, and Ami.

58 All the temple servants and the descendants of Solomon's servants were three hundred ninety-two.

59 The following were those who came up from Tel-melah, Tel-harsha, Cherub, Addan, and Immer, though they could not prove their families or their descent, whether they belonged to Israel: ⁶⁰the descendants of Delaiah, Tobiah, and Nekoda, six hundred fifty-two. ⁶¹Also, of the descendants of the priests: the descendants of Habaiah, Hakkoz, and Barzillai (who had married one of the daughters of Barzillai the Gileadite, and was called by their name). ⁶²These looked for their entries in the genealogical records, but they were not found there, and so they were excluded from the priesthood as unclean; ⁶³the

---

ᵃ Vg: Meaning of Heb uncertain

512 ...old them that they were not go ...e of the most holy food, until to ...uld be a priest to consult Urim to ...mmim.

...he whole assembly together was ...wo thousand three hundred sixty, ...des their male and female servants, ...hom there were seven thousand ...e hundred thirty-seven; and they had ...hundred male and female singers. They had seven hundred thirty-six ...orses, two hundred forty-five mules, ⁷four hundred thirty-five camels, and six thousand seven hundred twenty donkeys.

68 As soon as they came to the house of the LORD in Jerusalem, some of the heads of families made freewill offerings for the house of God, to erect it on its site. ⁶⁹According to their resources they gave to the building fund sixty-one thousand darics of gold, five thousand minas of silver, and one hundred priestly robes.

70 The priests, the Levites, and some of the people lived in Jerusalem and its vicinity;ᵇ and the singers, the gatekeepers, and the temple servants lived in their towns, and all Israel in their towns.

Worship Restored at Jerusalem

3 When the seventh month came, and the Israelites were in the towns, the people gathered together in Jerusalem. ²Then Jeshua son of Jozadak, with his fellow priests, and Zerubbabel son of Shealtiel with his kin set out to build the altar of the God of Israel, to offer burnt offerings on it, as prescribed in the law of Moses the man of God. ³They set up the altar on its foundation, because they were in dread of the neighboring peoples, and they offered burnt offerings upon it to the LORD, morning and evening. ⁴And they kept the festival of booths,ᶜ as prescribed, and offered the daily burnt offerings by number according to the ordinance, as required for each day, ⁵and after that the regular burnt offerings, the offerings at the new moon and at all the sacred festivals of the LORD, and the offerings of everyone who made a freewill offering to the LORD. ⁶From the first day of the seventh month they began to offer burnt offerings to the

LORD. But the foundation of the temple of the LORD was not yet laid. ⁷So they gave money to the masons and the carpenters, and food, drink, and oil to the Sidonians and the Tyrians to bring cedar trees from Lebanon to the sea, to Joppa, according to the grant that they had from King Cyrus of Persia.

Foundation Laid for the Temple

8 In the second year after their arrival at the house of God at Jerusalem, in the second month, Zerubbabel son of Shealtiel and Jeshua son of Jozadak made a beginning, together with the rest of their people, the priests and the Levites and all who had come to Jerusalem from the captivity. They appointed the Levites, from twenty years old and upward, to have the oversight of the work on the house of the LORD. ⁹And Jeshua with his sons and his kin, and Kadmiel and his sons, Binnui and Hodaviahᵈ along with the sons of Henadad, the Levites, their sons and kin, together took charge of the workers in the house of God.

10 When the builders laid the foundation of the temple of the LORD, the priests in their vestments were stationed to praise the LORD with trumpets, and the Levites, the sons of Asaph, with cymbals, according to the directions of King David of Israel; ¹¹and they sang responsively, praising and giving thanks to the LORD,

"For he is good,
    for his steadfast love endures
        forever toward Israel."

And all the people responded with a great shout when they praised the LORD, because the foundation of the house of the LORD was laid. ¹²But many of the priests and Levites and heads of families, old people who had seen the first house on its foundations, wept with a loud voice when they saw this house, though many shouted aloud for joy, ¹³so that the people could not distinguish the sound of the joyful shout from the sound of the people's weeping, for the people shouted so loudly that the sound was heard far away.

b 1 Esdras 5.46: Heb lacks *lived in Jerusalem and its vicinity*   c Or *tabernacles*; Heb *succoth*
d Compare 2.40; Neh 7.43; 1 Esdras 5.58: Heb *sons of Judah*

Resistance to Rebuilding the Temple

4 When the adversaries of Judah and Benjamin heard that the returned exiles were building a temple to the LORD, the God of Israel, 2they approached Zerubbabel and the heads of families and said to them, "Let us build with you, for we worship your God as you do, and we have been sacrificing to him ever since the days of King Esarhaddon of Assyria who brought us here." 3But Zerubbabel, Jeshua, and the rest of the heads of families in Israel said to them, "You shall have no part with us in building a house to our God; but we alone will build to the LORD, the God of Israel, as King Cyrus of Persia has commanded us."

WHEREVER SOULS ARE BEING TRIED AND RIPENED, IN WHATEVER COMMONPLACE AND HOMELY WAY, THERE GOD IS HEWING OUT THE PILLARS FOR HIS TEMPLE. —*Phillips Brooks*

---

4 Then the people of the land discouraged the people of Judah, and made them afraid to build, 5and they bribed officials to frustrate their plan throughout the reign of King Cyrus of Persia and until the reign of King Darius of Persia.

Rebuilding of Jerusalem Opposed

6 In the reign of Ahasuerus, in his accession year, they wrote an accusation against the inhabitants of Judah and Jerusalem.

7 And in the days of Artaxerxes, Bishlam and Mithredath and Tabeel and the rest of their associates wrote to King Artaxerxes of Persia; the letter was written in Aramaic and translated.*e* 8Rehum the royal deputy and Shimshai the scribe wrote a letter against Jerusalem to King Artaxerxes as follows 9(then Rehum the royal deputy, Shimshai the scribe, and the rest of their associates, the judges, the envoys, the officials, the Persians, the people of Erech, the Babylonians, the people of Susa, that is, the Elamites, 10and the rest of the nations whom the great and noble Osnappar deported and settled in the cities of Samaria and in the rest of the province Beyond the River wrote—and this is a copy of the letter that they sent):

11"To King Artaxerxes: Your servants, the people of the province Beyond the River, send greeting. And now 12let it be known to the king that the Jews who came up from you to us have come to Jerusalem. They are rebuilding the rebellious and wicked city; they are finishing the walls and repairing the foundations. 13Now may it be known to the king that, if this city is rebuilt and its walls finished, they will not pay tax, custom, or toll, and the royal revenue will be reduced. 14Now because we share the salt of the palace and it is not fitting for us to witness the king's dishonor, therefore we send and inform the king, 15so that a search may be made in the annals of your ancestors. You will discover in the annals that this is a rebellious city, hurtful to kings and provinces, and that sedition was stirred up in it from long ago. On that account this city was laid waste. 16We make known to the king that, if this city is rebuilt and its walls finished, you will then have no possession in the province Beyond the River."

17 The king sent an answer: "To Rehum the royal deputy and Shimshai the scribe and the rest of their associates who live in Samaria and in the rest of the province Beyond the River, greeting. And now 18the letter that you sent to us has been read in translation before me. 19So I made a decree, and someone searched and discovered that this city has risen against kings from long ago, and that rebellion and sedition have been made in it. 20Jerusalem has had mighty kings who ruled over the whole province Beyond the River, to whom tribute, custom, and toll were paid. 21Therefore issue an order that these people be made to cease, and that this city not be rebuilt, until I make a decree. 22Moreover, take care not to be slack in this matter; why should damage grow to the hurt of the king?"

23 Then when the copy of King Artaxerxes' letter was read before Rehum and the scribe Shimshai and their associates,

---

e Heb adds *in Aramaic,* indicating that 4.8-6.18 is in Aramaic. Another interpretation is *The letter was written in the Aramaic script and set forth in the Aramaic language*

514 ...d to the Jews in Jerusalem and ...and power made them cease. ...the time the work on the house of ...Jerusalem stopped and was dis-...ued until the second year of the ...f King Darius of Persia.

...ration of the Temple Resumed

5 Now the prophets, Haggai[f] and Zechariah son of Iddo, prophe-...d to the Jews who were in Judah and ...rusalem, in the name of the God of ...srael who was over them. 2Then Zerub-...babel son of Shealtiel and Jeshua son of Jozadak set out to rebuild the house of God in Jerusalem; and with them were the prophets of God, helping them.

3 At the same time Tattenai the governor of the province Beyond the River and Shethar-bozenai and their associates came to them and spoke to them thus, "Who gave you a decree to build this house and to finish this structure?" 4They[g] also asked them this, "What are the names of the men who are building this building?" 5But the eye of their God was upon the elders of the Jews, and they did not stop them until a report reached Darius and then answer was returned by letter in reply to it.

6 The copy of the letter that Tattenai the governor of the province Beyond the River and Shethar-bozenai and his associates the envoys who were in the province Beyond the River sent to King Darius; 7they sent him a report, in which was written as follows: "To Darius the king, all peace! 8May it be known to the king that we went to the province of Judah, to the house of the great God. It is being built of hewn stone, and timber is laid in the walls; this work is being done diligently and prospers in their hands. 9Then we spoke to those elders and asked them, 'Who gave you a decree to build this house and to finish this structure?' 10We also asked them their names, for your information, so that we might write down the names of the men at their head. 11This was their reply to us: 'We are the servants of the God of heaven and earth, and we are rebuilding the house that was built many years ago, which a great king of Israel built and finished. 12But because our ances-

tors had angered the God of heaven, he gave them into the hand of King Nebuchadnezzar of Babylon, the Chaldean, who destroyed this house and carried away the people to Babylonia. 13However, King Cyrus of Babylon, in the first year of his reign, made a decree that this house of God should be rebuilt. 14Moreover, the gold and silver vessels of the house of God, which Nebuchadnezzar had taken out of the temple in Jerusalem and had brought into the temple of Babylon, these King Cyrus took out of the temple of Babylon, and they were delivered to a man named Sheshbazzar, whom he had made governor. 15He said to him, "Take these vessels; go and put them in the temple in Jerusalem, and let the house of God be rebuilt on its site." 16Then this Sheshbazzar came and laid the foundations of the house of God in Jerusalem; and from that time until now it has been under construction, and it is not yet finished.' 17And now, if it seems good to the king, have a search made in the royal archives there in Babylon, to see whether a decree was issued by King Cyrus for the rebuilding of this house of God in Jerusalem. Let the king send us his pleasure in this matter."

The Decree of Darius

6 Then King Darius made a decree, and they searched the archives where the documents were stored in Babylon. 2But it was in Ecbatana, the capital in the province of Media, that a scroll was found on which this was written: "A record. 3In the first year of his reign, King Cyrus issued a decree: Concerning the house of God at Jerusalem, let the house be rebuilt, the place where sacrifices are offered and burnt offerings are brought;[h] its height shall be sixty cubits and its width sixty cubits, 4with three courses of hewn stones and one course of timber; let the cost be paid from the royal treasury. 5Moreover, let the gold and silver vessels of the house of God, which Nebuchadnezzar took out of the temple in Jerusalem and brought to Babylon, be restored and brought back to the temple in Jerusalem, each to its place; you shall put them in the house of God."

f Aram adds *the prophet*   g Gk Syr: Aram *We*   h Meaning of Aram uncertain

6 "Now you, Tattenai, governor of the province Beyond the River, Shethar-bozenai, and you, their associates, the envoys in the province Beyond the River, keep away; 7let the work on this house of God alone; let the governor of the Jews and the elders of the Jews rebuild this house of God on its site. 8Moreover I make a decree regarding what you shall do for these elders of the Jews for the rebuilding of this house of God: the cost is to be paid to these people, in full and without delay, from the royal revenue, the tribute of the province Beyond the River. 9Whatever is needed—young bulls, rams, or sheep for burnt offerings to the God of heaven, wheat, salt, wine, or oil, as the priests in Jerusalem require—let that be given to them day by day without fail, 10so that they may offer pleasing sacrifices to the God of heaven, and pray for the life of the king and his children. 11Furthermore I decree that if anyone alters this edict, a beam shall be pulled out of the house of the perpetrator, who then shall be impaled on it. The house shall be made a dunghill. 12May the God who has established his name there overthrow any king or people that shall put forth a hand to alter this, or to destroy this house of God in Jerusalem. I, Darius, make a decree; let it be done with all diligence."

Completion and Dedication of the Temple

13 Then, according to the word sent by King Darius, Tattenai, the governor of the province Beyond the River, Shethar-bozenai, and their associates did with all diligence what King Darius had ordered. 14So the elders of the Jews built and prospered, through the prophesying of the prophet Haggai and Zechariah son of Iddo. They finished their building by command of the God of Israel and by decree of Cyrus, Darius, and King Artaxerxes of Persia; 15and this house was finished on the third day of the month of Adar, in the sixth year of the reign of King Darius.

16 The people of Israel, the priests and the Levites, and the rest of the returned exiles, celebrated the dedication of this house of God with joy. 17They offered at the dedication of this house of God one

hundred bulls, two hundred ___ hundred lambs, and as a si___rs, four all Israel, twelve male goats___ing for the number of the tribes of I___ng to they set the priests in their ___then the Levites in their courses f___nd of God at Jerusalem, as it is v___e book of Moses.

The Passover Celebrated

19 On the fourteenth da___ month the returned exile___ passover. 20For both the prie___ Levites had purified themse___ them were clean. So they k___ passover lamb for all the returne___ for their fellow priests, and for ___ selves. 21It was eaten by the peop___ Israel who had returned from exile, a___ also by all who had joined them and sep___ arated themselves from the pollutions of the nations of the land to worship the LORD, the God of Israel. 22With joy they celebrated the festival of unleavened bread seven days; for the LORD had made them joyful, and had turned the heart of the king of Assyria to them, so that he aided them in the work on the house of God, the God of Israel.

The Coming and Work of Ezra

7 After this, in the reign of King Artaxerxes of Persia, Ezra son of Seraiah, son of Azariah, son of Hilkiah, 2son of Shallum, son of Zadok, son of Ahitub, 3son of Amariah, son of Azariah, son of Meraioth, 4son of Zerahiah, son of Uzzi, son of Bukki, 5son of Abishua, son of Phinehas, son of Eleazar, son of the chief priest Aaron— 6this Ezra went up from Babylonia. He was a scribe skilled in the law of Moses that the LORD the God of Israel had given; and the king granted him all that he asked, for the hand of the LORD his God was upon him.

7 Some of the people of Israel, and some of the priests and Levites, the singers and gatekeepers, and the temple servants also went up to Jerusalem, in the seventh year of King Artaxerxes. 8They came to Jerusalem in the fifth month, which was in the seventh year of the king. 9On the first day of the first month the journey up from Babylon was begun, and on the first day of the fifth month he came to Jerusalem, for the

516 and of his God was upon him. had set his heart to study the grac le LORD, and to do it, and to 10 e statutes and ordinances in

etter of Artaxerxes to Ezra

This is a copy of the letter that Artaxerxes gave to the priest Ezra, scribe, a scholar of the text of the mandments of the LORD and his utes for Israel: 12"Artaxerxes, king of gs, to the priest Ezra, the scribe of the w of the God of heaven: Peace.*i* And ow 13I decree that any of the people of srael or their priests or Levites in my kingdom who freely offers to go to Jerusalem may go with you. 14For you are sent by the king and his seven counselors to make inquiries about Judah and Jerusalem according to the law of your God, which is in your hand, 15and also to convey the silver and gold that the king and his counselors have freely offered to the God of Israel, whose dwelling is in Jerusalem, 16with all the silver and gold that you shall find in the whole province of Babylonia, and with the freewill offerings of the people and the priests, given willingly for the house of their God in Jerusalem. 17With this money, then, you shall with all diligence buy bulls, rams, and lambs, and their grain offerings and their drink offerings, and you shall offer them on the altar of the house of your God in Jerusalem. 18Whatever seems good to you and your colleagues to do with the rest of the silver and gold, you may do, according to the will of your God. 19The vessels that have been given you for the service of the house of your God, you shall deliver before the God of Jerusalem. 20And whatever else is required for the house of your God, which you are responsible for providing, you may provide out of the king's treasury.

21 "I, King Artaxerxes, decree to all the treasurers in the province Beyond the River: Whatever the priest Ezra, the scribe of the law of the God of heaven, requires of you, let it be done with all diligence, 22up to one hundred talents of silver, one hundred cors of wheat, one

hundred baths*j* of wine, one hundred baths*j* of oil, and unlimited salt. 23Whatever is commanded by the God of heaven, let it be done with zeal for the house of the God of heaven, or wrath will come upon the realm of the king and his heirs. 24We also notify you that it shall not be lawful to impose tribute, custom, or toll on any of the priests, the Levites, the singers, the doorkeepers, the temple servants, or other servants of this house of God.

25 "And you, Ezra, according to the God-given wisdom you possess, appoint magistrates and judges who may judge all the people in the province Beyond the River who know the laws of your God; and you shall teach those who do not know them. 26All who will not obey the law of your God and the law of the king, let judgment be strictly executed on them, whether for death or for banishment or for confiscation of their goods or for imprisonment."

27 Blessed be the LORD, the God of our ancestors, who put such a thing as this into the heart of the king to glorify the house of the LORD in Jerusalem, 28and who extended to me steadfast love before the king and his counselors, and before all the king's mighty officers. I took courage, for the hand of the LORD my God was upon me, and I gathered leaders from Israel to go up with me.

Heads of Families Who Returned with Ezra

8 These are their family heads, and this is the genealogy of those who went up with me from Babylonia, in the reign of King Artaxerxes: 2Of the descendants of Phinehas, Gershom. Of Ithamar, Daniel. Of David, Hattush, 3of the descendants of Shecaniah. Of Parosh, Zechariah, with whom were registered one hundred fifty males. 4Of the descendants of Pahath-moab, Eliehoenai son of Zerahiah, and with him two hundred males. 5Of the descendants of Zattu,*k* Shecaniah son of Jahaziel, and with him three hundred males. 6Of the descendants of Adin, Ebed son of Jonathan, and with him fifty males. 7Of the descendants of Elam, Jeshaiah son of

i Syr Vg 1 Esdras 8.9: Aram *Perfect*   *j* A Heb measure of volume   *k* Gk 1 Esdras 8.32: Heb lacks *of Zattu*

Athaliah, and with him seventy males. [8]Of the descendants of Shephatiah, Zebadiah son of Michael, and with him eighty males. [9]Of the descendants of Joab, Obadiah son of Jehiel, and with him two hundred eighteen males. [10]Of the descendants of Bani,[1] Shelomith son of Josiphiah, and with him one hundred sixty males. [11]Of the descendants of Bebai, Zechariah son of Bebai, and with him twenty-eight males. [12]Of the descendants of Azgad, Johanan son of Hakkatan, and with him one hundred ten males. [13]Of the descendants of Adonikam, those who came later, their names being Eliphelet, Jeuel, and Shemaiah, and with them sixty males. [14]Of the descendants of Bigvai, Uthai and Zaccur, and with them seventy males.

Servants for the Temple

15 I gathered them by the river that runs to Ahava, and there we camped three days. As I reviewed the people and the priests, I found there none of the descendants of Levi. [16]Then I sent for Eliezer, Ariel, Shemaiah, Elnathan, Jarib, Elnathan, Nathan, Zechariah, and Meshullam, who were leaders, and for Joiarib and Elnathan, who were wise, [17]and sent them to Iddo, the leader at the place called Casiphia, telling them what to say to Iddo and his colleagues the temple servants at Casiphia, namely, to send us ministers for the house of our God. [18]Since the gracious hand of our God was upon us, they brought us a man of discretion, of the descendants of Mahli son of Levi son of Israel, namely Sherebiah, with his sons and kin, eighteen; [19]also Hashabiah and with him Jeshaiah of the descendants of Merari, with his kin and their sons, twenty; [20]besides two hundred twenty of the temple servants, whom David and his officials had set apart to attend the Levites. These were all mentioned by name.

Fasting and Prayer for Protection

21 Then I proclaimed a fast there, at the river Ahava, that we might deny ourselves[m] before our God, to seek from him a safe journey for ourselves, our children, and all our possessions. [22]For I was ashamed to ask the king for a band of soldiers and cavalry to protect us against the enemy on our way, since we had told the king that the hand of our God is gracious to all who seek him, but his power and his wrath are against all who forsake him. [23]So we fasted and petitioned our God for this, and he listened to our entreaty.

Gifts for the Temple

24 Then I set apart twelve of the leading priests: Sherebiah, Hashabiah, and ten of their kin with them. [25]And I weighed out to them the silver and the gold and the vessels, the offering for the house of our God that the king, his counselors, his lords, and all Israel there present had offered; [26]I weighed out into their hand six hundred fifty talents of silver, and one hundred silver vessels worth . . . talents,[n] and one hundred talents of gold, [27]twenty gold bowls worth a thousand darics, and two vessels of fine polished bronze as precious as gold. [28]And I said to them, "You are holy to the LORD, and the vessels are holy; and the silver and the gold are a freewill offering to the LORD, the God of your ancestors. [29]Guard them and keep them until you weigh them before the chief priests and the Levites and the heads of families in Israel at Jerusalem, within the chambers of the house of the LORD." [30]So the priests and the Levites took over the silver, the gold, and the vessels as they were weighed out, to bring them to Jerusalem, to the house of our God.

The Return to Jerusalem

31 Then we left the river Ahava on the twelfth day of the first month, to go to Jerusalem; the hand of our God was upon us, and he delivered us from the hand of the enemy and from ambushes along the way. [32]We came to Jerusalem and remained there three days. [33]On the fourth day, within the house of our God, the silver, the gold, and the vessels were weighed into the hands of the priest Meremoth son of Uriah, and with him was Eleazar son of Phinehas, and with them were the Levites, Jozabad son of Jeshua and Noadiah son of Binnui. [34]The

---

l Gk 1 Esdras 8.36: Heb lacks *Bani*   *m* Or *might fast*   *n* The number of talents is lacking

518 s counted and weighed, and the of everything was recorded.

t that time those who had come captivity, the returned exiles, ed burnt offerings to the God of l, twelve bulls for all Israel, ninety- rams, seventy-seven lambs, and as a offering twelve male goats; all this as a burnt offering to the LORD. 36They lso delivered the king's commissions to the king's satraps and to the governors of the province Beyond the River; and they supported the people and the house of God.

Denunciation of Mixed Marriages

9 After these things had been done, the officials approached me and said, "The people of Israel, the priests, and the Levites have not separat- ed themselves from the peoples of the lands with their abominations, from the Canaanites, the Hittites, the Perizzites, the Jebusites, the Ammonites, the Moabites, the Egyptians, and the Amo- rites. 2For they have taken some of their daughters as wives for themselves and for their sons. Thus the holy seed has mixed itself with the peoples of the lands, and in this faithlessness the offi- cials and leaders have led the way." 3When I heard this, I tore my garment and my mantle, and pulled hair from my head and beard, and sat appalled. 4Then all who trembled at the words of the God of Israel, because of the faithless- ness of the returned exiles, gathered around me while I sat appalled until the evening sacrifice.

Ezra's Prayer

5 At the evening sacrifice I got up from my fasting, with my garments and my mantle torn, and fell on my knees, spread out my hands to the LORD my God, 6and said,

"O my God, I am too ashamed and embarrassed to lift my face to you, my God, for our iniquities have risen higher than our heads, and our guilt has mounted up to the heavens. 7From the days of our ancestors to this day we have been deep in guilt, and for our iniquities we, our kings, and our priests have been handed over to the kings of the lands, to

the sword, to captivity, to plundering, and to utter shame, as is now the case. 8But now for a brief moment favor has been shown by the LORD our God, who has left us a remnant, and given us a stake in his holy place, in order that he° may brighten our eyes and grant us a lit- tle sustenance in our slavery. 9For we are slaves; yet our God has not forsaken us in our slavery, but has extended to us his steadfast love before the kings of Per- sia, to give us new life to set up the house of our God, to repair its ruins, and to give us a wall in Judea and Jerusalem.

10 "And now, our God, what shall we say after this? For we have forsaken your commandments, 11which you com- manded by your servants the prophets, saying, 'The land that you are entering to possess is a land unclean with the pollutions of the peoples of the lands, with their abominations. They have filled it from end to end with their uncleanness. 12Therefore do not give your daughters to their sons, neither take their daughters for your sons, and never seek their peace or prosperity, so that you may be strong and eat the good of the land and leave it for an inheri- tance to your children forever.' 13After all that has come upon us for our evil deeds and for our great guilt, seeing that you, our God, have punished us less than our iniquities deserved and have given us such a remnant as this, 14shall we break your commandments again and intermarry with the peoples who practice these abominations? Would you not be angry with us until you destroy us without remnant or survivor? 15O LORD, God of Israel, you are just, but we have escaped as a remnant, as is now the case. Here we are before you in our guilt, though no one can face you because of this."

The People's Response

10 While Ezra prayed and made confession, weeping and throwing himself down before the house of God, a very great assembly of men, women, and children gathered to him out of Israel; the people also wept bitter- ly. 2Shecaniah son of Jehiel, of the descendants of Elam, addressed Ezra,

o Heb our God

saying, "We have broken faith with our God and have married foreign women from the peoples of the land, but even now there is hope for Israel in spite of this. ³So now let us make a covenant with our God to send away all these wives and their children, according to the counsel of my lord and of those who tremble at the commandment of our God; and let it be done according to the law. ⁴Take action, for it is your duty, and we are with you; be strong, and do it." ⁵Then Ezra stood up and made the leading priests, the Levites, and all Israel

swear that they would do said. So they swore.

Foreign Wives and Their (
Rejected

6 Then Ezra withdrew fr the house of God, and we chamber of Jehohanan son of where he spent the night.ᵖ He eat bread or drink water, for mourning over the faithlessnes exiles. ⁷They made a proclama throughout Judah and Jerusalem to

p 1 Esdras 9.2: Heb *where he went*

519

ad been

THURSDAY

HOPE EXPECTS . . .
John Calvin

VERSE: Ezra 10.2   **PASSAGE:** Ezra 10.1–4

f faith . . . is a sure persuasion of the truth of God which can neither lie nor deceive us and be neither vain nor false, those who have conceived this certainty surely expect likewise that God will accomplish his promises which, according to their conviction, cannot but be true. So that, in sum, hope is nothing else than the expectation of the things that faith has believed to be truly promised by God. Thus faith believes God to be truthful: Hope expects that he will show his veracity at the opportune time. Faith believes God to be our Father: Hope expects that he will always act as such toward us. Faith believes eternal life to be given to us: Hope expects that it shall at some time be revealed. Faith is the foundation on which hope rests: Hope nourishes and maintains faith. For, just as no one can expect and hope anything from God, except he who will have first believed his promises, so, on the other hand, it is necessary that our feeble faith (lest it grow weary and fail) be sustained and kept by patient hope and expectation.

ADDITIONAL SCRIPTURE READING:
Romans 5.3–5; 2 Thessalonians 2.16–17; Hebrews 10.23

Go to page 526 for your next devotional reading.

1500   1700

520

...med exiles that they should ...at Jerusalem, [8]and that if any ...the ...ome within three days, by order ...of the officials and the elders all their ...ty should be forfeited, and they ...selves banned from the congrega-...of the exiles.

...Then all the people of Judah and ...njamin assembled at Jerusalem with-...the three days; it was the ninth month, on the twentieth day of the month. All the people sat in the open square before the house of God, trembling because of this matter and because of the heavy rain. [10]Then Ezra the priest stood up and said to them, "You have trespassed and married foreign women, and so increased the guilt of Israel. [11]Now make confession to the LORD the God of your ancestors, and do his will; separate yourselves from the peoples of the land and from the foreign wives." [12]Then all the assembly answered with a loud voice, "It is so; we must do as you have said. [13]But the people are many, and it is a time of heavy rain; we cannot stand in the open. Nor is this a task for one day or for two, for many of us have transgressed in this matter. [14]Let our officials represent the whole assembly, and let all in our towns who have taken foreign wives come at appointed times, and with them the elders and judges of every town, until the fierce wrath of our God on this account is averted from us." [15]Only Jonathan son of Asahel and Jahzeiah son of Tikvah opposed this, and Meshullam and Shabbethai the Levites supported them.

16 Then the returned exiles did so. Ezra the priest selected men, [q] heads of families, according to their families, each of them designated by name. On the first day of the tenth month they sat down to examine the matter. [17]By the first day of the first month they had come to the end of all the men who had married foreign women.

18 There were found of the descendants of the priests who had married foreign women, of the descendants of Jeshua son of Jozadak and his brothers: Maaseiah, Eliezer, Jarib, and Gedaliah. [19]They pledged themselves to send away their wives, and their guilt offering was a ram of the flock for their guilt. [20]Of the descendants of Immer: Hanani and Zebadiah. [21]Of the descendants of Harim: Maaseiah, Elijah, Shemaiah, Jehiel, and Uzziah. [22]Of the descendants of Pashhur: Elioenai, Maaseiah, Ishmael, Nethanel, Jozabad, and Elasah.

23 Of the Levites: Jozabad, Shimei, Kelaiah (that is, Kelita), Pethahiah, Judah, and Eliezer. [24]Of the singers: Eliashib. Of the gatekeepers: Shallum, Telem, and Uri.

25 And of Israel: of the descendants of Parosh: Ramiah, Izziah, Malchijah, Mijamin, Eleazar, Hashabiah,[r] and Benaiah. [26]Of the descendants of Elam: Mattaniah, Zechariah, Jehiel, Abdi, Jeremoth, and Elijah. [27]Of the descendants of Zattu: Elioenai, Eliashib, Mattaniah, Jeremoth, Zabad, and Aziza. [28]Of the descendants of Bebai: Jehohanan, Hananiah, Zabbai, and Athlai. [29]Of the descendants of Bani: Meshullam, Malluch, Adaiah, Jashub, Sheal, and Jeremoth. [30]Of the descendants of Pahath-moab: Adna, Chelal, Benaiah, Maaseiah, Mattaniah, Bezalel, Binnui, and Manasseh. [31]Of the descendants of Harim: Eliezer, Isshijah, Malchijah, Shemaiah, Shimeon, [32]Benjamin, Malluch, and Shemariah. [33]Of the descendants of Hashum: Mattenai, Mattattah, Zabad, Eliphelet, Jeremai, Manasseh, and Shimei. [34]Of the descendants of Bani: Maadai, Amram, Uel, [35]Benaiah, Bedeiah, Cheluhi, [36]Vaniah, Meremoth, Eliashib, [37]Mattaniah, Mattenai, and Jaasu. [38]Of the descendants of Binnui:[s] Shimei, [39]Shelemiah, Nathan, Adaiah, [40]Machnadebai, Shashai, Sharai, [41]Azarel, Shelemiah, Shemariah, [42]Shallum, Amariah, and Joseph. [43]Of the descendants of Nebo: Jeiel, Mattithiah, Zabad, Zebina, Jaddai, Joel, and Benaiah. [44]All these had married foreign women, and they sent them away with their children.[t]

---

q 1 Esdras 9.16: Syr: Heb *And there were selected Ezra,*   r 1 Esdras 9.26 Gk: Heb *Malchijah*
s Gk: Heb *Bani, Binnui*   t 1 Esdras 9.36; Meaning of Heb uncertain.

NEHEMIAH

HE BOOK OF NEHEMIAH CONTIN-
UES THE HISTORY OF THE JEWS
WHO RETURNED FROM EXILE IN
BABYLON. NEHEMIAH WENT TO JERUSALEM
IN 445 B.C. AND LED THE PEOPLE IN REPAIR-
ING THE WALLS. WITH EZRA HE PROVIDED
LEADERSHIP FOR THE PEOPLE. A RECURRING
THEME OF THIS BOOK IS THE DESCRIPTION
OF THE IMPORTANCE OF PRAYER TO NEHE-
MIAH. AS YOU READ THIS BOOK, LEARN
FROM NEHEMIAH'S EXAMPLE OF BALANC-
ING SPIRITUALITY WITH DOWN-TO-EARTH
ACTION.

Nehemiah Prays for His People

1 The words of Nehemiah son of Hacaliah. In the month of Chislev, in the twentieth year, while I was in Susa the capital, 2one of my brothers, Hanani, came with certain men from Judah; and I asked them about the Jews that survived, those who had escaped the captivity, and about Jerusalem. 3They replied, "The survivors there in the province who escaped captivity are in great trouble and shame; the wall of Jerusalem is broken down, and its gates have been destroyed by fire."

4 When I heard these words I sat down and wept, and mourned for days, fasting and praying before the God of heaven. 5I said, "O LORD God of heaven, the great and awesome God who keeps covenant and steadfast love with those who love him and keep his commandments; 6let your ear be attentive and your eyes open to hear the prayer of your servant that I now pray before you day and night for your servants, the people of Israel, confessing the sins of the people of Israel, which we have sinned against you. Both I and my family have sinned. 7We have offended you deeply, failing to keep the commandments, the statutes, and the ordinances that you commanded your servant Moses. 8Remember the word that you commanded your servant Moses, 'If you are unfaithful, I will scatter you among the peoples; 9but if you return to me and keep my commandments and do them, though your outcasts are under the farthest skies, I will gather them from there and bring them to the place at

522

have chosen to establish my which [people], whom you redeemed by [great] power and your strong hand. [Lord], let your ear be attentive to the [prayer] of your servant, and to the prayer [of y]our servants who delight in revering [yo]ur name. Give success to your servant [to]day, and grant him mercy in the sight [o]f this man!"

At the time, I was cupbearer to the king.

MORE THINGS ARE WROUGHT BY PRAYER THAN THIS WORLD DREAMS OF. —*Alfred, Lord Tennyson*

Nehemiah Sent to Judah

2 In the month of Nisan, in the twentieth year of King Artaxerxes, when wine was served him, I carried the wine and gave it to the king. Now, I had never been sad in his presence before. ²So the king said to me, "Why is your face sad, since you are not sick? This can only be sadness of the heart." Then I was very much afraid. ³I said to the king, "May the king live forever! Why should my face not be sad, when the city, the place of my ancestors' graves, lies waste, and its gates have been destroyed by fire?" ⁴Then the king said to me, "What do you request?" So I prayed to the God of heaven. ⁵Then I said to the king, "If it pleases the king, and if your servant has found favor with you, I ask that you send me to Judah, to the city of my ancestors' graves, so that I may rebuild it." ⁶The king said to me (the queen also was sitting beside him), "How long will you be gone, and when will you return?" So it pleased the king to send me, and I set him a date. ⁷Then I said to the king, "If it pleases the king, let letters be given me to the governors of the province Beyond the River, that they may grant me passage until I arrive in Judah; ⁸and a letter to Asaph, the keeper of the king's forest, directing him to give me timber to make beams for the gates of the temple fortress, and for the wall of the city, and for the house that I shall occupy." And the king granted me what I asked, for the gracious hand of my God was upon me.

⁹Then I came to the governors of the province Beyond the River, and gave them the king's letters. Now the king had sent officers of the army and cavalry with me. ¹⁰When Sanballat the Horonite and Tobiah the Ammonite official heard this, it displeased them greatly that someone had come to seek the welfare of the people of Israel.

Nehemiah's Inspection of the Walls

11 So I came to Jerusalem and was there for three days. ¹²Then I got up during the night, I and a few men with me; I told no one what my God had put into my heart to do for Jerusalem. The only animal I took was the animal I rode. ¹³I went out by night by the Valley Gate past the Dragon's Spring and to the Dung Gate, and I inspected the walls of Jerusalem that had been broken down and its gates that had been destroyed by fire. ¹⁴Then I went on to the Fountain Gate and to the King's Pool; but there was no place for the animal I was riding to continue. ¹⁵So I went up by way of the valley by night and inspected the wall. Then I turned back and entered by the Valley Gate, and so returned. ¹⁶The officials did not know where I had gone or what I was doing; I had not yet told the Jews, the priests, the nobles, the officials, and the rest that were to do the work.

Decision to Restore the Walls

17 Then I said to them, "You see the trouble we are in, how Jerusalem lies in ruins with its gates burned. Come, let us rebuild the wall of Jerusalem, so that we may no longer suffer disgrace." ¹⁸I told them that the hand of my God had been gracious upon me, and also the words that the king had spoken to me. Then they said, "Let us start building!" So they committed themselves to the common good. ¹⁹But when Sanballat the Horonite and Tobiah the Ammonite official, and Geshem the Arab heard of it, they mocked and ridiculed us, saying, "What is this that you are doing? Are you rebelling against the king?" ²⁰Then I replied to them, "The God of heaven is the one who will give us success, and we his servants are going to start building;

but you have no share or claim or historic right in Jerusalem."

Organization of the Work

3 Then the high priest Eliashib set to work with his fellow priests and rebuilt the Sheep Gate. They consecrated it and set up its doors; they consecrated it as far as the Tower of the Hundred and as far as the Tower of Hananel. 2And the men of Jericho built next to him. And next to them*a* Zaccur son of Imri built.

3 The sons of Hassenaah built the Fish Gate; they laid its beams and set up its doors, its bolts, and its bars. 4Next to them Meremoth son of Uriah son of Hakkoz made repairs. Next to them Meshullam son of Berechiah son of Meshezabel made repairs. Next to them Zadok son of Baana made repairs. 5Next to them the Tekoites made repairs; but their nobles would not put their shoulders to the work of their Lord.*b*

6 Joiada son of Paseah and Meshullam son of Besodeiah repaired the Old Gate; they laid its beams and set up its doors, its bolts, and its bars. 7Next to them repairs were made by Melatiah the Gibeonite and Jadon the Meronothite— the men of Gibeon and of Mizpah—who were under the jurisdiction of*c* the governor of the province Beyond the River. 8Next to them Uzziel son of Harhaiah, one of the goldsmiths, made repairs. Next to him Hananiah, one of the perfumers, made repairs; and they restored Jerusalem as far as the Broad Wall. 9Next to them Rephaiah son of Hur, ruler of half the district of*d* Jerusalem, made repairs. 10Next to them Jedaiah son of Harumaph made repairs opposite his house; and next to him Hattush son of Hashabneiah made repairs. 11Malchijah son of Harim and Hasshub son of Pahath-moab repaired another section and the Tower of the Ovens. 12Next to him Shallum son of Hallohesh, ruler of half the district of*d* Jerusalem, made repairs, he and his daughters.

13 Hanun and the inhabitants of Zanoah repaired the Valley Gate; they rebuilt it and set up its doors, its bolts,

and its bars, and repaired ̶ ̶ ̶ ̶ cubits of the wall, as far a̶ ̶ ̶ ̶ Gate.

14 Malchijah son of Recl ̶ ̶ ̶ the district of*e* Beth-hacchere̶ ̶ ̶ the Dung Gate; he rebuilt it̶ ̶ ̶ its doors, its bolts, and its ba̶ ̶ ̶

15 And Shallum son of C̶ ̶ ̶ ruler of the district of*e* Mizpa̶ ̶ ̶ the Fountain Gate; he rebuilt i̶ ̶ ̶ ered it and set up its doors, its̶ ̶ ̶ its bars; and he built the wall o̶ ̶ ̶ of Shelah of the king's garden, ̶ ̶ ̶ the stairs that go down from the ̶ ̶ ̶ David. 16After him Nehemiah s̶ ̶ ̶ Azbuk, ruler of half the district of*d* Be̶ ̶ ̶ zur, repaired from a point opposite th̶ ̶ ̶ graves of David, as far as the artificial̶ ̶ ̶ pool and the house of the warriors. 17After him the Levites made repairs: Rehum son of Bani; next to him Hashabiah, ruler of half the district of*d* Keilah, made repairs for his district. 18After him their kin made repairs: Binnui,*f* son of Henadad, ruler of half the district of*d* Keilah; 19next to him Ezer son of Jeshua, ruler*g* of Mizpah, repaired another section opposite the ascent to the armory at the Angle. 20After him Baruch son of Zabbai repaired another section from the Angle to the door of the house of the high priest Eliashib. 21After him Meremoth son of Uriah son of Hakkoz repaired another section from the door of the house of Eliashib to the end of the house of Eliashib. 22After him the priests, the men of the surrounding area, made repairs. 23After them Benjamin and Hasshub made repairs opposite their house. After them Azariah son of Maaseiah son of Ananiah made repairs beside his own house. 24After him Binnui son of Henadad repaired another section, from the house of Azariah to the Angle and to the corner. 25Palal son of Uzai repaired opposite the Angle and the tower projecting from the upper house of the king at the court of the guard. After him Pedaiah son of Parosh 26and the temple servants living*h* on Ophel made repairs up to a point opposite the Water Gate on the east and the projecting tower. 27After him the Tekoites

---

a Heb *him*   *b* Or *lords*   *c* Meaning of Heb uncertain   *d* Or *supervisor of half the portion*
assigned to   *e* Or *supervisor of the portion assigned to*   *f* Gk Syr Compare verse 24, 10.9: Heb
Bavvai   *g* Or *supervisor*   *h* Cn: Heb *were living*

nother section opposite the projecting tower as far as the wall

...ove the Horse Gate the priests ...pairs, each one opposite his own [ ]29After them Zadok son of Immer repairs opposite his own house. ... him Shemaiah son of Shecaniah, ...keeper of the East Gate, made repairs. ...fter him Hananiah son of Shelemiah ...d Hanun sixth son of Zalaph repaired ...nother section. After him Meshullam ...on of Berechiah made repairs opposite ...his living quarters. 31After him Malchi-jah, one of the goldsmiths, made repairs as far as the house of the temple servants and of the merchants, opposite the Muster Gate, i and to the upper room of the corner. 32And between the upper room of the corner and the Sheep Gate the goldsmiths and the merchants made repairs.

Hostile Plots Thwarted

4 j Now when Sanballat heard that we were building the wall, he was angry and greatly enraged, and he mocked the Jews. 2He said in the presence of his associates and of the army of Samaria, "What are these feeble Jews doing? Will they restore things? Will they sacrifice? Will they finish it in a day? Will they revive the stones out of the heaps of rubbish—and burned ones at that?" 3Tobiah the Ammonite was beside him, and he said, "That stone wall they are building—any fox going up on it would break it down!" 4Hear, O our God, for we are despised; turn their taunt back on their own heads, and give them over as plunder in a land of captivity. 5Do not cover their guilt, and do not let their sin be blotted out from your sight; for they have hurled insults in the face of the builders.

6 So we rebuilt the wall, and all the wall was joined together to half its height; for the people had a mind to work.

7k But when Sanballat and Tobiah and the Arabs and the Ammonites and the Ashdodites heard that the repairing of the walls of Jerusalem was going forward and the gaps were beginning to be

closed, they were very angry, 8and all plotted together to come and fight against Jerusalem and to cause confusion in it. 9So we prayed to our God, and set a guard as a protection against them day and night.

10 But Judah said, "The strength of the burden bearers is failing, and there is too much rubbish so that we are unable to work on the wall." 11And our enemies said, "They will not know or see anything before we come upon them and kill them and stop the work." 12When the Jews who lived near them came, they said to us ten times, "From all the places where they live l they will come up against us."m 13So in the lowest parts of the space behind the wall, in open places, I stationed the people according to their families, n with their swords, their spears, and their bows. 14After I looked these things over, I stood up and said to the nobles and the officials and the rest of the people, "Do not be afraid of them. Remember the LORD, who is great and awesome, and fight for your kin, your sons, your daughters, your wives, and your homes."

15 When our enemies heard that their plot was known to us, and that God had frustrated it, we all returned to the wall, each to his work. 16From that day on, half of my servants worked on construction, and half held the spears, shields, bows, and body-armor; and the leaders posted themselves behind the whole house of Judah, 17who were building the wall. The burden bearers carried their loads in such a way that each labored on the work with one hand and with the other held a weapon. 18And each of the builders had his sword strapped at his side while he built. The man who sounded the trumpet was beside me. 19And I said to the nobles, the officials, and the rest of the people, "The work is great and widely spread out, and we are separated far from one another on the wall. 20Rally to us wherever you hear the sound of the trumpet. Our God will fight for us."

21 So we labored at the work, and half of them held the spears from break of dawn until the stars came out. 22I also said to the people at that time, "Let

i Or Hammiphkad Gate   j Ch 3.33 in Heb   k Ch 4.1 in Heb   l Cn: Heb you return
m Compare Gk Syr: Meaning of Heb uncertain   n Meaning of Heb uncertain

every man and his servant pass the night inside Jerusalem, so that they may be a guard for us by night and may labor by day." 23So neither I nor my brothers nor my servants nor the men of the guard who followed me ever took off our clothes; each kept his weapon in his right hand.o

Nehemiah Deals with Oppression

5 Now there was a great outcry of the people and of their wives against their Jewish kin. 2For there were those who said, "With our sons and our daughters, we are many; we must get grain, so that we may eat and stay alive." 3There were also those who said, "We are having to pledge our fields, our vineyards, and our houses in order to get grain during the famine." 4And there were those who said, "We are having to borrow money on our fields and vineyards to pay the king's tax. 5Now our flesh is the same as that of our kindred; our children are the same as their children; and yet we are forcing our sons and daughters to be slaves, and some of our daughters have been ravished; we are powerless, and our fields and vineyards now belong to others."

6 I was very angry when I heard their outcry and these complaints. 7After thinking it over, I brought charges against the nobles and the officials; I said to them, "You are all taking interest from your own people." And I called a great assembly to deal with them, 8and said to them, "As far as we were able, we have bought back our Jewish kindred who had been sold to other nations; but now you are selling your own kin, who must then be bought back by us!" They were silent, and could not find a word to say. 9So I said, "The thing that you are doing is not good. Should you not walk in the fear of our God, to prevent the taunts of the nations our enemies? 10Moreover I and my brothers and my servants are lending them money and grain. Let us stop this taking of interest. 11Restore to them, this very day, their fields, their vineyards, their olive orchards, and their houses, and the interest on money, grain, wine, and oil that you have been exacting from them."

12Then they said, "We will restore everything and demand nothing more from them. We will do as you require." And I called the priests, and made them take an oath to do as they had promised. 13I also shook out the fold of my garment and said, "So may God shake out everyone from house and from property who does not perform this promise. Thus may they be shaken out and emptied." And all the assembly said, "Amen," and praised the LORD. And the people did as they had promised.

The Generosity of Nehemiah

14 Moreover from the time that I was appointed to be their governor in the land of Judah, from the twentieth year to the thirty-second year of King Artaxerxes, twelve years, neither I nor my brothers ate the food allowance of the governor. 15The former governors who were before me laid heavy burdens on the people, and took food and wine from them, besides forty shekels of silver. Even their servants lorded it over the people. But I did not do so, because of the fear of God. 16Indeed, I devoted myself to the work on this wall, and acquired no land; and all my servants were gathered there for the work. 17Moreover there were at my table one hundred fifty people, Jews and officials, besides those who came to us from the nations around us. 18Now that which was prepared for one day was one ox and six choice sheep; also fowls were prepared for me, and every ten days skins of wine in abundance; yet with all this I did not demand the food allowance of the governor, because of the heavy burden of labor on the people. 19Remember for my good, O my God, all that I have done for this people.

Intrigues of Enemies Foiled

6 Now when it was reported to Sanballat and Tobiah and to Geshem the Arab and to the rest of our enemies that I had built the wall and that there was no gap left in it (though up to that time I had not set up the doors in the gates), 2Sanballat and Geshem sent to me, saying, "Come and let us meet together in one of the villages in

o Cn: Heb each his weapon the water

526

f Ono." But they intended to the p rm. ³So I sent messengers to do ying, "I am doing a great work k nnot come down. Why should k stop while I leave it to come to you?" ⁴They sent to me four in this way, and I answered them e same manner. ⁵In the same way allat for the fifth time sent his ser- t to me with an open letter in his d. ⁶In it was written, "It is reported nong the nations—and Geshem*p* also ys it—that you and the Jews intend to ebel; that is why you are building the wall; and according to this report you wish to become their king. ⁷You have also set up prophets to proclaim in Jerusalem concerning you, 'There is a king in Judah!' And now it will be reported to the king according to these words. So come, therefore, and let us confer together." ⁸Then I sent to him, saying, "No such things as you say have been done; you are inventing them out of your own mind" ⁹—for they all wanted to frighten us, thinking, "Their hands will drop from the work, and it will not be done." But now, O God, strengthen my hands.

p Heb *Gashmu*

FRIDAY

THE STRENGTH OF WEAKNESS
Oswald Chambers

VERSE: Nehemiah 6.9   **PASSAGE:** Nehemiah 6.9–16

 e was crucified in weakness" (2 Corinthians 13.4). Jesus Christ represents God limiting his own power for one purpose: he died for the weak, for the ungodly, for sinners, and for no one else. "I have come to call not the righteous but sinners to repentance" (Luke 5.32).

The "strong man" idea is the one that appeals to men, the strong man physically, morally, strong in every way; the kingdoms of men are to be founded on strong men and the weakest are to go to the wall. History proves, however, that it is the strongest that go to the wall, not the weakest.

In all trade and commerce there is oppression, and we try to justify it by saying that the weakest must go to the wall. But is that so? Where are the mighty civilizations of other days? Where are the prehistoric animals, those colossal powerful creatures? It is they that have gone to the wall. The great blunder in all kingdoms among men is that we will demand strong men, consequently, each kingdom in its turn goes to the wall because no chain is stronger than its weakest link.

ADDITIONAL SCRIPTURE READING:
Luke 5.30–32; 2 Corinthians 12.9–10; 13.3–4

Go to page 528 for your next devotional reading.

1900   Present

10 One day when I went into the house of Shemaiah son of Delaiah son of Mehetabel, who was confined to his house, he said, "Let us meet together in the house of God, within the temple, and let us close the doors of the temple, for they are coming to kill you; indeed, tonight they are coming to kill you." 11But I said, "Should a man like me run away? Would a man like me go into the temple to save his life? I will not go in!" 12Then I perceived and saw that God had not sent him at all, but he had pronounced the prophecy against me because Tobiah and Sanballat had hired him. 13He was hired for this purpose, to intimidate me and make me sin by acting in this way, and so they could give me a bad name, in order to taunt me. 14Remember Tobiah and Sanballat, O my God, according to these things that they did, and also the prophetess Noadiah and the rest of the prophets who wanted to make me afraid.

The Wall Completed

15 So the wall was finished on the twenty-fifth day of the month Elul, in fifty-two days. 16And when all our enemies heard of it, all the nations around us were afraid*q* and fell greatly in their own esteem; for they perceived that this work had been accomplished with the help of our God. 17Moreover in those days the nobles of Judah sent many letters to Tobiah, and Tobiah's letters came to them. 18For many in Judah were bound by oath to him, because he was the son-in-law of Shecaniah son of Arah: and his son Jehohanan had married the daughter of Meshullam son of Berechiah. 19Also they spoke of his good deeds in my presence, and reported my words to him. And Tobiah sent letters to intimidate me.

7 Now when the wall had been built and I had set up the doors, and the gatekeepers, the singers, and the Levites had been appointed, 2I gave my brother Hanani charge over Jerusalem, along with Hananiah the commander of the citadel—for he was a faithful man and feared God more than many. 3And I said to them, "The gates of Jerusalem are not to be opened until the sun is hot;

while the gatekeepers*r* are still standing guard, let them shut and bar the doors. Appoint guards from among the inhabitants of Jerusalem, some at their watch posts, and others before their own houses." 4The city was wide and large, but the people within it were few and no houses had been built.

Lists of the Returned Exiles

5 Then my God put it into my mind to assemble the nobles and the officials and the people to be enrolled by genealogy. And I found the book of the genealogy of those who were the first to come back, and I found the following written in it:

6 These are the people of the province who came up out of the captivity of those exiles whom King Nebuchadnezzar of Babylon had carried into exile; they returned to Jerusalem and Judah, each to his town. 7They came with Zerubbabel, Jeshua, Nehemiah, Azariah, Raamiah, Nahamani, Mordecai, Bilshan, Mispereth, Bigvai, Nehum, Baanah.

The number of the Israelite people: 8the descendants of Parosh, two thousand one hundred seventy-two. 9Of Shephatiah, three hundred seventy-two. 10Of Arah, six hundred fifty-two. 11Of Pahath-moab, namely the descendants of Jeshua and Joab, two thousand eight hundred eighteen. 12Of Elam, one thousand two hundred fifty-four. 13Of Zattu, eight hundred forty-five. 14Of Zaccai, seven hundred sixty. 15Of Binnui, six hundred forty-eight. 16Of Bebai, six hundred twenty-eight. 17Of Azgad, two thousand three hundred twenty-two. 18Of Adonikam, six hundred sixty-seven. 19Of Bigvai, two thousand sixty-seven. 20Of Adin, six hundred fifty-five. 21Of Ater, namely of Hezekiah, ninety-eight. 22Of Hashum, three hundred twenty-eight. 23Of Bezai, three hundred twenty-four. 24Of Hariph, one hundred twelve. 25Of Gibeon, ninety-five. 26The people of Bethlehem and Netophah, one hundred eighty-eight. 27Of Anathoth, one hundred twenty-eight. 28Of Beth-azmaveth, forty-two. 29Of Kiriath-jearim, Chephirah, and Beeroth, seven hundred forty-three. 30Of Ramah and Geba, six hundred twenty-one. 31Of Michmas,

---

q Another reading is *saw*   *r* Heb *while they*

WEEKEND

O FOR A THOUSAND TONGUES TO SING!
Charles Wesley

VERSE: Psalm 19.1   PASSAGE: Psalm 19.1–4

 for a thousand tongues to sing
My dear Redeemer's praise,
The glories of my God and King,
The triumphs of his grace!

My gracious Master and my God,
Assist me to proclaim
And spread through all the earth abroad
The honors of thy name.

Jesus! the name that charms our fears
And bids our sorrows cease;
'Tis music in the sinner's ears,
'Tis life and health and peace.

ADDITIONAL SCRIPTURE READING:
Psalms 35.28; 104.33–34

Go to page 531 for your next devotional reading.

one hundred twenty-two. 32Of Bethel and Ai, one hundred twenty-three. 33Of the other Nebo, fifty-two. 34The descendants of the other Elam, one thousand two hundred fifty-four. 35Of Harim, three hundred twenty. 36Of Jericho, three hundred forty-five. 37Of Lod, Hadid, and Ono, seven hundred twenty-one. 38Of Senaah, three thousand nine hundred thirty.

39 The priests: the descendants of Jedaiah, namely the house of Jeshua, nine hundred seventy-three. 40Of Immer, one thousand fifty-two. 41Of Pashhur, one thousand two hundred forty-seven. 42Of Harim, one thousand seventeen.

43 The Levites: the descendants of Jeshua, namely of Kadmiel of the descendants of Hodevah, seventy-four. 44The singers: the descendants of Asaph, one hundred forty-eight. 45The gate-keepers: the descendants of Shallum, of Ater, of Talmon, of Akkub, of Hatita, of Shobai, one hundred thirty-eight.

46 The temple servants: the descendants of Ziha, of Hasupha, of Tabbaoth, 47of Keros, of Sia, of Padon, 48of Lebana, of Hagaba, of Shalmai, 49of Hanan, of Giddel, of Gahar, 50of Reaiah, of Rezin, of Nekoda, 51of Gazzam, of Uzza, of Paseah, 52of Besai, of Meunim, of Nephushesim, 53of Bakbuk, of Hakupha, of Harhur, 54of Bazlith, of Mehida, of Harsha, 55of Barkos, of Sisera, of Temah, 56of Neziah, of Hatipha.

57 The descendants of Solomon's servants: of Sotai, of Sophereth, of Perida, 58of Jaala, of Darkon, of Giddel, 59of Shephatiah, of Hattil, of Pochereth-hazzebaim, of Amon.

60 All the temple servants and the descendants of Solomon's servants were three hundred ninety-two.

61 The following were those who came up from Tel-melah, Tel-harsha, Cherub, Addon, and Immer, but they could not prove their ancestral houses or their descent, whether they belonged to Israel: 62the descendants of Delaiah, of Tobiah, of Nekoda, six hundred forty-two. 63Also, of the priests: the descendants of Hobaiah, of Hakkoz, of Barzillai (who had married one of the daughters of Barzillai the Gileadite and was called by their name). 64These sought their reg-istration among those enrolled in the genealogies, but it was not found there, so they were excluded from the priesthood as unclean; 65the governor told them that they were not to partake of the most holy food, until a priest with Urim and Thummim should come.

66 The whole assembly together was forty-two thousand three hundred sixty, 67besides their male and female slaves, of whom there were seven thousand three hundred thirty-seven; and they had two hundred forty-five singers, male and female. 68They had seven hundred thirty-six horses, two hundred forty-five mules, *s* 69four hundred thirty-five camels, and six thousand seven hundred twenty donkeys.

70 Now some of the heads of ancestral houses contributed to the work. The governor gave to the treasury one thousand darics of gold, fifty basins, and five hundred thirty priestly robes. 71And some of the heads of ancestral houses gave into the building fund twenty thousand darics of gold and two thousand two hundred minas of silver. 72And what the rest of the people gave was twenty thousand darics of gold, two thousand minas of silver, and sixty-seven priestly robes.

73 So the priests, the Levites, the gatekeepers, the singers, some of the people, the temple servants, and all Israel settled in their towns.

Ezra Summons the People to Obey the Law

When the seventh month came—the people of Israel being settled in their towns— **8** 1all the people gathered together into the square before the Water Gate. They told the scribe Ezra to bring the book of the law of Moses, which the LORD had given to Israel. 2Accordingly, the priest Ezra brought the law before the assembly, both men and women and all who could hear with understanding. This was on the first day of the seventh month. 3He read from it facing the square before the Water Gate from early morning until midday, in the presence of the men and the women and those who could understand; and the ears of all the people were attentive to

---

s Ezra 2.66 and the margins of some Hebrew Mss: MT lacks *They had . . . forty-five mules*

the book of the law. 4The scribe Ezra stood on a wooden platform that had

---

THE BIBLE WAS NEVER INTENDED TO BE A BOOK FOR SCHOLARS AND SPECIALISTS ONLY. FROM THE VERY BEGINNING IT WAS INTENDED TO BE EVERYBODY'S BOOK, AND THAT IS WHAT IT CONTINUES TO BE.
—F. F. Bruce

---

been made for the purpose; and beside him stood Mattithiah, Shema, Anaiah, Uriah, Hilkiah, and Maaseiah on his right hand; and Pedaiah, Mishael, Malchijah, Hashum, Hash-baddanah, Zechariah, and Meshullam on his left hand. 5And Ezra opened the book in the sight of all the people, for he was standing above all the people; and when he opened it, all the people stood up. 6Then Ezra blessed the LORD, the great God, and all the people answered, "Amen, Amen," lifting up their hands. Then they bowed their heads and worshiped the LORD with their faces to the ground. 7Also Jeshua, Bani, Sherebiah, Jamin, Akkub, Shabbethai, Hodiah, Maaseiah, Kelita, Azariah, Jozabad, Hanan, Pelaiah, the Levites,*t* helped the people to understand the law, while the people remained in their places. 8So they read from the book, from the law of God, with interpretation. They gave the sense, so that the people understood the reading.

9 And Nehemiah, who was the governor, and Ezra the priest and scribe, and the Levites who taught the people said to all the people, "This day is holy to the LORD your God; do not mourn or weep." For all the people wept when they heard the words of the law. 10Then he said to them, "Go your way, eat the fat and drink sweet wine and send portions of them to those for whom nothing is prepared, for this day is holy to our LORD; and do not be grieved, for the joy of the LORD is your strength." 11So the Levites stilled all the people, saying, "Be quiet, for this day is holy; do not be grieved." 12And all the people went their way to eat and drink and to send portions and to make great rejoicing, because they had understood the words that were declared to them.

The Festival of Booths Celebrated

13 On the second day the heads of ancestral houses of all the people, with the priests and the Levites, came together to the scribe Ezra in order to study the words of the law. 14And they found it written in the law, which the LORD had commanded by Moses, that the people of Israel should live in booths*u* during the festival of the seventh month, 15and that they should publish and proclaim in all their towns and in Jerusalem as follows, "Go out to the hills and bring branches of olive, wild olive, myrtle, palm, and other leafy trees to make booths,*u* as it is written." 16So the people went out and brought them, and made booths*u* for themselves, each on the roofs of their houses, and in their courts and in the courts of the house of God, and in the square at the Water Gate and in the square at the Gate of Ephraim. 17And all the assembly of those who had returned from the captivity made booths*u* and lived in them; for from the days of Jeshua son of Nun to that day the people of Israel had not done so. And there was very great rejoicing. 18And day by day, from the first day to the last day, he read from the book of the law of God. They kept the festival seven days; and on the eighth day there was a solemn assembly, according to the ordinance.

National Confession

9 Now on the twenty-fourth day of this month the people of Israel were assembled with fasting and in sackcloth, and with earth on their heads.*v* 2Then those of Israelite descent separated themselves from all foreigners, and stood and confessed their sins and the iniquities of their ancestors. 3They stood up in their place and read from the book of the law of the LORD their God for a fourth part of the day, and for another fourth they made confession and worshiped the LORD their God. 4Then Jeshua, Bani, Kadmiel, Shebaniah, Bunni, Sherebiah, Bani, and Chenani stood on the stairs of the Levites and cried out with a loud voice to the LORD their God. 5Then the Levites, Jeshua, Kadmiel, Bani, Hashab-

---

t 1 Esdras 9.48 Vg: Heb *and the Levites*   *u* Or *tabernacles;* Heb *succoth*   *v* Heb *on them* neiah, Sherebiah, Hodiah, Shebaniah, and Pethahiah, said, "Stand up and bless the LORD your God from everlasting to everlasting. Blessed be your glorious name, which is exalted above all blessing and praise."

6 And Ezra said: w "You are the LORD, you alone; you have made heaven, the heaven of heavens, with all their host, the earth and all that is on it, the seas and all that is in them. To all of them you give life, and the host of heaven worships you. 7You are the LORD, the God who chose Abram and brought him out of Ur of the Chaldeans and gave him the name Abraham; 8and you found his heart faithful before you, and made with him a covenant to give to his descen-

dants the land of the Canaanite, the Hittite, the Amorite, the Perizzite, the Jebusite, and the Girgashite; and you have fulfilled your promise, for you are righteous.

9 "And you saw the distress of our ancestors in Egypt and heard their cry at the Red Sea. x 10You performed signs and wonders against Pharaoh and all his servants and all the people of his land, for you knew that they acted insolently against our ancestors. You made a name for yourself, which remains to this day. 11And you divided the sea before them, so that they passed through the sea on dry land, but you threw their pursuers into the depths, like a stone into mighty waters. 12Moreover, you led them by day

w Gk: Heb lacks *And Ezra said*   x Or *Sea of Reeds*

MONDAY

INNER INVINCIBILITY
Oswald Chambers

VERSE: Nehemiah 8.10   PASSAGE: Nehemiah 8.2–12

he joy of the LORD is your strength." Where do the saints get their joy? If we did not know some Christians well, we might think from just observing them that they have no burdens at all to bear. But we must lift the veil from our eyes. The fact that the peace, light, and joy of God is in them is proof that a burden is there as well. The burden that God places on us squeezes the grapes in our lives and produces the wine, but most of us see only the wine and not the burden. No power on earth or in hell can conquer the Spirit of God living within the human spirit; it creates an inner invincibility.

If your life is producing only a whine, instead of the wine, then ruthlessly kick it out. It is definitely a crime for a Christian to be weak in God's strength.

ADDITIONAL SCRIPTURE READING:
Psalm 28.7–8; Isaiah 12.1–3

Go to page 541 for your next devotional reading.

1900   Present

with a pillar of cloud, and by night with a pillar of fire, to give them light on the way in which they should go. 13 You came down also upon Mount Sinai, and spoke with them from heaven, and gave them right ordinances and true laws, good statutes and commandments, 14 and you made known your holy sabbath to them and gave them commandments and statutes and a law through your servant Moses. 15 For their hunger you gave them bread from heaven, and for their thirst you brought water for them out of the rock, and you told them to go in to possess the land that you swore to give them.

16 "But they and our ancestors acted presumptuously and stiffened their necks and did not obey your commandments; 17 they refused to obey, and were not mindful of the wonders that you performed among them; but they stiffened their necks and determined to return to their slavery in Egypt. But you are a God ready to forgive, gracious and merciful, slow to anger and abounding in steadfast love, and you did not forsake them. 18 Even when they had cast an image of a calf for themselves and said, 'This is your God who brought you up out of Egypt,' and had committed great blasphemies, 19 you in your great mercies did not forsake them in the wilderness; the pillar of cloud that led them in the way did not leave them by day, nor the pillar of fire by night that gave them light on the way by which they should go. 20 You gave your good spirit to instruct them, and did not withhold your manna from their mouths, and gave them water for their thirst. 21 Forty years you sustained them in the wilderness so that they lacked nothing; their clothes did not wear out and their feet did not swell. 22 And you gave them kingdoms and peoples, and allotted to them every corner, y so they took possession of the land of King Sihon of Heshbon and the land of King Og of Bashan. 23 You multiplied their descendants like the stars of heaven, and brought them into the land that you had told their ancestors to enter and possess. 24 So the descendants went in and possessed the land, and you subdued before them the inhabitants of the land,

the Canaanites, and gave them into their hands, with their kings and the peoples of the land, to do with them as they pleased. 25 And they captured fortress cities and a rich land, and took possession of houses filled with all sorts of goods, hewn cisterns, vineyards, olive orchards, and fruit trees in abundance; so they ate, and were filled and became fat, and delighted themselves in your great goodness.

26 "Nevertheless they were disobedient and rebelled against you and cast your law behind their backs and killed your prophets, who had warned them in order to turn them back to you, and they committed great blasphemies. 27 Therefore you gave them into the hands of their enemies, who made them suffer. Then in the time of their suffering they cried out to you and you heard them from heaven, and according to your great mercies you gave them saviors who saved them from the hands of their enemies. 28 But after they had rest, they again did evil before you, and you abandoned them to the hands of their enemies, so that they had dominion over them; yet when they turned and cried to you, you heard from heaven, and many times you rescued them according to your mercies. 29 And you warned them in order to turn them back to your law. Yet they acted presumptuously and did not obey your commandments, but sinned against your ordinances, by the observance of which a person shall live. They turned a stubborn shoulder and stiffened their neck and would not obey. 30 Many years you were patient with them, and warned them by your spirit through your prophets; yet they would not listen. Therefore you handed them over to the peoples of the lands. 31 Nevertheless, in your great mercies you did not make an end of them or forsake them, for you are a gracious and merciful God.

32 "Now therefore, our God—the great and mighty and awesome God, keeping covenant and steadfast love—do not treat lightly all the hardship that has come upon us, upon our kings, our officials, our priests, our prophets, our ancestors, and all your people, since the time of the kings of Assyria until today.

y Meaning of Heb uncertain

33You have been just in all that has come upon us, for you have dealt faithfully and we have acted wickedly; 34our kings, our officials, our priests, and our ancestors have not kept your law or heeded the commandments and the warnings that you gave them. 35Even in their own kingdom, and in the great goodness you bestowed on them, and in the large and rich land that you set before them, they did not serve you and did not turn from their wicked works. 36Here we are, slaves to this day—slaves in the land that you gave to our ancestors to enjoy its fruit and its good gifts. 37Its rich yield goes to the kings whom you have set over us because of our sins; they have power also over our bodies and over our livestock at their pleasure, and we are in great distress."

Those Who Signed the Covenant

38z Because of all this we make a firm agreement in writing, and on that sealed document are inscribed the names of our officials, our Levites, and our priests.

10 a Upon the sealed document are the names of Nehemiah the governor, son of Hacaliah, and Zedekiah; 2Seraiah, Azariah, Jeremiah, 3Pashhur, Amariah, Malchijah, 4Hattush, Shebaniah, Malluch, 5Harim, Meremoth; Obadiah, 6Daniel, Ginnethon, Baruch, 7Meshullam, Abijah, Mijamin, 8Maaziah, Bilgai, Shemaiah; these are the priests. 9And the Levites: Jeshua son of Azaniah, Binnui of the sons of Henadad, Kadmiel; 10and their associates, Shebaniah, Hodiah, Kelita, Pelaiah, Hanan, 11Mica, Rehob, Hashabiah, 12Zaccur, Sherebiah, Shebaniah, 13Hodiah, Bani, Beninu. 14The leaders of the people: Parosh, Pahath-moab, Elam, Zattu, Bani, 15Bunni, Azgad, Bebai, 16Adonijah, Bigvai, Adin, 17Ater, Hezekiah, Azzur, 18Hodiah, Hashum, Bezai, 19Hariph, Anathoth, Nebai, 20Magpiash, Meshullam, Hezir, 21Meshezabel, Zadok, Jaddua, 22Pelatiah, Hanan, Anaiah, 23Hoshea, Hananiah, Hasshub, 24Hallohesh, Pilha, Shobek, 25Rehum, Hashabnah, Maaseiah, 26Ahiah, Hanan, Anan, 27Malluch, Harim, and Baanah.

Summary of the Covenant

28 The rest of the people, the priests, the Levites, the gatekeepers, the singers, the temple servants, and all who have separated themselves from the peoples of the lands to adhere to the law of God, their wives, their sons, their daughters, all who have knowledge and understanding, 29join with their kin, their nobles, and enter into a curse and an oath to walk in God's law, which was given by Moses the servant of God, and to observe and do all the commandments of the LORD our Lord and his ordinances and his statutes. 30We will not give our daughters to the peoples of the land or take their daughters for our sons; 31and if the peoples of the land bring in merchandise or any grain on the sabbath day to sell, we will not buy it from them on the sabbath or on a holy day; and we will forego the crops of the seventh year and the exaction of every debt.

32 We also lay on ourselves the obligation to charge ourselves yearly one-third of a shekel for the service of the house of our God: 33for the rows of bread, the regular grain offering, the regular burnt offering, the sabbaths, the new moons, the appointed festivals, the sacred donations, and the sin offerings to make atonement for Israel, and for all the work of the house of our God. 34We have also cast lots among the priests, the Levites, and the people, for the wood offering, to bring it into the house of our God, by ancestral houses, at appointed times, year by year, to burn on the altar of the LORD our God, as it is written in the law. 35We obligate ourselves to bring the first fruits of our soil and the first fruits of all fruit of every tree, year by year, to the house of the LORD; 36also to bring to the house of our God, to the priests who minister in the house of our God, the firstborn of our sons and of our livestock, as it is written in the law, and the firstlings of our herds and of our flocks; 37and to bring the first of our dough, and our contributions, the fruit of every tree, the wine and the oil, to the priests, to the chambers of the house of our God; and to bring to the Levites the tithes from our soil, for it is the Levites who collect the tithes in all our rural

z Ch 10.1 in Heb   a Ch 10.2 in Heb

towns. 38And the priest, the descendant of Aaron, shall be with the Levites when the Levites receive the tithes; and the Levites shall bring up a tithe of the tithes to the house of our God, to the chambers of the storehouse. 39For the people of Israel and the sons of Levi shall bring the contribution of grain, wine, and oil to the storerooms where the vessels of the sanctuary are, and where the priests that minister, and the gatekeepers and the singers are. We will not neglect the house of our God.

Population of the City Increased

11 Now the leaders of the people lived in Jerusalem; and the rest of the people cast lots to bring one out of ten to live in the holy city Jerusalem, while nine-tenths remained in the other towns. 2And the people blessed all those who willingly offered to live in Jerusalem.

3 These are the leaders of the province who lived in Jerusalem; but in the towns of Judah all lived on their property in their towns: Israel, the priests, the Levites, the temple servants, and the descendants of Solomon's servants. 4And in Jerusalem lived some of the Judahites and of the Benjaminites. Of the Judahites: Athaiah son of Uzziah son of Zechariah son of Amariah son of Shephatiah son of Mahalalel, of the descendants of Perez; 5and Maaseiah son of Baruch son of Col-hozeh son of Hazaiah son of Adaiah son of Joiarib son of Zechariah son of the Shilonite. 6All the descendants of Perez who lived in Jerusalem were four hundred sixty-eight valiant warriors.

7 And these are the Benjaminites: Sallu son of Meshullam son of Joed son of Pedaiah son of Kolaiah son of Maaseiah son of Ithiel son of Jeshaiah. 8And his brothers[b] Gabbai, Sallai: nine hundred twenty-eight. 9Joel son of Zichri was their overseer; and Judah son of Hassenuah was second in charge of the city.

10 Of the priests: Jedaiah son of Joiarib, Jachin, 11Seraiah son of Hilkiah son of Meshullam son of Zadok son of Meraioth son of Ahitub, officer of the house of God, 12and their associates who did the work of the house, eight hundred twenty-two; and Adaiah son of Jeroham son of Pelaliah son of Amzi son of Zechariah son of Pashhur son of Malchijah, 13and his associates, heads of ancestral houses, two hundred forty-two; and Amashsai son of Azarel son of Ahzai son of Meshillemoth son of Immer, 14and their associates, valiant warriors, one hundred twenty-eight; their overseer was Zabdiel son of Haggedolim.

15 And of the Levites: Shemaiah son of Hasshub son of Azrikam son of Hashabiah son of Bunni; 16and Shabbethai and Jozabad, of the leaders of the Levites, who were over the outside work of the house of God; 17and Mattaniah son of Mica son of Zabdi son of Asaph, who was the leader to begin the thanksgiving in prayer, and Bakbukiah, the second among his associates; and Abda son of Shammua son of Galal son of Jeduthun. 18All the Levites in the holy city were two hundred eighty-four.

19 The gatekeepers, Akkub, Talmon and their associates, who kept watch at the gates, were one hundred seventy-two. 20And the rest of Israel, and of the priests and the Levites, were in all the towns of Judah, all of them in their inheritance. 21But the temple servants lived on Ophel; and Ziha and Gishpa were over the temple servants.

22 The overseer of the Levites in Jerusalem was Uzzi son of Bani son of Hashabiah son of Mattaniah son of Mica, of the descendants of Asaph, the singers, in charge of the work of the house of God. 23For there was a command from the king concerning them, and a settled provision for the singers, as was required every day. 24And Pethahiah son of Meshezabel, of the descendants of Zerah son of Judah, was at the king's hand in all matters concerning the people.

Villages outside Jerusalem

25 And as for the villages, with their fields, some of the people of Judah lived in Kiriath-arba and its villages, and in Dibon and its villages, and in Jekabzeel and its villages, 26and in Jeshua and in Moladah and Beth-pelet, 27in Hazarshual, in Beer-sheba and its villages, 28in Ziklag, in Meconah and its villages, 29in En-rimmon, in Zorah, in Jarmuth,

b Gk Mss: Heb *And after him*

30Zanoah, Adullam, and their villages, Lachish and its fields, and Azekah and its villages. So they camped from Beersheba to the valley of Hinnom. 31The people of Benjamin also lived from Geba onward, at Michmash, Aija, Bethel and its villages, 32Anathoth, Nob, Ananiah, 33Hazor, Ramah, Gittaim, 34Hadid, Zeboim, Neballat, 35Lod, and Ono, the valley of artisans. 36And certain divisions of the Levites in Judah were joined to Benjamin.

A List of Priests and Levites

12 These are the priests and the Levites who came up with Zerubbabel son of Shealtiel, and Jeshua: Seraiah, Jeremiah, Ezra, 2Amariah, Malluch, Hattush, 3Shecaniah, Rehum, Meremoth, 4Iddo, Ginnethoi, Abijah, 5Mijamin, Maadiah, Bilgah, 6Shemaiah, Joiarib, Jedaiah, 7Sallu, Amok, Hilkiah, Jedaiah. These were the leaders of the priests and of their associates in the days of Jeshua.

8 And the Levites: Jeshua, Binnui, Kadmiel, Sherebiah, Judah, and Mattaniah, who with his associates was in charge of the songs of thanksgiving. 9And Bakbukiah and Unno their associates stood opposite them in the service. 10Jeshua was the father of Joiakim, Joiakim the father of Eliashib, Eliashib the father of Joiada, 11Joiada the father of Jonathan, and Jonathan the father of Jaddua.

12 In the days of Joiakim the priests, heads of ancestral houses, were: of Seraiah, Meraiah; of Jeremiah, Hananiah; 13of Ezra, Meshullam; of Amariah, Jehohanan; 14of Malluchi, Jonathan; of Shebaniah, Joseph; 15of Harim, Adna; of Meraioth, Helkai; 16of Iddo, Zechariah; of Ginnethon, Meshullam; 17of Abijah, Zichri; of Miniamin, of Moadiah, Piltai; 18of Bilgah, Shammua; of Shemaiah, Jehonathan; 19of Joiarib, Mattenai; of Jedaiah, Uzzi; 20of Sallai, Kallai; of Amok, Eber; 21of Hilkiah, Hashabiah; of Jedaiah, Nethanel.

22 As for the Levites, in the days of Eliashib, Joiada, Johanan, and Jaddua, there were recorded the heads of ancestral houses; also the priests until the reign of Darius the Persian. 23The Levites, heads of ancestral houses, were recorded in the Book of the Annals until the days of Johanan son of Eliashib. 24And the leaders of the Levites: Hashabiah, Sherebiah, and Jeshua son of Kadmiel, with their associates over against them, to praise and to give thanks, according to the commandment of David the man of God, section opposite to section. 25Mattaniah, Bakbukiah, Obadiah, Meshullam, Talmon, and Akkub were gatekeepers standing guard at the storehouses of the gates. 26These were in the days of Joiakim son of Jeshua son of Jozadak, and in the days of the governor Nehemiah and of the priest Ezra, the scribe.

Dedication of the City Wall

27 Now at the dedication of the wall of Jerusalem they sought out the Levites in all their places, to bring them to Jerusalem to celebrate the dedication with rejoicing, with thanksgivings and with singing, with cymbals, harps, and lyres. 28The companies of the singers gathered together from the circuit around Jerusalem and from the villages of the Netophathites; 29also from Beth-gilgal and from the region of Geba and Azmaveth; for the singers had built for themselves villages around Jerusalem. 30And the priests and the Levites purified themselves; and they purified the people and the gates and the wall.

31 Then I brought the leaders of Judah up onto the wall, and appointed two great companies that gave thanks and went in procession. One went to the right on the wall to the Dung Gate; 32and after them went Hoshaiah and half the officials of Judah, 33and Azariah, Ezra, Meshullam, 34Judah, Benjamin, Shemaiah, and Jeremiah, 35and some of the young priests with trumpets: Zechariah son of Jonathan son of Shemaiah son of Mattaniah son of Micaiah son of Zaccur son of Asaph; 36and his kindred, Shemaiah, Azarel, Milalai, Gilalai, Maai, Nethanel, Judah, and Hanani, with the musical instruments of David the man of God; and the scribe Ezra went in front of them. 37At the Fountain Gate, in front of them, they went straight up by the stairs of the city of David, at the ascent of the wall, above the house of David, to the Water Gate on the east.

38 The other company of those who gave thanks went to the left,c and I followed them with half of the people on the wall, above the Tower of the Ovens, to the Broad Wall, 39and above the Gate of Ephraim, and by the Old Gate, and by the Fish Gate and the Tower of Hananel and the Tower of the Hundred, to the Sheep Gate; and they came to a halt at the Gate of the Guard. 40So both companies of those who gave thanks stood in the house of God, and I and half of the officials with me; 41and the priests Eliakim, Maaseiah, Miniamin, Micaiah, Elioenai, Zechariah, and Hananiah, with trumpets; 42and Maaseiah, Shemaiah, Eleazar, Uzzi, Jehohanan, Malchijah, Elam, and Ezer. And the singers sang with Jezrahiah as their leader. 43They offered great sacrifices that day and rejoiced, for God had made them rejoice with great joy; the women and children also rejoiced. The joy of Jerusalem was heard far away.

Temple Responsibilities

44 On that day men were appointed over the chambers for the stores, the contributions, the first fruits, and the tithes, to gather into them the portions required by the law for the priests and for the Levites from the fields belonging to the towns; for Judah rejoiced over the priests and the Levites who ministered. 45They performed the service of their God and the service of purification, as did the singers and the gatekeepers, according to the command of David and his son Solomon. 46For in the days of David and Asaph long ago there was a leader of the singers, and there were songs of praise and thanksgiving to God. 47In the days of Zerubbabel and in the days of Nehemiah all Israel gave the daily portions for the singers and the gatekeepers. They set apart that which was for the Levites; and the Levites set apart that which was for the descendants of Aaron.

Foreigners Separated from Israel

13 On that day they read from the book of Moses in the hearing of the people; and in it was found written that no Ammonite or Moabite should ever enter the assembly of God, 2because they did not meet the Israelites with bread and water, but hired Balaam against them to curse them—yet our God turned the curse into a blessing. 3When the people heard the law, they separated from Israel all those of foreign descent.

The Reforms of Nehemiah

4 Now before this, the priest Eliashib, who was appointed over the chambers of the house of our God, and who was related to Tobiah, 5prepared for Tobiah a large room where they had previously put the grain offering, the frankincense, the vessels, and the tithes of grain, wine, and oil, which were given by commandment to the Levites, singers, and gatekeepers, and the contributions for the priests. 6While this was taking place I was not in Jerusalem, for in the thirty-second year of King Artaxerxes of Babylon I went to the king. After some time I asked leave of the king 7and returned to Jerusalem. I then discovered the wrong that Eliashib had done on behalf of Tobiah, preparing a room for him in the courts of the house of God. 8And I was very angry, and I threw all the household furniture of Tobiah out of the room. 9Then I gave orders and they cleansed the chambers, and I brought back the vessels of the house of God, with the grain offering and the frankincense.

10 I also found out that the portions of the Levites had not been given to them; so that the Levites and the singers, who had conducted the service, had gone back to their fields. 11So I remonstrated with the officials and said, "Why is the house of God forsaken?" And I gathered them together and set them in their stations. 12Then all Judah brought the tithe of the grain, wine, and oil into the storehouses. 13And I appointed as treasurers over the storehouses the priest Shelemiah, the scribe Zadok, and Pedaiah of the Levites, and as their assistant Hanan son of Zaccur son of Mattaniah, for they were considered faithful; and their duty was to distribute to their associates. 14Remember me, O my God, concerning this, and do

c Cn: Heb opposite

not wipe out my good deeds that I have done for the house of my God and for his service.

Sabbath Reforms Begun

15 In those days I saw in Judah people treading wine presses on the sabbath, and bringing in heaps of grain and loading them on donkeys; and also wine, grapes, figs, and all kinds of burdens, which they brought into Jerusalem on the sabbath day; and I warned them at that time against selling food. 16Tyrians also, who lived in the city, brought in fish and all kinds of merchandise and sold them on the sabbath to the people of Judah, and in Jerusalem. 17Then I remonstrated with the nobles of Judah and said to them, "What is this evil thing that you are doing, profaning the sabbath day? 18Did not your ancestors act in this way, and did not our God bring all this disaster on us and on this city? Yet you bring more wrath on Israel by profaning the sabbath."

19 When it began to be dark at the gates of Jerusalem before the sabbath, I commanded that the doors should be shut and gave orders that they should not be opened until after the sabbath. And I set some of my servants over the gates, to prevent any burden from being brought in on the sabbath day. 20Then the merchants and sellers of all kinds of merchandise spent the night outside Jerusalem once or twice. 21But I warned them and said to them, "Why do you spend the night in front of the wall? If you do so again, I will lay hands on you." From that time on they did not come on the sabbath. 22And I commanded the Levites that they should purify themselves and come and guard the gates, to keep the sabbath day holy. Remember this also in my favor, O my God, and spare me according to the greatness of your steadfast love.

Mixed Marriages Condemned

23 In those days also I saw Jews who had married women of Ashdod, Ammon, and Moab; 24and half of their children spoke the language of Ashdod, and they could not speak the language of Judah, but spoke the language of various peoples. 25And I contended with them and cursed them and beat some of them and pulled out their hair; and I made them take an oath in the name of God, saying, "You shall not give your daughters to their sons, or take their daughters for your sons or for yourselves. 26Did not King Solomon of Israel sin on account of such women? Among the many nations there was no king like him, and he was beloved by his God, and God made him king over all Israel; nevertheless, foreign women made even him to sin. 27Shall we then listen to you and do all this great evil and act treacherously against our God by marrying foreign women?"

28 And one of the sons of Jehoiada, son of the high priest Eliashib, was the son-in-law of Sanballat the Horonite; I chased him away from me. 29Remember them, O my God, because they have defiled the priesthood, the covenant of the priests and the Levites.

30 Thus I cleansed them from everything foreign, and I established the duties of the priests and Levites, each in his work; 31and I provided for the wood offering, at appointed times, and for the first fruits. Remember me, O my God, for good.

ESTHER

THIS BOOK, NAMED AFTER ITS LEADING CHARACTER, A BEAUTIFUL JEWISH GIRL WHOM KING AHASUERUS OF PERSIA CHOSE TO BE HIS QUEEN, REMEMBERS THE GREAT DELIVERANCE OF THE JEWISH PEOPLE DURING THE REIGN OF AHASUERUS. ALTHOUGH THE NAME OF GOD DOES NOT APPEAR IN THE BOOK, HIS CARE FOR HIS CHOSEN PEOPLE IS CLEARLY SHOWN. BE ASSURED THAT HE IS AT WORK IN YOUR LIFE TODAY AS WELL.

King Ahasuerus Deposes Queen Vashti

1 This happened in the days of Ahasuerus, the same Ahasuerus who ruled over one hundred twenty-seven provinces from India to Ethiopia.[a] ²In those days when King Ahasuerus sat on his royal throne in the citadel of Susa, ³in the third year of his reign, he gave a banquet for all his officials and ministers. The army of Persia and Media and the nobles and governors of the provinces were present, ⁴while he displayed the great wealth of his kingdom and the splendor and pomp of his majesty for many days, one hundred eighty days in all.

5 When these days were completed, the king gave for all the people present in the citadel of Susa, both great and small, a banquet lasting for seven days, in the court of the garden of the king's palace. ⁶There were white cotton curtains and blue hangings tied with cords of fine linen and purple to silver rings[b] and marble pillars. There were couches of gold and silver on a mosaic pavement of porphyry, marble, mother-of-pearl, and colored stones. ⁷Drinks were served in golden goblets, goblets of different kinds, and the royal wine was lavished according to the bounty of the king. ⁸Drinking was by flagons, without restraint; for the king had given orders to all the officials of his palace to do as each one desired. ⁹Furthermore, Queen

a Or Nubia; Heb Cush   b Or rods

Vashti gave a banquet for the women in the palace of King Ahasuerus.

10 On the seventh day, when the king was merry with wine, he commanded Mehuman, Biztha, Harbona, Bigtha and Abagtha, Zethar and Carkas, the seven eunuchs who attended him, 11to bring Queen Vashti before the king, wearing the royal crown, in order to show the peoples and the officials her beauty; for she was fair to behold. 12But Queen Vashti refused to come at the king's command conveyed by the eunuchs. At this the king was enraged, and his anger burned within him.

13 Then the king consulted the sages who knew the lawsc (for this was the king's procedure toward all who were versed in law and custom, 14and those next to him were Carshena, Shethar, Admatha, Tarshish, Meres, Marsena, and Memucan, the seven officials of Persia and Media, who had access to the king, and sat first in the kingdom): 15"According to the law, what is to be done to Queen Vashti because she has not performed the command of King Ahasuerus conveyed by the eunuchs?" 16Then Memucan said in the presence of the king and the officials, "Not only has Queen Vashti done wrong to the king, but also to all the officials and all the peoples who are in all the provinces of King Ahasuerus. 17For this deed of the queen will be made known to all women, causing them to look with contempt on their husbands, since they will say, 'King Ahasuerus commanded Queen Vashti to be brought before him, and she did not come.' 18This very day the noble ladies of Persia and Media who have heard of the queen's behavior will rebel againstd the king's officials, and there will be no end of contempt and wrath! 19If it pleases the king, let a royal order go out from him, and let it be written among the laws of the Persians and the Medes so that it may not be altered, that Vashti is never again to come before King Ahasuerus; and let the king give her royal position to another who is better than she. 20So when the decree made by the king is proclaimed throughout all his kingdom, vast as it is,

all women will give honor to their husbands, high and low alike."

21 This advice pleased the king and the officials, and the king did as Memucan proposed; 22he sent letters to all the royal provinces, to every province in its own script and to every people in its own language, declaring that every man should be master in his own house.e

Esther Becomes Queen

2 After these things, when the anger of King Ahasuerus had abated, he remembered Vashti and what she had done and what had been decreed against her. 2Then the king's servants who attended him said, "Let beautiful young virgins be sought out for the king. 3And let the king appoint commissioners in all the provinces of his kingdom to gather all the beautiful young virgins to the harem in the citadel of Susa under custody of Hegai, the king's eunuch, who is in charge of the women; let their cosmetic treatments be given them. 4And let the girl who pleases the king be queen instead of Vashti." This pleased the king, and he did so.

5 Now there was a Jew in the citadel of Susa whose name was Mordecai son of Jair son of Shimei son of Kish, a Benjaminite. 6Kishf had been carried away from Jerusalem among the captives carried away with King Jeconiah of Judah, whom King Nebuchadnezzar of Babylon had carried away. 7Mordecaig had brought up Hadassah, that is Esther, his cousin, for she had neither father nor mother; the girl was fair and beautiful, and when her father and her mother died, Mordecai adopted her as his own daughter. 8So when the king's order and his edict were proclaimed, and when many young women were gathered in the citadel of Susa in custody of Hegai, Esther also was taken into the king's palace and put in custody of Hegai, who had charge of the women. 9The girl pleased him and won his favor, and he quickly provided her with her cosmetic treatments and her portion of food, and with seven chosen maids from the king's palace, and advanced her and her maids to the best place in the harem.

c Cn: Heb times   d Cn: Heb will tell   e Heb adds and speak according to the language of his people
f Heb a Benjamite 6who   g Heb He

¹⁰Esther did not reveal her people or kindred, for Mordecai had charged her not to tell. ¹¹Every day Mordecai would walk around in front of the court of the harem, to learn how Esther was and how she fared.

12 The turn came for each girl to go in to King Ahasuerus, after being twelve months under the regulations for the women, since this was the regular period of their cosmetic treatment, six months with oil of myrrh and six months with perfumes and cosmetics for women. ¹³When the girl went in to the king she was given whatever she asked for to take with her from the harem to the king's palace. ¹⁴In the evening she went in; then in the morning she came back to the second harem in custody of Shaashgaz, the king's eunuch, who was in charge of the concubines; she did not go in to the king again, unless the king delighted in her and she was summoned by name.

15 When the turn came for Esther daughter of Abihail the uncle of Mordecai, who had adopted her as his own daughter, to go in to the king, she asked for nothing except what Hegai the king's eunuch, who had charge of the women, advised. Now Esther was admired by all who saw her. ¹⁶When Esther was taken to King Ahasuerus in his royal palace in the tenth month, which is the month of Tebeth, in the seventh year of his reign, ¹⁷the king loved Esther more than all the other women; of all the virgins she won his favor and devotion, so that he set the royal crown on her head and made her queen instead of Vashti. ¹⁸Then the king gave a great banquet to all his officials and ministers—"Esther's banquet." He also granted a holiday[h] to the provinces, and gave gifts with royal liberality.

Mordecai Discovers a Plot

19 When the virgins were being gathered together,[i] Mordecai was sitting at the king's gate. ²⁰Now Esther had not revealed her kindred or her people, as Mordecai had charged her; for Esther obeyed Mordecai just as when she was brought up by him. ²¹In those days, while Mordecai was sitting at the king's gate, Bigthan and Teresh, two of the king's eunuchs, who guarded the threshold, became angry and conspired to assassinate[j] King Ahasuerus. ²²But the matter came to the knowledge of Mordecai, and he told it to Queen Esther, and Esther told the king in the name of Mordecai. ²³When the affair was investigated and found to be so, both the men were hanged on the gallows. It was recorded in the book of the annals in the presence of the king.

Haman Undertakes to Destroy the Jews

3 After these things King Ahasuerus promoted Haman son of Hammedatha the Agagite, and advanced him and set his seat above all the officials who were with him. ²And all the king's servants who were at the king's gate bowed down and did obeisance to Haman; for the king had so commanded concerning him. But Mordecai did not bow down or do obeisance. ³Then the king's servants who were at the king's gate said to Mordecai, "Why do you disobey the king's command?" ⁴When they spoke to him day after day and he would not listen to them, they told Haman, in order to see whether Mordecai's words would avail; for he had told them that he was a Jew. ⁵When Haman saw that Mordecai did not bow down or do obeisance to him, Haman was infuriated. ⁶But he thought it beneath him to lay hands on Mordecai alone. So, having been told who Mordecai's people were, Haman plotted to destroy all the Jews, the people of Mordecai, throughout the whole kingdom of Ahasuerus.

7 In the first month, which is the month of Nisan, in the twelfth year of King Ahasuerus, they cast Pur—which means "the lot"—before Haman for the day and for the month, and the lot fell on the thirteenth day[k] of the twelfth month, which is the month of Adar. ⁸Then Haman said to King Ahasuerus, "There is a certain people scattered and separated among the peoples in all the provinces of your kingdom; their laws are different from those of every other

h Or an amnesty   i Heb adds a second time   j Heb to lay hands on   k Cn Compare Gk and verse 13 below: Heb the twelfth month

PRIDE MEANS ENMITY
C. S. Lewis

VERSE: Esther 3.5–6   **PASSAGE:** Esther 3.1–15

 reed will certainly make a man want money, for the sake of a better house, better holidays, better things to eat and drink. But only up to a point. What is it that makes a man with £10,000 a year anxious to get £20,000 a year? It is not the greed for more pleasure. £10,000 will give all the luxuries that any man can really enjoy. It is pride—the wish to be richer than some other rich man, and (still more) the wish for power. For, of course, power is what pride really enjoys: there is nothing makes a man feel so superior to others as being able to move them about like toy soldiers. What makes a pretty girl spread misery wherever she goes by collecting admirers? Certainly not her sexual instinct: that kind of girl is quite often sexually frigid. It is pride. What is it that makes a political leader or a whole nation go on and on, demanding more and more? Pride again. Pride is competitive by its very nature: that is why it goes on and on. If I am a proud man, then, as long as there is one man in the whole world more powerful, or richer, or cleverer than I, he is my rival and my enemy.

The Christians are right: it is pride which has been the chief cause of misery in every nation and every family since the world began. Other vices may sometimes bring people together: you may find good fellowship and jokes and friendliness among drunken people or unchaste people. But pride always means enmity—it *is* enmity. And not only enmity between man and man, but enmity to God.

In God you come up against something which is in every respect immeasurably superior to yourself. Unless you know God as that—and, therefore, know yourself as nothing in comparison—you do not know God at all. As long as you are proud you cannot know God. A proud man is always looking down on things and people: and, of course, as long as you are looking down, you cannot see something that is above you.

ADDITIONAL SCRIPTURE READING:
Proverbs 11.2; Mark 9.33–37; James 4.1–3

Go to page 543 for your next devotional reading.

1900   Present

people, and they do not keep the king's laws, so that it is not appropriate for the king to tolerate them. 9If it pleases the king, let a decree be issued for their destruction, and I will pay ten thousand talents of silver into the hands of those who have charge of the king's business, so that they may put it into the king's treasuries." 10So the king took his signet ring from his hand and gave it to Haman son of Hammedatha the Agagite, the enemy of the Jews. 11The king said to Haman, "The money is given to you, and the people as well, to do with them as it seems good to you."

12 Then the king's secretaries were summoned on the thirteenth day of the first month, and an edict, according to all that Haman commanded, was written to the king's satraps and to the governors over all the provinces and to the officials of all the peoples, to every province in its own script and every people in its own language; it was written in the name of King Ahasuerus and sealed with the king's ring. 13Letters were sent by couriers to all the king's provinces, giving orders to destroy, to kill, and to annihilate all Jews, young and old, women and children, in one day, the thirteenth day of the twelfth month, which is the month of Adar, and to plunder their goods. 14A copy of the document was to be issued as a decree in every province by proclamation, calling on all the peoples to be ready for that day. 15The couriers went quickly by order of the king, and the decree was issued in the citadel of Susa. The king and Haman sat down to drink; but the city of Susa was thrown into confusion.

Esther Agrees to Help the Jews

4 When Mordecai learned all that had been done, Mordecai tore his clothes and put on sackcloth and ashes, and went through the city, wailing with a loud and bitter cry; 2he went up to the entrance of the king's gate, for no one might enter the king's gate clothed with sackcloth. 3In every province, wherever the king's command and his decree came, there was great mourning among the Jews, with fasting and weeping and lamenting, and most of them lay in sackcloth and ashes.

4 When Esther's maids and her eunuchs came and told her, the queen was deeply distressed; she sent garments to clothe Mordecai, so that he might take off his sackcloth; but he would not accept them. 5Then Esther called for Hathach, one of the king's eunuchs, who had been appointed to attend her, and ordered him to go to Mordecai to learn what was happening and why. 6Hathach went out to Mordecai in the open square of the city in front of the king's gate, 7and Mordecai told him all that had happened to him, and the exact sum of money that Haman had promised to pay into the king's treasuries for the destruction of the Jews. 8Mordecai also gave him a copy of the written decree issued in Susa for their destruction, that he might show it to Esther, explain it to her, and charge her to go to the king to make supplication to him and entreat him for her people.

9 Hathach went and told Esther what Mordecai had said. 10Then Esther spoke to Hathach and gave him a message for Mordecai, saying, 11"All the king's servants and the people of the king's provinces know that if any man or woman goes to the king inside the inner court without being called, there is but one law—all alike are to be put to death. Only if the king holds out the golden scepter to someone, may that person live. I myself have not been called to come in to the king for thirty days." 12When they told Mordecai what Esther had said, 13Mordecai told them to reply to Esther, "Do not think that in the king's palace you will escape any more than all the other Jews. 14For if you keep silence at such a time as this, relief and deliverance will rise for the Jews from another quarter, but you and your father's family will perish. Who knows? Perhaps you have come to royal dignity for just such a time as this." 15Then Esther said in reply to Mordecai, 16"Go, gather all the Jews to be found in Susa, and hold a fast on my behalf, and neither eat nor drink for three days, night or day. I and my maids will also fast as you do. After that I will go to the king, though it is against the law; and if I perish, I perish." 17Mordecai then went away and

did everything as Esther had ordered him.

Esther's Banquet

 5 On the third day Esther put on her royal robes and stood in the inner court of the king's palace, opposite the king's hall. The king was sitting on his royal throne inside the palace opposite the entrance to the palace. ²As soon as the king saw Queen Esther standing in the court, she won his favor and he held out to her the golden scepter that was in his hand. Then Esther approached

---

WEDNESDAY

THE MAGISTRATE OR CIVIL OFFICER
John Calvin

VERSE: Esther 4.17   **PASSAGE:** Esther 4.12–17

---

he mutual duty of subjects and citizens is not only to honor and to revere their superiors, but to recommend by prayers to the Lord their salvation and prosperity, to submit willingly to their rule, to obey their laws and constitutions, and not to refuse the charges imposed by them: be they taxes, tolls, tributes, and other contributions, or be they offices, civic commissions, and all the like. So that we must not only render ourselves obedient to superiors who rightly and dutifully administer their higher office, but also it is fit to endure those who tyrannically abuse their power, until, through legitimate order, we be freed from their yoke. For, just as a good prince is a testimony of the divine beneficence for maintaining the salvation of men, so a bad and evil prince is a plague of God for chastising the sins of the people. Yet, let this generally be held as certain that to both the power is given by God, and we cannot resist them without our resisting the ordinance of God.

But from obedience to superiors we must always except one thing: that it does not draw us away from obedience to him to whose edicts the commands of all kings must yield. The Lord, therefore, is the king of kings, and, once he has opened his sacred mouth, he must be listened to by all and above all. Only after that, we are subject to men who are constituted over us, but not otherwise than in him. If men command us to do something against him, we must do nothing, nor keep any account of such an order. On the contrary, let rather this sentence take place: that it is necessary to "obey God rather than men!" (Acts 5.29).

ADDITIONAL SCRIPTURE READING:
Romans 13.1–5; Titus 3.1; 1 Peter 2.13–17

Go to page 549 for your next devotional reading.

1500   1700

and touched the top of the scepter. ³The king said to her, "What is it, Queen Esther? What is your request? It shall be given you, even to the half of my kingdom." ⁴Then Esther said, "If it pleases the king, let the king and Haman come today to a banquet that I have prepared for the king." ⁵Then the king said, "Bring Haman quickly, so that we may do as Esther desires." So the king and Haman came to the banquet that Esther had prepared. ⁶While they were drinking wine, the king said to Esther, "What is your petition? It shall be granted you. And what is your request? Even to the half of my kingdom, it shall be fulfilled." ⁷Then Esther said, "This is my petition and request: ⁸If I have won the king's favor, and if it pleases the king to grant my petition and fulfill my request, let the king and Haman come tomorrow to the banquet that I will prepare for them, and then I will do as the king has said."

Haman Plans to Have Mordecai Hanged

9 Haman went out that day happy and in good spirits. But when Haman saw Mordecai in the king's gate, and observed that he neither rose nor trembled before him, he was infuriated with Mordecai; ¹⁰nevertheless Haman restrained himself and went home. Then he sent and called for his friends and his wife Zeresh, ¹¹and Haman recounted to them the splendor of his riches, the number of his sons, all the promotions with which the king had honored him, and how he had advanced him above the officials and the ministers of the king. ¹²Haman added, "Even Queen Esther let no one but myself come with the king to the banquet that she prepared. Tomorrow also I am invited by her, together with the king. ¹³Yet all this does me no good so long as I see the Jew Mordecai sitting at the king's gate." ¹⁴Then his wife Zeresh and all his friends said to him, "Let a gallows fifty cubits high be made, and in the morning tell the king to have Mordecai hanged on it; then go with the king to the banquet in good spirits." This advice pleased Haman, and he had the gallows made.

The King Honors Mordecai

6 On that night the king could not sleep, and he gave orders to bring the book of records, the annals, and they were read to the king. ²It was found written how Mordecai had told about Bigthana and Teresh, two of the king's eunuchs, who guarded the threshold, and who had conspired to assassinate[1] King Ahasuerus. ³Then the king said, "What honor or distinction has been bestowed on Mordecai for this?" The king's servants who attended him said, "Nothing has been done for him." ⁴The king said, "Who is in the court?" Now Haman had just entered the outer court of the king's palace to speak to the king about having Mordecai hanged on the gallows that he had prepared for him. ⁵So the king's servants told him, "Haman is there, standing in the court." The king said, "Let him come in." ⁶So Haman came in, and the king said to him, "What shall be done for the man whom the king wishes to honor?" Haman said to himself, "Whom would the king wish to honor more than me?" ⁷So Haman said to the king, "For the man whom the king wishes to honor, ⁸let royal robes be brought, which the king has worn, and a horse that the king has ridden, with a royal crown on its head. ⁹Let the robes and the horse be handed over to one of the king's most noble officials; let him[m] robe the man whom the king wishes to honor, and let him[m] conduct the man on horseback through the open square of the city, proclaiming before him: 'Thus shall it be done for the man whom the king wishes to honor.'" ¹⁰Then the king said to Haman, "Quickly, take the robes and the horse, as you have said, and do so to the Jew Mordecai who sits at the king's gate. Leave out nothing that you have mentioned." ¹¹So Haman took the robes and the horse and robed Mordecai and led him riding through the open square of the city, proclaiming, "Thus shall it be done for the man whom the king wishes to honor."

12 Then Mordecai returned to the king's gate, but Haman hurried to his house, mourning and with his head covered. ¹³When Haman told his wife Zeresh

l Heb to lay hands on　　m Heb them

and all his friends everything that had happened to him, his advisers and his wife Zeresh said to him, "If Mordecai, before whom your downfall has begun, is of the Jewish people, you will not prevail against him, but will surely fall before him."

Haman's Downfall and Mordecai's Advancement

14 While they were still talking with him, the king's eunuchs arrived and hurried Haman off to the banquet that Esther had prepared. **7** ¹So the king and Haman went in to feast with Queen Esther. ²On the second day, as they were drinking wine, the king again said to Esther, "What is your petition, Queen Esther? It shall be granted you. And what is your request? Even to the half of my kingdom, it shall be fulfilled." ³Then Queen Esther answered, "If I have won your favor, O king, and if it pleases the king, let my life be given me—that is my petition—and the lives of my people—that is my request. ⁴For we have been sold, I and my people, to be destroyed, to be killed, and to be annihilated. If we had been sold merely as slaves, men and women, I would have held my peace; but no enemy can compensate for this damage to the king."[n] ⁵Then King Ahasuerus said to Queen Esther, "Who is he, and where is he, who has presumed to do this?" ⁶Esther said, "A foe and enemy, this wicked Haman!" Then Haman was terrified before the king and the queen. ⁷The king rose from the feast in wrath and went into the palace garden, but Haman stayed to beg his life from Queen Esther, for he saw that the king had determined to destroy him. ⁸When the king returned from the palace garden to the banquet hall, Haman had thrown himself on the couch where Esther was reclining; and the king said, "Will he even assault the queen in my presence, in my own house?" As the words left the mouth of the king, they covered Haman's face. ⁹Then Harbona, one of the eunuchs in attendance on the king, said, "Look, the very gallows that Haman has prepared for Mordecai, whose word saved the king, stands at Haman's house, fifty cubits high." And the king said, "Hang him on that." ¹⁰So they hanged Haman on the gallows that he had prepared for Mordecai. Then the anger of the king abated.

Esther Saves the Jews

8 On that day King Ahasuerus gave to Queen Esther the house of Haman, the enemy of the Jews; and Mordecai came before the king, for Esther had told what he was to her. ²Then the king took off his signet ring, which he had taken from Haman, and gave it to Mordecai. So Esther set Mordecai over the house of Haman.

3 Then Esther spoke again to the king; she fell at his feet, weeping and pleading with him to avert the evil design of Haman the Agagite and the plot that he had devised against the Jews. ⁴The king held out the golden scepter to Esther, ⁵and Esther rose and stood before the king. She said, "If it pleases the king, and if I have won his favor, and if the thing seems right before the king, and I have his approval, let an order be written to revoke the letters devised by Haman son of Hammedatha the Agagite, which he wrote giving orders to destroy the Jews who are in all the provinces of the king. ⁶For how can I bear to see the calamity that is coming on my people? Or how can I bear to see the destruction of my kindred?" ⁷Then King Ahasuerus said to Queen Esther and to the Jew Mordecai, "See, I have given Esther the house of Haman, and they have hanged him on the gallows, because he plotted to lay hands on the Jews. ⁸You may write as you please with regard to the Jews, in the name of the king, and seal it with the king's ring; for an edict written in the name of the king and sealed with the king's ring cannot be revoked."

9 The king's secretaries were summoned at that time, in the third month, which is the month of Sivan, on the twenty-third day; and an edict was written, according to all that Mordecai commanded, to the Jews and to the satraps and the governors and the officials of the provinces from India to Ethiopia,[o] one hundred twenty-seven provinces, to

n Meaning of Heb uncertain *o* Or *Nubia;* Heb *Cush*

every province in its own script and to every people in its own language, and also to the Jews in their script and their language. 10He wrote letters in the name of King Ahasuerus, sealed them with the king's ring, and sent them by mounted couriers riding on fast steeds bred from the royal herd.*p* 11By these letters the king allowed the Jews who were in every city to assemble and defend their lives, to destroy, to kill, and to annihilate any armed force of any people or province that might attack them, with their children and women, and to plunder their goods 12on a single day throughout all the provinces of King Ahasuerus, on the thirteenth day of the twelfth month, which is the month of Adar. 13A copy of the writ was to be issued as a decree in every province and published to all peoples, and the Jews were to be ready on that day to take revenge on their enemies. 14So the couriers, mounted on their swift royal steeds, hurried out, urged by the king's command. The decree was issued in the citadel of Susa.

15 Then Mordecai went out from the presence of the king, wearing royal robes of blue and white, with a great golden crown and a mantle of fine linen and purple, while the city of Susa shouted and rejoiced. 16For the Jews there was light and gladness, joy and honor. 17In every province and in every city, wherever the king's command and his edict came, there was gladness and joy among the Jews, a festival and a holiday. Furthermore, many of the peoples of the country professed to be Jews, because the fear of the Jews had fallen upon them.

Destruction of the Enemies of the Jews

9 Now in the twelfth month, which is the month of Adar, on the thirteenth day, when the king's command and edict were about to be executed, on the very day when the enemies of the Jews hoped to gain power over them, but which had been changed to a day when the Jews would gain power over their foes, 2the Jews gathered in their cities throughout all the provinces of King Ahasuerus to lay hands on those who

had sought their ruin; and no one could withstand them, because the fear of them had fallen upon all peoples. 3All the officials of the provinces, the satraps and the governors, and the royal officials were supporting the Jews, because the fear of Mordecai had fallen upon them. 4For Mordecai was powerful in the king's house, and his fame spread throughout all the provinces as the man Mordecai grew more and more powerful. 5So the Jews struck down all their enemies with the sword, slaughtering, and destroying them, and did as they pleased to those who hated them. 6In the citadel of Susa the Jews killed and destroyed five hundred people. 7They killed Parshandatha, Dalphon, Aspatha, 8Poratha, Adalia, Aridatha, 9Parmashta, Arisai, Aridai, Vaizatha, 10the ten sons of Haman son of Hammedatha, the enemy of the Jews; but they did not touch the plunder.

11 That very day the number of those killed in the citadel of Susa was reported to the king. 12The king said to Queen Esther, "In the citadel of Susa the Jews have killed five hundred people and also the ten sons of Haman. What have they done in the rest of the king's provinces? Now what is your petition? It shall be granted you. And what further is your request? It shall be fulfilled." 13Esther said, "If it pleases the king, let the Jews who are in Susa be allowed tomorrow also to do according to this day's edict, and let the ten sons of Haman be hanged on the gallows." 14So the king commanded this to be done; a decree was issued in Susa, and the ten sons of Haman were hanged. 15The Jews who were in Susa gathered also on the fourteenth day of the month of Adar and they killed three hundred persons in Susa; but they did not touch the plunder.

16 Now the other Jews who were in the king's provinces also gathered to defend their lives, and gained relief from their enemies, and killed seventy-five thousand of those who hated them; but they laid no hands on the plunder. 17This was on the thirteenth day of the month of Adar, and on the fourteenth day they rested and made that a day of feasting and gladness.

p Meaning of Heb uncertain

The Feast of Purim Inaugurated

18 But the Jews who were in Susa gathered on the thirteenth day and on the fourteenth, and rested on the fifteenth day, making that a day of feasting and gladness. 19 Therefore the Jews of the villages, who live in the open towns, hold the fourteenth day of the month of Adar as a day for gladness and feasting, a holiday on which they send gifts of food to one another.

20 Mordecai recorded these things, and sent letters to all the Jews who were in all the provinces of King Ahasuerus, both near and far, 21 enjoining them that they should keep the fourteenth day of the month Adar and also the fifteenth day of the same month, year by year, 22 as the days on which the Jews gained relief from their enemies, and as the month that had been turned for them from sorrow into gladness and from mourning into a holiday; that they should make them days of feasting and gladness, days for sending gifts of food to one another and presents to the poor. 23 So the Jews adopted as a custom what they had begun to do, as Mordecai had written to them.

24 Haman son of Hammedatha the Agagite, the enemy of all the Jews, had plotted against the Jews to destroy them, and had cast Pur—that is "the lot"—to crush and destroy them; 25 but when Esther came before the king, he gave orders in writing that the wicked plot that he had devised against the Jews should come upon his own head, and that he and his sons should be hanged on the gallows. 26 Therefore these days are called Purim, from the word Pur. Thus because of all that was written in this letter, and of what they had faced in this matter, and of what had happened to them, 27 the Jews established and accepted as a custom for themselves and their descendants and all who joined them, that without fail they would continue to observe these two days every year, as it was written and at the time appointed. 28 These days should be remembered and kept throughout every generation, in every family, province, and city; and these days of Purim should never fall into disuse among the Jews, nor should the commemoration of these days cease among their descendants.

29 Queen Esther daughter of Abihail, along with the Jew Mordecai, gave full written authority, confirming this second letter about Purim. 30 Letters were sent wishing peace and security to all the Jews, to the one hundred twenty-seven provinces of the kingdom of Ahasuerus, 31 and giving orders that these days of Purim should be observed at their appointed seasons, as the Jew Mordecai and Queen Esther enjoined on the Jews, just as they had laid down for themselves and for their descendants regulations concerning their fasts and their lamentations. 32 The command of Queen Esther fixed these practices of Purim, and it was recorded in writing.

10 King Ahasuerus laid tribute on the land and on the islands of the sea. 2 All the acts of his power and might, and the full account of the high honor of Mordecai, to which the king advanced him, are they not written in the annals of the kings of Media and Persia? 3 For Mordecai the Jew was next in rank to King Ahasuerus, and he was powerful among the Jews and popular with his many kindred, for he sought the good of his people and interceded for the welfare of all his descendants.

JOB

THE BOOK OF JOB IS NAMED FOR ITS MAIN CHARACTER, A RIGHTEOUS MAN WHO WAS VERY RICH. EVEN AFTER LOSING EVERYTHING HE OWNED AND SUFFERING FROM A TERRIBLE SICKNESS, JOB STILL CONFESSED HIS TRUST IN GOD. THE BOOK PROVIDES A PROFOUND STATEMENT ON GOD'S JUSTICE IN LIGHT OF HUMAN SUFFERING. HOW CAN THE JUSTICE OF AN ALMIGHTY GOD BE DEFENDED IN THE FACE OF EVIL, ESPECIALLY HUMAN SUFFERING, AND EVEN MORE POIGNANTLY, THE SUFFERING OF THE INNOCENT? AS YOU READ THIS BOOK, REMEMBER THAT EVEN THOUGH YOU DON'T HAVE ALL THE ANSWERS TO QUESTIONS ABOUT SUFFERING, GOD IS STILL IN CONTROL.

Job and His Family

1 There was once a man in the land of Uz whose name was Job. That man was blameless and upright, one who feared God and turned away from evil. ²There were born to him seven sons and three daughters. ³He had seven thousand sheep, three thousand camels, five hundred yoke of oxen, five hundred donkeys, and very many servants; so that this man was the greatest of all the people of the east. ⁴His sons used to go and hold feasts in one another's houses in turn; and they would send and invite their three sisters to eat and drink with them. ⁵And when the feast days had run their course, Job would send and sanctify them, and he would rise early in the morning and offer burnt offerings according to the number of them all; for Job said, "It may be that my children have sinned, and cursed God in their hearts." This is what Job always did.

Attack on Job's Character

6 One day the heavenly beings[a] came to present themselves before the LORD, and Satan[b] also came among them. ⁷The LORD said to Satan,[b] "Where have you come from?" Satan[b] answered the LORD, "From going to and fro on the earth, and from walking up and down on it." ⁸The LORD said to Satan,[b] "Have you considered my servant Job? There is no one like him on the earth, a blameless and upright man who fears God and turns

a Heb *sons of God*   *b* Or *the Accuser*; Heb *ha-satan* away from evil." 9Then Satan*c* answered the LORD, "Does Job fear God for nothing? 10Have you not put a fence around him and his house and all that he has, on every side? You have blessed the work of his hands, and his possessions have increased in the land. 11But stretch out your hand now, and touch all that he has, and he will curse you to your face."

12The LORD said to Satan,*c* "Very well, all that he has is in your power; only do not stretch out your hand against him!" So Satan*c* went out from the presence of the LORD.

Job Loses Property and Children

13 One day when his sons and daughters were eating and drinking wine in

c Or *the Accuser;* Heb *ha-satan*

THURSDAY

ABUNDANT LIVING "IN SPITE OF"
E. Stanley Jones

VERSE: Job 1.21   **PASSAGE:** Job 1.13–22

bundant living is sometimes on account of, but more often, perhaps, in spite of. When circumstances are against us, we must be able to set the sails of our souls and use even adverse winds. The Christian faith does not offer exemption from sorrow and pain and frustration—it offers the power, not merely to bear, but to use these adversities. The secret of using pain and suffering and frustration is in many ways life's greatest secret. When you have learned that, you are unbeatable and unbreakable . . .

The Christian "can take it," because he can take hold of adversity and use it . . . [Christ] bore the cross, for he could use the cross. You cannot bear the cross long—it will break your spirit, unless you can take that cross and make it serve higher purposes. The stoic bears the cross; the Christian makes the cross bear fruit.

Any movement that has learned the secret of making the bitterest tree—the cross—bear the sweet fruit has learned the secret of abundant living.

O Christ, we begin to see thy secret. Thou didst lay hold of life when life was speaking its cruelest word and didst turn that very word into God's most redemptive word. Thou didst not bear the cross—thou didst use it. Give me power to do just that. Then, in thee, I am invincible. Amen.

ADDITIONAL SCRIPTURE READING:
Job 2.10; 1 Thessalonians 5.18; James 1.12

Go to page 565 for your next devotional reading.

1900   Present

the eldest brother's house, 14a messenger came to Job and said, "The oxen were plowing and the donkeys were feeding beside them, 15and the Sabeans fell on them and carried them off, and killed the servants with the edge of the sword; I alone have escaped to tell you." 16While he was still speaking, another came and said, "The fire of God fell from heaven and burned up the sheep and the servants, and consumed them; I alone have escaped to tell you." 17While he was still speaking, another came and said, "The Chaldeans formed three columns, made a raid on the camels and carried them off, and killed the servants with the edge of the sword; I alone have escaped to tell you." 18While he was still speaking, another came and said, "Your sons and daughters were eating and drinking wine in their eldest brother's house, 19and suddenly a great wind came across the desert, struck the four corners of the house, and it fell on the young people, and they are dead; I alone have escaped to tell you."

20 Then Job arose, tore his robe, shaved his head, and fell on the ground and worshiped. 21He said, "Naked I came from my mother's womb, and naked shall I return there; the LORD gave, and the LORD has taken away; blessed be the name of the LORD."

22 In all this Job did not sin or charge God with wrongdoing.

Attack on Job's Health

2 One day the heavenly beings[d] came to present themselves before the LORD, and Satan[e] also came among them to present himself before the LORD. 2The LORD said to Satan,[e] "Where have you come from?" Satan[e] answered the LORD, "From going to and fro on the earth, and from walking up and down on it." 3The LORD said to Satan,[e] "Have you considered my servant Job? There is no one like him on the earth, a blameless and upright man who fears God and turns away from evil. He still persists in his integrity, although you incited me against him, to destroy him for no reason." 4Then Satan[e] answered the LORD, "Skin for

skin! All that people have they will give to save their lives.[f] 5But stretch out your hand now and touch his bone and his flesh, and he will curse you to your face." 6The LORD said to Satan,[e] "Very well, he is in your power; only spare his life."

7 So Satan[e] went out from the presence of the LORD, and inflicted loathsome sores on Job from the sole of his foot to the crown of his head. 8Job[g] took a potsherd with which to scrape himself, and sat among the ashes.

9 Then his wife said to him, "Do you still persist in your integrity? Curse[h] God, and die." 10But he said to her, "You speak as any foolish woman would speak. Shall we receive the good at the hand of God, and not receive the bad?" In all this Job did not sin with his lips.

Job's Three Friends

11 Now when Job's three friends heard of all these troubles that had come upon him, each of them set out from his home—Eliphaz the Temanite, Bildad the Shuhite, and Zophar the Naamathite. They met together to go and console and comfort him. 12When they saw him from a distance, they did not recognize him, and they raised their voices and wept aloud; they tore their robes and threw dust in the air upon their heads. 13They sat with him on the ground seven days and seven nights, and no one spoke a word to him, for they saw that his suffering was very great.

Job Curses the Day He Was Born

3 After this Job opened his mouth and cursed the day of his birth. 2Job said:
3   "Let the day perish in which I was
           born,
       and the night that said,
       'A man-child is conceived.'
4   Let that day be darkness!
       May God above not seek it,
       or light shine on it.
5   Let gloom and deep darkness claim
           it.
       Let clouds settle upon it;
       let the blackness of the day
           terrify it.

---

d Heb sons of God   e Or the Accuser; Heb ha-satan   f Or All that the man has he will give for his
life   g Heb He   h Heb Bless

6 That night—let thick darkness
  seize it!
  let it not rejoice among the days
  of the year;
  let it not come into the number
  of the months.
7 Yes, let that night be barren;
  let no joyful cry be heard[i] in it.
8 Let those curse it who curse the
  Sea,[j]
  those who are skilled to rouse up
  Leviathan.
9 Let the stars of its dawn be dark;
  let it hope for light, but have
  none;
  may it not see the eyelids of the
  morning—
10 because it did not shut the doors of
  my mother's womb,
  and hide trouble from my eyes.

11 "Why did I not die at birth,
  come forth from the womb and
  expire?
12 Why were there knees to receive
  me,
  or breasts for me to suck?
13 Now I would be lying down and
  quiet;
  I would be asleep; then I would
  be at rest
14 with kings and counselors of the
  earth
  who rebuild ruins for
  themselves,
15 or with princes who have gold,
  who fill their houses with silver.
16 Or why was I not buried like a
  stillborn child,
  like an infant that never sees the
  light?
17 There the wicked cease from
  troubling,
  and there the weary are at rest.
18 There the prisoners are at ease
  together;
  they do not hear the voice of the
  taskmaster.
19 The small and the great are there,
  and the slaves are free from their
  masters.

20 "Why is light given to one in
  misery,
  and life to the bitter in soul,

21 who long for death, but it does not
  come,
  and dig for it more than for
  hidden treasures;
22 who rejoice exceedingly,
  and are glad when they find the
  grave?
23 Why is light given to one who
  cannot see the way,
  whom God has fenced in?
24 For my sighing comes like[k] my
  bread,
  and my groanings are poured out
  like water.
25 Truly the thing that I fear comes
  upon me,
  and what I dread befalls me.
26 I am not at ease, nor am I quiet;
  I have no rest; but trouble
  comes."

Eliphaz Speaks: Job Has Sinned

4 Then Eliphaz the Temanite
answered:
2 "If one ventures a word with you,
  will you be offended?
  But who can keep from speaking?
3 See, you have instructed many;
  you have strengthened the weak
  hands.
4 Your words have supported those
  who were stumbling,
  and you have made firm the
  feeble knees.
5 But now it has come to you, and
  you are impatient;
  it touches you, and you are
  dismayed.
6 Is not your fear of God your
  confidence,
  and the integrity of your ways
  your hope?

7 "Think now, who that was
  innocent ever perished?
  Or where were the upright cut
  off?
8 As I have seen, those who plow
  iniquity
  and sow trouble reap the same.
9 By the breath of God they perish,
  and by the blast of his anger they
  are consumed.
10 The roar of the lion, the voice of
  the fierce lion,

and the teeth of the young lions
are broken.
11 The strong lion perishes for lack of
prey,
and the whelps of the lioness are
scattered.

12 "Now a word came stealing to me,
my ear received the whisper of it.
13 Amid thoughts from visions of the
night,
when deep sleep falls on mortals,
14 dread came upon me, and
trembling,
which made all my bones shake.
15 A spirit glided past my face;
the hair of my flesh bristled.
16 It stood still,
but I could not discern its
appearance.
A form was before my eyes;
there was silence, then I heard a
voice:
17 'Can mortals be righteous before[l]
God?
Can human beings be pure
before[l] their Maker?
18 Even in his servants he puts no
trust,
and his angels he charges with
error;
19 how much more those who live in
houses of clay,
whose foundation is in the dust,
who are crushed like a moth.
20 Between morning and evening they
are destroyed;
they perish forever without any
regarding it.
21 Their tent-cord is plucked up
within them,
and they die devoid of wisdom.'

Job Is Corrected by God

5 "Call now; is there anyone
who will answer you?
To which of the holy ones will you
turn?
2 Surely vexation kills the fool,
and jealousy slays the simple.
3 I have seen fools taking root,
but suddenly I cursed their
dwelling.
4 Their children are far from safety,

they are crushed in the gate,
and there is no one to deliver
them.
5 The hungry eat their harvest,
and they take it even out of the
thorns;[m]
and the thirsty[n] pant after their
wealth.
6 For misery does not come from the
earth,
nor does trouble sprout from the
ground;
7 but human beings are born to
trouble
just as sparks[o] fly upward.

8 "As for me, I would seek God,
and to God I would commit my
cause.
9 He does great things and
unsearchable,
marvelous things without
number.
10 He gives rain on the earth
and sends waters on the fields;
11 he sets on high those who are
lowly,
and those who mourn are lifted
to safety.
12 He frustrates the devices of the
crafty,
so that their hands achieve no
success.
13 He takes the wise in their own
craftiness;
and the schemes of the wily are
brought to a quick end.
14 They meet with darkness in the
daytime,
and grope at noonday as in the
night.
15 But he saves the needy from the
sword of their mouth,
from the hand of the mighty.
16 So the poor have hope,
and injustice shuts its mouth.

17 "How happy is the one whom God
reproves;
therefore do not despise the
discipline of the Almighty.[p]
18 For he wounds, but he binds up;
he strikes, but his hands heal.

---

l Or *more than*   m Meaning of Heb uncertain   n Aquila Symmachus Syr Vg: Heb *snare*
o Or *birds*; Heb *sons of Resheph*   p Traditional rendering of Heb *Shaddai*

19 He will deliver you from six
   troubles;
      in seven no harm shall touch you.
20 In famine he will redeem you from
   death,
      and in war from the power of the
      sword.
21 You shall be hidden from the
   scourge of the tongue,
      and shall not fear destruction
      when it comes.
22 At destruction and famine you
   shall laugh,
      and shall not fear the wild
      animals of the earth.
23 For you shall be in league with the
   stones of the field,
      and the wild animals shall be at
      peace with you.
24 You shall know that your tent is
   safe,
      you shall inspect your fold and
      miss nothing.
25 You shall know that your
   descendants will be many,
      and your offspring like the grass
      of the earth.
26 You shall come to your grave in
   ripe old age,
      as a shock of grain comes up to
      the threshing floor in its
      season.
27 See, we have searched this out; it is
   true.
      Hear, and know it for yourself."

Job Replies: My Complaint Is Just

6 Then Job answered:
2 "O that my vexation were
   weighed,
      and all my calamity laid in the
      balances!
3 For then it would be heavier than
   the sand of the sea;
      therefore my words have been
      rash.
4 For the arrows of the Almighty*q* are
   in me;
      my spirit drinks their poison;
      the terrors of God are arrayed
      against me.
5 Does the wild ass bray over its grass,
   or the ox low over its fodder?

6 Can that which is tasteless be
   eaten without salt,
      or is there any flavor in the juice
      of mallows?*r*
7 My appetite refuses to touch them;
      they are like food that is
      loathsome to me.*r*

8 "O that I might have my request,
      and that God would grant my
      desire;
9 that it would please God to crush
   me,
      that he would let loose his hand
      and cut me off!
10 This would be my consolation;
      I would even exult*r* in
      unrelenting pain;
      for I have not denied the words of
      the Holy One.
11 What is my strength, that I should
   wait?
      And what is my end, that I
      should be patient?
12 Is my strength the strength of
   stones,
      or is my flesh bronze?
13 In truth I have no help in me,
      and any resource is driven from
      me.

14 "Those who withhold*s* kindness
   from a friend
      forsake the fear of the Almighty.*q*
15 My companions are treacherous
   like a torrent-bed,
      like freshets that pass away,
16 that run dark with ice,
      turbid with melting snow.
17 In time of heat they disappear;
      when it is hot, they vanish from
      their place.
18 The caravans turn aside from their
   course;
      they go up into the waste, and
      perish.
19 The caravans of Tema look,
      the travelers of Sheba hope.
20 They are disappointed because they
   were confident;
      they come there and are
      confounded.

---

q Traditional rendering of Heb *Shaddai*   *r* Meaning of Heb uncertain   *s* Syr Vg Compare Tg:
Meaning of Heb uncertain

21 Such you have now become to me;[t]
        you see my calamity, and are
        afraid.
22 Have I said, 'Make me a gift'?
        Or, 'From your wealth offer a
        bribe for me'?
23 Or, 'Save me from an opponent's
        hand'?
        Or, 'Ransom me from the hand of
        oppressors'?

24 "Teach me, and I will be silent;
        make me understand how I have
        gone wrong.
25 How forceful are honest words!
        But your reproof, what does it
        reprove?
26 Do you think that you can reprove
        words,
        as if the speech of the desperate
        were wind?
27 You would even cast lots over the
        orphan,
        and bargain over your friend.

28 "But now, be pleased to look at me;
        for I will not lie to your face.
29 Turn, I pray, let no wrong be done.
        Turn now, my vindication is at
        stake.
30 Is there any wrong on my tongue?
        Cannot my taste discern
        calamity?

Job: My Suffering Is without End

7 "Do not human beings have a
        hard service on earth,
        and are not their days like the
        days of a laborer?
2 Like a slave who longs for the
        shadow,
        and like laborers who look for
        their wages,
3 so I am allotted months of
        emptiness,
        and nights of misery are
        apportioned to me.
4 When I lie down I say, 'When shall
        I rise?'
        But the night is long,
        and I am full of tossing until
        dawn.
5 My flesh is clothed with worms
        and dirt;

my skin hardens, then breaks out
        again.
6 My days are swifter than a weaver's
        shuttle,
        and come to their end without
        hope.[u]

7 "Remember that my life is a breath;
        my eye will never again see good.
8 The eye that beholds me will see
        me no more;
        while your eyes are upon me, I
        shall be gone.
9 As the cloud fades and vanishes,
        so those who go down to Sheol
        do not come up;
10 they return no more to their houses,
        nor do their places know them
        any more.

11 "Therefore I will not restrain my
        mouth;
        I will speak in the anguish of my
        spirit;
        I will complain in the bitterness
        of my soul.
12 Am I the Sea, or the Dragon,
        that you set a guard over me?
13 When I say, 'My bed will comfort
        me,'
        my couch will ease my
        complaint,'
14 then you scare me with dreams
        and terrify me with visions,
15 so that I would choose strangling
        and death rather than this body.
16 I loathe my life; I would not live
        forever.
        Let me alone, for my days are a
        breath.
17 What are human beings, that you
        make so much of them,
        that you set your mind on them,
18 visit them every morning,
        test them every moment?
19 Will you not look away from me
        for a while,
        let me alone until I swallow my
        spittle?
20 If I sin, what do I do to you, you
        watcher of humanity?
        Why have you made me your
        target?
        Why have I become a burden to
        you?

t Cn Compare Gk Syr: Meaning of Heb uncertain   u Or as the thread runs out

21 Why do you not pardon my
transgression
and take away my iniquity?
For now I shall lie in the earth;
you will seek me, but I shall not
be.''

Bildad Speaks: Job Should Repent

8 Then Bildad the Shuhite answered:

2 "How long will you say these
things,
and the words of your mouth be a
great wind?

3 Does God pervert justice?
Or does the Almighty[v] pervert
the right?

4 If your children sinned against him,
he delivered them into the power
of their transgression.

5 If you will seek God
and make supplication to the
Almighty,[v]

6 if you are pure and upright,
surely then he will rouse himself
for you
and restore to you your rightful
place.

7 Though your beginning was small,
your latter days will be very
great.

8 "For inquire now of bygone
generations,
and consider what their ancestors
have found;

9 for we are but of yesterday, and we
know nothing,
for our days on earth are but a
shadow.

10 Will they not teach you and tell
you
and utter words out of their
understanding?

11 "Can papyrus grow where there is
no marsh?
Can reeds flourish where there is
no water?

12 While yet in flower and not cut
down,
they wither before any other
plant.

13 Such are the paths of all who forget
God;
the hope of the godless shall
perish.

14 Their confidence is gossamer,
a spider's house their trust.

15 If one leans against its house, it
will not stand;
if one lays hold of it, it will not
endure.

16 The wicked thrive[w] before the sun,
and their shoots spread over the
garden.

17 Their roots twine around the
stoneheap;
they live among the rocks.[x]

18 If they are destroyed from their
place,
then it will deny them, saying, 'I
have never seen you.'

19 See, these are their happy ways,[y]
and out of the earth still others
will spring.

20 "See, God will not reject a
blameless person,
nor take the hand of evildoers.

21 He will yet fill your mouth with
laughter,
and your lips with shouts of joy.

22 Those who hate you will be
clothed with shame,
and the tent of the wicked will
be no more."

Job Replies: There Is No Mediator

9 Then Job answered:

2 "Indeed I know that this is so;
but how can a mortal be just
before God?

3 If one wished to contend with him,
one could not answer him once
in a thousand.

4 He is wise in heart, and mighty in
strength
—who has resisted him, and
succeeded?—

5 he who removes mountains, and
they do not know it,
when he overturns them in his
anger;

6 who shakes the earth out of its
place,
and its pillars tremble;

v Traditional rendering of Heb *Shaddai*   w Heb *He thrives*   x Gk Vg: Meaning of Heb uncertain
y Meaning of Heb uncertain

7 who commands the sun, and it
  does not rise;
  who seals up the stars;
8 who alone stretched out the
  heavens
  and trampled the waves of the
  Sea;*z*
9 who made the Bear and Orion,
  the Pleiades and the chambers of
  the south;
10 who does great things beyond
  understanding,
  and marvelous things without
  number.
11 Look, he passes by me, and I do not
  see him;
  he moves on, but I do not
  perceive him.
12 He snatches away; who can stop
  him?
  Who will say to him, 'What are
  you doing?'

13 "God will not turn back his anger;
  the helpers of Rahab bowed
  beneath him.
14 How then can I answer him,
  choosing my words with him?
15 Though I am innocent, I cannot
  answer him;
  I must appeal for mercy to my
  accuser.*a*
16 If I summoned him and he
  answered me,
  I do not believe that he would
  listen to my voice.
17 For he crushes me with a tempest,
  and multiplies my wounds
  without cause;
18 he will not let me get my breath,
  but fills me with bitterness.
19 If it is a contest of strength, he is
  the strong one!
  If it is a matter of justice, who
  can summon him?*b*
20 Though I am innocent, my own
  mouth would condemn me;
  though I am blameless, he would
  prove me perverse.
21 I am blameless; I do not know
  myself;
  I loathe my life.
22 It is all one; therefore I say,

he destroys both the blameless
and the wicked.
23 When disaster brings sudden death,
  he mocks at the calamity*c* of the
  innocent.
24 The earth is given into the hand of
  the wicked;
  he covers the eyes of its judges—
  if it is not he, who then is it?

25 "My days are swifter than a runner;
  they flee away, they see no good.
26 They go by like skiffs of reed,
  like an eagle swooping on the
  prey.
27 If I say, 'I will forget my complaint;
  I will put off my sad countenance
  and be of good cheer,'
28 I become afraid of all my suffering,
  for I know you will not hold me
  innocent.
29 I shall be condemned;
  why then do I labor in vain?
30 If I wash myself with soap
  and cleanse my hands with lye,
31 yet you will plunge me into filth,
  and my own clothes will abhor
  me.
32 For he is not a mortal, as I am, that
  I might answer him,
  that we should come to trial
  together.
33 There is no umpire*d* between us,
  who might lay his hand on us
  both.
34 If he would take his rod away from
  me,
  and not let dread of him terrify
  me,
35 then I would speak without fear of
  him,
  for I know I am not what I am
  thought to be.*e*

Job: I Loathe My Life

10 "I loathe my life;
  I will give free utterance to
  my complaint;
  I will speak in the bitterness of
  my soul.
2 I will say to God, Do not condemn
  me;

---

z Or *trampled the back of the sea dragon*   *a* Or *for my right*   *b* Compare Gk: Heb *me*
c Meaning of Heb uncertain   *d* Another reading is *Would that there were an umpire*   *e* Cn: Heb *for I am not so in myself*

let me know why you contend
against me.
3 Does it seem good to you to oppress,
to despise the work of your hands
and favor the schemes of the
wicked?
4 Do you have eyes of flesh?
Do you see as humans see?
5 Are your days like the days of
mortals,
or your years like human years,
6 that you seek out my iniquity
and search for my sin,
7 although you know that I am not
guilty,
and there is no one to deliver out
of your hand?
8 Your hands fashioned and made
me;
and now you turn and destroy
me.*f*
9 Remember that you fashioned me
like clay;
and will you turn me to dust
again?
10 Did you not pour me out like milk
and curdle me like cheese?
11 You clothed me with skin and flesh,
and knit me together with bones
and sinews.
12 You have granted me life and
steadfast love,
and your care has preserved my
spirit.
13 Yet these things you hid in your
heart;
I know that this was your
purpose.
14 If I sin, you watch me,
and do not acquit me of my
iniquity.
15 If I am wicked, woe to me!
If I am righteous, I cannot lift up
my head,
for I am filled with disgrace
and look upon my affliction.
16 Bold as a lion you hunt me;
you repeat your exploits against
me.
17 You renew your witnesses against
me,

and increase your vexation
toward me;
you bring fresh troops against
me.*g*
18 "Why did you bring me forth from
the womb?
Would that I had died before any
eye had seen me,
19 and were as though I had not been,
carried from the womb to the
grave.
20 Are not the days of my life few?*h*
Let me alone, that I may find a
little comfort*i*
21 before I go, never to return,
to the land of gloom and deep
darkness,
22 the land of gloom*j* and chaos,
where light is like darkness."

Zophar Speaks: Job's Guilt Deserves Punishment

11 Then Zophar the Naamathite
answered:
2 "Should a multitude of words go
unanswered,
and should one full of talk be
vindicated?
3 Should your babble put others to
silence,
and when you mock, shall no
one shame you?
4 For you say, 'My conduct*k* is pure,
and I am clean in God's*l* sight.'
5 But O that God would speak,
and open his lips to you,
6 and that he would tell you the
secrets of wisdom!
For wisdom is many-sided.*m*
Know then that God exacts of you
less than your guilt deserves.

7 "Can you find out the deep things
of God?
Can you find out the limit of the
Almighty?*n*
8 It is higher than heaven*o*—what
can you do?
Deeper than Sheol—what can
you know?

---

f Cn Compare Gk Syr: Heb *made me together all around, and you destroy me*   *g* Cn Compare Gk: Heb *toward me; changes and a troop are with me*   *h* Cn Compare Gk Syr: Heb *Are not my days few? Let him cease!*   *i* Heb *that I may brighten up a little*   *j* Heb *gloom as darkness, deep darkness*   *k* Gk: Heb *teaching*   *l* Heb *your*   *m* Meaning of Heb uncertain   *n* Traditional rendering of Heb *Shaddai*   *o* Heb *The heights of heaven*

9 Its measure is longer than the
      earth,
   and broader than the sea.
10 If he passes through, and
      imprisons,
   and assembles for judgment, who
      can hinder him?
11 For he knows those who are
      worthless;
   when he sees iniquity, will he
      not consider it?
12 But a stupid person will get
      understanding,
   when a wild ass is born human.*p*

13 "If you direct your heart rightly,
   you will stretch out your hands
      toward him.
14 If iniquity is in your hand, put it far
      away,
   and do not let wickedness reside
      in your tents.
15 Surely then you will lift up your
      face without blemish;
   you will be secure, and will not
      fear.
16 You will forget your misery;
   you will remember it as waters
      that have passed away.
17 And your life will be brighter than
      the noonday;
   its darkness will be like the
      morning.
18 And you will have confidence,
      because there is hope;
   you will be protected*q* and take
      your rest in safety.
19 You will lie down, and no one will
      make you afraid;
   many will entreat your favor.
20 But the eyes of the wicked will fail;
   all way of escape will be lost to
      them,
   and their hope is to breathe their
      last."

Job Replies: I Am a Laughingstock

12 Then Job answered:
2 "No doubt you are the
      people,
   and wisdom will die with you.
3 But I have understanding as well as
      you;
   I am not inferior to you.

Who does not know such things
   as these?
4 I am a laughingstock to my friends;
   I, who called upon God and he
      answered me,
   a just and blameless man, I am a
      laughingstock.
5 Those at ease have contempt for
      misfortune,*p*
   but it is ready for those whose
      feet are unstable.
6 The tents of robbers are at peace,
   and those who provoke God are
      secure,
   who bring their god in their
      hands.*r*

7 "But ask the animals, and they will
      teach you;
   the birds of the air, and they will
      tell you;
8 ask the plants of the earth,*s* and
      they will teach you;
   and the fish of the sea will
      declare to you.
9 Who among all these does not
      know
   that the hand of the LORD has
      done this?
10 In his hand is the life of every
      living thing
   and the breath of every human
      being.
11 Does not the ear test words
   as the palate tastes food?
12 Is wisdom with the aged,
   and understanding in length of
      days?

13 "With God*t* are wisdom and
      strength;
   he has counsel and
      understanding.
14 If he tears down, no one can
      rebuild;
   if he shuts someone in, no one
      can open up.
15 If he withholds the waters, they dry
      up;
   if he sends them out, they
      overwhelm the land.
16 With him are strength and wisdom;
   the deceived and the deceiver are
      his.

p Meaning of Heb uncertain   *q* Or *you will look around*   *r* Or *whom God brought forth by his*
hand; Meaning of Heb uncertain   *s* Or *speak to the earth*   *t* Heb *him*

17 He leads counselors away stripped,
   and makes fools of judges.
18 He looses the sash of kings,
   and binds a waistcloth on their
   loins.
19 He leads priests away stripped,
   and overthrows the mighty.
20 He deprives of speech those who
   are trusted,
   and takes away the discernment
   of the elders.
21 He pours contempt on princes,
   and looses the belt of the strong.
22 He uncovers the deeps out of
   darkness,
   and brings deep darkness to light.
23 He makes nations great, then
   destroys them;
   he enlarges nations, then leads
   them away.
24 He strips understanding from the
   leaders[u] of the earth,
   and makes them wander in a
   pathless waste.
25 They grope in the dark without
   light;
   he makes them stagger like a
   drunkard.

ATHEISTS PUT ON A FALSE COURAGE AND
ALACRITY IN THE MIDST OF THEIR DARKNESS
AND APPREHENSIONS, LIKE CHILDREN WHO,
WHEN THEY FEAR TO GO INTO THE DARK, WILL
SING OR WHISTLE TO KEEP UP THEIR COURAGE.

—*Alexander Pope*

---

13 "Look, my eye has seen all this,
   my ear has heard and understood
   it.
2 What you know, I also know;
   I am not inferior to you.
3 But I would speak to the
   Almighty,[v]
   and I desire to argue my case
   with God.
4 As for you, you whitewash with
   lies;
   all of you are worthless
   physicians.

5 If you would only keep silent,
   that would be your wisdom!
6 Hear now my reasoning,
   and listen to the pleadings of my
   lips.
7 Will you speak falsely for God,
   and speak deceitfully for him?
8 Will you show partiality toward
   him,
   will you plead the case for God?
9 Will it be well with you when he
   searches you out?
   Or can you deceive him, as one
   person deceives another?
10 He will surely rebuke you
   if in secret you show partiality.
11 Will not his majesty terrify you,
   and the dread of him fall upon
   you?
12 Your maxims are proverbs of ashes,
   your defenses are defenses of
   clay.
13 "Let me have silence, and I will
   speak,
   and let come on me what may.
14 I will take my flesh in my teeth,
   and put my life in my hand.[w]
15 See, he will kill me; I have no
   hope;[x]
   but I will defend my ways to his
   face.
16 This will be my salvation,
   that the godless shall not come
   before him.
17 Listen carefully to my words,
   and let my declaration be in your
   ears.
18 I have indeed prepared my case;
   I know that I shall be vindicated.
19 Who is there that will contend
   with me?
   For then I would be silent and
   die.

Job's Despondent Prayer

20 Only grant two things to me,
   then I will not hide myself from
   your face:
21 withdraw your hand far from me,
   and do not let dread of you terrify
   me.

---

u Heb adds *of the people*   v Traditional rendering of Heb *Shaddai*   w Gk: Heb *Why should I take
. . . in my hand?*   x Or *Though he kill me, yet I will trust in him*

22   Then call, and I will answer;
        or let me speak, and you reply to
        me.
23   How many are my iniquities and
        my sins?
        Make me know my transgression
        and my sin.
24   Why do you hide your face,
        and count me as your enemy?
25   Will you frighten a windblown leaf
        and pursue dry chaff?
26   For you write bitter things against
        me,
        and make me reap[y] the iniquities
        of my youth.
27   You put my feet in the stocks,
        and watch all my paths;
        you set a bound to the soles of
        my feet.
28   One wastes away like a rotten
        thing,
        like a garment that is moth-eaten.

14   "A mortal, born of woman,
        few of days and full of
        trouble,
2   comes up like a flower and
        withers,
        flees like a shadow and does not
        last.
3   Do you fix your eyes on such a
        one?
        Do you bring me into judgment
        with you?
4   Who can bring a clean thing out of
        an unclean?
        No one can.
5   Since their days are determined,
        and the number of their months
        is known to you,
        and you have appointed the
        bounds that they cannot
        pass,
6   look away from them, and desist,[z]
        that they may enjoy, like
        laborers, their days.

7   "For there is hope for a tree,
        if it is cut down, that it will
        sprout again,
        and that its shoots will not cease.
8   Though its root grows old in the
        earth,
        and its stump dies in the ground,
9   yet at the scent of water it will bud

and put forth branches like a
        young plant.
10   But mortals die, and are laid low;
        humans expire, and where are
        they?
11   As waters fail from a lake,
        and a river wastes away and dries
        up,
12   so mortals lie down and do not rise
        again;
        until the heavens are no more,
        they will not awake
        or be roused out of their sleep.
13   O that you would hide me in Sheol,
        that you would conceal me until
        your wrath is past,
        that you would appoint me a set
        time, and remember me!
14   If mortals die, will they live again?
        All the days of my service I
        would wait
        until my release should come.
15   You would call, and I would answer
        you;
        you would long for the work of
        your hands.
16   For then you would not[a] number
        my steps,
        you would not keep watch over
        my sin;
17   my transgression would be sealed
        up in a bag,
        and you would cover over my
        iniquity.

18   "But the mountain falls and
        crumbles away,
        and the rock is removed from its
        place;
19   the waters wear away the stones;
        the torrents wash away the soil
        of the earth;
        so you destroy the hope of
        mortals.
20   You prevail forever against them,
        and they pass away;
        you change their countenance,
        and send them away.
21   Their children come to honor, and
        they do not know it;
        they are brought low, and it goes
        unnoticed.
22   They feel only the pain of their
        own bodies,
        and mourn only for themselves."

y Heb inherit   z Cn: Heb that they may desist   a Syr: Heb lacks not

Eliphaz Speaks: Job Undermines Religion

15 Then Eliphaz the Temanite answered:

2 "Should the wise answer with
        windy knowledge,
    and fill themselves with the east
        wind?
3 Should they argue in unprofitable
        talk,
    or in words with which they can
        do no good?
4 But you are doing away with the
        fear of God,
    and hindering meditation before
        God.
5 For your iniquity teaches your
        mouth,
    and you choose the tongue of the
        crafty.
6 Your own mouth condemns you,
        and not I;
    your own lips testify against you.

7 "Are you the firstborn of the
        human race?
    Were you brought forth before
        the hills?
8 Have you listened in the council of
        God?
    And do you limit wisdom to
        yourself?
9 What do you know that we do not
        know?
    What do you understand that is
        not clear to us?
10 The gray-haired and the aged are on
        our side,
    those older than your father.
11 Are the consolations of God too
        small for you,
    or the word that deals gently
        with you?
12 Why does your heart carry you
        away,
    and why do your eyes flash,[b]
13 so that you turn your spirit against
        God,
    and let such words go out of your
        mouth?
14 What are mortals, that they can be
        clean?
    Or those born of woman, that
        they can be righteous?

15 God puts no trust even in his holy
        ones,
    and the heavens are not clean in
        his sight;
16 how much less one who is
        abominable and corrupt,
    one who drinks iniquity like
        water!

17 "I will show you; listen to me;
    what I have seen I will declare—
18 what sages have told,
    and their ancestors have not
        hidden,
19 to whom alone the land was given,
    and no stranger passed among
        them.
20 The wicked writhe in pain all their
        days,
    through all the years that are laid
        up for the ruthless.
21 Terrifying sounds are in their ears;
    in prosperity the destroyer will
        come upon them.
22 They despair of returning from
        darkness,
    and they are destined for the
        sword.
23 They wander abroad for bread,
        saying, 'Where is it?'
    They know that a day of
        darkness is ready at hand;
24 distress and anguish terrify them;
    they prevail against them, like a
        king prepared for battle.
25 Because they stretched out their
        hands against God,
    and bid defiance to the
        Almighty,[c]
26 running stubbornly against him
    with a thick-bossed shield;
27 because they have covered their
        faces with their fat,
    and gathered fat upon their loins,
28 they will live in desolate cities,
    in houses that no one should
        inhabit,
    houses destined to become heaps
        of ruins;
29 they will not be rich, and their
        wealth will not endure,
    nor will they strike root in the
        earth;[d]

b Meaning of Heb uncertain   c Traditional rendering of Heb Shaddai   d Vg: Meaning of Heb uncertain

30 they will not escape from darkness;
    the flame will dry up their
      shoots,
    and their blossom*e* will be swept
      away*f* by the wind.
31 Let them not trust in emptiness,
    deceiving themselves;
    for emptiness will be their
      recompense.
32 It will be paid in full before their
    time,
    and their branch will not be
      green.
33 They will shake off their unripe
    grape, like the vine,
    and cast off their blossoms, like
      the olive tree.
34 For the company of the godless is
    barren,
    and fire consumes the tents of
      bribery.
35 They conceive mischief and bring
    forth evil
    and their heart prepares deceit."

Job Reaffirms His Innocence

16 Then Job answered:
2 "I have heard many such
    things;
    miserable comforters are you all.
3 Have windy words no limit?
    Or what provokes you that you
      keep on talking?
4 I also could talk as you do,
    if you were in my place;
    I could join words together against
      you,
    and shake my head at you.
5 I could encourage you with my
    mouth,
    and the solace of my lips would
      assuage your pain.

6 "If I speak, my pain is not assuaged,
    and if I forbear, how much of it
      leaves me?
7 Surely now God has worn me out;
    he has*g* made desolate all my
      company.
8 And he has*g* shriveled me up,
    which is a witness against me;
    my leanness has risen up against
      me,
    and it testifies to my face.

9 He has torn me in his wrath, and
    hated me;
    he has gnashed his teeth at me;
    my adversary sharpens his eyes
      against me.
10 They have gaped at me with their
    mouths;
    they have struck me insolently
      on the cheek;
    they mass themselves together
      against me.
11 God gives me up to the ungodly,
    and casts me into the hands of
      the wicked.
12 I was at ease, and he broke me in
    two;
    he seized me by the neck and
      dashed me to pieces;
    he set me up as his target;
13   his archers surround me.
He slashes open my kidneys, and
    shows no mercy;
    he pours out my gall on the
      ground.
14 He bursts upon me again and again;
    he rushes at me like a warrior.
15 I have sewed sackcloth upon my
    skin,
    and have laid my strength in the
      dust.
16 My face is red with weeping,
    and deep darkness is on my
      eyelids,
17 though there is no violence in my
    hands,
    and my prayer is pure.

18 "O earth, do not cover my blood;
    let my outcry find no resting
      place.
19 Even now, in fact, my witness is in
    heaven,
    and he that vouches for me is on
      high.
20 My friends scorn me;
    my eye pours out tears to God,
21 that he would maintain the right of
    a mortal with God,
    as*h* one does for a neighbor.
22 For when a few years have come,
    I shall go the way from which I
      shall not return.

---

e Gk: Heb *mouth*   *f* Cn: Heb *will depart*   *g* Heb *you have*   *h* Syr Vg Tg: Heb *and*

Job Prays for Relief

17 My spirit is broken, my days are extinct,
the grave is ready for me.
2 Surely there are mockers around me,
and my eye dwells on their provocation.

3 "Lay down a pledge for me with yourself;
who is there that will give surety for me?
4 Since you have closed their minds to understanding,
therefore you will not let them triumph.
5 Those who denounce friends for reward—
the eyes of their children will fail.

6 "He has made me a byword of the peoples,
and I am one before whom people spit.
7 My eye has grown dim from grief,
and all my members are like a shadow.
8 The upright are appalled at this,
and the innocent stir themselves up against the godless.
9 Yet the righteous hold to their way,
and they that have clean hands grow stronger and stronger.
10 But you, come back now, all of you,
and I shall not find a sensible person among you.
11 My days are past, my plans are broken off,
the desires of my heart.
12 They make night into day;
'The light,' they say, 'is near to the darkness.'[i]
13 If I look for Sheol as my house,
if I spread my couch in darkness,
14 if I say to the Pit, 'You are my father,'
and to the worm, 'My mother,' or 'My sister,'
15 where then is my hope?
Who will see my hope?
16 Will it go down to the bars of Sheol?
Shall we descend together into the dust?"

Bildad Speaks: God Punishes the Wicked

18 Then Bildad the Shuhite answered:
2 "How long will you hunt for words?
Consider, and then we shall speak.
3 Why are we counted as cattle?
Why are we stupid in your sight?
4 You who tear yourself in your anger—
shall the earth be forsaken because of you,
or the rock be removed out of its place?

5 "Surely the light of the wicked is put out,
and the flame of their fire does not shine.
6 The light is dark in their tent,
and the lamp above them is put out.
7 Their strong steps are shortened,
and their own schemes throw them down.
8 For they are thrust into a net by their own feet,
and they walk into a pitfall.
9 A trap seizes them by the heel;
a snare lays hold of them.
10 A rope is hid for them in the ground,
a trap for them in the path.
11 Terrors frighten them on every side,
and chase them at their heels.
12 Their strength is consumed by hunger,[j]
and calamity is ready for their stumbling.
13 By disease their skin is consumed,[k]
the firstborn of Death consumes their limbs.
14 They are torn from the tent in which they trusted,
and are brought to the king of terrors.
15 In their tents nothing remains;
sulfur is scattered upon their habitations.
16 Their roots dry up beneath,
and their branches wither above.

---

i Meaning of Heb uncertain   *j* Or *Disaster is hungry for them*   *k* Cn: Heb *It consumes the limbs of his skin*

17 Their memory perishes from the
earth,
and they have no name in the
street.
18 They are thrust from light into
darkness,
and driven out of the world.
19 They have no offspring or
descendant among their
people,
and no survivor where they used
to live.
20 They of the west are appalled at
their fate,
and horror seizes those of the east.
21 Surely such are the dwellings of the
ungodly,
such is the place of those who do
not know God."

Job Replies: I Know That My Redeemer Lives

19 Then Job answered:
2 "How long will you torment
me,
and break me in pieces with
words?
3 These ten times you have cast
reproach upon me;
are you not ashamed to wrong
me?
4 And even if it is true that I have
erred,
my error remains with me.
5 If indeed you magnify yourselves
against me,
and make my humiliation an
argument against me,
6 know then that God has put me in
the wrong,
and closed his net around me.
7 Even when I cry out, 'Violence!' I
am not answered;
I call aloud, but there is no justice.
8 He has walled up my way so that I
cannot pass,
and he has set darkness upon my
paths.
9 He has stripped my glory from me,
and taken the crown from my
head.
10 He breaks me down on every side,
and I am gone,
he has uprooted my hope like a
tree.

11 He has kindled his wrath against
me,
and counts me as his adversary.
12 His troops come on together;
they have thrown up siegeworks[1]
against me,
and encamp around my tent.

13 "He has put my family far from me,
and my acquaintances are wholly
estranged from me.
14 My relatives and my close friends
have failed me;
15 the guests in my house have
forgotten me;
my serving girls count me as a
stranger;
I have become an alien in their
eyes.
16 I call to my servant, but he gives
me no answer;
I must myself plead with him.
17 My breath is repulsive to my wife;
I am loathsome to my own
family.
18 Even young children despise me;
when I rise, they talk against me.
19 All my intimate friends abhor me,
and those whom I loved have
turned against me.
20 My bones cling to my skin and to
my flesh,
and I have escaped by the skin of
my teeth.
21 Have pity on me, have pity on me,
O you my friends,
for the hand of God has touched
me!
22 Why do you, like God, pursue me,
never satisfied with my flesh?

23 "O that my words were written
down!
O that they were inscribed in a
book!
24 O that with an iron pen and with
lead
they were engraved on a rock
forever!
25 For I know that my Redeemer[m]
lives,
and that at the last he[n] will stand
upon the earth;[o]
26 and after my skin has been thus
destroyed,

1 Cn: Heb their way   m Or Vindicator   n Or that he the Last   o Heb dust

then in[p] my flesh I shall see God,[q]
27 whom I shall see on my side,[r]
and my eyes shall behold, and
not another.
My heart faints within me!
28 If you say, 'How we will persecute
him!'

and, 'The root of the matter is
found in him';
29 be afraid of the sword,
for wrath brings the punishment
of the sword,
so that you may know there is a
judgment."

p Or *without*   q Meaning of Heb of this verse uncertain   r Or *for myself*

FRIDAY

LET US KNIT FAST OUR SOULS TO HIM
Clement of Rome

VERSE: Job 19.25   **PASSAGE:** Job 19.25–27

eed we find it such a great wonder that he has a resurrection in store for those who have served him in holiness and in the confidence of a sound faith? For in Scripture we read, *You will raise me up, and I will praise you;* and also, *After I had lain down and fallen asleep, I rose up again; for you are with me.* Job too, says, *You will raise up this flesh of mine which has had all these trials to endure.*

Seeing then that we have this hope, let us knit fast our souls to him who is ever true to his word and righteous in his judgments. He who has forbidden us to use any deception can much less be a deceiver himself; untruth is the only thing that is impossible to God. So let us rekindle the ardor of our belief in him, and also remind ourselves that there is nothing in the world with which he is not in close touch. With the word of his greatness has he assembled all that exists, and with a word he is able to overturn it again; for *who can say to him, What have you done? or who shall withstand the power of his might?* He will act at all times as, and when, he chooses; and not one of his decrees shall fail. The entire universe lies open before him; and there is nothing that is hidden from his counsel; for *the heavens are a proclamation of God's glory, and the firmament a declaration of his handiwork. Day utters the message to day, and night proclaims the knowledge though there are no words or speeches and their voices are inaudible* (see Psalm 19.1–3).

ADDITIONAL SCRIPTURE READING:
Numbers 23.19; John 5.24–29

Go to page 570 for your next devotional reading.
Go to page 570 for your next devotional reading.

100   500

Zophar Speaks: Wickedness Receives Just Retribution

20 Then Zophar the Naamathite answered:

2 "Pay attention! My thoughts urge me to answer,
 because of the agitation within me.

3 I hear censure that insults me,
 and a spirit beyond my understanding answers me.

4 Do you not know this from of old,
 ever since mortals were placed on earth,

5 that the exulting of the wicked is short,
 and the joy of the godless is but for a moment?

6 Even though they mount up high as the heavens,
 and their head reaches to the clouds,

7 they will perish forever like their own dung;
 those who have seen them will say, 'Where are they?'

8 They will fly away like a dream, and not be found;
 they will be chased away like a vision of the night.

9 The eye that saw them will see them no more,
 nor will their place behold them any longer.

10 Their children will seek the favor of the poor,
 and their hands will give back their wealth.

11 Their bodies, once full of youth, will lie down in the dust with them.

12 "Though wickedness is sweet in their mouth,
 though they hide it under their tongues,

13 though they are loath to let it go,
 and hold it in their mouths,

14 yet their food is turned in their stomachs;
 it is the venom of asps within them.

15 They swallow down riches and vomit them up again;
 God casts them out of their bellies.

16 They will suck the poison of asps;
 the tongue of a viper will kill them.

17 They will not look on the rivers,
 the streams flowing with honey and curds.

18 They will give back the fruit of their toil,
 and will not swallow it down;
 from the profit of their trading they will get no enjoyment.

19 For they have crushed and abandoned the poor,
 they have seized a house that they did not build.

20 "They knew no quiet in their bellies;
 in their greed they let nothing escape.

21 There was nothing left after they had eaten;
 therefore their prosperity will not endure.

22 In full sufficiency they will be in distress;
 all the force of misery will come upon them.

23 To fill their belly to the full
 God^s will send his fierce anger into them,
 and rain it upon them as their food.^{t}

24 They will flee from an iron weapon;
 a bronze arrow will strike them through.

25 It is drawn forth and comes out of their body,
 and the glittering point comes out of their gall;
 terrors come upon them.

26 Utter darkness is laid up for their treasures;
 a fire fanned by no one will devour them;
 what is left in their tent will be consumed.

27 The heavens will reveal their iniquity,
 and the earth will rise up against them.

s Heb *he*   t Cn: Meaning of Heb uncertain

28 The possessions of their house will
    be carried away,
    dragged off in the day of God's[u]
    wrath.

29 This is the portion of the wicked
    from God,
    the heritage decreed for them by
    God."

Job Replies: The Wicked Often Go Unpunished

21 Then Job answered:
2 "Listen carefully to my
    words,
    and let this be your consolation.

3 Bear with me, and I will speak;
    then after I have spoken, mock
    on.

4 As for me, is my complaint
    addressed to mortals?
    Why should I not be impatient?

5 Look at me, and be appalled,
    and lay your hand upon your
    mouth.

6 When I think of it I am dismayed,
    and shuddering seizes my flesh.

7 Why do the wicked live on,
    reach old age, and grow mighty
    in power?

8 Their children are established in
    their presence,
    and their offspring before their
    eyes.

9 Their houses are safe from fear,
    and no rod of God is upon them.

10 Their bull breeds without fail;
    their cow calves and never
    miscarries.

11 They send out their little ones like
    a flock,
    and their children dance around.

12 They sing to the tambourine and
    the lyre,
    and rejoice to the sound of the
    pipe.

13 They spend their days in prosperity,
    and in peace they go down to
    Sheol.

14 They say to God, 'Leave us alone!
    We do not desire to know your
    ways.

15 What is the Almighty,[v] that we
    should serve him?
    And what profit do we get if we
    pray to him?'

16 Is not their prosperity indeed their
    own achievement?[w]
    The plans of the wicked are
    repugnant to me.

17 "How often is the lamp of the
    wicked put out?
    How often does calamity come
    upon them?
    How often does God[x] distribute
    pains in his anger?

18 How often are they like straw
    before the wind,
    and like chaff that the storm
    carries away?

19 You say, 'God stores up their
    iniquity for their children.'
    Let it be paid back to them, so
    that they may know it.

20 Let their own eyes see their
    destruction,
    and let them drink of the wrath
    of the Almighty.[v]

21 For what do they care for their
    household after them,
    when the number of their
    months is cut off?

22 Will any teach God knowledge,
    seeing that he judges those that
    are on high?

23 One dies in full prosperity,
    being wholly at ease and secure,

24 his loins full of milk
    and the marrow of his bones
    moist.

25 Another dies in bitterness of soul,
    never having tasted of good.

26 They lie down alike in the dust,
    and the worms cover them.

27 "Oh, I know your thoughts,
    and your schemes to wrong me.

28 For you say, 'Where is the house of
    the prince?
    Where is the tent in which the
    wicked lived?'

29 Have you not asked those who
    travel the roads,
    and do you not accept their
    testimony,

30 that the wicked are spared in the
    day of calamity,
    and are rescued in the day of
    wrath?

u Heb *his*   v Traditional rendering of Heb *Shaddai*   w Heb *in their hand*   x Heb *he*

31 Who declares their way to their
        face,
    and who repays them for what
        they have done?
32 When they are carried to the grave,
    a watch is kept over their tomb.
33 The clods of the valley are sweet to
        them;
    everyone will follow after,
    and those who went before are
        innumerable.
34 How then will you comfort me
        with empty nothings?
    There is nothing left of your
        answers but falsehood."

Eliphaz Speaks: Job's Wickedness Is Great

22 Then Eliphaz the Temanite
    answered:
2 "Can a mortal be of use to God?
    Can even the wisest be of service
        to him?
3 Is it any pleasure to the Almighty^y
        if you are righteous,
    or is it gain to him if you make
        your ways blameless?
4 Is it for your piety that he reproves
        you,
    and enters into judgment with
        you?
5 Is not your wickedness great?
    There is no end to your
        iniquities.
6 For you have exacted pledges from
        your family for no reason,
    and stripped the naked of their
        clothing.
7 You have given no water to the
        weary to drink,
    and you have withheld bread
        from the hungry.
8 The powerful possess the land,
    and the favored live in it.
9 You have sent widows away
        empty-handed,
    and the arms of the orphans you
        have crushed.^z
10 Therefore snares are around you,
    and sudden terror overwhelms
        you,
11 or darkness so that you cannot see;
    a flood of water covers you.

12 "Is not God high in the heavens?
    See the highest stars, how lofty
        they are!
13 Therefore you say, 'What does God
        know?
    Can he judge through the deep
        darkness?
14 Thick clouds enwrap him, so that
        he does not see,
    and he walks on the dome of
        heaven.'
15 Will you keep to the old way
    that the wicked have trod?
16 They were snatched away before
        their time;
    their foundation was washed
        away by a flood.
17 They said to God, 'Leave us alone,'
    and 'What can the Almighty^y do
        to us?'^a
18 Yet he filled their houses with good
        things—
    but the plans of the wicked are
        repugnant to me.
19 The righteous see it and are glad;
    the innocent laugh them to
        scorn,
20 saying, 'Surely our adversaries are
        cut off,
    and what they left, the fire has
        consumed.'

21 "Agree with God,^b and be at peace;
    in this way good will come to
        you.
22 Receive instruction from his
        mouth,
    and lay up his words in your
        heart.
23 If you return to the Almighty,^y you
        will be restored,
    if you remove unrighteousness
        from your tents,
24 if you treat gold like dust,
    and gold of Ophir like the stones
        of the torrent-bed,
25 and if the Almighty^y is your gold
    and your precious silver,
26 then you will delight yourself in
        the Almighty,^y
    and lift up your face to God.
27 You will pray to him, and he will
        hear you,
    and you will pay your vows.

y Traditional rendering of Heb Shaddai   z Gk Syr Tg Vg: Heb were crushed   a Gk Syr: Heb them
b Heb him

28 You will decide on a matter, and it
will be established for you,
and light will shine on your ways.
29 When others are humiliated, you
say it is pride;
for he saves the humble.
30 He will deliver even those who are
guilty;
they will escape because of the
cleanness of your hands."*c*

Job Replies: My Complaint Is Bitter

23 Then Job answered:
2 "Today also my complaint
is bitter;*d*
his*e* hand is heavy despite my
groaning.
3 Oh, that I knew where I might find
him,
that I might come even to his
dwelling!
4 I would lay my case before him,
and fill my mouth with
arguments.
5 I would learn what he would
answer me,
and understand what he would
say to me.
6 Would he contend with me in the
greatness of his power?
No; but he would give heed to
me.
7 There an upright person could
reason with him,
and I should be acquitted forever
by my judge.

8 "If I go forward, he is not there;
or backward, I cannot perceive
him;
9 on the left he hides, and I cannot
behold him;
I turn*f* to the right, but I cannot
see him.
10 But he knows the way that I take;
when he has tested me, I shall
come out like gold.
11 My foot has held fast to his steps;
I have kept his way and have not
turned aside.
12 I have not departed from the
commandment of his lips;

I have treasured in*g* my bosom
the words of his mouth.
13 But he stands alone and who can
dissuade him?
What he desires, that he does.
14 For he will complete what he
appoints for me;
and many such things are in his
mind.
15 Therefore I am terrified at his
presence;
when I consider, I am in dread of
him.
16 God has made my heart faint;
the Almighty*h* has terrified me;
17 If only I could vanish in darkness,
and thick darkness would cover
my face!*i*

Job Complains of Violence on the Earth

24 "Why are times not kept by
the Almighty,*h*
and why do those who know him
never see his days?
2 The wicked*j* remove landmarks;
they seize flocks and pasture
them.
3 They drive away the donkey of the
orphan;
they take the widow's ox for a
pledge.
4 They thrust the needy off the road;
the poor of the earth all hide
themselves.
5 Like wild asses in the desert
they go out to their toil,
scavenging in the wasteland
food for their young.
6 They reap in a field not their own
and they glean in the vineyard of
the wicked.
7 They lie all night naked, without
clothing,
and have no covering in the cold.
8 They are wet with the rain of the
mountains,
and cling to the rock for want of
shelter.

9 "There are those who snatch the
orphan child from the breast,

c Meaning of Heb uncertain   *d* Syr Vg Tg: Heb *rebellious*   *e* Gk Syr: Heb *my*   *f* Syr Vg: Heb *he turns*   *g* Gk Vg: Heb *from*   *h* Traditional rendering of Heb *Shaddai*   *i* Or *But I am not destroyed by the darkness; he has concealed the thick darkness from me*   *j* Gk: Heb *they*

WEEKEND

BATTER MY HEART
John Donne

VERSE: Job 23.10   **PASSAGE:** Job 23.8–12

atter my heart, three-personed God, for you
As yet but knock, breathe, shine, and seek to
    mend;
That I may rise and stand, o'erthrow me, and
    bend
Your force to break, blow, burn and make me new.
I, like an usurped town, to another due,
Labour to admit you, but oh, to no end;
Reason your viceroy in me, me should defend,
But is captived, and proves weak or untrue.
Yet dearly I love you, and would be loved fain,
But am betrothed unto your enemy:
Divorce me, untie, or break that knot again,
Take me to you, imprison me, for I
Except you enthrall me, never shall be free,
Nor ever chaste, except you ravish me.

ADDITIONAL SCRIPTURE READING:
Job 1.11–12; Zechariah 13.9; James 1.2–4

Go to page 573 for your next devotional reading.

1500   1700

and take as a pledge the infant of
   the poor.
10 They go about naked, without
      clothing;
   though hungry, they carry the
      sheaves;
11 between their terraces*k* they press
      out oil;
   they tread the wine presses, but
      suffer thirst.
12 From the city the dying groan,
      and the throat of the wounded
      cries for help;
   yet God pays no attention to
      their prayer.

13 "There are those who rebel against
      the light,
   who are not acquainted with its
      ways,
   and do not stay in its paths.
14 The murderer rises at dusk
      to kill the poor and needy,
   and in the night is like a thief.
15 The eye of the adulterer also waits
      for the twilight,
   saying, 'No eye will see me';
   and he disguises his face.
16 In the dark they dig through
      houses;
   by day they shut themselves up;
   they do not know the light.
17 For deep darkness is morning to all
      of them;
   for they are friends with the
      terrors of deep darkness.

18 "Swift are they on the face of the
      waters;
   their portion in the land is cursed;
   no treader turns toward their
      vineyards.
19 Drought and heat snatch away the
      snow waters;
   so does Sheol those who have
      sinned.
20 The womb forgets them;
   the worm finds them sweet;
   they are no longer remembered;
   so wickedness is broken like a
      tree.

21 "They harm*l* the childless woman,
      and do no good to the widow.

22 Yet God*m* prolongs the life of the
      mighty by his power;
   they rise up when they despair of
      life.
23 He gives them security, and they
      are supported;
   his eyes are upon their ways.
24 They are exalted a little while, and
      then are gone;
   they wither and fade like the
      mallow;*n*
   they are cut off like the heads of
      grain.
25 If it is not so, who will prove me a
      liar,
   and show that there is nothing in
      what I say?"

Bildad Speaks: How Can a Mortal Be Righteous Before God?

25 Then Bildad the Shuhite
   answered:
2 "Dominion and fear are with God;*o*
   he makes peace in his high
      heaven.
3 Is there any number to his armies?
   Upon whom does his light not
      arise?
4 How then can a mortal be
      righteous before God?
   How can one born of woman be
      pure?
5 If even the moon is not bright
      and the stars are not pure in his
      sight,
6 how much less a mortal, who is a
      maggot,
   and a human being, who is a
      worm!"

Job Replies: God's Majesty Is Unsearchable

26 Then Job answered:
2 "How you have helped one
      who has no power!
   How you have assisted the arm
      that has no strength!
3 How you have counseled one who
      has no wisdom,
   and given much good advice!
4 With whose help have you uttered
      words,
   and whose spirit has come forth
      from you?

k Meaning of Heb uncertain   *l* Gk Tg: Heb *feed on* or *associate with*   *m* Heb *he*   *n* Gk: Heb *like all others*   *o* Heb *him*

5 The shades below tremble,
   the waters and their inhabitants.
6 Sheol is naked before God,
   and Abaddon has no covering.
7 He stretches out Zaphon*p* over the
      void,
   and hangs the earth upon
      nothing.
8 He binds up the waters in his thick
      clouds,
   and the cloud is not torn open by
      them.
9 He covers the face of the full moon,
   and spreads over it his cloud.
10 He has described a circle on the
      face of the waters,
   at the boundary between light
      and darkness.
11 The pillars of heaven tremble,
   and are astounded at his rebuke.
12 By his power he stilled the Sea;
   by his understanding he struck
      down Rahab.
13 By his wind the heavens were made
      fair;
   his hand pierced the fleeing
      serpent.
14 These are indeed but the outskirts
      of his ways;
   and how small a whisper do we
      hear of him!
   But the thunder of his power who
      can understand?"

Job Maintains His Integrity

27 Job again took up his discourse and said:
2 "As God lives, who has taken away
      my right,
   and the Almighty,*q* who has
      made my soul bitter,
3 as long as my breath is in me
   and the spirit of God is in my
      nostrils,
4 my lips will not speak falsehood,
   and my tongue will not utter
      deceit.
5 Far be it from me to say that you
      are right;
   until I die I will not put away my
      integrity from me.
6 I hold fast my righteousness, and
      will not let it go;
   my heart does not reproach me
      for any of my days.

7 "May my enemy be like the
      wicked,
   and may my opponent be like the
      unrighteous.
8 For what is the hope of the godless
      when God cuts them off,
   when God takes away their lives?
9 Will God hear their cry
   when trouble comes upon them?
10 Will they take delight in the
      Almighty?*q*
   Will they call upon God at all
      times?
11 I will teach you concerning the
      hand of God;
   that which is with the Almighty*q*
      I will not conceal.
12 All of you have seen it yourselves;
   why then have you become
      altogether vain?

13 "This is the portion of the wicked
      with God,
   and the heritage that oppressors
      receive from the Almighty:*q*
14 If their children are multiplied, it is
      for the sword;
   and their offspring have not
      enough to eat.
15 Those who survive them the
      pestilence buries,
   and their widows make no
      lamentation.
16 Though they heap up silver like
      dust,
   and pile up clothing like clay—
17 they may pile it up, but the just
      will wear it,
   and the innocent will divide the
      silver.
18 They build their houses like nests,
   like booths made by sentinels of
      the vineyard.
19 They go to bed with wealth, but
      will do so no more;
   they open their eyes, and it is
      gone.
20 Terrors overtake them like a flood;
   in the night a whirlwind carries
      them off.
21 The east wind lifts them up and
      they are gone;
   it sweeps them out of their place.
22 It*r* hurls at them without pity;

---

p Or *the North*   *q* Traditional rendering of Heb *Shaddai*   *r* Or *He* (that is God)

they flee from its[s] power in
    headlong flight.
23 It[t] claps its[s] hands at them,
    and hisses at them from its[s]
    place.

Interlude: Where Wisdom Is Found

 28 "Surely there is a mine for
    silver,
    and a place for gold to be refined.
2 Iron is taken out of the earth,
    and copper is smelted from ore.
3 Miners put[u] an end to darkness,

and search out to the farthest
    bound
the ore in gloom and deep
    darkness.
4 They open shafts in a valley away
    from human habitation;
they are forgotten by travelers,
they sway suspended, remote
    from people.
5 As for the earth, out of it comes
    bread;
but underneath it is turned up as
    by fire.

s Or *his*   t Or *He* (that is God)   u Heb *He puts*

MONDAY

THE TRIBULATIONS OF JOB
Martin Luther

VERSE: Job 27.5   **PASSAGE:** Job 27.1–6

ob had many tribulations; he was also plagued of his
own friends, who fiercely assaulted him. The text says,
that his friends fell upon him, and were full of wrath
against him; they tormented him thoroughly, but he
held his peace, suffered them to talk their talk, as if he should
say, you know not what you prate about. Job is an example of
God's goodness and mercy; for how upright and holy soever he
was, yet he sorely fell into temptation; but he was not forsaken,
he was again delivered and redeemed through God's grace and
mercy . . .
    When Satan will not leave off tempting thee, then bear with
patience, hold on hand and foot, nor faint, as if there would be no
end thereof, but stand courageously, and attend God's leisure,
knowing that what the devil cannot accomplish by his sudden
and powerful assaults, he thinks to gain by craft, by persevering
to vex and tempt thee, thereby to make thee faint and weary . . .
But be fully assured, that in this sport with the devil, God, with
all his holy angels, takes delight and joy; and assure thyself, also,
that the end thereof will be blessed and happy.

ADDITIONAL SCRIPTURE READING:
Job 13.15; 2 Corinthians 1.12

Go to page 580 for your next devotional reading.

1500   1700

6 Its stones are the place of
      sapphires,^{v}
      and its dust contains gold.

7 "That path no bird of prey knows,
      and the falcon's eye has not seen
      it.
8 The proud wild animals have not
      trodden it;
      the lion has not passed over it.

9 "They put their hand to the flinty
      rock,
      and overturn mountains by the
      roots.
10 They cut out channels in the rocks,
      and their eyes see every precious
      thing.
11 The sources of the rivers they
      probe;^{w}
      hidden things they bring to light.

12 "But where shall wisdom be found?
      And where is the place of
      understanding?
13 Mortals do not know the way to
      it,^{x}
      and it is not found in the land of
      the living.
14 The deep says, 'It is not in me,'
      and the sea says, 'It is not with
      me.'
15 It cannot be gotten for gold,
      and silver cannot be weighed out
      as its price.
16 It cannot be valued in the gold of
      Ophir,
      in precious onyx or sapphire.^{v}
17 Gold and glass cannot equal it,
      nor can it be exchanged for
      jewels of fine gold.
18 No mention shall be made of coral
      or of crystal;
      the price of wisdom is above
      pearls.
19 The chrysolite of Ethiopia^y cannot
      compare with it,
      nor can it be valued in pure gold.

20 "Where then does wisdom come
      from?
      And where is the place of
      understanding?

21 It is hidden from the eyes of all
      living,
      and concealed from the birds of
      the air.
22 Abaddon and Death say,
      'We have heard a rumor of it
      with our ears.'

23 "God understands the way to it,
      and he knows its place.
24 For he looks to the ends of the
      earth,
      and sees everything under the
      heavens.
25 When he gave to the wind its
      weight,
      and apportioned out the waters
      by measure;
26 when he made a decree for the rain,
      and a way for the thunderbolt;
27 then he saw it and declared it;
      he established it, and searched it
      out.
28 And he said to humankind,
      'Truly, the fear of the Lord, that is
      wisdom;
      and to depart from evil is
      understanding.' "

Job Finishes His Defense

29 Job again took up his discourse
      and said:
2 "O that I were as in the months of
      old,
      as in the days when God watched
      over me;
3 when his lamp shone over my head,
      and by his light I walked through
      darkness;
4 when I was in my prime,
      when the friendship of God was
      upon my tent;
5 when the Almighty^z was still with
      me,
      when my children were around
      me;
6 when my steps were washed with
      milk,
      and the rock poured out for me
      streams of oil!
7 When I went out to the gate of the
      city,
      when I took my seat in the
      square,

---

v Or *lapis lazuli*   w Gk Vg: Heb *bind*   x Gk: Heb *its price*   y Or *Nubia*; Heb *Cush*
z Traditional rendering of Heb *Shaddai*

8 the young men saw me and
withdrew,
and the aged rose up and stood;
9 the nobles refrained from talking,
and laid their hands on their
mouths;
10 the voices of princes were hushed,
and their tongues stuck to the
roof of their mouths.
11 When the ear heard, it commended
me,
and when the eye saw, it
approved;
12 because I delivered the poor who
cried,
and the orphan who had no
helper.
13 The blessing of the wretched came
upon me,
and I caused the widow's heart to
sing for joy.
14 I put on righteousness, and it
clothed me;
my justice was like a robe and a
turban.
15 I was eyes to the blind,
and feet to the lame.
16 I was a father to the needy,
and I championed the cause of
the stranger.
17 I broke the fangs of the
unrighteous,
and made them drop their prey
from their teeth.
18 Then I thought, 'I shall die in my
nest,
and I shall multiply my days like
the phoenix;*a*
19 my roots spread out to the waters,
with the dew all night on my
branches;
20 my glory was fresh with me,
and my bow ever new in my
hand.'
21 "They listened to me, and waited,
and kept silence for my counsel.
22 After I spoke they did not speak
again,
and my word dropped upon them
like dew.*b*
23 They waited for me as for the rain;
they opened their mouths as for
the spring rain.

24 I smiled on them when they had no
confidence;
and the light of my countenance
they did not extinguish.*c*
25 I chose their way, and sat as chief,
and I lived like a king among his
troops,
like one who comforts mourners.

30 "But now they make sport of
me,
those who are younger than I,
whose fathers I would have
disdained
to set with the dogs of my flock.
2 What could I gain from the
strength of their hands?
All their vigor is gone.
3 Through want and hard hunger
they gnaw the dry and desolate
ground,
4 they pick mallow and the leaves of
bushes,
and to warm themselves the
roots of broom.
5 They are driven out from society;
people shout after them as after a
thief.
6 In the gullies of wadis they must
live,
in holes in the ground, and in the
rocks.
7 Among the bushes they bray;
under the nettles they huddle
together.
8 A senseless, disreputable brood,
they have been whipped out of
the land.
9 "And now they mock me in song;
I am a byword to them.
10 They abhor me, they keep aloof
from me;
they do not hesitate to spit at the
sight of me.
11 Because God has loosed my
bowstring and humbled me,
they have cast off restraint in my
presence.
12 On my right hand the rabble rise up;
they send me sprawling,
and build roads for my ruin.
13 They break up my path,
they promote my calamity;
no one restrains*d* them.

a Or like sand   b Heb lacks like dew   c Meaning of Heb uncertain   d Cn: Heb helps

14 As through a wide breach they
       come;
   amid the crash they roll on.
15 Terrors are turned upon me;
   my honor is pursued as by the
       wind,
   and my prosperity has passed
       away like a cloud.

16 "And now my soul is poured out
       within me;
   days of affliction have taken hold
       of me.
17 The night racks my bones,
   and the pain that gnaws me takes
       no rest.
18 With violence he seizes my
       garment;*e*
   he grasps me by*f* the collar of my
       tunic.
19 He has cast me into the mire,
   and I have become like dust and
       ashes.
20 I cry to you and you do not answer
       me;
   I stand, and you merely look at
       me.
21 You have turned cruel to me;
   with the might of your hand you
       persecute me.
22 You lift me up on the wind, you
       make me ride on it,
   and you toss me about in the roar
       of the storm.
23 I know that you will bring me to
       death,
   and to the house appointed for all
       living.

24 "Surely one does not turn against
       the needy,*g*
   when in disaster they cry for
       help.*h*
25 Did I not weep for those whose day
       was hard?
   Was not my soul grieved for the
       poor?
26 But when I looked for good, evil
       came;
   and when I waited for light,
       darkness came.
27 My inward parts are in turmoil,
   and are never still;

days of affliction come to meet
   me.
28 I go about in sunless gloom;
   I stand up in the assembly and
       cry for help.
29 I am a brother of jackals,
   and a companion of ostriches.
30 My skin turns black and falls from
       me,
   and my bones burn with heat.
31 My lyre is turned to mourning,
   and my pipe to the voice of those
       who weep.

31 "I have made a covenant
       with my eyes;
   how then could I look upon a
       virgin?
2 What would be my portion from
       God above,
   and my heritage from the
       Almighty*i* on high?
3 Does not calamity befall the
       unrighteous,
   and disaster the workers of
       iniquity?
4 Does he not see my ways,
   and number all my steps?

5 "If I have walked with falsehood,
   and my foot has hurried to
       deceit—
6 let me be weighed in a just balance,
   and let God know my
       integrity!—
7 if my step has turned aside from
       the way,
   and my heart has followed my
       eyes,
   and if any spot has clung to my
       hands;
8 then let me sow, and another eat;
   and let what grows for me be
       rooted out.

9 "If my heart has been enticed by a
       woman,
   and I have lain in wait at my
       neighbor's door;
10 then let my wife grind for another,
   and let other men kneel over her.
11 For that would be a heinous crime;
   that would be a criminal offense;

e Gk: Heb *my garment is disfigured*   *f* Heb *like*   *g* Heb *ruin*   *h* Cn: Meaning of Heb uncertain
i Traditional rendering of Heb *Shaddai*

12 for that would be a fire consuming
       down to Abaddon,
    and it would burn to the root all
       my harvest.

13 "If I have rejected the cause of my
       male or female slaves,
    when they brought a complaint
       against me;
14 what then shall I do when God
       rises up?
    When he makes inquiry, what
       shall I answer him?
15 Did not he who made me in the
       womb make them?
    And did not one fashion us in the
       womb?

16 "If I have withheld anything that
       the poor desired,
    or have caused the eyes of the
       widow to fail,
17 or have eaten my morsel alone,
    and the orphan has not eaten
       from it—
18 for from my youth I reared the
       orphan*j* like a father,
    and from my mother's womb I
       guided the widow*k*—
19 if I have seen anyone perish for lack
       of clothing,
    or a poor person without covering,
20 whose loins have not blessed me,
    and who was not warmed with
       the fleece of my sheep;
21 if I have raised my hand against the
       orphan,
    because I saw I had supporters at
       the gate;
22 then let my shoulder blade fall
       from my shoulder,
    and let my arm be broken from
       its socket.
23 For I was in terror of calamity from
       God,
    and I could not have faced his
       majesty.

24 "If I have made gold my trust,
    or called fine gold my confidence;
25 if I have rejoiced because my
       wealth was great,
    or because my hand had gotten
       much;

26 if I have looked at the sun*l* when it
       shone,
    or the moon moving in splendor,
27 and my heart has been secretly
       enticed,
    and my mouth has kissed my
       hand;
28 this also would be an iniquity to be
       punished by the judges,
    for I should have been false to
       God above.

29 "If I have rejoiced at the ruin of
       those who hated me,
    or exulted when evil overtook
       them—
30 I have not let my mouth sin
    by asking for their lives with a
       curse—
31 if those of my tent ever said,
    'O that we might be sated with
       his flesh!'*m*—
32 the stranger has not lodged in the
       street;
    I have opened my doors to the
       traveler—
33 if I have concealed my
       transgressions as others do,*n*
    by hiding my iniquity in my
       bosom,
34 because I stood in great fear of the
       multitude,
    and the contempt of families
       terrified me,
    so that I kept silence, and did not
       go out of doors—
35 O that I had one to hear me!
    (Here is my signature! Let the
       Almighty*o* answer me!)
    O that I had the indictment
       written by my adversary!
36 Surely I would carry it on my
       shoulder;
    I would bind it on me like a
       crown;
37 I would give him an account of all
       my steps;
    like a prince I would approach
       him.

38 "If my land has cried out against
       me,
    and its furrows have wept
       together;

---

j Heb *him*   *k* Heb *her*   *l* Heb *the light*   *m* Meaning of Heb uncertain   *n* Or *as Adam did*
o Traditional rendering of Heb *Shaddai*

39 if I have eaten its yield without
payment,
and caused the death of its
owners;
40 let thorns grow instead of wheat,
and foul weeds instead of barley."

The words of Job are ended.

Elihu Rebukes Job's Friends

32 So these three men ceased to answer Job, because he was righteous in his own eyes. 2 Then Elihu son of Barachel the Buzite, of the family of Ram, became angry. He was angry at Job because he justified himself rather than God; 3 he was angry also at Job's three friends because they had found no answer, though they had declared Job to be in the wrong.p 4 Now Elihu had waited to speak to Job, because they were older than he. 5 But when Elihu saw that there was no answer in the mouths of these three men, he became angry.

6 Elihu son of Barachel the Buzite answered:
"I am young in years,
and you are aged;
therefore I was timid and afraid
to declare my opinion to you.
7 I said, 'Let days speak,
and many years teach wisdom.'
8 But truly it is the spirit in a mortal,
the breath of the Almighty,q that
makes for understanding.
9 It is not the oldr that are wise,
nor the aged that understand
what is right.
10 Therefore I say, 'Listen to me;
let me also declare my opinion.'

11 "See, I waited for your words,
I listened for your wise sayings,
while you searched out what to
say.
12 I gave you my attention,
but there was in fact no one that
confuted Job,
no one among you that answered
his words.
13 Yet do not say, 'We have found
wisdom;
God may vanquish him, not a
human.'

14 He has not directed his words
against me,
and I will not answer him with
your speeches.

15 "They are dismayed, they answer
no more;
they have not a word to say.
16 And am I to wait, because they do
not speak,
because they stand there, and
answer no more?
17 I also will give my answer;
I also will declare my opinion.
18 For I am full of words;
the spirit within me constrains
me.
19 My heart is indeed like wine that
has no vent;
like new wineskins, it is ready to
burst.
20 I must speak, so that I may find
relief;
I must open my lips and answer.
21 I will not show partiality to any
person
or use flattery toward anyone.
22 For I do not know how to flatter—
or my Maker would soon put an
end to me!

Elihu Rebukes Job

33 "But now, hear my speech,
O Job,
and listen to all my words.
2 See, I open my mouth;
the tongue in my mouth speaks.
3 My words declare the uprightness
of my heart,
and what my lips know they
speak sincerely.
4 The spirit of God has made me,
and the breath of the Almightyq
gives me life.
5 Answer me, if you can;
set your words in order before
me; take your stand.
6 See, before God I am as you are;
I too was formed from a piece of
clay.
7 No fear of me need terrify you;
my pressure will not be heavy on
you.

p Another ancient tradition reads answer, and had put God in the wrong　q Traditional rendering of Heb Shaddai　r Gk Syr Vg: Heb many

8 "Surely, you have spoken in my
     hearing,
   and I have heard the sound of
     your words.
9 You say, 'I am clean, without
     transgression;
   I am pure, and there is no
     iniquity in me.
10 Look, he finds occasions against
     me,
   he counts me as his enemy;
11 he puts my feet in the stocks,
   and watches all my paths.'

12 "But in this you are not right. I will
     answer you:
   God is greater than any mortal.
13 Why do you contend against him,
   saying, 'He will answer none of
     my[s] words'?
14 For God speaks in one way,
   and in two, though people do not
     perceive it.
15 In a dream, in a vision of the night,
   when deep sleep falls on mortals,
   while they slumber on their beds,
16 then he opens their ears,
   and terrifies them with warnings,
17 that he may turn them aside from
     their deeds,
   and keep them from pride,
18 to spare their souls from the Pit,
   their lives from traversing the
     River.
19 They are also chastened with pain
     upon their beds,
   and with continual strife in their
     bones,
20 so that their lives loathe bread,
   and their appetites dainty food.
21 Their flesh is so wasted away that
     it cannot be seen;
   and their bones, once invisible,
     now stick out.
22 Their souls draw near the Pit,
   and their lives to those who bring
     death.
23 Then, if there should be for one of
     them an angel,
   a mediator, one of a thousand,
   one who declares a person
     upright,
24 and he is gracious to that person,
     and says,

   'Deliver him from going down
     into the Pit;
   I have found a ransom;
25 let his flesh become fresh with
     youth;
   let him return to the days of his
     youthful vigor';
26 then he prays to God, and is
     accepted by him,
   he comes into his presence with
     joy,
   and God[t] repays him for his
     righteousness.
27 That person sings to others and
     says,
   'I sinned, and perverted what was
     right,
   and it was not paid back to me.
28 He has redeemed my soul from
     going down to the Pit,
   and my life shall see the light.'

29 "God indeed does all these things,
   twice, three times, with mortals,
30 to bring back their souls from the
     Pit,
   so that they may see the light of
     life.[u]
31 Pay heed, Job, listen to me;
   be silent, and I will speak.
32 If you have anything to say, answer
     me;
   speak, for I desire to justify you.
33 If not, listen to me;
   be silent, and I will teach you
     wisdom."

Elihu Proclaims God's Justice

34 Then Elihu continued and
   said:
2 "Hear my words, you wise men,
   and give ear to me, you who
     know;
3 for the ear tests words
   as the palate tastes food.
4 Let us choose what is right;
   let us determine among
     ourselves what is good.
5 For Job has said, 'I am innocent,
   and God has taken away my
     right;
6 in spite of being right I am counted
     a liar;
   my wound is incurable, though I
     am without transgression.'

s Compare Gk: Heb *his*   t Heb *he*   u Syr: Heb *to be lighted with the light of life*

7 Who is there like Job,
     who drinks up scoffing like
       water,

8 who goes in company with
     evildoers
   and walks with the wicked?

TUESDAY

RANSOMED TO BE ONE WITH CHRIST
James Hudson Taylor

VERSE: Job 33.24   **PASSAGE:** Job 33.22–28

 am no better than before (may I not say, in a sense, I do
not wish to be, nor am I striving to be); but I am dead
and buried with Christ—aye, and risen too and ascended; and now Christ lives in me, and "the life that I now
live in the flesh, I live by the faith of the Son of God, who loved
me, and gave himself for me" (Galatians 2.20, KJV). I now
believe I am dead to sin. God reckons me so, and tells me to
reckon myself so. He knows best. All my past experience may
have shown that it *was* not so; but I dare not say it *is* not now,
when he says it is. I feel and know that old things have passed
away. I am as capable of sinning as ever, but Christ is realized as
present as never before. He cannot sin; and he can keep me from
sinning. I cannot say (I am sorry to have to confess it) that since
I have seen this light I have not sinned; but I do feel there was no
need to have done so. And further—walking more in the light,
my conscience has been more tender; sin has been instantly
seen, confessed, pardoned; and peace and joy (with humility)
instantly restored; with one exception, when for several hours
peace and joy did not return—from want, as I had to learn, of full
confession, and from some attempt to justify self . . .

And now I must close, I have not said half I would, nor *as* I
would had I more time. May God give you to lay hold on these
blessed truths. Do not let us continue to say, in *effect*, "Who shall
ascend into heaven? that is, to bring Christ down from above"
(Romans 10.6, KJV). In other words, do not let us consider him as
afar off, when God has made us *one with him*, members of his
very body. Nor should we look upon this experience, these truths,
as for the few. They are the birthright of every child of God, and
no one can dispense with them without dishonor to our Lord. The
only power for deliverance from sin or for true service is Christ.

ADDITIONAL SCRIPTURE READING:
Romans 10.5–10; 2 Corinthians 5.7; Galatians 2.20

Go to page 583 for your next devotional reading.

1700   1900

9 For he has said, 'It profits one
    nothing
      to take delight in God.'

10 "Therefore, hear me, you who have
    sense;
      far be it from God that he should
      do wickedness,
      and from the Almighty[v] that he
      should do wrong.
11 For according to their deeds he will
    repay them,
      and according to their ways he
      will make it befall them.
12 Of a truth, God will not do
    wickedly,
      and the Almighty[v] will not
      pervert justice.
13 Who gave him charge over the
    earth
      and who laid on him[w] the whole
      world?
14 If he should take back his spirit[x] to
    himself,
      and gather to himself his breath,
15 all flesh would perish together,
      and all mortals return to dust.

16 "If you have understanding, hear
    this;
      listen to what I say.
17 Shall one who hates justice govern?
      Will you condemn one who is
      righteous and mighty,
18 who says to a king, 'You scoundrel!'
      and to princes, 'You wicked
      men!';
19 who shows no partiality to nobles,
      nor regards the rich more than
      the poor,
      for they are all the work of his
      hands?
20 In a moment they die;
      at midnight the people are
      shaken and pass away,
      and the mighty are taken away
      by no human hand.

21 "For his eyes are upon the ways of
    mortals,
      and he sees all their steps.
22 There is no gloom or deep darkness
      where evildoers may hide
      themselves.

23 For he has not appointed a time[y]
    for anyone
      to go before God in judgment.
24 He shatters the mighty without
    investigation,
      and sets others in their place.
25 Thus, knowing their works,
      he overturns them in the night,
      and they are crushed.
26 He strikes them for their
    wickedness
      while others look on,
27 because they turned aside from
    following him,
      and had no regard for any of his
      ways,
28 so that they caused the cry of the
    poor to come to him,
      and he heard the cry of the
      afflicted—
29 When he is quiet, who can
    condemn?
      When he hides his face, who can
      behold him,
      whether it be a nation or an
      individual?—
30 so that the godless should not
    reign,
      or those who ensnare the people.

31 "For has anyone said to God,
    'I have endured punishment; I
      will not offend any more;
32 teach me what I do not see;
      if I have done iniquity, I will do it
      no more'?
33 Will he then pay back to suit you,
      because you reject it?
      For you must choose, and not I;
      therefore declare what you know.[z]
34 Those who have sense will say to
    me,
      and the wise who hear me will
      say,
35 'Job speaks without knowledge,
      his words are without insight.'
36 Would that Job were tried to the
    limit,
      because his answers are those of
      the wicked.
37 For he adds rebellion to his sin;
      he claps his hands among us,
      and multiplies his words against
      God."

v Traditional rendering of Heb *Shaddai*   w Heb lacks *on him*   x Heb *his heart his spirit*
y Cn: Heb *yet*   z Meaning of Heb of verses 29-33 uncertain

Elihu Condemns Self-Righteousness

35 Elihu continued and said:
2 "Do you think this to be just?
    You say, 'I am in the right before God.'
3 If you ask, 'What advantage have I?
    How am I better off than if I had sinned?'
4 I will answer you
    and your friends with you.
5 Look at the heavens and see;
    observe the clouds, which are higher than you.
6 If you have sinned, what do you accomplish against him?
    And if your transgressions are multiplied, what do you do to him?
7 If you are righteous, what do you give to him;
    or what does he receive from your hand?
8 Your wickedness affects others like you,
    and your righteousness, other human beings.

9 "Because of the multitude of oppressions people cry out;
    they call for help because of the arm of the mighty.
10 But no one says, 'Where is God my Maker,
    who gives strength in the night,
11 who teaches us more than the animals of the earth,
    and makes us wiser than the birds of the air?'
12 There they cry out, but he does not answer,
    because of the pride of evildoers.
13 Surely God does not hear an empty cry,
    nor does the Almighty^a regard it.
14 How much less when you say that you do not see him,
    that the case is before him, and you are waiting for him!
15 And now, because his anger does not punish,
    and he does not greatly heed transgression,^b

16 Job opens his mouth in empty talk,
    he multiplies words without knowledge."

Elihu Exalts God's Goodness

36 Elihu continued and said:
2 "Bear with me a little, and I will show you,
    for I have yet something to say on God's behalf.
3 I will bring my knowledge from far away,
    and ascribe righteousness to my Maker.
4 For truly my words are not false;
    one who is perfect in knowledge is with you.

5 "Surely God is mighty and does not despise any;
    he is mighty in strength of understanding.
6 He does not keep the wicked alive,
    but gives the afflicted their right.
7 He does not withdraw his eyes from the righteous,
    but with kings on the throne he sets them forever, and they are exalted.
8 And if they are bound in fetters and caught in the cords of affliction,
9 then he declares to them their work
    and their transgressions, that they are behaving arrogantly.
10 He opens their ears to instruction,
    and commands that they return from iniquity.
11 If they listen, and serve him,
    they complete their days in prosperity,
    and their years in pleasantness.
12 But if they do not listen, they shall perish by the sword,
    and die without knowledge.

13 "The godless in heart cherish anger;
    they do not cry for help when he binds them.
14 They die in their youth,
    and their life ends in shame.^c

---

a Traditional rendering of Heb *Shaddai*   b Theodotion Symmachus Compare Vg: Meaning of Heb uncertain   c Heb *ends among the temple prostitutes*

15 He delivers the afflicted by their
      affliction,
   and opens their ear by adversity.

AFFLICTION IS ABLE TO DROWN OUT EVERY
EARTHLY VOICE . . . BUT THE VOICE OF ETERNITY
WITHIN A MAN IT CANNOT DROWN. WHEN BY
THE AID OF AFFLICTION ALL IRRELEVANT VOICES
ARE BROUGHT TO SILENCE, IT CAN BE HEARD,
THIS VOICE WITHIN.   —Søren Kierkegaard

16 He also allured you out of distress
      into a broad place where there
      was no constraint,

   and what was set on your table
      was full of fatness.

17 "But you are obsessed with the
      case of the wicked;
   judgment and justice seize you.
18 Beware that wrath does not entice
      you into scoffing,
   and do not let the greatness of
      the ransom turn you aside.
19 Will your cry avail to keep you
      from distress,
   or will all the force of your
      strength?
20 Do not long for the night,

WEDNESDAY

SONGS IN THE NIGHT
Charles H. Spurgeon

VERSE: Job 35.10   **PASSAGE:** Job 35.4–16

ny man can sing in the day. When the cup is full, man draws inspiration from it. When wealth rolls in abundance around him, any man can praise the God who gives a plenteous harvest or sends home a loaded argosy . . .

It is easy to sing when we can read the notes by daylight; but he is skillful who sings when there is not a ray of light to read by, who sings from his heart. No man can make a song in the night of himself; he may attempt it, but he will find that a song in the night must be divinely inspired. Let all things go well, I can weave songs, fashioning them wherever I go out of the flowers that grow on my path; but put me in a desert, where no green thing grows, and wherewith shall I frame a hymn of praise to God? . . .

No, it is not in man's power to sing when all is adverse . . . Since our Maker gives *songs in the night*, let us wait on him for the music . . . Let us not remain songless because affliction is upon us, but tune our lips to the melody of thanksgiving.

ADDITIONAL SCRIPTURE READING:
Psalms 42.8; 77.5–7; Acts 16.25

Go to page 586 for your next devotional reading.

1700   1900

when peoples are cut off in their
place.

21 Beware! Do not turn to iniquity;
because of that you have been
tried by affliction.

22 See, God is exalted in his power;
who is a teacher like him?

23 Who has prescribed for him his
way,
or who can say, 'You have done
wrong'?

Elihu Proclaims God's Majesty

24 "Remember to extol his work,
of which mortals have sung.

25 All people have looked on it;
everyone watches it from far
away.

26 Surely God is great, and we do not
know him;
the number of his years is
unsearchable.

27 For he draws up the drops of water;
he distills^d his mist in rain,

28 which the skies pour down
and drop upon mortals
abundantly.

29 Can anyone understand the
spreading of the clouds,
the thunderings of his pavilion?

30 See, he scatters his lightning
around him
and covers the roots of the sea.

31 For by these he governs peoples;
he gives food in abundance.

32 He covers his hands with the
lightning,
and commands it to strike the
mark.

33 Its crashing^e tells about him;
he is jealous^e with anger against
iniquity.

37 "At this also my heart
trembles,
and leaps out of its place.

2 Listen, listen to the thunder of his
voice
and the rumbling that comes
from his mouth.

3 Under the whole heaven he lets it
loose,
and his lightning to the corners
of the earth.

4 After it his voice roars;
he thunders with his majestic
voice
and he does not restrain the
lightnings^f when his voice is
heard.

5 God thunders wondrously with his
voice;
he does great things that we
cannot comprehend.

6 For to the snow he says, 'Fall on
the earth';
and the shower of rain, his heavy
shower of rain,

7 serves as a sign on everyone's hand,
so that all whom he has made
may know it.^{g}

8 Then the animals go into their lairs
and remain in their dens.

9 From its chamber comes the
whirlwind,
and cold from the scattering
winds.

10 By the breath of God ice is given,
and the broad waters are frozen
fast.

11 He loads the thick cloud with
moisture;
the clouds scatter his lightning.

12 They turn round and round by his
guidance,
to accomplish all that he
commands them
on the face of the habitable
world.

13 Whether for correction, or for his
land,
or for love, he causes it to
happen.

14 "Hear this, O Job;
stop and consider the wondrous
works of God.

15 Do you know how God lays his
command upon them,
and causes the lightning of his
cloud to shine?

16 Do you know the balancings of the
clouds,
the wondrous works of the one
whose knowledge is perfect,

17 you whose garments are hot
when the earth is still because of
the south wind?

d Cn: Heb they distill   e Meaning of Heb uncertain   f Heb them   g Meaning of Heb of verse 7
uncertain

18 Can you, like him, spread out the
skies,
hard as a molten mirror?
19 Teach us what we shall say to him;
we cannot draw up our case
because of darkness.
20 Should he be told that I want to
speak?
Did anyone ever wish to be
swallowed up?
21 Now, no one can look on the light
when it is bright in the skies,
when the wind has passed and
cleared them.
22 Out of the north comes golden
splendor;
around God is awesome majesty.
23 The Almighty[h]—we cannot find
him;
he is great in power and justice,
and abundant righteousness he
will not violate.
24 Therefore mortals fear him;
he does not regard any who are
wise in their own conceit."

The LORD Answers Job

38 Then the LORD answered Job
out of the whirlwind:
2 "Who is this that darkens counsel
by words without
knowledge?
3 Gird up your loins like a man,
I will question you, and you shall
declare to me.

4 "Where were you when I laid the
foundation of the earth?
Tell me, if you have
understanding.
5 Who determined its
measurements—surely you
know!
Or who stretched the line upon
it?
6 On what were its bases sunk,
or who laid its cornerstone
7 when the morning stars sang
together
and all the heavenly beings[i]
shouted for joy?

8 "Or who shut in the sea with doors
when it burst out from the
womb?—

9 when I made the clouds its
garment,
and thick darkness its swaddling
band,
10 and prescribed bounds for it,
and set bars and doors,
11 and said, 'Thus far shall you come,
and no farther,
and here shall your proud waves
be stopped'?

12 "Have you commanded the
morning since your days
began,
and caused the dawn to know its
place,
13 so that it might take hold of the
skirts of the earth,
and the wicked be shaken out of
it?
14 It is changed like clay under the
seal,
and it is dyed[j] like a garment.
15 Light is withheld from the wicked,
and their uplifted arm is broken.

16 "Have you entered into the springs
of the sea,
or walked in the recesses of the
deep?
17 Have the gates of death been
revealed to you,
or have you seen the gates of
deep darkness?
18 Have you comprehended the
expanse of the earth?
Declare, if you know all this.

19 "Where is the way to the dwelling
of light,
and where is the place of
darkness,
20 that you may take it to its territory
and that you may discern the
paths to its home?
21 Surely you know, for you were born
then,
and the number of your days is
great!

22 "Have you entered the storehouses
of the snow,
or have you seen the storehouses
of the hail,

h Traditional rendering of Heb Shaddai   i Heb sons of God   j Cn: Heb and they stand forth

23 which I have reserved for the time
      of trouble,
   for the day of battle and war?
24 What is the way to the place where
      the light is distributed,
   or where the east wind is
      scattered upon the earth?

25 "Who has cut a channel for the
      torrents of rain,
   and a way for the thunderbolt,
26 to bring rain on a land where no
      one lives,
   on the desert, which is empty of
      human life,

THURSDAY

THE RAYS OF THE NATURE OF GOD
Origen

VERSE: Job 38.12   **PASSAGE:** Job 38

 aving refuted, then, as well as we could, every notion
which might suggest that we were to think of God as
in any degree corporeal, we go on to say that, according
to strict truth, God is incomprehensible, and incapable
of being measured. For whatever be the knowledge which we are
able to obtain of God, either by perception or reflection, we must
of necessity believe that he is by many degrees far better than
what we perceive him to be . . . But among all intelligent, that is,
incorporeal beings, what is so superior to all others—so unspeak-
ably and incalculably superior—as God, whose nature cannot be
grasped or seen by the power of any human understanding, even
the purest and brightest?
   . . . Our eyes frequently cannot look upon the nature of the
light itself—that is, upon the substance of the sun; but when we
behold his splendor or his rays pouring in, perhaps, through windows or some small openings to admit the light, we can reflect
how great is the supply and source of the light of the body. So, in
like manner, the works of divine Providence and the plan of this
whole world are a sort of rays, as it were, of the nature of God, in
comparison with his real substance and being. As, therefore, our
understanding is unable of itself to behold God himself as he is,
it knows the Father of the world from the beauty of his works
and the comeliness of his creatures. God, therefore, is not to be
thought of as being either a body or as existing in a body, but as
an uncompounded intellectual nature, admitting within himself
no addition of any kind.

ADDITIONAL SCRIPTURE READING:
Isaiah 9.2; John 8.12; Acts 13.47

Go to page 590 for your next devotional reading.

100   500

27 to satisfy the waste and desolate
 land,
 and to make the ground put forth
 grass?

28 "Has the rain a father,
 or who has begotten the drops of
 dew?
29 From whose womb did the ice
 come forth,
 and who has given birth to the
 hoarfrost of heaven?
30 The waters become hard like stone,
 and the face of the deep is frozen.

31 "Can you bind the chains of the
 Pleiades,
 or loose the cords of Orion?
32 Can you lead forth the Mazzaroth
 in their season,
 or can you guide the Bear with its
 children?
33 Do you know the ordinances of the
 heavens?
 Can you establish their rule on
 the earth?

34 "Can you lift up your voice to the
 clouds,
 so that a flood of waters may
 cover you?
35 Can you send forth lightnings, so
 that they may go
 and say to you, 'Here we are'?
36 Who has put wisdom in the inward
 parts,k
 or given understanding to the
 mind?k
37 Who has the wisdom to number
 the clouds?
 Or who can tilt the waterskins of
 the heavens,
38 when the dust runs into a mass
 and the clods cling together?

39 "Can you hunt the prey for the lion,
 or satisfy the appetite of the
 young lions,
40 when they crouch in their dens,
 or lie in wait in their covert?
41 Who provides for the raven its prey,
 when its young ones cry to God,
 and wander about for lack of
 food?

39 "Do you know when the
 mountain goats give birth?
 Do you observe the calving of the
 deer?
2 Can you number the months that
 they fulfill,
 and do you know the time when
 they give birth,
3 when they crouch to give birth to
 their offspring,
 and are delivered of their young?
4 Their young ones become strong,
 they grow up in the open;
 they go forth, and do not return
 to them.

5 "Who has let the wild ass go free?
 Who has loosed the bonds of the
 swift ass,
6 to which I have given the steppe for
 its home,
 the salt land for its dwelling
 place?
7 It scorns the tumult of the city;
 it does not hear the shouts of the
 driver.
8 It ranges the mountains as its
 pasture,
 and it searches after every green
 thing.

9 "Is the wild ox willing to serve
 you?
 Will it spend the night at your
 crib?
10 Can you tie it in the furrow with
 ropes,
 or will it harrow the valleys after
 you?
11 Will you depend on it because its
 strength is great,
 and will you hand over your
 labor to it?
12 Do you have faith in it that it will
 return,
 and bring your grain to your
 threshing floor?l

13 "The ostrich's wings flap wildly,
 though its pinions lack
 plumage.k
14 For it leaves its eggs to the earth,
 and lets them be warmed on the
 ground,

---

k Meaning of Heb uncertain   l Heb *your grain and your threshing floor*

15 forgetting that a foot may crush
            them,
      and that a wild animal may
            trample them.
16 It deals cruelly with its young, as if
            they were not its own;
      though its labor should be in
            vain, yet it has no fear;
17 because God has made it forget
            wisdom,
      and given it no share in
            understanding.
18 When it spreads its plumes aloft,m
      it laughs at the horse and its
            rider.

19 "Do you give the horse its might?
      Do you clothe its neck with
            mane?
20 Do you make it leap like the
            locust?
      Its majestic snorting is terrible.
21 It pawsn violently, exults mightily;
      it goes out to meet the weapons.
22 It laughs at fear, and is not
            dismayed;
      it does not turn back from the
            sword.
23 Upon it rattle the quiver,
      the flashing spear, and the javelin.
24 With fierceness and rage it
            swallows the ground;
      it cannot stand still at the sound
            of the trumpet.
25 When the trumpet sounds, it says
            'Aha!'
      From a distance it smells the
            battle,
      the thunder of the captains, and
            the shouting.

26 "Is it by your wisdom that the
            hawk soars,
      and spreads its wings toward the
            south?
27 Is it at your command that the
            eagle mounts up
      and makes its nest on high?
28 It lives on the rock and makes its
            home
      in the fastness of the rocky crag.
29 From there it spies the prey;
      its eyes see it from far away.

30 Its young ones suck up blood;
      and where the slain are, there it
            is."

40 And the LORD said to Job:
2 "Shall a faultfinder contend
      with the Almighty?o
Anyone who argues with God
      must respond."

Job's Response to God

3 Then Job answered the LORD:
4 "See, I am of small account; what
            shall I answer you?
      I lay my hand on my mouth.
5 I have spoken once, and I will not
            answer;
      twice, but will proceed no
            further."

God's Challenge to Job

6 Then the LORD answered Job out of
the whirlwind:
7 "Gird up your loins like a man;
      I will question you, and you
            declare to me.
8 Will you even put me in the wrong?
      Will you condemn me that you
            may be justified?
9 Have you an arm like God,
      and can you thunder with a voice
            like his?

10 "Deck yourself with majesty and
            dignity;
      clothe yourself with glory and
            splendor.
11 Pour out the overflowings of your
            anger,
      and look on all who are proud,
            and abase them.
12 Look on all who are proud, and
            bring them low;
      tread down the wicked where
            they stand.
13 Hide them all in the dust together;
      bind their faces in the world
            below.p
14 Then I will also acknowledge to you
      that your own right hand can
            give you victory.

15 "Look at Behemoth,
      which I made just as I made you;

m Meaning of Heb uncertain   n Gk Syr Vg: Heb they dig   o Traditional rendering of Heb Shaddai
p Heb the hidden place

it eats grass like an ox.

16 Its strength is in its loins,
    and its power in the muscles of
      its belly.
17 It makes its tail stiff like a cedar;
    the sinews of its thighs are knit
      together.
18 Its bones are tubes of bronze,
    its limbs like bars of iron.

19 "It is the first of the great acts of
      God—
    only its Maker can approach it
      with the sword.
20 For the mountains yield food for it
    where all the wild animals play.
21 Under the lotus plants it lies,
    in the covert of the reeds and in
      the marsh.
22 The lotus trees cover it for shade;
    the willows of the wadi surround
      it.
23 Even if the river is turbulent, it is
      not frightened;
    it is confident though Jordan
      rushes against its mouth.
24 Can one take it with hooks^q
    or pierce its nose with a snare?

41 ^r "Can you draw out
    Leviathan^s with a fishhook,
    or press down its tongue with a
      cord?
2 Can you put a rope in its nose,
    or pierce its jaw with a hook?
3 Will it make many supplications to
      you?
    Will it speak soft words to you?
4 Will it make a covenant with you
    to be taken as your servant
      forever?
5 Will you play with it as with a bird,
    or will you put it on leash for
      your girls?
6 Will traders bargain over it?
    Will they divide it up among the
      merchants?
7 Can you fill its skin with harpoons,
    or its head with fishing spears?
8 Lay hands on it;
    think of the battle; you will not
      do it again!

9^t Any hope of capturing it^u will be
      disappointed;
    were not even the gods^v
      overwhelmed at the sight of
      it?
10 No one is so fierce as to dare to stir
      it up.
    Who can stand before it?^w
11 Who can confront it^w and be safe?^x
    —under the whole heaven, who?^y

12 "I will not keep silence concerning
      its limbs,
    or its mighty strength, or its
      splendid frame.
13 Who can strip off its outer garment?
    Who can penetrate its double
      coat of mail?^z
14 Who can open the doors of its face?
    There is terror all around its teeth.
15 Its back^a is made of shields in rows,
    shut up closely as with a seal.
16 One is so near to another
    that no air can come between
      them.
17 They are joined one to another;
    they clasp each other and cannot
      be separated.
18 Its sneezes flash forth light,
    and its eyes are like the eyelids of
      the dawn.
19 From its mouth go flaming torches;
    sparks of fire leap out.
20 Out of its nostrils comes smoke,
    as from a boiling pot and burning
      rushes.
21 Its breath kindles coals,
    and a flame comes out of its
      mouth.
22 In its neck abides strength,
    and terror dances before it.
23 The folds of its flesh cling together;
    it is firmly cast and immovable.
24 Its heart is as hard as stone,
    as hard as the lower millstone.
25 When it raises itself up the gods are
      afraid;
    at the crashing they are beside
      themselves.
26 Though the sword reaches it, it
      does not avail,
    nor does the spear, the dart, or
      the javelin.

27 It counts iron as straw,
   and bronze as rotten wood.
28 The arrow cannot make it flee;
   slingstones, for it, are turned to
   chaff.
29 Clubs are counted as chaff;
   it laughs at the rattle of javelins.
30 Its underparts are like sharp
   potsherds;
   it spreads itself like a threshing
   sledge on the mire.

31 It makes the deep boil like a pot;
   it makes the sea like a pot of
   ointment.
32 It leaves a shining wake behind it;
   one would think the deep to be
   white-haired.
33 On earth it has no equal,
   a creature without fear.
34 It surveys everything that is lofty;
   it is king over all that are
   proud."

FRIDAY

THE GREAT MYSTERY OF HUMAN LIFE
Fyodor Dostoyevsky

VERSE: Job 42.10   **PASSAGE:** Job 42.10–16

hat a book it is, and what lessons there are in it! What a book the Bible is, what a miracle, what strength is given with it to man. It is like a mold cast of the world and man and human nature, everything is there, and a law for everything for all the ages. And what mysteries are solved and revealed; God raises Job again, gives him wealth again. Many years pass by, and he has other children and loves them. But how could he love those new ones when those first children are no more, when he has lost them? Remembering them, how could he be fully happy with those new ones, however dear the new ones might be? But he could, he could. It's the great mystery of human life that old grief passes gradually into quiet, tender joy. The mild serenity of age takes the place of the riotous blood of youth. I bless the rising sun each day, and as before, my heart sings to meet it, but now I love even more its setting, its long slanting rays and the soft, tender, gentle memories that come with them, the dear images from the whole of my long happy life—and over all the divine truth, softening, reconciling, forgiving! My life is ending, I know that well, but every day that is left me I feel how my earthly life is in touch with a new, infinite, unknown, but approaching life, the nearness of which sets my soul quivering with rapture, my mind glowing and my heart weeping with joy.

ADDITIONAL SCRIPTURE READING:
Isaiah 61.7–8; 1 Timothy 6.17; James 5.11

Go to page 593 for your next devotional reading.

1700   1900

Job Is Humbled and Satisfied

42 Then Job answered the LORD:
2 "I know that you can do all things,
and that no purpose of yours can be thwarted.
3 'Who is this that hides counsel
without knowledge?'
Therefore I have uttered what I did not understand,
things too wonderful for me,
which I did not know.
4 'Hear, and I will speak;
I will question you, and you declare to me.'
5 I had heard of you by the hearing of the ear,
but now my eye sees you;
6 therefore I despise myself,
and repent in dust and ashes."

SEEING GOD, JOB FORGETS ALL HE WANTED TO SAY, ALL HE THOUGHT HE WOULD SAY IF HE COULD BUT SEE HIM.   —George MacDonald

---

Job's Friends Are Humiliated

7 After the LORD had spoken these words to Job, the LORD said to Eliphaz the Temanite: "My wrath is kindled against you and against your two friends; for you have not spoken of me what is right, as my servant Job has. 8Now therefore take seven bulls and seven rams, and go to my servant Job, and offer up for yourselves a burnt offering; and my servant Job shall pray for you, for I will accept his prayer not to deal with you according to your folly; for you have not spoken of me what is right, as my servant Job has done." 9So Eliphaz the Temanite and Bildad the Shuhite and Zophar the Naamathite went and did what the LORD had told them; and the LORD accepted Job's prayer.

Job's Fortunes Are Restored Twofold

10 And the LORD restored the fortunes of Job when he had prayed for his friends; and the LORD gave Job twice as much as he had before. 11Then there came to him all his brothers and sisters and all who had known him before, and they ate bread with him in his house; they showed him sympathy and comforted him for all the evil that the LORD had brought upon him; and each of them gave him a piece of money[b] and a gold ring. 12The LORD blessed the latter days of Job more than his beginning; and he had fourteen thousand sheep, six thousand camels, a thousand yoke of oxen, and a thousand donkeys. 13He also had seven sons and three daughters. 14He named the first Jemimah, the second Keziah, and the third Keren-happuch. 15In all the land there were no women so beautiful as Job's daughters; and their father gave them an inheritance along with their brothers. 16After this Job lived one hundred and forty years, and saw his children, and his children's children, four generations. 17And Job died, old and full of days.

b Heb a qesitah

PSALMS

T HE BOOK OF PSALMS GIVES VOICE TO HUMAN EMOTION. THIS IS NOT A BOOK OF CATECHISM OR DOCTRINE; IT IS FOR THE MOST PART A BOOK OF PRAYER AND PRAISE. IT SPEAKS TO GOD IN PRAYER AND OF GOD IN PRAISE AND IN PROFESSIONS OF FAITH AND TRUST. THINK OF THE PSALMS AS ENTRIES IN A DIARY, REFLECTING PEOPLE'S MOST INTIMATE DEALINGS WITH GOD. YOU'LL FIND COMFORT AND STRENGTH HERE WHEN YOU IDENTIFY WITH THE OLD TESTAMENT SAINTS WHO WROTE THESE PRAYERS AND SONGS.

BOOK I
(Psalms 1–41)

Psalm

The Two Ways

1 Happy are those
  who do not follow the advice of
    the wicked,
  or take the path that sinners tread,
    or sit in the seat of scoffers;
2 but their delight is in the law of the
    LORD,
  and on his law they meditate day
    and night.
3 They are like trees
  planted by streams of water,
  which yield their fruit in its season,
and their leaves do not wither.
  In all that they do, they prosper.

4 The wicked are not so,
  but are like chaff that the wind
    drives away.
5 Therefore the wicked will not
    stand in the judgment,
  nor sinners in the congregation of
    the righteous;

THE PSALMS ARE THE ANATOMY OF THE SOUL.

—*John Calvin*

---

6 for the LORD watches over the way
    of the righteous,
  but the way of the wicked will
    perish.

WEEKEND

MAY 13, 1657
Anne Bradstreet

VERSE: Psalm 84.6 **PASSAGE:** Psalm 84.1–7

s spring the winter doth succeed
And leaves the naked trees do dress,
The earth all black is clothed in green.
At sunshine each their joy express.

My sun's returned with healing wings,
My soul and body doth rejoice,
My heart exults and praises sings
To him that heard my wailing voice.

My winter's past, my storms are gone,
And former clouds seem now all fled,
But if they must eclipse again,
I'll run where I was succored.

I have a shelter from the storm,
A shadow from the fainting heat,
I have access unto his throne,
Who is a God so wondrous great.

O hath thou made my pilgrimage
Thus pleasant, fair, and good,
Blessed me in youth and elder age,
My Baca made a springing flood.

O studious am what I shall do
To show my duty with delight;
All I can give is but thine own
And at the most a simple mite.

ADDITIONAL SCRIPTURE READING:
Psalm 29.11; Isaiah 25.4; Romans 5.3–5

Go to page 594 for your next devotional reading.

1500   1700

Psalm

God's Promise to His Anointed

1   Why do the nations conspire,
    and the peoples plot in vain?

2   The kings of the earth set
    themselves,
    and the rulers take counsel
    together,
    against the LORD and his
    anointed, saying,

3   "Let us burst their bonds asunder,
    and cast their cords from us."

MONDAY

THE WELL-KNOWN TERRITORY
John Calvin

VERSE: Psalm 1.1   **PASSAGE:** Psalm 1.1–6

I t would make too long a story to tell of the conflicts of all sorts in which I was active and of the trials by which I was tested. I will merely repeat briefly what I said before, so as not to offend fastidious readers with unnecessary words. Since [in the Psalms] David showed me the way with his own footsteps, I felt myself greatly comforted. The holy king was hurt more seriously by the envy and dishonesty of treacherous men at home than he was by the Philistines and other enemies who harassed him from the outside. I also have been attacked on all sides and have had scarcely a moment's relief from both external and internal conflicts. Satan has undertaken all too often in many ways to corrupt the fabric of this church. The result has been that I, who am a peaceable and timid man, was compelled to break the force of the deadly attacks by interposing my own body as a shield . . .

But this also was David's experience. He deserved well of his people, yet he was hated by many, as he laments in Psalm 69.4 (KJV): *They hate me without a cause . . . I returned what I did not rob.* When I was assailed by the undeserved hatred of those whose duty it was to help me, I received no small comfort from knowing of the glorious example [set by David].

Now these experiences were a very great help to my understanding of the Psalms, since, as I read, I was going through well-known territory. And I hope my readers will realize that when I discuss David's thoughts more intimately than those of others, I am speaking not as a remote spectator but as one who knows all about these things from his own experience.

ADDITIONAL SCRIPTURE READING:
Psalms 32.7; 39.7–8; 142.7

Go to page 596 for your next devotional reading.

1500   1700

4 He who sits in the heavens laughs;
    the LORD has them in derision.
5 Then he will speak to them in his
        wrath,
    and terrify them in his fury,
        saying,
6 "I have set my king on Zion, my
        holy hill."

7 I will tell of the decree of the LORD:
    He said to me, "You are my son;
        today I have begotten you.
8 Ask of me, and I will make the
        nations your heritage,
    and the ends of the earth your
        possession.
9 You shall break them with a rod of
        iron,
    and dash them in pieces like a
        potter's vessel."

10 Now therefore, O kings, be wise;
    be warned, O rulers of the earth.
11 Serve the LORD with fear,
    with trembling ¹²kiss his feet,ᵃ
    or he will be angry, and you will
        perish in the way;
    for his wrath is quickly kindled.

    Happy are all who take refuge in
        him.

Psalm

Trust in God under Adversity

A Psalm of David, when he fled from
his son Absalom.

1 O LORD, how many are my foes!
    Many are rising against me;
2 many are saying to me,
    "There is no help for youᵇ in
        God."   Selah

3 But you, O LORD, are a shield
        around me,
    my glory, and the one who lifts
        up my head.
4 I cry aloud to the LORD,
    and he answers me from his holy
        hill.   Selah

5 I lie down and sleep;

I wake again, for the LORD
    sustains me.
6 I am not afraid of ten thousands of
        people
    who have set themselves against
        me all around.

7 Rise up, O LORD!
    Deliver me, O my God!
For you strike all my enemies on
        the cheek;
    you break the teeth of the
        wicked.

8 Deliverance belongs to the LORD;
    may your blessing be on your
        people!   Selah

Psalm

Confident Plea for Deliverance from Enemies

To the leader: with stringed instruments.
        A Psalm of David.

1 Answer me when I call, O God of
        my right!
    You gave me room when I was in
        distress.
    Be gracious to me, and hear my
        prayer.

2 How long, you people, shall my
        honor suffer shame?
    How long will you love vain
        words, and seek after lies?
                                 Selah
3 But know that the LORD has set
        apart the faithful for himself;
    the LORD hears when I call to
        him.

4 When you are disturbed,ᶜ do not
        sin;
    ponder it on your beds, and be
        silent.   Selah
5 Offer right sacrifices,
    and put your trust in the LORD.

6 There are many who say, "O that
        we might see some good!
    Let the light of your face shine
        on us, O LORD!"

ᵃ Cn: Meaning of Heb of verses 11b and 12a is uncertain   ᵇ Syr: Heb him   ᶜ Or are angry

IN THE SILENCE
Dag Hammarskjold

VERSE: Psalm 4.4   **PASSAGE:** Psalm 4.4–8

ave mercy
Upon us.
Have mercy
Upon our efforts,
That we
Before thee,
In love and in faith,
Righteousness and humility,
May follow thee,
With self-denial, steadfastness, and courage,
And meet thee
In the silence.

Give us
A pure heart
That we may see thee,
A humble heart
That we may hear thee,
A heart of love
That we may serve thee,
A heart of faith
That we may live thee,

Thou
Whom I do not know
But whose I am.

Thou
Whom I do not comprehend
But who hast dedicated me
To my fate.
Thou—

ADDITIONAL SCRIPTURE READING:
Exodus 34.5–8; 1 Kings 19.11–12

Go to page 598 for your next devotional reading.

1900   Present

7 You have put gladness in my heart
more than when their grain and
wine abound.

8 I will both lie down and sleep in
peace;
for you alone, O LORD, make me
lie down in safety.

Psalm

 5

*Trust in God for Deliverance
from Enemies*

To the leader: for the flutes.
A Psalm of David.

1 Give ear to my words, O LORD;
give heed to my sighing.
2 Listen to the sound of my cry,
my King and my God,
for to you I pray.
3 O LORD, in the morning you hear
my voice;
in the morning I plead my case to
you, and watch.

4 For you are not a God who delights
in wickedness;
evil will not sojourn with you.
5 The boastful will not stand before
your eyes;
you hate all evildoers.
6 You destroy those who speak lies;
the LORD abhors the bloodthirsty
and deceitful.

7 But I, through the abundance of
your steadfast love,
will enter your house,
I will bow down toward your holy
temple
in awe of you.
8 Lead me, O LORD, in your
righteousness
because of my enemies;
make your way straight before
me.

9 For there is no truth in their
mouths;
their hearts are destruction;
their throats are open graves;
they flatter with their tongues.

10 Make them bear their guilt,
O God;
let them fall by their own
counsels;
because of their many
transgressions cast them out,
for they have rebelled against
you.

11 But let all who take refuge in you
rejoice;
let them ever sing for joy.
Spread your protection over them,
so that those who love your
name may exult in you.
12 For you bless the righteous,
O LORD;
you cover them with favor as
with a shield.

Psalm

 6

*Prayer for Recovery from Grave
Illness*

To the leader: with stringed instruments;
according to The Sheminith.
A Psalm of David.

1 O LORD, do not rebuke me in your
anger,
or discipline me in your wrath.
2 Be gracious to me, O LORD, for I am
languishing;
O LORD, heal me, for my bones
are shaking with terror.
3 My soul also is struck with terror,
while you, O LORD—how long?

4 Turn, O LORD, save my life;
deliver me for the sake of your
steadfast love.
5 For in death there is no
remembrance of you;
in Sheol who can give you praise?

6 I am weary with my moaning;
every night I flood my bed with
tears;
I drench my couch with my
weeping.
7 My eyes waste away because of
grief;
they grow weak because of all
my foes.

8   Depart from me, all you workers of
        evil,
    for the LORD has heard the sound
        of my weeping.
9   The LORD has heard my supplication;
        the LORD accepts my prayer.
10 All my enemies shall be ashamed
        and struck with terror;
    they shall turn back, and in a
        moment be put to shame.

Psalm

 7

Plea for Help against Persecutors

A Shiggaion of David, which he sang to the
    LORD concerning Cush, a Benjaminite.

1   O LORD my God, in you I take
        refuge;

WEDNESDAY

HOW TO BEGIN MORNING DEVOTIONS
William Law

VERSE: Psalm 5.3   PASSAGE: Psalm 5.1–3

he first thing that you are to do, when you are upon
your knees, is to shut your eyes, and with a short
silence let your soul place itself in the presence of God;
that is, you are to use this, or some other better
method, to separate yourself from all common thoughts, and
make your heart as sensible as you can of the divine presence.

Now if this recollection of spirit is necessary—as who can say
it is not?—then how poorly must they perform their devotions,
who are always in a hurry; who begin them in haste, and hardly
allow themselves time to repeat their very form, with any gravity or attention! Theirs is properly saying prayers, instead of
praying . . .

When you begin your petitions, use such various expressions
of the attributes of God, as may make you most sensible of the
greatness and power of the divine nature.

Begin, therefore, in words like these: O Being of all beings,
Fountain of all light and glory, gracious Father of men and
angels, whose universal Spirit is everywhere present, giving life,
and light, and joy, to all angels in heaven, and all creatures upon
earth . . .

For these representations of the divine attributes, which show
us in some degree the majesty and greatness of God, are an excellent means of raising our hearts into lively acts of worship and
adoration.

ADDITIONAL SCRIPTURE READING:
Psalms 88.13; 130.6; Mark 1.35

Go to page 599 for your next devotional reading.

1700   1900

save me from all my pursuers,
and deliver me,

2 or like a lion they will tear me
apart;
they will drag me away, with no
one to rescue.

3 O Lord my God, if I have done
this,
if there is wrong in my hands,

4 if I have repaid my ally with harm
or plundered my foe without
cause,

5 then let the enemy pursue and
overtake me,

trample my life to the ground,
and lay my soul in the dust. *Selah*

6 Rise up, O Lord, in your anger;
lift yourself up against the fury of
my enemies;
awake, O my God;*d* you have
appointed a judgment.

7 Let the assembly of the peoples be
gathered around you,
and over it take your seat*e* on
high.

8 The Lord judges the peoples;
judge me, O Lord, according to
my righteousness

d Or *awake for me*   *e* Cn: Heb *return*

THURSDAY

GOD'S WATER
Teresa of Avila

VERSE: Psalm 6.6   PASSAGE: Psalm 6.6–10

et's not think that everything is accomplished through much weeping but set our hands to the task of hard work and virtue. These are what we must pay attention to; let the tears come when God sends them and without any effort on our part to induce them. These tears from God will irrigate this dry earth, and they are a great help in producing fruit. The less attention we pay to them the more there are, for they are the water that falls from heaven. The tears we draw out by tiring ourselves in digging cannot compare with the tears that come from God, for often in digging we shall get worn out and not find even a puddle of water, much less a flowing well. Therefore, sisters, I consider it better for us to place ourselves in the presence of the Lord and look at his mercy and grandeur and at our own lowliness, and let him give us what he wants, whether water or dryness. He knows best what is suitable for us. With such an attitude we shall go about refreshed, and the devil will not have so much chance to play tricks on us.

ADDITIONAL SCRIPTURE READING:
2 Kings 20.5; Psalms 56.8; 126.5–6

Go to page 601 for your next devotional reading.

1500   1700

and according to the integrity
    that is in me.

9 O let the evil of the wicked come
    to an end,
  but establish the righteous,
you who test the minds and hearts,
  O righteous God.
10 God is my shield,
  who saves the upright in heart.
11 God is a righteous judge,
  and a God who has indignation
    every day.

12 If one does not repent, God[f] will
  whet his sword;
  he has bent and strung his bow;
13 he has prepared his deadly weapons,
  making his arrows fiery shafts.
14 See how they conceive evil,
  and are pregnant with mischief,
  and bring forth lies.
15 They make a pit, digging it out,
  and fall into the hole that they
    have made.
16 Their mischief returns upon their
  own heads,
  and on their own heads their
    violence descends.

17 I will give to the LORD the thanks
  due to his righteousness,
  and sing praise to the name of
    the LORD, the Most High.

Psalm

Divine Majesty and Human Dignity

To the leader: according to The Gittith.
A Psalm of David.

1 O LORD, our Sovereign,
  how majestic is your name in all
    the earth!

You have set your glory above the
  heavens.
2 Out of the mouths of babes and
    infants
you have founded a bulwark
  because of your foes,
  to silence the enemy and the
    avenger.

3 When I look at your heavens, the
  work of your fingers,
  the moon and the stars that you
    have established;
4 what are human beings that you
  are mindful of them,
  mortals[g] that you care for them?

5 Yet you have made them a little
  lower than God,[h]
  and crowned them with glory
    and honor.
6 You have given them dominion
  over the works of your hands;
  you have put all things under
    their feet,
7 all sheep and oxen,
  and also the beasts of the field,
8 the birds of the air, and the fish of
  the sea,
  whatever passes along the paths
    of the seas.

9 O LORD, our Sovereign,
  how majestic is your name in all
    the earth!

Psalm

God's Power and Justice

To the leader: according to Muth-labben.
A Psalm of David.

1 I will give thanks to the LORD with
  my whole heart;
  I will tell of all your wonderful
    deeds.
2 I will be glad and exult in you;
  I will sing praise to your name,
    O Most High.

3 When my enemies turned back,
  they stumbled and perished
    before you.
4 For you have maintained my just
  cause;
  you have sat on the throne giving
    righteous judgment.

5 You have rebuked the nations, you
  have destroyed the wicked;
  you have blotted out their name
    forever and ever.

---

f Heb he   g Heb ben adam, lit. son of man   h Or than the divine beings or angels: Heb elohim

FRIDAY

A Prayer of Thanksgiving
South Africa, National Service of Thanksgiving

VERSE: Psalm 9.1   PASSAGE: Psalm 9.1–10

God our loving eternal Parent, we praise you with a great shout of joy! Your ruling power has provided victorious! For centuries our land seemed too dark for sunrise, too bloody for healing, too sick for recovery, too hateful for reconciliation. But you have brought us into the daylight of liberation; you have healed us with new hope; you have stirred us to believe our nation can be reborn; we see the eyes of our sisters and brothers shining with resolve to build a new South Africa. Accept our prayers of praise and thanksgiving.

We thank you for our grandmothers and grandfathers who taught us to believe in liberation. We thank you for those who are great names to all our country now: Luthuli, Sobukwe, Biko, Visser, Joseph, Ngoyi, Hani, Tambo, and a thousand others. Many are named with our own names, treasured in our hearts, honored in our memories. Many rest in graves in other lands so that South African love embraces the world. We remember those thousands of people overseas who gave themselves in solidarity that our nation might be changed.

For all of these we thank and praise you. We thank you that democracy has come, and for the wonder of a government of national unity. We thank you for the commitment among all people to seek justice and peace, homes and jobs, education and health, reconciliation and reconstruction. We thank you that because apartheid has gone we can turn from the days of destruction to the work of reconstruction together. For our rich variety, our rich vision and our rich land, we thank you.

We thank you for the spiritual power which gives us new birth. You have given us the courage to change our minds, to open our hearts to those we despised, and to discover we can disagree without being enemies. We are not winners and losers, but citizens who push and pull together to move the nation forward. We thank you for the good news that you will always be with us, and will always overcome: that love will conquer hatred; that tolerance will conquer antagonism; that cooperation will conquer conflict; that your Holy Spirit can empower our spirits; through Jesus Christ our Lord.

ADDITIONAL SCRIPTURE READING:
Psalms 107.15–16; 117

Go to page 609 for your next devotional reading.

1900   Present

6 The enemies have vanished in
 everlasting ruins;
 their cities you have rooted out;
 the very memory of them has
 perished.

7 But the LORD sits enthroned forever,
 he has established his throne for
 judgment.
8 He judges the world with
 righteousness;
 he judges the peoples with equity.

9 The LORD is a stronghold for the
 oppressed,
 a stronghold in times of trouble.
10 And those who know your name
 put their trust in you,
 for you, O LORD, have not
 forsaken those who seek you.

11 Sing praises to the LORD, who
 dwells in Zion.
 Declare his deeds among the
 peoples.
12 For he who avenges blood is
 mindful of them;
 he does not forget the cry of the
 afflicted.

13 Be gracious to me, O LORD.
 See what I suffer from those who
 hate me;
 you are the one who lifts me up
 from the gates of death,
14 so that I may recount all your
 praises,
 and, in the gates of daughter Zion,
 rejoice in your deliverance.

15 The nations have sunk in the pit
 that they made;
 in the net that they hid has their
 own foot been caught.
16 The LORD has made himself known,
 he has executed judgment;
 the wicked are snared in the
 work of their own hands.
 Higgaion. Selah

17 The wicked shall depart to Sheol,
 all the nations that forget God.

18 For the needy shall not always be
 forgotten,

nor the hope of the poor perish
 forever.

19 Rise up, O LORD! Do not let
 mortals prevail;
 let the nations be judged before
 you.
20 Put them in fear, O LORD;
 let the nations know that they
 are only human.   *Selah*

Psalm

 10

Prayer for Deliverance from Enemies

1 Why, O LORD, do you stand far off?
 Why do you hide yourself in
 times of trouble?
2 In arrogance the wicked persecute
 the poor—
 let them be caught in the
 schemes they have devised.

3 For the wicked boast of the desires
 of their heart,
 those greedy for gain curse and
 renounce the LORD.
4 In the pride of their countenance
 the wicked say, "God will
 not seek it out";
 all their thoughts are, "There is
 no God."

5 Their ways prosper at all times;
 your judgments are on high, out
 of their sight;
 as for their foes, they scoff at
 them.
6 They think in their heart, "We
 shall not be moved;
 throughout all generations we
 shall not meet adversity."

7 Their mouths are filled with cursing
 and deceit and oppression;
 under their tongues are mischief
 and iniquity.
8 They sit in ambush in the villages;
 in hiding places they murder the
 innocent.

Their eyes stealthily watch for the
 helpless;
9 they lurk in secret like a lion in
 its covert;

they lurk that they may seize the
    poor;
  they seize the poor and drag
    them off in their net.

10 They stoop, they crouch,
    and the helpless fall by their
    might.
11 They think in their heart, "God has
    forgotten,
    he has hidden his face, he will
    never see it."

12 Rise up, O Lord; O God, lift up
    your hand;
    do not forget the oppressed.
13 Why do the wicked renounce God,
    and say in their hearts, "You will
    not call us to account"?

14 But you do see! Indeed you note
    trouble and grief,
    that you may take it into your
    hands;
  the helpless commit themselves to
    you;
    you have been the helper of the
    orphan.

15 Break the arm of the wicked and
    evildoers;
    seek out their wickedness until
    you find none.
16 The Lord is king forever and ever;
    the nations shall perish from his
    land.

17 O Lord, you will hear the desire of
    the meek;
    you will strengthen their heart,
    you will incline your ear
18 to do justice for the orphan and the
    oppressed,
    so that those from earth may
    strike terror no more. *i*

Psalm

Song of Trust in God
To the leader. Of David.

1 In the Lord I take refuge; how can
    you say to me,

"Flee like a bird to the
    mountains; *j*
2 for look, the wicked bend the
    bow,
    they have fitted their arrow to
    the string,
    to shoot in the dark at the
    upright in heart.
3 If the foundations are destroyed,
    what can the righteous do?"

4 The Lord is in his holy temple;
    the Lord's throne is in heaven.
    His eyes behold, his gaze
    examines humankind.
5 The Lord tests the righteous and
    the wicked,
    and his soul hates the lover of
    violence.
6 On the wicked he will rain coals of
    fire and sulfur;
    a scorching wind shall be the
    portion of their cup.
7 For the Lord is righteous;
    he loves righteous deeds;
    the upright shall behold his face.

Psalm

Plea for Help in Evil Times
To the leader: according to The Sheminith.
A Psalm of David.

1 Help, O Lord, for there is no longer
    anyone who is godly;
    the faithful have disappeared
    from humankind.
2 They utter lies to each other;
    with flattering lips and a double
    heart they speak.

3 May the Lord cut off all flattering
    lips,
    the tongue that makes great
    boasts,
4 those who say, "With our tongues
    we will prevail;
    our lips are our own—who is our
    master?"

5 "Because the poor are despoiled,
    because the needy groan,

i Meaning of Heb uncertain   *j* Gk Syr Jerome Tg: Heb *flee to your mountain, O bird*

I will now rise up," says the
LORD;
"I will place them in the safety
for which they long."
6 The promises of the LORD are
promises that are pure,
silver refined in a furnace on the
ground,
purified seven times.

7 You, O LORD, will protect us;
you will guard us from this
generation forever.
8 On every side the wicked prowl,
as vileness is exalted among
humankind.

Psalm

 13

Prayer for Deliverance from Enemies

To the leader. A Psalm of David.

1 How long, O LORD? Will you forget
me forever?
How long will you hide your face
from me?
2 How long must I bear pain[k] in my
soul,
and have sorrow in my heart all
day long?
How long shall my enemy be
exalted over me?

3 Consider and answer me, O LORD
my God!
Give light to my eyes, or I will
sleep the sleep of death,
4 and my enemy will say, "I have
prevailed";
my foes will rejoice because I am
shaken.

5 But I trusted in your steadfast
love;
my heart shall rejoice in your
salvation.
6 I will sing to the LORD,
because he has dealt bountifully
with me.

k Syr: Heb *hold counsels*

Psalm

 14

Denunciation of Godlessness

To the leader. Of David.

1 Fools say in their hearts, "There is
no God."
They are corrupt, they do
abominable deeds;
there is no one who does good.

I WAS . . . LIVING, LIKE SO MANY ATHEISTS OR
ANTITHEISTS, IN A WHIRL OF CONTRADICTIONS. I
MAINTAINED THAT GOD DID NOT EXIST. I WAS
ALSO VERY ANGRY WITH GOD FOR NOT EXISTING.
I WAS EQUALLY ANGRY WITH HIM FOR CREATING
A WORLD.   —*C. S. Lewis*

---

2 The LORD looks down from heaven
on humankind
to see if there are any who are
wise,
who seek after God.

3 They have all gone astray, they are
all alike perverse;
there is no one who does good,
no, not one.

4 Have they no knowledge, all the
evildoers
who eat up my people as they eat
bread,
and do not call upon the LORD?

5 There they shall be in great
terror,
for God is with the company of
the righteous.
6 You would confound the plans of
the poor,
but the LORD is their refuge.

7 O that deliverance for Israel would
come from Zion!
When the LORD restores the
fortunes of his people,
Jacob will rejoice; Israel will be
glad.

Psalm

Who Shall Abide in God's Sanctuary?

A Psalm of David.

1 O LORD, who may abide in your
  tent?
  Who may dwell on your holy
  hill?

2 Those who walk blamelessly, and
    do what is right,
  and speak the truth from their
    heart;
3 who do not slander with their
    tongue,
  and do no evil to their friends,
  nor take up a reproach against
    their neighbors;
4 in whose eyes the wicked are
    despised,
  but who honor those who fear
    the LORD;
  who stand by their oath even to
    their hurt;
5 who do not lend money at interest,
  and do not take a bribe against
    the innocent.

  Those who do these things shall
    never be moved.

Psalm

Song of Trust and Security in God

A Miktam of David.

1 Protect me, O God, for in you I
  take refuge.
2 I say to the LORD, "You are my
  Lord;
  I have no good apart from you."[1]

3 As for the holy ones in the land,
    they are the noble,
  in whom is all my delight.

4 Those who choose another god
  multiply their sorrows;[m]

their drink offerings of blood I
  will not pour out
  or take their names upon my
  lips.

5 The LORD is my chosen portion and
    my cup;
  you hold my lot.
6 The boundary lines have fallen for
    me in pleasant places;
  I have a goodly heritage.

7 I bless the LORD who gives me
    counsel;
  in the night also my heart
    instructs me.
8 I keep the LORD always before me;
  because he is at my right hand, I
    shall not be moved.

9 Therefore my heart is glad, and my
    soul rejoices;
  my body also rests secure.
10 For you do not give me up to Sheol,
  or let your faithful one see the
    Pit.

11 You show me the path of life.
  In your presence there is fullness
    of joy;
  in your right hand are pleasures
    forevermore.

Psalm

Prayer for Deliverance from Persecutors

A Prayer of David.

1 Hear a just cause, O LORD; attend
    to my cry;
  give ear to my prayer from lips
    free of deceit.
2 From you let my vindication come;
  let your eyes see the right.

3 If you try my heart, if you visit me
    by night,
  if you test me, you will find no
    wickedness in me;
  my mouth does not transgress.

1 Jerome Tg: Meaning of Heb uncertain   m Cn: Meaning of Heb uncertain

4 As for what others do, by the word
   of your lips
     I have avoided the ways of the
       violent.
5 My steps have held fast to your
   paths;
     my feet have not slipped.

6 I call upon you, for you will answer
   me, O God;
     incline your ear to me, hear my
       words.
7 Wondrously show your steadfast
   love,
     O savior of those who seek refuge
     from their adversaries at your
       right hand.

8 Guard me as the apple of the eye;
     hide me in the shadow of your
       wings,
9 from the wicked who despoil me,
     my deadly enemies who
       surround me.
10 They close their hearts to pity;
     with their mouths they speak
       arrogantly.
11 They track me down;[n] now they
     surround me;
     they set their eyes to cast me to
       the ground.
12 They are like a lion eager to tear,
     like a young lion lurking in
       ambush.

13 Rise up, O LORD, confront them,
     overthrow them!
     By your sword deliver my life
       from the wicked,
14 from mortals—by your hand,
     O LORD—
     from mortals whose portion in
       life is in this world.
     May their bellies be filled with
       what you have stored up for
         them;
     may their children have more
       than enough;
     may they leave something over
       to their little ones.

15 As for me, I shall behold your face
     in righteousness;
     when I awake I shall be satisfied,
       beholding your likeness.

Psalm

18

Royal Thanksgiving for Victory

To the leader. A Psalm of David the servant
of the LORD, who addressed the words of this
song to the LORD on the day when the LORD
delivered him from the hand of all his
enemies, and from the hand of Saul. He said:

1 I love you, O LORD, my strength.
2 The LORD is my rock, my fortress,
     and my deliverer,
   my God, my rock in whom I take
     refuge,
   my shield, and the horn of my
     salvation, my stronghold.
3 I call upon the LORD, who is
     worthy to be praised,
   so I shall be saved from my
     enemies.

4 The cords of death encompassed me;
   the torrents of perdition assailed
     me;
5 the cords of Sheol entangled me;
   the snares of death confronted
     me.

6 In my distress I called upon the
     LORD;
   to my God I cried for help.
   From his temple he heard my voice,
   and my cry to him reached his
     ears.

7 Then the earth reeled and rocked;
   the foundations also of the
     mountains trembled
   and quaked, because he was
     angry.
8 Smoke went up from his nostrils,
   and devouring fire from his
     mouth;
   glowing coals flamed forth from
     him.
9 He bowed the heavens, and came
     down;
   thick darkness was under his feet.
10 He rode on a cherub, and flew;
   he came swiftly upon the wings
     of the wind.
11 He made darkness his covering
     around him,

n One Ms Compare Syr: MT *Our steps*

his canopy thick clouds dark
with water.
12 Out of the brightness before him
there broke through his clouds
hailstones and coals of fire.
13 The LORD also thundered in the
heavens,
and the Most High uttered his
voice.ᵒ
14 And he sent out his arrows, and
scattered them;
he flashed forth lightnings, and
routed them.
15 Then the channels of the sea were
seen,
and the foundations of the world
were laid bare
at your rebuke, O LORD,
at the blast of the breath of your
nostrils.

16 He reached down from on high, he
took me;
he drew me out of mighty waters.
17 He delivered me from my strong
enemy,
and from those who hated me;
for they were too mighty for me.
18 They confronted me in the day of
my calamity;
but the LORD was my support.
19 He brought me out into a broad
place;
he delivered me, because he
delighted in me.

20 The LORD rewarded me according
to my righteousness;
according to the cleanness of my
hands he recompensed me.
21 For I have kept the ways of the
LORD,
and have not wickedly departed
from my God.
22 For all his ordinances were before
me,
and his statutes I did not put
away from me.
23 I was blameless before him,
and I kept myself from guilt.
24 Therefore the LORD has
recompensed me according
to my righteousness,
according to the cleanness of my
hands in his sight.

25 With the loyal you show yourself
loyal;
with the blameless you show
yourself blameless;
26 with the pure you show yourself
pure;
and with the crooked you show
yourself perverse.
27 For you deliver a humble people,
but the haughty eyes you bring
down.
28 It is you who light my lamp;
the LORD, my God, lights up my
darkness.
29 By you I can crush a troop,
and by my God I can leap over a
wall.
30 This God—his way is perfect;
the promise of the LORD proves
true;
he is a shield for all who take
refuge in him.

31 For who is God except the LORD?
And who is a rock besides our
God?—
32 the God who girded me with
strength,
and made my way safe.
33 He made my feet like the feet of a
deer,
and set me secure on the heights.
34 He trains my hands for war,
so that my arms can bend a bow
of bronze.
35 You have given me the shield of
your salvation,
and your right hand has
supported me;
your helpᵖ has made me great.
36 You gave me a wide place for my
steps under me,
and my feet did not slip.
37 I pursued my enemies and
overtook them;
and did not turn back until they
were consumed.
38 I struck them down, so that they
were not able to rise;
they fell under my feet.
39 For you girded me with strength for
the battle;
you made my assailants sink
under me.

o Gk See 2 Sam 22.14: Heb adds *hailstones and coals of fire*   p Or *gentleness*

40 You made my enemies turn their
        backs to me,
    and those who hated me I
        destroyed.
41 They cried for help, but there was
        no one to save them;
    they cried to the LORD, but he did
        not answer them.
42 I beat them fine, like dust before
        the wind;
    I cast them out like the mire of
        the streets.

43 You delivered me from strife with
        the peoples;*q*
    you made me head of the nations;
    people whom I had not known
        served me.
44 As soon as they heard of me they
        obeyed me;
    foreigners came cringing to me.
45 Foreigners lost heart,
    and came trembling out of their
        strongholds.

46 The LORD lives! Blessed be my rock,
    and exalted be the God of my
        salvation,
47 the God who gave me vengeance
    and subdued peoples under me;
48 who delivered me from my enemies;
    indeed, you exalted me above my
        adversaries;
    you delivered me from the
        violent.

49 For this I will extol you, O LORD,
        among the nations,
    and sing praises to your name.
50 Great triumphs he gives to his king,
    and shows steadfast love to his
        anointed,
    to David and his descendants
        forever.

Psalm

God's Glory in Creation and the Law
    To the leader. A Psalm of David.

1   The heavens are telling the glory of
        God;

and the firmament*r* proclaims his
    handiwork.
2   Day to day pours forth speech,
    and night to night declares
        knowledge.
3   There is no speech, nor are there
        words;
    their voice is not heard;
4   yet their voice*s* goes out through all
        the earth,
    and their words to the end of the
        world.

In the heavens*t* he has set a tent for
    the sun,
5   which comes out like a bridegroom
        from his wedding canopy,
    and like a strong man runs its
        course with joy.
6   Its rising is from the end of the
        heavens,
    and its circuit to the end of them;
    and nothing is hid from its heat.

7   The law of the LORD is perfect,
        reviving the soul;
    the decrees of the LORD are sure,
        making wise the simple;
8   the precepts of the LORD are right,
        rejoicing the heart;
    the commandment of the LORD is
        clear,
        enlightening the eyes;
9   the fear of the LORD is pure,
        enduring forever;
    the ordinances of the LORD are true
        and righteous altogether.
10 More to be desired are they than
        gold,
    even much fine gold;
    sweeter also than honey,
        and drippings of the honeycomb.

11 Moreover by them is your servant
        warned;
    in keeping them there is great
        reward.
12 But who can detect their errors?
    Clear me from hidden faults.
13 Keep back your servant also from
        the insolent;*u*
    do not let them have dominion
        over me.
    Then I shall be blameless,

q Gk Tg: Heb people   r Or dome   s Gk Jerome Compare Syr: Heb line   t Heb In them
u Or from proud thoughts

WEEKEND

A SONG OF ASCENTS
Charles Wesley

VERSE: Psalm 133.1   **PASSAGE:** Psalm 133

ehold how good a thing
It is to dwell in peace;
How pleasing to our king,
This fruit of righteousness;
When brethren all in one agree,
They know the joy of unity!
They know the joy of unity!

When all are sweetly joined
(True followers of the Lamb),
They're one in heart and mind,
They think and speak the same;
When all in love together dwell;
The comfort is unspeakable!
The comfort is unspeakable!

Where unity takes place,
The joys of heav'n we prove;
This is the gospel grace,
The unction from above;
The Spirit on all saints is shed,
Descending swift from Christ the head.
Descending swift from Christ the head.

Where unity is found,
The sweet anointing grace
Extends to all around,
And shines from every face;
To every praising saint it comes,
And fills him with divine perfumes.
And fills him with divine perfumes.

ADDITIONAL SCRIPTURE READING:
Ephesians 4.3–7; Philippians 2.2–5; 1 Peter 3.8

Go to page 614 for your next devotional reading.

1700   1900

and innocent of great
transgression.

14 Let the words of my mouth and the
meditation of my heart
be acceptable to you,
O LORD, my rock and my
redeemer.

Psalm

Prayer for Victory

To the leader. A Psalm of David.

1 The LORD answer you in the day of
trouble!
The name of the God of Jacob
protect you!
2 May he send you help from the
sanctuary,
and give you support from Zion.
3 May he remember all your
offerings,
and regard with favor your burnt
sacrifices.   *Selah*

4 May he grant you your heart's
desire,
and fulfill all your plans.
5 May we shout for joy over your
victory,
and in the name of our God set
up our banners.
May the LORD fulfill all your
petitions.

6 Now I know that the LORD will
help his anointed;
he will answer him from his holy
heaven
with mighty victories by his
right hand.
7 Some take pride in chariots, and
some in horses,
but our pride is in the name of
the LORD our God.
8 They will collapse and fall,
but we shall rise and stand
upright.

9 Give victory to the king, O LORD;
answer us when we call. *v*

Psalm

Thanksgiving for Victory

To the leader. A Psalm of David.

1 In your strength the king rejoices,
O LORD,
and in your help how greatly he
exults!
2 You have given him his heart's
desire,
and have not withheld the
request of his lips.   *Selah*
3 For you meet him with rich
blessings;
you set a crown of fine gold on
his head.
4 He asked you for life; you gave it to
him—
length of days forever and ever.
5 His glory is great through your
help;
splendor and majesty you bestow
on him.
6 You bestow on him blessings
forever;
you make him glad with the joy
of your presence.
7 For the king trusts in the LORD,
and through the steadfast love of
the Most High he shall not
be moved.

8 Your hand will find out all your
enemies;
your right hand will find out
those who hate you.
9 You will make them like a fiery
furnace
when you appear.
The LORD will swallow them up in
his wrath,
and fire will consume them.
10 You will destroy their offspring
from the earth,
and their children from among
humankind.
11 If they plan evil against you,
if they devise mischief, they will
not succeed.
12 For you will put them to flight;
you will aim at their faces with
your bows.

v Gk: Heb *give victory, O LORD; let the King answer us when we call*

13 Be exalted, O LORD, in your
    strength!
  We will sing and praise your
    power.

Psalm

 22

Plea for Deliverance from Suffering and Hostility

To the leader: according to The Deer of the
  Dawn. A Psalm of David.

1 My God, my God, why have you
    forsaken me?
  Why are you so far from helping
    me, from the words of my
    groaning?
2 O my God, I cry by day, but you do
    not answer;
  and by night, but find no rest.

3 Yet you are holy,
    enthroned on the praises of
    Israel.
4 In you our ancestors trusted;
    they trusted, and you delivered
    them.
5 To you they cried, and were saved;
    in you they trusted, and were not
    put to shame.

6 But I am a worm, and not human;
    scorned by others, and despised
    by the people.
7 All who see me mock at me;
    they make mouths at me, they
    shake their heads;
8 "Commit your cause to the LORD;
    let him deliver—
  let him rescue the one in whom
    he delights!"

9 Yet it was you who took me from
    the womb;
  you kept me safe on my mother's
    breast.
10 On you I was cast from my birth,
    and since my mother bore me
    you have been my God.
11 Do not be far from me,
    for trouble is near
    and there is no one to help.

12 Many bulls encircle me,
    strong bulls of Bashan surround
    me;
13 they open wide their mouths at me,
    like a ravening and roaring lion.

14 I am poured out like water,
    and all my bones are out of joint;
  my heart is like wax;
    it is melted within my breast;
15 my mouth[w] is dried up like a
    potsherd,
  and my tongue sticks to my jaws;
  you lay me in the dust of death.

16 For dogs are all around me;
    a company of evildoers encircles
    me.
  My hands and feet have shriveled;[x]
17 I can count all my bones.
  They stare and gloat over me;
18 they divide my clothes among
    themselves,
  and for my clothing they cast
    lots.

19 But you, O LORD, do not be far
    away!
  O my help, come quickly to my
    aid!
20 Deliver my soul from the sword,
    my life[y] from the power of the
    dog!
21 Save me from the mouth of the
    lion!

From the horns of the wild oxen
    you have rescued[z] me.
22 I will tell of your name to my
    brothers and sisters;[a]
  in the midst of the congregation I
    will praise you:
23 You who fear the LORD, praise him!
  All you offspring of Jacob, glorify
    him;
  stand in awe of him, all you
    offspring of Israel!
24 For he did not despise or abhor
    the affliction of the afflicted;
  he did not hide his face from me,[b]
  but heard when I[c] cried to him.

25 From you comes my praise in the
    great congregation;

---

w Cn: Heb *strength*   x Meaning of Heb uncertain   y Heb *my only one*   z Heb *answered*
a Or *kindred*   b Heb *him*   c Heb *he*

my vows I will pay before those
who fear him.
26 The poor[d] shall eat and be satisfied;
those who seek him shall praise
the LORD.
May your hearts live forever!

27 All the ends of the earth shall
remember
and turn to the LORD;
and all the families of the nations
shall worship before him.[e]
28 For dominion belongs to the LORD,
and he rules over the nations.

29 To him,[f] indeed, shall all who sleep
in[g] the earth bow down;
before him shall bow all who go
down to the dust,
and I shall live for him.[h]
30 Posterity will serve him;
future generations will be told
about the Lord,
31 and[i] proclaim his deliverance to a
people yet unborn,
saying that he has done it.

Psalm

The Divine Shepherd

A Psalm of David.

1 The LORD is my shepherd, I shall
not want.
2 He makes me lie down in green
pastures;
he leads me beside still waters;[j]
3 he restores my soul.[k]
He leads me in right paths[l]
for his name's sake.

4 Even though I walk through the
darkest valley,[m]
I fear no evil;
for you are with me;
your rod and your staff—
they comfort me.

5 You prepare a table before me
in the presence of my enemies;

you anoint my head with oil;
my cup overflows.
6 Surely[n] goodness and mercy[o] shall
follow me
all the days of my life,
and I shall dwell in the house of the
LORD
my whole life long.[p]

THE TWENTY-THIRD PSALM IS THE NIGHTINGALE
OF THE PSALMS. IT IS SMALL, OF A HOMELY FEATH-
ER, SINGING SHYLY OUT OF OBSCURITY; BUT IT
HAS FILLED THE AIR OF THE WHOLE WORLD WITH
MELODIOUS JOY.   —*Henry Ward Beecher*

Psalm

Entrance into the Temple

Of David. A Psalm.

1 The earth is the LORD's and all that
is in it,
the world, and those who live in
it;
2 for he has founded it on the seas,
and established it on the rivers.

3 Who shall ascend the hill of the
LORD?
And who shall stand in his holy
place?
4 Those who have clean hands and
pure hearts,
who do not lift up their souls to
what is false,
and do not swear deceitfully.
5 They will receive blessing from the
LORD,
and vindication from the God of
their salvation.
6 Such is the company of those who
seek him,
who seek the face of the God of
Jacob.[q]   *Selah*

7 Lift up your heads, O gates!
and be lifted up, O ancient doors!

---

d Or *afflicted*   e Gk Syr Jerome: Heb *you*   f Cn: Heb *They have eaten and*   g Cn: Heb *all the fat
ones*   h Compare Gk Syr Vg: Heb *and he who cannot keep himself alive*   i Compare Gk: Heb *it will
be told about the Lord to the generation,* [31]*they will come and*   j Heb *waters of rest*   k Or *life*
l Or *paths of righteousness*   m Or *the valley of the shadow of death*   n Or *Only*   o Or *kindness*
p Heb *for length of days*   q Gk Syr: Heb *your face, O Jacob*

that the King of glory may come
in.
8 Who is the King of glory?
The LORD, strong and mighty,
the LORD, mighty in battle.
9 Lift up your heads, O gates!
and be lifted up, O ancient doors!
that the King of glory may come
in.
10 Who is this King of glory?
The LORD of hosts,
he is the King of glory.   *Selah*

Psalm

 25

Prayer for Guidance and for Deliverance

Of David.

1 To you, O LORD, I lift up my soul.
2 O my God, in you I trust;
do not let me be put to shame;
do not let my enemies exult over
me.
3 Do not let those who wait for you
be put to shame;
let them be ashamed who are
wantonly treacherous.

4 Make me to know your ways,
O LORD;
teach me your paths.
5 Lead me in your truth, and teach
me,
for you are the God of my
salvation;
for you I wait all day long.

6 Be mindful of your mercy, O LORD,
and of your steadfast love,
for they have been from of old.
7 Do not remember the sins of my
youth or my transgressions;
according to your steadfast love
remember me,
for your goodness' sake, O LORD!

8 Good and upright is the LORD;
therefore he instructs sinners in
the way.
9 He leads the humble in what is
right,
and teaches the humble his way.

10 All the paths of the LORD are
steadfast love and
faithfulness,
for those who keep his covenant
and his decrees.

11 For your name's sake, O LORD,
pardon my guilt, for it is great.
12 Who are they that fear the LORD?
He will teach them the way that
they should choose.
13 They will abide in prosperity,
and their children shall possess
the land.
14 The friendship of the LORD is for
those who fear him,
and he makes his covenant
known to them.
15 My eyes are ever toward the LORD,
for he will pluck my feet out of
the net.

16 Turn to me and be gracious to me,
for I am lonely and afflicted.
17 Relieve the troubles of my heart,
and bring me^r out of my distress.
18 Consider my affliction and my
trouble,
and forgive all my sins.

19 Consider how many are my foes,
and with what violent hatred
they hate me.
20 O guard my life, and deliver me;
do not let me be put to shame,
for I take refuge in you.
21 May integrity and uprightness
preserve me,
for I wait for you.

22 Redeem Israel, O God,
out of all its troubles.

Psalm

 26

Plea for Justice and Declaration of Righteousness

Of David.

1 Vindicate me, O LORD,
for I have walked in my integrity,

---

r Or *The troubles of my heart are enlarged; bring me*

and I have trusted in the LORD
without wavering.
2 Prove me, O LORD, and try me;
test my heart and mind.
3 For your steadfast love is before my
eyes,
and I walk in faithfulness to you.ˢ

4 I do not sit with the worthless,
nor do I consort with hypocrites;
5 I hate the company of evildoers,
and will not sit with the wicked.

6 I wash my hands in innocence,
and go around your altar, O LORD,

ˢ Or *in your faithfulness*

7 singing aloud a song of thanksgiving,
and telling all your wondrous
deeds.

8 O LORD, I love the house in which
you dwell,
and the place where your glory
abides.
9 Do not sweep me away with
sinners,
nor my life with the bloodthirsty,
10 those in whose hands are evil
devices,
and whose right hands are full of
bribes.

MONDAY

THE SECRETS OF PROVIDENCE
A. B. Simpson

VERSE: Psalm 25.14   **PASSAGE:** Psalm 25

here are secrets of providence which God's dear children may learn. His dealings with them often seem, to the outward eye, dark and terrible. Faith looks deeper and says, "This is God's secret. You look only on the outside; I can look deeper and see the hidden meaning."

Sometimes diamonds are done up in rough packages, so that their value cannot be seen. When the tabernacle was built in the wilderness there was nothing rich in its outside appearance. The costly things were all within, and its outward covering of rough badger skin gave no hint of the valuable things which it contained.

God may send you, dear friends, some costly packages. Do not worry if they are done up in rough wrappings. You may be sure there are treasures of love, and kindness, and wisdom hidden within. If we take what he sends, *and trust him* for the goodness in it, even in the dark, we shall learn the meaning of the secrets of providence.

ADDITIONAL SCRIPTURE READING:
Genesis 18.17–19; Proverbs 3.32; Matthew 13.11–12

Go to page 617 for your next devotional reading.

1900   Present

11 But as for me, I walk in my integrity;
    redeem me, and be gracious to me.
12 My foot stands on level ground;
    in the great congregation I will
       bless the LORD.

Psalm

Triumphant Song of Confidence
Of David.

1 The LORD is my light and my
       salvation;
    whom shall I fear?
  The LORD is the stronghold[t] of my
       life;
    of whom shall I be afraid?

2 When evildoers assail me
    to devour my flesh—
  my adversaries and foes—
    they shall stumble and fall.

3 Though an army encamp against
       me,
    my heart shall not fear;
  though war rise up against me,
    yet I will be confident.

4 One thing I asked of the LORD,
    that will I seek after:
  to live in the house of the LORD
    all the days of my life,
  to behold the beauty of the LORD,
    and to inquire in his temple.

5 For he will hide me in his shelter
    in the day of trouble;
  he will conceal me under the cover
       of his tent;
    he will set me high on a rock.

6 Now my head is lifted up
    above my enemies all around me,
  and I will offer in his tent
    sacrifices with shouts of joy;
  I will sing and make melody to the
       LORD.

7 Hear, O LORD, when I cry aloud,
    be gracious to me and answer me!
8 "Come," my heart says, "seek his
       face!"

  Your face, LORD, do I seek.
9   Do not hide your face from me.

  Do not turn your servant away in
       anger,
    you who have been my help.
  Do not cast me off, do not forsake
       me,
    O God of my salvation!
10 If my father and mother forsake
       me,
    the LORD will take me up.

11 Teach me your way, O LORD,
    and lead me on a level path
       because of my enemies.
12 Do not give me up to the will of
       my adversaries,
    for false witnesses have risen
       against me,
  and they are breathing out
       violence.

13 I believe that I shall see the
       goodness of the LORD
    in the land of the living.
14 Wait for the LORD;
    be strong, and let your heart take
       courage;
    wait for the LORD!

Psalm

Prayer for Help and Thanksgiving for It
Of David.

1 To you, O LORD, I call;
    my rock, do not refuse to hear
       me,
  for if you are silent to me,
    I shall be like those who go down
       to the Pit.
2 Hear the voice of my supplication,
    as I cry to you for help,
  as I lift up my hands
    toward your most holy
       sanctuary.[u]

3 Do not drag me away with the
       wicked,
    with those who are workers of
       evil,

---

t Or refuge   u Heb your innermost sanctuary

who speak peace with their
neighbors,
while mischief is in their hearts.
4 Repay them according to their
work,
and according to the evil of their
deeds;
repay them according to the work
of their hands;
render them their due reward.
5 Because they do not regard the
works of the LORD,
or the work of his hands,
he will break them down and build
them up no more.

6 Blessed be the LORD,
for he has heard the sound of my
pleadings.
7 The LORD is my strength and my
shield;
in him my heart trusts;
so I am helped, and my heart exults,
and with my song I give thanks
to him.

8 The LORD is the strength of his
people;
he is the saving refuge of his
anointed.
9 O save your people, and bless your
heritage;
be their shepherd, and carry
them forever.

Psalm

The Voice of God in a Great Storm

A Psalm of David.

1 Ascribe to the LORD, O heavenly
beings,ᵛ
ascribe to the LORD glory and
strength.
2 Ascribe to the LORD the glory of his
name;
worship the LORD in holy
splendor.

3 The voice of the LORD is over the
waters;
the God of glory thunders,
the LORD, over mighty waters.

4 The voice of the LORD is powerful;
the voice of the LORD is full of
majesty.

5 The voice of the LORD breaks the
cedars;
the LORD breaks the cedars of
Lebanon.
6 He makes Lebanon skip like a calf,
and Sirion like a young wild ox.

7 The voice of the LORD flashes forth
flames of fire.
8 The voice of the LORD shakes the
wilderness;
the LORD shakes the wilderness
of Kadesh.

9 The voice of the LORD causes the
oaks to whirl,ʷ
and strips the forest bare;
and in his temple all say, "Glory!"

10 The LORD sits enthroned over the
flood;
the LORD sits enthroned as king
forever.
11 May the LORD give strength to his
people!
May the LORD bless his people
with peace!

Psalm

Thanksgiving for Recovery from Grave Illness

A Psalm. A Song at the dedication of the
temple. Of David.

1 I will extol you, O LORD, for you
have drawn me up,
and did not let my foes rejoice
over me.
2 O LORD my God, I cried to you for
help,
and you have healed me.
3 O LORD, you brought up my soul
from Sheol,
restored me to life from among
those gone down to the Pit.ˣ

4 Sing praises to the LORD, O you his
faithful ones,

ᵛ Heb *sons of gods*   ʷ Or *causes the deer to calve*   ˣ Or *that I should not go down to the Pit*

THE DAWN WILL COME
Martin Luther King, Jr.

VERSE: Psalm 30.5   **PASSAGE:** Psalm 30.1–5

t the beginning of the bus boycott in Montgomery, Alabama, we set up a voluntary car pool to get the people to and from their jobs. For eleven long months our car pool functioned extraordinarily well. Then Mayor Gayle introduced a resolution instructing the city's legal department to file such proceedings as it might deem proper to stop the operation of the car pool or any transportation system growing out of the bus boycott. A hearing was set for Tuesday, November 13, 1956.

At our regular weekly mass meeting, scheduled the night before the hearing, . . . I [said] "We have moved all of these months . . . in the daring faith that God is with us in our struggle. The many experiences of days gone by have vindicated that faith in a marvelous way. Tonight we must believe that a way will be made out of no way." Yet I could feel the cold breeze of pessimism pass over the audience. The night was darker than a thousand midnights. The light of hope was about to fade and the lamp of faith to flicker . . .

At noon, during a brief recess, I noticed an unusual commotion in the courtroom. Mayor Gayle was called to the back room. Several reporters moved excitedly in and out of the room. Momentarily a reporter came to the table where, as chief defendant, I sat with the lawyers. "Here is the decision that you have been waiting for," he said. "Read this release."

In anxiety and hope, I read these words: "The United States Supreme Court today unanimously ruled bus segregation unconstitutional in Montgomery, Alabama." My heart throbbed with an inexpressible joy. The darkest hour of our struggle had become the first hour of victory. Someone shouted from the back of the courtroom, "God Almighty has spoken from Washington!"

The dawn will come. Disappointment, sorrow, and despair are born at midnight, but morning follows. "Weeping may linger for the night," says the psalmist, "but joy comes with the morning."

ADDITIONAL SCRIPTURE READING:
Psalms 6.6–9; 125.5–6

Go to page 623 for your next devotional reading.

1900   Present

and give thanks to his holy
name.

5 For his anger is but for a moment;
his favor is for a lifetime.
Weeping may linger for the night,
but joy comes with the morning.

6 As for me, I said in my prosperity,
"I shall never be moved."

7 By your favor, O LORD,
you had established me as a
strong mountain;
you hid your face;
I was dismayed.

8 To you, O LORD, I cried,
and to the LORD I made
supplication:

9 "What profit is there in my death,
if I go down to the Pit?
Will the dust praise you?
Will it tell of your faithfulness?

10 Hear, O LORD, and be gracious to
me!
O LORD, be my helper!"

11 You have turned my mourning into
dancing;
you have taken off my sackcloth
and clothed me with joy,

12 so that my soul[y] may praise you
and not be silent.
O LORD my God, I will give
thanks to you forever.

Psalm

*Prayer and Praise for Deliverance
from Enemies*

To the leader. A Psalm of David.

1 In you, O LORD, I seek refuge;
do not let me ever be put to
shame;
in your righteousness deliver me.

2 Incline your ear to me;
rescue me speedily.
Be a rock of refuge for me,
a strong fortress to save me.

3 You are indeed my rock and my
fortress;

for your name's sake lead me and
guide me,

4 take me out of the net that is
hidden for me,
for you are my refuge.

5 Into your hand I commit my spirit;
you have redeemed me, O LORD,
faithful God.

6 You hate[z] those who pay regard to
worthless idols,
but I trust in the LORD.

7 I will exult and rejoice in your
steadfast love,
because you have seen my
affliction;
you have taken heed of my
adversities,

8 and have not delivered me into the
hand of the enemy;
you have set my feet in a broad
place.

9 Be gracious to me, O LORD, for I am
in distress;
my eye wastes away from grief,
my soul and body also.

10 For my life is spent with sorrow,
and my years with sighing;
my strength fails because of my
misery,[a]
and my bones waste away.

11 I am the scorn of all my
adversaries,
a horror[b] to my neighbors,
an object of dread to my
acquaintances;
those who see me in the street
flee from me.

12 I have passed out of mind like one
who is dead;
I have become like a broken
vessel.

13 For I hear the whispering of many—
terror all around!—
as they scheme together against me,
as they plot to take my life.

14 But I trust in you, O LORD;
I say, "You are my God."

15 My times are in your hand;
deliver me from the hand of my
enemies and persecutors.

y Heb *that glory*   z One Heb Ms Gk Syr Jerome: MT *I hate*   a Gk Syr: Heb *my iniquity*
b Cn: Heb *exceedingly*

16 Let your face shine upon your
     servant;
   save me in your steadfast love.
17 Do not let me be put to shame,
     O LORD,
   for I call on you;
   let the wicked be put to shame;
   let them go dumbfounded to
     Sheol.
18 Let the lying lips be stilled
   that speak insolently against the
     righteous
   with pride and contempt.

19 O how abundant is your goodness
   that you have laid up for those
     who fear you,
   and accomplished for those who
     take refuge in you,
   in the sight of everyone!
20 In the shelter of your presence you
     hide them
   from human plots;
   you hold them safe under your
     shelter
   from contentious tongues.

21 Blessed be the LORD,
   for he has wondrously shown his
     steadfast love to me
   when I was beset as a city under
     siege.
22 I had said in my alarm,
   "I am driven far[c] from your
     sight."
   But you heard my supplications
   when I cried out to you for help.

23 Love the LORD, all you his saints.
   The LORD preserves the faithful,
   but abundantly repays the one
     who acts haughtily.
24 Be strong, and let your heart take
     courage,
   all you who wait for the LORD.

Psalm

32

The Joy of Forgiveness
Of David. A Maskil.

1 Happy are those whose
     transgression is forgiven,
   whose sin is covered.

2 Happy are those to whom the LORD
     imputes no iniquity,
   and in whose spirit there is no
     deceit.

3 While I kept silence, my body
     wasted away
   through my groaning all day long.
4 For day and night your hand was
     heavy upon me;
   my strength was dried up[d] as by
     the heat of summer.   Selah

5 Then I acknowledged my sin to you,
   and I did not hide my iniquity;
   I said, "I will confess my
     transgressions to the LORD,"
   and you forgave the guilt of my
     sin.   Selah

6 Therefore let all who are faithful
     offer prayer to you;
   at a time of distress,[e] the rush of
     mighty waters
   shall not reach them.
7 You are a hiding place for me;
   you preserve me from trouble;
   you surround me with glad cries
     of deliverance.   Selah

8 I will instruct you and teach you
     the way you should go;
   I will counsel you with my eye
     upon you.
9 Do not be like a horse or a mule,
     without understanding,
   whose temper must be curbed
     with bit and bridle,
   else it will not stay near you.

10 Many are the torments of the
     wicked,
   but steadfast love surrounds
     those who trust in the LORD.
11 Be glad in the LORD and rejoice,
     O righteous,
   and shout for joy, all you upright
     in heart.

Psalm

33

The Greatness and Goodness of God

1 Rejoice in the LORD, O you
     righteous.
   Praise befits the upright.

c Another reading is *cut off*   d Meaning of Heb uncertain   e Cn: Heb *at a time of finding* only

2 Praise the LORD with the lyre;
    make melody to him with the
      harp of ten strings.
3 Sing to him a new song;
    play skillfully on the strings,
      with loud shouts.

4 For the word of the LORD is upright,
    and all his work is done in
      faithfulness.
5 He loves righteousness and justice;
    the earth is full of the steadfast
      love of the LORD.

6 By the word of the LORD the
      heavens were made,
    and all their host by the breath of
      his mouth.
7 He gathered the waters of the sea as
      in a bottle;
    he put the deeps in storehouses.

8 Let all the earth fear the LORD;
    let all the inhabitants of the
      world stand in awe of him.
9 For he spoke, and it came to be;
    he commanded, and it stood
      firm.

10 The LORD brings the counsel of the
      nations to nothing;
    he frustrates the plans of the
      peoples.
11 The counsel of the LORD stands
      forever,
    the thoughts of his heart to all
      generations.
12 Happy is the nation whose God is
      the LORD,
    the people whom he has chosen
      as his heritage.

13 The LORD looks down from heaven;
    he sees all humankind.
14 From where he sits enthroned he
      watches
    all the inhabitants of the earth—
15 he who fashions the hearts of them
      all,
    and observes all their deeds.
16 A king is not saved by his great
      army;
    a warrior is not delivered by his
      great strength.

17 The war horse is a vain hope for
      victory,
    and by its great might it cannot
      save.

18 Truly the eye of the LORD is on
      those who fear him,
    on those who hope in his
      steadfast love,
19 to deliver their soul from death,
    and to keep them alive in famine.

20 Our soul waits for the LORD;
    he is our help and shield.
21 Our heart is glad in him,
    because we trust in his holy
      name.
22 Let your steadfast love, O LORD, be
      upon us,
    even as we hope in you.

Psalm 34

Praise for Deliverance from Trouble

*Of David, when he feigned madness before
Abimelech, so that he drove him out,
and he went away.*

1 I will bless the LORD at all times;
    his praise shall continually be in
      my mouth.
2 My soul makes its boast in the
      LORD;
    let the humble hear and be glad.
3 O magnify the LORD with me,
    and let us exalt his name
      together.

4 I sought the LORD, and he answered
      me,
    and delivered me from all my
      fears.
5 Look to him, and be radiant;
    so your^f faces shall never be
      ashamed.
6 This poor soul cried, and was heard
      by the LORD,
    and was saved from every
      trouble.
7 The angel of the LORD encamps
      around those who fear him, and
      delivers them.

f Gk Syr Jerome: Heb *their*

8   O taste and see that the LORD is
     good;
     happy are those who take refuge
     in him.
9   O fear the LORD, you his holy
     ones,
     for those who fear him have no
     want.
10   The young lions suffer want and
     hunger,
     but those who seek the LORD
     lack no good thing.

11   Come, O children, listen to me;
     I will teach you the fear of the
     LORD.
12   Which of you desires life,
     and covets many days to enjoy
     good?
13   Keep your tongue from evil,
     and your lips from speaking
     deceit.
14   Depart from evil, and do good;
     seek peace, and pursue it.

15   The eyes of the LORD are on the
     righteous,
     and his ears are open to their
     cry.
16   The face of the LORD is against
     evildoers,
     to cut off the remembrance of
     them from the earth.
17   When the righteous cry for help,
     the LORD hears,
     and rescues them from all their
     troubles.
18   The LORD is near to the
     brokenhearted,
     and saves the crushed in spirit.

19   Many are the afflictions of the
     righteous,
     but the LORD rescues them from
     them all.
20   He keeps all their bones;
     not one of them will be broken.
21   Evil brings death to the wicked,
     and those who hate the righteous
     will be condemned.
22   The LORD redeems the life of his
     servants;
     none of those who take refuge in
     him will be condemned.

Psalm

 35

Prayer for Deliverance from Enemies

Of David.

1   Contend, O LORD, with those who
     contend with me;
     fight against those who fight
     against me!
2   Take hold of shield and buckler,
     and rise up to help me!
3   Draw the spear and javelin
     against my pursuers;
     say to my soul,
     "I am your salvation."

4   Let them be put to shame and
     dishonor
     who seek after my life.
     Let them be turned back and
     confounded
     who devise evil against me.
5   Let them be like chaff before the
     wind,
     with the angel of the LORD
     driving them on.
6   Let their way be dark and slippery,
     with the angel of the LORD
     pursuing them.

7   For without cause they hid their
     net^g for me;
     without cause they dug a pit^h for
     my life.
8   Let ruin come on them unawares.
     And let the net that they hid
     ensnare them;
     let them fall in it—to their ruin.

9   Then my soul shall rejoice in the
     LORD,
     exulting in his deliverance.
10   All my bones shall say,
     "O LORD, who is like you?
     You deliver the weak
     from those too strong for them,
     the weak and needy from those
     who despoil them."

11   Malicious witnesses rise up;
     they ask me about things I do not
     know.
12   They repay me evil for good;

---

g   Heb *a pit, their net*   h   The word *pit* is transposed from the preceding line my soul is forlorn.

13 But as for me, when they were sick,
     I wore sackcloth;
     I afflicted myself with fasting.
   I prayed with head bowed[i] on my
        bosom,
14   as though I grieved for a friend or
        a brother;
   I went about as one who laments
        for a mother,
     bowed down and in mourning.

15 But at my stumbling they gathered
        in glee,
     they gathered together against me;
   ruffians whom I did not know
     tore at me without ceasing;
16 they impiously mocked more and
        more,[j]
     gnashing at me with their teeth.

17 How long, O LORD, will you look
        on?
     Rescue me from their ravages,
     my life from the lions!
18 Then I will thank you in the great
        congregation;
     in the mighty throng I will praise
        you.

19 Do not let my treacherous enemies
        rejoice over me,
     or those who hate me without
        cause wink the eye.
20 For they do not speak peace,
     but they conceive deceitful words
     against those who are quiet in
        the land.
21 They open wide their mouths
        against me;
     they say, "Aha, Aha,
     our eyes have seen it."

22 You have seen, O LORD; do not be
        silent!
     O Lord, do not be far from me!
23 Wake up! Bestir yourself for my
        defense,
     for my cause, my God and my
        Lord!
24 Vindicate me, O LORD, my God,
     according to your righteousness,
     and do not let them rejoice over
        me.

25 Do not let them say to themselves,
     "Aha, we have our heart's desire."
   Do not let them say, "We have
        swallowed you[k] up."

26 Let all those who rejoice at my
        calamity
     be put to shame and confusion;
   let those who exalt themselves
        against me
     be clothed with shame and
        dishonor.

27 Let those who desire my
        vindication
     shout for joy and be glad,
     and say evermore,
   "Great is the LORD,
     who delights in the welfare of his
        servant."
28 Then my tongue shall tell of your
        righteousness
     and of your praise all day long.

Psalm

36

*Human Wickedness and Divine
Goodness*

> To the leader. Of David, the servant
> of the LORD.

1 Transgression speaks to the wicked
     deep in their hearts;
   there is no fear of God
     before their eyes.
2 For they flatter themselves in their
        own eyes
     that their iniquity cannot be
        found out and hated.
3 The words of their mouths are
        mischief and deceit;
     they have ceased to act wisely
        and do good.
4 They plot mischief while on their
        beds;
     they are set on a way that is not
        good;
     they do not reject evil.

5 Your steadfast love, O LORD,
        extends to the heavens,
     your faithfulness to the clouds.

---

i Or *My prayer turned back*   *j* Cn Compare Gk: Heb *like the profanest of mockers of a cake*
k Heb *him*

6 Your righteousness is like the
   mighty mountains,
   your judgments are like the great
   deep;
   you save humans and animals
   alike, O LORD.

7 How precious is your steadfast
   love, O God!

   All people may take refuge in the
   shadow of your wings.
8 They feast on the abundance of
   your house,
   and you give them drink from
   the river of your delights.
9 For with you is the fountain
   of life;
   in your light we see light.

WEDNESDAY

SEA, LIGHT, FIRE
Catherine of Siena

VERSE: Psalm 36.9   PASSAGE: Psalm 36.5–10

ternal Trinity, you are like a deep sea, in which the more I seek, the more I find; and the more I find, the more eagerly I seek. You fill the soul, yet never fully satisfy it; the soul continues to hunger and thirst for you, desiring you, longing to see you who are the source of all light.

In your light, eternal Trinity, I have seen into the deep ocean of your love, and have rejoiced in the beauty of your creation. Then looking at myself in you, I have recognized that you have made me in your image. This is the most precious gift which I receive from you in your power and in your wisdom.

Eternal Trinity, you are the creator and I the creature. I have come to know you because you have created me anew in your Son Jesus Christ. You are in love with me out of your love for him. You have given yourself to me. What more could I ask?

You are a fire, ever burning and never consumed. You consume in your heart all the self-love within my soul, taking away all coldness. You are a light, ever shining and never fading. You drive away all the darkness within my heart, enabling me to see your glorious truth.

You are goodness beyond all goodness, beauty beyond all beauty, wisdom beyond all wisdom.

You are the garment that covers all nakedness. You are the food that satisfies all hunger.

ADDITIONAL SCRIPTURE READING:
Psalm 27.1; Colossians 1.16–17

Go to page 629 for your next devotional reading.

500   1500

10 O continue your steadfast love to
those who know you,
and your salvation to the upright
of heart!
11 Do not let the foot of the arrogant
tread on me,
or the hand of the wicked drive
me away.
12 There the evildoers lie prostrate;
they are thrust down, unable to
rise.

Psalm 37

Exhortation to Patience and Trust
Of David.

1 Do not fret because of the wicked;
do not be envious of wrongdoers,
2 for they will soon fade like the
grass,
and wither like the green herb.

3 Trust in the LORD, and do good;
so you will live in the land, and
enjoy security.
4 Take delight in the LORD,
and he will give you the desires
of your heart.

5 Commit your way to the LORD;
trust in him, and he will act.
6 He will make your vindication
shine like the light,
and the justice of your cause like
the noonday.

7 Be still before the LORD, and wait
patiently for him;
do not fret over those who
prosper in their way,
over those who carry out evil
devices.

FRETFULNESS SPRINGS FROM A DETERMINATION
TO GET MY OWN WAY.   —Oswald Chambers

---

8 Refrain from anger, and forsake
wrath.
Do not fret—it leads only to evil.
9 For the wicked shall be cut off,
but those who wait for the LORD
shall inherit the land.

10 Yet a little while, and the wicked
will be no more;
though you look diligently for
their place, they will not be
there.
11 But the meek shall inherit the land,
and delight themselves in
abundant prosperity.

12 The wicked plot against the
righteous,
and gnash their teeth at them;
13 but the LORD laughs at the wicked,
for he sees that their day is
coming.

14 The wicked draw the sword and
bend their bows
to bring down the poor and
needy,
to kill those who walk uprightly;
15 their sword shall enter their own
heart,
and their bows shall be broken.

16 Better is a little that the righteous
person has
than the abundance of many
wicked.
17 For the arms of the wicked shall be
broken,
but the LORD upholds the
righteous.

18 The LORD knows the days of the
blameless,
and their heritage will abide
forever;
19 they are not put to shame in evil
times,
in the days of famine they have
abundance.

20 But the wicked perish,
and the enemies of the LORD are
like the glory of the pastures;
they vanish—like smoke they
vanish away.

21 The wicked borrow, and do not pay
back,
but the righteous are generous
and keep giving;
22 for those blessed by the LORD shall
inherit the land,
but those cursed by him shall be
cut off.

23 Our steps*l* are made firm by the
    LORD,
      when he delights in our*m* way;
24 though we stumble,*n* we*o* shall not
    fall headlong,
      for the LORD holds us*p* by the
      hand.

25 I have been young, and now am old,
      yet I have not seen the righteous
      forsaken
    or their children begging bread.
26 They are ever giving liberally and
    lending,
      and their children become a
      blessing.

27 Depart from evil, and do good;
      so you shall abide forever.
28 For the LORD loves justice;
      he will not forsake his faithful
      ones.

    The righteous shall be kept safe
    forever,
      but the children of the wicked
      shall be cut off.
29 The righteous shall inherit the land,
      and live in it forever.

30 The mouths of the righteous utter
    wisdom,
      and their tongues speak justice.
31 The law of their God is in their
    hearts;
      their steps do not slip.

32 The wicked watch for the righteous,
      and seek to kill them.
33 The LORD will not abandon them
      to their power,
      or let them be condemned when
      they are brought to trial.

34 Wait for the LORD, and keep to his
    way,
      and he will exalt you to inherit
      the land;
      you will look on the destruction
      of the wicked.

35 I have seen the wicked oppressing,
      and towering like a cedar of
      Lebanon.*q*

36 Again I*r* passed by, and they were
    no more;
      though I sought them, they could
      not be found.
37 Mark the blameless, and behold the
    upright,
      for there is posterity for the
      peaceable.
38 But transgressors shall be
    altogether destroyed;
      the posterity of the wicked shall
      be cut off.

39 The salvation of the righteous is
      from the LORD;
      he is their refuge in the time of
      trouble.
40 The LORD helps them and rescues
    them;
      he rescues them from the
      wicked, and saves them,
      because they take refuge in him.

Psalm

38

A Penitent Sufferer's Plea
for Healing

A Psalm of David, for the memorial offering.

1 O LORD, do not rebuke me in your
    anger,
      or discipline me in your wrath.
2 For your arrows have sunk into me,
      and your hand has come down on
      me.

3 There is no soundness in my flesh
      because of your indignation;
    there is no health in my bones
      because of my sin.
4 For my iniquities have gone over
    my head;
      they weigh like a burden too
      heavy for me.

5 My wounds grow foul and fester
      because of my foolishness;
6 I am utterly bowed down and
    prostrate;
      all day long I go around
      mourning.

---

l Heb *A man's steps*   *m* Heb *his*   *n* Heb *he stumbles*   *o* Heb *he*   *p* Heb *him*
q Gk: Meaning of Heb uncertain   *r* Gk Syr Jerome: Heb *he*

7 For my loins are filled with burning,
   and there is no soundness in my
   flesh.
8 I am utterly spent and crushed;
   I groan because of the tumult of
   my heart.

9 O Lord, all my longing is known to
   you;
   my sighing is not hidden from
   you.
10 My heart throbs, my strength fails
   me;
   as for the light of my eyes—it
   also has gone from me.
11 My friends and companions stand
   aloof from my affliction,
   and my neighbors stand far off.

12 Those who seek my life lay their
   snares;
   those who seek to hurt me speak
   of ruin,
   and meditate treachery all day
   long.

13 But I am like the deaf, I do not hear;
   like the mute, who cannot speak.
14 Truly, I am like one who does not
   hear,
   and in whose mouth is no retort.

15 But it is for you, O Lord, that I
   wait;
   it is you, O Lord my God, who
   will answer.
16 For I pray, "Only do not let them
   rejoice over me,
   those who boast against me
   when my foot slips."

17 For I am ready to fall,
   and my pain is ever with me.
18 I confess my iniquity;
   I am sorry for my sin.
19 Those who are my foes without
   cause[s] are mighty,
   and many are those who hate me
   wrongfully.
20 Those who render me evil for good
   are my adversaries because I
   follow after good.

21 Do not forsake me, O Lord;
   O my God, do not be far from me;

22 make haste to help me,
   O Lord, my salvation.

Psalm

 39

Prayer for Wisdom and Forgiveness
To the leader: to Jeduthun. A Psalm of David.

1 I said, "I will guard my ways
   that I may not sin with my
   tongue;
   I will keep a muzzle on my mouth
   as long as the wicked are in my
   presence."
2 I was silent and still;
   I held my peace to no avail;
   my distress grew worse,
3   my heart became hot within me.
While I mused, the fire burned;
   then I spoke with my tongue:

4 "Lord, let me know my end,
   and what is the measure of my
   days;
   let me know how fleeting my life
   is.
5 You have made my days a few
   handbreadths,
   and my lifetime is as nothing in
   your sight.
Surely everyone stands as a mere
   breath.   *Selah*
6 Surely everyone goes about like a
   shadow.
Surely for nothing they are in
   turmoil;
   they heap up, and do not know
   who will gather.

7 "And now, O Lord, what do I wait
   for?
   My hope is in you.
8 Deliver me from all my
   transgressions.
   Do not make me the scorn of the
   fool.
9 I am silent; I do not open my
   mouth,
   for it is you who have done it.
10 Remove your stroke from me;
   I am worn down by the blows[t] of
   your hand.

s Q Ms: MT *my living foes*   t Heb *hostility*

11 "You chastise mortals
    in punishment for sin,
consuming like a moth what is
    dear to them;
    surely everyone is a mere breath.
                            Selah

12 "Hear my prayer, O LORD,
    and give ear to my cry;
    do not hold your peace at my
        tears.
For I am your passing guest,
    an alien, like all my forebears.
13 Turn your gaze away from me, that
        I may smile again,
    before I depart and am no more."

Psalm

 40

Thanksgiving for Deliverance and Prayer for Help

To the leader. Of David. A Psalm.

1 I waited patiently for the LORD;
    he inclined to me and heard my
        cry.
2 He drew me up from the desolate
        pit,*u*
    out of the miry bog,
and set my feet upon a rock,
    making my steps secure.

STARS MAY BE SEEN FROM THE BOTTOM OF A DEEP
WELL WHEN THEY CANNOT BE DISCERNED FROM
THE TOP OF A MOUNTAIN.   —*C. H. Spurgeon*

---

3 He put a new song in my mouth,
    a song of praise to our God.
Many will see and fear,
    and put their trust in the LORD.

4 Happy are those who make
    the LORD their trust,
who do not turn to the proud,
    to those who go astray after false
        gods.
5 You have multiplied, O LORD my
        God,
    your wondrous deeds and your
        thoughts toward us;
    none can compare with you.

Were I to proclaim and tell of them,
    they would be more than can be
        counted.
6 Sacrifice and offering you do not
        desire,
    but you have given me an open
        ear.*v*
Burnt offering and sin offering
    you have not required.
7 Then I said, "Here I am;
    in the scroll of the book it is
        written of me.*w*
8 I delight to do your will, O my
        God;
    your law is within my heart."

9 I have told the glad news of
        deliverance
    in the great congregation;
see, I have not restrained my lips,
    as you know, O LORD.
10 I have not hidden your saving help
        within my heart,
    I have spoken of your
        faithfulness and your
        salvation;
    I have not concealed your steadfast
        love and your faithfulness
    from the great congregation.

11 Do not, O LORD, withhold
        your mercy from me;
    let your steadfast love and your
        faithfulness
    keep me safe forever.
12 For evils have encompassed me
        without number;
    my iniquities have overtaken me,
        until I cannot see;
they are more than the hairs of my
        head,
    and my heart fails me.

13 Be pleased, O LORD, to deliver me;
    O LORD, make haste to help me.
14 Let all those be put to shame and
        confusion
    who seek to snatch away my life;
let those be turned back and
        brought to dishonor
    who desire my hurt.
15 Let those be appalled because of
        their shame
    who say to me, "Aha, Aha!"

u Cn: Heb *pit of tumult*   *v* Heb *ears you have dug for me*   *w* Meaning of Heb uncertain

16 But may all who seek you
    rejoice and be glad in you;
  may those who love your salvation
    say continually, "Great is the
    LORD!"
17 As for me, I am poor and needy,
    but the Lord takes thought for me.
  You are my help and my deliverer;
    do not delay, O my God.

Psalm

 41

Assurance of God's Help and a Plea for Healing

To the leader. A Psalm of David.

1 Happy are those who consider the
    poor;[x]
  the LORD delivers them in the
    day of trouble.
2 The LORD protects them and keeps
    them alive;
  they are called happy in the land.
  You do not give them up to the
    will of their enemies.
3 The LORD sustains them on their
    sickbed;
  in their illness you heal all their
    infirmities.[y]

4 As for me, I said, "O LORD, be
    gracious to me;
  heal me, for I have sinned against
    you."
5 My enemies wonder in malice
    when I will die, and my name
    perish.
6 And when they come to see me,
    they utter empty words,
  while their hearts gather
    mischief;
  when they go out, they tell it
    abroad.
7 All who hate me whisper together
    about me;
  they imagine the worst for me.
8 They think that a deadly thing has
    fastened on me,
  that I will not rise again from
    where I lie.
9 Even my bosom friend in whom I
    trusted,

who ate of my bread, has lifted
    the heel against me.
10 But you, O LORD, be gracious to
    me,
  and raise me up, that I may repay
    them.

11 By this I know that you are pleased
    with me;
  because my enemy has not
    triumphed over me.
12 But you have upheld me because of
    my integrity,
  and set me in your presence
    forever.

13 Blessed be the LORD, the God of
    Israel,
  from everlasting to everlasting.
    Amen and Amen.

BOOK II
(Psalms 42–72)

Psalm

 42

Longing for God and His Help in Distress

To the leader. A Maskil of the Korahites.

1 As a deer longs for flowing streams,
    so my soul longs for you, O God.
2 My soul thirsts for God,
    for the living God.
  When shall I come and behold
    the face of God?
3 My tears have been my food
    day and night,
  while people say to me continually,
    "Where is your God?"

4 These things I remember,
    as I pour out my soul:
  how I went with the throng,[z]
    and led them in procession to the
    house of God,
  with glad shouts and songs of
    thanksgiving,
  a multitude keeping festival.
5 Why are you cast down, O my soul,
    and why are you disquieted
    within me?

x Or weak   y Heb you change all his bed   z Meaning of Heb uncertain

Panting After God

A. W. Tozer

Verse: Psalm 42.1   **Passage:** Psalm 42

ithin the hearts of a growing number of evangelicals in recent days has arisen a new yearning after an above-average spiritual experience. Yet the greater number still shy away from it and raise objections that evidence misunderstanding or fear or plain unbelief. They point to the neurotic, the psychotic, the pseudo-Christian cultist and the intemperate fanatic, and lump them all together without discrimination as followers of the "deeper life."

While this is of course completely preposterous, the fact that such confusion exists obliges those who advocate the Spirit-filled life to define their terms and explain their position. Just what, then, do we mean? And what are we advocating?

For myself, I am reverently concerned that I teach nothing but Christ crucified. For me to accept a teaching or even an emphasis, I must be persuaded that it is scriptural and altogether apostolic in spirit and temper. And it must be in full harmony with the best in the historic church and in the tradition marked by the finest devotional works, the sweetest and most radiant hymnody and the loftiest experiences revealed in Christian biography . . .

To speak of the "deeper life" is . . . to insist that believers explore the depth of the Christian evangel for those riches it surely contains but which we are as surely missing. The "deeper life" is deeper only because the average Christian life is tragically shallow.

They who advocate the deeper life today might compare unfavorably with almost any of the Christians that surrounded Paul or Peter in early times. While they may not as yet have made much progress, their faces are toward the light and they are beckoning us on. It is hard to see how we can justify our refusal to heed their call.

What the deeper life advocates are telling us is that we should press on to enjoy in personal inward experience the exalted privileges that are ours in Christ Jesus; that we should insist upon tasting the sweetness of internal worship in spirit as well as in truth; that to reach this ideal we should if necessary push beyond our contented brethren and bring upon ourselves whatever opposition may follow as a result.

Additional Scripture Reading:

Jeremiah 9.23–24; Ephesians 1.17–18; Colossians 1.9–12

Go to page 632 for your next devotional reading.

1900   Present

Hope in God; for I shall again praise
  him,
    my help ⁶and my God.

My soul is cast down within me;
  therefore I remember you
from the land of Jordan and of
    Hermon,
  from Mount Mizar.
7 Deep calls to deep
    at the thunder of your cataracts;
  all your waves and your billows
    have gone over me.
8 By day the LORD commands his
    steadfast love,
  and at night his song is with me,
  a prayer to the God of my life.

9 I say to God, my rock,
  "Why have you forgotten me?
  Why must I walk about mournfully
    because the enemy oppresses
      me?"
10 As with a deadly wound in my
    body,
  my adversaries taunt me,
  while they say to me continually,
  "Where is your God?"

11 Why are you cast down, O my soul,
  and why are you disquieted
    within me?
  Hope in God; for I shall again praise
    him,
    my help and my God.

Psalm

 43

Prayer to God in Time of Trouble

1 Vindicate me, O God, and defend
    my cause
  against an ungodly people;
from those who are deceitful and
    unjust
  deliver me!
2 For you are the God in whom I take
    refuge;
  why have you cast me off?
  Why must I walk about mournfully
    because of the oppression of the
      enemy?

3 O send out your light and your
    truth;
    let them lead me;
  let them bring me to your holy hill
    and to your dwelling.
4 Then I will go to the altar of God,
    to God my exceeding joy;
  and I will praise you with the harp,
    O God, my God.

5 Why are you cast down, O my soul,
  and why are you disquieted
    within me?
  Hope in God; for I shall again praise
    him,
    my help and my God.

Psalm

 44

National Lament and Prayer
for Help

To the leader. Of the Korahites. A Maskil.

1 We have heard with our ears,
    O God,
  our ancestors have told us,
  what deeds you performed in their
    days,
    in the days of old:
2 you with your own hand drove out
    the nations,
  but them you planted;
you afflicted the peoples,
  but them you set free;
3 for not by their own sword did they
    win the land,
  nor did their own arm give them
    victory;
but your right hand, and your arm,
    and the light of your
      countenance,
  for you delighted in them.

4 You are my King and my God;
  you command^a victories for
    Jacob.
5 Through you we push down our
    foes;
  through your name we tread
    down our assailants.
6 For not in my bow do I trust,
  nor can my sword save me.

a Gk Syr: Heb *You are my King, O God; command*

7 But you have saved us from our
       foes,
   and have put to confusion those
       who hate us.
8 In God we have boasted continually,
   and we will give thanks to your
       name forever.   *Selah*

9 Yet you have rejected us and abased
       us,
   and have not gone out with our
       armies.
10 You made us turn back from the foe,
   and our enemies have gotten
       spoil.
11 You have made us like sheep for
       slaughter,
   and have scattered us among the
       nations.
12 You have sold your people for a
       trifle,
   demanding no high price for them.

13 You have made us the taunt of our
       neighbors,
   the derision and scorn of those
       around us.
14 You have made us a byword among
       the nations,
   a laughingstock[b] among the
       peoples.
15 All day long my disgrace is before
       me,
   and shame has covered my face
16 at the words of the taunters and
       revilers,
   at the sight of the enemy and the
       avenger.

17 All this has come upon us,
   yet we have not forgotten you,
   or been false to your covenant.
18 Our heart has not turned back,
   nor have our steps departed from
       your way,
19 yet you have broken us in the
       haunt of jackals,
   and covered us with deep
       darkness.

20 If we had forgotten the name of our
       God,
   or spread out our hands to a
       strange god,

21 would not God discover this?
   For he knows the secrets of the
       heart.
22 Because of you we are being killed
       all day long,
   and accounted as sheep for the
       slaughter.

23 Rouse yourself! Why do you sleep,
       O Lord?
   Awake, do not cast us off forever!
24 Why do you hide your face?
   Why do you forget our affliction
       and oppression?
25 For we sink down to the dust;
   our bodies cling to the ground.
26 Rise up, come to our help.
   Redeem us for the sake of your
       steadfast love.

Psalm 45

Ode for a Royal Wedding

To the leader: according to Lilies. Of the
Korahites. A Maskil. A love song.

1 My heart overflows with a goodly
       theme;
   I address my verses to the king;
   my tongue is like the pen of a
       ready scribe.

2 You are the most handsome of men;
   grace is poured upon your lips;
   therefore God has blessed you
       forever.
3 Gird your sword on your thigh,
       O mighty one,
   in your glory and majesty.

4 In your majesty ride on
       victoriously
   for the cause of truth and to
       defend[c] the right;
   let your right hand teach you
       dread deeds.
5 Your arrows are sharp
   in the heart of the king's enemies;
   the peoples fall under you.

6 Your throne, O God,[d] endures
       forever and ever.

---

b Heb *a shaking of the head*   c Cn: Heb *and the meekness of*   d Or *Your throne is a throne of*
God, it

Your royal scepter is a scepter of
   equity;
7 you love righteousness and hate
   wickedness.
Therefore God, your God, has
   anointed you
with the oil of gladness beyond
   your companions;

8 your robes are all fragrant with
   myrrh and aloes and cassia.
From ivory palaces stringed
   instruments make you glad;
9 daughters of kings are among
   your ladies of honor;
at your right hand stands the
   queen in gold of Ophir.

FRIDAY

THE CITY OF GLORIOUS WORKS
Augustine

VERSE: Psalm 46.4   **PASSAGE:** Psalm 46.4–7

 e give the name of the city of God unto that society
whereof that Scripture bears witness, which has got
the most excellent authority and preeminence of all
other works whatsoever, by the disposing of the
divine providence, not the affectation of men's judgments. For
there it is said: "Glorious things are said of you, O city of God"
and in another place, "Great is the LORD, and most worthy of
praise, in the city of our God, his holy mountain. It is beautiful
in its loftiness, the joy of the whole earth." And by and by in the
same psalm: "As we have heard, so have we seen in the city of
the LORD Almighty, in the city of our God: God makes her
secure forever." And in another: "There is a river whose streams
make glad the city of God, the holy place where the Most High
dwells. God is within her, she will not fall." These testimonies,
and thousands more, teach us that there is a city of God, whereof his inspired love makes us desire to be members. The earthly
citizens prefer their gods before this heavenly city's holy
founder, knowing not that he is the God of gods, not of those
false, wicked, and proud ones (which wanting his light so universal and unchangeable, and being thereby cast into an extreme
needy power, each one follows his own state, as it were, and begs
peculiar honors of his servants), but of the godly and holy ones,
who select their own submission to him, rather than the world's
to them, and love rather to worship him, their God, than to be
worshiped for gods themselves.

ADDITIONAL SCRIPTURE READING:
Psalm 48.1–3; Revelation 21.10–22

Go to page 635 for your next devotional reading.

100   500

10 Hear, O daughter, consider and
    incline your ear;
  forget your people and your
    father's house,
11 and the king will desire your
    beauty.
  Since he is your lord, bow to him;
12   the people*e* of Tyre will seek your
    favor with gifts,
  the richest of the people 13with
    all kinds of wealth.

  The princess is decked in her
    chamber with gold-woven
    robes;*f*
14   in many-colored robes she is led
    to the king;
  behind her the virgins, her
    companions, follow.
15 With joy and gladness they are led
    along
  as they enter the palace of the
    king.

16 In the place of ancestors you,
    O king,*g* shall have sons;
  you will make them princes in
    all the earth.
17 I will cause your name to be
    celebrated in all generations;
  therefore the peoples will praise
    you forever and ever.

Psalm

God's Defense of His City and People

To the leader. Of the Korahites. According to
    Alamoth. A Song.

1 God is our refuge and strength,
  a very present*h* help in trouble.
2 Therefore we will not fear, though
    the earth should change,
  though the mountains shake in
    the heart of the sea;
3 though its waters roar and foam,
  though the mountains tremble
    with its tumult.   *Selah*

4 There is a river whose streams
    make glad the city of God,

  the holy habitation of the Most
    High.
5 God is in the midst of the city;*i* it
    shall not be moved;
  God will help it when the
    morning dawns.
6 The nations are in an uproar, the
    kingdoms totter;
  he utters his voice, the earth
    melts.
7 The LORD of hosts is with us;
  the God of Jacob is our refuge.*j*
                              Selah

8 Come, behold the works of the
    LORD;
  see what desolations he has
    brought on the earth.
9 He makes wars cease to the end of
    the earth;
  he breaks the bow, and shatters
    the spear;
  he burns the shields with fire.
10 "Be still, and know that I am God!
  I am exalted among the nations,
  I am exalted in the earth."
11 The LORD of hosts is with us;
  the God of Jacob is our refuge.*j*
                              Selah

Psalm

God's Rule over the Nations

To the leader. Of the Korahites. A Psalm.

1 Clap your hands, all you peoples;
  shout to God with loud songs of
    joy.
2 For the LORD, the Most High, is
    awesome,
  a great king over all the earth.
3 He subdued peoples under us,
  and nations under our feet.
4 He chose our heritage for us,
  the pride of Jacob whom he loves.
                              Selah

5 God has gone up with a shout,
  the LORD with the sound of a
    trumpet.
6 Sing praises to God, sing praises;

sing praises to our King, sing
praises.
7 For God is the king of all the earth;
sing praises with a psalm.*k*

8 God is king over the nations;
God sits on his holy throne.
9 The princes of the peoples gather
as the people of the God of
Abraham.
For the shields of the earth belong
to God;
he is highly exalted.

Psalm

 48

The Glory and Strength of Zion

A Song. A Psalm of the Korahites.

1 Great is the LORD and greatly to be
praised
in the city of our God.
His holy mountain, 2beautiful in
elevation,
is the joy of all the earth,
Mount Zion, in the far north,
the city of the great King.
3 Within its citadels God
has shown himself a sure defense.

4 Then the kings assembled,
they came on together.
5 As soon as they saw it, they were
astounded;
they were in panic, they took to
flight;
6 trembling took hold of them there,
pains as of a woman in labor,
7 as when an east wind shatters
the ships of Tarshish.
8 As we have heard, so have we seen
in the city of the LORD of hosts,
in the city of our God,
which God establishes forever.
            Selah

9 We ponder your steadfast love,
O God,
in the midst of your temple.
10 Your name, O God, like your
praise,
reaches to the ends of the earth.

Your right hand is filled with
victory.
11 Let Mount Zion be glad,
let the towns*l* of Judah rejoice
because of your judgments.

12 Walk about Zion, go all around it,
count its towers,
13 consider well its ramparts;
go through its citadels,
that you may tell the next
generation
14 that this is God,
our God forever and ever.
He will be our guide forever.

Psalm

 49

The Folly of Trust in Riches

To the leader. Of the Korahites. A Psalm.

1 Hear this, all you peoples;
give ear, all inhabitants of the
world,
2 both low and high,
rich and poor together.
3 My mouth shall speak wisdom;
the meditation of my heart shall
be understanding.
4 I will incline my ear to a proverb;
I will solve my riddle to the
music of the harp.

5 Why should I fear in times of
trouble,
when the iniquity of my
persecutors surrounds me,
6 those who trust in their wealth
and boast of the abundance of
their riches?
7 Truly, no ransom avails for one's
life,*m*
there is no price one can give to
God for it.
8 For the ransom of life is costly,
and can never suffice,
9 that one should live on forever
and never see the grave.*n*

10 When we look at the wise, they die;
fool and dolt perish together
and leave their wealth to others.

---

k Heb *Maskil*   *l* Heb *daughters*   *m* Another reading is *no one can ransom a brother*
n Heb *the pit*

WEEKEND

BROTHER SUN, SISTER MOON
Francis of Assisi

VERSE: Psalm 50.1   **PASSAGE:** Psalm 50.1–15

ost high, omnipotent, righteous Lord, to you be all praise, glory, honor and blessing. To you alone are they due, and no man is worthy to mention you.

Praise be to you, my Lord, for all your creatures, above all Brother Sun, who gives us the light of day. He is beautiful and radiant with great splendor, and so is like you most high Lord.

Praise be to you, my Lord, for Sister Moon and the stars. In heaven you fashioned them, clear and precious and beautiful.

Praise be to you, my Lord, for Brother Wind, and for every kind of weather, cloudy or fair, stormy or serene, by which you cherish all that you have made.

Praise be to you, my Lord, for Sister Water, which is useful and humble and precious and pure.

Praise be to you, my Lord, for Brother Fire, by whom you lighten the night, for he is beautiful and playful and robust and strong.

Praise be to you, my Lord, for our Sister Earth, who sustains and governs us, and produces varied fruits with colored flowers and herbs.

Praise be to you, my Lord, for those who forgive sins in your love, and for those who bear sickness and tribulation.

Blessed are those who endure in peace, for by you, most high Lord, they shall be crowned.

Praise and bless my Lord, giving him thanks and serving him with great humility.

ADDITIONAL SCRIPTURE READING:
Job 11.7–8; Psalm 108.4–5; Acts 17.24

Go to page 638 for your next devotional reading.

11 Their graves*o* are their homes
        forever,
    their dwelling places to all
        generations,
    though they named lands their
        own.
12 Mortals cannot abide in their
        pomp;
    they are like the animals that
        perish.

13 Such is the fate of the foolhardy,
    the end of those*p* who are pleased
        with their lot.   *Selah*
14 Like sheep they are appointed for
        Sheol;
    Death shall be their shepherd;
    straight to the grave they descend,*q*
    and their form shall waste away;
    Sheol shall be their home.*r*
15 But God will ransom my soul from
        the power of Sheol,
    for he will receive me.   *Selah*

16 Do not be afraid when some
        become rich,
    when the wealth of their houses
        increases.
17 For when they die they will carry
        nothing away;
    their wealth will not go down
        after them.
18 Though in their lifetime they
        count themselves happy
    —for you are praised when you
        do well for yourself—
19 they*s* will go to the company of
        their ancestors,
    who will never again see the light.
20 Mortals cannot abide in their
        pomp;
    they are like the animals that
        perish.

Psalm

 50

The Acceptable Sacrifice
A Psalm of Asaph.

1 The mighty one, God the LORD,
    speaks and summons the earth

from the rising of the sun to its
        setting.
2 Out of Zion, the perfection of
        beauty,
    God shines forth.

3 Our God comes and does not keep
        silence,
    before him is a devouring fire,
    and a mighty tempest all around
        him.
4 He calls to the heavens above
    and to the earth, that he may
        judge his people:
5 "Gather to me my faithful ones,
    who made a covenant with me
        by sacrifice!"
6 The heavens declare his
        righteousness,
    for God himself is judge.   *Selah*

7 "Hear, O my people, and I will
        speak,
    O Israel, I will testify against you.
    I am God, your God.
8 Not for your sacrifices do I rebuke
        you;
    your burnt offerings are
        continually before me.
9 I will not accept a bull from your
        house,
    or goats from your folds.
10 For every wild animal of the forest
        is mine,
    the cattle on a thousand hills.
11 I know all the birds of the air,*t*
    and all that moves in the field is
        mine.

12 "If I were hungry, I would not tell
        you,
    for the world and all that is in it
        is mine.
13 Do I eat the flesh of bulls,
    or drink the blood of goats?
14 Offer to God a sacrifice of
        thanksgiving,*u*
    and pay your vows to the Most
        High.
15 Call on me in the day of trouble;
    I will deliver you, and you shall
        glorify me."

o Gk Syr Compare Tg: Heb *their inward* (thought)   *p* Tg: Heb *after them*   *q* Cn: Heb *the upright
shall have dominion over them in the morning*   *r* Meaning of Heb uncertain   *s* Cn: Heb *you*
t Gk Syr Tg: Heb *mountains*   *u* Or *make thanksgiving your sacrifice to God*

16 But to the wicked God says:
    "What right have you to recite
        my statutes,
    or take my covenant on your lips?
17 For you hate discipline,
    and you cast my words behind
        you.
18 You make friends with a thief
        when you see one,
    and you keep company with
        adulterers.

19 "You give your mouth free rein for
        evil,
    and your tongue frames deceit.
20 You sit and speak against your kin;
    you slander your own mother's
        child.
21 These things you have done and I
        have been silent;
    you thought that I was one just
        like yourself.
    But now I rebuke you, and lay the
        charge before you.

22 "Mark this, then, you who forget
        God,
    or I will tear you apart, and there
        will be no one to deliver.
23 Those who bring thanksgiving as
        their sacrifice honor me;
    to those who go the right way[v]
    I will show the salvation of
        God."

Psalm

Prayer for Cleansing and Pardon

To the leader. A Psalm of David, when the
prophet Nathan came to him, after he had
gone in to Bathsheba.

1 Have mercy on me, O God,
    according to your steadfast love;
    according to your abundant mercy
        blot out my transgressions.
2 Wash me thoroughly from my
        iniquity,
    and cleanse me from my sin.

3 For I know my transgressions,
    and my sin is ever before me.

4 Against you, you alone, have I
        sinned,
    and done what is evil in your
        sight,
    so that you are justified in your
        sentence
    and blameless when you pass
        judgment.
5 Indeed, I was born guilty,
    a sinner when my mother
        conceived me.

6 You desire truth in the inward
        being;[w]
    therefore teach me wisdom in
        my secret heart.
7 Purge me with hyssop, and I shall
        be clean;
    wash me, and I shall be whiter
        than snow.
8 Let me hear joy and gladness;
    let the bones that you have
        crushed rejoice.
9 Hide your face from my sins,
    and blot out all my iniquities.

10 Create in me a clean heart, O God,
    and put a new and right[x] spirit
        within me.
11 Do not cast me away from your
        presence,
    and do not take your holy spirit
        from me.
12 Restore to me the joy of your
        salvation,
    and sustain in me a willing[y]
        spirit.

13 Then I will teach transgressors
        your ways,
    and sinners will return to you.
14 Deliver me from bloodshed, O God,
    O God of my salvation,
    and my tongue will sing aloud of
        your deliverance.

15 O Lord, open my lips,
    and my mouth will declare your
        praise.
16 For you have no delight in sacrifice;
    if I were to give a burnt offering,
        you would not be pleased.
17 The sacrifice acceptable to God[z] is
    a broken spirit;

---

v Heb *who set a way*   *w* Meaning of Heb uncertain   *x* Or *steadfast*   *y* Or *generous*
z Or *My sacrifice, O God,*

JESUS CHRIST—THE MIDDLE WAY
Blaise Pascal

VERSE: Psalm 51.1   PASSAGE: Psalm 51.1–10

he God of Christians is not a God who is simply the author of mathematical truths, or of the order of the elements, as is the god of the pagans and of Epicureans. Nor is he merely a God who providentially disposes the life and fortunes of men, to crown his worshipers with length of happy years. Such was the portion of the Jews. But the God of Abraham, the God of Isaac, the God of Jacob, the God of Christians, is a God of love and consolation, a God who fills the souls and hearts of his own, a God who makes them feel their inward wretchedness and his infinite mercy, who unites himself to their inmost spirit, filling it with humility and joy, with confidence and love, rendering them incapable of any end other than himself.

All who seek God apart from Jesus Christ, and who rest in nature, either find no light to satisfy them, or form for themselves a means of knowing God and serving him without a mediator. Thus they fall either into atheism or into deism, two things which the Christian religion almost equally abhors.

The God of Christians is a God who makes the soul perceive that he is her only good, that her only rest is in him, her only joy in loving him; who makes her at the same time abhor the obstacles which withhold her from loving him with all her strength. Her two hindrances, self-love and lust, are insupportable to her. This God makes her perceive that the root of self-love destroys her, and that he alone can heal.

The knowledge of God without that of our wretchedness creates pride. The knowledge of our wretchedness without that of God creates despair. The knowledge of Jesus Christ is the middle way, because in him we find both God and our wretchedness.

ADDITIONAL SCRIPTURE READING:
Exodus 34.6–7; Micah 7.18–20; Romans 7.24–25

Go to page 646 for your next devotional reading.

1500   1700

a broken and contrite heart,
   O God, you will not despise.

18 Do good to Zion in your good
    pleasure;
   rebuild the walls of Jerusalem,
19 then you will delight in right
    sacrifices,
   in burnt offerings and whole
    burnt offerings;
   then bulls will be offered on your
    altar.

Psalm

Judgment on the Deceitful

To the leader. A Maskil of David,
when Doeg the Edomite came to Saul
and said to him, "David has come to the
house of Ahimelech."

1 Why do you boast, O mighty one,
   of mischief done against the
    godly?[a]
   All day long 2you are plotting
    destruction.
   Your tongue is like a sharp razor,
    you worker of treachery.
3 You love evil more than good,
   and lying more than speaking the
    truth.   *Selah*
4 You love all words that devour,
   O deceitful tongue.

5 But God will break you down
    forever;
   he will snatch and tear you from
    your tent;
   he will uproot you from the land
    of the living.   *Selah*
6 The righteous will see, and fear,
   and will laugh at the evildoer,[b]
    saying,
7 "See the one who would not take
    refuge in God,
   but trusted in abundant riches,
    and sought refuge in wealth!"[c]

8 But I am like a green olive tree
   in the house of God.

I trust in the steadfast love of God
   forever and ever.
9 I will thank you forever,
   because of what you have done.
In the presence of the faithful
   I will proclaim[d] your name, for it
    is good.

Psalm

Denunciation of Godlessness

To the leader: according to Mahalath.
A Maskil of David.

1 Fools say in their hearts, "There is
    no God."
   They are corrupt, they commit
    abominable acts;
   there is no one who does good.
2 God looks down from heaven on
    humankind
   to see if there are any who are
    wise,
   who seek after God.

3 They have all fallen away, they are
    all alike perverse;
   there is no one who does good,
   no, not one.

4 Have they no knowledge, those
    evildoers,
   who eat up my people as they eat
    bread,
   and do not call upon God?

5 There they shall be in great terror,
   in terror such as has not been.
For God will scatter the bones of
    the ungodly;[e]
   they will be put to shame,[f] for
    God has rejected them.

6 O that deliverance for Israel would
    come from Zion!
   When God restores the fortunes
    of his people,
   Jacob will rejoice; Israel will be
    glad.

---

a Cn Compare Syr: Heb *the kindness of God*   *b* Heb *him*   *c* Syr Tg: Heb *in his destruction*
d Cn: Heb *wait for*   *e* Cn Compare Gk Syr: Heb *him who encamps against you*   *f* Gk: Heb *you
have put (them) to shame*

Psalm

Prayer for Vindication

To the leader: with stringed instruments. A Maskil of David, when the Ziphites went and told Saul, "David is in hiding among us."

1 Save me, O God, by your name,
   and vindicate me by your might.
2 Hear my prayer, O God;
   give ear to the words of my
      mouth.

3 For the insolent have risen against
      me,
   the ruthless seek my life;
   they do not set God before them.
                              Selah

4 But surely, God is my helper;
   the Lord is the upholder ofᵍ my
      life.
5 He will repay my enemies for their
      evil.
   In your faithfulness, put an end
      to them.

6 With a freewill offering I will
      sacrifice to you;
   I will give thanks to your name,
      O Lᴏʀᴅ, for it is good.
7 For he has delivered me from every
      trouble,
   and my eye has looked in
      triumph on my enemies.

Psalm

Complaint about a Friend's Treachery

To the leader: with stringed instruments. A Maskil of David.

1 Give ear to my prayer, O God;
   do not hide yourself from my
      supplication.
2 Attend to me, and answer me;
   I am troubled in my complaint.
   I am distraught ³by the noise of the
      enemy,

because of the clamor of the
      wicked.
   For they bringʰ trouble upon me,
      and in anger they cherish enmity
         against me.

4 My heart is in anguish within me,
   the terrors of death have fallen
      upon me.
5 Fear and trembling come upon me,
   and horror overwhelms me.
6 And I say, "O that I had wings like
      a dove!
   I would fly away and be at rest;
7 truly, I would flee far away;
   I would lodge in the wilderness;
                              Selah
8 I would hurry to find a shelter for
      myself
   from the raging wind and
      tempest."

9 Confuse, O Lord, confound their
      speech;
   for I see violence and strife in the
      city.
10 Day and night they go around it
      on its walls,
   and iniquity and trouble are within
      it;
11 ruin is in its midst;
   oppression and fraud
      do not depart from its
         marketplace.

12 It is not enemies who taunt me—
   I could bear that;
   it is not adversaries who deal
      insolently with me—
   I could hide from them.
13 But it is you, my equal,
   my companion, my familiar
      friend,
14 with whom I kept pleasant
      company;
   we walked in the house of God
      with the throng.
15 Let death come upon them;
   let them go down alive to Sheol;
   for evil is in their homes and in
      their hearts.

16 But I call upon God,
   and the Lᴏʀᴅ will save me.

---

g Gk Syr Jerome: Heb *is of those who uphold* or *is with those who uphold*   h Cn. Compare Gk: Heb *they cause to totter*

17 Evening and morning and at noon
  I utter my complaint and moan,
  and he will hear my voice.
18 He will redeem me unharmed
  from the battle that I wage,
  for many are arrayed against me.
19 God, who is enthroned from of old,
                                    Selah
  will hear, and will humble them—
because they do not change,
  and do not fear God.

20 My companion laid hands on a
    friend
  and violated a covenant with me[i]
21 with speech smoother than butter,
  but with a heart set on war;
with words that were softer than oil,
  but in fact were drawn swords.

22 Cast your burden[j] on the LORD,
  and he will sustain you;
he will never permit
  the righteous to be moved.

23 But you, O God, will cast them
    down
  into the lowest pit;
the bloodthirsty and treacherous
  shall not live out half their days.
But I will trust in you.

Psalm

 56

Trust in God under Persecution

To the leader: according to The Dove on Far-
  off Terebinths. Of David. A Miktam, when
  the Philistines seized him in Gath.

1 Be gracious to me, O God, for
    people trample on me;
  all day long foes oppress me;
2 my enemies trample on me all day
    long,
  for many fight against me.
O Most High, 3when I am afraid,
  I put my trust in you.
4 In God, whose word I praise,
  in God I trust; I am not afraid;
  what can flesh do to me?

5 All day long they seek to injure my
    cause;

all their thoughts are against me
  for evil.
6 They stir up strife, they lurk,
  they watch my steps.
As they hoped to have my life,
7 so repay[k] them for their crime;
  in wrath cast down the peoples,
    O God!

8 You have kept count of my
    tossings;
  put my tears in your bottle.
  Are they not in your record?
9 Then my enemies will retreat
  in the day when I call.
This I know, that[l] God is for me.
10 In God, whose word I praise,
  in the LORD, whose word I praise,
11 in God I trust; I am not afraid.
  What can a mere mortal do to
    me?

12 My vows to you I must perform,
    O God;
  I will render thank offerings to
    you.
13 For you have delivered my soul
    from death,
  and my feet from falling,
so that I may walk before God
  in the light of life.

Psalm

 57

*Praise and Assurance
under Persecution*

To the leader: Do Not Destroy. Of David. A
  Miktam, when he fled from Saul, in the cave.

1 Be merciful to me, O God, be
    merciful to me,
  for in you my soul takes refuge;
in the shadow of your wings I will
    take refuge,
  until the destroying storms pass
    by.
2 I cry to God Most High,
  to God who fulfills his purpose
    for me.
3 He will send from heaven and save
    me,
  he will put to shame those who
    trample on me.   *Selah*

---

i Heb lacks *with me*   *j* Or *Cast what he has given you*   *k* Cn: Heb *rescue*   *l* Or *because*

God will send forth his steadfast
 love and his faithfulness.

4 I lie down among lions
 that greedily devour[m] human
  prey;
their teeth are spears and arrows,
 their tongues sharp swords.

5 Be exalted, O God, above the
 heavens.
Let your glory be over all the
 earth.

6 They set a net for my steps;
 my soul was bowed down.
They dug a pit in my path,
 but they have fallen into it
  themselves.   *Selah*
7 My heart is steadfast, O God,
 my heart is steadfast.
I will sing and make melody.
8 Awake, my soul!
Awake, O harp and lyre!
 I will awake the dawn.
9 I will give thanks to you, O Lord,
 among the peoples;
I will sing praises to you among
 the nations.
10 For your steadfast love is as high as
 the heavens;
 your faithfulness extends to the
  clouds.

11 Be exalted, O God, above the
 heavens.
Let your glory be over all the
 earth.

Psalm

Prayer for Vengeance

To the leader: Do Not Destroy. Of David.
   A Miktam.

1 Do you indeed decree what is right,
 you gods?[n]
Do you judge people fairly?
2 No, in your hearts you devise
 wrongs;
 your hands deal out violence on
  earth.

3 The wicked go astray from the
 womb;
they err from their birth,
 speaking lies.
4 They have venom like the venom
 of a serpent,
like the deaf adder that stops its
 ear,
5 so that it does not hear the voice of
 charmers
or of the cunning enchanter.

6 O God, break the teeth in their
 mouths;
tear out the fangs of the young
 lions, O Lord!
7 Let them vanish like water that
 runs away;
like grass let them be trodden
 down[o] and wither.
8 Let them be like the snail that
 dissolves into slime;
like the untimely birth that
 never sees the sun.
9 Sooner than your pots can feel the
 heat of thorns,
whether green or ablaze, may he
 sweep them away!

10 The righteous will rejoice when
 they see vengeance done;
they will bathe their feet in the
 blood of the wicked.
11 People will say, "Surely there is a
 reward for the righteous;
surely there is a God who judges
 on earth."

Psalm

Prayer for Deliverance from Enemies

To the leader: Do Not Destroy. Of David.
A Miktam, when Saul ordered his house to be
  watched in order to kill him.

1 Deliver me from my enemies,
 O my God;
protect me from those who rise
 up against me.
2 Deliver me from those who work
 evil;
from the bloodthirsty save me.

m Cn: Heb *are aflame for*   *n* Or *mighty lords*   *o* Cn: Meaning of Heb uncertain

3   Even now they lie in wait for my
        life;
      the mighty stir up strife against
        me.
      For no transgression or sin of mine,
        O Lord,
4   for no fault of mine, they run and
        make ready.

      Rouse yourself, come to my help
        and see!
5   You, Lord God of hosts, are God
        of Israel.
      Awake to punish all the nations;
        spare none of those who
          treacherously plot evil. *Selah*

6   Each evening they come back,
        howling like dogs
      and prowling about the city.
7   There they are, bellowing with
        their mouths,
      with sharp words[p] on their lips—
      for "Who," they think,[q] "will
        hear us?"

8   But you laugh at them, O Lord;
      you hold all the nations in
        derision.
9   O my strength, I will watch for
        you;
      for you, O God, are my fortress.
10 My God in his steadfast love will
        meet me;
      my God will let me look in
        triumph on my enemies.

11 Do not kill them, or my people
        may forget;
      make them totter by your power,
        and bring them down,
      O Lord, our shield.
12 For the sin of their mouths, the
        words of their lips,
      let them be trapped in their
        pride.
      For the cursing and lies that they
        utter,
13   consume them in wrath;
      consume them until they are no
        more.
      Then it will be known to the ends
        of the earth
      that God rules over Jacob. *Selah*

14 Each evening they come back,
      howling like dogs
      and prowling about the city.
15 They roam about for food,
      and growl if they do not get their
        fill.

16 But I will sing of your might;
      I will sing aloud of your steadfast
        love in the morning.
      For you have been a fortress for me
        and a refuge in the day of my
        distress.
17 O my strength, I will sing praises to
        you,
      for you, O God, are my fortress,
      the God who shows me steadfast
        love.

Psalm

 60

*Prayer for National Victory
after Defeat*

To the leader: according to the Lily of the
Covenant. A Miktam of David; for
instruction; when he struggled with Aram-
naharaim and with Aram-zobah, and when
Joab on his return killed twelve thousand
Edomites in the Valley of Salt.

1   O God, you have rejected us,
        broken our defenses;
      you have been angry; now restore
        us!
2   You have caused the land to quake;
        you have torn it open;
      repair the cracks in it, for it is
        tottering.
3   You have made your people suffer
        hard things;
      you have given us wine to drink
        that made us reel.

4   You have set up a banner for those
        who fear you,
      to rally to it out of bowshot.[r]
                                       Selah
5   Give victory with your right hand,
        and answer us,[s]
      so that those whom you love
        may be rescued.

---

p Heb *with swords*   q Heb lacks *they think*   r Gk Syr Jerome: Heb *because of the truth*
s Another reading is *me*

6 God has promised in his sanctuary:[t]
"With exultation I will divide up
Shechem,
and portion out the Vale of
Succoth.
7 Gilead is mine, and Manasseh is
mine;
Ephraim is my helmet;
Judah is my scepter.
8 Moab is my washbasin;
on Edom I hurl my shoe;
over Philistia I shout in triumph."

9 Who will bring me to the fortified
city?
Who will lead me to Edom?
10 Have you not rejected us, O God?
You do not go out, O God, with
our armies.
11 O grant us help against the foe,
for human help is worthless.
12 With God we shall do valiantly;
it is he who will tread down our
foes.

Psalm

Assurance of God's Protection

To the leader: with stringed instruments.
Of David.

1 Hear my cry, O God;
listen to my prayer.
2 From the end of the earth I call to
you,
when my heart is faint.

Lead me to the rock
that is higher than I;
3 for you are my refuge,
a strong tower against the enemy.

4 Let me abide in your tent forever,
find refuge under the shelter of
your wings. *Selah*
5 For you, O God, have heard my
vows;
you have given me the heritage
of those who fear your name.

6 Prolong the life of the king;
may his years endure to all
generations!

7 May he be enthroned forever before
God;
appoint steadfast love and
faithfulness to watch over
him!

8 So I will always sing praises to your
name,
as I pay my vows day after day.

Psalm

Song of Trust in God Alone

To the leader: according to Jeduthun.
A Psalm of David.

1 For God alone my soul waits in
silence;
from him comes my salvation.
2 He alone is my rock and my
salvation,
my fortress; I shall never be
shaken.

3 How long will you assail a person,
will you batter your victim, all of
you,
as you would a leaning wall, a
tottering fence?
4 Their only plan is to bring down a
person of prominence.
They take pleasure in falsehood;
they bless with their mouths,
but inwardly they curse. *Selah*

5 For God alone my soul waits in
silence,
for my hope is from him.
6 He alone is my rock and my
salvation,
my fortress; I shall not be shaken.
7 On God rests my deliverance and
my honor;
my mighty rock, my refuge is in
God.

8 Trust in him at all times, O people;
pour out your heart before him;
God is a refuge for us. *Selah*

9 Those of low estate are but a breath,
those of high estate are a
delusion;

t Or *by his holiness*

in the balances they go up;
　　they are together lighter than a
　　　breath.
10　Put no confidence in extortion,
　　and set no vain hopes on robbery;
　　if riches increase, do not set your
　　　heart on them.

11　Once God has spoken;
　　twice have I heard this:
　that power belongs to God,
12　and steadfast love belongs to you,
　　O Lord.
　For you repay to all
　　according to their work.

Psalm 63

Comfort and Assurance in God's Presence

A Psalm of David, when he was in the
Wilderness of Judah.

1　O God, you are my God, I seek you,
　　my soul thirsts for you;
　my flesh faints for you,
　　as in a dry and weary land where
　　　there is no water.
2　So I have looked upon you in the
　　sanctuary,
　　beholding your power and glory.
3　Because your steadfast love is
　　better than life,
　　my lips will praise you.
4　So I will bless you as long as I live;
　　I will lift up my hands and call
　　　on your name.

5　My soul is satisfied as with a rich
　　feast,^{u}
　　and my mouth praises you with
　　　joyful lips
6　when I think of you on my bed,
　　and meditate on you in the
　　　watches of the night;
7　for you have been my help,
　　and in the shadow of your wings
　　　I sing for joy.
8　My soul clings to you;
　　your right hand upholds me.

9　But those who seek to destroy my
　　life
　　shall go down into the depths of
　　　the earth;
10　they shall be given over to the
　　power of the sword,
　　they shall be prey for jackals.
11　But the king shall rejoice in God;
　　all who swear by him shall exult,
　　for the mouths of liars will be
　　　stopped.

Psalm 64

Prayer for Protection from Enemies

To the leader. A Psalm of David.

1　Hear my voice, O God, in my
　　complaint;
　　preserve my life from the dread
　　　enemy.
2　Hide me from the secret plots of
　　the wicked,
　　from the scheming of evildoers,
3　who whet their tongues like
　　swords,
　　who aim bitter words like arrows,
4　shooting from ambush at the
　　blameless;
　　they shoot suddenly and without
　　　fear.
5　They hold fast to their evil purpose;
　　they talk of laying snares
　　secretly,
　thinking, "Who can see us?^{v}
6　　Who can search out our crimes?^{w}
　We have thought out a cunningly
　　conceived plot."
　For the human heart and mind
　　are deep.

7　But God will shoot his arrow at
　　them;
　　they will be wounded suddenly.
8　Because of their tongue he will
　　bring them to ruin;^{x}
　　all who see them will shake with
　　　horror.
9　Then everyone will fear;
　　they will tell what God has
　　　brought about,
　　and ponder what he has done.

---

u　Heb *with fat and fatness*　v　Syr: Heb *them*　w　Cn: Heb *They search out crimes*　x　Cn: Heb
They will bring him to ruin, their tongue being against them

10 Let the righteous rejoice in the LORD
and take refuge in him.
Let all the upright in heart glory.

Psalm

 65

Thanksgiving for Earth's Bounty

To the leader. A Psalm of David. A Song.

1 Praise is due to you,
O God, in Zion;
and to you shall vows be performed,

2   O you who answer prayer!
To you all flesh shall come.
3 When deeds of iniquity overwhelm
us,
you forgive our transgressions.
4 Happy are those whom you choose
and bring near
to live in your courts.
We shall be satisfied with the
goodness of your house,
your holy temple.

5 By awesome deeds you answer us
with deliverance,
O God of our salvation;

TUESDAY

PERSONAL PRAYER AT NIGHT
Gregory of Nazianzus

VERSE: Psalm 63.6   **PASSAGE:** Psalm 63

 ord Jesus, you are light from eternal lights.
You have dissolved all spiritual darkness
And my soul is filled with your brightness.
Your light makes all things beautiful.

You lit the skies with the sun and the moon.
You ordered night and day to follow each other peaceably.
And so you made the sun and the moon friends.
May I be friends with all whom I meet.

At night you give rest to our bodies.
By day you spur us on to work.
May I work with diligence and devotion,
That at night my conscience is at peace.

As I lay down on my bed at night,
May your fingers draw down my eyelids.
Lay your hand of blessing on my head
That righteous sleep may descend upon me.

ADDITIONAL SCRIPTURE READING:
Psalms 42.8; 119.147–148; 139.17–18

Go to page 652 for your next devotional reading.

100   500

you are the hope of all the ends of
    the earth
  and of the farthest seas.
6 By your^y strength you established
    the mountains;
  you are girded with might.
7 You silence the roaring of the seas,
    the roaring of their waves,
    the tumult of the peoples.
8 Those who live at earth's farthest
      bounds are awed by your
      signs;
  you make the gateways of the
      morning and the evening
      shout for joy.

9 You visit the earth and water it,
    you greatly enrich it;
  the river of God is full of water;
    you provide the people with
      grain,
  for so you have prepared it.
10 You water its furrows abundantly,
    settling its ridges,
  softening it with showers,
    and blessing its growth.
11 You crown the year with your
      bounty;
  your wagon tracks overflow with
      richness.
12 The pastures of the wilderness
    overflow,
  the hills gird themselves with joy,
13 the meadows clothe themselves
    with flocks,
  the valleys deck themselves with
    grain,
  they shout and sing together for
    joy.

Psalm

 66

Praise for God's Goodness to Israel

To the leader. A Song. A Psalm.

1 Make a joyful noise to God, all the
    earth;
2   sing the glory of his name;
  give to him glorious praise.
3 Say to God, "How awesome are
    your deeds!
  Because of your great power, your
    enemies cringe before you.

4 All the earth worships you;
  they sing praises to you,
  sing praises to your name." *Selah*

5 Come and see what God has done:
  he is awesome in his deeds
    among mortals.
6 He turned the sea into dry land;
  they passed through the river on
    foot.
There we rejoiced in him,
7   who rules by his might forever,
  whose eyes keep watch on the
    nations—
  let the rebellious not exalt
    themselves.   *Selah*

8 Bless our God, O peoples,
  let the sound of his praise be
    heard,
9 who has kept us among the living,
  and has not let our feet slip.
10 For you, O God, have tested us;
  you have tried us as silver is tried.
11 You brought us into the net;
  you laid burdens on our backs;
12 you let people ride over our heads;
  we went through fire and
    through water;
  yet you have brought us out to a
    spacious place.^z

13 I will come into your house with
    burnt offerings;
  I will pay you my vows,
14 those that my lips uttered
  and my mouth promised when I
    was in trouble.
15 I will offer to you burnt offerings of
    fatlings,
  with the smoke of the sacrifice of
    rams;
  I will make an offering of bulls and
    goats.   *Selah*

16 Come and hear, all you who fear
    God,
  and I will tell what he has done
    for me.
17 I cried aloud to him,
  and he was extolled with my
    tongue.
18 If I had cherished iniquity in my
    heart,
  the Lord would not have listened.

y Gk Jerome: Heb *his*   z Cn Compare Gk Syr Jerome Tg: Heb *to a saturation*

19 But truly God has listened;
       he has given heed to the words of
          my prayer.

20 Blessed be God,
       because he has not rejected my
          prayer
       or removed his steadfast love
          from me.

Psalm

The Nations Called to Praise God

To the leader: with stringed instruments.
A Psalm. A Song.

1 May God be gracious to us and
       bless us
       and make his face to shine upon
          us,   *Selah*
2 that your way may be known upon
       earth,
       your saving power among all
          nations.
3 Let the peoples praise you, O God;
       let all the peoples praise you.

4 Let the nations be glad and sing for
       joy,
       for you judge the peoples with
          equity
       and guide the nations upon earth.
                                      Selah
5 Let the peoples praise you, O God;
       let all the peoples praise you.

6 The earth has yielded its increase;
       God, our God, has blessed us.
7 May God continue to bless us;
       let all the ends of the earth revere
          him.

Psalm

Praise and Thanksgiving

To the leader. Of David. A Psalm. A Song.

1 Let God rise up, let his enemies be
       scattered;
       let those who hate him flee
          before him.

2 As smoke is driven away, so drive
       them away;
       as wax melts before the fire,
       let the wicked perish before God.
3 But let the righteous be joyful;
       let them exult before God;
       let them be jubilant with joy.

4 Sing to God, sing praises to his
          name;
       lift up a song to him who rides
          upon the clouds*a*—
       his name is the LORD—
       be exultant before him.

5 Father of orphans and protector of
          widows
       is God in his holy habitation.
6 God gives the desolate a home to
          live in;
       he leads out the prisoners to
          prosperity,
       but the rebellious live in a
          parched land.

7 O God, when you went out before
          your people,
       when you marched through the
          wilderness,   *Selah*
8 the earth quaked, the heavens
          poured down rain
       at the presence of God, the God
          of Sinai,
       at the presence of God, the God
          of Israel.
9 Rain in abundance, O God, you
          showered abroad;
       you restored your heritage when
          it languished;
10 your flock found a dwelling in it;
       in your goodness, O God, you
          provided for the needy.

11 The Lord gives the command;
       great is the company of those*b*
          who bore the tidings:
12 "The kings of the armies, they
          flee, they flee!"
    The women at home divide the
          spoil,
13   though they stay among the
          sheepfolds—
    the wings of a dove covered with
          silver,
       its pinions with green gold.

a Or *cast up a highway for him who rides through the deserts*   *b* Or *company of the women*

14 When the Almighty[c] scattered
      kings there,
   snow fell on Zalmon.

15 O mighty mountain, mountain of
      Bashan;
   O many-peaked mountain,
      mountain of Bashan!
16 Why do you look with envy,
      O many-peaked mountain,
   at the mount that God desired for
      his abode,
   where the LORD will reside
      forever?

17 With mighty chariotry, twice ten
      thousand,
   thousands upon thousands,
   the Lord came from Sinai into
      the holy place.[d]
18 You ascended the high mount,
      leading captives in your train
   and receiving gifts from people,
   even from those who rebel against
      the LORD God's abiding there.
19 Blessed be the Lord,
      who daily bears us up;
   God is our salvation.   Selah
20 Our God is a God of salvation,
   and to GOD, the Lord, belongs
      escape from death.

21 But God will shatter the heads of
      his enemies,
   the hairy crown of those who
      walk in their guilty ways.
22 The Lord said,
   "I will bring them back from
      Bashan,
   I will bring them back from the
      depths of the sea,
23 so that you may bathe[e] your feet in
      blood,
   so that the tongues of your dogs
      may have their share from
      the foe."

24 Your solemn processions are seen,[f]
      O God,
   the processions of my God, my
      King, into the sanctuary—
25 the singers in front, the musicians
      last,
   between them girls playing
      tambourines:

26 "Bless God in the great
      congregation,
   the LORD, O you who are of
      Israel's fountain!"
27 There is Benjamin, the least of
      them, in the lead,
   the princes of Judah in a body,
   the princes of Zebulun, the
      princes of Naphtali.

28 Summon your might, O God;
   show your strength, O God, as
      you have done for us before.
29 Because of your temple at Jerusalem
   kings bear gifts to you.
30 Rebuke the wild animals that live
      among the reeds,
   the herd of bulls with the calves
      of the peoples.
   Trample[g] under foot those who lust
      after tribute;
   scatter the peoples who delight
      in war.[h]
31 Let bronze be brought from Egypt;
   let Ethiopia[i] hasten to stretch out
      its hands to God.

32 Sing to God, O kingdoms of the
      earth;
   sing praises to the Lord,   Selah
33 O rider in the heavens, the ancient
      heavens;
   listen, he sends out his voice, his
      mighty voice.
34 Ascribe power to God,
   whose majesty is over Israel;
   and whose power is in the skies.
35 Awesome is God in his[j] sanctuary,
   the God of Israel;
   he gives power and strength to
      his people.

   Blessed be God!

Psalm

69

*Prayer for Deliverance
from Persecution*

To the leader: according to Lilies. Of David.

1 Save me, O God,
   for the waters have come up to
      my neck.

---

c Traditional rendering of Heb *Shaddai*   d Cn: Heb *The Lord among them Sinai in the holy* (place)
e Gk Syr Tg: Heb *shatter*   f Or *have been seen*   g Cn: Heb *Trampling*   h Meaning of Heb of verse
30 is uncertain   i Or *Nubia*; Heb *Cush*   j Gk: Heb *from your*

2 I sink in deep mire,
 where there is no foothold;
I have come into deep waters,
 and the flood sweeps over me.
3 I am weary with my crying;
 my throat is parched.
My eyes grow dim
 with waiting for my God.

4 More in number than the hairs of
  my head
 are those who hate me without
  cause;
many are those who would destroy
  me,
 my enemies who accuse me
  falsely.
What I did not steal
 must I now restore?
5 O God, you know my folly;
 the wrongs I have done are not
  hidden from you.

6 Do not let those who hope in you be
  put to shame because of me,
 O Lord GOD of hosts;
do not let those who seek you be
  dishonored because of me,
 O God of Israel.
7 It is for your sake that I have borne
  reproach,
 that shame has covered my face.
8 I have become a stranger to my
  kindred,
 an alien to my mother's children.

9 It is zeal for your house that has
  consumed me;
 the insults of those who insult
  you have fallen on me.
10 When I humbled my soul with
  fasting,[k]
 they insulted me for doing so.
11 When I made sackcloth my
  clothing,
 I became a byword to them.
12 I am the subject of gossip for those
  who sit in the gate,
 and the drunkards make songs
  about me.

13 But as for me, my prayer is to you,
 O LORD.
At an acceptable time, O God,

 in the abundance of your
  steadfast love, answer me.
With your faithful help 14rescue me
 from sinking in the mire;
let me be delivered from my
  enemies
 and from the deep waters.
15 Do not let the flood sweep over me,
 or the deep swallow me up,
 or the Pit close its mouth over
  me.

16 Answer me, O LORD, for your
  steadfast love is good;
 according to your abundant
  mercy, turn to me.
17 Do not hide your face from your
  servant,
 for I am in distress—make haste
  to answer me.
18 Draw near to me, redeem me,
 set me free because of my
  enemies.

19 You know the insults I receive,
 and my shame and dishonor;
 my foes are all known to you.
20 Insults have broken my heart,
 so that I am in despair.
I looked for pity, but there was
  none;
 and for comforters, but I found
  none.
21 They gave me poison for food,
 and for my thirst they gave me
  vinegar to drink.

22 Let their table be a trap for them,
 a snare for their allies.
23 Let their eyes be darkened so that
  they cannot see,
 and make their loins tremble
  continually.
24 Pour out your indignation upon
  them,
 and let your burning anger
  overtake them.
25 May their camp be a desolation;
 let no one live in their tents.
26 For they persecute those whom you
  have struck down,
 and those whom you have
  wounded, they attack still
  more.[l]

k Gk Syr: Heb I wept, with fasting my soul, or I made my soul mourn with fasting   l Gk Syr: Heb
recount the pain of

27 Add guilt to their guilt;
   may they have no acquittal from
      you.
28 Let them be blotted out of the book
      of the living;
   let them not be enrolled among
      the righteous.
29 But I am lowly and in pain;
   let your salvation, O God, protect
      me.

30 I will praise the name of God with
      a song;
   I will magnify him with
      thanksgiving.
31 This will please the LORD more
      than an ox
   or a bull with horns and hoofs.
32 Let the oppressed see it and be glad;
   you who seek God, let your
      hearts revive.
33 For the LORD hears the needy,
   and does not despise his own that
      are in bonds.

34 Let heaven and earth praise him,
   the seas and everything that
      moves in them.
35 For God will save Zion
   and rebuild the cities of Judah;
   and his servants shall live[m] there
      and possess it;
36 the children of his servants shall
      inherit it,
   and those who love his name
      shall live in it.

Psalm

Prayer for Deliverance from Enemies

To the leader. Of David, for the memorial
offering.

1 Be pleased, O God, to deliver me.
   O LORD, make haste to help me!
2 Let those be put to shame and
      confusion
   who seek my life.
   Let those be turned back and
      brought to dishonor
   who desire to hurt me.
3 Let those who say, "Aha, Aha!"
   turn back because of their shame.

4 Let all who seek you
   rejoice and be glad in you.
   Let those who love your salvation
   say evermore, "God is great!"
5 But I am poor and needy;
   hasten to me, O God!
   You are my help and my deliverer;
   O LORD, do not delay!

Psalm

Prayer for Lifelong Protection and Help

1 In you, O LORD, I take refuge;
   let me never be put to shame.
2 In your righteousness deliver me
      and rescue me;
   incline your ear to me and save
      me.
3 Be to me a rock of refuge,
   a strong fortress,[n] to save me,
   for you are my rock and my
      fortress.

4 Rescue me, O my God, from the
      hand of the wicked,
   from the grasp of the unjust and
      cruel.
5 For you, O Lord, are my hope,
   my trust, O LORD, from my youth.
6 Upon you I have leaned from my
      birth;
   it was you who took me from my
      mother's womb.
   My praise is continually of you.

7 I have been like a portent to many,
   but you are my strong refuge.
8 My mouth is filled with your praise,
   and with your glory all day long.
9 Do not cast me off in the time of
      old age;
   do not forsake me when my
      strength is spent.
10 For my enemies speak concerning
      me,
   and those who watch for my life
      consult together.
11 They say, "Pursue and seize that
      person
   whom God has forsaken,
   for there is no one to deliver."

m Syr: Heb and they shall live   n Gk Compare 31.3: Heb to come continually you have commanded

12 O God, do not be far from me;
      O my God, make haste to help
      me!
13 Let my accusers be put to shame
      and consumed;
    let those who seek to hurt me
      be covered with scorn and
      disgrace.
14 But I will hope continually,
      and will praise you yet more and
      more.
15 My mouth will tell of your
      righteous acts,
    of your deeds of salvation all day
      long,
    though their number is past my
      knowledge.

16 I will come praising the mighty
      deeds of the Lord God,
    I will praise your righteousness,
      yours alone.

17 O God, from my youth you have
      taught me,
    and I still proclaim your
      wondrous deeds.
18 So even to old age and gray hairs,
      O God, do not forsake me,
    until I proclaim your might
      to all the generations to come.o
    Your power 19and your
      righteousness, O God,
    reach the high heavens.

o Gk Compare Syr: Heb *to a generation, to all that come*

WEDNESDAY

A MEDITATION OF IMMORTALITY
John Calvin

VERSE: Psalm 70.4   **PASSAGE:** Psalm 70.1–4

s no man is found, however barbarous and even savage he may be, who is not touched by some idea of religion, it is clear that we all are created in order that we may know the majesty of our Creator, that having known it, we may esteem it above all and honor it with all awe, love, and reverence.

But, leaving aside the unbelievers, who seek nothing but to efface from their memory that idea of God which is planted in their hearts, we, who make profession of personal religion, must reflect that this decrepit life of ours, which will soon end, must be nothing else but a meditation of immortality. Now, nowhere can eternal and immortal life be found except in God. It is necessary, therefore, that the principal care and solicitude of our life be to seek God, to aspire to him with all the affection of our heart, and to repose nowhere else but in him alone.

ADDITIONAL SCRIPTURE READING:
Ecclesiastes 3.11; Romans 1.18–23

Go to page 655 for your next devotional reading.

1500   1700

You who have done great things,
O God, who is like you?
20 You who have made me see many
troubles and calamities
will revive me again;
from the depths of the earth
you will bring me up again.
21 You will increase my honor,
and comfort me once again.

22 I will also praise you with the harp
for your faithfulness, O my God;
I will sing praises to you with the
lyre,
O Holy One of Israel.
23 My lips will shout for joy
when I sing praises to you;
my soul also, which you have
rescued.
24 All day long my tongue will talk of
your righteous help,
for those who tried to do me harm
have been put to shame, and
disgraced.

Psalm

 72

*Prayer for Guidance and Support
for the King*

Of Solomon.

1 Give the king your justice, O God,
and your righteousness to a
king's son.
2 May he judge your people with
righteousness,
and your poor with justice.
3 May the mountains yield
prosperity for the people,
and the hills, in righteousness.
4 May he defend the cause of the
poor of the people,
give deliverance to the needy,
and crush the oppressor.

5 May he live*p* while the sun endures,
and as long as the moon,
throughout all generations.
6 May he be like rain that falls on the
mown grass,
like showers that water the
earth.

7 In his days may righteousness
flourish
and peace abound, until the
moon is no more.

8 May he have dominion from sea to
sea,
and from the River to the ends of
the earth.
9 May his foes*q* bow down before him,
and his enemies lick the dust.
10 May the kings of Tarshish and of
the isles
render him tribute,
may the kings of Sheba and Seba
bring gifts.
11 May all kings fall down before him,
all nations give him service.

12 For he delivers the needy when
they call,
the poor and those who have no
helper.
13 He has pity on the weak and the
needy,
and saves the lives of the needy.
14 From oppression and violence he
redeems their life;
and precious is their blood in his
sight.

15 Long may he live!
May gold of Sheba be given to
him.
May prayer be made for him
continually,
and blessings invoked for him all
day long.
16 May there be abundance of grain in
the land;
may it wave on the tops of the
mountains;
may its fruit be like Lebanon;
and may people blossom in the
cities
like the grass of the field.
17 May his name endure forever,
his fame continue as long as the
sun.
May all nations be blessed in him;*r*
may they pronounce him happy.

18 Blessed be the LORD, the God of
Israel,

---

p Gk: Heb *may they fear you*   *q* Cn: Heb *those who live in the wilderness*   *r* Or *bless themselves
by him*

who alone does wondrous things.
19 Blessed be his glorious name
    forever;
    may his glory fill the whole
    earth.
        Amen and Amen.

20 The prayers of David son of Jesse
    are ended.

BOOK III
(Psalms 73–89)

Psalm
 73

Plea for Relief from Oppressors
A Psalm of Asaph.

1 Truly God is good to the upright,^{s}
    to those who are pure in heart.
2 But as for me, my feet had almost
    stumbled;
    my steps had nearly slipped.
3 For I was envious of the arrogant;
    I saw the prosperity of the
    wicked.

4 For they have no pain;
    their bodies are sound and sleek.
5 They are not in trouble as others
    are;
    they are not plagued like other
    people.
6 Therefore pride is their necklace;
    violence covers them like a
    garment.
7 Their eyes swell out with fatness;
    their hearts overflow with follies.
8 They scoff and speak with malice;
    loftily they threaten oppression.
9 They set their mouths against
    heaven,
    and their tongues range over the
    earth.

10 Therefore the people turn and
    praise them,^{t}
    and find no fault in them.^{u}
11 And they say, "How can God
    know?
    Is there knowledge in the Most
    High?"

12 Such are the wicked;
    always at ease, they increase in
    riches.
13 All in vain I have kept my heart
    clean
    and washed my hands in
    innocence.
14 For all day long I have been plagued,
    and am punished every morning.

15 If I had said, "I will talk on in this
    way,"
    I would have been untrue to the
    circle of your children.
16 But when I thought how to
    understand this,
    it seemed to me a wearisome
    task,
17 until I went into the sanctuary of
    God;
    then I perceived their end.
18 Truly you set them in slippery
    places;
    you make them fall to ruin.
19 How they are destroyed in a
    moment,
    swept away utterly by terrors!
20 They are^v like a dream when one
    awakes;
    on awaking you despise their
    phantoms.

21 When my soul was embittered,
    when I was pricked in heart,
22 I was stupid and ignorant;
    I was like a brute beast toward
    you.
23 Nevertheless I am continually with
    you;
    you hold my right hand.
24 You guide me with your counsel,
    and afterward you will receive
    me with honor.^{w}
25 Whom have I in heaven but you?
    And there is nothing on earth
    that I desire other than you.
26 My flesh and my heart may fail,
    but God is the strength^x of my
    heart and my portion forever.

27 Indeed, those who are far from you
    will perish;
    you put an end to those who are
    false to you.

s Or good to Israel   t Cn: Heb his people return here   u Cn: Heb abundant waters are drained by them   v Cn: Heb Lord   w Or to glory   x Heb rock

28 But for me it is good to be near
    God;
    I have made the Lord GOD my
      refuge,
    to tell of all your works.

Psalm

*Plea for Help in Time of National
Humiliation*

A Maskil of Asaph.

1 O God, why do you cast us off
    forever?

    Why does your anger smoke
      against the sheep of your
      pasture?
2 Remember your congregation,
    which you acquired long ago,
    which you redeemed to be the
      tribe of your heritage.
    Remember Mount Zion, where
      you came to dwell.
3 Direct your steps to the perpetual
      ruins;
    the enemy has destroyed
      everything in the sanctuary.
4 Your foes have roared within your
      holy place;

THURSDAY

GOD'S CONTINUAL PRESENCE
Martin Luther

VERSE: Psalm 73.23   PASSAGE: Psalm 73

f for the sake of God's Word hardship, sorrow, and persecution come to us, all which follow in the train of the holy cross, the following thoughts should, with God's help, comfort and console us, and should make us determine to be of good cheer, full of courage and confidence, and lead us to surrender the cause trustfully into God's gracious and fatherly will.

First, that our cause is in the hands of him who says so clearly, "No man shall pluck them from my hand" (see John 10.28). It would not be wise to take our cause into our own hands, for we could and should lose it by our loose ways. Likewise all the comfortable words are true and do not lie, which say, "God is our refuge and strength" (Psalm 46.1). Has any man who puts his trust in God ever been put to shame? All who trust in God will be saved, and again: "Thou Lord hast not forsaken them that seek thee" (Psalm 9.10, KJV). Thus it is really true that God gave his only-begotten Son for our salvation. If God gave his own Son for us, how could he ever bring himself to desert us in small things?

ADDITIONAL SCRIPTURE READING:
Psalms 16.8; 139.1–12; Matthew 28.20

Go to page 669 for your next devotional reading.

1500   1700

they set up their emblems there.

5 At the upper entrance they hacked
the wooden trellis with axes.*y*

6 And then, with hatchets and
hammers,
they smashed all its carved work.

7 They set your sanctuary on fire;
they desecrated the dwelling
place of your name,
bringing it to the ground.

8 They said to themselves, "We will
utterly subdue them";
they burned all the meeting
places of God in the land.

9 We do not see our emblems;
there is no longer any prophet,
and there is no one among us
who knows how long.

10 How long, O God, is the foe to
scoff?
Is the enemy to revile your name
forever?

11 Why do you hold back your hand;
why do you keep your hand in*z*
your bosom?

12 Yet God my King is from of old,
working salvation in the earth.

13 You divided the sea by your might;
you broke the heads of the
dragons in the waters.

14 You crushed the heads of
Leviathan;
you gave him as food*a* for the
creatures of the wilderness.

15 You cut openings for springs and
torrents;
you dried up ever-flowing
streams.

16 Yours is the day, yours also the
night;
you established the luminaries*b*
and the sun.

17 You have fixed all the bounds of
the earth;
you made summer and winter.

18 Remember this, O LORD, how the
enemy scoffs,
and an impious people reviles
your name.

19 Do not deliver the soul of your
dove to the wild animals;

do not forget the life of your poor
forever.

20 Have regard for your*c* covenant,
for the dark places of the land are
full of the haunts of violence.

21 Do not let the downtrodden be put
to shame;
let the poor and needy praise
your name.

22 Rise up, O God, plead your cause;
remember how the impious scoff
at you all day long.

23 Do not forget the clamor of your
foes,
the uproar of your adversaries
that goes up continually.

Psalm

75

Thanksgiving for God's Wondrous Deeds

To the leader: Do Not Destroy. A Psalm of
Asaph. A Song.

1 We give thanks to you, O God;
we give thanks; your name is
near.
People tell of your wondrous deeds.

2 At the set time that I appoint
I will judge with equity.

3 When the earth totters, with all its
inhabitants,
it is I who keep its pillars steady.
Selah

4 I say to the boastful, "Do not
boast,"
and to the wicked, "Do not lift
up your horn;

5 do not lift up your horn on high,
or speak with insolent neck."

6 For not from the east or from the
west
and not from the wilderness
comes lifting up;

7 but it is God who executes
judgment,
putting down one and lifting up
another.

---

y Cn Compare Gk Syr: Meaning of Heb uncertain
a Heb *food for the people*   *b* Or *moon;* Heb *light*

z Cn: Heb *do you consume your right hand from*
c Gk Syr: Heb *the*

8 For in the hand of the Lord there is
        a cup
      with foaming wine, well mixed;
    he will pour a draught from it,
      and all the wicked of the earth
        shall drain it down to the dregs.
9 But I will rejoice[d] forever;
      I will sing praises to the God of
        Jacob.

10 All the horns of the wicked I will
        cut off,
      but the horns of the righteous
        shall be exalted.

Psalm

Israel's God—Judge of All the Earth

To the leader: with stringed instruments.
        A Psalm of Asaph. A Song.

1 In Judah God is known,
      his name is great in Israel.
2 His abode has been established in
        Salem,
      his dwelling place in Zion.
3 There he broke the flashing arrows,
      the shield, the sword, and the
        weapons of war.   *Selah*

4 Glorious are you, more majestic
      than the everlasting mountains.[e]
5 The stouthearted were stripped of
        their spoil;
      they sank into sleep;
    none of the troops
      was able to lift a hand.
6 At your rebuke, O God of Jacob,
      both rider and horse lay stunned.

7 But you indeed are awesome!
      Who can stand before you
      when once your anger is roused?
8 From the heavens you uttered
        judgment;
      the earth feared and was still
9 when God rose up to establish
        judgment,
      to save all the oppressed of the
        earth.   *Selah*

10 Human wrath serves only to praise
        you,
      when you bind the last bit of
        your[f] wrath around you.
11 Make vows to the Lord your God,
        and perform them;
      let all who are around him bring
        gifts
      to the one who is awesome,
12 who cuts off the spirit of princes,
      who inspires fear in the kings of
        the earth.

Psalm

God's Mighty Deeds Recalled

To the leader: according to Jeduthun.
        Of Asaph. A Psalm.

1 I cry aloud to God,
      aloud to God, that he may hear
        me.
2 In the day of my trouble I seek the
        Lord;
      in the night my hand is stretched
        out without wearying;
      my soul refuses to be comforted.
3 I think of God, and I moan;
      I meditate, and my spirit faints.
                                 Selah

4 You keep my eyelids from closing;
      I am so troubled that I cannot
        speak.
5 I consider the days of old,
      and remember the years of long
        ago.
6 I commune[g] with my heart in the
        night;
      I meditate and search my spirit:[h]
7 "Will the Lord spurn forever,
      and never again be favorable?
8 Has his steadfast love ceased
        forever?
      Are his promises at an end for all
        time?
9 Has God forgotten to be gracious?
      Has he in anger shut up his
        compassion?"   *Selah*
10 And I say, "It is my grief
      that the right hand of the Most
        High has changed."

d Gk: Heb *declare*   e Gk: Heb *the mountains of prey*   f Heb lacks *your*   g Gk Syr: Heb *My music*
h Syr Jerome: Heb *my spirit searches*

11 I will call to mind the deeds of the
    LORD;
    I will remember your wonders of
        old.
12 I will meditate on all your work,
    and muse on your mighty deeds.
13 Your way, O God, is holy.
    What god is so great as our God?
14 You are the God who works
        wonders;
    you have displayed your might
        among the peoples.
15 With your strong arm you
        redeemed your people,
    the descendants of Jacob and
        Joseph.   *Selah*

16 When the waters saw you, O God,
    when the waters saw you, they
        were afraid;
    the very deep trembled.
17 The clouds poured out water;
    the skies thundered;
    your arrows flashed on every
        side.
18 The crash of your thunder was in
        the whirlwind;
    your lightnings lit up the world;
    the earth trembled and shook.
19 Your way was through the sea,
    your path, through the mighty
        waters;
    yet your footprints were unseen.
20 You led your people like a flock
    by the hand of Moses and Aaron.

Psalm

78

*God's Goodness and Israel's
Ingratitude*

A Maskil of Asaph.

1 Give ear, O my people, to my
        teaching;
    incline your ears to the words of
        my mouth.
2 I will open my mouth in a parable;
    I will utter dark sayings from of
        old,
3 things that we have heard and
        known,
    that our ancestors have told us.

4 We will not hide them from their
        children;
    we will tell to the coming
        generation
    the glorious deeds of the LORD, and
        his might,
    and the wonders that he has
        done.

5 He established a decree in Jacob,
    and appointed a law in Israel,
    which he commanded our
        ancestors
    to teach to their children;
6 that the next generation might
        know them,
    the children yet unborn,
    and rise up and tell them to their
        children,
7 so that they should set their hope
        in God,
    and not forget the works of God,
    but keep his commandments;
8 and that they should not be like
        their ancestors,
    a stubborn and rebellious
        generation,
    a generation whose heart was not
        steadfast,
    whose spirit was not faithful to
        God.

9 The Ephraimites, armed with[i] the
        bow,
    turned back on the day of battle.
10 They did not keep God's covenant,
    but refused to walk according to
        his law.
11 They forgot what he had done,
    and the miracles that he had
        shown them.
12 In the sight of their ancestors he
        worked marvels
    in the land of Egypt, in the fields
        of Zoan.
13 He divided the sea and let them
        pass through it,
    and made the waters stand like a
        heap.
14 In the daytime he led them with a
        cloud,
    and all night long with a fiery
        light.
15 He split rocks open in the
        wilderness,

i Heb *armed with shooting*

and gave them drink abundantly
  as from the deep.
16 He made streams come out of the
    rock,
    and caused waters to flow down
      like rivers.

17 Yet they sinned still more against
    him,
    rebelling against the Most High
      in the desert.
18 They tested God in their heart
    by demanding the food they
      craved.
19 They spoke against God, saying,
    "Can God spread a table in the
      wilderness?
20 Even though he struck the rock so
      that water gushed out
    and torrents overflowed,
    can he also give bread,
      or provide meat for his people?"

21 Therefore, when the LORD heard,
      he was full of rage;
    a fire was kindled against Jacob,
      his anger mounted against Israel,
22 because they had no faith in God,
    and did not trust his saving
      power.
23 Yet he commanded the skies above,
    and opened the doors of heaven;
24 he rained down on them manna to
      eat,
    and gave them the grain of
      heaven.
25 Mortals ate of the bread of angels;
    he sent them food in abundance.
26 He caused the east wind to blow in
      the heavens,
    and by his power he led out the
      south wind;
27 he rained flesh upon them like
      dust,
    winged birds like the sand of the
      seas;
28 he let them fall within their camp,
    all around their dwellings.
29 And they ate and were well filled,
    for he gave them what they
      craved.
30 But before they had satisfied their
      craving,
    while the food was still in their
      mouths,
31 the anger of God rose against them

and he killed the strongest of
    them,
    and laid low the flower of Israel.
32 In spite of all this they still sinned;
    they did not believe in his
      wonders.
33 So he made their days vanish like a
      breath,
    and their years in terror.
34 When he killed them, they sought
      for him;
    they repented and sought God
      earnestly.
35 They remembered that God was
      their rock,
    the Most High God their
      redeemer.
36 But they flattered him with their
      mouths;
    they lied to him with their
      tongues.
37 Their heart was not steadfast
      toward him;
    they were not true to his
      covenant.
38 Yet he, being compassionate,
    forgave their iniquity,
    and did not destroy them;
    often he restrained his anger,
    and did not stir up all his wrath.
39 He remembered that they were but
      flesh,
    a wind that passes and does not
      come again.
40 How often they rebelled against
      him in the wilderness
    and grieved him in the desert!
41 They tested God again and again,
    and provoked the Holy One of
      Israel.
42 They did not keep in mind his
      power,
    or the day when he redeemed
      them from the foe;
43 when he displayed his signs in
      Egypt,
    and his miracles in the fields of
      Zoan.
44 He turned their rivers to blood,
    so that they could not drink of
      their streams.
45 He sent among them swarms of
      flies, which devoured them,
    and frogs, which destroyed them.

46 He gave their crops to the
       caterpillar,
    and the fruit of their labor to the
       locust.
47 He destroyed their vines with hail,
    and their sycamores with frost.
48 He gave over their cattle to the
       hail,
    and their flocks to thunderbolts.
49 He let loose on them his fierce
       anger,
    wrath, indignation, and distress,
    a company of destroying angels.
50 He made a path for his anger;
    he did not spare them from
       death,
    but gave their lives over to the
       plague.
51 He struck all the firstborn in Egypt,
    the first issue of their strength in
       the tents of Ham.
52 Then he led out his people like
       sheep,
    and guided them in the
       wilderness like a flock.
53 He led them in safety, so that they
       were not afraid;
    but the sea overwhelmed their
       enemies.
54 And he brought them to his holy
       hill,
    to the mountain that his right
       hand had won.
55 He drove out nations before them;
    he apportioned them for a
       possession
    and settled the tribes of Israel in
       their tents.

56 Yet they tested the Most High God,
    and rebelled against him.
    They did not observe his decrees,
57 but turned away and were faithless
       like their ancestors;
    they twisted like a treacherous
       bow.
58 For they provoked him to anger
       with their high places;
    they moved him to jealousy with
       their idols.
59 When God heard, he was full of
       wrath,
    and he utterly rejected Israel.
60 He abandoned his dwelling at
       Shiloh,

    the tent where he dwelt among
       mortals,
61 and delivered his power to
       captivity,
    his glory to the hand of the foe.
62 He gave his people to the sword,
    and vented his wrath on his
       heritage.
63 Fire devoured their young men,
    and their girls had no marriage
       song.
64 Their priests fell by the sword,
    and their widows made no
       lamentation.
65 Then the Lord awoke as from sleep,
    like a warrior shouting because
       of wine.
66 He put his adversaries to rout;
    he put them to everlasting
       disgrace.

67 He rejected the tent of Joseph,
    he did not choose the tribe of
       Ephraim;
68 but he chose the tribe of Judah,
    Mount Zion, which he loves.
69 He built his sanctuary like the high
       heavens,
    like the earth, which he has
       founded forever.
70 He chose his servant David,
    and took him from the
       sheepfolds;
71 from tending the nursing ewes he
       brought him
    to be the shepherd of his people
       Jacob,
    of Israel, his inheritance.
72 With upright heart he tended them,
    and guided them with skillful
       hand.

Psalm

Plea for Mercy for Jerusalem
A Psalm of Asaph.

1   O God, the nations have come into
       your inheritance;
    they have defiled your holy
       temple;
    they have laid Jerusalem in ruins.
2   They have given the bodies of your
       servants

to the birds of the air for food,
  the flesh of your faithful to the
    wild animals of the earth.
3 They have poured out their blood
    like water
  all around Jerusalem,
  and there was no one to bury
    them.
4 We have become a taunt to our
    neighbors,
  mocked and derided by those
    around us.

5 How long, O LORD? Will you be
    angry forever?
  Will your jealous wrath burn like
    fire?
6 Pour out your anger on the nations
    that do not know you,
  and on the kingdoms
    that do not call on your name.
7 For they have devoured Jacob
  and laid waste his habitation.

8 Do not remember against us the
    iniquities of our ancestors;
  let your compassion come
    speedily to meet us,
  for we are brought very low.
9 Help us, O God of our salvation,
    for the glory of your name;
  deliver us, and forgive our sins,
    for your name's sake.
10 Why should the nations say,
    "Where is their God?"
  Let the avenging of the outpoured
    blood of your servants
  be known among the nations
    before our eyes.

11 Let the groans of the prisoners
    come before you;
  according to your great power
    preserve those doomed to
    die.
12 Return sevenfold into the bosom of
    our neighbors
  the taunts with which they
    taunted you, O Lord!
13 Then we your people, the flock of
    your pasture,
  will give thanks to you forever;
  from generation to generation we
    will recount your praise.

Prayer for Israel's Restoration

To the leader: on Lilies, a Covenant.
    Of Asaph. A Psalm.

1 Give ear, O Shepherd of Israel,
    you who lead Joseph like a flock!
  You who are enthroned upon the
    cherubim, shine forth
2   before Ephraim and Benjamin
    and Manasseh.
  Stir up your might,
    and come to save us!

3 Restore us, O God;
    let your face shine, that we may
    be saved.

4 O LORD God of hosts,
    how long will you be angry with
    your people's prayers?
5 You have fed them with the bread
    of tears,
  and given them tears to drink in
    full measure.
6 You make us the scorn*j* of our
    neighbors;
  our enemies laugh among
    themselves.

7 Restore us, O God of hosts;
    let your face shine, that we may
    be saved.

8 You brought a vine out of Egypt;
    you drove out the nations and
    planted it.
9 You cleared the ground for it;
    it took deep root and filled the
    land.
10 The mountains were covered with
    its shade,
  the mighty cedars with its
    branches;
11 it sent out its branches to the sea,
  and its shoots to the River.
12 Why then have you broken down
    its walls,
  so that all who pass along the
    way pluck its fruit?
13 The boar from the forest ravages it,

---

j Syr: Heb *strife*

and all that move in the field
feed on it.

14 Turn again, O God of hosts;
   look down from heaven, and see;
have regard for this vine,
15   the stock that your right hand
      planted.k
16 They have burned it with fire, they
   have cut it down;l
   may they perish at the rebuke of
      your countenance.
17 But let your hand be upon the one
   at your right hand,
   the one whom you made strong
      for yourself.
18 Then we will never turn back from
   you;
   give us life, and we will call on
      your name.

19 Restore us, O LORD God of hosts;
   let your face shine, that we may
      be saved.

Psalm

God's Appeal to Stubborn Israel

To the leader: according to The Gittith.
Of Asaph.

1 Sing aloud to God our strength;
   shout for joy to the God of Jacob.
2 Raise a song, sound the
   tambourine,
   the sweet lyre with the harp.
3 Blow the trumpet at the new
   moon,
   at the full moon, on our festal
      day.
4 For it is a statute for Israel,
   an ordinance of the God of Jacob.
5 He made it a decree in Joseph,
   when he went out overm the land
      of Egypt.

I hear a voice I had not known:
6 "I relieved yourn shoulder of the
   burden;
   yourn hands were freed from the
      basket.

7 In distress you called, and I rescued
   you;
   I answered you in the secret
      place of thunder;
   I tested you at the waters of
      Meribah.   Selah
8 Hear, O my people, while I
   admonish you;
   O Israel, if you would but listen
      to me!
9 There shall be no strange god
   among you;
   you shall not bow down to a
      foreign god.
10 I am the LORD your God,
   who brought you up out of the
      land of Egypt.
   Open your mouth wide and I will
      fill it.

11 "But my people did not listen to
   my voice;
   Israel would not submit to me.
12 So I gave them over to their
   stubborn hearts,
   to follow their own counsels.
13 O that my people would listen to
   me,
   that Israel would walk in my
      ways!
14 Then I would quickly subdue their
   enemies,
   and turn my hand against their
      foes.
15 Those who hate the LORD would
   cringe before him,
   and their doom would last
      forever.
16 I would feed youo with the finest of
   the wheat,
   and with honey from the rock I
      would satisfy you."

Psalm

A Plea for Justice

A Psalm of Asaph.

1 God has taken his place in the
   divine council;
   in the midst of the gods he holds
      judgment:

---

k Heb adds from verse 17 and upon the one whom you made strong for yourself   l Cn: Heb it is cut
down   m Or against   n Heb his   o Cn Compare verse 16b: Heb he would feed him

2 "How long will you judge unjustly
   and show partiality to the
   wicked?   *Selah*
3 Give justice to the weak and the
   orphan;
   maintain the right of the lowly
   and the destitute.
4 Rescue the weak and the needy;
   deliver them from the hand of
   the wicked."

5 They have neither knowledge nor
   understanding,
   they walk around in darkness;
   all the foundations of the earth
   are shaken.

6 I say, "You are gods,
   children of the Most High, all of
   you;
7 nevertheless, you shall die like
   mortals,
   and fall like any prince."*p*

8 Rise up, O God, judge the earth;
   for all the nations belong to you!

Psalm

 83

Prayer for Judgment on Israel's Foes
   A Song. A Psalm of Asaph.

1 O God, do not keep silence;
   do not hold your peace or be still,
   O God!
2 Even now your enemies are in
   tumult;
   those who hate you have raised
   their heads.
3 They lay crafty plans against your
   people;
   they consult together against
   those you protect.
4 They say, "Come, let us wipe them
   out as a nation;
   let the name of Israel be
   remembered no more."
5 They conspire with one accord;
   against you they make a
   covenant—
6 the tents of Edom and the
   Ishmaelites,
   Moab and the Hagrites,

7 Gebal and Ammon and Amalek,
   Philistia with the inhabitants of
   Tyre;
8 Assyria also has joined them;
   they are the strong arm of the
   children of Lot.   *Selah*

9 Do to them as you did to Midian,
   as to Sisera and Jabin at the Wadi
   Kishon,
10 who were destroyed at En-dor,
   who became dung for the ground.
11 Make their nobles like Oreb and
   Zeeb,
   all their princes like Zebah and
   Zalmunna,
12 who said, "Let us take the pastures
   of God
   for our own possession."

13 O my God, make them like
   whirling dust,*q*
   like chaff before the wind.
14 As fire consumes the forest,
   as the flame sets the mountains
   ablaze,
15 so pursue them with your tempest
   and terrify them with your
   hurricane.
16 Fill their faces with shame,
   so that they may seek your
   name, O LORD.
17 Let them be put to shame and
   dismayed forever;
   let them perish in disgrace.
18 Let them know that you alone,
   whose name is the LORD,
   are the Most High over all the
   earth.

Psalm

 84

The Joy of Worship in the Temple
   To the leader: according to The Gittith.
   Of the Korahites. A Psalm.

1 How lovely is your dwelling place,
   O LORD of hosts!
2 My soul longs, indeed it faints
   for the courts of the LORD;
   my heart and my flesh sing for joy
   to the living God.

p Or *fall as one man, O princes*   *q* Or *a tumbleweed*

3 Even the sparrow finds a home,
     and the swallow a nest for herself,
     where she may lay her young,
   at your altars, O LORD of hosts,
     my King and my God.
4 Happy are those who live in your
       house,
     ever singing your praise.   *Selah*

5 Happy are those whose strength is
       in you,
     in whose heart are the highways
       to Zion.*r*
6 As they go through the valley of
       Baca
     they make it a place of springs;
     the early rain also covers it with
       pools.
7 They go from strength to strength;
     the God of gods will be seen in
       Zion.

8 O LORD God of hosts, hear my
       prayer;
     give ear, O God of Jacob!   *Selah*
9 Behold our shield, O God;
     look on the face of your anointed.

10 For a day in your courts is better
      than a thousand elsewhere.
    I would rather be a doorkeeper in
      the house of my God
    than live in the tents of
      wickedness.
11 For the LORD God is a sun and
      shield;
      he bestows favor and honor.
    No good thing does the LORD
      withhold
      from those who walk uprightly.
12 O LORD of hosts,
      happy is everyone who trusts in
        you.

Psalm

 85

Prayer for the Restoration of God's Favor

To the leader. Of the Korahites. A Psalm.

1 LORD, you were favorable to your
     land;
     you restored the fortunes of Jacob.

2 You forgave the iniquity of your
     people;
     you pardoned all their sin.   *Selah*
3 You withdrew all your wrath;
     you turned from your hot anger.

4 Restore us again, O God of our
       salvation,
     and put away your indignation
       toward us.
5 Will you be angry with us forever?
     Will you prolong your anger to
       all generations?
6 Will you not revive us again,
     so that your people may rejoice
       in you?
7 Show us your steadfast love,
     O LORD,
     and grant us your salvation.

8 Let me hear what God the LORD
       will speak,
     for he will speak peace to his
       people,
     to his faithful, to those who turn
       to him in their hearts.*s*
9 Surely his salvation is at hand for
       those who fear him,
     that his glory may dwell in our
       land.

10 Steadfast love and faithfulness will
      meet;
      righteousness and peace will kiss
        each other.
11 Faithfulness will spring up from
        the ground,
      and righteousness will look
        down from the sky.
12 The LORD will give what is good,
      and our land will yield its
        increase.
13 Righteousness will go before him,
      and will make a path for his steps.

Psalm

 86

Supplication for Help against Enemies

A Prayer of David.

1 Incline your ear, O LORD, and
     answer me,
     for I am poor and needy.

r Heb lacks *to Zion*   *s* Gk: Heb *but let them not turn back to folly*

2 Preserve my life, for I am devoted
    to you;
  save your servant who trusts in
    you.
  You are my God; ³be gracious to
    me, O Lord,
  for to you do I cry all day long.
4 Gladden the soul of your servant,
  for to you, O Lord, I lift up my
    soul.
5 For you, O Lord, are good and
    forgiving,
  abounding in steadfast love to all
    who call on you.
6 Give ear, O Lᴏʀᴅ, to my prayer;
  listen to my cry of supplication.
7 In the day of my trouble I call on
    you,
  for you will answer me.

8 There is none like you among the
    gods, O Lord,
  nor are there any works like
    yours.
9 All the nations you have made
    shall come
  and bow down before you,
    O Lord,
  and shall glorify your name.
10 For you are great and do wondrous
    things;
  you alone are God.
11 Teach me your way, O Lᴏʀᴅ,
  that I may walk in your truth;
  give me an undivided heart to
    revere your name.
12 I give thanks to you, O Lord my
    God, with my whole heart,
  and I will glorify your name
    forever.
13 For great is your steadfast love
    toward me;
  you have delivered my soul from
    the depths of Sheol.

14 O God, the insolent rise up against
    me;
  a band of ruffians seeks my life,
  and they do not set you before
    them.
15 But you, O Lord, are a God
    merciful and gracious,
  slow to anger and abounding in
    steadfast love and
    faithfulness.

16 Turn to me and be gracious to me;
  give your strength to your servant;
  save the child of your serving girl.
17 Show me a sign of your favor,
  so that those who hate me may
    see it and be put to shame,
  because you, Lᴏʀᴅ, have helped
    me and comforted me.

Psalm

The Joy of Living in Zion

Of the Korahites. A Psalm. A Song.

1 On the holy mount stands the city
    he founded;
2 the Lᴏʀᴅ loves the gates of Zion
  more than all the dwellings of
    Jacob.
3 Glorious things are spoken of you,
  O city of God.   *Selah*

4 Among those who know me I
    mention Rahab and Babylon;
  Philistia too, and Tyre, with
    Ethiopiaᵗ—
  "This one was born there," they
    say.

5 And of Zion it shall be said,
  "This one and that one were
    born in it";
  for the Most High himself will
    establish it.
6 The Lᴏʀᴅ records, as he registers
    the peoples,
  "This one was born there." *Selah*

7 Singers and dancers alike say,
  "All my springs are in you."

Psalm

Prayer for Help in Despondency

A Song. A Psalm of the Korahites. To the
leader: according to Mahalath Leannoth.
A Maskil of Heman the Ezrahite.

1 O Lᴏʀᴅ, God of my salvation,
  when, at night, I cry out in your
    presence,

t Or *Nubia*; Heb *Cush*

2   let my prayer come before you;
    incline your ear to my cry.

3   For my soul is full of troubles,
    and my life draws near to Sheol.
4   I am counted among those who go
      down to the Pit;
    I am like those who have no
      help,
5   like those forsaken among the dead,
    like the slain that lie in the grave,
    like those whom you remember no
      more,
    for they are cut off from your
      hand.
6   You have put me in the depths of
      the Pit,
    in the regions dark and deep.
7   Your wrath lies heavy upon me,
    and you overwhelm me with all
      your waves.   *Selah*

8   You have caused my companions
      to shun me;
    you have made me a thing of
      horror to them.
    I am shut in so that I cannot escape;
9   my eye grows dim through
      sorrow.
    Every day I call on you, O LORD;
    I spread out my hands to you.
10   Do you work wonders for the dead?
    Do the shades rise up to praise
      you?   *Selah*
11   Is your steadfast love declared in
      the grave,
    or your faithfulness in Abaddon?
12   Are your wonders known in the
      darkness,
    or your saving help in the land of
      forgetfulness?

13   But I, O LORD, cry out to you;
    in the morning my prayer comes
      before you.
14   O LORD, why do you cast me off?
    Why do you hide your face from
      me?
15   Wretched and close to death from
      my youth up,
    I suffer your terrors; I am
      desperate.*u*
16   Your wrath has swept over me;
    your dread assaults destroy me.

17   They surround me like a flood all
      day long;
    from all sides they close in on me.
18   You have caused friend and
      neighbor to shun me;
    my companions are in darkness.

Psalm

89

God's Covenant with David

A Maskil of Ethan the Ezrahite.

1   I will sing of your steadfast love,
      O LORD,*v* forever;
    with my mouth I will proclaim
      your faithfulness to all
      generations.
2   I declare that your steadfast love is
      established forever;
    your faithfulness is as firm as the
      heavens.

3   You said, "I have made a covenant
      with my chosen one,
    I have sworn to my servant David:
4   'I will establish your descendants
      forever,
    and build your throne for all
      generations.' "   *Selah*

5   Let the heavens praise your
      wonders, O LORD,
    your faithfulness in the assembly
      of the holy ones.
6   For who in the skies can be
      compared to the LORD?
    Who among the heavenly beings
      is like the LORD,
7   a God feared in the council of the
      holy ones,
    great and awesome*w* above all
      that are around him?
8   O LORD God of hosts,
    who is as mighty as you,
      O LORD?
    Your faithfulness surrounds you.
9   You rule the raging of the sea;
    when its waves rise, you still
      them.
10   You crushed Rahab like a carcass;
    you scattered your enemies with
      your mighty arm.

u Meaning of Heb uncertain   *v* Gk: Heb *the steadfast love of the* LORD   *w* Gk Syr: Heb *greatly awesome*

11 The heavens are yours, the earth
        also is yours;
    the world and all that is in it—
        you have founded them.
12 The north and the south^x—you
        created them;
    Tabor and Hermon joyously
        praise your name.
13 You have a mighty arm;
        strong is your hand, high your
        right hand.
14 Righteousness and justice are the
        foundation of your throne;
    steadfast love and faithfulness go
        before you.
15 Happy are the people who know
        the festal shout,
    who walk, O LORD, in the light of
        your countenance;
16 they exult in your name all day long,
        and extol^y your righteousness.
17 For you are the glory of their
        strength;
    by your favor our horn is exalted.
18 For our shield belongs to the LORD,
        our king to the Holy One of Israel.

19 Then you spoke in a vision to your
        faithful one, and said:
    "I have set the crown^z on one
        who is mighty,
    I have exalted one chosen from
        the people.
20 I have found my servant David;
        with my holy oil I have anointed
        him;
21 my hand shall always remain with
        him;
    my arm also shall strengthen him.
22 The enemy shall not outwit him,
        the wicked shall not humble
        him.
23 I will crush his foes before him
        and strike down those who hate
        him.
24 My faithfulness and steadfast love
        shall be with him;
    and in my name his horn shall be
        exalted.
25 I will set his hand on the sea
        and his right hand on the rivers.
26 He shall cry to me, 'You are my
        Father,
    my God, and the Rock of my
        salvation!'

27 I will make him the firstborn,
        the highest of the kings of the
        earth.
28 Forever I will keep my steadfast
        love for him,
    and my covenant with him will
        stand firm.
29 I will establish his line forever,
        and his throne as long as the
        heavens endure.
30 If his children forsake my law
        and do not walk according to my
        ordinances,
31 if they violate my statutes
        and do not keep my
        commandments,
32 then I will punish their
        transgression with the rod
    and their iniquity with scourges;
33 but I will not remove from him my
        steadfast love,
    or be false to my faithfulness.
34 I will not violate my covenant,
        or alter the word that went forth
        from my lips.
35 Once and for all I have sworn by
        my holiness;
    I will not lie to David.
36 His line shall continue forever,
        and his throne endure before me
        like the sun.
37 It shall be established forever like
        the moon,
    an enduring witness in the
        skies."   *Selah*

38 But now you have spurned and
        rejected him;
    you are full of wrath against your
        anointed.
39 You have renounced the covenant
        with your servant;
    you have defiled his crown in the
        dust.
40 You have broken through all his
        walls;
    you have laid his strongholds in
        ruins.
41 All who pass by plunder him;
        he has become the scorn of his
        neighbors.
42 You have exalted the right hand of
        his foes;
    you have made all his enemies
        rejoice.

x Or *Zaphon and Yamin*   y Cn: Heb *are exalted in*   z Cn: Heb *help*

43 Moreover, you have turned back
the edge of his sword,
and you have not supported him
in battle.
44 You have removed the scepter from
his hand,[a]
and hurled his throne to the
ground.
45 You have cut short the days of his
youth;
you have covered him with
shame.   *Selah*

46 How long, O LORD? Will you hide
yourself forever?
How long will your wrath burn
like fire?
47 Remember how short my time is—[b]
for what vanity you have created
all mortals!
48 Who can live and never see death?
Who can escape the power of
Sheol?   *Selah*

49 Lord, where is your steadfast love
of old,
which by your faithfulness you
swore to David?
50 Remember, O Lord, how your
servant is taunted;
how I bear in my bosom the
insults of the peoples,[c]
51 with which your enemies taunt,
O LORD,
with which they taunted the
footsteps of your anointed.

52 Blessed be the LORD forever.
Amen and Amen.

BOOK IV
(Psalms 90–106)

Psalm
 90

God's Eternity and Human Frailty
A Prayer of Moses, the man of God.

1 Lord, you have been our dwelling
place[d]
in all generations.

2 Before the mountains were brought
forth,
or ever you had formed the earth
and the world,
from everlasting to everlasting
you are God.
3 You turn us[e] back to dust,
and say, "Turn back, you
mortals."
4 For a thousand years in your sight
are like yesterday when it is past,
or like a watch in the night.

5 You sweep them away; they are
like a dream,
like grass that is renewed in the
morning;
6 in the morning it flourishes and is
renewed;
in the evening it fades and
withers.

7 For we are consumed by your anger;
by your wrath we are
overwhelmed.
8 You have set our iniquities before
you,
our secret sins in the light of
your countenance.

9 For all our days pass away under
your wrath;
our years come to an end[f] like a
sigh.
10 The days of our life are seventy
years,
or perhaps eighty, if we are strong;
even then their span[g] is only toil
and trouble;
they are soon gone, and we fly
away.

11 Who considers the power of your
anger?
Your wrath is as great as the fear
that is due you.
12 So teach us to count our days
that we may gain a wise heart.

13 Turn, O LORD! How long?
Have compassion on your
servants!

a Cn: Heb *removed his cleanness*   b Meaning of Heb uncertain   c Cn: Heb *bosom all of many*
peoples   d Another reading is *our refuge*   e Heb *humankind*   f Syr: Heb *we bring our years to*
an end   g Cn Compare Gk Syr Jerome Tg: Heb *pride*

THE FIRST SIX VERSES OF THE NINETIETH PSALM

Robert Burns

VERSE: Psalm 90.1   **PASSAGE:** Psalm 90.1–6

 thou, the first, the greatest friend
    Of all the human race!
Whose strong right hand has ever been
    Their stay and dwelling place!

Before the mountains heaved their heads
    Beneath thy forming hand,
Before this ponderous globe itself
    Arose at thy command:

That power which raised and still upholds
    This universal frame,
From countless, unbeginning time
    Was ever still the same.

Those mighty periods of years
    Which seem to us so vast,
Appear no more before thy sight
    Than yesterday that's past.

Thou giv'st the word; thy creature, man,
    Is to existence brought;
Again thou sayst, 'Ye sons of men,
    'Return ye into nought!'

Thou layest them with all their cares
    In everlasting sleep;
As with a flood thou tak'st them off
    With overwhelming sweep.

They flourish like the morning flower
    In beauty's pride arrayed;
But long ere night cut down it lies
    All withered and decayed.

ADDITIONAL SCRIPTURE READING:

Deuteronomy 33.27; Psalm 91.1

Go to page 686 for your next devotional reading.

1700   1900

14   Satisfy us in the morning with your
      steadfast love,
        so that we may rejoice and be
        glad all our days.

15   Make us glad as many days as you
      have afflicted us,
        and as many years as we have
        seen evil.

16   Let your work be manifest to your
      servants,
        and your glorious power to their
        children.

17   Let the favor of the Lord our God
      be upon us,
        and prosper for us the work of
        our hands—
        O prosper the work of our hands!

Psalm

Assurance of God's Protection

1   You who live in the shelter of the
      Most High,
        who abide in the shadow of the
        Almighty,*h*

2   will say to the LORD, "My refuge
      and my fortress;
        my God, in whom I trust."

3   For he will deliver you from the
      snare of the fowler
        and from the deadly pestilence;

4   he will cover you with his pinions,
        and under his wings you will find
        refuge;
        his faithfulness is a shield and
        buckler.

5   You will not fear the terror of the
      night,
        or the arrow that flies by day,

6   or the pestilence that stalks in
      darkness,
        or the destruction that wastes at
        noonday.

7   A thousand may fall at your side,
        ten thousand at your right hand,
        but it will not come near you.

8   You will only look with your eyes
        and see the punishment of the
        wicked.

9   Because you have made the LORD
      your refuge,*i*
        the Most High your dwelling
        place,

10   no evil shall befall you,
        no scourge come near your tent.

11   For he will command his angels
      concerning you
        to guard you in all your ways.

12   On their hands they will bear you
      up,
        so that you will not dash your
        foot against a stone.

13   You will tread on the lion and the
      adder,
        the young lion and the serpent
        you will trample under foot.

14   Those who love me, I will deliver;
      I will protect those who know
        my name.

15   When they call to me, I will answer
      them;
      I will be with them in trouble,
      I will rescue them and honor
        them.

16   With long life I will satisfy them,
        and show them my salvation.

Psalm

Thanksgiving for Vindication

A Psalm. A Song for the Sabbath Day.

1   It is good to give thanks to the
      LORD,
        to sing praises to your name,
        O Most High;

2   to declare your steadfast love in the
      morning,
        and your faithfulness by night,

3   to the music of the lute and the
      harp,
        to the melody of the lyre.

4   For you, O LORD, have made me
      glad by your work;
        at the works of your hands I sing
        for joy.

5   How great are your works, O LORD!
        Your thoughts are very deep!

6   The dullard cannot know,

---

h Traditional rendering of Heb *Shaddai*   *i* Cn: Heb *Because you, LORD, are my refuge; you have made*

the stupid cannot understand
  this:
7 though the wicked sprout like grass
  and all evildoers flourish,
  they are doomed to destruction
  forever,
8 but you, O LORD, are on high
  forever.
9 For your enemies, O LORD,
  for your enemies shall perish;
  all evildoers shall be scattered.

10 But you have exalted my horn like
  that of the wild ox;
  you have poured over me[j] fresh
  oil.
11 My eyes have seen the downfall of
  my enemies;
  my ears have heard the doom of
  my evil assailants.

12 The righteous flourish like the
  palm tree,
  and grow like a cedar in Lebanon.
13 They are planted in the house of
  the LORD;
  they flourish in the courts of our
  God.
14 In old age they still produce fruit;
  they are always green and full of
  sap,
15 showing that the LORD is upright;
  he is my rock, and there is no
  unrighteousness in him.

Psalm
 93

The Majesty of God's Rule

1 The LORD is king, he is robed in
  majesty;
  the LORD is robed, he is girded
  with strength.
  He has established the world; it
  shall never be moved;
2 your throne is established from
  of old;
  you are from everlasting.

3 The floods have lifted up, O LORD,
  the floods have lifted up their
  voice;
  the floods lift up their roaring.

4 More majestic than the thunders of
  mighty waters,
  more majestic than the waves[k] of
  the sea,
  majestic on high is the LORD!
5 Your decrees are very sure;
  holiness befits your house,
  O LORD, forevermore.

Psalm
 94

God the Avenger of the Righteous

1 O LORD, you God of vengeance,
  you God of vengeance, shine
  forth!
2 Rise up, O judge of the earth;
  give to the proud what they
  deserve!
3 O LORD, how long shall the wicked,
  how long shall the wicked exult?

4 They pour out their arrogant words;
  all the evildoers boast.
5 They crush your people, O LORD,
  and afflict your heritage.
6 They kill the widow and the
  stranger,
  they murder the orphan,
7 and they say, "The LORD does not
  see;
  the God of Jacob does not
  perceive."

8 Understand, O dullest of the
  people;
  fools, when will you be wise?
9 He who planted the ear, does he
  not hear?
  He who formed the eye, does he
  not see?
10 He who disciplines the nations,
  he who teaches knowledge to
  humankind,
  does he not chastise?
11 The LORD knows our thoughts,[l]
  that they are but an empty breath.

12 Happy are those whom you
  discipline, O LORD,
  and whom you teach out of your
  law,

j Syr: Meaning of Heb uncertain   k Cn: Heb *majestic are the waves*   l Heb *the thoughts of humankind*

13 giving them respite from days of
      trouble,
        until a pit is dug for the wicked.
14 For the LORD will not forsake his
      people;
        he will not abandon his heritage;
15 for justice will return to the
      righteous,
        and all the upright in heart will
          follow it.

16 Who rises up for me against the
      wicked?
        Who stands up for me against
          evildoers?
17 If the LORD had not been my help,
        my soul would soon have lived in
          the land of silence.
18 When I thought, "My foot is
      slipping,"
        your steadfast love, O LORD, held
          me up.
19 When the cares of my heart are
      many,
        your consolations cheer my soul.
20 Can wicked rulers be allied with
      you,
        those who contrive mischief by
          statute?
21 They band together against the life
      of the righteous,
        and condemn the innocent to
          death.
22 But the LORD has become my
      stronghold,
        and my God the rock of my
          refuge.
23 He will repay them for their
      iniquity
        and wipe them out for their
          wickedness;
        the LORD our God will wipe
          them out.

Psalm

A Call to Worship and Obedience

1 O come, let us sing to the LORD;
        let us make a joyful noise to the
          rock of our salvation!
2 Let us come into his presence with
      thanksgiving;
        let us make a joyful noise to him
          with songs of praise!

3 For the LORD is a great God,
        and a great King above all gods.
4 In his hand are the depths of the
      earth;
        the heights of the mountains are
          his also.
5 The sea is his, for he made it,
        and the dry land, which his
          hands have formed.

6 O come, let us worship and bow
      down,
        let us kneel before the LORD, our
          Maker!
7 For he is our God,
        and we are the people of his
          pasture,
        and the sheep of his hand.

   O that today you would listen to
      his voice!
8 Do not harden your hearts, as at
      Meribah,
        as on the day at Massah in the
          wilderness,
9 when your ancestors tested me,
        and put me to the proof, though
          they had seen my work.
10 For forty years I loathed that
      generation
        and said, "They are a people
          whose hearts go astray,
        and they do not regard my ways."
11 Therefore in my anger I swore,
        "They shall not enter my rest."

Psalm

Praise to God Who Comes
in Judgment

1 O sing to the LORD a new song;
        sing to the LORD, all the earth.
2 Sing to the LORD, bless his name;
        tell of his salvation from day to
          day.
3 Declare his glory among the
      nations,
        his marvelous works among all
          the peoples.
4 For great is the LORD, and greatly to
      be praised;
        he is to be revered above all gods.
5 For all the gods of the peoples are
      idols,

but the LORD made the heavens.
6 Honor and majesty are before him;
   strength and beauty are in his
      sanctuary.

7 Ascribe to the LORD, O families of
      the peoples,
   ascribe to the LORD glory and
      strength.
8 Ascribe to the LORD the glory due
      his name;
   bring an offering, and come into
      his courts.
9 Worship the LORD in holy splendor;
   tremble before him, all the earth.

10 Say among the nations, "The LORD
      is king!
   The world is firmly established;
      it shall never be moved.
   He will judge the peoples with
      equity."
11 Let the heavens be glad, and let the
      earth rejoice;
   let the sea roar, and all that fills
      it;
12 let the field exult, and everything
      in it.
   Then shall all the trees of the forest
      sing for joy
13 before the LORD; for he is coming,
   for he is coming to judge the
      earth.
   He will judge the world with
      righteousness,
   and the peoples with his truth.

Psalm

The Glory of God's Reign

1 The LORD is king! Let the earth
      rejoice;
   let the many coastlands be glad!
2 Clouds and thick darkness are all
      around him;
   righteousness and justice are the
      foundation of his throne.
3 Fire goes before him,
   and consumes his adversaries on
      every side.
4 His lightnings light up the world;
   the earth sees and trembles.

5 The mountains melt like wax
      before the LORD,
   before the Lord of all the earth.

6 The heavens proclaim his
      righteousness;
   and all the peoples behold his
      glory.
7 All worshipers of images are put to
      shame,
   those who make their boast in
      worthless idols;
   all gods bow down before him.
8 Zion hears and is glad,
   and the towns*m* of Judah rejoice,
   because of your judgments,
      O God.
9 For you, O LORD, are most high
      over all the earth;
   you are exalted far above all gods.

10 The LORD loves those who hate*n*
      evil;
   he guards the lives of his faithful;
   he rescues them from the hand of
      the wicked.
11 Light dawns*o* for the righteous,
   and joy for the upright in heart.
12 Rejoice in the LORD, O you
      righteous,
   and give thanks to his holy
      name!

Psalm

Praise the Judge of the World

A Psalm.

1 O sing to the LORD a new song,
   for he has done marvelous
      things.
   His right hand and his holy arm
   have gotten him victory.
2 The LORD has made known his
      victory;
   he has revealed his vindication in
      the sight of the nations.
3 He has remembered his steadfast
      love and faithfulness
   to the house of Israel.
   All the ends of the earth have seen
      the victory of our God.

m Heb *daughters*   *n* Cn: Heb *You who love the* LORD *hate*   *o* Gk Syr Jerome: Heb *is sown*

4 Make a joyful noise to the LORD, all
    the earth;
   break forth into joyous song and
    sing praises.
5 Sing praises to the LORD with the
    lyre,
   with the lyre and the sound of
    melody.
6 With trumpets and the sound of
    the horn
   make a joyful noise before the
    King, the LORD.

7 Let the sea roar, and all that fills it;
   the world and those who live in
    it.
8 Let the floods clap their hands;
   let the hills sing together for joy
9 at the presence of the LORD, for he
    is coming
   to judge the earth.
   He will judge the world with
    righteousness,
   and the peoples with equity.

Psalm

99

Praise to God for His Holiness

1 The LORD is king; let the peoples
    tremble!
   He sits enthroned upon the
    cherubim; let the earth
    quake!
2 The LORD is great in Zion;
   he is exalted over all the peoples.
3 Let them praise your great and
    awesome name.
   Holy is he!
4 Mighty King,*p* lover of justice,
   you have established equity;
   you have executed justice
   and righteousness in Jacob.
5 Extol the LORD our God;
   worship at his footstool.
   Holy is he!

6 Moses and Aaron were among his
    priests,
   Samuel also was among those
    who called on his name.
   They cried to the LORD, and he
    answered them.

7 He spoke to them in the pillar of
    cloud;
   they kept his decrees,
   and the statutes that he gave
    them.

8 O LORD our God, you answered
    them;
   you were a forgiving God to them,
   but an avenger of their
    wrongdoings.
9 Extol the LORD our God,
   and worship at his holy mountain;
   for the LORD our God is holy.

Psalm

100

All Lands Summoned to Praise God

A Psalm of thanksgiving.

1 Make a joyful noise to the LORD, all
    the earth.
2 Worship the LORD with gladness;
   come into his presence with
    singing.

3 Know that the LORD is God.
   It is he that made us, and we are
    his;*q*
   we are his people, and the sheep
    of his pasture.

4 Enter his gates with thanksgiving,
   and his courts with praise.
   Give thanks to him, bless his
    name.

5 For the LORD is good;
   his steadfast love endures forever,
   and his faithfulness to all
    generations.

Psalm

101

A Sovereign's Pledge of Integrity and Justice

Of David. A Psalm.

1 I will sing of loyalty and of justice;
   to you, O LORD, I will sing.

---

p Cn: Heb *And a king's strength*   *q* Another reading is *and not we ourselves*

2 I will study the way that is
blameless.
When shall I attain it?

I will walk with integrity of heart
within my house;
3 I will not set before my eyes
anything that is base.

I hate the work of those who fall
away;
it shall not cling to me.
4 Perverseness of heart shall be far
from me;
I will know nothing of evil.

5 One who secretly slanders a
neighbor
I will destroy.
A haughty look and an arrogant
heart
I will not tolerate.

6 I will look with favor on the
faithful in the land,
so that they may live with me;
whoever walks in the way that is
blameless
shall minister to me.

7 No one who practices deceit
shall remain in my house;
no one who utters lies
shall continue in my presence.

8 Morning by morning I will destroy
all the wicked in the land,
cutting off all evildoers
from the city of the LORD.

Psalm

102

Prayer to the Eternal King for Help

A prayer of one afflicted, when faint and
pleading before the LORD.

1 Hear my prayer, O LORD;
let my cry come to you.
2 Do not hide your face from me
in the day of my distress.
Incline your ear to me;
answer me speedily in the day
when I call.

3 For my days pass away like smoke,
and my bones burn like a
furnace.
4 My heart is stricken and withered
like grass;
I am too wasted to eat my bread.
5 Because of my loud groaning
my bones cling to my skin.
6 I am like an owl of the wilderness,
like a little owl of the waste
places.
7 I lie awake;
I am like a lonely bird on the
housetop.
8 All day long my enemies taunt me;
those who deride me use my
name for a curse.
9 For I eat ashes like bread,
and mingle tears with my drink,
10 because of your indignation and
anger;
for you have lifted me up and
thrown me aside.
11 My days are like an evening
shadow;
I wither away like grass.

12 But you, O LORD, are enthroned
forever;
your name endures to all
generations.
13 You will rise up and have
compassion on Zion,
for it is time to favor it;
the appointed time has come.
14 For your servants hold its stones
dear,
and have pity on its dust.
15 The nations will fear the name of
the LORD,
and all the kings of the earth
your glory.
16 For the LORD will build up Zion;
he will appear in his glory.
17 He will regard the prayer of the
destitute,
and will not despise their prayer.

18 Let this be recorded for a
generation to come,
so that a people yet unborn may
praise the LORD:
19 that he looked down from his holy
height,
from heaven the LORD looked at
the earth,

20 to hear the groans of the prisoners,
    to set free those who were
        doomed to die;
21 so that the name of the LORD may
        be declared in Zion,
    and his praise in Jerusalem,
22 when peoples gather together,
    and kingdoms, to worship the
        LORD.

23 He has broken my strength in
        midcourse;
    he has shortened my days.
24 "O my God," I say, "do not take
        me away
    at the midpoint of my life,
    you whose years endure
        throughout all generations."

25 Long ago you laid the foundation of
        the earth,
    and the heavens are the work of
        your hands.
26 They will perish, but you endure;
    they will all wear out like a
        garment.
    You change them like clothing, and
        they pass away;
27 but you are the same, and your
        years have no end.
28 The children of your servants shall
        live secure;
    their offspring shall be
        established in your presence.

Psalm

103

Thanksgiving for God's Goodness
Of David.

1 Bless the LORD, O my soul,
    and all that is within me,
    bless his holy name.
2 Bless the LORD, O my soul,
    and do not forget all his
        benefits—
3 who forgives all your iniquity,
    who heals all your diseases,
4 who redeems your life from the Pit,
    who crowns you with steadfast
        love and mercy,
5 who satisfies you with good as long
        as you live[r]

r Meaning of Heb uncertain

so that your youth is renewed
    like the eagle's.

6 The LORD works vindication
    and justice for all who are
        oppressed.
7 He made known his ways to Moses,
    his acts to the people of Israel.
8 The LORD is merciful and gracious,
    slow to anger and abounding in
        steadfast love.
9 He will not always accuse,
    nor will he keep his anger forever.
10 He does not deal with us according
        to our sins,
    nor repay us according to our
        iniquities.
11 For as the heavens are high above
        the earth,
    so great is his steadfast love
        toward those who fear him;
12 as far as the east is from the west,
    so far he removes our
        transgressions from us.
13 As a father has compassion for his
        children,
    so the LORD has compassion for
        those who fear him.
14 For he knows how we were made;
    he remembers that we are dust.

15 As for mortals, their days are like
        grass;
    they flourish like a flower of the
        field;
16 for the wind passes over it, and it is
        gone,
    and its place knows it no more.
17 But the steadfast love of the LORD
        is from everlasting to
        everlasting
    on those who fear him,
    and his righteousness to
        children's children,
18 to those who keep his covenant
    and remember to do his
        commandments.

19 The LORD has established his
        throne in the heavens,
    and his kingdom rules over all.
20 Bless the LORD, O you his angels,
    you mighty ones who do his
        bidding,
    obedient to his spoken word.

21 Bless the LORD, all his hosts,
   his ministers that do his will.
22 Bless the LORD, all his works,
   in all places of his dominion.
Bless the LORD, O my soul.

Psalm

God the Creator and Provider

1 Bless the LORD, O my soul.
   O LORD my God, you are very
     great.
You are clothed with honor and
   majesty,
2   wrapped in light as with a
   garment.
You stretch out the heavens like a
   tent,
3   you set the beams of your[s]
   chambers on the waters,
you make the clouds your[s] chariot,
   you ride on the wings of the wind,
4   you make the winds your[s]
   messengers,
   fire and flame your[s] ministers.

5 You set the earth on its foundations,
   so that it shall never be shaken.
6 You cover it with the deep as with
   a garment;
   the waters stood above the
   mountains.
7 At your rebuke they flee;
   at the sound of your thunder they
   take to flight.
8 They rose up to the mountains, ran
   down to the valleys
   to the place that you appointed
   for them.
9 You set a boundary that they may
   not pass,
   so that they might not again
   cover the earth.

10 You make springs gush forth in the
   valleys;
   they flow between the hills,
11 giving drink to every wild animal;
   the wild asses quench their thirst.
12 By the streams[t] the birds of the air
   have their habitation;
   they sing among the branches.

13 From your lofty abode you water
   the mountains;
   the earth is satisfied with the
   fruit of your work.

14 You cause the grass to grow for the
   cattle,
   and plants for people to use,[u]
to bring forth food from the earth,
15   and wine to gladden the human
   heart,
oil to make the face shine,
   and bread to strengthen the
   human heart.
16 The trees of the LORD are watered
   abundantly,
   the cedars of Lebanon that he
   planted.
17 In them the birds build their nests;
   the stork has its home in the fir
   trees.
18 The high mountains are for the
   wild goats;
   the rocks are a refuge for the
   coneys.
19 You have made the moon to mark
   the seasons;
   the sun knows its time for setting.
20 You make darkness, and it is night,
   when all the animals of the forest
   come creeping out.
21 The young lions roar for their prey,
   seeking their food from God.
22 When the sun rises, they withdraw
   and lie down in their dens.
23 People go out to their work
   and to their labor until the
   evening.

24 O LORD, how manifold are your
   works!
   In wisdom you have made them
   all;
   the earth is full of your creatures.
25 Yonder is the sea, great and wide,
   creeping things innumerable are
   there,
   living things both small and great.
26 There go the ships,
   and Leviathan that you formed to
   sport in it.

27 These all look to you
   to give them their food in due
   season;

s Heb *his*   t Heb *By them*   u Or *to cultivate*

28 when you give to them, they gather
       it up;
    when you open your hand, they
       are filled with good things.
29 When you hide your face, they are
       dismayed;
    when you take away their breath,
       they die
    and return to their dust.
30 When you send forth your spirit,^{v}
       they are created;
    and you renew the face of the
       ground.

31 May the glory of the LORD endure
       forever;
    may the LORD rejoice in his
       works—
32 who looks on the earth and it
       trembles,
    who touches the mountains and
       they smoke.
33 I will sing to the LORD as long as I
       live;
    I will sing praise to my God
       while I have being.
34 May my meditation be pleasing to
       him,
    for I rejoice in the LORD.

CONTEMPLATION IS LIKE SLEEP IN THE ARMS OF
GOD.   —*Bernard of Clairvaux*

---

35 Let sinners be consumed from the
       earth,
    and let the wicked be no more.
    Bless the LORD, O my soul.
    Praise the LORD!

Psalm

105

God's Faithfulness to Israel

1 O give thanks to the LORD, call on
       his name;
    make known his deeds among
       the peoples.
2 Sing to him, sing praises to him;
       tell of all his wonderful works.
3 Glory in his holy name;

let the hearts of those who seek
   the LORD rejoice.
4 Seek the LORD and his strength;
    seek his presence continually.
5 Remember the wonderful works he
    has done,
    his miracles, and the judgments
    he has uttered,
6 O offspring of his servant
    Abraham,^{w}
    children of Jacob, his chosen ones.

7 He is the LORD our God;
    his judgments are in all the earth.
8 He is mindful of his covenant
    forever,
    of the word that he commanded,
    for a thousand generations,
9 the covenant that he made with
    Abraham,
    his sworn promise to Isaac,
10 which he confirmed to Jacob as a
    statute,
    to Israel as an everlasting
    covenant,
11 saying, "To you I will give the land
    of Canaan
    as your portion for an
    inheritance."

12 When they were few in number,
    of little account, and strangers in
    it,
13 wandering from nation to nation,
    from one kingdom to another
    people,
14 he allowed no one to oppress them;
    he rebuked kings on their
    account,
15 saying, "Do not touch my anointed
    ones;
    do my prophets no harm."

16 When he summoned famine
    against the land,
    and broke every staff of bread,
17 he had sent a man ahead of them,
    Joseph, who was sold as a slave.
18 His feet were hurt with fetters,
    his neck was put in a collar of
    iron;
19 until what he had said came to pass,
    the word of the LORD kept testing
    him.

---

v Or *your breath* w Another reading is *Israel* (compare 1 Chr 16.13)

20 The king sent and released him;
   the ruler of the peoples set him
     free.
21 He made him lord of his house,
   and ruler of all his possessions,
22 to instruct[x] his officials at his
     pleasure,
   and to teach his elders wisdom.

23 Then Israel came to Egypt;
   Jacob lived as an alien in the land
     of Ham.
24 And the LORD made his people very
     fruitful,
   and made them stronger than
     their foes,
25 whose hearts he then turned to
     hate his people,
   to deal craftily with his servants.

26 He sent his servant Moses,
   and Aaron whom he had chosen.
27 They performed his signs among
     them,
   and miracles in the land of Ham.
28 He sent darkness, and made the
     land dark;
   they rebelled[y] against his words.
29 He turned their waters into blood,
   and caused their fish to die.
30 Their land swarmed with frogs,
   even in the chambers of their
     kings.
31 He spoke, and there came swarms
     of flies,
   and gnats throughout their
     country.
32 He gave them hail for rain,
   and lightning that flashed
     through their land.
33 He struck their vines and fig trees,
   and shattered the trees of their
     country.
34 He spoke, and the locusts came,
   and young locusts without
     number;
35 they devoured all the vegetation in
     their land,
   and ate up the fruit of their
     ground.
36 He struck down all the firstborn in
     their land,
   the first issue of all their
     strength.

37 Then he brought Israel[z] out with
     silver and gold,
   and there was no one among
     their tribes who stumbled.
38 Egypt was glad when they departed,
   for dread of them had fallen upon
     it.
39 He spread a cloud for a covering,
   and fire to give light by night.
40 They asked, and he brought quails,
   and gave them food from heaven
     in abundance.
41 He opened the rock, and water
     gushed out;
   it flowed through the desert like
     a river.
42 For he remembered his holy
     promise,
   and Abraham, his servant.

43 So he brought his people out with
     joy,
   his chosen ones with singing.
44 He gave them the lands of the
     nations,
   and they took possession of the
     wealth of the peoples,
45 that they might keep his statutes
   and observe his laws.
Praise the LORD!

Psalm

106

A Confession of Israel's Sins

1 Praise the LORD!
   O give thanks to the LORD, for he
     is good;
   for his steadfast love endures
     forever.
2 Who can utter the mighty doings of
     the LORD,
   or declare all his praise?
3 Happy are those who observe
     justice,
   who do righteousness at all
     times.

4 Remember me, O LORD, when you
     show favor to your people;
   help me when you deliver them;
5 that I may see the prosperity of
     your chosen ones,

x Gk Syr Jerome: Heb to bind   y Cn Compare Gk Syr: Heb they did not rebel   z Heb them

that I may rejoice in the gladness
  of your nation,
  that I may glory in your heritage.

6 Both we and our ancestors have
     sinned;
   we have committed iniquity,
     have done wickedly.
7 Our ancestors, when they were in
     Egypt,
   did not consider your wonderful
     works;
   they did not remember the
     abundance of your steadfast
     love,
   but rebelled against the Most
     High[a] at the Red Sea.[b]
8 Yet he saved them for his name's
     sake,
   so that he might make known
     his mighty power.
9 He rebuked the Red Sea,[b] and it
     became dry;
   he led them through the deep as
     through a desert.
10 So he saved them from the hand of
     the foe,
   and delivered them from the
     hand of the enemy.
11 The waters covered their
     adversaries;
   not one of them was left.
12 Then they believed his words;
   they sang his praise.

13 But they soon forgot his works;
   they did not wait for his counsel.
14 But they had a wanton craving in
     the wilderness,
   and put God to the test in the
     desert;
15 he gave them what they asked,
   but sent a wasting disease among
     them.

16 They were jealous of Moses in the
     camp,
   and of Aaron, the holy one of the
     LORD.
17 The earth opened and swallowed
     up Dathan,
   and covered the faction of
     Abiram.

18 Fire also broke out in their
     company;
   the flame burned up the wicked.
19 They made a calf at Horeb
   and worshiped a cast image.
20 They exchanged the glory of God[c]
   for the image of an ox that eats
     grass.
21 They forgot God, their Savior,
   who had done great things in
     Egypt,
22 wondrous works in the land of
     Ham,
   and awesome deeds by the Red
     Sea.[b]
23 Therefore he said he would destroy
     them—
   had not Moses, his chosen one,
   stood in the breach before him,
   to turn away his wrath from
     destroying them.

24 Then they despised the pleasant
     land,
   having no faith in his promise.
25 They grumbled in their tents,
   and did not obey the voice of the
     LORD.
26 Therefore he raised his hand and
     swore to them
   that he would make them fall in
     the wilderness,
27 and would disperse[d] their
     descendants among the
     nations,
   scattering them over the lands.

28 Then they attached themselves to
     the Baal of Peor,
   and ate sacrifices offered to the
     dead;
29 they provoked the LORD to anger
     with their deeds,
   and a plague broke out among
     them.
30 Then Phinehas stood up and
     interceded,
   and the plague was stopped.
31 And that has been reckoned to him
     as righteousness
   from generation to generation
     forever.

a Cn Compare 78.17, 56: Heb *rebelled at the sea*   b Or *Sea of Reeds*   c Compare Gk Mss: Heb
exchanged their glory   d Syr Compare Ezek 20.23: Heb *cause to fall*

32 They angered the LORD[e] at the
waters of Meribah,
and it went ill with Moses on
their account;
33 for they made his spirit bitter,
and he spoke words that were
rash.

34 They did not destroy the peoples,
as the LORD commanded them,
35 but they mingled with the nations
and learned to do as they did.
36 They served their idols,
which became a snare to them.
37 They sacrificed their sons
and their daughters to the
demons;
38 they poured out innocent blood,
the blood of their sons and
daughters,
whom they sacrificed to the idols
of Canaan;
and the land was polluted with
blood.
39 Thus they became unclean by their
acts,
and prostituted themselves in
their doings.

40 Then the anger of the LORD was
kindled against his people,
and he abhorred his heritage;
41 he gave them into the hand of the
nations,
so that those who hated them
ruled over them.
42 Their enemies oppressed them,
and they were brought into
subjection under their power.
43 Many times he delivered them,
but they were rebellious in their
purposes,
and were brought low through
their iniquity.
44 Nevertheless he regarded their
distress
when he heard their cry.
45 For their sake he remembered his
covenant,
and showed compassion
according to the abundance
of his steadfast love.
46 He caused them to be pitied
by all who held them captive.

47 Save us, O LORD our God,
and gather us from among the
nations,
that we may give thanks to your
holy name
and glory in your praise.

48 Blessed be the LORD, the God of
Israel,
from everlasting to everlasting.
And let all the people say, "Amen."
Praise the LORD!

BOOK V
(Psalms 107–150)

Psalm

107

*Thanksgiving for Deliverance
from Many Troubles*

1 O give thanks to the LORD, for he is
good;
for his steadfast love endures
forever.
2 Let the redeemed of the LORD say
so,
those he redeemed from trouble
3 and gathered in from the lands,
from the east and from the west,
from the north and from the
south.[f]

4 Some wandered in desert wastes,
finding no way to an inhabited
town;
5 hungry and thirsty,
their soul fainted within them.
6 Then they cried to the LORD in
their trouble,
and he delivered them from their
distress;
7 he led them by a straight way,
until they reached an inhabited
town.
8 Let them thank the LORD for his
steadfast love,
for his wonderful works to
humankind.
9 For he satisfies the thirsty,
and the hungry he fills with good
things.

e Heb *him*   f Cn: Heb *sea*

10 Some sat in darkness and in gloom,
       prisoners in misery and in irons,
11 for they had rebelled against the
       words of God,
     and spurned the counsel of the
       Most High.
12 Their hearts were bowed down
       with hard labor;
     they fell down, with no one to
       help.
13 Then they cried to the LORD in
       their trouble,
     and he saved them from their
       distress;
14 he brought them out of darkness
       and gloom,
     and broke their bonds asunder.
15 Let them thank the LORD for his
       steadfast love,
     for his wonderful works to
       humankind.
16 For he shatters the doors of bronze,
       and cuts in two the bars of iron.

17 Some were sick[g] through their
       sinful ways,
     and because of their iniquities
       endured affliction;
18 they loathed any kind of food,
       and they drew near to the gates
       of death.
19 Then they cried to the LORD in
       their trouble,
     and he saved them from their
       distress;
20 he sent out his word and healed
       them,
     and delivered them from
       destruction.
21 Let them thank the LORD for his
       steadfast love,
     for his wonderful works to
       humankind.
22 And let them offer thanksgiving
       sacrifices,
     and tell of his deeds with songs
       of joy.

23 Some went down to the sea in ships,
       doing business on the mighty
       waters;
24 they saw the deeds of the LORD,
       his wondrous works in the deep.
25 For he commanded and raised the
       stormy wind,

       which lifted up the waves of the
       sea.
26 They mounted up to heaven, they
       went down to the depths;
     their courage melted away in
       their calamity;
27 they reeled and staggered like
       drunkards,
     and were at their wits' end.
28 Then they cried to the LORD in
       their trouble,
     and he brought them out from
       their distress;
29 he made the storm be still,
       and the waves of the sea were
       hushed.
30 Then they were glad because they
       had quiet,
     and he brought them to their
       desired haven.
31 Let them thank the LORD for his
       steadfast love,
     for his wonderful works to
       humankind.
32 Let them extol him in the
       congregation of the people,
     and praise him in the assembly of
       the elders.

33 He turns rivers into a desert,
       springs of water into thirsty
       ground,
34 a fruitful land into a salty waste,
       because of the wickedness of its
       inhabitants.
35 He turns a desert into pools of water,
       a parched land into springs of
       water.
36 And there he lets the hungry live,
       and they establish a town to live
       in;
37 they sow fields, and plant vineyards,
       and get a fruitful yield.
38 By his blessing they multiply
       greatly,
     and he does not let their cattle
       decrease.

39 When they are diminished and
       brought low
     through oppression, trouble, and
       sorrow,
40 he pours contempt on princes
       and makes them wander in
       trackless wastes;

g Cn: Heb *fools*

41 but he raises up the needy out of
distress,
and makes their families like
flocks.
42 The upright see it and are glad;
and all wickedness stops its
mouth.
43 Let those who are wise give heed to
these things,
and consider the steadfast love of
the LORD.

Psalm

Praise and Prayer for Victory

A Song. A Psalm of David.

1 My heart is steadfast, O God, my
heart is steadfast;[h]
I will sing and make melody.
Awake, my soul![i]
2 Awake, O harp and lyre!
I will awake the dawn.
3 I will give thanks to you, O LORD,
among the peoples,
and I will sing praises to you
among the nations.
4 For your steadfast love is higher
than the heavens,
and your faithfulness reaches to
the clouds.

5 Be exalted, O God, above the
heavens,
and let your glory be over all the
earth.
6 Give victory with your right hand,
and answer me,
so that those whom you love
may be rescued.

7 God has promised in his sanctuary:[j]
"With exultation I will divide up
Shechem,
and portion out the Vale of
Succoth.
8 Gilead is mine; Manasseh is mine;
Ephraim is my helmet;
Judah is my scepter.
9 Moab is my washbasin;
on Edom I hurl my shoe;
over Philistia I shout in triumph."

10 Who will bring me to the fortified
city?
Who will lead me to Edom?
11 Have you not rejected us, O God?
You do not go out, O God, with
our armies.
12 O grant us help against the foe,
for human help is worthless.
13 With God we shall do valiantly;
it is he who will tread down our
foes.

Psalm

Prayer for Vindication and Vengeance

To the leader. Of David. A Psalm.

1 Do not be silent, O God of my
praise.
2 For wicked and deceitful mouths
are opened against me,
speaking against me with lying
tongues.
3 They beset me with words of hate,
and attack me without cause.
4 In return for my love they accuse
me,
even while I make prayer for
them.[k]
5 So they reward me evil for good,
and hatred for my love.

6 They say,[l] "Appoint a wicked man
against him;
let an accuser stand on his right.
7 When he is tried, let him be found
guilty;
let his prayer be counted as sin.
8 May his days be few;
may another seize his position.
9 May his children be orphans,
and his wife a widow.
10 May his children wander about and
beg;
may they be driven out of[m] the
ruins they inhabit.
11 May the creditor seize all that he
has;
may strangers plunder the fruits
of his toil.

h Heb Mss Gk Syr: MT lacks *my heart is steadfast*   i Compare 57.8: Heb *also my soul*   j Or *by his holiness*   k Syr: Heb *I prayer*   l Heb lacks *They say*   m Gk: Heb *and seek*

12 May there be no one to do him a
    kindness,
        nor anyone to pity his orphaned
        children.
13 May his posterity be cut off;
        may his name be blotted out in
        the second generation.
14 May the iniquity of his father[n] be
        remembered before the LORD,
        and do not let the sin of his
        mother be blotted out.
15 Let them be before the LORD
        continually,
        and may his[o] memory be cut off
        from the earth.
16 For he did not remember to show
        kindness,
        but pursued the poor and needy
        and the brokenhearted to their
        death.
17 He loved to curse; let curses come
        on him.
        He did not like blessing; may it
        be far from him.
18 He clothed himself with cursing as
        his coat,
        may it soak into his body like
        water,
        like oil into his bones.
19 May it be like a garment that he
        wraps around himself,
        like a belt that he wears every
        day."

20 May that be the reward of my
        accusers from the LORD,
        of those who speak evil against
        my life.
21 But you, O LORD my Lord,
        act on my behalf for your name's
        sake;
        because your steadfast love is
        good, deliver me.
22 For I am poor and needy,
        and my heart is pierced within me.
23 I am gone like a shadow at evening;
        I am shaken off like a locust.
24 My knees are weak through fasting;
        my body has become gaunt.
25 I am an object of scorn to my
        accusers;
        when they see me, they shake
        their heads.

26 Help me, O LORD my God!
        Save me according to your
        steadfast love.
27 Let them know that this is your
        hand;
        you, O LORD, have done it.
28 Let them curse, but you will bless.
        Let my assailants be put to
        shame;[p] may your servant be
        glad.
29 May my accusers be clothed with
        dishonor;
        may they be wrapped in their
        own shame as in a mantle.
30 With my mouth I will give great
        thanks to the LORD;
        I will praise him in the midst of
        the throng.
31 For he stands at the right hand of
        the needy,
        to save them from those who
        would condemn them to
        death.

Psalm

 110

*Assurance of Victory for God's
Priest-King*

Of David. A Psalm.

1 The LORD says to my lord,
        "Sit at my right hand
    until I make your enemies your
        footstool."

2 The LORD sends out from Zion
        your mighty scepter.
        Rule in the midst of your foes.
3 Your people will offer themselves
        willingly
        on the day you lead your forces
        on the holy mountains.[q]
    From the womb of the morning,
        like dew, your youth[r] will come
        to you.
4 The LORD has sworn and will not
        change his mind,
        "You are a priest forever
        according to the order of
        Melchizedek."[s]

---

n Cn: Heb *fathers*   o Gk: Heb *their*   p Gk: Heb *They have risen up and have been put to shame*
q Another reading is *in holy splendor*   r Cn: Heb *the dew of your youth*   s Or *forever, a rightful
king by my edict*

5 The Lord is at your right hand;
  he will shatter kings on the day
    of his wrath.
6 He will execute judgment among
    the nations,
  filling them with corpses;
  he will shatter heads
    over the wide earth.
7 He will drink from the stream by
    the path;
  therefore he will lift up his head.

Psalm

 111

Praise for God's Wonderful Works

1 Praise the LORD!
  I will give thanks to the LORD with
    my whole heart,
    in the company of the upright, in
    the congregation.
2 Great are the works of the LORD,
    studied by all who delight in
    them.
3 Full of honor and majesty is his
    work,
  and his righteousness endures
    forever.
4 He has gained renown by his
    wonderful deeds;
  the LORD is gracious and merciful.
5 He provides food for those who fear
    him;
  he is ever mindful of his covenant.
6 He has shown his people the power
    of his works,
  in giving them the heritage of the
    nations.
7 The works of his hands are faithful
    and just;
  all his precepts are trustworthy.
8 They are established forever and
    ever,
  to be performed with faithfulness
    and uprightness.
9 He sent redemption to his people;
  he has commanded his covenant
    forever.
  Holy and awesome is his name.
10 The fear of the LORD is the
    beginning of wisdom;
  all those who practice it[t] have a
    good understanding.
  His praise endures forever.

t Gk Syr: Heb them

Psalm

 112

Blessings of the Righteous

1 Praise the LORD!
  Happy are those who fear the
    LORD,
  who greatly delight in his
    commandments.
2 Their descendants will be mighty
    in the land;
  the generation of the upright will
    be blessed.
3 Wealth and riches are in their
    houses,
  and their righteousness endures
    forever.
4 They rise in the darkness as a light
    for the upright;
  they are gracious, merciful, and
    righteous.
5 It is well with those who deal
    generously and lend,
  who conduct their affairs with
    justice.
6 For the righteous will never be
    moved;
  they will be remembered forever.
7 They are not afraid of evil tidings;
  their hearts are firm, secure in
    the LORD.
8 Their hearts are steady, they will
    not be afraid;
  in the end they will look in
    triumph on their foes.
9 They have distributed freely, they
    have given to the poor;
  their righteousness endures
    forever;
  their horn is exalted in honor.
10 The wicked see it and are angry;
  they gnash their teeth and melt
    away;
  the desire of the wicked comes to
    nothing.

Psalm

 113

God the Helper of the Needy

1 Praise the LORD!
  Praise, O servants of the LORD;
  praise the name of the LORD.

WEEKEND

DOST THOU NOT CARE?
Christina Rossetti

VERSE: Psalm 95.7   **PASSAGE:** Psalm 95.1–7

 love and love not: Lord, it breaks my heart
   To love and not to love.
Thou veiled within thy glory, gone apart
   Into thy shrine which is above,
Dost thou not love me, Lord, or care
   For this mine ill?—
I love thee here or there
   I will accept thy broken heart, lie still.

Lord, it was well with me in time gone by
   That cometh not again,
When I was fresh and cheerful, who but I?
   I fresh, I cheerful: worn with pain
Now, out of sight and out of heart;
   O Lord, how long?—
I watch thee as thou art,
   I will accept thy fainting heart, be strong.

'Lie still,' 'be strong,' today: but, Lord, to-morrow,
   What of to-morrow, Lord?
Shall there be rest from toil, be truce from sorrow,
   Be living green upon the sward
Now but a barren grave to me,
   Be joy for sorrow?—
Did I not die for thee?
   Do I not live for thee? Leave Me to-morrow.

ADDITIONAL SCRIPTURE READING:
Psalm 42.1–2; Romans 7.15,19–25

Go to page 691 for your next devotional reading.

1700   1900

2 Blessed be the name of the LORD
    from this time on and
        forevermore.
3 From the rising of the sun to its
    setting
    the name of the LORD is to be
        praised.
4 The LORD is high above all nations,
    and his glory above the heavens.

5 Who is like the LORD our God,
    who is seated on high,
6 who looks far down
    on the heavens and the earth?
7 He raises the poor from the dust,
    and lifts the needy from the ash
        heap,
8 to make them sit with princes,
    with the princes of his people.
9 He gives the barren woman a
        home,
    making her the joyous mother of
        children.
    Praise the LORD!

Psalm

God's Wonders at the Exodus

1 When Israel went out from Egypt,
    the house of Jacob from a people
        of strange language,
2 Judah became God's[u] sanctuary,
    Israel his dominion.

3 The sea looked and fled;
    Jordan turned back.
4 The mountains skipped like rams,
    the hills like lambs.

5 Why is it, O sea, that you flee?
    O Jordan, that you turn back?
6 O mountains, that you skip like
        rams?
    O hills, like lambs?

7 Tremble, O earth, at the presence
        of the LORD,
    at the presence of the God of
        Jacob,
8 who turns the rock into a pool of
        water,
    the flint into a spring of water.

Psalm

The Impotence of Idols and the Greatness of God

1 Not to us, O LORD, not to us, but to
    your name give glory,
    for the sake of your steadfast love
        and your faithfulness.
2 Why should the nations say,
    "Where is their God?"

3 Our God is in the heavens;
    he does whatever he pleases.
4 Their idols are silver and gold,
    the work of human hands.
5 They have mouths, but do not
        speak;
    eyes, but do not see.
6 They have ears, but do not hear;
    noses, but do not smell.
7 They have hands, but do not feel;
    feet, but do not walk;
    they make no sound in their
        throats.
8 Those who make them are like
        them;
    so are all who trust in them.

9 O Israel, trust in the LORD!
    He is their help and their shield.
10 O house of Aaron, trust in the LORD!
    He is their help and their shield.
11 You who fear the LORD, trust in the
        LORD!
    He is their help and their shield.

12 The LORD has been mindful of us;
    he will bless us;
    he will bless the house of Israel;
    he will bless the house of Aaron;
13 he will bless those who fear the
        LORD,
    both small and great.

14 May the LORD give you increase,
    both you and your children.
15 May you be blessed by the LORD,
    who made heaven and earth.

16 The heavens are the LORD's heavens,
    but the earth he has given to
        human beings.

u Heb his

17 The dead do not praise the LORD,
   nor do any that go down into
     silence.
18 But we will bless the LORD
   from this time on and
     forevermore.
   Praise the LORD!

Psalm

 116

*Thanksgiving for Recovery
from Illness*

1 I love the LORD, because he has
    heard
   my voice and my supplications.
2 Because he inclined his ear to me,
   therefore I will call on him as
    long as I live.
3 The snares of death encompassed
    me;
   the pangs of Sheol laid hold on
    me;
   I suffered distress and anguish.
4 Then I called on the name of the
    LORD:
   "O LORD, I pray, save my life!"

5 Gracious is the LORD, and
    righteous;
   our God is merciful.
6 The LORD protects the simple;
   when I was brought low, he saved
    me.
7 Return, O my soul, to your rest,
   for the LORD has dealt
    bountifully with you.

8 For you have delivered my soul
    from death,
   my eyes from tears,
   my feet from stumbling.
9 I walk before the LORD
   in the land of the living.
10 I kept my faith, even when I said,
   "I am greatly afflicted";
11 I said in my consternation,
   "Everyone is a liar."

12 What shall I return to the LORD
   for all his bounty to me?
13 I will lift up the cup of salvation
   and call on the name of the LORD,
14 I will pay my vows to the LORD
   in the presence of all his people.

15 Precious in the sight of the LORD
   is the death of his faithful ones.
16 O LORD, I am your servant;
   I am your servant, the child of
    your serving girl.
   You have loosed my bonds.
17 I will offer to you a thanksgiving
    sacrifice
   and call on the name of the LORD.
18 I will pay my vows to the LORD
   in the presence of all his people,
19 in the courts of the house of the
    LORD,
   in your midst, O Jerusalem.
   Praise the LORD!

Psalm

 117

Universal Call to Worship

1 Praise the LORD, all you nations!
   Extol him, all you peoples!
2 For great is his steadfast love
    toward us,
   and the faithfulness of the LORD
    endures forever.
   Praise the LORD!

Psalm

 118

A Song of Victory

1 O give thanks to the LORD, for he is
    good;
   his steadfast love endures forever!

2 Let Israel say,
   "His steadfast love endures
    forever."
3 Let the house of Aaron say,
   "His steadfast love endures
    forever."
4 Let those who fear the LORD say,
   "His steadfast love endures
    forever."

5 Out of my distress I called on the
    LORD;
   the LORD answered me and set
    me in a broad place.
6 With the LORD on my side I do not
    fear.
   What can mortals do to me?

7 The LORD is on my side to help me;
  I shall look in triumph on those
    who hate me.
8 It is better to take refuge in the
    LORD
  than to put confidence in
    mortals.
9 It is better to take refuge in the
    LORD
  than to put confidence in princes.

10 All nations surrounded me;
   in the name of the LORD I cut
     them off!
11 They surrounded me, surrounded
     me on every side;
   in the name of the LORD I cut
     them off!
12 They surrounded me like bees;
   they blazed*v* like a fire of thorns;
   in the name of the LORD I cut
     them off!
13 I was pushed hard,*w* so that I was
     falling,
   but the LORD helped me.
14 The LORD is my strength and my
     might;
   he has become my salvation.

15 There are glad songs of victory in
     the tents of the righteous:
   "The right hand of the LORD does
     valiantly;
16 the right hand of the LORD is
     exalted;
   the right hand of the LORD does
     valiantly."
17 I shall not die, but I shall live,
   and recount the deeds of the
     LORD.
18 The LORD has punished me
     severely,
   but he did not give me over to
     death.

19 Open to me the gates of
     righteousness,
   that I may enter through them
   and give thanks to the LORD.

20 This is the gate of the LORD;
   the righteous shall enter through
     it.

21 I thank you that you have
     answered me
   and have become my salvation.
22 The stone that the builders rejected
   has become the chief
     cornerstone.
23 This is the LORD's doing;
   it is marvelous in our eyes.
24 This is the day that the LORD has
     made;
   let us rejoice and be glad in it.*x*
25 Save us, we beseech you, O LORD!
   O LORD, we beseech you, give us
     success!

26 Blessed is the one who comes in
     the name of the LORD.*y*
   We bless you from the house of
     the LORD.
27 The LORD is God,
   and he has given us light.
   Bind the festal procession with
     branches,
   up to the horns of the altar.*z*

28 You are my God, and I will give
     thanks to you;
   you are my God, I will extol you.

29 O give thanks to the LORD, for he is
     good,
   for his steadfast love endures
     forever.

Psalm

119

The Glories of God's Law

1 Happy are those whose way is
     blameless,
   who walk in the law of the LORD.
2 Happy are those who keep his
     decrees,
   who seek him with their whole
     heart,
3 who also do no wrong,
   but walk in his ways.
4 You have commanded your
     precepts
   to be kept diligently.
5 O that my ways may be steadfast
   in keeping your statutes!
6 Then I shall not be put to shame,

---

v Gk: Heb *were extinguished*   *w* Gk Syr Jerome: Heb *You pushed me hard*   *x* Or *in him*
y Or *Blessed in the name of the LORD is the one who comes*   *z* Meaning of Heb uncertain

having my eyes fixed on all your
    commandments.
7 I will praise you with an upright
    heart,
    when I learn your righteous
    ordinances.
8 I will observe your statutes;
    do not utterly forsake me.

9 How can young people keep their
    way pure?
    By guarding it according to your
    word.
10 With my whole heart I seek you;
    do not let me stray from your
    commandments.
11 I treasure your word in my heart,
    so that I may not sin against you.
12 Blessed are you, O LORD;
    teach me your statutes.
13 With my lips I declare
    all the ordinances of your mouth.
14 I delight in the way of your decrees
    as much as in all riches.
15 I will meditate on your precepts,
    and fix my eyes on your ways.
16 I will delight in your statutes;
    I will not forget your word.

17 Deal bountifully with your servant,
    so that I may live and observe
    your word.
18 Open my eyes, so that I may behold
    wondrous things out of your law.
19 I live as an alien in the land;
    do not hide your commandments
    from me.
20 My soul is consumed with longing
    for your ordinances at all times.
21 You rebuke the insolent, accursed
    ones,
    who wander from your
    commandments;
22 take away from me their scorn and
    contempt,
    for I have kept your decrees.
23 Even though princes sit plotting
    against me,
    your servant will meditate on
    your statutes.
24 Your decrees are my delight,
    they are my counselors.

25 My soul clings to the dust;
    revive me according to your
    word.

26 When I told of my ways, you
    answered me;
    teach me your statutes.
27 Make me understand the way of
    your precepts,
    and I will meditate on your
    wondrous works.
28 My soul melts away for sorrow;
    strengthen me according to your
    word.
29 Put false ways far from me;
    and graciously teach me your law.
30 I have chosen the way of
    faithfulness;
    I set your ordinances before me.
31 I cling to your decrees, O LORD;
    let me not be put to shame.
32 I run the way of your
    commandments,
    for you enlarge my understanding.

33 Teach me, O LORD, the way of your
    statutes,
    and I will observe it to the end.
34 Give me understanding, that I may
    keep your law
    and observe it with my whole
    heart.
35 Lead me in the path of your
    commandments,
    for I delight in it.
36 Turn my heart to your decrees,
    and not to selfish gain.
37 Turn my eyes from looking at
    vanities;
    give me life in your ways.
38 Confirm to your servant your
    promise,
    which is for those who fear you.
39 Turn away the disgrace that I dread,
    for your ordinances are good.
40 See, I have longed for your precepts;
    in your righteousness give me
    life.

41 Let your steadfast love come to me,
    O LORD,
    your salvation according to your
    promise.
42 Then I shall have an answer for
    those who taunt me,
    for I trust in your word.
43 Do not take the word of truth
    utterly out of my mouth,
    for my hope is in your
    ordinances.

44 I will keep your law continually,
    forever and ever.
45 I shall walk at liberty,
    for I have sought your precepts.
46 I will also speak of your decrees
    before kings,
    and shall not be put to shame;

47 I find my delight in your
    commandments,
    because I love them.
48 I revere your commandments,
    which I love,
    and I will meditate on your
    statutes.

MONDAY

HYMN 15

Christopher Smart

VERSE: Psalm 119.11   **PASSAGE:** Psalm 119.9–16

 guide my judgment and my taste,
    Sweet Spirit, author of the book
Of wonders, told in language chaste
    And plainness, not to be mistook.

O let me muse, and yet at sight
    The page admire, the page believe;
"Let there be light, and there was light,
    Let there be Paradise and Eve!"

Who his soul's rapture can refrain?
    At Joseph's ever-pleasing tale
Of marvels, the prodigious train,
    To Sinai's hill from Goshen's vale.

The psalmist and proverbial seer,
    And all the prophets sons of song,
Make all things precious, all things dear,
    And bear the brilliant word along.

O take the book from off the shelf,
    And con it meekly on thy knees;
Best panegyric on itself,
    And self-avouch'd to teach and please.

Respect, adore it heart and mind.
    How greatly sweet, how sweetly grand,
Who reads the most, is most refin'd,
    And polish'd by the Master's hand.

ADDITIONAL SCRIPTURE READING:
2 Timothy 3.16–17; Hebrews 4.12; 2 Peter 1.19–21

Go to page 696 for your next devotional reading.

1700   1900

49 Remember your word to your
      servant,
    in which you have made me hope.
50 This is my comfort in my distress,
    that your promise gives me life.
51 The arrogant utterly deride me,
    but I do not turn away from your
      law.
52 When I think of your ordinances
      from of old,
    I take comfort, O LORD.
53 Hot indignation seizes me because
      of the wicked,
    those who forsake your law.
54 Your statutes have been my songs
    wherever I make my home.
55 I remember your name in the
      night, O LORD,
    and keep your law.
56 This blessing has fallen to me,
    for I have kept your precepts.

57 The LORD is my portion;
    I promise to keep your words.
58 I implore your favor with all my
      heart;
    be gracious to me according to
      your promise.
59 When I think of your ways,
    I turn my feet to your decrees;
60 I hurry and do not delay
    to keep your commandments.
61 Though the cords of the wicked
      ensnare me,
    I do not forget your law.
62 At midnight I rise to praise you,
    because of your righteous
      ordinances.
63 I am a companion of all who fear
      you,
    of those who keep your precepts.
64 The earth, O LORD, is full of your
      steadfast love;
    teach me your statutes.

65 You have dealt well with your
      servant,
    O LORD, according to your word.
66 Teach me good judgment and
      knowledge,
    for I believe in your
      commandments.
67 Before I was humbled I went astray,
    but now I keep your word.
68 You are good and do good;
    teach me your statutes.

69 The arrogant smear me with lies,
    but with my whole heart I keep
      your precepts.
70 Their hearts are fat and gross,
    but I delight in your law.
71 It is good for me that I was
      humbled,
    so that I might learn your
      statutes.
72 The law of your mouth is better to
      me
    than thousands of gold and silver
      pieces.

73 Your hands have made and
      fashioned me;
    give me understanding that I may
      learn your commandments.
74 Those who fear you shall see me
      and rejoice,
    because I have hoped in your
      word.
75 I know, O LORD, that your
      judgments are right,
    and that in faithfulness you have
      humbled me.
76 Let your steadfast love become my
      comfort
    according to your promise to
      your servant.
77 Let your mercy come to me, that I
      may live;
    for your law is my delight.
78 Let the arrogant be put to shame,
    because they have subverted me
      with guile;
    as for me, I will meditate on your
      precepts.
79 Let those who fear you turn to me,
    so that they may know your
      decrees.
80 May my heart be blameless in your
      statutes,
    so that I may not be put to shame.

81 My soul languishes for your
      salvation;
    I hope in your word.
82 My eyes fail with watching for
      your promise;
    I ask, "When will you comfort
      me?"
83 For I have become like a wineskin
      in the smoke,
    yet I have not forgotten your
      statutes.

84 How long must your servant
        endure?
    When will you judge those who
        persecute me?
85 The arrogant have dug pitfalls for
        me;
    they flout your law.
86 All your commandments are
        enduring;
    I am persecuted without cause;
        help me!
87 They have almost made an end of
        me on earth;
    but I have not forsaken your
        precepts.
88 In your steadfast love spare my life,
    so that I may keep the decrees of
        your mouth.

89 The LORD exists forever;
    your word is firmly fixed in
        heaven.
90 Your faithfulness endures to all
        generations;
    you have established the earth,
        and it stands fast.
91 By your appointment they stand
        today,
    for all things are your servants.
92 If your law had not been my
        delight,
    I would have perished in my
        misery.
93 I will never forget your precepts,
    for by them you have given me
        life.
94 I am yours; save me,
    for I have sought your precepts.
95 The wicked lie in wait to destroy
        me,
    but I consider your decrees.
96 I have seen a limit to all perfection,
    but your commandment is
        exceedingly broad.

97 Oh, how I love your law!
    It is my meditation all day long.
98 Your commandment makes me
        wiser than my enemies,
    for it is always with me.
99 I have more understanding than all
        my teachers,
    for your decrees are my
        meditation.
100 I understand more than the aged,
    for I keep your precepts.

101 I hold back my feet from every evil
        way,
    in order to keep your word.
102 I do not turn away from your
        ordinances,
    for you have taught me.
103 How sweet are your words to my
        taste,
    sweeter than honey to my
        mouth!
104 Through your precepts I get
        understanding;
    therefore I hate every false way.

105 Your word is a lamp to my feet
    and a light to my path.

THE BIBLE IS GOD'S CHART FOR YOU TO STEER BY,
TO KEEP YOU FROM THE BOTTOM OF THE SEA,
AND TO SHOW YOU WHERE THE HARBOR IS, AND
HOW TO REACH IT WITHOUT RUNNING ON ROCKS
AND BARS.   —*Henry Ward Beecher*

---

106 I have sworn an oath and
        confirmed it,
    to observe your righteous
        ordinances.
107 I am severely afflicted;
    give me life, O LORD, according
        to your word.
108 Accept my offerings of praise,
        O LORD,
    and teach me your ordinances.
109 I hold my life in my hand
        continually,
    but I do not forget your law.
110 The wicked have laid a snare for
        me,
    but I do not stray from your
        precepts.
111 Your decrees are my heritage
        forever;
    they are the joy of my heart.
112 I incline my heart to perform your
        statutes
    forever, to the end.

113 I hate the double-minded,
    but I love your law.
114 You are my hiding place and my
        shield;
    I hope in your word.
115 Go away from me, you evildoers,
    that I may keep the
        commandments of my God.

116 Uphold me according to your
        promise, that I may live,
    and let me not be put to shame
        in my hope.
117 Hold me up, that I may be safe
    and have regard for your statutes
        continually.
118 You spurn all who go astray from
        your statutes;
    for their cunning is in vain.
119 All the wicked of the earth you
        count as dross;
    therefore I love your decrees.
120 My flesh trembles for fear of you,
    and I am afraid of your
        judgments.

121 I have done what is just and right;
    do not leave me to my oppressors.
122 Guarantee your servant's well-being;
    do not let the godless oppress me.
123 My eyes fail from watching for
        your salvation,
    and for the fulfillment of your
        righteous promise.
124 Deal with your servant according
        to your steadfast love,
    and teach me your statutes.
125 I am your servant; give me
        understanding,
    so that I may know your decrees.
126 It is time for the LORD to act,
    for your law has been broken.
127 Truly I love your commandments
        more than gold, more than fine
        gold.
128 Truly I direct my steps by all your
        precepts;*a*
    I hate every false way.

129 Your decrees are wonderful;
    therefore my soul keeps them.
130 The unfolding of your words gives
        light;
    it imparts understanding to the
        simple.
131 With open mouth I pant,
    because I long for your
        commandments.
132 Turn to me and be gracious to me,
    as is your custom toward those
        who love your name.
133 Keep my steps steady according to
        your promise,

and never let iniquity have
    dominion over me.
134 Redeem me from human
        oppression,
    that I may keep your precepts.
135 Make your face shine upon your
        servant,
    and teach me your statutes.
136 My eyes shed streams of tears
    because your law is not kept.

137 You are righteous, O LORD,
    and your judgments are right.
138 You have appointed your decrees in
        righteousness
    and in all faithfulness.
139 My zeal consumes me
    because my foes forget your
        words.
140 Your promise is well tried,
    and your servant loves it.
141 I am small and despised,
    yet I do not forget your precepts.
142 Your righteousness is an
        everlasting righteousness,
    and your law is the truth.
143 Trouble and anguish have come
        upon me,
    but your commandments are my
        delight.
144 Your decrees are righteous forever;
    give me understanding that I may
        live.

145 With my whole heart I cry; answer
        me, O LORD.
    I will keep your statutes.
146 I cry to you; save me,
    that I may observe your decrees.
147 I rise before dawn and cry for help;
    I put my hope in your words.
148 My eyes are awake before each
        watch of the night,
    that I may meditate on your
        promise.
149 In your steadfast love hear my
        voice;
    O LORD, in your justice preserve
        my life.
150 Those who persecute me with evil
        purpose draw near;
    they are far from your law.
151 Yet you are near, O LORD,
    and all your commandments are
        true.

a Gk Jerome: Meaning of Heb uncertain

152 Long ago I learned from your decrees
   that you have established them
      forever.

153 Look on my misery and rescue me,
   for I do not forget your law.
154 Plead my cause and redeem me;
   give me life according to your
      promise.
155 Salvation is far from the wicked,
   for they do not seek your statutes.
156 Great is your mercy, O LORD;
   give me life according to your
      justice.
157 Many are my persecutors and my
      adversaries,
   yet I do not swerve from your
      decrees.
158 I look at the faithless with disgust,
   because they do not keep your
      commands.
159 Consider how I love your precepts;
   preserve my life according to
      your steadfast love.
160 The sum of your word is truth;
   and every one of your righteous
      ordinances endures forever.

161 Princes persecute me without cause,
   but my heart stands in awe of
      your words.
162 I rejoice at your word
   like one who finds great spoil.
163 I hate and abhor falsehood,
   but I love your law.
164 Seven times a day I praise you
   for your righteous ordinances.
165 Great peace have those who love
      your law;
   nothing can make them stumble.
166 I hope for your salvation, O LORD,
   and I fulfill your
      commandments.
167 My soul keeps your decrees;
   I love them exceedingly.
168 I keep your precepts and decrees,
   for all my ways are before you.

169 Let my cry come before you,
      O LORD;
   give me understanding according
      to your word.
170 Let my supplication come before
      you;
   deliver me according to your
      promise.

171 My lips will pour forth praise,
   because you teach me your
      statutes.
172 My tongue will sing of your
      promise,
   for all your commandments are
      right.
173 Let your hand be ready to help me,
   for I have chosen your precepts.
174 I long for your salvation, O LORD,
   and your law is my delight.
175 Let me live that I may praise you,
   and let your ordinances help me.
176 I have gone astray like a lost sheep;
   seek out your servant,
   for I do not forget your
      commandments.

Psalm

*Prayer for Deliverance
from Slanderers*

            A Song of Ascents.

1   In my distress I cry to the LORD,
    that he may answer me:
2   "Deliver me, O LORD,
    from lying lips,
    from a deceitful tongue."

3   What shall be given to you?
    And what more shall be done to
      you,
    you deceitful tongue?
4   A warrior's sharp arrows,
    with glowing coals of the broom
      tree!

5   Woe is me, that I am an alien in
      Meshech,
    that I must live among the tents
      of Kedar.

BELLIGERENTS ARE NOT RELUCTANT TO HAVE
PEACE, BUT THEY WANT A PEACE TO THEIR OWN
LIKING.   *—Augustine*

---

6   Too long have I had my dwelling
    among those who hate peace.
7   I am for peace;
    but when I speak,
    they are for war.

I FELT MY HEART STRANGELY WARMED
John Wesley

VERSE: Psalm 119.165   **PASSAGE:** Psalm 119.165–168

Wed. May 24, 1738

In the evening I went very unwillingly to a society in Aldersgate-street, where one was reading Luther's preface to the epistle to the Romans. About a quarter before nine, while he was describing the change which God works in the heart through faith in Christ, I felt my heart strangely warmed. I felt I did trust in Christ, Christ alone, for salvation; and an assurance was given me that he had taken away my sins, even mine, and saved me from the law of sin and death.

I began to pray with all my might for those who had in a more especial manner despitefully used me and persecuted me. I then testified openly to all there what I now first felt in my heart. But it was not long before the enemy suggested, "This cannot be faith; for where is thy joy?" Then was I taught that peace and victory over sin are essential to faith in the captain of our salvation; but that, as to the transports of joy that usually attend the beginning of it, especially in those who have mourned deeply, God sometimes giveth, sometimes withholdeth them, according to the counsels of his own will . . .

Thurs. May 25, 1738

The moment I awaked, "Jesus, Master," was in my heart and in my mouth; and I found all my strength lay in keeping my eye fixed upon him, and my soul waiting on him continually. Being again at St. Paul's in the afternoon, I could taste the good word of God in the anthem, which began, "My song shall be always of the lovingkindness of the Lord: with my mouth will I ever be showing forth thy truth from one generation to another." Yet the enemy injected a fear, "If thou dost believe, why is there not a more sensible change?" I answered (yet not I), "That I know not. But this I know, I have 'now peace with God.' And I sin not today, and Jesus my Master has forbid me to take thought for the morrow."

ADDITIONAL SCRIPTURE READING:
Isaiah 32.17; Romans 5.1–2; Ephesians 2.14–17

Go to page 704 for your next devotional reading.

1700   1900

Psalm

Assurance of God's Protection
A Song of Ascents.

1 I lift up my eyes to the hills—
      from where will my help come?
2 My help comes from the LORD,
      who made heaven and earth.

3 He will not let your foot be moved;
      he who keeps you will not
         slumber.
4 He who keeps Israel
      will neither slumber nor sleep.

5 The LORD is your keeper;
      the LORD is your shade at your
         right hand.
6 The sun shall not strike you by day,
      nor the moon by night.

7 The LORD will keep you from all
         evil;
      he will keep your life.
8 The LORD will keep
      your going out and your coming
         in
      from this time on and
         forevermore.

Psalm

Song of Praise and Prayer for Jerusalem
A Song of Ascents. Of David.

1 I was glad when they said to me,
      "Let us go to the house of the
         LORD!"
2 Our feet are standing
      within your gates, O Jerusalem.

3 Jerusalem—built as a city
      that is bound firmly together.
4 To it the tribes go up,
      the tribes of the LORD,
   as was decreed for Israel,
      to give thanks to the name of the
         LORD.
5 For there the thrones for judgment
      were set up,

the thrones of the house of
   David.

6 Pray for the peace of Jerusalem:
      "May they prosper who love you.
7 Peace be within your walls,
      and security within your
         towers."
8 For the sake of my relatives and
         friends
      I will say, "Peace be within you."
9 For the sake of the house of the
         LORD our God,
      I will seek your good.

Psalm

Supplication for Mercy
A Song of Ascents.

1 To you I lift up my eyes,
      O you who are enthroned in the
         heavens!
2 As the eyes of servants
      look to the hand of their master,
   as the eyes of a maid
      to the hand of her mistress,
   so our eyes look to the LORD our
         God,
      until he has mercy upon us.

3 Have mercy upon us, O LORD, have
         mercy upon us,
      for we have had more than
         enough of contempt.
4 Our soul has had more than its fill
      of the scorn of those who are at
         ease,
      of the contempt of the proud.

Psalm

Thanksgiving for Israel's Deliverance
A Song of Ascents. Of David.

1 If it had not been the LORD who
         was on our side
      —let Israel now say—
2 if it had not been the LORD who
         was on our side,
      when our enemies attacked us,

3 then they would have swallowed
       us up alive,
   when their anger was kindled
       against us;
4 then the flood would have swept us
       away,
   the torrent would have gone over
       us;
5 then over us would have gone
   the raging waters.

6 Blessed be the LORD,
   who has not given us
     as prey to their teeth.
7 We have escaped like a bird
   from the snare of the fowlers;
   the snare is broken,
     and we have escaped.

8 Our help is in the name of the
     LORD,
   who made heaven and earth.

Psalm

The Security of God's People

A Song of Ascents.

1 Those who trust in the LORD are
     like Mount Zion,
   which cannot be moved, but
     abides forever.
2 As the mountains surround
     Jerusalem,
   so the LORD surrounds his people,
   from this time on and
     forevermore.
3 For the scepter of wickedness shall
     not rest
   on the land allotted to the
     righteous,
   so that the righteous might not
     stretch out
   their hands to do wrong.
4 Do good, O LORD, to those who are
     good,
   and to those who are upright in
     their hearts.
5 But those who turn aside to their
     own crooked ways
   the LORD will lead away with
     evildoers.
   Peace be upon Israel!

Psalm

A Harvest of Joy

A Song of Ascents.

1 When the LORD restored the
     fortunes of Zion,[b]
   we were like those who dream.
2 Then our mouth was filled with
     laughter,
   and our tongue with shouts of
     joy;
   then it was said among the nations,
   "The LORD has done great things
     for them."
3 The LORD has done great things for
     us,
   and we rejoiced.

4 Restore our fortunes, O LORD,
   like the watercourses in the
     Negeb.
5 May those who sow in tears
   reap with shouts of joy.
6 Those who go out weeping,
   bearing the seed for sowing,
   shall come home with shouts of joy,
   carrying their sheaves.

Psalm

God's Blessings in the Home

A Song of Ascents. Of Solomon.

1 Unless the LORD builds the house,
   those who build it labor in vain.
   Unless the LORD guards the city,
   the guard keeps watch in vain.
2 It is in vain that you rise up early
   and go late to rest,
   eating the bread of anxious toil;
   for he gives sleep to his beloved.[c]

3 Sons are indeed a heritage from the
     LORD,
   the fruit of the womb a reward.
4 Like arrows in the hand of a
     warrior
   are the sons of one's youth.
5 Happy is the man who has
   his quiver full of them.

---

b Or brought back those who returned to Zion   c Or for he provides for his beloved during sleep

He shall not be put to shame
    when he speaks with his enemies
      in the gate.

Psalm

The Happy Home of the Faithful
A Song of Ascents.

1 Happy is everyone who fears the
    LORD,
    who walks in his ways.
2 You shall eat the fruit of the labor
    of your hands;
    you shall be happy, and it shall
      go well with you.

3 Your wife will be like a fruitful vine
    within your house;
    your children will be like olive
      shoots
    around your table.
4 Thus shall the man be blessed
    who fears the LORD.

5 The LORD bless you from Zion.
    May you see the prosperity of
      Jerusalem
    all the days of your life.
6 May you see your children's
      children.
    Peace be upon Israel!

Psalm

Prayer for the Downfall of Israel's Enemies

A Song of Ascents.

1 "Often have they attacked me from
    my youth"
    —let Israel now say—
2 "often have they attacked me from
    my youth,
    yet they have not prevailed
      against me.
3 The plowers plowed on my back;
    they made their furrows long."
4 The LORD is righteous;
    he has cut the cords of the wicked.
5 May all who hate Zion
    be put to shame and turned
      backward.

6 Let them be like the grass on the
      housetops
    that withers before it grows up,
7 with which reapers do not fill their
      hands
    or binders of sheaves their arms,
8 while those who pass by do not say,
    "The blessing of the LORD be
      upon you!
    We bless you in the name of the
      LORD!"

Psalm

Waiting for Divine Redemption
A Song of Ascents.

1 Out of the depths I cry to you,
    O LORD.
2 Lord, hear my voice!
    Let your ears be attentive
    to the voice of my supplications!

3 If you, O LORD, should mark
      iniquities,
    Lord, who could stand?
4 But there is forgiveness with you,
    so that you may be revered.

5 I wait for the LORD, my soul waits,
    and in his word I hope;
6 my soul waits for the Lord
    more than those who watch for
      the morning,
    more than those who watch for
      the morning.

7 O Israel, hope in the LORD!
    For with the LORD there is
      steadfast love,
    and with him is great power to
      redeem.
8 It is he who will redeem Israel
    from all its iniquities.

Psalm

Song of Quiet Trust
A Song of Ascents. Of David.

1 O LORD, my heart is not lifted up,
    my eyes are not raised too high;

I do not occupy myself with things
    too great and too marvelous for
    me.
2 But I have calmed and quieted my
    soul,
    like a weaned child with its
    mother;
    my soul is like the weaned child
    that is with me.*d*

3 O Israel, hope in the LORD
    from this time on and
    forevermore.

Psalm

The Eternal Dwelling of God in Zion

A Song of Ascents.

1 O LORD, remember in David's favor
    all the hardships he endured;
2 how he swore to the LORD
    and vowed to the Mighty One of
    Jacob,
3 "I will not enter my house
    or get into my bed;
4 I will not give sleep to my eyes
    or slumber to my eyelids,
5 until I find a place for the LORD,
    a dwelling place for the Mighty
    One of Jacob."

6 We heard of it in Ephrathah;
    we found it in the fields of Jaar.
7 "Let us go to his dwelling place;
    let us worship at his footstool."

8 Rise up, O LORD, and go to your
    resting place,
    you and the ark of your might.
9 Let your priests be clothed with
    righteousness,
    and let your faithful shout for joy.
10 For your servant David's sake
    do not turn away the face of your
    anointed one.

11 The LORD swore to David a sure
    oath
    from which he will not turn back:
    "One of the sons of your body
    I will set on your throne.
12 If your sons keep my covenant
    and my decrees that I shall teach
    them,

d Or my soul within me is like a weaned child

    their sons also, forevermore,
    shall sit on your throne."
13 For the LORD has chosen Zion;
    he has desired it for his habitation:
14 "This is my resting place forever;
    here I will reside, for I have
    desired it.
15 I will abundantly bless its
    provisions;
    I will satisfy its poor with bread.
16 Its priests I will clothe with
    salvation,
    and its faithful will shout for joy.
17 There I will cause a horn to sprout
    up for David;
    I have prepared a lamp for my
    anointed one.
18 His enemies I will clothe with
    disgrace,
    but on him, his crown will
    gleam."

Psalm

133

The Blessedness of Unity

A Song of Ascents.

1 How very good and pleasant it is
    when kindred live together in
    unity!
2 It is like the precious oil on the
    head,
    running down upon the beard,
  on the beard of Aaron,
    running down over the collar of
    his robes.
3 It is like the dew of Hermon,
    which falls on the mountains of
    Zion.
  For there the LORD ordained his
    blessing,
    life forevermore.

Psalm

134

Praise in the Night

A Song of Ascents.

1 Come, bless the LORD, all you
    servants of the LORD,
    who stand by night in the house
    of the LORD!

2 Lift up your hands to the holy
        place,
     and bless the LORD.

3 May the LORD, maker of heaven
        and earth,
     bless you from Zion.

Psalm

Praise for God's Goodness and Might

1 Praise the LORD!
     Praise the name of the LORD;
     give praise, O servants of the
        LORD,
2 you that stand in the house of the
        LORD,
     in the courts of the house of our
        God.
3 Praise the LORD, for the LORD is
        good;
     sing to his name, for he is
        gracious.
4 For the LORD has chosen Jacob for
        himself,
     Israel as his own possession.

5 For I know that the LORD is great;
     our Lord is above all gods.
6 Whatever the LORD pleases he does,
     in heaven and on earth,
     in the seas and all deeps.
7 He it is who makes the clouds rise
        at the end of the earth;
     he makes lightnings for the rain
     and brings out the wind from his
        storehouses.

8 He it was who struck down the
        firstborn of Egypt,
     both human beings and animals;
9 he sent signs and wonders
     into your midst, O Egypt,
     against Pharaoh and all his
        servants.
10 He struck down many nations
     and killed mighty kings—
11 Sihon, king of the Amorites,
     and Og, king of Bashan,
     and all the kingdoms of
        Canaan—
12 and gave their land as a heritage,
     a heritage to his people Israel.

13 Your name, O LORD, endures
        forever,
     your renown, O LORD,
        throughout all ages.
14 For the LORD will vindicate his
        people,
     and have compassion on his
        servants.

15 The idols of the nations are silver
        and gold,
     the work of human hands.
16 They have mouths, but they do not
        speak;
     they have eyes, but they do not
        see;
17 they have ears, but they do not hear,
     and there is no breath in their
        mouths.
18 Those who make them
     and all who trust them
     shall become like them.

19 O house of Israel, bless the LORD!
     O house of Aaron, bless the LORD!
20 O house of Levi, bless the LORD!
     You that fear the LORD, bless the
        LORD!
21 Blessed be the LORD from Zion,
     he who resides in Jerusalem.
    Praise the LORD!

Psalm

God's Work in Creation and in History

1 O give thanks to the LORD, for he is
        good,
     for his steadfast love endures
        forever.
2 O give thanks to the God of gods,
     for his steadfast love endures
        forever.
3 O give thanks to the Lord of lords,
     for his steadfast love endures
        forever;

4 who alone does great wonders,
     for his steadfast love endures
        forever;
5 who by understanding made the
        heavens,
     for his steadfast love endures
        forever;

6 who spread out the earth on the
    waters,
    for his steadfast love endures
        forever;
7 who made the great lights,
    for his steadfast love endures
        forever;
8 the sun to rule over the day,
    for his steadfast love endures
        forever;
9 the moon and stars to rule over the
    night,
    for his steadfast love endures
        forever;

10 who struck Egypt through their
    firstborn,
    for his steadfast love endures
        forever;
11 and brought Israel out from among
    them,
    for his steadfast love endures
        forever;
12 with a strong hand and an
    outstretched arm,
    for his steadfast love endures
        forever;
13 who divided the Red Sea*e* in two,
    for his steadfast love endures
        forever;
14 and made Israel pass through the
    midst of it,
    for his steadfast love endures
        forever;
15 but overthrew Pharaoh and his
    army in the Red Sea,*e*
    for his steadfast love endures
        forever;
16 who led his people through the
    wilderness,
    for his steadfast love endures
        forever;
17 who struck down great kings,
    for his steadfast love endures
        forever;
18 and killed famous kings,
    for his steadfast love endures
        forever;
19 Sihon, king of the Amorites,
    for his steadfast love endures
        forever;
20 and Og, king of Bashan,
    for his steadfast love endures
        forever;
21 and gave their land as a heritage,

for his steadfast love endures
    forever;
22 a heritage to his servant Israel,
    for his steadfast love endures
        forever.

23 It is he who remembered us in our
    low estate,
    for his steadfast love endures
        forever;
24 and rescued us from our foes,
    for his steadfast love endures
        forever;
25 who gives food to all flesh,
    for his steadfast love endures
        forever.

26 O give thanks to the God of heaven,
    for his steadfast love endures
        forever.

Psalm

137

*Lament over the Destruction
of Jerusalem*

1 By the rivers of Babylon—
    there we sat down and there we
        wept
    when we remembered Zion.
2 On the willows*f* there
    we hung up our harps.
3 For there our captors
    asked us for songs,
    and our tormentors asked for
        mirth, saying,
    "Sing us one of the songs of
        Zion!"

4 How could we sing the LORD's song
    in a foreign land?
5 If I forget you, O Jerusalem,
    let my right hand wither!
6 Let my tongue cling to the roof of
    my mouth,
    if I do not remember you,
    if I do not set Jerusalem
        above my highest joy.

7 Remember, O LORD, against the
        Edomites
    the day of Jerusalem's fall,

e Or *Sea of Reeds*   *f* Or *poplars*

how they said, "Tear it down! Tear
it down!
Down to its foundations!"
8 O daughter Babylon, you
devastator!g
Happy shall they be who pay you
back
what you have done to us!
9 Happy shall they be who take your
little ones
and dash them against the rock!

Psalm

Thanksgiving and Praise
Of David.

1 I give you thanks, O Lord, with my
whole heart;
before the gods I sing your praise;
2 I bow down toward your holy
temple
and give thanks to your name for
your steadfast love and your
faithfulness;
for you have exalted your name
and your word
above everything.h
3 On the day I called, you answered
me,
you increased my strength of
soul.i

4 All the kings of the earth shall
praise you, O Lord,
for they have heard the words of
your mouth.
5 They shall sing of the ways of the
Lord,
for great is the glory of the Lord.
6 For though the Lord is high, he
regards the lowly;
but the haughty he perceives
from far away.

7 Though I walk in the midst of
trouble,
you preserve me against the
wrath of my enemies;
you stretch out your hand,
and your right hand delivers me.

8 The Lord will fulfill his purpose
for me;
your steadfast love, O Lord,
endures forever.
Do not forsake the work of your
hands.

Psalm

The Inescapable God
To the leader. Of David. A Psalm.

1 O Lord, you have searched me and
known me.
2 You know when I sit down and
when I rise up;
you discern my thoughts from far
away.
3 You search out my path and my
lying down,
and are acquainted with all my
ways.
4 Even before a word is on my
tongue,
O Lord, you know it completely.
5 You hem me in, behind and before,
and lay your hand upon me.
6 Such knowledge is too wonderful
for me;
it is so high that I cannot attain
it.

7 Where can I go from your spirit?
Or where can I flee from your
presence?
8 If I ascend to heaven, you are there;
if I make my bed in Sheol, you
are there.
9 If I take the wings of the morning
and settle at the farthest limits of
the sea,
10 even there your hand shall lead me,
and your right hand shall hold
me fast.
11 If I say, "Surely the darkness shall
cover me,
and the light around me become
night,"
12 even the darkness is not dark to
you;
the night is as bright as the day,
for darkness is as light to you.

---

g Or *you who are devastated* h Cn: Heb *you have exalted your word above all your name*
i Syr Compare Gk Tg: Heb *you made me arrogant in my soul with strength*

SEARCH ME, O GOD
A. W. Tozer

VERSE: Psalm 139.23   **PASSAGE:** Psalm 139.1–7, 23–24

 he author of the celebrated devotional work, *The Cloud of Unknowing*, begins his little book with a prayer that expresses the spirit of the deeper life teaching: "God, unto whom all hearts be open . . . and unto whom no secret thing is hid, I beseech thee so for to cleanse the intent of mine heart with the unspeakable gift of thy grace, that I may perfectly love thee and worthily praise thee. Amen."

Who that is truly born of the Spirit, unless he has been prejudiced by wrong teaching, can object to such a thorough cleansing of the heart as will enable him perfectly to love God and worthily to praise him? Yet this is exactly what we mean when we speak about the "deeper life" experience. Only we mean that it should be literally fulfilled within the heart, not merely accepted by the head.

Nicephorus, a father of the Eastern Church, in a little treatise on the Spirit-filled life, begins with a call that sounds strange to us only because we have been for so long accustomed to following Jesus afar off and to living among a people that follow him afar off. "You, who desire to capture the wondrous divine illumination of our Savior Jesus Christ—who seek to feel the divine fire in your heart—who strive to sense and experience the feeling of reconciliation with God—who, in order to unearth the treasure buried in the field of your heart and to gain possession of it, have renounced everything worldly—who desire the candles of our souls to burn brightly even now, and who for this purpose have renounced all the world—who wish by conscious experience to know and to receive the kingdom of heaven existing within you—come and I will impart to you the science of eternal heavenly life—"

Such quotations as these might easily be multiplied till they filled half a dozen volumes. This yearning after God has never completely died in any generation. Always there were some who scorned the low paths and insisted upon walking the high road of spiritual perfection. Yet, strangely enough, that word perfection never meant a spiritual terminal point nor a state of purity that made watchfulness and prayer unnecessary. Exactly the opposite was true.

ADDITIONAL SCRIPTURE READING:
Psalm 26.2; Hebrews 4.13

Go to page 710 for your next devotional reading.

1900   Present

13 For it was you who formed my
    inward parts;
  you knit me together in my
    mother's womb.
14 I praise you, for I am fearfully and
    wonderfully made.
  Wonderful are your works;
  that I know very well.
15   My frame was not hidden from
      you,
  when I was being made in secret,
    intricately woven in the depths
      of the earth.
16 Your eyes beheld my unformed
    substance.
  In your book were written
    all the days that were formed for
      me,
    when none of them as yet existed.
17 How weighty to me are your
      thoughts, O God!
  How vast is the sum of them!
18 I try to count them—they are more
      than the sand;
  I come to the end[j]—I am still
      with you.

IT IS EASIER FOR US TO GET TO KNOW GOD THAN
TO KNOW OUR OWN SOUL . . . GOD IS NEARER TO
US THAN OUR OWN SOUL, FOR HE IS THE GROUND
IN WHICH IT STANDS . . . SO IF WE WANT TO KNOW
OUR OWN SOUL AND ENJOY ITS FELLOWSHIP, IT IS
NECESSARY TO SEEK IT IN OUR LORD GOD.

—Julian of Norwich

---

19 O that you would kill the wicked,
      O God,
  and that the bloodthirsty would
      depart from me—
20 those who speak of you maliciously,
  and lift themselves up against
      you for evil![k]
21 Do I not hate those who hate you,
      O LORD?
  And do I not loathe those who
      rise up against you?
22 I hate them with perfect hatred;
  I count them my enemies.
23 Search me, O God, and know my
      heart;

  test me and know my thoughts.
24 See if there is any wicked[l] way in
      me,
  and lead me in the way
      everlasting.[m]

Psalm

Prayer for Deliverance from Enemies

To the leader. A Psalm of David.

1 Deliver me, O LORD, from evildoers;
  protect me from those who are
      violent,
2 who plan evil things in their minds
  and stir up wars continually.
3 They make their tongue sharp as a
      snake's,
  and under their lips is the venom
      of vipers.　　　*Selah*

4 Guard me, O LORD, from the hands
      of the wicked;
  protect me from the violent
  who have planned my downfall.
5 The arrogant have hidden a trap for
      me,
  and with cords they have spread
      a net,[n]
  along the road they have set
      snares for me.　　　*Selah*

6 I say to the LORD, "You are my God;
  give ear, O LORD, to the voice of
      my supplications."
7 O LORD, my Lord, my strong
      deliverer,
  you have covered my head in the
      day of battle.
8 Do not grant, O LORD, the desires
      of the wicked;
  do not further their evil plot.[o]
      　　　Selah

9 Those who surround me lift up
      their heads;[p]
  let the mischief of their lips
      overwhelm them!
10 Let burning coals fall on them!
  Let them be flung into pits, no
      more to rise!

---

j Or *I awake*　k Cn: Meaning of Heb uncertain
Jer 6.16　n Or *they have spread cords as a net*　o Heb adds *they are exalted*　p Cn Compare Gk:
Heb *those who surround me are uplifted in head*; Heb divides verses 8 and 9 differently
l Heb *hurtful*　m Or *the ancient way.* Compare

11   Do not let the slanderer be
         established in the land;
      let evil speedily hunt down the
         violent!

12   I know that the LORD maintains
         the cause of the needy,
      and executes justice for the poor.
13   Surely the righteous shall give
         thanks to your name;
      the upright shall live in your
         presence.

Psalm

Prayer for Preservation from Evil
A Psalm of David.

1   I call upon you, O LORD; come
         quickly to me;
      give ear to my voice when I call
         to you.
2   Let my prayer be counted as
         incense before you,
      and the lifting up of my hands as
         an evening sacrifice.

3   Set a guard over my mouth, O LORD;
      keep watch over the door of my
         lips.
4   Do not turn my heart to any evil,
         to busy myself with wicked
         deeds
      in company with those who work
         iniquity;
      do not let me eat of their
         delicacies.

5   Let the righteous strike me;
      let the faithful correct me.
      Never let the oil of the wicked
         anoint my head,q
      for my prayer is continuallyr
         against their wicked deeds.
6   When they are given over to those
         who shall condemn them,
      then they shall learn that my
         words were pleasant.
7   Like a rock that one breaks apart
         and shatters on the land,
      so shall their bones be strewn at
         the mouth of Sheol.s

8   But my eyes are turned toward you,
         O GOD, my Lord;
      in you I seek refuge; do not leave
         me defenseless.
9   Keep me from the trap that they
         have laid for me,
      and from the snares of evildoers.
10   Let the wicked fall into their own
         nets,
      while I alone escape.

Psalm

Prayer for Deliverance from Persecutors
A Maskil of David. When he was in the cave. A Prayer.

1   With my voice I cry to the LORD;
      with my voice I make
         supplication to the LORD.
2   I pour out my complaint before
         him;
      I tell my trouble before him.
3   When my spirit is faint,
      you know my way.

      In the path where I walk
         they have hidden a trap for me.
4   Look on my right hand and see—
         there is no one who takes notice
         of me;
      no refuge remains to me;
         no one cares for me.

5   I cry to you, O LORD;
      I say, "You are my refuge,
         my portion in the land of the
         living."
6   Give heed to my cry,
         for I am brought very low.

      Save me from my persecutors,
         for they are too strong for me.
7   Bring me out of prison,
         so that I may give thanks to your
         name.
      The righteous will surround me,
         for you will deal bountifully with
         me.

q Gk: Meaning of Heb uncertain   r Cn: Heb for continually and my prayer   s Meaning of Heb of verses 5-7 is uncertain

Psalm

 143

Prayer for Deliverance from Enemies

A Psalm of David.

1 Hear my prayer, O LORD;
    give ear to my supplications in
      your faithfulness;
    answer me in your righteousness.
2 Do not enter into judgment with
      your servant,
    for no one living is righteous
      before you.

3 For the enemy has pursued me,
    crushing my life to the ground,
    making me sit in darkness like
      those long dead.
4 Therefore my spirit faints within
      me;
    my heart within me is appalled.

5 I remember the days of old,
    I think about all your deeds,
    I meditate on the works of your
      hands.
6 I stretch out my hands to you;
    my soul thirsts for you like a
      parched land.   *Selah*

7 Answer me quickly, O LORD;
    my spirit fails.
Do not hide your face from me,
    or I shall be like those who go
      down to the Pit.
8 Let me hear of your steadfast love
      in the morning,
    for in you I put my trust.
Teach me the way I should go,
    for to you I lift up my soul.

9 Save me, O LORD, from my enemies;
    I have fled to you for refuge.*t*
10 Teach me to do your will,
    for you are my God.
Let your good spirit lead me
    on a level path.

11 For your name's sake, O LORD,
    preserve my life.
In your righteousness bring me
    out of trouble.

12 In your steadfast love cut off my
      enemies,
    and destroy all my adversaries,
    for I am your servant.

Psalm

 144

*Prayer for National Deliverance
and Security*

Of David.

1 Blessed be the LORD, my rock,
    who trains my hands for war, and
      my fingers for battle;
2 my rock*u* and my fortress,
    my stronghold and my deliverer,
my shield, in whom I take refuge,
    who subdues the peoples*v* under
      me.

3 O LORD, what are human beings
      that you regard them,
    or mortals that you think of
      them?
4 They are like a breath;
    their days are like a passing
      shadow.

5 Bow your heavens, O LORD, and
      come down;
    touch the mountains so that they
      smoke.
6 Make the lightning flash and
      scatter them;
    send out your arrows and rout
      them.
7 Stretch out your hand from on high;
    set me free and rescue me from
      the mighty waters,
    from the hand of aliens,
8 whose mouths speak lies,
    and whose right hands are false.

9 I will sing a new song to you,
      O God;
    upon a ten-stringed harp I will
      play to you,
10 the one who gives victory to kings,
    who rescues his servant David.
11 Rescue me from the cruel sword,
    and deliver me from the hand of
      aliens,

---

t One Heb Ms Gk: MT *to you I have hidden*   *u* With 18.2 and 2 Sam 22.2: Heb *my steadfast love*
v Heb Mss Syr Aquila Jerome: MT *my people*

whose mouths speak lies,
and whose right hands are false.

12 May our sons in their youth
be like plants full grown,
our daughters like corner pillars,
cut for the building of a palace.
13 May our barns be filled,
with produce of every kind;
may our sheep increase by
thousands,
by tens of thousands in our fields,
14 and may our cattle be heavy with
young.
May there be no breach in the
walls,w no exile,
and no cry of distress in our
streets.

15 Happy are the people to whom
such blessings fall;
happy are the people whose God
is the LORD.

Psalm

145

The Greatness and the Goodness of God

Praise. Of David.

1 I will extol you, my God and King,
and bless your name forever and
ever.
2 Every day I will bless you,
and praise your name forever and
ever.
3 Great is the LORD, and greatly to be
praised;
his greatness is unsearchable.

4 One generation shall laud your
works to another,
and shall declare your mighty
acts.
5 On the glorious splendor of your
majesty,
and on your wondrous works, I
will meditate.
6 The might of your awesome deeds
shall be proclaimed,
and I will declare your greatness.

7 They shall celebrate the fame of
your abundant goodness,
and shall sing aloud of your
righteousness.

8 The LORD is gracious and merciful,
slow to anger and abounding in
steadfast love.
9 The LORD is good to all,
and his compassion is over all
that he has made.

10 All your works shall give thanks to
you, O LORD,
and all your faithful shall bless
you.
11 They shall speak of the glory of
your kingdom,
and tell of your power,
12 to make known to all people yourx
mighty deeds,
and the glorious splendor of
youry kingdom.
13 Your kingdom is an everlasting
kingdom,
and your dominion endures
throughout all generations.

The LORD is faithful in all his
words,
and gracious in all his deeds.z
14 The LORD upholds all who are
falling,
and raises up all who are bowed
down.
15 The eyes of all look to you,
and you give them their food in
due season.
16 You open your hand,
satisfying the desire of every
living thing.
17 The LORD is just in all his ways,
and kind in all his doings.
18 The LORD is near to all who call on
him,
to all who call on him in truth.
19 He fulfills the desire of all who fear
him;
he also hears their cry, and saves
them.
20 The LORD watches over all who
love him,
but all the wicked he will
destroy.

w Heb lacks in the walls   x Gk Jerome Syr: Heb his   y Heb his   z These two lines supplied by
Q Ms Gk Syr

21 My mouth will speak the praise of
        the LORD,
    and all flesh will bless his holy
        name forever and ever.

Psalm

Praise for God's Help

1   Praise the LORD!
    Praise the LORD, O my soul!
2   I will praise the LORD as long as I
        live;
    I will sing praises to my God all
        my life long.

3   Do not put your trust in princes,
        in mortals, in whom there is no
        help.
4   When their breath departs, they
        return to the earth;
    on that very day their plans
        perish.

5   Happy are those whose help is the
        God of Jacob,
    whose hope is in the LORD their
        God,
6   who made heaven and earth,
        the sea, and all that is in them;
    who keeps faith forever;
7   who executes justice for the
            oppressed;
    who gives food to the hungry.

    The LORD sets the prisoners free;
8   the LORD opens the eyes of the
            blind.
    The LORD lifts up those who are
        bowed down;
    the LORD loves the righteous.
9   The LORD watches over the
        strangers;
    he upholds the orphan and the
        widow,
    but the way of the wicked he
        brings to ruin.

10 The LORD will reign forever,
        your God, O Zion, for all
        generations.
    Praise the LORD!

Psalm

Praise for God's Care for Jerusalem

1   Praise the LORD!
    How good it is to sing praises to
        our God;
    for he is gracious, and a song of
        praise is fitting.
2   The LORD builds up Jerusalem;
        he gathers the outcasts of Israel.
3   He heals the brokenhearted,
        and binds up their wounds.
4   He determines the number of the
        stars;
    he gives to all of them their
        names.
5   Great is our Lord, and abundant in
        power;
    his understanding is beyond
        measure.
6   The LORD lifts up the downtrodden;
        he casts the wicked to the
            ground.

7   Sing to the LORD with thanksgiving;
        make melody to our God on the
            lyre.
8   He covers the heavens with clouds,
        prepares rain for the earth,
    makes grass grow on the hills.
9   He gives to the animals their food,
        and to the young ravens when
            they cry.
10 His delight is not in the strength of
        the horse,
    nor his pleasure in the speed of a
        runner;[a]
11 but the LORD takes pleasure in
        those who fear him,
    in those who hope in his
        steadfast love.

12 Praise the LORD, O Jerusalem!
        Praise your God, O Zion!
13 For he strengthens the bars of your
        gates;
    he blesses your children within
        you.
14 He grants peace[b] within your
        borders;
    he fills you with the finest of
        wheat.

---

a Heb *legs of a person*   b Or *prosperity*

15 He sends out his command to the
   earth;
   his word runs swiftly.
16 He gives snow like wool;
   he scatters frost like ashes.
17 He hurls down hail like crumbs—
   who can stand before his cold?
18 He sends out his word, and melts
   them;

he makes his wind blow, and the
   waters flow.
19 He declares his word to Jacob,
   his statutes and ordinances to
   Israel.
20 He has not dealt thus with any
   other nation;
   they do not know his ordinances.
Praise the LORD!

THURSDAY

BROKEN HEARTS AND NUMBERED STARS
J. Stuart Holden

VERSE: Psalm 147.3–4   **PASSAGE:** Psalm 147.1–6

 e healeth the broken in heart . . . He telleth the number of the stars" (KJV). What a surprising conjunction is found in this twin attribute of God—active pity in the small circles of human experience and unmeasured power in the great realms of creation! Here is God manifesting himself in both the remotest and the nearest things of which we have any knowledge—the universal and the personal.

At first sight, it seems incongruous to suggest that these two things have anything in common. Surely there can be little, if any, connection between the starry heavens above and the suffering hearts below; between that which is so infinitely great and that which is so infinitely little; between that of which no man knows much and that of which all men know a great deal; between that which transcends in its greatness all our thoughts, and that which in its bitterness touches all our lives.

But in this declaration of the majesty and mercy of God, the psalmist is not indulging in mere flights of fancy. Nor is he doing violence to the separate revelations of God's power and love, as though these could ever be in contrast.

Instead, he is pointing to an underlying relationship between stars and sorrows—one that unerringly points to the overruling care of God. If we can understand this truth as we should, it will direct our hearts into the safe anchor of his love as nothing else could do.

ADDITIONAL SCRIPTURE READING:
Job 5.17–18; Hosea 6.1; Romans 11.33

Go to page 716 for your next devotional reading.

1700   1900

Psalm

Praise for God's Universal Glory

1 Praise the LORD!
  Praise the LORD from the heavens;
    praise him in the heights!
2 Praise him, all his angels;
    praise him, all his host!

3 Praise him, sun and moon;
    praise him, all you shining stars!
4 Praise him, you highest heavens,
    and you waters above the
      heavens!

5 Let them praise the name of the
    LORD,
    for he commanded and they were
      created.
6 He established them forever and
    ever;
    he fixed their bounds, which
      cannot be passed.*c*

7 Praise the LORD from the earth,
    you sea monsters and all deeps,
8 fire and hail, snow and frost,
    stormy wind fulfilling his
      command!

9 Mountains and all hills,
    fruit trees and all cedars!
10 Wild animals and all cattle,
    creeping things and flying birds!

11 Kings of the earth and all peoples,
    princes and all rulers of the
      earth!
12 Young men and women alike,
    old and young together!

13 Let them praise the name of the
    LORD,
    for his name alone is exalted;
    his glory is above earth and
      heaven.
14 He has raised up a horn for his
    people,
    praise for all his faithful,
    for the people of Israel who are
      close to him.
  Praise the LORD!

Psalm

[149 emblem]

Praise for God's Goodness to Israel

1 Praise the LORD!
  Sing to the LORD a new song,
    his praise in the assembly of the
      faithful.
2 Let Israel be glad in its Maker;
    let the children of Zion rejoice in
      their King.
3 Let them praise his name with
    dancing,
    making melody to him with
      tambourine and lyre.
4 For the LORD takes pleasure in his
    people;
    he adorns the humble with
      victory.
5 Let the faithful exult in glory;
    let them sing for joy on their
      couches.
6 Let the high praises of God be in
    their throats
    and two-edged swords in their
      hands,
7 to execute vengeance on the
    nations
    and punishment on the peoples,
8 to bind their kings with fetters
    and their nobles with chains of
      iron,
9 to execute on them the judgment
    decreed.
    This is glory for all his faithful
      ones.
  Praise the LORD!

Psalm

Praise for God's Surpassing Greatness

1 Praise the LORD!
  Praise God in his sanctuary;
    praise him in his mighty
      firmament!*d*
2 Praise him for his mighty deeds;
    praise him according to his
      surpassing greatness!

c Or he set a law that cannot pass away   *d Or dome*

3 Praise him with trumpet sound;
     praise him with lute and harp!
4 Praise him with tambourine and
     dance;
     praise him with strings and
       pipe!

5 Praise him with clanging cymbals;
     praise him with loud clashing
       cymbals!
6 Let everything that breathes praise
     the LORD!
     Praise the LORD!

PROVERBS

ACCORDING TO THE PROLOGUE, PROVERBS WAS WRITTEN TO GIVE "SHREWDNESS TO THE SIMPLE, KNOWLEDGE AND PRUDENCE TO THE YOUNG" (1.4), AND TO MAKE THE WISE WISER (1.5). ACQUIRING WISDOM AND KNOWING HOW TO AVOID THE PITFALLS OF FOLLY WILL LEAD TO HEALTH AND SUCCESS. ALTHOUGH PROVERBS IS A PRACTICAL BOOK DEALING WITH THE ART OF LIVING, IT BASES WISDOM SOLIDLY ON THE FEAR OF THE LORD (1.7). HERE YOU WILL FIND WISDOM THAT WORKS AND INSIGHTS THAT WON'T WEAR OUT.

---

1 The proverbs of Solomon son of David, king of Israel:

Prologue

2 For learning about wisdom and instruction,
   for understanding words of insight,
3 for gaining instruction in wise dealing,
   righteousness, justice, and equity;
4 to teach shrewdness to the simple,
   knowledge and prudence to the young—
5 let the wise also hear and gain in learning,
   and the discerning acquire skill,
6 to understand a proverb and a figure,
   the words of the wise and their riddles.

7 The fear of the LORD is the beginning of knowledge;
   fools despise wisdom and instruction.

Warnings against Evil Companions

8 Hear, my child, your father's instruction,
   and do not reject your mother's teaching;
9 for they are a fair garland for your head,
   and pendants for your neck.
10 My child, if sinners entice you,
   do not consent.
11 If they say, "Come with us, let us lie in wait for blood;

let us wantonly ambush the innocent;

12 like Sheol let us swallow them alive and whole, like those who go down to the Pit.

13 We shall find all kinds of costly things;
we shall fill our houses with booty.

14 Throw in your lot among us;
we will all have one purse"—

15 my child, do not walk in their way,
keep your foot from their paths;

16 for their feet run to evil,
and they hurry to shed blood.

17 For in vain is the net baited
while the bird is looking on;

18 yet they lie in wait—to kill themselves!
and set an ambush—for their own lives!

19 Such is the end[a] of all who are greedy for gain;
it takes away the life of its possessors.

The Call of Wisdom

20 Wisdom cries out in the street;
in the squares she raises her voice.

21 At the busiest corner she cries out;
at the entrance of the city gates she speaks:

22 "How long, O simple ones, will you love being simple?
How long will scoffers delight in their scoffing
and fools hate knowledge?

23 Give heed to my reproof;
I will pour out my thoughts to you;
I will make my words known to you.

24 Because I have called and you refused,
have stretched out my hand and no one heeded,

25 and because you have ignored all my counsel
and would have none of my reproof,

26 I also will laugh at your calamity;
I will mock when panic strikes you,

27 when panic strikes you like a storm,
and your calamity comes like a whirlwind,

when distress and anguish come upon you.

28 Then they will call upon me, but I will not answer;
they will seek me diligently, but will not find me.

29 Because they hated knowledge
and did not choose the fear of the LORD,

30 would have none of my counsel,
and despised all my reproof,

31 therefore they shall eat the fruit of their way
and be sated with their own devices.

32 For waywardness kills the simple,
and the complacency of fools destroys them;

33 but those who listen to me will be secure
and will live at ease, without dread of disaster."

MOCK ON, MOCK ON, VOLTAIRE, ROUSSEAU;
MOCK ON, MOCK ON; 'TIS ALL IN VAIN!
YOU THROW THE SAND AGAINST THE WIND,
AND THE WIND BLOWS IT BACK AGAIN.

—*William Blake*

The Value of Wisdom

2 My child, if you accept my words
and treasure up my commandments within you,

2 making your ear attentive to wisdom
and inclining your heart to understanding;

3 if you indeed cry out for insight,
and raise your voice for understanding;

4 if you seek it like silver,
and search for it as for hidden treasures—

5 then you will understand the fear of the LORD
and find the knowledge of God.

6 For the LORD gives wisdom;
from his mouth come knowledge and understanding;

7 he stores up sound wisdom for the upright;

a Gk: Heb *are the ways*

he is a shield to those who walk
    blamelessly,
8   guarding the paths of justice
        and preserving the way of his
        faithful ones.
9   Then you will understand
        righteousness and justice
    and equity, every good path;
10 for wisdom will come into your
        heart,
        and knowledge will be pleasant
        to your soul;
11 prudence will watch over you;
        and understanding will guard you.
12 It will save you from the way of evil,
        from those who speak perversely,
13 who forsake the paths of
        uprightness
        to walk in the ways of darkness,
14 who rejoice in doing evil
        and delight in the perverseness of
        evil;
15 those whose paths are crooked,
        and who are devious in their ways.

16 You will be saved from the loose[b]
        woman,
        from the adulteress with her
        smooth words,
17 who forsakes the partner of her
        youth
        and forgets her sacred covenant;
18 for her way[c] leads down to death,
        and her paths to the shades;
19 those who go to her never come
        back,
        nor do they regain the paths of life.

20 Therefore walk in the way of the
        good,
        and keep to the paths of the just.
21 For the upright will abide in the
        land,
        and the innocent will remain in
        it;
22 but the wicked will be cut off from
        the land,
        and the treacherous will be
        rooted out of it.

Admonition to Trust and Honor God

3   My child, do not forget my
        teaching,
        but let your heart keep my
        commandments;

2   for length of days and years of life
        and abundant welfare they will
        give you.

3   Do not let loyalty and faithfulness
        forsake you;
        bind them around your neck,
        write them on the tablet of your
        heart.
4   So you will find favor and good
        repute
        in the sight of God and of people.

5   Trust in the LORD with all your
        heart,
        and do not rely on your own
        insight.
6   In all your ways acknowledge him,
        and he will make straight your
        paths.
7   Do not be wise in your own eyes;
        fear the LORD, and turn away
        from evil.
8   It will be a healing for your flesh
        and a refreshment for your body.

9   Honor the LORD with your
        substance
        and with the first fruits of all
        your produce;
10 then your barns will be filled with
        plenty,
        and your vats will be bursting
        with wine.

11 My child, do not despise the LORD's
        discipline
        or be weary of his reproof,
12 for the LORD reproves the one he
        loves,
        as a father the son in whom he
        delights.

The True Wealth

13 Happy are those who find wisdom,
        and those who get
        understanding,
14 for her income is better than silver,
        and her revenue better than gold.
15 She is more precious than jewels,
        and nothing you desire can
        compare with her.
16 Long life is in her right hand;
        in her left hand are riches and
        honor.

b Heb strange   c Cn: Heb house

17 Her ways are ways of pleasantness,
   and all her paths are peace.
18 She is a tree of life to those who lay
   hold of her;
   those who hold her fast are called
   happy.

God's Wisdom in Creation

19 The LORD by wisdom founded the
   earth;
   by understanding he established
   the heavens;

20 by his knowledge the deeps broke
   open,
   and the clouds drop down the
   dew.

The True Security

21 My child, do not let these escape
   from your sight:
   keep sound wisdom and
   prudence,
22 and they will be life for your soul
   and adornment for your neck.

FRIDAY

FOLLOW THIS PATH
G. Campbell Morgan

VERSE: Proverbs 3.5   **PASSAGE:** Proverbs 3.5–7

 o simple and so clear is the statement, that interpretation is unnecessary. The reader, then, will be patient if
for this once the writer becomes reminiscent, and so a
witness rather than an advocate. I distinctly remember
the day when I left home to face life, amid its crowded ways, for
myself. My father, whose philosophy was certainly that of the
Hebrew wisdom, gave me these verses as providing a complete
guide to life. Looking back over the intervening years I know he
was right. In them there has been much of failure, many turnings aside from the straight highway, many devious and sorrowful wanderings from the true paths of life. All such failure, such
turnings aside, such wanderings, have resulted from leaning to
one's own understanding. The measure in which I have trusted
Jehovah, and acknowledged him, has been the measure of walking in the paths of real life. Doubt of God, pride of intellect, and
independence in volition, these are the things which blight and
blast. Paths chosen for us by God all lead onward and upward,
even when they seem to us to turn about in inextricable confusion, and to move downward to the valleys of humiliation and
suffering. He is the All-Wise, and to him, wisdom is the way by
which Love gains his victory.

ADDITIONAL SCRIPTURE READING:
Proverbs 28.26; Jeremiah 9.23–24; 1 Corinthians 8.2–3

Go to page 719 for your next devotional reading.

1900   Present

23 Then you will walk on your way
       securely
     and your foot will not stumble.
24 If you sit down,*d* you will not be
       afraid;
     when you lie down, your sleep
       will be sweet.
25 Do not be afraid of sudden panic,
     or of the storm that strikes the
       wicked;
26 for the LORD will be your confidence
     and will keep your foot from
       being caught.

27 Do not withhold good from those
       to whom it is due,*e*
     when it is in your power to do it.
28 Do not say to your neighbor, "Go,
       and come again,
     tomorrow I will give it"—when
       you have it with you.
29 Do not plan harm against your
       neighbor
     who lives trustingly beside you.
30 Do not quarrel with anyone
       without cause,
     when no harm has been done to
       you.
31 Do not envy the violent
     and do not choose any of their
       ways;
32 for the perverse are an abomination
       to the LORD,
     but the upright are in his
       confidence.
33 The LORD's curse is on the house of
       the wicked,
     but he blesses the abode of the
       righteous.
34 Toward the scorners he is scornful,
     but to the humble he shows favor.
35 The wise will inherit honor,
     but stubborn fools, disgrace.

Parental Advice

4 Listen, children, to a father's
       instruction,
     and be attentive, that you may
       gain*f* insight;
2 for I give you good precepts:
     do not forsake my teaching.
3 When I was a son with my father,
     tender, and my mother's favorite,
4 he taught me, and said to me,
     "Let your heart hold fast my words;

keep my commandments, and
       live.
5 Get wisdom; get insight: do not
       forget, nor turn away
     from the words of my mouth.
6 Do not forsake her, and she will
       keep you;
     love her, and she will guard you.
7 The beginning of wisdom is this:
       Get wisdom,
     and whatever else you get, get
       insight.
8 Prize her highly, and she will exalt
       you;
     she will honor you if you
       embrace her.
9 She will place on your head a fair
       garland;
     she will bestow on you a
       beautiful crown."

Admonition to Keep to the Right Path

10 Hear, my child, and accept my
       words,
     that the years of your life may be
       many.
11 I have taught you the way of
       wisdom;
     I have led you in the paths of
       uprightness.
12 When you walk, your step will not
       be hampered;
     and if you run, you will not
       stumble.
13 Keep hold of instruction; do not let
       go;
     guard her, for she is your life.
14 Do not enter the path of the
       wicked,
     and do not walk in the way of
       evildoers.
15 Avoid it; do not go on it;
     turn away from it and pass on.
16 For they cannot sleep unless they
       have done wrong;
     they are robbed of sleep unless
       they have made someone
       stumble.
17 For they eat the bread of
       wickedness
     and drink the wine of violence.
18 But the path of the righteous is like
       the light of dawn,

---

d Gk: Heb *lie down*   *e* Heb *from its owners*   *f* Heb *know*

which shines brighter and
brighter until full day.
19 The way of the wicked is like deep
darkness;
they do not know what they
stumble over.
20 My child, be attentive to my words;
incline your ear to my sayings.
21 Do not let them escape from your
sight;
keep them within your heart.
22 For they are life to those who find
them,
and healing to all their flesh.
23 Keep your heart with all vigilance,
for from it flow the springs of
life.
24 Put away from you crooked speech,
and put devious talk far from you.
25 Let your eyes look directly forward,
and your gaze be straight before
you.
26 Keep straight the path of your feet,
and all your ways will be sure.
27 Do not swerve to the right or to the
left;
turn your foot away from evil.

Warning against Impurity and Infidelity

5 My child, be attentive to my
wisdom;
incline your ear to my
understanding,
2 so that you may hold on to
prudence,
and your lips may guard
knowledge.
3 For the lips of a loose^g woman drip
honey,
and her speech is smoother than
oil;
4 but in the end she is bitter as
wormwood,
sharp as a two-edged sword.
5 Her feet go down to death;
her steps follow the path to Sheol.
6 She does not keep straight to the
path of life;
her ways wander, and she does
not know it.

7 And now, my child,^{h} listen to me,
and do not depart from the words
of my mouth.

8 Keep your way far from her,
and do not go near the door of her
house;
9 or you will give your honor to
others,
and your years to the merciless,
10 and strangers will take their fill of
your wealth,
and your labors will go to the
house of an alien;
11 and at the end of your life you will
groan,
when your flesh and body are
consumed,
12 and you say, "Oh, how I hated
discipline,
and my heart despised reproof!
13 I did not listen to the voice of my
teachers
or incline my ear to my
instructors.
14 Now I am at the point of utter ruin
in the public assembly."

15 Drink water from your own cistern,
flowing water from your own
well.
16 Should your springs be scattered
abroad,
streams of water in the streets?
17 Let them be for yourself alone,
and not for sharing with
strangers.
18 Let your fountain be blessed,
and rejoice in the wife of your
youth,
19 a lovely deer, a graceful doe.
May her breasts satisfy you at all
times;
may you be intoxicated always
by her love.
20 Why should you be intoxicated, my
son, by another woman
and embrace the bosom of an
adulteress?
21 For human ways are under the eyes
of the LORD,
and he examines all their paths.
22 The iniquities of the wicked
ensnare them,
and they are caught in the toils of
their sin.
23 They die for lack of discipline,
and because of their great folly
they are lost.

g Heb strange   h Gk Vg: Heb children

WEEKEND

JESUS, THE VERY THOUGHT OF THEE
Bernard of Clairvaux

VERSE: Isaiah 26.3   **PASSAGE:** Isaiah 26.1–10

 esus, the very thought of thee
With sweetness fills the breast;
But sweeter far thy face to see,
And in thy presence rest.

No voice can sing, no heart can frame,
Nor can the memory find,
A sweeter sound than Jesus' name,
The Savior of mankind.

O hope of every contrite heart,
O joy of all the meek,
To those who fall, how kind thou art:
How good to those who seek!

But what to those who find? Ah, this
Nor tongue nor pen can show;
The love of Jesus, what it is,
None but who love him know.

Jesus, our only joy be thou,
As thou our prize wilt be;
In thee be all our glory now,
And through eternity.

ADDITIONAL SCRIPTURE READING:
Isaiah 12.2; Matthew 1.21–23; Luke 1.31–33

Go to page 723 for your next devotional reading.

Practical Admonitions

6 ¹ My child, if you have given
your pledge to your neighbor,
if you have bound yourself to
another,ⁱ

² you are snared by the utterance of
your lips,ʲ
caught by the words of your
mouth.

³ So do this, my child, and save
yourself,
for you have come into your
neighbor's power:
go, hurry,ᵏ and plead with your
neighbor.

⁴ Give your eyes no sleep
and your eyelids no slumber;

⁵ save yourself like a gazelle from the
hunter,ˡ
like a bird from the hand of the
fowler.

⁶ Go to the ant, you lazybones;
consider its ways, and be wise.

⁷ Without having any chief
or officer or ruler,

⁸ it prepares its food in summer,
and gathers its sustenance in
harvest.

⁹ How long will you lie there,
O lazybones?
When will you rise from your
sleep?

¹⁰ A little sleep, a little slumber,
a little folding of the hands to rest,

¹¹ and poverty will come upon you
like a robber,
and want, like an armed warrior.

¹² A scoundrel and a villain
goes around with crooked speech,

¹³ winking the eyes, shuffling the feet,
pointing the fingers,

¹⁴ with perverted mind devising evil,
continually sowing discord;

¹⁵ on such a one calamity will
descend suddenly;
in a moment, damage beyond
repair.

¹⁶ There are six things that the LORD
hates,
seven that are an abomination to
him:

¹⁷ haughty eyes, a lying tongue,
and hands that shed innocent
blood,

¹⁸ a heart that devises wicked plans,
feet that hurry to run to evil,

¹⁹ a lying witness who testifies falsely,
and one who sows discord in a
family.

²⁰ My child, keep your father's
commandment,
and do not forsake your mother's
teaching.

²¹ Bind them upon your heart always;
tie them around your neck.

²² When you walk, theyᵐ will lead
you;
when you lie down, theyᵐ will
watch over you;
and when you awake, theyᵐ will
talk with you.

²³ For the commandment is a lamp
and the teaching a light,
and the reproofs of discipline are
the way of life,

²⁴ to preserve you from the wife of
another,ⁿ
from the smooth tongue of the
adulteress.

²⁵ Do not desire her beauty in your
heart,
and do not let her capture you
with her eyelashes;

²⁶ for a prostitute's fee is only a loaf of
bread,ᵒ
but the wife of another stalks a
man's very life.

²⁷ Can fire be carried in the bosom
without burning one's clothes?

²⁸ Or can one walk on hot coals
without scorching the feet?

²⁹ So is he who sleeps with his
neighbor's wife;
no one who touches her will go
unpunished.

³⁰ Thieves are not despised who steal
only
to satisfy their appetite when
they are hungry.

³¹ Yet if they are caught, they will pay
sevenfold;
they will forfeit all the goods of
their house.

---

i Or *a stranger*   *j* Cn Compare Gk Syr: Heb *the words of your mouth*   *k* Or *humble yourself*
l Cn: Heb *from the hand*   *m* Heb *it*   *n* Gk: MT *the evil woman*   *o* Cn Compare Gk Syr Vg Tg:
Heb *for because of a harlot to a piece of bread*

32 But he who commits adultery has
      no sense;
   he who does it destroys himself.
33 He will get wounds and dishonor,
      and his disgrace will not be
      wiped away.
34 For jealousy arouses a husband's
      fury,
   and he shows no restraint when
      he takes revenge.
35 He will accept no compensation,
      and refuses a bribe no matter
      how great.

The False Attractions of Adultery

7 My child, keep my words
   and store up my
      commandments with you;
2 keep my commandments and live,
      keep my teachings as the apple of
      your eye;
3 bind them on your fingers,
      write them on the tablet of your
      heart.
4 Say to wisdom, "You are my sister,"
      and call insight your intimate
      friend,
5 that they may keep you from the
      loose*p* woman,
   from the adulteress with her
      smooth words.

6 For at the window of my house
      I looked out through my lattice,
7 and I saw among the simple ones,
      I observed among the youths,
   a young man without sense,
8 passing along the street near her
      corner,
   taking the road to her house
9 in the twilight, in the evening,
      at the time of night and darkness.

10 Then a woman comes toward him,
      decked out like a prostitute, wily
      of heart.*q*
11 She is loud and wayward;
      her feet do not stay at home;
12 now in the street, now in the
      squares,
   and at every corner she lies in
      wait.
13 She seizes him and kisses him,
      and with impudent face she says
      to him:

14 "I had to offer sacrifices,
      and today I have paid my vows;
15 so now I have come out to meet
      you,
   to seek you eagerly, and I have
      found you!
16 I have decked my couch with
      coverings,
   colored spreads of Egyptian linen;
17 I have perfumed my bed with
      myrrh,
   aloes, and cinnamon.
18 Come, let us take our fill of love
      until morning;
   let us delight ourselves with
      love.
19 For my husband is not at home;
      he has gone on a long journey.
20 He took a bag of money with him;
      he will not come home until full
      moon."

21 With much seductive speech she
      persuades him;
   with her smooth talk she
      compels him.
22 Right away he follows her,
      and goes like an ox to the
      slaughter,
   or bounds like a stag toward the
      trap*r*
23   until an arrow pierces its
      entrails.
   He is like a bird rushing into a
      snare,
   not knowing that it will cost him
      his life.

24 And now, my children, listen to
      me,
   and be attentive to the words of
      my mouth.
25 Do not let your hearts turn aside to
      her ways;
   do not stray into her paths.
26 for many are those she has laid low,
      and numerous are her victims.
27 Her house is the way to Sheol,
      going down to the chambers of
      death.

The Gifts of Wisdom

8 Does not wisdom call,
   and does not understanding
      raise her voice?

p Heb *strange*   q Meaning of Heb uncertain   r Cn Compare Gk: Meaning of Heb uncertain

2   On the heights, beside the way,
        at the crossroads she takes her
            stand;
3   beside the gates in front of the town,
        at the entrance of the portals she
            cries out:
4   "To you, O people, I call,
        and my cry is to all that live.
5   O simple ones, learn prudence;
        acquire intelligence, you who
            lack it.
6   Hear, for I will speak noble things,
        and from my lips will come what
            is right;
7   for my mouth will utter truth;
        wickedness is an abomination to
            my lips.
8   All the words of my mouth are
        righteous;
        there is nothing twisted or
            crooked in them.
9   They are all straight to one who
        understands
        and right to those who find
            knowledge.
10 Take my instruction instead of
        silver,
        and knowledge rather than
            choice gold;
11 for wisdom is better than jewels,
        and all that you may desire
            cannot compare with her.
12 I, wisdom, live with prudence,^{s}
        and I attain knowledge and
            discretion.
13 The fear of the LORD is hatred of
        evil.
        Pride and arrogance and the way of
            evil
        and perverted speech I hate.

O LORD OUR GOD, GRANT US GRACE TO DESIRE
THEE WITH OUR WHOLE HEART; THAT SO DESIR-
ING, WE MAY SEEK, AND SEEKING, FIND THEE; AND
SO FINDING THEE, MAY LOVE THEE; AND LOVING
THEE, MAY HATE THOSE SINS FROM WHICH THOU
HAST REDEEMED US. AMEN.   —Anselm

---

14 I have good advice and sound
        wisdom;
        I have insight, I have strength.
15 By me kings reign,
        and rulers decree what is just;

16 by me rulers rule,
        and nobles, all who govern rightly.
17 I love those who love me,
        and those who seek me diligently
            find me.
18 Riches and honor are with me,
        enduring wealth and prosperity.
19 My fruit is better than gold, even
        fine gold,
        and my yield than choice silver.
20 I walk in the way of righteousness,
        along the paths of justice,
21 endowing with wealth those who
        love me,
        and filling their treasuries.

I NEVER KNEW ALL THERE WAS IN THE BIBLE UNTIL
I SPENT THOSE YEARS IN JAIL. I WAS CONSTANTLY
FINDING NEW TREASURES.   —John Bunyan

Wisdom's Part in Creation

22 The LORD created me at the
        beginning^t of his work,^{u}
        the first of his acts of long ago.
23 Ages ago I was set up,
        at the first, before the beginning
            of the earth.
24 When there were no depths I was
        brought forth,
        when there were no springs
            abounding with water.
25 Before the mountains had been
        shaped,
        before the hills, I was brought
            forth—
26 when he had not yet made earth
        and fields,^{s}
        or the world's first bits of soil.
27 When he established the heavens, I
        was there,
        when he drew a circle on the face
            of the deep,
28 when he made firm the skies above,
        when he established the
            fountains of the deep,
29 when he assigned to the sea its
        limit,
        so that the waters might not
            transgress his command,
        when he marked out the
            foundations of the earth,
30 then I was beside him, like a
        master worker;^{v}

---

^{s} Meaning of Heb uncertain ^{t} Or me as the beginning ^{u} Heb way ^{v} Another reading is little child

and I was daily his[w] delight,
    rejoicing before him always,
31 rejoicing in his inhabited world
    and delighting in the human
        race.

32 "And now, my children, listen to
        me:
    happy are those who keep my
        ways.
33 Hear instruction and be wise,
    and do not neglect it.
34 Happy is the one who listens to me,
    watching daily at my gates,
    waiting beside my doors.
35 For whoever finds me finds life
    and obtains favor from the LORD;

36 but those who miss me injure
        themselves;
    all who hate me love death."

Wisdom's Feast

9 Wisdom has built her house,
    she has hewn her seven pillars.
2 She has slaughtered her animals,
    she has mixed her wine,
    she has also set her table.
3 She has sent out her servant-girls,
    she calls
    from the highest places in the
        town,
4 "You that are simple, turn in
        here!"
    To those without sense she says,

w Gk: Heb lacks his

MONDAY

CONTINUE IN HIS PRESENCE
Brother Lawrence

VERSE: Proverbs 8.30   PASSAGE: Proverbs 8.27–31

here is no sweeter manner of living in the world than
continuous communion with God . . .
    If I were a preacher, I would preach nothing but prac-
ticing the presence of God. If I were to be responsible
for guiding souls in the right direction, I would urge everyone to
be aware of God's constant presence, if for no other reason than
because his presence is a delight to our souls and spirits.
    It is, however, also necessary. If we only knew how much we
need God's grace, we would never lose touch with him. Believe
me. Make a commitment never to deliberately stray from him,
to live the rest of your life in his holy presence. Don't do this in
expectation of receiving heavenly comforts; simply do it out of
love for him.
    Put your hand to the task! If you do it right, you will soon see
the results.

ADDITIONAL SCRIPTURE READING:
Joshua 18.6–10; 2 Chronicles 34.31; Romans 8.38–39

Go to page 727 for your next devotional reading.

1500   1700

5 "Come, eat of my bread
  and drink of the wine I have
    mixed.
6 Lay aside immaturity,[x] and live,
  and walk in the way of insight."

General Maxims

7 Whoever corrects a scoffer wins
    abuse;
  whoever rebukes the wicked gets
    hurt.
8 A scoffer who is rebuked will only
    hate you;
  the wise, when rebuked, will
    love you.
9 Give instruction[y] to the wise, and
    they will become wiser still;
  teach the righteous and they will
    gain in learning.
10 The fear of the LORD is the
    beginning of wisdom,
  and the knowledge of the Holy
    One is insight.
11 For by me your days will be
    multiplied,
  and years will be added to your
    life.
12 If you are wise, you are wise for
    yourself;
  if you scoff, you alone will bear it.

Folly's Invitation and Promise

13 The foolish woman is loud;
  she is ignorant and knows
    nothing.
14 She sits at the door of her house,
  on a seat at the high places of the
    town,
15 calling to those who pass by,
  who are going straight on their
    way,
16 "You who are simple, turn in here!"
  And to those without sense she
    says,
17 "Stolen water is sweet,
  and bread eaten in secret is
    pleasant."

CHARACTER IS WHAT YOU ARE IN THE DARK.
              —Dwight L. Moody

---

18 But they do not know that the
    dead[z] are there,

that her guests are in the depths
  of Sheol.

Wise Sayings of Solomon

10 The proverbs of Solomon.

A wise child makes a glad father,
  but a foolish child is a mother's
    grief.
2 Treasures gained by wickedness do
    not profit,
  but righteousness delivers from
    death.
3 The LORD does not let the
    righteous go hungry,
  but he thwarts the craving of the
    wicked.
4 A slack hand causes poverty,
  but the hand of the diligent
    makes rich.
5 A child who gathers in summer is
    prudent,
  but a child who sleeps in harvest
    brings shame.
6 Blessings are on the head of the
    righteous,
  but the mouth of the wicked
    conceals violence.
7 The memory of the righteous is a
    blessing,
  but the name of the wicked will
    rot.
8 The wise of heart will heed
    commandments,
  but a babbling fool will come to
    ruin.
9 Whoever walks in integrity walks
    securely,
  but whoever follows perverse
    ways will be found out.
10 Whoever winks the eye causes
    trouble,
  but the one who rebukes boldly
    makes peace.[a]
11 The mouth of the righteous is a
    fountain of life,
  but the mouth of the wicked
    conceals violence.
12 Hatred stirs up strife,
  but love covers all offenses.
13 On the lips of one who has
    understanding wisdom is
    found,
  but a rod is for the back of one
    who lacks sense.

---

x Or simpleness   y Heb lacks instruction   z Heb shades   a Gk: Heb but a babbling fool will
come to ruin

14 The wise lay up knowledge,
    but the babbling of a fool brings
      ruin near.
15 The wealth of the rich is their
      fortress;
    the poverty of the poor is their
      ruin.
16 The wage of the righteous leads to
      life,
    the gain of the wicked to sin.
17 Whoever heeds instruction is on
      the path to life,
    but one who rejects a rebuke goes
      astray.
18 Lying lips conceal hatred,
    and whoever utters slander is a
      fool.
19 When words are many,
      transgression is not lacking,
    but the prudent are restrained in
      speech.
20 The tongue of the righteous is
      choice silver;
    the mind of the wicked is of little
      worth.
21 The lips of the righteous feed many,
    but fools die for lack of sense.
22 The blessing of the LORD makes
      rich,
    and he adds no sorrow with it.[b]
23 Doing wrong is like sport to a fool,
    but wise conduct is pleasure to a
      person of understanding.
24 What the wicked dread will come
      upon them,
    but the desire of the righteous
      will be granted.
25 When the tempest passes, the
      wicked are no more,
    but the righteous are established
      forever.
26 Like vinegar to the teeth, and
      smoke to the eyes,
    so are the lazy to their
      employers.
27 The fear of the LORD prolongs life,
    but the years of the wicked will
      be short.
28 The hope of the righteous ends in
      gladness,
    but the expectation of the wicked
      comes to nothing.
29 The way of the LORD is a
      stronghold for the upright,
    but destruction for evildoers.

30 The righteous will never be
      removed,
    but the wicked will not remain
      in the land.
31 The mouth of the righteous brings
      forth wisdom,
    but the perverse tongue will be
      cut off.
32 The lips of the righteous know
      what is acceptable,
    but the mouth of the wicked
      what is perverse.

11

A false balance is an
abomination to the LORD,
    but an accurate weight is his
      delight.
2 When pride comes, then comes
      disgrace;
    but wisdom is with the humble.
3 The integrity of the upright guides
      them,
    but the crookedness of the
      treacherous destroys them.
4 Riches do not profit in the day of
      wrath,
    but righteousness delivers from
      death.
5 The righteousness of the blameless
      keeps their ways straight,
    but the wicked fall by their own
      wickedness.
6 The righteousness of the upright
      saves them,
    but the treacherous are taken
      captive by their schemes.
7 When the wicked die, their hope
      perishes,
    and the expectation of the
      godless comes to nothing.
8 The righteous are delivered from
      trouble,
    and the wicked get into it instead.
9 With their mouths the godless
      would destroy their
      neighbors,
    but by knowledge the righteous
      are delivered.
10 When it goes well with the
      righteous, the city rejoices;
    and when the wicked perish,
      there is jubilation.
11 By the blessing of the upright a city
      is exalted,
    but it is overthrown by the
      mouth of the wicked.

b Or *and toil adds nothing to it*

12 Whoever belittles another lacks
sense,
but an intelligent person remains
silent.

13 A gossip goes about telling secrets,
but one who is trustworthy in
spirit keeps a confidence.

14 Where there is no guidance, a
nation^c falls,
but in an abundance of
counselors there is safety.

15 To guarantee loans for a stranger
brings trouble,
but there is safety in refusing to
do so.

16 A gracious woman gets honor,
but she who hates virtue is
covered with shame.^d
The timid become destitute,^e
but the aggressive gain riches.

17 Those who are kind reward
themselves,
but the cruel do themselves
harm.

18 The wicked earn no real gain,
but those who sow righteousness
get a true reward.

19 Whoever is steadfast in
righteousness will live,
but whoever pursues evil will
die.

20 Crooked minds are an abomination
to the LORD,
but those of blameless ways are
his delight.

21 Be assured, the wicked will not go
unpunished,
but those who are righteous will
escape.

22 Like a gold ring in a pig's snout
is a beautiful woman without
good sense.

23 The desire of the righteous ends
only in good;
the expectation of the wicked in
wrath.

24 Some give freely, yet grow all the
richer;
others withhold what is due, and
only suffer want.

25 A generous person will be enriched,
and one who gives water will get
water.

26 The people curse those who hold
back grain,
but a blessing is on the head of
those who sell it.

27 Whoever diligently seeks good
seeks favor,
but evil comes to the one who
searches for it.

28 Those who trust in their riches will
wither,^f
but the righteous will flourish
like green leaves.

29 Those who trouble their
households will inherit
wind,
and the fool will be servant to
the wise.

30 The fruit of the righteous is a tree
of life,
but violence^g takes lives away.

31 If the righteous are repaid on earth,
how much more the wicked and
the sinner!

12 Whoever loves discipline
loves knowledge,
but those who hate to be rebuked
are stupid.

2 The good obtain favor from the
LORD,
but those who devise evil he
condemns.

3 No one finds security by
wickedness,
but the root of the righteous will
never be moved.

4 A good wife is the crown of her
husband,
but she who brings shame is like
rottenness in his bones.

5 The thoughts of the righteous are
just;
the advice of the wicked is
treacherous.

6 The words of the wicked are a
deadly ambush,
but the speech of the upright
delivers them.

7 The wicked are overthrown and are
no more,
but the house of the righteous
will stand.

8 One is commended for good sense,
but a perverse mind is despised.

---

c Or *an army*   d Compare Gk Syr: Heb lacks *but she . . . shame*   e Gk: Heb lacks *The timid . . .
destitute*   f Cn: Heb *fall*   g Cn Compare Gk Syr: Heb *a wise man*

9 Better to be despised and have a
    servant,
    than to be self-important and
    lack food.
10 The righteous know the needs of
    their animals,
    but the mercy of the wicked is
    cruel.

11 Those who till their land will have
    plenty of food,
    but those who follow worthless
    pursuits have no sense.
12 The wicked covet the proceeds of
    wickedness,*h*
    but the root of the righteous
    bears fruit.

h Or covet the catch of the wicked

TUESDAY

WHAT IS THE VIRTUE OF A HORSE?
Chrysostom

VERSE: Proverbs 11.28   **PASSAGE:** Proverbs 11.27–31

hat then is the virtue of a horse? is it to have a bridle studded with gold and girths to match, and a band of silken threads to fasten the housing, and clothes wrought in divers colors and gold tissue, and head gear studded with jewels, and locks of hair plaited with gold cord? or is it to be swift and strong in its legs, and even in its paces, and to have hoofs suitable to a well bred horse, and courage fitted for long journeys and warfare, and to be able to behave with calmness in the battlefield, and if a rout takes place to save its rider? Is it not manifest that these are the things which constitute the virtue of the horse, not the others? . . . Well, let us act in the same way in the case of human beings also: let us determine what is the virtue of man, and let us regard that alone as an injury, which is destructive to it. What then is the virtue of man? not riches that thou shouldest fear poverty: nor health of body that thou shouldest dread sickness, nor the opinion of the public, that thou shouldest view an evil reputation with alarm, nor life simply for its own sake, that death should be terrible to thee: nor liberty that thou shouldest avoid servitude: but carefulness in holding true doctrine, and rectitude in life. Of these things not even the devil himself will be able to rob a man, if he who possesses them guards them with the needful carefulness.

ADDITIONAL SCRIPTURE READING:
Psalms 20.7; 33.16–17; Jeremiah 17.5–7

Go to page 730 for your next devotional reading.

100   500

13 The evil are ensnared by the
transgression of their lips,
but the righteous escape from
trouble.
14 From the fruit of the mouth one is
filled with good things,
and manual labor has its reward.
15 Fools think their own way is right,
but the wise listen to advice.
16 Fools show their anger at once,
but the prudent ignore an insult.

AN INSULT IS EITHER SUSTAINED OR DESTROYED,
NOT BY THE DISPOSITION OF THOSE WHO INSULT,
BUT IN THE DISPOSITION OF THOSE WHO BEAR IT.

—*John Chrysostom*

---

17 Whoever speaks the truth gives
honest evidence,
but a false witness speaks
deceitfully.
18 Rash words are like sword thrusts,
but the tongue of the wise brings
healing.
19 Truthful lips endure forever,
but a lying tongue lasts only a
moment.
20 Deceit is in the mind of those who
plan evil,
but those who counsel peace
have joy.
21 No harm happens to the righteous,
but the wicked are filled with
trouble.
22 Lying lips are an abomination to
the LORD,
but those who act faithfully are
his delight.
23 One who is clever conceals
knowledge,
but the mind of a fool[i] broadcasts
folly.
24 The hand of the diligent will rule,
while the lazy will be put to
forced labor.
25 Anxiety weighs down the human
heart,
but a good word cheers it up.
26 The righteous gives good advice to
friends,[j]
but the way of the wicked leads
astray.

27 The lazy do not roast[k] their game,
but the diligent obtain precious
wealth.[k]
28 In the path of righteousness there is
life,
in walking its path there is no
death.

13 A wise child loves discipline,[l]
but a scoffer does not listen
to rebuke.
2 From the fruit of their words good
persons eat good things,
but the desire of the treacherous
is for wrongdoing.
3 Those who guard their mouths
preserve their lives;
those who open wide their lips
come to ruin.
4 The appetite of the lazy craves, and
gets nothing,
while the appetite of the diligent
is richly supplied.
5 The righteous hate falsehood,
but the wicked act shamefully
and disgracefully.
6 Righteousness guards one whose
way is upright,
but sin overthrows the wicked.
7 Some pretend to be rich, yet have
nothing;
others pretend to be poor, yet
have great wealth.
8 Wealth is a ransom for a person's
life,
but the poor get no threats.
9 The light of the righteous rejoices,
but the lamp of the wicked goes
out.
10 By insolence the heedless make
strife,
but wisdom is with those who
take advice.
11 Wealth hastily gotten[m] will
dwindle,
but those who gather little by
little will increase it.
12 Hope deferred makes the heart sick,
but a desire fulfilled is a tree of
life.
13 Those who despise the word bring
destruction on themselves,
but those who respect the
commandment will be
rewarded.

---

i Heb *the heart of fools*   *j* Syr: Meaning of Heb uncertain   *k* Meaning of Heb uncertain
l Cn: Heb *A wise child the discipline of his father*   *m* Gk Vg: Heb *from vanity*

14 The teaching of the wise is a
     fountain of life,
        so that one may avoid the snares
           of death.
15 Good sense wins favor,
        but the way of the faithless is
           their ruin.[n]
16 The clever do all things intelligently,
        but the fool displays folly.
17 A bad messenger brings trouble,
        but a faithful envoy, healing.
18 Poverty and disgrace are for the one
        who ignores instruction,
        but one who heeds reproof is
           honored.
19 A desire realized is sweet to the
        soul,
        but to turn away from evil is an
           abomination to fools.
20 Whoever walks with the wise
        becomes wise,
        but the companion of fools
           suffers harm.
21 Misfortune pursues sinners,
        but prosperity rewards the
           righteous.
22 The good leave an inheritance to
        their children's children,
        but the sinner's wealth is laid up
           for the righteous.
23 The field of the poor may yield
        much food,
        but it is swept away through
           injustice.
24 Those who spare the rod hate their
        children,
        but those who love them are
           diligent to discipline them.
25 The righteous have enough to
        satisfy their appetite,
        but the belly of the wicked is
           empty.

14 The wise woman[o] builds her
     house,
        but the foolish tears it down with
           her own hands.
2 Those who walk uprightly fear the
        LORD,
        but one who is devious in
           conduct despises him.
3 The talk of fools is a rod for their
        backs,[p]
        but the lips of the wise preserve
           them.

4 Where there are no oxen, there is
        no grain;
        abundant crops come by the
           strength of the ox.
5 A faithful witness does not lie,
        but a false witness breathes out
           lies.
6 A scoffer seeks wisdom in vain,
        but knowledge is easy for one
           who understands.
7 Leave the presence of a fool,
        for there you do not find words of
           knowledge.
8 It is the wisdom of the clever to
        understand where they go,
        but the folly of fools misleads.
9 Fools mock at the guilt offering,[q]
        but the upright enjoy God's favor.
10 The heart knows its own
        bitterness,
        and no stranger shares its joy.
11 The house of the wicked is
        destroyed,
        but the tent of the upright
           flourishes.
12 There is a way that seems right to a
        person,
        but its end is the way to death.[r]
13 Even in laughter the heart is sad,
        and the end of joy is grief.
14 The perverse get what their ways
        deserve,
        and the good, what their deeds
           deserve.[s]
15 The simple believe everything,
        but the clever consider their steps.
16 The wise are cautious and turn
        away from evil,
        but the fool throws off restraint
           and is careless.
17 One who is quick-tempered acts
        foolishly,
        and the schemer is hated.
18 The simple are adorned with[t] folly,
        but the clever are crowned with
           knowledge.
19 The evil bow down before the good,
        the wicked at the gates of the
           righteous.
20 The poor are disliked even by their
        neighbors,
        but the rich have many friends.
21 Those who despise their neighbors
        are sinners,

---

n Cn Compare Gk Syr Vg Tg: Heb *is enduring*   o Heb *Wisdom of women*   p Cn: Heb *a rod of pride*
q Meaning of Heb uncertain   r Heb *ways of death*   s Cn: Heb *from upon him*   t Or *inherit*

but happy are those who are kind
    to the poor.
22 Do they not err that plan evil?
    Those who plan good find loyalty
        and faithfulness.
23 In all toil there is profit,

but mere talk leads only to
    poverty.
24 The crown of the wise is their
    wisdom,[u]
    but folly is the garland[v] of fools.
25 A truthful witness saves lives,

u Cn Compare Gk: Heb *riches*   v Cn: Heb *is the folly*

WEDNESDAY

A BETTER RESURRECTION
Christina Rossetti

VERSE: Proverbs 14.10   **PASSAGE:** Proverbs 14.10, 13

 have no wit, no words, no tears;
    My heart within me like a stone
Is numbed too much for hopes or fears;
    Look right, look left, I dwell alone;
I lift mine eyes, but dimmed with grief
    No everlasting hills I see;
My life is in the falling leaf:
    O Jesus, quicken me.

My life is like a faded leaf,
    My harvest dwindled to a husk;
Truly my life is void and brief
    And tedious in the barren dusk;
My life is like a frozen thing,
    No bud nor greenness can I see:
Yet rise it shall—the sap of spring;
    O Jesus, rise in me.

My life is like a broken bowl,
    A broken bowl that cannot hold
One drop of water for my soul
    Or cordial in the searching cold;
Cast in the fire the perished thing,
    Melt and remold it, till it be
A royal cup for him my king:
    O Jesus, drink of me.

ADDITIONAL SCRIPTURE READING:
Job 23.10; Proverbs 17.3; Isaiah 64.8

Go to page 732 for your next devotional reading.

1700   1900

but one who utters lies is a
    betrayer.
26 In the fear of the LORD one has
    strong confidence,
    and one's children will have a
        refuge.
27 The fear of the LORD is a fountain
    of life,
    so that one may avoid the snares
        of death.
28 The glory of a king is a multitude
    of people;
    without people a prince is ruined.
29 Whoever is slow to anger has great
    understanding,
    but one who has a hasty temper
        exalts folly.
30 A tranquil mind gives life to the
    flesh,
    but passion makes the bones rot.
31 Those who oppress the poor insult
    their Maker,
    but those who are kind to the
        needy honor him.
32 The wicked are overthrown by
    their evildoing,
    but the righteous find a refuge in
        their integrity.w
33 Wisdom is at home in the mind of
    one who has understanding,
    but it is notx known in the heart
        of fools.
34 Righteousness exalts a nation,
    but sin is a reproach to any
        people.
35 A servant who deals wisely has the
    king's favor,
    but his wrath falls on one who
        acts shamefully.

15 A soft answer turns away
    wrath,
    but a harsh word stirs up anger.
2 The tongue of the wise dispenses
    knowledge,y
    but the mouths of fools pour out
        folly.
3 The eyes of the LORD are in every
    place,
    keeping watch on the evil and
        the good.
4 A gentle tongue is a tree of life,
    but perverseness in it breaks the
        spirit.
5 A fool despises a parent's
    instruction,

but the one who heeds
    admonition is prudent.
6 In the house of the righteous there
    is much treasure,
    but trouble befalls the income of
        the wicked.
7 The lips of the wise spread
    knowledge;
    not so the minds of fools.
8 The sacrifice of the wicked is an
    abomination to the LORD,
    but the prayer of the upright is
        his delight.
9 The way of the wicked is an
    abomination to the LORD,
    but he loves the one who pursues
        righteousness.
10 There is severe discipline for one
    who forsakes the way,
    but one who hates a rebuke will
        die.
11 Sheol and Abaddon lie open before
    the LORD,
    how much more human hearts!
12 Scoffers do not like to be rebuked;
    they will not go to the wise.
13 A glad heart makes a cheerful
    countenance,
    but by sorrow of heart the spirit
        is broken.
14 The mind of one who has
    understanding seeks
    knowledge,
    but the mouths of fools feed on
        folly.
15 All the days of the poor are hard,
    but a cheerful heart has a
        continual feast.

CHEERFULNESS IS NO SIN, NOR IS THERE ANY
GRACE IN A SOLEMN CAST OF COUNTENANCE.

—John Newton

---

16 Better is a little with the fear of the
    LORD
    than great treasure and trouble
        with it.
17 Better is a dinner of vegetables
    where love is
    than a fatted ox and hatred with
        it.
18 Those who are hot-tempered stir
    up strife,

---

w Gk Syr: Heb *in their death*   x Gk Syr: Heb lacks *not*   y Cn: Heb *makes knowledge good*

but those who are slow to anger
    calm contention.
19 The way of the lazy is overgrown
    with thorns,

but the path of the upright is a
    level highway.
20 A wise child makes a glad
    father,

THURSDAY

TOUCHING HEAVEN IN PRAYER
A. W. Tozer

VERSE: Proverbs 15.8   PASSAGE: Proverbs 15.6–9

oo many praying persons seek to use prayer as a means to ends that are not wholly pure. Prayer is often conceived to be little more than a technique for self-advancement, a heavenly method of achieving earthly success.

Every kind of personal religious project these days is being made the object of prayer. Some of these projects are unscriptural, or at least extrascriptural, and many of them have no higher motive than to relieve the promoter of the unpleasant task of earning an honest living . . .

The Scriptures are very clear about the place of prayer in the economy of God . . . "The prayer of the righteous is powerful and effective," wrote the inspired James (James 5.16) . . . With this the whole Bible and Christian experience agree: *Prayer is effective.* When it is not answered something is wrong.

The same apostle who affirmed the effective power of prayer admitted also that prayer is sometimes ineffective: "You ask and do not receive, because you ask wrongly, in order to spend what you get on your pleasures" (James 4.3).

Prayer that slavishly follows the day-by-day development of world news may quite easily be wasted. Most world events as reported by various news media are like ping-pong balls being batted back and forth. They are lively enough, they make an attention-getting racket, but they lack significance.

Surely the God who presides over history knows how few things matter. But he knows also what things do matter; and if we are spiritual enough to hear his voice he will lead us to engage in the kind of praying that will be effective.

ADDITIONAL SCRIPTURE READING:
1 Chronicles 29.17; Psalm 17.1; Proverbs 15.29

Go to page 736 for your next devotional reading.

1900   Present

but the foolish despise their mothers.

21 Folly is a joy to one who has no sense,
but a person of understanding walks straight ahead.

22 Without counsel, plans go wrong,
but with many advisers they succeed.

23 To make an apt answer is a joy to anyone,
and a word in season, how good it is!

24 For the wise the path of life leads upward,
in order to avoid Sheol below.

25 The LORD tears down the house of the proud,
but maintains the widow's boundaries.

26 Evil plans are an abomination to the LORD,
but gracious words are pure.

27 Those who are greedy for unjust gain make trouble for their households,
but those who hate bribes will live.

28 The mind of the righteous ponders how to answer,
but the mouth of the wicked pours out evil.

29 The LORD is far from the wicked,
but he hears the prayer of the righteous.

30 The light of the eyes rejoices the heart,
and good news refreshes the body.

31 The ear that heeds wholesome admonition
will lodge among the wise.

32 Those who ignore instruction despise themselves,
but those who heed admonition gain understanding.

33 The fear of the LORD is instruction in wisdom,
and humility goes before honor.

16 The plans of the mind belong to mortals,
but the answer of the tongue is from the LORD.

2 All one's ways may be pure in one's own eyes,
but the LORD weighs the spirit.

3 Commit your work to the LORD,
and your plans will be established.

4 The LORD has made everything for its purpose,
even the wicked for the day of trouble.

5 All those who are arrogant are an abomination to the LORD;
be assured, they will not go unpunished.

6 By loyalty and faithfulness iniquity is atoned for,
and by the fear of the LORD one avoids evil.

7 When the ways of people please the LORD,
he causes even their enemies to be at peace with them.

WE MUST LEARN TO LIVE TOGETHER AS BROTHERS OR PERISH TOGETHER AS FOOLS.

—*Martin Luther King, Jr.*

---

8 Better is a little with righteousness
than large income with injustice.

9 The human mind plans the way,
but the LORD directs the steps.

10 Inspired decisions are on the lips of a king;
his mouth does not sin in judgment.

11 Honest balances and scales are the LORD's;
all the weights in the bag are his work.

12 It is an abomination to kings to do evil,
for the throne is established by righteousness.

13 Righteous lips are the delight of a king,
and he loves those who speak what is right.

14 A king's wrath is a messenger of death,
and whoever is wise will appease it.

15 In the light of a king's face there is life,
and his favor is like the clouds that bring the spring rain.

16 How much better to get wisdom than gold!
To get understanding is to be chosen rather than silver.

17 The highway of the upright avoids evil;

those who guard their way
    preserve their lives.
18 Pride goes before destruction,
    and a haughty spirit before a fall.
19 It is better to be of a lowly spirit
        among the poor
    than to divide the spoil with the
        proud.
20 Those who are attentive to a
        matter will prosper,
    and happy are those who trust in
        the LORD.
21 The wise of heart is called
        perceptive,
    and pleasant speech increases
        persuasiveness.
22 Wisdom is a fountain of life to one
        who has it,
    but folly is the punishment of
        fools.
23 The mind of the wise makes their
        speech judicious,
    and adds persuasiveness to their
        lips.
24 Pleasant words are like a
        honeycomb,
    sweetness to the soul and health
        to the body.
25 Sometimes there is a way that
        seems to be right,
    but in the end it is the way to
        death.
26 The appetite of workers works for
        them;
    their hunger urges them on.
27 Scoundrels concoct evil,
    and their speech is like a
        scorching fire.
28 A perverse person spreads strife,
    and a whisperer separates close
        friends.
29 The violent entice their neighbors,
    and lead them in a way that is
        not good.
30 One who winks the eyes plans[z]
        perverse things;
    one who compresses the lips
        brings evil to pass.
31 Gray hair is a crown of glory;
    it is gained in a righteous life.
32 One who is slow to anger is better
        than the mighty,
    and one whose temper is
        controlled than one who
        captures a city.

33 The lot is cast into the lap,
    but the decision is the LORD's
        alone.

17 Better is a dry morsel with
        quiet
    than a house full of feasting with
        strife.
2   A slave who deals wisely will rule
        over a child who acts
        shamefully,
    and will share the inheritance as
        one of the family.
3   The crucible is for silver, and the
        furnace is for gold,
    but the LORD tests the heart.
4   An evildoer listens to wicked lips;
    and a liar gives heed to a
        mischievous tongue.
5   Those who mock the poor insult
        their Maker;
    those who are glad at calamity
        will not go unpunished.
6   Grandchildren are the crown of the
        aged,
    and the glory of children is their
        parents.
7   Fine speech is not becoming to a
        fool;
    still less is false speech to a ruler.[a]
8   A bribe is like a magic stone in the
        eyes of those who give it;
    wherever they turn they prosper.
9   One who forgives an affront fosters
        friendship,
    but one who dwells on disputes
        will alienate a friend.
10 A rebuke strikes deeper into a
        discerning person
    than a hundred blows into a fool.
11 Evil people seek only rebellion,
    but a cruel messenger will be
        sent against them.
12 Better to meet a she-bear robbed of
        its cubs
    than to confront a fool immersed
        in folly.
13 Evil will not depart from the house
        of one who returns evil for good.
14 The beginning of strife is like
        letting out water;
    so stop before the quarrel breaks
        out.
15 One who justifies the wicked and
        one who condemns the
        righteous

z Gk Syr Vg Tg: Heb *to plan*   a Or *a noble person*

are both alike an abomination to
the LORD.

16 Why should fools have a price in
hand
to buy wisdom, when they have
no mind to learn?

17 A friend loves at all times,
and kinsfolk are born to share
adversity.

18 It is senseless to give a pledge,
to become surety for a neighbor.

19 One who loves transgression loves
strife;
one who builds a high threshold
invites broken bones.

20 The crooked of mind do not
prosper,
and the perverse of tongue fall
into calamity.

21 The one who begets a fool gets
trouble;
the parent of a fool has no joy.

22 A cheerful heart is a good
medicine,
but a downcast spirit dries up the
bones.

23 The wicked accept a concealed
bribe
to pervert the ways of justice.

24 The discerning person looks to
wisdom,
but the eyes of a fool to the ends
of the earth.

25 Foolish children are a grief to their
father
and bitterness to her who bore
them.

26 To impose a fine on the innocent is
not right,
or to flog the noble for their
integrity.

27 One who spares words is
knowledgeable;
one who is cool in spirit has
understanding.

28 Even fools who keep silent are
considered wise;
when they close their lips, they
are deemed intelligent.

18 The one who lives alone is
self-indulgent,
showing contempt for all who
have sound judgment. b

2 A fool takes no pleasure in
understanding,
but only in expressing personal
opinion.

3 When wickedness comes,
contempt comes also;
and with dishonor comes
disgrace.

4 The words of the mouth are deep
waters;
the fountain of wisdom is a
gushing stream.

5 It is not right to be partial to the
guilty,
or to subvert the innocent in
judgment.

6 A fool's lips bring strife,
and a fool's mouth invites a
flogging.

7 The mouths of fools are their ruin,
and their lips a snare to
themselves.

8 The words of a whisperer are like
delicious morsels;
they go down into the inner parts
of the body.

9 One who is slack in work
is close kin to a vandal.

10 The name of the LORD is a strong
tower;
the righteous run into it and are
safe.

11 The wealth of the rich is their
strong city;
in their imagination it is like a
high wall.

12 Before destruction one's heart is
haughty,
but humility goes before honor.

13 If one gives answer before hearing,
it is folly and shame.

14 The human spirit will endure
sickness;
but a broken spirit—who can
bear?

15 An intelligent mind acquires
knowledge,
and the ear of the wise seeks
knowledge.

16 A gift opens doors;
it gives access to the great.

17 The one who first states a case
seems right,
until the other comes and cross-
examines.

18 Casting the lot puts an end to
disputes

b Meaning of Heb uncertain

and decides between powerful contenders.

19 An ally offended is stronger than a city;*c*
such quarreling is like the bars of a castle.

20 From the fruit of the mouth one's stomach is satisfied;
the yield of the lips brings satisfaction.

21 Death and life are in the power of the tongue,
and those who love it will eat its fruits.

22 He who finds a wife finds a good thing,
and obtains favor from the LORD.

23 The poor use entreaties,
but the rich answer roughly.

24 Some*d* friends play at friendship*e*
but a true friend sticks closer than one's nearest kin.

19 Better the poor walking in integrity
than one perverse of speech who is a fool.

2 Desire without knowledge is not good,

c Gk Syr Vg Tg: Meaning of Heb uncertain   *d* Syr Tg: Heb *A man of*   *e* Cn Compare Syr Vg Tg: Meaning of Heb uncertain

---

FRIDAY

TRUSTWORTHY FRIENDSHIP
Charles Kingsley

VERSE: Proverbs 18.24   PASSAGE: Proverbs 18

 blessed thing it is for any man or woman to have a friend; one human soul whom we can trust utterly; who knows the best and the worst of us, and who loves us, in spite of our faults: who will speak the honest truth to us, while the world flatters us to our faces, and laughs at us behind our backs; who will give us counsel and reproof in the day of prosperity and self conceit; but who, again will comfort and encourage us in the day of difficulty and sorrow, when the world leaves us alone to fight our own battles as we can.

If we have had the good fortune to win such a friend, let us do anything rather than lose him. We must give and forgive; live and let live. If our friends have faults we must bear with them. We must hope all things, believe all things, endure all things rather than lose that most precious of all earthly possessions—a trusty friend. And a friend once won, need never be lost, if we will only be trusty and true ourselves.

ADDITIONAL SCRIPTURE READING:
2 Samuel 9.1–13; Proverbs 17.17; John 15.14–15

Go to page 739 for your next devotional reading.

1700   1900

and one who moves too hurriedly
   misses the way.
3 One's own folly leads to ruin,
   yet the heart rages against the
      LORD.
4 Wealth brings many friends,
   but the poor are left friendless.
5 A false witness will not go
     unpunished,
   and a liar will not escape.
6 Many seek the favor of the generous,
   and everyone is a friend to a giver
     of gifts.
7 If the poor are hated even by their
     kin,
   how much more are they
     shunned by their friends!
   When they call after them, they are
     not there.*f*
8 To get wisdom is to love oneself;
   to keep understanding is to
     prosper.
9 A false witness will not go
     unpunished,
   and the liar will perish.
10 It is not fitting for a fool to live in
     luxury,
   much less for a slave to rule over
     princes.
11 Those with good sense are slow to
     anger,
   and it is their glory to overlook
     an offense.
12 A king's anger is like the growling
     of a lion,
   but his favor is like dew on the
     grass.
13 A stupid child is ruin to a father,
   and a wife's quarreling is a
     continual dripping of rain.
14 House and wealth are inherited
     from parents,
   but a prudent wife is from the
     LORD.
15 Laziness brings on deep sleep;
   an idle person will suffer hunger.
16 Those who keep the
     commandment will live;
   those who are heedless of their
     ways will die.
17 Whoever is kind to the poor lends
     to the LORD,
   and will be repaid in full.
18 Discipline your children while
     there is hope;

do not set your heart on their
   destruction.
19 A violent tempered person will pay
     the penalty;
   if you effect a rescue, you will
     only have to do it again.*f*
20 Listen to advice and accept
     instruction,
   that you may gain wisdom for
     the future.
21 The human mind may devise many
     plans,
   but it is the purpose of the LORD
     that will be established.

MAN PROPOSES BUT GOD DISPOSES.
   —*Thomas à Kempis*

---

22 What is desirable in a person is
     loyalty,
   and it is better to be poor than a
     liar.
23 The fear of the LORD is life indeed;
   filled with it one rests secure
   and suffers no harm.
24 The lazy person buries a hand in
     the dish,
   and will not even bring it back to
     the mouth.
25 Strike a scoffer, and the simple will
     learn prudence;
   reprove the intelligent, and they
     will gain knowledge.
26 Those who do violence to their
     father and chase away their
     mother
   are children who cause shame
     and bring reproach.
27 Cease straying, my child, from the
     words of knowledge,
   in order that you may hear
     instruction.
28 A worthless witness mocks at
     justice,
   and the mouth of the wicked
     devours iniquity.
29 Condemnation is ready for scoffers,
   and flogging for the backs of
     fools.

20 Wine is a mocker, strong
     drink a brawler,
   and whoever is led astray by it is
     not wise.

f Meaning of Heb uncertain

2 The dread anger of a king is like the
     growling of a lion;
   anyone who provokes him to
     anger forfeits life itself.
3 It is honorable to refrain from
     strife,
   but every fool is quick to quarrel.
4 The lazy person does not plow in
     season;
   harvest comes, and there is
     nothing to be found.
5 The purposes in the human mind
     are like deep water,
   but the intelligent will draw
     them out.
6 Many proclaim themselves loyal,
   but who can find one worthy of
     trust?
7 The righteous walk in integrity—
   happy are the children who
     follow them!
8 A king who sits on the throne of
     judgment
   winnows all evil with his eyes.
9 Who can say, "I have made my
     heart clean;
   I am pure from my sin"?
10 Diverse weights and diverse
     measures
   are both alike an abomination to
     the LORD.
11 Even children make themselves
     known by their acts,
   by whether what they do is pure
     and right.
12 The hearing ear and the seeing eye—
   the LORD has made them both.
13 Do not love sleep, or else you will
     come to poverty;
   open your eyes, and you will
     have plenty of bread.
14 "Bad, bad," says the buyer,
   then goes away and boasts.
15 There is gold, and abundance of
     costly stones;
   but the lips informed by
     knowledge are a precious
     jewel.
16 Take the garment of one who has
     given surety for a stranger;
   seize the pledge given as surety
     for foreigners.
17 Bread gained by deceit is sweet,
   but afterward the mouth will be
     full of gravel.

18 Plans are established by taking
     advice;
   wage war by following wise
     guidance.
19 A gossip reveals secrets;
   therefore do not associate with a
     babbler.
20 If you curse father or mother,
   your lamp will go out in utter
     darkness.
21 An estate quickly acquired in the
     beginning
   will not be blessed in the end.
22 Do not say, "I will repay evil";
   wait for the LORD, and he will
     help you.
23 Differing weights are an
     abomination to the LORD,
   and false scales are not good.
24 All our steps are ordered by the
     LORD;
   how then can we understand our
     own ways?
25 It is a snare for one to say rashly,
     "It is holy,"
   and begin to reflect only after
     making a vow.
26 A wise king winnows the wicked,
   and drives the wheel over them.
27 The human spirit is the lamp of the
     LORD,
   searching every inmost part.
28 Loyalty and faithfulness preserve
     the king,
   and his throne is upheld by
     righteousness.g
29 The glory of youths is their
     strength,
   but the beauty of the aged is their
     gray hair.
30 Blows that wound cleanse away
     evil;
   beatings make clean the
     innermost parts.

21 The king's heart is a stream of
     water in the hand of the LORD;
   he turns it wherever he will.
2 All deeds are right in the sight of
     the doer,
   but the LORD weighs the heart.
3 To do righteousness and justice
   is more acceptable to the LORD
     than sacrifice.
4 Haughty eyes and a proud heart—
   the lamp of the wicked—are sin.

g Gk: Heb *loyalty*

WEEKEND

THE LOOM OF TIME
Author Unknown

VERSE: Proverbs 20.24   **PASSAGE:** Proverbs 20

an's life is laid in the loom of time
　　To a pattern he does not see,
While the weavers work and the shuttles fly
　　Till the dawn of eternity.

Some shuttles are filled with silver threads
　　And some with threads of gold,
While often but the darker hues
　　Are all that they may hold.

But the weaver watches with skillful eye
　　Each shuttle fly to and fro,
And sees the pattern so deftly wrought
　　As the loom moves sure and slow.

God surely planned the pattern:
　　Each thread, the dark and fair,
Is chosen by his master skill
　　And placed in the web with care.

He only knows its beauty,
　　And guides the shuttles which hold
The threads so unattractive,
　　As well as the threads of gold.

Not till each loom is silent
　　And the shuttles cease to fly,
Shall God reveal the pattern
　　And explain the reason why

The dark threads were as needful
　　In the weaver's skillful hand
As the threads of gold and silver
　　For the pattern which he planned.

ADDITIONAL SCRIPTURE READING:
Psalm 37.23; Jeremiah 10.23; Acts 17.28

Go to page 741 for your next devotional reading.

5 The plans of the diligent lead
surely to abundance,
but everyone who is hasty comes
only to want.

6 The getting of treasures by a lying
tongue
is a fleeting vapor and a snare[h] of
death.

7 The violence of the wicked will
sweep them away,
because they refuse to do what is
just.

8 The way of the guilty is crooked,
but the conduct of the pure is
right.

9 It is better to live in a corner of the
housetop
than in a house shared with a
contentious wife.

10 The souls of the wicked desire evil;
their neighbors find no mercy in
their eyes.

11 When a scoffer is punished, the
simple become wiser;
when the wise are instructed,
they increase in knowledge.

12 The Righteous One observes the
house of the wicked;
he casts the wicked down to ruin.

13 If you close your ear to the cry of
the poor,
you will cry out and not be heard.

14 A gift in secret averts anger;
and a concealed bribe in the
bosom, strong wrath.

15 When justice is done, it is a joy to
the righteous,
but dismay to evildoers.

16 Whoever wanders from the way of
understanding
will rest in the assembly of the
dead.

17 Whoever loves pleasure will suffer
want;
whoever loves wine and oil will
not be rich.

18 The wicked is a ransom for the
righteous,
and the faithless for the upright.

19 It is better to live in a desert land
than with a contentious and
fretful wife.

20 Precious treasure remains[i] in the
house of the wise,

but the fool devours it.

21 Whoever pursues righteousness
and kindness
will find life[j] and honor.

22 One wise person went up against a
city of warriors
and brought down the stronghold
in which they trusted.

23 To watch over mouth and tongue
is to keep out of trouble.

24 The proud, haughty person, named
"Scoffer,"
acts with arrogant pride.

25 The craving of the lazy person is
fatal,
for lazy hands refuse to labor.

26 All day long the wicked covet,[k]
but the righteous give and do not
hold back.

27 The sacrifice of the wicked is an
abomination;
how much more when brought
with evil intent.

28 A false witness will perish,
but a good listener will testify
successfully.

29 The wicked put on a bold face,
but the upright give thought to[l]
their ways.

30 No wisdom, no understanding, no
counsel,
can avail against the LORD.

31 The horse is made ready for the day
of battle,
but the victory belongs to the
LORD.

22 A good name is to be chosen
rather than great riches,
and favor is better than silver or
gold.

IT IS NOT THE BRAINS THAT MATTER MOST, BUT
THAT WHICH GUIDES THEM—THE CHARACTER,
THE HEART, GENEROUS QUALITIES, PROGRESSIVE
IDEAS.
                            —*Fyodor Dostoyevsky*

---

2 The rich and the poor have this in
common:
the LORD is the maker of them all.

3 The clever see danger and hide;
but the simple go on, and suffer
for it.

---

h Gk: Heb seekers   i Gk: Heb and oil   j Gk: Heb life and righteousness   k Gk: Heb all day long
one covets covetously   l Another reading is establish

4 The reward for humility and fear of
 the LORD
 is riches and honor and life.
5 Thorns and snares are in the way of
 the perverse;
 the cautious will keep far from
 them.
6 Train children in the right way,

and when old, they will not
 stray.
7 The rich rule over the poor,
 and the borrower is the slave of
 the lender.
8 Whoever sows injustice will reap
 calamity,
 and the rod of anger will fail.

MONDAY

THE HERB CALLED "HEARTS-EASE"
John Bunyan

VERSE: Proverbs 22.4   **PASSAGES:** Proverbs 15.33; 18.12

 ow as they were going along and talking, they espied a boy feeding his father's sheep. The boy was in very mean clothes, but of a very fresh and well-favored countenance, and as he sat by himself he sang. Hark, said Mr. Greatheart, to what the shepherd's boy saith. So they hearkened, and he said:

He that is down needs fear no fall,
 He that is low no pride:
He that is humble ever shall
 Have God to be his guide.

I am content with what I have,
 Little be it or much:
And, Lord, contentment still I crave,
 Because thou savest such.

Fullness to such a burden is
 That go on pilgrimage:
Here little, and hereafter bliss,
 Is best from age to age.

Then said their guide, Do you hear him? I will dare to say that this boy lives a merrier life, and wears more of that herb called hearts-ease in his bosom, than he that is clad in silk and velvet.

ADDITIONAL SCRIPTURE READING:
Philippians 4.11–13; 1 Timothy 6.6–8

Go to page 748 for your next devotional reading.

1500   1700

9　Those who are generous are blessed,
　　for they share their bread with
　　the poor.

10　Drive out a scoffer, and strife goes
　　out;
　　quarreling and abuse will cease.

11　Those who love a pure heart and
　　are gracious in speech
　　will have the king as a friend.

12　The eyes of the LORD keep watch
　　over knowledge,
　　but he overthrows the words of
　　the faithless.

13　The lazy person says, "There is a
　　lion outside!
　　I shall be killed in the streets!"

14　The mouth of a loose[m] woman is a
　　deep pit;
　　he with whom the LORD is angry
　　falls into it.

15　Folly is bound up in the heart of a
　　boy,
　　but the rod of discipline drives it
　　far away.

16　Oppressing the poor in order to
　　enrich oneself,
　　and giving to the rich, will lead
　　only to loss.

Sayings of the Wise

17　　The words of the wise:

　　Incline your ear and hear my
　　words,[n]
　　and apply your mind to my
　　teaching;

18　for it will be pleasant if you keep
　　them within you,
　　if all of them are ready on your
　　lips.

19　So that your trust may be in the
　　LORD,
　　I have made them known to you
　　today—yes, to you.

20　Have I not written for you thirty
　　sayings
　　of admonition and knowledge,

21　to show you what is right and true,
　　so that you may give a true answer
　　to those who sent you?

22　Do not rob the poor because they
　　are poor,
　　or crush the afflicted at the gate;

23　for the LORD pleads their cause
　　and despoils of life those who
　　despoil them.

24　Make no friends with those given
　　to anger,
　　and do not associate with
　　hotheads,

25　or you may learn their ways
　　and entangle yourself in a snare.

26　Do not be one of those who give
　　pledges,
　　who become surety for debts.

27　If you have nothing with which to
　　pay,
　　why should your bed be taken
　　from under you?

28　Do not remove the ancient
　　landmark
　　that your ancestors set up.

29　Do you see those who are skillful
　　in their work?
　　They will serve kings;
　　they will not serve common
　　people.

23　When you sit down to eat
　　with a ruler,
　　observe carefully what[o] is before
　　you,

2　and put a knife to your throat
　　if you have a big appetite.

3　Do not desire the ruler's[p] delicacies,
　　for they are deceptive food.

4　Do not wear yourself out to get rich;
　　be wise enough to desist.

5　When your eyes light upon it, it is
　　gone;
　　for suddenly it takes wings to
　　itself,
　　flying like an eagle toward heaven.

6　Do not eat the bread of the stingy;
　　do not desire their delicacies;

7　for like a hair in the throat, so are
　　they.[q]
　　"Eat and drink!" they say to you;
　　but they do not mean it.

8　You will vomit up the little you
　　have eaten,
　　and you will waste your pleasant
　　words.

9　Do not speak in the hearing of a
　　fool,
　　who will only despise the
　　wisdom of your words.

---

m Heb strange　n Cn Compare Gk: Heb Incline your ear, and hear the words of the wise　o Or who
p Heb his　q Meaning of Heb uncertain

10 Do not remove an ancient landmark
   or encroach on the fields of
      orphans;
11 for their redeemer is strong;
   he will plead their cause against
      you.
12 Apply your mind to instruction
   and your ear to words of
      knowledge.
13 Do not withhold discipline from
   your children;
   if you beat them with a rod, they
      will not die.
14 If you beat them with the rod,
   you will save their lives from
      Sheol.
15 My child, if your heart is wise,
   my heart too will be glad.
16 My soul will rejoice
   when your lips speak what is
      right.
17 Do not let your heart envy sinners,
   but always continue in the fear of
      the LORD.
18 Surely there is a future,
   and your hope will not be cut off.

19 Hear, my child, and be wise,
   and direct your mind in the way.
20 Do not be among winebibbers,
   or among gluttonous eaters of
      meat;
21 for the drunkard and the glutton
   will come to poverty,
   and drowsiness will clothe them
      with rags.

22 Listen to your father who begot
      you,
   and do not despise your mother
      when she is old.
23 Buy truth, and do not sell it;
   buy wisdom, instruction, and
      understanding.
24 The father of the righteous will
      greatly rejoice;
   he who begets a wise son will be
      glad in him.
25 Let your father and mother be glad;
   let her who bore you rejoice.

26 My child, give me your heart,
   and let your eyes observe[r] my
      ways.

27 For a prostitute is a deep pit;
   an adulteress[s] is a narrow well.
28 She lies in wait like a robber
   and increases the number of the
      faithless.

29 Who has woe? Who has sorrow?
   Who has strife? Who has
      complaining?
   Who has wounds without cause?
   Who has redness of eyes?
30 Those who linger late over wine,
   those who keep trying mixed
      wines.
31 Do not look at wine when it is red,
   when it sparkles in the cup
   and goes down smoothly.
32 At the last it bites like a serpent,
   and stings like an adder.
33 Your eyes will see strange things,
   and your mind utter perverse
      things.
34 You will be like one who lies down
      in the midst of the sea,
   like one who lies on the top of a
      mast.[t]
35 "They struck me," you will say,[u]
   "but I was not hurt;
   they beat me, but I did not feel it.
   When shall I awake?
   I will seek another drink."

24 Do not envy the wicked,
   nor desire to be with them;
2 for their minds devise violence,
   and their lips talk of mischief.

3 By wisdom a house is built,
   and by understanding it is
      established;
4 by knowledge the rooms are filled
   with all precious and pleasant
      riches.
5 Wise warriors are mightier than
      strong ones,[v]
   and those who have knowledge
      than those who have
      strength;
6 for by wise guidance you can wage
      your war,
   and in abundance of counselors
      there is victory.
7 Wisdom is too high for fools;
   in the gate they do not open their
      mouths.

r Another reading is *delight in*   s Heb *an alien woman*   t Meaning of Heb uncertain   u Gk Syr
Vg Tg: Heb lacks *you will say*   v Gk Compare Syr Tg: Heb *A wise man is strength*

8   Whoever plans to do evil
        will be called a mischief-maker.
9   The devising of folly is sin,
        and the scoffer is an abomination
            to all.

10 If you faint in the day of adversity,
        your strength being small;
11 if you hold back from rescuing
            those taken away to death,
        those who go staggering to the
            slaughter;
12 if you say, "Look, we did not know
            this"—
        does not he who weighs the heart
            perceive it?
    Does not he who keeps watch over
            your soul know it?
        And will he not repay all
            according to their deeds?

13 My child, eat honey, for it is good,
        and the drippings of the
            honeycomb are sweet to
            your taste.
14 Know that wisdom is such to your
            soul;
        if you find it, you will find a
            future,
        and your hope will not be cut off.

15 Do not lie in wait like an outlaw
            against the home of the
            righteous;
        do no violence to the place where
            the righteous live;
16 for though they fall seven times,
            they will rise again;
        but the wicked are overthrown
            by calamity.

17 Do not rejoice when your enemies
            fall,
        and do not let your heart be glad
            when they stumble,
18 or else the LORD will see it and be
            displeased,
        and turn away his anger from
            them.

19 Do not fret because of evildoers.
        Do not envy the wicked;
20 for the evil have no future;
        the lamp of the wicked will go
            out.

21 My child, fear the LORD and the
            king,
        and do not disobey either of
            them; w
22 for disaster comes from them
            suddenly,
        and who knows the ruin that
            both can bring?

Further Sayings of the Wise

23   These also are sayings of the wise:

    Partiality in judging is not good.
24 Whoever says to the wicked, "You
            are innocent,"
        will be cursed by peoples,
            abhorred by nations;
25 but those who rebuke the wicked
            will have delight,
        and a good blessing will come
            upon them.
26 One who gives an honest answer
        gives a kiss on the lips.

27 Prepare your work outside,
        get everything ready for you in
            the field;
        and after that build your house.

28 Do not be a witness against your
            neighbor without cause,
        and do not deceive with your lips.
29 Do not say, "I will do to others as
            they have done to me;
        I will pay them back for what
            they have done."

30 I passed by the field of one who was
            lazy,
        by the vineyard of a stupid
            person;
31 and see, it was all overgrown with
            thorns;
        the ground was covered with
            nettles,
        and its stone wall was broken
            down.
32 Then I saw and considered it;
        I looked and received instruction.
33 A little sleep, a little slumber,
        a little folding of the hands to
            rest,
34 and poverty will come upon you
            like a robber,
        and want, like an armed warrior.

w Gk: Heb *do not associate with those who change*

Further Wise Sayings of Solomon

25 These are other proverbs of Solomon that the officials of King Hezekiah of Judah copied.

2 It is the glory of God to conceal
    things,
  but the glory of kings is to search
    things out.
3 Like the heavens for height, like
    the earth for depth,
  so the mind of kings is
    unsearchable.
4 Take away the dross from the
    silver,
  and the smith has material for a
    vessel;
5 take away the wicked from the
    presence of the king,
  and his throne will be established
    in righteousness.
6 Do not put yourself forward in the
    king's presence
  or stand in the place of the great;
7 for it is better to be told, "Come up
    here,"
  than to be put lower in the
    presence of a noble.

  What your eyes have seen
8   do not hastily bring into court;
  for^x what will you do in the end,
    when your neighbor puts you to
    shame?
9 Argue your case with your
    neighbor directly,
  and do not disclose another's
    secret;
10 or else someone who hears you will
    bring shame upon you,
  and your ill repute will have no
    end.

11 A word fitly spoken
  is like apples of gold in a setting
    of silver.
12 Like a gold ring or an ornament of
    gold
  is a wise rebuke to a listening
    ear.
13 Like the cold of snow in the time of
    harvest
  are faithful messengers to those
    who send them;

  they refresh the spirit of their
    masters.
14 Like clouds and wind without rain
  is one who boasts of a gift never
    given.
15 With patience a ruler may be
    persuaded,
  and a soft tongue can break bones.
16 If you have found honey, eat only
    enough for you,
  or else, having too much, you
    will vomit it.
17 Let your foot be seldom in your
    neighbor's house,
  otherwise the neighbor will
    become weary of you and
    hate you.
18 Like a war club, a sword, or a sharp
    arrow
  is one who bears false witness
    against a neighbor.
19 Like a bad tooth or a lame foot
  is trust in a faithless person in
    time of trouble.
20 Like vinegar on a wound^y
  is one who sings songs to a heavy
    heart.
  Like a moth in clothing or a worm
    in wood,
  sorrow gnaws at the human
    heart.^z
21 If your enemies are hungry, give
    them bread to eat;
  and if they are thirsty, give them
    water to drink;
22 for you will heap coals of fire on
    their heads,
  and the LORD will reward you.
23 The north wind produces rain,
  and a backbiting tongue, angry
    looks.
24 It is better to live in a corner of the
    housetop
  than in a house shared with a
    contentious wife.
25 Like cold water to a thirsty soul,
  so is good news from a far
    country.
26 Like a muddied spring or a polluted
    fountain
  are the righteous who give way
    before the wicked.
27 It is not good to eat much honey,
  or to seek honor on top of honor.

x Cn: Heb or else   y Gk: Heb Like one who takes off a garment on a cold day, like vinegar on lye
z Gk Syr Tg: Heb lacks Like a moth . . . human heart

28 Like a city breached, without walls,
is one who lacks self-control.

26 Like snow in summer or rain
in harvest,
so honor is not fitting for a fool.

2 Like a sparrow in its flitting, like a
swallow in its flying,
an undeserved curse goes
nowhere.

3 A whip for the horse, a bridle for
the donkey,
and a rod for the back of fools.

4 Do not answer fools according to
their folly,
or you will be a fool yourself.

5 Answer fools according to their
folly,
or they will be wise in their own
eyes.

6 It is like cutting off one's foot and
drinking down violence,
to send a message by a fool.

7 The legs of a disabled person hang
limp;
so does a proverb in the mouth of
a fool.

8 It is like binding a stone in a sling
to give honor to a fool.

9 Like a thornbush brandished by the
hand of a drunkard
is a proverb in the mouth of a
fool.

10 Like an archer who wounds
everybody
is one who hires a passing fool or
drunkard.[a]

11 Like a dog that returns to its vomit
is a fool who reverts to his folly.

12 Do you see persons wise in their
own eyes?
There is more hope for fools than
for them.

13 The lazy person says, "There is a
lion in the road!
There is a lion in the streets!"

14 As a door turns on its hinges,
so does a lazy person in bed.

15 The lazy person buries a hand in
the dish,
and is too tired to bring it back to
the mouth.

16 The lazy person is wiser in self-
esteem
than seven who can answer
discreetly.

17 Like somebody who takes a passing
dog by the ears
is one who meddles in the
quarrel of another.

18 Like a maniac who shoots deadly
firebrands and arrows,

19 so is one who deceives a neighbor
and says, "I am only joking!"

20 For lack of wood the fire goes out,
and where there is no whisperer,
quarreling ceases.

21 As charcoal is to hot embers and
wood to fire,
so is a quarrelsome person for
kindling strife.

22 The words of a whisperer are like
delicious morsels;
they go down into the inner parts
of the body.

23 Like the glaze[b] covering an earthen
vessel
are smooth[c] lips with an evil
heart.

24 An enemy dissembles in speaking
while harboring deceit within;

25 when an enemy speaks graciously,
do not believe it,
for there are seven abominations
concealed within;

26 though hatred is covered with
guile,
the enemy's wickedness will be
exposed in the assembly.

SOME PEOPLE ARE CONTENT NOT TO DO MEAN
ACTIONS; I WANT TO BECOME INCAPABLE OF A
MEAN THOUGHT OR FEELING.

—*George MacDonald*

---

27 Whoever digs a pit will fall into it,
and a stone will come back on
the one who starts it rolling.

28 A lying tongue hates its victims,
and a flattering mouth works
ruin.

27 Do not boast about tomorrow,
for you do not know what a
day may bring.

2 Let another praise you, and not
your own mouth—
a stranger, and not your own lips.

3 A stone is heavy, and sand is
weighty,

---

a Meaning of Heb uncertain   *b* Cn: Heb *silver of dross*   *c* Gk: Heb *burning*

but a fool's provocation is heavier
than both.

4 Wrath is cruel, anger is
overwhelming,
but who is able to stand before
jealousy?

5 Better is open rebuke
than hidden love.

6 Well meant are the wounds a friend
inflicts,
but profuse are the kisses of an
enemy.

7 The sated appetite spurns honey,
but to a ravenous appetite even
the bitter is sweet.

8 Like a bird that strays from its nest
is one who strays from home.

9 Perfume and incense make the
heart glad,
but the soul is torn by trouble.*d*

10 Do not forsake your friend or the
friend of your parent;
do not go to the house of your
kindred in the day of your
calamity.
Better is a neighbor who is nearby
than kindred who are far away.

11 Be wise, my child, and make my
heart glad,
so that I may answer whoever
reproaches me.

12 The clever see danger and hide;
but the simple go on, and suffer
for it.

13 Take the garment of one who has
given surety for a stranger;
seize the pledge given as surety
for foreigners.*e*

14 Whoever blesses a neighbor with a
loud voice,
rising early in the morning,
will be counted as cursing.

15 A continual dripping on a rainy day
and a contentious wife are alike;

16 to restrain her is to restrain the wind
or to grasp oil in the right hand.*f*

17 Iron sharpens iron,
and one person sharpens the
wits*g* of another.

18 Anyone who tends a fig tree will
eat its fruit,
and anyone who takes care of a
master will be honored.

19 Just as water reflects the face,
so one human heart reflects
another.

20 Sheol and Abaddon are never
satisfied,
and human eyes are never
satisfied.

21 The crucible is for silver, and the
furnace is for gold,
so a person is tested*h* by being
praised.

22 Crush a fool in a mortar with a
pestle
along with crushed grain,
but the folly will not be driven
out.

23 Know well the condition of your
flocks,
and give attention to your herds;

24 for riches do not last forever,
nor a crown for all generations.

25 When the grass is gone, and new
growth appears,
and the herbage of the mountains
is gathered,

26 the lambs will provide your
clothing,
and the goats the price of a field;

27 there will be enough goats' milk for
your food,
for the food of your household
and nourishment for your
servant-girls.

28

The wicked flee when no one
pursues,
but the righteous are as bold as a
lion.

2 When a land rebels
it has many rulers;
but with an intelligent ruler
there is lasting order.*f*

3 A ruler*i* who oppresses the poor
is a beating rain that leaves no
food.

4 Those who forsake the law praise
the wicked,
but those who keep the law
struggle against them.

5 The evil do not understand justice,
but those who seek the LORD
understand it completely.

---

d Gk: Heb *the sweetness of a friend is better than one's own counsel*   *e* Vg and 20.16: Heb *for a foreign woman*   *f* Meaning of Heb uncertain   *g* Heb *face*   *h* Heb lacks *is tested*   *i* Cn: Heb *A poor person*

6 Better to be poor and walk in
  integrity
  than to be crooked in one's ways
  even though rich.

7 Those who keep the law are wise
  children,
  but companions of gluttons
  shame their parents.

TUESDAY

HOLY BOLDNESS
Charles H. Spurgeon

VERSE: Proverbs 28.1   **PASSAGE:** Proverbs 28

---

 oly boldness honors the gospel. In the olden times, when Oriental despots had things pretty much their own way, they expected all ambassadors from the West to lay their mouths in the dust if permitted to appear before . . . the [Emperor]. Money-loving traders agreed to all this and ate dust as readily as reptiles, but when England sent her ambassadors abroad, the daring islanders stood bolt upright. They were told that they could not be indulged with a vision of the [Emperor] without going down on their hands and knees. "Very well," said the Englishmen, " . . . But tell his Celestial Splendor that it is very likely that his serenity will hear our cannon at his palace gates before long, and that their booming is not quite so harmless as the cooing of his sublimity's doves." The ambassadors of the British Crown were no cringing petitioners; [and] the British empire rose in the respect of the Oriental nations.

Our cowardice has subjected the gospel to contempt. Jesus was humble, and his servants must not be proud, but Jesus was never mean or cowardly, nor must his servants be. There was no braver man than Christ. He could stoop to save a soul, but he would stoop to nothing by which his character might be compromised, or truth and righteousness insulted. To preach the gospel boldly is to deliver it as such a message ought to be delivered. Blush to preach of a dying Savior? Apologize for talking about the Son of God condescending to be made man, that he might redeem us from all iniquity? *Never!* Oh, by the grace of God let us purpose with Paul "to be yet more bold," that the gospel may be yet more fully preached throughout all ranks of mankind.

ADDITIONAL SCRIPTURE READING:
Psalms 27.1–2; 46.2–3; Acts 4.13

Go to page 754 for your next devotional reading.

1700   1900

8 One who augments wealth by
    exorbitant interest
  gathers it for another who is kind
    to the poor.

9 When one will not listen to the law,
  even one's prayers are an
    abomination.

10 Those who mislead the upright
    into evil ways
  will fall into pits of their own
    making,
  but the blameless will have a
    goodly inheritance.

11 The rich is wise in self-esteem,
  but an intelligent poor person
    sees through the pose.

12 When the righteous triumph, there
    is great glory,
  but when the wicked prevail,
    people go into hiding.

13 No one who conceals
    transgressions will prosper,
  but one who confesses and
    forsakes them will obtain
    mercy.

14 Happy is the one who is never
    without fear,
  but one who is hard-hearted will
    fall into calamity.

15 Like a roaring lion or a charging
    bear
  is a wicked ruler over a poor
    people.

16 A ruler who lacks understanding is
    a cruel oppressor;
  but one who hates unjust gain
    will enjoy a long life.

17 If someone is burdened with the
    blood of another,
  let that killer be a fugitive until
    death;
  let no one offer assistance.

18 One who walks in integrity will be
    safe,
  but whoever follows crooked
    ways will fall into the Pit. *j*

19 Anyone who tills the land will
    have plenty of bread,
  but one who follows worthless
    pursuits will have plenty of
    poverty.

20 The faithful will abound with
    blessings,
  but one who is in a hurry to be
    rich will not go unpunished.

21 To show partiality is not good—
  yet for a piece of bread a person
    may do wrong.

22 The miser is in a hurry to get rich
  and does not know that loss is
    sure to come.

23 Whoever rebukes a person will
    afterward find more favor
  than one who flatters with the
    tongue.

24 Anyone who robs father or mother
  and says, "That is no crime,"
  is partner to a thug.

25 The greedy person stirs up strife,
  but whoever trusts in the LORD
    will be enriched.

26 Those who trust in their own wits
    are fools;
  but those who walk in wisdom
    come through safely.

27 Whoever gives to the poor will lack
    nothing,
  but one who turns a blind eye
    will get many a curse.

28 When the wicked prevail, people go
    into hiding;
  but when they perish, the
    righteous increase.

29 One who is often reproved,
    yet remains stubborn,
  will suddenly be broken beyond
    healing.

2 When the righteous are in
    authority, the people rejoice;
  but when the wicked rule, the
    people groan.

3 A child who loves wisdom makes a
    parent glad,
  but to keep company with
    prostitutes is to squander
    one's substance.

4 By justice a king gives stability to
    the land,
  but one who makes heavy
    exactions ruins it.

5 Whoever flatters a neighbor
  is spreading a net for the
    neighbor's feet.

6 In the transgression of the evil
    there is a snare,
  but the righteous sing and rejoice.

7 The righteous know the rights of
    the poor;
  the wicked have no such
    understanding.

j Syr: Heb *fall all at once*

8 Scoffers set a city aflame,
   but the wise turn away wrath.
9 If the wise go to law with fools,
   there is ranting and ridicule
     without relief.
10 The bloodthirsty hate the
     blameless,
   and they seek the life of the
     upright.
11 A fool gives full vent to anger,
   but the wise quietly holds it
     back.
12 If a ruler listens to falsehood,
   all his officials will be wicked.
13 The poor and the oppressor have
     this in common:
   the LORD gives light to the eyes
     of both.
14 If a king judges the poor with
     equity,
   his throne will be established
     forever.
15 The rod and reproof give wisdom,
   but a mother is disgraced by a
     neglected child.
16 When the wicked are in authority,
     transgression increases,
   but the righteous will look upon
     their downfall.
17 Discipline your children, and they
     will give you rest;
   they will give delight to your
     heart.
18 Where there is no prophecy, the
     people cast off restraint,
   but happy are those who keep the
     law.
19 By mere words servants are not
     disciplined,
   for though they understand, they
     will not give heed.
20 Do you see someone who is hasty
     in speech?
   There is more hope for a fool
     than for anyone like that.
21 A slave pampered from childhood
   will come to a bad end. k
22 One given to anger stirs up strife,
   and the hothead causes much
     transgression.
23 A person's pride will bring
     humiliation,
   but one who is lowly in spirit
     will obtain honor.

24 To be a partner of a thief is to hate
     one's own life;
   one hears the victim's curse, but
     discloses nothing. l
25 The fear of others m lays a snare,
   but one who trusts in the LORD is
     secure.
26 Many seek the favor of a ruler,
   but it is from the LORD that one
     gets justice.
27 The unjust are an abomination to
     the righteous,
   but the upright are an
     abomination to the wicked.

Sayings of Agur

30 The words of Agur son of
   Jakeh. An oracle.

Thus says the man: I am weary,
     O God,
   I am weary, O God. How can I
     prevail? n
2 Surely I am too stupid to be
     human;
   I do not have human
     understanding.
3 I have not learned wisdom,
   nor have I knowledge of the holy
     ones. o
4 Who has ascended to heaven and
     come down?
   Who has gathered the wind in
     the hollow of the hand?
   Who has wrapped up the waters in
     a garment?
   Who has established all the ends
     of the earth?
   What is the person's name?
   And what is the name of the
     person's child?
   Surely you know!

5 Every word of God proves true;
   he is a shield to those who take
     refuge in him.
6 Do not add to his words,
   or else he will rebuke you, and
     you will be found a liar.

7 Two things I ask of you;
   do not deny them to me before I
     die:

k Vg: Meaning of Heb uncertain   l Meaning of Heb uncertain   m Or human fear   n Or I am
spent. Meaning of Heb uncertain   o Or Holy One

8   Remove far from me falsehood and
        lying;
    give me neither poverty nor
        riches;
    feed me with the food that I
        need,
9   or I shall be full, and deny you,
        and say, "Who is the LORD?"
    or I shall be poor, and steal,
        and profane the name of my God.

10 Do not slander a servant to a
        master,
    or the servant will curse you, and
        you will be held guilty.

11 There are those who curse their
        fathers
    and do not bless their mothers.
12 There are those who are pure in
        their own eyes
    yet are not cleansed of their
        filthiness.
13 There are those—how lofty are
        their eyes,
    how high their eyelids lift!—
14 there are those whose teeth are
        swords,
    whose teeth are knives,
    to devour the poor from off the
        earth,
    the needy from among mortals.

15 The leech[p] has two daughters;
    "Give, give," they cry.
    Three things are never satisfied;
    four never say, "Enough":
16 Sheol, the barren womb,
    the earth ever thirsty for water,
    and the fire that never says,
        "Enough."[p]

17 The eye that mocks a father
    and scorns to obey a mother
    will be pecked out by the ravens of
        the valley
    and eaten by the vultures.

18 Three things are too wonderful for
        me;
    four I do not understand:
19 the way of an eagle in the sky,
    the way of a snake on a rock,
    the way of a ship on the high seas,
    and the way of a man with a girl.

20 This is the way of an adulteress:
    she eats, and wipes her mouth,
    and says, "I have done no
        wrong."

21 Under three things the earth
        trembles;
    under four it cannot bear up:
22 a slave when he becomes king,
    and a fool when glutted with
        food;
23 an unloved woman when she gets a
        husband,
    and a maid when she succeeds
        her mistress.

24 Four things on earth are small,
    yet they are exceedingly wise:
25 the ants are a people without
        strength,
    yet they provide their food in the
        summer;
26 the badgers are a people without
        power,
    yet they make their homes in the
        rocks;
27 the locusts have no king,
    yet all of them march in rank;
28 the lizard[q] can be grasped in the
        hand,
    yet it is found in kings' palaces.

29 Three things are stately in their
        stride;
    four are stately in their gait:
30 the lion, which is mightiest among
        wild animals
    and does not turn back before
        any;
31 the strutting rooster,[r] the he-goat,
    and a king striding before[p] his
        people.

32 If you have been foolish, exalting
        yourself,
    or if you have been devising evil,
    put your hand on your mouth.
33 For as pressing milk produces
        curds,
    and pressing the nose produces
        blood,
    so pressing anger produces strife.

p Meaning of Heb uncertain   q Or spider   r Gk Syr Tg Compare Vg: Meaning of Heb uncertain

The Teaching of King Lemuel's Mother

31 The words of King Lemuel. An oracle that his mother taught him:

2 No, my son! No, son of my womb!
 No, son of my vows!
3 Do not give your strength to women,
  your ways to those who destroy kings.
4 It is not for kings, O Lemuel,
  it is not for kings to drink wine,
  or for rulers to desire*s* strong drink;
5 or else they will drink and forget what has been decreed,
  and will pervert the rights of all the afflicted.
6 Give strong drink to one who is perishing,
  and wine to those in bitter distress;
7 let them drink and forget their poverty,
  and remember their misery no more.
8 Speak out for those who cannot speak,
  for the rights of all the destitute.*t*
9 Speak out, judge righteously,
  defend the rights of the poor and needy.

Ode to a Capable Wife

10 A capable wife who can find?
  She is far more precious than jewels.
11 The heart of her husband trusts in her,
  and he will have no lack of gain.
12 She does him good, and not harm,
  all the days of her life.
13 She seeks wool and flax,
  and works with willing hands.
14 She is like the ships of the merchant,
  she brings her food from far away.
15 She rises while it is still night
  and provides food for her household
  and tasks for her servant-girls.

16 She considers a field and buys it;
  with the fruit of her hands she plants a vineyard.
17 She girds herself with strength,
  and makes her arms strong.
18 She perceives that her merchandise is profitable.
  Her lamp does not go out at night.
19 She puts her hands to the distaff,
  and her hands hold the spindle.
20 She opens her hand to the poor,
  and reaches out her hands to the needy.
21 She is not afraid for her household when it snows,
  for all her household are clothed in crimson.
22 She makes herself coverings;
  her clothing is fine linen and purple.
23 Her husband is known in the city gates,
  taking his seat among the elders of the land.
24 She makes linen garments and sells them;
  she supplies the merchant with sashes.
25 Strength and dignity are her clothing,
  and she laughs at the time to come.
26 She opens her mouth with wisdom,
  and the teaching of kindness is on her tongue.
27 She looks well to the ways of her household,
  and does not eat the bread of idleness.
28 Her children rise up and call her happy;
  her husband too, and he praises her:
29 "Many women have done excellently,
  but you surpass them all."
30 Charm is deceitful, and beauty is vain,
  but a woman who fears the LORD is to be praised.
31 Give her a share in the fruit of her hands,
  and let her works praise her in the city gates.

s Cn: Heb *where*   *t* Heb *all children of passing away*

ECCLESIASTES

THIS BOOK TEACHES THAT LIFE NOT CENTERED ON GOD IS PURPOSELESS AND MEANINGLESS. WITHOUT GOD, NOTHING CAN SATISFY (2.25). WITH HIM, ALL OF LIFE AND HIS GOOD GIFTS ARE TO BE GRATEFULLY RECEIVED AND USED AND ENJOYED TO THE FULL (2.26; 11.8). AS YOU READ THIS BOOK, YOU WILL CONFRONT HONEST CONFESSIONS OF DOUBTS AND STRUGGLES WITH DISILLUSIONMENT. THINK ABOUT YOUR OWN SENSE OF PURPOSE AS YOU SEEK TO CULTIVATE A GOD-FEARING ATTITUDE TOWARD LIFE.

Reflections of a Royal Philosopher

 1 The words of the Teacher,[a] the son of David, king in Jerusalem.

2 Vanity of vanities, says the Teacher,[a]
vanity of vanities! All is vanity.

3 What do people gain from all the toil
at which they toil under the sun?

4 A generation goes, and a generation comes,
but the earth remains forever.

5 The sun rises and the sun goes down,
and hurries to the place where it rises.

6 The wind blows to the south,
and goes around to the north;
round and round goes the wind,
and on its circuits the wind returns.

7 All streams run to the sea,
but the sea is not full;
to the place where the streams flow,
there they continue to flow.

8 All things[b] are wearisome;
more than one can express;
the eye is not satisfied with seeing,
or the ear filled with hearing.

9 What has been is what will be,
and what has been done is what will be done;
there is nothing new under the sun.

10 Is there a thing of which it is said,
"See, this is new"?

a Heb *Qoheleth*, traditionally rendered *Preacher*   b Or *words*

It has already been,
    in the ages before us.
11 The people of long ago are not
        remembered,

nor will there be any
    remembrance
of people yet to come
    by those who come after them.

WEDNESDAY

THE CONSECRATION OF TIME
Thomas Merton

VERSE: Ecclesiastes 1.9   PASSAGE: Ecclesiastes 1.1–11

 he fundamental theme of Ecclesiastes is the paradox that, although there is "nothing new under the sun," each new generation of mankind is condemned by nature to wear itself out in the pursuit of "novelties" that do not exist. This concept . . . contains in itself the one great enigma of paganism. Only Christ, only the incarnation, by which God emerged from his eternity to enter into time and consecrate it to himself, could save time from being an endless circle of frustrations. Only Christianity can, in Saint Paul's phrase, "redeem the times." Other religions can break out of the wheel of time as though from a prison: but they can make nothing of time itself.

Saint Gregory of Nyssa, pursuing his meditations on the psychology of attachment and illusion, vision and detachment, which constitute his commentary on Ecclesiastes, observes how time weaves about us this web of illusion. It is not enough to say that the man who is attached to this world has bound himself to it, once and for all, by a wrong choice. No: he spins a whole net of falsities around his spirit by the repeated consecration of his whole self to values that do not exist. He exhausts himself in the pursuit of mirages that ever fade and are renewed as fast as they have faded, drawing him further and further into the wilderness where he must die of thirst . . .

And so, that "vanity of vanities" which so exercised the ancient preacher of Ecclesiastes and his commentator is a life not merely of deluded thoughts and aspirations, but above all a life of ceaseless and sterile activity. What is more, in such a life the measure of illusion is the very intensity of activity itself. The less you have, the more you do. The final delusion is movement, change, and variety for their own sakes alone.

ADDITIONAL SCRIPTURE READING:
Psalm 39.5–6; Ecclesiastes 6.10

Go to page 757 for your next devotional reading.

1900   Present

The Futility of Seeking Wisdom

12 I, the Teacher,*c* when king over Israel in Jerusalem, 13applied my mind to seek and to search out by wisdom all that is done under heaven; it is an unhappy business that God has given to human beings to be busy with. 14I saw all the deeds that are done under the sun; and see, all is vanity and a chasing after wind.*d*

15   What is crooked cannot be made
            straight,
        and what is lacking cannot be
            counted.

16 I said to myself, "I have acquired great wisdom, surpassing all who were over Jerusalem before me; and my mind has had great experience of wisdom and knowledge." 17And I applied my mind to know wisdom and to know madness and folly. I perceived that this also is but a chasing after wind.*d*

18   For in much wisdom is much
            vexation,
        and those who increase knowledge
            increase sorrow.

The Futility of Self-Indulgence

2 I said to myself, "Come now, I will make a test of pleasure; enjoy yourself." But again, this also was vanity. 2I said of laughter, "It is mad," and of pleasure, "What use is it?" 3I searched with my mind how to cheer my body with wine—my mind still guiding me with wisdom—and how to lay hold on folly, until I might see what was good for mortals to do under heaven during the few days of their life. 4I made great works; I built houses and planted vineyards for myself; 5I made myself gardens and parks, and planted in them all kinds of fruit trees. 6I made myself pools from which to water the forest of growing trees. 7I bought male and female slaves, and had slaves who were born in my house; I also had great possessions of herds and flocks, more than any who had been before me in Jerusalem. 8I also gathered for myself silver and gold and the treasure of kings and of the provinces; I got singers, both men and women, and delights of the flesh, and many concubines.*e*

9 So I became great and surpassed all who were before me in Jerusalem; also my wisdom remained with me. 10Whatever my eyes desired I did not keep from them; I kept my heart from no pleasure, for my heart found pleasure in all my toil, and this was my reward for all my toil. 11Then I considered all that my hands had done and the toil I had spent in doing it, and again, all was vanity and a chasing after wind,*d* and there was nothing to be gained under the sun.

Wisdom and Joy Given to One Who Pleases God

12 So I turned to consider wisdom and madness and folly; for what can the one do who comes after the king? Only what has already been done. 13Then I saw that wisdom excels folly as light excels darkness.

14   The wise have eyes in their head,
        but fools walk in darkness.

Yet I perceived that the same fate befalls all of them. 15Then I said to myself, "What happens to the fool will happen to me also; why then have I been so very wise?" And I said to myself that this also is vanity. 16For there is no enduring remembrance of the wise or of fools, seeing that in the days to come all will have been long forgotten. How can the wise die just like fools? 17So I hated life, because what is done under the sun was grievous to me; for all is vanity and a chasing after wind.*d*

18 I hated all my toil in which I had toiled under the sun, seeing that I must leave it to those who come after me 19—and who knows whether they will be wise or foolish? Yet they will be master of all for which I toiled and used my wisdom under the sun. This also is vanity. 20So I turned and gave my heart up to despair concerning all the toil of my labors under the sun, 21because sometimes one who has toiled with wisdom and knowledge and skill must leave all to be enjoyed by another who did not toil for it. This also is vanity and a great evil. 22What do mortals get from all the toil and strain with which they toil under the sun? 23For all their days are full of pain, and their work is a vexation;

---

c Heb *Qoheleth*, traditionally rendered *Preacher* of Heb uncertain   *d* Or *a feeding on wind.* See Hos 12.1   *e* Meaning even at night their minds do not rest. This also is vanity.

24 There is nothing better for mortals than to eat and drink, and find enjoyment in their toil. This also, I saw, is from the hand of God; 25for apart from him*f* who can eat or who can have enjoyment? 26For to the one who pleases him God gives wisdom and knowledge and joy; but to the sinner he gives the work of gathering and heaping, only to give to one who pleases God. This also is vanity and a chasing after wind.*g*

Everything Has Its Time

3 For everything there is a season, and a time for every matter under heaven:

2 a time to be born, and a time to die;
   a time to plant, and a time to pluck
      up what is planted;
3 a time to kill, and a time to heal;
   a time to break down, and a time to
      build up;
4 a time to weep, and a time to laugh;
   a time to mourn, and a time to
      dance;
5 a time to throw away stones, and a
      time to gather stones
      together;
   a time to embrace, and a time to
      refrain from embracing;
6 a time to seek, and a time to lose;
   a time to keep, and a time to throw
      away;
7 a time to tear, and a time to sew;
   a time to keep silence, and a time
      to speak;
8 a time to love, and a time to hate;
   a time for war, and a time for
      peace.

The God-Given Task

9 What gain have the workers from their toil? 10I have seen the business that God has given to everyone to be busy with. 11He has made everything suitable for its time; moreover he has put a sense of past and future into their minds, yet they cannot find out what God has done from the beginning to the end. 12I know that there is nothing better for them than to be happy and enjoy themselves as long as they live; 13moreover, it is God's gift that all should eat and drink and take pleasure in all their toil. 14I know that whatever God does endures forever; nothing can be added to it, nor anything taken from it; God has done this, so that all should stand in awe before him. 15That which is, already has been; that which is to be, already is; and God seeks out what has gone by.*h*

Judgment and the Future Belong to God

16 Moreover I saw under the sun that in the place of justice, wickedness was there, and in the place of righteousness, wickedness was there as well. 17I said in my heart, God will judge the righteous and the wicked, for he has appointed a time for every matter, and for every work. 18I said in my heart with regard to human beings that God is testing them to show that they are but animals. 19For the fate of humans and the fate of animals is the same; as one dies, so dies the other. They all have the same breath, and humans have no advantage over the animals; for all is vanity. 20All go to one place; all are from the dust, and all turn to dust again. 21Who knows whether the human spirit goes upward and the spirit of animals goes downward to the earth? 22So I saw that there is nothing better than that all should enjoy their work, for that is their lot; who can bring them to see what will be after them?

4 Again I saw all the oppressions that are practiced under the sun. Look, the tears of the oppressed— with no one to comfort them! On the side of their oppressors there was power—with no one to comfort them. 2And I thought the dead, who have already died, more fortunate than the living, who are still alive; 3but better than both is the one who has not yet been, and has not seen the evil deeds that are done under the sun.

4 Then I saw that all toil and all skill in work come from one person's envy of another. This also is vanity and a chasing after wind.*g*

5 Fools fold their hands
      and consume their own flesh.
6 Better is a handful with quiet
      than two handfuls with toil,
      and a chasing after wind.*g*

---

f Gk Syr: Heb *apart from me*　　*g* Or *a feeding on wind.* See Hos 12.1　　*h* Heb *what is pursued*

PREFACES FOR SEASONS
Book of Common Prayer

VERSE: Ecclesiastes 3.1   **PASSAGE:** Ecclesiastes 3.1–8

Advent

 ecause thou didst send thy beloved Son to redeem us from sin and death, and to make us heirs in him of everlasting life; that when he shall come again in power and great triumph to judge the world, we may without shame or fear rejoice to behold his appearing.

Incarnation

Because thou didst give Jesus Christ, thine only Son, to be born for us; who, by the mighty power of the Holy Ghost, was made very man of the substance of the Virgin Mary his mother; that we might be delivered from the bondage of sin, and receive power to become thy children.

Easter

But chiefly are we bound to praise thee for the glorious resurrection of thy Son Jesus Christ our Lord; for he is the very paschal lamb, who was sacrificed for us, and hath taken away the sin of the world; who by his death hath destroyed death, and by his rising to life again hath won for us everlasting life.

Ascension

Through thy dearly beloved son Jesus Christ our Lord; who after his glorious resurrection manifestly appeared to his disciples; and in their sight ascended into heaven, to prepare a place for us; that where he is, there we might also be, and reign with him in glory.

Pentecost

Through Jesus Christ our Lord; according to whose true promise the Holy Ghost came down [on this day] from heaven, lighting upon the disciples, to teach them and to lead them into all truth; uniting peoples of many tongues in the confession of one faith, and giving to thy church the power to serve thee as a royal priesthood, and to preach the Gospel to all nations.

ADDITIONAL SCRIPTURE READING:
Ecclesiastes 8.5–6; Song of Solomon 2.12

Go to page 760 for your next devotional reading.

1700   1900

7 Again, I saw vanity under the sun:
8the case of solitary individuals, without
sons or brothers; yet there is no end to
all their toil, and their eyes are never
satisfied with riches. "For whom am I
toiling," they ask, "and depriving myself of pleasure?" This also is vanity and
an unhappy business.

The Value of a Friend

9 Two are better than one, because
they have a good reward for their toil.
10For if they fall, one will lift up the
other; but woe to one who is alone and
falls and does not have another to help.
11Again, if two lie together, they keep
warm; but how can one keep warm
alone? 12And though one might prevail
against another, two will withstand one.
A threefold cord is not quickly broken.

13 Better is a poor but wise youth
than an old but foolish king, who will
no longer take advice. 14One can indeed
come out of prison to reign, even though
born poor in the kingdom. 15I saw all the
living who, moving about under the
sun, follow that*i* youth who replaced the
king;*j* 16there was no end to all those
people whom he led. Yet those who
come later will not rejoice in him. Surely this also is vanity and a chasing after
wind.*k*

Reverence, Humility,
and Contentment

5 *l* Guard your steps when you go
to the house of God; to draw
near to listen is better than the sacrifice
offered by fools; for they do not know
how to keep from doing evil.*m* 2*n*Never
be rash with your mouth, nor let your
heart be quick to utter a word before
God, for God is in heaven, and you upon
earth; therefore let your words be few.

3 For dreams come with many cares,
and a fool's voice with many words.

4 When you make a vow to God, do
not delay fulfilling it; for he has no pleasure in fools. Fulfill what you vow. 5It is
better that you should not vow than
that you should vow and not fulfill it.
6Do not let your mouth lead you into
sin, and do not say before the messenger
that it was a mistake; why should God

be angry at your words, and destroy the
work of your hands?

7 With many dreams come vanities
and a multitude of words;*o* but fear God.

8 If you see in a province the oppression of the poor and the violation of justice and right, do not be amazed at the
matter; for the high official is watched
by a higher, and there are yet higher
ones over them. 9But all things considered, this is an advantage for a land: a
king for a plowed field.*o*

10 The lover of money will not be
satisfied with money; nor the lover of
wealth, with gain. This also is vanity.

11 When goods increase, those who
eat them increase; and what gain has
their owner but to see them with his
eyes?

12 Sweet is the sleep of laborers,
whether they eat little or much; but the
surfeit of the rich will not let them sleep.

13 There is a grievous ill that I have
seen under the sun: riches were kept by
their owners to their hurt, 14and those
riches were lost in a bad venture; though
they are parents of children, they have
nothing in their hands. 15As they came
from their mother's womb, so they shall
go again, naked as they came; they shall
take nothing for their toil, which they
may carry away with their hands. 16This
also is a grievous ill: just as they came, so
shall they go; and what gain do they have
from toiling for the wind? 17Besides, all
their days they eat in darkness, in much
vexation and sickness and resentment.

18 This is what I have seen to be
good: it is fitting to eat and drink and
find enjoyment in all the toil with
which one toils under the sun the few
days of the life God gives us; for this is
our lot. 19Likewise all to whom God
gives wealth and possessions and whom
he enables to enjoy them, and to accept
their lot and find enjoyment in their
toil—this is the gift of God. 20For they
will scarcely brood over the days of their
lives, because God keeps them occupied
with the joy of their hearts.

The Frustration of Desires

6 There is an evil that I have seen
under the sun, and it lies heavy

i Heb *the second*   *j* Heb *him*   *k* Or *a feeding on wind.* See Hos 12.1   *l* Ch 4.17 in Heb
m Cn: Heb *they do not know how to do evil*   *n* Ch 5.1 in Heb   *o* Meaning of Heb uncertain

upon humankind: 2those to whom God gives wealth, possessions, and honor, so that they lack nothing of all that they desire, yet God does not enable them to enjoy these things, but a stranger enjoys them. This is vanity; it is a grievous ill. 3A man may beget a hundred children, and live many years; but however many are the days of his years, if he does not enjoy life's good things, or has no burial, I say that a stillborn child is better off than he. 4For it comes into vanity and goes into darkness, and in darkness its name is covered; 5moreover it has not seen the sun or known anything; yet it finds rest rather than he. 6Even though he should live a thousand years twice over, yet enjoy no good—do not all go to one place?

7 All human toil is for the mouth, yet the appetite is not satisfied. 8For what advantage have the wise over fools? And what do the poor have who know how to conduct themselves before the living? 9Better is the sight of the eyes than the wandering of desire; this also is vanity and a chasing after wind.p

10 Whatever has come to be has already been named, and it is known what human beings are, and that they are not able to dispute with those who are stronger. 11The more words, the more vanity, so how is one the better? 12For who knows what is good for mortals while they live the few days of their vain life, which they pass like a shadow? For who can tell them what will be after them under the sun?

A Disillusioned View of Life

7 A good name is better than
precious ointment,
and the day of death, than the
day of birth.
2 It is better to go to the house of
mourning
than to go to the house of
feasting;
for this is the end of everyone,
and the living will lay it to heart.
3 Sorrow is better than laughter,
for by sadness of countenance the
heart is made glad.
4 The heart of the wise is in the
house of mourning;

but the heart of fools is in the
house of mirth.
5 It is better to hear the rebuke of the
wise
than to hear the song of fools.
6 For like the crackling of thorns
under a pot,
so is the laughter of fools;
this also is vanity.
7 Surely oppression makes the wise
foolish,
and a bribe corrupts the heart.
8 Better is the end of a thing than its
beginning;
the patient in spirit are better
than the proud in spirit.
9 Do not be quick to anger,
for anger lodges in the bosom of
fools.
10 Do not say, "Why were the former
days better than these?"
For it is not from wisdom that
you ask this.
11 Wisdom is as good as an
inheritance,
an advantage to those who see
the sun.
12 For the protection of wisdom is
like the protection of money,
and the advantage of knowledge
is that wisdom gives life to
the one who possesses it.
13 Consider the work of God;
who can make straight what he
has made crooked?

14 In the day of prosperity be joyful, and in the day of adversity consider; God has made the one as well as the other, so that mortals may not find out anything that will come after them.

The Riddles of Life

15 In my vain life I have seen everything; there are righteous people who perish in their righteousness, and there are wicked people who prolong their life in their evildoing. 16Do not be too righteous, and do not act too wise; why should you destroy yourself? 17Do not be too wicked, and do not be a fool; why should you die before your time? 18It is good that you should take hold of the one, without letting go of the other; for the one who fears God shall succeed with both.

p Or a feeding on wind. See Hos 12.1

19 Wisdom gives strength to the wise more than ten rulers that are in a city.

20 Surely there is no one on earth so righteous as to do good without ever sinning.

21 Do not give heed to everything that people say, or you may hear your servant cursing you; 22your heart knows that many times you have yourself cursed others.

23 All this I have tested by wisdom; I said, "I will be wise," but it was far from me. 24That which is, is far off, and deep, very deep; who can find it out? 25I

FRIDAY

ALL WE HAVE IS THE ALMIGHTY'S
William Penn

VERSE: Ecclesiastes 7.14   **PASSAGE:** Ecclesiastes 7.13–14

or disappointments that come not by our own folly, they are the trials or corrections of heaven: and it is our own fault if they prove not to our advantage.

To repine at them does not mend the matter: it is only to grumble at our Creator. But to see the hand of God in them, with a humble submission to his will, is the way to turn our water into wine and engage the greatest love and mercy on our side.

We must needs disorder ourselves if we look only at our losses. But if we consider how little we deserve what is left, our passion will cool, and our murmurs will turn into thankfulness.

If our hairs fall not to the ground, less do we or our substance without God's providence.

Nor can we fall below the arms of God, how low soever it be we fall. For though our Savior's passion is over, his compassion is not. That never fails his humble, sincere disciples. In him they find more than all that they lose in the world.

Is it reasonable to take it ill that anybody desires of us that which is their own? All we have is the Almighty's; and shall not God have his own when he calls for it?

Discontentedness is not only in such a case ingratitude, but injustice. For we are both unthankful for the time we had it, and not honest enough to restore it, if we could keep it.

But it is hard for us to look on things in such a glass, and at such a distance from this low world; and yet it is our duty, and would be our wisdom and our glory to do so.

ADDITIONAL SCRIPTURE READING:
2 Kings 17.17–22; Haggai 1.5–7; Acts 14.22

Go to page 762 for your next devotional reading.

1500   1700

turned my mind to know and to search out and to seek wisdom and the sum of things, and to know that wickedness is folly and that foolishness is madness. 26I found more bitter than death the woman who is a trap, whose heart is snares and nets, whose hands are fetters; one who pleases God escapes her, but the sinner is taken by her. 27See, this is what I found, says the Teacher,*q* adding one thing to another to find the sum, 28which my mind has sought repeatedly, but I have not found. One man among a thousand I found, but a woman among all these I have not found. 29See, this alone I found, that God made human beings straightforward, but they have devised many schemes.

Obey the King and Enjoy Yourself

8 Who is like the wise man?
  And who knows the
    interpretation of a thing?
Wisdom makes one's face shine,
  and the hardness of one's
    countenance is changed.

2 Keep*r* the king's command because of your sacred oath. 3Do not be terrified; go from his presence, do not delay when the matter is unpleasant, for he does whatever he pleases. 4For the word of the king is powerful, and who can say to him, "What are you doing?" 5Whoever obeys a command will meet no harm, and the wise mind will know the time and way. 6For every matter has its time and way, although the troubles of mortals lie heavy upon them. 7Indeed, they do not know what is to be, for who can tell them how it will be? 8No one has power over the wind*s* to restrain the wind,*s* or power over the day of death; there is no discharge from the battle, nor does wickedness deliver those who practice it. 9All this I observed, applying my mind to all that is done under the sun, while one person exercises authority over another to the other's hurt.

God's Ways Are Inscrutable

10 Then I saw the wicked buried; they used to go in and out of the holy place, and were praised in the city where they had done such things.*t* This also is vanity. 11Because sentence against an evil deed is not executed speedily, the human heart is fully set to do evil. 12Though sinners do evil a hundred times and prolong their lives, yet I know that it will be well with those who fear God, because they stand in fear before him, 13but it will not be well with the wicked, neither will they prolong their days like a shadow, because they do not stand in fear before God.

14 There is a vanity that takes place on earth, that there are righteous people who are treated according to the conduct of the wicked, and there are wicked people who are treated according to the conduct of the righteous. I said that this also is vanity. 15So I commend enjoyment, for there is nothing better for people under the sun than to eat, and drink, and enjoy themselves, for this will go with them in their toil through the days of life that God gives them under the sun.

16 When I applied my mind to know wisdom, and to see the business that is done on earth, how one's eyes see sleep neither day nor night, 17then I saw all the work of God, that no one can find out what is happening under the sun. However much they may toil in seeking, they will not find it out; even though those who are wise claim to know, they cannot find it out.

Take Life as It Comes

9 All this I laid to heart, examining it all, how the righteous and the wise and their deeds are in the hand of God; whether it is love or hate one does not know. Everything that confronts them 2is vanity,*u* since the same fate comes to all, to the righteous and the wicked, to the good and the evil,*v* to the clean and the unclean, to those who sacrifice and those who do not sacrifice. As are the good, so are the sinners; those who swear are like those who shun an oath. 3This is an evil in all that happens under the sun, that the same fate comes to everyone. Moreover, the hearts of all are full of evil; madness is in their hearts while they live, and after that they go to

q Qoheleth, traditionally rendered *Preacher*   *r* Heb *I keep*   *s* Or *breath*   *t* Meaning of Heb uncertain   *u* Syr Compare Gk: Heb *Everything that confronts them* 2is everything   *v* Gk Syr Vg: Heb lacks *and the evil*

WEEKEND

JESUS THE LORD, OUR RIGHTEOUSNESS
Count Nikolaus Ludwig von Zinzendorf

VERSE: Isaiah 61.10   **PASSAGE:** Isaiah 61.10–11

esus, thy blood and righteousness,
My beauty are, my glorious dress;
Midst flaming worlds, in these arrayed,
With joy shall I lift up my head.

Lord, I believe thy precious blood,
Which, at the mercy seat of God,
Forever doth for sinners plead,
For me, e'en for my soul, was shed.

Lord, I believe were sinners more
Than sands upon the ocean shore,
Thou hast for all a ransom paid,
For all a full redemption made.

Bold shall I stand in that great day,
For who aught to my charge shall lay?
Fully, by thee, absolved I am
From sin and fear, from guilt and shame.

This spotless robe the same appears,
When ruined nature sinks in years;
No age can change its glorious hue,
Its glory is forever new.

Thou God of power, thou God of love,
Let many more, thy mercy prove;
Their beauty this, their glorious dress,
Jesus the Lord, our righteousness.

ADDITIONAL SCRIPTURE READING:
Psalm 132.9; Romans 13.14; Revelation 7.9–14

Go to page 764 for your next devotional reading.

1700   1900

the dead. **4**But whoever is joined with all the living has hope, for a living dog is better than a dead lion. **5**The living know that they will die, but the dead know nothing; they have no more reward, and even the memory of them is lost. **6**Their love and their hate and their envy have already perished; never again will they have any share in all that happens under the sun.

7 Go, eat your bread with enjoyment, and drink your wine with a merry heart; for God has long ago approved what you do. **8**Let your garments always be white; do not let oil be lacking on your head. **9**Enjoy life with the wife whom you love, all the days of your vain life that are given you under the sun, because that is your portion in life and in your toil at which you toil under the sun. **10**Whatever your hand finds to do, do with your might; for there is no work or thought or knowledge or wisdom in Sheol, to which you are going.

11 Again I saw that under the sun the race is not to the swift, nor the battle to the strong, nor bread to the wise, nor riches to the intelligent, nor favor to the skillful; but time and chance happen to them all. **12**For no one can anticipate the time of disaster. Like fish taken in a cruel net, and like birds caught in a snare, so mortals are snared at a time of calamity, when it suddenly falls upon them.

Wisdom Superior to Folly

13 I have also seen this example of wisdom under the sun, and it seemed great to me. **14**There was a little city with few people in it. A great king came against it and besieged it, building great siegeworks against it. **15**Now there was found in it a poor wise man, and he by his wisdom delivered the city. Yet no one remembered that poor man. **16**So I said, "Wisdom is better than might; yet the poor man's wisdom is despised, and his words are not heeded."

17 The quiet words of the wise are
     more to be heeded
   than the shouting of a ruler
     among fools.
18 Wisdom is better than weapons of
     war,
   but one bungler destroys much
     good.

Miscellaneous Observations

10 Dead flies make the
     perfumer's ointment give off
     a foul odor;
   so a little folly outweighs
     wisdom and honor.
2 The heart of the wise inclines to
     the right,
   but the heart of a fool to the left.
3 Even when fools walk on the road,
     they lack sense,
   and show to everyone that they
     are fools.
4 If the anger of the ruler rises against
     you, do not leave your post,
   for calmness will undo great
     offenses.

5 There is an evil that I have seen under the sun, as great an error as if it proceeded from the ruler: **6**folly is set in many high places, and the rich sit in a low place. **7**I have seen slaves on horseback, and princes walking on foot like slaves.

8 Whoever digs a pit will fall into it;
   and whoever breaks through a
     wall will be bitten by a snake.
9 Whoever quarries stones will be
     hurt by them;
   and whoever splits logs will be
     endangered by them.
10 If the iron is blunt, and one does
     not whet the edge,
   then more strength must be
     exerted;
   but wisdom helps one to succeed.
11 If the snake bites before it is
     charmed,
   there is no advantage in a
     charmer.

12 Words spoken by the wise bring
     them favor,
   but the lips of fools consume
     them.
13 The words of their mouths begin in
     foolishness,
   and their talk ends in wicked
     madness;
14 yet fools talk on and on.
   No one knows what is to happen,
   and who can tell anyone what
     the future holds?
15 The toil of fools wears them out,
   for they do not even know the
     way to town.

IN FORESIGHT OF THE GRAVE
Christina Rossetti

VERSE: Ecclesiastes 9.10   **PASSAGE:** Ecclesiastes 9.7–10

ears ago a small party of us crossed the Alps into Italy by the Pass of Mount St. Gotthard . . .
At a certain point of the ascent the mountain bloomed into an actual garden of forget-me-nots.

Unforgotten and never to be forgotten that lovely lavish efflorescence which made earth cerulean as the sky.

Thus I remember the mountain. But without that flower of memory could I have forgotten it?

Surely not: yet there, not elsewhere, a countless multitude of forget-me-nots made their home.

Such oftentimes seems the principle of allotment (if reverently I may term it so) among the human family. Many persons whose chief gifts taken one by one would suffice to memorialize them, engross not those only but along with them the winning graces which endear. Forget-me-nots enamel the height.

And what shall they do who display neither loftiness nor loveliness? If "one member be honored, all the members rejoice with it" (1 Corinthians 12.26, KJV).

Or, if this standard appears too exalted for frail flesh and blood to attain, then send thought onwards.

The crowning summit of Mount St. Gotthard abides invested, not with flowers, but with perpetual snow: not with life, but with lifelessness.

In foresight of the grave, whither we all are hastening, is it worthwhile to envy any? "There is no work, nor device, nor knowledge, nor wisdom, in the grave whither thou goest" (Ecclesiastes 9.10, KJV). "Grudge not one against another, brethren, lest ye be condemned: behold the judge standeth before the door" (James 5.9, KJV).

ADDITIONAL SCRIPTURE READING:
Job 14.7–12; James 5.9

Go to page 769 for your next devotional reading.

1700   1900

16 Alas for you, O land, when your
　　king is a servant,[w]
　　and your princes feast in the
　　　morning!
17 Happy are you, O land, when your
　　king is a nobleman,
　　and your princes feast at the
　　　proper time—
　　for strength, and not for
　　　drunkenness!
18 Through sloth the roof sinks in,
　　and through indolence the house
　　　leaks.
19 Feasts are made for laughter;
　　wine gladdens life,
　　and money meets every need.
20 Do not curse the king, even in your
　　thoughts,
　　or curse the rich, even in your
　　　bedroom;
　　for a bird of the air may carry your
　　　voice,
　　or some winged creature tell the
　　　matter.

The Value of Diligence

11 Send out your bread upon the
waters,
　　for after many days you will get
　　　it back.
2 Divide your means seven ways, or
　　even eight,
　　for you do not know what
　　　disaster may happen on
　　　earth.
3 When clouds are full,
　　they empty rain on the earth;
　　whether a tree falls to the south or
　　　to the north,
　　in the place where the tree falls,
　　　there it will lie.
4 Whoever observes the wind will
　　not sow;
　　and whoever regards the clouds
　　　will not reap.

5 Just as you do not know how the
breath comes to the bones in the mother's womb, so you do not know the work
of God, who makes everything.
6 In the morning sow your seed, and
at evening do not let your hands be idle;
for you do not know which will prosper,
this or that, or whether both alike will
be good.

Youth and Old Age

7 Light is sweet, and it is pleasant for
the eyes to see the sun.
8 Even those who live many years
should rejoice in them all; yet let them
remember that the days of darkness will
be many. All that comes is vanity.
9 Rejoice, young man, while you are
young, and let your heart cheer you in
the days of your youth. Follow the inclination of your heart and the desire of
your eyes, but know that for all these
things God will bring you into judgment.
10 Banish anxiety from your mind,
and put away pain from your body; for
youth and the dawn of life are vanity.

> GIVE ME A PERSON WHO SAYS, "THIS ONE THING I
> DO," AND NOT, "THESE FIFTY THINGS I DABBLE
> IN."
> —*Dwight L. Moody*

12 Remember your creator in the
days of your youth, before the
days of trouble come, and the years draw
near when you will say, "I have no pleasure in them"; 2before the sun and the
light and the moon and the stars are
darkened and the clouds return with[x]
the rain; 3in the day when the guards of
the house tremble, and the strong men
are bent, and the women who grind
cease working because they are few, and
those who look through the windows
see dimly; 4when the doors on the street
are shut, and the sound of the grinding is
low, and one rises up at the sound of a
bird, and all the daughters of song are
brought low; 5when one is afraid of
heights, and terrors are in the road; the
almond tree blossoms, the grasshopper
drags itself along[y] and desire fails;
because all must go to their eternal
home, and the mourners will go about
the streets; 6before the silver cord is
snapped,[z] and the golden bowl is broken,
and the pitcher is broken at the fountain,
and the wheel broken at the cistern,
7and the dust returns to the earth as it
was, and the breath[a] returns to God who
gave it. 8Vanity of vanities, says the
Teacher;[b] all is vanity.

---

w Or *a child*　x Or *after;* Heb 'ahar　y Or *is a burden*　z Syr Vg Compare Gk: Heb *is removed*
a Or *the spirit*　b Qoheleth, traditionally rendered *Preacher*

Epilogue

9 Besides being wise, the Teacher[c] also taught the people knowledge, weighing and studying and arranging many proverbs. [10]The Teacher[c] sought to find pleasing words, and he wrote words of truth plainly.

11 The sayings of the wise are like goads, and like nails firmly fixed are the collected sayings that are given by one shepherd.[d] [12]Of anything beyond these, my child, beware. Of making many books there is no end, and much study is a weariness of the flesh.

13 The end of the matter; all has been heard. Fear God, and keep his commandments; for that is the whole duty of everyone. [14]For God will bring every deed into judgment, including[e] every secret thing, whether good or evil.

SONG OF SOLOMON

IN ANCIENT ISRAEL EVERYTHING HUMAN CAME TO EXPRESSION IN WORDS. IN THE SONG, LOVE FINDS WORDS—INSPIRED WORDS THAT DISCLOSE ITS EXQUISITE CHARM AND BEAUTY AS ONE OF GOD'S CHOICEST GIFTS. IT ILLUMINATES THE SPONTANEOUS AND EXCLUSIVE LOVE BETWEEN A LOVER AND HIS BELOVED, DEMONSTRATING AT THE SAME TIME THE KIND OF LOVE CHRIST HAS FOR HIS CHURCH. REJOICE IN THE GIFT OF LOVE, AS YOU READ THIS TIMELESS EXPRESSION OF THE JOY AND INTIMACY OF LOVE, THE GIFT OF OUR CREATOR.

 1 The Song of Songs, which is Solomon's.

Colloquy of Bride and Friends

2 Let him kiss me with the kisses of
his mouth!
For your love is better than wine,
3   your anointing oils are fragrant,
your name is perfume poured out;
therefore the maidens love you.

JOB—HOW TO SUFFER;
PSALMS—HOW TO PRAY;
PROVERBS—HOW TO ACT;
ECCLESIASTES—HOW TO ENJOY;
SONG OF SOLOMON—HOW TO LOVE.
                    —*Oswald Chambers*

---

4 Draw me after you, let us make
haste.
The king has brought me into his
chambers.
We will exult and rejoice in you;
we will extol your love more
than wine;
rightly do they love you.

5 I am black and beautiful,
O daughters of Jerusalem,
like the tents of Kedar,
like the curtains of Solomon.
6 Do not gaze at me because I am
dark,
because the sun has gazed on me.
My mother's sons were angry with
me;
they made me keeper of the
vineyards,

but my own vineyard I have not
    kept!
7 Tell me, you whom my soul loves,
    where you pasture your flock,
    where you make it lie down at
      noon;
for why should I be like one who is
    veiled
    beside the flocks of your
      companions?

8 If you do not know,
    O fairest among women,
follow the tracks of the flock,
    and pasture your kids
    beside the shepherds' tents.

Colloquy of Bridegroom, Friends, and Bride

9 I compare you, my love,
    to a mare among Pharaoh's
      chariots.
10 Your cheeks are comely with
      ornaments,
    your neck with strings of jewels.
11 We will make you ornaments of
      gold,
    studded with silver.

12 While the king was on his couch,
    my nard gave forth its fragrance.
13 My beloved is to me a bag of myrrh
    that lies between my breasts.
14 My beloved is to me a cluster of
      henna blossoms
    in the vineyards of En-gedi.

15 Ah, you are beautiful, my love;
    ah, you are beautiful;
    your eyes are doves.
16 Ah, you are beautiful, my beloved,
    truly lovely.
Our couch is green;
17   the beams of our house are cedar,
    our rafters[a] are pine.

2 I am a rose[b] of Sharon,
    a lily of the valleys.

2 As a lily among brambles,
    so is my love among maidens.

3 As an apple tree among the trees of
      the wood,
    so is my beloved among young
      men.

With great delight I sat in his
    shadow,
    and his fruit was sweet to my
      taste.
4 He brought me to the banqueting
    house,
    and his intention toward me was
      love.
5 Sustain me with raisins,
    refresh me with apples;
    for I am faint with love.
6 O that his left hand were under my
    head,
    and that his right hand embraced
      me!
7 I adjure you, O daughters of
    Jerusalem,
    by the gazelles or the wild does:
do not stir up or awaken love
    until it is ready!

Springtime Rhapsody

8 The voice of my beloved!
    Look, he comes,
leaping upon the mountains,
    bounding over the hills.
9 My beloved is like a gazelle
    or a young stag.
Look, there he stands
    behind our wall,
gazing in at the windows,
    looking through the lattice.
10 My beloved speaks and says to me:
    "Arise, my love, my fair one,
    and come away;
11 for now the winter is past,
    the rain is over and gone.
12 The flowers appear on the earth;
    the time of singing has come,
and the voice of the turtledove
    is heard in our land.
13 The fig tree puts forth its figs,
    and the vines are in blossom;
    they give forth fragrance.
Arise, my love, my fair one,
    and come away.
14 O my dove, in the clefts of the
    rock,
    in the covert of the cliff,
let me see your face,
    let me hear your voice;
for your voice is sweet,
    and your face is lovely.
15 Catch us the foxes,
    the little foxes,

a Meaning of Heb uncertain   b Heb crocus

that ruin the vineyards—
  for our vineyards are in
    blossom."

16 My beloved is mine and I am his;
  he pastures his flock among the
    lilies.
17 Until the day breathes
  and the shadows flee,

turn, my beloved, be like a gazelle
  or a young stag on the cleft
    mountains.[c]

Love's Dream

 Upon my bed at night
  I sought him whom my soul
    loves;
  I sought him, but found him not;

c Or *on the mountains of Bether*: meaning of Heb uncertain

TUESDAY

LATE HAVE I LOVED THEE
Augustine

VERSE: Song of Solomon 2.5   **PASSAGE:** Song of Solomon 2.3–13

Late Have I Loved Thee

ate have I love thee, O Beauty so ancient and so new; late have I loved thee: for behold thou wert within me, and I outside; and I sought thee outside and in my unloveliness fell upon those lovely things that thou hast made. Thou wert with me, and I was not with thee. I was kept from thee by those things, yet had they not been in thee, they would not have been at all. Thou didst call and cry to me to break open my deafness: and thou didst send forth thy beams and shine upon me and chase away my blindness: thou didst breathe fragrance upon me, and I drew in my breath and do now pant for thee: I tasted thee, and now hunger and thirst for thee: thou didst touch me, and I have burned for thy peace.

Now I Love Thee Alone

Now I love thee alone.
Thee alone do I follow.
Thee alone do I seek.
Thee alone am I ready to serve.
For thou alone hast just dominion.
Under thy sway I long to be.

ADDITIONAL SCRIPTURE READING:
Psalms 42.1–3; 63.1–3; 119.130–131

Go to page 772 for your next devotional reading.

100   500

I called him, but he gave no
answer.*d*
2 "I will rise now and go about the
city,
in the streets and in the squares;
I will seek him whom my soul
loves."
I sought him, but found him not.
3 The sentinels found me,
as they went about in the city.
"Have you seen him whom my
soul loves?"
4 Scarcely had I passed them,
when I found him whom my soul
loves.
I held him, and would not let him
go
until I brought him into my
mother's house,
and into the chamber of her that
conceived me.
5 I adjure you, O daughters of
Jerusalem,
by the gazelles or the wild does:
do not stir up or awaken love
until it is ready!

The Groom and His Party Approach

6 What is that coming up from the
wilderness,
like a column of smoke,
perfumed with myrrh and
frankincense,
with all the fragrant powders of
the merchant?
7 Look, it is the litter of Solomon!
Around it are sixty mighty men
of the mighty men of Israel,
8 all equipped with swords
and expert in war,
each with his sword at his thigh
because of alarms by night.
9 King Solomon made himself a
palanquin
from the wood of Lebanon.
10 He made its posts of silver,
its back of gold, its seat of purple;
its interior was inlaid with love.*e*
Daughters of Jerusalem,
11 come out.
Look, O daughters of Zion,
at King Solomon,
at the crown with which his
mother crowned him
on the day of his wedding,

on the day of the gladness of his
heart.

The Bride's Beauty Extolled

4 How beautiful you are, my
love,
how very beautiful!
Your eyes are doves
behind your veil.
Your hair is like a flock of goats,
moving down the slopes of
Gilead.
2 Your teeth are like a flock of shorn
ewes
that have come up from the
washing,
all of which bear twins,
and not one among them is
bereaved.
3 Your lips are like a crimson thread,
and your mouth is lovely.
Your cheeks are like halves of a
pomegranate
behind your veil.
4 Your neck is like the tower of
David,
built in courses;
on it hang a thousand bucklers,
all of them shields of warriors.
5 Your two breasts are like two
fawns,
twins of a gazelle,
that feed among the lilies.
6 Until the day breathes
and the shadows flee,
I will hasten to the mountain of
myrrh
and the hill of frankincense.
7 You are altogether beautiful, my
love;
there is no flaw in you.
8 Come with me from Lebanon, my
bride;
come with me from Lebanon.
Depart*f* from the peak of Amana,
from the peak of Senir and
Hermon,
from the dens of lions,
from the mountains of leopards.

9 You have ravished my heart, my
sister, my bride,
you have ravished my heart with
a glance of your eyes,
with one jewel of your necklace.

---

d Gk: Heb lacks this line   *e* Meaning of Heb uncertain   *f* Or *Look*

10 How sweet is your love, my sister,
        my bride!
    how much better is your love
        than wine,
    and the fragrance of your oils
        than any spice!
11 Your lips distill nectar, my bride;
    honey and milk are under your
        tongue;
    the scent of your garments is like
        the scent of Lebanon.
12 A garden locked is my sister, my
        bride,
    a garden locked, a fountain
        sealed.
13 Your channel$g$ is an orchard of
        pomegranates
    with all choicest fruits,
    henna with nard,
14 nard and saffron, calamus and
        cinnamon,
    with all trees of frankincense,
    myrrh and aloes,
    with all chief spices—
15 a garden fountain, a well of living
        water,
    and flowing streams from
        Lebanon.

16 Awake, O north wind,
    and come, O south wind!
    Blow upon my garden
        that its fragrance may be wafted
        abroad.
    Let my beloved come to his garden,
    and eat its choicest fruits.

5 I come to my garden, my sister,
        my bride;
    I gather my myrrh with my spice,
    I eat my honeycomb with my
        honey,
    I drink my wine with my milk.

    Eat, friends, drink,
    and be drunk with love.

Another Dream

2 I slept, but my heart was awake.
    Listen! my beloved is knocking.
    "Open to me, my sister, my love,
    my dove, my perfect one;
    for my head is wet with dew,
    my locks with the drops of the
        night."

3 I had put off my garment;
    how could I put it on again?
    I had bathed my feet;
    how could I soil them?
4 My beloved thrust his hand into
        the opening,
    and my inmost being yearned for
        him.
5 I arose to open to my beloved,
    and my hands dripped with
        myrrh,
    my fingers with liquid myrrh,
    upon the handles of the bolt.
6 I opened to my beloved,
    but my beloved had turned and
        was gone.
    My soul failed me when he spoke.
    I sought him, but did not find him;
    I called him, but he gave no
        answer.
7 Making their rounds in the city
    the sentinels found me;
    they beat me, they wounded me,
    they took away my mantle,
    those sentinels of the walls.
8 I adjure you, O daughters of
        Jerusalem,
    if you find my beloved,
    tell him this:
    I am faint with love.

Colloquy of Friends and Bride

9 What is your beloved more than
        another beloved,
    O fairest among women?
    What is your beloved more than
        another beloved,
    that you thus adjure us?

10 My beloved is all radiant and ruddy,
    distinguished among ten
        thousand.
11 His head is the finest gold;
    his locks are wavy,
    black as a raven.
12 His eyes are like doves
    beside springs of water,
    bathed in milk,
    fitly set.g
13 His cheeks are like beds of spices,
    yielding fragrance.
    His lips are lilies,
    distilling liquid myrrh.
14 His arms are rounded gold,
    set with jewels.

g Meaning of Heb uncertain

His body is ivory work,[h]
   encrusted with sapphires.[i]
15 His legs are alabaster columns,
   set upon bases of gold.
His appearance is like Lebanon,
   choice as the cedars.
16 His speech is most sweet,
   and he is altogether desirable.
This is my beloved and this is my
   friend,
O daughters of Jerusalem.

h Meaning of Heb uncertain   i Heb *lapis lazuli*

6 Where has your beloved gone,
   O fairest among women?
Which way has your beloved
   turned,
   that we may seek him with you?

2 My beloved has gone down to his
   garden,
   to the beds of spices,
to pasture his flock in the gardens,
   and to gather lilies.

WEDNESDAY

FAINT WITH LOVE FOR HIM
Francis of Assisi

VERSE: Song of Solomon 5.8   **PASSAGE:** Song of Solomon 5.2–8

et us all love with all our heart, with all our soul, with all our mind, with all our strength and fortitude, with all our understanding and with all our powers, with our whole might and whole affection, with our innermost parts, our whole desires, and wills, the Lord God, who has given and gives to us all, the whole body, the whole soul, and our life; who has created and redeemed us, and by his mercy alone will save us; who has done and does all good to us, miserable and wretched, vile, unclean, ungrateful, and evil.

Let us therefore desire nothing else, wish for nothing else, and let nothing please and delight us except our Creator and Redeemer, and Savior, the only true God, who is full of good, all good, entire good, the true and supreme good, who alone is good, merciful and kind, gentle and sweet, who alone is holy, just, true, and upright, who alone is benign, pure, and clean, from whom, and through whom, and in whom is all mercy, all grace, all glory of all penitents and of the just, and of all the blessed rejoicing in heaven. Let nothing therefore hinder us, let nothing separate us, let nothing come between us.

ADDITIONAL SCRIPTURE READING:
Psalm 42.1–3; Jude 24–25

Go to page 777 for your next devotional reading.

500   1500

3   I am my beloved's and my beloved
        is mine;
    he pastures his flock among the
        lilies.

The Bride's Matchless Beauty

4   You are beautiful as Tirzah, my
        love,
        comely as Jerusalem,
        terrible as an army with banners.
5   Turn away your eyes from me,
        for they overwhelm me!
    Your hair is like a flock of goats,
        moving down the slopes of
        Gilead.
6   Your teeth are like a flock of ewes,
        that have come up from the
        washing;
    all of them bear twins,
        and not one among them is
        bereaved.
7   Your cheeks are like halves of a
        pomegranate
        behind your veil.
8   There are sixty queens and eighty
        concubines,
        and maidens without number.
9   My dove, my perfect one, is the
        only one,
        the darling of her mother,
        flawless to her that bore her.
    The maidens saw her and called
        her happy;
        the queens and concubines also,
        and they praised her.
10 "Who is this that looks forth like
        the dawn,
        fair as the moon, bright as the
        sun,
        terrible as an army with
        banners?"

11 I went down to the nut orchard,
        to look at the blossoms of the
        valley,
    to see whether the vines had
        budded,
        whether the pomegranates were
        in bloom.
12 Before I was aware, my fancy set me
        in a chariot beside my prince.j

13k Return, return, O Shulammite!

Return, return, that we may look
    upon you.

Why should you look upon the
    Shulammite,
    as upon a dance before two
    armies?l

Expressions of Praise

7   How graceful are your feet in
        sandals,
        O queenly maiden!
    Your rounded thighs are like jewels,
        the work of a master hand.
2   Your navel is a rounded bowl
        that never lacks mixed wine.
    Your belly is a heap of wheat,
        encircled with lilies.
3   Your two breasts are like two
        fawns,
        twins of a gazelle.
4   Your neck is like an ivory tower.
    Your eyes are pools in Heshbon,
        by the gate of Bath-rabbim.
    Your nose is like a tower of
        Lebanon,
        overlooking Damascus.
5   Your head crowns you like Carmel,
        and your flowing locks are like
        purple;
        a king is held captive in the
        tresses.m

6   How fair and pleasant you are,
        O loved one, delectable maiden!n
7   You are statelyo as a palm tree,
        and your breasts are like its
        clusters.
8   I say I will climb the palm tree
        and lay hold of its branches.
    O may your breasts be like clusters
        of the vine,
        and the scent of your breath like
        apples,
9   and your kissesp like the best wine
        that goes downq smoothly,
        gliding over lips and teeth.r

10 I am my beloved's,
        and his desire is for me.
11 Come, my beloved,
        let us go forth into the fields,
        and lodge in the villages;

j Cn: Meaning of Heb uncertain   k Ch 7.1 in Heb   l Or dance of Mahanaim   m Meaning of Heb
uncertain   n Syr: Heb in delights   o Heb This your stature is   p Heb palate   q Heb down for
my lover   r Gk Syr Vg: Heb lips of sleepers

12 let us go out early to the vineyards,
and see whether the vines have
budded,
whether the grape blossoms have
opened
and the pomegranates are in
bloom.
There I will give you my love.
13 The mandrakes give forth
fragrance,
and over our doors are all choice
fruits,
new as well as old,
which I have laid up for you,
O my beloved.

8 O that you were like a brother
to me,
who nursed at my mother's
breast!
If I met you outside, I would kiss
you,
and no one would despise me.
2 I would lead you and bring you
into the house of my mother,
and into the chamber of the one
who bore me.*s*
I would give you spiced wine to
drink,
the juice of my pomegranates.
3 O that his left hand were under my
head,
and that his right hand embraced
me!
4 I adjure you, O daughters of
Jerusalem,
do not stir up or awaken love
until it is ready!

Homecoming

5 Who is that coming up from the
wilderness,
leaning upon her beloved?

Under the apple tree I awakened
you.
There your mother was in labor
with you;
there she who bore you was in
labor.

6 Set me as a seal upon your heart,
as a seal upon your arm;
for love is strong as death,
passion fierce as the grave.
Its flashes are flashes of fire,
a raging flame.
7 Many waters cannot quench love,
neither can floods drown it.
If one offered for love
all the wealth of one's house,
it would be utterly scorned.

8 We have a little sister,
and she has no breasts.
What shall we do for our sister,
on the day when she is spoken
for?
9 If she is a wall,
we will build upon her a
battlement of silver;
but if she is a door,
we will enclose her with boards
of cedar.
10 I was a wall,
and my breasts were like towers;
then I was in his eyes
as one who brings*t* peace.
11 Solomon had a vineyard at Baal-
hamon;
he entrusted the vineyard to
keepers;
each one was to bring for its fruit
a thousand pieces of silver.
12 My vineyard, my very own, is for
myself;
you, O Solomon, may have the
thousand,
and the keepers of the fruit two
hundred!

13 O you who dwell in the gardens,
my companions are listening for
your voice;
let me hear it.

14 Make haste, my beloved,
and be like a gazelle
or a young stag
upon the mountains of spices!

---

s Gk Syr: Heb *my mother; she* (or *you*) *will teach me*   *t* Or *finds*

ISAIAH

 SAIAH WROTE DURING THE STORMY
PERIOD MARKING THE EXPANSION OF
THE ASSYRIAN EMPIRE AND THE DECLINE
OF ISRAEL. ISAIAH UNVEILS THE FULL DIMENSIONS
OF GOD'S JUDGMENT, WARNING JUDAH THAT HER
SIN WOULD BRING CAPTIVITY AT THE HANDS OF
BABYLON. YET, FOLLOWING ROUND AFTER ROUND
OF WARNING, ISAIAH TURNS TO THE PROMISE OF
GOD'S COMFORT, FORGIVENESS AND RESTORA-
TION. THE RESTORED EARTH AND THE RESTORED
PEOPLE WILL THEN CONFORM TO THE DIVINE
IDEAL, AND ALL WILL RESULT IN THE PRAISE AND
GLORY OF THE HOLY GOD OF ISRAEL.

---

1 The vision of Isaiah son of
Amoz, which he saw concern-
ing Judah and Jerusalem in the days of
Uzziah, Jotham, Ahaz, and Hezekiah,
kings of Judah.

The Wickedness of Judah

2 Hear, O heavens, and listen,
O earth;
for the LORD has spoken:
I reared children and brought them
up,
but they have rebelled against me.
3 The ox knows its owner,
and the donkey its master's crib;
but Israel does not know,
my people do not understand.

4 Ah, sinful nation,
people laden with iniquity,
offspring who do evil,
children who deal corruptly,
who have forsaken the LORD,
who have despised the Holy One
of Israel,
who are utterly estranged!

5 Why do you seek further beatings?
Why do you continue to rebel?
The whole head is sick,
and the whole heart faint.
6 From the sole of the foot even to
the head,
there is no soundness in it,
but bruises and sores
and bleeding wounds;
they have not been drained, or
bound up,
or softened with oil.

7   Your country lies desolate,
        your cities are burned with fire;
    in your very presence
        aliens devour your land;
        it is desolate, as overthrown by
            foreigners.
8   And daughter Zion is left
        like a booth in a vineyard,
    like a shelter in a cucumber field,
    like a besieged city.
9   If the LORD of hosts
        had not left us a few survivors,
    we would have been like Sodom,
        and become like Gomorrah.

10 Hear the word of the LORD,
        you rulers of Sodom!
    Listen to the teaching of our God,
        you people of Gomorrah!
11 What to me is the multitude of
            your sacrifices?
        says the LORD;
    I have had enough of burnt
            offerings of rams
        and the fat of fed beasts;
    I do not delight in the blood of
            bulls,
        or of lambs, or of goats.

12 When you come to appear before
            me,*a*
        who asked this from your hand?
        Trample my courts no more;
13 bringing offerings is futile;
        incense is an abomination to me.
    New moon and sabbath and calling
            of convocation—
    I cannot endure solemn
            assemblies with iniquity.
14 Your new moons and your
            appointed festivals
        my soul hates;
    they have become a burden to me,
        I am weary of bearing them.
15 When you stretch out your hands,
        I will hide my eyes from you;
    even though you make many
            prayers,
        I will not listen;
    your hands are full of blood.
16 Wash yourselves; make yourselves
            clean;
        remove the evil of your doings
            from before my eyes;
        cease to do evil,

17   learn to do good;
        seek justice,
            rescue the oppressed,
        defend the orphan,
            plead for the widow.

18 Come now, let us argue it out,
            says the LORD:
    though your sins are like scarlet,
        they shall be like snow;
    though they are red like crimson,
        they shall become like wool.
19 If you are willing and obedient,
        you shall eat the good of the
            land;
20 but if you refuse and rebel,
        you shall be devoured by the
            sword;
    for the mouth of the LORD has
            spoken.

The Degenerate City

21 How the faithful city
        has become a whore!
    She that was full of justice,
        righteousness lodged in her—
        but now murderers!
22 Your silver has become dross,
        your wine is mixed with water.
23 Your princes are rebels
        and companions of thieves.
    Everyone loves a bribe
        and runs after gifts.
    They do not defend the orphan,
        and the widow's cause does not
            come before them.

24 Therefore says the Sovereign, the
            LORD of hosts, the Mighty
            One of Israel:
    Ah, I will pour out my wrath on
            my enemies,
        and avenge myself on my foes!
25 I will turn my hand against you;
        I will smelt away your dross as
            with lye
        and remove all your alloy.
26 And I will restore your judges as at
            the first,
        and your counselors as at the
            beginning.
    Afterward you shall be called the
            city of righteousness,
        the faithful city.

a Or *see my face*

THAT IN WHICH OUR RELIGION LIES
George Fox

VERSE: Isaiah 1.17   **PASSAGE:** Isaiah 1.14–17

hen the priests and professors raged exceedingly against us and printed books against us; and said that our religion lay in not wearing fine clothes, and lace, and ribands, and in not eating good cheer, when we could not make feasts for the priests or professors as we used to do, nor feasts for companies in the cities; but if they would join with us, when they made feasts, to feast such as could not feast them again, we would make a feast for all the poor of the parish that could not feast us and them again. And this was according to Christ's command, but in this their selfish principle would never join with us.

We told them that when they went to their sports, and games, and plays, and the like, they had better serve God than spend their time so vainly. And that costly apparel, with the lace that we formally had hung upon our backs that kept us not warm, with that we could maintain a company of poor people that had no clothes.

And so our religion lay not in meats, nor drinks, nor clothes, nor thee nor thou, nor putting off hats nor making curtseys (at which they were greatly offended because we thee'd and thou'd them and could not put off our hats nor bow to them), and therefore they said our religion lay in such things. But our answer was, "Nay; for though the Spirit of God led into that which was comely and decent, and from chambering and wantonness, and from sporting and pastimes and feasting as in the day of slaughter, and from wearing costly apparel, as the apostle commands, and from the world's honor, fashions and customs—our religion lies in that which brings to visit the poor, and fatherless, and widows, and keeps from the spots of the world (which religion is pure and undefiled before God [see James 1.27]). This is our religion which we own, which the apostles were in above 1600 years since; and we do deny all vain religions got up since, which are not only spotted with the world, but plead for a body of sin and death to the grave; and their widows and fatherless lie begging up and down the streets and countries."

ADDITIONAL SCRIPTURE READING:
Deuteronomy 10.12–13; Micah 6.8; James 1.27

Go to page 781 for your next devotional reading.

1700   1900

27 Zion shall be redeemed by justice,
    and those in her who repent, by
        righteousness.
28 But rebels and sinners shall be
        destroyed together,
    and those who forsake the LORD
        shall be consumed.
29 For you shall be ashamed of the
        oaks
    in which you delighted;
    and you shall blush for the gardens
        that you have chosen.
30 For you shall be like an oak
        whose leaf withers,
    and like a garden without water.
31 The strong shall become like tinder,
    and their work[b] like a spark;
    they and their work shall burn
        together,
    with no one to quench them.

The Future House of God

2 The word that Isaiah son of
Amoz saw concerning Judah
and Jerusalem.

2 In days to come
    the mountain of the LORD's house
    shall be established as the highest
        of the mountains,
    and shall be raised above the hills;
    all the nations shall stream to it.
3 Many peoples shall come and say,
    "Come, let us go up to the
        mountain of the LORD,
    to the house of the God of Jacob;
    that he may teach us his ways
        and that we may walk in his
            paths."
    For out of Zion shall go forth
        instruction,
    and the word of the LORD from
        Jerusalem.
4 He shall judge between the nations,
    and shall arbitrate for many
        peoples;
    they shall beat their swords into
        plowshares,
    and their spears into pruning
        hooks;
    nation shall not lift up sword
        against nation,
    neither shall they learn war any
        more.

Judgment Pronounced on Arrogance

5 O house of Jacob,
    come, let us walk
    in the light of the LORD!
6 For you have forsaken the ways of[c]
        your people,
    O house of Jacob.
    Indeed they are full of diviners[d]
        from the east
    and of soothsayers like the
        Philistines,
    and they clasp hands with
        foreigners.
7 Their land is filled with silver and
        gold,
    and there is no end to their
        treasures;
    their land is filled with horses,
    and there is no end to their
        chariots.
8 Their land is filled with idols;
    they bow down to the work of
        their hands,
    to what their own fingers have
        made.
9 And so people are humbled,
    and everyone is brought low—
    do not forgive them!
10 Enter into the rock,
    and hide in the dust
    from the terror of the LORD,
    and from the glory of his majesty.
11 The haughty eyes of people shall be
        brought low,
    and the pride of everyone shall be
        humbled;
    and the LORD alone will be exalted
        on that day.
12 For the LORD of hosts has a day
    against all that is proud and lofty,
    against all that is lifted up and
        high;[e]
13 against all the cedars of Lebanon,
        lofty and lifted up;
    and against all the oaks of
        Bashan;
14 against all the high mountains,
    and against all the lofty hills;
15 against every high tower,
    and against every fortified wall;
16 against all the ships of Tarshish,
    and against all the beautiful
        craft.[f]

b Or its makers   c Heb lacks the ways of   d Cn: Heb lacks of diviners   e Cn Compare Gk: Heb
low   f Compare Gk: Meaning of Heb uncertain

17 The haughtiness of people shall be
      humbled,
   and the pride of everyone shall be
      brought low;
   and the LORD alone will be
      exalted on that day.
18 The idols shall utterly pass away.
19 Enter the caves of the rocks
      and the holes of the ground,
   from the terror of the LORD,
      and from the glory of his majesty,
   when he rises to terrify the earth.
20 On that day people will throw away
      to the moles and to the bats
   their idols of silver and their idols
      of gold,
   which they made for themselves
      to worship,
21 to enter the caverns of the rocks
      and the clefts in the crags,
   from the terror of the LORD,
      and from the glory of his majesty,
   when he rises to terrify the earth.
22 Turn away from mortals,
      who have only breath in their
         nostrils,
   for of what account are they?

3 For now the Sovereign, the
   LORD of hosts,
      is taking away from Jerusalem
         and from Judah
   support and staff—
      all support of bread,
      and all support of water—
2 warrior and soldier,
      judge and prophet,
      diviner and elder,
3 captain of fifty
      and dignitary,
   counselor and skillful magician
      and expert enchanter.
4 And I will make boys their princes,
      and babes shall rule over them.
5 The people will be oppressed,
      everyone by another
      and everyone by a neighbor;
   the youth will be insolent to the
      elder,
   and the base to the honorable.

6 Someone will even seize a relative,
      a member of the clan, saying,
   "You have a cloak;
      you shall be our leader,

   and this heap of ruins
      shall be under your rule."
7 But the other will cry out on that
      day, saying,
   "I will not be a healer;
      in my house there is neither
         bread nor cloak;
   you shall not make me
      leader of the people."
8 For Jerusalem has stumbled
      and Judah has fallen,
   because their speech and their
         deeds are against the LORD,
   defying his glorious presence.

9 The look on their faces bears
         witness against them;
      they proclaim their sin like
         Sodom,
      they do not hide it.
   Woe to them!
      For they have brought evil on
         themselves.
10 Tell the innocent how fortunate
         they are,
      for they shall eat the fruit of their
         labors.
11 Woe to the guilty! How
         unfortunate they are,
      for what their hands have done
         shall be done to them.
12 My people—children are their
         oppressors,
      and women rule over them.
   O my people, your leaders mislead
         you,
      and confuse the course of your
         paths.

13 The LORD rises to argue his case;
      he stands to judge the peoples.
14 The LORD enters into judgment
      with the elders and princes of his
         people:
   It is you who have devoured the
         vineyard;
      the spoil of the poor is in your
         houses.
15 What do you mean by crushing my
         people,
      by grinding the face of the poor?
      says the Lord GOD of hosts.

16 The LORD said:
   Because the daughters of Zion are
      haughty

and walk with outstretched
  necks,
glancing wantonly with their
  eyes,
mincing along as they go,
  tinkling with their feet;
17   the Lord will afflict with scabs
        the heads of the daughters of
          Zion,
        and the LORD will lay bare their
          secret parts.

18 In that day the Lord will take away
the finery of the anklets, the headbands,
and the crescents; 19the pendants, the
bracelets, and the scarfs; 20the headdresses, the armlets, the sashes, the perfume boxes, and the amulets; 21the
signet rings and nose rings; 22the festal
robes, the mantles, the cloaks, and the
handbags; 23the garments of gauze, the
linen garments, the turbans, and the
veils.
24   Instead of perfume there will be a
        stench;
      and instead of a sash, a rope;
      and instead of well-set hair,
        baldness;
      and instead of a rich robe, a
        binding of sackcloth;
      instead of beauty, shame.g
25   Your men shall fall by the sword
        and your warriors in battle.
26   And her gates shall lament and
        mourn;
      ravaged, she shall sit upon the
        ground.

4 Seven women shall take hold of
   one man in that day, saying,
"We will eat our own bread and
    wear our own clothes;
just let us be called by your name;
  take away our disgrace."

The Future Glory of the Survivors
in Zion

2 On that day the branch of the LORD
shall be beautiful and glorious, and the
fruit of the land shall be the pride and
glory of the survivors of Israel. 3Whoever
is left in Zion and remains in Jerusalem
will be called holy, everyone who has
been recorded for life in Jerusalem, 4once
the Lord has washed away the filth of the
daughters of Zion and cleansed the

g Q Ms: MT lacks shame

bloodstains of Jerusalem from its midst
by a spirit of judgment and by a spirit of
burning. 5Then the LORD will create over
the whole site of Mount Zion and over
its places of assembly a cloud by day and
smoke and the shining of a flaming fire
by night. Indeed over all the glory there
will be a canopy. 6It will serve as a pavilion, a shade by day from the heat, and a
refuge and a shelter from the storm and
rain.

The Song of the Unfruitful Vineyard

5 Let me sing for my beloved
   my love-song concerning his
     vineyard:
My beloved had a vineyard
  on a very fertile hill.
2   He dug it and cleared it of stones,
      and planted it with choice vines;
    he built a watchtower in the midst
      of it,
      and hewed out a wine vat in it;
    he expected it to yield grapes,
      but it yielded wild grapes.

3   And now, inhabitants of Jerusalem
      and people of Judah,
    judge between me
      and my vineyard.
4   What more was there to do for my
        vineyard
      that I have not done in it?
    When I expected it to yield grapes,
      why did it yield wild grapes?

5   And now I will tell you
      what I will do to my vineyard.
    I will remove its hedge,
      and it shall be devoured;
    I will break down its wall,
      and it shall be trampled down.
6   I will make it a waste;
      it shall not be pruned or hoed,
      and it shall be overgrown with
        briers and thorns;
    I will also command the clouds
      that they rain no rain upon it.

7   For the vineyard of the LORD of hosts
      is the house of Israel,
    and the people of Judah
      are his pleasant planting;
    he expected justice,
      but saw bloodshed;

righteousness,
but heard a cry!

Social Injustice Denounced

8 Ah, you who join house to house,
who add field to field,
until there is room for no one but
you,

and you are left to live alone
in the midst of the land!
9 The LORD of hosts has sworn in my
hearing:
Surely many houses shall be
desolate,
large and beautiful houses,
without inhabitant.

FRIDAY

PERSONAL LIFE AND SOCIAL JUSTICE
Harry Emerson Fosdick

VERSE: Isaiah 5.7   **PASSAGE:** Isaiah 5.1–7

 nyone who cares about character must care about social conditions, for every unfair economic situation, every social evil left to run its course means ruin to character. And the God of the Bible, because he cares supremely for personal life at its best, is zealously in earnest about social justice; his prophets blazed with indignation at all inequity, and his Son made the coming kingdom, when God's will would be done on earth, the center of his message. To fellowship with this earnest purpose of God we all are summoned; God believes in the glorious possibilities of life on earth; he is counting on us to put away the sins that hold the kingdom back and to fight the abuses that crush character in men. To believe in God, therefore—the God who is fighting his way with his children up through ignorance, brutality, and selfishness to "new heavens and a new earth, where righteousness is at home"—is no weakly comfortable blessing (see 2 Peter 3.13). It means joining a moral war; it means devotion, sacrifice; its spirit is the Cross and its motive an undiscourageable faith. And our underlying assurance that this war for a better world can be won is not simply our belief that it can be done, but *our faith that God is, and that he believes that it can be done.* When we pray we say, "your kingdom come," and we are full of hope about the long, sacrificial struggle, for the purpose behind and through it all is first of all God's. Our earnestness is but an echo of his.

ADDITIONAL SCRIPTURE READING:
Isaiah 58.6–8; Zechariah 7.9–14; Matthew 3.8

Go to page 784 for your next devotional reading.

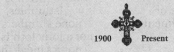

1900   Present

10   For ten acres of vineyard shall yield
             but one bath,
         and a homer of seed shall yield a
             mere ephah.*h*

11   Ah, you who rise early in the
             morning
         in pursuit of strong drink,
         who linger in the evening
             to be inflamed by wine,
12   whose feasts consist of lyre and
             harp,
         tambourine and flute and wine,
         but who do not regard the deeds of
             the LORD,
         or see the work of his hands!
13   Therefore my people go into exile
             without knowledge;
         their nobles are dying of hunger,
         and their multitude is parched
             with thirst.

14   Therefore Sheol has enlarged its
             appetite
         and opened its mouth beyond
             measure;
         the nobility of Jerusalem*i* and her
             multitude go down,
         her throng and all who exult in
             her.
15   People are bowed down, everyone
             is brought low,
         and the eyes of the haughty are
             humbled.
16   But the LORD of hosts is exalted by
             justice,
         and the Holy God shows himself
             holy by righteousness.
17   Then the lambs shall graze as in
             their pasture,
         fatlings and kids*j* shall feed
             among the ruins.

18   Ah, you who drag iniquity along
             with cords of falsehood,
         who drag sin along as with cart
             ropes,
19   who say, "Let him make haste,
         let him speed his work
         that we may see it;
         let the plan of the Holy One of
             Israel hasten to fulfillment,
         that we may know it!"
20   Ah, you who call evil good

         and good evil,
         who put darkness for light
             and light for darkness,
         who put bitter for sweet
             and sweet for bitter!

21   Ah, you who are wise in your own
             eyes,
         and shrewd in your own sight!
22   Ah, you who are heroes in drinking
             wine
         and valiant at mixing drink,
23   who acquit the guilty for a bribe,
         and deprive the innocent of their
             rights!

Foreign Invasion Predicted

24   Therefore, as the tongue of fire
             devours the stubble,
         and as dry grass sinks down in
             the flame,
         so their root will become rotten,
         and their blossom go up like
             dust;
         for they have rejected the
             instruction of the LORD of
             hosts,
         and have despised the word of
             the Holy One of Israel.

25   Therefore the anger of the LORD
             was kindled against his
             people,
         and he stretched out his hand
             against them and struck
             them;
         the mountains quaked,
         and their corpses were like refuse
             in the streets.
         For all this his anger has not turned
             away,
         and his hand is stretched out
             still.

26   He will raise a signal for a nation
             far away,
         and whistle for a people at the
             ends of the earth;
         Here they come, swiftly, speedily!
27   None of them is weary, none
             stumbles,
         none slumbers or sleeps,
         not a loincloth is loose,
         not a sandal-thong broken;

---

h The Heb *bath, homer,* and *ephah* are measures of quantity   *i* Heb *her nobility*   *j* Cn Compare
Gk: Heb *aliens*

28   their arrows are sharp,
     all their bows bent,
   their horses' hoofs seem like flint,
     and their wheels like the
      whirlwind.
29   Their roaring is like a lion,
     like young lions they roar;
   they growl and seize their prey,
     they carry it off, and no one can
      rescue.
30   They will roar over it on that day,
     like the roaring of the sea.
   And if one look to the land—
     only darkness and distress;
   and the light grows dark with
     clouds.

A Vision of God in the Temple

6 In the year that King Uzziah died, I saw the Lord sitting on a throne, high and lofty; and the hem of his robe filled the temple. 2Seraphs were in attendance above him; each had six wings: with two they covered their faces, and with two they covered their feet, and with two they flew. 3And one called to another and said:

   "Holy, holy, holy is the LORD of
     hosts;
   the whole earth is full of his glory."

4The pivots*k* on the thresholds shook at the voices of those who called, and the house filled with smoke. 5And I said: "Woe is me! I am lost, for I am a man of unclean lips, and I live among a people of unclean lips; yet my eyes have seen the King, the LORD of hosts!"

6 Then one of the seraphs flew to me, holding a live coal that had been taken from the altar with a pair of tongs. 7The seraph*l* touched my mouth with it and said: "Now that this has touched your lips, your guilt has departed and your sin is blotted out." 8Then I heard the voice of the Lord saying, "Whom shall I send, and who will go for us?" And I said, "Here am I; send me!" 9And he said, "Go and say to this people:

   'Keep listening, but do not
     comprehend;
   keep looking, but do not
     understand.'

10   Make the mind of this people dull,
     and stop their ears,

     and shut their eyes,
   so that they may not look with
     their eyes,
   and listen with their ears,
   and comprehend with their minds,
     and turn and be healed."
11   Then I said, "How long, O Lord?"
     And he said:
   "Until cities lie waste
     without inhabitant,
   and houses without people,
     and the land is utterly desolate;
12   until the LORD sends everyone far
     away,
   and vast is the emptiness in the
     midst of the land.
13   Even if a tenth part remain in it,
     it will be burned again,
   like a terebinth or an oak
     whose stump remains standing
     when it is felled."*k*
   The holy seed is its stump.

Isaiah Reassures King Ahaz

7 In the days of Ahaz son of Jotham son of Uzziah, king of Judah, King Rezin of Aram and King Pekah son of Remaliah of Israel went up to attack Jerusalem, but could not mount an attack against it. 2When the house of David heard that Aram had allied itself with Ephraim, the heart of Ahaz*m* and the heart of his people shook as the trees of the forest shake before the wind.

3 Then the LORD said to Isaiah, Go out to meet Ahaz, you and your son Shear-jashub,*n* at the end of the conduit of the upper pool on the highway to the Fuller's Field, 4and say to him, Take heed, be quiet, do not fear, and do not let your heart be faint because of these two smoldering stumps of firebrands, because of the fierce anger of Rezin and Aram and the son of Remaliah. 5Because Aram—with Ephraim and the son of Remaliah—has plotted evil against you, saying, 6Let us go up against Judah and cut off Jerusalem*o* and conquer it for ourselves and make the son of Tabeel king in it; 7therefore thus says the Lord GOD:

     It shall not stand,
      and it shall not come to pass.

k Meaning of Heb uncertain   *l* Heb *He*   *m* Heb *his heart*   *n* That is *A remnant shall return*
o Heb *cut it off*

WEEKEND

LORD, SPEAK TO ME, THAT I MAY SPEAK
Frances Ridley Havergal

VERSE: Isaiah 6.8   **PASSAGE:** Isaiah 6.1–8

 ord, speak to me, that I may speak
In living echoes of thy tone;
As thou hast sought, so let me seek
Thy erring children lost and lone.

O teach me, Lord, that I may teach
The precious things thou dost impart;
And wing my words, that they may reach
The hidden depths of many a heart.

O fill me with thy fullness, Lord,
Until my very heart o'erflow
In kindling thought and glowing word,
Thy love to tell, thy praise to show.

O use me, Lord, use even me,
Just as thou wilt, and when and where;
Until thy blessed face I see,
Thy rest, thy joy, thy glory share.

ADDITIONAL SCRIPTURE READING:
Exodus 4.10–13; Acts 26.16–18

Go to page 786 for your next devotional reading.

1700   1900

8 For the head of Aram is Damascus,
and the head of Damascus is
Rezin.
(Within sixty-five years Ephraim will
be shattered, no longer a people.)
9 The head of Ephraim is Samaria,
and the head of Samaria is the
son of Remaliah.
If you do not stand firm in faith,
you shall not stand at all.

Isaiah Gives Ahaz the Sign of Immanuel

10 Again the LORD spoke to Ahaz, saying, **11**Ask a sign of the LORD your God; let it be deep as Sheol or high as heaven. **12**But Ahaz said, I will not ask, and I will not put the LORD to the test. **13**Then Isaiah*p* said: "Hear then, O house of David! Is it too little for you to weary mortals, that you weary my God also? **14**Therefore the Lord himself will give you a sign. Look, the young woman*q* is with child and shall bear a son, and shall name him Immanuel.*r* **15**He shall eat curds and honey by the time he knows how to refuse the evil and choose the good. **16**For before the child knows how to refuse the evil and choose the good, the land before whose two kings you are in dread will be deserted. **17**The LORD will bring on you and on your people and on your ancestral house such days as have not come since the day that Ephraim departed from Judah—the king of Assyria."

18 On that day the LORD will whistle for the fly that is at the sources of the streams of Egypt, and for the bee that is in the land of Assyria. **19**And they will all come and settle in the steep ravines, and in the clefts of the rocks, and on all the thornbushes, and on all the pastures. **20** On that day the Lord will shave with a razor hired beyond the River— with the king of Assyria—the head and the hair of the feet, and it will take off the beard as well.

21 On that day one will keep alive a young cow and two sheep, **22**and will eat curds because of the abundance of milk that they give; for everyone that is left in the land shall eat curds and honey.

23 On that day every place where there used to be a thousand vines, worth a thousand shekels of silver, will become briers and thorns. **24**With bow and arrows one will go there, for all the land will be briers and thorns; **25**and as for all the hills that used to be hoed with a hoe, you will not go there for fear of briers and thorns; but they will become a place where cattle are let loose and where sheep tread.

Isaiah's Son a Sign of the Assyrian Invasion

8 Then the LORD said to me, Take a large tablet and write on it in common characters, "Belonging to Maher-shalal-hash-baz,"*s* **2**and have it attested*t* for me by reliable witnesses, the priest Uriah and Zechariah son of Jeberechiah. **3**And I went to the prophetess, and she conceived and bore a son. Then the LORD said to me, Name him Maher-shalal-hash-baz; **4**for before the child knows how to call "My father" or "My mother," the wealth of Damascus and the spoil of Samaria will be carried away by the king of Assyria.

5 The LORD spoke to me again: **6**Because this people has refused the waters of Shiloah that flow gently, and melt in fear before*u* Rezin and the son of Remaliah; **7**therefore, the Lord is bringing up against it the mighty flood waters of the River, the king of Assyria and all his glory; it will rise above all its channels and overflow all its banks; **8**it will sweep on into Judah as a flood, and, pouring over, it will reach up to the neck; and its outspread wings will fill the breadth of your land, O Immanuel.

9 Band together, you peoples, and be
dismayed;
listen, all you far countries;
gird yourselves and be dismayed;
gird yourselves and be dismayed!
10 Take counsel together, but it shall
be brought to naught;
speak a word, but it will not stand,
for God is with us.*v*

11 For the LORD spoke thus to me while his hand was strong upon me, and warned me not to walk in the way of

p Heb *he*   *q* Gk *the virgin*   *r* That is *God is with us*   *s* That is *The spoil speeds, the prey hastens*
t Q Ms Gk Syr: MT *and I caused to be attested*   *u* Cn: Meaning of Heb uncertain
v Heb *immanu el*

this people, saying: 12Do not call conspiracy all that this people calls conspiracy, and do not fear what it fears, or be in dread. 13But the LORD of hosts, him you shall regard as holy; let him be your fear, and let him be your dread. 14He will become a sanctuary, a stone one strikes against; for both houses of Israel he will become a rock one stumbles over—a trap and a snare for the inhabitants of Jerusalem. 15And many among them shall stumble; they shall fall and be broken; they shall be snared and taken.

Disciples of Isaiah

16 Bind up the testimony, seal the teaching among my disciples. 17I will wait for the LORD, who is hiding his face

---

MONDAY

OUT OF THE PICTURE
E. Stanley Jones

VERSE: Isaiah 7.14   **PASSAGE:** Isaiah 7.10–14

A little boy stood before the picture of his absent father, and then turned to his mother and wistfully said, "I wish father would step out of the picture."

This little boy expressed the deepest yearning of the human heart. We who have gazed upon the picture of God in nature are grateful, but not satisfied. We want our Father to step out of the impersonal picture and meet us as a person . . . The human heart is personal and wants a personal response.

"Why won't principles do? Why do we need a personal God?" someone asks. Well, suppose you go to a child crying for its mother and say, "Don't cry, little child; I'm giving to you the principle of motherhood." Would the tears dry and the face light up? Hardly. The child would brush aside your principle of motherhood and cry for its mother. We all want, not a principle nor a picture, but a person.

The Father *has* stepped out of the picture. The Word *has* become flesh (see John 1.14). That is the meaning of Christmas. Jesus is Immanuel—God with us. He is the personal approach from the unseen. We almost gasp as the Picture steps out of the frame . . . I look at the character and life of Jesus, and I know what God's character is like . . . [And] I too must become the word made flesh . . .

Gracious Father, as thou hast stepped out of the picture, help me this day to step out of the picture and let someone see in me the meaning of a Christian . . . Amen.

ADDITIONAL SCRIPTURE READING:
Matthew 1.23; Luke 1.35; John 1.14

Go to page 791 for your next devotional reading.

1900   Present

from the house of Jacob, and I will hope in him. ¹⁸See, I and the children whom the LORD has given me are signs and portents in Israel from the LORD of hosts, who dwells on Mount Zion. ¹⁹Now if people say to you, "Consult the ghosts and the familiar spirits that chirp and mutter; should not a people consult their gods, the dead on behalf of the living, ²⁰for teaching and for instruction?" surely, those who speak like this will have no dawn! ²¹They will pass through the land,ʷ greatly distressed and hungry; when they are hungry, they will be enraged and will curseˣ their king and their gods. They will turn their faces upward, ²²or they will look to the earth, but will see only distress and darkness, the gloom of anguish; and they will be thrust into thick darkness.ʸ

The Righteous Reign of the Coming King

9ᶻ But there will be no gloom for those who were in anguish. In the former time he brought into contempt the land of Zebulun and the land of Naphtali, but in the latter time he will make glorious the way of the sea, the land beyond the Jordan, Galilee of the nations.

2ᵃ The people who walked in
    darkness
    have seen a great light;
those who lived in a land of deep
    darkness—
    on them light has shined.
3 You have multiplied the nation,
    you have increased its joy;
they rejoice before you
    as with joy at the harvest,
    as people exult when dividing
    plunder.
4 For the yoke of their burden,
    and the bar across their
    shoulders,
    the rod of their oppressor,
    you have broken as on the day of
    Midian.
5 For all the boots of the tramping
    warriors
    and all the garments rolled in
    blood
    shall be burned as fuel for the fire.

6 For a child has been born for us,
    a son given to us;
authority rests upon his shoulders;
    and he is named
Wonderful Counselor, Mighty God,
    Everlasting Father, Prince of
    Peace.
7 His authority shall grow
    continually,
    and there shall be endless peace
for the throne of David and his
    kingdom.
He will establish and uphold it
with justice and with righteousness
    from this time onward and
    forevermore.
The zeal of the LORD of hosts will
    do this.

Judgment on Arrogance and Oppression

8 The Lord sent a word against Jacob,
    and it fell on Israel;
9 and all the people knew it—
    Ephraim and the inhabitants of
    Samaria—
    but in pride and arrogance of
    heart they said:
10 "The bricks have fallen,
    but we will build with dressed
    stones;
the sycamores have been cut down,
    but we will put cedars in their
    place."
11 So the LORD raised adversariesᵇ
    against them,
    and stirred up their enemies,
12 the Arameans on the east and the
    Philistines on the west,
    and they devoured Israel with
    open mouth.
For all this his anger has not turned
    away;
    his hand is stretched out still.

13 The people did not turn to him
    who struck them,
    or seek the LORD of hosts.
14 So the LORD cut off from Israel
    head and tail,
    palm branch and reed in one
    day—

w Heb *it*   x Or *curse by*   y Meaning of Heb uncertain   z Ch 8.23 in Heb   a Ch 9.1 in Heb
b Cn: Heb *the adversaries of Rezin*

15 elders and dignitaries are the head,
  and prophets who teach lies are
    the tail;
16 for those who led this people led
    them astray,
  and those who were led by them
    were left in confusion.
17 That is why the Lord did not have
    pity on[c] their young people,
  or compassion on their orphans
    and widows;
  for everyone was godless and an
    evildoer,
  and every mouth spoke folly.
  For all this his anger has not turned
    away;
  his hand is stretched out still.

18 For wickedness burned like a fire,
  consuming briers and thorns;
  it kindled the thickets of the forest,
  and they swirled upward in a
    column of smoke.
19 Through the wrath of the LORD of
    hosts
  the land was burned,
  and the people became like fuel for
    the fire;
  no one spared another.
20 They gorged on the right, but still
    were hungry,
  and they devoured on the left,
    but were not satisfied;
  they devoured the flesh of their
    own kindred;[d]
21 Manasseh devoured Ephraim, and
    Ephraim Manasseh,
  and together they were against
    Judah.
  For all this his anger has not turned
    away;
  his hand is stretched out still.

10 Ah, you who make
  iniquitous decrees,
  who write oppressive statutes,
2 to turn aside the needy from justice
  and to rob the poor of my people
    of their right,
  that widows may be your spoil,
  and that you may make the
    orphans your prey!

3 What will you do on the day of
    punishment,
  in the calamity that will come
    from far away?
  To whom will you flee for help,
  and where will you leave your
    wealth,
4 so as not to crouch among the
    prisoners
  or fall among the slain?
  For all this his anger has not turned
    away;
  his hand is stretched out still.

Arrogant Assyria Also Judged

5 Ah, Assyria, the rod of my anger—
  the club in their hands is my
    fury!
6 Against a godless nation I send
    him,
  and against the people of my
    wrath I command him,
  to take spoil and seize plunder,
  and to tread them down like the
    mire of the streets.
7 But this is not what he intends,
  nor does he have this in mind;
  but it is in his heart to destroy,
  and to cut off nations not a few.
8 For he says:
  "Are not my commanders all
    kings?
9 Is not Calno like Carchemish?
  Is not Hamath like Arpad?
  Is not Samaria like Damascus?
10 As my hand has reached to the
    kingdoms of the idols
  whose images were greater than
    those of Jerusalem and
    Samaria,
11 shall I not do to Jerusalem and her
    idols
  what I have done to Samaria and
    her images?"

12 When the Lord has finished all his
work on Mount Zion and on Jerusalem,
he[e] will punish the arrogant boasting of
the king of Assyria and his haughty
pride. 13For he says:
  "By the strength of my hand I have
    done it,

c Q Ms: MT *rejoice over*   d Or *arm*   e Heb *I*

and by my wisdom, for I have
    understanding;
I have removed the boundaries of
    peoples,
and have plundered their
    treasures;
like a bull I have brought down
    those who sat on thrones.
14 My hand has found, like a nest,
    the wealth of the peoples;
and as one gathers eggs that have
    been forsaken,
so I have gathered all the earth;
and there was none that moved a
    wing,
or opened its mouth, or chirped."

15 Shall the ax vaunt itself over the
    one who wields it,
or the saw magnify itself against
    the one who handles it?
As if a rod should raise the one who
    lifts it up,
or as if a staff should lift the one
    who is not wood!
16 Therefore the Sovereign, the LORD
    of hosts,
will send wasting sickness
    among his stout warriors,
and under his glory a burning will
    be kindled,
like the burning of fire.
17 The light of Israel will become a
    fire,
and his Holy One a flame;
and it will burn and devour
    his thorns and briers in one day.
18 The glory of his forest and his
    fruitful land
the LORD will destroy, both soul
    and body,
and it will be as when an invalid
    wastes away.
19 The remnant of the trees of his
    forest will be so few
that a child can write them
    down.

The Repentant Remnant of Israel

20 On that day the remnant of Israel
and the survivors of the house of Jacob
will no more lean on the one who struck
them, but will lean on the LORD, the
Holy One of Israel, in truth. 21A remnant will return, the remnant of Jacob,
to the mighty God. 22For though your
people Israel were like the sand of the
sea, only a remnant of them will return.
Destruction is decreed, overflowing
with righteousness. 23For the Lord GOD
of hosts will make a full end, as decreed,
in all the earth.f

24 Therefore thus says the Lord GOD
of hosts: O my people, who live in Zion,
do not be afraid of the Assyrians when
they beat you with a rod and lift up their
staff against you as the Egyptians did.
25For in a very little while my indignation will come to an end, and my anger
will be directed to their destruction.
26The LORD of hosts will wield a whip
against them, as when he struck Midian
at the rock of Oreb; his staff will be over
the sea, and he will lift it as he did in
Egypt. 27On that day his burden will be
removed from your shoulder, and his
yoke will be destroyed from your neck.

He has gone up from Rimmon,g
28   he has come to Aiath;
he has passed through Migron,
    at Michmash he stores his
    baggage;
29 they have crossed over the pass,
    at Geba they lodge for the night;
Ramah trembles,
    Gibeah of Saul has fled.
30 Cry aloud, O daughter Gallim!
    Listen, O Laishah!
    Answer her, O Anathoth!
31 Madmenah is in flight,
    the inhabitants of Gebim flee for
    safety.
32 This very day he will halt at Nob,
    he will shake his fist
    at the mount of daughter Zion,
    the hill of Jerusalem.

33 Look, the Sovereign, the LORD of
    hosts,
    will lop the boughs with
    terrifying power;
the tallest trees will be cut down,
    and the lofty will be brought low.
34 He will hack down the thickets of
    the forest with an ax,
    and Lebanon with its majestic
    treesh will fall.

f Or land   g Cn: Heb and his yoke from your neck, and a yoke will be destroyed because of fatness
h Cn Compare Gk Vg: Heb with a majestic one

The Peaceful Kingdom

11 A shoot shall come out from
the stump of Jesse,
and a branch shall grow out of
his roots.
2 The spirit of the LORD shall rest on
him,
the spirit of wisdom and
understanding,
the spirit of counsel and might,
the spirit of knowledge and the
fear of the LORD.
3 His delight shall be in the fear of
the LORD.

He shall not judge by what his eyes
see,
or decide by what his ears hear;
4 but with righteousness he shall
judge the poor,
and decide with equity for the
meek of the earth;
he shall strike the earth with the
rod of his mouth,
and with the breath of his lips he
shall kill the wicked.
5 Righteousness shall be the belt
around his waist,
and faithfulness the belt around
his loins.

6 The wolf shall live with the lamb,
the leopard shall lie down with
the kid,
the calf and the lion and the fatling
together,
and a little child shall lead them.
7 The cow and the bear shall graze,
their young shall lie down
together;
and the lion shall eat straw like
the ox.
8 The nursing child shall play over
the hole of the asp,
and the weaned child shall put
its hand on the adder's den.
9 They will not hurt or destroy
on all my holy mountain;
for the earth will be full of the
knowledge of the LORD
as the waters cover the sea.

Return of the Remnant of Israel and Judah

10 On that day the root of Jesse shall stand as a signal to the peoples; the nations shall inquire of him, and his dwelling shall be glorious.

11 On that day the Lord will extend his hand yet a second time to recover the remnant that is left of his people, from Assyria, from Egypt, from Pathros, from Ethiopia,*i* from Elam, from Shinar, from Hamath, and from the coastlands of the sea.
12 He will raise a signal for the
nations,
and will assemble the outcasts of
Israel,
and gather the dispersed of Judah
from the four corners of the earth.
13 The jealousy of Ephraim shall
depart,
the hostility of Judah shall be cut
off;
Ephraim shall not be jealous of
Judah,
and Judah shall not be hostile
towards Ephraim.
14 But they shall swoop down on the
backs of the Philistines in
the west,
together they shall plunder the
people of the east.
They shall put forth their hand
against Edom and Moab,
and the Ammonites shall obey
them.
15 And the LORD will utterly destroy
the tongue of the sea of Egypt;
and will wave his hand over the
River
with his scorching wind;
and will split it into seven
channels,
and make a way to cross on foot;
16 so there shall be a highway from
Assyria
for the remnant that is left of his
people,
as there was for Israel
when they came up from the
land of Egypt.

i Or *Nubia*; Heb *Cush*

Thanksgiving and Praise

12 You will say in that day:
I will give thanks to you,
O LORD,
for though you were angry with
me,
your anger turned away,
and you comforted me.

2 Surely God is my salvation;
I will trust, and will not be afraid,

j Heb *for Yah, the* LORD

for the LORD GOD*j* is my strength
and my might;
he has become my salvation.

3 With joy you will draw water from
the wells of salvation. 4 And you will say
in that day:
Give thanks to the LORD,
call on his name;
make known his deeds among the
nations;

TUESDAY

THE WELLS OF SALVATION
J. H. Jowett

VERSE: Isaiah 12.3   **PASSAGE:** Isaiah 12.1–3

he wells of the Lord are to be found where most I need them. The Lord of the way knows the pilgrim life, and the wells have been unsealed just where the soul is prone to become dry and faint. At the foot of the hill Difficulty was found a spring! Yes, these health-springs are lifting their crystal flood in the cheerless wastes of evil antagonisms and exhausting grief.

Sometimes I am foolish, and in my need I assume that the well is far away. I knew a farmer who for a generation had carried every pail of water from a distant well to meet the needs of his homestead. And one day he sunk a shaft by his own house door, and to his great joy he found that the water was waiting at his own gate! My soul, thy well is near, even here! Go not in search of him! Thy pilgrimage is ended, the waters are at thy feet!

But I must *"draw* the water out of the wells of salvation." The hand of faith must lift the gracious gift to the parched lips, and so refresh the panting soul. "I will *take* the cup of salvation." Stretch out thy "lame hand of faith," and take the holy, hallowing energy offered by the Lord.

ADDITIONAL SCRIPTURE READING:
Isaiah 55.1–3; John 4.10–14; 7.37–39

Go to page 804 for your next devotional reading.

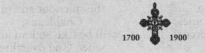

1700   1900

proclaim that his name is
  exalted.

5 Sing praises to the LORD, for he has
     done gloriously;
   let this be known[k] in all the
     earth.
6 Shout aloud and sing for joy,
     O royal[l] Zion,
   for great in your midst is the
     Holy One of Israel.

Proclamation against Babylon

13 The oracle concerning Babylon
       that Isaiah son of Amoz saw.

2 On a bare hill raise a signal,
     cry aloud to them;
   wave the hand for them to enter
     the gates of the nobles.
3 I myself have commanded my
     consecrated ones,
   have summoned my warriors,
     my proudly exulting ones,
   to execute my anger.

4 Listen, a tumult on the mountains
     as of a great multitude!
   Listen, an uproar of kingdoms,
     of nations gathering together!
   The LORD of hosts is mustering
     an army for battle.
5 They come from a distant land,
     from the end of the heavens,
   the LORD and the weapons of his
     indignation,
   to destroy the whole earth.

6 Wail, for the day of the LORD is
     near;
   it will come like destruction
     from the Almighty![m]
7 Therefore all hands will be feeble,
     and every human heart will melt,
8 and they will be dismayed.
   Pangs and agony will seize them;
     they will be in anguish like a
       woman in labor.
   They will look aghast at one
     another;
   their faces will be aflame.
9 See, the day of the LORD comes,
     cruel, with wrath and fierce
       anger,

to make the earth a desolation,
  and to destroy its sinners from it.
10 For the stars of the heavens and
     their constellations
   will not give their light;
   the sun will be dark at its rising,
     and the moon will not shed its
       light.
11 I will punish the world for its evil,
     and the wicked for their iniquity;
   I will put an end to the pride of the
     arrogant,
   and lay low the insolence of
     tyrants.
12 I will make mortals more rare than
     fine gold,
   and humans than the gold of
     Ophir.
13 Therefore I will make the heavens
     tremble,
   and the earth will be shaken out
     of its place,
   at the wrath of the LORD of hosts
     in the day of his fierce anger.
14 Like a hunted gazelle,
     or like sheep with no one to
       gather them,
   all will turn to their own people,
     and all will flee to their own
       lands.
15 Whoever is found will be thrust
     through,
   and whoever is caught will fall
     by the sword.
16 Their infants will be dashed to
     pieces
     before their eyes;
   their houses will be plundered,
     and their wives ravished.
17 See, I am stirring up the Medes
     against them,
   who have no regard for silver
     and do not delight in gold.
18 Their bows will slaughter the
     young men;
   they will have no mercy on the
     fruit of the womb;
   their eyes will not pity children.
19 And Babylon, the glory of
     kingdoms,
   the splendor and pride of the
     Chaldeans,
   will be like Sodom and Gomorrah
     when God overthrew them.

k Or this is made known   l Or O inhabitant of   m Traditional rendering of Heb Shaddai

20 It will never be inhabited
      or lived in for all generations;
   Arabs will not pitch their tents
         there,
      shepherds will not make their
         flocks lie down there.
21 But wild animals will lie down
         there,
      and its houses will be full of
         howling creatures;
   there ostriches will live,
      and there goat-demons will
         dance.
22 Hyenas will cry in its towers,
      and jackals in the pleasant
         palaces;
   its time is close at hand,
      and its days will not be prolonged.

Restoration of Judah

14 But the LORD will have compassion on Jacob and will
again choose Israel, and will set them in
their own land; and aliens will join them
and attach themselves to the house of
Jacob. 2 And the nations will take them
and bring them to their place, and the
house of Israel will possess the nations[n]
as male and female slaves in the LORD's
land; they will take captive those who
were their captors, and rule over those
who oppressed them.

Downfall of the King of Babylon

3 When the LORD has given you rest
from your pain and turmoil and the hard
service with which you were made to
serve, 4 you will take up this taunt
against the king of Babylon:
   How the oppressor has ceased!
      How his insolence[o] has ceased!
5   The LORD has broken the staff of
         the wicked,
      the scepter of rulers,
6   that struck down the peoples in
         wrath
      with unceasing blows,
   that ruled the nations in anger
      with unrelenting persecution.
7   The whole earth is at rest and
         quiet;
      they break forth into singing.
8   The cypresses exult over you,
      the cedars of Lebanon, saying,

"Since you were laid low,
   no one comes to cut us down."
9 Sheol beneath is stirred up
      to meet you when you come;
   it rouses the shades to greet you,
      all who were leaders of the earth;
   it raises from their thrones
      all who were kings of the
         nations.
10 All of them will speak
      and say to you:
   "You too have become as weak as
         we!
   You have become like us!"
11 Your pomp is brought down to
         Sheol,
      and the sound of your harps;
   maggots are the bed beneath you,
      and worms are your covering.

12 How you are fallen from heaven,
      O Day Star, son of Dawn!
   How you are cut down to the
         ground,
      you who laid the nations low!
13 You said in your heart,
      "I will ascend to heaven;
   I will raise my throne
      above the stars of God;
   I will sit on the mount of assembly
      on the heights of Zaphon;[p]
14 I will ascend to the tops of the
         clouds,
      I will make myself like the Most
         High."
15 But you are brought down to Sheol,
      to the depths of the Pit.
16 Those who see you will stare at
         you,
      and ponder over you:
   "Is this the man who made the
         earth tremble,
      who shook kingdoms,
17 who made the world like a desert
      and overthrew its cities,
      who would not let his prisoners
         go home?"
18 All the kings of the nations lie in
         glory,
      each in his own tomb;
19 but you are cast out, away from
         your grave,
      like loathsome carrion,[q]

n Heb them   o Q Ms Compare Gk Syr Vg: Meaning of MT uncertain   p Or assembly in the far
north   q Cn Compare Gk: Heb like a loathed branch

clothed with the dead, those
    pierced by the sword,
who go down to the stones of the
    Pit,
like a corpse trampled underfoot.
20 You will not be joined with them
    in burial,
because you have destroyed your
    land,
you have killed your people.

May the descendants of evildoers
    nevermore be named!
21 Prepare slaughter for his sons
    because of the guilt of their
      father.*r*
Let them never rise to possess the
    earth
    or cover the face of the world
      with cities.

22 I will rise up against them, says
the LORD of hosts, and will cut off from
Babylon name and remnant, offspring
and posterity, says the LORD. 23 And I
will make it a possession of the hedgehog, and pools of water, and I will sweep
it with the broom of destruction, says
the LORD of hosts.

An Oracle concerning Assyria

24 The LORD of hosts has sworn:
As I have designed,
    so shall it be;
and as I have planned,
    so shall it come to pass:
25 I will break the Assyrian in my
    land,
    and on my mountains trample
      him under foot;
his yoke shall be removed from
    them,
    and his burden from their
      shoulders.
26 This is the plan that is planned
    concerning the whole earth;
and this is the hand that is
    stretched out
    over all the nations.
27 For the LORD of hosts has planned,
    and who will annul it?
His hand is stretched out,
    and who will turn it back?

An Oracle concerning Philistia

28 In the year that King Ahaz died this
oracle came:

29 Do not rejoice, all you Philistines,
    that the rod that struck you is
      broken,
for from the root of the snake will
    come forth an adder,
    and its fruit will be a flying fiery
      serpent.
30 The firstborn of the poor will graze,
    and the needy lie down in safety;
but I will make your root die of
    famine,
    and your remnant I*s* will kill.
31 Wail, O gate; cry, O city;
    melt in fear, O Philistia, all of
      you!
For smoke comes out of the north,
    and there is no straggler in its
      ranks.

32 What will one answer the
    messengers of the nation?
"The LORD has founded Zion,
    and the needy among his people
    will find refuge in her."

An Oracle concerning Moab

15 An oracle concerning Moab.

Because Ar is laid waste in a night,
    Moab is undone;
because Kir is laid waste in a night,
    Moab is undone.
2 Dibon*t* has gone up to the temple,
    to the high places to weep;
over Nebo and over Medeba
    Moab wails.
On every head is baldness,
    every beard is shorn;
3 in the streets they bind on
      sackcloth;
    on the housetops and in the
      squares
    everyone wails and melts in
      tears.
4 Heshbon and Elealeh cry out,
    their voices are heard as far as
      Jahaz;
therefore the loins of Moab quiver;*u*
    his soul trembles.

r Syr Compare Gk: Heb *fathers*   *s* Q Ms Vg: MT *he*   *t* Cn: Heb *the house and Dibon*
u Cn Compare Gk Syr: Heb *the armed men of Moab cry aloud*

5 My heart cries out for Moab;
    his fugitives flee to Zoar,
    to Eglath-shelishiyah.
For at the ascent of Luhith
    they go up weeping;
on the road to Horonaim
    they raise a cry of destruction;
6 the waters of Nimrim
    are a desolation;
the grass is withered, the new
        growth fails,
    the verdure is no more.
7 Therefore the abundance they have
        gained
    and what they have laid up
they carry away
    over the Wadi of the Willows.
8 For a cry has gone
    around the land of Moab;
the wailing reaches to Eglaim,
    the wailing reaches to Beer-elim.
9 For the waters of Dibon^v are full of
        blood;
    yet I will bring upon Dibon^v even
        more—
    a lion for those of Moab who escape,
    for the remnant of the land.

16 Send lambs
    to the ruler of the land,
from Sela, by way of the desert,
    to the mount of daughter Zion.
2 Like fluttering birds,
    like scattered nestlings,
so are the daughters of Moab
    at the fords of the Arnon.
3 "Give counsel,
    grant justice;
make your shade like night
    at the height of noon;
hide the outcasts,
    do not betray the fugitive;
4 let the outcasts of Moab
    settle among you;
be a refuge to them
    from the destroyer."

When the oppressor is no more,
    and destruction has ceased,
and marauders have vanished from
        the land,
5 then a throne shall be established
        in steadfast love
    in the tent of David,

and on it shall sit in faithfulness
a ruler who seeks justice
    and is swift to do what is right.

6 We have heard of the pride of Moab
    —how proud he is!—
of his arrogance, his pride, and his
        insolence;
    his boasts are false.
7 Therefore let Moab wail,
    let everyone wail for Moab.
Mourn, utterly stricken,
    for the raisin cakes of Kir-
        hareseth.

8 For the fields of Heshbon languish,
    and the vines of Sibmah,
whose clusters once made drunk
    the lords of the nations,
reached to Jazer
    and strayed to the desert;
their shoots once spread abroad
    and crossed over the sea.
9 Therefore I weep with the weeping
        of Jazer
    for the vines of Sibmah;
I drench you with my tears,
    O Heshbon and Elealeh;
for the shout over your fruit harvest
    and your grain harvest has ceased.
10 Joy and gladness are taken away
        from the fruitful field;
and in the vineyards no songs are
        sung,
    no shouts are raised;
no treader treads out wine in the
        presses;
    the vintage-shout is hushed.^{w}
11 Therefore my heart throbs like a
        harp for Moab,
    and my very soul for Kir-heres.

12 When Moab presents himself, when he wearies himself upon the high place, when he comes to his sanctuary to pray, he will not prevail.

13 This was the word that the LORD spoke concerning Moab in the past. 14But now the LORD says, In three years, like the years of a hired worker, the glory of Moab will be brought into contempt, in spite of all its great multitude; and those who survive will be very few and feeble.

---

v Q Ms Vg Compare Syr: MT *Dimon* w Gk: Heb *I have hushed*

Cn Compare Gk: Heb *the cities of Aroer are deserted*
places of the wood and the highest bough   a Or *Nubia*; Heb *Cush*

4 For thus the LORD said to me:
   I will quietly look from my
      dwelling
      like clear heat in sunshine,
      like a cloud of dew in the heat of
         harvest.
5 For before the harvest, when the
      blossom is over
   and the flower becomes a
      ripening grape,
   he will cut off the shoots with
      pruning hooks,
   and the spreading branches he
      will hew away.
6 They shall all be left
      to the birds of prey of the
         mountains
   and to the animals of the earth.
   And the birds of prey will summer
      on them,
   and all the animals of the earth
      will winter on them.

7 At that time gifts will be brought to
the LORD of hosts from[b] a people tall and
smooth, from a people feared near and
far, a nation mighty and conquering,
whose land the rivers divide, to Mount
Zion, the place of the name of the LORD
of hosts.

An Oracle concerning Egypt

19 An oracle concerning Egypt.

See, the LORD is riding on a swift
   cloud
   and comes to Egypt;
the idols of Egypt will tremble at
   his presence,
   and the heart of the Egyptians
      will melt within them.
2 I will stir up Egyptians against
      Egyptians,
   and they will fight, one against
      the other,
   neighbor against neighbor,
   city against city, kingdom against
      kingdom;
3 the spirit of the Egyptians within
      them will be emptied out,
   and I will confound their plans;
   they will consult the idols and the
      spirits of the dead
   and the ghosts and the familiar
      spirits;

4 I will deliver the Egyptians
      into the hand of a hard master;
   a fierce king will rule over them,
      says the Sovereign, the LORD of
         hosts.
5 The waters of the Nile will be dried
      up,
   and the river will be parched and
      dry;
6 its canals will become foul,
   and the branches of Egypt's Nile
      will diminish and dry up,
   reeds and rushes will rot away.
7 There will be bare places by the
      Nile,
   on the brink of the Nile;
and all that is sown by the Nile
      will dry up,
   be driven away, and be no more.
8 Those who fish will mourn;
   all who cast hooks in the Nile
      will lament,
   and those who spread nets on the
      water will languish.
9 The workers in flax will be in
      despair,
   and the carders and those at the
      loom will grow pale.
10 Its weavers will be dismayed,
   and all who work for wages will
      be grieved.

11 The princes of Zoan are utterly
      foolish;
   the wise counselors of Pharaoh
      give stupid counsel.
How can you say to Pharaoh,
   "I am one of the sages,
   a descendant of ancient kings"?
12 Where now are your sages?
   Let them tell you and make
      known
   what the LORD of hosts has
      planned against Egypt.
13 The princes of Zoan have become
      fools,
   and the princes of Memphis are
      deluded;
   those who are the cornerstones of
      its tribes
   have led Egypt astray.
14 The LORD has poured into them[c]
   a spirit of confusion;

b Q Ms Gk Vg: MT *of*   c Gk Compare Tg: Heb *it*

and they have made Egypt stagger
    in all its doings
  as a drunkard staggers around in
    vomit.
15 Neither head nor tail, palm branch
    or reed,
  will be able to do anything for
    Egypt.

16 On that day the Egyptians will be like women, and tremble with fear before the hand that the LORD of hosts raises against them. 17 And the land of Judah will become a terror to the Egyptians; everyone to whom it is mentioned will fear because of the plan that the LORD of hosts is planning against them.

Egypt, Assyria, and Israel Blessed

18 On that day there will be five cities in the land of Egypt that speak the language of Canaan and swear allegiance to the LORD of hosts. One of these will be called the City of the Sun.

19 On that day there will be an altar to the LORD in the center of the land of Egypt, and a pillar to the LORD at its border. 20 It will be a sign and a witness to the LORD of hosts in the land of Egypt; when they cry to the LORD because of oppressors, he will send them a savior, and will defend and deliver them. 21 The LORD will make himself known to the Egyptians; and the Egyptians will know the LORD on that day, and will worship with sacrifice and burnt offering, and they will make vows to the LORD and perform them. 22 The LORD will strike Egypt, striking and healing; they will return to the LORD, and he will listen to their supplications and heal them.

23 On that day there will be a highway from Egypt to Assyria, and the Assyrian will come into Egypt, and the Egyptian into Assyria, and the Egyptians will worship with the Assyrians.

24 On that day Israel will be the third with Egypt and Assyria, a blessing in the midst of the earth, 25 whom the LORD of hosts has blessed, saying, "Blessed be Egypt my people, and Assyria the work of my hands, and Israel my heritage."

Isaiah Dramatizes the Conquest of Egypt and Ethiopia

20 In the year that the commander-in-chief, who was sent by King Sargon of Assyria, came to Ashdod and fought against it and took it— 2 at that time the LORD had spoken to Isaiah son of Amoz, saying, "Go, and loose the sackcloth from your loins and take your sandals off your feet," and he had done so, walking naked and barefoot. 3 Then the LORD said, "Just as my servant Isaiah has walked naked and barefoot for three years as a sign and a portent against Egypt and Ethiopia,d 4 so shall the king of Assyria lead away the Egyptians as captives and the Ethiopianse as exiles, both the young and the old, naked and barefoot, with buttocks uncovered, to the shame of Egypt. 5 And they shall be dismayed and confounded because of Ethiopiad their hope and of Egypt their boast. 6 In that day the inhabitants of this coastland will say, 'See, this is what has happened to those in whom we hoped and to whom we fled for help and deliverance from the king of Assyria! And we, how shall we escape?' "

Oracles concerning Babylon, Edom, and Arabia

21 The oracle concerning the wilderness of the sea.

  As whirlwinds in the Negeb sweep
    on,
    it comes from the desert,
    from a terrible land.
2 A stern vision is told to me;
    the betrayer betrays,
    and the destroyer destroys.
  Go up, O Elam,
    lay siege, O Media;
  all the sighing she has caused
    I bring to an end.
3 Therefore my loins are filled with
    anguish;
    pangs have seized me,
    like the pangs of a woman in
      labor;
  I am bowed down so that I cannot
    hear,
  I am dismayed so that I cannot
    see.

d Or Nubia; Heb Cush   e Or Nubians; Heb Cushites

4 My mind reels, horror has appalled
        me;
   the twilight I longed for
   has been turned for me into
        trembling.
5 They prepare the table,
   they spread the rugs,
   they eat, they drink.
   Rise up, commanders,
        oil the shield!
6 For thus the Lord said to me:
   "Go, post a lookout,
   let him announce what he sees.
7 When he sees riders, horsemen in
        pairs,
   riders on donkeys, riders on
        camels,
   let him listen diligently,
        very diligently."
8 Then the watcher*f* called out:
   "Upon a watchtower I stand,
        O Lord,
   continually by day,
   and at my post I am stationed
        throughout the night.
9 Look, there they come, riders,
        horsemen in pairs!"
   Then he responded,
   "Fallen, fallen is Babylon;
   and all the images of her gods
   lie shattered on the ground."
10 O my threshed and winnowed one,
    what I have heard from the LORD
        of hosts,
    the God of Israel, I announce to
        you.

11 The oracle concerning Dumah.

   One is calling to me from Seir,
   "Sentinel, what of the night?
   Sentinel, what of the night?"
12 The sentinel says:
   "Morning comes, and also the
        night.
   If you will inquire, inquire;
   come back again."

13 The oracle concerning the desert
        plain.

   In the scrub of the desert plain you
        will lodge,
   O caravans of Dedanites.

14 Bring water to the thirsty,
   meet the fugitive with bread,
   O inhabitants of the land of
        Tema.
15 For they have fled from the swords,
   from the drawn sword,
   from the bent bow,
   and from the stress of battle.

16 For thus the Lord said to me: Within a year, according to the years of a hired
worker, all the glory of Kedar will come
to an end; 17 and the remaining bows of
Kedar's warriors will be few; for the
LORD, the God of Israel, has spoken.

A Warning of Destruction of Jerusalem

22 The oracle concerning the
         valley of vision.

   What do you mean that you have
        gone up,
   all of you, to the housetops,
2 you that are full of shoutings,
   tumultuous city, exultant town?
   Your slain are not slain by the
        sword,
   nor are they dead in battle.
3 Your rulers have all fled together;
   they were captured without the
        use of a bow.*g*
   All of you who were found were
        captured,
   though they had fled far away.*h*
4 Therefore I said:
   Look away from me,
   let me weep bitter tears;
   do not try to comfort me
   for the destruction of my beloved
        people.

5 For the Lord GOD of hosts has a day
   of tumult and trampling and
        confusion
   in the valley of vision,
   a battering down of walls
   and a cry for help to the
        mountains.
6 Elam bore the quiver
   with chariots and cavalry,*i*
   and Kir uncovered the shield.
7 Your choicest valleys were full of
        chariots,

f Q Ms: MT *a lion*   *g* Or *without their bows*   *h* Gk Syr Vg: Heb *fled from far away*   *i* Meaning of
Heb uncertain

and the cavalry took their stand
at the gates.
8   He has taken away the covering of
Judah.

On that day you looked to the
weapons of the House of the Forest, 9and
you saw that there were many breaches
in the city of David, and you collected
the waters of the lower pool. 10You
counted the houses of Jerusalem, and
you broke down the houses to fortify the
wall. 11You made a reservoir between the
two walls for the water of the old pool.
But you did not look to him who did it,
or have regard for him who planned it
long ago.

12   In that day the Lord GOD of hosts
      called to weeping and mourning,
      to baldness and putting on
        sackcloth;
13   but instead there was joy and
      festivity,
      killing oxen and slaughtering
        sheep,
      eating meat and drinking wine.
      "Let us eat and drink,
      for tomorrow we die."
14   The LORD of hosts has revealed
      himself in my ears:
      Surely this iniquity will not be
      forgiven you until you die,
      says the Lord GOD of hosts.

Denunciation of Self-Seeking Officials

15 Thus says the Lord GOD of hosts:
Come, go to this steward, to Shebna, who
is master of the household, and say to
him: 16What right do you have here?
Who are your relatives here, that you
have cut out a tomb here for yourself,
cutting a tomb on the height, and carving
a habitation for yourself in the rock?
17The LORD is about to hurl you away
violently, my fellow. He will seize firm
hold on you, 18whirl you round and
round, and throw you like a ball into a
wide land; there you shall die, and there
your splendid chariots shall lie, O you
disgrace to your master's house! 19I will
thrust you from your office, and you will
be pulled down from your post.

20 On that day I will call my servant
Eliakim son of Hilkiah, 21and will clothe
him with your robe and bind your sash
on him. I will commit your authority to
his hand, and he shall be a father to the
inhabitants of Jerusalem and to the
house of Judah. 22I will place on his
shoulder the key of the house of David;
he shall open, and no one shall shut; he
shall shut, and no one shall open. 23I will
fasten him like a peg in a secure place,
and he will become a throne of honor to
his ancestral house. 24And they will
hang on him the whole weight of his
ancestral house, the offspring and issue,
every small vessel, from the cups to all
the flagons. 25On that day, says the LORD
of hosts, the peg that was fastened in a
secure place will give way; it will be cut
down and fall, and the load that was on it
will perish, for the LORD has spoken.

An Oracle concerning Tyre

23 The oracle concerning Tyre.

      Wail, O ships of Tarshish,
      for your fortress is destroyed.j
      When they came in from Cyprus
      they learned of it.
2   Be still, O inhabitants of the coast,
      O merchants of Sidon,
      your messengers crossed over the
        seak
3   and were on the mighty waters;
      your revenue was the grain of
        Shihor,
      the harvest of the Nile;
      you were the merchant of the
        nations.
4   Be ashamed, O Sidon, for the sea
      has spoken,
      the fortress of the sea, saying:
      "I have neither labored nor given
      birth,
      I have neither reared young men
      nor brought up young women."
5   When the report comes to Egypt,
      they will be in anguish over the
      report about Tyre.
6   Cross over to Tarshish—
      wail, O inhabitants of the coast!
7   Is this your exultant city
      whose origin is from days of old,

---

j Cn Compare verse 14: Heb for it is destroyed, without houses
they replenished you   k Q Ms: MT crossing over the sea,

whose feet carried her
    to settle far away?
8 Who has planned this
    against Tyre, the bestower of
        crowns,
    whose merchants were princes,
        whose traders were the honored
        of the earth?
9 The LORD of hosts has planned it—
    to defile the pride of all glory,
    to shame all the honored of the
        earth.
10 Cross over to your own land,
    O ships of[l] Tarshish;
    this is a harbor[m] no more.
11 He has stretched out his hand over
        the sea,
    he has shaken the kingdoms;
    the LORD has given command
        concerning Canaan
    to destroy its fortresses.
12 He said:
    You will exult no longer,
    O oppressed virgin daughter
        Sidon;
    rise, cross over to Cyprus—
    even there you will have no rest.

13 Look at the land of the Chaldeans! This is the people; it was not Assyria. They destined Tyre for wild animals. They erected their siege towers, they tore down her palaces, they made her a ruin.[n]
14   Wail, O ships of Tarshish,
    for your fortress is destroyed.
15 From that day Tyre will be forgotten for seventy years, the lifetime of one king. At the end of seventy years, it will happen to Tyre as in the song about the prostitute:
16   Take a harp,
    go about the city,
    you forgotten prostitute!
    Make sweet melody,
    sing many songs,
    that you may be remembered.
17 At the end of seventy years, the LORD will visit Tyre, and she will return to her trade, and will prostitute herself with all the kingdoms of the world on the face of the earth. 18 Her merchandise and her wages will be dedicated to the LORD; her profits[o] will not be stored or hoarded,

but her merchandise will supply abundant food and fine clothing for those who live in the presence of the LORD.

Impending Judgment on the Earth

24 Now the LORD is about to lay waste the earth and make it
    desolate,
    and he will twist its surface and
        scatter its inhabitants.
2 And it shall be, as with the people,
    so with the priest;
    as with the slave, so with his
        master;
    as with the maid, so with her
        mistress;
    as with the buyer, so with the
        seller;
    as with the lender, so with the
        borrower;
    as with the creditor, so with the
        debtor.
3 The earth shall be utterly laid
        waste and utterly despoiled;
    for the LORD has spoken this
        word.

4 The earth dries up and withers,
    the world languishes and
        withers;
    the heavens languish together
        with the earth.
5 The earth lies polluted
    under its inhabitants;
    for they have transgressed laws,
    violated the statutes,
    broken the everlasting covenant.
6 Therefore a curse devours the
        earth,
    and its inhabitants suffer for
        their guilt;
    therefore the inhabitants of the
        earth dwindled,
    and few people are left.
7 The wine dries up,
    the vine languishes,
    all the merry-hearted sigh.
8 The mirth of the timbrels is stilled,
    the noise of the jubilant has
        ceased,
    the mirth of the lyre is stilled.
9 No longer do they drink wine with
        singing;

---

l Cn Compare Gk: Heb *like the Nile, daughter*   m Cn: Heb *restraint*   n Meaning of Heb uncertain
o Heb *it*

strong drink is bitter to those
who drink it.

10 The city of chaos is broken down,
every house is shut up so that no
one can enter.

11 There is an outcry in the streets for
lack of wine;
all joy has reached its eventide;
the gladness of the earth is
banished.

12 Desolation is left in the city,
the gates are battered into ruins.

13 For thus it shall be on the earth
and among the nations,
as when an olive tree is beaten,
as at the gleaning when the grape
harvest is ended.

14 They lift up their voices, they sing
for joy;
they shout from the west over
the majesty of the LORD.

15 Therefore in the east give glory to
the LORD;
in the coastlands of the sea
glorify the name of the LORD,
the God of Israel.

16 From the ends of the earth we hear
songs of praise,
of glory to the Righteous One.
But I say, I pine away,
I pine away. Woe is me!
For the treacherous deal
treacherously,
the treacherous deal very
treacherously.

17 Terror, and the pit, and the snare
are upon you, O inhabitant of the
earth!

18 Whoever flees at the sound of the
terror
shall fall into the pit;
and whoever climbs out of the pit
shall be caught in the snare.
For the windows of heaven are
opened,
and the foundations of the earth
tremble.

19 The earth is utterly broken,
the earth is torn asunder,
the earth is violently shaken.

20 The earth staggers like a drunkard,
it sways like a hut;

its transgression lies heavy upon it,
and it falls, and will not rise
again.

21 On that day the LORD will punish
the host of heaven in heaven,
and on earth the kings of the
earth.

22 They will be gathered together
like prisoners in a pit;
they will be shut up in a prison,
and after many days they will be
punished.

23 Then the moon will be abashed,
and the sun ashamed;
for the LORD of hosts will reign
on Mount Zion and in Jerusalem,
and before his elders he will
manifest his glory.

Praise for Deliverance from Oppression

25 O LORD, you are my God;
I will exalt you, I will praise
your name;
for you have done wonderful
things,
plans formed of old, faithful and
sure.

2 For you have made the city a heap,
the fortified city a ruin;
the palace of aliens is a city no
more,
it will never be rebuilt.

3 Therefore strong peoples will
glorify you;
cities of ruthless nations will fear
you.

4 For you have been a refuge to the
poor,
a refuge to the needy in their
distress,
a shelter from the rainstorm and
a shade from the heat.
When the blast of the ruthless was
like a winter rainstorm,

5 the noise of aliens like heat in a
dry place,
you subdued the heat with the
shade of clouds;
the song of the ruthless was
stilled.

6 On this mountain the LORD of
hosts will make for all
peoples

a feast of rich food, a feast of
  well-aged wines,
of rich food filled with marrow,
  of well-aged wines strained
  clear.
7 And he will destroy on this
  mountain
the shroud that is cast over all
  peoples,
the sheet that is spread over all
  nations;
8 he will swallow up death forever.
Then the Lord GOD will wipe away
  the tears from all faces,
and the disgrace of his people he
  will take away from all the
  earth,
for the LORD has spoken.
9 It will be said on that day,
Lo, this is our God; we have
  waited for him, so that he
  might save us.
This is the LORD for whom we
  have waited;
let us be glad and rejoice in his
  salvation.
10 For the hand of the LORD will rest
  on this mountain.

The Moabites shall be trodden
  down in their place
as straw is trodden down in a
  dung-pit.
11 Though they spread out their hands
  in the midst of it,
as swimmers spread out their
  hands to swim,
their pride will be laid low
  despite the struggle*p* of their
  hands.
12 The high fortifications of his walls
  will be brought down,
laid low, cast to the ground, even
  to the dust.

Judah's Song of Victory

26 On that day this song will be
  sung in the land of Judah:
We have a strong city;
  he sets up victory
  like walls and bulwarks.
2 Open the gates,
  so that the righteous nation that
  keeps faith
  may enter in.

3 Those of steadfast mind you keep
  in peace—
in peace because they trust in
  you.
4 Trust in the LORD forever,
  for in the LORD GOD*q*
  you have an everlasting rock.
5 For he has brought low
  the inhabitants of the height;
  the lofty city he lays low.
He lays it low to the ground,
  casts it to the dust.
6 The foot tramples it,
  the feet of the poor,
  the steps of the needy.

7 The way of the righteous is level;
  O Just One, you make smooth
    the path of the righteous.
8 In the path of your judgments,
  O LORD, we wait for you;
your name and your renown
  are the soul's desire.
9 My soul yearns for you in the
  night,
  my spirit within me earnestly
    seeks you.
For when your judgments are in the
  earth,
  the inhabitants of the world
    learn righteousness.
10 If favor is shown to the wicked,
  they do not learn righteousness;
in the land of uprightness they deal
  perversely
and do not see the majesty of the
  LORD.
11 O LORD, your hand is lifted up,
  but they do not see it.
Let them see your zeal for your
  people, and be ashamed.
Let the fire for your adversaries
  consume them.
12 O LORD, you will ordain peace for
  us,
  for indeed, all that we have done,
    you have done for us.
13 O LORD our God,
  other lords besides you have
    ruled over us,
  but we acknowledge your name
    alone.
14 The dead do not live;
  shades do not rise—

p Meaning of Heb uncertain   q Heb in Yah, the LORD

because you have punished and
destroyed them,
and wiped out all memory of
them.
15 But you have increased the nation,
O LORD,
you have increased the nation;
you are glorified;
you have enlarged all the borders
of the land.

16 O LORD, in distress they sought
you,
they poured out a prayer[r]
when your chastening was on
them.
17 Like a woman with child,
who writhes and cries out in her
pangs
when she is near her time,
so were we because of you, O LORD;

r Meaning of Heb uncertain

WEDNESDAY

IS YOUR MIND STAYED ON GOD?
Oswald Chambers

VERSE: Isaiah 26.3   PASSAGE: Isaiah 26.1–6

s your mind stayed on God or is it starved? Starvation of the mind, caused by neglect, is one of the chief sources of exhaustion and weakness in a servant's life. If you have never used your mind to place yourself before God, begin to do it now. There is no reason to wait for God to come to you. You must turn your thoughts and your eyes away from the face of idols and look to him and be saved (see Isaiah 45.22).

Your mind is the greatest gift God has given you and it ought to be devoted entirely to him . . . When you have thoughts and ideas that are worthy of credit to God, learn to compare and associate them with all that happens in nature—the rising and the setting of the sun, the shining of the moon and the stars, and the changing of the seasons. You will begin to see that your thoughts are from God as well, and your mind will no longer be at the mercy of your impulsive thinking, but will always be used in service to God . . .

Remember whose you are and whom you serve. Encourage yourself to remember, and your affection for God will increase tenfold. Your mind will no longer be starved, but will be quick and enthusiastic, and your hope will be inexpressibly bright.

ADDITIONAL SCRIPTURE READING:
Isaiah 48.2; Jeremiah 17.7–8; Romans 4.18–21

Go to page 810 for your next devotional reading.

1900   Present

18 we were with child, we writhed,
but we gave birth only to wind.
We have won no victories on earth,
and no one is born to inhabit the
world.
19 Your dead shall live, their corpses*s*
shall rise.
O dwellers in the dust, awake
and sing for joy!
For your dew is a radiant dew,
and the earth will give birth to
those long dead.*t*

20 Come, my people, enter your
chambers,
and shut your doors behind you;
hide yourselves for a little while
until the wrath is past.
21 For the LORD comes out from his
place
to punish the inhabitants of the
earth for their iniquity;
the earth will disclose the blood
shed on it,
and will no longer cover its slain.

Israel's Redemption

27 On that day the LORD with
his cruel and great and strong
sword will punish Leviathan the fleeing
serpent, Leviathan the twisting serpent,
and he will kill the dragon that is in the
sea.

2 On that day:
A pleasant vineyard, sing about it!
3 I, the LORD, am its keeper;
every moment I water it.
I guard it night and day
so that no one can harm it;
4 I have no wrath.
If it gives me thorns and briers,
I will march to battle against it.
I will burn it up.
5 Or else let it cling to me for
protection,
let it make peace with me,
let it make peace with me.

6 In days to come*u* Jacob shall take
root,
Israel shall blossom and put forth
shoots,
and fill the whole world with fruit.

7 Has he struck them down as he
struck down those who
struck them?
Or have they been killed as their
killers were killed?
8 By expulsion,*v* by exile you
struggled against them;
with his fierce blast he removed
them in the day of the east
wind.
9 Therefore by this the guilt of Jacob
will be expiated,
and this will be the full fruit of
the removal of his sin:
when he makes all the stones of
the altars
like chalkstones crushed to pieces,
no sacred poles*w* or incense altars
will remain standing.
10 For the fortified city is solitary,
a habitation deserted and
forsaken, like the wilderness;
the calves graze there,
there they lie down, and strip its
branches.
11 When its boughs are dry, they are
broken;
women come and make a fire of
them.
For this is a people without
understanding;
therefore he that made them will
not have compassion on
them,
he that formed them will show
them no favor.

12 On that day the LORD will thresh
from the channel of the Euphrates to the
Wadi of Egypt, and you will be gathered
one by one, O people of Israel. 13 And on
that day a great trumpet will be blown,
and those who were lost in the land of
Assyria and those who were driven out
to the land of Egypt will come and worship the LORD on the holy mountain at
Jerusalem.

Judgment on Corrupt Rulers, Priests, and Prophets

28 Ah, the proud garland of the
drunkards of Ephraim,
and the fading flower of its
glorious beauty,

s Cn Compare Syr Tg: Heb *my corpse*   *t* Heb *to the shades*   *u* Heb *Those to come*   *v* Meaning of
Heb uncertain   *w* Heb *Asherim*

which is on the head of those
  bloated with rich food, of
  those overcome with wine!
2 See, the Lord has one who is
     mighty and strong;
   like a storm of hail, a destroying
     tempest,
   like a storm of mighty, overflowing
     waters;
   with his hand he will hurl them
     down to the earth.
3 Trampled under foot will be
     the proud garland of the
     drunkards of Ephraim.
4 And the fading flower of its
     glorious beauty,
   which is on the head of those
     bloated with rich food,
   will be like a first-ripe fig before
     the summer;
   whoever sees it, eats it up
     as soon as it comes to hand.

5 In that day the LORD of hosts will
     be a garland of glory,
   and a diadem of beauty, to the
     remnant of his people;
6 and a spirit of justice to the one
     who sits in judgment,
   and strength to those who turn
     back the battle at the gate.

7 These also reel with wine
     and stagger with strong drink;
   the priest and the prophet reel with
     strong drink,
     they are confused with wine,
     they stagger with strong drink;
   they err in vision,
     they stumble in giving
     judgment.
8 All tables are covered with filthy
     vomit;
   no place is clean.

9 "Whom will he teach knowledge,
     and to whom will he explain the
     message?
   Those who are weaned from milk,
     those taken from the breast?
10 For it is precept upon precept,
     precept upon precept,
   line upon line, line upon line,
     here a little, there a little."x

11 Truly, with stammering lip
     and with alien tongue
   he will speak to this people,
12   to whom he has said,
   "This is rest;
     give rest to the weary;
   and this is repose";
     yet they would not hear.
13 Therefore the word of the LORD
     will be to them,
   "Precept upon precept, precept
     upon precept,
   line upon line, line upon line,
     here a little, there a little;"x
   in order that they may go, and fall
     backward,
     and be broken, and snared, and
     taken.

14 Therefore hear the word of the
     LORD, you scoffers
   who rule this people in Jerusalem.
15 Because you have said, "We have
     made a covenant with death,
   and with Sheol we have an
     agreement;
   when the overwhelming scourge
     passes through
     it will not come to us;
   for we have made lies our refuge,
     and in falsehood we have taken
     shelter";
16 therefore thus says the Lord GOD,
   See, I am laying in Zion a
     foundation stone,
     a tested stone,
   a precious cornerstone, a sure
     foundation:
   "One who trusts will not panic."
17 And I will make justice the line,
     and righteousness the plummet;
   hail will sweep away the refuge of
     lies,
     and waters will overwhelm the
     shelter.
18 Then your covenant with death
     will be annulled,
   and your agreement with Sheol
     will not stand;
   when the overwhelming scourge
     passes through
     you will be beaten down by it.
19 As often as it passes through, it
     will take you;

x Meaning of Heb of this verse uncertain

for morning by morning it will
pass through,
by day and by night;
and it will be sheer terror to
understand the message.

20 For the bed is too short to stretch
oneself on it,
and the covering too narrow to
wrap oneself in it.

21 For the LORD will rise up as on
Mount Perazim,
he will rage as in the valley of
Gibeon
to do his deed—strange is his
deed!—
and to work his work—alien is
his work!

22 Now therefore do not scoff,
or your bonds will be made
stronger;
for I have heard a decree of
destruction
from the Lord GOD of hosts upon
the whole land.

23 Listen, and hear my voice;
Pay attention, and hear my
speech.

24 Do those who plow for sowing
plow continually?
Do they continually open and
harrow their ground?

25 When they have leveled its surface,
do they not scatter dill, sow
cummin,
and plant wheat in rows
and barley in its proper place,
and spelt as the border?

26 For they are well instructed;
their God teaches them.

27 Dill is not threshed with a
threshing sledge,
nor is a cart wheel rolled over
cummin;
but dill is beaten out with a stick,
and cummin with a rod.

28 Grain is crushed for bread,
but one does not thresh it
forever;
one drives the cart wheel and
horses over it,
but does not pulverize it.

29 This also comes from the LORD of
hosts;
he is wonderful in counsel,
and excellent in wisdom.

The Siege of Jerusalem

29 Ah, Ariel, Ariel,
the city where David
encamped!
Add year to year;
let the festivals run their round.

2 Yet I will distress Ariel,
and there shall be moaning and
lamentation,
and Jerusalem^y shall be to me
like an Ariel.^{z}

3 And like David^a I will encamp
against you;
I will besiege you with towers
and raise siegeworks against you.

4 Then deep from the earth you shall
speak,
from low in the dust your words
shall come;
your voice shall come from the
ground like the voice of a
ghost,
and your speech shall whisper
out of the dust.

5 But the multitude of your foes^b
shall be like small dust,
and the multitude of tyrants like
flying chaff.
And in an instant, suddenly,

6 you will be visited by the LORD of
hosts
with thunder and earthquake and
great noise,
with whirlwind and tempest, and
the flame of a devouring fire.

7 And the multitude of all the
nations that fight against
Ariel,
all that fight against her and her
stronghold, and who distress
her,
shall be like a dream, a vision of
the night.

8 Just as when a hungry person
dreams of eating
and wakes up still hungry,
or a thirsty person dreams of
drinking

---

y Heb *she*   z Probable meaning, *altar hearth*; compare Ezek 43.15   a Gk: Meaning of Heb uncertain
b Cn: Heb *strangers*

and wakes up faint, still thirsty,
so shall the multitude of all the
        nations be
    that fight against Mount Zion.

9   Stupefy yourselves and be in a
        stupor,
    blind yourselves and be blind!
    Be drunk, but not from wine;
    stagger, but not from strong
        drink!
10 For the LORD has poured out upon
        you
    a spirit of deep sleep;
    he has closed your eyes, you
        prophets,
    and covered your heads, you
        seers.

11 The vision of all this has become
for you like the words of a sealed document. If it is given to those who can
read, with the command, "Read this,"
they say, "We cannot, for it is sealed."
12 And if it is given to those who cannot
read, saying, "Read this," they say, "We
cannot read."

13 The Lord said:
    Because these people draw near
        with their mouths
    and honor me with their lips,
    while their hearts are far from
        me,
    and their worship of me is a human
        commandment learned by
        rote;
14 so I will again do
    amazing things with this people,
    shocking and amazing.
    The wisdom of their wise shall
        perish,
    and the discernment of the
        discerning shall be hidden.

15 Ha! You who hide a plan too deep
        for the LORD,
    whose deeds are in the dark,
    and who say, "Who sees us? Who
        knows us?"
16 You turn things upside down!
    Shall the potter be regarded as
        the clay?
    Shall the thing made say of its
        maker,
    "He did not make me";

or the thing formed say of the one
        who formed it,
    "He has no understanding"?

Hope for the Future

17 Shall not Lebanon in a very little
        while
    become a fruitful field,
    and the fruitful field be regarded
        as a forest?
18 On that day the deaf shall hear
    the words of a scroll,
    and out of their gloom and darkness
    the eyes of the blind shall see.
19 The meek shall obtain fresh joy in
        the LORD,
    and the neediest people shall
        exult in the Holy One of
        Israel.
20 For the tyrant shall be no more,
    and the scoffer shall cease to be;
    all those alert to do evil shall be
        cut off—
21 those who cause a person to lose a
        lawsuit,
    who set a trap for the arbiter in
        the gate,
    and without grounds deny justice
        to the one in the right.

22 Therefore thus says the LORD, who
redeemed Abraham, concerning the
house of Jacob:
    No longer shall Jacob be ashamed,
    no longer shall his face grow
        pale.
23 For when he sees his children,
    the work of my hands, in his
        midst,
    they will sanctify my name;
    they will sanctify the Holy One of
        Jacob,
    and will stand in awe of the God
        of Israel.
24 And those who err in spirit will
        come to understanding,
    and those who grumble will
        accept instruction.

The Futility of Reliance on Egypt

30 Oh, rebellious children, says
        the LORD,
    who carry out a plan, but not mine;
    who make an alliance, but against
        my will,
    adding sin to sin;

2 who set out to go down to Egypt
without asking for my counsel,
to take refuge in the protection of
Pharaoh,
and to seek shelter in the shadow
of Egypt;
3 Therefore the protection of
Pharaoh shall become your
shame,
and the shelter in the shadow of
Egypt your humiliation.
4 For though his officials are at Zoan
and his envoys reach Hanes,
5 everyone comes to shame
through a people that cannot
profit them,
that brings neither help nor profit,
but shame and disgrace.

6 An oracle concerning the animals
of the Negeb.
Through a land of trouble and
distress,
of lioness and roaring*c* lion,
of viper and flying serpent,
they carry their riches on the backs
of donkeys,
and their treasures on the humps
of camels,
to a people that cannot profit
them.
7 For Egypt's help is worthless and
empty,
therefore I have called her,
"Rahab who sits still."*d*

A Rebellious People

8 Go now, write it before them on a
tablet,
and inscribe it in a book,
so that it may be for the time to
come
as a witness forever.
9 For they are a rebellious people,
faithless children,
children who will not hear
the instruction of the LORD;
10 who say to the seers, "Do not see";
and to the prophets, "Do not
prophesy to us what is right;
speak to us smooth things,
prophesy illusions,
11 leave the way, turn aside from the
path,

let us hear no more about the
Holy One of Israel."
12 Therefore thus says the Holy One
of Israel:
Because you reject this word,
and put your trust in oppression
and deceit,
and rely on them;
13 therefore this iniquity shall
become for you
like a break in a high wall, bulging
out, and about to collapse,
whose crash comes suddenly, in
an instant;
14 its breaking is like that of a potter's
vessel
that is smashed so ruthlessly
that among its fragments not a
sherd is found
for taking fire from the hearth,
or dipping water out of the
cistern.

15 For thus said the Lord GOD, the
Holy One of Israel:
In returning and rest you shall be
saved;
in quietness and in trust shall be
your strength.
But you refused 16and said,
"No! We will flee upon horses"—
therefore you shall flee!
and, "We will ride upon swift
steeds"—
therefore your pursuers shall be
swift!
17 A thousand shall flee at the threat
of one,
at the threat of five you shall flee,
until you are left
like a flagstaff on the top of a
mountain,
like a signal on a hill.

God's Promise to Zion

18 Therefore the LORD waits to be
gracious to you;
therefore he will rise up to show
mercy to you.
For the LORD is a God of justice;
blessed are all those who wait for
him.
19 Truly, O people in Zion, inhabitants of Jerusalem, you shall weep no
more. He will surely be gracious to you

c Cn: Heb *from them*   *d* Meaning of Heb uncertain

at the sound of your cry; when he hears it, he will answer you. 20Though the Lord may give you the bread of adversity and the water of affliction, yet your Teacher will not hide himself any more, but your eyes shall see your Teacher. 21And when you turn to the right or when you turn to the left, your ears shall hear a word behind you, saying, "This is the way; walk in it." 22Then you will defile your silver-covered idols and your gold-plated images. You will scatter them like filthy rags; you will say to them, "Away with you!"

23 He will give rain for the seed with which you sow the ground, and grain, the produce of the ground, which will be rich and plenteous. On that day your cattle will graze in broad pastures; 24and the oxen and donkeys that till the ground will eat silage, which has been winnowed with shovel and fork. 25On every lofty mountain and every high hill there will be brooks running with water—on a day of the great slaughter, when the towers fall. 26Moreover the light of the moon will be like the light of the sun, and the light of the sun will be sevenfold, like the

---

THURSDAY

POURING OUT YOUR COMPLAINT
Martin Luther

VERSE: Isaiah 30.19   **PASSAGE:** Isaiah 30.15–19

ou must learn to pray and not sit alone or lie about, hanging your head and shaking it, brooding over your thoughts, worrying about how you can escape and looking at nothing but yourself and your sad and painful condition. Get up, you lazy villain, then fall upon your knees, lift your eyes and hands towards heaven, take a Psalm or the Lord's Prayer, and pour out your trouble with tears before God, lamenting and calling upon him . . .

The lifting up of hands, prayer, and the mentioning of trouble are sacrifices most pleasing to God. He desires it, and it is his will, that you should pour out your trouble before him, and not let it lie upon yourself, dragging it about with you and being chafed and tortured by it, so that in the end you make two, or even ten or a hundred calamities out of one. He wills that you should be too weak to bear and overcome such trouble, in order that you may learn to find strength in him, and that he may be praised through his strength in you. Behold, this is how Christians are made!

ADDITIONAL SCRIPTURE READING:
Isaiah 65.24; Jeremiah 29.11–13; 1 John 5.14–15

Go to page 813 for your next devotional reading.

1500   1700

light of seven days, on the day when the
LORD binds up the injuries of his people,
and heals the wounds inflicted by his
blow.

Judgment on Assyria

27 See, the name of the LORD comes
    from far away,
    burning with his anger, and in
      thick rising smoke;*e*
  his lips are full of indignation,
    and his tongue is like a devouring
      fire;
28 his breath is like an overflowing
    stream
    that reaches up to the neck—
  to sift the nations with the sieve of
    destruction,
    and to place on the jaws of the
      peoples a bridle that leads
      them astray.

29 You shall have a song as in the
night when a holy festival is kept; and
gladness of heart, as when one sets out
to the sound of the flute to go to the
mountain of the LORD, to the Rock of
Israel. 30 And the LORD will cause his
majestic voice to be heard and the
descending blow of his arm to be seen,
in furious anger and a flame of devouring fire, with a cloudburst and tempest
and hailstones. 31 The Assyrian will be
terror-stricken at the voice of the LORD,
when he strikes with his rod. 32 And
every stroke of the staff of punishment
that the LORD lays upon him will be to
the sound of timbrels and lyres; battling
with brandished arm he will fight with
him. 33 For his burning place*f* has long
been prepared; truly it is made ready for
the king,*g* its pyre made deep and wide,
with fire and wood in abundance; the
breath of the LORD, like a stream of sulfur, kindles it.

Alliance with Egypt Is Futile

31 Alas for those who go down
    to Egypt for help
  and who rely on horses,
  who trust in chariots because they
    are many
  and in horsemen because they
    are very strong,

  but do not look to the Holy One of
    Israel
    or consult the LORD!
2 Yet he too is wise and brings
    disaster;
  he does not call back his words,
  but will rise against the house of
    the evildoers,
  and against the helpers of those
    who work iniquity.
3 The Egyptians are human, and not
    God;
  their horses are flesh, and not
    spirit.
  When the LORD stretches out his
    hand,
  the helper will stumble, and the
    one helped will fall,
  and they will all perish together.

4 For thus the LORD said to me,
  As a lion or a young lion growls
    over its prey,
  and—when a band of shepherds
    is called out against it—
  is not terrified by their shouting
    or daunted at their noise,
  so the LORD of hosts will come
    down
    to fight upon Mount Zion and
      upon its hill.
5 Like birds hovering overhead, so
    the LORD of hosts
    will protect Jerusalem;
  he will protect and deliver it,
  he will spare and rescue it.

6 Turn back to him whom you*h* have
deeply betrayed, O people of Israel. 7 For
on that day all of you shall throw away
your idols of silver and idols of gold,
which your hands have sinfully made
for you.
8 "Then the Assyrian shall fall by a
    sword, not of mortals;
  and a sword, not of humans, shall
    devour him;
  he shall flee from the sword,
  and his young men shall be put
    to forced labor.
9 His rock shall pass away in terror,
  and his officers desert the
    standard in panic,"
  says the LORD, whose fire is in
    Zion,

---

e Meaning of Heb uncertain   *f* Or *Topheth*   *g* Or *Molech*   *h* Heb *they*

and whose furnace is in
Jerusalem.

Government with Justice Predicted

32 See, a king will reign in
righteousness,
and princes will rule with justice.
2 Each will be like a hiding place
from the wind,
a covert from the tempest,
like streams of water in a dry place,
like the shade of a great rock in a
weary land.
3 Then the eyes of those who have
sight will not be closed,
and the ears of those who have
hearing will listen.
4 The minds of the rash will have
good judgment,
and the tongues of stammerers
will speak readily and
distinctly.
5 A fool will no longer be called
noble,
nor a villain said to be honorable.
6 For fools speak folly,
and their minds plot iniquity:
to practice ungodliness,
to utter error concerning the
LORD,
to leave the craving of the hungry
unsatisfied,
and to deprive the thirsty of
drink.
7 The villainies of villains are evil;
they devise wicked devices
to ruin the poor with lying words,
even when the plea of the needy
is right.
8 But those who are noble plan noble
things,
and by noble things they stand.

Complacent Women Warned of Disaster

9 Rise up, you women who are at
ease, hear my voice;
you complacent daughters, listen
to my speech.
10 In little more than a year
you will shudder, you
complacent ones;
for the vintage will fail,
the fruit harvest will not come.

11 Tremble, you women who are at
ease,
shudder, you complacent ones;
strip, and make yourselves bare,
and put sackcloth on your loins.
12 Beat your breasts for the pleasant
fields,
for the fruitful vine,
13 for the soil of my people
growing up in thorns and briers;
yes, for all the joyous houses
in the jubilant city.
14 For the palace will be forsaken,
the populous city deserted;
the hill and the watchtower
will become dens forever,
the joy of wild asses,
a pasture for flocks;
15 until a spirit from on high is poured
out on us,
and the wilderness becomes a
fruitful field,
and the fruitful field is deemed a
forest.

The Peace of God's Reign

16 Then justice will dwell in the
wilderness,
and righteousness abide in the
fruitful field.
17 The effect of righteousness will be
peace,
and the result of righteousness,
quietness and trust forever.
18 My people will abide in a peaceful
habitation,
in secure dwellings, and in quiet
resting places.
19 The forest will disappear
completely,^{i}
and the city will be utterly laid
low.
20 Happy will you be who sow beside
every stream,
who let the ox and the donkey
range freely.

A Prophecy of Deliverance from Foes

33 Ah, you destroyer,
who yourself have not been
destroyed;
you treacherous one,
with whom no one has dealt
treacherously!

---

i Cn: Heb *And it will hail when the forest comes down*

I HAVE LOVED THE DOCTRINES OF THE GOSPEL
Jonathan Edwards

VERSE: Isaiah 32.2   PASSAGE: Isaiah 32.1–8

 n January 12, 1723, I made a solemn dedication of myself to God, and wrote it down; giving up myself, and all that I had to God; to be for the future, in no respect, my own; to act as one that had no right to himself, in any respect. And solemnly vowed, to take God for my whole portion and felicity; looking on nothing else, as any part of my happiness, nor acting as if it were; and his law for the constant rule of my obedience: engaging to fight, with all my might, against the world, the flesh, and the devil, to the end of my life. But I have reason to be infinitely humbled, when I consider, how much I have failed, of answering my obligation . . .

I have loved the doctrines of the gospel; they have been to my soul like green pastures. The gospel has seemed to me the richest treasure; the treasure that I have most desired, and longed that it might dwell richly in me. The way of salvation by Christ, has appeared, in a general way, glorious and excellent, most pleasant and most beautiful. It has often seemed to me, that it would, in a great measure, spoil heaven, to receive it in any other way. That text has often been affecting and delightful to me, Isaiah 32.2 (KJV), *A man shall be as an hiding place from the wind, and a covert from the tempest* . . .

Though it seems to me, that in some respects, I was a far better Christian, for two or three years after my first conversion, than I am now; and lived in a more constant delight and pleasure; yet of late years, I have had a more full and constant sense of the absolute sovereignty of God, and a delight in that sovereignty; and have had more of a sense of the glory of Christ, as a mediator revealed in the gospel. On one Saturday night, in particular, I had such a discovery of the excellency of the gospel above all other doctrines, that I could not but say to myself, "This is my chosen light, my chosen doctrine," and of Christ, "This is my chosen prophet." It appeared sweet, beyond all expression, to follow Christ, and to be taught, and enlightened, and instructed by him; to learn of him, and live to him.

ADDITIONAL SCRIPTURE READING:
Psalm 32.7; Isaiah 25.4

Go to page 817 for your next devotional reading.

1700   1900

When you have ceased to destroy,
    you will be destroyed;
and when you have stopped dealing
    treacherously,
you will be dealt with
    treacherously.

2 O Lord, be gracious to us; we wait
    for you.
Be our arm every morning,
    our salvation in the time of
    trouble.
3 At the sound of tumult, peoples
    fled;
    before your majesty, nations
    scattered.
4 Spoil was gathered as the
    caterpillar gathers;
    as locusts leap, they leaped*j* upon
    it.
5 The Lord is exalted, he dwells on
    high;
    he filled Zion with justice and
    righteousness;
6 he will be the stability of your
    times,
    abundance of salvation, wisdom,
    and knowledge;
    the fear of the Lord is Zion's
    treasure.*k*

7 Listen! the valiant*j* cry in the
    streets;
    the envoys of peace weep
    bitterly.
8 The highways are deserted,
    travelers have quit the road.
The treaty is broken,
    its oaths*l* are despised,
    its obligation*m* is disregarded.
9 The land mourns and languishes;
    Lebanon is confounded and
    withers away;
Sharon is like a desert;
    and Bashan and Carmel shake off
    their leaves.

10 "Now I will arise," says the Lord,
    "now I will lift myself up;
    now I will be exalted.
11 You conceive chaff, you bring forth
    stubble;
    your breath is a fire that will
    consume you.

12 And the peoples will be as if
    burned to lime,
    like thorns cut down, that are
    burned in the fire."

13 Hear, you who are far away, what I
    have done;
    and you who are near,
    acknowledge my might.
14 The sinners in Zion are afraid;
    trembling has seized the godless:
"Who among us can live with the
    devouring fire?
Who among us can live with
    everlasting flames?"
15 Those who walk righteously and
    speak uprightly,
    who despise the gain of
    oppression,
who wave away a bribe instead of
    accepting it,
who stop their ears from hearing
    of bloodshed
and shut their eyes from looking
    on evil,
16 they will live on the heights;
    their refuge will be the fortresses
    of rocks;
    their food will be supplied, their
    water assured.

The Land of the Majestic King

17 Your eyes will see the king in his
    beauty;
    they will behold a land that
    stretches far away.
18 Your mind will muse on the terror:
    "Where is the one who counted?
Where is the one who weighed
    the tribute?
Where is the one who counted
    the towers?"
19 No longer will you see the insolent
    people,
    the people of an obscure speech
    that you cannot
    comprehend,
stammering in a language that
    you cannot understand.
20 Look on Zion, the city of our
    appointed festivals!
Your eyes will see Jerusalem,
    a quiet habitation, an immovable
    tent,

---

j Meaning of Heb uncertain   *k* Heb *his treasure;* meaning of Heb uncertain   *l* Q Ms: MT *cities*
m Or *everyone*

whose stakes will never be pulled
up,
and none of whose ropes will be
broken.
21 But there the LORD in majesty will
be for us
a place of broad rivers and
streams,
where no galley with oars can go,
nor stately ship can pass.
22 For the LORD is our judge, the LORD
is our ruler,
the LORD is our king; he will save
us.

23 Your rigging hangs loose;
it cannot hold the mast firm in
its place,
or keep the sail spread out.

Then prey and spoil in abundance
will be divided;
even the lame will fall to
plundering.
24 And no inhabitant will say, "I am
sick";
the people who live there will be
forgiven their iniquity.

Judgment on the Nations

34 Draw near, O nations, to
hear;
O peoples, give heed!
Let the earth hear, and all that fills
it,
the world, and all that comes
from it.
2 For the LORD is enraged against all
the nations,
and furious against all their
hordes;
he has doomed them, has given
them over for slaughter.
3 Their slain shall be cast out,
and the stench of their corpses
shall rise;
the mountains shall flow with
their blood.
4 All the host of heaven shall rot
away,
and the skies roll up like a scroll.
All their host shall wither
like a leaf withering on a vine,
or fruit withering on a fig tree.

5 When my sword has drunk its fill
in the heavens,
lo, it will descend upon Edom,
upon the people I have doomed
to judgment.
6 The LORD has a sword; it is sated
with blood,
it is gorged with fat,
with the blood of lambs and
goats,
with the fat of the kidneys of
rams.
For the LORD has a sacrifice in
Bozrah,
a great slaughter in the land of
Edom.
7 Wild oxen shall fall with them,
and young steers with the mighty
bulls.
Their land shall be soaked with
blood,
and their soil made rich with fat.

8 For the LORD has a day of
vengeance,
a year of vindication by Zion's
cause.[n]
9 And the streams of Edom[o] shall be
turned into pitch,
and her soil into sulfur;
her land shall become burning
pitch.
10 Night and day it shall not be
quenched;
its smoke shall go up forever.
From generation to generation it
shall lie waste;
no one shall pass through it
forever and ever.
11 But the hawk[p] and the hedgehog[p]
shall possess it;
the owl[p] and the raven shall live
in it.
He shall stretch the line of
confusion over it,
and the plummet of chaos over[q]
its nobles.
12 They shall name it No Kingdom
There,
and all its princes shall be
nothing.
13 Thorns shall grow over its
strongholds,

n Or of recompense by Zion's defender   o Heb her streams   p Identification uncertain
q Heb lacks over

nettles and thistles in its
    fortresses.
It shall be the haunt of jackals,
    an abode for ostriches.
14 Wildcats shall meet with hyenas,
    goat-demons shall call to each
        other;
    there too Lilith shall repose,
    and find a place to rest.
15 There shall the owl nest
    and lay and hatch and brood in
        its shadow;
    there too the buzzards shall gather,
    each one with its mate.
16 Seek and read from the book of the
        LORD:
    Not one of these shall be missing;
    none shall be without its mate.
    For the mouth of the LORD has
        commanded,
    and his spirit has gathered them.
17 He has cast the lot for them,
    his hand has portioned it out to
        them with the line;
    they shall possess it forever,
    from generation to generation
        they shall live in it.

The Return of the Redeemed
to Zion

35 The wilderness and the dry
        land shall be glad,
    the desert shall rejoice and
        blossom;
    like the crocus 2it shall blossom
        abundantly,
    and rejoice with joy and singing.
    The glory of Lebanon shall be given
        to it,
    the majesty of Carmel and
        Sharon.
    They shall see the glory of the
        LORD,
    the majesty of our God.

3   Strengthen the weak hands,
    and make firm the feeble knees.
4   Say to those who are of a fearful
        heart,
    "Be strong, do not fear!
    Here is your God.
    He will come with vengeance,
    with terrible recompense.
    He will come and save you."

5   Then the eyes of the blind shall be
        opened,
    and the ears of the deaf unstopped;
6   then the lame shall leap like a deer,
    and the tongue of the speechless
        sing for joy.
    For waters shall break forth in the
        wilderness,
    and streams in the desert;
7   the burning sand shall become a
        pool,
    and the thirsty ground springs of
        water;
    the haunt of jackals shall become a
        swamp,*r*
    the grass shall become reeds and
        rushes.

8   A highway shall be there,
    and it shall be called the Holy
        Way;
    the unclean shall not travel on it,*s*
    but it shall be for God's people;*t*
    no traveler, not even fools, shall
        go astray.
9   No lion shall be there,
    nor shall any ravenous beast
        come up on it;
    they shall not be found there,
    but the redeemed shall walk
        there.
10 And the ransomed of the LORD
        shall return,
    and come to Zion with singing;
    everlasting joy shall be upon their
        heads;
    they shall obtain joy and
        gladness,
    and sorrow and sighing shall flee
        away.

Sennacherib Threatens Jerusalem

36 In the fourteenth year of King
        Hezekiah, King Sennacherib
of Assyria came up against all the fortified cities of Judah and captured them.
2The king of Assyria sent the Rabshakeh
from Lachish to King Hezekiah at Jerusalem, with a great army. He stood by
the conduit of the upper pool on the
highway to the Fuller's Field. 3And there
came out to him Eliakim son of Hilkiah,
who was in charge of the palace, and
Shebna the secretary, and Joah son of
Asaph, the recorder.

r Cn: Heb *in the haunt of jackals is her resting place*   *s* Or *pass it by*   *t* Cn: Heb *for them*

WEEKEND

NATIVITY
John Donne

VERSE: Matthew 1.18   **PASSAGE:** Matthew 1.18–25

mmensity cloistered in thy dear womb,
Now leaves his well-beloved imprisonment,
There he hath made himself to his intent
Weak enough, now into our world to come;
But Oh, for thee, for him, hath th' inn no room?
Yet lay him in this stall, and from the Orient,
Stars, and wisemen will travel to prevent
Th' effect of Herod's jealous general doom.
Seest thou, my soul, with thy faith's eyes, how he
Which fills all place, yet none holds him, doth lie?
Was not his pity towards thee wondrous high,
That would have need to be pitied by thee?
Kiss him, and with him into Egypt go,
With his kind mother, who partakes thy woe.

ADDITIONAL SCRIPTURE READING:
Luke 1.27–80; Galatians 4.4

Go to page 822 for your next devotional reading.

1500   1700

4 The Rabshakeh said to them, "Say to Hezekiah: Thus says the great king, the king of Assyria: On what do you base this confidence of yours? 5Do you think that mere words are strategy and power for war? On whom do you now rely, that you have rebelled against me? 6See, you are relying on Egypt, that broken reed of a staff, which will pierce the hand of anyone who leans on it. Such is Pharaoh king of Egypt to all who rely on him. 7But if you say to me, 'We rely on the LORD our God,' is it not he whose high places and altars Hezekiah has removed, saying to Judah and to Jerusalem, 'You shall worship before this altar'? 8Come now, make a wager with my master the king of Assyria: I will give you two thousand horses, if you are able on your part to set riders on them. 9How then can you repulse a single captain among the least of my master's servants, when you rely on Egypt for chariots and for horsemen? 10Moreover, is it without the LORD that I have come up against this land to destroy it? The LORD said to me, Go up against this land, and destroy it."

11 Then Eliakim, Shebna, and Joah said to the Rabshakeh, "Please speak to your servants in Aramaic, for we understand it; do not speak to us in the language of Judah within the hearing of the people who are on the wall." 12But the Rabshakeh said, "Has my master sent me to speak these words to your master and to you, and not to the people sitting on the wall, who are doomed with you to eat their own dung and drink their own urine?"

13 Then the Rabshakeh stood and called out in a loud voice in the language of Judah, "Hear the words of the great king, the king of Assyria! 14Thus says the king: 'Do not let Hezekiah deceive you, for he will not be able to deliver you. 15Do not let Hezekiah make you rely on the LORD by saying, The LORD will surely deliver us; this city will not be given into the hand of the king of Assyria.' 16Do not listen to Hezekiah; for thus says the king of Assyria: 'Make your peace with me and come out to me; then everyone of you will eat from your own vine and your own fig tree and drink water from your own cistern,

17until I come and take you away to a land like your own land, a land of grain and wine, a land of bread and vineyards. 18Do not let Hezekiah mislead you by saying, The LORD will save us. Has any of the gods of the nations saved their land out of the hand of the king of Assyria? 19Where are the gods of Hamath and Arpad? Where are the gods of Sepharvaim? Have they delivered Samaria out of my hand? 20Who among all the gods of these countries have saved their countries out of my hand, that the LORD should save Jerusalem out of my hand?' "

21 But they were silent and answered him not a word, for the king's command was, "Do not answer him." 22Then Eliakim son of Hilkiah, who was in charge of the palace, and Shebna the secretary, and Joah son of Asaph, the recorder, came to Hezekiah with their clothes torn, and told him the words of the Rabshakeh.

Hezekiah Consults Isaiah

37 When King Hezekiah heard it, he tore his clothes, covered himself with sackcloth, and went into the house of the LORD. 2And he sent Eliakim, who was in charge of the palace, and Shebna the secretary, and the senior priests, covered with sackcloth, to the prophet Isaiah son of Amoz. 3They said to him, "Thus says Hezekiah, This day is a day of distress, of rebuke, and of disgrace; children have come to the birth, and there is no strength to bring them forth. 4It may be that the LORD your God heard the words of the Rabshakeh, whom his master the king of Assyria has sent to mock the living God, and will rebuke the words that the LORD your God has heard; therefore lift up your prayer for the remnant that is left."

5 When the servants of King Hezekiah came to Isaiah, 6Isaiah said to them, "Say to your master, 'Thus says the LORD: Do not be afraid because of the words that you have heard, with which the servants of the king of Assyria have reviled me. 7I myself will put a spirit in him, so that he shall hear a rumor, and return to his own land; I will cause him to fall by the sword in his own land.' "

8 The Rabshakeh returned, and found the king of Assyria fighting against

Libnah; for he had heard that the king had left Lachish. ⁹Now the king^u heard concerning King Tirhakah of Ethiopia,^v "He has set out to fight against you." When he heard it, he sent messengers to Hezekiah, saying, ¹⁰"Thus shall you speak to King Hezekiah of Judah: Do not let your God on whom you rely deceive you by promising that Jerusalem will not be given into the hand of the king of Assyria. ¹¹See, you have heard what the kings of Assyria have done to all lands, destroying them utterly. Shall you be delivered? ¹²Have the gods of the nations delivered them, the nations that my predecessors destroyed, Gozan, Haran, Rezeph, and the people of Eden who were in Telassar? ¹³Where is the king of Hamath, the king of Arpad, the king of the city of Sepharvaim, the king of Hena, or the king of Ivvah?"

Hezekiah's Prayer

14 Hezekiah received the letter from the hand of the messengers and read it; then Hezekiah went up to the house of the LORD and spread it before the LORD. ¹⁵And Hezekiah prayed to the LORD, saying: ¹⁶"O LORD of hosts, God of Israel, who are enthroned above the cherubim, you are God, you alone, of all the kingdoms of the earth; you have made heaven and earth. ¹⁷Incline your ear, O LORD, and hear; open your eyes, O LORD, and see; hear all the words of Sennacherib, which he has sent to mock the living God. ¹⁸Truly, O LORD, the kings of Assyria have laid waste all the nations and their lands, ¹⁹and have hurled their gods into the fire, though they were no gods, but the work of human hands— wood and stone—and so they were destroyed. ²⁰So now, O LORD our God, save us from his hand, so that all the kingdoms of the earth may know that you alone are the LORD."

21 Then Isaiah son of Amoz sent to Hezekiah, saying: "Thus says the LORD, the God of Israel: Because you have prayed to me concerning King Sennacherib of Assyria, ²²this is the word that the LORD has spoken concerning him:

She despises you, she scorns you—
    virgin daughter Zion;

she tosses her head—behind your
    back,
    daughter Jerusalem.

23 "Whom have you mocked and
    reviled?
    Against whom have you raised
    your voice
and haughtily lifted your eyes?
    Against the Holy One of Israel!
24 By your servants you have mocked
    the Lord,
    and you have said, 'With my
    many chariots
I have gone up the heights of the
    mountains,
    to the far recesses of Lebanon;
I felled its tallest cedars,
    its choicest cypresses;
I came to its remotest height,
    its densest forest.
25 I dug wells
    and drank waters,
I dried up with the sole of my foot
    all the streams of Egypt.'

26 "Have you not heard
    that I determined it long ago?
I planned from days of old
    what now I bring to pass,
that you should make fortified cities
    crash into heaps of ruins,
27 while their inhabitants, shorn of
    strength,
    are dismayed and confounded;
they have become like plants of the
    field
    and like tender grass,
like grass on the housetops,
    blighted^w before it is grown.

28 "I know your rising up^x and your
    sitting down,
    your going out and coming in,
    and your raging against me.
29 Because you have raged against me
    and your arrogance has come to
    my ears,
I will put my hook in your nose
    and my bit in your mouth;
I will turn you back on the way
    by which you came.

30 "And this shall be the sign for you:

<hr>

u Heb *he*   v Or *Nubia;* Heb *Cush*   w With 2 Kings 19.26: Heb *field*   x Q Ms Gk: MT lacks *your rising up*

This year eat what grows of itself, and in the second year what springs from that; then in the third year sow, reap, plant vineyards, and eat their fruit. ³¹The surviving remnant of the house of Judah shall again take root downward, and bear fruit upward; ³²for from Jerusalem a remnant shall go out, and from Mount Zion a band of survivors. The zeal of the LORD of hosts will do this.

33 "Therefore thus says the LORD concerning the king of Assyria: He shall not come into this city, shoot an arrow there, come before it with a shield, or cast up a siege ramp against it. ³⁴By the way that he came, by the same he shall return; he shall not come into this city, says the LORD. ³⁵For I will defend this city to save it, for my own sake and for the sake of my servant David."

Sennacherib's Defeat and Death

36 Then the angel of the LORD set out and struck down one hundred eighty-five thousand in the camp of the Assyrians; when morning dawned, they were all dead bodies. ³⁷Then King Sennacherib of Assyria left, went home, and lived at Nineveh. ³⁸As he was worshiping in the house of his god Nisroch, his sons Adrammelech and Sharezer killed him with the sword, and they escaped into the land of Ararat. His son Esarhaddon succeeded him.

Hezekiah's Illness

38 In those days Hezekiah became sick and was at the point of death. The prophet Isaiah son of Amoz came to him, and said to him, "Thus says the LORD: Set your house in order, for you shall die; you shall not recover." ²Then Hezekiah turned his face to the wall, and prayed to the LORD: ³"Remember now, O LORD, I implore you, how I have walked before you in faithfulness with a whole heart, and have done what is good in your sight." And Hezekiah wept bitterly.

4 Then the word of the LORD came to Isaiah: ⁵"Go and say to Hezekiah, Thus says the LORD, the God of your ancestor David: I have heard your prayer, I have seen your tears; I will add fifteen years

to your life. ⁶I will deliver you and this city out of the hand of the king of Assyria, and defend this city.

7 "This is the sign to you from the LORD, that the LORD will do this thing that he has promised: ⁸See, I will make the shadow cast by the declining sun on the dial of Ahaz turn back ten steps." So the sun turned back on the dial the ten steps by which it had declined.ʸ

9 A writing of King Hezekiah of Judah, after he had been sick and had recovered from his sickness:

10   I said: In the noontide of my days
          I must depart;
      I am consigned to the gates of Sheol
          for the rest of my years.
11   I said, I shall not see the LORD
          in the land of the living;
      I shall look upon mortals no more
          among the inhabitants of the
          world.
12   My dwelling is plucked up and
          removed from me
      like a shepherd's tent;
      like a weaver I have rolled up my
          life;
      he cuts me off from the loom;
      from day to night you bring me to
          an end;ʸ
13   I cry for helpᶻ until morning;
      like a lion he breaks all my bones;
          from day to night you bring me
          to an end.ʸ

14   Like a swallow or a craneʸ I clamor,
          I moan like a dove.
      My eyes are weary with looking
          upward.
      O Lord, I am oppressed; be my
          security!
15   But what can I say? For he has
          spoken to me,
      and he himself has done it.
      All my sleep has fledᵃ
          because of the bitterness of my
          soul.

16   O Lord, by these things people live,
          and in all these is the life of my
          spirit.ʸ
      Oh, restore me to health and
          make me live!

ʸ Meaning of Heb uncertain   ᶻ Cn: Meaning of Heb uncertain   ᵃ Cn Compare Syr: Heb *I will walk slowly all my years*

17 Surely it was for my welfare
        that I had great bitterness;
    but you have held back[b] my life
        from the pit of destruction,
    for you have cast all my sins
        behind your back.
18 For Sheol cannot thank you,
        death cannot praise you;
    those who go down to the Pit
            cannot hope
        for your faithfulness.
19 The living, the living, they thank
            you,
        as I do this day;
    fathers make known to children
        your faithfulness.

20 The LORD will save me,
        and we will sing to stringed
            instruments[c]
    all the days of our lives,
        at the house of the LORD.

21 Now Isaiah had said, "Let them
take a lump of figs, and apply it to the
boil, so that he may recover." ²²Hezeki-
ah also had said, "What is the sign that I
shall go up to the house of the LORD?"

Envoys from Babylon Welcomed

39 At that time King Merodach-
baladan son of Baladan of Babylon sent envoys with letters and a
present to Hezekiah, for he heard that
he had been sick and had recovered.
²Hezekiah welcomed them; he showed
them his treasure house, the silver, the
gold, the spices, the precious oil, his
whole armory, all that was found in his
storehouses. There was nothing in his
house or in all his realm that Hezekiah
did not show them. ³Then the prophet
Isaiah came to King Hezekiah and said
to him, "What did these men say? From
where did they come to you?" Hezekiah
answered, "They have come to me from
a far country, from Babylon." ⁴He said,
"What have they seen in your house?"
Hezekiah answered, "They have seen all
that is in my house; there is nothing in
my storehouses that I did not show
them."
5 Then Isaiah said to Hezekiah,
"Hear the word of the LORD of hosts:
⁶Days are coming when all that is in

your house, and that which your ancestors have stored up until this day, shall
be carried to Babylon; nothing shall be
left, says the LORD. ⁷Some of your own
sons who are born to you shall be taken
away; they shall be eunuchs in the
palace of the king of Babylon." ⁸Then
Hezekiah said to Isaiah, "The word of
the LORD that you have spoken is good."
For he thought, "There will be peace
and security in my days."

God's People Are Comforted

40 Comfort, O comfort my
people,
    says your God.
2   Speak tenderly to Jerusalem,
        and cry to her
    that she has served her term,
        that her penalty is paid,
    that she has received from the
            LORD's hand
        double for all her sins.

3   A voice cries out:
    "In the wilderness prepare the way
            of the LORD,
        make straight in the desert a
            highway for our God.
4   Every valley shall be lifted up,
        and every mountain and hill be
            made low;
    the uneven ground shall become
            level,
        and the rough places a plain.
5   Then the glory of the LORD shall be
            revealed,
        and all people shall see it
            together,
    for the mouth of the LORD has
            spoken."

6   A voice says, "Cry out!"
        And I said, "What shall I cry?"
    All people are grass,
        their constancy is like the flower
            of the field.
7   The grass withers, the flower fades,
        when the breath of the LORD
            blows upon it;
        surely the people are grass.
8   The grass withers, the flower fades;
        but the word of our God will
            stand forever.

b Cn Compare Gk Vg: Heb loved   c Heb my stringed instruments

THE COMFORT OF THE SOVEREIGN PHYSICIAN
Brother Lawrence

VERSE: Isaiah 38.16   **PASSAGE:** Isaiah 38.12–17

 do not pray that you may be delivered from your pains, but I pray God earnestly that he would give you strength and patience to bear them as long as he pleases. Comfort yourself with him who holds you fastened to the cross. He will loose you when he thinks fit. Happy those who suffer with him. Accustom yourself to suffer in that manner, and seek from him the strength to endure as much, and as long, as he shall judge to be necessary for you. The men of the world do not comprehend these truths, nor is it to be wondered at, since they suffer like what they are, and not like Christians. They consider sickness as a pain to nature, and not as a favor from God; and seeing it only in that light, they find nothing in it but grief and distress. But those who consider sickness as coming from the hand of God, as the effect of his mercy, and the means which he employs for their salvation—such commonly find in it great sweetness and sensible consolation.

I wish you could convince yourself that God is often (in some sense) nearer to us, and more effectually present with us, in sickness than in health. Rely upon no other physician; for, according to my apprehension, he reserves your cure to himself. Put, then, all your trust in him, and you will soon find the effects of it in your recovery, which we often retard by putting greater confidence in physic than in God.

Whatever remedies you make use of, they will succeed only so far as he permits. When pains come from God, he only can cure them. He often sends diseases of the body to cure those of the soul. Comfort yourself with the sovereign Physician both of the soul and body.

Be satisfied with the condition in which God places you . . . Continue, then, always with God; it is the only support and comfort for your affliction. I shall beseech him to be with you. I present my service. I am,

Yours . . .

ADDITIONAL SCRIPTURE READING:
Psalm 71.20; Lamentations 3.25–26

Go to page 827 for your next devotional reading.

1500   1700

9 Get you up to a high mountain,
    O Zion, herald of good tidings;*d*
  lift up your voice with strength,
    O Jerusalem, herald of good
      tidings,*e*
    lift it up, do not fear;
  say to the cities of Judah,
    "Here is your God!"
10 See, the Lord GOD comes with
      might,
    and his arm rules for him;
  his reward is with him,
    and his recompense before him.
11 He will feed his flock like a
      shepherd;
    he will gather the lambs in his
      arms,
  and carry them in his bosom,
    and gently lead the mother
      sheep.

12 Who has measured the waters in
      the hollow of his hand
    and marked off the heavens with
      a span,
  enclosed the dust of the earth in a
      measure,
    and weighed the mountains in
      scales
    and the hills in a balance?
13 Who has directed the spirit of the
      LORD,
    or as his counselor has instructed
      him?
14 Whom did he consult for his
      enlightenment,
    and who taught him the path of
      justice?
  Who taught him knowledge,
    and showed him the way of
      understanding?
15 Even the nations are like a drop
      from a bucket,
    and are accounted as dust on the
      scales;
  see, he takes up the isles like fine
    dust.
16 Lebanon would not provide fuel
      enough,
    nor are its animals enough for a
      burnt offering.
17 All the nations are as nothing
    before him;

  they are accounted by him as less
    than nothing and emptiness.

18 To whom then will you liken God,
    or what likeness compare with
      him?
19 An idol? —A workman casts it,
    and a goldsmith overlays it with
      gold,
    and casts for it silver chains.
20 As a gift one chooses mulberry
      wood*f*
    —wood that will not rot—
  then seeks out a skilled artisan
    to set up an image that will not
      topple.

21 Have you not known? Have you
      not heard?
    Has it not been told you from the
      beginning?
  Have you not understood from
    the foundations of the earth?
22 It is he who sits above the circle of
      the earth,
    and its inhabitants are like
      grasshoppers;
  who stretches out the heavens like
      a curtain,
    and spreads them like a tent to
      live in;
23 who brings princes to naught,
    and makes the rulers of the earth
      as nothing.

24 Scarcely are they planted, scarcely
      sown,
    scarcely has their stem taken
      root in the earth,
  when he blows upon them, and
      they wither,
    and the tempest carries them off
      like stubble.

25 To whom then will you compare
      me,
    or who is my equal? says the
      Holy One.
26 Lift up your eyes on high and see:
    Who created these?
  He who brings out their host and
      numbers them,
    calling them all by name;
  because he is great in strength,

---

d Or *O herald of good tidings to Zion*   *e* Or *O herald of good tidings to Jerusalem*   *f* Meaning of Heb uncertain

mighty in power,
  not one is missing.

27 Why do you say, O Jacob,
    and speak, O Israel,
  "My way is hidden from the LORD,
    and my right is disregarded by
      my God"?
28 Have you not known? Have you
      not heard?
  The LORD is the everlasting God,
    the Creator of the ends of the
      earth.
  He does not faint or grow weary;
    his understanding is
      unsearchable.
29 He gives power to the faint,
    and strengthens the powerless.
30 Even youths will faint and be
      weary,
    and the young will fall
      exhausted;
31 but those who wait for the LORD
      shall renew their strength,
    they shall mount up with wings
      like eagles,
  they shall run and not be weary,
    they shall walk and not faint.

Israel Assured of God's Help

41 Listen to me in silence,
    O coastlands;
  let the peoples renew their
      strength;
  let them approach, then let them
      speak;
    let us together draw near for
      judgment.

2 Who has roused a victor from the
      east,
    summoned him to his service?
  He delivers up nations to him,
    and tramples kings under foot;
  he makes them like dust with his
      sword,
    like driven stubble with his bow.
3 He pursues them and passes on
      safely,
    scarcely touching the path with
      his feet.
4 Who has performed and done this,
    calling the generations from the
      beginning?
  I, the LORD, am first,

  and will be with the last.
5 The coastlands have seen and are
      afraid,
    the ends of the earth tremble;
    they have drawn near and come.
6 Each one helps the other,
    saying to one another, "Take
      courage!"
7 The artisan encourages the
      goldsmith,
    and the one who smooths with
      the hammer encourages the
      one who strikes the anvil,
  saying of the soldering, "It is good";
    and they fasten it with nails so
      that it cannot be moved.
8 But you, Israel, my servant,
    Jacob, whom I have chosen,
    the offspring of Abraham, my
      friend;
9 you whom I took from the ends of
      the earth,
    and called from its farthest
      corners,
  saying to you, "You are my servant,
    I have chosen you and not cast
      you off";
10 do not fear, for I am with you,
    do not be afraid, for I am your
      God;
  I will strengthen you, I will help you,
    I will uphold you with my
      victorious right hand.

11 Yes, all who are incensed against
      you
    shall be ashamed and disgraced;
  those who strive against you
    shall be as nothing and shall
      perish.
12 You shall seek those who contend
      with you,
    but you shall not find them;
  those who war against you
    shall be as nothing at all.
13 For I, the LORD your God,
    hold your right hand;
  it is I who say to you, "Do not fear,
    I will help you."

14 Do not fear, you worm Jacob,
    you insect[g] Israel!
  I will help you, says the LORD;
    your Redeemer is the Holy One
      of Israel.

g Syr: Heb men of

15 Now, I will make of you a
       threshing sledge,
    sharp, new, and having teeth;
    you shall thresh the mountains and
       crush them,
       and you shall make the hills like
          chaff.
16 You shall winnow them and the
       wind shall carry them away,
    and the tempest shall scatter
       them.
    Then you shall rejoice in the LORD;
       in the Holy One of Israel you
          shall glory.

17 When the poor and needy seek
       water,
       and there is none,
       and their tongue is parched with
          thirst,
    I the LORD will answer them,
    I the God of Israel will not
       forsake them.
18 I will open rivers on the bare
       heights,*h*
    and fountains in the midst of the
       valleys;
    I will make the wilderness a pool of
       water,
    and the dry land springs of water.
19 I will put in the wilderness the
       cedar,
       the acacia, the myrtle, and the
          olive;
    I will set in the desert the cypress,
       the plane and the pine together,
20 so that all may see and know,
       all may consider and understand,
    that the hand of the LORD has done
       this,
       the Holy One of Israel has
          created it.

The Futility of Idols

21 Set forth your case, says the LORD;
       bring your proofs, says the King
          of Jacob.
22 Let them bring them, and tell us
       what is to happen.
    Tell us the former things, what
       they are,
       so that we may consider them,
    and that we may know their
       outcome;

or declare to us the things to
       come.
23 Tell us what is to come hereafter,
       that we may know that you are
          gods;
    do good, or do harm,
       that we may be afraid and
          terrified.
24 You, indeed, are nothing
       and your work is nothing at all;
    whoever chooses you is an
       abomination.

25 I stirred up one from the north, and
       he has come,
    from the rising of the sun he was
       summoned by name.*i*
    He shall trample*j* on rulers as on
       mortar,
       as the potter treads clay.
26 Who declared it from the
       beginning, so that we might
          know,
    and beforehand, so that we might
       say, "He is right"?
    There was no one who declared it,
       none who proclaimed,
       none who heard your words.
27 I first have declared it to Zion,*k*
       and I give to Jerusalem a herald
          of good tidings.
28 But when I look there is no one;
       among these there is no
          counselor
    who, when I ask, gives an
       answer.
29 No, they are all a delusion;
       their works are nothing;
       their images are empty wind.

The Servant, a Light to the Nations

42 Here is my servant, whom I
       uphold,
    my chosen, in whom my soul
       delights;
    I have put my spirit upon him;
       he will bring forth justice to the
          nations.
2 He will not cry or lift up his voice,
    or make it heard in the street;
3 a bruised reed he will not break,
    and a dimly burning wick he will
       not quench;

h Or *trails*   *i* Cn Compare Q Ms Gk: MT *and he shall call on my name*   *j* Cn: Heb *come*
k Cn: Heb *First to Zion—Behold, behold them*

he will faithfully bring forth
  justice.
4 He will not grow faint or be
    crushed
  until he has established justice in
    the earth;
  and the coastlands wait for his
    teaching.

5 Thus says God, the LORD,
    who created the heavens and
      stretched them out,
    who spread out the earth and
      what comes from it,
  who gives breath to the people
    upon it
  and spirit to those who walk in
    it:
6 I am the LORD, I have called you in
    righteousness,
  I have taken you by the hand and
    kept you;
  I have given you as a covenant to
    the people,[1]
  a light to the nations,
7   to open the eyes that are blind,
  to bring out the prisoners from the
    dungeon,
  from the prison those who sit in
    darkness.
8 I am the LORD, that is my name;
  my glory I give to no other,
  nor my praise to idols.
9 See, the former things have come
    to pass,
  and new things I now declare;
  before they spring forth,
  I tell you of them.

A Hymn of Praise

10 Sing to the LORD a new song,
    his praise from the end of the
      earth!
  Let the sea roar[m] and all that fills
    it,
    the coastlands and their
      inhabitants.
11 Let the desert and its towns lift up
    their voice,
    the villages that Kedar inhabits;
  let the inhabitants of Sela sing for
    joy,
  let them shout from the tops of
    the mountains.

12 Let them give glory to the LORD,
    and declare his praise in the
      coastlands.
13 The LORD goes forth like a soldier,
    like a warrior he stirs up his fury;
  he cries out, he shouts aloud,
    he shows himself mighty against
      his foes.

14 For a long time I have held my
      peace,
    I have kept still and restrained
      myself;
  now I will cry out like a woman in
    labor,
    I will gasp and pant.
15 I will lay waste mountains and
      hills,
    and dry up all their herbage;
  I will turn the rivers into islands,
    and dry up the pools.
16 I will lead the blind
    by a road they do not know,
  by paths they have not known
    I will guide them.
  I will turn the darkness before
      them into light,
    the rough places into level
      ground.
  These are the things I will do,
    and I will not forsake them.
17 They shall be turned back and
      utterly put to shame—
    those who trust in carved
      images,
  who say to cast images,
    "You are our gods."

18 Listen, you that are deaf;
    and you that are blind, look up
      and see!
19 Who is blind but my servant,
    or deaf like my messenger whom
      I send?
  Who is blind like my dedicated
      one,
    or blind like the servant of the
      LORD?
20 He sees many things, but does[n] not
      observe them;
    his ears are open, but he does not
      hear.

---

1 Meaning of Heb uncertain   m Cn Compare Ps 96.11; 98.7: Heb *Those who go down to the sea*
n Heb *You see many things but do*

Israel's Disobedience

21 The LORD was pleased, for the sake
  of his righteousness,
  to magnify his teaching and
  make it glorious.
22 But this is a people robbed and
  plundered,
  all of them are trapped in holes
  and hidden in prisons;
  they have become a prey with no
  one to rescue,
  a spoil with no one to say,
  "Restore!"
23 Who among you will give heed to
  this,
  who will attend and listen for the
  time to come?

TUESDAY

GOD'S TERRIBLENESS AND GENTLENESS
Joseph Parker

VERSE: Isaiah 42.14   **PASSAGE:** Isaiah 42.14–16

he combination of great power and great restraint—
indeed, the combination of opposite qualities and uses
generally—is well-known in civilized life and in the
laws of nature. The fire that warms the room when
properly regulated, will, if abused, reduce the proudest palaces to
ashes. The river, which softens and refreshes the landscape, if
allowed to escape its banks, can devastate the most fruitful
fields . . .

In our text in Isaiah we are confronted with the highest
expression of the same truth: The mighty God is the everlasting
Father; the terrible One is more gentle than the gentlest friend;
he who rides in the chariot of thunder stoops to lead the blind by
a way that they know not and to gather the lambs in his bosom.

In pointing out the terribleness of God, I do not appeal to fear
. . . We do not say, "Be good, or God will crush you." That is not
virtue, that is not liberty—it is vice put on its good behavior. It is
iniquity with a sword suspended over its head . . .

The great truth to be learned is that all the terribleness of God
is the good man's security. When the good man sees God wasting the mountains and the hills, and drying up the rivers, he does
not say, "I must worship him or he will destroy me." He says,
"The beneficent side of that power is all mine. Because of that
power I am safe. The very lightning is my guardian, and in the
whirlwind I hear a pledge of benediction."

ADDITIONAL SCRIPTURE READING:
Psalms 107.33–34; 114.3–8; Nahum 1.5–8

Go to page 836 for your next devotional reading.

1700   1900

24 Who gave up Jacob to the spoiler,
      and Israel to the robbers?
   Was it not the LORD, against whom
      we have sinned,
      in whose ways they would not
        walk,
      and whose law they would not
        obey?
25 So he poured upon him the heat of
      his anger
      and the fury of war;
   it set him on fire all around, but he
      did not understand;
   it burned him, but he did not
      take it to heart.

Restoration and Protection Promised

43 But now thus says the LORD,
   he who created you, O Jacob,
   he who formed you, O Israel:
   Do not fear, for I have redeemed
      you;
      I have called you by name, you
        are mine.
2 When you pass through the waters,
      I will be with you;
      and through the rivers, they shall
        not overwhelm you;
   when you walk through fire you
      shall not be burned,
      and the flame shall not consume
        you.
3 For I am the LORD your God,
      the Holy One of Israel, your
        Savior.
   I give Egypt as your ransom,
      Ethiopia⁰ and Seba in exchange
        for you.
4 Because you are precious in my
      sight,
      and honored, and I love you,
   I give people in return for you,
      nations in exchange for your life.
5 Do not fear, for I am with you;
   I will bring your offspring from
      the east,
      and from the west I will gather
        you;
6 I will say to the north, "Give them
      up,"
      and to the south, "Do not
        withhold;
   bring my sons from far away
      and my daughters from the end
        of the earth—

7 everyone who is called by my
      name,
      whom I created for my glory,
      whom I formed and made."

8 Bring forth the people who are
        blind, yet have eyes,
      who are deaf, yet have ears!
9 Let all the nations gather together,
      and let the peoples assemble.
   Who among them declared this,
      and foretold to us the former
        things?
   Let them bring their witnesses to
      justify them,
      and let them hear and say, "It is
        true."
10 You are my witnesses, says the
      LORD,
      and my servant whom I have
        chosen,
   so that you may know and believe
        me
      and understand that I am he.
   Before me no god was formed,
      nor shall there be any after me.
11 I, I am the LORD,
      and besides me there is no savior.
12 I declared and saved and
        proclaimed,
      when there was no strange god
        among you;
      and you are my witnesses, says
        the LORD.
13 I am God, and also henceforth I am
      He;
      there is no one who can deliver
        from my hand;
      I work and who can hinder it?

14 Thus says the LORD,
      your Redeemer, the Holy One of
        Israel:
   For your sake I will send to Babylon
      and break down all the bars,
      and the shouting of the
        Chaldeans will be turned to
        lamentation.ᵖ
15 I am the LORD, your Holy One,
      the Creator of Israel, your King.
16 Thus says the LORD,
      who makes a way in the sea,
      a path in the mighty waters,
17 who brings out chariot and horse,
      army and warrior;

o Or *Nubia*; Heb *Cush*   p Meaning of Heb uncertain

they lie down, they cannot rise,
    they are extinguished, quenched
    like a wick:
18 Do not remember the former
    things,
    or consider the things of old.
19 I am about to do a new thing;
    now it springs forth, do you not
      perceive it?
    I will make a way in the wilderness
    and rivers in the desert.
20 The wild animals will honor me,
    the jackals and the ostriches;
    for I give water in the wilderness,
    rivers in the desert,
    to give drink to my chosen people,
21   the people whom I formed for
      myself
    so that they might declare my
      praise.

22 Yet you did not call upon me,
    O Jacob;
    but you have been weary of me,
    O Israel!
23 You have not brought me your
    sheep for burnt offerings,
    or honored me with your
    sacrifices.
    I have not burdened you with
    offerings,
    or wearied you with
    frankincense.
24 You have not bought me sweet
    cane with money,
    or satisfied me with the fat of
    your sacrifices.
    But you have burdened me with
    your sins;
    you have wearied me with your
    iniquities.

25 I, I am He
    who blots out your
    transgressions for my own
    sake,
    and I will not remember your
    sins.
26 Accuse me, let us go to trial;
    set forth your case, so that you
      may be proved right.
27 Your first ancestor sinned,
    and your interpreters
    transgressed against me.

28 Therefore I profaned the princes of
    the sanctuary,
    I delivered Jacob to utter
    destruction,
    and Israel to reviling.

God's Blessing on Israel

44 But now hear, O Jacob my
    servant,
    Israel whom I have chosen!
2 Thus says the LORD who made you,
    who formed you in the womb
    and will help you:
    Do not fear, O Jacob my servant,
    Jeshurun whom I have chosen.
3 For I will pour water on the thirsty
    land,
    and streams on the dry ground;
    I will pour my spirit upon your
    descendants,
    and my blessing on your
    offspring.
4 They shall spring up like a green
    tamarisk,
    like willows by flowing streams.
5 This one will say, "I am the
    LORD's,"
    another will be called by the
    name of Jacob,
    yet another will write on the hand,
    "The LORD's,"
    and adopt the name of Israel.

6 Thus says the LORD, the King of
    Israel,
    and his Redeemer, the LORD of
    hosts:
    I am the first and I am the last;
    besides me there is no god.
7 Who is like me? Let them proclaim
    it,
    let them declare and set it forth
    before me.
    Who has announced from of old the
    things to come?q
    Let them tell usr what is yet to
    be.
8 Do not fear, or be afraid;
    have I not told you from of old
    and declared it?
    You are my witnesses!
    Is there any god besides me?
    There is no other rock; I know
    not one.

q Cn: Heb *from my placing an eternal people and things to come*   r Tg: Heb *them*

The Absurdity of Idol Worship

9 All who make idols are nothing, and the things they delight in do not profit; their witnesses neither see nor know. And so they will be put to shame. 10Who would fashion a god or cast an image that can do no good? 11Look, all its devotees shall be put to shame; the artisans too are merely human. Let them all assemble, let them stand up; they shall be terrified, they shall all be put to shame.

12 The ironsmith fashions its and works it over the coals, shaping it with hammers, and forging it with his strong arm; he becomes hungry and his strength fails, he drinks no water and is faint. 13The carpenter stretches a line, marks it out with a stylus, fashions it with planes, and marks it with a compass; he makes it in human form, with human beauty, to be set up in a shrine. 14He cuts down cedars or chooses a holm tree or an oak and lets it grow strong among the trees of the forest. He plants a cedar and the rain nourishes it. 15Then it can be used as fuel. Part of it he takes and warms himself; he kindles a fire and bakes bread. Then he makes a god and worships it, makes it a carved image and bows down before it. 16Half of it he burns in the fire; over this half he roasts meat, eats it and is satisfied. He also warms himself and says, "Ah, I am warm, I can feel the fire!" 17The rest of it he makes into a god, his idol, bows down to it and worships it; he prays to it and says, "Save me, for you are my god!"

18 They do not know, nor do they comprehend; for their eyes are shut, so that they cannot see, and their minds as well, so that they cannot understand. 19No one considers, nor is there knowledge or discernment to say, "Half of it I burned in the fire; I also baked bread on its coals, I roasted meat and have eaten. Now shall I make the rest of it an abomination? Shall I fall down before a block of wood?" 20He feeds on ashes; a deluded mind has led him astray, and he cannot save himself or say, "Is not this thing in my right hand a fraud?"

s Cn: Heb an ax

Israel Is Not Forgotten

21 Remember these things, O Jacob,
    and Israel, for you are my
        servant;
  I formed you, you are my servant;
    O Israel, you will not be
        forgotten by me.
22 I have swept away your
        transgressions like a cloud,
    and your sins like mist;
  return to me, for I have redeemed
        you.

23 Sing, O heavens, for the LORD has
        done it;
    shout, O depths of the earth;
  break forth into singing,
        O mountains,
  O forest, and every tree in it!
  For the LORD has redeemed Jacob,
    and will be glorified in Israel.

24 Thus says the LORD, your
        Redeemer,
    who formed you in the womb:
  I am the LORD, who made all
        things,
    who alone stretched out the
        heavens,
    who by myself spread out the
        earth;
25 who frustrates the omens of liars,
    and makes fools of diviners;
  who turns back the wise,
    and makes their knowledge
        foolish;
26 who confirms the word of his
        servant,
    and fulfills the prediction of his
        messengers;
  who says of Jerusalem, "It shall be
        inhabited,"
    and of the cities of Judah, "They
        shall be rebuilt,
    and I will raise up their ruins";
27 who says to the deep, "Be dry—
    I will dry up your rivers";
28 who says of Cyrus, "He is my
        shepherd,
    and he shall carry out all my
        purpose";
  and who says of Jerusalem, "It shall
        be rebuilt,"
    and of the temple, "Your
        foundation shall be laid."

Cyrus, God's Instrument

45 Thus says the LORD to his
anointed, to Cyrus,
whose right hand I have grasped
to subdue nations before him
and strip kings of their robes,
to open doors before him—
and the gates shall not be closed:
2 I will go before you
and level the mountains, [t]
I will break in pieces the doors of
bronze
and cut through the bars of iron,
3 I will give you the treasures of
darkness
and riches hidden in secret
places,
so that you may know that it is I,
the LORD,
the God of Israel, who call you by
your name.
4 For the sake of my servant Jacob,
and Israel my chosen,
I call you by your name,
I surname you, though you do
not know me.
5 I am the LORD, and there is no
other;
besides me there is no god.
I arm you, though you do not
know me,
6 so that they may know, from the
rising of the sun
and from the west, that there is
no one besides me;
I am the LORD, and there is no
other.
7 I form light and create darkness,
I make weal and create woe;
I the LORD do all these things.

8 Shower, O heavens, from above,
and let the skies rain down
righteousness;
let the earth open, that salvation
may spring up, [u]
and let it cause righteousness to
sprout up also;
I the LORD have created it.

9 Woe to you who strive with your
Maker,
earthen vessels with the potter! [v]
Does the clay say to the one who
fashions it, "What are you
making"?
or "Your work has no handles"?
10 Woe to anyone who says to a father,
"What are you begetting?"
or to a woman, "With what are
you in labor?"
11 Thus says the LORD,
the Holy One of Israel, and its
Maker:
Will you question me [w] about my
children,
or command me concerning the
work of my hands?
12 I made the earth,
and created humankind upon it;
it was my hands that stretched out
the heavens,
and I commanded all their host.
13 I have aroused Cyrus [x] in
righteousness,
and I will make all his paths
straight;
he shall build my city
and set my exiles free,
not for price or reward,
says the LORD of hosts.
14 Thus says the LORD:
The wealth of Egypt and the
merchandise of Ethiopia, [y]
and the Sabeans, tall of stature,
shall come over to you and be yours,
they shall follow you;
they shall come over in chains
and bow down to you.
They will make supplication to
you, saying,
"God is with you alone, and
there is no other;
there is no god besides him."
15 Truly, you are a God who hides
himself,
O God of Israel, the Savior.
16 All of them are put to shame and
confounded,
the makers of idols go in
confusion together.
17 But Israel is saved by the LORD
with everlasting salvation;
you shall not be put to shame or
confounded
to all eternity.

t Q Ms Gk: MT the swellings   u Q Ms: MT that they may bring forth salvation   v Cn: Heb with
the potsherds, or with the potters   w Cn: Heb Ask me of things to come   x Heb him
y Or Nubia; Heb Cush

18 For thus says the LORD,
      who created the heavens
         (he is God!),
      who formed the earth and made it
         (he established it;
      he did not create it a chaos,
         he formed it to be inhabited!):
      I am the LORD, and there is no
         other.
19 I did not speak in secret,
      in a land of darkness;
      I did not say to the offspring of Jacob,
         "Seek me in chaos."
      I the LORD speak the truth,
         I declare what is right.

Idols Cannot Save Babylon

20 Assemble yourselves and come
         together,
      draw near, you survivors of the
         nations!
      They have no knowledge—
         those who carry about their
            wooden idols,
      and keep on praying to a god
         that cannot save.
21 Declare and present your case;
      let them take counsel together!
      Who told this long ago?
         Who declared it of old?
      Was it not I, the LORD?
         There is no other god besides me,
      a righteous God and a Savior;
         there is no one besides me.

22 Turn to me and be saved,
      all the ends of the earth!
      For I am God, and there is no
         other.
23 By myself I have sworn,
      from my mouth has gone forth in
         righteousness
      a word that shall not return:
      "To me every knee shall bow,
         every tongue shall swear."

24 Only in the LORD, it shall be said of
         me,
      are righteousness and strength;
      all who were incensed against him
         shall come to him and be
            ashamed.
25 In the LORD all the offspring of
         Israel
      shall triumph and glory.

46 Bel bows down, Nebo stoops,
      their idols are on beasts and
         cattle;
      these things you carry are loaded
         as burdens on weary animals.
2 They stoop, they bow down
         together;
      they cannot save the burden,
         but themselves go into captivity.

3 Listen to me, O house of Jacob,
      all the remnant of the house of
         Israel,
      who have been borne by me from
         your birth,
      carried from the womb;
4 even to your old age I am he,
      even when you turn gray I will
         carry you.
      I have made, and I will bear;
         I will carry and will save.

5 To whom will you liken me and
         make me equal,
      and compare me, as though we
         were alike?
6 Those who lavish gold from the
         purse,
      and weigh out silver in the
         scales—
      they hire a goldsmith, who makes
         it into a god;
      then they fall down and worship!
7 They lift it to their shoulders, they
         carry it,
      they set it in its place, and it
         stands there;
      it cannot move from its place.
      If one cries out to it, it does not
         answer
      or save anyone from trouble.

8 Remember this and consider,z
      recall it to mind, you
         transgressors,
9 remember the former things of
         old;
      for I am God, and there is no other;
         I am God, and there is no one
            like me,
10 declaring the end from the
         beginning
      and from ancient times things
         not yet done,

z Meaning of Heb uncertain

saying, "My purpose shall stand,
and I will fulfill my intention,"
11 calling a bird of prey from the east,
the man for my purpose from a
far country.
I have spoken, and I will bring it to
pass;
I have planned, and I will do it.

12 Listen to me, you stubborn of heart,
you who are far from deliverance:
13 I bring near my deliverance, it is
not far off,
and my salvation will not tarry;
I will put salvation in Zion,
for Israel my glory.

The Humiliation of Babylon

47 Come down and sit in the
dust,
virgin daughter Babylon!
Sit on the ground without a throne,
daughter Chaldea!
For you shall no more be called
tender and delicate.
2 Take the millstones and grind meal,
remove your veil,
strip off your robe, uncover your
legs,
pass through the rivers.
3 Your nakedness shall be uncovered,
and your shame shall be seen.
I will take vengeance,
and I will spare no one.
4 Our Redeemer—the LORD of hosts
is his name—
is the Holy One of Israel.

5 Sit in silence, and go into darkness,
daughter Chaldea!
For you shall no more be called
the mistress of kingdoms.
6 I was angry with my people,
I profaned my heritage;
I gave them into your hand,
you showed them no mercy;
on the aged you made your yoke
exceedingly heavy.
7 You said, "I shall be mistress
forever,"
so that you did not lay these
things to heart
or remember their end.

8 Now therefore hear this, you lover
of pleasures,
who sit securely,
who say in your heart,
"I am, and there is no one besides
me;
I shall not sit as a widow
or know the loss of children"—
9 both these things shall come upon
you
in a moment, in one day:
the loss of children and
widowhood
shall come upon you in full
measure,
in spite of your many sorceries
and the great power of your
enchantments.

10 You felt secure in your
wickedness;
you said, "No one sees me."
Your wisdom and your knowledge
led you astray,
and you said in your heart,
"I am, and there is no one besides
me."
11 But evil shall come upon you,
which you cannot charm away;
disaster shall fall upon you,
which you will not be able to
ward off;
and ruin shall come on you
suddenly,
of which you know nothing.

12 Stand fast in your enchantments
and your many sorceries,
with which you have labored
from your youth;
perhaps you may be able to
succeed,
perhaps you may inspire terror.
13 You are wearied with your many
consultations;
let those who study[a] the heavens
stand up and save you,
those who gaze at the stars,
and at each new moon predict
what[b] shall befall you.

14 See, they are like stubble,
the fire consumes them;
they cannot deliver themselves
from the power of the flame.

a Meaning of Heb uncertain   b Gk Syr Compare Vg: Heb from what

No coal for warming oneself is this,
    no fire to sit before!
15 Such to you are those with whom
        you have labored,
    who have trafficked with you
        from your youth;
    they all wander about in their own
        paths;
    there is no one to save you.

God the Creator and Redeemer

48 Hear this, O house of Jacob,
    who are called by the name
    of Israel,
    and who came forth from the
        loins*c* of Judah;
    who swear by the name of the LORD,
    and invoke the God of Israel,
    but not in truth or right.
2 For they call themselves after the
        holy city,
    and lean on the God of Israel;
    the LORD of hosts is his name.

3 The former things I declared long
        ago,
    they went out from my mouth
        and I made them known;
    then suddenly I did them and
        they came to pass.
4 Because I know that you are
        obstinate,
    and your neck is an iron sinew
    and your forehead brass,
5 I declared them to you from long
        ago,
    before they came to pass I
        announced them to you,
    so that you would not say, "My
        idol did them,
    my carved image and my cast
        image commanded them."

6 You have heard; now see all this;
    and will you not declare it?
    From this time forward I make you
        hear new things,
    hidden things that you have not
        known.
7 They are created now, not long ago;
    before today you have never
        heard of them,
    so that you could not say, "I
        already knew them."

8 You have never heard, you have
        never known,
    from of old your ear has not been
        opened.
    For I knew that you would deal
        very treacherously,
    and that from birth you were
        called a rebel.
9 For my name's sake I defer my
        anger,
    for the sake of my praise I
        restrain it for you,
    so that I may not cut you off.
10 See, I have refined you, but not
        like*d* silver;
    I have tested you in the furnace
        of adversity.
11 For my own sake, for my own sake,
        I do it,
    for why should my name*e* be
        profaned?
    My glory I will not give to
        another.

12 Listen to me, O Jacob,
    and Israel, whom I called:
    I am He; I am the first,
    and I am the last.
13 My hand laid the foundation of the
        earth,
    and my right hand spread out the
        heavens;
    when I summon them,
    they stand at attention.

14 Assemble, all of you, and hear!
    Who among them has declared
        these things?
    The LORD loves him;
    he shall perform his purpose on
        Babylon,
    and his arm shall be against the
        Chaldeans.
15 I, even I, have spoken and called
        him,
    I have brought him, and he will
        prosper in his way.
16 Draw near to me, hear this!
    From the beginning I have not
        spoken in secret,
    from the time it came to be I
        have been there.
    And now the Lord GOD has sent
        me and his spirit.

c Cn: Heb *waters*   *d* Cn: Heb *with*   *e* Gk Old Latin: Heb *for why should it*

17 Thus says the LORD,
   your Redeemer, the Holy One of
       Israel:
   I am the LORD your God,
     who teaches you for your own
         good,
     who leads you in the way you
         should go.
18 O that you had paid attention to
       my commandments!
     Then your prosperity would have
         been like a river,
     and your success like the waves
         of the sea;
19 your offspring would have been
       like the sand,
     and your descendants like its
         grains;
   their name would never be cut off
     or destroyed from before me.

20 Go out from Babylon, flee from
     Chaldea,
   declare this with a shout of joy,
       proclaim it,
   send it forth to the end of the earth;
     say, "The LORD has redeemed his
         servant Jacob!"
21 They did not thirst when he led
       them through the deserts;
   he made water flow for them
       from the rock;
   he split open the rock and the
       water gushed out.

22 "There is no peace," says the LORD,
     "for the wicked."

The Servant's Mission

49 Listen to me, O coastlands,
   pay attention, you peoples
       from far away!
   The LORD called me before I was
       born,
     while I was in my mother's
         womb he named me.
2 He made my mouth like a sharp
     sword,
   in the shadow of his hand he hid
       me;
   he made me a polished arrow,
     in his quiver he hid me away.
3 And he said to me, "You are my
       servant,

Israel, in whom I will be
   glorified."
4 But I said, "I have labored in vain,
     I have spent my strength for
         nothing and vanity;
   yet surely my cause is with the
       LORD,
     and my reward with my God."

5 And now the LORD says,
     who formed me in the womb to
       be his servant,
   to bring Jacob back to him,
     and that Israel might be gathered
       to him,
   for I am honored in the sight of the
       LORD,
     and my God has become my
       strength—
6 he says,
   "It is too light a thing that you
       should be my servant
     to raise up the tribes of Jacob
     and to restore the survivors of
         Israel;
   I will give you as a light to the
       nations,
     that my salvation may reach to
       the end of the earth."

7 Thus says the LORD,
   the Redeemer of Israel and his
       Holy One,
   to one deeply despised, abhorred by
       the nations,
   the slave of rulers,
   "Kings shall see and stand up,
     princes, and they shall prostrate
       themselves,
   because of the LORD, who is
       faithful,
   the Holy One of Israel, who has
       chosen you."

Zion's Children to Be Brought Home

8 Thus says the LORD:
   In a time of favor I have answered
       you,
     on a day of salvation I have
       helped you;
   I have kept you and given you
     as a covenant to the people,[f]
   to establish the land,

f Meaning of Heb uncertain

to apportion the desolate
  heritages;
9 saying to the prisoners, "Come
    out,"
  to those who are in darkness,
    "Show yourselves."
  They shall feed along the ways,
    on all the bare heights^g shall be
    their pasture;
10 they shall not hunger or thirst,

neither scorching wind nor sun
  shall strike them down,
for he who has pity on them will
  lead them,
and by springs of water will guide
  them.
11 And I will turn all my mountains
    into a road,
  and my highways shall be raised
    up.

g Or *the trails*

WEDNESDAY

BEFORE HIS DEATH AT THE STAKE
Thomas Cranmer

VERSE: Isaiah 49.7   **PASSAGE:** Isaiah 49.1–13

Father of heaven; O Son of God, Redeemer of the world; O Holy Ghost, proceeding from them both; three persons, and one God; have mercy upon me, most wretched caitiff and miserable sinner. I have offended both heaven and earth, more grievously than any tongue can express. Whither then may I go, or wither should I flee for succor? To heaven I may be ashamed to lift up mine eyes, and in earth I find no refuge or succor. What shall I then do? Shall I despair? God forbid. O good God, thou art merciful, and refusest none that cometh unto thee for succor. To thee, therefore, do I run; to thee do I humble myself; saying, O Lord God, my sins be great, but yet have mercy upon me for thy great mercy. O God the Son, this great mystery was not wrought (that God became man) for few or small offenses; nor thou didst not give thy Son unto death, O God the Father, for our little and small sins only, but for all the greatest sins of the world, so that the sinner return unto thee with a penitent heart, as I do here at this present. Wherefore have mercy upon me, O Lord, whose property is always to have mercy; for although my sins be great, yet thy mercy is greater. And I crave nothing, O Lord, for mine own merits, but for thy name's sake, that it may be glorified thereby.

ADDITIONAL SCRIPTURE READING:
Psalms 51.1; 86.3; Mark 10.47

Go to page 842 for your next devotional reading.

1500   1700

12 Lo, these shall come from far away,
    and lo, these from the north and
        from the west,
    and these from the land of
        Syene.*h*

13 Sing for joy, O heavens, and exult,
        O earth;
    break forth, O mountains, into
        singing!
    For the LORD has comforted his
        people,
    and will have compassion on his
        suffering ones.

14 But Zion said, "The LORD has
        forsaken me,
    my Lord has forgotten me."
15 Can a woman forget her nursing
        child,
    or show no compassion for the
        child of her womb?
    Even these may forget,
        yet I will not forget you.
16 See, I have inscribed you on the
        palms of my hands;
    your walls are continually before
        me.
17 Your builders outdo your
        destroyers,*i*
    and those who laid you waste go
        away from you.
18 Lift up your eyes all around and
        see;
    they all gather, they come to you.
    As I live, says the LORD,
        you shall put all of them on like
            an ornament,
    and like a bride you shall bind
        them on.

19 Surely your waste and your
        desolate places
    and your devastated land—
    surely now you will be too crowded
        for your inhabitants,
    and those who swallowed you up
        will be far away.
20 The children born in the time of
        your bereavement
    will yet say in your hearing:
    "The place is too crowded for me;
        make room for me to settle."
21 Then you will say in your heart,

"Who has borne me these?
    I was bereaved and barren,
        exiled and put away—
    so who has reared these?
    I was left all alone—
        where then have these come
            from?"

22 Thus says the Lord GOD:
    I will soon lift up my hand to the
        nations,
    and raise my signal to the
        peoples;
    and they shall bring your sons in
        their bosom,
    and your daughters shall be
        carried on their shoulders.
23 Kings shall be your foster fathers,
    and their queens your nursing
        mothers.
    With their faces to the ground they
        shall bow down to you,
    and lick the dust of your feet.
    Then you will know that I am the
        LORD;
    those who wait for me shall not
        be put to shame.

24 Can the prey be taken from the
        mighty,
    or the captives of a tyrant*j* be
        rescued?
25 But thus says the LORD:
    Even the captives of the mighty
        shall be taken,
    and the prey of the tyrant be
        rescued;
    for I will contend with those who
        contend with you,
    and I will save your children.
26 I will make your oppressors eat
        their own flesh,
    and they shall be drunk with
        their own blood as with
            wine.
    Then all flesh shall know
        that I am the LORD your Savior,
    and your Redeemer, the Mighty
        One of Jacob.

50 Thus says the LORD:
    Where is your mother's bill
        of divorce
    with which I put her away?

---

h Q Ms: MT *Sinim*   *i* Or *Your children come swiftly; your destroyers*   *j* Q Ms Syr Vg: MT *of a righteous person*

Or which of my creditors is it
    to whom I have sold you?
No, because of your sins you were
        sold,
    and for your transgressions your
        mother was put away.
2 Why was no one there when I came?
    Why did no one answer when I
        called?
    Is my hand shortened, that it
        cannot redeem?
    Or have I no power to deliver?
    By my rebuke I dry up the sea,
    I make the rivers a desert;
    their fish stink for lack of water,
    and die of thirst.*k*
3 I clothe the heavens with
        blackness,
    and make sackcloth their
        covering.

The Servant's Humiliation and Vindication

4 The Lord GOD has given me
        the tongue of a teacher,*l*
    that I may know how to sustain
        the weary with a word.
    Morning by morning he wakens—
        wakens my ear
    to listen as those who are taught.
5 The Lord GOD has opened my ear,
    and I was not rebellious,
    I did not turn backward.
6 I gave my back to those who struck
        me,
    and my cheeks to those who
        pulled out the beard;
    I did not hide my face
        from insult and spitting.

7 The Lord GOD helps me;
    therefore I have not been
        disgraced;
    therefore I have set my face like
        flint,
    and I know that I shall not be put
        to shame;
8 he who vindicates me is near.
    Who will contend with me?
    Let us stand up together.
    Who are my adversaries?
    Let them confront me.
9 It is the Lord GOD who helps me;
    who will declare me guilty?

All of them will wear out like a
        garment;
    the moth will eat them up.

10 Who among you fears the LORD
        and obeys the voice of his
        servant,
    who walks in darkness
        and has no light,
    yet trusts in the name of the LORD
        and relies upon his God?
11 But all of you are kindlers of fire,
        lighters of firebrands.*m*
    Walk in the flame of your fire,
        and among the brands that you
        have kindled!
    This is what you shall have from
        my hand:
    you shall lie down in torment.

Blessings in Store for God's People

51 Listen to me, you that pursue
        righteousness,
    you that seek the LORD.
    Look to the rock from which you
        were hewn,
    and to the quarry from which
        you were dug.
2 Look to Abraham your father
        and to Sarah who bore you;
    for he was but one when I called
        him,
    but I blessed him and made him
        many.
3 For the LORD will comfort Zion;
    he will comfort all her waste
        places,
    and will make her wilderness like
        Eden,
    her desert like the garden of the
        LORD;
    joy and gladness will be found in
        her,
    thanksgiving and the voice of
        song.

4 Listen to me, my people,
    and give heed to me, my nation;
    for a teaching will go out from me,
        and my justice for a light to the
        peoples.
5 I will bring near my deliverance
        swiftly,
    my salvation has gone out

---

k Or *die on the thirsty ground*   *l* Cn: Heb *of those who are taught*   *m* Syr: Heb *you gird yourselves with firebrands*

and my arms will rule the
peoples;
the coastlands wait for me,
and for my arm they hope.
6 Lift up your eyes to the heavens,
and look at the earth beneath;
for the heavens will vanish like
smoke,
the earth will wear out like a
garment,
and those who live on it will die
like gnats;[n]
but my salvation will be forever,
and my deliverance will never be
ended.

7 Listen to me, you who know
righteousness,
you people who have my
teaching in your hearts;
do not fear the reproach of others,
and do not be dismayed when
they revile you.
8 For the moth will eat them up like
a garment,
and the worm will eat them like
wool;
but my deliverance will be forever,
and my salvation to all
generations.

9 Awake, awake, put on strength,
O arm of the LORD!
Awake, as in days of old,
the generations of long ago!
Was it not you who cut Rahab in
pieces,
who pierced the dragon?
10 Was it not you who dried up the sea,
the waters of the great deep;
who made the depths of the sea a
way
for the redeemed to cross over?
11 So the ransomed of the LORD shall
return,
and come to Zion with singing;
everlasting joy shall be upon their
heads;
they shall obtain joy and gladness,
and sorrow and sighing shall flee
away.

12 I, I am he who comforts you;
why then are you afraid of a mere
mortal who must die,

a human being who fades like
grass?
13 You have forgotten the LORD, your
Maker,
who stretched out the heavens
and laid the foundations of the
earth.
You fear continually all day long
because of the fury of the
oppressor,
who is bent on destruction.
But where is the fury of the
oppressor?
14 The oppressed shall speedily be
released;
they shall not die and go down to
the Pit,
nor shall they lack bread.
15 For I am the LORD your God,
who stirs up the sea so that its
waves roar—
the LORD of hosts is his name.
16 I have put my words in your
mouth,
and hidden you in the shadow of
my hand,
stretching out[o] the heavens
and laying the foundations of the
earth,
and saying to Zion, "You are my
people."

17 Rouse yourself, rouse yourself!
Stand up, O Jerusalem,
you who have drunk at the hand of
the LORD
the cup of his wrath,
who have drunk to the dregs
the bowl of staggering.
18 There is no one to guide her
among all the children she has
borne;
there is no one to take her by the
hand
among all the children she has
brought up.
19 These two things have befallen you
—who will grieve with you?—
devastation and destruction,
famine and sword—
who will comfort you?[p]
20 Your children have fainted,
they lie at the head of every
street
like an antelope in a net;

n Or in like manner   o Syr: Heb planting   p Q Ms Gk Syr Vg: MT how may I comfort you?

they are full of the wrath of the
 LORD,
 the rebuke of your God.

21 Therefore hear this, you who are
 wounded,*q*
 who are drunk, but not with
 wine:
22 Thus says your Sovereign, the
 LORD,
 your God who pleads the cause of
 his people:
 See, I have taken from your hand
 the cup of staggering;
 you shall drink no more
 from the bowl of my wrath.
23 And I will put it into the hand of
 your tormentors,
 who have said to you,
 "Bow down, that we may walk
 on you";
 and you have made your back like
 the ground
 and like the street for them to
 walk on.

Let Zion Rejoice

52 Awake, awake,
 put on your strength, O Zion!
 Put on your beautiful garments,
 O Jerusalem, the holy city;
 for the uncircumcised and the
 unclean
 shall enter you no more.
2 Shake yourself from the dust, rise
 up,
 O captive*r* Jerusalem;
 loose the bonds from your neck,
 O captive daughter Zion!

3 For thus says the LORD: You were
sold for nothing, and you shall be
redeemed without money. 4For thus
says the Lord GOD: Long ago, my people
went down into Egypt to reside there as
aliens; the Assyrian, too, has oppressed
them without cause. 5Now therefore
what am I doing here, says the LORD,
seeing that my people are taken away
without cause? Their rulers howl, says
the LORD, and continually, all day long,
my name is despised. 6Therefore my
people shall know my name; therefore
in that day they shall know that it is I
who speak; here am I.

7 How beautiful upon the mountains
 are the feet of the messenger who
 announces peace,
 who brings good news,
 who announces salvation,
 who says to Zion, "Your God
 reigns."
8 Listen! Your sentinels lift up their
 voices,
 together they sing for joy;
 for in plain sight they see
 the return of the LORD to Zion.
9 Break forth together into singing,
 you ruins of Jerusalem;
 for the LORD has comforted his
 people,
 he has redeemed Jerusalem.
10 The LORD has bared his holy arm
 before the eyes of all the nations;
 and all the ends of the earth shall
 see
 the salvation of our God.

11 Depart, depart, go out from there!
 Touch no unclean thing;
 go out from the midst of it, purify
 yourselves,
 you who carry the vessels of the
 LORD.
12 For you shall not go out in haste,
 and you shall not go in flight;
 for the LORD will go before you,
 and the God of Israel will be your
 rear guard.

The Suffering Servant

13 See, my servant shall prosper;
 he shall be exalted and lifted up,
 and shall be very high.
14 Just as there were many who were
 astonished at him*s*
 —so marred was his appearance,
 beyond human semblance,
 and his form beyond that of
 mortals—
15 so he shall startle*t* many nations;
 kings shall shut their mouths
 because of him;
 for that which had not been told
 them they shall see,
 and that which they had not
 heard they shall
 contemplate.

q Or humbled   r Cn: Heb rise up, sit   s Syr Tg: Heb you   t Meaning of Heb uncertain

53

Who has believed what we have heard?
And to whom has the arm of the LORD been revealed?

2 For he grew up before him like a young plant,
and like a root out of dry ground;
he had no form or majesty that we should look at him,
nothing in his appearance that we should desire him.

3 He was despised and rejected by others;
a man of suffering[u] and acquainted with infirmity;
and as one from whom others hide their faces[v]
he was despised, and we held him of no account.

4 Surely he has borne our infirmities
and carried our diseases;
yet we accounted him stricken,
struck down by God, and afflicted.

5 But he was wounded for our transgressions,
crushed for our iniquities;
upon him was the punishment that made us whole,
and by his bruises we are healed.

6 All we like sheep have gone astray;
we have all turned to our own way,
and the LORD has laid on him the iniquity of us all.

7 He was oppressed, and he was afflicted,
yet he did not open his mouth;
like a lamb that is led to the slaughter,
and like a sheep that before its shearers is silent,
so he did not open his mouth.

8 By a perversion of justice he was taken away.
Who could have imagined his future?
For he was cut off from the land of the living,
stricken for the transgression of my people.

9 They made his grave with the wicked
and his tomb[w] with the rich,[x]
although he had done no violence,
and there was no deceit in his mouth.

10 Yet it was the will of the LORD to crush him with pain.[y]
When you make his life an offering for sin,[z]
he shall see his offspring, and shall prolong his days;
through him the will of the LORD shall prosper.

11 Out of his anguish he shall see light;[a]
he shall find satisfaction through his knowledge.
The righteous one,[b] my servant, shall make many righteous,
and he shall bear their iniquities.

12 Therefore I will allot him a portion with the great,
and he shall divide the spoil with the strong;
because he poured out himself to death,
and was numbered with the transgressors;
yet he bore the sin of many,
and made intercession for the transgressors.

The Eternal Covenant of Peace

54

Sing, O barren one who did not bear;
burst into song and shout,
you who have not been in labor!
For the children of the desolate woman will be more
than the children of her that is married, says the LORD.

2 Enlarge the site of your tent,
and let the curtains of your habitations be stretched out;
do not hold back; lengthen your cords
and strengthen your stakes.

u Or *a man of sorrows*   v Or *as one who hides his face from us*   w Q Ms: MT *and in his death*
x Cn: Heb *with a rich person*   y Or *by disease*; meaning of Heb uncertain   z Meaning of Heb uncertain   a Q Mss: MT lacks *light*   b Or *and he shall find satisfaction. Through his knowledge, the righteous one*

3   For you will spread out to the right
        and to the left,
    and your descendants will
        possess the nations
    and will settle the desolate
        towns.

4   Do not fear, for you will not be
        ashamed;

do not be discouraged, for you
    will not suffer disgrace;
for you will forget the shame of
    your youth,
and the disgrace of your
    widowhood you will
    remember no more.

5   For your Maker is your husband,
    the LORD of hosts is his name;

THURSDAY

HE HATH BORNE OUR GRIEFS
Martin Luther

VERSE: Isaiah 53.4   **PASSAGE:** Isaiah 53.1–6

 hese are clear and powerful words. The sufferings of this king are our griefs and sorrows. He carries the burden which ought to be ours for ever. The stripes and bruises which we have merited, namely, that we should suffer thirst and hunger, and die eternally, all this is laid on him. His suffering avails for me, and for you, and for us all; for it was undertaken for our good. But we esteemed him to be the one who was afflicted and smitten of God.

And that is true. For Moses himself says, "Cursed be the man that hangeth on the tree" (Deuteronomy 21.23, KJV). That is why he was railed at as one condemned and cursed. He cannot even help himself, how then can he heal others (see Matthew 27.42–43)? But they did not see properly. For lo, he is carrying our sorrows. According to the outward appearance he seems to be cursed, but according to the spirit he carries my sorrows and yours, and the sorrows of us all. "The chastisement of our peace was upon him, and with his stripes we are healed" (Isaiah 53.5, KJV). He is chastised, we are in peace. I and you, and all men have called forth God's wrath; he has atoned, that we, redeemed from sin, may rest in peace. He must suffer, we are set free.

We ought not so shamefully to forget such great love and mercy.

ADDITIONAL SCRIPTURE READING:
Isaiah 53.11–12; Matthew 8.17; Galatians 3.13

Go to page 853 for your next devotional reading.

1500   1700

the Holy One of Israel is your
   Redeemer,
   the God of the whole earth he is
   called.

6 For the LORD has called you
   like a wife forsaken and grieved
      in spirit,
   like the wife of a man's youth
      when she is cast off,
   says your God.

7 For a brief moment I abandoned
      you,
   but with great compassion I will
      gather you.

8 In overflowing wrath for a moment
      I hid my face from you,
   but with everlasting love I will
      have compassion on you,
   says the LORD, your Redeemer.

9 This is like the days of Noah to me:
   Just as I swore that the waters of
      Noah
   would never again go over the
      earth,
   so I have sworn that I will not be
      angry with you
   and will not rebuke you.

10 For the mountains may depart
      and the hills be removed,
   but my steadfast love shall not
      depart from you,
   and my covenant of peace shall
      not be removed,
   says the LORD, who has
      compassion on you.

11 O afflicted one, storm-tossed, and
      not comforted,
   I am about to set your stones in
      antimony,
   and lay your foundations with
      sapphires.c

12 I will make your pinnacles of
      rubies,
   your gates of jewels,
   and all your wall of precious
      stones.

13 All your children shall be taught by
      the LORD,
   and great shall be the prosperity
      of your children.

14 In righteousness you shall be
      established;

you shall be far from oppression,
   for you shall not fear;
   and from terror, for it shall not
      come near you.

15 If anyone stirs up strife,
   it is not from me;
   whoever stirs up strife with you
      shall fall because of you.

16 See it is I who have created the
      smith
   who blows the fire of coals,
   and produces a weapon fit for its
      purpose;
   I have also created the ravager to
      destroy.

17 No weapon that is fashioned
      against you shall prosper,
   and you shall confute every
      tongue that rises against you
      in judgment.
This is the heritage of the servants
      of the LORD
   and their vindication from me,
      says the LORD.

An Invitation to Abundant Life

55 Ho, everyone who thirsts,
      come to the waters;
and you that have no money,
   come, buy and eat!
Come, buy wine and milk
   without money and without
      price.

2 Why do you spend your money for
      that which is not bread,
   and your labor for that which
      does not satisfy?
Listen carefully to me, and eat
      what is good,
   and delight yourselves in rich
      food.

3 Incline your ear, and come to me;
   listen, so that you may live.
I will make with you an everlasting
      covenant,
   my steadfast, sure love for David.

4 See, I made him a witness to the
      peoples,
   a leader and commander for the
      peoples.

5 See, you shall call nations that you
      do not know,
   and nations that do not know
      you shall run to you,

c Or lapis lazuli

because of the LORD your God, the
Holy One of Israel,
for he has glorified you.

6 Seek the LORD while he may be
found,
call upon him while he is near;
7 let the wicked forsake their way,
and the unrighteous their
thoughts;
let them return to the LORD, that
he may have mercy on them,
and to our God, for he will
abundantly pardon.
8 For my thoughts are not your
thoughts,
nor are your ways my ways, says
the LORD.
9 For as the heavens are higher than
the earth,
so are my ways higher than your
ways
and my thoughts than your
thoughts.

10 For as the rain and the snow come
down from heaven,
and do not return there until
they have watered the earth,
making it bring forth and sprout,
giving seed to the sower and
bread to the eater,
11 so shall my word be that goes out
from my mouth;
it shall not return to me empty,
but it shall accomplish that which I
purpose,
and succeed in the thing for
which I sent it.

12 For you shall go out in joy,
and be led back in peace;
the mountains and the hills before
you
shall burst into song,
and all the trees of the field shall
clap their hands.
13 Instead of the thorn shall come up
the cypress;
instead of the brier shall come up
the myrtle;
and it shall be to the LORD for a
memorial,
for an everlasting sign that shall
not be cut off.

The Covenant Extended to All Who Obey

56 Thus says the LORD:
Maintain justice, and do
what is right,
for soon my salvation will come,
and my deliverance be revealed.

2 Happy is the mortal who does this,
the one who holds it fast,
who keeps the sabbath, not
profaning it,
and refrains from doing any evil.

3 Do not let the foreigner joined to
the LORD say,
"The LORD will surely separate
me from his people";
and do not let the eunuch say,
"I am just a dry tree."
4 For thus says the LORD:
To the eunuchs who keep my
sabbaths,
who choose the things that
please me
and hold fast my covenant,
5 I will give, in my house and within
my walls,
a monument and a name
better than sons and daughters;
I will give them an everlasting
name
that shall not be cut off.

6 And the foreigners who join
themselves to the LORD,
to minister to him, to love the
name of the LORD,
and to be his servants,
all who keep the sabbath, and do
not profane it,
and hold fast my covenant—
7 these I will bring to my holy
mountain,
and make them joyful in my
house of prayer;
their burnt offerings and their
sacrifices
will be accepted on my altar;
for my house shall be called a
house of prayer
for all peoples.
8 Thus says the Lord GOD,
who gathers the outcasts of
Israel,

I will gather others to them
    besides those already gathered.*d*

The Corruption of Israel's Rulers

9 All you wild animals,
    all you wild animals in the
        forest, come to devour!
10 Israel's*e* sentinels are blind,
    they are all without knowledge;
  they are all silent dogs
    that cannot bark;
  dreaming, lying down,
    loving to slumber.
11 The dogs have a mighty appetite;
    they never have enough.
  The shepherds also have no
    understanding;
  they have all turned to their own
    way,
    to their own gain, one and all.
12 "Come," they say, "let us*f* get
    wine;
  let us fill ourselves with strong
    drink.
  And tomorrow will be like today,
    great beyond measure."

Israel's Futile Idolatry

57 The righteous perish,
    and no one takes it to heart;
  the devout are taken away,
    while no one understands.
  For the righteous are taken away
    from calamity,
2   and they enter into peace;
  those who walk uprightly
    will rest on their couches.

A GREAT MANY PEOPLE ARE TRYING TO MAKE
PEACE, BUT THAT HAS ALREADY BEEN DONE. GOD
HAS NOT LEFT IT FOR US TO DO; ALL WE HAVE TO
DO IS TO ENTER INTO IT.   *—Dwight L. Moody*

---

3 But as for you, come here,
    you children of a sorceress,
  you offspring of an adulterer and
    a whore.*g*
4 Whom are you mocking?
    Against whom do you open your
        mouth wide
  and stick out your tongue?

Are you not children of
    transgression,
  the offspring of deceit—
5 you that burn with lust among the
    oaks,
    under every green tree;
  you that slaughter your children in
    the valleys,
    under the clefts of the rocks?
6 Among the smooth stones of the
    valley is your portion;
  they, they, are your lot;
  to them you have poured out a
    drink offering,
    you have brought a grain offering.
  Shall I be appeased for these
    things?
7 Upon a high and lofty mountain
    you have set your bed,
  and there you went up to offer
    sacrifice.
8 Behind the door and the doorpost
    you have set up your symbol;
  for, in deserting me,*h* you have
    uncovered your bed,
  you have gone up to it,
  you have made it wide;
  and you have made a bargain for
    yourself with them,
  you have loved their bed,
  you have gazed on their
    nakedness.*i*
9 You journeyed to Molech*j* with oil,
    and multiplied your perfumes;
  you sent your envoys far away,
    and sent down even to Sheol.
10 You grew weary from your many
    wanderings,
    but you did not say, "It is useless."
  You found your desire rekindled,
    and so you did not weaken.

11 Whom did you dread and fear
    so that you lied,
  and did not remember me
    or give me a thought?
  Have I not kept silent and closed
    my eyes,*k*
    and so you do not fear me?
12 I will concede your righteousness
    and your works,
  but they will not help you.

---

d Heb *besides his gathered ones*   *e* Heb *His*   *f* Q Ms Syr Vg Tg: MT *me*   *g* Heb *an adulterer and
she plays the whore*   *h* Meaning of Heb uncertain   *i* Or *their phallus*; Heb *the hand*   *j* Or *the
king*   *k* Gk Vg: Heb *silent even for a long time*

13 When you cry out, let your
    collection of idols deliver you!
The wind will carry them off,
    a breath will take them away.
But whoever takes refuge in me
    shall possess the land
    and inherit my holy mountain.

A Promise of Help and Healing

14 It shall be said,
    "Build up, build up, prepare the way,
    remove every obstruction from
        my people's way."
15 For thus says the high and lofty one
    who inhabits eternity, whose
        name is Holy:
I dwell in the high and holy place,
    and also with those who are
        contrite and humble in spirit,
to revive the spirit of the humble,
    and to revive the heart of the
        contrite.
16 For I will not continually accuse,
    nor will I always be angry;
for then the spirits would grow
    faint before me,
    even the souls that I have made.
17 Because of their wicked
    covetousness I was angry;
I struck them, I hid and was
    angry;
but they kept turning back to
    their own ways.
18 I have seen their ways, but I will
    heal them;
I will lead them and repay them
    with comfort,
creating for their mourners the
    fruit of the lips.[1]
19 Peace, peace, to the far and the
    near, says the LORD;
    and I will heal them.
20 But the wicked are like the tossing
    sea
that cannot keep still;
    its waters toss up mire and mud.
21 There is no peace, says my God, for
    the wicked.

False and True Worship

58 Shout out, do not hold back!
    Lift up your voice like a
        trumpet!
Announce to my people their
    rebellion,

    to the house of Jacob their sins.
2 Yet day after day they seek me
    and delight to know my ways,
as if they were a nation that
    practiced righteousness
    and did not forsake the ordinance
    of their God;
they ask of me righteous judgments,
    they delight to draw near to God.
3 "Why do we fast, but you do not
    see?
Why humble ourselves, but you
    do not notice?"
Look, you serve your own interest
    on your fast day,
    and oppress all your workers.
4 Look, you fast only to quarrel and
    to fight
    and to strike with a wicked fist.
Such fasting as you do today
    will not make your voice heard
        on high.
5 Is such the fast that I choose,
    a day to humble oneself?
Is it to bow down the head like a
    bulrush,
    and to lie in sackcloth and ashes?
Will you call this a fast,
    a day acceptable to the LORD?

6 Is not this the fast that I choose:
    to loose the bonds of injustice,
    to undo the thongs of the yoke,
to let the oppressed go free,
    and to break every yoke?
7 Is it not to share your bread with
    the hungry,
    and bring the homeless poor into
    your house;
when you see the naked, to cover
    them,
    and not to hide yourself from
    your own kin?

MY PIECE OF BREAD ONLY BELONGS TO ME
WHEN I KNOW THAT EVERYONE ELSE HAS A
SHARE AND THAT NO ONE STARVES WHILE I EAT.

—*Leo Tolstoy*

---

8 Then your light shall break forth
    like the dawn,
    and your healing shall spring up
    quickly;

---

1 Meaning of Heb uncertain

your vindicator[m] shall go before
    you,
    the glory of the LORD shall be
        your rear guard.
9   Then you shall call, and the LORD
        will answer;
    you shall cry for help, and he will
        say, Here I am.

If you remove the yoke from
    among you,
    the pointing of the finger, the
        speaking of evil,
10 if you offer your food to the hungry
    and satisfy the needs of the
        afflicted,
    then your light shall rise in the
        darkness
    and your gloom be like the
        noonday.
11 The LORD will guide you
        continually,
    and satisfy your needs in parched
        places,
    and make your bones strong;
and you shall be like a watered
        garden,
    like a spring of water,
    whose waters never fail.
12 Your ancient ruins shall be rebuilt;
    you shall raise up the
        foundations of many
        generations;
you shall be called the repairer of
        the breach,
    the restorer of streets to live in.

13 If you refrain from trampling the
        sabbath,
    from pursuing your own interests
        on my holy day;
    if you call the sabbath a delight
    and the holy day of the LORD
        honorable;
    if you honor it, not going your own
        ways,
    serving your own interests, or
        pursuing your own affairs;[n]
14 then you shall take delight in the
        LORD,
    and I will make you ride upon
        the heights of the earth;
    I will feed you with the heritage of
        your ancestor Jacob,

for the mouth of the LORD has
    spoken.

Injustice and Oppression to Be Punished

59 See, the LORD's hand is not
        too short to save,
    nor his ear too dull to hear.
2   Rather, your iniquities have been
        barriers
    between you and your God,
    and your sins have hidden his face
        from you
    so that he does not hear.
3   For your hands are defiled with
        blood,
    and your fingers with iniquity;
    your lips have spoken lies,
    your tongue mutters wickedness.
4   No one brings suit justly,
    no one goes to law honestly;
    they rely on empty pleas, they
        speak lies,
    conceiving mischief and
        begetting iniquity.
5   They hatch adders' eggs,
    and weave the spider's web;
    whoever eats their eggs dies,
    and the crushed egg hatches out a
        viper.
6   Their webs cannot serve as
        clothing;
    they cannot cover themselves
        with what they make.
    Their works are works of iniquity,
    and deeds of violence are in their
        hands.
7   Their feet run to evil,
    and they rush to shed innocent
        blood;
    their thoughts are thoughts of
        iniquity,
    desolation and destruction are in
        their highways.
8   The way of peace they do not know,
    and there is no justice in their
        paths.
    Their roads they have made
        crooked;
    no one who walks in them
        knows peace.

9   Therefore justice is far from us,
    and righteousness does not reach
        us;

m Or vindication   n Heb or speaking words

we wait for light, and lo! there is
   darkness;
and for brightness, but we walk
   in gloom.
10 We grope like the blind along a
   wall,
groping like those who have no
   eyes;
we stumble at noon as in the
   twilight,
among the vigorous*o* as though
   we were dead.
11 We all growl like bears;
   like doves we moan mournfully.
We wait for justice, but there is
   none;
for salvation, but it is far from us.
12 For our transgressions before you
   are many,
and our sins testify against us.
Our transgressions indeed are with
   us,
and we know our iniquities:
13 transgressing, and denying the
   Lord,
and turning away from following
   our God,
talking oppression and revolt,
conceiving lying words and
   uttering them from the
   heart.
14 Justice is turned back,
   and righteousness stands at a
   distance;
for truth stumbles in the public
   square,
and uprightness cannot enter.
15 Truth is lacking,
   and whoever turns from evil is
   despoiled.

The Lord saw it, and it displeased
   him
that there was no justice.
16 He saw that there was no one,
   and was appalled that there was
   no one to intervene;
so his own arm brought him
   victory,
and his righteousness upheld
   him.
17 He put on righteousness like a
   breastplate,
and a helmet of salvation on his
   head;

he put on garments of vengeance
   for clothing,
and wrapped himself in fury as in
   a mantle.
18 According to their deeds, so will he
   repay;
wrath to his adversaries, requital
   to his enemies;
to the coastlands he will render
   requital.
19 So those in the west shall fear the
   name of the Lord,
and those in the east, his glory;
for he will come like a pent-up
   stream
that the wind of the Lord drives
   on.

20 And he will come to Zion as
   Redeemer,
to those in Jacob who turn from
   transgression, says the Lord.
21 And as for me, this is my covenant
with them, says the Lord: my spirit that
is upon you, and my words that I have
put in your mouth, shall not depart out of
your mouth, or out of the mouths of your
children, or out of the mouths of your
children's children, says the Lord, from
now on and forever.

The Ingathering of the Dispersed

60 Arise, shine; for your light
   has come,
and the glory of the Lord has
   risen upon you.
2 For darkness shall cover the earth,
   and thick darkness the peoples;
but the Lord will arise upon you,
   and his glory will appear over
   you.
3 Nations shall come to your light,
   and kings to the brightness of
   your dawn.

4 Lift up your eyes and look around;
   they all gather together, they
   come to you;
your sons shall come from far
   away,
and your daughters shall be
   carried on their nurses' arms.
5 Then you shall see and be radiant;
   your heart shall thrill and
   rejoice,*p*

o Meaning of Heb uncertain   p Heb be enlarged

because the abundance of the sea
   shall be brought to you,
  the wealth of the nations shall
   come to you.
6 A multitude of camels shall cover
   you,
  the young camels of Midian and
   Ephah;
  all those from Sheba shall come.
They shall bring gold and
   frankincense,
  and shall proclaim the praise of
   the LORD.
7 All the flocks of Kedar shall be
   gathered to you,
  the rams of Nebaioth shall
   minister to you;
they shall be acceptable on my
   altar,
  and I will glorify my glorious
   house.

8 Who are these that fly like a cloud,
  and like doves to their windows?
9 For the coastlands shall wait for
   me,
  the ships of Tarshish first,
to bring your children from far
   away,
  their silver and gold with them,
for the name of the LORD your God,
  and for the Holy One of Israel,
  because he has glorified you.
10 Foreigners shall build up your
   walls,
  and their kings shall minister to
   you;
for in my wrath I struck you down,
  but in my favor I have had mercy
   on you.
11 Your gates shall always be open;
  day and night they shall not be
   shut,
so that nations shall bring you their
   wealth,
  with their kings led in
   procession.
12 For the nation and kingdom
  that will not serve you shall
   perish;
  those nations shall be utterly laid
   waste.
13 The glory of Lebanon shall come to
   you,

the cypress, the plane, and the
   pine,
to beautify the place of my
   sanctuary;
  and I will glorify where my feet
   rest.
14 The descendants of those who
   oppressed you
  shall come bending low to you,
and all who despised you
  shall bow down at your feet;
they shall call you the City of the
   LORD,
  the Zion of the Holy One of
   Israel.
15 Whereas you have been forsaken
   and hated,
  with no one passing through,
I will make you majestic forever,
  a joy from age to age.
16 You shall suck the milk of nations,
  you shall suck the breasts of
   kings;
and you shall know that I, the
   LORD, am your Savior
  and your Redeemer, the Mighty
   One of Jacob.

17 Instead of bronze I will bring gold,
  instead of iron I will bring silver;
instead of wood, bronze,
  instead of stones, iron.
I will appoint Peace as your
   overseer
  and Righteousness as your
   taskmaster.
18 Violence shall no more be heard in
   your land,
  devastation or destruction within
   your borders;
you shall call your walls Salvation,
  and your gates Praise.

God the Glory of Zion

19 The sun shall no longer be
  your light by day,
nor for brightness shall the moon
  give light to you by night;*q*
but the LORD will be your
  everlasting light,
  and your God will be your glory.
20 Your sun shall no more go down,
  or your moon withdraw itself;
for the LORD will be your
  everlasting light,

q Q Ms Gk Old Latin Tg: MT lacks *by night*

and your days of mourning shall
be ended.
21 Your people shall all be righteous;
they shall possess the land
forever.
They are the shoot that I planted,
the work of my hands,
so that I might be glorified.
22 The least of them shall become a
clan,
and the smallest one a mighty
nation;
I am the LORD;
in its time I will accomplish it
quickly.

The Good News of Deliverance

61 The spirit of the Lord GOD is
upon me,
because the LORD has anointed
me;
he has sent me to bring good news
to the oppressed,
to bind up the brokenhearted,
to proclaim liberty to the captives,
and release to the prisoners;
2 to proclaim the year of the LORD's
favor,
and the day of vengeance of our
God;
to comfort all who mourn;
3 to provide for those who mourn in
Zion—
to give them a garland instead of
ashes,
the oil of gladness instead of
mourning,
the mantle of praise instead of a
faint spirit.
They will be called oaks of
righteousness,
the planting of the LORD, to
display his glory.
4 They shall build up the ancient
ruins,
they shall raise up the former
devastations;
they shall repair the ruined cities,
the devastations of many
generations.

5 Strangers shall stand and feed your
flocks,
foreigners shall till your land and
dress your vines;

6 but you shall be called priests of
the LORD,
you shall be named ministers of
our God;
you shall enjoy the wealth of the
nations,
and in their riches you shall glory.
7 Because their[r] shame was double,
and dishonor was proclaimed as
their lot,
therefore they shall possess a
double portion;
everlasting joy shall be theirs.

8 For I the LORD love justice,
I hate robbery and wrongdoing;[s]
I will faithfully give them their
recompense,
and I will make an everlasting
covenant with them.
9 Their descendants shall be known
among the nations,
and their offspring among the
peoples;
all who see them shall acknowledge
that they are a people whom the
LORD has blessed.
10 I will greatly rejoice in the LORD,
my whole being shall exult in my
God;
for he has clothed me with the
garments of salvation,
he has covered me with the robe
of righteousness,
as a bridegroom decks himself with
a garland,
and as a bride adorns herself with
her jewels.
11 For as the earth brings forth its
shoots,
and as a garden causes what is
sown in it to spring up,
so the Lord GOD will cause
righteousness and praise
to spring up before all the
nations.

The Vindication and Salvation of Zion

62 For Zion's sake I will not
keep silent,
and for Jerusalem's sake I will
not rest,
until her vindication shines out
like the dawn,

r Heb your   s Or robbery with a burnt offering

and her salvation like a burning
　　torch.
2　The nations shall see your
　　　vindication,
　　and all the kings your glory;
　　and you shall be called by a new
　　　name
　　　that the mouth of the LORD will
　　　　give.
3　You shall be a crown of beauty in
　　　the hand of the LORD,
　　and a royal diadem in the hand of
　　　your God.
4　You shall no more be termed
　　　Forsaken,^t
　　and your land shall no more be
　　　termed Desolate;^u
　　but you shall be called My Delight
　　　Is in Her,^v
　　and your land Married;^w
　　for the LORD delights in you,
　　and your land shall be married.
5　For as a young man marries a
　　　young woman,
　　so shall your builder^x marry you,
　　and as the bridegroom rejoices over
　　　the bride,
　　so shall your God rejoice over you.
6　Upon your walls, O Jerusalem,
　　I have posted sentinels;
　　all day and all night
　　　they shall never be silent.
　　You who remind the LORD,
　　　take no rest,
7　and give him no rest
　　　until he establishes Jerusalem
　　and makes it renowned
　　　throughout the earth.
8　The LORD has sworn by his right
　　　hand
　　and by his mighty arm:
　　I will not again give your grain
　　　to be food for your enemies,
　　and foreigners shall not drink the
　　　wine
　　　for which you have labored;
9　but those who garner it shall eat it
　　　and praise the LORD,
　　and those who gather it shall drink
　　　it
　　　in my holy courts.

10　Go through, go through the gates,
　　　prepare the way for the people;
　　build up, build up the highway,

clear it of stones,
lift up an ensign over the peoples.
11　The LORD has proclaimed
　　　to the end of the earth:
　　Say to daughter Zion,
　　　"See, your salvation comes;
　　his reward is with him,
　　　and his recompense before him."
12　They shall be called, "The Holy
　　　People,
　　The Redeemed of the LORD";
　　and you shall be called, "Sought
　　　Out,
　　A City Not Forsaken."

Vengeance on Edom

63 "Who is this that comes
from Edom,
　　from Bozrah in garments stained
　　　crimson?
　　Who is this so splendidly robed,
　　　marching in his great might?"

　　"It is I, announcing vindication,
　　　mighty to save."

2　"Why are your robes red,
　　　and your garments like theirs
　　　　who tread the wine press?"

3　"I have trodden the wine press
　　　alone,
　　　and from the peoples no one was
　　　　with me;
　　I trod them in my anger
　　　and trampled them in my wrath;
　　their juice spattered on my
　　　garments,
　　　and stained all my robes.
4　For the day of vengeance was in my
　　　heart,
　　　and the year for my redeeming
　　　　work had come.
5　I looked, but there was no helper;
　　　I stared, but there was no one to
　　　　sustain me;
　　so my own arm brought me
　　　victory,
　　　and my wrath sustained me.
6　I trampled down peoples in my
　　　anger,
　　　I crushed them in my wrath,
　　　and I poured out their lifeblood
　　　　on the earth."

t Heb *Azubah*　u Heb *Shemamah*　v Heb *Hephzibah*　w Heb *Beulah*　x Cn: Heb *your sons*

God's Mercy Remembered

7 I will recount the gracious deeds of
   the LORD,
      the praiseworthy acts of the
      LORD,
   because of all that the LORD has
   done for us,
      and the great favor to the house
      of Israel
   that he has shown them according
   to his mercy,
      according to the abundance of his
      steadfast love.
8 For he said, "Surely they are my
   people,
      children who will not deal
      falsely";
   and he became their savior
9   in all their distress.
   It was no messenger[y] or angel
      but his presence that saved
      them;[z]
   in his love and in his pity he
   redeemed them;
      he lifted them up and carried
      them all the days of old.

10 But they rebelled
      and grieved his holy spirit;
   therefore he became their enemy;
      he himself fought against them.
11 Then they[a] remembered the days
   of old,
      of Moses his servant.[b]
   Where is the one who brought
      them up out of the sea
   with the shepherds of his flock?
   Where is the one who put within
   them
      his holy spirit,
12 who caused his glorious arm
      to march at the right hand of
      Moses,
   who divided the waters before
   them
      to make for himself an
      everlasting name,
13 who led them through the
   depths?
   Like a horse in the desert,
      they did not stumble.
14 Like cattle that go down into the
   valley,

the spirit of the LORD gave them
rest.
Thus you led your people,
   to make for yourself a glorious
   name.

A Prayer of Penitence

15 Look down from heaven and see,
      from your holy and glorious
      habitation.
   Where are your zeal and your
   might?
      The yearning of your heart and
      your compassion?
      They are withheld from me.
16 For you are our father,
      though Abraham does not know
      us
   and Israel does not acknowledge
   us;
   you, O LORD, are our father;
      our Redeemer from of old is your
      name.
17 Why, O LORD, do you make us
      stray from your ways
      and harden our heart, so that we
      do not fear you?
   Turn back for the sake of your
   servants,
      for the sake of the tribes that are
      your heritage.
18 Your holy people took possession
      for a little while;
   but now our adversaries have
      trampled down your
      sanctuary.
19 We have long been like those
      whom you do not rule,
   like those not called by your
      name.

64 O that you would tear open
the heavens and come down,
   so that the mountains would
   quake at your presence—
2[c] as when fire kindles brushwood
   and the fire causes water to
   boil—
to make your name known to your
adversaries,
   so that the nations might
   tremble at your presence!
3 When you did awesome deeds that
   we did not expect,

---

y Gk: Heb anguish   z Or savior. 9In all their distress he was distressed; the angel of his presence
saved them;   a Heb he   b Cn: Heb his people   c Ch 64.1 in Heb

you came down, the mountains
quaked at your presence.
4 From ages past no one has heard,
no ear has perceived,
no eye has seen any God besides
you,
who works for those who wait
for him.
5 You meet those who gladly do
right,

those who remember you in your
ways.
But you were angry, and we sinned;
because you hid yourself we
transgressed. *d*
6 We have all become like one who is
unclean,
and all our righteous deeds are
like a filthy cloth.
We all fade like a leaf,

d Meaning of Heb uncertain

FRIDAY

THE OVERRIDING FUNCTION OF THE FATHER
Hannah Whitall Smith

VERSE: Isaiah 64.8   PASSAGE: Isaiah 64.8–12

 ut you may say what about the other names of God . . .
this blessed name of Father . . . must underlie every
other name by which he has ever been known. Has he
been called a judge? Yes, but he is a father judge, one
who judges as a loving father would. Is he a king? Yes, but he is
a king who is at the same time the father of his subjects, and
who rules them with a father's tenderness. Is he a lawgiver? Yes,
but he is a lawgiver who gives laws as a father would, remembering the weakness and ignorance of his helpless children.
"Like as a father pitieth his children, so the Lord pitieth them
that fear him. For he knoweth our frame; he remembereth that
we are dust" (Psalm 103.13–14, KJV). It is not "as a judge judges,
so the Lord judges"; not "as a taskmaster controls, so the Lord
controls"; not "as a lawgiver imposes laws, so the Lord imposes
laws"; but, "as a father pitieth, so the Lord pitieth."

Never, never must we think of God in any other way than as
"our Father." All other attributes with which we endow him in
our conceptions must be based upon and limited by this one of
"our Father." What a good father could not do, God, who is our
Father, cannot do either; and what a good father ought to do,
God, who is our Father, is absolutely sure to do.

ADDITIONAL SCRIPTURE READING:
Deuteronomy 32.6; Isaiah 63.16; Galatians 3.26

Go to page 854 for your next devotional reading.

1700   1900

I ARISE TODAY
Patrick of Ireland

VERSE: Psalm 23.4   **PASSAGE:** Psalm 23

 arise today
Through God's strength to pilot me;
God's might to uphold me,
God's wisdom to guide me,
God's eye to look before me,
God's ear to hear me,
God's word to speak for me,
God's hand to guard me,
God's way to lie before me,
God's shield to protect me,
God's hosts to save me
From snares of the devil,
From temptations of vices,
From every one who desires me ill,
Afar or anear,
Alone or in a multitude.

ADDITIONAL SCRIPTURE READING:
Psalm 72.3–7; Daniel 6.26–27; Malachi 3.18

Go to page 858 for your next devotional reading.

and our iniquities, like the wind,
    take us away.
7 There is no one who calls on your
    name,
  or attempts to take hold of you;
for you have hidden your face from
    us,
  and have delivered*e* us into the
    hand of our iniquity.
8 Yet, O LORD, you are our Father;
  we are the clay, and you are our
    potter;
  we are all the work of your hand.
9 Do not be exceedingly angry,
    O LORD,
  and do not remember iniquity
    forever.
  Now consider, we are all your
    people.
10 Your holy cities have become a
    wilderness,
  Zion has become a wilderness,
  Jerusalem a desolation.
11 Our holy and beautiful house,
  where our ancestors praised you,
has been burned by fire,
  and all our pleasant places have
    become ruins.
12 After all this, will you restrain
    yourself, O LORD?
  Will you keep silent, and punish
    us so severely?

The Righteousness of God's Judgment

65 I was ready to be sought out
    by those who did not ask,
to be found by those who did not
    seek me.
I said, "Here I am, here I am,"
  to a nation that did not call on
    my name.
2 I held out my hands all day long
  to a rebellious people,
who walk in a way that is not good,
  following their own devices;
3 a people who provoke me
  to my face continually,
sacrificing in gardens
  and offering incense on bricks;
4 who sit inside tombs,
  and spend the night in secret
    places;
who eat swine's flesh,

with broth of abominable things
  in their vessels;
5 who say, "Keep to yourself,
  do not come near me, for I am
    too holy for you."
These are a smoke in my nostrils,
  a fire that burns all day long.
6 See, it is written before me:
  I will not keep silent, but I will
    repay;
I will indeed repay into their laps
7 their*f* iniquities and their*f*
    ancestors' iniquities
    together,
             says the LORD;
because they offered incense on the
    mountains
  and reviled me on the hills,
I will measure into their laps
  full payment for their actions.
8 Thus says the LORD:
As the wine is found in the cluster,
  and they say, "Do not destroy it,
  for there is a blessing in it,"
so I will do for my servants' sake,
  and not destroy them all.
9 I will bring forth descendants*g* from
    Jacob,
  and from Judah inheritors*h* of my
    mountains;
my chosen shall inherit it,
  and my servants shall settle
    there.
10 Sharon shall become a pasture for
    flocks,
  and the Valley of Achor a place
    for herds to lie down,
for my people who have sought
    me.
11 But you who forsake the LORD,
  who forget my holy mountain,
who set a table for Fortune
  and fill cups of mixed wine for
    Destiny;
12 I will destine you to the sword,
  and all of you shall bow down to
    the slaughter;
because, when I called, you did not
    answer,
  when I spoke, you did not listen,
but you did what was evil in my
    sight,
  and chose what I did not delight
    in.
13 Therefore thus says the Lord GOD:

e Gk Syr Old Latin Tg: Heb *melted*   *f* Gk Syr: Heb *your*   *g* Or *a descendant*   *h* Or *an inheritor*

My servants shall eat,
  but you shall be hungry;
my servants shall drink,
  but you shall be thirsty;
my servants shall rejoice,
  but you shall be put to shame;
14 my servants shall sing for gladness
    of heart,
  but you shall cry out for pain of
    heart,
  and shall wail for anguish of spirit.
15 You shall leave your name to my
    chosen to use as a curse,
  and the Lord GOD will put you to
    death;
  but to his servants he will give a
    different name.
16 Then whoever invokes a blessing
    in the land
  shall bless by the God of
    faithfulness,
  and whoever takes an oath in the
    land
  shall swear by the God of
    faithfulness;
because the former troubles are
    forgotten
  and are hidden from my sight.

The Glorious New Creation

17 For I am about to create new
    heavens
  and a new earth;
the former things shall not be
    remembered
  or come to mind.
18 But be glad and rejoice forever
  in what I am creating;
for I am about to create Jerusalem
    as a joy,
  and its people as a delight.
19 I will rejoice in Jerusalem,
  and delight in my people;
no more shall the sound of weeping
    be heard in it,
  or the cry of distress.
20 No more shall there be in it
  an infant that lives but a few days,
    or an old person who does not
    live out a lifetime;
for one who dies at a hundred years
    will be considered a youth,
  and one who falls short of a
    hundred will be considered
    accursed.

21 They shall build houses and
    inhabit them;
  they shall plant vineyards and eat
    their fruit.
22 They shall not build and another
    inhabit;
  they shall not plant and another
    eat;
for like the days of a tree shall the
    days of my people be,
  and my chosen shall long enjoy
    the work of their hands.
23 They shall not labor in vain,
  or bear children for calamity;*i*
for they shall be offspring blessed
    by the LORD—
  and their descendants as well.
24 Before they call I will answer,
  while they are yet speaking I will
    hear.
25 The wolf and the lamb shall feed
    together,
  the lion shall eat straw like the
    ox;
  but the serpent—its food shall be
    dust!
They shall not hurt or destroy
  on all my holy mountain,
                    says the LORD.

The Worship God Demands

66 Thus says the LORD:
  Heaven is my throne
  and the earth is my footstool;
what is the house that you would
    build for me,
  and what is my resting place?
2 All these things my hand has
    made,
  and so all these things are mine,*j*
                    says the LORD.
But this is the one to whom I will
    look,
  to the humble and contrite in
    spirit,
  who trembles at my word.

3 Whoever slaughters an ox is like
    one who kills a human
    being;
  whoever sacrifices a lamb, like
    one who breaks a dog's neck;
whoever presents a grain offering,
    like one who offers swine's
    blood;*k*

whoever makes a memorial
offering of frankincense, like
one who blesses an idol.
These have chosen their own ways,
and in their abominations they
take delight;
4 I also will choose to mock[1] them,
and bring upon them what they
fear;
because, when I called, no one
answered,
when I spoke, they did not listen;
but they did what was evil in my
sight,
and chose what did not please
me.

The LORD Vindicates Zion

5 Hear the word of the LORD,
you who tremble at his word:
Your own people who hate you
and reject you for my name's sake
have said, "Let the LORD be glorified,
so that we may see your joy";
but it is they who shall be put to
shame.

6 Listen, an uproar from the city!
A voice from the temple!
The voice of the LORD,
dealing retribution to his enemies!

7 Before she was in labor
she gave birth;
before her pain came upon her
she delivered a son.
8 Who has heard of such a thing?
Who has seen such things?
Shall a land be born in one day?
Shall a nation be delivered in one
moment?
Yet as soon as Zion was in labor
she delivered her children.
9 Shall I open the womb and not
deliver?
says the LORD;
shall I, the one who delivers, shut
the womb?
says your God.

10 Rejoice with Jerusalem, and be glad
for her,
all you who love her;
rejoice with her in joy,

all you who mourn over her—
11 that you may nurse and be satisfied
from her consoling breast;
that you may drink deeply with
delight
from her glorious bosom.

12 For thus says the LORD:
I will extend prosperity to her like
a river,
and the wealth of the nations
like an overflowing stream;
and you shall nurse and be carried
on her arm,
and dandled on her knees.
13 As a mother comforts her child,
so I will comfort you;
you shall be comforted in
Jerusalem.

The Reign and Indignation of God

14 You shall see, and your heart shall
rejoice;
your bodies[m] shall flourish like
the grass;
and it shall be known that the hand
of the LORD is with his
servants,
and his indignation is against his
enemies.
15 For the LORD will come in fire,
and his chariots like the
whirlwind,
to pay back his anger in fury,
and his rebuke in flames of fire.
16 For by fire will the LORD execute
judgment,
and by his sword, on all flesh;
and those slain by the LORD shall
be many.

17 Those who sanctify and purify
themselves to go into the gardens, following the one in the center, eating the
flesh of pigs, vermin, and rodents, shall
come to an end together, says the LORD.

18 For I know[n] their works and their
thoughts, and I am[o] coming to gather all
nations and tongues; and they shall
come and shall see my glory, 19 and I will
set a sign among them. From them I will
send survivors to the nations, to Tarshish, Put,[p] and Lud—which draw the

1 Or to punish   m Heb bones   n Gk Syr: Heb lacks know   o Gk Syr Vg Tg: Heb it is
p Gk: Heb Pul

bow—to Tubal and Javan, to the coastlands far away that have not heard of my fame or seen my glory; and they shall declare my glory among the nations. [20]They shall bring all your kindred from all the nations as an offering to the

MONDAY

THE HOPE OF FINDING THE GOD OF COMFORT
Henry Ward Beecher

VERSE: Isaiah 66.13   **PASSAGE:** Isaiah 66.10–13

h! What need there is that up out of this darkness and trouble and sadness, out of these calamities, there should be exalted, somewhere, an image that writes upon itself, "I am the God of comfort." That brings God right home to man's need. The world would die if it had no hope of finding such a God.

He penetrates and pervades the universe with his nature and with his disposition. My flagging faith has need of some such assurance. I have walked very much in thought with those old philosophers who believe that there was a God of evil, as well as one of good. I am more willingly a disciple, therefore, of that inspired teaching which declared that evil is not a personage. It is not even an empire.

Like the emery and sand with which we scour off rude surfaces, evil and trouble in this world are but instruments. And they are in the hands of God. If they bite with sharp attrition, it is because we need more scouring. It is because men's troubles need ruder handling and chiseling, that evils float in the air, swim in the sea, and spring up from out of the ground.

But all is under the control of *the God of consolation*, as it is said elsewhere; *the God of comfort* (see 2 Corinthians 1.3–4), *and the Father of mercies*, as it is said here. More are the tender thoughts, the inspired potential actions, in God, than in the stars in the heavens. Innumerable are the sweet influences that he sends down from his realm above. More and purer are his blessings than the drops of dew that night shakes down on the flowers and grass.

He penetrates and pervades the world with more saving mercies than does the sun with particles of light and heat. He declares that his nature in himself is boundless—that his heart of mercy is inexhaustible—that his work of comfort is endless.

ADDITIONAL SCRIPTURE READING:
Romans 15.5; 2 Corinthians 1.3–5; 2 Thessalonians 2.16–17

Go to page 873 for your next devotional reading.

1700   1900

LORD, on horses, and in chariots, and in litters, and on mules, and on dromedaries, to my holy mountain Jerusalem, says the LORD, just as the Israelites bring a grain offering in a clean vessel to the house of the LORD. ²¹And I will also take some of them as priests and as Levites, says the LORD.

22 For as the new heavens and the
new earth,
which I will make,
shall remain before me, says the
LORD;

so shall your descendants and
your name remain.
23 From new moon to new moon,
and from sabbath to sabbath,
all flesh shall come to worship
before me,
says the LORD.

24 And they shall go out and look at the dead bodies of the people who have rebelled against me; for their worm shall not die, their fire shall not be quenched, and they shall be an abhorrence to all flesh.

JEREMIAH

EREMIAH PROPHESIED IN JUDAH DURING
A PERIOD WHEN THE DOOM OF ENTIRE
NATIONS—INCLUDING JUDAH ITSELF—
WAS BEING SEALED. JEREMIAH'S PERSONAL LIFE
AND STRUGGLES ARE KNOWN TO US IN GREATER
DETAIL THAN THOSE OF ANY OTHER OLD TESTA-
MENT PROPHET. JUDGMENT IS ONE OF THE PERVA-
SIVE THEMES IN HIS WRITINGS, ALTHOUGH, LIKE
ISAIAH, HE WRITES STIRRING WORDS OF HOPE
ABOUT JUDAH'S FUTURE REDEMPTION. WATCH
FOR JEREMIAH'S ENCOURAGEMENT—PROPHECIES
THAT ARE BEING FULFILLED TODAY WHENEVER
SINFUL HEARTS ARE TRANSFORMED BY GOD.

1 The words of Jeremiah son of Hilkiah, of the priests who were in Anathoth in the land of Benjamin, ²to whom the word of the LORD came in the days of King Josiah son of Amon of Judah, in the thirteenth year of his reign. ³It came also in the days of King Jehoiakim son of Josiah of Judah, and until the end of the eleventh year of King Zedekiah son of Josiah of Judah, until the captivity of Jerusalem in the fifth month.

Jeremiah's Call and Commission

4 Now the word of the LORD came to me saying,

5 "Before I formed you in the womb I
      knew you,
   and before you were born I
      consecrated you;

   I appointed you a prophet to the
      nations."

⁶Then I said, "Ah, Lord GOD! Truly I do not know how to speak, for I am only a boy." ⁷But the LORD said to me,

   "Do not say, 'I am only a boy';
   for you shall go to all to whom I
      send you,
   and you shall speak whatever I
      command you.

8 Do not be afraid of them,
   for I am with you to deliver you,
                    says the LORD."

⁹Then the LORD put out his hand and touched my mouth; and the LORD said to me,

   "Now I have put my words in your
      mouth.

10 See, today I appoint you over
      nations and over kingdoms,

to pluck up and to pull down,
to destroy and to overthrow,
to build and to plant."

11 The word of the LORD came to me, saying, "Jeremiah, what do you see?" And I said, "I see a branch of an almond tree."*a* 12Then the LORD said to me, "You have seen well, for I am watching*b* over my word to perform it." 13The word of the LORD came to me a second time, saying, "What do you see?" And I said, "I see a boiling pot, tilted away from the north."

14 Then the LORD said to me: Out of the north disaster shall break out on all the inhabitants of the land. 15For now I am calling all the tribes of the kingdoms of the north, says the LORD; and they shall come and all of them shall set their thrones at the entrance of the gates of Jerusalem, against all its surrounding walls and against all the cities of Judah. 16And I will utter my judgments against them, for all their wickedness in forsaking me; they have made offerings to other gods, and worshiped the works of their own hands. 17But you, gird up your loins; stand up and tell them everything that I command you. Do not break down before them, or I will break you before them. 18And I for my part have made you today a fortified city, an iron pillar, and a bronze wall, against the whole land— against the kings of Judah, its princes, its priests, and the people of the land. 19They will fight against you; but they shall not prevail against you, for I am with you, says the LORD, to deliver you.

God Pleads with Israel to Repent

2 The word of the LORD came to me, saying: 2Go and proclaim in the hearing of Jerusalem, Thus says the LORD:
I remember the devotion of your
youth,
your love as a bride,
how you followed me in the
wilderness,
in a land not sown.
3 Israel was holy to the LORD,
the first fruits of his harvest.
All who ate of it were held guilty;
disaster came upon them,
says the LORD.

4 Hear the word of the LORD, O house of Jacob, and all the families of the house of Israel. 5Thus says the LORD:
What wrong did your ancestors find
in me
that they went far from me,
and went after worthless things,
and became worthless
themselves?
6 They did not say, "Where is the
LORD
who brought us up from the land
of Egypt,
who led us in the wilderness,
in a land of deserts and pits,
in a land of drought and deep
darkness,
in a land that no one passes
through,
where no one lives?"
7 I brought you into a plentiful land
to eat its fruits and its good
things.
But when you entered you defiled
my land,
and made my heritage an
abomination.
8 The priests did not say, "Where is
the LORD?"
Those who handle the law did
not know me;
the rulers*c* transgressed against me;
the prophets prophesied by Baal,
and went after things that do not
profit.

9 Therefore once more I accuse you,
says the LORD,
and I accuse your children's
children.
10 Cross to the coasts of Cyprus and
look,
send to Kedar and examine with
care;
see if there has ever been such a
thing.
11 Has a nation changed its gods,
even though they are no gods?
But my people have changed their
glory
for something that does not
profit.
12 Be appalled, O heavens, at this,
be shocked, be utterly desolate,
says the LORD,

---

a Heb *shaqed*   *b* Heb *shoqed*   *c* Heb *shepherds*

13 for my people have committed two
     evils:
   they have forsaken me,
   the fountain of living water,
     and dug out cisterns for
       themselves,
   cracked cisterns
     that can hold no water.

14 Is Israel a slave? Is he a homeborn
     servant?
   Why then has he become
     plunder?
15 The lions have roared against him,
     they have roared loudly.
   They have made his land a waste;
     his cities are in ruins, without
       inhabitant.
16 Moreover, the people of Memphis
     and Tahpanhes
   have broken the crown of your
     head.
17 Have you not brought this upon
     yourself
   by forsaking the LORD your God,
     while he led you in the way?
18 What then do you gain by going to
     Egypt,
   to drink the waters of the Nile?
   Or what do you gain by going to
     Assyria,
     to drink the waters of the
       Euphrates?
19 Your wickedness will punish you,
     and your apostasies will convict
       you.
   Know and see that it is evil and
     bitter
   for you to forsake the LORD your
     God;
     the fear of me is not in you,
       says the Lord GOD of hosts.

20 For long ago you broke your yoke
     and burst your bonds,
   and you said, "I will not serve!"
   On every high hill
     and under every green tree
     you sprawled and played the
       whore.
21 Yet I planted you as a choice vine,
     from the purest stock.
   How then did you turn degenerate
     and become a wild vine?
22 Though you wash yourself with lye
     and use much soap,

the stain of your guilt is still
   before me,
                 says the Lord GOD.
23 How can you say, "I am not
     defiled,
   I have not gone after the Baals"?
   Look at your way in the valley;
     know what you have done—
   a restive young camel interlacing
     her tracks,
24   a wild ass at home in the
        wilderness,
   in her heat sniffing the wind!
     Who can restrain her lust?
   None who seek her need weary
     themselves;
     in her month they will find her.
25 Keep your feet from going unshod
     and your throat from thirst.
   But you said, "It is hopeless,
     for I have loved strangers,
     and after them I will go."

26 As a thief is shamed when caught,
     so the house of Israel shall be
       shamed—
   they, their kings, their officials,
     their priests, and their prophets,
27 who say to a tree, "You are my
     father,"
   and to a stone, "You gave me
     birth."
   For they have turned their backs to
     me,
     and not their faces.
   But in the time of their trouble
     they say,
     "Come and save us!"
28 But where are your gods
     that you made for yourself?
   Let them come, if they can save
     you,
     in your time of trouble;
   for you have as many gods
     as you have towns, O Judah.

29 Why do you complain against me?
     You have all rebelled against me,
                 says the LORD.
30 In vain I have struck down your
     children;
     they accepted no correction.
   Your own sword devoured your
     prophets
     like a ravening lion.

31 And you, O generation, behold the
    word of the LORD!d
    Have I been a wilderness to Israel,
    or a land of thick darkness?
    Why then do my people say, "We
    are free,
    we will come to you no more"?
32 Can a girl forget her ornaments,
    or a bride her attire?
    Yet my people have forgotten me,
    days without number.

33 How well you direct your course
    to seek lovers!
    So that even to wicked women
    you have taught your ways.
34 Also on your skirts is found
    the lifeblood of the innocent
    poor,
    though you did not catch them
    breaking in.
    Yet in spite of all these thingsd
35 you say, "I am innocent;
    surely his anger has turned from
    me."
    Now I am bringing you to
    judgment
    for saying, "I have not sinned."
36 How lightly you gad about,
    changing your ways!
    You shall be put to shame by Egypt
    as you were put to shame by
    Assyria.
37 From there also you will come
    away
    with your hands on your head;
    for the LORD has rejected those in
    whom you trust,
    and you will not prosper through
    them.

Unfaithful Israel

3 Ife a man divorces his wife
    and she goes from him
    and becomes another man's wife,
    will he return to her?
    Would not such a land be greatly
    polluted?
    You have played the whore with
    many lovers;
    and would you return to me?
                        says the LORD.
2 Look up to the bare heights,f and
    see!

Where have you not been lain
    with?
By the waysides you have sat
    waiting for lovers,
    like a nomad in the wilderness.
You have polluted the land
    with your whoring and
    wickedness.
3 Therefore the showers have been
    withheld,
    and the spring rain has not come;
    yet you have the forehead of a
    whore,
    you refuse to be ashamed.
4 Have you not just now called to
    me,
    "My Father, you are the friend of
    my youth—
5 will he be angry forever,
    will he be indignant to the end?"
    This is how you have spoken,
    but you have done all the evil
    that you could.

A Call to Repentance

6 The LORD said to me in the days of
King Josiah: Have you seen what she
did, that faithless one, Israel, how she
went up on every high hill and under
every green tree, and played the whore
there? 7And I thought, "After she has
done all this she will return to me"; but
she did not return, and her false sister
Judah saw it. 8Sheg saw that for all the
adulteries of that faithless one, Israel, I
had sent her away with a decree of
divorce; yet her false sister Judah did not
fear, but she too went and played the
whore. 9Because she took her whoredom so lightly, she polluted the land,
committing adultery with stone and
tree. 10Yet for all this her false sister
Judah did not return to me with her
whole heart, but only in pretense, says
the LORD.

11 Then the LORD said to me: Faithless Israel has shown herself less guilty
than false Judah. 12Go, and proclaim
these words toward the north, and say:
    Return, faithless Israel,
                        says the LORD.
    I will not look on you in anger,
    for I am merciful,
                        says the LORD;

d Meaning of Heb uncertain   e Q Ms Gk Syr: MT Saying, If   f Or the trails   g Q Ms Gk Mss
Syr: MT I

I will not be angry forever.
13 Only acknowledge your guilt,
    that you have rebelled against
        the LORD your God,
    and scattered your favors among
        strangers under every green
        tree,
    and have not obeyed my voice,
                    says the LORD.
14 Return, O faithless children,
                    says the LORD,
    for I am your master;
    I will take you, one from a city and
        two from a family,
    and I will bring you to Zion.

15 I will give you shepherds after my own heart, who will feed you with knowledge and understanding. 16And when you have multiplied and increased in the land, in those days, says the LORD, they shall no longer say, "The ark of the covenant of the LORD." It shall not come to mind, or be remembered, or missed; nor shall another one be made. 17At that time Jerusalem shall be called the throne of the LORD, and all nations shall gather to it, to the presence of the LORD in Jerusalem, and they shall no longer stubbornly follow their own evil will. 18In those days the house of Judah shall join the house of Israel, and together they shall come from the land of the north to the land that I gave your ancestors for a heritage.

19 I thought
    how I would set you among my
        children,
    and give you a pleasant land,
        the most beautiful heritage of all
        the nations.
    And I thought you would call me,
        My Father,
    and would not turn from
        following me.
20 Instead, as a faithless wife leaves
        her husband,
    so you have been faithless to me,
        O house of Israel,
                    says the LORD.

21 A voice on the bare heights[h] is
        heard,

the plaintive weeping of Israel's
    children,
because they have perverted their
    way,
    they have forgotten the LORD
        their God:
22 Return, O faithless children,
    I will heal your faithlessness.

"Here we come to you;
    for you are the LORD our God.
23 Truly the hills are[i] a delusion,
    the orgies on the mountains.
Truly in the LORD our God
    is the salvation of Israel.

24 "But from our youth the shameful thing has devoured all for which our ancestors had labored, their flocks and their herds, their sons and their daughters. 25Let us lie down in our shame, and let our dishonor cover us; for we have sinned against the LORD our God, we and our ancestors, from our youth even to this day; and we have not obeyed the voice of the LORD our God."

4 If you return, O Israel,
                    says the LORD,
    if you return to me,
    if you remove your abominations
        from my presence,
        and do not waver,
2 and if you swear, "As the LORD
        lives!"
    in truth, in justice, and in
        uprightness,
    then nations shall be blessed[j] by
        him,
    and by him they shall boast.

3 For thus says the LORD to the people of Judah and to the inhabitants of Jerusalem:
    Break up your fallow ground,
        and do not sow among thorns.
4 Circumcise yourselves to the LORD,
        remove the foreskin of your
        hearts,
    O people of Judah and
        inhabitants of Jerusalem,
    or else my wrath will go forth like
        fire,
    and burn with no one to quench
        it,
    because of the evil of your
        doings.

h Or the trails   i Gk Syr Vg: Heb Truly from the hills is   j Or shall bless themselves

Invasion and Desolation of Judah Threatened

5 Declare in Judah, and proclaim in Jerusalem, and say:

Blow the trumpet through the land;
    shout aloud[k] and say,
"Gather together, and let us go
    into the fortified cities!"
6 Raise a standard toward Zion,
    flee for safety, do not delay,
for I am bringing evil from the
        north,
    and a great destruction.
7 A lion has gone up from its thicket,
    a destroyer of nations has set out;
he has gone out from his place
    to make your land a waste;
    your cities will be ruins
    without inhabitant.
8 Because of this put on sackcloth,
    lament and wail:
"The fierce anger of the LORD
    has not turned away from us."

9On that day, says the LORD, courage shall fail the king and the officials; the priests shall be appalled and the prophets astounded. 10Then I said, "Ah, Lord GOD, how utterly you have deceived this people and Jerusalem, saying, 'It shall be well with you,' even while the sword is at the throat!"

11 At that time it will be said to this people and to Jerusalem: A hot wind comes from me out of the bare heights[l] in the desert toward my poor people, not to winnow or cleanse— 12a wind too strong for that. Now it is I who speak in judgment against them.
13   Look! He comes up like clouds,
    his chariots like the whirlwind;
his horses are swifter than eagles—
    woe to us, for we are ruined!
14 O Jerusalem, wash your heart clean
        of wickedness
    so that you may be saved.
How long shall your evil schemes
    lodge within you?
15 For a voice declares from Dan
    and proclaims disaster from
        Mount Ephraim.
16 Tell the nations, "Here they are!"
    Proclaim against Jerusalem,

"Besiegers come from a distant
        land;
they shout against the cities of
        Judah.
17 They have closed in around her
    like watchers of a field,
because she has rebelled against
        me,
                    says the LORD.
18 Your ways and your doings
    have brought this upon you.
This is your doom; how bitter it is!
It has reached your very heart."

Sorrow for a Doomed Nation

19 My anguish, my anguish! I writhe
        in pain!
    Oh, the walls of my heart!
My heart is beating wildly;
    I cannot keep silent;
for I[m] hear the sound of the
        trumpet,
    the alarm of war.
20 Disaster overtakes disaster,
    the whole land is laid waste.
Suddenly my tents are destroyed,
    my curtains in a moment.
21 How long must I see the standard,
    and hear the sound of the
        trumpet?
22 "For my people are foolish,
    they do not know me;
they are stupid children,
    they have no understanding.
They are skilled in doing evil,
    but do not know how to do
        good."

23 I looked on the earth, and lo, it was
        waste and void;
    and to the heavens, and they had
        no light.
24 I looked on the mountains, and lo,
        they were quaking,
    and all the hills moved to and
        fro.
25 I looked, and lo, there was no one
        at all,
    and all the birds of the air had
        fled.
26 I looked, and lo, the fruitful land
        was a desert,
    and all its cities were laid in
        ruins

k Or shout, take your weapons: Heb shout, fill (your hand)   l Or the trails   m Another reading is for you, O my soul,

before the LORD, before his fierce anger.

27 For thus says the LORD: The whole land shall be a desolation; yet I will not make a full end.

28 Because of this the earth shall mourn,
and the heavens above grow black;
for I have spoken, I have purposed;
I have not relented nor will I turn back.

29 At the noise of horseman and archer
every town takes to flight;
they enter thickets; they climb among rocks;
all the towns are forsaken,
and no one lives in them.

30 And you, O desolate one,
what do you mean that you dress in crimson,
that you deck yourself with ornaments of gold,
that you enlarge your eyes with paint?
In vain you beautify yourself.
Your lovers despise you;
they seek your life.

31 For I heard a cry as of a woman in labor,
anguish as of one bringing forth her first child,
the cry of daughter Zion gasping for breath,
stretching out her hands,
"Woe is me! I am fainting before killers!"

The Utter Corruption of God's People

5 Run to and fro through the streets of Jerusalem,
look around and take note!
Search its squares and see
if you can find one person
who acts justly
and seeks truth—
so that I may pardon Jerusalem.[n]

2 Although they say, "As the LORD lives,"
yet they swear falsely.

3 O LORD, do your eyes not look for truth?

You have struck them,
but they felt no anguish;
you have consumed them,
but they refused to take correction.
They have made their faces harder than rock;
they have refused to turn back.

4 Then I said, "These are only the poor,
they have no sense;
for they do not know the way of the LORD,
the law of their God.

5 Let me go to the rich[o]
and speak to them;
surely they know the way of the LORD,
the law of their God."
But they all alike had broken the yoke,
they had burst the bonds.

6 Therefore a lion from the forest shall kill them,
a wolf from the desert shall destroy them.
A leopard is watching against their cities;
everyone who goes out of them shall be torn in pieces—
because their transgressions are many,
their apostasies are great.

7 How can I pardon you?
Your children have forsaken me,
and have sworn by those who are no gods.
When I fed them to the full,
they committed adultery
and trooped to the houses of prostitutes.

8 They were well-fed lusty stallions,
each neighing for his neighbor's wife.

9 Shall I not punish them for these things?
says the LORD;
and shall I not bring retribution on a nation such as this?

10 Go up through her vine-rows and destroy,

but do not make a full end;
strip away her branches,
    for they are not the LORD's.
11 For the house of Israel and the
        house of Judah
    have been utterly faithless to me,
                    says the LORD.
12 They have spoken falsely of the
        LORD,
    and have said, "He will do
        nothing.
    No evil will come upon us,
        and we shall not see sword or
        famine."
13 The prophets are nothing but wind,
    for the word is not in them.
    Thus shall it be done to them!

14 Therefore thus says the LORD, the
        God of hosts:
    Because they*p* have spoken this
        word,
    I am now making my words in
        your mouth a fire,
    and this people wood, and the
        fire shall devour them.
15 I am going to bring upon you
    a nation from far away, O house
        of Israel,
                    says the LORD.
    It is an enduring nation,
        it is an ancient nation,
    a nation whose language you do
        not know,
        nor can you understand what
        they say.
16 Their quiver is like an open tomb;
    all of them are mighty warriors.
17 They shall eat up your harvest and
        your food;
    they shall eat up your sons and
        your daughters;
    they shall eat up your flocks and
        your herds;
    they shall eat up your vines and
        your fig trees;
    they shall destroy with the sword
        your fortified cities in which you
        trust.

18 But even in those days, says the
LORD, I will not make a full end of you.
19 And when your people say, "Why has
the LORD our God done all these things
to us?" you shall say to them, "As you

have forsaken me and served foreign
gods in your land, so you shall serve
strangers in a land that is not yours."

20 Declare this in the house of Jacob,
        proclaim it in Judah:
21 Hear this, O foolish and senseless
        people,
    who have eyes, but do not see,
    who have ears, but do not hear.
22 Do you not fear me? says the LORD;
    Do you not tremble before me?
    I placed the sand as a boundary for
        the sea,
    a perpetual barrier that it cannot
        pass;
    though the waves toss, they cannot
        prevail,
    though they roar, they cannot
        pass over it.
23 But this people has a stubborn and
        rebellious heart;
    they have turned aside and gone
        away.
24 They do not say in their hearts,
    "Let us fear the LORD our God,
    who gives the rain in its season,
    the autumn rain and the spring
        rain,
    and keeps for us
        the weeks appointed for the
        harvest."
25 Your iniquities have turned these
        away,
    and your sins have deprived you
        of good.
26 For scoundrels are found among my
        people;
    they take over the goods of
        others.
    Like fowlers they set a trap;*q*
        they catch human beings.
27 Like a cage full of birds,
    their houses are full of treachery;
    therefore they have become great
        and rich,
28 they have grown fat and sleek.
    They know no limits in deeds of
        wickedness;
    they do not judge with justice
    the cause of the orphan, to make it
        prosper,
    and they do not defend the rights
        of the needy.

p Heb *you*   *q* Meaning of Heb uncertain

29 Shall I not punish them for these
        things?
                        says the LORD,
    and shall I not bring retribution
        on a nation such as this?

30 An appalling and horrible thing
        has happened in the land:
31 the prophets prophesy falsely,
        and the priests rule as the
            prophets direct; *r*
    my people love to have it so,
        but what will you do when the
            end comes?

The Imminence and Horror
of the Invasion

6 Flee for safety, O children of
        Benjamin,
    from the midst of Jerusalem!
    Blow the trumpet in Tekoa,
        and raise a signal on Beth-
            haccherem;
    for evil looms out of the north,
        and great destruction.
2   I have likened daughter Zion
        to the loveliest pasture. *s*
3   Shepherds with their flocks shall
        come against her.
    They shall pitch their tents
        around her;
    they shall pasture, all in their
        places.
4   "Prepare war against her;
        up, and let us attack at noon!"
    "Woe to us, for the day declines,
        the shadows of evening
            lengthen!"
5   "Up, and let us attack by night,
        and destroy her palaces!"
6   For thus says the LORD of hosts:
    Cut down her trees;
        cast up a siege ramp against
            Jerusalem.
    This is the city that must be
        punished; *t*
    there is nothing but oppression
        within her.
7   As a well keeps its water fresh,
        so she keeps fresh her
            wickedness;
    violence and destruction are heard
        within her;

sickness and wounds are ever
    before me.
8   Take warning, O Jerusalem,
        or I shall turn from you in
            disgust,
    and make you a desolation,
        an uninhabited land.

9   Thus says the LORD of hosts:
    Glean *u* thoroughly as a vine
        the remnant of Israel;
    like a grape-gatherer, pass your
        hand again
    over its branches.

10 To whom shall I speak and give
        warning,
        that they may hear?
    See, their ears are closed, *v*
        they cannot listen.
    The word of the LORD is to them an
        object of scorn;
        they take no pleasure in it.
11 But I am full of the wrath of the
        LORD;
        I am weary of holding it in.

    Pour it out on the children in the
        street,
    and on the gatherings of young
        men as well;
    both husband and wife shall be
        taken,
        the old folk and the very aged.
12 Their houses shall be turned over
        to others,
        their fields and wives together;
    for I will stretch out my hand
        against the inhabitants of the
            land,
                        says the LORD.

13 For from the least to the greatest of
        them,
    everyone is greedy for unjust
        gain;
    and from prophet to priest,
        everyone deals falsely.
14 They have treated the wound of my
        people carelessly,
    saying, "Peace, peace,"
        when there is no peace.
15 They acted shamefully, they
        committed abomination;

*r Or rule by their own authority   s Or I will destroy daughter Zion, the loveliest pasture   t Or the
city of license   u Cn: Heb They shall glean   v Heb are uncircumcised*

yet they were not ashamed,
   they did not know how to blush.
Therefore they shall fall among
   those who fall;
   at the time that I punish them,
   they shall be overthrown,
       says the LORD.

16 Thus says the LORD:
Stand at the crossroads, and look,
   and ask for the ancient paths,
   where the good way lies; and walk
     in it,
   and find rest for your souls.
But they said, "We will not walk in
   it."

17 Also I raised up sentinels for you:
   "Give heed to the sound of the
     trumpet!"
But they said, "We will not give
   heed."

18 Therefore hear, O nations,
   and know, O congregation, what
     will happen to them.

19 Hear, O earth; I am going to bring
   disaster on this people,
   the fruit of their schemes,
because they have not given heed
   to my words;
   and as for my teaching, they have
     rejected it.

20 Of what use to me is frankincense
   that comes from Sheba,
   or sweet cane from a distant
     land?
Your burnt offerings are not
     acceptable,
   nor are your sacrifices pleasing to
     me.

21 Therefore thus says the LORD:
See, I am laying before this people
   stumbling blocks against which
     they shall stumble;
parents and children together,
   neighbor and friend shall perish.

22 Thus says the LORD:
See, a people is coming from the
   land of the north,
   a great nation is stirring from the
     farthest parts of the earth.

23 They grasp the bow and the javelin,
   they are cruel and have no mercy,
   their sound is like the roaring
     sea;
   they ride on horses,

equipped like a warrior for battle,
   against you, O daughter Zion!

24 "We have heard news of them,
   our hands fall helpless;
anguish has taken hold of us,
   pain as of a woman in labor.

25 Do not go out into the field,
   or walk on the road;
for the enemy has a sword,
   terror is on every side."

26 O my poor people, put on
     sackcloth,
   and roll in ashes;
make mourning as for an only
     child,
   most bitter lamentation:
for suddenly the destroyer
   will come upon us.

27 I have made you a tester and a
     refiner[w] among my people
so that you may know and test
   their ways.

28 They are all stubbornly rebellious,
   going about with slanders;
they are bronze and iron,
   all of them act corruptly.

29 The bellows blow fiercely,
   the lead is consumed by the fire;
in vain the refining goes on,
   for the wicked are not removed.

30 They are called "rejected silver,"
   for the LORD has rejected them.

Jeremiah Proclaims God's Judgment on the Nation

7 The word that came to Jeremiah from the LORD: 2Stand in the gate of the LORD's house, and proclaim there this word, and say, Hear the word of the LORD, all you people of Judah, you that enter these gates to worship the LORD. 3Thus says the LORD of hosts, the God of Israel: Amend your ways and your doings, and let me dwell with you[x] in this place. 4Do not trust in these deceptive words: "This is[y] the temple of the LORD, the temple of the LORD, the temple of the LORD."

5 For if you truly amend your ways and your doings, if you truly act justly one with another, 6if you do not oppress the alien, the orphan, and the widow, or

shed innocent blood in this place, and if you do not go after other gods to your own hurt, 7then I will dwell with you in this place, in the land that I gave of old to your ancestors forever and ever.

8 Here you are, trusting in deceptive words to no avail. 9Will you steal, murder, commit adultery, swear falsely, make offerings to Baal, and go after other gods that you have not known, 10and then come and stand before me in this house, which is called by my name, and say, "We are safe!"—only to go on doing all these abominations? 11Has this house, which is called by my name, become a den of robbers in your sight? You know, I too am watching, says the LORD. 12Go now to my place that was in Shiloh, where I made my name dwell at first, and see what I did to it for the wickedness of my people Israel. 13And now, because you have done all these things, says the LORD, and when I spoke to you persistently, you did not listen, and when I called you, you did not answer, 14therefore I will do to the house that is called by my name, in which you trust, and to the place that I gave to you and to your ancestors, just what I did to Shiloh. 15And I will cast you out of my sight, just as I cast out all your kinsfolk, all the offspring of Ephraim.

The People's Disobedience

16 As for you, do not pray for this people, do not raise a cry or prayer on their behalf, and do not intercede with me, for I will not hear you. 17Do you not see what they are doing in the towns of Judah and in the streets of Jerusalem? 18The children gather wood, the fathers kindle fire, and the women knead dough, to make cakes for the queen of heaven; and they pour out drink offerings to other gods, to provoke me to anger. 19Is it I whom they provoke? says the LORD. Is it not themselves, to their own hurt? 20Therefore thus says the Lord GOD: My anger and my wrath shall be poured out on this place, on human beings and animals, on the trees of the field and the fruit of the ground; it will burn and not be quenched.

21 Thus says the LORD of hosts, the God of Israel: Add your burnt offerings to your sacrifices, and eat the flesh. 22For in the day that I brought your ancestors out of the land of Egypt, I did not speak to them or command them concerning burnt offerings and sacrifices. 23But this command I gave them, "Obey my voice, and I will be your God, and you shall be my people; and walk only in the way that I command you, so that it may be well with you." 24Yet they did not obey or incline their ear, but, in the stubbornness of their evil will, they walked in their own counsels, and looked backward rather than forward. 25From the day that your ancestors came out of the land of Egypt until this day, I have persistently sent all my servants the prophets to them, day after day; 26yet they did not listen to me, or pay attention, but they stiffened their necks. They did worse than their ancestors did.

27 So you shall speak all these words to them, but they will not listen to you. You shall call to them, but they will not answer you. 28You shall say to them: This is the nation that did not obey the voice of the LORD their God, and did not accept discipline; truth has perished; it is cut off from their lips.

29   Cut off your hair and throw it
         away;
     raise a lamentation on the bare
         heights,z
     for the LORD has rejected and
         forsaken
     the generation that provoked his
         wrath.

30 For the people of Judah have done evil in my sight, says the LORD; they have set their abominations in the house that is called by my name, defiling it. 31And they go on building the high placea of Topheth, which is in the valley of the son of Hinnom, to burn their sons and their daughters in the fire—which I did not command, nor did it come into my mind. 32Therefore, the days are surely coming, says the LORD, when it will no more be called Topheth, or the valley of the son of Hinnom, but the valley of Slaughter: for they will bury in Topheth until there is no more room. 33The corpses of this people will

z Or the trails   a Gk Tg: Heb high places

be food for the birds of the air, and for the animals of the earth; and no one will frighten them away. 34And I will bring to an end the sound of mirth and gladness, the voice of the bride and bridegroom in the cities of Judah and in the streets of Jerusalem; for the land shall become a waste.

8 At that time, says the LORD, the bones of the kings of Judah, the bones of its officials, the bones of the priests, the bones of the prophets, and the bones of the inhabitants of Jerusalem shall be brought out of their tombs; 2and they shall be spread before the sun and the moon and all the host of heaven, which they have loved and served, which they have followed, and which they have inquired of and worshiped; and they shall not be gathered or buried; they shall be like dung on the surface of the ground. 3Death shall be preferred to life by all the remnant that remains of this evil family in all the places where I have driven them, says the LORD of hosts.

The Blind Perversity of the Whole Nation

4 You shall say to them, Thus says the LORD:
When people fall, do they not get up again?
 If they go astray, do they not turn back?
5 Why then has this people[b] turned away
 in perpetual backsliding?
They have held fast to deceit,
 they have refused to return.
6 I have given heed and listened,
 but they do not speak honestly;
no one repents of wickedness,
 saying, "What have I done!"
All of them turn to their own course,
 like a horse plunging headlong into battle.
7 Even the stork in the heavens knows its times;
and the turtledove, swallow, and crane[c]
 . observe the time of their coming;

but my people do not know
 the ordinance of the LORD.

8 How can you say, "We are wise,
 and the law of the LORD is with us,"
when, in fact, the false pen of the scribes
 has made it into a lie?
9 The wise shall be put to shame,
 they shall be dismayed and taken;
since they have rejected the word of the LORD,
 what wisdom is in them?
10 Therefore I will give their wives to others
 and their fields to conquerors,
because from the least to the greatest
 everyone is greedy for unjust gain;
from prophet to priest
 everyone deals falsely.
11 They have treated the wound of my people carelessly,
 saying, "Peace, peace,"
 when there is no peace.
12 They acted shamefully, they committed abomination;
 yet they were not at all ashamed,
 they did not know how to blush.
Therefore they shall fall among those who fall;
 at the time when I punish them,
 they shall be overthrown,
 says the LORD.
13 When I wanted to gather them, says the LORD,
there are[d] no grapes on the vine,
 nor figs on the fig tree;
even the leaves are withered,
 and what I gave them has passed away from them.[c]

14 Why do we sit still?
Gather together, let us go into the fortified cities
 and perish there;
for the LORD our God has doomed us to perish,
 and has given us poisoned water to drink,
 because we have sinned against the LORD.

b One Ms Gk: MT this people, Jerusalem, of them, says the LORD. There are   c Meaning of Heb uncertain   d Or I will make an end

15 We look for peace, but find no
        good,
    for a time of healing, but there is
        terror instead.

16 The snorting of their horses is
        heard from Dan;
    at the sound of the neighing of
        their stallions
    the whole land quakes.
    They come and devour the land
        and all that fills it,
    the city and those who live in it.
17 See, I am letting snakes loose
        among you,
    adders that cannot be charmed,
    and they shall bite you,
                    says the LORD.

The Prophet Mourns for the People

18 My joy is gone, grief is upon me,
    my heart is sick.
19 Hark, the cry of my poor people
    from far and wide in the land:
    "Is the LORD not in Zion?
    Is her King not in her?"
    ("Why have they provoked me to
        anger with their images,
    with their foreign idols?")
20 "The harvest is past, the summer is
        ended,
    and we are not saved."
21 For the hurt of my poor people I am
        hurt,
    I mourn, and dismay has taken
        hold of me.

22 Is there no balm in Gilead?
    Is there no physician there?
    Why then has the health of my
        poor people
    not been restored?
9 e O that my head were a spring
        of water,
    and my eyes a fountain of tears,
    so that I might weep day and night
    for the slain of my poor people!
2f O that I had in the desert
    a traveler's lodging place,
    that I might leave my people
    and go away from them!
    For they are all adulterers,
    a band of traitors.

3 They bend their tongues like bows;
    they have grown strong in the
        land for falsehood, and not
        for truth;
    for they proceed from evil to evil,
    and they do not know me, says
        the LORD.

4 Beware of your neighbors,
    and put no trust in any of your
        kin;g
    for all your kinh are supplanters,
    and every neighbor goes around
        like a slanderer.
5 They all deceive their neighbors,
    and no one speaks the truth;
    they have taught their tongues to
        speak lies;
    they commit iniquity and are too
        weary to repent.i
6 Oppression upon oppression,
        deceitj upon deceit!
    They refuse to know me, says the
        LORD.

7 Therefore thus says the LORD of
        hosts:
    I will now refine and test them,
    for what else can I do with my
        sinful people?k
8 Their tongue is a deadly arrow;
    it speaks deceit through the
        mouth.
    They all speak friendly words to
        their neighbors,
    but inwardly are planning to lay
        an ambush.
9 Shall I not punish them for these
        things? says the LORD;
    and shall I not bring retribution
    on a nation such as this?

10 Take upl weeping and wailing for
        the mountains,
    and a lamentation for the
        pastures of the wilderness,
    because they are laid waste so that
        no one passes through,
    and the lowing of cattle is not
        heard;
    both the birds of the air and the
        animals
    have fled and are gone.

---

e Ch 8.23 in Heb   f Ch 9.1 in Heb   g Heb in a brother   h Heb for every brother   i Cn Compare
Gk: Heb they weary themselves with iniquity. 6Your dwelling   j Cn: Heb Your dwelling in the midst
of deceit   k Or my poor people   l Gk Syr: Heb I will take up

11 I will make Jerusalem a heap of
    ruins,
    a lair of jackals;
    and I will make the towns of Judah
    a desolation,
    without inhabitant.

12 Who is wise enough to understand this? To whom has the mouth of the LORD spoken, so that they may declare it? Why is the land ruined and laid waste like a wilderness, so that no one passes through? 13And the LORD says: Because they have forsaken my law that I set before them, and have not obeyed my voice, or walked in accordance with it, 14but have stubbornly followed their own hearts and have gone after the Baals, as their ancestors taught them. 15Therefore thus says the LORD of hosts,

the God of Israel: I am feeding this people with wormwood, and giving them poisonous water to drink. 16I will scatter them among nations that neither they nor their ancestors have known; and I will send the sword after them, until I have consumed them.

The People Mourn in Judgment

17 Thus says the LORD of hosts:
    Consider, and call for the mourning
    women to come;
    send for the skilled women to
    come;
18 let them quickly raise a dirge over
    us,
    so that our eyes may run down
    with tears,
    and our eyelids flow with water.

TUESDAY

A BALM IN GILEAD
African-American Spiritual

VERSE: Jeremiah 8.22   PASSAGE: Jeremiah 8.18–22

 here is a balm in Gilead
To make the wounded whole,
There is a balm in Gilead
To heal the sin-sick soul.

Sometimes I feel discouraged,
And think my work's in vain,
But then the Holy Spirit
Revives my soul again.

If you can't preach like Peter,
If you can't pray like Paul,
Just tell the love of Jesus,
And say he died for all.

ADDITIONAL SCRIPTURE READING:
Jeremiah 30.12–17; 46.11

Go to page 882 for your next devotional reading.

1700   1900

19 For a sound of wailing is heard
        from Zion:
    "How we are ruined!
    We are utterly shamed,
    because we have left the land,
        because they have cast down our
        dwellings."

20 Hear, O women, the word of the
        LORD,
    and let your ears receive the
        word of his mouth;
    teach to your daughters a dirge,
        and each to her neighbor a
        lament.
21 "Death has come up into our
        windows,
        it has entered our palaces,
    to cut off the children from the
        streets
        and the young men from the
        squares."
22 Speak! Thus says the LORD:
    "Human corpses shall fall
        like dung upon the open field,
    like sheaves behind the reaper,
        and no one shall gather them."

23 Thus says the LORD: Do not let the
wise boast in their wisdom, do not let
the mighty boast in their might, do not
let the wealthy boast in their wealth;
24but let those who boast boast in this,
that they understand and know me, that
I am the LORD; I act with steadfast love,
justice, and righteousness in the earth;
for in these things I delight, says the
LORD.

25 The days are surely coming, says
the LORD, when I will attend to all those
who are circumcised only in the foreskin: 26Egypt, Judah, Edom, the Ammonites, Moab, and all those with
shaven temples who live in the desert.
For all these nations are uncircumcised,
and all the house of Israel is uncircumcised in heart.

Idolatry Has Brought Ruin on Israel

10 Hear the word that the LORD
speaks to you, O house of
Israel. 2Thus says the LORD:
    Do not learn the way of the
        nations,
    or be dismayed at the signs of the
        heavens;
    for the nations are dismayed at
        them.
3 For the customs of the peoples are
        false:
    a tree from the forest is cut down,
        and worked with an ax by the
        hands of an artisan;
4 people deck it with silver and gold;
        they fasten it with hammer and
        nails
    so that it cannot move.
5 Their idolsm are like scarecrows in
        a cucumber field,
    and they cannot speak;
    they have to be carried,
        for they cannot walk.
    Do not be afraid of them,
        for they cannot do evil,
    nor is it in them to do good.

6 There is none like you, O LORD;
        you are great, and your name is
        great in might.
7 Who would not fear you, O King of
        the nations?
    For that is your due;
    among all the wise ones of the
        nations
        and in all their kingdoms
    there is no one like you.
8 They are both stupid and foolish;
        the instruction given by idols
        is no better than wood!n
9 Beaten silver is brought from
        Tarshish,
        and gold from Uphaz.
    They are the work of the artisan
        and of the hands of the
        goldsmith;
        their clothing is blue and purple;
    they are all the product of skilled
        workers.
10 But the LORD is the true God;
        he is the living God and the
        everlasting King.
    At his wrath the earth quakes,
        and the nations cannot endure
        his indignation.

11 Thus shall you say to them: The
gods who did not make the heavens and
the earth shall perish from the earth and
from under the heavens.o

m Heb They   n Meaning of Heb uncertain   o This verse is in Aramaic

12 It is he who made the earth by his
        power,
    who established the world by his
        wisdom,
    and by his understanding
        stretched out the heavens.
13 When he utters his voice, there is a
        tumult of waters in the
        heavens,
    and he makes the mist rise from
        the ends of the earth.
    He makes lightnings for the rain,
        and he brings out the wind from
        his storehouses.
14 Everyone is stupid and without
        knowledge;
    goldsmiths are all put to shame
        by their idols;
    for their images are false,
        and there is no breath in them.
15 They are worthless, a work of
        delusion;
    at the time of their punishment
        they shall perish.
16 Not like these is the LORD,^{p} the
        portion of Jacob,
    for he is the one who formed all
        things,
    and Israel is the tribe of his
        inheritance;
    the LORD of hosts is his name.

The Coming Exile

17 Gather up your bundle from the
        ground,
    O you who live under siege!
18 For thus says the LORD:
    I am going to sling out the
        inhabitants of the land
        at this time,
    and I will bring distress on them,
        so that they shall feel it.

19 Woe is me because of my hurt!
        My wound is severe.
    But I said, "Truly this is my
        punishment,
        and I must bear it."
20 My tent is destroyed,
        and all my cords are broken;
    my children have gone from me,
        and they are no more;
    there is no one to spread my tent
        again,
        and to set up my curtains.

21 For the shepherds are stupid,
        and do not inquire of the LORD;
    therefore they have not prospered,
        and all their flock is scattered.
22 Hear, a noise! Listen, it is coming—
        a great commotion from the land
        of the north
    to make the cities of Judah a
        desolation,
        a lair of jackals.

23 I know, O LORD, that the way of
        human beings is not in their
        control,
    that mortals as they walk cannot
        direct their steps.
24 Correct me, O LORD, but in just
        measure;
    not in your anger, or you will
        bring me to nothing.

25 Pour out your wrath on the nations
        that do not know you,
    and on the peoples that do not
        call on your name;
    for they have devoured Jacob;
        they have devoured him and
        consumed him,
    and have laid waste his
        habitation.

Israel and Judah Have Broken the Covenant

11 The word that came to Jeremiah from the LORD: 2Hear the words of this covenant, and speak to the people of Judah and the inhabitants of Jerusalem. 3You shall say to them, Thus says the LORD, the God of Israel: Cursed be anyone who does not heed the words of this covenant, 4which I commanded your ancestors when I brought them out of the land of Egypt, from the iron-smelter, saying, Listen to my voice, and do all that I command you. So shall you be my people, and I will be your God, 5that I may perform the oath that I swore to your ancestors, to give them a land flowing with milk and honey, as at this day. Then I answered, "So be it, LORD."

6 And the LORD said to me: Proclaim all these words in the cities of Judah, and in the streets of Jerusalem: Hear the

p Heb lacks the LORD

words of this covenant and do them. ⁷For I solemnly warned your ancestors when I brought them up out of the land of Egypt, warning them persistently, even to this day, saying, Obey my voice. ⁸Yet they did not obey or incline their ear, but everyone walked in the stubbornness of an evil will. So I brought upon them all the words of this covenant, which I commanded them to do, but they did not.

9 And the LORD said to me: Conspiracy exists among the people of Judah and the inhabitants of Jerusalem. ¹⁰They have turned back to the iniquities of their ancestors of old, who refused to heed my words; they have gone after other gods to serve them; the house of Israel and the house of Judah have broken the covenant that I made with their ancestors. ¹¹Therefore, thus says the LORD, assuredly I am going to bring disaster upon them that they cannot escape; though they cry out to me, I will not listen to them. ¹²Then the cities of Judah and the inhabitants of Jerusalem will go and cry out to the gods to whom they make offerings, but they will never save them in the time of their trouble. ¹³For your gods have become as many as your towns, O Judah; and as many as the streets of Jerusalem are the altars to shame you have set up, altars to make offerings to Baal.

14 As for you, do not pray for this people, or lift up a cry or prayer on their behalf, for I will not listen when they call to me in the time of their trouble. ¹⁵What right has my beloved in my house, when she has done vile deeds? Can vows*q* and sacrificial flesh avert your doom? Can you then exult? ¹⁶The LORD once called you, "A green olive tree, fair with goodly fruit"; but with the roar of a great tempest he will set fire to it, and its branches will be consumed. ¹⁷The LORD of hosts, who planted you, has pronounced evil against you, because of the evil that the house of Israel and the house of Judah have done, provoking me to anger by making offerings to Baal.

q Gk: Heb Can many

Jeremiah's Life Threatened

18   It was the LORD who made it
              known to me, and I knew;
         then you showed me their evil
              deeds.
19   But I was like a gentle lamb
         led to the slaughter.
      And I did not know it was against
              me
         that they devised schemes,
              saying,
      "Let us destroy the tree with its
              fruit,
         let us cut him off from the land
              of the living,
         so that his name will no longer
              be remembered!"
20   But you, O LORD of hosts, who
              judge righteously,
         who try the heart and the mind,
      let me see your retribution upon
              them,
         for to you I have committed my
              cause.

21 Therefore thus says the LORD concerning the people of Anathoth, who seek your life, and say, "You shall not prophesy in the name of the LORD, or you will die by our hand"— ²²therefore thus says the LORD of hosts: I am going to punish them; the young men shall die by the sword; their sons and their daughters shall die by famine; ²³and not even a remnant shall be left of them. For I will bring disaster upon the people of Anathoth, the year of their punishment.

Jeremiah Complains to God

12 You will be in the right,
         O LORD,
         when I lay charges against you;
         but let me put my case to you.
      Why does the way of the guilty
              prosper?
         Why do all who are treacherous
              thrive?
2   You plant them, and they take root;
         they grow and bring forth fruit;
      you are near in their mouths
         yet far from their hearts.
3   But you, O LORD, know me;
         You see me and test me—my
              heart is with you.

Pull them out like sheep for the
   slaughter,
and set them apart for the day of
   slaughter.
4 How long will the land mourn,
   and the grass of every field
      wither?
For the wickedness of those who
   live in it
   the animals and the birds are
      swept away,
and because people said, "He is
   blind to our ways."[r]

God Replies to Jeremiah

5 If you have raced with foot-runners
   and they have wearied you,
   how will you compete with
      horses?
And if in a safe land you fall down,
   how will you fare in the thickets
      of the Jordan?
6 For even your kinsfolk and your
      own family,
   even they have dealt
      treacherously with you;
they are in full cry after you;
   do not believe them,
   though they speak friendly words
      to you.

7 I have forsaken my house,
   I have abandoned my heritage;
I have given the beloved of my
      heart
   into the hands of her enemies.
8 My heritage has become to me
   like a lion in the forest;
she has lifted up her voice against
      me—
   therefore I hate her.
9 Is the hyena greedy[s] for my
      heritage at my command?
Are the birds of prey all around
      her?
Go, assemble all the wild animals;
   bring them to devour her.
10 Many shepherds have destroyed
      my vineyard,
   they have trampled down my
      portion,
they have made my pleasant
      portion
   a desolate wilderness.

11 They have made it a desolation;
   desolate, it mourns to me.
The whole land is made desolate,
   but no one lays it to heart.
12 Upon all the bare heights[t] in the
      desert
   spoilers have come;
for the sword of the LORD devours
   from one end of the land to the
      other;
   no one shall be safe.
13 They have sown wheat and have
      reaped thorns,
they have tired themselves out
   but profit nothing.
They shall be ashamed of their[u]
      harvests
   because of the fierce anger of the
      LORD.

14 Thus says the LORD concerning all my evil neighbors who touch the heritage that I have given my people Israel to inherit: I am about to pluck them up from their land, and I will pluck up the house of Judah from among them. 15And after I have plucked them up, I will again have compassion on them, and I will bring them again to their heritage and to their land, everyone of them. 16And then, if they will diligently learn the ways of my people, to swear by my name, "As the LORD lives," as they taught my people to swear by Baal, then they shall be built up in the midst of my people. 17But if any nation will not listen, then I will completely uproot it and destroy it, says the LORD.

The Linen Loincloth

13 Thus said the LORD to me, "Go and buy yourself a linen loincloth, and put it on your loins, but do not dip it in water." 2So I bought a loincloth according to the word of the LORD, and put it on my loins. 3And the word of the LORD came to me a second time, saying, 4"Take the loincloth that you bought and are wearing, and go now to the Euphrates,[v] and hide it there in a cleft of the rock." 5So I went, and hid it by the Euphrates,[w] as the LORD commanded me. 6And after many days the LORD said to me, "Go now to the

---

r Gk: Heb *to our future*   s Cn: Heb *Is the hyena, the bird of prey*   t Or *the trails*   u Heb *your*
v Or *to Parah*; Heb *perath*   w Or *by Parah*; Heb *perath*

Euphrates,ˣ and take from there the loincloth that I commanded you to hide there." ⁷Then I went to the Euphrates,ˣ and dug, and I took the loincloth from the place where I had hidden it. But now the loincloth was ruined; it was good for nothing.

8 Then the word of the LORD came to me: ⁹Thus says the LORD: Just so I will ruin the pride of Judah and the great pride of Jerusalem. ¹⁰This evil people, who refuse to hear my words, who stubbornly follow their own will and have gone after other gods to serve them and worship them, shall be like this loincloth, which is good for nothing. ¹¹For as the loincloth clings to one's loins, so I made the whole house of Israel and the whole house of Judah cling to me, says the LORD, in order that they might be for me a people, a name, a praise, and a glory. But they would not listen.

Symbol of the Wine-Jars

12 You shall speak to them this word: Thus says the LORD, the God of Israel: Every wine-jar should be filled with wine. And they will say to you, "Do you think we do not know that every wine-jar should be filled with wine?" ¹³Then you shall say to them: Thus says the LORD: I am about to fill all the inhabitants of this land—the kings who sit on David's throne, the priests, the prophets, and all the inhabitants of Jerusalem—with drunkenness. ¹⁴And I will dash them one against another, parents and children together, says the LORD. I will not pity or spare or have compassion when I destroy them.

Exile Threatened

15 Hear and give ear; do not be
    haughty,
  for the LORD has spoken.
16 Give glory to the LORD your God
    before he brings darkness,
  and before your feet stumble
    on the mountains at twilight;
  while you look for light,
  he turns it into gloom
    and makes it deep darkness.
17 But if you will not listen,

  my soul will weep in secret for
    your pride;
  my eyes will weep bitterly and run
    down with tears,
  because the LORD's flock has
    been taken captive.

18 Say to the king and the queen
    mother:
  "Take a lowly seat,
  for your beautiful crown
    has come down from your
    head."ʸ
19 The towns of the Negeb are shut
    up
  with no one to open them;
  all Judah is taken into exile,
    wholly taken into exile.

20 Lift up your eyes and see
    those who come from the north.
  Where is the flock that was given
    you,
    your beautiful flock?
21 What will you say when they set as
    head over you
    those whom you have trained
    to be your allies?
  Will not pangs take hold of you,
    like those of a woman in labor?
22 And if you say in your heart,
    "Why have these things come
    upon me?"
  it is for the greatness of your
    iniquity
    that your skirts are lifted up,
    and you are violated.
23 Can Ethiopiansᶻ change their skin
    or leopards their spots?
  Then also you can do good
    who are accustomed to do evil.
24 I will scatter youᵃ like chaff
    driven by the wind from the
    desert.
25 This is your lot,
    the portion I have measured out
    to you, says the LORD,
  because you have forgotten me
    and trusted in lies.
26 I myself will lift up your skirts over
    your face,
    and your shame will be seen.
27 I have seen your abominations,

x Or to Parah; Heb perath   y Gk Syr Vg: Meaning of Heb uncertain   z Or Nubians; Heb Cushites
a Heb them

your adulteries and neighings,
    your shameless prostitutions
on the hills of the countryside.
Woe to you, O Jerusalem!
    How long will it be
before you are made clean?

The Great Drought

14 The word of the LORD that came to Jeremiah concerning the drought:

2 Judah mourns
    and her gates languish;
they lie in gloom on the ground,
    and the cry of Jerusalem goes up.
3 Her nobles send their servants for
      water;
    they come to the cisterns,
they find no water,
    they return with their vessels
      empty.
They are ashamed and dismayed
    and cover their heads.
4 because the ground is cracked.
    Because there has been no rain
      on the land
the farmers are dismayed;
    they cover their heads.
5 Even the doe in the field forsakes
      her newborn fawn
because there is no grass.
6 The wild asses stand on the bare
      heights,*b*
    they pant for air like jackals;
their eyes fail
    because there is no herbage.

7 Although our iniquities testify
      against us,
    act, O LORD, for your name's
      sake;
our apostasies indeed are many,
    and we have sinned against you.
8 O hope of Israel,
    its savior in time of trouble,
why should you be like a stranger
      in the land,
    like a traveler turning aside for
      the night?
9 Why should you be like someone
      confused,
    like a mighty warrior who
      cannot give help?
Yet you, O LORD, are in the midst
    of us,

and we are called by your name;
    do not forsake us!

10 Thus says the LORD concerning
      this people:
Truly they have loved to wander,
    they have not restrained their
      feet;
therefore the LORD does not accept
      them,
now he will remember their
      iniquity
    and punish their sins.

11 The LORD said to me: Do not pray for the welfare of this people. 12 Although they fast, I do not hear their cry, and although they offer burnt offering and grain offering, I do not accept them; but by the sword, by famine, and by pestilence I consume them.

Denunciation of Lying Prophets

13 Then I said: "Ah, Lord GOD! Here are the prophets saying to them, 'You shall not see the sword, nor shall you have famine, but I will give you true peace in this place.' " 14 And the LORD said to me: The prophets are prophesying lies in my name; I did not send them, nor did I command them or speak to them. They are prophesying to you a lying vision, worthless divination, and the deceit of their own minds. 15 Therefore thus says the LORD concerning the prophets who prophesy in my name though I did not send them, and who say, "Sword and famine shall not come on this land": By sword and famine those prophets shall be consumed. 16 And the people to whom they prophesy shall be thrown out into the streets of Jerusalem, victims of famine and sword. There shall be no one to bury them—themselves, their wives, their sons, and their daughters. For I will pour out their wickedness upon them.

17 You shall say to them this word:
Let my eyes run down with tears
      night and day,
    and let them not cease,
for the virgin daughter—my
      people—is struck down with
      a crushing blow,
    with a very grievous wound.

b Or the trails

18 If I go out into the field,
        look—those killed by the sword!
    And if I enter the city,
        look—those sick with[c] famine!
    For both prophet and priest ply
        their trade throughout the
        land,
    and have no knowledge.

The People Plead for Mercy

19 Have you completely rejected
        Judah?
    Does your heart loathe Zion?
    Why have you struck us down
        so that there is no healing for us?
    We look for peace, but find no
        good;
    for a time of healing, but there is
        terror instead.
20 We acknowledge our wickedness,
        O LORD,
    the iniquity of our ancestors,
    for we have sinned against you.
21 Do not spurn us, for your name's
        sake;
    do not dishonor your glorious
        throne;
    remember and do not break your
        covenant with us.
22 Can any idols of the nations bring
        rain?
    Or can the heavens give showers?
    Is it not you, O LORD our God?
    We set our hope on you,
        for it is you who do all this.

Punishment Is Inevitable

15 Then the LORD said to me:
Though Moses and Samuel
stood before me, yet my heart would not
turn toward this people. Send them out
of my sight, and let them go! 2And when
they say to you, "Where shall we go?"
you shall say to them: Thus says the
LORD:
    Those destined for pestilence, to
        pestilence,
    and those destined for the sword,
        to the sword;
    those destined for famine, to
        famine,
    and those destined for captivity,
        to captivity.
3And I will appoint over them four
kinds of destroyers, says the LORD: the

sword to kill, the dogs to drag away, and
the birds of the air and the wild animals
of the earth to devour and destroy. 4I
will make them a horror to all the kingdoms of the earth because of what King
Manasseh son of Hezekiah of Judah did
in Jerusalem.

5   Who will have pity on you,
        O Jerusalem,
    or who will bemoan you?
    Who will turn aside
        to ask about your welfare?
6   You have rejected me, says the
        LORD,
    you are going backward;
    so I have stretched out my hand
        against you and destroyed
        you—
    I am weary of relenting.
7   I have winnowed them with a
        winnowing fork
    in the gates of the land;
    I have bereaved them, I have
        destroyed my people;
    they did not turn from their ways.
8   Their widows became more
        numerous
    than the sand of the seas;
    I have brought against the mothers
        of youths
    a destroyer at noonday;
    I have made anguish and terror
        fall upon her suddenly.
9   She who bore seven has languished;
        she has swooned away;
    her sun went down while it was
        yet day;
    she has been shamed and
        disgraced.
    And the rest of them I will give to
        the sword
    before their enemies,
                    says the LORD.

Jeremiah Complains Again and Is Reassured

10 Woe is me, my mother, that you
ever bore me, a man of strife and contention to the whole land! I have not
lent, nor have I borrowed, yet all of
them curse me. 11The LORD said: Surely
I have intervened in your life[d] for good,
surely I have imposed enemies on you in
a time of trouble and in a time of dis-

---

c Heb *look—the sicknesses of*   d Heb *intervened with you* tress.*e* 12Can iron and bronze break iron from the north?

13 Your wealth and your treasures I will give as plunder, without price, for all your sins, throughout all your territory. 14I will make you serve your enemies in a land that you do not know, for in my anger a fire is kindled that shall burn forever.

15 O LORD, you know;
   remember me and visit me,
     and bring down retribution for
      me on my persecutors.
In your forbearance do not take me
     away;
   know that on your account I
     suffer insult.
16 Your words were found, and I ate
     them,
   and your words became to me a
     joy
   and the delight of my heart;
for I am called by your name,
   O LORD, God of hosts.
17 I did not sit in the company of
     merrymakers,
   nor did I rejoice;
under the weight of your hand I sat
     alone,
   for you had filled me with
     indignation.
18 Why is my pain unceasing,
   my wound incurable,
     refusing to be healed?
Truly, you are to me like a deceitful
     brook,
   like waters that fail.

19 Therefore thus says the LORD:
If you turn back, I will take you
     back,
   and you shall stand before me.
If you utter what is precious, and
     not what is worthless,
   you shall serve as my mouth.
It is they who will turn to you,
   not you who will turn to them.
20 And I will make you to this people
     a fortified wall of bronze;
they will fight against you,
   but they shall not prevail over
     you,
for I am with you
   to save you and deliver you,
          says the LORD.

21 I will deliver you out of the hand of
     the wicked,
   and redeem you from the grasp of
     the ruthless.

Jeremiah's Celibacy and Message

16 The word of the LORD came to me: 2You shall not take a wife, nor shall you have sons or daughters in this place. 3For thus says the LORD concerning the sons and daughters who are born in this place, and concerning the mothers who bear them and the fathers who beget them in this land: 4They shall die of deadly diseases. They shall not be lamented, nor shall they be buried; they shall become like dung on the surface of the ground. They shall perish by the sword and by famine, and their dead bodies shall become food for the birds of the air and for the wild animals of the earth.

5 For thus says the LORD: Do not enter the house of mourning, or go to lament, or bemoan them; for I have taken away my peace from this people, says the LORD, my steadfast love and mercy. 6Both great and small shall die in this land; they shall not be buried, and no one shall lament for them; there shall be no gashing, no shaving of the head for them. 7No one shall break bread*f* for the mourner, to offer comfort for the dead; nor shall anyone give them the cup of consolation to drink for their fathers or their mothers. 8You shall not go into the house of feasting to sit with them, to eat and drink. 9For thus says the LORD of hosts, the God of Israel: I am going to banish from this place, in your days and before your eyes, the voice of mirth and the voice of gladness, the voice of the bridegroom and the voice of the bride.

10 And when you tell this people all these words, and they say to you, "Why has the LORD pronounced all this great evil against us? What is our iniquity? What is the sin that we have committed against the LORD our God?" 11then you shall say to them: It is because your ancestors have forsaken me, says the LORD, and have gone after other gods and have served and worshiped them, and have forsaken me and have not kept

e Meaning of Heb uncertain   *f* Two Mss Gk: MT *break for them*

my law; 12and because you have behaved worse than your ancestors, for
here you are, every one of you, following
your stubborn evil will, refusing to listen to me. 13Therefore I will hurl you
out of this land into a land that neither
you nor your ancestors have known, and
there you shall serve other gods day and
night, for I will show you no favor.

God Will Restore Israel

14 Therefore, the days are surely
coming, says the LORD, when it shall no
longer be said, "As the LORD lives who
brought the people of Israel up out of the
land of Egypt," 15but "As the LORD lives
who brought the people of Israel up out
of the land of the north and out of all the
lands where he had driven them." For I

WEDNESDAY

FOOD FOR THE INNER MAN
George Müller

VERSE: Jeremiah 15.16   **PASSAGE:** Jeremiah 15.10–21

he most important thing I had to do was to read the
Word of God and to meditate on it. Thus my heart
might be comforted, encouraged, warned, reproved,
and instructed.

Formerly, when I rose, I began to pray as soon as possible. But
I often spent a quarter of an hour to an hour on my knees struggling to pray while my mind wandered. Now I rarely have this
problem. As my heart is nourished by the truth of the Word, I am
brought into true fellowship with God. I speak to my Father and
to my Friend (although I am unworthy) about the things that he
has brought before me in his precious Word.

It often astonishes me that I did not see the importance of
meditation upon Scripture earlier in my Christian life. As the
outward man is not fit for work for any length of time unless he
eats, so it is with the inner man. What is the food for the inner
man? Not prayer, but *the Word of God*—not the simple reading
of the Word of God, so that it only passes through our minds,
just as water runs through a pipe. No, we must consider what we
read, ponder over it, and apply it to our hearts . . .

Meditation on God's Word has given me the help and
strength to pass peacefully through deep trials. What a difference
there is when the soul is refreshed in fellowship with God early
in the morning! Without spiritual preparation, the service, the
trials, and the temptations of the day can be overwhelming.

ADDITIONAL SCRIPTURE READING:
Ezekiel 3.1–3; 2 Timothy 3.16–17; Revelation 10.9

Go to page 885 for your next devotional reading.

1700   1900

will bring them back to their own land that I gave to their ancestors.

16 I am now sending for many fishermen, says the LORD, and they shall catch them; and afterward I will send for many hunters, and they shall hunt them from every mountain and every hill, and out of the clefts of the rocks. 17For my eyes are on all their ways; they are not hidden from my presence, nor is their iniquity concealed from my sight. 18Andᵍ I will doubly repay their iniquity and their sin, because they have polluted my land with the carcasses of their detestable idols, and have filled my inheritance with their abominations.

19 O LORD, my strength and my
        stronghold,
    my refuge in the day of trouble,
    to you shall the nations come
        from the ends of the earth and
            say:
    Our ancestors have inherited
            nothing but lies,
        worthless things in which there
            is no profit.
20 Can mortals make for themselves
            gods?
        Such are no gods!

21 "Therefore I am surely going to teach them, this time I am going to teach them my power and my might, and they shall know that my name is the LORD."

Judah's Sin and Punishment

17 The sin of Judah is written with an iron pen; with a diamond point it is engraved on the tablet of their hearts, and on the horns of their altars, 2while their children remember their altars and their sacred poles,ʰ beside every green tree, and on the high hills, 3on the mountains in the open country. Your wealth and all your treasures I will give for spoil as the price of your sinⁱ throughout all your territory. 4By your own act you shall lose the heritage that I gave you, and I will make you serve your enemies in a land that you do not know, for in my anger a fire is kindledʲ that shall burn forever.

5 Thus says the LORD:
    Cursed are those who trust in mere
            mortals
        and make mere flesh their
            strength,
        whose hearts turn away from the
            LORD.
6 They shall be like a shrub in the
            desert,
        and shall not see when relief
            comes.
    They shall live in the parched
            places of the wilderness,
        in an uninhabited salt land.

7 Blessed are those who trust in the
            LORD,
        whose trust is the LORD.

OUR CONFIDENCE IN CHRIST DOES NOT MAKE US LAZY, NEGLIGENT, OR CARELESS, BUT, ON THE CONTRARY, IT AWAKENS US, URGES US ON, AND MAKES US ACTIVE IN LIVING RIGHTEOUS LIVES AND DOING GOOD. THERE IS NO SELF-CONFIDENCE TO COMPARE WITH THIS. —*Ulrich Zwingli*

---

8 They shall be like a tree planted by
            water,
        sending out its roots by the
            stream.
    It shall not fear when heat comes,
        and its leaves shall stay green;
    in the year of drought it is not
            anxious,
        and it does not cease to bear
            fruit.

9 The heart is devious above all else;
        it is perverse—
        who can understand it?
10 I the LORD test the mind
        and search the heart,
    to give to all according to their
            ways,
        according to the fruit of their
            doings.

11 Like the partridge hatching what it
            did not lay,
        so are all who amass wealth
            unjustly;

---

g Gk: Heb *And first*   h Heb *Asherim*   i Cn: Heb *spoil your high places for sin*   j Two Mss Theodotion: *you kindled*

in mid-life it will leave them,
   and at their end they will prove
     to be fools.

12 O glorious throne, exalted from the
    beginning,
   shrine of our sanctuary!
13 O hope of Israel! O Lord!
   All who forsake you shall be put
    to shame;
   those who turn away from you[k]
    shall be recorded in the
    underworld,[l]
   for they have forsaken the
    fountain of living water, the
    Lord.

Jeremiah Prays for Vindication

14 Heal me, O Lord, and I shall be
    healed;
   save me, and I shall be saved;
   for you are my praise.
15 See how they say to me,
   "Where is the word of the Lord?
    Let it come!"
16 But I have not run away from being
    a shepherd[m] in your service,
   nor have I desired the fatal day.
   You know what came from my
    lips;
   it was before your face.
17 Do not become a terror to me;
   you are my refuge in the day of
    disaster;
18 Let my persecutors be shamed,
   but do not let me be shamed;
   let them be dismayed,
   but do not let me be dismayed;
   bring on them the day of disaster;
    destroy them with double
     destruction!

Hallow the Sabbath Day

19 Thus said the Lord to me: Go and stand in the People's Gate, by which the kings of Judah enter and by which they go out, and in all the gates of Jerusalem, 20and say to them: Hear the word of the Lord, you kings of Judah, and all Judah, and all the inhabitants of Jerusalem, who enter by these gates. 21Thus says the Lord: For the sake of your lives, take care that you do not bear a burden on the sabbath day or bring it in by the gates of Jerusalem. 22And do not carry a

burden out of your houses on the sabbath or do any work, but keep the sabbath day holy, as I commanded your ancestors. 23Yet they did not listen or incline their ear; they stiffened their necks and would not hear or receive instruction.

24 But if you listen to me, says the Lord, and bring in no burden by the gates of this city on the sabbath day, but keep the sabbath day holy and do no work on it, 25then there shall enter by the gates of this city kings[n] who sit on the throne of David, riding in chariots and on horses, they and their officials, the people of Judah and the inhabitants of Jerusalem; and this city shall be inhabited forever. 26And people shall come from the towns of Judah and the places around Jerusalem, from the land of Benjamin, from the Shephelah, from the hill country, and from the Negeb, bringing burnt offerings and sacrifices, grain offerings and frankincense, and bringing thank offerings to the house of the Lord. 27But if you do not listen to me, to keep the sabbath day holy, and to carry in no burden through the gates of Jerusalem on the sabbath day, then I will kindle a fire in its gates; it shall devour the palaces of Jerusalem and shall not be quenched.

The Potter and the Clay

18 The word that came to Jeremiah from the Lord: 2"Come, go down to the potter's house, and there I will let you hear my words." 3So I went down to the potter's house, and there he was working at his wheel. 4The vessel he was making of clay was spoiled in the potter's hand, and he reworked it into another vessel, as seemed good to him.

5 Then the word of the Lord came to me: 6Can I not do with you, O house of Israel, just as this potter has done? says the Lord. Just like the clay in the potter's hand, so are you in my hand, O house of Israel. 7At one moment I may declare concerning a nation or a kingdom, that I will pluck up and break down and destroy it, 8but if that nation, concerning which I have spoken, turns from its evil, I will change my mind about the disaster that I intended to bring on it. 9And at another moment I

---

k Heb me   l Or in the earth   m Meaning of Heb uncertain   n Cn: Heb kings and officials

may declare concerning a nation or a kingdom that I will build and plant it, [10]but if it does evil in my sight, not listening to my voice, then I will change my mind about the good that I had intended to do to it. [11]Now, therefore,

say to the people of Judah and the inhabitants of Jerusalem: Thus says the LORD: Look, I am a potter shaping evil against you and devising a plan against you. Turn now, all of you from your evil way, and amend your ways and your doings.

THURSDAY

PERPETUAL PROSPERITY?

Charles H. Spurgeon

VERSE: Jeremiah 17.11   **PASSAGE:** Jeremiah 17.11–18

he path of the Christian is not always bright with sunshine; he has his seasons of darkness and of storm. True, . . . religion is calculated to give a man happiness below as well as bliss above; but experience tells us that if the course of the just be "As the shining light that shineth more and more unto the perfect day," then sometimes *that* light is eclipsed (see Proverbs 4.18). At certain periods clouds cover the believer's sun, and he walks in darkness and sees no light.

There are many who have rejoiced in the presence of God for a season; they have basked in the sunshine in the earlier stages of their Christian career; they have walked along the "green pastures" by the side of the "still waters," but suddenly they find the glorious sky is clouded. Instead of the Land of Goshen, they have to tread the sandy desert: in the place of sweet waters, they find troubled streams, bitter to the taste, and they say, "Surely, if I were a child of God, this would not happen."

Oh! say not this, you who are walking in darkness . . . No Christian has enjoyed perpetual prosperity; no believer can always keep his harp from the willows. Perhaps the Lord allotted you at first a smooth and unclouded path because you were weak and timid. He tempered the wind to the shorn lamb, but now that you are stronger in the spiritual life, you must enter the riper and rougher experience of God's full-grown children. We need winds and tempests to exercise our faith, to tear off the rotten bough of self-dependence, and to root us more firmly in Christ. The day of evil reveals to us the value of our glorious hope.

ADDITIONAL SCRIPTURE READING:
Psalm 41.1; Jeremiah 16.19; Nahum 1.7

Go to page 898 for your next devotional reading.

1700   1900

Israel's Stubborn Idolatry

12 But they say, "It is no use! We will follow our own plans, and each of us will act according to the stubbornness of our evil will."

13 Therefore thus says the Lord:
Ask among the nations:
Who has heard the like of this?
The virgin Israel has done
a most horrible thing.

14 Does the snow of Lebanon leave
the crags of Sirion?[o]
Do the mountain[p] waters run dry,[q]
the cold flowing streams?

15 But my people have forgotten me,
they burn offerings to a delusion;
they have stumbled[r] in their ways,
in the ancient roads,
and have gone into bypaths,
not the highway,

16 making their land a horror,
a thing to be hissed at forever.
All who pass by it are horrified
and shake their heads.

17 Like the wind from the east,
I will scatter them before the
enemy.
I will show them my back, not my
face,
in the day of their calamity.

A Plot against Jeremiah

18 Then they said, "Come, let us make plots against Jeremiah—for instruction shall not perish from the priest, nor counsel from the wise, nor the word from the prophet. Come, let us bring charges against him,[s] and let us not heed any of his words."

19 Give heed to me, O Lord,
and listen to what my adversaries
say!

20 Is evil a recompense for good?
Yet they have dug a pit for my
life.
Remember how I stood before you
to speak good for them,
to turn away your wrath from
them.

21 Therefore give their children over
to famine;

hurl them out to the power of the
sword,
let their wives become childless
and widowed.
May their men meet death by
pestilence,
their youths be slain by the
sword in battle.

22 May a cry be heard from their
houses,
when you bring the marauder
suddenly upon them!
For they have dug a pit to catch me,
and laid snares for my feet.

23 Yet you, O Lord, know
all their plotting to kill me.
Do not forgive their iniquity,
do not blot out their sin from
your sight.
Let them be tripped up before you;
deal with them while you are
angry.

The Broken Earthenware Jug

19 Thus said the Lord: Go and buy a potter's earthenware jug. Take with you[t] some of the elders of the people and some of the senior priests, 2and go out to the valley of the son of Hinnom at the entry of the Potsherd Gate, and proclaim there the words that I tell you. 3You shall say: Hear the word of the Lord, O kings of Judah and inhabitants of Jerusalem. Thus says the Lord of hosts, the God of Israel: I am going to bring such disaster upon this place that the ears of everyone who hears of it will tingle. 4Because the people have forsaken me, and have profaned this place by making offerings in it to other gods whom neither they nor their ancestors nor the kings of Judah have known, and because they have filled this place with the blood of the innocent, 5and gone on building the high places of Baal to burn their children in the fire as burnt offerings to Baal, which I did not command or decree, nor did it enter my mind; 6therefore the days are surely coming, says the Lord, when this place shall no more be called Topheth, or the valley of the son of Hinnom, but the valley of Slaughter. 7And in this place I

o Cn: Heb *of the field*   p Cn: Heb *foreign*   q Cn: Heb *Are . . . plucked up?*   r Gk Syr Vg: Heb *they made them stumble*   s Heb *strike him with the tongue*   t Syr Tg Compare Gk: Heb lacks *take with you*

will make void the plans of Judah and Jerusalem, and will make them fall by the sword before their enemies, and by the hand of those who seek their life. I will give their dead bodies for food to the birds of the air and to the wild animals of the earth. 8 And I will make this city a horror, a thing to be hissed at; everyone who passes by it will be horrified and will hiss because of all its disasters. 9 And I will make them eat the flesh of their sons and the flesh of their daughters, and all shall eat the flesh of their neighbors in the siege, and in the distress with which their enemies and those who seek their life afflict them.

10 Then you shall break the jug in the sight of those who go with you, 11 and shall say to them: Thus says the LORD of hosts: So will I break this people and this city, as one breaks a potter's vessel, so that it can never be mended. In Topheth they shall bury until there is no more room to bury. 12 Thus will I do to this place, says the LORD, and to its inhabitants, making this city like Topheth. 13 And the houses of Jerusalem and the houses of the kings of Judah shall be defiled like the place of Topheth—all the houses upon whose roofs offerings have been made to the whole host of heaven, and libations have been poured out to other gods.

14 When Jeremiah came from Topheth, where the LORD had sent him to prophesy, he stood in the court of the LORD's house and said to all the people: 15 Thus says the LORD of hosts, the God of Israel: I am now bringing upon this city and upon all its towns all the disaster that I have pronounced against it, because they have stiffened their necks, refusing to hear my words.

Jeremiah Persecuted by Pashhur

20 Now the priest Pashhur son of Immer, who was chief officer in the house of the LORD, heard Jeremiah prophesying these things. 2 Then Pashhur struck the prophet Jeremiah, and put him in the stocks that were in the upper Benjamin Gate of the house of the LORD. 3 The next morning when Pashhur released Jeremiah from the stocks, Jeremiah said to him, The LORD has named you not Pashhur but "Terror-

all-around." 4 For thus says the LORD: I am making you a terror to yourself and to all your friends; and they shall fall by the sword of their enemies while you look on. And I will give all Judah into the hand of the king of Babylon; he shall carry them captive to Babylon, and shall kill them with the sword. 5 I will give all the wealth of this city, all its gains, all its prized belongings, and all the treasures of the kings of Judah into the hand of their enemies, who shall plunder them, and seize them, and carry them to Babylon. 6 And you, Pashhur, and all who live in your house, shall go into captivity, and to Babylon you shall go; there you shall die, and there you shall be buried, you and all your friends, to whom you have prophesied falsely.

Jeremiah Denounces His Persecutors

7 O LORD, you have enticed me,
   and I was enticed;
you have overpowered me,
   and you have prevailed.
I have become a laughingstock all
   day long;
   everyone mocks me.
8 For whenever I speak, I must cry
   out,
   I must shout, "Violence and
      destruction!"
For the word of the LORD has
   become for me
   a reproach and derision all day
      long.
9 If I say, "I will not mention him,
   or speak any more in his name,"
then within me there is something
   like a burning fire
   shut up in my bones;
I am weary with holding it in,
   and I cannot.
10 For I hear many whispering:
   "Terror is all around!
Denounce him! Let us denounce
      him!"
   All my close friends
   are watching for me to stumble.
"Perhaps he can be enticed,
   and we can prevail against him,
   and take our revenge on him."
11 But the LORD is with me like a
   dread warrior;

therefore my persecutors will
    stumble,
and they will not prevail.
They will be greatly shamed,
    for they will not succeed.
Their eternal dishonor
    will never be forgotten.
12 O LORD of hosts, you test the
        righteous,
    you see the heart and the mind;
let me see your retribution upon
        them,
    for to you I have committed my
        cause.

13 Sing to the LORD;
        praise the LORD!
For he has delivered the life of the
        needy
    from the hands of evildoers.

14 Cursed be the day
        on which I was born!
The day when my mother bore me,
        let it not be blessed!
15 Cursed be the man
        who brought the news to my
        father, saying,
    "A child is born to you, a son,"
        making him very glad.
16 Let that man be like the cities
        that the LORD overthrew without
        pity;
    let him hear a cry in the morning
        and an alarm at noon,
17 because he did not kill me in the
        womb;
    so my mother would have been
        my grave,
        and her womb forever great.
18 Why did I come forth from the
        womb
    to see toil and sorrow,
        and spend my days in shame?

Jerusalem Will Fall to Nebuchadrezzar

21 This is the word that came to
Jeremiah from the LORD,
when King Zedekiah sent to him Pashhur son of Malchiah and the priest
Zephaniah son of Maaseiah, saying,
2 "Please inquire of the LORD on our
behalf, for King Nebuchadrezzar of Babylon is making war against us; perhaps
the LORD will perform a wonderful deed

for us, as he has often done, and will
make him withdraw from us."
3 Then Jeremiah said to them: 4 Thus
you shall say to Zedekiah: Thus says the
LORD, the God of Israel: I am going to
turn back the weapons of war that are in
your hands and with which you are
fighting against the king of Babylon and
against the Chaldeans who are besieging
you outside the walls; and I will bring
them together into the center of this
city. 5 I myself will fight against you with
outstretched hand and mighty arm, in
anger, in fury, and in great wrath. 6 And I
will strike down the inhabitants of this
city, both human beings and animals;
they shall die of a great pestilence.
7 Afterward, says the LORD, I will give
King Zedekiah of Judah, and his servants, and the people in this city—those
who survive the pestilence, sword, and
famine—into the hands of King Nebuchadrezzar of Babylon, into the hands
of their enemies, into the hands of those
who seek their lives. He shall strike
them down with the edge of the sword;
he shall not pity them, or spare them, or
have compassion.
8 And to this people you shall say:
Thus says the LORD: See, I am setting
before you the way of life and the way of
death. 9 Those who stay in this city shall
die by the sword, by famine, and by
pestilence; but those who go out and
surrender to the Chaldeans who are
besieging you shall live and shall have
their lives as a prize of war. 10 For I have
set my face against this city for evil and
not for good, says the LORD: it shall be
given into the hands of the king of Babylon, and he shall burn it with fire.

Message to the House of David

11 To the house of the king of Judah
say: Hear the word of the LORD,
12 O house of David! Thus says the LORD:
    Execute justice in the morning,
        and deliver from the hand of the
        oppressor
    anyone who has been robbed,
        or else my wrath will go forth like
        fire,
        and burn, with no one to quench
        it,
        because of your evil doings.

13   See, I am against you, O inhabitant
        of the valley,
      O rock of the plain,
                  says the LORD;
      you who say, "Who can come
        down against us,
        or who can enter our places of
          refuge?"
14   I will punish you according to the
        fruit of your doings,
                  says the LORD;
      I will kindle a fire in its forest,
        and it shall devour all that is
          around it.

Exhortation to Repent

22 Thus says the LORD: Go down to the house of the king of Judah, and speak there this word, ²and say: Hear the word of the LORD, O King of Judah sitting on the throne of David—you, and your servants, and your people who enter these gates. ³Thus says the LORD: Act with justice and righteousness, and deliver from the hand of the oppressor anyone who has been robbed. And do no wrong or violence to the alien, the orphan, and the widow, or shed innocent blood in this place. ⁴For if you will indeed obey this word, then through the gates of this house shall enter kings who sit on the throne of David, riding in chariots and on horses, they, and their servants, and their people. ⁵But if you will not heed these words, I swear by myself, says the LORD, that this house shall become a desolation. ⁶For thus says the LORD concerning the house of the king of Judah:
      You are like Gilead to me,
        like the summit of Lebanon;
      but I swear that I will make you a
        desert,
        an uninhabited city.ᵘ
7   I will prepare destroyers against
        you,
      all with their weapons;
      they shall cut down your choicest
        cedars
      and cast them into the fire.

8 And many nations will pass by this city, and all of them will say one to another, "Why has the LORD dealt in this way with that great city?" ⁹And they will answer, "Because they abandoned the covenant of the LORD their God, and worshiped other gods and served them."

10   Do not weep for him who is dead,
        nor bemoan him;
      weep rather for him who goes
        away,
        for he shall return no more
          to see his native land.

Message to the Sons of Josiah

11 For thus says the LORD concerning Shallum son of King Josiah of Judah, who succeeded his father Josiah, and who went away from this place: He shall return here no more, ¹²but in the place where they have carried him captive he shall die, and he shall never see this land again.

13   Woe to him who builds his house
        by unrighteousness,
      and his upper rooms by injustice;
      who makes his neighbors work for
        nothing,
        and does not give them their
          wages;
14   who says, "I will build myself a
        spacious house
      with large upper rooms,"
      and who cuts out windows for it,
        paneling it with cedar,
        and painting it with vermilion.
15   Are you a king
        because you compete in cedar?
      Did not your father eat and drink
        and do justice and righteousness?
        Then it was well with him.
16   He judged the cause of the poor and
        needy;
        then it was well.
      Is not this to know me?
        says the LORD.
17   But your eyes and heart
        are only on your dishonest gain,
      for shedding innocent blood,
        and for practicing oppression and
          violence.

18 Therefore thus says the LORD concerning King Jehoiakim son of Josiah of Judah:
      They shall not lament for him,
        saying,
      "Alas, my brother!" or "Alas,
        sister!"

u Cn: Heb *uninhabited cities*

They shall not lament for him,
saying,
"Alas, lord!" or "Alas, his
majesty!"
19 With the burial of a donkey he
shall be buried—
dragged off and thrown out
beyond the gates of
Jerusalem.

20 Go up to Lebanon, and cry out,
and lift up your voice in Bashan;
cry out from Abarim,
for all your lovers are crushed.
21 I spoke to you in your prosperity,
but you said, "I will not listen."
This has been your way from your
youth,
for you have not obeyed my
voice.
22 The wind shall shepherd all your
shepherds,
and your lovers shall go into
captivity;
then you will be ashamed and
dismayed
because of all your wickedness.
23 O inhabitant of Lebanon,
nested among the cedars,
how you will groan^v when pangs
come upon you,
pain as of a woman in labor!

Judgment on Coniah (Jehoiachin)

24 As I live, says the LORD, even if
King Coniah son of Jehoiakim of Judah
were the signet ring on my right hand,
even from there I would tear you off
25 and give you into the hands of those
who seek your life, into the hands of
those of whom you are afraid, even into
the hands of King Nebuchadrezzar of
Babylon and into the hands of the
Chaldeans. 26 I will hurl you and the
mother who bore you into another
country, where you were not born, and
there you shall die. 27 But they shall not
return to the land to which they long to
return.
28 Is this man Coniah a despised
broken pot,
a vessel no one wants?
Why are he and his offspring hurled
out

and cast away in a land that they
do not know?
29 O land, land, land,
hear the word of the LORD!
30 Thus says the LORD:
Record this man as childless,
a man who shall not succeed in
his days;
for none of his offspring shall
succeed
in sitting on the throne of David,
and ruling again in Judah.

Restoration after Exile

23 Woe to the shepherds who
destroy and scatter the sheep
of my pasture! says the LORD. 2 Therefore
thus says the LORD, the God of Israel,
concerning the shepherds who shepherd
my people: It is you who have scattered
my flock, and have driven them away,
and you have not attended to them. So I
will attend to you for your evil doings,
says the LORD. 3 Then I myself will gather the remnant of my flock out of all the
lands where I have driven them, and I
will bring them back to their fold, and
they shall be fruitful and multiply. 4 I
will raise up shepherds over them who
will shepherd them, and they shall not
fear any longer, or be dismayed, nor
shall any be missing, says the LORD.

The Righteous Branch of David

5 The days are surely coming, says
the LORD, when I will raise up for David
a righteous Branch, and he shall reign as
king and deal wisely, and shall execute
justice and righteousness in the land. 6 In
his days Judah will be saved and Israel
will live in safety. And this is the name
by which he will be called: "The LORD is
our righteousness."
7 Therefore, the days are surely coming, says the LORD, when it shall no
longer be said, "As the LORD lives who
brought the people of Israel up out of the
land of Egypt," 8 but "As the LORD lives
who brought out and led the offspring of
the house of Israel out of the land of the
north and out of all the lands where he^w
had driven them." Then they shall live
in their own land.

v Gk Vg Syr: Heb *will be pitied*   w Gk: Heb *I*

False Prophets of Hope Denounced

9 Concerning the prophets:
My heart is crushed within me,
   all my bones shake;
I have become like a drunkard,
   like one overcome by wine,
because of the LORD
   and because of his holy words.
10 For the land is full of adulterers;
      because of the curse the land
         mourns,
      and the pastures of the
         wilderness are dried up.
   Their course has been evil,
      and their might is not right.
11 Both prophet and priest are
         ungodly;
      even in my house I have found
         their wickedness,
                     says the LORD.
12 Therefore their way shall be to
         them
      like slippery paths in the
         darkness,
      into which they shall be driven
         and fall;
   for I will bring disaster upon them
      in the year of their punishment,
                     says the LORD.
13 In the prophets of Samaria
      I saw a disgusting thing:
   they prophesied by Baal
      and led my people Israel astray.
14 But in the prophets of Jerusalem
      I have seen a more shocking
         thing:
   they commit adultery and walk in
         lies;
      they strengthen the hands of
         evildoers,
      so that no one turns from
         wickedness;
   all of them have become like
         Sodom to me,
      and its inhabitants like
         Gomorrah.
15 Therefore thus says the LORD of
         hosts concerning the
         prophets:
   "I am going to make them eat
         wormwood,
      and give them poisoned water to
         drink;
   for from the prophets of Jerusalem
      ungodliness has spread
         throughout the land."

16 Thus says the LORD of hosts: Do not listen to the words of the prophets who prophesy to you; they are deluding you. They speak visions of their own minds, not from the mouth of the LORD. 17They keep saying to those who despise the word of the LORD, "It shall be well with you"; and to all who stubbornly follow their own stubborn hearts, they say, "No calamity shall come upon you."

18 For who has stood in the council of
         the LORD
      so as to see and to hear his word?
   Who has given heed to his word
      so as to proclaim it?
19 Look, the storm of the LORD!
   Wrath has gone forth,
      a whirling tempest;
   it will burst upon the head of the
         wicked.
20 The anger of the LORD will not turn
         back
      until he has executed and
         accomplished
      the intents of his mind.
   In the latter days you will
      understand it clearly.

21 I did not send the prophets,
      yet they ran;
   I did not speak to them,
      yet they prophesied.
22 But if they had stood in my
         council,
      then they would have proclaimed
         my words to my people,
   and they would have turned them
         from their evil way,
      and from the evil of their doings.

23 Am I a God near by, says the LORD, and not a God far off? 24Who can hide in secret places so that I cannot see them? says the LORD. Do I not fill heaven and earth? says the LORD. 25I have heard what the prophets have said who prophesy lies in my name, saying, "I have dreamed, I have dreamed!" 26How long? Will the hearts of the prophets ever turn back—those who prophesy lies, and who prophesy the deceit of their own heart? 27They plan to make my people forget my name by their dreams that they tell one another, just as their ancestors forgot my name for

Baal. 28Let the prophet who has a dream tell the dream, but let the one who has my word speak my word faithfully. What has straw in common with wheat? says the LORD. 29Is not my word like fire, says the LORD, and like a hammer that breaks a rock in pieces? 30See, therefore, I am against the prophets, says the LORD, who steal my words from one another. 31See, I am against the prophets, says the LORD, who use their own tongues and say, "Says the LORD." 32See, I am against those who prophesy lying dreams, says the LORD, and who tell them, and who lead my people astray by their lies and their recklessness, when I did not send them or appoint them; so they do not profit this people at all, says the LORD.

33 When this people, or a prophet, or a priest asks you, "What is the burden of the LORD?" you shall say to them, "You are the burden,x and I will cast you off, says the LORD." 34And as for the prophet, priest, or the people who say, "The burden of the LORD," I will punish them and their households. 35Thus shall you say to one another, among yourselves, "What has the LORD answered?" or "What has the LORD spoken?" 36But "the burden of the LORD" you shall mention no more, for the burden is everyone's own word, and so you pervert the words of the living God, the LORD of hosts, our God. 37Thus you shall ask the prophet, "What has the LORD answered you?" or "What has the LORD spoken?" 38But if you say, "the burden of the LORD," thus says the LORD: Because you have said these words, "the burden of the LORD," when I sent to you, saying, You shall not say, "the burden of the LORD," 39therefore, I will surely lift you upy and cast you away from my presence, you and the city that I gave to you and your ancestors. 40And I will bring upon you everlasting disgrace and perpetual shame, which shall not be forgotten.

The Good and the Bad Figs

24 The LORD showed me two baskets of figs placed before the temple of the LORD. This was after King Nebuchadrezzar of Babylon had taken into exile from Jerusalem King Jeconiah son of Jehoiakim of Judah, together with the officials of Judah, the artisans, and the smiths, and had brought them to Babylon. 2One basket had very good figs, like first-ripe figs, but the other basket had very bad figs, so bad that they could not be eaten. 3And the LORD said to me, "What do you see, Jeremiah?" I said, "Figs, the good figs very good, and the bad figs very bad, so bad that they cannot be eaten."

4 Then the word of the LORD came to me: 5Thus says the LORD, the God of Israel: Like these good figs, so I will regard as good the exiles from Judah, whom I have sent away from this place to the land of the Chaldeans. 6I will set my eyes upon them for good, and I will bring them back to this land. I will build them up, and not tear them down; I will plant them, and not pluck them up. 7I will give them a heart to know that I am the LORD; and they shall be my people and I will be their God, for they shall return to me with their whole heart.

8 But thus says the LORD: Like the bad figs that are so bad they cannot be eaten, so will I treat King Zedekiah of Judah, his officials, the remnant of Jerusalem who remain in this land, and those who live in the land of Egypt. 9I will make them a horror, an evil thing, to all the kingdoms of the earth—a disgrace, a byword, a taunt, and a curse in all the places where I shall drive them. 10And I will send sword, famine, and pestilence upon them, until they are utterly destroyed from the land that I gave to them and their ancestors.

The Babylonian Captivity Foretold

25 The word that came to Jeremiah concerning all the people of Judah, in the fourth year of King Jehoiakim son of Josiah of Judah (that was the first year of King Nebuchadrezzar of Babylon), 2which the prophet Jeremiah spoke to all the people of Judah and all the inhabitants of Jerusalem: 3For twenty-three years, from the thirteenth year of King Josiah son of Amon of Judah, to this day, the word of the LORD has come to me, and I have spoken persistently to you, but you have not listened. 4And though the LORD persistent-

x Gk Vg: Heb What burden   y Heb Mss Gk Vg: MT forget you

ly sent you all his servants the prophets, you have neither listened nor inclined your ears to hear [5]when they said, "Turn now, everyone of you, from your evil way and wicked doings, and you will remain upon the land that the LORD has given to you and your ancestors from of old and forever; [6]do not go after other gods to serve and worship them, and do not provoke me to anger with the work of your hands. Then I will do you no harm." [7]Yet you did not listen to me, says the LORD, and so you have provoked me to anger with the work of your hands to your own harm.

8 Therefore thus says the LORD of hosts: Because you have not obeyed my words, [9]I am going to send for all the tribes of the north, says the LORD, even for King Nebuchadrezzar of Babylon, my servant, and I will bring them against this land and its inhabitants, and against all these nations around; I will utterly destroy them, and make them an object of horror and of hissing, and an everlasting disgrace.[z] [10]And I will banish from them the sound of mirth and the sound of gladness, the voice of the bridegroom and the voice of the bride, the sound of the millstones and the light of the lamp. [11]This whole land shall become a ruin and a waste, and these nations shall serve the king of Babylon seventy years. [12]Then after seventy years are completed, I will punish the king of Babylon and that nation, the land of the Chaldeans, for their iniquity, says the LORD, making the land an everlasting waste. [13]I will bring upon that land all the words that I have uttered against it, everything written in this book, which Jeremiah prophesied against all the nations. [14]For many nations and great kings shall make slaves of them also; and I will repay them according to their deeds and the work of their hands.

The Cup of God's Wrath

15 For thus the LORD, the God of Israel, said to me: Take from my hand this cup of the wine of wrath, and make all the nations to whom I send you drink it. [16]They shall drink and stagger and go out of their minds because of the sword that I am sending among them.

17 So I took the cup from the LORD's hand, and made all the nations to whom the LORD sent me drink it: [18]Jerusalem and the towns of Judah, its kings and officials, to make them a desolation and a waste, an object of hissing and of cursing, as they are today; [19]Pharaoh king of Egypt, his servants, his officials, and all his people; [20]all the mixed people;[a] all the kings of the land of Uz; all the kings of the land of the Philistines—Ashkelon, Gaza, Ekron, and the remnant of Ashdod; [21]Edom, Moab, and the Ammonites; [22]all the kings of Tyre, all the kings of Sidon, and the kings of the coastland across the sea; [23]Dedan, Tema, Buz, and all who have shaven temples; [24]all the kings of Arabia and all the kings of the mixed peoples[a] that live in the desert; [25]all the kings of Zimri, all the kings of Elam, and all the kings of Media; [26]all the kings of the north, far and near, one after another, and all the kingdoms of the world that are on the face of the earth. And after them the king of Sheshach[b] shall drink.

27 Then you shall say to them, Thus says the LORD of hosts, the God of Israel: Drink, get drunk and vomit, fall and rise no more, because of the sword that I am sending among you.

28 And if they refuse to accept the cup from your hand to drink, then you shall say to them: Thus says the LORD of hosts: You must drink! [29]See, I am beginning to bring disaster on the city that is called by my name, and how can you possibly avoid punishment? You shall not go unpunished, for I am summoning a sword against all the inhabitants of the earth, says the LORD of hosts.

30 You, therefore, shall prophesy against them all these words, and say to them:

The LORD will roar from on high,
and from his holy habitation
utter his voice;
he will roar mightily against his
fold,
and shout, like those who tread
grapes,

---

z Gk Compare Syr: Heb *and everlasting desolations* cryptogram for *Babel*, Babylon   a Meaning of Heb uncertain   b *Sheshach* is a against all the inhabitants of the earth.

31   The clamor will resound to the
        ends of the earth,
      for the LORD has an indictment
        against the nations;
      he is entering into judgment with
        all flesh,
      and the guilty he will put to the
        sword,
                            says the LORD.

32   Thus says the LORD of hosts:
      See, disaster is spreading
        from nation to nation,
      and a great tempest is stirring
        from the farthest parts of the
        earth!

33 Those slain by the LORD on that day shall extend from one end of the earth to the other. They shall not be lamented, or gathered, or buried; they shall become dung on the surface of the ground.

34   Wail, you shepherds, and cry out;
        roll in ashes, you lords of the
        flock,
      for the days of your slaughter have
        come—and your
        dispersions,c
      and you shall fall like a choice
        vessel.

35   Flight shall fail the shepherds,
      and there shall be no escape for
        the lords of the flock.

36   Hark! the cry of the shepherds,
      and the wail of the lords of the
        flock!
      For the LORD is despoiling their
        pasture,

37   and the peaceful folds are
        devastated,
      because of the fierce anger of the
        LORD.

38   Like a lion he has left his covert;
      for their land has become a waste
      because of the cruel sword,
      and because of his fierce anger.

Jeremiah's Prophecies in the Temple

26 At the beginning of the reign of King Jehoiakim son of Josiah of Judah, this word came from the LORD: 2Thus says the LORD: Stand in the court of the LORD's house, and speak to all the cities of Judah that come to worship in the house of the LORD; speak to them all the words that I command you; do not hold back a word. 3It may be that they will listen, all of them, and will turn from their evil way, that I may change my mind about the disaster that I intend to bring on them because of their evil doings. 4You shall say to them: Thus says the LORD: If you will not listen to me, to walk in my law that I have set before you, 5and to heed the words of my servants the prophets whom I send to you urgently—though you have not heeded— 6then I will make this house like Shiloh, and I will make this city a curse for all the nations of the earth.

7 The priests and the prophets and all the people heard Jeremiah speaking these words in the house of the LORD. 8And when Jeremiah had finished speaking all that the LORD had commanded him to speak to all the people, then the priests and the prophets and all the people laid hold of him, saying, "You shall die! 9Why have you prophesied in the name of the LORD, saying, 'This house shall be like Shiloh, and this city shall be desolate, without inhabitant'?" And all the people gathered around Jeremiah in the house of the LORD.

10 When the officials of Judah heard these things, they came up from the king's house to the house of the LORD and took their seat in the entry of the New Gate of the house of the LORD. 11Then the priests and the prophets said to the officials and to all the people, "This man deserves the sentence of death because he has prophesied against this city, as you have heard with your own ears."

12 Then Jeremiah spoke to all the officials and all the people, saying, "It is the LORD who sent me to prophesy against this house and this city all the words you have heard. 13Now therefore amend your ways and your doings, and obey the voice of the LORD your God, and the LORD will change his mind about the disaster that he has pronounced against you. 14But as for me, here I am in your hands. Do with me as seems good and right to you. 15Only know for certain that if you put me to death, you will be

c Meaning of Heb uncertain

bringing innocent blood upon yourselves and upon this city and its inhabitants, for in truth the LORD sent me to you to speak all these words in your ears."

16 Then the officials and all the people said to the priests and the prophets, "This man does not deserve the sentence of death, for he has spoken to us in the name of the LORD our God." 17And some of the elders of the land arose and said to all the assembled people, 18"Micah of Moresheth, who prophesied during the days of King Hezekiah of Judah, said to all the people of Judah: 'Thus says the LORD of hosts,

Zion shall be plowed as a field;
Jerusalem shall become a heap of
    ruins,
and the mountain of the house a
    wooded height.'

19Did King Hezekiah of Judah and all Judah actually put him to death? Did he not fear the LORD and entreat the favor of the LORD, and did not the LORD change his mind about the disaster that he had pronounced against them? But we are about to bring great disaster on ourselves!"

20 There was another man prophesying in the name of the LORD, Uriah son of Shemaiah from Kiriath-jearim. He prophesied against this city and against this land in words exactly like those of Jeremiah. 21And when King Jehoiakim, with all his warriors and all the officials, heard his words, the king sought to put him to death; but when Uriah heard of it, he was afraid and fled and escaped to Egypt. 22Then King Jehoiakim sent[d] Elnathan son of Achbor and men with him to Egypt, 23and they took Uriah from Egypt and brought him to King Jehoiakim, who struck him down with the sword and threw his dead body into the burial place of the common people.

24 But the hand of Ahikam son of Shaphan was with Jeremiah so that he was not given over into the hands of the people to be put to death.

The Sign of the Yoke

27 In the beginning of the reign of King Zedekiah[e] son of Josiah of Judah, this word came to Jeremiah

from the LORD. 2Thus the LORD said to me: Make yourself a yoke of straps and bars, and put them on your neck. 3Send word[f] to the king of Edom, the king of Moab, the king of the Ammonites, the king of Tyre, and the king of Sidon by the hand of the envoys who have come to Jerusalem to King Zedekiah of Judah. 4Give them this charge for their masters: Thus says the LORD of hosts, the God of Israel: This is what you shall say to your masters: 5It is I who by my great power and my outstretched arm have made the earth, with the people and animals that are on the earth, and I give it to whomever I please. 6Now I have given all these lands into the hand of King Nebuchadnezzar of Babylon, my servant, and I have given him even the wild animals of the field to serve him. 7All the nations shall serve him and his son and his grandson, until the time of his own land comes; then many nations and great kings shall make him their slave.

8 But if any nation or kingdom will not serve this king, Nebuchadnezzar of Babylon, and put its neck under the yoke of the king of Babylon, then I will punish that nation with the sword, with famine, and with pestilence, says the LORD, until I have completed its[g] destruction by his hand. 9You, therefore, must not listen to your prophets, your diviners, your dreamers,[h] your soothsayers, or your sorcerers, who are saying to you, "You shall not serve the king of Babylon." 10For they are prophesying a lie to you, with the result that you will be removed far from your land; I will drive you out, and you will perish. 11But any nation that will bring its neck under the yoke of the king of Babylon and serve him, I will leave on its own land, says the LORD, to till it and live there.

12 I spoke to King Zedekiah of Judah in the same way: Bring your necks under the yoke of the king of Babylon, and serve him and his people, and live. 13Why should you and your people die by the sword, by famine, and by pestilence, as the LORD has spoken concerning any nation that will not serve the king of Babylon? 14Do not listen to the

---

d Heb adds *men to Egypt*   *e* Another reading is *Jehoiakim*   *f* Cn: Heb *send them*   *g* Heb *their*
h Gk Syr Vg: Heb *dreams*

words of the prophets who are telling you not to serve the king of Babylon, for they are prophesying a lie to you. 15I have not sent them, says the LORD, but they are prophesying falsely in my name, with the result that I will drive you out and you will perish, you and the prophets who are prophesying to you.

16 Then I spoke to the priests and to all this people, saying, Thus says the LORD: Do not listen to the words of your prophets who are prophesying to you, saying, "The vessels of the LORD's house will soon be brought back from Babylon," for they are prophesying a lie to you. 17Do not listen to them; serve the king of Babylon and live. Why should this city become a desolation? 18If indeed they are prophets, and if the word of the LORD is with them, then let them intercede with the LORD of hosts, that the vessels left in the house of the LORD, in the house of the king of Judah, and in Jerusalem may not go to Babylon. 19For thus says the LORD of hosts concerning the pillars, the sea, the stands, and the rest of the vessels that are left in this city, 20which King Nebuchadnezzar of Babylon did not take away when he took into exile from Jerusalem to Babylon King Jeconiah son of Jehoiakim of Judah, and all the nobles of Judah and Jerusalem— 21thus says the LORD of hosts, the God of Israel, concerning the vessels left in the house of the LORD, in the house of the king of Judah, and in Jerusalem: 22They shall be carried to Babylon, and there they shall stay, until the day when I give attention to them, says the LORD. Then I will bring them up and restore them to this place.

Hananiah Opposes Jeremiah and Dies

28 In that same year, at the beginning of the reign of King Zedekiah of Judah, in the fifth month of the fourth year, the prophet Hananiah son of Azzur, from Gibeon, spoke to me in the house of the LORD, in the presence of the priests and all the people, saying, 2"Thus says the LORD of hosts, the God of Israel: I have broken the yoke of the king of Babylon. 3Within two years I will bring back to this place all the vessels of the LORD's house, which King Nebuchadnezzar of Babylon took away from this place and carried to Babylon. 4I will also bring back to this place King Jeconiah son of Jehoiakim of Judah, and all the exiles from Judah who went to Babylon, says the LORD, for I will break the yoke of the king of Babylon."

5 Then the prophet Jeremiah spoke to the prophet Hananiah in the presence of the priests and all the people who were standing in the house of the LORD; 6and the prophet Jeremiah said, "Amen! May the LORD do so; may the LORD fulfill the words that you have prophesied, and bring back to this place from Babylon the vessels of the house of the LORD, and all the exiles. 7But listen now to this word that I speak in your hearing and in the hearing of all the people. 8The prophets who preceded you and me from ancient times prophesied war, famine, and pestilence against many countries and great kingdoms. 9As for the prophet who prophesies peace, when the word of that prophet comes true, then it will be known that the LORD has truly sent the prophet."

10 Then the prophet Hananiah took the yoke from the neck of the prophet Jeremiah, and broke it. 11And Hananiah spoke in the presence of all the people, saying, "Thus says the LORD: This is how I will break the yoke of King Nebuchadnezzar of Babylon from the neck of all the nations within two years." At this, the prophet Jeremiah went his way.

12 Sometime after the prophet Hananiah had broken the yoke from the neck of the prophet Jeremiah, the word of the LORD came to Jeremiah: 13Go, tell Hananiah, Thus says the LORD: You have broken wooden bars only to forge iron bars in place of them! 14For thus says the LORD of hosts, the God of Israel: I have put an iron yoke on the neck of all these nations so that they may serve King Nebuchadnezzar of Babylon, and they shall indeed serve him; I have even given him the wild animals. 15And the prophet Jeremiah said to the prophet Hananiah, "Listen, Hananiah, the LORD has not sent you, and you made this people trust in a lie. 16Therefore thus says the LORD: I am going to send you off the face of the earth. Within this year you

will be dead, because you have spoken rebellion against the LORD."

17 In that same year, in the seventh month, the prophet Hananiah died.

Jeremiah's Letter to the Exiles in Babylon

29 These are the words of the letter that the prophet Jeremiah sent from Jerusalem to the remaining elders among the exiles, and to the priests, the prophets, and all the people, whom Nebuchadnezzar had taken into exile from Jerusalem to Babylon. 2This was after King Jeconiah, and the queen mother, the court officials, the leaders of Judah and Jerusalem, the artisans, and the smiths had departed from Jerusalem. 3The letter was sent by the hand of Elasah son of Shaphan and Gemariah son of Hilkiah, whom King Zedekiah of Judah sent to Babylon to King Nebuchadnezzar of Babylon. It said: 4Thus says the LORD of hosts, the God of Israel, to all the exiles whom I have sent into exile from Jerusalem to Babylon: 5Build houses and live in them; plant gardens and eat what they produce. 6Take wives and have sons and daughters; take wives for your sons, and give your daughters in marriage, that they may bear sons and daughters; multiply there, and do not decrease. 7But seek the welfare of the city where I have sent you into exile, and pray to the LORD on its behalf, for in its welfare you will find your welfare. 8For thus says the LORD of hosts, the God of Israel: Do not let the prophets and the diviners who are among you deceive you, and do not listen to the dreams that they dream,*i* 9for it is a lie that they are prophesying to you in my name; I did not send them, says the LORD.

10 For thus says the LORD: Only when Babylon's seventy years are completed will I visit you, and I will fulfill to you my promise and bring you back to this place. 11For surely I know the plans I have for you, says the LORD, plans for your welfare and not for harm, to give you a future with hope. 12Then when you call upon me and come and pray to me, I will hear you. 13When you search for me, you will find me; if you seek me with all your heart, 14I will let you find

me, says the LORD, and I will restore your fortunes and gather you from all the nations and all the places where I have driven you, says the LORD, and I will bring you back to the place from which I sent you into exile.

15 Because you have said, "The LORD has raised up prophets for us in Babylon,"— 16Thus says the LORD concerning the king who sits on the throne of David, and concerning all the people who live in this city, your kinsfolk who did not go out with you into exile: 17Thus says the LORD of hosts, I am going to let loose on them sword, famine, and pestilence, and I will make them like rotten figs that are so bad they cannot be eaten. 18I will pursue them with the sword, with famine, and with pestilence, and will make them a horror to all the kingdoms of the earth, to be an object of cursing, and horror, and hissing, and a derision among all the nations where I have driven them, 19because they did not heed my words, says the LORD, when I persistently sent to you my servants the prophets, but they*j* would not listen, says the LORD. 20But now, all you exiles whom I sent away from Jerusalem to Babylon, hear the word of the LORD: 21Thus says the LORD of hosts, the God of Israel, concerning Ahab son of Kolaiah and Zedekiah son of Maaseiah, who are prophesying a lie to you in my name: I am going to deliver them into the hand of King Nebuchadrezzar of Babylon, and he shall kill them before your eyes. 22And on account of them this curse shall be used by all the exiles from Judah in Babylon: "The LORD make you like Zedekiah and Ahab, whom the king of Babylon roasted in the fire," 23because they have perpetrated outrage in Israel and have committed adultery with their neighbors' wives, and have spoken in my name lying words that I did not command them; I am the one who knows and bears witness, says the LORD.

The Letter of Shemaiah

24 To Shemaiah of Nehelam you shall say: 25Thus says the LORD of hosts, the God of Israel: In your own name you sent a letter to all the people who are in Jerusalem, and to the priest Zephaniah

---

i Cn: Heb *your dreams that you cause to dream*   *j* Syr: Heb *you*

You Will Seek Me and Find Me

Mozarabic Sacramentary

VERSE: Jeremiah 29.11–12   **PASSAGE:** Jeremiah 29.10–14

For Hope

ord, when we think only of our own wants and desires, we are impatient to have them satisfied, yet in our hearts we know that such satisfaction will crumble to dust. Give us that spirit of hope which can enable us to want what you want, and to wait patiently on your time, in the knowledge that in you alone comes true and lasting pleasure.

For Love

O Lord, you have brought all your faithful people into a single, universal family, stretching across heaven and earth. Bind us together with a spiritual love which is stronger than any human love, that in serving one another we may neither count the cost nor seek reward, but think only of the common good.

For Peace

O God, through the death of your Son you reconciled us one to another, drawing us together in the bond of peace. In times of trouble and adversity, may your peace sustain us, calming our fretful and anxious hearts, and saving us from all hateful and violent activities.

For Purity

Make us, O Lord, flourish like pure, white lilies in the courts of your house, giving forth the sweet fragrance of your love to all who pass.

For Mercy

O God, in revealing to us the perfect spiritual beauty of your Son, you have shown the grotesque ugliness of our depravity, and so filled us with remorse. We beg you, Lord, to reach down to us in your mercy, re-creating us in the image of your Son, that we may be fit to live with him in your heavenly kingdom.

ADDITIONAL SCRIPTURE READING:
Isaiah 55.6–7; Amos 5.4–6; Luke 11.9–10

Go to page 900 for your next devotional reading.

son of Maaseiah, and to all the priests, saying, 26The LORD himself has made you priest instead of the priest Jehoiada, so that there may be officers in the house of the LORD to control any madman who plays the prophet, to put him in the stocks and the collar. 27So now why have you not rebuked Jeremiah of Anathoth who plays the prophet for you? 28For he has actually sent to us in Babylon, saying, "It will be a long time; build houses and live in them, and plant gardens and eat what they produce."

29 The priest Zephaniah read this letter in the hearing of the prophet Jeremiah. 30Then the word of the LORD came to Jeremiah: 31Send to all the exiles, saying, Thus says the LORD concerning Shemaiah of Nehelam: Because Shemaiah has prophesied to you, though I did not send him, and has led you to trust in a lie, 32therefore thus says the LORD: I am going to punish Shemaiah of Nehelam and his descendants; he shall not have anyone living among this people to see[k] the good that I am going to do to my people, says the LORD, for he has spoken rebellion against the LORD.

Restoration Promised for Israel and Judah

30 The word that came to Jeremiah from the LORD: 2Thus says the LORD, the God of Israel: Write in a book all the words that I have spoken to you. 3For the days are surely coming, says the LORD, when I will restore the fortunes of my people, Israel and Judah, says the LORD, and I will bring them back to the land that I gave to their ancestors and they shall take possession of it.

4 These are the words that the LORD spoke concerning Israel and Judah:

5 Thus says the LORD:
We have heard a cry of panic,
    of terror, and no peace.
6 Ask now, and see,
    can a man bear a child?
Why then do I see every man
    with his hands on his loins like a
        woman in labor?
    Why has every face turned pale?
7 Alas! that day is so great
    there is none like it;

it is a time of distress for Jacob;
    yet he shall be rescued from it.
8 On that day, says the LORD of hosts, I will break the yoke from off his[l] neck, and I will burst his[l] bonds, and strangers shall no more make a servant of him. 9But they shall serve the LORD their God and David their king, whom I will raise up for them.

10 But as for you, have no fear, my
        servant Jacob, says the LORD,
    and do not be dismayed, O Israel;
for I am going to save you from far
        away,
    and your offspring from the land
        of their captivity.
Jacob shall return and have quiet
        and ease,
    and no one shall make him
        afraid.
11 For I am with you, says the LORD,
        to save you;
I will make an end of all the
        nations
    among which I scattered you,
    but of you I will not make an
        end.
I will chastise you in just measure,
    and I will by no means leave you
        unpunished.

12 For thus says the LORD:
Your hurt is incurable,
    your wound is grievous.
13 There is no one to uphold your
        cause,
    no medicine for your wound,
    no healing for you.
14 All your lovers have forgotten you;
    they care nothing for you;
for I have dealt you the blow of an
        enemy,
    the punishment of a merciless
        foe,
because your guilt is great,
    because your sins are so
        numerous.
15 Why do you cry out over your hurt?
    Your pain is incurable.
Because your guilt is great,
    because your sins are so
        numerous,
    I have done these things to you.

k Gk: Heb and he shall not see   l Cn: Heb your

WEEKEND

A Rest Prepared for Me
John Wesley

Verse: Psalm 62.1   **Passage:** Psalm 62.1–2

ord, I believe a rest remains,
    To all thy people known;
A rest where pure enjoyment reigns
    And thou art loved alone,

A rest where all our soul's desire
    Is fix'd on things above;
Where doubt and pain and fear expire,
    Cast out by perfect love . . .

Come, O my Saviour, come away!
    Into my soul descend!
No longer from thy creature stay,
    My author and my end!

The bliss thou hast for me prepared,
    No longer be delay'd:
Come, my exceeding great reward,
    For whom I first was made.

Come, Father, Son, and Holy Ghost,
    And seal me thine abode!
Let all I am in thee be lost:
    Let all be lost in God!

ADDITIONAL SCRIPTURE READING:
Isaiah 43.1–3; Lamentations 3.22–23

Go to page 902 for your next devotional reading.

1700   1900

16 Therefore all who devour you shall
    be devoured,
    and all your foes, everyone of
      them, shall go into captivity;
  those who plunder you shall be
    plundered,
    and all who prey on you I will
      make a prey.
17 For I will restore health to you,
    and your wounds I will heal,
                    says the LORD,
  because they have called you an
    outcast:
    "It is Zion; no one cares for her!"

18 Thus says the LORD:
  I am going to restore the fortunes of
    the tents of Jacob,
    and have compassion on his
      dwellings;
  the city shall be rebuilt upon its
    mound,
    and the citadel set on its rightful
      site.
19 Out of them shall come
    thanksgiving,
    and the sound of merrymakers.
  I will make them many, and they
    shall not be few;
    I will make them honored, and
      they shall not be disdained.
20 Their children shall be as of old,
    their congregation shall be
      established before me;
    and I will punish all who oppress
      them.
21 Their prince shall be one of their
    own,
    their ruler shall come from their
      midst;
  I will bring him near, and he shall
    approach me,
    for who would otherwise dare to
      approach me?
                    says the LORD.
22 And you shall be my people,
    and I will be your God.

23 Look, the storm of the LORD!
    Wrath has gone forth,
  a whirling*m* tempest;
    it will burst upon the head of the
      wicked.

24 The fierce anger of the LORD will
    not turn back
    until he has executed and
      accomplished
    the intents of his mind.
  In the latter days you will
    understand this.

The Joyful Return of the Exiles

31 At that time, says the LORD, I will be the God of all the families of Israel, and they shall be my people.
2 Thus says the LORD:
  The people who survived the
    sword
    found grace in the wilderness;
  when Israel sought for rest,
3   the LORD appeared to him*n* from
        far away.*o*
  I have loved you with an
    everlasting love;
    therefore I have continued my
      faithfulness to you.
4 Again I will build you, and you
    shall be built,
    O virgin Israel!
  Again you shall take*p* your
    tambourines,
    and go forth in the dance of the
      merrymakers.
5 Again you shall plant vineyards
    on the mountains of Samaria;
  the planters shall plant,
    and shall enjoy the fruit.
6 For there shall be a day when
    sentinels will call
    in the hill country of Ephraim:
  "Come, let us go up to Zion,
    to the LORD our God."

7 For thus says the LORD:
  Sing aloud with gladness for
    Jacob,
    and raise shouts for the chief of
      the nations;
  proclaim, give praise, and say,
    "Save, O LORD, your people,
    the remnant of Israel."
8 See, I am going to bring them from
    the land of the north,
    and gather them from the
      farthest parts of the earth,

m One Ms: Meaning of MT uncertain   *n* Gk: Heb me   *o* Or to him long ago   *p* Or adorn
yourself with

among them the blind and the lame,
those with child and those in
labor, together;
a great company, they shall
return here.

⁹ With weeping they shall come,
and with consolations⁹ I will
lead them back,
I will let them walk by brooks of
water,

q Gk Compare Vg Tg: Heb *supplications*

MONDAY

A PERSONAL PRAYER FOR LOVINGKINDNESS
John Baillie

VERSE: Jeremiah 31.3   **PASSAGE:** Jeremiah 31.3–4

 God, immortal, eternal, invisible, I remember with gladness and thanksgiving all that thou hast been to this world of men:

Companion of the brave:
Upholder of the loyal:
Light of the wanderer:
Joy of the pilgrim:
Guide of the pioneer:
Helper of laboring men:
Refuge of the broken-hearted:
Deliverer of the oppressed:
Succor of the tempted:
Strength of the victorious:
Ruler of rulers:
Friend of the poor:
Rescuer of the perishing:
Hope of the dying.

Give me faith now to believe that thou canst be all in all to me, according to my need, if only I renounce all proud self-dependence and put my trust in thee . . .

Show thy lovingkindness tonight, O Lord, to all who stand in need of thy help. Be with the weak to make them strong and with the strong to make them gentle. Cheer the lonely with thy company and the distracted with thy solitude. Prosper thy church in the fulfillment of her mighty task, and grant thy blessing to all who have toiled today in Christ's name. Amen.

ADDITIONAL SCRIPTURE READING:
Hosea 11.4; 1 Peter 1.3

Go to page 936 for your next devotional reading.

1900   Present

in a straight path in which they
    shall not stumble;
for I have become a father to Israel,
    and Ephraim is my firstborn.

10 Hear the word of the LORD,
    O nations,
and declare it in the coastlands
    far away;
say, "He who scattered Israel will
    gather him,
and will keep him as a shepherd
    a flock."
11 For the LORD has ransomed Jacob,
    and has redeemed him from
    hands too strong for him.
12 They shall come and sing aloud on
    the height of Zion,
and they shall be radiant over the
    goodness of the LORD,
over the grain, the wine, and the
    oil,
and over the young of the flock
    and the herd;
their life shall become like a
    watered garden,
and they shall never languish
    again.
13 Then shall the young women
    rejoice in the dance,
and the young men and the old
    shall be merry.
I will turn their mourning into joy,
    I will comfort them, and give
    them gladness for sorrow.
14 I will give the priests their fill of
    fatness,
and my people shall be satisfied
    with my bounty,
            says the LORD.

15 Thus says the LORD:
A voice is heard in Ramah,
    lamentation and bitter weeping.
Rachel is weeping for her children;
    she refuses to be comforted for
    her children,
because they are no more.
16 Thus says the LORD:
Keep your voice from weeping,
    and your eyes from tears;
for there is a reward for your work,
            says the LORD:
they shall come back from the
    land of the enemy;

17 there is hope for your future,
            says the LORD:
your children shall come back to
    their own country.

18 Indeed I heard Ephraim pleading:
"You disciplined me, and I took the
    discipline;
I was like a calf untrained.
Bring me back, let me come back,
    for you are the LORD my God.
19 For after I had turned away I
    repented;
and after I was discovered, I
    struck my thigh;
I was ashamed, and I was dismayed
    because I bore the disgrace of my
    youth."
20 Is Ephraim my dear son?
    Is he the child I delight in?
As often as I speak against him,
    I still remember him.
Therefore I am deeply moved for
    him;
I will surely have mercy on him,
          says the LORD.

21 Set up road markers for yourself,
    make yourself guideposts;
consider well the highway,
    the road by which you went.
Return, O virgin Israel,
    return to these your cities.
22 How long will you waver,
    O faithless daughter?
For the LORD has created a new
    thing on the earth:
a woman encompasses[r] a man.

23 Thus says the LORD of hosts, the
God of Israel: Once more they shall use
these words in the land of Judah and in
its towns when I restore their fortunes:
"The LORD bless you, O abode of
    righteousness,
O holy hill!"
24 And Judah and all its towns shall live
there together, and the farmers and
those who wander[s] with their flocks.
25 I will satisfy the weary,
    and all who are faint I will
    replenish.
26 Thereupon I awoke and looked,
and my sleep was pleasant to me.

r Meaning of Heb uncertain   s Cn Compare Syr Vg Tg: Heb *and they shall wander*

Individual Retribution

27 The days are surely coming, says the LORD, when I will sow the house of Israel and the house of Judah with the seed of humans and the seed of animals. 28And just as I have watched over them to pluck up and break down, to overthrow, destroy, and bring evil, so I will watch over them to build and to plant, says the LORD. 29In those days they shall no longer say:

> "The parents have eaten sour
> grapes,
>   and the children's teeth are set
>   on edge."

30But all shall die for their own sins; the teeth of everyone who eats sour grapes shall be set on edge.

A New Covenant

31 The days are surely coming, says the LORD, when I will make a new covenant with the house of Israel and the house of Judah. 32It will not be like the covenant that I made with their ancestors when I took them by the hand to bring them out of the land of Egypt—a covenant that they broke, though I was their husband,*t* says the LORD. 33But this is the covenant that I will make with the house of Israel after those days, says the LORD: I will put my law within them, and I will write it on their hearts; and I will be their God, and they shall be my people. 34No longer shall they teach one another, or say to each other, "Know the LORD," for they shall all know me, from the least of them to the greatest, says the LORD; for I will forgive their iniquity, and remember their sin no more.

35   Thus says the LORD,
          who gives the sun for light by day
              and the fixed order of the moon
                  and the stars for light by
                      night,
          who stirs up the sea so that its
                  waves roar—
              the LORD of hosts is his name:
36   If this fixed order were ever to cease
              from my presence, says the LORD,
          then also the offspring of Israel
                  would cease
              to be a nation before me forever.

37   Thus says the LORD:
          If the heavens above can be
                  measured,
              and the foundations of the earth
                  below can be explored,
          then I will reject all the offspring of
                  Israel
              because of all they have done,
                          says the LORD.

Jerusalem to Be Enlarged

38 The days are surely coming, says the LORD, when the city shall be rebuilt for the LORD from the tower of Hananel to the Corner Gate. 39And the measuring line shall go out farther, straight to the hill Gareb, and shall then turn to Goah. 40The whole valley of the dead bodies and the ashes, and all the fields as far as the Wadi Kidron, to the corner of the Horse Gate toward the east, shall be sacred to the LORD. It shall never again be uprooted or overthrown.

Jeremiah Buys a Field During the Siege

32 The word that came to Jeremiah from the LORD in the tenth year of King Zedekiah of Judah, which was the eighteenth year of Nebuchadrezzar. 2At that time the army of the king of Babylon was besieging Jerusalem, and the prophet Jeremiah was confined in the court of the guard that was in the palace of the king of Judah, 3where King Zedekiah of Judah had confined him. Zedekiah had said, "Why do you prophesy and say: Thus says the LORD: I am going to give this city into the hand of the king of Babylon, and he shall take it; 4King Zedekiah of Judah shall not escape out of the hands of the Chaldeans, but shall surely be given into the hands of the king of Babylon, and shall speak with him face to face and see him eye to eye; 5and he shall take Zedekiah to Babylon, and there he shall remain until I attend to him, says the LORD; though you fight against the Chaldeans, you shall not succeed?"

6 Jeremiah said, The word of the LORD came to me: 7Hanamel son of your uncle Shallum is going to come to you and say, "Buy my field that is at Anathoth, for the right of redemption by

t Or master

purchase is yours." 8Then my cousin Hanamel came to me in the court of the guard, in accordance with the word of the LORD, and said to me, "Buy my field that is at Anathoth in the land of Benjamin, for the right of possession and redemption is yours; buy it for yourself." Then I knew that this was the word of the LORD.

9 And I bought the field at Anathoth from my cousin Hanamel, and weighed out the money to him, seventeen shekels of silver. 10I signed the deed, sealed it, got witnesses, and weighed the money on scales. 11Then I took the sealed deed of purchase, containing the terms and conditions, and the open copy; 12and I gave the deed of purchase to Baruch son of Neriah son of Mahseiah, in the presence of my cousin Hanamel, in the presence of the witnesses who signed the deed of purchase, and in the presence of all the Judeans who were sitting in the court of the guard. 13In their presence I charged Baruch, saying, 14Thus says the LORD of hosts, the God of Israel: Take these deeds, both this sealed deed of purchase and this open deed, and put them in an earthenware jar, in order that they may last for a long time. 15For thus says the LORD of hosts, the God of Israel: Houses and fields and vineyards shall again be bought in this land.

Jeremiah Prays for Understanding

16 After I had given the deed of purchase to Baruch son of Neriah, I prayed to the LORD, saying: 17Ah Lord GOD! It is you who made the heavens and the earth by your great power and by your outstretched arm! Nothing is too hard for you. 18You show steadfast love to the thousandth generation,u but repay the guilt of parents into the laps of their children after them, O great and mighty God whose name is the LORD of hosts, 19great in counsel and mighty in deed; whose eyes are open to all the ways of mortals, rewarding all according to their ways and according to the fruit of their doings. 20You showed signs and wonders in the land of Egypt, and to this day in Israel and among all humankind, and have made yourself a name that continues to this very day. 21You brought your people Israel out of the land of Egypt with signs and wonders, with a strong hand and outstretched arm, and with great terror; 22and you gave them this land, which you swore to their ancestors to give them, a land flowing with milk and honey; 23and they entered and took possession of it. But they did not obey your voice or follow your law; of all you commanded them to do, they did nothing. Therefore you have made all these disasters come upon them. 24See, the siege ramps have been cast up against the city to take it, and the city, faced with sword, famine, and pestilence, has been given into the hands of the Chaldeans who are fighting against it. What you spoke has happened, as you yourself can see. 25Yet you, O Lord GOD, have said to me, "Buy the field for money and get witnesses"—though the city has been given into the hands of the Chaldeans.

God's Assurance of the People's Return

26 The word of the LORD came to Jeremiah: 27See, I am the LORD, the God of all flesh; is anything too hard for me? 28Therefore, thus says the LORD: I am going to give this city into the hands of the Chaldeans and into the hand of King Nebuchadrezzar of Babylon, and he shall take it. 29The Chaldeans who are fighting against this city shall come, set it on fire, and burn it, with the houses on whose roofs offerings have been made to Baal and libations have been poured out to other gods, to provoke me to anger. 30For the people of Israel and the people of Judah have done nothing but evil in my sight from their youth; the people of Israel have done nothing but provoke me to anger by the work of their hands, says the LORD. 31This city has aroused my anger and wrath, from the day it was built until this day, so that I will remove it from my sight 32because of all the evil of the people of Israel and the people of Judah that they did to provoke me to anger—they, their kings and their officials, their priests and their prophets, the citizens of Judah and the inhabitants of Jerusalem. 33They have turned their backs to me, not their faces; though I

u Or to thousands

have taught them persistently, they would not listen and accept correction. 34They set up their abominations in the house that bears my name, and defiled it. 35They built the high places of Baal in the valley of the son of Hinnom, to offer up their sons and daughters to Molech, though I did not command them, nor did it enter my mind that they should do this abomination, causing Judah to sin.

36 Now therefore thus says the LORD, the God of Israel, concerning this city of which you say, "It is being given into the hand of the king of Babylon by the sword, by famine, and by pestilence": 37See, I am going to gather them from all the lands to which I drove them in my anger and my wrath and in great indignation; I will bring them back to this place, and I will settle them in safety. 38They shall be my people, and I will be their God. 39I will give them one heart and one way, that they may fear me for all time, for their own good and the good of their children after them. 40I will make an everlasting covenant with them, never to draw back from doing good to them; and I will put the fear of me in their hearts, so that they may not turn from me. 41I will rejoice in doing good to them, and I will plant them in this land in faithfulness, with all my heart and all my soul.

42 For thus says the LORD: Just as I have brought all this great disaster upon this people, so I will bring upon them all the good fortune that I now promise them. 43Fields shall be bought in this land of which you are saying, It is a desolation, without human beings or animals; it has been given into the hands of the Chaldeans. 44Fields shall be bought for money, and deeds shall be signed and sealed and witnessed, in the land of Benjamin, in the places around Jerusalem, and in the cities of Judah, of the hill country, of the Shephelah, and of the Negeb; for I will restore their fortunes, says the LORD.

Healing after Punishment

33 The word of the LORD came to Jeremiah a second time, while he was still confined in the court

of the guard: 2Thus says the LORD who made the earth,v the LORD who formed it to establish it—the LORD is his name: 3Call to me and I will answer you, and will tell you great and hidden things that you have not known. 4For thus says the LORD, the God of Israel, concerning the houses of this city and the houses of the kings of Judah that were torn down to make a defense against the siege ramps and before the sword:w 5The Chaldeans are coming in to fightx and to fill them with the dead bodies of those whom I shall strike down in my anger and my wrath, for I have hidden my face from this city because of all their wickedness. 6I am going to bring it recovery and healing; I will heal them and reveal to them abundancew of prosperity and security. 7I will restore the fortunes of Judah and the fortunes of Israel, and rebuild them as they were at first. 8I will cleanse them from all the guilt of their sin against me, and I will forgive all the guilt of their sin and rebellion against me. 9And this cityy shall be to me a name of joy, a praise and a glory before all the nations of the earth who shall hear of all the good that I do for them; they shall fear and tremble because of all the good and all the prosperity I provide for it.

10 Thus says the LORD: In this place of which you say, "It is a waste without human beings or animals," in the towns of Judah and the streets of Jerusalem that are desolate, without inhabitants, human or animal, there shall once more be heard 11the voice of mirth and the voice of gladness, the voice of the bridegroom and the voice of the bride, the voices of those who sing, as they bring thank offerings to the house of the LORD:

"Give thanks to the LORD of hosts,
    for the LORD is good,
    for his steadfast love endures
        forever!"

For I will restore the fortunes of the land as at first, says the LORD.

12 Thus says the LORD of hosts: In this place that is waste, without human beings or animals, and in all its towns there shall again be pasture for shepherds resting their flocks. 13In the towns

---

v Gk: Heb it   w Meaning of Heb uncertain   x Cn: Heb *They are coming in to fight against the Chaldeans*   y Heb *And it*

of the hill country, of the Shephelah, and of the Negeb, in the land of Benjamin, the places around Jerusalem, and in the towns of Judah, flocks shall again pass under the hands of the one who counts them, says the LORD.

The Righteous Branch and the Covenant with David

14 The days are surely coming, says the LORD, when I will fulfill the promise I made to the house of Israel and the house of Judah. 15In those days and at that time I will cause a righteous Branch to spring up for David; and he shall execute justice and righteousness in the land. 16In those days Judah will be saved and Jerusalem will live in safety. And this is the name by which it will be called: "The LORD is our righteousness."

17 For thus says the LORD: David shall never lack a man to sit on the throne of the house of Israel, 18and the levitical priests shall never lack a man in my presence to offer burnt offerings, to make grain offerings, and to make sacrifices for all time.

19 The word of the LORD came to Jeremiah: 20Thus says the LORD: If any of you could break my covenant with the day and my covenant with the night, so that day and night would not come at their appointed time, 21only then could my covenant with my servant David be broken, so that he would not have a son to reign on his throne, and my covenant with my ministers the Levites. 22Just as the host of heaven cannot be numbered and the sands of the sea cannot be measured, so I will increase the offspring of my servant David, and the Levites who minister to me.

23 The word of the LORD came to Jeremiah: 24Have you not observed how these people say, "The two families that the LORD chose have been rejected by him," and how they hold my people in such contempt that they no longer regard them as a nation? 25Thus says the LORD: Only if I had not established my covenant with day and night and the ordinances of heaven and earth, 26would I reject the offspring of Jacob and of my servant David and not choose any of his descendants as rulers over the offspring

of Abraham, Isaac, and Jacob. For I will restore their fortunes, and will have mercy upon them.

Death in Captivity Predicted for Zedekiah

34 The word that came to Jeremiah from the LORD, when King Nebuchadrezzar of Babylon and all his army and all the kingdoms of the earth and all the peoples under his dominion were fighting against Jerusalem and all its cities: 2Thus says the LORD, the God of Israel: Go and speak to King Zedekiah of Judah and say to him: Thus says the LORD: I am going to give this city into the hand of the king of Babylon, and he shall burn it with fire. 3And you yourself shall not escape from his hand, but shall surely be captured and handed over to him; you shall see the king of Babylon eye to eye and speak with him face to face; and you shall go to Babylon. 4Yet hear the word of the LORD, O King Zedekiah of Judah! Thus says the LORD concerning you: You shall not die by the sword; 5you shall die in peace. And as spices were burnedz for your ancestors, the earlier kings who preceded you, so they shall burn spicesa for you and lament for you, saying, "Alas, lord!" For I have spoken the word, says the LORD.

6 Then the prophet Jeremiah spoke all these words to Zedekiah king of Judah, in Jerusalem, 7when the army of the king of Babylon was fighting against Jerusalem and against all the cities of Judah that were left, Lachish and Azekah; for these were the only fortified cities of Judah that remained.

Treacherous Treatment of Slaves

8 The word that came to Jeremiah from the LORD, after King Zedekiah had made a covenant with all the people in Jerusalem to make a proclamation of liberty to them— 9that all should set free their Hebrew slaves, male and female, so that no one should hold another Judean in slavery. 10And they obeyed, all the officials and all the people who had entered into the covenant that all would set free their slaves, male or female, so that they would not be enslaved again;

z Heb as there was burning   a Heb shall burn

they obeyed and set them free. 11But afterward they turned around and took back the male and female slaves they had set free, and brought them again into subjection as slaves. 12The word of the LORD came to Jeremiah from the LORD: 13Thus says the LORD, the God of Israel: I myself made a covenant with your ancestors when I brought them out of the land of Egypt, out of the house of slavery, saying, 14"Every seventh year each of you must set free any Hebrews who have been sold to you and have served you six years; you must set them free from your service." But your ancestors did not listen to me or incline their ears to me. 15You yourselves recently repented and did what was right in my sight by proclaiming liberty to one another, and you made a covenant before me in the house that is called by my name; 16but then you turned around and profaned my name when each of you took back your male and female slaves, whom you had set free according to their desire, and you brought them again into subjection to be your slaves. 17Therefore, thus says the LORD: You have not obeyed me by granting a release to your neighbors and friends; I am going to grant a release to you, says the LORD—a release to the sword, to pestilence, and to famine. I will make you a horror to all the kingdoms of the earth. 18And those who transgressed my covenant and did not keep the terms of the covenant that they made before me, I will make like*b* the calf when they cut it in two and passed between its parts: 19the officials of Judah, the officials of Jerusalem, the eunuchs, the priests, and all the people of the land who passed between the parts of the calf 20shall be handed over to their enemies and to those who seek their lives. Their corpses shall become food for the birds of the air and the wild animals of the earth. 21And as for King Zedekiah of Judah and his officials, I will hand them over to their enemies and to those who seek their lives, to the army of the king of Babylon, which has withdrawn from you. 22I am going to command, says the LORD, and will bring them back to this city; and they will fight against it, and take it, and burn it

with fire. The towns of Judah I will make a desolation without inhabitant.

The Rechabites Commended

35 The word that came to Jeremiah from the LORD in the days of King Jehoiakim son of Josiah of Judah: 2Go to the house of the Rechabites, and speak with them, and bring them to the house of the LORD, into one of the chambers; then offer them wine to drink. 3So I took Jaazaniah son of Jeremiah son of Habazziniah, and his brothers, and all his sons, and the whole house of the Rechabites. 4I brought them to the house of the LORD into the chamber of the sons of Hanan son of Igdaliah, the man of God, which was near the chamber of the officials, above the chamber of Maaseiah son of Shallum, keeper of the threshold. 5Then I set before the Rechabites pitchers full of wine, and cups; and I said to them, "Have some wine." 6But they answered, "We will drink no wine, for our ancestor Jonadab son of Rechab commanded us, 'You shall never drink wine, neither you nor your children; 7nor shall you ever build a house, or sow seed; nor shall you plant a vineyard, or even own one; but you shall live in tents all your days, that you may live many days in the land where you reside.' 8We have obeyed the charge of our ancestor Jonadab son of Rechab in all that he commanded us, to drink no wine all our days, ourselves, our wives, our sons, or our daughters, 9and not to build houses to live in. We have no vineyard or field or seed; 10but we have lived in tents, and have obeyed and done all that our ancestor Jonadab commanded us. 11But when King Nebuchadrezzar of Babylon came up against the land, we said, 'Come, and let us go to Jerusalem for fear of the army of the Chaldeans and the army of the Arameans.' That is why we are living in Jerusalem."

12 Then the word of the LORD came to Jeremiah: 13Thus says the LORD of hosts, the God of Israel: Go and say to the people of Judah and the inhabitants of Jerusalem, Can you not learn a lesson and obey my words? says the LORD. 14The command has been carried out that Jonadab son of Rechab gave to his

b Cn: Heb lacks *like*

descendants to drink no wine; and they drink none to this day, for they have obeyed their ancestor's command. But I myself have spoken to you persistently, and you have not obeyed me. 15I have sent to you all my servants the prophets, sending them persistently, saying, "Turn now everyone of you from your evil way, and amend your doings, and do not go after other gods to serve them, and then you shall live in the land that I gave to you and your ancestors." But you did not incline your ear or obey me. 16The descendants of Jonadab son of Rechab have carried out the command that their ancestor gave them, but this people has not obeyed me. 17Therefore, thus says the Lord, the God of hosts, the God of Israel: I am going to bring on Judah and on all the inhabitants of Jerusalem every disaster that I have pronounced against them; because I have spoken to them and they have not listened, I have called to them and they have not answered.

18 But to the house of the Rechabites Jeremiah said: Thus says the Lord of hosts, the God of Israel: Because you have obeyed the command of your ancestor Jonadab, and kept all his precepts, and done all that he commanded you, 19therefore thus says the Lord of hosts, the God of Israel: Jonadab son of Rechab shall not lack a descendant to stand before me for all time.

The Scroll Read in the Temple

36 In the fourth year of King Jehoiakim son of Josiah of Judah, this word came to Jeremiah from the Lord: 2Take a scroll and write on it all the words that I have spoken to you against Israel and Judah and all the nations, from the day I spoke to you, from the days of Josiah until today. 3It may be that when the house of Judah hears of all the disasters that I intend to do to them, all of them may turn from their evil ways, so that I may forgive their iniquity and their sin.

4 Then Jeremiah called Baruch son of Neriah, and Baruch wrote on a scroll at Jeremiah's dictation all the words of the Lord that he had spoken to him. 5And Jeremiah ordered Baruch, saying, "I am prevented from entering the house of the Lord; 6so you go yourself, and on a fast day in the hearing of the people in the Lord's house you shall read the words of the Lord from the scroll that you have written at my dictation. You shall read them also in the hearing of all the people of Judah who come up from their towns. 7It may be that their plea will come before the Lord, and that all of them will turn from their evil ways, for great is the anger and wrath that the Lord has pronounced against this people." 8And Baruch son of Neriah did all that the prophet Jeremiah ordered him about reading from the scroll the words of the Lord in the Lord's house.

9 In the fifth year of King Jehoiakim son of Josiah of Judah, in the ninth month, all the people in Jerusalem and all the people who came from the towns of Judah to Jerusalem proclaimed a fast before the Lord. 10Then, in the hearing of all the people, Baruch read the words of Jeremiah from the scroll, in the house of the Lord, in the chamber of Gemariah son of Shaphan the secretary, which was in the upper court, at the entry of the New Gate of the Lord's house.

The Scroll Read in the Palace

11 When Micaiah son of Gemariah son of Shaphan heard all the words of the Lord from the scroll, 12he went down to the king's house, into the secretary's chamber; and all the officials were sitting there: Elishama the secretary, Delaiah son of Shemaiah, Elnathan son of Achbor, Gemariah son of Shaphan, Zedekiah son of Hananiah, and all the officials. 13And Micaiah told them all the words that he had heard, when Baruch read the scroll in the hearing of the people. 14Then all the officials sent Jehudi son of Nethaniah son of Shelemiah son of Cushi to say to Baruch, "Bring the scroll that you read in the hearing of the people, and come." So Baruch son of Neriah took the scroll in his hand and came to them. 15And they said to him, "Sit down and read it to us." So Baruch read it to them. 16When they heard all the words, they turned to one another in alarm, and said to Baruch, "We certainly must report all these words to the king." 17Then they questioned Baruch, "Tell us now, how did you write all these words?

Was it at his dictation?" 18Baruch answered them, "He dictated all these words to me, and I wrote them with ink on the scroll." 19Then the officials said to Baruch, "Go and hide, you and Jeremiah, and let no one know where you are."

Jehoiakim Burns the Scroll

20 Leaving the scroll in the chamber of Elishama the secretary, they went to the court of the king; and they reported all the words to the king. 21Then the king sent Jehudi to get the scroll, and he took it from the chamber of Elishama the secretary; and Jehudi read it to the king and all the officials who stood beside the king. 22Now the king was sitting in his winter apartment (it was the ninth month), and there was a fire burning in the brazier before him. 23As Jehudi read three or four columns, the king*c* would cut them off with a penknife and throw them into the fire in the brazier, until the entire scroll was consumed in the fire that was in the brazier. 24Yet neither the king, nor any of his servants who heard all these words, was alarmed, nor did they tear their garments. 25Even when Elnathan and Delaiah and Gemariah urged the king not to burn the scroll, he would not listen to them. 26And the king commanded Jerahmeel the king's son and Seraiah son of Azriel and Shelemiah son of Abdeel to arrest the secretary Baruch and the prophet Jeremiah. But the LORD hid them.

Jeremiah Dictates Another

27 Now, after the king had burned the scroll with the words that Baruch wrote at Jeremiah's dictation, the word of the LORD came to Jeremiah: 28Take another scroll and write on it all the former words that were in the first scroll, which King Jehoiakim of Judah has burned. 29And concerning King Jehoiakim of Judah you shall say: Thus says the LORD, You have dared to burn this scroll, saying, Why have you written in it that the king of Babylon will certainly come and destroy this land, and will cut off from it human beings and animals? 30Therefore thus says the LORD concerning King Jehoiakim of Judah: He shall have no one to sit upon the throne of David, and his dead body shall be cast out to the heat by day and the frost by night. 31And I will punish him and his offspring and his servants for their iniquity; I will bring on them, and on the inhabitants of Jerusalem, and on the people of Judah, all the disasters with which I have threatened them—but they would not listen.

32 Then Jeremiah took another scroll and gave it to the secretary Baruch son of Neriah, who wrote on it at Jeremiah's dictation all the words of the scroll that King Jehoiakim of Judah had burned in the fire; and many similar words were added to them.

Zedekiah's Vain Hope

37 Zedekiah son of Josiah, whom King Nebuchadrezzar of Babylon made king in the land of Judah, succeeded Coniah son of Jehoiakim. 2But neither he nor his servants nor the people of the land listened to the words of the LORD that he spoke through the prophet Jeremiah.

3 King Zedekiah sent Jehucal son of Shelemiah and the priest Zephaniah son of Maaseiah to the prophet Jeremiah saying, "Please pray for us to the LORD our God." 4Now Jeremiah was still going in and out among the people, for he had not yet been put in prison. 5Meanwhile, the army of Pharaoh had come out of Egypt; and when the Chaldeans who were besieging Jerusalem heard news of them, they withdrew from Jerusalem.

6 Then the word of the LORD came to the prophet Jeremiah: 7Thus says the LORD, God of Israel: This is what the two of you shall say to the king of Judah, who sent you to me to inquire of me: Pharaoh's army, which set out to help you, is going to return to its own land, to Egypt. 8And the Chaldeans shall return and fight against this city; they shall take it and burn it with fire. 9Thus says the LORD: Do not deceive yourselves, saying, "The Chaldeans will surely go away from us," for they will not go away. 10Even if you defeated the whole army of Chaldeans who are fighting against you, and there remained of them only wounded men in their tents, they would rise up and burn this city with fire.

c Heb he

Jeremiah Is Imprisoned

11 Now when the Chaldean army had withdrawn from Jerusalem at the approach of Pharaoh's army, 12Jeremiah set out from Jerusalem to go to the land of Benjamin to receive his share of property[d] among the people there. 13When he reached the Benjamin Gate, a sentinel there named Irijah son of Shelemiah son of Hananiah arrested the prophet Jeremiah saying, "You are deserting to the Chaldeans." 14And Jeremiah said, "That is a lie; I am not deserting to the Chaldeans." But Irijah would not listen to him, and arrested Jeremiah and brought him to the officials. 15The officials were enraged at Jeremiah, and they beat him and imprisoned him in the house of the secretary Jonathan, for it had been made a prison. 16Thus Jeremiah was put in the cistern house, in the cells, and remained there many days.

17 Then King Zedekiah sent for him, and received him. The king questioned him secretly in his house, and said, "Is there any word from the LORD?" Jeremiah said, "There is!" Then he said, "You shall be handed over to the king of Babylon." 18Jeremiah also said to King Zedekiah, "What wrong have I done to you or your servants or this people, that you have put me in prison? 19Where are your prophets who prophesied to you, saying, 'The king of Babylon will not come against you and against this land'? 20Now please hear me, my lord king: be good enough to listen to my plea, and do not send me back to the house of the secretary Jonathan to die there." 21So King Zedekiah gave orders, and they committed Jeremiah to the court of the guard; and a loaf of bread was given him daily from the bakers' street, until all the bread of the city was gone. So Jeremiah remained in the court of the guard.

Jeremiah in the Cistern

38 Now Shephatiah son of Mattan, Gedaliah son of Pashhur, Jucal son of Shelemiah, and Pashhur son of Malchiah heard the words that Jeremiah was saying to all the people, 2Thus says the LORD, Those who stay in this city shall die by the sword, by famine, and by pestilence; but those who go out to the Chaldeans shall live; they shall have their lives as a prize of war, and live. 3Thus says the LORD, This city shall surely be handed over to the army of the king of Babylon and be taken. 4Then the officials said to the king, "This man ought to be put to death, because he is discouraging the soldiers who are left in this city, and all the people, by speaking such words to them. For this man is not seeking the welfare of this people, but their harm." 5King Zedekiah said, "Here he is; he is in your hands; for the king is powerless against you." 6So they took Jeremiah and threw him into the cistern of Malchiah, the king's son, which was in the court of the guard, letting Jeremiah down by ropes. Now there was no water in the cistern, but only mud, and Jeremiah sank in the mud.

Jeremiah Is Rescued by Ebed-melech

7 Ebed-melech the Ethiopian,[e] a eunuch in the king's house, heard that they had put Jeremiah into the cistern. The king happened to be sitting at the Benjamin Gate, 8So Ebed-melech left the king's house and spoke to the king, 9"My lord king, these men have acted wickedly in all they did to the prophet Jeremiah by throwing him into the cistern to die there of hunger, for there is no bread left in the city." 10Then the king commanded Ebed-melech the Ethiopian,[e] "Take three men with you from here, and pull the prophet Jeremiah up from the cistern before he dies." 11So Ebed-melech took the men with him and went to the house of the king, to a wardrobe of[f] the storehouse, and took from there old rags and worn-out clothes, which he let down to Jeremiah in the cistern by ropes. 12Then Ebed-melech the Ethiopian[e] said to Jeremiah, "Just put the rags and clothes between your armpits and the ropes." Jeremiah did so. 13Then they drew Jeremiah up by the ropes and pulled him out of the cistern. And Jeremiah remained in the court of the guard.

Zedekiah Consults Jeremiah Again

14 King Zedekiah sent for the prophet Jeremiah and received him at the

---

d Meaning of Heb uncertain   *e* Or *Nubian*; Heb *Cushite*   *f* Cn: Heb *to under*

third entrance of the temple of the LORD. The king said to Jeremiah, "I have something to ask you; do not hide anything from me." 15Jeremiah said to Zedekiah, "If I tell you, you will put me to death, will you not? And if I give you advice, you will not listen to me." 16So King Zedekiah swore an oath in secret to Jeremiah, "As the LORD lives, who gave us our lives, I will not put you to death or hand you over to these men who seek your life."

17 Then Jeremiah said to Zedekiah, "Thus says the LORD, the God of hosts, the God of Israel, If you will only surrender to the officials of the king of Babylon, then your life shall be spared, and this city shall not be burned with fire, and you and your house shall live. 18But if you do not surrender to the officials of the king of Babylon, then this city shall be handed over to the Chaldeans, and they shall burn it with fire, and you yourself shall not escape from their hand." 19King Zedekiah said to Jeremiah, "I am afraid of the Judeans who have deserted to the Chaldeans, for I might be handed over to them and they would abuse me." 20Jeremiah said, "That will not happen. Just obey the voice of the LORD in what I say to you, and it shall go well with you, and your life shall be spared. 21But if you are determined not to surrender, this is what the LORD has shown me— 22a vision of all the women remaining in the house of the king of Judah being led out to the officials of the king of Babylon and saying,

'Your trusted friends have seduced
          you
     and have overcome you;
  Now that your feet are stuck in the
          mud,
     they desert you.'
23All your wives and your children shall be led out to the Chaldeans, and you yourself shall not escape from their hand, but shall be seized by the king of Babylon; and this city shall be burned with fire."

24 Then Zedekiah said to Jeremiah, "Do not let anyone else know of this conversation, or you will die. 25If the officials should hear that I have spoken with you, and they should come and say

to you, 'Just tell us what you said to the king; do not conceal it from us, or we will put you to death. What did the king say to you?' 26then you shall say to them, 'I was presenting my plea to the king not to send me back to the house of Jonathan to die there.' " 27All the officials did come to Jeremiah and questioned him; and he answered them in the very words the king had commanded. So they stopped questioning him, for the conversation had not been overheard. 28And Jeremiah remained in the court of the guard until the day that Jerusalem was taken.

The Fall of Jerusalem

39 In the ninth year of King Zedekiah of Judah, in the tenth month, King Nebuchadrezzar of Babylon and all his army came against Jerusalem and besieged it; 2in the eleventh year of Zedekiah, in the fourth month, on the ninth day of the month, a breach was made in the city. 3When Jerusalem was taken,g all the officials of the king of Babylon came and sat in the middle gate: Nergal-sharezer, Samgar-nebo, Sarsechim the Rabsaris, Nergal-sharezer the Rabmag, with all the rest of the officials of the king of Babylon. 4When King Zedekiah of Judah and all the soldiers saw them, they fled, going out of the city at night by way of the king's garden through the gate between the two walls; and they went toward the Arabah. 5But the army of the Chaldeans pursued them, and overtook Zedekiah in the plains of Jericho; and when they had taken him, they brought him up to King Nebuchadrezzar of Babylon, at Riblah, in the land of Hamath; and he passed sentence on him. 6The king of Babylon slaughtered the sons of Zedekiah at Riblah before his eyes; also the king of Babylon slaughtered all the nobles of Judah. 7He put out the eyes of Zedekiah, and bound him in fetters to take him to Babylon. 8The Chaldeans burned the king's house and the houses of the people, and broke down the walls of Jerusalem. 9Then Nebuzaradan the captain of the guard exiled to Babylon the rest of the people who were left in the city, those who had deserted to him, and the people

g This clause has been transposed from 38.28

who remained. [10]Nebuzaradan the captain of the guard left in the land of Judah some of the poor people who owned nothing, and gave them vineyards and fields at the same time.

Jeremiah, Set Free, Remembers Ebed-melech

11 King Nebuchadrezzar of Babylon gave command concerning Jeremiah through Nebuzaradan, the captain of the guard, saying, [12]"Take him, look after him well and do him no harm, but deal with him as he may ask you." [13]So Nebuzaradan the captain of the guard, Nebushazban the Rabsaris, Nergal-sharezer the Rabmag, and all the chief officers of the king of Babylon sent [14]and took Jeremiah from the court of the guard. They entrusted him to Gedaliah son of Ahikam son of Shaphan to be brought home. So he stayed with his own people.

15 The word of the LORD came to Jeremiah while he was confined in the court of the guard: [16]Go and say to Ebedmelech the Ethiopian:[h] Thus says the LORD of hosts, the God of Israel: I am going to fulfill my words against this city for evil and not for good, and they shall be accomplished in your presence on that day. [17]But I will save you on that day, says the LORD, and you shall not be handed over to those whom you dread. [18]For I will surely save you, and you shall not fall by the sword; but you shall have your life as a prize of war, because you have trusted in me, says the LORD.

Jeremiah with Gedaliah the Governor

40 The word that came to Jeremiah from the LORD after Nebuzaradan the captain of the guard had let him go from Ramah, when he took him bound in fetters along with all the captives of Jerusalem and Judah who were being exiled to Babylon. [2]The captain of the guard took Jeremiah and said to him, "The LORD your God threatened this place with this disaster; [3]and now the LORD has brought it about, and has done as he said, because all of you sinned against the LORD and did not obey his voice. Therefore this thing has come upon you. [4]Now look, I have just released

you today from the fetters on your hands. If you wish to come with me to Babylon, come, and I will take good care of you; but if you do not wish to come with me to Babylon, you need not come. See, the whole land is before you; go wherever you think it good and right to go. [5]If you remain,[i] then return to Gedaliah son of Ahikam son of Shaphan, whom the king of Babylon appointed governor of the towns of Judah, and stay with him among the people; or go wherever you think it right to go." So the captain of the guard gave him an allowance of food and a present, and let him go. [6]Then Jeremiah went to Gedaliah son of Ahikam at Mizpah, and stayed with him among the people who were left in the land.

7 When all the leaders of the forces in the open country and their troops heard that the king of Babylon had appointed Gedaliah son of Ahikam governor in the land, and had committed to him men, women, and children, those of the poorest of the land who had not been taken into exile to Babylon, [8]they went to Gedaliah at Mizpah—Ishmael son of Nethaniah, Johanan son of Kareah, Seraiah son of Tanhumeth, the sons of Ephai the Netophathite, Jezaniah son of the Maacathite, they and their troops. [9]Gedaliah son of Ahikam son of Shaphan swore to them and their troops, saying, "Do not be afraid to serve the Chaldeans. Stay in the land and serve the king of Babylon, and it shall go well with you. [10]As for me, I am staying at Mizpah to represent you before the Chaldeans who come to us; but as for you, gather wine and summer fruits and oil, and store them in your vessels, and live in the towns that you have taken over." [11]Likewise, when all the Judeans who were in Moab and among the Ammonites and in Edom and in other lands heard that the king of Babylon had left a remnant in Judah and had appointed Gedaliah son of Ahikam son of Shaphan as governor over them, [12]then all the Judeans returned from all the places to which they had been scattered and came to the land of Judah, to Gedaliah at Mizpah; and they gathered wine and summer fruits in great abundance.

13 Now Johanan son of Kareah and all the leaders of the forces in the open

h Or Nubian; Heb Cushite   i Syr: Meaning of Heb uncertain

country came to Gedaliah at Mizpah [14]and said to him, "Are you at all aware that Baalis king of the Ammonites has sent Ishmael son of Nethaniah to take your life?" But Gedaliah son of Ahikam would not believe them. [15]Then Johanan son of Kareah spoke secretly to Gedaliah at Mizpah, "Please let me go and kill Ishmael son of Nethaniah, and no one else will know. Why should he take your life, so that all the Judeans who are gathered around you would be scattered, and the remnant of Judah would perish?" [16]But Gedaliah son of Ahikam said to Johanan son of Kareah, "Do not do such a thing, for you are telling a lie about Ishmael."

Insurrection against Gedaliah

41 In the seventh month, Ishmael son of Nethaniah son of Elishama, of the royal family, one of the chief officers of the king, came with ten men to Gedaliah son of Ahikam, at Mizpah. As they ate bread together there at Mizpah, [2]Ishmael son of Nethaniah and the ten men with him got up and struck down Gedaliah son of Ahikam son of Shaphan with the sword and killed him, because the king of Babylon had appointed him governor in the land. [3]Ishmael also killed all the Judeans who were with Gedaliah at Mizpah, and the Chaldean soldiers who happened to be there.

[4] On the day after the murder of Gedaliah, before anyone knew of it, [5]eighty men arrived from Shechem and Shiloh and Samaria, with their beards shaved and their clothes torn, and their bodies gashed, bringing grain offerings and incense to present at the temple of the LORD. [6]And Ishmael son of Nethaniah came out from Mizpah to meet them, weeping as he came. As he met them, he said to them, "Come to Gedaliah son of Ahikam." [7]When they reached the middle of the city, Ishmael son of Nethaniah and the men with him slaughtered them, and threw them[j] into a cistern. [8]But there were ten men among them who said to Ishmael, "Do not kill us, for we have stores of wheat, barley, oil, and

honey hidden in the fields." So he refrained, and did not kill them along with their companions.

[9] Now the cistern into which Ishmael had thrown all the bodies of the men whom he had struck down was the large cistern[k] that King Asa had made for defense against King Baasha of Israel; Ishmael son of Nethaniah filled that cistern with those whom he had killed. [10]Then Ishmael took captive all the rest of the people who were in Mizpah, the king's daughters and all the people who were left at Mizpah, whom Nebuzaradan, the captain of the guard, had committed to Gedaliah son of Ahikam. Ishmael son of Nethaniah took them captive and set out to cross over to the Ammonites.

[11] But when Johanan son of Kareah and all the leaders of the forces with him heard of all the crimes that Ishmael son of Nethaniah had done, [12]they took all their men and went to fight against Ishmael son of Nethaniah. They came upon him at the great pool that is in Gibeon. [13]And when all the people who were with Ishmael saw Johanan son of Kareah and all the leaders of the forces with him, they were glad. [14]So all the people whom Ishmael had carried away captive from Mizpah turned around and came back, and went to Johanan son of Kareah. [15]But Ishmael son of Nethaniah escaped from Johanan with eight men, and went to the Ammonites. [16]Then Johanan son of Kareah and all the leaders of the forces with him took all the rest of the people whom Ishmael son of Nethaniah had carried away captive[l] from Mizpah after he had slain Gedaliah son of Ahikam—soldiers, women, children, and eunuchs, whom Johanan brought back from Gibeon.[m] [17]And they set out, and stopped at Geruth Chimham near Bethlehem, intending to go to Egypt [18]because of the Chaldeans; for they were afraid of them, because Ishmael son of Nethaniah had killed Gedaliah son of Ahikam, whom the king of Babylon had made governor over the land.

---

j Syr: Heb lacks *and threw them*; compare verse 9   *k* Gk: Heb *whom he had killed by the hand of Gedaliah*   *l* Cn: Heb *whom he recovered from Ishmael son of Nethaniah*   *m* Meaning of Heb uncertain

Jeremiah Advises Survivors Not to Migrate

42 Then all the commanders of the forces, and Johanan son of Kareah and Azariah[n] son of Hoshaiah, and all the people from the least to the greatest, approached ²the prophet Jeremiah and said, "Be good enough to listen to our plea, and pray to the LORD your God for us—for all this remnant. For there are only a few of us left out of many, as your eyes can see. ³Let the LORD your God show us where we should go and what we should do." ⁴The prophet Jeremiah said to them, "Very well: I am going to pray to the LORD your God as you request, and whatever the LORD answers you I will tell you; I will keep nothing back from you." ⁵They in their turn said to Jeremiah, "May the LORD be a true and faithful witness against us if we do not act according to everything that the LORD your God sends us through you. ⁶Whether it is good or bad, we will obey the voice of the LORD our God to whom we are sending you, in order that it may go well with us when we obey the voice of the LORD our God."

7 At the end of ten days the word of the LORD came to Jeremiah. ⁸Then he summoned Johanan son of Kareah and all the commanders of the forces who were with him, and all the people from the least to the greatest, ⁹and said to them, "Thus says the LORD, the God of Israel, to whom you sent me to present your plea before him: ¹⁰If you will only remain in this land, then I will build you up and not pull you down; I will plant you, and not pluck you up; for I am sorry for the disaster that I have brought upon you. ¹¹Do not be afraid of the king of Babylon, as you have been; do not be afraid of him, says the LORD, for I am with you, to save you and to rescue you from his hand. ¹²I will grant you mercy, and he will have mercy on you and restore you to your native soil. ¹³But if you continue to say, 'We will not stay in this land,' thus disobeying the voice of the LORD your God ¹⁴and saying, 'No, we will go to the land of Egypt, where we shall not see war, or hear the sound of the trumpet, or be hungry for bread,

and there we will stay,' ¹⁵then hear the word of the LORD, O remnant of Judah. Thus says the LORD of hosts, the God of Israel: If you are determined to enter Egypt and go to settle there, ¹⁶then the sword that you fear shall overtake you there, in the land of Egypt; and the famine that you dread shall follow close after you into Egypt; and there you shall die. ¹⁷All the people who have determined to go to Egypt to settle there shall die by the sword, by famine, and by pestilence; they shall have no remnant or survivor from the disaster that I am bringing upon them.

18 "For thus says the LORD of hosts, the God of Israel: Just as my anger and my wrath were poured out on the inhabitants of Jerusalem, so my wrath will be poured out on you when you go to Egypt. You shall become an object of execration and horror, of cursing and ridicule. You shall see this place no more. ¹⁹The LORD has said to you, O remnant of Judah, Do not go to Egypt. Be well aware that I have warned you today ²⁰that you have made a fatal mistake. For you yourselves sent me to the LORD your God, saying, 'Pray for us to the LORD our God, and whatever the LORD our God says, tell us and we will do it.' ²¹So I have told you today, but you have not obeyed the voice of the LORD your God in anything that he sent me to tell you. ²²Be well aware, then, that you shall die by the sword, by famine, and by pestilence in the place where you desire to go and settle."

Taken to Egypt, Jeremiah Warns of Judgment

43 When Jeremiah finished speaking to all the people all these words of the LORD their God, with which the LORD their God had sent him to them, ²Azariah son of Hoshaiah and Johanan son of Kareah and all the other insolent men said to Jeremiah, "You are telling a lie. The LORD our God did not send you to say, 'Do not go to Egypt to settle there'; ³but Baruch son of Neriah is inciting you against us, to hand us over to the Chaldeans, in order that they may kill us or take us into exile in Babylon." ⁴So Johanan son of Kareah and all

n Gk: Heb *Jezaniah*

the commanders of the forces and all the people did not obey the voice of the LORD, to stay in the land of Judah. 5But Johanan son of Kareah and all the commanders of the forces took all the remnant of Judah who had returned to settle in the land of Judah from all the nations to which they had been driven— 6the men, the women, the children, the princesses, and everyone whom Nebuzaradan the captain of the guard had left with Gedaliah son of Ahikam son of Shaphan; also the prophet Jeremiah and Baruch son of Neriah. 7And they came into the land of Egypt, for they did not obey the voice of the LORD. And they arrived at Tahpanhes.

8 Then the word of the LORD came to Jeremiah in Tahpanhes: 9Take some large stones in your hands, and bury them in the clay pavemento that is at the entrance to Pharaoh's palace in Tahpanhes. Let the Judeans see you do it, 10and say to them, Thus says the LORD of hosts, the God of Israel: I am going to send and take my servant King Nebuchadrezzar of Babylon, and hep will set his throne above these stones that I have buried, and he will spread his royal canopy over them. 11He shall come and ravage the land of Egypt, giving

those who are destined for
         pestilence, to pestilence,
and those who are destined for
         captivity, to captivity,
and those who are destined for
         the sword, to the sword.

12Heq shall kindle a fire in the temples of the gods of Egypt; and he shall burn them and carry them away captive; and he shall pick clean the land of Egypt, as a shepherd picks his cloak clean of vermin; and he shall depart from there safely. 13He shall break the obelisks of Heliopolis, which is in the land of Egypt; and the temples of the gods of Egypt he shall burn with fire.

Denunciation of Persistent Idolatry

44 The word that came to Jeremiah for all the Judeans living in the land of Egypt, at Migdol, at Tahpanhes, at Memphis, and in the land of Pathros, 2Thus says the LORD of hosts, the God of Israel: You yourselves have seen all the disaster that I have brought on Jerusalem and on all the towns of Judah. Look at them; today they are a desolation, without an inhabitant in them, 3because of the wickedness that they committed, provoking me to anger, in that they went to make offerings and serve other gods that they had not known, neither they, nor you, nor your ancestors. 4Yet I persistently sent to you all my servants the prophets, saying, "I beg you not to do this abominable thing that I hate!" 5But they did not listen or incline their ear, to turn from their wickedness and make no offerings to other gods. 6So my wrath and my anger were poured out and kindled in the towns of Judah and in the streets of Jerusalem; and they became a waste and a desolation, as they still are today. 7And now thus says the LORD God of hosts, the God of Israel: Why are you doing such great harm to yourselves, to cut off man and woman, child and infant, from the midst of Judah, leaving yourselves without a remnant? 8Why do you provoke me to anger with the works of your hands, making offerings to other gods in the land of Egypt where you have come to settle? Will you be cut off and become an object of cursing and ridicule among all the nations of the earth? 9Have you forgotten the crimes of your ancestors, of the kings of Judah, of theirr wives, your own crimes and those of your wives, which they committed in the land of Judah and in the streets of Jerusalem? 10They have shown no contrition or fear to this day, nor have they walked in my law and my statutes that I set before you and before your ancestors.

11 Therefore thus says the LORD of hosts, the God of Israel: I am determined to bring disaster on you, to bring all Judah to an end. 12I will take the remnant of Judah who are determined to come to the land of Egypt to settle, and they shall perish, everyone; in the land of Egypt they shall fall; by the sword and by famine they shall perish; from the least to the greatest, they shall die by the sword and by famine; and they shall become an object of execration and horror, of cursing and ridicule. 13I will punish those who live in the land of Egypt,

o Meaning of Heb uncertain   p Gk Syr: Heb I   q Gk Syr Vg: Heb I   r Heb his

as I have punished Jerusalem, with the sword, with famine, and with pestilence, [14]so that none of the remnant of Judah who have come to settle in the land of Egypt shall escape or survive or return to the land of Judah. Although they long to go back to live there, they shall not go back, except some fugitives.

15 Then all the men who were aware that their wives had been making offerings to other gods, and all the women who stood by, a great assembly, all the people who lived in Pathros in the land of Egypt, answered Jeremiah: [16]"As for the word that you have spoken to us in the name of the LORD, we are not going to listen to you. [17]Instead, we will do everything that we have vowed, make offerings to the queen of heaven and pour out libations to her, just as we and our ancestors, our kings and our officials, used to do in the towns of Judah and in the streets of Jerusalem. We used to have plenty of food, and prospered, and saw no misfortune. [18]But from the time we stopped making offerings to the queen of heaven and pouring out libations to her, we have lacked everything and have perished by the sword and by famine." [19]And the women said,[s] "Indeed we will go on making offerings to the queen of heaven and pouring out libations to her; do you think that we made cakes for her, marked with her image, and poured out libations to her without our husbands' being involved?"

20 Then Jeremiah said to all the people, men and women, all the people who were giving him this answer: [21]"As for the offerings that you made in the towns of Judah and in the streets of Jerusalem, you and your ancestors, your kings and your officials, and the people of the land, did not the LORD remember them? Did it not come into his mind? [22]The LORD could no longer bear the sight of your evil doings, the abominations that you committed; therefore your land became a desolation and a waste and a curse, without inhabitant, as it is to this day. [23]It is because you burned offerings, and because you sinned against the LORD and did not obey the voice of the LORD or walk in his law and in his statutes

and in his decrees, that this disaster has befallen you, as is still evident today."

24 Jeremiah said to all the people and all the women, "Hear the word of the LORD, all you Judeans who are in the land of Egypt, [25]Thus says the LORD of hosts, the God of Israel: You and your wives have accomplished in deeds what you declared in words, saying, 'We are determined to perform the vows that we have made, to make offerings to the queen of heaven and to pour out libations to her.' By all means, keep your vows and make your libations! [26]Therefore hear the word of the LORD, all you Judeans who live in the land of Egypt: Lo, I swear by my great name, says the LORD, that my name shall no longer be pronounced on the lips of any of the people of Judah in all the land of Egypt, saying, 'As the Lord GOD lives.' [27]I am going to watch over them for harm and not for good; all the people of Judah who are in the land of Egypt shall perish by the sword and by famine, until not one is left. [28]And those who escape the sword shall return from the land of Egypt to the land of Judah, few in number; and all the remnant of Judah, who have come to the land of Egypt to settle, shall know whose words will stand, mine or theirs! [29]This shall be the sign to you, says the LORD, that I am going to punish you in this place, in order that you may know that my words against you will surely be carried out: [30]Thus says the LORD, I am going to give Pharaoh Hophra, king of Egypt, into the hands of his enemies, those who seek his life, just as I gave King Zedekiah of Judah into the hand of King Nebuchadrezzar of Babylon, his enemy who sought his life."

A Word of Comfort to Baruch

45 The word that the prophet Jeremiah spoke to Baruch son of Neriah, when he wrote these words in a scroll at the dictation of Jeremiah, in the fourth year of King Jehoiakim son of Josiah of Judah: [2]Thus says the LORD, the God of Israel, to you, O Baruch: [3]You said, "Woe is me! The LORD has added sorrow to my pain; I am weary with my groaning, and I find no rest." [4]Thus you shall say to him, "Thus says the LORD: I

---

[s] Compare Syr: Heb lacks *And the women said*

am going to break down what I have
built, and pluck up what I have planted—
that is, the whole land. 5And you, do you
seek great things for yourself? Do not
seek them; for I am going to bring disaster upon all flesh, says the LORD; but I
will give you your life as a prize of war in
every place to which you may go."

Judgment on Egypt

46 The word of the LORD that
came to the prophet Jeremiah
concerning the nations.

2 Concerning Egypt, about the army
of Pharaoh Neco, king of Egypt, which
was by the river Euphrates at Carchemish and which King Nebuchadrezzar of
Babylon defeated in the fourth year of
King Jehoiakim son of Josiah of Judah:

3   Prepare buckler and shield,
        and advance for battle!
4   Harness the horses;
        mount the steeds!
    Take your stations with your
            helmets,
        whet your lances,
        put on your coats of mail!
5   Why do I see them terrified?
        They have fallen back;
    their warriors are beaten down,
        and have fled in haste.
    They do not look back—
        terror is all around!
                        says the LORD.
6   The swift cannot flee away,
        nor can the warrior escape;
    in the north by the river Euphrates
        they have stumbled and fallen.

7   Who is this, rising like the Nile,
        like rivers whose waters surge?
8   Egypt rises like the Nile,
        like rivers whose waters surge.
    It said, Let me rise, let me cover
            the earth,
        let me destroy cities and their
            inhabitants.
9   Advance, O horses,
        and dash madly, O chariots!
    Let the warriors go forth:
        Ethiopia[t] and Put who carry the
            shield,
        the Ludim, who draw[u] the bow.

10   That day is the day of the Lord GOD
        of hosts,
    a day of retribution,
        to gain vindication from his foes.
    The sword shall devour and be
            sated,
        and drink its fill of their blood.
    For the Lord GOD of hosts holds a
            sacrifice
    in the land of the north by the
        river Euphrates.
11   Go up to Gilead, and take balm,
        O virgin daughter Egypt!
    In vain you have used many
            medicines;
        there is no healing for you.
12   The nations have heard of your
            shame,
        and the earth is full of your cry;
    for warrior has stumbled against
            warrior;
        both have fallen together.

Babylonia Will Strike Egypt

13 The word that the LORD spoke to
the prophet Jeremiah about the coming
of King Nebuchadrezzar of Babylon to
attack the land of Egypt:

14   Declare in Egypt, and proclaim in
            Migdol;
        proclaim in Memphis and
            Tahpanhes;
    Say, "Take your stations and be
            ready,
        for the sword shall devour those
            around you."
15   Why has Apis fled?[v]
        Why did your bull not stand?
        —because the LORD thrust him
            down.
16   Your multitude stumbled[w] and fell,
        and one said to another,[x]
    "Come, let us go back to our own
            people
        and to the land of our birth,
        because of the destroying sword."
17   Give Pharaoh, king of Egypt, the
            name
        "Braggart who missed his
            chance."

18   As I live, says the King,
        whose name is the LORD of hosts,
    one is coming

---

t Or Nubia; Heb Cush   u Cn: Heb who grasp, who draw   v Gk: Heb Why was it swept away
w Gk: Meaning of Heb uncertain   x Gk: Heb and fell one to another and they said

like Tabor among the mountains,
and like Carmel by the sea.
19 Pack your bags for exile,
sheltered daughter Egypt!
For Memphis shall become a waste,
a ruin, without inhabitant.

20 A beautiful heifer is Egypt—
a gadfly from the north lights
upon her.
21 Even her mercenaries in her midst
are like fatted calves;
they too have turned and fled
together,
they did not stand;
for the day of their calamity has
come upon them,
the time of their punishment.

22 She makes a sound like a snake
gliding away;
for her enemies march in force,
and come against her with axes,
like those who fell trees.
23 They shall cut down her forest,
says the LORD,
though it is impenetrable,
because they are more numerous
than locusts;
they are without number.
24 Daughter Egypt shall be put to
shame;
she shall be handed over to a
people from the north.

25 The LORD of hosts, the God of Israel, said: See, I am bringing punishment
upon Amon of Thebes, and Pharaoh, and
Egypt and her gods and her kings, upon
Pharaoh and those who trust in him. 26I
will hand them over to those who seek
their life, to King Nebuchadrezzar of
Babylon and his officers. Afterward
Egypt shall be inhabited as in the days of
old, says the LORD.

God Will Save Israel

27 But as for you, have no fear, my
servant Jacob,
and do not be dismayed, O Israel;
for I am going to save you from far
away,
and your offspring from the land
of their captivity.

Jacob shall return and have quiet
and ease,
and no one shall make him afraid.
28 As for you, have no fear, my
servant Jacob,
says the LORD,
for I am with you.
I will make an end of all the nations
among which I have banished
you,
but I will not make an end of you!
I will chastise you in just measure,
and I will by no means leave you
unpunished.

Judgment on the Philistines

47 The word of the LORD that
came to the prophet Jeremiah
concerning the Philistines, before Pharaoh attacked Gaza:
2 Thus says the LORD:
See, waters are rising out of the
north
and shall become an overflowing
torrent;
they shall overflow the land and all
that fills it,
the city and those who live in it.
People shall cry out,
and all the inhabitants of the
land shall wail.
3 At the noise of the stamping of the
hoofs of his stallions,
at the clatter of his chariots, at
the rumbling of their wheels,
parents do not turn back for
children,
so feeble are their hands,
4 because of the day that is coming
to destroy all the Philistines,
to cut off from Tyre and Sidon
every helper that remains.
For the LORD is destroying the
Philistines,
the remnant of the coastland of
Caphtor.
5 Baldness has come upon Gaza,
Ashkelon is silenced.
O remnant of their power!y
How long will you gash
yourselves?
6 Ah, sword of the LORD!
How long until you are quiet?
Put yourself into your scabbard,
rest and be still!

y Gk: Heb *their valley*

7 How can it^z be quiet,
    when the LORD has given it an
      order?
Against Ashkelon and against the
    seashore—
    there he has appointed it.

Judgment on Moab

48 Concerning Moab.

Thus says the LORD of hosts, the God of
Israel:
    Alas for Nebo, it is laid waste!
      Kiriathaim is put to shame, it is
        taken;
    the fortress is put to shame and
      broken down;
2 the renown of Moab is no more.
In Heshbon they planned evil
      against her:
    "Come, let us cut her off from
      being a nation!"
You also, O Madmen, shall be
      brought to silence;^{a}
    the sword shall pursue you.

3 Hark! a cry from Horonaim,
    "Desolation and great
      destruction!"
4 "Moab is destroyed!"
    her little ones cry out.
5 For at the ascent of Luhith
    they go^b up weeping bitterly;
for at the descent of Horonaim
    they have heard the distressing
      cry of anguish.
6 Flee! Save yourselves!
    Be like a wild ass^c in the desert!

7 Surely, because you trusted in your
      strongholds^d and your
      treasures,
    you also shall be taken;
Chemosh shall go out into exile,
    with his priests and his
      attendants.
8 The destroyer shall come upon
      every town,
    and no town shall escape;
the valley shall perish,
    and the plain shall be destroyed,
      as the LORD has spoken.

9 Set aside salt for Moab,
    for she will surely fall;
her towns shall become a
      desolation,
    with no inhabitant in them.

10 Accursed is the one who is slack
in doing the work of the LORD; and
accursed is the one who keeps back the
sword from bloodshed.

11 Moab has been at ease from his
      youth,
    settled like wine^e on its dregs;
he has not been emptied from
      vessel to vessel,
    nor has he gone into exile;
therefore his flavor has remained
    and his aroma is unspoiled.
12 Therefore, the time is surely coming, says the LORD, when I shall send to
him decanters to decant him, and
empty his vessels, and break his^f jars in
pieces. 13Then Moab shall be ashamed
of Chemosh, as the house of Israel was
ashamed of Bethel, their confidence.

14 How can you say, "We are heroes
    and mighty warriors"?
15 The destroyer of Moab and his
      towns has come up,
    and the choicest of his young
      men have gone down to
      slaughter,
    says the King, whose name is the
      LORD of hosts.
16 The calamity of Moab is near at
      hand
    and his doom approaches swiftly.
17 Mourn over him, all you his
      neighbors,
    and all who know his name;
say, "How the mighty scepter is
      broken,
    the glorious staff!"

18 Come down from glory,
    and sit on the parched ground,
    enthroned daughter Dibon!
For the destroyer of Moab has come
      up against you;
he has destroyed your
      strongholds.

---

z Gk Vg: Heb *you*   a The place-name *Madmen* sounds like the Hebrew verb *to be silent*
b Cn: Heb *he goes*   c Gk Aquila: Heb *like Aroer*   d Gk: Heb *works*   e Heb lacks *like wine*
f Gk Aquila: Heb *their*

19 Stand by the road and watch,
    you inhabitant of Aroer!
Ask the man fleeing and the
    woman escaping;
    say, "What has happened?"
20 Moab is put to shame, for it is
    broken down;
    wail and cry!
Tell it by the Arnon,
    that Moab is laid waste.

21 Judgment has come upon the tableland, upon Holon, and Jahzah, and Mephaath, 22and Dibon, and Nebo, and Beth-diblathaim, 23and Kiriathaim, and Beth-gamul, and Beth-meon, 24and Kerioth, and Bozrah, and all the towns of the land of Moab, far and near. 25The horn of Moab is cut off, and his arm is broken, says the LORD.
26 Make him drunk, because he magnified himself against the LORD; let Moab wallow in his vomit; he too shall become a laughingstock. 27Israel was a laughingstock for you, though he was not caught among thieves; but whenever you spoke of him you shook your head!

28 Leave the towns, and live on the
    rock,
    O inhabitants of Moab!
Be like the dove that nests
    on the sides of the mouth of a
    gorge.
29 We have heard of the pride of
    Moab—
    he is very proud—
of his loftiness, his pride, and his
    arrogance,
    and the haughtiness of his heart.
30 I myself know his insolence, says
    the LORD;
    his boasts are false,
    his deeds are false.
31 Therefore I wail for Moab;
    I cry out for all Moab;
    for the people of Kir-heres I
    mourn.
32 More than for Jazer I weep for you,
    O vine of Sibmah!
Your branches crossed over the sea,
    reached as far as Jazer;*g*

upon your summer fruits and your
    vintage
    the destroyer has fallen.
33 Gladness and joy have been taken
    away
    from the fruitful land of Moab;
I have stopped the wine from the
    wine presses;
    no one treads them with shouts
    of joy;
    the shouting is not the shout of
    joy.

34 Heshbon and Elealeh cry out;*h* as far as Jahaz they utter their voice, from Zoar to Horonaim and Eglath-shelishiyah. For even the waters of Nimrim have become desolate. 35And I will bring to an end in Moab, says the LORD, those who offer sacrifice at a high place and make offerings to their gods. 36Therefore my heart moans for Moab like a flute, and my heart moans like a flute for the people of Kir-heres; for the riches they gained have perished.
37 For every head is shaved and every beard cut off; on all the hands there are gashes, and on the loins sackcloth. 38On all the housetops of Moab and in the squares there is nothing but lamentation; for I have broken Moab like a vessel that no one wants, says the LORD. 39How it is broken! How they wail! How Moab has turned his back in shame! So Moab has become a derision and a horror to all his neighbors.
40 For thus says the LORD:
    Look, he shall swoop down like an
    eagle,
    and spread his wings against
    Moab;
41 the towns*i* shall be taken
    and the strongholds seized.
The hearts of the warriors of Moab,
    on that day,
    shall be like the heart of a
    woman in labor.
42 Moab shall be destroyed as a people,
    because he magnified himself
    against the LORD.
43 Terror, pit, and trap
    are before you, O inhabitants of
    Moab!
                says the LORD.

g Two Mss and Isa 16.8: MT *the sea of Jazer*   h Cn: Heb *From the cry of Heshbon to Elealeh*
i Or *Kerioth*

44 Everyone who flees from the terror
 shall fall into the pit,
and everyone who climbs out of
 the pit
 shall be caught in the trap.
For I will bring these things*j* upon
 Moab
 in the year of their punishment,
 says the LORD.

45 In the shadow of Heshbon
 fugitives stop exhausted;
for a fire has gone out from
 Heshbon,
 a flame from the house of Sihon;
it has destroyed the forehead of
 Moab,
 the scalp of the people of tumult.*k*
46 Woe to you, O Moab!
 The people of Chemosh have
 perished,
for your sons have been taken
 captive,
 and your daughters into captivity.
47 Yet I will restore the fortunes of
 Moab
 in the latter days, says the LORD.
 Thus far is the judgment on Moab.

Judgment on the Ammonites

49 Concerning the Ammonites.

Thus says the LORD:
 Has Israel no sons?
 Has he no heir?
Why then has Milcom dispossessed
 Gad,
 and his people settled in its
 towns?
2 Therefore, the time is surely
 coming,
 says the LORD,
when I will sound the battle alarm
 against Rabbah of the
 Ammonites;
it shall become a desolate mound,
 and its villages shall be burned
 with fire;
then Israel shall dispossess those
 who dispossessed him,
 says the LORD.

3 Wail, O Heshbon, for Ai is laid
 waste!
 Cry out, O daughters*l* of Rabbah!

Put on sackcloth,
 lament, and slash yourselves
 with whips!*m*
For Milcom shall go into exile,
 with his priests and his
 attendants.
4 Why do you boast in your strength?
 Your strength is ebbing,
O faithless daughter.
 You trusted in your treasures,
 saying,
 "Who will attack me?"
5 I am going to bring terror upon you,
 says the Lord GOD of hosts,
 from all your neighbors,
and you will be scattered, each
 headlong,
 with no one to gather the
 fugitives.
6 But afterward I will restore the fortunes of the Ammonites, says the LORD.

Judgment on Edom

7 Concerning Edom.

Thus says the LORD of hosts:
 Is there no longer wisdom in
 Teman?
 Has counsel perished from the
 prudent?
 Has their wisdom vanished?
8 Flee, turn back, get down low,
 inhabitants of Dedan!
For I will bring the calamity of
 Esau upon him,
 the time when I punish him.
9 If grape-gatherers came to you,
 would they not leave gleanings?
If thieves came by night,
 even they would pillage only
 what they wanted.
10 But as for me, I have stripped Esau
 bare,
 I have uncovered his hiding
 places,
 and he is not able to conceal
 himself.
His offspring are destroyed, his
 kinsfolk
 and his neighbors; and he is no
 more.
11 Leave your orphans, I will keep
 them alive;
 and let your widows trust in me.
12 For thus says the LORD: If those

j Gk Syr: Heb *bring upon it*   *k* Or *of Shaon*   *l* Or *villages*   *m* Cn: Meaning of Heb uncertain

who do not deserve to drink the cup still have to drink it, shall you be the one to go unpunished? You shall not go unpunished; you must drink it. [13]For by myself I have sworn, says the LORD, that Bozrah shall become an object of horror and ridicule, a waste, and an object of cursing; and all her towns shall be perpetual wastes.

[14] I have heard tidings from the LORD,
  and a messenger has been sent
    among the nations:
  "Gather yourselves together and
    come against her,
  and rise up for battle!"
[15] For I will make you least among
    the nations,
  despised by humankind.
[16] The terror you inspire
  and the pride of your heart have
    deceived you,
  you who live in the clefts of the
    rock,[n]
  who hold the height of the hill.
  Although you make your nest as
    high as the eagle's,
  from there I will bring you down,
            says the LORD.

[17] Edom shall become an object of horror; everyone who passes by it will be horrified and will hiss because of all its disasters. [18]As when Sodom and Gomorrah and their neighbors were overthrown, says the LORD, no one shall live there, nor shall anyone settle in it. [19]Like a lion coming up from the thickets of the Jordan against a perennial pasture, I will suddenly chase Edom[o] away from it; and I will appoint over it whomever I choose.[p] For who is like me? Who can summon me? Who is the shepherd who can stand before me? [20]Therefore hear the plan that the LORD has made against Edom and the purposes that he has formed against the inhabitants of Teman: Surely the little ones of the flock shall be dragged away; surely their fold shall be appalled at their fate. [21]At the sound of their fall the earth shall tremble; the sound of their cry shall be heard at the Red Sea.[q] [22]Look, he shall mount up and swoop down like an eagle, and spread his wings

against Bozrah, and the heart of the warriors of Edom in that day shall be like the heart of a woman in labor.

Judgment on Damascus

23 Concerning Damascus.

  Hamath and Arpad are confounded,
    for they have heard bad news;
  they melt in fear, they are troubled
      like the sea[r]
    that cannot be quiet.
[24] Damascus has become feeble, she
      turned to flee,
    and panic seized her;
  anguish and sorrows have taken
      hold of her,
    as of a woman in labor.
[25] How the famous city is forsaken,[s]
    the joyful town![t]
[26] Therefore her young men shall fall
      in her squares,
  and all her soldiers shall be
      destroyed in that day,
          says the LORD of hosts.
[27] And I will kindle a fire at the wall
      of Damascus,
  and it shall devour the
      strongholds of Ben-hadad.

Judgment on Kedar and Hazor

28 Concerning Kedar and the kingdoms of Hazor that King Nebuchadrezzar of Babylon defeated.

  Thus says the LORD:
  Rise up, advance against Kedar!
  Destroy the people of the east!
[29] Take their tents and their flocks,
    their curtains and all their goods;
  carry off their camels for
      yourselves,
  and a cry shall go up: "Terror is
      all around!"
[30] Flee, wander far away, hide in deep
      places,
  O inhabitants of Hazor!
          says the LORD.
  For King Nebuchadrezzar of
      Babylon
  has made a plan against you
  and formed a purpose against
      you.

n Or of Sela   o Heb him   p Or and I will single out the choicest of his rams: Meaning of Heb
uncertain   q Or Sea of Reeds   r Cn: Heb there is trouble in the sea   s Vg: Heb is not forsaken
t Syr Vg Tg: Heb the town of my joy

31 Rise up, advance against a nation at
    ease,
      that lives secure,
                  says the LORD,
    that has no gates or bars,
      that lives alone.
32 Their camels shall become booty,
      their herds of cattle a spoil.
    I will scatter to every wind
      those who have shaven temples,
    and I will bring calamity
      against them from every side,
                says the LORD.
33 Hazor shall become a lair of
    jackals,
      an everlasting waste;
    no one shall live there,
      nor shall anyone settle in it.

Judgment on Elam

34 The word of the LORD that came
to the prophet Jeremiah concerning
Elam, at the beginning of the reign of
King Zedekiah of Judah.

35 Thus says the LORD of hosts: I am
going to break the bow of Elam, the
mainstay of their might; 36and I will
bring upon Elam the four winds from
the four quarters of heaven; and I will
scatter them to all these winds, and
there shall be no nation to which the
exiles from Elam shall not come. 37I will
terrify Elam before their enemies, and
before those who seek their life; I will
bring disaster upon them, my fierce
anger, says the LORD. I will send the
sword after them, until I have consumed
them; 38and I will set my throne in
Elam, and destroy their king and officials, says the LORD.

39 But in the latter days I will restore
the fortunes of Elam, says the LORD.

Judgment on Babylon

50 The word that the LORD
spoke concerning Babylon,
concerning the land of the Chaldeans,
by the prophet Jeremiah:
2 Declare among the nations and
    proclaim,
      set up a banner and proclaim,
      do not conceal it, say:
    Babylon is taken,
      Bel is put to shame,
      Merodach is dismayed.

    Her images are put to shame,
      her idols are dismayed.
3 For out of the north a nation has
come up against her; it shall make her
land a desolation, and no one shall live
in it; both human beings and animals
shall flee away.

4 In those days and in that time, says
the LORD, the people of Israel shall
come, they and the people of Judah
together; they shall come weeping as
they seek the LORD their God. 5They
shall ask the way to Zion, with faces
turned toward it, and they shall come
and join[u] themselves to the LORD by an
everlasting covenant that will never be
forgotten.

6 My people have been lost sheep;
their shepherds have led them astray,
turning them away on the mountains;
from mountain to hill they have gone,
they have forgotten their fold. 7All who
found them have devoured them, and
their enemies have said, "We are not
guilty, because they have sinned against
the LORD, the true pasture, the LORD, the
hope of their ancestors."

8 Flee from Babylon, and go out of
the land of the Chaldeans, and be like
male goats leading the flock. 9For I am
going to stir up and bring against Babylon a company of great nations from
the land of the north; and they shall
array themselves against her; from there
she shall be taken. Their arrows are like
the arrows of a skilled warrior who does
not return empty-handed. 10Chaldea
shall be plundered; all who plunder her
shall be sated, says the LORD.

11 Though you rejoice, though you
    exult,
      O plunderers of my heritage,
    though you frisk about like a heifer
      on the grass,
      and neigh like stallions,
12 your mother shall be utterly
    shamed,
      and she who bore you shall be
      disgraced.
    Lo, she shall be the last of the
      nations,

---

u Gk: Heb *toward it. Come! They shall join*

a wilderness, dry land, and a
    desert.
13 Because of the wrath of the LORD
        she shall not be inhabited,
    but shall be an utter desolation;
    everyone who passes by Babylon
        shall be appalled
    and hiss because of all her
        wounds.
14 Take up your positions around
        Babylon,
    all you that bend the bow;
    shoot at her, spare no arrows,
        for she has sinned against the
        LORD.
15 Raise a shout against her from all
        sides,
    "She has surrendered;
    her bulwarks have fallen,
        her walls are thrown down."
    For this is the vengeance of the
        LORD:
    take vengeance on her,
        do to her as she has done.
16 Cut off from Babylon the sower,
        and the wielder of the sickle in
        time of harvest;
    because of the destroying sword
        all of them shall return to their
        own people,
    and all of them shall flee to their
        own land.

17 Israel is a hunted sheep driven away by lions. First the king of Assyria devoured it, and now at the end King Nebuchadrezzar of Babylon has gnawed its bones. 18Therefore, thus says the LORD of hosts, the God of Israel: I am going to punish the king of Babylon and his land, as I punished the king of Assyria. 19I will restore Israel to its pasture, and it shall feed on Carmel and in Bashan, and on the hills of Ephraim and in Gilead its hunger shall be satisfied. 20In those days and at that time, says the LORD, the iniquity of Israel shall be sought, and there shall be none; and the sins of Judah, and none shall be found; for I will pardon the remnant that I have spared.

21 Go up to the land of Merathaim;ᵛ
        go up against her,
    and attack the inhabitants of
        Pekodʷ

and utterly destroy the last of
    them,ˣ
                        says the LORD;
    do all that I have commanded
        you.
22 The noise of battle is in the land,
        and great destruction!
23 How the hammer of the whole
        earth
    is cut down and broken!
    How Babylon has become
        a horror among the nations!
24 You set a snare for yourself and you
        were caught, O Babylon,
        but you did not know it;
    you were discovered and seized,
        because you challenged the
        LORD.
25 The LORD has opened his armory,
        and brought out the weapons of
        his wrath,
    for the Lord GOD of hosts has a task
        to do
    in the land of the Chaldeans.
26 Come against her from every
        quarter;
    open her granaries;
    pile her up like heaps of grain, and
        destroy her utterly;
    let nothing be left of her.
27 Kill all her bulls,
        let them go down to the
        slaughter.
    Alas for them, their day has come,
        the time of their punishment!

28 Listen! Fugitives and refugees from the land of Babylon are coming to declare in Zion the vengeance of the LORD our God, vengeance for his temple.

29 Summon archers against Babylon, all who bend the bow. Encamp all around her; let no one escape. Repay her according to her deeds; just as she has done, do to her—for she has arrogantly defied the LORD, the Holy One of Israel. 30Therefore her young men shall fall in her squares, and all her soldiers shall be destroyed on that day, says the LORD.

31 I am against you, O arrogant one,
        says the Lord GOD of hosts;
    for your day has come,
        the time when I will punish you.

v Or of Double Rebellion   w Or of Punishment   x Tg: Heb destroy after them

32 The arrogant one shall stumble and
    fall,
  with no one to raise him up,
and I will kindle a fire in his cities,
  and it will devour everything
    around him.

33 Thus says the LORD of hosts: The
people of Israel are oppressed, and so too
are the people of Judah; all their captors
have held them fast and refuse to let
them go. 34Their Redeemer is strong;
the LORD of hosts is his name. He will
surely plead their cause, that he may
give rest to the earth, but unrest to the
inhabitants of Babylon.

35 A sword against the Chaldeans,
    says the LORD,
  and against the inhabitants of
    Babylon,
  and against her officials and her
    sages!
36 A sword against the diviners,
    so that they may become fools!
  A sword against her warriors,
    so that they may be destroyed!
37 A sword against her[y] horses and
    against her[y] chariots,
  and against all the foreign troops
    in her midst,
  so that they may become
    women!
  A sword against all her treasures,
    that they may be plundered!
38 A drought[z] against her waters,
    that they may be dried up!
  For it is a land of images,
    and they go mad over idols.

39 Therefore wild animals shall live
with hyenas in Babylon,[a] and ostriches
shall inhabit her; she shall never again
be peopled, or inhabited for all generations. 40As when God overthrew Sodom
and Gomorrah and their neighbors, says
the LORD, so no one shall live there, nor
shall anyone settle in her.

41 Look, a people is coming from the
    north;
  a mighty nation and many kings

are stirring from the farthest
    parts of the earth.
42 They wield bow and spear,
    they are cruel and have no mercy.
  The sound of them is like the
    roaring sea;
  they ride upon horses,
set in array as a warrior for battle,
    against you, O daughter Babylon!

43 The king of Babylon heard news of
    them,
  and his hands fell helpless;
anguish seized him,
  pain like that of a woman in
    labor.

44 Like a lion coming up from the
thickets of the Jordan against a perennial pasture, I will suddenly chase them
away from her; and I will appoint over
her whomever I choose.[b] For who is like
me? Who can summon me? Who is the
shepherd who can stand before me?
45Therefore hear the plan that the LORD
has made against Babylon, and the purposes that he has formed against the
land of the Chaldeans: Surely the little
ones of the flock shall be dragged away;
surely their[c] fold shall be appalled at
their fate. 46At the sound of the capture
of Babylon the earth shall tremble, and
her cry shall be heard among the
nations.

51 Thus says the LORD:
  I am going to stir up a
    destructive wind[d]
  against Babylon
  and against the inhabitants of
    Leb-qamai;[e]
2 and I will send winnowers to
    Babylon,
  and they shall winnow her.
  They shall empty her land
  when they come against her from
    every side
  on the day of trouble.
3 Let not the archer bend his bow,
  and let him not array himself in
    his coat of mail.
  Do not spare her young men;
  utterly destroy her entire army.

y Cn: Heb his z Another reading is A sword
the choicest of her rams: Meaning of Heb uncertain
d Or stir up the spirit of a destroyer e Leb-qamai is a cryptogram for Kasdim, Chaldea
a Heb lacks in Babylon b Or and I will single out
c Syr Gk Tg Compare 49.20: Heb lacks their

4 They shall fall down slain in the
  land of the Chaldeans,
  and wounded in her streets.
5 Israel and Judah have not been
  forsaken
  by their God, the LORD of hosts,
  though their land is full of guilt
  before the Holy One of Israel.

6 Flee from the midst of Babylon,
  save your lives, each of you!
  Do not perish because of her guilt,
  for this is the time of the LORD's
  vengeance;
  he is repaying her what is due.
7 Babylon was a golden cup in the
  LORD's hand,
  making all the earth drunken;
  the nations drank of her wine,
  and so the nations went mad.
8 Suddenly Babylon has fallen and is
  shattered;
  wail for her!
  Bring balm for her wound;
  perhaps she may be healed.
9 We tried to heal Babylon,
  but she could not be healed.
  Forsake her, and let each of us go
  to our own country;
  for her judgment has reached up to
  heaven
  and has been lifted up even to the
  skies.
10 The LORD has brought forth our
  vindication;
  come, let us declare in Zion
  the work of the LORD our God.

11 Sharpen the arrows!
  Fill the quivers!
The LORD has stirred up the spirit of the
kings of the Medes, because his purpose
concerning Babylon is to destroy it, for
that is the vengeance of the LORD,
vengeance for his temple.
12 Raise a standard against the walls
  of Babylon;
  make the watch strong;
  post sentinels;
  prepare the ambushes;
  for the LORD has both planned and
  done
  what he spoke concerning the
  inhabitants of Babylon.

13 You who live by mighty waters,
  rich in treasures,
  your end has come,
  the thread of your life is cut.
14 The LORD of hosts has sworn by
  himself:
  Surely I will fill you with troops
  like a swarm of locusts,
  and they shall raise a shout of
  victory over you.

15 It is he who made the earth by his
  power,
  who established the world by his
  wisdom,
  and by his understanding stretched
  out the heavens.
16 When he utters his voice there is a
  tumult of waters in the
  heavens,
  and he makes the mist rise from
  the ends of the earth.
  He makes lightnings for the rain,
  and he brings out the wind from
  his storehouses.
17 Everyone is stupid and without
  knowledge;
  goldsmiths are all put to shame
  by their idols;
  for their images are false,
  and there is no breath in them.
18 They are worthless, a work of
  delusion;
  at the time of their punishment
  they shall perish.
19 Not like these is the LORD,f the
  portion of Jacob,
  for he is the one who formed all
  things,
  and Israel is the tribe of his
  inheritance;
  the LORD of hosts is his name.

Israel the Creator's Instrument
20 You are my war club, my weapon
  of battle:
  with you I smash nations;
  with you I destroy kingdoms;
21 with you I smash the horse and its
  rider;
  with you I smash the chariot and
  the charioteer;
22 with you I smash man and woman;
  with you I smash the old man
  and the boy;

f Heb lacks the LORD

with you I smash the young man
    and the girl;
23 with you I smash shepherds and
        their flocks;
    with you I smash farmers and their
        teams;
    with you I smash governors and
        deputies.

The Doom of Babylon

24 I will repay Babylon and all the
inhabitants of Chaldea before your very
eyes for all the wrong that they have
done in Zion, says the LORD.

25 I am against you, O destroying
        mountain,
                        says the LORD,
    that destroys the whole earth;
    I will stretch out my hand against
        you,
    and roll you down from the crags,
    and make you a burned-out
        mountain.
26 No stone shall be taken from you
        for a corner
    and no stone for a foundation,
    but you shall be a perpetual waste,
        says the LORD.

27 Raise a standard in the land,
    blow the trumpet among the
        nations;
    prepare the nations for war against
        her,
    summon against her the
        kingdoms,
    Ararat, Minni, and Ashkenaz;
    appoint a marshal against her,
    bring up horses like bristling
        locusts.
28 Prepare the nations for war against
        her,
    the kings of the Medes, with
        their governors and deputies,
    and every land under their
        dominion.
29 The land trembles and writhes,
    for the LORD's purposes against
        Babylon stand,
    to make the land of Babylon a
        desolation,
    without inhabitant.
30 The warriors of Babylon have given
        up fighting,
    they remain in their strongholds;

their strength has failed,
    they have become women;
her buildings are set on fire,
    her bars are broken.
31 One runner runs to meet another,
    and one messenger to meet
        another,
    to tell the king of Babylon
    that his city is taken from end to
        end:
32 the fords have been seized,
    the marshes have been burned
        with fire,
    and the soldiers are in panic.
33 For thus says the LORD of hosts, the
        God of Israel:
    Daughter Babylon is like a
        threshing floor
    at the time when it is trodden;
    yet a little while
    and the time of her harvest will
        come.

34 "King Nebuchadrezzar of Babylon
        has devoured me,
    he has crushed me;
    he has made me an empty vessel,
    he has swallowed me like a
        monster;
    he has filled his belly with my
        delicacies,
    he has spewed me out.
35 May my torn flesh be avenged on
        Babylon,"
    the inhabitants of Zion shall say.
    "May my blood be avenged on the
        inhabitants of Chaldea,"
    Jerusalem shall say.
36 Therefore thus says the LORD:
    I am going to defend your cause
    and take vengeance for you.
    I will dry up her sea
    and make her fountain dry;
37 and Babylon shall become a heap of
        ruins,
    a den of jackals,
    an object of horror and of hissing,
    without inhabitant.

38 Like lions they shall roar together;
    they shall growl like lions'
        whelps.
39 When they are inflamed, I will set
        out their drink
    and make them drunk, until they
        become merry

and then sleep a perpetual sleep
  and never wake, says the LORD.
40 I will bring them down like lambs
      to the slaughter,
    like rams and goats.

41 How Sheshach[g] is taken,
    the pride of the whole earth
      seized!
  How Babylon has become
    an object of horror among the
      nations!
42 The sea has risen over Babylon;
    she has been covered by its
      tumultuous waves.
43 Her cities have become an object of
      horror,
    a land of drought and a desert,
  a land in which no one lives,
    and through which no mortal
      passes.
44 I will punish Bel in Babylon,
    and make him disgorge what he
      has swallowed.
  The nations shall no longer stream
      to him;
    the wall of Babylon has fallen.

45 Come out of her, my people!
    Save your lives, each of you,
    from the fierce anger of the LORD!
46 Do not be fainthearted or fearful
      at the rumors heard in the land—
  one year one rumor comes,
    the next year another,
  rumors of violence in the land
    and of ruler against ruler.

47 Assuredly, the days are coming
    when I will punish the images of
      Babylon;
  her whole land shall be put to
      shame,
    and all her slain shall fall in her
      midst.
48 Then the heavens and the earth,
    and all that is in them,
  shall shout for joy over Babylon;
    for the destroyers shall come
      against them out of the
      north,
                     says the LORD.
49 Babylon must fall for the slain of
      Israel,

as the slain of all the earth have
    fallen because of Babylon.

50 You survivors of the sword,
    go, do not linger!
  Remember the LORD in a distant
      land,
    and let Jerusalem come into your
      mind:
51 We are put to shame, for we have
      heard insults;
    dishonor has covered our face,
  for aliens have come
    into the holy places of the LORD's
      house.

52 Therefore the time is surely
      coming, says the LORD,
    when I will punish her idols,
  and through all her land
    the wounded shall groan.
53 Though Babylon should mount up
      to heaven,
    and though she should fortify her
      strong height,
  from me destroyers would come
      upon her,
    says the LORD.

54 Listen!—a cry from Babylon!
    A great crashing from the land of
      the Chaldeans!
55 For the LORD is laying Babylon
      waste,
    and stilling her loud clamor.
  Their waves roar like mighty
      waters,
    the sound of their clamor
      resounds;
56 for a destroyer has come against
      her,
    against Babylon;
  her warriors are taken,
    their bows are broken;
  for the LORD is a God of
      recompense,
    he will repay in full.
57 I will make her officials and her
      sages drunk,
    also her governors, her deputies,
      and her warriors;
  they shall sleep a perpetual sleep
      and never wake,
    says the King, whose name is the
      LORD of hosts.

g Sheshach is a cryptogram for Babel, Babylon

58   Thus says the LORD of hosts:
    The broad wall of Babylon
       shall be leveled to the ground,
    and her high gates
       shall be burned with fire.
    The peoples exhaust themselves for
       nothing,
    and the nations weary
       themselves only for fire.h

Jeremiah's Command to Seraiah

59 The word that the prophet Jeremiah commanded Seraiah son of Neriah son of Mahseiah, when he went with King Zedekiah of Judah to Babylon, in the fourth year of his reign. Seraiah was the quartermaster. 60Jeremiah wrote in ai scroll all the disasters that would come on Babylon, all these words that are written concerning Babylon. 61And Jeremiah said to Seraiah: "When you come to Babylon, see that you read all these words, 62and say, 'O LORD, you yourself threatened to destroy this place so that neither human beings nor animals shall live in it, and it shall be desolate forever.' 63When you finish reading this scroll, tie a stone to it, and throw it into the middle of the Euphrates, 64and say, 'Thus shall Babylon sink, to rise no more, because of the disasters that I am bringing on her.'"j

Thus far are the words of Jeremiah.

The Destruction of Jerusalem Reviewed

52 Zedekiah was twenty-one years old when he began to reign; he reigned eleven years in Jerusalem. His mother's name was Hamutal daughter of Jeremiah of Libnah. 2He did what was evil in the sight of the LORD, just as Jehoiakim had done. 3Indeed, Jerusalem and Judah so angered the LORD that he expelled them from his presence.

Zedekiah rebelled against the king of Babylon. 4And in the ninth year of his reign, in the tenth month, on the tenth day of the month, King Nebuchadrezzar of Babylon came with all his army against Jerusalem, and they laid siege to it; they built siegeworks against it all around. 5So the city was besieged until

the eleventh year of King Zedekiah. 6On the ninth day of the fourth month the famine became so severe in the city that there was no food for the people of the land. 7Then a breach was made in the city wall;k and all the soldiers fled and went out from the city by night by the way of the gate between the two walls, by the king's garden, though the Chaldeans were all around the city. They went in the direction of the Arabah. 8But the army of the Chaldeans pursued the king, and overtook Zedekiah in the plains of Jericho; and all his army was scattered, deserting him. 9Then they captured the king, and brought him up to the king of Babylon at Riblah in the land of Hamath, and he passed sentence on him. 10The king of Babylon killed the sons of Zedekiah before his eyes, and also killed all the officers of Judah at Riblah. 11He put out the eyes of Zedekiah, and bound him in fetters, and the king of Babylon took him to Babylon, and put him in prison until the day of his death.

12 In the fifth month, on the tenth day of the month—which was the nineteenth year of King Nebuchadrezzar, king of Babylon—Nebuzaradan the captain of the bodyguard who served the king of Babylon, entered Jerusalem. 13He burned the house of the LORD, the king's house, and all the houses of Jerusalem; every great house he burned down. 14All the army of the Chaldeans, who were with the captain of the guard, broke down all the walls around Jerusalem. 15Nebuzaradan the captain of the guard carried into exile some of the poorest of the people and the rest of the people who were left in the city and the deserters who had defected to the king of Babylon, together with the rest of the artisans. 16But Nebuzaradan the captain of the guard left some of the poorest people of the land to be vinedressers and tillers of the soil.

17 The pillars of bronze that were in the house of the LORD, and the stands and the bronze sea that were in the house of the LORD, the Chaldeans broke in pieces, and carried all the bronze to Babylon. 18They took away the pots, the

---

h Gk Syr Compare Hab 2.13: Heb *and the nations for fire, and they are weary*   i Or *one*   j Gk: Heb *on her. And they shall weary themselves*   k Heb lacks *wall*

shovels, the snuffers, the basins, the ladles, and all the vessels of bronze used in the temple service. [19]The captain of the guard took away the small bowls also, the firepans, the basins, the pots, the lampstands, the ladles, and the bowls for libation, both those of gold and those of silver. [20]As for the two pillars, the one sea, the twelve bronze bulls that were under the sea, and the stands,[1] which King Solomon had made for the house of the LORD, the bronze of all these vessels was beyond weighing. [21]As for the pillars, the height of the one pillar was eighteen cubits, its circumference was twelve cubits; it was hollow and its thickness was four fingers. [22]Upon it was a capital of bronze; the height of the capital was five cubits; latticework and pomegranates, all of bronze, encircled the top of the capital. And the second pillar had the same, with pomegranates. [23]There were ninety-six pomegranates on the sides; all the pomegranates encircling the latticework numbered one hundred.

24 The captain of the guard took the chief priest Seraiah, the second priest Zephaniah, and the three guardians of the threshold; [25]and from the city he took an officer who had been in command of the soldiers, and seven men of the king's council who were found in the city; the secretary of the commander of the army who mustered the people of the land; and sixty men of the people of the land who were found inside the city.

[26]Then Nebuzaradan the captain of the guard took them, and brought them to the king of Babylon at Riblah. [27]And the king of Babylon struck them down, and put them to death at Riblah in the land of Hamath. So Judah went into exile out of its land.

28 This is the number of the people whom Nebuchadrezzar took into exile: in the seventh year, three thousand twenty-three Judeans; [29]in the eighteenth year of Nebuchadrezzar he took into exile from Jerusalem eight hundred thirty-two persons; [30]in the twenty-third year of Nebuchadrezzar, Nebuzaradan the captain of the guard took into exile of the Judeans seven hundred forty-five persons; all the persons were four thousand six hundred.

Jehoiachin Favored in Captivity

31 In the thirty-seventh year of the exile of King Jehoiachin of Judah, in the twelfth month, on the twenty-fifth day of the month, King Evil-merodach of Babylon, in the year he began to reign, showed favor to King Jehoiachin of Judah and brought him out of prison; [32]he spoke kindly to him, and gave him a seat above the seats of the other kings who were with him in Babylon. [33]So Jehoiachin put aside his prison clothes, and every day of his life he dined regularly at the king's table. [34]For his allowance, a regular daily allowance was given him by the king of Babylon, as long as he lived, up to the day of his death.

1 Cn: Heb that were under the stands

LAMENTATIONS

AMENTATIONS IS THE ONLY OLD TESTA-
MENT BOOK THAT CONSISTS SOLELY OF
LAMENTS. ITS AUTHOR, TRADITIONALLY
THOUGHT TO BE JEREMIAH, "LAMENTS" THE
INTENSE SUFFERING OF GOD'S PEOPLE AND THE
UTTER DEVASTATION OF THE TEMPLE. KNOWING
THAT GOD IS MERCIFUL, HE APPEALS FOR MERCY IN
PRAYER. IN THE MIDDLE OF THE BOOK, JEREMIAH
AFFIRMS GOD'S GOODNESS AND FAITHFULNESS IN
THE MIDST OF SUFFERING. HERE YOU FIND A FAITH
ROOTED IN GOD'S UNCHANGING CHARACTER—
A RINGING AFFIRMATION OF THE GOD WHOSE
"MERCIES NEVER COME TO AN END" (3.22).

The Deserted City

1 How lonely sits the city
    that once was full of people!
How like a widow she has become,
    she that was great among the
        nations!
She that was a princess among the
        provinces
    has become a vassal.

2 She weeps bitterly in the night,
    with tears on her cheeks;
among all her lovers
    she has no one to comfort her;
all her friends have dealt
        treacherously with her,
    they have become her enemies.

3 Judah has gone into exile with
        suffering
    and hard servitude;
she lives now among the nations,
    and finds no resting place;
her pursuers have all overtaken her
    in the midst of her distress.

4 The roads to Zion mourn,
    for no one comes to the festivals;
all her gates are desolate,
    her priests groan;
her young girls grieve, *a*
    and her lot is bitter.

5 Her foes have become the masters,
    her enemies prosper,
because the LORD has made her
        suffer

a Meaning of Heb uncertain

for the multitude of her
transgressions;
her children have gone away,
captives before the foe.

6 From daughter Zion has departed
all her majesty.
Her princes have become like stags
that find no pasture;
they fled without strength
before the pursuer.

7 Jerusalem remembers,
in the days of her affliction and
wandering,
all the precious things
that were hers in days of old.
When her people fell into the hand
of the foe,
and there was no one to help her,
the foe looked on mocking
over her downfall.

8 Jerusalem sinned grievously,
so she has become a mockery;
all who honored her despise her,
for they have seen her nakedness;
she herself groans,
and turns her face away.

9 Her uncleanness was in her skirts;
she took no thought of her future;
her downfall was appalling,
with none to comfort her.
"O LORD, look at my affliction,
for the enemy has triumphed!"

10 Enemies have stretched out their
hands
over all her precious things;
she has even seen the nations
invade her sanctuary,
those whom you forbade
to enter your congregation.

11 All her people groan
as they search for bread;
they trade their treasures for food
to revive their strength.
Look, O LORD, and see
how worthless I have become.

12 Is it nothing to you,[b] all you who
pass by?
Look and see

if there is any sorrow like my
sorrow,
which was brought upon me,
which the LORD inflicted
on the day of his fierce anger.

13 From on high he sent fire;
it went deep into my bones;
he spread a net for my feet;
he turned me back;
he has left me stunned,
faint all day long.

14 My transgressions were bound[b]
into a yoke;
by his hand they were fastened
together;
they weigh on my neck,
sapping my strength;
the Lord handed me over
to those whom I cannot
withstand.

15 The LORD has rejected
all my warriors in the midst of
me;
he proclaimed a time against me
to crush my young men;
the Lord has trodden as in a wine
press
the virgin daughter Judah.

16 For these things I weep;
my eyes flow with tears;
for a comforter is far from me,
one to revive my courage;
my children are desolate,
for the enemy has prevailed.

17 Zion stretches out her hands,
but there is no one to comfort her;
the LORD has commanded against
Jacob
that his neighbors should
become his foes;
Jerusalem has become
a filthy thing among them.

18 The LORD is in the right,
for I have rebelled against his
word;
but hear, all you peoples,
and behold my suffering;
my young women and young men
have gone into captivity.

b Meaning of Heb uncertain

19 I called to my lovers
  but they deceived me;
my priests and elders
  perished in the city
while seeking food
  to revive their strength.

20 See, O LORD, how distressed I am;
  my stomach churns,
my heart is wrung within me,
  because I have been very
    rebellious.
In the street the sword bereaves;
  in the house it is like death.

21 They heard how I was groaning,
  with no one to comfort me.
All my enemies heard of my
    trouble;
  they are glad that you have done
    it.
Bring on the day you have
    announced,
  and let them be as I am.

22 Let all their evil doing come before
    you;
  and deal with them
as you have dealt with me
  because of all my transgressions;
for my groans are many
  and my heart is faint.

God's Warnings Fulfilled

2 How the Lord in his anger
  has humiliated^c daughter Zion!
He has thrown down from heaven
    to earth
  the splendor of Israel;
he has not remembered his
    footstool
  in the day of his anger.

2 The Lord has destroyed without
    mercy
  all the dwellings of Jacob;
in his wrath he has broken down
  the strongholds of daughter
    Judah;
he has brought down to the ground
    in dishonor
  the kingdom and its rulers.

3 He has cut down in fierce anger
  all the might of Israel;

he has withdrawn his right hand
    from them
  in the face of the enemy;
he has burned like a flaming fire in
    Jacob,
  consuming all around.

4 He has bent his bow like an enemy,
  with his right hand set like a foe;
he has killed all in whom we took
    pride
  in the tent of daughter Zion;
he has poured out his fury like fire.

5 The Lord has become like an
    enemy;
  he has destroyed Israel.
He has destroyed all its palaces,
  laid in ruins its strongholds,
and multiplied in daughter Judah
  mourning and lamentation.

6 He has broken down his booth like
    a garden,
  he has destroyed his tabernacle;
the LORD has abolished in Zion
  festival and sabbath,
and in his fierce indignation has
    spurned
  king and priest.

7 The Lord has scorned his altar,
  disowned his sanctuary;
he has delivered into the hand of
    the enemy
  the walls of her palaces;
a clamor was raised in the house of
    the LORD
  as on a day of festival.

8 The LORD determined to lay in
    ruins
  the wall of daughter Zion;
he stretched the line;
  he did not withhold his hand
    from destroying;
he caused rampart and wall to
    lament;
  they languish together.

9 Her gates have sunk into the
    ground;
  he has ruined and broken her
    bars;

c Meaning of Heb uncertain

her king and princes are among the
  nations;
guidance is no more,
and her prophets obtain
  no vision from the LORD.

10 The elders of daughter Zion
    sit on the ground in silence;
  they have thrown dust on their
    heads
    and put on sackcloth;
  the young girls of Jerusalem
    have bowed their heads to the
    ground.

11 My eyes are spent with weeping;
    my stomach churns;
  my bile is poured out on the ground
    because of the destruction of my
    people,
  because infants and babes faint
    in the streets of the city.

12 They cry to their mothers,
    "Where is bread and wine?"
  as they faint like the wounded
    in the streets of the city,
  as their life is poured out
    on their mothers' bosom.

13 What can I say for you, to what
    compare you,
    O daughter Jerusalem?
  To what can I liken you, that I may
    comfort you,
    O virgin daughter Zion?
  For vast as the sea is your ruin;
    who can heal you?

14 Your prophets have seen for you
    false and deceptive visions;
  they have not exposed your iniquity
    to restore your fortunes,
  but have seen oracles for you
    that are false and misleading.

15 All who pass along the way
    clap their hands at you;
  they hiss and wag their heads
    at daughter Jerusalem;
  "Is this the city that was called
    the perfection of beauty,
    the joy of all the earth?"

16 All your enemies
    open their mouths against you;
  they hiss, they gnash their teeth,
    they cry: "We have devoured her!
  Ah, this is the day we longed for;
    at last we have seen it!"

17 The LORD has done what he
    purposed,
  he has carried out his threat;
  as he ordained long ago,
  he has demolished without pity;
  he has made the enemy rejoice over
    you,
    and exalted the might of your
    foes.

18 Cry aloud[d] to the Lord!
    O wall of daughter Zion!
  Let tears stream down like a torrent
    day and night!
  Give yourself no rest,
    your eyes no respite!

19 Arise, cry out in the night,
    at the beginning of the watches!
  Pour out your heart like water
    before the presence of the Lord!
  Lift your hands to him
    for the lives of your children,
  who faint for hunger
    at the head of every street.

20 Look, O LORD, and consider!
    To whom have you done this?
  Should women eat their offspring,
    the children they have borne?
  Should priest and prophet be killed
    in the sanctuary of the Lord?

21 The young and the old are lying
    on the ground in the streets;
  my young women and my young
    men
    have fallen by the sword;
  in the day of your anger you have
    killed them,
    slaughtering without mercy.

22 You invited my enemies from all
    around
    as if for a day of festival;
  and on the day of the anger of the
    LORD
    no one escaped or survived;
  those whom I bore and reared
    my enemy has destroyed.

d Cn: Heb *Their heart cried*

God's Steadfast Love Endures

 3 I am one who has seen affliction
under the rod of God's[e] wrath;
2 he has driven and brought me
into darkness without any light;
3 against me alone he turns his hand,
again and again, all day long.

4 He has made my flesh and my skin
waste away,
and broken my bones;
5 he has besieged and enveloped me
with bitterness and tribulation;
6 he has made me sit in darkness
like the dead of long ago.

e Heb *his*

TUESDAY

A TIME OF TEMPTATION
F. B. Meyer

VERSE: Lamentations 3.19   **PASSAGE:** Lamentations 3.19–26

You will be tempted to the end of your life, and the nearer you live to Christ the more you will be tempted . . . The [one] who sees the heavenly vision is the [one] whom the devil will tempt to the uttermost. God will permit it because temptation does for us what the storms do for the oaks—it roots us—and what the fire does for the painting on porcelain—it makes us permanent. You never know that you have a grip on Christ, or that he has a grip on you so well as when the devil is using all his force to attract you from him; then you feel the pull of Christ's right hand.

As long as the soldier slinks outside the battle, he faces little danger, but let him plunge in and follow the captain and he will soon have the bullets flying about him. Some of us have had a good time because there was no use in the devil wasting powder and shot upon us; we haven't been doing him any harm. But once we begin to wake up and set to work for God, the devil will set a thousand evils to worrying us . . .

The nearer you get to Christ the more you will have to do with temptation. The closer you get into the heart of the fight the more the devil will torment you . . . But the virulence of the temptation means not that you are declining into sin, but that you are advancing in holiness; that the devil is afraid of you and hopes only to wound Christ by hurting you.

ADDITIONAL SCRIPTURE READING:
Psalm 119.105; Jeremiah 15.16; Matthew 4.1–4

Go to page 938 for your next devotional reading.

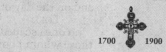

1700   1900

7 He has walled me about so that I
      cannot escape;
   he has put heavy chains on me;
8 though I call and cry for help,
   he shuts out my prayer;
9 he has blocked my ways with hewn
      stones,
   he has made my paths crooked.

10 He is a bear lying in wait for me,
   a lion in hiding;
11 he led me off my way and tore me
      to pieces;
   he has made me desolate;
12 he bent his bow and set me
   as a mark for his arrow.

13 He shot into my vitals
   the arrows of his quiver;
14 I have become the laughingstock of
      all my people,
   the object of their taunt-songs all
      day long.
15 He has filled me with bitterness,
   he has sated me with wormwood.

16 He has made my teeth grind on
      gravel,
   and made me cower in ashes;

AFFLICTION TEACHETH A WICKED PERSON SOME-
TIME TO PRAY: PROSPERITY NEVER. —Ben Johnson

---

17   my soul is bereft of peace;
      I have forgotten what happiness
         is;
18 so I say, "Gone is my glory,
      and all that I had hoped for from
         the LORD."

19 The thought of my affliction and
      my homelessness
   is wormwood and gall!
20 My soul continually thinks of it
   and is bowed down within me.
21 But this I call to mind,
   and therefore I have hope:

22 The steadfast love of the LORD
      never ceases,f
   his mercies never come to an end;
23 they are new every morning;
   great is your faithfulness.

24 "The LORD is my portion," says my
      soul,
   "therefore I will hope in him."

25 The LORD is good to those who
      wait for him,
   to the soul that seeks him.
26 It is good that one should wait
      quietly
   for the salvation of the LORD.
27 It is good for one to bear
   the yoke in youth,
28 to sit alone in silence
   when the Lord has imposed it,
29 to put one's mouth to the dust
   (there may yet be hope),
30 to give one's cheek to the smiter,
   and be filled with insults.

31 For the Lord will not
   reject forever.
32 Although he causes grief, he will
      have compassion
   according to the abundance of his
      steadfast love;
33 for he does not willingly afflict
   or grieve anyone.

34 When all the prisoners of the land
   are crushed under foot,
35 when human rights are perverted
   in the presence of the Most High,
36 when one's case is subverted
   —does the Lord not see it?

37 Who can command and have it
      done,
   if the Lord has not ordained it?
38 Is it not from the mouth of the
      Most High
   that good and bad come?
39 Why should any who draw breath
      complain
   about the punishment of their
      sins?

40 Let us test and examine our ways,
   and return to the LORD.
41 Let us lift up our hearts as well as
      our hands
   to God in heaven.
42 We have transgressed and rebelled,
   and you have not forgiven.

f Syr Tg: Heb LORD, we are not cut off

43 You have wrapped yourself with
    anger and pursued us,
  killing without pity;
44 you have wrapped yourself with a
    cloud
  so that no prayer can pass through.
45 You have made us filth and rubbish
  among the peoples.

46 All our enemies
  have opened their mouths
    against us;
47 panic and pitfall have come upon us,
  devastation and destruction.

48 My eyes flow with rivers of tears
  because of the destruction of my
    people.

49 My eyes will flow without ceasing,
  without respite,
50 until the LORD from heaven
  looks down and sees.
51 My eyes cause me grief
  at the fate of all the young
    women in my city.

52 Those who were my enemies
  without cause
  have hunted me like a bird;

WEDNESDAY

THE HAND OF GOD ALSO WAITS
Frances Ridley Havergal

VERSE: Lamentations 3.24   **PASSAGE:** Lamentations 3.24–27

 id you ever hear of anyone being much used for Christ who did not have some *special* waiting time, some complete *upset* of all his or her plans first; from St. Paul's being sent off into the desert of Arabia for three years, when he must have been boiling over with the glad tidings, down to the present day (see Galatians 1.17–18)?

You were looking forward to telling about trusting Jesus in Syria; now he says, "I want you to *show* what it is to trust me, without waiting for Syria."

My own case is far less severe, but the same in principle, that when I thought the door was flung open for me to go with a bound into literary work, it is opposed, and doctor steps in and says, simply, "Never! She must choose between writing and living; she can't do both" . . .

In 1869 [I] saw the evident wisdom of being kept waiting nine years in the shade. God's love being unchangeable, he is just as loving when we do not see or feel his love. Also his love and his sovereignty are co-equal and universal; so he withholds the enjoyment and conscious progress because he knows best what will really ripen and further his work in us.

ADDITIONAL SCRIPTURE READING:
1 Kings 17.3–6; Ezekiel 37.1; Acts 9.7–9

Go to page 958 for your next devotional reading.

1700   1900

53 they flung me alive into a pit
and hurled stones on me;
54 water closed over my head;
I said, "I am lost."

55 I called on your name, O LORD,
from the depths of the pit;
56 you heard my plea, "Do not close
your ear
to my cry for help, but give me
relief!"
57 You came near when I called on
you;
you said, "Do not fear!"

58 You have taken up my cause,
O Lord,
you have redeemed my life.
59 You have seen the wrong done to
me, O LORD;
judge my cause.
60 You have seen all their malice,
all their plots against me.

61 You have heard their taunts,
O LORD,
all their plots against me.
62 The whispers and murmurs of my
assailants
are against me all day long.
63 Whether they sit or rise—see,
I am the object of their taunt-
songs.

64 Pay them back for their deeds,
O LORD,
according to the work of their
hands!
65 Give them anguish of heart;
your curse be on them!
66 Pursue them in anger and destroy
them
from under the LORD's heavens.

The Punishment of Zion

4 How the gold has grown dim,
how the pure gold is changed!
The sacred stones lie scattered
at the head of every street.

2 The precious children of Zion,
worth their weight in fine gold—
how they are reckoned as earthen
pots,
the work of a potter's hands!

3 Even the jackals offer the breast
and nurse their young,
but my people has become cruel,
like the ostriches in the
wilderness.

4 The tongue of the infant sticks
to the roof of its mouth for thirst;
the children beg for food,
but no one gives them anything.

5 Those who feasted on delicacies
perish in the streets;
those who were brought up in
purple
cling to ash heaps.

6 For the chastisement g of my people
has been greater
than the punishment h of Sodom,
which was overthrown in a
moment,
though no hand was laid on it. i

7 Her princes were purer than snow,
whiter than milk;
their bodies were more ruddy than
coral,
their hair i like sapphire. j

8 Now their visage is blacker than
soot;
they are not recognized in the
streets.
Their skin has shriveled on their
bones;
it has become as dry as wood.

9 Happier were those pierced by the
sword
than those pierced by hunger,
whose life drains away, deprived
of the produce of the field.

10 The hands of compassionate
women
have boiled their own children;
they became their food
in the destruction of my people.

11 The LORD gave full vent to his
wrath;
he poured out his hot anger,
and kindled a fire in Zion
that consumed its foundations.

g Or iniquity   h Or sin   i Meaning of Heb uncertain   j Or lapis lazuli

12 The kings of the earth did not
    believe,
    nor did any of the inhabitants of
    the world,
    that foe or enemy could enter
    the gates of Jerusalem.

13 It was for the sins of her prophets
    and the iniquities of her priests,
    who shed the blood of the
    righteous
    in the midst of her.

14 Blindly they wandered through the
    streets,
    so defiled with blood
    that no one was able
    to touch their garments.

15 "Away! Unclean!" people shouted
    at them;
    "Away! Away! Do not touch!"
    So they became fugitives and
    wanderers;
    it was said among the nations,
    "They shall stay here no longer."

16 The LORD himself has scattered
    them,
    he will regard them no more;
    no honor was shown to the priests,
    no favor to the elders.

17 Our eyes failed, ever watching
    vainly for help;
    we were watching eagerly
    for a nation that could not save.

18 They dogged our steps
    so that we could not walk in our
    streets;
    our end drew near; our days were
    numbered;
    for our end had come.

19 Our pursuers were swifter
    than the eagles in the heavens;
    they chased us on the mountains,
    they lay in wait for us in the
    wilderness.

20 The LORD's anointed, the breath of
    our life,
    was taken in their pits—

the one of whom we said, "Under
    his shadow
    we shall live among the nations."

21 Rejoice and be glad, O daughter
    Edom,
    you that live in the land of Uz;
    but to you also the cup shall pass;
    you shall become drunk and strip
    yourself bare.

22 The punishment of your iniquity,
    O daughter Zion, is
    accomplished,
    he will keep you in exile no
    longer;
    but your iniquity, O daughter
    Edom, he will punish,
    he will uncover your sins.

A Plea for Mercy

5 Remember, O LORD, what has
    befallen us;
    look, and see our disgrace!
2 Our inheritance has been turned
    over to strangers,
    our homes to aliens.
3 We have become orphans,
    fatherless;
    our mothers are like widows.
4 We must pay for the water we
    drink;
    the wood we get must be bought.
5 With a yoke*k* on our necks we are
    hard driven;
    we are weary, we are given no
    rest.
6 We have made a pact with*l* Egypt
    and Assyria,
    to get enough bread.
7 Our ancestors sinned; they are no
    more,
    and we bear their iniquities.
8 Slaves rule over us;
    there is no one to deliver us from
    their hand.
9 We get our bread at the peril of our
    lives,
    because of the sword in the
    wilderness.
10 Our skin is black as an oven
    from the scorching heat of
    famine.
11 Women are raped in Zion,
    virgins in the towns of Judah.

k Symmachus: Heb lacks With a yoke   l Heb have given the hand to

12 Princes are hung up by their hands;
    no respect is shown to the elders.
13 Young men are compelled to grind,
    and boys stagger under loads of
        wood.
14 The old men have left the city gate,
    the young men their music.
15 The joy of our hearts has ceased;
    our dancing has been turned to
        mourning.
16 The crown has fallen from our
        head;
    woe to us, for we have sinned!
17 Because of this our hearts are sick,
    because of these things our eyes
        have grown dim:

18 because of Mount Zion, which lies
        desolate;
    jackals prowl over it.

19 But you, O LORD, reign forever;
    your throne endures to all
        generations.
20 Why have you forgotten us
        completely?
    Why have you forsaken us these
        many days?
21 Restore us to yourself, O LORD,
        that we may be restored;
    renew our days as of old—
22 unless you have utterly rejected us,
    and are angry with us beyond
        measure.

EZEKIEL

ZEKIEL WAS AMONG THE MORE THAN 3,000 JEWS EXILED TO BABYLON BY NEBU- CHADNEZZAR IN 597 B.C., AND THERE AMONG THE EXILES HE RECEIVED HIS CALL TO BECOME A PROPHET. AS A PRIEST-PROPHET CALLED TO MINISTER TO THE EXILES, HE USES WORDS, VISIONS AND "MINI-DRAMAS" TO URGE THE PEOPLE TO RENEW THEIR COMMITMENT TO GOD. NOWHERE IN THE BIBLE IS GOD'S CONTROL OVER ALL CRE- ATION EXPRESSED MORE CLEARLY THAN IN EZEKIEL. WATCH FOR THE MESSAGE OF GOD'S MAJESTY AND GLORY: ALL THIS WOULD HAPPEN SO THAT THEY WILL "KNOW THAT I AM THE LORD" (6.10).

The Vision of the Chariot

1 In the thirtieth year, in the fourth month, on the fifth day of the month, as I was among the exiles by the river Chebar, the heavens were opened, and I saw visions of God. ²On the fifth day of the month (it was the fifth year of the exile of King Jehoi-achin), ³the word of the LORD came to the priest Ezekiel son of Buzi, in the land of the Chaldeans by the river Chebar; and the hand of the LORD was on him there.

4 As I looked, a stormy wind came out of the north: a great cloud with brightness around it and fire flashing forth continually, and in the middle of the fire, something like gleaming amber. ⁵In the middle of it was something like four living creatures. This was their appearance: they were of human form. ⁶Each had four faces, and each of them had four wings. ⁷Their legs were straight, and the soles of their feet were like the sole of a calf's foot; and they sparkled like burnished bronze. ⁸Under their wings on their four sides they had human hands. And the four had their faces and their wings thus: ⁹their wings touched one another; each of them moved straight ahead, without turning as they moved. ¹⁰As for the appearance of their faces: the four had the face of a human being, the face of a lion on the right side, the face of an ox on the left side, and the face of an eagle; ¹¹such were their faces. Their wings were spread out above; each creature had two wings, each of which touched the wing of another, while two covered their bodies.

¹²Each moved straight ahead; wherever the spirit would go, they went, without turning as they went. ¹³In the middle of*ᵃ* the living creatures there was something that looked like burning coals of fire, like torches moving to and fro among the living creatures; the fire was bright, and lightning issued from the fire. ¹⁴The living creatures darted to and fro, like a flash of lightning.

15 As I looked at the living creatures, I saw a wheel on the earth beside the living creatures, one for each of the four of them.*ᵇ* ¹⁶As for the appearance of the wheels and their construction: their appearance was like the gleaming of beryl; and the four had the same form, their construction being something like a wheel within a wheel. ¹⁷When they moved, they moved in any of the four directions without veering as they moved. ¹⁸Their rims were tall and awesome, for the rims of all four were full of eyes all around. ¹⁹When the living creatures moved, the wheels moved beside them; and when the living creatures rose from the earth, the wheels rose. ²⁰Wherever the spirit would go, they went, and the wheels rose along with them; for the spirit of the living creatures was in the wheels. ²¹When they moved, the others moved; when they stopped, the others stopped; and when they rose from the earth, the wheels rose along with them; for the spirit of the living creatures was in the wheels.

22 Over the heads of the living creatures there was something like a dome, shining like crystal,*ᶜ* spread out above their heads. ²³Under the dome their wings were stretched out straight, one toward another; and each of the creatures had two wings covering its body. ²⁴When they moved, I heard the sound of their wings like the sound of mighty waters, like the thunder of the Almighty,*ᵈ* a sound of tumult like the sound of an army; when they stopped, they let down their wings. ²⁵And there came a voice from above the dome over their heads; when they stopped, they let down their wings.

26 And above the dome over their heads there was something like a throne, in appearance like sapphire;*ᵉ* and seated above the likeness of a throne was something that seemed like a human form. ²⁷Upward from what appeared like the loins I saw something like gleaming amber, something that looked like fire enclosed all around; and downward from what looked like the loins I saw something that looked like fire, and there was a splendor all around. ²⁸Like the bow in a cloud on a rainy day, such was the appearance of the splendor all around. This was the appearance of the likeness of the glory of the LORD.

When I saw it, I fell on my face, and I heard the voice of someone speaking.

The Vision of the Scroll

2 He said to me: O mortal,*ᶠ* stand up on your feet, and I will speak with you. ²And when he spoke to me, a spirit entered into me and set me on my feet; and I heard him speaking to me. ³He said to me, Mortal, I am sending you to the people of Israel, to a nation*ᵍ* of rebels who have rebelled against me; they and their ancestors have transgressed against me to this very day. ⁴The descendants are impudent and stubborn. I am sending you to them, and you shall say to them, "Thus says the Lord GOD." ⁵Whether they hear or refuse to hear (for they are a rebellious house), they shall know that there has been a prophet among them. ⁶And you, O mortal, do not be afraid of them, and do not be afraid of their words, though briers and thorns surround you and you live among scorpions; do not be afraid of their words, and do not be dismayed at their looks, for they are a rebellious house. ⁷You shall speak my words to them, whether they hear or refuse to hear; for they are a rebellious house.

8 But you, mortal, hear what I say to you; do not be rebellious like that rebellious house; open your mouth and eat what I give you. ⁹I looked, and a hand was stretched out to me, and a written scroll was in it. ¹⁰He spread it before me; it had writing on the front and on the

---

a Gk OL: Heb *And the appearance of*   *b* Heb *of their faces*   *c* Gk: Heb *like the awesome crystal*   *d* Traditional rendering of Heb *Shaddai*   *e* Or *lapis lazuli*   *f* Or *son of man;* Heb *ben adam* (and so throughout the book when Ezekiel is addressed)   *g* Syr: Heb *to nations*

back, and written on it were words of lamentation and mourning and woe.

3 He said to me, O mortal, eat what is offered to you; eat this scroll, and go, speak to the house of Israel. 2So I opened my mouth, and he gave me the scroll to eat. 3He said to me, Mortal, eat this scroll that I give you and fill your stomach with it. Then I ate it; and in my mouth it was as sweet as honey.

4 He said to me: Mortal, go to the house of Israel and speak my very words to them. 5For you are not sent to a people of obscure speech and difficult language, but to the house of Israel— 6not to many peoples of obscure speech and difficult language, whose words you cannot understand. Surely, if I sent you to them, they would listen to you. 7But the house of Israel will not listen to you, for they are not willing to listen to me; because all the house of Israel have a hard forehead and a stubborn heart. 8See, I have made your face hard against their faces, and your forehead hard against their foreheads. 9Like the hardest stone, harder than flint, I have made your forehead; do not fear them or be dismayed at their looks, for they are a rebellious house. 10He said to me: Mortal, all my words that I shall speak to you receive in your heart and hear with your ears; 11then go to the exiles, to your people, and speak to them. Say to them, "Thus says the Lord God"; whether they hear or refuse to hear.

Ezekiel at the River Chebar

12 Then the spirit lifted me up, and as the glory of the Lord rose[h] from its place, I heard behind me the sound of loud rumbling; 13it was the sound of the wings of the living creatures brushing against one another, and the sound of the wheels beside them, that sounded like a loud rumbling. 14The spirit lifted me up and bore me away; I went in bitterness in the heat of my spirit, the hand of the Lord being strong upon me. 15I came to the exiles at Tel-abib, who lived by the river Chebar.[i] And I sat there among them, stunned, for seven days.

16 At the end of seven days, the word of the Lord came to me: 17Mortal, I have made you a sentinel for the house of Israel; whenever you hear a word from my mouth, you shall give them warning from me. 18If I say to the wicked, "You shall surely die," and you give them no warning, or speak to warn the wicked from their wicked way, in order to save their life, those wicked persons shall die for their iniquity; but their blood I will require at your hand. 19But if you warn the wicked, and they do not turn from their wickedness, or from their wicked way, they shall die for their iniquity; but you will have saved your life. 20Again, if the righteous turn from their righteousness and commit iniquity, and I lay a stumbling block before them, they shall die; because you have not warned them, they shall die for their sin, and their righteous deeds that they have done shall not be remembered; but their blood I will require at your hand. 21If, however, you warn the righteous not to sin, and they do not sin, they shall surely live, because they took warning; and you will have saved your life.

Ezekiel Isolated and Silenced

22 Then the hand of the Lord was upon me there; and he said to me, Rise up, go out into the valley, and there I will speak with you. 23So I rose up and went out into the valley; and the glory of the Lord stood there, like the glory that I had seen by the river Chebar; and I fell on my face. 24The spirit entered into me, and set me on my feet; and he spoke with me and said to me: Go, shut yourself inside your house. 25As for you, mortal, cords shall be placed on you, and you shall be bound with them, so that you cannot go out among the people; 26and I will make your tongue cling to the roof of your mouth, so that you shall be speechless and unable to reprove them; for they are a rebellious house. 27But when I speak with you, I will open your mouth, and you shall say to them, "Thus says the Lord God"; let those who will hear, hear; and let those who refuse to hear, refuse; for they are a rebellious house.

---

h Cn: Heb and blessed be the glory of the Lord Another reading is Chebar, and I sat where they sat   i Two Mss Syr: Heb Chebar, and to where they lived.

The Siege of Jerusalem Portrayed

4 And you, O mortal, take a brick and set it before you. On it portray a city, Jerusalem; ²and put siege-works against it, and build a siege wall against it, and cast up a ramp against it; set camps also against it, and plant battering rams against it all around. ³Then take an iron plate and place it as an iron wall between you and the city; set your face toward it, and let it be in a state of siege, and press the siege against it. This is a sign for the house of Israel.

4 Then lie on your left side, and place the punishment of the house of Israel upon it; you shall bear their punishment for the number of the days that you lie there. ⁵For I assign to you a number of days, three hundred ninety days, equal to the number of the years of their punishment; and so you shall bear the punishment of the house of Israel. ⁶When you have completed these, you shall lie down a second time, but on your right side, and bear the punishment of the house of Judah; forty days I assign you, one day for each year. ⁷You shall set your face toward the siege of Jerusalem, and with your arm bared you shall prophesy against it. ⁸See, I am putting cords on you so that you cannot turn from one side to the other until you have completed the days of your siege.

9 And you, take wheat and barley, beans and lentils, millet and spelt; put them into one vessel, and make bread for yourself. During the number of days that you lie on your side, three hundred ninety days, you shall eat it. ¹⁰The food that you eat shall be twenty shekels a day by weight; at fixed times you shall eat it. ¹¹And you shall drink water by measure, one-sixth of a hin; at fixed times you shall drink. ¹²You shall eat it as a barley-cake, baking it in their sight on human dung. ¹³The LORD said, "Thus shall the people of Israel eat their bread, unclean, among the nations to which I will drive them." ¹⁴Then I said, "Ah Lord GOD! I have never defiled myself; from my youth up until now I have never eaten what died of itself or was torn by animals, nor has carrion flesh come into my mouth." ¹⁵Then he said to me, "See, I will let you have cow's dung instead of human dung, on which you may prepare your bread."

16 Then he said to me, Mortal, I am going to break the staff of bread in Jerusalem; they shall eat bread by weight and with fearfulness; and they shall drink water by measure and in dismay. ¹⁷Lacking bread and water, they will look at one another in dismay, and waste away under their punishment.

A Sword against Jerusalem

5 And you, O mortal, take a sharp sword; use it as a barber's razor and run it over your head and your beard; then take balances for weighing, and divide the hair. ²One third of the hair you shall burn in the fire inside the city, when the days of the siege are completed; one third you shall take and strike with the sword all around the city;ʲ and one third you shall scatter to the wind, and I will unsheathe the sword after them. ³Then you shall take from these a small number, and bind them in the skirts of your robe. ⁴From these, again, you shall take some, throw them into the fire and burn them up; from there a fire will come out against all the house of Israel.

5 Thus says the Lord GOD: This is Jerusalem; I have set her in the center of the nations, with countries all around her. ⁶But she has rebelled against my ordinances and my statutes, becoming more wicked than the nations and the countries all around her, rejecting my ordinances and not following my statutes. ⁷Therefore thus says the Lord GOD: Because you are more turbulent than the nations that are all around you, and have not followed my statutes or kept my ordinances, but have acted according to the ordinances of the nations that are all around you; ⁸therefore thus says the Lord GOD: I, I myself, am coming against you; I will execute judgments among you in the sight of the nations. ⁹And because of all your abominations, I will do to you what I have never yet done, and the like of which I will never do again. ¹⁰Surely, parents shall eat their children in your midst, and children shall eat their parents; I will execute judgments on you, and any of you who

j Heb *it*

survive I will scatter to every wind. [11]Therefore, as I live, says the Lord GOD, surely, because you have defiled my sanctuary with all your detestable things and with all your abominations—therefore I will cut you down;[k] my eye will not spare, and I will have no pity. [12]One third of you shall die of pestilence or be consumed by famine among you; one third shall fall by the sword around you; and one third I will scatter to every wind and will unsheathe the sword after them.

13 My anger shall spend itself, and I will vent my fury on them and satisfy myself; and they shall know that I, the LORD, have spoken in my jealousy, when I spend my fury on them. [14]Moreover I will make you a desolation and an object of mocking among the nations around you, in the sight of all that pass by. [15]You shall be[l] a mockery and a taunt, a warning and a horror, to the nations around you, when I execute judgments on you in anger and fury, and with furious punishments—I, the LORD, have spoken— [16]when I loose against you[m] my deadly arrows of famine, arrows for destruction, which I will let loose to destroy you, and when I bring more and more famine upon you, and break your staff of bread. [17]I will send famine and wild animals against you, and they will rob you of your children; pestilence and bloodshed shall pass through you; and I will bring the sword upon you. I, the LORD, have spoken.

Judgment on Idolatrous Israel

6 The word of the LORD came to me: [2]O mortal, set your face toward the mountains of Israel, and prophesy against them, [3]and say, You mountains of Israel, hear the word of the Lord GOD! Thus says the Lord GOD to the mountains and the hills, to the ravines and the valleys: I, I myself will bring a sword upon you, and I will destroy your high places. [4]Your altars shall become desolate, and your incense stands shall be broken; and I will throw down your slain in front of your idols. [5]I will lay the corpses of the people of Israel in front of their idols; and I will scatter your bones around your altars. [6]Wherev-

er you live, your towns shall be waste and your high places ruined, so that your altars will be waste and ruined,[n] your idols broken and destroyed, your incense stands cut down, and your works wiped out. [7]The slain shall fall in your midst; then you shall know that I am the LORD.

8 But I will spare some. Some of you shall escape the sword among the nations and be scattered through the countries. [9]Those of you who escape shall remember me among the nations where they are carried captive, how I was crushed by their wanton heart that turned away from me, and their wanton eyes that turned after their idols. Then they will be loathsome in their own sight for the evils that they have committed, for all their abominations. [10]And they shall know that I am the LORD; I did not threaten in vain to bring this disaster upon them.

11 Thus says the Lord GOD: Clap your hands and stamp your foot, and say, Alas for all the vile abominations of the house of Israel! For they shall fall by the sword, by famine, and by pestilence. [12]Those far off shall die of pestilence; those nearby shall fall by the sword; and any who are left and are spared shall die of famine. Thus I will spend my fury upon them. [13]And you shall know that I am the LORD, when their slain lie among their idols around their altars, on every high hill, on all the mountain tops, under every green tree, and under every leafy oak, wherever they offered pleasing odor to all their idols. [14]I will stretch out my hand against them, and make the land desolate and waste, throughout all their settlements, from the wilderness to Riblah.[o] Then they shall know that I am the LORD.

Impending Disaster

7 The word of the LORD came to me: [2]You, O mortal, thus says the Lord GOD to the land of Israel:
An end! The end has come
    upon the four corners of the land.
3 Now the end is upon you,
    I will let loose my anger upon
     you;

k Another reading is I will withdraw   l Gk Syr Vg Tg: Heb It shall be   m Heb them   n Syr Vg Tg: Heb and be made guilty   o Another reading is Diblah

I will judge you according to your
ways,
I will punish you for all your
abominations.
4   My eye will not spare you, I will
have no pity.
I will punish you for your ways,
while your abominations are
among you.
Then you shall know that I am the
LORD.
5   Thus says the Lord GOD:
Disaster after disaster! See, it
comes.
6   An end has come, the end has
come.
It has awakened against you; see, it
comes!
7   Your doom*p* has come to you,
O inhabitant of the land.
The time has come, the day is
near—
of tumult, not of reveling on the
mountains.
8   Soon now I will pour out my wrath
upon you;
I will spend my anger against
you.
I will judge you according to your
ways,
and punish you for all your
abominations.
9   My eye will not spare; I will have
no pity.
I will punish you according to
your ways,
while your abominations are
among you.
Then you shall know that it is I the
LORD who strike.
10 See, the day! See, it comes!
Your doom*p* has gone out.
The rod has blossomed, pride has
budded.
11   Violence has grown into a rod of
wickedness.
None of them shall remain,
not their abundance, not their
wealth;
no pre-eminence among them.*p*
12 The time has come, the day draws
near;
let not the buyer rejoice, nor the
seller mourn,

for wrath is upon all their
multitude.
13 For the sellers shall not return to what
has been sold as long as they remain
alive. For the vision concerns all their
multitude; it shall not be revoked.
Because of their iniquity, they cannot
maintain their lives.*p*
14   They have blown the horn and
made everything ready;
but no one goes to battle,
for my wrath is upon all their
multitude.
15   The sword is outside, pestilence
and famine are inside;
those in the field die by the
sword;
those in the city—famine and
pestilence devour them.
16   If any survivors escape,
they shall be found on the
mountains
like doves of the valleys,
all of them moaning over their
iniquity.
17   All hands shall grow feeble,
all knees turn to water.
18   They shall put on sackcloth,
horror shall cover them.
Shame shall be on all faces,
baldness on all their heads.
19   They shall fling their silver into the
streets,
their gold shall be treated as
unclean.
Their silver and gold cannot save them
on the day of the wrath of the LORD.
They shall not satisfy their hunger or fill
their stomachs with it. For it was the
stumbling block of their iniquity.
20 From their*q* beautiful ornament, in
which they took pride, they made their
abominable images, their detestable
things; therefore I will make of it an
unclean thing to them.
21   I will hand it over to strangers as
booty,
to the wicked of the earth as
plunder;
they shall profane it.
22   I will avert my face from them,
so that they may profane my
treasured*r* place;
the violent shall enter it,
they shall profane it.

---

p Meaning of Heb uncertain   *q* Syr Symmachus: Heb *its*   *r* Or *secret*

23   Make a chain!s
     For the land is full of bloody
         crimes;
         the city is full of violence.
24   I will bring the worst of the nations
         to take possession of their
         houses.
     I will put an end to the arrogance of
         the strong,
         and their holy places shall be
         profaned.
25   When anguish comes, they will
         seek peace,
         but there shall be none.
26   Disaster comes upon disaster,
         rumor follows rumor;
     they shall keep seeking a vision
         from the prophet;
         instruction shall perish from the
         priest,
         and counsel from the elders.
27   The king shall mourn,
         the prince shall be wrapped in
         despair,
         and the hands of the people of
         the land shall tremble.
     According to their way I will deal
         with them;
         according to their own
         judgments I will judge them.
And they shall know that I am the
LORD.

Abominations in the Temple

8   In the sixth year, in the sixth month, on the fifth day of the month, as I sat in my house, with the elders of Judah sitting before me, the hand of the Lord GOD fell upon me there. 2I looked, and there was a figure that looked like a human being;t below what appeared to be its loins it was fire, and above the loins it was like the appearance of brightness, like gleaming amber. 3It stretched out the form of a hand, and took me by a lock of my head; and the spirit lifted me up between earth and heaven, and brought me in visions of God to Jerusalem, to the entrance of the gateway of the inner court that faces north, to the seat of the image of jealousy, which provokes to jealousy. 4And the glory of the God of Israel was there, like the vision that I had seen in the valley.

5 Then Godu said to me, "O mortal, lift up your eyes now in the direction of the north." So I lifted up my eyes toward the north, and there, north of the altar gate, in the entrance, was this image of jealousy. 6He said to me, "Mortal, do you see what they are doing, the great abominations that the house of Israel are committing here, to drive me far from my sanctuary? Yet you will see still greater abominations."

7 And he brought me to the entrance of the court; I looked, and there was a hole in the wall. 8Then he said to me, "Mortal, dig through the wall"; and when I dug through the wall, there was an entrance. 9He said to me, "Go in, and see the vile abominations that they are committing here." 10So I went in and looked; there, portrayed on the wall all around, were all kinds of creeping things, and loathsome animals, and all the idols of the house of Israel. 11Before them stood seventy of the elders of the house of Israel, with Jaazaniah son of Shaphan standing among them. Each had his censer in his hand, and the fragrant cloud of incense was ascending. 12Then he said to me, "Mortal, have you seen what the elders of the house of Israel are doing in the dark, each in his room of images? For they say, 'The LORD does not see us, the LORD has forsaken the land.' " 13He said also to me, "You will see still greater abominations that they are committing."

14 Then he brought me to the entrance of the north gate of the house of the LORD; women were sitting there weeping for Tammuz. 15Then he said to me, "Have you seen this, O mortal? You will see still greater abominations than these."

16 And he brought me into the inner court of the house of the LORD; there, at the entrance of the temple of the LORD, between the porch and the altar, were about twenty-five men, with their backs to the temple of the LORD, and their faces toward the east, prostrating themselves to the sun toward the east. 17Then he said to me, "Have you seen this, O mortal? Is it not bad enough that the house of Judah commits the abominations done here? Must they fill the

s Meaning of Heb uncertain   t Gk: Heb like fire   u Heb he land with violence, and provoke my anger still further? See, they are putting the branch to their nose! **18**Therefore I will act in wrath; my eye will not spare, nor will I have pity; and though they cry in my hearing with a loud voice, I will not listen to them."

The Slaughter of the Idolaters

9 Then he cried in my hearing with a loud voice, saying, "Draw near, you executioners of the city, each with his destroying weapon in his hand." **2**And six men came from the direction of the upper gate, which faces north, each with his weapon for slaughter in his hand; among them was a man clothed in linen, with a writing case at his side. They went in and stood beside the bronze altar.

3 Now the glory of the God of Israel had gone up from the cherub on which it rested to the threshold of the house. The LORD called to the man clothed in linen, who had the writing case at his side; **4**and said to him, "Go through the city, through Jerusalem, and put a mark on the foreheads of those who sigh and groan over all the abominations that are committed in it." **5**To the others he said in my hearing, "Pass through the city after him, and kill; your eye shall not spare, and you shall show no pity. **6**Cut down old men, young men and young women, little children and women, but touch no one who has the mark. And begin at my sanctuary." So they began with the elders who were in front of the house. **7**Then he said to them, "Defile the house, and fill the courts with the slain. Go!" So they went out and killed in the city. **8**While they were killing, and I was left alone, I fell prostrate on my face and cried out, "Ah Lord GOD! will you destroy all who remain of Israel as you pour out your wrath upon Jerusalem?" **9**He said to me, "The guilt of the house of Israel and Judah is exceedingly great; the land is full of bloodshed and the city full of perversity; for they say, 'The LORD has forsaken the land, and the LORD does not see.' **10**As for me, my eye will not spare, nor will I have pity, but I will bring down their deeds upon their heads."

11 Then the man clothed in linen, with the writing case at his side, brought back word, saying, "I have done as you commanded me."

God's Glory Leaves Jerusalem

10 Then I looked, and above the dome that was over the heads of the cherubim there appeared above them something like a sapphire,ᵛ in form resembling a throne. **2**He said to the man clothed in linen, "Go within the wheelwork underneath the cherubim; fill your hands with burning coals from among the cherubim, and scatter them over the city." He went in as I looked on. **3**Now the cherubim were standing on the south side of the house when the man went in; and a cloud filled the inner court. **4**Then the glory of the LORD rose up from the cherub to the threshold of the house; the house was filled with the cloud, and the court was full of the brightness of the glory of the LORD. **5**The sound of the wings of the cherubim was heard as far as the outer court, like the voice of God Almightyʷ when he speaks.

6 When he commanded the man clothed in linen, "Take fire from within the wheelwork, from among the cherubim," he went in and stood beside a wheel. **7**And a cherub stretched out his hand from among the cherubim to the fire that was among the cherubim, took some of it and put it into the hands of the man clothed in linen, who took it and went out. **8**The cherubim appeared to have the form of a human hand under their wings.

9 I looked, and there were four wheels beside the cherubim, one beside each cherub; and the appearance of the wheels was like gleaming beryl. **10**And as for their appearance, the four looked alike, something like a wheel within a wheel. **11**When they moved, they moved in any of the four directions without veering as they moved; but in whatever direction the front wheel faced, the others followed without veering as they moved. **12**Their entire body, their rims, their spokes, their wings, and the wheels—the wheels of the four of them—were full of eyes all around. **13**As

v Or *lapis lazuli*   w Traditional rendering of Heb *El Shaddai*

for the wheels, they were called in my hearing "the wheelwork." 14Each one had four faces: the first face was that of the cherub, the second face was that of a human being, the third that of a lion, and the fourth that of an eagle.

15 The cherubim rose up. These were the living creatures that I saw by the river Chebar. 16When the cherubim moved, the wheels moved beside them; and when the cherubim lifted up their wings to rise up from the earth, the wheels at their side did not veer. 17When they stopped, the others stopped, and when they rose up, the others rose up with them; for the spirit of the living creatures was in them.

18 Then the glory of the LORD went out from the threshold of the house and stopped above the cherubim. 19The cherubim lifted up their wings and rose up from the earth in my sight as they went out with the wheels beside them. They stopped at the entrance of the east gate of the house of the LORD; and the glory of the God of Israel was above them.

20 These were the living creatures that I saw underneath the God of Israel by the river Chebar; and I knew that they were cherubim. 21Each had four faces, each four wings, and underneath their wings something like human hands. 22As for what their faces were like, they were the same faces whose appearance I had seen by the river Chebar. Each one moved straight ahead.

Judgment on Wicked Counselors

11 The spirit lifted me up and brought me to the east gate of the house of the LORD, which faces east. There, at the entrance of the gateway, were twenty-five men; among them I saw Jaazaniah son of Azzur, and Pelatiah son of Benaiah, officials of the people. 2He said to me, "Mortal, these are the men who devise iniquity and who give wicked counsel in this city; 3they say, 'The time is not near to build houses; this city is the pot, and we are the meat.' 4Therefore prophesy against them; prophesy, O mortal."

5 Then the spirit of the LORD fell upon me, and he said to me, "Say, Thus says the LORD: This is what you think, O house of Israel; I know the things that come into your mind. 6You have killed many in this city, and have filled its streets with the slain. 7Therefore thus says the Lord GOD: The slain whom you have placed within it are the meat, and this city is the pot; but you shall be taken out of it. 8You have feared the sword; and I will bring the sword upon you, says the Lord GOD. 9I will take you out of it and give you over to the hands of foreigners, and execute judgments upon you. 10You shall fall by the sword; I will judge you at the border of Israel. And you shall know that I am the LORD. 11This city shall not be your pot, and you shall not be the meat inside it; I will judge you at the border of Israel. 12Then you shall know that I am the LORD, whose statutes you have not followed, and whose ordinances you have not kept, but you have acted according to the ordinances of the nations that are around you."

13 Now, while I was prophesying, Pelatiah son of Benaiah died. Then I fell down on my face, cried with a loud voice, and said, "Ah Lord GOD! will you make a full end of the remnant of Israel?"

God Will Restore Israel

14 Then the word of the LORD came to me: 15Mortal, your kinsfolk, your own kin, your fellow exiles,x the whole house of Israel, all of them, are those of whom the inhabitants of Jerusalem have said, "They have gone far from the LORD; to us this land is given for a possession." 16Therefore say: Thus says the Lord GOD: Though I removed them far away among the nations, and though I scattered them among the countries, yet I have been a sanctuary to them for a little whiley in the countries where they have gone. 17Therefore say: Thus says the Lord GOD: I will gather you from the peoples, and assemble you out of the countries where you have been scattered, and I will give you the land of Israel. 18When they come there, they will remove from it all its detestable things and all its abominations. 19I will give them onez heart, and put a new spirit within them; I will remove the heart of stone from their flesh and give them a

---

x Gk Syr: Heb *people of your kindred*   y Or *to some extent*   z Another reading is *a new*

heart of flesh, 20so that they may follow my statutes and keep my ordinances and obey them. Then they shall be my people, and I will be their God. 21But as for those whose heart goes after their detestable things and their abominations,*a* I will bring their deeds upon their own heads, says the Lord GOD.

22 Then the cherubim lifted up their wings, with the wheels beside them; and the glory of the God of Israel was above them. 23And the glory of the LORD ascended from the middle of the city, and stopped on the mountain east of the city. 24The spirit lifted me up and brought me in a vision by the spirit of God into Chaldea, to the exiles. Then the vision that I had seen left me. 25And I told the exiles all the things that the LORD had shown me.

Judah's Captivity Portrayed

12 The word of the LORD came to me: 2Mortal, you are living in the midst of a rebellious house, who have eyes to see but do not see, who

---

NONE ARE SO DEAF AS THOSE WHO WILL NOT HEAR.   —*Matthew Henry*

---

have ears to hear but do not hear; 3for they are a rebellious house. Therefore, mortal, prepare for yourself an exile's baggage, and go into exile by day in their sight; you shall go like an exile from your place to another place in their sight. Perhaps they will understand, though they are a rebellious house. 4You shall bring out your baggage by day in their sight, as baggage for exile; and you shall go out yourself at evening in their sight, as those do who go into exile. 5Dig through the wall in their sight, and carry the baggage through it. 6In their sight you shall lift the baggage on your shoulder, and carry it out in the dark; you shall cover your face, so that you may not see the land; for I have made you a sign for the house of Israel.

7 I did just as I was commanded. I brought out my baggage by day, as baggage for exile, and in the evening I dug

through the wall with my own hands; I brought it out in the dark, carrying it on my shoulder in their sight.

8 In the morning the word of the LORD came to me: 9Mortal, has not the house of Israel, the rebellious house, said to you, "What are you doing?" 10Say to them, "Thus says the Lord GOD: This oracle concerns the prince in Jerusalem and all the house of Israel in it." 11Say, "I am a sign for you: as I have done, so shall it be done to them; they shall go into exile, into captivity." 12And the prince who is among them shall lift his baggage on his shoulder in the dark, and shall go out; he*b* shall dig through the wall and carry it through; he shall cover his face, so that he may not see the land with his eyes. 13I will spread my net over him, and he shall be caught in my snare; and I will bring him to Babylon, the land of the Chaldeans, yet he shall not see it; and he shall die there. 14I will scatter to every wind all who are around him, his helpers and all his troops; and I will unsheathe the sword behind them. 15And they shall know that I am the LORD, when I disperse them among the nations and scatter them through the countries. 16But I will let a few of them escape from the sword, from famine and pestilence, so that they may tell of all their abominations among the nations where they go; then they shall know that I am the LORD.

Judgment Not Postponed

17 The word of the LORD came to me: 18Mortal, eat your bread with quaking, and drink your water with trembling and with fearfulness; 19and say to the people of the land, Thus says the Lord GOD concerning the inhabitants of Jerusalem in the land of Israel: They shall eat their bread with fearfulness, and drink their water in dismay, because their land shall be stripped of all it contains, on account of the violence of all those who live in it. 20The inhabited cities shall be laid waste, and the land shall become a desolation; and you shall know that I am the LORD.

21 The word of the LORD came to me: 22Mortal, what is this proverb of yours

a Cn: Heb *And to the heart of their detestable things and their abominations their heart goes*
b Gk Syr: Heb *they*

about the land of Israel, which says, "The days are prolonged, and every vision comes to nothing"? 23 Tell them therefore, "Thus says the Lord GOD: I will put an end to this proverb, and they shall use it no more as a proverb in Israel." But say to them, The days are near, and the fulfillment of every vision. 24 For there shall no longer be any false vision or flattering divination within the house of Israel. 25 But I the LORD will speak the word that I speak, and it will be fulfilled. It will no longer be delayed; but in your days, O rebellious house, I will speak the word and fulfill it, says the Lord GOD.

26 The word of the LORD came to me: 27 Mortal, the house of Israel is saying, "The vision that he sees is for many years ahead; he prophesies for distant times." 28 Therefore say to them, Thus says the Lord GOD: None of my words will be delayed any longer, but the word that I speak will be fulfilled, says the Lord GOD.

False Prophets Condemned

13 The word of the LORD came to me: 2 Mortal, prophesy against the prophets of Israel who are prophesying; say to those who prophesy out of their own imagination: "Hear the word of the LORD!" 3 Thus says the Lord GOD, Alas for the senseless prophets who follow their own spirit, and have seen nothing! 4 Your prophets have been like jackals among ruins, O Israel. 5 You have not gone up into the breaches, or repaired a wall for the house of Israel, so that it might stand in battle on the day of the LORD. 6 They have envisioned falsehood and lying divination; they say, "Says the LORD," when the LORD has not sent them, and yet they wait for the fulfillment of their word! 7 Have you not seen a false vision or uttered a lying divination, when you have said, "Says the LORD," even though I did not speak?

8 Therefore thus says the Lord GOD: Because you have uttered falsehood and envisioned lies, I am against you, says the Lord GOD. 9 My hand will be against the prophets who see false visions and utter lying divinations; they shall not be in the council of my people, nor be enrolled in the register of the house of Israel, nor shall they enter the land of Israel; and you shall know that I am the Lord GOD. 10 Because, in truth, because they have misled my people, saying, "Peace," when there is no peace; and because, when the people build a wall, these prophets c smear whitewash on it. 11 Say to those who smear whitewash on it that it shall fall. There will be a deluge of rain, d great hailstones will fall, and a stormy wind will break out. 12 When the wall falls, will it not be said to you, "Where is the whitewash you smeared on it?" 13 Therefore thus says the Lord GOD: In my wrath I will make a stormy wind break out, and in my anger there shall be a deluge of rain, and hailstones in wrath to destroy it. 14 I will break down the wall that you have smeared with whitewash, and bring it to the ground, so that its foundation will be laid bare; when it falls, you shall perish within it; and you shall know that I am the LORD. 15 Thus I will spend my wrath upon the wall, and upon those who have smeared it with whitewash; and I will say to you, The wall is no more, nor those who smeared it— 16 the prophets of Israel who prophesied concerning Jerusalem and saw visions of peace for it, when there was no peace, says the Lord GOD.

17 As for you, mortal, set your face against the daughters of your people, who prophesy out of their own imagination; prophesy against them 18 and say, Thus says the Lord GOD: Woe to the women who sew bands on all wrists, and make veils for the heads of persons of every height, in the hunt for human lives! Will you hunt down lives among my people, and maintain your own lives? 19 You have profaned me among my people for handfuls of barley and for pieces of bread, putting to death persons who should not die and keeping alive persons who should not live, by your lies to my people, who listen to lies.

20 Therefore thus says the Lord GOD: I am against your bands with which you hunt lives; e I will tear them from your arms, and let the lives go free, the lives that you hunt down like birds. 21 I will tear off your veils, and save my people from your hands; they shall no longer

---

c Heb *they*   d Heb *rain and you*   e Gk Syr: Heb *lives for birds*

be prey in your hands; and you shall know that I am the LORD. 22Because you have disheartened the righteous falsely, although I have not disheartened them, and you have encouraged the wicked not to turn from their wicked way and save their lives; 23therefore you shall no longer see false visions or practice divination; I will save my people from your hand. Then you will know that I am the LORD.

God's Judgments Justified

14 Certain elders of Israel came to me and sat down before me. 2And the word of the LORD came to me: 3Mortal, these men have taken their idols into their hearts, and placed their iniquity as a stumbling block before them; shall I let myself be consulted by them? 4Therefore speak to them, and say to them, Thus says the Lord GOD: Any of those of the house of Israel who take their idols into their hearts and place their iniquity as a stumbling block before them, and yet come to the prophet—I the LORD will answer those who come with the multitude of their idols, 5in order that I may take hold of the hearts of the house of Israel, all of whom are estranged from me through their idols.

6 Therefore say to the house of Israel, Thus says the Lord GOD: Repent and turn away from your idols; and turn away your faces from all your abominations. 7For any of those of the house of Israel, or of the aliens who reside in Israel, who separate themselves from me, taking their idols into their hearts and placing their iniquity as a stumbling block before them, and yet come to a prophet to inquire of me by him, I the LORD will answer them myself. 8I will set my face against them; I will make them a sign and a byword and cut them off from the midst of my people; and you shall know that I am the LORD.

9 If a prophet is deceived and speaks a word, I, the LORD, have deceived that prophet, and I will stretch out my hand against him, and will destroy him from the midst of my people Israel. 10And they shall bear their punishment—the punishment of the inquirer and the pun-

ishment of the prophet shall be the same— 11so that the house of Israel may no longer go astray from me, nor defile themselves any more with all their transgressions. Then they shall be my people, and I will be their God, says the Lord GOD.

12 The word of the LORD came to me: 13Mortal, when a land sins against me by acting faithlessly, and I stretch out my hand against it, and break its staff of bread and send famine upon it, and cut off from it human beings and animals, 14even if Noah, Daniel,f and Job, these three, were in it, they would save only their own lives by their righteousness, says the Lord GOD. 15If I send wild animals through the land to ravage it, so that it is made desolate, and no one may pass through because of the animals; 16even if these three men were in it, as I live, says the Lord GOD, they would save neither sons nor daughters; they alone would be saved, but the land would be desolate. 17Or if I bring a sword upon that land and say, "Let a sword pass through the land," and I cut off human beings and animals from it; 18though these three men were in it, as I live, says the Lord GOD, they would save neither sons nor daughters, but they alone would be saved. 19Or if I send a pestilence into that land, and pour out my wrath upon it with blood, to cut off humans and animals from it; 20even if Noah, Daniel,f and Job were in it, as I live, says the Lord GOD, they would save neither son nor daughter; they would save only their own lives by their righteousness.

21 For thus says the Lord GOD: How much more when I send upon Jerusalem my four deadly acts of judgment, sword, famine, wild animals, and pestilence, to cut off humans and animals from it! 22Yet, survivors shall be left in it, sons and daughters who will be brought out; they will come out to you. When you see their ways and their deeds, you will be consoled for the evil that I have brought upon Jerusalem, for all that I have brought upon it. 23They shall console you, when you see their ways and their deeds; and you shall know that it

f Or, as otherwise read, Danel

was not without cause that I did all that I have done in it, says the Lord GOD.

The Useless Vine

15 The word of the LORD came to me:

2 O mortal, how does the wood of
    the vine surpass all other
    wood—
  the vine branch that is among
    the trees of the forest?
3 Is wood taken from it to make
    anything?
  Does one take a peg from it on
    which to hang any object?
4 It is put in the fire for fuel;
  when the fire has consumed both
    ends of it
  and the middle of it is charred,
  is it useful for anything?
5 When it was whole it was used for
    nothing;
  how much less—when the fire
    has consumed it,
  and it is charred—
  can it ever be used for anything!

6 Therefore thus says the Lord GOD: Like the wood of the vine among the trees of the forest, which I have given to the fire for fuel, so I will give up the inhabitants of Jerusalem. 7I will set my face against them; although they escape from the fire, the fire shall still consume them; and you shall know that I am the LORD, when I set my face against them. 8And I will make the land desolate, because they have acted faithlessly, says the Lord GOD.

God's Faithless Bride

16 The word of the LORD came to me: 2Mortal, make known to Jerusalem her abominations, 3and say, Thus says the Lord GOD to Jerusalem: Your origin and your birth were in the land of the Canaanites; your father was an Amorite, and your mother a Hittite. 4As for your birth, on the day you were born your navel cord was not cut, nor were you washed with water to cleanse you, nor rubbed with salt, nor wrapped in cloths. 5No eye pitied you, to do any of these things for you out of compassion for you; but you were thrown out in the

open field, for you were abhorred on the day you were born.

6 I passed by you, and saw you flailing about in your blood. As you lay in your blood, I said to you, "Live! 7and grow up g like a plant of the field." You grew up and became tall and arrived at full womanhood; h your breasts were formed, and your hair had grown; yet you were naked and bare.

8 I passed by you again and looked on you; you were at the age for love. I spread the edge of my cloak over you, and covered your nakedness: I pledged myself to you and entered into a covenant with you, says the Lord GOD, and you became mine. 9Then I bathed you with water and washed off the blood from you, and anointed you with oil. 10I clothed you with embroidered cloth and with sandals of fine leather; I bound you in fine linen and covered you with rich fabric. i 11I adorned you with ornaments: I put bracelets on your arms, a chain on your neck, 12a ring on your nose, earrings in your ears, and a beautiful crown upon your head. 13You were adorned with gold and silver, while your clothing was of fine linen, rich fabric, i and embroidered cloth. You had choice flour and honey and oil for food. You grew exceedingly beautiful, fit to be a queen. 14Your fame spread among the nations on account of your beauty, for it was perfect because of my splendor that I had bestowed on you, says the Lord GOD.

15 But you trusted in your beauty, and played the whore because of your fame, and lavished your whorings on any passer-by. i 16You took some of your garments, and made for yourself colorful shrines, and on them played the whore; nothing like this has ever been or ever shall be. i 17You also took your beautiful jewels of my gold and my silver that I had given you, and made for yourself male images, and with them played the whore; 18and you took your embroidered garments to cover them, and set my oil and my incense before them. 19Also my bread that I gave you—I fed you with choice flour and oil and honey—you set it before them as a pleasing odor; and so

g Gk Syr: Heb *Live! I made you a myriad*   h Cn: Heb *ornament of ornaments*   i Meaning of Heb uncertain   j Heb adds *let it be his*

it was, says the Lord GOD. 20You took your sons and your daughters, whom you had borne to me, and these you sacrificed to them to be devoured. As if your whorings were not enough! 21You slaughtered my children and delivered them up as an offering to them. 22And in all your abominations and your whorings you did not remember the days of your youth, when you were naked and bare, flailing about in your blood.

23 After all your wickedness (woe, woe to you! says the Lord GOD), 24you built yourself a platform and made yourself a lofty place in every square; 25at the head of every street you built your lofty place and prostituted your beauty, offering yourself to every passer-by, and multiplying your whoring. 26You played the whore with the Egyptians, your lustful neighbors, multiplying your whoring, to provoke me to anger. 27Therefore I stretched out my hand against you, reduced your rations, and gave you up to the will of your enemies, the daughters of the Philistines, who were ashamed of your lewd behavior. 28You played the whore with the Assyrians, because you were insatiable; you played the whore with them, and still you were not satisfied. 29You multiplied your whoring with Chaldea, the land of merchants; and even with this you were not satisfied.

30 How sick is your heart, says the Lord GOD, that you did all these things, the deeds of a brazen whore; 31building your platform at the head of every street, and making your lofty place in every square! Yet you were not like a whore, because you scorned payment. 32Adulterous wife, who receives strangers instead of her husband! 33Gifts are given to all whores; but you gave your gifts to all your lovers, bribing them to come to you from all around for your whorings. 34So you were different from other women in your whorings: no one solicited you to play the whore; and you gave payment, while no payment was given to you; you were different.

35 Therefore, O whore, hear the word of the LORD: 36Thus says the Lord GOD, Because your lust was poured out and your nakedness uncovered in your whoring with your lovers, and because of all your abominable idols, and

because of the blood of your children that you gave to them, 37therefore, I will gather all your lovers, with whom you took pleasure, all those you loved and all those you hated; I will gather them against you from all around, and will uncover your nakedness to them, so that they may see all your nakedness. 38I will judge you as women who commit adultery and shed blood are judged, and bring blood upon you in wrath and jealousy. 39I will deliver you into their hands, and they shall throw down your platform and break down your lofty places; they shall strip you of your clothes and take your beautiful objects and leave you naked and bare. 40They shall bring up a mob against you, and they shall stone you and cut you to pieces with their swords. 41They shall burn your houses and execute judgments on you in the sight of many women; I will stop you from playing the whore, and you shall also make no more payments. 42So I will satisfy my fury on you, and my jealousy shall turn away from you; I will be calm, and will be angry no longer. 43Because you have not remembered the days of your youth, but have enraged me with all these things; therefore, I have returned your deeds upon your head, says the Lord GOD.

Have you not committed lewdness beyond all your abominations? 44See, everyone who uses proverbs will use this proverb about you, "Like mother, like daughter." 45You are the daughter of your mother, who loathed her husband and her children; and you are the sister of your sisters, who loathed their husbands and their children. Your mother was a Hittite and your father an Amorite. 46Your elder sister is Samaria, who lived with her daughters to the north of you; and your younger sister, who lived to the south of you, is Sodom with her daughters. 47You not only followed their ways, and acted according to their abominations; within a very little time you were more corrupt than they in all your ways. 48As I live, says the Lord GOD, your sister Sodom and her daughters have not done as you and your daughters have done. 49This was the guilt of your sister Sodom: she and her daughters had pride, excess of food, and prosperous ease, but did not aid the poor and needy. 50They were haughty, and did abominable things before me; therefore I removed them when I saw it. 51Samaria has not committed half your sins; you have committed more abominations than they, and have made your sisters appear righteous by all the abominations that you have committed. 52Bear your disgrace, you also, for you have brought about for your sisters a more favorable judgment; because of your sins in which you acted more abominably than they, they are more in the right than you. So be ashamed, you also, and bear your disgrace, for you have made your sisters appear righteous.

53 I will restore their fortunes, the fortunes of Sodom and her daughters and the fortunes of Samaria and her daughters, and I will restore your own fortunes along with theirs, 54in order that you may bear your disgrace and be ashamed of all that you have done, becoming a consolation to them. 55As for your sisters, Sodom and her daughters shall return to their former state, Samaria and her daughters shall return to their former state, and you and your daughters shall return to your former state. 56Was not your sister Sodom a byword in your mouth in the day of your pride, 57before your wickedness was uncovered? Now you are a mockery to the daughters of Aramk and all her neighbors, and to the daughters of the Philistines, those all around who despise you. 58You must bear the penalty of your lewdness and your abominations, says the LORD.

An Everlasting Covenant

59 Yes, thus says the Lord GOD: I will deal with you as you have done, you who have despised the oath, breaking the covenant; 60yet I will remember my covenant with you in the days of your youth, and I will establish with you an everlasting covenant. 61Then you will remember your ways, and be ashamed when Il take your sisters, both your elder and your younger, and give them to you as daughters, but not on account of mym covenant with you. 62I will establish my covenant with you, and

you shall know that I am the LORD, 63in order that you may remember and be confounded, and never open your mouth again because of your shame, when I forgive you all that you have done, says the Lord GOD.

The Two Eagles and the Vine

17 The word of the LORD came to me: 2O mortal, propound a riddle, and speak an allegory to the house of Israel. 3Say: Thus says the Lord GOD:

A great eagle, with great wings and
    long pinions,
  rich in plumage of many colors,
    came to the Lebanon.
He took the top of the cedar,
4   broke off its topmost shoot;
  he carried it to a land of trade,
    set it in a city of merchants.
5 Then he took a seed from the land,
    placed it in fertile soil;
  a plantn by abundant waters,
    he set it like a willow twig.
6 It sprouted and became a vine
    spreading out, but low;
  its branches turned toward him,
    its roots remained where it stood.
  So it became a vine;
    it brought forth branches,
    put forth foliage.

7 There was another great eagle,
    with great wings and much
      plumage.
  And see! This vine stretched out
    its roots toward him;
  it shot out its branches toward him,
    so that he might water it.
  From the bed where it was planted
8   it was transplanted
  to good soil by abundant waters,
    so that it might produce branches
    and bear fruit
    and become a noble vine.
9Say: Thus says the Lord GOD:
  Will it prosper?
  Will he not pull up its roots,
    cause its fruit to rotn and wither,
    its fresh sprouting leaves to fade?
  No strong arm or mighty army will
      be needed
    to pull it from its roots.

k Another reading is Edom   l Syr: Heb you   m Heb lacks my   n Meaning of Heb uncertain

10   When it is transplanted, will it
          thrive?
      When the east wind strikes it,
          will it not utterly wither,
          wither on the bed where it grew?

11 Then the word of the LORD came
to me: 12Say now to the rebellious house:
Do you not know what these things
mean? Tell them: The king of Babylon
came to Jerusalem, took its king and its
officials, and brought them back with
him to Babylon. 13He took one of the
royal offspring and made a covenant
with him, putting him under oath (he
had taken away the chief men of the
land), 14so that the kingdom might be
humble and not lift itself up, and that by
keeping his covenant it might stand.
15But he rebelled against him by sending
ambassadors to Egypt, in order that they
might give him horses and a large army.
Will he succeed? Can one escape who
does such things? Can he break the covenant and yet escape? 16As I live, says
the Lord GOD, surely in the place where
the king resides who made him king,
whose oath he despised, and whose covenant with him he broke—in Babylon he
shall die. 17Pharaoh with his mighty
army and great company will not help
him in war, when ramps are cast up and
siege walls built to cut off many lives.
18Because he despised the oath and broke
the covenant, because he gave his hand
and yet did all these things, he shall not
escape. 19Therefore thus says the Lord
GOD: As I live, I will surely return upon
his head my oath that he despised, and
my covenant that he broke. 20I will
spread my net over him, and he shall be
caught in my snare; I will bring him to
Babylon and enter into judgment with
him there for the treason he has committed against me. 21All the picko of his
troops shall fall by the sword, and the
survivors shall be scattered to every
wind; and you shall know that I, the
LORD, have spoken.

Israel Exalted at Last

22 Thus says the Lord GOD:
      I myself will take a sprig
          from the lofty top of a cedar;
          I will set it out.
      I will break off a tender one

      from the topmost of its young
          twigs;
      I myself will plant it
          on a high and lofty mountain.
23   On the mountain height of Israel
          I will plant it,
      in order that it may produce
          boughs and bear fruit,
          and become a noble cedar.
      Under it every kind of bird will
          live;
      in the shade of its branches will
          nest
      winged creatures of every kind.
24   All the trees of the field shall know
          that I am the LORD.
      I bring low the high tree,
          I make high the low tree;
      I dry up the green tree
          and make the dry tree flourish.
      I the LORD have spoken;
          I will accomplish it.

Individual Retribution

18 The word of the LORD came
to me: 2What do you mean by
repeating this proverb concerning the
land of Israel, "The parents have eaten
sour grapes, and the children's teeth are
set on edge"? 3As I live, says the Lord
GOD, this proverb shall no more be used
by you in Israel. 4Know that all lives are
mine; the life of the parent as well as the
life of the child is mine: it is only the
person who sins that shall die.

5 If a man is righteous and does what
is lawful and right— 6if he does not eat
upon the mountains or lift up his eyes to
the idols of the house of Israel, does not
defile his neighbor's wife or approach a
woman during her menstrual period,
7does not oppress anyone, but restores
to the debtor his pledge, commits no
robbery, gives his bread to the hungry
and covers the naked with a garment,
8does not take advance or accrued interest, withholds his hand from iniquity,
executes true justice between contend-
ing parties, 9follows my statutes, and is
careful to observe my ordinances, acting
faithfully—such a one is righteous; he
shall surely live, says the Lord GOD.

10 If he has a son who is violent, a
shedder of blood, 11who does any of
these things (though his fatherp does

o Another reading is *fugitives*   p Heb *he*

none of them), who eats upon the mountains, defiles his neighbor's wife, ¹²oppresses the poor and needy, commits robbery, does not restore the pledge, lifts up his eyes to the idols, commits abomination, ¹³takes advance or accrued interest; shall he then live? He shall not. He has done all these abominable things; he shall surely die; his blood shall be upon himself.

14 But if this man has a son who sees all the sins that his father has done, considers, and does not do likewise, ¹⁵who does not eat upon the mountains or lift up his eyes to the idols of the house of Israel, does not defile his neighbor's wife, ¹⁶does not wrong anyone, exacts no pledge, commits no robbery, but gives his bread to the hungry and covers the naked with a garment, ¹⁷withholds his hand from iniquity,*q* takes no advance or accrued interest, observes my ordinances, and follows my statutes; he shall not die for his father's iniquity; he shall surely live. ¹⁸As for his father, because he practiced extortion, robbed his brother, and did what is not good among his people, he dies for his iniquity.

19 Yet you say, "Why should not the son suffer for the iniquity of the father?" When the son has done what is lawful and right, and has been careful to observe all my statutes, he shall surely live. ²⁰The person who sins shall die. A child shall not suffer for the iniquity of a parent, nor a parent suffer for the iniquity of

q Gk: Heb *the poor*

THURSDAY

ALL SOULS ARE GOD'S
G. Campbell Morgan

VERSE: Ezekiel 18.4   **PASSAGE:** Ezekiel 18.3–9

ll lives are mine. The great truth revealed is that every individual has a relationship with God available, which is mightier than all the facts resulting from physical relationships. It may be true that in my physical being I have inherited tendencies to some forms of evil from my father; but in the fact of my essential relation to God there are forces available to me more and mightier than all these tendencies. Therefore if I die, it is not because of the sin of my father, but because I fail to avail myself of my resources in God; and if I live, it is because I have availed myself of these resources . . . The former [righteousness] results from right relationship with God, and the latter [evil] from failure to realize that relationship. All souls are his, and that means that every soul is made for first-hand personal dealing with him.

ADDITIONAL SCRIPTURE READING:
Numbers 16.22–33; Hebrews 12.9–10

Go to page 978 for your next devotional reading.

1900   Present

a child; the righteousness of the righteous shall be his own, and the wickedness of the wicked shall be his own.

21 But if the wicked turn away from all their sins that they have committed and keep all my statutes and do what is lawful and right, they shall surely live; they shall not die. 22None of the transgressions that they have committed shall be remembered against them; for the righteousness that they have done they shall live. 23Have I any pleasure in the death of the wicked, says the Lord God, and not rather that they should turn from their ways and live? 24But when the righteous turn away from their righteousness and commit iniquity and do the same abominable things that the wicked do, shall they live? None of the righteous deeds that they have done shall be remembered; for the treachery of which they are guilty and the sin they have committed, they shall die.

25 Yet you say, "The way of the Lord is unfair." Hear now, O house of Israel: Is my way unfair? Is it not your ways that are unfair? 26When the righteous turn away from their righteousness and commit iniquity, they shall die for it; for the iniquity that they have committed they shall die. 27Again, when the wicked turn away from the wickedness they have committed and do what is lawful and right, they shall save their life. 28Because they considered and turned away from all the transgressions that they had committed, they shall surely live; they shall not die. 29Yet the house of Israel says, "The way of the Lord is unfair." O house of Israel, are my ways unfair? Is it not your ways that are unfair?

30 Therefore I will judge you, O house of Israel, all of you according to your ways, says the Lord God. Repent and turn from all your transgressions; otherwise iniquity will be your ruin.[r] 31Cast away from you all the transgressions that you have committed against me, and get yourselves a new heart and a new spirit! Why will you die, O house of Israel? 32For I have no pleasure in the death of anyone, says the Lord God. Turn, then, and live.

Israel Degraded

19 As for you, raise up a lamentation for the princes of Israel, 2and say:

What a lioness was your mother
  among lions!
She lay down among young lions,
  rearing her cubs.
3 She raised up one of her cubs;
  he became a young lion,
and he learned to catch prey;
  he devoured humans.
4 The nations sounded an alarm
  against him;
  he was caught in their pit;
and they brought him with hooks
  to the land of Egypt.
5 When she saw that she was
  thwarted,
  that her hope was lost,
she took another of her cubs
  and made him a young lion.
6 He prowled among the lions;
  he became a young lion,
and he learned to catch prey;
  he devoured people.
7 And he ravaged their strongholds,[s]
  and laid waste their towns;
the land was appalled, and all in it,
  at the sound of his roaring.
8 The nations set upon him
  from the provinces all around;
they spread their net over him;
  he was caught in their pit.
9 With hooks they put him in a cage,
  and brought him to the king of
    Babylon;
  they brought him into custody,
so that his voice should be heard no
    more
  on the mountains of Israel.
10 Your mother was like a vine in a
    vineyard[t]
  transplanted by the water,
fruitful and full of branches
  from abundant water.
11 Its strongest stem became
  a ruler's scepter;[u]
it towered aloft
  among the thick boughs;
it stood out in its height
  with its mass of branches.
12 But it was plucked up in fury,
  cast down to the ground;

r Or so that they shall not be a stumbling block of iniquity to you   s Heb his widows   t Cn: Heb in your blood   u Heb Its strongest stems became rulers' scepters

the east wind dried it up;
    its fruit was stripped off,
its strong stem was withered;
    the fire consumed it.
13 Now it is transplanted into the
    wilderness,
    into a dry and thirsty land.
14 And fire has gone out from its
    stem,
    has consumed its branches and
    fruit,
so that there remains in it no
    strong stem,
    no scepter for ruling.

This is a lamentation, and it is used as a lamentation.

Israel's Continuing Rebellion

20 In the seventh year, in the fifth month, on the tenth day of the month, certain elders of Israel came to consult the LORD, and sat down before me. 2And the word of the LORD came to me: 3Mortal, speak to the elders of Israel, and say to them: Thus says the Lord GOD: Why are you coming? To consult me? As I live, says the Lord GOD, I will not be consulted by you. 4Will you judge them, mortal, will you judge them? Then let them know the abominations of their ancestors, 5and say to them: Thus says the Lord GOD: On the day when I chose Israel, I swore to the offspring of the house of Jacob—making myself known to them in the land of Egypt—I swore to them, saying, I am the LORD your God. 6On that day I swore to them that I would bring them out of the land of Egypt into a land that I had searched out for them, a land flowing with milk and honey, the most glorious of all lands. 7And I said to them, Cast away the detestable things your eyes feast on, every one of you, and do not defile yourselves with the idols of Egypt; I am the LORD your God. 8But they rebelled against me and would not listen to me; not one of them cast away the detestable things their eyes feasted on, nor did they forsake the idols of Egypt.

Then I thought I would pour out my wrath upon them and spend my anger against them in the midst of the land of Egypt. 9But I acted for the sake of my name, that it should not be profaned in the sight of the nations among whom they lived, in whose sight I made myself known to them in bringing them out of the land of Egypt. 10So I led them out of the land of Egypt and brought them into the wilderness. 11I gave them my statutes and showed them my ordinances, by whose observance everyone shall live. 12Moreover I gave them my sabbaths, as a sign between me and them, so that they might know that I the LORD sanctify them. 13But the house of Israel rebelled against me in the wilderness; they did not observe my statutes but rejected my ordinances, by whose observance everyone shall live; and my sabbaths they greatly profaned.

Then I thought I would pour out my wrath upon them in the wilderness, to make an end of them. 14But I acted for the sake of my name, so that it should not be profaned in the sight of the nations, in whose sight I had brought them out. 15Moreover I swore to them in the wilderness that I would not bring them into the land that I had given them, a land flowing with milk and honey, the most glorious of all lands, 16because they rejected my ordinances and did not observe my statutes, and profaned my sabbaths; for their heart went after their idols. 17Nevertheless my eye spared them, and I did not destroy them or make an end of them in the wilderness.

18 I said to their children in the wilderness, Do not follow the statutes of your parents, nor observe their ordinances, nor defile yourselves with their idols. 19I the LORD am your God; follow my statutes, and be careful to observe my ordinances, 20and hallow my sabbaths that they may be a sign between me and you, so that you may know that I the LORD am your God. 21But the children rebelled against me; they did not follow my statutes, and were not careful to observe my ordinances, by whose observance everyone shall live; they profaned my sabbaths.

Then I thought I would pour out my wrath upon them and spend my anger against them in the wilderness. 22But I withheld my hand, and acted for the sake of my name, so that it should not be profaned in the sight of the nations, in whose sight I had brought them out. ²³Moreover I swore to them in the wilderness that I would scatter them among the nations and disperse them through the countries, ²⁴because they had not executed my ordinances, but had rejected my statutes and profaned my sabbaths, and their eyes were set on their ancestors' idols. ²⁵Moreover I gave them statutes that were not good and ordinances by which they could not live. ²⁶I defiled them through their very gifts, in their offering up all their firstborn, in order that I might horrify them, so that they might know that I am the LORD.

27 Therefore, mortal, speak to the house of Israel and say to them, Thus says the Lord GOD: In this again your ancestors blasphemed me, by dealing treacherously with me. ²⁸For when I had brought them into the land that I swore to give them, then wherever they saw any high hill or any leafy tree, there they offered their sacrifices and presented the provocation of their offering; there they sent up their pleasing odors, and there they poured out their drink offerings. ²⁹(I said to them, What is the high place to which you go? So it is called Bamah[v] to this day.) ³⁰Therefore say to the house of Israel, Thus says the Lord GOD: Will you defile yourselves after the manner of your ancestors and go astray after their detestable things? ³¹When you offer your gifts and make your children pass through the fire, you defile yourselves with all your idols to this day. And shall I be consulted by you, O house of Israel? As I live, says the Lord GOD, I will not be consulted by you.

32 What is in your mind shall never happen—the thought, "Let us be like the nations, like the tribes of the countries, and worship wood and stone."

God Will Restore Israel

33 As I live, says the Lord GOD, surely with a mighty hand and an outstretched arm, and with wrath poured out, I will be king over you. ³⁴I will bring you out from the peoples and gather you out of the countries where you are scattered, with a mighty hand and an outstretched arm, and with wrath poured out; ³⁵and I will bring you into the wilderness of the peoples, and there I will enter into judgment with you face to face. ³⁶As I entered into judgment with your ancestors in the wilderness of the land of Egypt, so I will enter into judgment with you, says the Lord GOD. ³⁷I will make you pass under the staff, and will bring you within the bond of the covenant. ³⁸I will purge out the rebels among you, and those who transgress against me; I will bring them out of the land where they reside as aliens, but they shall not enter the land of Israel. Then you shall know that I am the LORD.

39 As for you, O house of Israel, thus says the Lord GOD: Go serve your idols, everyone of you now and hereafter, if you will not listen to me; but my holy name you shall no more profane with your gifts and your idols.

40 For on my holy mountain, the mountain height of Israel, says the Lord GOD, there all the house of Israel, all of them, shall serve me in the land; there I will accept them, and there I will require your contributions and the choicest of your gifts, with all your sacred things. ⁴¹As a pleasing odor I will accept you, when I bring you out from the peoples, and gather you out of the countries where you have been scattered; and I will manifest my holiness among you in the sight of the nations. ⁴²You shall know that I am the LORD, when I bring you into the land of Israel, the country that I swore to give to your ancestors. ⁴³There you shall remember your ways and all the deeds by which you have polluted yourselves; and you shall loathe yourselves for all the evils that you have committed. ⁴⁴And you shall know that I am the LORD, when I deal with you for my name's sake, not according to your evil ways, or corrupt deeds, O house of Israel, says the Lord GOD.

A Prophecy against the Negeb

45[w] The word of the LORD came to me: ⁴⁶Mortal, set your face toward the south, preach against the south, and prophesy against the forest land in the Negeb; ⁴⁷say to the forest of the Negeb, Hear the word of the LORD: Thus says

v That is *High Place*   w Ch 21.1 in Heb

the Lord GOD, I will kindle a fire in you, and it shall devour every green tree in you and every dry tree; the blazing flame shall not be quenched, and all faces from south to north shall be scorched by it. 48All flesh shall see that I the LORD have kindled it; it shall not be quenched. 49Then I said, "Ah Lord GOD! they are saying of me, 'Is he not a maker of allegories?' "

The Drawn Sword of God

21 x The word of the LORD came to me: 2Mortal, set your face toward Jerusalem and preach against the sanctuaries; prophesy against the land of Israel 3and say to the land of Israel, Thus says the LORD: I am coming against you, and will draw my sword out of its sheath, and will cut off from you both righteous and wicked. 4Because I will cut off from you both righteous and wicked, therefore my sword shall go out of its sheath against all flesh from south to north; 5and all flesh shall know that I the LORD have drawn my sword out of its sheath; it shall not be sheathed again. 6Moan therefore, mortal; moan with breaking heart and bitter grief before their eyes. 7And when they say to you, "Why do you moan?" you shall say, "Because of the news that has come. Every heart will melt and all hands will be feeble, every spirit will faint and all knees will turn to water. See, it comes and it will be fulfilled," says the Lord GOD.

8 And the word of the LORD came to me: 9Mortal, prophesy and say: Thus says the Lord; Say:

A sword, a sword is sharpened,
    it is also polished;
10 it is sharpened for slaughter,
    honed to flash like lightning!
How can we make merry?
    You have despised the rod,
    and all discipline.y
11 The swordz is given to be polished,
    to be grasped in the hand;
it is sharpened, the sword is
    polished,
    to be placed in the slayer's hand.
12 Cry and wail, O mortal,
    for it is against my people;

it is against all Israel's princes;
    they are thrown to the sword,
    together with my people.
    Ah! Strike the thigh!
13For consider: What! If you despise the rod, will it not happen?y says the Lord GOD.
14 And you, mortal, prophesy;
    strike hand to hand.
Let the sword fall twice, thrice;
    it is a sword for killing.
A sword for great slaughter—
    it surrounds them;
15 therefore hearts melt
    and many stumble.
At all their gates I have set
    the pointy of the sword.
Ah! It is made for flashing,
    it is polisheda for slaughter.
16 Attack to the right!
    Engage to the left!
    —wherever your edge is directed.
17 I too will strike hand to hand,
    I will satisfy my fury;
    I the LORD have spoken.

18 The word of the LORD came to me: 19Mortal, mark out two roads for the sword of the king of Babylon to come; both of them shall issue from the same land. And make a signpost, make it for a fork in the road leading to a city; 20mark out the road for the sword to come to Rabbah of the Ammonites or to Judah and tob Jerusalem the fortified. 21For the king of Babylon stands at the parting of the way, at the fork in the two roads, to use divination; he shakes the arrows, he consults the teraphim,c he inspects the liver. 22Into his right hand comes the lot for Jerusalem, to set battering rams, to call out for slaughter, for raising the battle cry, to set battering rams against the gates, to cast up ramps, to build siege towers. 23But to them it will seem like a false divination; they have sworn solemn oaths; but he brings their guilt to remembrance, bringing about their capture.

24 Therefore thus says the Lord GOD: Because you have brought your guilt to remembrance, in that your transgressions are uncovered, so that in all your deeds your sins appear—because you

---

x Ch 21.6 in Heb   y Meaning of Heb uncertain
Heb Judah in   c Or the household gods   z Heb It   a Tg: Heb wrapped up   b Gk Syr:

have come to remembrance, you shall be taken in hand.[d]

25 As for you, vile, wicked prince of
        Israel,
      you whose day has come,
      the time of final punishment,
26 thus says the Lord GOD:
      Remove the turban, take off the
        crown;
        things shall not remain as they
          are.
      Exalt that which is low,
        abase that which is high.
27 A ruin, a ruin, a ruin—
        I will make it!
      (Such has never occurred.)
      Until he comes whose right it is;
        to him I will give it.

28 As for you, mortal, prophesy, and say, Thus says the Lord GOD concerning the Ammonites, and concerning their reproach; say:
      A sword, a sword! Drawn for
        slaughter,
        polished to consume,[e] to flash
          like lightning.
29 Offering false visions for you,
        divining lies for you,
      they place you over the necks
        of the vile, wicked ones—
      those whose day has come,
        the time of final punishment.
30 Return it to its sheath!
      In the place where you were
        created,
        in the land of your origin,
        I will judge you.
31 I will pour out my indignation
        upon you,
      with the fire of my wrath
        I will blow upon you.
      I will deliver you into brutish
        hands,
        those skillful to destroy.
32 You shall be fuel for the fire,
        your blood shall enter the earth;
      you shall be remembered no more,
        for I the LORD have spoken.

The Bloody City

22 The word of the LORD came to me: [2]You, mortal, will you judge, will you judge the bloody city? Then declare to it all its abominable deeds. [3]You shall say, Thus says the Lord GOD: A city! Shedding blood within itself; its time has come; making its idols, defiling itself. [4]You have become guilty by the blood that you have shed, and defiled by the idols that you have made; you have brought your day near, the appointed time of your years has come. Therefore I have made you a disgrace before the nations, and a mockery to all the countries. [5]Those who are near and those who are far from you will mock you, you infamous one, full of tumult.

6 The princes of Israel in you, everyone according to his power, have been bent on shedding blood. [7]Father and mother are treated with contempt in you; the alien residing within you suffers extortion; the orphan and the widow are wronged in you. [8]You have despised my holy things, and profaned my sabbaths. [9]In you are those who slander to shed blood, those in you who eat upon the mountains, who commit lewdness in your midst. [10]In you they uncover their fathers' nakedness; in you they violate women in their menstrual periods. [11]One commits abomination with his neighbor's wife; another lewdly defiles his daughter-in-law; another in you defiles his sister, his father's daughter. [12]In you, they take bribes to shed blood; you take both advance interest and accrued interest, and make gain of your neighbors by extortion; and you have forgotten me, says the Lord GOD.

13 See, I strike my hands together at the dishonest gain you have made, and at the blood that has been shed within you. [14]Can your courage endure, or can your hands remain strong in the days when I shall deal with you? I the LORD have spoken, and I will do it. [15]I will scatter you among the nations and disperse you through the countries, and I will purge your filthiness out of you. [16]And I[f] shall be profaned through you in the sight of the nations; and you shall know that I am the LORD.

17 The word of the LORD came to me: [18]Mortal, the house of Israel has become dross to me; all of them, silver,[g] bronze,

---

[d] Or *be taken captive*   [e] Cn: Heb *to contain*   [f] Gk Syr Vg: Heb *you*   [g] Transposed from the end
of the verse; compare verse 20

tin, iron, and lead. In the smelter they have become dross. ¹⁹Therefore thus says the Lord GOD: Because you have all become dross, I will gather you into the midst of Jerusalem. ²⁰As one gathers silver, bronze, iron, lead, and tin into a smelter, to blow the fire upon them in order to melt them; so I will gather you in my anger and in my wrath, and I will put you in and melt you. ²¹I will gather you and blow upon you with the fire of my wrath, and you shall be melted within it. ²²As silver is melted in a smelter, so you shall be melted in it; and you shall know that I the LORD have poured out my wrath upon you.

23 The word of the LORD came to me: ²⁴Mortal, say to it: You are a land that is not cleansed, not rained upon in the day of indignation. ²⁵Its princesʰ within it are like a roaring lion tearing the prey; they have devoured human lives; they have taken treasure and precious things; they have made many widows within it. ²⁶Its priests have done violence to my teaching and have profaned my holy things; they have made no distinction between the holy and the common, neither have they taught the difference between the unclean and the clean, and they have disregarded my sabbaths, so that I am profaned among them. ²⁷Its officials within it are like wolves tearing the prey, shedding blood, destroying lives to get dishonest gain. ²⁸Its prophets have smeared whitewash on their behalf, seeing false visions and divining lies for them, saying, "Thus says the Lord GOD," when the LORD has not spoken. ²⁹The people of the land have practiced extortion and committed robbery; they have oppressed the poor and needy, and have extorted from the alien without redress. ³⁰And I sought for anyone among them who would repair the wall and stand in the breach before me on behalf of the land, so that I would not destroy it; but I found no one. ³¹Therefore I have poured out my indignation upon them; I have consumed them with the fire of my wrath; I have returned their conduct upon their heads, says the Lord GOD.

Oholah and Oholibah

23 The word of the LORD came to me: ²Mortal, there were two women, the daughters of one mother; ³they played the whore in Egypt; they played the whore in their youth; their breasts were caressed there, and their virgin bosoms were fondled. ⁴Oholah was the name of the elder and Oholibah the name of her sister. They became mine, and they bore sons and daughters. As for their names, Oholah is Samaria, and Oholibah is Jerusalem.

5 Oholah played the whore while she was mine; she lusted after her lovers the Assyrians, warriorsⁱ ⁶clothed in blue, governors and commanders, all of them handsome young men, mounted horsemen. ⁷She bestowed her favors upon them, the choicest men of Assyria all of them; and she defiled herself with all the idols of everyone for whom she lusted. ⁸She did not give up her whorings that she had practiced since Egypt; for in her youth men had lain with her and fondled her virgin bosom and poured out their lust upon her. ⁹Therefore I delivered her into the hands of her lovers, into the hands of the Assyrians, for whom she lusted. ¹⁰These uncovered her nakedness; they seized her sons and her daughters; and they killed her with the sword. Judgment was executed upon her, and she became a byword among women.

11 Her sister Oholibah saw this, yet she was more corrupt than she in her lusting and in her whorings, which were worse than those of her sister. ¹²She lusted after the Assyrians, governors and commanders, warriorsⁱ clothed in full armor, mounted horsemen, all of them handsome young men. ¹³And I saw that she was defiled; they both took the same way. ¹⁴But she carried her whorings further; she saw male figures carved on the wall, images of the Chaldeans portrayed in vermilion, ¹⁵with belts around their waists, with flowing turbans on their heads, all of them looking like officers— a picture of Babylonians whose native land was Chaldea. ¹⁶When she saw them she lusted after them, and sent messengers to them in Chaldea. ¹⁷And the Babylonians came to her into the

ʰ Gk: Heb *indignation.* ²⁵*A conspiracy of its prophets*   ⁱ Meaning of Heb uncertain bed of love, and they defiled her with their lust; and after she defiled herself with them, she turned from them in disgust. [18]When she carried on her whorings so openly and flaunted her nakedness, I turned in disgust from her, as I had turned from her sister. [19]Yet she increased her whorings, remembering the days of her youth, when she played the whore in the land of Egypt [20]and lusted after her paramours there, whose members were like those of donkeys, and whose emission was like that of stallions. [21]Thus you longed for the lewdness of your youth, when the Egyptians[j] fondled your bosom and caressed[k] your young breasts.

22 Therefore, O Oholibah, thus says the Lord GOD: I will rouse against you your lovers from whom you turned in disgust, and I will bring them against you from every side: [23]the Babylonians and all the Chaldeans, Pekod and Shoa and Koa, and all the Assyrians with them, handsome young men, governors and commanders all of them, officers and warriors,[l] all of them riding on horses. [24]They shall come against you from the north[m] with chariots and wagons and a host of peoples; they shall set themselves against you on every side with buckler, shield, and helmet, and I will commit the judgment to them, and they shall judge you according to their ordinances. [25]I will direct my indignation against you, in order that they may deal with you in fury. They shall cut off your nose and your ears, and your survivors shall fall by the sword. They shall seize your sons and your daughters, and your survivors shall be devoured by fire. [26]They shall also strip you of your clothes and take away your fine jewels. [27]So I will put an end to your lewdness and your whoring brought from the land of Egypt; you shall not long for them, or remember Egypt any more. [28]For thus says the Lord GOD: I will deliver you into the hands of those whom you hate, into the hands of those from whom you turned in disgust; [29]and they shall deal with you in hatred, and take away all the fruit of your labor, and leave you naked and bare, and the nakedness of your whorings shall be exposed. Your lewdness and your whorings [30]have brought this upon you, because you played the whore with the nations, and polluted yourself with their idols. [31]You have gone the way of your sister; therefore I will give her cup into your hand. [32]Thus says the Lord GOD:

You shall drink your sister's cup,
    deep and wide;
you shall be scorned and derided,
    it holds so much.
33 You shall be filled with
        drunkenness and sorrow.
    A cup of horror and desolation
        is the cup of your sister Samaria;
34 you shall drink it and drain it out,
        and gnaw its sherds,
        and tear out your breasts;
for I have spoken, says the Lord GOD. [35]Therefore thus says the Lord GOD: Because you have forgotten me and cast me behind your back, therefore bear the consequences of your lewdness and whorings.

36 The LORD said to me: Mortal, will you judge Oholah and Oholibah? Then declare to them their abominable deeds. [37]For they have committed adultery, and blood is on their hands; with their idols they have committed adultery; and they have even offered up to them for food the children whom they had borne to me. [38]Moreover this they have done to me: they have defiled my sanctuary on the same day and profaned my sabbaths. [39]For when they had slaughtered their children for their idols, on the same day they came into my sanctuary to profane it. This is what they did in my house.

40 They even sent for men to come from far away, to whom a messenger was sent, and they came. For them you bathed yourself, painted your eyes, and decked yourself with ornaments; [41]you sat on a stately couch, with a table spread before it on which you had placed my incense and my oil. [42]The sound of a raucous multitude was around her, with many of the rabble brought in drunken from the wilderness; and they put bracelets on the arms[n] of the women, and beautiful crowns upon their heads.

43 Then I said, Ah, she is worn out

---

j Two Mss: MT *from Egypt*   k Cn: Heb *for the sake of*   l Compare verses 6 and 12 Heb *officers and called ones*   m Gk: Meaning of Heb uncertain   n Heb *hands*

with adulteries, but they carry on their sexual acts with her. 44For they have gone in to her, as one goes in to a whore. Thus they went in to Oholah and to Oholibah, wanton women. 45But righteous judges shall declare them guilty of adultery and of bloodshed; because they are adulteresses and blood is on their hands.

46 For thus says the Lord GOD: Bring up an assembly against them, and make them an object of terror and of plunder. 47The assembly shall stone them and with their swords they shall cut them down; they shall kill their sons and their daughters, and burn up their houses. 48Thus will I put an end to lewdness in the land, so that all women may take warning and not commit lewdness as you have done. 49They shall repay you for your lewdness, and you shall bear the penalty for your sinful idolatry; and you shall know that I am the Lord GOD.

The Boiling Pot

24 In the ninth year, in the tenth month, on the tenth day of the month, the word of the LORD came to me: 2Mortal, write down the name of this day, this very day. The king of Babylon has laid siege to Jerusalem this very day. 3And utter an allegory to the rebellious house and say to them, Thus says the Lord GOD:

Set on the pot, set it on,
  pour in water also;
4 put in it the pieces,
  all the good pieces, the thigh and
    the shoulder;
  fill it with choice bones.
5 Take the choicest one of the flock,
  pile the logs[o] under it;
  boil its pieces,[p]
  seethe[q] also its bones in it.

6 Therefore thus says the Lord GOD:
Woe to the bloody city,
  the pot whose rust is in it,
  whose rust has not gone out of it!
Empty it piece by piece,
  making no choice at all.[r]
7 For the blood she shed is inside it;
  she placed it on a bare rock;

she did not pour it out on the
  ground,
to cover it with earth.
8 To rouse my wrath, to take
  vengeance,
I have placed the blood she shed
  on a bare rock,
so that it may not be covered.
9Therefore thus says the Lord GOD:
Woe to the bloody city!
I will even make the pile great.
10 Heap up the logs, kindle the fire;
  boil the meat well, mix in the
    spices,
  let the bones be burned.
11 Stand it empty upon the coals,
  so that it may become hot, its
    copper glow,
  its filth melt in it, its rust be
    consumed.
12 In vain I have wearied myself;[s]
  its thick rust does not depart.
  To the fire with its rust![t]
13 Yet, when I cleansed you in your
    filthy lewdness,
  you did not become clean from
    your filth;
you shall not again be cleansed
  until I have satisfied my fury
    upon you.
14I the LORD have spoken; the time is coming, I will act. I will not refrain, I will not spare, I will not relent. According to your ways and your doings I will judge you, says the Lord GOD.

Ezekiel's Bereavement

15 The word of the LORD came to me: 16Mortal, with one blow I am about to take away from you the delight of your eyes; yet you shall not mourn or weep, nor shall your tears run down. 17Sigh, but not aloud; make no mourning for the dead. Bind on your turban, and put your sandals on your feet; do not cover your upper lip or eat the bread of mourners.[u] 18So I spoke to the people in the morning, and at evening my wife died. And on the next morning I did as I was commanded.

19 Then the people said to me, "Will you not tell us what these things mean for us, that you are acting this way?"

---

o Compare verse 10: Heb the bones   p Two Mss: Heb its boilings   q Cn: Heb its bones seethe
r Heb piece, no lot has fallen on it   s Cn: Meaning of Heb uncertain   t Meaning of Heb uncertain
u Vg Tg: Heb of men

20Then I said to them: The word of the LORD came to me: 21Say to the house of Israel, Thus says the Lord GOD: I will profane my sanctuary, the pride of your power, the delight of your eyes, and your heart's desire; and your sons and your daughters whom you left behind shall fall by the sword. 22And you shall do as I have done; you shall not cover your upper lip or eat the bread of mourners.v 23Your turbans shall be on your heads and your sandals on your feet; you shall not mourn or weep, but you shall pine away in your iniquities and groan to one another. 24Thus Ezekiel shall be a sign to you; you shall do just as he has done. When this comes, then you shall know that I am the Lord GOD.

25 And you, mortal, on the day when I take from them their stronghold, their joy and glory, the delight of their eyes and their heart's affection, and alsow their sons and their daughters, 26on that day, one who has escaped will come to you to report to you the news. 27On that day your mouth shall be opened to the one who has escaped, and you shall speak and no longer be silent. So you shall be a sign to them; and they shall know that I am the LORD.

Proclamation against Ammon

25 The word of the LORD came to me: 2Mortal, set your face toward the Ammonites and prophesy against them. 3Say to the Ammonites, Hear the word of the Lord GOD: Thus says the Lord GOD, Because you said, "Aha!" over my sanctuary when it was profaned, and over the land of Israel when it was made desolate, and over the house of Judah when it went into exile; 4therefore I am handing you over to the people of the east for a possession. They shall set their encampments among you and pitch their tents in your midst; they shall eat your fruit, and they shall drink your milk. 5I will make Rabbah a pasture for camels and Ammon a fold for flocks. Then you shall know that I am the LORD. 6For thus says the Lord GOD: Because you have clapped your hands and stamped your feet and rejoiced with all the malice within you against the land of Israel, 7therefore I have stretched out my hand against you, and will hand you over as plunder to the nations. I will cut you off from the peoples and will make you perish out of the countries; I will destroy you. Then you shall know that I am the LORD.

Proclamation against Moab

8 Thus says the Lord GOD: Because Moabx said, The house of Judah is like all the other nations, 9therefore I will lay open the flank of Moab from the townsy on its frontier, the glory of the country, Beth-jeshimoth, Baal-meon, and Kiriathaim. 10I will give it along with Ammon to the people of the east as a possession. Thus Ammon shall be remembered no more among the nations, 11and I will execute judgments upon Moab. Then they shall know that I am the LORD.

Proclamation against Edom

12 Thus says the Lord GOD: Because Edom acted revengefully against the house of Judah and has grievously offended in taking vengeance upon them, 13therefore thus says the Lord GOD, I will stretch out my hand against Edom, and cut off from it humans and animals, and I will make it desolate; from Teman even to Dedan they shall fall by the sword. 14I will lay my vengeance upon Edom by the hand of my people Israel; and they shall act in Edom according to my anger and according to my wrath; and they shall know my vengeance, says the Lord GOD.

Proclamation against Philistia

15 Thus says the Lord GOD: Because with unending hostilities the Philistines acted in vengeance, and with malice of heart took revenge in destruction; 16therefore thus says the Lord GOD, I will stretch out my hand against the Philistines, cut off the Cherethites, and destroy the rest of the seacoast. 17I will execute great vengeance on them with wrathful punishments. Then they shall know that I am the LORD, when I lay my vengeance on them.

---

v Vg Tg: Heb of men   w Heb lacks and also   x Gk Old Latin: Heb Moab and Seir   y Heb towns from its towns

Proclamation against Tyre

26 In the eleventh year, on the first day of the month, the word of the LORD came to me: 2Mortal, because Tyre said concerning Jerusalem, "Aha, broken is the gateway of the peoples;
it has swung open to me;
I shall be replenished,
now that it is wasted,"
3therefore, thus says the Lord GOD:
See, I am against you, O Tyre!
I will hurl many nations against you,
as the sea hurls its waves.
4 They shall destroy the walls of Tyre
and break down its towers.
I will scrape its soil from it
and make it a bare rock.
5 It shall become, in the midst of the sea,
a place for spreading nets.
I have spoken, says the Lord GOD.
It shall become plunder for the nations,
6 and its daughter-towns in the country
shall be killed by the sword.
Then they shall know that I am the LORD.

7 For thus says the Lord GOD: I will bring against Tyre from the north King Nebuchadrezzar of Babylon, king of kings, together with horses, chariots, cavalry, and a great and powerful army.
8 Your daughter-towns in the country
he shall put to the sword.
He shall set up a siege wall against you,
cast up a ramp against you,
and raise a roof of shields against you.
9 He shall direct the shock of his battering rams against your walls
and break down your towers with his axes.
10 His horses shall be so many
that their dust shall cover you.
At the noise of cavalry, wheels, and chariots
your very walls shall shake,
when he enters your gates
like those entering a breached city.
11 With the hoofs of his horses
he shall trample all your streets.
He shall put your people to the sword,
and your strong pillars shall fall to the ground.
12 They will plunder your riches
and loot your merchandise;
they shall break down your walls
and destroy your fine houses.
Your stones and timber and soil
they shall cast into the water.
13 I will silence the music of your songs;
the sound of your lyres shall be heard no more.
14 I will make you a bare rock;
you shall be a place for spreading nets.
You shall never again be rebuilt,
for I the LORD have spoken,
says the Lord GOD.

15 Thus says the Lord GOD to Tyre: Shall not the coastlands shake at the sound of your fall, when the wounded groan, when slaughter goes on within you? 16Then all the princes of the sea shall step down from their thrones; they shall remove their robes and strip off their embroidered garments. They shall clothe themselves with trembling, and shall sit on the ground; they shall tremble every moment, and be appalled at you. 17And they shall raise a lamentation over you, and say to you:
How you have vanished*z* from the seas,
O city renowned,
once mighty on the sea,
you and your inhabitants,*a*
who imposed your*b* terror
on all the mainland!*c*
18 Now the coastlands tremble
on the day of your fall;
the coastlands by the sea
are dismayed at your passing.

19 For thus says the Lord GOD: When I make you a city laid waste, like cities that are not inhabited, when I bring up the deep over you, and the great waters cover you, 20then I will thrust you down

---

z Gk OL Aquila: Heb *have vanished, O inhabited one,*   *a* Heb *it and its inhabitants*   *b* Heb *their*
c Cn: Heb *its inhabitants*

with those who descend into the Pit, to the people of long ago, and I will make you live in the world below, among primeval ruins, with those who go down to the Pit, so that you will not be inhabited or have a place[d] in the land of the living. ²¹I will bring you to a dreadful end, and you shall be no more; though sought for, you will never be found again, says the Lord GOD.

Lamentation over Tyre

27 The word of the LORD came to me: ²Now you, mortal, raise a lamentation over Tyre, ³and say to Tyre, which sits at the entrance to the sea, merchant of the peoples on many coastlands, Thus says the Lord GOD:

O Tyre, you have said,
"I am perfect in beauty."
4   Your borders are in the heart of the
        seas;
    your builders made perfect your
        beauty.
5   They made all your planks
        of fir trees from Senir;
    they took a cedar from Lebanon
        to make a mast for you.
6   From oaks of Bashan
        they made your oars;
    they made your deck of pines[e]
        from the coasts of Cyprus,
        inlaid with ivory.
7   Of fine embroidered linen from
        Egypt
    was your sail,
        serving as your ensign;
    blue and purple from the coasts of
        Elishah
    was your awning.
8   The inhabitants of Sidon and Arvad
        were your rowers;
    skilled men of Zemer[f] were within
        you,
        they were your pilots.
9   The elders of Gebal and its artisans
        were within you,
        caulking your seams;
    all the ships of the sea with their
        mariners were within you,
        to barter for your wares.
10 Paras[g] and Lud and Put
        were in your army,

    your mighty warriors;
    they hung shield and helmet in you;
        they gave you splendor.
11 Men of Arvad and Helech[h]
        were on your walls all around;
    men of Gamad were at your
        towers.
    They hung their quivers all around
        your walls;
        they made perfect your beauty.

12 Tarshish did business with you out of the abundance of your great wealth; silver, iron, tin, and lead they exchanged for your wares. ¹³Javan, Tubal, and Meshech traded with you; they exchanged human beings and vessels of bronze for your merchandise. ¹⁴Beth-togarmah exchanged for your wares horses, war horses, and mules. ¹⁵The Rhodians[i] traded with you; many coastlands were your own special markets; they brought you in payment ivory tusks and ebony. ¹⁶Edom[j] did business with you because of your abundant goods; they exchanged for your wares turquoise, purple, embroidered work, fine linen, coral, and rubies. ¹⁷Judah and the land of Israel traded with you; they exchanged for your merchandise wheat from Minnith, millet,[k] honey, oil, and balm. ¹⁸Damascus traded with you for your abundant goods—because of your great wealth of every kind—wine of Helbon, and white wool. ¹⁹Vedan and Javan from Uzal[k] entered into trade for your wares; wrought iron, cassia, and sweet cane were bartered for your merchandise. ²⁰Dedan traded with you in saddlecloths for riding. ²¹Arabia and all the princes of Kedar were your favored dealers in lambs, rams, and goats; in these they did business with you. ²²The merchants of Sheba and Raamah traded with you; they exchanged for your wares the best of all kinds of spices, and all precious stones, and gold. ²³Haran, Canneh, Eden, the merchants of Sheba, Asshur, and Chilmad traded with you. ²⁴These traded with you in choice garments, in clothes of blue and embroidered work, and in carpets of colored material, bound with cords and made secure; in these they traded with you.[l]

d Gk: Heb I will give beauty   e Or boxwood   f Cn Compare Gen 10.18: Heb your skilled men,
O Tyre   g Or Persia   h Or and your army   i Gk: Heb The Dedanites   j Another reading is
Aram   k Meaning of Heb uncertain   l Cn: Heb in your market

25The ships of Tarshish traveled for you in your trade.

So you were filled and heavily
    laden
    in the heart of the seas.

26 Your rowers have brought you
      into the high seas.
    The east wind has wrecked you
      in the heart of the seas.

27 Your riches, your wares, your
        merchandise,
      your mariners and your pilots,
    your caulkers, your dealers in
        merchandise,
      and all your warriors within you,
    with all the company
      that is with you,
    sink into the heart of the seas
      on the day of your ruin.

28 At the sound of the cry of your
        pilots
      the countryside shakes,

29 and down from their ships
      come all that handle the oar.
    The mariners and all the pilots of
        the sea
      stand on the shore

30 and wail aloud over you,
      and cry bitterly.
    They throw dust on their heads
      and wallow in ashes;

31 they make themselves bald for you,
      and put on sackcloth,
    and they weep over you in
        bitterness of soul,
      with bitter mourning.

32 In their wailing they raise a
        lamentation for you,
      and lament over you:
    "Who was ever destroyed[m] like Tyre
      in the midst of the sea?

33 When your wares came from the
        seas,
      you satisfied many peoples;
    with your abundant wealth and
        merchandise
      you enriched the kings of the
        earth.

34 Now you are wrecked by the seas,
      in the depths of the waters;
    your merchandise and all your
        crew
      have sunk with you.

35 All the inhabitants of the
        coastlands

are appalled at you;
    and their kings are horribly afraid,
      their faces are convulsed.

36 The merchants among the peoples
        hiss at you;
      you have come to a dreadful end
    and shall be no more forever."

Proclamation against the King of Tyre

28 The word of the LORD came
    to me: 2Mortal, say to the
prince of Tyre, Thus says the Lord GOD:
    Because your heart is proud
      and you have said, "I am a god;
    I sit in the seat of the gods,
      in the heart of the seas,"
    yet you are but a mortal, and no
        god,
      though you compare your mind
        with the mind of a god.

3   You are indeed wiser than Daniel;[n]
      no secret is hidden from you;

4   by your wisdom and your
        understanding
      you have amassed wealth for
        yourself,
    and have gathered gold and silver
      into your treasuries.

5   By your great wisdom in trade
      you have increased your wealth,
    and your heart has become proud
      in your wealth.

6   Therefore thus says the Lord GOD:
    Because you compare your mind
      with the mind of a god,

7   therefore, I will bring strangers
        against you,
      the most terrible of the nations;
    they shall draw their swords
        against the beauty of your
        wisdom
      and defile your splendor.

8   They shall thrust you down to the
        Pit,
      and you shall die a violent death
        in the heart of the seas.

9   Will you still say, "I am a god,"
      in the presence of those who kill
        you,
    though you are but a mortal, and
        no god,
      in the hands of those who wound
        you?

m Tg Vg: Heb *like silence*   n Or, as otherwise read, *Danel*

10 You shall die the death of the
         uncircumcised
      by the hand of foreigners;
      for I have spoken, says the Lord
         GOD.

Lamentation over the King of Tyre

11 Moreover the word of the LORD
came to me: 12Mortal, raise a lamentation over the king of Tyre, and say to
him, Thus says the Lord GOD:
      You were the signet of perfection,⁰
         full of wisdom and perfect in
         beauty.
13   You were in Eden, the garden of
         God;
      every precious stone was your
         covering,
      carnelian, chrysolite, and
         moonstone,
      beryl, onyx, and jasper,
      sapphire,ᵖ turquoise, and emerald;
      and worked in gold were your
         settings
      and your engravings.⁰
      On the day that you were created
      they were prepared.
14   With an anointed cherub as
         guardian I placed you;⁰
      you were on the holy mountain
         of God;
      you walked among the stones of
         fire.
15   You were blameless in your ways
      from the day that you were
         created,
      until iniquity was found in you.
16   In the abundance of your trade
      you were filled with violence,
         and you sinned;
      so I cast you as a profane thing
         from the mountain of God,
      and the guardian cherub drove
         you out
      from among the stones of fire.
17   Your heart was proud because of
         your beauty;
      you corrupted your wisdom for
         the sake of your splendor.
      I cast you to the ground;
      I exposed you before kings,
      to feast their eyes on you.
18   By the multitude of your iniquities,
      in the unrighteousness of your
         trade,
      you profaned your sanctuaries.
      So I brought out fire from within
         you;
      it consumed you,
      and I turned you to ashes on the
         earth
      in the sight of all who saw you.
19   All who know you among the
         peoples
      are appalled at you;
      you have come to a dreadful end
      and shall be no more forever.

Proclamation against Sidon

20 The word of the LORD came to me:
21Mortal, set your face toward Sidon,
and prophesy against it, 22and say, Thus
says the Lord GOD:
      I am against you, O Sidon,
      and I will gain glory in your
         midst.
      They shall know that I am the
         LORD
      when I execute judgments in it,
      and manifest my holiness in it;
23   for I will send pestilence into it,
      and bloodshed into its streets;
      and the dead shall fall in its midst,
      by the sword that is against it on
         every side.
      And they shall know that I am the
         LORD.

24 The house of Israel shall no longer
find a pricking brier or a piercing thorn
among all their neighbors who have
treated them with contempt. And they
shall know that I am the Lord GOD.

Future Blessing for Israel

25 Thus says the Lord GOD: When I
gather the house of Israel from the peoples among whom they are scattered,
and manifest my holiness in them in the
sight of the nations, then they shall settle on their own soil that I gave to my
servant Jacob. 26They shall live in safety
in it, and shall build houses and plant
vineyards. They shall live in safety,
when I execute judgments upon all their
neighbors who have treated them with
contempt. And they shall know that I
am the LORD their God.

o Meaning of Heb uncertain   p Or *lapis lazuli*

Proclamation against Egypt

29 In the tenth year, in the tenth month, on the twelfth day of the month, the word of the LORD came to me: [2]Mortal, set your face against Pharaoh king of Egypt, and prophesy against him and against all Egypt; [3]speak, and say, Thus says the Lord GOD:

I am against you,
　　Pharaoh king of Egypt,
the great dragon sprawling
　　in the midst of its channels,
saying, "My Nile is my own;
　　I made it for myself."
[4] I will put hooks in your jaws,
　　and make the fish of your
　　　　channels stick to your
　　　　scales.
I will draw you up from your
　　channels,
　　with all the fish of your
　　　　channels
　　sticking to your scales.
[5] I will fling you into the
　　wilderness,
　　you and all the fish of your
　　　　channels;
you shall fall in the open field,
　　and not be gathered and buried.
To the animals of the earth and to
　　the birds of the air
　　I have given you as food.
[6] Then all the inhabitants of Egypt
　　shall know
　　　that I am the LORD

because you[q] were a staff of reed
　　to the house of Israel;
[7] when they grasped you with the
　　hand, you broke,
　　and tore all their shoulders;
and when they leaned on you, you
　　broke,
　　and made all their legs unsteady.[r]

8 Therefore, thus says the Lord GOD: I will bring a sword upon you, and will cut off from you human being and animal; [9]and the land of Egypt shall be a desolation and a waste. Then they shall know that I am the LORD.

Because you[s] said, "The Nile is mine, and I made it," [10]therefore, I am against you, and against your channels, and I will make the land of Egypt an utter waste and desolation, from Migdol to Syene, as far as the border of Ethiopia.[t] [11]No human foot shall pass through it, and no animal foot shall pass through it; it shall be uninhabited forty years. [12]I will make the land of Egypt a desolation among desolated countries; and her cities shall be a desolation forty years among cities that are laid waste. I will scatter the Egyptians among the nations, and disperse them among the countries.

13 Further, thus says the Lord GOD: At the end of forty years I will gather the Egyptians from the peoples among whom they were scattered; [14]and I will restore the fortunes of Egypt, and bring them back to the land of Pathros, the land of their origin; and there they shall be a lowly kingdom. [15]It shall be the most lowly of the kingdoms, and never again exalt itself above the nations; and I will make them so small that they will never again rule over the nations. [16]The Egyptians[u] shall never again be the reliance of the house of Israel; they will recall their iniquity, when they turned to them for aid. Then they shall know that I am the Lord GOD.

Babylonia Will Plunder Egypt

17 In the twenty-seventh year, in the first month, on the first day of the month, the word of the LORD came to me: [18]Mortal, King Nebuchadrezzar of Babylon made his army labor hard against Tyre; every head was made bald and every shoulder was rubbed bare; yet neither he nor his army got anything from Tyre to pay for the labor that he had expended against it. [19]Therefore thus says the Lord GOD: I will give the land of Egypt to King Nebuchadrezzar of Babylon; and he shall carry off its wealth and despoil it and plunder it; and it shall be the wages for his army. [20]I have given him the land of Egypt as his payment for which he labored, because they worked for me, says the Lord GOD.

21 On that day I will cause a horn to sprout up for the house of Israel, and I will open your lips among them. Then they shall know that I am the LORD.

q Gk Syr Vg: Heb they　　r Syr: Heb stand　　s Gk Syr Vg: Heb he　　t Or Nubia; Heb Cush
u Heb It

Lamentation for Egypt

30 The word of the Lord came to me: 2Mortal, prophesy, and say, Thus says the Lord God:
Wail, "Alas for the day!"
3   For a day is near,
      the day of the Lord is near;
   it will be a day of clouds,
      a time of doom[v] for the nations.
4   A sword shall come upon Egypt,
      and anguish shall be in
         Ethiopia,[w]
   when the slain fall in Egypt,
      and its wealth is carried away,
      and its foundations are torn
         down.
5Ethiopia,[w] and Put, and Lud, and all Arabia, and Libya,[x] and the people of the allied land[y] shall fall with them by the sword.

6   Thus says the Lord:
   Those who support Egypt shall fall,
      and its proud might shall come
         down;
   from Migdol to Syene
      they shall fall within it by the
         sword,
   says the Lord God.
7   They shall be desolated among
         other desolated countries,
      and their cities shall lie among
         cities laid waste.
8   Then they shall know that I am the
         Lord,
      when I have set fire to Egypt,
      and all who help it are broken.
9 On that day, messengers shall go out from me in ships to terrify the unsuspecting Ethiopians;[z] and anguish shall come upon them on the day of Egypt's doom;[a] for it is coming!

10   Thus says the Lord God:
   I will put an end to the hordes of
         Egypt,
      by the hand of King
         Nebuchadrezzar of Babylon.
11   He and his people with him, the
         most terrible of the nations,
      shall be brought in to destroy the
         land;
      and they shall draw their swords
         against Egypt,
      and fill the land with the slain.
12   I will dry up the channels,
      and will sell the land into the
         hand of evildoers;
   I will bring desolation upon the
         land and everything in it
      by the hand of foreigners;
   I the Lord have spoken.

13 Thus says the Lord God:
   I will destroy the idols
      and put an end to the images in
         Memphis;
   there shall no longer be a prince in
         the land of Egypt;
      so I will put fear in the land of
         Egypt.
14   I will make Pathros a desolation,
      and will set fire to Zoan,
      and will execute acts of judgment
         on Thebes.
15   I will pour my wrath upon
         Pelusium,
      the stronghold of Egypt,
      and cut off the hordes of Thebes.
16   I will set fire to Egypt;
      Pelusium shall be in great agony;
   Thebes shall be breached,
      and Memphis face adversaries by
         day.
17   The young men of On and of Pi-
         beseth shall fall by the
         sword;
      and the cities themselves[b] shall
         go into captivity.
18   At Tehaphnehes the day shall be
         dark,
      when I break there the dominion
         of Egypt,
   and its proud might shall come to
         an end;
      the city[c] shall be covered by a
         cloud,
      and its daughter-towns shall go
         into captivity.
19   Thus I will execute acts of
         judgment on Egypt.
      Then they shall know that I am
         the Lord.

Proclamation against Pharaoh

20 In the eleventh year, in the first month, on the seventh day of the month, the word of the Lord came to

---

v Heb lacks *of doom*   w Or *Nubia*; Heb *Cush*   x Compare Gk Syr Vg: Heb *Cub*   y Meaning of Heb uncertain   z Or *Nubians*; Heb *Cush*   a Heb *the day of Egypt*   b Heb *and they*   c Heb *she*

me: 21Mortal, I have broken the arm of Pharaoh king of Egypt; it has not been bound up for healing or wrapped with a bandage, so that it may become strong to wield the sword. 22Therefore thus says the Lord GOD: I am against Pharaoh king of Egypt, and will break his arms, both the strong arm and the one that was broken; and I will make the sword fall from his hand. 23I will scatter the Egyptians among the nations, and disperse them throughout the lands. 24I will strengthen the arms of the king of Babylon, and put my sword in his hand; but I will break the arms of Pharaoh, and he will groan before him with the groans of one mortally wounded. 25I will strengthen the arms of the king of Babylon, but the arms of Pharaoh shall fall. And they shall know that I am the LORD, when I put my sword into the hand of the king of Babylon. He shall stretch it out against the land of Egypt, 26and I will scatter the Egyptians among the nations and disperse them throughout the countries. Then they shall know that I am the LORD.

The Lofty Cedar

31 In the eleventh year, in the third month, on the first day of the month, the word of the LORD came to me: 2Mortal, say to Pharaoh king of Egypt and to his hordes:

Whom are you like in your
   greatness?
3   Consider Assyria, a cedar of
      Lebanon,
with fair branches and forest shade,
   and of great height,
   its top among the clouds.d
4   The waters nourished it,
      the deep made it grow tall,
making its rivers flowe
   around the place it was planted,
sending forth its streams
   to all the trees of the field.
5   So it towered high
      above all the trees of the field;
its boughs grew large
   and its branches long,
   from abundant water in its
      shoots.
6   All the birds of the air
      made their nests in its boughs;

under its branches all the animals
   of the field
   gave birth to their young;
and in its shade
   all great nations lived.
7   It was beautiful in its greatness,
      in the length of its branches;
   for its roots went down
      to abundant water.
8   The cedars in the garden of God
      could not rival it,
   nor the fir trees equal its boughs;
   the plane trees were as nothing
      compared with its branches;
   no tree in the garden of God
      was like it in beauty.
9   I made it beautiful
      with its mass of branches,
   the envy of all the trees of Eden
      that were in the garden of God.

10 Therefore thus says the Lord GOD: Because itf towered high and set its top among the clouds,d and its heart was proud of its height, 11I gave it into the hand of the prince of the nations; he has dealt with it as its wickedness deserves. I have cast it out. 12Foreigners from the most terrible of the nations have cut it down and left it. On the mountains and in all the valleys its branches have fallen, and its boughs lie broken in all the watercourses of the land; and all the peoples of the earth went away from its shade and left it.
13   On its fallen trunk settle
      all the birds of the air,
   and among its boughs lodge
      all the wild animals.
14All this is in order that no trees by the waters may grow to lofty height or set their tops among the clouds,d and that no trees that drink water may reach up to them in height.
   For all of them are handed over to
      death,
   to the world below;
   along with all mortals,
      with those who go down to the
         Pit.
15 Thus says the Lord GOD: On the day it went down to Sheol I closed the deep over it and covered it; I restrained its rivers, and its mighty waters were checked. I clothed Lebanon in gloom for it, and all the trees of the field fainted

d Gk: Heb thick boughs   e Gk: Heb rivers going   f Syr Vg: Heb you because of it. ¹⁶I made the nations quake at the sound of its fall, when I cast it down to Sheol with those who go down to the Pit; and all the trees of Eden, the choice and best of Lebanon, all that were well watered, were consoled in the world below. ¹⁷They also went down to Sheol with it, to those killed by the sword, along with its allies,ᵍ those who lived in its shade among the nations.

18 Which among the trees of Eden was like you in glory and in greatness? Now you shall be brought down with the trees of Eden to the world below; you shall lie among the uncircumcised, with those who are killed by the sword. This is Pharaoh and all his horde, says the Lord GOD.

Lamentation over Pharaoh and Egypt

32 In the twelfth year, in the twelfth month, on the first day of the month, the word of the LORD came to me: ²Mortal, raise a lamentation over Pharaoh king of Egypt, and say to him:

You consider yourself a lion among
    the nations,
  but you are like a dragon in the
    seas;
you thrash about in your streams,
  trouble the water with your feet,
  and foul yourʰ streams.
3 Thus says the Lord GOD:
  In an assembly of many peoples
  I will throw my net over you;
  and Iⁱ will haul you up in my
    dragnet.
4 I will throw you on the ground,
  on the open field I will fling you,
  and will cause all the birds of the
    air to settle on you,
  and I will let the wild animals of
    the whole earth gorge
    themselves with you.
5 I will strew your flesh on the
    mountains,
  and fill the valleys with your
    carcass.ʲ
6 I will drench the land with your
    flowing blood
  up to the mountains,

  and the watercourses will be
    filled with you.
7 When I blot you out, I will cover
    the heavens,
  and make their stars dark;
  I will cover the sun with a cloud,
  and the moon shall not give its
    light.
8 All the shining lights of the
    heavens
  I will darken above you,
  and put darkness on your land,
      says the Lord GOD.
9 I will trouble the hearts of many
    peoples,
  as I carry you captiveᵏ among the
    nations,
  into countries you have not
    known.
10 I will make many peoples appalled
    at you;
  their kings shall shudder because
    of you.
When I brandish my sword before
    them,
  they shall tremble every moment
  for their lives, each one of them,
    on the day of your downfall.
11 For thus says the Lord GOD:
  The sword of the king of Babylon
    shall come against you.
12 I will cause your hordes to fall
  by the swords of mighty ones,
  all of them most terrible among
    the nations.
They shall bring to ruin the pride of
    Egypt,
  and all its hordes shall perish.
13 I will destroy all its livestock
  from beside abundant waters;
  and no human foot shall trouble
    them any more,
  nor shall the hoofs of cattle
    trouble them.
14 Then I will make their waters
    clear,
  and cause their streams to run
    like oil, says the Lord GOD.
15 When I make the land of Egypt
    desolate
  and when the land is stripped of
    all that fills it,
  when I strike down all who live in
    it,

---

g Heb *its arms*   h Heb *their*   i Gk Vg: Heb *they*   j Symmachus Syr Vg: Heb *your height*
k Gk: Heb *bring your destruction*

then they shall know that I am the LORD.

16 This is a lamentation; it shall be chanted.
    The women of the nations shall chant it.
    Over Egypt and all its hordes they shall chant it,
    says the Lord GOD.

Dirge over Egypt

17 In the twelfth year, in the first month,[1] on the fifteenth day of the month, the word of the LORD came to me:
18 Mortal, wail over the hordes of Egypt,
    and send them down,
    with Egypt[m] and the daughters of majestic nations,
    to the world below,
    with those who go down to the Pit.
19   "Whom do you surpass in beauty?
    Go down! Be laid to rest with the uncircumcised!"
20They shall fall among those who are killed by the sword. Egypt[n] has been handed over to the sword; carry away both it and its hordes. 21The mighty chiefs shall speak of them, with their helpers, out of the midst of Sheol: "They have come down, they lie still, the uncircumcised, killed by the sword."

22 Assyria is there, and all its company, their graves all around it, all of them killed, fallen by the sword. 23Their graves are set in the uttermost parts of the Pit. Its company is all around its grave, all of them killed, fallen by the sword, who spread terror in the land of the living.

24 Elam is there, and all its hordes around its grave; all of them killed, fallen by the sword, who went down uncircumcised into the world below, who spread terror in the land of the living. They bear their shame with those who go down to the Pit. 25They have made Elam[m] a bed among the slain with all its hordes, their graves all around it, all of them uncircumcised, killed by the sword; for terror of them was spread in the land of the living, and they bear their

shame with those who go down to the Pit; they are placed among the slain.

26 Meshech and Tubal are there, and all their multitude, their graves all around them, all of them uncircumcised, killed by the sword; for they spread terror in the land of the living. 27And they do not lie with the fallen warriors of long ago[o] who went down to Sheol with their weapons of war, whose swords were laid under their heads, and whose shields[p] are upon their bones; for the terror of the warriors was in the land of the living. 28So you shall be broken and lie among the uncircumcised, with those who are killed by the sword.

29 Edom is there, its kings and all its princes, who for all their might are laid with those who are killed by the sword; they lie with the uncircumcised, with those who go down to the Pit.

30 The princes of the north are there, all of them, and all the Sidonians, who have gone down in shame with the slain, for all the terror that they caused by their might; they lie uncircumcised with those who are killed by the sword, and bear their shame with those who go down to the Pit.

31 When Pharaoh sees them, he will be consoled for all his hordes—Pharaoh and all his army, killed by the sword, says the Lord GOD. 32For he[q] spread terror in the land of the living; therefore he shall be laid to rest among the uncircumcised, with those who are slain by the sword—Pharaoh and all his multitude, says the Lord GOD.

Ezekiel Israel's Sentry

33 The word of the LORD came to me: 2O Mortal, speak to your people and say to them, If I bring the sword upon a land, and the people of the land take one of their number as their sentinel; 3and if the sentinel sees the sword coming upon the land and blows the trumpet and warns the people; 4then if any who hear the sound of the trumpet do not take warning, and the sword comes and takes them away, their blood shall be upon their own heads. 5They heard the sound of the trumpet and did not take warning; their

---

1 Gk: Heb lacks *in the first month*   m Heb *it*   n Heb *It*   o Gk Old Latin: Heb *of the uncircumcised*   p Cn: Heb *iniquities*   q Cn: Heb *I*

blood shall be upon themselves. But if they had taken warning, they would have saved their lives. 6But if the sentinel sees the sword coming and does not blow the trumpet, so that the people are not warned, and the sword comes and takes any of them, they are taken away in their iniquity, but their blood I will require at the sentinel's hand.

7 So you, mortal, I have made a sentinel for the house of Israel; whenever you hear a word from my mouth, you shall give them warning from me. 8If I say to the wicked, "O wicked ones, you shall surely die," and you do not speak to warn the wicked to turn from their ways, the wicked shall die in their iniquity, but their blood I will require at your hand. 9But if you warn the wicked to turn from their ways, and they do not turn from their ways, the wicked shall die in their iniquity, but you will have saved your life.

God's Justice and Mercy

10 Now you, mortal, say to the house of Israel, Thus you have said: "Our transgressions and our sins weigh upon us, and we waste away because of them; how then can we live?" 11Say to them, As I live, says the Lord GOD, I have no pleasure in the death of the wicked, but that the wicked turn from their ways and live; turn back, turn back from your evil ways; for why will you die, O house of Israel? 12And you, mortal, say to your people, The righteousness of the righteous shall not save them when they transgress; and as for the wickedness of the wicked, it shall not make them stumble when they turn from their wickedness; and the righteous shall not be able to live by their righteousness^r when they sin. 13Though I say to the righteous that they shall surely live, yet if they trust in their righteousness and commit iniquity, none of their righteous deeds shall be remembered; but in the iniquity that they have committed they shall die. 14Again, though I say to the wicked, "You shall surely die," yet if they turn from their sin and do what is lawful and right— 15if the wicked restore the pledge, give back what they have taken by robbery, and walk in the statutes of life, committing no iniquity—they shall surely live, they shall not die. 16None of the sins that they have committed shall be remembered against them; they have done what is lawful and right, they shall surely live.

17 Yet your people say, "The way of the Lord is not just," when it is their own way that is not just. 18When the righteous turn from their righteousness, and commit iniquity, they shall die for it.^s 19And when the wicked turn from their wickedness, and do what is lawful and right, they shall live by it.^s 20Yet you say, "The way of the Lord is not just." O house of Israel, I will judge all of you according to your ways!

The Fall of Jerusalem

21 In the twelfth year of our exile, in the tenth month, on the fifth day of the month, someone who had escaped from Jerusalem came to me and said, "The city has fallen." 22Now the hand of the LORD had been upon me the evening before the fugitive came; but he had opened my mouth by the time the fugitive came to me in the morning; so my mouth was opened, and I was no longer unable to speak.

The Survivors in Judah

23 The word of the LORD came to me: 24Mortal, the inhabitants of these waste places in the land of Israel keep saying, "Abraham was only one man, yet he got possession of the land; but we are many; the land is surely given us to possess." 25Therefore say to them, Thus says the Lord GOD: You eat flesh with the blood, and lift up your eyes to your idols, and shed blood; shall you then possess the land? 26You depend on your swords, you commit abominations, and each of you defiles his neighbor's wife; shall you then possess the land? 27Say this to them, Thus says the Lord GOD: As I live, surely those who are in the waste places shall fall by the sword; and those who are in the open field I will give to the wild animals to be devoured; and those who are in strongholds and in caves shall die by pestilence. 28I will make the land a desolation and a waste, and its proud might shall come to an end; and the

r Heb by it   s Heb them

THE WATCHMAN OF THE SOCIETY OF FRIENDS
John Woolman

VERSE: Ezekiel 33.6   PASSAGE: Ezekiel 33.1–12

 bout the twenty-third year of my age, I had many fresh and heavenly openings, in respect to the care and providence of the Almighty over his creatures in general, and over man as the most noble amongst those which are visible. And being clearly convinced in my judgment, that to place my whole trust in God was best for me, I felt renewed engagements, that in all things I might act on an inward principle of virtue, and pursue worldly business no farther, than as truth opened my way therein.

About the time called *Christmas*, I observed many people from the country, and dwellers in town, who, resorting to public houses, spent their time in drinking and vain sports, tending to corrupt one another; on which account I was much troubled. At one house, in particular, there was much disorder; and I believed it was a duty incumbent on me to go and speak to the master of that house. I considered I was young, and that several elderly friends in town had opportunity to see these things; but though I would gladly have been excused, yet I could not feel my mind clear.

The exercise was heavy; and as I was reading what the Almighty said to *Ezekiel*, respecting his duty as a watchman, the matter was set home more clearly; and then, with prayers and tears, I besought the Lord for his assistance, who, in loving-kindness, gave me a resigned heart. Then, at a suitable opportunity, I went to the public house, and, seeing the man amongst much company, I went to him, and told him, I wanted to speak with him; so we went aside, and there, in the fear of the Almighty, I expressed to him what rested on my mind; which he took kindly, and afterward showed more regard to me than before. In a few years afterwards he died, middle-aged; and I often thought that, had I neglected my duty in that case, it would have given me great trouble; and I was humbly thankful to my gracious Father, who had supported me herein.

ADDITIONAL SCRIPTURE READING:
Nehemiah 7.3; Isaiah 62.6

Go to page 981 for your next devotional reading.

1700   1900

mountains of Israel shall be so desolate that no one will pass through. ²⁹Then they shall know that I am the LORD, when I have made the land a desolation and a waste because of all their abominations that they have committed.

30 As for you, mortal, your people who talk together about you by the walls, and at the doors of the houses, say to one another, each to a neighbor, "Come and hear what the word is that comes from the LORD." ³¹They come to you as people come, and they sit before you as my people, and they hear your words, but they will not obey them. For flattery is on their lips, but their heart is set on their gain. ³²To them you are like a singer of love songs,^t one who has a beautiful voice and plays well on an instrument; they hear what you say, but they will not do it. ³³When this comes— and come it will!—then they shall know that a prophet has been among them.

Israel's False Shepherds

34 The word of the LORD came to me: ²Mortal, prophesy against the shepherds of Israel: prophesy, and say to them—to the shepherds: Thus says the Lord GOD: Ah, you shepherds of Israel who have been feeding yourselves! Should not shepherds feed the sheep? ³You eat the fat, you clothe yourselves with the wool, you slaughter the fatlings; but you do not feed the sheep. ⁴You have not strengthened the weak, you have not healed the sick, you have not bound up the injured, you have not brought back the strayed, you have not sought the lost, but with force and harshness you have ruled them. ⁵So they were scattered, because there was no shepherd; and scattered, they became food for all the wild animals. ⁶My sheep were scattered, they wandered over all the mountains and on every high hill; my sheep were scattered over all the face of the earth, with no one to search or seek for them.

7 Therefore, you shepherds, hear the word of the LORD: ⁸As I live, says the Lord GOD, because my sheep have become a prey, and my sheep have become food for all the wild animals, since there was no shepherd; and

because my shepherds have not searched for my sheep, but the shepherds have fed themselves and have not fed my sheep; ⁹therefore, you shepherds, hear the word of the LORD: ¹⁰Thus says the Lord GOD, I am against the shepherds; and I will demand my sheep at their hand, and put a stop to their feeding the sheep; no longer shall the shepherds feed themselves. I will rescue my sheep from their mouths, so that they may not be food for them.

God, the True Shepherd

11 For thus says the Lord GOD: I myself will search for my sheep, and will seek them out. ¹²As shepherds seek out their flocks when they are among their scattered sheep, so I will seek out my sheep. I will rescue them from all the places to which they have been scattered on a day of clouds and thick darkness. ¹³I will bring them out from the peoples and gather them from the countries, and will bring them into their own land; and I will feed them on the mountains of Israel, by the watercourses, and in all the inhabited parts of the land. ¹⁴I will feed them with good pasture, and the mountain heights of Israel shall be their pasture; there they shall lie down in good grazing land, and they shall feed on rich pasture on the mountains of Israel. ¹⁵I myself will be the shepherd of my sheep, and I will make them lie down, says the Lord GOD. ¹⁶I will seek the lost, and I will bring back the strayed, and I will bind up the injured, and I will strengthen the weak, but the fat and the strong I will destroy. I will feed them with justice.

17 As for you, my flock, thus says the Lord GOD: I shall judge between sheep and sheep, between rams and goats: ¹⁸Is it not enough for you to feed on the good pasture, but you must tread down with your feet the rest of your pasture? When you drink of clear water, must you foul the rest with your feet? ¹⁹And must my sheep eat what you have trodden with your feet, and drink what you have fouled with your feet?

20 Therefore, thus says the Lord GOD to them: I myself will judge between the fat sheep and the lean sheep. ²¹Because

---

t Cn: Heb like a love song

you pushed with flank and shoulder, and butted at all the weak animals with your horns until you scattered them far and wide, 22I will save my flock, and they shall no longer be ravaged; and I will judge between sheep and sheep.

23 I will set up over them one shepherd, my servant David, and he shall feed them: he shall feed them and be their shepherd. 24And I, the LORD, will be their God, and my servant David shall be prince among them; I, the LORD, have spoken.

25 I will make with them a covenant of peace and banish wild animals from the land, so that they may live in the wild and sleep in the woods securely. 26I will make them and the region around my hill a blessing; and I will send down the showers in their season; they shall be showers of blessing. 27The trees of the field shall yield their fruit, and the earth shall yield its increase. They shall be secure on their soil; and they shall know that I am the LORD, when I break the bars of their yoke, and save them from the hands of those who enslaved them. 28They shall no more be plunder for the nations, nor shall the animals of the land devour them; they shall live in safety, and no one shall make them afraid. 29I will provide for them a splendid vegetation so that they shall no more be consumed with hunger in the land, and no longer suffer the insults of the nations. 30They shall know that I, the LORD their God, am with them, and that they, the house of Israel, are my people, says the Lord GOD. 31You are my sheep, the sheep of my pastureu and I am your God, says the Lord GOD.

Judgment on Mount Seir

35 The word of the LORD came to me: 2Mortal, set your face against Mount Seir, and prophesy against it, 3and say to it, Thus says the Lord GOD:

I am against you, Mount Seir;
   I stretch out my hand against you
      to make you a desolation and a
      waste.
4 I lay your towns in ruins;
   you shall become a desolation,

and you shall know that I am the LORD.

5Because you cherished an ancient enmity, and gave over the people of Israel to the power of the sword at the time of their calamity, at the time of their final punishment; 6therefore, as I live, says the Lord GOD, I will prepare you for blood, and blood shall pursue you; since you did not hate bloodshed, bloodshed shall pursue you. 7I will make Mount Seir a waste and a desolation; and I will cut off from it all who come and go. 8I will fill its mountains with the slain; on your hills and in your valleys and in all your watercourses those killed with the sword shall fall. 9I will make you a perpetual desolation, and your cities shall never be inhabited. Then you shall know that I am the LORD.

10 Because you said, "These two nations and these two countries shall be mine, and we will take possession of them,"—although the LORD was there— 11therefore, as I live, says the Lord GOD, I will deal with you according to the anger and envy that you showed because of your hatred against them; and I will make myself known among you,v when I judge you. 12You shall know that I, the LORD, have heard all the abusive speech that you uttered against the mountains of Israel, saying, "They are laid desolate, they are given us to devour." 13And you magnified yourselves against me with your mouth, and multiplied your words against me; I heard it. 14Thus says the Lord GOD: As the whole earth rejoices, I will make you desolate. 15As you rejoiced over the inheritance of the house of Israel, because it was desolate, so I will deal with you; you shall be desolate, Mount Seir, and all Edom, all of it. Then they shall know that I am the LORD.

Blessing on Israel

36 And you, mortal, prophesy to the mountains of Israel, and say: O mountains of Israel, hear the word of the LORD. 2Thus says the Lord GOD: Because the enemy said of you, "Aha!" and, "The ancient heights have become our possession," 3therefore prophesy, and say: Thus says the Lord

u Gk OL: Heb pasture, you are people   v Gk: Heb them

WEEKEND

THE SOWER
William Cowper

VERSE: Matthew 13.3   **PASSAGE:** Matthew 13.1–9

e sons of earth prepare the plough,
    Break up your fallow ground!
The sower is gone forth to sow,
    And scatter blessings round.

The seed that finds a stony soil,
    Shoots forth a hasty blade;
But ill repays the sower's toil,
    Soon withered, scorched, and dead.

The thorny ground is sure to balk
    All hopes of harvest there;
We find a tall and sickly stalk,
    But not the fruitful ear.

The beaten path and highway side
    Receive the trust in vain;
The watchful birds the spoil divide,
    And pick up all the grain.

But where the Lord of grace and power
    Has blessed the happy field;
How plenteous is the golden store
    The deep-wrought furrows yield!

Father of mercies we have need
    Of thy preparing grace;
Let the same hand that gives the seed,
    Provide a fruitful place.

ADDITIONAL SCRIPTURE READING:
Matthew 13.18–23; Mark 4.1–12; Luke 8.5–8

Go to page 1000 for your next devotional reading.

1700   1900

GOD: Because they made you desolate indeed, and crushed you from all sides, so that you became the possession of the rest of the nations, and you became an object of gossip and slander among the people; 4therefore, O mountains of Israel, hear the word of the Lord GOD: Thus says the Lord GOD to the mountains and the hills, the watercourses and the valleys, the desolate wastes and the deserted towns, which have become a source of plunder and an object of derision to the rest of the nations all around; 5therefore thus says the Lord GOD: I am speaking in my hot jealousy against the rest of the nations, and against all Edom, who, with wholehearted joy and utter contempt, took my land as their possession, because of its pasture, to plunder it. 6Therefore prophesy concerning the land of Israel, and say to the mountains and hills, to the watercourses and valleys, Thus says the Lord GOD: I am speaking in my jealous wrath, because you have suffered the insults of the nations; 7therefore thus says the Lord GOD: I swear that the nations that are all around you shall themselves suffer insults.

8 But you, O mountains of Israel, shall shoot out your branches, and yield your fruit to my people Israel; for they shall soon come home. 9See now, I am for you; I will turn to you, and you shall be tilled and sown; 10and I will multiply your population, the whole house of Israel, all of it; the towns shall be inhabited and the waste places rebuilt; 11and I will multiply human beings and animals upon you. They shall increase and be fruitful; and I will cause you to be inhabited as in your former times, and will do more good to you than ever before. Then you shall know that I am the LORD. 12I will lead people upon you—my people Israel—and they shall possess you, and you shall be their inheritance. No longer shall you bereave them of children.

13 Thus says the Lord GOD: Because they say to you, "You devour people, and you bereave your nation of children," 14therefore you shall no longer devour people and no longer bereave your nation of children, says the Lord GOD; 15and no longer will I let you hear the insults of the nations, no longer shall you bear the disgrace of the peoples; and no longer shall you cause your nation to stumble, says the Lord GOD.

The Renewal of Israel

16 The word of the LORD came to me: 17Mortal, when the house of Israel lived on their own soil, they defiled it with their ways and their deeds; their conduct in my sight was like the uncleanness of a woman in her menstrual period. 18So I poured out my wrath upon them for the blood that they had shed upon the land, and for the idols with which they had defiled it. 19I scattered them among the nations, and they were dispersed through the countries; in accordance with their conduct and their deeds I judged them. 20But when they came to the nations, wherever they came, they profaned my holy name, in that it was said of them, "These are the people of the LORD, and yet they had to go out of his land." 21But I had concern for my holy name, which the house of Israel had profaned among the nations to which they came.

22 Therefore say to the house of Israel, Thus says the Lord GOD: It is not for your sake, O house of Israel, that I am about to act, but for the sake of my holy name, which you have profaned among the nations to which you came. 23I will sanctify my great name, which has been profaned among the nations, and which you have profaned among them; and the nations shall know that I am the LORD, says the Lord GOD, when through you I display my holiness before their eyes. 24I will take you from the nations, and gather you from all the countries, and bring you into your own land. 25I will sprinkle clean water upon you, and you shall be clean from all your uncleannesses, and from all your idols I will cleanse you. 26A new heart I will give you, and a new spirit I will put within you; and I will remove from your body the heart of stone and give you a heart of flesh. 27I will put my spirit within you, and make you follow my statutes and be careful to observe my ordinances. 28Then you shall live in the land that I gave to your ancestors; and you shall be my people, and I will be your God. 29I

will save you from all your uncleanness-es, and I will summon the grain and make it abundant and lay no famine upon you. 30I will make the fruit of the tree and the produce of the field abundant, so that you may never again suffer the disgrace of famine among the nations. 31Then you shall remember your evil ways, and your dealings that were not good; and you shall loathe yourselves for your iniquities and your abominable deeds. 32It is not for your sake that I will act, says the Lord GOD; let that be known to you. Be ashamed and dismayed for your ways, O house of Israel.

33 Thus says the Lord GOD: On the day that I cleanse you from all your iniquities, I will cause the towns to be inhabited, and the waste places shall be rebuilt. 34The land that was desolate shall be tilled, instead of being the desolation that it was in the sight of all who passed by. 35And they will say, "This land that was desolate has become like the garden of Eden; and the waste and desolate and ruined towns are now inhabited and fortified." 36Then the nations that are left all around you shall know that I, the LORD, have rebuilt the ruined places, and replanted that which was desolate; I, the LORD, have spoken, and I will do it.

37 Thus says the Lord GOD: I will also let the house of Israel ask me to do this for them: to increase their population like a flock. 38Like the flock for sacrifices,w like the flock at Jerusalem during her appointed festivals, so shall the ruined towns be filled with flocks of people. Then they shall know that I am the LORD.

The Valley of Dry Bones

37 The hand of the LORD came upon me, and he brought me out by the spirit of the LORD and set me down in the middle of a valley; it was full of bones. 2He led me all around them; there were very many lying in the valley, and they were very dry. 3He said to me, "Mortal, can these bones live?" I answered, "O Lord GOD, you know." 4Then he said to me, "Prophesy to these bones, and say to them: O dry bones,

hear the word of the LORD. 5Thus says the Lord GOD to these bones: I will cause breathx to enter you, and you shall live. 6I will lay sinews on you, and will cause flesh to come upon you, and cover you with skin, and put breathx in you, and you shall live; and you shall know that I am the LORD."

7 So I prophesied as I had been commanded; and as I prophesied, suddenly there was a noise, a rattling, and the bones came together, bone to its bone. 8I looked, and there were sinews on them, and flesh had come upon them, and skin had covered them; but there was no breath in them. 9Then he said to me, "Prophesy to the breath, prophesy, mortal, and say to the breath:y Thus says the Lord GOD: Come from the four winds, O breath,y and breathe upon these slain, that they may live." 10I prophesied as he commanded me, and the breath came into them, and they lived, and stood on their feet, a vast multitude.

11 Then he said to me, "Mortal, these bones are the whole house of Israel. They say, 'Our bones are dried up, and our hope is lost; we are cut off completely.' 12Therefore prophesy, and say to them, Thus says the Lord GOD: I am going to open your graves, and bring you up from your graves, O my people; and I will bring you back to the land of Israel. 13And you shall know that I am the LORD, when I open your graves, and bring you up from your graves, O my people. 14I will put my spirit within you, and you shall live, and I will place you on your own soil; then you shall know that I, the LORD, have spoken and will act, says the LORD."

The Two Sticks

15 The word of the LORD came to me: 16Mortal, take a stick and write on it, "For Judah, and the Israelites associated with it"; then take another stick and write on it, "For Joseph (the stick of Ephraim) and all the house of Israel associated with it"; 17and join them together into one stick, so that they may become one in your hand. 18And when your people say to you, "Will you not show us what you mean by these?" 19say to them, Thus says the Lord GOD: I am

---

w Heb *flock of holy things*   x Or *spirit*   y Or *wind* or *spirit*

about to take the stick of Joseph (which is in the hand of Ephraim) and the tribes of Israel associated with it; and I will put the stick of Judah upon it,^{z} and make them one stick, in order that they may be one in my hand. 20When the sticks on which you write are in your hand before their eyes, 21then say to them, Thus says the Lord GOD: I will take the people of Israel from the nations among which they have gone, and will gather them from every quarter, and bring them to their own land. 22I will make them one nation in the land, on the mountains of Israel; and one king shall be king over them all. Never again shall they be two nations, and never again shall they be divided into two kingdoms. 23They shall never again defile themselves with their idols and their detestable things, or with any of their transgressions. I will save them from all the apostasies into which they have fallen,^{a} and will cleanse them. Then they shall be my people, and I will be their God.

24 My servant David shall be king over them; and they shall all have one shepherd. They shall follow my ordinances and be careful to observe my statutes. 25They shall live in the land that I gave to my servant Jacob, in which your ancestors lived; they and their children and their children's children shall live there forever; and my servant David shall be their prince forever. 26I will make a covenant of peace with them; it shall be an everlasting covenant with them; and I will bless^b them and multiply them, and will set my sanctuary among them forevermore. 27My dwelling place shall be with them; and I will be their God, and they shall be my people. 28Then the nations shall know that I the LORD sanctify Israel, when my sanctuary is among them forevermore.

Invasion by Gog

38 The word of the LORD came to me: 2Mortal, set your face toward Gog, of the land of Magog, the chief prince of Meshech and Tubal. Prophesy against him 3and say: Thus

says the Lord GOD: I am against you, O Gog, chief prince of Meshech and Tubal; 4I will turn you around and put hooks into your jaws, and I will lead you out with all your army, horses and horsemen, all of them clothed in full armor, a great company, all of them with shield and buckler, wielding swords. 5Persia, Ethiopia,^{c} and Put are with them, all of them with buckler and helmet; 6Gomer and all its troops; Beth-togarmah from the remotest parts of the north with all its troops—many peoples are with you.

7 Be ready and keep ready, you and all the companies that are assembled around you, and hold yourselves in reserve for them. 8After many days you shall be mustered; in the latter years you shall go against a land restored from war, a land where people were gathered from many nations on the mountains of Israel, which had long lain waste; its people were brought out from the nations and now are living in safety, all of them. 9You shall advance, coming on like a storm; you shall be like a cloud covering the land, you and all your troops, and many peoples with you.

10 Thus says the Lord GOD: On that day thoughts will come into your mind, and you will devise an evil scheme. 11You will say, "I will go up against the land of unwalled villages; I will fall upon the quiet people who live in safety, all of them living without walls, and having no bars or gates"; 12to seize spoil and carry off plunder; to assail the waste places that are now inhabited, and the people who were gathered from the nations, who are acquiring cattle and goods, who live at the center^d of the earth. 13Sheba and Dedan and the merchants of Tarshish and all its young warriors^e will say to you, "Have you come to seize spoil? Have you assembled your horde to carry off plunder, to carry away silver and gold, to take away cattle and goods, to seize a great amount of booty?"

14 Therefore, mortal, prophesy, and say to Gog: Thus says the Lord GOD: On that day when my people Israel are living securely, you will rouse yourself^f

15and come from your place out of the remotest parts of the north, you and many peoples with you, all of them riding on horses, a great horde, a mighty army; 16you will come up against my people Israel, like a cloud covering the earth. In the latter days I will bring you against my land, so that the nations may know me, when through you, O Gog, I display my holiness before their eyes.

Judgment on Gog

17 Thus says the Lord GOD: Are you he of whom I spoke in former days by my servants the prophets of Israel, who in those days prophesied for years that I would bring you against them? 18On that day, when Gog comes against the land of Israel, says the Lord GOD, my wrath shall be aroused. 19For in my jealousy and in my blazing wrath I declare: On that day there shall be a great shaking in the land of Israel; 20the fish of the sea, and the birds of the air, and the animals of the field, and all creeping things that creep on the ground, and all human beings that are on the face of the earth, shall quake at my presence, and the mountains shall be thrown down, and the cliffs shall fall, and every wall shall tumble to the ground. 21I will summon the sword against Gogg inh all my mountains, says the Lord GOD; the swords of all will be against their comrades. 22With pestilence and bloodshed I will enter into judgment with him; and I will pour down torrential rains and hailstones, fire and sulfur, upon him and his troops and the many peoples that are with him. 23So I will display my greatness and my holiness and make myself known in the eyes of many nations. Then they shall know that I am the LORD.

Gog's Armies Destroyed

39 And you, mortal, prophesy against Gog, and say: Thus says the Lord GOD: I am against you, O Gog, chief prince of Meshech and Tubal! 2I will turn you around and drive you forward, and bring you up from the remotest parts of the north, and lead you against the mountains of Israel. 3I will strike your bow from your left hand, and

will make your arrows drop out of your right hand. 4You shall fall upon the mountains of Israel, you and all your troops and the peoples that are with you; I will give you to birds of prey of every kind and to the wild animals to be devoured. 5You shall fall in the open field; for I have spoken, says the Lord GOD. 6I will send fire on Magog and on those who live securely in the coastlands; and they shall know that I am the LORD.

7 My holy name I will make known among my people Israel; and I will not let my holy name be profaned any more; and the nations shall know that I am the LORD, the Holy One in Israel. 8It has come! It has happened, says the Lord GOD. This is the day of which I have spoken.

9 Then those who live in the towns of Israel will go out and make fires of the weapons and burn them—bucklers and shields, bows and arrows, handpikes and spears—and they will make fires of them for seven years. 10They will not need to take wood out of the field or cut down any trees in the forests, for they will make their fires of the weapons; they will despoil those who despoiled them, and plunder those who plundered them, says the Lord GOD.

The Burial of Gog

11 On that day I will give to Gog a place for burial in Israel, the Valley of the Travelersi east of the sea; it shall block the path of the travelers, for there Gog and all his horde will be buried; it shall be called the Valley of Hamon-gog.j 12Seven months the house of Israel shall spend burying them, in order to cleanse the land. 13All the people of the land shall bury them; and it will bring them honor on the day that I show my glory, says the Lord GOD. 14They will set apart men to pass through the land regularly and bury any invadersk who remain on the face of the land, so as to cleanse it; for seven months they shall make their search. 15As the searchersk pass through the land, anyone who sees a human bone shall set up a sign by it, until the buriers have buried it in the Valley of

g Heb him   h Heb to or for   i Or of the Abarim   j That is, the Horde of Gog   k Heb travelers

Hamon-gog.[l] [16](A city Hamonah[m] is there also.) Thus they shall cleanse the land.

[17] As for you, mortal, thus says the Lord GOD: Speak to the birds of every kind and to all the wild animals: Assemble and come, gather from all around to the sacrificial feast that I am preparing for you, a great sacrificial feast on the mountains of Israel, and you shall eat flesh and drink blood. [18]You shall eat the flesh of the mighty, and drink the blood of the princes of the earth—of rams, of lambs, and of goats, of bulls, all of them fatlings of Bashan. [19]You shall eat fat until you are filled, and drink blood until you are drunk, at the sacrificial feast that I am preparing for you. [20]And you shall be filled at my table with horses and charioteers,[n] with warriors and all kinds of soldiers, says the Lord GOD.

Israel Restored to the Land

[21] I will display my glory among the nations; and all the nations shall see my judgment that I have executed, and my hand that I have laid on them. [22]The house of Israel shall know that I am the LORD their God, from that day forward. [23]And the nations shall know that the house of Israel went into captivity for their iniquity, because they dealt treacherously with me. So I hid my face from them and gave them into the hand of their adversaries, and they all fell by the sword. [24]I dealt with them according to their uncleanness and their transgressions, and hid my face from them.

[25] Therefore thus says the Lord GOD: Now I will restore the fortunes of Jacob, and have mercy on the whole house of Israel; and I will be jealous for my holy name. [26]They shall forget[o] their shame, and all the treachery they have practiced against me, when they live securely in their land with no one to make them afraid, [27]when I have brought them back from the peoples and gathered them from their enemies' lands, and through them have displayed my holiness in the sight of many nations. [28]Then they shall know that I am the LORD their God because I sent them into exile among the nations, and then gathered them into their own land. I will leave none of them behind; [29]and I will never again

---

FOR JUST AS BY THE COURTESY OF GOD HE FORGETTETH OUR SIN AFTER THE TIME THAT WE OURSELVES REPENT, SO WILLETH HE THAT WE FORGET OUR SIN IN REGARD TO OUR STUPID DEPRESSION AND OUR DOUBTFUL FEARS.

—*Julian of Norwich*

---

hide my face from them, when I pour out my spirit upon the house of Israel, says the Lord GOD.

The Vision of the New Temple

40 In the twenty-fifth year of our exile, at the beginning of the year, on the tenth day of the month, in the fourteenth year after the city was struck down, on that very day, the hand of the LORD was upon me, and he brought me there. [2]He brought me, in visions of God, to the land of Israel, and set me down upon a very high mountain, on which was a structure like a city to the south. [3]When he brought me there, a man was there, whose appearance shone like bronze, with a linen cord and a measuring reed in his hand; and he was standing in the gateway. [4]The man said to me, "Mortal, look closely and listen attentively, and set your mind upon all that I shall show you, for you were brought here in order that I might show it to you; declare all that you see to the house of Israel."

[5] Now there was a wall all around the outside of the temple area. The length of the measuring reed in the man's hand was six long cubits, each being a cubit and a handbreadth in length; so he measured the thickness of the wall, one reed; and the height, one reed. [6]Then he went into the gateway facing east, going up its steps, and measured the threshold of the gate, one reed deep.[p] There were [7]recesses, and each recess was one reed wide and one reed deep; and the space between the recesses, five cubits; and the threshold

---

l That is, *the Horde of Gog*　　*m* That is *The Horde*　　*n* Heb *chariots*　　*o* Another reading is *They shall bear*　　*p* Heb *deep, and one threshold, one reed deep*

of the gate by the vestibule of the gate at the inner end was one reed deep. 8Then he measured the inner vestibule of the gateway, one cubit. 9Then he measured the vestibule of the gateway, eight cubits; and its pilasters, two cubits; and the vestibule of the gate was at the inner end. 10There were three recesses on either side of the east gate; the three were of the same size; and the pilasters on either side were of the same size. 11Then he measured the width of the opening of the gateway, ten cubits; and the width of the gateway, thirteen cubits. 12There was a barrier before the recesses, one cubit on either side; and the recesses were six cubits on either side. 13Then he measured the gate from the back*q* of the one recess to the back*q* of the other, a width of twenty-five cubits, from wall to wall.*r* 14He measured*s* also the vestibule, twenty cubits; and the gate next to the pilaster on every side of the court.*t* 15From the front of the gate at the entrance to the end of the inner vestibule of the gate was fifty cubits. 16The recesses and their pilasters had windows, with shutters*t* on the inside of the gateway all around, and the vestibules also had windows on the inside all around; and on the pilasters were palm trees.

17 Then he brought me into the outer court; there were chambers there, and a pavement, all around the court; thirty chambers fronted on the pavement. 18The pavement ran along the side of the gates, corresponding to the length of the gates; this was the lower pavement. 19Then he measured the distance from the inner front of*u* the lower gate to the outer front of the inner court, one hundred cubits.*v*

20 Then he measured the gate of the outer court that faced north—its depth and width. 21Its recesses, three on either side, and its pilasters and its vestibule were of the same size as those of the first gate; its depth was fifty cubits, and its width twenty-five cubits. 22Its windows, its vestibule, and its palm trees were of the same size as those of the gate that faced toward the east. Seven

steps led up to it; and its vestibule was on the inside.*w* 23Opposite the gate on the north, as on the east, was a gate to the inner court; he measured from gate to gate, one hundred cubits.

24 Then he led me toward the south, and there was a gate on the south; and he measured its pilasters and its vestibule; they had the same dimensions as the others. 25There were windows all around in it and in its vestibule, like the windows of the others; its depth was fifty cubits, and its width twenty-five cubits. 26There were seven steps leading up to it; its vestibule was on the inside.*w* It had palm trees on its pilasters, one on either side. 27There was a gate on the south of the inner court; and he measured from gate to gate toward the south, one hundred cubits.

28 Then he brought me to the inner court by the south gate, and he measured the south gate; it was of the same dimensions as the others. 29Its recesses, its pilasters, and its vestibule were of the same size as the others; and there were windows all around in it and in its vestibule; its depth was fifty cubits, and its width twenty-five cubits. 30There were vestibules all around, twenty-five cubits deep and five cubits wide. 31Its vestibule faced the outer court, and palm trees were on its pilasters, and its stairway had eight steps.

32 Then he brought me to the inner court on the east side, and he measured the gate; it was of the same size as the others. 33Its recesses, its pilasters, and its vestibule were of the same dimensions as the others; and there were windows all around in it and in its vestibule; its depth was fifty cubits, and its width twenty-five cubits. 34Its vestibule faced the outer court, and it had palm trees on its pilasters, on either side; and its stairway had eight steps.

35 Then he brought me to the north gate, and he measured it; it had the same dimensions as the others. 36Its recesses, its pilasters, and its vestibule were of the same size as the others;*x* and it had windows all around. Its depth was fifty cubits, and its width twenty-five cubits.

---

q Gk: Heb *roof*   *r* Heb *opening facing opening*   *s* Heb *made*   *t* Meaning of Heb uncertain
u Compare Gk: Heb *from before*   *v* Heb adds *the east and the north*   *w* Gk: Heb *before them*
x One Ms: Compare verses 29 and 33: MT lacks *were of the same size as the others*

³⁷Its vestibule*y* faced the outer court, and it had palm trees on its pilasters, on either side; and its stairway had eight steps.

38 There was a chamber with its door in the vestibule of the gate,*z* where the burnt offering was to be washed. ³⁹And in the vestibule of the gate were two tables on either side, on which the burnt offering and the sin offering and the guilt offering were to be slaughtered. ⁴⁰On the outside of the vestibule*a* at the entrance of the north gate were two tables; and on the other side of the vestibule of the gate were two tables. ⁴¹Four tables were on the inside, and four tables on the outside of the side of the gate, eight tables, on which the sacrifices were to be slaughtered. ⁴²There were also four tables of hewn stone for the burnt offering, a cubit and a half long, and one cubit and a half wide, and one cubit high, on which the instruments were to be laid with which the burnt offerings and the sacrifices were slaughtered. ⁴³There were pegs, one handbreadth long, fastened all around the inside. And on the tables the flesh of the offering was to be laid.

44 On the outside of the inner gateway there were chambers for the singers in the inner court, one*b* at the side of the north gate facing south, the other at the side of the east gate facing north. ⁴⁵He said to me, "This chamber that faces south is for the priests who have charge of the temple, ⁴⁶and the chamber that faces north is for the priests who have charge of the altar; these are the descendants of Zadok, who alone among the descendants of Levi may come near to the LORD to minister to him." ⁴⁷He measured the court, one hundred cubits deep, and one hundred cubits wide, a square; and the altar was in front of the temple.

The Temple

48 Then he brought me to the vestibule of the temple and measured the pilasters of the vestibule, five cubits on either side; and the width of the gate was fourteen cubits; and the sidewalls of the

gate were three cubits*c* on either side. ⁴⁹The depth of the vestibule was twenty cubits, and the width twelve*d* cubits; ten steps led up*e* to it; and there were pillars beside the pilasters on either side.

41 Then he brought me to the nave, and measured the pilasters; on each side six cubits was the width of the pilasters.*f* ²The width of the entrance was ten cubits; and the sidewalls of the entrance were five cubits on either side. He measured the length of the nave, forty cubits, and its width, twenty cubits. ³Then he went into the inner room and measured the pilasters of the entrance, two cubits; and the width of the entrance, six cubits; and the sidewalls*g* of the entrance, seven cubits. ⁴He measured the depth of the room, twenty cubits, and its width, twenty cubits, beyond the nave. And he said to me, This is the most holy place.

5 Then he measured the wall of the temple, six cubits thick; and the width of the side chambers, four cubits, all around the temple. ⁶The side chambers were in three stories, one over another, thirty in each story. There were offsets*h* all around the wall of the temple to serve as supports for the side chambers, so that they should not be supported by the wall of the temple. ⁷The passageway*i* of the side chambers widened from story to story; for the structure was supplied with a stairway all around the temple. For this reason the structure became wider from story to story. One ascended from the bottom story to the uppermost story by way of the middle one. ⁸I saw also that the temple had a raised platform all around; the foundations of the side chambers measured a full reed of six long cubits. ⁹The thickness of the outer wall of the side chambers was five cubits; and the free space between the side chambers of the temple ¹⁰and the chambers of the court was a width of twenty cubits all around the temple on every side. ¹¹The side chambers opened onto the area left free, one door toward the north, and another door toward the south; and the width of the part that was left free was five cubits all around.

y Gk Vg Compare verses 26, 31, 34: Heb *pilasters*   *z* Cn: Heb *at the pilasters of the gates*
a Cn: Heb *to him who goes up*   *b* Heb lacks *one*   *c* Gk: Heb *and the width of the gate was three cubits*   *d* Gk: Heb *eleven*   *e* Gk: Heb *and by steps that went up*   *f* Compare Gk: Heb *tent*
g Gk: Heb *width*   *h* Gk Compare 1 Kings 6.6: Heb *they entered*   *i* Cn: Heb *it was surrounded*

12 The building that was facing the temple yard on the west side was seventy cubits wide; and the wall of the building was five cubits thick all around, and its depth ninety cubits.

13 Then he measured the temple, one hundred cubits deep; and the yard and the building with its walls, one hundred cubits deep; [14]also the width of the east front of the temple and the yard, one hundred cubits.

15 Then he measured the depth of the building facing the yard at the west, together with its galleries[j] on either side, one hundred cubits.

The nave of the temple and the inner room and the outer[k] vestibule [16]were paneled,[l] and, all around, all three had windows with recessed[m] frames. Facing the threshold the temple was paneled with wood all around, from the floor up to the windows (now the windows were covered), [17]to the space above the door, even to the inner room, and on the outside. And on all the walls all around in the inner room and the nave there was a pattern.[n] [18]It was formed of cherubim and palm trees, a palm tree between cherub and cherub. Each cherub had two faces: [19]a human face turned toward the palm tree on the one side, and the face of a young lion turned toward the palm tree on the other side. They were carved on the whole temple all around; [20]from the floor to the area above the door, cherubim and palm trees were carved on the wall.[o]

21 The doorposts of the nave were square. In front of the holy place was something resembling [22]an altar of wood, three cubits high, two cubits long, and two cubits wide;[p] its corners, its base,[q] and its walls were of wood. He said to me, "This is the table that stands before the LORD." [23]The nave and the holy place had each a double door. [24]The doors had two leaves apiece, two swinging leaves for each door. [25]On the doors of the nave were carved cherubim and palm trees, such as were carved on the walls; and there was a canopy of wood in front of the vestibule outside. [26]And there were recessed windows and palm trees on either side, on the sidewalls of the vestibule.[r]

The Holy Chambers and the Outer Wall

42 Then he led me out into the outer court, toward the north, and he brought me to the chambers that were opposite the temple yard and opposite the building on the north. [2]The length of the building that was on the north side[s] was[t] one hundred cubits, and the width fifty cubits. [3]Across the twenty cubits that belonged to the inner court, and facing the pavement that belonged to the outer court, the chambers rose[u] gallery[v] by gallery[v] in three stories. [4]In front of the chambers was a passage on the inner side, ten cubits wide and one hundred cubits deep,[w] and its[x] entrances were on the north. [5]Now the upper chambers were narrower, for the galleries[v] took more away from them than from the lower and middle chambers in the building. [6]For they were in three stories, and they had no pillars like the pillars of the outer[y] court; for this reason the upper chambers were set back from the ground more than the lower and the middle ones. [7]There was a wall outside parallel to the chambers, toward the outer court, opposite the chambers, fifty cubits long. [8]For the chambers on the outer court were fifty cubits long, while those opposite the temple were one hundred cubits long. [9]At the foot of these chambers ran a passage that one entered from the east in order to enter them from the outer court. [10]The width of the passage[z] was fixed by the wall of the court.

On the south[a] also, opposite the vacant area and opposite the building, there were chambers [11]with a passage in front of them; they were similar to the chambers on the north, of the same length and width, with the same exits[b]

---

j Cn: Meaning of Heb uncertain   k Gk: Heb of the court   l Gk: Heb the thresholds
m Cn Compare Gk 1 Kings 6.4: Meaning of Heb uncertain   n Heb measures   o Cn Compare verse 25: Heb and the wall   p Gk: Heb lacks two cubits wide   q Gk: Heb length   r Cn: Heb vestibule. And the side chambers of the temple and the canopies   s Gk: Heb door   t Gk: Heb before the length   u Heb lacks the chambers rose   v Meaning of Heb uncertain   w Gk Syr: Heb a way of one cubit   x Heb their   y Gk: Heb lacks outer   z Heb lacks of the passage   a Gk: Heb east
b Heb and all their exits

and arrangements and doors. 12So the entrances of the chambers to the south were entered through the entrance at the head of the corresponding passage, from the east, along the matching wall.c

13 Then he said to me, "The north chambers and the south chambers opposite the vacant area are the holy chambers, where the priests who approach the LORD shall eat the most holy offerings; there they shall deposit the most holy offerings—the grain offering, the sin offering, and the guilt offering—for the place is holy. 14When the priests enter the holy place, they shall not go out of it into the outer court without laying there the vestments in which they minister, for these are holy; they shall put on other garments before they go near to the area open to the people."

15 When he had finished measuring the interior of the temple area, he led me out by the gate that faces east, and measured the temple area all around. 16He measured the east side with the measuring reed, five hundred cubits by the measuring reed. 17Then he turned and measuredd the north side, five hundred cubits by the measuring reed. 18Then he turned and measuredd the south side, five hundred cubits by the measuring reed. 19Then he turned to the west side and measured, five hundred cubits by the measuring reed. 20He measured it on the four sides. It had a wall around it, five hundred cubits long and five hundred cubits wide, to make a separation between the holy and the common.

The Divine Glory Returns to the Temple

43 Then he brought me to the gate, the gate facing east. 2And there, the glory of the God of Israel was coming from the east; the sound was like the sound of mighty waters; and the earth shone with his glory. 3Thee vision I saw was like the vision that I had seen when he came to destroy the city, andf like the vision that I had seen by the river Chebar; and I fell upon my face. 4As the glory of the LORD entered the temple by the gate facing

east, 5the spirit lifted me up, and brought me into the inner court; and the glory of the LORD filled the temple.

6 While the man was standing beside me, I heard someone speaking to me out of the temple. 7He said to me: Mortal, this is the place of my throne and the place for the soles of my feet, where I will reside among the people of Israel forever. The house of Israel shall no more defile my holy name, neither they nor their kings, by their whoring, and by the corpses of their kings at their death.g 8When they placed their threshold by my threshold and their doorposts beside my doorposts, with only a wall between me and them, they were defiling my holy name by their abominations that they committed; therefore I have consumed them in my anger. 9Now let them put away their idolatry and the corpses of their kings far from me, and I will reside among them forever.

10 As for you, mortal, describe the temple to the house of Israel, and let them measure the pattern; and let them be ashamed of their iniquities. 11When they are ashamed of all that they have done, make known to them the plan of the temple, its arrangement, its exits and its entrances, and its whole form—all its ordinances and its entire plan and all its laws; and write it down in their sight, so that they may observe and follow the entire plan and all its ordinances. 12This is the law of the temple: the whole territory on the top of the mountain all around shall be most holy. This is the law of the temple.

The Altar

13 These are the dimensions of the altar by cubits (the cubit being one cubit and a handbreadth): its base shall be one cubit high,h and one cubit wide, with a rim of one span around its edge. This shall be the height of the altar: 14From the base on the ground to the lower ledge, two cubits, with a width of one cubit; and from the smaller ledge to the larger ledge, four cubits, with a width of one cubit; 15and the altar hearth, four cubits; and from the altar hearth projecting upward, four horns. 16The altar

hearth shall be square, twelve cubits long by twelve wide. [17]The ledge also shall be square, fourteen cubits long by fourteen wide, with a rim around it half a cubit wide, and its surrounding base, one cubit. Its steps shall face east.

18 Then he said to me: Mortal, thus says the Lord GOD: These are the ordinances for the altar: On the day when it is erected for offering burnt offerings upon it and for dashing blood against it, [19]you shall give to the levitical priests of the family of Zadok, who draw near to me to minister to me, says the Lord GOD, a bull for a sin offering. [20]And you shall take some of its blood, and put it on the four horns of the altar, and on the four corners of the ledge, and upon the rim all around; thus you shall purify it and make atonement for it. [21]You shall also take the bull of the sin offering, and it shall be burnt in the appointed place belonging to the temple, outside the sacred area.

22 On the second day you shall offer a male goat without blemish for a sin offering; and the altar shall be purified, as it was purified with the bull. [23]When you have finished purifying it, you shall offer a bull without blemish and a ram from the flock without blemish. [24]You shall present them before the LORD, and the priests shall throw salt on them and offer them up as a burnt offering to the LORD. [25]For seven days you shall provide daily a goat for a sin offering; also a bull and a ram from the flock, without blemish, shall be provided. [26]Seven days shall they make atonement for the altar and cleanse it, and so consecrate it. [27]When these days are over, then from the eighth day onward the priests shall offer upon the altar your burnt offerings and your offerings of well-being; and I will accept you, says the Lord GOD.

The Closed Gate

44 Then he brought me back to the outer gate of the sanctuary, which faces east; and it was shut. [2]The LORD said to me: This gate shall remain shut; it shall not be opened, and no one shall enter by it; for the LORD, the God of Israel, has entered by it; therefore it shall remain shut. [3]Only the prince, because he is a prince, may sit in it to eat food before the LORD; he shall enter by way of the vestibule of the gate, and shall go out by the same way.

Admission to the Temple

4 Then he brought me by way of the north gate to the front of the temple; and I looked, and lo! the glory of the LORD filled the temple of the LORD; and I fell upon my face. [5]The LORD said to me: Mortal, mark well, look closely, and listen attentively to all that I shall tell you concerning all the ordinances of the temple of the LORD and all its laws; and mark well those who may be admitted to[i] the temple and all those who are to be excluded from the sanctuary. [6]Say to the rebellious house,[j] to the house of Israel, Thus says the Lord GOD: O house of Israel, let there be an end to all your abominations [7]in admitting foreigners, uncircumcised in heart and flesh, to be in my sanctuary, profaning my temple when you offer to me my food, the fat and the blood. You[k] have broken my covenant with all your abominations. [8]And you have not kept charge of my sacred offerings; but you have appointed foreigners[l] to act for you in keeping my charge in my sanctuary.

9 Thus says the Lord GOD: No foreigner, uncircumcised in heart and flesh, of all the foreigners who are among the people of Israel, shall enter my sanctuary. [10]But the Levites who went far from me, going astray from me after their idols when Israel went astray, shall bear their punishment. [11]They shall be ministers in my sanctuary, having oversight at the gates of the temple, and serving in the temple; they shall slaughter the burnt offering and the sacrifice for the people, and they shall attend on them and serve them. [12]Because they ministered to them before their idols and made the house of Israel stumble into iniquity, therefore I have sworn concerning them, says the Lord GOD, that they shall bear their punishment. [13]They shall not come near to me, to serve me as priest, nor come near any of my sacred offerings, the things that are most sacred; but they shall bear their shame, and the consequences of the

---

i Cn: Heb *the entrance of*   *j* Gk: Heb lacks *house*   *k* Gk Syr Vg: Heb *They*   *l* Heb lacks *foreigners*

abominations that they have committed. [14]Yet I will appoint them to keep charge of the temple, to do all its chores, all that is to be done in it.

The Levitical Priests

15 But the levitical priests, the descendants of Zadok, who kept the charge of my sanctuary when the people of Israel went astray from me, shall come near to me to minister to me; and they shall attend me to offer me the fat and the blood, says the Lord GOD. [16]It is they who shall enter my sanctuary, it is they who shall approach my table, to minister to me, and they shall keep my charge. [17]When they enter the gates of the inner court, they shall wear linen vestments; they shall have nothing of wool on them, while they minister at the gates of the inner court, and within. [18]They shall have linen turbans on their heads, and linen undergarments on their loins; they shall not bind themselves with anything that causes sweat. [19]When they go out into the outer court to the people, they shall remove the vestments in which they have been ministering, and lay them in the holy chambers; and they shall put on other garments, so that they may not communicate holiness to the people with their vestments. [20]They shall not shave their heads or let their locks grow long; they shall only trim the hair of their heads. [21]No priest shall drink wine when he enters the inner court. [22]They shall not marry a widow, or a divorced woman, but only a virgin of the stock of the house of Israel, or a widow who is the widow of a priest. [23]They shall teach my people the difference between the holy and the common, and show them how to distinguish between the unclean and the clean. [24]In a controversy they shall act as judges, and they shall decide it according to my judgments. They shall keep my laws and my statutes regarding all my appointed festivals, and they shall keep my sabbaths holy. [25]They shall not defile themselves by going near to a dead person; for father or mother, however, and for son or daughter, and for brother or unmarried sister they may defile themselves. [26]After he has become clean, they shall count seven days for him. [27]On the day that he goes into the holy place, into the inner court, to minister in the holy place, he shall offer his sin offering, says the Lord GOD.

28 This shall be their inheritance: I am their inheritance; and you shall give them no holding in Israel; I am their holding. [29]They shall eat the grain offering, the sin offering, and the guilt offering; and every devoted thing in Israel shall be theirs. [30]The first of all the first fruits of all kinds, and every offering of all kinds from all your offerings, shall belong to the priests; you shall also give to the priests the first of your dough, in order that a blessing may rest on your house. [31]The priests shall not eat of anything, whether bird or animal, that died of itself or was torn by animals.

The Holy District

45 When you allot the land as an inheritance, you shall set aside for the LORD a portion of the land as a holy district, twenty-five thousand cubits long and twenty[m] thousand cubits wide; it shall be holy throughout its entire extent. [2]Of this, a square plot of five hundred by five hundred cubits shall be for the sanctuary, with fifty cubits for an open space around it. [3]In the holy district you shall measure off a section twenty-five thousand cubits long and ten thousand wide, in which shall be the sanctuary, the most holy place. [4]It shall be a holy portion of the land; it shall be for the priests, who minister in the sanctuary and approach the LORD to minister to him; and it shall be both a place for their houses and a holy place for the sanctuary. [5]Another section, twenty-five thousand cubits long and ten thousand cubits wide, shall be for the Levites who minister at the temple, as their holding for cities to live in.[n]

6 Alongside the portion set apart as the holy district you shall assign as a holding for the city an area five thousand cubits wide, and twenty-five thousand cubits long; it shall belong to the whole house of Israel.

7 And to the prince shall belong the land on both sides of the holy district and the holding of the city, alongside the

m Gk: Heb ten   n Gk: Heb as their holding, twenty chambers

holy district and the holding of the city, on the west and on the east, corresponding in length to one of the tribal portions, and extending from the western to the eastern boundary [8]of the land. It is to be his property in Israel. And my princes shall no longer oppress my people; but they shall let the house of Israel have the land according to their tribes.

9 Thus says the Lord GOD: Enough, O princes of Israel! Put away violence and oppression, and do what is just and right. Cease your evictions of my people, says the Lord GOD.

Weights and Measures

10 You shall have honest balances, an honest ephah, and an honest bath.[o] [11]The ephah and the bath shall be of the same measure, the bath containing one-tenth of a homer, and the ephah one-tenth of a homer; the homer shall be the standard measure. [12]The shekel shall be twenty gerahs. Twenty shekels, twenty-five shekels, and fifteen shekels shall make a mina for you.

Offerings

13 This is the offering that you shall make: one-sixth of an ephah from each homer of wheat, and one-sixth of an ephah from each homer of barley, [14]and as the fixed portion of oil,[p] one-tenth of a bath from each cor (the cor,[q] like the homer, contains ten baths); [15]and one sheep from every flock of two hundred, from the pastures of Israel. This is the offering for grain offerings, burnt offerings, and offerings of well-being, to make atonement for them, says the Lord GOD. [16]All the people of the land shall join with the prince in Israel in making this offering. [17]But this shall be the obligation of the prince regarding the burnt offerings, grain offerings, and drink offerings, at the festivals, the new moons, and the sabbaths, all the appointed festivals of the house of Israel: he shall provide the sin offerings, grain offerings, the burnt offerings, and the offerings of well-being, to make atonement for the house of Israel.

Festivals

18 Thus says the Lord GOD: In the first month, on the first day of the month, you shall take a young bull without blemish, and purify the sanctuary. [19]The priest shall take some of the blood of the sin offering and put it on the doorposts of the temple, the four corners of the ledge of the altar, and the posts of the gate of the inner court. [20]You shall do the same on the seventh day of the month for anyone who has sinned through error or ignorance; so you shall make atonement for the temple.

21 In the first month, on the fourteenth day of the month, you shall celebrate the festival of the passover, and for seven days unleavened bread shall be eaten. [22]On that day the prince shall provide for himself and all the people of the land a young bull for a sin offering. [23]And during the seven days of the festival he shall provide as a burnt offering to the LORD seven young bulls and seven rams without blemish, on each of the seven days; and a male goat daily for a sin offering. [24]He shall provide as a grain offering an ephah for each bull, an ephah for each ram, and a hin of oil to each ephah. [25]In the seventh month, on the fifteenth day of the month and for the seven days of the festival, he shall make the same provision for sin offerings, burnt offerings, and grain offerings, and for the oil.

Miscellaneous Regulations

46 Thus says the Lord GOD: The gate of the inner court that faces east shall remain closed on the six working days; but on the sabbath day it shall be opened and on the day of the new moon it shall be opened. [2]The prince shall enter by the vestibule of the gate from outside, and shall take his stand by the post of the gate. The priests shall offer his burnt offering and his offerings of well-being, and he shall bow down at the threshold of the gate. Then he shall go out, but the gate shall not be closed until evening. [3]The people of the land shall bow down at the entrance of that gate before the LORD on the sabbaths and on the new moons. [4]The burnt offering that the prince offers to the LORD on the sabbath day shall be six lambs without blemish and a ram

without blemish; 5and the grain offering with the ram shall be an ephah, and the grain offering with the lambs shall be as much as he wishes to give, together with a hin of oil to each ephah. 6On the day of the new moon he shall offer a young bull without blemish, and six lambs and a ram, which shall be without blemish; 7as a grain offering he shall provide an ephah with the bull and an ephah with the ram, and with the lambs as much as he wishes, together with a hin of oil to each ephah. 8When the prince enters, he shall come in by the vestibule of the gate, and he shall go out by the same way.

9 When the people of the land come before the LORD at the appointed festivals, whoever enters by the north gate to worship shall go out by the south gate; and whoever enters by the south gate shall go out by the north gate: they shall not return by way of the gate by which they entered, but shall go out straight ahead. 10When they come in, the prince shall come in with them; and when they go out, he shall go out.

11 At the festivals and the appointed seasons the grain offering with a young bull shall be an ephah, and with a ram an ephah, and with the lambs as much as one wishes to give, together with a hin of oil to an ephah. 12When the prince provides a freewill offering, either a burnt offering or offerings of well-being as a freewill offering to the LORD, the gate facing east shall be opened for him; and he shall offer his burnt offering or his offerings of well-being as he does on the sabbath day. Then he shall go out, and after he has gone out the gate shall be closed.

13 He shall provide a lamb, a yearling, without blemish, for a burnt offering to the LORD daily; morning by morning he shall provide it. 14And he shall provide a grain offering with it morning by morning regularly, one-sixth of an ephah, and one-third of a hin of oil to moisten the choice flour, as a grain offering to the LORD; this is the ordinance for all time. 15Thus the lamb and the grain offering and the oil shall be provided, morning by morning, as a regular burnt offering.

16 Thus says the Lord GOD: If the prince makes a gift to any of his sons out of his inheritance,r it shall belong to his sons, it is their holding by inheritance. 17But if he makes a gift out of his inheritance to one of his servants, it shall be his to the year of liberty; then it shall revert to the prince; only his sons may keep a gift from his inheritance. 18The prince shall not take any of the inheritance of the people, thrusting them out of their holding; he shall give his sons their inheritance out of his own holding, so that none of my people shall be dispossessed of their holding.

19 Then he brought me through the entrance, which was at the side of the gate, to the north row of the holy chambers for the priests; and there I saw a place at the extreme western end of them. 20He said to me, "This is the place where the priests shall boil the guilt offering and the sin offering, and where they shall bake the grain offering, in order not to bring them out into the outer court and so communicate holiness to the people."

21 Then he brought me out to the outer court, and led me past the four corners of the court; and in each corner of the court there was a court— 22in the four corners of the court were smalls courts, forty cubits long and thirty wide; the four were of the same size. 23On the inside, around each of the four courtst was a row of masonry, with hearths made at the bottom of the rows all around. 24Then he said to me, "These are the kitchens where those who serve at the temple shall boil the sacrifices of the people."

Water Flowing from the Temple

47 Then he brought me back to the entrance of the temple; there, water was flowing from below the threshold of the temple toward the east (for the temple faced east); and the water was flowing down from below the south end of the threshold of the temple, south of the altar. 2Then he brought me out by way of the north gate, and led me around on the outside to the outer gate that faces toward the

---

r Gk: Heb *it is his inheritance*   s Gk Syr Vg: Meaning of Heb uncertain   t Heb *the four of them*

east;ᵘ and the water was coming out on the south side.

3 Going on eastward with a cord in his hand, the man measured one thousand cubits, and then led me through the water; and it was ankle-deep. 4Again he measured one thousand, and led me through the water; and it was knee-deep. Again he measured one thousand, and led me through the water; and it was up to the waist. 5Again he measured one thousand, and it was a river that I could not cross, for the water had risen; it was deep enough to swim in, a river that could not be crossed. 6He said to me, "Mortal, have you seen this?"

Then he led me back along the bank of the river. 7As I came back, I saw on the bank of the river a great many trees on the one side and on the other. 8He said to me, "This water flows toward the eastern region and goes down into the Arabah; and when it enters the sea, the sea of stagnant waters, the water will become fresh. 9Wherever the river goes,ᵛ every living creature that swarms will live, and there will be very many fish, once these waters reach there. It will become fresh; and everything will live where the river goes. 10People will stand fishing beside the seaʷ from En-gedi to En-eglaim; it will be a place for the spreading of nets; its fish will be of a great many kinds, like the fish of the Great Sea. 11But its swamps and marshes will not become fresh; they are to be left for salt. 12On the banks, on both sides of the river, there will grow all kinds of trees for food. Their leaves will not wither nor their fruit fail, but they will bear fresh fruit every month, because the water for them flows from the sanctuary. Their fruit will be for food, and their leaves for healing."

The New Boundaries of the Land

13 Thus says the Lord GOD: These are the boundaries by which you shall divide the land for inheritance among the twelve tribes of Israel. Joseph shall have two portions. 14You shall divide it equally; I swore to give it to your ances-

tors, and this land shall fall to you as your inheritance.

15 This shall be the boundary of the land: On the north side, from the Great Sea by way of Hethlon to Lebo-hamath, and on to Zedad,ˣ 16Berothah, Sibraim (which lies between the border of Damascus and the border of Hamath), as far as Hazer-hatticon, which is on the border of Hauran. 17So the boundary shall run from the sea to Hazar-enon, which is north of the border of Damascus, with the border of Hamath to the north.ᵘ This shall be the north side.

18 On the east side, between Hauran and Damascus; along the Jordan between Gilead and the land of Israel; to the eastern sea and as far as Tamar.ʸ This shall be the east side.

19 On the south side, it shall run from Tamar as far as the waters of Meribath-kadesh, from there along the Wadi of Egyptᶻ to the Great Sea. This shall be the south side.

20 On the west side, the Great Sea shall be the boundary to a point opposite Lebo-hamath. This shall be the west side.

21 So you shall divide this land among you according to the tribes of Israel. 22You shall allot it as an inheritance for yourselves and for the aliens who reside among you and have begotten children among you. They shall be to you as citizens of Israel; with you they shall be allotted an inheritance among the tribes of Israel. 23In whatever tribe aliens reside, there you shall assign them their inheritance, says the Lord GOD.

The Tribal Portions

48 These are the names of the tribes: Beginning at the northern border, on the Hethlon road,ᵃ from Lebo-hamath, as far as Hazar-enon (which is on the border of Damascus, with Hamath to the north), andᵇ extending from the east side to the west,ᶜ Dan, one portion. 2Adjoining the territory of Dan, from the east side to the west, Asher, one portion. 3Adjoining the territory of Asher, from the east side to the west, Naphtali, one portion. 4Adjoining the territory of Naphtali, from the east side to the west, Manasseh, one portion. 5Adjoining the territory of Manasseh, from the east side to the west, Ephraim, one portion. 6Adjoining the territory of Ephraim, from the east side to the west, Reuben, one portion. 7Adjoining the territory of Reuben, from the east side to the west, Judah, one portion.

8 Adjoining the territory of Judah, from the east side to the west, shall be the portion that you shall set apart, twenty-five thousand cubits in width, and in length equal to one of the tribal portions, from the east side to the west, with the sanctuary in the middle of it. 9The portion that you shall set apart for the LORD shall be twenty-five thousand cubits in length, and twenty$d$ thousand in width. 10These shall be the allotments of the holy portion: the priests shall have an allotment measuring twenty-five thousand cubits on the northern side, ten thousand cubits in width on the western side, ten thousand in width on the eastern side, and twenty-five thousand in length on the southern side, with the sanctuary of the LORD in the middle of it. 11This shall be for the consecrated priests, the descendants$e$ of Zadok, who kept my charge, who did not go astray when the people of Israel went astray, as the Levites did. 12It shall belong to them as a special portion from the holy portion of the land, a most holy place, adjoining the territory of the Levites. 13Alongside the territory of the priests, the Levites shall have an allotment twenty-five thousand cubits in length and ten thousand in width. The whole length shall be twenty-five thousand cubits and the width twenty$f$ thousand. 14They shall not sell or exchange any of it; they shall not transfer this choice portion of the land, for it is holy to the LORD.

15 The remainder, five thousand cubits in width and twenty-five thousand in length, shall be for ordinary use for the city, for dwellings and for open country. In the middle of it shall be the city; 16and these shall be its dimensions: the north side four thousand five hun-

dred cubits, the south side four thousand five hundred, the east side four thousand five hundred, and the west side four thousand five hundred. 17The city shall have open land: on the north two hundred fifty cubits, on the south two hundred fifty, on the east two hundred fifty, on the west two hundred fifty. 18The remainder of the length alongside the holy portion shall be ten thousand cubits to the east, and ten thousand to the west, and it shall be alongside the holy portion. Its produce shall be food for the workers of the city. 19The workers of the city, from all the tribes of Israel, shall cultivate it. 20The whole portion that you shall set apart shall be twenty-five thousand cubits square, that is, the holy portion together with the property of the city.

21 What remains on both sides of the holy portion and of the property of the city shall belong to the prince. Extending from the twenty-five thousand cubits of the holy portion to the east border, and westward from the twenty-five thousand cubits to the west border, parallel to the tribal portions, it shall belong to the prince. The holy portion with the sanctuary of the temple in the middle of it, 22and the property of the Levites and of the city, shall be in the middle of that which belongs to the prince. The portion of the prince shall lie between the territory of Judah and the territory of Benjamin.

23 As for the rest of the tribes: from the east side to the west, Benjamin, one portion. 24Adjoining the territory of Benjamin, from the east side to the west, Simeon, one portion. 25Adjoining the territory of Simeon, from the east side to the west, Issachar, one portion. 26Adjoining the territory of Issachar, from the east side to the west, Zebulun, one portion. 27Adjoining the territory of Zebulun, from the east side to the west, Gad, one portion. 28And adjoining the territory of Gad to the south, the boundary shall run from Tamar to the waters of Meribath-kadesh, from there along the Wadi of Egypt$g$ to the Great Sea. 29This is the land that you shall allot as an inheritance among the tribes of Isra-

el, and these are their portions, says the Lord GOD.

30 These shall be the exits of the city: On the north side, which is to be four thousand five hundred cubits by measure, ³¹three gates, the gate of Reuben, the gate of Judah, and the gate of Levi, the gates of the city being named after the tribes of Israel. ³²On the east side, which is to be four thousand five hundred cubits, three gates, the gate of Joseph, the gate of Benjamin, and the gate of Dan. ³³On the south side, which is to be four thousand five hundred cubits by measure, three gates, the gate of Simeon, the gate of Issachar, and the gate of Zebulun. ³⁴On the west side, which is to be four thousand five hundred cubits, three gates,ʰ the gate of Gad, the gate of Asher, and the gate of Naphtali. ³⁵The circumference of the city shall be eighteen thousand cubits. And the name of the city from that time on shall be, The LORD is There.

---

h One Ms Gk Syr: MT *their gates three*

DANIEL

ANIEL RECORDS EVENTS THAT
TOOK PLACE DURING ISRAEL'S
CAPTIVITY AND ENCOURAGES THE
PEOPLE TO TRUST IN THE GOD WHO CON-
TROLS ALL OF HISTORY. DANIEL'S VISIONS
ALWAYS SHOW GOD AS TRIUMPHANT. AS
YOU READ THIS BOOK BE ENCOURAGED THAT
GOD STILL SHOWS HIS FAITHFULNESS AND
HIS PROTECTION TODAY, AS HE KEEPS HIS
PROMISE NEVER TO DESERT YOU. HE GIVES
YOU THE STRENGTH TO STAND FIRM IN HIM
AS YOU SERVE AND OBEY HIM DAY BY DAY.

Four Young Israelites at the Babylonian Court

1 In the third year of the reign of King Jehoiakim of Judah, King Nebuchadnezzar of Babylon came to Jerusalem and besieged it. 2 The Lord let King Jehoiakim of Judah fall into his power, as well as some of the vessels of the house of God. These he brought to the land of Shinar,*a* and placed the vessels in the treasury of his gods.

3 Then the king commanded his palace master Ashpenaz to bring some of the Israelites of the royal family and of the nobility, 4 young men without physical defect and handsome, versed in every branch of wisdom, endowed with knowledge and insight, and competent to serve in the king's palace; they were to be taught the literature and language of the Chaldeans. 5 The king assigned them a daily portion of the royal rations of food and wine. They were to be educated for three years, so that at the end of that time they could be stationed in the king's court. 6 Among them were Daniel, Hananiah, Mishael, and Azariah, from the tribe of Judah. 7 The palace master gave them other names: Daniel he called Belteshazzar, Hananiah he called Shadrach, Mishael he called Meshach, and Azariah he called Abednego.

8 But Daniel resolved that he would not defile himself with the royal rations of food and wine; so he asked the palace master to allow him not to defile himself. 9 Now God allowed Daniel to

a Gk Theodotion: Heb adds *to the house of his own gods*

receive favor and compassion from the palace master. 10The palace master said to Daniel, "I am afraid of my lord the king; he has appointed your food and your drink. If he should see you in poorer condition than the other young men of your own age, you would endanger my head with the king." 11Then Daniel asked the guard whom the palace master had appointed over Daniel, Hananiah, Mishael, and Azariah: 12"Please test your servants for ten days. Let us be given vegetables to eat and water to drink. 13You can then compare our appearance with the appearance of the young men who eat the royal rations, and deal with your servants according to what you observe." 14So he agreed to this proposal and tested them for ten days. 15At the end of ten days it was observed that they appeared better and fatter than all the young men who had been eating the royal rations. 16So the guard continued to withdraw their royal rations and the wine they were to drink, and gave them vegetables. 17To these four young men God gave knowledge and skill in every aspect of literature and wisdom; Daniel also had insight into all visions and dreams.

18 At the end of the time that the king had set for them to be brought in, the palace master brought them into the presence of Nebuchadnezzar, 19and the king spoke with them. And among them all, no one was found to compare with Daniel, Hananiah, Mishael, and Azariah; therefore they were stationed in the king's court. 20In every matter of wisdom and understanding concerning which the king inquired of them, he found them ten times better than all the magicians and enchanters in his whole kingdom. 21And Daniel continued there until the first year of King Cyrus.

Nebuchadnezzar's Dream

2 In the second year of Nebuchadnezzar's reign, Nebuchadnezzar dreamed such dreams that his spirit was troubled and his sleep left him. 2So the king commanded that the magicians, the enchanters, the sorcerers, and the Chaldeans be summoned to tell the king his dreams. When they came in and stood before the king, 3he said to them, "I have had such a dream that my spirit is troubled by the desire to understand it." 4The Chaldeans said to the king (in Aramaic),b "O king, live forever! Tell your servants the dream, and we will reveal the interpretation." 5The king answered the Chaldeans, "This is a public decree: if you do not tell me both the dream and its interpretation, you shall be torn limb from limb, and your houses shall be laid in ruins. 6But if you do tell me the dream and its interpretation, you shall receive from me gifts and rewards and great honor. Therefore tell me the dream and its interpretation." 7They answered a second time, "Let the king first tell his servants the dream, then we can give its interpretation." 8The king answered, "I know with certainty that you are trying to gain time, because you see I have firmly decreed: 9if you do not tell me the dream, there is but one verdict for you. You have agreed to speak lying and misleading words to me until things take a turn. Therefore, tell me the dream, and I shall know that you can give me its interpretation." 10The Chaldeans answered the king, "There is no one on earth who can reveal what the king demands! In fact no king, however great and powerful, has ever asked such a thing of any magician or enchanter or Chaldean. 11The thing that the king is asking is too difficult, and no one can reveal it to the king except the gods, whose dwelling is not with mortals."

12 Because of this the king flew into a violent rage and commanded that all the wise men of Babylon be destroyed. 13The decree was issued, and the wise men were about to be executed; and they looked for Daniel and his companions, to execute them. 14Then Daniel responded with prudence and discretion to Arioch, the king's chief executioner, who had gone out to execute the wise men of Babylon; 15he asked Arioch, the royal official, "Why is the decree of the king so urgent?" Arioch then explained the matter to Daniel. 16So Daniel went in and requested that the king give him time and he would tell the king the interpretation.

b The text from this point to the end of chapter 7 is in Aramaic

God Reveals Nebuchadnezzar's Dream

17 Then Daniel went to his home and informed his companions, Hananiah, Mishael, and Azariah, 18and told them to seek mercy from the God of heaven concerning this mystery, so that Daniel and his companions with the rest of the wise men of Babylon might not perish. 19Then the mystery was revealed to Daniel in a vision of the night, and Daniel blessed the God of heaven.
20 Daniel said:

"Blessed be the name of God from
    age to age,
    for wisdom and power are his.
21 He changes times and seasons,
    deposes kings and sets up kings;
    he gives wisdom to the wise
    and knowledge to those who
    have understanding.

MONDAY

THE HEARER AND ANSWERER OF PRAYER
Dwight L. Moody

VERSE: Daniel 2.22   PASSAGE: Daniel 2.1–23

 ne of [God's] greatest and most wonderful characteristics [is that] he is the hearer and answerer of prayer. As an instance of this, see Daniel 2.18, where there is a prayer that God would reveal to his servants, not only the interpretation of a dream, but even the dream itself. "Is there anything too hard for the LORD (see Genesis 18.14)?" No. In the very next verse we have the answer right back, as it were, by telegraph from heaven: "During the night the mystery was revealed to Daniel in a vision."

The Scripture is full of such answers; every page of it encourages prayer. God will have us pray, and he will answer prayer. Surely we have all found that out in our experience; if not, it is our own fault. "See, the LORD's hand is not too short to save, nor his ear too dull to hear" (Isaiah 59.1). It is our own prayers that are shortened and that are weak and faithless. Oh, let us "ask in faith, never doubting (James 1.6)!" Some people are like the disciples in Jerusalem praying for the release of Peter; their prayers were answered, and Peter stood at the door, but they could not believe it; they said it must be his spirit (see Acts 12.5–14). Oh, let us take God at his word! He says, "While they are yet speaking I will hear" (Isaiah 65.24). Is not that encouraging? He delights to hear our prayers; he will not weary with our often coming.

ADDITIONAL SCRIPTURE READING:
Daniel 4.9; Amos 3.7; 1 Corinthians 2.9–10

Go to page 1007 for your next devotional reading.

1900   Present

22   He reveals deep and hidden things;
    he knows what is in the
       darkness,
    and light dwells with him.
23   To you, O God of my ancestors,
    I give thanks and praise,
    for you have given me wisdom and
       power,
    and have now revealed to me
       what we asked of you,
    for you have revealed to us what
       the king ordered."

Daniel Interprets the Dream

24   Therefore Daniel went to Arioch, whom the king had appointed to destroy the wise men of Babylon, and said to him, "Do not destroy the wise men of Babylon; bring me in before the king, and I will give the king the interpretation." 25 Then Arioch quickly brought Daniel before the king and said to him: "I have found among the exiles from Judah a man who can tell the king the interpretation." 26 The king said to Daniel, whose name was Belteshazzar, "Are you able to tell me the dream that I have seen and its interpretation?" 27 Daniel answered the king, "No wise men, enchanters, magicians, or diviners can show to the king the mystery that the king is asking, 28 but there is a God in heaven who reveals mysteries, and he has disclosed to King Nebuchadnezzar what will happen at the end of days. Your dream and the visions of your head as you lay in bed were these: 29 To you, O king, as you lay in bed, came thoughts of what would be hereafter, and the revealer of mysteries disclosed to you what is to be. 30 But as for me, this mystery has not been revealed to me because of any wisdom that I have more than any other living being, but in order that the interpretation may be known to the king and that you may understand the thoughts of your mind.

31   "You were looking, O king, and lo! there was a great statue. This statue was huge, its brilliance extraordinary; it was standing before you, and its appearance was frightening. 32 The head of that statue was of fine gold, its chest and arms of silver, its middle and thighs of bronze, 33 its legs of iron, its feet partly of iron and partly of clay. 34 As you looked on, a stone was cut out, not by human hands, and it struck the statue on its feet of iron and clay and broke them in pieces. 35 Then the iron, the clay, the bronze, the silver, and the gold, were all broken in pieces and became like the chaff of the summer threshing floors; and the wind carried them away, so that not a trace of them could be found. But the stone that struck the statue became a great mountain and filled the whole earth.

36   "This was the dream; now we will tell the king its interpretation. 37 You, O king, the king of kings—to whom the God of heaven has given the kingdom, the power, the might, and the glory, 38 into whose hand he has given human beings, wherever they live, the wild animals of the field, and the birds of the air, and whom he has established as ruler over them all—you are the head of gold. 39 After you shall arise another kingdom inferior to yours, and yet a third kingdom of bronze, which shall rule over the whole earth. 40 And there shall be a fourth kingdom, strong as iron; just as iron crushes and smashes everything,[c] it shall crush and shatter all these. 41 As you saw the feet and toes partly of potter's clay and partly of iron, it shall be a divided kingdom; but some of the strength of iron shall be in it, as you saw the iron mixed with the clay. 42 As the toes of the feet were part iron and part clay, so the kingdom shall be partly strong and partly brittle. 43 As you saw the iron mixed with clay, so will they mix with one another in marriage,[d] but they will not hold together, just as iron does not mix with clay. 44 And in the days of those kings the God of heaven will set up a kingdom that shall never be destroyed, nor shall this kingdom be left to another people. It shall crush all these kingdoms and bring them to an end, and it shall stand forever; 45 just as you saw that a stone was cut from the mountain not by hands, and that it crushed the iron, the bronze, the clay, the silver, and the gold. The great God has informed the king what shall be hereafter. The dream is certain, and its interpretation trustworthy."

c Gk Theodotion Syr Vg: Aram adds *and like iron that crushes*   d Aram *by human seed*

Daniel and His Friends Promoted

46 Then King Nebuchadnezzar fell on his face, worshiped Daniel, and commanded that a grain offering and incense be offered to him. 47The king said to Daniel, "Truly, your God is God of gods and Lord of kings and a revealer of mysteries, for you have been able to reveal this mystery!" 48Then the king promoted Daniel, gave him many great gifts, and made him ruler over the whole province of Babylon and chief prefect over all the wise men of Babylon. 49Daniel made a request of the king, and he appointed Shadrach, Meshach, and Abednego over the affairs of the province of Babylon. But Daniel remained at the king's court.

The Golden Image

3 King Nebuchadnezzar made a golden statue whose height was sixty cubits and whose width was six cubits; he set it up on the plain of Dura in the province of Babylon. 2Then King Nebuchadnezzar sent for the satraps, the prefects, and the governors, the counselors, the treasurers, the justices, the magistrates, and all the officials of the provinces, to assemble and come to the dedication of the statue that King Nebuchadnezzar had set up. 3So the satraps, the prefects, and the governors, the counselors, the treasurers, the justices, the magistrates, and all the officials of the provinces, assembled for the dedication of the statue that King Nebuchadnezzar had set up. When they were standing before the statue that Nebuchadnezzar had set up, 4the herald proclaimed aloud, "You are commanded, O peoples, nations, and languages, 5that when you hear the sound of the horn, pipe, lyre, trigon, harp, drum, and entire musical ensemble, you are to fall down and worship the golden statue that King Nebuchadnezzar has set up. 6Whoever does not fall down and worship shall immediately be thrown into a furnace of blazing fire." 7Therefore, as soon as all the peoples heard the sound of the horn, pipe, lyre, trigon, harp, drum, and entire musical ensemble, all the peoples, nations, and languages fell down and worshiped the golden statue that King Nebuchadnezzar had set up.

8 Accordingly, at this time certain Chaldeans came forward and denounced the Jews. 9They said to King Nebuchadnezzar, "O king, live forever! 10You, O king, have made a decree, that everyone who hears the sound of the horn, pipe, lyre, trigon, harp, drum, and entire musical ensemble, shall fall down and worship the golden statue, 11and whoever does not fall down and worship shall be thrown into a furnace of blazing fire. 12There are certain Jews whom you have appointed over the affairs of the province of Babylon: Shadrach, Meshach, and Abednego. These pay no heed to you, O king. They do not serve your gods and they do not worship the golden statue that you have set up."

13 Then Nebuchadnezzar in furious rage commanded that Shadrach, Meshach, and Abednego be brought in; so they brought those men before the king. 14Nebuchadnezzar said to them, "Is it true, O Shadrach, Meshach, and Abednego, that you do not serve my gods and you do not worship the golden statue that I have set up? 15Now if you are ready when you hear the sound of the horn, pipe, lyre, trigon, harp, drum, and entire musical ensemble to fall down and worship the statue that I have made, well and good.e But if you do not worship, you shall immediately be thrown into a furnace of blazing fire, and who is the god that will deliver you out of my hands?"

16 Shadrach, Meshach, and Abednego answered the king, "O Nebuchadnezzar, we have no need to present a defense to you in this matter. 17If our God whom we serve is able to deliver us from the furnace of blazing fire and out of your hand, O king, let him deliver us.f 18But if not, be it known to you, O king, that we will not serve your gods and we will not worship the golden statue that you have set up."

The Fiery Furnace

19 Then Nebuchadnezzar was so filled with rage against Shadrach, Meshach, and Abednego that his face was

---

e Aram lacks *well and good*   f Or *If our God whom we serve is able to deliver us, he will deliver us from the furnace of blazing fire and out of your hand, O king.*

distorted. He ordered the furnace heated up seven times more than was customary, 20and ordered some of the strongest guards in his army to bind Shadrach, Meshach, and Abednego and to throw them into the furnace of blazing fire. 21So the men were bound, still wearing their tunics,g their trousers,g their hats, and their other garments, and they were thrown into the furnace of blazing fire. 22Because the king's command was urgent and the furnace was so overheated, the raging flames killed the men who lifted Shadrach, Meshach, and Abednego. 23But the three men, Shadrach, Meshach, and Abednego, fell down, bound, into the furnace of blazing fire.

24 Then King Nebuchadnezzar was astonished and rose up quickly. He said to his counselors, "Was it not three men that we threw bound into the fire?" They answered the king, "True, O king." 25He replied, "But I see four men unbound, walking in the middle of the fire, and they are not hurt; and the fourth has the appearance of a god."h

---

AS SURE AS EVER GOD PUTS HIS CHILDREN IN THE FURNACE, HE WILL BE IN THE FURNACE WITH THEM.   —*C. H. Spurgeon*

26Nebuchadnezzar then approached the door of the furnace of blazing fire and said, "Shadrach, Meshach, and Abednego, servants of the Most High God, come out! Come here!" So Shadrach, Meshach, and Abednego came out from the fire. 27And the satraps, the prefects, the governors, and the king's counselors gathered together and saw that the fire had not had any power over the bodies of those men; the hair of their heads was not singed, their tunicsg were not harmed, and not even the smell of fire came from them. 28Nebuchadnezzar said, "Blessed be the God of Shadrach, Meshach, and Abednego, who has sent his angel and delivered his servants who trusted in him. They disobeyed the king's command and yielded up their bodies rather than serve and worship

any god except their own God. 29Therefore I make a decree: Any people, nation, or language that utters blasphemy against the God of Shadrach, Meshach, and Abednego shall be torn limb from limb, and their houses laid in ruins; for there is no other god who is able to deliver in this way." 30Then the king promoted Shadrach, Meshach, and Abednego in the province of Babylon.

Nebuchadnezzar's Second Dream

4i King Nebuchadnezzar to all peoples, nations, and languages that live throughout the earth: May you have abundant prosperity! 2The signs and wonders that the Most High God has worked for me I am pleased to recount.

3   How great are his signs,
          how mighty his wonders!
        His kingdom is an everlasting
          kingdom,
          and his sovereignty is from
              generation to generation.

4j I, Nebuchadnezzar, was living at ease in my home and prospering in my palace. 5I saw a dream that frightened me; my fantasies in bed and the visions of my head terrified me. 6So I made a decree that all the wise men of Babylon should be brought before me, in order that they might tell me the interpretation of the dream. 7Then the magicians, the enchanters, the Chaldeans, and the diviners came in, and I told them the dream, but they could not tell me its interpretation. 8At last Daniel came in before me—he who was named Belteshazzar after the name of my god, and who is endowed with a spirit of the holy godsk—and I told him the dream: 9"O Belteshazzar, chief of the magicians, I know that you are endowed with a spirit of the holy godsk and that no mystery is too difficult for you. Hearl the dream that I saw; tell me its interpretation.

10m Upon my bed this is what I saw;
          there was a tree at the center of
              the earth,
          and its height was great.

---

g Meaning of Aram word uncertain   h Aram *a son of the gods*   i Ch 3.31 in Aram   j Ch 4.1 in Aram   k Or *a holy, divine spirit*   l Theodotion: Aram *The visions of*   m Theodotion Syr Compare Gk: Aram adds *The visions of my head*

11 The tree grew great and strong,
    its top reached to heaven,
    and it was visible to the ends of
      the whole earth.
12 Its foliage was beautiful,
    its fruit abundant,
    and it provided food for all.
  The animals of the field found
      shade under it,
    the birds of the air nested in its
      branches,
    and from it all living beings were
      fed.

13 "I continued looking, in the visions of my head as I lay in bed, and there was a holy watcher, coming down from heaven. 14He cried aloud and said:
  'Cut down the tree and chop off its
      branches,
    strip off its foliage and scatter its
      fruit.
  Let the animals flee from beneath
      it
    and the birds from its branches.
15 But leave its stump and roots in the
      ground,
    with a band of iron and bronze,
    in the tender grass of the field.
  Let him be bathed with the dew of
      heaven,
    and let his lot be with the
      animals of the field
    in the grass of the earth.
16 Let his mind be changed from that
      of a human,
    and let the mind of an animal be
      given to him.
  And let seven times pass over
      him.
17 The sentence is rendered by decree
      of the watchers,
    the decision is given by order of
      the holy ones,
  in order that all who live may know
    that the Most High is sovereign
      over the kingdom of mortals;
  he gives it to whom he will
    and sets over it the lowliest of
      human beings.'

18 "This is the dream that I, King Nebuchadnezzar, saw. Now you, Belteshazzar, declare the interpretation, since all the wise men of my kingdom are unable to tell me the interpretation. You are able, however, for you are endowed with a spirit of the holy gods."n

Daniel Interprets the Second Dream

19 Then Daniel, who was called Belteshazzar, was severely distressed for a while. His thoughts terrified him. The king said, "Belteshazzar, do not let the dream or the interpretation terrify you." Belteshazzar answered, "My lord, may the dream be for those who hate you, and its interpretation for your enemies! 20The tree that you saw, which grew great and strong, so that its top reached to heaven and was visible to the end of the whole earth, 21whose foliage was beautiful and its fruit abundant, and which provided food for all, under which animals of the field lived, and in whose branches the birds of the air had nests— 22it is you, O king! You have grown great and strong. Your greatness has increased and reaches to heaven, and your sovereignty to the ends of the earth. 23And whereas the king saw a holy watcher coming down from heaven and saying, 'Cut down the tree and destroy it, but leave its stump and roots in the ground, with a band of iron and bronze, in the grass of the field; and let him be bathed with the dew of heaven, and let his lot be with the animals of the field, until seven times pass over him'— 24this is the interpretation, O king, and it is a decree of the Most High that has come upon my lord the king: 25You shall be driven away from human society, and your dwelling shall be with the wild animals. You shall be made to eat grass like oxen, you shall be bathed with the dew of heaven, and seven times shall pass over you, until you have learned that the Most High has sovereignty over the kingdom of mortals, and gives it to whom he will. 26As it was commanded to leave the stump and roots of the tree, your kingdom shall be re-established for you from the time that you learn that Heaven is sovereign. 27Therefore, O king, may my counsel be acceptable to you: atone foro your sins with righteousness, and your iniquities with mercy to the oppressed, so that your prosperity may be prolonged."

n Or a holy, divine spirit   o Aram break off

Nebuchadnezzar's Humiliation

28 All this came upon King Nebuchadnezzar. ²⁹At the end of twelve months he was walking on the roof of the royal palace of Babylon, ³⁰and the king said, "Is this not magnificent Babylon, which I have built as a royal capital by my mighty power and for my glorious majesty?" ³¹While the words were still in the king's mouth, a voice came from heaven: "O King Nebuchadnezzar, to you it is declared: The kingdom has departed from you! ³²You shall be driven away from human society, and your dwelling shall be with the animals of the field. You shall be made to eat grass like oxen, and seven times shall pass over you, until you have learned that the Most High has sovereignty over the kingdom of mortals and gives it to whom he will." ³³Immediately the sentence was fulfilled against Nebuchadnezzar. He was driven away from human society, ate grass like oxen, and his body was bathed with the dew of heaven, until his hair grew as long as eagles' feathers and his nails became like birds' claws.

Nebuchadnezzar Praises God

34 When that period was over, I, Nebuchadnezzar, lifted my eyes to heaven, and my reason returned to me.
I blessed the Most High,
    and praised and honored the one
        who lives forever.
For his sovereignty is an everlasting
        sovereignty,
    and his kingdom endures from
        generation to generation.
35   All the inhabitants of the earth are
        accounted as nothing,
    and he does what he wills with
        the host of heaven
    and the inhabitants of the earth.
There is no one who can stay his
        hand
    or say to him, "What are you
        doing?"
³⁶At that time my reason returned to me; and my majesty and splendor were restored to me for the glory of my kingdom. My counselors and my lords sought me out, I was re-established over

my kingdom, and still more greatness was added to me. ³⁷Now I, Nebuchadnezzar, praise and extol and honor the King of heaven,
    for all his works are truth,
        and his ways are justice;
    and he is able to bring low
        those who walk in pride.

Belshazzar's Feast

5 King Belshazzar made a great festival for a thousand of his lords, and he was drinking wine in the presence of the thousand.
2 Under the influence of the wine, Belshazzar commanded that they bring in the vessels of gold and silver that his father Nebuchadnezzar had taken out of the temple in Jerusalem, so that the king and his lords, his wives, and his concubines might drink from them. ³So they brought in the vessels of gold and silverᵖ that had been taken out of the temple, the house of God in Jerusalem, and the king and his lords, his wives, and his concubines drank from them. ⁴They drank the wine and praised the gods of gold and silver, bronze, iron, wood, and stone.

The Writing on the Wall

5 Immediately the fingers of a human hand appeared and began writing on the plaster of the wall of the royal palace, next to the lampstand. The king was watching the hand as it wrote. ⁶Then the king's face turned pale, and his thoughts terrified him. His limbs gave way, and his knees knocked together. ⁷The king cried aloud to bring in the enchanters, the Chaldeans, and the diviners; and the king said to the wise men of Babylon, "Whoever can read this writing and tell me its interpretation shall be clothed in purple, have a chain of gold around his neck, and rank third in the kingdom." ⁸Then all the king's wise men came in, but they could not read the writing or tell the king the interpretation. ⁹Then King Belshazzar became greatly terrified and his face turned pale, and his lords were perplexed.
10 The queen, when she heard the discussion of the king and his lords,

---

ᵖ Theodotion Vg: Aram lacks *and silver*

came into the banqueting hall. The queen said, "O king, live forever! Do not let your thoughts terrify you or your face grow pale. 11There is a man in your kingdom who is endowed with a spirit of the holy gods.q In the days of your father he was found to have enlightenment, understanding, and wisdom like the wisdom of the gods. Your father, King Nebuchadnezzar, made him chief of the magicians, enchanters, Chaldeans, and diviners,r 12because an excellent spirit, knowledge, and understanding to interpret dreams, explain riddles, and solve problems were found in this Daniel, whom the king named Belteshazzar. Now let Daniel be called, and he will give the interpretation."

The Writing on the Wall Interpreted

13 Then Daniel was brought in before the king. The king said to Daniel, "So you are Daniel, one of the exiles of Judah, whom my father the king brought from Judah? 14I have heard of you that a spirit of the godss is in you, and that enlightenment, understanding, and excellent wisdom are found in you. 15Now the wise men, the enchanters, have been brought in before me to read this writing and tell me its interpretation, but they were not able to give the interpretation of the matter. 16But I have heard that you can give interpretations and solve problems. Now if you are able to read the writing and tell me its interpretation, you shall be clothed in purple, have a chain of gold around your neck, and rank third in the kingdom."

17 Then Daniel answered in the presence of the king, "Let your gifts be for yourself, or give your rewards to someone else! Nevertheless I will read the writing to the king and let him know the interpretation. 18O king, the Most High God gave your father Nebuchadnezzar kingship, greatness, glory, and majesty. 19And because of the greatness that he gave him, all peoples, nations, and languages trembled and feared before him. He killed those he wanted to kill, kept alive those he wanted to keep alive, honored those he wanted to honor, and degraded those he wanted to degrade.

20But when his heart was lifted up and his spirit was hardened so that he acted proudly, he was deposed from his kingly throne, and his glory was stripped from him. 21He was driven from human society, and his mind was made like that of an animal. His dwelling was with the wild asses, he was fed grass like oxen, and his body was bathed with the dew of heaven, until he learned that the Most High God has sovereignty over the kingdom of mortals, and sets over it whomever he will. 22And you, Belshazzar his son, have not humbled your heart, even though you knew all this! 23You have exalted yourself against the Lord of heaven! The vessels of his temple have been brought in before you, and you and your lords, your wives and your concubines have been drinking wine from them. You have praised the gods of silver and gold, of bronze, iron, wood, and stone, which do not see or hear or know; but the God in whose power is your very breath, and to whom belong all your ways, you have not honored.

24 "So from his presence the hand was sent and this writing was inscribed. 25And this is the writing that was inscribed: MENE, MENE, TEKEL, and PARSIN. 26This is the interpretation of the matter: MENE, God has numbered the days oft your kingdom and brought it to an end; 27TEKEL, you have been weighed on the scales and found wanting; 28PERES,u your kingdom is divided and given to the Medes and Persians."

29 Then Belshazzar gave the command, and Daniel was clothed in purple, a chain of gold was put around his neck, and a proclamation was made concerning him that he should rank third in the kingdom.

30 That very night Belshazzar, the Chaldean king, was killed. 31vAnd Darius the Mede received the kingdom, being about sixty-two years old.

The Plot against Daniel

6 It pleased Darius to set over the kingdom one hundred twenty satraps, stationed throughout the whole kingdom, 2and over them three presidents, including Daniel; to these the

---

q Or a holy, divine spirit   r Aram adds the king your father   s Or a divine spirit   t Aram lacks the days of   u The singular of Parsin   v Ch 6.1 in Aram

satraps gave account, so that the king might suffer no loss. ³Soon Daniel distinguished himself above all the other presidents and satraps because an excellent spirit was in him, and the king planned to appoint him over the whole kingdom. ⁴So the presidents and the satraps tried to find grounds for complaint against Daniel in connection with the kingdom. But they could find no grounds for complaint or any corruption, because he was faithful, and no

negligence or corruption could be found in him. ⁵The men said, "We shall not find any ground for complaint against this Daniel unless we find it in connection with the law of his God."

6 So the presidents and satraps conspired and came to the king and said to him, "O King Darius, live forever! ⁷All the presidents of the kingdom, the prefects and the satraps, the counselors and the governors are agreed that the king should establish an ordinance and

TUESDAY

ARE YOU FIT FOR HEAVEN?
J. C. Ryle

VERSE: Daniel 5.23   PASSAGE: Daniel 5.18–31

 elshazzar had Daniel the prophet hard by his door—Ananias and Sapphira joined the church in the days when the apostles were working miracles—Judas Iscariot was a chosen companion of our Lord Jesus Christ himself (see also Matthew 26.14; Acts 5.1–10). But they all sinned with a high hand against light and knowledge; and they were all suddenly destroyed without remedy. They had no time or space for repentance. As they lived, so they died: as they were, they hurried away to meet God. They went with all their sins upon them, unpardoned, unrenewed, and utterly unfit for heaven . . .

Oh, that you would be wise! Oh, that you would consider your latter end! . . . There is a love in God towards sinners which is unspeakable and unsearchable—but it is for those who "hear Christ's voice and follow him." Seek to have an interest in that love. Break off every known sin; come out boldly from the world; cry mightily to God in prayer; cast yourself wholly and unreservedly on the Lord Jesus for time and eternity; lay aside every weight. Cling to nothing, however dear, which interferes with your soul's salvation; give up everything, however precious, which comes between you and heaven. This old shipwrecked world is fast sinking beneath your feet: the one thing needful is to have a place in the lifeboat and get safe to shore.

ADDITIONAL SCRIPTURE READING:
Psalm 18.23; Daniel 2.47; Hebrews 12.1

Go to page 1013 for your next devotional reading.

1900   Present

enforce an interdict, that whoever prays to anyone, divine or human, for thirty days, except to you, O king, shall be thrown into a den of lions. 8Now, O king, establish the interdict and sign the document, so that it cannot be changed, according to the law of the Medes and the Persians, which cannot be revoked." 9Therefore King Darius signed the document and interdict.

Daniel in the Lions' Den

10 Although Daniel knew that the document had been signed, he continued to go to his house, which had windows in its upper room open toward Jerusalem, and to get down on his knees three times a day to pray to his God and praise him, just as he had done previously. 11The conspirators came and found Daniel praying and seeking mercy before his God. 12Then they approached the king and said concerning the interdict, "O king! Did you not sign an interdict, that anyone who prays to anyone, divine or human, within thirty days except to you, O king, shall be thrown into a den of lions?" The king answered, "The thing stands fast, according to the law of the Medes and Persians, which cannot be revoked." 13Then they responded to the king, "Daniel, one of the exiles from Judah, pays no attention to you, O king, or to the interdict you have signed, but he is saying his prayers three times a day."

14 When the king heard the charge, he was very much distressed. He was determined to save Daniel, and until the sun went down he made every effort to rescue him. 15Then the conspirators came to the king and said to him, "Know, O king, that it is a law of the Medes and Persians that no interdict or ordinance that the king establishes can be changed."

16 Then the king gave the command, and Daniel was brought and thrown into the den of lions. The king said to Daniel, "May your God, whom you faithfully serve, deliver you!" 17A stone was brought and laid on the mouth of the den, and the king sealed it with his own signet and with the signet of his lords, so that nothing might be changed concerning Daniel. 18Then the king went to his palace and spent the night fasting; no food was brought to him, and sleep fled from him.

Daniel Saved from the Lions

19 Then, at break of day, the king got up and hurried to the den of lions. 20When he came near the den where Daniel was, he cried out anxiously to Daniel, "O Daniel, servant of the living God, has your God whom you faithfully serve been able to deliver you from the lions?" 21Daniel then said to the king, "O king, live forever! 22My God sent his angel and shut the lions' mouths so that they would not hurt me, because I was found blameless before him; and also before you, O king, I have done no wrong." 23Then the king was exceedingly glad and commanded that Daniel be taken up out of the den. So Daniel was taken up out of the den, and no kind of harm was found on him, because he had trusted in his God. 24The king gave a command, and those who had accused Daniel were brought and thrown into the den of lions—they, their children, and their wives. Before they reached the bottom of the den the lions overpowered them and broke all their bones in pieces.

25 Then King Darius wrote to all peoples and nations of every language throughout the whole world: "May you have abundant prosperity! 26I make a decree, that in all my royal dominion people should tremble and fear before the God of Daniel:

For he is the living God,
    enduring forever.
His kingdom shall never be
    destroyed,
    and his dominion has no end.
27 He delivers and rescues,
    he works signs and wonders in
        heaven and on earth;
    for he has saved Daniel
        from the power of the lions."

28So this Daniel prospered during the reign of Darius and the reign of Cyrus the Persian.

Visions of the Four Beasts

7 In the first year of King Belshazzar of Babylon, Daniel had a dream and visions of his head as he lay in

bed. Then he wrote down the dream:[w] [2]I,[x] Daniel, saw in my vision by night the four winds of heaven stirring up the great sea, [3]and four great beasts came up out of the sea, different from one another. [4]The first was like a lion and had eagles' wings. Then, as I watched, its wings were plucked off, and it was lifted up from the ground and made to stand on two feet like a human being; and a human mind was given to it. [5]Another beast appeared, a second one, that looked like a bear. It was raised up on one side, had three tusks[y] in its mouth among its teeth and was told, "Arise, devour many bodies!" [6]After this, as I watched, another appeared, like a leopard. The beast had four wings of a bird on its back and four heads; and dominion was given to it. [7]After this I saw in the visions by night a fourth beast, terrifying and dreadful and exceedingly strong. It had great iron teeth and was devouring, breaking in pieces, and stamping what was left with its feet. It was different from all the beasts that preceded it, and it had ten horns. [8]I was considering the horns, when another horn appeared, a little one coming up among them; to make room for it, three of the earlier horns were plucked up by the roots. There were eyes like human eyes in this horn, and a mouth speaking arrogantly.

Judgment before the Ancient One

9 As I watched,
  thrones were set in place,
    and an Ancient One[z] took his
      throne,
  his clothing was white as snow,
    and the hair of his head like pure
      wool;
  his throne was fiery flames,
    and its wheels were burning fire.
10 A stream of fire issued
    and flowed out from his
      presence.
  A thousand thousands served him,
    and ten thousand times ten
      thousand stood attending
      him.
  The court sat in judgment,
    and the books were opened.

[11]I watched then because of the noise of the arrogant words that the horn was speaking. And as I watched, the beast was put to death, and its body destroyed and given over to be burned with fire. [12]As for the rest of the beasts, their dominion was taken away, but their lives were prolonged for a season and a time. [13]As I watched in the night visions,

  I saw one like a human being[a]
    coming with the clouds of
      heaven.
  And he came to the Ancient One[b]
    and was presented before him.
14 To him was given dominion
    and glory and kingship,
  that all peoples, nations, and
      languages
    should serve him.
  His dominion is an everlasting
      dominion
    that shall not pass away,
  and his kingship is one
    that shall never be destroyed.

Daniel's Visions Interpreted

15 As for me, Daniel, my spirit was troubled within me,[c] and the visions of my head terrified me. [16]I approached one of the attendants to ask him the truth concerning all this. So he said that he would disclose to me the interpretation of the matter: [17]"As for these four great beasts, four kings shall arise out of the earth. [18]But the holy ones of the Most High shall receive the kingdom and possess the kingdom forever—forever and ever."

19 Then I desired to know the truth concerning the fourth beast, which was different from all the rest, exceedingly terrifying, with its teeth of iron and claws of bronze, and which devoured and broke in pieces, and stamped what was left with its feet; [20]and concerning the ten horns that were on its head, and concerning the other horn, which came up and to make room for which three of them fell out—the horn that had eyes and a mouth that spoke arrogantly, and that seemed greater than the others. [21]As I looked, this horn made war with

---

w Q Ms Theodotion: MT adds *the beginning of the words; he said answered and said, "I* y Or *ribs* z Aram *an Ancient of Days* b Aram *the Ancient of Days* c Aram *troubled in its sheath* x Theodotion: Aram *Daniel* a Aram *one like a son of man*

the holy ones and was prevailing over them, 22until the Ancient One[d] came; then judgment was given for the holy ones of the Most High, and the time arrived when the holy ones gained possession of the kingdom.

23 This is what he said: "As for the fourth beast,

there shall be a fourth kingdom on earth
that shall be different from all the other kingdoms;
it shall devour the whole earth,
and trample it down, and break it to pieces.
24 As for the ten horns,
out of this kingdom ten kings shall arise,
and another shall arise after them.
This one shall be different from the former ones,
and shall put down three kings.
25 He shall speak words against the Most High,
shall wear out the holy ones of the Most High,
and shall attempt to change the sacred seasons and the law;
and they shall be given into his power
for a time, two times,[e] and half a time.
26 Then the court shall sit in judgment,
and his dominion shall be taken away,
to be consumed and totally destroyed.
27 The kingship and dominion
and the greatness of the kingdoms under the whole heaven
shall be given to the people of the holy ones of the Most High;
their kingdom shall be an everlasting kingdom,
and all dominions shall serve and obey them."

28 Here the account ends. As for me, Daniel, my thoughts greatly terrified me, and my face turned pale; but I kept the matter in my mind.

Vision of a Ram and a Goat

8 In the third year of the reign of King Belshazzar a vision appeared to me, Daniel, after the one that had appeared to me at first. 2In the vision I was looking and saw myself in Susa the capital, in the province of Elam,[f] and I was by the river Ulai.[g] 3I looked up and saw a ram standing beside the river.[h] It had two horns. Both horns were long, but one was longer than the other, and the longer one came up second. 4I saw the ram charging westward and northward and southward. All beasts were powerless to withstand it, and no one could rescue from its power; it did as it pleased and became strong.

5 As I was watching, a male goat appeared from the west, coming across the face of the whole earth without touching the ground. The goat had a horn[i] between its eyes. 6It came toward the ram with the two horns that I had seen standing beside the river,[h] and it ran at it with savage force. 7I saw it approaching the ram. It was enraged against it and struck the ram, breaking its two horns. The ram did not have power to withstand it; it threw the ram down to the ground and trampled upon it, and there was no one who could rescue the ram from its power. 8Then the male goat grew exceedingly great; but at the height of its power, the great horn was broken, and in its place there came up four prominent horns toward the four winds of heaven.

9 Out of one of them came another[j] horn, a little one, which grew exceedingly great toward the south, toward the east, and toward the beautiful land. 10It grew as high as the host of heaven. It threw down to the earth some of the host and some of the stars, and trampled on them. 11Even against the prince of the host it acted arrogantly; it took the regular burnt offering away from him and overthrew the place of his sanctuary. 12Because of wickedness, the host was given over to it together with the regular burnt offering;[k] it cast truth to the ground, and kept prospering in what it did. 13Then I heard a holy one

---

d Aram *the Ancient of Days*   e Aram *a time, times*   f Gk Theodotion: MT Q Ms repeat *in the vision I was looking*   g Or *the Ulai Gate*   h Or *gate*   i Theodotion: Gk *one horn*; Heb *a horn of vision*   j Cn Compare 7.8: Heb *one*   k Meaning of Heb uncertain

speaking, and another holy one said to the one that spoke, "For how long is this vision concerning the regular burnt offering, the transgression that makes desolate, and the giving over of the sanctuary and host to be trampled?"[1] [14]And he answered him,[m] "For two thousand three hundred evenings and mornings; then the sanctuary shall be restored to its rightful state."

Gabriel Interprets the Vision

15 When I, Daniel, had seen the vision, I tried to understand it. Then someone appeared standing before me, having the appearance of a man, [16]and I heard a human voice by the Ulai, calling, "Gabriel, help this man understand the vision." [17]So he came near where I stood; and when he came, I became frightened and fell prostrate. But he said to me, "Understand, O mortal,[n] that the vision is for the time of the end."

18 As he was speaking to me, I fell into a trance, face to the ground; then he touched me and set me on my feet. [19]He said, "Listen, and I will tell you what will take place later in the period of wrath; for it refers to the appointed time of the end. [20]As for the ram that you saw with the two horns, these are the kings of Media and Persia. [21]The male goat[o] is the king of Greece, and the great horn between its eyes is the first king. [22]As for the horn that was broken, in place of which four others arose, four kingdoms shall arise from his[p] nation, but not with his power.

23   At the end of their rule,
        when the transgressions have
            reached their full measure,
        a king of bold countenance shall
            arise,
        skilled in intrigue.
24   He shall grow strong in power,[q]
        shall cause fearful destruction,
        and shall succeed in what he does.
    He shall destroy the powerful
        and the people of the holy ones.
25   By his cunning
        he shall make deceit prosper
            under his hand,
        and in his own mind he shall be
            great.

Without warning he shall destroy
        many
        and shall even rise up against the
            Prince of princes.
    But he shall be broken, and not by
        human hands.
[26]The vision of the evenings and the mornings that has been told is true. As for you, seal up the vision, for it refers to many days from now."

27   So I, Daniel, was overcome and lay sick for some days; then I arose and went about the king's business. But I was dismayed by the vision and did not understand it.

Daniel's Prayer for the People

9 In the first year of Darius son of Ahasuerus, by birth a Mede, who became king over the realm of the Chaldeans— [2]in the first year of his reign, I, Daniel, perceived in the books the number of years that, according to the word of the LORD to the prophet Jeremiah, must be fulfilled for the devastation of Jerusalem, namely, seventy years.

3   Then I turned to the Lord God, to seek an answer by prayer and supplication with fasting and sackcloth and ashes. [4]I prayed to the LORD my God and made confession, saying,

---

YOU ART COMING TO A KING,

LARGE PETITIONS WITH YOU BRING

FOR HIS GRACE AND POWER ARE SUCH

NONE CAN EVER ASK TOO MUCH.   —John Newton

"Ah, Lord, great and awesome God, keeping covenant and steadfast love with those who love you and keep your commandments, [5]we have sinned and done wrong, acted wickedly and rebelled, turning aside from your commandments and ordinances. [6]We have not listened to your servants the prophets, who spoke in your name to our kings, our princes, and our ancestors, and to all the people of the land.

7   "Righteousness is on your side, O Lord, but open shame, as at this day, falls on us, the people of Judah, the inhabitants of Jerusalem, and all Israel,

---

l Meaning of Heb uncertain   *m* Gk Theodotion Syr Vg: Heb *me*   *n* Heb *son of man*   *o* Or *shaggy male goat*   *p* Gk Theodotion Vg: Heb *the*   *q* Theodotion and one Gk Ms: Heb repeats (from 8.22) *but not with his power*

those who are near and those who are far away, in all the lands to which you have driven them, because of the treachery that they have committed against you. 8Open shame, O Lord, falls on us, our kings, our officials, and our ancestors, because we have sinned against you. 9To the Lord our God belong mercy and forgiveness, for we have rebelled against him, 10and have not obeyed the voice of the Lord our God by following his laws, which he set before us by his servants the prophets.

11 "All Israel has transgressed your law and turned aside, refusing to obey your voice. So the curse and the oath written in the law of Moses, the servant of God, have been poured out upon us, because we have sinned against you. 12He has confirmed his words, which he spoke against us and against our rulers, by bringing upon us a calamity so great that what has been done against Jerusalem has never before been done under the whole heaven. 13Just as it is written in the law of Moses, all this calamity has come upon us. We did not entreat the favor of the Lord our God, turning from our iniquities and reflecting on his^r fidelity. 14So the Lord kept watch over this calamity until he brought it upon us. Indeed, the Lord our God is right in all that he has done; for we have disobeyed his voice.

15 "And now, O Lord our God, who brought your people out of the land of Egypt with a mighty hand and made your name renowned even to this day— we have sinned, we have done wickedly. 16O Lord, in view of all your righteous acts, let your anger and wrath, we pray, turn away from your city Jerusalem, your holy mountain; because of our sins and the iniquities of our ancestors, Jerusalem and your people have become a disgrace among all our neighbors. 17Now therefore, O our God, listen to the prayer of your servant and to his supplication, and for your own sake, Lord,^s let your face shine upon your desolated sanctuary. 18Incline your ear, O my God, and hear. Open your eyes and look at our desolation and the city that bears your name. We do not present

our supplication before you on the ground of our righteousness, but on the ground of your great mercies. 19O Lord, hear; O Lord, forgive; O Lord, listen and act and do not delay! For your own sake, O my God, because your city and your people bear your name!"

The Seventy Weeks

20 While I was speaking, and was praying and confessing my sin and the sin of my people Israel, and presenting my supplication before the Lord my God on behalf of the holy mountain of my God— 21while I was speaking in prayer, the man Gabriel, whom I had seen before in a vision, came to me in swift flight at the time of the evening sacrifice. 22He came^t and said to me, "Daniel, I have now come out to give you wisdom and understanding. 23At the beginning of your supplications a word went out, and I have come to declare it, for you are greatly beloved. So consider the word and understand the vision:

24 "Seventy weeks are decreed for your people and your holy city: to finish the transgression, to put an end to sin, and to atone for iniquity, to bring in everlasting righteousness, to seal both vision and prophet, and to anoint a most holy place.^u 25Know therefore and understand: from the time that the word went out to restore and rebuild Jerusalem until the time of an anointed prince, there shall be seven weeks; and for sixty-two weeks it shall be built again with streets and moat, but in a troubled time. 26After the sixty-two weeks, an anointed one shall be cut off and shall have nothing, and the troops of the prince who is to come shall destroy the city and the sanctuary. Its^v end shall come with a flood, and to the end there shall be war. Desolations are decreed. 27He shall make a strong covenant with many for one week, and for half of the week he shall make sacrifice and offering cease; and in their place^w shall be an abomination that desolates, until the decreed end is poured out upon the desolator."

r Heb your   s Theodotion Vg Compare Syr: Heb for the Lord's sake   t Gk Syr: Heb He made to understand   u Or thing or one   v Or His   w Cn: Meaning of Heb uncertain

Conflict of Nations and Heavenly Powers

10 In the third year of King Cyrus of Persia a word was revealed to Daniel, who was named Belteshazzar. The word was true, and it concerned a great conflict. He understood the word, having received understanding in the vision.

2 At that time I, Daniel, had been mourning for three weeks. ³I had eaten no rich food, no meat or wine had entered my mouth, and I had not anointed myself at all, for the full three weeks. ⁴On the twenty-fourth day of the first month, as I was standing on the bank of the great river (that is, the Tigris), ⁵I looked up and saw a man clothed in linen, with a belt of gold from Uphaz around his waist. ⁶His body was like beryl, his face like lightning, his eyes like flaming torches, his arms and legs like the gleam of burnished bronze, and the sound of his words like the roar of a multitude. ⁷I, Daniel, alone saw the vision; the people who were with me did not see the vision, though a great trembling fell upon them, and they fled and hid themselves. ⁸So I was left alone to see this great vision. My strength left me, and my complexion grew deathly pale, and I retained no strength. ⁹Then I heard the sound of his words; and when I heard the sound of his words, I fell into a trance, face to the ground.

10 But then a hand touched me and roused me to my hands and knees. ¹¹He

---

WEDNESDAY

THE PRESSURE OF HARD PLACES
A. B. Simpson

VERSE: Daniel 9.18   **PASSAGE:** Daniel 9.3–19

The pressure of hard places makes us value life. Every time our life is given back to us from such a trial, it is like a new beginning, and we learn better how much it is worth, and make more of it for God and man. The pressure helps us to understand the trials of others, and fits us to help and sympathize with them.

There is a shallow, superficial nature, that gets hold of a theory or a promise lightly, and talks very glibly about the distrust of those who shrink from every trial; but the man or woman who has suffered much never does this, but is very tender and gentle, and knows what suffering really means . . .

Trials and hard places are needed to press us forward, even as the furnace fires in the hold of that mighty ship give force that moves the piston, drives the engine, and propels that great vessel across the sea in the face of the winds and waves.

ADDITIONAL SCRIPTURE READING:

Romans 5.3–4; 2 Corinthians 4.17; James 1.2–4

Go to page 1016 for your next devotional reading.

1900   Present

said to me, "Daniel, greatly beloved, pay attention to the words that I am going to speak to you. Stand on your feet, for I have now been sent to you." So while he was speaking this word to me, I stood up trembling. 12He said to me, "Do not fear, Daniel, for from the first day that you set your mind to gain understanding and to humble yourself before your God, your words have been heard, and I have come because of your words. 13But the prince of the kingdom of Persia opposed me twenty-one days. So Michael, one of the chief princes, came to help me, and I left him there with the prince of the kingdom of Persia,ˣ 14and have come to help you understand what is to happen to your people at the end of days. For there is a further vision for those days."

15 While he was speaking these words to me, I turned my face toward the ground and was speechless. 16Then one in human form touched my lips, and I opened my mouth to speak, and said to the one who stood before me, "My lord, because of the vision such pains have come upon me that I retain no strength. 17How can my lord's servant talk with my lord? For I am shaking,ʸ no strength remains in me, and no breath is left in me."

18 Again one in human form touched me and strengthened me. 19He said, "Do not fear, greatly beloved, you are safe. Be strong and courageous!" When he spoke to me, I was strengthened and said, "Let my lord speak, for you have strengthened me." 20Then he said, "Do you know why I have come to you? Now I must return to fight against the prince of Persia, and when I am through with him, the prince of Greece will come. 21But I am to tell you what is inscribed in the book of truth. There is no one with me who contends against these princes except Michael, your prince.

11 1As for me, in the first year of Darius the Mede, I stood up to support and strengthen him.

2 "Now I will announce the truth to you. Three more kings shall arise in Persia. The fourth shall be far richer than all of them, and when he has become strong through his riches, he shall stir up all against the kingdom of Greece. 3Then a warrior king shall arise, who shall rule with great dominion and take action as he pleases. 4And while still rising in power, his kingdom shall be broken and divided toward the four winds of heaven, but not to his posterity, nor according to the dominion with which he ruled; for his kingdom shall be uprooted and go to others besides these.

5 "Then the king of the south shall grow strong, but one of his officers shall grow stronger than he and shall rule a realm greater than his own realm. 6After some years they shall make an alliance, and the daughter of the king of the south shall come to the king of the north to ratify the agreement. But she shall not retain her power, and his offspring shall not endure. She shall be given up, she and her attendants and her child and the one who supported her.

"In those times 7a branch from her roots shall rise up in his place. He shall come against the army and enter the fortress of the king of the north, and he shall take action against them and prevail. 8Even their gods, with their idols and with their precious vessels of silver and gold, he shall carry off to Egypt as spoils of war. For some years he shall refrain from attacking the king of the north; 9then the latter shall invade the realm of the king of the south, but will return to his own land.

10 "His sons shall wage war and assemble a multitude of great forces, which shall advance like a flood and pass through, and again shall carry the war as far as his fortress. 11Moved with rage, the king of the south shall go out and do battle against the king of the north, who shall muster a great multitude, which shall, however, be defeated by his enemy. 12When the multitude has been carried off, his heart shall be exalted, and he shall overthrow tens of thousands, but he shall not prevail. 13For the king of the north shall again raise a multitude, larger than the former, and after some yearsᶻ he shall advance with a great army and abundant supplies.

14 "In those times many shall rise against the king of the south. The law-

---

x Gk Theodotion: Heb I was left there with the kings of Persia　　　y Gk: Heb from now　　　z Heb and at the end of the times years less among your own people shall lift themselves up in order to fulfill the vision, but they shall fail. 15Then the king of the north shall come and throw up siegeworks, and take a well-fortified city. And the forces of the south shall not stand, not even his picked troops, for there shall be no strength to resist. 16But he who comes against him shall take the actions he pleases, and no one shall withstand him. He shall take a position in the beautiful land, and all of it shall be in his power. 17He shall set his mind to come with the strength of his whole kingdom, and he shall bring terms of peace*a* and perform them. In order to destroy the kingdom,*b* he shall give him a woman in marriage; but it shall not succeed or be to his advantage. 18Afterward he shall turn to the coastlands, and shall capture many. But a commander shall put an end to his insolence; indeed,*c* he shall turn his insolence back upon him. 19Then he shall turn back toward the fortresses of his own land, but he shall stumble and fall, and shall not be found.

20 "Then shall arise in his place one who shall send an official for the glory of the kingdom; but within a few days he shall be broken, though not in anger or in battle. 21In his place shall arise a contemptible person on whom royal majesty had not been conferred; he shall come in without warning and obtain the kingdom through intrigue. 22Armies shall be utterly swept away and broken before him, and the prince of the covenant as well. 23And after an alliance is made with him, he shall act deceitfully and become strong with a small party. 24Without warning he shall come into the richest parts*d* of the province and do what none of his predecessors had ever done, lavishing plunder, spoil, and wealth on them. He shall devise plans against strongholds, but only for a time. 25He shall stir up his power and determination against the king of the south with a great army, and the king of the south shall wage war with a much greater and stronger army. But he shall not succeed, for plots shall be devised against him 26by those who eat of the royal rations. They shall break him, his army shall be swept away, and many shall fall slain. 27The two kings, their minds bent on evil, shall sit at one table and exchange lies. But it shall not succeed, for there remains an end at the time appointed. 28He shall return to his land with great wealth, but his heart shall be set against the holy covenant. He shall work his will, and return to his own land.

29 "At the time appointed he shall return and come into the south, but this time it shall not be as it was before. 30For ships of Kittim shall come against him, and he shall lose heart and withdraw. He shall be enraged and take action against the holy covenant. He shall turn back and pay heed to those who forsake the holy covenant. 31Forces sent by him shall occupy and profane the temple and fortress. They shall abolish the regular burnt offering and set up the abomination that makes desolate. 32He shall seduce with intrigue those who violate the covenant; but the people who are loyal to their God shall stand firm and take action. 33The wise among the people shall give understanding to many; for some days, however, they shall fall by sword and flame, and suffer captivity and plunder. 34When they fall victim, they shall receive a little help, and many shall join them insincerely. 35Some of the wise shall fall, so that they may be refined, purified, and cleansed,*e* until the time of the end, for there is still an interval until the time appointed.

36 "The king shall act as he pleases. He shall exalt himself and consider himself greater than any god, and shall speak horrendous things against the God of gods. He shall prosper until the period of wrath is completed, for what is determined shall be done. 37He shall pay no respect to the gods of his ancestors, or to the one beloved by women; he shall pay no respect to any other god, for he shall consider himself greater than all. 38He shall honor the god of fortresses instead of these; a god whom his ancestors did not know he shall honor with gold and silver, with precious stones and costly

---

a Gk: Heb *kingdom, and upright ones with him*   *b* Heb *it*   *c* Meaning of Heb uncertain
d Or *among the richest men*   *e* Heb *made them white*

gifts. 39He shall deal with the strongest fortresses by the help of a foreign god. Those who acknowledge him he shall make more wealthy, and shall appoint them as rulers over many, and shall distribute the land for a price.

The Time of the End

40 "At the time of the end the king of the south shall attack him. But the king of the north shall rush upon him like a whirlwind, with chariots and horsemen,

and with many ships. He shall advance against countries and pass through like a flood. 41He shall come into the beautiful land, and tens of thousands shall fall victim, but Edom and Moab and the main part of the Ammonites shall escape from his power. 42He shall stretch out his hand against the countries, and the land of Egypt shall not escape. 43He shall become ruler of the treasures of gold and of silver, and all the riches of Egypt; and the Libyans and the Ethiopians*f* shall

f Or *Nubians;* Heb *Cushites*

THURSDAY

BLESSED IS THE ONE WHO WAITS
Charles H. Spurgeon

VERSE: Daniel 12.6   **PASSAGE:** Daniel 12.1–13

 t may seem an easy thing to *wait,* but it is one of the postures which a Christian soldier does not learn without years of teaching. Marching and quick-marching are much easier to God's warriors than standing still. There are hours of perplexity when the most willing spirit, anxiously desirous to serve the Lord, knows not what part to take. Then what shall it do? Vex itself by despair? Fly back in cowardice, turn to the right hand in fear, or rush forward in presumption? No, only simply wait.

Wait in prayer, however. Call on God, and spread the case before him; tell him your difficulty and plead his promise of aid. In dilemmas between one duty and another, it is sweet to be humble as a child and *wait with simplicity of soul* on the Lord. It is sure to be well with us when we feel and know our own folly, and are heartily willing to be guided by the will of God.

But *wait in faith.* Express your unstaggering confidence in him, for unfaithful, untrusting waiting is but an insult to the Lord. Believe that if he keeps you tarrying even till midnight, yet he will come at the right time; the vision will come and will not tarry.

ADDITIONAL SCRIPTURE READING:
Psalms 27.14; 37.34; 1 Corinthians 1.7

Go to page 1021 for your next devotional reading.

1700   1900

follow in his train. 44But reports from the east and the north shall alarm him, and he shall go out with great fury to bring ruin and complete destruction to many. 45He shall pitch his palatial tents between the sea and the beautiful holy mountain. Yet he shall come to his end, with no one to help him.

The Resurrection of the Dead

12 "At that time Michael, the great prince, the protector of your people, shall arise. There shall be a time of anguish, such as has never occurred since nations first came into existence. But at that time your people shall be delivered, everyone who is found written in the book. 2Many of those who sleep in the dust of the earth*g* shall awake, some to everlasting life, and some to shame and everlasting contempt. 3Those who are wise shall shine like the brightness of the sky,*h* and those who lead many to righteousness, like the stars forever and ever. 4But you, Daniel, keep the words secret and the book sealed until the time of the end. Many shall be running back and forth, and evil*i* shall increase."

5 Then I, Daniel, looked, and two others appeared, one standing on this bank of the stream and one on the other. 6One of them said to the man clothed in linen, who was upstream, "How long shall it be until the end of these wonders?" 7The man clothed in linen, who was upstream, raised his right hand and his left hand toward heaven. And I heard him swear by the one who lives forever that it would be for a time, two times, and half a time,*j* and that when the shattering of the power of the holy people comes to an end, all these things would be accomplished. 8I heard but could not understand; so I said, "My lord, what shall be the outcome of these things?" 9He said, "Go your way, Daniel, for the words are to remain secret and sealed until the time of the end. 10Many shall be purified, cleansed, and refined, but the wicked shall continue to act wickedly. None of the wicked shall understand, but those who are wise shall understand. 11From the time that the regular burnt offering is taken away and the abomination that desolates is set up, there shall be one thousand two hundred ninety days. 12Happy are those who persevere and attain the thousand three hundred thirty-five days. 13But you, go your way,*k* and rest; you shall rise for your reward at the end of the days."

g Or *the land of dust*   h Or *dome*   i Cn Compare Gk: Heb *knowledge*   j Heb *a time, times, and a half*   k Gk Theodotion: Heb adds *to the end*

HOSEA

THE BOOK IS NAMED AFTER THE PROPHET WHOSE MESSAGE IT PRESERVES. HOSEA PROPHESIED JUST BEFORE THE NORTHERN KINGDOM OF ISRAEL WAS CONQUERED BY THE ASSYRIANS. THE STORY OF HOSEA'S FAMILY LIFE ILLUSTRATES ANOTHER LOVE STORY—THAT GOD LOVES US, EVEN WHEN OUR SINS HAVE BROKEN HIS HEART. LOOK BEYOND HOSEA'S SUFFERING TO SEE A STARTLING EXAMPLE OF LOVE THAT WILL NOT QUIT. TAKE COURAGE IN KNOWING THAT GOD'S LOVE AND HEALING ARE AVAILABLE TO YOU TODAY.

1 The word of the LORD that came to Hosea son of Beeri, in the days of Kings Uzziah, Jotham, Ahaz, and Hezekiah of Judah, and in the days of King Jeroboam son of Joash of Israel.

The Family of Hosea

2 When the LORD first spoke through Hosea, the LORD said to Hosea, "Go, take for yourself a wife of whoredom and have children of whoredom, for the land commits great whoredom by forsaking the LORD." 3So he went and took Gomer daughter of Diblaim, and she conceived and bore him a son.

4 And the LORD said to him, "Name him Jezreel;*a* for in a little while I will punish the house of Jehu for the blood of Jezreel, and I will put an end to the kingdom of the house of Israel. 5On that day I will break the bow of Israel in the valley of Jezreel."

6 She conceived again and bore a daughter. Then the LORD said to him, "Name her Lo-ruhamah,*b* for I will no longer have pity on the house of Israel or forgive them. 7But I will have pity on the house of Judah, and I will save them by the LORD their God; I will not save them by bow, or by sword, or by war, or by horses, or by horsemen."

8 When she had weaned Lo-ruhamah, she conceived and bore a son. 9Then the LORD said, "Name him Lo-ammi,*c* for you are not my people and I am not your God."*d*

a That is *God sows*   *b* That is *Not pitied*   *c* That is *Not my people*   *d* Heb *I am not yours*

The Restoration of Israel

10[e] Yet the number of the people of Israel shall be like the sand of the sea, which can be neither measured nor numbered; and in the place where it was said to them, "You are not my people," it shall be said to them, "Children of the living God." 11 The people of Judah and the people of Israel shall be gathered together, and they shall appoint for themselves one head; and they shall take possession of[f] the land, for great shall be the day of Jezreel.

2 [g] Say to your brother,[h] Ammi,[i] and to your sister,[j] Ruhamah.[k]

Israel's Infidelity, Punishment, and Redemption

2 Plead with your mother, plead—
     for she is not my wife,
     and I am not her husband—
   that she put away her whoring
          from her face,
     and her adultery from between
          her breasts,
3 or I will strip her naked
     and expose her as in the day she
          was born,
   and make her like a wilderness,
     and turn her into a parched land,
     and kill her with thirst.
4 Upon her children also I will have
          no pity,
     because they are children of
          whoredom.
5 For their mother has played the
          whore;
     she who conceived them has
          acted shamefully.
   For she said, "I will go after my
          lovers;
     they give me my bread and my
          water,
     my wool and my flax, my oil and
          my drink."
6 Therefore I will hedge up her[l] way
          with thorns;
     and I will build a wall against
          her,
     so that she cannot find her paths.
7 She shall pursue her lovers,
     but not overtake them;
   and she shall seek them,
     but shall not find them.

   Then she shall say, "I will go
     and return to my first husband,
     for it was better with me then
          than now."
8 She did not know
     that it was I who gave her
     the grain, the wine, and the oil,
   and who lavished upon her silver
     and gold that they used for Baal.
9 Therefore I will take back
     my grain in its time,
     and my wine in its season;
   and I will take away my wool and
          my flax,
     which were to cover her
          nakedness.
10 Now I will uncover her shame
     in the sight of her lovers,
     and no one shall rescue her out of
          my hand.
11 I will put an end to all her mirth,
     her festivals, her new moons, her
          sabbaths,
     and all her appointed festivals.
12 I will lay waste her vines and her
          fig trees,
     of which she said,
   "These are my pay,
     which my lovers have given me."
   I will make them a forest,
     and the wild animals shall
          devour them.
13 I will punish her for the festival
          days of the Baals,
     when she offered incense to them
   and decked herself with her ring
          and jewelry,
     and went after her lovers,
     and forgot me, says the LORD.

14 Therefore, I will now allure her,
     and bring her into the
          wilderness,
     and speak tenderly to her.
15 From there I will give her her
          vineyards,
     and make the Valley of Achor a
          door of hope.
   There she shall respond as in the
          days of her youth,
     as at the time when she came out
          of the land of Egypt.
16 On that day, says the LORD, you will call me, "My husband," and no longer

---

e Ch 2.1 in Heb   f Heb rise up from   g Ch 2.3 in Heb   h Gk: Heb brothers   i That is My people   j Gk Vg: Heb sisters   k That is Pitied   l Gk Syr: Heb your

will you call me, "My Baal."*m* **17**For I will remove the names of the Baals from her mouth, and they shall be mentioned by name no more. **18**I will make for you*n* a covenant on that day with the wild animals, the birds of the air, and the creeping things of the ground; and I will abolish*o* the bow, the sword, and war from the land; and I will make you lie down in safety. **19**And I will take you for my wife forever; I will take you for my wife in righteousness and in justice, in steadfast love, and in mercy. **20**I will take you for my wife in faithfulness; and you shall know the LORD.

21 On that day I will answer, says the
LORD,
I will answer the heavens
and they shall answer the earth;
22 and the earth shall answer the
grain, the wine, and the oil,
and they shall answer Jezreel;*p*
23 and I will sow him*q* for myself in
the land.
And I will have pity on
Lo-ruhamah,*r*
and I will say to Lo-ammi,*s* "You
are my people";
and he shall say, "You are my
God."

Further Assurances of God's Redeeming Love

3 The LORD said to me again, "Go, love a woman who has a lover and is an adulteress, just as the LORD loves the people of Israel, though they turn to other gods and love raisin cakes." **2**So I bought her for fifteen shekels of silver and a homer of barley and a measure of wine.*t* **3**And I said to her, "You must remain as mine for many days; you shall not play the whore, you shall not have intercourse with a man, nor I with you." **4**For the Israelites shall remain many days without king or prince, without sacrifice or pillar, without ephod or teraphim. **5**Afterward the Israelites shall return and seek the LORD their God, and David their king; they shall come in awe to the LORD and to his goodness in the latter days.

God Accuses Israel

4 Hear the word of the LORD,
O people of Israel;
for the LORD has an indictment
against the inhabitants of the
land.
There is no faithfulness or loyalty,
and no knowledge of God in the
land.
2 Swearing, lying, and murder,
and stealing and adultery break
out;
bloodshed follows bloodshed.
3 Therefore the land mourns,
and all who live in it languish;
together with the wild animals
and the birds of the air,
even the fish of the sea are
perishing.

4 Yet let no one contend,
and let none accuse,
for with you is my contention,
O priest.*u*
5 You shall stumble by day;
the prophet also shall stumble
with you by night,
and I will destroy your mother.
6 My people are destroyed for lack of
knowledge;
because you have rejected
knowledge,
I reject you from being a priest to
me.
And since you have forgotten the
law of your God,
I also will forget your children.

7 The more they increased,
the more they sinned against me;
they changed*v* their glory into
shame.
8 They feed on the sin of my people;
they are greedy for their iniquity.
9 And it shall be like people, like
priest;
I will punish them for their ways,
and repay them for their deeds.
10 They shall eat, but not be satisfied;
they shall play the whore, but
not multiply;
because they have forsaken the
LORD

---

m That is, *"My master"*   *n* Heb *them*   *o* Heb *break*   *p* That is *God sows*   *q* Cn: Heb *her*
r That is *Not pitied*   *s* That is *Not my people*   *t* Gk: Heb *a homer of barley and a lethech of barley*
u Cn: Meaning of Heb uncertain   *v* Ancient Heb tradition: MT *I will change*

to devote themselves to [11]whoredom.

The Idolatry of Israel

Wine and new wine
  take away the understanding.
12 My people consult a piece of wood,
    and their divining rod gives them
      oracles.
  For a spirit of whoredom has led
    them astray,
    and they have played the whore,
      forsaking their God.
13 They sacrifice on the tops of the
      mountains,
    and make offerings upon the
      hills,

under oak, poplar, and terebinth,
  because their shade is good.

Therefore your daughters play the
    whore,
  and your daughters-in-law
    commit adultery.
14 I will not punish your daughters
    when they play the whore,
  nor your daughters-in-law when
    they commit adultery;
  for the men themselves go aside
    with whores,
    and sacrifice with temple
      prostitutes;
  thus a people without
    understanding comes to ruin.

FRIDAY

SENSITIVE SENSES
F. B. Meyer

VERSE: Hosea 4.6   **PASSAGE:** Hosea 4.4–9

ost of us never use our spiritual sense. God has given us a nose to smell with, eyes to see with, hands to feel with, a tongue to taste with. We are made in three parts—body, soul, and spirit. The soul has senses equivalent to those of the body, and the spirit behind that has a third set of senses that an unregenerate man has not commenced to use. But if you are a spiritual man you will use these spiritual senses to discriminate the thoughts as they come to your heart. "By reason of use" you will have your senses exercised to discern both good and evil . . .

If you live in the midst of bad people, bad books, and bad things, you lose your power of detecting bad thoughts when they come teeming about you like microbes. But if every day you spend an hour on God's mountains or upon the broad sea of the Bible, and get some of God's accurate senses into you, you will be able to detect things which are wrong that other people, even Christians, pass without seeing as wrong.

ADDITIONAL SCRIPTURE READING:
Psalm 119.105; Hebrews 4.12

Go to page 1024 for your next devotional reading.

1700   1900

15 Though you play the whore,
        O Israel,
    do not let Judah become guilty.
    Do not enter into Gilgal,
        or go up to Beth-aven,
        and do not swear, "As the LORD
            lives."
16 Like a stubborn heifer,
        Israel is stubborn;
    can the LORD now feed them
        like a lamb in a broad pasture?

17 Ephraim is joined to idols—
        let him alone.
18 When their drinking is ended, they
            indulge in sexual orgies;
        they love lewdness more than
            their glory.w
19 A wind has wrapped themx in its
            wings,
        and they shall be ashamed
            because of their altars.y

Impending Judgment on Israel and Judah

5 Hear this, O priests!
    Give heed, O house of Israel!
    Listen, O house of the king!
        For the judgment pertains to you;
    for you have been a snare at
            Mizpah,
        and a net spread upon Tabor,
2 and a pit dug deep in Shittim;z
        but I will punish all of them.

3 I know Ephraim,
        and Israel is not hidden from me;
    for now, O Ephraim, you have
            played the whore;
        Israel is defiled.
4 Their deeds do not permit them
        to return to their God.
    For the spirit of whoredom is
            within them,
        and they do not know the LORD.

5 Israel's pride testifies against him;
    Ephraima stumbles in his guilt;
        Judah also stumbles with them.
6 With their flocks and herds they
            shall go
        to seek the LORD,
    but they will not find him;

        he has withdrawn from them.
7 They have dealt faithlessly with
            the LORD;
        for they have borne illegitimate
            children.
    Now the new moon shall devour
        them along with their fields.

8 Blow the horn in Gibeah,
        the trumpet in Ramah.
    Sound the alarm at Beth-aven;
        look behind you, Benjamin!
9 Ephraim shall become a desolation
        in the day of punishment;
    among the tribes of Israel
        I declare what is sure.
10 The princes of Judah have become
        like those who remove the
            landmark;
    on them I will pour out
        my wrath like water.
11 Ephraim is oppressed, crushed in
            judgment,
        because he was determined to go
            after vanity.b
12 Therefore I am like maggots to
            Ephraim,
        and like rottenness to the house
            of Judah.
13 When Ephraim saw his sickness,
        and Judah his wound,
    then Ephraim went to Assyria,
        and sent to the great king.c
    But he is not able to cure you
        or heal your wound.
14 For I will be like a lion to Ephraim,
        and like a young lion to the
            house of Judah.
    I myself will tear and go away;
        I will carry off, and no one shall
            rescue.
15 I will return again to my place
        until they acknowledge their
            guilt and seek my face.
    In their distress they will beg my
        favor:

A Call to Repentance

6 "Come, let us return to the
            LORD;
        for it is he who has torn, and he
            will heal us;

---

w Cn Compare Gk: Meaning of Heb uncertain   x Heb *her*   y Gk Syr: Heb *sacrifices*
z Cn: Meaning of Heb uncertain   a Heb *Israel and Ephraim*   b Gk: Meaning of Heb uncertain
c Cn: Heb *to a king who will contend*

he has struck down, and he will
bind us up.
2 After two days he will revive us;
on the third day he will raise us
up,
that we may live before him.
3 Let us know, let us press on to
know the LORD;
his appearing is as sure as the
dawn;
he will come to us like the
showers,
like the spring rains that water
the earth."

Impenitence of Israel and Judah

4 What shall I do with you,
O Ephraim?
What shall I do with you,
O Judah?
Your love is like a morning cloud,
like the dew that goes away
early.
5 Therefore I have hewn them by the
prophets,
I have killed them by the words
of my mouth,
and my*d* judgment goes forth as
the light.
6 For I desire steadfast love and not
sacrifice,
the knowledge of God rather
than burnt offerings.

7 But at*e* Adam they transgressed the
covenant;
there they dealt faithlessly with
me.
8 Gilead is a city of evildoers,
tracked with blood.
9 As robbers lie in wait*f* for someone,
so the priests are banded
together;*g*
they murder on the road to
Shechem,
they commit a monstrous crime.
10 In the house of Israel I have seen a
horrible thing;
Ephraim's whoredom is there,
Israel is defiled.

11 For you also, O Judah, a harvest is
appointed.

When I would restore the fortunes
of my people,

7 ¹when I would heal Israel,
the corruption of Ephraim is
revealed,
and the wicked deeds of Samaria;
for they deal falsely,
the thief breaks in,
and the bandits raid outside.
2 But they do not consider
that I remember all their
wickedness.
Now their deeds surround them,
they are before my face.
3 By their wickedness they make the
king glad,
and the officials by their treachery.
4 They are all adulterers;
they are like a heated oven,
whose baker does not need to stir
the fire,
from the kneading of the dough
until it is leavened.
5 On the day of our king the officials
became sick with the heat of
wine;
he stretched out his hand with
mockers.
6 For they are kindled*h* like an oven,
their heart burns within
them;
all night their anger smolders;
in the morning it blazes like a
flaming fire.
7 All of them are hot as an oven,
and they devour their rulers.
All their kings have fallen;
none of them calls upon me.

8 Ephraim mixes himself with the
peoples;
Ephraim is a cake not turned.
9 Foreigners devour his strength,
but he does not know it;
gray hairs are sprinkled upon him,
but he does not know it.
10 Israel's pride testifies against*i* him;
yet they do not return to the
LORD their God,
or seek him, for all this.

Futile Reliance on the Nations

11 Ephraim has become like a dove,
silly and without sense;

---

d Gk Syr: Heb *your*   *e* Cn: Heb *like*   *f* Cn: Meaning of Heb uncertain   *g* Syr Heb *are a company*
h Gk Syr: Heb *brought near*   *i* Or *humbles*

WEEKEND

DEWDROP CHRISTIANITY
Horatius Bonar

VERSE: Hosea 6.4   **PASSAGE:** Hosea 6.1–6

 here is some danger of falling into a soft Christianity, under the plea of a lofty and ethereal theology. Christianity was born for endurance; it is not an exotic, but a hardy plant, braced by the keen wind; not languid, nor childish, nor cowardly. It walks with strong step and erect frame; it is kindly, but firm; it is gentle, but honest; it is calm, but not facile; decided, but not churlish. It does not fear to speak the stern word of condemnation against error, nor to raise its voice against surrounding evils, knowing that it is not of this world. It does not shrink from giving honest reproof, lest it come under the charge of displaying an unchristian spirit . . . The religion of both Old and New Testament is marked by fervent outspoken testimonies against evil. To speak smooth things in such a case may be sentimentalism, but it is not Christianity. It is a betrayal of the cause of truth and righteousness.

If anyone should be frank, manly, honest, cheerful (I do not say blunt or rude, for a Christian must be courteous and polite), it is he who has tasted that the Lord is gracious.

ADDITIONAL SCRIPTURE READING:
Hosea 13.3; Luke 8.13–15

Go to page 1029 for your next devotional reading.

1700   1900

they call upon Egypt, they go to
Assyria.
12 As they go, I will cast my net over
them;
I will bring them down like birds
of the air;
I will discipline them according
to the report made to their
assembly.*j*

13 Woe to them, for they have strayed
from me!
Destruction to them, for they
have rebelled against me!
I would redeem them,
but they speak lies against me.

14 They do not cry to me from the
heart,
but they wail upon their beds;
they gash themselves for grain and
wine;
they rebel against me.
15 It was I who trained and
strengthened their arms,
yet they plot evil against me.
16 They turn to that which does not
profit;*k*
they have become like a
defective bow;
their officials shall fall by the
sword
because of the rage of their
tongue.
So much for their babbling in the
land of Egypt.

Israel's Apostasy

8 Set the trumpet to your lips!
One like a vulture*j* is over the
house of the LORD,
because they have broken my
covenant,
and transgressed my law.
2 Israel cries to me,
"My God, we—Israel—know
you!"
3 Israel has spurned the good;
the enemy shall pursue him.

4 They made kings, but not through
me;
they set up princes, but without
my knowledge.
With their silver and gold they
made idols

for their own destruction.
5 Your calf is rejected, O Samaria.
My anger burns against them.
How long will they be incapable of
innocence?
6 For it is from Israel,
an artisan made it;
it is not God.
The calf of Samaria
shall be broken to pieces.*l*

7 For they sow the wind,
and they shall reap the
whirlwind.
The standing grain has no heads,
it shall yield no meal;
if it were to yield,
foreigners would devour it.
8 Israel is swallowed up;
now they are among the nations
as a useless vessel.
9 For they have gone up to Assyria,
a wild ass wandering alone;
Ephraim has bargained for lovers.
10 Though they bargain with the
nations,
I will now gather them up.
They shall soon writhe
under the burden of kings and
princes.

11 When Ephraim multiplied altars to
expiate sin,
they became to him altars for
sinning.
12 Though I write for him the
multitude of my
instructions,
they are regarded as a strange
thing.
13 Though they offer choice
sacrifices,*k*
though they eat flesh,
the LORD does not accept them.
Now he will remember their
iniquity,
and punish their sins;
they shall return to Egypt.
14 Israel has forgotten his Maker,
and built palaces;
and Judah has multiplied fortified
cities;
but I will send a fire upon his
cities,

---

j Meaning of Heb uncertain   *k* Cn: Meaning of Heb uncertain   *l* Or *shall go up in flames*

and it shall devour his
    strongholds.

Punishment for Israel's Sin

9 Do not rejoice, O Israel!
    Do not exult[m] as other nations
        do;
    for you have played the whore,
        departing from your God.
    You have loved a prostitute's pay
        on all threshing floors.
2   Threshing floor and wine vat shall
        not feed them,
    and the new wine shall fail them.
3   They shall not remain in the land
        of the Lord;
    but Ephraim shall return to Egypt,
    and in Assyria they shall eat
        unclean food.

4   They shall not pour drink offerings
        of wine to the Lord,
    and their sacrifices shall not
        please him.
    Such sacrifices shall be like
        mourners' bread;
    all who eat of it shall be defiled;
    for their bread shall be for their
        hunger only;
    it shall not come to the house of
        the Lord.

5   What will you do on the day of
        appointed festival,
    and on the day of the festival of
        the Lord?
6   For even if they escape destruction,
    Egypt shall gather them,
    Memphis shall bury them.
    Nettles shall possess their precious
        things of silver;[n]
    thorns shall be in their tents.

7   The days of punishment have come,
    the days of recompense have
        come;
    Israel cries,[o]
    "The prophet is a fool,
        the man of the spirit is mad!"
    Because of your great iniquity,
        your hostility is great.
8   The prophet is a sentinel for my
        God over Ephraim,
    yet a fowler's snare is on all his
        ways,

and hostility in the house of his
    God.
9   They have deeply corrupted
        themselves
    as in the days of Gibeah;
    he will remember their iniquity,
    he will punish their sins.

10 Like grapes in the wilderness,
        I found Israel.
    Like the first fruit on the fig tree,
        in its first season,
    I saw your ancestors.
    But they came to Baal-peor,
        and consecrated themselves to a
            thing of shame,
    and became detestable like the
        thing they loved.
11 Ephraim's glory shall fly away like
        a bird—
    no birth, no pregnancy, no
        conception!
12 Even if they bring up children,
    I will bereave them until no one
        is left.
    Woe to them indeed
        when I depart from them!
13 Once I saw Ephraim as a young
        palm planted in a lovely
            meadow,[n]
    but now Ephraim must lead out
        his children for slaughter.
14 Give them, O Lord—
        what will you give?
    Give them a miscarrying womb
        and dry breasts.

15 Every evil of theirs began at Gilgal;
        there I came to hate them.
    Because of the wickedness of their
        deeds
    I will drive them out of my
        house.
    I will love them no more;
        all their officials are rebels.

16 Ephraim is stricken,
        their root is dried up,
        they shall bear no fruit.
    Even though they give birth,
        I will kill the cherished offspring
            of their womb.
17 Because they have not listened to
        him,
    my God will reject them;

m Gk: Heb *To exultation*   n Meaning of Heb uncertain   o Cn Compare Gk: Heb *shall know*

they shall become wanderers
among the nations.

Israel's Sin and Captivity

10 Israel is a luxuriant vine
that yields its fruit.
The more his fruit increased
the more altars he built;
as his country improved,
he improved his pillars.
2 Their heart is false;
now they must bear their guilt.
The LORD[p] will break down their
altars,
and destroy their pillars.

3 For now they will say:
"We have no king,
for we do not fear the LORD,
and a king—what could he do for
us?"
4 They utter mere words;
with empty oaths they make
covenants;
so litigation springs up like
poisonous weeds
in the furrows of the field.
5 The inhabitants of Samaria tremble
for the calf[q] of Beth-aven.
Its people shall mourn for it,
and its idolatrous priests shall
wail[r] over it,
over its glory that has departed
from it.
6 The thing itself shall be carried to
Assyria
as tribute to the great king.[s]
Ephraim shall be put to shame,
and Israel shall be ashamed of his
idol.[t]

7 Samaria's king shall perish
like a chip on the face of the
waters.
8 The high places of Aven, the sin of
Israel,
shall be destroyed.
Thorn and thistle shall grow up
on their altars.
They shall say to the mountains,
Cover us,
and to the hills, Fall on us.

9 Since the days of Gibeah you have
sinned, O Israel;
there they have continued.
Shall not war overtake them in
Gibeah?
10 I will come[u] against the wayward
people to punish them;
and nations shall be gathered
against them
when they are punished[v] for their
double iniquity.

11 Ephraim was a trained heifer
that loved to thresh,
and I spared her fair neck;
but I will make Ephraim break the
ground;
Judah must plow;
Jacob must harrow for himself.
12 Sow for yourselves righteousness;
reap steadfast love;
break up your fallow ground;
for it is time to seek the LORD,
that he may come and rain
righteousness upon you.

13 You have plowed wickedness,
you have reaped injustice,
you have eaten the fruit of lies.
Because you have trusted in your
power
and in the multitude of your
warriors,
14 therefore the tumult of war shall
rise against your people,
and all your fortresses shall be
destroyed,
as Shalman destroyed Beth-arbel on
the day of battle
when mothers were dashed in
pieces with their children.
15 Thus it shall be done to you,
O Bethel,
because of your great wickedness.
At dawn the king of Israel
shall be utterly cut off.

God's Compassion Despite Israel's Ingratitude

11 When Israel was a child, I
loved him,
and out of Egypt I called my son.
2 The more I[w] called them,
the more they went from me;[x]

---

p Heb he   q Gk Syr: Heb calves   r Cn: Heb exult   s Cn: Heb to a king who will contend
t Cn: Heb counsel   u Cn Compare Gk: Heb In my desire   v Gk: Heb bound   w Gk: Heb they
x Gk: Heb them

they kept sacrificing to the Baals,
　and offering incense to idols.

3　Yet it was I who taught Ephraim to
　　walk,
　　I took them up in my[y] arms;
　but they did not know that I
　　healed them.
4　I led them with cords of human
　　kindness,
　　with bands of love.
　I was to them like those
　who lift infants to their cheeks.[z]
　I bent down to them and fed
　　them.

5　They shall return to the land of
　　Egypt,
　　and Assyria shall be their king,
　because they have refused to
　　return to me.
6　The sword rages in their cities,
　　it consumes their oracle-priests,
　　and devours because of their
　　schemes.
7　My people are bent on turning
　　away from me.
　　To the Most High they call,
　but he does not raise them up at
　　all.[a]

8　How can I give you up, Ephraim?
　　How can I hand you over,
　　　O Israel?
　How can I make you like Admah?
　　How can I treat you like Zeboiim?
　My heart recoils within me;
　　my compassion grows warm and
　　　tender.
9　I will not execute my fierce anger;
　　I will not again destroy Ephraim;
　for I am God and no mortal,
　　the Holy One in your midst,
　and I will not come in wrath.[a]

10　They shall go after the LORD,
　　who roars like a lion;
　when he roars,
　　his children shall come
　　　trembling from the west.
11　They shall come trembling like
　　　birds from Egypt,
　　and like doves from the land of
　　　Assyria;

and I will return them to their
　homes, says the LORD.

12b　Ephraim has surrounded me with
　　lies,
　　and the house of Israel with
　　　deceit;
　but Judah still walks[c] with God,
　　and is faithful to the Holy One.

12　Ephraim herds the wind,
　　and pursues the east wind all
　　　day long;
　they multiply falsehood and
　　violence;
　they make a treaty with
　　Assyria,
　and oil is carried to Egypt.

The Long History of Rebellion

2　The LORD has an indictment
　　against Judah,
　　and will punish Jacob according
　　　to his ways,
　and repay him according to his
　　deeds.
3　In the womb he tried to supplant
　　his brother,
　　and in his manhood he strove
　　　with God.
4　He strove with the angel and
　　prevailed,
　　he wept and sought his favor;
　he met him at Bethel,
　　and there he spoke with him.[d]
5　The LORD the God of hosts,
　　the LORD is his name!
6　But as for you, return to your God,
　　hold fast to love and justice,
　　and wait continually for your
　　　God.

7　A trader, in whose hands are false
　　balances,
　　he loves to oppress.
8　Ephraim has said, "Ah, I am rich,
　　I have gained wealth for myself;
　in all of my gain
　　no offense has been found in me
　　that would be sin."[a]
9　I am the LORD your God
　　from the land of Egypt;
　I will make you live in tents again,
　　as in the days of the appointed
　　　festival.

y　Gk Syr Vg: Heb his　　z　Or who ease the yoke on their jaws　　a　Meaning of Heb uncertain
b　Ch 12.1 in Heb　　c　Heb roams or rules　　d　Gk Syr: Heb us

10 I spoke to the prophets;
    it was I who multiplied visions,
    and through the prophets I will
        bring destruction.
11 In Gilead[e] there is iniquity,
    they shall surely come to
        nothing.
    In Gilgal they sacrifice bulls,
        so their altars shall be like stone
            heaps
        on the furrows of the field.
12 Jacob fled to the land of Aram,
    there Israel served for a wife,
    and for a wife he guarded sheep.[f]

e Compare Syr: Heb *Gilead*   f Heb lacks *sheep*

13 By a prophet the LORD brought
        Israel up from Egypt,
    and by a prophet he was guarded.
14 Ephraim has given bitter offense,
        so his Lord will bring his crimes
            down on him
        and pay him back for his insults.

Relentless Judgment on Israel

 13 When Ephraim spoke, there
            was trembling;
    he was exalted in Israel;
    but he incurred guilt through
        Baal and died.

MONDAY

THE DEPTHS OF HUMAN NATURE
Francis Schaeffer

VERSE: Hosea 12.8   PASSAGE: Hosea 11.12—12.8

The more the Holy Spirit puts his finger on my life and goes down deep into my life, the more I understand that there are deep wells to my nature. Modern psychology has dealt with these under the terms unconscious and subconscious, and though the philosophy behind modern psychology is often fundamentally wrong, surely it is right in pointing out that we are more than merely that which is on the surface. We are like the iceberg: one-tenth above and nine-tenths below. It is a very, very simple thing to fool ourselves, and that is why we must question this word "known." If I say I can have freedom from all "known" sin, surely I must acknowledge the meaningfulness of the question: *What do I know?* Until I can describe what I know, I cannot go on meaningfully to ask whether I can have freedom from "known" sin. As the Holy Spirit has wrestled with me down through the years, more and more I am aware of the depths of my own nature, and the depths of the results of that awful fall in the Garden of Eden. Man is separated from him.

ADDITIONAL SCRIPTURE READING:
Deuteronomy 8.17–18; Luke 16.15; Romans 8.26–27

Go to page 1031 for your next devotional reading.

1900   Present

2 And now they keep on sinning
  and make a cast image for
    themselves,
  idols of silver made according to
    their understanding,
  all of them the work of artisans.
  "Sacrifice to these," they say.g
  People are kissing calves!
3 Therefore they shall be like the
    morning mist
  or like the dew that goes away
    early,
  like chaff that swirls from the
    threshing floor
  or like smoke from a window.

4 Yet I have been the LORD your God
    ever since the land of Egypt;
  you know no God but me,
    and besides me there is no savior.
5 It was I who fedh you in the
    wilderness,
  in the land of drought.
6 When I fedi them, they were
    satisfied;
  they were satisfied, and their
    heart was proud;
  therefore they forgot me.
7 So I will become like a lion to
    them,
  like a leopard I will lurk beside
    the way.
8 I will fall upon them like a bear
    robbed of her cubs,
  and will tear open the covering of
    their heart;
  there I will devour them like a lion,
    as a wild animal would mangle
      them.

9 I will destroy you, O Israel;
    who can help you?j
10 Where now isk your king, that he
    may save you?
  Where in all your cities are your
    rulers,
  of whom you said,
    "Give me a king and rulers"?
11 I gave you a king in my anger,
    and I took him away in my wrath.

12 Ephraim's iniquity is bound up;
    his sin is kept in store.

13 The pangs of childbirth come for
    him,
  but he is an unwise son;
  for at the proper time he does not
    present himself
  at the mouth of the womb.

14 Shall I ransom them from the
    power of Sheol?
  Shall I redeem them from Death?
  O Death, where arel your plagues?
  O Sheol, where isl your
    destruction?
  Compassion is hidden from my
    eyes.

15 Although he may flourish among
    rushes,m
  the east wind shall come, a blast
    from the LORD,
  rising from the wilderness;
  and his fountain shall dry up,
    his spring shall be parched.
  It shall strip his treasury
    of every precious thing.
16n Samaria shall bear her guilt,
  because she has rebelled against
    her God;
  they shall fall by the sword,
    their little ones shall be dashed
      in pieces,
  and their pregnant women ripped
    open.

A Plea for Repentance

14 Return, O Israel, to the LORD
    your God,
  for you have stumbled because of
    your iniquity.
2 Take words with you
    and return to the LORD;
  say to him,
    "Take away all guilt;
  accept that which is good,
    and we will offer
  the fruito of our lips.
3 Assyria shall not save us;
  we will not ride upon horses;
  we will say no more, 'Our God,'
    to the work of our hands.
  In you the orphan finds mercy."

g Cn Compare Gk: Heb To these they say sacrifices of people   h Gk Syr: Heb knew   i Cn: Heb
according to their pasture   j Gk Syr: Heb for in me is your help   k Gk Syr Vg: Heb I will be
l Gk Syr: Heb I will be   m Or among brothers   n Ch 14.1 in Heb   o Gk Syr: Heb bulls

Assurance of Forgiveness

4 I will heal their disloyalty;
  I will love them freely,
     for my anger has turned from
     them.
5 I will be like the dew to Israel;
     he shall blossom like the lily,
     he shall strike root like the
        forests of Lebanon.*p*

6 His shoots shall spread out;
     his beauty shall be like the olive
        tree,
     and his fragrance like that of
        Lebanon.
7 They shall again live beneath my*q*
        shadow,
     they shall flourish as a garden;*r*
     they shall blossom like the vine,

p Cn: Heb *like Lebanon*   q Heb *his*   r Cn: Heb *they shall grow grain*

TUESDAY

GOD LOVES THE BACKSLIDER
Dwight L. Moody

VERSE: Hosea 14.4   **PASSAGE:** Hosea 14

 backslider came into the inquiry room night before last, and I was trying to tell him God loved him. He would hardly believe me. He thought because he had not kept up his love and faithfulness to God, and to his own vows, that God had stopped loving him.

Now, it says in John 13.1, "He loved them to the end," that is, his love was unchangeable. You may have forgotten him and betrayed him and denied him, but nevertheless, he loves you; he loves the backslider. There is not a man here who has wandered from God and betrayed him but what the Lord Jesus loves him and wants him to come back.

Now, in Hosea 14.4, God says that he will heal every backslider. "I will love them freely." So the Lord tells the backsliders, "If you will only come back to me, I will forgive you." It was thus with Peter who denied his Lord. The Savior forgave him and sent him to preach his glorious gospel on the day of Pentecost when 3,000 were won to Christ under one sermon of a backslider (see John 18.25–27; 21.15–19; Acts 2.14–39).

Don't let a backslider go out of this hall this evening with such hard talk about the Lord. No backslider can say God has left him. He may think so, but it is one of the devil's lies. The Lord has never left a man yet.

ADDITIONAL SCRIPTURE READING:
Isaiah 57.18; Jeremiah 3.22; 17.14

Go to page 1036 for your next devotional reading.

1900   Present

their fragrance shall be like the
     wine of Lebanon.

8   O Ephraim, what have I^s to do with
     idols?
   It is I who answer and look after
     you.^t
  I am like an evergreen cypress;
     your faithfulness^u comes from me.

9   Those who are wise understand
     these things;
   those who are discerning know
     them.
  For the ways of the LORD are
     right,
   and the upright walk in them,
   but transgressors stumble in
     them.

---

s Or *What more has Ephraim*   *t* Heb *him*   *u* Heb *your fruit*

JOEL

HE PROPHET JOEL URGED THE PEOPLE
OF JUDAH TO TURN AGAIN TO GOD
AND WARNED THEM THAT JUDGMENT
WAS AT HAND. HE DESCRIBED THIS JUDGMENT
AS "THE GREAT AND TERRIBLE DAY OF THE
LORD" (2.31). HE WARNED THAT THE DAY OF
PUNISHMENT WOULD COME NOT ONLY ON
OTHER NATIONS, BUT ON UNFAITHFUL ISRAEL AS
WELL, AND HE CALLED UPON EVERYONE TO
REPENT. AS YOU READ THE BOOK OF JOEL, YOU
WILL SEE GOD'S INTENSE DESIRE FOR INTIMACY
WITH ALL OF HIS PEOPLE.

1

The word of the LORD that
came to Joel son of Pethuel:

Lament over the Ruin of the Country

2 Hear this, O elders,
   give ear, all inhabitants of the
      land!
   Has such a thing happened in your
      days,
   or in the days of your ancestors?
3 Tell your children of it,
   and let your children tell their
      children,
   and their children another
      generation.

4 What the cutting locust left,
   the swarming locust has eaten.
   What the swarming locust left,
   the hopping locust has eaten,

and what the hopping locust left,
   the destroying locust has eaten.

5 Wake up, you drunkards, and weep;
   and wail, all you wine-drinkers,
over the sweet wine,
   for it is cut off from your mouth.
6 For a nation has invaded my land,
   powerful and innumerable;
its teeth are lions' teeth,
   and it has the fangs of a lioness.
7 It has laid waste my vines,
   and splintered my fig trees;
it has stripped off their bark and
      thrown it down;
   their branches have turned white.

8 Lament like a virgin dressed in
      sackcloth
   for the husband of her youth.

9 The grain offering and the drink
        offering are cut off
    from the house of the LORD.
    The priests mourn,
        the ministers of the LORD.
10 The fields are devastated,
        the ground mourns;
    for the grain is destroyed,
        the wine dries up,
        the oil fails.

11 Be dismayed, you farmers,
        wail, you vinedressers,
    over the wheat and the barley;
        for the crops of the field are
            ruined.
12 The vine withers,
        the fig tree droops.
    Pomegranate, palm, and apple—
        all the trees of the field are dried
            up;
    surely, joy withers away
        among the people.

A Call to Repentance and Prayer

13 Put on sackcloth and lament, you
        priests;
    wail, you ministers of the altar.
    Come, pass the night in sackcloth,
        you ministers of my God!
    Grain offering and drink offering
        are withheld from the house of
            your God.

14 Sanctify a fast,
        call a solemn assembly.
    Gather the elders
        and all the inhabitants of the land
    to the house of the LORD your God,
        and cry out to the LORD.

15 Alas for the day!
    For the day of the LORD is near,
        and as destruction from the
            Almighty[a] it comes.
16 Is not the food cut off
        before our eyes,
    joy and gladness
        from the house of our God?

17 The seed shrivels under the clods,[b]
        the storehouses are desolate;
    the granaries are ruined
        because the grain has failed.

18 How the animals groan!
    The herds of cattle wander about
    because there is no pasture for them;
        even the flocks of sheep are
            dazed.[c]

19 To you, O LORD, I cry.
    For fire has devoured
        the pastures of the wilderness,
    and flames have burned
        all the trees of the field.
20 Even the wild animals cry to you
        because the watercourses are
            dried up,
    and fire has devoured
        the pastures of the wilderness.

2 Blow the trumpet in Zion;
        sound the alarm on my holy
            mountain!
    Let all the inhabitants of the land
        tremble,
    for the day of the LORD is
        coming, it is near—
2 a day of darkness and gloom,
        a day of clouds and thick
            darkness!
    Like blackness spread upon the
        mountains
    a great and powerful army comes;
    their like has never been from of old,
        nor will be again after them
        in ages to come.

3 Fire devours in front of them,
        and behind them a flame burns.
    Before them the land is like the
        garden of Eden,
        but after them a desolate
            wilderness,
        and nothing escapes them.

4 They have the appearance of horses,
        and like war-horses they charge.
5 As with the rumbling of chariots,
        they leap on the tops of the
            mountains,
    like the crackling of a flame of fire
        devouring the stubble,
    like a powerful army
        drawn up for battle.

6 Before them peoples are in anguish,
        all faces grow pale.[b]

---

a Traditional rendering of Heb *Shaddai*   b Meaning of Heb uncertain   c Compare Gk Syr Vg:
Meaning of Heb uncertain

7 Like warriors they charge,
   like soldiers they scale the wall.
  Each keeps to its own course,
   they do not swerve from[d] their
    paths.
8 They do not jostle one another,
   each keeps to its own track;
  they burst through the weapons
   and are not halted.
9 They leap upon the city,
   they run upon the walls;
  they climb up into the houses,
   they enter through the windows
    like a thief.

10 The earth quakes before them,
    the heavens tremble.
   The sun and the moon are
    darkened,
    and the stars withdraw their
     shining.
11 The LORD utters his voice
    at the head of his army;
   how vast is his host!
    Numberless are those who obey
     his command.
   Truly the day of the LORD is great;
    terrible indeed—who can endure
     it?

12 Yet even now, says the LORD,
    return to me with all your heart,
   with fasting, with weeping, and
    with mourning;
13 rend your hearts and not your
    clothing.
   Return to the LORD, your God,
    for he is gracious and merciful,
   slow to anger, and abounding in
    steadfast love,
    and relents from punishing.
14 Who knows whether he will not
    turn and relent,
    and leave a blessing behind him,
   a grain offering and a drink offering
    for the LORD, your God?

15 Blow the trumpet in Zion;
    sanctify a fast;
   call a solemn assembly;
16 gather the people.
   Sanctify the congregation;
    assemble the aged;
   gather the children,
    even infants at the breast.

Let the bridegroom leave his room,
 and the bride her canopy.

17 Between the vestibule and the altar
    let the priests, the ministers of
     the LORD, weep.
   Let them say, "Spare your people,
    O LORD,
    and do not make your heritage a
     mockery,
    a byword among the nations.
   Why should it be said among the
     peoples,
    'Where is their God?' "

God's Response and Promise

18 Then the LORD became jealous for
     his land,
    and had pity on his people.
19 In response to his people the LORD
     said:
   I am sending you
    grain, wine, and oil,
    and you will be satisfied;
   and I will no more make you
    a mockery among the nations.

20 I will remove the northern army far
     from you,
    and drive it into a parched and
     desolate land,
   its front into the eastern sea,
    and its rear into the western sea;
   its stench and foul smell will rise up.
    Surely he has done great things!

21 Do not fear, O soil;
    be glad and rejoice,
    for the LORD has done great things!
22 Do not fear, you animals of the
     field,
    for the pastures of the wilderness
     are green;
   the tree bears its fruit,
    the fig tree and vine give their
     full yield.

23 O children of Zion, be glad
    and rejoice in the LORD your God;
   for he has given the early rain[e] for
     your vindication,
   he has poured down for you
    abundant rain,
    the early and the later rain, as
     before.

24 The threshing floors shall be full of
grain,
 the vats shall overflow with wine
and oil.

25 I will repay you for the years
 that the swarming locust has
eaten,
the hopper, the destroyer, and the
cutter,
 my great army, which I sent
against you.

26 You shall eat in plenty and be
satisfied,
 and praise the name of the LORD
your God,
 who has dealt wondrously with
you.
And my people shall never again be
put to shame.

27 You shall know that I am in the
midst of Israel,
 and that I, the LORD, am your
God and there is no other.

WEDNESDAY

WHEN THE AUTHOR WALKS ON THE STAGE
C. S. Lewis

VERSE: Joel 2.11   **PASSAGE:** Joel 2.1–11

 wonder whether people who ask God to interfere openly and directly in our world quite realize what it will be like when he does. When that happens, it is the end of the world. When the author walks on to the stage the play is over. God is going to invade, all right: but what is the good of saying you are on his side then, when you see the whole natural universe melting away like a dream and something else—something it never entered your head to conceive—comes crashing in; something so beautiful to some of us and so terrible to others that none of us will have any choice left? For this time it will be God without disguise; something so overwhelming that it will strike either irresistible love or irresistible horror into every creature. It will be too late then to choose your side. There is no use saying you choose to lie down when it has become impossible to stand up. That will not be the time for choosing: it will be the time when we discover which side we really have chosen, whether we realized it before or not. Now, today, this moment, is our chance to choose the right side. God is holding back to give us that chance. It will not last for ever. We must take it or leave it.

ADDITIONAL SCRIPTURE READING:
Isaiah 49.8; 2 Corinthians 6.2; Hebrews 4.7

Go to page 1044 for your next devotional reading.

1900 Present

And my people shall never again be
    put to shame.

God's Spirit Poured Out

28ᶠ Then afterward
    I will pour out my spirit on all
       flesh;
    your sons and your daughters shall
       prophesy,
       your old men shall dream dreams,
       and your young men shall see
         visions.
29 Even on the male and female slaves,
      in those days, I will pour out my
        spirit.

30 I will show portents in the heavens
and on the earth, blood and fire and
columns of smoke. 31The sun shall be
turned to darkness, and the moon to
blood, before the great and terrible day of
the LORD comes. 32Then everyone who
calls on the name of the LORD shall be
saved; for in Mount Zion and in Jerusalem there shall be those who escape, as
the LORD has said, and among the survivors shall be those whom the LORD
calls.

3 g For then, in those days and at
that time, when I restore the
fortunes of Judah and Jerusalem, 2I will
gather all the nations and bring them
down to the valley of Jehoshaphat, and I
will enter into judgment with them
there, on account of my people and my
heritage Israel, because they have scattered them among the nations. They
have divided my land, 3and cast lots for
my people, and traded boys for prostitutes, and sold girls for wine, and drunk
it down.

4 What are you to me, O Tyre and
Sidon, and all the regions of Philistia? Are
you paying me back for something? If
you are paying me back, I will turn your
deeds back upon your own heads swiftly
and speedily. 5For you have taken my silver and my gold, and have carried my
rich treasures into your temples.ʰ 6You
have sold the people of Judah and Jerusalem to the Greeks, removing them far
from their own border. 7But now I will
rouse them to leave the places to which
you have sold them, and I will turn your

deeds back upon your own heads. 8I will
sell your sons and your daughters into
the hand of the people of Judah, and they
will sell them to the Sabeans, to a nation
far away; for the LORD has spoken.

Judgment in the Valley of Jehoshaphat

9   Proclaim this among the nations:
    Prepare war,ⁱ
      stir up the warriors.
    Let all the soldiers draw near,
      let them come up.
10   Beat your plowshares into swords,
      and your pruning hooks into
        spears;
      let the weakling say, "I am a
        warrior."

11   Come quickly,ʲ
      all you nations all around,
      gather yourselves there.
    Bring down your warriors, O LORD.
12   Let the nations rouse themselves,
      and come up to the valley of
        Jehoshaphat;
    for there I will sit to judge
      all the neighboring nations.

13   Put in the sickle,
      for the harvest is ripe.
    Go in, tread,
      for the wine press is full.
    The vats overflow,
      for their wickedness is great.

14   Multitudes, multitudes,
      in the valley of decision!
    For the day of the LORD is near
      in the valley of decision.
15   The sun and the moon are darkened,
      and the stars withdraw their
        shining.

16   The LORD roars from Zion,
      and utters his voice from
        Jerusalem,
    and the heavens and the earth
        shake.
    But the LORD is a refuge for his
        people,
    a stronghold for the people of
        Israel.

f Ch 3.1 in Heb   g Ch 4.1 in Heb   h Or palaces   i Heb sanctify war   j Meaning of Heb
uncertain

The Glorious Future of Judah

17 So you shall know that I, the LORD
       your God,
    dwell in Zion, my holy
       mountain.
    And Jerusalem shall be holy,
       and strangers shall never again
       pass through it.

18 In that day
    the mountains shall drip sweet
       wine,
    the hills shall flow with milk,
    and all the stream beds of Judah
    shall flow with water;

a fountain shall come forth from
    the house of the LORD
and water the Wadi Shittim.

19 Egypt shall become a desolation
    and Edom a desolate wilderness,
    because of the violence done to the
       people of Judah,
    in whose land they have shed
       innocent blood.

20 But Judah shall be inhabited forever,
    and Jerusalem to all generations.

21 I will avenge their blood, and I will
       not clear the guilty,*k*
    for the LORD dwells in Zion.

k Gk Syr: Heb *I will hold innocent their blood that I have not held innocent*

AMOS

MOS, A SHEPHERD FROM THE SMALL TOWN OF TEKOA; WAS SENT TO ANNOUNCE GOD'S JUDGMENT ON THE NORTHERN KINGDOM OF ISRAEL. WITH STRONG POETIC IMAGERY, AMOS SPEAKS PASSIONATELY ABOUT GOD'S CONCERN FOR THE POOR AND URGES A RETURN TO RIGHTEOUSNESS AND JUSTICE. AS YOU READ THIS BOOK, LOOK FOR GOD'S PERSPECTIVE ON ISSUES OF SOCIAL JUSTICE, AND BE PREPARED TO RESPOND WITH A HEART OF COMPASSION.

1 The words of Amos, who was among the shepherds of Tekoa, which he saw concerning Israel in the days of King Uzziah of Judah and in the days of King Jeroboam son of Joash of Israel, two years[a] before the earthquake.

Judgment on Israel's Neighbors

2 And he said:

The LORD roars from Zion,
  and utters his voice from
    Jerusalem;
the pastures of the shepherds
    wither,
  and the top of Carmel dries up.

3 Thus says the LORD:
For three transgressions of
    Damascus,
and for four, I will not revoke the
    punishment;[b]
because they have threshed Gilead
    with threshing sledges of iron.
4 So I will send a fire on the house of
    Hazael,
  and it shall devour the
    strongholds of Ben-hadad.
5 I will break the gate bars of
    Damascus,
  and cut off the inhabitants from
    the Valley of Aven,
and the one who holds the scepter
    from Beth-eden;
  and the people of Aram shall go
    into exile to Kir,
                    says the LORD.

6 Thus says the LORD:

---

a Or *during two years*   b Heb *cause it to return*

For three transgressions of Gaza,
and for four, I will not revoke the
punishment;^c
because they carried into exile
entire communities,
to hand them over to Edom.
7 So I will send a fire on the wall of
Gaza,
fire that shall devour its
strongholds.
8 I will cut off the inhabitants from
Ashdod,
and the one who holds the
scepter from Ashkelon;
I will turn my hand against Ekron,
and the remnant of the
Philistines shall perish,
says the Lord GOD.

9 Thus says the LORD:
For three transgressions of Tyre,
and for four, I will not revoke the
punishment;^c
because they delivered entire
communities over to Edom,
and did not remember the
covenant of kinship.
10 So I will send a fire on the wall of
Tyre,
fire that shall devour its
strongholds.

11 Thus says the LORD:
For three transgressions of Edom,
and for four, I will not revoke the
punishment;^c
because he pursued his brother
with the sword
and cast off all pity;
he maintained his anger
perpetually,^d
and kept his wrath^e forever.
12 So I will send a fire on Teman,
and it shall devour the
strongholds of Bozrah.

13 Thus says the LORD:
For three transgressions of the
Ammonites,
and for four, I will not revoke the
punishment;^c
because they have ripped open
pregnant women in Gilead
in order to enlarge their territory.

14 So I will kindle a fire against the
wall of Rabbah,
fire that shall devour its
strongholds,
with shouting on the day of battle,
with a storm on the day of the
whirlwind;
15 then their king shall go into exile,
he and his officials together,
says the LORD.

2 Thus says the LORD:
For three transgressions of
Moab,
and for four, I will not revoke the
punishment;^c
because he burned to lime
the bones of the king of Edom.
2 So I will send a fire on Moab,
and it shall devour the
strongholds of Kerioth,
and Moab shall die amid uproar,
amid shouting and the sound of
the trumpet;
3 I will cut off the ruler from its midst,
and will kill all its officials with
him,
says the LORD.

Judgment on Judah

4 Thus says the LORD:
For three transgressions of Judah,
and for four, I will not revoke the
punishment;^c
because they have rejected the law
of the LORD,
and have not kept his statutes,
but they have been led astray by
the same lies
after which their ancestors
walked.
5 So I will send a fire on Judah,
and it shall devour the
strongholds of Jerusalem.

Judgment on Israel

6 Thus says the LORD:
For three transgressions of Israel,
and for four, I will not revoke the
punishment;^c
because they sell the righteous for
silver,
and the needy for a pair of
sandals—

c Heb cause it to return   d Syr Vg: Heb and his anger tore perpetually   e Gk Syr Vg: Heb and his
wrath kept

7 they who trample the head of the
    poor into the dust of the earth,
  and push the afflicted out of the
    way;
  father and son go in to the same
    girl,
  so that my holy name is
    profaned;
8 they lay themselves down beside
    every altar
  on garments taken in pledge;
  and in the house of their God they
    drink
  wine bought with fines they
    imposed.

9 Yet I destroyed the Amorite before
    them,
  whose height was like the height
    of cedars,
  and who was as strong as oaks;
  I destroyed his fruit above,
  and his roots beneath.
10 Also I brought you up out of the
    land of Egypt,
  and led you forty years in the
    wilderness,
  to possess the land of the
    Amorite.
11 And I raised up some of your
    children to be prophets
  and some of your youths to be
    nazirites.*f*
  Is it not indeed so, O people of
    Israel?
               says the LORD.

12 But you made the nazirites*f* drink
    wine,
  and commanded the prophets,
  saying, "You shall not prophesy."

13 So, I will press you down in your
    place,
  just as a cart presses down
  when it is full of sheaves.*g*
14 Flight shall perish from the swift,
  and the strong shall not retain
    their strength,
  nor shall the mighty save their
    lives;
15 those who handle the bow shall not
    stand,

  and those who are swift of foot
    shall not save themselves,
  nor shall those who ride horses
    save their lives;
16 and those who are stout of heart
    among the mighty
  shall flee away naked in that day,
            says the LORD.

Israel's Guilt and Punishment

3 Hear this word that the LORD
has spoken against you, O people of Israel, against the whole family
that I brought up out of the land of
Egypt:
2 You only have I known
  of all the families of the earth;
  therefore I will punish you
  for all your iniquities.

3 Do two walk together
  unless they have made an
    appointment?
4 Does a lion roar in the forest,
  when it has no prey?
  Does a young lion cry out from its
    den,
  if it has caught nothing?
5 Does a bird fall into a snare on the
    earth,
  when there is no trap for it?
  Does a snare spring up from the
    ground,
  when it has taken nothing?
6 Is a trumpet blown in a city,
  and the people are not afraid?
  Does disaster befall a city,
  unless the LORD has done it?
7 Surely the Lord GOD does nothing,
  without revealing his secret
  to his servants the prophets.
8 The lion has roared;
  who will not fear?
  The Lord GOD has spoken;
  who can but prophesy?

9 Proclaim to the strongholds in
    Ashdod,
  and to the strongholds in the
    land of Egypt,
  and say, "Assemble yourselves on
    Mount*h* Samaria,
  and see what great tumults are
    within it,

f That is, *those separated* or *those consecrated*   *g* Meaning of Heb uncertain   *h* Gk Syr: Heb *the*
mountains of

and what oppressions are in its
    midst."
10 They do not know how to do right,
    says the LORD,
    those who store up violence and
      robbery in their strongholds.
11 Therefore thus says the Lord GOD:
An adversary shall surround the
    land,
    and strip you of your defense;
    and your strongholds shall be
      plundered.

12 Thus says the LORD: As the shepherd rescues from the mouth of the lion
two legs, or a piece of an ear, so shall the
people of Israel who live in Samaria be
rescued, with the corner of a couch and
part*i* of a bed.

13 Hear, and testify against the house
    of Jacob,
    says the Lord GOD, the God of
      hosts:
14 On the day I punish Israel for its
    transgressions,
    I will punish the altars of Bethel,
and the horns of the altar shall be
    cut off
and fall to the ground.
15 I will tear down the winter house
    as well as the summer house;
    and the houses of ivory shall
      perish,
    and the great houses*j* shall come to
      an end,
          says the LORD.

4 Hear this word, you cows of
    Bashan
who are on Mount Samaria,
who oppress the poor, who crush
    the needy,
who say to their husbands,
    "Bring something to drink!"
2 The Lord GOD has sworn by his
    holiness:
The time is surely coming upon
    you,
when they shall take you away
    with hooks,
    even the last of you with
      fishhooks.
3 Through breaches in the wall you
    shall leave,

each one straight ahead;
and you shall be flung out into
    Harmon,*i*
          says the LORD.
4 Come to Bethel—and transgress;
    to Gilgal—and multiply
      transgression;
bring your sacrifices every
    morning,
    your tithes every three days;
5 bring a thank offering of leavened
    bread,
    and proclaim freewill offerings,
      publish them;
    for so you love to do, O people of
      Israel!
          says the Lord GOD.

Israel Rejects Correction

6 I gave you cleanness of teeth in all
    your cities,
    and lack of bread in all your
      places,
yet you did not return to me,
          says the LORD.

7 And I also withheld the rain from
    you
    when there were still three
      months to the harvest;
I would send rain on one city,
    and send no rain on another city;
one field would be rained upon,
    and the field on which it did not
      rain withered;
8 so two or three towns wandered to
    one town
    to drink water, and were not
      satisfied;
yet you did not return to me,
          says the LORD.

9 I struck you with blight and
    mildew;
    I laid waste*k* your gardens and
      your vineyards;
    the locust devoured your fig trees
      and your olive trees;
yet you did not return to me,
          says the LORD.

10 I sent among you a pestilence after
    the manner of Egypt;
    I killed your young men with the
      sword;

---

i Meaning of Heb uncertain   *j* Or *many houses*   *k* Cn: Heb *the multitude of*

I carried away your horses;[1]
　　and I made the stench of your
　　　camp go up into your
　　　nostrils;
yet you did not return to me,
　　　　　　　　says the LORD.

11 I overthrew some of you,
　　as when God overthrew Sodom
　　　and Gomorrah,
　　and you were like a brand
　　　snatched from the fire;
yet you did not return to me,
　　　　　　　　says the LORD.

12 Therefore thus I will do to you,
　　O Israel;
　　because I will do this to you,
　　prepare to meet your God,
　　　O Israel!

13 For lo, the one who forms the
　　　mountains, creates the wind,
　　reveals his thoughts to mortals,
　　makes the morning darkness,
　　and treads on the heights of the
　　　earth—
　　the LORD, the God of hosts, is his
　　　name!

A Lament for Israel's Sin

5 Hear this word that I take
up over you in lamentation,
O house of Israel:
2 Fallen, no more to rise,
　　is maiden Israel;
forsaken on her land,
　　with no one to raise her up.

3 For thus says the Lord GOD:
The city that marched out a
　　　thousand
　　shall have a hundred left,
and that which marched out a
　　hundred
　　shall have ten left.[m]

4 For thus says the LORD to the house
　　of Israel:
Seek me and live;
5 but do not seek Bethel,
and do not enter into Gilgal
　　or cross over to Beer-sheba;
for Gilgal shall surely go into exile,
　　and Bethel shall come to nothing.

6 Seek the LORD and live,
　　or he will break out against the
　　　house of Joseph like fire,
　　and it will devour Bethel, with
　　　no one to quench it.
7 Ah, you that turn justice to
　　　wormwood,
　　and bring righteousness to the
　　　ground!

8 The one who made the Pleiades
　　and Orion,
　　and turns deep darkness into the
　　　morning,
　　and darkens the day into night,
who calls for the waters of the sea,
　　and pours them out on the
　　　surface of the earth,
　　the LORD is his name,
9 who makes destruction flash out
　　　against the strong,
　　so that destruction comes upon
　　　the fortress.

10 They hate the one who reproves in
　　　the gate,
　　and they abhor the one who
　　　speaks the truth.
11 Therefore because you trample on
　　　the poor
　　and take from them levies of
　　　grain,
you have built houses of hewn
　　　stone,
　　but you shall not live in them;
you have planted pleasant
　　　vineyards,
　　but you shall not drink their
　　　wine.
12 For I know how many are your
　　　transgressions,
　　and how great are your sins—
you who afflict the righteous, who
　　take a bribe,
　　and push aside the needy in the
　　　gate.
13 Therefore the prudent will keep
　　　silent in such a time;
　　for it is an evil time.

14 Seek good and not evil,
　　that you may live;
and so the LORD, the God of hosts,
　　will be with you,
　　just as you have said.

---

1 Heb *with the captivity of your horses*　　*m* Heb adds *to the house of Israel*

HE WHO TURNS BLACKNESS INTO DAWN
Martin Luther King, Jr.

VERSE: Amos 5.8   PASSAGE: Amos 5.4–17

idnight is a confusing hour when it is difficult to be faithful. The most inspiring word that the church may speak is that no midnight long remains. The weary traveler by midnight who asks for bread is really seeking the dawn. Our eternal message of hope is that dawn will come. Our slave foreparents realized this. They were never unmindful of the fact of midnight, for always there was the rawhide whip of the overseer and the auction block where families were torn asunder to remind them of its reality. When they thought of the agonizing darkness of midnight, they sang:

> Oh, nobody knows de trouble I've seen,
>   Glory hallelujah!
> Sometimes I'm up, sometimes I'm down,
>   Oh, yes, Lord,
> Sometimes I'm almost to de groun',
>   Oh, yes, Lord,
> Oh, nobody knows de trouble I've seen,
>   Glory hallelujah!

Encompassed by a staggering midnight but believing that morning would come, they sang:

> I'm so glad trouble don't last alway.
> O my Lord, O my Lord, what shall I do?

Their positive belief in the dawn was the growing edge of hope that kept the slaves faithful amid the most barren and tragic circumstances.

Faith in the dawn arises from the faith that God is good and just. When one believes this, he knows that the contradictions of life are neither final nor ultimate. He can walk through the dark night and the radiant conviction that all things work together for good for those that love God. Even the most starless midnight may herald the dawn of some great fulfillment.

ADDITIONAL SCRIPTURE READING:
Psalms 30.5; 126.5–6; Amos 4.13

Go to page 1048 for your next devotional reading.

15 Hate evil and love good,
  and establish justice in the gate;
  it may be that the LORD, the God of
    hosts,
  will be gracious to the remnant
    of Joseph.

16 Therefore thus says the LORD, the
    God of hosts, the Lord:
  In all the squares there shall be
    wailing;
  and in all the streets they shall
    say, "Alas! alas!"
  They shall call the farmers to
    mourning,
  and those skilled in lamentation,
    to wailing;
17 in all the vineyards there shall be
    wailing,
  for I will pass through the midst
    of you,
                    says the LORD.

The Day of the LORD a Dark Day

18 Alas for you who desire the day of
    the LORD!
  Why do you want the day of the
    LORD?
  It is darkness, not light;
19   as if someone fled from a lion,
    and was met by a bear;
  or went into the house and rested a
    hand against the wall,
    and was bitten by a snake.
20 Is not the day of the LORD darkness,
    not light,
  and gloom with no brightness in
    it?

21 I hate, I despise your festivals,
  and I take no delight in your
    solemn assemblies.
22 Even though you offer me your
    burnt offerings and grain
    offerings,
  I will not accept them;
  and the offerings of well-being of
    your fatted animals
  I will not look upon.
23 Take away from me the noise of
    your songs;
  I will not listen to the melody of
    your harps.
24 But let justice roll down like
    waters,

and righteousness like an ever-
    flowing stream.

WE WILL NOT BE SATISFIED UNTIL JUSTICE ROLLS
DOWN LIKE WATERS, AND RIGHTEOUSNESS LIKE A
MIGHTY STREAM.   —*Martin Luther King, Jr.*

---

25 Did you bring to me sacrifices and
offerings the forty years in the wilderness, O house of Israel? 26 You shall take
up Sakkuth your king, and Kaiwan your
star-god, your images,[n] which you made
for yourselves; 27 therefore I will take you
into exile beyond Damascus, says the
LORD, whose name is the God of hosts.

Complacent Self-Indulgence Will Be Punished

6 Alas for those who are at ease
    in Zion,
  and for those who feel secure on
    Mount Samaria,
  the notables of the first of the
    nations,
  to whom the house of Israel
    resorts!
2 Cross over to Calneh, and see;
  from there go to Hamath the
    great;
  then go down to Gath of the
    Philistines.
  Are you better[o] than these
    kingdoms?
  Or is your[p] territory greater than
    their[q] territory,
3 O you that put far away the evil day,
  and bring near a reign of
    violence?

4 Alas for those who lie on beds of
    ivory,
  and lounge on their couches,
  and eat lambs from the flock,
  and calves from the stall;
5 who sing idle songs to the sound of
    the harp,
  and like David improvise on
    instruments of music;
6 who drink wine from bowls,
  and anoint themselves with the
    finest oils,
  but are not grieved over the ruin
    of Joseph!

---

n Heb *your images, your star-god*   o Or *Are they better*   p Heb *their*   q Heb *your*

7 Therefore they shall now be the
    first to go into exile,
  and the revelry of the loungers
    shall pass away.

8 The Lord GOD has sworn by
    himself
  (says the LORD, the God of hosts):
  I abhor the pride of Jacob
    and hate his strongholds;
  and I will deliver up the city and
    all that is in it.

9 If ten people remain in one house,
they shall die. 10And if a relative, one
who burns the dead,*r* shall take up the
body to bring it out of the house, and
shall say to someone in the innermost
parts of the house, "Is anyone else with
you?" the answer will come, "No."
Then the relative*s* shall say, "Hush! We
must not mention the name of the
LORD."

11 See, the LORD commands,
  and the great house shall be
    shattered to bits,
  and the little house to pieces.
12 Do horses run on rocks?
  Does one plow the sea with
    oxen?*t*
  But you have turned justice into
    poison
  and the fruit of righteousness
    into wormwood—
13 you who rejoice in Lo-debar,*u*
  who say, "Have we not by our
    own strength
  taken Karnaim*v* for ourselves?"
14 Indeed, I am raising up against you
    a nation,
  O house of Israel, says the LORD,
    the God of hosts,
  and they shall oppress you from
    Lebo-hamath
  to the Wadi Arabah.

Locusts, Fire, and a Plumb Line

7 This is what the Lord GOD
showed me: he was forming locusts at the time the latter growth began
to sprout (it was the latter growth after
the king's mowings). 2When they had

finished eating the grass of the land, I
said,
  "O Lord GOD, forgive, I beg you!
  How can Jacob stand?
  He is so small!"
3 The LORD relented concerning this;
  "It shall not be," said the LORD.

4 This is what the Lord GOD showed
me: the Lord GOD was calling for a
shower of fire,*w* and it devoured the great
deep and was eating up the land. 5Then I
said,
  "O Lord GOD, cease, I beg you!
  How can Jacob stand?
  He is so small!"
6 The LORD relented concerning this;
  "This also shall not be," said the
    Lord GOD.

7 This is what he showed me: the
Lord was standing beside a wall built
with a plumb line, with a plumb line in
his hand. 8And the LORD said to me,
"Amos, what do you see?" And I said,
"A plumb line." Then the Lord said,
  "See, I am setting a plumb line
    in the midst of my people Israel;
    I will never again pass them by;
9   the high places of Isaac shall be
    made desolate,
  and the sanctuaries of Israel shall
    be laid waste,
  and I will rise against the house
    of Jeroboam with the sword."

Amaziah Complains to the King

10 Then Amaziah, the priest of Bethel, sent to King Jeroboam of Israel, saying, "Amos has conspired against you in
the very center of the house of Israel; the
land is not able to bear all his words.
11For thus Amos has said,
  'Jeroboam shall die by the sword,
    and Israel must go into exile
    away from his land.' "
12And Amaziah said to Amos, "O seer,
go, flee away to the land of Judah, earn
your bread there, and prophesy there;
13but never again prophesy at Bethel, for
it is the king's sanctuary, and it is a temple of the kingdom."
14 Then Amos answered Amaziah, "I
am*x* no prophet, nor a prophet's son; but

r Or who makes a burning for him   *s Heb he*   *t Or Does one plow them with oxen*   *u Or in a
thing of nothingness*   *v Or horns*   *w Or for a judgment by fire*   *x Or was*

I am[y] a herdsman, and a dresser of syca-more trees, 15and the LORD took me from following the flock, and the LORD said to me, 'Go, prophesy to my people Israel.'
16 "Now therefore hear the word of
        the LORD.
    You say, 'Do not prophesy against
        Israel,
      and do not preach against the
        house of Isaac.'
17 Therefore thus says the LORD:
    'Your wife shall become a
        prostitute in the city,
      and your sons and your daughters
        shall fall by the sword,
      and your land shall be parceled
        out by line;
    you yourself shall die in an unclean
        land,
      and Israel shall surely go into
        exile away from its land.' "

The Basket of Fruit

8 This is what the Lord GOD showed me—a basket of sum-mer fruit.[z] 2He said, "Amos, what do you see?" And I said, "A basket of sum-mer fruit."[z] Then the LORD said to me,
    "The end[a] has come upon my
        people Israel;
      I will never again pass them by.
3   The songs of the temple[b] shall
        become wailings in that day,"
                  says the Lord GOD;
    "the dead bodies shall be many,
        cast out in every place. Be
        silent!"

4   Hear this, you that trample on the
        needy,
      and bring to ruin the poor of the
        land,
5   saying, "When will the new moon
        be over
      so that we may sell grain;
    and the sabbath,
      so that we may offer wheat for
        sale?
    We will make the ephah small and
        the shekel great,
      and practice deceit with false
        balances,
6   buying the poor for silver
      and the needy for a pair of
        sandals,

and selling the sweepings of the
    wheat."

7   The LORD has sworn by the pride of
        Jacob:
    Surely I will never forget any of
        their deeds.
8   Shall not the land tremble on this
        account,
      and everyone mourn who lives in
        it,
    and all of it rise like the Nile,
      and be tossed about and sink
        again, like the Nile of Egypt?

9   On that day, says the Lord GOD,
      I will make the sun go down at
        noon,
      and darken the earth in broad
        daylight.
10 I will turn your feasts into
        mourning,
      and all your songs into
        lamentation;
    I will bring sackcloth on all loins,
      and baldness on every head;
    I will make it like the mourning for
        an only son,
      and the end of it like a bitter day.

11 The time is surely coming, says the
        Lord GOD,
      when I will send a famine on the
        land;
    not a famine of bread, or a thirst for
        water,
      but of hearing the words of the
        LORD.
12 They shall wander from sea to sea,
      and from north to east;
    they shall run to and fro, seeking
        the word of the LORD,
      but they shall not find it.

13 In that day the beautiful young
        women and the young men
      shall faint for thirst.
14 Those who swear by Ashimah of
        Samaria,
      and say, "As your god lives,
        O Dan,"
    and, "As the way of Beer-sheba
        lives"—
      they shall fall, and never rise
        again.

y Or was   z Heb qayits   a Heb qets   b Or palace

The Destruction of Israel

 9 I saw the LORD standing
    beside[c] the altar, and he said:
Strike the capitals until the
    thresholds shake,

and shatter them on the heads of
    all the people;[d]
and those who are left I will kill
    with the sword;
not one of them shall flee away,
    not one of them shall escape.

c Or on   d Heb all of them

FRIDAY

THE ENDS ARE SWALLOWED IN THE MEANS
Martin Luther King, Jr.

VERSE: Amos 8.4   **PASSAGE:** Amos 8.4–7

nly an irrelevant religion fails to be concerned about man's economic well-being. Religion at its best realizes that the soul is crushed as long as the body is tortured with hunger pangs and harrowed with the need for shelter. Jesus realized that we need food, clothing, shelter, and economic security. He said in clear and concise terms: "Your Father knows what you need" (Matthew 6.8). But Jesus knew that man was more than a dog to be satisfied by a few economic bones. He realized that the internal of a man's life is as significant as the external. So he added, "Strive first for the kingdom of God and his righteousness, and all these things will be given to you as well" (v. 33). The tragedy of the rich man was that he sought the means first, and in the process the ends were swallowed in the means.

The richer this man became materially the poorer he became intellectually and spiritually. He may have been married, but he probably could not love his wife. It is possible that he gave her countless material gifts, but he could not give her that which she needed most, love and affection. He may have had children, but he probably did not appreciate them. He may have had the great books of the ages shelved neatly in his library, but he never read them. He may have had access to great music, but he did not listen. His eyes did not behold the majestic splendor of the skies. His ears were not attuned to the melodious sweetness of heavenly music. His mind was closed to the insights of poets, prophets, and philosophers. His title was justly merited—"You fool!"

ADDITIONAL SCRIPTURE READING:
Matthew 6.28–34; Luke 12.27–31

Go to page 1050 for your next devotional reading.

1900   Present

2 Though they dig into Sheol,
    from there shall my hand take
      them;
  though they climb up to heaven,
    from there I will bring them
      down.
3 Though they hide themselves on
    the top of Carmel,
    from there I will search out and
      take them;
  and though they hide from my
    sight at the bottom of the
      sea,
    there I will command the sea-
      serpent, and it shall bite
        them.
4 And though they go into captivity
    in front of their enemies,
    there I will command the sword,
      and it shall kill them;
  and I will fix my eyes on them
    for harm and not for good.

5 The Lord, GOD of hosts,
  he who touches the earth and it
    melts,
    and all who live in it mourn,
  and all of it rises like the Nile,
    and sinks again, like the Nile of
      Egypt;
6 who builds his upper chambers in
    the heavens,
    and founds his vault upon the
      earth;
  who calls for the waters of the sea,
    and pours them out upon the
      surface of the earth—
  the LORD is his name.

7 Are you not like the Ethiopians*e* to
    me,
    O people of Israel? says the LORD.
  Did I not bring Israel up from the
    land of Egypt,
    and the Philistines from Caphtor
      and the Arameans from Kir?
8 The eyes of the Lord GOD are upon
    the sinful kingdom,
    and I will destroy it from the face
      of the earth

—except that I will not utterly
    destroy the house of Jacob,
      says the LORD.

9 For lo, I will command,
    and shake the house of Israel
      among all the nations
  as one shakes with a sieve,
    but no pebble shall fall to the
      ground.
10 All the sinners of my people shall
    die by the sword,
    who say, "Evil shall not overtake
      or meet us."

The Restoration of David's Kingdom

11 On that day I will raise up
    the booth of David that is fallen,
  and repair its*f* breaches,
    and raise up its*g* ruins,
    and rebuild it as in the days of old;
12 in order that they may possess the
      remnant of Edom
    and all the nations who are called
      by my name,
      says the LORD who does this.

13 The time is surely coming, says the
      LORD,
    when the one who plows shall
      overtake the one who reaps,
    and the treader of grapes the one
      who sows the seed;
  the mountains shall drip sweet
    wine,
    and all the hills shall flow with it.
14 I will restore the fortunes of my
      people Israel,
    and they shall rebuild the ruined
      cities and inhabit them;
  they shall plant vineyards and
    drink their wine,
    and they shall make gardens and
      eat their fruit.
15 I will plant them upon their land,
    and they shall never again be
      plucked up
    out of the land that I have given
      them,
        says the LORD your God.

---

e Or *Nubians;* Heb *Cushites*   *f* Gk: Heb *their*   *g* Gk: Heb *his*

WEEKEND

WE GIVE THEE THANKS, O LORD
Horatius Bonar

VERSE: Matthew 26.26   **PASSAGE:** Matthew 26.26–30

 or the bread and for the wine,
For the pledge that seals him mine,
For the words of love divine,
We give thee thanks, O Lord.

Only bread and only wine,
Yet to faith, the solemn sign
Of the heav'nly and divine!
We give thee thanks, O Lord.

For the words that turn our eye
To the cross of Calvary,
Bidding us in faith draw nigh,
We give thee thanks, O Lord . . .

For thy words in Spirit shown,
For thy will to us made known.
"Do ye this until I come,"
We give thee thanks, O Lord.

Till he come we take the bread,
Type of him on whom we feed,
Him who liveth and was dead!
We give thee thanks, O Lord.

Till he come we take the cup;
As we at his table sup,
Eye and heart are lifted up!
We give thee thanks, O Lord.

For that coming, here foreshown,
For that day to man unknown,
For the glory and the throne,
We give thee thanks, O Lord.

ADDITIONAL SCRIPTURE READING:
John 6.33–35; 1 Corinthians 11.26–29

Go to page 1052 for your next devotional reading.

1700   1900

OBADIAH

BADIAH'S PROPHECY CENTERS
AROUND AN ANCIENT FEUD BE-
TWEEN EDOM AND ISRAEL. AS
DESCENDANTS OF ESAU, THE EDOMITES
HELD A GRUDGE AGAINST ISRAEL BECAUSE
JACOB HAD CHEATED THEIR ANCESTOR OUT
OF HIS BIRTHRIGHT. OBADIAH PROPHESIES
JUDGMENT AGAINST EDOM, REMINDING THE
PEOPLE OF EDOM THAT GOD IS IN CONTROL
OF THE WORLD. EDOM HERSELF WILL BE
DESTROYED, BUT MOUNT ZION AND ISRAEL
WILL BE DELIVERED, AND GOD'S KINGDOM
WILL TRIUMPH.

Proud Edom Will Be Brought Low

1 The vision of Obadiah.

Thus says the Lord GOD
concerning Edom:
We have heard a report from the
LORD,
and a messenger has been sent
among the nations:
"Rise up! Let us rise against it for
battle!"
2 I will surely make you least among
the nations;
you shall be utterly despised.
3 Your proud heart has deceived you,
you that live in the clefts of the
rock,[a]
whose dwelling is in the heights.

You say in your heart,
"Who will bring me down to the
ground?"

PRIDE, THE NEVER-FAILING VICE OF FOOLS.
—*Alexander Pope*

---

4 Though you soar aloft like the eagle,
though your nest is set among
the stars,
from there I will bring you down,
says the LORD.

Pillage and Slaughter Will Repay Edom's Cruelty

5 If thieves came to you,
if plunderers by night

---

a Or *clefts of Sela*

—how you have been
destroyed!—
would they not steal only what
they wanted?
If grape-gatherers came to you,
would they not leave gleanings?

6 How Esau has been pillaged,
his treasures searched out!

7 All your allies have deceived you,
they have driven you to the
border;
your confederates have prevailed
against you;
those who ate[b] your bread have
set a trap for you—
there is no understanding of it.

8 On that day, says the LORD,

I will destroy the wise out of
Edom,
and understanding out of Mount
Esau.

9 Your warriors shall be shattered,
O Teman,
so that everyone from Mount
Esau will be cut off.

Edom Mistreated His Brother

10 For the slaughter and violence done
to your brother Jacob,
shame shall cover you,
and you shall be cut off forever.

11 On the day that you stood aside,
on the day that strangers carried
off his wealth,
and foreigners entered his gates

b Cn: Heb lacks those who ate

MONDAY

THE VOICE OF THE PROPHET
Charles H. Spurgeon

VERSE: Obadiah 1   **PASSAGE:** Obadiah 1–4

 very skillful bowman went to the mountains in search
of game. All the beasts of the forest fled at his
approach. The lion alone challenged him to combat.
The bowman immediately let fly an arrow and said to
the lion, "I send you my messenger, that from him you might
learn what I myself will be when I assail you." The lion thus
wounded rushed away in great fear, and when a fox exhorted
him to be of good courage and not to run away at the first attack,
he said, "You counsel me in vain, for if he sends so fearful a messenger, how shall I abide the attack of the man himself?"

If the warning admonitions of God's ministers fill the conscience with terror, what must it be to face the Lord himself? If
one bolt of judgment brings a man into a cold sweat, what will
it be to stand before an angry God in the last great day?

ADDITIONAL SCRIPTURE READING:
Isaiah 34.1–17; 63.3–6

Go to page 1055 for your next devotional reading.

1700   1900

and cast lots for Jerusalem,
you too were like one of them.
12 But you should not have gloated[c]
over[d] your brother
on the day of his misfortune;
you should not have rejoiced over
the people of Judah
on the day of their ruin;
you should not have boasted
on the day of distress.
13 You should not have entered the
gate of my people
on the day of their calamity;
you should not have joined in the
gloating over Judah's[e] disaster
on the day of his calamity;
you should not have looted his goods
on the day of his calamity.
14 You should not have stood at the
crossings
to cut off his fugitives;
you should not have handed over
his survivors
on the day of distress.

15 For the day of the LORD is near
against all the nations.
As you have done, it shall be done
to you;
your deeds shall return on your
own head.
16 For as you have drunk on my holy
mountain,
all the nations around you shall
drink;
they shall drink and gulp down,[f]
and shall be as though they had
never been.

Israel's Final Triumph

17 But on Mount Zion there shall be
those that escape,
and it shall be holy;
and the house of Jacob shall take
possession of those who
dispossessed them.
18 The house of Jacob shall be a fire,
the house of Joseph a flame,
and the house of Esau stubble;
they shall burn them and consume
them,
and there shall be no survivor of
the house of Esau;
for the LORD has spoken.
19 Those of the Negeb shall possess
Mount Esau,
and those of the Shephelah the
land of the Philistines;
they shall possess the land of
Ephraim and the land of
Samaria,
and Benjamin shall possess
Gilead.
20 The exiles of the Israelites who are
in Halah[g]
shall possess[h] Phoenicia as far as
Zarephath;
and the exiles of Jerusalem who are
in Sepharad
shall possess the towns of the
Negeb.
21 Those who have been saved[i] shall
go up to Mount Zion
to rule Mount Esau;
and the kingdom shall be the
LORD's.

c Heb *But do not gloat* (and similarly through verse 14)   d Heb *on the day of*   e Heb *his*
f Meaning of Heb uncertain   g Cn: Heb *in this army*   h Cn: Meaning of Heb uncertain
i Or *Saviors*

JONAH

HEN GOD SENT HIM TO WARN THE PEOPLE OF NINEVEH TO REPENT, JONAH RAN IN THE OPPO-SITE DIRECTION. BUT GOD USED A RELUC-TANT PROPHET AS A VEHICLE OF HIS GRACE. AS YOU READ THIS BOOK, NOTE GOD'S GREAT COMPASSION FOR ALL PEOPLE AND HIS DESIRE FOR SINCERE REPENTANCE REGARD-LESS OF WHAT SOMEONE HAS DONE. AND THANK HIM FOR REACHING OUT TO YOU IN LOVE AND CALLING YOU TO TELL OTHERS ABOUT HIS GRACE FOR THEM.

Jonah Tries to Run Away from God

1 Now the word of the LORD came to Jonah son of Amittai, saying, [2]"Go at once to Nineveh, that great city, and cry out against it; for their wickedness has come up before me." [3]But Jonah set out to flee to Tarshish from the presence of the LORD. He went down to Joppa and found a ship going to Tarshish; so he paid his fare and went on board, to go with them to Tarshish, away from the presence of the LORD.

[4] But the LORD hurled a great wind upon the sea, and such a mighty storm came upon the sea that the ship threatened to break up. [5]Then the mariners were afraid, and each cried to his god. They threw the cargo that was in the ship into the sea, to lighten it for them. Jonah, meanwhile, had gone down into the hold of the ship and had lain down, and was fast asleep. [6]The captain came and said to him, "What are you doing sound asleep? Get up, call on your god! Perhaps the god will spare us a thought so that we do not perish."

[7] The sailors[a] said to one another, "Come, let us cast lots, so that we may know on whose account this calamity has come upon us." So they cast lots, and the lot fell on Jonah. [8]Then they said to him, "Tell us why this calamity has come upon us. What is your occupation? Where do you come from? What is your country? And of what people are you?" [9]"I am a Hebrew," he replied. "I worship the LORD, the God of heaven, who made

a Heb They

the sea and the dry land." ¹⁰Then the men were even more afraid, and said to him, "What is this that you have done!" For the men knew that he was fleeing from the presence of the LORD, because he had told them so.

11 Then they said to him, "What shall we do to you, that the sea may quiet down for us?" For the sea was growing more and more tempestuous. ¹²He said to them, "Pick me up and throw me into the sea; then the sea will quiet down for you;

TUESDAY

KEPT SECURE IN OUR STRUGGLES
Julian of Norwich

VERSE: Jonah 1.3   **PASSAGE:** Jonah 1.1–3

n this life there is within us who are to be saved a surprising mixture of good and bad. We have our risen Lord; we have the wretchedness and mischief done by Adam's fall and death. Kept secure by Christ we are assured, by his touch of grace, of salvation; broken by Adam's fall, and in many ways by our own sins and sorrows, we are so darkened and blinded that we can hardly find any comfort. But in our heart we abide in God, and confidently trust to his mercy and grace—and this is his working in us. And of his goodness he opens the eye of our understanding so that we can see; sometimes it is less, sometimes more, according to our God-given ability to receive it. Now we are uplifted by the one; now we are allowed to fall into the other. And this fluctuating is so baffling that we are hard put to know where we stand, whether we are thinking of ourselves or of our fellow believers. It certainly is a marvelous mix up! But the one thing that matters is that we always say "Yes" to God whenever we experience him, and really do will to be with him, with all our heart and soul and strength. It is then that we hate and despise our evil inclinations, and all else that might make us sin, physically or spiritually. Yet, when this sweetness vanishes, we fall back into our blind state, and so into all sorts of distress and trouble. At such a time this is our strength—we know by faith that, through the virtue of Christ our guardian, we never really accept this situation; but, protesting against it, we hang on and pray through all this trouble and grief, until such time as once again God will reveal himself to us.

ADDITIONAL SCRIPTURE READING:
Genesis 3.8–9; Psalm 139.7–12

Go to page 1057 for your next devotional reading.

500   1500

for I know it is because of me that this great storm has come upon you." ¹³Nevertheless the men rowed hard to bring the ship back to land, but they could not, for the sea grew more and more stormy against them. ¹⁴Then they cried out to the LORD, "Please, O LORD, we pray, do not let us perish on account of this man's life. Do not make us guilty of innocent blood; for you, O LORD, have done as it pleased you." ¹⁵So they picked Jonah up and threw him into the sea; and the sea ceased from its raging. ¹⁶Then the men feared the LORD even more, and they offered a sacrifice to the LORD and made vows.

17ᵇ But the LORD provided a large fish to swallow up Jonah; and Jonah was in the belly of the fish three days and three nights.

A Psalm of Thanksgiving

2 Then Jonah prayed to the LORD his God from the belly of the fish, ²saying,

"I called to the LORD out of my
    distress,
  and he answered me;
out of the belly of Sheol I cried,
  and you heard my voice.
³ You cast me into the deep,
    into the heart of the seas,
    and the flood surrounded me;
  all your waves and your billows
    passed over me.
⁴ Then I said, 'I am driven away
    from your sight;
  howᶜ shall I look again
    upon your holy temple?'
⁵ The waters closed in over me;
    the deep surrounded me;
  weeds were wrapped around my
    head
⁶   at the roots of the mountains.
  I went down to the land
    whose bars closed upon me
      forever;
  yet you brought up my life from
    the Pit,
  O LORD my God.
⁷ As my life was ebbing away,
    I remembered the LORD;
  and my prayer came to you,
    into your holy temple.
⁸ Those who worship vain idols
    forsake their true loyalty.

⁹ But I with the voice of thanksgiving
    will sacrifice to you;
  what I have vowed I will pay.
  Deliverance belongs to the LORD!"
¹⁰Then the LORD spoke to the fish, and it spewed Jonah out upon the dry land.

Conversion of Nineveh

3 The word of the LORD came to Jonah a second time, saying, ²"Get up, go to Nineveh, that great city, and proclaim to it the message that I tell you." ³So Jonah set out and went to Nineveh, according to the word of the LORD. Now Nineveh was an exceedingly large city, a three days' walk across. ⁴Jonah began to go into the city, going a day's walk. And he cried out, "Forty days more, and Nineveh shall be overthrown!" ⁵And the people of Nineveh believed God; they proclaimed a fast, and everyone, great and small, put on sackcloth.

6 When the news reached the king of Nineveh, he rose from his throne, removed his robe, covered himself with sackcloth, and sat in ashes. ⁷Then he had a proclamation made in Nineveh: "By the decree of the king and his nobles: No human being or animal, no herd or flock, shall taste anything. They shall not feed, nor shall they drink water. ⁸Human beings and animals shall be covered with sackcloth, and they shall cry mightily to God. All shall turn from their evil ways and from the violence that is in their hands. ⁹Who knows? God may relent and change his mind; he may turn from his fierce anger, so that we do not perish."

10 When God saw what they did, how they turned from their evil ways, God changed his mind about the calamity that he had said he would bring upon them; and he did not do it.

MAN MAY DISMISS COMPASSION FROM HIS HEART,
BUT GOD WILL NEVER.　　*—William Cowper*

Jonah's Anger

4 But this was very displeasing to Jonah, and he became angry. ²He prayed to the LORD and said, "O LORD! Is not this what I said while I was still in

b Ch 2.1 in Heb　c Theodotion: Heb *surely*

my own country? That is why I fled to Tarshish at the beginning, for I knew that you are a gracious God and merciful, slow to anger, and abounding in steadfast love, and ready to relent from punishing. ³And now, O LORD, please take my life from me, for it is better for me to die than to live." ⁴And the LORD said, "Is it right for you to be angry?" ⁵Then Jonah went out of the city and sat down east of the city, and made a booth for himself there. He sat under it in the shade, waiting to see what would become of the city.

6 The LORD God appointed a bush,ᵈ and made it come up over Jonah, to give shade over his head, to save him from his

---

ᵈ Heb *qiqayon,* possibly *the castor bean plant*

WEDNESDAY

ALWAYS PRAY
Sojourner Truth

VERSE: Jonah 2.7   **PASSAGE:** Jonah 2.1–9

 sabella avers that, in her darkest hours, she had no fear of any worse hell than the one she then carried in her bosom; though it had ever been pictured to her in its deepest colors, and threatened her as a reward for all her misdemeanors. Her vileness and God's holiness and all pervading presence, which filled immensity, and threatened her with instant annihilation, composed the burden of her vision of terror. Her faith in prayer is equal to her faith in the love of Jesus. Her language is, "Let others say what they will of the efficacy of prayer, *I* believe in it, and *I* shall pray. Thank God! Yes, *I shall always pray,*" she exclaims, putting her hands together with the greatest enthusiasm.

For some time subsequent to the happy change we have spoken of, Isabella's prayers partook largely of their former character; and while, in deep affliction, she labored for the recovery of her son, she prayed with constancy and fervor; and the following may be taken as a specimen:—"Oh, God, you know how much I am distressed, for I have told you again and again. Now, God, help me get my son. If you were in trouble, as I am, and I could help you, as you can me, think I wouldn't do it? Yes, God, you *know* I would do it. Oh, God, you know I have no money, but you can make the people do for me, and you must make the people do for me. I will never give you peace till you do, God. Oh, God, make the people hear me—don't let them turn me off, without hearing and helping me."

ADDITIONAL SCRIPTURE READING:
2 Chronicles 20.27; Psalm 18.6; Luke 18.1–8

Go to page 1066 for your next devotional reading.

1700   1900

discomfort; so Jonah was very happy about the bush. 7But when dawn came up the next day, God appointed a worm that attacked the bush, so that it withered. 8When the sun rose, God prepared a sultry east wind, and the sun beat down on the head of Jonah so that he was faint and asked that he might die. He said, "It is better for me to die than to live."

Jonah Is Reproved

9 But God said to Jonah, "Is it right for you to be angry about the bush?" And he said, "Yes, angry enough to die." 10Then the LORD said, "You are concerned about the bush, for which you did not labor and which you did not grow; it came into being in a night and perished in a night. 11And should I not be concerned about Nineveh, that great city, in which there are more than a hundred and twenty thousand persons who do not know their right hand from their left, and also many animals?"

MICAH

T HE PROPHET MICAH WROTE TO
THE PEOPLE OF JUDAH TO WARN
THEM THAT GOD'S JUDGMENT WAS
NEAR BECAUSE THEY HAD REJECTED GOD
AND HIS LAW. HIS MESSAGE ALTERNATED
BETWEEN ORACLES OF DOOM AND ORACLES
OF HOPE, STRESSING THAT GOD HATES IDOL-
ATRY, INJUSTICE, REBELLION AND EMPTY
RITUALISM, BUT HE DELIGHTS IN FORGIVING
THOSE WHO RETURN TO HIM. AS YOU READ
THIS BOOK, TAKE COMFORT THAT GOD
OFFERS HOPE FOR THOSE WHO REMAIN
FAITHFUL TO HIM.

---

1 The word of the LORD that came to Micah of Moresheth in the days of Kings Jotham, Ahaz, and Hezekiah of Judah, which he saw concerning Samaria and Jerusalem.

Judgment Pronounced against Samaria

2 Hear, you peoples, all of you;
    listen, O earth, and all that is in it;
and let the Lord GOD be a witness
    against you,
    the Lord from his holy temple.
3 For lo, the LORD is coming out of
    his place,
    and will come down and tread
    upon the high places of the
    earth.

4 Then the mountains will melt
    under him
    and the valleys will burst open,
like wax near the fire,
    like waters poured down a steep
    place.
5 All this is for the transgression of
    Jacob
    and for the sins of the house of
    Israel.
What is the transgression of Jacob?
    Is it not Samaria?
And what is the high place[a] of
    Judah?
    Is it not Jerusalem?
6 Therefore I will make Samaria a
    heap in the open country,
    a place for planting vineyards.

---

a Heb *what are the high places*

I will pour down her stones into
   the valley,
and uncover her foundations.
7 All her images shall be beaten to
   pieces,
all her wages shall be burned
   with fire,
and all her idols I will lay waste;
for as the wages of a prostitute she
   gathered them,
and as the wages of a prostitute
   they shall again be used.

The Doom of the Cities of Judah

8 For this I will lament and wail;
I will go barefoot and naked;
I will make lamentation like the
   jackals,
and mourning like the ostriches.
9 For her wound[b] is incurable.
It has come to Judah;
it has reached to the gate of my
   people,
to Jerusalem.

10 Tell it not in Gath,
weep not at all;
in Beth-leaphrah
roll yourselves in the dust.
11 Pass on your way,
inhabitants of Shaphir,
in nakedness and shame;
the inhabitants of Zaanan
do not come forth;
Beth-ezel is wailing
and shall remove its support
   from you.
12 For the inhabitants of Maroth
wait anxiously for good,
yet disaster has come down from
   the LORD
to the gate of Jerusalem.
13 Harness the steeds to the chariots,
inhabitants of Lachish;
it was the beginning of sin
to daughter Zion,
for in you were found
the transgressions of Israel.
14 Therefore you shall give parting
   gifts
to Moresheth-gath;
the houses of Achzib shall be a
   deception
to the kings of Israel.

15 I will again bring a conqueror upon
   you,
inhabitants of Mareshah;
the glory of Israel
shall come to Adullam.
16 Make yourselves bald and cut off
   your hair
for your pampered children;
make yourselves as bald as the eagle,
for they have gone from you into
   exile.

Social Evils Denounced

2 Alas for those who devise
   wickedness
and evil deeds[c] on their beds!
When the morning dawns, they
   perform it,
because it is in their power.
2 They covet fields, and seize them;
houses, and take them away;
they oppress householder and
   house,
people and their inheritance.
3 Therefore thus says the LORD:
Now, I am devising against this
   family an evil
from which you cannot remove
   your necks;
and you shall not walk haughtily,
for it will be an evil time.
4 On that day they shall take up a
   taunt song against you,
and wail with bitter lamentation,
and say, "We are utterly ruined;
the LORD[d] alters the inheritance
   of my people;
how he removes it from me!
Among our captors[e] he parcels
   out our fields."
5 Therefore you will have no one to
   cast the line by lot
in the assembly of the LORD.

6 "Do not preach"—thus they
   preach—
"one should not preach of such
   things;
disgrace will not overtake us."
7 Should this be said, O house of
   Jacob?
Is the LORD's patience exhausted?
Are these his doings?
Do not my words do good
to one who walks uprightly?

b Gk Syr Vg: Heb *wounds*   c Cn: Heb *work evil*   d Heb *he*   e Cn: Heb *the rebellious*

8 But you rise up against my people*f*
    as an enemy;
  you strip the robe from the
    peaceful,*g*
  from those who pass by trustingly
    with no thought of war.
9 The women of my people you drive
    out
  from their pleasant houses;
  from their young children you take
    away
  my glory forever.
10 Arise and go;
  for this is no place to rest,
  because of uncleanness that destroys
    with a grievous destruction.*h*
11 If someone were to go about
    uttering empty falsehoods,
  saying, "I will preach to you of
    wine and strong drink,"
  such a one would be the preacher
    for this people!

A Promise for the Remnant of Israel

12 I will surely gather all of you,
    O Jacob,
  I will gather the survivors of Israel;
  I will set them together
  like sheep in a fold,
  like a flock in its pasture;
  it will resound with people.
13 The one who breaks out will go up
    before them;
  they will break through and pass
    the gate,
  going out by it.
  Their king will pass on before them,
  the LORD at their head.

Wicked Rulers and Prophets

3 And I said:
  Listen, you heads of Jacob
  and rulers of the house of Israel!
  Should you not know justice?—
2   you who hate the good and love
    the evil,
  who tear the skin off my people,*i*
  and the flesh off their bones;
3 who eat the flesh of my people,
  flay their skin off them,
  break their bones in pieces,
    and chop them up like meat*j* in a
    kettle,
  like flesh in a caldron.

4 Then they will cry to the LORD,
  but he will not answer them;
  he will hide his face from them at
    that time,
  because they have acted wickedly.

5 Thus says the LORD concerning the
    prophets
  who lead my people astray,
  who cry "Peace"
    when they have something to eat,
  but declare war against those
  who put nothing into their
    mouths.
6 Therefore it shall be night to you,
    without vision,
  and darkness to you, without
    revelation.
  The sun shall go down upon the
    prophets,
  and the day shall be black over
    them;
7 the seers shall be disgraced,
  and the diviners put to shame;
  they shall all cover their lips,
  for there is no answer from God.
8 But as for me, I am filled with
    power,
  with the spirit of the LORD,
  and with justice and might,
  to declare to Jacob his transgression
  and to Israel his sin.

9 Hear this, you rulers of the house
    of Jacob
  and chiefs of the house of Israel,
  who abhor justice
  and pervert all equity,
10 who build Zion with blood
  and Jerusalem with wrong!
11 Its rulers give judgment for a bribe,
  its priests teach for a price,
  its prophets give oracles for
    money;
  yet they lean upon the LORD and
    say,
  "Surely the LORD is with us!
  No harm shall come upon us."
12 Therefore because of you
  Zion shall be plowed as a field;
  Jerusalem shall become a heap of
    ruins,
  and the mountain of the house a
    wooded height.

f Cn: Heb *But yesterday my people rose*   *g* Cn: Heb *from before a garment*   *h* Meaning of Heb
uncertain   *i* Heb *from them*   *j* Gk: Heb *as*

Peace and Security through Obedience

4 In days to come
the mountain of the LORD's house
shall be established as the highest of the mountains,
and shall be raised up above the hills.
Peoples shall stream to it,
2 and many nations shall come and say:
"Come, let us go up to the mountain of the LORD,
to the house of the God of Jacob;
that he may teach us his ways
and that we may walk in his paths."
For out of Zion shall go forth instruction,
and the word of the LORD from Jerusalem.
3 He shall judge between many peoples,
and shall arbitrate between strong nations far away;
they shall beat their swords into plowshares,
and their spears into pruning hooks;
nation shall not lift up sword against nation,
neither shall they learn war any more;
4 but they shall all sit under their own vines and under their own fig trees,
and no one shall make them afraid;
for the mouth of the LORD of hosts has spoken.

5 For all the peoples walk,
each in the name of its god,
but we will walk in the name of the LORD our God
forever and ever.

Restoration Promised after Exile

6 In that day, says the LORD,
I will assemble the lame
and gather those who have been driven away,
and those whom I have afflicted.

7 The lame I will make the remnant,
and those who were cast off, a strong nation;
and the LORD will reign over them in Mount Zion
now and forevermore.

8 And you, O tower of the flock,
hill of daughter Zion,
to you it shall come,
the former dominion shall come,
the sovereignty of daughter Jerusalem.

9 Now why do you cry aloud?
Is there no king in you?
Has your counselor perished,
that pangs have seized you like a woman in labor?
10 Writhe and groan,[k] O daughter Zion,
like a woman in labor;
for now you shall go forth from the city
and camp in the open country;
you shall go to Babylon.
There you shall be rescued,
there the LORD will redeem you
from the hands of your enemies.

11 Now many nations
are assembled against you,
saying, "Let her be profaned,
and let our eyes gaze upon Zion."
12 But they do not know
the thoughts of the LORD;
they do not understand his plan,
that he has gathered them as sheaves to the threshing floor.
13 Arise and thresh,
O daughter Zion,
for I will make your horn iron
and your hoofs bronze;
you shall beat in pieces many peoples,
and shall[l] devote their gain to the LORD,
their wealth to the Lord of the whole earth.

5 [m] Now you are walled around with a wall;[n]
siege is laid against us;

---

k Meaning of Heb uncertain　　l Gk Syr Tg: Heb *and I will*　　m Ch 4.14 in Heb　　n Cn Compare
Gk: Meaning of Heb uncertain

with a rod they strike the ruler of
Israel
upon the cheek.

The Ruler from Bethlehem

2 o But you, O Bethlehem of Ephrathah,
who are one of the little clans of
Judah,
from you shall come forth for me
one who is to rule in Israel,
whose origin is from of old,
from ancient days.
3 Therefore he shall give them up
until the time
when she who is in labor has
brought forth;
then the rest of his kindred shall
return
to the people of Israel.
4 And he shall stand and feed his
flock in the strength of the
LORD,
in the majesty of the name of the
LORD his God.
And they shall live secure, for now
he shall be great
to the ends of the earth;
5 and he shall be the one of peace.

If the Assyrians come into our
land
and tread upon our soil,*p*
we will raise against them seven
shepherds
and eight installed as rulers.
6 They shall rule the land of Assyria
with the sword,
and the land of Nimrod with the
drawn sword;*q*
they*r* shall rescue us from the
Assyrians
if they come into our land
or tread within our border.

The Future Role of the Remnant

7 Then the remnant of Jacob,
surrounded by many peoples,
shall be like dew from the LORD,
like showers on the grass,
which do not depend upon people
or wait for any mortal.
8 And among the nations the
remnant of Jacob,
surrounded by many peoples,

shall be like a lion among the
animals of the forest,
like a young lion among the
flocks of sheep,
which, when it goes through,
treads down
and tears in pieces, with no one
to deliver.
9 Your hand shall be lifted up over
your adversaries,
and all your enemies shall be cut
off.

10 In that day, says the LORD,
I will cut off your horses from
among you
and will destroy your chariots;
11 and I will cut off the cities of your
land
and throw down all your
strongholds;
12 and I will cut off sorceries from
your hand,
and you shall have no more
soothsayers;
13 and I will cut off your images
and your pillars from among you,
and you shall bow down no more
to the work of your hands;
14 and I will uproot your sacred poles*s*
from among you
and destroy your towns.
15 And in anger and wrath I will
execute vengeance
on the nations that did not obey.

God Challenges Israel

6 Hear what the LORD says:
Rise, plead your case before the
mountains,
and let the hills hear your voice.
2 Hear, you mountains, the
controversy of the LORD,
and you enduring foundations of
the earth;
for the LORD has a controversy with
his people,
and he will contend with Israel.

3 "O my people, what have I done to
you?
In what have I wearied you?
Answer me!

---

o Ch 5.1 in Heb   *p* Gk: Heb *in our palaces*   *q* Cn: Heb *in its entrances*   *r* Heb *he*
s Heb *Asherim*

4 For I brought you up from the land
of Egypt,
and redeemed you from the
house of slavery;
and I sent before you Moses,
Aaron, and Miriam.
5 O my people, remember now what
King Balak of Moab devised,
what Balaam son of Beor
answered him,
and what happened from Shittim to
Gilgal,
that you may know the saving
acts of the LORD."

What God Requires

6 "With what shall I come before the
LORD,
and bow myself before God on
high?
Shall I come before him with burnt
offerings,
with calves a year old?
7 Will the LORD be pleased with
thousands of rams,
with ten thousands of rivers of
oil?
Shall I give my firstborn for my
transgression,
the fruit of my body for the sin of
my soul?"
8 He has told you, O mortal, what is
good;
and what does the LORD require
of you
but to do justice, and to love
kindness,
and to walk humbly with your
God?

Cheating and Violence to Be Punished

9 The voice of the LORD cries to the
city
(it is sound wisdom to fear your
name):
Hear, O tribe and assembly of the
city![t]
10 Can I forget[u] the treasures of
wickedness in the house of
the wicked,
and the scant measure that is
accursed?

11 Can I tolerate wicked scales
and a bag of dishonest weights?
12 Your[v] wealthy are full of violence;
your[w] inhabitants speak lies,
with tongues of deceit in their
mouths.
13 Therefore I have begun[x] to strike
you down,
making you desolate because of
your sins.
14 You shall eat, but not be satisfied,
and there shall be a gnawing
hunger within you;
you shall put away, but not save,
and what you save, I will hand
over to the sword.
15 You shall sow, but not reap;
you shall tread olives, but not
anoint yourselves with oil;
you shall tread grapes, but not
drink wine.
16 For you have kept the statutes of
Omri[y]
and all the works of the house of
Ahab,
and you have followed their
counsels.
Therefore I will make you a
desolation, and your[z]
inhabitants an object of
hissing;
so you shall bear the scorn of my
people.

The Total Corruption of the People

7 Woe is me! For I have become
like one who,
after the summer fruit has been
gathered,
after the vintage has been gleaned,
finds no cluster to eat;
there is no first-ripe fig for which
I hunger.
2 The faithful have disappeared from
the land,
and there is no one left who is
upright;
they all lie in wait for blood,
and they hunt each other with
nets.
3 Their hands are skilled to do evil;
the official and the judge ask for a
bribe,

---

t Cn Compare Gk: Heb *tribe, and who has appointed it yet!*   u Cn: Meaning of Heb uncertain
v Heb *Whose*   w Heb *whose*   x Gk Syr Vg: Heb *have made sick*   y Gk Syr Vg Tg: Heb *the statutes of Omri are kept*   z Heb *its*

and the powerful dictate what they
        desire;
    thus they pervert justice.*a*

4   The best of them is like a brier,
        the most upright of them a thorn
        hedge.
    The day of their*b* sentinels, of their*b*
        punishment, has come;
    now their confusion is at hand.

5   Put no trust in a friend,
        have no confidence in a loved one;
    guard the doors of your mouth
        from her who lies in your
        embrace;

6   for the son treats the father with
        contempt,
    the daughter rises up against her
        mother,
    the daughter-in-law against her
        mother-in-law;
    your enemies are members of
        your own household.

7   But as for me, I will look to the
        LORD,
    I will wait for the God of my
        salvation;
    my God will hear me.

IF YOU DO NOT HOPE, YOU WILL NOT FIND WHAT
IS BEYOND YOUR HOPES.   —*Clement of Alexandria*

Penitence and Trust in God

8   Do not rejoice over me, O my
        enemy;
    when I fall, I shall rise;
    when I sit in darkness,
        the LORD will be a light to me.

9   I must bear the indignation of the
        LORD,
        because I have sinned against
        him,
    until he takes my side
        and executes judgment for me.
    He will bring me out to the light;
        I shall see his vindication.

10 Then my enemy will see,
        and shame will cover her who
        said to me,
    "Where is the LORD your God?"
    My eyes will see her downfall;*c*
    now she will be trodden down
        like the mire of the streets.

A Prophecy of Restoration

11 A day for the building of your walls!
        In that day the boundary shall be
        far extended.

MOST HIGH, GLORIOUS GOD, ENLIGHTEN THE
DARKNESS OF MY HEART AND GIVE ME, LORD, A
CORRECT FAITH, A CERTAIN HOPE, A PERFECT
CHARITY, SENSE AND KNOWLEDGE, SO THAT I MAY
CARRY OUT YOUR HOLY AND TRUE COMMAND.

        —*Francis of Assisi*

---

12 In that day they will come to you
        from Assyria to*d* Egypt,
    and from Egypt to the River,
        from sea to sea and from
        mountain to mountain.

13 But the earth will be desolate
        because of its inhabitants,
    for the fruit of their doings.

14 Shepherd your people with your staff,
        the flock that belongs to you,
    which lives alone in a forest
        in the midst of a garden land;
    let them feed in Bashan and Gilead
        as in the days of old.

15 As in the days when you came out
        of the land of Egypt,
    show us*e* marvelous things.

16 The nations shall see and be
        ashamed
        of all their might;
    they shall lay their hands on their
        mouths;
    their ears shall be deaf;

17 they shall lick dust like a snake,
        like the crawling things of the
        earth;
    they shall come trembling out of
        their fortresses;
    they shall turn in dread to the
        LORD our God,
    and they shall stand in fear of you.

God's Compassion and Steadfast Love

18 Who is a God like you, pardoning
        iniquity
        and passing over the transgression
        of the remnant of your*f*
        possession?

---

a Cn: Heb *they weave it*   *b* Heb *your*   *c* Heb lacks *downfall*   *d* One Ms: MT *Assyria and
cities of*   *e* Cn: Heb *I will show him*   *f* Heb *his*

He does not retain his anger forever,
  because he delights in showing
    clemency.
19 He will again have compassion
    upon us;
  he will tread our iniquities under
    foot.

You will cast all our[g] sins
  into the depths of the sea.
20 You will show faithfulness to Jacob
  and unswerving loyalty to
    Abraham,
  as you have sworn to our ancestors
    from the days of old.

g Gk Syr Vg Tg: Heb *their*

THURSDAY

LOOK TO THE LORD

Mrs. Charles E. Cowman

VERSE: Micah 7.7   PASSAGE: Micah 7.1–7

 everal years ago while visiting certain of the Northern European countries, it was necessary for me to cross the North Sea in a large ocean liner. During the first days of the voyage we sped along over calm seas, but suddenly we were overtaken by a frightening tempest. The waves were like great mountains, and we were lifted to their heights. The great ship rocked and rolled, creaked and groaned. The faces of the passengers were blanched white with fear. Even the little ones clung to their mothers, sensing the nearness of danger—the very air was surcharged by an ominous foreboding of impending destruction. When it seemed that surely the ship had endured to the very limit, a man appeared on the scene. There was no trace of anxiety or concern on his face. His presence radiated calmness, rest and peace. With a voice full of gentleness he assured us, "all's well," and our fears disappeared.

Who was that man? The captain. He had taken that vessel through many a long voyage, plowed rough seas, met terrible storms, and had always arrived safely into port . . .

What have we to fear? . . . Is not our Captain on board? . . . With Christ in the vessel we smile at the storm.

Yes, one whose faith is continually stimulated by *the upward look* gives no ground to the attempted encroachment of despair. No matter how great the trouble or how dark the outlook, a quick lifting of the heart to God in a moment of real actual faith in him will completely alter any situation and turn the darkness of midnight into glorious sunrise.

ADDITIONAL SCRIPTURE READING:
Psalms 31.5; 37.5; Isaiah 65.24

Go to page 1068 for your next devotional reading.

1900   Present

NAHUM

AHUM (MEANING "COMFORT")
PROPHESIES AGAINST THE CRUEL
NATION OF ASSYRIA. HE REMINDS
THE PEOPLE OF JUDAH THAT GOD IS IN CON-
TROL OF HISTORY AND WILL NOT ALLOW EVIL
TO PREVAIL FOREVER. NAHUM PROPHESIED
THAT NINEVEH WOULD FALL, WHICH DID
HAPPEN IN 612 B.C. KINGDOMS BUILT ON
WICKEDNESS AND TYRANNY MUST EVENTU-
ALLY FALL, AS ASSYRIA DID. AS YOU READ
THIS BOOK, TAKE COMFORT THAT GOD IS
THE LORD OF HISTORY AND HE WILL HAVE
HIS WAY.

---

1 An oracle concerning Nineveh. The book of the vision of Nahum of Elkosh.

The Consuming Wrath of God

2 A jealous and avenging God is the
    LORD,
    the LORD is avenging and
        wrathful;
    the LORD takes vengeance on his
        adversaries
    and rages against his enemies.
3 The LORD is slow to anger but great
        in power,
    and the LORD will by no means
        clear the guilty.

    His way is in whirlwind and storm,
        and the clouds are the dust of his
            feet.
4 He rebukes the sea and makes it
        dry,
    and he dries up all the rivers;
    Bashan and Carmel wither,
        and the bloom of Lebanon fades.
5 The mountains quake before him,
        and the hills melt;
    the earth heaves before him,
        the world and all who live in it.

6 Who can stand before his
        indignation?
    Who can endure the heat of his
        anger?
    His wrath is poured out like fire,
        and by him the rocks are broken
            in pieces.
7 The LORD is good,
    a stronghold in a day of trouble;

TRUST IN THE GOODNESS OF GOD
François Fénelon

VERSE: Nahum 1.7   **PASSAGE:** Nahum 1.2–8

he best and highest use of your mind is to learn to distrust yourself, to renounce your own will, to submit to the will of God, and to become as a little child. It is not of doing difficult things that I speak, but of performing the most common actions with your heart fixed on God, and as one who is accomplishing the end of his being. You will act as others do, except that you will never sin . . . You will be moderate at table, moderate in speaking, moderate in expense, moderate in judging, moderate in your diversions; sober even in your wisdom and foresight. It is this universal sobriety in the use of the best things that is taught us by the true love of God. We are neither austere, nor fretful, nor scrupulous, but have within ourselves a principle of love that enlarges the heart and sheds a gentle influence upon everything; that, without constraint or effort, inspires a delicate apprehension lest we should displease God; and that arrests us if we are tempted to do wrong.

In this state we suffer, as other people do, from fatigue, embarrassments, misfortunes, bodily infirmities, trials from ourselves and trials from others, temptations, disgusts, and sometimes discouragements. But though our crosses are the same with those of the rest of the world, our motives for supporting them are very different. We have learned from Jesus Christ how to endure. This can purify, this can detach us from self and renew the spirit of our minds. We see God in everything, but we have the clearest vision of him in suffering and in our humiliations . . .

Put your trust not in your resolutions or your own strength, but in the goodness of God, who has loved you when you thought not of him, and before you could love him.

ADDITIONAL SCRIPTURE READING:
2 Chronicles 32.8–11; Jeremiah 17.7–8

Go to page 1070 for your next devotional reading.

1500   1700

he protects those who take refuge
       in him,
8   even in a rushing flood.
He will make a full end of his
       adversaries,[a]
       and will pursue his enemies into
              darkness.
9 Why do you plot against the LORD?
       He will make an end;
       no adversary will rise up twice.
10 Like thorns they are entangled,
       like drunkards they are drunk;
       they are consumed like dry straw.
11 From you one has gone out
       who plots evil against the LORD,
       one who counsels wickedness.

Good News for Judah

12 Thus says the LORD,
       "Though they are at full strength
              and many,[b]
       they will be cut off and pass away.
       Though I have afflicted you,
       I will afflict you no more.
13 And now I will break off his yoke
              from you
       and snap the bonds that bind
              you."

14 The LORD has commanded
              concerning you:
       "Your name shall be perpetuated
              no longer;
       from the house of your gods I will
              cut off
       the carved image and the cast
              image.
       I will make your grave, for you are
              worthless."

15c Look! On the mountains the feet of
              one
       who brings good tidings,
       who proclaims peace!
Celebrate your festivals, O Judah,
       fulfill your vows,
       for never again shall the wicked
              invade you;
       they are utterly cut off.

The Destruction of the Wicked City

2 A shatterer[d] has come up
       against you.

Guard the ramparts;
       watch the road;
gird your loins;
       collect all your strength.
2 (For the LORD is restoring the
              majesty of Jacob,
       as well as the majesty of Israel,
       though ravagers have ravaged them
       and ruined their branches.)

3 The shields of his warriors are red;
       his soldiers are clothed in
              crimson.
The metal on the chariots flashes
       on the day when he musters
              them;
       the chargers[e] prance.
4 The chariots race madly through
              the streets,
       they rush to and fro through the
              squares;
       their appearance is like torches,
       they dart like lightning.
5 He calls his officers;
       they stumble as they come
              forward;
       they hasten to the wall,
       and the mantelet[b] is set up.
6 The river gates are opened,
       the palace trembles.
7 It is decreed[b] that the city[f] be
              exiled,
       its slave women led away,
       moaning like doves
       and beating their breasts.
8 Nineveh is like a pool
       whose waters[g] run away.
       "Halt! Halt!"—
       but no one turns back.
9 "Plunder the silver,
       plunder the gold!
There is no end of treasure!
       An abundance of every precious
              thing!"

10 Devastation, desolation, and
              destruction!
       Hearts faint and knees tremble,
       all loins quake,
       all faces grow pale!
11 What became of the lions' den,
       the cave[h] of the young lions,
       where the lion goes,

---

a Gk: Heb *of her place*   b Meaning of Heb uncertain   c Ch 2.1 in Heb   d Cn: Heb *scatterer*
e Cn Compare Gk Syr: Heb *cypresses*   f Heb *it*   g Cn Compare Gk: Heb *a pool, from the days that
she has become, and they*   h Cn: Heb *pasture*

WEEKEND

BEAUTIFUL FEET
Frances Ridley Havergal

VERSE: Nahum 1.15   PASSAGE: Nahum 1.14–15

 ur Lord has many uses for what is kept for himself. How beautiful are the feet of them that bring glad tidings of good things! That is the best use of all, and I expect the angels think those feet beautiful, even if they are cased in muddy boots or galoshes . . .

If we want to have these beautiful feet, we must have the tidings ready which they are to bear. Let us ask him to keep our hearts so freshly full of his good news of salvation that our mouths may speak out of their abundance. If the clouds be full of rain, they empty themselves upon the earth. May we be so filled with the Spirit that we may have much to pour out for others.

Besides the privilege of carrying water from the wells of salvation, there are plenty of cups of cold water to be carried in all directions; not to the poor only—ministries of love are often as much needed by a rich friend. But the feet must be kept for these; they will be too tired for them if they are tired out for self-pleasing. In such services we are treading in the blessed steps of Christ, who went about doing good.

ADDITIONAL SCRIPTURE READING:
Isaiah 52.7; Romans 10.15

Go to page 1075 for your next devotional reading.

1700   1900

and the lion's cubs, with no one
    to disturb them?
12 The lion has torn enough for his
    whelps
    and strangled prey for his
    lionesses;
he has filled his caves with prey
    and his dens with torn flesh.

13 See, I am against you, says the
LORD of hosts, and I will burn your[i]
chariots in smoke, and the sword shall
devour your young lions; I will cut off
your prey from the earth, and the voice
of your messengers shall be heard no
more.

Ruin Imminent and Inevitable

3 Ah! City of bloodshed,
    utterly deceitful, full of booty—
    no end to the plunder!
2 The crack of whip and rumble of
    wheel,
    galloping horse and bounding
    chariot!
3 Horsemen charging,
    flashing sword and glittering
    spear,
piles of dead,
    heaps of corpses,
dead bodies without end—
    they stumble over the bodies!
4 Because of the countless
    debaucheries of the
    prostitute,
    gracefully alluring, mistress of
    sorcery,
who enslaves[j] nations through her
    debaucheries,
    and peoples through her sorcery,
5 I am against you,
    says the LORD of hosts,
    and will lift up your skirts over
    your face;
and I will let nations look on your
    nakedness
    and kingdoms on your shame.
6 I will throw filth at you
    and treat you with contempt,
    and make you a spectacle.
7 Then all who see you will shrink
    from you and say,
    "Nineveh is devastated; who will
    bemoan her?"

Where shall I seek comforters for
    you?

8 Are you better than Thebes[k]
    that sat by the Nile,
with water around her,
    her rampart a sea,
    water her wall?

IF WE HAVE NOT QUIET IN OUR MINDS, OUTWARD
COMFORT WILL DO NO MORE FOR US THAN A
GOLDEN SLIPPER ON A GOUTY FOOT.
                              —*John Bunyan*

---

9 Ethiopia[l] was her strength,
    Egypt too, and that without
    limit;
    Put and the Libyans were her[m]
    helpers.
10 Yet she became an exile,
    she went into captivity;
even her infants were dashed in
    pieces
    at the head of every street;
lots were cast for her nobles,
    all her dignitaries were bound in
    fetters.
11 You also will be drunken,
    you will go into hiding;[n]
you will seek
    a refuge from the enemy.
12 All your fortresses are like fig trees
    with first-ripe figs—
if shaken they fall
    into the mouth of the eater.
13 Look at your troops:
    they are women in your midst.
The gates of your land
    are wide open to your foes;
fire has devoured the bars of your
    gates.

14 Draw water for the siege,
    strengthen your forts;
trample the clay,
    tread the mortar,
    take hold of the brick mold!
15 There the fire will devour you,
    the sword will cut you off.
It will devour you like the
    locust.

---

i Heb *her*   *j* Heb *sells*   *k* Heb *No-amon*   *l* Or *Nubia;* Heb *Cush*   *m* Gk: Heb *your*
n Meaning of Heb uncertain

Multiply yourselves like the
      locust,
  multiply like the grasshopper!
16 You increased your merchants
      more than the stars of the
      heavens.
    The locust sheds its skin and
      flies away.
17 Your guards are like grasshoppers,
    your scribes like swarms° of
      locusts
  settling on the fences
    on a cold day—
  when the sun rises, they fly
      away;

no one knows where they have
      gone.
18 Your shepherds are asleep,
    O king of Assyria;
    your nobles slumber.
  Your people are scattered on the
      mountains
    with no one to gather them.
19 There is no assuaging your hurt,
    your wound is mortal.
  All who hear the news about you
    clap their hands over you.
  For who has ever escaped
    your endless cruelty?

_o_ Meaning of Heb uncertain

HABAKKUK

ABAKKUK PRAYED AND PROPHESIED
IN TIMES OF CRISIS. THE INTERNA-
TIONAL SCENE WAS SHOCKED BY
EVENTS OF FAR-REACHING IMPORT. INTER-
NALLY THE PEOPLE OF GOD WERE CAUGHT
UP IN A CRISIS OF RELIGIOUS AND MORAL
BEWILDERMENT. IT WAS INTO THAT TROU-
BLED SCENE THAT HABAKKUK STEPPED WITH
HIS EXPRESSIONS OF CONFUSION AND COM-
PLAINT. AS YOU READ THIS BOOK, NOTICE
GOD'S UNEXPECTED ANSWER AND THE HOPE
HABAKKUK FINALLY DISCOVERED.

---

1 The oracle that the prophet
Habakkuk saw.

The Prophet's Complaint

2 O LORD, how long shall I cry for
help,
and you will not listen?
Or cry to you "Violence!"
and you will not save?
3 Why do you make me see
wrongdoing
and look at trouble?
Destruction and violence are before
me;
strife and contention arise.
4 So the law becomes slack
and justice never prevails.
The wicked surround the
righteous—

therefore judgment comes forth
perverted.

5 Look at the nations, and see!
Be astonished! Be astounded!
For a work is being done in your
days
that you would not believe if you
were told.
6 For I am rousing the Chaldeans,
that fierce and impetuous nation,
who march through the breadth of
the earth
to seize dwellings not their own.
7 Dread and fearsome are they;
their justice and dignity proceed
from themselves.
8 Their horses are swifter than
leopards,

more menacing than wolves at
   dusk;
their horses charge.
Their horsemen come from far
   away;
they fly like an eagle swift to
   devour.
9 They all come for violence,
   with faces pressing*a* forward;
they gather captives like sand.
10 At kings they scoff,
   and of rulers they make sport.
They laugh at every fortress,
   and heap up earth to take it.
11 Then they sweep by like the wind;
   they transgress and become
      guilty;
their own might is their god!

12 Are you not from of old,
   O LORD my God, my Holy One?
You*b* shall not die.
O LORD, you have marked them for
   judgment;
and you, O Rock, have
   established them for
   punishment.
13 Your eyes are too pure to behold
      evil,
   and you cannot look on
      wrongdoing;
why do you look on the
   treacherous,
   and are silent when the wicked
      swallow
those more righteous than they?
14 You have made people like the fish
      of the sea,
   like crawling things that have no
      ruler.

15 The enemy*c* brings all of them up
      with a hook;
   he drags them out with his net,
he gathers them in his seine;
   so he rejoices and exults.
16 Therefore he sacrifices to his net
   and makes offerings to his seine;
for by them his portion is lavish,
   and his food is rich.
17 Is he then to keep on emptying his
      net,
   and destroying nations without
      mercy?

God's Reply to the Prophet's Complaint

2 I will stand at my watchpost,
   and station myself on the
      rampart;
I will keep watch to see what he
   will say to me,
   and what he*d* will answer
      concerning my complaint.
2 Then the LORD answered me and
      said:
Write the vision;
   make it plain on tablets,
   so that a runner may read it.
3 For there is still a vision for the
      appointed time;
   it speaks of the end, and does not
      lie.
If it seems to tarry, wait for it;
   it will surely come, it will not
      delay.
4 Look at the proud!
   Their spirit is not right in them,
   but the righteous live by their
      faith.*e*
5 Moreover, wealth*f* is treacherous;
   the arrogant do not endure.
They open their throats wide as
      Sheol;
   like Death they never have
      enough.
They gather all nations for
      themselves,
   and collect all peoples as their
      own.

The Woes of the Wicked

6 Shall not everyone taunt such people and, with mocking riddles, say about
them,
   "Alas for you who heap up what is
      not your own!"
   How long will you load
      yourselves with goods taken
      in pledge?
7 Will not your own creditors
      suddenly rise,
   and those who make you tremble
      wake up?
   Then you will be booty for
      them.
8 Because you have plundered many
      nations,

all that survive of the peoples
shall plunder you—
because of human bloodshed, and
violence to the earth,
to cities and all who live in them.

9 "Alas for you who get evil gain for
your houses,
setting your nest on high
to be safe from the reach of
harm!"

MONDAY

IVAN HAS NO GOD. HE HAS AN IDEA.
Fyodor Dostoyevsky

VERSE: Habakkuk 1.11   **PASSAGE:** Habakkuk 1.5–11

ou see, I never had any of these doubts before, but it was all hidden away in me. It was perhaps just because I did not understand these ideas surging up in me that I used to drink and fight and rage. It was to stifle them in myself, to still them, to smother them. There is an idea in Ivan; he is not Rakitin. But Ivan is a sphinx and is silent; he is always silent. It's God that's worrying me. That's the only thing that's worrying me. What if he doesn't exist? What if Rakitin's right—that it's an idea made up by men? Then, if he doesn't exist, man is the chief of the earth, of the universe. Magnificent! Only how is he going to be good without God? That's the question. I always come back to that. For whom is man going to love then? To whom will he be thankful? To whom will he sing the hymn? Rakitin laughs, Rakitin says that one can love humanity without God. Well, only a sniveling idiot can maintain that. I can't understand it. Life's easy for Rakitin—"You'd better think about the extension of civic rights," he says, "or even of keeping down the price of meat. You will show your love for humanity more simply and directly by that than by philosophy." I answered him, "Well, but you without a God, are more likely to raise the price of meat if it suits you and make a ruble on every kopeck." He lost his temper. But after all, what is goodness? Answer me that, Alexey. Goodness is one thing with me and another with a Chinaman, so it's a relative thing. Or isn't it? Is it not relative? A treacherous question! You won't laugh if I tell you it's kept me awake two nights. I only wonder now how people can live and think nothing about it. Vanity! Ivan has no God. He has an idea.

ADDITIONAL SCRIPTURE READING:
Daniel 5.4; Lamentations 5.19; Hebrews 1.10–12

Go to page 1077 for your next devotional reading.

1700 1900

10   You have devised shame for your
house
by cutting off many peoples;
you have forfeited your life.
11   The very stones will cry out from
the wall,
and the plaster[g] will respond
from the woodwork.

12   "Alas for you who build a town by
bloodshed,
and found a city on iniquity!"
13   Is it not from the LORD of hosts
that peoples labor only to feed
the flames,
and nations weary themselves for
nothing?
14   But the earth will be filled
with the knowledge of the glory
of the LORD,
as the waters cover the sea.

15   "Alas for you who make your
neighbors drink,
pouring out your wrath[h] until
they are drunk,
in order to gaze on their
nakedness!"
16   You will be sated with contempt
instead of glory.
Drink, you yourself, and stagger![i]
The cup in the LORD's right hand
will come around to you,
and shame will come upon your
glory!
17   For the violence done to Lebanon
will overwhelm you;
the destruction of the animals
will terrify you—[j]
because of human bloodshed and
violence to the earth,
to cities and all who live in
them.

18   What use is an idol
once its maker has shaped it—
a cast image, a teacher of lies?
For its maker trusts in what has
been made,
though the product is only an
idol that cannot speak!
19   Alas for you who say to the wood,
"Wake up!"

to silent stone, "Rouse yourself!"
Can it teach?
See, it is gold and silver plated,
and there is no breath in it at all.

20   But the LORD is in his holy temple;
let all the earth keep silence
before him!

3   A prayer of the prophet Habakkuk according to Shigionoth.

The Prophet's Prayer

2   O LORD, I have heard of your
renown,
and I stand in awe, O LORD, of
your work.
In our own time revive it;
in our own time make it known;
in wrath may you remember
mercy.
3   God came from Teman,
the Holy One from Mount Paran.
                 Selah
His glory covered the heavens,
and the earth was full of his
praise.
4   The brightness was like the sun;
rays came forth from his hand,
where his power lay hidden.
5   Before him went pestilence,
and plague followed close behind.
6   He stopped and shook the earth;
he looked and made the nations
tremble.
The eternal mountains were
shattered;
along his ancient pathways
the everlasting hills sank low.
7   I saw the tents of Cushan under
affliction;
the tent-curtains of the land of
Midian trembled.
8   Was your wrath against the rivers,[k]
O LORD?
Or your anger against the rivers,[k]
or your rage against the sea,[l]
when you drove your horses,
your chariots to victory?
9   You brandished your naked bow,
sated[m] were the arrows at your
command.[n]   *Selah*
You split the earth with rivers.

---

g Or *beam*   h Or *poison*   i Q Ms Gk: MT *be uncircumcised*   j Gk Syr: Meaning of Heb
uncertain   k Or *against River*   l Or *against Sea*   m Cn: Heb *oaths*   n Meaning of Heb
uncertain

THE ARRIVAL AT THE HIGH PLACES
Hannah Hurnard

VERSE: Habakkuk 3.19   **PASSAGE:** Habakkuk 3.18–19

hen he had finished, Much-Afraid lifted her face toward the high places which were quite invisible and spoke quietly through the mist. "My Lord, behold me—here I am, in the place thou didst send me to—doing the thing thou didst tell me to do for 'where you die, I will die—there will I be buried. May the LORD do thus and so to me, and more as well, if even death parts me from you!' " (Ruth 1.17).

Still there was silence, a silence as of the grave, for indeed she was in the grave of her own hopes and still without the promised hinds' feet, still outside the high places with even the promise to be laid down on the altar. This was the place to which the long, heartbreaking journey had led her. Yet just once more before she laid it down on the altar, Much-Afraid repeated the glorious promise which had been the cause of her starting for the high places. "GOD, the Lord, is my strength; he makes my feet like the feet of a deer, he makes me tread upon the heights" (Habakkuk 3.19).

The priest put forth a hand of steel, right into her heart. There was a sound of rending and tearing, and the human love, with all its myriad rootlets and fibers, came forth. He held it for a moment and then said, "Yes, it was ripe for removal, the time had come. There is not a rootlet torn or missing."

When he had said this he cast it down on the altar and spread his hands above it. There came a flash of fire which seemed to rend the altar; after that, nothing but ashes remained, either of the love itself, which had been so deeply planted in her heart, or of the suffering and sorrow which had been her companions on that long, strange journey. A sense of utter, overwhelming rest and peace engulfed Much-Afraid. At last, the offering had been made and there was nothing left to be done. When the priest had unbound her she leaned forward over the ashes on the altar and said with complete thanksgiving, "It is finished."

Then, utterly exhausted, she fell asleep.

ADDITIONAL SCRIPTURE READING:
Deuteronomy 32.13; Isaiah 58.14; 2 Corinthians 12.9–10

Go to page 1081 for your next devotional reading.

1900   Present

10 The mountains saw you, and
          writhed;
    a torrent of water swept by;
the deep gave forth its voice.
    The sun*o* raised high its hands;
11 the moon*p* stood still in its exalted
          place,
    at the light of your arrows
        speeding by,
    at the gleam of your flashing
        spear.
12 In fury you trod the earth,
    in anger you trampled nations.
13 You came forth to save your people,
    to save your anointed.
You crushed the head of the wicked
      house,
    laying it bare from foundation to
      roof.*q*   *Selah*
14 You pierced with their own arrows
        the head*r* of his warriors,*s*
    who came like a whirlwind to
        scatter us,*t*
    gloating as if ready to devour the
      poor who were in hiding.
15 You trampled the sea with your
      horses,
    churning the mighty waters.

16 I hear, and I tremble within;
    my lips quiver at the sound.

Rottenness enters into my bones,
    and my steps tremble*u* beneath
      me.
I wait quietly for the day of
      calamity
    to come upon the people who
      attack us.

Trust and Joy in the Midst of Trouble

17 Though the fig tree does not
        blossom,
    and no fruit is on the vines;
though the produce of the olive
      fails,
    and the fields yield no food;
though the flock is cut off from the
      fold,
    and there is no herd in the stalls,
18 yet I will rejoice in the LORD;
    I will exult in the God of my
      salvation.
19 GOD, the Lord, is my strength;
    he makes my feet like the feet of
      a deer,
    and makes me tread upon the
      heights.*v*

To the leader: with stringed*w*
    instruments.

---

o Heb *It*   *p* Heb *sun, moon*   *q* Meaning of Heb uncertain   *r* Or *leader*   *s* Vg Compare Gk Syr: Meaning of Heb uncertain   *t* Heb *me*   *u* Cn Compare Gk: Meaning of Heb uncertain   *v* Heb *my heights*   *w* Heb *my stringed*

ZEPHANIAH

EPHANIAH WROTE TO THE PEOPLE OF JUDAH, WARNING THEM OF JUDGMENT AND A TERRIBLE "DAY OF THE LORD" THAT WAS TO COME—A DAY WHEN GOD WOULD SEVERELY PUNISH THE NATIONS. AS YOU READ THIS BOOK, LOOK FOR THE NOTE OF HOPE THAT GOD'S JUDGMENT WOULD PAVE THE WAY FOR A NEW SOCIETY IN WHICH JUSTICE WOULD PREVAIL AND ALL PEOPLE WOULD WORSHIP THE LORD.

1 The word of the LORD that came to Zephaniah son of Cushi son of Gedaliah son of Amariah son of Hezekiah, in the days of King Josiah son of Amon of Judah.

The Coming Judgment on Judah

2 I will utterly sweep away everything
   from the face of the earth, says
   the LORD.
3 I will sweep away humans and
   animals;
   I will sweep away the birds of the
   air
   and the fish of the sea.
   I will make the wicked stumble.a
   I will cut off humanity
   from the face of the earth, says
   the LORD.
4 I will stretch out my hand against
   Judah,
   and against all the inhabitants of
   Jerusalem;
   and I will cut off from this place
   every remnant of Baal
   and the name of the idolatrous
   priests;b
5 those who bow down on the roofs
   to the host of the heavens;
   those who bow down and swear to
   the LORD,
   but also swear by Milcom;c
6 those who have turned back from
   following the LORD,

---

a Cn: Heb *sea, and those who cause the wicked to stumble* b Compare Gk: Heb *the idolatrous priests with the priests* c Gk Mss Syr Vg: Heb *Malcam* (or, *their king*)

who have not sought the LORD or
    inquired of him.

7 Be silent before the Lord GOD!
    For the day of the LORD is at hand;
  the LORD has prepared a sacrifice,
    he has consecrated his guests.
8 And on the day of the LORD's
    sacrifice
  I will punish the officials and the
    king's sons
  and all who dress themselves in
    foreign attire.
9 On that day I will punish
    all who leap over the threshold,
  who fill their master's house
    with violence and fraud.

10 On that day, says the LORD,
    a cry will be heard from the Fish
    Gate,
  a wail from the Second Quarter,
    a loud crash from the hills.
11 The inhabitants of the Mortar wail,
    for all the traders have perished;
  all who weigh out silver are cut
    off.
12 At that time I will search
    Jerusalem with lamps,
  and I will punish the people
  who rest complacently[d] on their
    dregs,
    those who say in their hearts,
  "The LORD will not do good,
    nor will he do harm."
13 Their wealth shall be plundered,
    and their houses laid waste.
  Though they build houses,
    they shall not inhabit them;
  though they plant vineyards,
    they shall not drink wine from
    them.

The Great Day of the LORD

14 The great day of the LORD is near,
    near and hastening fast;
  the sound of the day of the LORD is
    bitter,
    the warrior cries aloud there.
15 That day will be a day of wrath,
    a day of distress and anguish,
  a day of ruin and devastation,
    a day of darkness and gloom,
    a day of clouds and thick darkness,

16 a day of trumpet blast and battle
    cry
  against the fortified cities
    and against the lofty battlements.

17 I will bring such distress upon
    people
    that they shall walk like the
    blind;
  because they have sinned against
    the LORD,
  their blood shall be poured out like
    dust,
    and their flesh like dung.
18 Neither their silver nor their gold
    will be able to save them
    on the day of the LORD's wrath;
  in the fire of his passion
    the whole earth shall be
    consumed;
  for a full, a terrible end
    he will make of all the
    inhabitants of the earth.

Judgment on Israel's Enemies

2 Gather together, gather,
    O shameless nation,
2 before you are driven away
    like the drifting chaff,[e]
  before there comes upon you
    the fierce anger of the LORD,
  before there comes upon you
    the day of the LORD's wrath.
3 Seek the LORD, all you humble of
    the land,
    who do his commands;
  seek righteousness, seek humility;
    perhaps you may be hidden
    on the day of the LORD's wrath.
4 For Gaza shall be deserted,
    and Ashkelon shall become a
    desolation;
  Ashdod's people shall be driven out
    at noon,
    and Ekron shall be uprooted.

5 Ah, inhabitants of the seacoast,
    you nation of the Cherethites!
  The word of the LORD is against
    you,
    O Canaan, land of the
    Philistines;
  and I will destroy you until no
    inhabitant is left.

---

d Heb *who thicken*   e Cn Compare Gk Syr: Heb *before a decree is born; like chaff a day has passed away*

THE MOMENT OF MEANING
T. S. Eliot

VERSE: Zephaniah 1.14   **PASSAGE:** Zephaniah 1.14—2.3

hen came, at a predetermined moment, a moment in
    time and of time,
A moment not out of time, but in time, in what we call
    history: transecting, bisecting the world of time,
    a moment in time but not like a moment of time,
A moment in time but time was made through that
    moment; for without the meaning there is no
    time, and that moment of time gave the
    meaning.
Then it seemed as if men must proceed from light to light,
    in the light of the Word,
Through the passion and sacrifice saved in spite of their
    negative being:
Bestial as ever before, carnal, self-seeking as always before,
    selfish and purblind as ever before,
Yet always struggling, always reaffirming, always resuming
    their march on the way that was lit by the light;
Often halting, loitering, straying, delaying, returning, yet
    following no other way.
But it seems that something has happened that has never
    happened before: though we know not just
    when, or why, or where.
Men have left God not for other gods, they say, but for no
    god; and this has never happened before
That men both deny gods and worship gods, professing first
    reason,
And then money, and power, and what they call life, or race,
    or dialectic.
The church disowned, the tower overthrown, the bells
    upturned, what have we to do
But stand with empty hands and palms turned upwards
In an age which advances progressively backwards?

ADDITIONAL SCRIPTURE READING:
Jeremiah 30.7; Zephaniah 1.7; Acts 2.20–21

Go to page 1086 for your next devotional reading.

1900   Present

6 And you, O seacoast, shall be
    pastures,
    meadows for shepherds
    and folds for flocks.
7 The seacoast shall become the
    possession
    of the remnant of the house of
      Judah,
    on which they shall pasture,
and in the houses of Ashkelon
    they shall lie down at evening.
For the Lord their God will be
    mindful of them
    and restore their fortunes.

8 I have heard the taunts of Moab
    and the revilings of the
      Ammonites,
how they have taunted my people
    and made boasts against their
      territory.
9 Therefore, as I live, says the Lord
    of hosts,
    the God of Israel,
Moab shall become like Sodom
    and the Ammonites like
      Gomorrah,
a land possessed by nettles and salt
    pits,
    and a waste forever.
The remnant of my people shall
    plunder them,
    and the survivors of my nation
    shall possess them.
10 This shall be their lot in return for
    their pride,
    because they scoffed and boasted
against the people of the Lord of
    hosts.
11 The Lord will be terrible against
    them;
    he will shrivel all the gods of the
      earth,
and to him shall bow down,
    each in its place,
    all the coasts and islands of the
    nations.

12 You also, O Ethiopians,*f*
    shall be killed by my sword.

13 And he will stretch out his hand
    against the north,
    and destroy Assyria;

and he will make Nineveh a
    desolation,
    a dry waste like the desert.
14 Herds shall lie down in it,
    every wild animal;*g*
the desert owl*h* and the screech
    owl*h*
    shall lodge on its capitals;
the owl*i* shall hoot at the window,
    the raven*j* croak on the
      threshold;
    for its cedar work will be laid
      bare.
15 Is this the exultant city
    that lived secure,
that said to itself,
    "I am, and there is no one else"?
What a desolation it has become,
    a lair for wild animals!
Everyone who passes by it
    hisses and shakes the fist.

The Wickedness of Jerusalem

3 Ah, soiled, defiled,
    oppressing city!
2 It has listened to no voice;
    it has accepted no correction.
It has not trusted in the Lord;
    it has not drawn near to its God.

3 The officials within it
    are roaring lions;
its judges are evening wolves
    that leave nothing until the
      morning.
4 Its prophets are reckless,
    faithless persons;
its priests have profaned what is
    sacred,
    they have done violence to the
      law.
5 The Lord within it is righteous;
    he does no wrong.
Every morning he renders his
    judgment,
    each dawn without fail;
    but the unjust knows no shame.

6 I have cut off nations;
    their battlements are in ruins;
I have laid waste their streets
    so that no one walks in them;
their cities have been made
    desolate,

---

f Or *Nubians;* Heb *Cushites*   *g* Tg Compare Gk: Heb *nation*   *h* Meaning of Heb uncertain
i Cn: Heb *a voice*   *j* Gk Vg: Heb *desolation*

without people, without
  inhabitants.
7 I said, "Surely the city[k] will fear
  me,
  it will accept correction;
it will not lose sight[l]
  of all that I have brought upon
  it."
But they were the more eager
  to make all their deeds corrupt.

Punishment and Conversion of the Nations

8 Therefore wait for me, says the
  LORD,
  for the day when I arise as a
  witness.
For my decision is to gather
  nations,
to assemble kingdoms,
to pour out upon them my
  indignation,
  all the heat of my anger;
for in the fire of my passion
  all the earth shall be consumed.

9 At that time I will change the
  speech of the peoples
  to a pure speech,
that all of them may call on the
  name of the LORD
and serve him with one accord.
10 From beyond the rivers of
  Ethiopia[m]
  my suppliants, my scattered
  ones,
  shall bring my offering.

11 On that day you shall not be put to
  shame
  because of all the deeds by which
  you have rebelled against
  me;
for then I will remove from your
  midst
  your proudly exultant ones,
and you shall no longer be haughty
  in my holy mountain.
12 For I will leave in the midst of you
  a people humble and lowly.
They shall seek refuge in the name
  of the LORD—
13   the remnant of Israel;

they shall do no wrong
  and utter no lies,
nor shall a deceitful tongue
  be found in their mouths.
Then they will pasture and lie
  down,
  and no one shall make them
  afraid.

A Song of Joy

14 Sing aloud, O daughter Zion;
  shout, O Israel!
Rejoice and exult with all your
  heart,
  O daughter Jerusalem!
15 The LORD has taken away the
  judgments against you,
  he has turned away your
  enemies.
The king of Israel, the LORD, is in
  your midst;
  you shall fear disaster no more.
16 On that day it shall be said to
  Jerusalem:
Do not fear, O Zion;
  do not let your hands grow weak.
17 The LORD, your God, is in your
  midst,
  a warrior who gives victory;
he will rejoice over you with
  gladness,
  he will renew you[n] in his love;
he will exult over you with loud
  singing
18   as on a day of festival.[o]
I will remove disaster from you,[p]
  so that you will not bear
  reproach for it.
19 I will deal with all your oppressors
  at that time.
And I will save the lame
  and gather the outcast,
and I will change their shame into
  praise
  and renown in all the earth.
20 At that time I will bring you home,
  at the time when I gather you;
for I will make you renowned and
  praised
  among all the peoples of the
  earth,
when I restore your fortunes
  before your eyes, says the LORD.

---

k Heb *it*   l Gk Syr: Heb *its dwelling will not be cut off*   m Or *Nubia;* Heb *Cush*   n Gk Syr: Heb *he will be silent*   o Gk Syr: Meaning of Heb uncertain   p Cn: Heb *I will remove from you; they were*

HAGGAI

 AGGAI WAS A PROPHET WHO, ALONG
WITH ZECHARIAH, ENCOURAGED THE
RETURNED EXILES TO REBUILD THE TEM-
PLE. THE MESSAGES OF HAGGAI WERE GIVEN DUR-
ING A FOUR-MONTH PERIOD IN 520 B.C. HAGGAI
CLEARLY SHOWS THE CONSEQUENCES OF DISOBE-
DIENCE AND THE BLESSINGS OF OBEDIENCE, AS HE
TELLS THE PEOPLE THAT THEY HAVE DEPRIVED
THEMSELVES OF GOD'S BLESSINGS BY FORSAKING
THE TEMPLE BUILDING PROJECT. WHEN THE PEO-
PLE GIVE PRIORITY TO GOD AND HIS HOUSE, THEY
ARE BLESSED. OBEDIENCE BRINGS THE ENCOUR-
AGEMENT AND STRENGTH OF GOD'S SPIRIT.

The Command to Rebuild the Temple

1 In the second year of King Darius, in the sixth month, on the first day of the month, the word of the LORD came by the prophet Haggai to Zerubbabel son of Shealtiel, governor of Judah, and to Joshua son of Jehozadak, the high priest: ²Thus says the LORD of hosts: These people say the time has not yet come to rebuild the LORD's house. ³Then the word of the LORD came by the prophet Haggai, saying: ⁴Is it a time for you yourselves to live in your paneled houses, while this house lies in ruins? ⁵Now therefore thus says the LORD of hosts: Consider how you have fared. ⁶You have sown much, and harvested little; you eat, but you never have enough; you drink, but you never have your fill; you clothe yourselves, but no one is warm; and you that earn wages earn wages to put them into a bag with holes.

7 Thus says the LORD of hosts: Consider how you have fared. ⁸Go up to the hills and bring wood and build the house, so that I may take pleasure in it and be honored, says the LORD. ⁹You have looked for much, and, lo, it came to little; and when you brought it home, I blew it away. Why? says the LORD of hosts. Because my house lies in ruins, while all of you hurry off to your own houses. ¹⁰Therefore the heavens above you have withheld the dew, and the earth has withheld its produce. ¹¹And I have called for a drought on the land and the hills, on the grain, the new wine, the oil, on what the soil produces, on

human beings and animals, and on all their labors.

12 Then Zerubbabel son of Shealtiel, and Joshua son of Jehozadak, the high priest, with all the remnant of the people, obeyed the voice of the LORD their God, and the words of the prophet Haggai, as the LORD their God had sent him; and the people feared the LORD. 13Then Haggai, the messenger of the LORD, spoke to the people with the LORD's message, saying, I am with you, says the LORD. 14And the LORD stirred up the spirit of Zerubbabel son of Shealtiel, governor of Judah, and the spirit of Joshua son of Jehozadak, the high priest, and the spirit of all the remnant of the people; and they came and worked on the house of the LORD of hosts, their God, 15on the twenty-fourth day of the month, in the sixth month.

The Future Glory of the Temple

2 In the second year of King Darius, 1in the seventh month, on the twenty-first day of the month, the word of the LORD came by the prophet Haggai, saying: 2Speak now to Zerubbabel son of Shealtiel, governor of Judah, and to Joshua son of Jehozadak, the high priest, and to the remnant of the people, and say, 3Who is left among you that saw this house in its former glory? How does it look to you now? Is it not in your sight as nothing? 4Yet now take courage, O Zerubbabel, says the LORD; take courage, O Joshua, son of Jehozadak, the high priest; take courage, all you people of the land, says the LORD; work, for I am with you, says the LORD of hosts, 5according to the promise that I made you when you came out of Egypt. My spirit abides among you; do not fear. 6For thus says the LORD of hosts: Once again, in a little while, I will shake the heavens and the earth and the sea and the dry land; 7and I will shake all the nations, so that the treasure of all nations shall come, and I will fill this house with splendor, says the LORD of hosts. 8The silver is mine, and the gold is mine, says the LORD of hosts. 9The latter splendor of this house shall be greater than the former, says the LORD of

hosts; and in this place I will give prosperity, says the LORD of hosts.

A Rebuke and a Promise

10 On the twenty-fourth day of the ninth month, in the second year of Darius, the word of the LORD came by the prophet Haggai, saying: 11Thus says the LORD of hosts: Ask the priests for a ruling: 12If one carries consecrated meat in the fold of one's garment, and with the fold touches bread, or stew, or wine, or oil, or any kind of food, does it become holy? The priests answered, "No." 13Then Haggai said, "If one who is unclean by contact with a dead body touches any of these, does it become unclean?" The priests answered, "Yes, it becomes unclean." 14Haggai then said, So is it with this people, and with this nation before me, says the LORD; and so with every work of their hands; and what they offer there is unclean. 15But now, consider what will come to pass from this day on. Before a stone was placed upon a stone in the LORD's temple, 16how did you fare?a When one came to a heap of twenty measures, there were but ten; when one came to the wine vat to draw fifty measures, there were but twenty. 17I struck you and all the products of your toil with blight and mildew and hail; yet you did not return to me, says the LORD. 18Consider from this day on, from the twenty-fourth day of the ninth month. Since the day that the foundation of the LORD's temple was laid, consider: 19Is there any seed left in the barn? Do the vine, the fig tree, the pomegranate, and the olive tree still yield nothing? From this day on I will bless you.

God's Promise to Zerubbabel

20 The word of the LORD came a second time to Haggai on the twenty-fourth day of the month: 21Speak to Zerubbabel, governor of Judah, saying, I am about to shake the heavens and the earth, 22and to overthrow the throne of kingdoms; I am about to destroy the strength of the kingdoms of the nations, and overthrow the chariots and their riders; and the horses and their riders shall fall, every one by the sword of a

a Gk: Heb since they were

comrade. ²³On that day, says the LORD of hosts, I will take you, O Zerubbabel my servant, son of Shealtiel, says the LORD, and make you like a signet ring; for I have chosen you, says the LORD of hosts.

THURSDAY

THE SHAKING OF THE THINGS THAT ARE MADE
Hannah Whitall Smith

VERSE: Haggai 2.6–7   **PASSAGE:** Haggai 2.6–9, 21–22

 he "foundation of God standeth sure" (2 Timothy 2.19, KJV), and it is the only foundation that does. Therefore, we need to be "shaken" from off every other foundation in order that we may be forced to rest on the foundation of God alone. And this explains the necessity for those "shakings" through which so many Christians seem called to pass. The Lord sees that they are building their spiritual houses on flimsy foundations, which will not be able to withstand the "vehement beating" of the storms of life; and not in anger but in tenderest love, he shakes our earth and our heaven until all that "can be shaken" is removed, and only those "things which cannot be shaken" are left behind.

The apostle tells us that the things that are shaken are the "things that are made" (Hebrews 12.27, KJV); that is, the things that are manufactured by our own efforts, feelings that we get up, doctrines that we elaborate, good works that we perform. It is not that these things are bad things in themselves. It is only when the soul begins to rest on them instead of upon the Lord that he is compelled to "shake" us from off them. And this shaking applies, we are told, "not to the earth only, but also to heaven." This means, I am sure, that it is possible to have "things that are made" even in religious matters.

How much of the so-called religiousness of many Christians consists of these "things that are made," I cannot say; but I sometimes think the great overturnings and tossings in matters of faith, which so distress Christians in these times, may be only the necessary shaking of the "things that are made," in order that only that which "cannot be shaken" may remain.

ADDITIONAL SCRIPTURE READING:
Psalm 125.1; Hebrews 12.27–28

Go to page 1088 for your next devotional reading.

1700   1900

ZECHARIAH

ECHARIAH'S PROPHETIC MINISTRY TOOK PLACE IN THE POSTEXILIC PERIOD, THE TIME OF THE JEWISH RESTORATION FROM BABYLONIAN CAPTIVITY. HIS PROPHECIES BEGAN TWO MONTHS AFTER HAGGAI'S FIRST MESSAGE. TO A PEOPLE DISCOURAGED ABOUT THEIR TASK OF REBUILDING THE TEMPLE, ZECHARIAH SPOKE WORDS OF ENCOURAGEMENT AND MOTIVATION. LOOK FOR THE MANY PREDICTIONS CONCERNING THE COMING MESSIAH, AS ZECHARIAH GAVE HIS PEOPLE A VISION OF GOD'S PURPOSES BEYOND THE RESTORED TEMPLE.

Israel Urged to Repent

1 In the eighth month, in the second year of Darius, the word of the LORD came to the prophet Zechariah son of Berechiah son of Iddo, saying: 2The LORD was very angry with your ancestors. 3Therefore say to them, Thus says the LORD of hosts: Return to me, says the LORD of hosts, and I will return to you, says the LORD of hosts. 4Do not be like your ancestors, to whom the former prophets proclaimed, "Thus says the LORD of hosts, Return from your evil ways and from your evil deeds." But they did not hear or heed me, says the LORD. 5Your ancestors, where are they? And the prophets, do they live forever? 6But my words and my statutes, which I commanded my servants the prophets, did they not overtake your ancestors? So they repented and said, "The LORD of hosts has dealt with us according to our ways and deeds, just as he planned to do."

First Vision: The Horsemen

7 On the twenty-fourth day of the eleventh month, the month of Shebat, in the second year of Darius, the word of the LORD came to the prophet Zechariah son of Berechiah son of Iddo; and Zechariah*a* said, 8In the night I saw a man riding on a red horse! He was standing among the myrtle trees in the glen; and behind him were red, sorrel, and white horses. 9Then I said, "What are these, my lord?" The angel who talked

a Heb *and he*

with me said to me, "I will show you what they are." 10So the man who was standing among the myrtle trees answered, "They are those whom the LORD has sent to patrol the earth." 11Then they spoke to the angel of the LORD who was standing among the myrtle trees, "We have patrolled the earth, and lo, the whole earth remains at peace." 12Then the angel of the LORD said, "O LORD of hosts, how long will you withhold mercy from Jerusalem and the cities of Judah, with which you have been angry these seventy years?" 13Then the LORD replied with gracious and comforting words to the angel who talked with me. 14So the angel who talked with me said to me, Proclaim this message: Thus says the LORD of hosts; I am very jealous for Jerusalem and for Zion. 15And I am extremely angry with the nations that are at ease; for while I was only a little angry, they made the disaster worse. 16Therefore, thus says the LORD, I have returned to Jerusalem with compassion; my house shall be built in it, says the LORD of hosts, and the measuring line shall be stretched out over Jerusalem. 17Proclaim further: Thus says the LORD of hosts: My cities shall again overflow with prosperity; the LORD will again comfort Zion and again choose Jerusalem.

Second Vision: The Horns and the Smiths

18*b* And I looked up and saw four horns. 19I asked the angel who talked

b Ch 2.1 in Heb

FRIDAY

GOD'S MERCY
Catherine of Siena

VERSE: Zechariah 1.16   **PASSAGE:** Zechariah 1.12–17

erciful Lord, it does not surprise me that you forget completely the sins of those who repent. I am not surprised that you remain faithful to those who hate and revile you. The mercy which pours forth from you fills the whole world.

It was by your mercy that we were created, and by your mercy that you redeemed us by sending your Son. Your mercy is the light in which sinners find you and good people come back to you. Your mercy is everywhere, even in the depths of hell where you offer to forgive the tortured souls. Your justice is constantly tempered with mercy, so you refuse to punish us as we deserve. O mad lover! It was not enough for you to take on our humanity; you had to die for us as well.

ADDITIONAL SCRIPTURE READING:
Jeremiah 33.10–11; Ezekiel 37.26–27

Go to page 1089 for your next devotional reading.

500   1500

WEEKEND

HIS SAVIOR'S WORDS, GOING TO THE CROSS
Robert Herrick

VERSE: Luke 23.27   **PASSAGE:** Luke 23.26–31

ave, have ye no regard, all ye
Who pass this way, to pity me,
Who am a man of misery!

A man both bruised, and broke, and one
Who suffers not here for mine own,
But for my friends' transgression!

Ah! Zion's Daughters, do not fear
The cross, the cords, the nails, the spear,
The myrrh, the gall, the vinegar:

For Christ, your loving Savior, hath
Drunk up the wine of God's fierce wrath;
Only, there's left a little froth,

Less for to taste, than for to show,
What bitter cups had been your due,
Had he not drank them up for you.

ADDITIONAL SCRIPTURE READING:
Matthew 27.33–37; Mark 15.22–26

Go to page 1091 for your next devotional reading.

1500   1700

with me, "What are these?" And he answered me, "These are the horns that have scattered Judah, Israel, and Jerusalem." [20]Then the LORD showed me four blacksmiths. [21]And I asked, "What are they coming to do?" He answered, "These are the horns that scattered Judah, so that no head could be raised; but these have come to terrify them, to strike down the horns of the nations that lifted up their horns against the land of Judah to scatter its people."[c]

Third Vision: The Man with a Measuring Line

[2][d]I looked up and saw a man with a measuring line in his hand. [2]Then I asked, "Where are you going?" He answered me, "To measure Jerusalem, to see what is its width and what is its length." [3]Then the angel who talked with me came forward, and another angel came forward to meet him, [4]and said to him, "Run, say to that young man: Jerusalem shall be inhabited like villages without walls, because of the multitude of people and animals in it. [5]For I will be a wall of fire all around it, says the LORD, and I will be the glory within it."

Interlude: An Appeal to the Exiles

6 Up, up! Flee from the land of the north, says the LORD; for I have spread you abroad like the four winds of heaven, says the LORD. [7]Up! Escape to Zion, you that live with daughter Babylon. [8]For thus said the LORD of hosts (after his glory[e] sent me) regarding the nations that plundered you: Truly, one who touches you touches the apple of my eye.[f] [9]See now, I am going to raise[g] my hand against them, and they shall become plunder for their own slaves. Then you will know that the LORD of hosts has sent me. [10]Sing and rejoice, O daughter Zion! For lo, I will come and dwell in your midst, says the LORD. [11]Many nations shall join themselves to the LORD on that day, and shall be my people; and I will dwell in your midst. And you shall know that the LORD of hosts has sent me to you. [12]The LORD will inherit Judah as his portion in the holy land, and will again choose Jerusalem. 13 Be silent, all people, before the LORD; for he has roused himself from his holy dwelling.

Fourth Vision: Joshua and Satan

[3] Then he showed me the high priest Joshua standing before the angel of the LORD, and Satan[h] standing at his right hand to accuse him. [2]And the LORD said to Satan,[h] "The LORD rebuke you, O Satan![h] The LORD who has chosen Jerusalem rebuke you! Is not this man a brand plucked from the fire?" [3]Now Joshua was dressed with filthy clothes as he stood before the angel. [4]The angel said to those who were standing before him, "Take off his filthy clothes." And to him he said, "See, I have taken your guilt away from you, and I will clothe you with festal apparel." [5]And I said, "Let them put a clean turban on his head." So they put a clean turban on his head and clothed him with the apparel; and the angel of the LORD was standing by.

6 Then the angel of the LORD assured Joshua, saying [7]"Thus says the LORD of hosts: If you will walk in my ways and keep my requirements, then you shall rule my house and have charge of my courts, and I will give you the right of access among those who are standing here. [8]Now listen, Joshua, high priest, you and your colleagues who sit before you! For they are an omen of things to come: I am going to bring my servant the Branch. [9]For on the stone that I have set before Joshua, on a single stone with seven facets, I will engrave its inscription, says the LORD of hosts, and I will remove the guilt of this land in a single day. [10]On that day, says the LORD of hosts, you shall invite each other to come under your vine and fig tree."

Fifth Vision: The Lampstand and Olive Trees

[4] The angel who talked with me came again, and wakened me, as one is wakened from sleep. [2]He said to me, "What do you see?" And I said, "I see a lampstand all of gold, with a bowl

---

c Heb it   d Ch 2.5 in Heb   e Cn: Heb after glory he   f Heb his eye   g Or wave   h Or the Accuser; Heb the Adversary

CHRISTIAN'S BURDEN IS LOOSED
John Bunyan

VERSE: Zechariah 3.4   PASSAGE: Zechariah 3.3–5

ow I saw in my dream, that the highway up which Christian was to go was fenced on either side with a wall; and that wall was called "Salvation" (Isaiah 26.1). Up this way, therefore, did burdened Christian run; but not without great difficulty, because of the load on his back.

He ran thus till he came at a place somewhat ascending; and upon that place stood a cross, and a little below, in the bottom, a sepulcher. So I saw in my dream, that just as Christian came up with the cross, his burden loosed from off his shoulders, and fell from off his back, and began to tumble; and so continued to do till it came to the mouth of the sepulcher, where it fell in, and I saw it no more.

Then was Christian glad and lightsome, and said, with a merry heart,

He hath given me rest by his sorrow,
And life by his death . . .

Now, as he stood looking and weeping, behold three shining ones came to him, and saluted him with, "Peace be to thee!" so the first said to him, "Your sins are forgiven" (Mark 2.5); the second stripped him of his rags, and clothed him with change of raiment (Zechariah 3.4); the third also set a mark in his forehead, and gave him a roll with a seal upon it (Ephesians 1.13), which he bade him look on as he ran, and that he should give it in the Celestial Gate: so they went their way. Then Christian gave three leaps for joy, and went on singing:

Thus far did I come laden with my sin,
Nor could aught ease the grief that I was in,
Till I came hither. What a place is this!
Must here be the beginning of my bliss!
Must here the burden fall from off my back!
Must here the strings that bound it to me crack!
Blest cross! blest sepulcher! blest rather be
The man that there was put to shame for me!

ADDITIONAL SCRIPTURE READING:
Psalm 32.1–2; Matthew 11.30

Go to page 1096 for your next devotional reading.

1500   1700

on the top of it; there are seven lamps on it, with seven lips on each of the lamps that are on the top of it. ³And by it there are two olive trees, one on the right of the bowl and the other on its left." ⁴I said to the angel who talked with me, "What are these, my lord?" ⁵Then the angel who talked with me answered me, "Do you not know what these are?" I said, "No, my lord." ⁶He said to me, "This is the word of the LORD to Zerubbabel: Not by might, nor by power, but by my spirit, says the LORD of hosts. ⁷What are you, O great mountain? Before Zerubbabel you shall become a plain; and he shall bring out the top stone amid shouts of 'Grace, grace to it!' "

8 Moreover the word of the LORD came to me, saying, ⁹"The hands of Zerubbabel have laid the foundation of this house; his hands shall also complete it. Then you will know that the LORD of hosts has sent me to you. ¹⁰For whoever has despised the day of small things shall rejoice, and shall see the plummet in the hand of Zerubbabel.

"These seven are the eyes of the LORD, which range through the whole earth." ¹¹Then I said to him, "What are these two olive trees on the right and the left of the lampstand?" ¹²And a second time I said to him, "What are these two branches of the olive trees, which pour out the oil^i through the two golden pipes?" ¹³He said to me, "Do you not know what these are?" I said, "No, my lord." ¹⁴Then he said, "These are the two anointed ones who stand by the Lord of the whole earth."

Sixth Vision: The Flying Scroll

5 Again I looked up and saw a flying scroll. ²And he said to me, "What do you see?" I answered, "I see a flying scroll; its length is twenty cubits, and its width ten cubits." ³Then he said to me, "This is the curse that goes out over the face of the whole land; for everyone who steals shall be cut off according to the writing on one side, and everyone who swears falsely^j shall be cut off according to the writing on the other side. ⁴I have sent it out, says the LORD of hosts, and it shall enter the

house of the thief, and the house of anyone who swears falsely by my name; and it shall abide in that house and consume it, both timber and stones."

Seventh Vision: The Woman in a Basket

5 Then the angel who talked with me came forward and said to me, "Look up and see what this is that is coming out." ⁶I said, "What is it?" He said, "This is a basket^k coming out." And he said, "This is their iniquity^l in all the land." ⁷Then a leaden cover was lifted, and there was a woman sitting in the basket!^{k} ⁸And he said, "This is Wickedness." So he thrust her back into the basket,^{k} and pressed the leaden weight down on its mouth. ⁹Then I looked up and saw two women coming forward. The wind was in their wings; they had wings like the wings of a stork, and they lifted up the basket^k between earth and sky. ¹⁰Then I said to the angel who talked with me, "Where are they taking the basket?"^{k} ¹¹He said to me, "To the land of Shinar, to build a house for it; and when this is prepared, they will set the basket^k down there on its base."

Eighth Vision: Four Chariots

6 And again I looked up and saw four chariots coming out from between two mountains—mountains of bronze. ²The first chariot had red horses, the second chariot black horses, ³the third chariot white horses, and the fourth chariot dappled gray^m horses. ⁴Then I said to the angel who talked with me, "What are these, my lord?" ⁵The angel answered me, "These are the four winds^n of heaven going out, after presenting themselves before the Lord of all the earth. ⁶The chariot with the black horses goes toward the north country, the white ones go toward the west country,^{o} and the dappled ones go toward the south country." ⁷When the steeds came out, they were impatient to get off and patrol the earth. And he said, "Go, patrol the earth." So they patrolled the earth. ⁸Then he cried out to me, "Lo, those who go toward the north country have set my spirit at rest in the north country."

---

i Cn: Heb gold j The word falsely added from verse 4 k Heb ephah l Gk Compare Syr: Heb their eye m Compare Gk: Meaning of Heb uncertain n Or spirits o Cn: Heb go after them

The Coronation of the Branch

9 The word of the LORD came to me:
[10]Collect silver and gold[p] from the exiles—from Heldai, Tobijah, and Jedaiah—who have arrived from Babylon; and go the same day to the house of Josiah son of Zephaniah. [11]Take the silver and gold and make a crown,[q] and set it on the head of the high priest Joshua son of Jehozadak; [12]say to him: Thus says the LORD of hosts: Here is a man whose name is Branch: for he shall branch out in his place, and he shall build the temple of the LORD. [13]It is he that shall build the temple of the LORD; he shall bear royal honor, and shall sit upon his throne and rule. There shall be a priest by his throne, with peaceful understanding between the two of them. [14]And the crown[r] shall be in the care of Heldai,[s] Tobijah, Jedaiah, and Josiah[t] son of Zephaniah, as a memorial in the temple of the LORD.

15 Those who are far off shall come and help to build the temple of the LORD; and you shall know that the LORD of hosts has sent me to you. This will happen if you diligently obey the voice of the LORD your God.

Hypocritical Fasting Condemned

7 In the fourth year of King Darius, the word of the LORD came to Zechariah on the fourth day of the ninth month, which is Chislev. [2]Now the people of Bethel had sent Sharezer and Regem-melech and their men, to entreat the favor of the LORD, [3]and to ask the priests of the house of the LORD of hosts and the prophets, "Should I mourn and practice abstinence in the fifth month, as I have done for so many years?" [4]Then the word of the LORD of hosts came to me: [5]Say to all the people of the land and the priests: When you fasted and lamented in the fifth month and in the seventh, for these seventy years, was it for me that you fasted? [6]And when you eat and when you drink, do you not eat and drink only for yourselves? [7]Were not these the words that the LORD proclaimed by the former prophets, when Jerusalem was inhabited and in prosperity, along with the towns around it, and when the Negeb and the Shephelah were inhabited?

Punishment for Rejecting God's Demands

8 The word of the LORD came to Zechariah, saying: [9]Thus says the LORD of hosts: Render true judgments, show kindness and mercy to one another; [10]do not oppress the widow, the orphan, the alien, or the poor; and do not devise evil

---

COMPASSION MEANS JUSTICE.
—*Meister Eckhart*

---

in your hearts against one another. [11]But they refused to listen, and turned a stubborn shoulder, and stopped their ears in order not to hear. [12]They made their hearts adamant in order not to hear the law and the words that the LORD of hosts had sent by his spirit through the former prophets. Therefore great wrath came from the LORD of hosts. [13]Just as, when I[u] called, they would not hear; so, when they called, I would not hear, says the LORD of hosts, [14]and I scattered them with a whirlwind among all the nations that they had not known. Thus the land they left was desolate, so that no one went to and fro, and a pleasant land was made desolate.

God's Promises to Zion

8 The word of the LORD of hosts came to me, saying: [2]Thus says the LORD of hosts: I am jealous for Zion with great jealousy, and I am jealous for her with great wrath. [3]Thus says the LORD: I will return to Zion, and will dwell in the midst of Jerusalem; Jerusalem shall be called the faithful city, and the mountain of the LORD of hosts shall be called the holy mountain. [4]Thus says the LORD of hosts: Old men and old women shall again sit in the streets of Jerusalem, each with staff in hand because of their great age. [5]And the streets of the city shall be full of boys and girls playing in its streets. [6]Thus says the LORD of hosts: Even though it seems impossible to the remnant of this

---

p Cn Compare verse 11: Heb lacks *silver and gold crowns*   q Gk Mss Syr Tg: Heb *crowns*   r Gk Syr: Heb
s Syr Compare verse 10: Heb *Helem*   t Syr Compare verse 10: Heb *Hen*   u Heb *he*

people in these days, should it also seem impossible to me, says the LORD of hosts? 7Thus says the LORD of hosts: I will save my people from the east country and from the west country; 8and I will bring them to live in Jerusalem. They shall be my people and I will be their God, in faithfulness and in righteousness.

9 Thus says the LORD of hosts: Let your hands be strong—you that have recently been hearing these words from the mouths of the prophets who were present when the foundation was laid for the rebuilding of the temple, the house of the LORD of hosts. 10For before those days there were no wages for people or for animals, nor was there any safety from the foe for those who went out or came in, and I set them all against one another. 11But now I will not deal with the remnant of this people as in the former days, says the LORD of hosts. 12For there shall be a sowing of peace; the vine shall yield its fruit, the ground shall give its produce, and the skies shall give their dew; and I will cause the remnant of this people to possess all these things. 13Just as you have been a cursing among the nations, O house of Judah and house of Israel, so I will save you and you shall be a blessing. Do not be afraid, but let your hands be strong.

14 For thus says the LORD of hosts: Just as I purposed to bring disaster upon you, when your ancestors provoked me to wrath, and I did not relent, says the LORD of hosts, 15so again I have purposed in these days to do good to Jerusalem and to the house of Judah; do not be afraid. 16These are the things that you shall do: Speak the truth to one another, render in your gates judgments that are true and make for peace, 17do not devise evil in your hearts against one another, and love no false oath; for all these are things that I hate, says the LORD.

Joyful Fasting

18 The word of the LORD of hosts came to me, saying: 19Thus says the LORD of hosts: The fast of the fourth month, and the fast of the fifth, and the fast of the seventh, and the fast of the tenth, shall be seasons of joy and gladness, and cheerful festivals for the house of Judah: therefore love truth and peace.

Many Peoples Drawn to Jerusalem

20 Thus says the LORD of hosts: Peoples shall yet come, the inhabitants of many cities; 21the inhabitants of one city shall go to another, saying, "Come, let us go to entreat the favor of the LORD, and to seek the LORD of hosts; I myself am going." 22Many peoples and strong nations shall come to seek the LORD of hosts in Jerusalem, and to entreat the favor of the LORD. 23Thus says the LORD of hosts: In those days ten men from nations of every language shall take hold of a Jew, grasping his garment and saying, "Let us go with you, for we have heard that God is with you."

Judgment on Israel's Enemies

9　　　An Oracle.

The word of the LORD is against the
　　land of Hadrach
　and will rest upon Damascus.
For to the LORD belongs the
　　capitalv of Aram,w
　as do all the tribes of Israel;
2　Hamath also, which borders on it,
　　Tyre and Sidon, though they are
　　　very wise.
3　Tyre has built itself a rampart,
　　and heaped up silver like dust,
　　and gold like the dirt of the streets.
4　But now, the Lord will strip it of its
　　　possessions
　　and hurl its wealth into the sea,
　　and it shall be devoured by fire.

5　Ashkelon shall see it and be afraid;
　　Gaza too, and shall writhe in
　　　anguish;
　　Ekron also, because its hopes are
　　　withered.
　The king shall perish from Gaza;
　　Ashkelon shall be uninhabited;
6　a mongrel people shall settle in
　　　Ashdod,
　　and I will make an end of the
　　　pride of Philistia.
7　I will take away its blood from its
　　　mouth,
　　and its abominations from
　　　between its teeth;

v Heb eye   w Cn: Heb of Adam (or of humankind)

it too shall be a remnant for our
    God;
  it shall be like a clan in Judah,
  and Ekron shall be like the
    Jebusites.
8 Then I will encamp at my house as
    a guard,
  so that no one shall march to and
    fro;
  no oppressor shall again overrun
    them,
  for now I have seen with my own
    eyes.

The Coming Ruler of God's People

9 Rejoice greatly, O daughter Zion!
  Shout aloud, O daughter
    Jerusalem!
  Lo, your king comes to you;
    triumphant and victorious is he,
  humble and riding on a donkey,
    on a colt, the foal of a donkey.
10 He[x] will cut off the chariot from
    Ephraim
  and the war-horse from
    Jerusalem;
  and the battle bow shall be cut off,
    and he shall command peace to
    the nations;
  his dominion shall be from sea to
    sea,
  and from the River to the ends of
    the earth.

11 As for you also, because of the
    blood of my covenant with
    you,
  I will set your prisoners free from
    the waterless pit.
12 Return to your stronghold,
    O prisoners of hope;
  today I declare that I will restore
    to you double.
13 For I have bent Judah as my bow;
  I have made Ephraim its arrow.
  I will arouse your sons, O Zion,
    against your sons, O Greece,
  and wield you like a warrior's
    sword.

14 Then the LORD will appear over
    them,
  and his arrow go forth like
    lightning;

the Lord GOD will sound the
    trumpet
  and march forth in the
    whirlwinds of the south.
15 The LORD of hosts will protect
    them,
  and they shall devour and tread
    down the slingers;[y]
  they shall drink their blood[z] like
    wine,
  and be full like a bowl,
  drenched like the corners of the
    altar.

16 On that day the LORD their God
    will save them
  for they are the flock of his
    people;
  for like the jewels of a crown
    they shall shine on his land.
17 For what goodness and beauty are
    his!
  Grain shall make the young men
    flourish,
  and new wine the young women.

Restoration of Judah and Israel

10 Ask rain from the LORD
    in the season of the spring
    rain,
  from the LORD who makes the
    storm clouds,
  who gives showers of rain to
    you,[a]
  the vegetation in the field to
    everyone.
2 For the teraphim[b] utter nonsense,
    and the diviners see lies;
  the dreamers tell false dreams,
    and give empty consolation.
  Therefore the people wander like
    sheep;
  they suffer for lack of a shepherd.

3 My anger is hot against the
    shepherds,
  and I will punish the leaders;[c]
  for the LORD of hosts cares for his
    flock, the house of Judah,
  and will make them like his
    proud war-horse.
4 Out of them shall come the
    cornerstone,
  out of them the tent peg,

---

x Gk: Heb I   y Cn: Heb the slingstones   z Gk: Heb shall drink   a Heb them   b Or household
gods   c Or male goats

out of them the battle bow,
  out of them every commander.
5 Together they shall be like warriors
    in battle,
  trampling the foe in the mud of
    the streets;
they shall fight, for the LORD is
    with them,
and they shall put to shame the
    riders on horses.

6 I will strengthen the house of Judah,
  and I will save the house of Joseph.
I will bring them back because I
    have compassion on them,

and they shall be as though I had
  not rejected them;
for I am the LORD their God and I
  will answer them.
7 Then the people of Ephraim shall
  become like warriors,
and their hearts shall be glad as
  with wine.
Their children shall see it and
  rejoice,
  their hearts shall exult in the
    LORD.

8 I will signal for them and gather
  them in,

TUESDAY

PRECIOUS JEWELS
William O. Cushing

VERSE: Zechariah 9.16   PASSAGE: Zechariah 9.15–17

hen he cometh, when he cometh
To make up his jewels,
All his jewels, precious jewels,
His loved and his own.

He will gather, he will gather
The gems for his kingdom,
All the pure ones, all the bright ones,
His loved and his own.

Little children, little children
Who love their Redeemer
Are the jewels, precious jewels,
His loved and his own.

Like the stars of the morning,
His bright crown adorning,
They shall shine in their beauty—
Bright gems for his crown.

ADDITIONAL SCRIPTURE READING:
Isaiah 25.6–8; 62.3; Haggai 2.23

Go to page 1098 for your next devotional reading.

1700   1900

for I have redeemed them,
and they shall be as numerous as
they were before.
9 Though I scattered them among
the nations,
yet in far countries they shall
remember me,
and they shall rear their children
and return.
10 I will bring them home from the
land of Egypt,
and gather them from Assyria;
I will bring them to the land of
Gilead and to Lebanon,
until there is no room for them.
11 They[d] shall pass through the sea of
distress,
and the waves of the sea shall be
struck down,
and all the depths of the Nile
dried up.
The pride of Assyria shall be laid
low,
and the scepter of Egypt shall
depart.
12 I will make them strong in the
LORD,
and they shall walk in his name,
says the LORD.

11 Open your doors, O Lebanon,
so that fire may devour your
cedars!
2 Wail, O cypress, for the cedar has
fallen,
for the glorious trees are ruined!
Wail, oaks of Bashan,
for the thick forest has been felled!
3 Listen, the wail of the shepherds,
for their glory is despoiled!
Listen, the roar of the lions,
for the thickets of the Jordan are
destroyed!

Two Kinds of Shepherds

4 Thus said the LORD my God: Be a
shepherd of the flock doomed to slaughter. 5 Those who buy them kill them and
go unpunished; and those who sell them
say, "Blessed be the LORD, for I have become rich"; and their own shepherds
have no pity on them. 6 For I will no
longer have pity on the inhabitants of the
earth, says the LORD. I will cause them,

every one, to fall each into the hand of a
neighbor, and each into the hand of the
king; and they shall devastate the earth,
and I will deliver no one from their hand.
7 So, on behalf of the sheep merchants, I became the shepherd of the
flock doomed to slaughter. I took two
staffs; one I named Favor, the other I
named Unity, and I tended the sheep.
8 In one month I disposed of the three
shepherds, for I had become impatient
with them, and they also detested me.
9 So I said, "I will not be your shepherd.
What is to die, let it die; what is to be destroyed, let it be destroyed; and let those
that are left devour the flesh of one another!" 10 I took my staff Favor and
broke it, annulling the covenant that I
had made with all the peoples. 11 So it
was annulled on that day, and the sheep
merchants, who were watching me,
knew that it was the word of the LORD.
12 I then said to them, "If it seems right
to you, give me my wages; but if not,
keep them." So they weighed out as my
wages thirty shekels of silver. 13 Then
the LORD said to me, "Throw it into the
treasury"[e]—this lordly price at which I
was valued by them. So I took the thirty
shekels of silver and threw them into
the treasury[e] in the house of the LORD.
14 Then I broke my second staff Unity,
annulling the family ties between Judah
and Israel.
15 Then the LORD said to me: Take
once more the implements of a worthless shepherd. 16 For I am now raising up
in the land a shepherd who does not care
for the perishing, or seek the wandering,[f] or heal the maimed, or nourish the
healthy,[g] but devours the flesh of the fat
ones, tearing off even their hoofs.
17 Oh, my worthless shepherd,
who deserts the flock!
May the sword strike his arm
and his right eye!
Let his arm be completely withered,
his right eye utterly blinded!

Jerusalem's Victory

12 An Oracle.

The word of the LORD concerning Israel: Thus says the LORD, who stretched

---

d Gk: Heb He   e Syr: Heb it to the potter   f Syr Compare Gk Vg: Heb the youth   g Meaning of
Heb uncertain

out the heavens and founded the earth and formed the human spirit within: ²See, I am about to make Jerusalem a cup of reeling for all the surrounding peoples; it will be against Judah also in the siege against Jerusalem. ³On that day I will make Jerusalem a heavy stone for all the peoples; all who lift it shall grievously hurt themselves. And all the nations of the earth shall come together against it. ⁴On that day, says the LORD, I will strike every horse with panic, and its rider with madness. But on the house of Judah I will keep a watchful eye, when I strike every horse of the peoples with blindness. ⁵Then the clans of Judah shall say to themselves, "The inhabitants of Jerusalem have strength through the LORD of hosts, their God."

6 On that day I will make the clans of Judah like a blazing pot on a pile of wood, like a flaming torch among sheaves; and they shall devour to the right and to the left all the surrounding peoples, while Jerusalem shall again be inhabited in its place, in Jerusalem.

7 And the LORD will give victory to the tents of Judah first, that the glory of the house of David and the glory of the inhabitants of Jerusalem may not be exalted over that of Judah. ⁸On that day the LORD will shield the inhabitants of Jerusalem so that the feeblest among them on that day shall be like David, and the house of David shall be like God, like the angel of the LORD, at their head. ⁹And on that day I will seek to destroy all the nations that come against Jerusalem.

WEDNESDAY

QUICKENING GRACE
Martin Luther

VERSE: Zechariah 12.10   **PASSAGE:** Zechariah 12.10–14

hen a Christian begins to know Christ as his Lord and Savior, through whom he is redeemed from death and brought into his kingdom and inheritance, his heart is aglow with a flaming love of God and he would gladly help everyone to the same experience. For he knows no greater joy than that he possesses this treasure, that he knows Christ. Therefore he goes out and teaches and exhorts other people, praising and testifying to it before all men, praying and yearning that they too might attain to such grace. That is a restless spirit enjoying the highest rest in the grace and peace of God, for it cannot be silent or idle, but is always striving with all its power to spread the honor and glory of God among the people, that others too may receive this Spirit of grace and may then help with the work of prayer. For where the Spirit of grace is, he quickens our hearts, so that we can, and may, and must begin to pray.

ADDITIONAL SCRIPTURE READING:
Psalm 51.12; Jeremiah 31.9; Romans 8.26

Go to page 1102 for your next devotional reading.

1500   1700

Mourning for the Pierced One

10 And I will pour out a spirit of compassion and supplication on the house of David and the inhabitants of Jerusalem, so that, when they look on the one[h] whom they have pierced, they shall mourn for him, as one mourns for an only child, and weep bitterly over him, as one weeps over a firstborn. 11On that day the mourning in Jerusalem will be as great as the mourning for Hadad-rimmon in the plain of Megiddo. 12The land shall mourn, each family by itself; the family of the house of David by itself, and their wives by themselves; the family of the house of Nathan by itself, and their wives by themselves; 13the family of the house of Levi by itself, and their wives by themselves; the family of the Shimeites by itself, and their wives by themselves; 14and all the families that are left, each by itself, and their wives by themselves.

13 On that day a fountain shall be opened for the house of David and the inhabitants of Jerusalem, to cleanse them from sin and impurity.

Idolatry Cut Off

2 On that day, says the LORD of hosts, I will cut off the names of the idols from the land, so that they shall be remembered no more; and also I will remove from the land the prophets and the unclean spirit. 3And if any prophets appear again, their fathers and mothers who bore them will say to them, "You shall not live, for you speak lies in the name of the LORD"; and their fathers and their mothers who bore them shall pierce them through when they prophesy. 4On that day the prophets will be ashamed, every one, of their visions when they prophesy; they will not put on a hairy mantle in order to deceive, 5but each of them will say, "I am no prophet, I am a tiller of the soil; for the land has been my possession[i] since my youth." 6And if anyone asks them, "What are these wounds on your chest?"[i] the answer will be "The wounds I received in the house of my friends."

The Shepherd Struck, the Flock Scattered

7 "Awake, O sword, against my
    shepherd,
  against the man who is my
    associate,"
        says the LORD of hosts.
  Strike the shepherd, that the sheep
    may be scattered;
  I will turn my hand against the
    little ones.
8 In the whole land, says the LORD,
  two-thirds shall be cut off and
    perish,
  and one-third shall be left alive.
9 And I will put this third into the
    fire,
  refine them as one refines silver,
  and test them as gold is tested.
  They will call on my name,
    and I will answer them.
  I will say, "They are my people";
  and they will say, "The LORD is
    our God."

Future Warfare and Final Victory

14 See, a day is coming for the LORD, when the plunder taken from you will be divided in your midst. 2For I will gather all the nations against Jerusalem to battle, and the city shall be taken and the houses looted and the women raped; half the city shall go into exile, but the rest of the people shall not be cut off from the city. 3Then the LORD will go forth and fight against those nations as when he fights on a day of battle. 4On that day his feet shall stand on the Mount of Olives, which lies before Jerusalem on the east; and the Mount of Olives shall be split in two from east to west by a very wide valley; so that one half of the Mount shall withdraw northward, and the other half southward. 5And you shall flee by the valley of the LORD's mountain,[k] for the valley between the mountains shall reach to Azal;[l] and you shall flee as you fled from the earthquake in the days of King Uzziah of Judah. Then the LORD my God will come, and all the holy ones with him.

6 On that day there shall not be[m] either cold or frost.[n] 7And there shall be

h Heb on me   i Cn: Heb for humankind has caused me to possess   j Heb wounds between your hands   k Heb my mountains   l Meaning of Heb uncertain   m Cn: Heb there shall not be light   n Compare Gk Syr Vg Tg: Meaning of Heb uncertain

continuous day (it is known to the
LORD), not day and not night, for at
evening time there shall be light.
8 On that day living waters shall flow
out from Jerusalem, half of them to the
eastern sea and half of them to the western sea; it shall continue in summer as
in winter.
9 And the LORD will become king
over all the earth; on that day the LORD
will be one and his name one.
10 The whole land shall be turned
into a plain from Geba to Rimmon
south of Jerusalem. But Jerusalem shall
remain aloft on its site from the Gate of
Benjamin to the place of the former gate,
to the Corner Gate, and from the Tower
of Hananel to the king's wine presses.
11 And it shall be inhabited, for never
again shall it be doomed to destruction;
Jerusalem shall abide in security.
12 This shall be the plague with
which the LORD will strike all the peoples that wage war against Jerusalem:
their flesh shall rot while they are still
on their feet; their eyes shall rot in their
sockets, and their tongues shall rot in
their mouths. 13 On that day a great
panic from the LORD shall fall on them,
so that each will seize the hand of a
neighbor, and the hand of the one will
be raised against the hand of the other;
14 even Judah will fight at Jerusalem.
And the wealth of all the surrounding
nations shall be collected—gold, silver,
and garments in great abundance. 15 And
a plague like this plague shall fall on the
horses, the mules, the camels, the donkeys, and whatever animals may be in
those camps.
16 Then all who survive of the nations that have come against Jerusalem
shall go up year after year to worship the
King, the LORD of hosts, and to keep the
festival of booths.[o] 17 If any of the families of the earth do not go up to Jerusalem to worship the King, the LORD of
hosts, there will be no rain upon them.
18 And if the family of Egypt do not go up
and present themselves, then on them
shall[p] come the plague that the LORD inflicts on the nations that do not go up to
keep the festival of booths.[o] 19 Such shall
be the punishment of Egypt and the
punishment of all the nations that do
not go up to keep the festival of booths.[o]
20 On that day there shall be inscribed on the bells of the horses, "Holy
to the LORD." And the cooking pots in
the house of the LORD shall be as holy
as[q] the bowls in front of the altar; 21 and
every cooking pot in Jerusalem and
Judah shall be sacred to the LORD of
hosts, so that all who sacrifice may
come and use them to boil the flesh of
the sacrifice. And there shall no longer
be traders[r] in the house of the LORD of
hosts on that day.

o Or *tabernacles*; Heb *succoth* p Gk Syr: Heb *shall not* q Heb *shall be like* r Or *Canaanites*

MALACHI

HE TEMPLE HAD BEEN REBUILT, BUT TIMES OF PROSPERITY HAD NOT COME. THE PEOPLE WERE SUFFERING DROUGHT AND FAMINE, AND THEY RESPONDED WITH INDIFFERENCE AND SPIRITUAL LETHARGY. THEY HAD FORGOTTEN GOD AND TREATED HIM WITH DISHONOR. AGAINST SUCH A BACKGROUND MALACHI, MEANING "MY MESSENGER," WAS WRITTEN. WHILE MALACHI'S MESSAGE IS FILLED WITH INDICTMENTS AND WARNINGS, BE ALERT TO GOD'S PASSIONATE LOVE FOR HIS PEOPLE AND HIS DESIRE THAT WE RETURN THAT LOVE WITH OUR OWN WHOLEHEARTED LOVE AND OBEDIENCE.

 1 An oracle. The word of the LORD to Israel by Malachi.*a*

Israel Preferred to Edom

2 I have loved you, says the LORD. But you say, "How have you loved us?" Is not Esau Jacob's brother? says the LORD. Yet I have loved Jacob ³but I have hated Esau; I have made his hill country a desolation and his heritage a desert for jackals. ⁴If Edom says, "We are shattered but we will rebuild the ruins," the LORD of hosts says: They may build, but I will tear down, until they are called the wicked country, the people with whom the LORD is angry forever. ⁵Your own eyes shall see this, and you shall say, "Great is the LORD beyond the borders of Israel!"

Corruption of the Priesthood

6 A son honors his father, and servants their master. If then I am a father, where is the honor due me? And if I am a master, where is the respect due me? says the LORD of hosts to you, O priests, who despise my name. You say, "How have we despised your name?" ⁷By offering polluted food on my altar. And you say, "How have we polluted it?"*b* By thinking that the LORD's table may be despised. ⁸When you offer blind animals in sacrifice, is that not wrong? And when you offer those that are lame or sick, is that not wrong? Try presenting that to your governor; will he be pleased with you or show you favor? says the LORD of hosts. ⁹And now implore the

a Or *by my messenger*   *b* Gk: Heb *you*

favor of God, that he may be gracious to us. The fault is yours. Will he show favor to any of you? says the LORD of hosts. [10]Oh, that someone among you would shut the temple[c] doors, so that you would not kindle fire on my altar in vain! I have no pleasure in you, says the LORD of hosts, and I will not accept an offering from your hands. [11]For from the rising of the sun to its setting my name is great among the nations, and in every place incense is offered to my name, and a pure offering; for my name is great among the nations, says the LORD of hosts. [12]But you profane it when you say that the Lord's table is polluted, and the food for it[d] may be despised. [13]"What a weariness this is," you say, and you sniff at me,[e] says the LORD of hosts. You bring what has been taken by violence or is lame or sick, and this you bring as your offering! Shall I accept that from your hand? says the LORD. [14]Cursed be the cheat who has a male in the flock and vows to give it, and yet sacrifices to the Lord what is blemished; for I am a great King, says the LORD of hosts, and my name is reverenced among the nations.

c Heb lacks temple   d Compare Syr Tg: Heb its fruit, its food   e Another reading is at it

---

THURSDAY

GOD IS IN LOVE WITH US
Catherine of Siena

VERSE: Malachi 1.2   PASSAGE: Malachi 2.10–12

ternal Father, you said, "Let us make humankind to our own image and likeness" (see Genesis 1.26). Thus you were willing to share with us your own greatness. You gave us the intellect to share your truth. You gave us the wisdom to share your goodness. And you gave us the free will to love that which is true and just.

Why did you so dignify us? It was because you looked upon us, and fell in love with us. It was love which first prompted you to create us; and it was love which caused you to share with us your truth and goodness.

Yet your heart must break when you see us turn against you. You must weep when you see us abusing our intellect in pursuit of that which is false. You must cry with pain when we distort our wisdom in order to justify evil.

But you never desert us. Out of the same love that caused you to create us, you have now sent your only Son to save us. He is your perfect image and likeness, and so through him we can be restored to your image and likeness.

ADDITIONAL SCRIPTURE READING:
Genesis 1.26–27; Isaiah 43.4; Jeremiah 31.3

Go to page 1104 for your next devotional reading.

500   1500

2 And now, O priests, this command is for you. 2If you will not listen, if you will not lay it to heart to give glory to my name, says the LORD of hosts, then I will send the curse on you and I will curse your blessings; indeed I have already cursed them,*f* because you do not lay it to heart. 3I will rebuke your offspring, and spread dung on your faces, the dung of your offerings, and I will put you out of my presence.*g*

4 Know, then, that I have sent this command to you, that my covenant with Levi may hold, says the LORD of hosts. 5My covenant with him was a covenant of life and well-being, which I gave him; this called for reverence, and he revered me and stood in awe of my name. 6True instruction was in his mouth, and no wrong was found on his lips. He walked with me in integrity and uprightness, and he turned many from iniquity. 7For the lips of a priest should guard knowledge, and people should seek instruction from his mouth, for he is the messenger of the LORD of hosts. 8But you have turned aside from the way; you have caused many to stumble by your instruction; you have corrupted the covenant of Levi, says the LORD of hosts, 9and so I make you despised and abased before all the people, inasmuch as you have not kept my ways but have shown partiality in your instruction.

The Covenant Profaned by Judah

10 Have we not all one father? Has not one God created us? Why then are we faithless to one another, profaning the covenant of our ancestors? 11Judah has been faithless, and abomination has been committed in Israel and in Jerusalem; for Judah has profaned the sanctuary of the LORD, which he loves, and has married the daughter of a foreign god. 12May the LORD cut off from the tents of Jacob anyone who does this— any to witness*h* or answer, or to bring an offering to the LORD of hosts. 13 And this you do as well: You cover the LORD's altar with tears, with weeping and groaning because he no longer regards the offering or accepts it with favor

at your hand. 14You ask, "Why does he not?" Because the LORD was a witness between you and the wife of your youth, to whom you have been faithless, though she is your companion and your wife by covenant. 15Did not one God make her?*i* Both flesh and spirit are his.*j* And what does the one God*k* desire? Godly offspring. So look to yourselves, and do not let anyone be faithless to the wife of his youth. 16For I hate*l* divorce,

---

THE FORM OF MARRIAGE LIES IN AN INSEPARABLE UNION OF MINDS BY WHICH EITHER IS UNALTERABLY PLIGHTED TO SERVE THE OTHER LOYALLY.

—*Thomas Aquinas*

---

says the LORD, the God of Israel, and covering one's garment with violence, says the LORD of hosts. So take heed to yourselves and do not be faithless.

17 You have wearied the LORD with your words. Yet you say, "How have we wearied him?" By saying, "All who do evil are good in the sight of the LORD, and he delights in them." Or by asking, "Where is the God of justice?"

The Coming Messenger

3 See, I am sending my messenger to prepare the way before me, and the Lord whom you seek will suddenly come to his temple. The messenger of the covenant in whom you delight—indeed, he is coming, says the LORD of hosts. 2But who can endure the day of his coming, and who can stand when he appears?

For he is like a refiner's fire and like fullers' soap; 3he will sit as a refiner and purifier of silver, and he will purify the descendants of Levi and refine them like gold and silver, until they present offerings to the LORD in righteousness.*m* 4Then the offering of Judah and Jerusalem will be pleasing to the LORD as in the days of old and as in former years.

5 Then I will draw near to you for judgment; I will be swift to bear witness against the sorcerers, against the adulterers, against those who swear falsely, against those who oppress the hired

---

f Heb *it*   *g* Cn Compare Gk Syr: Heb *and he shall bear you to it*   *h* Cn Compare Gk: Heb *arouse* *i* Or *Has he not made one?*   *j* Cn: Heb *and a remnant of spirit was his*   *k* Heb *he*   *l* Cn: Heb *he hates*   *m* Or *right offerings to the LORD*

workers in their wages, the widow and the orphan, against those who thrust aside the alien, and do not fear me, says the LORD of hosts.

6 For I the LORD do not change; therefore you, O children of Jacob, have not perished. 7Ever since the days of your ancestors you have turned aside from my statutes and have not kept them. Re-turn to me, and I will return to you, says the LORD of hosts. But you say, "How shall we return?"

Do Not Rob God

8 Will anyone rob God? Yet you are robbing me! But you say, "How are we robbing you?" In your tithes and offer-ings! 9You are cursed with a curse, for

---

FRIDAY

GOD THE REMEDY
Henry Ward Beecher

VERSE: Malachi 4.2   PASSAGE: Malachi 4.1–3

 od is himself a vast medicine. God's soul and nature are the blood of the universe. Ask the physician what it is that he trusts to throw out deadly influences from the human system. If there are diseased organs, what cures them? Do you think pills do the work? They do but little except to say to the lazy organ, "Wake up and go to work, and throw out the enemy that is preying upon you." What is medi-cine? It is merely a coaxer. Its business is to say to the part af-fected, "Lazy dog! Wake up and get well."

If a man gets well, he cures himself—often, thanks to the doc-tor; more often, thanks to the nurse; always, thanks to nature. That does the work, if it is done at all. What is the stream that carries reparation to the wasted parts, that carries stimulation to the dormant parts, that carries nutrition to the exhausted parts? What is it that fights? It is the blood.

And throughout the vast heaven, throughout time and the universe, the blood of the world comes from the heart of God. The mercies of the loving God throb everywhere—above and below, within and without, endless in circuits, vast in distribu-tion, infinitely potential. It is the heart of God that carries restoration, inspiration, aspiration, and final victory. And as long as God lives, and is what he is "the Father of mercies, and the God of all comfort" (see 2 Corinthians 1.3)—this world will not go to rack and ruin.

ADDITIONAL SCRIPTURE READING:
Psalm 103.1–3; Isaiah 53.5; Hosea 6.1–3

Go to page 1110 for your next devotional reading.

1700   1900

you are robbing me—the whole nation of you! [10]Bring the full tithe into the storehouse, so that there may be food in my house, and thus put me to the test, says the LORD of hosts; see if I will not open the windows of heaven for you and pour down for you an overflowing blessing. [11]I will rebuke the locust[n] for you, so that it will not destroy the produce of your soil; and your vine in the field shall not be barren, says the LORD of hosts. [12]Then all nations will count you happy, for you will be a land of delight, says the LORD of hosts.

13 You have spoken harsh words against me, says the LORD. Yet you say, "How have we spoken against you?" [14]You have said, "It is vain to serve God. What do we profit by keeping his command or by going about as mourners before the LORD of hosts? [15]Now we count the arrogant happy; evildoers not only prosper, but when they put God to the test they escape."

The Reward of the Faithful

16 Then those who revered the LORD spoke with one another. The LORD took note and listened, and a book of remembrance was written before him of those who revered the LORD and thought on his name. [17]They shall be mine, says the LORD of hosts, my special possession on the day when I act, and I will spare them as parents spare their children who serve them. [18]Then once more you shall see the difference between the righteous and the wicked, between one who serves God and one who does not serve him.

The Great Day of the LORD

4 [o] See, the day is coming, burning like an oven, when all the arrogant and all evildoers will be stubble; the day that comes shall burn them up, says the LORD of hosts, so that it will leave them neither root nor branch. [2]But for you who revere my name the sun of righteousness shall rise, with healing in its wings. You shall go out leaping like calves from the stall. [3]And you shall tread down the wicked, for they will be ashes under the soles of your feet, on the day when I act, says the LORD of hosts.

4 Remember the teaching of my servant Moses, the statutes and ordinances that I commanded him at Horeb for all Israel.

5 Lo, I will send you the prophet Elijah before the great and terrible day of the LORD comes. [6]He will turn the hearts of parents to their children and the hearts of children to their parents, so that I will not come and strike the land with a curse.[p]

---

n Heb *devourer*   o Ch 4.1-6 are Ch 3.19-24 in Heb   p Or *a ban of utter destruction*

NEW
TESTAMENT

MATTHEW

MATTHEW WRITES THIS GOSPEL TO REVEAL JESUS AS THE PROMISED MESSIAH AND KING. HE ALSO TELLS US MUCH ABOUT THE LIFE AND MINISTRY OF JESUS, ESPECIALLY HOW HE FULFILLS THE PROMISES OF THE OLD TESTAMENT, AND ABOUT HOW HIS FOLLOWERS SHOULD CONDUCT THEIR LIVES AS CITIZENS OF GOD'S KINGDOM. MATTHEW BEGINS HIS GOSPEL WITH THE BIRTH OF JESUS, WHO IS CALLED "EMMANUEL" (1.23), OR "GOD IS WITH US," AND CLOSES HIS STORY WITH JESUS' REASSURING PROMISE, "I AM WITH YOU ALWAYS" (28.20).

The Genealogy of Jesus the Messiah

1 An account of the genealogy*a* of Jesus the Messiah,*b* the son of David, the son of Abraham.

2 Abraham was the father of Isaac, and Isaac the father of Jacob, and Jacob the father of Judah and his brothers, ³and Judah the father of Perez and Zerah by Tamar, and Perez the father of Hezron, and Hezron the father of Aram, ⁴and Aram the father of Aminadab, and Aminadab the father of Nahshon, and Nahshon the father of Salmon, ⁵and Salmon the father of Boaz by Rahab, and Boaz the father of Obed by Ruth, and Obed the father of Jesse, ⁶and Jesse the father of King David.

And David was the father of Solomon by the wife of Uriah, ⁷and Solomon the father of Rehoboam, and Rehoboam the father of Abijah, and Abijah the father of Asaph,*c* ⁸and Asaph*c* the father of Jehoshaphat, and Jehoshaphat the father of Joram, and Joram the father of Uzziah, ⁹and Uzziah the father of Jotham, and Jotham the father of Ahaz, and Ahaz the father of Hezekiah, ¹⁰and Hezekiah the father of Manasseh, and Manasseh the father of Amos,*d* and Amos*d* the father of Josiah, ¹¹and Josiah the father of Jechoniah and his brothers, at the time of the deportation to Babylon.

12 And after the deportation to Babylon: Jechoniah was the father of Salathiel, and Salathiel the father of Zerubbabel, ¹³and Zerubbabel the father of Abiud,

WEEKEND

The Song of the Virgin Mary
Miles Coverdale

y soul doth magnify the Lord,
My spirit rejoiceth greatly
In God my Savior and his word;
For he hath seen the low degree
Of me his handmaiden truly.
Behold now, after this day,
All generations shall speak of me,
And call me blessed alway.

For he that is only of might
Hath done great things for me;
And holy is his name by right:
As for his endless mercy,
It endureth perpetually,
In every generation,
On them that fear him unfeignedly
Without dissimulation.

He showeth strength with his great arm,
Declaring himself to be of power;
He scattereth the proud to their own harm,
Even with the wicked behavior
Of their own hearts every hour
He putteth down the mighty
From their high seat and great honor,
Exalting them of low degree.

The hungry filleth he with good,
And letteth the rich go empty,
Where his own people want no food:
He thinketh upon his mercy,
And helpeth his servant truly,
Even Israel, as he promised
Unto our fathers perpetually,
Abraham and to his seed.

Additional Scripture Reading:
Exodus 15.21; 1 Samuel 2.1

Go to page 1112 for your next devotional reading.

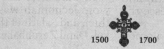

1500   1700

and Abiud the father of Eliakim, and Eliakim the father of Azor, 14and Azor the father of Zadok, and Zadok the father of Achim, and Achim the father of Eliud, 15and Eliud the father of Eleazar, and Eleazar the father of Matthan, and Matthan the father of Jacob, 16and Jacob the father of Joseph the husband of Mary, of whom Jesus was born, who is called the Messiah.*e*

17 So all the generations from Abraham to David are fourteen generations; and from David to the deportation to Babylon, fourteen generations; and from the deportation to Babylon to the Messiah,*e* fourteen generations.

The Birth of Jesus the Messiah

18 Now the birth of Jesus the Messiah*f* took place in this way. When his mother Mary had been engaged to Joseph, but before they lived together, she was found to be with child from the Holy Spirit. 19Her husband Joseph, being a righteous man and unwilling to expose her to public disgrace, planned to dismiss her quietly. 20But just when he had resolved to do this, an angel of the Lord appeared to him in a dream and said, "Joseph, son of David, do not be afraid to take Mary as your wife, for the child conceived in her is from the Holy Spirit. 21She will bear a son, and you are to name him Jesus, for he will save his people from their sins." 22All this took place to fulfill what had been spoken by the Lord through the prophet:

23   "Look, the virgin shall conceive
      and bear a son,
  and they shall name him
      Emmanuel,"

which means, "God is with us." 24When Joseph awoke from sleep, he did as the angel of the Lord commanded him; he took her as his wife, 25but had no marital relations with her until she had borne a son;*g* and he named him Jesus.

The Visit of the Wise Men

2 In the time of King Herod, after Jesus was born in Bethlehem of Judea, wise men*h* from the East came to Jerusalem, 2asking, "Where is the child who has been born king of the Jews? For we observed his star at its rising,*i* and have come to pay him homage." 3When King Herod heard this, he was frightened, and all Jerusalem with him; 4and calling together all the chief priests and scribes of the people, he inquired of them where the Messiah*e* was to be born. 5They told him, "In Bethlehem of Judea; for so it has been written by the prophet:

6   'And you, Bethlehem, in the land of
      Judah,
  are by no means least among the
      rulers of Judah;
  for from you shall come a ruler
    who is to shepherd*j* my people
      Israel.' "

7 Then Herod secretly called for the wise men*h* and learned from them the exact time when the star had appeared. 8Then he sent them to Bethlehem, saying, "Go and search diligently for the child; and when you have found him, bring me word so that I may also go and pay him homage." 9When they had heard the king, they set out; and there, ahead of them, went the star that they had seen at its rising,*i* until it stopped over the place where the child was. 10When they saw that the star had stopped,*k* they were overwhelmed with joy. 11On entering the house, they saw the child with Mary his mother; and they knelt down and paid him homage. Then, opening their treasure chests, they offered him gifts of gold, frankincense, and myrrh. 12And having been warned in a dream not to return to Herod, they left for their own country by another road.

The Escape to Egypt

13 Now after they had left, an angel of the Lord appeared to Joseph in a dream and said, "Get up, take the child and his mother, and flee to Egypt, and remain there until I tell you; for Herod is about to search for the child, to destroy him." 14Then Joseph*l* got up, took the child and his mother by night, and went to Egypt, 15and remained there until the death of Herod. This was to fulfill what had been spoken by the Lord through the prophet, "Out of Egypt I have called my son."

e Or *the Christ*   *f* Or *Jesus Christ*   *g* Other ancient authorities read *her firstborn son*
h Or *astrologers;* Gk *magi*   *i* Or *in the East*   *j* Or *rule*   *k* Gk *saw the star*   *l* Gk *he*

The Massacre of the Infants

16 When Herod saw that he had been tricked by the wise men,*m* he was infuriated, and he sent and killed all the children in and around Bethlehem who were two years old or under, according to the time that he had learned from the wise men.*m* 17 Then was fulfilled what had been spoken through the prophet Jeremiah:

18 "A voice was heard in Ramah,
      wailing and loud lamentation,
   Rachel weeping for her children;
      she refused to be consoled,
      because they are no more."

m Or *astrologers;* Gk *magi*

MONDAY

THE BOOK OF JOY
Henry Ward Beecher

VERSE: Matthew 2.10   **PASSAGE:** Matthew 2.9–12

 call the New Testament the Book of Joy. There is nowhere in the world another book that is pervaded with such a spirit of exhilaration. Nowhere does it pour forth a melancholy strain. Often pathetic, it is never gloomy. Full of sorrows, it is full of victory over sorrow.

In all the round of literature, there is not another book that can cast such cheer and inspire such hope. Yet it eschews humor, and forgoes wit. It is intensely earnest, and yet full of quiet. It is profoundly solemn, yet there is not a strain of morbid feeling in it.

Some books have recognized the wretchedness of man's condition on earth, and in some sense have produced exhilaration; but it was done rather by amusing their readers. These books have turned life into a comedy. They have held up men's weakness to mirth. They have turned men's passions to ridicule, sharply puncturing their folly by wit. They have sought to redeem them from suffering by taking out all earnestness, all faith, all urgent convictions.

Not so with the Christian Scriptures. They never jest; they never ridicule; they never deal in comic scenes. They disdain, in short, all those methods by which other writings have inspired cheer. Yet, by a method of their own, they produce in all who accept them a reasonable sympathy, elevation of mind, high hope, and cheerful resignation.

ADDITIONAL SCRIPTURE READING:
Romans 15.13; 1 Peter 1.8–9

Go to page 1114 for your next devotional reading.

1700   1900

The Return from Egypt

19 When Herod died, an angel of the Lord suddenly appeared in a dream to Joseph in Egypt and said, 20"Get up, take the child and his mother, and go to the land of Israel, for those who were seeking the child's life are dead." 21Then Joseph[n] got up, took the child and his mother, and went to the land of Israel. 22But when he heard that Archelaus was ruling over Judea in place of his father Herod, he was afraid to go there. And after being warned in a dream, he went away to the district of Galilee. 23There he made his home in a town called Nazareth, so that what had been spoken through the prophets might be fulfilled, "He will be called a Nazorean."

The Proclamation of John the Baptist

3 In those days John the Baptist appeared in the wilderness of Judea, proclaiming, 2"Repent, for the kingdom of heaven has come near."[o] 3This is the one of whom the prophet Isaiah spoke when he said,

"The voice of one crying out in the wilderness:
'Prepare the way of the Lord,
    make his paths straight.' "

4Now John wore clothing of camel's hair with a leather belt around his waist, and his food was locusts and wild honey. 5Then the people of Jerusalem and all Judea were going out to him, and all the region along the Jordan, 6and they were baptized by him in the river Jordan, confessing their sins.

7 But when he saw many Pharisees and Sadducees coming for baptism, he said to them, "You brood of vipers! Who warned you to flee from the wrath to come? 8Bear fruit worthy of repentance. 9Do not presume to say to yourselves, 'We have Abraham as our ancestor'; for I tell you, God is able from these stones to raise up children to Abraham. 10Even now the ax is lying at the root of the trees; every tree therefore that does not bear good fruit is cut down and thrown into the fire.

11 "I baptize you with[p] water for repentance, but one who is more powerful than I is coming after me; I am not worthy to carry his sandals. He will baptize you with[p] the Holy Spirit and fire. 12His winnowing fork is in his hand, and he will clear his threshing floor and will gather his wheat into the granary; but the chaff he will burn with unquenchable fire."

The Baptism of Jesus

13 Then Jesus came from Galilee to John at the Jordan, to be baptized by him. 14John would have prevented him, saying, "I need to be baptized by you, and do you come to me?" 15But Jesus answered him, "Let it be so now; for it is proper for us in this way to fulfill all righteousness." Then he consented. 16And when Jesus had been baptized, just as he came up from the water, suddenly the heavens were opened to him and he saw the Spirit of God descending like a dove and alighting on him. 17And a voice from heaven said, "This is my Son, the Beloved,[q] with whom I am well pleased."

The Temptation of Jesus

4 Then Jesus was led up by the Spirit into the wilderness to be tempted by the devil. 2He fasted forty days and forty nights, and afterwards he was famished. 3The tempter came and said to him, "If you are the Son of God, command these stones to become loaves of bread." 4But he answered, "It is written,

'One does not live by bread alone,
    but by every word that comes
        from the mouth of God.' "

5 Then the devil took him to the holy city and placed him on the pinnacle of the temple, 6saying to him, "If you are the Son of God, throw yourself down; for it is written,

'He will command his angels
        concerning you,'
and 'On their hands they will
        bear you up,
so that you will not dash your foot
        against a stone.' "

7Jesus said to him, "Again it is written, 'Do not put the Lord your God to the test.' "

8 Again, the devil took him to a very high mountain and showed him all the kingdoms of the world and their

splendor; ⁹and he said to him, "All these I will give you, if you will fall down and

---

THE ANGELS ARE THE DISPENSERS AND ADMINIS-
TRATORS OF THE DIVINE BENEFICENCE TOWARD
US; THEY REGARD OUR SAFETY, UNDERTAKE OUR
DEFENSE, DIRECT OUR WAYS, AND EXERCISE A
CONSTANT SOLICITUDE THAT NO EVIL BEFALL US.
—*John Calvin*

---

r Gk *he*

worship me." ¹⁰Jesus said to him, "Away with you, Satan! for it is written,

> 'Worship the Lord your God,
>   and serve only him.' "

¹¹Then the devil left him, and suddenly angels came and waited on him.

Jesus Begins His Ministry in Galilee

12 Now when Jesusʳ heard that John had been arrested, he withdrew to Galilee. ¹³He left Nazareth and made his

---

TUESDAY

THE SON OF GOD IS GOD AND MAN
From Athanasian Creed

VERSE: Matthew 3.17   **PASSAGE:** Matthew 3.13–17

The Father is made of none, neither created nor begotten. The Son is of the Father alone, not made, nor created, but begotten.

The Holy Ghost is of the Father and of the Son, neither made, nor created nor begotten, but proceeding.

So there is one Father, not three Fathers; one Son, not three Sons; one Holy Ghost, not three Holy Ghosts.

And in this Trinity none is afore, or after other; none is greater, or less than another; but the whole three persons are co-eternal together and co-equal . . .

He therefore that will be saved must thus think of the Trinity.

Furthermore, it is necessary to everlasting salvation that he also believe rightly the incarnation of our Lord Jesus Christ. For the right faith is, that we believe and confess, that our Lord Jesus Christ, the Son of God, is God and Man;

God, of the substance of the Father, begotten before the worlds; and Man, of the substance of his mother, born in the world; perfect God and perfect Man, of a reasonable soul and human flesh subsisting; equal to the Father, as touching his Godhead; and inferior to the Father, as touching his Manhood. Who although he be God and Man, yet he is not two, but one Christ . . .

ADDITIONAL SCRIPTURE READING:
Psalm 2.2–12; 1 John 5.20

Go to page 1116 for your next devotional reading.

100   500

home in Capernaum by the sea, in the territory of Zebulun and Naphtali, **14**so that what had been spoken through the prophet Isaiah might be fulfilled:

15 "Land of Zebulun, land of
          Naphtali,
      on the road by the sea, across the
          Jordan, Galilee of the
          Gentiles—
16 the people who sat in darkness
          have seen a great light,
      and for those who sat in the region
          and shadow of death
          light has dawned."

17From that time Jesus began to proclaim, "Repent, for the kingdom of heaven has come near."s

Jesus Calls the First Disciples

18 As he walked by the Sea of Galilee, he saw two brothers, Simon, who is called Peter, and Andrew his brother, casting a net into the sea—for they were fishermen. **19**And he said to them, "Follow me, and I will make you fish for people." **20**Immediately they left their nets and followed him. **21**As he went from there, he saw two other brothers, James son of Zebedee and his brother John, in the boat with their father Zebedee, mending their nets, and he called them. **22**Immediately they left the boat and their father, and followed him.

Jesus Ministers to Crowds of People

23 Jesust went throughout Galilee, teaching in their synagogues and proclaiming the good newsu of the kingdom and curing every disease and every sickness among the people. **24**So his fame spread throughout all Syria, and they brought to him all the sick, those who were afflicted with various diseases and pains, demoniacs, epileptics, and paralytics, and he cured them. **25**And great crowds followed him from Galilee, the Decapolis, Jerusalem, Judea, and from beyond the Jordan.

The Beatitudes

5 When Jesusv saw the crowds, he went up the mountain; and after he sat down, his disciples came to him. **2**Then he began to speak, and taught them, saying:

3 "Blessed are the poor in spirit, for theirs is the kingdom of heaven.

THE MAN WHO IS POOR IN SPIRIT IS THE MAN WHO HAS REALIZED THAT THINGS MEAN NOTHING, AND THAT GOD MEANS EVERYTHING.

—*William Barclay*

---

4 "Blessed are those who mourn, for they will be comforted.

5 "Blessed are the meek, for they will inherit the earth.

6 "Blessed are those who hunger and thirst for righteousness, for they will be filled.

7 "Blessed are the merciful, for they will receive mercy.

8 "Blessed are the pure in heart, for they will see God.

9 "Blessed are the peacemakers, for they will be called children of God.

10 "Blessed are those who are persecuted for righteousness' sake, for theirs is the kingdom of heaven.

11 "Blessed are you when people revile you and persecute you and utter all kinds of evil against you falselyw on my account. **12**Rejoice and be glad, for your reward is great in heaven, for in the same way they persecuted the prophets who were before you.

Salt and Light

13 "You are the salt of the earth; but if salt has lost its taste, how can its saltiness be restored? It is no longer good for anything, but is thrown out and trampled under foot.

14 "You are the light of the world. A city built on a hill cannot be hid. **15**No one after lighting a lamp puts it under the bushel basket, but on the lampstand, and it gives light to all in the house. **16**In the same way, let your light shine before others, so that they may see your good works and give glory to your Father in heaven.

The Law and the Prophets

17 "Do not think that I have come to abolish the law or the prophets; I have come not to abolish but to fulfill. **18**For truly I tell you, until heaven and earth

s Or *is at hand*   t Gk *He*   u Gk *gospel*   v Gk *he*   w Other ancient authorities lack *falsely*

pass away, not one letter,ˣ not one stroke of a letter, will pass from the law until all is accomplished. ¹⁹Therefore, whoever breaksʸ one of the least of these commandments, and teaches others to do the same, will be called least in the kingdom of heaven; but whoever does them and teaches them will be called great in the kingdom of heaven. ²⁰For I tell you, unless your righteousness exceeds that of

x Gk *one iota*   y Or *annuls*

WEDNESDAY

THE PROPERTY OF LIGHT
Dietrich Bonhoeffer

VERSE: Matthew 5.14   **PASSAGE:** Matthew 5.14–16

he call of Jesus makes the disciple community not only the salt but also the light of the world: their activity is visible, as well as imperceptible. "You *are* the light." Once again it is not: "You are to be the light," they are already the light because Christ has called them, they are a light which is seen of men, they cannot be otherwise, and if they were it would be a sign that they had not been called. How impossible, how utterly absurd it would be for the disciples—*these* disciples, such men as these!—to try and *become* the light of the world! No, they are already the light, and the call has made them so. Nor does Jesus say: "You *have* the light." The light is not an instrument which has been put into their hands, such as their preaching. It is the disciples themselves. The same Jesus who, speaking of himself, said, "I am the light," says to his followers: "You are the light in your whole existence, provided you remain faithful to your calling (see also John 8.12). And since you are that light, you can no longer remain hidden, even if you want to." It is the property of light to shine. A city set on a hill cannot be hid; it can be seen for miles away, whether it is a fortified burgh, a stronghold or a tottering ruin. This city set on the hill (the Israelite would instinctively think of "Jerusalem on high") is the disciple community. But this is not to say that the disciples have now to make their first decision. The only necessary decision has already been taken. Now they must be what they really are—otherwise they are not followers of Jesus. The followers are a visible community; their discipleship visible in action which lifts them out of the world—otherwise it would not be discipleship.

ADDITIONAL SCRIPTURE READING:
Luke 8.16; John 8.12

Go to page 1122 for your next devotional reading.

1900   Present

the scribes and Pharisees, you will never enter the kingdom of heaven.

Concerning Anger

21 "You have heard that it was said to those of ancient times, 'You shall not murder'; and 'whoever murders shall be liable to judgment.' 22But I say to you that if you are angry with a brother or sister,z you will be liable to judgment; and if you insulta a brother or sister,b you will be liable to the council; and if you say, 'You fool,' you will be liable to the hellc of fire. 23So when you are offering your gift at the altar, if you remember that your brother or sisterd has something against you, 24leave your gift there before the altar and go; first be reconciled to your brother or sister,d and then come and offer your gift. 25Come to terms quickly with your accuser while you are on the way to courte with him, or your accuser may hand you over to the judge, and the judge to the guard, and you will be thrown into prison. 26Truly I tell you, you will never get out until you have paid the last penny.

Concerning Adultery

27 "You have heard that it was said, 'You shall not commit adultery.' 28But I say to you that everyone who looks at a woman with lust has already committed adultery with her in his heart. 29If your right eye causes you to sin, tear it out and throw it away; it is better for you to lose one of your members than for your whole body to be thrown into hell.c 30And if your right hand causes you to sin, cut it off and throw it away; it is better for you to lose one of your members than for your whole body to go into hell.c

Concerning Divorce

31 "It was also said, 'Whoever divorces his wife, let him give her a certificate of divorce.' 32But I say to you that anyone who divorces his wife, except on the ground of unchastity, causes her to commit adultery; and whoever marries a divorced woman commits adultery.

Concerning Oaths

33 "Again, you have heard that it was said to those of ancient times, 'You shall not swear falsely, but carry out the vows you have made to the Lord.' 34But I say to you, Do not swear at all, either by heaven, for it is the throne of God, 35or by the earth, for it is his footstool, or by Jerusalem, for it is the city of the great King. 36And do not swear by your head, for you cannot make one hair white or black. 37Let your word be 'Yes, Yes' or 'No, No'; anything more than this comes from the evil one.f

Concerning Retaliation

38 "You have heard that it was said, 'An eye for an eye and a tooth for a tooth.' 39But I say to you, Do not resist an evildoer. But if anyone strikes you on the right cheek, turn the other also; 40and if anyone wants to sue you and take your coat, give your cloak as well; 41and if anyone forces you to go one mile, go also the second mile. 42Give to everyone who begs from you, and do not refuse anyone who wants to borrow from you.

Love for Enemies

43 "You have heard that it was said, 'You shall love your neighbor and hate your enemy.' 44But I say to you, Love your enemies and pray for those who persecute you, 45so that you may be children of your Father in heaven; for he makes his sun rise on the evil and on the good, and sends rain on the righteous and on the unrighteous. 46For if you love those who love you, what reward do you have? Do not even the tax collectors do the same? 47And if you greet only your brothers and sisters,g what more are you doing than others? Do not even the Gentiles do the same? 48Be perfect, therefore, as your heavenly Father is perfect.

Concerning Almsgiving

6 "Beware of practicing your piety before others in order to be seen by them; for then you have no reward from your Father in heaven.

---

z Gk a brother; other ancient authorities add without cause   a Gk say Raca to (an obscure term of abuse)   b Gk a brother   c Gk Gehenna   d Gk your brother   e Gk lacks to court   f Or evil   g Gk your brothers

2 "So whenever you give alms, do not sound a trumpet before you, as the hypocrites do in the synagogues and in the streets, so that they may be praised by others. Truly I tell you, they have received their reward. 3But when you give alms, do not let your left hand know what your right hand is doing, 4so that your alms may be done in secret; and your Father who sees in secret will reward you.*h*

Concerning Prayer

5 "And whenever you pray, do not be like the hypocrites; for they love to stand and pray in the synagogues and at the street corners, so that they may be seen by others. Truly I tell you, they have received their reward. 6But whenever you pray, go into your room and shut the door and pray to your Father who is in secret; and your Father who sees in secret will reward you.*h*

7 "When you are praying, do not heap up empty phrases as the Gentiles do; for they think that they will be heard because of their many words. 8Do not be like them, for your Father knows what you need before you ask him.

THE FEWER WORDS, THE BETTER PRAYER.

—*Martin Luther*

---

9 "Pray then in this way:
  Our Father in heaven,
    hallowed be your name.
10   Your kingdom come.
  Your will be done,
    on earth as it is in heaven.
11   Give us this day our daily bread.*i*
12   And forgive us our debts,
    as we also have forgiven our
      debtors.
13   And do not bring us to the time
    of trial,*j*
    but rescue us from the evil
      one.*k*

14For if you forgive others their trespasses, your heavenly Father will also forgive you; 15but if you do not forgive others, neither will your Father forgive your trespasses.

Concerning Fasting

16 "And whenever you fast, do not look dismal, like the hypocrites, for they disfigure their faces so as to show others that they are fasting. Truly I tell you, they have received their reward. 17But when you fast, put oil on your head and wash your face, 18so that your fasting may be seen not by others but by your Father who is in secret; and your Father who sees in secret will reward you.*h*

Concerning Treasures

19 "Do not store up for yourselves treasures on earth, where moth and rust*l* consume and where thieves break in and steal; 20but store up for yourselves treasures in heaven, where neither moth nor rust*l* consumes and where thieves do not break in and steal. 21For where your treasure is, there your heart will be also.

The Sound Eye

22 "The eye is the lamp of the body. So, if your eye is healthy, your whole body will be full of light; 23but if your eye is unhealthy, your whole body will be full of darkness. If then the light in you is darkness, how great is the darkness!

Serving Two Masters

24 "No one can serve two masters; for a slave will either hate the one and love the other, or be devoted to the one and despise the other. You cannot serve God and wealth.*m*

Do Not Worry

25 "Therefore I tell you, do not worry about your life, what you will eat or what you will drink,*n* or about your body, what you will wear. Is not life more than food, and the body more than clothing? 26Look at the birds of the air; they neither sow nor reap nor gather into barns, and yet your heavenly Father feeds them. Are you not of more value than they? 27And

---

h Other ancient authorities add *openly*   *i* Or *our bread for tomorrow*   *j* Or *us into temptation*
k Or *from evil.* Other ancient authorities add, in some form, *For the kingdom and the power and the glory are yours forever. Amen.*   *l* Gk *eating*   *m* Gk *mammon*   *n* Other ancient authorities lack or *what you will drink*

can any of you by worrying add a single hour to your span of life?o 28And why do you worry about clothing? Consider the lilies of the field, how they grow; they neither toil nor spin, 29yet I tell you, even Solomon in all his glory was not clothed like one of these. 30But if God so clothes the grass of the field, which is alive today and tomorrow is thrown into the oven, will he not much more clothe you—you of little faith? 31Therefore do not worry, saying, 'What will we eat?' or 'What will we drink?' or 'What will we wear?' 32For it is the Gentiles who strive for all these things; and indeed your heavenly Father knows that you need all these things. 33But strive first for the kingdom of Godp and hisq righteousness, and all these things will be given to you as well.

34 "So do not worry about tomorrow, for tomorrow will bring worries of its own. Today's trouble is enough for today.

ANXIETY DOES NOT EMPTY TOMORROW OF ITS SORROWS BUT ONLY EMPTIES TODAY OF ITS STRENGTH. —*C. H. Spurgeon*

Judging Others

7 "Do not judge, so that you may not be judged. 2For with the judgment you make you will be judged, and the measure you give will be the measure you get. 3Why do you see the speck in your neighbor'sr eye, but do not notice the log in your own eye? 4Or how can you say to your neighbor,s 'Let me take the speck out of your eye,' while the log is in your own eye? 5You hypocrite, first take the log out of your own eye, and then you will see clearly to take the speck out of your neighbor'sr eye.

Profaning the Holy

6 "Do not give what is holy to dogs; and do not throw your pearls before swine, or they will trample them under foot and turn and maul you.

Ask, Search, Knock

7 "Ask, and it will be given you; search, and you will find; knock, and the

door will be opened for you. 8For everyone who asks receives, and everyone who searches finds, and for everyone who knocks, the door will be opened. 9Is there anyone among you who, if your child asks for bread, will give a stone? 10Or if the child asks for a fish, will give a snake? 11If you then, who are evil, know how to give good gifts to your children, how much more will your Father in heaven give good things to those who ask him!

The Golden Rule

12 "In everything do to others as you would have them do to you; for this is the law and the prophets.

The Narrow Gate

13 "Enter through the narrow gate; for the gate is wide and the road is easyt that leads to destruction, and there are many who take it. 14For the gate is narrow and the road is hard that leads to life, and there are few who find it.

A Tree and Its Fruit

15 "Beware of false prophets, who come to you in sheep's clothing but inwardly are ravenous wolves. 16You will know them by their fruits. Are grapes gathered from thorns, or figs from thistles? 17In the same way, every good tree bears good fruit, but the bad tree bears bad fruit. 18A good tree cannot bear bad fruit, nor can a bad tree bear good fruit. 19Every tree that does not bear good fruit is cut down and thrown into the fire. 20Thus you will know them by their fruits.

Concerning Self-Deception

21 "Not everyone who says to me, 'Lord, Lord,' will enter the kingdom of heaven, but only the one who does the will of my Father in heaven. 22On that day many will say to me, 'Lord, Lord, did we not prophesy in your name, and cast out demons in your name, and do many deeds of power in your name?' 23Then I will declare to them, 'I never knew you; go away from me, you evildoers.'

---

o Or *add one cubit to your height*   p Other ancient authorities lack *of God*   q Or *its*
r Gk *brother's*   s Gk *brother*   t Other ancient authorities read *for the road is wide and easy*

Hearers and Doers

24 "Everyone then who hears these words of mine and acts on them will be like a wise man who built his house on rock. 25 The rain fell, the floods came, and the winds blew and beat on that house, but it did not fall, because it had been founded on rock. 26 And everyone who hears these words of mine and does not act on them will be like a foolish man who built his house on sand. 27 The rain fell, and the floods came, and the winds blew and beat against that house, and it fell—and great was its fall!"

28 Now when Jesus had finished saying these things, the crowds were astounded at his teaching, 29 for he taught them as one having authority, and not as their scribes.

Jesus Cleanses a Leper

8 When Jesus[u] had come down from the mountain, great crowds followed him; 2 and there was a leper[v] who came to him and knelt before him, saying, "Lord, if you choose, you can make me clean." 3 He stretched out his hand and touched him, saying, "I do choose. Be made clean!" Immediately his leprosy[v] was cleansed. 4 Then Jesus said to him, "See that you say nothing to anyone; but go, show yourself to the priest, and offer the gift that Moses commanded, as a testimony to them."

Jesus Heals a Centurion's Servant

5 When he entered Capernaum, a centurion came to him, appealing to him 6 and saying, "Lord, my servant is lying at home paralyzed, in terrible distress." 7 And he said to him, "I will come and cure him." 8 The centurion answered, "Lord, I am not worthy to have you come under my roof; but only speak the word, and my servant will be healed. 9 For I also am a man under authority, with soldiers under me; and I say to one, 'Go,' and he goes, and to another, 'Come,' and he comes, and to my slave, 'Do this,' and the slave does it." 10 When Jesus heard him, he was amazed and said to those who followed him, "Truly I tell you, in no one[w] in Israel have I found

such faith. 11 I tell you, many will come from east and west and will eat with Abraham and Isaac and Jacob in the kingdom of heaven, 12 while the heirs of the kingdom will be thrown into the outer darkness, where there will be weeping and gnashing of teeth." 13 And to the centurion Jesus said, "Go; let it be done for you according to your faith." And the servant was healed in that hour.

Jesus Heals Many at Peter's House

14 When Jesus entered Peter's house, he saw his mother-in-law lying in bed with a fever; 15 he touched her hand, and the fever left her, and she got up and began to serve him. 16 That evening they brought to him many who were possessed with demons; and he cast out the spirits with a word, and cured all who were sick. 17 This was to fulfill what had been spoken through the prophet Isaiah, "He took our infirmities and bore our diseases."

Would-Be Followers of Jesus

18 Now when Jesus saw great crowds around him, he gave orders to go over to the other side. 19 A scribe then approached and said, "Teacher, I will follow you wherever you go." 20 And Jesus said to him, "Foxes have holes, and birds of the air have nests; but the Son of Man has nowhere to lay his head." 21 Another of his disciples said to him, "Lord, first let me go and bury my father." 22 But Jesus said to him, "Follow me, and let the dead bury their own dead."

Jesus Stills the Storm

23 And when he got into the boat, his disciples followed him. 24 A windstorm arose on the sea, so great that the boat was being swamped by the waves; but he was asleep. 25 And they went and woke him up, saying, "Lord, save us! We are perishing!" 26 And he said to them, "Why are you afraid, you of little faith?" Then he got up and rebuked the winds and the sea; and there was a dead calm. 27 They were amazed, saying, "What sort of man is this, that even the winds and the sea obey him?"

u Gk he   v The terms leper and leprosy can refer to several diseases   w Other ancient authorities read Truly I tell you, not even

Jesus Heals the Gadarene Demoniacs

28 When he came to the other side, to the country of the Gadarenes,x two demoniacs coming out of the tombs met him. They were so fierce that no one could pass that way. 29Suddenly they shouted, "What have you to do with us, Son of God? Have you come here to torment us before the time?" 30Now a large herd of swine was feeding at some distance from them. 31The demons begged him, "If you cast us out, send us into the herd of swine." 32And he said to them, "Go!" So they came out and entered the swine; and suddenly, the whole herd rushed down the steep bank into the sea and perished in the water. 33The swineherds ran off, and on going into the town, they told the whole story about what had happened to the demoniacs. 34Then the whole town came out to meet Jesus; and when they saw him, they begged him to leave their neighborhood. 1And after getting into a boat he crossed the sea and came to his own town.

Jesus Heals a Paralytic

2 And just then some people were carrying a paralyzed man lying on a bed. When Jesus saw their faith, he said to the paralytic, "Take heart, son; your sins are forgiven." 3Then some of the scribes said to themselves, "This man is blaspheming." 4But Jesus, perceiving their thoughts, said, "Why do you think evil in your hearts? 5For which is easier, to say, 'Your sins are forgiven,' or to say, 'Stand up and walk'? 6But so that you may know that the Son of Man has authority on earth to forgive sins"—he then said to the paralytic—"Stand up, take your bed and go to your home." 7And he stood up and went to his home. 8When the crowds saw it, they were filled with awe, and they glorified God, who had given such authority to human beings.

The Call of Matthew

9 As Jesus was walking along, he saw a man called Matthew sitting at the tax booth; and he said to him, "Follow me." And he got up and followed him.

10 And as he sat at dinnery in the house, many tax collectors and sinners came and were sittingz with him and his disciples. 11When the Pharisees saw this, they said to his disciples, "Why does your teacher eat with tax collectors and sinners?" 12But when he heard this, he said, "Those who are well have no need of a physician, but those who are sick. 13Go and learn what this means, 'I desire mercy, not sacrifice.' For I have come to call not the righteous but sinners."

The Question about Fasting

14 Then the disciples of John came to him, saying, "Why do we and the Pharisees fast often,a but your disciples do not fast?" 15And Jesus said to them, "The wedding guests cannot mourn as long as the bridegroom is with them, can they? The days will come when the bridegroom is taken away from them, and then they will fast. 16No one sews a piece of unshrunk cloth on an old cloak, for the patch pulls away from the cloak, and a worse tear is made. 17Neither is new wine put into old wineskins; otherwise, the skins burst, and the wine is spilled, and the skins are destroyed; but new wine is put into fresh wineskins, and so both are preserved."

A Girl Restored to Life and a Woman Healed

18 While he was saying these things to them, suddenly a leader of the synagogueb came in and knelt before him, saying, "My daughter has just died; but come and lay your hand on her, and she will live." 19And Jesus got up and followed him, with his disciples. 20Then suddenly a woman who had been suffering from hemorrhages for twelve years came up behind him and touched the fringe of his cloak, 21for she said to herself, "If I only touch his cloak, I will be made well." 22Jesus turned, and seeing her he said, "Take heart, daughter; your faith has made you well." And instantly the woman was made well. 23When Jesus came to the leader's house and saw the flute players and the crowd making a commotion, 24he said, "Go away; for the girl is not dead but sleeping." And

---

x Other ancient authorities read Gergesenes ; others, Gerasenes   y Gk reclined   z Gk were reclining   a Other ancient authorities lack often   b Gk lacks of the synagogue

A TRUE RELATION WITH CHRIST
Dietrich Bonhoeffer

VERSE: Matthew 9.9   **PASSAGE:** Matthew 9.9–13

 hen we are called to follow Christ, we are summoned to an exclusive attachment to his person. The grace of his call bursts all the bonds of legalism. It is a gracious call, a gracious commandment. It transcends the difference between the law and the gospel. Christ calls, the disciple follows; that is grace and commandment in one. "I shall walk at liberty; for I have sought your precepts" (Psalm 119.45).

Discipleship means adherence to Christ, and, because Christ is the object of that adherence, it must take the form of discipleship. An abstract Christology, a doctrinal system, a general religious knowledge on the subject of grace or on the forgiveness of sins, render discipleship superfluous, and in fact they positively exclude any idea of discipleship whatever, and are essentially inimical to the whole conception of following Christ. With an abstract idea it is possible to enter into a relation of formal knowledge, to become enthusiastic about it, and perhaps even to put it into practice; but it can never be followed in personal obedience. Christianity without the living Christ is inevitably Christianity without discipleship, and Christianity without discipleship is always Christianity without Christ. It remains an abstract idea, a myth which has a place for the Fatherhood of God, but omits Christ as the living Son. And a Christianity of that kind is nothing more or less than the end of discipleship. In such a religion there is trust in God, but no following of Christ. Because the Son of God became man, because he is the mediator, for that reason alone the only true relation we can have with him is to follow him. Discipleship is bound to Christ as the mediator, and where it is properly understood, it necessarily implies faith in the Son of God as the mediator. Only the mediator, the God-man, can call men to follow him.

ADDITIONAL SCRIPTURE READING:
Luke 5.27–28; John 13.34–35

Go to page 1126 for your next devotional reading.

1900   Present

they laughed at him. 25But when the crowd had been put outside, he went in and took her by the hand, and the girl got up. 26And the report of this spread throughout that district.

Jesus Heals Two Blind Men

27 As Jesus went on from there, two blind men followed him, crying loudly, "Have mercy on us, Son of David!" 28When he entered the house, the blind men came to him; and Jesus said to them, "Do you believe that I am able to do this?" They said to him, "Yes, Lord." 29Then he touched their eyes and said, "According to your faith let it be done to you." 30And their eyes were opened. Then Jesus sternly ordered them, "See that no one knows of this." 31But they went away and spread the news about him throughout that district.

Jesus Heals One Who Was Mute

32 After they had gone away, a demoniac who was mute was brought to him. 33And when the demon had been cast out, the one who had been mute spoke; and the crowds were amazed and said, "Never has anything like this been seen in Israel." 34But the Pharisees said, "By the ruler of the demons he casts out the demons."c

The Harvest Is Great, the Laborers Few

35 Then Jesus went about all the cities and villages, teaching in their synagogues, and proclaiming the good news of the kingdom, and curing every disease and every sickness. 36When he saw the crowds, he had compassion for them, because they were harassed and helpless, like sheep without a shepherd. 37Then he said to his disciples, "The harvest is plentiful, but the laborers are few; 38therefore ask the Lord of the harvest to send out laborers into his harvest."

The Twelve Apostles

10 Then Jesusd summoned his twelve disciples and gave them authority over unclean spirits, to cast them out, and to cure every disease

and every sickness. 2These are the names of the twelve apostles: first, Simon, also known as Peter, and his brother Andrew; James son of Zebedee, and his brother John; 3Philip and Bartholomew; Thomas and Matthew the tax collector; James son of Alphaeus, and Thaddaeus;e 4Simon the Cananaean, and Judas Iscariot, the one who betrayed him.

The Mission of the Twelve

5 These twelve Jesus sent out with the following instructions: "Go nowhere among the Gentiles, and enter no town of the Samaritans, 6but go rather to the lost sheep of the house of Israel. 7As you go, proclaim the good news, 'The kingdom of heaven has come near.'f 8Cure the sick, raise the dead, cleanse the lepers,g cast out demons. You received without payment; give without payment. 9Take no gold, or silver, or copper in your belts, 10no bag for your journey, or two tunics, or sandals, or a staff; for laborers deserve their food. 11Whatever town or village you enter, find out who in it is worthy, and stay there until you leave. 12As you enter the house, greet it. 13If the house is worthy, let your peace come upon it; but if it is not worthy, let your peace return to you. 14If anyone will not welcome you or listen to your words, shake off the dust from your feet as you leave that house or town. 15Truly I tell you, it will be more tolerable for the land of Sodom and Gomorrah on the day of judgment than for that town.

Coming Persecutions

16 "See, I am sending you out like sheep into the midst of wolves; so be wise as serpents and innocent as doves. 17Beware of them, for they will hand you over to councils and flog you in their synagogues; 18and you will be dragged before governors and kings because of me, as a testimony to them and the Gentiles. 19When they hand you over, do not worry about how you are to speak or what you are to say; for what you are to say will be given to you at that time; 20for it is not you who speak, but the Spirit of your Father speaking through you. 21Brother will

---

c Other ancient authorities lack this verse   d Gk *he*   e Other ancient authorities read *Lebbaeus,* or *Lebbaeus called Thaddaeus*   f Or *is at hand*   g The terms *leper* and *leprosy* can refer to several diseases

betray brother to death, and a father his child, and children will rise against parents and have them put to death; 22and you will be hated by all because of my name. But the one who endures to the end will be saved. 23When they persecute you in one town, flee to the next; for truly I tell you, you will not have gone through all the towns of Israel before the Son of Man comes.

24 "A disciple is not above the teacher, nor a slave above the master; 25it is enough for the disciple to be like the teacher, and the slave like the master. If they have called the master of the house Beelzebul, how much more will they malign those of his household!

Whom to Fear

26 "So have no fear of them; for nothing is covered up that will not be uncovered, and nothing secret that will not become known. 27What I say to you in the dark, tell in the light; and what you hear whispered, proclaim from the housetops. 28Do not fear those who kill the body but cannot kill the soul; rather fear him who can destroy both soul and body in hell.*h* 29Are not two sparrows sold for a penny? Yet not one of them will fall to the ground apart from your Father. 30And even the hairs of your head are all counted. 31So do not be afraid; you are of more value than many sparrows.

32 "Everyone therefore who acknowledges me before others, I also will acknowledge before my Father in heaven; 33but whoever denies me before others, I also will deny before my Father in heaven.

Not Peace, but a Sword

34 "Do not think that I have come to bring peace to the earth; I have not come to bring peace, but a sword.
35   For I have come to set a man
            against his father,
     and a daughter against her mother,
     and a daughter-in-law against her
            mother-in-law;
36   and one's foes will be members of
            one's own household.
37Whoever loves father or mother more

than me is not worthy of me; and whoever loves son or daughter more than me is not worthy of me; 38and whoever does not take up the cross and follow me is not worthy of me. 39Those who find their life will lose it, and those who lose their life for my sake will find it.

Rewards

40 "Whoever welcomes you welcomes me, and whoever welcomes me welcomes the one who sent me. 41Whoever welcomes a prophet in the name of a prophet will receive a prophet's reward; and whoever welcomes a righteous person in the name of a righteous person will receive the reward of the righteous; 42and whoever gives even a cup of cold water to one of these little ones in the name of a disciple—truly I tell you, none of these will lose their reward."

11 Now when Jesus had finished instructing his twelve disciples, he went on from there to teach and proclaim his message in their cities.

Messengers from John the Baptist

2 When John heard in prison what the Messiah*i* was doing, he sent word by his*j* disciples 3and said to him, "Are you the one who is to come, or are we to wait for another?" 4Jesus answered them, "Go and tell John what you hear and see: 5the blind receive their sight, the lame walk, the lepers*k* are cleansed, the deaf hear, the dead are raised, and the poor have good news brought to them. 6And blessed is anyone who takes no offense at me."

Jesus Praises John the Baptist

7 As they went away, Jesus began to speak to the crowds about John: "What did you go out into the wilderness to look at? A reed shaken by the wind? 8What then did you go out to see? Someone*l* dressed in soft robes? Look, those who wear soft robes are in royal palaces. 9What then did you go out to see? A prophet?*m* Yes, I tell you, and more than a prophet. 10This is the one about whom it is written,

h Gk *Gehenna*   *i* Or *the Christ*   *j* Other ancient authorities read *two of his*   *k* The terms *leper* and *leprosy* can refer to several diseases   *l* Or *Why then did you go out? To see someone*   *m* Other ancient authorities read *Why then did you go out? To see a prophet?*

'See, I am sending my messenger
   ahead of you,
     who will prepare your way before
      you.'
11Truly I tell you, among those born of
women no one has arisen greater than
John the Baptist; yet the least in the
kingdom of heaven is greater than he.
12From the days of John the Baptist until
now the kingdom of heaven has suffered
violence,n and the violent take it by
force. 13For all the prophets and the law
prophesied until John came; 14and if you
are willing to accept it, he is Elijah who
is to come. 15Let anyone with earso listen!

16 "But to what will I compare this
generation? It is like children sitting in
the marketplaces and calling to one another,
17   'We played the flute for you, and
      you did not dance;
     we wailed, and you did not
      mourn.'
18For John came neither eating nor
drinking, and they say, 'He has a
demon'; 19the Son of Man came eating
and drinking, and they say, 'Look, a glutton and a drunkard, a friend of tax collectors and sinners!' Yet wisdom is vindicated by her deeds."p

Woes to Unrepentant Cities

20 Then he began to reproach the cities in which most of his deeds of power
had been done, because they did not repent. 21"Woe to you, Chorazin! Woe to
you, Bethsaida! For if the deeds of power
done in you had been done in Tyre and
Sidon, they would have repented long
ago in sackcloth and ashes. 22But I tell
you, on the day of judgment it will be
more tolerable for Tyre and Sidon than
for you. 23And you, Capernaum,
   will you be exalted to heaven?
     No, you will be brought down to
      Hades.
For if the deeds of power done in you
had been done in Sodom, it would have
remained until this day. 24But I tell you
that on the day of judgment it will be
more tolerable for the land of Sodom
than for you."

Jesus Thanks His Father

25 At that time Jesus said, "I thankq
you, Father, Lord of heaven and earth,
because you have hidden these things
from the wise and the intelligent and
have revealed them to infants; 26yes, Father, for such was your gracious will.r
27All things have been handed over to
me by my Father; and no one knows the
Son except the Father, and no one
knows the Father except the Son and
anyone to whom the Son chooses to reveal him.

28 "Come to me, all you that are
weary and are carrying heavy burdens,
and I will give you rest. 29Take my yoke
upon you, and learn from me; for I am
gentle and humble in heart, and you will
find rest for your souls. 30For my yoke is
easy, and my burden is light."

I HAVE READ IN PLATO AND CICERO SAYINGS
THAT ARE VERY WISE AND VERY BEAUTIFUL; BUT I
NEVER READ IN EITHER OF THEM: "COME UNTO
ME ALL YE THAT LABOR AND ARE HEAVY LADEN."

                   —*Augustine*

Plucking Grain on the Sabbath

12 At that time Jesus went
through the grainfields on the
sabbath; his disciples were hungry, and
they began to pluck heads of grain and
to eat. 2When the Pharisees saw it, they
said to him, "Look, your disciples are
doing what is not lawful to do on the
sabbath." 3He said to them, "Have you
not read what David did when he and
his companions were hungry? 4He entered the house of God and ate the bread
of the Presence, which it was not lawful
for him or his companions to eat, but
only for the priests. 5Or have you not
read in the law that on the sabbath the
priests in the temple break the sabbath
and yet are guiltless? 6I tell you, something greater than the temple is here.
7But if you had known what this means,
'I desire mercy and not sacrifice,' you
would not have condemned the guiltless. 8For the Son of Man is lord of the
sabbath."

---

n Or has been coming violently   o Other ancient authorities add to hear   p Other ancient
authorities read children   q Or praise   r Or for so it was well-pleasing in your sight

The Man with a Withered Hand

9 He left that place and entered their synagogue; 10a man was there with a withered hand, and they asked him, "Is it lawful to cure on the sabbath?" so that they might accuse him. 11He said to them, "Suppose one of you has only one sheep and it falls into a pit on the sabbath; will you not lay hold of it and lift it out? 12How much more valuable is a

---

FRIDAY

SELF-CONSCIOUSNESS VS. CHRIST-CONSCIOUSNESS
Oswald Chambers

VERSE: Matthew 11.28   **PASSAGE:** Matthew 11.25–30

 henever anything begins to disintegrate your life with Jesus Christ, turn to him at once, asking him to re-establish your rest. Never allow anything to remain in your life that is causing the unrest. Think of every detail of your life that is causing the disintegration as something to fight against, not as something you should allow to remain. Ask the Lord to put awareness of himself in you, and your self-awareness will disappear. Then he will be your all in all. Beware of allowing your self-awareness to continue, because slowly but surely it will awaken self-pity, and self-pity is satanic . . . Ask the Lord to give you Christ-awareness, and he will steady you until your completeness in him is absolute.

A complete life is the life of a child. When I am fully conscious of my awareness of Christ, there is something wrong. It is the sick person who really knows what health is. A child of God is not aware of the will of God because he *is* the will of God. When we have deviated even slightly from the will of God, we begin to ask, "Lord, what is your will?" A child of God never prays to be made aware of the fact that God answers prayer, because he is so restfully certain that God always answers prayer.

If we try to overcome self-awareness through any of our own commonsense methods, we will only serve to strengthen our self-awareness tremendously. Jesus says, "Come to me . . . and I will give you rest," that is, Christ-awareness will take the place of self-awareness. Wherever Jesus comes he establishes rest— the rest of the completion of activity in our lives that is never aware of itself.

ADDITIONAL SCRIPTURE READING:
Psalm 116.7–9; John 14.27

Go to page 1130 for your next devotional reading.

1900   Present

human being than a sheep! So it is lawful to do good on the sabbath." 13Then he said to the man, "Stretch out your hand." He stretched it out, and it was restored, as sound as the other. 14But the Pharisees went out and conspired against him, how to destroy him.

God's Chosen Servant

15 When Jesus became aware of this, he departed. Many crowds*s* followed him, and he cured all of them, 16and he ordered them not to make him known. 17This was to fulfill what had been spoken through the prophet Isaiah:

18   "Here is my servant, whom I have
          chosen,
      my beloved, with whom my soul
          is well pleased.
      I will put my Spirit upon him,
          and he will proclaim justice to
          the Gentiles.
19   He will not wrangle or cry aloud,
          nor will anyone hear his voice in
          the streets.
20   He will not break a bruised reed
          or quench a smoldering wick
      until he brings justice to victory.
21   And in his name the Gentiles
          will hope."

Jesus and Beelzebul

22 Then they brought to him a demoniac who was blind and mute; and he cured him, so that the one who had been mute could speak and see. 23All the crowds were amazed and said, "Can this be the Son of David?" 24But when the Pharisees heard it, they said, "It is only by Beelzebul, the ruler of the demons, that this fellow casts out the demons." 25He knew what they were thinking and said to them, "Every kingdom divided against itself is laid waste, and no city or house divided against itself will stand. 26If Satan casts out Satan, he is divided against himself; how then will his kingdom stand? 27If I cast out demons by Beelzebul, by whom do your own exorcists*t* cast them out? Therefore they will be your judges. 28But if it is by the Spirit of God that I cast out demons, then the kingdom of God has come to you. 29Or how can one enter a strong man's house and plunder his property, without first

tying up the strong man? Then indeed the house can be plundered. 30Whoever is not with me is against me, and whoever does not gather with me scatters. 31Therefore I tell you, people will be forgiven for every sin and blasphemy, but blasphemy against the Spirit will not be forgiven. 32Whoever speaks a word against the Son of Man will be forgiven, but whoever speaks against the Holy Spirit will not be forgiven, either in this age or in the age to come.

A Tree and Its Fruit

33 "Either make the tree good, and its fruit good; or make the tree bad, and its fruit bad; for the tree is known by its fruit. 34You brood of vipers! How can you speak good things, when you are evil? For out of the abundance of the heart the mouth speaks. 35The good person brings good things out of a good treasure, and the evil person brings evil things out of an evil treasure. 36I tell you, on the day of judgment you will have to give an account for every careless word you utter; 37for by your words you will be justified, and by your words you will be condemned."

The Sign of Jonah

38 Then some of the scribes and Pharisees said to him, "Teacher, we wish to see a sign from you." 39But he answered them, "An evil and adulterous generation asks for a sign, but no sign will be given to it except the sign of the prophet Jonah. 40For just as Jonah was three days and three nights in the belly of the sea monster, so for three days and three nights the Son of Man will be in the heart of the earth. 41The people of Nineveh will rise up at the judgment with this generation and condemn it, because they repented at the proclamation of Jonah, and see, something greater than Jonah is here! 42The queen of the South will rise up at the judgment with this generation and condemn it, because she came from the ends of the earth to listen to the wisdom of Solomon, and see, something greater than Solomon is here!

s Other ancient authorities lack crowds   t Gk sons

The Return of the Unclean Spirit

43 "When the unclean spirit has gone out of a person, it wanders through waterless regions looking for a resting place, but it finds none. 44 Then it says, 'I will return to my house from which I came.' When it comes, it finds it empty, swept, and put in order. 45 Then it goes and brings along seven other spirits more evil than itself, and they enter and live there; and the last state of that person is worse than the first. So will it be also with this evil generation."

The True Kindred of Jesus

46 While he was still speaking to the crowds, his mother and his brothers were standing outside, wanting to speak to him. 47 Someone told him, "Look, your mother and your brothers are standing outside, wanting to speak to you."[u] 48 But to the one who had told him this, Jesus[v] replied, "Who is my mother, and who are my brothers?" 49 And pointing to his disciples, he said, "Here are my mother and my brothers! 50 For whoever does the will of my Father in heaven is my brother and sister and mother."

The Parable of the Sower

13 That same day Jesus went out of the house and sat beside the sea. 2 Such great crowds gathered around him that he got into a boat and sat there, while the whole crowd stood on the beach. 3 And he told them many things in parables, saying: "Listen! A sower went out to sow. 4 And as he sowed, some seeds fell on the path, and the birds came and ate them up. 5 Other seeds fell on rocky ground, where they did not have much soil, and they sprang up quickly, since they had no depth of soil. 6 But when the sun rose, they were scorched; and since they had no root, they withered away. 7 Other seeds fell among thorns, and the thorns grew up and choked them. 8 Other seeds fell on good soil and brought forth grain, some a hundredfold, some sixty, some thirty. 9 Let anyone with ears[w] listen!"

The Purpose of the Parables

10 Then the disciples came and asked him, "Why do you speak to them in parables?" 11 He answered, "To you it has been given to know the secrets[x] of the kingdom of heaven, but to them it has not been given. 12 For to those who have, more will be given, and they will have an abundance; but from those who have nothing, even what they have will be taken away. 13 The reason I speak to them in parables is that 'seeing they do not perceive, and hearing they do not listen, nor do they understand.' 14 With them indeed is fulfilled the prophecy of Isaiah that says:

'You will indeed listen, but never
    understand,
  and you will indeed look, but
    never perceive.
15 For this people's heart has grown
    dull,
  and their ears are hard of hearing,
    and they have shut their eyes;
  so that they might not look
    with their eyes,
  and listen with their ears,
  and understand with their heart
    and turn—
  and I would heal them.'

16 But blessed are your eyes, for they see, and your ears, for they hear. 17 Truly I tell you, many prophets and righteous people longed to see what you see, but did not see it, and to hear what you hear, but did not hear it.

The Parable of the Sower Explained

18 "Hear then the parable of the sower. 19 When anyone hears the word of the kingdom and does not understand it, the evil one comes and snatches away what is sown in the heart; this is what was sown on the path. 20 As for what was sown on rocky ground, this is the one who hears the word and immediately receives it with joy; 21 yet such a person has no root, but endures only for a while, and when trouble or persecution arises on account of the word, that person immediately falls away.[y] 22 As for what was sown among thorns, this is the one who hears the word, but the cares of the world and the lure of wealth

u Other ancient authorities lack verse 47   v Gk he   w Other ancient authorities add to hear
x Or mysteries   y Gk stumbles

choke the word, and it yields nothing. [23]But as for what was sown on good soil, this is the one who hears the word and understands it, who indeed bears fruit and yields, in one case a hundredfold, in another sixty, and in another thirty."

The Parable of Weeds among the Wheat

24 He put before them another parable: "The kingdom of heaven may be compared to someone who sowed good seed in his field; [25]but while everybody was asleep, an enemy came and sowed weeds among the wheat, and then went away. [26]So when the plants came up and bore grain, then the weeds appeared as well. [27]And the slaves of the householder came and said to him, 'Master, did you not sow good seed in your field? Where, then, did these weeds come from?' [28]He answered, 'An enemy has done this.' The slaves said to him, 'Then do you want us to go and gather them?' [29]But he replied, 'No; for in gathering the weeds you would uproot the wheat along with them. [30]Let both of them grow together until the harvest; and at harvest time I will tell the reapers, Collect the weeds first and bind them in bundles to be burned, but gather the wheat into my barn.' "

The Parable of the Mustard Seed

31 He put before them another parable: "The kingdom of heaven is like a mustard seed that someone took and sowed in his field; [32]it is the smallest of all the seeds, but when it has grown it is the greatest of shrubs and becomes a tree, so that the birds of the air come and make nests in its branches."

The Parable of the Yeast

33 He told them another parable: "The kingdom of heaven is like yeast that a woman took and mixed in with[z] three measures of flour until all of it was leavened."

The Use of Parables

34 Jesus told the crowds all these things in parables; without a parable he told them nothing. [35]This was to fulfill what had been spoken through the prophet:[a]

"I will open my mouth to speak in parables;
I will proclaim what has been hidden from the foundation of the world."[b]

Jesus Explains the Parable of the Weeds

36 Then he left the crowds and went into the house. And his disciples approached him, saying, "Explain to us the parable of the weeds of the field." [37]He answered, "The one who sows the good seed is the Son of Man; [38]the field is the world, and the good seed are the children of the kingdom; the weeds are the children of the evil one, [39]and the enemy who sowed them is the devil; the harvest is the end of the age, and the reapers are angels. [40]Just as the weeds are collected and burned up with fire, so will it be at the end of the age. [41]The Son of Man will send his angels, and they will collect out of his kingdom all causes of sin and all evildoers, [42]and they will throw them into the furnace of fire, where there will be weeping and gnashing of teeth. [43]Then the righteous will shine like the sun in the kingdom of their Father. Let anyone with ears[c] listen!

Three Parables

44 "The kingdom of heaven is like treasure hidden in a field, which someone found and hid; then in his joy he goes and sells all that he has and buys that field.

COSTLY GRACE IS THE TREASURE HIDDEN IN THE FIELD; FOR THE SAKE OF IT A MAN WILL GLADLY GO AND SELL ALL THAT HE HAS. IT IS COSTLY BECAUSE IT COSTS A MAN HIS LIFE, AND IT IS GRACE BECAUSE IT GIVES A MAN THE ONLY TRUE LIFE.
—*Dietrich Bonhoeffer*

---

45 "Again, the kingdom of heaven is like a merchant in search of fine pearls; [46]on finding one pearl of great value, he went and sold all that he had and bought it.

---

z Gk *hid in of the world*   a Other ancient authorities read *the prophet Isaiah*   b Other ancient authorities lack
c Other ancient authorities add *to hear*

WEEKEND

A SONG FOR SIMEON
T. S. Eliot

VERSE: Luke 2.25   **PASSAGE:** Luke 2.25–34

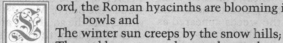ord, the Roman hyacinths are blooming in
    bowls and
The winter sun creeps by the snow hills;
The stubborn season has made stand.
My life is light, waiting for the death wind,
Like a feather on the back of my hand.
Dust in sunlight and memory in corners
Wait for the wind that chills towards the dead land . . .

Before the time of cords and scourges and lamentation
Grant us thy peace.
Before the stations of the mountain of desolation,
Before the certain hour of maternal sorrow,
Now at this birth season of decease,
Let the infant, the still unspeaking and unspoken
    Word,
Grant Israel's consolation
To one who has eighty years and no tomorrow . . .

I am tired with my own life and the lives of those
    after me,
I am dying in my own death and the deaths of those
    after me.
Let thy servant depart,
Having seen thy salvation.

ADDITIONAL SCRIPTURE READING:
Isaiah 44.23; 52.9

Go to page 1135 for your next devotional reading.

1900   Present

47 "Again, the kingdom of heaven is like a net that was thrown into the sea and caught fish of every kind; 48when it was full, they drew it ashore, sat down, and put the good into baskets but threw out the bad. 49So it will be at the end of the age. The angels will come out and separate the evil from the righteous 50and throw them into the furnace of fire, where there will be weeping and gnashing of teeth.

Treasures New and Old

51 "Have you understood all this?" They answered, "Yes." 52And he said to them, "Therefore every scribe who has been trained for the kingdom of heaven is like the master of a household who brings out of his treasure what is new and what is old." 53When Jesus had finished these parables, he left that place.

The Rejection of Jesus at Nazareth

54 He came to his hometown and began to teach the people*d* in their synagogue, so that they were astounded and said, "Where did this man get this wisdom and these deeds of power? 55Is not this the carpenter's son? Is not his mother called Mary? And are not his brothers James and Joseph and Simon and Judas? 56And are not all his sisters with us? Where then did this man get all this?" 57And they took offense at him. But Jesus said to them, "Prophets are not without honor except in their own country and in their own house." 58And he did not do many deeds of power there, because of their unbelief.

The Death of John the Baptist

14 At that time Herod the ruler*e* heard reports about Jesus; 2and he said to his servants, "This is John the Baptist; he has been raised from the dead, and for this reason these powers are at work in him." 3For Herod had arrested John, bound him, and put him in prison on account of Herodias, his brother Philip's wife,*f* 4because John had been telling him, "It is not lawful for you to have her." 5Though Herod*g* wanted to put him to death, he feared the crowd, because they regarded him as a prophet. 6But when Herod's birthday came, the daughter of Herodias danced before the company, and she pleased Herod 7so much that he promised on oath to grant her whatever she might ask. 8Prompted by her mother, she said, "Give me the head of John the Baptist here on a platter." 9The king was grieved, yet out of regard for his oaths and for the guests, he commanded it to be given; 10he sent and had John beheaded in the prison. 11The head was brought on a platter and given to the girl, who brought it to her mother. 12His disciples came and took the body and buried it; then they went and told Jesus.

Feeding the Five Thousand

13 Now when Jesus heard this, he withdrew from there in a boat to a deserted place by himself. But when the crowds heard it, they followed him on foot from the towns. 14When he went ashore, he saw a great crowd; and he had compassion for them and cured their sick. 15When it was evening, the disciples came to him and said, "This is a deserted place, and the hour is now late; send the crowds away so that they may go into the villages and buy food for themselves." 16Jesus said to them, "They need not go away; you give them something to eat." 17They replied, "We have nothing here but five loaves and two fish." 18And he said, "Bring them here to me." 19Then he ordered the crowds to sit down on the grass. Taking the five loaves and the two fish, he looked up to heaven, and blessed and broke the loaves, and gave them to the disciples, and the disciples gave them to the crowds. 20And all ate and were filled; and they took up what was left over of the broken pieces, twelve baskets full. 21And those who ate were about five thousand men, besides women and children.

Jesus Walks on the Water

22 Immediately he made the disciples get into the boat and go on ahead to the other side, while he dismissed the crowds. 23And after he had dismissed the crowds, he went up the mountain by himself to pray. When evening came, he was there alone, 24but by this time the boat, battered by the waves, was far from

---

d Gk *them*   *e* Gk *tetrarch*   *f* Other ancient authorities read *his brother's wife*   *g* Gk *he*

the land,[h] for the wind was against them. 25And early in the morning he came walking toward them on the sea. 26But when the disciples saw him walking on the sea, they were terrified, saying, "It is a ghost!" And they cried out in fear. 27But immediately Jesus spoke to them and said, "Take heart, it is I; do not be afraid."

28 Peter answered him, "Lord, if it is you, command me to come to you on the water." 29He said, "Come." So Peter got out of the boat, started walking on the water, and came toward Jesus. 30But when he noticed the strong wind,[i] he became frightened, and beginning to sink, he cried out, "Lord, save me!" 31Jesus immediately reached out his hand and caught him, saying to him, "You of little faith, why did you doubt?" 32When they got into the boat, the wind ceased. 33And those in the boat worshiped him, saying, "Truly you are the Son of God."

Jesus Heals the Sick in Gennesaret

34 When they had crossed over, they came to land at Gennesaret. 35After the people of that place recognized him, they sent word throughout the region and brought all who were sick to him, 36and begged him that they might touch even the fringe of his cloak; and all who touched it were healed.

The Tradition of the Elders

15 Then Pharisees and scribes came to Jesus from Jerusalem and said, 2"Why do your disciples break the tradition of the elders? For they do not wash their hands before they eat." 3He answered them, "And why do you break the commandment of God for the sake of your tradition? 4For God said,[j] 'Honor your father and your mother,' and, 'Whoever speaks evil of father or mother must surely die.' 5But you say that whoever tells father or mother, 'Whatever support you might have had from me is given to God,'[k] then that person need not honor the father.[l] 6So, for the sake of your tradition, you make void the word[m] of God. 7You hypocrites!

Isaiah prophesied rightly about you when he said:

8   'This people honors me with their
        lips,
        but their hearts are far from me;
9   in vain do they worship me,
        teaching human precepts as
        doctrines.' "

Things That Defile

10 Then he called the crowd to him and said to them, "Listen and understand: 11it is not what goes into the mouth that defiles a person, but it is what comes out of the mouth that defiles." 12Then the disciples approached and said to him, "Do you know that the Pharisees took offense when they heard what you said?" 13He answered, "Every plant that my heavenly Father has not planted will be uprooted. 14Let them alone; they are blind guides of the blind.[n] And if one blind person guides another, both will fall into a pit." 15But Peter said to him, "Explain this parable to us." 16Then he said, "Are you also still without understanding? 17Do you not see that whatever goes into the mouth enters the stomach, and goes out into the sewer? 18But what comes out of the mouth proceeds from the heart, and this is what defiles. 19For out of the heart come evil intentions, murder, adultery, fornication, theft, false witness, slander. 20These are what defile a person, but to eat with unwashed hands does not defile."

The Canaanite Woman's Faith

21 Jesus left that place and went away to the district of Tyre and Sidon. 22Just then a Canaanite woman from that region came out and started shouting, "Have mercy on me, Lord, Son of David; my daughter is tormented by a demon." 23But he did not answer her at all. And his disciples came and urged him, saying, "Send her away, for she keeps shouting after us." 24He answered, "I was sent only to the lost sheep of the house of Israel." 25But she came and knelt before him, saying, "Lord, help me." 26He answered,

---

h Other ancient authorities read *was out on the sea*   i Other ancient authorities read *the wind*
j Other ancient authorities read *commanded, saying*   k Or *is an offering*   l Other ancient
authorities add *or the mother*   m Other ancient authorities read *law* ; others, *commandment*
n Other ancient authorities lack *of the blind*

"It is not fair to take the children's food and throw it to the dogs." 27She said, "Yes, Lord, yet even the dogs eat the crumbs that fall from their masters' table." 28Then Jesus answered her, "Woman, great is your faith! Let it be done for you as you wish." And her daughter was healed instantly.

Jesus Cures Many People

29 After Jesus had left that place, he passed along the Sea of Galilee, and he went up the mountain, where he sat down. 30Great crowds came to him, bringing with them the lame, the maimed, the blind, the mute, and many others. They put them at his feet, and he cured them, 31so that the crowd was amazed when they saw the mute speaking, the maimed whole, the lame walking, and the blind seeing. And they praised the God of Israel.

Feeding the Four Thousand

32 Then Jesus called his disciples to him and said, "I have compassion for the crowd, because they have been with me now for three days and have nothing to eat; and I do not want to send them away hungry, for they might faint on the way." 33The disciples said to him, "Where are we to get enough bread in the desert to feed so great a crowd?" 34Jesus asked them, "How many loaves have you?" They said, "Seven, and a few small fish." 35Then ordering the crowd to sit down on the ground, 36he took the seven loaves and the fish; and after giving thanks he broke them and gave them to the disciples, and the disciples gave them to the crowds. 37And all of them ate and were filled; and they took up the broken pieces left over, seven baskets full. 38Those who had eaten were four thousand men, besides women and children. 39After sending away the crowds, he got into the boat and went to the region of Magadan.o

The Demand for a Sign

16 The Pharisees and Sadducees came, and to test Jesusp they asked him to show them a sign from heaven. 2He answered them, "When it is

evening, you say, 'It will be fair weather, for the sky is red.' 3And in the morning, 'It will be stormy today, for the sky is red and threatening.' You know how to interpret the appearance of the sky, but you cannot interpret the signs of the times.q 4An evil and adulterous generation asks for a sign, but no sign will be given to it except the sign of Jonah." Then he left them and went away.

The Yeast of the Pharisees and Sadducees

5 When the disciples reached the other side, they had forgotten to bring any bread. 6Jesus said to them, "Watch out, and beware of the yeast of the Pharisees and Sadducees." 7They said to one another, "It is because we have brought no bread." 8And becoming aware of it, Jesus said, "You of little faith, why are you talking about having no bread? 9Do you still not perceive? Do you not remember the five loaves for the five thousand, and how many baskets you gathered? 10Or the seven loaves for the four thousand, and how many baskets you gathered? 11How could you fail to perceive that I was not speaking about bread? Beware of the yeast of the Pharisees and Sadducees!" 12Then they understood that he had not told them to beware of the yeast of bread, but of the teaching of the Pharisees and Sadducees.

Peter's Declaration about Jesus

13 Now when Jesus came into the district of Caesarea Philippi, he asked his disciples, "Who do people say that the Son of Man is?" 14And they said, "Some say John the Baptist, but others Elijah, and still others Jeremiah or one of the prophets." 15He said to them, "But who do you say that I am?" 16Simon Peter answered, "You are the Messiah,r the Son of the living God." 17And Jesus answered him, "Blessed are you, Simon son of Jonah! For flesh and blood has not revealed this to you, but my Father in heaven. 18And I tell you, you are Peter,s and on this rockt I will build my church, and the gates of Hades will not prevail against it. 19I will give you the keys of the kingdom of heaven, and whatever

---

o Other ancient authorities read *Magdala* or *Magdalan*   p Gk *him*   q Other ancient authorities lack 2*When it is . . . of the times*   r Or *the Christ*   s Gk *Petros*   t Gk *petra*

you bind on earth will be bound in heaven, and whatever you loose on earth will be loosed in heaven." 20Then he sternly ordered the disciples not to tell anyone that he was[u] the Messiah.[v]

Jesus Foretells His Death and Resurrection

21 From that time on, Jesus began to show his disciples that he must go to Jerusalem and undergo great suffering at the hands of the elders and chief priests and scribes, and be killed, and on the third day be raised. 22And Peter took him aside and began to rebuke him, saying, "God forbid it, Lord! This must never happen to you." 23But he turned and said to Peter, "Get behind me, Satan! You are a stumbling block to me; for you are setting your mind not on divine things but on human things."

The Cross and Self-Denial

24 Then Jesus told his disciples, "If any want to become my followers, let them deny themselves and take up their cross and follow me. 25For those who want to save their life will lose it, and those who lose their life for my sake will find it. 26For what will it profit them if they gain the whole world but forfeit their life? Or what will they give in return for their life? 27 "For the Son of Man is to come with his angels in the glory of his Father, and then he will repay everyone for what has been done. 28Truly I tell you, there are some standing here who will not taste death before they see the Son of Man coming in his kingdom."

The Transfiguration

17 Six days later, Jesus took with him Peter and James and his brother John and led them up a high mountain, by themselves. 2And he was transfigured before them, and his face shone like the sun, and his clothes became dazzling white. 3Suddenly there appeared to them Moses and Elijah, talking with him. 4Then Peter said to Jesus, "Lord, it is good for us to be here; if you wish, I[w] will make three dwellings[x]

here, one for you, one for Moses, and one for Elijah." 5While he was still speaking, suddenly a bright cloud overshadowed them, and from the cloud a voice said, "This is my Son, the Beloved;[y] with him I am well pleased; listen to him!" 6When the disciples heard this, they fell to the ground and were overcome by fear. 7But Jesus came and touched them, saying, "Get up and do not be afraid." 8And when they looked up, they saw no one except Jesus himself alone.

9 As they were coming down the mountain, Jesus ordered them, "Tell no one about the vision until after the Son of Man has been raised from the dead." 10And the disciples asked him, "Why, then, do the scribes say that Elijah must come first?" 11He replied, "Elijah is indeed coming and will restore all things; 12but I tell you that Elijah has already come, and they did not recognize him, but they did to him whatever they pleased. So also the Son of Man is about to suffer at their hands." 13Then the disciples understood that he was speaking to them about John the Baptist.

Jesus Cures a Boy with a Demon

14 When they came to the crowd, a man came to him, knelt before him, 15and said, "Lord, have mercy on my son, for he is an epileptic and he suffers terribly; he often falls into the fire and often into the water. 16And I brought him to your disciples, but they could not cure him." 17Jesus answered, "You faithless and perverse generation, how much longer must I be with you? How much longer must I put up with you? Bring him here to me." 18And Jesus rebuked the demon,[z] and it[a] came out of him, and the boy was cured instantly. 19Then the disciples came to Jesus privately and said, "Why could we not cast it out?" 20He said to them, "Because of your little faith. For truly I tell you, if you have faith the size of a[b] mustard seed, you will say to this mountain, 'Move from here to there,' and it will move; and nothing will be impossible for you."[c]

---

u Other ancient authorities add *Jesus*   v Or *the Christ*   w Other ancient authorities read *we*
x Or *tents*   y Or *my beloved Son*   z Gk *it* or *him*   a Gk *the demon*   b Gk *faith as a grain of*
c Other ancient authorities add verse 21, *But this kind does not come out except by prayer and fasting*

Jesus Again Foretells His Death and Resurrection

22 As they were gathering[d] in Galilee, Jesus said to them, "The Son of Man is going to be betrayed into human hands, 23and they will kill him, and on the third day he will be raised." And they were greatly distressed.

Jesus and the Temple Tax

24 When they reached Capernaum, the collectors of the temple tax[e] came to Peter and said, "Does your teacher not pay the temple tax?"[e] 25He said, "Yes, he does." And when he came home, Jesus spoke of it first, asking, "What do you think, Simon? From whom do kings of

d Other ancient authorities read living   e Gk didrachma

MONDAY

EXPERIENCING THE LORD
A. B. Simpson

VERSE: Matthew 17.8   **PASSAGE:** Matthew 17.1–8

nce it was the blessing, now it is the Lord;
Once it was the feeling, now it is his word;
Once his gift I wanted, now, the Giver own;
Once I sought for healing, now himself alone.

Once 'twas painful trying, now 'tis perfect trust;
Once a half salvation, now the uttermost;
Once 'twas ceaseless holding, now he holds me fast;
Once 'twas constant drifting, now my anchor's cast.

Once 'twas busy planning, now 'tis trustful prayer;
Once 'twas anxious caring, now he has the care;
Once 'twas what I wanted, now what Jesus says;
Once 'twas constant asking, now 'tis ceaseless praise.

Once I hoped in Jesus, now I know he's mine;
Once my lamps were dying, now they brightly shine;
Once for death I waited, now his coming hail;
And my hopes are anchored safe within the veil.

All in all forever,
Only Christ I'll sing;
Ev'rything is in Christ,
And Christ is ev'rything.

ADDITIONAL SCRIPTURE READING:
Philippians 3.7–11; 1 Peter 5.7

Go to page 1138 for your next devotional reading.

1900   Present

the earth take toll or tribute? From their children or from others?" [26]When Peter[f] said, "From others," Jesus said to him, "Then the children are free. [27]However, so that we do not give offense to them, go to the sea and cast a hook; take the first fish that comes up; and when you open its mouth, you will find a coin;[g] take that and give it to them for you and me."

True Greatness

18 At that time the disciples came to Jesus and asked, "Who is the greatest in the kingdom of heaven?" [2]He called a child, whom he put among them, [3]and said, "Truly I tell you, unless you change and become like children, you will never enter the kingdom of heaven. [4]Whoever becomes humble like this child is the greatest in the kingdom of heaven. [5]Whoever welcomes one such child in my name welcomes me.

Temptations to Sin

6 "If any of you put a stumbling block before one of these little ones who believe in me, it would be better for you if a great millstone were fastened around your neck and you were drowned in the depth of the sea. [7]Woe to the world because of stumbling blocks! Occasions for stumbling are bound to come, but woe to the one by whom the stumbling block comes!

8 "If your hand or your foot causes you to stumble, cut it off and throw it away; it is better for you to enter life maimed or lame than to have two hands or two feet and to be thrown into the eternal fire. [9]And if your eye causes you to stumble, tear it out and throw it away; it is better for you to enter life with one eye than to have two eyes and to be thrown into the hell[h] of fire.

The Parable of the Lost Sheep

10 "Take care that you do not despise one of these little ones; for, I tell you, in heaven their angels continually see the face of my Father in heaven.[i] [12]What do

you think? If a shepherd has a hundred sheep, and one of them has gone astray, does he not leave the ninety-nine on the mountains and go in search of the one that went astray? [13]And if he finds it, truly I tell you, he rejoices over it more than over the ninety-nine that never went astray. [14]So it is not the will of your[i] Father in heaven that one of these little ones should be lost.

Reproving Another Who Sins

15 "If another member of the church[k] sins against you,[l] go and point out the fault when the two of you are alone. If the member listens to you, you have regained that one.[m] [16]But if you are not listened to, take one or two others along with you, so that every word may be confirmed by the evidence of two or three witnesses. [17]If the member refuses to listen to them, tell it to the church; and if the offender refuses to listen even to the church, let such a one be to you as a Gentile and a tax collector. [18]Truly I tell you, whatever you bind on earth will be bound in heaven, and whatever you loose on earth will be loosed in heaven. [19]Again, truly I tell you, if two of you agree on earth about anything you ask, it will be done for you by my Father in heaven. [20]For where two or three are gathered in my name, I am there among them."

Forgiveness

21 Then Peter came and said to him, "Lord, if another member of the church[n] sins against me, how often should I forgive? As many as seven times?" [22]Jesus said to him, "Not seven times, but, I tell you, seventy-seven[o] times.

The Parable of the Unforgiving Servant

23 "For this reason the kingdom of heaven may be compared to a king who wished to settle accounts with his slaves. [24]When he began the reckoning, one who owed him ten thousand talents[p] was brought to him; [25]and, as he could not

---

f Gk he   g Gk stater; the stater was worth two didrachmas   h Gk Gehenna   i Other ancient authorities add verse 11, For the Son of Man came to save the lost   j Other ancient authorities read my k Gk If your brother   l Other ancient authorities lack against you   m Gk the brother   n Gk if my brother   o Or seventy times seven   p A talent was worth more than fifteen years' wages of a laborer

pay, his lord ordered him to be sold, together with his wife and children and all his possessions, and payment to be made. 26So the slave fell on his knees before him, saying, 'Have patience with me, and I will pay you everything.' 27And out of pity for him, the lord of that slave released him and forgave him the debt. 28But that same slave, as he went out, came upon one of his fellow slaves who owed him a hundred denarii;*q* and seizing him by the throat, he said, 'Pay what you owe.' 29Then his fellow slave fell down and pleaded with him, 'Have patience with me, and I will pay you.' 30But he refused; then he went and threw him into prison until he would pay the debt. 31When his fellow slaves saw what had happened, they were greatly distressed, and they went and reported to their lord all that had taken place. 32Then his lord summoned him and said to him, 'You wicked slave! I forgave you all that debt because you pleaded with me. 33Should you not have had mercy on your fellow slave, as I had mercy on you?' 34And in anger his lord handed him over to be tortured until he would pay his entire debt. 35So my heavenly Father will also do to every one of you, if you do not forgive your brother or sister*r* from your heart."

Teaching about Divorce

19 When Jesus had finished saying these things, he left Galilee and went to the region of Judea beyond the Jordan. 2Large crowds followed him, and he cured them there.

3 Some Pharisees came to him, and to test him they asked, "Is it lawful for a man to divorce his wife for any cause?" 4He answered, "Have you not read that the one who made them at the beginning 'made them male and female,' 5and said, 'For this reason a man shall leave his father and mother and be joined to his wife, and the two shall become one flesh'? 6So they are no longer two, but one flesh. Therefore what God has joined together, let no one separate." 7They said to him, "Why then did Moses command us to give a certificate of dismissal and to

divorce her?" 8He said to them, "It was because you were so hard-hearted that Moses allowed you to divorce your wives, but from the beginning it was not so. 9And I say to you, whoever divorces his wife, except for unchastity, and marries another commits adultery."*s*

10 His disciples said to him, "If such is the case of a man with his wife, it is better not to marry." 11But he said to them, "Not everyone can accept this teaching, but only those to whom it is given. 12For there are eunuchs who have been so from birth, and there are eunuchs who have been made eunuchs by others, and there are eunuchs who have made themselves eunuchs for the sake of the kingdom of heaven. Let anyone accept this who can."

Jesus Blesses Little Children

13 Then little children were being brought to him in order that he might lay his hands on them and pray. The disciples spoke sternly to those who brought them; 14but Jesus said, "Let the little children come to me, and do not stop them; for it is to such as these that the kingdom of heaven belongs." 15And he laid his hands on them and went on his way.

The Rich Young Man

16 Then someone came to him and said, "Teacher, what good deed must I do to have eternal life?" 17And he said to him, "Why do you ask me about what is good? There is only one who is good. If you wish to enter into life, keep the commandments." 18He said to him, "Which ones?" And Jesus said, "You shall not murder; You shall not commit adultery; You shall not steal; You shall not bear false witness; 19Honor your father and mother; also, You shall love your neighbor as yourself." 20The young man said to

---

WHO IS FREE FROM DEFECTS? HE LACKS EVERYTHING WHO THINKS HE LACKS NOTHING.

—*Bernard of Clairvaux*

---

him, "I have kept all these;*t* what do I still lack?" 21Jesus said to him, "If you wish to

---

be perfect, go, sell your possessions, and give the money[u] to the poor, and you will have treasure in heaven; then come, follow me." [22]When the young man heard this word, he went away grieving, for he had many possessions.

[23] Then Jesus said to his disciples, "Truly I tell you, it will be hard for a rich person to enter the kingdom of heaven. [24]Again I tell you, it is easier for a camel to go through the eye of a needle than for someone who is rich to enter the kingdom of God." [25]When the disciples heard this, they were greatly astounded and said, "Then who can be saved?" [26]But Jesus looked at them and said, "For mortals it is impossible, but for God all things are possible."

[27] Then Peter said in reply, "Look, we have left everything and followed you. What then will we have?" [28]Jesus said to them, "Truly I tell you, at the

u Gk lacks *the money*

TUESDAY

THOU SHALT NOT COVET
Richard Pynson

VERSE: Matthew 19.21–22 **PASSAGE:** Matthew 19.16–24

he riches and wealth of this world are like the minstrel's horse. Once upon a time there came a proud thief into a stable and found a minstrel's horse standing next to his own. And since the minstrel's horse was the finer of the two, he took it and rode away on it, leaving his own feeble horse in the stable. The minstrel, who happened to see all this, ran by way of a short cut and met the thief as he was crossing a river. The minstrel cried, "Let us kneel!" The horse, who knew his master's voice well, kneeled down in the river, as he was accustomed to do when playing with his master. Then the minstrel said, "Arise!" and immediately the horse stood up, as he had been taught, and threw the proud thief into the water and ran again to his master.

This minstrel is the world, which plays with the folk of this world as does a minstrel or a juggler or a gambler. His horse is this world's wealth, which often, upon hearing the voice of its master, the world, plays "let us kneel" and brings people low and into great poverty and forsakes them in their greatest need and follows after the play of this world and not after the will of the covetous that would possess it. But often, those who toil most to be rich become the poorest.

ADDITIONAL SCRIPTURE READING:
Matthew 6.24; 1 Timothy 6.10

Go to page 1141 for your next devotional reading.

1500   1700

renewal of all things, when the Son of Man is seated on the throne of his glory,

you who have followed me will also sit on twelve thrones, judging the twelve tribes of Israel. 29 And everyone who has left houses or brothers or sisters or father or mother or children or fields, for my name's sake, will receive a hundredfold,*v* and will inherit eternal life. 30 But many who are first will be last, and the last will be first.

The Laborers in the Vineyard

20 "For the kingdom of heaven is like a landowner who went out early in the morning to hire laborers for his vineyard. 2 After agreeing with the laborers for the usual daily wage,*w* he sent them into his vineyard. 3 When he went out about nine o'clock, he saw others standing idle in the marketplace; 4 and he said to them, 'You also go into the vineyard, and I will pay you whatever is right.' So they went. 5 When he went out again about noon and about three o'clock, he did the same. 6 And about five o'clock he went out and found others standing around; and he said to them, 'Why are you standing here idle all day?' 7 They said to him, 'Because no one has hired us.' He said to them, 'You also go into the vineyard.' 8 When evening came, the owner of the vineyard said to his manager, 'Call the laborers and give them their pay, beginning with the last and then going to the first.' 9 When those hired about five o'clock came, each of them received the usual daily wage.*w* 10 Now when the first came, they thought they would receive more; but each of them also received the usual daily wage.*w* 11 And when they received it, they grumbled against the landowner, 12 saying, 'These last worked only one hour, and you have made them equal to us who have borne the burden

of the day and the scorching heat.' 13 But he replied to one of them, 'Friend, I am doing you no wrong; did you not agree with me for the usual daily wage?*w* 14 Take what belongs to you and go; I choose to give to this last the same as I give to you. 15 Am I not allowed to do what I choose with what belongs to me? Or are you envious because I am generous?'*x* 16 So the last will be first, and the first will be last."*y*

A Third Time Jesus Foretells His Death and Resurrection

17 While Jesus was going up to Jerusalem, he took the twelve disciples aside by themselves, and said to them on the way, 18 "See, we are going up to Jerusalem, and the Son of Man will be handed over to the chief priests and scribes, and they will condemn him to death; 19 then they will hand him over to the Gentiles to be mocked and flogged and crucified; and on the third day he will be raised."

The Request of the Mother of James and John

20 Then the mother of the sons of Zebedee came to him with her sons, and kneeling before him, she asked a favor of him. 21 And he said to her, "What do you want?" She said to him, "Declare that these two sons of mine will sit, one at your right hand and one at your left, in your kingdom." 22 But Jesus answered, "You do not know what you are asking. Are you able to drink the cup that I am about to drink?"*z* They said to him, "We are able." 23 He said to them, "You will indeed drink my cup, but to sit at my right hand and at my left, this is not mine to grant, but it is for those for whom it has been prepared by my Father."

24 When the ten heard it, they were angry with the two brothers. 25 But Jesus called them to him and said, "You know that the rulers of the Gentiles lord it over them, and their great ones are tyrants over them. 26 It will not be so among you; but whoever wishes to be great among you must be your servant,

---

v Other ancient authorities read *manifold*   *w* Gk *a denarius*   *x* Gk *is your eye evil because I am good?*   *y* Other ancient authorities add *for many are called but few are chosen*   *z* Other ancient authorities add *or to be baptized with the baptism that I am baptized with?*

27and whoever wishes to be first among you must be your slave; 28just as the Son of Man came not to be served but to serve, and to give his life a ransom for many."

Jesus Heals Two Blind Men

29 As they were leaving Jericho, a large crowd followed him. 30There were two blind men sitting by the roadside. When they heard that Jesus was passing by, they shouted, "Lord,*a* have mercy on us, Son of David!" 31The crowd sternly ordered them to be quiet; but they shouted even more loudly, "Have mercy on us, Lord, Son of David!" 32Jesus stood still and called them, saying, "What do you want me to do for you?" 33They said to him, "Lord, let our eyes be opened." 34Moved with compassion, Jesus touched their eyes. Immediately they regained their sight and followed him.

Jesus' Triumphal Entry into Jerusalem

21 When they had come near Jerusalem and had reached Bethphage, at the Mount of Olives, Jesus sent two disciples, 2saying to them, "Go into the village ahead of you, and immediately you will find a donkey tied, and a colt with her; untie them and bring them to me. 3If anyone says anything to you, just say this, 'The Lord needs them.' And he will send them immediately.*b*" 4This took place to fulfill what had been spoken through the prophet, saying,
5   "Tell the daughter of Zion,
     Look, your king is coming to you,
       humble, and mounted on a
         donkey,
       and on a colt, the foal of a
         donkey."
6The disciples went and did as Jesus had directed them; 7they brought the donkey and the colt, and put their cloaks on them, and he sat on them. 8A very large crowd*c* spread their cloaks on the road, and others cut branches from the trees and spread them on the road. 9The crowds that went ahead of him and that followed were shouting,

"Hosanna to the Son of David!
   Blessed is the one who comes in
     the name of the Lord!
Hosanna in the highest heaven!"
10When he entered Jerusalem, the whole city was in turmoil, asking, "Who is this?" 11The crowds were saying, "This is the prophet Jesus from Nazareth in Galilee."

Jesus Cleanses the Temple

12 Then Jesus entered the temple*d* and drove out all who were selling and buying in the temple, and he overturned the tables of the money changers and the seats of those who sold doves. 13He said to them, "It is written,
   'My house shall be called a house
     of prayer';
   but you are making it a den of
     robbers."

14 The blind and the lame came to him in the temple, and he cured them. 15But when the chief priests and the scribes saw the amazing things that he did, and heard*e* the children crying out in the temple, "Hosanna to the Son of David," they became angry 16and said to him, "Do you hear what these are saying?" Jesus said to them, "Yes; have you never read,
   'Out of the mouths of infants and
     nursing babies
   you have prepared praise for
     yourself'?"
17He left them, went out of the city to Bethany, and spent the night there.

Jesus Curses the Fig Tree

18 In the morning, when he returned to the city, he was hungry. 19And seeing a fig tree by the side of the road, he went to it and found nothing at all on it but leaves. Then he said to it, "May no fruit ever come from you again!" And the fig tree withered at once. 20When the disciples saw it, they were amazed, saying, "How did the fig tree wither at once?" 21Jesus answered them, "Truly I tell you, if you have faith and do not doubt, not only will you do what has been done to the fig tree, but even if you say to this mountain, 'Be lifted up and thrown into

---

a Other ancient authorities lack *Lord*   *b* Or '*The Lord needs them and will send them back immediately.'*   *c* Or *Most of the crowd*   *d* Other ancient authorities add *of God*   *e* Gk lacks *heard*

the sea,' it will be done. 22Whatever you ask for in prayer with faith, you will receive."

The Authority of Jesus Questioned

23 When he entered the temple, the chief priests and the elders of the people came to him as he was teaching, and said, "By what authority are you doing these things, and who gave you this authority?" 24Jesus said to them, "I will also ask you one question; if you tell me the answer, then I will also tell you by what authority I do these things. 25Did

---

WEDNESDAY

THE HOUSE OF PRAYER
William Cowper

VERSE: Matthew 21.13   **PASSAGE:** Matthew 21.12–17

hy mansion is the Christian's heart,
O Lord, thy dwelling-place secure!
Bid the unruly throng depart,
And leave the consecrated door.

Devoted as it is to thee,
A thievish swarm frequents the place;
They steal away my joys from me,
And rob my Savior of his praise.

There too a sharp designing trade
Sin, Satan, and the world maintain;
Nor cease to press me, and persuade,
To part with ease and purchase pain.

I know them, and I hate their din,
Am weary of the bustling crowd;
But while their voice is heard within,
I cannot serve thee as I would.

Oh! for the joy thy presence gives,
What peace shall reign when thou art here!
Thy presence makes this den of thieves,
A calm delightful house of prayer.

And if thou make thy temple shine,
Yet, self-abased, will I adore;
The gold and silver are not mine,
I give thee what was thine before.

ADDITIONAL SCRIPTURE READING:
Psalm 93.5; Isaiah 56.7

Go to page 1147 for your next devotional reading.

1700   1900

the baptism of John come from heaven, or was it of human origin?" And they argued with one another, "If we say, 'From heaven,' he will say to us, 'Why then did you not believe him?' 26But if we say, 'Of human origin,' we are afraid of the crowd; for all regard John as a prophet." 27So they answered Jesus, "We do not know." And he said to them, "Neither will I tell you by what authority I am doing these things.

The Parable of the Two Sons

28 "What do you think? A man had two sons; he went to the first and said, 'Son, go and work in the vineyard today.' 29He answered, 'I will not'; but later he changed his mind and went. 30The father*f* went to the second and said the same; and he answered, 'I go, sir'; but he did not go. 31Which of the two did the will of his father?" They said, "The first." Jesus said to them, "Truly I tell you, the tax collectors and the prostitutes are going into the kingdom of God ahead of you. 32For John came to you in the way of righteousness and you did not believe him, but the tax collectors and the prostitutes believed him; and even after you saw it, you did not change your minds and believe him.

The Parable of the Wicked Tenants

33 "Listen to another parable. There was a landowner who planted a vineyard, put a fence around it, dug a wine press in it, and built a watchtower. Then he leased it to tenants and went to another country. 34When the harvest time had come, he sent his slaves to the tenants to collect his produce. 35But the tenants seized his slaves and beat one, killed another, and stoned another. 36Again he sent other slaves, more than the first; and they treated them in the same way. 37Finally he sent his son to them, saying, 'They will respect my son.' 38But when the tenants saw the son, they said to themselves, 'This is the heir; come, let us kill him and get his inheritance.' 39So they seized him, threw him out of the vineyard, and killed him. 40Now when the owner of the vineyard comes, what will he do to those tenants?" 41They said to him, "He will put those wretches to a

miserable death, and lease the vineyard to other tenants who will give him the produce at the harvest time."

42 Jesus said to them, "Have you never read in the scriptures:

'The stone that the builders
    rejected
  has become the cornerstone;*g*
this was the Lord's doing,
  and it is amazing in our eyes'?

43Therefore I tell you, the kingdom of God will be taken away from you and given to a people that produces the fruits of the kingdom.*h* 44The one who falls on this stone will be broken to pieces; and it will crush anyone on whom it falls."*i*

45 When the chief priests and the Pharisees heard his parables, they realized that he was speaking about them. 46They wanted to arrest him, but they feared the crowds, because they regarded him as a prophet.

The Parable of the Wedding Banquet

22 Once more Jesus spoke to them in parables, saying: 2"The kingdom of heaven may be compared to a king who gave a wedding banquet for his son. 3He sent his slaves to call those who had been invited to the wedding banquet, but they would not come. 4Again he sent other slaves, saying, 'Tell those who have been invited: Look, I have prepared my dinner, my oxen and my fat calves have been slaughtered, and everything is ready; come to the wedding banquet.' 5But they made light of it and went away, one to his farm, another to his business, 6while the rest seized his slaves, mistreated them, and killed them. 7The king was enraged. He sent his troops, destroyed those murderers, and burned their city. 8Then he said to his slaves, 'The wedding is ready, but those invited were not worthy. 9Go therefore into the main streets, and invite everyone you find to the wedding banquet.' 10Those slaves went out into the streets and gathered all whom they found, both good and bad; so the wedding hall was filled with guests.

11 "But when the king came in to see the guests, he noticed a man there who was not wearing a wedding robe, 12and

f Gk He   *g* Or keystone   *h* Gk the fruits of it   *i* Other ancient authorities lack verse 44 he said to him, 'Friend, how did you get in here without a wedding robe?' And he was speechless. 13Then the king said to the attendants, 'Bind him hand and foot, and throw him into the outer darkness, where there will be weeping and gnashing of teeth.' 14For many are called, but few are chosen."

The Question about Paying Taxes

15 Then the Pharisees went and plotted to entrap him in what he said. 16So they sent their disciples to him, along with the Herodians, saying, "Teacher, we know that you are sincere, and teach the way of God in accordance with truth, and show deference to no one; for you do not regard people with partiality. 17Tell us, then, what you think. Is it lawful to pay taxes to the emperor, or not?" 18But Jesus, aware of their malice, said, "Why are you putting me to the test, you hypocrites? 19Show me the coin used for the tax." And they brought him a denarius. 20Then he said to them, "Whose head is this, and whose title?" 21They answered, "The emperor's." Then he said to them, "Give therefore to the emperor the things that are the emperor's, and to God the things that are God's." 22When they heard this, they were amazed; and they left him and went away.

The Question about the Resurrection

23 The same day some Sadducees came to him, saying there is no resurrection;j and they asked him a question, saying, 24"Teacher, Moses said, 'If a man dies childless, his brother shall marry the widow, and raise up children for his brother.' 25Now there were seven brothers among us; the first married, and died childless, leaving the widow to his brother. 26The second did the same, so also the third, down to the seventh. 27Last of all, the woman herself died. 28In the resurrection, then, whose wife of the seven will she be? For all of them had married her."

29 Jesus answered them, "You are wrong, because you know neither the scriptures nor the power of God. 30For in the resurrection they neither marry nor are given in marriage, but are like angelsk in heaven. 31And as for the resurrection of the dead, have you not read what was said to you by God, 32'I am the God of Abraham, the God of Isaac, and the God of Jacob'? He is God not of the dead, but of the living." 33And when the crowd heard it, they were astounded at his teaching.

The Greatest Commandment

34 When the Pharisees heard that he had silenced the Sadducees, they gathered together, 35and one of them, a lawyer, asked him a question to test him. 36"Teacher, which commandment in the law is the greatest?" 37He said to him, " 'You shall love the Lord your God with all your heart, and with all your soul, and with all your mind.' 38This is the greatest and first commandment. 39And a second is like it: 'You shall love your neighbor as yourself.' 40On these two commandments hang all the law and the prophets."

The Question about David's Son

41 Now while the Pharisees were gathered together, Jesus asked them this question: 42"What do you think of the Messiah?l Whose son is he?" They said to him, "The son of David." 43He said to them, "How is it then that David by the Spiritm calls him Lord, saying,
44 'The Lord said to my Lord,
    "Sit at my right hand,
       until I put your enemies under
          your feet" '?
45If David thus calls him Lord, how can he be his son?" 46No one was able to give him an answer, nor from that day did anyone dare to ask him any more questions.

Jesus Denounces Scribes and Pharisees

23 Then Jesus said to the crowds and to his disciples, 2"The scribes and the Pharisees sit on Moses' seat; 3therefore, do whatever they teach you and follow it; but do not do as they do, for they do not practice what they teach. 4They tie up heavy burdens, hard to bear,n and lay them on the shoulders of

---

j Other ancient authorities read *who say that there is no resurrection*   k Other ancient authorities add *of God*   l Or *Christ*   m Gk *in spirit*   n Other ancient authorities lack *hard to bear*

others; but they themselves are unwilling to lift a finger to move them. 5They do all their deeds to be seen by others; for they make their phylacteries broad and their fringes long. 6They love to have the place of honor at banquets and the best seats in the synagogues, 7and to be greeted with respect in the marketplaces, and to have people call them rabbi. 8But you are not to be called rabbi, for you have one teacher, and you are all students.o 9And call no one your father on earth, for you have one Father—the one in heaven. 10Nor are you to be called instructors, for you have one instructor, the Messiah.p 11The greatest among you will be your servant. 12All who exalt themselves will be humbled, and all who humble themselves will be exalted.

13 "But woe to you, scribes and Pharisees, hypocrites! For you lock people out of the kingdom of heaven. For you do not go in yourselves, and when others are going in, you stop them.q 15Woe to you, scribes and Pharisees, hypocrites! For you cross sea and land to make a single convert, and you make the new convert twice as much a child of hellr as yourselves.

16 "Woe to you, blind guides, who say, 'Whoever swears by the sanctuary is bound by nothing, but whoever swears by the gold of the sanctuary is bound by the oath.' 17You blind fools! For which is greater, the gold or the sanctuary that has made the gold sacred? 18And you say, 'Whoever swears by the altar is bound by nothing, but whoever swears by the gift that is on the altar is bound by the oath.' 19How blind you are! For which is greater, the gift or the altar that makes the gift sacred? 20So whoever swears by the altar, swears by it and by everything on it; 21and whoever swears by the sanctuary, swears by it and by the one who dwells in it; 22and whoever swears by heaven, swears by the throne of God and by the one who is seated upon it.

23 "Woe to you, scribes and Pharisees, hypocrites! For you tithe mint, dill, and cummin, and have neglected the weightier matters of the law: justice and mercy and faith. It is these you ought to have practiced without neglecting the others. 24You blind guides! You strain out a gnat but swallow a camel!

25 "Woe to you, scribes and Pharisees, hypocrites! For you clean the outside of the cup and of the plate, but inside they are full of greed and self-indulgence. 26You blind Pharisee! First clean the inside of the cup,s so that the outside also may become clean.

27 "Woe to you, scribes and Pharisees, hypocrites! For you are like whitewashed tombs, which on the outside look beautiful, but inside they are full of the bones of the dead and of all kinds of filth. 28So you also on the outside look righteous to others, but inside you are full of hypocrisy and lawlessness.

29 "Woe to you, scribes and Pharisees, hypocrites! For you build the tombs of the prophets and decorate the graves of the righteous, 30and you say, 'If we had lived in the days of our ancestors, we would not have taken part with them in shedding the blood of the prophets.' 31Thus you testify against yourselves that you are descendants of those who murdered the prophets. 32Fill up, then, the measure of your ancestors. 33You snakes, you brood of vipers! How can you escape being sentenced to hell?r 34Therefore I send you prophets, sages, and scribes, some of whom you will kill and crucify, and some you will flog in your synagogues and pursue from town to town, 35so that upon you may come all the righteous blood shed on earth, from the blood of righteous Abel to the blood of Zechariah son of Barachiah, whom you murdered between the sanctuary and the altar. 36Truly I tell you, all this will come upon this generation.

The Lament over Jerusalem

37 "Jerusalem, Jerusalem, the city that kills the prophets and stones those who are sent to it! How often have I desired to gather your children together as a hen gathers her brood under her wings, and you were not willing! 38See, your house is left to you, desolate.t 39For I tell

---

o Gk brothers　　p Or the Christ　　q Other authorities add here (or after verse 12) verse 14, Woe to you, scribes and Pharisees, hypocrites! For you devour widows' houses and for the sake of appearance you make long prayers; therefore you will receive the greater condemnation　　r Gk Gehenna
s Other ancient authorities add and of the plate　　t Other ancient authorities lack desolate

you, you will not see me again until you say, 'Blessed is the one who comes in the name of the Lord.' "

The Destruction of the Temple Foretold

24 As Jesus came out of the temple and was going away, his disciples came to point out to him the buildings of the temple. 2Then he asked them, "You see all these, do you not? Truly I tell you, not one stone will be left here upon another; all will be thrown down."

Signs of the End of the Age

3 When he was sitting on the Mount of Olives, the disciples came to him privately, saying, "Tell us, when will this be, and what will be the sign of your coming and of the end of the age?" 4Jesus answered them, "Beware that no one leads you astray. 5For many will come in my name, saying, 'I am the Messiah!'u and they will lead many astray. 6And you will hear of wars and rumors of wars; see that you are not alarmed; for this must take place, but the end is not yet. 7For nation will rise against nation, and kingdom against kingdom, and there will be faminesv and earthquakes in various places: 8all this is but the beginning of the birth pangs.

Persecutions Foretold

9 "Then they will hand you over to be tortured and will put you to death, and you will be hated by all nations because of my name. 10Then many will fall away,w and they will betray one another and hate one another. 11And many false prophets will arise and lead many astray. 12And because of the increase of lawlessness, the love of many will grow cold. 13But the one who endures to the end will be saved. 14And this good newsx of the kingdom will be proclaimed throughout the world, as a testimony to all the nations; and then the end will come.

The Desolating Sacrilege

15 "So when you see the desolating sacrilege standing in the holy place, as was spoken of by the prophet Daniel (let the reader understand), 16then those in Judea must flee to the mountains; 17the one on the housetop must not go down to take what is in the house; 18the one in the field must not turn back to get a coat. 19Woe to those who are pregnant and to those who are nursing infants in those days! 20Pray that your flight may not be in winter or on a sabbath. 21For at that time there will be great suffering, such as has not been from the beginning of the world until now, no, and never will be. 22And if those days had not been cut short, no one would be saved; but for the sake of the elect those days will be cut short. 23Then if anyone says to you, 'Look! Here is the Messiah!'u or 'There he is!'—do not believe it. 24For false messiahsy and false prophets will appear and produce great signs and omens, to lead astray, if possible, even the elect. 25Take note, I have told you beforehand. 26So, if they say to you, 'Look! He is in the wilderness,' do not go out. If they say, 'Look! He is in the inner rooms,' do not believe it. 27For as the lightning comes from the east and flashes as far as the west, so will be the coming of the Son of Man. 28Wherever the corpse is, there the vultures will gather.

The Coming of the Son of Man

29 "Immediately after the suffering of those days
  the sun will be darkened,
    and the moon will not give its
      light;
  the stars will fall from heaven,
    and the powers of heaven will be
      shaken.
30Then the sign of the Son of Man will appear in heaven, and then all the tribes of the earth will mourn, and they will see 'the Son of Man coming on the clouds of heaven' with power and great glory. 31And he will send out his angels with a loud trumpet call, and they will gather his elect from the four winds, from one end of heaven to the other.

The Lesson of the Fig Tree

32 "From the fig tree learn its lesson: as soon as its branch becomes tender

u Or the Christ   v Other ancient authorities add and pestilences   w Or stumble   x Or gospel
y Or christs

and puts forth its leaves, you know that summer is near. 33So also, when you see all these things, you know that he^z is near, at the very gates. 34Truly I tell you, this generation will not pass away until all these things have taken place. 35Heaven and earth will pass away, but my words will not pass away.

The Necessity for Watchfulness

36 "But about that day and hour no one knows, neither the angels of heaven, nor the Son,^a but only the Father. 37For as the days of Noah were, so will be the coming of the Son of Man. 38For as in those days before the flood they were eating and drinking, marrying and giving in marriage, until the day Noah entered the ark, 39and they knew nothing until the flood came and swept them all away, so too will be the coming of the Son of Man. 40Then two will be in the field; one will be taken and one will be left. 41Two women will be grinding meal together; one will be taken and one will be left. 42Keep awake therefore, for you do not know on what day^b your Lord is coming. 43But understand this: if the owner of the house had known in what part of the night the thief was coming, he would have stayed awake and would not have let his house be broken into. 44Therefore you also must be ready, for the Son of Man is coming at an unexpected hour.

The Faithful or the Unfaithful Slave

45 "Who then is the faithful and wise slave, whom his master has put in charge of his household, to give the other slaves^c their allowance of food at the proper time? 46Blessed is that slave whom his master will find at work when he arrives. 47Truly I tell you, he will put that one in charge of all his possessions. 48But if that wicked slave says to himself, 'My master is delayed,' 49and he begins to beat his fellow slaves, and eats and drinks with drunkards, 50the master of that slave will come on a day when he does not expect him and at an hour that he does not know. 51He will

cut him in pieces^d and put him with the hypocrites, where there will be weeping and gnashing of teeth.

The Parable of the Ten Bridesmaids

25 "Then the kingdom of heaven will be like this. Ten bridesmaids^e took their lamps and went to meet the bridegroom.^f 2Five of them were foolish, and five were wise. 3When the foolish took their lamps, they took no oil with them; 4but the wise took flasks of oil with their lamps. 5As the bridegroom was delayed, all of them became drowsy and slept. 6But at midnight there was a shout, 'Look! Here is the bridegroom! Come out to meet him.' 7Then all those bridesmaids^e got up and trimmed their lamps. 8The foolish said to the wise, 'Give us some of your oil, for our lamps are going out.' 9But the wise replied, 'No! there will not be enough for you and for us; you had better go to the dealers and buy some for yourselves.' 10And while they went to buy it, the bridegroom came, and those who were ready went with him into the wedding banquet; and the door was shut. 11Later the other bridesmaids^e came also, saying, 'Lord, lord, open to us.' 12But he replied, 'Truly I tell you, I do not know you.' 13Keep awake therefore, for you know neither the day nor the hour.^g

The Parable of the Talents

14 "For it is as if a man, going on a journey, summoned his slaves and entrusted his property to them; 15to one he gave five talents,^h to another two, to another one, to each according to his ability. Then he went away. 16The one who had received the five talents went off at once and traded with them, and made five more talents. 17In the same way, the one who had the two talents made two more talents. 18But the one who had received the one talent went off and dug a hole in the ground and hid his master's money. 19After a long time the master of those slaves came and settled accounts with them. 20Then the one who had received the five talents came forward,

---

z Or it   a Other ancient authorities lack nor the Son   b Other ancient authorities read at what hour   c Gk to give them   d Or cut him off   e Gk virgins   f Other ancient authorities add and the bride   g Other ancient authorities add in which the Son of Man is coming   h A talent was worth more than fifteen years' wages of a laborer

bringing five more talents, saying, 'Master, you handed over to me five talents; see, I have made five more talents.' 21His master said to him, 'Well done, good and trustworthy slave; you have been trustworthy in a few things, I will put you in charge of many things; enter into the joy of your master.' 22And the one with the two talents also came forward, saying, 'Master, you handed over to me two talents; see, I have made two more talents.' 23His master said to him, 'Well done, good and trustworthy slave; you have been trustworthy in a few things, I will put you in charge of many things; enter into the joy of your master.' 24Then the one who had received the one talent also came forward, saying, 'Master, I knew that you were a harsh man, reaping where you did not sow, and gathering where you did not scatter seed; 25so I was afraid, and I went and hid your talent in the ground. Here you have what is yours.' 26But his master replied, 'You wicked and lazy slave! You knew, did you, that I reap where I did not sow, and gather where I did not scatter? 27Then you ought to have invested my money with the bankers, and on my return I would have received what was my own with interest. 28So take the talent from him, and give it to the one with the ten talents. 29For to all those who have, more will be given, and they will have an abundance; but from those who have nothing, even what they have will be taken away. 30As for this worthless slave, throw him into the outer darkness, where there will be weeping and gnashing of teeth.'

THURSDAY

A SONNET
John Milton

VERSE: Matthew 25.10   **PASSAGE:** Matthew 25.1–30

ady that in the prime of earliest youth,
   Wisely hast shunned the broad way and the green,
   And with those few art eminently seen
   That labor up the hill of heavenly truth,
The better part with Mary and with Ruth
   Chosen thou hast; and they that overween,
   And at thy growing virtues fret their spleen,
   No anger find in thee, but pity and ruth.
Thy care is fixed and zealously attends
   To fill thy odorous lamp with deeds of light,
   And hope that reaps not shame. Therefore be sure
Thou, when the bridegroom with his feastful friends
   Passes to bliss at the mid-hour of night,
   Hast gained thy entrance, virgin wise and pure.

ADDITIONAL SCRIPTURE READING:
Psalm 18.28; 1 Timothy 4.12

Go to page 1149 for your next devotional reading.

1500   1700

The Judgment of the Nations

31 "When the Son of Man comes in his glory, and all the angels with him, then he will sit on the throne of his glory. 32All the nations will be gathered before him, and he will separate people one from another as a shepherd separates the sheep from the goats, 33and he will put the sheep at his right hand and the goats at the left. 34Then the king will say to those at his right hand, 'Come, you that are blessed by my Father, inherit the kingdom prepared for you from the foundation of the world; 35for I was hungry and you gave me food, I was thirsty and you gave me something to drink, I was a stranger and you welcomed me, 36I was naked and you gave me clothing, I was sick and you took care of me, I was in prison and you visited me.' 37Then the righteous will answer him, 'Lord, when was it that we saw you hungry and gave you food, or thirsty and gave you something to drink? 38And when was it that we saw you a stranger and welcomed you, or naked and gave you clothing? 39And when was it that we saw you sick or in prison and visited you?' 40And the king will answer them, 'Truly I tell you, just as you did it to one of the least of these who are members of my family,[i] you did it to me.' 41Then he will say to those at his left hand, 'You that are accursed, depart from me into the eternal fire prepared for the devil and his angels; 42for I was hungry and you gave me no food, I was thirsty and you gave me nothing to drink, 43I was a stranger and you did not welcome me, naked and you did not give me clothing, sick and in prison and you did not visit me.' 44Then they also will answer, 'Lord, when was it that we saw you hungry or thirsty or a stranger or naked or sick or in prison, and did not take care of you?' 45Then he will answer them, 'Truly I tell you, just as you did not do it to one of the least of these, you did not do it to me.' 46And these will go away into eternal punishment, but the righteous into eternal life."

The Plot to Kill Jesus

26 When Jesus had finished saying all these things, he said to his disciples, 2"You know that after two days the Passover is coming, and the Son of Man will be handed over to be crucified."

3 Then the chief priests and the elders of the people gathered in the palace of the high priest, who was called Caiaphas, 4and they conspired to arrest Jesus by stealth and kill him. 5But they said, "Not during the festival, or there may be a riot among the people."

The Anointing at Bethany

6 Now while Jesus was at Bethany in the house of Simon the leper,[j] 7a woman came to him with an alabaster jar of very costly ointment, and she poured it on his head as he sat at the table. 8But when the disciples saw it, they were angry and said, "Why this waste? 9For this ointment could have been sold for a large sum, and the money given to the poor." 10But Jesus, aware of this, said to them, "Why do you trouble the woman? She has performed a good service for me. 11For you always have the poor with you, but you will not always have me. 12By pouring this ointment on my body she has prepared me for burial. 13Truly I tell you, wherever this good news[k] is proclaimed in the whole world, what she has done will be told in remembrance of her."

Judas Agrees to Betray Jesus

14 Then one of the twelve, who was called Judas Iscariot, went to the chief priests 15and said, "What will you give me if I betray him to you?" They paid him thirty pieces of silver. 16And from that moment he began to look for an opportunity to betray him.

The Passover with the Disciples

17 On the first day of Unleavened Bread the disciples came to Jesus, saying, "Where do you want us to make the preparations for you to eat the Passover?" 18He said, "Go into the city to a certain man, and say to him, 'The Teacher says, My time is near; I will

---

i Gk *these my brothers*   *j* The terms *leper* and *leprosy* can refer to several diseases   *k* Or *gospel*

"WHATEVER YOU DID NOT DO"
William Temple

VERSE: Matthew 25.44–45   **PASSAGE:** Matthew 25.31–46

t is Christ who pines when the poor are hungry; it is Christ who is repulsed when strangers are not welcome; it is Christ who suffers when rags fail to keep out the cold; it is Christ who is in anguish in the long-drawn illness; it is Christ who waits behind the prison doors. You come upon one of those who have been broken by the tempests of life, and if you look with eyes of Christian faith and love, he will lift a brow "luminous and imperial from the rags," and you will know that you are standing before the King of kings, Lord of lords.

Christ brought to the world a new conception of royalty. He rules by love and not by force. That, as he expressly said, is the difference between his kingdom and the kingdoms of this world. His most regal act was the supreme self-sacrifice whereby he would draw all men to himself and make them willingly obedient to him forever (see John 12.32). In full harmony with this, he never speaks of himself as king except on one occasion only, . . . when, in the parable of the sheep and the goats, he identifies himself with the failures of the world and the outcasts of society. "Then the king will say to those on his right hand, . . . I was hungry and you gave me food, I was thirsty and you gave me something to drink, I was a stranger and you welcomed me, I was naked and you gave me clothing, I was sick and you took care of me, I was in prison and you visited me" (Matthew 25.34–36).

Civilization, as we know it, produces much human refuse. Slum dwellings, long hours of work, underpayment, child labor, lack of education, prostitution—all these evils are responsible for stunting and warping the development of souls. Things are improving, we hope. But unless we are exerting all the strength that Christ gives us in ending these bad conditions, then the responsibility for wasted lives lies at our door, and from the streets of cities or the lanes of countrysides the cry goes up through the lips of their Savior and our Judge: "Just as you did not do it to one of the least of these, you did not do it to me."

ADDITIONAL SCRIPTURE READING:
Luke 10.25–37; Hebrews 13.1–3

Go to page 1152 for your next devotional reading.

1900   Present

keep the Passover at your house with my disciples.' " ¹⁹So the disciples did as Jesus had directed them, and they prepared the Passover meal.

20 When it was evening, he took his place with the twelve;[1] ²¹and while they were eating, he said, "Truly I tell you, one of you will betray me." ²²And they became greatly distressed and began to say to him one after another, "Surely not I, Lord?" ²³He answered, "The one who has dipped his hand into the bowl with me will betray me. ²⁴The Son of Man goes as it is written of him, but woe to that one by whom the Son of Man is betrayed! It would have been better for that one not to have been born." ²⁵Judas, who betrayed him, said, "Surely not I, Rabbi?" He replied, "You have said so."

The Institution of the Lord's Supper

26 While they were eating, Jesus took a loaf of bread, and after blessing it he broke it, gave it to the disciples, and said, "Take, eat; this is my body." ²⁷Then he took a cup, and after giving thanks he gave it to them, saying, "Drink from it, all of you; ²⁸for this is my blood of the[m] covenant, which is poured out for many for the forgiveness of sins. ²⁹I tell you, I will never again drink of this fruit of the vine until that day when I drink it new with you in my Father's kingdom."

30 When they had sung the hymn, they went out to the Mount of Olives.

Peter's Denial Foretold

31 Then Jesus said to them, "You will all become deserters because of me this night; for it is written,
'I will strike the shepherd,
and the sheep of the flock will be scattered.'
³²But after I am raised up, I will go ahead of you to Galilee." ³³Peter said to him, "Though all become deserters because of you, I will never desert you." ³⁴Jesus said to him, "Truly I tell you, this very night, before the cock crows, you will deny me three times." ³⁵Peter said to him, "Even though I must die with you,

I will not deny you." And so said all the disciples.

Jesus Prays in Gethsemane

36 Then Jesus went with them to a place called Gethsemane; and he said to his disciples, "Sit here while I go over there and pray." ³⁷He took with him Peter and the two sons of Zebedee, and began to be grieved and agitated. ³⁸Then he said to them, "I am deeply grieved, even to death; remain here, and stay awake with me." ³⁹And going a little farther, he threw himself on the ground and prayed, "My Father, if it is possible, let this cup pass from me; yet not what I want but what you want." ⁴⁰Then he came to the disciples and found them sleeping; and he said to Peter, "So, could you not stay awake with me one hour? ⁴¹Stay awake and pray that you may not come into the time of trial;[n] the spirit indeed is willing, but the flesh is weak." ⁴²Again he went away for the second time and prayed, "My Father, if this cannot pass unless I drink it, your will be done." ⁴³Again he came and found them sleeping, for their eyes were heavy. ⁴⁴So leaving them again, he went away and prayed for the third time, saying the same words. ⁴⁵Then he came to the disciples and said to them, "Are you still sleeping and taking your rest? See, the hour is at hand, and the Son of Man is betrayed into the hands of sinners. ⁴⁶Get up, let us be going. See, my betrayer is at hand."

SPREAD OUT YOUR PETITION BEFORE GOD, AND THEN SAY, "THY WILL, NOT MINE, BE DONE." THE SWEETEST LESSON I HAVE LEARNED IN GOD'S SCHOOL IS TO LET THE LORD CHOOSE FOR ME.
—*Dwight L. Moody*

The Betrayal and Arrest of Jesus

47 While he was still speaking, Judas, one of the twelve, arrived; with him was a large crowd with swords and clubs, from the chief priests and the elders of the people. ⁴⁸Now the betrayer had given them a sign, saying, "The one I will kiss is the man; arrest him." ⁴⁹At

---

l Other ancient authorities add *disciples*   m Other ancient authorities add *new*   n Or *into temptation*

once he came up to Jesus and said, "Greetings, Rabbi!" and kissed him. [50]Jesus said to him, "Friend, do what you are here to do." Then they came and laid hands on Jesus and arrested him. [51]Suddenly, one of those with Jesus put his hand on his sword, drew it, and struck the slave of the high priest, cutting off his ear. [52]Then Jesus said to him, "Put your sword back into its place; for all who take the sword will perish by the sword. [53]Do you think that I cannot appeal to my Father, and he will at once send me more than twelve legions of angels? [54]But how then would the scriptures be fulfilled, which say it must happen in this way?" [55]At that hour Jesus said to the crowds, "Have you come out with swords and clubs to arrest me as though I were a bandit? Day after day I sat in the temple teaching, and you did not arrest me. [56]But all this has taken place, so that the scriptures of the prophets may be fulfilled." Then all the disciples deserted him and fled.

Jesus before the High Priest

57 Those who had arrested Jesus took him to Caiaphas the high priest, in whose house the scribes and the elders had gathered. [58]But Peter was following him at a distance, as far as the courtyard of the high priest; and going inside, he sat with the guards in order to see how this would end. [59]Now the chief priests and the whole council were looking for false testimony against Jesus so that they might put him to death, [60]but they found none, though many false witnesses came forward. At last two came forward [61]and said, "This fellow said, 'I am able to destroy the temple of God and to build it in three days.' " [62]The high priest stood up and said, "Have you no answer? What is it that they testify against you?" [63]But Jesus was silent.

WHENEVER ANYTHING DISAGREEABLE OR DISPLEASING HAPPENS TO YOU, REMEMBER CHRIST CRUCIFIED AND BE SILENT.   —*John of the Cross*

Then the high priest said to him, "I put you under oath before the living God,

tell us if you are the Messiah,[o] the Son of God." [64]Jesus said to him, "You have said so. But I tell you,

From now on you will see the Son
    of Man
seated at the right hand of Power
    and coming on the clouds of
    heaven."

[65]Then the high priest tore his clothes and said, "He has blasphemed! Why do we still need witnesses? You have now heard his blasphemy. [66]What is your verdict?" They answered, "He deserves death." [67]Then they spat in his face and struck him; and some slapped him, [68]saying, "Prophesy to us, you Messiah![o] Who is it that struck you?"

Peter's Denial of Jesus

69 Now Peter was sitting outside in the courtyard. A servant-girl came to him and said, "You also were with Jesus the Galilean." [70]But he denied it before all of them, saying, "I do not know what you are talking about." [71]When he went out to the porch, another servant-girl saw him, and she said to the bystanders, "This man was with Jesus of Nazareth."[p] [72]Again he denied it with an oath, "I do not know the man." [73]After a little while the bystanders came up and said to Peter, "Certainly you are also one of them, for your accent betrays you." [74]Then he began to curse, and he swore an oath, "I do not know the man!" At that moment the cock crowed. [75]Then Peter remembered what Jesus had said: "Before the cock crows, you will deny me three times." And he went out and wept bitterly.

Jesus Brought before Pilate

27 When morning came, all the chief priests and the elders of the people conferred together against Jesus in order to bring about his death. [2]They bound him, led him away, and handed him over to Pilate the governor.

The Suicide of Judas

3 When Judas, his betrayer, saw that Jesus[q] was condemned, he repented and brought back the thirty pieces of silver to the chief priests and the elders. [4]He said, "I have sinned by betraying innocent[r]

---

o Or *Christ*   p Gk *the Nazorean*   q Gk *he*   r Other ancient authorities read *righteous*

WEEKEND

TO HIS SAVIOR, A CHILD; A PRESENT, BY A CHILD
Robert Herrick

VERSE: Luke 2.27   **PASSAGE:** Luke 2.25–32

Go pretty child, and bear this flower
Unto thy little Savior;
And tell him, by that bud now blown,
He is the Rose of Sharon known:
When thou hast said so, stick it there
Upon his bib, or stomacher:
And tell him, (for good handsell too)
That thou hast brought a whistle new,
Made of a clean strait oaten reed,
To charm his cries, (at time of need:)
Tell him, for coral, thou hast none;
But if thou hadst, he should have one;
But poor thou art, and known to be
Even as moneyless, as he.
Lastly, if thou canst win a kiss
From those mellifluous lips of his;
Then never take a second on,
To spoil the first impression.

ADDITIONAL SCRIPTURE READING:
Acts 2.36; Hebrews 1.8

Go to page 1155 for your next devotional reading.

1500   1700

blood." But they said, "What is that to us? See to it yourself." 5Throwing down the pieces of silver in the temple, he departed; and he went and hanged himself. 6But the chief priests, taking the pieces of silver, said, "It is not lawful to put them into the treasury, since they are blood money." 7After conferring together, they used them to buy the potter's field as a place to bury foreigners. 8For this reason that field has been called the Field of Blood to this day. 9Then was fulfilled what had been spoken through the prophet Jeremiah,*s* "And they took*t* the thirty pieces of silver, the price of the one on whom a price had been set,*u* on whom some of the people of Israel had set a price, 10and they gave*v* them for the potter's field, as the Lord commanded me."

Pilate Questions Jesus

11 Now Jesus stood before the governor; and the governor asked him, "Are you the King of the Jews?" Jesus said, "You say so." 12But when he was accused by the chief priests and elders, he did not answer. 13Then Pilate said to him, "Do you not hear how many accusations they make against you?" 14But he gave him no answer, not even to a single charge, so that the governor was greatly amazed.

Barabbas or Jesus?

15 Now at the festival the governor was accustomed to release a prisoner for the crowd, anyone whom they wanted. 16At that time they had a notorious prisoner, called Jesus*w* Barabbas. 17So after they had gathered, Pilate said to them, "Whom do you want me to release for you, Jesus*w* Barabbas or Jesus who is called the Messiah?"*x* 18For he realized that it was out of jealousy that they had handed him over. 19While he was sitting on the judgment seat, his wife sent word to him, "Have nothing to do with that innocent man, for today I have suffered a great deal because of a dream about him." 20Now the chief priests and the elders persuaded the crowds to ask for Barabbas and to have Jesus killed. 21The governor again said to them, "Which of the two do you want me to release for you?" And they said, "Barabbas." 22Pilate said to them, "Then what should I do with Jesus who is called the Messiah?"*x* All of them said, "Let him be crucified!" 23Then he asked, "Why, what evil has he done?" But they shouted all the more, "Let him be crucified!"

Pilate Hands Jesus over to Be Crucified

24 So when Pilate saw that he could do nothing, but rather that a riot was beginning, he took some water and washed his hands before the crowd, saying, "I am innocent of this man's blood;*y* see to it yourselves." 25Then the people as a whole answered, "His blood be on us and on our children!" 26So he released Barabbas for them; and after flogging Jesus, he handed him over to be crucified.

The Soldiers Mock Jesus

27 Then the soldiers of the governor took Jesus into the governor's headquarters,*z* and they gathered the whole cohort around him. 28They stripped him and put a scarlet robe on him, 29and after twisting some thorns into a crown, they put it on his head. They put a reed in his right hand and knelt before him and mocked him, saying, "Hail, King of the Jews!" 30They spat on him, and took the reed and struck him on the head. 31After mocking him, they stripped him of the robe and put his own clothes on him. Then they led him away to crucify him.

The Crucifixion of Jesus

32 As they went out, they came upon a man from Cyrene named Simon; they compelled this man to carry his cross. 33And when they came to a place called Golgotha (which means Place of a Skull), 34they offered him wine to drink, mixed with gall; but when he tasted it, he would not drink it. 35And when they had crucified him, they divided his clothes

---

s Other ancient authorities read *Zechariah* or *Isaiah One*   v Other ancient authorities read *I gave*   w Other ancient authorities lack *Jesus*   x Or *the Christ*   y Other ancient authorities read *this righteous blood*, or *this righteous man's blood*   z Gk *the praetorium*   t Or *I took*   u Or *the price of the precious*

among themselves by casting lots;[a]
36then they sat down there and kept
watch over him. 37Over his head they
put the charge against him, which read,
"This is Jesus, the King of the Jews."

38 Then two bandits were crucified
with him, one on his right and one on
his left. 39Those who passed by derided[b]
him, shaking their heads 40and saying,
"You who would destroy the temple and
build it in three days, save yourself! If
you are the Son of God, come down
from the cross." 41In the same way the
chief priests also, along with the scribes
and elders, were mocking him, saying,
42"He saved others; he cannot save himself.[c] He is the King of Israel; let him
come down from the cross now, and we
will believe in him. 43He trusts in God;
let God deliver him now, if he wants to;
for he said, 'I am God's Son.' " 44The
bandits who were crucified with him
also taunted him in the same way.

The Death of Jesus

45 From noon on, darkness came over
the whole land[d] until three in the afternoon. 46And about three o'clock Jesus
cried with a loud voice, "Eli, Eli, lema
sabachthani?" that is, "My God, my
God, why have you forsaken me?"
47When some of the bystanders heard it,
they said, "This man is calling for Elijah." 48At once one of them ran and got a
sponge, filled it with sour wine, put it on
a stick, and gave it to him to drink. 49But
the others said, "Wait, let us see whether
Elijah will come to save him."[e] 50Then
Jesus cried again with a loud voice and
breathed his last.[f] 51At that moment the
curtain of the temple was torn in two,
from top to bottom. The earth shook,
and the rocks were split. 52The tombs
also were opened, and many bodies of
the saints who had fallen asleep were
raised. 53After his resurrection they
came out of the tombs and entered the
holy city and appeared to many. 54Now
when the centurion and those with him,
who were keeping watch over Jesus, saw
the earthquake and what took place,

they were terrified and said, "Truly this
man was God's Son!"[g]

55 Many women were also there,
looking on from a distance; they had followed Jesus from Galilee and had provided for him. 56Among them were
Mary Magdalene, and Mary the mother
of James and Joseph, and the mother of
the sons of Zebedee.

The Burial of Jesus

57 When it was evening, there came
a rich man from Arimathea, named Joseph, who was also a disciple of Jesus.
58He went to Pilate and asked for the
body of Jesus; then Pilate ordered it to be
given to him. 59So Joseph took the body
and wrapped it in a clean linen cloth
60and laid it in his own new tomb,
which he had hewn in the rock. He then
rolled a great stone to the door of the
tomb and went away. 61Mary Magdalene
and the other Mary were there, sitting
opposite the tomb.

The Guard at the Tomb

62 The next day, that is, after the day
of Preparation, the chief priests and the
Pharisees gathered before Pilate 63and
said, "Sir, we remember what that impostor said while he was still alive, 'After
three days I will rise again.' 64Therefore
command the tomb to be made secure
until the third day; otherwise his disciples may go and steal him away, and tell
the people, 'He has been raised from the
dead,' and the last deception would be
worse than the first." 65Pilate said to
them, "You have a guard[h] of soldiers; go,
make it as secure as you can."[i] 66So they
went with the guard and made the tomb
secure by sealing the stone.

The Resurrection of Jesus

28 After the sabbath, as the first
day of the week was dawning,
Mary Magdalene and the other Mary
went to see the tomb. 2And suddenly
there was a great earthquake; for an angel
of the Lord, descending from heaven,
came and rolled back the stone and sat on
it. 3His appearance was like lightning,

---

a Other ancient authorities add *in order that what had been spoken through the prophet might be
fulfilled, "They divided my clothes among themselves, and for my clothing they cast lots."*
b Or *blasphemed*   c Or *is he unable to save himself?*   d Or *earth*   e Other ancient authorities
add *And another took a spear and pierced his side, and out came water and blood*   f Or *gave up his
spirit*   g Or *a son of God*   h Or *Take a guard*   i Gk *you know how*

and his clothing white as snow. ⁴For fear of him the guards shook and became like dead men. ⁵But the angel said to the women, "Do not be afraid; I know that you are looking for Jesus who was crucified. ⁶He is not here; for he has been raised, as he said. Come, see the place where he𝑗 lay. ⁷Then go quickly and tell his disciples, 'He has been raised from the dead,ᵏ and indeed he is going ahead of you to Galilee; there you will see him.' This is my message for you." ⁸So they left the tomb quickly with fear and great joy, and ran to tell his disciples. ⁹Suddenly Jesus met them and said, "Greetings!" And they came to him, took hold of his feet, and worshiped him. ¹⁰Then Jesus said to them, "Do not be afraid; go and tell my brothers to go to Galilee; there they will see me."

𝑗 Other ancient authorities read *the Lord*   *k* Other ancient authorities lack *from the dead*

MONDAY

RESURRECTION, IMPERFECT
John Donne

VERSE: Matthew 28.1   PASSAGE: Matthew 28.1–10

leep sleep old sun, thou canst not have repast
As yet, the wound thou tookst on Friday last;
Sleep then, and rest; The world may bear thy stay,
A better sun rose before thee to day,
Who, not content to enlighten all that dwell
On the earth's face, as thou, enlightened hell,
And made the dark fire languish in that vale,
As, at thy presence here, our fires grow pale.
Whose body having walked on earth, and now
Hasting to heaven, would, that he might allow
Himself unto all stations, and fill all,
For these three days become a mineral;
He was all gold when he lay down, but rose
All tincture, and doth not alone dispose
Leaden and iron wills to good, but is
Of power to make even sinful flesh like his.
Had one of those, whose credulous piety
Thought, that a soul one might discern and see
Go from a body, at this sepulcher been,
And, issuing from the sheet, this body seen,
He would have justly thought this body a soul,
If not of any man, yet of the whole.

ADDITIONAL SCRIPTURE READING:
John 11.25; Philippians 2.5–11

Go to page 1160 for your next devotional reading.

1500   1700

The Report of the Guard

11 While they were going, some of the guard went into the city and told the chief priests everything that had happened. 12After the priests[1] had assembled with the elders, they devised a plan to give a large sum of money to the soldiers, 13telling them, "You must say, 'His disciples came by night and stole him away while we were asleep.' 14If this comes to the governor's ears, we will satisfy him and keep you out of trouble." 15So they took the money and did as they were directed. And this story is still told among the Jews to this day.

The Commissioning of the Disciples

16 Now the eleven disciples went to Galilee, to the mountain to which Jesus had directed them. 17When they saw him, they worshiped him; but some doubted. 18And Jesus came and said to them, "All authority in heaven and on earth has been given to me. 19Go therefore and make disciples of all nations, baptizing them in the name of the Father and of the Son and of the Holy Spirit, 20and teaching them to obey everything that I have commanded you. And remember, I am with you always, to the end of the age."[m]

---

1 Gk *they*   *m* Other ancient authorities add *Amen*

MARK

T HE GOSPEL OF MARK TAKES A FAST-PACED APPROACH TO INTRODUCING JESUS CHRIST, THE SON OF GOD. MARK SHOWS JESUS MOVING QUICKLY FROM TEACHING HIS DISCIPLES TO HEALING SICK PEOPLE TO CONFRONTING RELIGIOUS LEADERS ON HIS WAY TO DEATH ON THE CROSS. NOTE MARK'S SENSITIVE PORTRAYAL OF THE COMPASSIONATE SUFFERING SERVANT, JESUS, FULL OF LIFE AND EMOTION AND PURPOSE, AND OUR CALL TO BE DISCIPLES OF JESUS. KEEP IN MIND THE LOVE JESUS SHOWED HIS DISCIPLES AND ASK YOURSELF, "IF JESUS WAS WILLING TO SUFFER FOR ME, WHAT AM I WILLING TO DO AS HIS DISCIPLE?"

The Proclamation of John the Baptist

1 The beginning of the good news*a* of Jesus Christ, the Son of God.*b*

2 As it is written in the prophet Isaiah,*c*

"See, I am sending my messenger
    ahead of you,*d*
who will prepare your way;
3   the voice of one crying out in the
        wilderness:
    'Prepare the way of the Lord,
        make his paths straight,' "

4John the baptizer appeared*e* in the wilderness, proclaiming a baptism of repentance for the forgiveness of sins. 5And people from the whole Judean countryside and all the people of Jerusalem were going out to him, and were baptized by him in the river Jordan, confessing their sins. 6Now John was clothed with camel's hair, with a leather belt around his waist, and he ate locusts and wild honey. 7He proclaimed, "The one who is more powerful than I is coming after me; I am not worthy to stoop down and untie the thong of his sandals. 8I have baptized you with*f* water; but he will baptize you with*f* the Holy Spirit."

The Baptism of Jesus

9 In those days Jesus came from Nazareth of Galilee and was baptized by John in the Jordan. 10And just as he was coming up out of the water, he saw the heavens torn apart and the Spirit descending

---

a Or *gospel*   *b* Other ancient authorities lack *the Son of God*   *c* Other ancient authorities read *in*
the prophets   *d* Gk *before your face*   *e* Other ancient authorities read *John was baptizing*   *f* Or *in*

like a dove on him. [11]And a voice came from heaven, "You are my Son, the Beloved;[g] with you I am well pleased."

The Temptation of Jesus

12 And the Spirit immediately drove him out into the wilderness. [13]He was in the wilderness forty days, tempted by Satan; and he was with the wild beasts; and the angels waited on him.

The Beginning of the Galilean Ministry

14 Now after John was arrested, Jesus came to Galilee, proclaiming the good news[h] of God,[i] [15]and saying, "The time is fulfilled, and the kingdom of God has come near;[j] repent, and believe in the good news."[h]

Jesus Calls the First Disciples

16 As Jesus passed along the Sea of Galilee, he saw Simon and his brother Andrew casting a net into the sea—for they were fishermen. [17]And Jesus said to them, "Follow me and I will make you fish for people." [18]And immediately they left their nets and followed him.

ONE DAY THERE CAME ALONG THAT SILENT SHORE,

WHILE I MY NET WAS CASTING IN THE SEA,

A MAN WHO SPOKE AS NEVER MAN BEFORE,

I FOLLOWED HIM; NEW LIFE BEGAN IN ME.

MINE WAS THE BOAT, BUT HIS THE VOICE,

AND HIS THE CALL, YET MINE THE CHOICE.

—George MacDonald

---

[19]As he went a little farther, he saw James son of Zebedee and his brother John, who were in their boat mending the nets. [20]Immediately he called them; and they left their father Zebedee in the boat with the hired men, and followed him.

The Man with an Unclean Spirit

21 They went to Capernaum; and when the sabbath came, he entered the synagogue and taught. [22]They were astounded at his teaching, for he taught them as one having authority, and not as the scribes. [23]Just then there was in their synagogue a man with an unclean spirit, [24]and he cried out, "What have you to do with us, Jesus of Nazareth? Have you come to destroy us? I know who you are, the Holy One of God." [25]But Jesus rebuked him, saying, "Be silent, and come out of him!" [26]And the unclean spirit, convulsing him and crying with a loud voice, came out of him. [27]They were all amazed, and they kept on asking one another, "What is this? A new teaching—with authority! He[k] commands even the unclean spirits, and they obey him." [28]At once his fame began to spread throughout the surrounding region of Galilee.

Jesus Heals Many at Simon's House

29 As soon as they[l] left the synagogue, they entered the house of Simon and Andrew, with James and John. [30]Now Simon's mother-in-law was in bed with a fever, and they told him about her at once. [31]He came and took her by the hand and lifted her up. Then the fever left her, and she began to serve them.

32 That evening, at sundown, they brought to him all who were sick or possessed with demons. [33]And the whole city was gathered around the door. [34]And he cured many who were sick with various diseases, and cast out many demons; and he would not permit the demons to speak, because they knew him.

A Preaching Tour in Galilee

35 In the morning, while it was still very dark, he got up and went out to a deserted place, and there he prayed. [36]And Simon and his companions hunted for him. [37]When they found him, they said to him, "Everyone is searching for you." [38]He answered, "Let us go on to the neighboring towns, so that I may proclaim the message there also; for that is what I came out to do." [39]And he went throughout Galilee, proclaiming the message in their synagogues and casting out demons.

---

g Or my beloved Son   h Or gospel   i Other ancient authorities read of the kingdom   j Or is at hand   k Or A new teaching! With authority he   l Other ancient authorities read he

Jesus Cleanses a Leper

40 A leper[m] came to him begging him, and kneeling[n] he said to him, "If you choose, you can make me clean." [41]Moved with pity,[o] Jesus[p] stretched out his hand and touched him, and said to him, "I do choose. Be made clean!" [42]Immediately the leprosy[m] left him, and he was made clean. [43]After sternly warning him he sent him away at once, [44]saying to him, "See that you say nothing to anyone; but go, show yourself to the priest, and offer for your cleansing what Moses commanded, as a testimony to them." [45]But he went out and began to proclaim it freely, and to spread the word, so that Jesus[p] could no longer go into a town openly, but stayed out in the country; and people came to him from every quarter.

Jesus Heals a Paralytic

2 When he returned to Capernaum after some days, it was reported that he was at home. [2]So many gathered around that there was no longer room for them, not even in front of the door; and he was speaking the word to them. [3]Then some people[q] came, bringing to him a paralyzed man, carried by four of them. [4]And when they could not bring him to Jesus because of the crowd, they removed the roof above him; and after having dug through it, they let down the mat on which the paralytic lay. [5]When Jesus saw their faith, he said to the paralytic, "Son, your sins are forgiven." [6]Now some of the scribes were sitting there, questioning in their hearts, [7]"Why does this fellow speak in this way? It is blasphemy! Who can forgive sins but God alone?" [8]At once Jesus perceived in his spirit that they were discussing these questions among themselves; and he said to them, "Why do you raise such questions in your hearts? [9]Which is easier, to say to the paralytic, 'Your sins are forgiven,' or to say, 'Stand up and take your mat and walk'? [10]But so that you may know that the Son of Man has authority on earth to forgive sins"—he said to the paralytic— [11]"I say

to you, stand up, take your mat and go to your home." [12]And he stood up, and immediately took the mat and went out before all of them; so that they were all amazed and glorified God, saying, "We have never seen anything like this!"

Jesus Calls Levi

13 Jesus[r] went out again beside the sea; the whole crowd gathered around him, and he taught them. [14]As he was walking along, he saw Levi son of Alphaeus sitting at the tax booth, and he said to him, "Follow me." And he got up and followed him.

15 And as he sat at dinner[s] in Levi's[t] house, many tax collectors and sinners were also sitting[u] with Jesus and his disciples—for there were many who followed him. [16]When the scribes of[v] the Pharisees saw that he was eating with sinners and tax collectors, they said to his disciples, "Why does he eat[w] with tax collectors and sinners?" [17]When Jesus heard this, he said to them, "Those who are well have no need of a physician, but those who are sick; I have come to call not the righteous but sinners."

The Question about Fasting

18 Now John's disciples and the Pharisees were fasting; and people[q] came and said to him, "Why do John's disciples and the disciples of the Pharisees fast, but your disciples do not fast?" [19]Jesus said to them, "The wedding guests cannot fast while the bridegroom is with them, can they? As long as they have the bridegroom with them, they cannot fast. [20]The days will come when the bridegroom is taken away from them, and then they will fast on that day.

21 "No one sews a piece of unshrunk cloth on an old cloak; otherwise, the patch pulls away from it, the new from the old, and a worse tear is made. [22]And no one puts new wine into old wineskins; otherwise, the wine will burst the skins, and the wine is lost, and so are the skins; but one puts new wine into fresh wineskins."[x]

---

m The terms *leper* and *leprosy* can refer to several diseases   n Other ancient authorities lack *kneeling*
o Other ancient authorities read *anger*   p Gk *he*   q Gk *they*   r Gk *He*   s Gk *reclined*
t Gk *his*   u Gk *reclining*   v Other ancient authorities read *and*   w Other ancient authorities add *and drink*   x Other ancient authorities lack *but one puts new wine into fresh wineskins*

Pronouncement about the Sabbath

23 One sabbath he was going through the grainfields; and as they made their way his disciples began to pluck heads of grain. 24The Pharisees said to him, "Look, why are they doing what is not lawful on the sabbath?" 25And he said to them, "Have you never read what David did when he and his companions were hungry and in need of food? 26He entered the house of God, when Abiathar was high priest, and ate the bread of the Presence, which it is not lawful for any but the priests to eat, and he gave some to his companions." 27Then he said to them, "The sabbath was made for humankind, and not humankind for the sabbath; 28so the Son of Man is lord even of the sabbath."

TUESDAY

THE WINE OF THE SPIRITUAL LIFE
Charles H. Spurgeon

VERSE: Mark 2.22   PASSAGE: Mark 2.18–22

 ow like a Christian a person may be and yet posses no vital godliness! Walk through a museum and you will see all the orders of animals standing in their various places and exhibiting themselves with the utmost possible propriety. The rhinoceros demurely retains the position in which he was set at first, the eagle does not soar through the window, the wolf does not howl at night. Every creature, whether bird, beast, or fish, remains in the particular glass case allotted to it. But we know that these are not the creatures, but only the outward semblances of them. Yet in what do they differ? Certainly in nothing which you could readily see, for the well-stuffed animal is precisely like what the living animal would have been. That eye of glass even appears to have more brightness in it than the natural eye of the creature itself. But there is a secret inward something lacking, which, when it has once departed, you cannot restore. So in the churches of Christ, many professing believers are not living believers, but stuffed Christians. They possess all the externals of religion, and every outward morality that you could desire. They behave with great propriety, they keep their places, and there is no outward difference between them and the true believer, except upon the vital point, the life which no power on earth can possibly confer.

ADDITIONAL SCRIPTURE READING:
Isaiah 26.8; Matthew 23.27–28

Go to page 1165 for your next devotional reading.

1700   1900

The Man with a Withered Hand

3 Again he entered the synagogue, and a man was there who had a withered hand. ²They watched him to see whether he would cure him on the sabbath, so that they might accuse him. ³And he said to the man who had the withered hand, "Come forward." ⁴Then he said to them, "Is it lawful to do good or to do harm on the sabbath, to save life or to kill?" But they were silent. ⁵He looked around at them with anger; he was grieved at their hardness of heart and said to the man, "Stretch out your hand." He stretched it out, and his hand was restored. ⁶The Pharisees went out and immediately conspired with the Herodians against him, how to destroy him.

A Multitude at the Seaside

7 Jesus departed with his disciples to the sea, and a great multitude from Galilee followed him; ⁸hearing all that he was doing, they came to him in great numbers from Judea, Jerusalem, Idumea, beyond the Jordan, and the region around Tyre and Sidon. ⁹He told his disciples to have a boat ready for him because of the crowd, so that they would not crush him; ¹⁰for he had cured many, so that all who had diseases pressed upon him to touch him. ¹¹Whenever the unclean spirits saw him, they fell down before him and shouted, "You are the Son of God!" ¹²But he sternly ordered them not to make him known.

Jesus Appoints the Twelve

13 He went up the mountain and called to him those whom he wanted, and they came to him. ¹⁴And he appointed twelve, whom he also named apostles,ʸ to be with him, and to be sent out to proclaim the message, ¹⁵and to have authority to cast out demons. ¹⁶So he appointed the twelve:ᶻ Simon (to whom he gave the name Peter); ¹⁷James son of Zebedee and John the brother of James (to whom he gave the name Boanerges, that is, Sons of Thunder); ¹⁸and Andrew, and Philip, and Bartholomew, and Matthew, and Thomas, and James son of Alphaeus, and Thaddaeus, and Simon the Cananaean, ¹⁹and Judas Iscariot, who betrayed him.

Jesus and Beelzebul

Then he went home; ²⁰and the crowd came together again, so that they could not even eat. ²¹When his family heard it, they went out to restrain him, for people were saying, "He has gone out of his mind." ²²And the scribes who came down from Jerusalem said, "He has Beelzebul, and by the ruler of the demons he casts out demons." ²³And he called them to him, and spoke to them in parables, "How can Satan cast out Satan? ²⁴If a kingdom is divided against itself, that kingdom cannot stand. ²⁵And if a house is divided against itself, that house will not be able to stand. ²⁶And if Satan has risen up against himself and is divided, he cannot stand, but his end has come. ²⁷But no one can enter a strong man's house and plunder his property without first tying up the strong man; then indeed the house can be plundered.

28 "Truly I tell you, people will be forgiven for their sins and whatever blasphemies they utter; ²⁹but whoever blasphemes against the Holy Spirit can never have forgiveness, but is guilty of an eternal sin"— ³⁰for they had said, "He has an unclean spirit."

The True Kindred of Jesus

31 Then his mother and his brothers came; and standing outside, they sent to him and called him. ³²A crowd was sitting around him; and they said to him, "Your mother and your brothers and sistersᵃ are outside, asking for you." ³³And he replied, "Who are my mother and my brothers?" ³⁴And looking at those who sat around him, he said, "Here are my mother and my brothers! ³⁵Whoever does the will of God is my brother and sister and mother."

The Parable of the Sower

4 Again he began to teach beside the sea. Such a very large crowd gathered around him that he got into a boat on the sea and sat there, while the whole crowd was beside the sea on the

---

y Other ancient authorities lack *whom he also named apostles*   z Other ancient authorities lack *So he appointed the twelve*   a Other ancient authorities lack *and sisters*

land. 2He began to teach them many things in parables, and in his teaching he said to them: 3"Listen! A sower went out to sow. 4And as he sowed, some seed fell on the path, and the birds came and ate it up. 5Other seed fell on rocky ground, where it did not have much soil, and it sprang up quickly, since it had no depth of soil. 6And when the sun rose, it was scorched; and since it had no root, it withered away. 7Other seed fell among thorns, and the thorns grew up and choked it, and it yielded no grain. 8Other seed fell into good soil and brought forth grain, growing up and increasing and yielding thirty and sixty and a hundredfold." 9And he said, "Let anyone with ears to hear listen!"

The Purpose of the Parables

10 When he was alone, those who were around him along with the twelve asked him about the parables. 11And he said to them, "To you has been given the secret[b] of the kingdom of God, but for those outside, everything comes in parables; 12in order that

'they may indeed look, but not
        perceive,
    and may indeed listen, but not
        understand;
so that they may not turn again
    and be forgiven.' "

13 And he said to them, "Do you not understand this parable? Then how will you understand all the parables? 14The sower sows the word. 15These are the ones on the path where the word is sown: when they hear, Satan immediately comes and takes away the word that is sown in them. 16And these are the ones sown on rocky ground: when they hear the word, they immediately receive it with joy. 17But they have no root, and endure only for a while; then, when trouble or persecution arises on account of the word, immediately they fall away.[c] 18And others are those sown among the thorns: these are the ones who hear the word, 19but the cares of the world, and the lure of wealth, and the desire for other things come in and choke the word, and it yields nothing. 20And these are the ones sown on the good soil: they hear the word and accept it and bear fruit, thirty and sixty and a hundredfold."

A Lamp under a Bushel Basket

21 He said to them, "Is a lamp brought in to be put under the bushel basket, or under the bed, and not on the lampstand? 22For there is nothing hidden, except to be disclosed; nor is anything secret, except to come to light. 23Let anyone with ears to hear listen!" 24And he said to them, "Pay attention to what you hear; the measure you give will be the measure you get, and still more will be given you. 25For to those who have, more will be given; and from those who have nothing, even what they have will be taken away."

The Parable of the Growing Seed

26 He also said, "The kingdom of God is as if someone would scatter seed on the ground, 27and would sleep and rise night and day, and the seed would sprout and grow, he does not know how. 28The earth produces of itself, first the stalk, then the head, then the full grain in the head. 29But when the grain is ripe, at once he goes in with his sickle, because the harvest has come."

The Parable of the Mustard Seed

30 He also said, "With what can we compare the kingdom of God, or what parable will we use for it? 31It is like a mustard seed, which, when sown upon the ground, is the smallest of all the seeds on earth; 32yet when it is sown it grows up and becomes the greatest of all shrubs, and puts forth large branches, so that the birds of the air can make nests in its shade."

The Use of Parables

33 With many such parables he spoke the word to them, as they were able to hear it; 34he did not speak to them except in parables, but he explained everything in private to his disciples.

Jesus Stills a Storm

35 On that day, when evening had come, he said to them, "Let us go across to the other side." 36And leaving the crowd behind, they took him with them

b Or mystery   c Or stumble

in the boat, just as he was. Other boats were with him. [37] A great windstorm arose, and the waves beat into the boat, so that the boat was already being swamped. [38] But he was in the stern, asleep on the cushion; and they woke him up and said to him, "Teacher, do you not care that we are perishing?" [39] He woke up and rebuked the wind, and said to the sea, "Peace! Be still!" Then the wind ceased, and there was a dead calm. [40] He said to them, "Why are you afraid? Have you still no faith?" [41] And they were filled with great awe and said to one another, "Who then is this, that even the wind and the sea obey him?"

HOW OFTEN WE LOOK UPON GOD AS OUR LAST AND FEEBLEST RESOURCE! WE GO TO HIM BE-CAUSE WE HAVE NOWHERE ELSE TO GO. AND THEN WE LEARN THAT THE STORMS OF LIFE HAVE DRIVEN US, NOT UPON THE ROCKS, BUT INTO THE DESIRED HAVEN. —*George MacDonald*

Jesus Heals the Gerasene Demoniac

5 They came to the other side of the sea, to the country of the Gerasenes.[d] [2] And when he had stepped out of the boat, immediately a man out of the tombs with an unclean spirit met him. [3] He lived among the tombs; and no one could restrain him any more, even with a chain; [4] for he had often been re-strained with shackles and chains, but the chains he wrenched apart, and the shackles he broke in pieces; and no one had the strength to subdue him. [5] Night and day among the tombs and on the mountains he was always howling and bruising himself with stones. [6] When he saw Jesus from a distance, he ran and bowed down before him; [7] and he shout-ed at the top of his voice, "What have you to do with me, Jesus, Son of the Most High God? I adjure you by God, do not torment me." [8] For he had said to him, "Come out of the man, you un-clean spirit!" [9] Then Jesus[e] asked him, "What is your name?" He replied, "My name is Legion; for we are many." [10] He

begged him earnestly not to send them out of the country. [11] Now there on the hillside a great herd of swine was feed-ing; [12] and the unclean spirits[f] begged him, "Send us into the swine; let us enter them." [13] So he gave them permis-sion. And the unclean spirits came out and entered the swine; and the herd, numbering about two thousand, rushed down the steep bank into the sea, and were drowned in the sea.

14 The swineherds ran off and told it in the city and in the country. Then peo-ple came to see what it was that had happened. [15] They came to Jesus and saw the demoniac sitting there, clothed and in his right mind, the very man who had had the legion; and they were afraid. [16] Those who had seen what had hap-pened to the demoniac and to the swine reported it. [17] Then they began to beg Jesus[g] to leave their neighborhood. [18] As he was getting into the boat, the man who had been possessed by demons begged him that he might be with him. [19] But Jesus[e] refused, and said to him, "Go home to your friends, and tell them how much the Lord has done for you, and what mercy he has shown you." [20] And he went away and began to pro-claim in the Decapolis how much Jesus had done for him; and everyone was amazed.

A Girl Restored to Life and a Woman Healed

21 When Jesus had crossed again in the boat[h] to the other side, a great crowd gathered around him; and he was by the sea. [22] Then one of the leaders of the syn-agogue named Jairus came and, when he saw him, fell at his feet [23] and begged him repeatedly, "My little daughter is at the point of death. Come and lay your hands on her, so that she may be made well, and live." [24] So he went with him.

And a large crowd followed him and pressed in on him. [25] Now there was a woman who had been suffering from hemorrhages for twelve years. [26] She had endured much under many physicians, and had spent all that she had; and she was no better, but rather grew worse. [27] She had heard about Jesus, and came

---

d Other ancient authorities read Gergesenes; *others,* Gadarenes   *e Gk* he   *f Gk* they   *g Gk* him
h Other ancient authorities lack in the boat

up behind him in the crowd and touched his cloak, 28for she said, "If I but touch his clothes, I will be made well." 29Immediately her hemorrhage stopped; and she felt in her body that she was healed of her disease. 30Immediately aware that power had gone forth from him, Jesus turned about in the crowd and said, "Who touched my clothes?" 31And his disciples said to him, "You see the crowd pressing in on you; how can you say, 'Who touched me?' " 32He looked all around to see who had done it. 33But the woman, knowing what had happened to her, came in fear and trembling, fell down before him, and told him the whole truth. 34He said to her, "Daughter, your faith has made you well; go in peace, and be healed of your disease."

35 While he was still speaking, some people came from the leader's house to say, "Your daughter is dead. Why trouble the teacher any further?" 36But overhearing[i] what they said, Jesus said to the leader of the synagogue, "Do not fear, only believe." 37He allowed no one to follow him except Peter, James, and John, the brother of James. 38When they came to the house of the leader of the synagogue, he saw a commotion, people weeping and wailing loudly. 39When he had entered, he said to them, "Why do you make a commotion and weep? The child is not dead but sleeping." 40And they laughed at him. Then he put them all outside, and took the child's father and mother and those who were with him, and went in where the child was. 41He took her by the hand and said to her, "Talitha cum," which means, "Little girl, get up!" 42And immediately the girl got up and began to walk about (she was twelve years of age). At this they were overcome with amazement. 43He strictly ordered them that no one should know this, and told them to give her something to eat.

The Rejection of Jesus at Nazareth

6 He left that place and came to his hometown, and his disciples followed him. 2On the sabbath he began to teach in the synagogue, and many who heard him were astounded. They said, "Where did this man get all this? What is this wisdom that has been given to him? What deeds of power are being done by his hands! 3Is not this the carpenter, the son of Mary[j] and brother of James and Joses and Judas and Simon, and are not his sisters here with us?" And they took offense[k] at him. 4Then Jesus said to them, "Prophets are not without honor, except in their hometown, and among their own kin, and in their own house." 5And he could do no deed of power there, except that he laid his hands on a few sick people and cured them. 6And he was amazed at their unbelief.

The Mission of the Twelve

Then he went about among the villages teaching. 7He called the twelve and began to send them out two by two, and gave them authority over the unclean spirits. 8He ordered them to take nothing for their journey except a staff; no bread, no bag, no money in their belts; 9but to wear sandals and not to put on two tunics. 10He said to them, "Wherever you enter a house, stay there until you leave the place. 11If any place will not welcome you and they refuse to hear you, as you leave, shake off the dust that is on your feet as a testimony against them." 12So they went out and proclaimed that all should repent. 13They cast out many demons, and anointed with oil many who were sick and cured them.

The Death of John the Baptist

14 King Herod heard of it, for Jesus'[l] name had become known. Some were[m] saying, "John the baptizer has been raised from the dead; and for this reason these powers are at work in him." 15But others said, "It is Elijah." And others said, "It is a prophet, like one of the prophets of old." 16But when Herod heard of it, he said, "John, whom I beheaded, has been raised."

17 For Herod himself had sent men who arrested John, bound him, and put him in prison on account of Herodias,

---

i Or ignoring; other ancient authorities read hearing
carpenter and of Mary   k Or stumbled   l Gk his

j Other ancient authorities read son of the
m Other ancient authorities read He was

his brother Philip's wife, because Herod[n] had married her. [18]For John had been telling Herod, "It is not lawful for you to have your brother's wife." [19]And Herodias had a grudge against him, and wanted to kill him. But she could not, [20]for Herod feared John, knowing that he was a righteous and holy man, and he protected him. When he heard him, he was greatly perplexed;[o] and yet he liked to listen to him. [21]But an opportunity came when Herod on his birthday gave a banquet for his courtiers and officers and for the leaders of Galilee. [22]When

n Gk he   o Other ancient authorities read *he did many things*

THE REPENTANCE OF THOMAS MORE
Thomas More

VERSE: Mark 6.12   PASSAGE: Mark 6.7–12

ood and gracious Lord, as you give me grace to acknowledge my sins, so give me grace in both word and heart to repent them and utterly forsake them. And forgive me those sins which my pride blinds me from discerning.

Glorious God, give me your grace to turn my back on the things of this world, and to fix my heart solely on you.

Give me your grace to amend my life, so that I can approach death without resentment, knowing that in you it is the gateway to eternal riches.

Glorious God, take from me all sinful fear, all sinful sorrow and self-pity, all sinful hope and all sinful desire. Instead give me such fear, such sorrow, such pity, such hope and such desire as may be profitable for my soul.

Good Lord, give me this grace, in all my fear and agony, to find strength in that great fear and agony which you, sweet Savior, had on the Mount of Olives before your bitter passion.

Almighty God, take from me all desire for worldly praise, and all emotions of anger and revenge. Give me a humble, lowly, quiet, peaceable, patient, generous, kind, tender and compassionate mind.

Grant me, good Lord, a full faith, a firm hope and a fervent love, that I may desire only that which gives you pleasure and conforms to your will.

And, above all, look upon me with your love and your favor.

ADDITIONAL SCRIPTURE READING:
Jeremiah 15.19; John 14.1–4

Go to page 1171 for your next devotional reading.

1500   1700

his daughter Herodias[p] came in and danced, she pleased Herod and his guests; and the king said to the girl, "Ask me for whatever you wish, and I will give it." 23And he solemnly swore to her, "Whatever you ask me, I will give you, even half of my kingdom." 24She went out and said to her mother, "What should I ask for?" She replied, "The head of John the baptizer." 25Immediately she rushed back to the king and requested, "I want you to give me at once the head of John the Baptist on a platter." 26The king was deeply grieved; yet out of regard for his oaths and for the guests, he did not want to refuse her. 27Immediately the king sent a soldier of the guard with orders to bring John's[q] head. He went and beheaded him in the prison, 28brought his head on a platter, and gave it to the girl. Then the girl gave it to her mother. 29When his disciples heard about it, they came and took his body, and laid it in a tomb.

Feeding the Five Thousand

30 The apostles gathered around Jesus, and told him all that they had done and taught. 31He said to them, "Come away to a deserted place all by yourselves and rest a while." For many were coming and going, and they had no leisure even to eat. 32And they went away in the boat to a deserted place by themselves. 33Now many saw them going and recognized them, and they hurried there on foot from all the towns and arrived ahead of them. 34As he went ashore, he saw a great crowd; and he had compassion for them, because they were like sheep without a shepherd; and he began to teach them many things. 35When it grew late, his disciples came to him and said, "This is a deserted place, and the hour is now very late; 36send them away so that they may go into the surrounding country and villages and buy something for themselves to eat." 37But he answered them, "You give them something to eat." They said to him, "Are we to go and buy two hundred denarii[r] worth of bread, and give it to them to eat?" 38And he said to them, "How many

loaves have you? Go and see." When they had found out, they said, "Five, and two fish." 39Then he ordered them to get all the people to sit down in groups on the green grass. 40So they sat down in groups of hundreds and of fifties. 41Taking the five loaves and the two fish, he looked up to heaven, and blessed and broke the loaves, and gave them to his disciples to set before the people; and he divided the two fish among them all. 42And all ate and were filled; 43and they took up twelve baskets full of broken pieces and of the fish. 44Those who had eaten the loaves numbered five thousand men.

Jesus Walks on the Water

45 Immediately he made his disciples get into the boat and go on ahead to the other side, to Bethsaida, while he dismissed the crowd. 46After saying farewell to them, he went up on the mountain to pray.

47 When evening came, the boat was out on the sea, and he was alone on the land. 48When he saw that they were straining at the oars against an adverse wind, he came towards them early in the morning, walking on the sea. He intended to pass them by. 49But when they saw him walking on the sea, they thought it was a ghost and cried out; 50for they all saw him and were terrified. But immediately he spoke to them and said, "Take heart, it is I; do not be afraid." 51Then he got into the boat with them and the wind ceased. And they were utterly astounded, 52for they did not understand about the loaves, but their hearts were hardened.

Healing the Sick in Gennesaret

53 When they had crossed over, they came to land at Gennesaret and moored the boat. 54When they got out of the boat, people at once recognized him, 55and rushed about that whole region and began to bring the sick on mats to wherever they heard he was. 56And wherever he went, into villages or cities or farms, they laid the sick in the marketplaces, and begged him that they

might touch even the fringe of his cloak; and all who touched it were healed.

The Tradition of the Elders

7 Now when the Pharisees and some of the scribes who had come from Jerusalem gathered around him, 2they noticed that some of his disciples were eating with defiled hands, that is, without washing them. 3(For the Pharisees, and all the Jews, do not eat unless they thoroughly wash their hands,s thus observing the tradition of the elders; 4and they do not eat anything from the market unless they wash it;t and there are also many other traditions that they observe, the washing of cups, pots, and bronze kettles.u) 5So the Pharisees and the scribes asked him, "Why do your disciples not livev according to the tradition of the elders, but eat with defiled hands?" 6He said to them, "Isaiah prophesied rightly about you hypocrites, as it is written,

'This people honors me with their lips,
    but their hearts are far from me;
7   in vain do they worship me,
        teaching human precepts as doctrines.'

8You abandon the commandment of God and hold to human tradition."

9 Then he said to them, "You have a fine way of rejecting the commandment of God in order to keep your tradition! 10For Moses said, 'Honor your father and your mother'; and, 'Whoever speaks evil of father or mother must surely die.' 11But you say that if anyone tells father or mother, 'Whatever support you might have had from me is Corban' (that is, an offering to Godw)— 12then you no longer permit doing anything for a father or mother, 13thus making void the word of God through your tradition that you have handed on. And you do many things like this."

14 Then he called the crowd again and said to them, "Listen to me, all of you, and understand: 15there is nothing outside a person that by going in can defile, but the things that come out are what defile."x

17 When he had left the crowd and entered the house, his disciples asked him about the parable. 18He said to them, "Then do you also fail to understand? Do you not see that whatever goes into a person from outside cannot defile, 19since it enters, not the heart but the stomach, and goes out into the sewer?" (Thus he declared all foods clean.) 20And he said, "It is what comes out of a person that defiles. 21For it is from within, from the human heart, that evil intentions come: fornication, theft, murder, 22adultery, avarice, wickedness, deceit, licentiousness, envy, slander, pride, folly. 23All these evil things come from within, and they defile a person."

The Syrophoenician Woman's Faith

24 From there he set out and went away to the region of Tyre.y He entered a house and did not want anyone to know he was there. Yet he could not escape notice, 25but a woman whose little daughter had an unclean spirit immediately heard about him, and she came and bowed down at his feet. 26Now the woman was a Gentile, of Syrophoenician origin. She begged him to cast the demon out of her daughter. 27He said to her, "Let the children be fed first, for it is not fair to take the children's food and throw it to the dogs." 28But she answered him, "Sir,z even the dogs under the table eat the children's crumbs." 29Then he said to her, "For saying that, you may go—the demon has left your daughter." 30So she went home, found the child lying on the bed, and the demon gone.

Jesus Cures a Deaf Man

31 Then he returned from the region of Tyre, and went by way of Sidon towards the Sea of Galilee, in the region of the Decapolis. 32They brought to him a deaf man who had an impediment in his speech; and they begged him to lay his hand on him. 33He took him aside in private, away from the crowd, and put

---

s Meaning of Gk uncertain   t Other ancient authorities read *and when they come from the marketplace, they do not eat unless they purify themselves*   u Other ancient authorities add *and beds*   v Gk *walk*   w Gk lacks *to God*   x Other ancient authorities add verse 16, "*Let anyone with ears to hear listen*"   y Other ancient authorities add *and Sidon*   z Or *Lord*; other ancient authorities prefix *Yes*

his fingers into his ears, and he spat and touched his tongue. 34 Then looking up to heaven, he sighed and said to him, "Ephphatha," that is, "Be opened." 35 And immediately his ears were opened, his tongue was released, and he spoke plainly. 36 Then Jesus*a* ordered them to tell no one; but the more he ordered them, the more zealously they proclaimed it. 37 They were astounded beyond measure, saying, "He has done everything well; he even makes the deaf to hear and the mute to speak."

Feeding the Four Thousand

8 In those days when there was again a great crowd without anything to eat, he called his disciples and said to them, 2 "I have compassion for the crowd, because they have been with me now for three days and have nothing to eat. 3 If I send them away hungry to their homes, they will faint on the way—and some of them have come from a great distance." 4 His disciples replied, "How can one feed these people with bread here in the desert?" 5 He asked them, "How many loaves do you have?" They said, "Seven." 6 Then he ordered the crowd to sit down on the ground; and he took the seven loaves, and after giving thanks he broke them and gave them to his disciples to distribute; and they distributed them to the crowd. 7 They had also a few small fish; and after blessing them, he ordered that these too should be distributed. 8 They ate and were filled; and they took up the broken pieces left over, seven baskets full. 9 Now there were about four thousand people. And he sent them away. 10 And immediately he got into the boat with his disciples and went to the district of Dalmanutha.*b*

The Demand for a Sign

11 The Pharisees came and began to argue with him, asking him for a sign from heaven, to test him. 12 And he sighed deeply in his spirit and said, "Why does this generation ask for a sign? Truly I tell you, no sign will be given to this generation." 13 And he left them, and getting into the boat again, he went across to the other side.

The Yeast of the Pharisees and of Herod

14 Now the disciples*c* had forgotten to bring any bread; and they had only one loaf with them in the boat. 15 And he cautioned them, saying, "Watch out— beware of the yeast of the Pharisees and the yeast of Herod."*d* 16 They said to one another, "It is because we have no bread." 17 And becoming aware of it, Jesus said to them, "Why are you talking about having no bread? Do you still not perceive or understand? Are your hearts hardened? 18 Do you have eyes, and fail to see? Do you have ears, and fail to hear? And do you not remember? 19 When I broke the five loaves for the five thousand, how many baskets full of broken pieces did you collect?" They said to him, "Twelve." 20 "And the seven for the four thousand, how many baskets full of broken pieces did you collect?" And they said to him, "Seven." 21 Then he said to them, "Do you not yet understand?"

Jesus Cures a Blind Man at Bethsaida

22 They came to Bethsaida. Some people*e* brought a blind man to him and begged him to touch him. 23 He took the blind man by the hand and led him out of the village; and when he had put saliva on his eyes and laid his hands on him, he asked him, "Can you see anything?" 24 And the man*f* looked up and said, "I can see people, but they look like trees, walking." 25 Then Jesus*f* laid his hands on his eyes again; and he looked intently and his sight was restored, and he saw everything clearly. 26 Then he sent him away to his home, saying, "Do not even go into the village."*g*

Peter's Declaration about Jesus

27 Jesus went on with his disciples to the villages of Caesarea Philippi; and on the way he asked his disciples, "Who do people say that I am?" 28 And they an-

---

a Gk *he*　　*b* Other ancient authorities read *Mageda* or *Magdala*　　*c* Gk *they*　　*d* Other ancient authorities read *the Herodians*　　*e* Gk *They*　　*f* Gk *he*　　*g* Other ancient authorities add *or tell anyone in the village*

swered him, "John the Baptist; and others, Elijah; and still others, one of the prophets." 29He asked them, "But who do you say that I am?" Peter answered him, "You are the Messiah."*h* 30And he sternly ordered them not to tell anyone about him.

Jesus Foretells His Death and Resurrection

31 Then he began to teach them that the Son of Man must undergo great suffering, and be rejected by the elders, the chief priests, and the scribes, and be killed, and after three days rise again. 32He said all this quite openly. And Peter took him aside and began to rebuke him. 33But turning and looking at his disciples, he rebuked Peter and said, "Get behind me, Satan! For you are setting your mind not on divine things but on human things."

34 He called the crowd with his disciples, and said to them, "If any want to become my followers, let them deny themselves and take up their cross and follow me. 35For those who want to save their life will lose it, and those who lose their life for my sake, and for the sake of the gospel,*i* will save it. 36For what will it profit them to gain the whole world and forfeit their life? 37Indeed, what can they give in return for their life? 38Those who are ashamed of me and of my words*j* in this adulterous and sinful generation, of them the Son of Man will also be ashamed when he comes in the glory of his Father with the holy angels."

THE CHRISTIAN HAS GREATLY THE ADVANTAGE OF THE UNBELIEVER, HAVING EVERYTHING TO GAIN AND NOTHING TO LOSE.   —Lord Byron

---

9 1And he said to them, "Truly I tell you, there are some standing here who will not taste death until they see that the kingdom of God has come with*k* power."

The Transfiguration

2 Six days later, Jesus took with him Peter and James and John, and led them up a high mountain apart, by themselves. And he was transfigured before them, 3and his clothes became dazzling white, such as no one*l* on earth could bleach them. 4And there appeared to them Elijah with Moses, who were talking with Jesus. 5Then Peter said to Jesus, "Rabbi, it is good for us to be here; let us make three dwellings,*m* one for you, one for Moses, and one for Elijah." 6He did not know what to say, for they were terrified. 7Then a cloud overshadowed them, and from the cloud there came a voice, "This is my Son, the Beloved;*n* listen to him!" 8Suddenly when they looked around, they saw no one with them any more, but only Jesus.

The Coming of Elijah

9 As they were coming down the mountain, he ordered them to tell no one about what they had seen, until after the Son of Man had risen from the dead. 10So they kept the matter to themselves, questioning what this rising from the dead could mean. 11Then they asked him, "Why do the scribes say that Elijah must come first?" 12He said to them, "Elijah is indeed coming first to restore all things. How then is it written about the Son of Man, that he is to go through many sufferings and be treated with contempt? 13But I tell you that Elijah has come, and they did to him whatever they pleased, as it is written about him."

The Healing of a Boy with a Spirit

14 When they came to the disciples, they saw a great crowd around them, and some scribes arguing with them. 15When the whole crowd saw him, they were immediately overcome with awe, and they ran forward to greet him. 16He asked them, "What are you arguing about with them?" 17Someone from the crowd answered him, "Teacher, I brought you my son; he has a spirit that makes him unable to speak; 18and whenever it seizes him, it dashes him down; and he foams and grinds his teeth and becomes rigid; and I asked your disciples to cast it out,

---

h Or *the Christ*   *i* Other ancient authorities read *lose their life for the sake of the gospel*   *j* Other ancient authorities read *and of mine*   *k* Or *in*   *l* Gk *no fuller*   *m* Or *tents*   *n* Or *my beloved Son*

but they could not do so." [19]He answered them, "You faithless generation, how much longer must I be among you? How much longer must I put up with you? Bring him to me." [20]And they brought the boy[o] to him. When the spirit saw him, immediately it convulsed the boy,[o] and he fell on the ground and rolled about, foaming at the mouth. [21]Jesus[p] asked the father, "How long has this been happening to him?" And he said, "From childhood. [22]It has often cast him into the fire and into the water, to destroy him; but if you are able to do anything, have pity on us and help us." [23]Jesus said to him, "If you are able!—All things can be done for the one who believes." [24]Immediately the father of the child cried out,[q] "I believe; help my unbelief!" [25]When Jesus saw that a crowd came running together, he rebuked the unclean spirit, saying to it, "You spirit that keeps this boy from speaking and hearing, I command you, come out of him, and never enter him again!" [26]After crying out and convulsing him terribly, it came out, and the boy was like a corpse, so that most of them said, "He is dead." [27]But Jesus took him by the hand and lifted him up, and he was able to stand. [28]When he had entered the house, his disciples asked him privately, "Why could we not cast it out?" [29]He said to them, "This kind can come out only through prayer."[r]

Jesus Again Foretells His Death and Resurrection

30 They went on from there and passed through Galilee. He did not want anyone to know it; [31]for he was teaching his disciples, saying to them, "The Son of Man is to be betrayed into human hands, and they will kill him, and three days after being killed, he will rise again." [32]But they did not understand what he was saying and were afraid to ask him.

Who Is the Greatest?

33 Then they came to Capernaum; and when he was in the house he asked them, "What were you arguing about on the way?" [34]But they were silent, for on the way they had argued with one another who was the greatest. [35]He sat down, called the twelve, and said to them, "Whoever wants to be first must be last of all and servant of all." [36]Then he took a little child and put it among them; and taking it in his arms, he said to them, [37]"Whoever welcomes one such child in my name welcomes me, and whoever welcomes me welcomes not me but the one who sent me."

Another Exorcist

38 John said to him, "Teacher, we saw someone[s] casting out demons in your name, and we tried to stop him, because he was not following us." [39]But Jesus said, "Do not stop him; for no one who does a deed of power in my name will be able soon afterward to speak evil of me. [40]Whoever is not against us is for us. [41]For truly I tell you, whoever gives you a cup of water to drink because you bear the name of Christ will by no means lose the reward.

Temptations to Sin

42 "If any of you put a stumbling block before one of these little ones who believe in me,[t] it would be better for you if a great millstone were hung around your neck and you were thrown into the sea. [43]If your hand causes you to stumble, cut it off; it is better for you to enter life maimed than to have two hands and to go to hell,[u] to the unquenchable fire.[v] [45]And if your foot causes you to stumble, cut it off; it is better for you to enter life lame than to have two feet and to be thrown into hell.[u,v] [47]And if your eye causes you to stumble, tear it out; it is better for you to enter the kingdom of God with one eye than to have two eyes and to be thrown into hell,[u] [48]where their worm never dies, and the fire is never quenched.

49 "For everyone will be salted with fire.[w] [50]Salt is good; but if salt has lost its saltiness, how can you season it?[x] Have salt in yourselves, and be at peace with one another."

---

o Gk *him*   p Gk *He*   q Other ancient authorities add *with tears*   r Other ancient authorities add *and fasting*   s Other ancient authorities add *who does not follow us*   t Other ancient authorities lack *in me*   u Gk *Gehenna*   v Verses 44 and 46 (which are identical with verse 48) are lacking in the best ancient authorities   w Other ancient authorities either add or substitute *and every sacrifice will be salted with salt*   x Or *how can you restore its saltiness?*

Teaching about Divorce

 10 He left that place and went to the region of Judea and[y] beyond the Jordan. And crowds again gathered around him; and, as was his custom, he again taught them.

2 Some Pharisees came, and to test him they asked, "Is it lawful for a man to divorce his wife?" 3He answered them, "What did Moses command you?" 4They said, "Moses allowed a man to write a certificate of dismissal and to divorce her." 5But Jesus said to them, "Because of your hardness of heart he wrote this commandment for you. 6But from the beginning of creation, 'God made

[y] Other ancient authorities lack *and*

THURSDAY

MAKE US LIKE CHILDREN AGAIN
Peter Marshall

VERSE: Mark 9.37   PASSAGE: Mark 9.35–37

orgive us, Lord, that as we grow to maturity, our faith is blighted with doubts, withered with worry, tainted with sophistication. We pray that thou wilt make us like children again in faith—not childish, but childlike in the simplicity of a faith that is willing to trust thee even though we cannot see what tomorrow will bring.

We ask thee to give to each of us that childlike faith, that simplicity of mind which is willing to lay aside all egotism and conceit, which recognizes vanity for what it is—an empty show, which knows that we are incapable of thinking the thoughts of God, which is willing to be humble again.

Then may we feel once more as do our children who whisper their love to thee, who trace with chubby little fingers the pictures of Jesus in a picture book—those pictures that portray thee, Lord Jesus, with a hurt lamb in thy arms or a child on thy knee. Help us, even now, to feel again like that, that we may be as loving, as trusting, as innocent, as grateful, as affectionate.

And as we are willing to kneel again as children, then shall we discover for ourselves the glory thou hast revealed, and find the wonder of it gripping our hearts and preparing them for thy peace. So shall we, along with our children, enter into the kingdom of God, and know it, and feel it, and rejoice in it. In thy name, who didst dare to come to earth as a little child, we pray. Amen.

ADDITIONAL SCRIPTURE READING:
Matthew 18.3; 1 John 3.1

Go to page 1176 for your next devotional reading.

1900   Present

them male and female.' 7'For this reason a man shall leave his father and mother and be joined to his wife,z 8and the two shall become one flesh.' So they are no longer two, but one flesh. 9Therefore what God has joined together, let no one separate."

10 Then in the house the disciples asked him again about this matter. 11He said to them, "Whoever divorces his wife and marries another commits adultery against her; 12and if she divorces her husband and marries another, she commits adultery."

Jesus Blesses Little Children

13 People were bringing little children to him in order that he might touch them; and the disciples spoke sternly to them. 14But when Jesus saw this, he was indignant and said to them, "Let the little children come to me; do not stop them; for it is to such as these that the kingdom of God belongs. 15Truly I tell you, whoever does not receive the kingdom of God as a little child will never enter it." 16And he took them up in his arms, laid his hands on them, and blessed them.

The Rich Man

17 As he was setting out on a journey, a man ran up and knelt before him, and asked him, "Good Teacher, what must I do to inherit eternal life?" 18Jesus said to him, "Why do you call me good? No one is good but God alone. 19You know the commandments: 'You shall not murder; You shall not commit adultery; You shall not steal; You shall not bear false witness; You shall not defraud; Honor your father and mother.' " 20He said to him, "Teacher, I have kept all these since my youth." 21Jesus, looking at him, loved him and said, "You lack one thing; go, sell what you own, and give the moneya to the poor, and you will have treasure in heaven; then come, follow me." 22When he heard this, he was shocked and went away grieving, for he had many possessions.

23 Then Jesus looked around and said to his disciples, "How hard it will be for those who have wealth to enter the kingdom of God!" 24And the disciples were perplexed at these words. But Jesus said to them again, "Children, how hard it isb to enter the kingdom of God! 25It is easier for a camel to go through the eye of a needle than for someone who is rich to enter the kingdom of God." 26They were greatly astounded and said to one another,c "Then who can be saved?" 27Jesus looked at them and said, "For mortals it is impossible, but not for God; for God all things are possible."

28 Peter began to say to him, "Look, we have left everything and followed you." 29Jesus said, "Truly I tell you, there is no one who has left house or brothers or sisters or mother or father or children or fields, for my sake and for the sake of the good news,d 30who will not receive a hundredfold now in this age—houses, brothers and sisters, mothers and children, and fields, with persecutions—and in the age to come eternal life. 31But many who are first will be last, and the last will be first."

A Third Time Jesus Foretells His Death and Resurrection

32 They were on the road, going up to Jerusalem, and Jesus was walking ahead of them; they were amazed, and those who followed were afraid. He took the twelve aside again and began to tell them what was to happen to him, 33saying, "See, we are going up to Jerusalem, and the Son of Man will be handed over to the chief priests and the scribes, and they will condemn him to death; then they will hand him over to the Gentiles; 34they will mock him, and spit upon him, and flog him, and kill him; and after three days he will rise again."

The Request of James and John

35 James and John, the sons of Zebedee, came forward to him and said to him, "Teacher, we want you to do for us whatever we ask of you." 36And he said to them, "What is it you want me to do for you?" 37And they said to him, "Grant us to sit, one at your right hand and one at your left, in your glory." 38But Jesus said to them, "You do not know what you are asking. Are you able

---

z Other ancient authorities lack *and be joined to his wife*   a Gk lacks *the money*   b Other ancient authorities add *for those who trust in riches*   c Other ancient authorities read *to him*   d Or *gospel*

to drink the cup that I drink, or be baptized with the baptism that I am baptized with?" [39]They replied, "We are able." Then Jesus said to them, "The cup that I drink you will drink; and with the baptism with which I am baptized, you will be baptized; [40]but to sit at my right hand or at my left is not mine to grant, but it is for those for whom it has been prepared."

41 When the ten heard this, they began to be angry with James and John. [42]So Jesus called them and said to them, "You know that among the Gentiles those whom they recognize as their rulers lord it over them, and their great ones are tyrants over them. [43]But it is not so among you; but whoever wishes to become great among you must be your servant, [44]and whoever wishes to be first among you must be slave of all. [45]For the Son of Man came not to be served but to serve, and to give his life a ransom for many."

The Healing of Blind Bartimaeus

46 They came to Jericho. As he and his disciples and a large crowd were leaving Jericho, Bartimaeus son of Timaeus, a blind beggar, was sitting by the roadside. [47]When he heard that it was Jesus of Nazareth, he began to shout out and say, "Jesus, Son of David, have mercy on me!" [48]Many sternly ordered him to be quiet, but he cried out even more loudly, "Son of David, have mercy on me!" [49]Jesus stood still and said, "Call him here." And they called the blind man, saying to him, "Take heart; get up, he is calling you." [50]So throwing off his cloak, he sprang up and came to Jesus. [51]Then Jesus said to him, "What do you want me to do for you?" The blind man said to him, "My teacher,[e] let me see again." [52]Jesus said to him, "Go; your faith has made you well." Immediately he regained his sight and followed him on the way.

Jesus' Triumphal Entry into Jerusalem

11 When they were approaching Jerusalem, at Bethphage and Bethany, near the Mount of Olives, he sent two of his disciples [2]and said to them, "Go into the village ahead of you, and immediately as you enter it, you will find tied there a colt that has never been ridden; untie it and bring it. [3]If anyone says to you, 'Why are you doing this?' just say this, 'The Lord needs it and will send it back here immediately.' " [4]They went away and found a colt tied near a door, outside in the street. As they were untying it, [5]some of the bystanders said to them, "What are you doing, untying the colt?" [6]They told them what Jesus had said; and they allowed them to take it. [7]Then they brought the colt to Jesus and threw their cloaks on it; and he sat on it. [8]Many people spread their cloaks on the road, and others spread leafy branches that they had cut in the fields. [9]Then those who went ahead and those who followed were shouting,

"Hosanna!
    Blessed is the one who comes in
        the name of the Lord!
10   Blessed is the coming kingdom of
        our ancestor David!
    Hosanna in the highest heaven!"

11 Then he entered Jerusalem and went into the temple; and when he had looked around at everything, as it was already late, he went out to Bethany with the twelve.

Jesus Curses the Fig Tree

12 On the following day, when they came from Bethany, he was hungry. [13]Seeing in the distance a fig tree in leaf, he went to see whether perhaps he would find anything on it. When he came to it, he found nothing but leaves, for it was not the season for figs. [14]He said to it, "May no one ever eat fruit from you again." And his disciples heard it.

Jesus Cleanses the Temple

15 Then they came to Jerusalem. And he entered the temple and began to drive out those who were selling and those who were buying in the temple, and he overturned the tables of the money changers and the seats of those who sold doves; [16]and he would not allow anyone to carry anything through

e Aramaic *Rabbouni*

the temple. **17**He was teaching and saying, "Is it not written,

'My house shall be called a house
        of prayer for all the nations'?
But you have made it a den of
        robbers.''

18And when the chief priests and the scribes heard it, they kept looking for a way to kill him; for they were afraid of him, because the whole crowd was spellbound by his teaching. **19**And when evening came, Jesus and his disciples*f* went out of the city.

The Lesson from the Withered Fig Tree

20 In the morning as they passed by, they saw the fig tree withered away to its roots. **21**Then Peter remembered and said to him, "Rabbi, look! The fig tree that you cursed has withered." **22**Jesus answered them, "Have*g* faith in God. **23**Truly I tell you, if you say to this mountain, 'Be taken up and thrown into the sea,' and if you do not doubt in your heart, but believe that what you say will come to pass, it will be done for you. **24**So I tell you, whatever you ask for in prayer, believe that you have received*h* it, and it will be yours.

25 "Whenever you stand praying, forgive, if you have anything against anyone; so that your Father in heaven may also forgive you your trespasses."*i*

I FIRMLY BELIEVE A GREAT MANY PRAYERS ARE
NOT ANSWERED BECAUSE WE ARE NOT WILLING
TO FORGIVE SOMEONE.   *—Dwight L. Moody*

Jesus' Authority Is Questioned

27 Again they came to Jerusalem. As he was walking in the temple, the chief priests, the scribes, and the elders came to him **28**and said, "By what authority are you doing these things? Who gave you this authority to do them?" **29**Jesus said to them, "I will ask you one question; answer me, and I will tell you by what authority I do these things. **30**Did the baptism of John come from heaven, or was it of human origin? Answer me."

31They argued with one another, "If we say, 'From heaven,' he will say, 'Why then did you not believe him?' **32**But shall we say, 'Of human origin'?"—they were afraid of the crowd, for all regarded John as truly a prophet. **33**So they answered Jesus, "We do not know." And Jesus said to them, "Neither will I tell you by what authority I am doing these things."

The Parable of the Wicked Tenants

12 Then he began to speak to them in parables. "A man planted a vineyard, put a fence around it, dug a pit for the wine press, and built a watchtower; then he leased it to tenants and went to another country. **2**When the season came, he sent a slave to the tenants to collect from them his share of the produce of the vineyard. **3**But they seized him, and beat him, and sent him away empty-handed. **4**And again he sent another slave to them; this one they beat over the head and insulted. **5**Then he sent another, and that one they killed. And so it was with many others; some they beat, and others they killed. **6**He had still one other, a beloved son. Finally he sent him to them, saying, 'They will respect my son.' **7**But those tenants said to one another, 'This is the heir; come, let us kill him, and the inheritance will be ours.' **8**So they seized him, killed him, and threw him out of the vineyard. **9**What then will the owner of the vineyard do? He will come and destroy the tenants and give the vineyard to others. **10**Have you not read this scripture:

'The stone that the builders
        rejected
    has become the cornerstone;*j*
11   this was the Lord's doing,
        and it is amazing in our eyes'?"

12 When they realized that he had told this parable against them, they wanted to arrest him, but they feared the crowd. So they left him and went away.

The Question about Paying Taxes

13 Then they sent to him some Pharisees and some Herodians to trap him in

---

f Gk *they*: other ancient authorities read *he*   *g* Other ancient authorities read *"If you have*   *h* Other ancient authorities read *are receiving*   *i* Other ancient authorities add verse 26, "But if you do not forgive, neither will your Father in heaven forgive your trespasses."   *j* Or *keystone*

what he said. 14And they came and said to him, "Teacher, we know that you are sincere, and show deference to no one; for you do not regard people with partiality, but teach the way of God in accordance with truth. Is it lawful to pay taxes to the emperor, or not? 15Should we pay them, or should we not?" But knowing their hypocrisy, he said to them, "Why are you putting me to the test? Bring me a denarius and let me see it." 16And they brought one. Then he said to them, "Whose head is this, and whose title?" They answered, "The emperor's." 17Jesus said to them, "Give to the emperor the things that are the emperor's, and to God the things that are God's." And they were utterly amazed at him.

The Question about the Resurrection

18 Some Sadducees, who say there is no resurrection, came to him and asked him a question, saying, 19"Teacher, Moses wrote for us that if a man's brother dies, leaving a wife but no child, the man*k* shall marry the widow and raise up children for his brother. 20There were seven brothers; the first married and, when he died, left no children; 21and the second married the widow*l* and died, leaving no children; and the third likewise; 22none of the seven left children. Last of all the woman herself died. 23In the resurrection*m* whose wife will she be? For the seven had married her."

24 Jesus said to them, "Is not this the reason you are wrong, that you know neither the scriptures nor the power of God? 25For when they rise from the dead, they neither marry nor are given in marriage, but are like angels in heaven. 26And as for the dead being raised, have you not read in the book of Moses, in the story about the bush, how God said to him, 'I am the God of Abraham, the God of Isaac, and the God of Jacob'? 27He is God not of the dead, but of the living; you are quite wrong."

The First Commandment

28 One of the scribes came near and heard them disputing with one another, and seeing that he answered them well,

he asked him, "Which commandment is the first of all?" 29Jesus answered, "The first is, 'Hear, O Israel: the Lord our God, the Lord is one; 30you shall love the Lord your God with all your heart, and with all your soul, and with all your mind, and with all your strength.' 31The second is this, 'You shall love your neighbor as yourself.' There is no other commandment greater than these." 32Then the scribe said to him, "You are right, Teacher; you have truly said that 'he is one, and besides him there is no other'; 33and 'to love him with all the heart, and with all the understanding, and with all the strength,' and 'to love one's neighbor as oneself,'—this is much more important than all whole burnt offerings and sacrifices." 34When Jesus saw that he answered wisely, he said to him, "You are not far from the kingdom of God." After that no one dared to ask him any question.

The Question about David's Son

35 While Jesus was teaching in the temple, he said, "How can the scribes say that the Messiah*n* is the son of David? 36David himself, by the Holy Spirit, declared,

'The Lord said to my Lord,
"Sit at my right hand,
    until I put your enemies under
        your feet." '
37David himself calls him Lord; so how can he be his son?" And the large crowd was listening to him with delight.

Jesus Denounces the Scribes

38 As he taught, he said, "Beware of the scribes, who like to walk around in long robes, and to be greeted with respect in the marketplaces, 39and to have the best seats in the synagogues and places of honor at banquets! 40They devour widows' houses and for the sake of appearance say long prayers. They will receive the greater condemnation."

The Widow's Offering

41 He sat down opposite the treasury, and watched the crowd putting money into the treasury. Many rich people put in large sums. 42A poor widow came and

---

k Gk *his brother*   *l* Gk *her*   *m* Other ancient authorities add *when they rise*   *n* Or *the Christ*

put in two small copper coins, which are worth a penny. 43Then he called his disciples and said to them, "Truly I tell you, this poor widow has put in more than all those who are contributing to the treasury. 44For all of them have contributed out of their abundance; but she out of her poverty has put in everything she had, all she had to live on."

The Destruction of the Temple Foretold

13 As he came out of the temple, one of his disciples said to him, "Look, Teacher, what large stones and what large buildings!" 2Then Jesus asked him, "Do you see these great buildings? Not one stone will be left here upon another; all will be thrown down."

FRIDAY

THE LAW OF LOVE IS GOOD AND SWEET
Bernard of Clairvaux

VERSE: Mark 12.30   **PASSAGE:** Mark 12.28–31

he law of love is good and sweet. It is not only borne lightly and easily, but it also makes bearable the laws which make men into slaves and hirelings. It does not destroy them; it fulfills them. As the Lord says, "I have not come to take away the law but to fulfill it" (Matthew 5.17). It tempers the slave's law and makes the hireling's law orderly. It lightens both. For there will never be any love without fear but chaste love. There will never be love without greed unless it is kept within bounds. Therefore love fulfills the slave's law when it overflows in devotion. It fulfills the hireling's law when it sets limits to greed.

Devotion mixed with fear does not remove the fear but purifies it. Punishment is lifted, for while law was servitude it could not function without it. Fear remains forever, but a pure and filial fear. For we read that "perfect love casts out fear" (1 John 4.18). This is to be understood to refer to the punishment which is never absent from servile fear, as I have said—by that mode of speaking by which the cause is often given for the effect.

Greed is brought to order when love overshadows it and evils are condemned and what is better is preferred to what is merely good, and the good is desired only for the sake of what is better. When by the grace of God this is fully achieved, the body is loved, and all the goods of the body for the sake of the soul, and the goods of the soul for the sake of God, and God for his own sake.

ADDITIONAL SCRIPTURE READING:
Matthew 5.17; 1 John 4.18

Go to page 1178 for your next devotional reading.

500   1500

3 When he was sitting on the Mount of Olives opposite the temple, Peter, James, John, and Andrew asked him privately, 4"Tell us, when will this be, and what will be the sign that all these things are about to be accomplished?" 5Then Jesus began to say to them, "Beware that no one leads you astray. 6Many will come in my name and say, 'I am he!'o and they will lead many astray. 7When you hear of wars and rumors of wars, do not be alarmed; this must take place, but the end is still to come. 8For nation will rise against nation, and kingdom against kingdom; there will be earthquakes in various places; there will be famines. This is but the beginning of the birth pangs.

Persecution Foretold

9 "As for yourselves, beware; for they will hand you over to councils; and you will be beaten in synagogues; and you will stand before governors and kings because of me, as a testimony to them. 10And the good newsp must first be proclaimed to all nations. 11When they bring you to trial and hand you over, do not worry beforehand about what you are to say; but say whatever is given you at that time, for it is not you who speak, but the Holy Spirit. 12Brother will betray brother to death, and a father his child, and children will rise against parents and have them put to death; 13and you will be hated by all because of my name. But the one who endures to the end will be saved.

The Desolating Sacrilege

14 "But when you see the desolating sacrilege set up where it ought not to be (let the reader understand), then those in Judea must flee to the mountains; 15the one on the housetop must not go down or enter the house to take anything away; 16the one in the field must not turn back to get a coat. 17Woe to those who are pregnant and to those who are nursing infants in those days! 18Pray that it may not be in winter. 19For in those days there will be suffering, such as has not been from the beginning of the creation that God created until now,

no, and never will be. 20And if the Lord had not cut short those days, no one would be saved; but for the sake of the elect, whom he chose, he has cut short those days. 21And if anyone says to you at that time, 'Look! Here is the Messiah!'q or 'Look! There he is!'—do not believe it. 22False messiahsr and false prophets will appear and produce signs and omens, to lead astray, if possible, the elect. 23But be alert; I have already told you everything.

The Coming of the Son of Man

24 "But in those days, after that suffering,
the sun will be darkened,
    and the moon will not give its
        light,
25   and the stars will be falling from
        heaven,
    and the powers in the heavens
        will be shaken.
26Then they will see 'the Son of Man coming in clouds' with great power and glory. 27Then he will send out the angels, and gather his elect from the four winds, from the ends of the earth to the ends of heaven.

The Lesson of the Fig Tree

28 "From the fig tree learn its lesson: as soon as its branch becomes tender and puts forth its leaves, you know that summer is near. 29So also, when you see these things taking place, you know that hes is near, at the very gates. 30Truly I tell you, this generation will not pass away until all these things have taken place. 31Heaven and earth will pass away, but my words will not pass away.

The Necessity for Watchfulness

32 "But about that day or hour no one knows, neither the angels in heaven, nor the Son, but only the Father. 33Beware, keep alert;t for you do not know when the time will come. 34It is like a man going on a journey, when he leaves home and puts his slaves in charge, each with his work, and commands the doorkeeper to be on the watch. 35Therefore, keep awake—for you do not know when the master of the

o Gk I am   p Gk gospel   q Or the Christ   r Or christs   s Or it   t Other ancient authorities add and pray

WEEKEND

A Hymn on the Nativity of My Savior

Ben Jonson

Verse: Luke 2.7   **Passage:** Luke 2.1–7

 sing the birth, was born tonight,
  The author both of life, and light;
    The angels so did sound it,
  And like the ravished shepherds said,
Who saw the light, and were afraid,
    Yet searched, and true they found it.

The Son of God, th' Eternal King,
That did us all salvation bring,
    And freed the soul from danger;
He whom the whole world could not take,
The Word, which heaven, and earth did make,
    Was now laid in a manger.

The Father's wisdom willed it so,
The Son's obedience knew no No,
    Both wills were in one stature,
And as that wisdom had decreed,
The Word was now made flesh indeed,
    And took on him our nature.

What comfort by him do we win?
Who made himself the prince of sin,
    To make us heirs of glory?
To see this babe, all innocence;
A martyr born in our defense;
    Can man forget this story?

Additional Scripture Reading:
Isaiah 7.14; Galatians 4.4

Go to page 1180 for your next devotional reading.

1500 🕂 1700

house will come, in the evening, or at midnight, or at cockcrow, or at dawn, **36**or else he may find you asleep when he comes suddenly. **37**And what I say to you I say to all: Keep awake."

The Plot to Kill Jesus

14 It was two days before the Passover and the festival of Unleavened Bread. The chief priests and the scribes were looking for a way to arrest Jesus[u] by stealth and kill him; **2**for they said, "Not during the festival, or there may be a riot among the people."

The Anointing at Bethany

3 While he was at Bethany in the house of Simon the leper,[v] as he sat at the table, a woman came with an alabaster jar of very costly ointment of nard, and she broke open the jar and poured the ointment on his head. **4**But some were there who said to one another in anger, "Why was the ointment wasted in this way? **5**For this ointment could have been sold for more than three hundred denarii,[w] and the money given to the poor." And they scolded her. **6**But Jesus said, "Let her alone; why do you trouble her? She has performed a good service for me. **7**For you always have the poor with you, and you can show kindness to them whenever you wish; but you will not always have me. **8**She has done what she could; she has anointed my body beforehand for its burial. **9**Truly I tell you, wherever the good news[x] is proclaimed in the whole world, what she has done will be told in remembrance of her."

Judas Agrees to Betray Jesus

10 Then Judas Iscariot, who was one of the twelve, went to the chief priests in order to betray him to them. **11**When they heard it, they were greatly pleased, and promised to give him money. So he began to look for an opportunity to betray him.

The Passover with the Disciples

12 On the first day of Unleavened Bread, when the Passover lamb is sacri-ficed, his disciples said to him, "Where do you want us to go and make the preparations for you to eat the Passover?" **13**So he sent two of his disciples, saying to them, "Go into the city, and a man carrying a jar of water will meet you; follow him, **14**and wherever he enters, say to the owner of the house, 'The Teacher asks, Where is my guest room where I may eat the Passover with my disciples?' **15**He will show you a large room upstairs, furnished and ready. Make preparations for us there." **16**So the disciples set out and went to the city, and found everything as he had told them; and they prepared the Passover meal.

17 When it was evening, he came with the twelve. **18**And when they had taken their places and were eating, Jesus said, "Truly I tell you, one of you will betray me, one who is eating with me." **19**They began to be distressed and to say to him one after another, "Surely, not I?" **20**He said to them, "It is one of the twelve, one who is dipping bread[y] into the bowl[z] with me. **21**For the Son of Man goes as it is written of him, but woe to that one by whom the Son of Man is betrayed! It would have been better for that one not to have been born."

The Institution of the Lord's Supper

22 While they were eating, he took a loaf of bread, and after blessing it he broke it, gave it to them, and said, "Take; this is my body." **23**Then he took

---

BREAKING ONE BREAD, WHICH IS THE MEDICINE OF IMMORTALITY, THE ANTIDOTE AGAINST DEATH WHICH GIVES ETERNAL LIFE IN JESUS CHRIST.
                                        —*Irenaeus of Lyons*

---

a cup, and after giving thanks he gave it to them, and all of them drank from it. **24**He said to them, "This is my blood of the[a] covenant, which is poured out for many. **25**Truly I tell you, I will never again drink of the fruit of the vine until that day when I drink it new in the kingdom of God."

---

u Gk *him*   *v* The terms *leper* and *leprosy* can refer to several diseases   *w* The denarius was the usual day's wage for a laborer   *x* Or *gospel*   *y* Gk lacks *bread*   *z* Other ancient authorities read *same bowl*   *a* Other ancient authorities add *new*

Peter's Denial Foretold

26 When they had sung the hymn, they went out to the Mount of Olives. 27 And Jesus said to them, "You will all become deserters; for it is written,

'I will strike the shepherd,
and the sheep will be scattered.'

28 But after I am raised up, I will go before you to Galilee." 29 Peter said to him, "Even though all become deserters, I will not." 30 Jesus said to him, "Truly I tell you, this day, this very night, before the cock crows twice, you will deny me three times." 31 But he said vehemently, "Even though I must die with you, I will not deny you." And all of them said the same.

Jesus Prays in Gethsemane

32 They went to a place called Gethsemane; and he said to his disciples, "Sit here while I pray." 33 He took with him Peter and James and John, and began to be distressed and agitated. 34 And he said to them, "I am deeply grieved, even to death; remain here, and keep awake." 35 And going a little farther, he threw himself on the ground and prayed that,

---

MONDAY

HUMBLY I ADORE THEE, VERITY UNSEEN
Thomas Aquinas

VERSE: Mark 14.22   PASSAGE: Mark 14.22–26

umbly I adore thee, verity unseen,
who thy glory hidest 'neath these shadows mean;
lo, to thee surrendered, my whole heart is bowed,
tranced as it beholds thee, shrined within the cloud.

Taste and touch and vision to discern thee fail;
faith, that comes by hearing, pierces through the veil.
I believe whate'er the Son of God hath told;
what the truth hath spoken, that for truth I hold.

O memorial wondrous of the Lord's own death;
living bread that givest all thy creatures breath,
grant my spirit ever by the life may live,
to my taste thy sweetness never failing give.

Jesus, whom now hidden, I by faith behold,
what my soul doth long for, that thy word foretold:
face to face thy splendor, I at last shall see,
in the glorious vision, blessed Lord, of thee.

ADDITIONAL SCRIPTURE READING:
John 6.48–51; 1 Corinthians 11.23–28

Go to page 1183 for your next devotional reading.

500   1500

if it were possible, the hour might pass from him. 36He said, "Abba,*b* Father, for you all things are possible; remove this cup from me; yet, not what I want, but what you want." 37He came and found them sleeping; and he said to Peter, "Simon, are you asleep? Could you not keep awake one hour? 38Keep awake and pray that you may not come into the time of trial;*c* the spirit indeed is willing, but the flesh is weak." 39And again he went away and prayed, saying the same words. 40And once more he came and found them sleeping, for their eyes were very heavy; and they did not know what to say to him. 41He came a third time and said to them, "Are you still sleeping and taking your rest? Enough! The hour has come; the Son of Man is betrayed into the hands of sinners. 42Get up, let us be going. See, my betrayer is at hand."

The Betrayal and Arrest of Jesus

43 Immediately, while he was still speaking, Judas, one of the twelve, arrived; and with him there was a crowd with swords and clubs, from the chief priests, the scribes, and the elders. 44Now the betrayer had given them a sign, saying, "The one I will kiss is the man; arrest him and lead him away under guard." 45So when he came, he went up to him at once and said, "Rabbi!" and kissed him. 46Then they laid hands on him and arrested him. 47But one of those who stood near drew his sword and struck the slave of the high priest, cutting off his ear. 48Then Jesus said to them, "Have you come out with swords and clubs to arrest me as though I were a bandit? 49Day after day I was with you in the temple teaching, and you did not arrest me. But let the scriptures be fulfilled." 50All of them deserted him and fled.

51 A certain young man was following him, wearing nothing but a linen cloth. They caught hold of him, 52but he left the linen cloth and ran off naked.

Jesus before the Council

53 They took Jesus to the high priest; and all the chief priests, the elders, and the scribes were assembled. 54Peter had followed him at a distance, right into the courtyard of the high priest; and he was sitting with the guards, warming himself at the fire. 55Now the chief priests and the whole council were looking for testimony against Jesus to put him to death; but they found none. 56For many gave false testimony against him, and their testimony did not agree. 57Some stood up and gave false testimony against him, saying, 58"We heard him say, 'I will destroy this temple that is made with hands, and in three days I will build another, not made with hands.' " 59But even on this point their testimony did not agree. 60Then the high priest stood up before them and asked Jesus, "Have you no answer? What is it that they testify against you?" 61But he was silent and did not answer. Again the high priest asked him, "Are you the Messiah,*d* the Son of the Blessed One?" 62Jesus said, "I am; and

'you will see the Son of Man
    seated at the right hand of the
        Power,'
and 'coming with the clouds of
        heaven.' "

63Then the high priest tore his clothes and said, "Why do we still need witnesses? 64You have heard his blasphemy! What is your decision?" All of them condemned him as deserving death. 65Some began to spit on him, to blindfold him, and to strike him, saying to him, "Prophesy!" The guards also took him over and beat him.

Peter Denies Jesus

66 While Peter was below in the courtyard, one of the servant-girls of the high priest came by. 67When she saw Peter warming himself, she stared at him and said, "You also were with Jesus, the man from Nazareth." 68But he denied it, saying, "I do not know or understand what you are talking about." And he went out into the forecourt.*e* Then the cock crowed.*f* 69And the servant-girl, on seeing him, began again to say to the bystanders, "This man is one of them." 70But again he denied it. Then after a little while the bystanders again said to

b Aramaic for *Father*   *c* Or *into temptation*   *d* Or *the Christ*   *e* Or *gateway*   *f* Other ancient authorities lack *Then the cock crowed*

Peter, "Certainly you are one of them; for you are a Galilean." 71But he began to curse, and he swore an oath, "I do not know this man you are talking about." 72At that moment the cock crowed for the second time. Then Peter remembered that Jesus had said to him, "Before the cock crows twice, you will deny me three times." And he broke down and wept.

Jesus before Pilate

15 As soon as it was morning, the chief priests held a consultation with the elders and scribes and the whole council. They bound Jesus, led him away, and handed him over to Pilate. 2Pilate asked him, "Are you the King of the Jews?" He answered him, "You say so." 3Then the chief priests accused him of many things. 4Pilate asked him again, "Have you no answer? See how many charges they bring against you." 5But Jesus made no further reply, so that Pilate was amazed.

Pilate Hands Jesus over to Be Crucified

6 Now at the festival he used to release a prisoner for them, anyone for whom they asked. 7Now a man called Barabbas was in prison with the rebels who had committed murder during the insurrection. 8So the crowd came and began to ask Pilate to do for them according to his custom. 9Then he answered them, "Do you want me to release for you the King of the Jews?" 10For he realized that it was out of jealousy that the chief priests had handed him over. 11But the chief priests stirred up the crowd to have him release Barabbas for them instead. 12Pilate spoke to them again, "Then what do you wish me to do*g* with the man you call*h* the King of the Jews?" 13They shouted back, "Crucify him!" 14Pilate asked them, "Why, what evil has he done?" But they shouted all the more, "Crucify him!" 15So Pilate, wishing to satisfy the crowd, released Barabbas for them; and after flogging Jesus, he handed him over to be crucified.

The Soldiers Mock Jesus

16 Then the soldiers led him into the courtyard of the palace (that is, the governor's headquarters*i*); and they called together the whole cohort. 17And they clothed him in a purple cloak; and after twisting some thorns into a crown, they put it on him. 18And they began saluting him, "Hail, King of the Jews!" 19They struck his head with a reed, spat upon him, and knelt down in homage to him. 20After mocking him, they stripped him of the purple cloak and put his own clothes on him. Then they led him out to crucify him.

The Crucifixion of Jesus

21 They compelled a passer-by, who was coming in from the country, to carry his cross; it was Simon of Cyrene, the father of Alexander and Rufus. 22Then they brought Jesus*j* to the place called Golgotha (which means the place of a skull). 23And they offered him wine mixed with myrrh; but he did not take it. 24And they crucified him, and divided his clothes among them, casting lots to decide what each should take.

25 It was nine o'clock in the morning when they crucified him. 26The inscription of the charge against him read, "The King of the Jews." 27And with him they crucified two bandits, one on his right and one on his left.*k* 29Those who passed by derided*l* him, shaking their heads and saying, "Aha! You who would destroy the temple and build it in three days, 30save yourself, and come down from the cross!" 31In the same way the chief priests, along with the scribes, were also mocking him among themselves and saying, "He saved others; he cannot save himself. 32Let the Messiah,*m* the King of Israel, come down from the cross now, so that we may see and believe." Those who were crucified with him also taunted him.

The Death of Jesus

33 When it was noon, darkness came over the whole land*n* until three in the afternoon. 34At three o'clock Jesus cried

g Other ancient authorities read what should I do   h Other ancient authorities lack the man you call   i Gk the praetorium   j Gk him   k Other ancient authorities add verse 28, And the scripture was fulfilled that says, "And he was counted among the lawless."   l Or blasphemed   m Or the Christ   n Or earth

GOOD FRIDAY, 1613. RIDING WESTWARD
John Donne

VERSE: Mark 15.37   **PASSAGE:** Mark 15.33–41

ence is't, that I am carried towards the West
This day, when my soul's form bends towards the East.
There I should see a sun, by rising, set,
And by that setting endless day beget:
But that Christ on this cross did rise and fall,
Sin had eternally benighted all.
Yet dare I almost be glad I do not see
That spectacle, of too much weight for me.
Who sees God's face, that is self life, must die;
What a death were it then to see God die?
It made his own lieutenant nature, shrink;
It made his footstool crack, and the sun wink.
Could I behold those hands which span the poles,
And tune all spheres at once, pierced with those holes?
Could I behold that endless height which is
Zenith to us, and our Antipodes,
Humbled below us? Or that blood which is
The seat of all our souls, if not of his,
Make dirt of dust, or that flesh which was worn
By God, for his apparel, ragged and torn?
If on these things I durst not look, durst I
Upon his miserable mother cast mine eye,
Who was God's partner here, and furnished thus
Half of that sacrifice which ransomed us?
Though these things, as I ride, be from mine eye,
They are present yet unto my memory,
For that looks towards them; and thou lookst towards me,
O Savior, as thou hangst upon the tree.
I turn my back to thee but to receive
Corrections, till thy mercies bid thee leave.
O think me worth thine anger; punish me;
Burn off my rusts, and my deformity,
Restore thine Image so much, by thy grace
That thou mayst know me, and I'll turn my face.

ADDITIONAL SCRIPTURE READING:
Exodus 40.21; Hebrews 4.14–16

Go to page 1188 for your next devotional reading.

1500   1700

out with a loud voice, "Eloi, Eloi, lema sabachthani?" which means, "My God, my God, why have you forsaken me?"*o* 35When some of the bystanders heard it, they said, "Listen, he is calling for Elijah." 36And someone ran, filled a sponge with sour wine, put it on a stick, and gave it to him to drink, saying, "Wait, let us see whether Elijah will come to take him down." 37Then Jesus gave a loud cry and breathed his last. 38And the curtain of the temple was torn in two, from top to bottom. 39Now when the centurion, who stood facing him, saw that in this way he*p* breathed his last, he said, "Truly this man was God's Son!"*q*

40 There were also women looking on from a distance; among them were Mary Magdalene, and Mary the mother of James the younger and of Joses, and Salome. 41These used to follow him and provided for him when he was in Galilee; and there were many other women who had come up with him to Jerusalem.

The Burial of Jesus

42 When evening had come, and since it was the day of Preparation, that is, the day before the sabbath, 43Joseph of Arimathea, a respected member of the council, who was also himself waiting expectantly for the kingdom of God, went boldly to Pilate and asked for the body of Jesus. 44Then Pilate wondered if he were already dead; and summoning the centurion, he asked him whether he had been dead for some time. 45When he learned from the centurion that he was dead, he granted the body to Joseph. 46Then Joseph*r* bought a linen cloth, and taking down the body,*s* wrapped it in the linen cloth, and laid it in a tomb that had been hewn out of the rock. He then rolled a stone against the door of the tomb. 47Mary Magdalene and Mary the mother of Joses saw where the body*s* was laid.

The Resurrection of Jesus

16 When the sabbath was over, Mary Magdalene, and Mary

the mother of James, and Salome bought spices, so that they might go and anoint him. 2And very early on the first day of the week, when the sun had risen, they went to the tomb. 3They had been saying to one another, "Who will roll away the stone for us from the entrance to the tomb?" 4When they looked up, they saw that the stone, which was very large, had already been rolled back. 5As they entered the tomb, they saw a young man, dressed in a white robe, sitting on the right side; and they were alarmed. 6But he said to them, "Do not be alarmed; you are looking for Jesus of Nazareth, who was crucified. He has been raised; he is not here. Look, there is the place they laid him. 7But go, tell his disciples and Peter that he is going ahead of you to Galilee; there you will see him, just as he told you." 8So they went out and fled from the tomb, for terror and amazement had seized them; and they said nothing to anyone, for they were afraid.*t*

THE SHORTER ENDING OF MARK

⟦And all that had been commanded them they told briefly to those around Peter. And afterward Jesus himself sent out through them, from east to west, the sacred and imperishable proclamation of eternal salvation.*u*⟧

THE LONGER ENDING OF MARK

Jesus Appears to Mary Magdalene

9 ⟦Now after he rose early on the first day of the week, he appeared first to Mary Magdalene, from whom he had cast out seven demons. 10She went out and told those who had been with him, while they were mourning and weeping. 11But when they heard that he was alive and had been seen by her, they would not believe it.

Jesus Appears to Two Disciples

12 After this he appeared in another form to two of them, as they were walk-

---

o Other ancient authorities read *made me a reproach*   *p* Other ancient authorities add *cried out and* *q* Or *a son of God*   *r* Gk *he*   *s* Gk *it*   *t* Some of the most ancient authorities bring the book to a close at the end of verse 8. One authority concludes the book with the shorter ending; others include the shorter ending and then continue with verses 9-20. In most authorities verses 9-20 follow immediately after verse 8, though in some of these authorities the passage is marked as being doubtful.   *u* Other ancient authorities add *Amen*

ing into the country. 13 And they went back and told the rest, but they did not believe them.

Jesus Commissions the Disciples

14 Later he appeared to the eleven themselves as they were sitting at the table; and he upbraided them for their lack of faith and stubbornness, because they had not believed those who saw him after he had risen.ᵛ 15 And he said to them, "Go into all the world and proclaim the good newsʷ to the whole creation. 16 The one who believes and is baptized will be saved; but the one who does not believe will be condemned. 17 And these signs will accompany those who believe: by using my name they will cast out demons; they will speak in new tongues; 18 they will pick up snakes in their hands,ˣ and if they drink any deadly thing, it will not hurt them; they will lay their hands on the sick, and they will recover."

The Ascension of Jesus

19 So then the Lord Jesus, after he had spoken to them, was taken up into heaven and sat down at the right hand of God. 20 And they went out and proclaimed the good news everywhere, while the Lord worked with them and confirmed the message by the signs that accompanied it.ʸ]]

---

v Other ancient authorities add, in whole or in part, And they excused themselves, saying, "This age of lawlessness and unbelief is under Satan, who does not allow the truth and power of God to prevail over the unclean things of the spirits. Therefore reveal your righteousness now"—thus they spoke to Christ. And Christ replied to them, "The term of years of Satan's power has been fulfilled, but other terrible things draw near. And for those who have sinned I was handed over to death, that they may return to the truth and sin no more, that they may inherit the spiritual and imperishable glory of righteousness that is in heaven."   w Or gospel   x Other ancient authorities lack in their hands   y Other ancient authorities add Amen

LUKE

LUKE WRITES HIS GOSPEL TO SHARE THE GOOD NEWS OF SALVATION—A MESSAGE INTENDED FOR EVERYONE. A PHYSICIAN BY PROFESSION, LUKE DISPLAYS GOOD "BEDSIDE MANNERS" BY SHOWING COMPASSION FOR PEOPLE CONSIDERED OUTCASTS, INCLUDING TAX COLLECTORS, WOMEN, CHILDREN AND THE POOR. NOT ONLY DOES LUKE SHOW GREAT REGARD FOR PEOPLE, BUT HE ALSO SHOWS A DEEP CONCERN FOR PRAYER, DISCIPLESHIP, JOY AND THE MINISTRY OF THE SPIRIT. AS YOU READ LUKE'S ACCOUNT OF THE LIFE OF JESUS, MAY YOU BE LIKE HIM WHO "REJOICED IN THE HOLY SPIRIT" (10.21).

Dedication to Theophilus

1 Since many have undertaken to set down an orderly account of the events that have been fulfilled among us, ²just as they were handed on to us by those who from the beginning were eyewitnesses and servants of the word, ³I too decided, after investigating everything carefully from the very first,ᵃ to write an orderly account for you, most excellent Theophilus, ⁴so that you may know the truth concerning the things about which you have been instructed.

The Birth of John the Baptist Foretold

5 In the days of King Herod of Judea, there was a priest named Zechariah, who belonged to the priestly order of Abijah. His wife was a descendant of Aaron, and her name was Elizabeth. ⁶Both of them were righteous before God, living blamelessly according to all the commandments and regulations of the Lord. ⁷But they had no children, because Elizabeth was barren, and both were getting on in years.

8 Once when he was serving as priest before God and his section was on duty, ⁹he was chosen by lot, according to the custom of the priesthood, to enter the sanctuary of the Lord and offer incense. ¹⁰Now at the time of the incense offering, the whole assembly of the people was praying outside. ¹¹Then there appeared to him an angel of the Lord, standing at the right side of the altar of

a Or *for a long time*

incense. 12When Zechariah saw him, he was terrified; and fear overwhelmed him. 13But the angel said to him, "Do not be afraid, Zechariah, for your prayer has been heard. Your wife Elizabeth will bear you a son, and you will name him John. 14You will have joy and gladness, and many will rejoice at his birth, 15for he will be great in the sight of the Lord. He must never drink wine or strong drink; even before his birth he will be filled with the Holy Spirit. 16He will turn many of the people of Israel to the Lord their God. 17With the spirit and power of Elijah he will go before him, to turn the hearts of parents to their children, and the disobedient to the wisdom of the righteous, to make ready a people prepared for the Lord." 18Zechariah said to the angel, "How will I know that this is so? For I am an old man, and my wife is getting on in years." 19The angel replied, "I am Gabriel. I stand in the presence of God, and I have been sent to speak to you and to bring you this good news. 20But now, because you did not believe my words, which will be fulfilled in their time, you will become mute, unable to speak, until the day these things occur."

21 Meanwhile the people were waiting for Zechariah, and wondered at his delay in the sanctuary. 22When he did come out, he could not speak to them, and they realized that he had seen a vision in the sanctuary. He kept motioning to them and remained unable to speak. 23When his time of service was ended, he went to his home.

24 After those days his wife Elizabeth conceived, and for five months she remained in seclusion. She said, 25"This is what the Lord has done for me when he looked favorably on me and took away the disgrace I have endured among my people."

The Birth of Jesus Foretold

26 In the sixth month the angel Gabriel was sent by God to a town in Galilee called Nazareth, 27to a virgin engaged to a man whose name was Joseph, of the house of David. The virgin's name was Mary. 28And he came to her and said,

"Greetings, favored one! The Lord is with you."b 29But she was much perplexed by his words and pondered what sort of greeting this might be. 30The angel said to her, "Do not be afraid, Mary, for you have found favor with God. 31And now, you will conceive in your womb and bear a son, and you will name him Jesus. 32He will be great, and will be called the Son of the Most High, and the Lord God will give to him the throne of his ancestor David. 33He will reign over the house of Jacob forever, and of his kingdom there will be no end." 34Mary said to the angel, "How can this be, since I am a virgin?"c 35The angel said to her, "The Holy Spirit will come upon you, and the power of the Most High will overshadow you; therefore the child to be bornd will be holy; he will be called Son of God. 36And now, your relative Elizabeth in her old age has also conceived a son; and this is the sixth month for her who was said to be barren. 37For nothing will be impossible with God." 38Then Mary said, "Here am I, the servant of the Lord; let it be with me according to your word." Then the angel departed from her.

Mary Visits Elizabeth

39 In those days Mary set out and went with haste to a Judean town in the hill country, 40where she entered the house of Zechariah and greeted Elizabeth. 41When Elizabeth heard Mary's greeting, the child leaped in her womb. And Elizabeth was filled with the Holy Spirit 42and exclaimed with a loud cry, "Blessed are you among women, and blessed is the fruit of your womb. 43And why has this happened to me, that the mother of my Lord comes to me? 44For as soon as I heard the sound of your greeting, the child in my womb leaped for joy. 45And blessed is she who believed that there would bee a fulfillment of what was spoken to her by the Lord."

Mary's Song of Praise

46 And Maryf said,
"My soul magnifies the Lord,
47   and my spirit rejoices in God my Savior,

---

b Other ancient authorities add *Blessed are you among women*   c Gk *I do not know a man*
d Other ancient authorities add *of you*   e Or *believed, for there will be*   f Other ancient authorities read *Elizabeth*

48   for he has looked with favor on the
      lowliness of his servant.
     Surely, from now on all
      generations will call me
      blessed;
49   for the Mighty One has done great
      things for me,
     and holy is his name.
50   His mercy is for those who fear him
     from generation to generation.
51   He has shown strength with his
      arm;
     he has scattered the proud in the
      thoughts of their hearts.
52   He has brought down the powerful
      from their thrones,
     and lifted up the lowly;

53   he has filled the hungry with good
      things,
     and sent the rich away empty.
54   He has helped his servant Israel,
     in remembrance of his mercy,
55   according to the promise he made
      to our ancestors,
     to Abraham and to his
      descendants forever."

56 And Mary remained with her about three months and then returned to her home.

The Birth of John the Baptist

57 Now the time came for Elizabeth to give birth, and she bore a son. 58 Her neighbors and relatives heard that the

WEDNESDAY

A GOD-MAN BORN OF A VIRGIN WOMAN
Anselm of Canterbury

VERSE: Luke 1.26–27   **PASSAGE:** Luke 1.26–38

 xercise your pictorial art, then, not on an empty fiction, but upon a solid truth, and say that it is extremely fitting that, as the sin of man and the cause of our condemnation took their origin from a woman, so the cure for sin and the cause of our salvation must be born of a woman. And so that women may not despair of attaining to the lot of the blessed, because such great evil has issued from a woman, it was fitting that such a great good should issue from a woman, to revitalize their hope. Add this to your painting: If it was a virgin who was the cause of all evil to the human race, it is far more fitting that it be a virgin who will be the cause of all good. Depict this also: If the woman whom God made from a man without a woman was made from a virgin, it is also extremely fitting that the man who will originate from a woman without a man be born of a virgin. But for the present let these examples suffice of the pictures that can be depicted on the fact that the God-man must be born of a virgin woman.

ADDITIONAL SCRIPTURE READING:
Genesis 3.11–13; Luke 1.46–55

Go to page 1196 for your next devotional reading.

500   1500

Lord had shown his great mercy to her, and they rejoiced with her.

59 On the eighth day they came to circumcise the child, and they were going to name him Zechariah after his father. 60But his mother said, "No; he is to be called John." 61They said to her, "None of your relatives has this name." 62Then they began motioning to his father to find out what name he wanted to give him. 63He asked for a writing tablet and wrote, "His name is John." And all of them were amazed. 64Immediately his mouth was opened and his tongue freed, and he began to speak, praising God. 65Fear came over all their neighbors, and all these things were talked about throughout the entire hill country of Judea. 66All who heard them pondered them and said, "What then will this child become?" For, indeed, the hand of the Lord was with him.

Zechariah's Prophecy

67 Then his father Zechariah was filled with the Holy Spirit and spoke this prophecy:
68 "Blessed be the Lord God of Israel,
    for he has looked favorably on his
        people and redeemed them.
69 He has raised up a mighty savior*g*
    for us
    in the house of his servant David,
70 as he spoke through the mouth of
    his holy prophets from of old,
71 that we would be saved from our
    enemies and from the hand
    of all who hate us.
72 Thus he has shown the mercy
    promised to our ancestors,
    and has remembered his holy
      covenant,
73 the oath that he swore to our
    ancestor Abraham,
    to grant us 74that we, being
      rescued from the hands of
      our enemies,
    might serve him without fear, 75in
      holiness and righteousness
    before him all our days.
76 And you, child, will be called the
    prophet of the Most High;
    for you will go before the Lord to
      prepare his ways,

77 to give knowledge of salvation to
    his people
    by the forgiveness of their sins.
78 By the tender mercy of our God,
    the dawn from on high will break
      upon*h* us,
79 to give light to those who sit in
    darkness and in the shadow
    of death,
    to guide our feet into the way of
      peace."

80 The child grew and became strong in spirit, and he was in the wilderness until the day he appeared publicly to Israel.

The Birth of Jesus

2 In those days a decree went out from Emperor Augustus that all the world should be registered. 2This was the first registration and was taken while Quirinius was governor of Syria. 3All went to their own towns to be registered. 4Joseph also went from the town of Nazareth in Galilee to Judea, to the city of David called Bethlehem, because he was descended from the house and family of David. 5He went to be registered with Mary, to whom he was engaged and who was expecting a child. 6While they were there, the time came for her to deliver her child. 7And she gave birth to her firstborn son and wrapped him in bands of cloth, and laid him in a manger, because there was no place for them in the inn.

The Shepherds and the Angels

8 In that region there were shepherds living in the fields, keeping watch over their flock by night. 9Then an angel of the Lord stood before them, and the glory of the Lord shone around them, and they were terrified. 10But the angel said to them, "Do not be afraid; for see— I am bringing you good news of great joy for all the people: 11to you is born this day in the city of David a Savior, who is the Messiah,*i* the Lord. 12This will be a sign for you: you will find a child wrapped in bands of cloth and lying in a manger." 13And suddenly there was with the angel a multitude of the heavenly host,*j* praising God and saying,

g Gk *a horn of salvation*   *h* Other ancient authorities read *has broken upon*   *i* Or *the Christ*   *j* Gk *army*

14   "Glory to God in the highest
            heaven,
     and on earth peace among those
            whom he favors!"[k]

15 When the angels had left them and gone into heaven, the shepherds said to one another, "Let us go now to Bethlehem and see this thing that has taken place, which the Lord has made known to us." [16]So they went with haste and found Mary and Joseph, and the child lying in the manger. [17]When they saw this, they made known what had been told them about this child; [18]and all who heard it were amazed at what the shepherds told them. [19]But Mary treasured all these words and pondered them in her heart. [20]The shepherds returned, glorifying and praising God for all they had heard and seen, as it had been told them.

Jesus Is Named

21 After eight days had passed, it was time to circumcise the child; and he was called Jesus, the name given by the angel before he was conceived in the womb.

Jesus Is Presented in the Temple

22 When the time came for their purification according to the law of Moses, they brought him up to Jerusalem to present him to the Lord [23](as it is written in the law of the Lord, "Every firstborn male shall be designated as holy to the Lord"), [24]and they offered a sacrifice according to what is stated in the law of the Lord, "a pair of turtledoves or two young pigeons."

25 Now there was a man in Jerusalem whose name was Simeon;[l] this man was righteous and devout, looking forward to the consolation of Israel, and the Holy Spirit rested on him. [26]It had been revealed to him by the Holy Spirit that he would not see death before he had seen the Lord's Messiah.[m] [27]Guided by the Spirit, Simeon[n] came into the temple; and when the parents brought in the child Jesus, to do for him what was customary under the law, [28]Simeon[o] took him in his arms and praised God, saying,

29   "Master, now you are dismissing
            your servant[p] in peace,
       according to your word;
30   for my eyes have seen your
            salvation,
31   which you have prepared in the
            presence of all peoples,
32   a light for revelation to the
            Gentiles
       and for glory to your people
            Israel."

33 And the child's father and mother were amazed at what was being said about him. [34]Then Simeon[l] blessed them and said to his mother Mary, "This child is destined for the falling and the rising of many in Israel, and to be a sign that will be opposed [35]so that the inner thoughts of many will be revealed—and a sword will pierce your own soul too."

36 There was also a prophet, Anna[q] the daughter of Phanuel, of the tribe of Asher. She was of a great age, having lived with her husband seven years after her marriage, [37]then as a widow to the age of eighty-four. She never left the temple but worshiped there with fasting and prayer night and day. [38]At that moment she came, and began to praise God and to speak about the child[r] to all who were looking for the redemption of Jerusalem.

The Return to Nazareth

39 When they had finished everything required by the law of the Lord, they returned to Galilee, to their own town of Nazareth. [40]The child grew and became strong, filled with wisdom; and the favor of God was upon him.

The Boy Jesus in the Temple

41 Now every year his parents went to Jerusalem for the festival of the Passover. [42]And when he was twelve years old, they went up as usual for the festival. [43]When the festival was ended and they started to return, the boy Jesus stayed behind in Jerusalem, but his parents did not know it. [44]Assuming that he was in the group of travelers, they went a day's journey. Then they started to look for him among their relatives

---

k Other ancient authorities read peace, goodwill among people   l Gk Symeon   m Or the Lord's Christ   n Gk In the Spirit, he   o Gk he   p Gk slave   q Gk Hanna   r Gk him

and friends. [45]When they did not find him, they returned to Jerusalem to search for him. [46]After three days they found him in the temple, sitting among the teachers, listening to them and asking them questions. [47]And all who heard him were amazed at his understanding and his answers. [48]When his parents[s] saw him they were astonished; and his mother said to him, "Child, why have you treated us like this? Look, your father and I have been searching for you in great anxiety." [49]He said to them, "Why were you searching for me? Did you not know that I must be in my Father's house?"[t] [50]But they did not understand what he said to them. [51]Then he went down with them and came to Nazareth, and was obedient to them. His mother treasured all these things in her heart.

[52] And Jesus increased in wisdom and in years,[u] and in divine and human favor.

The Proclamation of John the Baptist

3 In the fifteenth year of the reign of Emperor Tiberius, when Pontius Pilate was governor of Judea, and Herod was ruler[v] of Galilee, and his brother Philip ruler[v] of the region of Ituraea and Trachonitis, and Lysanias ruler[v] of Abilene, [2]during the high priesthood of Annas and Caiaphas, the word of God came to John son of Zechariah in the wilderness. [3]He went into all the region around the Jordan, proclaiming a baptism of repentance for the forgiveness of sins, [4]as it is written in the book of the words of the prophet Isaiah,

"The voice of one crying out in the wilderness:
'Prepare the way of the Lord,
    make his paths straight.
[5] Every valley shall be filled,
    and every mountain and hill
        shall be made low,
and the crooked shall be made
        straight,
    and the rough ways made
        smooth;
[6] and all flesh shall see the salvation
        of God.' "

[7] John said to the crowds that came out to be baptized by him, "You brood of vipers! Who warned you to flee from the wrath to come? [8]Bear fruits worthy of repentance. Do not begin to say to yourselves, 'We have Abraham as our ancestor'; for I tell you, God is able from these stones to raise up children to Abraham. [9]Even now the ax is lying at the root of the trees; every tree therefore that does not bear good fruit is cut down and thrown into the fire."

[10] And the crowds asked him, "What then should we do?" [11]In reply he said to them, "Whoever has two coats must share with anyone who has none; and whoever has food must do likewise." [12]Even tax collectors came to be baptized, and they asked him, "Teacher, what should we do?" [13]He said to them, "Collect no more than the amount prescribed for you." [14]Soldiers also asked him, "And we, what should we do?" He said to them, "Do not extort money from anyone by threats or false accusation, and be satisfied with your wages."

[15] As the people were filled with expectation, and all were questioning in their hearts concerning John, whether he might be the Messiah,[w] [16]John answered all of them by saying, "I baptize you with water; but one who is more powerful than I is coming; I am not worthy to untie the thong of his sandals. He will baptize you with[x] the Holy Spirit and fire. [17]His winnowing fork is in his hand, to clear his threshing floor and to gather the wheat into his granary; but the chaff he will burn with unquenchable fire."

[18] So, with many other exhortations, he proclaimed the good news to the people. [19]But Herod the ruler,[v] who had been rebuked by him because of Herodias, his brother's wife, and because of all the evil things that Herod had done, [20]added to them all by shutting up John in prison.

The Baptism of Jesus

[21] Now when all the people were baptized, and when Jesus also had been baptized and was praying, the heaven was opened, [22]and the Holy Spirit descended upon him in bodily form like a

---

s Gk *they*   t Or *be about my Father's interests?*   u Or *in stature*   v Gk *tetrarch*   w Or *the Christ*   x Or *in*

dove. And a voice came from heaven, "You are my Son, the Beloved;[y] with you I am well pleased."[z]

The Ancestors of Jesus

23 Jesus was about thirty years old when he began his work. He was the son (as was thought) of Joseph son of Heli, [24]son of Matthat, son of Levi, son of Melchi, son of Jannai, son of Joseph, [25]son of Mattathias, son of Amos, son of Nahum, son of Esli, son of Naggai, [26]son of Maath, son of Mattathias, son of Semein, son of Josech, son of Joda, [27]son of Joanan, son of Rhesa, son of Zerubbabel, son of Shealtiel,[a] son of Neri, [28]son of Melchi, son of Addi, son of Cosam, son of Elmadam, son of Er, [29]son of Joshua, son of Eliezer, son of Jorim, son of Matthat, son of Levi, [30]son of Simeon, son of Judah, son of Joseph, son of Jonam, son of Eliakim, [31]son of Melea, son of Menna, son of Mattatha, son of Nathan, son of David, [32]son of Jesse, son of Obed, son of Boaz, son of Sala,[b] son of Nahshon, [33]son of Amminadab, son of Admin, son of Arni,[c] son of Hezron, son of Perez, son of Judah, [34]son of Jacob, son of Isaac, son of Abraham, son of Terah, son of Nahor, [35]son of Serug, son of Reu, son of Peleg, son of Eber, son of Shelah, [36]son of Cainan, son of Arphaxad, son of Shem, son of Noah, son of Lamech, [37]son of Methuselah, son of Enoch, son of Jared, son of Mahalaleel, son of Cainan, [38]son of Enos, son of Seth, son of Adam, son of God.

The Temptation of Jesus

4 Jesus, full of the Holy Spirit, returned from the Jordan and was led by the Spirit in the wilderness, [2]where for forty days he was tempted by the devil. He ate nothing at all during those days, and when they were over, he was famished. [3]The devil said to him, "If you are the Son of God, command this stone to become a loaf of bread." [4]Jesus answered him, "It is written, 'One does not live by bread alone.' "

5 Then the devil[d] led him up and showed him in an instant all the kingdoms of the world. [6]And the devil[d] said

to him, "To you I will give their glory and all this authority; for it has been given over to me, and I give it to anyone I please. [7]If you, then, will worship me, it will all be yours." [8]Jesus answered him, "It is written,

'Worship the Lord your God,
    and serve only him.' "

9 Then the devil[d] took him to Jerusalem, and placed him on the pinnacle of the temple, saying to him, "If you are the Son of God, throw yourself down from here, [10]for it is written,

'He will command his angels
        concerning you,
    to protect you,'

[11]and

'On their hands they will bear you
        up,
    so that you will not dash your
        foot against a stone.' "

[12]Jesus answered him, "It is said, 'Do not put the Lord your God to the test.' " [13]When the devil had finished every test, he departed from him until an opportune time.

The Beginning of the Galilean Ministry

14 Then Jesus, filled with the power of the Spirit, returned to Galilee, and a report about him spread through all the surrounding country. [15]He began to teach in their synagogues and was praised by everyone.

The Rejection of Jesus at Nazareth

16 When he came to Nazareth, where he had been brought up, he went to the synagogue on the sabbath day, as was his custom. He stood up to read, [17]and the scroll of the prophet Isaiah was given to him. He unrolled the scroll and found the place where it was written:
[18]   "The Spirit of the Lord is upon me,
        because he has anointed me
            to bring good news to the poor.
    He has sent me to proclaim release
            to the captives
        and recovery of sight to the blind,
            to let the oppressed go free,
[19]   to proclaim the year of the Lord's
            favor."

---

y Or *my beloved Son*   z Other ancient authorities read *You are my Son, today I have begotten you*   a Gk *Salathiel*   b Other ancient authorities read *Salmon*   c Other ancient authorities read *Amminadab, son of Aram*; others vary widely   d Gk *he*

20And he rolled up the scroll, gave it back to the attendant, and sat down. The eyes of all in the synagogue were fixed on him. 21Then he began to say to them, "Today this scripture has been fulfilled in your hearing." 22All spoke well of him and were amazed at the gracious words that came from his mouth. They said, "Is not this Joseph's son?" 23He said to them, "Doubtless you will quote to me this proverb, 'Doctor, cure yourself!' And you will say, 'Do here also in your hometown the things that we have heard you did at Capernaum.' " 24And he said, "Truly I tell you, no prophet is accepted in the prophet's hometown. 25But the truth is, there were many widows in Israel in the time of Elijah, when the heaven was shut up three years and six months, and there was a severe famine over all the land; 26yet Elijah was sent to none of them except to a widow at Zarephath in Sidon. 27There were also many lepers*e* in Israel in the time of the prophet Elisha, and none of them was cleansed except Naaman the Syrian." 28When they heard this, all in the synagogue were filled with rage. 29They got up, drove him out of the town, and led him to the brow of the hill on which their town was built, so that they might hurl him off the cliff. 30But he passed through the midst of them and went on his way.

The Man with an Unclean Spirit

31 He went down to Capernaum, a city in Galilee, and was teaching them on the sabbath. 32They were astounded at his teaching, because he spoke with authority. 33In the synagogue there was a man who had the spirit of an unclean demon, and he cried out with a loud voice, 34"Let us alone! What have you to do with us, Jesus of Nazareth? Have you come to destroy us? I know who you are, the Holy One of God." 35But Jesus rebuked him, saying, "Be silent, and come out of him!" When the demon had thrown him down before them, he came out of him without having done him any harm. 36They were all amazed and kept saying to one another, "What kind of utterance is this? For with authority

and power he commands the unclean spirits, and out they come!" 37And a report about him began to reach every place in the region.

Healings at Simon's House

38 After leaving the synagogue he entered Simon's house. Now Simon's mother-in-law was suffering from a high fever, and they asked him about her. 39Then he stood over her and rebuked the fever, and it left her. Immediately she got up and began to serve them.

40 As the sun was setting, all those who had any who were sick with various kinds of diseases brought them to him; and he laid his hands on each of them and cured them. 41Demons also came out of many, shouting, "You are the Son of God!" But he rebuked them and would not allow them to speak, because they knew that he was the Messiah.*f*

Jesus Preaches in the Synagogues

42 At daybreak he departed and went into a deserted place. And the crowds were looking for him; and when they reached him, they wanted to prevent him from leaving them. 43But he said to them, "I must proclaim the good news of the kingdom of God to the other cities also; for I was sent for this purpose." 44So he continued proclaiming the message in the synagogues of Judea.*g*

Jesus Calls the First Disciples

5 Once while Jesus*h* was standing beside the lake of Gennesaret, and the crowd was pressing in on him to hear the word of God, 2he saw two boats there at the shore of the lake; the fishermen had gone out of them and were washing their nets. 3He got into one of the boats, the one belonging to Simon, and asked him to put out a little way from the shore. Then he sat down and taught the crowds from the boat. 4When he had finished speaking, he said to Simon, "Put out into the deep water and let down your nets for a catch." 5Simon answered, "Master, we have worked all night long but have caught nothing. Yet if you say so, I will let down the nets."

---

e The terms *leper* and *leprosy* can refer to several diseases   *f* Or *the Christ*   *g* Other ancient authorities read *Galilee*   *h* Gk *he*

6When they had done this, they caught so many fish that their nets were beginning to break. 7So they signaled their partners in the other boat to come and help them. And they came and filled both boats, so that they began to sink. 8But when Simon Peter saw it, he fell down at Jesus' knees, saying, "Go away from me, Lord, for I am a sinful man!" 9For he and all who were with him were amazed at the catch of fish that they had taken; 10and so also were James and John, sons of Zebedee, who were partners with Simon. Then Jesus said to Simon, "Do not be afraid; from now on you will be catching people." 11When they had brought their boats to shore, they left everything and followed him.

Jesus Cleanses a Leper

12 Once, when he was in one of the cities, there was a man covered with leprosy.[i] When he saw Jesus, he bowed with his face to the ground and begged him, "Lord, if you choose, you can make me clean." 13Then Jesus[j] stretched out his hand, touched him, and said, "I do choose. Be made clean." Immediately the leprosy[i] left him. 14And he ordered him to tell no one. "Go," he said, "and show yourself to the priest, and, as Moses commanded, make an offering for your cleansing, for a testimony to them." 15But now more than ever the word about Jesus[k] spread abroad; many crowds would gather to hear him and to be cured of their diseases. 16But he would withdraw to deserted places and pray.

Jesus Heals a Paralytic

17 One day, while he was teaching, Pharisees and teachers of the law were sitting near by (they had come from every village of Galilee and Judea and from Jerusalem); and the power of the Lord was with him to heal.[l] 18Just then some men came, carrying a paralyzed man on a bed. They were trying to bring him in and lay him before Jesus;[k] 19but finding no way to bring him in because of the crowd, they went up on the roof and let him down with his bed through the tiles into the middle of the crowd[m]

in front of Jesus. 20When he saw their faith, he said, "Friend,[n] your sins are forgiven you." 21Then the scribes and the Pharisees began to question, "Who is this who is speaking blasphemies? Who can forgive sins but God alone?" 22When Jesus perceived their questionings, he answered them, "Why do you raise such questions in your hearts? 23Which is easier, to say, 'Your sins are forgiven you,' or to say, 'Stand up and walk'? 24But so that you may know that the Son of Man has authority on earth to forgive sins"—he said to the one who was paralyzed—"I say to you, stand up and take your bed and go to your home." 25Immediately he stood up before them, took what he had been lying on, and went to his home, glorifying God. 26Amazement seized all of them, and they glorified God and were filled with awe, saying, "We have seen strange things today."

Jesus Calls Levi

27 After this he went out and saw a tax collector named Levi, sitting at the tax booth; and he said to him, "Follow me." 28And he got up, left everything, and followed him.

29 Then Levi gave a great banquet for him in his house; and there was a large crowd of tax collectors and others sitting at the table[o] with them. 30The Pharisees and their scribes were complaining to his disciples, saying, "Why do you eat and drink with tax collectors and sinners?" 31Jesus answered, "Those who are well have no need of a physician, but those who are sick; 32I have come to call not the righteous but sinners to repentance."

The Question about Fasting

33 Then they said to him, "John's disciples, like the disciples of the Pharisees, frequently fast and pray, but your disciples eat and drink." 34Jesus said to them, "You cannot make wedding guests fast while the bridegroom is with them, can you? 35The days will come when the bridegroom will be taken away from them, and then they will fast in those days." 36He also told them a parable:

---

i The terms *leper* and *leprosy* can refer to several diseases   j Gk *he*   k Gk *him*   l Other ancient authorities read *was present to heal them*   m Gk *into the midst*   n Gk *Man*   o Gk *reclining*

"No one tears a piece from a new garment and sews it on an old garment; otherwise the new will be torn, and the piece from the new will not match the old. 37And no one puts new wine into old wineskins; otherwise the new wine will burst the skins and will be spilled, and the skins will be destroyed. 38But new wine must be put into fresh wineskins. 39And no one after drinking old wine desires new wine, but says, 'The old is good.' "*p*

The Question about the Sabbath

6 One sabbath*q* while Jesus*r* was going through the grainfields, his disciples plucked some heads of grain, rubbed them in their hands, and ate them. 2But some of the Pharisees said, "Why are you doing what is not lawful*s* on the sabbath?" 3Jesus answered, "Have you not read what David did when he and his companions were hungry? 4He entered the house of God and took and ate the bread of the Presence, which it is not lawful for any but the priests to eat, and gave some to his companions?" 5Then he said to them, "The Son of Man is lord of the sabbath."

The Man with a Withered Hand

6 On another sabbath he entered the synagogue and taught, and there was a man there whose right hand was withered. 7The scribes and the Pharisees watched him to see whether he would cure on the sabbath, so that they might find an accusation against him. 8Even though he knew what they were thinking, he said to the man who had the withered hand, "Come and stand here." He got up and stood there. 9Then Jesus said to them, "I ask you, is it lawful to do good or to do harm on the sabbath, to save life or to destroy it?" 10After looking around at all of them, he said to him, "Stretch out your hand." He did so, and his hand was restored. 11But they were filled with fury and discussed with one another what they might do to Jesus.

Jesus Chooses the Twelve Apostles

12 Now during those days he went out to the mountain to pray; and he spent the night in prayer to God. 13And when day came, he called his disciples and chose twelve of them, whom he also named apostles: 14Simon, whom he named Peter, and his brother Andrew, and James, and John, and Philip, and Bartholomew, 15and Matthew, and Thomas, and James son of Alphaeus, and Simon, who was called the Zealot, 16and Judas son of James, and Judas Iscariot, who became a traitor.

Jesus Teaches and Heals

17 He came down with them and stood on a level place, with a great crowd of his disciples and a great multitude of people from all Judea, Jerusalem, and the coast of Tyre and Sidon. 18They had come to hear him and to be healed of their diseases; and those who were troubled with unclean spirits were cured. 19And all in the crowd were trying to touch him, for power came out from him and healed all of them.

Blessings and Woes

20 Then he looked up at his disciples and said:
"Blessed are you who are poor,
    for yours is the kingdom of God.
21 "Blessed are you who are hungry
        now,
    for you will be filled.
"Blessed are you who weep now,
    for you will laugh.
22 "Blessed are you when people hate you, and when they exclude you, revile you, and defame you*t* on account of the Son of Man. 23Rejoice in that day and leap for joy, for surely your reward is great in heaven; for that is what their ancestors did to the prophets.
24 "But woe to you who are rich,
        for you have received your
            consolation.
25 "Woe to you who are full now,
    for you will be hungry.
"Woe to you who are laughing
        now,
    for you will mourn and weep.
26 "Woe to you when all speak well

---

p Other ancient authorities read *better*; others lack verse 39   *q* Other ancient authorities read *On the second first sabbath*   *r* Gk *he*   *s* Other ancient authorities add *to do*   *t* Gk *cast out your name as evil*

of you, for that is what their ancestors did to the false prophets.

Love for Enemies

27 "But I say to you that listen, Love your enemies, do good to those who hate you, 28bless those who curse you, pray for those who abuse you. 29If anyone strikes you on the cheek, offer the other also; and from anyone who takes away your coat do not withhold even your shirt. 30Give to everyone who begs from you; and if anyone takes away your goods, do not ask for them again. 31Do to others as you would have them do to you.

32 "If you love those who love you, what credit is that to you? For even sinners love those who love them. 33If you do good to those who do good to you,

---

THURSDAY

PRAYER OF A PEACEMAKER
Martin Luther King, Jr.

VERSE: Luke 6.31   **PASSAGE:** Luke 6.27–36

 God, our Heavenly Father, we thank thee for this golden privilege to worship thee, the only true God of the universe. We come to thee today, grateful that thou hast kept us through the long night of the past and ushered us into the challenge of the present and the bright hope of the future. We are mindful, O God, that man cannot save himself, for man is not the measure of things and humanity is not God. Bound by our chains of sins and finiteness, we know we need a Savior. We thank thee, O God, for the spiritual nature of man. We are in nature but we live above nature. Help us never to let anybody or any condition pull us so low as to cause us to hate. Give us strength to love our enemies and to do good to those who despitefully use us and persecute us. We thank thee for thy church, founded upon thy Word, that challenges us to do more than sing and pray, but go out and work as though the very answer to our prayers depended on us and not upon thee. Then, finally, help us to realize that man was created to shine like stars and live on through all eternity. Keep us, we pray, in perfect peace, help us to walk together, pray together, sing together, and live together until that day when all God's children, Black, White, Red, and Yellow will rejoice in one common band of humanity in the kingdom of our Lord and of our God, we pray. Amen.

ADDITIONAL SCRIPTURE READING:
Matthew 5.9; Titus 3.1–2

Go to page 1199 for your next devotional reading.

1900   Present

what credit is that to you? For even sinners do the same. 34If you lend to those from whom you hope to receive, what credit is that to you? Even sinners lend to sinners, to receive as much again. 35But love your enemies, do good, and lend, expecting nothing in return.*u* Your reward will be great, and you will be children of the Most High; for he is kind to the ungrateful and the wicked. 36Be merciful, just as your Father is merciful.

Judging Others

37 "Do not judge, and you will not be judged; do not condemn, and you will not be condemned. Forgive, and you will be forgiven; 38give, and it will be given to you. A good measure, pressed down, shaken together, running over, will be put into your lap; for the measure you give will be the measure you get back."

39 He also told them a parable: "Can a blind person guide a blind person? Will not both fall into a pit? 40A disciple is not above the teacher, but everyone who is fully qualified will be like the teacher. 41Why do you see the speck in your neighbor's*v* eye, but do not notice the log in your own eye? 42Or how can you say to your neighbor,*w* 'Friend,*w* let me take out the speck in your eye,' when you yourself do not see the log in your own eye? You hypocrite, first take the log out of your own eye, and then you will see clearly to take the speck out of your neighbor's*v* eye.

BE NOT ANGRY THAT YOU CANNOT MAKE OTHERS AS YOU WISH THEM TO BE SINCE YOU CANNOT MAKE YOURSELF AS YOU WISH TO BE.

—*Thomas à Kempis*

A Tree and Its Fruit

43 "No good tree bears bad fruit, nor again does a bad tree bear good fruit; 44for each tree is known by its own fruit. Figs are not gathered from thorns, nor are grapes picked from a bramble bush. 45The good person out of the good treasure of the heart produces good, and the evil person out of evil treasure produces

evil; for it is out of the abundance of the heart that the mouth speaks.

The Two Foundations

46 "Why do you call me 'Lord, Lord,' and do not do what I tell you? 47I will show you what someone is like who comes to me, hears my words, and acts on them. 48That one is like a man building a house, who dug deeply and laid the foundation on rock; when a flood arose, the river burst against that house but could not shake it, because it had been well built.*x* 49But the one who hears and does not act is like a man who built a house on the ground without a foundation. When the river burst against it, immediately it fell, and great was the ruin of that house."

Jesus Heals a Centurion's Servant

7 After Jesus*y* had finished all his sayings in the hearing of the people, he entered Capernaum. 2A centurion there had a slave whom he valued highly, and who was ill and close to death. 3When he heard about Jesus, he sent some Jewish elders to him, asking him to come and heal his slave. 4When they came to Jesus, they appealed to him earnestly, saying, "He is worthy of having you do this for him, 5for he loves our people, and it is he who built our synagogue for us." 6And Jesus went with them, but when he was not far from the house, the centurion sent friends to say to him, "Lord, do not trouble yourself, for I am not worthy to have you come under my roof; 7therefore I did not presume to come to you. But only speak the word, and let my servant be healed. 8For I also am a man set under authority, with soldiers under me; and I say to one, 'Go,' and he goes, and to another, 'Come,' and he comes, and to my slave, 'Do this,' and the slave does it." 9When Jesus heard this he was amazed at him, and turning to the crowd that followed him, he said, "I tell you, not even in Israel have I found such faith." 10When those who had been sent returned to the house, they found the slave in good health.

---

u Other ancient authorities read *despairing of no one*   *v* Gk *brother's*   *w* Gk *brother*   *x* Other ancient authorities read *founded upon the rock*   *y* Gk *he*

Jesus Raises the Widow's Son at Nain

11 Soon afterwards[z] he went to a town called Nain, and his disciples and a large crowd went with him. 12As he approached the gate of the town, a man who had died was being carried out. He was his mother's only son, and she was a widow; and with her was a large crowd from the town. 13When the Lord saw her, he had compassion for her and said to her, "Do not weep." 14Then he came forward and touched the bier, and the bearers stood still. And he said, "Young man, I say to you, rise!" 15The dead man sat up and began to speak, and Jesus[a] gave him to his mother. 16Fear seized all of them; and they glorified God, saying, "A great prophet has risen among us!" and "God has looked favorably on his people!" 17This word about him spread throughout Judea and all the surrounding country.

Messengers from John the Baptist

18 The disciples of John reported all these things to him. So John summoned two of his disciples 19and sent them to the Lord to ask, "Are you the one who is to come, or are we to wait for another?" 20When the men had come to him, they said, "John the Baptist has sent us to you to ask, 'Are you the one who is to come, or are we to wait for another?' " 21Jesus[b] had just then cured many people of diseases, plagues, and evil spirits, and had given sight to many who were blind. 22And he answered them, "Go and tell John what you have seen and heard: the blind receive their sight, the lame walk, the lepers[c] are cleansed, the deaf hear, the dead are raised, the poor have good news brought to them. 23And blessed is anyone who takes no offense at me."

24 When John's messengers had gone, Jesus[a] began to speak to the crowds about John:[d] "What did you go out into the wilderness to look at? A reed shaken by the wind? 25What then did you go out to see? Someone[e] dressed in soft robes? Look, those who put on fine clothing and live in luxury are in royal palaces. 26What then did you go out to see? A

prophet? Yes, I tell you, and more than a prophet. 27This is the one about whom it is written,

'See, I am sending my messenger ahead of you,
who will prepare your way before you.'

28I tell you, among those born of women no one is greater than John; yet the least in the kingdom of God is greater than he." 29(And all the people who heard this, including the tax collectors, acknowledged the justice of God,[f] because they had been baptized with John's baptism. 30But by refusing to be baptized by him, the Pharisees and the lawyers rejected God's purpose for themselves.)

31 "To what then will I compare the people of this generation, and what are they like? 32They are like children sitting in the marketplace and calling to one another,

'We played the flute for you, and you did not dance;
we wailed, and you did not weep.'

33For John the Baptist has come eating no bread and drinking no wine, and you say, 'He has a demon'; 34the Son of Man has come eating and drinking, and you say, 'Look, a glutton and a drunkard, a friend of tax collectors and sinners!' 35Nevertheless, wisdom is vindicated by all her children."

A Sinful Woman Forgiven

36 One of the Pharisees asked Jesus[d] to eat with him, and he went into the Pharisee's house and took his place at the table. 37And a woman in the city, who was a sinner, having learned that he was eating in the Pharisee's house, brought an alabaster jar of ointment. 38She stood behind him at his feet, weeping, and began to bathe his feet with her tears and to dry them with her hair. Then she continued kissing his feet and anointing them with the ointment. 39Now when the Pharisee who had invited him saw it, he said to himself, "If this man were a prophet, he would have known who and what kind of woman this is who is touching him—that she is a sinner." 40Jesus spoke up and said to

---

z Other ancient authorities read *Next day*   a Gk *he*   b Gk *He*   c The terms *leper* and *leprosy* can refer to several diseases   d Gk *him*   e Or *Why then did you go out? To see someone*   f Or *praised God*

TEMPERANCE: ONE OF THE "CARDINAL VIRTUES"
C. S. Lewis

VERSE: Luke 7.34   **PASSAGE:** Luke 7.31–35

 emperance is, unfortunately, one of those words that has changed its meaning. It now usually means teetotalism. But in the days when the second cardinal virtue was christened "temperance," it meant nothing of the sort. Temperance referred not specially to drink, but to all pleasures; and it meant not abstaining, but going the right length and no further. It is a mistake to think that Christians ought all to be teetotallers; Mohammedanism, not Christianity, is the teetotal religion. Of course it may be the duty of a particular Christian or of any Christian, at a particular time, to abstain from strong drink, either because he is the sort of man who cannot drink at all without drinking too much, or because he wants to give the money to the poor, or because he is with people who are inclined to drunkenness and must not encourage them by drinking himself. But the whole point is that he is abstaining, for a good reason, from something which he does not condemn and which he likes to see other people enjoying. One of the marks of a certain type of bad man is that he cannot give up a thing himself without wanting every one else to give it up. That is not the Christian way. An individual Christian may see fit to give up all sorts of things for special reasons—marriage, or meat, or beer, or the cinema; but the moment he starts saying the things are bad in themselves, or looking down his nose at other people who do use them, he has taken the wrong turning.

One great piece of mischief has been done by the modern restriction of the word temperance to the question of drink. It helps people to forget that you can be just as intemperate about lots of other things. A man who makes his golf or his motor-bicycle the center of his life, or a woman who devotes all her thoughts to clothes or bridge or her dog, is being just as "intemperate" as someone who gets drunk every evening. Of course, it does not show on the outside so easily: bridge-mania or golf-mania do not make you fall down in the middle of the road. But God is not deceived by externals.

ADDITIONAL SCRIPTURE READING:
Proverbs 25.28; Titus 3.3–5

Go to page 1202 for your next devotional reading.

1900   Present

him, "Simon, I have something to say to you." "Teacher," he replied, "speak." [41]"A certain creditor had two debtors; one owed five hundred denarii,[g] and the other fifty. [42]When they could not pay, he canceled the debts for both of them. Now which of them will love him more?" [43]Simon answered, "I suppose the one for whom he canceled the greater debt." And Jesus[h] said to him, "You have judged rightly." [44]Then turning toward the woman, he said to Simon, "Do you see this woman? I entered your house; you gave me no water for my feet, but she has bathed my feet with her tears and dried them with her hair. [45]You gave me no kiss, but from the time I came in she has not stopped kissing my feet. [46]You did not anoint my head with oil, but she has anointed my feet with ointment. [47]Therefore, I tell you, her sins, which were many, have been forgiven; hence she has shown great love. But the one to whom little is forgiven, loves little." [48]Then he said to her, "Your sins are forgiven." [49]But those who were at the table with him began to say among themselves, "Who is this who even forgives sins?" [50]And he said to the woman, "Your faith has saved you; go in peace."

Some Women Accompany Jesus

8 Soon afterwards he went on through cities and villages, proclaiming and bringing the good news of the kingdom of God. The twelve were with him, [2]as well as some women who had been cured of evil spirits and infirmities: Mary, called Magdalene, from whom seven demons had gone out, [3]and Joanna, the wife of Herod's steward Chuza, and Susanna, and many others, who provided for them[i] out of their resources.

The Parable of the Sower

4 When a great crowd gathered and people from town after town came to him, he said in a parable: [5]"A sower went out to sow his seed; and as he sowed, some fell on the path and was trampled on, and the birds of the air ate it up. [6]Some fell on the rock; and as it grew up, it withered for lack of moisture. [7]Some fell among thorns, and the thorns grew with it and choked it. [8]Some fell into good soil, and when it grew, it produced a hundredfold." As he said this, he called out, "Let anyone with ears to hear listen!"

The Purpose of the Parables

9 Then his disciples asked him what this parable meant. [10]He said, "To you it has been given to know the secrets[i] of the kingdom of God; but to others I speak[k] in parables, so that

'looking they may not perceive,
    and listening they may not
      understand.'

The Parable of the Sower Explained

11 "Now the parable is this: The seed is the word of God. [12]The ones on the path are those who have heard; then the devil comes and takes away the word from their hearts, so that they may not believe and be saved. [13]The ones on the rock are those who, when they hear the word, receive it with joy. But these have no root; they believe only for a while and in a time of testing fall away. [14]As for what fell among the thorns, these are the ones who hear; but as they go on their way, they are choked by the cares and riches and pleasures of life, and their fruit does not mature. [15]But as for that in the good soil, these are the ones who,

---

I HAVE NOW DISPOSED OF ALL MY PROPERTY TO MY FAMILY. THERE IS ONE THING MORE I WISH I COULD GIVE THEM AND THAT IS THE CHRISTIAN RELIGION. IF THEY HAD THAT, AND I HAD NOT GIVEN THEM ONE SHILLING, THEY WOULD HAVE BEEN RICH; AND IF THEY HAD NOT THAT, AND I HAD GIVEN THEM ALL THE WORLD, THEY WOULD BE POOR.   —*Patrick Henry*

---

when they hear the word, hold it fast in an honest and good heart, and bear fruit with patient endurance.

A Lamp under a Jar

16 "No one after lighting a lamp

---

g The denarius was the usual day's wage for a laborer   *h* Gk he   *i* Other ancient authorities read *him*   *j* Or *mysteries*   *k* Gk lacks *I speak*

hides it under a jar, or puts it under a bed, but puts it on a lampstand, so that those who enter may see the light. [17] For nothing is hidden that will not be disclosed, nor is anything secret that will not become known and come to light. [18] Then pay attention to how you listen; for to those who have, more will be given; and from those who do not have, even what they seem to have will be taken away."

The True Kindred of Jesus

19 Then his mother and his brothers came to him, but they could not reach him because of the crowd. [20] And he was told, "Your mother and your brothers are standing outside, wanting to see you." [21] But he said to them, "My mother and my brothers are those who hear the word of God and do it."

Jesus Calms a Storm

22 One day he got into a boat with his disciples, and he said to them, "Let us go across to the other side of the lake." So they put out, [23] and while they were sailing he fell asleep. A windstorm swept down on the lake, and the boat was filling with water, and they were in danger. [24] They went to him and woke him up, shouting, "Master, Master, we are perishing!" And he woke up and rebuked the wind and the raging waves; they ceased, and there was a calm. [25] He said to them, "Where is your faith?" They were afraid and amazed, and said to one another, "Who then is this, that he commands even the winds and the water, and they obey him?"

Jesus Heals the Gerasene Demoniac

26 Then they arrived at the country of the Gerasenes,[1] which is opposite Galilee. [27] As he stepped out on land, a man of the city who had demons met him. For a long time he had worn[m] no clothes, and he did not live in a house but in the tombs. [28] When he saw Jesus, he fell down before him and shouted at the top of his voice, "What have you to do with me, Jesus, Son of the Most High God? I beg you, do not torment me"—

[29] for Jesus[n] had commanded the unclean spirit to come out of the man. (For many times it had seized him; he was kept under guard and bound with chains and shackles, but he would break the bonds and be driven by the demon into the wilds.) [30] Jesus then asked him, "What is your name?" He said, "Legion"; for many demons had entered him. [31] They begged him not to order them to go back into the abyss.

32 Now there on the hillside a large herd of swine was feeding; and the demons[o] begged Jesus[p] to let them enter these. So he gave them permission. [33] Then the demons came out of the man and entered the swine, and the herd rushed down the steep bank into the lake and was drowned.

34 When the swineherds saw what had happened, they ran off and told it in the city and in the country. [35] Then people came out to see what had happened, and when they came to Jesus, they found the man from whom the demons had gone sitting at the feet of Jesus, clothed and in his right mind. And they were afraid. [36] Those who had seen it told them how the one who had been possessed by demons had been healed. [37] Then all the people of the surrounding country of the Gerasenes[1] asked Jesus[p] to leave them; for they were seized with great fear. So he got into the boat and returned. [38] The man from whom the demons had gone begged that he might be with him; but Jesus[n] sent him away, saying, [39] "Return to your home, and declare how much God has done for you." So he went away, proclaiming throughout the city how much Jesus had done for him.

A Girl Restored to Life and a Woman Healed

40 Now when Jesus returned, the crowd welcomed him, for they were all waiting for him. [41] Just then there came a man named Jairus, a leader of the synagogue. He fell at Jesus' feet and begged him to come to his house, [42] for he had an only daughter, about twelve years old, who was dying.

---

1 Other ancient authorities read *Gadarenes*; others, *Gergesenes*   m Other ancient authorities read *a man of the city who had had demons for a long time met him. He wore*   n Gk *he*   o Gk *they* p Gk *him*

WEEKEND

GODHEAD HERE IN HIDING
Thomas Aquinas

VERSE: Luke 23.42   **PASSAGE:** Luke 23.39–43

 odhead here in hiding, whom I do adore
Masked by these bare shadows, shape and
   nothing more,
 See, Lord, at thy service low lies here a heart
Lost, all lost in wonder at the God thou art.

Seeing, touching, tasting are in thee deceived;
How says trusty hearing? that shall be believed;
What God's Son has told me, take for true I do;
Truth himself speaks truly or there's nothing true.

On the cross thy godhead made no sign to men;
Here thy very manhood steals from human ken:
Both are my confession, both are my belief,
And I pray the prayer of the dying thief.

I am not like Thomas, wounds I cannot see,
But can plainly call thee God and Lord as he:
This faith each day deeper be my holding of,
Daily make me harder hope and dearer love.

O thou our reminder of Christ crucified,
Living Bread the life of us for whom he died,
Lend this life to me then: feed and feast my mind,
There be thou the sweetness man was meant to find . . .

Jesu, whom I look at shrouded here below,
I beseech thee send me what I thirst for so,
Some day to gaze on thee face to face in light,
And be blest for ever with thy glory's light.

ADDITIONAL SCRIPTURE READING:
John 3.16; 20.24–29

Go to page 1206 for your next devotional reading.

500 1500

As he went, the crowds pressed in on him. ⁴³Now there was a woman who had been suffering from hemorrhages for twelve years; and though she had spent all she had on physicians,*q* no one could cure her. ⁴⁴She came up behind him and touched the fringe of his clothes, and immediately her hemorrhage stopped. ⁴⁵Then Jesus asked, "Who touched me?" When all denied it, Peter*r* said, "Master, the crowds surround you and press in on you." ⁴⁶But Jesus said, "Someone touched me; for I noticed that power had gone out from me." ⁴⁷When the woman saw that she could not remain hidden, she came trembling; and falling down before him, she declared in the presence of all the people why she had touched him, and how she had been immediately healed. ⁴⁸He said to her, "Daughter, your faith has made you well; go in peace."

49 While he was still speaking, someone came from the leader's house to say, "Your daughter is dead; do not trouble the teacher any longer." ⁵⁰When Jesus heard this, he replied, "Do not fear. Only believe, and she will be saved." ⁵¹When he came to the house, he did not allow anyone to enter with him, except Peter, John, and James, and the child's father and mother. ⁵²They were all weeping and wailing for her; but he said, "Do not weep; for she is not dead but sleeping." ⁵³And they laughed at him, knowing that she was dead. ⁵⁴But he took her by the hand and called out, "Child, get up!" ⁵⁵Her spirit returned, and she got up at once. Then he directed them to give her something to eat. ⁵⁶Her parents were astounded; but he ordered them to tell no one what had happened.

The Mission of the Twelve

9 Then Jesus*s* called the twelve together and gave them power and authority over all demons and to cure diseases, ²and he sent them out to proclaim the kingdom of God and to heal. ³He said to them, "Take nothing for your journey, no staff, nor bag, nor bread, nor money—not even an extra tunic. ⁴Whatever house you enter, stay there, and leave from there. ⁵Wherever they do not welcome you, as you are leaving that town shake the dust off your feet as a testimony against them." ⁶They departed and went through the villages, bringing the good news and curing diseases everywhere.

Herod's Perplexity

7 Now Herod the ruler*t* heard about all that had taken place, and he was perplexed, because it was said by some that John had been raised from the dead, ⁸by some that Elijah had appeared, and by others that one of the ancient prophets had arisen. ⁹Herod said, "John I beheaded; but who is this about whom I hear such things?" And he tried to see him.

Feeding the Five Thousand

10 On their return the apostles told Jesus*u* all they had done. He took them with him and withdrew privately to a city called Bethsaida. ¹¹When the crowds found out about it, they followed him; and he welcomed them, and spoke to them about the kingdom of God, and healed those who needed to be cured.

12 The day was drawing to a close, and the twelve came to him and said, "Send the crowd away, so that they may go into the surrounding villages and countryside, to lodge and get provisions; for we are here in a deserted place." ¹³But he said to them, "You give them something to eat." They said, "We have no more than five loaves and two fish— unless we are to go and buy food for all these people." ¹⁴For there were about five thousand men. And he said to his disciples, "Make them sit down in groups of about fifty each." ¹⁵They did so and made them all sit down. ¹⁶And taking the five loaves and the two fish, he looked up to heaven, and blessed and broke them, and gave them to the disciples to set before the crowd. ¹⁷And all ate and were filled. What was left over was gathered up, twelve baskets of broken pieces.

Peter's Declaration about Jesus

18 Once when Jesus*s* was praying alone, with only the disciples near him, he asked them, "Who do the crowds say

q Other ancient authorities lack and though she had spent all she had on physicians   r Other ancient authorities add *and those who were with him*   s Gk *he*   t Gk *tetrarch*   u Gk *him*

that I am?" [19]They answered, "John the Baptist; but others, Elijah; and still others, that one of the ancient prophets has arisen." [20]He said to them, "But who do you say that I am?" Peter answered, "The Messiah[v] of God."

Jesus Foretells His Death and Resurrection

21 He sternly ordered and commanded them not to tell anyone, [22]saying, "The Son of Man must undergo great suffering, and be rejected by the elders, chief priests, and scribes, and be killed, and on the third day be raised."

23 Then he said to them all, "If any want to become my followers, let them deny themselves and take up their cross daily and follow me. [24]For those who want to save their life will lose it, and those who lose their life for my sake will save it. [25]What does it profit them if they gain the whole world, but lose or forfeit themselves? [26]Those who are ashamed of me and of my words, of them the Son of Man will be ashamed when he comes in his glory and the glory of the Father and of the holy angels. [27]But truly I tell you, there are some standing here who will not taste death before they see the kingdom of God."

The Transfiguration

28 Now about eight days after these sayings Jesus[w] took with him Peter and John and James, and went up on the mountain to pray. [29]And while he was praying, the appearance of his face changed, and his clothes became dazzling white. [30]Suddenly they saw two men, Moses and Elijah, talking to him. [31]They appeared in glory and were speaking of his departure, which he was about to accomplish at Jerusalem. [32]Now Peter and his companions were weighed down with sleep; but since they had stayed awake,[x] they saw his glory and the two men who stood with him. [33]Just as they were leaving him, Peter said to Jesus, "Master, it is good for us to be here; let us make three dwellings,[y] one for you, one for Moses, and one for Elijah"—not knowing what

he said. [34]While he was saying this, a cloud came and overshadowed them; and they were terrified as they entered the cloud. [35]Then from the cloud came a voice that said, "This is my Son, my Chosen;[z] listen to him!" [36]When the voice had spoken, Jesus was found alone. And they kept silent and in those days told no one any of the things they had seen.

Jesus Heals a Boy with a Demon

37 On the next day, when they had come down from the mountain, a great crowd met him. [38]Just then a man from the crowd shouted, "Teacher, I beg you to look at my son; he is my only child. [39]Suddenly a spirit seizes him, and all at once he[a] shrieks. It convulses him until he foams at the mouth; it mauls him and will scarcely leave him. [40]I begged your disciples to cast it out, but they could not." [41]Jesus answered, "You faithless and perverse generation, how much longer must I be with you and bear with you? Bring your son here." [42]While he was coming, the demon dashed him to the ground in convulsions. But Jesus rebuked the unclean spirit, healed the boy, and gave him back to his father. [43]And all were astounded at the greatness of God.

Jesus Again Foretells His Death

While everyone was amazed at all that he was doing, he said to his disciples, [44]"Let these words sink into your ears: The Son of Man is going to be betrayed into human hands." [45]But they did not understand this saying; its meaning was concealed from them, so that they could not perceive it. And they were afraid to ask him about this saying.

True Greatness

46 An argument arose among them as to which one of them was the greatest. [47]But Jesus, aware of their inner thoughts, took a little child and put it by his side, [48]and said to them, "Whoever welcomes this child in my name welcomes me, and whoever welcomes me welcomes the one who sent me; for the least among all of you is the greatest."

v Or *The Christ*　w Gk *he*　x Or *but when they were fully awake*　y Or *tents*　z Other ancient authorities read *my Beloved*　a Or *it*

Another Exorcist

49 John answered, "Master, we saw someone casting out demons in your name, and we tried to stop him, because he does not follow with us." 50But Jesus said to him, "Do not stop him; for whoever is not against you is for you."

A Samaritan Village Refuses to Receive Jesus

51 When the days drew near for him to be taken up, he set his face to go to Jerusalem. 52And he sent messengers ahead of him. On their way they entered a village of the Samaritans to make ready for him; 53but they did not receive him, because his face was set toward Jerusalem. 54When his disciples James and John saw it, they said, "Lord, do you want us to command fire to come down from heaven and consume them?"*b* 55But he turned and rebuked them. 56Then*c* they went on to another village.

Would-Be Followers of Jesus

57 As they were going along the road, someone said to him, "I will follow you wherever you go." 58And Jesus said to him, "Foxes have holes, and birds of the air have nests; but the Son of Man has nowhere to lay his head." 59To another he said, "Follow me." But he said, "Lord, first let me go and bury my father." 60But Jesus*d* said to him, "Let the dead bury their own dead; but as for you,

---

TO HOLD ON TO THE PLOUGH WHILE WIPING OUR TEARS—THIS IS CHRISTIANITY.   —*Watchman Nee*

---

go and proclaim the kingdom of God." 61Another said, "I will follow you, Lord; but let me first say farewell to those at my home." 62Jesus said to him, "No one who puts a hand to the plow and looks back is fit for the kingdom of God."

The Mission of the Seventy

10 After this the Lord appointed seventy*e* others and sent them on ahead of him in pairs to every town and place where he himself intended to go. 2He said to them, "The harvest is plentiful, but the laborers are few; therefore ask the Lord of the harvest to send out laborers into his harvest. 3Go on your way. See, I am sending you out like lambs into the midst of wolves. 4Carry no purse, no bag, no sandals; and greet no one on the road. 5Whatever house you enter, first say, 'Peace to this house!' 6And if anyone is there who shares in peace, your peace will rest on that person; but if not, it will return to you. 7Remain in the same house, eating and drinking whatever they provide, for the laborer deserves to be paid. Do not move about from house to house. 8Whenever you enter a town and its people welcome you, eat what is set before you; 9cure the sick who are there, and say to them, 'The kingdom of God has come near to you.'*f* 10But whenever you enter a town and they do not welcome you, go out into its streets and say, 11'Even the dust of your town that clings to our feet, we wipe off in protest against you. Yet know this: the kingdom of God has come near.'*g* 12I tell you, on that day it will be more tolerable for Sodom than for that town.

Woes to Unrepentant Cities

13 "Woe to you, Chorazin! Woe to you, Bethsaida! For if the deeds of power done in you had been done in Tyre and Sidon, they would have repented long ago, sitting in sackcloth and ashes. 14But at the judgment it will be more tolerable for Tyre and Sidon than for you. 15And you, Capernaum,
    will you be exalted to heaven?
    No, you will be brought down to
        Hades.
16 "Whoever listens to you listens to me, and whoever rejects you rejects me, and whoever rejects me rejects the one who sent me."

The Return of the Seventy

17 The seventy*e* returned with joy, saying, "Lord, in your name even the demons submit to us!" 18He said to

---

b Other ancient authorities add *as Elijah did*   *c* Other ancient authorities read *rebuked them, and said, "You do not know what spirit you are of, 56for the Son of Man has not come to destroy the lives of human beings but to save them." Then*   *d* Gk *he*   *e* Other ancient authorities read *seventy-two*
f Or *is at hand for you*   *g* Or *is at hand*

WHO IS A LOVABLE NEIGHBOR?
Thomas Merton

VERSE: Luke 10.29   PASSAGE: Luke 10.25–37

onsider the question that was asked: "Who is my neighbor?" This was, in fact, the second question which a lawyer asked of Christ. His first, intended as a temptation or an embarrassment, was, "How shall I obtain eternal life?" This is an important question, and so important that nobody can be without the answer to it. And note that he asks this question of him of whom we read: "This is eternal life, that they may know you, the only true God, and Jesus Christ whom you have sent" (John 17.3). Since the answer to the most important of questions is accessible to everyone, the lawyer should have known it. And he did know it. He had no need to ask it at all. The Lord made this clear, for he said: "What is the first commandment?" When the lawyer replied, saying that the first commandment was the love of God and of our neighbor, then Christ told him to keep that commandment and he would have eternal life. In this way it became clear that the question was not necessary. But in order to prove that he had a real problem, the lawyer asked again: "Who is my neighbor?"

We can perhaps assume that he meant by this he had no problem about loving God, since "God is good," but that he was perplexed about loving his neighbor, since some men are better than others and all are imperfect. This being the case, in order to protect himself against loving an unworthy object and thus wasting his love, he wanted to know where to draw the line. Who is the neighbor to be loved, who is the alien not to be loved? The question is a matter of classification. Therefore it is a matter of judgment also, for to classify is to judge. How then does one classify people, and judge them accurately as worthy of love, or of hatred, or of indifference? This is a pretty question. But to the Lord it was a question that had no meaning, for he said, "Do not judge, so that you may not be judged" (Matthew 7.1). Do not classify, and do not be classified.

ADDITIONAL SCRIPTURE READING:
Matthew 7.1; Mark 12.30–31

Go to page 1208 for your next devotional reading.

1900   Present

them, "I watched Satan fall from heaven like a flash of lightning. [19]See, I have given you authority to tread on snakes and scorpions, and over all the power of the enemy; and nothing will hurt you. [20]Nevertheless, do not rejoice at this, that the spirits submit to you, but rejoice that your names are written in heaven."

Jesus Rejoices

21 At that same hour Jesus[h] rejoiced in the Holy Spirit[i] and said, "I thank[j] you, Father, Lord of heaven and earth, because you have hidden these things from the wise and the intelligent and have revealed them to infants; yes, Father, for such was your gracious will.[k] [22]All things have been handed over to me by my Father; and no one knows who the Son is except the Father, or who the Father is except the Son and anyone to whom the Son chooses to reveal him."

23 Then turning to the disciples, Jesus[h] said to them privately, "Blessed are the eyes that see what you see! [24]For I tell you that many prophets and kings desired to see what you see, but did not see it, and to hear what you hear, but did not hear it."

The Parable of the Good Samaritan

25 Just then a lawyer stood up to test Jesus.[l] "Teacher," he said, "what must I do to inherit eternal life?" [26]He said to him, "What is written in the law? What do you read there?" [27]He answered, "You shall love the Lord your God with all your heart, and with all your soul, and with all your strength, and with all your mind; and your neighbor as yourself." [28]And he said to him, "You have given the right answer; do this, and you will live."

29 But wanting to justify himself, he asked Jesus, "And who is my neighbor?" [30]Jesus replied, "A man was going down from Jerusalem to Jericho, and fell into the hands of robbers, who stripped him, beat him, and went away, leaving him half dead. [31]Now by chance a priest was going down that road; and when he saw him, he passed by on the other side. [32]So likewise a Levite, when he came to the place and saw him, passed by on the other side. [33]But a Samaritan while traveling came near him; and when he saw him, he was moved with pity. [34]He went to him and bandaged his wounds, having poured oil and wine on them. Then he put him on his own animal, brought him to an inn, and took care of him. [35]The next day he took out two denarii,[m] gave them to the innkeeper, and said, 'Take care of him; and when I come back, I will repay you whatever more you spend.' [36]Which of these three, do you think, was a neighbor to the man who fell into the hands of the robbers?" [37]He said, "The one who showed him mercy." Jesus said to him, "Go and do likewise."

Jesus Visits Martha and Mary

38 Now as they went on their way, he entered a certain village, where a woman named Martha welcomed him into her home. [39]She had a sister named Mary, who sat at the Lord's feet and listened to what he was saying. [40]But Martha was distracted by her many tasks; so she came to him and asked, "Lord, do you not care that my sister has left me to do all the work by myself? Tell her then to help me." [41]But the Lord answered her, "Martha, Martha, you are worried and distracted by many things; [42]there is need of only one thing.[n] Mary has chosen the better part, which will not be taken away from her."

The Lord's Prayer

11 He was praying in a certain place, and after he had finished, one of his disciples said to him, "Lord, teach us to pray, as John taught his disciples." [2]He said to them, "When you pray, say:

Father,[o] hallowed be your name.
    Your kingdom come.[p]
3   Give us each day our daily
        bread.[q]
4   And forgive us our sins,

---

h Gk he   i Other authorities read in the spirit   j Or praise   k Or for so it was well-pleasing in your sight   l Gk him   m The denarius was the usual day's wage for a laborer   n Other ancient authorities read few things are necessary, or only one   o Other ancient authorities read Our Father in heaven   p A few ancient authorities read Your Holy Spirit come upon us and cleanse us. Other ancient authorities add Your will be done, on earth as in heaven   q Or our bread for tomorrow for we ourselves forgive everyone indebted to us. And do not bring us to the time of trial."[r]

Perseverance in Prayer

5 And he said to them, "Suppose one of you has a friend, and you go to him at midnight and say to him, 'Friend, lend me three loaves of bread; 6for a friend of mine has arrived, and I have nothing to set before him.' 7And he answers from within, 'Do not bother me; the door has already been locked, and my children are with me in bed; I cannot get up and give you anything.' 8I tell you, even though he will not get up and give him anything because he is his friend, at least because of his persistence he will get up and give him whatever he needs.

9 "So I say to you, Ask, and it will be given you; search, and you will find; knock, and the door will be opened for you. 10For everyone who asks receives, and everyone who searches finds, and for everyone who knocks, the door will

---

r Or us into temptation. Other ancient authorities add but rescue us from the evil one (or from evil)

TUESDAY

EMPTINESS BEFORE FULLNESS
A. W. Tozer

VERSE: Luke 11.13   **PASSAGE:** Luke 11.11–13

efore there can be fullness there must be emptiness. Before God can fill us with himself we must first be emptied of ourselves. It is this emptying that brings the painful disappointment and despair of self of which so many persons have complained just prior to their new and radiant experience.

There must come a total of self-devaluation, a death to all things without us and within us, or there can never be real filling with the Holy Spirit . . .

While I shy away from "how to" formulas in spiritual things, I believe the answer to the question "How can I be filled?" may be answered in four words, all of them active verbs. They are these: (1) *surrender* (Romans 12.1–2), (2) *ask* (Luke 11.13), (3) *obey* (Acts 5.32), (4) believe (Galatians 3.2) . . .

Complete and ungrudging obedience to the will of God is absolutely indispensable to the reception of the Spirit's anointing. As we wait before God we should reverently search the Scriptures and listen for the voice of gentle stillness to learn what our heavenly Father expects of us. Then, trusting in his enabling, we should obey to the best of our ability and understanding.

ADDITIONAL SCRIPTURE READING:
Ezekiel 36.26–27; John 7.37–39; Ephesians 5.18

Go to page 1218 for your next devotional reading.

1900   Present

be opened. 11Is there anyone among you who, if your child asks for*s* a fish, will give a snake instead of a fish? 12Or if the child asks for an egg, will give a scorpion? 13If you then, who are evil, know how to give good gifts to your children, how much more will the heavenly Father give the Holy Spirit*t* to those who ask him!"

THAT GIFT OF HIS, FROM GOD DESCENDED:

AH FRIEND, WHAT GIFT OF MAN'S DOES NOT?

—Robert Browning

Jesus and Beelzebul

14 Now he was casting out a demon that was mute; when the demon had gone out, the one who had been mute spoke, and the crowds were amazed. 15But some of them said, "He casts out demons by Beelzebul, the ruler of the demons." 16Others, to test him, kept demanding from him a sign from heaven. 17But he knew what they were thinking and said to them, "Every kingdom divided against itself becomes a desert, and house falls on house. 18If Satan also is divided against himself, how will his kingdom stand? —for you say that I cast out the demons by Beelzebul. 19Now if I cast out the demons by Beelzebul, by whom do your exorcists*u* cast them out? Therefore they will be your judges. 20But if it is by the finger of God that I cast out the demons, then the kingdom of God has come to you. 21When a strong man, fully armed, guards his castle, his property is safe. 22But when one stronger than he attacks him and overpowers him, he takes away his armor in which he trusted and divides his plunder. 23Whoever is not with me is against me, and whoever does not gather with me scatters.

The Return of the Unclean Spirit

24 "When the unclean spirit has gone out of a person, it wanders through waterless regions looking for a resting place, but not finding any, it says, 'I will return to my house from which I came.' 25When it comes, it finds it swept and put in order. 26Then it goes and brings seven other spirits more evil than itself, and they enter and live there; and the last state of that person is worse than the first."

True Blessedness

27 While he was saying this, a woman in the crowd raised her voice and said to him, "Blessed is the womb that bore you and the breasts that nursed you!" 28But he said, "Blessed rather are those who hear the word of God and obey it!"

The Sign of Jonah

29 When the crowds were increasing, he began to say, "This generation is an evil generation; it asks for a sign, but no sign will be given to it except the sign of Jonah. 30For just as Jonah became a sign to the people of Nineveh, so the Son of Man will be to this generation. 31The queen of the South will rise at the judgment with the people of this generation and condemn them, because she came from the ends of the earth to listen to the wisdom of Solomon, and see, something greater than Solomon is here! 32The people of Nineveh will rise up at the judgment with this generation and condemn it, because they repented at the proclamation of Jonah, and see, something greater than Jonah is here!

The Light of the Body

33 "No one after lighting a lamp puts it in a cellar,*v* but on the lampstand so that those who enter may see the light. 34Your eye is the lamp of your body. If your eye is healthy, your whole body is full of light; but if it is not healthy, your body is full of darkness. 35Therefore consider whether the light in you is not darkness. 36If then your whole body is full of light, with no part of it in darkness, it will be as full of light as when a lamp gives you light with its rays."

Jesus Denounces Pharisees and Lawyers

37 While he was speaking, a Pharisee invited him to dine with him; so he

---

s Other ancient authorities add *bread, will give a stone;* or *if your child asks for*   t Other ancient authorities read *the Father give the Holy Spirit from heaven*   u Gk *sons*   v Other ancient authorities add *or under the bushel basket*

went in and took his place at the table. 38The Pharisee was amazed to see that he did not first wash before dinner. 39Then the Lord said to him, "Now you Pharisees clean the outside of the cup and of the dish, but inside you are full of greed and wickedness. 40You fools! Did not the one who made the outside make the inside also? 41So give for alms those things that are within; and see, everything will be clean for you.

42 "But woe to you Pharisees! For you tithe mint and rue and herbs of all kinds, and neglect justice and the love of God; it is these you ought to have practiced, without neglecting the others. 43Woe to you Pharisees! For you love to have the seat of honor in the synagogues and to be greeted with respect in the marketplaces. 44Woe to you! For you are like unmarked graves, and people walk over them without realizing it."

45 One of the lawyers answered him, "Teacher, when you say these things, you insult us too." 46And he said, "Woe also to you lawyers! For you load people with burdens hard to bear, and you yourselves do not lift a finger to ease them. 47Woe to you! For you build the tombs of the prophets whom your ancestors killed. 48So you are witnesses and approve of the deeds of your ancestors; for they killed them, and you build their tombs. 49Therefore also the Wisdom of God said, 'I will send them prophets and apostles, some of whom they will kill and persecute,' 50so that this generation may be charged with the blood of all the prophets shed since the foundation of the world, 51from the blood of Abel to the blood of Zechariah, who perished between the altar and the sanctuary. Yes, I tell you, it will be charged against this generation. 52Woe to you lawyers! For you have taken away the key of knowledge; you did not enter yourselves, and you hindered those who were entering."

53 When he went outside, the scribes and the Pharisees began to be very hostile toward him and to cross-examine him about many things, 54lying in wait for him, to catch him in something he might say.

A Warning against Hypocrisy

12 Meanwhile, when the crowd gathered by the thousands, so that they trampled on one another, he began to speak first to his disciples, "Beware of the yeast of the Pharisees, that is, their hypocrisy. 2Nothing is covered up that will not be uncovered, and nothing secret that will not become known. 3Therefore whatever you have said in the dark will be heard in the light, and what you have whispered behind closed doors will be proclaimed from the housetops.

Exhortation to Fearless Confession

4 "I tell you, my friends, do not fear those who kill the body, and after that can do nothing more. 5But I will warn you whom to fear: fear him who, after he has killed, has authorityw to cast into hell.x Yes, I tell you, fear him! 6Are not five sparrows sold for two pennies? Yet not one of them is forgotten in God's sight. 7But even the hairs of your head are all counted. Do not be afraid; you are of more value than many sparrows.

8 "And I tell you, everyone who acknowledges me before others, the Son of Man also will acknowledge before the angels of God; 9but whoever denies me before others will be denied before the angels of God. 10And everyone who speaks a word against the Son of Man will be forgiven; but whoever blasphemes against the Holy Spirit will not be forgiven. 11When they bring you before the synagogues, the rulers, and the authorities, do not worry about howy you are to defend yourselves or what you are to say; 12for the Holy Spirit will teach you at that very hour what you ought to say."

The Parable of the Rich Fool

13 Someone in the crowd said to him, "Teacher, tell my brother to divide the family inheritance with me." 14But he said to him, "Friend, who set me to be a judge or arbitrator over you?" 15And he said to them, "Take care! Be on your guard against all kinds of greed; for one's life does not consist in the abundance of possessions." 16Then he told them a par-

w Or power   x Gk Gehenna   y Other ancient authorities add or what able: "The land of a rich man produced abundantly. 17And he thought to himself, 'What should I do, for I have no place to store my crops?' 18Then he said, 'I will do this: I will pull down my barns and build larger ones, and there I will store all my grain and my goods. 19And I will say to my soul, Soul, you have ample goods laid up for many years; relax, eat, drink, be merry.' 20But God said to him, 'You fool! This very night your life is being demanded of you. And the things you have prepared, whose will they be?' 21So it is with those who store up treasures for themselves but are not rich toward God."

Do Not Worry

22 He said to his disciples, "Therefore I tell you, do not worry about your life, what you will eat, or about your body, what you will wear. 23For life is more than food, and the body more than clothing. 24Consider the ravens: they neither sow nor reap, they have neither storehouse nor barn, and yet God feeds them. Of how much more value are you than the birds! 25And can any of you by worrying add a single hour to your span of life?z 26If then you are not able to do so small a thing as that, why do you worry about the rest? 27Consider the lilies, how they grow: they neither toil nor spin;a yet I tell you, even Solomon in all his glory was not clothed like one of these. 28But if God so clothes the grass of the field, which is alive today and tomorrow is thrown into the oven, how much more will he clothe you—you of little faith! 29And do not keep striving for what you are to eat and what you are to drink, and do not keep worrying. 30For it is the nations of the world that strive after all these things, and your Father knows that you need them. 31Instead, strive for hisb kingdom, and these things will be given to you as well.

32 "Do not be afraid, little flock, for it is your Father's good pleasure to give you the kingdom. 33Sell your possessions, and give alms. Make purses for yourselves that do not wear out, an unfailing treasure in heaven, where no

thief comes near and no moth destroys. 34For where your treasure is, there your heart will be also.

ANXIETY IS NOT ONLY A PAIN WHICH WE MUST ASK GOD TO ASSUAGE BUT ALSO A WEAKNESS WE MUST ASK HIM TO PARDON—FOR HE'S TOLD US TO TAKE NO CARE FOR THE MORROW.   —C. S. Lewis

---

Watchful Slaves

35 "Be dressed for action and have your lamps lit; 36be like those who are waiting for their master to return from the wedding banquet, so that they may open the door for him as soon as he comes and knocks. 37Blessed are those slaves whom the master finds alert when he comes; truly I tell you, he will fasten his belt and have them sit down to eat, and he will come and serve them. 38If he comes during the middle of the night, or near dawn, and finds them so, blessed are those slaves.

39 "But know this: if the owner of the house had known at what hour the thief was coming, hec would not have let his house be broken into. 40You also must be ready, for the Son of Man is coming at an unexpected hour."

The Faithful or the Unfaithful Slave

41 Peter said, "Lord, are you telling this parable for us or for everyone?" 42And the Lord said, "Who then is the faithful and prudent manager whom his master will put in charge of his slaves, to give them their allowance of food at the proper time? 43Blessed is that slave whom his master will find at work when he arrives. 44Truly I tell you, he will put that one in charge of all his possessions. 45But if that slave says to himself, 'My master is delayed in coming,' and if he begins to beat the other slaves, men and women, and to eat and drink and get drunk, 46the master of that slave will come on a day when he does not expect him and at an hour that he does not know, and will cut him in pieces,d and put him with the unfaithful. 47That slave who knew what his master wanted, but

---

z Or add a cubit to your stature   a Other ancient authorities read Consider the lilies; they neither spin nor weave   b Other ancient authorities read God's   c Other ancient authorities add would have watched and   d Or cut him off

did not prepare himself or do what was wanted, will receive a severe beating. 48But the one who did not know and did what deserved a beating will receive a light beating. From everyone to whom much has been given, much will be required; and from the one to whom much has been entrusted, even more will be demanded.

Jesus the Cause of Division

49 "I came to bring fire to the earth, and how I wish it were already kindled! 50I have a baptism with which to be baptized, and what stress I am under until it is completed! 51Do you think that I have come to bring peace to the earth? No, I tell you, but rather division! 52From now on five in one household will be divided, three against two and two against three; 53they will be divided:

father against son
  and son against father,
mother against daughter
  and daughter against mother,
mother-in-law against her
    daughter-in-law
  and daughter-in-law against
    mother-in-law."

Interpreting the Time

54 He also said to the crowds, "When you see a cloud rising in the west, you immediately say, 'It is going to rain'; and so it happens. 55And when you see the south wind blowing, you say, 'There will be scorching heat'; and it happens. 56You hypocrites! You know how to interpret the appearance of earth and sky, but why do you not know how to interpret the present time?

Settling with Your Opponent

57 "And why do you not judge for yourselves what is right? 58Thus, when you go with your accuser before a magistrate, on the way make an effort to settle the case,e or you may be dragged before the judge, and the judge hand you over to the officer, and the officer throw you in prison. 59I tell you, you will never get out until you have paid the very last penny."

e Gk settle with him

Repent or Perish

13 At that very time there were some present who told him about the Galileans whose blood Pilate had mingled with their sacrifices. 2He asked them, "Do you think that because these Galileans suffered in this way they were worse sinners than all other Galileans? 3No, I tell you; but unless you repent, you will all perish as they did. 4Or those eighteen who were killed when the tower of Siloam fell on them—do you think that they were worse offenders than all the others living in Jerusalem? 5No, I tell you; but unless you repent, you will all perish just as they did."

The Parable of the Barren Fig Tree

6 Then he told this parable: "A man had a fig tree planted in his vineyard; and he came looking for fruit on it and found none. 7So he said to the gardener, 'See here! For three years I have come looking for fruit on this fig tree, and still I find none. Cut it down! Why should it be wasting the soil?' 8He replied, 'Sir, let it alone for one more year, until I dig around it and put manure on it. 9If it bears fruit next year, well and good; but if not, you can cut it down.' "

Jesus Heals a Crippled Woman

10 Now he was teaching in one of the synagogues on the sabbath. 11And just then there appeared a woman with a spirit that had crippled her for eighteen years. She was bent over and was quite unable to stand up straight. 12When Jesus saw her, he called her over and said, "Woman, you are set free from your ailment." 13When he laid his hands on her, immediately she stood up straight and began praising God. 14But the leader of the synagogue, indignant because Jesus had cured on the sabbath, kept saying to the crowd, "There are six days on which work ought to be done; come on those days and be cured, and not on the sabbath day." 15But the Lord answered him and said, "You hypocrites! Does not each of you on the sabbath untie his ox or his donkey from the manger, and lead it away to give it

water? 16And ought not this woman, a daughter of Abraham whom Satan bound for eighteen long years, be set free from this bondage on the sabbath day?" 17When he said this, all his opponents were put to shame; and the entire crowd was rejoicing at all the wonderful things that he was doing.

The Parable of the Mustard Seed

18 He said therefore, "What is the kingdom of God like? And to what should I compare it? 19It is like a mustard seed that someone took and sowed in the garden; it grew and became a tree, and the birds of the air made nests in its branches."

The Parable of the Yeast

20 And again he said, "To what should I compare the kingdom of God? 21It is like yeast that a woman took and mixed in with*f* three measures of flour until all of it was leavened."

The Narrow Door

22 Jesus*g* went through one town and village after another, teaching as he made his way to Jerusalem. 23Someone asked him, "Lord, will only a few be saved?" He said to them, 24"Strive to enter through the narrow door; for many, I tell you, will try to enter and will not be able. 25When once the owner of the house has got up and shut the door, and you begin to stand outside and to knock at the door, saying, 'Lord, open to us,' then in reply he will say to you, 'I do not know where you come from.' 26Then you will begin to say, 'We ate and drank with you, and you taught in our streets.' 27But he will say, 'I do not know where you come from; go away from me, all you evildoers!' 28There will be weeping and gnashing of teeth when you see Abraham and Isaac and Jacob and all the prophets in the kingdom of God, and you yourselves thrown out. 29Then people will come from east and west, from north and south, and will eat in the kingdom of God. 30Indeed, some are last who will be first, and some are first who will be last."

The Lament over Jerusalem

31 At that very hour some Pharisees came and said to him, "Get away from here, for Herod wants to kill you." 32He said to them, "Go and tell that fox for me,*h* 'Listen, I am casting out demons and performing cures today and tomorrow, and on the third day I finish my work. 33Yet today, tomorrow, and the next day I must be on my way, because it is impossible for a prophet to be killed outside of Jerusalem.' 34Jerusalem, Jerusalem, the city that kills the prophets and stones those who are sent to it! How often have I desired to gather your children together as a hen gathers her brood under her wings, and you were not willing! 35See, your house is left to you. And I tell you, you will not see me until the time comes when*i* you say, 'Blessed is the one who comes in the name of the Lord.' "

Jesus Heals the Man with Dropsy

14 On one occasion when Jesus*j* was going to the house of a leader of the Pharisees to eat a meal on the sabbath, they were watching him closely. 2Just then, in front of him, there was a man who had dropsy. 3And Jesus asked the lawyers and Pharisees, "Is it lawful to cure people on the sabbath, or not?" 4But they were silent. So Jesus*j* took him and healed him, and sent him away. 5Then he said to them, "If one of you has a child*k* or an ox that has fallen into a well, will you not immediately pull it out on a sabbath day?" 6And they could not reply to this.

Humility and Hospitality

7 When he noticed how the guests chose the places of honor, he told them a parable. 8"When you are invited by someone to a wedding banquet, do not sit down at the place of honor, in case someone more distinguished than you has been invited by your host; 9and the host who invited both of you may come and say to you, 'Give this person your place,' and then in disgrace you would start to take the lowest place. 10But when you are invited, go and sit down at the lowest place, so that when your host

---

f Gk *hid in*   *g* Gk *He*   *h* Gk lacks *for me*   *i* Other ancient authorities lack *the time comes when*   *j* Gk *he*   *k* Other ancient authorities read *a donkey*

comes, he may say to you, 'Friend, move up higher'; then you will be honored in the presence of all who sit at the table with you. [11]For all who exalt themselves will be humbled, and those who humble themselves will be exalted."

12 He said also to the one who had invited him, "When you give a luncheon or a dinner, do not invite your friends or your brothers or your relatives or rich neighbors, in case they may invite you in return, and you would be repaid. [13]But when you give a banquet, invite the poor, the crippled, the lame, and the blind. [14]And you will be blessed, because they cannot repay you, for you will be repaid at the resurrection of the righteous."

The Parable of the Great Dinner

15 One of the dinner guests, on hearing this, said to him, "Blessed is anyone who will eat bread in the kingdom of God!" [16]Then Jesus[l] said to him, "Someone gave a great dinner and invited many. [17]At the time for the dinner he sent his slave to say to those who had been invited, 'Come; for everything is ready now.' [18]But they all alike began to make excuses. The first said to him, 'I have bought a piece of land, and I must go out and see it; please accept my regrets.' [19]Another said, 'I have bought five yoke of oxen, and I am going to try them out; please accept my regrets.' [20]Another said, 'I have just been married, and therefore I cannot come.' [21]So the slave returned and reported this to his master. Then the owner of the house became angry and said to his slave, 'Go out at once into the streets and lanes of the town and bring in the poor, the crippled, the blind, and the lame.' [22]And the slave said, 'Sir, what you ordered has been done, and there is still room.' [23]Then the master said to the slave, 'Go out into the roads and lanes, and compel people to come in, so that my house may be filled. [24]For I tell you,[m] none of those who were invited will taste my dinner.' "

The Cost of Discipleship

25 Now large crowds were traveling with him; and he turned and said to them, [26]"Whoever comes to me and does not hate father and mother, wife and children, brothers and sisters, yes, and even life itself, cannot be my disciple. [27]Whoever does not carry the cross and follow me cannot be my disciple.

I DO NOT PRAY FOR A LIGHTER LOAD, BUT FOR A STRONGER BACK. —*Phillips Brooks*

---

[28]For which of you, intending to build a tower, does not first sit down and estimate the cost, to see whether he has enough to complete it? [29]Otherwise, when he has laid a foundation and is not able to finish, all who see it will begin to ridicule him, [30]saying, 'This fellow began to build and was not able to finish.' [31]Or what king, going out to wage war against another king, will not sit down first and consider whether he is able with ten thousand to oppose the one who comes against him with twenty thousand? [32]If he cannot, then, while the other is still far away, he sends a delegation and asks for the terms of peace. [33]So therefore, none of you can become my disciple if you do not give up all your possessions.

About Salt

34 "Salt is good; but if salt has lost its taste, how can its saltiness be restored?[n] [35]It is fit neither for the soil nor for the manure pile; they throw it away. Let anyone with ears to hear listen!"

The Parable of the Lost Sheep

15 Now all the tax collectors and sinners were coming near to listen to him. [2]And the Pharisees and the scribes were grumbling and saying, "This fellow welcomes sinners and eats with them."

3 So he told them this parable: [4]"Which one of you, having a hundred sheep and losing one of them, does not leave the ninety-nine in the wilderness and go after the one that is lost until he finds it? [5]When he has found it, he lays it on his shoulders and rejoices. [6]And when he comes home, he calls together his friends and neighbors, saying to

---

l Gk *he*   *m* The Greek word for *you* here is plural   *n* Or *how can it be used for seasoning?*

them, 'Rejoice with me, for I have found my sheep that was lost.' [7]Just so, I tell you, there will be more joy in heaven over one sinner who repents than over ninety-nine righteous persons who need no repentance.

The Parable of the Lost Coin

8 "Or what woman having ten silver coins,[o] if she loses one of them, does not light a lamp, sweep the house, and search carefully until she finds it? [9]When she has found it, she calls together her friends and neighbors, saying, 'Rejoice with me, for I have found the coin that I had lost.' [10]Just so, I tell you, there is joy in the presence of the angels of God over one sinner who repents."

The Parable of the Prodigal and His Brother

11 Then Jesus[p] said, "There was a man who had two sons. [12]The younger of them said to his father, 'Father, give me the share of the property that will belong to me.' So he divided his property between them. [13]A few days later the younger son gathered all he had and traveled to a distant country, and there he squandered his property in dissolute living. [14]When he had spent everything, a severe famine took place throughout that country, and he began to be in need. [15]So he went and hired himself out to one of the citizens of that country, who sent him to his fields to feed the pigs. [16]He would gladly have filled himself with[q] the pods that the pigs were eating; and no one gave him anything. [17]But when he came to himself he said, 'How many of my father's hired hands have bread enough and to spare, but here I am dying of hunger! [18]I will get up and go to my father, and I will say to him, "Father, I have sinned against heaven and before you; [19]I am no longer worthy to be called your son; treat me like one of your hired hands." ' [20]So he set off and went to his father. But while he was still far off, his father saw him and was filled with compassion; he ran and put his arms around him and kissed him. [21]Then the son said to him, 'Father, I have sinned against heaven and before

you; I am no longer worthy to be called your son.'[r] [22]But the father said to his slaves, 'Quickly, bring out a robe—the best one—and put it on him; put a ring on his finger and sandals on his feet. [23]And get the fatted calf and kill it, and let us eat and celebrate; [24]for this son of mine was dead and is alive again; he was lost and is found!' And they began to celebrate.

25 "Now his elder son was in the field; and when he came and approached the house, he heard music and dancing. [26]He called one of the slaves and asked what was going on. [27]He replied, 'Your brother has come, and your father has killed the fatted calf, because he has got him back safe and sound.' [28]Then he became angry and refused to go in. His father came out and began to plead with him. [29]But he answered his father, 'Listen! For all these years I have been working like a slave for you, and I have never disobeyed your command; yet you have never given me even a young goat so that I might celebrate with my friends. [30]But when this son of yours came back, who has devoured your property with prostitutes, you killed the fatted calf for him!' [31]Then the father[p] said to him, 'Son, you are always with me, and all that is mine is yours. [32]But we had to celebrate and rejoice, because this brother of yours was dead and has come to life; he was lost and has been found.' "

The Parable of the Dishonest Manager

16 Then Jesus[p] said to the disciples, "There was a rich man who had a manager, and charges were brought to him that this man was squandering his property. [2]So he summoned him and said to him, 'What is this that I hear about you? Give me an accounting of your management, because you cannot be my manager any longer.' [3]Then the manager said to himself, 'What will I do, now that my master is taking the position away from me? I am not strong enough to dig, and I am ashamed to beg. [4]I have decided what to do so that, when I am dismissed as manager, people may

---

o Gk *drachmas*, each worth about a day's wage for a laborer   p Gk *he*   q Other ancient authorities
read *filled his stomach with*   r Other ancient authorities add *Treat me like one of your hired servants*

welcome me into their homes.' ⁵So, summoning his master's debtors one by one, he asked the first, 'How much do you owe my master?' ⁶He answered, 'A hundred jugs of olive oil.' He said to him, 'Take your bill, sit down quickly, and make it fifty.' ⁷Then he asked another, 'And how much do you owe?' He replied, 'A hundred containers of wheat.' He said to him, 'Take your bill and make it eighty.' ⁸And his master commended the dishonest manager because he had acted shrewdly; for the children of this age are more shrewd in dealing with their own generation than are the children of light. ⁹And I tell you, make friends for yourselves by means of dishonest wealthˢ so that when it is gone, they may welcome you into the eternal homes.ᵗ

10 "Whoever is faithful in a very little is faithful also in much; and whoever is dishonest in a very little is dishonest also in much. ¹¹If then you have not been faithful with the dishonest wealth,ˢ who will entrust to you the true riches? ¹²And if you have not been faithful with what belongs to another, who will give you what is your own? ¹³No slave can serve two masters; for a slave will either hate the one and love the other, or be devoted to the one and despise the other. You cannot serve God and wealth."ˢ

The Law and the Kingdom of God

14 The Pharisees, who were lovers of money, heard all this, and they ridiculed him. ¹⁵So he said to them, "You are those who justify yourselves in the sight of others; but God knows your hearts; for what is prized by human beings is an abomination in the sight of God.

16 "The law and the prophets were in effect until John came; since then the good news of the kingdom of God is proclaimed, and everyone tries to enter it by force.ᵘ ¹⁷But it is easier for heaven and earth to pass away, than for one stroke of a letter in the law to be dropped.

18 "Anyone who divorces his wife and marries another commits adultery,

and whoever marries a woman divorced from her husband commits adultery.

The Rich Man and Lazarus

19 "There was a rich man who was dressed in purple and fine linen and who feasted sumptuously every day. ²⁰And at his gate lay a poor man named Lazarus, covered with sores, ²¹who longed to satisfy his hunger with what fell from the rich man's table; even the dogs would come and lick his sores. ²²The poor man died and was carried away by the angels to be with Abraham.ᵛ The rich man also died and was buried. ²³In Hades, where he was being tormented, he looked up and saw Abraham far away with Lazarus by his side.ʷ ²⁴He called out, 'Father Abraham, have mercy on me, and send Lazarus to dip the tip of his finger in water and cool my tongue; for I am in agony in these flames.' ²⁵But Abraham said, 'Child, remember that during your lifetime you received your good things, and Lazarus in like manner evil things; but now he is comforted here, and you are in agony. ²⁶Besides all this, between you and us a great chasm has been fixed, so that those who might want to pass from here to you cannot do so, and no one can cross from there to us.' ²⁷He said, 'Then, father, I beg you to send him to my father's house— ²⁸for I have five brothers—that he may warn them, so that they will not also come into this place of torment.' ²⁹Abraham replied, 'They have Moses and the prophets; they should listen to them.' ³⁰He said, 'No, father Abraham; but if someone goes to them from the dead, they will repent.' ³¹He said to him, 'If they do not listen to Moses and the prophets, neither will they be convinced even if someone rises from the dead.' "

Some Sayings of Jesus

17 Jesusˣ said to his disciples, "Occasions for stumbling are bound to come, but woe to anyone by whom they come! ²It would be better for you if a millstone were hung around your neck and you were thrown into the sea than for you to cause one of these little ones to stumble. ³Be on your guard!

---

s Gk mammon   t Gk tents   u Or everyone is strongly urged to enter it   v Gk to Abraham's bosom   w Gk in his bosom   x Gk He

If another disciple[y] sins, you must rebuke the offender, and if there is repentance, you must forgive. [4]And if the same person sins against you seven times a day, and turns back to you seven times and says, 'I repent,' you must forgive."

5 The apostles said to the Lord, "Increase our faith!" [6]The Lord replied, "If you had faith the size of a[z] mustard seed, you could say to this mulberry tree, 'Be uprooted and planted in the sea,' and it would obey you.

7 "Who among you would say to your slave who has just come in from plowing or tending sheep in the field, 'Come here at once and take your place at the table'? [8]Would you not rather say to him, 'Prepare supper for me, put on your apron and serve me while I eat and drink; later you may eat and drink'? [9]Do you thank the slave for doing what was commanded? [10]So you also, when you have done all that you were ordered to do, say, 'We are worthless slaves; we have done only what we ought to have done!' "

Jesus Cleanses Ten Lepers

11 On the way to Jerusalem Jesus[a] was going through the region between Samaria and Galilee. [12]As he entered a village, ten lepers[b] approached him. Keeping their distance, [13]they called out, saying, "Jesus, Master, have mercy on us!" [14]When he saw them, he said to them, "Go and show yourselves to the priests." And as they went, they were made clean. [15]Then one of them, when he saw that he was healed, turned back, praising God with a loud voice. [16]He prostrated himself at Jesus'[c] feet and thanked him. And he was a Samaritan. [17]Then Jesus asked, "Were not ten made clean? But the other nine, where are they? [18]Was none of them found to return and give praise to God except this foreigner?" [19]Then he said to him, "Get up and go on your way; your faith has made you well."

The Coming of the Kingdom

20 Once Jesus[a] was asked by the Pharisees when the kingdom of God was coming, and he answered, "The kingdom of God is not coming with things that can be observed; [21]nor will they say, 'Look, here it is!' or 'There it is!' For, in fact, the kingdom of God is among[d] you."

22 Then he said to the disciples, "The days are coming when you will long to see one of the days of the Son of Man, and you will not see it. [23]They will say to you, 'Look there!' or 'Look here!' Do not go, do not set off in pursuit. [24]For as the lightning flashes and lights up the sky from one side to the other, so will the Son of Man be in his day.[e] [25]But first he must endure much suffering and be rejected by this generation. [26]Just as it was in the days of Noah, so too it will be in the days of the Son of Man. [27]They were eating and drinking, and marrying and being given in marriage, until the day Noah entered the ark, and the flood came and destroyed all of them. [28]Likewise, just as it was in the days of Lot: they were eating and drinking, buying and selling, planting and building, [29]but on the day that Lot left Sodom, it rained fire and sulfur from heaven and destroyed all of them [30]—it will be like that on the day that the Son of Man is revealed. [31]On that day, anyone on the housetop who has belongings in the house must not come down to take them away; and likewise anyone in the field must not turn back. [32]Remember Lot's wife. [33]Those who try to make their life secure will lose it, but those who lose their life will keep it. [34]I tell you, on that night there will be two in one bed; one will be taken and the other left. [35]There will be two women grinding meal together; one will be taken and the other left."[f]

WE OUGHT NOT TO TOLERATE FOR A MINUTE THE GHASTLY AND GRIEVOUS THOUGHT THAT GOD WILL NOT ANSWER PRAYER. HISTORY, AS MANIFESTED IN CHRIST JESUS, DEMANDS IT.

—*C. H. Spurgeon*

---

[37]Then they asked him, "Where, Lord?" He said to them, "Where the corpse is, there the vultures will gather."

---

y Gk *your brother*   z Gk *faith as a grain of*   a Gk *he*   b The terms *leper* and *leprosy* can refer to several diseases   c Gk *his*   d Or *within*   e Other ancient authorities lack *in his day*   f Other ancient authorities add verse 36, *"Two will be in the field; one will be taken and the other left."*

The Parable of the Widow and the Unjust Judge

 18 Then Jesus[g] told them a parable about their need to pray always and not to lose heart. ²He said,

"In a certain city there was a judge who neither feared God nor had respect for people. ³In that city there was a widow who kept coming to him and saying, 'Grant me justice against my opponent.' ⁴For a while he refused; but later he said

g Gk *he*

WEDNESDAY

LUTHER ON PRAYER
Martin Luther

VERSE: Luke 18.1   **PASSAGE:** Luke 18.1–14

pright Christians pray without ceasing; though they pray not always with their mouths, yet their hearts pray continually, sleeping and waking; for the sigh of a true Christian is a prayer. As the Psalm saith: "Because of the deep sighing of the poor, I will rise up, saith the Lord," etc. (see Psalm 12.5, KJV). In like manner a true Christian always carries the cross, though he feel it not always.

The Lord's Prayer binds the people together, and knits them one to another, so that one prays for another and together one with another; and it is so strong and powerful that it even drives away the fear of death.

Prayer preserves the church, and hitherto has done the best for the church; therefore we must continually pray. Hence Christ says: "Ask, and ye shall have; seek, and ye shall find; knock, and it shall be opened unto you" (see Luke 11.9, KJV).

First, when we are in trouble, he will have us to pray; for God often, as it were, hides himself, and will not hear; yea, will not suffer himself to be found. Then we must seek him; that is, we must continue in prayer. When we seek him, he often locks himself up, as it were, in a private chamber; if we intend to come in unto him, then we must knock, and when we have knocked once or twice, then he begins a little to hear. At last, when we make much knocking, then he opens, and says: What will ye have? Lord, say we, we would have this or that; then, says he, Take it unto you. In such sort must we persist in praying, and waken God up.

ADDITIONAL SCRIPTURE READING:
Matthew 7.7–11; 1 Thessalonians 5.16–18

Go to page 1227 for your next devotional reading.

1500   1700

to himself, 'Though I have no fear of God and no respect for anyone, [5]yet because this widow keeps bothering me, I will grant her justice, so that she may not wear me out by continually coming.' "[h] [6]And the Lord said, "Listen to what the unjust judge says. [7]And will not God grant justice to his chosen ones who cry to him day and night? Will he delay long in helping them? [8]I tell you, he will quickly grant justice to them. And yet, when the Son of Man comes, will he find faith on earth?"

The Parable of the Pharisee and the Tax Collector

[9] He also told this parable to some who trusted in themselves that they were righteous and regarded others with contempt: [10]"Two men went up to the temple to pray, one a Pharisee and the other a tax collector. [11]The Pharisee, standing by himself, was praying thus, 'God, I thank you that I am not like other people: thieves, rogues, adulterers, or even like this tax collector. [12]I fast twice a week; I give a tenth of all my income.' [13]But the tax collector, standing

IF YOUR PRAYER IS SELFISH, THE ANSWER WILL BE SOMETHING THAT WILL REBUKE YOUR SELFISHNESS. YOU MAY NOT RECOGNIZE IT AS HAVING COME AT ALL, BUT IT IS SURE TO BE THERE.
                              —William Temple

far off, would not even look up to heaven, but was beating his breast and saying, 'God, be merciful to me, a sinner!' [14]I tell you, this man went down to his home justified rather than the other; for all who exalt themselves will be humbled, but all who humble themselves will be exalted."

Jesus Blesses Little Children

[15] People were bringing even infants to him that he might touch them; and when the disciples saw it, they sternly ordered them not to do it. [16]But Jesus called for them and said, "Let the little children come to me, and do not stop them; for it is to such as these that the kingdom of God belongs. [17]Truly I tell

you, whoever does not receive the kingdom of God as a little child will never enter it."

The Rich Ruler

[18] A certain ruler asked him, "Good Teacher, what must I do to inherit eternal life?" [19]Jesus said to him, "Why do you call me good? No one is good but God alone. [20]You know the commandments: 'You shall not commit adultery; You shall not murder; You shall not steal; You shall not bear false witness; Honor your father and mother.' " [21]He replied, "I have kept all these since my youth." [22]When Jesus heard this, he said to him, "There is still one thing lacking. Sell all that you own and distribute the money[i] to the poor, and you will have treasure in heaven; then come, follow me." [23]But when he heard this, he became sad; for he was very rich. [24]Jesus looked at him and said, "How hard it is for those who have wealth to enter the kingdom of God! [25]Indeed, it is easier for a camel to go through the eye of a needle than for someone who is rich to enter the kingdom of God."

[26] Those who heard it said, "Then who can be saved?" [27]He replied, "What is impossible for mortals is possible for God."

[28] Then Peter said, "Look, we have left our homes and followed you." [29]And he said to them, "Truly I tell you, there is no one who has left house or wife or brothers or parents or children, for the sake of the kingdom of God, [30]who will not get back very much more in this age, and in the age to come eternal life."

A Third Time Jesus Foretells His Death and Resurrection

[31] Then he took the twelve aside and said to them, "See, we are going up to Jerusalem, and everything that is written about the Son of Man by the prophets will be accomplished. [32]For he will be handed over to the Gentiles; and he will be mocked and insulted and spat upon. [33]After they have flogged him, they will kill him, and on the third day he will rise again." [34]But they understood nothing about all these things; in

h Or so that she may not finally come and slap me in the face   i Gk lacks the money

fact, what he said was hidden from them, and they did not grasp what was said.

Jesus Heals a Blind Beggar Near Jericho

35 As he approached Jericho, a blind man was sitting by the roadside begging. 36When he heard a crowd going by, he asked what was happening. 37They told him, "Jesus of Nazareth[j] is passing by." 38Then he shouted, "Jesus, Son of David, have mercy on me!" 39Those who were in front sternly ordered him to be quiet; but he shouted even more loudly, "Son of David, have mercy on me!" 40Jesus stood still and ordered the man to be brought to him; and when he came near, he asked him, 41"What do you want me to do for you?" He said, "Lord, let me see again." 42Jesus said to him, "Receive your sight; your faith has saved you." 43Immediately he regained his sight and followed him, glorifying God; and all the people, when they saw it, praised God.

Jesus and Zacchaeus

19 He entered Jericho and was passing through it. 2A man was there named Zacchaeus; he was a chief tax collector and was rich. 3He was trying to see who Jesus was, but on account of the crowd he could not, because he was short in stature. 4So he ran ahead and climbed a sycamore tree to see him, because he was going to pass that way. 5When Jesus came to the place, he looked up and said to him, "Zacchaeus, hurry and come down; for I must stay at your house today." 6So he hurried down and was happy to welcome him. 7All who saw it began to grumble and said, "He has gone to be the guest of one who is a sinner." 8Zacchaeus stood there and said to the Lord, "Look, half of my possessions, Lord, I will give to the poor; and if I have defrauded anyone of anything, I will pay back four times as much." 9Then Jesus said to him, "Today salvation has come to this house, because he too is a son of Abraham. 10For the Son of Man came to seek out and to save the lost."

The Parable of the Ten Pounds

11 As they were listening to this, he went on to tell a parable, because he was near Jerusalem, and because they supposed that the kingdom of God was to appear immediately. 12So he said, "A nobleman went to a distant country to get royal power for himself and then return. 13He summoned ten of his slaves, and gave them ten pounds,[k] and said to them, 'Do business with these until I come back.' 14But the citizens of his country hated him and sent a delegation after him, saying, 'We do not want this man to rule over us.' 15When he returned, having received royal power, he ordered these slaves, to whom he had given the money, to be summoned so that he might find out what they had gained by trading. 16The first came forward and said, 'Lord, your pound has made ten more pounds.' 17He said to him, 'Well done, good slave! Because you have been trustworthy in a very small thing, take charge of ten cities.' 18Then the second came, saying, 'Lord, your pound has made five pounds.' 19He said to him, 'And you, rule over five cities.' 20Then the other came, saying, 'Lord, here is your pound. I wrapped it up in a piece of cloth, 21for I was afraid of you, because you are a harsh man; you take what you did not deposit, and reap what you did not sow.' 22He said to him, 'I will judge you by your own words, you wicked slave! You knew, did you, that I was a harsh man, taking what I did not deposit and reaping what I did not sow? 23Why then did you not put my money into the bank? Then when I returned, I could have collected it with interest.' 24He said to the bystanders, 'Take the pound from him and give it to the one who has ten pounds.' 25(And they said to him, 'Lord, he has ten pounds!') 26'I tell you, to all those who have, more will be given; but from those who have nothing, even what they have will be taken away. 27But as for these enemies of mine who did not want me to be king over them—bring them here and slaughter them in my presence.' "

---

j Gk *the Nazorean*   k The mina, rendered here by *pound*, was about three months' wages for a laborer

Jesus' Triumphal Entry into Jerusalem

28 After he had said this, he went on ahead, going up to Jerusalem.

29 When he had come near Bethphage and Bethany, at the place called the Mount of Olives, he sent two of the disciples, 30saying, "Go into the village ahead of you, and as you enter it you will find tied there a colt that has never been ridden. Untie it and bring it here. 31If anyone asks you, 'Why are you untying it?' just say this, 'The Lord needs it.' " 32So those who were sent departed and found it as he had told them. 33As they were untying the colt, its owners asked them, "Why are you untying the colt?" 34They said, "The Lord needs it." 35Then they brought it to Jesus; and after throwing their cloaks on the colt, they set Jesus on it. 36As he rode along, people kept spreading their cloaks on the road. 37As he was now approaching the path down from the Mount of Olives, the whole multitude of the disciples began to praise God joyfully with a loud voice for all the deeds of power that they had seen, 38saying,

"Blessed is the king
who comes in the name of the Lord!
Peace in heaven,
and glory in the highest heaven!"

39Some of the Pharisees in the crowd said to him, "Teacher, order your disciples to stop." 40He answered, "I tell you, if these were silent, the stones would shout out."

Jesus Weeps over Jerusalem

41 As he came near and saw the city, he wept over it, 42saying, "If you, even you, had only recognized on this day the things that make for peace! But now they are hidden from your eyes. 43Indeed, the days will come upon you, when your enemies will set up ramparts around you and surround you, and hem you in on every side. 44They will crush you to the ground, you and your children within you, and they will not leave within you one stone upon another; because you did not recognize the time of your visitation from God."1

Jesus Cleanses the Temple

45 Then he entered the temple and began to drive out those who were selling things there; 46and he said, "It is written,

'My house shall be a house of prayer';
but you have made it a den of robbers."

47 Every day he was teaching in the temple. The chief priests, the scribes, and the leaders of the people kept looking for a way to kill him; 48but they did not find anything they could do, for all the people were spellbound by what they heard.

The Authority of Jesus Questioned

20 One day, as he was teaching the people in the temple and telling the good news, the chief priests and the scribes came with the elders 2and said to him, "Tell us, by what authority are you doing these things? Who is it who gave you this authority?" 3He answered them, "I will also ask you a question, and you tell me: 4Did the baptism of John come from heaven, or was it of human origin?" 5They discussed it with one another, saying, "If we say, 'From heaven,' he will say, 'Why did you not believe him?' 6But if we say, 'Of human origin,' all the people will stone us; for they are convinced that John was a prophet." 7So they answered that they did not know where it came from. 8Then Jesus said to them, "Neither will I tell you by what authority I am doing these things."

The Parable of the Wicked Tenants

9 He began to tell the people this parable: "A man planted a vineyard, and leased it to tenants, and went to another country for a long time. 10When the season came, he sent a slave to the tenants in order that they might give him his share of the produce of the vineyard; but the tenants beat him and sent him away empty-handed. 11Next he sent another slave; that one also they beat and insulted and sent away empty-handed. 12And he sent still a third; this one also they wounded and threw out. 13Then the

1 Gk lacks from God

owner of the vineyard said, 'What shall I do? I will send my beloved son; perhaps they will respect him.' [14]But when the tenants saw him, they discussed it among themselves and said, 'This is the heir; let us kill him so that the inheritance may be ours.' [15]So they threw him out of the vineyard and killed him. What then will the owner of the vineyard do to them? [16]He will come and destroy those tenants and give the vineyard to others." When they heard this, they said, "Heaven forbid!" [17]But he looked at them and said, "What then does this text mean:

'The stone that the builders rejected
has become the cornerstone'?[m]
[18]Everyone who falls on that stone will be broken to pieces; and it will crush anyone on whom it falls." [19]When the scribes and chief priests realized that he had told this parable against them, they wanted to lay hands on him at that very hour, but they feared the people.

The Question about Paying Taxes

20 So they watched him and sent spies who pretended to be honest, in order to trap him by what he said, so as to hand him over to the jurisdiction and authority of the governor. [21]So they asked him, "Teacher, we know that you are right in what you say and teach, and you show deference to no one, but teach the way of God in accordance with truth. [22]Is it lawful for us to pay taxes to the emperor, or not?" [23]But he perceived their craftiness and said to them, [24]"Show me a denarius. Whose head and whose title does it bear?" They said, "The emperor's." [25]He said to them, "Then give to the emperor the things that are the emperor's, and to God the things that are God's." [26]And they were not able in the presence of the people to trap him by what he said; and being amazed by his answer, they became silent.

The Question about the Resurrection

27 Some Sadducees, those who say there is no resurrection, came to him [28]and asked him a question, "Teacher, Moses wrote for us that if a man's broth-

er dies, leaving a wife but no children, the man[n] shall marry the widow and raise up children for his brother. [29]Now there were seven brothers; the first married, and died childless; [30]then the second [31]and the third married her, and so in the same way all seven died childless. [32]Finally the woman also died. [33]In the resurrection, therefore, whose wife will the woman be? For the seven had married her."

34 Jesus said to them, "Those who belong to this age marry and are given in marriage; [35]but those who are considered worthy of a place in that age and in the resurrection from the dead neither marry nor are given in marriage. [36]Indeed they cannot die anymore, because they are like angels and are children of God, being children of the resurrection. [37]And the fact that the dead are raised Moses himself showed, in the story about the bush, where he speaks of the Lord as the God of Abraham, the God of Isaac, and the God of Jacob. [38]Now he is God not of the dead, but of the living; for to him all of them are alive." [39]Then some of the scribes answered, "Teacher, you have spoken well." [40]For they no longer dared to ask him another question.

The Question about David's Son

41 Then he said to them, "How can they say that the Messiah[o] is David's son? [42]For David himself says in the book of Psalms,

'The Lord said to my Lord,
"Sit at my right hand,
43   until I make your enemies your
footstool." '
[44]David thus calls him Lord; so how can he be his son?"

Jesus Denounces the Scribes

45 In the hearing of all the people he said to the[p] disciples, [46]"Beware of the scribes, who like to walk around in long robes, and love to be greeted with respect in the marketplaces, and to have the best seats in the synagogues and places of honor at banquets. [47]They devour widows' houses and for the sake of appearance say long prayers. They will receive the greater condemnation."

m Or keystone   n Gk his brother   o Or the Christ   p Other ancient authorities read his

The Widow's Offering

21 He looked up and saw rich people putting their gifts into the treasury; 2he also saw a poor widow put in two small copper coins. 3He said, "Truly I tell you, this poor widow has put in more than all of them; 4for all of them have contributed out of their abundance, but she out of her poverty has put in all she had to live on."

The Destruction of the Temple Foretold

5 When some were speaking about the temple, how it was adorned with beautiful stones and gifts dedicated to God, he said, 6"As for these things that you see, the days will come when not one stone will be left upon another; all will be thrown down."

Signs and Persecutions

7 They asked him, "Teacher, when will this be, and what will be the sign that this is about to take place?" 8And he said, "Beware that you are not led astray; for many will come in my name and say, 'I am he!'q and, 'The time is near!'r Do not go after them.

9 "When you hear of wars and insurrections, do not be terrified; for these things must take place first, but the end will not follow immediately." 10Then he said to them, "Nation will rise against nation, and kingdom against kingdom; 11there will be great earthquakes, and in various places famines and plagues; and there will be dreadful portents and great signs from heaven.

12 "But before all this occurs, they will arrest you and persecute you; they will hand you over to synagogues and prisons, and you will be brought before kings and governors because of my name. 13This will give you an opportunity to testify. 14So make up your minds not to prepare your defense in advance; 15for I will give you wordss and a wisdom that none of your opponents will be able to withstand or contradict. 16You will be betrayed even by parents and brothers, by relatives and friends; and they will put some of you to death. 17You will be hated by all because of my name. 18But not a hair of your head will perish. 19By your endurance you will gain your souls.

The Destruction of Jerusalem Foretold

20 "When you see Jerusalem surrounded by armies, then know that its desolation has come near.t 21Then those in Judea must flee to the mountains, and those inside the city must leave it, and those out in the country must not enter it; 22for these are days of vengeance, as a fulfillment of all that is written. 23Woe to those who are pregnant and to those who are nursing infants in those days! For there will be great distress on the earth and wrath against this people; 24they will fall by the edge of the sword and be taken away as captives among all nations; and Jerusalem will be trampled on by the Gentiles, until the times of the Gentiles are fulfilled.

The Coming of the Son of Man

25 "There will be signs in the sun, the moon, and the stars, and on the earth distress among nations confused by the roaring of the sea and the waves. 26People will faint from fear and foreboding of what is coming upon the world, for the powers of the heavens will be shaken. 27Then they will see 'the Son of Man coming in a cloud' with power and great glory. 28Now when these things begin to take place, stand up and raise your heads, because your redemption is drawing near."

The Lesson of the Fig Tree

29 Then he told them a parable: "Look at the fig tree and all the trees; 30as soon as they sprout leaves you can see for yourselves and know that summer is already near. 31So also, when you see these things taking place, you know that the kingdom of God is near. 32Truly I tell you, this generation will not pass away until all things have taken place. 33Heaven and earth will pass away, but my words will not pass away.

Exhortation to Watch

34 "Be on guard so that your hearts are not weighed down with dissipation

q Gk I am   r Or at hand   s Gk a mouth   t Or is at hand

and drunkenness and the worries of this life, and that day does not catch you unexpectedly, 35like a trap. For it will come upon all who live on the face of the whole earth. 36Be alert at all times, praying that you may have the strength to escape all these things that will take place, and to stand before the Son of Man."

37 Every day he was teaching in the temple, and at night he would go out and spend the night on the Mount of Olives, as it was called. 38And all the people would get up early in the morning to listen to him in the temple.

The Plot to Kill Jesus

22 Now the festival of Unleavened Bread, which is called the Passover, was near. 2The chief priests and the scribes were looking for a way to put Jesus*u* to death, for they were afraid of the people.

3 Then Satan entered into Judas called Iscariot, who was one of the twelve; 4he went away and conferred with the chief priests and officers of the temple police about how he might betray him to them. 5They were greatly pleased and agreed to give him money. 6So he consented and began to look for an opportunity to betray him to them when no crowd was present.

The Preparation of the Passover

7 Then came the day of Unleavened Bread, on which the Passover lamb had to be sacrificed. 8So Jesus*v* sent Peter and John, saying, "Go and prepare the Passover meal for us that we may eat it." 9They asked him, "Where do you want us to make preparations for it?" 10"Listen," he said to them, "when you have entered the city, a man carrying a jar of water will meet you; follow him into the house he enters 11and say to the owner of the house, 'The teacher asks you, "Where is the guest room, where I may eat the Passover with my disciples?" ' 12He will show you a large room upstairs, already furnished. Make preparations for us there." 13So they went and found everything as he had told them; and they prepared the Passover meal.

The Institution of the Lord's Supper

14 When the hour came, he took his place at the table, and the apostles with him. 15He said to them, "I have eagerly desired to eat this Passover with you before I suffer; 16for I tell you, I will not eat it*w* until it is fulfilled in the kingdom of God." 17Then he took a cup, and after giving thanks he said, "Take this and divide it among yourselves; 18for I tell you that from now on I will not drink of the fruit of the vine until the kingdom of God comes." 19Then he took a loaf of bread, and when he had given thanks, he broke it and gave it to them, saying, "This is my body, which is given for you. Do this in remembrance of me." 20And he did the same with the cup after supper, saying, "This cup that is poured out for you is the new covenant in my blood.*x* 21But see, the one who betrays me is with me, and his hand is on the table. 22For the Son of Man is going as it has been determined, but woe to that one by whom he is betrayed!" 23Then they began to ask one another which one of them it could be who would do this.

The Dispute about Greatness

24 A dispute also arose among them as to which one of them was to be regarded as the greatest. 25But he said to them, "The kings of the Gentiles lord it over them; and those in authority over them are called benefactors. 26But not so with you; rather the greatest among you must become like the youngest, and the leader like one who serves. 27For who is greater, the one who is at the table or the one who serves? Is it not the one at the table? But I am among you as one who serves.

28 "You are those who have stood by me in my trials; 29and I confer on you, just as my Father has conferred on me, a kingdom, 30so that you may eat and drink at my table in my kingdom, and you will sit on thrones judging the twelve tribes of Israel.

Jesus Predicts Peter's Denial

31 "Simon, Simon, listen! Satan has

u Gk *him*　v Gk *he*　w Other ancient authorities read *never eat it again*　x Other ancient authorities lack, in whole or in part, verses 19b-20 (*which is given . . . in my blood*)

demanded[y] to sift all of you like wheat, [32]but I have prayed for you that your own faith may not fail; and you, when once you have turned back, strengthen your brothers." [33]And he said to him, "Lord, I am ready to go with you to prison and to death!" [34]Jesus[z] said, "I tell you, Peter, the cock will not crow this day, until you have denied three times that you know me."

Purse, Bag, and Sword

35 He said to them, "When I sent you out without a purse, bag, or sandals, did you lack anything?" They said, "No, not a thing." [36]He said to them, "But now, the one who has a purse must take it, and likewise a bag. And the one who has no sword must sell his cloak and buy one. [37]For I tell you, this scripture must be fulfilled in me, 'And he was counted among the lawless'; and indeed what is written about me is being fulfilled." [38]They said, "Lord, look, here are two swords." He replied, "It is enough."

Jesus Prays on the Mount of Olives

39 He came out and went, as was his custom, to the Mount of Olives; and the disciples followed him. [40]When he reached the place, he said to them, "Pray that you may not come into the time of trial."[a] [41]Then he withdrew from them about a stone's throw, knelt down, and prayed, [42]"Father, if you are willing, remove this cup from me; yet, not my will but yours be done." [[43]Then an angel from heaven appeared to him and gave him strength. [44]In his anguish he prayed more earnestly, and his sweat became like great drops of blood falling down on the ground.]][b] [45]When he got up from prayer, he came to the disciples and found them sleeping because of grief, [46]and he said to them, "Why are you sleeping? Get up and pray that you may not come into the time of trial."[a]

The Betrayal and Arrest of Jesus

47 While he was still speaking, suddenly a crowd came, and the one called Judas, one of the twelve, was leading them. He approached Jesus to kiss him; [48]but Jesus said to him, "Judas, is it with a kiss that you are betraying the Son of Man?" [49]When those who were around him saw what was coming, they asked, "Lord, should we strike with the sword?" [50]Then one of them struck the slave of the high priest and cut off his right ear. [51]But Jesus said, "No more of this!" And he touched his ear and healed him. [52]Then Jesus said to the chief priests, the officers of the temple police, and the elders who had come for him, "Have you come out with swords and clubs as if I were a bandit? [53]When I was with you day after day in the temple, you did not lay hands on me. But this is your hour, and the power of darkness!"

Peter Denies Jesus

54 Then they seized him and led him away, bringing him into the high priest's house. But Peter was following at a distance. [55]When they had kindled a fire in the middle of the courtyard and sat down together, Peter sat among them. [56]Then a servant-girl, seeing him in the firelight, stared at him and said, "This man also was with him." [57]But he denied it, saying, "Woman, I do not know him." [58]A little later someone else, on seeing him, said, "You also are one of them." But Peter said, "Man, I am not!" [59]Then about an hour later still another kept insisting, "Surely this man also was with him; for he is a Galilean." [60]But Peter said, "Man, I do not know what you are talking about!" At that moment, while he was still speaking, the cock crowed. [61]The Lord turned and looked at Peter. Then Peter remembered the word of the Lord, how he had said to him, "Before the cock crows today, you will deny me three times." [62]And he went out and wept bitterly.

The Mocking and Beating of Jesus

63 Now the men who were holding Jesus began to mock him and beat him; [64]they also blindfolded him and kept asking him, "Prophesy! Who is it that struck you?" [65]They kept heaping many other insults on him.

Jesus before the Council

66 When day came, the assembly of

---

y Or has obtained permission   z Gk He   a Or into temptation   b Other ancient authorities lack verses 43 and 44

the elders of the people, both chief priests and scribes, gathered together, and they brought him to their council. [67]They said, "If you are the Messiah,[c] tell us." He replied, "If I tell you, you will not believe; [68]and if I question you, you will not answer. [69]But from now on the Son of Man will be seated at the right hand of the power of God." [70]All of them asked, "Are you, then, the Son of God?" He said to them, "You say that I am." [71]Then they said, "What further testimony do we need? We have heard it ourselves from his own lips!"

Jesus before Pilate

23 Then the assembly rose as a body and brought Jesus[d] before Pilate. [2]They began to accuse him, saying, "We found this man perverting our nation, forbidding us to pay taxes to the emperor, and saying that he himself is the Messiah, a king."[e] [3]Then Pilate asked him, "Are you the king of the Jews?" He answered, "You say so." [4]Then Pilate said to the chief priests and the crowds, "I find no basis for an accusation against this man." [5]But they were insistent and said, "He stirs up the people by teaching throughout all Judea, from Galilee where he began even to this place."

Jesus before Herod

6 When Pilate heard this, he asked whether the man was a Galilean. [7]And when he learned that he was under Herod's jurisdiction, he sent him off to Herod, who was himself in Jerusalem at that time. [8]When Herod saw Jesus, he was very glad, for he had been wanting to see him for a long time, because he had heard about him and was hoping to see him perform some sign. [9]He questioned him at some length, but Jesus[f] gave him no answer. [10]The chief priests and the scribes stood by, vehemently accusing him. [11]Even Herod with his soldiers treated him with contempt and mocked him; then he put an elegant robe on him, and sent him back to Pilate. [12]That same day Herod and Pilate became friends with each other; before this they had been enemies.

Jesus Sentenced to Death

13 Pilate then called together the chief priests, the leaders, and the people, [14]and said to them, "You brought me this man as one who was perverting the people; and here I have examined him in your presence and have not found this man guilty of any of your charges against him. [15]Neither has Herod, for he sent him back to us. Indeed, he has done nothing to deserve death. [16]I will therefore have him flogged and release him."[g]

18 Then they all shouted out together, "Away with this fellow! Release Barabbas for us!" [19](This was a man who had been put in prison for an insurrection that had taken place in the city, and for murder.) [20]Pilate, wanting to release Jesus, addressed them again; [21]but they kept shouting, "Crucify, crucify him!" [22]A third time he said to them, "Why, what evil has he done? I have found in him no ground for the sentence of death; I will therefore have him flogged and then release him." [23]But they kept urgently demanding with loud shouts that he should be crucified; and their voices prevailed. [24]So Pilate gave his verdict that their demand should be granted. [25]He released the man they asked for, the one who had been put in prison for insurrection and murder, and he handed Jesus over as they wished.

The Crucifixion of Jesus

26 As they led him away, they seized a man, Simon of Cyrene, who was coming from the country, and they laid the cross on him, and made him carry it behind Jesus. [27]A great number of the people followed him, and among them were women who were beating their breasts and wailing for him. [28]But Jesus turned to them and said, "Daughters of Jerusalem, do not weep for me, but weep for yourselves and for your children. [29]For the days are surely coming when they will say, 'Blessed are the barren, and the wombs that never bore, and the breasts that never nursed.' [30]Then they will begin to say to the mountains, 'Fall on us'; and to the hills, 'Cover us.' [31]For if they do this when the wood is green, what will happen when it is dry?"

---

c Or *the Christ*   d Gk *him*   e Or *is an anointed king*   f Gk *he*   g Here, or after verse 19, other ancient authorities add verse 17, *Now he was obliged to release someone for them at the festival*

GOOD AND EVIL CHANGED PLACES
Leo Tolstoy

VERSE: Luke 23.43   **PASSAGE:** Luke 23.39–43

 ive years ago I came to believe in Christ's teaching, and my life suddenly changed; I ceased to desire what I had previously desired, and began to desire what I formerly did not want. What had previously seemed to me good seemed evil, and what had seemed evil seemed good. It happened to me as it happens to a man who goes out on some business and on the way suddenly decides that the business is unnecessary and returns home. All that was on his right is now on his left, and all that was on his left is now on his right; his former wish to get as far as possible from home has changed into a wish to be as near as possible to it. The direction of my life and my desires became different, and good and evil changed places . . .

I, like that thief on the cross, have believed Christ's teaching and been saved. And this is no far-fetched comparison, but the closest expression of the condition of spiritual despair and horror at the problem of life and death in which I lived formerly, and of the condition of peace and happiness in which I am now. I, like the thief, knew that I was unhappy and suffering . . . I, like the thief to the cross, was nailed by some force to that life of suffering and evil. And as, after the meaningless sufferings and evils of life, the thief awaited the terrible darkness of death, so did I await the same thing.

In all this I was exactly like the thief, but the difference was that the thief was already dying, while I was still living. The thief might believe that his salvation lay there beyond the grave, but I could not be satisfied with that, because besides a life beyond the grave life still awaited me here. But I did not understand that life. It seemed to me terrible. And suddenly I heard the words of Christ and understood them, and life and death ceased to seem to me evil, and instead of despair I experienced happiness and the joy of life undisturbed by death.

ADDITIONAL SCRIPTURE READING:
Psalm 56.13; 1 Peter 1.8–9

Go to page 1229 for your next devotional reading.

1700   1900

32 Two others also, who were criminals, were led away to be put to death with him. 33When they came to the place that is called The Skull, they crucified Jesus[h] there with the criminals, one on his right and one on his left. [[34Then Jesus said, "Father, forgive them; for they do not know what they are doing."]][i] And they cast lots to divide his clothing. 35And the people stood by, watching; but the leaders scoffed at him, saying, "He saved others; let him save himself if he is the Messiah[j] of God, his chosen one!" 36The soldiers also mocked him, coming up and offering him sour wine, 37and saying, "If you are the King of the Jews, save yourself!" 38There was also an inscription over him,[k] "This is the King of the Jews."

39 One of the criminals who were hanged there kept deriding[l] him and saying, "Are you not the Messiah?[j] Save yourself and us!" 40But the other rebuked him, saying, "Do you not fear God, since you are under the same sentence of condemnation? 41And we indeed have been condemned justly, for we are getting what we deserve for our deeds, but this man has done nothing wrong." 42Then he said, "Jesus, remember me when you come into[m] your kingdom." 43He replied, "Truly I tell you, today you will be with me in Paradise."

The Death of Jesus

44 It was now about noon, and darkness came over the whole land[n] until three in the afternoon, 45while the sun's light failed;[o] and the curtain of the temple was torn in two. 46Then Jesus, crying with a loud voice, said, "Father, into your hands I commend my spirit." Having said this, he breathed his last. 47When the centurion saw what had taken place, he praised God and said, "Certainly this man was innocent."[p] 48And when all the crowds who had gathered there for this spectacle saw what had taken place, they returned home, beating their breasts. 49But all his acquaintances, including the women who had followed him from Galilee, stood at a distance, watching these things.

The Burial of Jesus

50 Now there was a good and righteous man named Joseph, who, though a member of the council, 51had not agreed to their plan and action. He came from the Jewish town of Arimathea, and he was waiting expectantly for the kingdom of God. 52This man went to Pilate and asked for the body of Jesus. 53Then he took it down, wrapped it in a linen cloth, and laid it in a rock-hewn tomb where no one had ever been laid. 54It was the day of Preparation, and the sabbath was beginning.[q] 55The women who had come with him from Galilee followed, and they saw the tomb and how his body was laid. 56Then they returned, and prepared spices and ointments.

On the sabbath they rested according to the commandment.

The Resurrection of Jesus

24 But on the first day of the week, at early dawn, they came to the tomb, taking the spices that they had prepared. 2They found the stone rolled away from the tomb, 3but when they went in, they did not find the body.[r] 4While they were perplexed about this, suddenly two men in dazzling clothes stood beside them. 5The women[s] were terrified and bowed their

---

TOMB, THOU SHALT NOT HOLD HIM LONGER;

DEATH IS STRONG, BUT LIFE IS STRONGER;

STRONGER THAN THE DARK, THE LIGHT;

STRONGER THAN THE WRONG, THE RIGHT;

FAITH AND HOPE TRIUMPHANT SAY

CHRIST WILL RISE ON EASTER DAY.

　　　—*Phillips Brooks*

---

faces to the ground, but the men[t] said to them, "Why do you look for the living among the dead? He is not here, but has risen.[u] 6Remember how he told you,

---

h Gk *him*　i Other ancient authorities lack the sentence *Then Jesus . . . what they are doing*
j Or *the Christ*　k Other ancient authorities add *written in Greek and Latin and Hebrew* (that is, Aramaic)　l Or *blaspheming*　m Other ancient authorities read *in*　n Or *earth*　o Or *the sun was eclipsed.* Other ancient authorities read *the sun was darkened*　p Or *righteous*　q Gk *was dawning*　r Other ancient authorities add *of the Lord Jesus*　s Gk *They*　t Gk *but they*
u Other ancient authorities lack *He is not here, but has risen*

FRIDAY

WALKING WITH JESUS
Jacob Boehme

VERSE: Luke 24.15   PASSAGE: Luke 24.13–16

At Noon

 God, the source of eternal light, you provide temporal light for the earth, ruling over the sun and the moon that all creatures may live and thrive. The warmth and brightness of the sun makes the flowers bloom and the crops grow. And the gentle beams of the moon and stars remind us that your Word is alive and active even when we can see only dimly. Guide me to find my rightful place in your creation, that in some small way I may add to the beauty of your handiwork. And may your eternal light shine in the darkest corners of my soul, that all shadow of sin may be expelled.

At Evening

I thank you, O God, for your care and protection this day, keeping me from physical harm and spiritual corruption. I now place the work of the day into your hands, trusting that you will redeem my errors and turn my achievements to your glory. And I now ask you to work within me, trusting that you will use the hours of rest to create in me a new heart and new soul. Let my mind, which through the day has been directed to my work, through the evening be wholly directed at you.

At Bedtime

As I take off my dusty, dirty clothes, let me also be stripped of the sins I have committed this day. I confess, dear Lord, that in so many ways my thoughts and actions have been impure. Now I come before you, naked in body and bare in soul, to be washed clean. Let me rest tonight in your arms, and so may the dreams that pass through my mind be holy. And let me awake tomorrow, strong and eager to serve you.

ADDITIONAL SCRIPTURE READING:
Psalms 15.1–3; 43.3

Go to page 1233 for your next devotional reading.

1500   1700

while he was still in Galilee, [7]that the Son of Man must be handed over to sinners, and be crucified, and on the third day rise again." [8]Then they remembered his words, [9]and returning from the tomb, they told all this to the eleven and to all the rest. [10]Now it was Mary Magdalene, Joanna, Mary the mother of James, and the other women with them who told this to the apostles. [11]But these words seemed to them an idle tale, and they did not believe them. [12]But Peter got up and ran to the tomb; stooping and looking in, he saw the linen cloths by themselves; then he went home, amazed at what had happened.[v]

The Walk to Emmaus

13 Now on that same day two of them were going to a village called Emmaus, about seven miles[w] from Jerusalem, [14]and talking with each other about all these things that had happened. [15]While they were talking and discussing, Jesus himself came near and went with them, [16]but their eyes were kept from recognizing him. [17]And he said to them, "What are you discussing with each other while you walk along?" They stood still, looking sad.[x] [18]Then one of them, whose name was Cleopas, answered him, "Are you the only stranger in Jerusalem who does not know the things that have taken place there in these days?" [19]He asked them, "What things?" They replied, "The things about Jesus of Nazareth,[y] who was a prophet mighty in deed and word before God and all the people, [20]and how our chief priests and leaders handed him over to be condemned to death and crucified him. [21]But we had hoped that he was the one to redeem Israel.[z] Yes, and besides all this, it is now the third day since these things took place. [22]Moreover, some women of our group astounded us. They were at the tomb early this morning, [23]and when they did not find his body there, they came back and told us that they had indeed seen a vision of angels who said that he was alive. [24]Some of those who were with us

went to the tomb and found it just as the women had said; but they did not see him." [25]Then he said to them, "Oh, how foolish you are, and how slow of heart to believe all that the prophets have declared! [26]Was it not necessary that the Messiah[a] should suffer these things and then enter into his glory?" [27]Then beginning with Moses and all the prophets, he interpreted to them the things about himself in all the scriptures.

28 As they came near the village to which they were going, he walked ahead as if he were going on. [29]But they urged him strongly, saying, "Stay with us, because it is almost evening and the day is now nearly over." So he went in to stay with them. [30]When he was at the table with them, he took bread, blessed and broke it, and gave it to them. [31]Then their eyes were opened, and they recognized him; and he vanished from their sight. [32]They said to each other, "Were not our hearts burning within us[b] while he was talking to us on the road, while he was opening the scriptures to us?" [33]That same hour they got up and returned to Jerusalem; and they found the eleven and their companions gathered together. [34]They were saying, "The Lord has risen indeed, and he has appeared to Simon!" [35]Then they told what had happened on the road, and how he had been made known to them in the breaking of the bread.

Jesus Appears to His Disciples

36 While they were talking about this, Jesus himself stood among them and said to them, "Peace be with you."[c] [37]They were startled and terrified, and thought that they were seeing a ghost. [38]He said to them, "Why are you frightened, and why do doubts arise in your hearts? [39]Look at my hands and my feet; see that it is I myself. Touch me and see; for a ghost does not have flesh and bones as you see that I have." [40]And when he had said this, he showed them his hands and his feet.[d] [41]While in their joy they were disbelieving and still wondering, he said to them, "Have you anything

v Other ancient authorities lack verse 12   w Gk sixty stadia; other ancient authorities read a hundred sixty stadia   x Other ancient authorities read walk along, looking sad?   y Other ancient authorities read Jesus the Nazorean   z Or to set Israel free   a Or the Christ   b Other ancient authorities lack within us   c Other ancient authorities lack and said to them, "Peace be with you." d Other ancient authorities lack verse 40

here to eat?" [42]They gave him a piece of broiled fish, [43]and he took it and ate in their presence.

44 Then he said to them, "These are my words that I spoke to you while I was still with you—that everything written about me in the law of Moses, the prophets, and the psalms must be fulfilled." [45]Then he opened their minds to understand the scriptures, [46]and he said to them, "Thus it is written, that the Messiah[e] is to suffer and to rise from the dead on the third day, [47]and that repentance and forgiveness of sins is to be proclaimed in his name to all nations, beginning from Jerusalem. [48]You are witnesses[f] of these things. [49]And see, I am sending upon you what my Father promised; so stay here in the city until you have been clothed with power from on high."

IN THE OLD TESTAMENT THE NEW LIES HIDDEN, IN THE NEW TESTAMENT THE OLD IS LAID OPEN.

—Augustine

The Ascension of Jesus

50 Then he led them out as far as Bethany, and, lifting up his hands, he blessed them. [51]While he was blessing them, he withdrew from them and was carried up into heaven.[g] [52]And they worshiped him, and[h] returned to Jerusalem with great joy; [53]and they were continually in the temple blessing God.[i]

---

e Or the Christ   f Or nations. Beginning from Jerusalem [48]you are witnesses   g Other ancient authorities lack and was carried up into heaven   h Other ancient authorities lack worshiped him, and   i Other ancient authorities add Amen

JOHN

HY DID GOD'S SON COME TO EARTH? JOHN'S GOSPEL HAS THE ANSWER. "FOR GOD SO LOVED THE WORLD THAT HE GAVE HIS ONLY SON, SO THAT EVERYONE WHO BELIEVES IN HIM MAY NOT PERISH BUT MAY HAVE ETERNAL LIFE" (3.16). JOHN'S WRITINGS ARE DESIGNED TO CONVINCE PEOPLE TO BELIEVE IN JESUS AS GOD IN HUMAN FORM AND TO "HAVE LIFE" AS A RESULT (20.31). REFLECT ON THE ONE WHO ONCE LIVED AMONG PEOPLE LIKE US, AND RENEW YOUR TRUST THAT HE WILL GIVE YOU LIFE TO THE FULL.

The Word Became Flesh

1 In the beginning was the Word, and the Word was with God, and the Word was God. ²He was in the beginning with God. ³All things came into being through him, and without him not one thing came into being. What has come into being ⁴in him was life,ᵃ and the life was the light of all people. ⁵The light shines in the darkness, and the darkness did not overcome it.

6 There was a man sent from God, whose name was John. ⁷He came as a witness to testify to the light, so that all might believe through him. ⁸He himself was not the light, but he came to testify to the light. ⁹The true light, which enlightens everyone, was coming into the world.ᵇ

10 He was in the world, and the world came into being through him; yet the world did not know him. ¹¹He came to what was his own,ᶜ and his own people did not accept him. ¹²But to all who received him, who believed in his name, he gave power to become children of God, ¹³who were born, not of blood or of the will of the flesh or of the will of man, but of God.

DEITY INDWELLING MEN! THAT, I SAY IS CHRISTIANITY!
—*A. W. Tozer*

---

a Or ³through him. And without him not one thing came into being that has come into being. ⁴In him was life   b Or He was the true light that enlightens everyone coming into the world   c Or to his own home

WEEKEND

THE WORD OF GOD IS GOD IN ACTION
F. F. Bruce

VERSE: John 1.1   **PASSAGE:** John 1.1–2

n the beginning," . . . when the universe was brought into existence, the divine Word by which it was brought into existence was already there. And the language which follows shows that our Evangelist has no mere literary personification in mind. The personal status which he ascribes to the Word is a matter of real existence; the relation which the Word bears to God is a personal relation: "the Word was with God."

This statement has profound theological implications . . . The Word of God is distinguished from God himself, and yet exists in a close personal relation with him; moreover, the Word shares the very nature of God, for "the Word was *God.*"

The structure of the third clause in verse 1 . . . demands the translation "the Word was God." Since *logos* [Word] has the article preceding it, it is marked out as the subject . . . Had *theos* [God] as well as *logos* been preceded by the article the meaning would have been that the Word was completely identical with God, which is impossible if the Word was also "with God." What is meant is that the Word shared the nature and being of God, or (to use a piece of modern jargon) was an extension of the personality of God . . .

So, when heaven and earth were created, there was the Word of God, already existing in the closest association with God and partaking of the essence of God. No matter how far back we may try to push our imagination, we can never reach a point at which we could say of the Divine Word, as Arius did, "There was once when he was not."

ADDITIONAL SCRIPTURE READING:
Isaiah 55.11; Revelation 1.8

Go to page 1236 for your next devotional reading.

1900   Present

14 And the Word became flesh and lived among us, and we have seen his glory, the glory as of a father's only son,d full of grace and truth. 15(John testified to him and cried out, "This was he of whom I said, 'He who comes after me ranks ahead of me because he was before me.' ") 16From his fullness we have all received, grace upon grace. 17The law indeed was given through Moses; grace and truth came through Jesus Christ. 18No one has ever seen God. It is God the only Son,e who is close to the Father's heart,f who has made him known.

The Testimony of John the Baptist

19 This is the testimony given by John when the Jews sent priests and Levites from Jerusalem to ask him, "Who are you?" 20He confessed and did not deny it, but confessed, "I am not the Messiah."g 21And they asked him, "What then? Are you Elijah?" He said, "I am not." "Are you the prophet?" He answered, "No." 22Then they said to him, "Who are you? Let us have an answer for those who sent us. What do you say about yourself?" 23He said,

"I am the voice of one crying out in the wilderness,
'Make straight the way of the Lord,'

as the prophet Isaiah said.

24 Now they had been sent from the Pharisees. 25They asked him, "Why then are you baptizing if you are neither the Messiah,g nor Elijah, nor the prophet?" 26John answered them, "I baptize with water. Among you stands one whom you do not know, 27the one who is coming after me; I am not worthy to untie the thong of his sandal." 28This took place in Bethany across the Jordan where John was baptizing.

The Lamb of God

29 The next day he saw Jesus coming toward him and declared, "Here is the Lamb of God who takes away the sin of the world! 30This is he of whom I said, 'After me comes a man who ranks ahead of me because he was before me.' 31I myself did not know him; but I came

baptizing with water for this reason, that he might be revealed to Israel." 32And John testified, "I saw the Spirit descending from heaven like a dove, and it remained on him. 33I myself did not know him, but the one who sent me to baptize with water said to me, 'He on whom you see the Spirit descend and remain is the one who baptizes with the Holy Spirit.' 34And I myself have seen and have testified that this is the Son of God."h

The First Disciples of Jesus

35 The next day John again was standing with two of his disciples, 36and as he watched Jesus walk by, he exclaimed, "Look, here is the Lamb of God!"· 37The two disciples heard him say this, and they followed Jesus. 38When Jesus turned and saw them following, he said to them, "What are you looking for?" They said to him, "Rabbi" (which translated means Teacher), "where are you staying?" 39He said to them, "Come and see." They came and saw where he was staying, and they remained with him that day. It was about four o'clock in the afternoon. 40One of the two who heard John speak and followed him was Andrew, Simon Peter's brother. 41He first found his brother Simon and said to him, "We have found the Messiah" (which is translated Anointedi). 42He brought Simonj to Jesus, who looked at him and said, "You are Simon son of John. You are to be called Cephas" (which is translated Peterk).

Jesus Calls Philip and Nathanael

43 The next day Jesus decided to go to Galilee. He found Philip and said to him, "Follow me." 44Now Philip was from Bethsaida, the city of Andrew and Peter. 45Philip found Nathanael and said to him, "We have found him about whom Moses in the law and also the prophets wrote, Jesus son of Joseph from Nazareth." 46Nathanael said to him, "Can anything good come out of Nazareth?" Philip said to him, "Come and see." 47When Jesus saw Nathanael coming toward him, he said of him, "Here is truly an Israelite in whom there is no deceit!" 48Nathanael asked him, "Where did you

d Or the Father's only Son   e Other ancient authorities read It is an only Son, God, or It is the only Son   f Gk bosom   g Or the Christ   h Other ancient authorities read is God's chosen one   i Or Christ   j Gk him   k From the word for rock in Aramaic (kepha) and Greek (petra), respectively

get to know me?" Jesus answered, "I saw you under the fig tree before Philip called you." 49Nathanael replied, "Rabbi, you are the Son of God! You are the King of Israel!" 50Jesus answered, "Do you believe because I told you that I saw you under the fig tree? You will see greater things than these." 51And he said to him, "Very truly, I tell you,*l* you will see heaven opened and the angels of God ascending and descending upon the Son of Man."

The Wedding at Cana

2 On the third day there was a wedding in Cana of Galilee, and the mother of Jesus was there. 2Jesus and his disciples had also been invited to the wedding. 3When the wine gave out, the mother of Jesus said to him, "They have no wine." 4And Jesus said to her, "Woman, what concern is that to you and to me? My hour has not yet come." 5His mother said to the servants, "Do whatever he tells you." 6Now standing there were six stone water jars for the Jewish rites of purification, each holding twenty or thirty gallons. 7Jesus said to them, "Fill the jars with water." And they filled them up to the brim. 8He said to them, "Now draw some out, and take it to the chief steward." So they took it. 9When the steward tasted the water that had become wine, and did not know where it came from (though the servants who had drawn the water knew), the steward called the bridegroom 10and said to him, "Everyone serves the good wine first, and then the inferior wine after the guests have become drunk. But you have kept the good wine until now." 11Jesus did this, the first of his signs, in Cana of Galilee, and revealed his glory; and his disciples believed in him.

12 After this he went down to Capernaum with his mother, his brothers, and his disciples; and they remained there a few days.

Jesus Cleanses the Temple

13 The Passover of the Jews was near, and Jesus went up to Jerusalem. 14In the temple he found people selling cattle, sheep, and doves, and the money chang-

ers seated at their tables. 15Making a whip of cords, he drove all of them out of the temple, both the sheep and the cattle. He also poured out the coins of the money changers and overturned their tables. 16He told those who were selling the doves, "Take these things out of here! Stop making my Father's house a marketplace!" 17His disciples remembered that it was written, "Zeal for your house will consume me." 18The Jews then said to him, "What sign can you show us for doing this?" 19Jesus answered them, "Destroy this temple, and in three days I will raise it up." 20The Jews then said, "This temple has been under construction for forty-six years, and will you raise it up in three days?" 21But he was speaking of the temple of his body. 22After he was raised from the dead, his disciples remembered that he had said this; and they believed the scripture and the word that Jesus had spoken.

23 When he was in Jerusalem during the Passover festival, many believed in his name because they saw the signs that he was doing. 24But Jesus on his part would not entrust himself to them, because he knew all people 25and needed no one to testify about anyone; for he himself knew what was in everyone.

Nicodemus Visits Jesus

3 Now there was a Pharisee named Nicodemus, a leader of the Jews. 2He came to Jesus*m* by night and said to him, "Rabbi, we know that you are a teacher who has come from God; for no one can do these signs that you do apart from the presence of God." 3Jesus answered him, "Very truly, I tell you, no one can see the kingdom of God without being born from above."*n* 4Nicodemus said to him, "How can anyone be born after having grown old? Can one enter a second time into the mother's womb and be born?" 5Jesus answered, "Very truly, I tell you, no one can enter the kingdom of God without being born of water and Spirit. 6What is born of the flesh is flesh, and what is born of the Spirit is spirit.*o* 7Do not be astonished that I said to you, 'You*p* must be born from

---

l Both instances of the Greek word for *you* in this verse are plural   *m* Gk *him*   *n* Or *born anew*
o The same Greek word means both *wind* and *spirit*   *p* The Greek word for *you* here is plural

above.'*q* ⁸The wind*r* blows where it chooses, and you hear the sound of it, but you do not know where it comes from or where it goes. So it is with everyone who is born of the Spirit." ⁹Nicodemus said to him, "How can these things be?" ¹⁰Jesus

q Or *anew*   *r* The same Greek word means both *wind* and *spirit*

MONDAY

A WAY OF LIFE
Sir William Osler

VERSE: John 3.5   **PASSAGE:** John 3.1–7

o you remember that most touching of all incidents in Christ's ministry, when the anxious ruler Nicodemus came by night, worried lest the things that pertained to his everlasting peace were not a part of his busy and successful life? Christ's message to him is his message to the world—never more needed than at present: "You must be born of the Spirit." You wish to be with the leaders . . . know the great souls that make up the moral radium of the world. You must be born of their spirit, initiated into their fraternity, whether of the spiritually minded followers of the Nazarene or of that larger company, elect from every nation, seen by St. John.

Begin the day with Christ and [the Lord's] prayer—you need no other. Creedless, with it you have religion; creed-stuffed, it will leaven any theological dough in which you stick. As the soul is dyed by the thoughts, let no day pass without contact with the best literature of the world. Learn to know your Bible, though not perhaps as your fathers did. In forming character and in shaping conduct, its touch has still its ancient power. Of the kindred of Ram and sons of Elihu, you should know its beauties and its strength. Fifteen or twenty minutes day by day will give you fellowship with the great minds of the race, and little by little as the years pass you extend your friendship with the immortal dead. They will give you faith in your own day. Listen while they speak to you of the fathers . . . Mankind, it has been said, is always advancing, man is always the same. The love, hope, fear, and faith that make humanity, and the elemental passions of the human heart, remain unchanged, and the secret of inspiration in any literature is the capacity to touch the cord that vibrates in a sympathy that knows no time nor place . . .

ADDITIONAL SCRIPTURE READING:
2 Timothy 3.16; James 1.22–25

Go to page 1239 for your next devotional reading.

1900   Present

answered him, "Are you a teacher of Israel, and yet you do not understand these things?

---

11 "Very truly, I tell you, we speak of what we know and testify to what we have seen; yet yous do not receive our testimony. 12If I have told you about earthly things and you do not believe, how can you believe if I tell you about heavenly things? 13No one has ascended into heaven except the one who descended from heaven, the Son of Man.t 14And just as Moses lifted up the serpent in the wilderness, so must the Son of Man be lifted up, 15that whoever believes in him may have eternal life.u

16 "For God so loved the world that he gave his only Son, so that everyone who believes in him may not perish but may have eternal life.

17 "Indeed, God did not send the Son into the world to condemn the world, but in order that the world might be saved through him. 18Those who believe in him are not condemned; but those who do not believe are condemned already, because they have not believed in the name of the only Son of God. 19And this is the judgment, that the light has come into the world, and people loved darkness rather than light because their deeds were evil. 20For all who do evil hate the light and do not come to the light, so that their deeds may not be exposed. 21But those who do what is true come to the light, so that it may be clearly seen that their deeds have been done in God."u

Jesus and John the Baptist

22 After this Jesus and his disciples went into the Judean countryside, and he spent some time there with them and baptized. 23John also was baptizing at Aenon near Salim because water was abundant there; and people kept coming and were being baptized 24—John, of course, had not yet been thrown into prison.

25 Now a discussion about purification arose between John's disciples and a Jew.v 26They came to John and said to him, "Rabbi, the one who was with you across the Jordan, to whom you testified, here he is baptizing, and all are going to him." 27John answered, "No one can receive anything except what has been given from heaven. 28You yourselves are my witnesses that I said, 'I am not the Messiah,w but I have been sent ahead of him.' 29He who has the bride is the bridegroom. The friend of the bridegroom, who stands and hears him, rejoices greatly at the bridegroom's voice. For this reason my joy has been fulfilled. 30He must increase, but I must decrease."x

The One Who Comes from Heaven

31 The one who comes from above is above all; the one who is of the earth belongs to the earth and speaks about earthly things. The one who comes from heaven is above all. 32He testifies to what he has seen and heard, yet no one accepts his testimony. 33Whoever has accepted his testimony has certifiedy this, that God is true. 34He whom God has sent speaks the words of God, for he gives the Spirit without measure. 35The Father loves the Son and has placed all things in his hands. 36Whoever believes in the Son has eternal life; whoever disobeys the Son will not see life, but must endure God's wrath.

Jesus and the Woman of Samaria

4 Now when Jesusz learned that the Pharisees had heard, "Jesus is making and baptizing more disciples than John" 2— although it was not Jesus himself but his disciples who baptized— 3he left Judea and started back to Galilee. 4But he had to go through Samaria. 5So he came to a Samaritan city called Sychar, near the plot of ground that Jacob had given to his son Joseph.

---

s The Greek word for *you* here and in verse 12 is plural   t Other ancient authorities add *who is in heaven*   u Some interpreters hold that the quotation concludes with verse 15   v Other ancient authorities read *the Jews*   w Or *the Christ*   x Some interpreters hold that the quotation continues through verse 36   y Gk *set a seal to*   z Other ancient authorities read *the Lord*

⁶Jacob's well was there, and Jesus, tired out by his journey, was sitting by the well. It was about noon.

7 A Samaritan woman came to draw water, and Jesus said to her, "Give me a drink." ⁸(His disciples had gone to the city to buy food.) ⁹The Samaritan woman said to him, "How is it that you, a Jew, ask a drink of me, a woman of Samaria?" (Jews do not share things in common with Samaritans.)ᵃ ¹⁰Jesus answered her, "If you knew the gift of God, and who it is that is saying to you, 'Give me a drink,' you would have asked him, and he would have given you living water." ¹¹The woman said to him, "Sir, you have no bucket, and the well is deep. Where do you get that living water? ¹²Are you greater than our ancestor Jacob, who gave us the well, and with his sons and his flocks drank from it?" ¹³Jesus said to her, "Everyone who drinks of this water will be thirsty again, ¹⁴but those who drink of the water that I will give them will never be thirsty. The water that I will give will become in them a spring of water gushing up to eternal life." ¹⁵The woman said to him, "Sir, give me this water, so that I may never be thirsty or have to keep coming here to draw water."

16 Jesus said to her, "Go, call your husband, and come back." ¹⁷The woman answered him, "I have no husband." Jesus said to her, "You are right in saying, 'I have no husband'; ¹⁸for you have had five husbands, and the one you have now is not your husband. What you have said is true!" ¹⁹The woman said to him, "Sir, I see that you are a prophet. ²⁰Our ancestors worshiped on this mountain, but youᵇ say that the place where people must worship is in Jerusalem." ²¹Jesus said to her, "Woman, believe me, the hour is coming when you will worship the Father neither on this mountain nor in Jerusalem. ²²You worship what you do not know; we worship what we know, for salvation is from the Jews. ²³But the hour is coming, and is now here, when the true worshipers will worship the Father in spirit and truth, for the Father seeks such as these to

worship him. ²⁴God is spirit, and those who worship him must worship in spirit and truth." ²⁵The woman said to him, "I know that Messiah is coming" (who is called Christ). "When he comes, he will proclaim all things to us." ²⁶Jesus said to her, "I am he,ᶜ the one who is speaking to you."

27 Just then his disciples came. They were astonished that he was speaking with a woman, but no one said, "What do you want?" or, "Why are you speaking with her?" ²⁸Then the woman left her water jar and went back to the city. She said to the people, ²⁹"Come and see a man who told me everything I have ever done! He cannot be the Messiah,ᵈ can he?" ³⁰They left the city and were on their way to him.

31 Meanwhile the disciples were urging him, "Rabbi, eat something." ³²But he said to them, "I have food to eat that you do not know about." ³³So the disciples said to one another, "Surely no one has brought him something to eat?" ³⁴Jesus said to them, "My food is to do the will of him who sent me and to complete his work. ³⁵Do you not say, 'Four months more, then comes the harvest'? But I tell you, look around you, and see how the fields are ripe for harvesting. ³⁶The reaper is already receivingᵉ wages and is gathering fruit for eternal life, so that sower and reaper may rejoice together. ³⁷For here the saying holds true, 'One sows and another reaps.' ³⁸I sent you to reap that for which you did not labor. Others have labored, and you have entered into their labor."

39 Many Samaritans from that city believed in him because of the woman's testimony, "He told me everything I have ever done." ⁴⁰So when the Samaritans came to him, they asked him to stay with them; and he stayed there two days. ⁴¹And many more believed because of his word. ⁴²They said to the woman, "It is no longer because of what you said that we believe, for we have heard for ourselves, and we know that this is truly the Savior of the world."

---

a Other ancient authorities lack this sentence   b The Greek word for *you* here and in verses 21 and 22 is plural   c Gk *I am*   d Or *the Christ*   e Or ³⁵. . . *the fields are already ripe for harvesting.* ³⁶*The reaper is receiving*

Jesus Returns to Galilee

43 When the two days were over, he went from that place to Galilee 44(for Jesus himself had testified that a prophet has no honor in the prophet's own country). 45When he came to Galilee, the Galileans welcomed him, since they had seen all that he had done in Jerusalem at the festival; for they too had gone to the festival.

TUESDAY

THE ESSENCE OF TRUE WORSHIP
F. F. Bruce

VERSE: John 4.24   **PASSAGE:** John 4.21–24

he answer [about worship] that the Samaritan woman received was quite different from anything that she could have expected. The time when there was any point in the argument about the claims of Gerizim versus those of Zion had come to an end. A new order was now being introduced which rendered such questions out-of-date and meaningless. The important question is not *where* people worship God but *how* they worship him . . .

The prophets had spoken of a coming day when not one central sanctuary alone, but the whole earth, would be the habitation of the name and glory of God (see Isaiah 6.3; Habakkuk 2.14). While the manifest consummation of this hope, associated as it is with the universal knowledge of God, lies in the future even from our perspective, yet to faith the conditions of that coming age are present already . . . Spiritual worship, genuine worship, cannot be tied to set places and seasons. And such worship is seen to be the more appropriate when we consider the nature of the God to whom it is offered.

"God is spirit": it is not merely that he is *a* spirit among other spirits; rather, God himself is pure spirit, and the worship in which he takes delight is accordingly spiritual worship—the sacrifice of a humble, contrite, grateful and adoring spirit. This affirmation of our Lord's was not entirely new; it but crowns the witness of psalmists and prophets in earlier ages, who saw that material things could at best be the vehicle of true worship but could never belong to its essence. Sincere heart-devotion, whenever and wherever found, is indispensable if men and woman would present to God worship which he can accept.

ADDITIONAL SCRIPTURE READING:
Psalm 86.9; Romans 12.1

Go to page 1246 for your next devotional reading.

1900   Present

Jesus Heals an Official's Son

46 Then he came again to Cana in Galilee where he had changed the water into wine. Now there was a royal official whose son lay ill in Capernaum. 47When he heard that Jesus had come from Judea to Galilee, he went and begged him to come down and heal his son, for he was at the point of death. 48Then Jesus said to him, "Unless you*f* see signs and wonders you will not believe." 49The official said to him, "Sir, come down before my little boy dies." 50Jesus said to him, "Go; your son will live." The man believed the word that Jesus spoke to him and started on his way. 51As he was going down, his slaves met him and told him that his child was alive. 52So he asked them the hour when he began to recover, and they said to him, "Yesterday at one in the afternoon the fever left him." 53The father realized that this was the hour when Jesus had said to him, "Your son will live." So he himself believed, along with his whole household. 54Now this was the second sign that Jesus did after coming from Judea to Galilee.

Jesus Heals on the Sabbath

5 After this there was a festival of the Jews, and Jesus went up to Jerusalem.

2 Now in Jerusalem by the Sheep Gate there is a pool, called in Hebrew*g* Bethzatha,*h* which has five porticoes. 3In these lay many invalids—blind, lame, and paralyzed.*i* 5One man was there who had been ill for thirty-eight years. 6When Jesus saw him lying there and knew that he had been there a long time, he said to him, "Do you want to be made well?" 7The sick man answered him, "Sir, I have no one to put me into the pool when the water is stirred up; and while I am making my way, someone else steps down ahead of me." 8Jesus said to him, "Stand up, take your mat and walk." 9At once the man was made well, and he took up his mat and began to walk.

Now that day was a sabbath. 10So the Jews said to the man who had been cured, "It is the sabbath; it is not lawful for you to carry your mat." 11But he answered them, "The man who made me well said to me, 'Take up your mat and walk.'" 12They asked him, "Who is the man who said to you, 'Take it up and walk'?" 13Now the man who had been healed did not know who it was, for Jesus had disappeared in*j* the crowd that was there. 14Later Jesus found him in the temple and said to him, "See, you have been made well! Do not sin any more, so that nothing worse happens to you." 15The man went away and told the Jews that it was Jesus who had made him well. 16Therefore the Jews started persecuting Jesus, because he was doing such things on the sabbath. 17But Jesus answered them, "My Father is still working, and I also am working." 18For this reason the Jews were seeking all the more to kill him, because he was not only breaking the sabbath, but was also calling God his own Father, thereby making himself equal to God.

The Authority of the Son

19 Jesus said to them, "Very truly, I tell you, the Son can do nothing on his own, but only what he sees the Father doing; for whatever the Father*k* does, the Son does likewise. 20The Father loves the Son and shows him all that he himself is doing; and he will show him greater works than these, so that you will be astonished. 21Indeed, just as the Father raises the dead and gives them life, so also the Son gives life to whomever he wishes. 22The Father judges no one but has given all judgment to the Son, 23so that all may honor the Son just as they honor the Father. Anyone who does not honor the Son does not honor the Father who sent him. 24Very truly, I tell you, anyone who hears my word and believes him who sent me has eternal life, and does not come under judgment, but has passed from death to life.

25 "Very truly, I tell you, the hour is coming, and is now here, when the dead will hear the voice of the Son of God,

---

f Both instances of the Greek word for *you* in this verse are plural   *g* That is, *Aramaic*   *h* Other ancient authorities read *Bethesda*, others *Bethsaida*   *i* Other ancient authorities add, wholly or in part, *waiting for the stirring of the water;* *4for an angel of the Lord went down at certain seasons into the pool, and stirred up the water; whoever stepped in first after the stirring of the water was made well from whatever disease that person had.*   *j* Or *had left because of*   *k* Gk *that one*

and those who hear will live. 26For just as the Father has life in himself, so he has granted the Son also to have life in himself; 27and he has given him authority to execute judgment, because he is the Son of Man. 28Do not be astonished at this; for the hour is coming when all who are in their graves will hear his voice 29and will come out—those who have done good, to the resurrection of life, and those who have done evil, to the resurrection of condemnation.

Witnesses to Jesus

30 "I can do nothing on my own. As I hear, I judge; and my judgment is just, because I seek to do not my own will but the will of him who sent me.

31 "If I testify about myself, my testimony is not true. 32There is another who testifies on my behalf, and I know that his testimony to me is true. 33You sent messengers to John, and he testified to the truth. 34Not that I accept such human testimony, but I say these things so that you may be saved. 35He was a burning and shining lamp, and you were willing to rejoice for a while in his light. 36But I have a testimony greater than John's. The works that the Father has given me to complete, the very works that I am doing, testify on my behalf that the Father has sent me. 37And the Father who sent me has himself testified on my behalf. You have never heard his voice or seen his form, 38and you do not have his word abiding in you, because you do not believe him whom he has sent.

39 "You search the scriptures because you think that in them you have eternal life; and it is they that testify on my behalf. 40Yet you refuse to come to me to have life. 41I do not accept glory from human beings. 42But I know that you do not have the love of God in*l* you. 43I have come in my Father's name, and you do not accept me; if another comes in his own name, you will accept him. 44How can you believe when you accept glory from one another and do not seek the glory that comes from the one who alone is God? 45Do not think that I will accuse you before the Father; your accuser is Moses, on whom you have set your hope.

46If you believed Moses, you would believe me, for he wrote about me. 47But if you do not believe what he wrote, how will you believe what I say?"

Feeding the Five Thousand

6 After this Jesus went to the other side of the Sea of Galilee, also called the Sea of Tiberias.*m* 2A large crowd kept following him, because they saw the signs that he was doing for the sick. 3Jesus went up the mountain and sat down there with his disciples. 4Now the Passover, the festival of the Jews, was near. 5When he looked up and saw a large crowd coming toward him, Jesus said to Philip, "Where are we to buy bread for these people to eat?" 6He said this to test him, for he himself knew what he was going to do. 7Philip answered him, "Six months' wages*n* would not buy enough bread for each of them to get a little." 8One of his disciples, Andrew, Simon Peter's brother, said to him, 9"There is a boy here who has five barley loaves and two fish. But what are they among so many people?" 10Jesus said, "Make the people sit down." Now there was a great deal of grass in the place; so they*o* sat down, about five thousand in all. 11Then Jesus took the loaves, and when he had given thanks, he distributed them to those who were seated; so also the fish, as much as they wanted. 12When they were satisfied, he told his disciples, "Gather up the fragments left over, so that nothing may be lost." 13So they gathered them up, and from the fragments of the five barley loaves, left by those who had eaten, they filled twelve baskets. 14When the people saw the sign that he had done, they began to say, "This is indeed the prophet who is to come into the world."

15 When Jesus realized that they were about to come and take him by force to make him king, he withdrew again to the mountain by himself.

Jesus Walks on the Water

16 When evening came, his disciples went down to the sea, 17got into a boat, and started across the sea to Capernaum. It was now dark, and Jesus had not yet

l Or among   m Gk of Galilee of Tiberias   n Gk Two hundred denarii; the denarius was the usual day's wage for a laborer   o Gk the men come to them. 18The sea became rough because a strong wind was blowing. 19When they had rowed about three or four miles,p they saw Jesus walking on the sea and coming near the boat, and they were terrified. 20But he said to them, "It is I;q do not be afraid." 21Then they wanted to take him into the boat, and immediately the boat reached the land toward which they were going.

The Bread from Heaven

22 The next day the crowd that had stayed on the other side of the sea saw that there had been only one boat there. They also saw that Jesus had not got into the boat with his disciples, but that his disciples had gone away alone. 23Then some boats from Tiberias came near the place where they had eaten the bread after the Lord had given thanks.r 24So when the crowd saw that neither Jesus nor his disciples were there, they themselves got into the boats and went to Capernaum looking for Jesus.

25 When they found him on the other side of the sea, they said to him, "Rabbi, when did you come here?" 26Jesus answered them, "Very truly, I tell you, you are looking for me, not because you saw signs, but because you ate your fill of the loaves. 27Do not work for the food that perishes, but for the food that endures for eternal life, which the Son of Man will give you. For it is on him that God the Father has set his seal." 28Then they said to him, "What must we do to perform the works of God?" 29Jesus answered them, "This is the work of God, that you believe in him whom he has sent." 30So they said to him, "What sign are you going to give us then, so that we may see it and believe you? What work are you performing? 31Our ancestors ate the manna in the wilderness; as it is written, 'He gave them bread from heaven to eat.' " 32Then Jesus said to them, "Very truly, I tell you, it was not Moses who gave you the bread from heaven, but it is my Father who gives you the true bread from heaven. 33For the bread of God is that whichs comes down from heaven and

gives life to the world." 34They said to him, "Sir, give us this bread always."

MY SPIRIT HAS BECOME DRY BECAUSE IT FORGETS TO FEED ON YOU.   —John of the Cross

---

35 Jesus said to them, "I am the bread of life. Whoever comes to me will never be hungry, and whoever believes in me will never be thirsty. 36But I said to you that you have seen me and yet do not believe. 37Everything that the Father gives me will come to me, and anyone who comes to me I will never drive away; 38for I have come down from heaven, not to do my own will, but the will of him who sent me. 39And this is the will of him who sent me, that I should lose nothing of all that he has given me, but raise it up on the last day. 40This is indeed the will of my Father, that all who see the Son and believe in him may have eternal life; and I will raise them up on the last day."

41 Then the Jews began to complain about him because he said, "I am the bread that came down from heaven." 42They were saying, "Is not this Jesus, the son of Joseph, whose father and mother we know? How can he now say, 'I have come down from heaven'?" 43Jesus answered them, "Do not complain among yourselves. 44No one can come to me unless drawn by the Father who sent me; and I will raise that person up on the last day. 45It is written in the prophets, 'And they shall all be taught by God.' Everyone who has heard and learned from the Father comes to me. 46Not that anyone has seen the Father except the one who is from God; he has seen the Father. 47Very truly, I tell you, whoever believes has eternal life. 48I am the bread of life. 49Your ancestors ate the manna in the wilderness, and they died. 50This is the bread that comes down from heaven, so that one may eat of it and not die. 51I am the living bread that came down from heaven. Whoever eats of this bread will live forever; and the bread that I will give for the life of the world is my flesh."

---

p Gk about twenty-five or thirty stadia   q Gk I am   r Other ancient authorities lack after the Lord had given thanks   s Or he who

52 The Jews then disputed among themselves, saying, "How can this man give us his flesh to eat?" 53So Jesus said to them, "Very truly, I tell you, unless you eat the flesh of the Son of Man and drink his blood, you have no life in you. 54Those who eat my flesh and drink my blood have eternal life, and I will raise them up on the last day; 55for my flesh is true food and my blood is true drink. 56Those who eat my flesh and drink my blood abide in me, and I in them. 57Just as the living Father sent me, and I live because of the Father, so whoever eats me will live because of me. 58This is the bread that came down from heaven, not like that which your ancestors ate, and they died. But the one who eats this bread will live forever." 59He said these things while he was teaching in the synagogue at Capernaum.

The Words of Eternal Life

60 When many of his disciples heard it, they said, "This teaching is difficult; who can accept it?" 61But Jesus, being aware that his disciples were complaining about it, said to them, "Does this offend you? 62Then what if you were to see the Son of Man ascending to where he was before? 63It is the spirit that gives life; the flesh is useless. The words that I have spoken to you are spirit and life. 64But among you there are some who do not believe." For Jesus knew from the first who were the ones that did not believe, and who was the one that would betray him. 65And he said, "For this reason I have told you that no one can come to me unless it is granted by the Father."

66 Because of this many of his disciples turned back and no longer went about with him. 67So Jesus asked the twelve, "Do you also wish to go away?" 68Simon Peter answered him, "Lord, to whom can we go? You have the words of eternal life. 69We have come to believe and know that you are the Holy One of God."t 70Jesus answered them, "Did I not choose you, the twelve? Yet one of you is a devil." 71He was speaking of Judas son of Simon Iscariot,u for he,

though one of the twelve, was going to betray him.

The Unbelief of Jesus' Brothers

7 After this Jesus went about in Galilee. He did not wishv to go about in Judea because the Jews were looking for an opportunity to kill him. 2Now the Jewish festival of Boothsw was near. 3So his brothers said to him, "Leave here and go to Judea so that your disciples also may see the works you are doing; 4for no one who wantsx to be widely known acts in secret. If you do these things, show yourself to the world." 5(For not even his brothers believed in him.) 6Jesus said to them, "My time has not yet come, but your time is always here. 7The world cannot hate you, but it hates me because I testify against it that its works are evil. 8Go to the festival yourselves. I am noty going to this festival, for my time has not yet fully come." 9After saying this, he remained in Galilee.

Jesus at the Festival of Booths

10 But after his brothers had gone to the festival, then he also went, not publicly but as it werez in secret. 11The Jews were looking for him at the festival and saying, "Where is he?" 12And there was considerable complaining about him among the crowds. While some were saying, "He is a good man," others were saying, "No, he is deceiving the crowd." 13Yet no one would speak openly about him for fear of the Jews.

14 About the middle of the festival Jesus went up into the temple and began to teach. 15The Jews were astonished at it, saying, "How does this man have such learning,a when he has never been taught?" 16Then Jesus answered them, "My teaching is not mine but his who sent me. 17Anyone who resolves to do the will of God will know whether the teaching is from God or whether I am speaking on my own. 18Those who speak on their own seek their own glory; but the one who seeks the glory of him who sent him is true, and there is nothing false in him.

19 "Did not Moses give you the law? Yet none of you keeps the law. Why are you looking for an opportunity to kill me?" 20The crowd answered, "You have a demon! Who is trying to kill you?" 21Jesus answered them, "I performed one work, and all of you are astonished. 22Moses gave you circumcision (it is, of course, not from Moses, but from the patriarchs), and you circumcise a man on the sabbath. 23If a man receives circumcision on the sabbath in order that the law of Moses may not be broken, are you angry with me because I healed a man's whole body on the sabbath? 24Do not judge by appearances, but judge with right judgment."

Is This the Christ?

25 Now some of the people of Jerusalem were saying, "Is not this the man whom they are trying to kill? 26And here he is, speaking openly, but they say nothing to him! Can it be that the authorities really know that this is the Messiah?b 27Yet we know where this man is from; but when the Messiahb comes, no one will know where he is from." 28Then Jesus cried out as he was teaching in the temple, "You know me, and you know where I am from. I have not come on my own. But the one who sent me is true, and you do not know him. 29I know him, because I am from him, and he sent me." 30Then they tried to arrest him, but no one laid hands on him, because his hour had not yet come. 31Yet many in the crowd believed in him and were saying, "When the Messiahb comes, will he do more signs than this man has done?"c

Officers Are Sent to Arrest Jesus

32 The Pharisees heard the crowd muttering such things about him, and the chief priests and Pharisees sent temple police to arrest him. 33Jesus then said, "I will be with you a little while longer, and then I am going to him who sent me. 34You will search for me, but you will not find me; and where I am, you cannot come." 35The Jews said to one another, "Where does this man intend to go that we will not find him? Does he intend to go to the Dispersion among the Greeks and teach the Greeks? 36What does he mean by saying, 'You will search for me and you will not find me' and 'Where I am, you cannot come'?"

Rivers of Living Water

37 On the last day of the festival, the great day, while Jesus was standing there, he cried out, "Let anyone who is thirsty come to me, 38and let the one who believes in me drink. Asd the scripture has said, 'Out of the believer's hearte shall flow rivers of living water.' " 39Now he said this about the Spirit, which believers in him were to receive; for as yet there was no Spirit,f because Jesus was not yet glorified.

Division among the People

40 When they heard these words, some in the crowd said, "This is really the prophet." 41Others said, "This is the Messiah."b But some asked, "Surely the Messiahb does not come from Galilee, does he? 42Has not the scripture said that the Messiahb is descended from David and comes from Bethlehem, the village where David lived?" 43So there was a division in the crowd because of him. 44Some of them wanted to arrest him, but no one laid hands on him.

The Unbelief of Those in Authority

45 Then the temple police went back to the chief priests and Pharisees, who asked them, "Why did you not arrest him?" 46The police answered, "Never has anyone spoken like this!" 47Then the Pharisees replied, "Surely you have not been deceived too, have you? 48Has any one of the authorities or of the Pharisees believed in him? 49But this crowd, which does not know the law—they are accursed." 50Nicodemus, who had gone to Jesusg before, and who was one of them, asked, 51"Our law does not judge people without first giving them a hearing to find out what they are doing, does it?" 52They replied, "Surely you are not also from Galilee, are you? Search and you will see that no prophet is to arise from Galilee."

b Or the Christ   c Other ancient authorities read is doing   d Or come to me and drink. 38The one who believes in me, as   e Gk out of his belly   f Other ancient authorities read for as yet the Spirit (others, Holy Spirit) had not been given   g Gk him

The Woman Caught in Adultery

⟦ 53 Then each of them went home,
8 1 while Jesus went to the Mount
of Olives. 2 Early in the morning
he came again to the temple. All the people
came to him and he sat down and
began to teach them. 3 The scribes and
the Pharisees brought a woman who had
been caught in adultery; and making her
stand before all of them, 4 they said to
him, "Teacher, this woman was caught
in the very act of committing adultery.
5 Now in the law Moses commanded us
to stone such women. Now what do you
say?" 6 They said this to test him, so that
they might have some charge to bring
against him. Jesus bent down and wrote
with his finger on the ground. 7 When
they kept on questioning him, he
straightened up and said to them, "Let
anyone among you who is without sin be
the first to throw a stone at her." 8 And
once again he bent down and wrote on
the ground.*h* 9 When they heard it, they
went away, one by one, beginning with
the elders; and Jesus was left alone with
the woman standing before him. 10 Jesus
straightened up and said to her, "Woman,
where are they? Has no one condemned
you?" 11 She said, "No one, sir."*i* And
Jesus said, "Neither do I condemn you.
Go your way, and from now on do not sin
again."⟧*j*

Jesus the Light of the World

12 Again Jesus spoke to them, saying,
"I am the light of the world. Whoever follows
me will never walk in darkness but
will have the light of life." 13 Then the
Pharisees said to him, "You are testifying
on your own behalf; your testimony is
not valid." 14 Jesus answered, "Even if I
testify on my own behalf, my testimony
is valid because I know where I have
come from and where I am going, but you
do not know where I come from or where
I am going. 15 You judge by human standards;*k*
I judge no one. 16 Yet even if I do
judge, my judgment is valid; for it is not I
alone who judge, but I and the Father*l*
who sent me. 17 In your law it is written
that the testimony of two witnesses is

valid. 18 I testify on my own behalf, and
the Father who sent me testifies on my
behalf." 19 Then they said to him, "Where
is your Father?" Jesus answered, "You
know neither me nor my Father. If you
knew me, you would know my Father
also." 20 He spoke these words while he
was teaching in the treasury of the temple,
but no one arrested him, because his
hour had not yet come.

Jesus Foretells His Death

21 Again he said to them, "I am going
away, and you will search for me, but
you will die in your sin. Where I am
going, you cannot come." 22 Then the
Jews said, "Is he going to kill himself? Is
that what he means by saying, 'Where I
am going, you cannot come'?" 23 He said
to them, "You are from below, I am from
above; you are of this world, I am not of
this world. 24 I told you that you would
die in your sins, for you will die in your
sins unless you believe that I am he."*m*
25 They said to him, "Who are you?"
Jesus said to them, "Why do I speak to
you at all?*n* 26 I have much to say about
you and much to condemn; but the one
who sent me is true, and I declare to the
world what I have heard from him."
27 They did not understand that he was
speaking to them about the Father. 28 So
Jesus said, "When you have lifted up the
Son of Man, then you will realize that I
am he,*m* and that I do nothing on my
own, but I speak these things as the Father
instructed me. 29 And the one who
sent me is with me; he has not left me
alone, for I always do what is pleasing to
him." 30 As he was saying these things,
many believed in him.

True Disciples

31 Then Jesus said to the Jews who
had believed in him, "If you continue in
my word, you are truly my disciples;
32 and you will know the truth, and the
truth will make you free." 33 They answered
him, "We are descendants of
Abraham and have never been slaves to
anyone. What do you mean by saying,
'You will be made free'?"

---

h Other ancient authorities add *the sins of each of them*   *i* Or *Lord*   *j* The most ancient authorities
lack 7.53—8.11; other authorities add the passage here or after 7.36 or after 21.25 or after Luke 21.38,
with variations of text; some mark the passage as doubtful.   *k* Gk *according to the flesh*   *l* Other
ancient authorities read *he*   *m* Gk *I am*   *n* Or *What I have told you from the beginning*

34 Jesus answered them, "Very truly, I tell you, everyone who commits sin is a slave to sin. 35 The slave does not have a permanent place in the household; the son has a place there forever. 36 So if the Son makes you free, you will be free

---

WEDNESDAY

THE WHOLESOME PRECEPT OF OUR LORD
Cyprian

VERSE: John 8.31   **PASSAGE:** John 8.31–41

t is the wholesome precept of our Lord and Master: "He that endureth," saith he, "unto the end the same shall be saved" (see Matthew 10.22); and again, "If ye continue," saith he, "in my word ye shall be truly my disciples; and ye shall know the truth, and the truth shall make you free." We must endure and persevere, beloved brethren, in order that, being admitted to the hope of truth and liberty, we may attain to the truth and liberty itself; for that very fact that we are Christians is the substance of faith and hope. But that hope and faith may attain to their result, there is need of patience. For we are not following after present glory, but future, according to what Paul the apostle also warns us, and says, "We are saved by hope; but hope that is seen is not hope: for what a man seeth, why doth he hope for? But if we hope for that which we see not, then do we by patience wait for it" (see Romans 8.24). Therefore, waiting and patience are needful, that we may fulfill that which we have begun to be, and may receive that which we believe and hope for, according to God's own showing . . . [Paul] admonishes that no man should impatiently faint in his labor, that none should be either called off or overcome by temptations and desist in the midst of the praise and in the way of glory; and the things that are past perish, while those which have begun cease to be perfect; as it is written, "The righteousness of the righteous shall not deliver him in whatever day he shall transgress" (see Ezekiel 33.12); and again, "Hold that which thou hast, that another take not thy crown" (see Revelation 3.11). Which word exhorts us to persevere with patience and courage, so that he who strives towards the crown with the praise now near at hand, may be crowned by the continuance of patience.

ADDITIONAL SCRIPTURE READING:
2 Chronicles 20.17; 2 Thessalonians 2.15

Go to page 1250 for your next devotional reading.

100   500

indeed. 37I know that you are descendants of Abraham; yet you look for an opportunity to kill me, because there is no place in you for my word. 38I declare what I have seen in the Father's presence; as for you, you should do what you have heard from the Father."o

Jesus and Abraham

39 They answered him, "Abraham is our father." Jesus said to them, "If you were Abraham's children, you would be doingp what Abraham did, 40but now you are trying to kill me, a man who has told you the truth that I heard from God. This is not what Abraham did. 41You are indeed doing what your father does." They said to him, "We are not illegitimate children; we have one father, God himself." 42Jesus said to them, "If God were your Father, you would love me, for I came from God and now I am here. I did not come on my own, but he sent me. 43Why do you not understand what I say? It is because you cannot accept my word. 44You are from your father the devil, and you choose to do your father's desires. He was a murderer from the beginning and does not stand in the truth, because there is no truth in him. When he lies, he speaks according to his own nature, for he is a liar and the father of lies. 45But because I tell the truth, you do not believe me. 46Which of you convicts me of sin? If I tell the truth, why do you not believe me? 47Whoever is from God hears the words of God. The reason you do not hear them is that you are not from God."

48 The Jews answered him, "Are we not right in saying that you are a Samaritan and have a demon?" 49Jesus answered, "I do not have a demon; but I honor my Father, and you dishonor me. 50Yet I do not seek my own glory; there is one who seeks it and he is the judge. 51Very truly, I tell you, whoever keeps my word will never see death." 52The Jews said to him, "Now we know that you have a demon. Abraham died, and so did the prophets; yet you say, 'Whoever keeps my word will never taste death.' 53Are you greater than our father Abraham, who died? The prophets also died. Who do you claim to be?" 54Jesus answered, "If I glorify myself, my glory is nothing. It is my Father who glorifies me, he of whom you say, 'He is our God,' 55though you do not know him. But I know him; if I would say that I do not know him, I would be a liar like you. But I do know him and I keep his word. 56Your ancestor Abraham rejoiced that he would see my day; he saw it and was glad." 57Then the Jews said to him, "You are not yet fifty years old, and have you seen Abraham?"q 58Jesus said to them, "Very truly, I tell you, before Abraham was, I am." 59So they picked up stones to throw at him, but Jesus hid himself and went out of the temple.

A Man Born Blind Receives Sight

9 As he walked along, he saw a man blind from birth. 2His disciples asked him, "Rabbi, who sinned, this man or his parents, that he was born blind?" 3Jesus answered, "Neither this man nor his parents sinned; he was born blind so that God's works might be revealed in him. 4Wer must work the works of him who sent mes while it is day; night is coming when no one can work. 5As long as I am in the world, I am the light of the world." 6When he had said this, he spat on the ground and made mud with the saliva and spread the mud on the man's eyes, 7saying to him, "Go, wash in the pool of Siloam" (which means Sent). Then he went and washed and came back able to see. 8The neighbors and those who had seen him before as a beggar began to ask, "Is this not the man who used to sit and beg?" 9Some were saying, "It is he." Others were saying, "No, but it is someone like him." He kept saying, "I am the man." 10But they kept asking him, "Then how were your eyes opened?" 11He answered, "The man called Jesus made mud, spread it on my eyes, and said to me, 'Go to Siloam and wash.' Then I went and washed and received my sight." 12They said to him, "Where is he?" He said, "I do not know."

o Other ancient authorities read you do what you have heard from your father   p Other ancient authorities read If you are Abraham's children, then do   q Other ancient authorities read has Abraham seen you?   r Other ancient authorities read I   s Other ancient authorities read us

The Pharisees Investigate the Healing

13 They brought to the Pharisees the man who had formerly been blind. [14]Now it was a sabbath day when Jesus made the mud and opened his eyes. [15]Then the Pharisees also began to ask him how he had received his sight. He said to them, "He put mud on my eyes. Then I washed, and now I see." [16]Some of the Pharisees said, "This man is not from God, for he does not observe the sabbath." But others said, "How can a man who is a sinner perform such signs?" And they were divided. [17]So they said again to the blind man, "What do you say about him? It was your eyes he opened." He said, "He is a prophet."

18 The Jews did not believe that he had been blind and had received his sight until they called the parents of the man who had received his sight [19]and asked them, "Is this your son, who you say was born blind? How then does he now see?" [20]His parents answered, "We know that this is our son, and that he was born blind; [21]but we do not know how it is that now he sees, nor do we know who opened his eyes. Ask him; he is of age. He will speak for himself." [22]His parents said this because they were afraid of the Jews; for the Jews had already agreed that anyone who confessed Jesus[t] to be the Messiah[u] would be put out of the synagogue. [23]Therefore his parents said, "He is of age; ask him."

24 So for the second time they called the man who had been blind, and they said to him, "Give glory to God! We know that this man is a sinner." [25]He answered, "I do not know whether he is a sinner. One thing I do know, that though I was blind, now I see." [26]They said to him, "What did he do to you? How did he open your eyes?" [27]He answered them, "I have told you already, and you would not listen. Why do you want to hear it again? Do you also want to become his disciples?" [28]Then they reviled him, saying, "You are his disciple, but we are disciples of Moses. [29]We know that God has spoken to Moses, but as for this man, we do not know where he comes from." [30]The man answered,

"Here is an astonishing thing! You do not know where he comes from, and yet he opened my eyes. [31]We know that God does not listen to sinners, but he does listen to one who worships him and obeys his will. [32]Never since the world began has it been heard that anyone opened the eyes of a person born blind. [33]If this man were not from God, he could do nothing." [34]They answered him, "You were born entirely in sins, and are you trying to teach us?" And they drove him out.

Spiritual Blindness

35 Jesus heard that they had driven him out, and when he found him, he said, "Do you believe in the Son of Man?"[v] [36]He answered, "And who is he, sir?[w] Tell me, so that I may believe in him." [37]Jesus said to him, "You have seen him, and the one speaking with you is he." [38]He said, "Lord,[w] I believe." And he worshiped him. [39]Jesus said, "I came into this world for judgment so that those who do not see may see, and those who do see may become blind." [40]Some of the Pharisees near him heard this and said to him, "Surely we are not blind, are we?" [41]Jesus said to them, "If you were blind, you would not have sin. But now that you say, 'We see,' your sin remains.

Jesus the Good Shepherd

10 "Very truly, I tell you, anyone who does not enter the sheepfold by the gate but climbs in by another way is a thief and a bandit. [2]The one who enters by the gate is the shepherd of the sheep. [3]The gatekeeper opens the gate for him, and the sheep hear his voice. He calls his own sheep by name and leads them out. [4]When he has brought out all his own, he goes ahead of them, and the sheep follow him because they know his voice. [5]They will not follow a stranger, but they will run from him because they do not know the voice of strangers." [6]Jesus used this figure of speech with them, but they did not understand what he was saying to them.

7 So again Jesus said to them, "Very truly, I tell you, I am the gate for the sheep. [8]All who came before me are thieves and bandits; but the sheep did

---

t Gk *him*   u Or *the Christ*   v Other ancient authorities read *the Son of God*   w *Sir* and *Lord* translate the same Greek word

not listen to them. 9I am the gate. Whoever enters by me will be saved, and will come in and go out and find pasture. 10The thief comes only to steal and kill and destroy. I came that they may have life, and have it abundantly.

11 "I am the good shepherd. The good shepherd lays down his life for the sheep. 12The hired hand, who is not the shepherd and does not own the sheep, sees the wolf coming and leaves the sheep and runs away—and the wolf snatches them and scatters them. 13The hired hand runs away because a hired hand does not care for the sheep. 14I am the good shepherd. I know my own and my own know me, 15just as the Father knows me and I know the Father. And I lay down my life for the sheep. 16I have other sheep that do not belong to this fold. I must bring them also, and they will listen to my voice. So there will be one flock, one shepherd. 17For this reason the Father loves me, because I lay down my life in order to take it up again. 18No one takes× it from me, but I lay it down of my own accord. I have power to lay it down, and I have power to take it up again. I have received this command from my Father."

19 Again the Jews were divided because of these words. 20Many of them were saying, "He has a demon and is out of his mind. Why listen to him?" 21Others were saying, "These are not the words of one who has a demon. Can a demon open the eyes of the blind?"

Jesus Is Rejected by the Jews

22 At that time the festival of the Dedication took place in Jerusalem. It was winter, 23and Jesus was walking in the temple, in the portico of Solomon. 24So the Jews gathered around him and said to him, "How long will you keep us in suspense? If you are the Messiah,y tell us plainly." 25Jesus answered, "I have told you, and you do not believe. The works that I do in my Father's name testify to me; 26but you do not believe, because you do not belong to my sheep. 27My sheep hear my voice. I know them,

and they follow me. 28I give them eternal life, and they will never perish. No one will snatch them out of my hand. 29What my Father has given me is greater than all else, and no one can snatch it out of the Father's hand.z 30The Father and I are one."

31 The Jews took up stones again to stone him. 32Jesus replied, "I have shown you many good works from the Father. For which of these are you going to stone me?" 33The Jews answered, "It is not for a good work that we are going to stone you, but for blasphemy, because you, though only a human being, are making yourself God." 34Jesus answered, "Is it not written in your law,a 'I said, you are gods'? 35If those to whom the word of God came were called 'gods'—and the scripture cannot be annulled— 36can you say that the one whom the Father has sanctified and sent into the world is blaspheming because I said, 'I am God's Son'? 37If I am not doing the works of my Father, then do not believe me. 38But if I do them, even though you do not believe me, believe the works, so that you may know and understandb that the Father is in me and I am in the Father." 39Then they tried to arrest him again, but he escaped from their hands.

40 He went away again across the Jordan to the place where John had been baptizing earlier, and he remained there. 41Many came to him, and they were saying, "John performed no sign, but everything that John said about this man was true." 42And many believed in him there.

The Death of Lazarus

11 Now a certain man was ill, Lazarus of Bethany, the village of Mary and her sister Martha. 2Mary was the one who anointed the Lord with perfume and wiped his feet with her hair; her brother Lazarus was ill. 3So the sisters sent a message to Jesus,c "Lord, he whom you love is ill." 4But when Jesus heard it, he said, "This illness does not lead to death; rather it is for God's glory, so that the Son of God may be glorified

x Other ancient authorities read has taken   y Or the Christ   z Other ancient authorities read My Father who has given them to me is greater than all, and no one can snatch them out of the Father's hand   a Other ancient authorities read in the law   b Other ancient authorities lack and understand; others read and believe   c Gk him

through it." [5] Accordingly, though Jesus loved Martha and her sister and Lazarus, [6] after having heard that Lazarus*d* was ill, he stayed two days longer in the place where he was.

[7] Then after this he said to the disciples, "Let us go to Judea again." [8] The disciples said to him, "Rabbi, the Jews were just now trying to stone you, and are you going there again?" [9] Jesus answered,

d Gk *he*

THURSDAY

THE MELDING OF MARTHA AND MARY
Evelyn Underhill

VERSE: John 11.20   **PASSAGE:** John 11.17–31

t. Theresa said that to give our Lord a perfect service, Martha and Mary must combine. The modern tendency is to turn from the attitude and the work of Mary; and even call it—as I have heard it called by busy social Christians—a form of spiritual selfishness. Thousands of devoted men and women today believe that the really good part is to keep busy, and give themselves no time to take what is offered to those who abide quietly with Christ; because there seem such a lot of urgent jobs for Martha to do. The result of this can only be a maiming of their human nature, exhaustion, loss of depth and of vision; and it is seen in the vagueness and ineffectuality of a great deal of the work that is done for God. It means a total surrender to the busy click-click of the life of succession; nowhere, in the end, more deadly than in the religious sphere. I insist on this because I feel, more and more, the danger in which we stand of developing a lopsided Christianity; so concentrated on service, and on this-world obligations, as to forget the needs of constant willed and quiet contact with that other world, wherefrom the sanctions of service and the power in which to do it proceed. We mostly spend those lives conjugating three verbs: to Want, to Have, and to Do. Craving, clutching, and fussing, on the material, political, social, emotional, intellectual—even on the religious—plane, we are kept in perpetual unrest: forgetting that none of these verbs has ultimate significance, except so far as they are transcended by and included in, the fundamental verb, to Be: and that Being, not wanting, having, and doing, is the essence of a spiritual life.

ADDITIONAL SCRIPTURE READING:
Luke 10.38–42; John 15.4

Go to page 1252 for your next devotional reading.

1900   Present

"Are there not twelve hours of daylight? Those who walk during the day do not stumble, because they see the light of this world. 10But those who walk at night stumble, because the light is not in them." 11After saying this, he told them, "Our friend Lazarus has fallen asleep, but I am going there to awaken him." 12The disciples said to him, "Lord, if he has fallen asleep, he will be all right." 13Jesus, however, had been speaking about his death, but they thought that he was referring merely to sleep. 14Then Jesus told them plainly, "Lazarus is dead. 15For your sake I am glad I was not there, so that you may believe. But let us go to him." 16Thomas, who was called the Twin,e said to his fellow disciples, "Let us also go, that we may die with him."

Jesus the Resurrection and the Life

17 When Jesus arrived, he found that Lazarusf had already been in the tomb four days. 18Now Bethany was near Jerusalem, some two milesg away, 19and many of the Jews had come to Martha and Mary to console them about their brother. 20When Martha heard that Jesus was coming, she went and met him, while Mary stayed at home. 21Martha said to Jesus, "Lord, if you had been here, my brother would not have died. 22But even now I know that God will give you whatever you ask of him." 23Jesus said to her, "Your brother will rise again." 24Martha said to him, "I know that he will rise again in the resurrection on the last day." 25Jesus said to her, "I am the resurrection and the life.h Those who believe in me, even though they die, will live, 26and everyone who lives and believes in me will never die. Do you believe this?" 27She said to him, "Yes, Lord, I believe that you are the Messiah,i the Son of God, the one coming into the world."

Jesus Weeps

28 When she had said this, she went back and called her sister Mary, and told her privately, "The Teacher is here and is calling for you." 29And when she heard it, she got up quickly and went to him. 30Now Jesus had not yet come to the

village, but was still at the place where Martha had met him. 31The Jews who were with her in the house, consoling her, saw Mary get up quickly and go out. They followed her because they thought that she was going to the tomb to weep there. 32When Mary came where Jesus was and saw him, she knelt at his feet and said to him, "Lord, if you had been here, my brother would not have died." 33When Jesus saw her weeping, and the Jews who came with her also weeping, he was greatly disturbed in spirit and deeply moved. 34He said, "Where have you laid him?" They said to him, "Lord, come and see." 35Jesus began to weep. 36So the Jews said, "See how he loved him!" 37But some of them said, "Could not he who opened the eyes of the blind man have kept this man from dying?"

Jesus Raises Lazarus to Life

38 Then Jesus, again greatly disturbed, came to the tomb. It was a cave, and a stone was lying against it. 39Jesus said, "Take away the stone." Martha, the sister of the dead man, said to him, "Lord, already there is a stench because he has been dead four days." 40Jesus said to her, "Did I not tell you that if you believed, you would see the glory of God?" 41So they took away the stone. And Jesus looked upward and said, "Father, I thank you for having heard me. 42I knew that you always hear me, but I have said this for the sake of the crowd standing here, so that they may believe that you sent me." 43When he had said this, he cried with a loud voice, "Lazarus, come out!" 44The dead man came out, his hands and feet bound with strips of cloth, and his face wrapped in a cloth. Jesus said to them, "Unbind him, and let him go."

WHAT IS SO INTRICATE, SO ENTANGLING AS DEATH? WHOEVER GOT OUT OF A WINDING SHEET?   —John Donne

---

The Plot to Kill Jesus

45 Many of the Jews therefore, who had come with Mary and had seen what

---

e Gk Didymus   f Gk he   g Gk fifteen stadia   h Other ancient authorities lack and the life
i Or the Christ

Jesus did, believed in him. ⁴⁶But some of them went to the Pharisees and told them what he had done. ⁴⁷So the chief priests and the Pharisees called a meeting of the council, and said, "What are we to do? This man is performing many signs. ⁴⁸If we let him go on like this, everyone will believe in him, and the Romans will

FRIDAY

THE FRAGRANCE OF GOD
Watchman Nee

VERSE: John 12.3   **PASSAGE:** John 12.1–8

There must be something—a willingness to yield, a breaking and a pouring out of everything to him—which gives release to that fragrance of Christ and produces in other lives an awareness of need, drawing them out and on to know the Lord. This is what I feel to be the heart of everything. The gospel has as its one object the producing in us sinners of a condition that will satisfy the heart of our God. In order that he may have that, we come to him with all we have, all we are—yes, even the most cherished things in our spiritual experience—and we make known to him: "Lord, I am willing to let go all of this for you: not just for your work, not for your children, not for anything else at all, but altogether and only for yourself!"

Oh, to be wasted! It is a blessed thing to be wasted for the Lord. So many who have been prominent in the Christian world know nothing of this. Many of us have been used to the full—have been used, I would say, too much—but we do not know what it means to be "wasted on God." We like to be always "on the go": the Lord would sometimes prefer to have us in prison. We think in terms of apostolic journeys: God dares to put his greatest ambassadors in chains.

"But thanks be to God, who in Christ always leads us in triumphal procession and through us spreads in every place the fragrance that comes from knowing him" (2 Corinthians 2.14).

"The house was filled with the fragrance of the perfume" (John 12.3).

The Lord grant us grace that we may learn how to please him. When, like Paul, we make this our supreme aim (2 Corinthians 5.9), the gospel will have achieved its end.

ADDITIONAL SCRIPTURE READING:
Philippians 2.14–18; Hebrews 13.15

Go to page 1254 for your next devotional reading.

1900   Present

come and destroy both our holy place[j] and our nation." [49]But one of them, Caiaphas, who was high priest that year, said to them, "You know nothing at all! [50]You do not understand that it is better for you to have one man die for the people than to have the whole nation destroyed." [51]He did not say this on his own, but being high priest that year he prophesied that Jesus was about to die for the nation, [52]and not for the nation only, but to gather into one the dispersed children of God. [53]So from that day on they planned to put him to death.

[54] Jesus therefore no longer walked about openly among the Jews, but went from there to a town called Ephraim in the region near the wilderness; and he remained there with the disciples.

[55] Now the Passover of the Jews was near, and many went up from the country to Jerusalem before the Passover to purify themselves. [56]They were looking for Jesus and were asking one another as they stood in the temple, "What do you think? Surely he will not come to the festival, will he?" [57]Now the chief priests and the Pharisees had given orders that anyone who knew where Jesus[k] was should let them know, so that they might arrest him.

Mary Anoints Jesus

12 Six days before the Passover Jesus came to Bethany, the home of Lazarus, whom he had raised from the dead. [2]There they gave a dinner for him. Martha served, and Lazarus was one of those at the table with him. [3]Mary took a pound of costly perfume made of pure nard, anointed Jesus' feet, and wiped them[l] with her hair. The house was filled with the fragrance of the perfume. [4]But Judas Iscariot, one of his disciples (the one who was about to betray him), said, [5]"Why was this perfume not sold for three hundred denarii[m] and the money given to the poor?" [6](He said this not because he cared about the poor, but because he was a thief; he kept the common purse and used to steal what was put into it.) [7]Jesus said, "Leave her alone. She bought it[n] so that she might

keep it for the day of my burial. [8]You always have the poor with you, but you do not always have me."

The Plot to Kill Lazarus

[9] When the great crowd of the Jews learned that he was there, they came not only because of Jesus but also to see Lazarus, whom he had raised from the dead. [10]So the chief priests planned to put Lazarus to death as well, [11]since it was on account of him that many of the Jews were deserting and were believing in Jesus.

Jesus' Triumphal Entry into Jerusalem

[12] The next day the great crowd that had come to the festival heard that Jesus was coming to Jerusalem. [13]So they took branches of palm trees and went out to meet him, shouting,

"Hosanna!
    Blessed is the one who comes in
        the name of the Lord—
        the King of Israel!"

[14]Jesus found a young donkey and sat on it; as it is written:

[15] "Do not be afraid, daughter of
        Zion.
    Look, your king is coming,
        sitting on a donkey's colt!"

[16]His disciples did not understand these things at first; but when Jesus was glorified, then they remembered that these things had been written of him and had been done to him. [17]So the crowd that had been with him when he called Lazarus out of the tomb and raised him from the dead continued to testify.[o] [18]It was also because they heard that he had performed this sign that the crowd went to meet him. [19]The Pharisees then said to one another, "You see, you can do nothing. Look, the world has gone after him!"

Some Greeks Wish to See Jesus

[20] Now among those who went up to worship at the festival were some Greeks. [21]They came to Philip, who was from Bethsaida in Galilee, and said to him, "Sir, we wish to see Jesus." [22]Philip went and told Andrew; then Andrew and Philip went and told Jesus. [23]Jesus

---

[j] Or *our temple*; Greek *our place*   [k] Gk *he*   [l] Gk *his feet*   [m] Three hundred denarii would be nearly a year's wages for a laborer   [n] Gk lacks *She bought it*   [o] Other ancient authorities read *with him began to testify that he had called. . .from the dead*

WEEKEND

THE DONKEY
G. K. Chesterton

VERSE: John 12.14   **PASSAGE:** John 12.12–16

hen fishes flew and forests walked
    And figs grew upon thorn,
Some moment when the moon was blood,
    Then surely I was born;

With monstrous head and sickening cry
    And ears like errant wings,
The devil's walking parody
    On all four-footed things.

The tattered outlaw of the earth,
    Of ancient crooked will;
Starve, scourge, deride me: I am dumb,
    I keep my secret still.

Fools! For I also had my hour;
    One far fierce hour and sweet:
There was a shout about my ears,
    And palms before my feet!

ADDITIONAL SCRIPTURE READING:
Zechariah 9.9; Matthew 21.5–6

Go to page 1257 for your next devotional reading.

1900   Present

answered them, "The hour has come for the Son of Man to be glorified. 24 Very truly, I tell you, unless a grain of wheat falls into the earth and dies, it remains just a single grain; but if it dies, it bears much fruit. 25 Those who love their life lose it, and those who hate their life in this world will keep it for eternal life. 26 Whoever serves me must follow me, and where I am, there will my servant be also. Whoever serves me, the Father will honor.

Jesus Speaks about His Death

27 "Now my soul is troubled. And what should I say—'Father, save me from this hour'? No, it is for this reason that I have come to this hour. 28 Father, glorify your name." Then a voice came from heaven, "I have glorified it, and I will glorify it again." 29 The crowd standing there heard it and said that it was thunder. Others said, "An angel has spoken to him." 30 Jesus answered, "This voice has come for your sake, not for mine. 31 Now is the judgment of this world; now the ruler of this world will be driven out. 32 And I, when I am lifted up from the earth, will draw all people$p$ to myself." 33 He said this to indicate the kind of death he was to die. 34 The crowd answered him, "We have heard from the law that the Messiah$q$ remains forever. How can you say that the Son of Man must be lifted up? Who is this Son of Man?" 35 Jesus said to them, "The light is with you for a little longer. Walk while you have the light, so that the darkness may not overtake you. If you walk in the darkness, you do not know where you are going. 36 While you have the light, believe in the light, so that you may become children of light."

The Unbelief of the People

After Jesus had said this, he departed and hid from them. 37 Although he had performed so many signs in their presence, they did not believe in him. 38 This was to fulfill the word spoken by the prophet Isaiah:

"Lord, who has believed our
    message,
and to whom has the arm of the
    Lord been revealed?"

39 And so they could not believe, because Isaiah also said,

40   "He has blinded their eyes
        and hardened their heart,
    so that they might not look with
        their eyes,
    and understand with their heart
        and turn—
    and I would heal them."

41 Isaiah said this because$r$ he saw his glory and spoke about him. 42 Nevertheless many, even of the authorities, believed in him. But because of the Pharisees they did not confess it, for fear that they would be put out of the synagogue; 43 for they loved human glory more than the glory that comes from God.

Summary of Jesus' Teaching

44 Then Jesus cried aloud: "Whoever believes in me believes not in me but in him who sent me. 45 And whoever sees me sees him who sent me. 46 I have come as light into the world, so that everyone who believes in me should not remain in the darkness. 47 I do not judge anyone who hears my words and does not keep them, for I came not to judge the world, but to save the world. 48 The one who rejects me and does not receive my word has a judge; on the last day the word that I have spoken will serve as judge, 49 for I have not spoken on my own, but the Father who sent me has himself given me a commandment about what to say and what to speak. 50 And I know that his commandment is eternal life. What I speak, therefore, I speak just as the Father has told me."

Jesus Washes the Disciples' Feet

13 Now before the festival of the Passover, Jesus knew that his hour had come to depart from this world and go to the Father. Having loved his own who were in the world, he loved them to the end. 2 The devil had already put it into the heart of Judas son of Simon Iscariot to betray him. And during supper 3 Jesus, knowing that the Father had given all things into his hands, and that he had come from God and was going to God, 4 got up from the table,s took off his outer robe, and tied a towel

---

p Other ancient authorities read *all things* q Or *the Christ* r Other ancient witnesses read *when*
s Gk *from supper*

around himself. [5]Then he poured water into a basin and began to wash the disciples' feet and to wipe them with the towel that was tied around him. [6]He came to Simon Peter, who said to him, "Lord, are you going to wash my feet?" [7]Jesus answered, "You do not know now what I am doing, but later you will understand." [8]Peter said to him, "You will never wash my feet." Jesus answered, "Unless I wash you, you have no share with me." [9]Simon Peter said to him, "Lord, not my feet only but also my hands and my head!" [10]Jesus said to him, "One who has bathed does not need to wash, except for the feet,[t] but is entirely clean. And you[u] are clean, though not all of you." [11]For he knew who was to betray him; for this reason he said, "Not all of you are clean."

12 After he had washed their feet, had put on his robe, and had returned to the table, he said to them, "Do you know what I have done to you? [13]You call me Teacher and Lord—and you are right, for that is what I am. [14]So if I, your Lord and Teacher, have washed your feet, you also ought to wash one another's feet. [15]For I have set you an example, that you also should do as I have done to you. [16]Very truly, I tell you, servants[v] are not greater than their master, nor are messengers greater than the one who sent them. [17]If you know these things, you are blessed if you do them. [18]I am not speaking of all of you; I know whom I have chosen. But it is to fulfill the scripture, 'The one who ate my bread[w] has lifted his heel against me.' [19]I tell you this now, before it occurs, so that when it does occur, you may believe that I am he.[x] [20]Very truly, I tell you, whoever receives one whom I send receives me; and whoever receives me receives him who sent me."

Jesus Foretells His Betrayal

21 After saying this Jesus was troubled in spirit, and declared, "Very truly, I tell you, one of you will betray me." [22]The disciples looked at one another, uncertain of whom he was speaking.

[23]One of his disciples—the one whom Jesus loved—was reclining next to him; [24]Simon Peter therefore motioned to him to ask Jesus of whom he was speaking. [25]So while reclining next to Jesus, he asked him, "Lord, who is it?" [26]Jesus answered, "It is the one to whom I give this piece of bread when I have dipped it in the dish."[y] So when he had dipped the piece of bread, he gave it to Judas son of Simon Iscariot.[z] [27]After he received the piece of bread,[a] Satan entered into him. Jesus said to him, "Do quickly what you are going to do." [28]Now no one at the table knew why he said this to him. [29]Some thought that, because Judas had the common purse, Jesus was telling him, "Buy what we need for the festival"; or, that he should give something to the poor. [30]So, after receiving the piece of bread, he immediately went out. And it was night.

The New Commandment

31 When he had gone out, Jesus said, "Now the Son of Man has been glorified, and God has been glorified in him. [32]If God has been glorified in him,[b] God will also glorify him in himself and will glorify him at once. [33]Little children, I am with you only a little longer. You will look for me; and as I said to the Jews so now I say to you, 'Where I am going, you cannot come.' [34]I give you a new commandment, that you love one another. Just as I have loved you, you also should love one another. [35]By this everyone will know that you are my disciples, if you have love for one another."

Jesus Foretells Peter's Denial

36 Simon Peter said to him, "Lord, where are you going?" Jesus answered, "Where I am going, you cannot follow me now; but you will follow afterward." [37]Peter said to him, "Lord, why can I not follow you now? I will lay down my life for you." [38]Jesus answered, "Will you lay down your life for me? Very truly, I tell you, before the cock crows, you will have denied me three times.

---

t Other ancient authorities lack *except for the feet*   u The Greek word for *you* here is plural
v Gk *slaves*   w Other ancient authorities read *ate bread with me*   x Gk *I am*   y Gk *dipped it*
z Other ancient authorities read *Judas Iscariot son of Simon*; others, *Judas son of Simon from Karyot* (Kerioth)   a Gk *After the piece of bread*   b Other ancient authorities lack *If God has been glorified in him*

THE INCARNATE TRUTH AND LIFE
F. F. Bruce

VERSE: John 14.6   **PASSAGE:** John 14.5–14

homas's bewildered question, like many questions in the Fourth Gospel, provides Jesus with the opportunity of expanding and elucidating what he has just said. Jesus is going to the Father, and his disciples are to follow him; for them he is himself the way to the Father. He is, in fact, the only way by which men and women may come to the Father; there is no other way. If this seems offensively exclusive, let it be borne in mind that the one who makes this claim is the incarnate Word, the revealer of the Father. If God has no avenue of communication with mankind apart from his Word (incarnate or otherwise), mankind has no avenue of approach to God apart from that same Word, who became flesh and dwelt among us in order to supply such an avenue of approach. Jesus' claim, understood in the light of the prologue to the Gospel, is inclusive, not exclusive. All truth is God's truth, as all life is God's life; but God's truth and God's life are incarnate in Jesus.

It has been suggested that, in the Semitic language which Jesus spoke, the nouns "truth" and "life" were governed by "the way," as though he said, "I am the way of truth and life"— "I am the true and living way." This is no doubt an attractive suggestion . . . but that is not how [John] understood the words. For him the three nouns are co-ordinate, and are best understood by us as they were by him: "I am the way and the truth and the life." Jesus is not only the way to God; he is the truth of God—how could he be otherwise, since he is the embodiment of God's self-revelation?—and he is the life of God, "the true God and eternal life" (1 John 5.20), manifested on earth to give his flesh "for the life of the world" (John 6.51) . . .

To come to God by this way is to know him. The disciples have already begun to know the Father because they have come to know the Son; in fact (although they do not realize it yet) in the Son they have seen the Father.

ADDITIONAL SCRIPTURE READING:
John 10.9; Hebrews 10.19–22

Go to page 1259 for your next devotional reading.

1900   Present

Jesus the Way to the Father

14 "Do not let your hearts be troubled. Believe*c* in God, believe also in me. ²In my Father's house there are many dwelling places. If it were not so, would I have told you that I go to prepare a place for you?*d* ³And if I go and prepare a place for you, I will come again and will take you to myself, so that where I am, there you may be also. ⁴And you know the way to the place where I am going."*e* ⁵Thomas said to him, "Lord, we do not know where you are going. How can we know the way?" ⁶Jesus said to him, "I am the way, and the truth, and the life. No one comes to the Father except through me. ⁷If you know me, you will know*f* my Father also. From now on you do know him and have seen him."

8 Philip said to him, "Lord, show us the Father, and we will be satisfied." ⁹Jesus said to him, "Have I been with you all this time, Philip, and you still do not know me? Whoever has seen me has seen the Father. How can you say, 'Show us the Father'? ¹⁰Do you not believe that I am in the Father and the Father is in me? The words that I say to you I do not speak on my own; but the Father who dwells in me does his works. ¹¹Believe me that I am in the Father and the Father is in me; but if you do not, then believe me because of the works themselves. ¹²Very truly, I tell you, the one who believes in me will also do the works that I do and, in fact, will do greater works than these, because I am going to the Father. ¹³I will do whatever you ask in my name, so that the Father may be glorified in the Son. ¹⁴If in my name you ask me*g* for anything, I will do it.

The Promise of the Holy Spirit

15 "If you love me, you will keep*h* my commandments. ¹⁶And I will ask the Father, and he will give you another Advocate,*i* to be with you forever. ¹⁷This is the Spirit of truth, whom the world cannot receive, because it neither sees him nor knows him. You know him, because he abides with you, and he will be in*j* you.

18 "I will not leave you orphaned; I am coming to you. ¹⁹In a little while the world will no longer see me, but you will see me; because I live, you also will live. ²⁰On that day you will know that I am in my Father, and you in me, and I in you. ²¹They who have my commandments and keep them are those who love me; and those who love me will be loved by my Father, and I will love them and reveal myself to them." ²²Judas (not Iscariot) said to him, "Lord, how is it that you will reveal yourself to us, and not to the world?" ²³Jesus answered him, "Those who love me will keep my word, and my Father will love them, and we will come to them and make our home with them. ²⁴Whoever does not love me does not keep my words; and the word that you hear is not mine, but is from the Father who sent me.

25 "I have said these things to you while I am still with you. ²⁶But the Advocate,*i* the Holy Spirit, whom the Father will send in my name, will teach you everything, and remind you of all that I have said to you. ²⁷Peace I leave with you; my peace I give to you. I do not give to you as the world gives. Do not let your hearts be troubled, and do not let them be afraid. ²⁸You heard me say to you, 'I am going away, and I am coming to you.' If you loved me, you would rejoice that I am going to the Father, because the Father is greater than I. ²⁹And now I have told you this before it occurs, so that when it does occur, you may believe. ³⁰I will no longer talk much with you, for the ruler of this world is coming. He has no power over me; ³¹but I do as the Father has commanded me, so that the world may know that I love the Father. Rise, let us be on our way.

Jesus the True Vine

15 "I am the true vine, and my Father is the vinegrower. ²He removes every branch in me that bears no fruit. Every branch that bears fruit he

---

c Or *You believe*   *d* Or *If it were not so, I would have told you; for I go to prepare a place for you*
e Other ancient authorities read *Where I am going you know, and the way you know*   *f* Other ancient authorities read *If you had known me, you would have known*   *g* Other ancient authorities lack *me*
h Other ancient authorities read *me, keep*   *i* Or *Helper*   *j* Or *among*

prunes[k] to make it bear more fruit. 3You have already been cleansed[k] by the word that I have spoken to you. 4Abide in me as I abide in you. Just as the branch cannot bear fruit by itself unless it abides in the vine, neither can you unless you abide in me. 5I am the vine, you are the branches. Those who abide in me and I in them bear much fruit, because apart from me you can do nothing. 6Whoever does not abide in me is thrown away like a branch and withers; such branches are gathered, thrown into the fire, and burned. 7If you abide in me, and my words abide in you, ask for whatever you wish, and it will be done for you. 8My Father is glorified by this, that you bear much fruit and become[l] my disciples. 9As the Father has loved me, so I have loved you; abide in my love. 10If you keep

k The same Greek root refers to pruning and cleansing   l Or be

---

TUESDAY

WITHOUT ME YOU CAN DO NOTHING
Andrew Murray

VERSE: John 15.5   **PASSAGE:** John 15.1–8

ithout the vine the branch can do nothing. To the vine it owes its right of place in the vineyard, its life and its fruitfulness. And so the Lord says, "Apart from me you can do nothing." The believer can each day be pleasing to God only in that which he does through the power of Christ dwelling in him. The daily inflowing of the life-sap of the Holy Spirit is his only power to bring forth fruit. He lives alone in him and is for each moment dependent on him alone.

Without the branch the vine can also do nothing. A vine without the branches can bear no fruit. No less indispensable than the vine to the branch, is the branch to the vine. Such is the wonderful condescension of the grace of Jesus, that just as his people are dependent on him, he has made himself dependent on them. Without his disciples he cannot dispense his blessing to the world . . . This is the high honor to which he has called his redeemed ones, that as indispensable as he is to them in heaven, that *from* him their fruit may be found, so indispensable are they to him on earth, that *through* them his fruit may be found. Believers, meditate on this until your soul bows to worship in presence of the mystery of the perfect union between Christ and the believer.

ADDITIONAL SCRIPTURE READING:
Psalm 1.1–3; Colossians 3.3

Go to page 1263 for your next devotional reading.

1900   Present

my commandments, you will abide in my love, just as I have kept my Father's commandments and abide in his love. [11]I have said these things to you so that my joy may be in you, and that your joy may be complete.

12 "This is my commandment, that you love one another as I have loved you. [13]No one has greater love than this, to lay down one's life for one's friends. [14]You are my friends if you do what I command you. [15]I do not call you servants[m] any longer, because the servant[n] does not know what the master is doing; but I have called you friends, because I have made known to you everything that I have heard from my Father. [16]You did not choose me but I chose you. And I appointed you to go and bear fruit, fruit that will last, so that the Father will give you whatever you ask him in my name. [17]I am giving you these commands so that you may love one another.

The World's Hatred

18 "If the world hates you, be aware that it hated me before it hated you. [19]If you belonged to the world,[o] the world would love you as its own. Because you do not belong to the world, but I have chosen you out of the world—therefore the world hates you. [20]Remember the word that I said to you, 'Servants[p] are not greater than their master.' If they persecuted me, they will persecute you; if they kept my word, they will keep yours also. [21]But they will do all these things to you on account of my name, because they do not know him who sent me. [22]If I had not come and spoken to them, they would not have sin; but now they have no excuse for their sin. [23]Whoever hates me hates my Father also. [24]If I had not done among them the works that no one else did, they would not have sin. But now they have seen and hated both me and my Father. [25]It was to fulfill the word that is written in their law, 'They hated me without a cause.'

26 "When the Advocate[q] comes, whom I will send to you from the Father, the Spirit of truth who comes from the Father, he will testify on my behalf.

[27]You also are to testify because you have been with me from the beginning.

16 "I have said these things to you to keep you from stumbling. [2]They will put you out of the synagogues. Indeed, an hour is coming when those who kill you will think that by doing so they are offering worship to God. [3]And they will do this because they have not known the Father or me. [4]But I have said these things to you so that when their hour comes you may remember that I told you about them.

The Work of the Spirit

"I did not say these things to you from the beginning, because I was with you. [5]But now I am going to him who sent me; yet none of you asks me, 'Where are you going?' [6]But because I have said these things to you, sorrow has filled your hearts. [7]Nevertheless I tell you the truth: it is to your advantage that I go away, for if I do not go away, the Advocate[q] will not come to you; but if I go, I will send him to you. [8]And when he comes, he will prove the world wrong about[r] sin and righteousness and judgment: [9]about sin, because they do not believe in me; [10]about righteousness, because I am going to the Father and you will see me no longer; [11]about judgment, because the ruler of this world has been condemned.

12 "I still have many things to say to you, but you cannot bear them now.

COME, HOLY GHOST, FOR MOVED BY THEE
  THE PROPHET WROTE AND SPOKE;
UNLOCK THE TRUTH, THYSELF THE KEY,
  UNSEAL THE SACRED BOOK.

—John Calvin

---

[13]When the Spirit of truth comes, he will guide you into all the truth; for he will not speak on his own, but will speak whatever he hears, and he will declare to you the things that are to come. [14]He will glorify me, because he will take what is mine and declare it to you. [15]All that the Father has is mine. For

---

m Gk *slaves*   n Gk *slave*   o Gk *were of the world*   p Gk *Slaves*   q Or *Helper*   r Or *convict the world of*

this reason I said that he will take what is mine and declare it to you.

Sorrow Will Turn into Joy

16 "A little while, and you will no longer see me, and again a little while, and you will see me." 17Then some of his disciples said to one another, "What does he mean by saying to us, 'A little while, and you will no longer see me, and again a little while, and you will see me'; and 'Because I am going to the Father'?" 18They said, "What does he mean by this 'a little while'? We do not know what he is talking about." 19Jesus knew that they wanted to ask him, so he said to them, "Are you discussing among yourselves what I meant when I said, 'A little while, and you will no longer see me, and again a little while, and you will see me'? 20Very truly, I tell you, you will weep and mourn, but the world will rejoice; you will have pain, but your pain will turn into joy. 21When a woman is in labor, she has pain, because her hour has come. But when her child is born, she no longer remembers the anguish because of the joy of having brought a human being into the world. 22So you have pain now; but I will see you again, and your hearts will rejoice, and no one will take your joy from you. 23On that day you will ask nothing of me.s Very truly, I tell you, if you ask anything of the Father in my name, he will give it to you.t 24Until now you have not asked for anything in my name. Ask and you will receive, so that your joy may be complete.

Peace for the Disciples

25 "I have said these things to you in figures of speech. The hour is coming when I will no longer speak to you in figures, but will tell you plainly of the Father. 26On that day you will ask in my name. I do not say to you that I will ask the Father on your behalf; 27for the Father himself loves you, because you have loved me and have believed that I came from God.u 28I came from the Father and have come into the world; again, I am leaving the world and am going to the Father."

29 His disciples said, "Yes, now you are speaking plainly, not in any figure of speech! 30Now we know that you know all things, and do not need to have anyone question you; by this we believe that you came from God." 31Jesus answered them, "Do you now believe? 32The hour is coming, indeed it has come, when you will be scattered, each one to his home, and you will leave me alone. Yet I am not alone because the Father is with me. 33I have said this to you, so that in me you may have peace. In the world you face persecution. But take courage; I have conquered the world!"

Jesus Prays for His Disciples

17 After Jesus had spoken these words, he looked up to heaven and said, "Father, the hour has come; glorify your Son so that the Son may glorify you, 2since you have given him authority over all people,v to give eternal life to all whom you have given him. 3And this is eternal life, that they may know you, the only true God, and Jesus Christ whom you have sent. 4I glorified you on earth by finishing the work that you gave me to do. 5So now, Father, glorify me in your own presence with the glory that I had in your presence before the world existed.

6 "I have made your name known to those whom you gave me from the world. They were yours, and you gave them to me, and they have kept your word. 7Now they know that everything you have given me is from you; 8for the words that you gave to me I have given to them, and they have received them and know in truth that I came from you; and they have believed that you sent me. 9I am asking on their behalf; I am not asking on behalf of the world, but on behalf of those whom you gave me, because they are yours. 10All mine are yours, and yours are mine; and I have been glorified in them. 11And now I am no longer in the world, but they are in the world, and I am coming to you. Holy Father, protect them in your name that you have given me, so that they may be one, as we are one. 12While I was with them, I protected them in your name thatw you have given me. I guarded them,

---

s Or will ask me no question   t Other ancient authorities read Father, he will give it to you in my name   u Other ancient authorities read the Father   v Gk flesh   w Other ancient authorities read protected in your name those whom

and not one of them was lost except the one destined to be lost,^{x} so that the scripture might be fulfilled. 13But now I am coming to you, and I speak these things in the world so that they may have my joy made complete in themselves.^{y} 14I have given them your word, and the world has hated them because they do not belong to the world, just as I do not belong to the world. 15I am not asking you to take them out of the world, but I ask you to protect them from the evil one.^{z} 16They do not belong to the world, just as I do not belong to the world. 17Sanctify them in the truth; your word is truth. 18As you have sent me into the world, so I have sent them into the world. 19And for their sakes I sanctify myself, so that they also may be sanctified in truth.

20 "I ask not only on behalf of these, but also on behalf of those who will believe in me through their word, 21that they may all be one. As you, Father, are in me and I am in you, may they also be in us,^{a} so that the world may believe that you have sent me. 22The glory that you have given me I have given them, so that they may be one, as we are one, 23I in them and you in me, that they may become completely one, so that the world may know that you have sent me and have loved them even as you have loved me. 24Father, I desire that those also, whom you have given me, may be with me where I am, to see my glory, which you have given me because you loved me before the foundation of the world.

25 "Righteous Father, the world does not know you, but I know you; and these know that you have sent me. 26I made your name known to them, and I will make it known, so that the love with which you have loved me may be in them, and I in them."

The Betrayal and Arrest of Jesus

18 After Jesus had spoken these words, he went out with his disciples across the Kidron valley to a place where there was a garden, which he and his disciples entered. 2Now Judas, who betrayed him, also knew the place, because Jesus often met there with his disciples. 3So Judas brought a detach-

ment of soldiers together with police from the chief priests and the Pharisees, and they came there with lanterns and torches and weapons. 4Then Jesus, knowing all that was to happen to him, came forward and asked them, "Whom are you looking for?" 5They answered, "Jesus of Nazareth."^{b} Jesus replied, "I am he."^{c} Judas, who betrayed him, was standing with them. 6When Jesus^d said to them, "I am he,"^{c} they stepped back and fell to the ground. 7Again he asked them, "Whom are you looking for?" And they said, "Jesus of Nazareth."^{b} 8Jesus answered, "I told you that I am he.^{c} So if you are looking for me, let these men go." 9This was to fulfill the word that he had spoken, "I did not lose a single one of those whom you gave me." 10Then Simon Peter, who had a sword, drew it, struck the high priest's slave, and cut off his right ear. The slave's name was Malchus. 11Jesus said to Peter, "Put your sword back into its sheath. Am I not to drink the cup that the Father has given me?"

Jesus before the High Priest

12 So the soldiers, their officer, and the Jewish police arrested Jesus and bound him. 13First they took him to Annas, who was the father-in-law of Caiaphas, the high priest that year. 14Caiaphas was the one who had advised the Jews that it was better to have one person die for the people.

Peter Denies Jesus

15 Simon Peter and another disciple followed Jesus. Since that disciple was known to the high priest, he went with Jesus into the courtyard of the high priest, 16but Peter was standing outside at the gate. So the other disciple, who was known to the high priest, went out, spoke to the woman who guarded the gate, and brought Peter in. 17The woman said to Peter, "You are not also one of this man's disciples, are you?" He said, "I am not." 18Now the slaves and the police had made a charcoal fire because it was cold, and they were standing around it and warming themselves. Peter also was standing with them and warming himself.

x Gk except the son of destruction   y Or among themselves   z Or from evil   a Other ancient authorities read be one in us   b Gk the Nazorean   c Gk I am   d Gk he

The High Priest Questions Jesus

19 Then the high priest questioned Jesus about his disciples and about his teaching. 20Jesus answered, "I have spoken openly to the world; I have always taught in synagogues and in the temple, where all the Jews come together. I have said nothing in secret. 21Why

---

WEDNESDAY

A SPLENDOR OF HOPE
George MacDonald

VERSE: John 17.24   PASSAGE: John 17.20–26

et us note . . . that the dwelling of Jesus in us is the power of the Spirit of God upon us; for "the Lord is the Spirit," and "this comes from the Lord, who is the Spirit" (2 Corinthians 3.18). When we think Christ, Christ comes; when we receive his image into our spiritual mirror, he enters with it.

When our hearts turn to him, that is opening the door to him, that is holding up our mirror to him; then he comes in, not by our thought only, not in our idea only, but he comes himself, and of his own will. Thus the Lord, the Spirit, becomes the soul of our souls, becomes spiritually what he always was creatively; and as our spirit informs, gives shape to our bodies, in like manner his soul informs, gives shape to our souls.

In this there is nothing unnatural, nothing at conflict with our being. It is but that the deeper soul that willed and wills our souls, rises up, the infinite Life, into the self we call *I* and *me*, makes the *I* and *me* more and more his, and himself more and more ours; until at length the glory of our existence flashes upon us, we face full to the sun that enlightens what it sent forth, and know ourselves alive with an infinite life, even the life of the Father. Then indeed we *are*; then indeed we have life; the life of Jesus has, through light, become life in us; the glory of God in the face of Jesus, mirrored in our hearts, has made us alive; we are one with God for ever and ever.

What less than such a splendor of hope would be worthy the revelation of Jesus? Filled with the soul of their Father, men shall inherit the glory of their Father; filled with themselves, they cast him out, and rot. No other saving can save them. They must receive the Son and through the Son the Father.

ADDITIONAL SCRIPTURE READING:
Colossians 2.13; Revelation 3.20

Go to page 1266 for your next devotional reading.

1700   1900

do you ask me? Ask those who heard what I said to them; they know what I said." 22When he had said this, one of the police standing nearby struck Jesus on the face, saying, "Is that how you answer the high priest?" 23Jesus answered, "If I have spoken wrongly, testify to the wrong. But if I have spoken rightly, why do you strike me?" 24Then Annas sent him bound to Caiaphas the high priest.

Peter Denies Jesus Again

25 Now Simon Peter was standing and warming himself. They asked him, "You are not also one of his disciples, are you?" He denied it and said, "I am not." 26One of the slaves of the high priest, a relative of the man whose ear Peter had cut off, asked, "Did I not see you in the garden with him?" 27Again Peter denied it, and at that moment the cock crowed.

Jesus before Pilate

28 Then they took Jesus from Caiaphas to Pilate's headquarters.e It was early in the morning. They themselves did not enter the headquarters,e so as to avoid ritual defilement and to be able to eat the Passover. 29So Pilate went out to them and said, "What accusation do you bring against this man?" 30They answered, "If this man were not a criminal, we would not have handed him over to you." 31Pilate said to them, "Take him yourselves and judge him according to your law." The Jews replied, "We are not permitted to put anyone to death." 32(This was to fulfill what Jesus had said when he indicated the kind of death he was to die.)

33 Then Pilate entered the headquarterse again, summoned Jesus, and asked him, "Are you the King of the Jews?" 34Jesus answered, "Do you ask this on your own, or did others tell you about me?" 35Pilate replied, "I am not a Jew, am I? Your own nation and the chief priests have handed you over to me. What have you done?" 36Jesus answered, "My kingdom is not from this world. If my kingdom were from this world, my followers would be fighting to keep me from being handed over to the Jews. But as it is, my kingdom is not from here." 37Pilate asked him, "So you are a king?" Jesus an-

swered, "You say that I am a king. For this I was born, and for this I came into the world, to testify to the truth. Everyone who belongs to the truth listens to my voice." 38Pilate asked him, "What is truth?"

Jesus Sentenced to Death

After he had said this, he went out to the Jews again and told them, "I find no case against him. 39But you have a custom that I release someone for you at the Passover. Do you want me to release for you the King of the Jews?" 40They shouted in reply, "Not this man, but Barabbas!" Now Barabbas was a bandit.

19 Then Pilate took Jesus and had him flogged. 2And the soldiers wove a crown of thorns and put it on his head, and they dressed him in a purple robe. 3They kept coming up to him, saying, "Hail, King of the Jews!" and striking him on the face. 4Pilate went out again and said to them, "Look, I am bringing him out to you to let you know that I find no case against him." 5So Jesus came out, wearing the crown of thorns and the purple robe. Pilate said to them, "Here is the man!" 6When the chief priests and the police saw him, they shouted, "Crucify him! Crucify him!" Pilate said to them, "Take him yourselves and crucify him; I find no case against him." 7The Jews answered him, "We have a law, and according to that law he ought to die because he has claimed to be the Son of God."

8 Now when Pilate heard this, he was more afraid than ever. 9He entered his headquarterse again and asked Jesus, "Where are you from?" But Jesus gave him no answer. 10Pilate therefore said to him, "Do you refuse to speak to me? Do you not know that I have power to release you, and power to crucify you?" 11Jesus answered him, "You would have no power over me unless it had been given you from above; therefore the one who handed me over to you is guilty of a greater sin." 12From then on Pilate tried to release him, but the Jews cried out, "If you release this man, you are no friend of the emperor. Everyone who claims to be a king sets himself against the emperor."

13 When Pilate heard these words, he brought Jesus outside and satf on the

judge's bench at a place called The Stone Pavement, or in Hebrew$g$ Gabbatha. 14Now it was the day of Preparation for the Passover; and it was about noon. He said to the Jews, "Here is your King!" 15They cried out, "Away with him! Away with him! Crucify him!" Pilate asked them, "Shall I crucify your King?" The chief priests answered, "We have no king but the emperor." 16Then he handed him over to them to be crucified.

The Crucifixion of Jesus

So they took Jesus; 17and carrying the cross by himself, he went out to what is called The Place of the Skull, which in Hebrew$g$ is called Golgotha. 18There they crucified him, and with him two others, one on either side, with Jesus between them. 19Pilate also had an inscription

---

WHERE LIFE WAS SLAIN AND TRUTH WAS

SLANDERED

ON THAT ONE HOLIER HILL THAN ROME.

—G. K. Chesterton

---

written and put on the cross. It read, "Jesus of Nazareth,h the King of the Jews." 20Many of the Jews read this inscription, because the place where Jesus was crucified was near the city; and it was written in Hebrew,g in Latin, and in Greek. 21Then the chief priests of the Jews said to Pilate, "Do not write, 'The King of the Jews,' but, 'This man said, I am King of the Jews.'" 22Pilate answered, "What I have written I have written." 23When the soldiers had crucified Jesus, they took his clothes and divided them into four parts, one for each soldier. They also took his tunic; now the tunic was seamless, woven in one piece from the top. 24So they said to one another, "Let us not tear it, but cast lots for it to see who will get it." This was to fulfill what the scripture says,

"They divided my clothes among
        themselves,
    and for my clothing they cast
        lots."

25And that is what the soldiers did.

Meanwhile, standing near the cross of Jesus were his mother, and his mother's sister, Mary the wife of Clopas, and Mary Magdalene. 26When Jesus saw his mother and the disciple whom he loved standing beside her, he said to his mother, "Woman, here is your son." 27Then he said to the disciple, "Here is your mother." And from that hour the disciple took her into his own home.

28 After this, when Jesus knew that all was now finished, he said (in order to fulfill the scripture), "I am thirsty." 29A jar full of sour wine was standing there. So they put a sponge full of the wine on a branch of hyssop and held it to his mouth. 30When Jesus had received the wine, he said, "It is finished." Then he bowed his head and gave up his spirit.

Jesus' Side Is Pierced

31 Since it was the day of Preparation, the Jews did not want the bodies left on the cross during the sabbath, especially because that sabbath was a day of great solemnity. So they asked Pilate to have the legs of the crucified men broken and the bodies removed. 32Then the soldiers came and broke the legs of the first and of the other who had been crucified with him. 33But when they came to Jesus and saw that he was already dead, they did not break his legs. 34Instead, one of the soldiers pierced his side with a spear, and at once blood and water came out. 35(He who saw this has testified so that you also may believe. His testimony is true, and he knows$i$ that he tells the truth.) 36These things occurred so that the scripture might be fulfilled, "None of his bones shall be broken." 37And again another passage of scripture says, "They will look on the one whom they have pierced."

NO PAIN, NO PALM; NO THORNS, NO THRONE; NO

GALL, NO GLORY; NO CROSS, NO CROWN.

—William Penn

The Burial of Jesus

38 After these things, Joseph of Arimathea, who was a disciple of Jesus, though a secret one because of his fear of the Jews, asked Pilate to let him take away the body of Jesus. Pilate gave him permission; so he came and removed his

---

g That is, *Aramaic*   h Gk *the Nazorean*   i Or *there is one who knows*

PRAYERS ON THE DEATH OF CHRIST
Bonaventura

VERSE: John 19.30   **PASSAGE:** John 19.28–42

Gethsemane

ord Jesus, you have shaped our faith, by making us believe you shared our mortal nature. In Gethsemane real drops of sweat fell from your body.

Lord Jesus, you have given us hope, because you endured all the spiritual and physical hardships which mortal nature can suffer. In Gethsemane your soul was in torment, and your heart shook at the prospect of the physical pain to come.

You showed all the natural weaknesses of the flesh, that we might know that you have truly borne our sorrows.

Trial

Sweet Jesus, what soul can be so hardened as not to cry out at your plight?

Sweet Jesus, what heart can be so hardened as not to groan with compassion for you?

Sweet Jesus, my ears can hardly bear to hear those horrible shouts:

"Away with him. Away with him. Crucify him."

Crucifixion

O Lord, holy Father, show us what kind of man it is who is hanging for our sakes on the cross, whose suffering causes the rocks themselves to crack and crumble with compassion, whose death brings the dead back to life.

Let my heart crack and crumble at the sight of him. Let my soul break apart with compassion for his suffering. Let it be shattered with grief at my sins for which he dies. And finally let it be softened with devoted love for him.

Burial

O my God, Jesus, I am in every way unworthy of you. Yet, like Joseph of Arimathea, I want to offer a space for you. He offered his own tomb; I offer my heart.

Enter the darkness of my heart, as your body entered the darkness of Joseph's tomb. And make me worthy to receive you, driving out all sin that I may be filled with your spiritual light.

ADDITIONAL SCRIPTURE READING:
Psalm 22; 1 Peter 2.21–24

Go to page 1268 for your next devotional reading.

500   1500

body. ³⁹Nicodemus, who had at first come to Jesus by night, also came, bringing a mixture of myrrh and aloes, weighing about a hundred pounds. ⁴⁰They took the body of Jesus and wrapped it with the spices in linen cloths, according to the burial custom of the Jews. ⁴¹Now there was a garden in the place where he was crucified, and in the garden there was a new tomb in which no one had ever been laid. ⁴²And so, because it was the Jewish day of Preparation, and the tomb was nearby, they laid Jesus there.

The Resurrection of Jesus

20 Early on the first day of the week, while it was still dark, Mary Magdalene came to the tomb and saw that the stone had been removed from the tomb. ²So she ran and went to Simon Peter and the other disciple, the one whom Jesus loved, and said to them, "They have taken the Lord out of the tomb, and we do not know where they have laid him." ³Then Peter and the other disciple set out and went toward the tomb. ⁴The two were running together, but the other disciple outran Peter and reached the tomb first. ⁵He bent down to look in and saw the linen wrappings lying there, but he did not go in. ⁶Then Simon Peter came, following him, and went into the tomb. He saw the linen wrappings lying there, ⁷and the cloth that had been on Jesus' head, not lying with the linen wrappings but rolled up in a place by itself. ⁸Then the other disciple, who reached the tomb first, also went in, and he saw and believed; ⁹for as yet they did not understand the scripture, that he must rise from the dead. ¹⁰Then the disciples returned to their homes.

Jesus Appears to Mary Magdalene

11 But Mary stood weeping outside the tomb. As she wept, she bent over to look^j into the tomb; ¹²and she saw two angels in white, sitting where the body of Jesus had been lying, one at the head and the other at the feet. ¹³They said to her, "Woman, why are you weeping?" She said to them, "They have taken away my Lord, and I do not know where

they have laid him." ¹⁴When she had said this, she turned around and saw Jesus standing there, but she did not know that it was Jesus. ¹⁵Jesus said to her, "Woman, why are you weeping? Whom are you looking for?" Supposing him to be the gardener, she said to him, "Sir, if you have carried him away, tell me where you have laid him, and I will take him away." ¹⁶Jesus said to her, "Mary!" She turned and said to him in Hebrew,^k "Rabbouni!" (which means Teacher). ¹⁷Jesus said to her, "Do not hold on to me, because I have not yet ascended to the Father. But go to my brothers and say to them, 'I am ascending to my Father and your Father, to my God and your God.' " ¹⁸Mary Magdalene went and announced to the disciples, "I have seen the Lord"; and she told them that he had said these things to her.

Jesus Appears to the Disciples

19 When it was evening on that day, the first day of the week, and the doors of the house where the disciples had met were locked for fear of the Jews, Jesus came and stood among them and said, "Peace be with you." ²⁰After he said this, he showed them his hands and his side. Then the disciples rejoiced when they saw the Lord. ²¹Jesus said to them again, "Peace be with you. As the Father has sent me, so I send you." ²²When he had said this, he breathed on them and said to them, "Receive the Holy Spirit. ²³If you forgive the sins of any, they are forgiven them; if you retain the sins of any, they are retained."

Jesus and Thomas

24 But Thomas (who was called the Twin^l), one of the twelve, was not with them when Jesus came. ²⁵So the other disciples told him, "We have seen the Lord." But he said to them, "Unless I see the mark of the nails in his hands, and put my finger in the mark of the nails and my hand in his side, I will not believe."

26 A week later his disciples were again in the house, and Thomas was with them. Although the doors were shut, Jesus came and stood among them and said, "Peace be with you." ²⁷Then he said to Thomas, "Put your finger here

j Gk lacks to look   k That is, Aramaic   l Gk Didymus

THE HOLINESS OF HOME
Gregory of Nyssa

VERSE: John 20.29   **PASSAGE:** John 20.24–29

e confessed that the Christ who was manifested is very God, as much before as after our sojourn at Jerusalem; our faith in him was not increased afterwards any more than it was diminished. Before we saw Bethlehem we knew his being made man by means of the Virgin; before we saw his grave we believed in his resurrection from the dead; apart from seeing the Mount of Olives, we confessed that his ascension into heaven was real. We derived only thus much of profit from our traveling thither, namely that we came to know by being able to compare them, that our own places are far holier than those abroad. Wherefore, O ye who fear the Lord, praise him in the places where ye now are. Change of place does not effect any drawing nearer unto God, but wherever thou mayest be, God will come to thee, if the chambers of thy soul be found of such a sort that he can dwell in thee and walk in thee. But if thou keepest thine inner man full of wicked thoughts, even if thou wast on Golgotha, even if thou wast on the Mount of Olives, even if thou stoodest on the memorial-rock of the resurrection, thou wilt be as far away from receiving Christ into thyself, as one who has not even begun to confess him . . . Inasmuch as the gift and the distribution of the Holy Spirit had not yet passed upon the apostles, our Lord commanded them to remain in the same place, until they should have been endued with power from on high (see Acts 1.4). Now, if that which happened at the beginning, when the Holy Spirit was dispensing each of his gifts under the appearance of a flame, continued until now, it would be right for all to remain in that place where that dispensing took place; but if the Spirit "bloweth" where he "listeth," those, too, who have become believers here are made partakers of that gift; and that according to the proportion of their faith, not in consequence of their pilgrimage to Jerusalem.

ADDITIONAL SCRIPTURE READING:
1 Chronicles 17.4–6; Revelation 21.1–3

Go to page 1270 for your next devotional reading.

100   500

and see my hands. Reach out your hand and put it in my side. Do not doubt but believe." 28Thomas answered him, "My Lord and my God!" 29Jesus said to him, "Have you believed because you have seen me? Blessed are those who have not seen and yet have come to believe."

The Purpose of This Book

30 Now Jesus did many other signs in the presence of his disciples, which are not written in this book. 31But these are written so that you may come to believem that Jesus is the Messiah,n the Son of God, and that through believing you may have life in his name.

CHRISTIANITY, IF FALSE, IS OF NO IMPORTANCE, AND, IF TRUE, OF INFINITE IMPORTANCE. THE ONE THING IT CANNOT BE IS MODERATELY IMPORTANT.
                                        —C. S. Lewis

Jesus Appears to Seven Disciples

21 After these things Jesus showed himself again to the disciples by the Sea of Tiberias; and he showed himself in this way. 2Gathered there together were Simon Peter, Thomas called the Twin,o Nathanael of Cana in Galilee, the sons of Zebedee, and two others of his disciples. 3Simon Peter said to them, "I am going fishing." They said to him, "We will go with you." They went out and got into the boat, but that night they caught nothing.

4 Just after daybreak, Jesus stood on the beach; but the disciples did not know that it was Jesus. 5Jesus said to them, "Children, you have no fish, have you?" They answered him, "No." 6He said to them, "Cast the net to the right side of the boat, and you will find some." So they cast it, and now they were not able to haul it in because there were so many fish. 7That disciple whom Jesus loved said to Peter, "It is the Lord!" When Simon Peter heard that it was the Lord, he put on some clothes, for he was naked, and jumped into the sea. 8But the other disciples came in the boat, dragging the net full of fish, for

they were not far from the land, only about a hundred yardsp off.

9 When they had gone ashore, they saw a charcoal fire there, with fish on it, and bread. 10Jesus said to them, "Bring some of the fish that you have just caught." 11So Simon Peter went aboard and hauled the net ashore, full of large fish, a hundred fifty-three of them; and though there were so many, the net was not torn. 12Jesus said to them, "Come and have breakfast." Now none of the disciples dared to ask him, "Who are you?" because they knew it was the Lord. 13Jesus came and took the bread and gave it to them, and did the same with the fish. 14This was now the third time that Jesus appeared to the disciples after he was raised from the dead.

Jesus and Peter

15 When they had finished breakfast, Jesus said to Simon Peter, "Simon son of John, do you love me more than these?" He said to him, "Yes, Lord; you know that I love you." Jesus said to him, "Feed my lambs." 16A second time he said to him, "Simon son of John, do you love me?" He said to him, "Yes, Lord; you know that I love you." Jesus said to him, "Tend my sheep." 17He said to him the third time, "Simon son of John, do you love me?" Peter felt hurt because he said to him the third time, "Do you love me?" And he said to him, "Lord, you know everything; you know that I love you." Jesus said to him, "Feed my sheep. 18Very truly, I tell you, when you were younger, you used to fasten your own belt and to go wherever you wished. But when you grow old, you will stretch out your hands, and someone else will fasten a belt around you and take you where you do not wish to go." 19(He said this to indicate the kind of death by which he would glorify God.) After this he said to him, "Follow me."

Jesus and the Beloved Disciple

20 Peter turned and saw the disciple whom Jesus loved following them; he was the one who had reclined next to

---

m Other ancient authorities read *may continue to believe*   n Or *the Christ*   o Gk *Didymus*
p Gk *two hundred cubits*

WEEKEND

AN HYMNE OF HEAVENLY LOVE
Edmund Spenser

VERSE: John 21.15   **PASSAGE:** John 21.15–17

im first to love great right and reason is,
Who first to us our life and being gave,
And after, when we fared had amiss,
   Us wretches from the second death did save;
And last the food of life, which now we have,
Even he himself, in his dear sacrament,
To feed our hungry souls, unto us lent.

Then next, to love our brethren that were made
Of that self mould, and that self Maker's hand,
That we, and to the same again shall fade,
Where they shall have like heritage of land,
However here on higher steps we stand;
Which also were with self-same price redeemed
That we, however of us light esteemed.

And were they not, yet since that loving Lord
Commanded us to love them for his sake,
Even for his sake, and for his sacred word,
Which in his last bequest he to us spake,
We should them love, and with their needs partake;
Knowing that whatso'er to them we give,
We give to him by whom we all do live.

Such mercy he by his most holy rede
Unto us taught, and to approve it true,
Ensampled it by his most righteous deed,
Showing us mercy (miserable crew!)
That we the like should to the wretches show,
And love our brethren; thereby to approve
How much himself that loved us we love.

ADDITIONAL SCRIPTURE READING:
Ephesians 3.14–19; 1 John 4.19–21

Go to page 1275 for your next devotional reading.

1500   1700

Jesus at the supper and had said, "Lord, who is it that is going to betray you?" 21When Peter saw him, he said to Jesus, "Lord, what about him?" 22Jesus said to him, "If it is my will that he remain until I come, what is that to you? Follow me!" 23So the rumor spread in the community*q* that this disciple would not die. Yet Jesus did not say to him that he would not die, but, "If it is my will that

he remain until I come, what is that to you?"*r*

24 This is the disciple who is testifying to these things and has written them, and we know that his testimony is true. 25But there are also many other things that Jesus did; if every one of them were written down, I suppose that the world itself could not contain the books that would be written.

---

q Gk *among the brothers*   *r* Other ancient authorities lack *what is that to you*

ACTS

IKE A SEQUEL TO A MOVIE, ACTS PICKS UP THE ACTION BEGUN IN LUKE'S GOSPEL. SOME REFER TO THE BOOK OF ACTS AS "THE ACTS OF THE HOLY SPIRIT," BECAUSE IT FOCUSES ON THE COMING OF THE SPIRIT ON GOD'S PEOPLE, THE CHURCH, IN A NEW AND POWERFUL WAY. IN THIS BOOK LUKE RECORDS CHRISTIANITY'S AMAZING GROWTH, SHOWING HOW REVIVAL COMES NOT BY HUMAN EFFORT BUT BY THE POWER OF THE HOLY SPIRIT. THE SPIRIT SO ACTIVE IN ACTS IS THE SAME SPIRIT AT WORK IN YOUR LIFE TODAY.

The Promise of the Holy Spirit

1 In the first book, Theophilus, I wrote about all that Jesus did and taught from the beginning 2until the day when he was taken up to heaven, after giving instructions through the Holy Spirit to the apostles whom he had chosen. 3After his suffering he presented himself alive to them by many convincing proofs, appearing to them during forty days and speaking about the kingdom of God. 4While staying*a* with them, he ordered them not to leave Jerusalem, but to wait there for the promise of the Father. "This," he said, "is what you have heard from me; 5for John baptized with water, but you will be baptized with*b* the Holy Spirit not many days from now."

The Ascension of Jesus

6 So when they had come together, they asked him, "Lord, is this the time when you will restore the kingdom to Israel?" 7He replied, "It is not for you to know the times or periods that the Father has set by his own authority. 8But you will receive power when the Holy Spirit has come upon you; and you will be my witnesses in Jerusalem, in all Judea and Samaria, and to the ends of the earth." 9When he had said this, as they were watching, he was lifted up, and a cloud took him out of their sight. 10While he was going and they were gazing up toward heaven, suddenly two men in white robes stood by them. 11They said, "Men of Galilee, why do

a Or *eating*   *b* Or *by*

you stand looking up toward heaven? This Jesus, who has been taken up from you into heaven, will come in the same way as you saw him go into heaven."

JESUS DEPARTED FROM OUR SIGHT THAT HE MIGHT RETURN TO OUR HEART. HE DEPARTED, AND BEHOLD, HE IS HERE.   —*Augustine*

Matthias Chosen to Replace Judas

12 Then they returned to Jerusalem from the mount called Olivet, which is near Jerusalem, a sabbath day's journey away. [13]When they had entered the city, they went to the room upstairs where they were staying, Peter, and John, and James, and Andrew, Philip and Thomas, Bartholomew and Matthew, James son of Alphaeus, and Simon the Zealot, and Judas son of[c] James. [14]All these were constantly devoting themselves to prayer, together with certain women, including Mary the mother of Jesus, as well as his brothers.

15 In those days Peter stood up among the believers[d] (together the crowd numbered about one hundred twenty persons) and said, [16]"Friends,[e] the scripture had to be fulfilled, which the Holy Spirit through David foretold concerning Judas, who became a guide for those who arrested Jesus— [17]for he was numbered among us and was allotted his share in this ministry." [18](Now this man acquired a field with the reward of his wickedness; and falling headlong,[f] he burst open in the middle and all his bowels gushed out. [19]This became known to all the residents of Jerusalem, so that the field was called in their language Hakeldama, that is, Field of Blood.) [20]"For it is written in the book of Psalms,

'Let his homestead become desolate,
   and let there be no one to live in
      it';

and

'Let another take his position of
      overseer.'

[21]So one of the men who have accompanied us during all the time that the Lord Jesus went in and out among us, [22]beginning from the baptism of John until the day when he was taken up from us— one of these must become a witness with us to his resurrection." [23]So they proposed two, Joseph called Barsabbas, who was also known as Justus, and Matthias. [24]Then they prayed and said, "Lord, you know everyone's heart. Show us which one of these two you have chosen [25]to take the place[g] in this ministry and apostleship from which Judas turned aside to go to his own place." [26]And they cast lots for them, and the lot fell on Matthias; and he was added to the eleven apostles.

The Coming of the Holy Spirit

2 When the day of Pentecost had come, they were all together in one place. [2]And suddenly from heaven there came a sound like the rush of a violent wind, and it filled the entire house where they were sitting. [3]Divided tongues, as of fire, appeared among them, and a tongue rested on each of them. [4]All of them were filled with the Holy Spirit and began to speak in other languages, as the Spirit gave them ability.

5 Now there were devout Jews from every nation under heaven living in Jerusalem. [6]And at this sound the crowd gathered and was bewildered, because each one heard them speaking in the native language of each. [7]Amazed and astonished, they asked, "Are not all these who are speaking Galileans? [8]And how is it that we hear, each of us, in our own native language? [9]Parthians, Medes, Elamites, and residents of Mesopotamia, Judea and Cappadocia, Pontus and Asia, [10]Phrygia and Pamphylia, Egypt and the parts of Libya belonging to Cyrene, and visitors from Rome, both Jews and proselytes, [11]Cretans and Arabs—in our own languages we hear them speaking about God's deeds of power." [12]All were amazed and perplexed, saying to one another, "What does this mean?" [13]But others sneered and said, "They are filled with new wine."

Peter Addresses the Crowd

14 But Peter, standing with the eleven, raised his voice and addressed them, "Men of Judea and all who live in

---

c Or *the brother of*   *d* Gk *brothers*   *e* Gk *Men, brothers*   *f* Or *swelling up*   *g* Other ancient authorities read *the share*

Jerusalem, let this be known to you, and listen to what I say. 15Indeed, these are not drunk, as you suppose, for it is only nine o'clock in the morning. 16No, this is what was spoken through the prophet Joel:

17 'In the last days it will be, God declares,
that I will pour out my Spirit upon all flesh,
and your sons and your daughters shall prophesy,
and your young men shall see visions,
and your old men shall dream dreams.
18 Even upon my slaves, both men and women,
in those days I will pour out my Spirit;
and they shall prophesy.
19 And I will show portents in the heaven above
and signs on the earth below,
blood, and fire, and smoky mist.
20 The sun shall be turned to darkness and the moon to blood,
before the coming of the Lord's great and glorious day.
21 Then everyone who calls on the name of the Lord shall be saved.'

22 "You that are Israelites,h listen to what I have to say: Jesus of Nazareth,i a man attested to you by God with deeds of power, wonders, and signs that God did through him among you, as you yourselves know— 23this man, handed over to you according to the definite plan and foreknowledge of God, you crucified and killed by the hands of those outside the law. 24But God raised him up, having freed him from death,j because it was impossible for him to be held in its power. 25For David says concerning him,

'I saw the Lord always before me,
for he is at my right hand so that I will not be shaken;
26 therefore my heart was glad, and my tongue rejoiced;
moreover my flesh will live in hope.

27 For you will not abandon my soul to Hades,
or let your Holy One experience corruption.
28 You have made known to me the ways of life;
you will make me full of gladness with your presence.'

29 "Fellow Israelites,k I may say to you confidently of our ancestor David that he both died and was buried, and his tomb is with us to this day. 30Since he was a prophet, he knew that God had sworn with an oath to him that he would put one of his descendants on his throne. 31Foreseeing this, Davidl spoke of the resurrection of the Messiah,m saying,

'He was not abandoned to Hades,
nor did his flesh experience corruption.'

32This Jesus God raised up, and of that all of us are witnesses. 33Being therefore exalted atn the right hand of God, and having received from the Father the promise of the Holy Spirit, he has poured out this that you both see and hear. 34For David did not ascend into the heavens, but he himself says,

'The Lord said to my Lord,
"Sit at my right hand,
35 until I make your enemies your footstool." '

36Therefore let the entire house of Israel know with certainty that God has made him both Lord and Messiah,o this Jesus whom you crucified."

The First Converts

37 Now when they heard this, they were cut to the heart and said to Peter and to the other apostles, "Brothers,k what should we do?" 38Peter said to them, "Repent, and be baptized every one of you in the name of Jesus Christ so that your sins may be forgiven; and you will receive the gift of the Holy Spirit. 39For the promise is for you, for your children, and for all who are far away, everyone whom the Lord our God calls to him." 40And he testified with many other arguments and exhorted them, saying, "Save yourselves from this corrupt generation." 41So those who welcomed his message were baptized, and

DEVOTED TO THE BREAKING OF BREAD
The Didache

VERSE: Acts 2.42

PASSAGE: Acts 2.42–47

 ow about the Eucharist: This is how to give thanks: First in connection with the cup: "We thank you, our Father, for the holy vine of David, your child, which you have revealed through Jesus, your child. To you be glory forever."

Then in connection with the piece [broken off the loaf]: "We thank you, our Father, for the life and knowledge which you have revealed through Jesus, your child. To you be glory forever. As this piece [of bread] was scattered over the hills and then was brought together and made one, so let your church be brought together from the ends of the earth into your kingdom. For yours is the glory and the power through Jesus Christ forever."

You must not let anyone eat or drink of your Eucharist except those baptized in the Lord's name. For in reference to this the Lord said, "Do not give what is sacred to dogs" (see Matthew 7.6).

After you have finished your meal, say grace in this way: "We thank you, holy Father, for your sacred name which you have lodged in our hearts, and for the knowledge and faith and immortality which you have revealed through Jesus, your child. To you be glory forever. Almighty Master, you have created everything for the sake of your name, and have given men food and drink to enjoy that they may thank you. But to us you have given spiritual food and drink and eternal life through Jesus, your child. Above all, we thank you that you are mighty. To you be glory forever.

"Remember, Lord, your church, to save it from all evil and to make it perfect by your love. Make it holy, and gather it together from the four winds into your kingdom which you have made ready for it. For yours is the power and the glory forever.

"Let grace come and let this world pass away.

"Hosanna to the God of David!

"If anyone is holy, let him come. If not, let him repent.

"Our Lord, come!

"Amen."

ADDITIONAL SCRIPTURE READING:
Matthew 26.26–29; 1 Corinthians 11.17–34

Go to page 1278 for your next devotional reading.

that day about three thousand persons were added. 42They devoted themselves to the apostles' teaching and fellowship, to the breaking of bread and the prayers.

Life among the Believers

43 Awe came upon everyone, because many wonders and signs were being done by the apostles. 44All who believed were together and had all things in common; 45they would sell their possessions and goods and distribute the proceeds$p$ to all, as any had need. 46Day by day, as they spent much time together in the temple, they broke bread at home$q$ and ate their food with glad and generous$r$ hearts, 47praising God and having the goodwill of all the people. And day by day the Lord added to their number those who were being saved.

THERE IS NO LIFE THAT IS NOT IN COMMUNITY. AND NO COMMUNITY NOT LIVED IN PRAISE OF GOD. —T. S. Eliot

---

Peter Heals a Crippled Beggar

3 One day Peter and John were going up to the temple at the hour of prayer, at three o'clock in the afternoon. 2And a man lame from birth was being carried in. People would lay him daily at the gate of the temple called the Beautiful Gate so that he could ask for alms from those entering the temple. 3When he saw Peter and John about to go into the temple, he asked them for alms. 4Peter looked intently at him, as did John, and said, "Look at us." 5And he fixed his attention on them, expecting to receive something from them. 6But Peter said, "I have no silver or gold, but what I have I give you; in the name of Jesus Christ of Nazareth,s stand up and walk." 7And he took him by the right hand and raised him up; and immediately his feet and ankles were made strong. 8Jumping up, he stood and began to walk, and entered the temple with them, walking and leaping and praising God. 9All the people saw him walking and praising God, 10and they recognized him as the one who used to sit and ask for alms at

the Beautiful Gate of the temple; and they were filled with wonder and amazement at what had happened to him.

Peter Speaks in Solomon's Portico

11 While he clung to Peter and John, all the people ran together to them in the portico called Solomon's Portico, utterly astonished. 12When Peter saw it, he addressed the people, "You Israelites,t why do you wonder at this, or why do you stare at us, as though by our own power or piety we had made him walk? 13The God of Abraham, the God of Isaac, and the God of Jacob, the God of our ancestors has glorified his servant$u$ Jesus, whom you handed over and rejected in the presence of Pilate, though he had decided to release him. 14But you rejected the Holy and Righteous One and asked to have a murderer given to you, 15and you killed the Author of life, whom God raised from the dead. To this we are witnesses. 16And by faith in his name, his name itself has made this man strong, whom you see and know; and the faith that is through Jesus$v$ has given him this perfect health in the presence of all of you.

17 "And now, friends,w I know that you acted in ignorance, as did also your rulers. 18In this way God fulfilled what he had foretold through all the prophets, that his Messiah$x$ would suffer. 19Repent therefore, and turn to God so that your sins may be wiped out, 20so that times of refreshing may come from the presence of the Lord, and that he may send the Messiah$y$ appointed for you, that is, Jesus, 21who must remain in heaven until the time of universal restoration that God announced long ago through his holy prophets. 22Moses said, 'The Lord your God will raise up for you from your own people$w$ a prophet like me. You must listen to whatever he tells you. 23And it will be that everyone who does not listen to that prophet will be utterly rooted out of the people.' 24And all the prophets, as many as have spoken, from Samuel and those after him, also predicted these days. 25You are the descendants of the prophets and of the covenant that God gave to your an-

---

p Gk them　q Or from house to house　r Or sincere　s Gk the Nazorean　t Gk Men, Israelites
u Or child　v Gk him　w Gk brothers　x Or his Christ　y Or the Christ

cestors, saying to Abraham, 'And in your descendants all the families of the earth shall be blessed.' 26When God raised up his servant,z he sent him first to you, to bless you by turning each of you from your wicked ways."

Peter and John before the Council

4 While Peter and John*a* were speaking to the people, the priests, the captain of the temple, and the Sadducees came to them, 2much annoyed because they were teaching the people and proclaiming that in Jesus there is the resurrection of the dead. 3So they arrested them and put them in custody until the next day, for it was already evening. 4But many of those who heard the word believed; and they numbered about five thousand.

5 The next day their rulers, elders, and scribes assembled in Jerusalem, 6with Annas the high priest, Caiaphas, John,*b* and Alexander, and all who were of the high-priestly family. 7When they had made the prisoners*c* stand in their midst, they inquired, "By what power or by what name did you do this?" 8Then Peter, filled with the Holy Spirit, said to them, "Rulers of the people and elders, 9if we are questioned today because of a good deed done to someone who was sick and are asked how this man has been healed, 10let it be known to all of you, and to all the people of Israel, that this man is standing before you in good health by the name of Jesus Christ of Nazareth,*d* whom you crucified, whom God raised from the dead. 11This Jesus*e* is
'the stone that was rejected by you,
   the builders;
it has become the cornerstone.'*f*
12There is salvation in no one else, for there is no other name under heaven given among mortals by which we must be saved."

13 Now when they saw the boldness of Peter and John and realized that they were uneducated and ordinary men, they were amazed and recognized them as companions of Jesus. 14When they saw the man who had been cured standing beside them, they had nothing to say

in opposition. 15So they ordered them to leave the council while they discussed the matter with one another. 16They said, "What will we do with them? For it is obvious to all who live in Jerusalem that a notable sign has been done through them; we cannot deny it. 17But to keep it from spreading further among the people, let us warn them to speak no more to anyone in this name." 18So they called them and ordered them not to speak or teach at all in the name of Jesus. 19But Peter and John answered them, "Whether it is right in God's sight to listen to you rather than to God, you must judge; 20for we cannot keep from speaking about what we have seen and heard." 21After threatening them again, they let them go, finding no way to punish them because of the people, for all of them praised God for what had happened. 22For the man on whom this sign of healing had been performed was more than forty years old.

The Believers Pray for Boldness

23 After they were released, they went to their friends*g* and reported what the chief priests and the elders had said to them. 24When they heard it, they raised their voices together to God and said, "Sovereign Lord, who made the heaven and the earth, the sea, and everything in them, 25it is you who said by the Holy Spirit through our ancestor David, your servant:*z*
'Why did the Gentiles rage,
  and the peoples imagine vain
    things?
26   The kings of the earth took their
    stand,
  and the rulers have gathered
    together
    against the Lord and against his
     Messiah.'*h*
27For in this city, in fact, both Herod and Pontius Pilate, with the Gentiles and the peoples of Israel, gathered together against your holy servant*z* Jesus, whom you anointed, 28to do whatever your hand and your plan had predestined to take place. 29And now, Lord, look at their threats, and grant to your servants*i*

z Or *child*   a Gk *While they*   b Other ancient authorities read *Jonathan*   c Gk *them*
d Gk *the Nazorean*   e Gk *This*   f Or *keystone*   g Gk *their own*   h Or *his Christ*
i Gk *slaves*

to speak your word with all boldness, ³⁰while you stretch out your hand to heal, and signs and wonders are per- formed through the name of your holy servant^j Jesus." ³¹When they had prayed, the place in which they were

j Or *child*

TUESDAY

ARRESTED IN THE STEEPLEHOUSE
George Fox

VERSE: Acts 4.3   **PASSAGE:** Acts 4.1–4

ow while I was at Mansfield-Woodhouse, I was moved to go to the steeplehouse there on a First-day, out of the meeting in Mansfield, and when the priest had done I declared the truth to the priest and people. But the people fell upon me with their fists, books, and without compassion or mercy beat me down in the steeplehouse and almost smothered me in it, being under them . . . Then they punched and thrust and struck me up and down and they set me in the stocks and brought a whip to whip me, but did not. And as I sat in the stocks they threw stones at me, and my head, arms, breast, shoulders, back, and sides were so bruised that I was mazed and dazzled with the blows . . .

After some time they had me before the magistrate, at a knight's house and examined me, where were many great persons, and I reasoned with them of the things of God and his teachings, and Christ's, and how that God that made the world did not well in temples made with hands (see Acts 17.24); and of divers things of the truth I spake to them, and they, seeing how evilly I had been used, set me at liberty. The rude people were ready to fall upon me with staves but the constable kept them off. And when they had set me at liberty, they threatened me with pistols, if ever I came again they would kill me and shoot me; and they would carry their pistols to the steeplehouse . . . I was scarce able to go or well to stand, by reason of ill-usage. Yet with much ado I got about a mile from the town, and as I was passing along the fields friends met me. I was so bruised that I could not turn in my bed, and bruised inwardly at my heart, but after a while the power of the Lord went through me and healed me, that I was well, glory be to the Lord forever.

ADDITIONAL SCRIPTURE READING:
2 Corinthians 6.4–10; 2 Timothy 3.12–14

Go to page 1282 for your next devotional reading.

1500   1700

gathered together was shaken; and they were all filled with the Holy Spirit and spoke the word of God with boldness.

The Believers Share Their Possessions

32 Now the whole group of those who believed were of one heart and soul, and no one claimed private ownership of any possessions, but everything they owned was held in common. 33With great power the apostles gave their testimony to the resurrection of the Lord Jesus, and great grace was upon them all. 34There was not a needy person among them, for as many as owned lands or houses sold them and brought the proceeds of what was sold. 35They laid it at the apostles' feet, and it was distributed to each as any had need. 36There was a Levite, a native of Cyprus, Joseph, to whom the apostles gave the name Barnabas (which means "son of encouragement"). 37He sold a field that belonged to him, then brought the money, and laid it at the apostles' feet.

Ananias and Sapphira

5 But a man named Ananias, with the consent of his wife Sapphira, sold a piece of property; 2with his wife's knowledge, he kept back some of the proceeds, and brought only a part and laid it at the apostles' feet. 3"Ananias," Peter asked, "why has Satan filled your heart to lie to the Holy Spirit and to keep back part of the proceeds of the land? 4While it remained unsold, did it not remain your own? And after it was sold, were not the proceeds at your disposal? How is it that you have contrived this deed in your heart? You did not lie to us*k* but to God!" 5Now when Ananias heard these words, he fell down and died. And great fear seized all who heard of it. 6The young men came and wrapped up his body,*l* then carried him out and buried him.

7 After an interval of about three hours his wife came in, not knowing what had happened. 8Peter said to her, "Tell me whether you and your husband sold the land for such and such a price." And she said, "Yes, that was the price." 9Then Peter said to her, "How is it that you have agreed together to put the Spirit of the Lord to the test? Look, the feet of those who have buried your husband are at the door, and they will carry you out." 10Immediately she fell down at his feet and died. When the young men came in they found her dead, so they carried her out and buried her beside her husband. 11And great fear seized the whole church and all who heard of these things.

The Apostles Heal Many

12 Now many signs and wonders were done among the people through the apostles. And they were all together in Solomon's Portico. 13None of the rest dared to join them, but the people held them in high esteem. 14Yet more than ever believers were added to the Lord, great numbers of both men and women, 15so that they even carried out the sick into the streets, and laid them on cots and mats, in order that Peter's shadow might fall on some of them as he came by. 16A great number of people would also gather from the towns around Jerusalem, bringing the sick and those tormented by unclean spirits, and they were all cured.

The Apostles Are Persecuted

17 Then the high priest took action; he and all who were with him (that is, the sect of the Sadducees), being filled with jealousy, 18arrested the apostles and put them in the public prison. 19But during the night an angel of the Lord opened the prison doors, brought them out, and said, 20"Go, stand in the temple and tell the people the whole message about this life." 21When they heard this, they entered the temple at daybreak and went on with their teaching.

When the high priest and those with him arrived, they called together the council and the whole body of the elders of Israel, and sent to the prison to have them brought. 22But when the temple police went there, they did not find them in the prison; so they returned and reported, 23"We found the prison securely locked and the guards standing at the doors, but when we opened them, we found no one inside." 24Now when the

---

k Gk *to men*   *l* Meaning of Gk uncertain

captain of the temple and the chief priests heard these words, they were perplexed about them, wondering what might be going on. 25Then someone arrived and announced, "Look, the men whom you put in prison are standing in the temple and teaching the people!" 26Then the captain went with the temple police and brought them, but without violence, for they were afraid of being stoned by the people.

27 When they had brought them, they had them stand before the council. The high priest questioned them, 28saying, "We gave you strict orders not to teach in this name,m yet here you have filled Jerusalem with your teaching and you are determined to bring this man's blood on us." 29But Peter and the apostles answered, "We must obey God rather than any human authority.n 30The God of our ancestors raised up Jesus, whom you had killed by hanging him on a tree. 31God exalted him at his right hand as Leader and Savior that he might give repentance to Israel and forgiveness of sins. 32And we are witnesses to these things, and so is the Holy Spirit whom God has given to those who obey him."

33 When they heard this, they were enraged and wanted to kill them. 34But a Pharisee in the council named Gamaliel, a teacher of the law, respected by all the people, stood up and ordered the men to be put outside for a short time. 35Then he said to them, "Fellow Israelites,o consider carefully what you propose to do to these men. 36For some time ago Theudas rose up, claiming to be somebody, and a number of men, about four hundred, joined him; but he was killed, and all who followed him were dispersed and disappeared. 37After him Judas the Galilean rose up at the time of the census and got people to follow him; he also perished, and all who followed him were scattered. 38So in the present case, I tell you, keep away from these men and let them alone; because if this plan or this undertaking is of human origin, it will fail; 39but if it is of God, you will not be able to overthrow

them—in that case you may even be found fighting against God!"

They were convinced by him, 40and when they had called in the apostles, they had them flogged. Then they ordered them not to speak in the name of Jesus, and let them go. 41As they left the council, they rejoiced that they were considered worthy to suffer dishonor for the sake of the name. 42And every day in the temple and at homep they did not cease to teach and proclaim Jesus as the Messiah.q

Seven Chosen to Serve

6 Now during those days, when the disciples were increasing in number, the Hellenists complained against the Hebrews because their widows were being neglected in the daily distribution of food. 2And the twelve called together the whole community of the disciples and said, "It is not right that we should neglect the word of God in order to wait on tables.r 3Therefore, friends,s select from among yourselves seven men of good standing, full of the Spirit and of wisdom, whom we may appoint to this task, 4while we, for our part, will devote ourselves to prayer and to serving the word." 5What they said pleased the whole community, and they chose Stephen, a man full of faith and the Holy Spirit, together with Philip, Prochorus, Nicanor, Timon, Parmenas, and Nicolaus, a proselyte of Antioch. 6They had these men stand before the apostles, who prayed and laid their hands on them.

7 The word of God continued to spread; the number of the disciples increased greatly in Jerusalem, and a great many of the priests became obedient to the faith.

The Arrest of Stephen

8 Stephen, full of grace and power, did great wonders and signs among the people. 9Then some of those who belonged to the synagogue of the Freedmen (as it was called), Cyrenians, Alexandrians, and others of those from Cilicia and Asia, stood up and argued

m Other ancient authorities read Did we not give you strict orders not to teach in this name?
n Gk than men   o Gk Men, Israelites   p Or from house to house   q Or the Christ   r Or keep accounts   s Gk brothers

with Stephen. 10But they could not withstand the wisdom and the Spirit[t] with which he spoke. 11Then they secretly instigated some men to say, "We have heard him speak blasphemous words against Moses and God." 12They stirred up the people as well as the elders and the scribes; then they suddenly confronted him, seized him, and brought him before the council. 13They set up false witnesses who said, "This man never stops saying things against this holy place and the law; 14for we have heard him say that this Jesus of Nazareth[u] will destroy this place and will change the customs that Moses handed on to us." 15And all who sat in the council looked intently at him, and they saw that his face was like the face of an angel.

Stephen's Speech to the Council

7 Then the high priest asked him, "Are these things so?" 2And Stephen replied:

"Brothers[v] and fathers, listen to me. The God of glory appeared to our ancestor Abraham when he was in Mesopotamia, before he lived in Haran, 3and said to him, 'Leave your country and your relatives and go to the land that I will show you.' 4Then he left the country of the Chaldeans and settled in Haran. After his father died, God had him move from there to this country in which you are now living. 5He did not give him any of it as a heritage, not even a foot's length, but promised to give it to him as his possession and to his descendants after him, even though he had no child. 6And God spoke in these terms, that his descendants would be resident aliens in a country belonging to others, who would enslave them and mistreat them during four hundred years. 7'But I will judge the nation that they serve,' said God, 'and after that they shall come out and worship me in this place.' 8Then he gave him the covenant of circumcision. And so Abraham[w] became the father of Isaac and circumcised him on the eighth day; and Isaac became the father of Jacob, and Jacob of the twelve patriarchs.

9 "The patriarchs, jealous of Joseph, sold him into Egypt; but God was with him, 10and rescued him from all his afflictions, and enabled him to win favor and to show wisdom when he stood before Pharaoh, king of Egypt, who appointed him ruler over Egypt and over all his household. 11Now there came a famine throughout Egypt and Canaan, and great suffering, and our ancestors could find no food. 12But when Jacob heard that there was grain in Egypt, he sent our ancestors there on their first visit. 13On the second visit Joseph made himself known to his brothers, and Joseph's family became known to Pharaoh. 14Then Joseph sent and invited his father Jacob and all his relatives to come to him, seventy-five in all; 15so Jacob went down to Egypt. He himself died there as well as our ancestors, 16and their bodies[x] were brought back to Shechem and laid in the tomb that Abraham had bought for a sum of silver from the sons of Hamor in Shechem.

17 "But as the time drew near for the fulfillment of the promise that God had made to Abraham, our people in Egypt increased and multiplied 18until another king who had not known Joseph ruled over Egypt. 19He dealt craftily with our race and forced our ancestors to abandon their infants so that they would die. 20At this time Moses was born. and he was beautiful before God. For three months he was brought up in his father's house; 21and when he was abandoned, Pharaoh's daughter adopted him and brought him up as her own son. 22So Moses was instructed in all the wisdom of the Egyptians and was powerful in his words and deeds.

23 "When he was forty years old, it came into his heart to visit his relatives, the Israelites.[y] 24When he saw one of them being wronged, he defended the oppressed man and avenged him by striking down the Egyptian. 25He supposed that his kinsfolk would understand that God through him was rescuing them, but they did not understand. 26The next day he came to some of them as they were quarreling and tried to reconcile them, saying, 'Men, you are brothers; why do you wrong each other?'

t Or spirit   u Gk the Nazorean   v Gk Men, brothers   w Gk he   x Gk they   y Gk his brothers, the sons of Israel

27But the man who was wronging his neighbor pushed Moses[z] aside, saying, 'Who made you a ruler and a judge over us? 28Do you want to kill me as you killed the Egyptian yesterday?' 29When he heard this, Moses fled and became a resident alien in the land of Midian. There he became the father of two sons.

30 "Now when forty years had passed, an angel appeared to him in the wilderness of Mount Sinai, in the flame of a burning bush. 31When Moses saw it,

z Gk him

he was amazed at the sight; and as he approached to look, there came the voice of the Lord: 32'I am the God of your ancestors, the God of Abraham, Isaac, and Jacob.' Moses began to tremble and did not dare to look. 33Then the Lord said to him, 'Take off the sandals from your feet, for the place where you are standing is holy ground. 34I have surely seen the mistreatment of my people who are in Egypt and have heard their groaning, and I have come down to

WEDNESDAY

A MARTYR'S PRAYER
Polycarp of Smyrna

VERSE: Acts 7.60   PASSAGE: Acts 7.54—8.1

At the Stake

ord God Almighty, we have come to know you through that dear child of yours, Jesus Christ, and he has led us to you. I bless you because you have thought me worthy of this day and hour, worthy to be numbered among the martyrs and then to drink out of the cup that Jesus has drunk from; so with him you have counted me worthy to rise and live for ever.

May I be admitted to your presence today, a satisfactory and welcome sacrifice. You have made my life a preparation for this. You showed me that this was my destiny, and now, true to your word, you have brought it about. For this and all your blessings I praise you and give you glory.

As the Flames Rose

Lord Jesus Christ, receive my soul.
    Blessings to you, Lord Jesus Christ, that you have thought me
        fit to share this fate with you, sinner that I am.
    Lord, Lord, Lord, come to my help; I turn to you for refuge.

ADDITIONAL SCRIPTURE READING:
Romans 14.8; Philippians 1.21

Go to page 1288 for your next devotional reading.

100   500

rescue them. Come now, I will send you to Egypt.'

35 "It was this Moses whom they rejected when they said, 'Who made you a ruler and a judge?' and whom God now sent as both ruler and liberator through the angel who appeared to him in the bush. 36He led them out, having performed wonders and signs in Egypt, at the Red Sea, and in the wilderness for forty years. 37This is the Moses who said to the Israelites, 'God will raise up a prophet for you from your own people*a* as he raised me up.' 38He is the one who was in the congregation in the wilderness with the angel who spoke to him at Mount Sinai, and with our ancestors; and he received living oracles to give to us. 39Our ancestors were unwilling to obey him; instead, they pushed him aside, and in their hearts they turned back to Egypt, 40saying to Aaron, 'Make gods for us who will lead the way for us; as for this Moses who led us out from the land of Egypt, we do not know what has happened to him.' 41At that time they made a calf, offered a sacrifice to the idol, and reveled in the works of their hands. 42But God turned away from them and handed them over to worship the host of heaven, as it is written in the book of the prophets:

'Did you offer to me slain victims
    and sacrifices
    forty years in the wilderness,
        O house of Israel?
43   No; you took along the tent of
        Moloch,
    and the star of your god Rephan,
        the images that you made to
        worship;
    so I will remove you beyond
        Babylon.'

44 "Our ancestors had the tent of testimony in the wilderness, as God*b* directed when he spoke to Moses, ordering him to make it according to the pattern he had seen. 45Our ancestors in turn brought it in with Joshua when they dispossessed the nations that God drove out before our ancestors. And it was there until the time of David, 46who found favor with God and asked that he might find a dwelling place for the house of Jacob.*c* 47But it was Solomon who built a house for him. 48Yet the Most High does not dwell in houses made with human hands;*d* as the prophet says,

49   'Heaven is my throne,
        and the earth is my footstool.
    What kind of house will you build
        for me, says the Lord,
    or what is the place of my rest?
50   Did not my hand make all these
        things?'

51 "You stiff-necked people, uncircumcised in heart and ears, you are forever opposing the Holy Spirit, just as your ancestors used to do. 52Which of the prophets did your ancestors not persecute? They killed those who foretold the coming of the Righteous One, and now you have become his betrayers and murderers. 53You are the ones that received the law as ordained by angels, and yet you have not kept it."

The Stoning of Stephen

54 When they heard these things, they became enraged and ground their teeth at Stephen.*e* 55But filled with the Holy Spirit, he gazed into heaven and saw the glory of God and Jesus standing at the right hand of God. 56"Look," he said, "I see the heavens opened and the Son of Man standing at the right hand of God!" 57But they covered their ears, and with a loud shout all rushed together against him. 58Then they dragged him out of the city and began to stone him; and the witnesses laid their coats at the feet of a young man named Saul. 59While they were stoning Stephen, he prayed, "Lord Jesus, receive my spirit." 60Then he knelt down and cried out in a loud voice, "Lord, do not hold this sin against them." When he had said this, he died.*f* 1And Saul approved of their killing him.

Saul Persecutes the Church

That day a severe persecution began against the church in Jerusalem, and all except the apostles were scattered throughout the countryside of Judea and Samaria. 2Devout men buried Stephen and made loud lamentation over him.

---

a Gk *your brothers*   *b* Gk *he*   *c* Other ancient authorities read *for the God of Jacob*   *d* Gk *with hands*   *e* Gk *him*   *f* Gk *fell asleep*

3But Saul was ravaging the church by entering house after house; dragging off both men and women, he committed them to prison.

Philip Preaches in Samaria

4 Now those who were scattered went from place to place, proclaiming the word. 5Philip went down to the city*g* of Samaria and proclaimed the Messiah*h* to them. 6The crowds with one accord listened eagerly to what was said by Philip, hearing and seeing the signs that he did, 7for unclean spirits, crying with loud shrieks, came out of many who were possessed; and many others who were paralyzed or lame were cured. 8So there was great joy in that city.

9 Now a certain man named Simon had previously practiced magic in the city and amazed the people of Samaria, saying that he was someone great. 10All of them, from the least to the greatest, listened to him eagerly, saying, "This man is the power of God that is called Great." 11And they listened eagerly to him because for a long time he had amazed them with his magic. 12But when they believed Philip, who was proclaiming the good news about the kingdom of God and the name of Jesus Christ, they were baptized, both men and women. 13Even Simon himself believed. After being baptized, he stayed constantly with Philip and was amazed when he saw the signs and great miracles that took place.

HOW SWEET THE NAME OF JESUS SOUNDS
  IN A BELIEVER'S EAR!
IT SOOTHES HIS SORROWS, HEALS HIS WOUNDS,
  AND DRIVES AWAY HIS FEAR!

—*John Newton*

---

14 Now when the apostles at Jerusalem heard that Samaria had accepted the word of God, they sent Peter and John to them. 15The two went down and prayed for them that they might receive the Holy Spirit 16(for as yet the Spirit had not come*i* upon any of them; they had only been baptized in the name of the Lord Jesus). 17Then Peter and John*j* laid their hands on them, and they received the Holy Spirit. 18Now when Simon saw that the Spirit was given through the laying on of the apostles' hands, he offered them money, 19saying, "Give me also this power so that anyone on whom I lay my hands may receive the Holy Spirit." 20But Peter said to him, "May your silver perish with you, because you thought you could obtain God's gift with money! 21You have no part or share in this, for your heart is not right before God. 22Repent therefore of this wickedness of yours, and pray to the Lord that, if possible, the intent of your heart may be forgiven you. 23For I see that you are in the gall of bitterness and the chains of wickedness." 24Simon answered, "Pray for me to the Lord, that nothing of what you*k* have said may happen to me."

25 Now after Peter and John*l* had testified and spoken the word of the Lord, they returned to Jerusalem, proclaiming the good news to many villages of the Samaritans.

Philip and the Ethiopian Eunuch

26 Then an angel of the Lord said to Philip, "Get up and go toward the south*m* to the road that goes down from Jerusalem to Gaza." (This is a wilderness road.) 27So he got up and went. Now there was an Ethiopian eunuch, a court official of the Candace, queen of the Ethiopians, in charge of her entire treasury. He had come to Jerusalem to worship 28and was returning home; seated in his chariot, he was reading the prophet Isaiah. 29Then the Spirit said to Philip, "Go over to this chariot and join it." 30So Philip ran up to it and heard him reading the prophet Isaiah. He asked, "Do you understand what you are reading?" 31He replied, "How can I, unless someone guides me?" And he invited Philip to get in and sit beside him. 32Now the passage of the scripture that he was reading was this:

"Like a sheep he was led to the
    slaughter,
  and like a lamb silent before its
    shearer,
    so he does not open his mouth.

---

g Other ancient authorities read *a city*   h Or *the Christ*   i Gk *fallen*   j Gk *they*   k The Greek word for *you* and the verb *pray* are plural   l Gk *after they*   m Or *go at noon*

33   In his humiliation justice was
         denied him.
       Who can describe his generation?
         For his life is taken away from
         the earth."

34The eunuch asked Philip, "About whom, may I ask you, does the prophet say this, about himself or about someone else?" 35Then Philip began to speak, and starting with this scripture, he proclaimed to him the good news about Jesus. 36As they were going along the road, they came to some water; and the eunuch said, "Look, here is water! What is to prevent me from being baptized?"n 38He commanded the chariot to stop, and both of them, Philip and the eunuch, went down into the water, and Philipo baptized him. 39When they came up out of the water, the Spirit of the Lord snatched Philip away; the eunuch saw him no more, and went on his way rejoicing. 40But Philip found himself at Azotus, and as he was passing through the region, he proclaimed the good news to all the towns until he came to Caesarea.

The Conversion of Saul

9 Meanwhile Saul, still breathing threats and murder against the disciples of the Lord, went to the high priest 2and asked him for letters to the synagogues at Damascus, so that if he found any who belonged to the Way, men or women, he might bring them bound to Jerusalem. 3Now as he was going along and approaching Damascus, suddenly a light from heaven flashed around him. 4He fell to the ground and heard a voice saying to him, "Saul, Saul, why do you persecute me?" 5He asked, "Who are you, Lord?" The reply came, "I am Jesus, whom you are persecuting. 6But get up and enter the city, and you will be told what you are to do." 7The men who were traveling with him stood speechless because they heard the voice but saw no one. 8Saul got up from the ground, and though his eyes were open, he could see nothing; so they led him by the hand and brought him into Damas-

cus. 9For three days he was without sight, and neither ate nor drank.

10 Now there was a disciple in Damascus named Ananias. The Lord said to him in a vision, "Ananias." He answered, "Here I am, Lord." 11The Lord said to him, "Get up and go to the street called Straight, and at the house of Judas look for a man of Tarsus named Saul. At this moment he is praying, 12and he has seen in a visionp a man named Ananias come in and lay his hands on him so that he might regain his sight." 13But Ananias answered, "Lord, I have heard from many about this man, how much evil he has done to your saints in Jerusalem; 14and here he has authority from the chief priests to bind all who invoke your name." 15But the Lord said to him, "Go, for he is an instrument whom I have chosen to bring my name before Gentiles and kings and before the people of Israel; 16I myself will show him how much he must suffer for the sake of my name." 17So Ananias went and entered the house. He laid his hands on Saulq and said, "Brother Saul, the Lord Jesus, who appeared to you on your way here, has sent me so that you may regain your sight and be filled with the Holy Spirit." 18And immediately something like scales fell from his eyes, and his sight was restored. Then he got up and was baptized, 19and after taking some food, he regained his strength.

Saul Preaches in Damascus

For several days he was with the disciples in Damascus, 20and immediately he began to proclaim Jesus in the synagogues, saying, "He is the Son of God." 21All who heard him were amazed and said, "Is not this the man who made havoc in Jerusalem among those who invoked this name? And has he not come here for the purpose of bringing them bound before the chief priests?" 22Saul became increasingly more powerful and confounded the Jews who lived in Damascus by proving that Jesusr was the Messiah.s

n Other ancient authorities add all or most of verse 37, *And Philip said, "If you believe with all your heart, you may." And he replied, "I believe that Jesus Christ is the Son of God."*   o Gk *he*   p Other ancient authorities lack *in a vision*   q Gk *him*   r Gk *that this*   s Or *the Christ*

Saul Escapes from the Jews

23 After some time had passed, the Jews plotted to kill him, 24but their plot became known to Saul. They were watching the gates day and night so that they might kill him; 25but his disciples took him by night and let him down through an opening in the wall,^{t} lowering him in a basket.

Saul in Jerusalem

26 When he had come to Jerusalem, he attempted to join the disciples; and they were all afraid of him, for they did not believe that he was a disciple. 27But Barnabas took him, brought him to the apostles, and described for them how on the road he had seen the Lord, who had spoken to him, and how in Damascus he had spoken boldly in the name of Jesus. 28So he went in and out among them in Jerusalem, speaking boldly in the name of the Lord. 29He spoke and argued with the Hellenists; but they were attempting to kill him. 30When the believers^u learned of it, they brought him down to Caesarea and sent him off to Tarsus.

31 Meanwhile the church throughout Judea, Galilee, and Samaria had peace and was built up. Living in the fear of the Lord and in the comfort of the Holy Spirit, it increased in numbers.

The Healing of Aeneas

32 Now as Peter went here and there among all the believers,^{v} he came down also to the saints living in Lydda. 33There he found a man named Aeneas, who had been bedridden for eight years, for he was paralyzed. 34Peter said to him, "Aeneas, Jesus Christ heals you; get up and make your bed!" And immediately he got up. 35And all the residents of Lydda and Sharon saw him and turned to the Lord.

Peter in Lydda and Joppa

36 Now in Joppa there was a disciple whose name was Tabitha, which in Greek is Dorcas.^{w} She was devoted to good works and acts of charity. 37At that time she became ill and died. When they had washed her, they laid her in a room upstairs. 38Since Lydda was near Joppa, the disciples, who heard that Peter was there, sent two men to him with the request, "Please come to us without delay." 39So Peter got up and went with them; and when he arrived, they took him to the room upstairs. All the widows stood beside him, weeping and showing tunics and other clothing that Dorcas had made while she was with them. 40Peter put all of them outside, and then he knelt down and prayed. He turned to the body and said, "Tabitha, get up." Then she opened her eyes, and seeing Peter, she sat up. 41He gave her his hand and helped her up. Then calling the saints and widows, he showed her to be alive. 42This became known throughout Joppa, and many believed in the Lord. 43Meanwhile he stayed in Joppa for some time with a certain Simon, a tanner.

Peter and Cornelius

10 In Caesarea there was a man named Cornelius, a centurion of the Italian Cohort, as it was called. 2He was a devout man who feared God with all his household; he gave alms generously to the people and prayed constantly to God. 3One afternoon at about three o'clock he had a vision in which he clearly saw an angel of God coming in and saying to him, "Cornelius." 4He stared at him in terror and said, "What is it, Lord?" He answered, "Your prayers and your alms have ascended as a memorial before God. 5Now send men to Joppa for a certain Simon who is called Peter; 6he is lodging with Simon, a tanner, whose house is by the seaside." 7When the angel who spoke to him had left, he called two of his slaves and a devout soldier from the ranks of those who served him, 8and after telling them everything, he sent them to Joppa.

9 About noon the next day, as they were on their journey and approaching the city, Peter went up on the roof to pray. 10He became hungry and wanted something to eat; and while it was being prepared, he fell into a trance. 11He saw the heaven opened and something like a large sheet coming down, being lowered

t Gk through the wall   u Gk brothers   v Gk all of them   w The name Tabitha in Aramaic and the name Dorcas in Greek mean a gazelle to the ground by its four corners. [12]In it were all kinds of four-footed creatures and reptiles and birds of the air. [13]Then he heard a voice saying, "Get up, Peter; kill and eat." [14]But Peter said, "By no means, Lord; for I have never eaten anything that is profane or unclean." [15]The voice said to him again, a second time, "What God has made clean, you must not call profane." [16]This happened three times, and the thing was suddenly taken up to heaven.

17 Now while Peter was greatly puzzled about what to make of the vision that he had seen, suddenly the men sent by Cornelius appeared. They were asking for Simon's house and were standing by the gate. [18]They called out to ask whether Simon, who was called Peter, was staying there. [19]While Peter was still thinking about the vision, the Spirit said to him, "Look, three[x] men are searching for you. [20]Now get up, go down, and go with them without hesitation; for I have sent them." [21]So Peter went down to the men and said, "I am the one you are looking for; what is the reason for your coming?" [22]They answered, "Cornelius, a centurion, an upright and God-fearing man, who is well spoken of by the whole Jewish nation, was directed by a holy angel to send for you to come to his house and to hear what you have to say." [23]So Peter[y] invited them in and gave them lodging.

The next day he got up and went with them, and some of the believers[z] from Joppa accompanied him. [24]The following day they came to Caesarea. Cornelius was expecting them and had called together his relatives and close friends. [25]On Peter's arrival Cornelius met him, and falling at his feet, worshiped him. [26]But Peter made him get up, saying, "Stand up; I am only a mortal." [27]And as he talked with him, he went in and found that many had assembled; [28]and he said to them, "You yourselves know that it is unlawful for a Jew to associate with or to visit a Gentile; but God has shown me that I should not call anyone profane or unclean. [29]So when I was sent for, I came without objection. Now may I ask why you sent for me?"

30 Cornelius replied, "Four days ago at this very hour, at three o'clock, I was praying in my house when suddenly a man in dazzling clothes stood before me. [31]He said, 'Cornelius, your prayer has been heard and your alms have been remembered before God. [32]Send therefore to Joppa and ask for Simon, who is called Peter; he is staying in the home of Simon, a tanner, by the sea.' [33]Therefore I sent for you immediately, and you have been kind enough to come. So now all of us are here in the presence of God to listen to all that the Lord has commanded you to say."

Gentiles Hear the Good News

34 Then Peter began to speak to them: "I truly understand that God shows no partiality, [35]but in every nation anyone who fears him and does what is right is acceptable to him. [36]You know the message he sent to the people of Israel, preaching peace by Jesus Christ—he is Lord of all. [37]That message spread throughout Judea, beginning in Galilee after the baptism that John announced: [38]how God anointed Jesus of Nazareth with the Holy Spirit and with power; how he went about doing good and healing all who were oppressed by the devil, for God was with him. [39]We are witnesses to all that he did both in Judea and in Jerusalem. They put him to death by hanging him on a tree; [40]but God raised him on the third day and allowed him to appear, [41]not to all the people but to us who were chosen by God as witnesses, and who ate and drank with him after he rose from the dead. [42]He commanded us to preach to the people and to testify that he is the one ordained by God as judge of the living and the dead. [43]All the prophets testify about him that everyone who believes in him receives forgiveness of sins through his name."

Gentiles Receive the Holy Spirit

44 While Peter was still speaking, the Holy Spirit fell upon all who heard the word. [45]The circumcised believers who had come with Peter were astounded that the gift of the Holy Spirit had been poured out even on the Gentiles, [46]for they heard them speaking in tongues and extolling God. Then Peter said,

x One ancient authority reads two; others lack the word   y Gk he   z Gk brothers

AT THE CENTER
Thomas R. Kelly

VERSE: Acts 10.34   **PASSAGE:** Acts 10.24–35

n the Fellowship, cultural and educational and national and racial differences are leveled. Unlettered men are at ease with the truly humble scholar . . . , and the scholar listens with joy and openness to the precious experiences of God's dealing with the workingman. We find men with chilly theologies but with glowing hearts. We overleap the boundaries of church membership and find Lutherans and Roman Catholics, Jews and Christians, within the Fellowship. We reread the poets and the saints, and the Fellowship is enlarged. With urgent hunger we read the Scriptures, with no thought of pious exercise, but in order to find more friends for the soul. We brush past our historical learning in the Scriptures, to seize upon those writers who lived in the Center, in the Life and in the Power. Particularly does devotional literature become illuminated, for *The Imitation of Christ*, and Augustine's *Confessions*, and Brother Lawrence's *Practice of the Presence of God* speak the language of the souls who live at the Center. Time telescopes and vanishes, centuries and creeds are overleaped. The incident of death puts no boundaries to the Blessed Community, wherein men and women live and love and work and pray in that Life and Power which gave forth the Scriptures. And we wonder and grieve at the overwhelmingly heady preoccupation of religious people with problems, problems, unless they have first come into the Fellowship of the Light.

The final grounds of holy Fellowship are in God. Lives immersed and drowned in God are drowned in love, and know one another in him, and know one another in love. God is the medium, the matrix, the focus, the solvent. As Meister Eckhart suggests, he who is wholly surrounded by God, enveloped by God, clothed with God, glowing in selfless love toward him—such a man no one can touch except he touch God also.

ADDITIONAL SCRIPTURE READING:
John 3.16; Colossians 3.12–15

Go to page 1293 for your next devotional reading.

Go to page 1293 for your next devotional reading.

1900   Present

47 "Can anyone withhold the water for baptizing these people who have received the Holy Spirit just as we have?" 48So he ordered them to be baptized in the name of Jesus Christ. Then they invited him to stay for several days.

Peter's Report to the Church at Jerusalem

11 Now the apostles and the believers*a* who were in Judea heard that the Gentiles had also accepted the word of God. 2So when Peter went up to Jerusalem, the circumcised believers*b* criticized him, 3saying, "Why did you go to uncircumcised men and eat with them?" 4Then Peter began to explain it to them, step by step, saying, 5"I was in the city of Joppa praying, and in a trance I saw a vision. There was something like a large sheet coming down from heaven, being lowered by its four corners; and it came close to me. 6As I looked at it closely I saw four-footed animals, beasts of prey, reptiles, and birds of the air. 7I also heard a voice saying to me, 'Get up, Peter; kill and eat.' 8But I replied, 'By no means, Lord; for nothing profane or unclean has ever entered my mouth.' 9But a second time the voice answered from heaven, 'What God has made clean, you must not call profane.' 10This happened three times; then everything was pulled up again to heaven. 11At that very moment three men, sent to me from Caesarea, arrived at the house where we were. 12The Spirit told me to go with them and not to make a distinction between them and us.*c* These six brothers also accompanied me, and we entered the man's house. 13He told us how he had seen the angel standing in his house and saying, 'Send to Joppa and bring Simon, who is called Peter; 14he will give you a message by which you and your entire household will be saved.' 15And as I began to speak, the Holy Spirit fell upon them just as it had upon us at the beginning. 16And I remembered the word of the Lord, how he had said, 'John baptized with water, but you will be baptized with the Holy Spirit.' 17If then God gave them the same gift that he gave us when we believed in the Lord Jesus Christ, who was I that I could hinder God?" 18When they heard this, they were silenced. And they praised God, saying, "Then God has given even to the Gentiles the repentance that leads to life."

The Church in Antioch

19 Now those who were scattered because of the persecution that took place over Stephen traveled as far as Phoenicia, Cyprus, and Antioch, and they spoke the word to no one except Jews. 20But among them were some men of Cyprus and Cyrene who, on coming to Antioch, spoke to the Hellenists*d* also, proclaiming the Lord Jesus. 21The hand of the Lord was with them, and a great number became believers and turned to the Lord. 22News of this came to the ears of the church in Jerusalem, and they sent Barnabas to Antioch. 23When he came and saw the grace of God, he rejoiced, and he exhorted them all to remain faithful to the Lord with steadfast devotion; 24for he was a good man, full of the Holy Spirit and of faith. And a great many people were brought to the Lord. 25Then Barnabas went to Tarsus to look for Saul, 26and when he had found him, he brought him to Antioch. So it was that for an entire year they met with*e* the church and taught a great many people, and it was in Antioch that the disciples were first called "Christians."

27 At that time prophets came down from Jerusalem to Antioch. 28One of them named Agabus stood up and predicted by the Spirit that there would be a severe famine over all the world; and this took place during the reign of Claudius. 29The disciples determined that according to their ability, each would send relief to the believers*a* living in Judea; 30this they did, sending it to the elders by Barnabas and Saul.

James Killed and Peter Imprisoned

12 About that time King Herod laid violent hands upon some who belonged to the church. 2He had James, the brother of John, killed with the sword. 3After he saw that it pleased

a Gk brothers   *b* Gk lacks *believers*   *c* Or *not to hesitate*   *d* Other ancient authorities read *Greeks*   *e* Or *were guests of*

the Jews, he proceeded to arrest Peter also. (This was during the festival of Unleavened Bread.) 4When he had seized him, he put him in prison and handed him over to four squads of soldiers to guard him, intending to bring him out to the people after the Passover. 5While Peter was kept in prison, the church prayed fervently to God for him.

Peter Delivered from Prison

6 The very night before Herod was going to bring him out, Peter, bound with two chains, was sleeping between two soldiers, while guards in front of the door were keeping watch over the prison. 7Suddenly an angel of the Lord appeared and a light shone in the cell. He tapped Peter on the side and woke him, saying, "Get up quickly." And the chains fell off his wrists. 8The angel said to him, "Fasten your belt and put on your sandals." He did so. Then he said to him, "Wrap your cloak around you and follow me." 9Peter*f* went out and followed him; he did not realize that what was happening with the angel's help was real; he thought he was seeing a vision. 10After they had passed the first and the second guard, they came before the iron gate leading into the city. It opened for them of its own accord, and they went outside and walked along a lane, when suddenly the angel left him. 11Then Peter came to himself and said, "Now I am sure that the Lord has sent his angel and rescued me from the hands of Herod and from all that the Jewish people were expecting."

12 As soon as he realized this, he went to the house of Mary, the mother of John whose other name was Mark, where many had gathered and were praying. 13When he knocked at the outer gate, a maid named Rhoda came to answer. 14On recognizing Peter's voice, she was so overjoyed that, instead of opening the gate, she ran in and announced that Peter was standing at the gate. 15They said to her, "You are out of your mind!" But she insisted that it was so. They said, "It is his angel." 16Meanwhile Peter continued knocking; and when they opened the gate, they saw him and were amazed. 17He motioned to them with his hand to be silent, and described for them how the Lord had brought him out of the prison. And he added, "Tell this to James and to the believers."*g* Then he left and went to another place.

18 When morning came, there was no small commotion among the soldiers over what had become of Peter. 19When Herod had searched for him and could not find him, he examined the guards and ordered them to be put to death. Then he went down from Judea to Caesarea and stayed there.

The Death of Herod

20 Now Herod*h* was angry with the people of Tyre and Sidon. So they came to him in a body; and after winning over Blastus, the king's chamberlain, they asked for a reconciliation, because their country depended on the king's country for food. 21On an appointed day Herod put on his royal robes, took his seat on the platform, and delivered a public address to them. 22The people kept shouting, "The voice of a god, and not of a mortal!" 23And immediately, because he had not given the glory to God, an angel of the Lord struck him down, and he was eaten by worms and died.

24 But the word of God continued to advance and gain adherents. 25Then after completing their mission Barnabas and Saul returned to*i* Jerusalem and brought with them John, whose other name was Mark.

Barnabas and Saul Commissioned

13 Now in the church at Antioch there were prophets and teachers: Barnabas, Simeon who was called Niger, Lucius of Cyrene, Manaen a member of the court of Herod the ruler,*j* and Saul. 2While they were worshiping the Lord and fasting, the Holy Spirit said, "Set apart for me Barnabas and Saul for the work to which I have called them." 3Then after fasting and praying they laid their hands on them and sent them off.

The Apostles Preach in Cyprus

4 So, being sent out by the Holy Spirit, they went down to Seleucia; and from

---

f Gk *He*   *g* Gk *brothers*   *h* Gk *he*   *i* Other ancient authorities read *from*   *j* Gk *tetrarch*

there they sailed to Cyprus. [5]When they arrived at Salamis, they proclaimed the word of God in the synagogues of the Jews. And they had John also to assist them. [6]When they had gone through the whole island as far as Paphos, they met a certain magician, a Jewish false prophet, named Bar-Jesus. [7]He was with the proconsul, Sergius Paulus, an intelligent man, who summoned Barnabas and Saul and wanted to hear the word of God. [8]But the magician Elymas (for that is the translation of his name) opposed them and tried to turn the proconsul away from the faith. [9]But Saul, also known as Paul, filled with the Holy Spirit, looked intently at him [10]and said, "You son of the devil, you enemy of all righteousness, full of all deceit and villainy, will you not stop making crooked the straight paths of the Lord? [11]And now listen—the hand of the Lord is against you, and you will be blind for a while, unable to see the sun." Immediately mist and darkness came over him, and he went about groping for someone to lead him by the hand. [12]When the proconsul saw what had happened, he believed, for he was astonished at the teaching about the Lord.

Paul and Barnabas in Antioch of Pisidia

13 Then Paul and his companions set sail from Paphos and came to Perga in Pamphylia. John, however, left them and returned to Jerusalem; [14]but they went on from Perga and came to Antioch in Pisidia. And on the sabbath day they went into the synagogue and sat down. [15]After the reading of the law and the prophets, the officials of the synagogue sent them a message, saying, "Brothers, if you have any word of exhortation for the people, give it." [16]So Paul stood up and with a gesture began to speak:

"You Israelites,[k] and others who fear God, listen. [17]The God of this people Israel chose our ancestors and made the people great during their stay in the land of Egypt, and with uplifted arm he led them out of it. [18]For about forty years he put up with[l] them in the wilderness.

[19]After he had destroyed seven nations in the land of Canaan, he gave them their land as an inheritance [20]for about four hundred fifty years. After that he gave them judges until the time of the prophet Samuel. [21]Then they asked for a king; and God gave them Saul son of Kish, a man of the tribe of Benjamin, who reigned for forty years. [22]When he had removed him, he made David their king. In his testimony about him he said, 'I have found David, son of Jesse, to be a man after my heart, who will carry out all my wishes.' [23]Of this man's posterity God has brought to Israel a Savior, Jesus, as he promised; [24]before his coming John had already proclaimed a baptism of repentance to all the people of Israel. [25]And as John was finishing his work, he said, 'What do you suppose that I am? I am not he. No, but one is coming after me; I am not worthy to untie the thong of the sandals[m] on his feet.'

26 "My brothers, you descendants of Abraham's family, and others who fear God, to us[n] the message of this salvation has been sent. [27]Because the residents of Jerusalem and their leaders did not recognize him or understand the words of the prophets that are read every sabbath, they fulfilled those words by condemning him. [28]Even though they found no cause for a sentence of death, they asked Pilate to have him killed. [29]When they had carried out everything that was written about him, they took him down from the tree and laid him in a tomb. [30]But God raised him from the dead; [31]and for many days he appeared to those who came up with him from Galilee to Jerusalem, and they are now his witnesses to the people. [32]And we bring you the good news that what God promised to our ancestors [33]he has fulfilled for us, their children, by raising Jesus; as also it is written in the second psalm,

'You are my Son;
    today I have begotten you.'

[34]As to his raising him from the dead, no more to return to corruption, he has spoken in this way,

'I will give you the holy promises
    made to David.'

k Gk Men, Israelites   l Other ancient authorities read cared for   m Gk untie the sandals
n Other ancient authorities read you

35Therefore he has also said in another psalm,

'You will not let your Holy One
   experience corruption.'

36For David, after he had served the purpose of God in his own generation, died, *o* was laid beside his ancestors, and experienced corruption; 37but he whom God raised up experienced no corruption. 38Let it be known to you therefore, my brothers, that through this man forgiveness of sins is proclaimed to you; 39by this Jesus*p* everyone who believes is set free from all those sins*q* from which you could not be freed by the law of Moses. 40Beware, therefore, that what the prophets said does not happen to you:

41   'Look, you scoffers!
      Be amazed and perish,
   for in your days I am doing a work,
      a work that you will never
         believe, even if someone tells
            you.' "

42 As Paul and Barnabas*r* were going out, the people urged them to speak about these things again the next sabbath. 43When the meeting of the synagogue broke up, many Jews and devout converts to Judaism followed Paul and Barnabas, who spoke to them and urged them to continue in the grace of God.

44 The next sabbath almost the whole city gathered to hear the word of the Lord.*s* 45But when the Jews saw the crowds, they were filled with jealousy; and blaspheming, they contradicted what was spoken by Paul. 46Then both Paul and Barnabas spoke out boldly, saying, "It was necessary that the word of God should be spoken first to you. Since you reject it and judge yourselves to be unworthy of eternal life, we are now turning to the Gentiles. 47For so the Lord has commanded us, saying,

'I have set you to be a light for the
      Gentiles,
   so that you may bring salvation
      to the ends of the earth.' "

48 When the Gentiles heard this, they were glad and praised the word of the Lord; and as many as had been destined for eternal life became believers. 49Thus the word of the Lord spread throughout the region. 50But the Jews incited the devout women of high standing and the leading men of the city, and stirred up persecution against Paul and Barnabas, and drove them out of their region. 51So they shook the dust off their feet in protest against them, and went to Iconium. 52And the disciples were filled with joy and with the Holy Spirit.

Paul and Barnabas in Iconium

14 The same thing occurred in Iconium, where Paul and Barnabas*r* went into the Jewish synagogue and spoke in such a way that a great number of both Jews and Greeks became believers. 2But the unbelieving Jews stirred up the Gentiles and poisoned their minds against the brothers. 3So they remained for a long time, speaking boldly for the Lord, who testified to the word of his grace by granting signs and wonders to be done through them. 4But the residents of the city were divided; some sided with the Jews, and some with the apostles. 5And when an attempt was made by both Gentiles and Jews, with their rulers, to mistreat them and to stone them, 6the apostles*r* learned of it and fled to Lystra and Derbe, cities of Lycaonia, and to the surrounding country; 7and there they continued proclaiming the good news.

Paul and Barnabas in Lystra and Derbe

8 In Lystra there was a man sitting who could not use his feet and had never walked, for he had been crippled from birth. 9He listened to Paul as he was speaking. And Paul, looking at him intently and seeing that he had faith to be healed, 10said in a loud voice, "Stand upright on your feet." And the man*t* sprang up and began to walk. 11When the crowds saw what Paul had done, they shouted in the Lycaonian language, "The gods have come down to us in human form!" 12Barnabas they called Zeus, and Paul they called Hermes, because he was the chief speaker. 13The priest of Zeus, whose temple was just outside the city, *u* brought oxen and garlands to the gates; he and the crowds

---

o Gk *fell asleep*   *p* Gk *this*   *q* Gk *all*   *r* Gk *they*   *s* Other ancient authorities read *God*
t Gk *he*   *u* Or *The priest of Zeus-Outside-the-City*

FRIDAY

FAITH AND ELECTION
John Calvin

VERSE: Acts 13.48   **PASSAGE:** Acts 13.46–52

I t is objected by some, that God will be inconsistent with himself, if he invites all men universally to come to him, and receives only a few elect, . . . that by external preaching all are called to repentance and faith, and yet that the spirit of repentance and faith is not given to all . . . What they assume, I deny as being false in two respects. For he who threatens drought to one city while it rains upon another, and who denounces to another place a famine of doctrine, lays himself under no positive obligation to call all men alike. And he who, forbidding Paul to preach the word in Asia, and suffering him not to go into Bithynia, calls him into Macedonia, demonstrates his right to distribute this treasure to whom he pleases (see Acts 16.7–9). In Isaiah, he still more fully declares his destination of the promises of salvation exclusively for the elect (see Isaiah 26.19); for of them only, and not indiscriminately of all mankind, he declares that they shall be his disciples. Whence it appears, that when the doctrine of salvation is offered to all for their effectual benefit, it is a corrupt prostitution of that which is declared to be reserved particularly for the children of the church . . . Let this suffice, that though the voice of the gospel addresses all men generally, yet the gift of faith is bestowed on few . . . It is no new thing for the seed to fall among thorns or in stony places; not only because most men are evidently in actual rebellion against God, but because they are not all endued with eyes and ears. Where, then, will be the consistency of God's calling to himself such as he knows will never come? . . . Faith, indeed, is properly connected with election, provided it occupies the second place. This order is clearly expressed in these words of Christ: "This is the Father's will, that of all which he hath given me, I should lose nothing . . . And this is the will of him that sent me, that every one which believeth on the son, may have everlasting life" (John 6.39–40, KJV).

ADDITIONAL SCRIPTURE READING:
Isaiah 42.1, 6–7; 2 Thessalonians 2.13–15

Go to page 1295 for your next devotional reading.

1500   1700

wanted to offer sacrifice. 14When the apostles Barnabas and Paul heard of it, they tore their clothes and rushed out into the crowd, shouting, 15"Friends,v why are you doing this? We are mortals just like you, and we bring you good news, that you should turn from these worthless things to the living God, who made the heaven and the earth and the sea and all that is in them. 16In past generations he allowed all the nations to follow their own ways; 17yet he has not left himself without a witness in doing good—giving you rains from heaven and fruitful seasons, and filling you with food and your hearts with joy." 18Even with these words, they scarcely restrained the crowds from offering sacrifice to them.

19 But Jews came there from Antioch and Iconium and won over the crowds. Then they stoned Paul and dragged him out of the city, supposing that he was dead. 20But when the disciples surrounded him, he got up and went into the city. The next day he went on with Barnabas to Derbe.

The Return to Antioch in Syria

21 After they had proclaimed the good news to that city and had made many disciples, they returned to Lystra, then on to Iconium and Antioch. 22There they strengthened the souls of the disciples and encouraged them to continue in the faith, saying, "It is through many persecutions that we must enter the kingdom of God." 23And after they had appointed elders for them in each church, with prayer and fasting they entrusted them to the Lord in whom they had come to believe.

24 Then they passed through Pisidia and came to Pamphylia. 25When they had spoken the word in Perga, they went down to Attalia. 26From there they sailed back to Antioch, where they had been commended to the grace of God for the workw that they had completed. 27When they arrived, they called the church together and related all that God had done with them, and how he had opened a door of faith for the Gentiles.

28And they stayed there with the disciples for some time.

The Council at Jerusalem

15 Then certain individuals came down from Judea and were teaching the brothers, "Unless you are circumcised according to the custom of Moses, you cannot be saved." 2And after Paul and Barnabas had no small dissension and debate with them, Paul and Barnabas and some of the others were appointed to go up to Jerusalem to discuss this question with the apostles and the elders. 3So they were sent on their way by the church, and as they passed through both Phoenicia and Samaria, they reported the conversion of the Gentiles, and brought great joy to all the believers.x 4When they came to Jerusalem, they were welcomed by the church and the apostles and the elders, and they reported all that God had done with them. 5But some believers who belonged to the sect of the Pharisees stood up and said, "It is necessary for them to be circumcised and ordered to keep the law of Moses."

6 The apostles and the elders met together to consider this matter. 7After there had been much debate, Peter stood up and said to them, "My brothers,y you know that in the early days God made a choice among you, that I should be the one through whom the Gentiles would hear the message of the good news and become believers. 8And God, who knows the human heart, testified to them by giving them the Holy Spirit, just as he did to us; 9and in cleansing their hearts by faith he has made no distinction between them and us. 10Now therefore why are you putting God to the test by placing on the neck of the disciples a yoke that neither our ancestors nor we have been able to bear? 11On the contrary, we believe that we will be saved through the grace of the Lord Jesus, just as they will."

12 The whole assembly kept silence, and listened to Barnabas and Paul as they told of all the signs and wonders that God had done through them among the Gentiles. 13After they finished

---

v Gk Men   w Or committed in the grace of God to the work   x Gk brothers   y Gk Men, brothers

WEEKEND

EVENING ON CALAIS BEACH
William Wordsworth

VERSE: John 20.13–14   **PASSAGE:** John 20

I t is a beauteous evening, calm and free,
  The holy time is quiet as a Nun
  Breathless with adoration; the broad sun
Is sinking down in its tranquility;
The gentleness of heaven broods o'er the sea:
  Listen! the mighty Being is awake,
  And doth with his eternal motion make
A sound like thunder—everlastingly.
Dear child! dear girl! that walkest with me here,
  If thou appear untouched by solemn thought,
  Thy nature is not therefore less divine:
Thou liest in Abraham's bosom all the year;
  And worship'st at the Temple's inner shrine,
  God being with thee when we know it not.

ADDITIONAL SCRIPTURE READING:
Matthew 27.55–56; Luke 8.1–3

Go to page 1300 for your next devotional reading.

1700   1900

speaking, James replied, "My brothers,z listen to me. 14Simeon has related how God first looked favorably on the Gentiles, to take from among them a people for his name. 15This agrees with the words of the prophets, as it is written,

16 'After this I will return,
and I will rebuild the dwelling of
David, which has fallen;
from its ruins I will rebuild it,
and I will set it up,
17 so that all other peoples may seek
the Lord—
even all the Gentiles over whom
my name has been called.
Thus says the Lord, who has
been making these things
18known from long ago.'a

19Therefore I have reached the decision that we should not trouble those Gentiles who are turning to God, 20but we should write to them to abstain only from things polluted by idols and from fornication and from whatever has been strangledb and from blood. 21For in every city, for generations past, Moses has had those who proclaim him, for he has been read aloud every sabbath in the synagogues."

The Council's Letter to Gentile Believers

22 Then the apostles and the elders, with the consent of the whole church, decided to choose men from among their membersc and to send them to Antioch with Paul and Barnabas. They sent Judas called Barsabbas, and Silas, leaders among the brothers, 23with the following letter: "The brothers, both the apostles and the elders, to the believersd of Gentile origin in Antioch and Syria and Cilicia, greetings. 24Since we have heard that certain persons who have gone out from us, though with no instructions from us, have said things to disturb you and have unsettled your minds,e 25we have decided unanimously to choose representativesf and send them to you, along with our beloved Barnabas and Paul, 26who have risked their lives for the sake of our Lord Jesus Christ. 27We have therefore

sent Judas and Silas, who themselves will tell you the same things by word of mouth. 28For it has seemed good to the Holy Spirit and to us to impose on you no further burden than these essentials: 29that you abstain from what has been sacrificed to idols and from blood and from what is strangledg and from fornication. If you keep yourselves from these, you will do well. Farewell."

30 So they were sent off and went down to Antioch. When they gathered the congregation together, they delivered the letter. 31When its membersh read it, they rejoiced at the exhortation. 32Judas and Silas, who were themselves prophets, said much to encourage and strengthen the believers.d 33After they had been there for some time, they were sent off in peace by the believersd to those who had sent them.i 35But Paul and Barnabas remained in Antioch, and there, with many others, they taught and proclaimed the word of the Lord.

Paul and Barnabas Separate

36 After some days Paul said to Barnabas, "Come, let us return and visit the believersd in every city where we proclaimed the word of the Lord and see how they are doing." 37Barnabas wanted to take with them John called Mark. 38But Paul decided not to take with them one who had deserted them in Pamphylia and had not accompanied them in the work. 39The disagreement became so sharp that they parted company; Barnabas took Mark with him and sailed away to Cyprus. 40But Paul chose Silas and set out, the believersd commending him to the grace of the Lord. 41He went through Syria and Cilicia, strengthening the churches.

Timothy Joins Paul and Silas

16 Paulj went on also to Derbe and to Lystra, where there was a disciple named Timothy, the son of a Jewish woman who was a believer; but his father was a Greek. 2He was well spoken of by the believersd in Lystra and Iconium. 3Paul wanted Timothy to ac-

---

z Gk Men, brothers   a Other ancient authorities read things. 18Known to God from of old are all his works.'   b Other ancient authorities lack and from whatever has been strangled   c Gk from among them   d Gk brothers   e Other ancient authorities add saying, 'You must be circumcised and keep the law,'   f Gk men   g Other ancient authorities lack and from what is strangled   h Gk When they   i Other ancient authorities add verse 34, But it seemed good to Silas to remain there   j Gk He

company him; and he took him and had him circumcised because of the Jews who were in those places, for they all knew that his father was a Greek. 4As they went from town to town, they delivered to them for observance the decisions that had been reached by the apostles and elders who were in Jerusalem. 5So the churches were strengthened in the faith and increased in numbers daily.

Paul's Vision of the Man of Macedonia

6 They went through the region of Phrygia and Galatia, having been forbidden by the Holy Spirit to speak the word in Asia. 7When they had come opposite Mysia, they attempted to go into Bithynia, but the Spirit of Jesus did not allow them; 8so, passing by Mysia, they went down to Troas. 9During the night Paul had a vision: there stood a man of Macedonia pleading with him and saying, "Come over to Macedonia and help us." 10When he had seen the vision, we immediately tried to cross over to Macedonia, being convinced that God had called us to proclaim the good news to them.

The Conversion of Lydia

11 We set sail from Troas and took a straight course to Samothrace, the following day to Neapolis, 12and from there to Philippi, which is a leading city of the district[k] of Macedonia and a Roman colony. We remained in this city for some days. 13On the sabbath day we went outside the gate by the river, where we supposed there was a place of prayer; and we sat down and spoke to the women who had gathered there. 14A certain woman named Lydia, a worshiper of God, was listening to us; she was from the city of Thyatira and a dealer in purple cloth. The Lord opened her heart to listen eagerly to what was said by Paul. 15When she and her household were baptized, she urged us, saying, "If you have judged me to be faithful to the Lord, come and stay at my home." And she prevailed upon us.

Paul and Silas in Prison

16 One day, as we were going to the place of prayer, we met a slave-girl who had a spirit of divination and brought her owners a great deal of money by fortune-telling. 17While she followed Paul and us, she would cry out, "These men are slaves of the Most High God, who proclaim to you[l] a way of salvation." 18She kept doing this for many days. But Paul, very much annoyed, turned and said to the spirit, "I order you in the name of Jesus Christ to come out of her." And it came out that very hour.

19 But when her owners saw that their hope of making money was gone, they seized Paul and Silas and dragged them into the marketplace before the authorities. 20When they had brought them before the magistrates, they said, "These men are disturbing our city; they are Jews 21and are advocating customs that are not lawful for us as Romans to adopt or observe." 22The crowd joined in attacking them, and the magistrates had them stripped of their clothing and ordered them to be beaten with rods. 23After they had given them a severe flogging, they threw them into prison and ordered the jailer to keep them securely. 24Following these instructions, he put them in the innermost cell and fastened their feet in the stocks.

25 About midnight Paul and Silas were praying and singing hymns to God, and the prisoners were listening to them. 26Suddenly there was an earthquake, so violent that the foundations of the prison were shaken; and immediately all the doors were opened and everyone's chains were unfastened. 27When the jailer woke up and saw the prison doors wide open, he drew his sword and was about to kill himself, since he supposed that the prisoners had escaped. 28But Paul shouted in a loud voice, "Do not harm yourself, for we are all here." 29The jailer[m] called for lights, and rushing in, he fell down trembling before Paul and Silas. 30Then he brought them outside and said, "Sirs, what must I do to be saved?" 31They answered, "Believe on the Lord Jesus, and you will be saved, you and your household." 32They spoke the word of the Lord[n] to him and to all who were in his house. 33At the same

k Other authorities read *a city of the first district*   l Other ancient authorities read *to us*   m Gk *He*
n Other ancient authorities read *word of God*

hour of the night he took them and washed their wounds; then he and his entire family were baptized without delay. 34He brought them up into the house and set food before them; and he and his entire household rejoiced that he had become a believer in God.

35 When morning came, the magistrates sent the police, saying, "Let those men go." 36And the jailer reported the message to Paul, saying, "The magistrates sent word to let you go; therefore come out now and go in peace." 37But Paul replied, "They have beaten us in public, uncondemned, men who are Roman citizens, and have thrown us into prison; and now are they going to discharge us in secret? Certainly not! Let them come and take us out themselves." 38The police reported these words to the magistrates, and they were afraid when they heard that they were Roman citizens; 39so they came and apologized to them. And they took them out and asked them to leave the city. 40After leaving the prison they went to Lydia's home; and when they had seen and encouraged the brothers and sisters*o* there, they departed.

The Uproar in Thessalonica

17 After Paul and Silas*p* had passed through Amphipolis and Apollonia, they came to Thessalonica, where there was a synagogue of the Jews. 2And Paul went in, as was his custom, and on three sabbath days argued with them from the scriptures, 3explaining and proving that it was necessary for the Messiah*q* to suffer and to rise from the dead, and saying, "This is the Messiah,*q* Jesus whom I am proclaiming to you." 4Some of them were persuaded and joined Paul and Silas, as did a great many of the devout Greeks and not a few of the leading women. 5But the Jews became jealous, and with the help of some ruffians in the marketplaces they formed a mob and set the city in an uproar. While they were searching for Paul and Silas to bring them out to the assembly, they attacked Jason's house. 6When they could not find them, they dragged Jason and some believers*o* before the city authorities,*r* shouting,

"These people who have been turning the world upside down have come here also, 7and Jason has entertained them as guests. They are all acting contrary to the decrees of the emperor, saying that there is another king named Jesus." 8The people and the city officials were disturbed when they heard this, 9and after they had taken bail from Jason and the others, they let them go.

Paul and Silas in Beroea

10 That very night the believers*o* sent Paul and Silas off to Beroea; and when they arrived, they went to the Jewish synagogue. 11These Jews were more receptive than those in Thessalonica, for they welcomed the message very eagerly and examined the scriptures every day to see whether these things were so. 12Many of them therefore believed, including not a few Greek women and men of high standing. 13But when the Jews of Thessalonica learned that the word of God had been proclaimed by Paul in Beroea as well, they came there too, to stir up and incite the crowds. 14Then the believers*o* immediately sent Paul away to the coast, but Silas and Timothy remained behind. 15Those who conducted Paul brought him as far as Athens; and after receiving instructions to have Silas and Timothy join him as soon as possible, they left him.

Paul in Athens

16 While Paul was waiting for them in Athens, he was deeply distressed to see that the city was full of idols. 17So he argued in the synagogue with the Jews and the devout persons, and also in the marketplace*s* every day with those who happened to be there. 18Also some Epicurean and Stoic philosophers debated with him. Some said, "What does this babbler want to say?" Others said, "He seems to be a proclaimer of foreign divinities." (This was because he was telling the good news about Jesus and the resurrection.) 19So they took him and brought him to the Areopagus and asked him, "May we know what this new teaching is that you are presenting? 20It sounds rather strange to us, so we would like to know what it means."

o Gk *brothers*   *p* Gk *they*   *q* Or *the Christ*   *r* Gk *politarchs*   *s* Or *civic center;* Gk *agora*

21Now all the Athenians and the foreigners living there would spend their time in nothing but telling or hearing something new.

22 Then Paul stood in front of the Areopagus and said, "Athenians, I see how extremely religious you are in every way. 23For as I went through the city and looked carefully at the objects of your worship, I found among them an altar with the inscription, 'To an unknown god.' What therefore you worship as unknown, this I proclaim to you. 24The God who made the world and everything in it, he who is Lord of heaven and earth, does not live in shrines made by human hands, 25nor is he served by human hands, as though he needed anything, since he himself gives to all mortals life and breath and all things. 26From one ancestort he made all nations to inhabit the whole earth, and he allotted the times of their existence and the boundaries of the places where they would live, 27so that they would search for Godu and perhaps grope for him and find him—though indeed he is not far from each one of us. 28For 'In him we live and move and have our being'; as even some of your own poets have said,
'For we too are his offspring.'
29Since we are God's offspring, we ought not to think that the deity is like gold, or silver, or stone, an image formed by the art and imagination of mortals. 30While God has overlooked the times of human ignorance, now he commands all people everywhere to repent, 31because he has fixed a day on which he

---

GOD, OF YOUR GOODNESS, GIVE ME YOURSELF FOR YOU ARE SUFFICIENT FOR ME. I CANNOT PROPERLY ASK ANYTHING LESS, TO BE WORTHY OF YOU. IF I WERE TO ASK LESS, I SHOULD ALWAYS BE IN WANT. IN YOU ALONE DO I HAVE ALL.

—Julian of Norwich

---

will have the world judged in righteousness by a man whom he has appointed, and of this he has given assurance to all by raising him from the dead."

32 When they heard of the resurrection of the dead, some scoffed; but others said, "We will hear you again about this." 33At that point Paul left them. 34But some of them joined him and became believers, including Dionysius the Areopagite and a woman named Damaris, and others with them.

Paul in Corinth

18 After this Paulv left Athens and went to Corinth. 2There he found a Jew named Aquila, a native of Pontus, who had recently come from Italy with his wife Priscilla, because Claudius had ordered all Jews to leave Rome. Paulw went to see them, 3and, because he was of the same trade, he stayed with them, and they worked together—by trade they were tentmakers. 4Every sabbath he would argue in the synagogue and would try to convince Jews and Greeks.

5 When Silas and Timothy arrived from Macedonia, Paul was occupied with proclaiming the word,x testifying to the Jews that the Messiahy was Jesus. 6When they opposed and reviled him, in protest he shook the dust from his clothesz and said to them, "Your blood be on your own heads! I am innocent. From now on I will go to the Gentiles." 7Then he left the synagoguea and went to the house of a man named Titiusb Justus, a worshiper of God; his house was next door to the synagogue. 8Crispus, the official of the synagogue, became a believer in the Lord, together with all his household; and many of the Corinthians who heard Paul became believers and were baptized. 9One night the Lord said to Paul in a vision, "Do not be afraid, but speak and do not be silent; 10for I am with you, and no one will lay a hand on you to harm you, for there are many in this city who are my people." 11He stayed there a year and six months, teaching the word of God among them.

12 But when Gallio was proconsul of Achaia, the Jews made a united attack on Paul and brought him before the tribunal. 13They said, "This man is persuading people to worship God in ways

---

t Gk From one; other ancient authorities read From one blood   u Other ancient authorities read the Lord   v Gk he   w Gk He   x Gk with the word   y Or the Christ   z Gk reviled him, he shook out his clothes   a Gk left there   b Other ancient authorities read Titus

WHY CHRISTIANS LOSE REALITY
Francis Schaeffer

VERSE: Acts 17.29   **PASSAGE:** Acts 17.22–31

ur generation is overwhelmingly naturalistic. There is an almost complete commitment to the concept of the uniformity of natural causes in a closed system. This is its distinguishing mark. If we are not careful, even though we say we are Biblical Christians and supernaturalists, nevertheless the naturalism of our generation tends to come in upon us. It may infiltrate our thinking without our recognizing its coming, like a fog creeping in through a window opened only half an inch. As soon as this happens, Christians begin to lose the reality of their Christian lives . . . All too often the reality is lost because the "ceiling" is down too close upon our heads. It is too low. And the "ceiling" which closes us in is the naturalistic type of thinking.

Now the Christian's spirituality . . . does not stand alone. It is related to the unity of the Bible's view of the universe. This means that we must understand—intellectually, with the windows open—that the universe is not what our generation says it is, seeing only the naturalistic universe . . . For example, we have said that we are to love God enough to say, "Thank you" even for the difficult things. We must immediately understand, as we say this, that this has no meaning whatsoever unless we live in a personal universe in which there is a personal God who objectively exists . . .

We have also considered Christ's redemptive death, which has no meaning whatsoever outside the relationship of a supernatural world. The only reason the words "redemptive death" have any meaning is that there is a personal God who exists and, more than that, has a character. He is not morally neutral. When man sins against that character, which is the law of the universe, he is guilty, and God will judge that man on the basis of true moral guilt. In such a setting, the words "the redemptive death of Christ" have meaning, otherwise they cannot.

ADDITIONAL SCRIPTURE READING:
2 Kings 6.15–23; Titus 2.11–14

Go to page 1304 for your next devotional reading.

1900   Present

that are contrary to the law." [14]Just as Paul was about to speak, Gallio said to the Jews, "If it were a matter of crime or serious villainy, I would be justified in accepting the complaint of you Jews; [15]but since it is a matter of questions about words and names and your own law, see to it yourselves; I do not wish to be a judge of these matters." [16]And he dismissed them from the tribunal. [17]Then all of them[c] seized Sosthenes, the official of the synagogue, and beat him in front of the tribunal. But Gallio paid no attention to any of these things.

Paul's Return to Antioch

18 After staying there for a considerable time, Paul said farewell to the believers[d] and sailed for Syria, accompanied by Priscilla and Aquila. At Cenchreae he had his hair cut, for he was under a vow. [19]When they reached Ephesus, he left them there, but first he himself went into the synagogue and had a discussion with the Jews. [20]When they asked him to stay longer, he declined; [21]but on taking leave of them, he said, "I[e] will return to you, if God wills." Then he set sail from Ephesus.

22 When he had landed at Caesarea, he went up to Jerusalem[f] and greeted the church, and then went down to Antioch. [23]After spending some time there he departed and went from place to place through the region of Galatia[g] and Phrygia, strengthening all the disciples.

Ministry of Apollos

24 Now there came to Ephesus a Jew named Apollos, a native of Alexandria. He was an eloquent man, well-versed in the scriptures. [25]He had been instructed in the Way of the Lord; and he spoke with burning enthusiasm and taught accurately the things concerning Jesus, though he knew only the baptism of John. [26]He began to speak boldly in the synagogue; but when Priscilla and Aquila heard him, they took him aside and explained the Way of God to him more accurately. [27]And when he wished to cross over to Achaia, the believers[d] encouraged him and wrote to the disciples to welcome him. On his arrival he greatly helped those who through grace had become believers, [28]for he powerfully refuted the Jews in public, showing by the scriptures that the Messiah[h] is Jesus.

Paul in Ephesus

19 While Apollos was in Corinth, Paul passed through the interior regions and came to Ephesus, where he found some disciples. [2]He said to them, "Did you receive the Holy Spirit when you became believers?" They replied, "No, we have not even heard that there is a Holy Spirit." [3]Then he said, "Into what then were you baptized?" They answered, "Into John's baptism." [4]Paul said, "John baptized with the baptism of repentance, telling the people to believe in the one who was to come after him, that is, in Jesus." [5]On hearing this, they were baptized in the name of the Lord Jesus. [6]When Paul had laid his hands on them, the Holy Spirit came upon them, and they spoke in tongues and prophesied— [7]altogether there were about twelve of them.

8 He entered the synagogue and for three months spoke out boldly, and argued persuasively about the kingdom of God. [9]When some stubbornly refused to believe and spoke evil of the Way before the congregation, he left them, taking the disciples with him, and argued daily in the lecture hall of Tyrannus.[i] [10]This continued for two years, so that all the residents of Asia, both Jews and Greeks, heard the word of the Lord.

The Sons of Sceva

11 God did extraordinary miracles through Paul, [12]so that when the handkerchiefs or aprons that had touched his skin were brought to the sick, their diseases left them, and the evil spirits came out of them. [13]Then some itinerant Jewish exorcists tried to use the name of the Lord Jesus over those who had evil spirits, saying, "I adjure you by the Jesus whom Paul proclaims." [14]Seven sons of a Jewish high priest named Sceva were

c Other ancient authorities read all the Greeks   d Gk brothers   e Other ancient authorities read I must at all costs keep the approaching festival in Jerusalem, but I   f Gk went up   g Gk the Galatian region   h Or the Christ   i Other ancient authorities read of a certain Tyrannus, from eleven o'clock in the morning to four in the afternoon

doing this. 15But the evil spirit said to them in reply, "Jesus I know, and Paul I know; but who are you?" 16Then the man with the evil spirit leaped on them, mastered them all, and so overpowered them that they fled out of the house naked and wounded. 17When this became known to all residents of Ephesus, both Jews and Greeks, everyone was awestruck; and the name of the Lord Jesus was praised. 18Also many of those who became believers confessed and disclosed their practices. 19A number of those who practiced magic collected their books and burned them publicly; when the value of these books*j* was calculated, it was found to come to fifty thousand silver coins. 20So the word of the Lord grew mightily and prevailed.

The Riot in Ephesus

21 Now after these things had been accomplished, Paul resolved in the Spirit to go through Macedonia and Achaia, and then to go on to Jerusalem. He said, "After I have gone there, I must also see Rome." 22So he sent two of his helpers, Timothy and Erastus, to Macedonia, while he himself stayed for some time longer in Asia.

23 About that time no little disturbance broke out concerning the Way. 24A man named Demetrius, a silversmith who made silver shrines of Artemis, brought no little business to the artisans. 25These he gathered together, with the workers of the same trade, and said, "Men, you know that we get our wealth from this business. 26You also see and hear that not only in Ephesus but in almost the whole of Asia this Paul has persuaded and drawn away a considerable number of people by saying that gods made with hands are not gods. 27And there is danger not only that this trade of ours may come into disrepute but also that the temple of the great goddess Artemis will be scorned, and she will be deprived of her majesty that brought all Asia and the world to worship her."

28 When they heard this, they were enraged and shouted, "Great is Artemis of the Ephesians!" 29The city was filled with the confusion; and people*k* rushed together to the theater, dragging with them Gaius and Aristarchus, Macedonians who were Paul's travel companions. 30Paul wished to go into the crowd, but the disciples would not let him; 31even some officials of the province of Asia,*l* who were friendly to him, sent him a message urging him not to venture into the theater. 32Meanwhile, some were shouting one thing, some another; for the assembly was in confusion, and most of them did not know why they had come together. 33Some of the crowd gave instructions to Alexander, whom the Jews had pushed forward. And Alexander motioned for silence and tried to make a defense before the people. 34But when they recognized that he was a Jew, for about two hours all of them shouted in unison, "Great is Artemis of the Ephesians!" 35But when the town clerk had quieted the crowd, he said, "Citizens of Ephesus, who is there that does not know that the city of the Ephesians is the temple keeper of the great Artemis and of the statue that fell from heaven?*m* 36Since these things cannot be denied, you ought to be quiet and do nothing rash. 37You have brought these men here who are neither temple robbers nor blasphemers of our*n* goddess. 38If therefore Demetrius and the artisans with him have a complaint against anyone, the courts are open, and there are proconsuls; let them bring charges there against one another. 39If there is anything further*o* you want to know, it must be settled in the regular assembly. 40For we are in danger of being charged with rioting today, since there is no cause that we can give to justify this commotion." 41When he had said this, he dismissed the assembly.

Paul Goes to Macedonia and Greece

20 After the uproar had ceased, Paul sent for the disciples; and after encouraging them and saying farewell, he left for Macedonia. 2When he had gone through those regions and had given the believers*p* much encour-

---

j Gk them   *k* Gk they   *l* Gk some of the Asiarchs   *m* Meaning of Gk uncertain   *n* Other ancient authorities read your   *o* Other ancient authorities read about other matters   *p* Gk given them

agement, he came to Greece, ³where he stayed for three months. He was about to set sail for Syria when a plot was made against him by the Jews, and so he decided to return through Macedonia. ⁴He was accompanied by Sopater son of Pyrrhus from Beroea, by Aristarchus and Secundus from Thessalonica, by Gaius from Derbe, and by Timothy, as well as by Tychicus and Trophimus from Asia. ⁵They went ahead and were waiting for us in Troas; ⁶but we sailed from Philippi after the days of Unleavened Bread, and in five days we joined them in Troas, where we stayed for seven days.

Paul's Farewell Visit to Troas

7 On the first day of the week, when we met to break bread, Paul was holding a discussion with them; since he intended to leave the next day, he continued speaking until midnight. ⁸There were many lamps in the room upstairs where we were meeting. ⁹A young man named Eutychus, who was sitting in the window, began to sink off into a deep sleep while Paul talked still longer. Overcome by sleep, he fell to the ground three floors below and was picked up dead. ¹⁰But Paul went down, and bending over him took him in his arms, and said, "Do not be alarmed, for his life is in him." ¹¹Then Paul went upstairs, and after he had broken bread and eaten, he continued to converse with them until dawn; then he left. ¹²Meanwhile they had taken the boy away alive and were not a little comforted.

The Voyage from Troas to Miletus

13 We went ahead to the ship and set sail for Assos, intending to take Paul on board there; for he had made this arrangement, intending to go by land himself. ¹⁴When he met us in Assos, we took him on board and went to Mitylene. ¹⁵We sailed from there, and on the following day we arrived opposite Chios. The next day we touched at Samos, and*q* the day after that we came to Miletus. ¹⁶For Paul had decided to sail past Ephesus, so that he might not have to spend time in Asia; he was eager to be

in Jerusalem, if possible, on the day of Pentecost.

Paul Speaks to the Ephesian Elders

17 From Miletus he sent a message to Ephesus, asking the elders of the church to meet him. ¹⁸When they came to him, he said to them:

"You yourselves know how I lived among you the entire time from the first day that I set foot in Asia, ¹⁹serving the Lord with all humility and with tears, enduring the trials that came to me through the plots of the Jews. ²⁰I did not shrink from doing anything helpful, proclaiming the message to you and teaching you publicly and from house to house, ²¹as I testified to both Jews and Greeks about repentance toward God and faith toward our Lord Jesus. ²²And now, as a captive to the Spirit,*r* I am on my way to Jerusalem, not knowing what will happen to me there, ²³except that the Holy Spirit testifies to me in every city that imprisonment and persecutions are waiting for me. ²⁴But I do not count my life of any value to myself, if only I may finish my course and the ministry that I received from the Lord Jesus, to testify to the good news of God's grace.

25 "And now I know that none of you, among whom I have gone about proclaiming the kingdom, will ever see my face again. ²⁶Therefore I declare to you this day that I am not responsible for the blood of any of you, ²⁷for I did not shrink from declaring to you the whole purpose of God. ²⁸Keep watch over yourselves and over all the flock, of which the Holy Spirit has made you overseers, to shepherd the church of God*s* that he obtained with the blood of his own Son.*t* ²⁹I know that after I have gone, savage wolves will come in among you, not sparing the flock. ³⁰Some even from your own group will come distorting the truth in order to entice the disciples to follow them. ³¹Therefore be alert, remembering that for three years I did not cease night or day to warn everyone with tears. ³²And now I commend you to God and to the message of his grace, a message that is able to build you up and

---

q Other ancient authorities add *after remaining at Trogyllium*   r Or *And now, bound in the spirit*
s Other ancient authorities read *of the Lord*   t Or *with his own blood;* Gk *with the blood of his Own*

to give you the inheritance among all who are sanctified. 33I coveted no one's silver or gold or clothing. 34You know for yourselves that I worked with my own hands to support myself and my companions. 35In all this I have given you an example that by such work we must support the weak, remembering

TUESDAY

SATURATED WITH THE SPIRIT
Hilary of Poitiers

VERSE: Acts 20.24   **PASSAGE:** Acts 20.17–24

Hoisting My Sails

he chief service I owe you, O God, is that every thought and word of mine should speak of you. The power of speech which you have bestowed on me can give me no greater pleasure than to serve you by preaching your gospel.

But in saying this, I am merely expressing what I want to do. If I am actually to use this gift, I must ask you for your help—ask you to fill the sails I have hoisted for you with the wind of your Holy Spirit, inspiring my mind and my voice. I know that I am often heavy with stupor, so that I am too lazy to speak of you. And I do not spend sufficient time studying your Scriptures, to ensure that my words conform to your Word. Give me the energy and the courage to share the spirit of the apostles, that like them I may truly be an ambassador of your grace.

Saturated in His Love

Although I am dust and ashes, Lord, I am tied to you by bonds of love. Therefore I feel I can speak freely to you. Before I came to know you, I was nothing. I did not know the meaning of life, and I had no understanding of myself. I have no doubt that you had a purpose in causing me to be born; yet you had no need of me, and on my own I was of no use to you.

But then you decided that I should hear the words of your Son, Jesus Christ. And that as I heard his words, you enabled his love to penetrate my heart. Now I am completely saturated in his love and faith, and there is no remedy. Now, Lord, I cannot change my attitude to my faith; I can only die for it.

ADDITIONAL SCRIPTURE READING:
Psalm 139; Philippians 1.21–26

Go to page 1308 for your next devotional reading.

100   500

the words of the Lord Jesus, for he himself said, 'It is more blessed to give than to receive.' "

36 When he had finished speaking, he knelt down with them all and prayed. 37There was much weeping among them all; they embraced Paul and kissed him, 38grieving especially because of what he had said, that they would not see him again. Then they brought him to the ship.

Paul's Journey to Jerusalem

21 When we had parted from them and set sail, we came by a straight course to Cos, and the next day to Rhodes, and from there to Patara.ᵘ 2When we found a ship bound for Phoenicia, we went on board and set sail. 3We came in sight of Cyprus; and leaving it on our left, we sailed to Syria and landed at Tyre, because the ship was to unload its cargo there. 4We looked up the disciples and stayed there for seven days. Through the Spirit they told Paul not to go on to Jerusalem. 5When our days there were ended, we left and proceeded on our journey; and all of them, with wives and children, escorted us outside the city. There we knelt down on the beach and prayed 6and said farewell to one another. Then we went on board the ship, and they returned home.

7 When we had finishedᵛ the voyage from Tyre, we arrived at Ptolemais; and we greeted the believersʷ and stayed with them for one day. 8The next day we left and came to Caesarea; and we went into the house of Philip the evangelist, one of the seven, and stayed with him. 9He had four unmarried daughtersˣ who had the gift of prophecy. 10While we were staying there for several days, a prophet named Agabus came down from Judea. 11He came to us and took Paul's belt, bound his own feet and hands with it, and said, "Thus says the Holy Spirit, 'This is the way the Jews in Jerusalem will bind the man who owns this belt and will hand him over to the Gentiles.' " 12When we heard this, we and the people there urged him not to go up to Jerusalem. 13Then Paul answered,

"What are you doing, weeping and breaking my heart? For I am ready not only to be bound but even to die in Jerusalem for the name of the Lord Jesus." 14Since he would not be persuaded, we remained silent except to say, "The Lord's will be done."

15 After these days we got ready and started to go up to Jerusalem. 16Some of the disciples from Caesarea also came along and brought us to the house of Mnason of Cyprus, an early disciple, with whom we were to stay.

Paul Visits James at Jerusalem

17 When we arrived in Jerusalem, the brothers welcomed us warmly. 18The next day Paul went with us to visit James; and all the elders were present. 19After greeting them, he related one by one the things that God had done among the Gentiles through his ministry. 20When they heard it, they praised God. Then they said to him, "You see, brother, how many thousands of believers there are among the Jews, and they are all zealous for the law. 21They have been told about you that you teach all the Jews living among the Gentiles to forsake Moses, and that you tell them not to circumcise their children or observe the customs. 22What then is to be done? They will certainly hear that you have come. 23So do what we tell you. We have four men who are under a vow. 24Join these men, go through the rite of purification with them, and pay for the shaving of their heads. Thus all will know that there is nothing in what they have been told about you, but that you yourself observe and guard the law. 25But as for the Gentiles who have become believers, we have sent a letter with our judgment that they should abstain from what has been sacrificed to idols and from blood and from what is strangledʸ and from fornication." 26Then Paul took the men, and the next day, having purified himself, he entered the temple with them, making public the completion of the days of purification when the sacrifice would be made for each of them.

---

u Other ancient authorities add *and Myra*   v Or *continued*   w Gk *brothers*   x Gk *four daughters, virgins,*   y Other ancient authorities lack *and from what is strangled*

Paul Arrested in the Temple

27 When the seven days were almost completed, the Jews from Asia, who had seen him in the temple, stirred up the whole crowd. They seized him, 28shouting, "Fellow Israelites, help! This is the man who is teaching everyone everywhere against our people, our law, and this place; more than that, he has actually brought Greeks into the temple and has defiled this holy place." 29For they had previously seen Trophimus the Ephesian with him in the city, and they supposed that Paul had brought him into the temple. 30Then all the city was aroused, and the people rushed together. They seized Paul and dragged him out of the temple, and immediately the doors were shut. 31While they were trying to kill him, word came to the tribune of the cohort that all Jerusalem was in an uproar. 32Immediately he took soldiers and centurions and ran down to them. When they saw the tribune and the soldiers, they stopped beating Paul. 33Then the tribune came, arrested him, and ordered him to be bound with two chains; he inquired who he was and what he had done. 34Some in the crowd shouted one thing, some another; and as he could not learn the facts because of the uproar, he ordered him to be brought into the barracks. 35When Paul[z] came to the steps, the violence of the mob was so great that he had to be carried by the soldiers. 36The crowd that followed kept shouting, "Away with him!"

Paul Defends Himself

37 Just as Paul was about to be brought into the barracks, he said to the tribune, "May I say something to you?" The tribune[a] replied, "Do you know Greek? 38Then you are not the Egyptian who recently stirred up a revolt and led the four thousand assassins out into the wilderness?" 39Paul replied, "I am a Jew, from Tarsus in Cilicia, a citizen of an important city; I beg you, let me speak to the people." 40When he had given him permission, Paul stood on the steps and motioned to the people for silence; and when there was a great hush, he addressed them in the Hebrew[b] language, saying:

22 "Brothers and fathers, listen to the defense that I now make before you."

2 When they heard him addressing them in Hebrew,[b] they became even more quiet. Then he said:

3 "I am a Jew, born in Tarsus in Cilicia, but brought up in this city at the feet of Gamaliel, educated strictly according to our ancestral law, being zealous for God, just as all of you are today. 4I persecuted this Way up to the point of death by binding both men and women and putting them in prison, 5as the high priest and the whole council of elders can testify about me. From them I also received letters to the brothers in Damascus, and I went there in order to bind those who were there and to bring them back to Jerusalem for punishment.

Paul Tells of His Conversion

6 "While I was on my way and approaching Damascus, about noon a great light from heaven suddenly shone about me. 7I fell to the ground and heard a voice saying to me, 'Saul, Saul, why are you persecuting me?' 8I answered, 'Who are you, Lord?' Then he said to me, 'I am Jesus of Nazareth[c] whom you are persecuting.' 9Now those who were with me saw the light but did not hear the voice of the one who was speaking to me. 10I asked, 'What am I to do, Lord?' The Lord said to me, 'Get up and go to Damascus; there you will be told everything that has been assigned to you to do.' 11Since I could not see because of the brightness of that light, those who were with me took my hand and led me to Damascus.

12 "A certain Ananias, who was a devout man according to the law and well spoken of by all the Jews living there, 13came to me; and standing beside me, he said, 'Brother Saul, regain your sight!' In that very hour I regained my sight and saw him. 14Then he said, 'The God of our ancestors has chosen you to know his will, to see the Righteous One and to hear his own voice; 15for you will be his witness to all the world of what you have seen and heard. 16And now why do you delay? Get up, be baptized, and have

z Gk he a Gk He b That is, Aramaic c Gk the Nazorean

your sins washed away, calling on his name.'

Paul Sent to the Gentiles

17 "After I had returned to Jerusalem and while I was praying in the temple, I fell into a trance [18]and saw Jesus[d] saying to me, 'Hurry and get out of Jerusalem quickly, because they will not accept your testimony about me.' [19]And I said, 'Lord, they themselves know that in every synagogue I imprisoned and beat those who believed in you. [20]And while the blood of your witness Stephen was shed, I myself was standing by, approving and keeping the coats of those who killed him.' [21]Then he said to me, 'Go, for I will send you far away to the Gentiles.' "

Paul and the Roman Tribune

22 Up to this point they listened to him, but then they shouted, "Away with such a fellow from the earth! For he should not be allowed to live." [23]And while they were shouting, throwing off their cloaks, and tossing dust into the air, [24]the tribune directed that he was to be brought into the barracks, and ordered him to be examined by flogging, to find out the reason for this outcry against him. [25]But when they had tied him up with thongs,[e] Paul said to the centurion who was standing by, "Is it legal for you to flog a Roman citizen who is uncondemned?" [26]When the centurion heard that, he went to the tribune and said to him, "What are you about to do? This man is a Roman citizen." [27]The tribune came and asked Paul,[d] "Tell me, are you a Roman citizen?" And he said, "Yes." [28]The tribune answered, "It cost me a large sum of money to get my citizenship." Paul said, "But I was born a citizen." [29]Immediately those who were about to examine him drew back from him; and the tribune also was afraid, for he realized that Paul was a Roman citizen and that he had bound him.

Paul before the Council

30 Since he wanted to find out what Paul[f] was being accused of by the Jews,

the next day he released him and ordered the chief priests and the entire council to meet. He brought Paul down and had him stand before them.

23 While Paul was looking intently at the council he said, "Brothers,[g] up to this day I have lived my life with a clear conscience before God." [2]Then the high priest Ananias ordered those standing near him to strike him on the mouth. [3]At this Paul said to him, "God will strike you, you whitewashed wall! Are you sitting there to judge me according to the law, and yet in violation of the law you order me to be struck?" [4]Those standing nearby said, "Do you dare to insult God's high priest?" [5]And Paul said, "I did not realize, brothers, that he was high priest; for it is written, 'You shall not speak evil of a leader of your people.' "

6 When Paul noticed that some were Sadducees and others were Pharisees, he called out in the council, "Brothers, I am a Pharisee, a son of Pharisees. I am on trial concerning the hope of the resurrection[h] of the dead." [7]When he said this, a dissension began between the Pharisees and the Sadducees, and the assembly was divided. [8](The Sadducees say that there is no resurrection, or angel, or spirit; but the Pharisees acknowledge all three.) [9]Then a great clamor arose, and certain scribes of the Pharisees' group stood up and contended, "We find nothing wrong with this man. What if a spirit or an angel has spoken to him?" [10]When the dissension became violent, the tribune, fearing that they would tear Paul to pieces, ordered the soldiers to go down, take him by force, and bring him into the barracks.

11 That night the Lord stood near him and said, "Keep up your courage! For just as you have testified for me in Jerusalem, so you must bear witness also in Rome."

The Plot to Kill Paul

12 In the morning the Jews joined in a conspiracy and bound themselves by an oath neither to eat nor drink until they had killed Paul. [13]There were more than forty who joined in this conspiracy.

---

d Gk him   e Or up for the lashes   f Gk he   g Gk Men, brothers   h Gk concerning hope and resurrection

¹⁴They went to the chief priests and elders and said, "We have strictly bound ourselves by an oath to taste no food until we have killed Paul. ¹⁵Now then, you and the council must notify the tribune to bring him down to you, on the

WEDNESDAY

THE HOPE OF THE RESURRECTION
Reinhold Niebuhr

VERSE: Acts 23.6   **PASSAGE:** Acts 23.6–8

he idea of the resurrection of the body is a Biblical symbol in which modern minds take the greatest offense and which has long since been displaced in most modern versions of the Christian faith by the idea of the immortality of the soul. The latter idea is regarded as a more plausible expression of the hope of everlasting life. It is true of course that the idea of the resurrection transcends the limits of the conceivable; but it is not always appreciated that this is equally true of the idea of an immortal soul. The fact is that the unity of historical existence, despite its involvement in and transcendence over nature, makes it no more possible to conceive transcendent spirit, completely freed of the conditions of nature, than to conceive the conditions of nature transmuted into an eternal consummation. Either idea, as every other idea, which points to the consummation beyond history, is beyond logical conception. The hope of the resurrection nevertheless embodies the very genius of the Christian idea of the historical. On the one hand it implies that eternity will fulfill and not annul the richness and variety which the temporal process has elaborated. On the other it implies that the condition of finiteness and freedom, which lies at the basis of historical existence, is a problem for which there is no solution by any human power. Only God can save this problem. From the human perspective it can only be solved by faith. All structures of meaning and realms of coherence, which human reason constructs, face the chasm of meaninglessness when men discover that the tangents of meaning transcend the limits of existence. Only faith has an answer for this problem. The Christian answer is faith in the God who is revealed in Christ and from whose love neither life nor death can separate us.

ADDITIONAL SCRIPTURE READING:
1 Corinthians 15.12–14; Philippians 3.8–11

Go to page 1314 for your next devotional reading.

1900   Present

pretext that you want to make a more thorough examination of his case. And we are ready to do away with him before he arrives."

16 Now the son of Paul's sister heard about the ambush; so he went and gained entrance to the barracks and told Paul. 17Paul called one of the centurions and said, "Take this young man to the tribune, for he has something to report to him." 18So he took him, brought him to the tribune, and said, "The prisoner Paul called me and asked me to bring this young man to you; he has something to tell you." 19The tribune took him by the hand, drew him aside privately, and asked, "What is it that you have to report to me?" 20He answered, "The Jews have agreed to ask you to bring Paul down to the council tomorrow, as though they were going to inquire more thoroughly into his case. 21But do not be persuaded by them, for more than forty of their men are lying in ambush for him. They have bound themselves by an oath neither to eat nor drink until they kill him. They are ready now and are waiting for your consent." 22So the tribune dismissed the young man, ordering him, "Tell no one that you have informed me of this."

Paul Sent to Felix the Governor

23 Then he summoned two of the centurions and said, "Get ready to leave by nine o'clock tonight for Caesarea with two hundred soldiers, seventy horsemen, and two hundred spearmen. 24Also provide mounts for Paul to ride, and take him safely to Felix the governor." 25He wrote a letter to this effect:

26 "Claudius Lysias to his Excellency the governor Felix, greetings. 27This man was seized by the Jews and was about to be killed by them, but when I had learned that he was a Roman citizen, I came with the guard and rescued him. 28Since I wanted to know the charge for which they accused him, I had him brought to their council. 29I found that he was accused concerning questions of their law, but was charged

with nothing deserving death or imprisonment. 30When I was informed that there would be a plot against the man, I sent him to you at once, ordering his accusers also to state before you what they have against him.*i*"

31 So the soldiers, according to their instructions, took Paul and brought him during the night to Antipatris. 32The next day they let the horsemen go on with him, while they returned to the barracks. 33When they came to Caesarea and delivered the letter to the governor, they presented Paul also before him. 34On reading the letter, he asked what province he belonged to, and when he learned that he was from Cilicia, 35he said, "I will give you a hearing when your accusers arrive." Then he ordered that he be kept under guard in Herod's headquarters.*j*

Paul before Felix at Caesarea

24 Five days later the high priest Ananias came down with some elders and an attorney, a certain Tertullus, and they reported their case against Paul to the governor. 2When Paul*k* had been summoned, Tertullus began to accuse him, saying:

"Your Excellency,*l* because of you we have long enjoyed peace, and reforms have been made for this people because of your foresight. 3We welcome this in every way and everywhere with utmost gratitude. 4But, to detain you no further, I beg you to hear us briefly with your customary graciousness. 5We have, in fact, found this man a pestilent fellow, an agitator among all the Jews throughout the world, and a ringleader of the sect of the Nazarenes.*m* 6He even tried to profane the temple, and so we seized him.*n* 8By examining him yourself you will be able to learn from him concerning everything of which we accuse him."

9 The Jews also joined in the charge by asserting that all this was true.

Paul's Defense before Felix

10 When the governor motioned to him to speak, Paul replied:

i Other ancient authorities add *Farewell*   *j* Gk *praetorium*   *k* Gk *he*   *l* Gk lacks *Your Excellency*
m Gk *Nazoreans*   *n* Other ancient authorities add *and we would have judged him according to our
law.* 7*But the chief captain Lysias came and with great violence took him out of our hands,*
8*commanding his accusers to come before you.*

"I cheerfully make my defense, knowing that for many years you have been a judge over this nation. 11As you can find out, it is not more than twelve days since I went up to worship in Jerusalem. 12They did not find me disputing with anyone in the temple or stirring up a crowd either in the synagogues or throughout the city. 13Neither can they prove to you the charge that they now bring against me. 14But this I admit to you, that according to the Way, which they call a sect, I worship the God of our ancestors, believing everything laid down according to the law or written in the prophets. 15I have a hope in God—a hope that they themselves also accept—that there will be a resurrection of both° the righteous and the unrighteous. 16Therefore I do my best always to have a clear conscience toward God and all people. 17Now after some years I

AND I WILL PLACE WITHIN THEM AS A GUIDE
MY UMPIRE CONSCIENCE, WHOM IF THEY WILL
HEAR,
LIGHT AFTER LIGHT WELL US'D THEY SHALL
ATTAIN,
AND TO THE END PERSISTING, SAFE ARRIVE.
—*John Milton*

came to bring alms to my nation and to offer sacrifices. 18While I was doing this, they found me in the temple, completing the rite of purification, without any crowd or disturbance. 19But there were some Jews from Asia—they ought to be here before you to make an accusation, if they have anything against me. 20Or let these men here tell what crime they had found when I stood before the council, 21unless it was this one sentence that I called out while standing before them, 'It is about the resurrection of the dead that I am on trial before you today.'"

22 But Felix, who was rather well informed about the Way, adjourned the hearing with the comment, "When Lysias the tribune comes down, I will decide your case." 23Then he ordered the centurion to keep him in custody, but to let him have some liberty and not to

prevent any of his friends from taking care of his needs.

Paul Held in Custody

24 Some days later when Felix came with his wife Drusilla, who was Jewish, he sent for Paul and heard him speak concerning faith in Christ Jesus. 25And as he discussed justice, self-control, and the coming judgment, Felix became frightened and said, "Go away for the present; when I have an opportunity, I will send for you." 26At the same time he hoped that money would be given him by Paul, and for that reason he used to send for him very often and converse with him.

27 After two years had passed, Felix was succeeded by Porcius Festus; and since he wanted to grant the Jews a favor, Felix left Paul in prison.

Paul Appeals to the Emperor

25 Three days after Festus had arrived in the province, he went up from Caesarea to Jerusalem 2where the chief priests and the leaders of the Jews gave him a report against Paul. They appealed to him 3and requested, as a favor to them against Paul,ᵖ to have him transferred to Jerusalem. They were, in fact, planning an ambush to kill him along the way. 4Festus replied that Paul was being kept at Caesarea, and that he himself intended to go there shortly. 5"So," he said, "let those of you who have the authority come down with me, and if there is anything wrong about the man, let them accuse him."

6 After he had stayed among them not more than eight or ten days, he went down to Caesarea; the next day he took his seat on the tribunal and ordered Paul to be brought. 7When he arrived, the Jews who had gone down from Jerusalem surrounded him, bringing many serious charges against him, which they could not prove. 8Paul said in his defense, "I have in no way committed an offense against the law of the Jews, or against the temple, or against the emperor." 9But Festus, wishing to do the Jews a favor, asked Paul, "Do you wish to go up to Jerusalem and be tried there

o Other ancient authorities read *of the dead, both of* p Gk *him* before me on these charges?" 10Paul said, "I am appealing to the emperor's tribunal; this is where I should be tried. I have done no wrong to the Jews, as you very well know. 11Now if I am in the wrong and have committed something for which I deserve to die, I am not trying to escape death; but if there is nothing to their charges against me, no one can turn me over to them. I appeal to the emperor." 12Then Festus, after he had conferred with his council, replied, "You have appealed to the emperor; to the emperor you will go."

Festus Consults King Agrippa

13 After several days had passed, King Agrippa and Bernice arrived at Caesarea to welcome Festus. 14Since they were staying there several days, Festus laid Paul's case before the king, saying, "There is a man here who was left in prison by Felix. 15When I was in Jerusalem, the chief priests and the elders of the Jews informed me about him and asked for a sentence against him. 16I told them that it was not the custom of the Romans to hand over anyone before the accused had met the accusers face to face and had been given an opportunity to make a defense against the charge. 17So when they met here, I lost no time, but on the next day took my seat on the tribunal and ordered the man to be brought. 18When the accusers stood up, they did not charge him with any of the crimes*q* that I was expecting. 19Instead they had certain points of disagreement with him about their own religion and about a certain Jesus, who had died, but whom Paul asserted to be alive. 20Since I was at a loss how to investigate these questions, I asked whether he wished to go to Jerusalem and be tried there on these charges.*r* 21But when Paul had appealed to be kept in custody for the decision of his Imperial Majesty, I ordered him to be held until I could send him to the emperor." 22Agrippa said to Festus, "I would like to hear the man myself." "Tomorrow," he said, "you will hear him."

Paul Brought before Agrippa

23 So on the next day Agrippa and Bernice came with great pomp, and they entered the audience hall with the military tribunes and the prominent men of the city. Then Festus gave the order and Paul was brought in. 24And Festus said, "King Agrippa and all here present with us, you see this man about whom the whole Jewish community petitioned me, both in Jerusalem and here, shouting that he ought not to live any longer. 25But I found that he had done nothing deserving death; and when he appealed to his Imperial Majesty, I decided to send him. 26But I have nothing definite to write to our sovereign about him. Therefore I have brought him before all of you, and especially before you, King Agrippa, so that, after we have examined him, I may have something to write— 27for it seems to me unreasonable to send a prisoner without indicating the charges against him."

Paul Defends Himself before Agrippa

26 Agrippa said to Paul, "You have permission to speak for yourself." Then Paul stretched out his hand and began to defend himself:

2 "I consider myself fortunate that it is before you, King Agrippa, I am to make my defense today against all the accusations of the Jews, 3because you are especially familiar with all the customs and controversies of the Jews; therefore I beg of you to listen to me patiently.

4 "All the Jews know my way of life from my youth, a life spent from the beginning among my own people and in Jerusalem. 5They have known for a long time, if they are willing to testify, that I have belonged to the strictest sect of our religion and lived as a Pharisee. 6And now I stand here on trial on account of my hope in the promise made by God to our ancestors, 7a promise that our twelve tribes hope to attain, as they earnestly worship day and night. It is for this hope, your Excellency,*s* that I am accused by Jews! 8Why is it thought incredible by any of you that God raises the dead?

9 "Indeed, I myself was convinced that I ought to do many things against the name of Jesus of Nazareth.*t* 10And that is what I did in Jerusalem; with au-

---

q Other ancient authorities read *with anything*   *r* Gk *on them*   *s* Gk *O king*   *t* Gk *the Nazorean* thority received from the chief priests, I not only locked up many of the saints in prison, but I also cast my vote against them when they were being condemned to death. 11By punishing them often in all the synagogues I tried to force them to blaspheme; and since I was so furiously enraged at them, I pursued them even to foreign cities.

Paul Tells of His Conversion

12 "With this in mind, I was traveling to Damascus with the authority and commission of the chief priests, 13when at midday along the road, your Excellency,u I saw a light from heaven, brighter than the sun, shining around me and my companions. 14When we had all fallen to the ground, I heard a voice saying to me in the Hebrewv language, 'Saul, Saul, why are you persecuting me? It hurts you to kick against the goads.' 15I asked, 'Who are you, Lord?' The Lord answered, 'I am Jesus whom you are persecuting. 16But get up and stand on your feet; for I have appeared to you for this purpose, to appoint you to serve and testify to the things in which you have seen mew and to those in which I will appear to you. 17I will rescue you from your people and from the Gentiles—to whom I am sending you 18to open their eyes so that they may turn from darkness to light and from the power of Satan to God, so that they may receive forgiveness of sins and a place among those who are sanctified by faith in me.'

Paul Tells of His Preaching

19 "After that, King Agrippa, I was not disobedient to the heavenly vision, 20but declared first to those in Damascus, then in Jerusalem and throughout the countryside of Judea, and also to the Gentiles, that they should repent and turn to God and do deeds consistent with repentance. 21For this reason the Jews seized me in the temple and tried to kill me. 22To this day I have had help from God, and so I stand here, testifying to both small and great, saying nothing but what the prophets and Moses said would take place: 23that the Messiahx must suffer, and that, by being the first

to rise from the dead, he would proclaim light both to our people and to the Gentiles."

Paul Appeals to Agrippa to Believe

24 While he was making this defense, Festus exclaimed, "You are out of your mind, Paul! Too much learning is driving you insane!" 25But Paul said, "I am not out of my mind, most excellent Festus, but I am speaking the sober truth. 26Indeed the king knows about these things, and to him I speak freely; for I am certain that none of these things has escaped his notice, for this was not done in a corner. 27King Agrippa, do you believe the prophets? I know that you believe." 28Agrippa said to Paul, "Are you so quickly persuading me to become a Christian?"y 29Paul replied, "Whether

---

THERE ARE TWO KINDS OF PEOPLE IN THIS WORLD, THE CONSCIOUS DOGMATISTS AND THE UNCONSCIOUS DOGMATISTS. I HAVE ALWAYS FOUND MYSELF THAT THE UNCONSCIOUS DOGMATISTS WERE BY FAR THE MOST DOGMATIC.

—G. K. Chesterton

---

quickly or not, I pray to God that not only you but also all who are listening to me today might become such as I am—except for these chains."

30 Then the king got up, and with him the governor and Bernice and those who had been seated with them; 31and as they were leaving, they said to one another, "This man is doing nothing to deserve death or imprisonment." 32Agrippa said to Festus, "This man could have been set free if he had not appealed to the emperor."

Paul Sails for Rome

27 When it was decided that we were to sail for Italy, they transferred Paul and some other prisoners to a centurion of the Augustan Cohort, named Julius. 2Embarking on a ship of Adramyttium that was about to set sail to the ports along the coast of Asia, we put to sea, accompanied by Aristarchus, a Macedonian from Thessa-

---

u Gk O king   v That is, Aramaic   w Other ancient authorities read the things that you have seen
x Or the Christ   y Or Quickly you will persuade me to play the Christian

lonica. ³The next day we put in at Sidon; and Julius treated Paul kindly, and allowed him to go to his friends to be cared for. ⁴Putting out to sea from there, we sailed under the lee of Cyprus, because the winds were against us. ⁵After we had sailed across the sea that is off Cilicia and Pamphylia, we came to Myra in Lycia. ⁶There the centurion found an Alexandrian ship bound for Italy and put us on board. ⁷We sailed slowly for a number of days and arrived with difficulty off Cnidus, and as the wind was against us, we sailed under the lee of Crete off Salmone. ⁸Sailing past it with difficulty, we came to a place called Fair Havens, near the city of Lasea.

9 Since much time had been lost and sailing was now dangerous, because even the Fast had already gone by, Paul advised them, ¹⁰saying, "Sirs, I can see that the voyage will be with danger and much heavy loss, not only of the cargo and the ship, but also of our lives." ¹¹But the centurion paid more attention to the pilot and to the owner of the ship than to what Paul said. ¹²Since the harbor was not suitable for spending the winter, the majority was in favor of putting to sea from there, on the chance that somehow they could reach Phoenix, where they could spend the winter. It was a harbor of Crete, facing southwest and northwest.

The Storm at Sea

13 When a moderate south wind began to blow, they thought they could achieve their purpose; so they weighed anchor and began to sail past Crete, close to the shore. ¹⁴But soon a violent wind, called the northeaster, rushed down from Crete.ᶻ ¹⁵Since the ship was caught and could not be turned head-on into the wind, we gave way to it and were driven. ¹⁶By running under the lee of a small island called Caudaᵃ we were scarcely able to get the ship's boat under control. ¹⁷After hoisting it up they took measuresᵇ to undergird the ship; then, fearing that they would run on the Syrtis, they lowered the sea anchor and so were driven. ¹⁸We were being pounded by the storm so violently that on the

next day they began to throw the cargo overboard, ¹⁹and on the third day with their own hands they threw the ship's tackle overboard. ²⁰When neither sun nor stars appeared for many days, and no small tempest raged, all hope of our being saved was at last abandoned.

21 Since they had been without food for a long time, Paul then stood up among them and said, "Men, you should have listened to me and not have set sail from Crete and thereby avoided this damage and loss. ²²I urge you now to keep up your courage, for there will be no loss of life among you, but only of the ship. ²³For last night there stood by me an angel of the God to whom I belong and whom I worship, ²⁴and he said, 'Do not be afraid, Paul; you must stand before the emperor; and indeed, God has granted safety to all those who are sailing with you.' ²⁵So keep up your courage, men, for I have faith in God that it will be exactly as I have been told. ²⁶But we will have to run aground on some island."

27 When the fourteenth night had come, as we were drifting across the sea of Adria, about midnight the sailors suspected that they were nearing land. ²⁸So they took soundings and found twenty fathoms; a little farther on they took soundings again and found fifteen fathoms. ²⁹Fearing that we might run on the rocks, they let down four anchors from the stern and prayed for day to come. ³⁰But when the sailors tried to escape from the ship and had lowered the boat into the sea, on the pretext of putting out anchors from the bow, ³¹Paul said to the centurion and the soldiers, "Unless these men stay in the ship, you cannot be saved." ³²Then the soldiers cut away the ropes of the boat and set it adrift.

33 Just before daybreak, Paul urged all of them to take some food, saying, "Today is the fourteenth day that you have been in suspense and remaining without food, having eaten nothing. ³⁴Therefore I urge you to take some food, for it will help you survive; for none of you will lose a hair from your heads." ³⁵After he had said this, he took bread; and giving thanks to God in the presence of all, he broke it and began to

---

z Gk it   a Other ancient authorities read *Clauda*   b Gk *helps*

THE MINISTER IN HIS STUDY
W. W. Staley

VERSE: Acts 27.23–24   **PASSAGE:** Acts 27.1–42

 mighty host surrounds me in my library. Peter, James, and John did not see as much nor hear as much as the minister in his library. Jesus is here too, in the Bible and by the Spirit. There are more people in my library than in my church. They speak to me; they kindle the fires of my imagination; they quicken my faith, humble my pride, rebuke my wrong-doing and wrong-thinking, warn me against sin, and point my soul to the living Christ. I find tombs with angels, deserts with fountains, gardens with Saviors, prisons with praises, and crosses with crowns. Above the roar of the tempest, the flap of the split sails, the creak of the breaking timbers, and the cry of endangered men, I hear Jesus say, "Peace! Be still" (Mark 4.39). I hear Nebuchadnezzar say, "I see four men unbound, walking in the middle of the fire, and they are not hurt; and the fourth has the appearance of a god" (Daniel 3.25). I hear Paul, in the midst of darkness and the raging sea, say, "Last night there stood by me an angel of the God to whom I belong and whom I worship, and he said, 'Do not be afraid'" (Acts 27.23–24). The past is a mighty host, their thought, faith, love, and lives still speaking to our own.

The library is a transfiguration scene, crowning lofty summits, silently and sweetly speaking to the minister so as to inspire him with renewed strength and satisfaction that arms him for the good fight of faith. Beyond this teeming past are the living millions moving to and fro, loving and hating, helping and hindering, neglecting age, crushing childhood, desecrating the Sabbath, greedily preying upon their fellows, preparing for war, and killing the flower of age . . . The minister should seek to interpret the present age in the light of the Gospel and past civilizations. From his study as a tower, he should get his vision of mankind and God, and then go forth to preach salvation to a sinning world. His sermon should be a message from God, supported by His word, fired by His Spirit, and delivered in the spirit of love.

ADDITIONAL SCRIPTURE READING:
Matthew 28.19; Ephesians 4.11–16

Go to page 1318 for your next devotional reading.

1900   Present

eat. 36Then all of them were encouraged and took food for themselves. 37(We were in all two hundred seventy-six*c* persons in the ship.) 38After they had satisfied their hunger, they lightened the ship by throwing the wheat into the sea.

The Shipwreck

39 In the morning they did not recognize the land, but they noticed a bay with a beach, on which they planned to run the ship ashore, if they could. 40So they cast off the anchors and left them in the sea. At the same time they loosened the ropes that tied the steering-oars; then hoisting the foresail to the wind, they made for the beach. 41But striking a reef,*d* they ran the ship aground; the bow stuck and remained immovable, but the stern was being broken up by the force of the waves. 42The soldiers' plan was to kill the prisoners, so that none might swim away and escape; 43but the centurion, wishing to save Paul, kept them from carrying out their plan. He ordered those who could swim to jump overboard first and make for the land, 44and the rest to follow, some on planks and others on pieces of the ship. And so it was that all were brought safely to land.

Paul on the Island of Malta

28 After we had reached safety, we then learned that the island was called Malta. 2The natives showed us unusual kindness. Since it had begun to rain and was cold, they kindled a fire and welcomed all of us around it. 3Paul had gathered a bundle of brushwood and was putting it on the fire, when a viper, driven out by the heat, fastened itself on his hand. 4When the natives saw the creature hanging from his hand, they said to one another, "This man must be a murderer; though he has escaped from the sea, justice has not allowed him to live." 5He, however, shook off the creature into the fire and suffered no harm. 6They were expecting him to swell up or drop dead, but after they had waited a long time and saw that nothing unusual had happened to

him, they changed their minds and began to say that he was a god.

7 Now in the neighborhood of that place were lands belonging to the leading man of the island, named Publius, who received us and entertained us hospitably for three days. 8It so happened that the father of Publius lay sick in bed with fever and dysentery. Paul visited him and cured him by praying and putting his hands on him. 9After this happened, the rest of the people on the island who had diseases also came and were cured. 10They bestowed many honors on us, and when we were about to sail, they put on board all the provisions we needed.

Paul Arrives at Rome

11 Three months later we set sail on a ship that had wintered at the island, an Alexandrian ship with the Twin Brothers as its figurehead. 12We put in at Syracuse and stayed there for three days; 13then we weighed anchor and came to Rhegium. After one day there a south wind sprang up, and on the second day we came to Puteoli. 14There we found believers*e* and were invited to stay with them for seven days. And so we came to Rome. 15The believers*e* from there, when they heard of us, came as far as the Forum of Appius and Three Taverns to meet us. On seeing them, Paul thanked God and took courage.

16 When we came into Rome, Paul was allowed to live by himself, with the soldier who was guarding him.

Paul and Jewish Leaders in Rome

17 Three days later he called together the local leaders of the Jews. When they had assembled, he said to them, "Brothers, though I had done nothing against our people or the customs of our ancestors, yet I was arrested in Jerusalem and handed over to the Romans. 18When they had examined me, the Romans*f* wanted to release me, because there was no reason for the death penalty in my case. 19But when the Jews objected, I was compelled to appeal to the emperor—even though I had no charge to bring against my nation. 20For this reason

---

c Other ancient authorities read *seventy-six;* others, *about seventy-six*   *d* Gk *place of two seas*
e Gk *brothers*   *f* Gk *they*

therefore I have asked to see you and speak with you,g since it is for the sake of the hope of Israel that I am bound with this chain." 21They replied, "We have received no letters from Judea about you, and none of the brothers coming here has reported or spoken anything evil about you. 22But we would like to hear from you what you think, for with regard to this sect we know that everywhere it is spoken against."

Paul Preaches in Rome

23 After they had set a day to meet with him, they came to him at his lodgings in great numbers. From morning until evening he explained the matter to them, testifying to the kingdom of God and trying to convince them about Jesus both from the law of Moses and from the prophets. 24Some were convinced by what he had said, while others refused to believe. 25So they disagreed with each other; and as they were leaving, Paul made one further statement: "The Holy Spirit was right in saying to your ancestors through the prophet Isaiah,

26 'Go to this people and say,
      You will indeed listen, but never
         understand,
      and you will indeed look, but
         never perceive.
27 For this people's heart has grown
         dull,
      and their ears are hard of hearing,
      and they have shut their eyes;
      so that they might not look
         with their eyes,
      and listen with their ears,
      and understand with their heart
         and turn—
      and I would heal them.'
28Let it be known to you then that this salvation of God has been sent to the Gentiles; they will listen."h

30 He lived there two whole years at his own expensei and welcomed all who came to him, 31proclaiming the kingdom of God and teaching about the Lord Jesus Christ with all boldness and without hindrance.

---

g Or I have asked you to see me and speak with me when he had said these words, the Jews departed, arguing vigorously among themselves   h Other ancient authorities add verse 29, And own hired dwelling   i Or in his

ROMANS

HE BOOK OF ROMANS OFFERS SOME OF THE MOST LIVELY TEACHING ON FAITH AND LIFE EVER RECORDED. IN THIS LETTER PAUL TELLS OF GOD'S WONDERFUL PLAN FOR REDEEMING HIS PEOPLE AND SETTING THEM FREE FOR SERVICE THROUGH THE POWER OF HIS SPIRIT. AS YOU READ ABOUT THE RICHES OF GOD'S GRACE, BE COMFORTED THAT NOTHING "WILL BE ABLE TO SEPARATE US FROM THE LOVE OF GOD IN CHRIST JESUS OUR LORD" (8.39). THEN RESPOND TO HIS LOVE WITH A TRANSFORMED LIFE OF SERVICE.

Salutation

1 Paul, a servant*a* of Jesus Christ, called to be an apostle, set apart for the gospel of God, 2which he promised beforehand through his prophets in the holy scriptures, 3the gospel concerning his Son, who was descended from David according to the flesh 4and was declared to be Son of God with power according to the spirit*b* of holiness by resurrection from the dead, Jesus Christ our Lord, 5through whom we have received grace and apostleship to bring about the obedience of faith among all the Gentiles for the sake of his name, 6including yourselves who are called to belong to Jesus Christ,

7 To all God's beloved in Rome, who are called to be saints:

Grace to you and peace from God our Father and the Lord Jesus Christ.

Prayer of Thanksgiving

8 First, I thank my God through Jesus Christ for all of you, because your faith is proclaimed throughout the world. 9For God, whom I serve with my spirit by announcing the gospel*c* of his Son, is my witness that without ceasing I remember you always in my prayers, 10asking that by God's will I may somehow at last succeed in coming to you. 11For I am longing to see you so that I may share with you some spiritual gift to strengthen you— 12or rather so that we may be mutually encouraged by each

a Gk *slave*   *b* Or *Spirit*   *c* Gk *my spirit in the gospel*

THE IMPEACHMENT OF ST. PAUL

C. S. Lewis

VERSE: Romans 1.1–2   PASSAGE: Romans 1.1–7

 most astonishing misconception has long dominated the modern mind on the subject of St. Paul. It is to this effect: that Jesus preached a kindly and simple religion (found in the gospels) and that St. Paul afterwards corrupted it into a cruel and complicated religion (found in the epistles). This is really quite untenable. All the most terrifying texts came from the mouth of our Lord: all the texts on which we can base such warrant as we have for hoping that all men will be saved come from St. Paul . . . There is no real evidence for a pre-Pauline doctrine different from St. Paul's. The epistles are, for the most part, the earliest Christian documents we possess. The gospels come later. They are not "the gospel," the statement of the Christian belief. They were written for those who had already been converted, who had already accepted "the gospel." They leave out many of the "complications" (that is, the theology) because they are intended for readers who have already been instructed in it. In that sense the epistles are more primitive and more central than the gospels—though not, of course, than the great events which the gospels recount . . . In the earlier history of every rebellion there is a stage at which you do not yet attack the King in person. You say: "The King is all right. It is his ministers who are wrong. They misrepresent him and corrupt all his plans—which, I'm sure, are good plans if only the ministers would let them take effect." And the first victory consists in beheading a few ministers: only at a later stage do you go on and behead the King himself. In the same way, the nineteenth-century attack on St. Paul was really only a stage in the revolt against Christ . . . It was unfortunate that [the attack] could not impress anyone who had really read the gospels and the epistles with attention: but apparently few people had, and so the first victory was won. St. Paul was impeached and banished and the world went on to the next step—the attack on the King himself.

ADDITIONAL SCRIPTURE READING:
Psalm 14.1–5; Acts 9.1–19

Go to page 1320 for your next devotional reading.

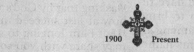

1900   Present

other's faith, both yours and mine. 13I want you to know, brothers and sisters,*d* that I have often intended to come to you (but thus far have been prevented), in order that I may reap some harvest among you as I have among the rest of the Gentiles. 14I am a debtor both to Greeks and to barbarians, both to the wise and to the foolish 15— hence my eagerness to proclaim the gospel to you also who are in Rome.

The Power of the Gospel

16 For I am not ashamed of the gospel; it is the power of God for salvation to everyone who has faith, to the Jew first and also to the Greek. 17For in it the righteousness of God is revealed through faith for faith; as it is written, "The one who is righteous will live by faith."*e*

The Guilt of Humankind

18 For the wrath of God is revealed from heaven against all ungodliness and wickedness of those who by their wickedness suppress the truth. 19For what can be known about God is plain to them, because God has shown it to them. 20Ever since the creation of the world his eternal power and divine nature, invisible though they are, have been understood and seen through the things he has made. So they are without excuse; 21for though they knew God,

---

REALLY, A YOUNG ATHEIST CANNOT GUARD HIS FAITH TOO CAREFULLY.   —*C. S. Lewis*

---

they did not honor him as God or give thanks to him, but they became futile in their thinking, and their senseless minds were darkened. 22Claiming to be wise, they became fools; 23and they exchanged the glory of the immortal God for images resembling a mortal human being or birds or four-footed animals or reptiles.

24 Therefore God gave them up in the lusts of their hearts to impurity, to the degrading of their bodies among themselves, 25because they exchanged the truth about God for a lie and worshiped

and served the creature rather than the Creator, who is blessed forever! Amen.

26 For this reason God gave them up to degrading passions. Their women exchanged natural intercourse for unnatural, 27and in the same way also the men, giving up natural intercourse with women, were consumed with passion for one another. Men committed shameless acts with men and received in their own persons the due penalty for their error.

28 And since they did not see fit to acknowledge God, God gave them up to a debased mind and to things that should not be done. 29They were filled with every kind of wickedness, evil, covetousness, malice. Full of envy, murder, strife, deceit, craftiness, they are gossips, 30slanderers, God-haters,*f* insolent, haughty, boastful, inventors of evil, rebellious toward parents, 31foolish, faithless, heartless, ruthless. 32They know God's decree, that those who practice such things deserve to die—yet they not only do them but even applaud others who practice them.

The Righteous Judgment of God

2 Therefore you have no excuse, whoever you are, when you judge others; for in passing judgment on another you condemn yourself, because you, the judge, are doing the very same things. 2You say,*g* "We know that God's judgment on those who do such things is in accordance with truth." 3Do you imagine, whoever you are, that when you judge those who do such things and yet do them yourself, you will escape the judgment of God? 4Or do you despise the riches of his kindness and forbearance and patience? Do you not realize that God's kindness is meant to lead you to repentance? 5But by your hard and impenitent heart you are storing up wrath for yourself on the day of wrath, when God's righteous judgment will be revealed. 6For he will repay according to each one's deeds: 7to those who by patiently doing good seek for glory and honor and immortality, he will give eternal life; 8while for those who are self-seeking and who obey not the truth but wickedness, there will be wrath and

---

d Gk *brothers*   *e* Or *The one who is righteous through faith will live*   *f* Or *God-hated*
g Gk lacks *You say*

WEEKEND

St. Paul
Thomas Merton

VERSE: Acts 9.3–4   PASSAGE: Acts 9.1–16

hen I was Saul, and sat among the cloaks,
My eyes were stones, I saw no sight of heaven
Open to take the spirit of the twisting Stephen.
When I was Saul, and sat among the rocks,
I locked my eyes, and made my brain my tomb,
Sealed with what boulders rolled across my reason!

When I was Saul and walked upon the blazing desert
My road was quiet as a trap.
I feared what word would split high noon with light
And lock my life, and try to drive me mad:
And thus I saw the Voice that struck me dead.

Tie up my breath, and wind me in white sheets of
　　　　　anguish,
And lay me in my three days' sepulchre
Until I find my Easter in a vision.

Oh Christ! Give back my life, go, cross Damascus,
Find out my Ananias in that other room:
Command him, as you do, in this my dream;
He knows my locks, and owns my ransom,
Waits for Your word to take his keys and come.

Additional Scripture Reading:
Acts 7.54—8.1; Philippians 1.21–24

Go to page 1323 for your next devotional reading.

1900　　　Present

fury. 9There will be anguish and distress for everyone who does evil, the Jew first and also the Greek, 10but glory and honor and peace for everyone who does good, the Jew first and also the Greek. 11For God shows no partiality.

12 All who have sinned apart from the law will also perish apart from the law, and all who have sinned under the law will be judged by the law. 13For it is not the hearers of the law who are righteous in God's sight, but the doers of the law who will be justified. 14When Gentiles, who do not possess the law, do instinctively what the law requires, these, though not having the law, are a law to themselves. 15They show that what the law requires is written on their hearts, to which their own conscience also bears witness; and their conflicting thoughts will accuse or perhaps excuse them 16on the day when, according to my gospel, God, through Jesus Christ, will judge the secret thoughts of all.

The Jews and the Law

17 But if you call yourself a Jew and rely on the law and boast of your relation to God 18and know his will and determine what is best because you are instructed in the law, 19and if you are sure that you are a guide to the blind, a light to those who are in darkness, 20a corrector of the foolish, a teacher of children, having in the law the embodiment of knowledge and truth, 21you, then, that teach others, will you not teach yourself? While you preach against stealing, do you steal? 22You that forbid adultery, do you commit adultery? You that abhor idols, do you rob temples? 23You that boast in the law, do you dishonor God by breaking the law? 24For, as it is written, "The name of God is blasphemed among the Gentiles because of you."

25 Circumcision indeed is of value if you obey the law; but if you break the law, your circumcision has become uncircumcision. 26So, if those who are uncircumcised keep the requirements of the law, will not their uncircumcision be regarded as circumcision? 27Then those who are physically uncircumcised but keep the law will condemn you that have the written code and circumcision but break the law. 28For a person is not a Jew who is one outwardly, nor is true circumcision something external and physical. 29Rather, a person is a Jew who is one inwardly, and real circumcision is a matter of the heart—it is spiritual and not literal. Such a person receives praise not from others but from God.

3 Then what advantage has the Jew? Or what is the value of circumcision? 2Much, in every way. For in the first place the Jews*h* were entrusted with the oracles of God. 3What if some were unfaithful? Will their faithlessness nullify the faithfulness of God? 4By no means! Although everyone is a liar, let God be proved true, as it is written,

"So that you may be justified in
    your words,
  and prevail in your judging."*i*

5But if our injustice serves to confirm the justice of God, what should we say? That God is unjust to inflict wrath on us? (I speak in a human way.) 6By no means! For then how could God judge the world? 7But if through my falsehood God's truthfulness abounds to his glory, why am I still being condemned as a sinner? 8And why not say (as some people slander us by saying that we say), "Let us do evil so that good may come"? Their condemnation is deserved!

None Is Righteous

9 What then? Are we any better off?*j* No, not at all; for we have already charged that all, both Jews and Greeks, are under the power of sin, 10as it is written:

"There is no one who is righteous,
    not even one;
11   there is no one who has
      understanding,
    there is no one who seeks God.
12   All have turned aside, together
      they have become worthless;
    there is no one who shows
      kindness,
    there is not even one."
13   "Their throats are opened graves;
    they use their tongues to
      deceive."
   "The venom of vipers is under
    their lips."
14   "Their mouths are full of cursing
      and bitterness."

---

h Gk they   *i* Gk when you are being judged   *j* Or at any disadvantage?

15 "Their feet are swift to shed blood;
16   ruin and misery are in their
         paths,
17   and the way of peace they have not
         known."
18   "There is no fear of God before
         their eyes."

19 Now we know that whatever the law says, it speaks to those who are under the law, so that every mouth may be silenced, and the whole world may be held accountable to God. 20For "no human being will be justified in his sight" by deeds prescribed by the law, for through the law comes the knowledge of sin.

Righteousness through Faith

21 But now, apart from law, the righteousness of God has been disclosed, and is attested by the law and the prophets, 22the righteousness of God through faith in Jesus Christ[k] for all who believe. For there is no distinction, 23since all have sinned and fall short of the glory of God; 24they are now justified by his grace as a gift, through the redemption that is in Christ Jesus, 25whom God put forward as a sacrifice of atonement[l] by his blood, effective through faith. He did this to show his righteousness, because in his divine forbearance he had passed over the sins previously committed; 26it was to prove at the present time that he himself is righteous and that he justifies the one who has faith in Jesus.[m]

27 Then what becomes of boasting? It is excluded. By what law? By that of works? No, but by the law of faith. 28For we hold that a person is justified by faith apart from works prescribed by the law. 29Or is God the God of Jews only? Is he not the God of Gentiles also? Yes, of Gentiles also, 30since God is one; and he will justify the circumcised on the ground of faith and the uncircumcised through that same faith. 31Do we then overthrow the law by this faith? By no means! On the contrary, we uphold the law.

The Example of Abraham

4 What then are we to say was gained by[n] Abraham, our ancestor according to the flesh? 2For if Abraham was justified by works, he has

something to boast about, but not before God. 3For what does the scripture say? "Abraham believed God, and it was reckoned to him as righteousness." 4Now to one who works, wages are not reckoned as a gift but as something due. 5But to one who without works trusts him who justifies the ungodly, such faith is reckoned as righteousness. 6So also David speaks of the blessedness of those to whom God reckons righteousness apart from works:
7   "Blessed are those whose iniquities
         are forgiven,
      and whose sins are covered;
8   blessed is the one against whom
         the Lord will not reckon
         sin."

9 Is this blessedness, then, pronounced only on the circumcised, or also on the uncircumcised? We say, "Faith was reckoned to Abraham as righteousness." 10How then was it reckoned to him? Was it before or after he had been circumcised? It was not after, but before he was circumcised. 11He received the sign of circumcision as a seal of the righteousness that he had by faith while he was still uncircumcised. The purpose was to make him the ancestor of all who believe without being circumcised and who thus have righteousness reckoned to them, 12and likewise the ancestor of the circumcised who are not only circumcised but who also follow the example of the faith that our ancestor Abraham had before he was circumcised.

God's Promise Realized through Faith

13 For the promise that he would inherit the world did not come to Abraham or to his descendants through the law but through the righteousness of faith. 14If it is the adherents of the law who are to be the heirs, faith is null and the promise is void. 15For the law brings wrath; but where there is no law, neither is there violation.

16 For this reason it depends on faith, in order that the promise may rest on grace and be guaranteed to all his descendants, not only to the adherents of the

k Or through the faith of Jesus Christ   l Or a place of atonement   m Or who has the faith of Jesus
n Other ancient authorities read say about

law but also to those who share the faith of Abraham (for he is the father of all of us, [17]as it is written, "I have made you the father of many nations")—in the presence of the God in whom he believed, who gives life to the dead and calls into existence the things that do not exist. [18]Hoping against hope, he believed

MONDAY

GOD'S JUSTICE AND HUMAN SIGNIFICANCE
Francis Schaeffer

VERSE: Romans 3.26   **PASSAGE:** Romans 3.21–26

f there is true moral guilt in the presence of a personal God (rather than a metaphysical intrinsic situation of what is and always has been), then perhaps there will be a solution from God's side. And God says to man that there is a solution. That solution rests upon God saying that he is holy and he is love, and in his love he has loved the world, and he sent his son. Now in history, there on Calvary's cross, in space and time, Jesus died. And we should never speak of Jesus' death without linking it to his person. This is the eternal Second Person of the Trinity. When he died, with the division that man has caused by his revolt now carried up into the Trinity itself, there in expiation, in propitiation and substitution, the true moral guilt is met by the *infinite* value of Jesus' death. Thus Jesus says: "It is finished" (John 19.30).

Romans 3.26 is a verse that we tend to pass by too quickly in the midst of the structure of the first three chapters of Romans. These chapters tell us first why man is lost, and then the solution in the propitiatory death of Jesus Christ. At this point Paul can say: "that he himself might be just and *yet* (the force of the Greek construction) the justifier of him who has faith in Jesus." On the one hand, because of the infinite value of Christ's holy death, God does not have to surrender his absolute holy character; and on the other, he does not have to violate man's significance in order for him to be able to pardon guilt and restore man's broken relationship to himself. This is the very opposite of the denial of antithesis and significance in modern man's leap into the dark, which says that somehow we must believe, without reason, that God is love. A moral absolute remains, and yet there is a solution to man's dilemma.

ADDITIONAL SCRIPTURE READING:
Matthew 27.50–54; 1 John 4.8–10

Go to page 1326 for your next devotional reading.

1900   Present

that he would become "the father of many nations," according to what was said, "So numerous shall your descendants be."* 19He did not weaken in faith when he considered his own body, which was already*o* as good as dead (for he was about a hundred years old), or when he considered the barrenness of Sarah's womb. 20No distrust made him waver concerning the promise of God, but he grew strong in his faith as he gave glory to God, 21being fully convinced that God was able to do what he had promised. 22Therefore his faith*p* "was reckoned to him as righteousness." 23Now the words, "it was reckoned to him," were written not for his sake alone, 24but for ours also. It will be reckoned to us who believe in him who raised Jesus our Lord from the dead, 25who was handed over to death for our trespasses and was raised for our justification.

Results of Justification

5 Therefore, since we are justified by faith, we*q* have peace with God through our Lord Jesus Christ, 2through whom we have obtained access*r* to this grace in which we stand; and we*s* boast in our hope of sharing the glory of God. 3And not only that, but we*s* also boast in our sufferings, knowing that suffering produces endurance, 4and endurance produces character, and character produces hope, 5and hope does not disappoint us, because God's love has been poured into our hearts through the Holy Spirit that has been given to us.

WE ARE ALWAYS IN THE FORGE, OR ON THE ANVIL; BY TRIALS GOD IS SHAPING US FOR HIGHER THINGS. —*Henry Ward Beecher*

---

6 For while we were still weak, at the right time Christ died for the ungodly. 7Indeed, rarely will anyone die for a righteous person—though perhaps for a good person someone might actually dare to die. 8But God proves his love for us in that while we still were sinners Christ died for us. 9Much more surely then, now that we have been justified by his blood, will we be saved through him from the wrath of God.*t* 10For if while we were enemies, we were reconciled to God through the death of his Son, much more surely, having been reconciled, will we be saved by his life. 11But more than that, we even boast in God through our Lord Jesus Christ, through whom we have now received reconciliation.

Adam and Christ

12 Therefore, just as sin came into the world through one man, and death came through sin, and so death spread to all because all have sinned— 13sin was indeed in the world before the law, but sin is not reckoned when there is no law. 14Yet death exercised dominion from Adam to Moses, even over those whose sins were not like the transgression of Adam, who is a type of the one who was to come.

15 But the free gift is not like the trespass. For if the many died through the one man's trespass, much more surely have the grace of God and the free gift in the grace of the one man, Jesus Christ, abounded for the many. 16And the free gift is not like the effect of the one man's sin. For the judgment following one trespass brought condemnation, but the free gift following many trespasses brings justification. 17If, because of the one man's trespass, death exercised dominion through that one, much more surely will those who receive the abundance of grace and the free gift of righteousness exercise dominion in life through the one man, Jesus Christ.

18 Therefore just as one man's trespass led to condemnation for all, so one man's act of righteousness leads to justification and life for all. 19For just as by the one man's disobedience the many were made sinners, so by the one man's obedience the many will be made righteous. 20But law came in, with the result that the trespass multiplied; but where sin increased, grace abounded all the more, 21so that, just as sin exercised dominion in death, so grace might also exercise dominion through justification*u* leading to eternal life through Jesus Christ our Lord.

---

o Other ancient authorities lack *already* p Gk *Therefore it* q Other ancient authorities read *let us*
r Other ancient authorities add *by faith* s Or *let us* t Gk *the wrath* u Or *righteousness*

Dying and Rising with Christ

6 What then are we to say? Should we continue in sin in order that grace may abound? 2By no means! How can we who died to sin go on living in it? 3Do you not know that all of us who have been baptized into Christ Jesus were baptized into his death? 4Therefore we have been buried with him by baptism into death, so that, just as Christ was raised from the dead by the glory of the Father, so we too might walk in newness of life.

5 For if we have been united with him in a death like his, we will certainly be united with him in a resurrection like his. 6We know that our old self was crucified with him so that the body of sin might be destroyed, and we might no longer be enslaved to sin. 7For whoever has died is freed from sin. 8But if we have died with Christ, we believe that we will also live with him. 9We know that Christ, being raised from the dead, will never die again; death no longer has dominion over him. 10The death he died, he died to sin, once for all; but the life he lives, he lives to God. 11So you also must consider yourselves dead to sin and alive to God in Christ Jesus.

12 Therefore, do not let sin exercise dominion in your mortal bodies, to make you obey their passions. 13No longer present your members to sin as instruments[v] of wickedness, but present yourselves to God as those who have been brought from death to life, and present your members to God as instruments[v] of righteousness. 14For sin will have no dominion over you, since you are not under law but under grace.

Slaves of Righteousness

15 What then? Should we sin because we are not under law but under grace? By no means! 16Do you not know that if you present yourselves to anyone as obedient slaves, you are slaves of the one whom you obey, either of sin, which leads to death, or of obedience, which leads to righteousness? 17But thanks be to God that you, having once been slaves of sin, have become obedient from the heart to the form of teaching to which you were entrusted, 18and that you, having been set free from sin, have become

---

WHAT CAN I GIVE HIM,
  POOR AS I AM?
IF I WERE A SHEPHERD,
  I WOULD BRING A LAMB;
IF I WERE A WISE MAN,
  I WOULD DO MY PART;
YET WHAT I CAN I GIVE HIM—
  GIVE MY HEART.   —*Christina Georgina Rossetti*

---

slaves of righteousness. 19I am speaking in human terms because of your natural limitations.[w] For just as you once presented your members as slaves to impurity and to greater and greater iniquity, so now present your members as slaves to righteousness for sanctification.

20 When you were slaves of sin, you were free in regard to righteousness. 21So what advantage did you then get from the things of which you now are ashamed? The end of those things is death. 22But now that you have been freed from sin and enslaved to God, the advantage you get is sanctification. The end is eternal life. 23For the wages of sin is death, but the free gift of God is eternal life in Christ Jesus our Lord.

An Analogy from Marriage

7 Do you not know, brothers and sisters[x]—for I am speaking to those who know the law—that the law is binding on a person only during that person's lifetime? 2Thus a married woman is bound by the law to her husband as long as he lives; but if her husband dies, she is discharged from the law concerning the husband. 3Accordingly, she will be called an adulteress if she lives with another man while her husband is alive. But if her husband dies, she is free from that law, and if she marries another man, she is not an adulteress.

4 In the same way, my friends,[x] you have died to the law through the body of Christ, so that you may belong to another, to him who has been raised from the dead in order that we may bear fruit for God. 5While we were living in the flesh,

---

v Or *weapons*   w Gk *the weakness of your flesh*   x Gk *brothers*

A CIVIL WAR WITHIN THE SELF
E. Stanley Jones

VERSE: Romans 7.19   **PASSAGE:** Romans 7.7–25

 nto the conscious mind is introduced by conversion a new sense of conscious cleanness, a new loyalty, a new love. This introduction is so real, so satisfying, so conduct-determining, that the converted think the battle is over, that life is now to be one glad song of victory. Those honeymoon days come to an end, usually within a year. The subconscious urges, which have been laying low, apparently stunned into insensibility by the introduction of this new and different and authoritative life in the conscious mind, now begin to reassert themselves. Tempers, moods, fears, resentments, which we thought were gone forever, now lift their heads from the storm cellars of the subconscious, and the struggle between the conscious and the subconscious ensues. Paul calls it the war between "spirit" and "flesh" . . .

Many take it for granted that this stalemate is the best that the Christian faith offers. So they settle down to the state of being canceled out by this inevitable conflict. The seventh chapter of Romans is their escape and their excuse—Paul had this conflict, why shouldn't we? If the seventh of Romans were the only gospel Paul had to preach we would never have heard of him again. But the seventh of Romans is pre-Christian and sub-Christian—a man under the law fighting with sin in the subconscious with no resources of Christ at his disposal. It depicts the whole world experience without Christ. Does the Christian faith provide a way out of this dilemma? It can only if it provides for the conversion of the subconscious, and it does provide for just that. The area of the work of the Holy Spirit is largely, if not entirely, in the subconscious. He who made the subconscious has made plans for its redemption, its conversion, its sanctification. What kind of Creator would he have been if he had created the subconscious and then had not provided for its redemption in case evil should invade it?

ADDITIONAL SCRIPTURE READING:
Galatians 5.13–18; James 1.13–15

Go to page 1328 for your next devotional reading.

1900   Present

our sinful passions, aroused by the law, were at work in our members to bear fruit for death. 6But now we are discharged from the law, dead to that which held us captive, so that we are slaves not under the old written code but in the new life of the Spirit.

The Law and Sin

7 What then should we say? That the law is sin? By no means! Yet, if it had not been for the law, I would not have known sin. I would not have known what it is to covet if the law had not said, "You shall not covet." 8But sin, seizing an opportunity in the commandment, produced in me all kinds of covetousness. Apart from the law sin lies dead. 9I was once alive apart from the law, but when the commandment came, sin revived 10and I died, and the very commandment that promised life proved to be death to me. 11For sin, seizing an opportunity in the commandment, deceived me and through it killed me. 12So the law is holy, and the commandment is holy and just and good.

13 Did what is good, then, bring death to me? By no means! It was sin, working death in me through what is good, in order that sin might be shown to be sin, and through the commandment might become sinful beyond measure.

The Inner Conflict

14 For we know that the law is spiritual; but I am of the flesh, sold into slavery under sin.y 15I do not understand my own actions. For I do not do what I want, but I do the very thing I hate. 16Now if I do what I do not want, I agree that the law is good. 17But in fact it is no longer I that do it, but sin that dwells within me. 18For I know that nothing good dwells within me, that is, in my flesh. I can will what is right, but I cannot do it. 19For I do not do the good I want, but the evil I do not want is what I do. 20Now if I do what I do not want, it is no longer I that do it, but sin that dwells within me.

21 So I find it to be a law that when I want to do what is good, evil lies close at hand. 22For I delight in the law of God in

my inmost self, 23but I see in my members another law at war with the law of my mind, making me captive to the law of sin that dwells in my members. 24Wretched man that I am! Who will rescue me from this body of death? 25Thanks be to God through Jesus Christ our Lord!

So then, with my mind I am a slave to the law of God, but with my flesh I am a slave to the law of sin.

Life in the Spirit

8 There is therefore now no condemnation for those who are in Christ Jesus. 2For the law of the Spiritz of life in Christ Jesus has set youa free from the law of sin and of death. 3For God has done what the law, weakened by the flesh, could not do: by sending his own Son in the likeness of sinful flesh, and to deal with sin,b he condemned sin in the flesh, 4so that the just requirement of the law might be fulfilled in us, who walk not according to the flesh but according to the Spirit.z 5For those who live according to the flesh set their minds on the things of the flesh, but those who live according to the Spiritz set their minds on the things of the Spirit.z 6To set the mind on the flesh is death, but to set the mind on the Spiritz is life and peace. 7For this reason the mind that is set on the flesh is hostile to God; it does not submit to God's law— indeed it cannot, 8and those who are in the flesh cannot please God.

9 But you are not in the flesh; you are in the Spirit,z since the Spirit of God dwells in you. Anyone who does not have the Spirit of Christ does not belong to him. 10But if Christ is in you, though the body is dead because of sin, the Spiritz is life because of righteousness. 11If the Spirit of him who raised Jesus from the dead dwells in you, he who raised Christc from the dead will give life to your mortal bodies also throughd his Spirit that dwells in you.

12 So then, brothers and sisters,e we are debtors, not to the flesh, to live according to the flesh— 13for if you live according to the flesh, you will die; but if by

the Spirit you put to death the deeds of the body, you will live. **14**For all who are led by the Spirit of God are children of God. **15**For you did not receive a spirit of slavery to fall back into fear, but you have received a spirit of adoption. When we cry, "Abba!*f* Father!" **16**it is that very Spirit bearing witness*g* with our spirit that we are children of God, **17**and if children, then heirs, heirs of God and joint

f Aramaic for *Father*   *g* Or *15a spirit of adoption, by which we cry, "Abba! Father!"* *16The Spirit itself bears witness*

WEDNESDAY

FROM ASLEEP IN JESUS
Abraham Kuyper

VERSE: Romans 8.29   PASSAGE: Romans 8.28–34

o one on earth has ever fathomed his own being. Until we die we remain to ourselves the *deepest* mystery.

But this then is the glory that awaits us after dying—that the veil will be taken away from our face, and as in a clear mirror God will show us our own being (see 1 Corinthians 13.12).

Then only. Not before.

And herein is grace. If here on earth we were ever to have a sight of our own being as we actually are, we would be terrified at ourselves. Even as the loving wife, hastening to the hospital to see her husband who had been wounded on the field of battle—when she saw his misshapen, bandaged face, involuntarily recoiled; so would our soul shrink back from ourselves if we were to see in clearness our own being soiled by sin and enwound by grace.

And therefore Jesus tarries. And he will only let you see yourself when the latest trace of sin is gone and the last bandage has been removed and you can see yourself as a model of Christ's redeeming love, altogether sound and altogether healed.

Then the mystery of your person falls away from before you.

And God who *alone* knows your being, because he himself has foreordained and created you and has kept you and has restored you, will then discover you to yourself, reveal your own being to you and in your own being, *for God's sake,* make you rich.

ADDITIONAL SCRIPTURE READING:
Galatians 4.1–6; Ephesians 2.1–10

Go to page 1331 for your next devotional reading.

1900   Present

heirs with Christ—if, in fact, we suffer with him so that we may also be glorified with him.

Future Glory

18 I consider that the sufferings of this present time are not worth comparing with the glory about to be revealed to us. 19For the creation waits with eager longing for the revealing of the children of God; 20for the creation was subjected to futility, not of its own will but by the will of the one who subjected it, in hope 21that the creation itself will be set free from its bondage to decay and will obtain the freedom of the glory of the children of God. 22We know that the whole creation has been groaning in labor pains until now; 23and not only the creation, but we ourselves, who have the first fruits of the Spirit, groan inwardly while we wait for adoption, the redemption of our bodies. 24For in*h* hope we were saved. Now hope that is seen is not hope. For who hopes*i* for what is seen? 25But if we hope for what we do not see, we wait for it with patience.

26 Likewise the Spirit helps us in our weakness; for we do not know how to pray as we ought, but that very Spirit intercedes*j* with sighs too deep for words. 27And God,*k* who searches the heart, knows what is the mind of the Spirit, because the Spirit*l* intercedes for the saints according to the will of God.*m* 28 We know that all things work together for good*n* for those who love God, who are called according to his purpose. 29For those whom he foreknew he also predestined to be conformed to the image of his Son, in order that he might be the firstborn within a large family.*o* 30And those whom he predestined he also called; and those whom he called he also justified; and those whom he justified he also glorified.

God's Love in Christ Jesus

31 What then are we to say about these things? If God is for us, who is against us? 32He who did not withhold his own Son, but gave him up for all of us, will he not with him also give us everything else? 33Who will bring any charge against God's elect? It is God who justifies. 34Who is to condemn? It is Christ Jesus, who died, yes, who was raised, who is at the right hand of God, who indeed intercedes for us.*p* 35Who will separate us from the love of Christ? Will hardship, or distress, or persecution, or famine, or nakedness, or peril, or sword? 36As it is written,

"For your sake we are being killed
    all day long;
we are accounted as sheep to be
    slaughtered."

37No, in all these things we are more than conquerors through him who loved us. 38For I am convinced that neither death, nor life, nor angels, nor rulers, nor things present, nor things to come, nor powers, 39nor height, nor depth, nor anything else in all creation, will be able to separate us from the love of God in Christ Jesus our Lord.

God's Election of Israel

9 I am speaking the truth in Christ—I am not lying; my conscience confirms it by the Holy Spirit— 2I have great sorrow and unceasing anguish in my heart. 3For I could wish that I myself were accursed and cut off from Christ for the sake of my own people,*q* my kindred according to the flesh. 4They are Israelites, and to them belong the adoption, the glory, the covenants, the giving of the law, the worship, and the promises; 5to them belong the patriarchs, and from them, according to the flesh, comes the Messiah,*r* who is over all, God blessed forever.*s* Amen.

6 It is not as though the word of God had failed. For not all Israelites truly belong to Israel, 7and not all of Abraham's children are his true descendants; but "It is through Isaac that descendants shall be named for you." 8This means that it is not the children of the flesh who are the children of God, but the children of the promise are counted as descendants. 9For this is what the promise said,

h Or *by*   *i* Other ancient authorities read *awaits*   *j* Other ancient authorities add *for us* *k* Gk *the one*   *l* Gk *he* or *it*   *m* Gk *according to God*   *n* Other ancient authorities read *God makes all things work together for good,* or *in all things God works for good*   *o* Gk *among many brothers*   *p* Or *Is it Christ Jesus . . . for us?*   *q* Gk *my brothers*   *r* Or *the Christ*   *s* Cr *Messiah, who is God over all, blessed forever;* or *Messiah. May he who is God over all be blessed forever*

"About this time I will return and Sarah shall have a son." 10Nor is that all; something similar happened to Rebecca when she had conceived children by one husband, our ancestor Isaac. 11Even before they had been born or had done anything good or bad (so that God's purpose of election might continue, 12not by works but by his call) she was told, "The elder shall serve the younger." 13As it is written,

> "I have loved Jacob,
>> but I have hated Esau."

14 What then are we to say? Is there injustice on God's part? By no means! 15For he says to Moses,

> "I will have mercy on whom I have
>> mercy,
>> and I will have compassion on
>>> whom I have compassion."

16So it depends not on human will or exertion, but on God who shows mercy. 17For the scripture says to Pharaoh, "I have raised you up for the very purpose of showing my power in you, so that my name may be proclaimed in all the earth." 18So then he has mercy on whomever he chooses, and he hardens the heart of whomever he chooses.

God's Wrath and Mercy

19 You will say to me then, "Why then does he still find fault? For who can resist his will?" 20But who indeed are you, a human being, to argue with God? Will what is molded say to the one who molds it, "Why have you made me like this?" 21Has the potter no right over the clay, to make out of the same lump one object for special use and another for ordinary use? 22What if God, desiring to show his wrath and to make known his power, has endured with much patience the objects of wrath that are made for destruction; 23and what if he has done so in order to make known the riches of his glory for the objects of mercy, which he has prepared beforehand for glory— 24including us whom he has called, not from the Jews only but also from the Gentiles? 25As indeed he says in Hosea,

> "Those who were not my people I
>> will call 'my people,'
>> and her who was not beloved I
>>> will call 'beloved.' "
> 26 "And in the very place where it
>> was said to them, 'You are
>> not my people,'
>> there they shall be called
>>> children of the living God."

27 And Isaiah cries out concerning Israel, "Though the number of the children of Israel were like the sand of the sea, only a remnant of them will be saved; 28for the Lord will execute his sentence on the earth quickly and decisively."t 29And as Isaiah predicted,

> "If the Lord of hosts had not left
>> survivorsu to us,
>> we would have fared like Sodom
>>> and been made like Gomorrah."

Israel's Unbelief

30 What then are we to say? Gentiles, who did not strive for righteousness, have attained it, that is, righteousness through faith; 31but Israel, who did strive for the righteousness that is based on the law, did not succeed in fulfilling that law. 32Why not? Because they did not strive for it on the basis of faith, but as if it were based on works. They have stumbled over the stumbling stone, 33as it is written,

> "See, I am laying in Zion a stone
>> that will make people
>> stumble, a rock that will
>>> make them fall,
>> and whoever believes in himv
>>> will not be put to shame."

10 Brothers and sisters,w my heart's desire and prayer to God for them is that they may be saved. 2I can testify that they have a zeal for God, but it is not enlightened. 3For, being ignorant of the righteousness that comes from God, and seeking to establish their own, they have not submitted to God's righteousness. 4For Christ is the end of the law so that there may be righteousness for everyone who believes.

---

t Other ancient authorities read *for he will finish his work and cut it short in righteousness, because the Lord will make the sentence shortened on the earth*   u Or *descendants*; Gk *seed*   v Or *trusts in it*   w Gk *Brothers*

Salvation Is for All

5 Moses writes concerning the righteousness that comes from the law, that "the person who does these things will live by them." [6]But the righteousness that comes from faith says, "Do not say in your heart, 'Who will ascend into heaven?'" (that is, to bring Christ down) [7]"or 'Who will descend into the abyss?'" (that is, to bring Christ up from the dead). [8]But what does it say?

"The word is near you,
    on your lips and in your heart"
(that is, the word of faith that we proclaim); [9]because[x] if you confess with your lips that Jesus is Lord and believe in your heart that God raised him from the dead, you will be saved. [10]For one believes with the heart and so is justified, and one confesses with the mouth and so is saved. [11]The scripture says, "No one who believes in him will be

x Or namely, that

THURSDAY

YOU HAVE BEEN SAVED
Karl Barth

VERSE: Romans 10.9   **PASSAGE:** Romans 10.9–13

ou probably all know the legend of the rider who crossed the frozen Lake of Constance by night without knowing it. When he reached the opposite shore and was told whence he came, he broke down, horrified. This is the human situation when the sky opens and the earth is bright, when we may hear: *By grace you have been saved!* In such a moment we are like that terrified rider. When we hear this word we involuntarily look back, do we not, asking ourselves: Where have I been? Over an abyss, in mortal danger! What did I do? The most foolish thing I ever attempted! What happened? I was doomed and miraculously escaped and now I am safe! You ask: "Do we really live in such danger?" Yes, we live on the brink of death. But we have been saved. Look at our Savior and at our Salvation! Look at Jesus Christ on the cross, accused, sentenced, and punished instead of us! Do you know for whose sake he is hanging there? For *our* sake—because of *our* sin—sharing *our* captivity—burdened with *our* suffering! He nails *our* life to the cross. This is how God had to deal with *us*. From this darkness he has saved *us*. He who is not shattered after hearing this news may not yet have grasped the word of God: *By grace you have been saved.*

ADDITIONAL SCRIPTURE READING:
Psalm 23; Ephesians 2.8–9

Go to page 1333 for your next devotional reading.

1900   Present

put to shame." ¹²For there is no distinction between Jew and Greek; the same Lord is Lord of all and is generous to all who call on him. ¹³For, "Everyone who calls on the name of the Lord shall be saved."

14 But how are they to call on one in whom they have not believed? And how are they to believe in one of whom they have never heard? And how are they to hear without someone to proclaim him? ¹⁵And how are they to proclaim him unless they are sent? As it is written, "How beautiful are the feet of those who bring good news!" ¹⁶But not all have obeyed the good news;ʸ for Isaiah says, "Lord, who has believed our message?" ¹⁷So faith comes from what is heard, and what is heard comes through the word of Christ.ᶻ

18 But I ask, have they not heard? Indeed they have; for

"Their voice has gone out to all the earth,
    and their words to the ends of the world."

¹⁹Again I ask, did Israel not understand? First Moses says,

"I will make you jealous of those who are not a nation;
    with a foolish nation I will make you angry."

²⁰Then Isaiah is so bold as to say,

"I have been found by those who did not seek me;
    I have shown myself to those who did not ask for me."

²¹But of Israel he says, "All day long I have held out my hands to a disobedient and contrary people."

Israel's Rejection Is Not Final

11 I ask, then, has God rejected his people? By no means! I myself am an Israelite, a descendant of Abraham, a member of the tribe of Benjamin. ²God has not rejected his people whom he foreknew. Do you not know what the scripture says of Elijah, how he pleads with God against Israel? ³"Lord, they have killed your prophets, they have demolished your altars; I alone am left, and they are seeking my life." ⁴But

what is the divine reply to him? "I have kept for myself seven thousand who have not bowed the knee to Baal." ⁵So too at the present time there is a remnant, chosen by grace. ⁶But if it is by grace, it is no longer on the basis of works, otherwise grace would no longer be grace.ᵃ

7 What then? Israel failed to obtain what it was seeking. The elect obtained it, but the rest were hardened, ⁸as it is written,

"God gave them a sluggish spirit,
    eyes that would not see
    and ears that would not hear,
    down to this very day."

⁹And David says,

"Let their table become a snare and a trap,
    a stumbling block and a retribution for them;
10 let their eyes be darkened so that they cannot see,
    and keep their backs forever bent."

The Salvation of the Gentiles

11 So I ask, have they stumbled so as to fall? By no means! But through their stumblingᵇ salvation has come to the Gentiles, so as to make Israelᶜ jealous. ¹²Now if their stumblingᵇ means riches for the world, and if their defeat means riches for Gentiles, how much more will their full inclusion mean!

13 Now I am speaking to you Gentiles. Inasmuch then as I am an apostle to the Gentiles, I glorify my ministry ¹⁴in order to make my own peopleᵈ jealous, and thus save some of them. ¹⁵For if their rejection is the reconciliation of the world, what will their acceptance be but life from the dead! ¹⁶If the part of the dough offered as first fruits is holy, then the whole batch is holy; and if the root is holy, then the branches also are holy.

17 But if some of the branches were broken off, and you, a wild olive shoot, were grafted in their place to share the rich rootᵉ of the olive tree, ¹⁸do not boast over the branches. If you do boast, remember that it is not you that support the root, but the root that supports you.

y Or gospel   z Or about Christ; other ancient authorities read of God   a Other ancient authorities add But if it is by works, it is no longer on the basis of grace, otherwise work would no longer be work   b Gk transgression   c Gk them   d Gk my flesh   e Other ancient authorities read the richness

¹⁹You will say, "Branches were broken off so that I might be grafted in." ²⁰That is true. They were broken off because of their unbelief, but you stand only through faith. So do not become proud, but stand in awe. ²¹For if God did not

---

FRIDAY

FROM PAUL'S LETTER TO AMERICAN CHRISTIANS
Martin Luther King, Jr.

VERSE: Romans 12.2   PASSAGE: Romans 12.1–2

 find it necessary to remind you of the responsibility laid upon you to represent the ethical principles of Christianity amid a time that popularly disregards them. That was a task laid on me. I understand that there are many Christians in America who give their ultimate allegiance to man-made systems and customs. They are afraid to be different. Their great concern is to be accepted socially. They live by some such principle as this: "Everybody is doing it, so it must be all right." For so many of you morality merely reflects group consensus. In your modern sociological lingo, the mores are accepted as the right ways. You have unconsciously come to believe that what is right is determined by Gallup polls.

American Christians, I must say to you what I wrote to the Roman Christians years ago: "Do not be conformed to this world, but be transformed by the renewing of your minds" (Romans 12.2). You have a duel citizenry. You live both in time and eternity. Your highest loyalty is to God, and not to the mores or the folkways, the state or the nation, or any man-made institution. If any earthly institution or custom conflicts with God's will, it is your Christian duty to oppose it. You must never allow the transitory, evanescent demands of man-made institutions to take precedence over the eternal demands of the Almighty God. In a time when men are surrendering the high values of the faith you must cling to them, and despite the pressure of an alien generation preserve them for children yet unborn. You must be willing to challenge unjust mores, to champion unpopular causes, and to buck the status quo. You are called to be the salt of the earth. You are to be the light of the world. You are to be that vitally active leaven in the lump of the nation.

ADDITIONAL SCRIPTURE READING:
Matthew 5.11–16; Ephesians 4.21–24

Go to page 1335 for your next devotional reading.

1900   Present

spare the natural branches, perhaps he will not spare you.*f* 22Note then the kindness and the severity of God: severity toward those who have fallen, but God's kindness toward you, provided you continue in his kindness; otherwise you also will be cut off. 23And even those of Israel,*g* if they do not persist in unbelief, will be grafted in, for God has the power to graft them in again. 24For if you have been cut from what is by nature a wild olive tree and grafted, contrary to nature, into a cultivated olive tree, how much more will these natural branches be grafted back into their own olive tree.

All Israel Will Be Saved

25 So that you may not claim to be wiser than you are, brothers and sisters,*h* I want you to understand this mystery: a hardening has come upon part of Israel, until the full number of the Gentiles has come in. 26And so all Israel will be saved; as it is written,

> "Out of Zion will come the
> Deliverer;
> he will banish ungodliness from
> Jacob."

27   "And this is my covenant with
> them,
> when I take away their sins."

28As regards the gospel they are enemies of God*i* for your sake; but as regards election they are beloved, for the sake of their ancestors; 29for the gifts and the calling of God are irrevocable. 30Just as you were once disobedient to God but have now received mercy because of their disobedience, 31so they have now been disobedient in order that, by the mercy shown to you, they too may now*j* receive mercy. 32For God has imprisoned all in disobedience so that he may be merciful to all.

33 O the depth of the riches and wisdom and knowledge of God! How unsearchable are his judgments and how inscrutable his ways!

34   "For who has known the mind of
> the Lord?
> Or who has been his counselor?"

35   "Or who has given a gift to him,
> to receive a gift in return?"

36For from him and through him and to him are all things. To him be the glory forever. Amen.

The New Life in Christ

12 I appeal to you therefore, brothers and sisters,*h* by the mercies of God, to present your bodies as a living sacrifice, holy and acceptable to God, which is your spiritual*k* worship. 2Do not be conformed to this world,*l* but be transformed by the renewing of your minds, so that you may discern what is the will of God—what is good and acceptable and perfect.*m*

3 For by the grace given to me I say to everyone among you not to think of yourself more highly than you ought to think, but to think with sober judgment, each according to the measure of faith that God has assigned. 4For as in one body we have many members, and not all the members have the same function, 5so we, who are many, are one body in Christ, and individually we are members one of another. 6We have gifts that differ according to the grace given to us: prophecy, in proportion to faith; 7ministry, in ministering; the teacher, in teaching; 8the exhorter, in exhortation; the giver, in generosity; the leader, in diligence; the compassionate, in cheerfulness.

Marks of the True Christian

9 Let love be genuine; hate what is evil, hold fast to what is good; 10love one

---

IT IS VERY EASY TO OVERESTIMATE THE IMPORTANCE OF OUR OWN ACHIEVEMENTS IN COMPARISON WITH WHAT WE OWE OTHERS.

—*Dietrich Bonhoeffer*

---

another with mutual affection; outdo one another in showing honor. 11Do not lag in zeal, be ardent in spirit, serve the Lord.*n* 12Rejoice in hope, be patient in suffering, persevere in prayer. 13Contribute to the needs of the saints; extend hospitality to strangers.

14 Bless those who persecute you;

---

f Other ancient authorities read *neither will he spare you*   *g* Gk lacks *of Israel*   *h* Gk *brothers*
i Gk lacks *of God*   *j* Other ancient authorities lack *now*   *k* Or *reasonable*   *l* Gk *age*
m Or *what is the good and acceptable and perfect will of God*   *n* Other ancient authorities read *serve the opportune time*

WEEKEND

THE SOUND OF THE BELL
John Donne

VERSE: Acts 17.26   **PASSAGE:** Acts 17.24–28

ow, this Bell tolling softly for another, saies to me, Thou must die.
Perchance hee for whom this *Bell* tolls, may bee so ill, as that he knowes not it *tolls* for him; And perchance I may thinke my selfe so much better than I am, as that they who are about mee, and see my state, may have caused it to toll for mee, and I know not that . . . As therefore the *Bell* that rings to a *Sermon*, calls not upon the *Preacher* onely, but upon the *Congregation* to come; so this *Bell* calls us all: but how much more *mee*, who am brought so neere the *doore* by this *sicknesse* . . . No man is an *Iland*, intire of it selfe; every man is a peece of the *Continent*, a part of the *maine*; if a *Clod* bee washed away by the *Sea*, *Europe* is the lesse, as well as if a *Promontorie* were, as well as if a *Mannor* of thy *friends*, or of *thine owne* were; Any Mans *deathe* diminishes *me*, because I am involved in *Mankinde*; And therefore never send to know for whom the *bell* tolls; It tolls for *thee*.

ADDITIONAL SCRIPTURE READING:
Psalm 13.1–6; Revelation 21.1–4

Go to page 1337 for your next devotional reading.

1500   1700

bless and do not curse them. 15Rejoice with those who rejoice, weep with those who weep. 16Live in harmony with one another; do not be haughty, but associate with the lowly;*o* do not claim to be wiser than you are. 17Do not repay anyone evil for evil, but take thought for what is noble in the sight of all. 18If it is possible, so far as it depends on you, live peaceably with all. 19Beloved, never avenge yourselves, but leave room for the wrath of God;*p* for it is written, "Vengeance is mine, I will repay, says the Lord." 20No, "if your enemies are hungry, feed them; if they are thirsty, give them something to drink; for by doing this you will heap burning coals on their heads." 21Do not be overcome by evil, but overcome evil with good.

Being Subject to Authorities

13 Let every person be subject to the governing authorities; for there is no authority except from God, and those authorities that exist have been instituted by God. 2Therefore whoever resists authority resists what God has appointed, and those who resist will incur judgment. 3For rulers are not a terror to good conduct, but to bad. Do you wish to have no fear of the authority? Then do what is good, and you will receive its approval; 4for it is God's servant for your good. But if you do what is wrong, you should be afraid, for the authority*q* does not bear the sword in vain! It is the servant of God to execute wrath on the wrongdoer. 5Therefore one must be subject, not only because of wrath but also because of conscience. 6For the same reason you also pay taxes, for the authorities are God's servants, busy with this very thing. 7Pay to all that is due them—taxes to whom taxes are due, revenue to whom revenue is due, respect to whom respect is due, honor to whom honor is due.

Love for One Another

8 Owe no one anything, except to love one another; for the one who loves another has fulfilled the law. 9The commandments, "You shall not commit adultery; You shall not murder; You shall not steal; You shall not covet"; and any other commandment, are summed up in this word, "Love your neighbor as yourself." 10Love does no wrong to a neighbor; therefore, love is the fulfilling of the law.

An Urgent Appeal

11 Besides this, you know what time it is, how it is now the moment for you to wake from sleep. For salvation is nearer to us now than when we became believers; 12the night is far gone, the day is near. Let us then lay aside the works of darkness and put on the armor of light; 13let us live honorably as in the day, not in reveling and drunkenness, not in debauchery and licentiousness, not in quarreling and jealousy. 14Instead, put on the Lord Jesus Christ, and make no provision for the flesh, to gratify its desires.

IF THERE IS NO ELEMENT OF ASCETICISM IN OUR LIVES, IF WE GIVE FREE REIN TO THE DESIRES OF THE FLESH . . . WE SHALL FIND IT HARD TO TRAIN FOR THE SERVICE OF CHRIST. —*Dietrich Bonhoeffer*

Do Not Judge Another

14 Welcome those who are weak in faith,*r* but not for the purpose of quarreling over opinions. 2Some believe in eating anything, while the weak eat only vegetables. 3Those who eat must not despise those who abstain, and those who abstain must not pass judgment on those who eat; for God has welcomed them. 4Who are you to pass judgment on servants of another? It is before their own lord that they stand or fall. And they will be upheld, for the Lord*s* is able to make them stand.

5 Some judge one day to be better than another, while others judge all days to be alike. Let all be fully convinced in their own minds. 6Those who observe the day, observe it in honor of the Lord. Also those who eat, eat in honor of the Lord, since they give thanks to God; while those who abstain, abstain in

---

o Or *give yourselves to humble tasks*   *p* Gk *the wrath*   *q* Gk *it*   *r* Or *conviction*   *s* Other ancient authorities read *for God*

honor of the Lord and give thanks to God.

7 We do not live to ourselves, and we do not die to ourselves. 8If we live, we live to the Lord, and if we die, we die to the Lord; so then, whether we live or whether we die, we are the Lord's. 9For to this end Christ died and lived again, so that he might be Lord of both the dead and the living.

MONDAY

SCREWTAPE'S STRATEGY
C. S. Lewis

VERSE: Romans 13.8   **PASSAGE:** Romans 13.8–10

[Satan writes to one of his minions:]

y Dear Wormwood,
. . . The "Historical Jesus," however dangerous he may seem to be to us at some particular point, is always to be encouraged. About the general connection between Christianity and politics, our position is more delicate. Certainly we do not want men to allow their Christianity to flow over into their political life, for the establishment of anything like a really just society would be a major disaster. On the other hand we do want, and want very much, to make men treat Christianity as a means; preferably, of course, as a means to their own advancement, but, failing that, as a means to anything— even to social justice. The thing to do is get a man at first to value social justice as a thing which the Enemy [God] demands, and then work him on to the stage at which he values Christianity because it may produce social justice. For the Enemy will not be used as a convenience. Men or nations who think they can revive the faith in order to make a good society might just as well think they can use the stairs of heaven as a short cut to the nearest chemist's shop. Fortunately it is quite easy to coax humans round this little corner. Only today I have found a passage in a Christian writer where he recommends his own version of Christianity on the ground that "only such a faith can outlast the death of old cultures and the birth of new civilizations." You see the little rift? "Believe this, not because it is true, but for some other reason." That's the game,

Your affectionate uncle
Screwtape

ADDITIONAL SCRIPTURE READING:
Galatians 6.7–8; Hebrews 10.22–24

Go to page 1339 for your next devotional reading.

1900   Present

10 Why do you pass judgment on your brother or sister?[t] Or you, why do you despise your brother or sister?[t] For we will all stand before the judgment seat of God.[u] 11For it is written,

"As I live, says the Lord, every
      knee shall bow to me,
   and every tongue shall give praise
      to[v] God."

12So then, each of us will be accountable to God.[w]

AT THE DAY OF JUDGMENT WE SHALL NOT BE ASKED WHAT WE HAVE READ BUT WHAT WE HAVE DONE.   —Thomas à Kempis

---

Do Not Make Another Stumble

13 Let us therefore no longer pass judgment on one another, but resolve instead never to put a stumbling block or hindrance in the way of another.[x] 14I know and am persuaded in the Lord Jesus that nothing is unclean in itself; but it is unclean for anyone who thinks it unclean. 15If your brother or sister[t] is being injured by what you eat, you are no longer walking in love. Do not let what you eat cause the ruin of one for whom Christ died. 16So do not let your good be spoken of as evil. 17For the kingdom of God is not food and drink but righteousness and peace and joy in the Holy Spirit. 18The one who thus serves Christ is acceptable to God and has human approval. 19Let us then pursue what makes for peace and for mutual upbuilding. 20Do not, for the sake of food, destroy the work of God. Everything is indeed clean, but it is wrong for you to make others fall by what you eat; 21it is good not to eat meat or drink wine or do anything that makes your brother or sister[t] stumble.[y] 22The faith that you have, have as your own conviction before God. Blessed are those who have no reason to condemn themselves because of what they approve. 23But those who have doubts are condemned if they eat, because they do not act from faith;[z] for whatever does not proceed from faith[z] is sin.[a]

Please Others, Not Yourselves

15 We who are strong ought to put up with the failings of the weak, and not to please ourselves. 2Each of us must please our neighbor for the good purpose of building up the neighbor. 3For Christ did not please himself; but, as it is written, "The insults of those who insult you have fallen on me." 4For whatever was written in former days was written for our instruction, so that by steadfastness and by the encouragement of the scriptures we might have hope. 5May the God of steadfastness and encouragement grant you to live in harmony with one another, in accordance with Christ Jesus, 6so that together you may with one voice glorify the God and Father of our Lord Jesus Christ.

The Gospel for Jews and Gentiles Alike

7 Welcome one another, therefore, just as Christ has welcomed you, for the glory of God. 8For I tell you that Christ has become a servant of the circumcised on behalf of the truth of God in order that he might confirm the promises given to the patriarchs, 9and in order that the Gentiles might glorify God for his mercy. As it is written,

"Therefore I will confess[b] you
      among the Gentiles,
   and sing praises to your name";

10and again he says,

"Rejoice, O Gentiles, with his
      people";

11and again,

"Praise the Lord, all you Gentiles,
   and let all the peoples praise
      him";

12and again Isaiah says,

"The root of Jesse shall come,
   the one who rises to rule the
      Gentiles;
   in him the Gentiles shall hope."

13May the God of hope fill you with all joy and peace in believing, so that you may abound in hope by the power of the Holy Spirit.

---

t Gk brother   u Other ancient authorities read of Christ   v Or confess   w Other ancient authorities lack to God   x Gk of a brother   y Other ancient authorities add or be upset or be weakened   z Or conviction   a Other authorities, some ancient, add here 16.25-27   b Or thank

THE WIDENING CIRCLE OF RIPPLES IN THE POOL OF HISTORY

Karl Barth

VERSE: Romans 15.20   **PASSAGE:** Romans 15.17–21

e all know the curiosity that comes over us when from a window we see the people in the street suddenly stop and look up—shade their eyes with their hands and look straight up into the sky toward something which is hidden from us by the roof. Our curiosity is superfluous, for what they see is doubtless an airplane. But as to the sudden stopping, looking up, and tense attention characteristic of the people of the Bible, our wonder will not be so lightly dismissed. To me personally it came first with Paul: this man evidently sees and hears something which is above everything, which is absolutely beyond the range of my observation and the measure of my thought. Let me place myself as I will to this coming something that in enigmatical words he insists he sees and hears, I am still taken by the fact that he, Paul, or whoever it was who wrote the epistle to the Ephesians, for example, is eye and ear in a state which expressions such as inspiration, alarm, or stirring or overwhelming emotion, do not satisfactorily describe. I seem to see within so transparent a piece of literature a personality who is actually thrown out of his course by seeing and hearing what I for my part do not see and hear—who is, so to speak, captured, in order to be dragged as a prisoner from land to land for strange, intense, uncertain, and yet mysteriously well-planned service.

And if ever I come to fear lest mine is a case of self-hallucination, one glance at the secular events of those times, one glance at the widening circle of ripples in the pool of history, tells me of a certainty that a stone of unusual weight must have been dropped into deep water somewhere—tells me that, among all the hundreds of peripatetic preachers and miracle-workers from the Near East who in that day must have gone along the same Appian Way into imperial Rome, it was this one Paul, seeing and hearing what he did, who was the cause, if not of all, yet of the most important developments in that city's future.

ADDITIONAL SCRIPTURE READING:
Galatians 1.13–17; Ephesians 3.7–10

Go to page 1341 for your next devotional reading.

1900   Present

Paul's Reason for Writing So Boldly

14 I myself feel confident about you, my brothers and sisters,c that you yourselves are full of goodness, filled with all knowledge, and able to instruct one another. 15Nevertheless on some points I have written to you rather boldly by way of reminder, because of the grace given me by God 16to be a minister of Christ Jesus to the Gentiles in the priestly service of the gospel of God, so that the offering of the Gentiles may be acceptable, sanctified by the Holy Spirit. 17In Christ Jesus, then, I have reason to boast of my work for God. 18For I will not venture to speak of anything except what Christ has accomplishedd through me to win obedience from the Gentiles, by word and deed, 19by the power of signs and wonders, by the power of the Spirit of God,e so that from Jerusalem and as far around as Illyricum I have fully proclaimed the good newsf of Christ. 20Thus I make it my ambition to proclaim the good news,f not where Christ has already been named, so that I do not build on someone else's foundation, 21but as it is written,

"Those who have never been told
　　of him shall see,
and those who have never heard
　　of him shall understand."

Paul's Plan to Visit Rome

22 This is the reason that I have so often been hindered from coming to you. 23But now, with no further place for me in these regions, I desire, as I have for many years, to come to you 24when I go to Spain. For I do hope to see you on my journey and to be sent on by you, once I have enjoyed your company for a little while. 25At present, however, I am going to Jerusalem in a ministry to the saints; 26for Macedonia and Achaia have been pleased to share their resources with the poor among the saints at Jerusalem. 27They were pleased to do this, and indeed they owe it to them; for if the Gentiles have come to share in their spiritual blessings, they ought also to be of service to them in material things.

28So, when I have completed this, and have delivered to them what has been collected,g I will set out by way of you to Spain; 29and I know that when I come to you, I will come in the fullness of the blessingh of Christ.

30 I appeal to you, brothers and sisters,c by our Lord Jesus Christ and by the love of the Spirit, to join me in earnest prayer to God on my behalf, 31that I may be rescued from the unbelievers in Judea, and that my ministryi to Jerusalem may be acceptable to the saints, 32so that by God's will I may come to you with joy and be refreshed in your company. 33The God of peace be with all of you.j Amen.

Personal Greetings

16 I commend to you our sister Phoebe, a deacnk of the church at Cenchreae, 2so that you may welcome her in the Lord as is fitting for the saints, and help her in whatever she may require from you, for she has been a benefactor of many and of myself as well.

3 Greet Prisca and Aquila, who work with me in Christ Jesus, 4and who risked their necks for my life, to whom not only I give thanks, but also all the churches of the Gentiles. 5Greet also the church in their house. Greet my beloved Epaenetus, who was the first convertl in Asia for Christ. 6Greet Mary, who has worked very hard among you. 7Greet Andronicus and Junia,m my relativesn who were in prison with me; they are prominent among the apostles, and they were in Christ before I was. 8Greet Ampliatus, my beloved in the Lord. 9Greet Urbanus, our co-worker in Christ, and my beloved Stachys. 10Greet Apelles, who is approved in Christ. Greet those who belong to the family of Aristobulus. 11Greet my relativeo Herodion. Greet those in the Lord who belong to the family of Narcissus. 12Greet those workers in the Lord, Tryphaena and Tryphosa. Greet the beloved Persis, who has worked hard in the Lord. 13Greet Rufus, chosen in the Lord; and greet his mother—a mother to

---

c Gk brothers　d Gk speak of those things that Christ has not accomplished　e Other ancient authorities read of the Spirit or of the Holy Spirit　f Or gospel　g Gk have sealed to them this fruit　h Other ancient authorities add of the gospel　i Other ancient authorities read my bringing of a gift　j One ancient authority adds 16.25-27 here　k Or minister　l Gk first fruits　m Or Junias; other ancient authorities read Julia　n Or compatriots　o Or compatriot

me also. [14]Greet Asyncritus, Phlegon, Hermes, Patrobas, Hermas, and the brothers and sisters[p] who are with them. [15]Greet Philologus, Julia, Nereus and his sister, and Olympas, and all the saints who are with them. [16]Greet one another with a holy kiss. All the churches of Christ greet you.

Final Instructions

17 I urge you, brothers and sisters,[p] to keep an eye on those who cause dissensions and offenses, in opposition to the teaching that you have learned; avoid them. [18]For such people do not serve our Lord Christ, but their own appetites,[q] and by smooth talk and flattery they deceive the hearts of the simple-minded. [19]For while your obedience is known to all, so that I rejoice over you, I want you to be wise in what is good and guileless in what is evil. [20]The God of peace will shortly crush Satan under your feet. The grace of our Lord Jesus Christ be with you.[r]

21 Timothy, my co-worker, greets you; so do Lucius and Jason and Sosipater, my relatives.[s]

p Gk brothers   q Gk their own belly   r Other ancient authorities lack this sentence
s Or compatriots

WEDNESDAY

CHRIST, OUR DELIVERER
Hippolytus

VERSE: Romans 16.20   PASSAGE: Romans 16.20, 25–27

e give you thanks, O God, through your dear child, Jesus Christ, who in these last days you sent to save us and instruct us. He is your word, inseparable from you; you made all things through him, and you were well pleased with him.

You sent him from heaven to a virgin's womb. He lay in that womb and took flesh, and you were presented with a son, born of the Holy Spirit and of a virgin. He did what you wanted him to do. When he suffered, he stretched out his hands to free those who believed in you from suffering. When he died he destroyed death, breaking the chains of the devil which held us and crushing hell beneath his feet. When he rose again he gave light to the righteous, revealing his new covenant with mankind.

Thus, calling to mind his death and resurrection, we offer you bread and wine, thanking you for enabling us to stand before you and serve you. We ask you to send down your Holy Spirit on the offering which we make to you, uniting all who receive Holy Communion in the bond of your truth.

ADDITIONAL SCRIPTURE READING:
Luke 22.14–20; John 1.1–3,14

Go to page 1345 for your next devotional reading.

100   500

22 I Tertius, the writer of this letter, greet you in the Lord.[t]

23 Gaius, who is host to me and to the whole church, greets you. Erastus, the city treasurer, and our brother Quartus, greet you.[u]

Final Doxology

25 Now to God[v] who is able to strengthen you according to my gospel and the proclamation of Jesus Christ, according to the revelation of the mystery that was kept secret for long ages [26]but is now disclosed, and through the prophetic writings is made known to all the Gentiles, according to the command of the eternal God, to bring about the obedience of faith— [27]to the only wise God, through Jesus Christ, to whom[w] be the glory forever! Amen.[x]

---

t Or I Tertius, writing this letter in the Lord, greet you grace of our Lord Jesus Christ be with all of you. Amen.   u Other ancient authorities add verse 24, The   v Gk the one   w Other ancient authorities lack to whom. The verse then reads, to the only wise God be the glory through Jesus Christ forever. Amen.   x Other ancient authorities lack 16.25-27 or include it after 14.23 or 15.33; others put verse 24 after verse 27

1 CORINTHIANS

AUL WROTE TO THE CHURCH HE'D STARTED IN CORINTH (ACTS 18.1–17), A CHURCH NOW STRUGGLING TO LIVE IN OBEDIENCE. IN A LETTER MARKED BY LOVING CONCERN AND A TRUE PASTOR'S HEART, PAUL ADDRESSES PROBLEMS IN CHRISTIAN CONDUCT AND CHARACTER. LOOK FOR PRACTICAL INFORMATION RELEVANT TO CHRISTIAN LIVING AND RELATIONSHIPS, AS WELL AS UPLIFTING WORDS ABOUT LOVE (CHAPTER 13) AND THE RESURRECTION (CHAPTER 15).

Salutation

1 Paul, called to be an apostle of Christ Jesus by the will of God, and our brother Sosthenes,

2 To the church of God that is in Corinth, to those who are sanctified in Christ Jesus, called to be saints, together with all those who in every place call on the name of our Lord Jesus Christ, both their Lord[a] and ours:

3 Grace to you and peace from God our Father and the Lord Jesus Christ.

4 I give thanks to my[b] God always for you because of the grace of God that has been given you in Christ Jesus, 5for in every way you have been enriched in him, in speech and knowledge of every kind— 6just as the testimony of[c] Christ has been strengthened among you— 7so that you are not lacking in any spiritual gift as you wait for the revealing of our Lord Jesus Christ. 8He will also strengthen you to the end, so that you may be blameless on the day of our Lord Jesus Christ. 9God is faithful; by him you were called into the fellowship of his Son, Jesus Christ our Lord.

Divisions in the Church

10 Now I appeal to you, brothers and sisters,[d] by the name of our Lord Jesus Christ, that all of you be in agreement and that there be no divisions among you, but that you be united in the same mind and the same purpose. 11For it has been reported to me by Chloe's people

that there are quarrels among you, my brothers and sisters.*e* **12**What I mean is that each of you says, "I belong to Paul," or "I belong to Apollos," or "I belong to Cephas," or "I belong to Christ." **13**Has Christ been divided? Was Paul crucified for you? Or were you baptized in the name of Paul? **14**I thank God*f* that I baptized none of you except Crispus and Gaius, **15**so that no one can say that you were baptized in my name. **16**(I did baptize also the household of Stephanas; beyond that, I do not know whether I baptized anyone else.) **17**For Christ did not send me to baptize but to proclaim the gospel, and not with eloquent wisdom, so that the cross of Christ might not be emptied of its power.

Christ the Power and Wisdom of God

18 For the message about the cross is foolishness to those who are perishing, but to us who are being saved it is the power of God. **19**For it is written,

"I will destroy the wisdom of the
     wise,
and the discernment of the
     discerning I will thwart."

20Where is the one who is wise? Where is the scribe? Where is the debater of this age? Has not God made foolish the wisdom of the world? **21**For since, in the wisdom of God, the world did not know God through wisdom, God decided, through the foolishness of our proclamation, to save those who believe. **22**For Jews demand signs and Greeks desire wisdom, **23**but we proclaim Christ crucified, a stumbling block to Jews and foolishness to Gentiles, **24**but to those who are the called, both Jews and Greeks, Christ the power of God and the wisdom of God. **25**For God's foolishness is wiser than human wisdom, and God's weakness is stronger than human strength.

I BELIEVE IT TO BE A GRAVE MISTAKE TO PRESENT CHRISTIANITY AS SOMETHING CHARMING AND POPULAR WITH NO OFFENSE IN IT.

—*Dorothy L. Sayers*

---

26 Consider your own call, brothers and sisters:*g* not many of you were wise by human standards,*h* not many were powerful, not many were of noble birth. **27**But God chose what is foolish in the world to shame the wise; God chose what is weak in the world to shame the strong; **28**God chose what is low and despised in the world, things that are not, to reduce to nothing things that are, **29**so that no one*i* might boast in the presence of God. **30**He is the source of your life in Christ Jesus, who became for us wisdom from God, and righteousness and sanctification and redemption, **31**in order that, as it is written, "Let the one who boasts, boast in*j* the Lord."

Proclaiming Christ Crucified

2 When I came to you, brothers and sisters,*g* I did not come proclaiming the mystery*k* of God to you in lofty words or wisdom. **2**For I decided to know nothing among you except Jesus Christ, and him crucified. **3**And I came to you in weakness and in fear and in much trembling. **4**My speech and my proclamation were not with plausible words of wisdom,*l* but with a demonstration of the Spirit and of power, **5**so that your faith might rest not on human wisdom but on the power of God.

The True Wisdom of God

6 Yet among the mature we do speak wisdom, though it is not a wisdom of this age or of the rulers of this age, who are doomed to perish. **7**But we speak God's wisdom, secret and hidden, which God decreed before the ages for our glory. **8**None of the rulers of this age understood this; for if they had, they would not have crucified the Lord of glory. **9**But, as it is written,

"What no eye has seen, nor ear
     heard,
nor the human heart conceived,
what God has prepared for those
     who love him"—

10these things God has revealed to us through the Spirit; for the Spirit searches everything, even the depths of God. **11**For what human being knows what is truly

---

e Gk *my brothers*   *f* Other ancient authorities read *I am thankful*   *g* Gk *brothers*
h Gk *according to the flesh*   *i* Gk *no flesh*   *j* Or *of*   *k* Other ancient authorities read *testimony*
l Other ancient authorities read *the persuasiveness of wisdom*

human except the human spirit that is within? So also no one comprehends what is truly God's except the Spirit of God. ¹²Now we have received not the spirit of the world, but the Spirit that is from God, so that we may understand the gifts bestowed on us by God. ¹³And we speak of these things in words not

---

THURSDAY

CHRIST IS OUR WISDOM
George Whitefield

VERSE: 1 Corinthians 1.30   **PASSAGE:** 1 Corinthians 1.26–31

herein does true wisdom consist? Were I to ask some of you, perhaps you would say, in indulging the lust of the flesh, and saying to your souls, eat, drink, and be merry: but this is only the wisdom of brutes; they have as good a gust and relish for sensual pleasures, as the greatest epicure on earth. Others would tell me, true wisdom consisted in adding house to house, and field to field, and calling lands after their own names: but this cannot be true wisdom; for riches often take to themselves wings, and fly away, like an eagle towards heaven . . .

But perhaps you despise riches and pleasure, and therefore place wisdom in the knowledge of books: but . . . learned men are not always wise; nay, our common learning, so much cried up, makes men only so many accomplished fools; to keep you therefore no longer in suspense, and withal to humble you, I will send you to a heathen to school, to learn what true wisdom is: "Know thyself," was a saying of one of the wise men of Greece; this is certainly true wisdom, and this is that wisdom spoken of in the text, and which Jesus Christ is made to all elect sinners—they are made to know themselves, so as not to think more highly of themselves than they ought to think. Before, they were darkness; now, they are light in the Lord; and in that light they see their own darkness; they now bewail themselves as fallen creatures by nature, dead in trespasses and sins, sons and heirs of hell, and children of wrath; they now see that all their righteousnesses are but as filthy rags; that there is no health in their souls; that they are poor and miserable, blind and naked; and that there is no name given under heaven, whereby they can be saved, but that of Jesus Christ . . . thus Christ is made to them wisdom.

ADDITIONAL SCRIPTURE READING:
Proverbs 1.7–9; Ecclesiastes 12.13

Go to page 1347 for your next devotional reading.

1700   1900

taught by human wisdom but taught by the Spirit, interpreting spiritual things to those who are spiritual.[m]

14 Those who are unspiritual[n] do not receive the gifts of God's Spirit, for they are foolishness to them, and they are unable to understand them because they are spiritually discerned. 15 Those who are spiritual discern all things, and they are themselves subject to no one else's scrutiny.

16 "For who has known the mind of
      the Lord
        so as to instruct him?"
But we have the mind of Christ.

On Divisions in the Corinthian Church

3 And so, brothers and sisters,[o] I could not speak to you as spiritual people, but rather as people of the flesh, as infants in Christ. 2 I fed you with milk, not solid food, for you were not ready for solid food. Even now you are still not ready, 3 for you are still of the flesh. For as long as there is jealousy and quarreling among you, are you not of the flesh, and behaving according to human inclinations? 4 For when one says, "I belong to Paul," and another, "I belong to Apollos," are you not merely human?

5 What then is Apollos? What is Paul? Servants through whom you came to believe, as the Lord assigned to each. 6 I planted, Apollos watered, but God gave the growth. 7 So neither the one who plants nor the one who waters is anything, but only God who gives the growth. 8 The one who plants and the one who waters have a common purpose, and each will receive wages according to the labor of each. 9 For we are God's servants, working together; you are God's field, God's building.

10 According to the grace of God given to me, like a skilled master builder I laid a foundation, and someone else is building on it. Each builder must choose with care how to build on it. 11 For no one can lay any foundation other than the one that has been laid; that foundation is Jesus Christ. 12 Now if

anyone builds on the foundation with gold, silver, precious stones, wood, hay, straw— 13 the work of each builder will become visible, for the Day will disclose it, because it will be revealed with fire, and the fire will test what sort of work each has done. 14 If what has been built on the foundation survives, the builder will receive a reward. 15 If the work is burned up, the builder will suffer loss; the builder will be saved, but only as through fire.

> NO MATTER WHAT A MAN DOES, NO MATTER HOW SUCCESSFUL HE SEEMS TO BE IN ANY FIELD, IF THE HOLY SPIRIT IS NOT THE CHIEF ENERGIZER OF HIS ACTIVITY, IT WILL ALL FALL APART WHEN HE DIES.
> —A. W. Tozer

16 Do you not know that you are God's temple and that God's Spirit dwells in you?[p] 17 If anyone destroys God's temple, God will destroy that person. For God's temple is holy, and you are that temple.

18 Do not deceive yourselves. If you think that you are wise in this age, you should become fools so that you may become wise. 19 For the wisdom of this world is foolishness with God. For it is written,
  "He catches the wise in their
      craftiness,"
20 and again,
  "The Lord knows the thoughts of
      the wise,
    that they are futile."
21 So let no one boast about human leaders. For all things are yours, 22 whether Paul or Apollos or Cephas or the world or life or death or the present or the future— all belong to you, 23 and you belong to Christ, and Christ belongs to God.

The Ministry of the Apostles

4 Think of us in this way, as servants of Christ and stewards of God's mysteries. 2 Moreover, it is required of stewards that they be found trustworthy. 3 But with me it is a very small thing that I should be judged by you or by any human court. I do not

even judge myself. ⁴I am not aware of anything against myself, but I am not thereby acquitted. It is the Lord who judges me. ⁵Therefore do not pronounce judgment before the time, before the Lord comes, who will bring to light the things now hidden in darkness and will disclose the purposes of the heart. Then each one will receive commendation from God.

FRIDAY

FROM APOLOGY FOR MY FLIGHT
Athanasius

VERSE: 1 Corinthians 4.9   **PASSAGE:** 1 Corinthians 4.9–13

he flight of the saints was neither blamable nor unprofitable. If they had not avoided their persecutors, who would have preached the glad tiding of the Word of Truth? It was for this that the persecutors sought after the saints—that there might be no one to teach [the Word]. For this cause the saints endured all things, that the Gospel might be preached. Behold, while they were thus engaged in conflict with their enemies, they passed not the time of their flight unprofitably; nor while they were persecuted, did they forget the welfare of others. But as ministers of the Good Word, they grudged not to communicate it to all men; so that even while they fled, they preached the Gospel and gave warning of the wickedness of those who conspired against them and confirmed the faithful by their exhortations. Thus, the blessed Paul, having found it so by experience, declared, "All that will live godly in Christ shall suffer persecution" (2 Timothy 3.12, KJV). And straightway he prepared those who fled for the trial, saying, "Let us run with patience the race that is set before us" (Hebrews 12.1, KJV); for although there be continual tribulations, yet "tribulation worketh patience, and patience experience, and experience hope, and hope maketh not ashamed" (Romans 5.3–5, KJV) . . .

Thus the saints were abundantly preserved in their flight by the providence of God, as physicians for the sake of them that had need . . . This rule the blessed martyrs observed in their persecutions: When persecuted they fled; while concealing themselves they showed fortitude; and when discovered they submitted to martyrdom.

ADDITIONAL SCRIPTURE READING:
1 Peter 4.12–19; James 1.12

Go to page 1348 for your next devotional reading.

100   500

WEEKEND

THE WONDROUS CROSS
Isaac Watts

VERSE: 1 Corinthians 1.18   **PASSAGE:** 1 Corinthians 1.18–25

 hen I survey the wondrous cross
On which the Prince of glory died,
My richest gain I count but loss,
And pour contempt on all my pride.

Forbid it, Lord, that I should boast,
Save in the cross of Christ my God;
All the vain things that charm me most,
I sacrifice them to his blood.

See from his head, his hands, his feet,
Sorrow and love flow mingled down;
Did e'er such love and sorrow meet,
Or thorns compose so rich a crown?

His dying crimson like a robe,
Spreads o'er his body on the tree;
Then am I dead to all the globe,
And all the globe is dead to me.

Were the whole realm of nature mine,
That were an offering far too small;
Love so amazing, so divine,
Demands my heart, my life, my all!

ADDITIONAL SCRIPTURE READING:
Isaiah 29.14; Mark 15.37–39

Go to page 1351 for your next devotional reading.

1700   1900

6 I have applied all this to Apollos and myself for your benefit, brothers and sisters,q so that you may learn through us the meaning of the saying, "Nothing beyond what is written," so that none of you will be puffed up in favor of one against another. 7For who sees anything different in you?r What do you have that you did not receive? And if you received it, why do you boast as if it were not a gift?

8 Already you have all you want! Already you have become rich! Quite apart from us you have become kings! Indeed, I wish that you had become kings, so that we might be kings with you! 9For I think that God has exhibited us apostles as last of all, as though sentenced to death, because we have become a spectacle to the world, to angels and to mortals. 10We are fools for the sake of Christ, but you are wise in Christ. We are weak, but you are strong. You are held in honor, but we in disrepute. 11To the present hour we are hungry and thirsty, we are poorly clothed and beaten and homeless, 12and we grow weary from the work of our own hands. When reviled, we bless; when persecuted, we endure; 13when slandered, we speak kindly. We have become like the rubbish of the world, the dregs of all things, to this very day.

Fatherly Admonition

14 I am not writing this to make you ashamed, but to admonish you as my beloved children. 15For though you might have ten thousand guardians in Christ, you do not have many fathers. Indeed, in Christ Jesus I became your father through the gospel. 16I appeal to you, then, be imitators of me. 17For this reason I sents you Timothy, who is my beloved and faithful child in the Lord, to remind you of my ways in Christ Jesus, as I teach them everywhere in every church. 18But some of you, thinking that I am not coming to you, have become arrogant. 19But I will come to you soon, if the Lord wills, and I will find out not the talk of these arrogant people but their power. 20For the kingdom of God depends not on talk but on power. 21What would you prefer? Am I to come to you with a stick, or with love in a spirit of gentleness?

Sexual Immorality Defiles the Church

5 It is actually reported that there is sexual immorality among you, and of a kind that is not found even among pagans; for a man is living with his father's wife. 2And you are arrogant! Should you not rather have mourned, so that he who has done this would have been removed from among you?

3 For though absent in body, I am present in spirit; and as if present I have already pronounced judgment 4in the name of the Lord Jesus on the man who has done such a thing.t When you are assembled, and my spirit is present with the power of our Lord Jesus, 5you are to hand this man over to Satan for the destruction of the flesh, so that his spirit may be saved in the day of the Lord.u

6 Your boasting is not a good thing. Do you not know that a little yeast leavens the whole batch of dough? 7Clean out the old yeast so that you may be a new batch, as you really are unleavened. For our paschal lamb, Christ, has been sacrificed. 8Therefore, let us celebrate the festival, not with the old yeast, the yeast of malice and evil, but with the unleavened bread of sincerity and truth.

Sexual Immorality Must Be Judged

9 I wrote to you in my letter not to associate with sexually immoral persons— 10not at all meaning the immoral of this world, or the greedy and robbers, or idolaters, since you would then need to go out of the world. 11But now I am writing to you not to associate with anyone who bears the name of brother or sisterv who is sexually immoral or greedy, or is an idolater, reviler, drunkard, or robber. Do not even eat with such a one. 12For what have I to do with judging those outside? Is it not those who are inside that you are to judge? 13God will judge those outside. "Drive out the wicked person from among you."

q Gk brothers   r Or Who makes you different from another?   s Or am sending   t Or on the man who has done such a thing in the name of the Lord Jesus   u Other ancient authorities add Jesus
v Gk brother

Lawsuits among Believers

6 When any of you has a grievance against another, do you dare to take it to court before the unrighteous, instead of taking it before the saints? 2Do you not know that the saints will judge the world? And if the world is to be judged by you, are you incompetent to try trivial cases? 3Do you not know that we are to judge angels—to say nothing of ordinary matters? 4If you have ordinary cases, then, do you appoint as judges those who have no standing in the church? 5I say this to your shame. Can it be that there is no one among you wise enough to decide between one believerᵂ and another, 6but a believerᵂ goes to court against a believerᵂ—and before unbelievers at that?

7 In fact, to have lawsuits at all with one another is already a defeat for you. Why not rather be wronged? Why not rather be defrauded? 8But you yourselves wrong and defraud—and believersˣ at that.

9 Do you not know that wrongdoers will not inherit the kingdom of God? Do not be deceived! Fornicators, idolaters, adulterers, male prostitutes, sodomites, 10thieves, the greedy, drunkards, revilers, robbers—none of these will inherit the kingdom of God. 11And this is what some of you used to be. But you were washed, you were sanctified, you were justified in the name of the Lord Jesus Christ and in the Spirit of our God.

Glorify God in Body and Spirit

12 "All things are lawful for me," but not all things are beneficial. "All things are lawful for me," but I will not be dominated by anything. 13"Food is meant for the stomach and the stomach for food,"ʸ and God will destroy both one and the other. The body is meant not for fornication but for the Lord, and the Lord for the body. 14And God raised the Lord and will also raise us by his power. 15Do you not know that your bodies are members of Christ? Should I therefore take the members of Christ and make them members of a prostitute? Never! 16Do you not know that whoever is united to a prostitute becomes one body with her? For it is said, "The two shall be one flesh." 17But anyone united to the Lord becomes one spirit with him. 18Shun fornication! Every sin that a person commits is outside the body; but the fornicator sins against the body itself. 19Or do you not know that your body is a templeᶻ of the Holy Spirit within you, which you have from God, and that you are not your own? 20For you were bought with a price; therefore glorify God in your body.

Directions concerning Marriage

7 Now concerning the matters about which you wrote: "It is well for a man not to touch a woman." 2But because of cases of sexual immorality, each man should have his own wife and each woman her own husband. 3The husband should give to his wife her conjugal rights, and likewise the wife to her husband. 4For the wife does not have authority over her own body, but the husband does; likewise the husband does not have authority over his own body, but the wife does. 5Do not deprive one another except perhaps by agreement for a set time, to devote yourselves to prayer, and then come together again, so that Satan may not tempt you because of your lack of self-control. 6This I say by way of concession, not of command. 7I wish that all were as I myself am. But each has a particular gift from God, one having one kind and another a different kind.

8 To the unmarried and the widows I say that it is well for them to remain unmarried as I am. 9But if they are not practicing self-control, they should marry. For it is better to marry than to be aflame with passion.

10 To the married I give this command—not I but the Lord—that the wife should not separate from her husband 11(but if she does separate, let her remain unmarried or else be reconciled to her husband), and that the husband should not divorce his wife.

12 To the rest I say—I and not the Lord—that if any believerᵂ has a wife who is an unbeliever, and she consents to live with him, he should not divorce her. 13And if any woman has a husband who is an unbeliever, and he consents to live with her, she should not divorce

him. ¹⁴For the unbelieving husband is her husband. Otherwise, your children made holy through his wife, and the would be unclean, but as it is, they are unbelieving wife is made holy through holy. ¹⁵But if the unbelieving partner

MONDAY

THE EXHORTATION OF A FATHER TO HIS CHILDREN
Robert Smith

VERSE: 1 Corinthians 6.19   **PASSAGE:** 1 Corinthians 6.19–20

 e are the temples of the Lord,
        For ye are dearly bought;
  And they that do defile the same
        Shall surely come to naught.

Possess not pride in any wise,
      Build not your house too high;
But have always before your eyes
      That ye be born to die.

Defraud not him that hired is,
      Your labor to sustain
But give him always out of hand,
      His penny for his pain.

And as you would that other men
      Against you should proceed,
Do you the same to them again
      When they do stand in need.

And part your portion with the poor
      In money and in meat;
And feed the fainted feeble soul
      With that which ye should eat.

Ask counsel always of the wise,
      Give ear unto the end;
Refuse not you the sweet rebuke
      of him that is your friend.

Be thankful always to the Lord,
      With prayer and with praise,
Desiring him in all your works
      For to direct your ways.

ADDITIONAL SCRIPTURE READING:
2 Corinthians 6.16–18; Romans 15.5–6

Go to page 1353 for your next devotional reading.

1500   1700

separates, let it be so; in such a case the brother or sister is not bound. It is to peace that God has called you.*a* **16**Wife, for all you know, you might save your husband. Husband, for all you know, you might save your wife.

The Life That the Lord Has Assigned

17 However that may be, let each of you lead the life that the Lord has assigned, to which God called you. This is my rule in all the churches. **18**Was anyone at the time of his call already circumcised? Let him not seek to remove the marks of circumcision. Was anyone at the time of his call uncircumcised? Let him not seek circumcision. **19**Circumcision is nothing, and uncircumcision is nothing; but obeying the commandments of God is everything. **20**Let each of you remain in the condition in which you were called.

21 Were you a slave when called? Do not be concerned about it. Even if you can gain your freedom, make use of your present condition now more than ever.*b* **22**For whoever was called in the Lord as a slave is a freed person belonging to the Lord, just as whoever was free when called is a slave of Christ. **23**You were bought with a price; do not become slaves of human masters. **24**In whatever condition you were called, brothers and sisters,*c* there remain with God.

The Unmarried and the Widows

25 Now concerning virgins, I have no command of the Lord, but I give my opinion as one who by the Lord's mercy is trustworthy. **26**I think that, in view of the impending*d* crisis, it is well for you to remain as you are. **27**Are you bound to a wife? Do not seek to be free. Are you free from a wife? Do not seek a wife. **28**But if you marry, you do not sin, and if a virgin marries, she does not sin. Yet those who marry will experience distress in this life,*e* and I would spare you that. **29**I mean, brothers and sisters,*c* the appointed time has grown short; from now on, let even those who have wives be as though they had none, **30**and those who mourn as though they were not mourning, and those who rejoice as though

they were not rejoicing, and those who buy as though they had no possessions, **31**and those who deal with the world as though they had no dealings with it. For the present form of this world is passing away.

32 I want you to be free from anxieties. The unmarried man is anxious about the affairs of the Lord, how to please the Lord; **33**but the married man is anxious about the affairs of the world, how to please his wife, **34**and his interests are divided. And the unmarried woman and the virgin are anxious about the affairs of the Lord, so that they may be holy in body and spirit; but the married woman is anxious about the affairs of the world, how to please her husband. **35**I say this for your own benefit, not to put any restraint upon you, but to promote good order and unhindered devotion to the Lord.

36 If anyone thinks that he is not behaving properly toward his fiancée,*f* if his passions are strong, and so it has to be, let him marry as he wishes; it is no sin. Let them marry. **37**But if someone stands firm in his resolve, being under no necessity but having his own desire under control, and has determined in his own mind to keep her as his fiancée,*f* he will do well. **38**So then, he who marries his fiancée*f* does well; and he who refrains from marriage will do better.

39 A wife is bound as long as her husband lives. But if the husband dies,*g* she is free to marry anyone she wishes, only in the Lord. **40**But in my judgment she is more blessed if she remains as she is. And I think that I too have the Spirit of God.

Food Offered to Idols

8 Now concerning food sacrificed to idols: we know that "all of us possess knowledge." Knowledge puffs up, but love builds up. **2**Anyone who claims to know something does not yet have the necessary knowledge; **3**but anyone who loves God is known by him.

4 Hence, as to the eating of food offered to idols, we know that "no idol in the world really exists," and that "there is no God but one." **5**Indeed, even though there may be so-called gods in heaven or

---

a Other ancient authorities read *us*   *b* Or *avail yourself of the opportunity*   *c* Gk *brothers*
d Or *present*   *e* Gk *in the flesh*   *f* Gk *virgin*   *g* Gk *falls asleep*

on earth—as in fact there are many gods and many lords— ⁶yet for us there is one God, the Father, from whom are all things and for whom we exist, and one Lord, Jesus Christ, through whom are all things and through whom we exist.

7 It is not everyone, however, who

has this knowledge. Since some have become so accustomed to idols until now, they still think of the food they eat as food offered to an idol; and their conscience, being weak, is defiled. ⁸"Food will not bring us close to God."ʰ We are no worse off if we do not eat, and no

h The quotation may extend to the end of the verse

TUESDAY

UNITED WITH THE LORD
Teresa of Avila

VERSE: 1 Corinthians 7.32, 34   **PASSAGE:** 1 Corinthians 7.25–40

he spiritual betrothal is different, for the two often separate. And the union is also different because, even though it is the joining of two things into one, in the end the two can be separated and each remains by itself. We observe this ordinarily, for the favor of union with the Lord passes quickly, and afterward the soul remains without that company; I mean, without the awareness of it. In this other favor from the Lord, no. The soul always remains with its God in that center. Let us say that the union is like the joining of two wax candles to such an extent that the flame coming from them is but one, or that the wick, the flame, and the wax are all one. But afterward one candle can be easily separated from the other and there are two candles; the same holds for the wick. In the spiritual marriage the union is like what we have when rain falls from the sky into a river or fount; all is water, for the rain that fell from heaven cannot be divided or separated from the water of the river. Or it is like what we have when a little stream enters the sea, there is no means of separating the two. Or, like the bright light entering a room through two different windows; although the streams of light are separate when entering the room, they become one.

Perhaps this is what Saint Paul means in saying *he that is joined or united to the Lord becomes one Spirit with him* (see 1 Corinthians 6.17), and is referring to this sovereign marriage, presupposing that his majesty has brought the soul to it through union.

ADDITIONAL SCRIPTURE READING:
Romans 8.9–11; Ephesians 4.4–6

Go to page 1355 for your next devotional reading.

1500   1700

better off if we do. ⁹But take care that this liberty of yours does not somehow become a stumbling block to the weak. ¹⁰For if others see you, who possess knowledge, eating in the temple of an idol, might they not, since their conscience is weak, be encouraged to the point of eating food sacrificed to idols? ¹¹So by your knowledge those weak believers for whom Christ died are destroyed.ⁱ ¹²But when you thus sin against members of your family,ʲ and wound their conscience when it is weak, you sin against Christ. ¹³Therefore, if food is a cause of their falling,ᵏ I will never eat meat, so that I may not cause one of themˡ to fall.

The Rights of an Apostle

9 Am I not free? Am I not an apostle? Have I not seen Jesus our Lord? Are you not my work in the Lord? ²If I am not an apostle to others, at least I am to you; for you are the seal of my apostleship in the Lord.

3 This is my defense to those who would examine me. ⁴Do we not have the right to our food and drink? ⁵Do we not have the right to be accompanied by a believing wife,ᵐ as do the other apostles and the brothers of the Lord and Cephas? ⁶Or is it only Barnabas and I who have no right to refrain from working for a living? ⁷Who at any time pays the expenses for doing military service? Who plants a vineyard and does not eat any of its fruit? Or who tends a flock and does not get any of its milk?

8 Do I say this on human authority? Does not the law also say the same? ⁹For it is written in the law of Moses, "You shall not muzzle an ox while it is treading out the grain." Is it for oxen that God is concerned? ¹⁰Or does he not speak entirely for our sake? It was indeed written for our sake, for whoever plows should plow in hope and whoever threshes should thresh in hope of a share in the crop. ¹¹If we have sown spiritual good among you, is it too much if we reap your material benefits? ¹²If others share this rightful claim on you, do not we still more?

Nevertheless, we have not made use

of this right, but we endure anything rather than put an obstacle in the way of the gospel of Christ. ¹³Do you not know that those who are employed in the temple service get their food from the temple, and those who serve at the altar share in what is sacrificed on the altar? ¹⁴In the same way, the Lord commanded that those who proclaim the gospel should get their living by the gospel.

15 But I have made no use of any of these rights, nor am I writing this so that they may be applied in my case. Indeed, I would rather die than that—no one will deprive me of my ground for boasting! ¹⁶If I proclaim the gospel, this gives me no ground for boasting, for an obligation is laid on me, and woe to me if I do not proclaim the gospel! ¹⁷For if I do this of my own will, I have a reward; but if not of my own will, I am entrusted with a commission. ¹⁸What then is my reward? Just this: that in my proclamation I may make the gospel free of charge, so as not to make full use of my rights in the gospel.

19 For though I am free with respect to all, I have made myself a slave to all, so that I might win more of them. ²⁰To the Jews I became as a Jew, in order to win Jews. To those under the law I became as one under the law (though I myself am not under the law) so that I might win those under the law. ²¹To those outside the law I became as one outside the law (though I am not free from God's law but am under Christ's law) so that I might win those outside the law. ²²To the weak I became weak, so that I might win the weak. I have become all things to all people, that I might by all means save some. ²³I do it all for the sake of the gospel, so that I may share in its blessings.

24 Do you not know that in a race the runners all compete, but only one

WHEN THE FIGHT BEGINS WITHIN HIMSELF, A MAN'S WORTH SOMETHING. —Robert Browning

receives the prize? Run in such a way that you may win it. ²⁵Athletes exercise

ⁱ Gk the weak brother . . . is destroyed   ʲ Gk against the brothers   ᵏ Gk my brother's falling
ˡ Gk cause my brother   ᵐ Gk a sister as wife

self-control in all things; they do it to receive a perishable wreath, but we an imperishable one. 26So I do not run aimlessly, nor do I box as though beating the air; 27but I punish my body and enslave it, so that after proclaiming to others I myself should not be disqualified.

n Gk brothers

Warnings from Israel's History

10 I do not want you to be unaware, brothers and sisters,[n] that our ancestors were all under the cloud, and all passed through the sea, 2and all were baptized into Moses in the cloud and in the sea, 3and all ate the

---

WEDNESDAY

WHY IS THERE NO LAW FOR THOSE WHO ARE GOOD?
Bernard of Clairvaux

VERSE: 1 Corinthians 9.21   PASSAGE: 1 Corinthians 9.19–23

nd so the sons are not outside the law, unless perhaps someone wants to put a different interpretation on the text "The law is not made for the righteous" (1 Timothy 1.9, KJV). But you must know that law given in a spirit of slavery by fear is different from the law of freedom given in gentleness. Children are not under fear, but they cannot survive without love.

Do you wish to hear why there is no law for those who are good? Scripture says, "You have not received the spirit of slavery again in fear" (Romans 8.15, KJV). Hear then the just man saying of himself that he is not under the law and yet not free of the law. "I have become," he says, "as if I were under the law with those who are bound by the law, although I am not outside the law of God but bound by that of Christ" (1 Corinthians 9.20–21, KJV). So it is not right to say, "The just have no law," or, "The just are outside the law," but "The law is not made for the just," that is, it is not imposed on them against their will, but freely given to them when they are willing, and inspired by goodness (1 Timothy 1.9). So the Lord says beautifully, "Take my yoke upon you" (Matthew 11.29), as if he said, "I do not impose it on the unwilling; but you take it if you want to; otherwise you will find not rest but labor for your souls."

ADDITIONAL SCRIPTURE READING:
Joshua 22.5; Galatians 5.14

Go to page 1357 for your next devotional reading.

500   1500

same spiritual food, 4and all drank the same spiritual drink. For they drank from the spiritual rock that followed them, and the rock was Christ. 5Nevertheless, God was not pleased with most of them, and they were struck down in the wilderness.

6 Now these things occurred as examples for us, so that we might not desire evil as they did. 7Do not become idolaters as some of them did; as it is written, "The people sat down to eat and drink, and they rose up to play." 8We must not indulge in sexual immorality as some of them did, and twenty-three thousand fell in a single day. 9We must not put Christ*o* to the test, as some of them did, and were destroyed by serpents. 10And do not complain as some of them did, and were destroyed by the destroyer. 11These things happened to them to serve as an example, and they were written down to instruct us, on whom the ends of the ages have come. 12So if you think you are standing, watch out that you do not fall. 13No testing has overtaken you that is not common to everyone. God is faithful, and he will not let you be tested beyond your strength, but with the testing he will also provide the way out so that you may be able to endure it.

HE SAID NOT, THOU SHALL NOT BE TEMPESTED,
THOU SHALL NOT BE TRAVAILED,
THOU SHALL NOT BE AFFLICTED,
BUT HE SAID, THOU SHALL NOT BE OVERCOME.
—*Julian of Norwich*

14 Therefore, my dear friends,*p* flee from the worship of idols. 15I speak as to sensible people; judge for yourselves what I say. 16The cup of blessing that we bless, is it not a sharing in the blood of Christ? The bread that we break, is it not a sharing in the body of Christ? 17Because there is one bread, we who are many are one body, for we all partake of the one bread. 18Consider the people of Israel;*q* are not those who eat the sacrifices partners in the altar? 19What do I imply then? That food sacrificed to idols

is anything, or that an idol is anything? 20No, I imply that what pagans sacrifice, they sacrifice to demons and not to God. I do not want you to be partners with demons. 21You cannot drink the cup of the Lord and the cup of demons. You cannot partake of the table of the Lord and the table of demons. 22Or are we provoking the Lord to jealousy? Are we stronger than he?

Do All to the Glory of God

23 "All things are lawful," but not all things are beneficial. "All things are lawful," but not all things build up. 24Do not seek your own advantage, but that of the other. 25Eat whatever is sold in the meat market without raising any question on the ground of conscience, 26for "the earth and its fullness are the Lord's." 27If an unbeliever invites you to a meal and you are disposed to go, eat whatever is set before you without raising any question on the ground of conscience. 28But if someone says to you, "This has been offered in sacrifice," then do not eat it, out of consideration for the one who informed you, and for the sake of conscience— 29I mean the other's conscience, not your own. For why should my liberty be subject to the judgment of someone else's conscience? 30If I partake with thankfulness, why should I be denounced because of that for which I give thanks?

31 So, whether you eat or drink, or whatever you do, do everything for the glory of God. 32Give no offense to Jews or to Greeks or to the church of God, 33just as I try to please everyone in everything I do, not seeking my own advantage, but that of many, so that they may be saved. 11 1Be imitators of me, as I am of Christ.

Head Coverings

2 I commend you because you remember me in everything and maintain the traditions just as I handed them on to you. 3But I want you to understand that Christ is the head of every man, and the husband*r* is the head of his wife,*s* and God is the head of Christ. 4Any man who

o Other ancient authorities read *the Lord*   p Gk *my beloved*   q Gk *Israel according to the flesh*
r The same Greek word means *man* or *husband*   s Or *head of the woman*

prays or prophesies with something on his head disgraces his head, [5]but any woman who prays or prophesies with her head unveiled disgraces her head—it is one and the same thing as having her head shaved. [6]For if a woman will not veil herself, then she should cut off her hair; but if it is disgraceful for a woman to

---

THURSDAY

EATING AND DRINKING JUDGMENT
Dietrich Bonhoeffer

VERSE: 1 Corinthians 11.29   **PASSAGE:** 1 Corinthians 11.23–32

You think the Bible hasn't much to say about health, fortune, vigor, etc . . . It's certainly not true of the Old Testament. The intermediate theological category between God and human fortune is, as far as I can see, that of blessing. In the Old Testament—for example among the patriarchs—there's a concern not for fortune, but for God's blessing, which includes in itself all earthly good. In that blessing the whole of the earthly life is claimed for God, and it includes all his promises. It would be natural to suppose that, as usual, the New Testament spiritualizes the teaching of the Old Testament here, and therefore to regard the Old Testament blessing as superseded in the New. But is it an accident that sickness and death are mentioned in connection with the misuse of the Lord's Supper ("the cup of *blessing*," 1 Corinthians 10.16, KJV; 11.30, emphasis added), that Jesus restored people's health, and that while his disciples were with him they "lacked nothing"? Now, is it right to set the Old Testament blessing against the cross? That is what Kierkegaard did. That makes the cross, or at least suffering, an abstract principle; and that is just what gives rise to an unhealthy methodism, which deprives suffering of its element of contingency as a divine ordinance. It is true that in the Old Testament the person who receives the blessing has to endure a great deal of suffering (e.g. Abraham, Isaac, Jacob, and Joseph), but this never leads to the idea that fortune and suffering, blessing and cross are mutually exclusive and contradictory—nor does it in the New Testament. Indeed, the only difference between the Old and New Testaments in this respect is that in the Old blessing includes the cross, and in the New the cross includes the blessing . . .

ADDITIONAL SCRIPTURE READING:
Malachi 4.2; Acts 3.16

Go to page 1359 for your next devotional reading.

1900   Present

have her hair cut off or to be shaved, she should wear a veil. 7For a man ought not to have his head veiled, since he is the image and reflection[t] of God; but woman is the reflection[t] of man. 8Indeed, man was not made from woman, but woman from man. 9Neither was man created for the sake of woman, but woman for the sake of man. 10For this reason a woman ought to have a symbol of[u] authority on her head,[v] because of the angels. 11Nevertheless, in the Lord woman is not independent of man or man independent of woman. 12For just as woman came from man, so man comes through woman; but all things come from God. 13Judge for yourselves: is it proper for a woman to pray to God with her head unveiled? 14Does not nature itself teach you that if a man wears long hair, it is degrading to him, 15but if a woman has long hair, it is her glory? For her hair is given to her for a covering. 16But if anyone is disposed to be contentious—we have no such custom, nor do the churches of God.

Abuses at the Lord's Supper

17 Now in the following instructions I do not commend you, because when you come together it is not for the better but for the worse. 18For, to begin with, when you come together as a church, I hear that there are divisions among you; and to some extent I believe it. 19Indeed, there have to be factions among you, for only so will it become clear who among you are genuine. 20When you come together, it is not really to eat the Lord's supper. 21For when the time comes to eat, each of you goes ahead with your own supper, and one goes hungry and another becomes drunk. 22What! Do you not have homes to eat and drink in? Or do you show contempt for the church of God and humiliate those who have nothing? What should I say to you? Should I commend you? In this matter I do not commend you!

The Institution of the Lord's Supper

23 For I received from the Lord what I also handed on to you, that the Lord Jesus

on the night when he was betrayed took a loaf of bread, 24and when he had given thanks, he broke it and said, "This is my body that is for[w] you. Do this in remembrance of me." 25In the same way he took the cup also, after supper, saying, "This cup is the new covenant in my blood. Do this, as often as you drink it, in remembrance of me." 26For as often as you eat this bread and drink the cup, you proclaim the Lord's death until he comes.

Partaking of the Supper Unworthily

27 Whoever, therefore, eats the bread or drinks the cup of the Lord in an unworthy manner will be answerable for the body and blood of the Lord. 28Examine yourselves, and only then eat of the bread and drink of the cup. 29For all who eat and drink[x] without discerning the body,[y] eat and drink judgment against themselves. 30For this reason many of you are weak and ill, and some have died.[z] 31But if we judged ourselves, we would not be judged. 32But when we are judged by the Lord, we are disciplined[a] so that we may not be condemned along with the world.

33 So then, my brothers and sisters,[b] when you come together to eat, wait for one another. 34If you are hungry, eat at home, so that when you come together, it will not be for your condemnation. About the other things I will give instructions when I come.

Spiritual Gifts

12 Now concerning spiritual gifts,[c] brothers and sisters,[b] I do not want you to be uninformed. 2You know that when you were pagans, you were enticed and led astray to idols that could not speak. 3Therefore I want you to understand that no one speaking by the Spirit of God ever says "Let Jesus be cursed!" and no one can say "Jesus is Lord" except by the Holy Spirit.

4 Now there are varieties of gifts, but the same Spirit; 5and there are varieties of services, but the same Lord; 6and there are varieties of activities, but it is the same God who activates all of them in

---

t Or glory   u Gk lacks a symbol of   v Or have freedom of choice regarding her head   w Other ancient authorities read is broken for   x Other ancient authorities add in an unworthy manner,   y Other ancient authorities read the Lord's body   z Gk fallen asleep   a Or When we are judged, we are being disciplined by the Lord   b Gk brothers   c Or spiritual persons

everyone. 7To each is given the manifestation of the Spirit for the common good. 8To one is given through the Spirit the utterance of wisdom, and to another the utterance of knowledge according to the same Spirit, 9to another faith by the

FROM THE SAINTS' EVERLASTING REST
Richard Baxter

VERSE: 1 Corinthians 13.8   PASSAGE: 1 Corinthians 13.8–10

t is a question with some whether or not we shall know each other in heaven. Surely, no knowledge shall cease that we now have, but only that which implies our imperfection; and what imperfection can this imply? Nay, our present knowledge shall be increased beyond belief. It shall indeed be done away, but only as the light of candles and stars is done away by the rising of the sun; which is more properly a doing away of our ignorance than of our knowledge.

Indeed, we shall not know each other after the flesh, not by stature, voice, color, complexion, visage, or outward shape. If we had so known Christ, we should know him no more; not by parts and gifts of learning, nor titles of honor or worldly dignity; nor by terms of affinity and consanguinity, nor benefits, nor such relations; nor by youth or age; nor, I think, by sex; but by the image of Christ and spiritual relation and former faithfulness in improving our talents, beyond doubt, we shall know and be known.

Nor is it only our old acquaintance, but all the saints of all the ages, whose faces in the flesh we never saw, whom we shall there both know and comfortably enjoy . . . Those who now are willingly ministering spirits for our good will willingly then be our companions in joy for the perfecting of our good; and they who had such joy in heaven for our conversion will gladly rejoice with us in our glorification. I think, Christian, this will be a more honorable assembly than ever you beheld and a more happy society than you were ever in before . . .

What a day will it be when we shall join with them in praises to our Lord in and for that kingdom! So then I conclude, this is one singular excellency of the Rest of heaven, that we are "fellow citizens with the saints, and of the household of God" (Ephesians 2.19, KJV).

ADDITIONAL SCRIPTURE READING:
Isaiah 29.13–14; 1 Corinthians 13.2

Go to page 1361 for your next devotional reading.

1500   1700

same Spirit, to another gifts of healing by the one Spirit, 10to another the working of miracles, to another prophecy, to another the discernment of spirits, to another various kinds of tongues, to another the interpretation of tongues. 11All these are activated by one and the same Spirit, who allots to each one individually just as the Spirit chooses.

One Body with Many Members

12 For just as the body is one and has many members, and all the members of the body, though many, are one body, so it is with Christ. 13For in the one Spirit we were all baptized into one body— Jews or Greeks, slaves or free—and we were all made to drink of one Spirit.

14 Indeed, the body does not consist of one member but of many. 15If the foot would say, "Because I am not a hand, I do not belong to the body," that would not make it any less a part of the body. 16And if the ear would say, "Because I am not an eye, I do not belong to the body," that would not make it any less a part of the body. 17If the whole body were an eye, where would the hearing be? If the whole body were hearing, where would the sense of smell be? 18But as it is, God arranged the members in the body, each one of them, as he chose. 19If all were a single member, where would the body be? 20As it is, there are many members, yet one body. 21The eye cannot say to the hand, "I have no need of you," nor again the head to the feet, "I have no need of you." 22On the contrary, the members of the body that seem to be weaker are indispensable, 23and those members of the body that we think less honorable we clothe with greater honor, and our less respectable members are treated with greater respect; 24whereas our more respectable members do not need this. But God has so arranged the body, giving the greater honor to the inferior member, 25that there may be no dissension within the body, but the members may have the same care for one another. 26If one member suffers, all suffer together with it; if one member is honored, all rejoice together with it.

27 Now you are the body of Christ and individually members of it. 28And God has appointed in the church first apostles, second prophets, third teachers; then deeds of power, then gifts of healing, forms of assistance, forms of leadership, various kinds of tongues. 29Are all apostles? Are all prophets? Are all teachers? Do all work miracles? 30Do all possess gifts of healing? Do all speak in tongues? Do all interpret? 31But strive for the greater gifts. And I will show you a still more excellent way.

The Gift of Love

13 If I speak in the tongues of mortals and of angels, but do not have love, I am a noisy gong or a clanging cymbal. 2And if I have prophetic powers, and understand all mysteries and all knowledge, and if I have all faith, so as to remove mountains, but do not have love, I am nothing. 3If I give away all my possessions, and if I hand over my body so that I may boast,d but do not have love, I gain nothing.

4 Love is patient; love is kind; love is not envious or boastful or arrogant 5or rude. It does not insist on its own way; it is not irritable or resentful; 6it does not rejoice in wrongdoing, but rejoices in the truth. 7It bears all things, believes all things, hopes all things, endures all things.

8 Love never ends. But as for prophecies, they will come to an end; as for tongues, they will cease; as for knowledge, it will come to an end. 9For we know only in part, and we prophesy only in part; 10but when the complete comes, the partial will come to an end. 11When I was a child, I spoke like a child, I thought like a child, I reasoned like a child; when I became an adult, I put an end to childish ways. 12For now we see in a mirror, dimly,e but then we will see face to face. Now I know only in part; then I will know fully, even as I have been fully known. 13And now faith, hope, and love abide, these three; and the greatest of these is love.

CHARITY IS THE SCOPE OF ALL GOD'S COMMANDS.
—*John Chrysostom*

---

d Other ancient authorities read *body to be burned*   e Gk *in a riddle*

WEEKEND

THE HABIT OF PERFECTION
Gerard Manley Hopkins

VERSE: 1 Corinthians 13.10   **PASSAGE:** 1 Corinthians 13.1–10

lected Silence, sing to me
And beat upon my whorlèd ear,
Pipe me to measures still and be
The music that I care to hear.

Shape nothing, lips; be lovely-dumb:
It is the shut, the curfew sent
From there where all surrenders come
Which only makes you eloquent.

Be shellèd, eyes, with double dark
And find the uncreated light:
This ruck and reel which you remark
Coils, keeps, and teases simple sight.

Palate, the hutch of tasty lust,
Desire not to be rinsed with wine:
The can must be so sweet, the crust
So fresh that come in fasts divine!

Nostrils, your careless breath that spend
Upon the stir and keep of pride,
What relish shall the censers send
Along the sanctuary side!

O feel-of-primrose hands, O feet
That want the yield of plushy sward,
But you shall walk the golden street
And you unhouse and house the Lord.

And, Poverty, be thou the bride
And now the marriage feast begun,
And lily-colored clothes provide
Your spouse not labored-at nor spun.

ADDITIONAL SCRIPTURE READING:
Colossians 1.28; Hebrews 12.22–23

Go to page 1364 for your next devotional reading.

1700   1900

Gifts of Prophecy and Tongues

14 Pursue love and strive for the spiritual gifts, and especially that you may prophesy. 2For those who speak in a tongue do not speak to other people but to God; for nobody understands them, since they are speaking mysteries in the Spirit. 3On the other hand, those who prophesy speak to other people for their upbuilding and encouragement and consolation. 4Those who speak in a tongue build up themselves, but those who prophesy build up the church. 5Now I would like all of you to speak in tongues, but even more to prophesy. One who prophesies is greater than one who speaks in tongues, unless someone interprets, so that the church may be built up.

6 Now, brothers and sisters,f if I come to you speaking in tongues, how will I benefit you unless I speak to you in some revelation or knowledge or prophecy or teaching? 7It is the same way with lifeless instruments that produce sound, such as the flute or the harp. If they do not give distinct notes, how will anyone know what is being played? 8And if the bugle gives an indistinct sound, who will get ready for battle? 9So with yourselves; if in a tongue you utter speech that is not intelligible, how will anyone know what is being said? For you will be speaking into the air. 10There are doubtless many different kinds of sounds in the world, and nothing is without sound. 11If then I do not know the meaning of a sound, I will be a foreigner to the speaker and the speaker a foreigner to me. 12So with yourselves; since you are eager for spiritual gifts, strive to excel in them for building up the church.

13 Therefore, one who speaks in a tongue should pray for the power to interpret. 14For if I pray in a tongue, my spirit prays but my mind is unproductive. 15What should I do then? I will pray with the spirit, but I will pray with the mind also; I will sing praise with the spirit, but I will sing praise with the mind also. 16Otherwise, if you say a blessing with the spirit, how can anyone in the position of an outsider say the "Amen" to your thanksgiving, since the outsider does not know what you are

saying? 17For you may give thanks well enough, but the other person is not built up. 18I thank God that I speak in tongues more than all of you; 19nevertheless, in church I would rather speak five words with my mind, in order to instruct others also, than ten thousand words in a tongue.

20 Brothers and sisters,f do not be children in your thinking; rather, be infants in evil, but in thinking be adults. 21In the law it is written,

"By people of strange tongues
    and by the lips of foreigners
I will speak to this people;
    yet even then they will not listen
        to me,"

says the Lord. 22Tongues, then, are a sign not for believers but for unbelievers, while prophecy is not for unbelievers but for believers. 23If, therefore, the whole church comes together and all speak in tongues, and outsiders or unbelievers enter, will they not say that you are out of your mind? 24But if all prophesy, an unbeliever or outsider who enters is reproved by all and called to account by all. 25After the secrets of the unbeliever's heart are disclosed, that person will bow down before God and worship him, declaring, "God is really among you."

Orderly Worship

26 What should be done then, my friends?f When you come together, each one has a hymn, a lesson, a revelation, a tongue, or an interpretation. Let all things be done for building up. 27If anyone speaks in a tongue, let there be only two or at most three, and each in turn; and let one interpret. 28But if there is no one to interpret, let them be silent in church and speak to themselves and to God. 29Let two or three prophets speak, and let the others weigh what is said. 30If a revelation is made to someone else sitting nearby, let the first person be silent. 31For you can all prophesy one by one, so that all may learn and all be encouraged. 32And the spirits of prophets are subject to the prophets, 33for God is a God not of disorder but of peace.

(As in all the churches of the saints, 34women should be silent in the

f Gk brothers

churches. For they are not permitted to speak, but should be subordinate, as the law also says. 35If there is anything they desire to know, let them ask their husbands at home. For it is shameful for a woman to speak in church.g 36Or did the word of God originate with you? Or are you the only ones it has reached?)

37 Anyone who claims to be a prophet, or to have spiritual powers, must acknowledge that what I am writing to you is a command of the Lord. 38Anyone who does not recognize this is not to be recognized. 39So, my friends,h be eager to prophesy, and do not forbid speaking in tongues; 40but all things should be done decently and in order.

The Resurrection of Christ

15 Now I would remind you, brothers and sisters,i of the good newsj that I proclaimed to you, which you in turn received, in which also you stand, 2through which also you are being saved, if you hold firmly to the message that I proclaimed to you—unless you have come to believe in vain.

3 For I handed on to you as of first importance what I in turn had received: that Christ died for our sins in accordance with the scriptures, 4and that he was buried, and that he was raised on the third day in accordance with the scriptures, 5and that he appeared to Cephas, then to the twelve. 6Then he appeared to more than five hundred brothers and sistersi at one time, most of whom are still alive, though some have died.k 7Then he appeared to James, then to all the apostles. 8Last of all, as to one untimely born, he appeared also to me. 9For I am the

---

THE PRIMARY DECLARATION OF CHRISTIANITY IS NOT "THIS DO!" BUT "THIS HAPPENED!"

—Evelyn Underhill

---

least of the apostles, unfit to be called an apostle, because I persecuted the church of God. 10But by the grace of God I am what I am, and his grace toward me has not been in vain. On the contrary, I worked harder than any of them—

though it was not I, but the grace of God that is with me. 11Whether then it was I or they, so we proclaim and so you have come to believe.

The Resurrection of the Dead

12 Now if Christ is proclaimed as raised from the dead, how can some of you say there is no resurrection of the dead? 13If there is no resurrection of the dead, then Christ has not been raised; 14and if Christ has not been raised, then our proclamation has been in vain and your faith has been in vain. 15We are even found to be misrepresenting God, because we testified of God that he raised Christ—whom he did not raise if it is true that the dead are not raised. 16For if the dead are not raised, then Christ has not been raised. 17If Christ has not been raised, your faith is futile and you are still in your sins. 18Then those also who have diedk in Christ have perished. 19If for this life only we have hoped in Christ, we are of all people most to be pitied.

WHAT REASON HAVE ATHEISTS FOR SAYING THAT WE CANNOT RISE AGAIN? WHICH IS THE MORE DIFFICULT, TO BE BORN, OR TO RISE AGAIN? THAT WHAT HAS NEVER BEEN, SHOULD BE, OR THAT WHAT HAS BEEN SHOULD BE AGAIN? IS IT MORE DIFFICULT TO COME INTO BEING THAN TO RETURN TO IT?   —Blaise Pascal

---

20 But in fact Christ has been raised from the dead, the first fruits of those who have died.k 21For since death came through a human being, the resurrection of the dead has also come through a human being; 22for as all die in Adam, so all will be made alive in Christ. 23But each in his own order: Christ the first fruits, then at his coming those who belong to Christ. 24Then comes the end,l when he hands over the kingdom to God the Father, after he has destroyed every ruler and every authority and power. 25For he must reign until he has put all his enemies under his feet. 26The last enemy to be destroyed is death.

---

g Other ancient authorities put verses 34-35 after verse 40   h Gk my brothers   i Gk brothers
j Or gospel   k Gk fallen asleep   l Or Then come the rest

27For "God*m* has put all things in subjection under his feet." But when it says, "All things are put in subjection," it is plain that this does not include the one who put all things in subjection under him. 28When all things are subjected to him, then the Son himself will also be subjected to the one who put all things in subjection under him, so that God may be all in all.

29 Otherwise, what will those people do who receive baptism on behalf of the dead? If the dead are not raised at all, why are people baptized on their behalf? 30 And why are we putting ourselves in danger every hour? 31I die every day! That is as certain, brothers and sisters,*n* as my boasting of you—a boast that I make in Christ Jesus our Lord. 32If with merely human hopes I fought with wild

m Gk *he*   *n* Gk *brothers*

MONDAY

THE REALITY OF CHRIST
Ignatius of Antioch

VERSE: 1 Corinthians 15.32   PASSAGE: 1 Corinthians 15.29–34

e deaf, therefore, whenever anyone speaks to you apart from Jesus Christ, who was of the family of David, who was the son of Mary; who really was born, who both ate and drank; who really was persecuted under Pontius Pilate, who really was crucified and died while those in heaven and on earth looked on; who, moreover, really was raised from the dead when his Father raised him up, who—his Father, that is—in the same way will likewise also raise us up in Christ Jesus who believe in him, apart from whom we have no true life.

But if, as some atheists (that is, unbelievers) say, he suffered in appearance only (while they exist in appearance only!), why am I in chains? And why do I want to fight with wild beasts? If that is the case, I die for no reason; what is more, I am telling lies about the Lord.

Flee, therefore, from these wicked offshoots that bear deadly fruit; if anyone even tastes it, he dies on the spot. These people are not the Father's planting. For if they were, they would appear as branches of the cross, and their fruit would be imperishable—the same cross by which he, through his suffering, calls you who are his members. The head, therefore, cannot be born without members, since God promises unity, which he himself is.

ADDITIONAL SCRIPTURE READING:
2 Corinthians 4.14; Colossians 1.21–22

Go to page 1369 for your next devotional reading.

100   500

animals at Ephesus, what would I have gained by it? If the dead are not raised,.

"Let us eat and drink,
for tomorrow we die."

33Do not be deceived:

"Bad company ruins good morals."

34Come to a sober and right mind, and sin no more; for some people have no knowledge of God. I say this to your shame.

The Resurrection Body

35 But someone will ask, "How are the dead raised? With what kind of body do they come?" 36Fool! What you sow does not come to life unless it dies. 37And as for what you sow, you do not sow the body that is to be, but a bare seed, perhaps of wheat or of some other grain. 38But God gives it a body as he has chosen, and to each kind of seed its own body. 39Not all flesh is alike, but there is one flesh for human beings, another for animals, another for birds, and another for fish. 40There are both heavenly bodies and earthly bodies, but the glory of the heavenly is one thing, and that of the earthly is another. 41There is one glory of the sun, and another glory of the moon, and another glory of the stars; indeed, star differs from star in glory.

42 So it is with the resurrection of the dead. What is sown is perishable, what is raised is imperishable. 43It is sown in dishonor, it is raised in glory. It is sown in weakness, it is raised in power. 44It is sown a physical body, it is raised a spiritual body. If there is a physical body, there is also a spiritual body. 45Thus it is written, "The first man, Adam, became a living being"; the last Adam became a life-giving spirit. 46But it is not the spiritual that is first, but the physical, and then the spiritual. 47The first man was from the earth, a man of dust; the second man iso from heaven. 48As was the man of dust, so are those who are of the dust; and as is the man of heaven, so are those who are of heaven. 49Just as we have borne the image of the man of dust, we willp also bear the image of the man of heaven.

50 What I am saying, brothers and sisters,q is this: flesh and blood cannot inherit the kingdom of God, nor does the perishable inherit the imperishable. 51Listen, I will tell you a mystery! We will not all die,r but we will all be changed, 52in a moment, in the twinkling of an eye, at the last trumpet. For the trumpet will sound, and the dead will be raised imperishable, and we will be changed. 53For this perishable body must put on imperishability, and this mortal body must put on immortality. 54When this perishable body puts on imperishability, and this mortal body puts on immortality, then the saying that is written will be fulfilled:

"Death has been swallowed up in victory."

55 "Where, O death, is your victory?
Where, O death, is your sting?"

56The sting of death is sin, and the power of sin is the law. 57But thanks be

---

ONE SHORT SLEEP PAST, WE WAKE ETERNALLY,

AND DEATH SHALL BE NO MORE: DEATH, THOU

SHALT DIE!

—*John Donne*

---

to God, who gives us the victory through our Lord Jesus Christ.

58 Therefore, my beloved,s be steadfast, immovable, always excelling in the work of the Lord, because you know that in the Lord your labor is not in vain.

The Collection for the Saints

16 Now concerning the collection for the saints: you should follow the directions I gave to the churches of Galatia. 2On the first day of every week, each of you is to put aside and save whatever extra you earn, so that collections need not be taken when I come. 3And when I arrive, I will send any whom you approve with letters to take your gift to Jerusalem. 4If it seems advisable that I should go also, they will accompany me.

Plans for Travel

5 I will visit you after passing through Macedonia—for I intend to pass through Macedonia— 6and perhaps I

---

o Other ancient authorities add *the Lord*   p Other ancient authorities read *let us*   q Gk *brothers*
r Gk *fall asleep*   s Gk *beloved brothers*

will stay with you or even spend the winter, so that you may send me on my way, wherever I go. 7I do not want to see you now just in passing, for I hope to spend some time with you, if the Lord permits. 8But I will stay in Ephesus until Pentecost, 9for a wide door for effective work has opened to me, and there are many adversaries.

10 If Timothy comes, see that he has nothing to fear among you, for he is doing the work of the Lord just as I am; 11therefore let no one despise him. Send him on his way in peace, so that he may come to me; for I am expecting him with the brothers.

12 Now concerning our brother Apollos, I strongly urged him to visit you with the other brothers, but he was not at all willing*t* to come now. He will come when he has the opportunity.

Final Messages and Greetings

13 Keep alert, stand firm in your faith, be courageous, be strong. 14Let all that you do be done in love.

15 Now, brothers and sisters,*u* you know that members of the household of Stephanas were the first converts in Achaia, and they have devoted themselves to the service of the saints; 16I urge you to put yourselves at the service of such people, and of everyone who works and toils with them. 17I rejoice at the coming of Stephanas and Fortunatus and Achaicus, because they have made up for your absence; 18for they refreshed my spirit as well as yours. So give recognition to such persons.

19 The churches of Asia send greetings. Aquila and Prisca, together with the church in their house, greet you warmly in the Lord. 20All the brothers and sisters*u* send greetings. Greet one another with a holy kiss.

21 I, Paul, write this greeting with my own hand. 22Let anyone be accursed who has no love for the Lord. Our Lord, come!*v* 23The grace of the Lord Jesus be with you. 24My love be with all of you in Christ Jesus.*w*

---

t Or *it was not at all God's will for him*   *u* Gk *brothers*   *v* Gk *Marana tha*. These Aramaic words can also be read *Maran atha*, meaning *Our Lord has come*   *w* Other ancient authorities add *Amen*

2 CORINTHIANS

P AUL WROTE THIS SECOND LETTER TO THE CORINTHIANS A FEW MONTHS AFTER THE FIRST LETTER. THE DIVISIONS AND PROBLEMS ADDRESSED IN 1 CORINTHIANS WERE STILL PRESENT IN THE CHURCH AND FALSE TEACHERS WERE CHALLENGING PAUL'S INTEGRITY AND HIS AUTHORITY AS AN APOSTLE. WITH PASSIONATE EMOTION, PAUL MOVES BACK AND FORTH BETWEEN DESPAIR AND ECSTATIC JOY. WATCH FOR PRACTICAL ADVICE ON RESOLVING CONFLICT WITHIN THE CHURCH AND PROVIDING FINANCIAL SUPPORT FOR THE CHURCH AND FOR THE POOR.

Salutation

1 Paul, an apostle of Christ Jesus by the will of God, and Timothy our brother,

To the church of God that is in Corinth, including all the saints throughout Achaia:

2 Grace to you and peace from God our Father and the Lord Jesus Christ.

Paul's Thanksgiving after Affliction

3 Blessed be the God and Father of our Lord Jesus Christ, the Father of mercies and the God of all consolation, 4who consoles us in all our affliction, so that we may be able to console those who are in any affliction with the consolation with which we ourselves are con-soled by God. 5For just as the sufferings of Christ are abundant for us, so also our consolation is abundant through Christ. 6If we are being afflicted, it is for your consolation and salvation; if we are being consoled, it is for your consolation, which you experience when you patiently endure the same sufferings that we are also suffering. 7Our hope for you is unshaken; for we know that as you share in our sufferings, so also you share in our consolation.

8 We do not want you to be unaware, brothers and sisters,*a* of the affliction we experienced in Asia; for we were so utterly, unbearably crushed that we despaired of life itself. 9Indeed, we felt that we had received the sentence of death so that we would rely not on ourselves but

a Gk *brothers*

on God who raises the dead. [10]He who rescued us from so deadly a peril will continue to rescue us; on him we have set our hope that he will rescue us again, [11]as you also join in helping us by your prayers, so that many will give thanks on our[b] behalf for the blessing granted us through the prayers of many.

The Postponement of Paul's Visit

12 Indeed, this is our boast, the testimony of our conscience: we have behaved in the world with frankness[c] and godly sincerity, not by earthly wisdom but by the grace of God—and all the more toward you. [13]For we write you nothing other than what you can read and also understand; I hope you will understand until the end— [14]as you have already understood us in part—that on the day of the Lord Jesus we are your boast even as you are our boast.

15 Since I was sure of this, I wanted to come to you first, so that you might have a double favor;[d] [16]I wanted to visit you on my way to Macedonia, and to come back to you from Macedonia and have you send me on to Judea. [17]Was I vacillating when I wanted to do this? Do I make my plans according to ordinary human standards,[e] ready to say "Yes, yes" and "No, no" at the same time? [18]As surely as God is faithful, our word to you has not been "Yes and No." [19]For the Son of God, Jesus Christ, whom we proclaimed among you, Silvanus and Timothy and I, was not "Yes and No"; but in him it is always "Yes." [20]For in him every one of God's promises is a "Yes." For this reason it is through him that we say the "Amen," to the glory of God. [21]But it is God who establishes us with you in Christ and has anointed us, [22]by putting his seal on us and giving us his Spirit in our hearts as a first installment.

23 But I call on God as witness against me: it was to spare you that I did not come again to Corinth. [24]I do not mean to imply that we lord it over your faith; rather, we are workers with you for your joy, because you stand firm in the faith. 2 [1]So I made up my mind not to make you another painful visit. [2]For if I cause you pain, who is there to make me glad but the one whom I have pained? [3]And I wrote as I did, so that when I came, I might not suffer pain from those who should have made me rejoice; for I am confident about all of you, that my joy would be the joy of all of you. [4]For I wrote you out of much distress and anguish of heart and with many tears, not to cause you pain, but to let you know the abundant love that I have for you.

Forgiveness for the Offender

5 But if anyone has caused pain, he has caused it not to me, but to some extent—not to exaggerate it—to all of you. [6]This punishment by the majority is enough for such a person; [7]so now instead you should forgive and console him, so that he may not be overwhelmed by excessive sorrow. [8]So I urge you to reaffirm your love for him. [9]I wrote for this reason: to test you and to know whether you are obedient in everything. [10]Anyone whom you forgive, I also forgive. What I have forgiven, if I have forgiven anything, has been for your sake in the presence of Christ. [11]And we do this so that we may not be outwitted by Satan; for we are not ignorant of his designs.

Paul's Anxiety in Troas

12 When I came to Troas to proclaim the good news of Christ, a door was opened for me in the Lord; [13]but my mind could not rest because I did not find my brother Titus there. So I said farewell to them and went on to Macedonia.

14 But thanks be to God, who in Christ always leads us in triumphal procession, and through us spreads in every place the fragrance that comes from knowing him. [15]For we are the aroma of Christ to God among those who are being saved and among those who are perishing; [16]to the one a fragrance from death to death, to the other a fragrance from life to life. Who is sufficient for these things? [17]For we are not peddlers of God's word like so many;[f] but in

---

b Other ancient authorities read *your*   c Other ancient authorities read *holiness*   d Other ancient authorities read *pleasure*   e Gk *according to the flesh*   f Other ancient authorities read *like the others*

THE DIVINE *YES* HAS SOUNDED

E. Stanley Jones

VERSE: 2 Corinthians 1.20   **PASSAGE:** 2 Corinthians 1.18–22

 all the roll of the ancient philosophies—and the modern—and they nearly all come out to a *No*. The note of pessimism about life sounds in them all. Take Buddhism: Buddha, in his meditation under the Bo tree at Gaya, India, came to the startling conclusion: "Existence and suffering are one," inextricably bound up together. The only way to get out of suffering is to get out of life. So cut the root of desire and become desireless, even for life, and then you go out into that state, literally, "of the snuffed-out candle"—Nirvana. This is the most decisive No ever uttered about life. And yet hundreds of millions cling to this vast No as emancipation, for they feel life is saying the same, life is a No. Take the Vedanta philosophy, the outstanding philosophy of India. It says that you are to lose your separate individual personality and be absorbed into the impersonal essence, called Brahma. So you as a person are wiped out—like a raindrop you are lost in the ocean of the impersonal. It, too, is a vast No. Take Islam: Fundamentally Islam means submission—submission to the sovereign will of God. Your will is gone; his will is the all. For all intents and purposes the individual is swamped in the divine. This, too, is a vast No. Take Stoicism: To shut out sorrow and suffering, the Stoic had to shut out love and pity too, for if love and pity came in, then sorrow and suffering would come trooping in behind. This, too, is a No to the "greatest thing in the world"—love. Schopenhauer, the apostle of pessimism, seated on a park bench was asked by a policeman who thought him a tramp: "Who are you, and what are you here for?" Schopenhauer replied sadly, "I wish I knew." His was a No—a sad question mark. The loudest and saddest No that has been sounded on our planet is the latest: "God is dead." It is not only a No to life, but to God, the author of life; both God and life are dead. This is the nadir of the No.

Now in the midst of this world chorus of No, at last—at long last—"the divine 'yes' has sounded." And Jesus is that Yes.

ADDITIONAL SCRIPTURE READING:
John 14.6; 1 Timothy 4.9–10

Go to page 1371 for your next devotional reading.

1900   Present

Christ we speak as persons of sincerity, as persons sent from God and standing in his presence.

Ministers of the New Covenant

3 Are we beginning to commend ourselves again? Surely we do not need, as some do, letters of recommendation to you or from you, do we? 2You yourselves are our letter, written on ourᵍ hearts, to be known and read by all; 3and you show that you are a letter of Christ, prepared by us, written not with ink but with the Spirit of the living God, not on tablets of stone but on tablets of human hearts.

4 Such is the confidence that we have through Christ toward God. 5Not that we are competent of ourselves to claim anything as coming from us; our competence is from God, 6who has made us competent to be ministers of a new covenant, not of letter but of spirit; for the letter kills, but the Spirit gives life.

7 Now if the ministry of death, chiseled in letters on stone tablets,ʰ came in glory so that the people of Israel could not gaze at Moses' face because of the glory of his face, a glory now set aside, 8how much more will the ministry of the Spirit come in glory? 9For if there was glory in the ministry of condemnation, much more does the ministry of justification abound in glory! 10Indeed, what once had glory has lost its glory because of the greater glory; 11for if what was set aside came through glory, much more has the permanent come in glory!

12 Since, then, we have such a hope, we act with great boldness, 13not like Moses, who put a veil over his face to keep the people of Israel from gazing at the end of the glory thatⁱ was being set aside. 14But their minds were hardened. Indeed, to this very day, when they hear the reading of the old covenant, that same veil is still there, since only in Christ is it set aside. 15Indeed, to this very day whenever Moses is read, a veil lies over their minds; 16but when one turns to the Lord, the veil is removed. 17Now the Lord is the Spirit, and where the Spirit of the Lord is, there is freedom. 18And all of us, with unveiled faces, seeing the glory of the Lord as though reflected in a mirror, are being transformed into the same image from one degree of glory to another; for this comes from the Lord, the Spirit.

Treasure in Clay Jars

4 Therefore, since it is by God's mercy that we are engaged in this ministry, we do not lose heart. 2We have renounced the shameful things that

---

A DOG BARKS WHEN HIS MASTER IS ATTACKED. I WOULD BE A COWARD IF I SAW THAT GOD'S TRUTH IS ATTACKED AND YET WOULD REMAIN SILENT.
            —*John Calvin*

---

one hides; we refuse to practice cunning or to falsify God's word; but by the open statement of the truth we commend ourselves to the conscience of everyone in the sight of God. 3And even if our gospel is veiled, it is veiled to those who are perishing. 4In their case the god of this world has blinded the minds of the unbelievers, to keep them from seeing the light of the gospel of the glory of Christ, who is the image of God. 5For we do not proclaim ourselves; we proclaim Jesus Christ as Lord and ourselves as your slaves for Jesus' sake. 6For it is the God who said, "Let light shine out of darkness," who has shone in our hearts to give the light of the knowledge of the glory of God in the face of Jesus Christ.

7 But we have this treasure in clay jars, so that it may be made clear that this extraordinary power belongs to God and does not come from us. 8We are afflicted in every way, but not crushed; perplexed, but not driven to despair; 9persecuted, but not forsaken; struck down, but not destroyed; 10always carrying in the body the death of Jesus, so that the life of Jesus may also be made visible in our bodies. 11For while we live, we are always being given up to death for Jesus' sake, so that the life of Jesus may be made visible in our mortal flesh. 12So death is at work in us, but life in you.

13 But just as we have the same spirit of faith that is in accordance with scripture—"I believed, and so I spoke"—

---

g Other ancient authorities read your   *h Gk on stones*   *i Gk of what*

we also believe, and so we speak, 14because we know that the one who raised

---

the Lord Jesus will raise us also with Jesus, and will bring us with you into his presence. 15Yes, everything is for your sake, so that grace, as it extends to more and more people, may increase thanksgiving, to the glory of God.

Living by Faith

16 So we do not lose heart. Even though our outer nature is wasting away, our inner nature is being renewed day by

---

WEDNESDAY

WHERE THE SPIRIT-LORD IS, THERE IS LIBERTY
George MacDonald

VERSE: 2 Corinthians 3.17   **PASSAGE:** 2 Corinthians 3.17–18

hat it cost the Son to get so near to us that we could say *Come in*, is the story of his life. He stands at the door and knocks, and when we open to him he comes in, and dwells with us, and we are transformed to the same image of truth and purity and heavenly childhood (see Revelation 3.20). Where power dwells, there is no force; where the spirit-Lord is, there is liberty.

The Lord Jesus, by free, potent communion with their inmost being, will change his obedient brethren till in every thought and impulse they are good like him, unselfish, neighborly, brotherly like him, loving the Father perfectly like him, ready to die for the truth like him, caring like him for nothing in the universe but the will of God, which is love, harmony, liberty, beauty, and joy.

I do not know if we may call this having life in ourselves; but it is the waking up, the perfecting in us of the divine life inherited from our Father in heaven, who made us in his own image, whose nature remains in us, and makes it the deepest reproach to a man that he has neither heard his voice at any time, nor seen his shape. He who would thus live must, as a mirror draws into its bosom an outward glory, receive into his "heart of hearts" the inward glory of Jesus Christ, the truth.

ADDITIONAL SCRIPTURE READING:
Matthew 7.7–8; 2 Peter 1.4

Go to page 1373 for your next devotional reading.

1700   1900

day. ¹⁷For this slight momentary affliction is preparing us for an eternal weight
of glory beyond all measure, ¹⁸because
we look not at what can be seen but at
what cannot be seen; for what can be
seen is temporary, but what cannot be
seen is eternal.

5 For we know that if the earthly
tent we live in is destroyed, we
have a building from God, a house not
made with hands, eternal in the heavens.
²For in this tent we groan, longing to be
clothed with our heavenly dwelling— ³if
indeed, when we have taken it off*ʲ* we
will not be found naked. ⁴For while we
are still in this tent, we groan under our
burden, because we wish not to be un-
clothed but to be further clothed, so that
what is mortal may be swallowed up by
life. ⁵He who has prepared us for this
very thing is God, who has given us the
Spirit as a guarantee.

6 So we are always confident; even
though we know that while we are at
home in the body we are away from the
Lord— ⁷for we walk by faith, not by
sight. ⁸Yes, we do have confidence, and
we would rather be away from the body
and at home with the Lord. ⁹So whether
we are at home or away, we make it our
aim to please him. ¹⁰For all of us must
appear before the judgment seat of
Christ, so that each may receive recompense for what has been done in the
body, whether good or evil.

The Ministry of Reconciliation

11 Therefore, knowing the fear of the
Lord, we try to persuade others; but we
ourselves are well known to God, and I
hope that we are also well known to
your consciences. ¹²We are not commending ourselves to you again, but giving you an opportunity to boast about
us, so that you may be able to answer
those who boast in outward appearance
and not in the heart. ¹³For if we are beside ourselves, it is for God; if we are in
our right mind, it is for you. ¹⁴For the
love of Christ urges us on, because we
are convinced that one has died for all;
therefore all have died. ¹⁵And he died for
all, so that those who live might live no

longer for themselves, but for him who
died and was raised for them.

16 From now on, therefore, we regard
no one from a human point of view;ᵏ
even though we once knew Christ from
a human point of view,ᵏ we know him
no longer in that way. ¹⁷So if anyone is
in Christ, there is a new creation: everything old has passed away; see, everything has become new! ¹⁸All this is from
God, who reconciled us to himself
through Christ, and has given us the
ministry of reconciliation; ¹⁹that is, in
Christ God was reconciling the world to
himself,ˡ not counting their trespasses
against them, and entrusting the message of reconciliation to us. ²⁰So we are
ambassadors for Christ, since God is
making his appeal through us; we entreat you on behalf of Christ, be reconciled to God. ²¹For our sake he made
him to be sin who knew no sin, so that
in him we might become the righteousness of God.

6 As we work together with him,ᵐ
we urge you also not to accept
the grace of God in vain. ²For he says,

"At an acceptable time I have
listened to you,
and on a day of salvation I have
helped you."

See, now is the acceptable time; see,
now is the day of salvation! ³We are
putting no obstacle in anyone's way, so
that no fault may be found with our
ministry, ⁴but as servants of God we
have commended ourselves in every
way: through great endurance, in afflictions, hardships, calamities, ⁵beatings,
imprisonments, riots, labors, sleepless
nights, hunger; ⁶by purity, knowledge,
patience, kindness, holiness of spirit,
genuine love, ⁷truthful speech, and the
power of God; with the weapons of righteousness for the right hand and for the
left; ⁸in honor and dishonor, in ill repute
and good repute. We are treated as impostors, and yet are true; ⁹as unknown,
and yet are well known; as dying, and
see—we are alive; as punished, and yet
not killed; ¹⁰as sorrowful, yet always rejoicing; as poor, yet making many rich;
as having nothing, and yet possessing
everything.

---

j Other ancient authorities read *put it on*　　*k* Gk *according to the flesh*　　*l* Or *God was in Christ*
reconciling the world to himself　　*m* Gk *As we work together*

11 We have spoken frankly to you Corinthians; our heart is wide open to you. 12There is no restriction in our affections, but only in yours. 13In return—I speak as to children—open wide your hearts also.

The Temple of the Living God

14 Do not be mismatched with unbelievers. For what partnership is there between righteousness and lawlessness? Or what fellowship is there between light and darkness? 15What agreement does Christ have with Beliar? Or what does a believer share with an unbeliever? 16What agreement has the temple of God with idols? For we[n] are the temple of the living God; as God said,

"I will live in them and walk
among them,
and I will be their God,
and they shall be my people.

n Other ancient authorities read you

THURSDAY

THE CONSOLATIONS WHICH THE WORLD KNOWS NOT
Anne Bradstreet

VERSE: 2 Corinthians 6.18   **PASSAGE:** 2 Corinthians 6.14–18

ord, why should I doubt any more when thou hast given me such assured pledges of thy love? First, thou art my Creator, I thy creature, thou my master, I thy servant. But hence arises not my comfort, thou art my Father, I thy child; "Ye shall be my sons and daughters" (Romans 9.26, KJV) saith the Lord Almighty. Christ is my brother, I ascend unto my Father, and your Father, unto my God and your God; but lest this should not be enough, thy maker is thy husband. Nay more, I am a member of his body, he my head. Such privileges had not the Word of truth made them known, who or where is the man that durst in his heart have presumed to have thought it? So wonderful are these thoughts that my spirit fails in me at the consideration thereof, and I am confounded to think that God, who hath done so much for me, should have so little from me. But this is my comfort, when I come to heaven, I shall understand perfectly what he hath done for me, and then shall I be able to praise him as I ought. Lord, having this hope, let me purify myself as thou art pure, and let me be no more afraid of death, but even desire to be dissolved and be with thee, which is best of all.

ADDITIONAL SCRIPTURE READING:
Psalm 51.10; Romans 9.26

Go to page 1375 for your next devotional reading.

1500   1700

17 Therefore come out from them,
     and be separate from them, says
          the Lord,
and touch nothing unclean;
     then I will welcome you,
18 and I will be your father,
     and you shall be my sons and
          daughters,
says the Lord Almighty."

7 Since we have these promises, beloved, let us cleanse ourselves from every defilement of body and of spirit, making holiness perfect in the fear of God.

Paul's Joy at the Church's Repentance

2 Make room in your hearts*o* for us; we have wronged no one, we have corrupted no one, we have taken advantage of no one. 3I do not say this to condemn you, for I said before that you are in our hearts, to die together and to live together. 4I often boast about you; I have great pride in you; I am filled with consolation; I am overjoyed in all our affliction.

5 For even when we came into Macedonia, our bodies had no rest, but we were afflicted in every way—disputes without and fears within. 6But God, who consoles the downcast, consoled us by the arrival of Titus, 7and not only by his coming, but also by the consolation with which he was consoled about you, as he told us of your longing, your mourning, your zeal for me, so that I rejoiced still more. 8For even if I made you sorry with my letter, I do not regret it (though I did regret it, for I see that I grieved you with that letter, though only briefly). 9Now I rejoice, not because you were grieved, but because your grief led to repentance; for you felt a godly grief, so that you were not harmed in any way by us. 10For godly grief produces a repentance that leads to salvation and brings no regret, but worldly grief produces death. 11For see what earnestness this godly grief has produced in you, what eagerness to clear yourselves, what indignation, what alarm, what longing, what zeal, what punishment! At every point you have proved yourselves guiltless in the matter. 12So although I wrote to you, it was not on account of the one who did

the wrong, nor on account of the one who was wronged, but in order that your zeal for us might be made known to you before God. 13In this we find comfort.

In addition to our own consolation, we rejoiced still more at the joy of Titus, because his mind has been set at rest by all of you. 14For if I have been somewhat boastful about you to him, I was not disgraced; but just as everything we said to you was true, so our boasting to Titus has proved true as well. 15And his heart goes out all the more to you, as he remembers the obedience of all of you, and how you welcomed him with fear and trembling. 16I rejoice, because I have complete confidence in you.

Encouragement to Be Generous

8 We want you to know, brothers and sisters,*p* about the grace of God that has been granted to the churches of Macedonia; 2for during a severe ordeal of affliction, their abundant joy and their extreme poverty have overflowed in a wealth of generosity on their part. 3For, as I can testify, they voluntarily gave according to their means, and even beyond their means, 4begging us earnestly for the privilege*q* of sharing in this ministry to the saints— 5and this, not merely as we expected; they gave themselves first to the Lord and, by the will of God, to us, 6so that we might urge Titus that, as he had already made a beginning, so he should also complete this generous undertaking*r* among you. 7Now as you excel in everything—in faith, in speech, in knowledge, in utmost eagerness, and in our love for you*s*—so we want you to excel also in this generous undertaking.*t*

8 I do not say this as a command, but I am testing the genuineness of your love against the earnestness of others. 9For you know the generous act*t* of our Lord Jesus Christ, that though he was rich, yet for your sakes he became poor, so that by his poverty you might become rich. 10And in this matter I am giving my advice: it is appropriate for you who began last year not only to do something but even to desire to do something— 11now finish doing it, so that your eagerness

o Gk lacks *in your hearts*   p Gk *brothers*   q Gk *grace*   r Gk *this grace*   s Other ancient
authorities read *your love for us*   t Gk *the grace*

THE MEMORIAL TO THE MACEDONIANS' LIBERALITY

W. J. Conybeare and J. S. Howson

VERSE: 2 Corinthians 8.1   **PASSAGE:** 2 Corinthians 8.1–5

In writing to the Corinthians, [Paul] delicately contrasts their wealth with the poverty of the Macedonians. In speaking to the Macedonians themselves, such a mode of appeal was less natural, for they were poorer and more generous. Yet them also he endeavored to rouse to a generous rivalry, by telling them of the zeal of Achaia (2 Corinthians 8.24, 9.2) . . . Nor ought we, when speaking of the instruction to be gathered from this charitable undertaking, to leave unnoticed the calmness and deliberation of the method which he recommends of laying aside, week by week, what is devoted to God (1 Corinthians 16.2),—a practice equally remote from the excitement of popular appeals, and the mere impulse of instinctive benevolence.

The Macedonian Christians responded nobly to the appeal which was made to them by St. Paul. The zeal of their brethren in Achaia "stirred most of them to action" (2 Corinthians 9.2). God's grace was abundantly "manifested in the churches" on the north of the Aegean (2 Corinthians 8.1). Their conduct in this matter, as described to us by the apostle's pen, rises to the point of the highest praise. It was a time, not of prosperity, but of great affliction, to the Macedonian churches; nor were they wealthy communities like the church of Corinth; yet, "out of the most severe trial, their overflowing joy and their extreme poverty welled up in rich generosity" (v. 2). Their contribution was no niggardly gift, wrung from their covetousness (v. 5); but they gave honestly "as much as they were able" (v. 3), and not only so, but even "beyond their ability" (v. 3); nor did they give grudgingly, under the pressure of the apostle's urgency, but "entirely on their own, they urgently pleaded with us for the privilege of sharing in this service to the saints" (8.3–4). And this liberality arose from that which is the basis of all true Christian charity. "They gave themselves first to the Lord Jesus Christ, by the will of God" (see v. 5).

ADDITIONAL SCRIPTURE READING:
Luke 21.1–4; 1 Corinthians 16.2

Go to page 1378 for your next devotional reading.

1700   1900

may be matched by completing it according to your means. 12For if the eagerness is there, the gift is acceptable according to what one has—not according to what one does not have. 13I do not mean that there should be relief for others and pressure on you, but it is a question of a fair balance between 14your present abundance and their need, so that their abundance may be for your need, in order that there may be a fair balance. 15As it is written,

> "The one who had much did not
> have too much,
> and the one who had little did
> not have too little."

Commendation of Titus

16 But thanks be to God who put in the heart of Titus the same eagerness for you that I myself have. 17For he not only accepted our appeal, but since he is more eager than ever, he is going to you of his own accord. 18With him we are sending the brother who is famous among all the churches for his proclaiming the good news;u 19and not only that, but he has also been appointed by the churches to travel with us while we are administering this generous undertakingv for the glory of the Lord himselfw and to show our goodwill. 20We intend that no one should blame us about this generous gift that we are administering, 21for we intend to do what is right not only in the Lord's sight but also in the sight of others. 22And with them we are sending our brother whom we have often tested and found eager in many matters, but who is now more eager than ever because of his great confidence in you. 23As for Titus, he is my partner and co-worker in your service; as for our brothers, they are messengersx of the churches, the glory of Christ. 24Therefore openly before the churches, show them the proof of your love and of our reason for boasting about you.

The Collection for Christians at Jerusalem

9 Now it is not necessary for me to write you about the ministry to the saints, 2for I know your eagerness, which is the subject of my boasting

about you to the people of Macedonia, saying that Achaia has been ready since last year; and your zeal has stirred up most of them. 3But I am sending the brothers in order that our boasting about you may not prove to have been empty in this case, so that you may be ready, as I said you would be; 4otherwise, if some Macedonians come with me and find that you are not ready, we would be humiliated—to say nothing of you—in this undertaking.y 5So I thought it necessary to urge the brothers to go on ahead to you, and arrange in advance for this bountiful gift that you have promised, so that it may be ready as a voluntary gift and not as an extortion.

6 The point is this: the one who sows sparingly will also reap sparingly, and the one who sows bountifully will also reap bountifully. 7Each of you must give as you have made up your mind, not reluctantly or under compulsion, for God loves a cheerful giver. 8And God is able to provide you with every blessing in abundance, so that by always having enough of everything, you may share abundantly in every good work. 9As it is written,

---

IT IS NOT MY ABILITY, BUT MY RESPONSE TO GOD'S ABILITY, THAT COUNTS. —*Corrie ten Boom*

> "He scatters abroad, he gives to the
> poor;
> his righteousnessz endures
> forever."

10He who supplies seed to the sower and bread for food will supply and multiply your seed for sowing and increase the harvest of your righteousness.z 11You will be enriched in every way for your great generosity, which will produce thanksgiving to God through us; 12for the rendering of this ministry not only supplies the needs of the saints but also overflows with many thanksgivings to God. 13Through the testing of this ministry you glorify God by your obedience to the confession of the gospel of Christ and by the generosity of your sharing with them and with all others, 14while

---

u Or *the gospel*　v Gk *this grace*　w Other ancient authorities lack *himself*　x Gk *apostles*
y Other ancient authorities add *of boasting*　z Or *benevolence*

they long for you and pray for you because of the surpassing grace of God that he has given you. [15]Thanks be to God for his indescribable gift!

Paul Defends His Ministry

10 I myself, Paul, appeal to you by the meekness and gentleness of Christ—I who am humble when face to face with you, but bold toward you when I am away!— [2]I ask that when I am present I need not show boldness by daring to oppose those who think we are acting according to human standards.[a] [3]Indeed, we live as human beings,[b] but we do not wage war according to human standards;[a] [4]for the weapons of our warfare are not merely human,[c] but they have divine power to destroy strongholds. We destroy arguments [5]and every proud obstacle raised up against the knowledge of God, and we take every thought captive to obey Christ.

WE ARE CALLED TO BE GOD'S TRANSMITTERS, TO BE COMPLETELY SEPARATED FROM ALL THOUGHTS WHICH ARE CONTRARY TO HIS THINKING, SO THAT WE MAY TRANSMIT HIS THOUGHTS TO OTHERS.   —*Hannah Hurnard*

---

[6]We are ready to punish every disobedience when your obedience is complete.

7 Look at what is before your eyes. If you are confident that you belong to Christ, remind yourself of this, that just as you belong to Christ, so also do we. [8]Now, even if I boast a little too much of our authority, which the Lord gave for building you up and not for tearing you down, I will not be ashamed of it. [9]I do not want to seem as though I am trying to frighten you with my letters. [10]For they say, "His letters are weighty and strong, but his bodily presence is weak, and his speech contemptible." [11]Let such people understand that what we say by letter when absent, we will also do when present.

12 We do not dare to classify or compare ourselves with some of those who commend themselves. But when they measure themselves by one another, and compare themselves with one another, they do not show good sense. [13]We, however, will not boast beyond limits, but will keep within the field that God has assigned to us, to reach out even as far as you. [14]For we were not overstepping our limits when we reached you; we were the first to come all the way to you with the good news[d] of Christ. [15]We do not boast beyond limits, that is, in the labors of others; but our hope is that, as your faith increases, our sphere of action among you may be greatly enlarged, [16]so that we may proclaim the good news[d] in lands beyond you, without boasting of work already done in someone else's sphere of action. [17]"Let the one who boasts, boast in the Lord." [18]For it is not those who commend themselves that are approved, but those whom the Lord commends.

Paul and the False Apostles

11 I wish you would bear with me in a little foolishness. Do bear with me! [2]I feel a divine jealousy for you, for I promised you in marriage to one husband, to present you as a chaste virgin to Christ. [3]But I am afraid that as the serpent deceived Eve by its cunning, your thoughts will be led astray from a sincere and pure[e] devotion to Christ. [4]For if someone comes and proclaims another Jesus than the one we proclaimed, or if you receive a different spirit from the one you received, or a different gospel from the one you accepted, you submit to it readily enough. [5]I think that I am not in the least inferior to these super-apostles. [6]I may be untrained in speech, but not in knowledge; certainly in every way and in all things we have made this evident to you.

7 Did I commit a sin by humbling myself so that you might be exalted, because I proclaimed God's good news[f] to you free of charge? [8]I robbed other churches by accepting support from them in order to serve you. [9]And when I was with you and was in need, I did not burden anyone, for my needs were supplied by the friends[g] who came from Macedonia. So I refrained and will continue to refrain from burdening you in any way. [10]As the truth of Christ is in

---

a Gk *according to the flesh*   *b* Gk *in the flesh*   *c* Gk *fleshly*   *d* Or *the gospel*   *e* Other ancient authorities lack *and pure*   *f* Gk *the gospel of God*   *g* Gk *brothers*

WEEKEND

AT THE LORD'S TABLE
Horatius Bonar

VERSE: 1 Corinthians 11.26   **PASSAGE:** 1 Corinthians 11.23–26

Here, O my Lord, I see thee face to face;
　　Here would I touch and handle things unseen,
Here grasp with firmer hand the eternal grace,
　　And all my weariness upon thee lean.

Here would I feed upon the bread of God,
　　Here drink with thee the royal wine of heaven;
Here would I lay aside each earthly load,
　　Here taste afresh the calm of sin forgiven.

This is the hour of banquet and of song;
　　This is the heavenly table spread for me;
Here let me feast, and feasting, still prolong
　　The brief bright hour of fellowship with thee.

Too soon we rise; the symbols disappear;
　　The feast, though not the love, is past and gone;
The bread and wine remove, but thou are here,
　　Nearer than ever; still my Shield and Sun.

I have no help but thine; nor do I need
　　Another arm save thine to lean upon;
It is enough, my Lord, enough indeed;
　　My strength is in thy might, thy might alone.

Mine is the sin, but thine the righteousness;
　　Mine is the guilt, but thine the cleansing blood;
Here is my robe, my refuge, and my peace,—
　　Thy blood, thy righteousness, O Lord my God.

Feast after feast thus comes and passes by,
　　Yet, passing, points to the glad feast above,
Giving sweet foretaste of the festal joy,
　　The Lamb's great bridal feast of bliss and love.

ADDITIONAL SCRIPTURE READING:
John 6.35; Ephesians 1.7–8

Go to page 1380 for your next devotional reading.

1700　1900

me, this boast of mine will not be silenced in the regions of Achaia. 11And why? Because I do not love you? God knows I do!

12 And what I do I will also continue to do, in order to deny an opportunity to those who want an opportunity to be recognized as our equals in what they boast about. 13For such boasters are false apostles, deceitful workers, disguising themselves as apostles of Christ. 14And no wonder! Even Satan disguises himself as an angel of light. 15So it is not strange if his ministers also disguise themselves as ministers of righteousness. Their end will match their deeds.

Paul's Sufferings as an Apostle

16 I repeat, let no one think that I am a fool; but if you do, then accept me as a fool, so that I too may boast a little. 17What I am saying in regard to this boastful confidence, I am saying not with the Lord's authority, but as a fool; 18since many boast according to human standards,h I will also boast. 19For you gladly put up with fools, being wise yourselves! 20For you put up with it when someone makes slaves of you, or preys upon you, or takes advantage of you, or puts on airs, or gives you a slap in the face. 21To my shame, I must say, we were too weak for that!

But whatever anyone dares to boast of—I am speaking as a fool—I also dare to boast of that. 22Are they Hebrews? So am I. Are they Israelites? So am I. Are they descendants of Abraham? So am I. 23Are they ministers of Christ? I am talking like a madman—I am a better one: with far greater labors, far more imprisonments, with countless floggings, and often near death. 24Five times I have received from the Jews the forty lashes minus one. 25Three times I was beaten with rods. Once I received a stoning. Three times I was shipwrecked; for a night and a day I was adrift at sea; 26on frequent journeys, in danger from rivers, danger from bandits, danger from my own people, danger from Gentiles, danger in the city, danger in the wilderness, danger at sea, danger from false brothers and sisters;i 27in toil and hardship, through many a sleepless night, hungry and thirsty, often without food, cold and naked. 28And, besides other things, I am under daily pressure because of my anxiety for all the churches. 29Who is weak, and I am not weak? Who is made to stumble, and I am not indignant?

30 If I must boast, I will boast of the things that show my weakness. 31The God and Father of the Lord Jesus (blessed be he forever!) knows that I do not lie. 32In Damascus, the governorj under King Aretas guarded the city of Damascus in order tok seize me, 33but I was let down in a basket through a window in the wall,l and escaped from his hands.

Paul's Visions and Revelations

12 It is necessary to boast; nothing is to be gained by it, but I will go on to visions and revelations of the Lord. 2I know a person in Christ who fourteen years ago was caught up to the third heaven—whether in the body or out of the body I do not know; God knows. 3And I know that such a person—whether in the body or out of the body I do not know; God knows— 4was caught up into Paradise and heard things that are not to be told, that no mortal is permitted to repeat. 5On behalf of such a one I will boast, but on my own behalf I will not boast, except of my weaknesses. 6But if I wish to boast, I will not be a fool, for I will be speaking the truth. But I refrain from it, so that no one may think better of me than what is seen in me or heard from me, 7even considering the exceptional character of the revelations. Therefore, to keepm me from being too elated, a thorn was given me in the flesh, a messenger of Satan to torment me, to keep me from being too elated.n 8Three times I appealed to the Lord about this, that it would leave me, 9but he said to me, "My grace is sufficient for you, for powero is made perfect in weakness." So, I will boast all the more gladly of my weaknesses, so that the power of Christ may dwell in me. 10Therefore I am content with weaknesses, insults, hardships, persecutions,

---

h Gk *according to the flesh* i Gk *brothers* j Gk *ethnarch* k Other ancient authorities read *and wanted to* l Gk *through the wall* m Other ancient authorities read *To keep* n Other ancient authorities lack *to keep me from being too elated* o Other ancient authorities read *my power*

and calamities for the sake of Christ; for whenever I am weak, then I am strong.

GOD IS SUFFICIENT FOR ALL OUR NEEDS, FOR EVERY PROBLEM, AND FOR EVERY DIFFICULTY, FOR EVERY BROKEN HEART, AND FOR EVERY HUMAN SORROW.   —*Peter Marshall*

Paul's Concern for the Corinthian Church

11 I have been a fool! You forced me to it. Indeed you should have been the ones commending me, for I am not at all inferior to these super-apostles, even though I am nothing. 12 The signs of a true apostle were performed among you with utmost patience, signs and wonders and mighty works. 13 How have you been worse off than the other churches, except that I myself did not burden you? Forgive me this wrong!

14 Here I am, ready to come to you this third time. And I will not be a burden, because I do not want what is yours but you; for children ought not to lay up for their parents, but parents for their children. 15 I will most gladly spend and

---

MONDAY

SIX WORDS ARE ENOUGH
Karl Barth

VERSE: 2 Corinthians 12.9   **PASSAGE:** 2 Corinthians 12.7–10

y grace is sufficient for you" (2 Corinthians 12.9). This is a very short text—a mere six words—the shortest I have ever preached on. The brevity is an advantage for you; you can retain it better. I might say in passing that every time I come here I am very concerned that not so much my sermon but the text that it follows may really sink in and go with you. This time then: "My grace is sufficient for you." The wonderful spice of this saying lies in its brevity. The six words are enough. Some of you may have heard that in the last forty years I have written many books, some large. I will freely and frankly and gladly admit that these six words say much more and much better things than all the heaps of paper with which I have surrounded myself. They are enough—which cannot be said even remotely of my books. What may be good in my books can be at most that from afar they point to what these six words say. And when my books are long since outdated and forgotten, and every book in the world with them, these words will still shine with everlasting fullness: "My grace is sufficient for you."

ADDITIONAL SCRIPTURE READING:
Romans 5.20–21; Hebrews 4.16

Go to page 1383 for your next devotional reading.

1900   Present

be spent for you. If I love you more, am I to be loved less? 16Let it be assumed that I did not burden you. Nevertheless (you say) since I was crafty, I took you in by deceit. 17Did I take advantage of you through any of those whom I sent to you? 18I urged Titus to go, and sent the brother with him. Titus did not take advantage of you, did he? Did we not conduct ourselves with the same spirit? Did we not take the same steps?

19 Have you been thinking all along that we have been defending ourselves before you? We are speaking in Christ before God. Everything we do, beloved, is for the sake of building you up. 20For I fear that when I come, I may find you not as I wish, and that you may find me not as you wish; I fear that there may perhaps be quarreling, jealousy, anger, selfishness, slander, gossip, conceit, and disorder. 21I fear that when I come again, my God may humble me before you, and that I may have to mourn over many who previously sinned and have not repented of the impurity, sexual immorality, and licentiousness that they have practiced.

Further Warning

13 This is the third time I am coming to you. "Any charge must be sustained by the evidence of two or three witnesses." 2I warned those who sinned previously and all the others, and I warn them now while absent, as I did when present on my second visit, that if I come again, I will not be lenient— 3since you desire proof that Christ is speaking in me. He is not weak in dealing with you, but is powerful in you. 4For he was crucified in weakness, but lives by the power of God. For we are weak in him,*p* but in dealing with you we will live with him by the power of God.

5 Examine yourselves to see whether you are living in the faith. Test yourselves. Do you not realize that Jesus Christ is in you?—unless, indeed, you fail to meet the test! 6I hope you will find out that we have not failed. 7But we pray to God that you may not do anything wrong—not that we may appear to have met the test, but that you may do what is right, though we may seem to have failed. 8For we cannot do anything against the truth, but only for the truth. 9For we rejoice when we are weak and you are strong. This is what we pray for, that you may become perfect. 10So I write these things while I am away from you, so that when I come, I may not have to be severe in using the authority that the Lord has given me for building up and not for tearing down.

Final Greetings and Benediction

11 Finally, brothers and sisters,*q* farewell.*r* Put things in order, listen to my appeal,*s* agree with one another, live in peace; and the God of love and peace will be with you. 12Greet one another with a holy kiss. All the saints greet you.

13 The grace of the Lord Jesus Christ, the love of God, and the communion of*t* the Holy Spirit be with all of you.

p Other ancient authorities read *with him*   q Gk *brothers*   r Or *rejoice*   s Or *encourage one another*   t Or *and the sharing in*

GALATIANS

PAUL'S LETTER TO THE CHURCHES HE ESTABLISHED IN GALATIA (ACTS 13.13—14.28) CONTAINS HIS CLASSIC STATEMENT OF THE FOUNDATIONAL BIBLICAL TRUTH THAT A PERSON IS JUSTIFIED BY FAITH IN CHRIST. AFTER WARNING THE GALATIANS NOT TO DESERT THE GOSPEL, PAUL ENCOURAGES THEM TO LIVE OUT THE FREEDOM THEY HAVE IN CHRIST. AS YOU READ THIS LETTER, ASK GOD TO HELP YOU ENJOY THE FREEDOM YOU HAVE IN CHRIST AS YOU LIVE A SPIRIT-FILLED LIFE (5.22–23).

Salutation

1 Paul an apostle—sent neither by human commission nor from human authorities, but through Jesus Christ and God the Father, who raised him from the dead— 2and all the members of God's family*a* who are with me,

To the churches of Galatia:

3 Grace to you and peace from God our Father and the Lord Jesus Christ, 4who gave himself for our sins to set us free from the present evil age, according to the will of our God and Father, 5to whom be the glory forever and ever. Amen.

There Is No Other Gospel

6 I am astonished that you are so quickly deserting the one who called you in the grace of Christ and are turning to a different gospel— 7not that there is another gospel, but there are some who are confusing you and want to pervert the gospel of Christ. 8But even if we or an angel*b* from heaven should proclaim to you a gospel contrary to what we proclaimed to you, let that one be accursed! 9As we have said

---

YOU CANNOT HAVE CHRISTIAN PRINCIPLES WITHOUT CHRIST.   —Dorothy L. Sayers

---

before, so now I repeat, if anyone proclaims to you a gospel contrary to what you received, let that one be accursed!

---

a Gk *all the brothers*   *b* Or *a messenger*

10 Am I now seeking human approval, or God's approval? Or am I trying to please people? If I were still pleasing people, I would not be a servant[c] of Christ.

c Gk *slave*   d Gk *brothers*

Paul's Vindication of His Apostleship

11 For I want you to know, brothers and sisters,[d] that the gospel that was proclaimed by me is not of human origin; 12for I did not receive it from a human

---

TUESDAY

NO OTHER GOD
Karl Barth

VERSE: Galatians 1.9   **PASSAGE:** Galatians 1.6–9

hey [the German Christians] tell us as unequivocally as possible that the proclamation of the gospel both draws and must draw from two different sources. Holy Scripture is one, and the other is the "historical hour," the present political situation, the experience of the German revolution of 1933. With one eye the church must learn from this what God's word is, just as it learns it with the other eye from the Bible. As the Roman Catholic church has always said, there is the book of nature and the book of grace. For the German Christians the book of nature is the event of January 30 and all that it implies . . . We cannot understand this enterprise as reformation. It is deformation, not reformation. In it the church does not have the single eye that is demanded. It is squinting. Alongside God it sets a second god with an independent authority, namely, the Germans and their understanding of themselves and their concerns. But alongside God there can be no other God, or God ceases to be God, and all that we really have are two idols. The gospel preached by the German Christians is in classical form an unfree gospel. Faith is not decided by the call of God alone, nor is it our only comfort in life and in death. Alongside God the giver, Germans are honored as the necessary and proper vessel for saving grace. But if the gospel is no longer free, it has ceased to be gospel. Hence we have to say at this point a radical and unconditional no: no to the starting point of this thinking, and no to all that follows therefrom.

ADDITIONAL SCRIPTURE READING:
John 14.6; 1 Timothy 6.3

Go to page 1387 for your next devotional reading.

1900   Present

source, nor was I taught it, but I received it through a revelation of Jesus Christ.

13 You have heard, no doubt, of my earlier life in Judaism. I was violently persecuting the church of God and was trying to destroy it. 14I advanced in Judaism beyond many among my people of the same age, for I was far more zealous for the traditions of my ancestors. 15But when God, who had set me apart before I was born and called me through his grace, was pleased 16to reveal his Son to me,*e* so that I might proclaim him among the Gentiles, I did not confer with any human being, 17nor did I go up to Jerusalem to those who were already apostles before me, but I went away at once into Arabia, and afterwards I returned to Damascus.

18 Then after three years I did go up to Jerusalem to visit Cephas and stayed with him fifteen days; 19but I did not see any other apostle except James the Lord's brother. 20In what I am writing to you, before God, I do not lie! 21Then I went into the regions of Syria and Cilicia, 22and I was still unknown by sight to the churches of Judea that are in Christ; 23they only heard it said, "The one who formerly was persecuting us is now proclaiming the faith he once tried to destroy." 24And they glorified God because of me.

Paul and the Other Apostles

2 Then after fourteen years I went up again to Jerusalem with Barnabas, taking Titus along with me. 2I went up in response to a revelation. Then I laid before them (though only in a private meeting with the acknowledged leaders) the gospel that I proclaim among the Gentiles, in order to make sure that I was not running, or had not run, in vain. 3But even Titus, who was with me, was not compelled to be circumcised, though he was a Greek. 4But because of false believers*f* secretly brought in, who slipped in to spy on the freedom we have in Christ Jesus, so that they might enslave us— 5we did not submit to them even for a moment, so that the truth of the gospel might always remain with you. 6And

from those who were supposed to be acknowledged leaders (what they actually were makes no difference to me; God shows no partiality)—those leaders contributed nothing to me. 7On the contrary, when they saw that I had been entrusted with the gospel for the uncircumcised, just as Peter had been entrusted with the gospel for the circumcised 8(for he who worked through Peter making him an apostle to the circumcised also worked through me in sending me to the Gentiles), 9and when James and Cephas and John, who were acknowledged pillars, recognized the grace that had been given to me, they gave to Barnabas and me the right hand of fellowship, agreeing that we should go to the Gentiles and they to the circumcised. 10They asked only one thing, that we remember the poor, which was actually what I was*g* eager to do.

Paul Rebukes Peter at Antioch

11 But when Cephas came to Antioch, I opposed him to his face, because he stood self-condemned; 12for until certain people came from James, he used to eat with the Gentiles. But after they came, he drew back and kept himself separate for fear of the circumcision faction. 13And the other Jews joined him in this hypocrisy, so that even Barnabas was led astray by their hypocrisy. 14But when I saw that they were not acting consistently with the truth of the gospel, I said to Cephas before them all, "If you, though a Jew, live like a Gentile and not like a Jew, how can you compel the Gentiles to live like Jews?"*h*

Jews and Gentiles Are Saved by Faith

15 We ourselves are Jews by birth and not Gentile sinners; 16yet we know that a person is justified*i* not by the works of the law but through faith in Jesus Christ.*j* And we have come to believe in Christ Jesus, so that we might be justified by faith in Christ,*k* and not by doing the works of the law, because no one will be justified by the works of the law. 17But if, in our effort to be justified in Christ, we ourselves have been found to

---

e Gk *in me*   *f* Gk *false brothers*   *g* Or *had been* extends into the following paragraph   *i* Or *reckoned as righteous; and so elsewhere*   *h* Some interpreters hold that the quotation   *j* Or *the faith of Jesus Christ*   *k* Or *the faith of Christ*

be sinners, is Christ then a servant of sin? Certainly not! [18]But if I build up again the very things that I once tore down, then I demonstrate that I am a transgressor. [19]For through the law I died to the law, so that I might live to God. I have been crucified with Christ; [20]and it is no longer I who live, but it is Christ who lives in me. And the life I now live in the flesh I live by faith in the Son of God,[l] who loved me and gave himself for me. [21]I do not nullify the grace of God; for if justification[m] comes through the law, then Christ died for nothing.

IT IS THROUGH ACCEPTING THE CIRCUMSTANCES THAT COME TO US IN LIFE THAT SELF IS CRUCIFIED. —*Hannah Hurnard*

Law or Faith

3 You foolish Galatians! Who has bewitched you? It was before your eyes that Jesus Christ was publicly exhibited as crucified! [2]The only thing I want to learn from you is this: Did you receive the Spirit by doing the works of the law or by believing what you heard? [3]Are you so foolish? Having started with the Spirit, are you now ending with the flesh? [4]Did you experience so much for nothing?—if it really was for nothing. [5]Well then, does God[n] supply you with the Spirit and work miracles among you by your doing the works of the law, or by your believing what you heard?

6 Just as Abraham "believed God, and it was reckoned to him as righteousness," [7]so, you see, those who believe are the descendants of Abraham. [8]And the scripture, foreseeing that God would justify the Gentiles by faith, declared the gospel beforehand to Abraham, saying, "All the Gentiles shall be blessed in you." [9]For this reason, those who believe are blessed with Abraham who believed.

10 For all who rely on the works of the law are under a curse; for it is written, "Cursed is everyone who does not observe and obey all the things written in the book of the law." [11]Now it is evident that no one is justified before God

by the law; for "The one who is righteous will live by faith."[o] [12]But the law does not rest on faith; on the contrary, "Whoever does the works of the law[p] will live by them." [13]Christ redeemed us from the curse of the law by becoming a curse for us—for it is written, "Cursed is everyone who hangs on a tree"— [14]in order that in Christ Jesus the blessing of Abraham might come to the Gentiles, so that we might receive the promise of the Spirit through faith.

The Promise to Abraham

15 Brothers and sisters,[q] I give an example from daily life: once a person's will[r] has been ratified, no one adds to it or annuls it. [16]Now the promises were made to Abraham and to his offspring;[s] it does not say, "And to offsprings,"[t] as of many; but it says, "And to your offspring,"[s] that is, to one person, who is Christ. [17]My point is this: the law, which came four hundred thirty years later, does not annul a covenant previously ratified by God, so as to nullify the promise. [18]For if the inheritance comes from the law, it no longer comes from the promise; but God granted it to Abraham through the promise.

The Purpose of the Law

19 Why then the law? It was added because of transgressions, until the offspring[s] would come to whom the promise had been made; and it was ordained through angels by a mediator. [20]Now a mediator involves more than one party; but God is one.

21 Is the law then opposed to the promises of God? Certainly not! For if a law had been given that could make alive, then righteousness would indeed come through the law. [22]But the scripture has imprisoned all things under the power of sin, so that what was promised through faith in Jesus Christ[u] might be given to those who believe.

23 Now before faith came, we were imprisoned and guarded under the law until faith would be revealed. [24]Therefore the law was our disciplinarian until Christ came, so that we might be justified

---

l Or *by the faith of the Son of God*   *m* Or *righteousness*   *n* Gk *he*   *o* Or *The one who is righteous through faith will live*   *p* Gk *does them*   *q* Gk *Brothers*   *r* Or *covenant* (as in verse 17)   *s* Gk *seed*   *t* Gk *seeds*   *u* Or *through the faith of Jesus Christ*

by faith. 25But now that faith has come, we are no longer subject to a disciplinarian, 26for in Christ Jesus you are all children of God through faith. 27As many of you as were baptized into Christ have clothed yourselves with Christ. 28There is no longer Jew or Greek, there is no longer slave or free, there is no longer male and female; for all of you are one in Christ Jesus. 29And if you belong to Christ, then you are Abraham's offspring,*v* heirs according to the promise.

4 My point is this: heirs, as long as they are minors, are no better than slaves, though they are the owners of all the property; 2but they remain under guardians and trustees until the date set by the father. 3So with us; while we were minors, we were enslaved to the elemental spirits*w* of the world. 4But when the fullness of time had come, God sent his Son, born of a woman, born under the law, 5in order to redeem those who were under the law, so that we might receive adoption as children. 6And because you are children, God has sent the Spirit of his Son into our*x* hearts, crying, "Abba!*y* Father!" 7So you are no longer a slave but a child, and if a child then also an heir, through God.*z*

Paul Reproves the Galatians

8 Formerly, when you did not know God, you were enslaved to beings that by nature are not gods. 9Now, however, that you have come to know God, or rather to be known by God, how can you turn back again to the weak and beggarly elemental spirits?*a* How can you want to be enslaved to them again? 10You are observing special days, and months, and seasons, and years. 11I am afraid that my work for you may have been wasted.

12 Friends,*b* I beg you, become as I am, for I also have become as you are. You have done me no wrong. 13You know that it was because of a physical infirmity that I first announced the gospel to you; 14though my condition put you to the test, you did not scorn or despise me, but welcomed me as an angel of God, as Christ Jesus. 15What has become of the goodwill you felt? For I testify that, had it been possible, you would have torn out your eyes and given them to me. 16Have I now become your enemy by telling you the truth? 17They make much of you, but for no good purpose; they want to exclude you, so that you may make much of them. 18It is good to be made much of for a good purpose at all times, and not only when I am present with you. 19My little children, for whom I am again in the pain of childbirth until Christ is formed in you, 20I wish I were present with you now and could change my tone, for I am perplexed about you.

The Allegory of Hagar and Sarah

21 Tell me, you who desire to be subject to the law, will you not listen to the law? 22For it is written that Abraham had two sons, one by a slave woman and the other by a free woman. 23One, the child of the slave, was born according to the flesh; the other, the child of the free woman, was born through the promise. 24Now this is an allegory: these women are two covenants. One woman, in fact, is Hagar, from Mount Sinai, bearing children for slavery. 25Now Hagar is Mount Sinai in Arabia*c* and corresponds to the present Jerusalem, for she is in slavery with her children. 26But the other woman corresponds to the Jerusalem above; she is free, and she is our mother. 27For it is written,

"Rejoice, you childless one, you
    who bear no children;
burst into song and shout, you
    who endure no birth pangs;
for the children of the desolate
    woman are more numerous
than the children of the one who
    is married."

28Now you,*d* my friends,*e* are children of the promise, like Isaac. 29But just as at that time the child who was born according to the flesh persecuted the child who was born according to the Spirit, so it is now also. 30But what does the scripture say? "Drive out the slave and her child; for the child of the slave will not share the inheritance with the child of the free woman." ³¹So then, friends,ᶠ we are children, not of the slave but of

 5 the free woman. ¹For freedom Christ has set us free. Stand firm, therefore, and do not submit again to a yoke of slavery.

ᶠ Gk *brothers*

The Nature of Christian Freedom

2 Listen! I, Paul, am telling you that if you let yourselves be circumcised,

---

WHAT HAVE WE, SONS OF GOD, TO DO WITH LAW?

—*John Milton*

WEDNESDAY

CHARACTERISTICS OF THE CHRISTIAN COMMUNITY
Epistle to Diognetus

VERSE: Galatians 5.16   **PASSAGE:** Galatians 5.16–26

---

he relation of Christians to the world is that of a soul to the body. As the soul is diffused through every part of the body, so are Christians through all the cities of the world. The soul, too, inhabits the body, while at the same time forming no part of it; and Christians inhabit the world, but they are not part of the world. The soul, invisible herself, is immured within a visible body; so Christians can be recognized in the world, but their Christianity itself remains hidden from the eye. The flesh hates the soul, and wars against her without any provocation, because she is an obstacle to its own self-indulgence; and the world similarly hates the Christians without provocation, because they are opposed to its pleasures. All the same, the soul loves the flesh and all its members, despite their hatred for her; and Christians, too, love those who hate them. The soul, shut up inside the body, nevertheless holds the body together; and though they are confined within the world as in a dungeon, it is Christians who hold the world together. The soul, which is immortal, must dwell in a mortal tabernacle; and Christians, as they sojourn for a while in the midst of corruptibility here, look for incorruptibility in the heavens. Finally, just as to be stinted of food and drink makes for the soul's improvement, so when Christians are every day subjected to ill-treatment, they increase the more in numbers. Such is the high post of duty in which God has placed them, and it is their moral duty not to shrink from it.

ADDITIONAL SCRIPTURE READING:
John 18.36; 1 John 2.15–17

Go to page 1391 for your next devotional reading.

100   500

Christ will be of no benefit to you. 3Once again I testify to every man who lets himself be circumcised that he is obliged to obey the entire law. 4You who want to be justified by the law have cut yourselves off from Christ; you have fallen away from grace. 5For through the Spirit, by faith, we eagerly wait for the hope of righteousness. 6For in Christ Jesus neither circumcision nor uncircumcision counts for anything; the only thing that counts is faith working[g] through love.

7 You were running well; who prevented you from obeying the truth? 8Such persuasion does not come from the one who calls you. 9A little yeast leavens the whole batch of dough. 10I am confident about you in the Lord that you will not think otherwise. But whoever it is that is confusing you will pay the penalty. 11But my friends,[h] why am I still being persecuted if I am still preaching circumcision? In that case the offense of the cross has been removed. 12I wish those who unsettle you would castrate themselves!

13 For you were called to freedom, brothers and sisters;[h] only do not use your freedom as an opportunity for self-indulgence,[i] but through love become slaves to one another. 14For the whole law is summed up in a single commandment, "You shall love your neighbor as yourself." 15If, however, you bite and devour one another, take care that you are not consumed by one another.

The Works of the Flesh

16 Live by the Spirit, I say, and do not gratify the desires of the flesh. 17For what the flesh desires is opposed to the Spirit, and what the Spirit desires is opposed to the flesh; for these are opposed to each other, to prevent you from doing what you want. 18But if you are led by the Spirit, you are not subject to the law. 19Now the works of the flesh are obvious: fornication, impurity, licentiousness, 20idolatry, sorcery, enmities, strife, jealousy, anger, quarrels, dissensions, factions, 21envy,[j] drunkenness, carousing, and things like these. I am warning you, as I warned you before: those who

do such things will not inherit the kingdom of God.

The Fruit of the Spirit

22 By contrast, the fruit of the Spirit is love, joy, peace, patience, kindness, generosity, faithfulness, 23gentleness, and self-control. There is no law against such things. 24And those who belong to Christ Jesus have crucified the flesh with its passions and desires. 25If we live by the Spirit, let us also be guided by the Spirit. 26Let us not become conceited, competing against one another, envying one another.

Bear One Another's Burdens

6 My friends,[k] if anyone is detected in a transgression, you who have received the Spirit should restore such a one in a spirit of gentleness. Take care that you yourselves are not tempted. 2Bear one another's burdens, and in this way you will fulfill[l] the law of Christ. 3For if those who are nothing think they are something, they deceive themselves. 4All must test their own work; then that work, rather than their neighbor's work, will become a cause for pride. 5For all must carry their own loads.

6 Those who are taught the word must share in all good things with their teacher.

7 Do not be deceived; God is not mocked, for you reap whatever you sow. 8If you sow to your own flesh, you will reap corruption from the flesh; but if you sow to the Spirit, you will reap eternal life from the Spirit. 9So let us not grow weary in doing what is right, for we will reap at harvest time, if we do not give up. 10So then, whenever we have an opportunity, let us work for the good of all, and especially for those of the family of faith.

Final Admonitions and Benediction

11 See what large letters I make when I am writing in my own hand! 12It is those who want to make a good showing in the flesh that try to compel you to be circumcised—only that they may not be persecuted for the cross of Christ. 13Even the circumcised do not themselves obey the law, but they want you to be circumcised so that they may

g Or made effective   h Gk brothers   i Gk the flesh   j Other ancient authorities add murder
k Gk Brothers   l Other ancient authorities read in this way fulfill

boast about your flesh. [14]May I never boast of anything except the cross of our Lord Jesus Christ, by which[m] the world has been crucified to me, and I to the world. [15]For[n] neither circumcision nor uncircumcision is anything; but a new creation is everything! [16]As for those who will follow this rule—peace be upon them, and mercy, and upon the Israel of God.

17 From now on, let no one make trouble for me; for I carry the marks of Jesus branded on my body.

18 May the grace of our Lord Jesus Christ be with your spirit, brothers and sisters.[o] Amen.

m Or through whom   n Other ancient authorities add in Christ Jesus   o Gk brothers

EPHESIANS

PAUL WRITES THIS LETTER SO THAT HIS READERS MIGHT BETTER UNDERSTAND GOD'S ETERNAL PURPOSES FOR THE CHURCH. ONE OF THOSE PURPOSES IS TO RECONCILE PEOPLE TO GOD AND TO EACH OTHER THROUGH THE WORK OF JESUS ON THE CROSS. THINK ABOUT YOUR OWN RELATIONSHIP TO GOD AND OTHERS AND YOUR OWN NEED FOR RECONCILIATION. LOOK FOR PAUL'S PRACTICAL ADVICE ON HOW TO LIVE IN UNITY WITH GOD AND ONE ANOTHER.

Salutation

1 Paul, an apostle of Christ Jesus by the will of God,

To the saints who are in Ephesus and are faithful*a* in Christ Jesus:

2 Grace to you and peace from God our Father and the Lord Jesus Christ.

Spiritual Blessings in Christ

3 Blessed be the God and Father of our Lord Jesus Christ, who has blessed us in Christ with every spiritual blessing in the heavenly places, 4just as he chose us in Christ*b* before the foundation of the world to be holy and blameless before him in love. 5He destined us for adoption as his children through Jesus Christ, according to the good pleasure of his will, 6to the praise of his glorious grace that he freely bestowed on us in the Beloved. 7In him we have redemption through his blood, the forgiveness of our trespasses, according to the riches of his grace 8that he lavished on us. With all wisdom and insight 9he has made known to us the mystery of his will, according to his good pleasure that he set forth in Christ, 10as a plan for the fullness of time, to gather up all things in him, things in heaven and things on earth. 11In Christ we have also obtained an inheritance,*c* having been destined according to the purpose of him who accomplishes all things according to his counsel and will, 12so that we, who were

---

a Other ancient authorities lack *in Ephesus*, reading *saints who are also faithful*   *b* Gk *in him*
c Or *been made a heritage*

HYMN TO CHRIST
Clement of Alexandria

VERSE: Ephesians 1.17   **PASSAGE:** Ephesians 1.15–23

ou who bridles untamed colts,
Who gives flight to birds,
Who steers ships along their course,
Tame our wild hearts,
Lift our souls to you,
Steer us towards the safe harbor of your love.

King of the saints,
Invincible Lord of the Father,
Prince of wisdom,
Source of joy,
Savior of our race,
Cultivator of all life,
Guardian of our desires.
Whose sure hand guides us to heaven.

Fisher of men,
You cast out the sweet bait of your gospel,
You draw us out of the waters of sin,
Shepherd of men,
You call us with your sweet, gentle voice,
You invite us into your eternal sheepfold.

Fountain of mercy,
Light of truth,
Faith without limits,
Love without end,
Exemplar of virtue,
Proclaimer of justice,
Leader of men,
Your footprints show the way to heaven.

Mother of your people,
Your celestial breasts give pure spiritual milk.
You slake the thirst of all who have faith.
Bridegroom of your people,
Your celestial beauty inspires us to sing your praises,
You lift our voices with hymns of everlasting praise.

ADDITIONAL SCRIPTURE READING:
Psalms 19.14; 23.3

Go to page 1393 for your next devotional reading.

100   500

the first to set our hope on Christ, might live for the praise of his glory. 13In him you also, when you had heard the word of truth, the gospel of your salvation, and had believed in him, were marked with the seal of the promised Holy Spirit; 14this*d* is the pledge of our inheritance toward redemption as God's own people, to the praise of his glory.

Paul's Prayer

15 I have heard of your faith in the Lord Jesus and your love*e* toward all the saints, and for this reason 16I do not cease to give thanks for you as I remember you in my prayers. 17I pray that the God of our Lord Jesus Christ, the Father of glory, may give you a spirit of wisdom and revelation as you come to know him, 18so that, with the eyes of your heart enlightened, you may know what is the hope to which he has called you, what are the riches of his glorious inheritance among the saints, 19and what is the immeasurable greatness of his power for us who believe, according to the working of his great power. 20God*f* put this power to work in Christ when he raised him from the dead and seated him at his right hand in the heavenly places, 21far above all rule and authority and power and dominion, and above every name that is named, not only in this age but also in the age to come. 22And he has put all things under his feet and has made him the head over all things for the church, 23which is his body, the fullness of him who fills all in all.

From Death to Life

2 You were dead through the trespasses and sins 2in which you once lived, following the course of this world, following the ruler of the power of the air, the spirit that is now at work among those who are disobedient. 3All of us once lived among them in the passions of our flesh, following the desires of flesh and senses, and we were by nature children of wrath, like everyone else. 4But God, who is rich in mercy, out of the great love with which he loved us 5even when we were dead through our

trespasses, made us alive together with Christ*g*—by grace you have been saved— 6and raised us up with him and seated us with him in the heavenly places in Christ Jesus, 7so that in the ages to come he might show the immeasurable riches of his grace in kindness toward us in Christ Jesus. 8For by grace you have been saved through faith, and this is not your own doing; it is the gift of God— 9not the result of works, so that no one may boast. 10For we are what he has made us, created in Christ Jesus for good works, which God prepared beforehand to be our way of life.

NO MAN EVER BELIEVES WITH A TRUE AND SAVING FAITH UNLESS GOD INCLINES HIS HEART; AND NO MAN WHEN GOD DOES INCLINE HIS HEART CAN REFRAIN FROM BELIEVING.   *—Blaise Pascal*

One in Christ

11 So then, remember that at one time you Gentiles by birth,*h* called "the uncircumcision" by those who are called "the circumcision"—a physical circumcision made in the flesh by human hands— 12remember that you were at that time without Christ, being aliens from the commonwealth of Israel, and strangers to the covenants of promise, having no hope and without God in the world. 13But now in Christ Jesus you who once were far off have been brought near by the blood of Christ. 14For he is our peace; in his flesh he has made both groups into one and has broken down the dividing wall, that is, the hostility between us. 15He has abolished the law with its commandments and ordinances, that he might create in himself one new humanity in place of the two, thus making peace, 16and might reconcile both groups to God in one body*i* through the cross, thus putting to death that hostility through it.*j* 17So he came and proclaimed peace to you who were far off and peace to those who were near; 18for through him both of us have access in one Spirit to the Father. 19So then you are no longer strangers and aliens, but

---

d Other ancient authorities read *who*   *e* Other ancient authorities lack *and your love*   *f* Gk *He*
g Other ancient authorities read *in Christ*   *h* Gk *in the flesh*   *i* Or *reconcile both of us in one body*
for God   *j* Or *in him,* or *in himself*

THE UNSEARCHABLE RICHES OF CHRIST

James Hudson Taylor

VERSE: Ephesians 3.8   **PASSAGE:** Ephesians 3.7–13

t is a wonderful thing to be really one with a risen and exalted Savior, to be a member of Christ! Think what it involves. Can Christ be rich and I poor? Can your right hand be rich and the left poor? or your head be well fed while your body starves? Again, think of its bearing on prayer. Could a bank clerk say to a customer, "It was only your hand, not you that wrote that check"; or "I cannot pay this sum to your hand, but only to yourself"? No more can your prayers or mine be discredited if offered in the name of Jesus (i.e., not for the sake of Jesus merely, but on the ground that we are his, his members) so long as we keep within the limits of Christ's credit—a tolerably wide limit! If we ask for anything unscriptural, or not in accordance with the will of God, Christ himself could not do that. But "if we ask anything according to his will . . . we know that we have the petitions that we desired of him" (1 John 5.14–15, KJV).

The sweetest part, if one may speak of one part being sweeter than another, is the rest which full identification with Christ brings. I am no longer anxious about anything, as I realize this; for he, I know, is able to carry out his will, and his will is mine. It makes no matter where he places me, or how. That is rather for him to consider than for me; for in the easiest position he must give me his grace, and in the most difficult his grace is sufficient . . . If God should place me in serious perplexity, must he not give me much guidance; in positions of great difficulty, much grace; in circumstances of great pressure and trial, much strength? No fear that his resources will prove unequal to the emergency! And his resources are mine, for he is mine, and is with me and dwells in me.

ADDITIONAL SCRIPTURE READING:
2 Corinthians 9.1; Philippians 4.6

Go to page 1395 for your next devotional reading.

1700   1900

you are citizens with the saints and also members of the household of God, [20]built upon the foundation of the apostles and prophets, with Christ Jesus himself as the cornerstone.[k] [21]In him the whole structure is joined together and grows into a holy temple in the Lord; [22]in whom you also are built together spiritually[l] into a dwelling place for God.

Paul's Ministry to the Gentiles

3 This is the reason that I Paul am a prisoner for[m] Christ Jesus for the sake of you Gentiles— [2]for surely you have already heard of the commission of God's grace that was given me for you, [3]and how the mystery was made known to me by revelation, as I wrote above in a few words, [4]a reading of which will enable you to perceive my understanding of the mystery of Christ. [5]In former generations this mystery[n] was not made known to humankind, as it has now been revealed to his holy apostles and prophets by the Spirit: [6]that is, the Gentiles have become fellow heirs, members of the same body, and sharers in the promise in Christ Jesus through the gospel.

7 Of this gospel I have become a servant according to the gift of God's grace that was given me by the working of his power. [8]Although I am the very least of all the saints, this grace was given to me to bring to the Gentiles the news of the boundless riches of Christ, [9]and to make everyone see[o] what is the plan of the mystery hidden for ages in[p] God who created all things; [10]so that through the church the wisdom of God in its rich variety might now be made known to the rulers and authorities in the heavenly places. [11]This was in accordance with the eternal purpose that he has carried out in Christ Jesus our Lord, [12]in whom we have access to God in boldness and confidence through faith in him.[q] [13]I pray therefore that you[r] may not lose heart over my sufferings for you; they are your glory.

Prayer for the Readers

14 For this reason I bow my knees before the Father,[s] [15]from whom every family[t] in heaven and on earth takes its name. [16]I pray that, according to the riches of his glory, he may grant that you may be strengthened in your inner being with power through his Spirit, [17]and that Christ may dwell in your hearts through faith, as you are being rooted and grounded in love. [18]I pray that you may have the power to comprehend, with all the saints, what is the breadth and length and height and depth, [19]and to know the love of Christ that surpasses knowledge, so that you may be filled with all the fullness of God.

AH! DEAREST JESUS, HOLY CHILD,

   MAKE THEE A BED, SOFT, UNDEFILED,

WITHIN MY HEART, THAT IT MAY BE

   A QUIET CHAMBER KEPT FOR THEE.

          —*Martin Luther*

---

20 Now to him who by the power at work within us is able to accomplish abundantly far more than all we can ask or imagine, [21]to him be glory in the church and in Christ Jesus to all generations, forever and ever. Amen.

Unity in the Body of Christ

4 I therefore, the prisoner in the Lord, beg you to lead a life worthy of the calling to which you have been called, [2]with all humility and gentleness, with patience, bearing with one another in love, [3]making every effort to maintain the unity of the Spirit in the bond of peace. [4]There is one body and one Spirit, just as you were called to the one hope of your calling, [5]one Lord, one faith, one baptism, [6]one God and Father of all, who is above all and through all and in all.

7 But each of us was given grace according to the measure of Christ's gift. [8]Therefore it is said,

"When he ascended on high he
    made captivity itself a
    captive;
he gave gifts to his people."
[9](When it says, "He ascended," what

---

k Or *keystone*   l Gk *in the Spirit*   m Or *of*   n Gk *it*   o Other ancient authorities read *to bring to light*   p Or *by*   q Or *the faith of him*   r Or *I*   s Other ancient authorities add *of our Lord Jesus Christ*   t Gk *fatherhood*

WEEKEND

THE NICENE CREED

VERSE: Galatians 4.4   **PASSAGE:** Galatians 4.4–6

e believe in one God,
the Father, the Almighty,
maker of heaven and earth,
of all that is, seen and unseen.

We believe in one Lord, Jesus Christ,
the only Son of God,
eternally begotten of the Father,
God from God, light from light,
true God from true God,
begotten, not made,
of one being with the Father.
Through him all things were made.
For us and for our salvation
he came down from heaven:
by the power of the Holy Spirit
he became incarnate from the Virgin Mary,
and was made man.
For our sake he was crucified under Pontius Pilate;
he suffered death and was buried.
On the third day he rose again
in accordance with the Scriptures;
he ascended into heaven
and is seated at the right hand of the Father.
He will come again in glory to judge the living and
the dead,
and his kingdom will have no end.

We believe in the Holy Spirit, the Lord, the giver of life,
who proceeds from the Father and the Son
With the Father and the Son he is worshiped and
glorified.
He has spoken through the Prophets.
We believe in one holy catholic and apostolic church.
We acknowledge one baptism for the forgiveness
of sins,
We look for the resurrection of the dead,
and the life of the world to come. Amen.

ADDITIONAL SCRIPTURE READING:
Ephesians 4.3–6; Philippians 2.5–11

Go to page 1397 for your next devotional reading.

does it mean but that he had also descended[u] into the lower parts of the earth? [10]He who descended is the same one who ascended far above all the heavens, so that he might fill all things.) [11]The gifts he gave were that some would be apostles, some prophets, some evangelists, some pastors and teachers, [12]to equip the saints for the work of ministry, for building up the body of Christ, [13]until all of us come to the unity of the faith and of the knowledge of the Son of God, to maturity, to the measure of the full stature of Christ. [14]We must no longer be children, tossed to and fro and blown about by every wind of doctrine, by people's trickery, by their craftiness in deceitful scheming. [15]But speaking the truth in love, we must grow up in every way into him who is the head, into Christ, [16]from whom the whole body, joined and knit together by every ligament with which it is equipped, as each part is working properly, promotes the body's growth in building itself up in love.

The Old Life and the New

17 Now this I affirm and insist on in the Lord: you must no longer live as the Gentiles live, in the futility of their minds. [18]They are darkened in their understanding, alienated from the life of God because of their ignorance and hardness of heart. [19]They have lost all sensitivity and have abandoned themselves to licentiousness, greedy to practice every kind of impurity. [20]That is not the way you learned Christ! [21]For surely you have heard about him and were taught in him, as truth is in Jesus. [22]You were taught to put away your former way of life, your old self, corrupt and deluded by its lusts, [23]and to be renewed in the spirit of your minds, [24]and to clothe yourselves with the new self, created according to the likeness of God in true righteousness and holiness.

Rules for the New Life

25 So then, putting away falsehood, let all of us speak the truth to our neighbors, for we are members of one another. [26]Be angry but do not sin; do not let the sun go down on your anger, [27]and do not make room for the devil. [28]Thieves must give up stealing; rather let them labor and work honestly with their own hands, so as to have something to share with the needy. [29]Let no evil talk come out of your mouths, but only what is useful for building up,[v] as there is need, so that your words may give grace to those who hear. [30]And do not grieve the Holy Spirit of God, with which you were marked with a seal for the day of redemption. [31]Put away from you all bitterness and wrath and anger and wrangling and slander, together with all malice, [32]and be

---

WHEN ANGER ENTERS THE MIND, WISDOM DEPARTS. —*Thomas à Kempis*

---

kind to one another, tenderhearted, forgiving one another, as God in Christ has forgiven you.[w] [1]Therefore be imitators of God, as beloved children, [2]and live in love, as Christ loved us[x] and gave himself up for us, a fragrant offering and sacrifice to God.

Renounce Pagan Ways

3 But fornication and impurity of any kind, or greed, must not even be mentioned among you, as is proper among saints. [4]Entirely out of place is obscene, silly, and vulgar talk; but instead, let there be thanksgiving. [5]Be sure of this, that no fornicator or impure person, or one who is greedy (that is, an idolater), has any inheritance in the kingdom of Christ and of God.

6 Let no one deceive you with empty words, for because of these things the wrath of God comes on those who are disobedient. [7]Therefore do not be associated with them. [8]For once you were darkness, but now in the Lord you are light. Live as children of light— [9]for the fruit of the light is found in all that is good and right and true. [10]Try to find out what is pleasing to the Lord. [11]Take no part in the unfruitful works of darkness, but instead expose them. [12]For it is shameful even to mention what such people do secretly; [13]but everything exposed by the light

---

u Other ancient authorities add *first*　　v Other ancient authorities read *building up faith*　　w Other ancient authorities read *us*　　x Other ancient authorities read *you*

THE LORD'S INVITATION
Benedict of Nursia

VERSE: Ephesians 5.14   PASSAGE: Ephesians 5.8–14

et us then rise at length, since the Scripture arouseth us, saying: "It is now the hour for us to rise from sleep;" and having opened our eyes to the deifying light, let us hear with awestruck ears what the divine voice, crying our daily, doth admonish us, saying: "Today, if you shall hear his voice, harden not your hearts" (Hebrews 3.15, KJV). And again: "He that hath ears to hear let him hear what the Spirit saith to the churches" (see Revelation 2.7). And what doth he say?—"Come, children, hearken unto me, I will teach you the fear of the Lord" (Psalm 34.11). "Run whilst you have the light of life, that the darkness of death overtake you not."

And the Lord seeking his workman in the multitude of the people, to whom he proclaimeth these words, saith again: "Who is the man that desireth life and loveth to see good days?" (see 1 Peter 3.10). If hearing this thou answerest, "I am he," God saith to thee: "If thou wilt have true and everlasting life, keep thy tongue from evil, and thy lips from speaking guile; turn away from evil and do good; seek after peace and pursue it" (see Psalm 34.12–14). And when you shall have done these things, my eyes shall be upon you, and my ears unto your prayers. And before you shall call upon me I will say: "Behold, I am here."

What, dearest brethren, can be sweeter to us than this voice of the Lord inviting us? See, in his loving kindness, the Lord showeth us the way to life. Therefore, having our loins girt with faith and the performance of good works, let us walk his ways under the guidance of the gospel, that we may be found worthy of seeing him who hath called us to his kingdom. If we desire to dwell in the tabernacle of his kingdom, we cannot reach it in any way, unless we run thither by good works. But let us ask the Lord with the prophet, saying to him: "Lord, who shall dwell in thy tabernacle, or who shall rest in thy holy hill?" (Psalm 15.1).

ADDITIONAL SCRIPTURE READING:
Psalm 23.6; 1 Peter 3.11

Go to page 1402 for your next devotional reading.

500   1500

becomes visible, [14]for everything that becomes visible is light. Therefore it says,
"Sleeper, awake!
Rise from the dead,
and Christ will shine on you."

15 Be careful then how you live, not as unwise people but as wise, [16]making the most of the time, because the days are evil. [17]So do not be foolish, but understand what the will of the Lord is. [18]Do not get drunk with wine, for that is debauchery; but be filled with the Spirit, [19]as you sing psalms and hymns and spiritual songs among yourselves, singing and making melody to the Lord in your hearts, [20]giving thanks to God the Father at all times and for everything in the name of our Lord Jesus Christ.

The Christian Household

21 Be subject to one another out of reverence for Christ.

22 Wives, be subject to your husbands as you are to the Lord. [23]For the husband is the head of the wife just as Christ is the head of the church, the body of which he is the Savior. [24]Just as the church is subject to Christ, so also wives ought to be, in everything, to their husbands.

25 Husbands, love your wives, just as Christ loved the church and gave himself up for her, [26]in order to make her holy by cleansing her with the washing of water by the word, [27]so as to present the church to himself in splendor, without a spot or wrinkle or anything of the kind—yes, so that she may be holy and without blemish. [28]In the same way, husbands should love their wives as they do their own bodies. He who loves his wife loves himself. [29]For no one ever hates his own body, but he nourishes and tenderly cares for it, just as Christ does for the church, [30]because we are members of his body.[y] [31]"For this reason a man will leave his father and mother and be joined to his wife, and the two will become one flesh." [32]This is a great mystery, and I am applying it to Christ and the church. [33]Each of you, however, should love his wife as himself, and a wife should respect her husband.

Children and Parents

6 Children, obey your parents in the Lord,[z] for this is right. [2]"Honor your father and mother"—this is the first commandment with a promise: [3]"so that it may be well with you and you may live long on the earth."

4 And, fathers, do not provoke your children to anger, but bring them up in the discipline and instruction of the Lord.

Slaves and Masters

5 Slaves, obey your earthly masters with fear and trembling, in singleness of heart, as you obey Christ; [6]not only while being watched, and in order to please them, but as slaves of Christ, doing the will of God from the heart. [7]Render service with enthusiasm, as to the Lord and not to men and women, [8]knowing that whatever good we do, we will receive the same again from the Lord, whether we are slaves or free.

9 And, masters, do the same to them. Stop threatening them, for you know that both of you have the same Master in heaven, and with him there is no partiality.

The Whole Armor of God

10 Finally, be strong in the Lord and in the strength of his power. [11]Put on the whole armor of God, so that you may be able to stand against the wiles of the devil. [12]For our[a] struggle is not against enemies of blood and flesh, but against the rulers, against the authorities, against the cosmic powers of this present darkness, against the spiritual forces of evil in the heavenly places. [13]Therefore take up the whole armor of God, so that you may be able to withstand on that evil day, and having done everything, to stand firm. [14]Stand therefore, and fasten the belt of truth around your waist, and put on the breastplate of righteousness. [15]As shoes for your feet put on whatever will make you ready to proclaim the gospel of peace. [16]With all of these,[b] take the shield of faith, with which you will be able to quench all the flaming arrows of the evil one. [17]Take

---

y Other ancient authorities add *of his flesh and of his bones*   z Other ancient authorities lack *in the Lord*   a Other ancient authorities read *your*   b Or *In all circumstances*

the helmet of salvation, and the sword of the Spirit, which is the word of God.

18 Pray in the Spirit at all times in every prayer and supplication. To that end keep alert and always persevere in supplication for all the saints. [19]Pray

---

THE CHRISTIAN PRAYS IN EVERY SITUATION, IN HIS WALKS FOR RECREATION, IN HIS DEALINGS WITH OTHERS, IN SILENCE, IN READING, IN ALL RATIONAL PURSUITS. *—Clement of Alexandria*

---

also for me, so that when I speak, a message may be given to me to make known with boldness the mystery of the gospel,[c] [20]for which I am an ambassador in chains. Pray that I may declare it boldly, as I must speak.

Personal Matters and Benediction

21 So that you also may know how I am and what I am doing, Tychicus will tell you everything. He is a dear brother and a faithful minister in the Lord. [22]I am sending him to you for this very purpose, to let you know how we are, and to encourage your hearts.

23 Peace be to the whole community,[d] and love with faith, from God the Father and the Lord Jesus Christ. [24]Grace be with all who have an undying love for our Lord Jesus Christ.[e]

---

c Other ancient authorities lack *of the gospel*   d Gk *to the brothers*   e Other ancient authorities add *Amen*

PHILIPPIANS

P AUL WROTE TO THE PHILIPPIANS DURING HIS FIRST ROMAN IMPRISONMENT TO THANK THEM FOR THEIR LOVE AND HELP AND TO WARN THEM AGAINST FALSE TEACHERS. THE THEME OF THE BOOK IS "JOY" (THE WORD "JOY" IN ITS VARIOUS FORMS OCCURS 16 TIMES). BE ALERT TO PAUL'S WARNINGS AGAINST PRIDE AND A SELF-SEEKING ATTITUDE THAT CAN LEAD TO HARMFUL DIVISIONS. HOLD ON TO THE PRACTICAL TOOLS PAUL PROVIDES TO HELP YOU RESHAPE YOUR THINKING ACCORDING TO GOD'S WAYS.

Salutation

1 Paul and Timothy, servants*a* of Christ Jesus,

To all the saints in Christ Jesus who are in Philippi, with the bishops*b* and deacons:*c*

2 Grace to you and peace from God our Father and the Lord Jesus Christ.

Paul's Prayer for the Philippians

3 I thank my God every time I remember you, 4constantly praying with joy in every one of my prayers for all of you, 5because of your sharing in the gospel from the first day until now. 6I am confident of this, that the one who began a good work among you will bring it to completion by the day of Jesus Christ. 7It is right for me to think this

---

A CHRISTIAN IS NEVER IN A STATE OF COMPLETION BUT ALWAYS IN THE PROCESS OF BECOMING.
—*Martin Luther*

---

way about all of you, because you hold me in your heart,*d* for all of you share in God's grace*e* with me, both in my imprisonment and in the defense and confirmation of the gospel. 8For God is my witness, how I long for all of you with the compassion of Christ Jesus. 9And this is my prayer, that your love may overflow more and more with knowl-

---

a Gk *slaves*   *b* Or *overseers*   *c* Or *overseers and helpers*   *d* Or *because I hold you in my heart*
e Gk *in grace*

edge and full insight [10]to help you to determine what is best, so that in the day of Christ you may be pure and blameless, [11]having produced the harvest of righteousness that comes through Jesus Christ for the glory and praise of God.

Paul's Present Circumstances

12 I want you to know, beloved,[f] that what has happened to me has actually helped to spread the gospel, [13]so that it has become known throughout the whole imperial guard[g] and to everyone else that my imprisonment is for Christ; [14]and most of the brothers and sisters,[f] having been made confident in the Lord by my imprisonment, dare to speak the word[h] with greater boldness and without fear.

15 Some proclaim Christ from envy and rivalry, but others from goodwill. [16]These proclaim Christ out of love, knowing that I have been put here for the defense of the gospel; [17]the others proclaim Christ out of selfish ambition, not sincerely but intending to increase my suffering in my imprisonment. [18]What does it matter? Just this, that Christ is proclaimed in every way, whether out of false motives or true; and in that I rejoice.

WHEREVER THE WORD OF GOD IS PREACHED AND HEARD, THERE A CHURCH OF GOD EXISTS, EVEN IF IT SWARMS WITH MANY FAULTS.   —*John Calvin*

Yes, and I will continue to rejoice, [19]for I know that through your prayers and the help of the Spirit of Jesus Christ this will turn out for my deliverance. [20]It is my eager expectation and hope that I will not be put to shame in any way, but that by my speaking with all boldness, Christ will be exalted now as always in my body, whether by life or by death. [21]For to me, living is Christ and dying is gain. [22]If I am to live in the flesh, that means fruitful labor for me; and I do not know which I prefer. [23]I am hard pressed between the two: my desire is to depart and be with Christ, for that is far better; [24]but to remain in the flesh is more necessary for you. [25]Since I am

convinced of this, I know that I will remain and continue with all of you for your progress and joy in faith, [26]so that I may share abundantly in your boasting in Christ Jesus when I come to you again.

27 Only, live your life in a manner worthy of the gospel of Christ, so that, whether I come and see you or am absent and hear about you, I will know that you are standing firm in one spirit, striving side by side with one mind for the faith of the gospel, [28]and are in no way intimidated by your opponents. For them this is evidence of their destruction, but of your salvation. And this is God's doing. [29]For he has graciously granted you the privilege not only of believing in Christ, but of suffering for him as well— [30]since you are having the same struggle that you saw I had and now hear that I still have.

Imitating Christ's Humility

2 If then there is any encouragement in Christ, any consolation from love, any sharing in the Spirit, any compassion and sympathy, [2]make my joy complete: be of the same mind, having the same love, being in full accord and of one mind. [3]Do nothing from selfish ambition or conceit, but in humility regard others as better than yourselves. [4]Let each of you look not to your own interests, but to the interests of others. [5]Let the same mind be in you that was[i] in Christ Jesus,

6   who, though he was in the form of
        God,
        did not regard equality with God
        as something to be exploited,
7   but emptied himself,
        taking the form of a slave,
        being born in human likeness.
    And being found in human form,
8   he humbled himself
        and became obedient to the point
            of death—
        even death on a cross.

9   Therefore God also highly exalted
        him
        and gave him the name
        that is above every name,

---

f Gk *brothers*   *g* Gk *whole praetorium*   *h* Other ancient authorities read *word of God*   *i* Or *that you have*

10   so that at the name of Jesus
         every knee should bend,
      in heaven and on earth and under
         the earth,
11   and every tongue should confess
         that Jesus Christ is Lord,
      to the glory of God the Father.

Shining as Lights in the World

12 Therefore, my beloved, just as you
have always obeyed me, not only in my
presence, but much more now in my absence, work out your own salvation with
fear and trembling; 13for it is God who is

HE LEFT HIS FATHER'S THRONE ABOVE,
   SO FREE, SO INFINITE HIS GRACE!
EMPTIED HIMSELF OF ALL BUT LOVE,
   AND BLED FOR ADAM'S HELPLESS RACE.
                              —*Charles Wesley*

TUESDAY

THE WONDERFUL, UNSPEAKABLE MYSTERY
Martin Luther

VERSE: Philippians 2.8   PASSAGE: Philippians 2.6–10

ll the wisdom of the world is childish foolishness in
comparison with the acknowledgment of Christ. For
what is more wonderful than the unspeakable mystery, that the Son of God, the image of the eternal Father, took upon him the nature of man. Doubtless, he helped his
supposed father, Joseph, to build houses; for Joseph was a carpenter. What will they of Nazareth think at the day of judgment,
when they shall see Christ sitting in his divine majesty; surely
they will be astonished, and say: Lord, thou helpest build my
house, how comest thou now to this high honor?

When Jesus was born, doubtless, he cried and wept like other
children, and his mother tended him as other mothers tend their
children. As he grew up, he was submissive to his parents, and
waited on them, and carried his supposed father's dinner to him,
and when he came back, Mary, no doubt, often said: "My dear
little Jesus, where hast thou been?" (see Luke 2.48). He that
takes not offense at the simple, lowly, and mean course of the
life of Christ, is endued with high divine art and wisdom; yea,
has a special gift of God in the Holy Ghost. Let us ever bear in
mind, that our blessed Savior thus humbled and abased himself,
yielding even to the contumelious death of the cross, for the
comfort of us poor, miserable, and damned creatures.

ADDITIONAL SCRIPTURE READING:
John 10.9–10; 1 Corinthians 2.1–10

Go to page 1404 for your next devotional reading.

1500   1700

at work in you, enabling you both to will and to work for his good pleasure.

14 Do all things without murmuring and arguing, 15so that you may be blameless and innocent, children of God without blemish in the midst of a crooked and perverse generation, in which you shine like stars in the world. 16It is by your holding fast to the word of life that I can boast on the day of Christ that I did not run in vain or labor in vain. 17But even if I am being poured out as a libation over the sacrifice and the offering of your faith, I am glad and rejoice with all of you— 18and in the same way you also must be glad and rejoice with me.

Timothy and Epaphroditus

19 I hope in the Lord Jesus to send Timothy to you soon, so that I may be cheered by news of you. 20I have no one like him who will be genuinely concerned for your welfare. 21All of them are seeking their own interests, not those of Jesus Christ. 22But Timothy's^j worth you know, how like a son with a father he has served with me in the work of the gospel. 23I hope therefore to send him as soon as I see how things go with me; 24and I trust in the Lord that I will also come soon.

25 Still, I think it necessary to send to you Epaphroditus—my brother and co-worker and fellow soldier, your messenger^k and minister to my need; 26for he has been longing for^l all of you, and has been distressed because you heard that he was ill. 27He was indeed so ill that he nearly died. But God had mercy on him, and not only on him but on me also, so that I would not have one sorrow after another. 28I am the more eager to send him, therefore, in order that you may rejoice at seeing him again, and that I may be less anxious. 29Welcome him then in the Lord with all joy, and honor such people, 30because he came close to death for the work of Christ,^{m} risking his life to make up for those services that you could not give me.

3 Finally, my brothers and sisters,^{n} rejoice^o in the Lord.

Breaking with the Past

To write the same things to you is not troublesome to me, and for you it is a safeguard.

2 Beware of the dogs, beware of the evil workers, beware of those who mutilate the flesh!^{p} 3For it is we who are the circumcision, who worship in the Spirit of God^q and boast in Christ Jesus and have no confidence in the flesh— 4even though I, too, have reason for confidence in the flesh.

If anyone else has reason to be confident in the flesh, I have more: 5circumcised on the eighth day, a member of the people of Israel, of the tribe of Benjamin, a Hebrew born of Hebrews; as to the law, a Pharisee; 6as to zeal, a persecutor of the church; as to righteousness under the law, blameless.

7 Yet whatever gains I had, these I have come to regard as loss because of Christ. 8More than that, I regard everything as loss because of the surpassing value of knowing Christ Jesus my Lord. For his sake I have suffered the loss of all things, and I regard them as rubbish, in order that I may gain Christ 9and be found in him, not having a righteousness of my own that comes from the law, but one that comes through faith in Christ,^{r} the righteousness from God based on faith. 10I want to know Christ^s and the power of his resurrection and the sharing of his sufferings by becoming like him in his death, 11if somehow I may attain the resurrection from the dead.

Pressing toward the Goal

12 Not that I have already obtained this or have already reached the goal;^{t} but I press on to make it my own, because Christ Jesus has made me his own. 13Beloved,^{u} I do not consider that I have made it my own;^{v} but this one thing I do: forgetting what lies behind and straining forward to what lies ahead, 14I press on toward the goal for the prize of the heavenly^w call of God in Christ Jesus. 15Let those of us then who are mature be of the same mind; and if you

---

^{j} Gk his ^{k} Gk apostle ^{l} Other ancient authorities read longing to see ^{m} Other ancient authorities read of the Lord ^{n} Gk my brothers ^{o} Or farewell ^{p} Gk the mutilation ^{q} Other ancient authorities read worship God in spirit ^{r} Or through the faith of Christ ^{s} Gk him ^{t} Or have already been made perfect ^{u} Gk Brothers ^{v} Other ancient authorities read my own yet ^{w} Gk upward

think differently about anything, this too God will reveal to you. ¹⁶Only let us hold fast to what we have attained.

17 Brothers and sisters,ˣ join in imitating me, and observe those who live according to the example you have in us. ¹⁸For many live as enemies of the cross of Christ; I have often told you of them, and now I tell you even with tears.

¹⁹Their end is destruction; their god is the belly; and their glory is in their shame; their minds are set on earthly things. ²⁰But our citizenshipʸ is in heaven, and it is from there that we are expecting a Savior, the Lord Jesus Christ. ²¹He will transform the body of our humiliationᶻ that it may be conformed to the body of his glory,ᵃ by the power that

x Gk Brothers   y Or commonwealth   z Or our humble bodies   a Or his glorious body

WEDNESDAY

MEMORIAL
Blaise Pascal

VERSE: Philippians 3.8   PASSAGE: Philippians 3.7–11

ire.
God of Abraham, God of Isaac, God of Jacob,
not of the philosophers and the scholars.
Certainty, certainty, feeling, joy, peace.
(God of Jesus Christ) . . .
Your God will be my God.
Forgetfulness of the world and everything except God.
He is only found by the ways taught in the Gospel.
Grandeur of the human soul.
Righteous Father, the world has not known you, but I knew you.
Joy, joy, joy, tears of joy.
I separated myself from him . . .
My God, will you abandon me?
Let me not be eternally separated from him.
This is life eternal, that they might know you,
the only true God, and the one that you sent, Jesus Christ.
Jesus Christ. Jesus Christ.
I separated myself from him; I fled, renounced, crucified him.
Let me never be separated from him.
He can only be kept by the ways taught in the Gospel.
Total and sweet renunciation, etc.
Total submission to Jesus Christ and to my guide.
Eternal joy for one day of effort on earth . . . Amen.

ADDITIONAL SCRIPTURE READING:
Romans 8.1–2; Colossians 3.1–4

Go to page 1406 for your next devotional reading.

1500   1700

also enables him to make all things

4 subject to himself. ¹Therefore, my brothers and sisters,ᵇ whom I love and long for, my joy and crown, stand firm in the Lord in this way, my beloved.

Exhortations

2 I urge Euodia and I urge Syntyche to be of the same mind in the Lord. ³Yes, and I ask you also, my loyal companion,ᶜ help these women, for they have struggled beside me in the work of the gospel, together with Clement and the rest of my co-workers, whose names are in the book of life.

4 Rejoiceᵈ in the Lord always; again I will say, Rejoice.ᵈ ⁵Let your gentleness be known to everyone. The Lord is near. ⁶Do not worry about anything, but in everything by prayer and supplication with thanksgiving let your requests be made known to God. ⁷And the peace of God, which surpasses all understanding, will guard your hearts and your minds in Christ Jesus.

THE BEGINNING OF ANXIETY IS THE END OF FAITH; AND THE BEGINNING OF TRUE FAITH IS THE END OF ANXIETY.   —*George Muller*

8 Finally, beloved,ᵉ whatever is true, whatever is honorable, whatever is just, whatever is pure, whatever is pleasing, whatever is commendable, if there is any excellence and if there is anything worthy of praise, think aboutᶠ these things. ⁹Keep on doing the things that you have learned and received and heard and seen in me, and the God of peace will be with you.

Acknowledgment of the Philippians' Gift

10 I rejoiceᵍ in the Lord greatly that now at last you have revived your con-

cern for me; indeed, you were concerned for me, but had no opportunity to show it.ʰ ¹¹Not that I am referring to being in need; for I have learned to be content with whatever I have. ¹²I know what it is to have little, and I know what it is to have plenty. In any and all circumstances I have learned the secret of being well-fed and of going hungry, of having plenty and of being in need. ¹³I can do all

IF WE HAD NOT WINTER, THE SPRING WOULD NOT BE SO PLEASANT; IF WE DID NOT SOMETIMES TASTE OF ADVERSITY, PROSPERITY WOULD NOT BE SO WELCOME.   —*Anne Bradstreet*

things through him who strengthens me. ¹⁴In any case, it was kind of you to share my distress.

15 You Philippians indeed know that in the early days of the gospel, when I left Macedonia, no church shared with me in the matter of giving and receiving, except you alone. ¹⁶For even when I was in Thessalonica, you sent me help for my needs more than once. ¹⁷Not that I seek the gift, but I seek the profit that accumulates to your account. ¹⁸I have been paid in full and have more than enough; I am fully satisfied, now that I have received from Epaphroditus the gifts you sent, a fragrant offering, a sacrifice acceptable and pleasing to God. ¹⁹And my God will fully satisfy every need of yours according to his riches in glory in Christ Jesus. ²⁰To our God and Father be glory forever and ever. Amen.

Final Greetings and Benediction

21 Greet every saint in Christ Jesus. The friendsᵉ who are with me greet you. ²²All the saints greet you, especially those of the emperor's household.

23 The grace of the Lord Jesus Christ be with your spirit.ⁱ

b Gk *my brothers*   c Or *loyal Syzygus*   d Or *Farewell*   e Gk *brothers*   f Gk *take account of*   g Gk *I rejoiced*   h Gk lacks *to show it*   i Other ancient authorities add *Amen*

THE ESSENCE OF THE GOSPEL
Dietrich Bonhoeffer

VERSE: Philippians 4.6   **PASSAGE:** Philippians 4.4–7

nxiety is characteristic of the Gentiles for they rely on their own strength and work instead of relying on God. They do not know that the Father knows that we have need of all these things, and so they try to do for themselves what they do not expect from God. But the disciples know that the rule is "Strive first for the kingdom of God and his righteousness, and all these things will be given to you as well" (Matthew 6.33). Anxiety for food and clothing is clearly not the same thing as anxiety for the kingdom of God, however much we should like to persuade ourselves that when we are working for our families and concerning ourselves with bread and houses we are thereby building the kingdom, as though the kingdom could be realized only through our worldly cares. The kingdom of God and his righteousness are sharply distinguished from the gifts of the world which come our way. That kingdom is none other than the righteousness of Matthew 5 and 6, the righteousness of the cross and of following Christ beneath that cross. Fellowship with Jesus and obedience to his commandment come first, and all else follows. Worldly cares are not a part of our discipleship, but distinct and subordinate concerns. Before we start taking thought for our life, our food and clothing, our work and families, we must seek the righteousness of Christ . . . If we follow Jesus and look only to his righteousness, we are in his hands and under the protection of him and his Father. And if we are in communion with the Father, nought can harm us. We shall always be assured that he can feed his children and will not suffer them to hunger. God will help us in the hour of need, and he knows our needs.

ADDITIONAL SCRIPTURE READING:
Psalm 111.5; 1 Peter 5.7

Go to page 1410 for your next devotional reading.

1900   Present

COLOSSIANS

DURING PAUL'S THREE-YEAR MINISTRY IN EPHESUS, EPAPHRAS HAD BEEN CONVERTED AND HAD CARRIED THE GOSPEL TO COLOSSAE. THE YOUNG CHURCH THAT RESULTED THEN BECAME THE TARGET OF HERETICAL ATTACK, WHICH LED TO THE PENNING OF THIS LETTER. PAUL'S PURPOSE IS TO REFUTE THE FALSE TEACHERS, WHICH HE DOES BY ASSERTING THE SUPREMACY OF CHRIST AND EXAMINING WHAT THAT MEANS FOR EVERYDAY LIVING. AS YOU READ THIS LETTER, LOOK FOR INSIGHTS ON WAYS TO FORM ATTITUDES AND CARRY OUT ACTIONS THAT HONOR THE LORD.

Salutation

1 Paul, an apostle of Christ Jesus by the will of God, and Timothy our brother,

2 To the saints and faithful brothers and sisters[a] in Christ in Colossae:

Grace to you and peace from God our Father.

Paul Thanks God for the Colossians

3 In our prayers for you we always thank God, the Father of our Lord Jesus Christ, 4for we have heard of your faith in Christ Jesus and of the love that you have for all the saints, 5because of the hope laid up for you in heaven. You have heard of this hope before in the word of the truth, the gospel 6that has come to you. Just as it is bearing fruit and growing in the whole world, so it has been bearing fruit among yourselves from the day you heard it and truly comprehended the grace of God. 7This you learned from Epaphras, our beloved fellow servant.[b] He is a faithful minister of Christ on your[c] behalf, 8and he has made known to us your love in the Spirit.

9 For this reason, since the day we heard it, we have not ceased praying for you and asking that you may be filled with the knowledge of God's[d] will in all spiritual wisdom and understanding, 10so that you may lead lives worthy of the Lord, fully pleasing to him, as you bear fruit in every good work and as you grow in the knowledge of God. 11May you be made strong with all the strength

a Gk brothers   b Gk slave   c Other ancient authorities read our   d Gk his that comes from his glorious power, and may you be prepared to endure everything with patience, while joyfully [12]giving thanks to the Father, who has enabled[e] you[f] to share in the inheritance of the saints in the light. [13]He has rescued us from the power of darkness and transferred us into the kingdom of his beloved Son, [14]in whom we have redemption, the forgiveness of sins.[g]

I BELIEVE IN THE FORGIVENESS OF SINS.

—*The Apostles' Creed*

The Supremacy of Christ

15 He is the image of the invisible God, the firstborn of all creation; [16]for in[h] him all things in heaven and on earth were created, things visible and invisible, whether thrones or dominions or rulers or powers—all things have been created through him and for him. [17]He himself is before all things, and in[h] him all things hold together. [18]He is the head of the body, the church; he is the beginning, the firstborn from the dead, so that he might come to have first place in everything. [19]For in him all the fullness of God was pleased to dwell, [20]and through him God was pleased to reconcile to himself all things, whether on earth or in heaven, by making peace through the blood of his cross.

21 And you who were once estranged and hostile in mind, doing evil deeds, [22]he has now reconciled[i] in his fleshly body[j] through death, so as to present you holy and blameless and irreproachable before him— [23]provided that you continue securely established and steadfast in the faith, without shifting from the hope promised by the gospel that you heard, which has been proclaimed to every creature under heaven. I, Paul, became a servant of this gospel.

Paul's Interest in the Colossians

24 I am now rejoicing in my sufferings for your sake, and in my flesh I am completing what is lacking in Christ's afflictions for the sake of his body, that is, the church. [25]I became its servant according to God's commission that was given to me for you, to make the word of God fully known, [26]the mystery that has been hidden throughout the ages and generations but has now been revealed to his saints. [27]To them God chose to make known how great among the Gentiles are the riches of the glory of this mystery, which is Christ in you, the hope of glory. [28]It is he whom we proclaim, warning everyone and teaching everyone in all wisdom, so that we may present everyone mature in Christ. [29]For this I toil and struggle with all the energy that he powerfully inspires within me.

2 For I want you to know how much I am struggling for you, and for those in Laodicea, and for all who have not seen me face to face. [2]I want their hearts to be encouraged and united in love, so that they may have all the riches of assured understanding and have the knowledge of God's mystery, that is, Christ himself,[k] [3]in whom are hidden all the treasures of wisdom and knowledge. [4]I am saying this so that no one may deceive you with plausible arguments. [5]For though I am absent in body, yet I am with you in spirit, and I rejoice to see your morale and the firmness of your faith in Christ.

Fullness of Life in Christ

6 As you therefore have received Christ Jesus the Lord, continue to live your lives[l] in him, [7]rooted and built up in him and established in the faith, just as you were taught, abounding in thanksgiving.

8 See to it that no one takes you captive through philosophy and empty deceit, according to human tradition, according to the elemental spirits of the universe,[m] and not according to Christ. [9]For in him the whole fullness of deity dwells bodily, [10]and you have come to fullness in him, who is the head of every ruler and authority. [11]In him also you

---

e Other ancient authorities read *called*   *f* Other ancient authorities read *us*   *g* Other ancient authorities add *through his blood*   *h* Or *by*   *i* Other ancient authorities read *you have now been reconciled*   *j* Gk *in the body of his flesh*   *k* Other ancient authorities read *of the mystery of God, both of the Father and of Christ*   *l* Gk *to walk*   *m* Or *the rudiments of the world*

were circumcised with a spiritual circumcision,[n] by putting off the body of the flesh in the circumcision of Christ; [12]when you were buried with him in baptism, you were also raised with him through faith in the power of God, who raised him from the dead. [13]And when you were dead in trespasses and the uncircumcision of your flesh, God[o] made you[p] alive together with him, when he forgave us all our trespasses, [14]erasing the record that stood against us with its legal demands. He set this aside, nailing it to the cross. [15]He disarmed[q] the rulers and authorities and made a public example of them, triumphing over them in it.

16 Therefore do not let anyone condemn you in matters of food and drink or of observing festivals, new moons, or sabbaths. [17]These are only a shadow of what is to come, but the substance belongs to Christ. [18]Do not let anyone disqualify you, insisting on self-abasement and worship of angels, dwelling[r] on visions,[s] puffed up without cause by a human way of thinking,[t] [19]and not holding fast to the head, from whom the whole body, nourished and held together by its ligaments and sinews, grows with a growth that is from God.

Warnings against False Teachers

20 If with Christ you died to the elemental spirits of the universe,[u] why do you live as if you still belonged to the world? Why do you submit to regulations, [21]"Do not handle, Do not taste, Do not touch"? [22]All these regulations refer to things that perish with use; they are simply human commands and teachings. [23]These have indeed an appearance of wisdom in promoting self-imposed piety, humility, and severe treatment of the body, but they are of no value in checking self-indulgence.[v]

The New Life in Christ

3 So if you have been raised with Christ, seek the things that are above, where Christ is, seated at the right hand of God. [2]Set your minds on things that are above, not on things that are on earth, [3]for you have died, and your life is hidden with Christ in God. [4]When Christ who is your[w] life is revealed, then you also will be revealed with him in glory.

5 Put to death, therefore, whatever in you is earthly: fornication, impurity, passion, evil desire, and greed (which is idolatry). [6]On account of these the wrath of God is coming on those who are disobedient.[x] [7]These are the ways you also once followed, when you were living that life.[y] [8]But now you must get rid of all such things—anger, wrath, malice, slander, and abusive[z] language from your mouth. [9]Do not lie to one another, seeing that you have stripped off the old self with its practices [10]and have clothed yourselves with the new self, which is being renewed in knowledge according to the image of its creator. [11]In that renewal[a] there is no longer Greek and Jew, circumcised and uncircumcised, barbarian, Scythian, slave and free; but Christ is all and in all!

12 As God's chosen ones, holy and beloved, clothe yourselves with compassion, kindness, humility, meekness, and patience. [13]Bear with one another and, if anyone has a complaint against another, forgive each other; just as the Lord[b] has forgiven you, so you also must forgive. [14]Above all, clothe yourselves with love, which binds everything together in perfect harmony. [15]And let the peace of

---

TO ERR IS HUMAN, TO FORGIVE DIVINE.

—Alexander Pope

Christ rule in your hearts, to which indeed you were called in the one body. And be thankful. [16]Let the word of Christ[c] dwell in you richly; teach and admonish one another in all wisdom; and with gratitude in your hearts sing psalms, hymns, and spiritual songs to

---

n Gk *a circumcision made without hands*   o Gk *he*   p Other ancient authorities read *made us;* others, *made*   q Or *divested himself of*   r Other ancient authorities read *not dwelling*
s Meaning of Gk uncertain   t Gk *by the mind of his flesh*   u Or *the rudiments of the world*
v Or *are of no value, serving only to indulge the flesh*   w Other ancient authorities read *our*   x Other ancient authorities lack *on those who are disobedient* (Gk *the children of disobedience*)   y Or *living among such people*   z Or *filthy*   a Gk *its creator,* [11]*where*   b Other ancient authorities read *just as Christ*   c Other ancient authorities read *of God,* or *of the Lord*

God.*d* 17And whatever you do, in word or deed, do everything in the name of the Lord Jesus, giving thanks to God the Father through him.

Rules for Christian Households

18 Wives, be subject to your husbands, as is fitting in the Lord. 19Husbands, love your wives and never treat them harshly.

20 Children, obey your parents in everything, for this is your acceptable duty in the Lord. 21Fathers, do not provoke your children, or they may lose heart. 22Slaves, obey your earthly masters*e* in everything, not only while being watched and in order to please them, but wholeheartedly, fearing the Lord.*e* 23Whatever your task, put yourselves into it, as done for the Lord and not for your masters,*f* 24since you know that from the Lord you will receive the inheritance as your reward; you serve*g* the Lord Christ. 25For the wrongdoer will be paid back for whatever wrong has been done, and there is no partiality.

 1Masters, treat your slaves justly and fairly, for you know that you also have a Master in heaven.

Further Instructions

2 Devote yourselves to prayer, keeping alert in it with thanksgiving. 3At the

---

d Other ancient authorities read *to the Lord*   *e* In Greek the same word is used for *master* and *Lord*
f Gk *not for men*   *g* Or *you are slaves of,* or *be slaves of*

FRIDAY

TO MY DEAR AND LOVING HUSBAND
Anne Bradstreet

VERSE: Colossians 3.18   **PASSAGE:** Colossians 3.18–19

I
f ever two were one, then surely we.
If ever man were loved by wife, then thee;
If ever wife was happy in a man,
Compare with me, ye women, if you can.
I prize thy love more than whole mines of gold
Or all the riches that the East doth hold.
My love is such that rivers cannot quench,
Nor ought but love from thee, give recompense.
Thy love is such I can no way repay,
The heavens reward thee manifold, I pray.
Then while we live, in love let's so persevere
That when we live no more, we may live ever.

ADDITIONAL SCRIPTURE READING:
Genesis 2.42; Song of Solomon 1.1–3

Go to page 1411 for your next devotional reading.

1500   1700

WEEKEND

SAVED BY GRACE
Fanny Crosby

VERSE: Ephesians 2.8　　　　　**PASSAGE:** Ephesians 2.4–10

omeday the silver cord will break,
And I no more as now shall sing.
But, oh, the joy when I shall wake
Within the palace of the King!

Someday my earthly house will fall;
I cannot tell how soon 'twill be,
But this I know—my All in All
Has now a place in heav'n for me.

Someday, when fades the golden sun
Beneath the rosy-tinted west,
My blessed Lord will say, "Well done!"
And I shall enter into rest.

Someday, till then I'll watch and wait,
My lamp all trimmed and burning bright,
That when my Savior opes the gate,
My soul to him may take its flight.

And I shall see him face to face,
And tell the story—saved by grace:
And I shall see him face to face,
And tell the story—saved by grace.

ADDITIONAL SCRIPTURE READING:
John 14.23; 1 Corinthians 13.12

Go to page 1414 for your next devotional reading.

same time pray for us as well that God will open to us a door for the word, that we may declare the mystery of Christ, for which I am in prison, 4so that I may reveal it clearly, as I should.

5 Conduct yourselves wisely toward outsiders, making the most of the time.*h* 6Let your speech always be gracious, seasoned with salt, so that you may know how you ought to answer everyone.

Final Greetings and Benediction

7 Tychicus will tell you all the news about me; he is a beloved brother, a faithful minister, and a fellow servant*i* in the Lord. 8I have sent him to you for this very purpose, so that you may know how we are*j* and that he may encourage your hearts; 9he is coming with Onesimus, the faithful and beloved brother, who is one of you. They will tell you about everything here.

10 Aristarchus my fellow prisoner greets you, as does Mark the cousin of Barnabas, concerning whom you have received instructions—if he comes to you, welcome him. 11And Jesus who is called Justus greets you. These are the only ones of the circumcision among my co-workers for the kingdom of God, and they have been a comfort to me. 12Epaphras, who is one of you, a servant*i* of Christ Jesus, greets you. He is always wrestling in his prayers on your behalf, so that you may stand mature and fully assured in everything that God wills. 13For I testify for him that he has worked hard for you and for those in Laodicea and in Hierapolis. 14Luke, the beloved physician, and Demas greet you. 15Give my greetings to the brothers and sisters*k* in Laodicea, and to Nympha and the church in her house. 16And when this letter has been read among you, have it read also in the church of the Laodiceans; and see that you read also the letter from Laodicea. 17And say to Archippus, "See that you complete the task that you have received in the Lord."

18 I, Paul, write this greeting with my own hand. Remember my chains. Grace be with you.*l*

---

h Or *opportunity*   i Gk *slave*   j Other authorities read *that I may know how you are*
k Gk *brothers*   l Other ancient authorities add *Amen*

1 THESSALONIANS

 AUL FOUNDED THE CHURCH AT THESSALONICA DURING HIS SECOND MISSIONARY JOURNEY. HE WRITES THIS LETTER TO COMMEND THE BELIEVERS THERE FOR GROWING IN THE LORD AND ALSO TO CORRECT SOME MISUNDERSTANDINGS. THE SUBJECT OF CHRIST'S SECOND COMING PERMEATES THE LETTER, WITH EVERY CHAPTER REFERRING TO IT. LOOK FOR GUIDELINES ON CHRISTIAN RELATIONSHIPS AND FOR A PERSPECTIVE ON LIFE THAT IS SHAPED BY PAUL'S EMPHASIS ON ETERNITY.

Salutation

1 Paul, Silvanus, and Timothy,
To the church of the Thessalonians in God the Father and the Lord Jesus Christ:
Grace to you and peace.

The Thessalonians' Faith and Example

2 We always give thanks to God for all of you and mention you in our prayers, constantly ³remembering before our God and Father your work of faith and labor of love and steadfastness of hope in our Lord Jesus Christ. ⁴For we know, brothers and sisters*a* beloved by God, that he has chosen you, ⁵because our message of the gospel came to you not in word only, but also in power and in the Holy Spirit and with full conviction; just as you know what kind of persons we proved to be among you for your sake. ⁶And you became imitators of us and of the Lord, for in spite of persecution you received the word with joy inspired by the Holy Spirit, ⁷so that you became an example to all the believers in Macedonia and in Achaia. ⁸For the word of the Lord has sounded forth from you not only in Macedonia and Achaia, but in every place your faith in God has become known, so that we have no need to speak about it. ⁹For the people of those regions*b* report about us what kind of welcome we had among you, and how you turned to God from idols, to serve a living and true God, ¹⁰and to

a Gk brothers   *b* Gk For they

wait for his Son from heaven, whom he raised from the dead—Jesus, who rescues us from the wrath that is coming.

Paul's Ministry in Thessalonica

 2 You yourselves know, brothers and sisters,*c* that our coming to you was not in vain, 2but though we had already suffered and been shamefully mistreated at Philippi, as you know, we had courage in our God to declare to you the gospel of God in spite of great opposition. 3For our appeal does not spring from deceit or impure motives or trickery,

c Gk *brothers*

MONDAY

INTERCESSION AND HOLY FRIENDSHIP
William Law

VERSE: 1 Thessalonians 1.2   **PASSAGE:** 1 Thessalonians 1.1–3

 oly intercession . . . raised Christians to such a state of mutual love, as far exceeded all that has been praised and admired in human friendship. And when the same spirit of intercession is again in the world, when Christianity has the same power over the hearts of people that it then had, this holy friendship will be again in fashion, and Christians will be again the wonder of the world, for that exceeding love which they bear to one another.

For a frequent intercession with God, earnestly beseeching him to forgive the sins of all mankind, to bless them with his Spirit, and bring them to everlasting happiness, is the divinest exercise that the heart of man can be engaged in.

Be daily, therefore, on your knees, in a solemn deliberate performance of this devotion, praying for others in such forms, with such length, importunity, and earnestness, as you use for yourself; and you will find all little, ill-natured passions die away, your heart grow great and generous, delighting in the common happiness of others, as you used only to delight in your own.

For he that daily prays to God, that all men may be happy in heaven, takes the liveliest way to make him wish for, and delight in their happiness on earth. And it is hardly possible for you to beseech and entreat God to make any one happy in the highest enjoyments of his glory to all eternity, and yet be troubled to see him enjoy the much smaller gifts of God in his short and low state of human life.

ADDITIONAL SCRIPTURE READING:
Romans 8.26–27; Hebrews 7.24–25

Go to page 1417 for your next devotional reading.

1700   1900

4but just as we have been approved by God to be entrusted with the message of the gospel, even so we speak, not to please mortals, but to please God who tests our hearts. 5As you know and as God is our witness, we never came with words of flattery or with a pretext for greed; 6nor did we seek praise from mortals, whether from you or from others,

---

WHAT MEN CALL FAME IS, AFTER ALL, BUT A VERY WINDY THING. A MAN THINKS THAT MANY ARE PRAISING HIM, AND TALKING OF HIM ALONE, AND YET THEY SPEND BUT A VERY SMALL PART OF THE DAY THINKING OF HIM, BEING OCCUPIED WITH THINGS OF THEIR OWN.   —*Thomas More*

7though we might have made demands as apostles of Christ. But we were gentle*d* among you, like a nurse tenderly caring for her own children. 8So deeply do we care for you that we are determined to share with you not only the gospel of God but also our own selves, because you have become very dear to us.

9 You remember our labor and toil, brothers and sisters;*e* we worked night and day, so that we might not burden any of you while we proclaimed to you the gospel of God. 10You are witnesses, and God also, how pure, upright, and blameless our conduct was toward you believers. 11As you know, we dealt with each one of you like a father with his children, 12urging and encouraging you and pleading that you lead a life worthy of God, who calls you into his own kingdom and glory.

13 We also constantly give thanks to God for this, that when you received the word of God that you heard from us, you accepted it not as a human word but as what it really is, God's word, which is also at work in you believers. 14For you, brothers and sisters,*e* became imitators of the churches of God in Christ Jesus that are in Judea, for you suffered the same things from your own compatriots as they did from the Jews, 15who killed both the Lord Jesus and the prophets,*f* and drove us out; they displease God and oppose everyone 16by hindering us

from speaking to the Gentiles so that they may be saved. Thus they have constantly been filling up the measure of their sins; but God's wrath has overtaken them at last.*g*

Paul's Desire to Visit the Thessalonians Again

17 As for us, brothers and sisters,*e* when, for a short time, we were made orphans by being separated from you—in person, not in heart—we longed with great eagerness to see you face to face. 18For we wanted to come to you—certainly I, Paul, wanted to again and again—but Satan blocked our way. 19For what is our hope or joy or crown of boasting before our Lord Jesus at his coming? Is it not you? 20Yes, you are our glory and joy!

3 Therefore when we could bear it no longer, we decided to be left alone in Athens; 2and we sent Timothy, our brother and co-worker for God in proclaiming*h* the gospel of Christ, to strengthen and encourage you for the sake of your faith, 3so that no one would be shaken by these persecutions. Indeed, you yourselves know that this is what we are destined for. 4In fact, when we were with you, we told you beforehand that we were to suffer persecution; so it turned out, as you know. 5For this reason, when I could bear it no longer, I sent to find out about your faith; I was afraid that somehow the tempter had tempted you and that our labor had been in vain.

Timothy's Encouraging Report

6 But Timothy has just now come to us from you, and has brought us the good news of your faith and love. He has told us also that you always remember us kindly and long to see us—just as we long to see you. 7For this reason, brothers and sisters,*e* during all our distress and persecution we have been encouraged about you through your faith. 8For we now live, if you continue to stand firm in the Lord. 9How can we thank God enough for you in return for all the joy that we feel before our God because

---

d Other ancient authorities read *infants*   *e* Gk *brothers*   *f* Other ancient authorities read *their own prophets*   *g* Or *completely* or *forever*   *h* Gk lacks *proclaiming*

of you? 10Night and day we pray most earnestly that we may see you face to face and restore whatever is lacking in your faith.

11 Now may our God and Father himself and our Lord Jesus direct our way to you. 12And may the Lord make you increase and abound in love for one another and for all, just as we abound in love for you. 13And may he so strengthen your hearts in holiness that you may be blameless before our God and Father at the coming of our Lord Jesus with all his saints.

A Life Pleasing to God

4 Finally, brothers and sisters,*i* we ask and urge you in the Lord Jesus that, as you learned from us how you ought to live and to please God (as, in fact, you are doing), you should do so more and more. 2For you know what instructions we gave you through the Lord Jesus. 3For this is the will of God, your sanctification: that you abstain from fornication; 4that each one of you know how to control your own body*j* in holiness and honor, 5not with lustful passion, like the Gentiles who do not know God; 6that no one wrong or exploit a brother or sister*k* in this matter, because the Lord is an avenger in all these things, just as we have already told you beforehand and solemnly warned you. 7For God did not call us to impurity but in holiness. 8Therefore whoever rejects this rejects not human authority but God, who also gives his Holy Spirit to you.

IF YOU BELIEVE WHAT YOU LIKE IN THE GOSPEL, AND REJECT WHAT YOU DON'T LIKE, IT IS NOT THE GOSPEL YOU BELIEVE, BUT YOURSELF.

—*Augustine*

---

9 Now concerning love of the brothers and sisters,*i* you do not need to have anyone write to you, for you yourselves have been taught by God to love one another; 10and indeed you do love all the brothers and sisters*i* throughout Macedonia. But we urge you, beloved,*i* to do so more and more, 11to aspire to live quietly, to mind your own affairs, and to

work with your hands, as we directed you, 12so that you may behave properly toward outsiders and be dependent on no one.

The Coming of the Lord

13 But we do not want you to be uninformed, brothers and sisters,*i* about those who have died,*l* so that you may not grieve as others do who have no hope. 14For since we believe that Jesus died and rose again, even so, through Jesus, God will bring with him those who have died.*l* 15For this we declare to you by the word of the Lord, that we who are alive, who are left until the coming of the Lord, will by no means precede those who have died.*l* 16For the Lord himself, with a cry of command, with the archangel's call and with the sound of God's trumpet, will descend from heaven, and the dead in Christ will rise first. 17Then we who are alive, who are left, will be caught up in the clouds together with them to meet the Lord in the air; and so we will be with the Lord forever. 18Therefore encourage one another with these words.

5 Now concerning the times and the seasons, brothers and sisters,*i* you do not need to have anything written to you. 2For you yourselves know very well that the day of the Lord will come like a thief in the night. 3When they say, "There is peace and security," then sudden destruction will come upon them, as labor pains come upon a pregnant woman, and there will be no escape! 4But you, beloved,*i* are not in darkness, for that day to surprise you like a thief; 5for you are all children of light and children of the day; we are not of the night or of darkness. 6So then let us not fall asleep as others do, but let us keep awake and be sober; 7for those who sleep sleep at night, and those who are drunk get drunk at night. 8But since we belong to the day, let us be sober, and put on the breastplate of faith and love, and for a helmet the hope of salvation. 9For God has destined us not for wrath but for obtaining salvation through our Lord Jesus Christ, 10who died for us, so that whether we are awake or asleep we may live with him. 11Therefore encourage

---

i Gk *brothers*   *j* Or *how to take a wife for himself*   *k* Gk *brother*   *l* Gk *fallen asleep*

THE NEEDLE TOUCHED WITH THE LODESTONE
John Owen

VERSE: 1 Thessalonians 4.17   **PASSAGE:** 1 Thessalonians 4.13–18

las! we cannot here think of Christ but we are quickly ashamed of and troubled at our own thoughts: so confused are they, so unsteady, so imperfect. Commonly they issue in a groan or a sigh: "Oh when shall we come unto him? When shall we be ever with him? When shall we see him as he is?" And if at any time he begins to give more than ordinary evidences and intimations of his glory and love unto our souls, we are not able to bear them, so as to give them any abiding residence in our minds. But ordinarily this trouble and groaning is amongst our best attainments in this world, a trouble which, I pray God, I may never be delivered from until deliverance does come at once from this state of mortality. Yea, the good Lord increases this trouble more and more in all that believe.

The heart of a believer affected with the glory of Christ is like the needle touched with the lodestone. It can no longer be quiet, no longer be satisfied in a distance from him. It is put into a continual motion towards him. The motion indeed is weak and tremulous. Pantings, breathings, sighings, groanings, in prayer, in meditations, in the secret recesses of our minds, are the life of it. However, it is continually pressing towards him. But it obtains not its point, it comes not to its center and rest in this world.

But now above, all things are clear and serene, all plain and evident in our beholding the glory of Christ; we shall be ever with him, and see him as he is. This is heaven, this is blessedness, this is eternal rest . . .

But alas! here at present our minds recoil, our meditations fail, our hearts are overcome, our thoughts confused, and our eyes turn aside from the luster of this glory. But there, an immediate, constant view of it will bring in everlasting refreshment and joy unto our whole souls.

ADDITIONAL SCRIPTURE READING:
Job 19.25–27; Philippians 3.12–14

Go to page 1419 for your next devotional reading.

1500   1700

one another and build up each other, as indeed you are doing.

IT IS STILL ONE OF THE TRAGEDIES OF HUMAN HISTORY THAT THE "CHILDREN OF DARKNESS" ARE FREQUENTLY MORE DETERMINED AND ZEALOUS THAN THE "CHILDREN OF LIGHT."

—*Martin Luther King, Jr.*

Final Exhortations, Greetings, and Benediction

12 But we appeal to you, brothers and sisters,[m] to respect those who labor among you, and have charge of you in the Lord and admonish you; 13esteem them very highly in love because of their work. Be at peace among yourselves. 14And we urge you, beloved,[m] to admonish the idlers, encourage the fainthearted, help the weak, be patient with all of them. 15See that none of you repays evil for evil, but always seek to do good to one another and to all. 16Rejoice always, 17pray without ceasing, 18give thanks in all circumstances; for this is the will of God in Christ Jesus for you. 19Do not quench the Spirit. 20Do not despise the words of prophets,[n] 21but test everything; hold fast to what is good; 22abstain from every form of evil.

23 May the God of peace himself sanctify you entirely; and may your spirit and soul and body be kept sound[o] and blameless at the coming of our Lord Jesus Christ. 24The one who calls you is faithful, and he will do this.

25 Beloved,[p] pray for us.

26 Greet all the brothers and sisters[m] with a holy kiss. 27I solemnly command you by the Lord that this letter be read to all of them.[q]

28 The grace of our Lord Jesus Christ be with you.[r]

---

m Gk *brothers*   n Gk *despise prophecies*   o Or *complete*   p Gk *Brothers*   q Gk *to all the brothers*   r Other ancient authorities add *Amen*

CHRIST IS OUR SANCTIFICATION
George Whitefield

VERSE: 1 Thessalonians 5.23   **PASSAGE:** 1 Thessalonians 5.23–24

y sanctification I mean a total renovation of the whole man: by the righteousness of Christ, believers come legally, by sanctification they are made spiritually, alive; by the one they are entitled to, by the other they are made meet for, glory. They are sanctified, therefore, throughout, in spirit, soul, and body.

Their understandings, which were dark before, now become light in the Lord; and their wills, before contrary to, now become one with the will of God; their affections are now set on things above; their memory is now filled with divine things; their natural consciences are now enlightened; their members, which were before instruments of uncleanness, and of iniquity into iniquity, are now new creatures; "old things are passed away; all things are become new" (2 Corinthians 5.17, KJV) in their hearts: sin has now no longer dominion over them; they are freed from the power, though not the indwelling and being, of it; they are holy both in heart and life, in all manner of conversation; they are made partakers of a divine nature, and from Jesus Christ, they receive grace; and every grace that is in Christ, is copied and transcribed into their souls; they are transformed into his likeness; he is formed within them; they dwell in him, and he in them; they are led by the Spirit, and bring forth the fruits thereof; they know that Christ is their Emmanuel, God with and in them; they are living temples of the Holy Ghost. And therefore, being a holy habitation unto the Lord, the whole Trinity dwells and walks in them; even here, they sit together with Christ in heavenly places, and are vitally united to him, their head, by a living faith; their Redeemer, their Maker, is their husband; they are flesh of his flesh, bone of his bone; they talk, they walk with him, as a man talketh and walketh with his friend; in short, they are one with Christ, even as Jesus Christ and the Father are one.

ADDITIONAL SCRIPTURE READING:
1 Corinthians 6.11; 1 Thessalonians 5.23

Go to page 1421 for your next devotional reading.

1700   1900

2 THESSALONIANS

PAUL WRITES THIS SECOND LETTER TO THOSE BELIEVERS AT THESSALONICA WHO NEED CLARIFICATION ON THE ADVICE GIVEN IN HIS FIRST LETTER. SOME PEOPLE MISUNDERSTOOD PAUL AND WERE SO SURE JESUS WAS COMING SOON THAT THEY STOPPED WORKING. WHILE ASSURING THE THESSALONIANS THAT JESUS IS IN FACT COMING AGAIN, PAUL URGES HIS READERS TO TAKE RESPONSIBILITY FOR WHAT THEY NEED TO DO TODAY.

Salutation

1 Paul, Silvanus, and Timothy,
To the church of the Thessalonians in God our Father and the Lord Jesus Christ:
2 Grace to you and peace from God our*a* Father and the Lord Jesus Christ.

Thanksgiving

3 We must always give thanks to God for you, brothers and sisters,*b* as is right, because your faith is growing abundantly, and the love of everyone of you for one another is increasing. 4Therefore we ourselves boast of you among the churches of God for your steadfastness and faith during all your persecutions and the afflictions that you are enduring.

The Judgment at Christ's Coming

5 This is evidence of the righteous judgment of God, and is intended to make you worthy of the kingdom of God, for which you are also suffering. 6For it is indeed just of God to repay with affliction those who afflict you, 7and to give relief to the afflicted as well as to us, when the Lord Jesus is revealed from heaven with his mighty angels 8in flaming fire, inflicting vengeance on those who do not know God and on those who do not obey the gospel of our Lord Jesus. 9These will suffer the punishment of eternal destruction, separated from the presence of the Lord and from the glory of his might, 10when he comes to be glorified by his saints and to be marveled at

---

a Other ancient authorities read *the*　*b* Gk *brothers*

on that day among all who have believed, because our testimony to you was believed. 11To this end we always pray for you, asking that our God will make you worthy of his call and will fulfill by his power every good resolve and work of faith, 12so that the name of our Lord Jesus may be glorified in you, and you in him, according to the grace of our God and the Lord Jesus Christ.

The Man of Lawlessness

 As to the coming of our Lord Jesus Christ and our being gathered together to him, we beg you, brothers and sisters,c 2not to be quickly shaken in mind or alarmed, either by spirit or by word or by letter, as though from us, to the effect that the day of the Lord is already here. 3Let no one deceive you in any way; for that day will not come unless the rebellion comes first and the lawless oned is revealed, the one destined for destruction.e 4He opposes and exalts himself above every so-called god or object of worship, so that he takes his seat in the temple of God, declaring himself to be God. 5Do you not remember that I told you these things when I was still with you? 6And you know

c Gk brothers   d Gk the man of lawlessness; other ancient authorities read the man of sin
e Gk the son of destruction

THURSDAY

WHAT IS THE TRUE CHURCH?
A. W. Tozer

VERSE: 2 Thessalonians 1.4   PASSAGE: 2 Thessalonians 1.1–12

he true church is . . . composed of regenerated persons who differ from other human beings in that they have a superior kind of life imparted to them at the time of their inward renewal . . .

They have espoused the cause of a rejected and crucified man who claimed to be God and who has pledged his sacred honor that he will prepare a place for them in his Father's house and return again to conduct them there with rejoicing.

In the meantime they carry his cross, suffer whatever indignities men may heap upon them for his sake, act as his ambassadors and do good to all men in his name.

They steadfastly believe that they will share his triumph, and for this reason they are perfectly willing to share his rejection by a society that does not understand them.

And they have no hard feelings—only charity and compassion and a strong desire that all men may come to repentance and be reconciled to God.

ADDITIONAL SCRIPTURE READING:
James 5.10–11; 1 Peter 2.9–12; 4.12–19

Go to page 1423 for your next devotional reading.

1900   Present

what is now restraining him, so that he may be revealed when his time comes. 7For the mystery of lawlessness is already at work, but only until the one who now restrains it is removed. 8And then the lawless one will be revealed, whom the Lord Jesus*f* will destroy*g* with the breath of his mouth, annihilating him by the manifestation of his coming. 9The coming of the lawless one is apparent in the working of Satan, who uses all power, signs, lying wonders, 10and every kind of wicked deception for those who are perishing, because they refused to love the truth and so be saved. 11For this reason God sends them a powerful delusion, leading them to believe what is false, 12so that all who have not believed the truth but took pleasure in unrighteousness will be condemned.

Chosen for Salvation

13 But we must always give thanks to God for you, brothers and sisters*h* beloved by the Lord, because God chose you as the first fruits*i* for salvation through sanctification by the Spirit and through belief in the truth. 14For this purpose he called you through our proclamation of the good news,*j* so that you may obtain the glory of our Lord Jesus Christ. 15So then, brothers and sisters,*h* stand firm and hold fast to the traditions that you were taught by us, either by word of mouth or by our letter.

IF A MAN CANNOT BE A CHRISTIAN IN THE PLACE
WHERE HE IS, HE CANNOT BE A CHRISTIAN ANY-
WHERE.   —*Henry Ward Beecher*

---

16 Now may our Lord Jesus Christ himself and God our Father, who loved us and through grace gave us eternal comfort and good hope, 17comfort your hearts and strengthen them in every good work and word.

Request for Prayer

3 Finally, brothers and sisters,*h* pray for us, so that the word of the Lord may spread rapidly and be glo-

rified everywhere, just as it is among you, 2and that we may be rescued from wicked and evil people; for not all have faith. 3But the Lord is faithful; he will strengthen you and guard you from the evil one.*k* 4And we have confidence in the Lord concerning you, that you are doing and will go on doing the things that we command. 5May the Lord direct your hearts to the love of God and to the steadfastness of Christ.

Warning against Idleness

6 Now we command you, beloved,*h* in the name of our Lord Jesus Christ, to keep away from believers who are*l* living in idleness and not according to the tradition that they*m* received from us. 7For you yourselves know how you ought to imitate us; we were not idle when we were with you, 8and we did not eat anyone's bread without paying for it; but with toil and labor we worked night and day, so that we might not burden any of you. 9This was not because we do not have that right, but in order to give you an example to imitate. 10For even when we were with you, we gave you this command: Anyone unwilling to work should not eat. 11For we hear that some of you are living in idleness, mere busybodies, not doing any work. 12Now such persons we command and exhort in the Lord Jesus Christ to do their work quietly and to earn their own living. 13Brothers and sisters,*n* do not be weary in doing what is right.

14 Take note of those who do not obey what we say in this letter; have nothing to do with them, so that they may be ashamed. 15Do not regard them as enemies, but warn them as believers.*o*

Final Greetings and Benediction

16 Now may the Lord of peace himself give you peace at all times in all ways. The Lord be with all of you.

17 I, Paul, write this greeting with my own hand. This is the mark in every letter of mine; it is the way I write. 18The grace of our Lord Jesus Christ be with all of you.*p*

---

f Other ancient authorities lack *Jesus*   g Other ancient authorities read *consume*   h Gk *brothers*
i Other ancient authorities read *from the beginning*   j Or *through our gospel*   k Or *from evil*
l Gk *from every brother who is*   m Other ancient authorities read *you*   n Gk *Brothers*
o Gk *a brother*   p Other ancient authorities add *Amen*

CHRIST OUR HOPE
Dietrich Bonhoeffer

VERSE: 2 Thessalonians 2.16   **PASSAGE:** 2 Thessalonians 2.16–17

ear Eberhard,
I like to write to you as often as I can now, because I think you're always glad to hear from me. There's nothing special to report about myself nor about the family, as far as I know . . . I expect that Aunt Elisabeth will soon be visiting my parents.

During the last few nights it's been our turn again round here. When the bombs come shrieking down, I always think how trivial it all is compared with what you're going through over there. It often makes me downright angry to see how some people behave in such situations, and how little they think of what is happening to other people. The danger here never lasts more than a few minutes. I wonder how things are with Jochen Kanitz now? He was on the central front.

I've now finished *Memoirs from the House of Dead*. It contains a great deal that is wise and good. I'm still thinking about the assertion, which in his case is certainly not a mere conventional dictum, that a man cannot live without hope, and that men who have really lost all hope often become wild and wicked. It may be an open question whether in this case hope is an illusion. The importance of illusion to one's life should certainly not be underestimated; but for a Christian there must be hope based on a firm foundation. And even if illusion has so much power in people's lives that it can keep life moving, how great a power there is in a hope that is based on certainty, and how invincible a life with such a hope is. "Christ our hope"— this Pauline formula is the strength of our lives.

They've just come to take me off to my exercise, but I will just finish this letter, to make sure that it goes today. I think of you every day with true gratitude. God bless you and Renate and your boy and all of us.

Your Dietrich

ADDITIONAL SCRIPTURE READING:
Psalm 42; 2 Corinthians 10.3–4

Go to page 1425 for your next devotional reading.

1900   Present

1 TIMOTHY

PAUL WROTE TO TIMOTHY WITH AF-
FIRMATION AND ADVICE ON HOW
TO LEAD THE CHURCH AT EPHE-
SUS. HERE YOU WILL FIND GUIDELINES FOR
RUNNING A CHURCH, PRACTICAL HELP FOR
BELIEVERS IN THEIR RELATIONSHIPS WITH
OTHERS AND ADVICE ON DEALING WITH
FALSE TEACHERS. LOOK FOR THE UNDERLY-
ING PRINCIPLES THAT YOU CAN APPLY IN
YOUR EVERYDAY LIFE AS YOU SEEK TO BE
TRUE TO THE FAITH.

Salutation

1 Paul, an apostle of Christ Jesus by the command of God our Savior and of Christ Jesus our hope,

2 To Timothy, my loyal child in the faith:

Grace, mercy, and peace from God the Father and Christ Jesus our Lord.

Warning against False Teachers

3 I urge you, as I did when I was on my way to Macedonia, to remain in Ephesus so that you may instruct certain people not to teach any different doctrine, 4and not to occupy themselves with myths and endless genealogies that promote speculations rather than the divine training*a* that is known by faith.

5But the aim of such instruction is love that comes from a pure heart, a good conscience, and sincere faith. 6Some people have deviated from these and turned to meaningless talk, 7desiring to be teachers of the law, without understanding either what they are saying or the things about which they make assertions.

8 Now we know that the law is good, if one uses it legitimately. 9This means understanding that the law is laid down not for the innocent but for the lawless and disobedient, for the godless and sinful, for the unholy and profane, for those who kill their father or mother, for murderers, 10fornicators, sodomites, slave traders, liars, perjurers, and whatever else is contrary to the sound teaching 11that

a Or plan

WEEKEND

TO HEAVEN
Ben Jonson

VERSE: Philippians 1.23   **PASSAGE:** Philippians 1.20–26

ood and great God, can I not think of thee
    But it must, straight, my melancholy be?
Is it interpreted in my disease
    That, laden with my sins, I seek for ease?
O be thou witness, that the reins dost know
    And hearts of all, if I be sad for show,
And judge me after, if I dare pretend
    To aught but grace, or aim at other end.
As thou art all, so be thou all to me,
    First, midst, and last, converted, one and three;
My faith, my hope, my love; and in this state
    My judge, my witness, and my advocate.
Where have I been this while exil'd from thee,
    And whither rap'd, now thou but stoop'st to
      me?
Dwell, dwell here still, O being everywhere,
    How can I doubt to find thee ever, here?
I know my state, both full of shame and scorn
    Conceiv'd in sin, and unto labor born,
Standing with fear, and must with horror fall,
    And destin'd unto judgment, after all.
I feel my griefs too, and there scarce is ground
    Upon my flesh t'inflict another wound.
Yet dare I not complain, or wish for death
    With holy Paul, lest it be thought the breath
Of discontent; or that these prayers be
    For weariness of life, not love of thee.

ADDITIONAL SCRIPTURE READING:
Matthew 11.28; Galatians 6.9

Go to page 1427 for your next devotional reading.

1500   1700

conforms to the glorious gospel of the blessed God, which he entrusted to me.

Gratitude for Mercy

12 I am grateful to Christ Jesus our Lord, who has strengthened me, because he judged me faithful and appointed me to his service, 13even though I was formerly a blasphemer, a persecutor, and a man of violence. But I received mercy because I had acted ignorantly in unbelief, 14and the grace of our Lord overflowed for me with the faith and love that are in Christ Jesus. 15The saying is sure and worthy of full acceptance, that Christ Jesus came into the world to save sinners—of whom I am the foremost. 16But for that very reason I received mercy, so that in me, as the foremost, Jesus Christ might display the utmost patience, making me an example to those who would come to believe in him for eternal life. 17To the King of the ages, immortal, invisible, the only God, be honor and glory forever and ever.b Amen.

18 I am giving you these instructions, Timothy, my child, in accordance with the prophecies made earlier about you, so that by following them you may fight the good fight, 19having faith and a good conscience. By rejecting conscience, certain persons have suffered shipwreck in the faith; 20among them are Hymenaeus and Alexander, whom I have turned over to Satan, so that they may learn not to blaspheme.

Instructions concerning Prayer

2 First of all, then, I urge that supplications, prayers, intercessions, and thanksgivings be made for everyone, 2for kings and all who are in high positions, so that we may lead a quiet and peaceable life in all godliness and dignity. 3This is right and is acceptable in the sight of God our Savior, 4who desires everyone to be saved and to come to the knowledge of the truth. 5For

there is one God;
    there is also one mediator
        between God and
        humankind,

Christ Jesus, himself human,
6   who gave himself a ransom for all
—this was attested at the right time. 7For this I was appointed a herald and an apostle (I am telling the truth,c I am not lying), a teacher of the Gentiles in faith and truth.

8 I desire, then, that in every place the men should pray, lifting up holy hands without anger or argument; 9also

---

TO LIFT UP THE HANDS IN PRAYER GIVES GOD GLORY, BUT A MAN WITH A DUNGFORK IN HIS HAND, A WOMAN WITH A SLOP PAIL, GIVES HIM GLORY TOO. HE IS SO GREAT THAT ALL THINGS GIVE HIM GLORY IF YOU MEAN THEY SHOULD.

        —Gerard Manley Hopkins

---

that the women should dress themselves modestly and decently in suitable clothing, not with their hair braided, or with gold, pearls, or expensive clothes, 10but with good works, as is proper for women who profess reverence for God. 11Let a womand learn in silence with full submission. 12I permit no womand to teach or to have authority over a man;e she is to keep silent. 13For Adam was formed first, then Eve; 14and Adam was not deceived, but the woman was deceived and became a transgressor. 15Yet she will be saved through childbearing, provided they continue in faith and love and holiness, with modesty.

Qualifications of Bishops

3 The saying is sure:f whoever aspires to the office of bishopg desires a noble task. 2Now a bishoph must be above reproach, married only once,i temperate, sensible, respectable, hospitable, an apt teacher, 3not a drunkard, not violent but gentle, not quarrelsome, and not a lover of money. 4He must manage his own household well, keeping his

---

IF I TAKE CARE OF MY CHARACTER, MY REPUTATION WILL TAKE CARE OF ITSELF.

        —Dwight L. Moody

---

b Gk *to the ages of the ages*   *c* Other ancient authorities add *in Christ*   *d* Or *wife*   *e* Or *her husband*   *f* Some interpreters place these words at the end of the previous paragraph. Other ancient authorities read *The saying is commonly accepted*   *g* Or *overseer*   *h* Or *an overseer*   *i* Gk *the husband of one wife*

children submissive and respectful in every way— [5]for if someone does not know how to manage his own household, how can he take care of God's church? [6]He must not be a recent convert, or he may be puffed up with conceit and fall into the condemnation of the devil. [7]Moreover, he must be well thought of by

---

MONDAY

THE MAN-GOD
Anselm of Canterbury

VERSE: 1 Timothy 2.5   **PASSAGE:** 1 Timothy 2.5–6

e must inquire now, how there can be a God-man. For divine nature and human nature cannot be changed into each other, so that the divine nature would become human or the human divine. Neither can they be so mingled that the two would constitute some third sort of nature which is neither entirely divine nor entirely human. In brief, if it were possible that one were changed into the other, it would be only God and not man, or only man and not God . . . The man-God we are looking for cannot arise out of divine and human nature either by change of one into the other, or by a corruptive mingling of both into a third, because these things are impossible; or if they are possible, they are totally unable to explain our problem.

Now, if we say these two complete natures are joined in some way or other, yet in such a way that the human nature is one being and the divine nature is another, and it is not the same person who is both God and man, it is impossible for the two natures to accomplish what must be accomplished. God, surely, will not accomplish it because it is not his obligation; and man will not accomplish it because he has not the ability. In order that a God-man accomplish it, therefore, it is necessary that one and the same person be perfect God and perfect man to make this satisfaction. For no one can make the satisfaction unless he is truly God, and no one has the obligation unless he is truly man. While therefore, it is necessary to find a God-man, with the integrity of both natures preserved, it is no less necessary that these two complete natures be united in one person—just as the body and rational soul are united in one man—because otherwise it is impossible for the same person to be perfect God and perfect man.

ADDITIONAL SCRIPTURE READING:
John 1.1; Hebrews 4.15

Go to page 1433 for your next devotional reading.

500   1500

outsiders, so that he may not fall into disgrace and the snare of the devil.

Qualifications of Deacons

8 Deacons likewise must be serious, not double-tongued, not indulging in much wine, not greedy for money; 9they must hold fast to the mystery of the faith with a clear conscience. 10And let them first be tested; then, if they prove themselves blameless, let them serve as deacons. 11Women*j* likewise must be serious, not slanderers, but temperate, faithful in all things. 12Let deacons be married only once,*k* and let them manage their children and their households well; 13for those who serve well as deacons gain a good standing for themselves and great boldness in the faith that is in Christ Jesus.

The Mystery of Our Religion

14 I hope to come to you soon, but I am writing these instructions to you so that, 15if I am delayed, you may know how one ought to behave in the household of God, which is the church of the living God, the pillar and bulwark of the truth. 16Without any doubt, the mystery of our religion is great:

He*l* was revealed in flesh,
vindicated*m* in spirit,*n*
seen by angels,
proclaimed among Gentiles,
believed in throughout the world,
taken up in glory.

False Asceticism

4 Now the Spirit expressly says that in later*o* times some will renounce the faith by paying attention to deceitful spirits and teachings of demons, 2through the hypocrisy of liars whose consciences are seared with a hot iron. 3They forbid marriage and demand abstinence from foods, which God created to be received with thanksgiving by those who believe and know the truth. 4For everything created by God is good, and nothing is to be rejected, provided it is received with thanksgiving; 5for it is sanctified by God's word and by prayer.

A Good Minister of Jesus Christ

6 If you put these instructions before the brothers and sisters,*p* you will be a good servant*q* of Christ Jesus, nourished on the words of the faith and of the sound teaching that you have followed. 7Have nothing to do with profane myths and old wives' tales. Train yourself in godliness, 8for, while physical training is of some value, godliness is valuable in every way, holding promise for both the present life and the life to come. 9The saying is sure and worthy of full acceptance. 10For to this end we toil and struggle,*r* because we have our hope set on the living God, who is the Savior of all people, especially of those who believe.

11 These are the things you must insist on and teach. 12Let no one despise your youth, but set the believers an example in speech and conduct, in love, in faith, in purity. 13Until I arrive, give attention to the public reading of scripture,*s* to exhorting, to teaching. 14Do not neglect the gift that is in you, which was given to you through prophecy with the laying on of hands by the council of elders.*t* 15Put these things into practice, devote yourself to them, so that all may see your progress. 16Pay close attention to yourself and to your teaching; continue in these things, for in doing this you will save both yourself and your hearers.

Duties toward Believers

5 Do not speak harshly to an older man,*u* but speak to him as to a father, to younger men as brothers, 2to older women as mothers, to younger women as sisters—with absolute purity.

3 Honor widows who are really widows. 4If a widow has children or grandchildren, they should first learn their religious duty to their own family and make some repayment to their parents; for this is pleasing in God's sight. 5The real widow, left alone, has set her hope on God and continues in supplications and prayers night and day; 6but the widow*v* who lives for pleasure is dead even while she lives. 7Give these com-

mands as well, so that they may be above reproach. 8And whoever does not provide for relatives, and especially for family members, has denied the faith and is worse than an unbeliever.

9 Let a widow be put on the list if she is not less than sixty years old and has been married only once;*w* 10she must be well attested for her good works, as one who has brought up children, shown hospitality, washed the saints' feet, helped the afflicted, and devoted herself to doing good in every way. 11But refuse to put younger widows on the list; for when their sensual desires alienate them from Christ, they want to marry, 12and so they incur condemnation for having violated their first pledge. 13Besides that, they learn to be idle, gadding about from house to house; and they are not merely idle, but also gossips and busybodies, saying what they should not

---

---

say. 14So I would have younger widows marry, bear children, and manage their households, so as to give the adversary no occasion to revile us. 15For some have already turned away to follow Satan. 16If any believing woman*x* has relatives who are really widows, let her assist them; let the church not be burdened, so that it can assist those who are real widows.

17 Let the elders who rule well be considered worthy of double honor,*y* especially those who labor in preaching and teaching; 18for the scripture says, "You shall not muzzle an ox while it is treading out the grain," and, "The laborer deserves to be paid." 19Never accept any accusation against an elder except on the evidence of two or three witnesses. 20As for those who persist in sin, rebuke them in the presence of all, so that the rest also may stand in fear. 21In the presence of God and of Christ Jesus and of the elect angels, I warn you to

keep these instructions without prejudice, doing nothing on the basis of partiality. 22Do not ordain*z* anyone hastily, and do not participate in the sins of others; keep yourself pure.

23 No longer drink only water, but take a little wine for the sake of your stomach and your frequent ailments.

24 The sins of some people are conspicuous and precede them to judgment, while the sins of others follow them there. 25So also good works are conspicuous; and even when they are not, they cannot remain hidden.

6 Let all who are under the yoke of slavery regard their masters as worthy of all honor, so that the name of God and the teaching may not be blasphemed. 2Those who have believing masters must not be disrespectful to them on the ground that they are members of the church;*a* rather they must serve them all the more, since those who benefit by their service are believers and beloved.*b*

False Teaching and True Riches

Teach and urge these duties. 3Whoever teaches otherwise and does not agree with the sound words of our Lord Jesus Christ and the teaching that is in accordance with godliness, 4is conceited, understanding nothing, and has a morbid craving for controversy and for disputes about words. From these come envy, dissension, slander, base suspicions, 5and wrangling among those who are depraved in mind and bereft of the truth, imagining that godliness is a means of gain.*c* 6Of course, there is great gain in godliness combined with contentment; 7for we brought nothing into the world, so that*d* we can take nothing out of it; 8but if we have food and clothing, we will be content with these. 9But those who want to be rich fall into temptation and are trapped by many senseless and harmful desires that plunge people into ruin and destruction. 10For the love of money is a root of all kinds of evil, and in their eagerness to be rich some have

---

w Gk *the wife of one husband*   x Other ancient authorities read *believing man or woman*; others, *believing man*   y Or *compensation*   z Gk *Do not lay hands on*   a Gk *are brothers*   b Or *since they are believers and beloved, who devote themselves to good deeds*   c Other ancient authorities add *Withdraw yourself from such people*   d Other ancient authorities read *world—it is certain that*

wandered away from the faith and pierced themselves with many pains.

The Good Fight of Faith

11 But as for you, man of God, shun all this; pursue righteousness, godliness, faith, love, endurance, gentleness. 12Fight the good fight of the faith; take hold of the eternal life, to which you were called and for which you made*e* the good confession in the presence of many witnesses. 13In the presence of God, who gives life to all things, and of Christ Jesus, who in his testimony before Pontius Pilate made the good confession, I charge you 14to keep the commandment without spot or blame until the manifestation of our Lord Jesus Christ, 15which he will bring about at the right time—he who is the blessed and only Sovereign, the King of kings and Lord of lords. 16It is he alone who has immortality and dwells in unapproachable light, whom no one has ever

seen or can see; to him be honor and eternal dominion. Amen.

17 As for those who in the present age are rich, command them not to be haughty, or to set their hopes on the uncertainty of riches, but rather on God who richly provides us with everything for our enjoyment. 18They are to do good, to be rich in good works, generous, and ready to share, 19thus storing up for themselves the treasure of a good foundation for the future, so that they may take hold of the life that really is life.

Personal Instructions and Benediction

20 Timothy, guard what has been entrusted to you. Avoid the profane chatter and contradictions of what is falsely called knowledge; 21by professing it some have missed the mark as regards the faith.

Grace be with you.*f*

---

e Gk *confessed*   *f* The Greek word for *you* here is plural; in other ancient authorities it is singular. Other ancient authorities add *Amen*

2 TIMOTHY

AUL'S SECOND LETTER TO TIMOTHY, WRITTEN SHORTLY BEFORE PAUL'S DEATH, REPRESENTS THE ADVICE OF SOMEONE WHO KNOWS HE'S AT THE END OF HIS LIFE. LANGUISHING IN A COLD DUNGEON, CHAINED LIKE A COMMON CRIMINAL, PAUL KNOWS THAT HIS WORK IS DONE. HE CHALLENGES TIMOTHY TO A MORE EFFECTIVE MINISTRY AND ENCOURAGES HIM TO PERSEVERE IN HIS WALK WITH GOD. ASK GOD TO GIVE YOU DAILY STRENGTH TO KEEP WALKING WITH HIM, SECURE IN THE HOPE THAT IS YOURS IN CHRIST.

Salutation

1 Paul, an apostle of Christ Jesus by the will of God, for the sake of the promise of life that is in Christ Jesus,

2 To Timothy, my beloved child:

Grace, mercy, and peace from God the Father and Christ Jesus our Lord.

Thanksgiving and Encouragement

3 I am grateful to God—whom I worship with a clear conscience, as my ancestors did—when I remember you constantly in my prayers night and day. 4Recalling your tears, I long to see you so that I may be filled with joy. 5I am reminded of your sincere faith, a faith that lived first in your grandmother Lois and your mother Eunice and now, I am sure, lives in you. 6For this reason I remind you to rekindle the gift of God that is within you through the laying on of my hands; 7for God did not give us a spirit of cowardice, but rather a spirit of power and of love and of self-discipline.

8 Do not be ashamed, then, of the testimony about our Lord or of me his prisoner, but join with me in suffering for the gospel, relying on the power of God, 9who saved us and called us with a holy calling, not according to our works but according to his own purpose and grace. This grace was given to us in Christ Jesus before the ages began, 10but it has now been revealed through the appearing of our Savior Christ Jesus, who abolished death and brought life and immortality to light through the gospel. 11For this gospel I was appointed a herald

and an apostle and a teacher,*a* 12and for this reason I suffer as I do. But I am not ashamed, for I know the one in whom I have put my trust, and I am sure that he is able to guard until that day what I have entrusted to him.*b* 13Hold to the standard of sound teaching that you have heard from me, in the faith and love that are in Christ Jesus. 14Guard the good treasure entrusted to you, with the help of the Holy Spirit living in us.

15 You are aware that all who are in Asia have turned away from me, including Phygelus and Hermogenes. 16May the Lord grant mercy to the household of Onesiphorus, because he often refreshed me and was not ashamed of my chain; 17when he arrived in Rome, he eagerly*c* searched for me and found me 18—may the Lord grant that he will find mercy from the Lord on that day! And you know very well how much service he rendered in Ephesus.

A Good Soldier of Christ Jesus

2 You then, my child, be strong in the grace that is in Christ Jesus; 2and what you have heard from me through many witnesses entrust to faithful people who will be able to teach others as well. 3Share in suffering like a good soldier of Christ Jesus. 4No one serving in the army gets entangled in everyday affairs; the soldier's aim is to please the enlisting officer. 5And in the case of an athlete, no one is crowned without competing according to the rules. 6It is the farmer who does the work who ought to have the first share of the crops. 7Think over what I say, for the Lord will give you understanding in all things.

8 Remember Jesus Christ, raised from the dead, a descendant of David— that is my gospel, 9for which I suffer hardship, even to the point of being chained like a criminal. But the word of God is not chained. 10Therefore I endure everything for the sake of the elect, so that they may also obtain the salvation that is in Christ Jesus, with eternal glory. 11The saying is sure:

If we have died with him, we will
  also live with him;

12   if we endure, we will also reign
         with him;
      if we deny him, he will also deny us;
13   if we are faithless, he remains
         faithful—
      for he cannot deny himself.

A Worker Approved by God

14 Remind them of this, and warn them before God*d* that they are to avoid wrangling over words, which does no good but only ruins those who are listening. 15Do your best to present yourself to God as one approved by him, a worker who has no need to be ashamed, rightly explaining the word of truth. 16Avoid profane chatter, for it will lead people into more and more impiety,

---

IT IS OUR BEST WORK THAT GOD WANTS, NOT THE DREGS OF OUR EXHAUSTION. I THINK HE MUST PREFER QUALITY TO QUANTITY.

—*George MacDonald*

17and their talk will spread like gangrene. Among them are Hymenaeus and Philetus, 18who have swerved from the truth by claiming that the resurrection has already taken place. They are upsetting the faith of some. 19But God's firm foundation stands, bearing this inscription: "The Lord knows those who are his," and, "Let everyone who calls on the name of the Lord turn away from wickedness."

20 In a large house there are utensils not only of gold and silver but also of wood and clay, some for special use, some for ordinary. 21All who cleanse themselves of the things I have mentioned*e* will become special utensils, dedicated and useful to the owner of the house, ready for every good work. 22Shun youthful passions and pursue righteousness, faith, love, and peace, along with those who call on the Lord from a pure heart. 23Have nothing to do with stupid and senseless controversies; you know that they breed quarrels. 24And the Lord's servant*f* must not be quarrelsome but kindly to everyone, an apt teacher, patient, 25correcting opponents with

---

a Other ancient authorities add *of the Gentiles*   *b* Or *what has been entrusted to me*   *c* Or *promptly*   *d* Other ancient authorities read *the Lord*   *e* Gk *of these things*   *f* Gk *slave*

AS I READ, I SAW IT ALL!

James Hudson Taylor

VERSE: 2 Timothy 2.13 **PASSAGE:** 2 Timothy 2.11–13

 ctober 17th, 1869: . . . My mind has been greatly exercised for six or eight months past, feeling the need personally, and for our mission, of more holiness, life, power in our souls. But personal need stood first and was the greatest. I felt the ingratitude, the danger, the sin of not living nearer to God. I prayed, agonized, fasted, strove, made resolutions, read the Word more diligently, sought more time for retirement and meditation—but all was without effect. Every day, almost every hour, the consciousness of sin oppressed me. I knew that if I could only abide in Christ all would be well, but I *could not* . . . Each day brought its register of sin and failure, of lack of power. To will was indeed present with me, but how to perform I found not.

Then came the question, "Is there *no* rescue? Must it be thus to the end—constant conflict and, instead of victory, too often defeat?" How, too, could I preach with sincerity that to those who receive Jesus, "to them gave he power to become the sons of God" (*i.e.,* God-like) (John 1.12, KJV) when it was not so in my own experience? . . .

When my agony of soul was at its height, a sentence in a letter from dear McCarthy was used to remove the scales from my eyes, and the Spirit of God revealed the truth of *our oneness* with *Jesus* as I had never known it before. McCarthy, who had been much exercised by the same sense of failure, but saw the light before I did, wrote (I quote from memory):

> But how to get faith strengthened? Not by striving after faith, but by resting on the Faithful One.

As I read I saw it all! "If we believe not, *yet* he abideth" (2 Timothy 2.13, KJV). I looked to Jesus and saw (and when I saw, oh, how the joy flowed!) that he had said, "*I* will never leave *you*" (Hebrews 13.5). "Ah, *there* is rest!" I thought. "I have striven in vain to rest in him. I'll strive no more. For has *he* not promised to abide with me—never to leave me, never to fail me?" And, dearie, *he never will!*

ADDITIONAL SCRIPTURE READING:
Isaiah 40.29–31; Ephesians 6.10–11

Go to page 1435 for your next devotional reading.

1700   1900

gentleness. God may perhaps grant that they will repent and come to know the truth, 26and that they may escape from the snare of the devil, having been held captive by him to do his will.g

Godlessness in the Last Days

3 You must understand this, that in the last days distressing times will come. 2For people will be lovers of themselves, lovers of money, boasters, arrogant, abusive, disobedient to their parents, ungrateful, unholy, 3inhuman, implacable, slanderers, profligates, brutes, haters of good, 4treacherous, reckless, swollen with conceit, lovers of pleasure rather than lovers of God, 5holding to the outward form of godliness but denying its power. Avoid them! 6For among them are those who make their way into households and captivate silly women, overwhelmed by their sins and swayed by all kinds of desires, 7who are always being instructed and can never arrive at a knowledge of the truth. 8As Jannes and Jambres opposed Moses, so these people, of corrupt mind and counterfeit faith, also oppose the truth. 9But they will not make much progress, because, as in the case of those two men,h their folly will become plain to everyone.

Paul's Charge to Timothy

10 Now you have observed my teaching, my conduct, my aim in life, my faith, my patience, my love, my steadfastness, 11my persecutions, and my suffering the things that happened to me in Antioch, Iconium, and Lystra. What persecutions I endured! Yet the Lord rescued me from all of them. 12Indeed, all who want to live a godly life in Christ Jesus will be persecuted. 13But wicked people and impostors will go from bad to worse, deceiving others and being deceived. 14But as for you, continue in what you have learned and firmly believed, knowing from whom you learned it, 15and how from childhood you have known the sacred writings that are able to instruct you for salvation through faith in Christ Jesus. 16All scripture is inspired by God and isi use-

ful for teaching, for reproof, for correction, and for training in righteousness, 17so that everyone who belongs to God may be proficient, equipped for every good work.

4 In the presence of God and of Christ Jesus, who is to judge the living and the dead, and in view of his appearing and his kingdom, I solemnly urge you: 2proclaim the message; be persistent whether the time is favorable or unfavorable; convince, rebuke, and encourage, with the utmost patience in teaching. 3For the time is coming when people will not put up with sound doctrine, but having itching ears, they will accumulate for themselves teachers to suit their own desires, 4and will turn away from listening to the truth and wander away to myths. 5As for you, always be sober, endure suffering, do the work of an evangelist, carry out your ministry fully.

6 As for me, I am already being poured out as a libation, and the time of my departure has come. 7I have fought the good fight, I have finished the race, I have kept the faith. 8From now on there is reserved for me the crown of righteousness, which the Lord, the righteous judge, will give me on that day, and not only to me but also to all who have longed for his appearing.

> YOU ARE BUT A POOR SOLDIER OF CHRIST IF YOU THINK YOU CAN OVERCOME WITHOUT FIGHTING, AND SUPPOSE YOU CAN HAVE THE CROWN WITHOUT THE CONFLICT. —John Chrysostom

Personal Instructions

9 Do your best to come to me soon, 10for Demas, in love with this present world, has deserted me and gone to Thessalonica; Crescens has gone to Galatia,j Titus to Dalmatia. 11Only Luke is with me. Get Mark and bring him with you, for he is useful in my ministry. 12I have sent Tychicus to Ephesus. 13When you come, bring the cloak that I left with Carpus at Troas, also the books, and above all the parchments. 14Alexander the coppersmith did me great harm;

g Or by him, to do his (that is, God's) will   h Gk lacks two men   i Or Every scripture inspired by God is also   j Other ancient authorities read Gaul

INVOLVED WITH INSPIRATION

F. F. Bruce

VERSE: 2 Timothy 3.16   **PASSAGE:** 2 Timothy 3.14–17

or many years now the greater part of my time has been devoted to the study and interpretation of the Bible, in academic and non-academic settings alike. I regard this as a most worthwhile and rewarding occupation. There is only one form of ministry which I should rate more highly; that is the work of an evangelist, to which I have not been called. (About a hundred years ago, J. N. Darby remarked, in the course of a Bible reading in Edinburgh, that he considered the gift of an evangelist to be the highest gift in the church today. He was heard with keen delight by W. T. P. Wolston, who thought that some of his brethren should take this to heart and accordingly interposed: "Would you please say that again, Mr. Darby?" "No, my dear young brother," said the great man; "I won't flatter your vanity.")

I should not find the career of a Bible teacher so satisfying as I do if I were not persuaded that the Bible is God's word written. The fact that I am so persuaded means that I must not come to the Bible with my own preconceptions of what the Bible, as God's word written, can or cannot say. It is important to determine, by the canons of grammatical, textual, historical and literary study, what it actually does say. Occasionally, when I have expounded the meaning of some Biblical passage in a particular way, I have been asked, "But how does that square with inspiration?" But inspiration is not a concept of which I have a clear understanding before I come to the study of the text, so that I know in advance what limits are placed on the meaning of the text by the requirements of inspiration. On the contrary, it is by the patient study of the text that I come to understand better not only what the text itself means but also what is involved in biblical inspiration. My doctrine of Scripture is based on my study of Scripture, not *vice versa*.

ADDITIONAL SCRIPTURE READING:
Psalm 119.105; 2 Peter 1.21

Go to page 1436 for your next devotional reading.

1900   Present

the Lord will pay him back for his deeds. ¹⁵You also must beware of him, for he strongly opposed our message.

16 At my first defense no one came to my support, but all deserted me. May it not be counted against them! ¹⁷But the Lord stood by me and gave me strength, so that through me the message might be fully proclaimed and all the Gentiles might hear it. So I was rescued from the lion's mouth. ¹⁸The Lord will rescue me from every evil attack and save me for his heavenly kingdom. To him be the glory forever and ever. Amen.

Final Greetings and Benediction

19 Greet Prisca and Aquila, and the

T H U R S D A Y

FROM REVELATIONS OF DIVINE LOVE
Julian of Norwich

VERSE: 2 Timothy 4.18   **PASSAGE:** 2 Timothy 4.17–18

 ne time our Lord said to me, "All things shall be well." And another time he said, "You yourself shall see that all manner of things shall be well," and my soul understood these two sayings to mean several different things.

One meaning was that his will is for us to know that he takes notice not only of great and noble things, but of little and small things as well, low and simple things, one and the other. And so this is what he meant by saying, "All manner of things shall be well." For it is his will that we know even the smallest of things will not be forgotten.

Another meaning was this: We see many evil deeds done all around us, deeds that cause great harm, and sometimes it seems impossible that they should ever result in anything good. Sometimes when we see these evils, sorrowing and mourning because of them, we find it difficult to concentrate on beholding God blissfully, which is something we should do. And the cause of this is that our reasoning capacity is now so blind, low, and simple that we cannot know his high and marvelous wisdom, the power and the goodness of the blissful Trinity. And this is what he meant when he said, "You yourself shall see that all manner of things shall be well." It was as if he had said, "Take heed faithfully and trustingly now, and at the end of all things, you will truly see them in the fullness of joy."

ADDITIONAL SCRIPTURE READING:
Psalm 121; Romans 8.28, 37–39

Go to page 1439 for your next devotional reading.

500   1500

household of Onesiphorus. 20Erastus remained in Corinth; Trophimus I left ill in Miletus. 21Do your best to come before winter. Eubulus sends greetings to you, as do Pudens and Linus and Claudia and all the brothers and sisters.*k*

22 The Lord be with your spirit. Grace be with you.*l*

TITUS

ITUS, A CLOSE FRIEND OF PAUL, HELPED PAUL ORGANIZE AND LEAD CHURCHES IN THE EASTERN HALF OF THE ROMAN EMPIRE. PAUL WROTE THIS LETTER TO TITUS TO HELP HIM LEAD THE TROUBLED CHURCH ON THE ISLAND OF CRETE. PAUL COVERS SUCH MATTERS AS QUALIFICATIONS OF CHURCH LEADERS, GUIDELINES FOR A GODLY LIFE AND AN EMPHASIS ON FAITH THAT OVERCOMES DIVISION AMONG BELIEVERS.

Salutation

1 Paul, a servant*a* of God and an apostle of Jesus Christ, for the sake of the faith of God's elect and the knowledge of the truth that is in accordance with godliness, 2in the hope of

---

THE SERVANT OF GOD HAS A GOOD MASTER.

—*Blaise Pascal*

---

eternal life that God, who never lies, promised before the ages began— 3in due time he revealed his word through the proclamation with which I have been entrusted by the command of God our Savior,

4 To Titus, my loyal child in the faith we share:

Grace*b* and peace from God the Father and Christ Jesus our Savior.

Titus in Crete

5 I left you behind in Crete for this reason, so that you should put in order what remained to be done, and should appoint elders in every town, as I directed you: 6someone who is blameless, married only once,*c* whose children are believers, not accused of debauchery and not rebellious. 7For a bishop,*d* as God's steward, must be blameless; he must not be arrogant or quick-tempered or addicted to wine or violent or greedy for gain; 8but he must be hospitable, a lover

a Gk *slave*   *b* Other ancient authorities read *Grace, mercy,*   *c* Gk *husband of one wife*   *d* Or *an overseer*

of goodness, prudent, upright, devout, and self-controlled. [9]He must have a firm grasp of the word that is trustworthy in accordance with the teaching, so that he may be able both to preach with sound doctrine and to refute those who contradict it.

10 There are also many rebellious people, idle talkers and deceivers, especially those of the circumcision; [11]they must be silenced, since they are upsetting whole families by teaching for sordid gain what it is not right to teach. [12]It was one of them, their very own prophet, who said,

> "Cretans are always liars, vicious
> brutes, lazy gluttons."

[13]That testimony is true. For this reason rebuke them sharply, so that they may become sound in the faith, [14]not paying attention to Jewish myths or to commandments of those who reject the truth. [15]To the pure all things are pure, but to the corrupt and unbelieving nothing is pure. Their very minds and consciences are corrupted. [16]They profess to know God, but they deny him by their actions. They are detestable, disobedient, unfit for any good work.

Teach Sound Doctrine

 But as for you, teach what is consistent with sound doctrine. [2]Tell the older men to be temperate, serious, prudent, and sound in faith, in love, and in endurance.

3 Likewise, tell the older women to

WEEKEND

STRONG SON OF GOD
Alfred, Lord Tennyson

VERSE: Colossians 1.16   **PASSAGE:** Colossians 1.15–20

trong Son of God, immortal Love,
  Whom we, that have not seen thy face,
  By faith, and faith alone, embrace,
Believing where we cannot prove;

Thine are these orbs of light and shade;
  Thou madest Life in man and brute;
  Thou madest Death; and lo, thy foot
Is on the skull that thou hast made.

Thou wilt not leave us in the dust;
  Thou madest man, he knows not why,
  He thinks he was not made to die;
And thou hast made him: thou art just.

Thou seemest human and divine,
  The highest, holiest manhood, thou.
  Our wills are ours, we know not how,
Our wills are ours, to make them thine.

Our little systems have their day;
  They have their day and cease to be:
  They are but broken lights of thee,
And thou, O Lord, art more than they. . .

Let knowledge grow from more to more,
  But more of reverence in us dwell;
  That mind and soul, according well,
May make one music as before,

But vaster. We are fools and slight;
  We mock thee when we do not fear:
  But help thy foolish ones to bear;
Help thy vain worlds to bear thy light . . .

ADDITIONAL SCRIPTURE READING:
Hebrews 11.1; Revelation 2.10

Go to page 1442 for your next devotional reading.

1700   1900

be reverent in behavior, not to be slanderers or slaves to drink; they are to teach what is good, 4so that they may encourage the young women to love their husbands, to love their children, 5to be self-controlled, chaste, good managers of the household, kind, being submissive to their husbands, so that the word of God may not be discredited.

6 Likewise, urge the younger men to be self-controlled. 7Show yourself in all respects a model of good works, and in your teaching show integrity, gravity, 8and sound speech that cannot be censured; then any opponent will be put to shame, having nothing evil to say of us.

9 Tell slaves to be submissive to their masters and to give satisfaction in every respect; they are not to talk back, 10not to pilfer, but to show complete and perfect fidelity, so that in everything they may be an ornament to the doctrine of God our Savior.

11 For the grace of God has appeared, bringing salvation to all,e 12training us to renounce impiety and worldly passions, and in the present age to live lives that are self-controlled, upright, and godly, 13while we wait for the blessed hope and the manifestation of the glory of our great God and Savior,f Jesus Christ. 14He it is who gave himself for us that he might redeem us from all iniquity and purify for himself a people of his own who are zealous for good deeds.

15 Declare these things; exhort and reprove with all authority.g Let no one look down on you.

THE CHURCH IS NOT A GALLERY FOR THE EXHIBITION OF EMINENT CHRISTIANS, BUT A SCHOOL FOR THE EDUCATION OF IMPERFECT ONES.

—Henry Ward Beecher

Maintain Good Deeds

 3 Remind them to be subject to rulers and authorities, to be obedient, to be ready for every good work, 2to speak evil of no one, to avoid quarreling, to be gentle, and to show every courtesy to everyone. 3For we ourselves were once foolish, disobedient, led astray, slaves to various passions and pleasures, passing our days in malice and envy, despicable, hating one another. 4But when the goodness and loving kindness of God our Savior appeared, 5he saved us, not because of any works of righteousness that we had done, but according to his mercy, through the waterh of rebirth and renewal by the Holy Spirit. 6This Spirit he poured out on us richly through Jesus Christ our Savior, 7so that, having been justified by his grace, we might become heirs according to the hope of eternal life. 8The saying is sure.

I desire that you insist on these things, so that those who have come to believe in God may be careful to devote themselves to good works; these things are excellent and profitable to everyone. 9But avoid stupid controversies, genealogies, dissensions, and quarrels about the law, for they are unprofitable and worthless. 10After a first and second admonition, have nothing more to do with anyone who causes divisions, 11since you know that such a person is perverted and sinful, being self-condemned.

Final Messages and Benediction

12 When I send Artemas to you, or Tychicus, do your best to come to me at Nicopolis, for I have decided to spend the winter there. 13Make every effort to send Zenas the lawyer and Apollos on their way, and see that they lack nothing. 14And let people learn to devote themselves to good works in order to meet urgent needs, so that they may not be unproductive.

15 All who are with me send greetings to you. Greet those who love us in the faith.

Grace be with all of you.i

---

e Or has appeared to all, bringing salvation   f Or of the great God and our Savior
g Gk commandment   h Gk washing   i Other ancient authorities add Amen

THE EXAMPLE OF GOD'S ADORNMENT
Clement of Rome

VERSE: Titus 3.14   PASSAGE: Titus 3.12–15

hat must we do, then, my brothers? Should we relax our efforts at well-doing, and cease to exercise Christian love? God forbid that we, at least, should ever come to such a pass. On the contrary, let us be earnestly, even passionately, eager to set about any kind of activity that is good. Even the Architect and Lord of the universe himself takes a delight in working. In his supreme power he has established the heavens, and in his unsearchable wisdom set them in order. He divided the earth from the waters around it, and settled it securely on the firm foundation of his will, and at his word he called to life the beasts of the field that roam its surface. He formed the sea and its creatures, and confined them by his power. Above all, with his own sacred and immaculate hands he fashioned man, who in virtue of his intelligence is the chiefest and greatest of all his works and the very likeness of his own image; for God said, *Let us make man in our image and likeness; and God created man, male and female he created them* (Genesis 1.26–27, KJV). And when he had made an end of all his works, he gave them his approval and his blessing, saying, *Increase and multiply* (Genesis 1.28). We see, then, that good works have not only embellished the lives of all just men, but are an adornment with which even the Lord has delighted to deck himself; and therefore, with such an example before us, let us spare no effort to obey his will, but put all our energies into the work of righteousness.

ADDITIONAL SCRIPTURE READING:
Matthew 5.6; 2 Timothy 2.22

Go to page 1444 for your next devotional reading.

100   500

PHILEMON

HILEMON, A BELIEVER IN COLOSSAE, OWNED A SLAVE NAMED ONESIMUS WHO HAD APPARENTLY STOLEN FROM HIM AND THEN RUN AWAY. BUT ONESIMUS MET PAUL AND THROUGH HIS MINISTRY BECAME A CHRISTIAN. NOW HE WAS WILLING TO RETURN TO HIS MASTER. PAUL WRITES THIS PERSONAL APPEAL TO ASK PHILEMON TO ACCEPT ONESIMUS AS A CHRISTIAN BROTHER, NOT AS A SLAVE. READ THIS LETTER AS A CASE STUDY IN THE COST OF ASKING FOR FORGIVENESS AND OF GRANTING IT.

Salutation

1 Paul, a prisoner of Christ Jesus, and Timothy our brother,*a*

To Philemon our dear friend and co-worker, 2to Apphia our sister,*b* to Archippus our fellow soldier, and to the church in your house:

3 Grace to you and peace from God our Father and the Lord Jesus Christ.

Philemon's Love and Faith

4 When I remember you*c* in my prayers, I always thank my God 5because I hear of your love for all the saints and your faith toward the Lord Jesus. 6I pray that the sharing of your faith may become effective when you perceive all the good that we*d* may do for Christ. 7I have indeed received much joy and encouragement from your love, because the hearts of the saints have been refreshed through you, my brother.

Paul's Plea for Onesimus

8 For this reason, though I am bold enough in Christ to command you to do your duty, 9yet I would rather appeal to you on the basis of love—and I, Paul, do this as an old man, and now also as a prisoner of Christ Jesus.*e* 10I am appealing to you for my child, Onesimus, whose father I have become during my imprisonment. 11Formerly he was useless to you, but now he is indeed

a Gk *the brother*   *b* Gk *the sister*   *c* From verse 4 through verse 21, *you* is singular   *d* Other ancient authorities read *you* (plural)   *e* Or *as an ambassador of Christ Jesus, and now also his prisoner*

TUESDAY

PRAYER OF A SLAVE
Frederick Douglass

VERSE: Philemon 17   **PASSAGE:** Philemon 8–21

ur house stood within a few rods of the Chesapeake Bay, whose broad bosom was ever white with sails from every quarter of the habitable globe. Those beautiful vessels, robed in white, and so delightful to the eyes of freemen, were to me so many shrouded ghosts, to terrify and torment me with thoughts of my wretched condition. I have often, in the deep stillness of a summer's Sabbath, stood all alone upon the banks of that noble bay, and traced, with saddened heart and tearful eye, the countless number of sails moving off to the mighty ocean. The sight of these always affected me powerfully. My thoughts would compel utterance; and there, with no audience but the Almighty, I would pour out my soul's complaint in my rude way with an apostrophe to the multitude of ships.

"You are loosed from your moorings, and free. I am fast in my chains, and am a slave! You move merrily before the gentle gale, and I sadly before the bloody whip. You are freedom's swift-winged angels, that fly around the world; I am confined in bonds of iron. O, that I were free! O, that I were one of your gallant decks, and under your protecting wing. Alas! betwixt me and you the turbid waters roll. Go on, go on; O, that I could also go! Could I but swim! If I could fly! O, why was I born a man, of whom to make a brute! The glad ship is gone: she hides in the dim distance. I am left in the hell of unending slavery. O, God, save me! God, deliver me! Let me be free!—Is there any God? Why am I a slave? I will run away. I will not stand it. Get caught or get clear, I'll try it. I had as well die with ague as with fever. I have only one life to lose. I had as well be killed running as die standing. Only think of it: one hundred miles north, and I am free! Try it? Yes! God helping me, I will. It cannot be that I shall live and die a slave. I will take to the water. This very bay shall yet bear me into freedom."

ADDITIONAL SCRIPTURE READING:
Romans 7.24–25; 1 Corinthians 7.21–23

Go to page 1449 for your next devotional reading.

1700   1900

useful*f* both to you and to me. **12**I am sending him, that is, my own heart, back to you. **13**I wanted to keep him with me, so that he might be of service to me in your place during my imprisonment for the gospel; **14**but I preferred to do nothing without your consent, in order that your good deed might be voluntary and not something forced. **15**Perhaps this is the reason he was separated from you for a while, so that you might have him back forever, **16**no longer as a slave but more than a slave, a beloved brother—especially to me but how much more to you, both in the flesh and in the Lord.

17 So if you consider me your partner, welcome him as you would welcome me. **18**If he has wronged you in any way, or owes you anything, charge that to my account. **19**I, Paul, am writing this with my own hand: I will repay it. I say nothing about your owing me even your own self. **20**Yes, brother, let me have this benefit from you in the Lord! Refresh my heart in Christ. **21**Confident of your obedience, I am writing to you, knowing that you will do even more than I say.

22 One thing more—prepare a guest room for me, for I am hoping through your prayers to be restored to you.

Final Greetings and Benediction

23 Epaphras, my fellow prisoner in Christ Jesus, sends greetings to you,*g* **24**and so do Mark, Aristarchus, Demas, and Luke, my fellow workers.

25 The grace of the Lord Jesus Christ be with your spirit.*h*

---

f The name Onesimus means *useful* or (compare verse 20) *beneficial*   *g* Here *you* is singular
h Other ancient authorities add *Amen*

HEBREWS

THE FIRST-CENTURY CHURCH SUFFERED SEVERE PERSECUTION, AND THIS LETTER WAS WRITTEN IN THAT SETTING. THE INTENDED READERS SEEM TO HAVE BEEN JEWISH CHRISTIANS WHO WERE THINKING OF ABANDONING THEIR FAITH AND LAPSING BACK INTO JUDAISM. SO THE AUTHOR EXHORTS THEM TO HOLD FAST TO THEIR CONFESSION OF CHRIST AS SAVIOR AND LORD. THE THEME OF HEBREWS IS THE ABSOLUTE SUPREMACY AND SUFFICIENCY OF JESUS CHRIST AS REVEALER AND AS MEDIATOR OF GOD'S GRACE. AS YOU READ THIS BOOK, LOOK FOR THE INSPIRATION TO KEEP GOING IN THE FAITH.

God Has Spoken by His Son

1 Long ago God spoke to our ancestors in many and various ways by the prophets, ²but in these last days he has spoken to us by a Son,ᵃ whom he appointed heir of all things, through whom he also created the worlds. ³He is the reflection of God's glory and the exact imprint of God's very being, and he sustainsᵇ all things by his powerful word. When he had made purification for sins, he sat down at the right hand of the Majesty on high, ⁴having become as much superior to angels as the name he has inherited is more excellent than theirs.

The Son Is Superior to Angels

5 For to which of the angels did God ever say,

"You are my Son;
    today I have begotten you"?

Or again,

"I will be his Father,
    and he will be my Son"?

⁶And again, when he brings the firstborn into the world, he says,

"Let all God's angels worship him."

⁷Of the angels he says,

"He makes his angels winds,
    and his servants flames of fire."

⁸But of the Son he says,

"Your throne, O God, isᶜ forever
    and ever,

---

a Or *the Son*   *b* Or *bears along*   *c* Or *God is your throne*

and the righteous scepter is the
     scepter of your[d] kingdom.
9 You have loved righteousness and
     hated wickedness;
   therefore God, your God, has
     anointed you
   with the oil of gladness beyond
     your companions."
10 And,
   "In the beginning, Lord, you
     founded the earth,
   and the heavens are the work of
     your hands;
11 they will perish, but you remain;
   they will all wear out like
     clothing;
12 like a cloak you will roll them up,
   and like clothing[e] they will be
     changed.
   But you are the same,
     and your years will never end."
13 But to which of the angels has he ever
said,
   "Sit at my right hand
     until I make your enemies a
       footstool for your feet"?
14 Are not all angels[f] spirits in the divine
service, sent to serve for the sake of
those who are to inherit salvation?

Warning to Pay Attention

2 Therefore we must pay greater
attention to what we have
heard, so that we do not drift away from
it. 2 For if the message declared through
angels was valid, and every transgression or disobedience received a just
penalty, 3 how can we escape if we neglect so great a salvation? It was declared at first through the Lord, and it
was attested to us by those who heard
him, 4 while God added his testimony by
signs and wonders and various miracles,
and by gifts of the Holy Spirit, distributed according to his will.

Exaltation through Abasement

5 Now God[g] did not subject the coming world, about which we are speaking,
to angels. 6 But someone has testified
somewhere,

   "What are human beings that you
     are mindful of them,[h]
   or mortals, that you care for
     them?[i]
7 You have made them for a little
     while lower[j] than the angels;
   you have crowned them with
     glory and honor,[k]
8   subjecting all things under their
       feet."
Now in subjecting all things to them,
God[g] left nothing outside their control.
As it is, we do not yet see everything in
subjection to them, 9 but we do see Jesus,
who for a little while was made lower[l]
than the angels, now crowned with
glory and honor because of the suffering
of death, so that by the grace of God[m] he
might taste death for everyone.

10 It was fitting that God,[g] for whom
and through whom all things exist, in
bringing many children to glory, should
make the pioneer of their salvation perfect through sufferings. 11 For the one
who sanctifies and those who are sanctified all have one Father.[n] For this reason
Jesus[g] is not ashamed to call them
brothers and sisters,[o] 12 saying,

   "I will proclaim your name to my
     brothers and sisters,[o]
   in the midst of the congregation I
     will praise you."
13 And again,
   "I will put my trust in him."
And again,
   "Here am I and the children whom
     God has given me."

14 Since, therefore, the children
share flesh and blood, he himself likewise shared the same things, so that
through death he might destroy the one
who has the power of death, that is, the
devil, 15 and free those who all their lives
were held in slavery by the fear of death.
16 For it is clear that he did not come to
help angels, but the descendants of
Abraham. 17 Therefore he had to become
like his brothers and sisters[o] in every respect, so that he might be a merciful and
faithful high priest in the service of God,
to make a sacrifice of atonement for the

---

d Other ancient authorities read *his*   e Other ancient authorities lack *like clothing*   f Gk *all of
them*   g Gk *he*   h Gk *What is man that you are mindful of him?*   i Gk *or the son of man that
you care for him?* In the Hebrew of Psalm 8.4-6 both *man* and *son of man* refer to all humankind
j Or *them only a little lower*   k Other ancient authorities add *and set them over the works of your
hands*   l Or *who was made a little lower*   m Other ancient authorities read *apart from God*
n Gk *are all of one*   o Gk *brothers*

sins of the people. ¹⁸Because he himself was tested by what he suffered, he is able to help those who are being tested.

Moses a Servant, Christ a Son

3 Therefore, brothers and sisters,ᵖ holy partners in a heavenly calling, consider that Jesus, the apostle and high priest of our confession, ²was faithful to the one who appointed him, just as Moses also "was faithful in allᵠ God'sʳ house." ³Yet Jesusˢ is worthy of more glory than Moses, just as the builder of a house has more honor than the house itself. ⁴(For every house is built by someone, but the builder of all things is God.) ⁵Now Moses was faithful in all God'sʳ house as a servant, to testify to the things that would be spoken later. ⁶Christ, however, was faithful over God'sʳ house as a son, and we are his house if we hold firmᵗ the confidence and the pride that belong to hope.

Warning against Unbelief

7 Therefore, as the Holy Spirit says,
"Today, if you hear his voice,
8   do not harden your hearts as in the rebellion,
   as on the day of testing in the wilderness,
9   where your ancestors put me to the test,
   though they had seen my works
¹⁰for forty years.
Therefore I was angry with that generation,
and I said, 'They always go astray in their hearts,
and they have not known my ways.'
11   As in my anger I swore,
'They will not enter my rest.' "
¹²Take care, brothers and sisters,ᵖ that none of you may have an evil, unbelieving heart that turns away from the living God. ¹³But exhort one another every day, as long as it is called "today," so that none of you may be hardened by the deceitfulness of sin. ¹⁴For we have become partners of Christ, if only we hold our first confidence firm to the end. ¹⁵As it is said,

"Today, if you hear his voice,
do not harden your hearts as in the rebellion."
¹⁶Now who were they who heard and yet were rebellious? Was it not all those who left Egypt under the leadership of Moses? ¹⁷But with whom was he angry forty years? Was it not those who sinned, whose bodies fell in the wilderness? ¹⁸And to whom did he swear that they would not enter his rest, if not to those who were disobedient? ¹⁹So we see that they were unable to enter because of unbelief.

The Rest That God Promised

4 Therefore, while the promise of entering his rest is still open, let us take care that none of you should seem to have failed to reach it. ²For indeed the good news came to us just as to them; but the message they heard did not benefit them, because they were not united by faith with those who listened.ᵘ ³For we who have believed enter that rest, just as Godᵛ has said,

"As in my anger I swore,
'They shall not enter my rest,' "
though his works were finished at the foundation of the world. ⁴For in one place it speaks about the seventh day as follows, "And God rested on the seventh day from all his works." ⁵And again in this place it says, "They shall not enter my rest." ⁶Since therefore it remains open for some to enter it, and those who formerly received the good news failed to enter because of disobedience, ⁷again he sets a certain day— "today"—saying through David much later, in the words already quoted,

"Today, if you hear his voice,
do not harden your hearts."
⁸For if Joshua had given them rest, Godᵛ would not speak later about another day. ⁹So then, a sabbath rest still remains for the people of God; ¹⁰for those who enter God's rest also cease from their labors as God did from his. ¹¹Let us therefore make every effort to enter that rest, so that no one may fall through such disobedience as theirs.

12 Indeed, the word of God is living

---

p Gk *brothers*   q Other ancient authorities lack *all*   r Gk *his*   s Gk *this one*   t Other ancient authorities add *to the end*   u Other ancient authorities read *it did not meet with faith in those who listened*   v Gk *he*

CONCERNING SAVING FAITH
Nikolaus Ludwig Count von Zinzendorf

VERSE: Hebrews 3.12   **PASSAGE:** Hebrews 3.12–15

n the Savior's affairs [Peter] was not just a natural, unconverted, unfamiliar man (which indeed is in itself sin enough), but rather he was a deliberate denier, what today is called a renegade. He would rather not know his Lord; he was ashamed of his Lord; he abjured his Lord three times. And a few days later his Lord came up and rose from the dead and was loved by those people who had followed him to death itself, by the women who had helped to place him into the grave and who came back at early dawn and looked for him out of love. "Ah," says the Savior to them, "you dear children, I absolutely beg of you not to delay here with me, but go and tell my Peter that I am here again" (see Mark 16.7).

This must have been an astonishing message to Peter. Was this all his punishment, to be notified that his Lord is risen again? And if so, should he have been the very first who was comforted, whose heart was revived? Thus, when the Savior said to him afterward, "Do you love me more than these do?" he said, "You know all things; you know how much I love you" (see John 21.15–17). And at that time he really did love him more than all the others. Before he had loved him in his imagination; he had honored him and out of esteem for him had rashly claimed to be ready to suffer death for him rather than forsake him. He did make a bold beginning, but he got stuck, because his love was dry and intellectual. But when the Savior forgave him everything, when he acquitted him of his sins, when he declared a renegade to be his apostle, then Peter could hold back no longer. If anyone said anything about his Lord to him, tears filled his eyes, and his body and soul were humbled. Already in the high priest's palace the bare presentiment of the character of his Lord had made his eyes fountains of tears.

ADDITIONAL SCRIPTURE READING:
Mark 16.7; John 21.15

Go to page 1451 for your next devotional reading.

1700   1900

and active, sharper than any two-edged sword, piercing until it divides soul from spirit, joints from marrow; it is able to judge the thoughts and intentions of the heart. 13And before him no creature is hidden, but all are naked and laid bare to the eyes of the one to whom we must render an account.

THE WORD OF GOD IS NOT A SOUNDING BUT A PIERCING WORD, NOT PRONOUNCEABLE BY THE TONGUE BUT EFFICACIOUS IN THE MIND, NOT SENSIBLE TO THE EAR BUT FASCINATING TO THE AFFECTION.   —Bernard of Clairvaux

---

Jesus the Great High Priest

14 Since, then, we have a great high priest who has passed through the heavens, Jesus, the Son of God, let us hold fast to our confession. 15For we do not have a high priest who is unable to sympathize with our weaknesses, but we have one who in every respect has been tested[w] as we are, yet without sin. 16Let us therefore approach the throne of grace with boldness, so that we may receive mercy and find grace to help in time of need.

PRAY, ALWAYS PRAY; THOUGH WEARY, FAINT, AND LONE,
PRAYER NESTLES BY THE FATHER'S SHELTERING THRONE.
                              —A. B. Simpson

---

5 Every high priest chosen from among mortals is put in charge of things pertaining to God on their behalf, to offer gifts and sacrifices for sins. 2He is able to deal gently with the ignorant and wayward, since he himself is subject to weakness; 3and because of this he must offer sacrifice for his own sins as well as for those of the people. 4And one does not presume to take this honor, but takes it only when called by God, just as Aaron was.

5 So also Christ did not glorify himself in becoming a high priest, but was appointed by the one who said to him,

"You are my Son,
    today I have begotten you";
6as he says also in another place,
"You are a priest forever,
    according to the order of
        Melchizedek."

7 In the days of his flesh, Jesus[x] offered up prayers and supplications, with loud cries and tears, to the one who was able to save him from death, and he was heard because of his reverent submission. 8Although he was a Son, he learned obedience through what he suffered; 9and having been made perfect, he became the source of eternal salvation for all who obey him, 10having been designated by God a high priest according to the order of Melchizedek.

Warning against Falling Away

11 About this[y] we have much to say that is hard to explain, since you have become dull in understanding. 12For though by this time you ought to be teachers, you need someone to teach you again the basic elements of the oracles of God. You need milk, not solid food; 13for everyone who lives on milk, being still an infant, is unskilled in the word of righteousness. 14But solid food is for the mature, for those whose faculties have been trained by practice to distinguish good from evil.

The Peril of Falling Away

6 Therefore let us go on toward perfection,[z] leaving behind the basic teaching about Christ, and not laying again the foundation: repentance from dead works and faith toward God, 2instruction about baptisms, laying on of hands, resurrection of the dead, and eternal judgment. 3And we will do[a] this, if God permits. 4For it is impossible to restore again to repentance those who have once been enlightened, and have tasted the heavenly gift, and have shared in the Holy Spirit, 5and have tasted the goodness of the word of God and the powers of the age to come, 6and then have fallen away, since on their own they are crucifying again the Son of God and are holding him up to contempt. 7Ground that drinks up the rain falling

---

w Or tempted   x Gk he   y Or him   z Or toward maturity   a Other ancient authorities read let us do

on it repeatedly, and that produces a crop useful to those for whom it is cultivated, receives a blessing from God. [8]But if it produces thorns and thistles, it is worthless and on the verge of being cursed; its end is to be burned over.

9 Even though we speak in this way, beloved, we are confident of better things in your case, things that belong to salvation. [10]For God is not unjust; he will not overlook your work and the love that you showed for his sake[b] in serving the saints, as you still do. [11]And we want each one of you to show the same diligence so as to realize the full assurance of hope to the very end, [12]so

b Gk for his name

THURSDAY

THE PRIESTHOOD OF CHRIST
Jacobus Arminius

VERSE: Hebrews 4.15   **PASSAGE:** Hebrews 4.14–16

isdom was again desired in the Divine Council. She declared that [to resolve the conflict between Justice and Mercy] a man must be born from among men, who might have a nature in common with the rest of his brethren, that, being in all things tempted as they were, he might be able to sympathize with others in their suffering; and yet, that he should . . . not be under dominion of sin; that he should be one in whom Satan could find nothing worthy of condemnation, who should not be tormented by a consciousness of sin, and who should not even know sin, that is, one who should be "born in the likeness of sinful flesh, and yet without sin. For such a high priest became us, who is holy, harmless, undefiled, and separate from sinners" (Hebrews 7.26, KJV). But that he might have a community of nature with men, he ought to be born of a human being; and that he might have no participation in crime with them, but might be holy, he ought to be conceived by the Holy Ghost, because sanctification is his proper work . . . Therefore, the Word of God, who from the beginning was with God and by whom the worlds and all things visible and invisible were created, ought himself to be made flesh, to undertake the office of the priesthood, and to offer his own flesh to God as a sacrifice for the life of the world.

We now have the person who was entrusted with the priesthood and to whom the province was assigned of atoning for the common offense: it is Jesus Christ, the Son of God and of man.

ADDITIONAL SCRIPTURE READING:
John 1.1–5, 14; Hebrews 7.23–28

Go to page 1454 for your next devotional reading.

1500   1700

that you may not become sluggish, but imitators of those who through faith and patience inherit the promises.

The Certainty of God's Promise

13 When God made a promise to Abraham, because he had no one greater by whom to swear, he swore by himself, [14]saying, "I will surely bless you and multiply you." [15]And thus Abraham,[c] having patiently endured, obtained the promise. [16]Human beings, of course, swear by someone greater than themselves, and an oath given as confirmation puts an end to all dispute. [17]In the same way, when God desired to show even more clearly to the heirs of the promise the unchangeable character of his purpose, he guaranteed it by an oath, [18]so that through two unchangeable things, in which it is impossible that God would prove false, we who have taken refuge might be strongly encouraged to seize the hope set before us. [19]We have this hope, a sure and steadfast anchor of the soul, a hope that enters the inner shrine behind the curtain, [20]where Jesus, a forerunner on our behalf, has entered, having become a high priest forever according to the order of Melchizedek.

The Priestly Order of Melchizedek

7 This "King Melchizedek of Salem, priest of the Most High God, met Abraham as he was returning from defeating the kings and blessed him"; [2]and to him Abraham apportioned "one-tenth of everything." His name, in the first place, means "king of righteousness"; next he is also king of Salem, that is, "king of peace." [3]Without father, without mother, without genealogy, having neither beginning of days nor end of life, but resembling the Son of God, he remains a priest forever.

4 See how great he is! Even[d] Abraham the patriarch gave him a tenth of the spoils. [5]And those descendants of Levi who receive the priestly office have a commandment in the law to collect tithes[e] from the people, that is, from their kindred,[f] though these also are descended from Abraham. [6]But this man, who does not belong to their ancestry, collected tithes[e] from Abraham and

blessed him who had received the promises. [7]It is beyond dispute that the inferior is blessed by the superior. [8]In the one case, tithes are received by those who are mortal; in the other, by one of whom it is testified that he lives. [9]One might even say that Levi himself, who receives tithes, paid tithes through Abraham, [10]for he was still in the loins of his ancestor when Melchizedek met him.

Another Priest, Like Melchizedek

11 Now if perfection had been attainable through the levitical priesthood— for the people received the law under this priesthood—what further need would there have been to speak of another priest arising according to the order of Melchizedek, rather than one according to the order of Aaron? [12]For when there is a change in the priesthood, there is necessarily a change in the law as well. [13]Now the one of whom these things are spoken belonged to another tribe, from which no one has ever served at the altar. [14]For it is evident that our Lord was descended from Judah, and in connection with that tribe Moses said nothing about priests.

15 It is even more obvious when another priest arises, resembling Melchizedek, [16]one who has become a priest, not through a legal requirement concerning physical descent, but through the power of an indestructible life. [17]For it is attested of him,

"You are a priest forever,
    according to the order of
        Melchizedek."

[18]There is, on the one hand, the abrogation of an earlier commandment because it was weak and ineffectual [19](for the law made nothing perfect); there is, on the other hand, the introduction of a better hope, through which we approach God.

20 This was confirmed with an oath; for others who became priests took their office without an oath, [21]but this one became a priest with an oath, because of the one who said to him,

"The Lord has sworn
    and will not change his mind,
'You are a priest forever' "—
[22]accordingly Jesus has also become the guarantee of a better covenant.

c Gk he   d Other ancient authorities lack Even   e Or a tenth   f Gk brothers

23 Furthermore, the former priests were many in number, because they were prevented by death from continuing in office; 24but he holds his priesthood permanently, because he continues forever. 25Consequently he is able for all time to save[g] those who approach God through him, since he always lives to make intercession for them.

26 For it was fitting that we should have such a high priest, holy, blameless, undefiled, separated from sinners, and exalted above the heavens. 27Unlike the other[h] high priests, he has no need to offer sacrifices day after day, first for his own sins, and then for those of the people; this he did once for all when he offered himself. 28For the law appoints as high priests those who are subject to weakness, but the word of the oath, which came later than the law, appoints a Son who has been made perfect forever.

Mediator of a Better Covenant

8 Now the main point in what we are saying is this: we have such a high priest, one who is seated at the right hand of the throne of the Majesty in the heavens, 2a minister in the sanctuary and the true tent[i] that the Lord, and not any mortal, has set up. 3For every high priest is appointed to offer gifts and sacrifices; hence it is necessary for this priest also to have something to offer. 4Now if he were on earth, he would not be a priest at all, since there are priests who offer gifts according to the law. 5They offer worship in a sanctuary that is a sketch and shadow of the heavenly one; for Moses, when he was about to erect the tent,[i] was warned, "See that you make everything according to the pattern that was shown you on the mountain." 6But Jesus[j] has now obtained a more excellent ministry, and to that degree he is the mediator of a better covenant, which has been enacted through better promises. 7For if that first covenant had been faultless, there would have been no need to look for a second one.

8 God[k] finds fault with them when he says:

"The days are surely coming, says the Lord,
when I will establish a new covenant with the house of Israel
and with the house of Judah;
9   not like the covenant that I made with their ancestors,
on the day when I took them by the hand to lead them out of the land of Egypt;
for they did not continue in my covenant,
and so I had no concern for them, says the Lord.
10 This is the covenant that I will make with the house of Israel after those days, says the Lord:
I will put my laws in their minds,
and write them on their hearts,
and I will be their God,
and they shall be my people.
11 And they shall not teach one another
or say to each other, 'Know the Lord,'
for they shall all know me,
from the least of them to the greatest.
12 For I will be merciful toward their iniquities,
and I will remember their sins no more."

13In speaking of "a new covenant," he has made the first one obsolete. And what is obsolete and growing old will soon disappear.

The Earthly and the Heavenly Sanctuaries

9 Now even the first covenant had regulations for worship and an earthly sanctuary. 2For a tent[i] was constructed, the first one, in which were the lampstand, the table, and the bread of the Presence;[l] this is called the Holy Place. 3Behind the second curtain was a tent[i] called the Holy of Holies. 4In it stood the golden altar of incense and the ark of the covenant overlaid on all sides with gold, in which there were a golden urn holding the manna, and Aaron's rod that budded, and the tablets of the covenant; 5above it were the cherubim of

g Or able to save completely   h Gk lacks other   i Or tabernacle   j Gk he   k Gk He
l Gk the presentation of the loaves

glory overshadowing the mercy seat.*m* Of these things we cannot speak now in detail.

6 Such preparations having been made, the priests go continually into the first tent*n* to carry out their ritual du-

ties; 7but only the high priest goes into the second, and he but once a year, and not without taking the blood that he offers for himself and for the sins committed unintentionally by the people. 8By this the Holy Spirit indicates that the

m Or *the place of atonement*   *n* Or *tabernacle*

FRIDAY

THE DOUBLE DEBT
Bernard of Clairvaux

VERSE: Hebrews 9.14   PASSAGE: Hebrews 9.11–28

 od certainly is well within his rights in claiming to himself the works of his own hands, the gifts himself has given! How should the thing made fail to love the maker, provided that it have from him the power to love at all? How should it not love him with all its powers, since only by his gift has it got anything? Man, called into being out of nothing by God's free act and raised to such high honor, how patent is his debt of love to God's most just demand! How vastly God has multiplied his mercy too, in saving man and beast in such a way! Why, we had turned our glory into the likeness of a calf that eateth hay; our sin had brought us to the level of the beasts that know not God at all! If then I owe myself entire to my Creator, what shall I give my Re-creator more? The means of our remaking too, think what they cost! It was far easier to make than to redeem; for God had but to speak the word and all things were created, I included; but he who made me by a word, and made me once for all, spent on the task of my remaking many words and many marvelous deeds, and suffered grievous and humiliating wrongs.

What reward therefore shall I give the Lord for all the benefits that he has done to me? By his first work he gave me to myself; and by the next he gave himself to me. And when he gave himself, he gave me back myself that I had lost. Myself for myself, given and restored, I doubly owe to him. But what shall I return for himself? A thousand of myself would be as nothing in respect of him.

ADDITIONAL SCRIPTURE READING:
Romans 12.1; Hebrews 13.15–16

Go to page 1456 for your next devotional reading.

500   1500

way into the sanctuary has not yet been disclosed as long as the first tent[o] is still standing. [9]This is a symbol[p] of the present time, during which gifts and sacrifices are offered that cannot perfect the conscience of the worshiper, [10]but deal only with food and drink and various baptisms, regulations for the body imposed until the time comes to set things right.

11 But when Christ came as a high priest of the good things that have come,[q] then through the greater and perfect[r] tent[o] (not made with hands, that is, not of this creation), [12]he entered once for all into the Holy Place, not with the blood of goats and calves, but with his own blood, thus obtaining eternal redemption. [13]For if the blood of goats and bulls, with the sprinkling of the ashes of a heifer, sanctifies those who have been defiled so that their flesh is purified, [14]how much more will the blood of Christ, who through the eternal Spirit[s] offered himself without blemish to God, purify our[t] conscience from dead works to worship the living God!

15 For this reason he is the mediator of a new covenant, so that those who are called may receive the promised eternal inheritance, because a death has occurred that redeems them from the transgressions under the first covenant.[u] [16]Where a will[u] is involved, the death of the one who made it must be established. [17]For a will[u] takes effect only at death, since it is not in force as long as the one who made it is alive. [18]Hence not even the first covenant was inaugurated without blood. [19]For when every commandment had been told to all the people by Moses in accordance with the law, he took the blood of calves and goats,[v] with water and scarlet wool and hyssop, and sprinkled both the scroll itself and all the people, [20]saying, "This is the blood of the covenant that God has ordained for you." [21]And in the same way he sprinkled with the blood both the tent[o] and all the vessels used in worship. [22]Indeed, under the law almost everything is purified with blood, and without the shedding of blood there is no forgiveness of sins.

Christ's Sacrifice Takes Away Sin

23 Thus it was necessary for the sketches of the heavenly things to be purified with these rites, but the heavenly things themselves need better sacrifices than these. [24]For Christ did not enter a sanctuary made by human hands, a mere copy of the true one, but he entered into heaven itself, now to appear in the presence of God on our behalf. [25]Nor was it to offer himself again and again, as the high priest enters the Holy Place year after year with blood that is not his own; [26]for then he would have had to suffer again and again since the foundation of the world. But as it is, he has appeared once for all at the end of the age to remove sin by the sacrifice of himself. [27]And just as it is appointed for mortals to die once, and after that the judgment, [28]so Christ, having been offered once to bear the sins of many, will appear a second time, not to deal with sin, but to save those who are eagerly waiting for him.

Christ's Sacrifice Once for All

10 Since the law has only a shadow of the good things to come and not the true form of these realities, it[w] can never, by the same sacrifices that are continually offered year after year, make perfect those who approach. [2]Otherwise, would they not have ceased being offered, since the worshipers, cleansed once for all, would no longer have any consciousness of sin? [3]But in these sacrifices there is a reminder of sin year after year. [4]For it is impossible for the blood of bulls and goats to take away sins. [5]Consequently, when Christ[x] came into the world, he said,

"Sacrifices and offerings you have
            not desired,
    but a body you have prepared for
            me;
6   in burnt offerings and sin offerings
            you have taken no pleasure.
7   Then I said, 'See, God, I have come
            to do your will, O God'
    (in the scroll of the book[y] it is
            written of me)."

---

o Or tabernacle   p Gk parable   q Other ancient authorities read good things to come
r Gk more perfect   s Other ancient authorities read Holy Spirit   t Other ancient authorities read
your   u The Greek word used here means both covenant and will   v Other ancient authorities lack
and goats   w Other ancient authorities read they   x Gk he   y Meaning of Gk uncertain

WEEKEND

MY KING WILL SOON COME BACK AGAIN
Watchman Nee

VERSE: 2 Timothy 4.8   **PASSAGE:** 2 Timothy 4.6–8

y King will soon come back again,
The sky be filled with him;
The universe to be redeemed
Will see his light therein.
The Lord will soon fulfill his plan,
His footsteps now I hear;
His glorious frame I faintly see
Beginning to appear.

I'm longing for his presence blest
And dare not slothful be
While waiting for my Lord's return,
His own dear self to see.
My only hope—that he may come
And change my faith to sight;
There is no other joy on earth
Which gives my heart delight . . .

My Savior, all thy holy words
Can never doubted be;
With them encouraged day by day,
I'm faithful unto thee.
Oh, may thy glory soon appear,
The foe be overthrown;
Thy promises be realized,
And we brought to thy throne.

ADDITIONAL SCRIPTURE READING:
Matthew 25.31; Hebrews 9.28

Go to page 1460 for your next devotional reading.

1900   Present

8When he said above, "You have neither desired nor taken pleasure in sacrifices and offerings and burnt offerings and sin offerings" (these are offered according to the law), 9then he added, "See, I have come to do your will." He abolishes the first in order to establish the second. 10And it is by God's will[z] that we have been sanctified through the offering of the body of Jesus Christ once for all.

11 And every priest stands day after day at his service, offering again and again the same sacrifices that can never take away sins. 12But when Christ[a] had offered for all time a single sacrifice for sins, "he sat down at the right hand of God," 13and since then has been waiting "until his enemies would be made a footstool for his feet." 14For by a single offering he has perfected for all time those who are sanctified. 15And the Holy Spirit also testifies to us, for after saying,

16   "This is the covenant that I will
          make with them
      after those days, says the Lord:
      I will put my laws in their hearts,
          and I will write them on their
              minds,"
17he also adds,
      "I will remember[b] their sins and
          their lawless deeds no
              more."
18Where there is forgiveness of these, there is no longer any offering for sin.

A Call to Persevere

19 Therefore, my friends,[c] since we have confidence to enter the sanctuary by the blood of Jesus, 20by the new and living way that he opened for us through the curtain (that is, through his flesh), 21and since we have a great priest over the house of God, 22let us approach with a true heart in full assurance of faith, with our hearts sprinkled clean from an evil conscience and our bodies washed with pure water. 23Let us hold fast to the confession of our hope without wavering, for he who has promised is faithful. 24And let us consider how to provoke one another to love and good deeds, 25not neglecting to meet together, as is the habit of some, but encouraging one another, and all the more as you see the Day approaching.

26 For if we willfully persist in sin after having received the knowledge of the truth, there no longer remains a sacrifice for sins, 27but a fearful prospect of judgment, and a fury of fire that will consume the adversaries. 28Anyone who has violated the law of Moses dies without mercy "on the testimony of two or three witnesses." 29How much worse punishment do you think will be deserved by those who have spurned the Son of God, profaned the blood of the covenant by which they were sanctified, and outraged the Spirit of grace? 30For we know the one who said, "Vengeance is mine, I will repay." And again, "The Lord will judge his people." 31It is a fearful thing to fall into the hands of the living God.

32 But recall those earlier days when, after you had been enlightened, you endured a hard struggle with sufferings, 33sometimes being publicly exposed to abuse and persecution, and sometimes being partners with those so treated. 34For you had compassion for those who were in prison, and you cheerfully accepted the plundering of your possessions, knowing that you yourselves possessed something better and more lasting. 35Do not, therefore, abandon that confidence of yours; it brings a great reward. 36For you need endurance, so that when you have done the will of God, you may receive what was promised. 37For yet
      "in a very little while,
          the one who is coming will come
              and will not delay;
38   but my righteous one will live by
          faith.
      My soul takes no pleasure in
          anyone who shrinks back."
39But we are not among those who shrink back and so are lost, but among those who have faith and so are saved.

The Meaning of Faith

11 Now faith is the assurance of things hoped for, the conviction of things not seen. 2Indeed, by faith[d] our ancestors received approval. 3By

z Gk by that will   a Gk this one   b Gk on their minds and I will remember   c Gk Therefore, brothers   d Gk by this faith we understand that the worlds were prepared by the word of God, so that what is seen was made from things that are not visible.*e*

The Examples of Abel, Enoch, and Noah

4 By faith Abel offered to God a more acceptable*f* sacrifice than Cain's. Through this he received approval as righteous, God himself giving approval to his gifts; he died, but through his faith*g* he still speaks. 5By faith Enoch was taken so that he did not experience death; and "he was not found, because God had taken him." For it was attested before he was taken away that "he had pleased God." 6And without faith it is impossible to please God, for whoever would approach him must believe that he exists and that he rewards those who seek him. 7By faith Noah, warned by God about events as yet unseen, respected the warning and built an ark to save his household; by this he condemned the world and became an heir to the righteousness that is in accordance with faith.

The Faith of Abraham

8 By faith Abraham obeyed when he was called to set out for a place that he was to receive as an inheritance; and he set out, not knowing where he was going. 9By faith he stayed for a time in the land he had been promised, as in a foreign land, living in tents, as did Isaac and Jacob, who were heirs with him of the same promise. 10For he looked forward to the city that has foundations, whose architect and builder is God. 11By faith he received power of procreation, even though he was too old—and Sarah herself was barren—because he considered him faithful who had promised.*h* 12Therefore from one person, and this one as good as dead, descendants were born, "as many as the stars of heaven and as the innumerable grains of sand by the seashore."

13 All of these died in faith without having received the promises, but from a distance they saw and greeted them. They confessed that they were strangers and foreigners on the earth, 14for people who speak in this way make it clear that they are seeking a homeland. 15If they had been thinking of the land that they had left behind, they would have had opportunity to return. 16But as it is, they desire a better country, that is, a heavenly one. Therefore God is not ashamed to be called their God; indeed, he has prepared a city for them.

17 By faith Abraham, when put to the test, offered up Isaac. He who had received the promises was ready to offer up his only son, 18of whom he had been told, "It is through Isaac that descendants shall be named for you." 19He considered the fact that God is able even to raise someone from the dead—and figuratively speaking, he did receive him back. 20By faith Isaac invoked blessings for the future on Jacob and Esau. 21By faith Jacob, when dying, blessed each of the sons of Joseph, "bowing in worship over the top of his staff." 22By faith Joseph, at the end of his life, made mention of the exodus of the Israelites and gave instructions about his burial.*i*

The Faith of Moses

23 By faith Moses was hidden by his parents for three months after his birth, because they saw that the child was beautiful; and they were not afraid of the king's edict.*j* 24By faith Moses, when he was grown up, refused to be called a son of Pharaoh's daughter, 25choosing rather to share ill-treatment with the people of

---

e Or *was not made out of visible things*   *f* Gk *greater*   *g* Gk *through it*   *h* Or *By faith Sarah herself, though barren, received power to conceive, even when she was too old, because she considered him faithful who had promised.*   *i* Gk *his bones*   *j* Other ancient authorities add *By faith Moses, when he was grown up, killed the Egyptian, because he observed the humiliation of his people* (Gk *brothers*)

God than to enjoy the fleeting pleasures of sin. 26He considered abuse suffered for the Christ[k] to be greater wealth than the treasures of Egypt, for he was looking ahead to the reward. 27By faith he left Egypt, unafraid of the king's anger; for he persevered as though[l] he saw him who is invisible. 28By faith he kept the Passover and the sprinkling of blood, so that the destroyer of the firstborn would not touch the firstborn of Israel.[m]

The Faith of Other Israelite Heroes

29 By faith the people passed through the Red Sea as if it were dry land, but when the Egyptians attempted to do so they were drowned. 30By faith the walls of Jericho fell after they had been encircled for seven days. 31By faith Rahab the prostitute did not perish with those who were disobedient,[n] because she had received the spies in peace.

32 And what more should I say? For time would fail me to tell of Gideon, Barak, Samson, Jephthah, of David and Samuel and the prophets— 33who through faith conquered kingdoms, administered justice, obtained promises, shut the mouths of lions, 34quenched raging fire, escaped the edge of the sword, won strength out of weakness, became mighty in war, put foreign armies to flight. 35Women received their dead by resurrection. Others were tortured, refusing to accept release, in order to obtain a better resurrection. 36Others suffered mocking and flogging, and even chains and imprisonment. 37They were stoned to death, they were sawn in two,[o] they were killed by the sword; they went about in skins of sheep and goats, destitute, persecuted, tormented— 38of whom the world was not worthy. They wandered in deserts and mountains, and in caves and holes in the ground.

39 Yet all these, though they were commended for their faith, did not receive what was promised, 40since God had provided something better so that they would not, apart from us, be made perfect.

The Example of Jesus

12 Therefore, since we are surrounded by so great a cloud of witnesses, let us also lay aside every weight and the sin that clings so closely,[p] and let us run with perseverance the race that is set before us, 2looking to Jesus the pioneer and perfecter of our faith, who for the sake of[q] the joy that was set before him endured the cross, disregarding its shame, and has taken his seat at the right hand of the throne of God.

3 Consider him who endured such hostility against himself from sinners,[r] so that you may not grow weary or lose heart. 4In your struggle against sin you have not yet resisted to the point of shedding your blood. 5And you have forgotten the exhortation that addresses you as children—

"My child, do not regard lightly the
    discipline of the Lord,
  or lose heart when you are
    punished by him;
6   for the Lord disciplines those
    whom he loves,
  and chastises every child whom
    he accepts."

7Endure trials for the sake of discipline. God is treating you as children; for what child is there whom a parent does not discipline? 8If you do not have that discipline in which all children share, then you are illegitimate and not his children. 9Moreover, we had human parents to discipline us, and we respected them. Should we not be even more willing to be subject to the Father of spirits and live? 10For they disciplined us for a short time as seemed best to them, but he disciplines us for our good, in order that we may share his holiness. 11Now, discipline always seems painful rather than pleasant at the time, but later it yields the peaceful fruit of righteousness to those who have been trained by it.

12 Therefore lift your drooping hands and strengthen your weak knees, 13and make straight paths for your feet, so that what is lame may not be put out of joint, but rather be healed.

---

k Or the Messiah   l Or because   m Gk would not touch them   n Or unbelieving   o Other ancient authorities add they were tempted   p Other ancient authorities read sin that easily distracts   q Or who instead of   r Other ancient authorities read such hostility from sinners against themselves

NOW IT IS OUR TURN
Cardinal John Henry Newman

VERSE: Hebrews 12.1   **PASSAGE:** Hebrews 12.1–3

 nce it was the apostles' turn. It was St. Paul's turn once. He had all cares upon him all at once; covered from head to foot with cares, as Job with sores. And, as if all this were not enough, he had a thorn in the flesh added—some personal discomfort ever with him. Yet he did his part well—he was as a strong and bold wrestler in his day, and at the close of it was able to say, "I have fought a good fight, I have finished my course, I have kept the faith" (2 Timothy 4.7, KJV). And after him, the excellent of the earth, the white-robed army of martyrs, and the cheerful company of confessors, each in his turn, each in his day, have likewise played the man. And so down to this very time, when faith has wellnigh failed, first one and then another have been called out to exhibit before the Great King. It is as though all of us were allowed to stand round his throne at once, and he called on first this man, and then that, to take up the chant by himself, each in his turn having to repeat the melody which his brethren have before gone through. Or as if we held a solemn dance to his honor in the courts of heaven, and each had by himself to perform some one and the same solemn and graceful movement at a signal given. Or as if it were some trial of strength or of agility, and, while the ring of bystanders beheld and applauded, we in succession, one by one, were actors in the pageant. Such is our state; angels are looking on, Christ has gone before—Christ has given us an example, that we may follow in his steps. He went through far more, infinitely more, than we can be called to suffer. Our brethren have gone through much more; and they seem to encourage us by their success, and to sympathize in our essay. Now it is our turn; and all ministering spirits keep silence and look on. O let not your foot slip, or your eye be false, or your ear dull, or your attention flagging!

ADDITIONAL SCRIPTURE READING:
John 13.15; 1 Peter 2.20–21

Go to page 1465 for your next devotional reading.

1700   1900

Warnings against Rejecting God's Grace

14 Pursue peace with everyone, and the holiness without which no one will see the Lord. ¹⁵See to it that no one fails to obtain the grace of God; that no root of bitterness springs up and causes trouble, and through it many become defiled. ¹⁶See to it that no one becomes like Esau, an immoral and godless person, who sold his birthright for a single meal. ¹⁷You know that later, when he wanted to inherit the blessing, he was rejected, for he found no chance to repent,ˢ even though he sought the blessingᵗ with tears.

18 You have not come to somethingᵘ that can be touched, a blazing fire, and darkness, and gloom, and a tempest, ¹⁹and the sound of a trumpet, and a voice whose words made the hearers beg that not another word be spoken to them. ²⁰(For they could not endure the order that was given, "If even an animal touches the mountain, it shall be stoned to death." ²¹Indeed, so terrifying was the sight that Moses said, "I tremble with fear.") ²²But you have come to Mount Zion and to the city of the living God, the heavenly Jerusalem, and to innumerable angels in festal gathering, ²³and to the assemblyᵛ of the firstborn who are enrolled in heaven, and to God the judge of all, and to the spirits of the righteous made perfect, ²⁴and to Jesus, the mediator of a new covenant, and to the sprinkled blood that speaks a better word than the blood of Abel.

25 See that you do not refuse the one who is speaking; for if they did not escape when they refused the one who warned them on earth, how much less will we escape if we reject the one who warns from heaven! ²⁶At that time his voice shook the earth; but now he has promised, "Yet once more I will shake not only the earth but also the heaven." ²⁷This phrase, "Yet once more," indicates the removal of what is shaken— that is, created things—so that what cannot be shaken may remain. ²⁸Therefore, since we are receiving a kingdom that cannot be shaken, let us give thanks, by which we offer to God an acceptable worship with reverence and awe; ²⁹for indeed our God is a consuming fire.

Service Well-Pleasing to God

13 Let mutual love continue. ²Do not neglect to show hospitality to strangers, for by doing that some have entertained angels without knowing it. ³Remember those who are in prison, as though you were in prison with them; those who are being tortured, as though you yourselves were being tortured.ʷ ⁴Let marriage be held in honor by all, and let the marriage bed be kept undefiled; for God will judge fornicators and adulterers. ⁵Keep your lives free from the love of money, and be content with what you have; for he has said, "I will never leave you or forsake you." ⁶So we can say with confidence,

"The Lord is my helper;
    I will not be afraid.
What can anyone do to me?"

7 Remember your leaders, those who spoke the word of God to you; consider the outcome of their way of life, and imitate their faith. ⁸Jesus Christ is the same yesterday and today and forever. ⁹Do not be carried away by all kinds of strange teachings; for it is well for the heart to be strengthened by grace, not by regulations about food,ˣ which have not benefited those who observe them. ¹⁰We have an altar from which those who officiate in the tentʸ have no right to eat. ¹¹For the bodies of those animals whose blood is brought into the sanctuary by the high priest as a sacrifice for sin are burned outside the camp. ¹²Therefore Jesus also suffered outside the city gate in order to sanctify the people by his own blood. ¹³Let us then go to him outside the camp and bear the abuse he endured. ¹⁴For here we have no lasting city, but we are looking for the city that is to come. ¹⁵Through him, then, let us continually offer a sacrifice of praise to God, that is, the fruit of lips that confess his name. ¹⁶Do not neglect to do good and to share what you have, for such sacrifices are pleasing to God.

---

s Or no chance to change his father's mind   t Gk it   u Other ancient authorities read a mountain
v Or angels, and to the festal gathering ²³and assembly   w Gk were in the body   x Gk not by
foods   y Or tabernacle

17 Obey your leaders and submit to them, for they are keeping watch over your souls and will give an account. Let them do this with joy and not with sighing—for that would be harmful to you.

18 Pray for us; we are sure that we have a clear conscience, desiring to act honorably in all things. 19I urge you all the more to do this, so that I may be restored to you very soon.

Benediction

20 Now may the God of peace, who brought back from the dead our Lord Jesus, the great shepherd of the sheep, by the blood of the eternal covenant, 21make you complete in everything good so that you may do his will, working among us[z] that which is pleasing in his sight, through Jesus Christ, to whom be the glory forever and ever. Amen.

Final Exhortation and Greetings

22 I appeal to you, brothers and sisters,[a] bear with my word of exhortation, for I have written to you briefly. 23I want you to know that our brother Timothy has been set free; and if he comes in time, he will be with me when I see you. 24Greet all your leaders and all the saints. Those from Italy send you greetings. 25Grace be with all of you.[b]

JAMES

THE AUTHOR OF THIS LETTER IDEN-
TIFIES HIMSELF AS JAMES, PROBABLY
THE BROTHER OF JESUS AND THE
LEADER OF THE JERUSALEM COUNCIL. THE
BOOK OF JAMES HAS A DISTINCTIVELY JEWISH
NATURE THAT SUGGESTS IT WAS COMPOSED
WHEN THE CHURCH WAS STILL PREDOMI-
NANTLY JEWISH. THE LETTER DEALS PRIMAR-
ILY WITH THE PRACTICAL ASPECTS OF THE
CHRISTIAN FAITH, CONSISTING OF HARD-
HITTING COUNSEL FOR EVERYDAY CONDUCT.

Salutation

1 James, a servant*a* of God and of
the Lord Jesus Christ,
To the twelve tribes in the Dispersion:
Greetings.

Faith and Wisdom

2 My brothers and sisters,*b* whenever
you face trials of any kind, consider it

ADVERSITIES DO NOT MAKE A MAN FRAIL; THEY
SHOW WHAT SORT OF MAN HE IS.

—*Thomas à Kempis*

---

nothing but joy, ³because you know that
the testing of your faith produces endurance; ⁴and let endurance have its full

effect, so that you may be mature and
complete, lacking in nothing.

5 If any of you is lacking in wisdom,
ask God, who gives to all generously and
ungrudgingly, and it will be given you.
⁶But ask in faith, never doubting, for the
one who doubts is like a wave of the sea,
driven and tossed by the wind; ⁷, ⁸for the
doubter, being double-minded and unstable in every way, must not expect to
receive anything from the Lord.

Poverty and Riches

9 Let the believer*c* who is lowly boast
in being raised up, ¹⁰and the rich in
being brought low, because the rich will
disappear like a flower in the field. ¹¹For
the sun rises with its scorching heat and
withers the field; its flower falls, and its

a Gk *slave*   *b* Gk *brothers*   *c* Gk *brother*

beauty perishes. It is the same way with the rich; in the midst of a busy life, they will wither away.

Trial and Temptation

12 Blessed is anyone who endures temptation. Such a one has stood the test and will receive the crown of life that the Lord[d] has promised to those who love him. [13]No one, when tempted, should say, "I am being tempted by God"; for God cannot be tempted by evil and he himself tempts no one. [14]But one is tempted by one's own desire, being lured and enticed by it; [15]then, when that desire has conceived, it gives birth to sin, and that sin, when it is fully grown, gives birth to death. [16]Do not be deceived, my beloved.[e]

17 Every generous act of giving, with every perfect gift, is from above, coming down from the Father of lights, with whom there is no variation or shadow due to change.[f] [18]In fulfillment of his own purpose he gave us birth by the word of truth, so that we would become a kind of first fruits of his creatures.

Hearing and Doing the Word

19 You must understand this, my beloved:[e] let everyone be quick to listen, slow to speak, slow to anger; [20]for your anger does not produce God's righteousness. [21]Therefore rid yourselves of all sordidness and rank growth of wickedness, and welcome with meekness the implanted word that has the power to save your souls.

ANGER IS A WEED; HATE IS THE TREE.

—Augustine

---

22 But be doers of the word, and not merely hearers who deceive themselves. [23]For if any are hearers of the word and not doers, they are like those who look at themselves[g] in a mirror; [24]for they look at themselves and, on going away, immediately forget what they were like. [25]But those who look into the perfect law, the law of liberty, and persevere, being not hearers who forget but doers who act—they will be blessed in their doing.

26 If any think they are religious, and do not bridle their tongues but deceive their hearts, their religion is worthless. [27]Religion that is pure and undefiled before God, the Father, is this: to care for orphans and widows in their distress, and to keep oneself unstained by the world.

Warning against Partiality

2 My brothers and sisters,[h] do you with your acts of favoritism really believe in our glorious Lord Jesus Christ?[i] [2]For if a person with gold rings and in fine clothes comes into your assembly, and if a poor person in dirty clothes also comes in, [3]and if you take notice of the one wearing the fine clothes and say, "Have a seat here, please," while to the one who is poor you say, "Stand there," or, "Sit at my feet,"[j] [4]have you not made distinctions among yourselves, and become judges with evil thoughts? [5]Listen, my beloved brothers and sisters.[k] Has not God chosen the poor in the world to be rich in faith and to be heirs of the kingdom that he has promised to those who love him? [6]But you have dishonored the poor. Is it not the rich who oppress you? Is it not they who drag you into court? [7]Is it not they who blaspheme the excellent name that was invoked over you?

8 You do well if you really fulfill the royal law according to the scripture, "You shall love your neighbor as yourself." [9]But if you show partiality, you commit sin and are convicted by the law as transgressors. [10]For whoever keeps the whole law but fails in one point has become accountable for all of it. [11]For the one who said, "You shall not commit adultery," also said, "You shall not murder." Now if you do not commit adultery but if you murder, you have become a transgressor of the law. [12]So speak and so act as those who are to be judged by the law of liberty. [13]For judgment will be without mercy to anyone

---

d Gk he; other ancient authorities read *God*   e Gk *my beloved brothers*   f Other ancient authorities read *variation due to a shadow of turning*   g Gk *at the face of his birth*   h Gk *My brothers*   i Or *hold the faith of our glorious Lord Jesus Christ without acts of favoritism*   j Gk *Sit under my footstool*   k Gk *brothers*

GOD'S WORD IS TALKING TO ME
Søren Kierkegaard

VERSE: James 1.23–24   **PASSAGE:** James 1.22–25

hat is required in order to look at oneself with true blessing in the mirror of the Word?

The first requirement is that you do not look at the mirror, in order to inspect it, but that you look at yourself in the mirror . . . If there were only a single passage in the Bible which you understood—well, that is your first concern. You need not sit down and ponder over the obscure passages. God's Word is given in order that you may act according to it, not in order that you may practice the interpretation of what you find obscure . . . The second requirement is that, in order to see yourself in the mirror when you read God's Word, you must remember to be constantly saying to yourself, "It is speaking to me; I am the one it is talking about" . . . If God's Word is only a doctrine to you, it is no mirror. It is just as impossible to be mirrored in a doctrine as in a wall . . . No, when you read God's Word, you must constantly be saying to yourself, "It is talking to me, and about me." Finally, if you desire to observe yourself in the mirror of the Word with real blessing, you must not at once begin to forget how you looked. You must not be the forgetful hearer (or reader) of whom the apostle says that he carefully looked at his own face in a mirror and straightway forgot what manner of man he was . . . The right thing to do is to say to yourself at once: "I shall begin now to prevent myself from forgetting. Now, this very moment, I make this promise to myself and to God, even if it be but for the next hour or for today. For that length of time it shall be certain that I do not forget" . . . Doing it this way is much better than taking too big a bite to begin with, and saying "I shall never forget." It is much better never to forget to remember immediately than immediately to say that you will never forget.

ADDITIONAL SCRIPTURE READING:
Hebrews 4.12; 2 Timothy 2.1–19

Go to page 1467 for your next devotional reading.

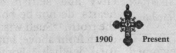

1900   Present

who has shown no mercy; mercy triumphs over judgment.

TEACH ME TO FEEL ANOTHER'S WOE,

TO HIDE THE FAULT I SEE;

THAT MERCY I TO OTHERS SHOW,

THAT MERCY SHOWN TO ME.

—*Alexander Pope*

Faith without Works Is Dead

14 What good is it, my brothers and sisters,[1] if you say you have faith but do not have works? Can faith save you? 15If a brother or sister is naked and lacks daily food, 16and one of you says to them, "Go in peace; keep warm and eat your fill," and yet you do not supply their bodily needs, what is the good of that? 17So faith by itself, if it has no works, is dead.

18 But someone will say, "You have faith and I have works." Show me your faith apart from your works, and I by my works will show you my faith. 19You believe that God is one; you do well. Even the demons believe—and shudder. 20Do you want to be shown, you senseless person, that faith apart from works is barren? 21Was not our ancestor Abraham justified by works when he offered his son Isaac on the altar? 22You see that faith was active along with his works, and faith was brought to completion by the works. 23Thus the scripture was fulfilled that says, "Abraham believed God, and it was reckoned to him as righteousness," and he was called the friend of God. 24You see that a person is justified by works and not by faith alone. 25Likewise, was not Rahab the prostitute also

---

MANY CAN SPEAK WELL, BUT FEW CAN DO WELL.
WE ARE BETTER SCHOLARS IN THE THEORY THAN
THE PRACTICE PART, BUT HE IS A TRUE CHRISTIAN
THAT IS PROFICIENT IN BOTH.   —*Anne Bradstreet*

---

justified by works when she welcomed the messengers and sent them out by another road? 26For just as the body without the spirit is dead, so faith without works is also dead.

Taming the Tongue

3 Not many of you should become teachers, my brothers and sisters,[1] for you know that we who teach will be judged with greater strictness. 2For all of us make many mistakes. Anyone who makes no mistakes in speaking is perfect, able to keep the whole body in check with a bridle. 3If we put bits into the mouths of horses to make them obey us, we guide their whole bodies. 4Or look at ships: though they are so large that it takes strong winds to drive them, yet they are guided by a very small rudder wherever the will of the pilot directs. 5So also the tongue is a small member, yet it boasts of great exploits.

How great a forest is set ablaze by a small fire! 6And the tongue is a fire. The tongue is placed among our members as a world of iniquity; it stains the whole body, sets on fire the cycle of nature,[m] and is itself set on fire by hell.[n] 7For every species of beast and bird, of reptile and sea creature, can be tamed and has been tamed by the human species, 8but no one can tame the tongue—a restless evil, full of deadly poison. 9With it we bless the Lord and Father, and with it we curse those who are made in the likeness of God. 10From the same mouth come blessing and cursing. My brothers and sisters,[o] this ought not to be so. 11Does a spring pour forth from the same opening both fresh and brackish water? 12Can a fig tree, my brothers and sisters,[p] yield olives, or a grapevine figs? No more can salt water yield fresh.

Two Kinds of Wisdom

13 Who is wise and understanding among you? Show by your good life that your works are done with gentleness born of wisdom. 14But if you have bitter envy and selfish ambition in your hearts, do not be boastful and false to the truth. 15Such wisdom does not come down from above, but is earthly, unspiritual, devilish. 16For where there is envy and selfish ambition, there will also be disorder and wickedness of every kind. 17But the wisdom from above is first pure, then peaceable, gentle, willing to

---

l Gk *brothers*   *m* Or *wheel of birth*   *n* Gk *Gehenna*   *o* Gk *My brothers*   *p* Gk *my brothers*

WHO SHALL CONVERT ME?

John Wesley

VERSE: James 2.18   **PASSAGE:** James 2.14–19

went to America, to convert the Indians; but O! who shall convert me? who, what is he that will deliver me from this evil heart of mischief? I have a fair summer religion. I can talk well; nay, and believe myself, while no danger is near; but let death look me in the face, and my spirit is troubled. Nor can I say, "To die is gain!" (see Philippians 1.21).

> I have a sin of fear, that when I've spun
> My last thread, I shall perish on the shore!

I think, verily, if the gospel be true, I am safe: for I not only have given, and do give, all my goods to feed the poor; I not only give my body to be burned, drowned, or whatever God shall appoint for me; but I follow after charity (though not as I ought, yet as I can), if haply I may attain it. I now believe the gospel is true. "I show my faith by my works," by staking my all upon it. I would do so again and again a thousand times, if the choice were still to make.

Whoever sees me, sees I would be a Christian. Therefore "are my ways not like other men's ways." Therefore I have been, I am, I am content to be, "a by-word, a proverb of reproach." But in a storm I think, "What, if the gospel be not true? Then thou art of all men most foolish. For what hast thou given thy goods, thy ease, thy friends, thy reputation, thy country, thy life? For what art thou wandering over the face of the earth?—A dream! a cunningly-devised fable!"

O! who will deliver me from this fear of death? What shall I do? Where shall I fly from it? Should I fight against it by thinking, or by not thinking of it? A wise man advised me some time since, "Be still and go on." Perhaps this is the best, to look upon it as my cross; when it comes, to let it humble me, and quicken all my good resolutions, especially that of praying without ceasing; and at other times, to take no thought about it, but quietly to go on "in the work of the Lord."

ADDITIONAL SCRIPTURE READING:
1 Corinthians 15.58; Ephesians 6.18

Go to page 1469 for your next devotional reading.

1700   1900

yield, full of mercy and good fruits, without a trace of partiality or hypocrisy. [18]And a harvest of righteousness is sown in peace for[q] those who make peace.

Friendship with the World

4 Those conflicts and disputes among you, where do they come from? Do they not come from your cravings that are at war within you? [2]You want something and do not have it; so you commit murder. And you covet[r] something and cannot obtain it; so you engage in disputes and conflicts. You do not have, because you do not ask. [3]You ask and do not receive, because you ask wrongly, in order to spend what you get on your pleasures. [4]Adulterers! Do you not know that friendship with the world is enmity with God? Therefore whoever wishes to be a friend of the world becomes an enemy of God. [5]Or do you suppose that it is for nothing that the scripture says, "God[s] yearns jealously for the spirit that he has made to dwell in us"? [6]But he gives all the more grace; therefore it says,

"God opposes the proud,
        but gives grace to the humble."

[7]Submit yourselves therefore to God. Resist the devil, and he will flee from you. [8]Draw near to God, and he will draw near to you. Cleanse your hands, you sinners, and purify your hearts, you double-minded. [9]Lament and mourn and weep. Let your laughter be turned into mourning and your joy into dejection. [10]Humble yourselves before the Lord, and he will exalt you.

Warning against Judging Another

11 Do not speak evil against one another, brothers and sisters.[t] Whoever speaks evil against another or judges another, speaks evil against the law and judges the law; but if you judge the law, you are not a doer of the law but a judge. [12]There is one lawgiver and judge who is able to save and to destroy. So who, then, are you to judge your neighbor?

Boasting about Tomorrow

13 Come now, you who say, "Today or tomorrow we will go to such and such a town and spend a year there, doing business and making money." [14]Yet you do not even know what tomorrow will bring. What is your life? For you are a mist that appears for a little while and then vanishes. [15]Instead you ought to say, "If the Lord wishes, we will live and do this or that." [16]As it is, you boast in your arrogance; all such boasting is evil. [17]Anyone, then, who knows the right thing to do and fails to do it, commits sin.

I READ MY BIBLE TO KNOW WHAT PEOPLE OUGHT TO DO, AND MY NEWSPAPER TO KNOW WHAT THEY ARE DOING.   —*John Henry Newman*

Warning to Rich Oppressors

5 Come now, you rich people, weep and wail for the miseries that are coming to you. [2]Your riches have rotted, and your clothes are moth-eaten. [3]Your gold and silver have rusted, and their rust will be evidence against you, and it will eat your flesh like fire. You have laid up treasure[u] for the last days. [4]Listen! The wages of the laborers who mowed your fields, which you kept back by fraud, cry out, and the cries of the harvesters have reached the ears of the Lord of hosts. [5]You have lived on the earth in luxury and in pleasure; you have fattened your hearts in a day of slaughter. [6]You have condemned and murdered the righteous one, who does not resist you.

Patience in Suffering

7 Be patient, therefore, beloved,[t] until the coming of the Lord. The farmer waits for the precious crop from the earth, being patient with it until it receives the early and the late rains. [8]You also must be patient. Strengthen your hearts, for the coming of the Lord is near.[v] [9]Beloved,[w] do not grumble against one another, so that you may not be judged. See, the Judge is standing at the doors! [10]As an example of suffering and patience, beloved,[t] take the prophets who spoke in the name of the

---

q Or *by*   *r* Or *you murder and you covet*   *s* Gk *He*   *t* Gk *brothers*   *u* Or *will eat your flesh, since you have stored up fire*   *v* Or *is at hand*   *w* Gk *Brothers*

WHERE, FOR WHOM, AND AT WHAT TIME WE OUGHT TO PRAY
John Knox

VERSE: James 5.16   **PASSAGE:** James 5.13–18

rivate prayer, such as men offer by themselves to God in secret, does not require any special place. Jesus Christ, indeed, commands us when we pray to enter into our chamber and close the door, and so to pray secretly unto our Father (see Matthew 6.6). By this he means that we should choose for our prayers such places as will offer least distraction; and also that in our times of prayer we should expel from our minds all vain thoughts. Otherwise, Jesus Christ himself observed no special place of prayer; for we find him sometimes praying on the Mount of Olives, sometimes in the desert, sometimes in the temple, and also in the Garden of Gethsemane. Peter prayed on a housetop; Paul prayed in prison and was heard of God; and he commands men to pray in all places, lifting up to God pure and clean hands, as we find that the prophets and other holy men did, whenever danger or necessity might require.

But public prayers should be made in places appointed for the assembling of Christians; and it is inexcusable willfully to absent oneself from these exercises of worship. I do not mean that to be absent from that particular place is sinful, because that place is more holy than any other; for the whole earth which God has created is equally holy. But the promise clearly made that, "For where two or three are gathered together in my name, there am I in the midst of them" (Matthew 18.20, KJV), condemns all those who neglect to join the congregation gathered in his name.

To be gathered in the name of Jesus Christ means this, to praise and magnify God, the Father, for the infinite blessings which he has given by his only Son, our Lord . . . Within such a congregation common prayers should be offered such as all men who hear may understand, that the hearts of all, joining with the voice of one, might unfeignedly and fervently say, "Amen!"

ADDITIONAL SCRIPTURE READING:
Matthew 6.6; Acts 4.31

Go to page 1473 for your next devotional reading.

1500   1700

Lord. ¹¹Indeed we call blessed those who showed endurance. You have heard of the endurance of Job, and you have seen the purpose of the Lord, how the Lord is compassionate and merciful.

12 Above all, my beloved,ˣ do not swear, either by heaven or by earth or by any other oath, but let your "Yes" be yes and your "No" be no, so that you may not fall under condemnation.

The Prayer of Faith

13 Are any among you suffering? They should pray. Are any cheerful?

TROUBLE AND PERPLEXITY DRIVE ME TO PRAYER AND PRAYER DRIVES AWAY PERPLEXITY AND TROUBLE.   —*Philip Melanchthon*

They should sing songs of praise. ¹⁴Are any among you sick? They should call for the elders of the church and have them pray over them, anointing them with oil in the name of the Lord. ¹⁵The prayer of faith will save the sick, and the Lord will raise them up; and anyone who has committed sins will be forgiven. ¹⁶Therefore confess your sins to one another, and pray for one another, so that you may be healed. The prayer of the righteous is powerful and effective. ¹⁷Elijah was a human being like us, and he prayed fervently that it might not rain, and for three years and six months it did not rain on the earth. ¹⁸Then he prayed again, and the heaven gave rain and the earth yielded its harvest.

19 My brothers and sisters,ʸ if anyone among you wanders from the truth and is brought back by another, ²⁰you should know that whoever brings back a sinner from wandering will save the sinner'sᶻ soul from death and will cover a multitude of sins.

1 PETER

HE RECIPIENTS OF THIS LETTER HAD BEEN SUFFERING VARIOUS TRIALS AND AFFLICTIONS, WITH THE THREAT OF MORE SEVERE DIFFICULTIES BEING VERY REAL. PETER TOUCHES ON VARIOUS DOCTRINES AND HAS MUCH TO SAY ABOUT CHRISTIAN LIFE AND DUTIES. 1 PETER HAS BEEN CHARACTERIZED AS A LETTER OF SUFFERING AND PERSECUTION, OF SUFFERING AND GLORY, OF HOPE AND COURAGE. NO OTHER NEW TESTAMENT BOOK SO REFLECTS THE REAL NATURE AND EFFECT OF GOD'S LOVE IN JESUS CHRIST.

Salutation

1 Peter, an apostle of Jesus Christ, To the exiles of the Dispersion in Pontus, Galatia, Cappadocia, Asia, and Bithynia, ²who have been chosen and destined by God the Father and sanctified by the Spirit to be obedient to Jesus Christ and to be sprinkled with his blood:

May grace and peace be yours in abundance.

A Living Hope

3 Blessed be the God and Father of our Lord Jesus Christ! By his great mercy he has given us a new birth into a living hope through the resurrection of Jesus Christ from the dead, ⁴and into an inheritance that is imperishable, undefiled, and unfading, kept in heaven for you, ⁵who are being protected by the power of God through faith for a salvation ready to be revealed in the last

TRIALS ARE MEDICINES WHICH OUR GRACIOUS AND WISE PHYSICIAN PRESCRIBES BECAUSE WE NEED THEM; AND HE PROPORTIONS THE FREQUENCY AND WEIGHT OF THEM TO WHAT THE CASE REQUIRES. LET US TRUST IN HIS SKILL AND THANK HIM FOR HIS PRESCRIPTION.

—John Newton

time. ⁶In this you rejoice,ᵃ even if now for a little while you have had to suffer various trials, ⁷so that the genuineness

ᵃ Or *Rejoice in this*

of your faith—being more precious than gold that, though perishable, is tested by fire—may be found to result in praise and glory and honor when Jesus Christ is revealed. 8Although you have not seen[b] him, you love him; and even though you do not see him now, you believe in him and rejoice with an indescribable and glorious joy, 9for you are receiving the outcome of your faith, the salvation of your souls.

10 Concerning this salvation, the prophets who prophesied of the grace that was to be yours made careful search and inquiry, 11inquiring about the person or time that the Spirit of Christ within them indicated when it testified in advance to the sufferings destined for Christ and the subsequent glory. 12It was revealed to them that they were serving not themselves but you, in regard to the things that have now been announced to you through those who brought you good news by the Holy Spirit sent from heaven—things into which angels long to look!

A Call to Holy Living

13 Therefore prepare your minds for action;[c] discipline yourselves; set all your hope on the grace that Jesus Christ will bring you when he is revealed. 14Like obedient children, do not be conformed to the desires that you formerly had in ignorance. 15Instead, as he who called you is holy, be holy yourselves in all your conduct; 16for it is written, "You shall be holy, for I am holy."

AS MAN BECOMES HOLY, JUST, MERCIFUL, PATIENT, . . . BY THE COPY HE WILL KNOW THE ORIGINAL, AND BY THE WORKMANSHIP IN HIMSELF HE WILL BE ACQUAINTED WITH THE HOLY WORKMAN.

—*William Penn*

---

17 If you invoke as Father the one who judges all people impartially according to their deeds, live in reverent fear during the time of your exile. 18You know that you were ransomed from the futile ways inherited from your ances-

tors, not with perishable things like silver or gold, 19but with the precious blood of Christ, like that of a lamb without defect or blemish. 20He was destined before the foundation of the world, but was revealed at the end of the ages for your sake. 21Through him you have come to trust in God, who raised him from the dead and gave him glory, so that your faith and hope are set on God.

22 Now that you have purified your souls by your obedience to the truth[d] so that you have genuine mutual love, love one another deeply[e] from the heart.[f] 23You have been born anew, not of perishable but of imperishable seed, through the living and enduring word of God.[g] 24For

"All flesh is like grass
   and all its glory like the flower of
      grass.
The grass withers,
   and the flower falls,
25   but the word of the Lord endures
      forever."

That word is the good news that was announced to you.

The Living Stone and a Chosen People

2 Rid yourselves, therefore, of all malice, and all guile, insincerity, envy, and all slander. 2Like newborn infants, long for the pure, spiritual milk, so that by it you may grow into salvation— 3if indeed you have tasted that the Lord is good.

4 Come to him, a living stone, though rejected by mortals yet chosen and precious in God's sight, and 5like living stones, let yourselves be built[h] into a spiritual house, to be a holy priesthood, to offer spiritual sacrifices acceptable to God through Jesus Christ. 6For it stands in scripture:

"See, I am laying in Zion a stone,
   a cornerstone chosen and
      precious;
and whoever believes in him[i] will
   not be put to shame."

7To you then who believe, he is precious; but for those who do not believe,

---

b Other ancient authorities read *known*   c Gk *gird up the loins of your mind*   d Other ancient authorities add *through the Spirit*   e Or *constantly*   f Other ancient authorities read *a pure heart*   g Or *through the word of the living and enduring God*   h Or *you yourselves are being built*   i Or *it*

"The stone that the builders
rejected
has become the very head of the
corner,"
8and
"A stone that makes them stumble,

and a rock that makes them
fall."
They stumble because they disobey the
word, as they were destined to do.
9 But you are a chosen race, a royal
priesthood, a holy nation, God's own

FRIDAY

FROM THE AGONY OF CHRISTIANITY
Miguel de Unamuno

VERSE: 1 Peter 2.17   PASSAGE: 1 Peter 2.13–17

 hat is all this talk about social Christianity? What is all this noise about the social kingdom of Christ . . . and what about the much-heralded Christian democracy? . . .

Those who persecuted Christ in order to destroy him agreed among themselves to ask him whether it was lawful to pay tribute to Caesar, the invader, the enemy of the Jewish fatherland, who represented political authority. If he answered in the affirmative, they would then picture him to the people as a bad Jew, as a bad patriot; and if he answered in the negative, they would accuse him of sedition in the face of the imperial authorities. Once the question had been posed, Jesus asked for a piece of money, and, pointing to the image depicted on the coin, he inquired, "Whose picture is this?" "Caesar's," they replied. And then he said, "Very well: give to Caesar what is Caesar's, and to God what is God's." The meaning is clear: give to Caesar, to this world, to society, the money which belongs to Caesar, to the world, to society; and to God give the soul which is destined to rise with its body. Christ thus detached himself from every problem of social economy; the same Christ who said that it is more difficult for a rich man to enter into the kingdom of heaven than for a camel to pass through the eye of a needle (see Matthew 19.24); and he showed clearly that his glad tidings have nothing to do with socio-economical or national questions, nothing to do with democracy or international demagogy, nothing to do with nationalism.

ADDITIONAL SCRIPTURE READING:
Luke 20.25; John 18.36

Go to page 1475 for your next devotional reading.

1900   Present

people,[j] in order that you may proclaim the mighty acts of him who called you out of darkness into his marvelous light. 10 Once you were not a people,
but now you are God's people;
once you had not received mercy,
but now you have received mercy.

Live as Servants of God

11 Beloved, I urge you as aliens and exiles to abstain from the desires of the flesh that wage war against the soul. 12Conduct yourselves honorably among the Gentiles, so that, though they malign you as evildoers, they may see your honorable deeds and glorify God when he comes to judge.[k]

13 For the Lord's sake accept the authority of every human institution,[l] whether of the emperor as supreme, 14or of governors, as sent by him to punish those who do wrong and to praise those who do right. 15For it is God's will that by doing right you should silence the ignorance of the foolish. 16As servants[m] of God, live as free people, yet do not use your freedom as a pretext for evil. 17Honor everyone. Love the family of believers.[n] Fear God. Honor the emperor.

THE CHRISTIAN LIFE WAS NOT MEANT TO LIVE IN A SOLITUDE FOREVER, NOR IS IT SUITED TO IT. IT IS A SOCIAL LIFE. ALL ITS MOVEMENTS SUGGEST AND PROPHESY A BROTHERHOOD. THAT BROTHERHOOD OF BELIEVERS IS THE CHRISTIAN CHURCH.   —*Phillips Brooks*

The Example of Christ's Suffering

18 Slaves, accept the authority of your masters with all deference, not only those who are kind and gentle but also those who are harsh. 19For it is a credit to you if, being aware of God, you endure pain while suffering unjustly. 20If you endure when you are beaten for doing wrong, what credit is that? But if you endure when you do right and suffer for it, you have God's approval. 21For to this you have been called, because Christ also suffered for you, leaving you

an example, so that you should follow in his steps.
22   "He committed no sin,
        and no deceit was found in his mouth."
23When he was abused, he did not return abuse; when he suffered, he did not threaten; but he entrusted himself to the one who judges justly. 24He himself bore our sins in his body on the cross,[o] so that, free from sins, we might live for righteousness; by his wounds[p] you have been healed. 25For you were going astray like sheep, but now you have returned to the shepherd and guardian of your souls.

Wives and Husbands

3 Wives, in the same way, accept the authority of your husbands, so that, even if some of them do not obey the word, they may be won over without a word by their wives' conduct, 2when they see the purity and reverence of your lives. 3Do not adorn yourselves outwardly by braiding your hair, and by wearing gold ornaments or fine clothing; 4rather, let your adornment be the inner self with the lasting beauty of a gentle and quiet spirit, which is very precious in God's sight. 5It was in this way long ago that the holy women who hoped in God used to adorn themselves by accepting the authority of their husbands. 6Thus Sarah obeyed Abraham and called him lord. You have become her daughters as long as you do what is good and never let fears alarm you.

7 Husbands, in the same way, show consideration for your wives in your life together, paying honor to the woman as the weaker sex,[q] since they too are also heirs of the gracious gift of life—so that nothing may hinder your prayers.

Suffering for Doing Right

8 Finally, all of you, have unity of spirit, sympathy, love for one another, a tender heart, and a humble mind. 9Do not repay evil for evil or abuse for abuse; but, on the contrary, repay with a blessing. It is for this that you were called— that you might inherit a blessing. 10For

---

j Gk *a people for his possession*   *k* Gk *God on the day of visitation*   *l* Or *every institution ordained for human beings*   *m* Gk *slaves*   *n* Gk *Love the brotherhood*   *o* Or *carried up our sins in his body to the tree*   *p* Gk *bruise*   *q* Gk *vessel*

WEEKEND

STANDING BY THE SEA
Søren Kierkegaard

VERSE: Matthew 10.31   **PASSAGE:** Matthew 10.29–31

t has always been one of my favorite places. As I stood there one quiet evening as the sea struck up its song with a deep and calm solemnity, whilst my eye met not a single sail on the vast expanse of water, and the sea set bounds to the heavens, and the heavens to the sea; whilst on the other side the busy noise of life subsided and the birds sang their evening prayer . . . and the hoarse screech of the gulls reminded me that I stood alone, and everything vanished before my eyes, and I turned back with a heavy heart to mix in the busy world, yet without forgetting such blessed moments . . .

As I stood there alone and forsaken, and the power of the sea and the battle of the elements reminded me of my own nothingness, and on the other hand the sure flight of the birds recalled the words spoken by Christ: "Not a sparrow shall fall to the ground without your Father knowing" (see Matthew 10.29): then all at once I felt how great and how small I was; then did those two mighty forces, pride and humility, happily unite in friendship. Lucky is the man to whom *that* is possible at every moment of his life; in whose breast those two factors have not only come to an agreement but have joined hands and been wedded . . . His life will flow on peacefully and quietly and he will neither drain the intoxicating cup of pride nor the bitter chalice of despair. He has found what the great philosopher . . . desired, but did not find: that Archimedean point from which he could lift the whole world, the point which for that very reason must lie outside the world, outside the limitations of time and space.

ADDITIONAL SCRIPTURE READING:
Psalm 19.1–4; James 3.13

Go to page 1477 for your next devotional reading.

1700   1900

"Those who desire life
and desire to see good days,
let them keep their tongues from evil
and their lips from speaking deceit;
11 let them turn away from evil and do good;
let them seek peace and pursue it.
12 For the eyes of the Lord are on the righteous,
and his ears are open to their prayer.
But the face of the Lord is against those who do evil."

13 Now who will harm you if you are eager to do what is good? 14But even if you do suffer for doing what is right, you are blessed. Do not fear what they fear,[r] and do not be intimidated, 15but in your hearts sanctify Christ as Lord. Always be ready to make your defense to anyone who demands from you an accounting for the hope that is in you; 16yet do it with gentleness and reverence.[s] Keep your conscience clear, so that, when you are maligned, those who abuse you for your good conduct in Christ may be put to shame. 17For it is better to suffer for doing good, if suffering should be God's will, than to suffer for doing evil. 18For Christ also suffered[t] for sins once for all, the righteous for the unrighteous, in order to bring you[u] to God. He was put to death in the flesh, but made alive in the spirit, 19in which also he went and made a proclamation to the spirits in prison, 20who in former times did not obey, when God waited patiently in the days of Noah, during the building of the ark, in which a few, that is, eight persons, were saved through water. 21And baptism, which this prefigured, now saves you—not as a removal of dirt from the body, but as an appeal to God for[v] a good conscience, through the resurrection of Jesus Christ, 22who has gone into heaven and is at the right hand of God, with angels, authorities, and powers made subject to him.

Good Stewards of God's Grace

4 Since therefore Christ suffered in the flesh,[w] arm yourselves also with the same intention (for whoever has suffered in the flesh has finished with sin), 2so as to live for the rest of your earthly life[x] no longer by human desires but by the will of God. 3You have already spent enough time in doing what the Gentiles like to do, living in licentiousness, passions, drunkenness, revels, carousing, and lawless idolatry. 4They are surprised that you no longer join them in the same excesses of dissipation, and so they blaspheme.[y] 5But they will have to give an accounting to him who stands ready to judge the living and the dead. 6For this is the reason the gospel was proclaimed even to the dead, so that, though they had been judged in the flesh as everyone is judged, they might live in the spirit as God does.

7 The end of all things is near;[z] therefore be serious and discipline yourselves for the sake of your prayers. 8Above all, maintain constant love for one another, for love covers a multitude of sins. 9Be hospitable to one another without complaining. 10Like good stewards of the manifold grace of God, serve one another with whatever gift each of you has received. 11Whoever speaks must do so as one speaking the very words of God; whoever serves must do so with the strength that God supplies, so that God may be glorified in all things through Jesus Christ. To him belong the glory and the power forever and ever. Amen.

Suffering as a Christian

12 Beloved, do not be surprised at the fiery ordeal that is taking place among you to test you, as though something strange were happening to you. 13But rejoice insofar as you are sharing Christ's sufferings, so that you may also be glad and shout for joy when his glory is revealed. 14If you are reviled for the name of Christ, you are blessed, because the spirit of glory,[a] which is the Spirit of God, is resting on you.[b] 15But let none of

r Gk their fear   s Or respect   t Other ancient authorities read died   u Other ancient authorities read us   v Or a pledge to God from   w Other ancient authorities add for us; others, for you   x Gk rest of the time in the flesh   y Or they malign you   z Or is at hand   a Other ancient authorities add and of power   b Other ancient authorities add On their part he is blasphemed, but on your part he is glorified

you suffer as a murderer, a thief, a criminal, or even as a mischief maker. [16]Yet
if any of you suffers as a Christian, do
not consider it a disgrace, but glorify
God because you bear this name. [17]For
the time has come for judgment to begin
with the household of God; if it begins
with us, what will be the end for those
who do not obey the gospel of God?
[18]And

> "If it is hard for the righteous to be
> saved,

MONDAY

A BRANCH OF BLESSEDNESS
John Newton

VERSE: 1 Peter 5.7   **PASSAGE:** 1 Peter 5.6–11

lessedness is a power of reposing ourselves and our
concerns upon the Lord's faithfulness and care, and
may be considered in two respects: a reliance upon
him that he will surely provide for us, guide us, protect
us, be our help in trouble, our shield in danger, so that, however
poor, weak, and defenseless in ourselves, we may rejoice in his
all-sufficiency as our own; and further, in consequence of this, a
peaceful, humble submission to his will under all events which,
upon their first impression, are contrary to our own views and
desires. Surely, in a world like this, where every thing is uncertain, where we are exposed to trials on every hand, and know not
but a single hour may bring forth something painful, yea dreadful, to our natural sensations, there can be no blessedness but so
far as we are thus enabled to entrust and resign all to the direction and faithfulness of the Lord our Shepherd. For want of more
of this spirit multitudes of professing Christians perplex and
wound themselves and dishonor their high calling by continual
anxieties, alarms, and complaints. They think nothing safe
under the Lord's keeping unless their own eye is likewise upon
it, and are seldom satisfied with any of his dispensations: for
though he gratify their desires in nine instances, a refusal in the
tenth spoils the relish of all, and they show the truths of the
gospel can afford them little comfort, if self is crossed. But
blessed is the man who trusteth in the Lord, and whose hope the
Lord is. He shall not be afraid of evil tidings: he shall be kept in
perfect peace, though the earth be moved, and the mountains
cast into the midst of the sea.

ADDITIONAL SCRIPTURE READING:
Psalm 55.22; 2 Timothy 4.5

Go to page 1482 for your next devotional reading.

1700   1900

what will become of the ungodly and the sinners?" ¹⁹Therefore, let those suffering in accordance with God's will entrust themselves to a faithful Creator, while continuing to do good.

Tending the Flock of God

5 Now as an elder myself and a witness of the sufferings of Christ, as well as one who shares in the glory to be revealed, I exhort the elders among you ²to tend the flock of God that is in your charge, exercising the oversight,ᶜ not under compulsion but willingly, as God would have you do itᵈ—not for sordid gain but eagerly. ³Do not lord it over those in your charge, but be examples to the flock. ⁴And when the chief shepherd appears, you will win the crown of glory that never fades away. ⁵In the same way, you who are younger must accept the authority of the elders.ᵉ And all of you must clothe yourselves with humility in your dealings with one another, for

"God opposes the proud,
    but gives grace to the humble."

6 Humble yourselves therefore under the mighty hand of God, so that he may exalt you in due time. ⁷Cast all your anxiety on him, because he cares for you. ⁸Discipline yourselves, keep alert.ᶠ Like a roaring lion your adversary the devil prowls around, looking for someone to devour. ⁹Resist him, steadfast in your faith, for you know that your brothers and sistersᵍ in all the world are undergoing the same kinds of suffering. ¹⁰And after you have suffered for a little while, the God of all grace, who has called you to his eternal glory in Christ, will himself restore, support, strengthen, and establish you. ¹¹To him be the power forever and ever. Amen.

Final Greetings and Benediction

12 Through Silvanus, whom I consider a faithful brother, I have written this short letter to encourage you and to testify that this is the true grace of God. Stand fast in it. ¹³Your sister churchʰ in Babylon, chosen together with you, sends you greetings; and so does my son Mark. ¹⁴Greet one another with a kiss of love.

Peace to all of you who are in Christ.ⁱ

---

c Other ancient authorities lack *exercising the oversight*   d Other ancient authorities lack *as God would have you do it*   e Or *of those who are older*   f Or *be vigilant*   g Gk *your brotherhood*   h Gk *She who is*   i Other ancient authorities add *Amen*

2 PETER

THE SAME GROUP OF CHRISTIANS ADDRESSED IN PETER'S FIRST LETTER WERE IN DANGER OF BEING MISLED BY FALSE TEACHERS. PETER, AS A "SHEPHERD" OF CHRIST'S SHEEP, TEACHES THE CHURCH HOW TO DEAL WITH THESE FALSE TEACHERS BUT ALSO SEEKS TO COMMEND TO HIS READERS A WHOLESOME COMBINATION OF CHRISTIAN FAITH AND PRACTICE. LOOK FOR GUIDELINES ON DEVELOPING CHRISTIAN CHARACTER AND ADMONITIONS ON HOW TO LIVE IN VIEW OF THE LORD'S COMING AGAIN.

Salutation

1 Simeon*a* Peter, a servant*b* and apostle of Jesus Christ,

To those who have received a faith as precious as ours through the righteousness of our God and Savior Jesus Christ:*c*

2 May grace and peace be yours in abundance in the knowledge of God and of Jesus our Lord.

The Christian's Call and Election

3 His divine power has given us everything needed for life and godliness, through the knowledge of him who called us by*d* his own glory and goodness. 4Thus he has given us, through these things, his precious and very great promises, so that through them you may escape from the corruption that is in the world because of lust, and may become participants of the divine nature. 5For this very reason, you must make every effort to support your faith with goodness, and goodness with knowledge, 6and knowledge with self-control, and self-control with endurance, and endurance with godliness, 7and godliness with mutual*e* affection, and mutual*e* affection with love. 8For if these things are yours and are increasing among you, they keep you from being ineffective and unfruitful in the knowledge of our Lord Jesus Christ. 9For anyone who lacks these things is nearsighted and blind, and is forgetful of the cleansing of past

a Other ancient authorities read *Simon*   *b* Gk *slave*   *c* Or *of our God and the Savior Jesus Christ*
d Other ancient authorities read *through*   *e* Gk *brotherly*

sins. 10Therefore, brothers and sisters,*f* be all the more eager to confirm your call and election, for if you do this, you will never stumble. 11For in this way, entry into the eternal kingdom of our Lord and Savior Jesus Christ will be richly provided for you.

12 Therefore I intend to keep on reminding you of these things, though you know them already and are established in the truth that has come to you. 13I think it right, as long as I am in this body,*g* to refresh your memory, 14since I know that my death*h* will come soon, as indeed our Lord Jesus Christ has made clear to me. 15And I will make every effort so that after my departure you may be able at any time to recall these things.

Eyewitnesses of Christ's Glory

16 For we did not follow cleverly devised myths when we made known to you the power and coming of our Lord Jesus Christ, but we had been eyewitnesses of his majesty. 17For he received honor and glory from God the Father when that voice was conveyed to him by the Majestic Glory, saying, "This is my Son, my Beloved,*i* with whom I am well pleased." 18We ourselves heard this voice come from heaven, while we were with him on the holy mountain.

19 So we have the prophetic message more fully confirmed. You will do well to be attentive to this as to a lamp shining in a dark place, until the day dawns and the morning star rises in your hearts. 20First of all you must understand this, that no prophecy of scripture is a matter of one's own interpretation, 21because no prophecy ever came by human will, but men and women moved by the Holy Spirit spoke from God.*j*

False Prophets and Their Punishment

2 But false prophets also arose among the people, just as there will be false teachers among you, who will secretly bring in destructive opinions. They will even deny the Master who bought them—bringing swift destruction on themselves. 2Even so, many will follow their licentious ways, and because of these teachers*k* the way of truth will be maligned. 3And in their greed they will exploit you with deceptive words. Their condemnation, pronounced against them long ago, has not been idle, and their destruction is not asleep.

4 For if God did not spare the angels when they sinned, but cast them into hell*l* and committed them to chains*m* of deepest darkness to be kept until the judgment; 5and if he did not spare the ancient world, even though he saved Noah, a herald of righteousness, with seven others, when he brought a flood on a world of the ungodly; 6and if by turning the cities of Sodom and Gomorrah to ashes he condemned them to extinction*n* and made them an example of what is coming to the ungodly;*o* 7and if he rescued Lot, a righteous man greatly distressed by the licentiousness of the lawless 8(for that righteous man, living among them day after day, was tormented in his righteous soul by their lawless deeds that he saw and heard), 9then the Lord knows how to rescue the godly from trial, and to keep the unrighteous under punishment until the day of judgment 10—especially those who indulge their flesh in depraved lust, and who despise authority.

Bold and willful, they are not afraid to slander the glorious ones,*p* 11whereas angels, though greater in might and power, do not bring against them a slanderous judgment from the Lord.*q* 12These people, however, are like irrational animals, mere creatures of instinct, born to be caught and killed. They slander what they do not understand, and when those creatures are destroyed,*r* they also will be destroyed, 13suffering*s* the penalty for doing wrong. They count it a pleasure to revel in the daytime. They are blots and blemishes, reveling in their dissipation*t*

f Gk *brothers*   g Gk *tent*   h Gk *the putting off of my tent*   i Other ancient authorities read *my beloved Son*   j Other ancient authorities read *but moved by the Holy Spirit saints of God spoke*   k Gk *because of them*   l Gk *Tartaros*   m Other ancient authorities read *pits*   n Other ancient authorities lack *to extinction*   o Other ancient authorities read *an example to those who were to be ungodly*   p Or *angels;* Gk *glories*   q Other ancient authorities read *before the Lord;* others lack the phrase   r Gk *in their destruction*   s Other ancient authorities read *receiving*   t Other ancient authorities read *love-feasts* while they feast with you. [14]They have eyes full of adultery, insatiable for sin. They entice unsteady souls. They have hearts trained in greed. Accursed children! [15]They have left the straight road and have gone astray, following the road of Balaam son of Bosor,[u] who loved the wages of doing wrong, [16]but was rebuked for his own transgression; a speechless donkey spoke with a human voice and restrained the prophet's madness.

17 These are waterless springs and mists driven by a storm; for them the deepest darkness has been reserved. [18]For they speak bombastic nonsense, and with licentious desires of the flesh they entice people who have just[v] escaped from those who live in error. [19]They promise them freedom, but they themselves are slaves of corruption; for people are slaves to whatever masters them. [20]For if, after they have escaped the defilements of the world through the knowledge of our Lord and Savior Jesus Christ, they are again entangled in them and overpowered, the last state has become worse for them than the first. [21]For it would have been better for them never to have known the way of righteousness than, after knowing it, to turn back from the holy commandment that was passed on to them. [22]It has happened to them according to the true proverb,

"The dog turns back to its own vomit,"

and,

"The sow is washed only to wallow in the mud."

The Promise of the Lord's Coming

3 This is now, beloved, the second letter I am writing to you; in them I am trying to arouse your sincere intention by reminding you [2]that you should remember the words spoken in the past by the holy prophets, and the commandment of the Lord and Savior spoken through your apostles. [3]First of all you must understand this, that in the last days scoffers will come, scoffing and indulging their own lusts [4]and saying, "Where is the promise of his coming?

For ever since our ancestors died,[w] all things continue as they were from the beginning of creation!" [5]They deliberately ignore this fact, that by the word of God heavens existed long ago and an earth was formed out of water and by means of water, [6]through which the world of that time was deluged with water and perished. [7]But by the same word the present heavens and earth have been reserved for fire, being kept until the day of judgment and destruction of the godless.

8 But do not ignore this one fact, beloved, that with the Lord one day is like a thousand years, and a thousand years are like one day. [9]The Lord is not slow about his promise, as some think of slowness, but is patient with you,[x] not wanting any to perish, but all to come to repentance. [10]But the day of the Lord will come like a thief, and then the heavens will pass away with a loud noise, and the elements will be dissolved with fire, and the earth and everything that is done on it will be disclosed.[y]

11 Since all these things are to be dissolved in this way, what sort of persons ought you to be in leading lives of holiness and godliness, [12]waiting for and hastening[z] the coming of the day of God, because of which the heavens will be set ablaze and dissolved, and the elements will melt with fire? [13]But, in accordance with his promise, we wait for new heavens and a new earth, where righteousness is at home.

Final Exhortation and Doxology

14 Therefore, beloved, while you are waiting for these things, strive to be found by him at peace, without spot or blemish; [15]and regard the patience of our Lord as salvation. So also our beloved brother Paul wrote to you according to the wisdom given him, [16]speaking of this as he does in all his letters. There are some things in them hard to understand, which the ignorant and unstable twist to their own destruction, as they do the other scriptures. [17]You therefore, beloved, since you are forewarned, be-

---

u Other ancient authorities read *Beor*   v Other ancient authorities read *actually*   w Gk *our fathers fell asleep*   x Other ancient authorities read *on your account*   y Other ancient authorities read *will be burned up*   z Or *earnestly desiring*

ware that you are not carried away with the error of the lawless and lose your own stability. [18]But grow in the grace and knowledge of our Lord and Savior Jesus Christ. To him be the glory both now and to the day of eternity. Amen.*a*

a Other ancient authorities lack *Amen*

TUESDAY

GROW BY THE POWER OF AN INWARD LIFE
Hannah Whitall Smith

VERSE: 2 Peter 3.18   **PASSAGE:** 2 Peter 3.17–18

o grow in grace is opposed to all growth in self-dependence or self-effort—to all legality, in fact, of every kind. It is to put our growing, as well as everything else, into the hands of the Lord and leave it with him. It is to be so satisfied with our husbandman, and with his skill and wisdom, that not a question will cross our minds as to his mode of treatment or his plan of cultivation. It is to grow as the lilies grow, or as the babies grow, without care and without anxiety; to grow by the power of an inward life-principle that cannot help but grow; to grow because we live, and therefore must grow; to grow because he who has planted us has planted a growing thing, and has made us on purpose to grow.

Surely this is what our Lord meant when he said, "Consider the lilies, how they grow: they toil not, neither do they spin: and yet I say unto you, that even Solomon in all his glory was not arrayed like one of these" (Matthew 6.28–29, KJV). Or, when he says again, "Which of you by taking thought can add one cubit unto his stature?" (Matthew 6.27). There is no effort in the growing of a babe or of a lily. The lily does not toil nor spin, it does not stretch nor strain, it does not make any effort of any kind to grow, it is not conscious even that it is growing; but by an inward life-principle, and through the nurturing care of God's providence and the fostering of caretaker or gardener, by the heat of the sun and the falling of the rain, it grows and buds and blossoms into the beautiful plant God meant it to be.

ADDITIONAL SCRIPTURE READING:
1 Kings 10.1–13; Luke 12.27

Go to page 1484 for your next devotional reading.

1700   1900

1 JOHN

T HE AUTHOR OF THIS LETTER IS JOHN THE SON OF ZEBEDEE—THE AUTHOR OF THE GOSPEL OF JOHN AND THE BOOK OF REVELATION. JOHN HAD TWO BASIC PURPOSES IN MIND IN THIS LETTER: (1) TO EXPOSE FALSE TEACHERS WHO DENIED, AMONG OTHER THINGS, JESUS' HUMANITY, AND (2) TO GIVE BELIEVERS ASSURANCE OF SALVATION. JOHN STRESSES GOD'S LOVE AS AN EXAMPLE FOR US TO FOLLOW IN OUR RELATIONSHIPS WITH EACH OTHER. HE ENCOURAGES BELIEVERS TO LIVE RIGHT AND TO MAINTAIN TRUTH BY MAINTAINING FELLOWSHIP WITH THE LORD.

The Word of Life

1 We declare to you what was from the beginning, what we have heard, what we have seen with our eyes, what we have looked at and touched with our hands, concerning the word of life— 2this life was revealed, and we have seen it and testify to it, and declare to you the eternal life that was with the Father and was revealed to us— 3we declare to you what we have seen and heard so that you also may have fellowship with us; and truly our fellowship is with the Father and with his Son Jesus Christ. 4We are writing these things so that our*a* joy may be complete.

God Is Light

5 This is the message we have heard from him and proclaim to you, that God is light and in him there is no darkness at all. 6If we say that we have fellowship with him while we are walking in darkness, we lie and do not do what is true; 7but if we walk in the light as he himself is in the light, we have fellowship with one another, and the blood of

SIN WILL KEEP YOU FROM THIS BOOK. THIS BOOK WILL KEEP YOU FROM SIN. —*Dwight L. Moody*

Jesus his Son cleanses us from all sin. 8If we say that we have no sin, we deceive

a Other ancient authorities read *your*

ourselves, and the truth is not in us. 9If we confess our sins, he who is faithful and just will forgive us our sins and cleanse us from all unrighteousness. 10If we say that we have not sinned, we make him a liar, and his word is not in us.

Christ Our Advocate

 2 My little children, I am writing these things to you so that you

may not sin. But if anyone does sin, we have an advocate with the Father, Jesus Christ the righteous; 2and he is the atoning sacrifice for our sins, and not for ours only but also for the sins of the whole world.

3 Now by this we may be sure that we know him, if we obey his commandments. 4Whoever says, "I have come to know him," but does not obey his commandments, is a liar, and in such a per-

---

WEDNESDAY

ANSELM'S CONFESSION
Anselm of Canterbury

VERSE: 1 John 1.9   **PASSAGE:** 1 John 1.8–10

 am frightened of living, Lord.
My whole life seems sinful or sterile.
Any fruits I bear are either false or rotten.
Nothing I do seems pleasing to you.
I am a barren tree that deserves
To be chopped down, cut and burnt.
I bear only the sharp and bitter thorns of sin.
If only those thorns could prick me into repentance.
Inside me my conscience burns.
I dare not show myself, yet I have nowhere to hide.
What will happen to me?
Who will protect me from your wrath?
Where can I find safety?
Lord, you are my judge in whose hands I tremble.
Yet you also are the one who can save me.
Though I fear you, I trust you.
Though I want to flee from you, I flee towards you.
Jesus, Jesus, deal with me according to your love.
Jesus, Jesus, forget the sin by which I have provoked you,
    And see only the misery which invokes you.
Most kind Lord,
Confirm in me all that belongs to you,
And cast away all that is alien to you.

ADDITIONAL SCRIPTURE READING:
Galatians 5.24; Colossians 2.11

Go to page 1487 for your next devotional reading.

500   1500

son the truth does not exist; 5but whoever obeys his word, truly in this person the love of God has reached perfection. By this we may be sure that we are in him: 6whoever says, "I abide in him," ought to walk just as he walked.

A New Commandment

7 Beloved, I am writing you no new commandment, but an old commandment that you have had from the beginning; the old commandment is the word that you have heard. 8Yet I am writing you a new commandment that is true in him and in you, becauseb the darkness is passing away and the true light is already shining. 9Whoever says, "I am in the light," while hating a brother or sister,c is still in the darkness. 10Whoever loves a brother or sisterd lives in the light, and in such a persone there is no cause for stumbling. 11But whoever hates another believerf is in the darkness, walks in the darkness, and does not know the way to go, because the darkness has brought on blindness.
12   I am writing to you, little children,
      because your sins are forgiven on
         account of his name.
13   I am writing to you, fathers,
      because you know him who is
         from the beginning.
   I am writing to you, young people,
      because you have conquered the
         evil one.
14   I write to you, children,
      because you know the Father.
   I write to you, fathers,
      because you know him who is
         from the beginning.
   I write to you, young people,
      because you are strong
      and the word of God abides in
         you,
      and you have overcome the
         evil one.
15 Do not love the world or the things in the world. The love of the Father is not in those who love the world; 16for all that is in the world—the desire of the flesh, the desire of the eyes, the pride in riches—comes not from the Father but from the world. 17And the world and its

desireg are passing away, but those who do the will of God live forever.

Warning against Antichrists

18 Children, it is the last hour! As you have heard that antichrist is coming, so now many antichrists have come. From this we know that it is the last hour. 19They went out from us, but they did not belong to us; for if they had belonged to us, they would have remained with us. But by going out they made it plain that none of them belongs to us. 20But you have been anointed by the Holy One, and all of you have knowledge.h 21I write to you, not because you do not know the truth, but because you know it, and you know that no lie comes from the truth. 22Who is the liar but the one who denies that Jesus is the Christ?i This is the antichrist, the one who denies the Father and the Son. 23No one who denies the Son has the Father; everyone who confesses the Son has the Father also. 24Let what you heard from the beginning abide in you. If what you heard from the beginning abides in you, then you will abide in the Son and in the Father. 25And this is what he has promised us,j eternal life.
26 I write these things to you concerning those who would deceive you. 27As for you, the anointing that you received from him abides in you, and so you do not need anyone to teach you. But as his anointing teaches you about all things, and is true and is not a lie, and just as it has taught you, abide in him.k
28 And now, little children, abide in him, so that when he is revealed we may have confidence and not be put to shame before him at his coming.

Children of God

29 If you know that he is righteous, you may be sure that everyone who does right has been born of him. 1See what love the Father has given us, that we should be called children of God; and that is what we are. The reason the world does not know us is that it did not know him. 2Beloved, we are

b Or that   c Gk hating a brother   d Gk loves a brother   e Or in it   f Gk hates a brother
g Or the desire for it   h Other ancient authorities read you know all things   i Or the Messiah
j Other ancient authorities read you   k Or it

God's children now; what we will be has not yet been revealed. What we do know is this: when he[1] is revealed, we will be like him, for we will see him as he is. [3]And all who have this hope in him purify themselves, just as he is pure.

4 Everyone who commits sin is guilty of lawlessness; sin is lawlessness. [5]You know that he was revealed to take away sins, and in him there is no sin. [6]No one who abides in him sins; no one who sins has either seen him or known him. [7]Little children, let no one deceive you. Everyone who does what is right is righteous, just as he is righteous. [8]Everyone who commits sin is a child of the devil; for the devil has been sinning from the beginning. The Son of God was revealed for this purpose, to destroy the works of the devil. [9]Those who have been born of God do not sin, because God's seed abides in them;[m] they cannot sin, because they have been born of God. [10]The children of God and the children of the devil are revealed in this way: all who do not do what is right are not from God, nor are those who do not love their brothers and sisters.[n]

Love One Another

11 For this is the message you have heard from the beginning, that we should love one another. [12]We must not be like Cain who was from the evil one and murdered his brother. And why did he murder him? Because his own deeds were evil and his brother's righteous. [13]Do not be astonished, brothers and sisters,[o] that the world hates you. [14]We know that we have passed from death to life because we love one another. Whoever does not love abides in death. [15]All who hate a brother or sister[n] are murderers, and you know that murderers do not have eternal life abiding in them. [16]We know love by this, that he laid down his life for us—and we ought to lay down our lives for one another. [17]How does God's love abide in anyone who has the world's goods and sees a brother or sister[p] in need and yet refuses help?

18 Little children, let us love, not in word or speech, but in truth and action.

[19]And by this we will know that we are from the truth and will reassure our hearts before him [20]whenever our hearts condemn us; for God is greater than our hearts, and he knows everything. [21]Beloved, if our hearts do not condemn us, we have boldness before God; [22]and we receive from him whatever we ask, because we obey his commandments and do what pleases him.

23 And this is his commandment, that we should believe in the name of his Son Jesus Christ and love one another, just as he has commanded us. [24]All who obey his commandments abide in him, and he abides in them. And by this we know that he abides in us, by the Spirit that he has given us.

Testing the Spirits

4 Beloved, do not believe every spirit, but test the spirits to see whether they are from God; for many false prophets have gone out into the world. [2]By this you know the Spirit of God: every spirit that confesses that Jesus Christ has come in the flesh is from God, [3]and every spirit that does not confess Jesus[q] is not from God. And this is the spirit of the antichrist, of which you have heard that it is coming; and now it is already in the world. [4]Little children, you are from God, and have conquered them; for the one who is in you is greater than the one who is in the world. [5]They are from the world; therefore what they say is from the world, and the world listens to them. [6]We are from God. Whoever knows God listens to us, and whoever is not from God does not listen to us. From this we know the spirit of truth and the spirit of error.

God Is Love

7 Beloved, let us love one another, because love is from God; everyone who loves is born of God and knows God. [8]Whoever does not love does not know God, for God is love. [9]God's love was revealed among us in this way: God sent his only Son into the world so that we might live through him. [10]In this is love, not that we loved God but that he loved us and sent his Son to be the atoning sac-

---

1 Or it   m Or because the children of God abide in him   n Gk his brother   o Gk brothers
p Gk brother   q Other ancient authorities read does away with Jesus (Gk dissolves Jesus)

rifice for our sins. ¹¹Beloved, since God loved us so much, we also ought to love one another. ¹²No one has ever seen God; if we love one another, God lives in us, and his love is perfected in us.

13 By this we know that we abide in him and he in us, because he has given us of his Spirit. ¹⁴And we have seen and do testify that the Father has sent his Son as the Savior of the world. ¹⁵God abides in those who confess that Jesus is the Son of God, and they abide in God. ¹⁶So we have known and believe the love that God has for us.

God is love, and those who abide in love abide in God, and God abides in them. ¹⁷Love has been perfected among us in this: that we may have boldness on the day of judgment, because as he is, so are we in this world. ¹⁸There is no fear in love, but perfect love casts out fear; for fear has to do with punishment, and whoever fears has not reached perfection in love. ¹⁹We love*r* because he first loved us. ²⁰Those who say, "I love God," and hate their brothers or sisters,*s* are liars; for those who do not love a brother or sister*t* whom they have seen, cannot

r Other ancient authorities add *him*; others add *God*   *s* Gk *brothers*   *t* Gk *brother*

THURSDAY

THE MYSTERY OF THE SON
Athenagoras

VERSE: 1 John 4.15   PASSAGE: 1 John 4.13–16

 et no one think it stupid for me to say that God has a Son. For we do not think of God the Father or of the Son in the way of the poets, who weave their myths by showing that gods are no better than men. But the Son of God is his Word in idea and in actuality; for by him and through him all things were made, the Father and the Son being one. And since the Son is in the Father and the Father in the Son by the unity and power of the Spirit, the Son of God is the mind and Word of the Father.

But if, owing to your sharp intelligence, it occurs to you to inquire further what is meant by the Son, I shall briefly explain. He is the first offspring of the Father. I do not mean that he was created, for, since God is eternal mind, he had his Word within himself from the beginning, being eternally wise. Rather did the Son come forth from God to give form and actuality to all material things, which essentially have a sort of formless nature and inert quality, the heavier particles being mixed up with the lighter.

ADDITIONAL SCRIPTURE READING:
Mark 14.61–62; John 9.35–39

Go to page 1490 for your next devotional reading.

100   500

love God whom they have not seen. [21]The commandment we have from him is this: those who love God must love their brothers and sisters[u] also.

Faith Conquers the World

5 Everyone who believes that Jesus is the Christ[v] has been born of God, and everyone who loves the parent loves the child. [2]By this we know that we love the children of God, when we love God and obey his commandments. [3]For the love of God is this, that we obey his commandments. And his commandments are not burdensome, [4]for whatever is born of God conquers the world. And this is the victory that conquers the world, our faith. [5]Who is it that conquers the world but the one who believes that Jesus is the Son of God?

Testimony concerning the Son of God

6 This is the one who came by water and blood, Jesus Christ, not with the water only but with the water and the blood. And the Spirit is the one that testifies, for the Spirit is the truth. [7]There are three that testify:[w] [8]the Spirit and the water and the blood, and these three agree. [9]If we receive human testimony, the testimony of God is greater; for this is the testimony of God that he has testified to his Son. [10]Those who believe in the Son of God have the testimony in their hearts. Those who do not believe in God[x] have made him a liar by not believing in the testimony that God has given concerning his Son. [11]And this is the testimony: God gave us eternal life, and this life is in his Son. [12]Whoever has the Son has life; whoever does not have the Son of God does not have life.

Epilogue

13 I write these things to you who believe in the name of the Son of God, so that you may know that you have eternal life.

14 And this is the boldness we have in him, that if we ask anything according to his will, he hears us. [15]And if we know that he hears us in whatever we ask, we know that we have obtained the requests made of him. [16]If you see your brother or sister[y] committing what is not a mortal sin, you will ask, and God[z] will give life to such a one—to those whose sin is not mortal. There is sin that is mortal; I do not say that you should pray about that. [17]All wrongdoing is sin, but there is sin that is not mortal.

18 We know that those who are born of God do not sin, but the one who was born of God protects them, and the evil one does not touch them. [19]We know that we are God's children, and that the whole world lies under the power of the evil one. [20]And we know that the Son of God has come and has given us understanding so that we may know him who is true;[a] and we are in him who is true, in his Son Jesus Christ. He is the true God and eternal life.

21 Little children, keep yourselves from idols.[b]

---

u Gk *brothers*   v Or *the Messiah*   w A few other authorities read (with variations) [7]*There are three that testify in heaven, the Father, the Word, and the Holy Spirit, and these three are one.* [8]*And there are three that testify on earth:*   x Other ancient authorities read *in the Son*   y Gk *your brother* z Gk *he*   a Other ancient authorities read *know the true God*   b Other ancient authorities add *Amen*

2 JOHN

URING THE FIRST TWO CENTURIES A.D. THE GOSPEL WAS TAKEN FROM PLACE TO PLACE BY TRAVELING EVANGELISTS. BELIEVERS CUSTOMARILY TOOK THESE MISSIONARIES INTO THEIR HOMES AND GAVE THEM PROVISIONS WHEN THEY LEFT. BECAUSE FALSE TEACHERS ALSO RELIED ON THIS PRACTICE, 2 JOHN WAS WRITTEN TO URGE DISCERNMENT IN SUPPORTING TRAVELING TEACHERS. LOOK FOR THE CHALLENGE TO BE CERTAIN ABOUT WHAT YOU BELIEVE AND HOW YOU LIVE.

Salutation

1 The elder to the elect lady and her children, whom I love in the truth, and not only I but also all who know the truth, 2because of the truth that abides in us and will be with us forever:

3 Grace, mercy, and peace will be with us from God the Father and from*a* Jesus Christ, the Father's Son, in truth and love.

Truth and Love

4 I was overjoyed to find some of your children walking in the truth, just as we have been commanded by the Father. 5But now, dear lady, I ask you, not as though I were writing you a new commandment, but one we have had from the beginning, let us love one another. 6And this is love, that we walk according to his commandments; this is the commandment just as you have heard it from the beginning—you must walk in it.

7 Many deceivers have gone out into the world, those who do not confess that Jesus Christ has come in the flesh; any such person is the deceiver and the antichrist! 8Be on your guard, so that you do not lose what we*b* have worked for, but may receive a full reward. 9Everyone who does not abide in the teaching of Christ, but goes beyond it, does not have God; whoever abides in the teaching has both the Father and the Son. 10Do not receive into the house or welcome anyone who comes to you and does not

a Other ancient authorities add *the Lord*   b Other ancient authorities read *you* bring this teaching; [11]for to welcome is to participate in the evil deeds of such a person.

Final Greetings

12 Although I have much to write to

c Other ancient authorities add *Amen*

you, I would rather not use paper and ink; instead I hope to come to you and talk with you face to face, so that our joy may be complete.

13 The children of your elect sister send you their greetings.[c]

FRIDAY

ABIDING IN THE TEACHING OF CHRIST
John Calvin

VERSE: 2 John 9   **PASSAGE:** 2 John 7–11

ll that Jesus Christ has done and suffered for our redemption, we veritably hold without any doubt, as it is contained in the Creed . . . that is to say, "I believe in God, the Father Almighty," and so on.

Therefore we acknowledge the things which are consequently given to us by God in Jesus Christ: First, that being in our own nature enemies of God and subject to his wrath and judgment, we are reconciled with him and received again in grace through the intercession of Jesus Christ, so that by his righteousness and guiltlessness we have remission of our sins, and by the shedding of his blood we are cleansed and purified from all our stains.

Second, we acknowledge that by his spirit we are regenerated into a new spiritual nature. That is to say, the evil desires of our flesh are mortified by grace, so that they rule us no longer. On the contrary, our will is rendered conformable to God's will, to follow in his way and to seek what is pleasing to him. Therefore we are by him delivered from the servitude of sin, under whose power we were of ourselves held captive, and by this deliverance we are made capable and able to do good works.

Finally, we acknowledge that this regeneration is so effected in us that, until we slough off this mortal body, there remains always in us much imperfection and infirmity, so that we always remain poor and wretched sinners in the presence of God. And however much we ought day by day to increase and grow in God's righteousness, there will never be plenitude or perfection while we live here . . . And so we ought always to look for our righteousness in Jesus Christ, and not at all in ourselves, and in him be confident and assured, putting no faith in our works.

ADDITIONAL SCRIPTURE READING:
Psalm 14.1–3; Romans 3.9–24

Go to page 1491 for your next devotional reading.

1500   1700

WEEKEND

BE STILL, MY HEART!
John Newton

VERSE: Hebrews 10.22   **PASSAGE:** Hebrews 10.19–25

e still, my heart! these anxious cares
To thee are burdens, thorns and snares;
They cast dishonor on the Lord,
And contradict his gracious word.

Brought safely by his hand thus far,
Why wilt thou now give place to fear?
How canst thou want if he provide,
Or lose thy way with such a guide?

When first before his mercy-seat
Thou didst to him thine all commit;
He gave thee warrant from that hour
To trust his wisdom, love, and power.

Did ever trouble yet befall,
And he refuse to hear thy call?
And has he not his promise passed,
That thou shalt overcome at last?

He who has helped me hitherto
Will help me all my journey through,
And give me daily cause to raise
New Ebenezers to his praise.

Though rough and thorny be the road,
It leads thee on, apace, to God;
Then count thy present trials small,
For God will make amends for all.

ADDITIONAL SCRIPTURE READING:
Psalm 91.1–2; James 5.7–8

Go to page 1493 for your next devotional reading.

1700   1900

3 JOHN

ITINERANT TEACHERS SENT OUT BY JOHN WERE REJECTED IN ONE OF THE CHURCHES IN THE PROVINCE OF ASIA BY A DICTATORIAL LEADER, DIOTREPHES. JOHN WROTE TO GAIUS, HIS FRIEND AND A LEADER IN THE CHURCH, TO THANK GAIUS FOR HIS HELP AND TO ENCOURAGE HIM IN HIS SUPPORT OF LEGITIMATE TEACHERS. HE ALSO REPROVES DIOTREPHES FOR NOT COOPERATING AND FOR REBELLING AGAINST JOHN'S LEADERSHIP.

Salutation

1 The elder to the beloved Gaius, whom I love in truth.

Gaius Commended for His Hospitality

2 Beloved, I pray that all may go well with you and that you may be in good health, just as it is well with your soul. ³I was overjoyed when some of the friends*a* arrived and testified to your faithfulness to the truth, namely how you walk in the truth. ⁴I have no greater joy than this, to hear that my children are walking in the truth.

5 Beloved, you do faithfully whatever you do for the friends,*a* even though they are strangers to you; ⁶they have tes-tified to your love before the church. You will do well to send them on in a manner worthy of God; ⁷for they began their journey for the sake of Christ,*b* accepting no support from non-believers.*c* ⁸Therefore we ought to support such people, so that we may become co-workers with the truth.

Diotrephes and Demetrius

9 I have written something to the church; but Diotrephes, who likes to put himself first, does not acknowledge our authority. ¹⁰So if I come, I will call attention to what he is doing in spreading false charges against us. And not content with those charges, he refuses to welcome the friends,*a* and even prevents

a Gk *brothers*   *b* Gk *for the sake of the name*   *c* Gk *the Gentiles*

FROM MARY MAGDALEN'S FUNERAL TEARS
Robert Southwell

VERSE: 3 John 11   **PASSAGE:** 3 John

 Christian soul, take Mary for your mirror; . . . learn, O sinful man, from this once-sinful woman, that sinners may find Christ if their sins be amended. Learn that those who are lost to sin may be recovered by love, that those who have been chased away by faintness of faith may be recalled by firmness of hope, and that which no mortal force, favor, or policy can grasp may be obtained by the continued tears of constant love.

Learn of Mary [to] rise early in the morning . . . Run with repentance to your sinful heart, which was meant to be a temple, but, through your own fault, was no better than a tomb for Christ, since, being unable to feel him living in you, he seems as if he were dead. Roll away the stone of your former hardness; remove all the heavy loads that oppress you in sin; and look into your soul to see if you can find the Lord. If he is not within you, then stand outside weeping . . .

Seek him only and nothing beside him. And if at first search he does not appear, then persevere in tears and continue your seeking. Stand upon the earth, treading upon all your earthly vanities, touching them with no more than the soles of your feet, that is, with the lowest and least part of your affection. To look better into the tomb, bow down your neck with the yoke of humility and stoop from lofty and proud conceits, so that with humbled and lowly looks you may find him whom your swelling and haughty thoughts had driven away . . .

And if he grants you the glorious sight of himself to your inward eyes, presume not to know him, but as his unworthy suppliant prostrate your petitions before him that you may truly discern him and faithfully serve him . . . If with Mary you crave no other solace from Jesus but Jesus himself, he will answer your tears with his presence and assure you of that presence with his own words, so that having seen him for yourself you may make him known to others, saying, with Mary, "I have seen our Lord, and these things he said to me" (see John 20.18).

ADDITIONAL SCRIPTURE READING:
Mark 16.9–10; Ephesians 1.3–10

Go to page 1496 for your next devotional reading.

1500   1700

those who want to do so and expels them from the church.

11 Beloved, do not imitate what is evil but imitate what is good. Whoever does good is from God; whoever does evil has not seen God. 12Everyone has testified favorably about Demetrius, and so has the truth itself. We also testify for him,[d] and you know that our testimony is true.

Final Greetings

13 I have much to write to you, but I would rather not write with pen and ink; 14instead I hope to see you soon, and we will talk together face to face.

15 Peace to you. The friends send you their greetings. Greet the friends there, each by name.

[d] Gk lacks *for him*

JUDE

JUDE ORIGINATED AS A PERSONAL LET-
TER TO ONE OR MORE OF THE CON-
GREGATIONS DISPERSED THROUGHOUT
THE ROMAN EMPIRE. THE DANGERS FACING
THE CHURCH AT THIS TIME WERE NOT THOSE OF
OUTRIGHT PERSECUTION BUT OF HERETICS AND
DISTORTERS OF THE FAITH. ALTHOUGH JUDE IS
EAGER TO WRITE TO HIS READERS ABOUT SALVA-
TION, HE MUST INSTEAD WARN THEM ABOUT
CERTAIN IMMORAL MEN WHO ARE PERVERTING
GOD'S GRACE. THE LETTER ADVISES BELIEVERS
TO STRENGTHEN THEIR RELATIONSHIP TO GOD
WITH PRAYER AND MUTUAL SUPPORT.

Salutation

1 Jude,[a] a servant[b] of Jesus Christ and brother of James,

To those who are called, who are beloved[c] in[d] God the Father and kept safe for[d] Jesus Christ:

2 May mercy, peace, and love be yours in abundance.

Occasion of the Letter

3 Beloved, while eagerly preparing to write to you about the salvation we share, I find it necessary to write and appeal to you to contend for the faith that was once for all entrusted to the saints. 4For certain intruders have stolen in among you, people who long ago were designated for this condemnation as ungodly, who pervert the grace of our God into licentiousness and deny our only Master and Lord, Jesus Christ.[e]

Judgment on False Teachers

5 Now I desire to remind you, though you are fully informed, that the Lord, who once for all saved[f] a people out of the land of Egypt, afterward destroyed those who did not believe. 6And the angels who did not keep their own position, but left their proper dwelling, he has kept in eternal chains in deepest darkness for the judgment of the great day. 7Likewise, Sodom and Gomorrah and the surrounding cities, which, in the

a Gk Judas   b Gk slave   c Other ancient authorities read sanctified   d Or by   e Or the only Master and our Lord Jesus Christ   f Other ancient authorities read though you were once for all fully informed, that Jesus (or Joshua) who saved

CHRISTIANITY AND

C. S. Lewis

VERSE: Jude 3   **PASSAGE:** Jude 3–4

[Satan writes to one of his minions:]

My Dear Wormwood,

The real trouble about the set your patient is living in is that it is *merely* Christian. They all have individual interests, of course, but the bond remains mere Christianity. What we want, if men become Christians at all, is to keep them in the state of mind I call "Christianity And." You know—Christianity and the Crisis, Christianity and the New Psychology, Christianity and the New Order, Christianity and Faith Healing, Christianity and Psychical Research, Christianity and Vegetarianism, Christianity and Spelling Reform. If they must be Christians let them at least be Christians with a difference. Substitute for the faith itself some fashion with a Christian coloring. Work on their horror of the Same Old Thing.

The horror of the Same Old Thing is one of the most valuable passions we have produced in the human heart—an endless source of heresies in religion, folly in counsel, infidelity in marriage, and inconstancy in friendship. The humans live in time, and experience reality successively. To experience much of it, therefore, they must experience many different things; in other words, they must experience change . . .

Now just as we pick out and exaggerate the pleasure of eating to produce gluttony, so we pick out this natural pleasantness of change and twist it into a demand for absolute novelty. This demand is entirely our workmanship. If we neglect our duty, men will be not only contented but transported by the mixed novelty and familiarity of snowdrops *this* January, sunrise *this* morning, plum pudding *this* Christmas. Children, until we have taught them better, will be perfectly happy with a seasonal round of games in which conkers succeed hopscotch as regularly as autumn follows summer. Only by our incessant efforts is the demand for infinite, or unrhythmical, change kept up.

ADDITIONAL SCRIPTURE READING:
Psalm 17.3; Acts 1.7–8

Go to page 1499 for your next devotional reading.

1900   Present

same manner as they, indulged in sexual immorality and pursued unnatural lust,[g] serve as an example by undergoing a punishment of eternal fire.

8 Yet in the same way these dreamers also defile the flesh, reject authority, and slander the glorious ones.[h] 9But when the archangel Michael contended with the devil and disputed about the body of Moses, he did not dare to bring a condemnation of slander[i] against him, but said, "The Lord rebuke you!" 10But these people slander whatever they do not understand, and they are destroyed by those things that, like irrational animals, they know by instinct. 11Woe to them! For they go the way of Cain, and abandon themselves to Balaam's error for the sake of gain, and perish in Korah's rebellion. 12These are blemishes[j] on your love-feasts, while they feast with you without fear, feeding themselves.[k] They are waterless clouds carried along by the winds; autumn trees without fruit, twice dead, uprooted; 13wild waves of the sea, casting up the foam of their own shame; wandering stars, for whom the deepest darkness has been reserved forever.

14 It was also about these that Enoch, in the seventh generation from Adam, prophesied, saying, "See, the Lord is coming[l] with ten thousands of his holy ones, 15to execute judgment on all, and to convict everyone of all the deeds of ungodliness that they have committed in such an ungodly way, and of all the harsh things that ungodly sinners have spoken against him." 16These are grumblers and malcontents; they indulge their own lusts; they are bombastic in speech, flattering people to their own advantage.

Warnings and Exhortations

17 But you, beloved, must remember the predictions of the apostles of our Lord Jesus Christ; 18for they said to you, "In the last time there will be scoffers, indulging their own ungodly lusts." 19It is these worldly people, devoid of the Spirit, who are causing divisions. 20But you, beloved, build yourselves up on your most holy faith; pray in the Holy Spirit; 21keep yourselves in the love of God; look forward to the mercy of our Lord Jesus Christ that leads to[m] eternal life. 22And have mercy on some who are wavering; 23save others by snatching them out of the fire; and have mercy on still others with fear, hating even the tunic defiled by their bodies.[n]

Benediction

24 Now to him who is able to keep you from falling, and to make you stand without blemish in the presence of his glory with rejoicing, 25to the only God our Savior, through Jesus Christ our Lord, be glory, majesty, power, and authority, before all time and now and forever. Amen.

AND NOW UNTO HIM WHO IS ABLE TO KEEP US FROM FALLING AND LIFT US FROM THE DARK VALLEY OF DESPAIR TO THE BRIGHT MOUNTAIN OF HOPE, FROM THE MIDNIGHT OF DESPERATION TO THE DAYBREAK OF JOY; TO HIM BE POWER AND AUTHORITY, FOR EVER AND EVER.

—*Martin Luther King, Jr.*

---

g Gk *went after other flesh*   h Or *angels;* Gk *glories*   i Or *condemnation for blasphemy*
j Or *reefs*   k Or *without fear. They are shepherds who care only for themselves*   l Gk *came*
m Gk *Christ to*   n Gk *by the flesh.* The Greek text of verses 22-23 is uncertain at several points

REVELATION

OHN WRITES A MESSAGE THAT
JESUS CHRIST REVEALS TO HIM.
HE WRITES TO COMFORT BELIEVERS
WHO ARE SUFFERING FOR THEIR FAITH. IT IS
A BOOK OF HOPE, FOR ITS CENTRAL MESSAGE
IS THAT GOD AND GOOD WILL TRIUMPH
OVER EVIL. LOOK FOR A COMBINATION OF
WARNINGS AND ENCOURAGEMENTS HERE—
WARNINGS AGAINST FALLING AWAY FROM
FAITH IN CHRIST AND ASSURANCES OF ULTI-
MATE VICTORY FOR THOSE WHO ARE ON
GOD'S SIDE.

Introduction and Salutation

1 The revelation of Jesus Christ, which God gave him to show his servants*a* what must soon take place; he made*b* it known by sending his angel to his servant*c* John, 2who testified to the word of God and to the testimony of Jesus Christ, even to all that he saw.

3 Blessed is the one who reads aloud the words of the prophecy, and blessed are those who hear and who keep what is written in it; for the time is near.

4 John to the seven churches that are in Asia:

Grace to you and peace from him who is and who was and who is to come, and from the seven spirits who are before his throne, 5and from Jesus Christ, the faithful witness, the firstborn of the dead, and the ruler of the kings of the earth.

To him who loves us and freed*d* us from our sins by his blood, 6and made*b* us to be a kingdom, priests serving*e* his God and Father, to him be glory and dominion forever and ever. Amen.

7   Look! He is coming with the
        clouds;
    every eye will see him,
    even those who pierced him;
        and on his account all the tribes
        of the earth will wail.
So it is to be. Amen.

8 "I am the Alpha and the Omega," says the Lord God, who is and who was and who is to come, the Almighty.

a Gk *slaves*   *b* Gk *and he made*   *c* Gk *slave*   *d* Other ancient authorities read *washed*
e Gk *priests to*

A Vision of Christ

9 I, John, your brother who share with you in Jesus the persecution and the kingdom and the patient endurance, was on the island called Patmos because of the word of God and the testimony of Jesus.*f* 10 I was in the spirit*g* on the Lord's day, and I heard behind me a loud voice

f Or *testimony to Jesus*   *g* Or *in the Spirit*

WEDNESDAY

LOVE BEFORE CLEANSING
Dwight L. Moody

VERSE: Revelation 1.5   **PASSAGE:** Revelation 1.4–6

 here was a boy, a great many years ago, who was kidnapped in London. Long months and years passed and the mother had prayed and prayed. All her efforts had failed, and they had given up all hope. But the mother did not quite give up her hope.

One day a boy was sent into the neighboring house to sweep the chimney, and by some mistake he got down through the wrong chimney. When he came down he came in by the sitting-room chimney.

His memory began at once to travel back through the years that had passed. He thought that things looked strangely familiar. The scenes of the early days of youth were dawning upon him; and as he stood there surveying the place, his mother came into the room.

He stood there, covered with rags and soot. Did she wait until she had sent him to be washed before she rushed and took him in her arms? No, indeed; it was her own boy. She took him to her arms, all black and sooty, hugged him to her bosom, and shed tears of joy on his head.

You have wandered very far from him, and there may not be a sound spot on you; but if you will just come to God he will forgive and receive you.

I think a good deal of Isaiah 38.17. It reads: "In your love you kept me from the pit of destruction; you have put all my sins behind your back" (NIV). Notice, the love comes first. [God] did not say that he had taken away sins and cast them behind him. He loved us first, and then he took our sins away.

ADDITIONAL SCRIPTURE READING:
Isaiah 38.17; John 3.16

Go to page 1501 for your next devotional reading.

1900   Present

like a trumpet [11]saying, "Write in a book what you see and send it to the seven churches, to Ephesus, to Smyrna, to Pergamum, to Thyatira, to Sardis, to Philadelphia, and to Laodicea."

12 Then I turned to see whose voice it was that spoke to me, and on turning I saw seven golden lampstands, [13]and in the midst of the lampstands I saw one like the Son of Man, clothed with a long robe and with a golden sash across his chest. [14]His head and his hair were white as white wool, white as snow; his eyes were like a flame of fire, [15]his feet were like burnished bronze, refined as in a furnace, and his voice was like the sound of many waters. [16]In his right hand he held seven stars, and from his mouth came a sharp, two-edged sword, and his face was like the sun shining with full force.

17 When I saw him, I fell at his feet as though dead. But he placed his right hand on me, saying, "Do not be afraid; I am the first and the last, [18]and the living one. I was dead, and see, I am alive forever and ever; and I have the keys of Death and of Hades. [19]Now write what you have seen, what is, and what is to take place after this. [20]As for the mystery of the seven stars that you saw in my right hand, and the seven golden lampstands: the seven stars are the angels of the seven churches, and the seven lampstands are the seven churches.

The Message to Ephesus

2 "To the angel of the church in Ephesus write: These are the words of him who holds the seven stars in his right hand, who walks among the seven golden lampstands:

2 "I know your works, your toil and your patient endurance. I know that you cannot tolerate evildoers; you have tested those who claim to be apostles but are not, and have found them to be false. [3]I also know that you are enduring patiently and bearing up for the sake of my name, and that you have not grown weary. [4]But I have this against you, that you have abandoned the love you had at first. [5]Remember then from what you have fallen; repent, and do the works

you did at first. If not, I will come to you and remove your lampstand from its place, unless you repent. [6]Yet this is to your credit: you hate the works of the Nicolaitans, which I also hate. [7]Let anyone who has an ear listen to what the Spirit is saying to the churches. To everyone who conquers, I will give permission to eat from the tree of life that is in the paradise of God.

The Message to Smyrna

8 "And to the angel of the church in Smyrna write: These are the words of the first and the last, who was dead and came to life:

9 "I know your affliction and your poverty, even though you are rich. I know the slander on the part of those who say that they are Jews and are not, but are a synagogue of Satan. [10]Do not fear what you are about to suffer. Beware, the devil is about to throw some of you into prison so that you may be tested, and for ten days you will have affliction. Be faithful until death, and I will give you the crown of life. [11]Let anyone who has an ear listen to what the Spirit is saying to the churches. Whoever conquers will not be harmed by the second death.

The Message to Pergamum

12 "And to the angel of the church in Pergamum write: These are the words of him who has the sharp two-edged sword:

13 "I know where you are living, where Satan's throne is. Yet you are holding fast to my name, and you did not deny your faith in me[h] even in the days of Antipas my witness, my faithful one, who was killed among you, where Satan lives. [14]But I have a few things against you: you have some there who hold to the teaching of Balaam, who taught Balak to put a stumbling block before the people of Israel, so that they would eat food sacrificed to idols and practice fornication. [15]So you also have some who hold to the teaching of the Nicolaitans. [16]Repent then. If not, I will come to you soon and make war against them with the sword of my mouth. [17]Let anyone who has an ear listen to what the Spirit is saying to the churches.

h Or deny my faith

THURSDAY

FOR THE RENEWAL OF GOD'S CHURCH
Isabella Graham

VERSE: Revelation 2.4   **PASSAGE:** Revelation 2.1–7

"O you who are Alpha and Omega, . . ." write with power, speak with power, in the heart of the angel of this church. Have you not in former days had your dwelling among them? In days of trouble did you not work in them the fruits of labor and patience, so that for your name's sake they labored and fainted not? You blessed them and gave them peace, and they rejoiced in the light of your countenance . . . Alas, Lord, we have . . . left our first love; we have not watched and prayed as you gave us command; . . . we have forsaken the counsel of our old men and given heed to flatterers; we have forgotten our dependence on you . . .

We are poor and blind and miserable and naked, rich in our fancied wisdom, seeing by our own light, compassing ourselves about with our own sparks, and flaunting our rags. "We feed on ashes . . ."

"Your covenant is well ordered in all things, and it is sure" (see 2 Samuel 23.5, KJV). Here, O Lord, I take my stand; here I lay my foundation, and on this your covenant I build; or rather here you yourself have laid my foundation, and on this rock you have set my soul and built my hopes, you subduing my enmity. I acquiesce. I will now "remember the years of your right hand" (see Psalm 77.10, KJV) . . .

O Lord, ever, ever, and again did you deliver [your people] and send provision for them by your own covenant: "chose David your servant and took him from the sheepfolds, from following the ewes great with young. You brought him to feed Jacob, your people, and Israel, your inheritance. So he fed them according to the integrity of his heart and guided them by the skillfulness of his hands . . ." (Psalm 78.70–71).

"This God is our God; we will make mention of his righteousness, and his only." By his own covenant, in his own time, and by means of his own providing, he will revive us. Amen.

ADDITIONAL SCRIPTURE READING:
Psalm 105.6–10; Isaiah 40.31

Go to page 1503 for your next devotional reading.

1700   1900

To everyone who conquers I will give some of the hidden manna, and I will give a white stone, and on the white stone is written a new name that no one knows except the one who receives it.

The Message to Thyatira

18 "And to the angel of the church in Thyatira write: These are the words of the Son of God, who has eyes like a flame of fire, and whose feet are like burnished bronze:

19 "I know your works—your love, faith, service, and patient endurance. I know that your last works are greater than the first. 20But I have this against you: you tolerate that woman Jezebel, who calls herself a prophet and is teaching and beguiling my servants[i] to practice fornication and to eat food sacrificed to idols. 21I gave her time to repent, but she refuses to repent of her fornication. 22Beware, I am throwing her on a bed, and those who commit adultery with her I am throwing into great distress, unless they repent of her doings; 23and I will strike her children dead. And all the churches will know that I am the one who searches minds and hearts, and I will give to each of you as your works deserve. 24But to the rest of you in Thyatira, who do not hold this teaching, who have not learned what some call 'the deep things of Satan,' to you I say, I do not lay on you any other burden; 25only hold fast to what you have until I come. 26To everyone who conquers and continues to do my works to the end,

I will give authority over the
nations;
27   to rule[j] them with an iron rod,
as when clay pots are shattered—
28even as I also received authority from my Father. To the one who conquers I will also give the morning star. 29Let anyone who has an ear listen to what the Spirit is saying to the churches.

The Message to Sardis

3 "And to the angel of the church in Sardis write: These are the words of him who has the seven spirits of God and the seven stars:

"I know your works; you have a name of being alive, but you are dead. 2Wake up, and strengthen what remains and is on the point of death, for I have not found your works perfect in the sight of my God. 3Remember then what you received and heard; obey it, and repent. If you do not wake up, I will come like a thief, and you will not know at what hour I will come to you. 4Yet you have still a few persons in Sardis who have not soiled their clothes; they will walk with me, dressed in white, for they are worthy. 5If you conquer, you will be clothed like them in white robes, and I will not blot your name out of the book of life; I will confess your name before my Father and before his angels. 6Let anyone who has an ear listen to what the Spirit is saying to the churches.

The Message to Philadelphia

7 "And to the angel of the church in Philadelphia write:
These are the words of the holy
one, the true one,
who has the key of David,
who opens and no one will shut,
who shuts and no one opens:
8 "I know your works. Look, I have set before you an open door, which no one is able to shut. I know that you have but little power, and yet you have kept my word and have not denied my name. 9I will make those of the synagogue of Satan who say that they are Jews and are not, but are lying—I will make them come and bow down before your feet, and they will learn that I have loved you. 10Because you have kept my word of patient endurance, I will keep you from the hour of trial that is coming on the whole world to test the inhabitants of the earth. 11I am coming soon; hold fast to what you have, so that no one may seize your crown. 12If you conquer, I will make you a pillar in the temple of my God; you will never go out of it. I will write on you the name of my God, and the name of the city of my God, the new Jerusalem that comes down from my God out of heaven, and my own new name. 13Let anyone who has an ear listen to what the Spirit is saying to the churches.

The Message to Laodicea

14 "And to the angel of the church in

Laodicea write: The words of the Amen, the faithful and true witness, the origin[k] of God's creation:

15 "I know your works; you are nei-

ther cold nor hot. I wish that you were either cold or hot. [16]So, because you are lukewarm, and neither cold nor hot, I am about to spit you out of my mouth.

k Or *beginning*

FRIDAY

BE FAITHFUL, EVEN TO THE POINT OF DEATH
Ignatius of Antioch

VERSE: Revelation 3.12   **PASSAGE:** Revelation 3.10–13

rom Syria all the way to Rome I am fighting with wild beasts, on land and sea, by night and day, chained amidst ten leopards (that is, a company of soldiers) who only get worse when they are well treated. Yet because of their mistreatment I am becoming more of a disciple; nevertheless "I am not thereby justified" (see 1 Corinthians 4.4). May I have the pleasure of the wild beasts that have been prepared for me; and I pray that they prove to be prompt with me. I will even coax them to devour me promptly, not as they have done with some, whom they were too timid to touch. And if when I am willing and ready they are not, I will force them. Bear with me— I know what is best for me. Now at last I am beginning to be a disciple. May nothing visible or invisible envy me, so that I may reach Jesus Christ. Fire and cross and battles with wild beasts, mutilation, mangling, wrenching of bones, the hacking of limbs, the crushing of my whole body, cruel tortures of the devil—let these come upon me, only let me reach Jesus Christ!

Neither the ends of the earth nor the kingdoms of this age are of any use to me. It is better for me to die for Jesus Christ than to rule over the ends of the earth. Him I seek, who died on our behalf; him I long for, who rose again for our sake. The pains of birth are upon me. Bear with me, brothers: do not keep me from living; do not desire my death. Do not give to the world one who wants to belong to God, nor tempt him with material things. Let me receive the pure light, for when I arrive there I will be a man. Allow me to be an imitator of the suffering of my God. If anyone has him within himself, let him understand what I long for and sympathize with me, knowing what constrains me.

ADDITIONAL SCRIPTURE READING:
John 11.25–26; Philippians 1.20–21

Go to page 1505 for your next devotional reading.

100   500

17For you say, 'I am rich, I have prospered, and I need nothing.' You do not realize that you are wretched, pitiable, poor, blind, and naked. 18Therefore I counsel you to buy from me gold refined by fire so that you may be rich; and white robes to clothe you and to keep the shame of your nakedness from being seen; and salve to anoint your eyes so that you may see. 19I reprove and discipline those whom I love. Be earnest, therefore, and repent. 20Listen! I am standing at the door, knocking; if you hear my voice and open the door, I will come in to you and eat with you, and you with me. 21To the one who conquers I will give a place with me on my throne, just as I myself conquered and sat down with my Father on his throne. 22Let anyone who has an ear listen to what the Spirit is saying to the churches."

The Heavenly Worship

4 After this I looked, and there in heaven a door stood open! And the first voice, which I had heard speaking to me like a trumpet, said, "Come up here, and I will show you what must take place after this." 2At once I was in the spirit,1 and there in heaven stood a throne, with one seated on the throne! 3And the one seated there looks like jasper and carnelian, and around the throne is a rainbow that looks like an emerald. 4Around the throne are twenty-four thrones, and seated on the thrones are twenty-four elders, dressed in white robes, with golden crowns on their heads. 5Coming from the throne are flashes of lightning, and rumblings and peals of thunder, and in front of the throne burn seven flaming torches, which are the seven spirits of God; 6and in front of the throne there is something like a sea of glass, like crystal.

Around the throne, and on each side of the throne, are four living creatures, full of eyes in front and behind: 7the first living creature like a lion, the second living creature like an ox, the third living creature with a face like a human face, and the fourth living creature like a flying eagle. 8And the four living creatures, each of them with six wings, are full of eyes all around and inside. Day and night without ceasing they sing,

"Holy, holy, holy,
  the Lord God the Almighty,
    who was and is and is to come."

9And whenever the living creatures give glory and honor and thanks to the one who is seated on the throne, who lives forever and ever, 10the twenty-four elders fall before the one who is seated on the throne and worship the one who lives forever and ever; they cast their crowns before the throne, singing,

11   "You are worthy, our Lord and God,
    to receive glory and honor and power,
  for you created all things,
    and by your will they existed and were created."

The Scroll and the Lamb

5 Then I saw in the right hand of the one seated on the throne a scroll written on the inside and on the back, sealedm with seven seals; 2and I saw a mighty angel proclaiming with a loud voice, "Who is worthy to open the scroll and break its seals?" 3And no one in heaven or on earth or under the earth was able to open the scroll or to look into it. 4And I began to weep bitterly because no one was found worthy to open the scroll or to look into it. 5Then one of the elders said to me, "Do not weep. See, the Lion of the tribe of Judah, the Root of David, has conquered, so that he can open the scroll and its seven seals."

6 Then I saw between the throne and the four living creatures and among the elders a Lamb standing as if it had been slaughtered, having seven horns and seven eyes, which are the seven spirits of God sent out into all the earth. 7He went and took the scroll from the right hand of the one who was seated on the throne. 8When he had taken the scroll, the four living creatures and the twenty-four elders fell before the Lamb, each holding a harp and golden bowls full of incense, which are the prayers of the saints. 9They sing a new song:

"You are worthy to take the scroll
  and to open its seals,

1 Or *in the Spirit*   m Or *written on the inside, and sealed on the back*

WEEKEND

THE ENCOUNTER
John Newton

VERSE: Revelation 5.9   **PASSAGE:** Revelation 5.9–12

n evil long I took delight,
    Unawed by shame or fear,
Till a new object struck my sight,
    And stopped my wild career:
I saw One hanging on a tree
    In agonies and blood,
Who fixed his languid eyes on me,
    As near his cross I stood.

Sure never till my latest breath
    Can I forget that look:
It seemed to charge me with his death,
    Though not a word he spoke:
My conscience felt and owned the guilt,
    And plunged me in despair;
I saw my sins his blood had spilt
    And helped to nail him there.

Alas! I knew not what I did!
    But now my tears are vain:
Where shall my trembling soul be hid?
    For I the Lord have slain!
A second look he gave, which said,
    'I freely all forgive;
This blood is for thy ransom paid.
    I die, that thou mayst live.'

Thus, while his death my sin displays
    In all its blackest hue,
Such is the mystery of grace,
    It seals my pardon too . . .

ADDITIONAL SCRIPTURE READING:
Philippians 2.8; Colossians 2.13–15

Go to page 1508 for your next devotional reading.

1700   1900

for you were slaughtered and by
　　your blood you ransomed for
　　God
　　saints from[n] every tribe and
　　language and people and
　　nation;
10　you have made them to be a
　　kingdom and priests serving[o]
　　our God,
　　and they will reign on earth."

11 Then I looked, and I heard the voice of many angels surrounding the throne and the living creatures and the elders; they numbered myriads of myriads and thousands of thousands, [12]singing with full voice,
　　"Worthy is the Lamb that was
　　slaughtered
　　to receive power and wealth and
　　wisdom and might
　　and honor and glory and blessing!"
[13]Then I heard every creature in heaven and on earth and under the earth and in the sea, and all that is in them, singing,
　　"To the one seated on the throne
　　and to the Lamb
　　be blessing and honor and glory and
　　might
　　forever and ever!"
[14]And the four living creatures said, "Amen!" And the elders fell down and worshiped.

The Seven Seals

6 Then I saw the Lamb open one of the seven seals, and I heard one of the four living creatures call out, as with a voice of thunder, "Come!"[p] [2]I looked, and there was a white horse! Its rider had a bow; a crown was given to him, and he came out conquering and to conquer.

3 When he opened the second seal, I heard the second living creature call out, "Come!"[p] [4]And out came[q] another horse, bright red; its rider was permitted to take peace from the earth, so that people would slaughter one another; and he was given a great sword.

5 When he opened the third seal, I heard the third living creature call out, "Come!"[p] I looked, and there was a black horse! Its rider held a pair of scales in his hand, [6]and I heard what seemed to

be a voice in the midst of the four living creatures saying, "A quart of wheat for a day's pay,[r] and three quarts of barley for a day's pay,[r] but do not damage the olive oil and the wine!"

7 When he opened the fourth seal, I heard the voice of the fourth living creature call out, "Come!"[p] [8]I looked and there was a pale green horse! Its rider's name was Death, and Hades followed with him; they were given authority over a fourth of the earth, to kill with sword, famine, and pestilence, and by the wild animals of the earth.

9 When he opened the fifth seal, I saw under the altar the souls of those who had been slaughtered for the word of God and for the testimony they had given; [10]they cried out with a loud voice, "Sovereign Lord, holy and true, how long will it be before you judge and avenge our blood on the inhabitants of the earth?" [11]They were each given a white robe and told to rest a little longer, until the number would be complete both of their fellow servants[s] and of their brothers and sisters,[t] who were soon to be killed as they themselves had been killed.

12 When he opened the sixth seal, I looked, and there came a great earthquake; the sun became black as sackcloth, the full moon became like blood, [13]and the stars of the sky fell to the earth as the fig tree drops its winter fruit when shaken by a gale. [14]The sky vanished like a scroll rolling itself up, and every mountain and island was removed from its place. [15]Then the kings of the earth and the magnates and the generals and the rich and the powerful, and everyone, slave and free, hid in the caves and among the rocks of the mountains, [16]calling to the mountains and rocks, "Fall on us and hide us from the face of the one seated on the throne and from the wrath of the Lamb; [17]for the great day of their wrath has come, and who is able to stand?"

The 144,000 of Israel Sealed

7 After this I saw four angels standing at the four corners of the earth, holding back the four winds of

---

n Gk ransomed for God from　o Gk priests to　p Or "Go!"　q Or went　r Gk a denarius
s Gk slaves　t Gk brothers

the earth so that no wind could blow on earth or sea or against any tree. ²I saw another angel ascending from the rising of the sun, having the seal of the living God, and he called with a loud voice to the four angels who had been given power to damage earth and sea, ³saying, "Do not damage the earth or the sea or the trees, until we have marked the servants^u of our God with a seal on their foreheads."

4 And I heard the number of those who were sealed, one hundred forty-four thousand, sealed out of every tribe of the people of Israel:

5 From the tribe of Judah twelve thousand sealed,
from the tribe of Reuben twelve thousand,
from the tribe of Gad twelve thousand,
6 from the tribe of Asher twelve thousand,
from the tribe of Naphtali twelve thousand,
from the tribe of Manasseh twelve thousand,
7 from the tribe of Simeon twelve thousand,
from the tribe of Levi twelve thousand,
from the tribe of Issachar twelve thousand,
8 from the tribe of Zebulun twelve thousand,
from the tribe of Joseph twelve thousand,
from the tribe of Benjamin twelve thousand sealed.

The Multitude from Every Nation

9 After this I looked, and there was a great multitude that no one could count, from every nation, from all tribes and peoples and languages, standing before the throne and before the Lamb, robed in white, with palm branches in their hands. ¹⁰They cried out in a loud voice, saying,

"Salvation belongs to our God who is seated on the throne, and to the Lamb!"

¹¹And all the angels stood around the throne and around the elders and the four living creatures, and they fell on

their faces before the throne and worshiped God, ¹²singing,

"Amen! Blessing and glory and wisdom
and thanksgiving and honor
and power and might
be to our God forever and ever! Amen."

13 Then one of the elders addressed me, saying, "Who are these, robed in white, and where have they come from?" ¹⁴I said to him, "Sir, you are the one that knows." Then he said to me, "These are they who have come out of the great ordeal; they have washed their robes and made them white in the blood of the Lamb.

15 For this reason they are before the throne of God,
and worship him day and night within his temple,
and the one who is seated on the throne will shelter them.
16 They will hunger no more, and thirst no more;
the sun will not strike them, nor any scorching heat;
17 for the Lamb at the center of the throne will be their shepherd,
and he will guide them to springs of the water of life,
and God will wipe away every tear from their eyes."

The Seventh Seal and the Golden Censer

8 When the Lamb opened the seventh seal, there was silence in heaven for about half an hour. ²And I saw the seven angels who stand before God, and seven trumpets were given to them.

3 Another angel with a golden censer came and stood at the altar; he was given a great quantity of incense to offer with the prayers of all the saints on the golden altar that is before the throne. ⁴And the smoke of the incense, with the prayers of the saints, rose before God from the hand of the angel. ⁵Then the angel took the censer and filled it with fire from the altar and threw it on the earth; and there were peals of thunder,

EVENING PRAYER
Thomas Merton

VERSE: Revelation 8.4   **PASSAGE:** Revelation 8.3–5

ord, receive my prayer
Sweet as incense smoke
Rising from my heart
Full of care
I lift up my hands
In evening sacrifice
Lord, receive my prayer.

When I meet the man
On my way
When he starts to curse
And threatens me,
Lord, guard my lips
I will not reply
Guide my steps in the night
As I go my way.

Maybe he belongs
To some other Lord
Who is not so wise and good
Maybe that is why those bones
Lie scattered on his road.

When I look to right and left
No one cares to know
Who I am, where I go . . .

Lord, to you I raise
Wide and bright
Faith-filled eyes
In the night
You are my protection
Bring me home.

And receive my prayer
Sweet as incense smoke
Rising from my heart
Free of care.

ADDITIONAL SCRIPTURE READING:
Matthew 6.9–13; John 14.14

Go to page 1512 for your next devotional reading.

1900   Present

rumblings, flashes of lightning, and an earthquake.

PRAYER IS THE INCENSE OF A HOLY HEART
  RISING TO GOD FROM BRUISED AND BROKEN
    THINGS,
WHEN KINDLED BY THE SPIRIT'S BURNING
  BREATH
  AND UPWARD BORNE BY FAITH'S ASCENDING
    WINGS.
                              —A. B. Simpson

The Seven Trumpets

6 Now the seven angels who had the seven trumpets made ready to blow them.

7 The first angel blew his trumpet, and there came hail and fire, mixed with blood, and they were hurled to the earth; and a third of the earth was burned up, and a third of the trees were burned up, and all green grass was burned up.

8 The second angel blew his trumpet, and something like a great mountain, burning with fire, was thrown into the sea. 9A third of the sea became blood, a third of the living creatures in the sea died, and a third of the ships were destroyed.

10 The third angel blew his trumpet, and a great star fell from heaven, blazing like a torch, and it fell on a third of the rivers and on the springs of water. 11The name of the star is Wormwood. A third of the waters became wormwood, and many died from the water, because it was made bitter.

12 The fourth angel blew his trumpet, and a third of the sun was struck, and a third of the moon, and a third of the stars, so that a third of their light was darkened; a third of the day was kept from shining, and likewise the night.

13 Then I looked, and I heard an eagle crying with a loud voice as it flew in midheaven, "Woe, woe, woe to the inhabitants of the earth, at the blasts of the other trumpets that the three angels are about to blow!"

9 And the fifth angel blew his trumpet, and I saw a star that had fallen from heaven to earth, and he was given the key to the shaft of the bottomless pit; 2he opened the shaft of the bottomless pit, and from the shaft rose smoke like the smoke of a great furnace, and the sun and the air were darkened with the smoke from the shaft. 3Then from the smoke came locusts on the earth, and they were given authority like the authority of scorpions of the earth. 4They were told not to damage the grass of the earth or any green growth or any tree, but only those people who do not have the seal of God on their foreheads. 5They were allowed to torture them for five months, but not to kill them, and their torture was like the torture of a scorpion when it stings someone. 6And in those days people will seek death but will not find it; they will long to die, but death will flee from them.

7 In appearance the locusts were like horses equipped for battle. On their heads were what looked like crowns of gold; their faces were like human faces, 8their hair like women's hair, and their teeth like lions' teeth; 9they had scales like iron breastplates, and the noise of their wings was like the noise of many chariots with horses rushing into battle. 10They have tails like scorpions, with stingers, and in their tails is their power to harm people for five months. 11They have as king over them the angel of the bottomless pit; his name in Hebrew is Abaddon,v and in Greek he is called Apollyon.w

12 The first woe has passed. There are still two woes to come.

13 Then the sixth angel blew his trumpet, and I heard a voice from the fourx horns of the golden altar before God, 14saying to the sixth angel who had the trumpet, "Release the four angels who are bound at the great river Euphrates." 15So the four angels were released, who had been held ready for the hour, the day, the month, and the year, to kill a third of humankind. 16The number of the troops of cavalry was two hundred million; I heard their number. 17And this was how I saw the horses in my vision: the riders wore breastplates the color of fire and of sapphirey and of

---

v That is, Destruction   w That is, Destroyer   x Other ancient authorities lack four
y Gk hyacinth

sulfur; the heads of the horses were like lions' heads, and fire and smoke and sulfur came out of their mouths. 18By these three plagues a third of humankind was killed, by the fire and smoke and sulfur coming out of their mouths. 19For the power of the horses is in their mouths and in their tails; their tails are like serpents, having heads; and with them they inflict harm.

20 The rest of humankind, who were not killed by these plagues, did not repent of the works of their hands or give up worshiping demons and idols of gold and silver and bronze and stone and wood, which cannot see or hear or walk. 21And they did not repent of their murders or their sorceries or their fornication or their thefts.

The Angel with the Little Scroll

10 And I saw another mighty angel coming down from heaven, wrapped in a cloud, with a rainbow over his head; his face was like the sun, and his legs like pillars of fire. 2He held a little scroll open in his hand. Setting his right foot on the sea and his left foot on the land, 3he gave a great shout, like a lion roaring. And when he shouted, the seven thunders sounded. 4And when the seven thunders had sounded, I was about to write, but I heard a voice from heaven saying, "Seal up what the seven thunders have said, and do not write it down." 5Then the angel whom I saw standing on the sea and the land raised his right hand to heaven

6   and swore by him who lives
     forever and ever,
who created heaven and what is in it, the earth and what is in it, and the sea and what is in it: "There will be no more delay, 7but in the days when the seventh angel is to blow his trumpet, the mystery of God will be fulfilled, as he announced to his servants*z* the prophets."

8 Then the voice that I had heard from heaven spoke to me again, saying, "Go, take the scroll that is open in the hand of the angel who is standing on the sea and on the land." 9So I went to the angel and told him to give me the little scroll; and he said to me, "Take it, and eat; it will be bitter to your stomach, but

sweet as honey in your mouth." 10So I took the little scroll from the hand of the angel and ate it; it was sweet as honey in my mouth, but when I had eaten it, my stomach was made bitter.

11 Then they said to me, "You must prophesy again about many peoples and nations and languages and kings."

The Two Witnesses

11 Then I was given a measuring rod like a staff, and I was told, "Come and measure the temple of God and the altar and those who worship there, 2but do not measure the court outside the temple; leave that out, for it is given over to the nations, and they will trample over the holy city for forty-two months. 3And I will grant my two witnesses authority to prophesy for one thousand two hundred sixty days, wearing sackcloth."

4 These are the two olive trees and the two lampstands that stand before the Lord of the earth. 5And if anyone wants to harm them, fire pours from their mouth and consumes their foes; anyone who wants to harm them must be killed in this manner. 6They have authority to shut the sky, so that no rain may fall during the days of their prophesying, and they have authority over the waters to turn them into blood, and to strike the earth with every kind of plague, as often as they desire.

7 When they have finished their testimony, the beast that comes up from the bottomless pit will make war on them and conquer them and kill them, 8and their dead bodies will lie in the street of the great city that is prophetically*a* called Sodom and Egypt, where also their Lord was crucified. 9For three and a half days members of the peoples and tribes and languages and nations will gaze at their dead bodies and refuse to let them be placed in a tomb; 10and the inhabitants of the earth will gloat over them and celebrate and exchange presents, because these two prophets had been a torment to the inhabitants of the earth.

11 But after the three and a half days, the breath*b* of life from God entered them, and they stood on their feet, and

z Gk *slaves*   a Or *allegorically;* Gk *spiritually*   b Or *the spirit* those who saw them were terrified. [c]Then they heard a loud voice from heaven saying to them, "Come up here!" And they went up to heaven in a cloud while their enemies watched them. 13 At that moment there was a great earthquake, and a tenth of the city fell; seven thousand people were killed in the earthquake, and the rest were terrified and gave glory to the God of heaven.

14 The second woe has passed. The third woe is coming very soon.

The Seventh Trumpet

15 Then the seventh angel blew his trumpet, and there were loud voices in heaven, saying,

"The kingdom of the world has
      become the kingdom of our
      Lord
   and of his Messiah,[d]
   and he will reign forever and ever."

16 Then the twenty-four elders who sit on their thrones before God fell on their faces and worshiped God, 17 singing,

"We give you thanks, Lord God
      Almighty,
   who are and who were,
   for you have taken your great power
      and begun to reign.
18 The nations raged,
   but your wrath has come,
   and the time for judging the dead,
   for rewarding your servants,[e] the
      prophets
   and saints and all who fear your
      name,
   both small and great,
   and for destroying those who
      destroy the earth."

19 Then God's temple in heaven was opened, and the ark of his covenant was seen within his temple; and there were flashes of lightning, rumblings, peals of thunder, an earthquake, and heavy hail.

The Woman and the Dragon

12 A great portent appeared in heaven: a woman clothed with the sun, with the moon under her feet, and on her head a crown of twelve stars. 2 She was pregnant and was crying out in birth pangs, in the agony of giving birth. 3 Then another portent appeared in

heaven: a great red dragon, with seven heads and ten horns, and seven diadems on his heads. 4 His tail swept down a third of the stars of heaven and threw them to the earth. Then the dragon stood before the woman who was about to bear a child, so that he might devour her child as soon as it was born. 5 And she gave birth to a son, a male child, who is to rule[f] all the nations with a rod of iron. But her child was snatched away and taken to God and to his throne; 6 and the woman fled into the wilderness, where she has a place prepared by God, so that there she can be nourished for one thousand two hundred sixty days.

Michael Defeats the Dragon

7 And war broke out in heaven; Michael and his angels fought against the dragon. The dragon and his angels fought back, 8 but they were defeated, and there was no longer any place for them in heaven. 9 The great dragon was thrown down, that ancient serpent, who is called the Devil and Satan, the deceiver of the whole world—he was thrown down to the earth, and his angels were thrown down with him.

10 Then I heard a loud voice in heaven, proclaiming,

"Now have come the salvation and
      the power
   and the kingdom of our God
   and the authority of his
      Messiah,[d]
   for the accuser of our comrades[g]
      has been thrown down,
   who accuses them day and night
      before our God.
11 But they have conquered him by
      the blood of the Lamb
   and by the word of their
      testimony,
   for they did not cling to life even in
      the face of death.
12 Rejoice then, you heavens
      and those who dwell in them!
   But woe to the earth and the sea,
   for the devil has come down to
      you
   with great wrath,
      because he knows that his time
         is short!"

c Other ancient authorities read I   d Gk Christ   e Gk slaves   f Or to shepherd
g Gk brothers

The Dragon Fights Again on Earth

13 So when the dragon saw that he had been thrown down to the earth, he pursued[h] the woman who had given birth to the male child. 14But the woman was given the two wings of the great eagle, so that she could fly from the serpent into the wilderness, to her place where she is nourished for a time, and times, and half a time. 15Then from his mouth the serpent poured water like a river after the woman, to sweep her away with the flood. 16But the earth came to the help of the woman; it opened its mouth and swallowed the river that the dragon had poured from his mouth. 17Then the dragon was angry

h Or *persecuted*

TUESDAY

FROM LUCIFER
Joost van den Vondel

VERSE: Revelation 12.7   **PASSAGE:** Revelation 12.7–9

ICHAEL: Praise be to God! The state of things above
Has changed. Our Grand Foe has met his defeat;
And in our hands he leaves his standard, helm,
And morning-star, and shield and banners bold.
Which spoil, gained in pursuit, even now does hang,
'Mid joys triumphant, honors, songs of praise,
And sounds of trump, on Heaven's axis bright,
The mirror clear of all rebelliousness,
Of all ambition that would rear its crest
'Gainst God, the stem immovable—grand fount,
Prime source, and Father of all things that are,
Which from his hand their nature did receive.
And various attributes. No more shall we
Behold the glow of Majesty Supreme
Dimmed by the damp of base ingratitude.
There, deep beneath our sight and these high thrones,
They wander through the air and restlessly
Move to and fro, all blind and overcast
With shrouding clouds, and horribly deformed.
Thus is his fate, who would assail God's Throne.
CHORUS: Thus is his fate, who would assail God's Throne.
Thus his fate, who would, through envy, man,
In God's own image made, deprive of light.

ADDITIONAL SCRIPTURE READING:
Isaiah 14.12–15; Romans 16.20

Go to page 1516 for your next devotional reading.

1500   1700

with the woman, and went off to make war on the rest of her children, those who keep the commandments of God and hold the testimony of Jesus.

The First Beast

18 Then the dragon[i] took his stand on the sand of the seashore. **13** ¹And I saw a beast rising out of the sea, having ten horns and seven heads; and on its horns were ten diadems, and on its heads were blasphemous names. ²And the beast that I saw was like a leopard, its feet were like a bear's, and its mouth was like a lion's mouth. And the dragon gave it his power and his throne and great authority. ³One of its heads seemed to have received a death-blow, but its mortal wound[j] had been healed. In amazement the whole earth followed the beast. ⁴They worshiped the dragon, for he had given his authority to the beast, and they worshiped the beast, saying, "Who is like the beast, and who can fight against it?"

5 The beast was given a mouth uttering haughty and blasphemous words, and it was allowed to exercise authority for forty-two months. ⁶It opened its mouth to utter blasphemies against God, blaspheming his name and his dwelling, that is, those who dwell in heaven. ⁷Also it was allowed to make war on the saints and to conquer them.[k] It was given authority over every tribe and people and language and nation, ⁸and all the inhabitants of the earth will worship it, everyone whose name has not been written from the foundation of the world in the book of life of the Lamb that was slaughtered.[l]

9 Let anyone who has an ear listen:
10 If you are to be taken captive,
        into captivity you go;
    if you kill with the sword,
        with the sword you must be
        killed.
Here is a call for the endurance and faith of the saints.

The Second Beast

11 Then I saw another beast that rose out of the earth; it had two horns like a lamb and it spoke like a dragon. ¹²It exercises all the authority of the first beast on its behalf, and it makes the earth and its inhabitants worship the first beast, whose mortal wound[m] had been healed. ¹³It performs great signs, even making fire come down from heaven to earth in the sight of all; ¹⁴and by the signs that it is allowed to perform on behalf of the beast, it deceives the inhabitants of earth, telling them to make an image for the beast that had been wounded by the sword[n] and yet lived; ¹⁵and it was allowed to give breath[o] to the image of the beast so that the image of the beast could even speak and cause those who would not worship the image of the beast to be killed. ¹⁶Also it causes all, both small and great, both rich and poor, both free and slave, to be marked on the right hand or the forehead, ¹⁷so that no one can buy or sell who does not have the mark, that is, the name of the beast or the number of its name. ¹⁸This calls for wisdom: let anyone with understanding calculate the number of the beast, for it is the number of a person. Its number is six hundred sixty-six.[p]

The Lamb and the 144,000

14 Then I looked, and there was the Lamb, standing on Mount Zion! And with him were one hundred forty-four thousand who had his name and his Father's name written on their foreheads. ²And I heard a voice from heaven like the sound of many waters and like the sound of loud thunder; the voice I heard was like the sound of harpists playing on their harps, ³and they sing a new song before the throne and before the four living creatures and before the elders. No one could learn that song except the one hundred forty-four thousand who have been redeemed from the earth. ⁴It is these who have not defiled themselves with women, for they are virgins; these follow the Lamb wherever he goes. They have been redeemed from humankind as first fruits for God and the

---

i Gk *Then he;* other ancient authorities read *Then I stood*   *j* Gk *the plague of its death*   *k* Other ancient authorities lack this sentence   *l* Or *written in the book of life of the Lamb that was slaughtered from the foundation of the world*   *m* Gk *whose plague of its death*   *n* Or *that had received the plague of the sword*   *o* Or *spirit*   *p* Other ancient authorities read *six hundred sixteen*

Lamb, 5and in their mouth no lie was found; they are blameless.

The Messages of the Three Angels

6 Then I saw another angel flying in midheaven, with an eternal gospel to proclaim to those who live*q* on the earth—to every nation and tribe and language and people. 7He said in a loud voice, "Fear God and give him glory, for the hour of his judgment has come; and worship him who made heaven and earth, the sea and the springs of water."

8 Then another angel, a second, followed, saying, "Fallen, fallen is Babylon the great! She has made all nations drink of the wine of the wrath of her fornication."

9 Then another angel, a third, followed them, crying with a loud voice, "Those who worship the beast and its image, and receive a mark on their foreheads or on their hands, 10they will also drink the wine of God's wrath, poured unmixed into the cup of his anger, and they will be tormented with fire and sulfur in the presence of the holy angels and in the presence of the Lamb. 11And the smoke of their torment goes up forever and ever. There is no rest day or night for those who worship the beast and its image and for anyone who receives the mark of its name."

12 Here is a call for the endurance of the saints, those who keep the commandments of God and hold fast to the faith of*r* Jesus.

13 And I heard a voice from heaven saying, "Write this: Blessed are the dead who from now on die in the Lord." "Yes," says the Spirit, "they will rest from their labors, for their deeds follow them."

Reaping the Earth's Harvest

14 Then I looked, and there was a white cloud, and seated on the cloud was one like the Son of Man, with a golden crown on his head, and a sharp sickle in his hand! 15Another angel came out of the temple, calling with a loud voice to the one who sat on the cloud, "Use your sickle and reap, for the hour to reap has come, because the harvest of the earth is fully ripe." 16So the one who sat on the cloud swung his sickle over the earth, and the earth was reaped.

17 Then another angel came out of the temple in heaven, and he too had a sharp sickle. 18Then another angel came out from the altar, the angel who has authority over fire, and he called with a loud voice to him who had the sharp sickle, "Use your sharp sickle and gather the clusters of the vine of the earth, for its grapes are ripe." 19So the angel swung his sickle over the earth and gathered the vintage of the earth, and he threw it into the great wine press of the wrath of God. 20And the wine press was trodden outside the city, and blood flowed from the wine press, as high as a horse's bridle, for a distance of about two hundred miles.*s*

The Angels with the Seven Last Plagues

15 Then I saw another portent in heaven, great and amazing: seven angels with seven plagues, which are the last, for with them the wrath of God is ended.

2 And I saw what appeared to be a sea of glass mixed with fire, and those who had conquered the beast and its image and the number of its name, standing beside the sea of glass with harps of God in their hands. 3And they sing the song of Moses, the servant*t* of God, and the song of the Lamb:

"Great and amazing are your deeds,
　　Lord God the Almighty!
Just and true are your ways,
　　King of the nations!*u*
4 Lord, who will not fear
　　and glorify your name?
For you alone are holy.
　　All nations will come
　　and worship before you,
for your judgments have been
　　revealed."

5 After this I looked, and the temple of the tent*v* of witness in heaven was opened, 6and out of the temple came the seven angels with the seven plagues, robed in pure bright linen,*w* with golden sashes across their chests. 7Then one of

---

q Gk *sit*　　*r* Or *to their faith in*　　*s* Gk *one thousand six hundred stadia*　　*t* Gk *slave*　　*u* Other ancient authorities read *the ages*　　*v* Or *tabernacle*　　*w* Other ancient authorities read *stone*

the four living creatures gave the seven angels seven golden bowls full of the wrath of God, who lives forever and ever; 8and the temple was filled with smoke from the glory of God and from his power, and no one could enter the temple until the seven plagues of the seven angels were ended.

The Bowls of God's Wrath

16 Then I heard a loud voice from the temple telling the seven angels, "Go and pour out on the earth the seven bowls of the wrath of God."

2 So the first angel went and poured his bowl on the earth, and a foul and painful sore came on those who had the mark of the beast and who worshiped its image.

3 The second angel poured his bowl into the sea, and it became like the blood of a corpse, and every living thing in the sea died.

4 The third angel poured his bowl into the rivers and the springs of water, and they became blood. 5And I heard the angel of the waters say,

> "You are just, O Holy One, who are and were,
>   for you have judged these things;
> 6   because they shed the blood of
>   saints and prophets,
>   you have given them blood to
>   drink.
> It is what they deserve!"

7And I heard the altar respond,

> "Yes, O Lord God, the Almighty,
>   your judgments are true and just!"

8 The fourth angel poured his bowl on the sun, and it was allowed to scorch people with fire; 9they were scorched by the fierce heat, but they cursed the name of God, who had authority over these plagues, and they did not repent and give him glory.

10 The fifth angel poured his bowl on the throne of the beast, and its kingdom was plunged into darkness; people gnawed their tongues in agony, 11and cursed the God of heaven because of their pains and sores, and they did not repent of their deeds.

12 The sixth angel poured his bowl on the great river Euphrates, and its water was dried up in order to prepare the way for the kings from the east. 13And I saw three foul spirits like frogs coming from the mouth of the dragon, from the mouth of the beast, and from the mouth of the false prophet. 14These are demonic spirits, performing signs, who go abroad to the kings of the whole world, to assemble them for battle on the great day of God the Almighty. 15("See, I am coming like a thief! Blessed is the one who stays awake and is clothed,x not going about naked and exposed to shame.") 16And they assembled them at the place that in Hebrew is called Harmagedon.

17 The seventh angel poured his bowl into the air, and a loud voice came out of the temple, from the throne, saying, "It is done!" 18And there came flashes of lightning, rumblings, peals of thunder, and a violent earthquake, such as had not occurred since people were upon the earth, so violent was that earthquake. 19The great city was split into three parts, and the cities of the nations fell. God remembered great Babylon and gave her the wine-cup of the fury of his wrath. 20And every island fled away, and no mountains were to be found; 21and huge hailstones, each weighing about a hundred pounds,y dropped from heaven on people, until they cursed God for the plague of the hail, so fearful was that plague.

The Great Whore and the Beast

17 Then one of the seven angels who had the seven bowls came and said to me, "Come, I will show you the judgment of the great whore who is seated on many waters, 2with whom the kings of the earth have committed fornication, and with the wine of whose fornication the inhabitants of the earth have become drunk." 3So he carried me away in the spiritz into a wilderness, and I saw a woman sitting on a scarlet beast that was full of blasphemous names, and it had seven heads and ten horns. 4The woman was clothed in purple and scarlet, and adorned with gold and jewels and pearls, holding in her hand a golden cup full of abominations and the impurities of her fornication;

---

x Gk *and keeps his robes*   y Gk *weighing about a talent*   z Or *in the Spirit*

⁵and on her forehead was written a name, a mystery: "Babylon the great, mother of whores and of earth's abominations." ⁶And I saw that the woman was drunk with the blood of the saints and the blood of the witnesses to Jesus.

When I saw her, I was greatly amazed. ⁷But the angel said to me, "Why are you so amazed? I will tell you the mystery of the woman, and of the beast with seven heads and ten horns that carries her. ⁸The beast that you saw was, and is not, and is about to ascend from the bottomless pit and go to destruction. And the inhabitants of the earth, whose names have not been written in the book of life from the foundation of the world, will be amazed when they see the beast, because it was and is not and is to come.

9 "This calls for a mind that has wis-

WEDNESDAY

THE ROCKS AND THE MOUNTAINS
African-American Spiritual

VERSE: Revelation 16.20   **PASSAGE:** Revelation 16.17–21

h, the rocks and the mountains
    shall flee away,
And you shall have a new
    hiding place that day.
Seeker, seeker,
    Give up your heart to God,
Doubter, doubter,
    Give up your heart to God,
Mourner, mourner,
    Give up your heart to God,
Sinner, sinner,
    Give up your heart to God,
Sister, sister,
    Give up your heart to God,
Mother, mother,
    Give up your heart to God,
Children, children,
    Give up your heart to God,
And you shall have a new
    hiding place that day.
Oh, the rocks and the mountains
    shall flee away,
And you shall have a new
    hiding place that day.

ADDITIONAL SCRIPTURE READING:
Matthew 4.17; Revelation 6.15–17

Go to page 1518 for your next devotional reading.

1700   1900

dom: the seven heads are seven mountains on which the woman is seated; also, they are seven kings, 10of whom five have fallen, one is living, and the other has not yet come; and when he comes, he must remain only a little while. 11As for the beast that was and is not, it is an eighth but it belongs to the seven, and it goes to destruction. 12And the ten horns that you saw are ten kings who have not yet received a kingdom, but they are to receive authority as kings for one hour, together with the beast. 13These are united in yielding their power and authority to the beast; 14they will make war on the Lamb, and the Lamb will conquer them, for he is Lord of lords and King of kings, and those with him are called and chosen and faithful."

15 And he said to me, "The waters that you saw, where the whore is seated, are peoples and multitudes and nations and languages. 16And the ten horns that you saw, they and the beast will hate the whore; they will make her desolate and naked; they will devour her flesh and burn her up with fire. 17For God has put it into their hearts to carry out his purpose by agreeing to give their kingdom to the beast, until the words of God will be fulfilled. 18The woman you saw is the great city that rules over the kings of the earth."

The Fall of Babylon

18 After this I saw another angel coming down from heaven, having great authority; and the earth was made bright with his splendor. 2He called out with a mighty voice,

"Fallen, fallen is Babylon the great!
It has become a dwelling place of demons,
a haunt of every foul spirit,
a haunt of every foul bird,
a haunt of every foul and hateful beast.a
3　For all the nations have drunkb
of the wine of the wrath of her fornication,
and the kings of the earth have committed fornication with her,

and the merchants of the earth have grown rich from the powerc of her luxury."

4 Then I heard another voice from heaven saying,

"Come out of her, my people,
so that you do not take part in her sins,
and so that you do not share in her plagues;
5　for her sins are heaped high as heaven,
and God has remembered her iniquities.
6　Render to her as she herself has rendered,
and repay her double for her deeds;
mix a double draught for her in the cup she mixed.
7　As she glorified herself and lived luxuriously,
so give her a like measure of torment and grief.
Since in her heart she says,
'I rule as a queen;
I am no widow,
and I will never see grief,'
8　therefore her plagues will come in a single day—
pestilence and mourning and famine—
and she will be burned with fire;
for mighty is the Lord God who judges her."

9 And the kings of the earth, who committed fornication and lived in luxury with her, will weep and wail over her when they see the smoke of her burning; 10they will stand far off, in fear of her torment, and say,

"Alas, alas, the great city,
Babylon, the mighty city!
For in one hour your judgment has come."

11 And the merchants of the earth weep and mourn for her, since no one buys their cargo anymore, 12cargo of gold, silver, jewels and pearls, fine linen, purple, silk and scarlet, all kinds of scented wood, all articles of ivory, all articles of costly wood, bronze, iron, and marble, 13cinnamon, spice, incense, myrrh,

a Other ancient authorities lack the words a haunt of every foul beast and attach the words and hateful to the previous line so as to read a haunt of every foul and hateful bird　b Other ancient authorities read She has made all nations drink　c Or resources

frankincense, wine, olive oil, choice flour and wheat, cattle and sheep, horses and chariots, slaves—and human lives. *d*

¹⁴ "The fruit for which your soul
longed
has gone from you,

d Or chariots, and human bodies and souls

THURSDAY

SONNET XIII & SONNET XIV
Edmund Spenser

VERSE: Revelation 17.3   PASSAGE: Revelation 17.1–18

 saw a woman sitting on a beast
Before mine eyes, of orange color hue:
Horror and dreadful name of blasphemy
Filled her with pride. And seven heads I saw,
Ten horns also the stately beast did bear.
She seemed with glory of the scarlet fair,
And with fine pearl and gold puffed up in heart.
The wine of whoredom in a cup she bare.
The name of Mystery writ in her face.
The blood of martyrs dear were her delight.
Most fierce and fell this woman seemed to me.
An angel then descending down from heaven,
With thundering voice cried out aloud, and said,
Now for a truth great Babylon is fallen.

Then might I see upon a white horse set
The faithful man with flaming countenance,
His head did shine with crowns set thereupon.
The word of God made him a noble name.
His precious robe I saw embrewed with blood.
Then saw I from the heaven on horses white,
A puissant army come the self-same way.
Then cried a shining angel as me thought,
That birds from air descending down on earth
Should war upon the kings, and eat their flesh.
Then did I see the beast and kings also
Joining their force to slay the faithful man.
But this fierce hateful beast and all her train,
Is pitiless thrown down in pit of fire.

ADDITIONAL SCRIPTURE READING:
Psalm 103.1–3; Revelation 19.11–16

Go to page 1522 for your next devotional reading.

1500   1700

and all your dainties and your
    splendor
  are lost to you,
  never to be found again!"
15 The merchants of these wares, who
gained wealth from her, will stand far
off, in fear of her torment, weeping and
mourning aloud,
16 "Alas, alas, the great city,
    clothed in fine linen,
      in purple and scarlet,
    adorned with gold,
      with jewels, and with pearls!
17 For in one hour all this wealth has
      been laid waste!"

And all shipmasters and seafarers,
sailors and all whose trade is on the sea,
stood far off 18 and cried out as they saw
the smoke of her burning,
  "What city was like the great
    city?"
19 And they threw dust on their heads, as
they wept and mourned, crying out,
  "Alas, alas, the great city,
    where all who had ships at sea
    grew rich by her wealth!
  For in one hour she has been laid
    waste."

20 Rejoice over her, O heaven, you
saints and apostles and prophets! For
God has given judgment for you against
her.

21 Then a mighty angel took up a
stone like a great millstone and threw it
into the sea, saying,
  "With such violence Babylon the
    great city
    will be thrown down,
    and will be found no more;
22 and the sound of harpists and
      minstrels and of flutists and
      trumpeters
    will be heard in you no more;
  and an artisan of any trade
    will be found in you no more;
  and the sound of the millstone
    will be heard in you no more;
23 and the light of a lamp
    will shine in you no more;
  and the voice of bridegroom and
    bride
    will be heard in you no more;
  for your merchants were the
    magnates of the earth,

and all nations were deceived by
    your sorcery.
24 And in you^e was found the blood of
      prophets and of saints,
  and of all who have been
    slaughtered on earth."

The Rejoicing in Heaven

19 After this I heard what
seemed to be the loud voice of
a great multitude in heaven, saying,
  "Hallelujah!
  Salvation and glory and power to
    our God,
2   for his judgments are true and
      just;
  he has judged the great whore
    who corrupted the earth with her
      fornication,
  and he has avenged on her the
    blood of his servants."^{f}
3 Once more they said,
  "Hallelujah!
  The smoke goes up from her
    forever and ever."
4 And the twenty-four elders and the four
living creatures fell down and worshiped
God who is seated on the throne, saying,
  "Amen. Hallelujah!"
5 And from the throne came a voice
saying,
  "Praise our God,
  all you his servants,^{f}
  and all who fear him,
  small and great."
6 Then I heard what seemed to be the
voice of a great multitude, like the sound
of many waters and like the sound of
mighty thunderpeals, crying out,
  "Hallelujah!
  For the Lord our God
    the Almighty reigns.
7 Let us rejoice and exult
    and give him the glory,
  for the marriage of the Lamb has
    come,
    and his bride has made herself
      ready;
8 to her it has been granted to be
      clothed
    with fine linen, bright and
      pure"—
for the fine linen is the righteous deeds
of the saints.
9 And the angel said^g to me, "Write

e Gk *her*   *f* Gk *slaves*   *g* Gk *he said*

this: Blessed are those who are invited to the marriage supper of the Lamb." And he said to me, "These are true words of God." 10Then I fell down at his feet to worship him, but he said to me, "You must not do that! I am a fellow servant[h] with you and your comrades[i] who hold the testimony of Jesus.[j] Worship God! For the testimony of Jesus[j] is the spirit of prophecy."

The Rider on the White Horse

11 Then I saw heaven opened, and there was a white horse! Its rider is called Faithful and True, and in righteousness he judges and makes war. 12His eyes are like a flame of fire, and on his head are many diadems; and he has a name inscribed that no one knows but himself. 13He is clothed in a robe dipped in[k] blood, and his name is called The Word of God. 14And the armies of heaven, wearing fine linen, white and pure, were following him on white horses. 15From his mouth comes a sharp sword with which to strike down the nations, and he will rule[l] them with a rod of iron; he will tread the wine press of the fury of the wrath of God the Almighty. 16On his robe and on his thigh he has a name inscribed, "King of kings and Lord of lords."

The Beast and Its Armies Defeated

17 Then I saw an angel standing in the sun, and with a loud voice he called to all the birds that fly in midheaven, "Come, gather for the great supper of God, 18to eat the flesh of kings, the flesh of captains, the flesh of the mighty, the flesh of horses and their riders—flesh of all, both free and slave, both small and great." 19Then I saw the beast and the kings of the earth with their armies gathered to make war against the rider on the horse and against his army. 20And the beast was captured, and with it the false prophet who had performed in its presence the signs by which he deceived those who had received the mark of the beast and those who worshiped its image. These two were thrown alive into the lake of fire that burns with sulfur. 21And the rest were killed by the sword

of the rider on the horse, the sword that came from his mouth; and all the birds were gorged with their flesh.

The Thousand Years

20 Then I saw an angel coming down from heaven, holding in his hand the key to the bottomless pit and a great chain. 2He seized the dragon, that ancient serpent, who is the Devil and Satan, and bound him for a thousand years, 3and threw him into the pit, and locked and sealed it over him, so that he would deceive the nations no more, until the thousand years were ended. After that he must be let out for a little while.

4 Then I saw thrones, and those seated on them were given authority to judge. I also saw the souls of those who had been beheaded for their testimony to Jesus[m] and for the word of God. They had not worshiped the beast or its image and had not received its mark on their foreheads or their hands. They came to life and reigned with Christ a thousand years. 5(The rest of the dead did not come to life until the thousand years were ended.) This is the first resurrection. 6Blessed and holy are those who share in the first resurrection. Over these the second death has no power, but they will be priests of God and of Christ, and they will reign with him a thousand years.

Satan's Doom

7 When the thousand years are ended, Satan will be released from his prison 8and will come out to deceive the nations at the four corners of the earth, Gog and Magog, in order to gather them for battle; they are as numerous as the sands of the sea. 9They marched up over the breadth of the earth and surrounded the camp of the saints and the beloved city. And fire came down from heaven[n] and consumed them. 10And the devil who had deceived them was thrown into the lake of fire and sulfur, where the beast and the false prophet were, and they will be tormented day and night forever and ever.

h Gk slave   i Gk brothers   j Or to Jesus   k Other ancient authorities read sprinkled with
l Or will shepherd   m Or for the testimony of Jesus   n Other ancient authorities read from God,
out of heaven, or out of heaven from God

The Dead Are Judged

11 Then I saw a great white throne and the one who sat on it; the earth and the heaven fled from his presence, and no place was found for them. 12 And I saw the dead, great and small, standing before the throne, and books were opened. Also another book was opened, the book of life. And the dead were judged according to their works, as recorded in the books. 13 And the sea gave up the dead that were in it, Death and Hades gave up the dead that were in them, and all were judged according to what they had done. 14 Then Death and Hades were thrown into the lake of fire. This is the second death, the lake of fire; 15 and anyone whose name was not found written in the book of life was thrown into the lake of fire.

The New Heaven and the New Earth

21 Then I saw a new heaven and a new earth; for the first heaven and the first earth had passed away, and the sea was no more. 2 And I saw the holy city, the new Jerusalem, coming down out of heaven from God, prepared as a bride adorned for her husband. 3 And I heard a loud voice from the throne saying,

"See, the home*o* of God is among
    mortals.
He will dwell*p* with them;
they will be his peoples,*q*
and God himself will be with
    them;*r*

4   he will wipe every tear from their
    eyes.
Death will be no more;
mourning and crying and pain will
    be no more,
for the first things have passed
    away."

5 And the one who was seated on the throne said, "See, I am making all things new." Also he said, "Write this, for these words are trustworthy and true." 6 Then he said to me, "It is done! I am the Alpha and the Omega, the beginning and the end. To the thirsty I will give water as a gift from the spring of the water of life. 7 Those who conquer will inherit these things, and I will be their God and they will be my children. 8 But as for the cowardly, the faithless,*s* the polluted, the murderers, the fornicators, the sorcerers, the idolaters, and all liars, their place will be in the lake that burns with fire and sulfur, which is the second death."

Vision of the New Jerusalem

9 Then one of the seven angels who had the seven bowls full of the seven last plagues came and said to me, "Come, I will show you the bride, the wife of the Lamb." 10 And in the spirit*t* he carried me away to a great, high mountain and showed me the holy city Jerusalem coming down out of heaven from God. 11 It has the glory of God and a radiance like a very rare jewel, like jasper, clear as crystal. 12 It has a great, high wall with twelve gates, and at the gates twelve angels, and on the gates are inscribed the names of the twelve tribes of the Israelites; 13 on the east three gates, on the north three gates, on the south three gates, and on the west three gates. 14 And the wall of the city has twelve foundations, and on them are the twelve names of the twelve apostles of the Lamb.

15 The angel*u* who talked to me had a measuring rod of gold to measure the city and its gates and walls. 16 The city lies foursquare, its length the same as its width; and he measured the city with his rod, fifteen hundred miles;*v* its length and width and height are equal. 17 He also measured its wall, one hundred forty-four cubits*w* by human measurement, which the angel was using. 18 The wall is built of jasper, while the city is pure gold, clear as glass. 19 The foundations of the wall of the city are adorned with every jewel; the first was jasper, the second sapphire, the third agate, the fourth emerald, 20 the fifth onyx, the sixth carnelian, the seventh chrysolite, the eighth beryl, the ninth topaz, the tenth chrysoprase, the eleventh jacinth, the twelfth amethyst. 21 And the twelve gates are twelve pearls, each of the gates is a single pearl,

---

o Gk *the tabernacle*   *p* Gk *will tabernacle*   *q* Other ancient authorities read *people*   *r* Other ancient authorities add *and be their God*   *s* Or *the unbelieving*   *t* Or *in the Spirit*   *u* Gk *He*
v Gk *twelve thousand stadia*   *w* That is, almost seventy-five yards

WALK IN JERUSALEM JUST LIKE JOHN
African-American Spiritual

VERSE: Revelation 21.10   **PASSAGE:** Revelation 21.9–27

Version 1

 want to be ready,
I want to be ready,
I want to be ready,
To walk in Jerusalem just like John.

John said the city was just four square,
And he declared he'd meet me there;
John! Oh, John! what do you say?
That I'll be there in the coming day.
When Peter was preaching at Pentecost
He was endowed with the Holy Ghost.

I want to be ready,
I want to be ready,
I want to be ready,
To walk in Jerusalem just like John.

Version 2

Last Sunday morning, last Sunday morning,
    last Sunday morning,
Walk in Jerusalem, just like John.
Walk in Jerusalem, all God's people,
Walk in Jerusalem, tell the angels,
Walk in Jerusalem, just like John.

Train is a-coming, train is a-coming,
Walk in Jerusalem, just like John,
Walk in Jerusalem, all my brethren,
Walk in Jerusalem, all my sisters,
Walk in Jerusalem, just like John.
She is loaded down with angels,
    loaded down with angels,
Walk in Jerusalem, just like John,
Walk in Jerusalem, see my father,
Walk in Jerusalem, see my mother,
Walk in Jerusalem, just like John.

ADDITIONAL SCRIPTURE READING:
Matthew 24.42; John 14.2

Go to page 1524 for your next devotional reading.

1700   1900

and the street of the city is pure gold, transparent as glass.

22 I saw no temple in the city, for its temple is the Lord God the Almighty and the Lamb. 23And the city has no need of sun or moon to shine on it, for the glory of God is its light, and its lamp is the Lamb. 24The nations will walk by its light, and the kings of the earth will bring their glory into it. 25Its gates will never be shut by day—and there will be no night there. 26People will bring into it the glory and the honor of the nations. 27But nothing unclean will enter it, nor anyone who practices abomination or falsehood, but only those who are written in the Lamb's book of life.

The River of Life

22 Then the angel[x] showed me the river of the water of life, bright as crystal, flowing from the throne of God and of the Lamb 2through the middle of the street of the city. On either side of the river is the tree of life[y] with its twelve kinds of fruit, producing its fruit each month; and the leaves of the tree are for the healing of the nations. 3Nothing accursed will be found there any more. But the throne of God and of the Lamb will be in it, and his servants[z] will worship him; 4they will see his face, and his name will be on their foreheads. 5And there will be no more night; they need no light of lamp or sun, for the Lord God will be their light, and they will reign forever and ever.

6 And he said to me, "These words are trustworthy and true, for the Lord, the God of the spirits of the prophets, has sent his angel to show his servants[z] what must soon take place."

7 "See, I am coming soon! Blessed is the one who keeps the words of the prophecy of this book."

Epilogue and Benediction

8 I, John, am the one who heard and saw these things. And when I heard and saw them, I fell down to worship at the feet of the angel who showed them to me; 9but he said to me, "You must not do that! I am a fellow servant[a] with you and your comrades[b] the prophets, and with those who keep the words of this book. Worship God!"

10 And he said to me, "Do not seal up the words of the prophecy of this book, for the time is near. 11Let the evildoer still do evil, and the filthy still be filthy, and the righteous still do right, and the holy still be holy."

12 "See, I am coming soon; my reward is with me, to repay according to everyone's work. 13I am the Alpha and the Omega, the first and the last, the beginning and the end."

14 Blessed are those who wash their robes,[c] so that they will have the right to the tree of life and may enter the city by the gates. 15Outside are the dogs and sorcerers and fornicators and murderers and idolaters, and everyone who loves and practices falsehood.

16 "It is I, Jesus, who sent my angel to you with this testimony for the churches. I am the root and the descendant of David, the bright morning star."

17   The Spirit and the bride say,
        "Come."
    And let everyone who hears say,
        "Come."
    And let everyone who is thirsty
        come.
    Let anyone who wishes take the
        water of life as a gift.

18 I warn everyone who hears the words of the prophecy of this book: if anyone adds to them, God will add to that person the plagues described in this book; 19if anyone takes away from the words of the book of this prophecy, God will take away that person's share in the tree of life and in the holy city, which are described in this book.

20 The one who testifies to these things says, "Surely I am coming soon." Amen. Come, Lord Jesus!

21 The grace of the Lord Jesus be with all the saints. Amen.[d]

---

x Gk he   y Or the Lamb. 2In the middle of the street of the city, and on either side of the river, is the tree of life   z Gk slaves   a Gk slave   b Gk brothers   c Other ancient authorities read do his commandments   d Other ancient authorities lack all; others lack the saints; others lack Amen

WEEKEND

CHRIST IS OUR REDEMPTION
George Whitefield

VERSE: Revelation 22.7   **PASSAGE:** Revelation 22.1–7

oes it not often dazzle your eyes, O ye children of God, to look at your own brightness, when the candle of the Lord shines out, and your Redeemer lifts up the light of his blessed countenance upon your souls? Are not you astonished, when you feel the love of God shed abroad in your hearts by the Holy Ghost, and God holds out the golden scepter of his mercy, and bids you ask what you will, and it shall be given you? Does not that peace of God, which keeps and rules your hearts, surpass the utmost limits of your understandings? And is not the joy you feel unspeakable? Is it not full of glory? I am persuaded it is; and in your secret communion, when the Lord's love flows in upon your souls, you are as it were swallowed up in, or, to use the apostle's phrase, "filled with all the fullness of God" (Ephesians 3.19, KJV). Are not you ready to cry out with Solomon, "And will the Lord, indeed, dwell thus with men!" (see 2 Chronicles 6.18). How is it that we should be thus thy sons and daughters, O Lord God Almighty!

If you are children of God, and know what it is to have fellowship with the Father and the Son; if you walk by faith, and not by sight; I am assured this is frequently the language of your hearts.

But look forward, and see an unbounded prospect of eternal happiness lying before thee, O believer! what thou hast already received are only the first-fruits, like the cluster of grapes brought out of the land of Canaan; only an earnest and pledge of yet infinitely better things to come: the harvest is to follow; thy grace is hereafter to be swallowed up in glory. Thy great Joshua, and merciful high priest, shall administer an abundant entrance to thee into the land of promise, that rest which awaits the children of God: for Christ is not only made to believers wisdom, righteousness, and sanctification, but also *redemption*.

ADDITIONAL SCRIPTURE READING:
John 12.35–36; Ephesians 1.13–14

1700   1900

ACKNOWLEDGMENTS

SUBJECT GUIDE

AUTHOR BIOGRAPHIES

READING PLANS

ACKNOWLEDGMENTS

Page 2: Taken from THE EVERLASTING MAN by G. K. Chesterton. Copyright © 1993 by Ignatius Press. Used by permission.

Page 15: Taken from MY UTMOST FOR HIS HIGHEST by Oswald Chambers. Copyright © 1935 by Dodd Mead & Co., renewed (c) 1963 by the Oswald Chambers Publications Assn. Ltd., and is used by permission of Discovery House Publishers, Box 3566, Grand Rapids MI 49501. All rights reserved.

Page 17: Taken from MY UTMOST FOR HIS HIGHEST by Oswald Chambers. Copyright © 1935 by Dodd Mead & Co., renewed (c) 1963 by the Oswald Chambers Publications Assn. Ltd., and is used by permission of Discovery House Publishers, Box 3566, Grand Rapids MI 49501. All rights reserved.

Page 25: Taken from CLASSIC SERMONS ON THE ATTRIBUTES OF GOD by Warren W. Wiersbe, ed. Copyright © 1989 by Kregel Publications, a division of Kregel Inc., Grand Rapids, Michigan. Used by permission.

Page 62: Taken from CAROLING DUSK by Countee Cullen. Copyright © 1993 by Carol Publishing Group. Used by permission of HarperCollins Publishers, Inc.

Page 72: Taken from SEARCHLIGHTS FROM THE WORD by G. Campbell Morgan. Copyright © 1977 by Fleming H. Revell, Co., a division of Baker Book House, Grand Rapids, Michigan. Used by permission.

Page 74: Taken from THE HYMNAL 1982 by Episcopal Church. Copyright © 1985 by The Church Pension Fund. Published by Church Hymnal Corporation. Used by permission.

Page 78: Reprinted by arrangement with The Heirs to the Estate of Martin Luther King, Jr., c/o Writers House, Inc. as agent for the proprietor. Copyright 1963 by Martin Luther King, Jr., copyright renewed 1991 by Coretta Scott King.

Page 92: Taken from CHRIST IN THE TABERNACLE by A. B. Simpson. Copyright © 1985 by Christian Publications, Inc., Camp Hill, Pennsylvania. Used by permission.

Page 97: Taken from CHRIST IN THE TABERNACLE by A. B. Simpson. Copyright © 1985 by Christian Publications, Inc., Camp Hill, Pennsylvania. Used by permission.

Page 201: Taken from KEYS TO THE DEEPER LIFE by A. W. Tozer. Copyright © 1957 by Sunday Magazine. Copyright © 1987 by Zondervan Publishing House. Used by permission of Zondervan Publishing House.

Page 231: Taken from A TESTAMENT OF DEVOTION. Copyright © 1941 by Harper & Row Publishers, Inc. Renewed 1969 by Lois Lael Kelly Statler. New introduction copyright © 1992 by HarperCollins Publishers, Inc. Reprinted by permission of HarperCollins Publishers, Inc.

Page 270: Reprinted with the permission of Scribner, a Division of Simon & Schuster from A DIARY OF PRIVATE PRAYER by John Baillie. Copyright 1949 by Charles Scribner's Sons; copyright renewed © 1977 by Ian Fowler Baillie.

Page 272: Taken from SEARCHLIGHTS FROM THE WORD by G. Campbell Morgan. Copyright © 1977 by Fleming H. Revell, a division of Baker Book House, Grand Rapids, Michigan. Used by permission.

Page 277: Taken from THE PRAYERS OF PETER MARSHALL by Catherine Marshall, ed. Copyright © 1982 by Catherine Marshall. Published by Chosen Books, a division of Baker Book House, Grand Rapids, Michigan. Used by permission.

Page 305: Taken from MY UTMOST FOR HIS HIGHEST by Oswald Chambers. Copyright © 1935 by Dodd Mead & Co., renewed (c) 1963 by the Oswald Chambers Publications Assn. Ltd., and is used by permission of Discovery House Publishers, Box 3566, Grand Rapids MI 49501. All rights reserved.

Page 314: Taken from GREAT DEVOTIONAL CLASSICS by Douglas V. Steere, arr. and ed. Copyright © 1961 by Upper Room Books. Used by permission of Dutton, an imprint of Penguin USA.

Page 346: Taken from MY UTMOST FOR HIS HIGHEST by Oswald Chambers. Copyright © 1935 by Dodd Mead & Co., renewed (c) 1963 by the Oswald Chambers Publications Assn. Ltd., and is used by permission of Discovery House Publishers, Box 3566, Grand Rapids MI 49501. All rights reserved.

Page 359: Taken from SEARCHLIGHTS FROM THE WORD by G. Campbell Morgan. Copyright © 1977 by Fleming H. Revell, a division of Baker Book House, Grand Rapids, Michigan. Used by permission.

Page 367: Taken from THE PLACE OF HELP by Oswald Chambers. Copyright © 1936 by Dodd Mead & Co., Grosset & Dunlap; © 1989 by the Oswald Chambers Publications Assoc. Ltd., and is used by permission of Discovery House Publishers, Box 3566, Grand Rapids MI 49501. All rights reserved.

Page 410: Taken from THE NORMAL CHRISTIAN LIFE by Watchman Nee. Copyright © 1977 by Angus I. Kinnear. Published by Tyndale House Publishers, Wheaton, Illinois. Used by permission.

Page 413: Taken from THEY WALKED WITH GOD by James S. Bell, Jr., comp. Copyright © 1993 by the Moody Bible Institute of Chicago. Published by Moody Press. Used by permission.

Page 469: Taken from TRUE SPIRITUALITY by Francis Schaeffer. Copyright © 1979 by Tyndale House Publishers, Wheaton, Illinois. Used by permission.

Page 472: Taken from THE SCHOOL OF CHARITY by Evelyn Underhill. Copyright © 1934 by Evelyn Underhill. Published by Longmans, Green, and Co. Used by permission.

Page 526: Taken from THE PLACE OF HELP by Oswald Chambers. Copyright © 1936 by Dodd Mead & Co., Grosset & Dunlap; © 1989 by the Oswald Chambers Publications Assoc. Ltd., and is used by permission of Discovery House Publishers, Box 3566, Grand Rapids MI 49501. All rights reserved.

Page 531: Taken from MY UTMOST FOR HIS HIGHEST by Oswald Chambers. Copyright © 1935 by Dodd Mead & Co., renewed (c) 1963 by the Oswald Chambers Publications Assn. Ltd., and is used by permission of Discovery House Publishers, Box 3566, Grand Rapids MI 49501. All rights reserved.

Page 541: Taken from MERE CHRISTIANITY by C. S. Lewis. Copyright © 1952 by Macmillan Publishing. Reprinted by permission of HarperCollins Publishers Limited.

Page 549: Taken from ABUNDANT LIVING by E. Stanley Jones. Copyright © 1942 by Abingdon Press. Used by permission.

Page 596: Taken from MARKINGS by Dag Hammarskjold. Copyright © 1972 Alfred A. Knopf, Inc. Used by permission.

Page 601: Taken from AFRICAN PRAYER BOOK by Desmond Tutu, ed. Copyright © 1995 by Desmond Tutu. Published by Doubleday and Company, Inc. Used by permission.

Page 617: Reprinted by arrangement with The Heirs to the Estate of Martin Luther King, Jr., c/o Writers House, Inc. as agent for the proprietor. Copyright 1963 by Martin Luther King, Jr., copyright renewed 1991 by Coretta Scott King.

Page 629: Taken from KEYS TO THE DEEPER LIFE by A. W. Tozer. Copyright © 1957 by Sunday Magazine. Copyright © 1987 by Zondervan Publishing House. Used by permission of Zondervan Publishing House.

Page 704: Taken from KEYS TO THE DEEPER LIFE by A. W. Tozer. Copyright © 1957 by Sunday Magazine. Copyright © 1987 by Zondervan Publishing House. Used by permission of Zondervan Publishing House.

Page 716: Taken from SEARCHLIGHTS FROM THE WORD by G. Campbell Morgan. Copyright © 1977 by Fleming H. Revell, Co., a division of Baker Book House, Grand Rapids, Michigan. Used by permission.

Page 732: Taken from KEYS TO THE DEEPER LIFE by A. W. Tozer. Copyright © 1957 by Sunday Magazine. Copyright © 1987 by Zondervan Publishing House. Used by permission of Zondervan Publishing House.

Page 754: Taken from THOMAS MERTON READER by Thomas Merton. Copyright © 1974 by Trustees of the Merton Legacy Fund. Published by Bantam Doubleday Dell. Used by permission.

Page 786: Taken from ABUNDANT LIVING by E. Stanley Jones. Copyright © 1942 by Whitmore & Stone. Published by Abingdon Press. Used by permission.

Page 804: Taken from MY UTMOST FOR HIS HIGHEST by Oswald Chambers. Copyright © 1935 by Dodd Mead & Co., renewed (c) 1963 by the Oswald Chambers Publications Assn. Ltd., and is used by permission of Discovery House Publishers, Box 3566, Grand Rapids MI 49501. All rights reserved.

Page 902: Reprinted with the permission of Scribner, a Division of Simon & Schuster from A DIARY OF PRIVATE PRAYER by John Baillie. Copyright 1949 by Charles Scribner's Sons; copyright renewed © 1977 by Ian Fowler Baillie.

Page 958: Taken from SEARCHLIGHTS FROM THE WORD by G. Campbell Morgan. Copyright © 1977 by Fleming H. Revell, a division of Baker Book House, Grand Rapids, Michigan. Used by permission.

Page 1000: Taken from THEY WALKED WITH GOD by James S. Bell, Jr., comp. Copyright © 1993 by The Moody Bible Institute of Chicago. Published by Moody Press. Used by permission.

Page 1029: Taken from TRUE SPIRITUALITY by Francis Schaeffer. Copyright © 1979 by Tyndale House Publishers, Wheaton, Illinois. Used by permission.

Page 1031: Taken from CLASSIC SERMONS ON THE ATTRIBUTES OF GOD by Warren W. Wiersbe, ed. Copyright © 1989 by Kregel Publications, a division of Kregel, Inc., Grand Rapids, Michigan. Used by permission.

Page 1036: Taken from MERE CHRISTIANITY by C. S. Lewis. Copyright © 1952 by Macmillan Publishing. Reprinted by permission of HarperCollins Publishers Limited.

Page 1044: Reprinted by arrangement with The Heirs to the Estate of Martin Luther King, Jr., c/o Writers House, Inc. as agent for the proprietor. Copyright 1963 by Martin Luther King, Jr., copyright renewed 1991 by Coretta Scott King.

Page 1048: Reprinted by arrangement with The Heirs to the Estate of Martin Luther King, Jr., c/o Writers House, Inc. as agent for the proprietor. Copyright 1963 by Martin Luther King, Jr., copyright renewed 1991 by Coretta Scott King.

Page 1066: Taken from STREAMS IN THE DESERT, VOL. 2 by Mrs. Charles E. Cowman. Copyright © 1966 by Cowman Publishing Co. Published by Zondervan Publishing House. Used by permission.

Page 1077: Taken from HINDS' FEET ON HIGH PLACES by Hannah Hurnard. Copyright © 1977 by Tyndale House Publishers. Published by Barbour and Company. Used by permission.

Page 1081: Taken from A TREASURY OF CHRISTIAN VERSE by Hugh Martin, ed. Copyright © 1959 by SCM Press, Ltd. (UK). Published by Fortress Press/Augsburg Fortress Publications. Used by permission.

Page 1096: Taken from GREAT HYMNS OF THE FAITH by John W. Peterson, ed. Copyright © 1968 by Zondervan Publishing House/Singspiration Music. Used by permission.

Page 1116: Taken from COST OF DISCIPLESHIP by Dietrich Bonhoeffer. Copyright © 1948 by SCM Press, Ltd. Published by Macmillan Publishing. Used by permission.

Page 1122: Taken from COST OF DISCIPLESHIP by Dietrich Bonhoeffer. Copyright © 1948 by SCM Press, Ltd. Published by Macmillan Publishing. Used by permission.

Page 1126: Taken from MY UTMOST FOR HIS HIGHEST by Oswald Chambers. Copyright © 1935 by Dodd Mead & Co., renewed (c) 1963 by the Oswald Chambers Publications Assn. Ltd., and is used by permission of Discovery House Publishers, Box 3566, Grand Rapids MI 49501. All rights reserved.

Page 1130: Taken from THE NEW OXFORD BOOK OF CHRISTIAN VERSE by Donald Davie, ed. Copyright © 1981 by Donald Davie. Published by Oxford University Press. Used by permission.

Page 1135: Taken from SELECTED HYMNS AND SONG. Copyright © 1992 by Tree of Life Publishers. Used by permission.

Page 1171: Taken from THE PRAYERS OF PETER MARSHALL by Catherine Marshall, ed. Copyright © 1982 by Catherine Marshall. Published by Chosen Books, a division of Baker Book House, Grand Rapids, Michigan. Used by permission.

Page 1185: Reprinted by arrangement with The Heirs to the Estate of Martin Luther King, Jr., c/o Writers House, Inc. as agent for the proprietor. Copyright 1963 by Martin Luther King, Jr., copyright renewed 1991 by Coretta Scott King.

Page 1196: Taken from MERE CHRISTIANITY by C. S. Lewis. Copyright © 1952 by Macmillan Publishing. Reprinted by permission of HarperCollins Publishers Limited.

Page 1206: Taken from THOMAS MERTON READER by Thomas Merton. Copyright © 1974 by Trustees of the Merton Legacy Fund. Published by Bantam Doubleday Dell. Used by permission.

Page 1208: Taken from KEYS TO THE DEEPER LIFE by A. W. Tozer. Copyright © 1957 by Sunday Magazine. Copyright © 1987 by Zondervan Publishing House. Used by permission of Zondervan Publishing House.

Page 1229: Taken from THE GOSPEL OF JOHN by F. F. Bruce. Copyright © 1983 by F. F. Bruce. Published by Eerdmans Publishing Co. Used by permission.

Page 1239: Taken from THE GOSPEL OF JOHN by F. F. Bruce. Copyright © 1983 by F. F Bruce. Published by Eerdmans Publishing Co. Used by permission.

Page 1246: Taken from AN ANTHOLOGY OF DEVOTIONAL LITERATURE by Thomas S. Kepler, ed. Copyright © 1947 by Stone and Pierce. Published by Baker Book House, Grand Rapids, Michigan. Used by permission.

Page 1250: Taken from GREAT DEVOTIONAL CLASSICS by Douglas V. Steere, arr. and ed. Copyright © 1961 by Upper Room Books. Used by permission of Dutton, an imprint of Penguin USA.

Page 1380: Taken from A KARL BARTH READER by Geoffrey W. Bromiley, ed. Copyright © 1986 by Eerdmans Publishing Co. Used by permission.

Page 1383: Taken from A KARL BARTH READER by Geoffrey W. Bromiley, ed. Copyright © 1986 by Eerdmans Publishing Co. Used by permission.

Page 1406: Taken from COST OF DISCIPLESHIP by Dietrich Bonhoeffer. Copyright © 1948 by SCM Press, Ltd. Published by Macmillan Publishing. Used by permission.

Page 1421: Taken from KEYS TO THE DEEPER LIFE by A. W. Tozer. Copyright © 1957 by Sunday Magazine. Copyright © 1987 by Zondervan Publishing House. Used by permission of Zondervan Publishing House.

Page 1423: Taken from LETTERS AND PAPERS FROM PRISON by Dietrich Bonhoeffer. Copyright © 1956 by SCM Press, Ltd. Published by Macmillan Publishing. Used by permission.

Page 1435: Taken from IN RETROSPECT by F. F. Bruce. Copyright © 1993 by F. F. Bruce. Published by Baker Book House Company. Used by permission.

Page 1456: Taken from SELECTED HYMNS AND SONGS. Copyright © 1992 by Tree of Life Publishers. Used by permission of Benson Music Group.

Page 1465: Taken from A DIARY OF READINGS by John Baillie. Copyright © 1955 by John Baillie. Published by Charles Scribner's Sons. Used by permission of Princeton University Press.

Page 1475: Taken from THE JOURNALS OF KIERKEGAARD. Translated by Alexander Dru. Copyright 1939 by Oxford University Press. Used by permission.

Page 1496: Taken from SCREWTAPE LETTERS by C. S. Lewis. Copyright © 1956 by Macmillan Publishing. Used by permission.

Page 1499: Taken from CLASSIC SERMONS ON THE ATTRIBUTES OF GOD by Warren W. Wiersbe, ed. Copyright © 1989 by Kregel Publications, a division of Kregel, Inc., Grand Rapids, Michigan. Used by permission.

Page 1508: Taken from COLLECTED POEMS OF THOMAS MERTON. Copyright © 1946 by New Directions, 1968, 1969, 1977 by the Trustees of the Merton Legacy Trust.

Every effort has been made to trace the ownership of copyright items in this collection and to obtain permission for their use. The publisher would appreciate notification of, and copyright details for, any instances where further acknowledgment is due, so that adjustments may be made in a future reprint.

SUBJECT GUIDE

AUTHOR BIOGRAPHIES

à Kempis, Thomas (c. 1380–1471). Born in Kempen near Köln (Cologne), Germany, and educated in the school at Deventer run by the Brethren of the Common Life, he later entered the Augustinian Convent of Mt. Saint Agnes near Zwolle. Ordained as a priest in 1413, he became subprior in 1429. He worked as a copyist and purportedly copied the entire Bible at least four times. All of this German mystic's writings—letters, poems, homilies, etc.—are devotional in nature. He is known best for *The Imitation of Christ*, which is a manual of devotion to help the soul achieve communion with God. *A devotion by this author can be found on page 6.*

African-American Spirituals. *These devotions can be found on pages 70, 192, 873, 1516, 1522.*

Anselm of Canterbury (c. 1033–1109). Born in Aosta, Italy, Anselm was directed towards a political career but chose the life of a Benedictine monk at Bec, Normandy, where he became prior in 1063. After the Norman conquest in 1066, Anselm visited England and reluctantly accepted the appointment as Archbishop of Canterbury in 1089. As a scholar, Anselm reintroduced an Augustinian spirit into theology. He sought to demonstrate the existence and attributes of God by an appeal to reason alone. Anselm insisted, however, that faith must precede reason. "I do not seek to understand in order that I may believe," he said, "But I believe in order to understand." His most famous work is *Cur Deus homo?* *(Why Did God Become Man?)* completed in Italy in 1098. *Devotions by this author can be found on pages 1188, 1427, 1484.*

Aquinas, Thomas (1225–1274). Born in Italy, he studied at the University of Naples and became a Dominican in 1244. He had such a large physique that he was nicknamed "dumb ox." Later, his theological thought and Christian devotion grew so large that he was dubbed "angelic doctor." Maintaining that theology is the "queen of the sciences" and philosophy is its servant, he attempted to synthesize Aristotelian philosophy and Biblical theology. His theology has had a great stabilizing effect on Catholic thought through the centuries. Held in high regard as a philosopher both within and outside a Christian context, the prolific Aquinas left two major works: the *Summa Theologica* and *Summa contra Gentiles*. *Devotions by this author can be found on pages 1180, 1202.*

Arminius, Jacobus (1560–1609). This Dutch Reformation theologian's writings influenced the Wesleyans and Methodists and enraged the Calvinists, especially on the issue of predestination. The University of Leyden in Holland conferred upon Arminius the degree of Doctor of Divinity, and, by way of acceptance, he delivered an oration on the "Priesthood of Christ." Arminius vividly paints an imagined scene in heaven in which Justice and Mercy debate over the best way to deal with a sinful people. Justice demands a payment of a blood sacrifice for sin. Mercy cries out for forgiveness. That both might be satisfied, Wisdom steps in. *A devotion by this author can be found on page 1454.*

Athanasian Creed. This profession of faith, named after the great fourth-century defender of the faith Athanasius (see below), was probably written by Ambrose (339–97) and has been commonly used by liturgical churches of the West. Composed in two parts, the creed is devoted respectively to the doctrines of the Trinity and of the incarnation. Its preface and conclusion both assert that belief in the truths it declares is necessary for salvation. *A devotion from this creed can be found on page 1114.*

Athanasius (c. 295–373). Exiled five times, Athanasius devoted 45 years to the church's successful struggle against Arianism. A native of Alexandria, Egypt, Athanasius became an advisor there to Bishop Alexander, who condemned Arius for his heretical views in 319. Arius advocated that Christ was not eternal but was created by the Father. This view spread rapidly in the Eastern church and threatened to turn the faith into a philosophy mixed with pagan thought. Emperor Constantine called the Council of Nicea to settle this issue (325). Athanasius' main work, *The Three Orations against the Arians* (c. 335), emphasizes that it was necessary for the Word to be as eternal as God if he was to form the divine image in man. *A devotion by this author can be found on page 1347.*

Athenagoras (2d century). It is said that this philosopher and apologist from Athens became a Christian while reading the Scriptures in order to argue against them. In his *Apology* (177), addressed to Roman Emperor Marcus Aurelius and his son Commodus, Athenagoras refuted the allegations that Christians were atheists, that they practiced incestuous immorality, and that they ate human flesh as part of their ritual. He also wrote a pamphlet, *On the Resurrection of the Body. A devotion by this author can be found on page 1487.*

Augustine of Hippo (354–430). Born in North Africa as the son of a pagan father and a Christian mother, the brilliant Augustine began a quest for religious truth at age 19. From the dualistic system of Manicheism through Neo-Platonism he searched until his longing was satisfied in the Epistle to the Romans. Augustine was baptized in Milan in 387 and became bishop of Hippo, North Africa, in 395. He is a figure of major importance to the church. In his *Confessions* (c. 397) he gives a Biblical understanding of a person's life under grace. In his *City of God* (c. 413–26) he is the first to give a Biblical view of history, time, and the state. He established the doctrine of the church, gave a clear statement concerning the person of Christ, and made the grace of God the theme of theology in the West. *Devotions by this author can be found on pages 632, 769.*

Baillie, John (1886–1960). The devotional classic *A Diary of Private Prayer* (1936) is this Scottish theologian, educator, and ecumenical leader's enduring gift to the church. He served as a professor of divinity at Edinburgh University, moderator of the Church of Scotland General Assembly, and as a member of the central committee of the first assembly of the World Council of Churches (1948), which he later served as one of its six world presidents (1954). *Devotions by this author can be found on pages 270, 902.*

Barnabas, Epistle of. Although Clement of Alexandria attributed this treatise to the apostle Barnabas, this is quite improbable. Rather its author was most likely a Christian in Alexandria, Egypt, writing between A.D. 70 and 100. *The Epistle of Barnabas* attempts to show Christ in types and figures of the Old Testament. This approach is also used in the New Testament book of Hebrews and is a refreshing way to view the Scriptures. Unfortunately, *Barnabas* is stridently polemic in tone and contains a strong attack on Judaism. The author succeeds in finding in the Old Testament convincing testimonies for the Christian faith. However, because these are presented in the context of an denunciation of Judaism, it is likely that the author was sowing seeds of anti-Semitism. *A devotion from this epistle can be found on page 130.*

Barth, Karl (1886–1968). Born in Basel, this Swiss theologian's writings strengthened many European Christian leaders to stand under persecution. Ordained in the Swiss Reformed Church in 1909, he was driven to reconsider his liberal theological training when, in 1914, his teachers supported German militarism. In 1933, when Adolf Hitler's National Socialism gained power in Germany, Barth and his associate Eduard Thurneysen published a series of pamphlets entitled *Theological Existence Today.* These opposed Hitler's cultural perversion of the Christian faith. He fled Germany for Switzerland in 1935. Barth's theology emphasized God's sovereignty, placing him firmly in the Reformed tradition. Central among his major writings is his multivolume, systematic theology *Church Dogmatics* (1932–67), which runs nearly 7,500 pages. *Devotions by this author can be found on pages 1331, 1339, 1380, 1383.*

Baxter, Richard (1615–1691). A renowned Puritan divine and one of England's most prolific religious authors, Baxter wrote more than 100 books. Due to spending much time at home because of ill-health, he became a largely self-taught scholar and preacher.

During one particularly severe illness, he wrote his most famous and influential work, *The Saints' Everlasting Rest*. In this lengthy and profound treatise, Baxter ponders the nature of life after death. *A devotion by this author can be found on page 1359.*

Beecher, Henry Ward (1813–1887). The brother of author Harriet Beecher Stowe, this Congregational clergyman, reformer, and political activist was one of the most popular and widely known preachers and lecturers in America. Beecher served in the pulpit of the Plymouth Congregational Church, Brooklyn, NY, for 40 years. Theologically he departed from Calvinism and radically reinterpreted the Bible in moralistic terms, stressing greatly the love of God. His sermons are published in several volumes entitled *The Plymouth Pulpit*. *Devotions by this author can be found on pages 858, 1104, 1112.*

Benedict of Nursia (c. 480–c. 547). Around 529 Benedict established a monastery at Monte Cassino, Italy, where he wrote the *Benedictine Rule*, which has been used until the present day as a pattern for monastic life. Through the *Rule* Benedict attempted to create an environment where ordinary men could pursue the service of God and their own spiritual improvement through a balanced life of manual labor, reading, prayer, and worship. *A devotion by this author can be found on page 1397.*

Bernard of Clairvaux (1090–1153). "Jesus the very thought of thee, with sweetness fills my soul." These words, written by this monk, mystic, leader, and spokesman for medieval Christianity, echo in churches even to this day. Bernard challenged all of Christendom, popes and princes, to examine their practice and develop lives of mystical devotion to God. His *Twelve Steps to Humility* describes a union of the divine and human wills that would not confuse the distinction between God and man. *Devotions by this author can be found on pages 719, 1176, 1355, 1451.*

Boehme, Jacob (1575–1624). An influential German Lutheran mystic, Jacob Boehme addressed diverse topics in his writing, including the person of God, the divine nature, the Fall, sin, death, and time and space. A modern reader may wish to refer to his *The Way to Christ*. He stated that his writings were based on divine revelation and spiritual experience. Boheme did not shy away from difficult and nontraditional concepts and language. This caused considerable controversy during his lifetime, yet Boheme's influence extended to William Law, John Milton, Issac Newton, and the Pietist movement. *Devotions by this author can be found on pages 478, 1229.*

Bonar, Horatius (1808–1889). Ira D. Sankey, musical associate of Dwight L. Moody acknowledged a debt of gratitude to this Scottish minister and hymn writer. Bonar published several volumes of hymns, which number about 600 songs. Bonar also wrote tracts and books, including significant contributions in the field of biography. His tract "Believe and Live," printed in more than a million copies, is said to have provided spiritual help to Queen Victoria. Bonar's hymns include "I Heard the Voice of Jesus Say," "Here, O My Lord, I See Thee Face to Face," "Upon a Life I Have Not Lived," and "For the Bread and For the Wine." *Devotions by this author can be found on pages 429, 1024, 1050, 1378.*

Bonaventura (1221–1274). Born in Italy and educated in France Bonaventura was a philosopher, theologian, and mystic whose ideas were akin to those of Augustine and the Protestant Reformers. The author of *The Journey of the Soul unto God*, he was one of the outstanding minds of the Middle Ages. More than a theologian, Bonaventura was also known for his piety and administrative ability. He has been called the second founder of the Franciscan order. *A devotion by this author can be found on page 1266.*

Bonhoeffer, Dietrich (1906–1945). This German theologian and modern Christian martyr refused to accept Hitler's interference in church affairs. So, with Karl Barth and others, Bonhoeffer helped found the Confessing Church in Germany. In 1935 he began an illegal seminary in Finkenwalde and early-on identified himself with the resistance against Nazism. After the arrest of 35,000 Jews on Krystalnacht (November 9, 1938), Bonhoeffer and others conspired to assassinate Hitler. When the plot failed, Bonhoeffer was arrested in April, 1943, and hung two years later. During his two-year prison stay, he wrote his two most widely read books: *The Cost of Discipleship* and *Letters and Papers from Prison*. *Devotions by this author can be found on pages 1116, 1122, 1357, 1406, 1423.*

Book of Common Prayer. The official prayer book of the Church of England and of Anglican churches in other countries, including the Episcopal church in the U.S., its full title is *The Book of Common Prayer and Administration of the Sacraments and Other Rites and Ceremonies of the Church*. It is the work of Thomas Cranmer and Nicholas Ridley and first appeared in 1549 during the reign of Edward VI. This book was a unified and simplified equivalent of Roman Catholic liturgical books yet in the common vernacular. It passed through suppression, restoration, amendments, and revisions until 1662. The Protestant Episcopal Church was formed in the U.S. in 1783 and a revised book for American use was produced and ratified in 1789. It was further revised in 1892, 1928, and 1979. *Devotions from this book can be found on pages 384, 757, 1394.*

Booth, William (1829–1912). The title of Booth's book *Darkest England and the Way Out* aptly describes the evangelist's view of conditions in his native land and his hope for its improvement. Booth was the founder and first general of the Salvation Army, which has been described as one of the most successful religious revivals of modern times. Converted in 1844, he became a Methodist minister only to resign in 1861. In 1865 he and his wife Catherine began a mission to slum-dwellers in Whitechapel, London, where he held open-air meetings accompanied by a lively band. He preached in taverns and jails, theaters and factories, and eventually built a network of agencies for social relief and rehabilitation. *A devotion by this author can be found on page 116.*

Bradstreet, Anne (1612–1672). "I have not studied in this you read to show my skill, but to declare the truth," wrote Anne Bradstreet to her children, "Not to set forth myself, but the glory of God." The Puritan poet arrived in the new world relatively early (1630) and lived in Massachusetts. Bradstreet's poetry was first published, unbeknownst to her, in London in 1650 (*The Tenth Muse, Lately Sprung Up in America*). Little direct information about America's first woman poet is recorded in historical sources. What is known can be amply found in Bradstreet's own poems, which are still in print through the Harvard University Press. *Devotions by this author can be found on pages 593, 1373, 1410.*

Brother Lawrence (c. 1605–1691). Nicholas Herman spent 18 years in the French army and later was an aide to the treasurer of France. In Paris when he was over 50 years old, he joined the Carmelite order. There he became known as Brother Lawrence. He never sought to advance beyond the status of lay brother but served the community as a cook for 30 years. His sparse and simple writings were published after his death (1691). A portion of these have been published in English as *The Practice of the Presence of God*. Despite his life of Catholic religious service, the orthodox mystical spirituality of Brother Lawrence has been received more widely in Protestant churches than in the Roman Catholic Church. *Devotions by this author can be found on pages 723, 822.*

Bruce, F. F. (1910–1990). A Scotsman, Bruce was the preeminent evangelical scholar of the post-World War II era. Although a lifelong member of the Plymouth Brethren, he disliked partisan labels. Acclaimed across the Christian spectrum, Dr. Bruce was president of both the Society for Old Testament Studies and its New Testament complement. His works are quite numerous and include *The Books and the Parchments* (1950), *Paul: Apostle of the Soul Set Free* (1977), *History of the Bible in English* (1979), and *The Canon of Scripture* (1988). *Devotions by this author can be found on pages 1233, 1239, 1257, 1435.*

Bunyan, John (1628–1688). This son of a tinker was the author of *The Pilgrim's Progress*, one of the most famous religious allegories in the English language. After experiencing conversion through the influence of his wife, Margaret Bentley, Bunyan became one of the leaders of a congregation of Nonconformists (Puritans) in Bedford, giving sermons as a lay preacher. After the restoration of Charles II (1660), Puritans lost the freedom of worship. Bunyan persisted in his unlicensed preaching and was confined to Bedford county jail (1660–72). There he wrote religious tracts and pamphlets and the first of his major works, the spiritual autobiography *Grace Abounding to the Chief of Sinners* (1666). In 1675 Bunyan was imprisoned again for six months. During that time he probably wrote the major part of his masterpiece, *The Pilgrim's Progress from This World to That Which Is to Come*, a prose allegory of the pilgrimage of a soul in search of salvation. It became the most widely read book in English after the Bible. *Devotions by this author can be found on pages 231, 741, 1091.*

Burns, Robert (1759–1796). A Scottish poet, whose works are known and loved wherever the English language is read. Although the poet was unjustly represented after his death as a drunkard and a reprobate, Burns touched the traditional folk songs of Scotland with his genius, transforming them into great poetry. Thus he immortalized Scotland's countryside and humble farm life. He was a keen and discerning satirist who reserved his sharpest barbs for sham, hypocrisy, and cruelty. For example, "Holy Willie's Prayer" satirized local ecclesiastical squabbles and attacked Calvinist theology, bringing him into conflict with the church. Burns also wrote approximately 100 songs, including such favorites as "Auld Lang Syne," "Comin' Thro' the Rye," and "A Red, Red Rose." *A devotion by this author can be found on page 669.*

Calvin, John (1509–1564). Along with Martin Luther, this French Protestant Reformer is regarded as one of the key figures of the Protestant Reformation. Calvin's *Institutes of the Christian Religion* is considered one of the most influential works in world literature. In Strassburg and Geneva Calvin labored to organize evangelical churches and in so doing developed an adaptable model of church government. This earned him the appellation "organizer of Protestantism." As social institutions deteriorated in the sixteenth century, many new institutions developed under the influence of Calvin's model. From there his "presbyterian" example has extended to influence modern democratic political theory. Calvin expounded Biblical teaching on various issues of his day in light of particular controversies within the church. Theologically, in the Pauline-Augustinian tradition, he tried to navigate a middle course between an exclusive emphasis on either divine providence or human responsibility. *Devotions by this author can be found on pages 301, 519, 543, 594, 652, 1293, 1490.*

Catherine of Siena (1347–1380). Although nearly illiterate, Catherine of Siena was quite influential in the church of her day. Born in Florence she became a Dominican at age 16. She worked for ecclesiastical reform and exercised great authority over her followers through her dictated letters. She is prominent among the church's mystics. *The Dialogue* is her spiritual testament. *Devotions by this author can be found on pages 623, 1088, 1102.*

Chambers, Oswald (1874–1917). "I feel I shall be buried for a time, hidden away in obscurity; then suddenly I shall flame out, do my work and be gone." Oswald Chambers prophecy about his ministry was accurate. Converted through his father after a meeting directed by Charles Spurgeon, Chambers studied art in London and Edinburgh, but eventually responded to God's call to the ministry. After graduation from Dunoon College, Chambers traveled in America and Japan with the Japanese evangelist Juji Nakada. In 1911 he started the Bible Training College in London. But in 1915 he closed the college and sailed for Egypt to minister to the troops at the large YMCA encampment at Zeitoun, Egypt. There, until his death, Chambers ministered to the soldiers. His wife, Gertrude, took notes as he spoke and these have since been published in over 30 volumes, including the best-selling *My Utmost for His Highest* (1935). *Devotions by this author can be found on pages 15, 17, 305, 346, 367, 526, 531, 804, 1126.*

Chesterton, G. K. (1874–1936). Playwright, novelist, poet, literary commentator, pamphleteer, essayist, lecturer, apologist, and editor, the Englishman G. K Chesterton was phenomenally prolific. Of his 100 books, four are considered foremost—*Orthodoxy*, *The Everlasting Man*, *St. Thomas Aquinas*, and *St. Francis of Assisi*. With his typical brilliant wit, Chesterton describes *Orthodoxy* as his "elephantine adventures in pursuit of the obvious." Written in 1908, *Orthodoxy* is typical of the humor, crispness, and pace of Chesterton's best work. He is also the author of the well-known Father Brown series of detective stories. *Devotions by this author can be found on pages 2, 1254.*

Chrysostom, John (c. 344/354–407). A tax revolt in Antioch gave this gifted and popular preacher the opportunity to deliver his most famous series of sermons, *On the Statues* (387). Chrysostom's sound Biblical exposition combined with practical application calmly brought the city through its crisis. Chrysostom was an eloquent speaker (his name means "golden-mouthed") and his careful methods of Biblical exegesis—a grammatical examination of the exact literal meaning of each verse from the original languages—were revived by the Protestant Reformers. In 397 the patriarch of Constantinople died and Chrysostom was designated his replacement. But the unwilling appointee had to be arrested by imperial troops in order to be consecrated bishop in 398. He then vigorously attacked the vices of the church and even antagonized the empress. Exiled in 403, Chrysostom was soon recalled and resumed his offensive ways. He died in banishment three years later. *A devotion by this author can be found on page 727.*

Clement of Alexandria (c. 155–c. 220). This Athenian pagan became a Christian through his study of philosophy. As a Christian Clement studied with Pantaenus at his school in Alexandria and became the school's head in 190. (Pantaenus's school later became Alexandria's official church catechetical school under Origen.) During these years (190–202) Clement wrote most of his works. His approach to the Scriptures was influenced by the Jewish writer Philo who used Greek philosophy to interpret the Old Testament. Through Clement of Alexandria, Philo's allegorical method of scriptural interpretation became fashionable and is identified with Alexandria to this day. Counted among the church fathers, Clement was significant as the forerunner and teacher of Origen—a chief influence upon the theology of the East. *A devotion by this author can be found on page 1391.*

Clement of Rome (fl. c. 90–100). As bishop of Rome and perhaps the third bishop after Peter, he is assumed to be the presbyter and bishop who wrote a letter on behalf of the church in Rome to the church at Corinth (96). This is probably the earliest Christian writing outside the New Testament and provides important evidence that canonical New Testament books were in circulation among first-century churches. His letter quotes from the Old Testament, uses sayings found in Matthew, Mark, and Luke, and also quotes Romans, 1 Corinthians, and Hebrews. *Devotions by this author can be found on pages 170, 565, 1439, 1442.*

Conybeare, William John (1815–1857). Educated at Cambridge, he was principal of Liverpool Collegiate Institute (1842–48). Later his friend J. S. Howson joined him and they both began to write the two-volume work, *The Life and Epistles of St. Paul* (1852), an extensive treatment that incorporated theological, geographical, and historical studies on Paul and his writings. *A devotion by this author can be found on page 1375.*

Coverdale, Miles (1488–1569). Fleeing persecution, this Englishman translated and published the Bible in the safety of Europe. In 1534 he published a paraphrase of the Psalms and the first complete English Bible in 1535. Under the protection of the king's vice regent Thomas Cromwell, a friend of Coverdale, this Bible was published by English printers. Cromwell then convinced Henry VIII of the need of an official English Bible. Coverdale was commissioned to revise his translation for this purpose in 1538. Called the "Great Bible" (1539), it is Coverdale's greatest achievement. Together with the work of William Tyndale it had significant influence on the translators of the King James Version of the Bible (1611). *A devotion by this author can be found on page 1110.*

Cowman, Lettie B. (1870–1960). Better known as "Mrs. Cowman," she was one of the best-selling devotional writers and compilers of the twentieth century, second only to Oswald Chambers. She drew largely on other sources to compile her devotionals, the most famous of which is her *Streams in the Desert*. A devotion by this author can be found on page 1066.

Cowper, William (1731–1800). An English hymn writer and poet, whose mother, Anne Donne, belonged to the same family as John Donne, the seventeenth-century poet and preacher. William Cowper studied law, was called to the Bar in 1754, and nominated to administrative posts in the House of Lords. This turned into an ordeal that left him suicidal and mentally unbalanced. While hospitalized he began to read the Bible and was converted to Christianity. In time Cowper moved to Olney, Buckinghamshire. In 1779 he and his friend John Newton published *Olney Hymns*, "for the use of the plain people." Of the 348 hymns in this collection, Cowper wrote 68, including "O for a Closer Walk with God!," "There is a Fountain Filled with Blood," "Hark, My Soul! It is the Lord," "Jesus! Where'er Thy People Meet," and "God Moves in a Mysterious Way." *Devotions by this author can be found on pages 981, 1141.*

Cranmer, Thomas (1489–1556). This Archbishop of Canterbury and leader of the English Reformation became such by being embroiled in the marital maneuvers of Henry VIII. In an age when the English clergy was celibate, he married a niece of the Lutheran theologian Andreas Osiander (1532). When Cranmer renounced allegiance to the pope, he directed that the pope's name be erased from every prayer book in England. It was Cranmer who pronounced the king of England head of the English church. He also simplified distribution of Miles Coverdale's English translation of the Bible. The fruit of Cranmer's genius as an editor, translator, and composer of prayers and formulae was an English prayer book called *The Book of Common Prayer* (1548), which is used to this day in churches of the Anglican Communion. Political and religious shifts in England caused Cranmer to be condemned as a heretic and he was burned at the stake on March 21, 1556. *A devotion by this author can be found on page 836.*

Crosby, Fanny (1820–1915). Although she was 41 years old when she penned her first hymn, this beloved American hymn writer wrote over 2000 gospel songs. Blinded at the age of six weeks, Crosby attended the New York City Institution for the Blind and later taught there (1847–58). She was devoted to service in New York's Bowery missions and many of her hymns were written for their use. This explains why her songs emphasize conversion, hope, and new life in Christ. Most English language hymnals contain hymns by Fanny Crosby such as "Blessed Assurance, Jesus is Mine," "Rescue the Perishing," "All the Way My Savior Leads Me," "Sweet Hour of Prayer," and "To God Be the Glory." *A devotion by this author can be found on page 1411.*

Cushing, William O. (1823–1902). American writer of Christian hymns. *A devotion by this author can be found on page 1096.*

Cyprian (c. 200–258). The leader of the Christian church in Africa became a Christian late in life (c. 245) In 248 he was chosen bishop of Carthage. During persecution by Decius, Cyprian fled from there. When the persecution ended, the church was divided over the treatment of those who had left the faith under duress and also of those who had been baptized by heretics. Cyprian was inclined toward a middle road of leniency toward apostates. He was adamantly against accepting into the communion those baptized by heretics. Stephen of Rome disagreed with this view and for the first time a bishop of Rome used his reputation as successor to the apostle Peter to claim authority over the other bishops. During the persecution conducted by Emperor Valerian, Cyprian was tried and martyred by beheading. Cyprian's *On the Unity of the Catholic Church*, an exposition of the hierarchical organization of the church written in response to Stephen, seals his position as one of the most authoritative of church fathers. *A devotion by this author can be found on page 1246.*

Didache, The. The title of this ancient manual of instruction for Christian converts comes from a Greek term that means *teaching*. It is a summary of moral principles, instructions on the organization of Christian communities, and rules on worship. Probably written in Syria during the first century A.D., it is also known as the *Teaching of the Twelve Apostles*. Discovered in 1873, this document contains the oldest recorded eucharistic prayers and orders on baptism, fasting, prayer, and the treatment of bishops, deacons, and prophets. Many early Christians regarded *The Didache* as equal to the books of the New Testament. Today it is valuable as a resource about early Christian life and belief. *A devotion from this book can be found on page 1275.*

Diognetus, Epistle to. Both the author and recipient of this letter are unknown. It probably dates from the second or third century A.D. and provides information on three matters of import to the church of that day: (1) reflecting the defensive position the church held in the days before Constantine, *The Epistle to Diognetus* explains why paganism and Judaism cannot be tolerated; (2) describes Christians as the soul of the world; and (3) declares firmly that Christianity is the unique revelation of God and of his love. *A devotion from this letter can be found on page 1387.*

Donne, John (1572–1631). The seventeenth-century religious writers referred to as the metaphysical poets (including Richard Crashaw, George Herbert, and Henry Vaughan) drew inspiration from the religious poetry of John Donne. Thereafter his work was almost forgotten until the nineteenth century. Then, in the 1920s, Ezra Pound and T. S. Eliot cited the influence of this English poet, prose writer, and clergyman. Now Donne is considered the greatest of the metaphysical poets and a peerless writer of love poetry. Donne became a priest of the Anglican church in 1615 and was appointed royal chaplain later that year. He attained eminence as a preacher, delivering sermons regarded as the most brilliant and eloquent of his time. A modern edition of his sermons runs ten volumes. *Devotions by this author can be found on pages 570, 817, 1155, 1183, 1335.*

Dostoyevsky, Fyodor (1821–1881). A promising literary career seemed to await the young atheistic socialist, Fyodor Dostoyevsky. But in 1849 he and other Russian intellectuals were arrested for studying the forbidden subject of French socialist utopianism. Four years of Siberian exile and imprisonment left Dostoyevsky with psychological scars, epilepsy, and the Christian faith. His Siberian experiences are fictionalized in *The House of the Dead* (1861). Dostoyevsky's life was characterized by physical hardship, poverty, and great literary productivity. The novels *Crime and Punishment* (1866), *The Idiot* (1868–69), and *The Possessed* (1871–72) brought him world recognition by 1873. His last novel, *The Brothers Karamazov* was published in 1880. In it, four brothers struggle in their relationships with both a rancorous, degenerate earthly father and a distant, mysterious heavenly Father. Dostoyevsky was concerned with the justice of God and the idea that "if God does not exist, then everything is permitted." *Devotions by this author can be found on pages 590, 1075.*

Douglass, Frederick (1817–1895). This self-educated son of an American slave escaped his owners in 1838. A career as an abolitionist began in 1841 when an impromptu speech to an antislavery convention in Nantucket, Massachusetts, revealed Douglass' verbal eloquence. He referred to himself as "a recent graduate from the institution of slavery with his diploma on his back." Under threat of arrest under the fugitive slave laws, he escaped to England in 1845. There he aroused sympathy for the abolitionists' cause and admirers purchased his freedom. Back in the U.S. by 1847, Douglass was the "station-master and conductor" of the Underground Railroad in Rochester, New York, and established the abolitionist newspaper North Star. He campaigned for Abraham Lincoln in 1860 and helped raise the Massachusetts 54th and 55th regiments of African-American soldiers. The pro-slavery retinue refused to believe that Douglass had been a slave. They called him an impostor invented by abolitionists. In their opinion no slave could be so intelligent and articulate. In reply, Douglass wrote *Narrative of the Life of Frederick Douglass, an American Slave* (1845), later published as the *Life and Times of Frederick Douglass* (1882). *A devotion by this author can be found on page 1444.*

Du Bois, W. E. B. (1868–1963). William Edward Burghardt Du Bois was an American writer and sociologist. He was the first African-American to be awarded a Ph.D. degree from Harvard University (1895). As an advocate for complete racial equality, he helped found the National Association for the Advancement of Colored People (NAACP) in 1910 and served as its director of publications until 1932. After a visit to the Soviet Union, he was convinced that advancement of African-Americans could be achieved through socialism. Du Bois was awarded the Lenin Peace Prize (1959), joined the Communist party (1961) and settled in Ghana where he edited the Encyclopedia Africana. His books include The Philadelphia Negro (1899), Black Reconstruction (1935), and the trilogy, Black Flame: The Ordeal of Mansart (1957), Mansart Builds a School (1959), and Worlds of Color (1961). A devotion by this author can be found on page 62.

Edwards, Jonathan (1703–1758). It has been said that "the whole of [Jonathan Edwards] thought might be viewed as one magnificent answer to the question, 'What is true religion?' " At age 13 he entered the Collegiate School of Connecticut (now Yale University) and graduated valedictorian (1720). At age 26 Edwards, a firm believer in Calvinism and the doctrine of predestination, became pastor at Northampton, Massachusetts, where a religious revival occurred in 1734 as a result of Edwards preaching. The British evangelist George Whitefield visited Edwards in 1740 and together they started the revival known as the Great Awakening, which engulfed all New England. At that time Edward's sermon "Sinners in the Hands of an Angry God" caused the congregation of Enfield, Connecticut, to rise weeping and moaning from their seats. This was typical throughout the revival. Edwards was a stern religious disciplinarian. So much so that a council representing ten congregations in the region dismissed Edwards in 1750. After a time serving in Stockbridge, Massachusetts, Edwards accepted the presidency of the College of New Jersey (later Princeton University, 1757). There he died as the result of an inoculation against smallpox (1758). His works include A Treatise Concerning Religious Affections (1746), Dissertation Concerning the End for Which God Created the World (1754), and The Great Christian Doctrine of Original Sin Defended (1758). Devotions by this author can be found on pages 235, 813.

Eliot, T. S. (1888–1965). "Those who talk of the Bible as a 'monument of English prose' are merely admiring it as a monument over the grave of Christianity." So wrote the Nobel Laureate Thomas Stearns Eliot, arguably the most influential English writer in the twentieth century. American-born and a graduate of Harvard, Eliot settled in London and became a British citizen. His first notable poem, "The Love Song of J. Alfred Prufrock" (1911), offered the title character as a symbol of an age morally adrift. "The Waste Land" (1922), a landmark of modern poetry, concerns the sterility of modern societies. Eliot's Christian convictions are seen in "The Journey of the Magi" (1930), which traces the poet's spiritual journey; and "Ash Wednesday" (1930), which depicts the need for repentance. "The Four Quartets" (1934–43) is Eliot at the apex of his poetic strength. It deals with the relationship between time and eternity. Notable among his works is Murder in the Cathedral (1930), a drama about the martyrdom of Archbishop Thomas ö Becket in Canterbury Cathedral. Eliot received the Nobel Prize for literature in 1948 and the U.S. Presidential Medal of Freedom in 1964. Devotions by this author can be found on pages 1081, 1130.

Elliot, Charlotte (1789–1871). This discouraged invalid and minister's daughter was once visited by an evangelist who told her, "You must go to God just as you are." She did this and found the truth in God's loving acceptance. Later she wrote what may be the best known invitation in Christian hymnody—"Just As I Am Without One Plea." Over 100 of her hymns appeared first in The Invalid's Hymn Book (1854) and then in Hymns for Public, Private and Social Worship, edited by her brother Henry Elliot. A devotion by this author can be found on page 74.

Fénelon, François (1651–1715). An archbishop of Cambrai and ardent follower of Madame Jeannne Guyon in the French quietistic movement, Fénelon was condemned by Pope Innocent XII for Fénelon's book Maxims of the Saints (1697), a book that supported Guyon's mysticism. Fénelon's subsequent submission to the pope seemed to lack sincerity but was accepted nonetheless. He was known in his diocese as a diligent, benevolent, and autocratic administrator, an effective and influential preacher, and through his writings, deeply devotional. *Devotions by this author can be found on pages 135, 143, 1068.*

Finney, Charles P. (1792–1875). An American lawyer, Finney first began reading the Bible because he noticed how often his law books referred to it. Then he had a powerful conversion experience that redirected the entire course of his life. He eventually became one of the most renowned revivalists of the nineteenth century as well as a lecturer, minister, and educator. Later in his life, he wrote about his extremely mystical conversion experience. *A devotion by this author can be found on page 424.*

Fosdick, Harry Emerson (1878–1969). "I would rather live in a world where my life is surrounded by mystery than live in a world so small that my mind could comprehend it." So spoke this American clergyman in his *Riverside Sermons*. Born in Buffalo, New York, Fosdick was ordained in the Baptist ministry (1903) and was pastor in Montclair, New Jersey (1904–15). He then became professor of practical theology at Union Theological Seminary (1915–46) and pastor of New York City's Riverside Church (1926–46). Fosdick became a national figure partially through preaching on his "National Vespers" radio program. Among his books are *The Second Mile* (1908), *The Manhood of the Master* (1913), and *On Being a Real Person* (1943). *A devotion by this author can be found on page 781.*

Fox, George (1624–1691). At Derby in 1650 this English religious leader and founder of the Society of Friends was convicted on a trumped-up charge of blasphemy by Justice Gervase Bennet. The preacher warned the judge to "tremble at the word of the Lord." Bennet responded contemptuously, calling Fox and his followers "quakers." This, together with their agitated movements during times of revelation, caused them to be known by that name. Born to a Puritan family, Fox was 19 when he left home and traveled in search of religious enlightenment. Eventually he came to rely on the "Inner Light of the Living Christ." Fox stressed the priesthood of all believers and advocated a simple life-style. He objected to political and religious authority and opposed war and slavery. According to Fox, all human actions should be directed by inner contemplation and a social conscience inspired by God. His writings include the *Journal* (1694), which is a comprehensive account of the origins of Quakerism. *Devotions by this author can be found on pages 777, 1278.*

Foxe, John (1516–1587). It has been said that *Foxe's Book of Martyrs* helped to give to England a sense of being an "elect Protestant nation." This Protestant clergyman studied at the University of Oxford and was a fellow of Magdalen College. When the Roman Catholic Mary I ascended to the English throne, Foxe and his wife fled to the Continent. There he began to work on a history of Christian persecutions. After Elizabeth I became queen, Foxe returned and published his history of the Protestant martyrs (1559). In 1570 *Foxe's Book of Martyrs* was placed in every collegiate church in England. *A devotion by this author can be found on page 493.*

Francis of Assisi (1182–1226). As a reckless, materialistic young soldier, Francis began a spiritual struggle. In 1205 he performed charities among lepers and began working on the restoration of dilapidated churches. Francis' father was angered by this change of character and the expenditures for charity. So he legally disinherited his son. Thus Francis began his life as a preacher, mystic, and founder of monastic communities devoted to poverty and service to the poor known as *Franciscans.* However, by 1222 the Franciscan friars, who had formerly renounced wealth to find true freedom to serve God and the needy, were entering politics and the universities. Francis pleaded against this because he felt it would betray the simplicity of the gospel. Yet finding the direction of the order was beyond his control, Francis retired to Assisi in what is now northern Italy. *Devotions by this author can be found on pages 635, 772.*

Gordon, George Noel, Lord Byron (1788–1824). In literature there is something known as the Byronic hero. This is an emotional young man who eschews humankind wandering through life weighed down by a sense of guilt for mysterious past transgressions. The hero of Lord Byron's poem "Childe Harold" was the first example of such a character and is to some extent patterned after Byron himself. During his short life this English poet became one of the most important and versatile writers of the romantic movement. He died in Greece as commander in chief of forces fighting the Turks. *A devotion by this author can be found on page 240.*

Graham, Isabella (1742–1814). This Scottish church worker helped to found many charities for the disenfranchised of society: the poor, orphans and widows, the homeless, and prisoners. Published posthumously under the title *Devotional Exercises* (1819), her journal is a classic of prayer and devotional thought. *A devotion by this author can be found on page 1501.*

Gregory of Nazianzus (330–389). The son of the bishop of Nazianzus in Cappadocia, Gregory studied in the Middle East, Alexandria, and Athens. He wanted to be a hermit, but his father wanted him to be a leader of the church. As it turned out, Gregory did both. His eloquent preaching and scholarly writing earned him the title "the theologian." An active participant in the Council of Constantinople (381), Gregory defended the Nicene council's view of the Trinity, condemned the Apollinarian view that Christ's humanity was passive, and denounced the Emperor Julian for restricting the rights of Christians. *A devotion by this author can be found on page 646.*

Gregory of Nyssa (330–c. 395). This theological prodigy elaborated the doctrines of resurrection, divine grace, and Christology, wrote on ascetic piety and mystic communion with God, and served as bishop of Nyssa. He, his older brother Basil, and Gregory of Nazianzus—the "three Cappadocians"—greatly influenced the fourth-century Eastern church. *A devotion by this author can be found on page 1268.*

Hammarskjöld, Dag (1905–1961). This Swedish economist and diplomat helped to organize the European Recovery Program (1947) and was vice-chairman of the executive committee of the Organization for European Economic Cooperation (1948–49). Hammarskjöld was chief of the Swedish delegation to the United Nations, elected secretary-general of the UN in 1953, and died in this capacity in a plane crash while on a diplomatic mission in Africa. In 1961 he was posthumously awarded the Nobel Peace Prize. Hammarskjöld's deeply religious and ethical philosophy is expressed in his book of meditations, *Markings* (1964). *A devotion by this author can be found on page 596.*

Havergal, Frances R. (1836–79). An English woman, Havergal who wrote many remarkable religious poems and hymns, one of which is "Take My Life and Let It Be." Her most enduring collection is called *Ministry of Song*, published in 1870. *Devotions by this author can be found on pages 784, 938, 1070.*

Henry, Matthew (1662–1714). As a Biblical expositor, his multivolume *Commentary on the Bible* still enjoy popularity, even though they were written almost 300 years ago. Under the Act of Uniformity of 1662, Henry was expelled from the Church of England. He considered a career in law but instead studied for the ministry. Ordained as a Presbyterian, he served two English parishes until his early death. *Devotions by this author can be found on pages 319, 500.*

Herrick, Robert (1591–1674). The chief work of this English Cavalier poet is *Hesperides; or, the Works Both Human and Divine of Robert Herrick, Esq.* (1648). Within this book, though with a separate title page, is a group of religious poems, *His Noble Numbers* (1647). The collection includes more than 1200 short poems with pastoral themes concerning English country life and village customs. Educated at the University of Cambridge, Herrick became vicar of Dean Prior in Devonshire (1629), but the Great Rebellion did not tolerate his Royalist views and his position was taken away (1647). When Charles II was restored to the throne, Herrick returned to Dean Prior (1662) where he lived until his death. *Devotions by this author can be found on pages 1089, 1152.*

Hilary of Poitiers (c. 315–368). Born into a prominent pagan family France, Hilary was educated in philosophy and rhetoric, converted to Christianity about 350 and, although married, was elected bishop of Poitiers three years later. When the embattled Athanasius was banished for his orthodox opposition to Arianism in 355, Hilary rallied the leaders of the churches in Gaul to counter those who supported the Arian position, including the emperor. For this Hilary was exiled to Asia Minor where he wrote *On the Trinity* (356–59), a cogent defense of the divinity of Christ against those who did not hold the Son to be eternal but created by the Father (Arianism). Hilary understood that the Father and the Son have identity of substance yet are two. *A devotion by this author can be found on page 1304.*

Hippolytus (c. 160–236). This presbyter of the Roman church was the most important theologian in third-century Rome where a disagreement over the absolution of sins caused him to withdraw from the church, thus becoming the first anti-pope in history. Because of this schism and the fact that he wrote in Greek instead of Latin, Hippolytus was soon forgotten in the West. He is significant for upholding the Logos doctrine against modalism. This doctrine distinguishes the persons of the Trinity as opposed to the modalistic belief that the three of the Trinity are simply different manifestations of the same person. Hippollytus' *Refutation of All Heresies* is significant in that it makes evident that all Christian heresies find their source in pagan philosophies. *A devotion by this author can be found on page 1341.*

Holden, J. Stuart (1874–1934). This gifted and personable Anglican preacher served as the vicar of St. Paul's Church in London. For nearly 30 years, he also provided leadership for the Keswick movement. *A devotion by this author can be found on page 710.*

Hopkins, Gerard Manley (1844–1889). Born near London and educated at Oxford, this talented poet converted to Roman Catholicism in 1866. Two years later, upon becoming a Jesuit, he burned all his poetry and vowed only to write if instructed to do so by his superiors. But his talent compelled him instead and by 1875 he was writing once again. *A devotion by this author can be found on page 1361.*

Howson, John Saul (1816–1885). A New Testament scholar, he was educated at Cambridge, where he served as a teacher until becoming the headmaster of Liverpool Collegiate Institute. There he joined his friend W. J. Conybeare, with whom he worked together on *The Life and Epistles of St. Paul* (2 vols., 1852), an extensive treatment that incorporated theological, geographical, and historical studies on Paul and his writings. *A devotion by this author can be found on page 1375.*

Hurnard, Hannah (1905–1990). In 1929 she traveled to Palestine on what would be the first of many mission trips to the Middle East. Here she ministered both to Arab as well as Jewish settlements and spent several years seving in missionary hospitals in Jerusalem. From 1949 until her death, Hurnard devoted herself to writing and speaking on behalf of her mission work. Among her well-read inspirational titles are *Watchmen of the Walls*, *Hinds' Feet on High Places*, and *Thou Shalt Remember*. *A devotion by this author can be found on page 1077.*

Ignatius of Antioch (d. c. 116). During the reign of the Roman Emperor Trajan, Ignatius was condemned to be devoured by wild beasts. He wrote seven letters while en route under armed guard from Antioch to Rome for execution. Of these, five were addressed to the Christian communities of Ephesus, Magnesia, Tralles, Philadelphia, and Smyrna cities in Asia Minor that had sent representatives to greet him as he passed through. The sixth was addressed to Polycarp, bishop of Smyrna. In the seventh he wrote ahead to the Christian community of Rome to prevent their intervention with the authorities. He wanted nothing to stand in the way of his martyrdom. These letters show the early development of the episcopal structure in the early church. Except for the Old and New Testaments Ignatius was the first to speak of the virgin birth of Jesus. He emphasized that the disciples touched the body of the risen Christ and first described the church as *catholic* in reference to her universal quality. *Devotions by this author can be found on pages 1364, 1503.*

Jones, E. Stanley (1884–1973). Twice nominated for the Nobel Peace Prize, he received seven honorary doctorates and wrote 29 books, the first of which is entitled *The Christ* *of the Indian Road.* An evangelist to Indian intellectuals, Jones was acquainted with Mahatma Gandhi, Jawaharlal Nehru, and Rabindranath Tagore, and negotiated between President Franklin Roosevelt and Japanese envoys. The preaching of E. Stanley Jones in his numerous worldwide evangelistic crusades was marked by his advocacy of the uniqueness of Christ, the gospel, and church union. *Devotions by this author can be found on pages 549, 786, 1326, 1369.*

Jonson, Ben (1572–1637). An English dramatist, poet and great figure of English literature, his first original play, "Every Man in His Humour," was performed in 1598 by the Lord Chamberlain's Company with William Shakespeare in the cast. Jonson was the acknowledged leader of the men of letters of his time and his creative talents were many and varied. English literature of the Jacobean and Carolinian periods was formed in part by his critical theories which advanced English drama as a form of literature and conscious art through adherence to classical forms and rules. *Devotions by this author can be found on pages 1178, 1425.*

Jowett, John Henry (1864–1923). This Scotsman was a popular preacher and writer who served as minister in Newcastle, Birmingham, and other cities in England. In 1911 he came to the United States to assume the pulpit of the Fifth Avenue Presbyterian Church in New York City, a pastorate that lasted until 1918. He soon became one of the most colorful and popular preachers in New York at the time. During his American stay he wrote and published a daily devotional book called *My Daily Meditation for the Circling Year. A devotion by this author can be found on page 791.*

Julian of Norwich (c. 1342–c. 1413). One of the greatest English mystics, Julian summarized her doctrine of God in this way: "I saw full surely that ere God made us he loved us; which love was never slacked nor ever shall be. And in this love he hath done all his works and in this love he hath made all things profitable to us and in this love our life is everlasting." Although very little is known with certainty about her, it is thought that Julian lived a solitary life of prayer and mediation near St. Julian's church, Norwich. In 1393 she wrote *The Sixteen Revelations of Divine Love,* the first book to be published by a female author in English. It sets forth the visions of Christ's suffering and the Trinity, which she claimed to have received in the course of two days in 1373. She spent the remainder of her life meditating on these ecstatic visions and her book expresses these insightful meditations with conviction, intelligence, and beauty. *Devotions by this author can be found on pages 1055, 1436.*

Kelly, Thomas R. (1893–1941). His *Testament of Devotion* is one of the most beloved devotional books of our time. Douglas V. Steere, a friend of his, compiled the book from Kelly's articles about the deeper life and published it three months after Kelly's death. In the most sublime terms Kelly describes the fellowship of true believers as those who live "at the Center." *A devotion by this author can be found on page 1288.*

Kierkegaard, Søren (1813–1855). Stressing that Christianity sees the incarnation as an actual historical event, this Danish Christian philosopher asserted that a Christian acquires salvation not through trying to live a moral life but through faith in the Jesus of history. The Danish edition of Kierkegaard's collected works runs 14 volumes, including essays, aphorisms, parables, fictional letters and diaries, and other literary forms. He applied the term *existential* to his philosophy because to him it was the expression of an intensely examined individual life, not the construction of a monolithic system. At the end of his life Kierkegaard attacked the Danish state church, which he claimed had reduced the Christian way of life to being a "nice person" conformed to acceptable manners. For Kierkegaard, being a Christian required a radical, courageous decision to follow Christ. It was this Christianity that he sought to reintroduce into Christendom. *Devotions by this author can be found on pages 1465, 1475.*

King, Martin Luther, Jr. (1929–1968). The eldest son of a prominent Baptist minister, he entered Morehouse College at the age of 15, was ordained a Baptist minister at the age of 17, graduated from Crozer Theological Seminary as class president in 1951, and received his Ph.D. from Boston University. The year the U.S. Supreme Court outlawed all segregated public education, King accepted an appointment as pastor in Montgomery, Alabama. There he organized a successful bus boycott (1955–56) to protest enforced racial segregation in public transportation. This catapulted King into national prominence as a leader for civil rights. In 1963 he led a massive civil rights campaign in Birmingham, Alabama, organized drives for black voter registration, desegregation, and better education and housing throughout the South. He led the historic March on Washington on August 28, 1963. There he delivered his famous "I Have a Dream" speech. In 1964 King was awarded the Nobel Peace Prize. In a speech in Memphis, Tennessee, on April 3, 1968, King said he had "been to the mountain top and seen the Promised Land." The following day he was assassinated. *Devotions by this author can be found on pages 78, 617, 1044, 1048, 1196, 1333.*

Kingsley, Charles (1819–1875). As an English minister, author, and social reformer, he was ferociously outspoken about the social ills of the day; as one man remarked, "Kingsley delivered sermons like a man wrestling with demons." In a message entitled "A Message of the Church to Laboring Men," he delivered a sermon at St. John's Church in London in which he denounced the social system that allowed the wealthy and educated to make money at the expense of the poor. *A devotion by this author can be found on page 736.*

Knox, John (1514–1572). This Scottish religious Reformer was the founder of Presbyterianism in Scotland. Originally a Roman Catholic priest, Knox became attracted to the preachings of the Scottish Protestant preacher George Wishart. When Wishart was executed in 1546, Knox preached in his place. Taken prisoner in 1547, Knox spent a year and a half in French galleys. When Edward VI, king of England interceded, he was released, joined the ministry of the Church of England, and was appointed a royal chaplain (1551). But the Roman Catholic Mary Tudor soon became Mary I, queen of England (1553) and the English Reformation came to a sudden halt. Knox then fled to Geneva where he studied under the French Protestant Reformer John Calvin. Knox returned to Scotland in 1559. When the Scottish parliment abolished papal authority and banned the Mass, it adopted a Reformed Confession of Faith that was largely written by Knox. Political and religious conflict continued for the remainder of his life. John Knox is still a figure who inspires countroversy, yet none can deny his powerful influence on the Reformation. *A devotion by this author can be found on page 1469.*

Kuyper, Abraham (1837–1920). Kuyper was a famed Dutch Calvinist theologian and statesman, who, while spending an active life in politics, was able to write warm and compelling works of theology that proved popular among scholars and lay readers alike. *A devotion by this author can be found on page 1328.*

Law, William (1686–1761). When William Law refused to take an oath of allegiance to the Hanoverian English King George I, he was banned permanently from preaching in the Church of England. Through his writing on Christian ethics and mysticism, however, he influenced many, including John Wesley and George Whitefield. Law's best work is the still accessible *A Serious Call to a Devout and Holy Life* (1728). It delineates the Christian ideal of an ascetic life and sets a standard of honoring God in outward affairs. With simplicity and beauty Law asserts that such a life is realized through self-denial, humility, and self-control. Law's other important works are *A Practical Treatise upon Christian Perfection* (1726), *The Spirit of Prayer* (1749), and *The Spirit of Love* (1752). *Devotions by this author can be found on pages 598, 1414.*

Lewis, C. S. (1898–1963). *Surprised by Joy* is a title befitting the autobiography of Clive Staples Lewis. He was a tutor, lecturer, and classics scholar in the insular world of Oxford and Cambridge Universities. Slowly he realized that the Christian faith is the only way to understand the human existence and came to believe at the age of 30. The author of more than 25 Christian works, his books have sold many millions of copies. The best known of these may be *Mere Christianity* (1952) and *The Screwtape Letters* (1942). The latter consists of imaginative letters written from a major devil named Screwtape to his nephew, Wormwood, a lesser devil who is charged with undermining a young man's soul. *Mere Christianity* simply and eloquently portrays the Christian faith without directly quoting Scripture. A perennial favorite of children (and their parents) is the *Chronicles of Narnia* (1950–56). The title of this seven-volume set refers to a land watched over by a marvelous lion named Aslan where a group of children find amazing (and allegorical) adventures. *The Perelandra Trilogy* (1938–45) is an unique fusion of science fiction, fantasy, and allegory involving space flight, the temptation of Eve, and the second coming of Christ. *Devotions by this author can be found on pages 541, 1036, 1199, 1318, 1337, 1496.*

Luther, Martin (1483–1546). Arguably the most crucial figure in modern European history, this German theologian and religious Reformer not only initiated the Protestant Reformation, but he directly influenced politics, economics, education, and language as well. Although descended from peasants, Luther was a promising young law student when he suddenly abandoned his studies and entered an Augustinian monastery (1505). Ordained in 1507, he was assigned as a lecturer in moral philosophy at the University of Wittenburg (1508) where he received his doctorate and the chair of Biblical theology in 1512. Within the next five years Luther came to understand that God's free grace is the unique source of salvation. This seed of truth bore abundant fruit in his fertile heart and on October 31, 1517, he published his *Ninety-five Theses* opposing certain beliefs and practices of the Catholic Church. The Reformation had begun. As it proceeded Luther came into his own as a leader and innovator. While in hiding he translated the New Testament into the common German tongue. In all of its significance, this was also a seminal contribution to the development of a standard German language. In translation the collected works of Martin Luther runs 56 volumes. His most popular book, published in 1529, is the *Small Catechism*. Luther was preacher, professor, theologian, linguist, educator, political theorist, pastor, husband, and more. Although his faults were as visible as his virtues, Martin Luther was the gifted and versatile man of the hour chosen to usher in a truly new era in human history. *Devotions by this author can be found on pages 206, 330, 506, 573, 655, 810, 842, 1098, 1218, 1402.*

MacDonald, George (1824–1905). A Scotsman, MacDonald was among the great writers of his time and knew many of his contemporaries such as Dickens, Emerson, Longfellow, Tennyson, Thackeray, and Whittier. MacDonald's *Phantastes* (1858) is the mythopoetic novel that helped start C. S. Lewis on his journey to God. MacDonald's so-called fairy tales are still enjoyed at many a bedtime. They include *At the Back of the North Wind* (1871), *The Princess and the Goblin* (1872), *The Lost Princess* (1875), and *The Princess and Curdie* (1883). *Devotions by this author can be found on pages 102, 1263, 1371.*

Marshall, Peter (1902–1949). This Scottish emigrant to America served as chaplain to the United States Senate for two years until his untimely death in 1949. Prior to this he had graduated from Columbia Theological Seminary in Decatur, Georgia (1931), served churches in Georgia, and was called to the New York Avenue Presbyterian Church of Washington, D.C., in 1937. Some of Marshall's sermons and prayers were posthumously published under the title *Mr. Jones, Meet the Master* (1949). His widow, Catherine Marshall, made her husband's story known when she published his biography, *A Man Called Peter* (1951). This book was later produced as a popular film. *Devotions by this author can be found on pages 277, 1171.*

Merton, Thomas (1915–1968). Born in France, Merton's father was an English landscape painter and his mother an American Quaker. While teaching English at Columbia University, Merton also worked at a Roman Catholic center in the Harlem area of New York City. In his popular autobiography, *The Seven Storey Mountain* (1941), Merton tells of his dramatic conversion to Roman Catholicism (1938) while in the midst of living a full and worldly life. Two years later he entered the Trappist Monastery of Gethsemani in Kentucky. The autobiographical *The Waters of Siloe* (1949), and *The Sign of Jonas* (1952) are vivid descriptions of his life there. Merton was a poet of personal Christian mysticism. His volumes of verse include *Figures for an Apocalypse*

(1947), *The Tears of the Blind Lions* (1949), and *The Strange Islands* (1957). His sensitivity to things contemporary such as the peace movement, the civil rights movement, and liturgical revival were remarkable. Merton died as a result of an accident while attending a Christian-Buddhist conference in Bangkok. *Devotions by this author can be found on pages 754, 1206, 1320, 1508.*

Meyer, F. B. (1847–1929). Born in London into a wealthy family, Frederick Brotherton Meyer was educated at London University and later studied theology at Regent's Park College. He held several successful pastorates and helped introduce churches to the then-unknown D. L. Moody. During much of Meyer's ministry he engaged in social work and temperance work. In 1904 he served as president of the Free Church Council and retired in 1921. For many years he was a popular convention speaker at Northfield, Keswick, and Portstewart. He also published a number of devotional studies on Biblical characters. *Devotions by this author can be found on pages 208, 259, 936, 1021.*

Milton, John (1608–1674). This extraordinary man, the greatest English poet after Shakespeare, spent the central years of his life writing prose tracts on religious, social, educational, and domestic responsibility. During the English Civil War (1640–60), Milton worked in government service. But he also wrote pamphlets on many pertinent topics: He attacked the institution of bishops, argued for divorce on the basis of incompatibility, for freedom of the press, for quality and balanced education, for constitutional rights of the people, for governmental reform, and for abolishment of the professional clergy. At the same time, he wrote some of the most notable sonnets in the English language and began the composition of *Paradise Lost*. He became totally blind in 1652. Milton's fields of study were extensive and he was fluent in, or familiar with, many ancient and modern languages, but the keystone of all his learning was the Bible. *Paradise Lost*, his masterpiece and one of the greatest poems in world literature, was completed in 1667. Milton himself said that with this work he aimed to "justify the ways of God to men." Composed of 12 cantos, the epic depicts the vast cosmic drama and focuses on God's acts in creation and Adam's fall. In it the reader soars to the apogee of John Milton's poetic imagination, intellect, and style. *Devotions by this author can be found on pages 4, 1147.*

Moody, Dwight L. (1837–1899). First a successful shoe salesman, Moody converted from Unitarianism to Congregationalism and became one of America's greatest evangelists. In 1860 he started missionary work in Chicago. There he did evangelistic work for the YMCA and started a Sunday school, which eventually became the Chicago Avenue Church. Later it was named the Moody Memorial Church. Joined by the American singer and hymn composer Ira Sankey (1840–1908), Moody mounted revival meetings. When his meetings met with great success in Britain, Moody and Sankey returned to America as heroes. Thereafter they were enthusiastically received in all quarters of the country. In 1879 Moody opened the Northfield Seminary for Young Women and in 1881 the Mount Hermon School for Boys in his hometown of Northfield, Massachusetts. In order to better train Christian workers, Moody founded a Bible school in Chicago, now known as the Moody Bible Institute (1889). *Devotions by this author can be found on pages 25, 413, 1000, 1031, 1499.*

More, Thomas (1478–1535). A religious stance against King Henry VIII cost this English statesman and writer his life. As a young man More wrote comedies and studied Greek and Latin literature. In 1499 he became a Carthusian monk. Giving this up, he entered Parliament (1504). More ran afoul of King Henry VII because of his legislative activities, but upon the ascension of Henry VIII, he was appointed undersheriff of London. In 1518 he became a member of the Privy Council and was knighted in 1521. Two years later he was made speaker of the House of Commons, and became lord chancellor in 1529. When Henry VIII requested a divorce from Catherine of Aragon, More refused because he was not willing to sanction defiance of papal authority. Thus the king had his former friend imprisoned in 1534. After his trial the following year, More contended that Parliament did not have the right to usurp papal authority in favor of the king. Condemned for this stand, More was decapitated on July 7, 1535. *A devotion by this author can be found on page 1165.*

Morgan, G. Campbell (1863–1945). Born in England, this son of a Baptist preacher preached his first sermon at 13. As a famous Bible teacher and evangelist, George Campbell Morgan pastored various churches in England, including Westminster Chapel in London (1904–17; 1933–45). He also served as president of Cheshunt College, Cambridge (1911–14). His published works on Bible sermons and commentaries number approximately 50 books. *Devotions by this author can be found on pages 72, 272, 359, 716, 958.*

Mozarabic Sacramentary (3rd century). From the third through the eleventh century this liturgy was used by believers inhabitating parts of the Iberian peninsula comprising Spain and Portugal. *A devotion from this liturgy can be found on page 898.*

Müller, George (1805–1898). Of German birth, Müller was a naturalized British citizen and converted in 1825. He eventually became a successful preacher at Ebenezer Chapel, a Plymouth Brethren meeting place in Devon. He firmly believed that his material needs could be supplied through faith and prayer alone. Inspired by the work of A. H. Francke in Germany, Müller started an orphanage in Bristol. He was eventually providing for the physical, educational, and spiritual needs of over 2000 boys and girls. Müller's testimony of faith and prayer has caused the establishment of many orphanages and other Christian endeavors throughout the world. *A devotion by this author can be found on page 882.*

Murray, Andrew (1828–1917). Some titles among Andrew Murray's 240 publications are dear to the hearts of Christians who draw on devotional literature to enhance their spiritual life. Among these are *Abide in Christ, Absolute Surrender, With Christ in the School of Prayer*, and *The Spirit of Christ.* Murray was a leader of the South African Dutch Reformed Church with a strong ecumenical spirit. He promoted the call to missions in South Africa and helped to found the University College of the Orange Free State and the Stellenbosch Seminary. His abiding legacy, however, is his body of devotional writings that emphasize the need for a rich, personal devotional life and its outworking in a Christian's life. *Devotions by this author can be found on pages 132, 165, 1259.*

Nee, Watchman (1903–1972). The indigenous church movement formed and fostered by Watchman Nee in pre-World War II China helped lay the foundation for many of the house churches that today maintain Christ's testimony in Communist China. When still a promising student, the eighteen-year-old Nee began to devote himself entirely to Bible study and preaching. This bore fruit in what was to be known to outsiders as the "Little Flock" movement with many assemblies spread across China. Arrested and tried on false charges, Nee was imprisoned in 1952 and died in prison in 1972. Nee's many books continue to enrich the church. They include a book on Romans entitled *The Normal Christian Life*, and a book on Ephesians called *Sit, Walk, Stand. Devotions by this author can be found on pages 410, 1252, 1456.*

Newman, John Henry (1801–1890). Newman graduated from Oxford and was ordained an Anglican in 1824. Thereafter, he became leader of the Oxford movement. This opposed the growth of theological liberalism within the Church of England and advocated the return to the theology and ritual of the period following the Reformation. Newman was well-known and influential when in 1845 he converted to the Roman Catholicism. A year later in Rome he was ordained as a priest. On his return to England he retired to a monastic life outside Oxford. When the British novelist Charles Kingsley charged that Roman Catholicism was indifferent to the truth, In 1864 Newman published his masterpiece, *Apologia Pro Vita Sua*, to explain his spiritual development. This is acknowledged as a classic of both religious autobiography and English prose. Newman was elevated to cardinal in 1879. *Devotions by this author can be found on pages 138, 1460.*

Newton, John (1725–1807). As a young man Newton was forced to join the British navy where he attained the position of midshipman. But he deserted and spent ten years in the African slave trade, becoming the master of a slave ship. During a storm at sea he experienced conversion to Christ. Later, while a tide surveyor at Liverpool (1755–60), Newton met George Whitefield and later John Wesley. Their influence was so profound that he studied for the ministry. After some resistance from the Church of England, Newton became curate at Olney where at age 39 he was ordained (1764). There he became an intimate friend of the poet William Cowper and together they produced the *Olney Hymns* (1779), containing Newton's "Glorious Things of Thee Are Spoken" and "One There Is Above All Others." Newton is most remembered for these and other hymns, including "How Sweet the Name of Jesus Sounds in a Believer's Ear." His "Amazing Grace, How Sweet the Sound" may be one of the most frequently sung and best loved of all English songs. *Devotions by this author can be found on pages 1477, 1491, 1505.*

Niebuhr, Reinhold (1892–1971). Born in Wright City, Missouri, this Protestant theologian was educated at Elmhurst College, Illinois; Eden Theological Seminary, Missouri; and Yale Divinity School. After ordination into the ministry of the Evangelical Synod of North America (1915), he became pastor of the Bethel Evangelical Church of Detroit. This harsh industrial environment forced Neibuhr to examine the interrelationships between religion, individuals, and modern society. A concern with the nature of man as a contact point for religion and society has been called "theological anthropology." Niebuhr's social doctrines profoundly influenced American theological and political thought. In 1928 he joined the faculty of the Union Theological Seminary, New York City, where he taught for 30 years. Reinhold Niebuhr received the U.S. Presidential Medal of Freedom in 1964 and was made a member of the American Academy of Arts and Letters. His works include *Moral Man and Immoral Society* (1932), *Interpretation of Christian Ethics* (1935), and *The Nature and Destiny of Man* (2 vols., 1941, 1943). *A devotion by this author can be found on page 1308.*

Origen (c. 185–c. 254). Jerome called this writer, teacher, and theologian the second teacher of the church after Paul. Born in Alexandria, Egypt, Origen was a student of Clement of Alexandria and taught both Christians and pagans for about 28 years. When in 230 the bishop of Jerusalem and the bishop of Caesarea ordained him a presbyter without consulting Origen's own bishop, Origen was forbidden to teach in his home city and deprived of his priesthood. Thereafter Origen lived in Caesarea where he founded a school of literature, philosophy, and theology. During the persecutions under Emperor Decius (250), Origen was imprisoned and tortured. Although freed, it is thought that he died of complications from his injuries. Origen was an incredibly productive writer of letters, theological treatises, apologetics, exegeses, and textual criticism and is regarded as the father of the allegorical method of scriptural interpretation. *Devotions by this author can be found on pages 56, 586.*

Osler, Sir William (1849–1919). A renowned Canadian physician and teacher, Osler served at Johns Hopkins University and completed his career as a professor of medicine at Oxford University, England. *A devotion by this author can be found on page 1236.*

Owen, John (1616–1683). During the civil war in England, parliament was at war with the king and so had removed the bishops from the Church of England. At this time the English theologian John Owen had the opportunity to practice the Congregational form of church government at Coggeshall, Essex, and became its great advocate. He was chaplain to Oliver Cromwell (1649–51), vice chancellor of Oxford (1652–57), and dean of Christ Church Cathedral (1651–60), and thus prominent in the religious, political, and academic life of the nation. Owen refused invitations to the ministry in Boston (1663) and the presidency of Harvard (1670) and instead rebuked the Congregationalists of New England for their intolerance. *Devotions by this author can be found on pages 183, 1417.*

Parker, Joseph (1830–1902). Born in Hexham, Parker preached with authority and appeal and became one of England's most popular preachers. Largely self-educated, Parker had pulpit gifts that soon moved him into leadership among the Congregationalists. He was a fearless and imaginative preacher who attracted both common people and the aristocracy, and he was particularly a "man's preacher." His *People's Bible* is a collection of the short-hand reports of the sermons and prayers Parker delivered as he preached through the entire Bible in seven years (1884–92). *A devotion by this author can be found on page 827.*

Parkhurst, Charles Henry (1842–1933). Actively involved in mission work, this medical doctor wrote a variety of devotional pieces, some of which appear in the devotional classic, *Streams in the Desert*. *A devotion by this author can be found on page 322.*

Pascal, Blaise (1623–1662). "The last function of reason is to recognize that there are an infinity of things which surpass it," wrote Blaise Pascal in *Pens es* (1670), his posthumous classic of literature and Christian apologetics. This statement came from one of the great minds in Western intellectual history, an eminent mathematician and physicist who was at the same time one of the greatest mystical writers in Christian literature. By the age of 12 Pascal had worked out the equivalent of many of Euclid's geometrical theorems. At 19 he invented the first practical calculating machine. Later he verified the theory of atmospheric pressure and formulated the mathematical theory of probability, a fundamental element of modern theoretical physics. Pascal was an adherent of the Roman Catholic reform movement known as Jansenism. His *Provincial Letters* (1657) is at once a classic in the literature of irony and satire, and a demand for a reemphasis on Augustine's doctrine of grace within the Catholic church. *Devotions by this author can be found on pages 456, 638, 1404.*

Patrick of Ireland (c. 390–c. 461). Apart from what we know from his own writings (*The Confession* and *The Letter to the Christian Subjects of the Tyrant Coroticus*), little is known with certainty about Patrick. Despite various traditions, he probably had no connections with Rome but rather was born in Britain, the son of Calpurnius, a Roman magistrate living in Britain. After Patrick's conversion he managed to escape from bondage as a slave and traveled to Scotland. Shortly after this, however, he returned to Ireland about 432. For the next 30 years he ministered throughout Ireland where he successfully shared the Good News. *A devotion by this author can be found on page 854.*

Penn, William (1644–1718). The United States boasts a rich and varied heritage. One of its jewels is this founder of Pennsylvania (1681), which at the time was the most secure home for religious toleration in the world. While imprisoned in the tower of London for a tract attacking the doctrines of the Church of England, Penn wrote the devotional classic *No Cross, No Crown* (1669). This book vindicated its author while expounding on Christian suffering. In it Penn wrote, "No pain, no palm; no thorns, no throne; no gall, no glory; no cross, no crown." In 1671, imprisoned in Newgate prison, Penn wrote *The Great Cause of Liberty of Conscience*, a defense of the doctrine of toleration. Given the appellation "the Renaissance Quaker," modern historians have called Penn a "compassionate humanitarian, mystic, theologian, and profound political theorist." *A devotion by this author can be found on page 760.*

Polycarp of Smyrna (c. 70–155/160). This apostolic father of the church was bishop at Smyrna (now Izmir, Turkey). Ignatius of Antioch, another of the apostolic fathers, visited Polycarp and addressed an epistle to him just prior to Ignatius's martyrdom (c. 116). According to his pupil Irenaeus, Polycarp was a disciple of John the Evangelist and acquainted with the other disciples of Christ. He had a gift of preaching, a devout character, and a position of great authority among the Asian churches. Polycarp was martyred at Smyrna at the age of 86. *A devotion by this author can be found on page 1282.*

Pynson, Richard (c. 1470–1530). Norman printer Richard Pynson completed the printing of an anonymous treatise on the Ten Commandments called *Dives and Pauper* (1493). Written in the form of a dialogue, this entertaining book details the discussion between a rich man, Dives, and a poor man, Pauper. Pauper is the wise hero of this book; with his homespun humor and wisdom, he catechizes Dives on the true meaning of the Commandments, often using folk tales to illustrate his points. *A devotion by this author can be found on page 1138.*

Rossetti, Christina (1830–1894). This English lyric poet was a devout High Church Anglican. Her devotion to God is seen in the collections *Goblin Market and Other Poems* (1862), considered her finest poetry, and *The Prince's Progress and Other Poems* (1866). Sister to Dante Gabriel Rossetti, the pre-Raphaelite painter and poet, Christina also wrote delightful verse for children, such as the charming lyrics in *Sing-Song: A Nursery Rhyme Book* (1872). *Devotions by this author can be found on pages 686, 730, 764.*

Ryle, J. C. (1816–1900). Born in England and educated at Oxford, John Charles Ryle was the son of a wealthy banker. Converted at the age of 22, he was ordained four years later. He was a prolific writer, a strong leader of the evangelicals, and a capable administrator. At the age of 64, upon the recommendation of Disraeli, he was appointed bishop of Liverpool in 1880. *A devotion by this author can be found on page 1007.*

Schaeffer, Francis (1912–1984). Ordained into the Presbyterian ministry, Francis Schaeffer had served various churches in Pennsylvania and St. Louis, Missouri when, in 1948, he was sent to Switzerland by the Presbyterian Board for Foreign Missions. Together with his wife Edith, Schaeffer founded an international study and ministry community in the Swiss Alps (1955). All were welcome at L'Abri (shelter), regardless of culture or beliefs, and thousands visited the Schaeffers to live, study, pray, and discuss secular culture. The work eventually spread to Milan, London, Amsterdam, and Rochester, Minnesota. Schaeffer wrote 23 books, of which he considered three to be essential to the understanding of his thought: *The God Who is There* (1968) shows how modern thought has forsaken the idea of truth and describes the tragic consequences of this abandonment; *Escape From Reason* (1968) explores and explains the sources of the disintegration of modern life; and *He Is There and He Is Not Silent* (1972) contrasts the despair of modern life with the Christian gospel of the knowable God. *Devotions by this author can be found on pages 469, 1029, 1300, 1323.*

Simpson, A. B. (1844–1919). The founder of the Christian and Missionary Alliance had his roots on the shores of Prince Edward Island, Canada. After serving various churches, A. B. Simpson built a congregation in New York City where he emphasized evangelism and pastoral visitation. He wrote some 70 books, numerous poems, and with his daughter Margaret composed a large number of songs featuring the sanctified life and confidence in divine healing. His books include *The Gospel of Healing, Holy Spirit, Christ in the Tabernacle,* and *The Life of Prayer. Devotions by this author can be found on pages 92, 97, 614, 1013, 1135.*

Smart, Christopher (1722–1771). After this English poet published his *Poems on Several Occasions,* including "The Hop Garden" (1752), and satirized the criticism of it in *Hilliad* (1753), his mental illness caused him to be confined to an asylum. There he produced the original and powerful poem, *A Song to David* (1763). Smart's other writings include *Hymns for Amusement of Children* (1775), and *Rejoice in the Lamb,* which was not published until 1939. *A devotion by this author can be found on page 691.*

Smith, Hannah Whitall (1832–1911). Raised in a strict Quaker home, this beloved author was married to Robert Piersall Smith (1851) and converted by the Plymouth Brethren (1858). An experience of faith caused this husband and wife team to embark on speaking tours in America and Europe. An outgrowth of their "Higher Christian Life" conferences in Great Britain were the ongoing Keswick Conventions (1874). Smith wrote the spiritual classic *The Christian's Secret of a Happy Life* (1875). *Devotions by this author can be found on pages 52, 243, 853, 1086, 1482.*

Smith, Robert (c. 1500–1555). Instead of directing recrimination toward his persecutors, this English clergyman and martyr left behind a poetic work entitled "The Exhortation of a Father to His Children." Written for his own children, he penned its gentle advice shortly before his execution. *A devotion by this author can be found on page 1351.*

Southwell, Robert (c. 1561–1595). Born in England and educated on the Continent, Southwell became a Jesuit and in 1586 returned to England where he served as a chaplain to the countess of Arundel. *St. Mary Magdalene's Funeral Tears* is the most famous sermon by this English Jesuit poet and martyr. It is a beautifully poetic exposition of John 20, in which Mary Magdalene comes to the empty tomb of Jesus. In the closing paragraphs, the author exhorts the reader to be more like Mary. Arrested in 1592, he was executed three years later. *A devotion by this author can be found on page 1493.*

Spenser, Edmund (1552–1599). This English poet spanned the divide between the medieval and Elizabethan periods and is most famous for his long allegorical romance, *The Faerie Queene* (1590). The poet, courtier, and explorer Sir Walter Raleigh brought Spenser and his poem to the attention of Queen Elizabeth I and *The Faerie Queene* received an enthusiastic reception. Gloriana, the poem's title character, queen of Fairyland, represents both glory and Queen Elizabeth I. In her honor, 12 knights engage in a series of adventures. Throughout the narrative, Arthur, the perfect knight, also appears. The six completed books (out of a planned twelve) relate the adventures of the knights who represent the qualities of holiness, temperance, chastity, friendship, justice, and courtesy. *Devotions by this author can be found on pages 1270, 1518.*

Spurgeon, Charles Haddon (1834–1892). The great English Baptist preacher and orator had difficulty finding a hall large enough to accommodate the crowds of people who desired to hear him. Although only 20 when he arrived at the New Park Street Chapel, London, he was soon preaching at the Surrey Gardens Music Hall while the Metropolitan Tabernacle was being built (1859–61). Seating 6000, this building provided a pulpit for Spurgeon until his death. A decided Calvinist, he could preach with power and humor while carefully expounding the Scriptures and presenting the gospel. Spurgeon's sermons, published weekly in his lifetime and eventually collected into 50 volumes, are still eminently readable today. *Devotions by this author can be found on pages 12, 104, 163, 255, 297, 349, 379, 583, 748, 885, 1016, 1052, 1160.*

Staley, W. W. (c. 1865–1940). In 1914 an American minister named W. W. Staley, pastor of Suffolk Christian Church in Virginia, delivered an address at a conference for ministers. Called "A Seaside Chautauqua and School of Methods," the conference was held in Virginia Beach. That address and four others by Staley that deal with ministerial lifestyle were later published in the book *The Minister.* Though meant for ministers, his talk on the subject of his love for books, "The Minister in His Study," is certainly true for many believers. *A devotion by this author can be found on page 1314.*

Taylor, James Hudson (1832–1905). This pioneer missionary and founder of the China Inland Mission is nearly the archetype of the ideal worker for God. At age five he indicated he wanted to be a missionary to China and was called by God to that work in 1849. Taylor prepared by studying medicine, theology, and Biblical languages, and practicing complete dependence on God for his material needs. After a short time in China, Taylor adopted native dress, a scandal to the other missionaries. Soon he had severed ties with his home mission and set off by faith to evangelize the interior—a task never before considered. Hudson Taylor proved to be one of the most profound pioneering spiritual influences in China and whatever Christian vitality exists there today is due in great part to his work. *Devotions by this author can be found on pages 398, 580, 1393, 1433.*

Temple, William (1881–1944). The son of Frederick Temple (archbishop of Canterbury, 1896–1902), William was ordained in 1908 by Randall Davidson (archbishop of Canterbury, 1903–28) and himself served as archbishop at Canterbury (1942–44). Temple's leadership of the Church of England had a threefold emphasis. First, in *Christian Faith and Life* (1931), *Nature, Man, and God* (1934), and *Reading in St. John's Gospel* (1939–40), he attempted to set forth a reasoned exposition of the Christian faith. Second, he also labored for the union of the churches as president of the Edinburgh Ecumenical Conference (1937 and 1942) and had a hand in initiating the British Council of Churches. Third, Temple's *Christianity and the Social Order* (1942), which sold 139,000 copies during World War II, expressed his passionate concern for national and social righteousness. *Devotions by this author can be found on pages 120, 1149.*

Tennyson, Lord Alfred (1809–1892). The foremost poet of his day and a great representative figure of the Victorian Age, Tennyson produced acknowledged masterpieces in many different poetic genres. The sequence of elegies for his dear deceased friend Henry Hallam, titled *In Memoriam* and published in 1850, is considered to be Tennyson's finest work and portions of it have found their way into the church's hymnody. The year 1850 was a watershed in the poet's life when he was appointed Poet Laureate, successor to William Wordsworth. Tennyson's work is not particularly doctrinal, but his hope for the afterlife is quite evident. For example, the final lines of "Crossing the Bar" read, "I hope to see my pilot face to face/when I have crossed the bar." An oft-quoted poem by Tennyson is "The Charge of the Light Brigade" (1854) and the lyrics to the hymn "Strong Son of God, Immortal Love" (1850) come from his pen. *Devotions by this author can be found on pages 373, 1440.*

Teresa of Avila (1515–1582). The spiritual depth of this Spanish mystic was balanced by her extraordinary organizational skills. While the Reformation was transforming other parts of Europe, her labors to purify the Spanish religious life strengthened the forces that reformed the Spanish Roman Catholic church from within. In 1562 she helped found a convent at Avila under the original Carmelite Rule. Her writings include *The Way of Perfection* (after 1565), instruction for her nuns; *The Interior Castle* (1577), an eloquent description of the contemplative life; and *The Foundations* (1573–82), an account of the origins of the Discalced Carmelites. *Devotions by this author can be found on pages 599, 1353.*

Tolstoy, Leo (1828–1910). This orphaned son of a Russian nobleman left his university studies without a degree, fought in the Crimean War, wrote several acclaimed short novels, and experimented in the progressive education of children, all before he wed the eighteen-year-old Sofya Andreyevna Bers in 1862. While the couple raised their 19 children, Tolstoy successfully managed his considerable estate and wrote his two greatest novels, *War and Peace* (1865–99), considered one of the greatest novels ever written, and *Anna Karenina* (1875–77), which is among the foremost modern psychological novels. The epic *War and Peace* depicts the national catastrophe of the Napoleonic invasion of Russia. Set in the years 1805–15, it tells a vast story of war between the two halves of Europe using 559 characters. It tells of the struggle of human souls from war to peace and of love between men and women, love of country, and above all, Christian love. Late in his life Tolstoy was excommunicated by the Russian Orthodox Church. At that time he said, "I believe that the will of God is most intelligibly expressed in the teachings of the man Jesus." *A devotion by this author can be found on page 1227.*

Tozer, A. W. (1897–1963). A lifelong pastor in the Christian and Missionary Alliance with a rich pulpit ministry, A. W. Tozer was without any formal education beyond grade school. He was intensely devotional, mystical and well-read. He drew from the writings of others, including François Fénelon, Bernard of Clairvaux, Julian of Norwich, as well as Emerson and Shakespeare. Readers still feel the impact of Tozer's ministry through his books in which he encourages his readers to know God personally and experientially. They include *The Pursuit of God* (1948), *The Divine Conquest* (1950), and *The Knowledge of the Holy* (1961). *Devotions by this author can be found on pages 201, 629, 704, 732, 1208, 1421.*

Truth, Sojourner (c. 1797–1883). Born into slavery in Ulster County, New York, Truth (originally named Isabella) was freed when New York State emancipated slaves in 1828. A mystic, she immediately began to preach in the streets of New York City. In 1843 she took the name Sojourner Truth, started preaching along the eastern seaboard, and came into contact with the abolitionist movement. For the next few years she toured the country speaking on its behalf. Then in 1850 she encountered the women's rights movement. President Abraham Lincoln received her in the White House in 1864. Though illiterate, Truth was a charismatic speaker who often drew large crowds to her gatherings that continued until 1875. *A devotion by this author can be found on page 1057.*

Unamuno, Miguel de (1864–1936). This Spanish novelist and philosopher underwent a spiritual crisis while assisting in services at a Greek Orthodox church in Paris in 1924. At the time, he was exiled from Spain by an often tyrannical government that had the support of many Christians. The crisis Unamuno experienced led him to write his book *The Agony of Christianity,* in which he took exception with those who equate various "isms" (nationalism, socialism, capitalism, etc.) with Christianity. *A devotion by this author can be found on page 1473.*

Underhill, Evelyn (1875–1941). Underhill's classic evaluation of spirituality, *Mysticism: A Study in the Nature and Development of Man's Spiritual Consciousness* (1911), examines the church from the first through the nineteenth centuries. An Anglican educated at King's College for Women in London, she soon became noted lecturer on mysticism and religious life and from 1924 led regular retreats. Underhill authored prose and verse works on mystical religion, including *The Mystical Way* (1913), *Life of the Spirit and Life of Today* (1922), and *Worship* (1937), an acclaimed study in liturgical practices in various church traditions. *Devotions by this author can be found on pages 314, 472, 1250.*

Vondel, Joost van den (1587–1679). In 1653 a group of Dutch artists, known as the Guild of St. Luke, held a feast in honor of Dutch dramatist and poet Joost van den Vondel, one of the most renowned writers of the Dutch Renaissance. At that very moment, Vondel's crowning achievement, a poetic drama called *Lucifer,* was in the process of being printed. It appeared the next year and would soon influence another landmark of Christian literature, namely, Milton's *Paradise Lost* (1667). *A devotion by this author can be found on page 1512.*

Watts, Issac (1674–1748). Prior to the eighteenth century, a strong prejudice existed in England against singing hymns that were composed in modern times. But the English theologian and pastor Issac Watts succeeded in overcoming these objections. Educated at an academy for dissenters at Stoke Newington, he eventually became minister of a dissenting church in London (1702) and published *Hymns* in 1707. This collection included "When I Survey the Wondrous Cross," "O God, Our Help in Ages Past," "Joy to the World," "Jesus Shall Reign Where'er the Sun," and other hymns seldom omitted from hymnals to this day. Religious conservatives at the time called them "Watts' whims," but independent congregations sang no other songs for most of the century. Watts' books on theological subjects were well known, as, for example, his *Scripture History* (1732). Yet it is his more than 500 hymns that have made a lasting impact on the devotion and worship of the church. *A devotion by this author can be found on page 1348.*

Wesley, Charles (1707–1788). The spiritual awakening of Charles Wesley preceded that of his brother John by three days (1738) and together they lead the great Methodist revival that revolutionized English society. Charles wrote the hymns that objectified his rich faith in order to provide the church with sound teaching and material for praise and worship. He produced about three hymns per week for 57 years—more than 8000 hymns. Among the most widely known are "Jesus, Lover of My Soul" and "Love Divine, All Love Excelling." Hymns that celebrate important dates on the Christian include "Lo, He Comes" for the Advent season; "Hark! The Herald Angels Sing" for Christmas; "Christ the Lord is Risen Today" is for Easter; and "Hail the Day that Sees Him Rise" for Ascension. *Devotions by this author can be found on pages 528, 609.*

Wesley, John (1703–1791). The fifteenth child of a British clergyman, this theologian, evangelist, and founder of Methodism, did more than any single person of his era to transform English society and change the nature of its religion. Educated at Oxford,

Wesley joined a group of students that adhered strictly and methodically to religious precepts and practices. They were derisively called "methodists" by their schoolmates. Disappointed by a failed attempt to be a missionary in Georgia, he returned to England where he experienced the "change which God works in the heart through faith in Christ," which would empower the remainder of his life. That power took him by horseback 250,000 miles on the roads of Great Britain to preach 42,000 sermons and write and publish 233 books. These included educational treatises, translations, histories, Biblical commentaries, an English dictionary, 23 collections of hymns, and a medical handbook, *Primitive Physick*, which went through 32 editions. By his own admission Wesley wanted to reform the nation. This he did through initiating or participating in legal and prison reform, the abolition of slavery, civil rights, and popular education. The last act of his life was the dictation of a letter to William Wilberforce to encourage him in the parliamentary fight over slavery. At John Wesley's death a popular secular magazine eulogized: "Instead of being 'an ornament to literature,' he was a blessing to his fellow creatures; instead of 'the genius of the age,' he was the servant of God!" *Devotions by this author can be found on pages 696, 900, 1467.*

Whitefield, George (1714–1770). The church in America is indebted to this great British evangelist and orator for participating with Jonathan Edwards in inaugurating the revival movement known as the Great Awakening (1739). In fact, Whitefield made seven trips to evangelize the American colonies and died in Newburyport, Massachusetts. Born in Gloucester, England, Whitefield became friends with John and Charles Wesley while a student at Oxford. Due to his unconventional manner of preaching and conducting services, many Church of England pulpits were closed to him. For this reason he preached in whatever venue was available, including open fields. Whitefield attracted vast crowds by his eloquence. People from every rank and station in life were held by the power of his preaching. Benjamin Franklin once estimated that Whitefield's voice could be heard by up to 30,000 people at one time. Because he believed that education was indispensable to a Christian, Whitefield helped found the American institutions that are now Princeton University, the University of Pennsylvania, and Dartmouth. *Devotions by this author can be found on pages 387, 1345, 1419, 1524.*

Woolman, John (1720–1772). One of the first abolitionist documents written in America, *Some Considerations on the Keeping of Negroes*(1754), came from the pen of John Woolman, the American Quaker leader, writer, and social reformer. Born near Mount Holly, New Jersey, self-educated, and deeply pious, Woolman worked as a tailor. He traveled through the colonies spreading the teachings of the Quakers and in time persuaded American Quakers to oppose slaveholding. John Woolman's *Journal* (1774), which gives an account of his spiritual life, greatly influenced abolitionists of the nineteenth century. Considered a classic of American literature, its 1871 edition was edited by the American poet John Greenleaf Whittier. While visiting the Society of Friends in England, Woolman died of smallpox and is buried in Kent. *A devotion by this author can be found on page 978.*

Wordsworth, William (1770–1850). This English poet collaborated with Samuel Taylor Coleridge on a slender book of poems entitled *Lyrical Ballads* (1798). It marked the beginning of the romantic movement in English poetry. The volume includes Wordsworth's memorable "Tintern Abbey" and Coleridge's famous "Rime of the Ancient Mariner." Most of the poems were written by Wordsworth. *Lyrical Ballads* was greeted with hostility by critics because it represented a revolt against the artificial classicism of contemporary English verse. But the theories and style of William Wordsworth created a new tradition in poetry. The greatest and most influential of England's romantic poets was born in Cockermouth, Cumberland, and educated at Cambridge. He developed a keen love of nature as a youth and the lyrical power and grace of his conversational blank verse is infused with an intense religious sense of the human relationship to nature. To Wordsworth, an orthodox member of the Church of England, God was manifest in the harmony of nature and his verse expresses the kinship between nature and the human soul. *A devotion by this author can be found on page 1295.*

Zinzendorf, Nicholaus Ludwig, Count Von (1700–1760). In 1722 this German-born member of Austrian nobility granted refuge on his estate in Bohemia to a group of persecuted Bohemian Brethren from Moravia. The community they formed there, called "Herrnhut," eventually became a refuge for Christians from other lands and religious backgrounds. In 1727 they formed a new denomination known as the Renewed Church of the Unity of the Brethren (known as the Moravian Brethren). Herrnhut missionaries were dispatched to many parts of the world. John Wesley encountered one such group of missionaries in passage to Georgia and was deeply moved by their faith. Zinzendorf himself visited the American colonies (1741–43) and worked among the Native Americans. Count Zinzendorf devoted his life, wealth, and labor to bring Christians of all persuasions together on the common ground of saving faith in Christ. He desired that this would be a visible expression of Christian love to the world. His writings include about 2000 hymns, many sermons, and various polemical treatises. An English volume entitled *Zinzendorf: Nine Public Lectures on Important Subjects in Religion* (1973) by George W. Forell provides a good introduction to Zinzendorf's views. *Devotions by this author can be found on pages 762, 1449.*

READING PLANS

GOD'S Word is his personal message of love to you today. The best way to grow as a Christian and get to know God in a more personal way is to spend time in his Word. Here are three ways for you to read through the Bible.

1. If you are reading the Bible for the first time:
   - Begin by reading the Gospel of Mark or the Gospel of John in the New Testament.
   - After reading one of these gospels, read the book of Acts or the book of Romans.
   - After reading Acts or Romans, pick an Old Testament book like Genesis or perhaps Psalms.

2. If you want to read through the entire Bible in one year:
   - Read three chapters each day, Monday through Saturday, and five chapters on Sunday.

3. If you want to read through the entire Bible in two years:
   - Read two chapters each day, Sunday through Saturday.

The following chart covers every book and chapter of the Bible. To keep track of what you have read, mark off each chapter as you complete it.

GENESIS *3/20/02*

□1	□2	□3	□4	□5	□6
□7	□8	□9 *9/4*	□10	□11	□12
□13	□14	□15	□16	□17	□18 *4/8*
□19	□20	□21 *4/16*	□22	□23	□24 *4/17*
□25	□26	□27	□28	□29	□30
□31	□32	□33	□34	□35	□36
□37	□38	□39	□40	□41	□42
□43	□44	□45	□46	□47	□48
□49	□50				

EXODUS

□1	□2	□3	□4	□5	□6
□7	□8	□9	□10	□11	□12
□13	□14	□15	□16	□17	□18
□19	□20	□21	□22	□23	□24
□25	□26	□27	□28	□29	□30
□31	□32	□33	□34	□35	□36
□37	□38	□39	□40		

LEVITICUS

□1	□2	□3	□4	□5	□6
□7	□8	□9	□10	□11	□12

□13	□14	□15	□16	□17	□18
□19	□20	□21	□22	□23	□24
□25	□26	□27			

NUMBERS

□1	□2	□3	□4	□5	□6
□7	□8	□9	□10	□11	□12
□13	□14	□15	□16	□17	□18
□19	□20	□21	□22	□23	□24
□25	□26	□27	□28	□29	□30
□31	□32	□33	□34	□35	□36

DEUTERONOMY

□1	□2	□3	□4	□5	□6
□7	□8	□9	□10	□11	□12
□13	□14	□15	□16	□17	□18
□19	□20	□21	□22	□23	□24
□25	□26	□27	□28	□29	□30
□31	□32	□33	□34		

JOSHUA

□1	□2	□3	□4	□5	□6
□7	□8	□9	□10	□11	□12
□13	□14	□15	□16	□17	□18

☐ 19   ☐ 20   ☐ 21   ☐ 22   ☐ 23   ☐ 24   ☐ 31   ☐ 32   ☐ 33   ☐ 34   ☐ 35   ☐ 36

JUDGES

☐ 1   ☐ 2   ☐ 3   ☐ 4   ☐ 5   ☐ 6
☐ 7   ☐ 8   ☐ 9   ☐ 10   ☐ 11   ☐ 12
☐ 13   ☐ 14   ☐ 15   ☐ 16   ☐ 17   ☐ 18
☐ 19   ☐ 20   ☐ 21

RUTH

☐ 1   ☐ 2   ☐ 3   ☐ 4

1 SAMUEL

☐ 1   ☐ 2   ☐ 3   ☐ 4   ☐ 5   ☐ 6
☐ 7   ☐ 8   ☐ 9   ☐ 10   ☐ 11   ☐ 12
☐ 13   ☐ 14   ☐ 15   ☐ 16   ☐ 17   ☐ 18
☐ 19   ☐ 20   ☐ 21   ☐ 22   ☐ 23   ☐ 24
☐ 25   ☐ 26   ☐ 27   ☐ 28   ☐ 29   ☐ 30
☐ 31

2 SAMUEL

☐ 1   ☐ 2   ☐ 3   ☐ 4   ☐ 5   ☐ 6
☐ 7   ☐ 8   ☐ 9   ☐ 10   ☐ 11   ☐ 12
☐ 13   ☐ 14   ☐ 15   ☐ 16   ☐ 17   ☐ 18
☐ 19   ☐ 20   ☐ 21   ☐ 22   ☐ 23   ☐ 24

1 KINGS

☐ 1   ☐ 2   ☐ 3   ☐ 4   ☐ 5   ☐ 6
☐ 7   ☐ 8   ☐ 9   ☐ 10   ☐ 11   ☐ 12
☐ 13   ☐ 14   ☐ 15   ☐ 16   ☐ 17   ☐ 18
☐ 19   ☐ 20   ☐ 21   ☐ 22

2 KINGS

☐ 1   ☐ 2   ☐ 3   ☐ 4   ☐ 5   ☐ 6
☐ 7   ☐ 8   ☐ 9   ☐ 10   ☐ 11   ☐ 12
☐ 13   ☐ 14   ☐ 15   ☐ 16   ☐ 17   ☐ 18
☐ 19   ☐ 20   ☐ 21   ☐ 22   ☐ 23   ☐ 24
☐ 25

1 CHRONICLES

☐ 1   ☐ 2   ☐ 3   ☐ 4   ☐ 5   ☐ 6
☐ 7   ☐ 8   ☐ 9   ☐ 10   ☐ 11   ☐ 12
☐ 13   ☐ 14   ☐ 15   ☐ 16   ☐ 17   ☐ 18
☐ 19   ☐ 20   ☐ 21   ☐ 22   ☐ 23   ☐ 24
☐ 25   ☐ 26   ☐ 27   ☐ 28   ☐ 29

2 CHRONICLES

☐ 1   ☐ 2   ☐ 3   ☐ 4   ☐ 5   ☐ 6
☐ 7   ☐ 8   ☐ 9   ☐ 10   ☐ 11   ☐ 12
☐ 13   ☐ 14   ☐ 15   ☐ 16   ☐ 17   ☐ 18
☐ 19   ☐ 20   ☐ 21   ☐ 22   ☐ 23   ☐ 24
☐ 25   ☐ 26   ☐ 27   ☐ 28   ☐ 29   ☐ 30

EZRA

☐ 1   ☐ 2   ☐ 3   ☐ 4   ☐ 5   ☐ 6
☐ 7   ☐ 8   ☐ 9   ☐ 10

NEHEMIAH

☐ 1   ☐ 2   ☐ 3   ☐ 4   ☐ 5   ☐ 6
☐ 7   ☐ 8   ☐ 9   ☐ 10   ☐ 11   ☐ 12
☐ 13

ESTHER

☐ 1   ☐ 2   ☐ 3   ☐ 4   ☐ 5   ☐ 6
☐ 7   ☐ 8   ☐ 9   ☐ 10

JOB

☐ 1   ☐ 2   ☐ 3   ☐ 4   ☐ 5   ☐ 6
☐ 7   ☐ 8   ☐ 9   ☐ 10   ☐ 11   ☐ 12
☐ 13   ☐ 14   ☐ 15   ☐ 16   ☐ 17   ☐ 18
☐ 19   ☐ 20   ☐ 21   ☐ 22   ☐ 23   ☐ 24
☐ 25   ☐ 26   ☐ 27   ☐ 28   ☐ 29   ☐ 30
☐ 31   ☐ 32   ☐ 33   ☐ 34   ☐ 35   ☐ 36
☐ 37   ☐ 38   ☐ 39   ☐ 40   ☐ 41   ☐ 42

PSALMS

☐ 1   ☐ 2   ☐ 3   ☐ 4   ☐ 5   ☐ 6
☐ 7   ☐ 8   ☐ 9   ☐ 10   ☐ 11   ☐ 12
☐ 13   ☐ 14   ☐ 15   ☐ 16   ☐ 17   ☐ 18
☐ 19   ☐ 20   ☐ 21   ☐ 22   ☐ 23   ☐ 24
☐ 25   ☐ 26   ☐ 27   ☐ 28   ☐ 29   ☐ 30
☐ 31   ☐ 32   ☐ 33   ☐ 34   ☐ 35   ☐ 36
☐ 37   ☐ 38   ☐ 39   ☐ 40   ☐ 41   ☐ 42
☐ 43   ☐ 44   ☐ 45   ☐ 46   ☐ 47   ☐ 48
☐ 49   ☐ 50   ☐ 51   ☐ 52   ☐ 53   ☐ 54
☐ 55   ☐ 56   ☐ 57   ☐ 58   ☐ 59   ☐ 60
☐ 61   ☐ 62   ☐ 63   ☐ 64   ☐ 65   ☐ 66
☐ 67   ☐ 68   ☐ 69   ☐ 70   ☐ 71   ☐ 72
☐ 73   ☐ 74   ☐ 75   ☐ 76   ☐ 77   ☐ 78
☐ 79   ☐ 80   ☐ 81   ☐ 82   ☐ 83   ☐ 84
☐ 85   ☐ 86   ☐ 87   ☐ 88   ☐ 89   ☐ 90
☐ 91   ☐ 92   ☐ 93   ☐ 94   ☐ 95   ☐ 96
☐ 97   ☐ 98   ☐ 99   ☐ 100   ☐ 101   ☐ 102
☐ 103   ☐ 104   ☐ 105   ☐ 106   ☐ 107   ☐ 108
☐ 109   ☐ 110   ☐ 111   ☐ 112   ☐ 113   ☐ 114
☐ 115   ☐ 116   ☐ 117   ☐ 118   ☐ 119   ☐ 120
☐ 121   ☐ 122   ☐ 123   ☐ 124   ☐ 125   ☐ 126
☐ 127   ☐ 128   ☐ 129   ☐ 130   ☐ 131   ☐ 132
☐ 133   ☐ 134   ☐ 135   ☐ 136   ☐ 137   ☐ 138
☐ 139   ☐ 140   ☐ 141   ☐ 142   ☐ 143   ☐ 144

☐ 145 ☐ 146 ☐ 147 ☐ 148 ☐ 149 ☐ 150

PROVERBS

☐ 1 ☐ 2 ☐ 3 ☐ 4 ☐ 5 ☐ 6
☐ 7 ☐ 8 ☐ 9 ☐ 10 ☐ 11 ☐ 12
☐ 13 ☐ 14 ☐ 15 ☐ 16 ☐ 17 ☐ 18
☐ 19 ☐ 20 ☐ 21 ☐ 22 ☐ 23 ☐ 24
☐ 25 ☐ 26 ☐ 27 ☐ 28 ☐ 29 ☐ 30
☐ 31

ECCLESIASTES

☐ 1 ☐ 2 ☐ 3 ☐ 4 ☐ 5 ☐ 6
☐ 7 ☐ 8 ☐ 9 ☐ 10 ☐ 11 ☐ 12

SONG OF SONGS

☐ 1 ☐ 2 ☐ 3 ☐ 4 ☐ 5 ☐ 6
☐ 7 ☐ 8

ISAIAH

☐ 1 ☐ 2 ☐ 3 ☐ 4 ☐ 5 ☐ 6
☐ 7 ☐ 8 ☐ 9 ☐ 10 ☐ 11 ☐ 12
☐ 13 ☐ 14 ☐ 15 ☐ 16 ☐ 17 ☐ 18
☐ 19 ☐ 20 ☐ 21 ☐ 22 ☐ 23 ☐ 24
☐ 25 ☐ 26 ☐ 27 ☐ 28 ☐ 29 ☐ 30
☐ 31 ☐ 32 ☐ 33 ☐ 34 ☐ 35 ☐ 36
☐ 37 ☐ 38 ☐ 39 ☐ 40 ☐ 41 ☐ 42
☐ 43 ☐ 44 ☐ 45 ☐ 46 ☐ 47 ☐ 48
☐ 49 ☐ 50 ☐ 51 ☐ 52 ☐ 53 ☐ 54
☐ 55 ☐ 56 ☐ 57 ☐ 58 ☐ 59 ☐ 60
☐ 61 ☐ 62 ☐ 63 ☐ 64 ☐ 65 ☐ 66

JEREMIAH

☐ 1 ☐ 2 ☐ 3 ☐ 4 ☐ 5 ☐ 6
☐ 7 ☐ 8 ☐ 9 ☐ 10 ☐ 11 ☐ 12
☐ 13 ☐ 14 ☐ 15 ☐ 16 ☐ 17 ☐ 18
☐ 19 ☐ 20 ☐ 21 ☐ 22 ☐ 23 ☐ 24
☐ 25 ☐ 26 ☐ 27 ☐ 28 ☐ 29 ☐ 30
☐ 31 ☐ 32 ☐ 33 ☐ 34 ☐ 35 ☐ 36
☐ 37 ☐ 38 ☐ 39 ☐ 40 ☐ 41 ☐ 42
☐ 43 ☐ 44 ☐ 45 ☐ 46 ☐ 47 ☐ 48
☐ 49 ☐ 50 ☐ 51 ☐ 52

LAMENTATIONS

☐ 1 ☐ 2 ☐ 3 ☐ 4 ☐ 5

EZEKIEL

☐ 1 ☐ 2 ☐ 3 ☐ 4 ☐ 5 ☐ 6
☐ 7 ☐ 8 ☐ 9 ☐ 10 ☐ 11 ☐ 12
☐ 13 ☐ 14 ☐ 15 ☐ 16 ☐ 17 ☐ 18
☐ 19 ☐ 20 ☐ 21 ☐ 22 ☐ 23 ☐ 24

☐ 25 ☐ 26 ☐ 27 ☐ 28 ☐ 29 ☐ 30
☐ 31 ☐ 32 ☐ 33 ☐ 34 ☐ 35 ☐ 36
☐ 37 ☐ 38 ☐ 39 ☐ 40 ☐ 41 ☐ 42
☐ 43 ☐ 44 ☐ 45 ☐ 46 ☐ 47 ☐ 48

DANIEL

☐ 1 ☐ 2 ☐ 3 ☐ 4 ☐ 5 ☐ 6
☐ 7 ☐ 8 ☐ 9 ☐ 10 ☐ 11 ☐ 12

HOSEA

☐ 1 ☐ 2 ☐ 3 ☐ 4 ☐ 5 ☐ 6
☐ 7 ☐ 8 ☐ 9 ☐ 10 ☐ 11 ☐ 12
☐ 13 ☐ 14

JOEL

☐ 1 ☐ 2 ☐ 3

AMOS

☐ 1 ☐ 2 ☐ 3 ☐ 4 ☐ 5 ☐ 6
☐ 7 ☐ 8 ☐ 9

OBADIAH

☐ OBADIAH

JONAH

☐ 1 ☐ 2 ☐ 3 ☐ 4

MICAH

☐ 1 ☐ 2 ☐ 3 ☐ 4 ☐ 5 ☐ 6
☐ 7

NAHUM

☐ 1 ☐ 2 ☐ 3

HABAKKUK

☐ 1 ☐ 2 ☐ 3

ZEPHANIAH

☐ 1 ☐ 2 ☐ 3

HAGGAI

☐ 1 ☐ 2

ZECHARIAH

☐ 1 ☐ 2 ☐ 3 ☐ 4 ☐ 5 ☐ 6
☐ 7 ☐ 8 ☐ 9 ☐ 10 ☐ 11 ☐ 12
☐ 13 ☐ 14

MALACHI

☐ 1 ☐ 2 ☐ 3 ☐ 4

MATTHEW

☐ 1 ☐ 2 ☐ 3 ☐ 4 ☐ 5 ☐ 6
☐ 7 ☐ 8 ☐ 9 ☐ 10 ☐ 11 ☐ 12

□13 □14 □15 □16 □17 □18
□19 □20 □21 □22 □23 □24
□25 □26 □27 □28

MARK

□1 □2 □3 □4 □5 □6
□7 □8 □9 □10 □11 □12
□13 □14 □15 □16

LUKE

□1 □2 □3 □4 □5 □6
□7 □8 □9 □10 □11 □12
□13 □14 □15 □16 □17 □18
□19 □20 □21 □22 □23 □24

JOHN

□1 □2 □3 □4 □5 □6
□7 □8 □9 □10 □11 □12
□13 □14 □15 □16 □17 □18
□19 □20 □21

ACTS

□1 □2 □3 □4 □5 □6
□7 □8 □9 □10 □11 □12
□13 □14 □15 □16 □17 □18
□19 □20 □21 □22 □23 □24
□25 □26 □27 □28

ROMANS

□1 □2 □3 □4 □5 □6
□7 □8 □9 □10 □11 □12
□13 □14 □15 □16

1 CORINTHIANS

□1 □2 □3 □4 □5 □6
□7 □8 □9 □10 □11 □12
□13 □14 □15 □16

2 CORINTHIANS

□1 □2 □3 □4 □5 □6
□7 □8 □9 □10 □11 □12
□13

GALATIANS

□1 □2 □3 □4 □5 □6

EPHESIANS

□1 □2 □3 □4 □5 □6

PHILIPPIANS

□1 □2 □3 □4

COLOSSIANS

□1 □2 □3 □4

1 THESSALONIANS

□1 □2 □3 □4 □5

2 THESSALONIANS

□1 □2 □3

1 TIMOTHY

□1 □2 □3 □4 □5 □6

2 TIMOTHY

□1 □2 □3 □4

TITUS

□1 □2 □3

PHILEMON

□PHILEMON

HEBREWS

□1 □2 □3 □4 □5 □6
□7 □8 □9 □10 □11 □12
□13

JAMES

□1 □2 □3 □4 □5

1 PETER

□1 □2 □3 □4 □5

2 PETER

□1 □2 □3

1 JOHN

□1 □2 □3 □4 □5

2 JOHN

□2 JOHN

3 JOHN

□3 JOHN

JUDE

□JUDE

REVELATION

□1 □2 □3 □4 □5 □6
□7 □8 □9 □10 □11 □12
□13 □14 □15 □16 □17 □18
□19 □20 □21 □22

The Classics
Devotional Bible

PROJECT MANAGEMENT AND EDITORIAL
BY GARY KNAPP

EDITORIAL ASSISTANCE BY SARAH HUPP
AND DANIEL PARTNER

INTERIOR DESIGN BY SHARON WRIGHT,
BELMONT, MI

INTERIOR TYPESETTING BY MULTOMAH GRAPHICS,
TROUTDALE, OR

INTERIOR PROOFREADNG BY PEACHTREE EDITORIAL
AND PROOFREADING SERVICE,
PEACHTREE CITY, GA

COVER DESIGN BY JAGER ASSOCIATES, INC.

PRINTED BY R.R. DONNELLEY & SONS COMPANY,
CRAWFORDSVILLE, IN

REFLECTIONS

REFLECTIONS

REFLECTIONS

REFLECTIONS

REFLECTIONS

REFLECTIONS

REFLECTIONS

REFLECTIONS

REFLECTIONS

REFLECTIONS